Here is what the critics say about Merriam-Webster:

"It is the closest we can get, in America, to the Voice of Authority." — *The New York Times*
WEBSTER'S THIRD NEW INTERNATIONAL DICTIONARY, UNABRIDGED

"It is the most up-to-the-minute dictionary in America today, one that keeps up with the headlines." — John Barkham
WEBSTER'S NINTH NEW COLLEGIATE DICTIONARY

"It is so ample and easy to use that for many it will largely supersede Roget..." — *The Wall Street Journal*
WEBSTER'S COLLEGIATE THESAURUS

"...one of the great books on language in this generation..."
—William Safire, *The New York Times*
WEBSTER'S DICTIONARY OF ENGLISH USAGE

"A must for every writer's library." — *The Boston Globe*
WEBSTER'S NEW DICTIONARY OF SYNONYMS

The Merriam-Webster Concise School and Office Dictionary

A Merriam-Webster®

Merriam-Webster Inc., Publishers
Springfield, Massachusetts

A GENUINE MERRIAM-WEBSTER

The name *Webster* alone is no guarantee of excellence. It is used by a number of publishers and may serve mainly to mislead an unwary buyer.

A Merriam-Webster® is the registered trademark you should look for when you consider the purchase of dictionaries or other fine reference books. It carries the reputation of a company that has been publishing since 1831 and is your assurance of quality and authority.

Library of Congress Cataloging in Publication Data
Main entry under title:
The Merriam-Webster concise school and office dictionary.
p. cm.
ISBN 0-87779-600-9
1. English language—Dictionaries I. Merriam-Webster, Inc.
PE1628.M35 1991
423—dc20 91-9382
CIP

Made in the United States of America

12345RRD939291

Contents

Preface

THE MERRIAM-WEBSTER CONCISE SCHOOL AND OFFICE DICTIONARY is the latest in the line of Merriam-Webster® paperback dictionaries designed to meet the day-to-day needs of dictionary users in the home, school, or office. It is firmly within the tradition of previous editions in its emphasis on practicality, range of material offered, and ease of use, but it also draws much new information—including new vocabulary—from Webster's Ninth New Collegiate Dictionary, the latest in our Collegiate® line of dictionaries.

The heart of this book is the A-Z vocabulary. Within this section, one finds the core of the English vocabulary; obsolete, rare, and highly technical words and obsolete meanings of common words have been omitted. The vocabulary is thus a compilation of the words most likely to be looked up by any person searching for a meaning, pronunciation, or end-of-line division point. Every definition in this section is based on examples of actual usage found among the more than 14,000,000 citations in the Merriam-Webster files.

The A-Z vocabulary is followed by several sections that dictionary users have long found helpful: a list of common English given names; a list of foreign words and phrases that often occur in English texts but that have not yet become part of the English vocabulary; a list of nations of the world; a list of places in the United States having 16,500 or more inhabitants, with a summary by states; a similar list of places in Canada, with a summary by provinces and territories; a section devoted to widely used signs and symbols; a Handbook of Style section that summarizes common conventions of punctuation, capitalization, and the use of italics; and a section on footnotes and other kinds of bibliographical references. All are listed on the Contents page.

The A-Z vocabulary is preceded by a section of Explanatory Notes that should be read carefully by every user of the dictionary. An understanding of the information contained in these notes will add markedly to the satisfaction and pleasure that come from looking into the pages of the dictionary. Following these notes is a page that lists and explains the pronunciation symbols used in this dictionary.

The Merriam-Webster Concise School and Office Dictionary is the product of a company that has been publishing dictionaries for nearly 150 years. It has been edited by an experienced staff of professional lexicographers, who believe that it will serve well those who want an easy-to-read record of today's English words.

Explanatory Notes

Entries

A boldface letter or a combination of such letters set flush with the left-hand margin of each column of type is a main entry. The main entry may consist of letters set solid, of letters joined by a hyphen, or of letters separated by one or more spaces:

hot . . . *adj*

hot–blood•ed . . . *adj*

hot dog . . . *n*

The material in lightface type that follows each main entry on the same line and on succeeding indented lines presents information about the main entry.

The main entries follow one another in alphabetical order letter by letter: *bill of exchange* follows *billion; Day of Atonement* follows *daylight saving time*. Those containing an Arabic numeral are alphabetized as if the numeral were spelled out: *4-H* comes between *fourfold* and *Four Hundred; 3-D* comes between *three* and *three-dimensional*. Those derived from proper names beginning with abbreviated forms of *Mac-* are alphabetized as if spelled *mac-*: *McCoy* comes after *Maccabees* and before *mace*.

A pair of guide words is printed at the top of each page. These indicate that the entries falling alphabetically between the words at the top of the outer column of each page are found on that page.

The guide words are usually the alphabetically first and the alphabetically last entries on the page:

alto • amends

Occasionally the last printed entry is not the alphabetically last entry. On page 34, for example, *³average* is the last main entry, but *averring*, an inflected form at *aver*, is the alphabetically last entry and is therefore the second guide word. The alphabetically last entry is not used, however, if it follows alphabetically the first guide word on the succeeding page. Thus on page 18 *anchoring* is not a guide word because it follows alphabetically the entry *anchorage* which is the first guide word on page 19.

Any boldface word—a main entry with definition, a variant, an inflected form, a defined or undefined run-on—may be used as a guide word.

When one main entry has exactly the same written form as another, the two are distinguished by superscript numerals preceding each word:

¹egg . . . *vb* **¹rash** . . . *adj*

²egg *n* **²rash** *n*

Words precede word elements made up of the same letters; solid compounds precede hyphenated compounds; hyphenated compounds precede open compounds; and lowercase entries precede those with an initial capital:

self . . . *n*

self- *comb form*

run•down . . . *n*

run–down . . . *adj*

run down . . . *vb*

fed•er•al . . . *adj*

Federal *n*

The centered dots within entry words indicate division points at which a hyphen may be put at the end of a line of print or writing. Thus the noun *res•er•va•tion* may be ended on one line and continued on the next in this manner:

res-
ervation

reser-
vation

reserva-
tion

Centered dots are not shown after a single initial letter or before a single terminal letter because typesetters seldom cut off a single letter:

evict . . . *vb*

mighty . . . *adj*

oleo . . . *n*

Nor are they usually shown at the second and succeeding homographs of a word:

¹pi•lot . . . *n*

²pilot *vb*

³pilot *adj*

There are acceptable alternative end-of-line divisions just as there are acceptable variant spellings and pronunciations, but no more than one division is shown for any entry in this dictionary.

A double hyphen at the end of a line in this dictionary (as in the definition at **dromedary**) stands for a hyphen that is retained when the word is written as a unit on one line. This kind of hyphen is represented in boldface words in this dictionary with an en dash, which appears whether or not it falls at the end of a line.

When a main entry is followed by the word *or* and another spelling, the two spellings are equal variants. Both are standard, and either one may be used according to personal inclination:

lou•ver *or* **lou•vre**

If two variants joined by *or* are out of alphabetical order, they remain equal variants. The one printed first is, however, slightly more common than the second:

coun•sel•or *or* **coun•sel•lor**

When another spelling is joined to the main entry by the word *also*, the spelling after *also* is a secondary variant and occurs less frequently than the first:

fo•gy *also* **fo•gey**

Secondary variants belong to standard usage and may be used according to personal inclination. If there are two secondary variants, the second is joined to the first by *or*. Once the word *also* is used to signal a secondary variant, all following variants are joined by *or:*

²wool•ly *also* **wool•ie** *or* **wooly**

Variants whose spelling puts them alphabetically more than a column away from the main entry are entered at their own alphabetical places and usually not at the main entry:

tsar . . . *var of* CZAR

Variants having a usage label appear only at their own alphabetical places:

la•bour *chiefly Brit var of* LABOR

To show all the stylings that are found for English compounds would require space that can be better used for other information. So this dictionary limits itself to a single styling for a compound:

book•sell•er
yes–man
home run

When a compound is widely used and one styling predominates, that styling is shown. When a compound is uncommon or when the evidence indicates that two or three stylings are approximately equal in frequency, the styling shown is based on the analogy of parallel compounds.

A main entry may be followed by one or more derivatives or by a homograph with a different functional label. These are run-on entries. Each is introduced by a lightface dash and each has a functional label. They are not defined, however, since their meanings are readily understood from the meaning of the root word:

healthy . . . *adj* . . . — **health•i•ly** . . . *adv* — **health•i•ness** . . . *n*
as•sent . . . *vb* . . . — **assent** *n*

A main entry may be followed by one or more phrases containing the entry word or an inflected form of it. These are also run-on entries. Each is introduced by a lightface dash but there is no functional label. They are, however, defined since their meanings are more than the sum of the meanings of their elements:

¹go . . . *vb* . . . — **go to bat for :** . . .
¹hand . . . *n* . . . — **at hand :** . . .

Defined phrases of this sort are run on at the entry constituting the first major element in the phrase. When there are variants, however, the run-on appears at the entry constituting the first major invariable element in the phrase:

¹seed . . . *n* . . . — **go to seed** *or* **run to seed 1:** . . .

Boldface words that appear within parentheses (as **co•ca** at **co•caine** and **jet engine** and **jet propulsion** at **jet–propelled**) are run-in entries.

Attention is called to the definition of *vocabulary entry* on page 585. The term *dictionary entry* includes all vocabulary entries as well as all boldface entries in the section headed "Foreign Words and Phrases."

Pronunciation

The matter between a pair of reversed virgules \ \ following the entry word indicates the pronunciation. The symbols used are explained in the chart printed inside the back cover.

A hyphen is used in the pronunciation to show syllabic division. These hyphens sometimes coincide with the centered dots in the entry word that indicate end-of-line division:

vol•ca•no \väl-ˈkā-nō\

Sometimes they do not:

grind•er \ˈgrīn-dər\

A high-set mark ˈ indicates major (primary) stress or accent; a low-set mark ˌ indicates minor (secondary) stress or accent:

cat•bird \ˈkat-ˌbərd\

The stress mark stands at the beginning of the syllable that receives the stress.

A syllable with neither a high-set mark nor a low-set mark is unstressed:

fig•ment \ˈfig-mənt\

The presence of variant pronunciations indicates that not all educated speakers pronounce words the same way. A second-place variant is not to be regarded as less acceptable than the pronunciation that is given first. It may, in fact, be used by as many educated speakers as the first variant, but the requirements of the printed page are such that one must precede the other:

eco•nom•ic \ˌek-ə-ˈnäm-ik, ˌē-kə-\
flac•cid \ˈflak-səd, ˈflas-əd\

Symbols enclosed by parentheses represent elements that are present in the pronunciation of some speakers but are absent from the pronunciation of other speakers, elements that are present in some but absent from other utterances of the same speaker, or elements whose presence or absence is uncertain:

fo•liage \ˈfō-l(ē-)ij\
duke \ˈd(y)ük\

Thus, the above parentheses indicate that some people say \ˈfō-lē-ij\ and others say \ˈfō-lij\; some \ˈdük\, others \ˈdyük\.

When a main entry has less than a full pronunciation, the missing part is to be supplied from a pronunciation in a preceding entry or within the same pair of reversed virgules:

out•er•most \-ˌmōst\
pa•la•ver \pə-ˈlav-ər, -ˈläv-\

The pronunciation of the first two syllables of *outermost* is found at the main entry *outer*. The hyphens before and after \ˈläv\ in the pronunciation of *palaver* indicate that both the first and the last parts of the pronunciation are to be taken from the immediately preceding pronunciation.

In general, no pronunciation is indicated for open compounds consisting of two or more English words that have own-place entry:

motor vehicle *n*

Only the first entry in a sequence of numbered homographs is given a pronunciation if their pronunciations are the same:

[1]**mea•sure** \'mezh-ər, 'māzh-\ *n*
[2]**measure** *vb*

The pronunciation of unpronounced derivatives and compounds run on at a main entry is a combination of the pronunciation at the main entry and the pronunciation of the other element as given at its alphabetical place in the vocabulary:

— **nar•row•ness** *n*
— **at last**

Thus, the pronunciation of *narrowness* is the sum of the pronunciations given at *narrow* and *-ness;* that of *at last*, the sum of the pronunciations of the two elements that make up the phrase.

Functional Labels

An italic label indicating a part of speech or some other functional classification follows the pronunciation or, if no pronunciation is given, the main entry. The eight traditional parts of speech are indicated as follows:

fa•ce•tious . . . *adj*
al•to•geth•er . . . *adv*
if . . . *conj*
amen . . . *interj*
log•ger•head . . . *n*
in•to . . . *prep*
we . . . *pron*
stul•ti•fy . . . *vb*

Other italicized labels used to indicate functional classifications that are not traditional parts of speech include:

blvd *abbr*
self- *comb form*
super- . . . *prefix*
-ous . . . *adj suffix*
-al•ly . . . *adv suffix*
-hood . . . *n suffix*
-fy . . . *vb suffix*
Na *symbol*
ought . . . *verbal auxiliary*

Functional labels are sometimes combined:

can•ta•bi•le . . . *adv or adj*

Inflected Forms

Nouns

The plurals of nouns are shown in this dictionary when suffixation brings about a change of final *-y* to *-i-*, when the noun ends in a consonant plus *-o* or in *-ey*, when the noun ends in *-oo*, when the noun has an irregular plural or a zero plural or a foreign plural, when the noun is a compound that pluralizes any element but the last, when the noun has variant plurals, and when it is believed that the dictionary user might have reasonable doubts about the spelling of the plural or when the plural is spelled in a way contrary to what is expected:

dairy . . . *n, pl* **dair•ies**
po•ta•to . . . *n, pl* **-toes**
lack•ey . . . *n, pl* **lackeys**
zoo . . . *n, pl* **zoos**
tooth . . . *n, pl* **teeth**
deer . . . *n, pl* **deer**
al•ga . . . *n, pl* **al•gae**
broth•er–in–law . . . *n, pl* **brothers–in–law**
[1]**fish** . . . *n, pl* **fish** *or* **fish•es**
[2]**pi** . . . *n, pl* **pis**

Cutback inflected forms are used when the noun has three or more syllables:

atroc•i•ty . . . *n, pl* **-ties**

The plurals of nouns are usually not shown when the base word is unchanged by suffixation, when the noun is a compound whose second element is readily recognizable as a regular free form entered at its own place, or when the noun is unlikely to occur in the plural:

car•rot . . . *n*
horse•fly . . . *n*
po•lyg•a•my . . . *n*

Nouns that are plural in form and that regularly occur in plural construction are labeled *n pl*:

bifocals . . . *n pl*

Nouns that are plural in form but that are not always construed as plurals are appropriately labeled:

taps . . . *n sing or pl*

Verbs

The principal parts of verbs are shown in this dictionary when suffixation brings about a doubling of a final consonant or an elision of a final *-e* or a change of final *-y* to *-i-*, when final *-c* changes to *-ck-* in suffixation, when the verb ends in *-ey*, when the inflection is irregular, when there are variant inflected forms, and when it is believed that the dictionary user might have reasonable doubts about the spelling of an inflected form or when the inflected form is spelled in a way contrary to what is expected:

beg . . . *vb* **begged; beg•ging**
equate . . . *vb* **equat•ed; equat•ing**
[1]**fry** . . . *vb* **fried; fry•ing**
[2]**panic** *vb* **pan•icked** . . .; **pan•ick•ing**
obey . . . *vb* **obeyed**; **obey•ing**
[1]**break** . . . *vb* **broke** . . .; **bro•ken** . . .; **break•ing**
[1]**trav•el** . . . *vb* **-eled** *or* **-elled**; **-el•ing** *or* **-el•ling**
[2]**visa** *vb* **vi•saed** . . .; **vi•sa•ing**
[2]**chagrin** *vb* **cha•grined** . . .; **cha•grin•ing**

The principal parts of a regularly inflected verb are shown when it is desirable to indicate the pronunciation of one of the inflected forms:

[2]**spell** *vb* **spelled** \'speld\; **spell•ing**
[2]**season** *vb* **sea•soned**; **sea•son•ing** \'sēz-(ᵊ-)niŋ\

Cutback inflected forms are usually used when the verb has

three or more syllables, when it is a two-syllable word that ends in *-l* and has variant spellings, and when it is a compound whose second element is readily recognized as an irregular verb:

mul•ti•ply . . . *vb* **-plied**; **-ply•ing**
cav•il . . . *vb* **-iled** *or* **-illed**; **-il•ing** *or* **-il•ling**
for•go *or* **fore•go** . . . *vb* **-went** . . .; **-gone** . . .; **-go•ing**

The principal parts of verbs are usually not shown when the base word is unchanged by suffixation or when the verb is a compound whose second element is readily recognizable as a regular free form entered at its own place:

[2]**shield** *vb*
[1]**out•reach** . . . *vb*

Adjectives & Adverbs

The comparative and superlative forms of adjectives and adverbs are shown in this dictionary when suffixation brings about a doubling of a final consonant or an elision of a final *-e* or a change of final *-y* to *-i-*, when the word ends in *-ey*, when the inflection is irregular, and when there are variant inflected forms:

[1]**fat** . . . *adj* **fat•ter**; **fat•test**
[1]**sure** . . . *adj* **sur•er**; **sur•est**
[1]**dry** . . . *adj* **dri•er** . . .; **dri•est**
hors•ey *or* **horsy** . . . *adj* **hors•i•er**; **-est**
bad . . . *adj* **worse** . . .; **worst**
sly . . . *adj* **sli•er** *also* **sly•er** . . .; **sli•est** *also* **sly•est**

The superlative forms of adjectives and adverbs of two or more syllables are usually cut back:

scanty . . . *adj* **scant•i•er**; **-est**
[1]**ear•ly** . . . *adv* **ear•li•er**; **-est**

The comparative and superlative forms of regularly inflected adjectives and adverbs are shown when it is desirable to indicate the pronunciation of the inflected forms:

strong \'strȯŋ\ *adj* **stron•ger** \'strȯŋ-gər\; **stron•gest** \'strȯŋ-gəst\

The inclusion of inflected forms in *-er* and *-est* at adjective and adverb entries means nothing more about the use of *more* and *most* with these adjectives and adverbs than that their comparative and superlative degrees may be expressed in either way: *kindlier* or *more kindly; kindliest* or *most kindly*.

At a few adjective entries only the superlative form is shown:

[2]**mere** *adj* **mer•est**

The absence of the comparative form indicates that there is no evidence of its use.

The comparative and superlative forms of adjectives and adverbs are usually not shown when the base word is unchanged by suffixation or when the word is a compound whose second element is readily recognizable as a regular free form entered at its own place:

[2]**quiet** *adj*
un•hap•py . . . *adj*

Inflected forms are not shown at undefined run-ons.

Capitalization

Most entries in this dictionary begin with a lowercase letter. A few of these have an italicized label *often cap*, which indicates that the word is as likely to be capitalized as not and that it is as acceptable with an uppercase initial as it is with one in lowercase. Some entries begin with an uppercase letter, which indicates that the word is usually capitalized. The absence of an initial capital or of an *often cap* label indicates that the word is not ordinarily capitalized:

spice . . . *n*
ba•bel . . . *n, often cap*
Quak•er . . . *n*

The capitalization of entries that are open or hyphenated compounds is similarly indicated by the form of the entry or by an italicized label:

living room *n*
in•dia ink . . . *n, often cap 1st I*
all–Amer•i•can . . . *adj*
German shepherd *n*
lazy Su•san . . . *n*
Jack Frost *n*

A word that is capitalized in some senses and lowercase in others shows variations from the form of the main entry by the use of italicized labels at the appropriate senses:

Apoc•ry•pha . . . *n* **1** *not cap*
[1]**Pres•by•te•ri•an** . . . *adj* **1** *often not cap*
cath•o•lic . . . *adj* . . . **2** *cap*
east•ern . . . *adj* **1** *often cap* . . . **2** *cap*

Etymology

This dictionary gives the etymologies for a number of the vocabulary entries. These etymologies are in boldface square brackets preceding the definition. Meanings given in roman type within these brackets are not definitions of the entry, but are meanings of the Middle English, Old English, or non-English words within the brackets.

The etymology gives the language from which words borrowed into English have come. It also gives the form of the word in that language or a representation of the word in our alphabet if the form in that language differs from that in English:

ae•gis . . . [L, fr. Gk *aigis* goatskin]
[1]**sav•age** . . . [ME *sauvage*, fr. MF, fr. ML *salvaticus*, fr. L *silvaticus* of the woods, wild . . .]

An etymology beginning with the name of a language (including ME or OE) and not giving the foreign (or Middle English or Old English) form indicates that this form is the same as the form of the entry word:

ibi•dem . . . [L]
na•dir . . . [ME, fr. MF . . .]

An etymology beginning with the name of a language (including ME or OE) and not giving the foreign (or Middle English or Old English) meaning indicates that this meaning is the same as the meaning expressed in the first definition in the entry:

tur•quoise . . . [ME *turkeis, turcas,* fr. MF *turquoyse* . . .]

Small superscript figures following words or syllables in an etymology refer to the tone of the word or syllable they follow. They are used only with forms cited for languages in which tonal variations distinguish words of different meaning that would otherwise sound alike.

kow•tow . . . [Chin *k'o*[1] *t'ou*[2], fr. *k'o*[1] to bump + *t'ou*[2] head]

Usage

Three types of status labels are used in this dictionary—temporal, regional, and stylistic—to signal that a word or a sense of a word is not part of the standard vocabulary of English.

The temporal label *obs* for "obsolete" means that there is no evidence of use since 1755:

[3]**post** *n* **1** *obs*

The label *obs* is a comment on the word being defined. When a thing, as distinguished from the word used to designate it, is obsolete, appropriate orientation is usually given in the definition:

far•thin•gale . . . *n* . . . **:** a support (as of hoops) worn esp. in the 16th century to swell out a skirt

The temporal label *archaic* means that a word or sense once in common use is found today only sporadically or in special contexts:

com•mon•weal . . . *n* . . . **1** *archaic*
[1]**thou** . . . *pron, archaic*

A word or sense limited in use to a specific region of the U.S. has an appropriate label. The adverb *chiefly* precedes a label when the word has some currency outside the specified region, and a double label is used to indicate considerable currency in each of two specific regions:

[2]**wash** *n* . . . **5** *West*
do•gie . . . *n, chiefly West*
goo•ber . . . *n, South & Midland*

Words current in all regions of the U.S. have no label.

A word or sense limited in use to one of the other countries of the English-speaking world has an appropriate regional label:

chem•ist . . . *n* . . . **2** *Brit*
loch . . . *n, Scot*
[2]**wireless** *n* . . . **2** *chiefly Brit*

The label *dial* for "dialect" indicates that the pattern of use of a word or sense is too complex for summary labeling: it usually includes several regional varieties of American English or of American and British English:

[1]**boot** . . . *n, chiefly dial*
cal•a•boose . . . *n* . . . *dial*

The stylistic label *slang* is used with words or senses that are especially appropriate in contexts of extreme informality:

[1]**rap** . . . *n* . . . **3** *slang*
tick•er . . . **n** . . . **3** *slang*

There is no satisfactory objective test for slang, especially with reference to a word out of context. No word, in fact, is invariably slang, and many standard words can be given slang applications.

Definitions are sometimes followed by verbal illustrations that show a typical use of the word in context. These illustrations are enclosed in angle brackets, and the word being illustrated is usually replaced by a lightface swung dash. The swung dash stands for the boldface entry word, and it may be followed by an italicized suffix:

[1]**let•ter** . . . *n* . . . **4** . . . ⟨the ~ of the law⟩
deep–seated . . . *adj* . . . **2** . . . ⟨~ convictions⟩
depth . . . *n* . . . **2** . . . ⟨the ~*s* of the woods⟩
[1]**fill** . . . *vb* . . . **6** . . . ⟨laughter ~*ed* the room⟩

The swung dash is not used when the form of the boldface entry word is changed in suffixation, and it is not used for open compounds:

en•gage . . . *vb* . . . **3** . . . ⟨*engaged* his friend's attention⟩
drum up *vb* **1** . . . ⟨*drum up* business⟩

Definitions are sometimes followed by usage notes that give supplementary information about such matters as idiom, syntax, and semantic relationship. A usage note is introduced by a lightface dash:

fro . . . *adv* . . . — used in the phrase *to and fro*
[2]**gang** *vb* **1** . . . — usu. used with *up*
[1]**jaw** . . . *n* . . . **2** . . . — usu. used in pl.
[1]**ada•gio** . . . *adv or adj* . . . — used as a direction in music
blast off . . . *vb* . . . — used esp. of rocket-propelled devices

Sometimes a usage note is used in place of a definition. Some function words (as conjunctions and prepositions) have chiefly grammatical meaning and little or no lexical meaning; most interjections express feelings but are otherwise untranslatable into lexical meaning; and some other words (as honorific titles) are more amenable to comment than to definition:

or . . . *conj* — used as a function word to indicate an alternative
[1]**in** . . . *prep* **1** — used to indicate physical surroundings
hal•le•lu•jah . . . *interj* . . . — used to express praise, joy, or thanks
ex•cel•len•cy . . . *n* . . . **2** — used as a title of honor

Sense Division

A boldface colon is used in this dictionary to introduce a definition:

found•ry . . . *n* . . . **:** a building or works where metal is cast

It is also used to separate two or more definitions of a single sense:

[2]**yellow** *n* **1** : a color between green and orange in the spectrum : the color of ripe lemons or sunflowers

Boldface Arabic numerals separate the senses of a word that has more than one sense:

idol . . . *n* **1** : an image worshiped as a god **2** : a false god **3** : an object of passionate devotion

A particular semantic relationship between senses is sometimes suggested by the use of one of the two italic sense dividers *esp* or *also.*

The sense divider *esp* (for *especially*) is used to introduce the most common meaning included in the more general preceding definition:

no•to•ri•ous . . . *adj* : generally known and talked of; *esp* : widely and unfavorably known

The sense divider *also* is used to introduce a meaning related to the preceding sense by an easily understood extension of that sense:

[1]**flour** . . . *n* : finely ground and sifted meal of a grain (as wheat); *also* : a fine soft powder

The order of senses is historical: the sense known to have been first used in English is entered first. This is not to be taken to mean, however, that each sense of a multisense word developed from the immediately preceding sense. It is altogether possible that sense 1 of a word has given rise to sense 2 and sense 2 to sense 3, but frequently sense 2 and sense 3 may have developed independently of one another from sense 1.

When an italicized label follows a boldface numeral, the label applies only to that specific numbered sense. It does not apply to any other boldface numbered senses:

craft . . . *n* . . . **3** *pl usu* **craft**
[1]**fa•ther** . . . *n* . . . **2** *cap* . . . **5** *often cap*
[2]**preview** *n* . . . **2** *also* **pre•vue** \\-ˌvyü\\
pub•li•can . . . *n* . . . **2** *chiefly Brit*

At *craft* the *pl* label applies to sense **3** but to none of the other numbered senses. At *father* the *cap* label applies only to sense **2** and the *often cap* label only to sense **5**. At *preview* the variant spelling and pronunciation apply only to sense **2**, as does the *chiefly Brit* label at *publican*.

Cross-Reference

Four different kinds of cross-references are used in this dictionary: directional, synonymous, cognate, and inflectional. In each instance the cross-reference is readily recognized by the lightface small capitals in which it is printed.

A cross-reference following a lightface dash and beginning with *see* is a directional cross-reference. It directs the dictionary user to look elsewhere for further information:

[1]**yen** . . . *n* . . . — see MONEY table

A cross-reference following a boldface colon is a synonymous cross-reference. It may stand alone as the only definition for an entry or for a sense of an entry; it may follow an analytical definition; it may be one of two or more synonymous cross-references separated by commas:

maize . . . *n* : INDIAN CORN
chap•let . . . *n* . . . **2** : a string of beads : NECKLACE
[2]**dress** *n* . . . **2** : FROCK, GOWN
cheek . . . *n* . . . **2** : IMPUDENCE, BOLDNESS, AUDACITY

A synonymous cross-reference indicates that a definition at the entry cross-referred to can be substituted as a definition for the entry or the sense in which the cross-reference appears.

A cross-reference following an italic *var of* ("variant of") is a cognate cross-reference:

Gipsy *var of* GYPSY

Occasionally a cognate cross-reference has a limiting label preceding *var of* as an indication that the variant is not standard English:

har•bour *chiefly Brit var of* HARBOR

A cross-reference following an italic label that identifies an entry as an inflected form (as of a noun or verb) is an inflectional cross-reference:

feet *pl of* FOOT
worn *past part of* WEAR

Inflectional cross-references appear only when the inflected form falls at least a column away from the entry cross-referred to.

Synonyms

A boldface **syn** near the end of an entry introduces words that are synonymous with the word being defined:

[2]**fear** . . . *n* . . . **syn** dread, fright, alarm, panic, terror, trepidation

Synonyms are not definitions although they may often be substituted for each other in context.

Combining Forms, Prefixes, & Suffixes

An entry that begins or ends with a hyphen is a word element that forms part of an English compound:

maxi- *comb form* **1** . . . ⟨*maxi*-kilt⟩
ex- . . . *prefix* . . . ⟨*ex*-president⟩
-ship . . . *n suffix* **1** . . . ⟨friend*ship*⟩

Combining forms, prefixes, and suffixes are entered in this dictionary for two reasons: to make understandable the meaning of many undefined run-ons and to make recognizable the meaningful elements of words that are not entered in the dictionary.

Lists of Undefined Words

Lists of undefined words occur after the entries *anti-*, *in-*, *non-*, *over-*, *re-*, *self-*, *semi-*, *sub-*, *super-*, and *un-*. These words are undefined because they are self-explanatory: their meanings are simply the sum of a meaning of the prefix or combining form and a meaning of the second element.

Abbreviations & Symbols

Abbreviations and symbols for chemical elements are included as main entries in the vocabulary:

govt *abbr* government
Fe *symbol* . . . iron

Abbreviations have been normalized to one form. In practice, however, there is considerable variation in the use of periods and in capitalization (as *vhf*, *v.h.f.*, *VHF*, and *V.H.F.*), and stylings other than those given in this dictionary are often acceptable.

Symbols that are not capable of being alphabetized are included in a separate section of the back matter headed "Signs and Symbols."

Abbreviations Used in This Work

ab	about
abbr	abbreviation
abl	ablative
acc	accusative
A.D.	anno Domini
adj	adjective
adv	adverb
AF	Anglo-French
alter	alteration
Am	American
AmerF	American French
AmerInd	American Indian
AmerSp	American Spanish
Ar	Arabic
Aram	Aramaic
B.C.	before Christ
Brit	British
C	Celsius
Calif	California
CanF	Canadian French
cap	capital, capitalized
Celt	Celtic
cent	century
Chin	Chinese
comb	combining
compar	comparative
conj	conjunction
Dan	Danish
dat	dative
deriv	derivative
dial	dialect
dim	diminutive
E	English
Egypt	Egyptian
Eng	English
Esk	Eskimo
esp	especially
F	Fahrenheit, French
fem	feminine
Flem	Flemish
fr	from
G	German
Gael	Gaelic
Gk	Greek
Gmc	Germanic
Heb	Hebrew
Hung	Hungarian
Icel	Icelandic
imit	imitative
imper	imperative
interj	interjection
Ir	Irish
IrGael	Irish Gaelic
irreg	irregular
It, Ital	Italian
Jp	Japanese
K	Kelvin
L	Latin
LaF	Louisiana French
LG	Low German
LGk	Late Greek
LHeb	Late Hebrew
lit	literally
LL	Late Latin
masc	masculine
ME	Middle English
MexSp	Mexican Spanish
MF	Middle French
MGk	Middle Greek
ML	Medieval Latin
modif	modification
MS	manuscript
n	noun
neut	neuter
NGk	New Greek
NHeb	New Hebrew
NL	New Latin
No	North
Norw	Norwegian
n pl	noun plural
obs	obsolete
OE	Old English
OF	Old French
OIt	Old Italian
ON	Old Norse
OPer	Old Persian
OProv	Old Provençal
orig	originally
OW	Old Welsh
part	participle
Per	Persian
perh	perhaps
Pg	Portuguese
pl	plural
Pol	Polish
pp	past participle
prep	preposition
pres	present
prob	probably
pron	pronoun, pronunciation
prp	present participle
Russ	Russian
Sc	Scotch, Scots
Scand	Scandinavian
ScGael	Scottish Gaelic
Scot	Scottish
Serb	Serbian
sing	singular
Skt	Sanskrit
Slav	Slavic
So	South
Sp	Spanish
St	Saint
superl	superlative
Sw	Swedish
syn	synonym, synonymy
trans	translation
Turk	Turkish
US	United States
USSR	Union of Soviet Socialist Republics
usu	usually
var	variant
vb	verb
vi	verb intransitive
VL	Vulgar Latin
vt	verb transitive
W	Welsh

Pronunciation Symbols

ə. . . .**a**but, c**o**llect, s**u**ppose

ˈə,ˌə. . . .h**u**mdr**u**m

ᵊ. . . .(in ᵊl, ᵊn) batt**le**, cott**on**; (in lᵊ, mᵊ, rᵊ) French tab**le**, pris**me**, tit**re**

ər. . . .op**er**ation, f**ur**th**er**

a. . . .m**a**p, p**a**tch

ā. . . .d**ay**, f**a**te

ä. . . .b**o**ther, c**o**t, f**a**ther

á. . . .a sound between \a\ and \ä\, as in an Eastern New England pronunciation of **au**nt, **a**sk

aů. . . .n**ow**, **ou**t

b. . . .**b**a**b**y, ri**b**

ch. . . .**ch**in, ca**tch**

d. . . .**d**i**d**, a**dd**er

e. . . .s**e**t, r**e**d

ē. . . .b**ea**t, **ea**s**y**

f. . . .**f**i**f**ty, cu**ff**

g. . . .**g**o, bi**g**

h. . . .**h**at, a**h**ead

hw. . . .**wh**ale

i. . . .t**i**p, ban**i**sh

ī. . . .s**i**te, b**uy**

j. . . .**j**ob, e**dge**

k. . . .**k**in, **c**oo**k**

k̲. . . .German Ba**ch**, Scots lo**ch**

l. . . .**l**i**l**y, coo**l**

m. . . .**m**ur**m**ur, di**m**

n. . . .**n**i**n**e, ow**n**

ⁿ. . . .indicates that a preceding vowel is pronounced through both nose and mouth, as in French bon \bōⁿ\

ŋ. . . .si**ng**, si**ng**er, fi**n**ger, i**n**k

ō. . . .b**o**ne, holl**ow**

ȯ. . . .s**aw**

œ. . . .French b**œu**f, German H**ö**lle

œ̄. . . .French f**eu**, German H**öh**le

ȯi. . . .t**oy**

p. . . .**p**e**pp**er, li**p**

r. . . .**r**a**r**ity

s. . . .**s**our**ce**, le**ss**

sh. . . .**sh**y, mi**ss**ion

t. . . .**t**ie, a**tt**ack

th. . . .**th**in, e**th**er

th̲. . . .**th**en, ei**th**er

ü. . . .b**oo**t, few \ˈfyü\

u̇. . . .p**u**t, pure \ˈpyu̇r\

ue. . . .German f**ü**llen

u̅e̅. . . .French r**ue**, German f**üh**len

v. . . .**v**i**v**id, gi**v**e

w. . . .**w**e, a**w**ay

y. . . .**y**ard, cue \ˈkyü\

ʸ. . . .indicates that a preceding \l\, \n\, or \w\ is modified by having the tongue approximate the position for \y\, as in French di**gne** \dēnʸ\

z. . . .**z**one, rai**se**

zh. . . .vi**s**ion, plea**s**ure

\\. . . .slant line used in pairs to mark the beginning and end of a transcription: \ˈpen\

ˈ. . . .mark at the beginning of a syllable that has primary (strongest) stress: \ˈshəf-əl-ˌbōrd\

ˌ. . . .mark at the beginning of a syllable that has secondary (next-strongest) stress: \ˈshəf-əl-ˌbōrd\

-. . . .mark of syllable division in pronunciations (the mark of end-of-line division in boldface entries is a centered dot •)

( ). . . .indicate that what is symbolized between sometimes occurs and sometimes does not occur in the pronunciation of the word: **fac·tory** \ˈfak-t(ə-)rē\ = \ˈfak-tə-rē, ˈfak-trē\

A

[1]a \ˈā\ *n, pl* **a's** *or* **as** \ˈāz\ *often cap* **1 :** the 1st letter of the English alphabet **2 :** a grade rating a student's work as superior

[2]a \ə, (ˈ)ā\ *indefinite article* **:** ONE, SOME — used to indicate an unspecified or unidentified individual ⟨there's ~ man outside⟩

[3]a *abbr, often cap* **1** absent **2** acre **3** alto **4** answer **5** are **6** area

AA *abbr* **1** Alcoholics Anonymous **2** antiaircraft **3** associate in arts

AAA *abbr* American Automobile Association

A and M *abbr* agricultural and mechanical

A and R *abbr* artists and repertory

aard·vark \ˈärd-ˌvärk\ *n* [obs. Afrikaans, fr. Afrikaans *aard* earth + *vark* pig] **:** a large burrowing African mammal that feeds on ants and termites with its sticky tongue

ab *abbr* about

AB *abbr* **1** able-bodied seaman **2** airman basic **3** [NL *artium baccalaureus*] bachelor of arts

ABA *abbr* American Bar Association

aback \ə-ˈbak\ *adv* **:** by surprise ⟨taken ~⟩

aba·cus \ˈab-ə-kəs\ *n, pl* **aba·ci** \ˈab-ə-ˌsī, -ˌkē\ *or* **aba·cus·es :** an instrument for making calculations by sliding counters along rods or grooves

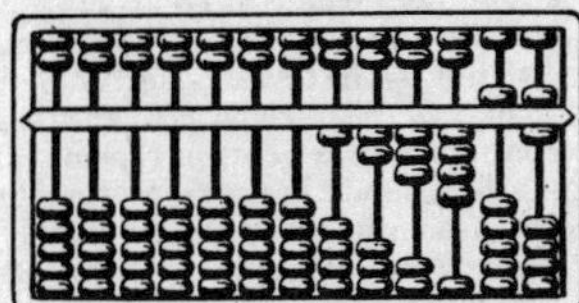

abacus

[1]**abaft** \ə-ˈbaft\ *prep* **:** to the rear of

[2]**abaft** *adv* **:** toward or at the stern **:** AFT

ab·a·lo·ne \ˌab-ə-ˈlō-nē\ *n* **:** a large edible sea mollusk with a flattened slightly spiral shell with holes along the edge

[1]**aban·don** \ə-ˈban-dən\ *vb* [ME *abandounen,* fr. MF *abandoner,* fr. *abandon,* n., surrender, fr. *a bandon* in one's power] **:** to give up completely **:** FORSAKE, DESERT — **aban·don·ment** *n*

[2]**abandon** *n* **:** a thorough yielding to natural impulses; *esp* **:** ENTHUSIASM, EXUBERANCE

aban·doned \ə-ˈban-dənd\ *adj* **:** morally unrestrained **syn** profligate, dissolute, reprobate

abase \ə-ˈbās\ *vb* **abased; abas·ing :** HUMBLE, DEGRADE — **abase·ment** *n*

abash \ə-ˈbash\ *vb* **:** to destroy the composure of **:** EMBARRASS — **abash·ment** *n*

abate \ə-ˈbāt\ *vb* **abat·ed; abat·ing 1 :** to put an end to ⟨~ a nuisance⟩ **2 :** to decrease in amount, number, or degree

abate·ment \ə-ˈbāt-mənt\ *n* **1 :** DECREASE **2 :** an amount abated; *esp* **:** a deduction from the full amount of a tax

ab·at·toir \ˈab-ə-ˌtwär\ *n* [F] **:** SLAUGHTERHOUSE

ab·ba·cy \ˈab-ə-sē\ *n, pl* **-cies :** the office or term of office of an abbot or abbess

ab·bé \a-ˈbā, ˈab-ˌā\ *n* **:** a member of the French secular clergy — used as a title

ab·bess \ˈab-əs\ *n* **:** the superior of a convent for nuns

ab·bey \ˈab-ē\ *n, pl* **abbeys 1 :** MONASTERY, CONVENT **2 :** an abbey church

ab·bot \ˈab-ət\ *n* [ME *abbod,* fr. OE, fr. LL *abbat-, abbas,* fr. LGk *abbas,* fr. Aramaic *abbā* father] **:** the superior of a monastery for men

abbr *abbr* abbreviation

ab·bre·vi·ate \ə-ˈbrē-vē-ˌāt\ *vb* **-at·ed; -at·ing :** SHORTEN, CURTAIL; *esp* **:** to reduce to an abbreviation

ab·bre·vi·a·tion \ə-ˌbrē-vē-ˈā-shən\ *n* **1 :** the act or result of abbreviating **2 :** a shortened form of a word or phrase used for brevity esp. in writing

[1]**ABC** \ˌā-ˌbē-ˈsē\ *n, pl* **ABC's** *or* **ABCs** \-ˈsēz\ **1 :** ALPHABET — usu. used in pl. **2 :** RUDIMENTS

[2]**ABC** *abbr* American Broadcasting Company

Ab·di·as \ab-ˈdī-əs\ *n* — see BIBLE table

ab·di·cate \ˈab-di-ˌkāt\ *vb* **-cat·ed; -cat·ing :** to give up (as a throne) formally — **ab·di·ca·tion** \ˌab-di-ˈkā-shən\ *n*

ab·do·men \ˈab-də-mən, ab-ˈdō-mən\ *n* **1 :** the cavity in or area of the body between the chest and the pelvis **2 :** the part of the body posterior to the thorax in an arthropod — **ab·dom·i·nal** \ab-ˈdäm-ən-ᵊl\ *adj* — **ab·dom·i·nal·ly** \-ē\ *adv*

ab·duct \ab-ˈdəkt\ *vb* **:** to take away (a person) by force **:** KIDNAP — **ab·duc·tion** \-ˈdək-shən\ *n* — **ab·duc·tor** \-tər\ *n*

abeam \ə-ˈbēm\ *adv or adj* **:** on a line at right angles to a ship's keel

abed \ə-ˈbed\ *adv or adj* **:** in bed

ab·er·ra·tion \ˌab-ə-ˈrā-shən\ *n* **1 :** deviation esp. from a moral standard or normal state **2 :** unsoundness of mind **:** DERANGEMENT **3 :** failure of a mirror or lens to produce exact point-to-point correspondence between an object and its image — **ab·er·rant** \a-ˈber-ənt\ *adj*

abet \ə-ˈbet\ *vb* **abet·ted; abet·ting** [ME *abetten,* fr. MF *abeter,* fr. OF *beter* to bait] **1 :** INCITE, ENCOURAGE **2 :** to assist or support in the achievement of a purpose — **abet·tor** *or* **abet·ter** \-ər\ *n*

abey·ance \ə-ˈbā-əns\ *n* **:** a condition of suspended activity

ab·hor \əb-ˈhȯr, ab-\ *vb* **ab·horred; ab·hor·ring** [ME *abhorren,* fr. L *abhorrēre,* fr. *ab-* + *horrēre* to shudder] **:** LOATHE, DETEST — **ab·hor·rence** \-əns\ *n*

ab·hor·rent \-ənt\ *adj* **:** LOATHSOME, DETESTABLE

abide \ə-ˈbīd\ *vb* **abode** \-ˈbōd\ *or* **abid·ed; abid·ing 1 :** BEAR, ENDURE **2 :** DWELL, REMAIN, LAST

abil·i·ty \ə-ˈbil-ət-ē\ *n, pl* **-ties :** the quality of being able **:** POWER, SKILL

ab·ject \ˈab-ˌjekt, ab-ˈjekt\ *adj* **:** low in spirit or hope **:** CRINGING — **ab·jec·tion** \ab-ˈjek-shən\ *n* — **ab·ject·ly** \ˈab-jekt-lē, ab-ˈjekt-\ *adv* — **ab·ject·ness** *n*

ab·jure \ab-ˈju̇r\ *vb* **ab·jured; ab·jur·ing 1 :** to renounce solemnly **:** RECANT **2 :** to abstain from — **ab·ju·ra·tion** \ˌab-jə-ˈrā-shən\ *n*

abl *abbr* ablative

ab·late \a-ˈblāt\ *vb* **ab·lat·ed; ab·lat·ing :** to remove or become removed by cutting, eating or wearing away, evaporating, or vaporizing

ab·la·tion \a-ˈblā-shən\ *n* **1 :** surgical cutting and removal **2 :** removal of a part (as the outside of a nose cone) by melting or vaporization

---

\ə\abut \ᵊ\kitten \ər\further \a\ash \ā\ace \ä\cot, cart \au̇\out \ch\chin \e\bet \ē\easy \g\go \i\hit \ī\ice \j\job \ŋ\sing \ō\go \ȯ\law \ȯi\boy \th\thin \th\the \ü\loot \u̇\foot \y\yet \zh\vision *see also* Pronunciation Symbols page

ab·la·tive \ˈab-lət-iv\ *adj* : of, relating to, or constituting a grammatical case (as in Latin) expressing typically the relation of separation and source — **ablative** *n*

ablaze \ə-ˈblāz\ *adj or adv* : being on fire : BLAZING

able \ˈā-bəl\ *adj* **abler** \-b(ə-)lər\; **ablest** \-b(ə-)ləst\ **1** : having sufficient power, skill, or resources to accomplish an object **2** : marked by skill or efficiency — **ably** \-blē\ *adv*

-able *also* **-ible** \ə-bəl\ *adj suffix* **1** : capable of, fit for, or worthy of (being so acted upon or toward) ⟨break*able*⟩ ⟨collect*ible*⟩ **2** : tending, given, or liable to ⟨knowledge*able*⟩ ⟨perish*able*⟩

able–bod·ied \ˌā-bəl-ˈbäd-ēd\ *adj* : having a sound strong body

abloom \ə-ˈblüm\ *adj* : BLOOMING

ab·lu·tion \ə-ˈblü-shən, a-ˈblü-\ *n* : the washing of one's body or part of it

ABM \ˌā-(ˌ)bē-ˈem\ *n, pl* **ABM's** *or* **ABMs** : ANTIBALLISTIC MISSILE

Ab·na·ki \ab-ˈnäk-ē\ *n, pl* **Abnaki** *or* **Abnakis** : a member of an American Indian people of Maine and southern Quebec

ab·ne·gate \ˈab-ni-ˌgāt\ *vb* **-gat·ed; -gat·ing 1** : SURRENDER, RELINQUISH **2** : DENY, RENOUNCE — **ab·ne·ga·tion** \ˌab-ni-ˈgā-shən\ *n*

ab·nor·mal \ab-ˈnȯr-məl\ *adj* : deviating from the normal or average — **ab·nor·mal·i·ty** \ˌab-nər-ˈmal-ət-ē, -(ˌ)nȯr-\ *n* — **ab·nor·mal·ly** \ab-ˈnȯr-mə-lē\ *adv*

[1]**aboard** \ə-ˈbōrd\ *adv* **1** : ALONGSIDE **2** : on, onto, or within a car, ship, or aircraft **3** : in or into a group or association ⟨welcome new workers ~⟩

[2]**aboard** *prep* : ON, ONTO, WITHIN

abode \ə-ˈbōd\ *n* **1** : STAY, SOJOURN **2** : HOME, RESIDENCE

abol·ish \ə-ˈbäl-ish\ *vb* : to do away with : ANNUL — **ab·o·li·tion** \ˌab-ə-ˈlish-ən\ *n*

ab·o·li·tion·ism \ˌab-ə-ˈlish-ə-ˌniz-əm\ *n* : advocacy of the abolition of slavery — **ab·o·li·tion·ist** \-ˈlish-(ə-)nəst\ *n or adj*

A–bomb \ˈā-ˌbäm\ *n* : ATOM BOMB — **A–bomb** *vb*

abom·i·na·ble \ə-ˈbäm-(ə-)nə-bəl\ *adj* : ODIOUS, LOATHSOME, DETESTABLE

abominable snow·man \-ˈsnō-mən, -ˌman\ *n, often cap A&S* : a mysterious animal reported as existing in the high Himalayas and usu. thought to be a bear

abom·i·nate \ə-ˈbäm-ə-ˌnāt\ *vb* **-nat·ed; -nat·ing** [L *abominari*, lit., to deprecate as an ill omen, fr. *ab-* away + *omen* omen] : LOATHE, DETEST

abom·i·na·tion \ə-ˌbäm-ə-ˈnā-shən\ *n* **1** : something abominable **2** : DISGUST, LOATHING

ab·orig·i·nal \ˌab-ə-ˈrij-(ə-)nəl\ *adj* : ORIGINAL, INDIGENOUS, PRIMITIVE

ab·orig·i·ne \ˌab-ə-ˈrij-ə-nē\ *n* : a member of the original race of inhabitants of a region : NATIVE

aborn·ing \ə-ˈbȯr-niŋ\ *adv* : while being born or produced

[1]**abort** \ə-ˈbȯrt\ *vb* **1** : to cause or undergo abortion **2** : to terminate prematurely ⟨~ a spaceflight⟩ — **abor·tive** \-ˈbȯrt-iv\ *adj*

[2]**abort** *n* : the premature termination of a mission of or a procedure relating to an aircraft or spacecraft

abor·tion \ə-ˈbȯr-shən\ *n* : a premature birth occurring before the fetus can survive; *also* : an induced expulsion of a fetus after, accompanied by, or followed by its death

abor·tion·ist \-sh(ə-)nəst\ *n* : one who induces abortions

abound \ə-ˈbau̇nd\ *vb* **1** : to be plentiful : TEEM **2** : to be fully supplied

[1]**about** \ə-ˈbau̇t\ *adv* **1** : on all sides **2** : AROUND **3** : NEARBY

[2]**about** *prep* **1** : on every side of **2** : near to **3** : on the verge of : GOING ⟨he was just ~ to go⟩ **4** : CONCERNING

about–face \-ˈfās\ *n* : a reversal of direction or attitude — **about–face** *vb*

[1]**above** \ə-ˈbəv\ *adv* **1** : in the sky; *also* : in or to heaven **2** : in or to a higher place; *also* : higher on the same page or on a preceding page

[2]**above** *prep* **1** : in or to a higher place than : OVER ⟨storm clouds ~ the bay⟩ **2** : superior to ⟨he thought her far ~ him⟩ **3** : more than : EXCEEDING

above·board \-ˌbōrd\ *adv or adj* : without concealment or deception : OPENLY

abp *abbr* archbishop

abr *abbr* abridged; abridgment

ab·ra·ca·dab·ra \ˌab-rə-kə-ˈdab-rə\ *n* **1** : a magical charm or incantation against calamity **2** : GIBBERISH

abrade \ə-ˈbrād\ *vb* **abrad·ed; abrad·ing 1** : to wear away by rubbing **2** : to wear down in spirit : IRRITATE — **abra·sion** \-ˈbrā-zhən\ *n*

[1]**abra·sive** \ə-ˈbrā-siv\ *n* : a substance (as pumice) for grinding, smoothing, or polishing

[2]**abrasive** *adj* : tending to abrade : causing irritation ⟨~ relationships⟩ — **abra·sive·ly** *adv* — **abra·sive·ness** *n*

abreast \ə-ˈbrest\ *adv or adj* **1** : side by side **2** : up to a standard or level esp. of knowledge

abridge \ə-ˈbrij\ *vb* **abridged; abridg·ing** [ME *abregen*, fr. MF *abregier*, fr. LL *abbreviare*, fr. L *ad* to + *brevis* short] : to lessen in length or extent : SHORTEN — **abridg·ment** *or* **abridge·ment** *n*

abroad \ə-ˈbrȯd\ *adv or adj* **1** : over a wide area **2** : away from one's home **3** : outside one's country

ab·ro·gate \ˈab-rə-ˌgāt\ *vb* **-gat·ed; -gat·ing** : ANNUL, REVOKE — **ab·ro·ga·tion** \ˌab-rə-ˈgā-shən\ *n*

abrupt \ə-ˈbrəpt\ *adj* **1** : broken or as if broken off **2** : SUDDEN, HASTY **3** : so quick as to seem rude **4** : DISCONNECTED **5** : STEEP — **abrupt·ly** *adv*

abs *abbr* absolute

ab·scess \ˈab-ˌses\ *n, pl* **ab·scess·es** [L *abscessus*, lit., act of going away, fr. *abscedere* to go away, fr. *abs-*, *ab-* away + *cedere* to go] : a collection of pus surrounded by inflamed tissue — **ab·scessed** \-ˌsest\ *adj*

ab·scis·sa \ab-ˈsis-ə\ *n, pl* **abscissas** *also* **ab·scis·sae** \-ˈsis-(ˌ)ē\ : the coordinate of a point in a plane coordinate system that is the distance of the point from the vertical axis found by measuring along the horizontal axis

ab·scis·sion \ab-ˈsizh-ən\ *n* **1** : the act or process of cutting off **2** : the natural separation of flowers, fruits, or leaves from plants — **ab·scise** \ab-ˈsīz\ *vb*

ab·scond \ab-ˈskänd\ *vb* : to depart secretly and hide oneself

ab·sence \ˈab-səns\ *n* **1** : the state or time of being absent **2** : WANT, LACK **3** : INATTENTION

[1]**ab·sent** \ˈab-sənt\ *adj* **1** : not present **2** : LACKING **3** : INATTENTIVE

[2]**ab·sent** \ab-ˈsent\ *vb* : to keep (oneself) away

[3]**ab·sent** \ˈab-sənt\ *prep* : in the absence of : WITHOUT

ab·sen·tee \ˌab-sən-ˈtē\ *n* : one that is absent or absents himself

absentee ballot *n* : a ballot submitted (as by mail) in advance of an election by a voter who is unable to be present at the polls

ab·sen·tee·ism \ˌab-sən-ˈtē-ˌiz-əm\ *n* : chronic absence (as from work or school)

ab·sent·mind·ed \ˌab-sənt-ˈmīn-dəd\ *adj* : unaware of one's surroundings or action : INATTENTIVE — **ab·sent·mind·ed·ly** *adv* — **ab·sent·mind·ed·ness** *n*

ab·sinthe *also* **ab·sinth** \ˈab-ˌsinth\ *n* [F] : a liqueur flavored esp. with wormwood and anise

ab·so·lute \ˈab-sə-ˌlüt, ˌab-sə-ˈlüt\ *adj* **1** : free from imperfection or mixture **2** : free from control, restriction, or qualification **3** : lacking grammatical connection with any other word in a sentence ⟨~ construction⟩ **4** : POSITIVE ⟨~ proof⟩ **5** : relating to the fundamental units of length, mass, and time **6** : relating to a temperature scale on which the zero point (**absolute zero**) corresponds to complete absence of heat equal to −273.15°C **7** : FUNDAMENTAL, ULTIMATE — **ab·so·lute·ly** *adv*

absolute pitch *n* **1** : the position of a tone in a standard scale independently determined by its rate of vibration **2** : the ability to sing or name a note asked for or heard

absolute value *n* : the numerical value of a real number that for a positive number or zero is equal to the number itself and for a negative number is equal to the positive number which when added to it is equal to zero

ab·so·lu·tion \ˌab-sə-ˈlü-shən\ *n* : the act of absolving; *esp* : a remission of sins pronounced by a priest in the sacrament of penance

ab·so·lut·ism \ˈab-sə-ˌlüt-ˌiz-əm\ *n* **1** : the theory that a ruler or government should have unlimited power **2** : government by an absolute ruler or authority

ab·solve \əb-ˈzälv, -ˈsälv\ *vb* **ab·solved; ab·solv·ing** : to set free from an obligation or the consequences of guilt

ab·sorb \əb-ˈsórb, -ˈzórb\ *vb* **1** : ASSIMILATE, INCORPORATE **2** : to suck up or take in in the manner of a sponge **3** : to engage (one's attention) : ENGROSS **4** : to receive without recoil or echo ⟨a ceiling that ~*s* sound⟩ **5** : to transform (radiant energy) into a different form usu. with a resulting rise in temperature — **ab·sorb·ing** *adj* — **ab·sorb·ing·ly** *adv*

ab·sor·bent *also* **ab·sor·bant** \əb-ˈsór-bənt, ˈ-zór-\ *adj* : able to absorb ⟨~ cotton⟩ — **ab·sor·ben·cy** \-bən-sē\ *n* — **absorbent** *also* **absorbant** *n*

ab·sorp·tion \əb-ˈsórp-shən, -ˈzórp-\ *n* **1** : a process of absorbing or being absorbed **2** : concentration of attention — **ab·sorp·tive** \-tiv\ *adj*

ab·stain \əb-ˈstān\ *vb* : to restrain oneself **syn** refrain, forbear — **ab·stain·er** *n* — **ab·sten·tion** \-ˈsten-chən\ *n*

ab·ste·mi·ous \ab-ˈstē-mē-əs\ *adj* [L *abstemius*, fr. *abs-* away + *temetum* mead] : sparing in use of food or drink : TEMPERATE — **ab·ste·mi·ous·ly** *adv*

ab·sti·nence \ˈab-stə-nəns\ *n* : voluntary refraining esp. from eating certain foods or drinking liquor — **ab·sti·nent** \-nənt\ *adj*

abstr *abbr* abstract

[1]**ab·stract** \ab-ˈstrakt, ˈab-ˌstrakt\ *adj* **1** : considered apart from a particular instance **2** : expressing a quality apart from an object ⟨*whiteness* is an ~ word⟩ **3** : having only intrinsic form with little or no pictorial representation ⟨~ painting⟩ — **ab·stract·ly** *adv* — **ab·stract·ness** \-ˈstrak(t)-nəs, -ˌstrak(t)-\ *n*

[2]**ab·stract** \ˈab-ˌstrakt; *2 also* ab-ˈstrakt\ *n* **1** : SUMMARY, EPITOME **2** : an abstract thing or state

[3]**ab·stract** \ab-ˈstrakt, ˈab-ˌstrakt; *2 usu* ˈab-ˌstrakt\ *vb* **1** : REMOVE, SEPARATE **2** : to make an abstract of : SUMMARIZE **3** : to draw away the attention of **4** : STEAL — **ab·stract·ed·ly** \ab-ˈstrak-təd-lē, ˈab-ˌstrak-\ *adv*

abstract expressionism *n* : art that expresses the artist's attitudes and emotions through abstract forms — **abstract expressionist** *n*

ab·strac·tion \ab-ˈstrak-shən\ *n* **1** : the act of abstracting : the state of being abstracted **2** : an abstract idea **3** : an abstract work of art

ab·struse \əb-ˈstrüs, ab-\ *adj* : hard to understand : RECONDITE — **ab·struse·ly** *adv* — **ab·struse·ness** *n*

ab·surd \əb-ˈsərd, -ˈzərd\ *adj* [MF *absurde*, fr. L *absurdus*, fr. *ab-* from + *surdus* deaf, stupid] : RIDICULOUS, UNREASONABLE — **ab·sur·di·ty** \-ət-ē\ *n* — **ab·surd·ly** *adv*

abun·dant \ə-ˈbən-dənt\ *adj* [ME, fr. MF, fr. L *abundant-, abundans*, prp. of *abundare* to abound, fr. *ab-* from + *unda* wave] : more than enough : amply sufficient **syn** copious, plentiful, ample, bountiful — **abundance** \-dəns\ *n* — **abun·dant·ly** *adv*

[1]**abuse** \ə-ˈbyüs\ *n* **1** : a corrupt practice **2** : MISUSE **3** : coarse and insulting speech **4** : MISTREATMENT

[2]**abuse** \ə-ˈbyüz\ *vb* **abused; abus·ing 1** : to attack in words : REVILE **2** : to put to a wrong use : MISUSE **3** : MISTREAT — **abus·er** *n* — **abu·sive** \-ˈbyü-siv\ *adj* — **abu·sive·ly** *adv* — **abu·sive·ness** *n*

abut \ə-ˈbət\ *vb* **abut·ted; abut·ting** : to touch along a border : border on

abut·ment \ə-ˈbət-mənt\ *n* : a structure that supports weight or withstands lateral pressure (as at the end of a bridge)

abysm \ə-ˈbiz-əm\ *n* : ABYSS

abys·mal \ə-ˈbiz-məl\ *adj* **1** : immeasurably deep : BOTTOMLESS **2** : absolutely wretched ⟨~ living conditions of the poor⟩ — **abys·mal·ly** *adv*

abyss \ə-ˈbis\ *n* **1** : the bottomless pit in old accounts of the universe **2** : an immeasurable depth

abys·sal \ə-ˈbis-əl\ *adj* : of or relating to the bottom waters of the ocean depths

ac *abbr* account

Ac *symbol* actinium

AC *abbr* **1** air-conditioning **2** alternating current **3** [L *ante Christum*] before Christ **4** [L *ante cibum*] before meals **5** area code

aca·cia \ə-ˈkā-shə\ *n* : any of numerous leguminous trees or shrubs with round white or yellow flower clusters and often fernlike leaves

acad *abbr* academic; academy

ac·a·deme \ˈak-ə-ˌdēm\ *n* : SCHOOL; *also* : academic environment

ac·a·dem·ic \ˌak-ə-ˈdem-ik\ *adj* **1** : of or relating to schools or colleges **2** : literary or general rather than technical **3** : theoretical rather than practical — **ac·a·dem·i·cal·ly** \-i-k(ə-)lē\ *adv*

ac·a·de·mi·cian \ˌak-əd-ə-ˈmish-ən, ə-ˌkad-ə-\ *n* : a member of a society of scholars or artists

ac·a·dem·i·cism \ˌak-ə-ˈdem-ə-ˌsiz-əm\ *also* **acad·e·mism** \ə-ˈkad-ə-ˌmiz-əm\ *n* : manner, style, or content conforming to the traditions or rules of an academy or movement

acad·e·my \ə-ˈkad-ə-mē\ *n, pl* **-mies** [Gk *Akadēmeia*, school of philosophy founded by Plato, fr. *Akadēmeia*, gymnasium where Plato taught, fr. *Akadēmos* Greek mythological hero] **1** : a school above the elementary level; *esp* : a private high school **2** : a society of scholars or artists

acan·thus \ə-ˈkan-thəs\ *n, pl* **acan·thus·es** *also* **acan·thi** \-ˈkan-ˌthī\ **1** : any of a genus of prickly herbs of the Mediterranean region **2** : an ornamentation (as on a column) representing the leaves of the acanthus

a cap·pel·la *also* **a ca·pel·la** \ˌäk-ə-ˈpel-ə\ *adv or adj* [It *a cappella* in chapel style] : without instrumental accompaniment ⟨the choir sang *a cappella*⟩

acc *abbr* accusative

ac·cede \ak-ˈsēd\ *vb* **ac·ced·ed; ac·ced·ing 1** : to become a party to an agreement **2** : to express approval **3** : to enter upon an office **syn** agree, acquiesce, assent, consent, subscribe

ac·ce·le·ran·do \ä-ˌchel-ə-ˈrän-dō\ *adv or adj* [It] : gradually faster — used as a direction in music

ac·cel·er·ate \ik-ˈsel-ə-ˌrāt, ak-\ *vb* **-at·ed; -at·ing 1** : to bring about earlier **2** : to speed up : QUICKEN — **ac·cel·er·a·tion** \-ˌsel-ə-ˈrā-shən\ *n*

ac·cel·er·a·tor \ik-ˈsel-ə-ˌrāt-ər, ak-\ *n* **1** : one that accelerates **2** : a pedal for controlling the speed of a motor-vehicle engine **3** : an apparatus for imparting high velocities to charged particles

ac·cel·er·om·e·ter \ik-ˌsel-ə-ˈräm-ət-ər, ak-\ *n* : an instrument for measuring acceleration or vibrations

[1]**ac·cent** \ˈak-ˌsent, ak-ˈsent\ *vb* : STRESS, EMPHASIZE

[2]**ac·cent** \ˈak-ˌsent\ *n* **1** : a distinctive manner of pronunciation ⟨a foreign ~⟩ **2** : prominence given to one syllable of a word esp. by stress **3** : a mark (as ´, `, ˆ) over a vowel in writing or printing used usu. to indicate a difference in pronunciation (as stress) from a vowel not so marked — **ac·cen·tu·al** \ak-ˈsench-(ə-)wəl\ *adj*

---

ac·cen·tu·ate \ak-ˈsen-chə-ˌwāt\ *vb* **-at·ed; -at·ing** : ACCENT — **ac·cen·tu·a·tion** \-ˌsen-chə-ˈwā-shən\ *n*
ac·cept \ik-ˈsept, ak-\ *vb* **1** : to receive willingly **2** : to agree to **3** : to assume an obligation to pay
ac·cept·able \ik-ˈsep-tə-bəl, ak-\ *adj* : capable or worthy of being accepted — **ac·cept·abil·i·ty** \ik-ˌsep-tə-ˈbil-ət-ē, ak-\ *n*
ac·cep·tance \ik-ˈsep-təns, ak-\ *n* **1** : the act of accepting **2** : the state of being accepted or acceptable **3** : an accepted bill of exchange
ac·cep·ta·tion \ˌak-ˌsep-ˈtā-shən\ *n* : the generally understood meaning of a word
[1]**ac·cess** \ˈak-ˌses\ *n* **1** : capacity to enter or approach **2** : a way of approach : ENTRANCE
[2]**access** *vb* : to get at : gain access to
ac·ces·si·ble \ik-ˈses-ə-bəl, ak-, ek-\ *adj* **1** : capable of being reached ⟨~ by train⟩ **2** : capable of being used, seen, or known : OBTAINABLE ⟨~ information⟩ — **ac·ces·si·bil·i·ty** \-ˌses-ə-ˈbil-ət-ē\ *n*
ac·ces·sion \ik-ˈsesh-ən, ak-\ *n* **1** : something added **2** : increase by something added **3** : the act of acceding to an office or position
ac·ces·so·ry *also* **ac·ces·sa·ry** \ik-ˈses-(ə-)rē, ak-\ *n, pl* **-ries** **1** : something helpful but not essential **2** : a person who though not present abets or assists in the commission of an offense **syn** appurtenance, adjunct, appendage, appendix — **accessory** *adj*
ac·ci·dence \ˈak-səd-əns\ *n* : a part of grammar that deals with inflections
ac·ci·dent \ˈak-səd-ənt\ *n* **1** : an event occurring by chance or unintentionally **2** : CHANCE ⟨met by ~⟩ **3** : a nonessential property
ac·ci·den·tal \ˌak-sə-ˈdent-ᵊl\ *adj* **1** : happening unexpectedly or by chance **2** : happening without intent or through carelessness **syn** casual, fortuitous, incidental, chance — **ac·ci·den·tal·ly** \-ˈdent-(ᵊ-)lē\ *also* **ac·ci·dent·ly** \-ˈdent-lē\ *adv*
ac·claim \ə-ˈklām\ *vb* **1** : APPLAUD, PRAISE **2** : to declare by acclamation **syn** extol, laud, commend, hail — **acclaim** *n*
ac·cla·ma·tion \ˌak-lə-ˈmā-shən\ *n* **1** : loud eager applause **2** : an overwhelming affirmative vote by shouting or applause rather than by ballot
ac·cli·mate \ˈak-lə-ˌmāt, ə-ˈklī-mət\ *vb* **-mat·ed; -mat·ing** : to accustom to a new climate or situation — **ac·cli·ma·tion** \ˌak-lə-ˈmā-shən, ˌak-ˌlī-\ *n*
ac·cli·ma·tize \ə-ˈklī-mə-ˌtīz\ *vb* **-tized; -tiz·ing** **1** : ACCLIMATE **2** : to become acclimated — **ac·cli·ma·ti·za·tion** \-ˌklī-mət-ə-ˈzā-shən\ *n*
ac·cliv·i·ty \ə-ˈkliv-ət-ē\ *n, pl* **-ties** : an ascending slope
ac·co·lade \ˈak-ə-ˌlād\ *n* [F, fr. *accoler* to embrace, fr. L *ad-* to + *collum* neck] : a recognition of merit : AWARD
ac·com·mo·date \ə-ˈkäm-ə-ˌdāt\ *vb* **-dat·ed; -dat·ing** **1** : to make fit or suitable : ADAPT, ADJUST **2** : HARMONIZE, RECONCILE **3** : to provide with something needed **4** : to hold without crowding **5** : to undergo visual accommodation
ac·com·mo·dat·ing *adj* : OBLIGING
ac·com·mo·da·tion \ə-ˌkäm-ə-ˈdā-shən\ *n* **1** : something supplied to satisfy a need; *esp* : LODGINGS — usu. used in pl. **2** : the act of accommodating : ADJUSTMENT **3** : the automatic adjustment of the eye for seeing at different distances
ac·com·pa·ni·ment \ə-ˈkəmp-(ə-)nē-mənt\ *n* : something that accompanies another; *esp* : subordinate music to support a principal voice or instrument
ac·com·pa·ny \ə-ˈkəmp-(ə-)nē\ *vb* **-nied; -ny·ing** **1** : to go or occur with : ATTEND **2** : to play an accompaniment for — **ac·com·pa·nist** \-(ə-)nəst\ *n*
ac·com·plice \ə-ˈkäm-pləs, -ˈkəm-\ *n* : an associate in crime
ac·com·plish \ə-ˈkäm-plish, -ˈkəm-\ *vb* : to bring to completion **syn** achieve, effect, execute, perform — **ac·com·plish·er** *n*
ac·com·plished \-plisht\ *adj* **1** : EXPERT, SKILLED **2** : established beyond doubt
ac·com·plish·ment \ə-ˈkäm-plish-mənt, -ˈkəm-\ *n* **1** : COMPLETION **2** : something completed or effected **3** : an acquired excellence or skill
[1]**ac·cord** \ə-ˈkȯrd\ *vb* [ME *accorden*, fr. OF *acorder*, fr. L *ad-* to + *cord-*, *cor* heart] **1** : GRANT, CONCEDE **2** : AGREE, HARMONIZE — **ac·cor·dant** \-ˈkȯrd-ᵊnt\ *adj*
[2]**accord** *n* : AGREEMENT, HARMONY
ac·cor·dance \ə-ˈkȯrd-ᵊns\ *n* **1** : ACCORD **2** : the act of granting
ac·cord·ing·ly \ə-ˈkȯrd-iŋ-lē\ *adv* **1** : in accordance **2** : CONSEQUENTLY, SO
according to *prep* **1** : in conformity with ⟨paid *according to* ability⟩ **2** : as stated or attested by ⟨*according to* her he wasn't home⟩
[1]**ac·cor·di·on** \ə-ˈkȯrd-ē-ən\ *n* [G *akkordion*, fr. *akkord* chord] : a portable keyboard instrument with a bellows and reeds
[2]**accordion** *adj* : folding like the bellows of an accordion ⟨~ pleats⟩
ac·cost \ə-ˈkȯst\ *vb* [MF *accoster*, deriv. of L *ad-* to + *costa* rib, side] : to approach and speak to esp. aggressively
[1]**ac·count** \ə-ˈkau̇nt\ *n* **1** : a statement of business transactions **2** : an arrangement with a vendor to supply credit **3** : a statement of reasons, causes, or motives **4** : VALUE, IMPORTANCE ⟨a person of no ~⟩ **5** : a sum of money deposited in a bank and subject to withdrawal by the depositor — **on account of** : BECAUSE OF — **on no account** : under no circumstances — **on one's own account** : on one's own behalf
[2]**account** *vb* **1** : CONSIDER ⟨I ~ him lucky⟩ **2** : to give an explanation — used with *for*
ac·count·able \ə-ˈkau̇nt-ə-bəl\ *adj* **1** : ANSWERABLE, RESPONSIBLE **2** : EXPLICABLE — **ac·count·abil·i·ty** \-ˌkau̇nt-ə-ˈbil-ət-ē\ *n*
ac·coun·tant \ə-ˈkau̇nt-ᵊnt\ *n* : a person skilled in accounting — **ac·coun·tan·cy** \-ᵊn-sē\ *n*
account executive *n* : a business executive (as in an advertising agency) in charge of a client's account
ac·count·ing \ə-ˈkau̇nt-iŋ\ *n* : the art or system of keeping and analyzing financial records
ac·cou·tre *or* **ac·cou·ter** \ə-ˈküt-ər\ *vb* **-cou·tred** *or* **-cou·tered; -cou·tring** *or* **-cou·ter·ing** \-ˈküt-ə-riŋ, ˈkü-triŋ\ : EQUIP, OUTFIT
ac·cou·tre·ment *or* **ac·cou·ter·ment** \ə-ˈkü-trə-mənt, -ˈküt-ər-mənt\ *n* [F] **1** : the act of equipping **2** : an accessory item — usu. used in pl. **3** : an identifying characteristic
ac·cred·it \ə-ˈkred-ət\ *vb* **1** : to endorse or approve officially **2** : CREDIT — **ac·cred·i·ta·tion** \-ˌkred-ə-ˈtā-shən\ *n*
ac·cre·tion \ə-ˈkrē-shən\ *n* **1** : growth or enlargement esp. by addition from without **2** : a product of accretion
ac·crue \ə-ˈkrü\ *vb* **ac·crued; ac·cru·ing** **1** : to come by way of increase **2** : to be added by periodic growth — **ac·cru·al** \-əl\ *n*
acct *abbr* account; accountant
ac·cul·tur·a·tion \ə-ˌkəl-chə-ˈrā-shən\ *n* : cultural modification of an individual or group by borrowing and adapting traits from another culture
ac·cu·mu·late \ə-ˈkyü-myə-ˌlāt\ *vb* **-lat·ed; -lat·ing** [L *accumulare*, fr. *ad-* to + *cumulare* to heap up] : to heap or pile up **syn** amass, gather, collect, stockpile — **ac·cu·mu·la·tion** \-ˌkyü-myə-ˈlā-shən\ *n* — **ac·cu·mu·la·tor** \-ˈkyü-myə-ˌlāt-ər\ *n*
ac·cu·rate \ˈak-yə-rət\ *adj* : free from error : EXACT, PRECISE — **ac·cu·ra·cy** \-rə-sē\ *n* — **ac·cu·rate·ly** *adv* — **ac·cu·rate·ness** *n*
ac·cursed \ə-ˈkərst, -ˈkər-səd\ *or* **ac·curst** \ə-ˈkərst\ *adj* **1** : being under a curse **2** : DAMNABLE, EXECRABLE
ac·cus·al \ə-ˈkyü-zəl\ *n* : ACCUSATION
ac·cu·sa·tive \ə-ˈkyü-zət-iv\ *adj* : of, relating to, or being

a grammatical case marking the direct object of a verb or the object of a preposition — **accusative** *n*

ac·cuse \ə-ˈkyüz\ *vb* **ac·cused; ac·cus·ing** : to charge with an offense : BLAME — **ac·cu·sa·tion** \ˌak-yə-ˈzā-shən\ *n* — **ac·cus·er** *n*

ac·cused \ə-ˈkyüzd\ *n, pl* **accused** : the defendant in a criminal case

ac·cus·tom \ə-ˈkəs-təm\ *vb* : to make familiar through use or experience

ac·cus·tomed \ə-ˈkəs-təmd\ *adj* : USUAL, CUSTOMARY

[1]**ace** \ˈās\ *n* [ME *as* a die face marked with one spot, fr. OF, fr. L, unit, a copper coin] **1** : a playing card bearing a single large pip in its center **2** : a point (as in tennis) won by a single stroke **3** : a golf score of one stroke on a hole **4** : a combat pilot who has brought down five or more enemy planes **5** : one that excels

[2]**ace** *vb* **aced; ac·ing 1** : to score an ace against (an opponent) **2** : to defeat decisively

[3]**ace** *adj* : of first rank or quality

ac·er·bate \ˈas-ər-ˌbāt\ *vb* **-bat·ed; -bat·ing** : IRRITATE, EXASPERATE

acer·bic \ə-ˈsər-bik, a-\ *adj* : acid in temper, mood, or tone

acer·bi·ty \ə-ˈsər-bət-ē\ *n, pl* **-ties** : SOURNESS, BITTERNESS

ac·e·tate \ˈas-ə-ˌtāt\ *n* **1** : a salt or ester of acetic acid **2** : a textile fiber made from cellulose and acetic acid; *also* : a fabric or plastic made of this fiber

ace·tic \ə-ˈsēt-ik\ *adj* : of, relating to, or producing acetic acid or vinegar

acetic acid *n* : a colorless pungent liquid acid that is the chief acid of vinegar and is used esp. in making chemical compounds

ac·e·tone \ˈas-ə-ˌtōn\ *n* : a volatile flammable fragrant liquid compound used in making other chemical compounds and as a solvent

ace·tyl·cho·line \ə-ˌsēt-ᵊl-ˈkō-ˌlēn\ *n* : a compound that is released at nerve endings of the autonomic nervous system and is active in the transmission of nerve impulses

acet·y·lene \ə-ˈset-ᵊl-ən, -ᵊl-ˌēn\ *n* : a colorless flammable gas used as a fuel (as in welding and soldering)

ace·tyl·sal·i·cyl·ic acid \ə-ˈsēt-ᵊl-ˌsal-ə-ˌsil-ik-\ *n* : ASPIRIN 1

ache \ˈāk\ *vb* **ached; ach·ing 1** : to suffer a usu. dull persistent pain **2** : LONG, YEARN — **ache** *n*

achieve \ə-ˈchēv\ *vb* **achieved; achiev·ing** [ME *acheven*, fr. MF *achever* to finish, fr. *a-* to (fr. L *ad-*) + *chief* end, head, fr. L *caput*] : to gain by work or effort **syn** accomplish, attain, realize — **achieve·ment** *n* — **achiev·er** *n*

Achil·les' heel \ə-ˌkil-ēz-\ *n* [fr. the story that the Gk. warrior Achilles was vulnerable only in the heel] : a vulnerable point

Achilles tendon \ə-ˌkil-ēz-\ *n* : the strong tendon joining the muscles in the calf of the leg to the bone of the heel

ach·ro·mat·ic \ˌak-rə-ˈmat-ik\ *adj* : giving an image almost free from extraneous colors ⟨∼ lens⟩

achy \ˈā-kē\ *adj* **ach·i·er; ach·i·est** : afflicted with aches — **ach·i·ness** *n*

[1]**ac·id** \ˈas-əd\ *adj* **1** : sour or biting to the taste; *also* : sharp or sour in manner **2** : of or relating to an acid — **acid·i·ty** \ə-ˈsid-ət-ē\ *n*

[2]**acid** *n* **1** : a sour substance **2** : a usu. water-soluble chemical compound that has a sour taste, reacts with a base to form a salt, and reddens litmus **3** : LSD — **acid·ic** \ə-ˈsid-ik\ *adj*

acid·i·fy \ə-ˈsid-ə-ˌfī\ *vb* **-fied; -fy·ing 1** : to make or become acid **2** : to change into an acid — **acid·i·fi·ca·tion** \-ˌsid-ə-fə-ˈkā-shən\ *n*

ac·i·do·sis \ˌas-ə-ˈdō-səs\ *n, pl* **-do·ses** \-ˈdō-ˌsēz\ : an abnormal state of reduced alkalinity of the blood and body tissues

acid precipitation *n* : precipitation with above normal acidity that is caused esp. by atmospheric pollutants

acid rain *n* : acid precipitation in the form of rain

acid test *n* : a severe or crucial test

acid·u·lous \ə-ˈsij-ə-ləs\ *adj* : somewhat acid in taste or manner

ack *abbr* acknowledge; acknowledgment

ack–ack \ˈak-ˌak\ *n* [Brit. signalmen's telephone pron. of *AA*, abbr. of *antiaircraft*] : an antiaircraft gun; *also* : antiaircraft fire

ac·knowl·edge \ik-ˈnäl-ij, ak-\ *vb* **-edged; -edg·ing 1** : to recognize the rights or authority of **2** : to admit as true **3** : to express thanks for; *also* : to report receipt of **4** : to recognize as valid — **ac·knowl·edg·ment** *also* **ac·knowl·edge·ment** *n*

ACLU *abbr* American Civil Liberties Union

ac·me \ˈak-mē\ *n* [Gk *akmē*] : the highest point

ac·ne \ˈak-nē\ *n* [Gk *aknē*, MS var. of *akmē*, lit., point] : a skin disorder marked by inflammation of skin glands and hair follicles and by pimple formation esp. on the face

ac·o·lyte \ˈak-ə-ˌlīt\ *n* **1** : one who assists the clergyman in a liturgical service **2** : FOLLOWER

ac·o·nite \ˈak-ə-ˌnīt\ *n* **1** : MONKSHOOD **2** : a drug obtained from a common Old World monkshood

acorn \ˈā-ˌkorn, -kərn\ *n* : the nut of the oak

acorn squash *n* : an acorn-shaped dark green winter squash with a ridged surface and sweet yellow to orange flesh

acous·tic \ə-ˈkü-stik\ *or* **acous·ti·cal** \-sti-kəl\ *adj* **1** : of or relating to the sense or organs of hearing, to sound, or to the science of sounds **2** : deadening sound ⟨∼ tile⟩ **3** : operated by or utilizing sound waves — **acous·ti·cal·ly** \-k(ə-)lē\ *adv*

acous·tics \ə-ˈkü-stiks\ *n sing or pl* **1** : the science of sound **2** : the qualities in a room that make it easy or hard for a person in it to hear distinctly

ac·quaint \ə-ˈkwānt\ *vb* [ME *acquainten*, deriv. of L *ad-* + *cognoscere* to know] **1** : to cause to know personally **2** : INFORM

ac·quain·tance \ə-ˈkwānt-ᵊns\ *n* **1** : personal knowledge **2** : a person with whom one is acquainted — **ac·quain·tance·ship** *n*

ac·qui·esce \ˌak-wē-ˈes\ *vb* **-esced; -esc·ing** : to accept or comply without open opposition **syn** consent, agree, assent, accede — **ac·qui·es·cence** \-ˈes-ᵊns\ *n* — **ac·qui·es·cent** \-ᵊnt\ *adj* — **ac·qui·es·cent·ly** *adv*

ac·quire \ə-ˈkwī(ə)r\ *vb* **ac·quired; ac·quir·ing** : to come into possession of : GET

ac·quired \ə-ˈkwī(ə)rd\ *adj* **1** : gained by or as a result of effort or experience **2** : caused by environmental forces and not passed from parent to offspring in the genes ⟨∼ characteristics⟩

acquired immune deficiency syndrome *n* : AIDS

acquired immunodeficiency syndrome *n* : AIDS

ac·quire·ment \-mənt\ *n* **1** : ATTAINMENT, ACCOMPLISHMENT **2** : the act of acquiring

ac·qui·si·tion \ˌak-wə-ˈzish-ən\ *n* **1** : ACQUIREMENT **2** : something acquired

ac·quis·i·tive \ə-ˈkwiz-ət-iv\ *adj* : eager to acquire : GREEDY — **ac·quis·i·tive·ly** *adv* — **ac·quis·i·tive·ness** *n*

ac·quit \ə-ˈkwit\ *vb* **ac·quit·ted; ac·quit·ting 1** : to pronounce not guilty **2** : to conduct (oneself) usu. satisfactorily — **ac·quit·tal** \-ᵊl\ *n*

acre \ˈā-kər\ *n* **1** *pl* : LANDS, ESTATE **2** — see WEIGHT table

acre·age \ˈā-k(ə-)rij\ *n* : area in acres

ac·rid \ˈak-rəd\ *adj* **1** : sharp and biting in taste or odor **2** : bitterly irritating : CAUSTIC — **acrid·i·ty** \a-ˈkrid-ət-ē, ə-\ *n* — **ac·rid·ness** *n*

ac·ri·mo·ny \ˈak-rə-ˌmō-nē\ *n, pl* **-nies** : harsh or biting sharpness of language or feeling — **ac·ri·mo·ni·ous** \ˌak-rə-ˈmō-nē-əs\ *adj*

ac·ro·bat \ˈak-rə-ˌbat\ *n* [F *acrobate*, fr. Gk *akrobatēs*, fr. *akrobatos* walking up high, fr. *akros* topmost + *bainein* to go] : a performer of gymnastic feats — **ac·ro·bat·ic** \ˌak-rə-ˈbat-ik\ *adj*

ac·ro·bat·ics \ˌak-rə-ˈbat-iks\ *n sing or pl* : the performance of an acrobat

ac·ro·nym \ˈak-rə-ˌnim\ *n* : a word (as *radar*) formed from the initial letter or letters of each of the successive parts or major parts of a compound term

ac·ro·pho·bia \ˌak-rə-ˈfō-bē-ə\ *n* : abnormal dread of being at a great height

acrop·o·lis \ə-ˈkräp-ə-ləs\ *n* [Gk *akropolis*, fr. *akros* topmost + *polis* city] : the upper fortified part of an ancient Greek city

[1]**across** \ə-ˈkrȯs\ *adv* **1** : to or on the opposite side **2** : so as to be understandable or acceptable : OVER ⟨get the point ~⟩

[2]**across** *prep* **1** : to or on the opposite side of ⟨ran ~ the street⟩ ⟨standing ~ the street⟩ **2** : on at an angle ⟨slapped him ~ the face⟩; *esp* : on so as to cross ⟨a log ~ the road⟩

across–the–board *adj* **1** : placed to win if a competitor wins, places, or shows ⟨an ~ bet⟩ **2** : including all classes or categories ⟨an ~ wage increase⟩

acros·tic \ə-ˈkrȯs-tik\ *n* **1** : a composition usu. in verse in which the initial or final letters of the lines taken in order form a word or phrase **2** : a series of words of equal length arranged to read the same horizontally or vertically — **acrostic** *adj*

acryl·ic \ə-ˈkril-ik\ *n* **1** : ACRYLIC RESIN **2** : a paint in which the vehicle is acrylic resin **3** : a quick-drying synthetic fiber used for woven and knitted cloth

acrylic resin *n* : a glassy thermoplastic used for cast and molded parts or as coatings and adhesives

[1]**act** \ˈakt\ *n* **1** : a thing done : DEED **2** : STATUTE, DECREE **3** : a main division of a play; *also* : an item on a variety program **4** : an instance of insincere behavior : PRETENSE

[2]**act** *vb* **1** : to perform by action esp. on the stage; *also* : FEIGN, SIMULATE, PRETEND **2** : to conduct oneself : BEHAVE **3** : to perform a specified function **4** : to produce an effect

[3]**act** *abbr* **1** active **2** actual

ACT *abbr* Australian Capital Territory

actg *abbr* acting

ACTH \ˌā-ˌsē-(ˌ)tē-ˈāch\ *n* : a protein hormone of the pituitary gland that stimulates the adrenal cortex

act·ing \ˈak-tiŋ\ *adj* : doing duty temporarily or for another ⟨~ president⟩

ac·tin·i·um \ak-ˈtin-ē-əm\ *n* : a radioactive metallic chemical element — see ELEMENT table

ac·tion \ˈak-shən\ *n* **1** : a legal proceeding **2** : the manner or method of performing **3** : ACTIVITY **4** : ACT, DEED **5** : the accomplishment of a thing usu. over a period of time, in stages, or with the possibility of repetition **6** *pl* : CONDUCT **7** : COMBAT, BATTLE **8** : the events of a literary plot **9** : an operating mechanism ⟨the ~ of a gun⟩; *also* : the way it operates ⟨stiff ~⟩

ac·tion·able \ˈak-sh(ə-)nə-bəl\ *adj* : affording ground for an action or suit at law

ac·ti·vate \ˈak-tə-ˌvāt\ *vb* **-vat·ed; -vat·ing** **1** : to spur into action; *also* : to make active, reactive, or radioactive **2** : to treat (as carbon) so as to improve adsorptive properties **3** : to aerate (sewage) to favor the growth of organisms that cause decomposition **4** : to set up (a military unit) formally; *also* : to call to active duty — **ac·ti·va·tion** \ˌak-tə-ˈvā-shən\ *n*

ac·tive \ˈak-tiv\ *adj* **1** : causing action or change **2** : asserting that the grammatical subject performs the action represented by the verb ⟨~ voice⟩ **3** : BRISK, LIVELY **4** : presently in operation or use **5** : tending to progress or to cause degeneration ⟨~ tuberculosis⟩ — **active** *n* — **ac·tive·ly** *adv*

ac·tiv·ism \ˈak-ti-ˌviz-əm\ *n* : a doctrine or practice that emphasizes vigorous action for political ends — **ac·tiv·ist** \-vəst\ *n or adj*

ac·tiv·i·ty \ak-ˈtiv-ət-ē\ *n, pl* **-ties** **1** : the quality or state of being active **2** : an occupation in which one is engaged

ac·tor \ˈak-tər\ *n* : one that acts in a play or motion picture

ac·tress \ˈak-trəs\ *n* : a woman who is an actor

Acts \ˈak(t)s\ *or* **Acts of the Apostles** — see BIBLE table

ac·tu·al \ˈak-ch(ə-w)əl\ *adj* : really existing : REAL — **ac·tu·al·i·ty** \ˌak-chə-ˈwal-ət-ē\ *n* — **ac·tu·al·iza·tion** \ˌak-ch(ə-w)ə-lə-ˈzā-shən\ *n* — **ac·tu·al·ize** \ˈak-ch(ə-w)ə-ˌlīz\ *vb*

ac·tu·al·ly \ˈak-ch(ə-w)ə-lē\ *adv* : in fact or in truth : REALLY

ac·tu·ary \ˈak-chə-ˌwer-ē\ *n, pl* **-ar·ies** : one who calculates insurance risks and premiums — **ac·tu·ar·i·al** \ˌak-chə-ˈwer-ē-əl\ *adj*

ac·tu·ate \ˈak-chə-ˌwāt\ *vb* **-at·ed; -at·ing** **1** : to put into action **2** : to move to action — **ac·tu·a·tor** \-ˌwāt-ər\ *n*

act up *vb* **1** : MISBEHAVE **2** : to function improperly

acu·ity \ə-ˈkyü-ət-ē\ *n, pl* **-ities** : keenness of perception

acu·men \ə-ˈkyü-mən\ *n* : mental keenness and penetration **syn** discernment, insight, percipience, perspicacity

acu·pres·sure \ˈak-yu̇-ˌpresh-ər\ *n* : SHIATSU

acu·punc·ture \ˈak-yu̇-ˌpəŋk-chər\ *n* : an orig. Chinese practice of puncturing the body (as with needles) at specific points to cure disease or relieve pain — **acu·punc·tur·ist** \ˌak-yu̇-ˈpəŋk-chə-rəst\ *n*

acute \ə-ˈkyüt\ *adj* **acut·er; acut·est** [L *acutus*, pp. of *acuere* to sharpen, fr. *acus* needle] **1** : SHARP, POINTED **2** : containing less than 90 degrees ⟨an ~ angle⟩ **3** : sharply perceptive; *esp* : mentally keen **4** : SEVERE ⟨~ distress⟩; *also* : having a sudden onset, sharp rise, and short duration ⟨~ inflammation⟩ **5** : of, marked by, or being an accent mark having the form ´ — **acute·ly** *adv* — **acute·ness** *n*

ad \ˈad\ *n* : ADVERTISEMENT

AD *abbr* **1** after date **2** [L *anno Domini*] in the year of our Lord — often printed in small capitals

ad·age \ˈad-ij\ *n* : an old familiar saying : PROVERB, MAXIM

[1]**ada·gio** \ə-ˈdäj-(ē-ˌ)ō, -ˈdäzh-\ *adv or adj* [It] : in slow time — used as a direction in music

[2]**adagio** *n, pl* **-gios** **1** : an adagio movement **2** : a ballet duet or trio displaying feats of lifting and balancing

[1]**ad·a·mant** \ˈad-ə-mənt, -ˌmant\ *n* [ME, fr. OF, fr. L *adamant-, adamas* hardest metal, diamond, fr. Gk] : a stone believed to be impenetrably hard — **ad·a·man·tine** \ˌad-ə-ˈman-ˌtēn, -ˌtīn\ *adj*

[2]**adamant** *adj* : INFLEXIBLE, UNYIELDING — **ad·a·mant·ly** *adv*

Ad·am's apple \ˈad-əmz-\ *n* : the projection in front of the neck formed by the largest cartilage of the larynx

adapt \ə-ˈdapt\ *vb* : to make suitable or fit (as for a new use or for different conditions) **syn** adjust, accommodate, conform — **adapt·abil·i·ty** \ə-ˌdap-tə-ˈbil-ət-ē\ *n* — **adapt·able** *adj* — **ad·ap·ta·tion** \ˌad-ˌap-ˈtā-shən, -əp-\ *n* — **adap·tive** \ə-ˈdap-tiv\ *adj*

adapt·er *also* **adap·tor** \ə-ˈdap-tər\ *n* **1** : one that adapts **2** : a device for connecting two dissimilar parts of an apparatus **3** : an attachment for adapting apparatus for uses not orig. intended

ADC *abbr* **1** aide-de-camp **2** Aid to Dependent Children

add \ˈad\ *vb* **1** : to join to something else so as to increase in number or amount **2** : to combine (numbers) into one sum

ad·dend \ˈad-ˌend\ *n* : a number to be added to another

ad·den·dum \ə-ˈden-dəm\ *n, pl* **-da** \-də\ [L] : something added; *esp* : a supplement to a book

[1]**ad·der** \ˈad-ər\ *n* **1** : a poisonous European viper or a

related snake 2 : any of various harmless No. American snakes (as the hognose snake)

[2]**add·er** \ˈad-ər\ *n* : one that adds; *esp* : a device that performs addition

[1]**ad·dict** \ə-ˈdikt\ *vb* **1** : to devote or surrender (oneself) to something habitually or excessively **2** : to cause (a person) to become physiologically dependent upon a drug — **ad·dic·tive** \-ˈdik-tiv\ *adj*

[2]**ad·dict** \ˈad-(ˌ)ikt\ *n* : one who is addicted (as to a drug)

ad·dic·tion \ə-ˈdik-shən\ *n* : the quality or state of being addicted; *esp* : compulsive need for habit-forming drugs

ad·di·tion \ə-ˈdish-ən\ *n* **1** : the act or process of adding; *also* : something added **2** : the operation of combining numbers to obtain their sum **syn** accretion, increment, accession, augmentation

ad·di·tion·al \ə-ˈdish-(ə-)nəl\ *adj* : coming by way of addition : ADDED, EXTRA — **ad·di·tion·al·ly** \-ē\ *adv*

[1]**ad·di·tive** \ˈad-ət-iv\ *adj* **1** : of, relating to, or characterized by addition **2** : produced by addition — **ad·di·tiv·i·ty** \ˌad-ə-ˈtiv-ət-ē\ *n*

[2]**additive** *n* : a substance added to another in small quantities to effect a desired change in properties ⟨food ~*s*⟩

ad·dle \ˈad-ᵊl\ *vb* **ad·dled; ad·dling** \ˈad-(ə-)liŋ\ **1** : to throw into confusion : MUDDLE **2** : to become rotten ⟨*addled* eggs⟩

addn *abbr* addition

addnl *abbr* additional

add–on \ˈad-ˌȯn, -ˌän\ *n* : something added as a supplement; *esp* : a component (as of a computer system) that increases capability

[1]**ad·dress** \ə-ˈdres\ *vb* **1** : to direct the attention of (oneself) **2** : to direct one's remarks to : deliver an address to **3** : to mark directions for delivery on **4** : to identify (as a memory location) by an address

[2]**ad·dress** \ə-ˈdres, ˈad-ˌres\ *n* **1** : skillful management **2** : a formal speech : LECTURE **3** : the place where a person or organization may be communicated with **4** : the directions for delivery placed on mail **5** : a location (as in a computer's memory) where particular data is stored

ad·dress·ee \ˌad-ˌres-ˈē, ə-ˌdres-ˈē\ *n* : one to whom something is addressed

ad·duce \ə-ˈd(y)üs\ *vb* **ad·duced; ad·duc·ing** : to offer as argument, reason, or proof **syn** advance, allege, cite, submit

-ade \ˈād\ *n suffix* **1** : act : action ⟨block*ade*⟩ **2** : product; *esp* : sweet drink ⟨lime*ade*⟩

ad·e·nine \ˈad-ᵊn-ˌēn\ *n* : one of the purine bases that make up the genetic code of DNA and RNA

ad·e·noid \ˈad-(ᵊ-)ˌnȯid\ *n* : an enlarged mass of tissue near the opening of the nose into the throat — usu. used in pl. — **adenoid** *or* **ad·e·noi·dal** \ˌad-(ᵊ-)ˈnȯid-əl\ *adj*

aden·o·sine tri·phos·phate \ə-ˈden-ə-ˌsēn-trī-ˈfäs-ˌfāt\ *n* : ATP

[1]**ad·ept** \ˈad-ˌept\ *n* : EXPERT

[2]**adept** \ə-ˈdept\ *adj* : highly skilled : EXPERT — **adept·ly** *adv* — **adept·ness** *n*

ad·e·quate \ˈad-i-kwət\ *adj* : equal to or sufficient for a specific requirement — **ad·e·qua·cy** \-kwə-sē\ *n* — **ad·e·quate·ly** *adv*

ad·here \ad-ˈhiər, əd-\ *vb* **ad·hered; ad·her·ing 1** : to give support : maintain loyalty **2** : to stick fast : CLING — **ad·her·ence** \-ˈhir-əns\ *n* — **ad·her·ent** \-ənt\ *adj or n*

ad·he·sion \ad-ˈhē-zhən, əd-\ *n* **1** : the act or state of adhering **2** : the union of bodily tissues abnormally grown together after inflammation; *also* : the newly formed uniting tissue **3** : the molecular attraction between the surfaces of bodies in contact

[1]**ad·he·sive** \-ˈhē-siv, -ziv\ *adj* **1** : tending to adhere : STICKY **2** : prepared for adhering

[2]**adhesive** *n* : an adhesive substance

adhesive tape *n* : tape coated on one side with an adhesive mixture; *esp* : one used to secure bandages and cover wounds

[1]**ad hoc** \ˈad-ˈhäk, -ˈhōk\ *adv* [L, for this] : for the case at hand apart from other applications

[2]**ad hoc** *adj* : concerned with or formed for a particular purpose ⟨an *ad hoc* committee⟩ ⟨*ad hoc* solutions⟩

adi·a·bat·ic \ˌad-ē-ə-ˈbat-ik\ *adj* : occurring without loss or gain of heat — **adi·a·bat·i·cal·ly** \-i-k(ə-)lē\ *adv*

adieu \ə-ˈd(y)ü\ *n, pl* **adieus** *or* **adieux** \ə-ˈd(y)üz\ : FAREWELL — often used interjectionally

ad in·fi·ni·tum \ˌad-ˌin-fə-ˈnīt-əm\ *adv or adj* : without end or limit

ad in·ter·im \ad-ˈin-tə-rəm, -ˌrim\ *adv* : for the intervening time — **ad interim** *adj*

adi·os \ˌad-ē-ˈōs, ˌäd-\ *interj* [Sp *adiós*, lit., to God] — used to express farewell

ad·i·pose \ˈad-ə-ˌpōs\ *adj* : of or relating to animal fat : FATTY

adj *abbr* **1** adjective **2** adjutant

ad·ja·cent \ə-ˈjās-ᵊnt\ *adj* : situated near or next **syn** adjoining, contiguous, abutting, juxtaposed, conterminous

ad·jec·tive \ˈaj-ik-tiv\ *n* : a word that typically serves as a modifier of a noun — **ad·jec·ti·val** \ˌaj-ik-ˈtī-vəl\ *adj* — **ad·jec·ti·val·ly** \-ē\ *adv*

ad·join \ə-ˈjȯin\ *vb* : to be situated next to

ad·join·ing *adj* : touching or bounding at a point or line

ad·journ \ə-ˈjərn\ *vb* **1** : to suspend indefinitely or until a stated time **2** : to transfer to another place — **ad·journ·ment** *n*

ad·judge \ə-ˈjəj\ *vb* **ad·judged; ad·judg·ing 1** : JUDGE, ADJUDICATE **2** : to hold or pronounce to be : DEEM **3** : to award by judicial decision

ad·ju·di·cate \ə-ˈjüd-i-ˌkāt\ *vb* **-cat·ed; -cat·ing** : to settle judicially — **ad·ju·di·ca·tion** \ə-ˌjüd-i-ˈkā-shən\ *n*

ad·junct \ˈaj-ˌəŋkt\ *n* : something joined or added to another but not essentially a part of it **syn** appendage, appurtenance, accessory, appendix

ad·jure \ə-ˈju̇r\ *vb* **ad·jured; ad·jur·ing** : to command solemnly : urge earnestly **syn** beg, beseech, implore — **ad·ju·ra·tion** \ˌaj-ə-ˈrā-shən\ *n*

ad·just \ə-ˈjəst\ *vb* **1** : to bring to agreement : SETTLE **2** : to cause to conform : ADAPT, FIT **3** : REGULATE ⟨~ a watch⟩ — **ad·just·able** *adj* — **ad·just·er** *also* **ad·jus·tor** \ə-ˈjəs-tər\ *n* — **ad·just·ment** \ə-ˈjəs(t)-mənt\ *n*

ad·ju·tant \ˈaj-ət-ənt\ *n* : one who assists; *esp* : an officer who assists a commanding officer by handling correspondence and keeping records

ad·ju·vant \ˈaj-ə-vənt\ *n* : one that helps or facilitates; *esp* : something that enhances the effectiveness of medical treatment — **adjuvant** *adj*

[1]**ad–lib** \ˈad-ˈlib\ *vb* **ad–libbed; ad–lib·bing** : IMPROVISE — **ad–lib** *n*

[2]**ad–lib** *adj* : spoken, composed, or performed without preparation

ad lib \ˈad-ˈlib\ *adv* [NL *ad libitum*] **1** : at one's pleasure **2** : without limit

ad li·bi·tum \ad-ˈlib-ət-əm\ *adj* [NL, in accordance with desire] : omissible according to a performer's wishes — used as a direction in music

adm *abbr* administration; administrative

ADM *abbr* admiral

ad·man \ˈad-ˌman\ *n* : one who writes, solicits, or places advertisements

admin *abbr* administration

ad·min·is·ter \əd-ˈmin-ə-stər\ *vb* **-tered; -ter·ing** \-st(ə-)riŋ\ **1** : MANAGE, SUPERINTEND **2** : to mete out : DISPENSE **3** : to give ritually or remedially ⟨~ quinine for malaria⟩ **4** : to perform the office of administrator — **ad·min·is·tra·ble** \-strə-bəl\ *adj* — **ad·min·is·trant** \-strənt\ *n*

ad·min·is·tra·tion \əd-ˌmin-ə-ˈstrā-shən, (ˌ)ad-\ *n* **1** : the act or process of administering **2** : MANAGEMENT **3** : the body of persons directing the government of a country **4** : the term of office of an administrative officer or body — **ad·min·is·tra·tive** \əd-ˈmin-ə-ˌstrāt-iv\ *adj* — **ad·min·is·tra·tive·ly** *adv*

ad·min·is·tra·tor \əd-ˈmin-ə-ˌstrāt-ər\ *n* : one that administers; *esp* : one who settles an intestate estate

ad·mi·ra·ble \ˈad-m(ə-)rə-bəl\ *adj* : worthy of admiration : EXCELLENT — **ad·mi·ra·bly** \-blē\ *adv*

ad·mi·ral \ˈad-m(ə-)rəl\ *n* [ME, fr. MF *amiral* admiral & ML *admiralis* emir, *admirallus* admiral, deriv. of Ar *amīr* commander] : a commissioned officer in the navy ranking next below a fleet admiral

ad·mi·ral·ty \ˈad-m(ə-)rəl-tē\ *n* **1** *cap* : a British government department formerly having authority over naval affairs **2** : the court having jurisdiction over maritime questions

ad·mire \əd-ˈmī(ə)r\ *vb* **ad·mired; ad·mir·ing** [MF *admirer*, fr. L *admirari*, fr. *ad-* to + *mirari* to wonder] : to regard with high esteem — **ad·mi·ra·tion** \ˌad-mə-ˈrā-shən\ *n* — **ad·mir·er** *n* — **ad·mir·ing·ly** \-ˈmī-riŋ-lē\ *adv*

ad·mis·si·ble \əd-ˈmis-ə-bəl\ *adj* : that can be or is worthy to be admitted or allowed : ALLOWABLE ⟨~ evidence⟩ — **ad·mis·si·bil·i·ty** \-ˌmis-ə-ˈbil-ət-ē\ *n*

ad·mis·sion \əd-ˈmish-ən\ *n* **1** : the granting of an argument **2** : the acknowledgment of a fact **3** : the act of admitting **4** : the privilege of being admitted **5** : a fee paid for admission

ad·mit \əd-ˈmit\ *vb* **ad·mit·ted; ad·mit·ting** **1** : PERMIT, ALLOW **2** : to allow to enter **3** : to recognize as genuine or valid — **ad·mit·ted·ly** *adv*

ad·mit·tance \əd-ˈmit-ᵊns\ *n* : permission to enter

ad·mix \ad-ˈmiks\ *vb* : MINGLE, MIX

ad·mix·ture \ad-ˈmiks-chər\ *n* **1** : something added in mixing **2** : MIXTURE

ad·mon·ish \ad-ˈmän-ish\ *vb* : to warn gently : reprove with a warning **syn** chide, reproach, rebuke, reprimand, reprove — **ad·mo·ni·tion** \ˌad-mə-ˈnish-ən\ *n* — **ad·mon·i·to·ry** \ad-ˈmän-ə-ˌtōr-ē\ *adj*

ad nau·se·am \ad-ˈnȯ-zē-əm\ *adv* [L] : to a sickening degree

ado \ə-ˈdü\ *n* **1** : bustling excitement : FUSS **2** : TROUBLE

ado·be \ə-ˈdō-bē\ *n* [Sp, fr. Ar *aṭ-ṭūb*, fr. Coptic *tōbe*] **1** : sun-dried brick; *also* : clay for making such bricks **2** : a structure made of adobe bricks — **adobe** *adj*

ad·o·les·cence \ˌad-ᵊl-ˈes-ᵊns\ *n* : the process or period of growth between childhood and maturity — **ad·o·les·cent** \-ᵊnt\ *adj or n*

adopt \ə-ˈdäpt\ *vb* **1** : to take (a child of other parents) as one's own child **2** : to take up and practice as one's own **3** : to accept formally and put into effect — **adop·tion** \-ˈdäp-shən\ *n*

adop·tive \ə-ˈdäp-tiv\ *adj* : made or acquired by adoption ⟨~ father⟩ — **adop·tive·ly** *adv*

ador·able \ə-ˈdōr-ə-bəl\ *adj* **1** : worthy of adoration **2** : extremely charming — **ador·ably** \-blē\ *adv*

adore \ə-ˈdōr\ *vb* **adored; ador·ing** [MF *adorer*, fr. L *adorare*, fr. *ad-* to + *orare* to speak, pray] **1** : WORSHIP **2** : to regard with reverent admiration **3** : to be extremely fond of — **ad·o·ra·tion** \ˌad-ə-ˈrā-shən\ *n*

adorn \ə-ˈdȯrn\ *vb* : to decorate with ornaments — **adorn·ment** *n*

ad·re·nal \ə-ˈdrēn-ᵊl\ *adj* : of, relating to, or being a pair of endocrine organs (**adrenal glands**) that are located near the kidneys and produce several hormones and esp. epinephrine

adren·a·line \ə-ˈdren-ᵊl-ən\ *n* : EPINEPHRINE

adrift \ə-ˈdrift\ *adv or adj* **1** : afloat without motive power or moorings **2** : without guidance or purpose

adroit \ə-ˈdrȯit\ *adj* [F, fr. OF, fr. *a-* to + *droit* right] **1** : dexterous with one's hands **2** : SHREWD, RESOURCEFUL **syn** canny, clever, cunning, ingenious — **adroit·ly** *adv* — **adroit·ness** *n*

ad·sorb \ad-ˈsȯrb, -ˈzȯrb\ *vb* : to take up (as molecules of gases) and hold on the surface of a solid or liquid — **ad·sorp·tion** \-ˈsȯrp-shən, -ˈzȯrp-\ *n* — **ad·sorp·tive** \-ˈsȯrp-tiv, -ˈzȯrp-\ *adj*

ad·u·late \ˈaj-ə-ˌlāt\ *vb* **-lat·ed; -lat·ing** : to flatter or admire excessively — **ad·u·la·tion** \ˌaj-ə-ˈlā-shən\ *n*

[1]**adult** \ə-ˈdəlt, ˈad-ˌəlt\ *adj* [L *adultus*, pp. of *adolescere* to grow up, fr. *ad-* to + *-olescere* (fr. *alescere* to grow)] : fully developed and mature — **adult·hood** *n*

[2]**adult** *n* : one that is adult; *esp* : a human being after an age (as 18) specified by law

adul·ter·ant \ə-ˈdəl-tə-rənt\ *n* : something used to adulterate another

adul·ter·ate \ə-ˈdəl-tə-ˌrāt\ *vb* **-at·ed; -at·ing** [L *adulterare*, fr. *ad-* to + *alter* other] : to make impure by mixing in a foreign or inferior substance — **adul·ter·a·tion** \-ˌdəl-tə-ˈrā-shən\ *n*

adul·tery \ə-ˈdəl-t(ə-)rē\ *n, pl* **-ter·ies** : sexual unfaithfulness of a married person — **adul·ter·er** \-tər-ər\ *n* — **adul·ter·ess** \-t(ə-)rəs\ *n* — **adul·ter·ous** \-t(ə-)rəs\ *adj*

ad·um·brate \ˈad-əm-ˌbrāt\ *vb* **-brat·ed; -brat·ing** **1** : to foreshadow vaguely : INTIMATE **2** : to suggest or disclose partially **3** : SHADE, OBSCURE — **ad·um·bra·tion** \ˌad-əm-ˈbrā-shən\ *n*

adv *abbr* **1** adverb **2** advertisement

ad va·lor·em \ˌad-və-ˈlōr-əm\ *adj* [L, according to the value] : imposed at a percentage of the value ⟨an *ad valorem* tax⟩

[1]**ad·vance** \əd-ˈvans\ *vb* **ad·vanced; ad·vanc·ing** **1** : to bring or move forward **2** : to assist the progress of **3** : to promote in rank **4** : to make earlier in time **5** : LEND **6** : PROPOSE **7** : to raise in rate : INCREASE — **ad·vance·ment** *n*

[2]**advance** *n* **1** : a forward movement **2** : IMPROVEMENT **3** : a rise esp. in price or value **4** : OFFER — **in advance** : BEFOREHAND

[3]**advance** *adj* : made, sent, or furnished ahead of time

ad·van·tage \əd-ˈvant-ij\ *n* **1** : superiority of position **2** : BENEFIT, GAIN **3** : the 1st point won in tennis after deuce — **ad·van·ta·geous** \ˌad-ˌvan-ˈtā-jəs, -vən-\ *adj* — **ad·van·ta·geous·ly** *adv*

ad·vent \ˈad-ˌvent\ *n* **1** *cap* : a penitential period beginning four Sundays before Christmas **2** : ARRIVAL; *esp, cap* : the coming of Christ

ad·ven·ti·tious \ˌad-vən-ˈtish-əs\ *adj* **1** : ACCIDENTAL, INCIDENTAL **2** : arising or occurring sporadically or in other than the usual location ⟨~ buds⟩ — **ad·ven·ti·tious·ly** *adv*

[1]**ad·ven·ture** \əd-ˈven-chər\ *n* **1** : a risky undertaking **2** : a remarkable and exciting experience — **ad·ven·tur·ous** \-ˈvench-(ə-)rəs\ *adj*

[2]**adventure** *vb* **-ven·tured; -ven·tur·ing** \-ˈvench-(ə-)riŋ\ : RISK, HAZARD

ad·ven·tur·er \əd-ˈvench-(ə-)rər\ *n* **1** : a person who engages in new and risky undertakings **2** : a person who follows a military career for adventure or profit **3** : a person who tries to gain wealth by questionable means

ad·ven·ture·some \əd-ˈven-chər-səm\ *adj* : inclined to take risks

ad·ven·tur·ess \əd-ˈvench-(ə-)rəs\ *n* : a female adventurer

ad·verb \ˈad-ˌvərb\ *n* : a word that typically serves as a modifier of a verb, an adjective, or another adverb — **ad·ver·bi·al** \ad-ˈvər-bē-əl\ *adj* — **ad·ver·bi·al·ly** \-ē\ *adv*

[1]**ad·ver·sary** \ˈad-və(r)-ˌser-ē\ *n, pl* **-sar·ies** : FOE

[2]**adversary** *adj* : involving antagonistic parties or interests

ad·verse \ad-ˈvərs, ˈad-ˌvərs\ *adj* **1** : acting against or in a contrary direction **2** : UNFAVORABLE — **ad·verse·ly** *adv*

ad·ver·si·ty \ad-ˈvər-sət-ē\ *n, pl* **-ties** : hard times : MISFORTUNE

ad·vert \ad-ˈvərt\ *vb* : REFER

ad·ver·tise \ˈad-vər-ˌtīz\ *vb* **-tised; -tis·ing 1** : INFORM, NOTIFY **2** : to call public attention to esp. in order to sell — **ad·ver·tis·er** *n*

ad·ver·tise·ment \ˌad-vər-ˈtīz-mənt; əd-ˈvərt-əs-mənt\ *n* **1** : the act of advertising **2** : a public notice intended to advertise something

ad·ver·tis·ing \ˈad-vər-ˌtī-ziŋ\ *n* : the business of preparing advertisements

ad·vice \əd-ˈvīs\ *n* **1** : recommendation with regard to a course of action : COUNSEL **2** : INFORMATION, REPORT

ad·vis·able \əd-ˈvī-zə-bəl\ *adj* : proper to be done : EXPEDIENT — **ad·vis·abil·i·ty** \-ˌvī-zə-ˈbil-ət-ē\ *n*

ad·vise \əd-ˈvīz\ *vb* **ad·vised; ad·vis·ing 1** : to give advice to : COUNSEL **2** : INFORM, NOTIFY **3** : CONSULT, CONFER — **ad·vis·er** *or* **ad·vi·sor** \-ˈvī-zər\ *n*

ad·vised \əd-ˈvīzd\ *adj* : thought out : CONSIDERED ⟨well-advised⟩ — **ad·vis·ed·ly** \-ˈvī-zəd-lē\ *adv*

ad·vise·ment \əd-ˈvīz-mənt\ *n* : careful consideration

ad·vi·so·ry \əd-ˈvīz-(ə-)rē\ *adj* **1** : having or exercising power to advise **2** : containing advice

¹**ad·vo·cate** \ˈad-və-kət, -ˌkāt\ *n* [deriv. of L *advocare* to summon, fr. *ad-* to + *vocare* to call] **1** : one who pleads another's cause **2** : one who argues or pleads for a cause or proposal — **ad·vo·ca·cy** \-və-kə-sē\ *n*

²**ad·vo·cate** \-ˌkāt\ *vb* **-cat·ed; -cat·ing** : to plead in favor of — **ad·vo·ca·tion** \ˌad-və-ˈkā-shən\ *n*

advt *abbr* advertisement

adz *or* **adze** \ˈadz\ *n* : a cutting tool that has a curved blade set at right angles to the handle and is used in shaping wood

AEC *abbr* Atomic Energy Commission

ae·gis \ˈē-jəs\ *n* [L, fr. Gk *aigis* goatskin] **1** : SHIELD, PROTECTION **2** : PATRONAGE, SPONSORSHIP

ae·o·li·an harp \ē-ˌō-lē-ən-\ *n* : a box with strings that produce musical sounds when wind blows on them

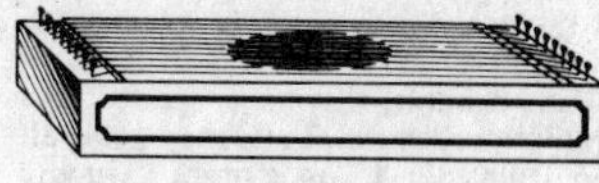

aeolian harp

ae·on \ˈē-ən, ˈē-ˌän\ *n* : an indefinitely long time : AGE

aer·ate \ˈa(-ə)r-ˌāt\ *vb* **aer·at·ed; aer·at·ing 1** : to supply (blood) with oxygen by respiration **2** : to supply or impregnate with air **3** : to combine or charge with gas — **aer·a·tion** \ˌa(-ə)r-ˈā-shən\ *n* — **aer·a·tor** \ˈa(-ə)r-ˌāt-ər\ *n*

¹**ae·ri·al** \ˈar-ē-əl, ā-ˈir-ē-əl\ *adj* **1** : inhabiting, occurring in, or done in the air **2** : AIRY **3** : of or relating to aircraft

²**aer·i·al** \ˈar-ē-əl\ *n* : ANTENNA 2

ae·ri·al·ist \ˈar-ē-ə-ləst, ā-ˈir-\ *n* : a performer of feats above the ground esp. on a flying trapeze

ae·rie \ˈa(ə)r-ē, ˈi(ə)r-ē\ *n* : a highly placed nest (as of an eagle)

aer·o·bat·ics \ˌar-ə-ˈbat-iks\ *n sing or pl* : spectacular flying feats and maneuvers

aer·o·bic \ˌa(-ə)r-ˈō-bik\ *adj* : living or active only in the presence of oxygen ⟨~ bacteria⟩ — **aer·obe** \ˈa(-ə)r-ˌōb\ *n* — **aer·o·bi·cal·ly** \-bi-k(ə-)lē\ *adv*

aer·o·bics \-biks\ *n sing or pl* : a system of exercises designed to improve the body's ability to take in and use oxygen

aero·drome \ˈar-ə-ˌdrōm\ *n, chiefly Brit* : AIRFIELD, AIRPORT

aero·dy·nam·ics \ˌar-ō-dī-ˈnam-iks\ *n* : the science dealing with the forces acting on bodies in motion in a gas (as air) — **aero·dy·nam·ic** \-ik\ *or* **aero·dy·nam·i·cal** \-i-kəl\ *adj* — **aero·dy·nam·i·cal·ly** \-i-k(ə-)lē\ *adv*

aero·naut \ˈar-ə-ˌnȯt\ *n* : one who operates or travels in an airship or balloon

aero·nau·tics \ˌar-ə-ˈnȯt-iks\ *n* : the science of aircraft operation — **aero·nau·ti·cal** \-i-kəl\ *or* **aero·nau·tic** \-ik\ *adj*

aero·plane \ˈar-ə-ˌplān\ *chiefly Brit var of* AIRPLANE

aero·sol \ˈar-ə-ˌsäl, -ˌsȯl\ *n* **1** : a suspension of fine solid or liquid particles in a gas **2** : a substance (as an insecticide or cosmetic) dispensed from a pressurized container as an aerosol

aero·space \ˈar-ō-ˌspās\ *n* : the earth's atmosphere and the space beyond — **aerospace** *adj*

aery \ˈa(ə)r-ē\ *adj* **aer·i·er; -est** : having an aerial quality : ETHEREAL

aes·thete \ˈes-ˌthēt\ *n* : a person having or affecting sensitivity to beauty esp. in art

aes·thet·ic \es-ˈthet-ik\ *adj* **1** : of or relating to aesthetics : ARTISTIC **2** : appreciative of the beautiful — **aes·thet·i·cal·ly** \-i-k(ə-)lē\ *adv*

aes·thet·ics \-ˈthet-iks\ *n* : a branch of philosophy dealing with the nature, creation, and appreciation of beauty

aes·ti·vate *var of* ESTIVATE

AF *abbr* **1** air force **2** audio frequency

¹**afar** \ə-ˈfär\ *adv* : from, at, or to a great distance

²**afar** *n* : a great distance

AFB *abbr* air force base

AFC *abbr* **1** American Football Conference **2** automatic frequency control

AFDC *abbr* Aid to Families with Dependent Children

af·fa·ble \ˈaf-ə-bəl\ *adj* : courteous and agreeable in conversation — **af·fa·bil·i·ty** \ˌaf-ə-ˈbil-ət-ē\ *n* — **af·fa·bly** \ˈaf-ə-blē\ *adv*

af·fair \ə-ˈfaər\ *n* [ME *affaire*, fr. MF, fr. *a faire* to do] **1** : something that relates to or involves one : CONCERN **2** : a romantic or sexual attachment of limited duration

¹**af·fect** \ə-ˈfekt, a-\ *vb* **1** : to be fond of using or wearing **2** : SIMULATE, ASSUME, PRETEND

²**affect** *vb* : to produce an effect on : INFLUENCE, IMPRESS

af·fec·ta·tion \ˌaf-ˌek-ˈtā-shən\ *n* : an attitude or mode of behavior assumed by a person in an effort to impress others

af·fect·ed \ə-ˈfek-təd, a-\ *adj* **1** : pretending to some trait which is not natural **2** : artificially assumed to impress others — **af·fect·ed·ly** *adv*

af·fect·ing \ə-ˈfek-tiŋ, a-\ *adj* : arousing pity, sympathy, or sorrow ⟨an ~ story⟩ — **af·fect·ing·ly** *adv*

¹**af·fec·tion** \ə-ˈfek-shən\ *n* : tender attachment : LOVE — **af·fec·tion·ate** \-sh(ə-)nət\ *adj* — **af·fec·tion·ate·ly** *adv*

²**affection** *n* : DISEASE, DISORDER ⟨an ~ of the brain⟩

af·fer·ent \ˈaf-ə-rənt, -ˌer-ənt\ *adj* : bearing or conducting inward toward a more central part and esp. a nerve center (as the brain or spinal cord) ⟨~ nerves⟩

af·fi·ance \ə-ˈfī-əns\ *vb* **-anced; -anc·ing** : BETROTH, ENGAGE

af·fi·da·vit \ˌaf-ə-ˈdā-vət\ *n* [ML, he has made an oath] : a sworn statement in writing

¹**af·fil·i·ate** \ə-ˈfil-ē-ˌāt\ *vb* **-at·ed; -at·ing** : to associate as a member or branch — **af·fil·i·a·tion** \-ˌfil-ē-ˈā-shən\ *n*

²**af·fil·i·ate** \ə-ˈfil-ē-ət\ *n* : an affiliated person or organization

af·fin·i·ty \ə-ˈfin-ət-ē\ *n, pl* **-ties 1** : KINSHIP, RELATIONSHIP **2** : attractive force : ATTRACTION, SYMPATHY

af·firm \ə-ˈfərm\ *vb* **1a** : CONFIRM, RATIFY **b** : to assert positively **2** : to make a solemn and formal declaration or assertion in place of an oath **syn** aver, avow, avouch, declare, assert — **af·fir·ma·tion** \ˌaf-ər-ˈmā-shən\ *n*

¹**af·fir·ma·tive** \ə-ˈfər-mət-iv\ *adj* : asserting that the fact is so : POSITIVE

[2]**affirmative** *n* **1** : an expression of affirmation or assent **2** : the side that upholds the proposition stated in a debate
affirmative action *n* : an active effort to improve the employment or educational opportunities of members of minority groups and women
[1]**af·fix** \ə-ˈfiks\ *vb* : ATTACH, ADD
[2]**af·fix** \ˈaf-ˌiks\ *n* : one or more sounds or letters attached to the beginning or end of a word and serving to produce a derivative word or an inflectional form
af·fla·tus \ə-ˈflāt-əs\ *n* : divine inspiration
af·flict \ə-ˈflikt\ *vb* : to cause pain and distress to **syn** rack, try, torment, torture — **af·flic·tion** \-ˈflik-shən\ *n*
af·flic·tive \ə-ˈflik-tiv\ *adj* : causing affliction : DISTRESSING — **af·flic·tive·ly** *adv*
af·flu·ence \ˈaf-ˌlü-ən(t)s; a-ˈflü-, ə-\ *n* : abundant supply; *also* : WEALTH, RICHES — **af·flu·ent** \-ənt\ *adj*
af·ford \ə-ˈfōrd\ *vb* **1** : to manage to bear or bear the cost of without serious harm or loss **2** : PROVIDE, FURNISH
af·for·es·ta·tion \a-ˌfòr-ə-ˈstā-shən\ *n* : the act or process of establishing forest cover — **af·for·est** \a-ˈfòr-əst, -ˈfär-\ *vb*
af·fray \ə-ˈfrā\ *n* : FIGHT, FRAY
af·fright \ə-ˈfrīt\ *vb* : FRIGHTEN, ALARM — **affright** *n*
af·front \ə-ˈfrənt\ *vb* **1** : INSULT **2** : CONFRONT — **affront** *n*
af·ghan \ˈaf-ˌgan\ *n* : a blanket or shawl of colored wool knitted or crocheted in sections
Af·ghan \ˈaf-ˌgan\ *n* : a native or inhabitant of Afghanistan — **Afghan** *adj*
Afghan hound *n* : any of a breed of tall slim swift hunting dogs with a coat of silky thick hair and a long silky top knot
af·ghani \af-ˈgan-ē\ *n* — see MONEY table
afi·cio·na·do \ə-ˌfish(-ē)-ə-ˈnäd-ō, -ˌfis-ē-\ *n, pl* **-dos** [Sp, deriv. of *afición* affection] : DEVOTEE, FAN
afield \ə-ˈfēld\ *adv or adj* **1** : to, in, or on the field **2** : away from home **3** : out of the way : ASTRAY
afire \ə-ˈfī(ə)r\ *adj or adv* : being on fire : BURNING
AFL *abbr* American Football League
aflame \ə-ˈflām\ *adj or adv* : FLAMING
AFL-CIO *abbr* American Federation of Labor and Congress of Industrial Organizations
afloat \ə-ˈflōt\ *adj or adv* **1** : borne on or as if on the water **2** : being on board ship **3** : ADRIFT
aflut·ter \ə-ˈflət-ər\ *adj* **1** : FLUTTERING **2** : nervously excited
afoot \ə-ˈfu̇t\ *adv or adj* **1** : on foot **2** : in action : in progress
afore·men·tioned \ə-ˈfōr-ˈmen-chənd\ *adj* : mentioned previously
afore·said \-ˌsed\ *adj* : said or named before
afore·thought \-ˌthȯt\ *adj* : PREMEDITATED ⟨with malice ~⟩
a for·ti·o·ri \ˌä-ˌfȯrt-ē-ˈōr-ē\ *adv* [NL, lit., from the stronger (argument)] : with even greater reason
afoul of \ə-ˈfau̇l-əv\ *prep* **1** : in or into collision or entanglement with **2** : in or into conflict with
Afr *abbr* Africa; African
afraid \ə-ˈfrād, *South also* ə-ˈfre(ə)d\ *adj* : FRIGHTENED, FEARFUL
A–frame \ˈā-ˌfrām\ *n* : a building having triangular front and rear walls with the roof reaching to the ground
afresh \ə-ˈfresh\ *adv* : ANEW, AGAIN
Af·ri·can \ˈaf-ri-kən\ *n* **1** : a native or inhabitant of Africa **2** : NEGRO — **African** *adj*
African violet *n* : a tropical African plant widely grown indoors for its velvety fleshy leaves and showy purple, pink, or white flowers
Af·ri·kaans \ˌaf-ri-ˈkäns\ *n* : a language developed from 17th century Dutch that is one of the official languages of the Republic of So. Africa
[1]**Af·ro** \ˈaf-rō\ *adj* : having the hair shaped into a round bushy mass
[2]**Afro** *n, pl* **Afros** : an Afro hairstyle
Af·ro–Amer·i·can \ˌaf-rō-ə-ˈmer-ə-kən\ *n* : an American of African and esp. of Negroid descent — **Afro–American** *adj*
aft \ˈaft\ *adv* : near, toward, or in the stern of a ship or the tail of an aircraft
AFT *abbr* American Federation of Teachers
[1]**af·ter** \ˈaf-tər\ *adv* : AFTERWARD, SUBSEQUENTLY
[2]**after** *prep* **1** : behind in place **2** : later than **3** : intent on the seizure, mastery, or achievement of ⟨he's ~ your job⟩
[3]**after** *conj* : following the time when
[4]**after** *adj* **1** : LATER **2** : located toward the rear
af·ter·birth \ˈaf-tər-ˌbərth\ *n* : the placenta and membranes of the fetus that are expelled after childbirth
af·ter·burn·er \-ˌbər-nər\ *n* : a device incorporated in the tail pipe of a turbojet engine for injecting fuel into the hot exhaust gases and burning it to provide extra thrust
af·ter·care \-ˌkeər\ *n* : the care, nursing, or treatment of a convalescent patient
af·ter·deck \-ˌdek\ *n* : the rear half of the deck of a ship
af·ter·ef·fect \ˈaf-tə-rə-ˌfekt\ *n* : an effect that follows its cause after an interval
af·ter·glow \ˈaf-tər-ˌglō\ *n* : a glow remaining where a light has disappeared
af·ter·im·age \ˈaf-tə-ˌrim-ij\ *n* : a usu. visual sensation continuing after the stimulus causing it has ended
af·ter·life \ˈaf-tər-ˌlīf\ *n* : an existence after death
af·ter·math \-ˌmath\ *n* **1** : a second-growth crop esp. of hay **2** : CONSEQUENCES, EFFECTS **syn** aftereffect, upshot, result, outcome
af·ter·noon \ˌaf-tər-ˈnün\ *n* : the time between noon and evening
af·ter–shave \ˈaf-tər-ˌshāv\ *n* : a usu. scented lotion for the face after shaving
af·ter·taste \-ˌtāst\ *n* : a sensation (as of flavor) continuing after the stimulus causing it has ended
af·ter–tax \ˈaf-tər-ˌtaks\ *adj* : remaining after payment of taxes and esp. of income tax ⟨an ~ profit⟩
af·ter·thought \-ˌthȯt\ *n* : a later thought; *also* : something thought of later
af·ter·ward \ˈaf-tə(r)-wərd\ *or* **af·ter·wards** \-wərdz\ *adv* : at a later time
Ag *symbol* [L *argentum*] silver
AG *abbr* **1** adjutant general **2** attorney general
again \ə-ˈgen, -ˈgin\ *adv* **1** : once more : ANEW **2** : on the other hand **3** : in addition : BESIDES
against \ə-ˈgenst\ *prep* **1** : directly opposite to : FACING **2** : in opposition to **3** : as defense from **4** : so as to touch or strike ⟨threw him ~ the wall⟩; *also* : TOUCHING
[1]**agape** \ə-ˈgāp\ *adj or adv* : having the mouth open in wonder or surprise : GAPING
[2]**aga·pe** \ä-ˈgä-pā, ˈäg-ə-ˌpā\ *n* [Gk, lit., love] : self-giving loyal concern that freely accepts another and seeks his or her good
agar \ˈäg-ˌär\ *n* **1** : a jellylike substance extracted from a red alga and used esp. as a gelling and stabilizing agent in foods **2** : a culture medium containing agar
agar–agar \ˌäg-ˌär-ˈäg-ˌär\ *n* : AGAR
ag·ate \ˈag-ət\ *n* **1** : a striped or clouded quartz **2** : a playing marble of agate or of glass
aga·ve \ə-ˈgäv-ē\ *n* : any of a genus of spiny-leaved plants (as a century plant) related to the amaryllis
agcy *abbr* agency
[1]**age** \ˈāj\ *n* **1** : the length of time during which a being or thing has lived or existed **2** : the time of life at which some particular qualification is achieved; *esp* : MAJORITY **3** : the latter part of life **4** : a long time **5** : a period in history
[2]**age** *vb* **aged; ag·ing** *or* **age·ing 1** : to grow old or cause to grow old **2** : to become or cause to become mature or mellow
-age \ij\ *n suffix* **1** : aggregate : collection ⟨track*age*⟩ **2** : action : process ⟨haul*age*⟩ **3** : cumulative result of ⟨break*age*⟩ **4** : rate of ⟨dos*age*⟩ **5** : house or place of

⟨orphan*age*⟩ **6** : state : rank ⟨vassal*age*⟩ **7** : fee : charge ⟨post*age*⟩

aged \ˈā-jəd *for 1;* ˈājd *for 2*\ *adj* **1** : of advanced age **2** : having attained a specified age ⟨a man ~ 40 years⟩

age·less \ˈāj-ləs\ *adj* **1** : not growing old or showing the effects of age **2** : TIMELESS, ETERNAL ⟨an ~ story⟩

agen·cy \ˈā-jən-sē\ *n, pl* **-cies** **1** : one through which something is accomplished : INSTRUMENTALITY **2** : the office or function of an agent **3** : an establishment doing business for another **4** : an administrative division (as of a government) **syn** means, medium, vehicle

agen·da \ə-ˈjən-də\ *n* : a list of things to be done : PROGRAM

agent \ˈā-jənt\ *n* **1** : one that acts **2** : MEANS, INSTRUMENT **3** : a person acting or doing business for another **syn** attorney, deputy, proxy, delegate

Agent Orange *n* : an herbicide widely used in the Vietnam War that is composed of 2,4-D and 2,4,5-T and contains a toxic contaminant

agent pro·vo·ca·teur \ˈäzh-ˌäⁿ-prō-ˌväk-ə-ˈtər, ˈā-jənt-\ *n, pl* **agents provocateurs** \ˈäzh-ˌäⁿ-prō-ˌväk-ə-ˈtər, ˈā-jənts-prō-\ [F] : a person hired to infiltrate a group and incite its members to illegal action

age of consent : the age at which one is legally competent to give consent (as to marriage)

age–old \ˈāj-ˈōld\ *adj* : having existed for ages : ANCIENT

ag·er·a·tum \ˌaj-ə-ˈrāt-əm\ *n, pl* **-tums** : any of a large genus of tropical American plants that are related to the daisies and have small showy heads of blue or white flowers

Ag·ge·us \a-ˈgē-əs\ *n* — see BIBLE table

¹ag·glom·er·ate \ə-ˈgläm-ə-ˌrāt\ *vb* **-at·ed; -at·ing** [L *agglomerare* to heap up, join, fr. *ad-* to + *glomer-, glomus* ball] : to gather into a mass : CLUSTER — **ag·glom·er·a·tion** \-ˌgläm-ə-ˈrā-shən\ *n*

²ag·glom·er·ate \-rət\ *n* : rock composed of volcanic fragments

ag·glu·ti·nate \ə-ˈglüt-ᵊn-ˌāt\ *vb* **-nat·ed; -nat·ing** **1** : to cause to adhere : gather into a group or mass **2** : to cause (as red blood cells or bacteria) to collect into clumps — **ag·glu·ti·na·tion** \-ˌglüt-ᵊn-ˈā-shən\ *n*

ag·gran·dize \ə-ˈgran-ˌdīz, ˈag-rən-\ *vb* **-dized; -diz·ing** : to make great or greater — **ag·gran·dize·ment** \ə-ˈgran-dəz-mənt, -ˌdīz-; ˌag-rən-ˈdīz-\ *n*

ag·gra·vate \ˈag-rə-ˌvāt\ *vb* **-vat·ed; -vat·ing** **1** : to make more severe : INTENSIFY **2** : IRRITATE — **ag·gra·va·tion** \ˌag-rə-ˈvā-shən\ *n*

¹ag·gre·gate \ˈag-ri-gət\ *adj* : formed by the gathering of units into one mass

²ag·gre·gate \-ˌgāt\ *vb* **-gat·ed; -gat·ing** : to collect into one mass

³ag·gre·gate \-gət\ *n* : a mass or body of units or parts somewhat loosely associated with one another; *also* : the whole amount

ag·gre·ga·tion \ˌag-ri-ˈgā-shən\ *n* **1** : a group, body, or mass composed of many distinct parts **2** : the collecting of units or parts into a mass or whole

ag·gres·sion \ə-ˈgresh-ən\ *n* **1** : an unprovoked attack **2** : the practice of making attacks **3** : hostile, injurious, or destructive behavior or outlook esp. when caused by frustration — **ag·gres·sor** \-ˈgres-ər\ *n*

ag·gres·sive \ə-ˈgres-iv\ *adj* **1** : tending toward or exhibiting aggression; *esp* : marked by combative readiness **2** : marked by driving energy or initiative : ENTERPRISING — **ag·gres·sive·ly** *adv* — **ag·gres·sive·ness** *n*

ag·grieve \ə-ˈgrēv\ *vb* **ag·grieved; ag·griev·ing** **1** : to cause grief to **2** : to inflict injury on : WRONG

aghast \ə-ˈgast\ *adj* : struck with amazement or horror

ag·ile \ˈaj-əl\ *adj* : able to move quickly and easily — **agil·i·ty** \ə-ˈjil-ət-ē\ *n*

ag·i·tate \ˈaj-ə-ˌtāt\ *vb* **-tat·ed; -tat·ing** **1** : to move with an irregular rapid motion **2** : to stir up : EXCITE **3** : to discuss earnestly **4** : to attempt to arouse public feeling — **ag·i·ta·tion** \ˌaj-ə-ˈtā-shən\ *n* — **ag·i·ta·tor** \ˈaj-ə-ˌtāt-ər\ *n*

ag·it·prop \ˈaj-ət-ˌpräp\ *n* [Russ] : political propaganda promulgated esp. through the arts

agleam \ə-ˈglēm\ *adj* : GLEAMING

aglit·ter \ə-ˈglit-ər\ *adj* : GLITTERING

aglow \ə-ˈglō\ *adj* : GLOWING

ag·nos·tic \ag-ˈnäs-tik, əg-\ *adj* [Gk *agnōstos* unknown, unknowable, fr. *a-* un- + *gnōstos* known] : of or relating to the belief that the existence of any ultimate reality (as God) is unknown and prob. unknowable — **agnostic** *n* — **ag·nos·ti·cism** \-ˈnäs-tə-ˌsiz-əm\ *n*

ago \ə-ˈgō\ *adj or adv* : earlier than the present time

agog \ə-ˈgäg\ *adj* [MF *en gogues* in mirth] : full of excitement : EAGER

¹a–go–go \ä-ˈgō-ˌgō\ *n* [*Whisky à Gogo*, café and discotheque in Paris, France, fr. F *à gogo* galore] : a nightclub for dancing to pop music : DISCOTHEQUE

²a–go–go *adj* : GO-GO

ag·o·nize \ˈag-ə-ˌnīz\ *vb* **-nized; -niz·ing** : to suffer or cause to suffer agony — **ag·o·niz·ing·ly** *adv*

ag·o·ny \ˈag-ə-nē\ *n, pl* **-nies** [ME *agonie*, fr. L *agonia*, fr. Gk *agōnia* struggle, anguish, fr. *agōn* gathering, contest for a prize] : extreme pain of mind or body **syn** suffering, distress, misery

agony column *n* : a newspaper column of personal advertisements relating esp. to missing relatives or friends

ago·ra \ˌäg-ə-ˈrä\ *n, pl* **ago·rot** \-ˈrōt\ — see *shekel* at MONEY table

ag·o·ra·pho·bia \ˌag-ə-rə-ˈfō-bē-ə\ *n* : abnormal fear of being in open spaces — **ag·o·ra·pho·bic** \-ˈfō-bik, -ˈfäb-ik\ *adj or n*

agr *abbr* agricultural; agriculture

agrar·i·an \ə-ˈgrer-ē-ən\ *adj* **1** : of or relating to land or its ownership ⟨~ reforms⟩ **2** : of or relating to farmers or farming interests — **agrarian** *n* — **agrar·i·an·ism** *n*

agree \ə-ˈgrē\ *vb* **agreed; agree·ing** **1** : ADMIT, CONCEDE **2** : to be similar : CORRESPOND **3** : to express agreement or approval **4** : to be in harmony **5** : to settle by common consent **6** : to be fitting or healthful : SUIT

agree·able \ə-ˈgrē-ə-bəl\ *adj* **1** : PLEASING, PLEASANT **2** : ready to consent **3** : being in harmony : CONSONANT — **agree·able·ness** *n* — **agree·ably** \-blē\ *adv*

agree·ment \ə-ˈgrē-mənt\ *n* **1** : harmony of opinion or action **2** : mutual understanding or arrangement; *also* : a document containing such an arrangement

agric *abbr* agricultural; agriculture

ag·ri·cul·ture \ˈag-ri-ˌkəl-chər\ *n* : FARMING, HUSBANDRY — **ag·ri·cul·tur·al** \ˌag-ri-ˈkəlch-(ə-)rəl\ *adj* — **ag·ri·cul·tur·ist** \-rəst\ *or* **ag·ri·cul·tur·al·ist** \-(ə-)rə-ləst\ *n*

agron·o·my \ə-ˈgrän-ə-mē\ *n* : a branch of agriculture that deals with the raising of crops and the care of the soil — **ag·ro·nom·ic** \ˌag-rə-ˈnäm-ik\ *adj* — **agron·o·mist** \ə-ˈgrän-ə-məst\ *n*

aground \ə-ˈgraünd\ *adv or adj* : on or onto the bottom or shore ⟨ran ~⟩

agt *abbr* agent

ague \ˈā-gyü\ *n* : a fever (as malaria) with recurrent chills and sweating

ahead \ə-ˈhed\ *adv or adj* **1** : in or toward the front **2** : into or for the future ⟨plan ~⟩ **3** : in or toward a more advantageous position

ahead of *prep* **1** : in front or advance of **2** : in excess of : ABOVE

AHL *abbr* American Hockey League

ahoy \ə-ˈhȯi\ *interj* — used in hailing ⟨ship ~⟩

AI *abbr* artificial intelligence

[1]**aid** \ˈād\ *vb* : to provide with what is useful in achieving an end : ASSIST
[2]**aid** *n* **1** : ASSISTANCE **2** : ASSISTANT
AID *abbr* Agency for International Development
aide \ˈād\ *n* : a person who acts as an assistant; *esp* : a military officer assisting a superior
aide–de–camp \ˌād-di-ˈkamp, -ˈkäⁿ\ *n, pl* **aides–de–camp** \ˌādz-di-\ [F] : AIDE
aid·man \ˈād-ˌman\ *n* : an army medical corpsman attached to a field unit
AIDS \ˈādz\ *n* [*a*cquired *i*mmuno*d*eficiency *s*yndrome] : a serious disease associated with infection of the cells of the immune system by a retrovirus, occurring esp. in homosexual and bisexual men and in intravenous drug abusers, and recognized clinically usu. by a life-threatening infection (as pneumonia) or Kaposi's sarcoma or both in addition to marked depression of the immune system
AIDS–related complex *n* : a collection of symptoms (as fever, weight loss, and lymphadenopathy) that is associated with the presence of antibodies to the AIDS virus and is followed by the development of AIDS in a certain proportion of cases
AIDS virus *n* : the retrovirus associated with AIDS and the AIDS-related complex
ai·grette \ā-ˈgret, ˈā-ˌgret\ *n* [F, plume, egret] : a plume or decorative tuft for the head
ail \ˈāl\ *vb* **1** : to be the matter with : TROUBLE **2** : to be unwell
ai·lan·thus \ā-ˈlan-thəs\ *n* : any of a genus of Asian trees or shrubs with pinnate leaves and ill-scented greenish flowers
ai·le·ron \ˈā-lə-ˌrän\ *n* : a movable part of an airplane wing used in banking
ail·ment \ˈāl-mənt\ *n* : a bodily disorder
[1]**aim** \ˈām\ *vb* [ME *aimen*, fr. MF *aesmer* & *esmer;* MF *aesmer*, fr. OF, fr. *a-* to (fr. L *ad-*) + *esmer* to estimate, fr. L *aestimare*] **1** : to point a weapon at an object **2** : to direct one's efforts : ASPIRE **3** : to direct to or toward a specified object or goal
[2]**aim** *n* **1** : the direction of a weapon **2** : OBJECT, PURPOSE — **aim·less** \-ləs\ *adj* — **aim·less·ly** *adv* — **aim·less·ness** *n*
AIM *abbr* American Indian Movement
ain't \ˈānt\ **1** : are not **2** : is not **3** : am not — though disapproved by many and more common in less educated speech, used orally in most parts of the U.S. by many educated speakers esp. in the phrase *ain't I*
Ai·nu \ˈī-nü\ *n, pl* **Ainu** *or* **Ainus** **1** : a member of an indigenous Caucasoid people of Japan **2** : the language of the Ainu people
[1]**air** \ˈaər\ *n* **1** : the gaseous mixture surrounding the earth **2** : a light breeze **3** : COMPRESSED AIR ⟨~ sprayer⟩ **4** : AIRCRAFT ⟨~ patrol⟩ **5** : AVIATION ⟨~ safety⟩ **6** : the medium of transmission of radio waves; *also* : RADIO, TELEVISION **7** : the outward appearance of a person or thing : MANNER **8** : an artificial manner **9** : MELODY, TUNE
[2]**air** *vb* **1** : to expose to the air **2** : to expose to public view
air bag *n* : a bag designed to fill automatically with gas to protect automobile passengers in case of accident
air·boat *n* : a shallow-draft boat driven by an airplane propeller
air·borne \ˈaər-ˌbōrn\ *adj* : supported or transported by air
air brake *n* **1** : a brake operated by a piston driven by compressed air **2** : a surface for lowering an airplane's speed
air·brush \-ˌbrəsh\ *n* : a device for applying a fine spray (as of paint) by compressed air — **airbrush** *vb*
air–con·di·tion \ˌaər-kən-ˈdish-ən\ *vb* : to equip with an apparatus for filtering air and controlling its humidity and temperature — **air con·di·tion·er** \-ˈdish-(ə-)nər\ *n*
air·craft \ˈaər-ˌkraft\ *n, pl* **aircraft** : a vehicle for traveling through the air
aircraft carrier *n* : a warship with a deck on which airplanes can be launched and landed
air·drome \-ˌdrōm\ *n* : AIRPORT
air·drop \-ˌdräp\ *n* : delivery of cargo or personnel by parachute from an airplane in flight — **air–drop** *vb*
Aire·dale terrier \ˈaər-ˌdāl-\ *n* : any of a breed of large terriers with a hard wiry coat
air·fare \-ˌfaər\ *n* : fare for travel by airplane
air·field \ˈaər-ˌfēld\ *n* **1** : the landing field of an airport **2** : AIRPORT
air·flow \-ˌflō\ *n* : the motion of air relative to a body in it
air·foil \-ˌfȯil\ *n* : an airplane surface (as a wing or rudder) designed to produce reaction from the air
air force *n* : the military organization of a nation for air warfare
air·frame \-ˌfrām\ *n* : the structure of an airplane or rocket without the power plant
air·freight \-ˈfrāt\ *n* : freight transport by air in volume; *also* : the charge for this service
air gun *n* **1** : a gun operated by compressed air **2** : a hand tool that works by compressed air; *esp* : AIRBRUSH
air lane *n* : AIRWAY 1
air·lift \ˈaər-ˌlift\ *n* : transportation (as of supplies or passengers) by aircraft — **airlift** *vb*
air·line \-ˌlīn\ *n* : a transportation system using airplanes
air·lin·er \ˈaər-ˌlī-nər\ *n* : a large passenger airplane operated by an airline
air lock *n* : an airtight chamber separating areas of different pressure
air·mail \ˈaər-ˈmāl, -ˌmāl\ *n* : the system of transporting mail by airplane; *also* : mail so transported — **airmail** *vb*
air·man \-mən\ *n* **1** : an enlisted man in the air force in one of the three ranks below sergeant **2** : AVIATOR, PILOT
airman basic *n* : an enlisted man of the lowest rank in the air force
airman first class *n* : an enlisted person in the air force with a rank just below that of sergeant
air mass *n* : a large horizontally homogeneous body of air
air·mo·bile \ˈaər-ˌmō-bəl, -ˌbēl\ *adj* : of, relating to, or being a military unit whose members are transported to combat areas usu. by helicopter
air·plane \-ˌplān\ *n* : a fixed-wing aircraft heavier than air that is driven by a propeller or jet engine and supported by the reaction of the air against its wings
air·play \-ˌplā\ *n* : the playing of recorded material on the air by a radio station
air pocket *n* : a condition of the atmosphere that causes an airplane to drop suddenly
air police *n* : the military police of an air force
air·port \ˈaər-ˌpōrt\ *n* : a place maintained for the landing and takeoff of aircraft and for receiving and discharging passengers and cargo
air raid *n* : an attack by armed airplanes on a surface target
air·ship \ˈaər-ˌship\ *n* : a lighter-than-air aircraft having propulsion and steering systems
air·sick \-ˌsik\ *adj* : affected with motion sickness associated with flying — **air·sick·ness** *n*
air·space \-ˌspās\ *n* : the space above a nation and under its jurisdiction
air·speed \-ˌspēd\ *n* : the speed (as of an airplane) with relation to the air as distinguished from its speed relative to the earth
air·strip \-ˌstrip\ *n* : a runway without normal airport facilities
air·tight \ˈaər-ˈtīt\ *adj* **1** : so tightly sealed that no air can enter or escape **2** : leaving no opening for attack
air–to–air *adj* : launched from one airplane in flight at another; *also* : involving aircraft in flight
air·wave \ˈaər-ˌwāv\ *n* : AIR 6 — usu. used in pl.

air·way \ˈ-ˌwā\ *n* **1** : a regular route for airplanes **2** : AIRLINE

air·wor·thy \ˈ-ˌwər-thē\ *adj* : fit or safe for operation in the air ⟨an ~ plane⟩ — **air·wor·thi·ness** *n*

airy \ˈa(ə)r-ē\ *adj* **air·i·er; -est** **1** : LOFTY **2** : lacking in reality : EMPTY **3** : DELICATE **4** : BREEZY

aisle \ˈīl\ *n* [ME *ile*, fr. MF *aile* wing, fr. L *ala*] **1** : the side of a church nave separated by piers from the nave proper **2** : a passage between sections of seats

ajar \ə-ˈjär\ *adj or adv* : partly open

AK *abbr* Alaska

aka *abbr* also known as

AKC *abbr* American Kennel Club

akim·bo \ə-ˈkim-bō\ *adj or adv* : having the hand on the hip and the elbow turned outward

akin \ə-ˈkin\ *adj* **1** : related by blood **2** : similar in kind

Al *symbol* aluminum

AL *abbr* **1** Alabama **2** American League **3** American Legion

[1]**-al** \əl\ *adj suffix* : of, relating to, or characterized by ⟨direction*al*⟩

[2]**-al** *n suffix* : action : process ⟨rehears*al*⟩

Ala *abbr* Alabama

ALA *abbr* Automobile Legal Association

al·a·bas·ter \ˈal-ə-ˌbas-tər\ *n* **1** : a compact fine-textured usu. white and translucent gypsum mineral often carved into objects (as vases) **2** : a hard translucent calcite

à la carte \ˌal-ə-ˈkärt, ˌäl-\ *adv or adj* [F] : with a separate price for each item on the menu

alac·ri·ty \ə-ˈlak-rət-ē\ *n* : cheerful readiness : BRISKNESS

à la mode \ˌal-ə-ˈmōd, ˌäl-\ *adj* [F, according to the fashion] **1** : FASHIONABLE, STYLISH **2** : topped with ice cream

[1]**alarm** \ə-ˈlärm\ *also* **ala·rum** \ə-ˈlär-əm, -ˈlar-\ *n* [ME *alarme*, fr. MF, fr. It *all'arme*, lit., to the weapon] **1** : a warning signal **2** : the terror caused by sudden danger

[2]**alarm** *also* **alarum** *vb* **1** : to warn of danger **2** : to arouse to a sense of danger : FRIGHTEN

alarm·ist \ə-ˈlär-məst\ *n* : a person who alarms others esp. needlessly

alas \ə-ˈlas\ *interj* — used to express unhappiness, pity, or concern

al·ba·core \ˈal-bə-ˌkōr\ *n, pl* **-core** *or* **-cores** : any of several tunas

Al·ba·nian \al-ˈbā-nē-ən\ *n* : a native or inhabitant of Albania

al·ba·tross \ˈal-bə-ˌtrȯs, -ˌträs\ *n, pl* **-tross** *or* **-tross·es** : a large web-footed seabird related to the petrels

al·be·it \ȯl-ˈbē-ət, al-\ *conj* : even though : ALTHOUGH

al·bi·no \al-ˈbī-nō\ *n, pl* **-nos** : a person or lower animal lacking coloring matter in the skin, hair, and eyes — **al·bi·nism** \ˈal-bə-ˌniz-əm\ *n*

al·bum \ˈal-bəm\ *n* **1** : a book with blank pages used for making a collection (as of stamps) **2** : one or more phonograph records or tape recordings produced as a single unit

al·bu·men \al-ˈbyü-mən\ *n* **1** : the white of an egg **2** : ALBUMIN

al·bu·min \al-ˈbyü-mən\ *n* : any of numerous water-soluble proteins of blood, milk, egg white, and plant and animal tissues

al·bu·min·ous \al-ˈbyü-mə-nəs\ *adj* : containing or resembling albumen or albumin

alc *abbr* alcohol

al·cal·de \al-ˈkäl-dē\ *n* : the chief administrative and judicial officer of a Spanish or Spanish-American town

al·ca·zar \al-ˈkäz-ər, -ˈkaz-\ *n* [Sp *alcázar*, fr. Ar *al-qaṣr* the castle] : a Spanish fortress or palace

al·che·my \ˈal-kə-mē\ *n* : medieval chemistry chiefly concerned with efforts to turn base metals into gold — **al·che·mist** \ˈal-kə-məst\ *n*

al·co·hol \ˈal-kə-ˌhȯl\ *n* [NL, fr. ML, powdered antimony, fr. Sp, fr. Ar *al-kuḥul* the powdered antimony] **1** : a colorless flammable liquid that is the intoxicating element in fermented and distilled liquors **2** : any of various carbon compounds similar to alcohol **3** : beverages containing alcohol

[1]**al·co·hol·ic** \ˌal-kə-ˈhȯl-ik, -ˈhäl-\ *adj* **1** : of, relating to, caused by, or containing alcohol **2** : affected with alcoholism — **al·co·hol·i·cal·ly** \-i-k(ə-)lē\ *adv*

[2]**alcoholic** *n* : a person affected with alcoholism

al·co·hol·ism \ˈal-kə-ˌhȯl-ˌiz-əm\ *n* : continued excessive and usu. uncontrollable use of alcoholic drinks; *also* : the abnormal state associated with such use

al·cove \ˈal-ˌkōv\ *n* **1** : a nook or small recess opening off a larger room **2** : a niche or arched opening (as in a wall)

ald *abbr* alderman

al·der \ˈȯl-dər\ *n* : a tree or shrub related to the birches and growing in wet areas

al·der·man \ˈȯl-dər-mən\ *n* : a member of a city legislative body

ale \ˈāl\ *n* : an alcoholic beverage brewed from malt and hops that is usu. more bitter than beer

ale·a·tor·ic \ˌā-lē-ə-ˈtȯr-ik\ *adj* : improvised or random in character ⟨~ music⟩

ale·a·to·ry \ˈā-lē-ə-ˌtōr-ē\ *adj* : ALEATORIC

alee \ə-ˈlē\ *adv* : on or toward the lee

ale·house \ˈāl-ˌhau̇s\ *n* : a place where ale is sold to be drunk on the premises

[1]**alert** \ə-ˈlərt\ *adj* [It *all' erta*, lit., on the ascent] **1** : watchful against danger **2** : quick to perceive and act — **alert·ly** *adv* — **alert·ness** *n*

[2]**alert** *n* **1** : a signal given to warn of danger **2** : the period during which an alert is in effect

[3]**alert** *vb* **1** : WARN **2** : to make aware of

Aleut \ˌal-ē-ˈüt, ə-ˈlüt\ *n* **1** : a member of a people of the Aleutian and Shumagin islands and the western part of Alaska peninsula **2** : the language of the Aleuts

ale·wife \ˈāl-ˌwīf\ *n* : a food fish of the herring family abundant esp. on the Atlantic coast

Al·ex·an·dri·an \ˌal-ig-ˈzan-drē-ən\ *adj* **1** : of or relating to Alexander the Great **2** : HELLENISTIC

al·ex·an·drine \-ˈzan-drən\ *n, often cap* : a line of six iambic feet

al·fal·fa \al-ˈfal-fə\ *n* : a leguminous plant widely grown for hay and forage

al·fres·co \al-ˈfres-kō\ *adj or adv* [It] : taking place in the open air

alg *abbr* algebra

al·ga \ˈal-gə\ *n, pl* **al·gae** \ˈal-(ˌ)jē\ : any of a group of lower plants having chlorophyll but no vascular system and including seaweeds and related freshwater plants — **al·gal** \-gəl\ *adj*

al·ge·bra \ˈal-jə-brə\ *n* [ML, fr. Ar *al-jabr*] : a branch of mathematics using symbols (as letters) to explore the relationships between numbers and the operations used to work with them — **al·ge·bra·ic** \ˌal-jə-ˈbrā-ik\ *adj* — **al·ge·bra·ical·ly** \-ˈbrā-ə-k(ə-)lē\ *adv*

Al·ge·ri·an \al-ˈjir-ē-ən\ *n* : a native or inhabitant of Algeria — **Algerian** *adj*

AL·GOL *or* **Al·gol** \ˈal-ˌgäl, -ˌgȯl\ *n* [*algo*rithmic *l*anguage] : a language for programming a computer esp. to work scientific problems

Al·gon·qui·an \al-ˈgän-kwē-ən, -ˈgäŋ-\ *n* : a member of an American Indian people of the Ottawa river valley

al·go·rithm \ˈal-gə-ˌrith-əm\ *n* : a procedure for solving a problem (as in mathematics)

[1]**alias** \ˈā-lē-əs, ˈāl-yəs\ *adv* [L, otherwise, fr. *alius* other] : otherwise called

[2]**alias** *n* : an assumed or additional name

[1]**al·i·bi** \ˈal-ə-ˌbī\ *n* [L, elsewhere, fr. *alius* other] **1** : a plea offered by an accused person of not having been at the

scene of commission of an offense **2** : an excuse (as for failure)

²alibi *vb* **-bied; -bi·ing 1** : to make an excuse for **2** : to offer an excuse

¹alien \ˈā-lē-ən, ˈāl-yən\ *adj* : FOREIGN

²alien *n* : a foreign-born resident who has not been naturalized

alien·able \ˈāl-yə-nə-bəl, ˈā-lē-ə-nə-\ *adj* : transferable to the ownership of another ⟨~ property⟩

alien·ate \ˈā-lē-ə-ˌnāt, ˈāl-yə-\ *vb* **-at·ed; -at·ing 1** : to transfer (property) to another **2** : to make hostile where previously friendship had existed : ESTRANGE — **alien·ation** \ˌā-lē-ə-ˈnā-shən, ˌāl-yə-\ *n*

alien·ist \-nəst\ *n* : PSYCHIATRIST; *esp* : one specializing in the legal aspects of psychology

¹alight \ə-ˈlīt\ *vb* **alight·ed** *also* **alit** \ə-ˈlit\ **alight·ing 1** : to get down (as from a vehicle) **2** : to come to rest from the air **syn** settle, land, perch

²alight *adj* : lighted up

align *also* **aline** \ə-ˈlīn\ *vb* **1** : to bring into line **2** : to array on the side of or against a cause — **align·ment** *also* **aline·ment** *n*

¹alike \ə-ˈlīk\ *adj* : LIKE **syn** akin, analogous, similar, comparable

²alike *adv* : EQUALLY

al·i·ment \ˈal-ə-mənt\ *n* : FOOD, NUTRIMENT

al·i·men·ta·ry \ˌal-ə-ˈmen-t(ə-)rē\ *adj* : of, relating to, or functioning in nourishment or nutrition

alimentary canal *n* : a tube that extends from the mouth to the anus and functions in the digestion and absorption of food and the elimination of residues

al·i·mo·ny \ˈal-ə-ˌmō-nē\ *n, pl* **-nies** [L *alimonia* sustenance, fr. *alere* to nourish] : an allowance made to one spouse by the other for support pending or after legal separation or divorce

A–line \ˈā-ˌlīn\ *adj* : having a flared bottom and a close-fitting top ⟨an ~ skirt⟩

alive \ə-ˈlīv\ *adj* **1** : having life : LIVING **2** : being in force or operation **3** : SENSITIVE ⟨~ to the danger⟩ **4** : ANIMATED ⟨streets ~ with traffic⟩

aliz·a·rin \ə-ˈliz-ə-rən\ *n* : an orange or red crystalline compound made synthetically and used as a red dye

alk *abbr* alkaline

al·ka·li \ˈal-kə-ˌlī\ *n, pl* **-lies** *or* **-lis 1** : a substance (as a hydroxide) that has a bitter taste and neutralizes acids **2** : a mixture of salts in the soil of some dry regions in such amount as to make ordinary farming impossible — **al·ka·line** \-kə-lən, -ˌlīn\ *adj* — **al·ka·lin·i·ty** \ˌal-kə-ˈlin-ət-ē\ *n*

al·ka·loid \ˈal-kə-ˌlȯid\ *n* : any of various usu. basic and bitter organic compounds found esp. in seed plants

al·kane \ˈal-ˌkān\ *n* : a hydrocarbon in which each carbon atom is bonded to 4 other atoms

al·kyd \ˈal-kəd\ *n* : any of numerous thermoplastic synthetic resins used esp. for protective coatings

¹all \ˈȯl\ *adj* **1** : the whole of **2** : the greatest possible **3** : every one of

²all *adv* **1** : WHOLLY **2** : so much ⟨~ the better for it⟩ **3** : for each side ⟨the score is two ~⟩

³all *pron* **1** : every one : the whole number, quantity, or amount ⟨~ of you are welcome⟩ ⟨~ of the money is gone⟩ **2** : EVERYTHING

Al·lah \ˈal-ə, ä-ˈlä\ *n* [Ar] : the supreme being of Islam

all–Amer·i·can \ˌȯl-ə-ˈmer-ə-kən\ *adj* **1** : composed wholly of American elements **2** : representative of the U.S. as a whole; *esp* : selected as the best in the U.S. — **all–American** *n*

all–around \ˌȯl-ə-ˈrau̇nd\ *adj* : having ability in many fields : VERSATILE

al·lay \ə-ˈlā\ *vb* **1** : to reduce in severity **2** : to put at rest **syn** alleviate, lighten, relieve, ease, assuage

all clear *n* : a signal that a danger has passed

al·lege \ə-ˈlej\ *vb* **al·leged; al·leg·ing 1** : to state as a fact without proof **2** : to bring forward as a reason or excuse — **al·le·ga·tion** \ˌal-i-ˈgā-shən\ *n* — **al·leg·ed·ly** \ə-ˈlej-əd-lē\ *adv*

al·le·giance \ə-ˈlē-jəns\ *n* **1** : loyalty owed by a citizen to his government **2** : loyalty to a person or cause

al·le·go·ry \ˈal-ə-ˌgōr-ē\ *n, pl* **-ries** : the expression through symbolic figures and actions of truths or generalizations about human conduct or experience — **al·le·gor·i·cal** \ˌal-ə-ˈgȯr-i-kəl\ *adj*

¹al·le·gro \ə-ˈleg-rō, -ˈlā-grō\ *adv or adj* [It, merry] : in a brisk lively tempo — used as a direction in music

²allegro *n, pl* **-gros** : an allegro movement

al·le·lu·ia \ˌal-ə-ˈlü-yə\ *interj* : HALLELUJAH

al·ler·gen \ˈal-ər-jən\ *n* : something that causes allergy — **al·ler·gen·ic** \ˌal-ər-ˈjen-ik\ *adj*

al·ler·gist \ˈal-ər-jəst\ *n* : a specialist in allergies

al·ler·gy \ˈal-ər-jē\ *n, pl* **-gies** [G *allergie*, fr. Gk *allos* other + *ergon* work] : exaggerated or abnormal reaction (as by sneezing, itching, or rashes) to substances, situations, or physical states harmless to most people — **al·ler·gic** \ə-ˈlər-jik\ *adj*

al·le·vi·ate \ə-ˈlē-vē-ˌāt\ *vb* **-at·ed; -at·ing** : to make easier to be endured **syn** lighten, mitigate, relieve, allay — **al·le·vi·a·tion** \ə-ˌlē-vē-ˈā-shən\ *n*

al·ley \ˈal-ē\ *n, pl* **alleys 1** : a place for bowling; *esp* : a hardwood lane **2** : a narrow street or passageway esp. between buildings

al·ley·way \ˈal-ē-ˌwā\ *n* : ALLEY 2

All·hal·lows \ȯl-ˈhal-ōz\ *n, pl* **Allhallows** : ALL SAINTS' DAY

al·li·ance \ə-ˈlī-əns\ *n* : a union to promote common interests **syn** league, coalition, confederacy, federation

al·lied \ə-ˈlīd, ˈal-ˌīd\ *adj* : joined in alliance

al·li·ga·tor \ˈal-ə-ˌgāt-ər\ *n* [Sp *el lagarto* the lizard, fr. L *lacertus* lizard] : either of two large short-legged reptiles resembling crocodiles but having a shorter and broader snout

alligator

alligator pear *n* : AVOCADO

al·lit·er·ate \ə-ˈlit-ə-ˌrāt\ *vb* **-at·ed; -at·ing 1** : to form an alliteration **2** : to arrange so as to make alliteration

al·lit·er·a·tion \ə-ˌlit-ə-ˈrā-shən\ *n* : the repetition of initial sounds in adjacent words or syllables — **al·lit·er·a·tive** \-ˈlit-ə-ˌrāt-iv\ *adj*

al·lo·cate \ˈal-ə-ˌkāt\ *vb* **-cat·ed; -cat·ing** : ALLOT, ASSIGN — **al·lo·ca·tion** \ˌal-ə-ˈkā-shən\ *n*

al·lot \ə-ˈlät\ *vb* **al·lot·ted; al·lot·ting** : to distribute as a share or portion **syn** assign, apportion, allocate — **al·lot·ment** *n*

all–out \ˈȯl-ˈau̇t\ *adj* : using maximum energy or resources ⟨an ~ offensive⟩

all over *adv* : EVERYWHERE

al·low \ə-ˈlau̇\ *vb* **1** : to assign as a share ⟨~ time for rest⟩ **2** : to reckon as a deduction **3** : ADMIT, CONCEDE **4** : PERMIT **5** : to make allowance ⟨~ for expansion⟩ — **al·low·able** *adj*

al·low·ance \-əns\ *n* **1** : an allotted share **2** : money given regularly for expenses **3** : the taking into account of mitigating circumstances

al·loy \ˈal-ˌȯi, ə-ˈlȯi\ *n* **1** : a substance composed of metals fused together **2** : an admixture of something that debases — **al·loy** \ə-ˈlȯi, ˈal-ˌȯi\ *vb*

all right *adv* **1** : beyond doubt : CERTAINLY **2** : SATISFACTORILY **3** : YES — **all right** *adj*

All Saints' Day *n* : a church feast observed November 1 in honor of all the saints

All Souls' Day *n* : a day of prayer observed November 2 for the souls of the faithful departed

all·spice \ˈȯl-ˌspīs\ *n* : the berry of a West Indian tree of the myrtle family; *also* : the mildly pungent and aromatic spice made from it

[1]**all–star** \ˌȯl-ˌstär\ *adj* : composed wholly or chiefly of star performers

[2]**all–star** \ˈȯl-ˌstär\ *n* : a member of an all-star team

all told *adv* : with everything counted

al·lude \ə-ˈlüd\ *vb* **al·lud·ed; al·lud·ing** [L *alludere*, lit., to play with] : to refer indirectly or by suggestion — **al·lu·sion** \-ˈlü-zhən\ *n* — **al·lu·sive** \-ˈlü-siv\ *adj* — **al·lu·sive·ly** *adv* — **al·lu·sive·ness** *n*

al·lure \ə-ˈlu̇r\ *vb* **al·lured; al·lur·ing** : to entice by charm or attraction — **allure** *n* — **al·lure·ment** *n*

al·lu·vi·um \ə-ˈlü-vē-əm\ *n, pl* **-vi·ums** *or* **-via** \-vē-ə\ : soil material (as clay or gravel) deposited by running water — **al·lu·vi·al** \-vē-əl\ *adj or n*

[1]**al·ly** \ə-ˈlī, ˈal-ˌī\ *vb* **al·lied; al·ly·ing** : to unite in alliance

[2]**al·ly** \ˈal-ˌī, ə-ˈlī\ *n, pl* **allies** : one united with another in an alliance

-al·ly \(ə-)lē\ *adv suffix* : [2]-LY ⟨terrific*ally*⟩

al·ma ma·ter \ˌal-mə-ˈmät-ər\ *n* [L, fostering mother] **1** : a school, college, or university that one has attended **2** : the song or hymn of a school, college, or university

al·ma·nac \ˈȯl-mə-ˌnak, ˈal-\ *n* : a publication containing astronomical and meteorological data and often a miscellany of other information

al·man·dite \ˈal-mən-ˌdīt\ *n* : a deep red garnet containing iron and aluminum

al·mighty \ȯl-ˈmīt-ē\ *adj* **1** *often cap* : having absolute power over all ⟨*Almighty* God⟩ **2** : relatively unlimited in power

Almighty *n* : GOD 1

al·mond \ˈäm-ənd, ˈam-; ˈal-mənd\ *n* : a small tree related to the peach; *also* : the edible nutlike kernel of its fruit

al·mo·ner \ˈal-mə-nər, ˈäm-ə-\ *n* : a person who distributes alms

al·most \ˈȯl-ˌmōst, ȯl-ˈmōst\ *adv* : only a little less than : NEARLY

alms \ˈämz, ˈälmz\ *n, pl* **alms** [ME *almesse, almes*, fr. OE *ǣlmesse, ǣlms*, fr. L *eleemosyna* alms, fr. Gk *eleēmosynē* pity, alms, fr. *eleēmōn* merciful] : something given freely to relieve the poor

alms·house \-ˌhau̇s\ *n, Brit* : a privately financed home for the poor

al·oe \ˈal-ō\ *n* **1** : any of a large genus of succulent chiefly southern African plants related to the lilies **2** *pl* : the dried juice of the leaves of an aloe used as a strong laxative and tonic

aloft \ə-ˈlȯft\ *adv* **1** : high in the air **2** : on or to the higher rigging of a ship

alo·ha \ə-ˈlō-ə, ä-ˈlō-hä\ *interj* [Hawaiian] — used to express greeting or farewell

alone \ə-ˈlōn\ *adj* **1** : separated from others **2** : not including anyone or anything else : ONLY **syn** lonely, lonesome, lone, solitary — **alone** *adv*

[1]**along** \ə-ˈlȯŋ\ *prep* **1** : on or near in a lengthwise direction ⟨walk ~ the street⟩ ⟨sail ~ the coast⟩ **2** : at a point on or during ⟨stopped ~ the way⟩

[2]**along** *adv* **1** : FORWARD, ON **2** : as a companion or associate ⟨bring her ~⟩ **3** : all the time ⟨knew it all ~⟩

along·shore \ə-ˈloŋ-ˈshōr\ *adv or adj* : along the shore or coast

[1]**along·side** \-ˌsīd\ *adv* : along or by the side

[2]**alongside** *prep* : side by side with; *specif* : parallel to

alongside of *prep* : ALONGSIDE

aloof \ə-ˈlüf\ *adj* : removed or distant in interest or feeling : reserved — **aloof·ness** *n*

al·o·pe·cia \ˌal-ə-ˈpē-sh(ē-)ə\ *n* : BALDNESS

aloud \ə-ˈlau̇d\ *adv* : using the voice so as to be clearly heard

alp \ˈalp\ *n* : a high rugged mountain

al·paca \al-ˈpak-ə\ *n* : a So. American mammal related to the llama; *also* : its fine long woolly hair or cloth made from this

al·pha·bet \ˈal-fə-ˌbet, -bət\ *n* : the set of letters used in writing a language arranged in a conventional order

al·pha·bet·i·cal \ˌal-fə-ˈbet-i-kəl\ *or* **al·pha·bet·ic** \-ˈbet-ik\ *adj* **1** : arranged in the order of the letters of the alphabet **2** : of or employing an alphabet — **al·pha·bet·i·cal·ly** \-i-k(ə-)lē\ *adv*

al·pha·bet·ize \ˈal-fə-bə-ˌtīz\ *vb* **-ized; -iz·ing** : to arrange in alphabetical order — **al·pha·bet·iz·er** *n*

al·pha·nu·mer·ic \ˌal-fə-n(y)u̇-ˈmer-ik\ *adj* : consisting of letters and numbers and often other symbols ⟨an ~ code⟩ *also* : being a character in an alphanumeric system

al·pha particle \ˌal-fə-\ *n* : a positively charged particle identical with the nucleus of a helium atom that is ejected at high speed in certain radioactive transformations

alpha ray *n* : a stream of alpha particles

alpha rhythm *n* : ALPHA WAVE

alpha wave *n* : an electrical rhythm of the brain often associated with a state of wakeful relaxation

Al·pine \ˈal-ˌpīn\ *adj* **1** : relating to, located in, or resembling the Alps mountains of south central Europe **2** *often not cap* : of, relating to, or growing on upland slopes above the highest elevation where trees grow

al·ready \ȯl-ˈred-ē\ *adv* : prior to a specified or implied time : PREVIOUSLY

al·right \ȯl-ˈrīt\ *adv* : ALL RIGHT

al·so \ˈȯl-sō\ *adv* : in addition : TOO

al·so–ran \-ˌran\ *n* **1** : a horse or dog that finishes out of the money in a race **2** : a contestant that does not win

alt *abbr* **1** alternate **2** altitude

Alta *abbr* Alberta

al·tar \ˈȯl-tər\ *n* **1** : a structure on which sacrifices are offered or incense is burned in worship **2** : a table used as a center of ritual

al·tar·piece \ˈȯl-tər-ˌpēs\ *n* : a work of art that decorates the space above and behind the altar

[1]**al·ter** \ˈȯl-tər\ *vb* **al·tered; al·ter·ing** \-t(ə-)riŋ\ **1** : to make or become different **2** : CASTRATE, SPAY — **al·ter·a·tion** \ˌȯl-tə-ˈrā-shən\ *n*

[2]**alter** *abbr* alteration

al·ter·ca·tion \ˌȯl-tər-ˈkā-shən\ *n* : a noisy or angry dispute

al·ter ego \ˌȯl-tər-ˈē-gō\ *n* [L, lit., second I] : a second self; *esp* : a trusted friend

[1]**al·ter·nate** \ˈȯl-tər-ˌnāt, ˈal-\ *vb* **-nat·ed; -nat·ing** : to occur or cause to occur by turns — **al·ter·na·tion** \ˌȯl-tər-ˈnā-shən, ˌal-\ *n*

[2]**al·ter·nate** \-nət\ *adj* **1** : arranged or succeeding by turns **2** : every other **3** : being an alternative ⟨an ~ route⟩ — **al·ter·nate·ly** *adv*

[3]**alternate** *n* : SUBSTITUTE

alternating current *n* : an electric current that reverses its direction at regular intervals

al·ter·na·tive \ȯl-ˈtər-nət-iv, al-\ *adj* : that may be chosen in place of something else — **alternative** *n*

al·ter·na·tor \ˈȯl-tər-ˌnāt-ər, ˈal-\ *n* : an electric generator for producing alternating current

al·though *also* **al·tho** \ȯl-ˈt͟hō\ *conj* : in spite of the fact that : even though

al·tim·e·ter \al-ˈtim-ət-ər, ˈal-tə-ˌmēt-ər\ *n* : an instrument for measuring altitude

al·ti·tude \ˈal-tə-ˌt(y)üd\ *n* **1** : angular distance above the horizon **2** : vertical distance : HEIGHT **3** : the perpendicular distance in a geometric figure from the vertex to the base, from the vertex of an angle to the side opposite, or from the base to a parallel side or face

al·to \ˈal-tō\ *n, pl* **altos** [It, lit., high, fr. L *altus*] : the lowest female voice; *also* : a singer or instrument having the range of such a voice

al·to·geth·er \ˌȯl-tə-ˈgeth-ər\ *adv* **1** : WHOLLY **2** : on the whole

al·tru·ism \ˈal-trü-ˌiz-əm\ *n* : unselfish interest in the welfare of others — **al·tru·ist** \-əst\ *n* — **al·tru·is·tic** \ˌal-trü-ˈis-tik\ *adj* — **al·tru·is·ti·cal·ly** \-ti-k(ə-)lē\ *adv*

al·um \ˈal-əm\ *n* **1** : either of two colorless crystalline aluminum-containing compounds having a sweetish-sour taste and used esp. as an emetic or as an astringent and styptic **2** : a colorless aluminum salt used in purifying water and in tanning and dyeing

alu·mi·na \ə-ˈlü-mə-nə\ *n* : the oxide of aluminum occurring in nature as corundum and in bauxite

al·u·min·i·um \ˌal-yə-ˈmin-ē-əm\ *n, chiefly Brit* : ALUMINUM

alu·mi·nize \ə-ˈlü-mə-ˌnīz\ *vb* **-nized; -niz·ing** : to treat or coat with aluminum

alu·mi·num \ə-ˈlü-mə-nəm\ *n* : a silver-white malleable ductile light metallic element that is the most abundant metal in the earth's crust — see ELEMENT table

alum·na \ə-ˈləm-nə\ *n, pl* **-nae** \-(ˌ)nē\ : a woman graduate or former student of a college or school

alum·nus \ə-ˈləm-nəs\ *n, pl* **-ni** \-ˌnī\ [L, foster son, pupil, fr. *alere* to nourish] : a graduate or former student of a college or school

al·ways \ˈȯl-wēz, -wəz, -(ˌ)wāz\ *adv* **1** : at all times : INVARIABLY **2** : FOREVER

Alz·hei·mer's disease \ˈälts-ˌhī-mərz-, ˈalz-\ *n* : a degenerative disease of the central nervous system characterized esp. by premature senile mental deterioration

am *pres 1st sing of* BE

[1]**Am** *abbr* America; American

[2]**Am** *symbol* americium

[1]**AM** \ˈā-ˌem\ *n* : a broadcasting system using amplitude modulation; *also* : a radio receiver for broadcasts made by such a system — **AM** *adj*

[2]**AM** *abbr* **1** ante meridiem — often not cap. **2** [NL *artium magister*] master of arts

AMA *abbr* American Medical Association

amah \ˈäm-(ˌ)ä\ *n* : an Oriental female servant; *esp* : a Chinese nurse

amain \ə-ˈmān\ *adv, archaic* : with full force or speed

amal·gam \ə-ˈmal-gəm\ *n* **1** : an alloy of mercury with another metal used in making dental cements **2** : a mixture of different elements

amal·gam·ate \ə-ˈmal-gə-ˌmāt\ *vb* **-at·ed; -at·ing** : to unite into one body or organization — **amal·ga·ma·tion** \-ˌmal-gə-ˈmā-shən\ *n*

aman·u·en·sis \ə-ˌman-yə-ˈwen-səs\ *n, pl* **-en·ses** \-ˌsēz\ : one employed to write from dictation or to copy what another has written : SECRETARY

am·a·ranth \ˈam-ə-ˌranth\ *n* **1** : any of a large genus of coarse herbs sometimes grown for their showy flowers **2** : a flower that never fades

am·a·ran·thine \ˌam-ə-ˈran-thən, -ˌthīn\ *adj* : relating to or resembling an amaranth : UNFADING, UNDYING

am·a·ryl·lis \ˌam-ə-ˈril-əs\ *n* : any of various plants of a group related to the lilies; *esp* : any of several African herbs having bulbs and grown for their clusters of large showy flowers

amass \ə-ˈmas\ *vb* : ACCUMULATE

am·a·teur \ˈam-ə-ˌtər, -ət-ər, -ə-ˌt(y)u̇r, -ə-ˌchu̇r, -ə-chər\ *n* [F, fr. L *amator* lover, fr. *amare* to love] **1** : a person who engages in a pursuit for pleasure and not as a profession **2** : a person who is not expert — **amateur** *adj* — **am·a·teur·ish** \ˌam-ə-ˈtər-ish, -ˈt(y)u̇r-\ *adj* — **am·a·teur·ism** \ˈam-ə-ˌtər-ˌiz-əm, -ət-ə-ˌriz-, -ə-ˌt(y)u̇r-ˌiz-, -ˌchu̇r-ˌiz-, -chə-ˌriz-\ *n*

am·a·tive \ˈam-ət-iv\ *adj* : disposed or disposing to love : AMOROUS — **am·a·tive·ly** *adv* — **am·a·tive·ness** *n*

am·a·to·ry \ˈam-ə-ˌtōr-ē\ *adj* : of or expressing sexual love

amaze \ə-ˈmāz\ *vb* **amazed; amaz·ing** : to overwhelm with wonder : ASTOUND **syn** astonish, surprise, dumbfound — **amaze·ment** *n* — **amaz·ing·ly** *adv*

am·a·zon \ˈam-ə-ˌzän, -ə-zən\ *n* **1** *cap* : a member of a race of female warriors repeatedly warring with the ancient Greeks of mythology **2** : a tall strong masculine woman — **am·a·zo·ni·an** \ˌam-ə-ˈzō-nē-ən\ *adj, often cap*

amb *abbr* ambassador

am·bas·sa·dor \am-ˈbas-əd-ər\ *n* : a country's representative in a foreign land — **am·bas·sa·do·ri·al** \-ˌbas-ə-ˈdōr-ē-əl\ *adj* — **am·bas·sa·dor·ship** *n*

am·ber \ˈam-bər\ *n* : a yellowish or brownish fossil resin used esp. for ornamental objects; *also* : the color of this resin

am·ber·gris \ˈam-bər-ˌgris, -ˌgrēs\ *n* : a waxy substance from the sperm whale used in making perfumes

am·bi·dex·trous \ˌam-bi-ˈdek-strəs\ *adj* : using both hands with equal ease — **am·bi·dex·trous·ly** *adv*

am·bi·ence *or* **am·bi·ance** \ˈam-bē-əns, äⁿ-byäⁿs\ *n* : a surrounding or pervading atmosphere

am·bi·ent \ˈam-bē-ənt\ *adj* : SURROUNDING

am·big·u·ous \am-ˈbig-yə-wəs\ *adj* : capable of being understood in more than one way — **am·bi·gu·i·ty** \ˌam-bə-ˈgyü-ət-ē\ *n*

am·bi·tion \am-ˈbish-ən\ *n* [ME, fr. MF or L; MF, fr. L *ambition- ambitio*, lit., going around, fr. *ambitus*, pp. of *ambire*, fr. *ambi-* around + *ire* to go] : eager desire for success or power

am·bi·tious \am-ˈbish-əs\ *adj* : characterized by ambition — **am·bi·tious·ly** *adv*

am·biv·a·lence \am-ˈbiv-ə-ləns\ *n* : simultaneous attraction toward and repulsion from a person, object, or action — **am·biv·a·lent** \-lənt\ *adj*

[1]**am·ble** \ˈam-bəl\ *vb* **am·bled; am·bling** \-b(ə-)liŋ\ : to go at an amble

[2]**amble** *n* : an easy gait esp. of a horse

am·bro·sia \am-ˈbrō-zh(ē-)ə\ *n* : the food of the Greek and Roman gods — **am·bro·sial** \-zh(ē-)əl\ *adj*

am·bu·lance \ˈam-byə-ləns\ *n* : a vehicle equipped for carrying the injured or sick

am·bu·lant \ˈam-byə-lənt\ *adj* : moving about : AMBULATORY

[1]**am·bu·la·to·ry** \ˈam-byə-lə-ˌtōr-ē\ *adj* **1** : of, relating to, or adapted to walking **2** : able to walk about

[2]**ambulatory** *n, pl* **-ries** : a sheltered place (as in a cloister) for walking

am·bus·cade \ˈam-bə-ˌskād\ *n* : AMBUSH

am·bush \ˈam-ˌbu̇sh\ *n* : a trap by which concealed persons attack an enemy by surprise — **ambush** *vb*

amdt *abbr* amendment

ame·ba, ame·bic, ame·boid *var of* AMOEBA, AMOEBIC, AMOEBOID

ame·lio·rate \ə-ˈmēl-yə-ˌrāt\ *vb* **-rat·ed; -rat·ing** : to make or grow better : IMPROVE — **ame·lio·ra·tion** \-ˌmēl-yə-ˈrā-shən\ *n*

amen \(ˈ)ā-ˈmen, (ˈ)ä-\ *interj* — used esp. at the end of prayers to express solemn ratification or approval

ame·na·ble \ə-ˈmē-nə-bəl, -ˈmen-ə-\ *adj* **1** : ANSWERABLE **2** : easily managed : TRACTABLE

amend \ə-ˈmend\ *vb* **1** : to change for the better : IMPROVE **2** : to alter formally in phraseology

amend·ment \ə-ˈmen(d)-mənt\ *n* **1** : correction of faults **2** : the process of amending a parliamentary motion or a constitution; *also* : the alteration so proposed or made

amends \ə-ˈmen(d)z\ *n sing or pl* : compensation for injury or loss

ame·ni·ty \ə-ˈmen-ət-ē, -ˈmē-nət-\ *n, pl* **-ties** **1** : AGREEABLENESS **2** : something serving to comfort or convenience **3** : a gesture observed in social relationships

Amer *abbr* America; American

amerce \ə-ˈmərs\ *vb* **amerced; amerc·ing** **1** : to penalize by a fine determined by the court **2** : PUNISH — **amercement** *n*

Amer·i·can \ə-ˈmer-ə-kən\ *n* **1** : a native or inhabitant of No. or So. America **2** : a citizen of the U.S. — **American** *adj* — **Amer·i·can·ism** \-ə-kə-ˌniz-əm\ *n* — **Amer·i·can·iza·tion** \ə-ˌmer-ə-kə-nə-ˈzā-shən\ *n* — **Amer·i·can·ize** \ə-ˈmer-ə-kə-ˌnīz\ *vb*

Amer·i·ca·na \ə-ˌmer-ə-ˈkan-ə, -ˈkän-\ *n pl* : materials concerning or characteristic of America, its civilization, or its culture; *also* : a collection of these

American Indian *n* : a member of any of the aboriginal peoples of No. and So. America except the Eskimos

American plan *n* : a hotel plan whereby the daily rates cover the cost of room and meals

American Sign Language *n* : a sign language for the deaf in which meaning is conveyed by a system of hand gestures and placement

am·er·i·ci·um \ˌam-ə-ˈris(h)-ē-əm\ *n* : a radioactive metallic chemical element produced artificially from plutonium — see ELEMENT table

AmerInd *abbr* American Indian

Am·er·in·di·an \ˌam-ə-ˈrin-dē-ən\ *adj* : of or relating to American Indians or their culture — **Amerindian** *n*

am·e·thyst \ˈam-ə-thəst\ *n* [ME *amatiste,* fr. OF & L; OF, fr. L *amethystus,* fr. Gk *amethystos,* lit., remedy against drunkenness, fr. *a-* not + *methyein* to be drunk, fr. *methy* wine] : a gemstone consisting of clear purple or bluish violet quartz

ami·a·ble \ˈā-mē-ə-bəl\ *adj* **1** : AGREEABLE **2** : having a friendly and sociable disposition — **ami·a·bil·i·ty** \ˌā-mē-ə-ˈbil-ət-ē\ *n* — **ami·a·bly** \ˈā-mē-ə-blē\ *adv*

am·i·ca·ble \ˈam-i-kə-bəl\ *adj* : FRIENDLY, PEACEABLE — **am·i·ca·bly** \-blē\ *adv*

amid \ə-ˈmid\ *or* **amidst** \-ˈmidst\ *prep* : in or into the middle of : AMONG

amid·ships \ə-ˈmid-ˌships\ *adv* : in or near the middle of a ship

ami·no acid \ə-ˌmē-nō-\ *n* : any of numerous nitrogen-containing acids that include some which are used by cells to build proteins

[1]**amiss** \ə-ˈmis\ *adv* **1** : WRONGLY **2** : ASTRAY **3** : IMPERFECTLY

[2]**amiss** *adj* **1** : WRONG **2** : out of place

am·i·ty \ˈam-ət-ē\ *n, pl* **-ties** : FRIENDSHIP; *esp* : friendly relations between nations

am·me·ter \ˈam-ˌēt-ər\ *n* : an instrument for measuring electric current in amperes

am·mo \ˈam-ō\ *n* : AMMUNITION

am·mo·nia \ə-ˈmō-nyə\ *n* [NL, fr. L *sal ammoniacus* sal ammoniac (ammonium chloride), lit., salt of Ammon, fr. Gk *ammōniakos* of Ammon, fr. *Ammōn* Ammon, Amen, an Egyptian god near one of whose temples it was prepared] **1** : a colorless gaseous compound of nitrogen and hydrogen used in refrigeration and in the making of fertilizers and explosives **2** : a solution (**ammonia water**) of ammonia in water

am·mo·ni·um \ə-ˈmō-nē-əm\ *n* : an ion or chemical group derived from ammonia by combination with hydrogen

ammonium chloride *n* : a white crystalline volatile salt used in batteries and as an expectorant

am·mu·ni·tion \ˌam-yə-ˈnish-ən\ *n* **1** : projectiles fired from guns **2** : explosive items used in war **3** : material for use in attack or defense

Amn *abbr* airman

am·ne·sia \am-ˈnē-zhə\ *n* : abnormal loss of memory — **am·ne·si·ac** \-z(h)ē-ˌak\ *or* **am·ne·sic** \-zik, -sik\ *adj or n*

am·nes·ty \ˈam-nə-stē\ *n, pl* **-ties** : an act granting a pardon to a group of individuals — **amnesty** *vb*

am·nio·cen·te·sis \ˌam-nē-ō-ˌsen-ˈtē-səs\ *n, pl* **-te·ses** \-ˈtē-ˌsēz\ : the surgical insertion of a hollow needle through the abdominal wall and uterus of a pregnant female esp. to obtain fluid used to check for chromosomal abnormality and to determine sex

amoe·ba \ə-ˈmē-bə\ *n, pl* **-bas** *or* **-bae** \-(ˌ)bē\ : any of various tiny one-celled protozoans that lack permanent cell organs and occur esp. in water and soil — **amoe·bic** \-bik\ *adj*

amoe·boid \-ˌbȯid\ *adj* : resembling an amoeba esp. in moving or readily changing shape

amok \ə-ˈmək, -ˈmäk\ *or* **amuck** \-ˈmək\ *adv* : in a violently excited state ⟨run ~⟩

among \ə-ˈməŋ\ *also* **amongst** \-ˈməŋst\ *prep* **1** : in or through the midst of **2** : in the number or class of **3** : in shares to each of **4** : by common action of

amon·til·la·do \ə-ˌmän-tə-ˈläd-ō\ *n, pl* **-dos** [Sp] : a medium dry sherry

amor·al \ā-ˈmȯr-əl\ *adj* : neither moral nor immoral; *esp* : being outside the sphere to which moral judgments apply — **amor·al·ly** *adv*

am·o·rous \ˈam-(ə-)rəs\ *adj* **1** : inclined to love **2** : being in love — **am·o·rous·ly** *adv* — **am·o·rous·ness** *n*

amor·phous \ə-ˈmȯr-fəs\ *adj* **1** : SHAPELESS, FORMLESS **2** : not crystallized

am·or·tize \ˈam-ər-ˌtīz, ə-ˈmȯr-\ *vb* **-tized; -tiz·ing** : to extinguish (as a mortgage) usu. by payment on the principal at the time of each periodic interest payment — **amor·ti·za·tion** \ˌam-ərt-ə-ˈzā-shən, ə-ˌmȯrt-\ *n*

Amos \ˈā-məs\ — see BIBLE table

[1]**amount** \ə-ˈmau̇nt\ *vb* **1** : to reach as a total **2** : to be equivalent

[2]**amount** *n* **1** : the total number or quantity **2** : a principal sum plus the interest on it

amour \ə-ˈmu̇r, ä-, a-\ *n* : a love affair esp. when illicit

amour pro·pre \ˌam-ˌu̇r-ˈprōprᵊ, ˌäm-ˌu̇r-ˈprȯprᵊ\ *n* [F] : SELF-ESTEEM

[1]**amp** \ˈamp\ *n* : AMPLIFIER; *also* : a unit consisting of an electronic amplifier and a loudspeaker

[2]**amp** *abbr* ampere

am·per·age \ˈam-p(ə-)rij\ *n* : the strength of a current of electricity expressed in amperes

am·pere \ˈam-ˌpiər\ *n* : a unit of electric current equivalent to a steady current produced by one volt applied across a resistance of one ohm

am·per·sand \ˈam-pər-ˌsand\ *n* [fr. *and per se and,* spoken form of the phrase *& per se and,* lit., (the character) & by itself (stands for the word) *and*] : a character & used for the word *and*

am·phet·amine \am-ˈfet-ə-ˌmēn, -mən\ *n* : a compound or one of its derivatives used esp. as a stimulant of the nervous system

am·phib·i·an \am-ˈfib-ē-ən\ *n* **1** : an amphibious organism; *esp* : any of a class of animals (as frogs and newts) intermediate between fishes and reptiles **2** : a vehicle designed to operate on both land and water

am·phib·i·ous \am-ˈfib-ē-əs\ *adj* [Gk *amphibios,* lit., living a double life, fr. *amphi-* on both sides + *bios* mode of *life*] **1** : able to live both on land and in water **2** : adapted for both land and water **3** : made by joint action of land, sea, and air forces invading from the sea; *also* : trained for such action

am·phi·bole \ˈam-fə-ˌbōl\ *n* : any of a group of rock-forming minerals containing calcium, magnesium, iron, aluminum, and sodium combined with silica

am·phi·the·ater \ˈam-fə-ˌthē-ət-ər\ *n* : an oval or circular structure with rising tiers of seats around an arena

am·pho·ra \ˈam-fə-rə\ *n, pl* **-rae** \-ˌrē\ *or* **-ras** : an ancient

Greek jar or vase with two handles that rise almost to the level of the mouth

am·ple \ˈam-pəl\ *adj* **am·pler** \-plər\ **am·plest** \-pləst\ **1** : LARGE, CAPACIOUS **2** : enough to satisfy : ABUNDANT — **am·ply** \-plē\ *adv*

am·pli·fy \ˈam-plə-ˌfī\ *vb* **-fied; -fy·ing 1** : to expand by extended treatment **2** : to increase (voltage, current, or power) in magnitude or strength **3** : to make louder — **am·pli·fi·ca·tion** \ˌam-plə-fə-ˈkā-shən\ *n* — **am·pli·fi·er** \ˈam-plə-ˌfī(-ə)r\ *n*

am·pli·tude \-ˌt(y)üd\ *n* **1** : ample extent : FULLNESS **2** : the extent of a vibratory movement (as of a pendulum) or of an oscillation (as of an alternating current or a radio wave)

amplitude modulation *n* **1** : modulation of the amplitude of a radio carrier wave in accordance with the strength of the signal **2** : a broadcasting system using amplitude modulation

am·poule *or* **am·pule** *also* **am·pul** \ˈam-ˌpyül, -pül\ *n* : a small sealed bulbous glass vessel used to hold a solution for hypodermic injection

am·pu·tate \ˈam-pyə-ˌtāt\ *vb* **-tat·ed; -tat·ing** : to cut off ⟨~ a leg⟩ — **am·pu·ta·tion** \ˌam-pyə-ˈtā-shən\ *n*

am·pu·tee \ˌam-pyə-ˈtē\ *n* : one who has had a limb amputated

amt *abbr* amount

amuck \ə-ˈmək\ *var of* AMOK

am·u·let \ˈam-yə-lət\ *n* : an ornament worn as a charm against evil

amuse \ə-ˈmyüz\ *vb* **amused; amus·ing** : to entertain in a light or playful manner : DIVERT — **amuse·ment** *n*

AMVETS \ˈam-ˌvets\ *abbr* American Veterans (of World War II)

am·y·lase \ˈam-ə-ˌlās, -ˌlāz\ *n* : any of several enzymes that accelerate the breakdown of starch and glycogen

an \ən, (ˈ)an\ *indefinite article* : A — used before words beginning with a vowel sound

[1]**-an** \ən\ *or* **-ian** \(ē-)ən\ *also* **-ean** \(ē-)ən, ˈē-ən\ *n suffix* **1** : one that belongs to ⟨Americ*an*⟩ ⟨Boston*ian*⟩ ⟨crusta*cean*⟩ **2** : one skilled in or specializing in ⟨phonetic*ian*⟩

[2]**-an** *or* **-ian** *also* **-ean** *adj suffix* **1** : of or belonging to ⟨Americ*an*⟩ ⟨Florid*ian*⟩ **2** : characteristic of : resembling ⟨Mozart*ean*⟩

AN *abbr* airman (Navy)

an·a·bol·ic steroid \ˌan-ə-ˌbäl-ik-\ *n* : any of a group of synthetic hormones sometimes taken by athletes in training to increase temporarily the size of their muscles

anach·ro·nism \ə-ˈnak-rə-ˌniz-əm\ *n* **1** : the error of placing a person or thing in the wrong period **2** : one that is chronologically out of place — **anach·ro·nis·tic** \ə-ˌnak-rə-ˈnis-tik\ *adj*

an·a·con·da \ˌan-ə-ˈkän-də\ *n* : a large So. American snake that suffocates and kills its prey by constriction

an·a·dem \ˈan-ə-ˌdem\ *n, archaic* : GARLAND, CHAPLET

anae·mia, anae·mic *var of* ANEMIA, ANEMIC

an·aer·obe \ˈan-ə-ˌrōb\ *n* : an anaerobic organism

an·aer·o·bic \ˌan-ə-ˈrō-bik\ *adj* : living, active, or occurring in the absence of free oxygen

an·aes·the·sia, an·aes·thet·ic *var of* ANESTHESIA, ANESTHETIC

ana·gram \ˈan-ə-ˌgram\ *n* : a word or phrase made by transposing the letters of another word or phrase

[1]**anal** \ˈān-ᵊl\ *adj* **1** : of, relating to, or situated near the anus **2** : of, relating to, or characterized by the stage of psychosexual development in psychoanalytic theory during which one is concerned esp. with feces **3** : of, relating to, or characterized by personality traits (as parsimony and ill humor) considered typical of fixation at the anal stage of development

[2]**anal** *abbr* **1** analogy **2** analysis; analytic

an·al·ge·sia \ˌan-ᵊl-ˈjē-zhə\ *n* : insensibility to pain — **an·al·ge·sic** \-ˈjē-zik, -sik\ *adj*

an·al·ge·sic \-ˈjē-zik, -sik\ *n* : an agent for producing analgesia

analog computer \ˌan-ᵊl-ˌȯg-, -ˌäg-\ *n* : a computer that operates with numbers represented by directly measurable quantities (as voltages)

anal·o·gous \ə-ˈnal-ə-gəs\ *adj* : similar in one or more respects but not homologous

an·a·logue *or* **an·a·log** \ˈan-ᵊl-ˌȯg, -ˌag\ *n* **1** : something that is analogous or similar to something else **2** : an organ similar in function to one of another animal or plant but different in structure or origin

anal·o·gy \ə-ˈnal-ə-jē\ *n, pl* **-gies 1** : inference that if two or more things agree in some respects they will probably agree in others **2** : a likeness in one or more ways between things otherwise unlike — **an·a·log·i·cal** \ˌan-ᵊl-ˈäj-i-kəl\ *adj* — **an·a·log·i·cal·ly** \-i-k(ə-)lē\ *adv*

anal·y·sis \ə-ˈnal-ə-səs\ *n, pl* **-y·ses** \-ˌsēz\ [NL, fr. Gk, fr. *analyein* to break up, fr. *ana-* up + *lyein* to loosen] **1** : separation of a thing into the parts or elements of which it is composed **2** : an examination of a thing to determine its parts or elements; *also* : a statement showing the results of such an examination **3** : PSYCHOANALYSIS — **an·a·lyst** \ˈan-ᵊl-əst\ *n* — **an·a·lyt·ic** \ˌan-ᵊl-ˈit-ik\ *or* **an·a·lyt·i·cal** \-i-kəl\ *adj*

an·a·lyze \ˈan-ᵊl-ˌīz\ *vb* **-lyzed; -lyz·ing** : to make an analysis of

an·a·pest \ˈan-ə-ˌpest\ *n* : a metrical foot of two unaccented syllables followed by one accented syllable — **an·a·pes·tic** \ˌan-ə-ˈpes-tik\ *adj or n*

an·ar·chism \ˈan-ər-ˌkiz-əm\ *n* : the theory that all government is undesirable — **an·ar·chist** \-kəst\ *n or adj* — **an·ar·chis·tic** \ˌan-ər-ˈkis-tik\ *adj*

an·ar·chy \ˈan-ər-kē\ *n* **1** : a social structure without government or law and order **2** : utter confusion — **an·ar·chic** \a-ˈnär-kik\ *adj*

anas·to·mo·sis \ə-ˌnas-tə-ˈmō-səs\ *n, pl* **-mo·ses** \-ˌsēz\ **1** : the union of parts or branches (as of blood vessels) **2** : NETWORK

anat *abbr* anatomical; anatomy

anath·e·ma \ə-ˈnath-ə-mə\ *n* **1** : a solemn curse **2** : a person or thing accursed; *also* : one intensely disliked

anath·e·ma·tize \-ˌtīz\ *vb* **-tized; -tiz·ing** : to pronounce an anathema against : CURSE

anat·o·mize \ə-ˈnat-ə-ˌmīz\ *vb* **-mized; -miz·ing** : to dissect so as to examine the structure and parts; *also* : ANALYZE

anat·o·my \ə-ˈnat-ə-mē\ *n, pl* **-mies** [LL *anatomia* dissection, fr. Gk *anatomē*, fr. *anatemnein* to dissect, fr. *ana-* up + *temnein* to cut] **1** : a branch of science dealing with the structure of organisms **2** : structural makeup esp. of an organism or any of its parts **3** : a separating into parts for detailed study : ANALYSIS, ANATOMIZING — **an·a·tom·ic** \ˌan-ə-ˈtäm-ik\ *or* **an·a·tom·i·cal** \-i-kəl\ *adj* — **an·a·tom·i·cal·ly** \-i-k(ə-)lē\ *adv* — **anat·o·mist** \ə-ˈnat-ə-məst\ *n*

anc *abbr* ancient

-ance \əns\ *n suffix* **1** : action or process ⟨further*ance*⟩ : instance of an action or process ⟨perform*ance*⟩ **2** : quality or state : instance of a quality or state ⟨protuber*ance*⟩ **3** : amount or degree ⟨conduct*ance*⟩

an·ces·tor \ˈan-ˌses-tər\ *n* [ME *ancestre*, fr. OF, fr. L *antecessor* one that goes before, fr. *antecedere* to go before, fr. *ante-* before + *cedere* to go] : one from whom an individual is descended

an·ces·tress \ˈan-ˌses-trəs\ *n* : a female ancestor

an·ces·try \ˈan-ˌses-trē\ *n* **1** : line of descent : LINEAGE **2** : ANCESTORS — **an·ces·tral** \an-ˈses-trəl\ *adj*

[1]**an·chor** \ˈaŋ-kər\ *n* **1** : a heavy metal device attached to a ship that catches hold of the bottom and holds the ship in place **2** : ANCHORPERSON

[2]**anchor** *vb* **an·chored; an·chor·ing** \-k(ə-)riŋ\ : to hold or become held in place by or as if by an anchor

an·chor·age \ˈaŋ-k(ə-)rij\ *n* : a place suitable for ships to anchor

an·cho·rite \ˈaŋ-kə-ˌrīt\ *n* : HERMIT

an·chor·man \ˈaŋ-kər-ˌman\ *n* **1** : the member of a team who competes last **2** : an anchorperson who is a man

an·chor·per·son \-ˌpər-sən\ *n* : a broadcaster who reads the news and introduces the reports of other broadcasters

an·chor·wom·an \-ˌwu̇m-ən\ *n* **1** : a woman who competes last **2** : an anchorperson who is a woman

an·cho·vy \ˈan-ˌchō-vē, an-ˈchō-\ *n, pl* **-vies** *or* **-vy** : a small herringlike fish used esp. for sauces and relishes

an·cien ré·gime \äⁿs-yaⁿ-rā-zhēm\ *n* **1** : the political and social system of France before the Revolution of 1789 **2** : a system no longer prevailing

[1]**an·cient** \ˈān-shənt\ *adj* **1** : having existed for many years **2** : belonging to times long past; *esp* : belonging to the period before the Middle Ages

[2]**ancient** *n* **1** : an aged person **2** *pl* : the peoples of ancient Greece and Rome

an·cil·lary \ˈan-sə-ˌler-ē\ *adj* **1** : SUBORDINATE, SUBSIDIARY **2** : AUXILIARY, SUPPLEMENTARY

-ancy \ən-sē\ *n suffix* : quality or state ⟨flamboy*ancy*⟩

and \ən(d), (ˈ)and\ *conj* — used to indicate connection or addition esp. of items within the same class or type or to join words or phrases of the same grammatical rank or function

[1]**an·dan·te** \än-ˈdän-ˌtā, -ˈdänt-ē\ *adv or adj* [It, lit., going, prp. of *andare* to go] : moderately slow — used as a direction in music

[2]**andante** *n* : an andante movement

and·iron \ˈan-ˌdī(-ə)rn\ *n* : one of a pair of metal supports for firewood in a fireplace

and/or \ˈan-ˈdȯr\ *conj* — used to indicate that either *and* or *or* may apply ⟨men ~ women means men *and* women or men *or* women⟩

an·dro·gen \ˈan-drə-jən\ *n* : a male sex hormone

an·droid \ˈan-ˌdrȯid\ *n* : an automaton with human form

an·ec·dote \ˈan-ik-ˌdōt\ *n* [F, fr. Gk *anekdota* unpublished items, fr. *a-* not + *ekdidonai* to publish] : a brief story of an interesting usu. biographical incident — **an·ec·dot·al** \ˌan-ik-ˈdōt-ᵊl\ *adj*

ane·mia \ə-ˈnē-mē-ə\ *n* **1** : a condition in which blood is deficient in quantity, in red blood cells, or in hemoglobin and which is marked by pallor, weakness, and irregular heart action **2** : lack of vitality — **ane·mic** \ə-ˈnē-mik\ *adj*

an·e·mom·e·ter \ˌan-ə-ˈmäm-ət-ər\ *n* : an instrument for measuring the force or speed of the wind

anem·o·ne \ə-ˈnem-ə-nē\ *n* : any of a large genus of herbs related to the buttercups that have showy flowers without petals but with conspicuous often colored sepals

anent \ə-ˈnent\ *prep* : ABOUT, CONCERNING

an·es·the·sia \ˌan-əs-ˈthē-zhə\ *n* : loss of bodily sensation

an·es·the·si·ol·o·gy \-ˌthē-zē-ˈäl-ə-jē\ *n* : a branch of medical science dealing with anesthesia and anesthetics — **an·es·the·si·ol·o·gist** \-jəst\ *n*

[1]**an·es·thet·ic** \ˌan-əs-ˈthet-ik\ *adj* : of, relating to, or capable of producing anesthesia

[2]**anesthetic** *n* : an agent that produces anesthesia — **anes·the·tist** \ə-ˈnes-thət-əst\ *n* — **anes·the·tize** \-thə-ˌtīz\ *vb*

anew \ə-ˈn(y)ü\ *adv* : over again : from a new start

an·gel \ˈān-jəl\ *n* [ME, fr. OF *angele*, fr. L *angelus*, fr. Gk *angelos*, lit., messenger] **1** : a spiritual being superior to man **2** : an attendant spirit ⟨guardian ~⟩ **3** : a winged figure of human form in art **4** : MESSENGER, HARBINGER **5** : a person held to resemble an angel **6** : a financial backer — **an·gel·ic** \an-ˈjel-ik\ *or* **an·gel·i·cal** \-i-kəl\ *adj* — **an·gel·i·cal·ly** \-i-k(ə-)lē\ *adv*

an·gel·fish \ˈān-jəl-ˌfish\ *n* : any of several bright-colored tropical fishes that are flattened from side to side

an·gel·i·ca \an-ˈjel-i-kə\ *n* : a biennial herb related to the carrot whose roots and fruit furnish a flavoring oil

[1]**an·ger** \ˈaŋ-gər\ *n* [ME, affliction, anger, fr. ON *angr* grief] : a strong feeling of displeasure **syn** wrath, ire, rage, fury, indignation

[2]**anger** *vb* **an·gered; an·ger·ing** \-g(ə-)riŋ\ : to make angry

an·gi·na \an-ˈjī-nə\ *n* [L, quinsy] : a disorder (as of the heart) marked by attacks of intense pain; *esp* : ANGINA PECTORIS — **an·gi·nal** \an-ˈjīn-ᵊl\ *adj*

angina pec·to·ris \-ˈpek-t(ə-)rəs\ *n* : a heart disease marked by brief attacks of sharp chest pain caused by deficient oxygenation of heart muscles

an·gio·sperm \ˈan-jē-ə-ˌspərm\ *n* : any of a class of vascular plants (as orchids or roses) having the seeds in a closed ovary

[1]**an·gle** \ˈaŋ-gəl\ *n* **1** : a sharp projecting corner **2** : the figure formed by the meeting of two lines in a point **3** : a point of view **4** : a special technique or plan : GIMMICK

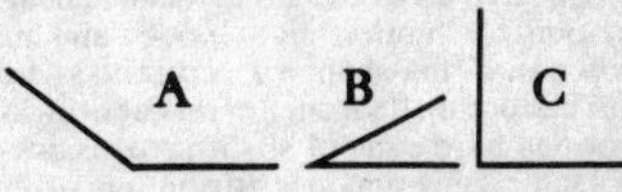

angle 2: *A* obtuse, *B* acute, *C* right

[2]**angle** *vb* **an·gled; an·gling** \-g(ə-)liŋ\ : to turn, move, or direct at an angle

[3]**angle** *vb* **an·gled; an·gling** \-g(ə-)liŋ\ : to fish with a hook and line — **an·gler** \-glər\ *n* — **an·gling** \-gliŋ\ *n*

an·gle·worm \ˈaŋ-gəl-ˌwərm\ *n* : EARTHWORM

An·gli·can \ˈaŋ-gli-kən\ *adj* **1** : of or relating to the established episcopal Church of England **2** : of or relating to England or the English nation — **Anglican** *n* — **An·gli·can·ism** \-kə-ˌniz-əm\ *n*

an·gli·cize \ˈaŋ-glə-ˌsīz\ *vb* **-cized; -ciz·ing** *often cap* **1** : to make English (as in habits, speech, character, or outlook) **2** : to borrow (a foreign word or phrase) into English without changing form or spelling and sometimes without changing pronunciation — **an·gli·ci·za·tion** \ˌaŋ-glə-sə-ˈzā-shən\ *n, often cap*

An·glo \ˈaŋ-glō\ *n, pl* **Anglos** : a non-Latin Caucasian inhabitant of the U.S.

An·glo–French \ˌaŋ-glō-ˈfrench\ *n* : the French language used in medieval England

An·glo·phile \ˈaŋ-glə-ˌfīl\ *also* **An·glo·phil** \-ˌfil\ *n* : one who greatly admires England and things English

An·glo·phobe \ˈaŋ-glə-ˌfōb\ *n* : one who is averse to England and things English

An·glo–Sax·on \ˌaŋ-glō-ˈsak-sən\ *n* **1** : a member of any of the Germanic peoples who invaded England in the 5th century A.D. **2** : a member of the English people **3** : Old English — **Anglo–Saxon** *adj*

an·go·ra \aŋ-ˈgōr-ə, an-\ *n* **1** : yarn or cloth made from the hair of an Angora goat or rabbit **2** *cap* : any of a breed of cats, goats, or rabbits with a long silky coat

an·gry \ˈaŋ-grē\ *adj* **an·gri·er; -est** : feeling or showing anger **syn** enraged, wrathful, irate, indignant, mad — **an·gri·ly** \-grə-lē\ *adv*

angst \ˈäŋst\ *n* [G] : a feeling of anxiety

ang·strom \ˈaŋ-strəm\ *n* : a unit of length equal to one ten-billionth of a meter

an·guish \ˈaŋ-gwish\ *n* : extreme pain or distress esp. of mind — **an·guished** \-gwisht\ *adj*

an·gu·lar \ˈaŋ-gyə-lər\ *adj* **1** : having one or more angles **2** : sharp-cornered **3** : being thin and bony — **an·gu·lar·i·ty** \ˌaŋ-gyə-ˈlar-ət-ē\ *n*

An·gus \ˈaŋ-gəs\ *n* : any of a breed of usu. black hornless beef cattle originating in Scotland

an·hy·drous \an-ˈhī-drəs\ *adj* : free from water

an·i·line \ˈan-ᵊl-ən\ *n* : an oily poisonous liquid used in making dyes, medicines, and explosives

an·i·mad·vert \ˌan-ə-ˌmad-ˈvərt\ *vb* : to remark critically : express censure — **an·i·mad·ver·sion** \-ˈvər-zhən\ *n*

[1]**an·i·mal** \ˈan-ə-məl\ *n* **1** : any of a kingdom of living things typically differing from plants in capacity for active movement, in rapid response to stimulation, and in lack of cellulose cell walls **2** : a lower animal as distinguished from man; *also* : MAMMAL

[2]**animal** *adj* **1** : of, relating to, or derived from animals **2** : of or relating to the physical as distinguished from the mental or spiritual **syn** carnal, fleshly, sensual

an·i·mal·cule \ˌan-ə-ˈmal-kyül\ *n* : a tiny animal usu. invisible to the naked eye

[1]**an·i·mate** \ˈan-ə-mət\ *adj* : having life

[2]**an·i·mate** \-ˌmāt\ *vb* **-mat·ed; -mat·ing 1** : to impart life to **2** : to give spirit and vigor to **3** : to make appear to move ⟨~ a cartoon for motion pictures⟩ — **an·i·mat·ed** *adj*

an·i·ma·tion \ˌan-ə-ˈmā-shən\ *n* **1** : LIVELINESS, VIVACITY **2** : a motion picture made from a series of drawings simulating motions by means of slight progressive changes

an·i·mism \ˈan-ə-ˌmiz-əm\ *n* : attribution of conscious life to nature as a whole or to inanimate objects — **an·i·mist** \-məst\ *n* — **an·i·mis·tic** \ˌan-ə-ˈmis-tik\ *adj*

an·i·mos·i·ty \ˌan-ə-ˈmäs-ət-ē\ *n, pl* **-ties** : ILL WILL, RESENTMENT

an·i·mus \ˈan-ə-məs\ *n* : deep-seated resentment and hostility

an·ion \ˈan-ˌī-ən, -ˌī-ˌän\ *n* : a negatively charged ion

an·ise \ˈan-əs\ *n* : an herb related to the carrot with aromatic seeds **(aniseed** \-ə(s)-ˌsēd**)** used in flavoring

an·is·ette \ˌan-ə-ˈset, -ˈzet\ *n* [F] : a usu. colorless sweet liqueur flavored with aniseed

ankh \ˈaŋk\ *n* : a cross having a loop for its upper vertical arm and serving esp. in ancient Egypt as an emblem of life

an·kle \ˈaŋ-kəl\ *n* : the joint or region between the foot and the leg

an·kle·bone \ˌan-kəl-ˈbōn, ˈaŋ-kəl-ˌbōn\ *n* : the bone that in human beings bears the weight of the body and with the tibia and fibula forms the ankle joint

an·klet \ˈaŋ-klət\ *n* **1** : something (as an ornament) worn around the ankle **2** : a short sock reaching slightly above the ankle

ann *abbr* **1** annals **2** annual

an·nals \ˈan-ᵊlz\ *n pl* **1** : a record of events in chronological order **2** : historical records — **an·nal·ist** \-ᵊl-əst\ *n*

an·neal \ə-ˈnēl\ *vb* : to make (as glass or steel) less brittle by heating and then cooling

[1]**an·nex** \ə-ˈneks, ˈan-ˌeks\ *vb* **1** : to attach as an addition **2** : to incorporate (as a territory) within a political domain — **an·nex·a·tion** \ˌan-ˌek-ˈsā-shən\ *n*

[2]**an·nex** \ˈan-ˌeks, -iks\ *n* : a subsidiary or supplementary structure

an·ni·hi·late \ə-ˈnī-ə-ˌlāt\ *vb* **-lat·ed; -lat·ing** : to destroy completely — **an·ni·hi·la·tion** \-ˌnī-ə-ˈlā-shən\ *n*

an·ni·ver·sa·ry \ˌan-ə-ˈvərs-(ə-)rē\ *n, pl* **-ries** : the annual return of the date of some notable event and esp. a wedding

an·no Do·mi·ni \ˌan-ō-ˈdäm-ə-nē, -ˈdō-mə-, -ˌnī\ *adv, often cap A* [ML, in the year of the Lord] — used to indicate that a time division falls within the Christian era

an·no·tate \ˈan-ə-ˌtāt\ *vb* **-tat·ed; -tat·ing** : to furnish with notes — **an·no·ta·tion** \ˌan-ə-ˈtā-shən\ *n* — **an·no·ta·tor** \ˈan-ə-ˌtāt-ər\ *n*

an·nounce \ə-ˈnau̇ns\ *vb* **-nounced; -nounc·ing 1** : to make known publicly **2** : to give notice of the arrival or presence of — **an·nounce·ment** *n*

an·nounc·er \ə-ˈnau̇n-sər\ *n* : a person who introduces radio or television programs, reads commercials and news summaries, and gives station identification

an·noy \ə-ˈnȯi\ *vb* : to disturb or irritate esp. by repeated acts : VEX **syn** irk, bother, pester, tease, harass — **an·noy·ing·ly** \-ˈnȯi-iŋ-lē\ *adv*

an·noy·ance \ə-ˈnȯi-əns\ *n* **1** : the act of annoying **2** : the state of being annoyed **3** : NUISANCE

[1]**an·nu·al** \ˈan-yə(-wə)l\ *adj* **1** : covering the period of a year **2** : occurring once a year : YEARLY **3** : completing the life cycle in one growing season ⟨~ plants⟩ — **an·nu·al·ly** \-ē\ *adv*

[2]**annual** *n* **1** : a publication appearing once a year **2** : an annual plant

annual ring *n* : the layer of wood produced by a single year's growth of a woody plant

an·nu·i·tant \ə-ˈn(y)ü-ət-ənt\ *n* : a beneficiary of an annuity

an·nu·i·ty \ə-ˈn(y)ü-ət-ē\ *n, pl* **-i·ties** : an amount payable annually; *also* : the right to receive such a payment

an·nul \ə-ˈnəl\ *vb* **an·nulled; an·nul·ling** : to make legally void — **an·nul·ment** *n*

an·nu·lar \ˈan-yə-lər\ *adj* : ring-shaped

annular eclipse *n* : an eclipse in which a thin outer ring of the sun's disk is not covered by the moon's disk

an·nun·ci·ate \ə-ˈnən-sē-ˌāt\ *vb* **-at·ed; -at·ing** : ANNOUNCE

an·nun·ci·a·tion \ə-ˌnən-sē-ˈā-shən\ *n* **1** : ANNOUNCEMENT **2** *cap* : March 25 observed as a church festival commemorating the announcement of the Incarnation

an·nun·ci·a·tor \ə-ˈnən-sē-ˌāt-ər\ *n* : one that annunciates; *specif* : a usu. electrically controlled signal board or indicator

an·ode \ˈan-ˌōd\ *n* **1** : the positive electrode of an electrolytic cell **2** : the negative terminal of a battery **3** : the electron-collecting electrode of an electron tube — **an·od·ic** \a-ˈnäd-ik\ *or* **an·od·al** \-ˈnōd-ᵊl\ *adj*

an·od·ize \ˈan-ə-ˌdīz\ *vb* **-ized; -iz·ing** : to subject (a metal) to electrolytic action as the anode of a cell in order to coat with a protective or decorative film

an·o·dyne \ˈan-ə-ˌdīn\ *n* : something that relieves pain : a soothing agent

anoint \ə-ˈnȯint\ *vb* **1** : to apply oil to esp. as a sacred rite **2** : CONSECRATE — **anoint·ment** *n*

anom·a·lous \ə-ˈnäm-ə-ləs\ *adj* : deviating from a general rule : ABNORMAL

anom·a·ly \ə-ˈnäm-ə-lē\ *n, pl* **-lies** : something anomalous : IRREGULARITY

[1]**anon** \ə-ˈnän\ *adv, archaic* : SOON

[2]**anon** *abbr* anonymous; anonymously

anon·y·mous \ə-ˈnän-ə-məs\ *adj* : of unknown or undeclared origin or authorship — **an·o·nym·i·ty** \ˌan-ə-ˈnim-ət-ē\ *n* — **anon·y·mous·ly** \ə-ˈnän-ə-məs-lē\ *adv*

anoph·e·les \ə-ˈnäf-ə-ˌlēz\ *n* [NL, genus name, fr. Gk *anōphelēs* useless, fr. *a-* not + *ophelos* advantage, help] : any of a genus of mosquitoes that includes all mosquitoes which transmit malaria to human beings

an·o·rec·tic \ˌan-ə-ˈrek-tik\ *also* **an·o·ret·ic** \-ˈret-ik\ *adj* : ANOREXIC — **anorectic** *n*

an·orex·ia \ˌan-ə-ˈrek-sē-ə\ *n* : loss of appetite esp. when prolonged

anorexia ner·vo·sa \-nər-ˈvō-sə\ *n* : a psychological and endocrine disorder primarily of young women marked esp. by faulty eating patterns, malnutrition, and usu. excessive weight loss

an·orex·ic \ˌan-ə-ˈrek-sik\ *adj* **1** : lacking or causing loss of appetite **2** : affected with or as if with anorexia nervosa — **anorexic** *n*

[1]**an·oth·er** \ə-ˈnəth-ər\ *adj* **1** : some other **2** : being one in addition : one more

[2]**another** *pron* **1** : an additional one : one more **2** : one that is different from the first or present one

ans *abbr* answer

[1]**an·swer** \ˈan-sər\ *n* **1** : something spoken or written in reply to a question **2** : a solution of a problem

[2]**answer** *vb* **an·swered; an·swer·ing** \ˈans-(ə-)riŋ\ **1** : to speak or write in reply to **2** : to be responsible **3** : to be adequate — **an·swer·er** *n*

an·swer·able \ˈans-(ə-)rə-bəl\ *adj* **1** : subject to taking blame or responsibility **2** : capable of being refuted

answering service *n* : a commercial service that answers telephone calls for its clients

[1]**ant** \ˈant\ *n* : any of a family of small social insects related to the bees and living in communities usu. in earth or wood

[2]**ant** *abbr* antonym

Ant *abbr* Antarctica

ant- — see ANTI-

[1]**-ant** \ənt\ *n suffix* **1** : one that performs or promotes (a specified action) ⟨cool*ant*⟩ **2** : thing that is acted upon (in a specified manner) ⟨inhal*ant*⟩

[2]**-ant** *adj suffix* **1** : performing (a specified action) or being (in a specified condition) ⟨propell*ant*⟩ **2** : promoting (a specified action or process) ⟨expector*ant*⟩

ant·ac·id \ant-ˈas-əd\ *n* : an agent that counteracts acidity — **antacid** *adj*

an·tag·o·nism \an-ˈtag-ə-ˌniz-əm\ *n* **1** : active opposition or hostility **2** : opposition in physiological action — **an·tag·o·nis·tic** \-ˌtag-ə-ˈnis-tik\ *adj*

an·tag·o·nist \-nəst\ *n* : ADVERSARY, OPPONENT

an·tag·o·nize \an-ˈtag-ə-ˌnīz\ *vb* **-nized; -niz·ing** : to provoke the hostility of

ant·arc·tic \ant-ˈärk-tik, -ˈärt-ik\ *adj, often cap* : of or relating to the south pole or the region near it

antarctic circle *n, often cap A&C* : the parallel of latitude that is approximately 66½ degrees south of the equator

[1]**an·te** \ˈant-ē\ *n* : a poker stake put up by each player before he sees his hand; *also* : an amount paid : PRICE

[2]**ante** *vb* **an·ted; an·te·ing 1** : to put up (an ante) **2** : PAY

ant·eat·er \ˈant-ˌēt-ər\ *n* : any of several mammals (as an aardvark) that feed on ants

an·te·bel·lum \ˌant-i-ˈbel-əm\ *adj* : existing before a war; *esp* : existing before the U.S. Civil War of 1861-65

an·te·ced·ent \ˌant-ə-ˈsēd-ᵊnt\ *n* **1** : a noun, pronoun, phrase, or clause referred to by a personal or relative pronoun **2** : a preceding event or cause **3** *pl* : the significant conditions of one's earlier life **4** *pl* : ANCESTORS — **antecedent** *adj*

an·te·cham·ber \ˈant-i-ˌchām-bər\ *n* : ANTEROOM

an·te·date \ˈant-i-ˌdāt\ *vb* **1** : to date (a paper) as of an earlier day than that on which the actual writing or signing is done **2** : to precede in time

an·te·di·lu·vi·an \ˌant-i-də-ˈlü-vē-ən, -dī-\ *adj* **1** : of the period before the biblical flood **2** : ANTIQUATED, OBSOLETE

an·te·lope \ˈant-ᵊl-ˌōp\ *n, pl* **-lope** *or* **-lopes** [ME, fabulous heraldic beast, prob. fr. MF *antelop* savage animal with sawlike horns, fr. ML *anthalopus*, fr. LGk *antholops*] **1** : any of various Old World cud-chewing mammals related to the oxen but with smaller lighter bodies and horns that extend upward and backward **2** : PRONGHORN

an·te me·ri·di·em \ˈant-i-mə-ˈrid-ē-əm\ *adj* [L] : being before noon

an·ten·na \an-ˈten-ə\ *n, pl* **-nae** \-(ˌ)ē\ *or* **-nas** [ML, fr. L, sail yard] **1** : one of the long slender paired segmented sensory organs on the head of an arthropod (as an insect or crab) **2** *pl usu -nas* : a metallic device (as a rod or wire) for sending out or receiving radio waves

an·te·pe·nult \ˌant-i-ˈpē-ˌnəlt\ *also* **an·te·pen·ul·ti·ma** \-pi-ˈnəl-tə-mə\ *n* : the 3d syllable of a word counting from the end — **an·te·pen·ul·ti·mate** \-pi-ˈnəl-tə-mət\ *adj or n*

an·te·ri·or \an-ˈtir-ē-ər\ *adj* **1** : situated before or toward the front **2** : situated near or nearer to the head **3** : coming before in time **syn** preceding, previous, prior, antecedent

an·te·room \ˈant-i-ˌrüm, -ˌru̇m\ *n* : a room forming the entrance to another and often used as a waiting room

an·them \ˈan-thəm\ *n* **1** : a sacred vocal composition **2** : a song or hymn of praise or gladness

an·ther \ˈan-thər\ *n* : the part of a stamen of a seed plant that contains pollen

ant·hill \ˈant-ˌhil\ *n* : a mound thrown up by ants or termites in digging their nest

an·thol·o·gy \an-ˈthäl-ə-jē\ *n, pl* **-gies** [NL *anthologia* collection of epigrams, fr. MGk, fr. Gk, flower gathering, fr. *anthos* flower + *logia* collecting, fr. *legein* to gather] : a collection of literary selections — **an·thol·o·gist** \-jəst\ *n* — **an·thol·o·gize** \-ˌjīz\ *vb*

an·thra·cite \ˈan-thrə-ˌsīt\ *n* : a hard glossy coal that burns without much smoke

an·thrax \ˈan-ˌthraks\ *n* : an infectious and usu. fatal bacterial disease of warm-blooded animals (as cattle and sheep); *also* : a bacterium causing anthrax

an·thro·po·cen·tric \ˌan-thrə-pə-ˈsen- trik\ *adj* : interpreting or regarding the world in terms of human values and experiences

[1]**an·thro·poid** \ˈan-thrə-ˌpȯid\ *n* : any of several large tailless apes (as a gorilla)

[2]**anthropoid** *adj* **1** : resembling a human being esp. in shape **2** : resembling an ape esp. in action

an·thro·pol·o·gy \ˌan-thrə-ˈpäl-ə-jē\ *n* : the science of human beings and esp. of their physical characteristics, their origin and the distribution of races, their environment and social relations, and their culture — **an·thro·po·log·i·cal** \-pə-ˈläj-i-kəl\ *adj* — **an·thro·pol·o·gist** \-ˈpäl-ə-jəst\ *n*

an·thro·po·mor·phism \ˌan-thrə-pə-ˈmȯr-ˌfiz-əm\ *n* : an interpretation of what is not human or personal in terms of human or personal characteristics : HUMANIZATION — **an·thro·po·mor·phic** \-fik\ *adj*

an·ti \ˈan-ˌtī, ˈant-ē\ *n, pl* **antis** : one who is opposed

anti- \ˌant-i, -ē; ˌan-ˌtī\ *or* **ant-** *or* **anth-** *prefix* **1** : opposite in kind, position, or action **2** : opposing : hostile toward **3** : counteractive **4** : preventive of : curative of

antiaircraft	**anti–imperialism**
anti–American	**anti–imperialist**
antibacterial	**antilabor**
anticapitalist	**antimalarial**
anti–Catholic	**antimicrobial**
anticlerical	**antislavery**
anticolonial	**antispasmodic**
anticommunism	**antistatic**
anticommunist	**antisubmarine**
antidemocractic	**antitank**
antiestablishment	**antitrust**
antifascist	**antiviral**

an·ti·abor·tion \ˌant-ē-ə-ˈbȯr-shən, ˌan-ˌtī-\ *adj* : opposed to abortion

an·ti·bal·lis·tic missile \ˌant-i-bə-ˌlis-tik-, ˌan-ˌtī-\ *n* : a missile for intercepting and destroying ballistic missiles

an·ti·bi·ot·ic \-bī-ˈät-ik, -bē-\ *n* : a substance produced by or derived by chemical alteration of a substance produced by a microorganism (as a fungus or bacterium) that in dilute solution inhibits or kills another microorganism — **antibiotic** *adj*

an·ti·body \ˈant-i-ˌbäd-ē\ *n* : any of the bodily substances produced in response to specific foreign substances or organisms (as a disease-producing microorganism) and counteracting their effects

[1]**an·tic** \ˈant-ik\ *n* : an often wildly playful or funny act or action

[2]**antic** *adj* [It *antico* ancient, fr. L *antiquus*] **1** *archaic* : GROTESQUE **2** : PLAYFUL

an·ti·can·cer \ˌant-i-ˈkan-sər, ˌan-ˌtī-\ *adj* : used or effective against cancer ⟨~ drugs⟩

An·ti·christ \ˈant-i-ˌkrīst\ *n* **1** : one who denies or opposes Christ **2** : a false Christ

an·tic·i·pate \an-ˈtis-ə-ˌpāt\ *vb* **-pat·ed; -pat·ing 1** : to foresee and provide for beforehand **2** : to look forward to —

an·tic·i·pa·tion \-ˌtis-ə-ˈpā-shən\ *n* — **an·tic·i·pa·to·ry** \-ˈtis-ə-pə-ˌtōr-ē\ *adj*
an·ti·cli·max \ˌant-i-ˈklī-ˌmaks\ *n* : something closing a series that is strikingly less important than what has preceded it — **an·ti·cli·mac·tic** \-klī-ˈmak-tik\ *adj*
an·ti·cline \ˈant-i-ˌklīn\ *n* : an arch of layers of rock in the earth's crust
an·ti·co·ag·u·lant \ˌant-i-kō-ˈag-yə-lənt\ *n* : a substance that hinders the clotting of blood — **anticoagulant** *adj*
an·ti·cy·clone \ˌant-i-ˈsī-ˌklōn\ *n* : a system of winds that rotates about a center of high atmospheric pressure — **an·ti·cy·clon·ic** \-sī-ˈklän-ik\ *adj*
[1]**an·ti·de·pres·sant** \ˌant-i-di-ˈpres-ᵊnt, ˌan-ˌtī-\ *adj* : used or tending to relieve psychic depression ⟨~ drugs⟩
[2]**antidepressant** *n* : an antidepressant drug
an·ti·dote \ˈant-i-ˌdōt\ *n* : a remedy to counteract the effects of poison
an·ti·fer·til·i·ty \-fər-ˈtil-ət-ē\ *adj* : tending to control excess or unwanted fertility : CONTRACEPTIVE ⟨~ agents⟩
an·ti·freeze \ˈant-i-ˌfrēz\ *n* : a substance that prevents a liquid from freezing
an·ti·gen \ˈant-i-jən\ *n* : a usu. protein or carbohydrate substance (as a toxin or an enzyme) capable of stimulating an immune response — **an·ti·gen·ic** \ˌant-i-ˈjen-ik\ *adj* — **an·ti·ge·nic·i·ty** \-jə-ˈnis-ət-ē\ *n*
an·ti·grav·i·ty \ˌant-i-ˈgrav-ət-ē, ˌan-ˌtī-\ *adj* : reducing or canceling the effect of gravity
an·ti·he·ro \ˈant-i-ˌhē-rō, ˈan-ˌtī-\ *n* : a protagonist who is notably lacking in heroic qualities (as courage)
an·ti·his·ta·mine \ˌant-i-ˈhis-tə-ˌmēn, ˌan-ˌtī-, -mən\ *n* : any of various drugs used in treating allergies and colds
an·ti·hy·per·ten·sive \-ˌhī-pər-ˈten-siv\ *n* : a substance that is effective against high blood pressure — **antihypertensive** *adj*
an·ti–in·flam·ma·to·ry \-in-ˈflam-ə-ˌtōr-ē\ *adj* : counteracting inflammation — **anti–inflammatory** *n*
an·ti–in·tel·lec·tu·al \-ˌint-ᵊl-ˈek-chə-wəl\ *adj* : opposing or hostile to intellectuals or to an intellectual view or approach
an·ti·knock \ˌant-i-ˈnäk\ *n* : a fuel additive to prevent knocking in an internal-combustion engine
an·ti·log·a·rithm \ˌant-i-ˈlȯg-ə-ˌrit͟h-əm, ˌan-ˌtī-, -ˈläg-\ *n* : the number corresponding to a given logarithm
an·ti·ma·cas·sar \ˌant-i-mə-ˈkas-ər\ *n* : a cover to protect the back or arms of furniture
an·ti·mag·net·ic \ˌant-i-mag-ˈnet-ik, ˌan-ˌtī-\ *adj* : having a balance unit composed of alloys that will not remain magnetized ⟨an ~ watch⟩
an·ti·mat·ter \ˈant-i-ˌmat-ər\ *n* : matter composed of the counterparts of ordinary matter
an·ti·mo·ny \ˈant-ə-ˌmō-nē\ *n* : a brittle silvery white metallic chemical element used in alloys — see ELEMENT table
an·ti·neu·tron \-ˈn(y)ü-ˌträn\ *n* : the uncharged antiparticle of the neutron
an·ti·no·mi·an \ˌant-i-ˈnō-mē-ən\ *n* : one who denies the validity of moral laws
an·tin·o·my \an-ˈtin-ə-mē\ *n, pl* **-mies** : a contradiction between two seemingly true statements
an·ti·nov·el \ˈant-i-ˌnäv-əl, ˈan-ˌtī-\ *n* : a work of fiction that lacks all or most of the traditional features of the novel
an·ti·nu·cle·ar \ˌant-i-ˈn(y)ü-klē-ər\ *adj* : opposing the use or production of nuclear power plants
an·ti·ox·i·dant \ˌant-ē-ˈäk-səd-ənt, ˌan-ˌtī-\ *n* : a substance that inhibits oxidation — **antioxidant** *adj*
an·ti·par·ti·cle \ˈant-i-ˌpärt-i-kəl, ˈan-ˌtī-\ *n* : an elementary particle identical to another elementary particle in mass but opposite to it in electric and magnetic properties
an·ti·pas·to \ˌant-i-ˈpas-tō, ˌänt-i-ˈpäs-\ *n, pl* **-ti** : any of various typically Italian hors d'oeuvres
an·tip·a·thy \an-ˈtip-ə-thē\ *n, pl* **-thies 1** : settled aversion or dislike **2** : an object of aversion — **an·ti·pa·thet·ic** \ˌant-i-pə-ˈthet-ik\ *adj*
an·ti·per·son·nel \ˌant-i-ˌpərs-ᵊn-ˈel, ˌan-ˌtī-\ *adj* : designed for use against military personnel ⟨~ mine⟩
an·ti·per·spi·rant \-ˈpər-spə-rənt\ *n* : a cosmetic preparation used to check excessive perspiration
an·tiph·o·nal \an-ˈtif-ən-ᵊl\ *adj* : performed by two alternating groups — **an·tiph·o·nal·ly** \-ē\ *adv*
an·ti·pode \ˈant-ə-ˌpōd\ *n, pl* **an·tip·o·des** \an-ˈtip-ə-ˌdēz\ [ME *antipodes,* pl., persons dwelling at opposite points on the globe, fr. L, fr. Gk, fr. pl. of *antipod-, antipous* with feet opposite, fr. *anti-* against + *pod-, pous* foot] : the parts of the earth diametrically opposite — usu. used in pl. — **an·tip·o·dal** \an-ˈtip-əd-ᵊl\ *adj* — **an·tip·o·de·an** \(ˌ)an-ˌtip-ə-ˈdē-ən\ *adj*
an·ti·pol·lu·tion \ˌant-i-pə-ˈlü-shən\ *adj* : designed to prevent, reduce, or eliminate pollution ⟨~ laws⟩
an·ti·pope \ˈant-i-ˌpōp\ *n* : one elected or claiming to be pope in opposition to the pope canonically chosen
an·ti·pov·er·ty \ˌant-i-ˈpäv-ərt-ē, ˌan-ˌtī-\ *adj* : of or relating to legislation designed to relieve poverty
an·ti·pro·ton \-ˈprō-ˌtän\ *n* : the antiparticle of the proton
an·ti·quar·i·an \ˌant-ə-ˈkwer-ē-ən\ *adj* **1** : of or relating to antiquities **2** : dealing in old books — **antiquarian** *n* — **an·ti·quar·i·an·ism** *n*
an·ti·quary \ˈant-ə-ˌkwer-ē\ *n, pl* **-quar·ies** : a person who collects or studies antiquities
an·ti·quat·ed \ˈant-ə-ˌkwāt-əd\ *adj* : OUT-OF-DATE, OLD-FASHIONED
[1]**an·tique** \an-ˈtēk\ *n* : an object made in a bygone period
[2]**antique** *adj* **1** : belonging to antiquity **2** : OLD-FASHIONED **3** : of a bygone style or period
[3]**antique** *vb* **-tiqued; -tiqu·ing** : to finish or refinish in antique style : give an appearance of age to
an·tiq·ui·ty \an-ˈtik-wət-ē\ *n, pl* **-ties 1** : ancient times **2** : great age **3** *pl* : relics of ancient times **4** *pl* : matters relating to ancient culture
an·ti–Sem·i·tism \ˌant-i-ˈsem-ə-ˌtiz-əm, ˌan-ˌtī-\ *n* : hostility toward Jews as a religious or social minority — **an·ti–Se·mit·ic** \-sə-ˈmit-ik\ *adj*
an·ti·sep·tic \ˌant-ə-ˈsep-tik\ *adj* **1** : killing or checking the growth of germs that cause decay or infection **2** : scrupulously clean : ASEPTIC — **antiseptic** *n* — **an·ti·sep·ti·cal·ly** \-ti-k(ə-)lē\ *adv*
an·ti·se·rum \ˈant-i-ˌsir-əm, ˈan-ˌtī-\ *n* : a serum containing antibodies
an·ti·so·cial \-ˈsō-shəl\ *adj* **1** : disliking the society of others **2** : contrary or hostile to the well-being of society ⟨crime is ~⟩
an·tith·e·sis \an-ˈtith-ə-səs\ *n, pl* **-e·ses** \-ˌsēz\ **1** : the opposition or contrast of ideas **2** : the direct opposite
an·ti·thet·i·cal \ˌant-ə-ˈthet-i-kəl\ *also* **an·ti·thet·ic** \-ik\ *adj* : constituting or marked by antithesis — **an·ti·thet·i·cal·ly** \-i-k(ə-)lē\ *adv*
an·ti·tox·in \ˌant-i-ˈtäk-sən\ *n* : an antibody that is able to neutralize a particular toxin, is formed when the toxin is introduced into the body, and is produced in lower animals for use in treating human diseases (as diphtheria); *also* : a serum containing antitoxin
an·ti·tu·mor \ˌant-i-ˈt(y)ü-mər, ˌan-ˌtī-\ *adj* : ANTICANCER
an·ti·ven·in \-ˈven-ən\ *n* : an antitoxin to a venom; *also* : a serum containing such antitoxin
ant·ler \ˈant-lər\ *n* [ME *aunteler,* fr. MF *antoillier,* fr. L *anteocularis* located before the eye, fr. *ante-* before + *oculus* eye] : the solid usu. branched horn of a deer; *also* : a branch of this horn — **ant·lered** \-lərd\ *adj*
ant lion *n* : any of various insects having a long-jawed larva that digs a conical pit in which it lies in wait for insects (as ants) on which it feeds
ant·onym \ˈant-ə-ˌnim\ *n* : a word of opposite meaning
anus \ˈā-nəs\ *n* [L] : the lower or posterior opening of the alimentary canal

an·vil \ˈan-vəl\ *n* **1** : a heavy iron block on which metal is shaped **2** : INCUS
anx·i·ety \aŋ-ˈzī-ət-ē\ *n, pl* **-et·ies** **1** : painful uneasiness of mind usu. over an anticipated ill **2** : abnormal apprehension and fear often accompanied by physiological signs (as sweating and increased pulse), by doubt about the nature and reality of the threat itself, and by self-doubt
anx·ious \ˈaŋk-shəs\ *adj* **1** : uneasy in mind : WORRIED **2** : earnestly wishing : EAGER — **anx·ious·ly** *adv*
¹any \ˈen-ē\ *adj* **1** : one chosen at random **2** : of whatever number or quantity
²any *pron* **1** : any one or ones ⟨take ~ of the books you like⟩ **2** : any amount ⟨~ of the money not used is to be returned⟩
³any *adv* : to any extent or degree : AT ALL ⟨could not walk ~ farther⟩
any·body \-ˌbäd-ē, -bəd-\ *pron* : ANYONE
any·how \-ˌhau̇\ *adv* **1** : in any way **2** : NEVERTHELESS; *also* : in any case
any·more \ˌen-ē-ˈmōr\ *adv* **1** : any longer **2** : at the present time
any·one \-(ˌ)wən\ *pron* : any person
any·place \-ˌplās\ *adv* : ANYWHERE
any·thing \-ˌthiŋ\ *pron* : any thing whatever
any·time \ˈen-ē-ˌtīm\ *adv* : at any time whatever
any·way \-ˌwā\ *adv* : ANYHOW
any·where \-ˌhweər\ *adv* : in or to any place
any·wise \-ˌwīz\ *adv* : in any way whatever
A–OK \ˌā-ō-ˈkā\ *adv or adj* : very definitely OK
A1 \ˈā-ˈwən\ *adj* : of the finest quality
A/1C *abbr* airman first class
aor·ta \ā-ˈȯrt-ə\ *n, pl* **-tas** *or* **-tae** \-ē\ : the main artery that carries blood from the heart — **aor·tic** \-ˈȯrt-ik\ *adj*
ap *abbr* **1** apostle **2** apothecaries
AP *abbr* **1** American plan **2** Associated Press
apace \ə-ˈpās\ *adv* : SWIFTLY
Apache \ə-ˈpach-ē *for 1;* ə-ˈpash *for 2*\ *n, pl* **Apache** *or* **Apach·es** \-ˈpach-ēz, -ˈpash(-əz)\ **1** : a member of an American Indian people of the southwestern U.S.; *also* : any of the languages of the Apache people **2** *not cap* : a member of a gang of criminals esp. in Paris
ap·a·nage *var of* APPANAGE
apart \ə-ˈpärt\ *adv* **1** : separately in place or time **2** : ASIDE **3** : in two or more parts : to pieces
apart·heid \ə-ˈpär-ˌtāt, -ˌtīt\ *n* [Afrikaans] : a policy of racial segregation practiced in the Republic of So. Africa
apart·ment \ə-ˈpärt-mənt\ *n* : a room or set of rooms occupied as a dwelling; *also* : a building divided into individual dwelling units
ap·a·thy \ˈap-ə-thē\ *n* **1** : lack of emotion **2** : lack of interest : INDIFFERENCE — **ap·a·thet·ic** \ˌap-ə-ˈthet-ik\ *adj* — **ap·a·thet·i·cal·ly** \-i-k(ə-)lē\ *adv*
ap·a·tite \ˈap-ə-ˌtīt\ *n* : any of a group of minerals that are phosphates of calcium and are used as a source of phosphorus
APB *abbr* all points bulletin
¹ape \ˈāp\ *n* **1** : any of the larger tailless primates (as a baboon or gorilla); *also* : MONKEY **2** : MIMIC, IMITATOR; *also* : a large uncouth person
²ape *vb* **aped; ap·ing** : IMITATE, MIMIC
ape–man \ˈāp-ˌman\ *n* : a primate intermediate in character between true man and the higher apes
aper·çu \â-per-sᵫ, ˌap-ər-ˈsü\ *n, pl* **aperçus** \-sᵫ(z), -ˈsüz\ : an immediate impression; *esp* : INSIGHT
aper·i·tif \ˌäp-ˌer-ə-ˈtēf\ *n* : an alcoholic drink taken as an appetizer
ap·er·ture \ˈap-ə(r)-ˌchu̇r, -chər\ *n* : OPENING, HOLE
apex \ˈā-ˌpeks\ *n, pl* **apex·es** *or* **api·ces** \ˈā-pə-ˌsēz, ˈap-ə-\ : the highest point : PEAK
apha·sia \ə-ˈfā-zh(ē-)ə\ *n* : loss or impairment of the power to use or comprehend words — **apha·sic** \-zik\ *adj or n*
aph·elion \a-ˈfēl-yən\ *n, pl* **-elia** \-yə\ [NL, fr. *apo-* away from + Gk *hēlios* sun] : the point in an object's orbit most distant from the sun
aphid \ˈā-fəd, ˈaf-əd\ *n* : a small insect that sucks the juices of plants
aphis \ˈā-fəs, ˈaf-əs\ *n, pl* **aphi·des** \ˈā-fə-ˌdēz, ˈaf-ə-\ : APHID
aph·o·rism \ˈaf-ə-ˌriz-əm\ *n* : a short saying stating a general truth : MAXIM — **aph·o·ris·tic** \ˌaf-ə-ˈris-tik\ *adj*
aph·ro·di·si·ac \ˌaf-rə-ˈdiz-ē-ˌak, -ˈdē-zē-\ *adj* : exciting sexual desire — **aphrodisiac** *n*
api·ary \ˈā-pē-ˌer-ē\ *n, pl* **-ar·ies** : a place where bees are kept — **api·a·rist** \-pē-ə-rəst\ *n*
api·cal \ˈā-pi-kəl, ˈap-i-\ *adj* : of, relating to, or situated at an apex — **api·cal·ly** \-k(ə-)lē\ *adv*
apiece \ə-ˈpēs\ *adv* : for each one
aplomb \ə-ˈpläm, -ˈpləm\ *n* [F, lit., perpendicularity, fr. MF, fr. *a plomb,* lit., according to the plummet] : complete composure or self-assurance
APO *abbr* army post office
Apoc *abbr* **1** Apocalypse **2** Apocrypha
apoc·a·lypse \ə-ˈpäk-ə-ˌlips\ *n* **1** : a writing prophesying a cataclysm in which evil forces are destroyed **2** *cap* — see BIBLE table — **apoc·a·lyp·tic** \-ˌpäk-ə-ˈlip-tik\ *also* **apoc·a·lyp·ti·cal** \-ti-kəl\ *adj*
Apoc·ry·pha \ə-ˈpäk-rə-fə\ *n* **1** *not cap* : writings of dubious authenticity **2** : books included in the Septuagint and Vulgate but excluded from the Jewish and Protestant canons of the Old Testament — see BIBLE table **3** : early Christian writings not included in the New Testament
apoc·ry·phal \-fəl\ *adj* **1** *often cap* : of or resembling the Apocrypha **2** : not canonical : SPURIOUS — **apoc·ry·phal·ly** \-ē\ *adv*
apo·gee \ˈap-ə-(ˌ)jē\ *n* [F *apogée,* fr. NL *apogaeum,* fr. Gk *apogaion,* fr. *apo* away from + *gē* earth] : the point at which an orbiting object is farthest from the body being orbited
apo·lit·i·cal \ˌā-pə-ˈlit-i-kəl\ *adj* **1** : having an aversion for or no interest in political affairs **2** : having no political significance — **apo·lit·i·cal·ly** \-k(ə-)lē\ *adv*
apol·o·get·ic \ə-ˌpäl-ə-ˈjet-ik\ *adj* : expressing apology — **apol·o·get·i·cal·ly** \-i-k(ə-)lē\ *adv*
ap·o·lo·gia \ˌap-ə-ˈlō-j(ē-)ə\ *n* : APOLOGY; *esp* : an argument in support or justification
apol·o·gize \ə-ˈpäl-ə-ˌjīz\ *vb* **-gized; -giz·ing** : to make an apology : express regret — **apol·o·gist** \-jəst\ *n*
apol·o·gy \ə-ˈpäl-ə-jē\ *n, pl* **-gies** **1** : a formal justification : DEFENSE **2** : an expression of regret for a wrong
apo·lune \ˈap-ə-ˌlün\ *n* : the point in a lunar orbit farthest from the moon's surface
ap·o·plexy \ˈap-ə-ˌplek-sē\ *n* : STROKE 3 — **ap·o·plec·tic** \ˌap-ə-ˈplek-tik\ *adj*
aport \ə-ˈpōrt\ *adv* : on or toward the left side of a ship
apos·ta·sy \ə-ˈpäs-tə-sē\ *n, pl* **-sies** : a renunciation or abandonment of a former loyalty (as to a religion) — **apos·tate** \ə-ˈpäs-ˌtāt, -tət\ *adj or n*
a pos·te·ri·o·ri \ˌä-pō-ˌstir-ē-ˈōr-ē\ *adj* [L, lit., from the latter] : relating to or derived by reasoning from observed facts — **a posteriori** *adv*
apos·tle \ə-ˈpäs-əl\ *n* **1** : one of the group composed of Jesus' 12 original disciples and Paul **2** : the first prominent missionary to a region or group **3** : one who initiates or first advocates a great reform — **apos·tle·ship** *n*
ap·os·tol·ic \ˌap-ə-ˈstäl-ik\ *adj* **1** : of or relating to an apostle or to the New Testament apostles **2** : of or

relating to a succession of spiritual authority from the apostles **3** : PAPAL

¹apos·tro·phe \ə-ˈpäs-trə-(ˌ)fē\ *n* : the rhetorical addressing of a usu. absent person or a usu. personified thing (as in "O grave, where is thy victory?")

²apostrophe *n* : a punctuation mark ' used esp. to indicate the possessive case or the omission of a letter or figure

apos·tro·phize \ə-ˈpäs-trə-ˌfīz\ *vb* **-phized; -phiz·ing** : to address as if present or capable of understanding

apothecaries' weight *n* : a system of weights based on the troy pound and ounce and used chiefly by pharmacists — see WEIGHT table

apoth·e·cary \ə-ˈpäth-ə-ˌker-ē\ *n, pl* **-car·ies** [ME *apothecarie,* fr. ML *apothecarius,* fr. LL, shopkeeper, fr. L *apotheca* storehouse, fr. Gk *apothēkē,* fr. *apotithenai* to put away] : DRUGGIST

ap·o·thegm \ˈap-ə-ˌthem\ *n* : APHORISM, MAXIM

apo·the·o·sis \ə-ˌpäth-ē-ˈō-səs, ˌap-ə-ˈthē-ə-səs\ *n, pl* **-o·ses** \-ˌsēz\ **1** : DEIFICATION **2** : the perfect example

app *abbr* **1** apparatus **2** appendix

ap·pall *also* **ap·pal** \ə-ˈpȯl\ *vb* **ap·palled; ap·pall·ing** : to overcome with horror : DISMAY

Ap·pa·loo·sa \ˌap-ə-ˈlü-sə\ *n* : any of a breed of saddle horses developed in northwestern No. America that have small dark spots or blotches on a white coat

ap·pa·nage \ˈap-ə-nij\ *n* **1** : provision (as a grant of land) made by a sovereign or legislative body for dependent members of the royal family **2** : a rightful adjunct

ap·pa·ra·tus \ˌap-ə-ˈrat-əs, -ˈrāt-\ *n, pl* **-tus·es** *or* **-tus** [L] **1** : a set of materials or equipment for a particular use **2** : a complex machine or device : MECHANISM **3** : the organization of a political party or underground movement

¹ap·par·el \ə-ˈpar-əl\ *vb* **-eled** *or* **-elled; -el·ing** *or* **-el·ling** **1** : CLOTHE, DRESS **2** : ADORN

²apparel *n* : CLOTHING, DRESS

ap·par·ent \ə-ˈpar-ənt\ *adj* **1** : open to view : VISIBLE **2** : EVIDENT, OBVIOUS **3** : appearing as real or true : SEEMING — **ap·par·ent·ly** *adv*

ap·pa·ri·tion \ˌap-ə-ˈrish-ən\ *n* : a supernatural appearance : GHOST

ap·peal \ə-ˈpēl\ *vb* **1** : to take steps to have (a case) reheard in a higher court **2** : to plead for help, corroboration, or decision **3** : to arouse a sympathetic response — **appeal** *n*

ap·pear \ə-ˈpiər\ *vb* **1** : to become visible **2** : to come formally before an authority **3** : SEEM **4** : to become evident **5** : to come before the public

ap·pear·ance \ə-ˈpir-əns\ *n* **1** : the act of appearing **2** : outward aspect : LOOK **3** : PHENOMENON

ap·pease \ə-ˈpēz\ *vb* **ap·peased; ap·peas·ing** **1** : to cause to subside : ALLAY **2** : PACIFY, CONCILIATE; *esp* : to buy off by concessions — **ap·pease·ment** *n*

ap·pel·lant \ə-ˈpel-ənt\ *n* : one who appeals esp. from a judicial decision

ap·pel·late \ə-ˈpel-ət\ *adj* : having power to review decisions of a lower court

ap·pel·la·tion \ˌap-ə-ˈlā-shən\ *n* : NAME, DESIGNATION

ap·pel·lee \ˌap-ə-ˈlē\ *n* : one against whom an appeal is taken

ap·pend \ə-ˈpend\ *vb* : to attach esp. as something additional : AFFIX

ap·pend·age \ə-ˈpen-dij\ *n* **1** : something appended to a principal or greater thing **2** : a projecting part of the body (as an antenna) esp. when paired with one on each side **syn** accessory, adjunct, appendix, appurtenance

ap·pen·dec·to·my \ˌap-ən-ˈdek-tə-mē\ *n, pl* **-mies** : surgical removal of the intestinal appendix

ap·pen·di·ci·tis \ə-ˌpen-də-ˈsīt-əs\ *n* : inflammation of the intestinal appendix

ap·pen·dix \ə-ˈpen-diks\ *n, pl* **-dix·es** *or* **-di·ces** \-də-ˌsēz\ [L] **1** : supplementary matter added at the end of a book **2** : a narrow blind tube usu. about three or four inches long that extends from the cecum in the lower right-hand part of the abdomen

ap·per·tain \ˌap-ər-ˈtān\ *vb* : to belong as a rightful part or privilege

ap·pe·tite \ˈap-ə-ˌtīt\ *n* [ME *apetit,* fr. MF, fr. L *appetitus,* fr. *appetere* to strive after, fr. *ad-* to + *petere* to go to] **1** : natural desire for satisfying some want or need esp. for food **2** : TASTE, PREFERENCE

ap·pe·tiz·er \ˈap-ə-ˌtī-zər\ *n* : a food or drink taken just before a meal to stimulate the appetite

ap·pe·tiz·ing \-ziŋ\ *adj* : tempting to the appetite — **ap·pe·tiz·ing·ly** *adv*

appl *abbr* applied

ap·plaud \ə-ˈplȯd\ *vb* : to show approval esp. by clapping

ap·plause \ə-ˈplȯz\ *n* : approval publicly expressed (as by clapping)

ap·ple \ˈap-əl\ *n* : a rounded fruit with firm white flesh and a seedy core; *also* : a tree that bears this fruit

ap·ple·jack \-ˌjak\ *n* : a liquor distilled from fermented cider

ap·pli·ance \ə-ˈplī-əns\ *n* **1** : INSTRUMENT, DEVICE **2** : a piece of household equipment (as a stove or toaster) operated by gas or electricity

ap·pli·ca·ble \ˈap-li-kə-bəl, ə-ˈplik-ə-\ *adj* : capable of being applied : RELEVANT — **ap·pli·ca·bil·i·ty** \ˌap-li-kə-ˈbil-ət-ē, ə-ˌplik-ə-\ *n*

ap·pli·cant \ˈap-li-kənt\ *n* : one who applies

ap·pli·ca·tion \ˌap-lə-ˈkā-shən\ *n* **1** : the act of applying **2** : assiduous attention **3** : REQUEST; *also* : a form used in making a request **4** : something placed or spread on a surface **5** : capacity for use

ap·pli·ca·tor \ˈap-lə-ˌkāt-ər\ *n* : one that applies; *esp* : a device for applying a substance (as medicine or polish)

ap·plied \ə-ˈplīd\ *adj* : put to practical use

ap·pli·qué \ˌap-lə-ˈkā\ *n* [F] : a fabric decoration cut out and fastened to a larger piece of material — **appliqué** *vb*

ap·ply \ə-ˈplī\ *vb* **ap·plied; ap·ply·ing** **1** : to put to practical use **2** : to place in contact : put or spread on a surface **3** : to employ with close attention **4** : to submit a request **5** : to have reference or connection

ap·point \ə-ˈpȯint\ *vb* **1** : to fix or set officially ⟨~ a day for trial⟩ **2** : to name officially **3** : to fit out : EQUIP

ap·poin·tee \ə-ˌpȯin-ˈtē, ˌa-\ *n* : a person appointed

ap·point·ive \ə-ˈpȯint-iv\ *adj* : subject to appointment

ap·point·ment \ə-ˈpȯint-mənt\ *n* **1** : the act of appointing **2** : a nonelective office or position **3** : an arrangement for a meeting **4** *pl* : FURNISHINGS, EQUIPMENT

ap·por·tion \ə-ˈpōr-shən\ *vb* **-tioned; -tion·ing** \-sh(ə-)niŋ\ : to distribute proportionately : ALLOT — **ap·por·tion·ment** *n*

ap·po·site \ˈap-ə-zət\ *adj* : APPROPRIATE, RELEVANT — **ap·po·site·ly** *adv* — **ap·po·site·ness** *n*

ap·po·si·tion \ˌap-ə-ˈzish-ən\ *n* : a grammatical construction in which a noun or pronoun is followed by another that explains it (as *the poet* and *Burns* in "a biography of the poet Burns")

ap·pos·i·tive \ə-ˈpäz-ət-iv, a-\ *adj* : of, relating to, or standing in grammatical apposition — **appositive** *n*

ap·praise \ə-ˈprāz\ *vb* **ap·praised; ap·prais·ing** : to set a value on — **ap·prais·al** \-ˈprā-zəl\ *n* — **ap·prais·er** *n*

ap·pre·cia·ble \ə-ˈprē-shə-bəl\ *adj* : large enough to be recognized and measured — **ap·pre·cia·bly** \-blē\ *adv*

ap·pre·ci·ate \ə-ˈprē-shē-ˌāt\ *vb* **-at·ed; -at·ing** **1** : to value justly **2** : to be aware of **3** : to be grateful for **4** : to increase in value — **ap·pre·ci·a·tion** \-ˌprē-shē-ˈā-shən\ *n*

ap·pre·cia·tive \ə-ˈprē-shət-iv, -shē-ˌāt-\ *adj* : having or showing appreciation

ap·pre·hend \ˌap-ri-ˈhend\ *vb* **1** : ARREST **2** : to become aware of **3** : to look forward to with dread **4** : UNDERSTAND — **ap·pre·hen·sion** \-ˈhen-chən\ *n*

ap·pre·hen·sive \-ˈhen-siv\ *adj* : viewing the future with anxiety — **ap·pre·hen·sive·ly** *adv* — **ap·pre·hen·sive·ness** *n*

[1]**ap·pren·tice** \ə-ˈprent-əs\ *n* **1** : a person learning a craft under a skilled worker **2** : BEGINNER — **ap·pren·tice·ship** *n*

[2]**apprentice** *vb* **-ticed; -tic·ing** : to bind or set at work as an apprentice

ap·prise \ə-ˈprīz\ *vb* **ap·prised; ap·pris·ing** : INFORM

ap·proach \ə-ˈprōch\ *vb* **1** : to move nearer to **2** : to be almost the same as **3** : to make advances to esp. for the purpose of creating a desired result **4** : to take preliminary steps toward — **approach** *n* — **ap·proach·able** *adj*

ap·pro·ba·tion \ˌap-rə-ˈbā-shən\ *n* : APPROVAL

[1]**ap·pro·pri·ate** \ə-ˈprō-prē-ˌāt\ *vb* **-at·ed; -at·ing 1** : to take possession of **2** : to set apart for a particular use

[2]**ap·pro·pri·ate** \ə-ˈprō-prē-ət\ *adj* : fitted to a purpose or use : SUITABLE **syn** proper, fit, apt, befitting — **ap·pro·pri·ate·ly** *adv* — **ap·pro·pri·ate·ness** *n*

ap·pro·pri·a·tion \ə-ˌprō-prē-ˈā-shən\ *n* **1** : an act or instance of appropriating **2** : money set aside by formal action for a specific use

ap·prov·al \ə-ˈprü-vəl\ *n* : an act of approving — **on approval** : subject to a prospective buyer's acceptance or refusal

ap·prove \ə-ˈprüv\ *vb* **ap·proved; ap·prov·ing 1** : to have or express a favorable opinion of **2** : to accept as satisfactory : RATIFY

approx *abbr* approximate; approximately

[1]**ap·prox·i·mate** \ə-ˈpräk-sə-mət\ *adj* : nearly correct or exact — **ap·prox·i·mate·ly** *adv*

[2]**ap·prox·i·mate** \-ˌmāt\ *vb* **-mat·ed; -mat·ing** : to come near : APPROACH — **ap·prox·i·ma·tion** \ə-ˌpräk-sə-ˈmā-shən\ *n*

appt *abbr* appoint; appointed; appointment

ap·pur·te·nance \ə-ˈpərt-(ᵊ)nəns\ *n* : something that belongs to or goes with another thing **syn** accessory, adjunct, appendage, appendix — **ap·pur·te·nant** \-(ᵊ)nənt\ *adj*

Apr *abbr* April

APR *abbr* annual percentage rate

apri·cot \ˈap-rə-ˌkät, ˈā-prə-\ *n* [deriv. of Ar *al-birqūq*] : an oval orange-colored fruit resembling the related peach and plum in flavor; *also* : a tree bearing apricots

April \ˈā-prəl\ *n* [ME, fr. OF & L; OF *avrill*, fr. L *Aprilis*] : the 4th month of the year having 30 days

a pri·o·ri \ˌä-prē-ˈōr-ē\ *adj* [L, from the former] **1** : characterized by or derived by reasoning from self-evident propositions **2** : independent of experience — **a priori** *adv*

apron \ˈā-prən, -pərn\ *n* [ME, alter. (resulting fr. incorrect division of *a napron*) of *napron*, fr. MF *naperon*, dim. of *nape* cloth, modif. of L *mappa* napkin] **1** : a garment tied over the front of the body to protect the clothes **2** : a paved area for parking or handling airplanes

[1]**ap·ro·pos** \ˌap-rə-ˈpō, ˈap-rə-ˌpō\ *adv* [F *à propos*, lit., to the purpose] **1** : OPPORTUNELY **2** : BY THE WAY

[2]**apropos** *adj* : being to the point

apropos of *prep* : with regard to

apse \ˈaps\ *n* : a projecting usu. semi–circular and vaulted part of a building (as a church)

[1]**apt** \ˈapt\ *adj* **1** : well adapted : SUITABLE **2** : having an habitual tendency : LIKELY **3** : quick to learn — **apt·ly** *adv* — **apt·ness** \ˈap(t)-nəs\ *n*

[2]**apt** *abbr* **1** apartment **2** aptitude

ap·ti·tude \ˈap-tə-ˌt(y)üd\ *n* **1** : natural ability : TALENT **2** : capacity for learning **3** : APPROPRIATENESS

aqua \ˈak-wə, ˈäk-\ *n* : a light greenish blue color

aqua·cul·ture *also* **aqui·cul·ture** \ˈak-wə-ˌkəl-chər, ˈäk-\ *n* : the cultivation of aquatic plants or animals (as fish or shellfish) for human use

aqua·ma·rine \ˌak-wə-mə-ˈrēn, ˌäk-\ *n* **1** : a bluish green gem **2** : a pale blue to light greenish blue

aqua·naut \ˈak-wə-ˌnȯt, ˈäk-\ *n* : a person who lives in an underwater shelter for an extended period

aqua·plane \-ˌplān\ *n* : a board towed behind a motorboat and ridden by a person standing on it — **aquaplane** *vb*

aqua re·gia \ˌak-wə-ˈrē-j(ē-)ə\ *n* [NL, lit., royal water] : a mixture of nitric and hydrochloric acids that dissolves gold or platinum

aquar·i·um \ə-ˈkwar-ē-əm\ *n, pl* **-i·ums** *or* **-ia** \-ē-ə\ **1** : a container (as a glass tank) in which living aquatic animals and plants are kept **2** : a place where aquatic animals and plants are kept and shown

Aquar·i·us \ə-ˈkwar-ē-əs\ *n* [L, lit., water carrier] **1** : a zodiacal constellation between Capricorn and Pisces usu. pictured as a man pouring water **2** : the 11th sign of the zodiac in astrology; *also* : one born under this sign

[1]**aquat·ic** \ə-ˈkwät-ik, -ˈkwat-\ *adj* **1** : growing or living in or frequenting water **2** : performed in or on water

[2]**aquatic** *n* : an aquatic animal or plant

aqua·vit \ˈäk-wə-ˌvēt\ *n* : a clear liquor flavored with caraway seeds

aqua vi·tae \ˌak-wə-ˈvīt-ē, ˌäk-\ *n* [ME, fr. ML, lit., water of life] : a strong alcoholic liquor (as brandy)

aq·ue·duct \ˈak-wə-ˌdəkt\ *n* **1** : a conduit for carrying running water **2** : a structure carrying a canal over a river or hollow **3** : a passage in a bodily part

aqueduct 1

aque·ous \ˈā-kwē-əs, ˈak-wē-\ *adj* **1** : WATERY **2** : made of, by, or with water

aqueous humor *n* : a clear fluid occupying the space between the lens and the cornea of the eye

aqui·fer \ˈak-wə-fər, ˈäk-\ *n* : a water-bearing stratum of permeable rock, sand, or gravel

aq·ui·line \ˈak-wə-ˌlīn, -lən\ *adj* **1** : of or resembling an eagle **2** : hooked like an eagle's beak ⟨an ~ nose⟩

ar *abbr* arrival; arrive

Ar *symbol* argon

AR *abbr* Arkansas

-ar \ər\ *adj suffix* : of or relating to ⟨molecul*ar*⟩ : being ⟨spectacul*ar*⟩ : resembling ⟨oracul*ar*⟩

Ar·ab \ˈar-əb\ *n* **1** : a member of a Semitic people of the Arabian peninsula in southwestern Asia **2** : a member of an Arabic-speaking people — **Arab** *adj* — **Ara·bi·an** \ə-ˈrā-bē-ən\ *adj or n*

ar·a·besque \ˌar-ə-ˈbesk\ *n* : a design of interlacing lines forming figures of flowers, foliage, and sometimes animals

[1]**Ar·a·bic** \ˈar-ə-bik\ *n* : a Semitic language of southwestern Asia and north Africa

[2]**Arabic** *adj* **1** : of or relating to the Arabs, Arabic, or the Arabian peninsula in southwestern Asia **2** : expressed in or making use of Arabic numerals

Arabic numeral *n* : one of the number symbols 1, 2, 3, 4, 5, 6, 7, 8, 9, and 0

ar·a·ble \ˈar-ə-bəl\ *adj* : fit for or cultivated by plowing : suitable for crops

arach·nid \ə-ˈrak-nəd\ *n* : any of a class of usu. 8-legged

\ə\abut \ᵊ\kitten \ər\further \a\ash \ā\ace \ä\cot, cart \au̇\out \ch\chin \e\bet \ē\easy \g\go \i\hit \ī\ice \j\job \ŋ\sing \ō\go \ȯ\law \ȯi\boy \th\thin \t͟h\the \ü\loot \u̇\foot \y\yet \zh\vision *see also* Pronunciation Symbols page

arthropods comprising the spiders, scorpions, mites, and ticks — **arachnid** *adj*

Ar·a·ma·ic \ˌar-ə-ˈmā-ik\ *n* : an ancient Semitic language

Arap·a·ho *or* **Arap·a·hoe** \ə-ˈrap-ə-ˌhō\ *n, pl* **Arapaho** *or* **Arapahos** *or* **Arapahoe** *or* **Arapahoes** : a member of an American Indian people of the western U.S.

ar·bi·ter \ˈär-bət-ər\ *n* : one having power to decide : JUDGE

ar·bi·trage \ˈär-bə-ˌträzh\ *n* [F, fr. MF, arbitration] : the purchase and sale of the same or equivalent security in different markets in order to profit from price discrepancies

ar·bi·tra·geur \ˌär-bə-(ˌ)trä-ˈzhər\ *or* **ar·bi·trag·er** \ˈär-bə-ˌträzh-ər\ *n* : one who practices arbitrage

ar·bit·ra·ment \är-ˈbit-rə-mənt\ *n* **1** : the act of deciding a dispute **2** : the judgment given by an arbitrator

ar·bi·trary \ˈär-bə-ˌtrer-ē\ *adj* **1** : AUTOCRATIC, DESPOTIC **2** : determined by will or caprice : selected at random — **ar·bi·trari·ly** \ˌär-bə-ˈtrer-ə-lē\ *adv* — **ar·bi·trari·ness** \ˈär-bə-ˌtrer-ē-nəs\ *n*

ar·bi·trate \ˈär-bə-ˌtrāt\ *vb* **-trat·ed; -trat·ing 1** : to act as arbitrator **2** : to act on as arbitrator **3** : to submit for decision to an arbitrator — **ar·bi·tra·tion** \ˌär-bə-ˈtrā-shən\ *n*

ar·bi·tra·tor \ˈär-bə-ˌtrāt-ər\ *n* : one chosen to settle differences between two parties in a controversy

ar·bor \ˈär-bər\ *n* [ME *erber* plot of grass, arbor, fr. OF *herbier* plot of grass, fr. *herbe* herb, grass] : a shelter formed of or covered with vines or branches

ar·bo·re·al \är-ˈbōr-ē-əl\ *adj* **1** : of, relating to, or resembling a tree **2** : living in trees ⟨~ monkeys⟩

ar·bo·re·tum \ˌär-bə-ˈrēt-əm\ *n, pl* **-retums** *or* **-re·ta** \-ˈrēt-ə\ [L, place grown with trees, fr. *arbor* tree] : a place where trees and plants are grown for scientific and educational purposes

ar·bor·vi·tae \ˌär-bər-ˈvīt-ē\ *n* : any of various evergreen trees with scalelike leaves that are related to the pines

ar·bu·tus \är-ˈbyüt-əs\ *n* : TRAILING ARBUTUS

¹arc \ˈärk\ *n* **1** : a sustained luminous discharge of electricity (as between two electrodes) **2** : a continuous portion of a curved line (as part of the circumference of a circle)

²arc *vb* : to form an electric arc

ARC *abbr* **1** American Red Cross **2** AIDS-related complex

ar·cade \är-ˈkād\ *n* **1** : an arched or covered passageway; *esp* : one lined with shops **2** : a row of arches with their supporting columns

ar·cane \är-ˈkān\ *adj* : SECRET, MYSTERIOUS

¹arch \ˈärch\ *n* **1** : a curved structure spanning an opening (as a door or window) **2** : something resembling an arch **3** : ARCHWAY

²arch *vb* **1** : to cover with an arch **2** : to form or bend into an arch

³arch *adj* **1** : CHIEF, EMINENT **2** : ROGUISH, MISCHIEVOUS — **arch·ly** *adv* — **arch·ness** *n*

⁴arch *abbr* architect; architectural; architecture

ar·chae·ol·o·gy *or* **ar·che·ol·o·gy** \ˌär-kē-ˈäl-ə-jē\ *n* : the study of past human life as revealed by relics left by ancient peoples — **ar·chae·o·log·i·cal** \-kē-ə-ˈläj-i-kəl\ *adj* — **ar·chae·ol·o·gist** \-kē-ˈäl-ə-jəst\ *n*

ar·cha·ic \är-ˈkā-ik\ *adj* **1** : belonging to an earlier time : ANTIQUATED **2** : having the characteristics of the language of the past and surviving chiefly in specialized uses ⟨~ words⟩ — **ar·cha·i·cal·ly** \-i-k(ə-)lē\ *adv*

arch·an·gel \ˈärk-ˌān-jəl\ *n* : an angel of high rank

arch·bish·op \ärch-ˈbish-əp\ *n* : a bishop of high rank — **arch·bish·op·ric** \-ə-(ˌ)prik\ *n*

arch·dea·con \-ˈdē-kən\ *n* : a clergyman who assists a diocesan bishop in ceremonial or administrative functions

arch·di·o·cese \-ˈdī-ə-səs, -ˌsēz, -ˌsēs\ *n* : the diocese of an archbishop

arch·duke \-ˈd(y)ük\ *n* **1** : a sovereign prince **2** : a prince of the imperial family of Austria

arch·en·e·my \ˈärch-ˈen-ə-mē\ *n, pl* **-mies** : a principal enemy

Ar·cheo·zo·ic \ˌär-kē-ə-ˈzō-ik\ *adj* : of, relating to, or being the earliest era of geologic history extending from the formation of the earth almost 4 billion years ago to about 1.4 billion years ago — **Archeozoic** *n*

ar·chery \ˈärch-(ə-)rē\ *n* : the art or practice of shooting with bow and arrows — **ar·cher** \ˈär-chər\ *n*

ar·che·type \ˈär-ki-ˌtīp\ *n* : the original pattern or model of all things of the same type

arch·fiend \ˈärch-ˈfēnd\ *n* : a chief fiend; *esp* : SATAN

ar·chi·epis·co·pal \ˌär-kē-ə-ˈpis-kə-pəl\ *adj* : of or relating to an archbishop

ar·chi·man·drite \ˌär-kə-ˈman-ˌdrīt\ *n* : a dignitary in an Eastern church ranking below a bishop

ar·chi·pel·a·go \ˌär-kə-ˈpel-ə-ˌgō, ˌär-chə-\ *n, pl* **-goes** *or* **-gos 1** : a sea dotted with islands **2** : a group of islands

ar·chi·tect \ˈär-kə-ˌtekt\ *n* : a person who plans buildings and oversees their construction

ar·chi·tec·ture \ˈär-kə-ˌtek-chər\ *n* **1** : the art or science of planning and building structures **2** : method or style of building — **ar·chi·tec·tur·al** \ˌar-kə-ˈtek-chə-rəl, -ˈtek-shrəl\ *adj* — **ar·chi·tec·tur·al·ly** \-ē\ *adv*

ar·chi·trave \ˈär-kə-ˌtrāv\ *n* : the supporting horizontal member just above the columns in a building in the classical style of architecture

ar·chive \ˈär-ˌkīv\ *n* : a place for keeping public records; *also* : public records — often used in pl.

ar·chi·vist \ˈär-kə-vəst, -ˌkī-\ *n* : a person in charge of archives

ar·chon \ˈär-ˌkän, -kən\ *n* : a chief magistrate of ancient Athens

arch·way \ˈärch-ˌwā\ *n* : a passageway under an arch; *also* : an arch over a passage

arc lamp *n* : a gas-filled electric lamp that produces light when a current arcs between incandescent electrodes

¹arc·tic \ˈärk-tik, ˈärt-ik\ *adj* [ME *artik*, fr. L *articus*, fr. Gk *arktikos*, fr. *arktos* bear, Ursa Major, north] **1** *often cap* : of or relating to the north pole or the region near it **2** : FRIGID

²arc·tic \ˈärt-ik, ˈärk-tik\ *n* : a rubber overshoe that reaches to the ankle or above

arctic circle *n, often cap A&C* : the parallel of latitude that is approximately 66½ degrees north of the equator

-ard \ərd\ *also* **-art** \ərt\ *n suffix* : one that is characterized by performing some action, possessing some quality, or being associated with some thing esp. conspicuously or excessively ⟨brагg*art*⟩ ⟨dull*ard*⟩

ar·dent \ˈärd-ᵊnt\ *adj* **1** : characterized by warmth of feeling : PASSIONATE **2** : FIERY, HOT **3** : GLOWING — **ar·dent·ly** *adv*

ar·dor \ˈärd-ər\ *n* **1** : warmth of feeling : ZEAL **2** : burning heat

ar·du·ous \ˈärj-(ə-)wəs\ *adj* : DIFFICULT, LABORIOUS — **ar·du·ous·ly** *adv* — **ar·du·ous·ness** *n*

¹are *pres 2d sing or pres pl of* BE

²are \ˈa(ə)r\ *n* — see METRIC SYSTEM table

ar·ea \ˈar-ē-ə\ *n* **1** : a flat surface or space **2** : the amount of surface included (as within the lines of a geometric figure) **3** : REGION **4** : range or extent of some thing or concept : FIELD

area code *n* : a 3-digit number that identifies each telephone service area in a country (as the U.S. or Canada)

area·way \-ˌwā\ *n* : a sunken space for giving access, air, and light to a basement

are·na \ə-ˈrē-nə\ *n* [L *harena*, *arena* sand, sandy place] **1** : an enclosed area used for public entertainment **2** : a sphere of activity or competition

ar·gent \ˈär-jənt\ *adj* : of or resembling silver : SILVERY

Ar·gen·tine \ˈär-jən-ˌtēn, -ˌtīn\ *or* **Ar·gen·tin·ean** *or* **Ar·gen·tin·i·an** \ˌär-jən-ˈtin-ē-ən\ *n* : a native or inhabitant of Argentina — **Argentine** *or* **Argentinean** *or* **Argentinian** *adj*

ar·gen·tite \ˈär-jən-ˌtīt\ *n* : a dark gray mineral that is an important ore of silver

ar·gil·la·ceous \ˌär-jə-ˈlā-shəs\ *adj* : CLAYEY

ar·gon \ˈär-ˌgän\ *n* [Gk, neut. of *argos* idle, lazy, fr. *a-* not + *ergon* work; fr. its relative inertness] : a colorless odorless gaseous chemical element found in the air and used for filling electric bulbs — see ELEMENT table

ar·go·sy \ˈär-gə-sē\ *n, pl* **-sies** **1** : a large merchant ship **2** : FLEET

ar·got \ˈär-gət, -ˌgō\ *n* : the language of a particular group or class esp. of the underworld

argu·able \ˈär-gyə-wə-bəl\ *adj* : open to argument, dispute, or question

ar·gue \ˈär-gyü\ *vb* **ar·gued; ar·gu·ing** **1** : to give reasons for or against something **2** : to contend in words : DISPUTE **3** : DEBATE **4** : to persuade by giving reasons

ar·gu·ment \ˈär-gyə-mənt\ *n* **1** : a reason offered in proof **2** : discourse intended to persuade **3** : QUARREL

ar·gu·men·ta·tion \ˌär-gyə-mən-ˈtā- shən\ *n* : the art of formal discussion

ar·gu·men·ta·tive \ˌär-gyə-ˈment-ət-iv\ *adj* : inclined to argue

ar·gyle *also* **ar·gyll** \ˈär-ˌgīl\ *n, often cap* : a geometric knitting pattern of varicolored diamonds on a single background color; *also* : a sock knit in this pattern

aria \ˈär-ē-ə\ *n* : an accompanied elaborate vocal solo forming part of a larger work

ar·id \ˈar-əd\ *adj* **1** : DRY, BARREN **2** : having insufficient rainfall to support agriculture — **arid·i·ty** \ə-ˈrid-ət-ē\ *n*

Ar·i·es \ˈar-(ē-)ˌēz\ *n* [L, lit., ram] **1** : a zodiacal constellation between Pisces and Taurus usu. pictured as a ram **2** : the 1st sign of the zodiac in astrology; *also* : one born under this sign

aright \ə-ˈrīt\ *adv* : RIGHTLY, CORRECTLY

arise \ə-ˈrīz\ *vb* **arose** \-ˈrōz\; **aris·en** \-ˈriz-ᵊn\; **aris·ing** \-ˈrī-ziŋ\ **1** : to get up **2** : ORIGINATE **3** : ASCEND **syn** rise, derive, spring, issue

ar·is·toc·ra·cy \ˌar-ə-ˈstäk-rə-sē\ *n, pl* **-cies** **1** : government by a noble or privileged class; *also* : a state so governed **2** : the governing class of an aristocracy **3** : UPPER CLASS — **aris·to·crat** \ə-ˈris-tə-ˌkrat\ *n* — **aris·to·crat·ic** \ə-ˌris-tə-ˈkrat-ik\ *adj*

arith *abbr* arithmetic; arithmetical

arith·me·tic \ə-ˈrith-mə-ˌtik\ *n* **1** : a branch of mathematics that deals with computations with numbers **2** : COMPUTATION, CALCULATION — **ar·ith·met·ic** \ˌar-ith-ˈmet-ik\ *or* **ar·ith·met·i·cal** \-i-kəl\ *adj* — **ar·ith·met·i·cal·ly** \-i-k(ə-)lē\ *adv* — **arith·me·ti·cian** \ə-ˌrith-mə-ˈtish-ən\ *n*

arithmetic mean *n* : the sum of a set of numbers divided by the number of numbers in the set

Ariz *abbr* Arizona

ark \ˈärk\ *n* **1** : a boat held to resemble that of Noah at the time of the Deluge **2** : the sacred chest in which the ancient Hebrews kept the tablets of the Law

Ark *abbr* Arkansas

¹arm \ˈärm\ *n* **1** : a human upper limb; *also* : a corresponding limb of a lower animal with a backbone **2** : something resembling an arm in shape or position ⟨an ~ of a chair⟩ **3** : POWER, MIGHT ⟨the ~ of the law⟩ — **armed** \ˈärmd\ *adj* — **arm·less** *adj*

²arm *vb* : to furnish with weapons

³arm *n* **1** : WEAPON **2** : a branch of the military forces **3** *pl* : the hereditary heraldic devices of a family

ar·ma·da \är-ˈmäd-ə, -ˈmād-\ *n* : a fleet of armed ships

ar·ma·dil·lo \ˌär-mə-ˈdil-ō\ *n, pl* **-los** : any of several small burrowing mammals with the head and body protected by an armor of bony plates

Ar·ma·ged·don \ˌär-mə-ˈged-ᵊn\ *n* : a final conclusive battle between the forces of good and evil; *also* : the site or time of this

ar·ma·ment \ˈär-mə-mənt\ *n* **1** : military strength **2** : arms and equipment (as of a tank or combat unit) **3** : the process of preparing for war

ar·ma·ture \ˈär-mə-ˌchu̇r, -chər\ *n* **1** : a protective covering or structure (as the spines of a cactus) **2** : the part including the conductors in an electric generator or motor in which the current is induced; *also* : the movable part in an electromagnetic device (as an electric bell or a loudspeaker)

arm·chair \ˈärm-ˌcheər\ *n* : a chair with supports for the arms

armed forces *n pl* : the combined military, naval, and air forces of a nation

arm·ful \ˈärm-ˌfu̇l\ *n, pl* **armfuls** *or* **arms·ful** \ˈärmz-ˌfu̇l\ : as much as the arm can hold

arm·hole \ˈärm-ˌhōl\ *n* : an opening for the arm in a garment

ar·mi·stice \ˈär-mə-stəs\ *n* : temporary suspension of hostilities by mutual agreement : TRUCE

arm·let \ˈärm-lət\ *n* : a band worn around the upper arm

ar·mor \ˈär-mər\ *n* **1** : protective covering **2** : armored forces and vehicles — **ar·mored** \-mərd\ *adj*

ar·mor·er \ˈär-mər-ər\ *n* **1** : one that makes arms and armor **2** : one that services firearms

ar·mo·ri·al \är-ˈmōr-ē-əl\ *adj* : of or bearing heraldic arms

ar·mory \ˈärm-(ə-)rē\ *n, pl* **ar·mor·ies** **1** : a place where arms are stored **2** : a factory where arms are made

arm·pit \ˈärm-ˌpit\ *n* : the hollow under the junction of the arm and shoulder

arm·rest \-ˌrest\ *n* : a support for the arm

ar·my \ˈär-mē\ *n, pl* **armies** **1** : a body of men organized for war **2** *often cap* : the complete military organization of a country for land warfare **3** : a great number **4** : a body of persons organized to advance a cause

army ant *n* : any of various nomadic social ants

ar·my·worm \ˈär-mē-ˌwərm\ *n* : any of numerous moths whose larvae move about destroying crops

ar·ni·ca \ˈär-ni-kə\ *n* **1** : any of several herbs related to the daisies **2** : a soothing preparation of dried arnica flowers used on bruises and sprains; *also* : dried arnica flowers

aro·ma \ə-ˈrō-mə\ *n* : a usu. pleasing odor : FRAGRANCE — **ar·o·mat·ic** \ˌar-ə-ˈmat-ik\ *adj*

arose *past of* ARISE

¹around \ə-ˈrau̇nd\ *adv* **1** : in or along a circuit **2** : on all sides **3** : NEARBY **4** : from one place to another **5** : in an opposite direction ⟨turn ~⟩

²around *prep* **1** : SURROUNDING ⟨trees ~ the house⟩ **2** : to or on the other side of ⟨~ the corner⟩ **3** : NEAR ⟨stayed right ~ home⟩ **4** : along the circuit of ⟨go ~ the world⟩

arouse \ə-ˈrau̇z\ *vb* **aroused; arous·ing** **1** : to awaken from sleep **2** : to stir up — **arous·al** \-ˈrau̇-zəl\ *n*

ar·peg·gio \är-ˈpej-(ē-ˌ)ō\ *n, pl* **-gios** [It fr. *arpeggiare* to play on the harp, fr. *arpa* harp] : a chord whose notes are performed in succession and not simultaneously

arr *abbr* **1** arranged **2** arrival; arrive

ar·raign \ə-ˈrān\ *vb* **1** : to call before a court to answer to an indictment **2** : to accuse of wrong or imperfection — **ar·raign·ment** *n*

ar·range \ə-ˈrānj\ *vb* **ar·ranged; ar·rang·ing** **1** : to put in order **2** : to come to an agreement about : SETTLE **3** : to adapt (a musical composition) to voices or instruments other than those for which it was orig. written — **ar·range·ment** *n* — **ar·rang·er** *n*

ar·rant \ˈar-ənt\ *adj* : being notoriously without moderation : EXTREME

ar·ras \ˈar-əs\ *n, pl* **arras** **1** : TAPESTRY **2** : a wall hanging or screen of tapestry

---

[1]**ar·ray** \ə-ˈrā\ *vb* **1** : to arrange in order **2** : to dress esp. splendidly

[2]**array** *n* **1** : a regular arrangement **2** : rich apparel **3** : an imposing group

ar·rears \ə-ˈriərz\ *n pl* **1** : a state of being behind in the discharge of obligations ⟨in ~ with the payments⟩ **2** : overdue debts

[1]**ar·rest** \ə-ˈrest\ *vb* **1** : STOP, CHECK **2** : to take into legal custody

[2]**arrest** *n* **1** : the act of stopping; *also* : the state of being stopped **2** : the act of taking into custody by legal authority

ar·riv·al \ə-ˈrī-vəl\ *n* **1** : the act of arriving **2** : one that arrives

ar·rive \ə-ˈrīv\ *vb* **ar·rived; ar·riv·ing 1** : to reach a destination **2** : to be near or at hand ⟨the time to go finally *arrived*⟩ **3** : to attain success

ar·ro·gant \ˈar-ə-gənt\ *adj* : offensively exaggerating one's own importance — **ar·ro·gance** \-gəns\ *n* — **ar·ro·gant·ly** *adv*

ar·ro·gate \-ˌgāt\ *vb* **-gat·ed; -gat·ing** : to claim or seize without justification as one's right

ar·row \ˈar-ō\ *n* **1** : a missile shot from a bow and usu. having a slender shaft, a pointed head, and feathers at the butt **2** : a pointed mark used to indicate direction

ar·row·head \ˈar-ō-ˌhed\ *n* : the pointed end of an arrow

ar·row·root \-ˌrüt, -ˌru̇t\ *n* : an edible starch from the roots of any of several tropical American plants; *also* : a plant yielding arrowroot

ar·royo \ə-ˈrȯi-ə, -ō\ *n, pl* **-royos** [Sp] **1** : a watercourse in a dry region **2** : a water-carved gully or channel

ar·se·nal \ˈärs-nəl, -ᵊn-əl\ *n* [deriv. of Ar *dār ṣināʿah* house of manufacture] **1** : a place for making and storing arms and military equipment **2** : STORE, REPERTORY

ar·se·nic \ˈärs-nik, -ᵊn-ik\ *n* **1** : a solid brittle poisonous chemical element of grayish color and metallic luster —see ELEMENT table **2** : a very poisonous oxygen compound of arsenic used in making glass and insecticides

ar·son \ˈärs-ᵊn\ *n* : the malicious burning of property

[1]**art** \ˈärt\ *n* **1** : skill acquired by experience or study **2** : a branch of learning; *esp* : one of the humanities **3** : an occupation requiring knowledge or skill **4** : the use of skill and imagination in the production of things of beauty; *also* : works so produced **5** : ARTFULNESS

[2]**art** *abbr* **1** article **2** artificial **3** artillery

-art — see -ARD

ar·te·ri·al \är-ˈtir-ē-əl\ *adj* **1** : of or relating to an artery; *also* : relating to or being the bright red oxygenated blood found in most arteries **2** : of, relating to, or being a route for through traffic

ar·te·ri·ole \är-ˈtir-ē-ˌōl\ *n* : one of the small terminal twigs of an artery that ends in capillaries — **ar·te·ri·o·lar** \-ˌtir-ē-ˈō-lər\ *adj*

ar·te·rio·scle·ro·sis \är-ˌtir-ē-ō-sklə-ˈrō-səs\ *n* : a chronic disease in which arterial walls are abnormally thickened and hardened — **ar·te·rio·scle·rot·ic** \-ˈrät-ik\ *adj or n*

ar·tery \ˈärt-ə-rē\ *n, pl* **-ter·ies 1** : one of the tubular vessels that carry the blood from the heart **2** : a main channel of transportation or communication; *esp* : a principal channel in a branching system

ar·te·sian well \är-ˌtē-zhən-\ *n* **1** : a bored well gushing water like a fountain **2** : a relatively deep-bored well

art·ful \ˈärt-fəl\ *adj* **1** : INGENIOUS **2** : CRAFTY — **art·ful·ly** \-ē\ *adv* — **art·ful·ness** *n*

ar·thri·tis \är-ˈthrīt-əs\ *n, pl* **-thri·ti·des** \-ˈthrit-ə-ˌdēz\ : inflammation of the joints — **ar·thrit·ic** \-ˈthrit-ik\ *adj or n*

ar·thro·pod \ˈär-thrə-ˌpäd\ *n* : any of a phylum of invertebrate animals comprising those (as insects, spiders, or crabs) with segmented bodies and jointed limbs — **arthropod** *adj*

ar·thros·co·py \är-ˈthräs-kə-pē\ *n, pl* **-pies** : visual examination of the interior of a joint (as the knee) with a special surgical instrument — **ar·thro·scope** \ˈär-thrə-ˌskōp\ *n* — **ar·thro·scop·ic** \ˌär-thrə-ˈskäp-ik\ *adj*

ar·ti·choke \ˈärt-ə-ˌchōk\ *n* [It dial. *articiocco*, fr. Ar *al-khurshūf*] : a tall herb related to the daisies; *also* : its edible flower head

ar·ti·cle \ˈärt-i-kəl\ *n* [ME, fr. OF, fr. L *articulus* joint, division, dim. of *artus* joint] **1** : a distinct part of a written document **2** : a nonfictional prose composition forming an independent part of a publication **3** : a word (as *an, the*) used with a noun to limit or give definiteness to its application **4** : a member of a class of things; *esp* : COMMODITY

ar·tic·u·lar \är-ˈtik-yə-lər\ *adj* : of or relating to a joint

[1]**ar·tic·u·late** \är-ˈtik-yə-lət\ *adj* **1** : divided into meaningful parts : INTELLIGIBLE **2** : able to speak; *also* : expressing oneself readily and effectively **3** : JOINTED — **ar·tic·u·late·ly** *adv* — **ar·tic·u·late·ness** *n*

[2]**ar·tic·u·late** \-ˌlāt\ *vb* **-lat·ed; -lat·ing 1** : to utter distinctly **2** : to unite by or as if by joints — **ar·tic·u·la·tion** \-ˌtik-yə-ˈlā-shən\ *n*

ar·ti·fact \ˈärt-ə-ˌfakt\ *n* : a usu. simple object (as a tool) showing human workmanship or modification

ar·ti·fice \ˈärt-ə-fəs\ *n* **1** : TRICK; *also* : TRICKERY **2** : an ingenious device; *also* : INGENUITY

ar·ti·fi·cer \är-ˈtif-ə-sər, ˈärt-ə-fə-sər\ *n* : a skilled workman

ar·ti·fi·cial \ˌärt-ə-ˈfish-əl\ *adj* **1** : produced by art rather than nature; *also* : made by man to imitate nature **2** : not genuine : FEIGNED — **ar·ti·fi·ci·al·i·ty** \-ˌfish-ē-ˈal-ət-ē\ *n* — **ar·ti·fi·cial·ly** \-ˈfish(-ə-)lē\ *adv* — **ar·ti·fi·cial·ness** \-ˈfish-əl-nəs\ *n*

artificial insemination *n* : introduction of semen into the uterus or oviduct by other than natural means

artificial intelligence *n* : the capability of a machine to imitate intelligent human behavior

artificial respiration *n* : the rhythmic forcing of air into and out of the lungs of a person whose breathing has stopped

ar·til·lery \är-ˈtil-(ə-)rē\ *n, pl* **-ler·ies 1** : large-bore mounted firearms usu. operated by crews **2** : a branch of the army armed with artillery — **ar·til·ler·ist** \-ˈtil-ə-rəst\ *n*

ar·ti·san \ˈärt-ə-zən, -sən\ *n* : a skilled manual worker

art·ist \ˈärt-əst\ *n* **1** : one who practices an art; *esp* : one who creates objects of beauty **2** : ARTISTE

ar·tiste \är-ˈtēst\ *n* : a skilled public performer

ar·tis·tic \är-ˈtis-tik\ *adj* : showing taste and skill — **ar·tis·ti·cal·ly** \-ti-k(ə-)lē\ *adv*

art·ist·ry \ˈärt-ə-strē\ *n* : artistic quality or ability

art·less \ˈärt-ləs\ *adj* **1** : lacking art or skill **2** : free from artificiality : NATURAL **3** : free from guile : SINCERE — **art·less·ly** *adv* — **art·less·ness** *n*

art nou·veau \ˌär(t)-nü-ˈvō\ *n, often cap A & N* [F, lit., new art] : a late 19th century decorative style characterized by sinuous lines and leaf-shaped forms

arty \ˈärt-ē\ *adj* **art·i·er; -est** : showily or pretentiously artistic — **art·i·ly** \ˈärt-ᵊl-ē\ *adv* — **art·i·ness** \-ē-nəs\ *n*

ar·um \ˈar-əm\ *n* : any of a genus of plants (as the jack-in-the-pulpit or a skunk cabbage) with flowers in a fleshy enclosed spike

ARV *abbr* American Revised Version

[1]**-ary** \ˌer-ē\ *n suffix* : thing or person belonging to or connected with ⟨function*ary*⟩

[2]**-ary** *adj suffix* : of, relating to, or connected with ⟨budget*ary*⟩

Ary·an \ˈar-ē-ən, ˈer-; ˈär-yən\ *adj* **1** : INDO-EUROPEAN **2** : NORDIC — **Aryan** *n*

[1]**as** \əz, (ˌ)az\ *adv* **1** : to the same degree or amount : EQUALLY ⟨~ green as grass⟩ **2** : for instance ⟨various trees, ~ oak or pine⟩ **3** : when considered in a specified relation ⟨my opinion ~ distinguished from his⟩

[2]**as** *conj* **1** : in the same amount or degree in which ⟨green ~ grass⟩ **2** : in the same way that ⟨farmed ~ his father before him had farmed⟩ **3** : WHILE, WHEN ⟨spoke to me

~ I was leaving⟩ **4** : THOUGH ⟨improbable ~ it seems⟩ **5** : SINCE, BECAUSE ⟨~ I'm not wanted, I'll go⟩ **6** : that the result is ⟨so guilty ~ to leave no doubt⟩

[3]as *pron* **1** : THAT — used after *same* or *such* ⟨it's the same price ~ before⟩ **2** : a fact that ⟨he's rich, ~ you know⟩

[4]as *prep* : in the capacity or character of ⟨this will serve ~ a substitute⟩

As *symbol* arsenic

AS *abbr* **1** American Samoa **2** Anglo-Saxon

asa·fet·i·da *or* **asa·foe·ti·da** \ˌas-ə-ˈfit-əd-ē, -ˈfet-əd-ə\ *n* : an ill-smelling plant gum formerly used in medicine

ASAP *abbr* as soon as possible

as·bes·tos \as-ˈbes-təs, az-\ *n* : a noncombustible grayish mineral that occurs in fibrous form and is used as a fireproof material

as·cend \ə-ˈsend\ *vb* **1** : to move upward : MOUNT, CLIMB **2** : to succeed to : OCCUPY ⟨he ~*ed* the throne⟩

as·cen·dan·cy *also* **as·cen·den·cy** \ə-ˈsen-dən-sē\ *n* : controlling influence : DOMINATION

[1]as·cen·dant *also* **as·cen·dent** \ə-ˈsen-dənt\ *n* : a dominant position

[2]ascendant *also* **ascendent** *adj* **1** : moving upward **2** : DOMINANT

as·cen·sion \ə-ˈsen-chən\ *n* : the act or process of ascending

Ascension Day *n* : the Thursday 40 days after Easter observed in commemoration of Christ's ascension into heaven

as·cent \ə-ˈsent\ *n* **1** : the act of mounting upward : CLIMB **2** : degree of upward slope

as·cer·tain \ˌas-ər-ˈtān\ *vb* : to learn by inquiry — **as·cer·tain·able** *adj*

as·cet·ic \ə-ˈset-ik\ *adj* : practicing self-denial esp. for religious reasons : AUSTERE — **ascetic** *n* — **as·cet·i·cism** \-ˈset-ə-ˌsiz-əm\ *n*

ASCII \ˈas-kē\ *n* [*A*merican *S*tandard *C*ode for *I*nformation *I*nterchange] : a computer code for representing alphanumeric information

ascor·bic acid \ə-ˌskȯr-bik-\ *n* : VITAMIN C

as·cot \ˈas-kət, -ˌkät\ *n* [*Ascot* Heath, racetrack near Ascot, England] : a broad neck scarf that is looped under the chin

as·cribe \ə-ˈskrīb\ *vb* **as·cribed; as·crib·ing** : to refer to a supposed cause, source, or author : ATTRIBUTE — **as·crib·able** *adj* — **as·crip·tion** \-ˈskrip-shən\ *n*

asep·tic \ā-ˈsep-tik\ *adj* : free or freed from disease-causing germs

asex·u·al \ā-ˈsek-sh(ə-w)əl\ *adj* **1** : lacking sex or functional sex organs **2** : occurring or formed without the production and union of two kinds of germ cells ⟨~ reproduction⟩ — **asex·u·al·ly** \(ˈ)ā-ˈseksh-(ə-)wə-lē\ *adv*

as for *prep* : with regard to : CONCERNING ⟨*as for* the others, they were late⟩

[1]ash \ˈash\ *n* **1** : any of a genus of trees related to the olive and having winged seeds and bark with grooves and ridges **2** : the tough elastic wood of an ash

[2]ash *n* **1** : the solid matter left when material is burned **2** : fine mineral particles from a volcano **3** *pl* : the remains of the dead human body

ashamed \ə-ˈshāmd\ *adj* **1** : feeling shame **2** : restrained by anticipation of shame ⟨~ to say anything⟩ — **asham·ed·ly** \-ˈshā-məd-lē\ *adv*

ash·en \ˈash-ən\ *adj* : resembling ashes (as in color); *esp* : deadly pale

ash·lar \ˈash-lər\ *n* : hewn or squared stone; *also* : masonry of such stone

ashore \ə-ˈshōr\ *adv* : on or to the shore

as how *conj* : THAT ⟨allowed *as how* she was glad to be here⟩

ash·ram \ˈäsh-rəm\ *n* : a religious retreat esp. of a Hindu sage

ash·tray \ˈash-ˌtrā\ *n* : a receptacle for tobacco ashes

Ash Wednesday *n* : the 1st day of Lent

ashy \ˈash-ē\ *adj* **ash·i·er; -est** : ASHEN

Asian \ˈā-zhən, -shən\ *adj* : of, relating to, or characteristic of the continent of Asia or its people — **Asian** *n*

Asi·at·ic \ˌā-z(h)ē-ˈat-ik\ *adj* : ASIAN — sometimes taken to be offensive — **Asiatic** *n*

[1]aside \ə-ˈsīd\ *adv* **1** : to or toward the side **2** : out of the way : AWAY

[2]aside *n* : an actor's words heard by the audience but supposedly not by other characters on stage

aside from *prep* **1** : BESIDES ⟨*aside from* being pretty, she's intelligent⟩ **2** : with the exception of ⟨*aside from* one D his grades are excellent⟩

as if *conj* **1** : as it would be if ⟨it's *as if* nothing had changed⟩ **2** : as one would if ⟨he acts *as if* he'd never been away⟩ **3** : THAT ⟨it seems *as if* nothing ever happens around here⟩

as·i·nine \ˈas-ᵊn-ˌīn\ *adj* [L *asininus*, fr. *asinus* ass] : STUPID, FOOLISH — **as·i·nin·i·ty** \ˌas-ᵊn-ˈin-ət-ē\ *n*

ask \ˈask\ *vb* **asked** \ˈas(k)t\ **ask·ing** **1** : to call on for an answer **2** : UTTER ⟨~ a question⟩ **3** : to make a request of ⟨~ him for help⟩ **4** : to make a request for ⟨~ help of her⟩ **5** : to set as a price ⟨~*ed* $800 for the car⟩ **6** : INVITE

askance \ə-ˈskans\ *adv* **1** : with a side glance **2** : with distrust

askew \ə-ˈskyü\ *adv or adj* : out of line : AWRY

ASL *abbr* American Sign Language

[1]aslant \ə-ˈslant\ *adv or adj* : in a slanting direction

[2]aslant *prep* : over or across in a slanting direction

asleep \ə-ˈslēp\ *adv or adj* **1** : in or into a state of sleep **2** : DEAD **3** : NUMB **4** : INACTIVE

as long as *conj* **1** : provided that ⟨do as you like *as long as* you get home on time⟩ **2** : INASMUCH AS, SINCE ⟨*as long as* you're up, turn on the light⟩

as of *prep* : AT, DURING, FROM, ON ⟨takes effect *as of* July 1⟩

asp \ˈasp\ *n* : a small poisonous African snake

as·par·a·gus \ə-ˈspar-ə-gəs\ *n* : a tall branching perennial herb related to the lilies; *also* : its edible young stalks

as·par·tame \as-ˈpär-ˌtām\ *n* : a crystalline low-calorie sweetener

as·pect \ˈas-ˌpekt\ *n* **1** : a position facing a particular direction **2** : APPEARANCE, LOOK **3** : PHASE

as·pen \ˈas-pən\ *n* : any of several poplars with leaves that flutter in the slightest breeze

as·per·i·ty \a-ˈsper-ət-ē, ə-\ *n, pl* **-ties** **1** : ROUGHNESS **2** : harshness of temper

as·per·sion \ə-ˈspər-zhən\ *n* : the act of calumniating; *also* : a calumnious remark

as·phalt \ˈas-ˌfȯlt\ *or* **as·phal·tum** \as-ˈfȯl-təm\ *n* : a dark solid or somewhat plastic substance that is found in natural beds or obtained as a residue in petroleum refining and is used in paving streets, in roofing houses, and in paints

asphalt jungle *n* : a big city or a specified part of a big city

as·pho·del \ˈas-fə-ˌdel\ *n* : any of several Old World herbs related to the lilies and bearing flowers in long erect spikes

as·phyx·ia \as-ˈfik-sē-ə\ *n* : a lack of oxygen or excess of carbon dioxide in the body usu. caused by interruption of breathing and causing unconsciousness

as·phyx·i·ate \-sē-ˌāt\ *vb* **-at·ed; -at·ing** : SUFFOCATE — **as·phyx·i·a·tion** \-ˌfik-sē-ˈā-shən\ *n*

as·pic \ˈas-pik\ *n* [F, lit., asp] : a savory meat jelly

as·pi·rant \ˈas-p(ə-)rənt, ə-ˈspī-rənt\ *n* : one who aspires **syn** candidate, applicant, seeker

as·pi·rate \ˈas-p(ə-)rət\ *n* **1** : an independent sound \h\ or a character (as the letter *h*) representing it **2** : a consonant having aspiration as its final component

as·pi·ra·tion \ˌas-pə-ˈrā-shən\ *n* **1** : the pronunciation or addition of an aspirate; *also* : the aspirate or its symbol **2** : a drawing of something in, out, up, or through by or as if by suction **3** : a strong desire to achieve something noble; *also* : an object of this desire

as·pire \ə-ˈspī(ə)r\ *vb* **as·pired; as·pir·ing** **1** : to have a noble desire or ambition **2** : to rise aloft

as·pi·rin \ˈas-p(ə-)rən\ *n, pl* **aspirin** *or* **aspirins** **1** : a white crystalline drug used to relieve pain and fever **2** : a tablet of aspirin

as regards *or* **as respects** *prep* : in regard to : with respect to

ass \ˈas\ *n* **1** : any of several long-eared animals smaller than the related horses; *esp* : DONKEY **2** : a stupid person

as·sail \ə-ˈsāl\ *vb* : to attack violently — **as·sail·able** *adj* — **as·sail·ant** *n*

as·sas·sin \ə-ˈsas-ᵊn\ *n* [deriv. of Ar *ḥashshāshīn,* pl. of *ḥashshāsh* hashish-user, fr. *hashīsh* hashish] : a murderer esp. for hire or fanatical reasons

as·sas·si·nate \ə-ˈas-ᵊn-ˌāt\ *vb* **-nat·ed; -nat·ing** : to murder by sudden or secret attack — **as·sas·si·na·tion** \-ˌsas-ᵊn-ˈā-shən\ *n*

as·sault \ə-ˈsȯlt\ *n* **1** : a violent attack **2** : an unlawful attempt or threat to do harm to another — **assault** *vb*

[1]**as·say** \ˈas-ˌā, a-ˈsā\ *n* : analysis to determine the quantity of one or more components present in a sample (as of an ore or drug)

[2]**as·say** \a-ˈsā, ˈas-ˌā\ *vb* **1** : TRY, ATTEMPT **2** : to subject (as an ore or drug) to an assay **3** : to make a critical estimate of

as·sem·blage \ə-ˈsem-blij, *3 & 4 also* ˌas-ˌäm-ˈbläzh\ *n* **1** : a collection of persons or things : GATHERING **2** : the act of assembling **3** : an artistic composition made from scraps, junk, and odds and ends **4** : the art of making assemblages

as·sem·ble \ə-ˈsem-bəl\ *vb* **-bled; -bling** \-b(ə-)liŋ\ **1** : to collect into one place : CONGREGATE **2** : to fit together the parts of **3** : to meet together : CONVENE

as·sem·bly \ə-ˈsem-blē\ *n, pl* **-blies** **1** : a gathering of persons : MEETING **2** *cap* : a legislative body; *esp* : the lower house of a legislature **3** : a signal for troops to assemble **4** : the fitting together of parts (as of a machine)

assembly language *n* : a symbolic language for programming a computer that is a close approximation of machine language

assembly line *n* : an arrangement of machines, equipment, and workers in which work passes from operation to operation in a direct line

as·sem·bly·man \ə-ˈsem-blē-mən\ *n* : a member of a legislative assembly

as·sem·bly·wom·an \-ˌwu̇m-ən\ *n* : a woman who is a member of an assembly

as·sent \ə-ˈsent\ *vb* : AGREE, CONCUR — **assent** *n*

as·sert \ə-ˈsərt\ *vb* **1** : to state positively **2** : to demonstrate the existence of **syn** declare, affirm, protest, avow, claim — **as·ser·tive** \-ˈsərt-iv\ *adj* — **as·ser·tive·ness** *n*

as·ser·tion \ə-ˈsər-shən\ *n* : a positive statement

as·sess \ə-ˈses\ *vb* **1** : to fix the rate or amount of **2** : to impose (as a tax) at a specified rate **3** : to evaluate for taxation — **as·sess·ment** *n* — **as·ses·sor** \-ər\ *n*

as·set \ˈas-ˌet\ *n* **1** *pl* : the entire property of a person or company that may be used to pay debts **2** : ADVANTAGE, RESOURCE

as·sev·er·ate \ə-ˈsev-ə-ˌrāt\ *vb* **-at·ed; -at·ing** : to assert earnestly — **as·sev·er·a·tion** \-ˌsev-ə-ˈrā-shən\ *n*

as·sid·u·ous \ə-ˈsij-(ə-)wəs\ *adj* : steadily attentive : DILIGENT — **as·si·du·i·ty** \ˌas-ə-ˈd(y)ü-ət-ē\ *n* — **as·sid·u·ous·ly** *adv* — **as·sid·u·ous·ness** *n*

as·sign \ə-ˈsīn\ *vb* **1** : to transfer (property) to another **2** : to appoint to a duty **3** : PRESCRIBE ⟨~ a lesson⟩ **4** : FIX, SPECIFY ⟨~ a limit⟩ **5** : ASCRIBE ⟨~ a reason⟩ — **as·sign·able** *adj*

as·sig·na·tion \ˌas-ig-ˈnā-shən\ *n* : an appointment for a lovers' meeting; *also* : the resulting meeting

assigned risk *n* : a poor risk (as an accident-prone motorist) that an insurance company is forced to insure by state law

as·sign·ment \ə-ˈsīn-mənt\ *n* **1** : the act of assigning **2** : something assigned

as·sim·i·late \ə-ˈsim-ə-ˌlāt\ *vb* **-lat·ed; -lat·ing** **1** : to take up and absorb as nourishment; *also* : to absorb into a cultural tradition **2** : COMPREHEND **3** : to make or become similar — **as·sim·i·la·tion** \-ˌsim-ə-ˈlā-shən\ *n*

[1]**as·sist** \ə-ˈsist\ *vb* : HELP, AID — **as·sis·tance** \-ˈsis-təns\ *n*

[2]**assist** *n* **1** : an act of assistance **2** : the act of a player who enables a teammate to make a putout (as in baseball) or score a goal (as in hockey)

as·sis·tant \ə-ˈsis-tənt\ *n* : one who assists : HELPER

as·size \ə-ˈsīz\ *n* **1** : a judicial inquest **2** *pl* : the former regular sessions of the superior courts in English counties

assn *abbr* association

assoc *abbr* associate; associated; association

[1]**as·so·ci·ate** \ə-ˈsō-s(h)ē-ˌāt\ *vb* **-at·ed; -at·ing** **1** : to join in companionship or partnership **2** : to connect in thought

[2]**as·so·ciate** \-s(h)ē-ət, -shət\ *n* **1** : a fellow worker : PARTNER **2** : COMPANION **3** *often cap* : a degree conferred esp. by a junior college ⟨~ in arts⟩ — **associate** *adj*

as·so·ci·a·tion \ə-ˌsō-s(h)ē-ˈā-shən\ *n* **1** : the act of associating **2** : an organization of persons : SOCIETY

as·so·cia·tive \ə-ˈsō-s(h)ē-ˌāt-iv, -shət-iv\ *adj* : of, relating to, or involved in association and esp. mental association

as·so·nance \ˈas-ə-nəns\ *n* : repetition of vowels esp. as an alternative to rhyme in verse

as soon as *conj* : immediately at or just after the time that ⟨we'll start *as soon as* he comes⟩

as·sort \ə-ˈsȯrt\ *vb* **1** : to distribute into like groups **2** : HARMONIZE

as·sort·ed \-ˈsȯrt-əd\ *adj* : consisting of various kinds

as·sort·ment \-ˈsȯrt-mənt\ *n* : a collection of assorted things or persons

asst *abbr* assistant

as·suage \ə-ˈswāj\ *vb* **as·suaged; as·suag·ing** **1** : to make (as pain or grief) less : EASE **2** : SATISFY **syn** alleviate, relieve, lighten, mitigate

as·sume \ə-ˈsüm\ *vb* **as·sumed; as·sum·ing** **1** : to take upon oneself **2** : to pretend to have **3** : to take as granted though not proved

as·sump·tion \ə-ˈsəmp-shən\ *n* **1** : the taking up of a person into heaven **2** *cap* : a church festival commemorating the Assumption of Mary and celebrated on August 15 **3** : a taking upon oneself **4** : PRETENSION **5** : SUPPOSITION

as·sur·ance \ə-ˈshu̇r-əns\ *n* **1** : PLEDGE **2** *chiefly Brit* : INSURANCE **3** : SECURITY **4** : SELF-CONFIDENCE; *also*: AUDACITY

as·sure \ə-ˈshu̇r\ *vb* **as·sured; as·sur·ing** **1** : INSURE **2** : to give confidence to **3** : to state confidently to **4** : to make certain the attainment of

as·sured \ə-ˈshu̇rd\ *n, pl* **assured** *or* **assureds** : the beneficiary of an insurance policy

as·ta·tine \ˈas-tə-ˌtēn\ *n* : an unstable radioactive chemical element — see ELEMENT table

as·ter \ˈas-tər\ *n* : any of various mostly fall-blooming leafy-stemmed herbs with daisylike purple, white, pink, or yellow flower heads

as·ter·isk \ˈas-tə-ˌrisk\ *n* [L *asteriscus,* fr. Gk *asteriskos,* lit., little star, dim. of *astēr*] : a character * used as a reference mark or as an indication of the omission of letters or words

astern \ə-ˈstərn\ *adv or adj* **1** : in, at, or toward the stern **2** : BACKWARD

as·ter·oid \ˈas-tə-ˌrȯid\ *n* : one of thousands of small planets between Mars and Jupiter with diameters under 500 miles (800 kilometers)

asth·ma \ˈaz-mə\ *n* : an often allergic disorder marked by difficulty in breathing and a cough — **asth·mat·ic** \az-ˈmat-ik\ *adj or n*

as though *conj* : AS IF

astig·ma·tism \ə-ˈstig-mə-ˌtiz-əm\ *n* : a defect in a lens or an eye causing improper focusing — **as·tig·mat·ic** \ˌas-tig-ˈmat-ik\ *adj*

astir \ə-ˈstər\ *adj* : being in action : MOVING

as to *prep* **1** : ABOUT, CONCERNING ⟨uncertain *as to* what went on⟩ **2** : ACCORDING TO ⟨graded *as to* size⟩

as·ton·ish \ə-ˈstän-ish\ *vb* : to strike with sudden and usu. great wonder : AMAZE — **as·ton·ish·ing·ly** *adv* — **as·ton·ish·ment** *n*

as·tound \ə-ˈstau̇nd\ *vb* : to fill with bewilderment or wonder — **as·tound·ing·ly** *adv*

¹astrad·dle \ə-ˈstrad-ᵊl\ *adv* : on or above and extending onto both sides

²astraddle *prep* : ASTRIDE

as·tra·khan \ˈas-trə-kən, -ˌkan\ *n, often cap* **1** : karakul of Russian origin **2** : a cloth with a usu. wool, curled, and looped pile resembling karakul

as·tral \ˈas-trəl\ *adj* : of or relating to the stars

astray \ə-ˈstrā\ *adv or adj* **1** : off the right way or route **2** : into error

¹astride \ə-ˈstrīd\ *adv* **1** : with one leg on each side **2** : with legs apart

²astride *prep* : with one leg on each side of

¹as·trin·gent \ə-ˈstrin-jənt\ *adj* : able or tending to shrink body tissues — **as·trin·gen·cy** \-jən-sē\ *n*

²astringent *n* : an astringent agent or substance

astrol *abbr* astrologer; astrology

as·tro·labe \ˈas-trə-ˌlāb\ *n* : an instrument for observing the positions of celestial bodies

as·trol·o·gy \ə-ˈsträl-ə-jē\ *n* : divination based on the supposed influence of the stars upon human events — **as·trol·o·ger** \-ə-jər\ *n* — **as·tro·log·i·cal** \ˌas-trə-ˈläj-i-kəl\ *adj*

astron *abbr* astronomer; astronomy

as·tro·naut \ˈas-trə-ˌnȯt\ *n* : a traveler in a spacecraft

as·tro·nau·tics \as-trə-ˈnȯt-iks\ *n* : the science of the construction and operation of spacecraft — **as·tro·nau·tic** \-ik\ *or* **as·tro·nau·ti·cal** \-i-kəl\ *adj*

as·tro·nom·i·cal \ˌas-trə-ˈnäm-i-kəl\ *also* **as·tro·nom·ic** \-ik\ *adj* **1** : of or relating to astronomy **2** : extremely large ⟨an ~ amount of money⟩

astronomical unit *n* : a unit of length used in astronomy equal to the mean distance of the earth from the sun or about 93 million miles (150 million kilometers)

as·tron·o·my \ə-ˈsträn-ə-mē\ *n, pl* **-mies** : the science of the celestial bodies and of their magnitudes, motions, and constitution — **as·tron·o·mer** \-ə-mər\ *n*

as·tro·phys·ics \ˌas-trə-ˈfiz-iks\ *n* : astronomy dealing esp. with the physical properties and dynamic processes of celestial objects — **as·tro·phys·i·cal** \-i-kəl\ *adj* — **as·tro·phys·i·cist** \-ˈfiz-(ə-)səst\ *n*

as·tute \ə-ˈst(y)üt, a-\ *adj* [L *astutus*, fr. *astus* craft] : shrewdly discerning; *also* : WILY — **as·tute·ly** *adv* — **as·tute·ness** *n*

asun·der \ə-ˈsən-dər\ *adv or adj* **1** : into separate pieces ⟨torn ~⟩ **2** : separated in position

ASV *abbr* American Standard Version

¹as well as *conj* : and in addition : and moreover ⟨brave *as well as* loyal⟩

²as well as *prep* : in addition to : BESIDES ⟨the coach, *as well as* the team, is ready⟩

asy·lum \ə-ˈsī-ləm\ *n* [ME, fr. L, fr. Gk *asylon*, neut. of *asylos* inviolable, fr. *a-* not + *sylon* right of seizure] **1** : a place of refuge **2** : protection given to esp. political fugitives **3** : an institution for the care of the needy or afflicted and esp. of the insane

asym·met·ri·cal \ˌā-sə-ˈme-tri-kəl\ *or* **asym·met·ric** \-trik\ *adj* : not symmetrical — **asym·me·try** \(ˈ)ā-ˈsim-ə-trē\ *n*

as·ymp·tote \ˈas-əm(p)-ˌtōt\ *n* : a straight line that is associated with a curve and tends to approximate it along an infinite branch — **as·ymp·tot·ic** \ˌas-əm(p)-ˈtät-ik\ *adj* — **as·ymp·tot·i·cal·ly** \-i-k(ə-)lē\ *adv*

¹at \ət, (ˈ)at\ *prep* **1** — used to indicate a point in time or space ⟨be here ~ 3 o'clock⟩ ⟨he is ~ the hotel⟩ **2** — used to indicate a goal ⟨swung ~ the ball⟩ ⟨laugh ~ him⟩ **3** — used to indicate position or condition ⟨~ rest⟩ **4** — used to indicate means, cause, or manner ⟨sold ~ auction⟩

²at \ˈät\ *n, pl* **at** — see *kip* at MONEY table

At *symbol* astatine

AT *abbr* automatic transmission

at all \ət-ˈȯl, ə-ˈtȯl, at-ˈȯl\ *adv* : in any way : in any circumstances ⟨not *at all* likely⟩

at·a·vism \ˈat-ə-ˌviz-əm\ *n* : appearance in an individual of a character typical of ancestors more remote than its parents; *also* : such an individual or character — **at·a·vis·tic** \ˌat-ə-ˈvis-tik\ *adj*

ate *past of* EAT

¹-ate \ət, ˌāt\ *n suffix* **1** : one acted upon (in a specified way) ⟨distill*ate*⟩ **2** : chemical compound or complex derived from a (specified) compound or element ⟨acet*ate*⟩

²-ate *n suffix* **1** : office : function : rank : group of persons holding a (specified) office or rank ⟨episcop*ate*⟩ **2** : state : dominion : jurisdiction ⟨emir*ate*⟩

³-ate *adj suffix* **1** : acted on (in a specified way) : being in a (specified) state ⟨temper*ate*⟩ ⟨degener*ate*⟩ **2** : marked by having ⟨vertebr*ate*⟩

⁴-ate \ˌāt\ *vb suffix* : cause to be modified or affected by ⟨pollin*ate*⟩ : cause to become ⟨activ*ate*⟩ : furnish with ⟨aer*ate*⟩

ate·lier \ˌat-ᵊl-ˈyā\ *n* **1** : an artist's studio **2** : WORKSHOP

athe·ist \ˈā-thē-əst\ *n* : one who denies the existence of God — **athe·ism** \-ˌiz-əm\ *n* — **athe·is·tic** \ˌā-thē-ˈis-tik\ *adj*

ath·e·nae·um *or* **ath·e·ne·um** \ˌath-ə-ˈnē-əm\ *n* : LIBRARY 1

ath·ero·scle·ro·sis \ˌath-ə-rō-sklə-ˈrō-səs\ *n* : arteriosclerosis characterized by the deposition of fatty substances in and the hardening of the inner layer of the arteries — **ath·ero·scle·rot·ic** \-ˈrät-ik\ *adj*

athirst \ə-ˈthərst\ *adj* **1** *archaic* : THIRSTY **2** : EAGER, LONGING

ath·lete \ˈath-ˌlēt\ *n* [ME, fr. L *athleta*, fr. Gk *athlētēs*, fr. *athlein* to contend for a prize, fr. *athlon* prize, contest] : one trained to compete in athletics

athlete's foot *n* : ringworm of the feet

ath·let·ic \ath-ˈlet-ik\ *adj* **1** : of or relating to athletes or athletics **2** : VIGOROUS, ACTIVE **3** : STURDY, MUSCULAR

ath·let·ics \ath-ˈlet-iks\ *n sing or pl* : exercises and games requiring physical skill, strength, and endurance

athletic supporter *n* : an elastic pouch used to support the male genitals and worn esp. during athletic activity

¹athwart \ə-ˈthwȯrt\ *prep* **1** : ACROSS **2** : in opposition to

²athwart *adv* : obliquely across

atilt \ə-ˈtilt\ *adv or adj* **1** : in a tilted position **2** : with lance in hand

Atl *abbr* Atlantic

at·las \ˈat-ləs\ *n* : a book of maps

atm *abbr* atmosphere; atmospheric

at·mo·sphere \ˈat-mə-ˌsfiər\ *n* **1** : the mass of air surrounding the earth **2** : a surrounding influence **3** : a unit of pressure equal to the pressure of air at sea level or about 14.7 pounds per square inch (10 newtons per square centimeter) **4** : a dominant effect — **at·mo·spher-**

ic \ˌat-mə-ˈsfir-ik, -ˈsfer-\ *adj* — **at·mo·spher·i·cal·ly** \-i-k(ə-)lē\ *adv*

at·mo·spher·ics \ˌat-mə-ˈsfir-iks, -ˈsfer-\ *n pl* : disturbances produced in a radio receiver by atmospheric electrical phenomena

atoll \ˈa-ˌtȯl, -ˌtäl, ˈā-\ *n* : a coral island consisting of a reef surrounding a lagoon

atoll

at·om \ˈat-əm\ *n* [ME, fr. L *atomus*, fr. Gk *atomos*, fr. *atomos* indivisible, fr. *a-* not + *temnein* to cut] **1** : a tiny particle : BIT **2** : the smallest particle of a chemical element that can exist alone or in combination

atom bomb *n* : a very destructive bomb utilizing the energy released by splitting the atom

atom·ic \ə-ˈtäm-ik\ *adj* **1** : of or relating to atoms, atomic energy, or atom bombs **2** : extremely small

atomic clock *n* : a precision clock regulated by the natural vibration of atoms or molecules (as of cesium or ammonia)

atomic energy *n* : energy that can be liberated by changes (as by fission or fusion) in the nucleus of an atom

atomic number *n* : the number of protons in the nucleus of an element

at·om·ize \ˈat-ə-ˌmīz\ *vb* **-ized; -iz·ing** : to reduce to minute particles

at·om·iz·er \ˈat-ə-ˌmī-zər\ *n* : a device for reducing a liquid to a very fine spray (as for spraying the throat)

atom smasher *n* : ACCELERATOR 3

aton·al \ā-ˈtōn-ᵊl\ *adj* : marked by avoidance of traditional musical tonality — **ato·nal·i·ty** \ˌā-tō-ˈnal-ət-ē\ *n* — **aton·al·ly** \ā-ˈtōn-ᵊl-ē\ *adv*

atone \ə-ˈtōn\ *vb* **atoned; aton·ing** **1** : to make amends **2** : EXPIATE

atone·ment \ə-ˈtōn-mənt\ *n* **1** : the reconciliation of God and man through the death of Jesus Christ **2** : reparation for an offense

atop \ə-ˈtäp\ *prep* : on top of

ATP \ˌā-ˌtē-ˈpē\ *n* [*a*denosine *t*ri*p*hosphate] : a compound that occurs widely in living tissue and supplies energy for many cellular processes by undergoing enzymatic hydrolysis

atri·um \ˈā-trē-əm\ *n, pl* **atria** \-trē-ə\ *also* **atri·ums** **1** : the central hall of a Roman house **2** : an anatomical cavity or passage; *esp* : one of the chambers of the heart that receives blood from the veins — **atri·al** \-trē-əl\ *adj*

atro·cious \ə-ˈtrō-shəs\ *adj* **1** : savagely brutal, cruel, or wicked **2** : very bad : ABOMINABLE — **atro·cious·ly** *adv* — **atro·cious·ness** *n*

atroc·i·ty \ə-ˈträs-ət-ē\ *n, pl* **-ties** **1** : ATROCIOUSNESS **2** : an atrocious act or object

[1]**at·ro·phy** \ˈa-trə-fē\ *n, pl* **-phies** : decrease in size or wasting away of a bodily part or tissue

[2]**atrophy** *vb* **-phied; -phy·ing** : to cause or undergo atrophy

at·ro·pine \ˈa-trə-ˌpēn\ *n* : a drug from belladonna and related plants used esp. to relieve spasms and to dilate the pupil of the eye

att *abbr* **1** attached **2** attention **3** attorney

at·tach \ə-ˈtach\ *vb* **1** : to seize legally in order to force payment of a debt **2** : to bind by personal ties **3** : FASTEN, CONNECT **4** : to be fastened or connected

at·ta·ché \ˌat-ə-ˈshā, ˌa-ˌta-, ə-ˌta-\ *n* [F] : a technical expert on the diplomatic staff of an ambassador

at·ta·ché case \ə-ˈtash-ā-, ˌat-ə-ˈshā-\ *n* : a small thin suitcase used esp. for carrying papers and documents

at·tach·ment \ə-ˈtach-mənt\ *n* **1** : legal seizure of property **2** : connection by ties of affection and regard **3** : a device attached to a machine or implement **4** : a connection by which one thing is attached to another

[1]**at·tack** \ə-ˈtak\ *vb* **1** : to set upon with force or words : ASSAIL, ASSAULT **2** : to set to work on

[2]**attack** *n* **1** : an offensive action **2** : a fit of sickness

at·tain \ə-ˈtān\ *vb* **1** : ACHIEVE, ACCOMPLISH **2** : to arrive at : REACH — **at·tain·abil·i·ty** \ə-ˈtā-nə-ˈbil-ət-ē\ *n* — **at·tain·able** *adj*

at·tain·der \ə-ˈtān-dər\ *n* : extinction of the civil rights of a person upon sentence of death or outlawry

at·tain·ment \ə-ˈtān-mənt\ *n* **1** : the act of attaining **2** : ACCOMPLISHMENT

at·taint \ə-ˈtānt\ *vb* : to condemn to loss of civil rights

at·tar \ˈat-ər\ *n* [Per *ʿatir* perfumed, fr. Ar, fr. *ʿitr* perfume] : a fragrant floral oil

at·tempt \ə-ˈtempt\ *vb* : to make an effort toward : TRY — **attempt** *n*

at·tend \ə-ˈtend\ *vb* **1** : to look after : TEND **2** : to be present with : ACCOMPANY **3** : to be present at **4** : to apply oneself **5** : to pay attention **6** : to take charge ⟨I'll ~ to that⟩

at·ten·dance \ə-ˈten-dəns\ *n* **1** : the act or fact of attending **2** : the number of persons present

[1]**at·ten·dant** \ə-ˈten-dənt\ *n* : one that attends another to render a service

[2]**attendant** *adj* : ACCOMPANYING ⟨~ circumstances⟩

at·ten·tion \ə-ˈten-chən\ *n* **1** : the act or state of applying the mind to an object **2** : CONSIDERATION **3** : an act of courtesy **4** : a position of readiness for further orders assumed on command by a soldier — **at·ten·tive** \-ˈtent-iv\ *adj* — **at·ten·tive·ly** *adv* — **at·ten·tive·ness** *n*

at·ten·u·ate \ə-ˈten-yə-ˌwāt\ *vb* **-at·ed; -at·ing** **1** : to make or become thin **2** : WEAKEN — **at·ten·u·a·tion** \-ˌten-yə-ˈwā-shən\ *n*

at·test \ə-ˈtest\ *vb* **1** : to certify as genuine by signing as a witness **2** : MANIFEST **3** : TESTIFY — **at·tes·ta·tion** \ˌa-ˌtes-ˈtā-shən\ *n*

at·tic \ˈat-ik\ *n* : the space or room in a building immediately below the roof

[1]**at·tire** \ə-ˈtī(ə)r\ *vb* **at·tired; at·tir·ing** : DRESS, ARRAY

[2]**attire** *n* : DRESS, CLOTHES

at·ti·tude \ˈat-ə-ˌt(y)üd\ *n* **1** : the arrangement of the parts of a body : POSTURE **2** : a mental position or feeling with regard to a fact or state **3** : the position of something in relation to something else

at·ti·tu·di·nize \ˌat-ə-ˈt(y)üd-ᵊn-ˌīz\ *vb* **-nized; -niz·ing** : to assume an affected mental attitude : POSE

attn *abbr* attention

at·tor·ney \ə-ˈtər-nē\ *n, pl* **-neys** : a legal agent qualified to act for persons in legal proceedings

attorney general *n, pl* **attorneys general** *or* **attorney generals** : the chief legal representative and adviser of a nation or state

at·tract \ə-ˈtrakt\ *vb* **1** : to draw to or toward oneself : cause to approach **2** : to draw by emotional or aesthetic appeal **syn** charm, fascinate, allure, captivate, enchant — **at·trac·tive** \-ˈtrak-tiv\ *adj* — **at·trac·tive·ly** *adv* — **at·trac·tive·ness** *n*

at·trac·tant \ə-ˈtrak-tənt\ *n* : a substance used to attract insects or other animals

at·trac·tion \ə-ˈtrak-shən\ *n* **1** : the act or power of attracting; *esp* : personal charm **2** : an attractive quality, object, or feature **3** : a force tending to draw particles together

attrib *abbr* attributive; attributively

[1]**at·tri·bute** \ˈa-trə-ˌbyüt\ *n* **1** : an inherent characteristic **2** : a word ascribing a quality; *esp* : ADJECTIVE

[2]**at·trib·ute** \ə-ˈtrib-yət\ *vb* **-ut·ed; -ut·ing** **1** : to explain as to cause or origin ⟨~ the illness to fatigue⟩ **2** : to regard

as a characteristic **syn** ascribe, credit, charge, impute — **at·trib·ut·able** *adj* — **at·tri·bu·tion** \ˌa-trə-ˈbyü-shən\ *n*

at·trib·u·tive \ə-ˈtrib-yət-iv\ *adj* : joined directly to a modified noun without a linking verb ⟨*red* in *red hair* is an ~ adjective⟩ — **attributive** *n*

at·tri·tion \ə-ˈtrish-ən\ *n* **1** : the act of wearing away by or as if by rubbing **2** : a reduction (as in personnel) as a result of resignation, retirement, or death

at·tune \ə-ˈt(y)ün\ *vb* : to bring into harmony : TUNE

atty *abbr* attorney

atyp·i·cal \ā-ˈtip-i-kəl\ *adj* : not typical : IRREGULAR

Au *symbol* [L *aurum*] gold

au·burn \ˈȯ-bərn\ *adj* : reddish brown — **auburn** *n*

au cou·rant \ˌō-kü-ˈrän^{n}\ *adj* [F, lit., in the current] : UP-TO-DATE

[1]**auc·tion** \ˈȯk-shən\ *n* [L *auction-*, *auctio*, lit., increase, fr. *auctus*, pp. of *augēre* to increase] : public sale of property to the highest bidder

[2]**auction** *vb* **auc·tioned; auc·tion·ing** \-sh(ə-)niŋ\ : to sell at auction

auction bridge *n* : a bridge game in which tricks made in excess of the contract are scored toward game

auc·tion·eer \ˌȯk-shə-ˈniər\ *n* : an agent who conducts an auction

auc·to·ri·al \ȯk-ˈtōr-ē-əl\ *adj* : of or relating to an author

aud *abbr* audit; auditor

au·da·cious \ȯ-ˈdā-shəs\ *adj* **1** : DARING, BOLD **2** : INSOLENT — **au·da·cious·ly** *adv* — **au·da·cious·ness** *n* — **au·dac·i·ty** \ȯ-ˈdas-ət-ē\ *n*

[1]**au·di·ble** \ˈȯd-ə-bəl\ *adj* : capable of being heard — **au·di·bil·i·ty** \ˌȯd-ə-ˈbil-ət-ē\ *n* — **au·di·bly** \ˈȯd-ə-blē\ *adv*

[2]**audible** *n* : AUTOMATIC 2

au·di·ence \ˈȯd-ē-əns\ *n* **1** : a formal interview **2** : an opportunity of being heard **3** : an assembly of listeners or spectators

[1]**au·dio** \ˈȯd-ē-ˌō\ *adj* **1** : of or relating to frequencies (as of radio waves) corresponding to those of audible sound waves **2** : of or relating to sound or its reproduction and esp. high-fidelity reproduction **3** : relating to or used in the transmission or reception of sound

[2]**audio** *n* **1** : the transmission, reception, or reproduction of sound **2** : the section of television or motion-picture equipment that deals with sound

au·di·ol·o·gy \ˌȯd-ē-ˈäl-ə-jē\ *n* : a branch of science dealing with hearing and esp. with the treatment of individuals having trouble with hearing — **au·di·o·log·i·cal** \-ē-ə-ˈläj-i-kəl\ *adj* — **au·di·ol·o·gist** \-ē-ˈäl-ə-jəst\ *n*

au·dio·phile \ˈȯd-ē-ō-ˌfīl\ *n* : one who is enthusiastic about high-fidelity sound reproduction

au·dio·vi·su·al \ˌȯd-ē-ō-ˈvizh-(ə-w)əl\ *adj* : of, relating to, or making use of both hearing and sight

au·dio·vi·su·als \-wəlz\ *n pl* : audiovisual materials (as filmstrips)

[1]**au·dit** \ˈȯd-ət\ *n* : a formal examination and verification of financial accounts

[2]**audit** *vb* **1** : to perform an audit on or for **2** : to attend (a course) without expecting formal credit

[1]**au·di·tion** \ȯ-ˈdish-ən\ *n* : HEARING; *esp* : a trial performance to appraise an entertainer's merits

[2]**audition** *vb* **-tioned; -tion·ing** \-ˈdish-(ə-)niŋ\ : to give an audition to; *also* : to give a trial performance

au·di·tor \ˈȯd-ət-ər\ *n* **1** : LISTENER **2** : a person who audits

au·di·to·ri·um \ˌȯd-ə-ˈtōr-ē-əm\ *n* **1** : the part of a public building where an audience sits **2** : a hall or building used for public gatherings

au·di·to·ry \ˈȯd-ə-ˌtōr-ē\ *adj* : of or relating to hearing or to the sense or organs of hearing

auf Wie·der·seh·en \au̇f-ˈvēd-ər-ˌzān\ *interj* [G] — used to express farewell

Aug *abbr* August

au·ger \ˈȯ-gər\ *n* : a boring tool

aught \ˈȯt, ˈät\ *n* : ZERO, CIPHER

aug·ment \ȯg-ˈment\ *vb* : ENLARGE, INCREASE — **aug·men·ta·tion** \ˌȯg-mən-ˈtā-shən\ *n*

au gra·tin \ō-ˈgrat-ᵊn, ȯ-, -ˈgrät-\ *adj* [F, lit., with the burnt scrapings from the pan] : covered with bread crumbs or grated cheese and browned

[1]**au·gur** \ˈȯ-gər\ *n* : DIVINER, SOOTHSAYER

[2]**augur** *vb* **1** : to foretell esp. from omens **2** : to give promise of : PRESAGE

au·gu·ry \ˈȯ-g(y)ə-rē\ *n, pl* **-ries 1** : divination from omens **2** : OMEN, PORTENT

au·gust \ȯ-ˈgəst\ *adj* : marked by majestic dignity or grandeur — **au·gust·ly** *adv* — **au·gust·ness** *n*

Au·gust \ˈȯ-gəst\ *n* [ME, fr. OE, fr. L *Augustus*, fr. *Augustus* Caesar] : the eighth month of the year having 31 days

au jus \ō-ˈzhü(s), -ˈjüs; ō-zhᵫ\ *adj* [F] : served in the juice obtained from roasting

auk \ˈȯk\ *n* : any of several stocky black-and-white diving seabirds that breed in colder parts of the northern hemisphere

auld \ˈȯl(d), ˈäl(d)\ *adj, chiefly Scot* : OLD

aunt \ˈant, ˈánt\ *n* **1** : the sister of one's father or mother **2** : the wife of one's uncle

au pair \ˈō-ˈpaər\ *n* [F, on even terms] : a foreign girl who does domestic work for a family in return for room and board and the opportunity to learn the family's language

au·ra \ˈȯr-ə\ *n* **1** : a distinctive atmosphere surrounding a given source **2** : a luminous radiation

au·ral \ˈȯr-əl\ *adj* : of or relating to the ear or to the sense of hearing

aurar *pl of* EYRIR

au·re·ate \ˈȯr-ē-ət\ *adj* **1** : of a golden color or brilliance **2** : RESPLENDENT, ORNATE

au·re·ole \ˈȯr-ē-ˌōl\ *or* **au·re·o·la** \ȯ-ˈrē-ə-lə\ *n* : HALO, NIMBUS

au re·voir \ˌōr-əv-ˈwär\ *n* [F, lit., till seeing again] : GOOD-BYE

au·ri·cle \ˈȯr-i-kəl\ *n* : an atrium of the heart

au·ric·u·lar \ȯ-ˈrik-yə-lər\ *adj* **1** : told privately ⟨~ confession⟩ **2** : known by the sense of hearing

au·ro·ra \ə-ˈrōr-ə\ *n, pl* **auroras** *or* **au·ro·rae** \-(ˌ)ē\ : a luminous phenomenon of streamers or arches of light appearing in the upper atmosphere esp. of a planet's polar regions — **au·ro·ral** \-əl\ *adj*

aurora aus·tra·lis \-ȯ-ˈstrā-ləs\ *n* : an aurora that occurs in earth's southern hemisphere

aurora bo·re·al·is \-ˌbōr-ē-ˈal-əs\ *n* : an aurora that occurs in earth's northern hemisphere

AUS *abbr* Army of the United States

aus·pice \ˈȯ-spəs\ *n, pl* **aus·pic·es** \-spə-səz, -ˌsēz\ [L *auspicium*, fr. *auspic-*, *auspex* diviner by birds, fr. *avis* bird + *specere* to look, look at] **1** : observation in augury **2** : a prophetic sign or omen **3** *pl* : kindly patronage and protection

aus·pi·cious \ȯ-ˈspish-əs\ *adj* **1** : promising success : FAVORABLE **2** : FORTUNATE, PROSPEROUS — **aus·pi·cious·ly** *adv*

aus·tere \ȯ-ˈstiər\ *adj* **1** : STERN, SEVERE, STRICT **2** : ABSTEMIOUS **3** : UNADORNED ⟨~ style⟩ — **aus·tere·ly** *adv* — **aus·ter·i·ty** \ȯ-ˈster-ət-ē\ *n*

[1]**aus·tral** \ˈȯs-trəl\ *adj* : SOUTHERN

[2]**aus·tral** \au̇-ˈsträl\ *n, pl* **aus·tral·es** \-ˈsträl-ās\ *also* **australs** — see MONEY table

Aus·tra·lian \ȯ-ˈstrāl-yən\ *n* : a native or inhabitant of Australia — **Australian** *adj*

Aus·tri·an \ˈȯ-strē-ən\ *n* : a native or inhabitant of Austria — **Austrian** *adj*

Aus·tro·ne·sian \ˌȯs-trə-ˈnē-zhən\ *adj* : of, relating to, or constituting a family of languages spoken in the area extending from Madagascar eastward through the Malay peninsula to Hawaii and Easter Island

auth *abbr* **1** authentic **2** author **3** authorized

au·then·tic \ə-ˈthent-ik, ȯ-\ *adj* : GENUINE, REAL — **au·then·ti·cal·ly** \-i- k(ə-)lē\ *adv* — **au·then·tic·i·ty** \ˌȯ-ˌthen-ˈtis-ət-ē\ *n*

au·then·ti·cate \ə-ˈthent-i-ˌkāt, ȯ-\ *vb* **-cat·ed; -cat·ing** : to prove genuine — **au·then·ti·ca·tion** \-ˌthent-i-ˈkā-shən\ *n*

au·thor \ˈȯ-thər\ *n* [ME *auctour,* deriv. of L *auctor* originator, author, fr. *auctus,* pp. of *augēre* to increase] **1** : one that writes or composes a literary work **2** : one that originates or creates

au·thor·ess \ˈȯ-th(ə-)rəs\ *n* : a woman author

au·thor·i·tar·i·an \ə-ˌthär-ə-ˈter-ē-ən, ə-, -ˌthȯr-\ *adj* **1** : characterized by or favoring the principle of blind obedience to authority **2** : characterized by or favoring concentration of political power in an authority not responsible to the people

au·thor·i·ta·tive \ə-ˈthär-ə-ˌtāt-iv, ȯ-, -ˈthȯr-\ *adj* : supported by, proceeding from, or being an authority : TRUSTWORTHY — **au·thor·i·ta·tive·ly** *adv*

au·thor·i·ty \ə-ˈthär-ət-ē, ȯ-, -ˈthȯr-\ *n, pl* **-ties** **1** : a citation used in support of a statement or in defense of an action; *also* : the source of such a citation **2** : one appealed to as an expert **3** : power to influence thought or behavior **4** : freedom granted : RIGHT **5** : persons in command; *esp* : GOVERNMENT

au·tho·rize \ˈȯ-thə-ˌrīz\ *vb* **-rized; -riz·ing** **1** : SANCTION **2** : to give legal power to — **au·tho·ri·za·tion** \ˌȯ-th(ə-)rə-ˈzā-shən\ *n*

au·thor·ship \ˈȯ-thər-ˌship\ *n* **1** : the state of being an author **2** : the source of a piece of writing, music, or art

au·tism \ˈȯ-ˌtiz-əm\ *n* : absorption in self-centered subjective mental activity (as daydreaming, fantasies, delusions, and hallucinations) esp. when accompanied by marked withdrawal from reality — **au·tis·tic** \ȯ-ˈtis-tik\ *adj*

au·to \ˈȯt-ō\ *n, pl* **autos** : AUTOMOBILE

au·to·bahn \ˈȯt-ō-ˌbän, ˈaůt-\ *n* : a German expressway

au·to·bi·og·ra·phy \ˌȯt-ə-bī-ˈäg-rə-fē, -bē-\ *n* : the biography of a person narrated by himself — **au·to·bi·og·ra·pher** \-fər\ *n* — **au·to·bi·o·graph·i·cal** \-ˌbī-ə-ˈgraf-i-kəl\ *adj*

au·toch·tho·nous \ȯ-ˈtäk-thə-nəs\ *adj* : INDIGENOUS, NATIVE

au·toc·ra·cy \ȯ-ˈtäk-rə-sē\ *n, pl* **-cies** : government by one person having unlimited power — **au·to·crat** \ˈȯt-ə-ˌkrat\ *n* — **au·to·crat·ic** \ˌȯt-ə-ˈkrat-ik\ *adj* — **au·to·crat·i·cal·ly** \-i-k(ə-)lē\ *adv*

¹au·to·graph \ˈȯt-ə-ˌgraf\ *n* **1** : an original manuscript **2** : a person's signature written by hand

²autograph *vb* : to write one's signature on

au·to·im·mune \ˌȯt-ō-im-ˈyün\ *adj* : of, relating to, or caused by antibodies or lymphocytes that attack molecules, cells, or tissues of the organism producing them ⟨~ diseases⟩ — **au·to·im·mu·ni·ty** \-im-ˈyün-ət-ē\ *n*

au·to·mate \ˈȯt-ə-ˌmāt\ *vb* **-mat·ed; -mat·ing** **1** : to operate by automation **2** : to convert to automatic operation

¹au·to·mat·ic \ˌȯt-ə-ˈmat-ik\ *adj* **1** : INVOLUNTARY **2** : made so that certain parts act in a desired manner at the proper time : SELF-ACTING — **au·to·mat·i·cal·ly** \-i-k(ə-)lē\ *adv*

²automatic *n* **1** : an automatic device; *esp* : an automatic firearm **2** : a substitute play called by a football quarterback at the line of scrimmage

au·to·ma·tion \ˌȯt-ə-ˈmā-shən\ *n* **1** : the technique of making an apparatus, a process, or a system operate automatically **2** : the state of being operated automatically **3** : automatic operation of an apparatus, process, or system by mechanical or electronic devices that replace human operators

au·tom·a·tize \ȯ-ˈtäm-ə-ˌtīz\ *vb* **-tized; -tiz·ing** : to make automatic — **au·tom·a·ti·za·tion** \-ˌtäm-ət-ə-ˈzā-shən\ *n*

au·tom·a·ton \ȯ-ˈtäm-ət-ən, -ə-ˌtän\ *n, pl* **-atons** *or* **-a·ta** \-ət-ə, -ə-ˌtä\ **1** : an automatic machine; *esp* : ROBOT **2** : an individual who acts mechanically

au·to·mo·bile \ˈȯt-ə-mō-ˌbēl, ˌȯt-ə-mə-ˈbēl\ *n* : a usu. 4-wheeled automotive vehicle for passenger transportation on streets and roadways — **au·to·mo·bil·ist** \-ˌbē-ləst, -ˈbē-\ *n*

au·to·mo·tive \ˌȯt-ə-ˈmōt-iv\ *adj* **1** : of or relating to automobiles, trucks, or buses **2** : SELF-PROPELLED

au·to·nom·ic nervous system \ˌȯt-ə-ˈnäm-ik-\ *n* : a part of the vertebrate nervous system that governs involuntary actions and that consists of the sympathetic nervous system and the parasympathetic nervous system

au·ton·o·mous \ȯ-ˈtän-ə-məs\ *adj* : having the right or power of self-government — **au·ton·o·mous·ly** *adv* — **au·ton·o·my** \-mē\ *n*

au·top·sy \ˈȯ-ˌtäp-sē, ˈȯt-əp-\ *n, pl* **-sies** [Gk *autopsia* act of seeing with one's own eyes, fr. *autos* self + *opsis* sight] : examination of a dead body usu. with dissection sufficient to determine the cause of death or extent of change produced by disease — **autopsy** *vb*

au·tumn \ˈȯt-əm\ *n* : the season between summer and winter — **au·tum·nal** \ȯ-ˈtəm-nəl\ *adj*

aux *or* **auxil** *abbr* auxiliary

¹aux·il·ia·ry \ȯg-ˈzil-yə-rē, -ˈzil-(ə-)rē\ *adj* **1** : providing help **2** : functioning in a subsidiary capacity **3** : accompanying a verb form to express person, number, mood, or tense ⟨~ verbs⟩

²auxiliary *n, pl* **-ries** **1** : an auxiliary person, group, or device **2** : an auxiliary verb

aux·in \ˈȯk-sən\ *n* : a plant hormone that stimulates growth in length

av *abbr* **1** avenue **2** average **3** avoirdupois

AV *abbr* **1** ad valorem **2** audiovisual **3** Authorized Version

¹avail \ə-ˈvāl\ *vb* : to be of use or advantage : HELP, BENEFIT

²avail *n* : USE ⟨effort was of no ~⟩

avail·able \ə-ˈvā-lə-bəl\ *adj* **1** : USABLE **2** : ACCESSIBLE — **avail·abil·i·ty** \-ˌvā-lə-ˈbil-ət-ē\ *n*

av·a·lanche \ˈav-ə-ˌlanch\ *n* : a mass of snow, ice, earth, or rock sliding down a mountainside

avant–garde \ˌäv-ˌän(t)-ˈgärd\ *n* [F, vanguard] : those esp. in the arts who create or apply new or experimental ideas and techniques — **avant–garde** *adj*

av·a·rice \ˈav-(ə-)rəs\ *n* : excessive desire for wealth : GREED — **av·a·ri·cious** \ˌav-ə-ˈrish-əs\ *adj*

avast \ə-ˈvast\ *vb imper* — a nautical command to stop or cease

av·a·tar \ˈav-ə-ˌtär\ *n* [Skt *avatāra* descent] : INCARNATION

avaunt \ə-ˈvȯnt\ *adv* : AWAY, HENCE

avdp *abbr* avoirdupois

ave *abbr* avenue

Ave Ma·ria \ˌäv-ˌā-mə-ˈrē-ə\ *n* : HAIL MARY

avenge \ə-ˈvenj\ *vb* **avenged; aveng·ing** : to take vengeance for — **aveng·er** *n*

av·e·nue \ˈav-ə-ˌn(y)ü\ *n* **1** : a way or route to a place or goal : PATH **2** : a broad street esp. when bordered by trees

aver \ə-ˈvər\ *vb* **averred; aver·ring** : to declare positively

¹av·er·age \ˈav-(ə-)rij\ *n* [modif. of MF *avarie* damage to ship or cargo, fr. It *avaria,* fr. Ar *ʽawārīyah* damaged merchandise] **1** : ARITHMETIC MEAN **2** : a ratio (as a rate per thousand) of successful tries to total tries ⟨batting ~ of .303⟩

²average *adj* **1** : equaling or approximating an arithmetic mean **2** : being about midway between extremes **3** : not out of the ordinary : COMMON

³average *vb* **av·er·aged; av·er·ag·ing** **1** : to be at or come to an average **2** : to be usually **3** : to find the average of

averse \ə-ˈvərs\ *adj* : having an active feeling of dislike or reluctance ⟨~ to exercise⟩
aver·sion \ə-ˈvər-zhən\ *n* **1** : a feeling of repugnance for something with a desire to avoid it **2** : something decidedly disliked
avert \ə-ˈvərt\ *vb* **1** : to turn aside or away ⟨~ the eyes⟩ **2** : to ward off
avg *abbr* average
avi·an \ˈā-vē-ən\ *adj* [L *avis* bird] : of, relating to, or derived from birds
avi·ary \ˈā-vē-ˌer-ē\ *n, pl* **-ar·ies** : a place where live birds are kept usu. for exhibition
avi·a·tion \ˌā-vē-ˈā-shən, ˌav-ē-\ *n* **1** : the operation of heavier-than-air aircraft **2** : aircraft manufacture, development, and design — **avi·a·tor** \ˈā-vē-ˌāt-ər, ˈav-ē-\ *n*
avi·a·trix \ˌā-vē-ˈā-triks, ˌav-ē-\ *n, pl* **-trix·es** \-trik-səz\ *or* **-tri·ces** \-trə-ˌsēz\ : a woman airplane pilot
av·id \ˈav-əd\ *adj* **1** : craving eagerly : GREEDY **2** : enthusiastic in pursuit of an interest — **avid·i·ty** \ə-ˈvid-ət-ē, a-\ *n* — **av·id·ly** *adv*
avi·on·ics \ˌā-vē-ˈän-iks, ˌav-ē-\ *n pl* : electronics designed for use in aerospace vehicles — **avi·on·ic** \-ik\ *adj*
avi·ta·min·osis \ˌā-ˌvīt-ə-mə-ˈnō-səs\ *n, pl* **-o·ses** \-ˌsēz\ : disease resulting from vitamin deficiency
avo \ˈav-(ˌ)ü\ *n, pl* **avos** — see *pataca* at MONEY table
av·o·ca·do \ˌav-ə-ˈkäd-ō, ˌäv-\ *n, pl* **-dos** *also* **-does** [modif. of Sp *aguacate*, fr. Nahuatl *ahuacatl*, lit., testicle] : a usu. green pear-shaped fruit with rich oily flesh that is produced by a tropical American tree; *also* : this tree
av·o·ca·tion \ˌav-ə-ˈkā-shən\ *n* : a subordinate occupation pursued esp. for pleasure : HOBBY
av·o·cet \ˈav-ə-ˌset\ *n* : any of several long-legged shorebirds with webbed feet and slender upward-curving bills
avoid \ə-ˈvȯid\ *vb* **1** : to keep away from : SHUN **2** : to prevent the occurrence of **3** : to refrain from — **avoid·able** *adj* — **avoid·ance** \-ᵊns\ *n*
av·oir·du·pois \ˌav-ərd-ə-ˈpȯiz\ *n* [ME *avoir de pois* goods sold by weight, fr. OF, lit., goods of weight] **1** : AVOIRDUPOIS WEIGHT **2** : WEIGHT, HEAVINESS; *esp* : personal weight
avoirdupois weight *n* : a system of weights based on a pound of 16 ounces and an ounce of 16 drams — see WEIGHT table
avouch \ə-ˈvau̇ch\ *vb* **1** : to declare positively : AVER **2** : GUARANTEE
avow \ə-ˈvau̇\ *vb* : to declare openly — **avow·al** \-ˈvau̇(-ə)l\ *n*
avun·cu·lar \ə-ˈvəŋ-kyə-lər\ *adj* : of, relating to, or resembling an uncle
await \ə-ˈwāt\ *vb* : to wait for : EXPECT
[1]**awake** \ə-ˈwāk\ *vb* **awoke** \-ˈwōk\ *also* **awaked** \-ˈwākt\; **awaked** *or* **awo·ken** \-ˈwō-kən\ *also* **awoke; awak·ing** : to bring back to consciousness after sleep : wake up
[2]**awake** *adj* : not asleep; *also* : ALERT
awak·en \ə-ˈwā-kən\ *vb* **awak·ened; awak·en·ing** \-ˈwāk-(ə-)niŋ\ : AWAKE
[1]**award** \ə-ˈwȯrd\ *vb* **1** : to give by judicial decision ⟨~ damages⟩ **2** : to give in recognition of merit or achievement ⟨~ a prize⟩
[2]**award** *n* **1** : a final decision : JUDGMENT **2** : something awarded : PRIZE
aware \ə-ˈwaər\ *adj* : having perception or knowledge : CONSCIOUS, INFORMED — **aware·ness** *n*
awash \ə-ˈwȯsh, -ˈwäsh\ *adj* **1** : washed by waves or tide **2** : AFLOAT **3** : FLOODED
[1]**away** \ə-ˈwā\ *adv* **1** : from this or that place ⟨go ~⟩ **2** : out of the way **3** : in another direction ⟨turn ~⟩ **4** : out of existence ⟨fade ~⟩ **5** : from one's possession ⟨give ~⟩ **6** : without interruption ⟨chatter ~⟩ **7** : at a distance in space or time ⟨far ~⟩ ⟨~ back in 1910⟩
[2]**away** *adj* **1** : ABSENT **2** : distant in space or time ⟨a lake 10 miles ~⟩
[1]**awe** \ˈȯ\ *n* **1** : profound and reverent dread of the supernatural **2** : respectful fear inspired by authority
[2]**awe** *vb* **awed; aw·ing** : to inspire with awe
aweigh \ə-ˈwā\ *adj* : just clear of the bottom and hanging perpendicularly ⟨anchors ~⟩
awe·some \ˈȯ-səm\ *adj* **1** : expressive of awe **2** : inspiring awe
awe·struck \-ˌstrək\ *also* **awe·strick·en** \-ˌstrik-ən\ *adj* : filled with awe
aw·ful \ˈȯ-fəl\ *adj* **1** : inspiring awe **2** : extremely disagreeable **3** : very great — **aw·ful·ly** \-ē\ *adv*
awhile \ə-ˈhwīl\ *adv* : for a while
awhirl \ə-ˈhwərl\ *adj* : in a whirl : WHIRLING
awk·ward \ˈȯ-kwərd\ *adj* **1** : CLUMSY **2** : UNGRACEFUL **3** : difficult to explain : EMBARRASSING **4** : difficult to deal with — **awk·ward·ly** *adv* — **awk·ward·ness** *n*
awl \ˈȯl\ *n* : a pointed instrument for making small holes
aw·ning \ˈȯn-iŋ\ *n* : a rooflike cover (as of canvas) extended over or in front of a place as a shelter
AWOL \ˈā-ˌwȯl, ˌā-ˌdəb-əl-yü-ˌō-ˈel\ *n* : a person who is absent without leave — **AWOL** *adj or adv*
awry \ə-ˈrī\ *adv or adj* **1** : ASKEW **2** : out of the right course : AMISS
ax *or* **axe** \ˈaks\ *n* : a chopping or cutting tool with an edged head fitted parallel to a handle
ax·i·al \ˈak-sē-əl\ *adj* **1** : of, relating to, or functioning as an axis **2** : situated around, in the direction of, on, or along an axis — **ax·i·al·ly** \ˈak-sē-ə-lē\ *adv*
ax·i·om \ˈak-sē-əm\ *n* [L *axioma*, fr. Gk *axioma*, lit., honor, fr. *axioun* to think worthy, fr. *axios* worth, worthy] **1** : a statement generally accepted as true : MAXIM **2** : a proposition regarded as a self-evident truth — **ax·i·om·at·ic** \ˌak-sē-ə-ˈmat-ik\ *adj* — **ax·i·om·at·i·cal·ly** \-i-k(ə-)lē\ *adv*
ax·is \ˈak-səs\ *n, pl* **ax·es** \-ˌsēz\ **1** : a real or imaginary straight line passing through a body that actually or supposedly revolves upon it ⟨the earth's ~⟩ **2** : one of the reference lines of a system of coordinates **3** : a straight line with respect to which a body or figure is symmetrical **4** : a bodily structure around which parts are arranged in a symmetrical way; *esp* : the main stem of a plant from which leaves and branches arise **5** : an alliance between major powers
ax·le \ˈak-səl\ *n* : a shaft on which a wheel revolves
ayah \ˈī-ə\ *n* [Hindi *āyā*, fr. Pg *aia*, fr. L *avia* grandmother] : a native nurse or maid in India
aya·tol·lah \ˌī-ə-ˈtō-lə, -ˈtäl-ə, -ˈtəl-ə, ˈī-ə-ˌ; ˌī-ə-tə-ˈlä\ *n* [Per, lit., sign of God, fr. Ar *ayat* sign, miracle + *allāh* God] : an Islamic religious leader — used as a title of respect
[1]**aye** *also* **ay** \ˈā\ *adv* : ALWAYS, EVER
[2]**aye** *also* **ay** \ˈī\ *adv* : YES
[3]**aye** *also* **ay** \ˈī\ *n, pl* **ayes** : an affirmative vote
AZ *abbr* Arizona
aza·lea \ə-ˈzāl-yə\ *n* : any of numerous rhododendrons with funnel-shaped blossoms and usu. deciduous leaves
az·i·muth \ˈaz-(ə-)məth\ *n* : horizontal direction expressed as an angular distance
Az·tec \ˈaz-ˌtek\ *n* : a member of an American Indian people that founded the Mexican empire and were conquered by Hernan Cortes in 1519 — **Az·tec·an** *adj*
azure \ˈazh-ər\ *n* : the blue of the clear sky — **azure** *adj*

B

¹b \ˈbē\ *n, pl* **b's** *or* **bs** \ˈbēz\ *often cap* **1** : the 2d letter of the English alphabet **2** : a grade rating a student's work as good

²b *abbr, often cap* **1** bachelor **2** bass **3** bishop **4** book **5** born

B *symbol* boron

Ba *symbol* barium

BA *abbr* **1** bachelor of arts **2** batting average

bab·bitt metal \ˈbab-ət-\ *n* : an alloy used for lining bearings; *esp* : one containing tin, copper, and antimony

bab·ble \ˈbab-əl\ *vb* **bab·bled; bab·bling** \-(ə-)liŋ\ **1** : to utter meaningless sounds **2** : to talk foolishly or excessively — **babble** *n* — **bab·bler** \-(ə-)lər\ *n*

babe \ˈbāb\ *n* **1** : BABY **2** *slang* : GIRL, WOMAN

ba·bel \ˈbā-bəl, ˈbab-əl\ *n, often cap* [fr. the Tower of *Babel,* Gen 11:4–9] : a place or scene of noise and confusion; *also* : a confused sound **syn** hubbub, racket, din, uproar, clamor

ba·boon \ba-ˈbün\ *n* [ME *babewin,* fr. MF *babouin,* fr. *baboue* grimace] : any of several large apes of Asia and Africa with doglike muzzles

ba·bush·ka \bə-ˈbüsh-kə, -ˈbu̇sh-\ *n* [Russ, grandmother, dim. of *baba* old woman] : a kerchief for the head

¹ba·by \ˈbā-bē\ *n, pl* **babies** **1** : a very young child : INFANT **2** : the youngest or smallest of a group **3** : a childish person — **baby** *adj* — **ba·by·hood** *n* — **ba·by·ish** *adj*

²baby *vb* **ba·bied; ba·by·ing** : to tend or treat often with excessive care

baby's breath *n* : any of a genus of herbs that are related to the pinks and have small delicate flowers

ba·by–sit \ˈbā-bē-ˌsit\ *vb* **-sat** \-ˌsat\; **-sit·ting** : to care for children usu. during a short absence of the parents — **ba·by–sit·ter** *n*

bac·ca·lau·re·ate \ˌbak-ə-ˈlȯr-ē-ət\ *n* **1** : the degree of bachelor conferred by colleges and universities **2** : a sermon delivered to a graduating class

bac·ca·rat \ˌbäk-ə-ˈrä, ˌbak-\ *n* : a card game played esp. in European casinos

bac·cha·nal \ˈbak-ən-ᵊl, ˌbak-ə-ˈnal, ˌbäk-ə-ˈnäl\ *n* **1** : REVELER **2** : drunken revelry : BACCHANALIA

bac·cha·na·lia \ˌbak-ə-ˈnāl-yə\ *n, pl* **bacchanalia** : a drunken orgy — **bac·cha·na·lian** \-ˈnāl-yən\ *adj or n*

bach·e·lor \ˈbach-(ə-)lər\ *n* **1** : a person who has received the usu. lowest degree conferred by a 4-year college **2** : a man who has not married — **bach·e·lor·hood** *n*

bach·e·lor·ette \ˌbach(-ə)-lə-ˈret\ *n* : a young unmarried woman

bachelor's button *n* : a European plant related to the daisies and having blue, pink, or white flower heads

ba·cil·lus \bə-ˈsil-əs\ *n, pl* **-li** \-ˌī\ [NL, fr. ML, small staff, dim. of L *baculus* staff] : any of numerous rod-shaped bacteria; *also* : a disease-producing bacterium — **bac·il·lary** \ˈbas-ə-ˌler-ē\ *adj*

¹back \ˈbak\ *n* **1** : the rear or dorsal part of the human body; *also* : the corresponding part of a lower animal **2** : the part or surface opposite the front **3** : a player in the backfield in football — **back·less** \-ləs\ *adj*

²back *adv* **1** : to, toward, or at the rear **2** : AGO **3** : so as to be restrained or retarded **4** : to, toward, or in a former place or state **5** : in return or reply

³back *adj* **1** : located at or in the back; *also* : REMOTE **2** : OVERDUE **3** : moving or operating backward **4** : not current **syn** posterior, hind, rear

⁴back *vb* **1** : SUPPORT, UPHOLD **2** : to go or cause to go backward or in reverse **3** : to furnish with a back : form the back of

back·ache \ˈbak-ˌāk\ *n* : pain in the back; *esp* : a dull persistent pain in the lower back

back–bench·er \-ˈben-chər\ *n* : a rank-and-file member of a British legislature

back·bite \-ˌbīt\ *vb* **-bit** \-ˌbit\; **-bit·ten** \-ˌbit-ᵊn\; **-bit·ing** \-ˌbīt-iŋ\ : to say mean or spiteful things about someone who is absent — **back·bit·er** *n*

back·board \-ˌbōrd\ *n* : a board or construction placed at the back or serving as a back

back·bone \-ˈbōn, -ˌbōn\ *n* **1** : the bony column in the back of a vertebrate that is the chief support of the trunk and consists of a jointed series of vertebrae enclosing and protecting the spinal cord **2** : firm resolute character

back·drop \ˈbak-ˌdräp\ *n* : a painted cloth hung across the rear of a stage

back·er \ˈbak-ər\ *n* : one that supports **syn** upholder, guarantor, sponsor, patron

back·field \-ˌfēld\ *n* : the football players whose positions are behind the line

¹back·fire \-ˌfī(ə)r\ *n* : a loud noise caused by the improperly timed explosion of fuel in the cylinder of an internal-combustion engine

²backfire *vb* **1** : to make or undergo a backfire **2** : to have a result opposite to what was intended

back·gam·mon \ˈbak-ˌgam-ən\ *n* : a game played with pieces on a double board in which the moves are determined by throwing dice

back·ground \ˈbak-ˌgrau̇nd\ *n* **1** : the scenery behind something **2** : the setting within which something takes place; *also* : the sum of a person's experience, training, and understanding

back·hand \ˈbak-ˌhand\ *n* : a stroke (as in tennis) made with the back of the hand turned in the direction in which the hand is moving; *also* : the side on which such a stroke is made — **back·hand** *vb*

back·hand·ed \ˈbak-ˈhan-dəd\ *adj* **1** : using or made with a backhand **2** : INDIRECT, DEVIOUS; *esp* : SARCASTIC

back·hoe \ˈbak-ˌhō\ *n* : an excavating machine having a bucket that is drawn toward the machine in operation

back·ing \ˈbak-iŋ\ *n* **1** : something forming a back **2** : SUPPORT, AID; *also* : a body of supporters

back·lash \ˈbak-ˌlash\ *n* **1** : a sudden violent backward movement or reaction **2** : a strong adverse reaction

¹back·log \-ˌlȯg, -ˌläg\ *n* **1** : a large log at the back of a hearth fire **2** : an accumulation of tasks unperformed or materials not processed

²backlog *vb* : to accumulate in reserve

back of *prep* : BEHIND

back out *vb* : to withdraw esp. from a commitment or contest

¹back·pack \ˈbak-ˌpak\ *n* : a camping pack supported by an aluminum frame and carried on the back

²backpack *vb* : to hike with a backpack — **back·pack·er** *n*

back·ped·al \ˈbak-ˌped-ᵊl\ *vb* : RETREAT

back·rest \-ˌrest\ *n* : a rest for the back

back·side \-ˈsīd\ *n* : BUTTOCKS

back·slap \-ˌslap\ *vb* : to display excessive cordiality — **back·slap·per** *n*

back·slide \-ˌslīd\ *vb* **-slid** \-ˌslid\; **-slid** *or* **-slid·den** \-ˌslid-ᵊn\; **-slid·ing** \-ˌslīd-iŋ\ : to lapse morally or in religious practice — **back·slid·er** *n*

back·spin \-ˌspin\ *n* : a backward rotary motion of a ball

¹back·stage \ˈbak-ˌstāj\ *adj* **1** : relating to or occurring in the area behind a stage **2** : of or relating to the private lives of theater people **3** : of or relating to the inner working or operation

²back·stage \ˈbak-ˈstāj\ *adv* **1** : in or to a backstage area **2** : SECRETLY

back·stairs \-ˌstaərz\ *adj* : SECRET, FURTIVE; *also* : SORDID, SCANDALOUS

[1]**back·stop** \-ˌstäp\ *n* : something serving as a stop behind something else; *esp* : a screen or fence to keep a ball from leaving the field of play

[2]**backstop** *vb* **1** : to serve as a backstop to **2** : SUPPORT

back·stretch \ˈbak-ˈstrech\ *n* : the side opposite the homestretch on a racecourse

back·stroke \-ˌstrōk\ *n* : a swimming stroke executed on the back

back talk *n* : an impudent, insolent, or argumentative reply

back·track \ˈbak-ˌtrak\ *vb* **1** : to retrace one's course **2** : to reverse a position or stand

back·up \-ˌəp\ *n* : one that serves as a substitute or alternative

[1]**back·ward** \ˈbak-wərd\ *or* **back·wards** \-wərdz\ *adv* **1** : toward the back **2** : with the back foremost **3** : in a reverse or contrary direction or way **4** : toward the past; *also* : toward a worse state

[2]**backward** *adj* **1** : directed, turned, or done backward **2** : DIFFIDENT, SHY **3** : retarded in development — **back·ward·ness** *n*

back·wash \ˈbak-ˌwȯsh, -ˌwäsh\ *n* : backward movement (as of water or air) produced by a propelling force (as the motion of oars)

back·wa·ter \-ˌwȯt-ər, -ˌwät-\ *n* **1** : water held or turned back in its course **2** : an isolated or backward place or condition

back·woods \-ˈwu̇dz\ *n pl* **1** : wooded or partly cleared areas far from cities **2** : a remote or isolated place

ba·con \ˈbā-kən\ *n* : salted and smoked meat from the sides or back of a pig

bacteria *pl of* BACTERIUM

bac·te·ri·cid·al \bak-ˌtir-ə-ˈsīd-ᵊl\ *adj* : destroying bacteria — **bac·te·ri·cide** \-ˈtir-ə-ˌsīd\ *n*

bac·te·ri·ol·o·gy \bak-ˌtir-ē-ˈäl-ə-jē\ *n* **1** : a science dealing with bacteria **2** : bacterial life and phenomena — **bac·te·ri·o·log·ic** \bak-ˌtir-ē-ə-ˈläj-ik\ *or* **bac·te·ri·o·log·i·cal** \-ˈläj-i-kəl\ *adj* — **bac·te·ri·ol·o·gist** \bak-ˌtir-ē-ˈäl-ə-jəst\ *n*

bac·te·rio·phage \bak-ˈtir-ē-ə-ˌfāj\ *n* : any of various viruses that attack specific bacteria

bac·te·ri·um \bak-ˈtir-ē-əm\ *n, pl* **-ria** \-ē-ə\ [NL, fr. Gk *baktērion* staff] : any of a class of microscopic plants including some that are disease producers and others that are valued esp. for their chemical effects (as fermentation) — **bac·te·ri·al** \-ē-əl\ *adj*

bad \ˈbad\ *adj* **worse** \ˈwərs\; **worst** \ˈwərst\ **1** : below standard : POOR; *also* : UNFAVORABLE ⟨a ~ report⟩ **2** : SPOILED, DECAYED **3** : WICKED; *also* : not well-behaved : NAUGHTY **4** : DISAGREEABLE ⟨a ~ taste⟩; *also* : HARMFUL **5** : DEFECTIVE, FAULTY ⟨~ wiring⟩; *also* : not valid ⟨a ~ check⟩ **6** : UNWELL, ILL **7** : SORRY, REGRETFUL **syn** evil, wrong, immoral, iniquitous, wicked — **bad·ly** *adv* — **bad·ness** *n*

bade *past and past part of* BID

badge \ˈbaj\ *n* : a device or token usu. worn as a sign of status

[1]**bad·ger** \ˈbaj-ər\ *n* : any of several sturdy burrowing mammals with long claws on their forefeet

[2]**badger** *vb* **bad·gered; bad·ger·ing** \ˈbaj-(ə-)riŋ\ : to harass or annoy persistently

ba·di·nage \ˌbad-ᵊn-ˈäzh\ *n* [F] : playful talk back and forth : BANTER

bad·land \ˈbad-ˌland\ *n* : a region marked by intricate erosional sculpturing and scanty vegetation — usu. used in pl.

bad·min·ton \ˈbad-ˌmint-ᵊn\ *n* : a court game played with light rackets and a shuttlecock volleyed over a net

Bae·de·ker \ˈbād-i-kər, ˈbed-\ *n* : GUIDEBOOK

[1]**baf·fle** \ˈbaf-əl\ *vb* **baf·fled; baf·fling** \-(ə-)liŋ\ : FRUSTRATE, THWART, FOIL; *also* : PERPLEX

[2]**baffle** *n* : a device (as a wall or screen) to deflect, check, or regulate flow (as of liquid or sound)

[1]**bag** \ˈbag\ *n* : a flexible usu. closable container (as for storing or carrying)

[2]**bag** *vb* **bagged; bag·ging 1** : DISTEND, BULGE **2** : to put in a bag **3** : to get possession of; *esp* : to take in hunting **syn** trap, snare, catch, capture, collar

ba·gasse \bə-ˈgas\ *n* [F] : plant residue (as of sugarcane) left after a product (as juice) has been extracted

bag·a·telle \ˌbag-ə-ˈtel\ *n* [F] : TRIFLE

ba·gel \ˈbā-gəl\ *n* [Yiddish *beygel*, deriv. of Old High German *boug* ring] : a hard glazed doughnut-shaped roll

bag·gage \ˈbag-ij\ *n* **1** : the traveling bags and personal belongings of a traveler : LUGGAGE **2** : a worthless or contemptible woman

bag·gy \ˈbag-ē\ *adj* **bag·gi·er; -est** : puffed out or hanging like a bag — **bag·gi·ly** \ˈbag-ə-lē\ *adv* — **bag·gi·ness** \-ē-nəs\ *n*

bag·man \-mən\ *n* : a person who collects or distributes illicitly gained money on behalf of another

ba·gnio \ˈban-yō\ *n, pl* **bagnios** [It *bagno*, lit., public baths] : BROTHEL

bag of waters : a double-walled fluid-filled sac that encloses and protects the fetus in the womb and that breaks releasing its fluid during the process of birth

bag·pipe \ˈbag-ˌpīp\ *n* : a musical wind instrument consisting of a bag, a tube with valves, and sounding pipes — often used in pl.

ba·guette \ba-ˈget\ *n* [F, lit., rod] : a gem having the shape of a long narrow rectangle; *also* : the shape itself

baht \ˈbät\ *n, pl* **baht** *also* **bahts** — see MONEY table

[1]**bail** \ˈbāl\ *n* : a container for ladling water out of a boat

[2]**bail** *vb* : to dip and throw out water from a boat

[3]**bail** *n* : security given to guarantee a prisoner's appearance when legally required; *also* : one giving such security or the release secured

[4]**bail** *vb* : to release under bail; *also* : to procure the release of by giving bail — **bail·able** \ˈbā-lə-bəl\ *adj*

[5]**bail** *n* : the arched handle of a pail or kettle

bai·liff \ˈbā-ləf\ *n* **1** : an aide of a British sheriff who serves writs and makes arrests; *also* : a minor officer of a U.S. court **2** : an estate or farm manager esp. in Britain : STEWARD

bai·li·wick \ˈbā-li-ˌwik\ *n* : one's special province or domain **syn** territory, field, sphere, domain, province

bails·man \ˈbālz-mən\ *n* : one who gives bail for another

bairn \ˈbaərn\ *n, chiefly Scot* : CHILD

[1]**bait** \ˈbāt\ *vb* **1** : to persecute by continued attacks **2** : to harass with dogs usu. for sport ⟨~ a bear⟩ **3** : to furnish (as a hook) with bait **4** : ALLURE, ENTICE **5** : to give food and drink to (as an animal) **syn** badger, heckle, hound

[2]**bait** *n* **1** : a lure for catching animals (as fish) **2** : LURE, TEMPTATION **syn** snare, trap, decoy, come-on, enticement

bai·za \ˈbī-(ˌ)zä\ *n* — see *rial* at MONEY table

baize \ˈbāz\ *n* : a coarse feltlike fabric

[1]**bake** \ˈbāk\ *vb* **baked; bak·ing 1** : to cook or become cooked in dry heat esp. in an oven **2** : to dry and harden by heat ⟨~ bricks⟩ — **bak·er** *n*

[2]**bake** *n* : a social gathering featuring baked food

baker's dozen *n* : THIRTEEN

bak·ery \ˈbā-k(ə-)rē\ *n, pl* **-er·ies** : a place for baking or selling baked goods

bake·shop \ˈbāk-ˌshäp\ *n* : BAKERY

baking powder *n* : a powder that consists of a carbonate, an acid, and a starch and that makes the dough rise in baking cakes and biscuits

baking soda *n* : SODIUM BICARBONATE

bak·sheesh \ˈbak-ˌshēsh\ *n* : payment (as a tip or bribe) to expedite service
bal *abbr* balance
bal·a·lai·ka \ˌbal-ə-ˈlī-kə\ *n* : a triangular wooden instrument related to the guitar and used esp. in the U.S.S.R.
[1]**bal·ance** \ˈbal-əns\ *n* [ME, fr. OF, fr. LL *bilanc-, bilanx* having two scalepans, fr. L *bi* two + *lanc-, lanx* plate] **1** : a weighing device : SCALE **2** : a weight, force, or influence counteracting the effect of another **3** : an oscillating wheel used to regulate a watch or clock **4** : a state of equilibrium **5** : REMAINDER, REST; *esp* : an amount in excess esp. on the credit side of an account — **bal·anced** \-ənst\ *adj*
[2]**balance** *vb* **bal·anced; bal·anc·ing 1** : to compute the balance of an account **2** : to arrange so that one set of elements equals another; *also* : to equal or equalize in weight, number, or proportions **3** : WEIGH **4** : to bring or come to a state or position of equipoise; *also* : to bring into harmony or proportion
balance wheel *n* : a wheel that regulates or stabilizes the motion of a mechanism
bal·boa \bal-ˈbō-ə\ *n* — see MONEY table
bal·brig·gan \bal-ˈbrig-ən\ *n* : a knitted cotton fabric used esp. for underwear
bal·co·ny \ˈbal-kə-nē\ *n, pl* **-nies 1** : a platform projecting from the side of a building and enclosed by a railing **2** : a gallery inside a building
[1]**bald** \ˈbȯld\ *adj* **1** : lacking a natural or usual covering (as of hair) **2** : UNADORNED, PLAIN **syn** bare, barren, naked, nude — **bald·ness** *n*
[2]**bald** *vb* : to become bald
bal·da·chin \ˈbȯl-də-kən, ˈbal-\ *or* **bal·da·chi·no** \ˌbal-də-ˈkē-nō\ *n, pl* **baldachins** *or* **baldachinos** : a canopylike structure over an altar
bald eagle *n* : an eagle of No. America that when mature has white head and neck feathers and a white tail
bal·der·dash \ˈbȯl-dər-ˌdash\ *n* : NONSENSE
bal·dric \ˈbȯl-drik\ *n* : a belt worn over the shoulder to carry a sword or bugle
[1]**bale** \ˈbāl\ *n* : a large bundle or closely packed package
[2]**bale** *vb* **baled; bal·ing** : to pack in a bale — **bal·er** *n*
ba·leen \bə-ˈlēn\ *n* : WHALEBONE
bale·ful \ˈbāl-fəl\ *adj* : DEADLY, HARMFUL; *also* : OMINOUS **syn** sinister, malefic, maleficent, malign
[1]**balk** \ˈbȯk\ *n* **1** : HINDRANCE, CHECK, SETBACK **2** : an illegal motion of the pitcher in baseball while in position
[2]**balk** *vb* **1** : BLOCK, THWART **2** : to stop short and refuse to go on **3** : to commit a balk in sports **syn** frustrate, baffle, foil, thwart
balky \ˈbȯ-kē\ *adj* **balk·i·er; -est** : likely to balk
[1]**ball** \ˈbȯl\ *n* **1** : a rounded body or mass (as at the base of the thumb or for use as a missile or in a game) **2** : a game played with a ball **3** : a pitched baseball that misses the strike zone and is not swung at by the batter **4** : a hit or thrown ball in various games ⟨foul ~⟩
[2]**ball** *vb* : to form into a ball
[3]**ball** *n* : a large formal dance
bal·lad \ˈbal-əd\ *n* **1** : a simple song : AIR **2** : a narrative poem of strongly marked rhythm suitable for singing **3** : a slow romantic dance song
bal·lad·eer \ˌbal-ə-ˈdiər\ *n* : a singer of ballads
[1]**bal·last** \ˈbal-əst\ *n* **1** : heavy material used to stabilize a ship or control a balloon's ascent **2** : crushed stone laid in a railroad bed or used in making concrete
[2]**ballast** *vb* : to provide with ballast **syn** balance, stabilize, steady
ball bearing *n* : a bearing in which the revolving part turns upon steel balls that roll easily in a groove; *also* : one of the balls in such a bearing
ball·car·ri·er \ˈbȯl-ˌkar-ē-ər\ *n* : the football player carrying the ball in an offensive play
bal·le·ri·na \ˌbal-ə-ˈrē-nə\ *n* : a female ballet dancer
bal·let \ˈba-ˌlā, ba-ˈlā\ *n* **1** : dancing in which fixed poses and steps are combined with light flowing movements often to convey a story; *also* : a theatrical art form using ballet dancing **2** : a company of ballet dancers
bal·let·o·mane \ba-ˈlet-ə-ˌmān\ *n* : a devotee of ballet
bal·lis·tic missile \bə-ˈlis-tik-\ *n* : a self-propelled missile that is guided during ascent and that falls freely during descent
bal·lis·tics \-tiks\ *n sing or pl* **1** : the science of the motion of projectiles (as bullets) in flight **2** : the flight characteristics of a projectile — **ballistic** *adj*
ball of fire : an unusually energetic person
[1]**bal·loon** \bə-ˈlün\ *n* **1** : a bag filled with gas or heated air so as to rise and float in the atmosphere **2** : a toy consisting of an inflatable rubber bag — **bal·loon·ist** *n*
[2]**balloon** *vb* **1** : to travel in a balloon **2** : to swell or puff out **3** : to increase rapidly
[1]**bal·lot** \ˈbal-ət\ *n* [It *ballotta* small ball used in secret voting, fr. It dial., dim. of *balla* ball] **1** : a piece of paper used to cast a vote **2** : the action or a system of voting; *also* : the right to vote
[2]**ballot** *vb* : to decide by ballot : VOTE
[1]**ball·park** \ˈbȯl-ˌpark\ *n* : a park in which ball games are played
[2]**ballpark** *adj* : approximately correct ⟨~ estimate⟩
ball·point \ˈbȯl-ˌpȯint\ *n* : a pen whose writing point is a small rotating metal ball that inks itself from an inner container
ball·room \ˈbȯl-ˌrüm, -ˌru̇m\ *n* : a large room for dances
bal·ly·hoo \ˈbal-ē-ˌhü\ *n, pl* **-hoos** : extravagant statements and claims made for publicity — **ballyhoo** *vb*
balm \ˈbäm, ˈbälm\ *n* **1** : a fragrant healing or soothing lotion or ointment **2** : any of several spicy fragrant herbs **3** : something that comforts or soothes
balmy \ˈbäm-ē, ˈbäl-mē\ *adj* **balm·i·er; -est 1** : gently soothing : MILD **2** : FOOLISH, ABSURD **syn** soft, bland, mild, gentle — **balm·i·ness** *n*
ba·lo·ney \bə-ˈlō-nē\ *n* : NONSENSE
bal·sa \ˈbȯl-sə\ *n* : the extremely light strong wood of a tropical American tree; *also* : the tree
bal·sam \ˈbȯl-səm\ *n* **1** : a fragrant aromatic and usu. resinous substance oozing from various plants; *also* : a preparation containing or smelling like balsam **2** : a balsam-yielding tree (as balsam fir) **3** : a common garden ornamental plant
balsam fir *n* : a resinous American evergreen tree that is widely used for pulpwood and as a Christmas tree
Bal·ti·more oriole \ˌbȯl-tə-ˌmōr-\ *n* : a common American oriole in which the male is brightly colored with orange, black, and white
bal·us·ter \ˈbal-ə-stər\ *n* [F *balustre,* fr. It *balaustro,* fr. *balaustra* wild pomegranate flower, fr. L *balaustium;* fr. its shape] : an upright support of a rail (as of a staircase)
bal·us·trade \-ə-ˌstrād\ *n* : a row of balusters topped by a rail
bam·boo \bam-ˈbü\ *n, pl* **bamboos** : any of various woody mostly tall tropical grasses including some with strong hollow stems used for building, furniture, or utensils
bamboo curtain *n, often cap B&C* : a political, military, and ideological barrier in the Orient
bam·boo·zle \bam-ˈbü-zəl\ *vb* **-boo·zled; -boo·zling** \-ˈbüz-(ə-)liŋ\ : TRICK, HOODWINK
[1]**ban** \ˈban\ *vb* **banned; ban·ning** : PROHIBIT, FORBID
[2]**ban** *n* **1** : CURSE **2** : a legal or formal prohibiting
[3]**ban** \ˈbän\ *n, pl* **ba·ni** \ˈbän-ē\ — see *leu* at MONEY table
ba·nal \bə-ˈnäl, -ˈnal; ˈbān-ᵊl\ *adj* [F] : COMMONPLACE, TRITE — **ba·nal·i·ty** \bā-ˈnal-ət-ē\ *n*
ba·nana \bə-ˈnan-ə\ *n* : a treelike tropical plant bearing thick clusters of yellow or reddish finger-shaped fruit; *also* : this fruit
[1]**band** \ˈband\ *n* **1** : something that binds, ties, or goes around **2** : a strip or stripe that can be distinguished (as by color or texture) from nearby matter **3** : a range of

wavelengths (as in radio) **4** : a group of grooves on a phonograph record containing recorded sound

²band *vb* **1** : to tie up, finish, or enclose with a band **2** : to gather or unite in a company or for some common end — **band·er** *n*

³band *n* : a group of persons, animals, or things; *esp* : a group of musicians organized for playing together

¹ban·dage \ˈban-dij\ *n* : a strip of material used esp. in dressing wounds

²bandage *vb* **ban·daged; ban·dag·ing** : to dress or cover with a bandage

ban·dan·na *or* **ban·dana** \ban-ˈdan-ə\ *n* : a large colored figured handkerchief

B and B *abbr* bed-and-breakfast

band·box \ˈban(d)-ˌbäks\ *n* : a usu. cylindrical box for carrying clothing

band·ed \ˈban-dəd\ *adj* : having or marked with bands

ban·de·role *or* **ban·de·rol** \ˈban-də-ˌrōl\ *n* : a long narrow forked flag or streamer

ban·dit \ˈban-dət\ *n* [It *bandito*, fr. *bandire* to banish] **1** *pl also* **ban·dit·ti** \ban-ˈdit-ē\ : an outlaw who lives by plunder; *esp* : a member of a band of marauders **2** : ROBBER — **ban·dit·ry** \ˈban-də-trē\ *n*

ban·do·lier *or* **ban·do·leer** \ˌban-də-ˈliər\ *n* : a belt slung over the shoulder esp. to carry ammunition

band saw *n* : a saw in the form of an endless steel belt running over pulleys

band·stand \ˈban(d)-ˌstand\ *n* : a usu. roofed platform on which a band or orchestra performs outdoors

b and w *abbr* black and white

band·wag·on \ˈband-ˌwag-ən\ *n* **1** : a wagon carrying musicians in a parade **2** : a movement that attracts support because it seems to be gaining popularity

¹ban·dy \ˈban-dē\ *vb* **ban·died; ban·dy·ing** **1** : to exchange (as blows or quips) esp. in rapid succession **2** : to use in a glib or offhand way

²bandy *adj* : curved outward ⟨~ legs⟩

bane \ˈbān\ *n* **1** : POISON **2** : WOE, HARM; *also* : a source of this — **bane·ful** *adj*

¹bang \ˈbaŋ\ *vb* **1** : BUMP ⟨fell and ~*ed* his knee⟩ **2** : to strike, thrust, or move usu. with a loud noise

²bang *n* **1** : a resounding blow **2** : a sudden loud noise

³bang *adv* : DIRECTLY, RIGHT

⁴bang *n* : a fringe of hair cut short (as across the forehead) — usu. used in pl.

⁵bang *vb* : to cut a bang in

Ban·gla·deshi \ˌbäŋ-glə-ˈdesh-ē\ *n* : a native or inhabitant of Bangladesh — **Bangladeshi** *adj*

ban·gle \ˈbaŋ-gəl\ *n* : BRACELET; *also* : a loose-hanging ornament

bang–up \ˈbaŋ-ˌəp\ *adj* : FIRST-RATE, EXCELLENT ⟨a ~ job⟩

bani *pl of* ³BAN

ban·ish \ˈban-ish\ *vb* **1** : to require by authority to leave a country **2** : to drive out : EXPEL **syn** exile, ostracize, deport, expel, relegate — **ban·ish·ment** *n*

ban·is·ter \ˈban-ə-stər\ *n* **1** : one of the upright supports of a handrail along a staircase **2** : the handrail of a staircase

ban·jo \ˈban-ˌjō\ *n, pl* **banjos** *also* **banjoes** : a musical instrument with a long neck, a drumlike body, and usu. five strings — **ban·jo·ist** *n*

¹bank \ˈbaŋk\ *n* **1** : a piled-up mass (as of cloud or earth) **2** : an undersea elevation **3** : rising ground bordering a lake, river, or sea **4** : the sideways slope of a surface along a curve or of a vehicle as it rounds a curve

²bank *vb* **1** : to form a bank about **2** : to cover (as a fire) with fuel to keep inactive **3** : to build (a curve) with the roadbed or track inclined laterally upward from the inside edge **4** : to pile or heap in a bank; *also* : to arrange in a tier **5** : to incline (an airplane) laterally

³bank *n* [ME, fr. MF or It; MF *banque*, fr. It *banca*, lit., bench] **1** : an establishment concerned esp. with the custody, loan, exchange, or issue of money, the extension of credit, and the transmission of funds **2** : a stock of or a place for holding something in reserve ⟨a blood ~⟩

⁴bank *vb* **1** : to conduct the business of a bank **2** : to deposit money or have an account in a bank — **bank·er** *n* — **bank·ing** *n*

⁵bank *n* : a group of objects arranged close together (as in a row or tier) ⟨a ~ of file drawers⟩

bank·book \ˈbaŋk-ˌbu̇k\ *n* : the depositor's book in which a bank records deposits and withdrawals

bank·card \-ˌkärd\ *n* : a credit card issued by a bank

bank note *n* : a promissory note issued by a bank and circulating as money

bank·roll \ˈbaŋk-ˌrōl\ *n* : supply of money : FUNDS

¹bank·rupt \ˈbaŋk-(ˌ)rəpt\ *n* : an insolvent person; *esp* : one whose property is turned over by court action to a trustee to be handled for the benefit of his creditors — **bankrupt** *vb*

²bankrupt *adj* **1** : reduced to financial ruin; *esp* : legally declared a bankrupt **2** : wholly lacking in or deprived of some essential ⟨~ soils⟩ — **bank·rupt·cy** \ˈbaŋk-(ˌ)rəp-(t)sē\ *n*

¹ban·ner \ˈban-ər\ *n* **1** : a piece of cloth attached to a staff and used by a leader as his standard **2** : FLAG

²banner *adj* : distinguished from all others esp. in excellence ⟨a ~ year⟩

ban·nock \ˈban-ək\ *n* : a flat oatmeal or barley cake usu. cooked on a griddle

banns \ˈbanz\ *n pl* : public announcement esp. in church of a proposed marriage

ban·quet \ˈbaŋ-kwət\ *n* [MF, fr. It *banchetto*, fr. dim. of *banca* bench, bank] : a ceremonial dinner — **banquet** *vb*

ban·quette \baŋ-ˈket\ *n* : a long upholstered bench esp. along a wall

ban·shee \ˈban-shē\ *n* [ScGael *bean-sīth*, fr. or akin to Old Irish *ben sīde* woman of fairyland] : a female spirit in Gaelic folklore whose wailing warns a family that one of them will soon die

ban·tam \ˈbant-əm\ *n* **1** : any of numerous small domestic fowls that are often miniatures of standard breeds **2** : a small but pugnacious person

¹ban·ter \ˈbant-ər\ *vb* : to speak to in a witty and teasing manner

²banter *n* : good-natured witty joking

bant·ling \ˈbant-liŋ\ *n* : a young child

Ban·tu \ˈban-ˌtü\ *n, pl* **Bantu** *or* **Bantus** **1** : a member of a family of Negroid peoples occupying equatorial and southern Africa **2** : a group of African languages spoken generally in equatorial and southern Africa

Ban·tu·stan \ˌban-tu̇-ˈstan, ˌbän-tu̇-ˈstän\ *n* : an all-black enclave in the Republic of So. Africa with a limited degree of self-government

ban·yan \ˈban-yən\ *n* [earlier *banyan* Hindu merchant, fr.

banyan

Hindi *baniyā;* fr. a merchant's pagoda erected under a tree of the species in Iran] : a large East Indian tree whose aerial roots grow downward to the ground and form new trunks

ban·zai \bän-ˈzī\ *n* : a Japanese cheer or cry of triumph

bao·bab \ˈbau̇-ˌbab, ˈbā-ə-\ *n* : an Old World tropical tree with short swollen trunk and sour edible gourdlike fruits

bap·tism \ˈbap-ˌtiz-əm\ *n* **1** : a Christian sacrament signifying spiritual rebirth and symbolized by the ritual use of water **2** : an act of baptizing — **bap·tis·mal** \bap-ˈtiz-məl\ *adj*

baptismal name *n* : GIVEN NAME

Bap·tist \ˈbap-təst\ *n* : a member of any of several Protestant denominations emphasizing baptism by immersion

bap·tis·tery *or* **bap·tis·try** \ˈbap-tə-strē\ *n, pl* **-ter·ies** *or* **-tries** : a place esp. in a church used for baptism

bap·tize \bap-ˈtīz, ˈbap-ˌtīz\ *vb* **bap·tized; bap·tiz·ing** [ME *baptizen,* fr. OF *baptiser,* fr. L *baptizare,* fr. Gk *baptizein* to dip, baptize, fr. *baptos* dipped, fr. *baptein* to dip] **1** : to administer baptism to; *also* : CHRISTEN **2** : to purify esp. by an ordeal

[1]**bar** \ˈbär\ *n* **1** : a long narrow piece of material (as wood or metal) used esp. for a lever, fastening, or support **2** : BARRIER, OBSTACLE **3** : the railing in a law court at which prisoners are stationed; *also* : the legal profession or the whole body of lawyers **4** : a stripe, band, or line much longer than wide **5** : a counter at which food or esp. drink is served; *also* : BARROOM **6** : a vertical line across the musical staff

[2]**bar** *vb* **barred; bar·ring** **1** : to fasten, confine, or obstruct with or as if with a bar or bars **2** : to mark with bars : STRIPE **3** : to shut or keep out : EXCLUDE **4** : FORBID, PREVENT

[3]**bar** *prep* : EXCEPT

[4]**bar** *abbr* barometer; barometric

Bar *abbr* Baruch

barb \ˈbärb\ *n* **1** : a sharp projection extending backward (as from the point of an arrow) **2** : a biting critical remark — **barbed** \ˈbärbd\ *adj*

bar·bar·ian \bär-ˈber-ē-ən\ *adj* **1** : of, relating to, or being a land, culture, or people alien to and usu. believed to be inferior to one's own **2** : lacking refinement, learning, or artistic or literary culture — **barbarian** *n*

bar·bar·ic \bär-ˈbar-ik\ *adj* **1** : BARBARIAN **2** : marked by a lack of restraint : WILD **3** : PRIMITIVE, UNSOPHISTICATED

bar·ba·rism \ˈbär-bə-ˌriz-əm\ *n* **1** : the social condition of barbarians; *also* : the use or display of barbarian or barbarous acts, attitudes, or ideas **2** : a word or expression that offends standards of correctness or purity

bar·ba·rous \ˈbär-b(ə-)rəs\ *adj* **1** : lacking culture or refinement **2** : using linguistic barbarisms **3** : mercilessly harsh or cruel — **bar·bar·i·ty** \bär-ˈbar-ət-ē\ *n* — **bar·ba·rous·ly** *adv*

[1]**bar·be·cue** \ˈbär-bi-ˌkyü\ *n* : a social gathering at which barbecued food is served

[2]**barbecue** *vb* **-cued; -cu·ing** **1** : to cook over hot coals or on a revolving spit **2** : to cook in a highly seasoned vinegar sauce

bar·bell \ˈbär-ˌbel\ *n* : a bar with adjustable weights attached to each end used for exercise and in weight-lifting competition

bar·ber \ˈbär-bər\ *n* [ME, fr. MF *barbeor,* fr. *barbe* beard, fr. L *barba*] : one whose business is cutting and dressing hair and shaving and trimming beards

bar·ber·ry \ˈbär-ˌber-ē\ *n* : any of a genus of spiny shrubs bearing yellow flowers followed by oblong red berries

bar·bi·tal \ˈbär-bə-ˌtȯl\ *n* : a white crystalline addictive hypnotic often administered in the form of its soluble sodium salt

bar·bi·tu·rate \bär-ˈbich-ə-rət\ *n* : any of various compounds (as a salt or ester) formed from an organic acid (**bar·bi·tu·ric acid** \ˌbär-bə-ˌt(y)u̇r- ik-\); *esp* : one used as a sedative or hypnotic

bar·ca·role *or* **bar·ca·rolle** \ˈbär-kə-ˌrōl\ *n* : a Venetian boat song characterized by a beat suggesting a rowing rhythm; *also* : a piece of music imitating this

bar chart *n* : BAR GRAPH

bar code *n* : a set of printed and variously spaced bars and sometimes numerals that is designed to be scanned to identify the object it labels

bard \ˈbärd\ *n* : POET

[1]**bare** \ˈbaər\ *adj* **bar·er; bar·est** **1** : NAKED **2** : UNCONCEALED, EXPOSED **3** : EMPTY **4** : leaving nothing to spare : MERE **5** : PLAIN, UNADORNED **syn** nude, bald, naked — **bare·ness** *n*

[2]**bare** *vb* **bared; bar·ing** : to make or lay bare : UNCOVER

bare·back \-ˌbak\ *or* **bare·backed** \-ˈbakt\ *adv or adj* : without a saddle

bare·faced \-ˈfāst\ *adj* **1** : having the face uncovered; *esp* : BEARDLESS **2** : not concealed : OPEN

bare·foot \-ˌfu̇t\ *or* **bare·foot·ed** \-ˈfu̇t-əd\ *adv or adj* : with bare feet

bare–hand·ed \-ˈhan-dəd\ *adv or adj* **1** : without gloves **2** : without tools or weapons

bare·head·ed \-ˈhed-əd\ *adv or adj* : without a hat

bare·ly \ˈbaər-lē\ *adv* **1** : PLAINLY, MEAGERLY **2** : by a narrow margin : only just ⟨~ enough money⟩ **syn** hardly, scarcely

bar·fly \ˈbär-ˌflī\ *n* : a drinker who frequents bars

[1]**bar·gain** \ˈbär-gən\ *n* **1** : AGREEMENT **2** : an advantageous purchase **3** : a transaction, situation, or event regarded in the light of its results

[2]**bargain** *vb* **1** : to negotiate over the terms of an agreement; *also* : to come to terms **2** : BARTER

[1]**barge** \ˈbärj\ *n* **1** : a broad flat-bottomed boat usu. moved by towing **2** : a motorboat supplied to a flagship (as for an admiral) **3** : a ceremonial boat elegantly furnished — **barge·man** \-mən\ *n*

[2]**barge** *vb* **barged; barg·ing** **1** : to carry by barge **2** : to move or thrust oneself clumsily or rudely

bari·tone \ˈbar-ə-ˌtōn\ *n* [F *baryton* or It *baritono,* fr. Gk *barytonos* deep sounding, fr. *barys* heavy + *tonos* tone] : a male voice between bass and tenor; *also* : a man with such a voice

bar·i·um \ˈbar-ē-əm\ *n* : a silver-white metallic chemical element that occurs only in combination — see ELEMENT table

[1]**bark** \ˈbärk\ *vb* **1** : to make the short loud cry of a dog **2** : to speak or utter in a curt loud tone : SNAP

[2]**bark** *n* : the sound made by a barking dog

[3]**bark** *n* : the tough corky outer covering of a woody stem or root

[4]**bark** *vb* **1** : to strip the bark from **2** : to rub the skin from : ABRADE

[5]**bark** *n* : a 3-masted ship with foremast and mainmast square-rigged and mizzenmast fore-and-aft rigged

bar·keep \ˈbär-ˌkēp\ *or* **bar·keep·er** \-ˌkē-pər\ *n* : BARTENDER

bark·er \ˈbär-kər\ *n* : a person who stands at the entrance esp. to a show and tries to attract customers to it

bar·ley \ˈbär-lē\ *n* : a cereal grass with seeds used as food and in making malt liquors; *also* : its seed

bar mitz·vah \bär-ˈmits-və\ *n, often cap B&M* [Heb *bar miṣwāh,* lit., son of the (divine) law] **1** : a Jewish boy who at about 13 years of age assumes religious responsibilities **2** : the ceremony recognizing a boy as a bar mitzvah

barn \ˈbärn\ *n* [ME *bern,* fr. OE *bereærn,* fr. *bere* barley + *ærn* place] : a building used esp. for storing hay and grain and for housing livestock or farm equipment

bar·na·cle \ˈbär-ni-kəl\ *n* : any of numerous small marine crustaceans free-swimming when young but fixed (as to rocks, whales, or ships) when adult

barn·storm \ˈbärn-ˌstȯrm\ *vb* : to travel through the country making brief stops to entertain (as with shows or flying stunts) or to campaign for political office

barn·yard \-ˌyärd\ *n* : a usu. fenced area adjoining a barn

baro·graph \ˈbar-ə-ˌgraf\ *n* : a recording barometer

ba·rom·e·ter \bə-ˈräm-ət-ər\ *n* : an instrument for measuring atmospheric pressure — **baro·met·ric** \ˌbar-ə-ˈme-trik\ *adj*

bar·on \ˈbar-ən\ *n* : a member of the lowest grade of the British peerage — **ba·ro·ni·al** \bə-ˈrō-nē-əl\ *adj* — **bar·ony** \ˈbar-ə-nē\ *n*

bar·on·age \-ə-nij\ *n* : PEERAGE

bar·on·ess \-ə-nəs\ *n* **1** : the wife or widow of a baron **2** : a woman holding a baronial title in her own right

bar·on·et \ˈbar-ə-nət\ *n* : a man holding a rank of honor below a baron but above a knight — **bar·on·et·cy** \-sē\ *n*

ba·roque \bə-ˈrōk, -ˈräk\ *adj* : marked by elaborate and sometimes grotesque ornamentation and esp. by curved and plastic figures

ba·rouche \bə-ˈrüsh\ *n* [G *barutsche,* fr. It *biroccio,* deriv. of LL *birotus* two-wheeled, fr. L *bi* two + *rota* wheel] : a 4-wheeled carriage with a high driver's seat in front and a folding top

bar·racks \ˈbar-əks\ *n sing or pl* : a building or group of buildings for lodging soldiers

bar·ra·cu·da \ˌbar-ə-ˈküd-ə\ *n, pl* **-da** *or* **-das** : any of several large predaceous sea fishes including some used for food

bar·rage \bə-ˈräzh, -ˈräj\ *n* : a heavy concentration of fire (as of artillery)

bar·ra·try \ˈbar-ə-trē\ *n, pl* **-tries 1** : the purchase or sale of office or preferment in church or state **2** : a fraudulent breach of duty by the master or crew of a ship intended to harm the owner or cargo **3** : the practice of inciting lawsuits or quarrels

barred \ˈbärd\ *adj* : STRIPED

[1]**bar·rel** \ˈbar-əl\ *n* **1** : a round bulging cask with flat ends of equal diameter **2** : the amount contained in a barrel **3** : a cylindrical or tubular part ⟨gun ~⟩

[2]**barrel** *vb* **-reled** *or* **-relled; -rel·ing** *or* **-rel·ling 1** : to pack in a barrel **2** : to travel at high speed

barrel roll *n* : an airplane maneuver in which a complete revolution about the longitudinal axis is made

[1]**bar·ren** \ˈbar-ən\ *adj* **1** : STERILE, UNFRUITFUL **2** : unproductive of results ⟨a ~ scheme⟩ **3** : lacking interest or charm **4** : DULL, STUPID — **bar·ren·ness** \-ən-nəs\ *n*

[2]**barren** *n* : a tract of barren land

bar·rette \bä-ˈret, bə-\ *n* : a clasp or bar for holding the hair in place

[1]**bar·ri·cade** \ˈbar-ə-ˌkād, ˌbar-ə-ˈkād\ *vb* **-cad·ed; -cad·ing** : to block, obstruct, or fortify with a barricade

[2]**barricade** *n* [F, fr. MF, fr. *barriquer* to barricade, fr. *barrique* barrel] **1** : a hastily thrown-up obstruction or fortification **2** : BARRIER, OBSTACLE

bar·ri·er \ˈbar-ē-ər\ *n* : something that separates, demarcates, or serves as a barricade ⟨racial ~*s*⟩

barrier reef *n* : a coral reef roughly parallel to a shore and separated from it by a lagoon

bar·ring \ˈbär-iŋ\ *prep* : excluding by exception : EXCEPTING

bar·rio \ˈbär-ē-ˌō, ˈbar-\ *n, pl* **-ri·os 1** : a district of a city or town in a Spanish-speaking country **2** : a Spanish-speaking quarter in a U.S. city

bar·ris·ter \ˈbar-ə-stər\ *n* : a British counselor admitted to plead in the higher courts

bar·room \ˈbär-ˌrüm, -ˌrům\ *n* : a room or establishment whose main feature is a bar for the sale of liquor

[1]**bar·row** \ˈbar-ō\ *n* : a large burial mound of earth and stones

[2]**barrow** *n* : a male hog castrated while young

[3]**barrow** *n* **1** : HANDBARROW **2** : WHEELBARROW **3** : a cart with a boxlike body and two shafts for pushing it

Bart *abbr* baronet

bar·tend·er \ˈbär-ˌten-dər\ *n* : one that serves liquor at a bar

bar·ter \ˈbärt-ər\ *vb* : to trade by exchange of goods — **barter** *n*

Ba·ruch \ˈbär-ˌük, bə-ˈrük\ *n* — see BIBLE table

bas·al \ˈbā-səl\ *adj* **1** : situated at or forming the base **2** : BASIC

basal metabolism *n* : the turnover of energy in a fasting and resting organism using energy solely to maintain vital cellular activity, respiration, and circulation as measured by the rate at which heat is given off

ba·salt \bə-ˈsȯlt, ˈbā-ˌsȯlt\ *n* : a dark fine-grained igneous rock — **ba·sal·tic** \bə-ˈsȯl-tik\ *adj*

[1]**base** \ˈbās\ *n, pl* **bas·es** \ˈbā-səz\ **1** : BOTTOM, FOUNDATION **2** : a side or face on which a geometrical figure stands; *also* : the length of a base **3** : a main ingredient or fundamental part **4** : the point of beginning an act or operation **5** : a place on which a force depends for supplies **6** : the number of units in a given digit's place of a number system that is required to give the numeral 1 in the next higher place ⟨the decimal system uses a ~ of 10⟩; *also* : such a system using an indicated base ⟨convert from ~ 10 to ~ 2⟩ **7** : any of the four stations at the corners of a baseball diamond **8** : a chemical compound (as lime or ammonia) that reacts with an acid to form a salt, has a salty taste, and turns litmus blue **syn** basis, ground, groundwork, footing, foundation

[2]**base** *vb* **based; bas·ing 1** : to form or serve as a base for **2** : ESTABLISH

[3]**base** *adj* **1** : of inferior quality : DEBASED, ALLOYED **2** : CONTEMPTIBLE, IGNOBLE **3** : MENIAL, DEGRADING **4** : of little value **syn** low, vile, despicable, wretched — **base·ly** *adv* — **base·ness** *n*

base·ball \ˈbās-ˌbȯl\ *n* : a game played with a bat and ball by two teams on a field with four bases arranged in a diamond; *also* : the ball used in this game

base·board \-ˌbōrd\ *n* : a line of boards or molding covering the joint of a wall and the adjoining floor

base·born \-ˈbȯrn\ *adj* **1** : of humble birth **2** : of illegitimate birth **3** : MEAN, IGNOBLE

base exchange *n* : a post exchange at a naval or air force base

base hit *n* : a hit in baseball that enables the batter to reach base safely with no error made and no base runner forced out

base·less \-ləs\ *adj* : having no base or basis : GROUNDLESS

base·line \ˈbās-ˌlīn\ *n* **1** : a line serving as a basis esp. to calculate or locate something **2** : the area within which a baseball player must keep when running between bases

base·ment \-mənt\ *n* **1** : the part of a building that is wholly or partly below ground level **2** : the lowest or fundamental part of something

base on balls : an advance to first base given to a baseball player who receives four balls

base runner *n* : a baseball player who is on base or is attempting to reach a base

[1]**bash** \ˈbash\ *vb* **1** : to strike violently : BEAT **2** : to smash by a blow

[2]**bash** *n* **1** : a heavy blow **2** : a festive social gathering : PARTY

bash·ful \ˈbash-fəl\ *adj* : inclined to shrink from public attention — **bash·ful·ness** *n*

ba·sic \ˈbā-sik\ *adj* **1** : of, relating to, or forming the base or essence : FUNDAMENTAL **2** : of, relating to, or having the character of a chemical base ⟨a ~ substance⟩ **syn** underlying, basal, fundamental, primary — **ba·si·cal·ly** \-si-k(ə-)lē\ *adv* — **ba·sic·i·ty** \bā-ˈsis-ət-ē\ *n*

ba·sil \ˈbaz-əl, ˈbās-\ *n* : either of two mints with fragrant leaves used in cooking

\ə\abut \ᵊ\kitten \ər\further \a\ash \ā\ace \ä\cot, cart \au̇\out \ch\chin \e\bet \ē\easy \g\go \i\hit \ī\ice \j\job \ŋ\sing \ō\go \ȯ\law \ȯi\boy \th\thin \t͟h\the \ü\loot \u̇\foot \y\yet \zh\vision *see also* Pronunciation Symbols page

ba·sil·i·ca \bə-ˈsil-i-kə, -ˈzil-\ *n* [L, fr. Gk *basilikē*, fr. fem. of *basilikos* royal, fr. *basileus* king] **1** : an early Christian church building consisting of nave and aisles with clerestory and apse **2** : a Roman Catholic church given ceremonial privileges

bas·i·lisk \ˈbas-ə-ˌlisk, ˈbaz-\ *n* [ME, fr. L *basiliscus*, fr. Gk *basiliskos*, fr. dim. of *basileus* king] : a legendary reptile with fatal breath and glance

ba·sin \ˈbās-ᵊn\ *n* **1** : an open usu. circular vessel with sloping sides for holding liquid (as water) **2** : a hollow or enclosed place containing water; *also* : the region drained by a river

ba·sis \ˈbā-səs\ *n, pl* **ba·ses** \-ˌsēz\ **1** : FOUNDATION, BASE **2** : a fundamental principle

bask \ˈbask\ *vb* **1** : to expose oneself to comfortable heat **2** : to enjoy something warmly comforting ⟨~*ing* in his friends' admiration⟩

bas·ket \ˈbas-kət\ *n* : a container made of woven material (as twigs or grasses); *also* : any of various lightweight usu. wood containers — **bas·ket·ful** *n*

bas·ket·ball \-ˌbȯl\ *n* : a game played on a court by two teams who try to throw an inflated ball through a raised goal; *also* : the ball used in this game

basket case *n* **1** : one who has all four limbs amputated **2** : one that is totally incapacitated or inoperative

basket weave *n* : a textile weave resembling the checkered pattern of a plaited basket

bas mitz·vah \bäs-ˈmits-və\ *n, often cap B&M* [Heb *bath miṣwāh*, lit., daughter of the (divine) law] **1** : a Jewish girl who at about 13 years of age assumes religious responsibilities **2** : the ceremony recognizing a girl as a bas mitzvah

Basque \ˈbask\ *n* **1** : a member of a people inhabiting a region bordering on the Bay of Biscay in northern Spain and southwestern France **2** : the language of the Basque people — **Basque** *adj*

bas–re·lief \ˌbä-ri-ˈlēf\ *n* [F] : a sculpture in relief with the design raised very slightly from the background

¹**bass** \ˈbas\ *n, pl* **bass** *or* **bass·es** : any of numerous sport and food fishes (as a striped bass)

²**bass** \ˈbās\ *adj* : of low pitch

³**bass** \ˈbās\ *n* **1** : a deep sound or tone **2** : the lower half of the musical pitch range **3** : the lowest male singing voice **4** : a singer or instrument having a bass voice or part

bas·set hound \ˈbas-ət-\ *n* : any of an old French breed of short-legged dogs with long ears and crooked front legs

bas·si·net \ˌbas-ə-ˈnet\ *n* : a baby's bed that resembles a basket and often has a hood over one end

bas·so \ˈbas-ō\ *n, pl* **bassos** *or* **bas·si** \ˈbäs-ˌē\ [It] : a bass singer

bas·soon \bə-ˈsün\ *n* : a musical wind instrument lower in pitch than the oboe

bass·wood \ˈbas-ˌwu̇d\ *n* : any of several New World lindens or their wood

bast \ˈbast\ *n* : BAST FIBER

¹**bas·tard** \ˈbas-tərd\ *n* **1** : an illegitimate child **2** : an offensive or disagreeable person

²**bastard** *adj* **1** : ILLEGITIMATE **2** : of an inferior or nontypical kind, size, or form; *also* : SPURIOUS — **bas·tardy** *n*

bas·tard·ize \ˈbas-tər-ˌdīz\ *vb* **-ized; -iz·ing** : to reduce from a higher to a lower state : DEBASE

¹**baste** \ˈbāst\ *vb* **bast·ed; bast·ing** : to sew with long stitches so as to keep temporarily in place

²**baste** *vb* **bast·ed; bast·ing** : to moisten (as meat) at intervals with liquid while cooking

bast fiber *n* : a strong woody plant fiber obtained chiefly from phloem and used esp. in making ropes

bas·ti·na·do \ˌbas-tə-ˈnād-ō, -ˈnäd-\ *or* **bas·ti·nade** \ˌbas-tə-ˈnād, -ˈnäd\ *n, pl* **-na·does** *or* **-nades** **1** : a blow or beating esp. with a stick **2** : a punishment consisting of beating the soles of the feet

bas·tion \ˈbas-chən\ *n* : a projecting part of a fortification; *also* : a fortified position — **bas·tioned** \-chənd\ *adj*

¹**bat** \ˈbat\ *n* **1** : a stout stick : CLUB **2** : a sharp blow **3** : an implement (as of wood) used to hit a ball (as in baseball) **4** : a turn at batting — usu. used with *at*

²**bat** *vb* **bat·ted; bat·ting** : to hit with or as if with a bat

³**bat** *n* : any of an order of night-flying mammals with forelimbs modified to form wings

⁴**bat** *vb* **bat·ted; bat·ting** : WINK, BLINK

batch \ˈbach\ *n* **1** : a quantity (as of bread) baked at one time **2** : a quantity of material for use at one time or produced at one operation

bate \ˈbāt\ *vb* **bat·ed; bat·ing** : MODERATE, REDUCE

bath \ˈbath, ˈbȧth\ *n, pl* **baths** \ˈba<u>th</u>z, ˈbaths, ˈbȧ<u>th</u>z, ˈbȧths\ **1** : a washing of the body **2** : water for washing the body **3** : a liquid in which objects are immersed so that it can act on them **4** : BATHROOM

bathe \ˈbā<u>th</u>\ *vb* **bathed; bath·ing** **1** : to wash in liquid and esp. water; *also* : to apply water or a medicated liquid to ⟨*bathed* her eyes⟩ **2** : to take a bath; *also* : to take a swim **3** : to wash along, over, or against so as to wet **4** : to suffuse with or as if with light — **bath·er** *n*

bath·house \ˈbath-ˌhau̇s, ˈbȧth-\ *n* **1** : a building equipped for bathing **2** : a building containing dressing rooms for bathers

bathing suit *n* : SWIMSUIT

batho·lith \ˈbath-ə-ˌlith\ *n* : a great mass of igneous rock that forced its way into or between other rocks and that stopped in its rise a considerable distance below the surface

ba·thos \ˈbā-ˌthäs\ *n* [Gk, lit., depth] **1** : the sudden appearance of the commonplace in otherwise elevated matter or style **2** : insincere or overdone pathos — **ba·thet·ic** \bə-ˈthet-ik\ *adj*

bath·robe \ˈbath-ˌrōb, ˈbȧth-\ *n* : a loose usu. absorbent robe worn before and after bathing or as a dressing gown

bath·room \-ˌrüm, -ˌru̇m\ *n* : a room containing a bathtub or shower and usu. a washbowl and toilet

bath·tub \-ˌtəb\ *n* : a usu. fixed tub for bathing

bathy·scaphe \ˈbath-i-ˌskaf, -ˌskāf\ *also* **bathy·scaph** \-ˌskaf\ *n* : a navigable undersea craft for deep-sea exploration

bathy·sphere \-ˌsfiər\ *n* : a steel diving sphere for deep-sea observation

bathy·ther·mo·graph \ˌbath-i-ˈthər-mə-ˌgraf\ *n* : an instrument that records water temperature as a function of depth

ba·tik \bə-ˈtēk, ˈbat-ik\ *n* [Malay] **1** : an Indonesian method of hand-printing textiles by coating with wax the parts not to be dyed; *also* : a design so executed **2** : a fabric printed by batik

ba·tiste \bə-ˈtēst\ *n* : a fine sheer fabric of plain weave

bat·man \ˈbat-mən\ *n* : an orderly of a British military officer

ba·ton \bə-ˈtän\ *n* : STAFF, ROD; *esp* : a stick with which the leader directs an orchestra or band

bats·man \ˈbats-mən\ *n* : a batter esp. in cricket

bat·tal·ion \bə-ˈtal-yən\ *n* **1** : a large body of troops organized to act together : ARMY **2** : a military unit composed of a headquarters and two or more units (as companies)

¹**bat·ten** \ˈbat-ᵊn\ *vb* **bat·tened; bat·ten·ing** \ˈbat-(ᵊ-)niŋ\ **1** : to grow or make fat **2** : THRIVE

²**batten** *n* : a strip of wood used esp. to seal or strengthen a joint

³**batten** *vb* **bat·tened; bat·ten·ing** \ˈbat-(ᵊ-)niŋ\ : to fasten with battens

¹**bat·ter** \ˈbat-ər\ *vb* : to beat or damage with repeated blows

²**batter** *n* : a soft mixture (as for cake) basically of flour and liquid

[3]**batter** *n* : one that bats; *esp* : the player whose turn it is to bat

battering ram *n* : an ancient military machine for battering down walls

bat·tery \ˈbat-(ə-)rē\ *n, pl* **-ter·ies 1** : BEATING; *esp* : unlawful beating or use of force on a person **2** : a grouping of artillery pieces for tactical purposes; *also* : the guns of a warship **3** : a group of electric cells for furnishing electric current; *also* : a single electric cell ⟨a flashlight ~⟩ **4** : a number of similar items grouped or used as a unit ⟨a ~ of tests⟩ **5** : the pitcher and catcher of a baseball team

bat·ting \ˈbat-iŋ\ *n* : layers or sheets of cotton or wool (as for lining quilts)

[1]**bat·tle** \ˈbat-ᵊl\ *n* [ME *batel*, fr. OF *bataille* battle, fortifying tower, battalion, fr. LL *battalia* combat, alter. of *battualia* fencing exercises, fr. L *battuere* to beat] : a general military engagement; *also* : an extended contest or controversy

[2]**battle** *vb* **bat·tled; bat·tling** \ˈbat-(ᵊ-)liŋ\ : to engage in battle : CONTEND, FIGHT

bat·tle–ax \ˈbat-ᵊl-ˌaks\ *n* **1** : a long-handled ax formerly used as a weapon **2** : a quarrelsome domineering woman

battle fatigue *n* : COMBAT FATIGUE

bat·tle·field \ˈbat-ᵊl-ˌfēld\ *n* : a place where a battle is fought

bat·tle·ment \-mənt\ *n* : a decorative or defensive parapet on top of a wall

bat·tle·ship \-ˌship\ *n* : a warship of the most heavily armed and armored class

bat·tle·wag·on \-ˌwag-ən\ *n* : BATTLESHIP

bat·ty \ˈbat-ē\ *adj* **bat·ti·er; -est** : CRAZY, FOOLISH

bau·ble \ˈbȯ-bəl\ *n* : TRINKET

baux·ite \ˈbȯk-ˌsīt\ *n* : a clayey substance that is the chief ore of aluminum

bawd \ˈbȯd\ *n* **1** : MADAM 2 **2** : PROSTITUTE

bawdy \ˈbȯd-ē\ *adj* **bawd·i·er; -est** : OBSCENE, LEWD — **bawd·i·ly** \ˈbȯd-ᵊl-ē\ *adv* — **bawd·i·ness** \-ē-nəs\ *n*

[1]**bawl** \ˈbȯl\ *vb* : to cry or cry out loudly; *also* : to scold harshly

[2]**bawl** *n* : a long loud cry : BELLOW

[1]**bay** \ˈbā\ *adj* : reddish brown

[2]**bay** *n* **1** : a bay-colored animal **2** : a reddish brown

[3]**bay** *n* : the European laurel; *also* : a shrub or tree resembling this

[4]**bay** *n* **1** : a section or compartment of a building or vehicle **2** : a compartment projecting outward from the wall of a building and containing a window (**bay window**)

[5]**bay** *vb* : to bark with deep long tones

[6]**bay** *n* **1** : the position of one unable to escape and forced to face danger **2** : a baying of dogs

[7]**bay** *n* : an inlet of a body of water (as the sea) usu. smaller than a gulf

bay·ber·ry \ˈbā-ˌber-ē\ *n* : a hardy deciduous shrub of coastal eastern No. America bearing small hard berries coated with a white wax used for candles; *also* : its fruit

bay leaf *n* : the dried leaf of the European laurel used in cooking

[1]**bay·o·net** \ˈbā-ə-nət, ˌbā-ə-ˈnet\ *n* : a daggerlike weapon made to fit on the muzzle end of a rifle

[2]**bayonet** *vb* **-net·ed** *also* **-net·ted; -net·ing** *also* **-net·ting** : to use or stab with a bayonet

bay·ou \ˈbī-ō, -ü\ *n* [Louisiana French, fr. Choctaw *bayuk*] : a marshy or sluggish body of water

bay rum *n* : a fragrant liquid used esp. as a cologne or after-shave lotion

ba·zaar \bə-ˈzär\ *n* **1** : a group of shops : MARKETPLACE **2** : a fair for the sale of articles usu. for charity

ba·zoo·ka \bə-ˈzü-kə\ *n* [*bazooka* (a crude musical instrument made of pipes and a funnel)] : a weapon consisting of a tube and launching an explosive rocket able to pierce armor

[1]**BB** \ˈbē-(ˌ)bē\ *n* : a small round shot pellet

[2]**BB** *abbr* base on balls

BBB *abbr* Better Business Bureau

BBC *abbr* British Broadcasting Corporation

bbl *abbr* barrel; barrels

BC *abbr* **1** before Christ — often printed in small capitals **2** British Columbia

BCD \ˌbē-ˌsē-ˈdē\ *n* [*b*inary *c*oded *d*ecimal] : a computer code for representing alphanumeric information

B cell *n* [bone-marrow-derived *cell*] : any of the lymphocytes that secrete antibodies when mature

B complex *n* : VITAMIN B COMPLEX

bd *abbr* **1** board **2** bound

bdl *or* **bdle** *abbr* bundle

bdrm *abbr* bedroom

be \(ˈ)bē\ *vb, past 1st & 3d sing* **was** \(ˈ)wəz, ˈwäz\; *2d sing* **were** \(ˈ)wər\; *pl* **were;** *past subjunctive* **were;** *past part* **been** \(ˈ)bin\; *pres part* **be·ing** \ˈbē-iŋ\; *pres 1st sing* **am** \əm, (ˈ)am\; *2d sing* **are** \ər, (ˈ)är\; *3d sing* **is** \(ˈ)iz, əz\; *pl* **are;** *pres subjunctive* **be 1** : to equal in meaning or symbolically ⟨God *is* love⟩; *also* : to have a specified qualification or relationship ⟨leaves *are* green⟩ ⟨this fish *is* a trout⟩ **2** : to have objective existence ⟨there *was* once an old woman⟩; *also* : to have or occupy a particular place ⟨here *is* your pen⟩ **3** : to take place : OCCUR ⟨the meeting *is* tonight⟩ **4** — used with the past participle of transitive verbs as a passive voice auxiliary ⟨the door *was* opened⟩ **5** — used as the auxiliary of the present participle in expressing continuous action ⟨he *is* sleeping⟩ **6** — used as an auxiliary with the past participle of some intransitive verbs to form archaic perfect tenses **7** — used as an auxiliary with *to* and the infinitive to express futurity, prearrangement, or obligation ⟨he *is* to come when called⟩

Be *symbol* beryllium

[1]**beach** \ˈbēch\ *n* : a sandy or gravelly part of the shore of an ocean or lake

[2]**beach** *vb* : to run or drive ashore

beach buggy *n* : DUNE BUGGY

beach·comb·er \ˈbēch-ˌkō-mər\ *n* : one who searches along a shore for useful or salable flotsam and refuse

beach·head \ˈbēch-ˌhed\ *n* : an area on an enemy-held shore occupied by an advance attacking force to protect the later landing of troops or supplies

bea·con \ˈbē-kən\ *n* **1** : a signal fire **2** : a guiding or warning signal (as a lighthouse) **3** : a radio transmitter emitting signals for guidance of aircraft

[1]**bead** \ˈbēd\ *n* [ME *bede* prayer, prayer bead, fr. OE *bed*, *gebed* prayer] **1** *pl* : a series of prayers and meditations made with a rosary **2** : a small piece of material pierced for threading on a line (as in a rosary) **3** : a small globular body **4** : a narrow projecting rim or band — **bead·ing** *n* — **beady** *adj*

[2]**bead** *vb* : to form into a bead

bea·dle \ˈbēd-ᵊl\ *n* : a usu. English parish officer whose duties include keeping order in church

bea·gle \ˈbē-gəl\ *n* : a small short-legged smooth-coated hound

beak \ˈbēk\ *n* : the bill of a bird and esp. of a bird of prey; *also* : a pointed projecting part — **beaked** \ˈbēkt\ *adj*

bea·ker \ˈbē-kər\ *n* **1** : a large drinking cup with a wide mouth **2** : a thin-walled laboratory vessel with a wide mouth

[1]**beam** \ˈbēm\ *n* **1** : a large long piece of timber or metal **2** : the bar of a balance from which the scales hang **3** : the breadth of a ship at its widest part **4** : a ray or shaft of light **5** : a collection of nearly parallel rays (as X rays) or particles (as electrons) **6** : a constant radio signal

transmitted for the guidance of pilots; *also* : the course indicated by this signal

²**beam** *vb* **1** : to send out light **2** : to aim (a broadcast) by directional antennas **3** : to smile with joy

¹**bean** \ˈbēn\ *n* : the edible seed borne in pods by some leguminous plants; *also* : a plant or a pod bearing these

²**bean** *vb* : to strike on the head with an object

bean·bag \ˈbēn-ˌbag\ *n* : a cloth bag partially filled typically with dried beans and used as a toy

bean·ball \ˈbēn-ˌbȯl\ *n* : a pitched baseball thrown at a batter's head

bean curd *n* : a food like soft cheese made from soybeans

bean·ie \ˈbē-nē\ *n* : a small round tight-fitting skullcap

beano \ˈbē-nō\ *n, pl* **beanos** : BINGO

¹**bear** \ˈbaər\ *n, pl* **bears 1** *or pl* **bear** : any of a family of large heavy mammals with shaggy hair and small tails **2** : a gruff or sullen person **3** : one who sells (as securities) in expectation of a price decline — **bear·ish** *adj*

²**bear** *vb* **bore** \ˈbōr\; **borne** \ˈbōrn\ *also* **born** \ˈbȯrn\; **bear·ing 1** : CARRY **2** : to be equipped with **3** : to give as testimony ⟨~ witness to the facts of the case⟩ **4** : to give birth to; *also* : PRODUCE, YIELD ⟨a tree that ~*s* regularly⟩ **5** : ENDURE, SUSTAIN ⟨~ pain⟩ ⟨*bore* the weight on piles⟩; *also* : to exert pressure or influence **6** : to be or become directed ⟨~ to the right⟩ — **bear·able** *adj* — **bear·er** *n*

¹**beard** \ˈbiərd\ *n* **1** : the hair that grows on the face of a man **2** : a growth of bristly hairs (as on rye or the chin of a goat) — **beard·ed** \-əd\ *adj* — **beard·less** *adj*

²**beard** *vb* : to confront boldly

bear·ing \ˈba(ə)r-iŋ\ *n* **1** : manner of carrying oneself : COMPORTMENT **2** : a supporting object, purpose, or point **3** : a machine part in which another part (as an axle or pin) turns **4** : an emblem in a coat of arms **5** : the position or direction of one point with respect to another or to the compass; *also* : a determination of position **6** *pl* : comprehension of one's situation **7** : connection with or influence on something; *also* : SIGNIFICANCE

bear·skin \ˈbaər-ˌskin\ *n* : an article made of the skin of a bear

beast \ˈbēst\ *n* **1** : ANIMAL 1; *esp* : a 4-footed mammal **2** : a contemptible person **syn** brute, animal, creature

¹**beast·ly** \ˈbēst-lē\ *adj* **beast·li·er; -est 1** : of, relating to, or resembling a beast **2** : ABOMINABLE, DISAGREEABLE — **beast·li·ness** \-lē-nəs\ *n*

²**beastly** *adv* : VERY

¹**beat** \ˈbēt\ *vb* **beat; beat·en** \ˈbēt-ᵊn\ *or* **beat; beat·ing 1** : to strike repeatedly **2** : TREAD **3** : to affect or alter by beating ⟨~ metal into sheets⟩ **4** : to sound (as an alarm) on a drum **5** : OVERCOME; *also* : SURPASS **6** : to act or arrive before ⟨~ his brother home⟩ **7** : THROB — **beat·er** *n*

²**beat** *n* **1** : a single stroke or blow esp. of a series; *also* : PULSATION **2** : a rhythmic stress in poetry or music or the rhythmic effect of these **3** : a regularly traversed course

³**beat** *adj* **1** : EXHAUSTED **2** : of or relating to beatniks

⁴**beat** *n* : BEATNIK

be·atif·ic \ˌbē-ə-ˈtif-ik\ *adj* : giving or indicative of great joy or bliss

be·at·i·fy \bē-ˈat-ə-ˌfī\ *vb* **-fied; -fy·ing 1** : to make supremely happy **2** : to declare to have attained the blessedness of heaven and authorize the title "Blessed" for — **be·at·i·fi·ca·tion** \-ˌat-ə-fə-ˈkā-shən\ *n*

be·at·i·tude \bē-ˈat-ə-ˌt(y)üd\ *n* **1** : a state of utmost bliss **2** : any of the declarations made in the Sermon on the Mount (Mt 5:3–12) beginning "Blessed are"

beat·nik \ˈbēt-nik\ *n* : a person who behaves and dresses unconventionally and is inclined to exotic philosophizing and extreme self-expression

beau \ˈbō\ *n, pl* **beaux** \ˈbōz\ *or* **beaus** [F, fr. *beau* beautiful, fr. L *bellus* pretty] **1** : a man of fashion : DANDY **2** : SUITOR, LOVER

beau geste \bō-ˈzhest\ *n, pl* **beaux gestes** *or* **beau gestes** \bō-ˈzhest\ : a graceful or magnanimous gesture

beau ide·al \ˌbō-ī-ˈdē(-ə)l\ *n, pl* **beau ideals** : the perfect type or model

Beau·jo·lais \ˌbō-zhō-ˈlā\ *n* : a French red table wine

beau monde \bō-ˈmänd, -mōⁿd\ *n, pl* **beau mondes** \-ˈmän(d)z\ *or* **beaux mondes** \bō-mōⁿd\ : the world of high society and fashion

beau·te·ous \ˈbyüt-ē-əs\ *adj* : BEAUTIFUL — **beau·te·ous·ly** *adv*

beau·ti·cian \byü-ˈtish-ən\ *n* : COSMETOLOGIST

beau·ti·ful \ˈbyüt-i-fəl\ *adj* : characterized by beauty : LOVELY **syn** pretty, fair, comely, lovely — **beau·ti·ful·ly** \-f(ə-)lē\ *adv*

beautiful people *n pl, often cap B&P* : people who are identified with international society

beau·ti·fy \ˈbyüt-ə-ˌfī\ *vb* **-fied; -fy·ing** : to make more beautiful — **beau·ti·fi·ca·tion** \ˌbyüt-ə-fə-ˈkā-shən\ *n* — **beau·ti·fi·er** *n*

beau·ty \ˈbyüt-ē\ *n, pl* **beauties** : qualities that give pleasure to the senses or exalt the mind : LOVELINESS; *also* : something having such qualities

beauty shop *n* : an establishment where hairdressing, facials, and manicures are done

beaux arts \bō-ˈzär\ *n pl* [F] : FINE ARTS

bea·ver \ˈbē-vər\ *n, pl* **beavers** : a large fur-bearing rodent that builds dams and underwater houses of mud and sticks; *also* : its fur

beaver

be·calm \bi-ˈkäm, -ˈkälm\ *vb* : to keep (as a ship) motionless by lack of wind

be·cause \bi-ˈkȯz, -ˈkəz\ *conj* : for the reason that

because of *prep* : by reason of

beck \ˈbek\ *n* : a beckoning gesture; *also* : SUMMONS

beck·on \ˈbek-ən\ *vb* **beck·oned; beck·on·ing** \ˈbek-(ə-)niŋ\ : to summon or signal esp. by a nod or gesture; *also* : ATTRACT

be·cloud \bi-ˈklau̇d\ *vb* : OBSCURE

be·come \bi-ˈkəm\ *vb* **-came** \-ˈkām\; **-come; -com·ing 1** : to come to be ⟨~ tired⟩ **2** : to suit or be suitable to ⟨her dress ~*s* her⟩

be·com·ing \-ˈkəm-iŋ\ *adj* : SUITABLE, FIT; *also* : ATTRACTIVE — **be·com·ing·ly** *adv*

¹**bed** \ˈbed\ *n* **1** : an article of furniture to sleep on **2** : a plot of ground prepared for plants **3** : FOUNDATION, BOTTOM ⟨river ~⟩ **4** : LAYER, STRATUM

²**bed** *vb* **bed·ded; bed·ding 1** : to put or go to bed **2** : to fix in a foundation : EMBED **3** : to plant in beds **4** : to lay or lie flat or in layers

bed–and–breakfast *adj* : offering lodging and breakfast ⟨a ~ place⟩ — **bed–and–breakfast** *n*

be·daub \bi-ˈdȯb\ *vb* : SMEAR

be·daz·zle \bi-ˈdaz-əl\ *vb* : to confuse by or as if by a strong light — **be·daz·zle·ment** *n*

bed·bug \ˈbed-ˌbəg\ *n* : a wingless bloodsucking bug infesting houses and esp. beds

bed·clothes \ˈbed-ˌklō(th)z\ *n pl* : BEDDING 1

bed·ding \ˈbed-iŋ\ *n* **1** : materials for making up a bed **2** : FOUNDATION

be·deck \bi-ˈdek\ *vb* : ADORN

be·dev·il \bi-ˈdev-əl\ *vb* **1** : HARASS, TORMENT **2** : CONFUSE, MUDDLE

be·dew \bi-ˈd(y)ü\ *vb* : to wet with or as if with dew

bed·fast \ˈbed-ˌfast\ *adj* : BEDRIDDEN

bed·fel·low \ˈbed-ˌfel-ō\ *n* **1** : one sharing the bed of another **2** : a close associate : ALLY

be·di·zen \bi-ˈdīz-ᵊn, -ˈdiz-\ *vb* [*be-* + *dizen,* fr. earlier *disen* to dress a distaff with flax, fr. Dutch] : to dress or adorn with showy or vulgar finery

bed·lam \ˈbed-ləm\ *n* [*Bedlam,* popular name for the Hospital of St. Mary of Bethlehem, London, an insane asylum, fr. ME *Bedlem* Bethlehem] **1** : an insane asylum **2** : a scene of uproar and confusion

bed·ou·in *or* **bed·u·in** \ˈbed(-ə)-wən\ *n, pl* **bedouin** *or* **bedouins** *or* **beduin** *or* **beduins** *often cap* : a nomadic Arab of the Arabian, Syrian, or No. African deserts

bed·pan \ˈbed-ˌpan\ *n* : a shallow vessel used by a person in bed for urination or defecation

bed·post \-ˌpōst\ *n* : the post of a bed

be·drag·gled \bi-ˈdrag-əld\ *adj* : soiled and disordered as if by being drenched

bed·rid·den \ˈbed-ˌrid-ᵊn\ *adj* : kept in bed by illness or weakness

bed·rock \-ˈräk\ *n* : the solid rock underlying surface materials (as soil) — **bedrock** *adj*

bed·roll \-ˌrōl\ *n* : bedding rolled up for carrying

bed·room \-ˌrüm, -ˌru̇m\ *n* : a room containing a bed and used esp. for sleeping

bed·side \ˈbed-ˌsīd\ *n* : the place beside a bed esp. of a sick or dying person

bed·sore \ˈbed-ˌsōr\ *n* : an ulceration of tissue deprived of nutrition by prolonged pressure

bed·spread \-ˌspred\ *n* : a usu. ornamental outer cover for a bed

bed·stead \-ˌsted, -ˌstid\ *n* : the framework of a bed

bed·time \-ˌtīm\ *n* : time for going to bed

bed–wet·ting \-ˌwet-iŋ\ *n* : involuntary discharge of urine esp. in bed during sleep — **bed–wet·ter** *n*

[1]**bee** \ˈbē\ *n* : a social and colonial 4-winged insect often kept in hives for the honey it produces; *also* : any of various related insects

[2]**bee** *n* : a gathering of people for a specific purpose

beech \ˈbēch\ *n, pl* **beech·es** *or* **beech** : any of a genus of deciduous hardwood trees with smooth gray bark and small sweet triangular nuts; *also* : the wood of a beech — **beech·en** \ˈbē-chən\ *adj*

beech·nut \ˈbēch-ˌnət\ *n* : the nut of a beech

[1]**beef** \ˈbēf\ *n, pl* **beefs** \ˈbēfs\ *or* **beeves** \ˈbēvz\ **1** : the flesh of a steer, cow, or bull; *also* : the dressed carcass of a beef animal **2** : a steer, cow, or bull esp. when fattened for food **3** : MUSCLE, BRAWN **4** *pl beefs* : COMPLAINT

[2]**beef** *vb* **1** : STRENGTHEN — usu. used with *up* **2** : COMPLAIN

beef·eat·er \-ˌēt-ər\ *n* : a yeoman of the guard of an English monarch

beef·steak \ˈbēf-ˌstāk\ *n* : a slice of beef suitable for broiling or frying

beefy \ˈbē-fē\ *adj* **beef·i·er; -est** : THICKSET, BRAWNY

bee·hive \ˈbē-ˌhīv\ *n* : HIVE 1, 3

bee·keep·er \-ˌkē-pər\ *n* : a raiser of bees — **bee·keep·ing** *n*

bee·line \-ˌlīn\ *n* : a straight direct course

been *past part of* BE

beep·er \ˈbē-pər\ *n* : a portable electronic device that alerts the person carrying it when it receives a special radio signal

beer \ˈbiər\ *n* : an alcoholic beverage brewed from malt and hops — **beery** *adj*

bees·wax \ˈbēz-ˌwaks\ *n* : WAX 1

beet \ˈbēt\ *n* : a garden plant with edible leaves and a thick sweet root used as a vegetable, as a source of sugar, or as forage; *also* : its root

[1]**bee·tle** \ˈbēt-ᵊl\ *n* : any of an order of insects having four wings of which the stiff outer pair covers the membranous inner pair when not in flight

[2]**beetle** *vb* **bee·tled; bee·tling** : to jut out : PROJECT

be·fall \bi-ˈfȯl\ *vb* **-fell** \-ˈfel\; **-fall·en** \-ˈfȯ-lən\ : to happen to : OCCUR

be·fit \bi-ˈfit\ *vb* : to be suitable to

be·fog \bi-ˈfȯg, -ˈfäg\ *vb* : OBSCURE; *also* : CONFUSE

[1]**be·fore** \bi-ˈfōr\ *adv or adj* **1** : in front **2** : EARLIER

[2]**before** *prep* **1** : in front of ⟨stood ~ him⟩ **2** : earlier than ⟨got there ~ me⟩ **3** : in a more important category than ⟨put quality ~ quantity⟩

[3]**before** *conj* **1** : earlier than the time when ⟨he got here ~ I did⟩ **2** : more willingly than ⟨he'd starve ~ he'd steal⟩

be·fore·hand \bi-ˈfōr-ˌhand\ *adv or adj* : in advance

be·foul \bi-ˈfau̇l\ *vb* : SOIL

be·friend \bi-ˈfrend\ *vb* : to act as friend to

be·fud·dle \bi-ˈfəd-ᵊl\ *vb* : MUDDLE, CONFUSE

beg \ˈbeg\ *vb* **begged; beg·ging** **1** : to ask as a charity; *also* : ENTREAT **2** : EVADE; *also* : assume as established ⟨~ the question⟩

be·get \bi-ˈget\ *vb* **-got** \-ˈgät\; **-got·ten** \-ˈgät-ᵊn\ *or* **-got; -get·ting** : to become the father of : SIRE

[1]**beg·gar** \ˈbeg-ər\ *n* : one that begs esp. as a way of life

[2]**beggar** *vb* **beg·gared; beg·gar·ing** \ˈbeg-(ə-)riŋ\ : IMPOVERISH

beg·gar·ly \ˈbeg-ər-lē\ *adj* **1** : marked by unrelieved poverty ⟨a ~ life⟩ **2** : contemptibly mean or inadequate

beg·gary \ˈbeg-ə-rē\ *n* : extreme poverty

be·gin \bi-ˈgin\ *vb* **be·gan** \-ˈgan\; **be·gun** \-ˈgən\; **be·gin·ning** **1** : to do the first part of an action; *also* : to undertake or undergo initial steps : COMMENCE **2** : to come into being : ARISE; *also* : FOUND **3** : ORIGINATE, INVENT — **be·gin·ner** *n*

be·gone \bi-ˈgȯn\ *vb* : to go away : DEPART — used esp. in the imperative

be·go·nia \bi-ˈgōn-yə\ *n* : any of a genus of tropical herbs widely grown for their showy leaves and waxy flowers

be·grime \bi-ˈgrīm\ *vb* **be·grimed; be·grim·ing** : to make dirty

be·grudge \bi-ˈgrəj\ *vb* **1** : to give or concede reluctantly **2** : to take little pleasure in : be annoyed by **3** : to envy the pleasure or enjoyment of

be·guile \-ˈgīl\ *vb* **be·guiled; be·guil·ing** **1** : DECEIVE, CHEAT **2** : to while away **3** : to coax by wiles

be·guine \bi-ˈgēn\ *n* [AmerF *béguine,* fr. F *béguin* flirtation] : a vigorous popular dance of the islands of Saint Lucia and Martinique

be·gum \ˈbā-gəm, ˈbē-\ *n* : a Muslim woman of high rank

be·half \bi-ˈhaf, -ˈhȧf\ *n* : BENEFIT, SUPPORT, DEFENSE

be·have \bi-ˈhāv\ *vb* **be·haved; be·hav·ing** **1** : to bear, comport, or conduct oneself in a particular and esp. a proper way **2** : to act, function, or react in a particular way

be·hav·ior \bi-ˈhā-vyər\ *n* : way of behaving; *esp* : personal conduct — **be·hav·ior·al** \-vyə-rəl\ *adj*

be·hav·ior·ism \bi-ˈhā-vyə-ˌriz-əm\ *n* : a school of psychology concerned with the objective evidence of behavior without reference to conscious experience

be·head \bi-ˈhed\ *vb* : to cut off the head of

be·he·moth \bi-ˈhē-məth, ˈbē-ə-ˌmäth\ *n* : a huge powerful animal described in Job 40:15–24 that is probably the hippopotamus; *also* : something of monstrous size or power

be·hest \bi-ˈhest\ *n* **1** : COMMAND **2** : an urgent prompting

[1]**be·hind** \bi-ˈhīnd\ *adv or adj* **1** : BACK, BACKWARD **2** : LATE, SLOW

[2]**behind** *prep* **1** : in or to a place or situation in back of or to the rear of ⟨look ~ you⟩ ⟨the staff stayed ~ the troops⟩ **2** : inferior to (as in rank) : BELOW ⟨three games ~ the first-place team⟩ **3** : in support of : SUPPORTING ⟨we're ~ you all the way⟩

---

be·hind·hand \bi-ˈhīnd-ˌhand\ *adj* **1** : being in arrears **2** : lagging behind the times **syn** tardy, late, overdue, belated

be·hold \bi-ˈhōld\ *vb* **-held** \-ˈheld\; **-hold·ing 1** : to have in sight : SEE **2** — used imperatively to direct the attention **syn** view, observe, notice, espy — **be·hold·er** *n*

be·hold·en \bi-ˈhōl-dən\ *adj* : OBLIGATED, INDEBTED

be·hoof \bi-ˈhüf\ *n* : ADVANTAGE, PROFIT

be·hoove \bi-ˈhüv\ *or* **be·hove** \-ˈhōv\ *vb* **be·hooved** *or* **be·hoved; be·hoov·ing** *or* **be·hov·ing** : to be necessary, proper, or advantageous for

beige \ˈbāzh\ *n* : a pale dull yellowish brown — **beige** *adj*

be·ing \ˈbē-iŋ\ *n* **1** : EXISTENCE; *also* : LIFE **2** : the qualities or constitution of an existent thing **3** : a living thing; *esp* : PERSON

be·la·bor \bi-ˈlā-bər\ *vb* **1** : to assail (as with words) tiresomely or at length **2** : to beat soundly

be·lat·ed \bi-ˈlāt-əd\ *adj* : DELAYED, LATE

be·lay \bi-ˈlā\ *vb* **1** : to wind (a rope) around a pin or cleat in order to hold secure **2** : QUIT, STOP — used in the imperative

belch \ˈbelch\ *vb* **1** : to expel (gas) from the stomach through the mouth **2** : to gush forth ⟨a volcano *~ing* lava⟩ — **belch** *n*

bel·dam *or* **bel·dame** \ˈbel-dəm\ *n* [ME *beldam* grandmother, fr. MF *bel* beautiful + ME *dam* lady, mother] : an old woman; *esp* : HAG

be·lea·guer \bi-ˈlē-gər\ *vb* **1** : BESIEGE **2** : HARASS ⟨*~ed* parents⟩

bel·fry \ˈbel-frē\ *n, pl* **belfries** [ME *belfrey,* alter. of *berfrey,* fr. MF *berfrei,* deriv. of Gk *pyrgos phorētos* movable war tower] : a tower for a bell (as on a church); *also* : the part of the tower in which the bell hangs

Belg *abbr* Belgian; Belgium

Bel·gian \ˈbel-jən\ *n* : a native or inhabitant of Belgium — **Belgian** *adj*

be·lie \bi-ˈlī\ *vb* **-lied; -ly·ing 1** : MISREPRESENT **2** : to prove (something) false **3** : to run counter to

be·lief \bə-ˈlēf\ *n* **1** : CONFIDENCE, TRUST **2** : something (as a tenet or creed) believed **syn** conviction, opinion, persuasion, sentiment

be·lieve \bə-ˈlēv\ *vb* **be·lieved; be·liev·ing 1** : to have religious convictions **2** : to have a firm conviction about something : accept as true **3** : to hold as an opinion : SUPPOSE — **be·liev·able** *adj* — **be·liev·er** *n*

be·like \bi-ˈlīk\ *adv, archaic* : PROBABLY

be·lit·tle \bi-ˈlit-ᵊl\ *vb* **-lit·tled; -lit·tling** \-ˈlit-(ᵊ-)liŋ\ : to make seem little or less; *also* : DISPARAGE

[1]**bell** \ˈbel\ *n* **1** : a hollow metallic device that makes a ringing sound when struck **2** : the sounding or stroke of a bell (as on shipboard to tell the time); *also* : time so indicated **3** : something with the flared form of a typical bell

[2]**bell** *vb* : to provide with a bell

bel·la·don·na \ˌbel-ə-ˈdän-ə\ *n* [It, lit., beautiful lady; fr. its cosmetic use] : a drug or extract used esp. to relieve spasms and pain or to dilate the eye and obtained from a poisonous European herb related to the potato; *also* : this herb

bell–bot·toms \ˈbel-ˈbät-əmz\ *n pl* : pants with wide flaring bottoms — **bell–bottom** *adj*

bell·boy \ˈbel-ˌbȯi\ *n* : BELLHOP

belle \ˈbel\ *n* : an attractive and popular girl or woman

belles let·tres \bel-letrᵊ\ *n pl* [F] : literature that is an end in itself and not practical or purely informative — **bel·le·tris·tic** \ˌbel-ə-ˈtris-tik\ *adj*

bell·hop \ˈbel-ˌhäp\ *n* : a hotel or club employee who takes guests to rooms, carries luggage, and runs errands

bel·li·cose \ˈbel-i-ˌkōs\ *adj* : WARLIKE, PUGNACIOUS **syn** belligerent, quarrelsome, combative, contentious, pugnacious — **bel·li·cos·i·ty** \ˌbel-i-ˈkäs-ət-ē\ *n*

bel·lig·er·en·cy \bə-ˈlij(-ə)-rən-sē\ *n* **1** : the status of a nation engaged in war **2** : BELLIGERENCE, TRUCULENCE

bel·lig·er·ent \-rənt\ *adj* **1** : waging war **2** : TRUCULENT **syn** bellicose, pugnacious, combative, contentious, warlike — **bel·lig·er·ence** \-rəns\ *n* — **belligerent** *n*

bel·low \ˈbel-ō\ *vb* **1** : to make the deep hollow sound characteristic of a bull **2** : to call or utter in a loud deep voice — **bellow** *n*

bel·lows \-ōz, -əz\ *n sing or pl* : a closed boxlike device with sides that can be spread apart and then pressed together to draw in air and expel it through a tube

bells \ˈbelz\ *n pl* : BELL-BOTTOMS

bell·weth·er \ˈbel-ˈweth-ər, -ˌweth-\ *n* : one that takes the lead or initiative

[1]**bel·ly** \ˈbel-ē\ *n, pl* **bellies** [ME *bely* bellows, belly, fr. OE *belg* bag, skin] **1** : ABDOMEN; *also* : STOMACH **2** : the underpart of an animal's body

[2]**belly** *vb* **bel·lied; bel·ly·ing** : BULGE

[1]**bel·ly·ache** \ˈbel-ē-ˌāk\ *n* : pain in the abdomen

[2]**bellyache** *vb* : COMPLAIN

belly button *n* : NAVEL

belly dance *n* : a usu. solo dance emphasizing movement of the belly — **belly dance** *vb* — **belly dancer** *n*

belly laugh *n* : a deep hearty laugh

be·long \bi-ˈlȯŋ\ *vb* **1** : to be suitable or appropriate; *also* : to be properly situated ⟨shoes ~ in the closet⟩ **2** : to be the property ⟨this *~s* to me⟩; *also* : to be attached (as through birth or membership) ⟨~ to a club⟩ **3** : to form an attribute or part ⟨this wheel *~s* to the cart⟩ **4** : to be classified ⟨whales ~ among the mammals⟩

be·long·ings \-ˈlȯŋ-iŋz\ *n pl* : GOODS, EFFECTS, POSSESSIONS

be·loved \bi-ˈləv(-ə)d\ *adj* : dearly loved — **beloved** *n*

[1]**be·low** \bi-ˈlō\ *adv* **1** : in or to a lower place or rank **2** : on earth **3** : in hell **syn** under, beneath, underneath

[2]**below** *prep* **1** : in or to a lower place than **2** : inferior to (as in rank)

[1]**belt** \ˈbelt\ *n* **1** : a strip (as of leather) worn about the waist **2** : an endless band passing around pulleys or cylinders to communicate motion or convey material **3** : a region marked by some distinctive feature; *esp* : one suited to a particular crop

[2]**belt** *vb* **1** : to encircle or secure with a belt **2** : to beat with or as if with a belt **3** : to mark with an encircling band

[3]**belt** *n* **1** : a jarring blow : WHACK **2** : DRINK ⟨a ~ of whiskey⟩

belt–tightening *n* : a reduction in spending

belt·way \ˈbelt-ˌwā\ *n* : a highway skirting an urban area

be·lu·ga \bə-ˈlü-gə\ *n* : a white sturgeon of the Black sea, Caspian sea, and their tributaries that is a source of caviar

bel·ve·dere \ˈbel-və-ˌdiər\ *n* [It, lit., beautiful view] : a structure (as a summerhouse) designed to command a view

be·mire \bi-ˈmī(ə)r\ *vb* : to cover or soil with or sink in mire

be·moan \bi-ˈmōn\ *vb* : LAMENT, DEPLORE **syn** bewail, grieve, moan, weep

be·muse \bi-ˈmyüz\ *vb* : BEWILDER, CONFUSE

[1]**bench** \ˈbench\ *n* **1** : a long seat for two or more persons **2** : the seat of a judge in court; *also* : the office or dignity of a judge **3** : COURT; *also* : JUDGES **4** : a table for holding work and tools ⟨a carpenter's ~⟩

[2]**bench** \ˈbench\ *vb* **1** : to furnish with benches **2** : to seat on a bench **3** : to remove from or keep out of a game

bench mark *n* **1** : a mark on a permanent object serving as an elevation reference in topographical surveys **2** *usu* **bench·mark** : a point of reference for measurement; *also* : STANDARD

bench warrant *n* : a warrant issued by a presiding judge or by a court against a person guilty of contempt or indicted for a crime

[1]**bend** \ˈbend\ *vb* **bent** \ˈbent\; **bend·ing 1** : to draw (as a bow) taut **2** : to curve or cause a change of shape in ⟨~ a bar⟩ **3** : to turn in a certain direction ⟨*bent* his steps toward town⟩ **4** : to make fast : SECURE **5** : SUBDUE **6**

: RESOLVE, DETERMINE ⟨*bent* on self-destruction⟩; *also* : APPLY ⟨*bent* themselves to the task⟩ **7** : DEFLECT **8** : to curve downward **9** : YIELD, SUBMIT

2**bend** *n* : a knot by which a rope is fastened (as to another rope)

3**bend** *n* **1** : an act or process of bending **2** : something bent; *esp* : CURVE **3** *pl* : a painful and dangerous disorder caused by release of gas bubbles in the tissues upon too rapid decrease in air pressure after a stay in a compressed atmosphere

bend·er \ˈben-dər\ *n* : SPREE

1**be·neath** \bi-ˈnēth\ *adv* : BELOW, UNDERNEATH **syn** under, underneath, below

2**beneath** *prep* **1** : BELOW, UNDER ⟨stood ~ a tree⟩ **2** : unworthy of ⟨considered such behavior ~ her⟩

bene·dic·tion \ˌben-ə-ˈdik-shən\ *n* : the invocation of a blessing esp. at the close of a public worship service

bene·fac·tion \-ˈfak-shən\ *n* : a charitable donation **syn** contribution, alms, beneficence, offering

bene·fac·tor \ˈben-ə-ˌfak-tər\ *n* : one that confers a benefit and esp. a benefaction

bene·fac·tress \-ˌfak-trəs\ *n* : a woman who is a benefactor

ben·e·fice \ˈben-ə-fəs\ *n* : an ecclesiastical office to which the revenue from an endowment is attached

be·nef·i·cence \bə-ˈnef-ə-səns\ *n* **1** : beneficent quality **2** : BENEFACTION

be·nef·i·cent \-sənt\ *adj* : doing or producing good (as by acts of kindness or charity); *also* : productive of benefit

ben·e·fi·cial \ˌben-ə-ˈfish-əl\ *adj* : being of benefit or help : HELPFUL **syn** advantageous, profitable, favorable, propitious — **ben·e·fi·cial·ly** \-ē\ *adv*

ben·e·fi·cia·ry \ˌben-ə-ˈfish-ē-ˌer-ē, -ˈfish-(ə-)rē\ *n, pl* **-ries** : one that receives a benefit (as the income of a trust or the proceeds of an insurance)

1**ben·e·fit** \ˈben-ə-ˌfit\ *n* **1** : ADVANTAGE ⟨the ~*s* of exercise⟩ **2** : useful aid : HELP; *also* : material aid provided or due (as in sickness or unemployment) as a right **3** : a performance or event to raise funds for some person or cause

2**benefit** *vb* **-fit·ed** \-ˌfit-əd\ *also* **-fit·ted; -fit·ing** *also* **-fit·ting 1** : to be useful or profitable to **2** : to receive benefit

be·nev·o·lence \bə-ˈnev(-ə)-ləns\ *n* **1** : charitable nature **2** : an act of kindness : CHARITY — **be·nev·o·lent** \-lənt\ *adj*

be·night·ed \bi-ˈnīt-əd\ *adj* **1** : overtaken by darkness or night **2** : living in ignorance

be·nign \bi-ˈnīn\ *adj* **1** : of a gentle disposition; *also* : showing kindness **2** : of a mild kind; *esp* : not malignant ⟨~ tumors⟩ **syn** benignant, kind, kindly, good-hearted — **be·nig·ni·ty** \-ˈnig-nət-ē\ *n*

be·nig·nant \-ˈnig-nənt\ *adj* : BENIGN 1 **syn** kind, kindly, good-hearted

ben·i·son \ˈben-ə-sən, -zən\ *n* : BLESSING, BENEDICTION

bent \ˈbent\ *n* **1** : strong inclination or interest; *also* : TALENT **2** : power of endurance **syn** talent, aptitude, gift, flair, knack, genius

ben·thic \ˈben-thik\ *adj* : of, relating to, or occurring at the bottom of a body of water

ben·thos \ˈben-ˌthäs\ *n* : organisms that live on or in the bottom of bodies of water

ben·ton·ite \ˈbent-ᵊn-ˌīt\ *n* : an absorptive clay used esp. as a filler (as in paper)

bent·wood \ˈbent-ˌwu̇d\ *adj* : made of wood bent into shape ⟨a ~ rocker⟩

be·numb \bi-ˈnəm\ *vb* **1** : DULL, DEADEN **2** : to make numb esp. by cold

ben·zene \ˈben-ˌzēn\ *n* : a colorless volatile flammable liquid hydrocarbon used in organic synthesis and as a solvent

ben·zine \ˈben-ˌzēn\ *n* : any of various flammable petroleum distillates used as solvents for fats or as motor fuels

ben·zo·ate \ˈben-zə-ˌwāt\ *n* : a salt or ester of benzoic acid

ben·zo·ic acid \ben-ˌzō-ik-\ *n* : a white crystalline acid used as a preservative and antiseptic and in synthesizing chemicals

ben·zo·in \ˈben-zə-wən, -ˌzȯin\ *n* : a balsamlike resin from trees of southern Asia used esp. in medicine and perfumes

be·queath \bi-ˈkwēth, -ˈkwēt͟h\ *vb* [ME *bequethen,* fr. OE *becwethan,* fr. *be-* + *cwethan* to say] **1** : to leave by will **2** : to hand down

be·quest \bi-ˈkwest\ *n* **1** : the action of bequeathing **2** : something bequeathed : LEGACY

be·rate \-ˈrāt\ *vb* : to scold harshly

Ber·ber \ˈbər-bər\ *n* : a member of a Caucasoid people of northwestern Africa

ber·ceuse \ber-ˈsə(r)z\ *n, pl* **berceuses** \-ˈsə(r)z(-əz)\ [F, fr. *bercer* to rock] **1** : LULLABY **2** : a musical composition that resembles a lullaby

1**be·reaved** \bi-ˈrēvd\ *adj* : suffering the death of a loved one — **be·reave·ment** *n*

2**bereaved** *n, pl* **bereaved** : one who is bereaved

be·reft \-ˈreft\ *adj* **1** : deprived of or lacking something — usu. used with *of* **2** : BEREAVED

be·ret \bə-ˈrā\ *n* : a round soft cap with no visor

berg \ˈbərg\ *n* : ICEBERG

beri·beri \ˌber-ē-ˈber-ē\ *n* : a deficiency disease marked by weakness, wasting, and nerve damage and caused by lack of thiamine

berke·li·um \ˈbər-klē-əm\ *n* : an artificially prepared radioactive chemical element — see ELEMENT table

Ber·mu·das \bər-ˈmyüd-əz\ *n pl* : BERMUDA SHORTS

Bermuda shorts *n pl* : knee-length walking shorts

ber·ry \ˈber-ē\ *n, pl* **berries 1** : a small pulpy fruit (as a strawberry) **2** : a simple fruit (as a grape, tomato, or banana) with the wall of the ripened ovary thick and pulpy **3** : the dry seed of some plants (as coffee)

ber·serk \bə(r)-ˈsərk, -ˈzərk\ *adj* [ON *berserkr* warrior frenzied in battle, fr. *björn* bear + *serkr* shirt] : FRENZIED, CRAZED — **berserk** *adv*

1**berth** \ˈbərth\ *n* **1** : room enough for a ship to maneuver **2** : the place where a ship lies at anchor **3** : a place to sit or sleep esp. on a ship or vehicle **4** : JOB, POSITION **syn** post, situation, office, appointment

2**berth** *vb* **1** : to bring or come into a berth **2** : to allot a berth to

ber·yl \ˈber-əl\ *n* : a hard silicate mineral occurring as green, yellow, pink, or white crystals

be·ryl·li·um \bə-ˈril-ē-əm\ *n* : a light strong metallic chemical element used as a hardener in alloys — see ELEMENT table

be·seech \bi-ˈsēch\ *vb* **-sought** \-ˈsȯt\ *or* **-seeched; -seech·ing** : to ask earnestly : ENTREAT **syn** implore, beg, plead, supplicate, importune

be·seem \bi-ˈsēm\ *vb, archaic* : to be seemly or fitting : BEFIT

be·set \-ˈset\ *vb* **1** : TROUBLE, HARASS **2** : ASSAIL; *also* : to hem in : SURROUND

be·set·ting *adj* : persistently present or assailing

1**be·side** \bi-ˈsīd\ *adv, archaic* : BESIDES

2**beside** *prep* **1** : by the side of ⟨sit ~ me⟩ **2** : BESIDES **3** : not relevant to

1**be·sides** \bi-ˈsīdz\ *prep* **1** : other than ⟨there's nobody here ~ me⟩ **2** : together with ⟨~ being pretty, she's intelligent⟩

2**besides** *adv* **1** : in addition : ALSO **2** : MOREOVER

be·siege \bi-ˈsēj\ *vb* : to lay siege to; *also* : IMPORTUNE — **be·sieg·er** *n*

be·smear \-ˈsmiər\ *vb* : SMEAR
be·smirch \-ˈsmərch\ *vb* : SMIRCH, SOIL
be·som \ˈbē-zəm\ *n* : BROOM
be·sot \bi-ˈsät\ *vb* **be·sot·ted; be·sot·ting** : to make dull or stupid; *esp* : to muddle with drunkenness
be·spat·ter \-ˈspat-ər\ *vb* : SPATTER
be·speak \bi-ˈspēk\ *vb* **-spoke** \-ˈspōk\; **-spo·ken** \-ˈspō-kən\; **-speak·ing** **1** : to hire or arrange for beforehand **2** : INDICATE, SIGNIFY **3** : FORETELL
be·sprin·kle \-ˈspriŋ-kəl\ *vb* : SPRINKLE
[1]**best** \ˈbest\ *adj, superlative of* GOOD **1** : excelling all others **2** : most productive (as of good or satisfaction) **3** : LARGEST, MOST
[2]**best** *adv, superlative of* WELL **1** : in the best way **2** : MOST
[3]**best** *n* : something that is best
[4]**best** *vb* : to get the better of : OUTDO
bes·tial \ˈbes-chəl\ *adj* **1** : of or relating to beasts **2** : resembling a beast esp. in lack of intelligence or reason
bes·ti·al·i·ty \ˌbes-chē-ˈal-ət-ē\ *n, pl* **-ties** **1** : the condition or status of a lower animal **2** : display or gratification of bestial traits or impulses
bes·ti·ary \ˈbes-chē-ˌer-ē\ *n, pl* **-ar·ies** : a medieval allegorical or moralizing work on the appearance and habits of animals
be·stir \bi-ˈstər\ *vb* : to rouse to action
best man *n* : the principal groomsman at a wedding
be·stow \bi-ˈstō\ *vb* **1** : PUT, PLACE, STOW **2** : to present as a gift : CONFER — **be·stow·al** *n*
be·stride \bi-ˈstrīd\ *vb* **-strode** \-ˈstrōd\; **-strid·den** \-ˈstrid-ᵊn\; **-strid·ing** \-ˈstrīd-iŋ\ : to ride, sit, or stand astride
[1]**bet** \ˈbet\ *n* **1** : something that is risked or pledged on the outcome of a contest **2** : an agreement requiring the person whose guess about a result proves wrong to give something to a person whose guess proves right; *also* : the making of such an agreement
[2]**bet** *vb* **bet** *also* **bet·ted; bet·ting** **1** : to stake on the outcome of an issue ⟨*bet* $2 on the race⟩ **2** : to make a bet with **3** : to lay a bet
[3]**bet** *abbr* between
be·take \bi-ˈtāk\ *vb* **-took** \-ˈtu̇k\; **-tak·en** \-ˈtā-kən\; **-tak·ing** : to cause (oneself) to go
be·ta particle \ˈbāt-ə-\ *n* : an electron or positron ejected from an atomic nucleus during radioactive transformation; *also* : a high-speed electron or positron
beta ray *n* **1** : BETA PARTICLE **2** : a stream of beta particles
be·ta·tron \ˈbāt-ə-ˌträn\ *n* : an electron accelerator
be·tel \ˈbēt-ᵊl\ *n* : a climbing pepper whose leaves are chewed together with lime and betel nut as a stimulant esp. by southern Asians
betel nut *n* : the astringent seed of an Asian palm that is chewed with betel leaves
bête noire \ˌbet-nə-ˈwär, ˌbāt-\ *n, pl* **bêtes noires** \ˌbet-nə-ˈwär(z), ˌbāt-\ [F, lit., black beast] : a person or thing strongly disliked or feared
beth·el \ˈbeth-əl\ *n* [Heb *bēth'ēl* house of God] : a place of worship esp. for seamen
be·think \bi-ˈthiŋk\ *vb* **-thought** \-ˈthȯt\; **-think·ing** : to cause (oneself) to call to mind or consider
be·tide \bi-ˈtīd\ *vb* : to happen to
be·times \bi-ˈtīmz\ *adv* : in good time : EARLY **syn** soon, seasonably, timely
be·to·ken \bi-ˈtō-kən\ *vb* **-to·kened; -to·ken·ing** \-ˈtōk-(ə-)niŋ\ **1** : to give evidence of **2** : PRESAGE **syn** indicate, attest, bespeak, testify
be·tray \bi-ˈtrā\ *vb* **1** : to lead astray; *esp* : SEDUCE **2** : to deliver to an enemy by treachery **3** : to prove unfaithful to **4** : to reveal unintentionally; *also* : SHOW, INDICATE **syn** mislead, delude, deceive, beguile — **be·tray·al** *n* — **be·tray·er** *n*
be·troth \bi-ˈträth, -ˈtrȯth, -ˈtrōth, *or with* th\ *vb* : to promise to marry : AFFIANCE — **be·troth·al** *n*
be·trothed *n* : the person to whom one is betrothed
[1]**bet·ter** \ˈbet-ər\ *adj, comparative of* GOOD **1** : more than half **2** : improved in health **3** : more attractive, favorable, or commendable **4** : more advantageous or effective **5** : improved in accuracy or performance
[2]**better** *vb* **1** : to make or become better **2** : SURPASS, EXCEL
[3]**better** *adv, comparative of* WELL **1** : in a superior manner **2** : to a higher or greater degree; *also* : MORE
[4]**better** *n* **1** : something better; *also* : a superior esp. in merit or rank **2** : ADVANTAGE
bet·ter·ment \ˈbet-ər-mənt\ *n* : IMPROVEMENT
bet·tor *or* **bet·ter** \ˈbet-ər\ *n* : one that bets
[1]**be·tween** \bi-ˈtwēn\ *prep* **1** : by the common action of ⟨earned $10,000 ~ the two of them⟩ **2** : in the interval separating ⟨an alley ~ two buildings⟩ **3** : marking or constituting the interrelation or interaction of ⟨hostility ~ nations⟩ **4** : in point of comparison of ⟨choose ~ two cars⟩
[2]**between** *adv* : in an intervening space or interval
be·twixt \bi-ˈtwikst\ *adv or prep* : BETWEEN
[1]**bev·el** \ˈbev-əl\ *n* **1** : a device for adjusting the slant of the surfaces of a piece of work **2** : the angle or slant that one surface or line makes with another when not at right angles
[2]**bevel** *vb* **-eled** *or* **-elled; -el·ing** *or* **-el·ling** \ˈbev-(ə-)liŋ\ **1** : to cut or shape (as an edge or surface) to a bevel **2** : INCLINE, SLANT
bev·er·age \ˈbev-(ə-)rij\ *n* : a drinkable liquid
bevy \ˈbev-ē\ *n, pl* **bev·ies** **1** : a large group or collection **2** : a group of animals and esp. quail together
be·wail \bi-ˈwāl\ *vb* : LAMENT **syn** deplore, bemoan, grieve, moan, weep
be·ware \-ˈwaər\ *vb* : to be on one's guard : be wary of
be·wil·der \bi-ˈwil-dər\ *vb* **-wil·dered; -wil·der·ing** \-d(ə-)riŋ\ : PERPLEX, CONFUSE **syn** mystify, distract, puzzle — **be·wil·der·ment** *n*
be·witch \-ˈwich\ *vb* **1** : to affect by witchcraft **2** : CHARM, FASCINATE **syn** enchant, attract, captivate — **be·witch·ment** *n*
bey \ˈbā\ *n* **1** : a former Turkish provincial governor **2** : the former native ruler of Tunis or Tunisia
[1]**be·yond** \bē-ˈänd\ *adv* **1** : FARTHER **2** : BESIDES
[2]**beyond** *prep* **1** : on or to the farther side of **2** : out of the reach or sphere of **3** : BESIDES
be·zel \ˈbē-zəl, ˈbez-əl\ *n* **1** : a sloping edge on a cutting tool **2** : the faceted part of a cut gem that rises above the setting **3** : a usu. grooved rim holding a transparent covering (as on a watch)
bf *abbr* boldface
BG *or* **B Gen** *abbr* brigadier general
bhang \ˈbaŋ\ *n* : a narcotic and intoxicant product of the hemp plant
Bi *symbol* bismuth
BIA *abbr* Bureau of Indian Affairs
bi·an·nu·al \(ˈ)bī-ˈan-yə(-wə)l\ *adj* : occurring twice a year — **bi·an·nu·al·ly** \-ē\ *adv*
[1]**bi·as** \ˈbī-əs\ *n* **1** : a line diagonal to the grain of a fabric **2** : PREJUDICE, BENT
[2]**bias** *adv* : on the bias : DIAGONALLY
[3]**bias** *vb* **bi·ased** *or* **bi·assed; bi·as·ing** *or* **bi·as·sing** : PREJUDICE
bi·as–ply tire \ˈbī-əs-ˌplī-\ *n* : a pneumatic tire having crossed layers of ply cord set diagonally to the center line of the tread
bi·ath·lon \bī-ˈath-lən, -ˌlän\ *n* : a composite athletic contest consisting of cross-country skiing and target shooting with a rifle
[1]**bib** \ˈbib\ *n* : a protective cover tied under a child's chin to protect the clothes
[2]**bib** *abbr* Bible; biblical
bi·be·lot \ˈbē-bə-ˌlō\ *n, pl* **bibelots** \-ˌlō(z)\ : a small household ornament or decorative object
Bi·ble \ˈbī-bəl\ *n* [ME, fr. OF, fr. ML *biblia*, fr. Gk, pl. of *biblion* book, fr. *byblos* papyrus, book, fr. *Byblos*, ancient Phoenician city from which papyrus was export-

ed] **1** : the sacred scriptures of Christians comprising the Old and New Testaments **2** : the sacred scriptures of Judaism or of some other religion — **bib·li·cal** \ˈbib-li-kəl\ *adj*

BOOKS OF THE OLD TESTAMENT

ROMAN CATHOLIC CANON	PROTESTANT CANON	ROMAN CATHOLIC CANON	PROTESTANT CANON
Genesis	Genesis	Wisdom	
Exodus	Exodus	Ecclesiasticus	
Leviticus	Leviticus	Isaias	Isaiah
Numbers	Numbers	Jeremias	Jeremiah
Deuteronomy	Deuteronomy	Lamentations	Lamentations
Josue	Joshua	Baruch	
Judges	Judges	Ezechiel	Ezekiel
Ruth	Ruth	Daniel	Daniel
1 & 2 Kings	1 & 2 Samuel	Osee	Hosea
3 & 4 Kings	1 & 2 Kings	Joel	Joel
1 & 2 Paralipomenon	1 & 2 Chronicles	Amos	Amos
		Abdias	Obadiah
1 Esdras	Ezra	Jonas	Jonah
2 Esdras	Nehemiah	Micheas	Micah
Tobias		Nahum	Nahum
Judith		Habacuc	Habakkuk
Esther	Esther	Sophonias	Zephaniah
Job	Job	Aggeus	Haggai
Psalms	Psalms	Zacharias	Zechariah
Proverbs	Proverbs	Malachias	Malachi
Ecclesiastes	Ecclesiastes	1 & 2 Machabees	
Canticle of Canticles	Song of Solomon		

JEWISH SCRIPTURE

Law	1 & 2 Kings	Nahum	Song of Songs
Genesis	Isaiah	Habakkuk	Ruth
Exodus	Jeremiah	Zephaniah	Lamentations
Leviticus	Ezekiel	Haggai	Ecclesiastes
Numbers	Hosea	Zechariah	Esther
Deuteronomy	Joel	Malachi	Daniel
Prophets	Amos	*Hagiographa*	Ezra
Joshua	Obadiah	Psalms	Nehemiah
Judges	Jonah	Proverbs	1 & 2 Chronicles
1 & 2 Samuel	Micah	Job	

PROTESTANT APOCRYPHA

1 & 2 Esdras	Wisdom of Solomon	Baruch	Susanna
Tobit	Ecclesiasticus or the Wisdom of Jesus Son of Sirach	Prayer of Azariah and the Song of the Three Holy Children	Bel and the Dragon
Judith			The Prayer of Manasses
Additions to Esther			1 & 2 Maccabees

BOOKS OF THE NEW TESTAMENT

Matthew	Romans	1 & 2 Thessalonians	1 & 2 Peter
Mark	1 & 2 Corinthians	1 & 2 Timothy	1, 2, 3 John
Luke	Galatians	Titus	Jude
John	Ephesians	Philemon	Revelation (Roman Catholic canon: Apocalypse)
Acts of the Apostles	Philippians	Hebrews	
	Colossians	James	

bib·li·og·ra·phy \ˌbib-lē-ˈäg-rə-fē\ *n, pl* **-phies 1** : the history or description of writings or publications **2** : a list of writings (as on a subject or of an author) — **bib·li·og·ra·pher** \-fər\ *n* — **bib·li·o·graph·ic** \-lē-ə-ˈgraf-ik\ *also* **bib·li·o·graph·i·cal** \-i-kəl\ *adj*

bib·lio·phile \ˈbib-lē-ə-ˌfīl\ *n* : a lover of books

bib·u·lous \ˈbib-yə-ləs\ *adj* **1** : highly absorbent **2** : fond of alcoholic beverages

bi·cam·er·al \ˈbī-ˈkam-(ə-)rəl\ *adj* : having or consisting of two legislative branches

bi·car·bon·ate \ˈbī-ˈkär-bə-ˌnāt, -nət\ *n* : an acid carbonate

bicarbonate of soda : SODIUM BICARBONATE

bi·cen·te·na·ry \ˌbī-sen-ˈten-ə-rē, bī-ˈsent-ᵊn-ˌer-ē\ *n* : BICENTENNIAL — **bicentenary** *adj*

bi·cen·ten·ni·al \ˌbī-sen-ˈten-ē-əl\ *n* : a 200th anniversary or its celebration — **bicentennial** *adj*

bi·ceps \ˈbī-ˌseps\ *n, pl* **biceps** *also* **bicepses** [NL, fr. L, two-headed, fr. *bi-* two + *caput* head] : a muscle (as in the front of the upper arm) having two points of origin

bi·chlo·ride of mercury \bī-ˈklōr-ˌīd-\ : MERCURIC CHLORIDE

[1]bick·er \ˈbik-ər\ *n* : QUARRELING, ALTERCATION

[2]bicker *vb* **bick·ered; bick·er·ing** \-(ə-)riŋ\ : to contend in petty altercation : SQUABBLE

bi·con·cave \ˌbī-(ˌ)kän-ˈkāv, bī-ˈkän-ˌkāv\ *adj* : concave on both sides ⟨red blood cells are ~⟩

bi·con·vex \ˌbī-(ˌ)kän-ˈveks, ˈbī-ˈkän-ˌveks\ *adj* : convex on both sides

bi·cus·pid \bī-ˈkəs-pəd\ *n* : PREMOLAR

[1]bi·cy·cle \ˈbī-ˌsik-əl\ *n* : a light 2-wheeled vehicle with a steering handle, saddle, and pedals

[2]bicycle *vb* **-cy·cled; -cy·cling** \-ˌsik-(ə-)liŋ, -ˌsīk-\ : to ride a bicycle — **bi·cy·cler** \-lər\ *n* — **bi·cy·clist** \-ləst\ *n*

[1]bid \ˈbid\ *vb* **bade** \ˈbad, ˈbād\ *or* **bid; bid·den** \ˈbid-ᵊn\ *or* **bid** *also* **bade; bid·ding 1** : COMMAND, ORDER **2** : INVITE **3** : to give expression to **4** : to make a bid : OFFER — **bid·der** *n*

[2]bid *n* **1** : an act of bidding; *also* : a chance or turn to bid **2** : an offer (as at an auction) of what one will give for something; *also* : the thing or sum offered **3** : INVITATION **4** : an announcement by a player in a card game of what he or she proposes to accomplish; *also* : an attempt to win or gain

bid·da·ble \ˈbid-ə-bəl\ *adj* **1** : OBEDIENT, DOCILE **2** : capable of being bid

bid·dy \ˈbid-ē\ *n, pl* **biddies** : a hen or young chicken

bide \ˈbīd\ *vb* **bode** \ˈbōd\ *or* **bid·ed; bided; bid·ing 1** : WAIT, TARRY **2** : DWELL **3** : to wait for

bi·det \bi-ˈdā\ *n* : a fixture about the height of a chair seat used esp. for bathing the external genitals and the posterior parts of the body

bi·di·rec·tion·al \ˌbī-də-ˈrek-sh(ə-)nəl\ *adj* : involving, moving, or taking place in two usu. opposite directions — **bi·di·rec·tion·al·ly** *adv*

bi·en·ni·al \bī-ˈen-ē-əl\ *adj* **1** : taking place once in two years **2** : lasting two years **3** : producing leaves the first year and fruiting and dying the second year — **biennial** *n* — **bi·en·ni·al·ly** \-ē\ *adv*

bi·en·ni·um \bī-ˈen-ē-əm\ *n, pl* **-niums** *or* **-nia** \-ē-ə\ [L, fr. *bi-* two + *annus* year] : a period of two years

bier \ˈbiər\ *n* : a stand bearing a coffin or corpse

bi·fo·cal \bī-ˈfō-kəl\ *adj* : having two focal lengths

bifocals \bī-ˈfō-kəlz\ *n pl* : eyeglasses with lenses that have one part that corrects for near vision and one for distant vision

bi·fur·cate \ˈbī-fər-ˌkāt, bī-ˈfər-\ *vb* **-cat·ed; -cat·ing** : to divide into two branches or parts — **bi·fur·ca·tion** \ˌbī-fər-ˈkā-shən\ *n*

big \ˈbig\ *adj* **big·ger; big·gest 1** : large in size, amount, or scope **2** : PREGNANT; *also* : SWELLING **3** : IMPORTANT, IMPOSING **syn** great, large, oversize — **big·ness** *n*

big·a·my \ˈbig-ə-mē\ *n* : the act of marrying one person while still legally married to another — **big·a·mist** \-məst\ *n* — **big·a·mous** \-məs\ *adj*

big bang theory *n* : a theory in astronomy: the universe originated from the explosion of a single mass of material so that the pieces are still flying apart

big brother *n* **1** : an older brother **2** : a man who befriends a delinquent or friendless boy **3** *cap both Bs* : the leader of an authoritarian state or movement

Big Dipper *n* : DIPPER 3

big·foot \ˈbig-ˌfu̇t\ *n* : SASQUATCH

big·horn \ˈbig-ˌhȯrn\ *n, pl* **bighorn** *or* **bighorns** : a wild sheep of mountainous western No. America

bight \ˈbīt\ *n* **1** : a curve in a coast; *also* : the bay formed by such a curve **2** : a slack part in a rope

big–name \ˈbig-ˈnām\ *adj* : widely popular ⟨a ~ performer⟩ — **big name** *n*
big·ot \ˈbig-ət\ *n* : one intolerantly devoted to his or her own church, party, or opinion **syn** fanatic, enthusiast, zealot — **big·ot·ed** \-ət-əd\ *adj* — **big·ot·ry** \-ə-trē\ *n*
big shot \ˈbig-ˌshät\ *n* : an important person
big time \-ˌtīm\ *n* **1** : a high-paying vaudeville circuit requiring only two performances a day **2** : the top rank of an activity or enterprise — **big–tim·er** \-ˌtī-mər\ *n*
big top *n* **1** : the main tent of a circus **2** : CIRCUS
big·wig \ˈbig-ˌwig\ *n* : BIG SHOT
bike \ˈbīk\ *n* **1** : BICYCLE **2** : MOTORCYCLE
bik·er *n* : MOTORCYCLIST; *esp* : one who is a member of an organized gang
bike·way \ˈbīk-ˌwā\ *n* : a thoroughfare for bicycles
bi·ki·ni \bə-ˈkē-nē\ *n* : a woman's brief 2-piece bathing suit
bi·lat·er·al \bī-ˈlat-(ə-)rəl\ *adj* **1** : having or involving two sides **2** : affecting reciprocally two sides or parties — **bi·lat·er·al·ly** \-ē\ *adv*
bile \ˈbīl\ *n* **1** : a bitter greenish fluid secreted by the liver that aids in the digestion of fats **2** : an ill-humored mood
bilge \ˈbilj\ *n* **1** : the part of a ship that lies between the bottom and the point where the sides go straight up **2** : stale or worthless remarks or ideas
bi·lin·gual \bī-ˈliŋ-gwəl\ *adj* : expressed in, knowing, or using two languages
bil·ious \ˈbil-yəs\ *adj* **1** : marked by or suffering from disordered liver function **2** : IRRITABLE, CHOLERIC — **bil·ious·ness** *n*
bilk \ˈbilk\ *vb* : CHEAT, SWINDLE
[1]**bill** \ˈbil\ *n* : the jaws of a bird together with their horny covering; *also* : a mouth structure (as of a turtle) resembling these

[1]bill: *1* flamingo, *2* falcon, *3* pigeon, *4* thrush, *5* merganser, *6* toucan, *7* finch, *8* spoonbill, *9* pelican

[2]**bill** *vb* : to caress fondly
[3]**bill** *n* **1** : a written document or note; *esp* : a draft of a law presented to a legislature for enactment **2** : a written statement of a legal wrong suffered or of some breach of law **3** : an itemized statement of particulars **4** : an itemized account of the separate cost of goods sold, services performed, or work done **5** : an advertisement (as a poster or handbill) displayed or distributed **6** : a piece of paper money
[4]**bill** *vb* **1** : to enter in or prepare a bill; *also* : to submit a bill or account to **2** : to advertise by bills or posters
bill·board \-ˌbōrd\ *n* : a flat surface on which advertising bills are posted
[1]**bil·let** \ˈbil-ət\ *n* **1** : an order requiring a person to provide lodging for a soldier; *also* : quarters assigned by or as if by such an order **2** : POSITION, APPOINTMENT
[2]**billet** *vb* : to assign lodging to by billet
bil·let–doux \ˌbil-ā-ˈdü\ *n, pl* **billets–doux** \-ā-ˈdü(z)\ [F *billet doux,* lit., sweet letter] : a love letter
bill·fold \ˈbil-ˌfōld\ *n* : WALLET
bil·liards \ˈbil-yərdz\ *n* : any of several games played on a rectangular table by driving balls against each other or into pockets with a cue
bil·lings·gate \ˈbil-iŋz-ˌgāt, *Brit usu* -git\ *n* [*Billingsgate,* old gate and fish market, London, England] : coarsely abusive language
bil·lion \ˈbil-yən\ *n* **1** : a thousand millions **2** *Brit* : a million millions — **billion** *adj* — **bil·lionth** \-yənth\ *adj or n*
bill of exchange : a written order from one party to another to pay to a person named in the bill a specified sum of money
[1]**bil·low** \ˈbil-ō\ *n* **1** : WAVE; *esp* : a great wave **2** : a rolling mass (as of fog or flame) like a great wave — **bil·lowy** \ˈbil-ə-wē\ *adj*
[2]**billow** *vb* : to rise and roll in waves; *also* : to swell out ⟨~*ing* sails⟩
bil·ly \ˈbil-ē\ *n, pl* **billies** : BILLY CLUB
billy club *n* : a heavy usu. wooden club; *esp* : a policeman's club
bil·ly goat \ˈbil-ē-\ *n* : a male goat
bi·met·al \ˈbī-ˌmet-ᵊl\ *adj* : BIMETALLIC — **bimetal** *n*
bi·me·tal·lic \ˌbī-mə-ˈtal-ik\ *adj* : made of two different metals — often used of devices having a bonded expansive part — **bimetallic** *n*
bi·met·al·lism \bī-ˈmet-ᵊl-ˌiz-əm\ *n* : the policy of using two metals at fixed ratios to form a standard of value for a monetary system
[1]**bi·month·ly** \bī-ˈmənth-lē\ *adj* **1** : occurring every two months **2** : occurring twice a month : SEMIMONTHLY — **bimonthly** *adv*
[2]**bimonthly** *n* : a bimonthly publication
bin \ˈbin\ *n* : a box, crib, or enclosure used for storage
bi·na·ry \ˈbī-nə-rē\ *adj* **1** : consisting of two things or parts : DOUBLE **2** : relating to, being, or belonging to a system of numbers having 2 as its base ⟨the ~ digits 0 and 1⟩ **3** : involving a choice between or condition of two alternatives only (as on-off, yes-no) — **binary** *n*
binary star *n* : a system of two stars revolving around each other
bin·au·ral \bī-ˈnȯr-əl\ *adj* : of or relating to sound reproduction involving the use of two separated microphones and two transmission channels to achieve a stereophonic effect
bind \ˈbīnd\ *vb* **bound** \ˈbau̇nd\; **bind·ing** **1** : TIE; *also* : to restrain as if by tying **2** : to put under an obligation; *also* : to constrain with legal authority **3** : BANDAGE **4** : to unite into a mass **5** : to compel as if by a pledge **6** : to strengthen or decorate with a band **7** : to fasten together and enclose in a cover ⟨~ books⟩ **8** : to exert a tying, restraining, or compelling effect — **bind·er** *n*
bind·ing \ˈbīn-diŋ\ *n* : something (as a ski fastening, a cover, or an edging fabric) used to bind
binge \ˈbinj\ *n* : SPREE
bin·go \ˈbiŋ-gō\ *n, pl* **bingos** : a game of chance played with cards having numbered squares corresponding to numbered balls drawn at random and won by covering five squares in a row
bin·na·cle \ˈbin-i-kəl\ *n* [alter. of ME *bitakle,* fr. Pg or Sp; Pg *bitácola* & Sp *bitácula,* fr. L *habitaculum* dwelling place, fr. *habitare* to inhabit] : a container holding a ship's compass
[1]**bin·oc·u·lar** \bī-ˈnäk-yə-lər, bə-\ *adj* : of, relating to, or adapted to the use of both eyes — **bin·oc·u·lar·ly** *adv*
[2]**bin·oc·u·lar** \bə-ˈnäk-yə-lər, bī-\ *n* **1** : a binocular optical instrument (as a microscope) **2** : a hand-held optical instrument composed of two telescopes and a focusing device — usu. used in pl.
bi·no·mi·al \bī-ˈnō-mē-əl\ *n* **1** : a mathematical expression consisting of two terms connected by the sign plus (+) or minus (−) **2** : a biological species name consisting of two terms — **binomial** *adj*
bio·chem·is·try \ˌbī-ō-ˈkem-ə-strē\ *n* : chemistry that deals with the chemical compounds and processes occurring in living things — **bio·chem·i·cal** \-i-kəl\ *adj or n* — **bio·chem·ist** \-əst\ *n*
bio·de·grad·able \-di-ˈgrād-ə-bəl\ *adj* : capable of being

broken down esp. into innocuous products by the actions of living things (as microorganisms) ⟨a ~ detergent⟩ — **bio·de·grad·abil·i·ty** \-ˌgrād-ə-ˈbil-ət-ē\ *n* — **bio·deg·ra·da·tion** \-ˌdeg-rə-ˈdā-shən\ *n* — **bio·de·grade** \-di-ˈgrād\ *vb*

bio·feed·back \-ˈfēd-ˌbak\ *n* : the technique of making unconscious or involuntary bodily processes (as heartbeat or brain waves) objectively perceptible to the senses (as by use of an oscilloscope) in order to manipulate them by conscious mental control

biog *abbr* biographer; biographical; biography

bio·ge·og·ra·phy \ˌbī-ō-jē-ˈäg-rə-fē\ *n* : a branch of biology that deals with the distribution of plants and animals — **bio·ge·og·ra·pher** \-fər\ *n*

bi·og·ra·phy \bī-ˈäg-rə-fē, bē-\ *n, pl* **-phies** : a written history of a person's life; *also* : such writings in general — **bi·og·ra·pher** \-fər\ *n* — **bi·o·graph·i·cal** \ˌbī-ə-ˈgraf-i-kəl\ *also* **bi·o·graph·ic** \-ik\ *adj*

biol *abbr* biologic; biological; biologist; biology

biological clock *n* : an inherent timing mechanism inferred to exist in some living systems (as a cell) in order to explain various cyclical physiological and behavioral responses

biological warfare *n* : warfare in which living organisms (as bacteria) are used to harm the enemy or his livestock and crops

bi·ol·o·gy \bī-ˈäl-ə-jē\ *n* [G *biologie,* fr. Gk *bios* mode of life + *logos* word] **1** : a science that deals with living beings and life processes **2** : the life processes of an organism or group — **bi·o·log·i·cal** \ˌbī-ə-ˈläj-i-kəl\ *also* **bi·o·log·ic** \-ik\ *adj* — **bi·ol·o·gist** \bī-ˈäl-ə-jəst\ *n*

bio·med·i·cal \ˌbī-ō-ˈmed-i-kəl\ *adj* : of, relating to, or involving biological, medical, and physical science

bi·on·ic \bī-ˈän-ik\ *adj* : having normal biological capability or performance enhanced by or as if by electronic or mechanical devices

bio·phys·ics \ˌbī-ō-ˈfiz-iks\ *n* : a branch of science concerned with the application of physical principles and methods to biological problems — **bio·phys·i·cal** \-i-kəl\ *adj* — **bio·phys·i·cist** \-ˈfiz-ə-səst\ *n*

bi·op·sy \ˈbī-ˌäp-sē\ *n, pl* **-sies** : the removal of tissue, cells, or fluids from the living body for examination

bio·rhythm \ˈbī-ō-ˌrith-əm\ *n* : an inherent rhythm that appears to control or initiate various biological processes

bio·sphere \ˈbī-ə-ˌsfiər\ *n* **1** : the part of the world in which life can exist **2** : living beings together with their environment

bi·ot·ic \bī-ˈät-ik\ *adj* : of or relating to life; *esp* : caused by living beings

bi·o·tin \ˈbī-ə-tən\ *n* : a member of the vitamin B complex found esp. in yeast, liver, and egg yolk and active in growth promotion

bi·o·tite \ˈbī-ə-ˌtīt\ *n* : a dark mica containing iron, magnesium, potassium, and aluminum

bi·par·ti·san \bī-ˈpärt-ə-zən\ *adj* : representing or composed of members of two parties

bi·par·tite \-ˈpär-ˌtīt\ *adj* **1** : being in two parts **2** : shared by two ⟨~ treaty⟩

bi·ped \ˈbī-ˌped\ *n* : a 2-footed animal

bi·plane \ˈbī-ˌplān\ *n* : an airplane with two wings placed one above the other

bi·po·lar \bī-ˈpō-lər\ *adj* : having or involving the use of two poles — **bi·po·lar·i·ty** \ˌbī-pō-ˈlar-ət-ē\ *n*

bi·ra·cial \bī-ˈrā-shəl\ *adj* : of, relating to, or involving members of two races

[1]**birch** \ˈbərch\ *n* **1** : any of a genus of mostly short-lived deciduous shrubs and trees with membranous outer bark and pale close-grained wood; *also* : this wood **2** : a birch rod or bundle of twigs for flogging — **birch** *or* **birch·en** \ˈbər-chən\ *adj*

[2]**birch** *vb* : WHIP, FLOG

Birch·er \ˈbər-chər\ *n* : a member or adherent of the John Birch Society — **Birch·ism** \ˈbər-ˌchiz-əm\ *n* — **Birch·ist** \-chəst\ *or* **Birch·ite** \-ˌchīt\ *n*

bird \ˈbərd\ *n* : any of a class of warm-blooded egg-laying vertebrates having the body feathered and the forelimbs modified to form wings

bird·bath \ˈbərd-ˌbath, -ˌbȧth\ *n* : a usu. ornamental basin set up for birds to bathe in

bird·house \-ˌhau̇s\ *n* : an artificial nesting place for birds; *also* : AVIARY

bird·ie \ˈbərd-ē\ *n* : a score of one under par on a hole in golf

bird·lime \-ˌlīm\ *n* : a sticky substance smeared on twigs to snare small birds

bird of paradise : any of numerous brilliantly colored plumed birds of the New Guinea area

bird of prey : a carnivorous bird that feeds wholly or chiefly on carrion or on meat taken by hunting

bird·seed \ˈbərd-ˌsēd\ *n* : a mixture of small seeds (as of hemp or millet) used for feeding birds

bird's–eye \ˈbərd-ˌzī\ *adj* **1** : seen from above as if by a flying bird ⟨~ view⟩; *also* : CURSORY **2** : marked with spots resembling birds' eyes ⟨~ maple⟩; *also* : made of bird's-eye wood

bi·ret·ta \bə-ˈret-ə\ *n* : a square cap with three ridges on top worn esp. by Roman Catholic clergymen

birr \ˈbir, ˈbər\ *n* — see MONEY table

birth \ˈbərth\ *n* **1** : the act or fact of being born or of bringing forth young **2** : LINEAGE, DESCENT **3** : ORIGIN, BEGINNING

birth control *n* : control of the number of children born esp. by preventing or lessening the frequency of conception

birth·day \ˈbərth-ˌdā\ *n* : the day or anniversary of one's birth

birth defect *n* : a physical or biochemical defect present at birth and inherited or environmentally induced

birth·mark \ˈbərth-ˌmärk\ *n* : an unusual mark or blemish on the skin at birth

birth·place \-ˌplās\ *n* : place of birth or origin

birth·rate \-ˌrāt\ *n* : the number of births for every 100 or every 1000 persons in a given area or group during a given time

birth·right \-ˌrīt\ *n* : a right, privilege, or possession to which one is entitled by birth **syn** legacy, patrimony, heritage, inheritance

birth·stone \-ˌstōn\ *n* : a gemstone associated symbolically with the month of one's birth

bis·cuit \ˈbis-kət\ *n* [ME *bisquite,* fr. MF *bescuit,* fr. (*pain*) *bescuit* twice-cooked bread] **1** : a crisp flat cake; *esp, Brit* : CRACKER 2 **2** : a small quick bread made from dough that has been rolled and cut or dropped from a spoon

bi·sect \ˈbī-ˌsekt\ *vb* : to divide into two usu. equal parts; *also* : CROSS, INTERSECT — **bi·sec·tion** \ˈbī-ˌsek-shən\ *n* — **bi·sec·tor** \-tər\ *n*

bi·sex·u·al \bī-ˈsek-sh(ə-w)əl\ *adj* **1** : possessing characters of or having sexual desire for both sexes **2** : of, relating to, or involving two sexes — **bisexual** *n* — **bi·sex·u·al·i·ty** \ˌbī-ˌsek-shə-ˈwal-ət-ē\ *n*

bish·op \ˈbish-əp\ *n* [ME *bisshop,* fr. OE *bisceop,* fr. L *episcopus,* fr. Gk *episkopos,* lit., overseer, fr. *epi-* on, over + *skeptesthai* to look] **1** : a clergyman ranking above a priest and typically governing a diocese **2** : any of various Protestant church officials who superintend other clergy **3** : a chess piece that can move diagonally across any number of adjoining unoccupied squares

bish·op·ric \ˈbish-ə-prik\ *n* **1** : DIOCESE **2** : the office of bishop

bis·muth \ˈbiz-məth\ *n* : a heavy brittle grayish white metallic chemical element used in alloys and medicine — see ELEMENT table
bi·son \ˈbīs-ᵊn, ˈbīz-\ *n, pl* **bison** : BUFFALO 2
bisque \ˈbisk\ *n* : a thick cream soup
bis·tro \ˈbēs-trō, ˈbis-\ *n, pl* **bistros** [F] **1** : a small or unpretentious European restaurant **2** : BAR; *also* : NIGHTCLUB
[1]**bit** \ˈbit\ *n* **1** : the part of a bridle that is placed in a horse's mouth **2** : the biting or cutting edge or part of a tool
[2]**bit** *n* **1** : a morsel of food; *also* : a small piece or quantity of something **2** : a small coin; *also* : a unit of value equal to 12½ cents **3** : something small or trivial; *also* : an indefinite usu. small degree or extent ⟨a ~ tired⟩
[3]**bit** *n* [*bi*nary digi*t*] : a unit of computer information equivalent to the result of a choice between two alternatives; *also* : its physical representation
[1]**bitch** \ˈbich\ *n* **1** : a female canine; *esp* : a female dog **2** : a malicious, spiteful, and domineering woman
[2]**bitch** *vb* : COMPLAIN
[1]**bite** \ˈbīt\ *vb* **bit** \ˈbit\; **bit·ten** \ˈbit-ᵊn\ *also* **bit; bit·ing** \ˈbīt-iŋ\ **1** : to grip with teeth or jaws; *also* : to wound or sting with or as if with fangs **2** : to cut or pierce with or as if with a sharp-edged instrument **3** : to cause to smart or sting **4** : CORRODE **5** : to take bait
[2]**bite** *n* **1** : the act or manner of biting **2** : MORSEL, SNACK **3** : a wound made by biting; *also* : a biting sensation
bit·ing \ˈbīt-iŋ\ *adj* : SHARP, CUTTING
bit·ter \ˈbit-ər\ *adj* **1** : being or inducing the one of the basic taste sensations that is acrid, astringent, or disagreeable and is suggestive of hops **2** : marked by intensity or severity (as of distress or hatred) **3** : extremely harsh or cruel — **bit·ter·ly** *adv* — **bit·ter·ness** *n*
bit·tern \ˈbit-ərn\ *n* : any of various small or medium-sized herons with a booming cry
bit·ters \ˈbit-ərz\ *n sing or pl* : a usu. alcoholic solution of bitter and often aromatic plant products used in mixing drinks and as a mild tonic
[1]**bit·ter·sweet** \ˈbit-ər-ˌswēt\ *n* **1** : a poisonous nightshade with purple flowers and orange-red berries **2** : a woody vine with yellow capsules that open when ripe and disclose scarlet seed coverings
[2]**bittersweet** *adj* : being at once both bitter and sweet
bi·tu·mi·nous coal \bə-ˈt(y)ü-mə-nəs-, bī-\ *n* : a coal that when heated yields considerable volatile waste matter
bi·valve \ˈbī-ˌvalv\ *n* : an animal (as a clam) with a shell composed of two separate parts that open and shut — **bivalve** *adj*
[1]**biv·ouac** \ˈbiv(-ə)-ˌwak\ *n* [F, fr. LG *biwake,* fr. *bi* at + *wake* guard] : a temporary encampment or shelter
[2]**bivouac** *vb* **-ouacked; -ouack·ing** : to form a bivouac : CAMP
[1]**bi·week·ly** \bī-ˈwē-klē\ *adj* **1** : occurring every two weeks : FORTNIGHTLY **2** : occurring twice a week — **biweekly** *adv*
[2]**biweekly** *n* : a biweekly publication
bi·year·ly \-ˈyiər-lē\ *adj* **1** : BIENNIAL **2** : BIANNUAL
bi·zarre \bə-ˈzär\ *adj* : ODD, ECCENTRIC, FANTASTIC — **bi·zarre·ly** *adv*
bk *abbr* **1** bank **2** book
Bk *symbol* berkelium
bkg *abbr* banking
bkgd *abbr* background
bks *abbr* barracks
bkt *abbr* **1** basket **2** bracket
bl *abbr* **1** bale **2** barrel **3** blue
blab \ˈblab\ *vb* **blabbed; blab·bing** : TATTLE, GOSSIP
[1]**black** \ˈblak\ *adj* **1** : of the color black; *also* : very dark **2** : SWARTHY **3** : of or relating to a group of dark-haired dark-skinned people **4** : NEGRO; *also* : AFRO-AMERICAN **5** : SOILED, DIRTY **6** : lacking light ⟨a ~ night⟩ **7** : WICKED, EVIL ⟨~ deeds⟩ ⟨~ magic⟩ **8** : DISMAL, GLOOMY ⟨a ~ outlook⟩ **9** : SULLEN ⟨a ~ mood⟩ — **black·ish** *adj* — **black·ly** *adv* — **black·ness** *n*
[2]**black** *n* **1** : a black pigment or dye; *also* : something (as clothing) that is black **2** : the color characteristic of soot or coal **3** : a person of a dark-skinned race; *esp* : NEGRO
[3]**black** *vb* : BLACKEN
black·a·moor \ˈblak-ə-ˌmu̇r\ *n* : NEGRO
black–and–blue \ˌblak-ən-ˈblü\ *adj* : darkly discolored from blood effused by bruising
black art *n* : MAGIC, WITCHCRAFT
black·ball \ˈblak-ˌbȯl\ *n* : a black object used to cast a negative vote; *also* : such a vote — **black·ball** *vb*
black bass *n* : any of several freshwater sunfishes native to eastern and central No. America
[1]**black belt** \ˈblak-ˌbelt\ *n, often cap both Bs* : an area densely populated by blacks
[2]**black belt** \-ˈbelt\ *n* **1** : a rating of expert (as in judo or karate) **2** : one who holds a black belt
black·ber·ry \ˈblak-ˌber-ē\ *n* : the usu. black or purple juicy but seedy edible fruit of various brambles; *also* : a plant bearing this fruit
black·bird \ˈblak-ˌbərd\ *n* : any of various birds (as the red-winged blackbird) of which the male is largely or wholly black
black·board \-ˌbōrd\ *n* : a dark smooth surface (as of slate) used for writing or drawing on usu. with chalk
black·body \ˈblak-ˈbäd-ē\ *n* : a body or surface that completely absorbs incident radiation
black box *n* : a usu. complicated electronic device whose components and workings are unknown or mysterious to the user
black death *n* : a form of bacterial plague that spread rapidly in Europe and Asia in the 14th century
black·en \ˈblak-ən\ *vb* **black·ened; black·en·ing** \-(ə-)niŋ\ **1** : to make or become black **2** : DEFAME, SULLY
black eye *n* : a discoloration of the skin around the eye from bruising
black–eyed Su·san \ˌblak-ˌīd-ˈsüz-ᵊn\ *n* : either of two No. American plants that are related to the daisies and have deep yellow to orange flower heads with dark conical centers
Black·foot \ˈblak-ˌfu̇t\ *n, pl* **Black·feet** *or* **Blackfoot** : a member of an American Indian people of Montana, Alberta, and Saskatchewan
black·guard \ˈblag-ərd, -ˌärd\ *n* : SCOUNDREL, RASCAL
black·head \ˈblak-ˌhed\ *n* : a small oily mass plugging the outlet of a skin gland
black·ing \ˈblak-iŋ\ *n* : a substance applied to something to make it black
[1]**black·jack** \-ˌjak\ *n* **1** : a leather-covered club with a flexible handle **2** : a card game in which the object is to be dealt cards having a higher count than the dealer but not exceeding 21
[2]**blackjack** *vb* : to hit with or as if with a blackjack
black light *n* : invisible ultraviolet or infrared radiation
black·list \ˈblak-ˌlist\ *n* : a list of persons who are disapproved of and are to be punished (as by refusal of jobs or a boycott) — **blacklist** *vb*
black·mail \ˈblak-ˌmāl\ *n* : extortion by threats esp. of public exposure; *also* : something so extorted — **blackmail** *vb* — **black·mail·er** *n*
black market *n* : illicit trade in goods; *also* : a place where such trade is carried on
Black Mass *n* : a travesty of the Christian mass ascribed to worshipers of Satan
Black Muslim *n* : a member of a chiefly black group that professes Islamic religious belief
black nationalist *n, often cap B&N* : a member of a group of militant blacks who advocate separatism from whites and the formation of self-governing black communities — **black nationalism** *n, often cap B&N*
black·out \ˈblak-ˌau̇t\ *n* **1** : a period of darkness due to electrical power failure **2** : a transitory loss or dulling of

vision or consciousness **3** : the prohibition or restriction of the telecasting of sports events to ensure ticket sales — **black out** \-ˈau̇t\ *vb*

Black Panther *n* : a member of an organization of militant black Americans

black power *n* : the mobilization of the political and economic power of black Americans esp. to further racial equality

black sheep *n* : a discreditable member of an otherwise respectable group

black·smith \ˈblak-ˌsmith\ *n* : a worker who shapes heated iron by hammering it

black·thorn \-ˌthȯrn\ *n* : a European thorny plum

black·top \ˈblak-ˌtäp\ *n* : a very dark material containing mixtures of hydrocarbons (as asphalt) used esp. for surfacing roads — **blacktop** *vb*

black widow *n* : a venomous New World spider having the female black with an hourglass-shaped red mark on the underside of the abdomen

blad·der \ˈblad-ər\ *n* : a sac in which liquid or gas is stored; *esp* : one in a vertebrate into which urine passes from the kidneys

blade \ˈblād\ *n* **1** : a leaf of a plant and esp. of a grass; *also* : the flat part of a leaf as distinguished from its stalk **2** : something (as the flat part of an oar or an arm of a propeller) resembling the blade of a leaf **3** : the cutting part of an instrument or tool **4** : SWORD; *also* : SWORDSMAN **5** : a dashing fellow ⟨a gay ~⟩ **6** : the runner of an ice skate

blain \ˈblān\ *n* : an inflammatory swelling or sore

[1]**blame** \ˈblām\ *vb* **blamed; blam·ing** [ME *blamen,* fr. OF *blamer,* fr. L *blasphemare* to blaspheme, fr. Gk *blasphēmein*] **1** : to find fault with **2** : to hold responsible or responsible for **syn** censure, denounce, condemn, criticize — **blam·able** *adj*

[2]**blame** *n* **1** : CENSURE, REPROOF **2** : responsibility for fault or error **syn** guilt, fault, culpability, onus — **blame·less** *adj* — **blame·less·ly** *adv*

blame·wor·thy \-ˌwər-t͟hē\ *adj* : deserving blame — **blame·wor·thi·ness** *n*

blanch \ˈblanch\ *vb* **1** : BLEACH **2** : to make or become white or pale

blanc·mange \blə-ˈmänj, -ˈmänzh\ *n* [ME *blancmanger,* fr. MF *blanc manger,* lit., white food] : a dessert made from gelatin or a starchy substance and milk usu. sweetened and flavored

bland \ˈbland\ *adj* **1** : smooth in manner : SUAVE **2** : gently soothing ⟨a ~ diet⟩; *also* : INSIPID **syn** gentle, mild, soft, balmy — **bland·ly** *adv* — **bland·ness** *n*

blan·dish·ment \ˈblan-dish-mənt\ *n* : flattering or coaxing speech or action : CAJOLERY

[1]**blank** \ˈblaŋk\ *adj* **1** : showing or causing an appearance of dazed dismay; *also* : EXPRESSIONLESS **2** : DULL, EMPTY ⟨~ moments⟩ **3** : free from writing or marks; *also* : having spaces to be filled in **4** : ABSOLUTE, DOWNRIGHT ⟨a ~ refusal⟩ **5** : not shaped in final form — **blank·ly** *adv* — **blank·ness** *n*

[2]**blank** *n* **1** : an empty space **2** : a form with spaces for the entry of data **3** : the center of a target **4** : an unfinished form (as of a key) **5** : a cartridge with propellant and a wad but no projectile

[3]**blank** *vb* **1** : to cover or close up : OBSCURE **2** : to keep from scoring

blank check *n* **1** : a signed check with the amount unspecified **2** : complete freedom of action

[1]**blan·ket** \ˈblaŋ-kət\ *n* **1** : a heavy woven often woolen covering **2** : a covering layer ⟨a ~ of snow⟩

[2]**blanket** *vb* : to cover with a blanket

[3]**blanket** *adj* : covering a group or class ⟨~ insurance⟩; *also* : applicable in all instances ⟨~ rules⟩

blank verse *n* : unrhymed iambic pentameter

blare \ˈblaər\ *vb* **blared; blar·ing** : to sound loud and harsh; *also* : to proclaim loudly — **blare** *n*

blar·ney \ˈblär-nē\ *n* [*Blarney stone,* a stone in Blarney Castle, near Cork, Ireland, held to bestow skill in flattery on those who kiss it] : skillful flattery : BLANDISHMENT

bla·sé \blä-ˈzā\ *adj* [F] : not responsive to pleasure or excitement as a result of excessive indulgence; *also* : SOPHISTICATED

blas·pheme \blas-ˈfēm\ *vb* **blas·phemed; blas·phem·ing 1** : to speak of or address with irreverence **2** : to utter blasphemy

blas·phe·my \ˈblas-fə-mē\ *n, pl* **-mies 1** : the act of expressing lack of reverence for God **2** : irreverence toward something considered sacred — **blas·phe·mous** \-məs\ *adj*

[1]**blast** \ˈblast\ *n* **1** : a violent gust of wind; *also* : its effect **2** : sound made by a wind instrument **3** : a current of air forced at high pressure through a hole in a furnace (**blast furnace**) **4** : a sudden withering esp. of plants : BLIGHT **5** : EXPLOSION; *also* : the often destructive wave of increased air pressure that moves outward from an explosion

[2]**blast** *vb* **1** : BLIGHT **2** : to shatter by or as if by an explosive

blast off \(ˈ)blast-ˈȯf\ *vb* : TAKE OFF 4 — used esp. of rocket-propelled devices — **blast–off** \ˈblast-ˌȯf\ *n*

bla·tant \ˈblāt-ᵊnt\ *adj* : offensively obtrusive : vulgarly showy **syn** vociferous, boisterous, clamorous, obstreperous — **bla·tan·cy** \-ᵊn-sē\ *n* — **bla·tant·ly** *adv*

blath·er \ˈblat͟h-ər\ *vb* **blath·ered; blath·er·ing** \-(ə-)riŋ\ : to talk foolishly — **blather** *n*

blath·er·skite \ˈblat͟h-ər-ˌskīt\ *n* : a blustering talkative person

[1]**blaze** \ˈblāz\ *n* **1** : FIRE **2** : intense direct light accompanied by heat **3** : something (as a dazzling display or sudden outburst) suggesting fire ⟨a ~ of autumn leaves⟩ **syn** glare, glow, flame

[2]**blaze** *vb* **blazed; blaz·ing 1** : to burn brightly; *also* : to flare up **2** : to be conspicuously bright : GLITTER

[3]**blaze** *vb* **blazed; blaz·ing** : to make public

[4]**blaze** *n* **1** : a white mark on the face of an animal **2** : a mark made on a tree or other fixed object usu. to leave a trail

[5]**blaze** *vb* **blazed; blaz·ing** : to mark (as a tree or trail) with blazes

blaz·er \ˈblā-zər\ *n* : a sports jacket often with notched collar and pockets that are stitched on

[1]**bla·zon** \ˈblāz-ᵊn\ *n* **1** : COAT OF ARMS **2** : ostentatious display

[2]**blazon** *vb* **bla·zoned; bla·zon·ing** \ˈblāz-(ə-)niŋ\ **1** : to publish widely : PROCLAIM **2** : DECK, ADORN

bldg *abbr* building

bldr *abbr* builder

[1]**bleach** \ˈblēch\ *vb* : WHITEN, BLANCH

[2]**bleach** *n* : a preparation used in bleaching

bleach·ers \ˈblē-chərz\ *n sing or pl* : a usu. uncovered stand containing lower-priced tiered seats for spectators

bleak \ˈblēk\ *adj* **1** : desolately barren and windswept **2** : lacking warm or cheering qualities — **bleak·ish** *adj* — **bleak·ly** *adv* — **bleak·ness** *n*

blear \ˈbliər\ *adj* : dim with water or tears ⟨~ eyes⟩

bleary \ˈbli(ə)r-ē\ *adj* **1** : dull or dimmed esp. from fatigue or sleep **2** : poorly outlined or defined

bleat \ˈblēt\ *n* : the cry of a sheep or goat or a sound like it — **bleat** *vb*

bleed \ˈblēd\ *vb* **bled** \ˈbled\; **bleed·ing 1** : to lose or shed blood **2** : to be wounded; *also* : to feel pain or distress **3** : to flow or ooze from a wounded surface; *also* : to draw fluid from ⟨~ a tire⟩ **4** : to extort money from

bleed·er \ˈblēd-ər\ *n* : one that bleeds; *esp* : HEMOPHILIAC

bleeding heart *n* **1** : a garden plant related to the poppies that has deep pink drooping heart-shaped flowers **2** : one who shows extreme sympathy esp. for an object of alleged persecution

¹blem·ish \ˈblem-ish\ *vb* : to spoil by a flaw : MAR

²blemish *n* : a noticeable flaw

¹blench \ˈblench\ *vb* [ME *blenchen* to deceive, blench, fr. OE *blencan* to deceive] : FLINCH, QUAIL **syn** shrink, recoil, wince, start

²blench *vb* : to grow or make pale

¹blend \ˈblend\ *vb* **blend·ed; blend·ing** **1** : to mix thoroughly **2** : to prepare (as coffee) by mixing different varieties **3** : to combine into an integrated whole **4** : HARMONIZE **syn** fuse, merge, mingle, coalesce — **blend·er** *n*

²blend *n* : a product of blending **syn** compound, composite, alloy, mixture

bless \ˈbles\ *vb* **blessed** \ˈblest\ *also* **blest** \ˈblest\; **bless·ing** [ME *blessen,* fr. OE *blētsian,* fr. *blōd* blood; fr. the use of blood in consecration] **1** : to hallow or consecrate by religious rite or word **2** : to make the sign of the cross over **3** : to invoke divine care for **4** : PRAISE, GLORIFY **5** : to confer happiness upon

bless·ed \ˈbles-əd\ *also* **blest** \ˈblest\ *adj* **1** : HOLY **2** : BEATIFIED **3** : DELIGHTFUL — **bless·ed·ness** *n*

bless·ing \ˈbles-iŋ\ *n* **1** : the act or words of one who blesses **2** : a thing conducive to happiness **3** : grace said at a meal

blew *past of* BLOW

¹blight \ˈblīt\ *n* **1** : a plant disease or injury marked by withering; *also* : an organism causing a blight **2** : an impairing or frustrating influence; *also* : an impaired or damaged condition

²blight *vb* : to affect with or suffer from blight

blimp \ˈblimp\ *n* : a nonrigid airship

¹blind \ˈblīnd\ *adj* **1** : lacking or grossly deficient in ability to see; *also* : intended for blind persons **2** : not based on reason, evidence, or knowledge ⟨~ faith⟩ **3** : not intelligently controlled or directed ⟨~ chance⟩ **4** : performed solely by the aid of instruments within an airplane ⟨a ~ landing⟩ **5** : hard to discern or make out : HIDDEN ⟨a ~ seam⟩ **6** : lacking an opening or outlet ⟨a ~ alley⟩ — **blind·ly** *adv* — **blind·ness** \ˈblīn(d)-nəs\ *n*

²blind *vb* **1** : to make blind **2** : DAZZLE **3** : DARKEN; *also* : HIDE

³blind *n* **1** : something (as a shutter) to hinder vision or keep out light **2** : a place of concealment **3** : SUBTERFUGE

blind date *n* : a date between persons who have not previously met; *also* : either of these persons

blind·er \ˈblīn-dər\ *n* : either of two flaps on a horse's bridle to prevent it from seeing to the side

blind·fold \ˈblīn(d)-ˌfōld\ *vb* : to cover the eyes of with or as if with a bandage — **blindfold** *n*

¹blink \ˈbliŋk\ *vb* **1** : WINK **2** : TWINKLE **3** : EVADE, IGNORE

²blink *n* **1** : GLIMMER, SPARKLE **2** : a usu. involuntary shutting and opening of the eye

blink·er \ˈbliŋ-kər\ *n* : a blinking light used as a signal

blin·tze \ˈblint-sə\ *or* **blintz** \ˈblints\ *n* [Yiddish *blintse*] : a thin rolled pancake with a filling usu. of cream cheese

blip \ˈblip\ *n* **1** : an image on a radar screen **2** : ABERRATION 1

bliss \ˈblis\ *n* : complete happiness : JOY **syn** beatitude, blessedness — **bliss·ful** \-fəl\ *adj* — **bliss·ful·ly** \-fə-lē\ *adv*

¹blis·ter \ˈblis-tər\ *n* **1** : a raised area of skin containing watery fluid; *also* : an agent that causes blisters **2** : something (as a raised spot in paint) suggesting a blister **3** : a disease of plants marked by large swollen patches on the leaves

²blister *vb* **blis·tered; blis·ter·ing** \-t(ə-)riŋ\ : to develop a blister; *also* : to cause blisters

blithe \ˈblīth, ˈblīth\ *adj* **blith·er; blith·est** : happily lighthearted **syn** merry, jovial, jolly, jocund — **blithe·ly** *adv* — **blithe·some** \-səm\ *adj*

blitz \ˈblits\ *n* **1** : an intensive series of air raids **2** : a fast intensive campaign **3** : a rush of the passer by the defensive linebackers in football — **blitz** *vb*

blitz·krieg \-ˌkrēg\ *n* [G, lit., lightning war, fr. *blitz* lightning + *krieg* war] : a sudden violent enemy attack

bliz·zard \ˈbliz-ərd\ *n* : a long severe snowstorm

blk *abbr* **1** black **2** block

bloat \ˈblōt\ *vb* : to swell by or as if by filling with water or air

bloat·er \ˈblōt-ər\ *n* : a fat herring or mackerel lightly salted and smoked

blob \ˈbläb\ *n* : a small lump or drop of a thick consistency

bloc \ˈbläk\ *n* [F, lit., block] : a combination of individuals or groups (as nations) working for a common purpose

¹block \ˈbläk\ *n* **1** : a solid piece of substantial material (as wood or stone) **2** : HINDRANCE, OBSTRUCTION; *also* : interruption of normal function of body or mind ⟨heart ~⟩ **3** : a frame enclosing one or more pulleys and having a hook or strap by which it may be attached to objects **4** : a quantity of things considered as a unit ⟨a ~ of seats⟩ **5** : a large building divided into separate units (as apartments or offices) **6** : a row of houses or shops **7** : a city square; *also* : the distance along one of the sides of such a square **8** : a piece of material with a hand-cut design on its surface from which copies are to be made

²block *vb* **1** : OBSTRUCT, CHECK **2** : to outline roughly ⟨~ out a statue⟩ **3** : to provide or support with a block ⟨~ up a wheel⟩ **syn** bar, impede, hinder, obstruct

¹block·ade \blä-ˈkād\ *vb* **block·ad·ed; block·ad·ing** : to subject to a blockade

²blockade *n* : the shutting off of a place usu. by troops or ships to prevent entrance or exit

block·bust·er \ˈbläk-ˌbəs-tər\ *n* : one that is very large, successful, or violent ⟨a ~ of a movie⟩

block·head \ˈbläk-ˌhed\ *n* : DOLT, DUNCE

block·house \-ˌhau̇s\ *n* : a small strong building used as a shelter (as from enemy fire) or observation post

¹blond *or* **blonde** \ˈbländ\ *adj* : fair in complexion; *also* : of a light or bleached color ⟨~ mahogany⟩ — **blond·ish** \-ish\ *adj*

²blond *or* **blonde** *n* : a person having blond hair

blood \ˈbləd\ *n* **1** : the red liquid that circulates in the heart, arteries, and veins of animals **2** : LIFEBLOOD; *also* : LIFE **3** : LINEAGE, STOCK **4** : KINSHIP; *also* : KINDRED **5** : the taking of life **6** : TEMPER, PASSION **7** : DANDY 1 — **blood·less** *adj* — **bloody** *adj*

blood bank *n* : a place where blood or plasma is stored

blood·bath \ˈbləd-ˌbath, -ˌbȧth\ *n* : MASSACRE

blood count *n* : the determination of the number of blood cells in a specific volume of blood; *also* : the number of cells so determined

blood·cur·dling \-ˌkərd-(ᵊ-)liŋ\ *adj* : causing great horror or fear : TERRIFYING

blood·ed \ˈbləd-əd\ *adj* **1** : entirely or largely purebred ⟨~ horses⟩ **2** : having blood of a specified kind ⟨warm-*blooded* animals⟩

blood group *n* : one of the classes into which human beings can be separated by the presence or absence in their blood of specific antigens

blood·hound \ˈbləd-ˌhau̇nd\ *n* : a large powerful hound with long drooping ears, a wrinkled face, and keen sense of smell

blood·let·ting \-ˌlet-iŋ\ *n* **1** : PHLEBOTOMY **2** : BLOODSHED

blood·line \-ˌlīn\ *n* : a sequence of direct ancestors esp. in a pedigree

blood·mo·bile \-mō-ˌbēl\ *n* : a motor vehicle equipped for collecting blood from donors

blood poisoning *n* : invasion of the bloodstream by virulent microorganisms from a focus of infection accompanied esp. by chills, fever, and prostration

blood pressure *n* : pressure of the blood on the walls of blood vessels and esp. arteries

blood·root \ˈbləd-ˌrüt, -ˌru̇t\ *n* : a plant related to the poppy that has a red root and sap, a solitary leaf, and a white flower in early spring

blood·shed \-ˌshed\ *n* : wounding or taking of life : CARNAGE, SLAUGHTER

blood·shot \-ˌshät\ *adj* : inflamed to redness ⟨~ eyes⟩

blood·stain \-ˌstān\ *n* : a discoloration caused by blood — **blood·stained** \-ˌstānd\ *adj*

blood·stone \-ˌstōn\ *n* : a green quartz sprinkled with red spots

blood·stream \-ˌstrēm\ *n* : the flowing blood in a circulatory system

blood·suck·er \-ˌsək-ər\ *n* : an animal that sucks blood; *esp* : LEECH — **blood·suck·ing** \-iŋ\ *adj*

blood test *n* : a test of the blood; *esp* : one for syphilis

blood·thirsty \ˈbləd-ˌthər-stē\ *adj* : eager to shed blood — **blood·thirst·i·ly** \-ˌthər-stə-lē\ *adv* — **blood·thirst·i·ness** \-stē-nəs\ *n*

blood type *n* : BLOOD GROUP — **blood–typ·ing** \-ˌtī-piŋ\ *n*

blood vessel *n* : a vessel (as a vein or artery) in which blood circulates in an animal

Bloody Mary \-ˈme(ə)r-ē\ *n, pl* **Bloody Marys** : a drink made essentially of vodka and tomato juice

[1]**bloom** \ˈblüm\ *n* **1** : FLOWER 1; *also* : flowers or amount of flowers (as of a plant) **2** : the period or state of flowering **3** : a state or time of beauty and vigor **4** : a powdery coating esp. on fruits and leaves **5** : rosy color; *also* : an appearance of freshness or health — **bloomy** *adj*

[2]**bloom** *vb* **1** : to produce or yield flowers **2** : to glow esp. with healthy color **syn** flower, blossom

bloo·mers \ˈblü-mərz\ *n pl* [Amelia *Bloomer* †1894 Am. pioneer in feminism] : a woman's garment of short loose trousers gathered at the knee

bloop·er \ˈblü-pər\ *n* **1** : an embarrassing blunder made in public **2** : a fly ball hit barely beyond a baseball infield

[1]**blos·som** \ˈbläs-əm\ *n* : the flower of a plant : BLOOM

[2]**blossom** *vb* : FLOWER, BLOOM

[1]**blot** \ˈblät\ *n* **1** : SPOT, STAIN ⟨ink ~*s*⟩ **2** : BLEMISH **syn** stigma, brand, slur

[2]**blot** *vb* **blot·ted; blot·ting 1** : SPOT, STAIN **2** : OBSCURE, ECLIPSE ⟨~ out the sun⟩ **3** *obs* : MAR; *esp* : DISGRACE **4** : to dry or remove with or as if with blotting paper **5** : to make a blot

blotch \ˈbläch\ *n* : a usu. large and irregular spot or mark (as of ink or color) — **blotch** *vb* — **blotchy** *adj*

blot·ter \ˈblät-ər\ *n* **1** : a piece of blotting paper **2** : a book for preliminary records (as of sales or arrests)

blot·ting paper *n* : a soft spongy paper used to absorb ink

blouse \ˈblau̇s, ˈblau̇z\ *n* **1** : a loose outer garment like a smock **2** : a usu. loose garment reaching from the neck to about the waist level

[1]**blow** \ˈblō\ *vb* **blew** \ˈblü\; **blown** \ˈblōn\; **blow·ing 1** : to move forcibly ⟨the wind *blew*⟩ **2** : to send forth a current of gas (as air) **3** : to act on with a current of gas or vapor; *esp* : to drive with such a current **4** : to sound or cause to sound ⟨~ a horn⟩ **5** : PANT, GASP; *also* : to expel moist air in breathing ⟨the whale *blew*⟩ **6** : BOAST; *also* : BLUSTER **7** : MELT — used of an electrical fuse **8** : to shape or form by blown or injected air ⟨~ glass⟩ **9** : to shatter or destroy by or as if by explosion **10** : to make breathless by exertion **11** : to spend recklessly — **blow·er** *n*

[2]**blow** *n* **1** : a usu. strong blowing of air : GALE **2** : BOASTING, BRAG **3** : a blowing from the mouth or nose or through or from an instrument

[3]**blow** *vb* **blew** \ˈblü\; **blown** \ˈblōn\; **blow·ing** : FLOWER, BLOOM

[4]**blow** *n* **1** : a forcible stroke **2** : COMBAT ⟨come to ~*s*⟩ **3** : a severe and usu. unexpected calamity

blow–by–blow \-bī-, -bə-\ *adj* : minutely detailed ⟨~ account⟩

blow·fly \ˈblō-ˌflī\ *n* : any of various two-winged flies (as a bluebottle) that deposit their eggs or maggots on meat or in wounds

blow·gun \-ˌgən\ *n* : a tube from which an arrow or a dart may be shot by the force of the breath

blow·out \ˈblō-ˌau̇t\ *n* : a bursting of something (as a tire) because of pressure of the contents (as air)

blow·pipe \ˈblō-ˌpīp\ *n* : a small tube for blowing gas (as air) into a flame so as to concentrate and increase the heat

blow·sy *also* **blow·zy** \ˈblau̇-zē\ *adj* : DISHEVELED, SLOVENLY

blow·torch \ˈblō-ˌtȯrch\ *n* : a small portable burner whose flame is made hotter by a blast of air or oxygen

blow·up \ˈblō-ˌəp\ *n* **1** : EXPLOSION **2** : an outburst of temper **3** : a photographic enlargement

blowy \ˈblō-ē\ *adj* : WINDY

BLT \ˌbē-ˌel-ˈtē\ *n* : a bacon, lettuce, and tomato sandwich

[1]**blub·ber** \ˈbləb-ər\ *vb* **blub·bered; blub·ber·ing** \ˈbləb-(ə-)riŋ\ : to cry noisily

[2]**blubber** *n* **1** : the fat of large sea mammals (as whales) **2** : a noisy crying

[1]**blud·geon** \ˈbləj-ən\ *n* : a short often loaded club

[2]**bludgeon** *vb* : to strike with or as if with a bludgeon

[1]**blue** \ˈblü\ *adj* **blu·er; blu·est 1** : of the color blue; *also* : BLUISH **2** : MELANCHOLY; *also* : DEPRESSING **3** : PURITANICAL **4** : INDECENT

[2]**blue** *n* **1** : a color between green and violet in the spectrum : the color of the clear daytime sky **2** : something (as clothing or the sky) that is blue

blue baby *n* : a baby with bluish skin due to faulty circulation caused by a heart defect

blue·bell \-ˌbel\ *n* : any of various plants with blue bell-shaped flowers

blue·ber·ry \ˈblü-ˌber-ē, -b(ə-)rē\ *n* : the edible blue or blackish berry of various shrubs of the heath family; *also* : one of these shrubs

blue·bird \-ˌbərd\ *n* : any of several small songbirds related to the robin but with blue above esp. in the male

blue–black \-ˈblak\ *adj* : being of a dark bluish hue

blue·bon·net \ˈblü-ˌbän-ət\ *n* : a low-growing annual lupine of Texas with silky foliage and blue flowers

blue·bot·tle \ˈblü-ˌbät-ᵊl\ *n* : any of several blowflies with iridescent blue bodies or abdomens

blue cheese *n* : cheese marked with veins of greenish blue mold

blue–col·lar \ˈblü-ˈkäl-ər\ *adj* : of, relating to, or being the class of workers whose duties call for work clothes

blue·fish \-ˌfish\ *n* : a marine sport and food fish bluish above and silvery below

blue·grass \-ˌgras\ *n* : KENTUCKY BLUEGRASS

blue jay \-ˌjā\ *n* : an American crested jay with upper parts bright blue that occurs east of the Rocky mountains

blue jeans *n pl* : pants usu. made of blue denim

blue·nose \ˈblü-ˌnōz\ *n* : one who advocates a rigorous moral code

blue·point \ˈblü-ˌpȯint\ *n* : a small delicate oyster orig. from Long Island, New York

blue·print \-ˌprint\ *n* **1** : a photographic print in white on a blue ground used esp. for copying mechanical drawings and architects' plans **2** : a detailed plan of action — **blueprint** *vb*

blues \ˈblüz\ *n pl* **1** : MELANCHOLY **2** : music in a style marked by recurrent minor intervals and melancholy lyrics

blue·stock·ing \ˈblü-ˌstäk-iŋ\ *n* : a woman having intellectual interests

blu·et \ˈblü-ət\ *n* : a low American herb with dainty solitary bluish flowers

blue whale *n* : a very large whalebone whale that may reach a weight of 100 tons (90 metric tons) and a length of 100 feet (30 meters)

¹**bluff** \ˈbləf\ *adj* **1** : having a broad flattened front **2** : rising steeply with a broad flat front **3** : OUTSPOKEN, FRANK **syn** abrupt, blunt, brusque, curt, gruff

²**bluff** *n* : a high steep bank : CLIFF

³**bluff** *vb* : to frighten or deceive by pretense or a mere show of strength

⁴**bluff** *n* : an act or instance of bluffing; *also* : one who bluffs

blu·ing *or* **blue·ing** \ˈblü-iŋ\ *n* : a preparation of blue or violet dyes used in laundering to counteract yellowing of white fabrics

blu·ish \ˈblü-ish\ *adj* : somewhat blue

¹**blun·der** \ˈblən-dər\ *vb* **blun·dered; blun·der·ing** \-d(ə-)riŋ\ **1** : to move clumsily or unsteadily **2** : to make a stupid or needless mistake

²**blunder** *n* : an avoidable and usu. serious mistake

blun·der·buss \ˈblən-dər-ˌbəs\ *n* [fr. obs. Dutch *donderbus,* fr. Dutch *donder* thunder + obs. Dutch *bus* gun] : an obsolete short-barreled firearm with a flaring muzzle

¹**blunt** \ˈblənt\ *adj* **1** : not sharp : DULL **2** : lacking in tact : BLUFF **syn** brusque, curt, gruff, abrupt, crusty — **blunt·ly** *adv* — **blunt·ness** *n*

²**blunt** *vb* : to make or become dull

¹**blur** \ˈblər\ *n* **1** : a smear or stain that obscures **2** : something vaguely seen or perceived — **blur·ry** \-ē\ *adj*

²**blur** *vb* **blurred; blur·ring** : DIM, CLOUD, OBSCURE

blurb \ˈblərb\ *n* : a short publicity notice (as on a book jacket)

blurt \ˈblərt\ *vb* : to utter suddenly and impulsively

blush \ˈbləsh\ *n* : a reddening of the face (as from modesty or confusion) : FLUSH — **blush** *vb* — **blush·ful** *adj*

blus·ter \ˈbləs-tər\ *vb* **blus·tered; blus·ter·ing** \-t(ə-)riŋ\ **1** : to blow in stormy noisy gusts **2** : to talk or act with noisy swaggering threats — **bluster** *n* — **blus·tery** \-t(ə-)rē\ *adj*

blvd *abbr* boulevard

B lymphocyte *n* : B CELL

BM *abbr* **1** basal metabolism **2** bowel movement

BMR *abbr* basal metabolic rate

BO *abbr* **1** body odor **2** box office **3** branch office

boa \ˈbō-ə\ *n* **1** : a large snake (as the **boa con·stric·tor** \ˌbō-ə-kən-ˈstrik-tər\ or the related anaconda) that suffocates and kills its prey by constriction **2** : a fluffy scarf usu. of fur or feathers

boar \ˈbōr\ *n* : a male swine; *also* : WILD BOAR

¹**board** \ˈbōrd\ *n* **1** : the side of a ship **2** : a thin flat length of sawed lumber; *also* : material (as cardboard) or a piece of material formed as a thin flat firm sheet **3** *pl* : STAGE 1 **4** : a table spread with a meal; *also* : daily meals esp. when furnished for pay **5** : a table at which a council or magistrates sit **6** : a group or association of persons organized for a special responsibility (as the management of a business or institution); *also* : an organized commercial exchange

²**board** *vb* **1** : to go aboard ⟨~ a boat⟩ **2** : to cover with boards **3** : to provide or be provided with meals and often lodging — **board·er** *n*

board·ing·house \ˈbōrd-iŋ-ˌhau̇s\ *n* : a house at which persons are boarded

board·walk \ˈbōrd-ˌwȯk\ *n* : a promenade (as of planking) along a beach

boast \ˈbōst\ *vb* **1** : to praise oneself **2** : to mention or assert with excessive pride **3** : to prize as a possession; *also* : HAVE ⟨the house ~*s* a fireplace⟩ — **boast** *n* — **boast·ful** \-fəl\ *adj* — **boast·ful·ly** \-ē\ *adv*

boat \ˈbōt\ *n* : a vessel (as a canoe or ship) for traveling through water

boat·er \ˈbōt-ər\ *n* **1** : one that travels in a boat **2** : a stiff straw hat

boat·man \ˈbōt-mən\ *n* : a man who manages, works on, or deals in boats

boat·swain \ˈbōs-ᵊn\ *n* : a subordinate officer of a ship in charge of the hull and related equipment

¹**bob** \ˈbäb\ *vb* **bobbed; bob·bing 1** : to move up and down jerkily or repeatedly **2** : to emerge, arise, or appear suddenly or unexpectedly

²**bob** *n* : a bobbing movement

³**bob** *n* **1** : a knob, knot, twist, or curl esp. of ribbons, yarn, or hair **2** : a short haircut of a woman or child **3** : FLOAT 2 **4** : a weight hanging from a line

⁴**bob** *vb* **bobbed; bob·bing** : to cut hair in a bob

⁵**bob** *n, pl* **bob** *slang Brit* : SHILLING

bob·bin \ˈbäb-ən\ *n* : a cylinder or spindle for holding or dispensing thread (as in a sewing machine)

bob·ble \ˈbäb-əl\ *vb* **bob·bled; bob·bling** \-(ə-)liŋ\ : FUMBLE — **bobble** *n*

bob·by \ˈbäb-ē\ *n, pl* **bobbies** [*Bobby,* nickname for *Robert,* after Sir *Robert* Peel, who organized the London police force] *Brit* : POLICEMAN

bob·by pin \ˈbäb-ē-\ *n* : a flat wire hairpin with prongs that press close together

bob·cat \ˈbäb-ˌkat\ *n* : a small usu. rusty-colored No. American lynx

bobcat

bob·o·link \ˈbäb-ə-ˌliŋk\ *n* : an American migratory songbird related to the meadowlarks

bob·sled \ˈbäb-ˌsled\ *n* **1** : a short sled usu. used as one of a joined pair **2** : a racing sled with two pairs of runners, a steering wheel, and a hand brake — **bobsled** *vb*

bob·white \(ˈ)bäb-ˈhwīt\ *n* : any of a genus of quail; *esp* : one of the eastern and central U.S.

boc·cie *or* **boc·ci** *or* **boc·ce** \ˈbäch-ē\ *n* : Italian lawn bowling played on a long narrow court

bock \ˈbäk\ *n* : a dark heavy beer usu. sold in early spring

bod \ˈbäd\ *n* : BODY

¹**bode** \ˈbōd\ *vb* **bod·ed; bod·ing** : to indicate by signs : PRESAGE

²**bode** *past of* BIDE

bo·de·ga \bō-ˈdā-gə\ *n* [Sp, fr. L *apotheca* storehouse] : a store specializing in Hispanic groceries

bod·ice \ˈbäd-əs\ *n* [alter. of *bodies,* pl. of *body*] : the usu. close-fitting part of a dress above the waist

bodi·less \ˈbäd-i-ləs, ˈbäd-ᵊl-əs\ *adj* : lacking a body or material form

¹**bodi·ly** \ˈbäd-ᵊl-ē\ *adj* : of or relating to the body ⟨~ welfare⟩

²**bodily** *adv* **1** : in the flesh **2** : as a whole ⟨lifted the crate up ~⟩

bod·kin \ˈbäd-kən\ *n* **1** : DAGGER **2** : a pointed implement for punching holes in cloth **3** : a blunt needle for drawing tape or ribbon through a loop or hem

body \ˈbäd-ē\ *n, pl* **bod·ies 1** : the physical whole of a living or dead organism; *also* : the trunk or main mass of an organism as distinguished from its appendages **2**

: a human being : PERSON **3** : the main part of something **4** : a mass of matter distinct from other masses **5** : GROUP **6** : VISCOSITY, FIRMNESS **7** : richness of flavor — used esp. of wines — **bod·ied** \ˈbäd-ēd\ *adj*

body English *n* : bodily motions made in a usu. unconscious effort to influence the movement of a propelled object (as a ball)

body·guard \ˈbäd-ē-ˌgärd\ *n* : a personal guard; *also* : RETINUE

body stocking *n* : a sheer close-fitting one-piece garment for the torso that often has sleeves and legs

body·work \ˈbäd-ē-ˌwərk\ *n* : the making or repairing of vehicle bodies

Boer \ˈbōr, ˈbu̇r\ *n* [Dutch, lit., farmer] : a South African of Dutch or Huguenot descent

[1]**bog** \ˈbäg, ˈbȯg\ *n* : wet, spongy, poorly drained, and usu. acid ground — **bog·gy** *adj*

[2]**bog** *vb* **bogged; bog·ging** : to sink into or as if into a bog

bo·gey *also* **bo·gie** *or* **bo·gy** \ˈbu̇g-ē, ˈbō-gē *for 1*; ˈbō-gē *for 2*\ *n, pl* **bogeys** *also* **bogies 1** : SPECTER, HOBGOBLIN; *also* : a source of fear or annoyance **2** : a score of one over par on a hole in golf

bo·gey·man \ˈbu̇g-ē-ˌman, ˈbō-gē-, ˈbü-gē-\ *n* : an imaginary monster used in threatening children

bog·gle \ˈbäg-əl\ *vb* **bog·gled; bog·gling** \-(ə-)liŋ\ : to overwhelm or be overwhelmed with fright or amazement

bo·gus \ˈbō-gəs\ *adj* : SPURIOUS, SHAM

Bo·he·mi·an \bō-ˈhē-mē-ən\ *n* **1** : a native or inhabitant of Bohemia **2** *often not cap* : VAGABOND, WANDERER **3** *often not cap* : a person (as a writer or artist) living an unconventional life — **bohemian** *adj, often cap*

[1]**boil** \ˈbȯil\ *n* : an inflamed swelling on the skin containing pus

[2]**boil** *vb* **1** : to heat or become heated to a temperature **(boiling point)** at which vapor is formed and rises in bubbles ⟨water ∼*s* and changes to steam⟩; *also* : to act on or be acted on by a boiling liquid ⟨∼ eggs⟩ **2** : to be in a state of seething agitation

[3]**boil** *n* : the act or state of boiling

boil·er \ˈbȯi-lər\ *n* **1** : a container in which something is boiled **2** : a strong vessel used in making steam **3** : a tank holding hot water

boil·er·mak·er \ˈbȯi-lər-ˌmā-kər\ *n* : whiskey with a beer chaser

bois·ter·ous \ˈbȯi-st(ə-)rəs\ *adj* : noisily turbulent or exuberant — **bois·ter·ous·ly** *adv*

bok choy \ˈbäk-ˈchȯi\ *n* : a Chinese vegetable related to the mustards that forms a loose head of green leaves with long thick white stalks

bo·la \ˈbō-lə\ *or* **bo·las** \-ləs\ *n, pl* **bolas** \-ləz\ *also* **bo·las·es** [AmerSp *bolas*, fr. Sp *bola* ball] : a cord with weights attached to the ends for hurling at and entangling an animal

bold \ˈbōld\ *adj* **1** : COURAGEOUS, INTREPID **2** : IMPUDENT **3** : STEEP **4** : ADVENTUROUS, FREE ⟨a ∼ thinker⟩ **syn** dauntless, brave, valiant — **bold·ly** *adv* — **bold·ness** \ˈbol(d)-nəs\ *n*

bold·face \ˈbōl(d)-ˌfās\ *n* : a heavy-faced type; *also* : printing in boldface — **bold–faced** \-ˈfāst\ *adj*

bole \ˈbōl\ *n* : the trunk of a tree

bo·le·ro \bə-ˈle(ə)r-ō\ *n, pl* **-ros 1** : a Spanish dance or its music **2** : a short loose jacket open at the front

bo·li·var \bə-ˈlē-ˌvär, ˈbäl-ə-vər\ *n, pl* **-vars** *or* **-va·res** \ˌbäl-ə-ˈvär-ˌās, ˌbō-li-\ — see MONEY table

boll \ˈbōl\ *n* : a seed pod (as of cotton)

boll weevil *n* : a small grayish weevil that infests the cotton plant both as a larva and as an adult

boll·worm \ˈbōl-ˌwərm\ *n* : any of several moths and esp. the corn earworm whose larvae feed on cotton bolls

bo·lo \ˈbō-lō\ *n, pl* **bolos** : a long heavy single-edged knife of Philippine origin

bo·lo·gna \bə-ˈlō-nē\ *n* [short for *Bologna sausage*, fr. *Bologna*, Italy] : a large smoked sausage of beef, veal, and pork

Bol·she·vik \ˈbōl-shə-ˌvik\ *n, pl* **Bolsheviks** *also* **Bol·she·vi·ki** \ˌbōl-shə-ˈvik-ē\ [Russ *bol'shevik*, fr. *bol'she* larger] **1** : a member of the party that seized power in Russia in the revolution of November 1917 **2** : COMMUNIST — **Bolshevik** *adj*

bol·she·vism \ˈbōl-shə-ˌviz-əm\ *n, often cap* : the doctrine or program of the Bolsheviks advocating violent overthrow of capitalism

[1]**bol·ster** \ˈbōl-stər\ *n* : a long pillow or cushion extending from side to side of a bed

[2]**bolster** *vb* **bol·stered; bol·ster·ing** \-st(ə-)riŋ\ : to support with or as if with a bolster; *also* : REINFORCE

[1]**bolt** \ˈbōlt\ *n* **1** : a missile (as an arrow) for a crossbow or catapult **2** : a flash of lightning : THUNDERBOLT **3** : a sliding bar used to fasten a door **4** : a roll of cloth or wallpaper of specified length **5** : a rod with a head at one end and a screw thread at the other used to hold objects in place **6** : a metal cylinder that drives the cartridge into the chamber of a firearm

[2]**bolt** *vb* **1** : to move suddenly (as in fright or hurry) : START, DASH **2** : to break away (as from association) ⟨∼ a political convention⟩ **3** : to secure or fasten with a bolt **4** : to swallow hastily or without chewing

[3]**bolt** *n* : an act of bolting

[4]**bolt** *vb* : SIFT ⟨∼ flour⟩

bo·lus \ˈbō-ləs\ *n* **1** : a large pill **2** : a soft mass of chewed food

[1]**bomb** \ˈbäm\ *n* **1** : a fused explosive device designed to detonate under specified conditions (as impact) **2** : a container of material (as insecticide) under pressure for release in a fine spray **3** : a long pass in football

[2]**bomb** *vb* : to attack with bombs

bom·bard \bäm-ˈbärd, bəm-\ *vb* **1** : to attack esp. with artillery or bombers **2** : to assail persistently **3** : to subject to the impact of rapidly moving particles (as electrons) — **bom·bard·ment** *n*

bom·bar·dier \ˌbäm-bə(r)-ˈdiər\ *n* : a bomber-crew member who releases the bombs

bom·bast \ˈbäm-ˌbast\ *n* [fr. *bombast* cotton padding, fr. MF *bombace*, fr. ML *bombax* cotton, alter. of L *bombyx* silkworm, silk, fr. Gk] : pretentious wordy speech or writing — **bom·bas·tic** \bäm-ˈbas-tik\ *adj*

bom·ba·zine \ˌbäm-bə-ˈzēn\ *n* **1** : a silk fabric in twill weave dyed black **2** : a twilled fabric with silk warp and worsted filling

bomb·er \ˈbäm-ər\ *n* : one that bombs; *esp* : an airplane for dropping bombs

bomb·proof \ˈbäm-ˌprüf\ *adj* : safe against the explosive force of bombs

bomb·shell \ˈbäm-ˌshel\ *n* **1** : BOMB 1 **2** : one that stuns, amazes, or completely upsets

bona fide \ˈbō-nə-ˌfīd, ˈbän-ə-; ˌbō-nə-ˈfīd-ē, -ˈfīd-ə\ *adj* [L, in good faith] **1** : made in good faith ⟨a *bona fide* agreement⟩ **2** : GENUINE, REAL ⟨a *bona fide* bargain⟩ **syn** authentic

bo·nan·za \bə-ˈnan-zə\ *n* [Sp, lit., fair weather, fr. ML *bonacia*, alter. of L *malacia* calm at sea, fr. Gk *malakia*, lit., softness, fr. *malakos* soft] : something yielding a rich return

bon·bon \ˈbän-ˌbän\ *n* : a candy with a creamy center and a soft covering (as of chocolate)

[1]**bond** \ˈbänd\ *n* **1** : FETTER **2** : a binding or uniting force or tie ⟨∼*s* of friendship⟩ **3** : an agreement or obligation often made binding by a pledge of money or goods **4** : a person who acts as surety for another **5** : an interest-bearing certificate of public or private indebtedness **6**

: the state of goods subject to supervision pending payment of taxes or duties due ⟨imports held in ~⟩

[2]**bond** *vb* **1** : to assure payment of duties or taxes on (goods) by giving a bond **2** : to insure against losses caused by the acts of ⟨~ a bank teller⟩ **3** : to make or become firmly united as if by bonds ⟨~ iron to copper⟩

bond·age \ˈbän-dij\ *n* : SLAVERY, SERVITUDE

bond·hold·er \ˈbänd-ˌhōl-dər\ *n* : one that owns a government or corporation bond

bond·ing *n* : the formation of a close personal relationship esp. through frequent or constant association ⟨~ of mother and child⟩

bond·man \ˈbän(d)-mən\ *n* : SLAVE, SERF

[1]**bonds·man** \ˈbän(d)z-mən\ *n* : BONDMAN

[2]**bondsman** *n* : SURETY 3

bond·wom·an \ˈbänd-ˌwu̇m-ən\ *n* : a female slave or serf

[1]**bone** \ˈbōn\ *n* **1** : a hard largely calcareous tissue forming most of the skeleton of a vertebrate animal; *also* : one of the pieces of bone making up a vertebrate skeleton **2** : a hard animal substance (as ivory or whalebone) similar to true bone **3** : something made of bone — **bone·less** *adj* — **bony** *also* **bon·ey** \ˈbō-nē\ *adj*

[2]**bone** *vb* **boned; bon·ing** : to free from bones ⟨~ a chicken⟩

bone black *n* : the black carbon residue from calcined bones used esp. as a pigment

bone meal *n* : fertilizer or feed made of crushed or ground bone

bon·er \ˈbō-nər\ *n* : a stupid and ridiculous blunder

bone up *vb* **1** : CRAM 3 **2** : to refresh one's memory ⟨*boned up* on the speech before giving it⟩

bon·fire \ˈbän-ˌfī(ə)r\ *n* [ME *bonefire* a fire of bones, fr. *bon* bone + *fire*] : a large fire built in the open air

bon·go \ˈbäŋ-gō\ *n, pl* **bongos** *also* **bongoes** [AmerSp *bongó*] : one of a pair of small tuned drums played with the hands

bon·ho·mie \ˌbän-ə-ˈmē\ *n* [F *bonhomie,* fr. *bonhomme* good-natured man, fr. *bon* good + *homme* man] : good-natured easy friendliness

bo·ni·to \bə-ˈnēt-ō\ *n, pl* **-tos** *or* **-to** : any of several medium-sized tunas

bon mot \bōⁿ-ˈmō\ *n, pl* **bons mots** \bōⁿ-ˈmō(z)\ *or* **bon mots** \-ˈmō(z)\ [F, lit., good word] : a clever remark

bon·net \ˈbän-ət\ *n* : a covering (as a cap) for the head; *esp* : a hat for a woman or infant tied under the chin

bon·ny \ˈbän-ē\ *adj* **bon·ni·er; -est** *chiefly Brit* : ATTRACTIVE, FAIR; *also* : FINE, EXCELLENT

bon·sai \bōn-ˈsī\ *n, pl* **bonsai** [Jp] : a potted plant (as a tree) dwarfed by special methods of culture; *also* : the art of growing such a plant

bo·nus \ˈbō-nəs\ *n* : something in addition to what is expected

bon vi·vant \ˌbän-vē-ˈvänt, ˌbōⁿ-vē-ˈväⁿ\ *n, pl* **bons vivants** \ˌbän-vē-ˈvänts, ˌbōⁿ-vē-ˈväⁿ(z)\ *or* **bon vivants** *same*\ [F, lit., good liver] : a person having cultivated, refined, and sociable tastes esp. in food and drink

bon voy·age \ˌbōⁿv-ˌwī-ˈäzh, -ˌwä-ˈyäzh; ˌbän-\ *n* : FAREWELL — often used as an interjection

bonze \ˈbänz\ *n* : a Buddhist monk

boo \ˈbü\ *n, pl* **boos** : a shout of disapproval or contempt — **boo** *vb*

boo·by \ˈbü-bē\ *n, pl* **boobies** : an awkward ineffective person : DOPE

booby hatch *n* : an insane asylum

booby prize *n* : an award for the poorest performance in a contest

booby trap *n* : a trap for the unwary; *esp* : a concealed explosive device set to go off when some harmless-looking object is touched

boo·dle \ˈbüd-ᵊl\ *n* **1** : bribe money **2** : a large amount of money

[1]**book** \ˈbu̇k\ *n* **1** : a set of sheets bound into a volume **2** : a long written or printed narrative or record **3** : a major division of a long literary work **4** *cap* : BIBLE

[2]**book** *vb* **1** : to engage, reserve, or schedule by or as if by writing in a book ⟨~ seats on a plane⟩ **2** : to enter charges against in a police register

book·case \-ˌkās\ *n* : a piece of furniture consisting of shelves to hold books

book·end \-ˌend\ *n* : a support to hold up a row of books

book·ie \ˈbu̇k-ē\ *n* : BOOKMAKER

book·ish \ˈbu̇k-ish\ *adj* **1** : fond of books and reading **2** : inclined to rely unduly on book knowledge

book·keep·er \ˈbu̇k-ˌkē-pər\ *n* : one who records the accounts or transactions of a business — **book·keep·ing** \-piŋ\ *n*

book·let \ˈbu̇k-lət\ *n* : PAMPHLET

book·mak·er \ˈbu̇k-ˌmā-kər\ *n* : one who determines odds and receives and pays off bets — **book·mak·ing** \-kiŋ\ *n*

book·mark \-ˌmärk\ *or* **book·mark·er** \-ˌmär-kər\ *n* : a marker for finding a place in a book

book·mo·bile \ˈbu̇k-mō-ˌbēl\ *n* : a truck that serves as a traveling library

book·plate \ˈbu̇k-ˌplāt\ *n* : a label pasted in a book to show who owns it

book·sell·er \ˈbu̇k-ˌsel-ər\ *n* : one who sells books; *esp* : the proprietor of a bookstore

book·shelf \-ˌshelf\ *n* : a shelf for books

book·worm \ˈbu̇k-ˌwərm\ *n* **1** : a person unusually devoted to reading and study **2** : an insect larva (as of a beetle) that feeds on the binding and paste of a book

[1]**boom** \ˈbüm\ *n* **1** : a long spar used to extend the bottom of a sail **2** : a beam projecting from the upright pole of a derrick to support or guide the object lifted **3** : a line of floating timbers used to obstruct passage or catch floating objects

[2]**boom** *vb* **1** : to make a deep hollow sound : RESOUND **2** : to grow or cause to grow rapidly esp. in value, esteem, or importance

[3]**boom** *n* **1** : a booming sound or cry **2** : a rapid expansion or increase esp. of economic activity

boo·mer·ang \ˈbü-mə-ˌraŋ\ *n* [native name in Australia] : a bent or angular club that can be so thrown as to return near the starting point

[1]**boon** \ˈbün\ *n* [ME, fr. ON *bōn* petition] : BENEFIT, BLESSING **syn** favor, gift, largess, present

[2]**boon** *adj* [ME *bon,* fr. MF, good] : INTIMATE, CONGENIAL

boon·docks \ˈbün-ˌdäks\ *n pl* [Tagalog (language of the Philippines) *bundok* mountain] **1** : rough country filled with dense brush **2** : a rural area

boon·dog·gle \ˈbün-ˌdäg-əl, -ˌdȯg-\ *n* : a useless or wasteful project or activity

boor \ˈbu̇r\ *n* **1** : YOKEL **2** : a rude or insensitive person **syn** churl, lout, clown, clodhopper — **boor·ish** *adj*

boost \ˈbüst\ *vb* **1** : to push up from below **2** : INCREASE, RAISE ⟨~ prices⟩ **3** : AID, PROMOTE ⟨voted a bonus to ~ morale⟩ — **boost** *n* — **boost·er** *n*

[1]**boot** \ˈbüt\ *n, chiefly dial* : something to equalize a trade — **to boot** : BESIDES

[2]**boot** *vb, archaic* : AVAIL, PROFIT

[3]**boot** *n* **1** : a covering for the foot and leg **2** : a protective sheath (as of a flower) **3** *Brit* : an automobile trunk **4** : KICK; *also* : a discharge from employment **5** : a navy or marine corps trainee

[4]**boot** *vb* **1** : KICK **2** : to eject or discharge summarily

boot·black \ˈbüt-ˌblak\ *n* : a person who shines shoes

boo·tee *or* **boo·tie** \ˈbüt-ē\ *n* : an infant's knitted or crocheted sock

booth \ˈbüth\ *n, pl* **booths** \ˈbüt͟hz, ˈbüths\ **1** : a small enclosed stall (as at a fair) **2** : a small enclosure giving privacy for a person ⟨voting ~⟩ ⟨telephone ~⟩ **3** : a restaurant accommodation having a table between backed benches

boot·leg \ˈbüt-ˌleg\ *vb* : to make, transport, or sell (as liquor) illegally — **boot·leg** *adj or n* — **boot·leg·ger** *n*

boot·less \ˈbüt-ləs\ *adj* : USELESS **syn** futile, vain, abortive, fruitless — **boot·less·ly** *adv*

boo·ty \ˈbüt-ē\ *n, pl* **booties** : PLUNDER, SPOIL

[1]**booze** \ˈbüz\ *vb* **boozed; booz·ing** : to drink liquor to excess — **booz·er** *n*

[2]**booze** *n* : intoxicating liquor — **boozy** *adj*

bop \ˈbäp\ *vb* **bopped; bop·ping** : HIT, SOCK — **bop** *n*

BOQ *abbr* bachelor officers' quarters

bor *abbr* borough

bo·rate \ˈbōr-ˌāt\ *n* : a salt or ester of boric acid

bo·rax \ˈbōr-ˌaks\ *n* : a crystalline borate of sodium that occurs as a mineral and is used as a flux and cleanser

bor·del·lo \bȯr-ˈdel-ō\ *n, pl* **-los** [It] : BROTHEL

[1]**bor·der** \ˈbȯrd-ər\ *n* **1** : EDGE, MARGIN **2** : BOUNDARY, FRONTIER **syn** rim, brim, brink, fringe, perimeter

[2]**border** *vb* **bor·dered; bor·der·ing** \ˈbȯrd-(ə-)riŋ\ **1** : to put a border on **2** : ADJOIN **3** : VERGE

bor·der·land \ˈbȯrd-ər-ˌland\ *n* **1** : territory at or near a border **2** : an outlying or intermediate region often not clearly defined

bor·der·line \-ˌlīn\ *adj* : being in an intermediate position or state; *esp* : not quite up to what is standard or expected ⟨~ intelligence⟩

[1]**bore** \ˈbōr\ *vb* **bored; bor·ing** **1** : to make a hole in with or as if with a drill **2** : to make (as a well) by boring or digging away material **syn** perforate, drill, prick, puncture — **bor·er** *n*

[2]**bore** *n* **1** : a hole made by or as if by boring **2** : a cylindrical cavity **3** : the diameter of a hole or tube; *esp* : the interior diameter of a gun barrel or engine cylinder

[3]**bore** *past of* BEAR

[4]**bore** *n* : a tidal flood with a high abrupt front

[5]**bore** *n* : one that causes boredom

[6]**bore** *vb* **bored; bor·ing** : to weary with tedious dullness

bo·re·al \ˈbōr-ē-əl\ *adj* : of, relating to, or located in northern regions

bore·dom \ˈbōrd-əm\ *n* : the condition of being bored

bo·ric acid \ˌbōr-ik-\ *n* : a white crystalline weak acid that contains boron and is used as an antiseptic

born \ˈbȯrn\ *adj* **1** : brought into life by birth **2** : NATIVE ⟨American-*born*⟩ **3** : having special natural abilities or character from birth ⟨a ~ leader⟩

born–again *adj* : having experienced a revival of a personal faith or conviction ⟨~ believer⟩ ⟨~ liberal⟩

borne *past part of* BEAR

bo·ron \ˈbōr-ˌän\ *n* : a chemical element that occurs in nature only in combination (as in borax) — see ELEMENT table

bor·ough \ˈbər-ō\ *n* **1** : a British town that sends one or more members to Parliament; *also* : an incorporated British urban area **2** : an incorporated town or village in some U.S. states; *also* : any of the five political divisions of New York City **3** : a civil division of the state of Alaska corresponding to a county in most other states

bor·row \ˈbär-ō\ *vb* **1** : to take or receive (something) temporarily and with intent to return **2** : to take into possession or use from another source : DERIVE, APPROPRIATE ⟨~ a metaphor⟩

borscht *or* **borsch** \ˈbȯrsh(t)\ *n* [Russ *borshch*] : a soup made mainly from beets

bosh \ˈbäsh\ *n* [Turk *boş* empty] : foolish talk or action : NONSENSE

bosky \ˈbäs-kē\ *adj* : covered with trees or shrubs

[1]**bo·som** \ˈbu̇z-əm, ˈbüz-\ *n* **1** : the front of the human chest; *esp* : the female breasts **2** : the part of a garment covering the breast **3** : the seat of secret thoughts and feelings — **bo·somed** \-əmd\ *adj*

[2]**bosom** *adj* : CLOSE, INTIMATE

[1]**boss** \ˈbäs, ˈbȯs\ *n* : a knoblike ornament : STUD

[2]**boss** *vb* : to ornament with bosses

[3]**boss** \ˈbȯs\ *n* **1** : one (as a foreman or manager) exercising control or supervision **2** : a politician who controls votes or dictates policies — **bossy** *adj*

[4]**boss** \ˈbȯs\ *vb* : to act as a boss : SUPERVISE

bo·sun \ˈbōs-ᵊn\ *var of* BOATSWAIN

bot *abbr* botanical; botanist; botany

bot·a·ny \ˈbät-(ᵊ-)nē\ *n, pl* **-nies** **1** : a branch of biology dealing with plants and plant life **2** : plant life (as of a given region); *also* : the biology of a plant or plant group — **bo·tan·i·cal** \bə-ˈtan-i-kəl\ *adj* — **bot·a·nist** \ˈbät-(ᵊ-)nəst\ *n* — **bot·a·nize** \-ᵊn-ˌīz\ *vb*

botch \ˈbäch\ *vb* : to foul up hopelessly : BUNGLE — **botch** *n*

[1]**both** \ˈbōth\ *adj* : being the two : affecting the one and the other

[2]**both** *pron* : both ones : the one as well as the other

[3]**both** *conj* — used as a function word to indicate and stress the inclusion of each of two or more things specified by coordinated words, phrases, or clauses ⟨~ New York and London⟩

both·er \ˈbät͟h-ər\ *vb* **-ered; -er·ing** \-(ə-)riŋ\ : WORRY, PESTER, TROUBLE **syn** vex, annoy, irk, provoke — **bother** *n* — **both·er·some** \-səm\ *adj*

[1]**bot·tle** \ˈbät-ᵊl\ *n* **1** : a container (as of glass) with a narrow neck and usu. no handles **2** : the quantity held by a bottle **3** : intoxicating liquor

[2]**bottle** *vb* **bot·tled; bot·tling** \ˈbät-(ᵊ-)liŋ\ **1** : to confine as if in a bottle : RESTRAIN **2** : to put into a bottle

bot·tle·neck \ˈbät-ᵊl-ˌnek\ *n* **1** : a narrow passage or point of congestion **2** : something that obstructs or impedes

bot·tom \ˈbät-əm\ *n* **1** : an under or supporting surface; *also* : BUTTOCKS **2** : the surface on which a body of water lies **3** : the lowest part or place; *also* : an inferior position ⟨start at the ~⟩ **4** : low land along a river — **bottom** *adj* — **bot·tom·less** *adj*

bot·tom·land \ˈbät-əm-ˌland\ *n* : BOTTOM 4

bottom line *n* **1** : the essential point : CRUX **2** : the final result : OUTCOME

bottom out *vb* : to reach a low point before rebounding ⟨a security market that *bottoms out*⟩

bot·u·lism \ˈbäch-ə-ˌliz-əm\ *n* : acute food poisoning caused by a bacterial toxin in food

bou·doir \ˈbüd-ˌwär, ˈbu̇d-\ *n* [F, fr. *bouder* to pout] : a woman's private room

bouf·fant \bü-ˈfänt, ˈbü-ˌfänt\ *adj* [F] : puffed out ⟨~ hairdos⟩

bough \ˈbau̇\ *n* : a usu. large or main branch of a tree

bought *past and past part of* BUY

bouil·la·baisse \ˌbü-yə-ˈbās\ *n* [F] : a highly seasoned fish stew made with at least two kinds of fish

bouil·lon \ˈbü-ˌyän; ˈbu̇l-ˌyän, -yən\ *n* : a clear soup made usu. from beef

boul·der \ˈbōl-dər\ *n* : a large detached rounded or worn mass of rock — **boul·dered** \-dərd\ *adj*

bou·le·vard \ˈbu̇l-ə-ˌvärd, ˈbül-\ *n* [F, modif. of Middle Dutch *bolwerc* bulwark; so called because the first boulevards were laid out on the sites of razed city fortifications] : a broad often landscaped thoroughfare

bounce \ˈbau̇ns\ *vb* **bounced; bounc·ing** **1** : to cause to rebound ⟨~ a ball⟩ **2** : to rebound after striking — **bounce** *n*

bounc·er \ˈbau̇n-sər\ *n* : someone employed in a public place to remove disorderly persons

[1]**bound** \ˈbau̇nd\ *adj* : intending to go

[2]**bound** *n* : LIMIT, BOUNDARY — **bound·less** *adj* — **bound·less·ness** *n*

[3]**bound** *vb* **1** : to set limits to **2** : to form the boundary of **3** : to name the boundaries of

[4]**bound** *past and past part of* BIND

[5]**bound** *adj* **1** : constrained by or as if by bonds : CONFINED, OBLIGED **2** : enclosed in a binding or cover **3** : RESOLVED, DETERMINED; *also* : SURE

[6]**bound** *n* **1** : LEAP, JUMP **2** : REBOUND, BOUNCE

[7]**bound** *vb* : SPRING, BOUNCE

bound·ary \ˈbau̇n-d(ə-)rē\ *n, pl* **-aries** : something that marks or fixes a limit (as of territory) **syn** border, frontier, march

bound·en \ˈbau̇n-dən\ *adj* : BINDING

boun·te·ous \ˈbau̇nt-ē-əs\ *adj* **1** : GENEROUS **2** : ABUNDANT — **boun·te·ous·ly** *adv*

boun·ti·ful \ˈbau̇nt-i-fəl\ *adj* **1** : giving freely **2** : PLENTIFUL — **boun·ti·ful·ly** *adv*

boun·ty \ˈbau̇nt-ē\ *n, pl* **bounties** [ME *bounte* goodness, fr. OF *bonté*, fr. L *bonitas*, fr. *bonus* good] **1** : GENEROSITY **2** : something given liberally **3** : a reward, premium, or subsidy given usu. for doing something

bou·quet \bō-ˈkā, bü-\ *n* [F, fr. MF, thicket, fr. OF *bosc* forest] **1** : flowers picked and fastened together in a bunch **2** : a distinctive aroma (as of wine) **syn** scent, fragrance, perfume, redolence

bour·bon \ˈbər-bən\ *n* : a whiskey distilled from a corn mash

bour·geois \ˈbu̇rzh-ˌwä, bu̇rzh-ˈwä\ *n, pl* **bourgeois** \-ˌwä(z), -ˈwä(z)\ [MF, lit., citizen of a town, fr. *borc* town, borough, fr. L *burgus* fortified place, of Gmc origin] : a middle-class person — **bourgeois** *adj*

bour·geoi·sie \ˌbu̇rzh-ˌwä-ˈzē\ *n* : a social order dominated by bourgeois

bourn *or* **bourne** \ˈbōrn, ˈbu̇rn\ *n, archaic* : BOUNDARY; *also* : DESTINATION

bourse \ˈbu̇rs\ *n* : a European stock exchange

bout \ˈbau̇t\ *n* **1** : CONTEST, MATCH **2** : OUTBREAK, ATTACK ⟨a ~ of measles⟩ **3** : SESSION

bou·tique \bü-ˈtēk\ *n* : a fashionable specialty shop

bou·ton·niere \ˌbüt-ᵊn-ˈiər\ *n* : a flower or bouquet worn in a buttonhole

bo·vine \ˈbō-ˌvīn, -ˌvēn\ *adj* : of, relating to, or resembling the ox or cow — **bovine** *n*

[1]**bow** \ˈbau̇\ *vb* **1** : SUBMIT, YIELD **2** : to bend the head or body (as in submission, courtesy, or assent)

[2]**bow** *n* : an act or posture of bowing

[3]**bow** \ˈbō\ *n* **1** : BEND, ARCH; *esp* : RAINBOW **2** : a weapon for shooting arrows; *also* : ARCHER **3** : a knot formed by doubling a line into two or more loops **4** : a wooden rod strung with horsehairs for playing an instrument of the violin family

[4]**bow** \ˈbō\ *vb* **1** : BEND, CURVE **2** : to play (an instrument) with a bow

[5]**bow** \ˈbau̇\ *n* : the forward part of a ship — **bow** *adj*

bowd·ler·ize \ˈbōd-lə-ˌrīz, ˈbau̇d-\ *vb* **-ized; -iz·ing** : to expurgate by omitting parts considered vulgar

bow·el \ˈbau̇(-ə)l\ *n* **1** : INTESTINE — usu. used in pl. **2** : one of the divisions of the intestine **3** *pl* : the inmost parts ⟨the ~*s* of the earth⟩

bow·er \ˈbau̇(-ə)r\ *n* : a shelter of boughs or vines : ARBOR

[1]**bowl** \ˈbōl\ *n* **1** : a concave vessel used to hold liquids **2** : a drinking vessel **3** : a bowl-shaped part or structure — **bowl·ful** \-ˌfu̇l\ *n*

[2]**bowl** *n* **1** : a ball for rolling on a level surface in bowling **2** : a cast of the ball in bowling

[3]**bowl** *vb* **1** : to play a game of bowling; *also* : to roll a ball in bowling **2** : to travel (as in a vehicle) rapidly and smoothly **3** : to strike or knock down with a moving object; *also* : to overwhelm with surprise

bowlder *var of* BOULDER

bow·legged \ˈbō-ˌleg-əd\ *adj* : having legs that bow outward at or below the knee — **bow·leg** \ˈbō-ˌleg\ *n*

[1]**bowl·er** \ˈbō-lər\ *n* : one that bowls

[2]**bow·ler** \ˈbō-lər\ *n* : DERBY 3

bow·line \ˈbō-lən, -ˌlīn\ *n* : a knot used to form a loop that neither slips nor jams

bowl·ing \ˈbō-liŋ\ *n* : any of various games in which balls are rolled on a green or alley at an object or a group of objects; *esp* : TENPINS

bow·man \ˈbō-mən\ *n* : ARCHER

bow·sprit \ˈbau̇-ˌsprit\ *n* : a spar projecting forward from the prow of a ship

bow·string \ˈbō-ˌstriŋ\ *n* : the cord connecting the two ends of a bow

[1]**box** \ˈbäks\ *n, pl* **box** *or* **box·es** : an evergreen shrub or small tree used esp. for hedges

[2]**box** *n* **1** : a rigid typically rectangular receptacle often with a cover; *also* : the quantity held by a box **2** : a small compartment (as for a group of theater patrons); *also* : a boxlike receptacle or division **3** : any of six spaces on a baseball diamond where the batter, pitcher, coaches, and catcher stand **4** : PREDICAMENT

[3]**box** *vb* : to furnish with or enclose in or as if in a box

[4]**box** *n* : a punch or slap esp. on the ear

[5]**box** *vb* **1** : to strike with the hand **2** : to engage in boxing with : fight with the fists **syn** smack, cuff, strike, slap

box·car \ˈbäks-ˌkär\ *n* : a roofed freight car usu. with sliding doors in the sides

[1]**box·er** \ˈbäk-sər\ *n* : one that engages in boxing

[2]**boxer** *n* : a compact short-haired usu. fawn or brindled dog of a breed of German origin

box·ing \ˈbäk-siŋ\ *n* : the sport of fighting with the fists

box office *n* : an office (as in a theater) where admission tickets are sold

box·wood \ˈbäks-ˌwu̇d\ *n* : the tough hard wood of the box; *also* : a box tree or shrub

boy \ˈbȯi\ *n* **1** : a male child : YOUTH **2** : SON — **boy·hood** \-ˌhu̇d\ *n* — **boy·ish** *adj* — **boy·ish·ly** *adv* — **boy·ish·ness** *n*

boy·cott \ˈbȯi-ˌkät\ *vb* [Charles C. *Boycott* †1897 E land agent in Ireland who was ostracized for refusing to reduce rents] : to refrain from having any dealings with — **boycott** *n*

Boy Scout *n* : a member of the Boy Scouts of America

boy·sen·ber·ry \ˈbȯiz-ᵊn-ˌber-ē, ˈbȯis-\ *n* : a large bramble fruit with a raspberry flavor; *also* : the hybrid plant bearing it developed by crossing blackberries and raspberries

bp *abbr* bishop

BP *abbr* **1** blood pressure **2** boiling point

bpl *abbr* birthplace

BPOE *abbr* Benevolent and Protective Order of Elks

br *abbr* **1** branch **2** brass **3** brown

[1]**Br** *abbr* Britain; British

[2]**Br** *symbol* bromine

BR *abbr* bedroom

bra \ˈbrä\ *n* : BRASSIERE

[1]**brace** \ˈbrās\ *vb* **braced; brac·ing 1** *archaic* : to make fast : BIND **2** : to tighten preparatory to use; *also* : to get ready for : prepare oneself **3** : INVIGORATE **4** : to furnish or support with a brace; *also* : STRENGTHEN **5** : to set firmly; *also* : to gain courage or confidence

[2]**brace** *n, pl* **brac·es 1** *or pl* **brace** : two of a kind ⟨~ of dogs⟩ **2** : a crank-shaped device for turning a bit **3** : something (as a tie, prop, or clamp) that distributes, directs, or resists pressure or weight **4** *pl* : SUSPENDERS **5** : an appliance for supporting a body part (as the shoulders) **6** *pl* : dental appliances used to exert pressure to straighten misaligned teeth **7** : a mark { or } or ⏞ used to connect words or items to be considered together

brace·let \ˈbrā-slət\ *n* [ME, fr. MF, dim. of *bras* arm, fr. L *bracchium*, fr. Gk *brachiōn*] : an ornamental band or chain worn around the wrist

bra·ce·ro \brä-ˈser-ō\ *n, pl* **-ros** : a Mexican laborer admitted to the U.S. esp. for seasonal farm work

brack·en \ˈbrak-ən\ *n* : a large coarse fern; *also* : a growth of such ferns

[1]**brack·et** \ˈbrak-ət\ *n* **1** : a projecting framework or arm designed to support weight; *also* : a shelf on such framework **2** : one of a pair of punctuation marks [ ]

used esp. to enclose interpolated matter **3** : a continuous section of a series; *esp* : one of a graded series of income groups

2bracket *vb* **1** : to furnish or fasten with brackets **2** : to place within brackets; *also* : to separate or group with or as if with brackets

brack·ish \ˈbrak-ish\ *adj* : somewhat salty — **brack·ish·ness** *n*

bract \ˈbrakt\ *n* : an often modified leaf on or at the base of a flower stalk

brad \ˈbrad\ *n* : a slender nail with a small head

brae \ˈbrā\ *n, chiefly Scot* : a hillside esp. along a river

brag \ˈbrag\ *vb* **bragged; brag·ging** : to talk or assert boastfully — **brag** *n*

brag·ga·do·cio \ˌbrag-ə-ˈdō-s(h)ē-ˌō, -(ˌ)shō\ *n, pl* **-cios 1** : BRAGGART, BOASTER **2** : empty boasting **3** : arrogant pretension : COCKINESS

brag·gart \ˈbrag-ərt\ *n* : one who brags

Brah·man *or* **Brah·min** \ˈbräm-ən *for 1;* ˈbrām-, ˈbräm-, ˈbram- *for 2*\ *n* **1** : a Hindu of the highest caste traditionally assigned to the priesthood **2** : any of a breed of large vigorous humped cattle developed in the southern U.S. from Indian stock **3** *usu Brahmin* : a person of high social standing and cultivated intellect and taste

Brah·man·ism \ˈbräm-ə-ˌniz-əm\ *n* : orthodox Hinduism

1braid \ˈbrād\ *vb* **1** : to form (strands) into a braid : PLAIT; *also* : to make by braiding **2** : to ornament with braid

2braid *n* **1** : a cord or ribbon of three or more interwoven strands; *also* : a length of braided hair **2** : a narrow ornamental fabric of intertwined threads

braille \ˈbrāl\ *n, often cap* : a system of writing for the blind that uses characters made up of raised dots

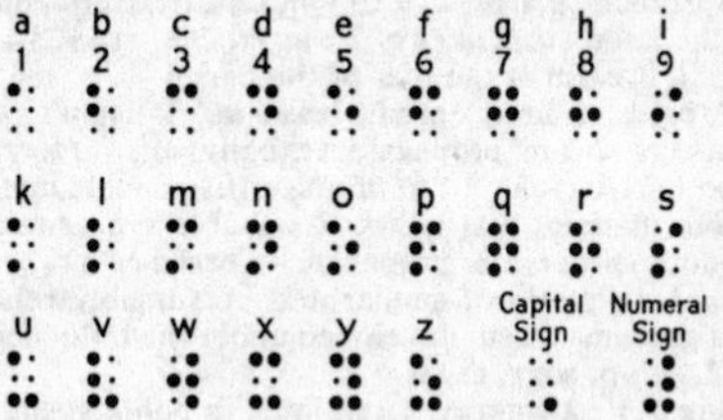

a b c d e f g h i j
1 2 3 4 5 6 7 8 9 0
k l m n o p q r s t
u v w x y z Capital Sign Numeral Sign

braille alphabet

1brain \ˈbrān\ *n* **1** : the part of the vertebrate nervous system that is the organ of thought and nervous coordination, is made up of nerve cells and their fibers, and is enclosed in the skull; *also* : a centralized mass of nerve tissue in an invertebrate **2** : INTELLECT, INTELLIGENCE — often used in pl. — **brained** \ˈbrānd\ *adj* — **brain·less** *adj* — **brainy** *adj*

2brain *vb* **1** : to kill by smashing the skull **2** : to hit on the head

brain·child \-ˌchīld\ *n* : a product of one's creative imagination

brain death *n* : final cessation of activity in the central nervous system esp. as indicated by a flat electroencephalogram

brain drain *n* : a migration of professional people (as scientists) from one country to another usu. for higher pay

brain·storm \-ˌstȯrm\ *n* : a sudden burst of inspiration

brain·wash·ing \ˈbrān-ˌwȯsh-iŋ, -ˌwäsh-\ *n* **1** : a forcible attempt by indoctrination to induce someone to give up his basic political, social, or religious beliefs and attitudes and to accept contrasting regimented ideas **2** : persuasion by propaganda or salesmanship — **brainwash** *vb*

brain wave *n* : rhythmic fluctuation of voltage between parts of the brain; *also* : a current produced by brain waves

braise \ˈbrāz\ *vb* **braised; brais·ing** : to cook (meat) slowly in fat and little moisture in a closed pot

1brake \ˈbrāk\ *n* : any of a genus of tall coarse ferns with compound fronds

2brake *n* : a device for slowing or stopping motion esp. by friction — **brake·less** *adj*

3brake *vb* **braked; brak·ing 1** : to slow or stop by or as if by a brake **2** : to apply a brake

4brake *n* : rough or wet land heavily overgrown (as with thickets or reeds)

brake·man \ˈbrāk-mən\ *n* : a train crew member who inspects the train and assists the conductor

bram·ble \ˈbram-bəl\ *n* : any of a large genus of prickly shrubs (as a blackberry) related to the roses; *also* : any rough prickly shrub or vine

bran \ˈbran\ *n* : broken husks of cereal grain sifted from flour or meal

1branch \ˈbranch\ *n* [ME, fr. OF *branche,* fr. L *branca* paw] **1** : a natural subdivision (as a bough or twig) of a plant stem **2** : a division (as of an antler or a river) related to a whole like a plant branch to its stem **3** : a discrete unit or element of a complex system (as of knowledge, people, or business); *esp* : a division of a family descended from one ancestor — **branched** \ˈbrancht\ *adj*

2branch *vb* **1** : to develop branches **2** : DIVERGE

1brand \ˈbrand\ *n* **1** : a piece of charred or burning wood **2** : a mark made (as by burning) usu. to identify; *also* : a mark of disgrace : STIGMA **3** : a class of goods identified as the product of a particular firm or producer **4** : a distinctive kind ⟨his own ~ of humor⟩

2brand *vb* **1** : to mark with a brand **2** : STIGMATIZE

bran·dish \ˈbran-dish\ *vb* : to shake or wave menacingly **syn** flourish, flash, flaunt

brand–new \ˈbran-ˈn(y)ü\ *adj* : conspicuously new and unused

bran·dy \ˈbran-dē\ *n, pl* **brandies** [short for *brandywine,* fr. Dutch *brandewijn,* fr. Middle Dutch *brantwijn,* fr. *brant* distilled + *wijn* wine] : a liquor distilled from wine or fermented fruit juice — **brandy** *vb*

brash \ˈbrash\ *adj* **1** : IMPETUOUS **2** : aggressively self-assertive

brass \ˈbras\ *n* **1** : an alloy of copper and zinc; *also* : an object of brass **2** : brazen self-assurance — **brassy** *adj*

bras·se·rie \ˌbras-(ə-)ˈrē\ *n* : an informal usu. French restaurant serving simple hearty food

brass hat *n* : a high-ranking military officer

bras·siere \brə-ˈziər\ *n* : a woman's close-fitting undergarment designed to support the breasts

brat \ˈbrat\ *n* : an ill-behaved child — **brat·ty** *adj*

bra·va·do \brə-ˈväd-ō\ *n, pl* **-does** *or* **-dos 1** : blustering swaggering conduct **2** : a show of bravery

1brave \ˈbrāv\ *adj* **brav·er; brav·est** [MF, fr. It & Sp *bravo* courageous, wild, fr. L *barbarus* barbarous] **1** : showing courage **2** : EXCELLENT, SPLENDID **syn** bold, intrepid, courageous, valiant — **brave·ly** *adv*

2brave *vb* **braved; brav·ing** : to face or endure bravely

3brave *n* : an American Indian warrior

brav·ery \ˈbrāv-(ə-)rē\ *n, pl* **-er·ies** : COURAGE

bra·vo \ˈbräv-ō\ *n, pl* **bravos** : a shout of approval — often used as an interjection in applauding

bra·vu·ra \brə-ˈv(y)ůr-ə\ *n* **1** : a florid brilliant musical style **2** : self-assured brilliant performance

brawl \ˈbrȯl\ *n* : a noisy quarrel **syn** fracas, row, rumpus, scrap, fray, melee — **brawl** *vb* — **brawl·er** *n*

\ə\abut \ᵊ\kitten \ər\further \a\ash \ā\ace \ä\cot, cart \aů\out \ch\chin \e\bet \ē\easy \g\go \i\hit \ī\ice \j\job \ŋ\sing \ō\go \ȯ\law \ȯi\boy \th\thin \th\the \ü\loot \ů\foot \y\yet \zh\vision *see also* Pronunciation Symbols page

brawn \ˈbrȯn\ *n* : strong muscles; *also* : muscular strength — **brawny** *adj*

bray \ˈbrā\ *n* : the characteristic harsh cry of a donkey — **bray** *vb*

braze \ˈbrāz\ *vb* **brazed; braz·ing** : to solder with an alloy (as brass) that melts at a lower temperature than that of the metals being joined — **braz·er** *n*

bra·zen \ˈbrāz-ᵊn\ *adj* **1** : made of brass **2** : sounding harsh and loud **3** : of the color of brass **4** : marked by contemptuous boldness — **bra·zen·ly** *adv* — **bra·zen·ness** \ˈbrāz-ᵊn-(n)əs\ *n*

¹**bra·zier** \ˈbrā-zhər\ *n* : a worker in brass

²**brazier** *n* **1** : a vessel holding burning coals (as for heating) **2** : a device on which food is grilled

Bra·zil·ian \brə-ˈzil-yən\ *n* : a native or inhabitant of Brazil — **Brazilian** *adj*

Bra·zil nut \brə-ˈzil-\ *n* : a triangular oily edible nut borne in large capsules by a tall So. American tree; *also* : the tree

¹**breach** \ˈbrēch\ *n* **1** : a breaking of a law, obligation, tie (as of friendship), or standard (as of conduct) **2** : an interruption or opening made by or as if by breaking through **syn** violation, transgression, infringement, trespass

²**breach** *vb* : to make a breach in

¹**bread** \ˈbred\ *n* **1** : baked food made basically of flour or meal **2** : FOOD

²**bread** *vb* : to cover with bread crumbs before cooking

bread·bas·ket \ˈbred-ˌbas-kət\ *n* : a major cereal-producing region

bread·fruit \-ˌfrüt\ *n* : a round usu. seedless fruit resembling bread in color and texture when baked; *also* : a tall tropical tree related to the mulberry and bearing breadfruit

bread·stuff \-ˌstəf\ *n* : GRAIN, FLOUR

breadth \ˈbredth, ˈbretth\ *n* **1** : WIDTH **2** : SPACIOUSNESS; *also* : liberality of taste or views

bread·win·ner \ˈbred-ˌwin-ər\ *n* : a member of a family whose wages supply its livelihood

¹**break** \ˈbrāk\ *vb* **broke** \ˈbrōk\; **bro·ken** \ˈbrō-kən\; **break·ing** **1** : to separate into parts usu. suddenly or violently : come or force apart **2** : TRANSGRESS ⟨~ a law⟩ **3** : to force a way into, out of, or through **4** : to disrupt the order or unity of ⟨~ ranks⟩ ⟨~ up a gang⟩; *also* : to bring to submission or helplessness **5** : EXCEED, SURPASS ⟨~ a record⟩ **6** : RUIN **7** : to make known **8** : HALT, INTERRUPT; *also* : to act or change abruptly (as a course or activity) **9** : to come esp. suddenly into being or notice ⟨as day ~*s*⟩ **10** : to fail under stress **11** : HAPPEN, DEVELOP — **break·able** *adj or n*

²**break** *n* **1** : an act of breaking **2** : a result of breaking; *esp* : an interruption of continuity ⟨coffee ~⟩ ⟨a ~ for the commercial⟩ **3** : a stroke of good luck

break·age \ˈbrā-kij\ *n* **1** : the action of breaking **2** : articles or amount broken **3** : loss due to things broken

break·down \ˈbrāk-ˌdau̇n\ *n* **1** : functional failure; *esp* : a physical, mental, or nervous collapse **2** : DISINTEGRATION **3** : DECOMPOSITION **4** : ANALYSIS, CLASSIFICATION — **break down** \(ˈ)brāk-ˈdau̇n\ *vb*

break·er \ˈbrā-kər\ *n* **1** : one that breaks **2** : a wave that breaks into foam (as against the shore)

break·fast \ˈbrek-fəst\ *n* : the first meal of the day — **breakfast** *vb*

break·front \ˈbrāk-ˌfrənt\ *n* : a large cabinet whose center section projects beyond the flanking end sections

break in \(ˈ)brāk-ˈin\ *vb* **1** : to enter a building by force **2** : INTERRUPT; *also* : INTRUDE **3** : TRAIN

break out \(ˈ)brāk-ˈau̇t\ *vb* **1** : to develop or erupt suddenly and with force **2** : to develop a skin rash

break·through \ˈbrāk-ˌthrü\ *n* **1** : an act or instance of breaking through an obstruction or defensive line **2** : a sudden advance in knowledge or technique

break·up \ˈbrāk-ˌəp\ *n* **1** : DISSOLUTION **2** : a division into smaller units — **break up** *vb*

break·wa·ter \ˈbrāk-ˌwȯt-ər, -ˌwät-\ *n* : a structure built to protect a harbor or beach from the force of waves

bream \ˈbrim, brēm\ *n, pl* **bream** *or* **breams** : any of various small freshwater sunfishes

breast \ˈbrest\ *n* **1** : either of two milk-producing glandular organs situated on the front of the chest esp. in the human female **2** : the front part of the body between the neck and the abdomen **3** : the seat of emotion and thought

breast·bone \ˈbres(t)-ˈbōn, -ˌbōn\ *n* : STERNUM

breast–feed \ˈbrest-ˌfēd\ *vb* : to feed (a baby) from a mother's breast rather than from a bottle

breast·plate \ˈbres(t)-ˌplāt\ *n* : a metal plate of armor for protecting the breast

breast·stroke \-ˌstrōk\ *n* : a swimming stroke executed by extending the arms in front of the head while drawing the knees forward and outward and then sweeping the arms back with palms out while kicking backward and outward

breast·work \ˈbrest-ˌwərk\ *n* : a temporary fortification

breath \ˈbreth\ *n* **1** : the act or power of breathing **2** : a slight breeze **3** : air inhaled or exhaled in breathing **4** : spoken sound **5** : SPIRIT — **breath·less** *adj* — **breath·less·ly** *adv*

breathe \ˈbrēth\ *vb* **breathed; breath·ing** **1** : to inhale and exhale **2** : LIVE **3** : to halt for rest **4** : to utter softly or secretly

breath·tak·ing \ˈbreth-ˌtā-kiŋ\ *adj* **1** : making one out of breath **2** : EXCITING, THRILLING ⟨~ beauty⟩

brec·cia \ˈbrech-(ē-)ə\ *n* : a rock consisting of sharp fragments held in fine-grained material

breech \ˈbrēch\ *n* **1** *pl* *usu* ˈbrich-əz\ : trousers ending near the knee; *also* : PANTS **2** : BUTTOCKS, RUMP **3** : the part of a firearm at the rear of the barrel

¹**breed** \ˈbrēd\ *vb* **bred** \ˈbred\; **breed·ing** **1** : BEGET; *also* : ORIGINATE **2** : to propagate sexually; *also* : MATE **3** : BRING UP, NURTURE **4** : to produce (fissionable material) from material that is not fissionable **syn** generate, reproduce, procreate, propagate — **breed·er** *n*

²**breed** *n* **1** : a strain of similar and presumably related plants or animals usu. developed under the influence of man **2** : KIND, SORT, CLASS

breed·ing *n* **1** : ANCESTRY **2** : training in polite social interaction **3** : sexual propagation of plants or animals

¹**breeze** \ˈbrēz\ *n* : a light wind — **breezy** *adj*

²**breeze** *vb* **breezed; breez·ing** : to progress quickly and easily

breeze·way \ˈbrēz-ˌwā\ *n* : a roofed open passage connecting two buildings (as a house and garage)

breth·ren \ˈbreth-(ə-)rən, -ərn\ *pl of* BROTHER — used esp. in formal or solemn address

Brethren *n pl* : members of one of several Protestant denominations originating chiefly in a German religious movement and stressing personal religious experience

bre·vet \bri-ˈvet\ *n* : a commission giving a military officer higher nominal rank than that for which he receives pay — **brevet** *vb*

bre·via·ry \ˈbrē-vyə-rē, -vē-ˌer-ē\ *n, pl* **-ries** : a book of prayers, hymns, psalms, and readings used by Roman Catholic priests

brev·i·ty \ˈbrev-ət-ē\ *n, pl* **-ties** : shortness of duration; *esp* : shortness or conciseness of expression

brew \ˈbrü\ *vb* **1** : to prepare (as beer) by steeping, boiling, and fermenting **2** : to prepare (as tea) by soaking in hot water — **brew** *n* — **brew·er** *n* — **brew·ery** \ˈbrü-ə-rē, ˈbru̇(-ə)r-ē\ *n*

bri·ar \ˈbrī(-ə)r\ *n* : a tobacco pipe made from the root of a brier

¹**bribe** \ˈbrīb\ *n* [ME, something stolen, fr. MF, bread given to a beggar] : something (as money or a favor) given or promised to a person to influence conduct

[2]**bribe** *vb* **bribed; brib·ing** : to corrupt or influence by offering a bribe — **brib·ery** \ˈbrī-b(ə-)rē\ *n*

bric–a–brac \ˈbrik-ə-ˌbrak\ *n pl* [F] : small ornamental articles

[1]**brick** \ˈbrik\ *n* : a block molded from moist clay and hardened by heat used esp. for building

[2]**brick** *vb* : to close, cover, or pave with bricks

brick·bat \ˈbrik-ˌbat\ *n* **1** : a piece of a broken brick esp. when thrown as a missile **2** : an uncomplimentary remark

brick·lay·er \ˈbrik-ˌlā-ər\ *n* : a person who builds or paves with bricks — **brick·lay·ing** \-ˌlā-iŋ\ *n*

[1]**brid·al** \ˈbrīd-ᵊl\ *n* [ME *bridale,* fr. OE *brȳdealu,* fr. *brȳd* bride + *ealu* ale] : MARRIAGE, WEDDING

[2]**bridal** *adj* : of or relating to a bride or a wedding

bride \ˈbrīd\ *n* : a woman just married or about to be married

bride·groom \ˈbrīd-ˌgrüm, -ˌgrům\ *n* : a man just married or about to be married

brides·maid \ˈbrīdz-ˌmād\ *n* : a woman who attends a bride at her wedding

[1]**bridge** \ˈbrij\ *n* **1** : a structure built over a depression or obstacle for use as a passageway **2** : something (as the upper part of the nose) resembling a bridge in form or function; *esp* : a platform over the deck of a ship **3** : an artificial replacement for missing teeth

[2]**bridge** *vb* **bridged; bridg·ing** : to build a bridge over — **bridge·able** *adj*

[3]**bridge** *n* : a card game for four players developed from whist

bridge·head \-ˌhed\ *n* : an advanced position seized in enemy territory as a foothold

bridge·work \-ˌwərk\ *n* : dental bridges

[1]**bri·dle** \ˈbrīd-ᵊl\ *n* **1** : headgear with which a horse is controlled **2** : CURB, RESTRAINT

[2]**bridle** *vb* **bri·dled; bri·dling** \ˈbrīd-(ᵊ-)liŋ\ **1** : to put a bridle on; *also* : to restrain with or as if with a bridle **2** : to show hostility or scorn usu. by tossing the head

[1]**brief** \ˈbrēf\ *adj* **1** : short in duration or extent **2** : CONCISE; *also* : CURT — **brief·ly** *adv* — **brief·ness** *n*

[2]**brief** *n* **1** : a concise statement or document; *esp* : one summarizing a law client's case or a legal argument **2** *pl* : short snug underpants

[3]**brief** *vb* : to give final instructions or essential information to

brief·case \ˈbrēf-ˌkās\ *n* : a flat flexible case for carrying papers

[1]**bri·er** *or* **bri·ar** \ˈbrī(-ə)r\ *n* : a plant (as a bramble or rose) with a thorny or prickly woody stem; *also* : a group or mass of brier bushes — **bri·ery** \ˈbrī(-ə)r-ē\ *adj*

[2]**brier** *or* **briar** *n* : a heath of southern Europe with a root used for making pipes

[1]**brig** \ˈbrig\ *n* : a 2-masted square-rigged sailing ship

[2]**brig** *n* : the place of confinement for offenders on a naval ship

[3]**brig** *abbr* **1** brigade **2** brigadier

bri·gade \brig-ˈād\ *n* **1** : a military unit composed of a headquarters, one or more units of infantry or armored forces, and supporting units **2** : a group organized for a particular purpose (as fire-fighting)

brig·a·dier general \ˌbrig-ə-ˌdiər-\ *n* : a commissioned officer (as in the army) ranking next below a major general

brig·and \ˈbrig-ənd\ *n* : BANDIT — **brig·and·age** \-ən-dij\ *n*

brig·an·tine \ˈbrig-ən-ˌtēn\ *n* : a 2-masted square-rigged ship not carrying a square mainsail

Brig Gen *abbr* brigadier general

bright \ˈbrīt\ *adj* **1** : SHINING, RADIANT **2** : ILLUSTRIOUS, GLORIOUS **3** : INTELLIGENT, CLEVER; *also* : LIVELY, CHEERFUL **syn** brilliant, lustrous, beaming, radiant — **bright·ly** *adv* — **bright·ness** *n*

bright·en \ˈbrīt-ᵊn\ *vb* **bright·ened; bright·en·ing** \ˈbrīt-(ᵊ-)niŋ\ : to make or become bright or brighter — **bright·en·er** \-(ᵊ-)nər\ *n*

[1]**bril·liant** \ˈbril-yənt\ *adj* [F *brillant,* prp. of *briller* to shine, fr. It *brillare,* fr. *brillo* beryl, fr. L *beryllus*] **1** : very bright **2** : STRIKING, DISTINCTIVE **3** : very intelligent **syn** radiant, lustrous, beaming, lucid, bright, lambent — **bril·liance** \-yəns\ *or* **bril·lian·cy** \-yən-sē\ *n* — **bril·liant·ly** *adv*

[2]**brilliant** *n* : a gem cut in a particular form with many facets

bril·lian·tine \ˈbril-yən-ˌtēn\ *n* : a usu. oily dressing for the hair

brim \ˈbrim\ *n* : EDGE, RIM **syn** brink, border, verge, fringe — **brim·less** *adj*

brim·ful \-ˈfůl\ *adj* : full to the brim

brim·stone \ˈbrim-ˌstōn\ *n* : SULFUR

brin·dled \ˈbrin-dᵊld\ *adj* : having dark streaks or flecks on a gray or tawny ground ⟨a ~ Great Dane⟩

brine \ˈbrīn\ *n* **1** : water saturated with salt **2** : OCEAN — **brin·i·ness** \ˈbrī-nē-nəs\ *n* — **briny** \ˈbrī-nē\ *adj*

bring \ˈbriŋ\ *vb* **brought** \ˈbrȯt\; **bring·ing** \ˈbriŋ-iŋ\ **1** : to cause to come with one **2** : INDUCE, PERSUADE, LEAD **3** : PRODUCE, EFFECT **4** : to sell for — **bring·er** *n*

bring about *vb* : to cause to take place : EFFECT

bring up *vb* **1** : to give a parent's fostering care to **2** : to come or bring to a sudden halt **3** : to call to notice **4** : VOMIT

brink \ˈbriŋk\ *n* **1** : an edge at the top of a steep place **2** : the point of onset

brio \ˈbrē-ō\ *n* : VIVACITY, SPIRIT

bri·oche \brē-ˈōsh, -ˈȯsh\ *n* [F] : a roll baked from light yeast dough rich with eggs and butter

bri·quette *or* **bri·quet** \brik-ˈet\ *n* : a compacted often brick-shaped mass of fine material ⟨a charcoal ~⟩

brisk \ˈbrisk\ *adj* **1** : ALERT, LIVELY **2** : INVIGORATING **syn** agile, spry, nimble — **brisk·ly** *adv* — **brisk·ness** *n*

bris·ket \ˈbris-kət\ *n* : the breast or lower chest of a quadruped

bris·ling *or* **bris·tling** \ˈbriz-liŋ, ˈbris-\ *n* : a small sardine-like herring

[1]**bris·tle** \ˈbris-əl\ *n* : a short stiff coarse hair — **bris·tly** \-(ə-)lē\ *adj*

[2]**bristle** *vb* **bris·tled; bris·tling** \ˈbris-(ə-)liŋ\ **1** : to stand stiffly erect **2** : to show angry defiance **3** : to appear as if covered with bristles

Brit *abbr* Britain; British

Bri·tan·nia metal \bri-ˌtan-yə-, -ˌtan-ē-ə-\ *n* : a silver-white alloy of tin, antimony, and copper similar to pewter

Bri·tan·nic \bri-ˈtan-ik\ *adj* : BRITISH

britch·es \ˈbrich-əz\ *n pl* : BREECHES, TROUSERS

Brit·ish \ˈbrit-ish\ *n pl* : the people of Great Britain or the Commonwealth — **British** *adj*

British thermal unit *n* : the quantity of heat needed to raise the temperature of one pound of water one degree Fahrenheit

Brit·on \ˈbrit-ᵊn\ *n* **1** : a member of a people inhabiting Britain before the Anglo-Saxon invasion **2** : a native or inhabitant of Great Britain

brit·tle \ˈbrit-ᵊl\ *adj* **brit·tler** \ˈbrit-(ᵊ-)lər\; **brit·tlest** \-ləst, -ᵊl-əst\ : easily broken or snapped : FRAGILE **syn** crisp, crumbly, friable

bro *abbr* brother

[1]**broach** \ˈbrōch\ *n* : a pointed tool

[2]**broach** *vb* **1** : to pierce (as a cask) in order to draw the contents **2** : to introduce as a topic of conversation

[1]**broad** \ˈbrȯd\ *adj* **1** : WIDE **2** : SPACIOUS **3** : CLEAR, OPEN **4** : OBVIOUS **5** : COARSE, CRUDE ⟨~ stories⟩ **6** : liberal in outlook **7** : GENERAL **8** : dealing with essential points — **broad·ly** *adv* — **broad·ness** *n*

[2]**broad** *n, slang* : WOMAN

[1]**broad·cast** \ˈbrȯd-ˌkast\ *vb* **broadcast** *also* **broad·cast·ed; broad·cast·ing 1** : to scatter or sow broadcast **2** : to make widely known **3** : to transmit a broadcast — **broad·cast·er** *n*

[2]**broadcast** *adv* : to or over a wide area

[3]**broadcast** *n* **1** : the transmission of sound or images by radio or television **2** : a single radio or television program

broad·cloth \-ˌklȯth\ *n* **1** : a smooth dense woolen cloth **2** : a fine soft cloth of cotton, silk, or synthetic fiber

broad·en \ˈbrȯd-ᵊn\ *vb* **broad·ened; broad·en·ing** \ˈbrȯd-(ᵊ-)niŋ\ : WIDEN

broad·loom \-ˌlüm\ *adj* : woven on a wide loom esp. in a solid color ⟨a ~ carpet⟩

broad–mind·ed \-ˈmīn-dəd\ *adj* : free from prejudice — **broad–mind·ed·ly** *adv* — **broad–mind·ed·ness** *n*

broad·side \-ˌsīd\ *n* **1** : a sheet of paper printed usu. on one side (as an advertisement) **2** : the part of a ship's side above the waterline **3** : all of the guns on one side of a ship; *also* : their simultaneous firing **4** : a volley of abuse or denunciation

broad–spectrum *adj* : having a wide range esp. of effectiveness ⟨~ antibiotics⟩

broad·sword \ˈbrȯd-ˌsōrd\ *n* : a broad-bladed sword

broad·tail \-ˌtāl\ *n* : a flat and wavy fur or skin of a very young or premature karakul lamb

bro·cade \brō-ˈkād\ *n* : a usu. silk fabric with a raised design

broc·co·li \ˈbräk-(ə-)lē\ *n* [It, pl. of *broccolo* flowering top of a cabbage, dim. of *brocco* small nail, sprout, fr. L *broccus* projecting] : an open branching cauliflower whose young flowering shoots are used as a vegetable

bro·chette \brō-ˈshet\ *n* : SKEWER

bro·chure \brō-ˈshu̇r\ *n* [F, fr. *brocher* to sew, fr. MF, to prick, fr. OF *brochier,* fr. *broche* pointed tool] : PAMPHLET, BOOKLET

bro·gan \ˈbrō-gən, brō-ˈgan\ *n* : a heavy shoe; *esp* : a work shoe reaching to the ankle

brogue \ˈbrōg\ *n* : a dialect or regional pronunciation; *esp* : an Irish accent

broi·der \ˈbrȯid-ər\ *vb* : EMBROIDER — **broi·dery** \ˈbrȯid-(ə-)rē\ *n*

broil \ˈbrȯil\ *vb* : to cook by exposure to radiant heat : GRILL — **broil** *n*

broil·er \ˈbrȯi-lər\ *n* **1** : a utensil for broiling **2** : a young chicken fit for broiling

[1]**broke** \ˈbrōk\ *past of* BREAK

[2]**broke** *adj* : PENNILESS

bro·ken \ˈbrō-kən\ *adj* **1** : SHATTERED **2** : having gaps or breaks : INTERRUPTED, DISRUPTED **3** : SUBDUED, CRUSHED **4** : BANKRUPT **5** : imperfectly spoken — **bro·ken·ly** *adv*

bro·ken·heart·ed \ˌbrō-kən-ˈhärt-əd\ *adj* : overcome by grief or despair

bro·ker \ˈbrō-kər\ *n* : an agent who negotiates contracts of purchase and sale

bro·ker·age \ˈbrō-k(ə-)rij\ *n* **1** : the business of a broker **2** : the fee or commission charged by a broker

bro·mide \ˈbrō-ˌmīd\ *n* **1** : a compound of bromine and another element or chemical group including some (as potassium bromide) used as sedatives **2** : a trite remark or notion

bro·mid·ic \brō-ˈmid-ik\ *adj* : DULL, TIRESOME ⟨~ remarks⟩

bro·mine \ˈbrō-ˌmēn\ *n* [F *brome* bromine, fr. Gk *brōmos* stink] : a deep red liquid corrosive chemical element that gives off an irritating vapor — see ELEMENT table

bronc \ˈbräŋk\ *n* : BRONCO

bron·chi·al \ˈbräŋ-kē-əl\ *adj* : of, relating to, or affecting the bronchi or their branches

bron·chi·tis \brän-ˈkīt-əs, bräŋ-\ *n* : inflammation of the bronchi and their branches — **bron·chit·ic** \-ˈkit-ik\ *adj*

bron·chus \ˈbräŋ-kəs\ *n, pl* **bron·chi** \ˈbräŋ-ˌkī, -ˌkē\ : either of the main divisions of the windpipe each leading to a lung

bron·co \ˈbräŋ-kō\ *n, pl* **broncos** [MexSp, fr. Sp, rough, wild] : an unbroken or partly broken range horse of western No. America; *also* : MUSTANG

bron·to·sau·rus \ˌbränt-ə-ˈsȯr-əs\ *or* **bron·to·saur** \ˈbränt-ə-ˌsȯr\ *n* [deriv. of Gk *brontē* thunder + *sauros* lizard] : any of various large 4-footed and probably herbivorous dinosaurs

Bronx cheer \ˈbräŋks-\ *n* : RASPBERRY 2

[1]**bronze** \ˈbränz\ *vb* **bronzed; bronz·ing** : to give the appearance of bronze to

[2]**bronze** *n* **1** : an alloy of copper and tin and sometimes other elements; *also* : something made of bronze **2** : a yellowish brown color — **bronzy** \ˈbrän-zē\ *adj*

brooch \ˈbrōch, ˈbrüch\ *n* : an ornamental clasp or pin

[1]**brood** \ˈbrüd\ *n* : a family of young animals or children and esp. of birds

[2]**brood** *vb* **1** : to sit on eggs to hatch them; *also* : to shelter (hatched young) with the wings **2** : to think anxiously or gloomily about something : PONDER

[3]**brood** *adj* : kept for breeding ⟨a ~ mare⟩

brood·er \ˈbrüd-ər\ *n* **1** : one that broods **2** : a heated structure for raising young birds

[1]**brook** \ˈbru̇k\ *vb* : TOLERATE, BEAR

[2]**brook** *n* : a small natural stream of water

brook·let \-lət\ *n* : a small brook

brook trout *n* : a common speckled cold-water char of eastern No. America

broom \ˈbrüm, ˈbru̇m\ *n* **1** : any of several shrubs of the legume family with long slender branches and usu. yellow flowers **2** : an implement for sweeping orig. made from twigs — **broom·stick** \-ˌstik\ *n*

bros *abbr* brothers

broth \ˈbrȯth\ *n, pl* **broths** \ˈbrȯths, ˈbrȯt͟hz\ **1** : liquid in which meat or sometimes vegetable food has been cooked **2** : a fluid culture medium

broth·el \ˈbräth-əl, ˈbrȯth-\ *n* : an establishment where prostitutes are available

broth·er \ˈbrət͟h-ər\ *n, pl* **brothers** *also* **breth·ren** \ˈbret͟h-(ə-)rən, ˈbret͟h-ərn\ **1** : a male having one or both parents in common with another individual; *also* : KINSMAN **2** : a kindred human being **3** : a man who is a religious but not a priest — **broth·er·li·ness** \-lē-nəs\ *n* — **broth·er·ly** \-lē\ *adj*

broth·er·hood \ˈbrət͟h-ər-ˌhu̇d\ *n* **1** : the state of being brothers or a brother **2** : ASSOCIATION, FRATERNITY **3** : the whole body of persons in a business or profession

broth·er–in–law \ˈbrət͟h-(ə-)rən-ˌlȯ, ˈbrət͟h-ərn-ˌlȯ\ *n, pl* **brothers–in–law** \ˈbrət͟h-ərz-ən-\ : the brother of one's spouse; *also* : the husband of one's sister or of one's spouse's sister

brougham \ˈbrü(-ə)m, ˈbrō(-ə)m\ *n* **1** : a light closed horse-drawn carriage with the driver outside in front **2** : COUPÉ 2 **3** : a sedan having no roof over the driver's seat

brought *past and past part of* BRING

brou·ha·ha \ˈbrü-ˌhä-ˌhä\ *n* : HUBBUB, UPROAR

brow \ˈbrau̇\ *n* **1** : the eyebrow or the ridge on which it grows; *also* : FOREHEAD **2** : the projecting upper part of a steep place

brow·beat \ˈbrau̇-ˌbēt\ *vb* **-beat; -beat·en** \-ˈbēt-ᵊn\ *or* **-beat; -beat·ing** : to intimidate by sternness or arrogance : BULLY **syn** intimidate, hector

[1]**brown** \ˈbrau̇n\ *adj* : of the color brown; *also* : of dark or tanned complexion

[2]**brown** *n* : a color like that of coffee or chocolate that is a blend of red and yellow darkened by black — **brown·ish** *adj*

[3]**brown** *vb* : to make or become brown

brown bag·ging \-ˈbag-iŋ\ *n* : the practice of carrying one's lunch usu. in a brown bag — **brown bag·ger** \-ˈbag-ər\ *n*

brown·ie \ˈbrau̇-nē\ *n* **1 :** a legendary cheerful elf who performs good deeds at night **2** *cap* **:** a member of the Girl Scouts from 6 through 8 years of age

brown·out \ˈbrau̇n-ˌau̇t\ *n* **:** a curtailment in electrical power; *also* **:** a period of reduced illumination due to such curtailment

brown rice *n* **:** hulled but unpolished rice that retains most of the bran layers

brown·stone \ˈbrau̇n-ˌstōn\ *n* **:** a dwelling faced with reddish brown sandstone

[1]**browse** \ˈbrau̇z\ *vb* **browsed; brows·ing 1 :** to feed on browse; *also* **:** GRAZE **2 :** to read bits at random in a book or collection of books

[2]**browse** *n* **:** tender shoots, twigs, and leaves fit for food for cattle

bru·in \ˈbrü-ən\ *n* **:** BEAR

[1]**bruise** \ˈbrüz\ *vb* **bruised; bruis·ing 1 :** to inflict a bruise on; *also* **:** to become bruised **2 :** to break down by pounding ⟨~ garlic for a salad⟩

[2]**bruise** *n* **:** a surface injury to flesh **:** CONTUSION

bruis·er \ˈbrü-zər\ *n* **:** a big husky man

bruit \ˈbrüt\ *vb* **:** to noise abroad

brunch \ˈbrənch\ *n* **:** a meal that combines a late breakfast and an early lunch

bru·net *or* **bru·nette** \brü-ˈnet\ *adj* [F *brunet*, masc., *brunette*, fem., brownish, fr. OF, fr. *brun* brown] **:** of dark or relatively dark pigmentation; *esp* **:** having brown or black hair and eyes — **brunet** *or* **brunette** *n*

brunt \ˈbrənt\ *n* **:** the main shock, force, or stress esp. of an attack

[1]**brush** \ˈbrəsh\ *n* **1 :** BRUSHWOOD **2 :** scrub vegetation or land covered with it

[2]**brush** *n* **1 :** a device composed of bristles set in a handle and used esp. for cleaning or painting **2 :** a bushy tail (as of a fox) **3 :** an electrical conductor that makes contact between a stationary and a moving part of a generator or motor **4 :** a light rubbing or touching

[3]**brush** *vb* **1 :** to treat (as in cleaning or painting) with a brush **2 :** to remove with or as if with a brush; *also* **:** to dispose of in an offhand manner **3 :** to touch gently in passing

[4]**brush** *n* **:** SKIRMISH **syn** encounter, run-in

brush–off \ˈbrəsh-ˌȯf\ *n* **:** an abrupt or offhand dismissal

brush up *vb* **:** to renew one's skill

brush·wood \ˈbrəsh-ˌwu̇d\ *n* **1 :** small branches lopped from trees or shrubs **2 :** a thicket of shrubs and small trees

brusque \ˈbrəsk\ *adj* [F *brusque*, fr. It *brusco*, fr. ML *bruscus* a plant with stiff twigs used for brooms] **:** CURT, BLUNT, ABRUPT **syn** gruff, bluff, crusty, short — **brusque·ly** *adv*

brus·sels sprout \ˌbrəs-əl(z)-\ *n*, *often cap B* **:** one of the edible small heads borne on the stalk of a cabbagelike plant; *also*, *pl* **:** this plant

bru·tal \ˈbrüt-ᵊl\ *adj* **1 :** resembling or befitting a brute (as in coarseness or cruelty) **2 :** HARSH, SEVERE ⟨~ weather⟩ — **bru·tal·i·ty** \brü-ˈtal-ət-ē\ *n* — **bru·tal·ly** \ˈbrüt-ᵊl-ē\ *adv*

bru·tal·ize \ˈbrüt-ᵊl-ˌīz\ *vb* **-ized; -iz·ing 1 :** to make brutal **2 :** to treat brutally

[1]**brute** \ˈbrüt\ *adj* [ME, fr. MF *brut* rough, fr. L *brutus* stupid, lit., heavy] **1 :** of, relating to, or typical of beasts **2 :** BRUTAL **3 :** UNREASONING; *also* **:** purely physical

[2]**brute** *n* **1 :** BEAST 1 **2 :** a brutal person **syn** animal, creature

brut·ish \ˈbrüt-ish\ *adj* **1 :** BRUTE 1 **2 :** stupidly cruel or sensual; *also* **:** UNREASONING

BS *abbr* bachelor of science

BSA *abbr* Boy Scouts of America

BSc *abbr* bachelor of science

bskt *abbr* basket

Bt *abbr* baronet

btry *abbr* battery

Btu *abbr* British thermal unit

bu *abbr* bushel

[1]**bub·ble** \ˈbəb-əl\ *n* **1 :** a globule of gas in a liquid **2 :** a thin film of liquid filled with gas **3 :** something lacking firmness or solidity — **bub·bly** \-(ə-)lē\ *adj*

[2]**bubble** *vb* **bub·bled; bub·bling** \ˈbəb-(ə-)liŋ\ **:** to form, rise in, or give off bubbles

bu·bo \ˈb(y)ü-bō\ *n*, *pl* **buboes :** an inflammatory swelling of a lymph gland

bu·bon·ic plague \b(y)ü-ˌbän-ik-\ *n* **:** a plague caused by a bacterium transmitted to human beings by flea bites and marked esp. by chills and fever and by buboes usu. in the groin

buc·ca·neer \ˌbək-ə-ˈniər\ *n* **:** PIRATE

[1]**buck** \ˈbək\ *n*, *pl* **bucks 1** *or pl* **buck :** a male animal (as a deer or antelope) **2 :** DANDY **3 :** DOLLAR

[2]**buck** *vb* **1 :** to spring with a quick plunging leap ⟨a *~ing* horse⟩ **2 :** to charge against something; *also* **:** to strive for advancement sometimes without regard to ethical behavior

buck·board \-ˌbōrd\ *n* **:** a 4-wheeled vehicle with a floor of long springy boards

buckboard

buck·et \ˈbək-ət\ *n* **1 :** PAIL **2 :** an object resembling a bucket in collecting, scooping, or carrying something — **buck·et·ful** *n*

bucket seat *n* **:** a low separate seat for one person (as in an automobile)

buck·eye \ˈbək-ˌī\ *n* **:** a tree related to the horse chestnut that occurs chiefly in the central U.S.; *also* **:** its large nutlike seed

buck fever *n* **:** nervous excitement of an inexperienced hunter at the sight of game

[1]**buck·le** \ˈbək-əl\ *n* **:** a clasp (as on a belt) for two loose ends

[2]**buckle** *vb* **buck·led; buck·ling** \ˈbək-(ə-)liŋ\ **1 :** to fasten with a buckle **2 :** to apply oneself with vigor **3 :** to crumple up **:** BEND, COLLAPSE

[3]**buckle** *n* **:** BEND, FOLD, KINK

buck·ler \ˈbək-lər\ *n* **:** SHIELD

buck·ram \ˈbək-rəm\ *n* **:** a coarse stiff cloth used esp. for binding books

buck·saw \ˈbək-ˌsȯ\ *n* **:** a saw set in a usu. H-shaped frame and used for sawing wood

buck·shot \ˈbək-ˌshät\ *n* **:** lead shot that is from .24 to .33 inch (about 6.1 to 8.4 millimeters) in diameter

buck·skin \-ˌskin\ *n* **1 :** the skin of a buck **2 :** a soft usu. suede-finished leather — **buckskin** *adj*

buck·tooth \-ˈtüth\ *n* **:** a large projecting front tooth — **buck–toothed** \-ˈtütht\ *adj*

buck·wheat \-ˌhwēt\ *n* **:** either of two plants grown for their triangular seeds which are used as a cereal grain; *also* **:** these seeds

bu·col·ic \byü-ˈkäl-ik\ *adj* [L *bucolicus*, fr. Gk *boukolikos*, fr. *boukolos* one who tends cattle, fr. *bous* head of

\ə\abut \ᵊ\kitten \ər\further \a\ash \ā\ace \ä\cot, cart \au̇\out \ch\chin \e\bet \ē\easy \g\go \i\hit \ī\ice \j\job \ŋ\sing \ō\go \ȯ\law \ȯi\boy \th\thin \t͟h\the \ü\loot \u̇\foot \y\yet \zh\vision *see also* Pronunciation Symbols page

cattle + *-kolos* (akin to L *colere* to cultivate)] : RURAL, RUSTIC

¹**bud** \ˈbəd\ *n* **1** : an undeveloped plant shoot (as of a leaf or a flower); *also* : a partly opened flower **2** : an asexual reproductive structure **3** : something not yet mature

²**bud** *vb* **bud·ded; bud·ding 1** : to form or put forth buds; *also* : to reproduce by asexual buds **2** : to be or develop like a bud **3** : to propagate a desired variety (as of peach) by inserting a bud in a plant of a different variety

Bud·dhism \ˈbü-ˌdiz-əm, ˈbu̇d-ˌiz-\ *n* : a religion of eastern and central Asia growing out of the teachings of Gautama Buddha — **Bud·dhist** \ˈbüd-əst, ˈbu̇d-\ *n or adj*

bud·dy \ˈbəd-ē\ *n, pl* **buddies** : COMPANION; *esp* : a fellow soldier

budge \ˈbəj\ *vb* **budged; budg·ing** : MOVE, STIR, SHIFT

bud·ger·i·gar \ˈbəj-(ə-)rē-ˌgär, ˌbəj-ə-ˈrē-\ *n* : a small brightly colored Australian parrot often kept as a pet

¹**bud·get** \ˈbəj-ət\ *n* [ME *bowgette*, fr. MF *bougette*, dim. of *bouge* leather bag, fr. L *bulga*] **1** : STOCK, SUPPLY **2** : a financial report containing estimates of income and expenses; *also* : a plan for coordinating income and expenses

²**budget** *vb* **1** : to allow for in a budget **2** : to draw up a budget

³**budget** *adj* : INEXPENSIVE

bud·gie \ˈbəj-ē\ *n* : BUDGERIGAR

¹**buff** \ˈbəf\ *n* **1** : a dull yellow-orange color **2** : FAN, ENTHUSIAST

²**buff** *adj* : of the color buff

³**buff** *vb* : POLISH, SHINE

buf·fa·lo \ˈbəf-ə-ˌlō\ *n, pl* **-lo** *or* **-loes** *also* **-los 1** : WATER BUFFALO **2** : a large shaggy-maned No. American wild bovine mammal with short horns and heavy forequarters with a large muscular hump

¹**buf·fer** \ˈbəf-ər\ *n* : something that lessens shock (as from a physical or financial blow)

²**buffer** *n* : one that buffs

¹**buf·fet** \ˈbəf-ət\ *n* : BLOW, SLAP

²**buffet** *vb* **1** : to strike with the hand; *also* : to pound repeatedly **2** : to struggle against or on **syn** beat, batter, drub, pummel, thrash

³**buf·fet** \(ˌ)bə-ˈfā, bü-\ *n* **1** : SIDEBOARD **2** : a counter for refreshments; *also* : a meal at which people serve themselves (as from a buffet)

buff leather *n* : a strong supple oil-tanned leather

buf·foon \(ˌ)bə-ˈfün\ *n* [MF *bouffon*, fr. It *buffone*, fr. ML *bufon-*, *bufo*, fr. L, toad] : CLOWN 2 **syn** fool, jester — **buf·foon·ery** \-(ə-)rē\ *n*

¹**bug** \ˈbəg\ *n* **1** : an insect or other creeping or crawling invertebrate animal; *esp* : an insect pest (as a bedbug) **2** : any of an order of insects with sucking mouthparts and incomplete metamorphosis that includes many plant pests **3** : an unexpected mistake or imperfection ⟨a ~ in a computer program⟩ **4** : a disease-producing germ; *also* : a disease caused by it **5** : a concealed listening device

²**bug** *vb* **bugged; bug·ging 1** : BOTHER, ANNOY **2** : to plant a concealed microphone in

bug·a·boo \ˈbəg-ə-ˌbü\ *n, pl* **-boos** : BOGEY 1

bug·bear \ˈbəg-ˌbaər\ *n* : BOGEY 1; *also* : a source of dread

bug·gy \ˈbəg-ē\ *n, pl* **buggies** : a light carriage

bu·gle \ˈbyü-gəl\ *n* [ME, buffalo, instrument made of buffalo horn, bugle, fr. OF, fr. L *buculus*, dim. of *bos* head of cattle] : a valveless brass wind instrument resembling a trumpet and used esp. for military calls — **bu·gler** \-glər\ *n*

¹**build** \ˈbild\ *vb* **built** \ˈbilt\; **build·ing 1** : to form or have formed by ordering and uniting materials ⟨~ a house⟩; *also* : to bring into being or develop **2** : to produce or create gradually ⟨~ an argument on facts⟩ **3** : INCREASE, ENLARGE; *also* : ENHANCE **4** : to engage in building — **build·er** *n*

²**build** *n* : form or mode of structure; *esp* : PHYSIQUE

build·ing \ˈbil-diŋ\ *n* **1** : a usu. roofed and walled structure (as a house) for permanent use **2** : the art or business of constructing buildings

build·up \ˈbild-ˌəp\ *n* : the act or process of building up; *also* : something produced by this

built–in \ˈbil-ˈtin\ *adj* **1** : forming an integral part of a structure **2** : INHERENT

bulb \ˈbəlb\ *n* **1** : an underground resting stage of a plant (as a lily or an onion) consisting of a short stem base bearing one or more buds enclosed in overlapping leaves; *also* : a fleshy plant structure (as a tuber) resembling a bulb **2** : a plant having or growing from a bulb **3** : a rounded more or less bulb-shaped object or part (as for an electric lamp) — **bul·bous** \ˈbəl-bəs\ *adj*

Bul·gar·i·an \ˌbəl-ˈgar-ē-ən, bu̇l-\ *n* : a native or inhabitant of Bulgaria — **Bulgarian** *adj*

¹**bulge** \ˈbəlj\ *vb* **bulged; bulg·ing** : to become or cause to become protuberant

²**bulge** *n* : a swelling projecting part

bu·li·mia \b(y)ü-ˈlim-ē-ə, -ˈlēm-\ *n* : an abnormal and constant craving for food — **bu·lim·ic** \-ˈlim-ik\ *adj or n*

¹**bulk** \ˈbəlk\ *n* **1** : MAGNITUDE, VOLUME **2** : material (as indigestible fibrous residues of food) that forms a mass in the intestine **3** : a large mass **4** : the major portion

²**bulk** *vb* **1** : to have a bulky appearance **2** : to appear as a factor : LOOM

bulk·head \ˈbəlk-ˌhed\ *n* **1** : a partition separating compartments **2** : a structure built to cover a shaft or a cellar stairway

bulky \ˈbəl-kē\ *adj* **bulk·i·er; -est** : having bulk; *esp* : being large and unwieldy

¹**bull** \ˈbu̇l\ *n* **1** : the adult male of a bovine animal; *also* : a usu. adult male of various other large animals (as the elephant or walrus) **2** : one who buys securities or commodities in expectation of a price increase — **bull·ish** *adj*

²**bull** *adj* **1** : MALE **2** : large of its kind **3** : RISING ⟨a ~ market⟩

³**bull** *n* [ME *bulle*, fr. ML *bulla*, fr. L, bubble, amulet] : a papal letter

⁴**bull** *n, slang* : NONSENSE

⁵**bull** *abbr* bulletin

¹**bull·dog** \ˈbu̇l-ˌdȯg\ *n* : any of a breed of compact muscular short-haired dogs of English origin

²**bulldog** *vb* : to throw (a steer) by seizing the horns and twisting the neck

bull·doze \-ˌdōz\ *vb* **1** : to move, clear, or level with a tractor-driven machine (**bull·doz·er**) having a broad blade for pushing **2** : to force as if by using a bulldozer

bul·let \ˈbu̇l-ət\ *n* [MF *boulette* small ball & *boulet* missile, dims. of *boule* ball] : a missile to be shot from a firearm — **bul·let·proof** \ˌbu̇l-ət-ˈprüf\ *adj*

bul·le·tin \ˈbu̇l-ət-ᵊn\ *n* **1** : a brief public report intended for immediate release on a matter of public interest **2** : a periodical publication (as of a college) — **bulletin** *vb*

bull·fight \ˈbu̇l-ˌfīt\ *n* : a spectacle in which people ceremonially fight with and usu. kill bulls in an arena — **bull·fight·er** *n*

bull·frog \-ˌfrȯg, -ˌfräg\ *n* : FROG; *esp* : a large deep-voiced frog

bull·head \-ˌhed\ *n* : any of several common freshwater catfishes of the U.S.

bull·head·ed \-ˈhed-əd\ *adj* : stupidly stubborn : HEADSTRONG

bul·lion \ˈbu̇l-yən\ *n* : gold or silver esp. in bars or ingots

bull·ock \ˈbu̇l-ək\ *n* : a young bull; *also* : STEER

bull pen *n* : a place on a baseball field where relief pitchers warm up; *also* : the relief pitchers of a baseball team

bull session *n* : an informal discussion

bull's–eye \ˈbu̇l-ˌzī\ *n, pl* **bull's–eyes** : the center of a target; *also* : a shot that hits the bull's-eye

¹**bul·ly** \ˈbu̇l-ē\ *n, pl* **bullies** : a person habitually cruel to others who are weaker

[2]**bully** *adj* : EXCELLENT, FIRST-RATE — often used interjectionally
[3]**bully** *vb* **bul·lied; bul·ly·ing** : to behave as a bully toward : DOMINEER **syn** browbeat, intimidate, hector
bul·rush \ˈbu̇l-ˌrəsh\ *n* : any of several large rushes or sedges of wetlands
bul·wark \ˈbu̇l-(ˌ)wərk, -ˌwȯrk; ˈbəl-(ˌ)wərk\ *n* **1** : a wall-like defensive structure **2** : a strong support or protection in danger
[1]**bum** \ˈbəm\ *adj* **1** : WORTHLESS ⟨~ advice⟩ **2** : DISABLED ⟨a ~ knee⟩
[2]**bum** *vb* **bummed; bum·ming 1** : to wander as a tramp; *also* : LOAF **2** : to seek or gain by begging
[3]**bum** *n* : an idle worthless fellow : LOAFER
bum·ble·bee \ˈbəm-bəl-ˌbē\ *n* : any of numerous large hairy social bees
bum·mer \ˈbəm-ər\ *n* : an unpleasant experience
[1]**bump** \ˈbəmp\ *n* **1** : a local bulge; *esp* : a swelling of tissue **2** : a sudden forceful blow or impact — **bumpy** *adj*
[2]**bump** *vb* **1** : to strike or knock forcibly; *also* : to move or alter by bumping **2** : to collide with
[1]**bum·per** \ˈbəm-pər\ *n* **1** : a cup or glass filled to the brim **2** : something unusually large — **bumper** *adj*
[2]**bump·er** \ˈbəm-pər\ *n* : a device for absorbing shock or preventing damage; *esp* : a metal bar at either end of an automobile
bump·kin \ˈbəmp-kən\ *n* : an awkward and unsophisticated country person
bump·tious \ˈbəmp-shəs\ *adj* : obtusely and often noisily self-assertive
bun \ˈbən\ *n* : a sweet biscuit or roll
[1]**bunch** \ˈbənch\ *n* **1** : SWELLING **2** : CLUSTER, GROUP — **bunchy** *adj*
[2]**bunch** *vb* : to form into a group or bunch
bun·co *or* **bun·ko** \ˈbəŋ-kō\ *n, pl* **buncos** *or* **bunkos** : a swindling scheme — **bunco** *vb*
[1]**bun·dle** \ˈbən-dᵊl\ *n* **1** : several items bunched and fastened together; *also* : something wrapped for carrying **2** : a considerable amount : LOT **3** : a small group esp. of mostly parallel nerve or muscle fibers
[2]**bundle** *vb* **bun·dled; bun·dling** \ˈbənd-(ᵊ-)liŋ\ : to gather or tie in a bundle
bun·dling \ˈbənd-(ᵊ-)liŋ\ *n* : a former custom of a courting couple's occupying the same bed without undressing
bung \ˈbəŋ\ *n* : the stopper in the bunghole of a cask
bun·ga·low \ˈbəŋ-gə-ˌlō\ *n* : a one-storied house with a low-pitched roof
bung·hole \ˈbəŋ-ˌhōl\ *n* : a hole for emptying or filling a cask
bun·gle \ˈbəŋ-gəl\ *vb* **bun·gled; bun·gling** \-g(ə-)liŋ\ : to do badly : BOTCH — **bungle** *n* — **bun·gler** \-g(ə-)lər\ *n*
bun·ion \ˈbən-yən\ *n* : an inflamed swelling of the first joint of the big toe
[1]**bunk** \ˈbəŋk\ *n* : BED; *esp* : a built-in bed that is often one of a tier
[2]**bunk** *n* : BUNKUM, NONSENSE
bun·ker \ˈbəŋ-kər\ *n* **1** : a bin or compartment for storage (as for coal on a ship) **2** : a protective embankment or dugout **3** : a sand trap or embankment constituting a hazard on a golf course
bun·kum *or* **bun·combe** \ˈbəŋ-kəm\ *n* [*Buncombe* County, N.C.; fr. the defense of a seemingly irrelevant speech made by its congressional representative that he was speaking to Buncombe] : insincere or foolish talk
bun·ny \ˈbən-ē\ *n, pl* **-nies** : RABBIT
Bun·sen burner \ˌbən-sən-\ *n* : a gas burner usu. consisting of a straight tube with air holes at the bottom
[1]**bunt** \ˈbənt\ *vb* **1** : BUTT **2** : to push or tap a baseball lightly without swinging the bat
[2]**bunt** *n* : an act or instance of bunting; *also* : a bunted ball
[1]**bun·ting** \ˈbənt-iŋ\ *n* : any of numerous small stout-billed finches
[2]**bunting** *n* : a thin fabric used esp. for flags; *also* : FLAGS
[1]**buoy** \ˈbü-ē, ˈbȯi\ *n* **1** : a floating object anchored in water to mark something (as a channel, shoal, or rock) **2** : a float consisting of a ring of buoyant material to support a person who has fallen into the water
[2]**buoy** *vb* **1** : to mark by a buoy **2** : to keep afloat **3** : to raise the spirits of
buoy·an·cy \ˈbȯi-ən-sē, ˈbü-yən-\ *n* **1** : the tendency of a body to float or rise when submerged in a fluid **2** : the power of a fluid to exert an upward force on a body placed in it **3** : resilience of spirit — **buoy·ant** \-ənt, -yənt\ *adj*
[1]**bur** \ˈbər\ *var of* BURR
[2]**bur** *abbr* bureau
[1]**bur·den** \ˈbərd-ᵊn\ *n* **1** : LOAD; *also* : CARE, RESPONSIBILITY **2** : something oppressive : ENCUMBRANCE **3** : CARGO; *also* : capacity for cargo
[2]**burden** *vb* **bur·dened; bur·den·ing** \ˈbərd-(ᵊ-)niŋ\ : LOAD, OPPRESS — **bur·den·some** \-səm\ *adj*
[3]**burden** *n* **1** : REFRAIN, CHORUS **2** : a main theme or idea : GIST
bur·dock \ˈbər-ˌdäk\ *n* : any of a genus of coarse composite herbs with globe-shaped flower heads surrounded by prickly bracts
bu·reau \ˈbyu̇r-ō\ *n, pl* **bureaus** *also* **bu·reaux** \-ōz\ [F, desk, cloth covering for desks, fr. OF *burel* woolen cloth, fr. L *burra* shaggy cloth] **1** : a chest of drawers for bedroom use **2** : an administrative unit (as of a government department) **3** : a branch of a publication or wire service in an important news center
bu·reau·cra·cy \byu̇-ˈräk-rə-sē\ *n, pl* **-cies 1** : a body of appointive government officials **2** : administration characterized by specialization of functions under fixed rules and a hierarchy of authority; *also* : an unwieldy administrative system deficient in initiative and flexibility — **bu·reau·crat** \ˈbyu̇r-ə-ˌkrat\ *n* — **bu·reau·crat·ic** \ˌbyu̇r-ə-ˈkrat-ik\ *adj*
bur·geon \ˈbər-jən\ *vb* : to put forth fresh growth (as from buds) : grow vigorously : FLOURISH
bur·gess \ˈbər-jəs\ *n* **1** : a citizen of a borough **2** : an official or representative usu. of a borough
burgh \ˈbər-ō\ *n* : a Scottish town
bur·gher \ˈbər-gər\ *n* **1** : TOWNSMAN **2** : a prosperous solid citizen
bur·glary \ˈbər-glə-rē\ *n, pl* **-glar·ies** : forcible entry into a building and esp. a dwelling with intent to steal — **bur·glar** \-glər\ *n* — **bur·glar·ize** \ˈbər-glə-ˌrīz\ *vb*
bur·gle \ˈbər-gəl\ *vb* **bur·gled; bur·gling** \-g(ə-)liŋ\ : to commit burglary on
bur·go·mas·ter \ˈbər-gə-ˌmas-tər\ *n* : the chief magistrate of a town in some European countries
Bur·gun·dy \ˈbər-gən-dē\ *n, pl* **-dies** : a red or white table wine
buri·al \ˈber-ē-əl\ *n* : the act or process of burying
burl \ˈbərl\ *n* : a hard woody often flattened hemispherical outgrowth on a tree
bur·lap \ˈbər-ˌlap\ *n* : a coarse fabric usu. of jute or hemp used esp. for bags
[1]**bur·lesque** \(ˌ)bər-ˈlesk\ *n* [*burlesque*, adj. (comic, droll), fr. F, fr. It *burlesco*, fr. *burla* joke, fr. Sp] **1** : a witty or derisive literary or dramatic imitation **2** : broadly humorous theatrical entertainment consisting of several items (as songs, skits, or dances)
[2]**burlesque** *vb* **bur·lesqued; bur·lesqu·ing** : to make ludicrous by burlesque : MOCK **syn** caricature, parody, travesty
bur·ly \ˈbər-lē\ *adj* **bur·li·er; -est** : strongly and heavily built : HUSKY **syn** muscular, brawny, beefy, hefty

Bur·mese \ˌbər-ˈmēz, -ˈmēs\ *n, pl* **Burmese** : a native or inhabitant of Burma — **Burmese** *adj*

[1]**burn** \ˈbərn\ *vb* **burned** \ˈbərnd, ˈbərnt\ *or* **burnt** \ˈbərnt\; **burn·ing 1** : to be on fire **2** : to feel or look as if on fire **3** : to alter or become altered by or as if by the action of fire or heat **4** : to use as fuel ⟨~ coal⟩; *also* : to destroy by fire ⟨~ trash⟩ **5** : to cause or make by fire ⟨~ a hole⟩; *also* : to affect as if by heat

[2]**burn** *n* : an injury or effect produced by or as if by burning

burn·er \ˈbər-nər\ *n* : the part of a fuel-burning or heat-producing device where the flame or heat is produced

bur·nish \ˈbər-nish\ *vb* : to make shiny esp. by rubbing : POLISH — **bur·nish·er** *n* — **bur·nish·ing** *adj or n*

bur·noose *or* **bur·nous** \(ˌ)bər-ˈnüs\ *n* : a hooded cloak worn esp. by Arabs

burn·out \ˈbər-ˌnau̇t\ *n* **1** : the cessation of operation of a jet or rocket engine **2** : exhaustion of one's physical or emotional strength

burp \ˈbərp\ *n* : an act of belching — **burp** *vb*

burp gun *n* : a small submachine gun

burr \ˈbər\ *n* **1** *usu* **bur** : a rough or prickly envelope of a fruit; *also* : a plant that bears burs **2** : roughness left in cutting or shaping metal **3** : WHIR — **bur·ry** *adj*

bur·ri·to \bə-ˈrēt-ō\ *n* [AmerSp, fr. Sp, lit., little donkey, dim. of *burro*] : a flour tortilla rolled around a filling and baked

bur·ro \ˈbər-ō, ˈbu̇r-\ *n, pl* **burros** [Sp] : a usu. small donkey

[1]**bur·row** \ˈbər-ō\ *n* : a hole in the ground made by an animal (as a rabbit)

[2]**burrow** *vb* **1** : to form by tunneling ⟨~ a way through the snow⟩; *also* : to make a burrow **2** : to progress by or as if by digging — **bur·row·er** *n*

bur·sar \ˈbər-sər\ *n* : a treasurer esp. of a college

bur·si·tis \(ˌ)bər-ˈsīt-əs\ *n* : inflammation of the serous sac (**bur·sa** \ˈbər-sə\) of a joint (as the elbow or shoulder)

[1]**burst** \ˈbərst\ *vb* **burst** *or* **burst·ed; burst·ing 1** : to fly apart or into pieces **2** : to show one's feelings suddenly; *also* : PLUNGE ⟨~ into song⟩ **3** : to enter or emerge suddenly : SPRING **4** : to be filled to the breaking point

[2]**burst** *n* **1** : a sudden outbreak or effort : SPURT **2** : EXPLOSION **3** : an act or result of bursting

Bu·run·di·an \bu̇-ˈrün-dē-ən\ *n* : a native or inhabitant of Burundi

bury \ˈber-ē\ *vb* **bur·ied; bury·ing 1** : to deposit in the earth; *also* : to inter with funeral ceremonies **2** : CONCEAL, HIDE

[1]**bus** \ˈbəs\ *n, pl* **bus·es** *or* **bus·ses** [short for *omnibus*, fr. F, fr. L, for all, dat. pl. of *omnis* all] : a large motor-driven passenger vehicle

[2]**bus** *vb* **bused** *or* **bussed; bus·ing** *or* **bus·sing 1** : to travel or transport by bus **2** : to work as a busboy

[3]**bus** *abbr* business

bus·boy \ˈbəs-ˌbȯi\ *n* : a waiter's helper

bus·by \ˈbəz-bē\ *n, pl* **busbies** : a military full-dress fur hat

bush \ˈbu̇sh\ *n* **1** : SHRUB **2** : rough uncleared country **3** : a thick tuft or mat — **bushy** *adj*

bushed \ˈbu̇sht\ *adj* : TIRED, EXHAUSTED

bush·el \ˈbu̇sh-əl\ *n* — see WEIGHT table

bush·ing \ˈbu̇sh-iŋ\ *n* : a usu. removable cylindrical lining in an opening of a mechanical part to limit the size of the opening, resist wear (as in a bearing for an axle), or serve as a guide

bush·mas·ter \ˈbu̇sh-ˌmas-tər\ *n* : a large venomous tropical American snake

bush·whack \-ˌhwak\ *vb* **1** : to live or hide out in the woods **2** : AMBUSH — **bush·whack·er** *n*

busi·ly \ˈbiz-ə-lē\ *adv* : in a busy manner

busi·ness \ˈbiz-nəs, -nəz\ *n* **1** : OCCUPATION, CALLING; *also* : TASK, MISSION **2** : a commercial or industrial enterprise; *also* : TRADE ⟨~ is good⟩ **3** : AFFAIR, MATTER **4** : personal concerns **syn** commerce, industry, trade, traffic

busi·ness·man \-ˌman\ *n* : a man engaged in business esp. as an executive

busi·ness·per·son \-ˌpərs-ᵊn\ *n* : a businessman or businesswoman

busi·ness·wom·an \-ˌwu̇m-ən\ *n* : a woman engaged in business esp. as an executive

bus·kin \ˈbəs-kən\ *n* **1** : a laced boot reaching halfway to the knee **2** : tragic drama

buss \ˈbəs\ *n* : KISS — **buss** *vb*

[1]**bust** \ˈbəst\ *n* [F *buste*, fr. It *busto*, fr. L *bustum* tomb] **1** : sculpture representing the upper part of the human figure **2** : the part of the human torso between the neck and the waist; *esp* : the breasts of a woman

[2]**bust** *vb* **bust·ed** *also* **bust; bust·ing 1** : BREAK, SMASH; *also* : BURST **2** : to ruin financially **3** : DEMOTE **4** : TAME **5** *slang* : ARREST

[3]**bust** *n* **1** : a drinking session **2** : a complete failure : FLOP **3** : a business depression **4** : PUNCH, SOCK **5** *slang* : a police raid

[1]**bus·tle** \ˈbəs-əl\ *vb* **bus·tled; bus·tling** \ˈbəs-(ə-)liŋ\ : to move or work in a brisk fussy way

[2]**bustle** *n* : briskly energetic activity

[3]**bustle** *n* : a pad or frame formerly worn to swell out the fullness at the back of a woman's skirt

[1]**busy** \ˈbiz-ē\ *adj* **busi·er; -est 1** : engaged in action : not idle **2** : being in use ⟨~ telephones⟩ **3** : full of activity ⟨~ streets⟩ **4** : OFFICIOUS **syn** employed, engaged, occupied

[2]**busy** *vb* **bus·ied; busy·ing** : to make or keep busy : OCCUPY

busy·body \ˈbiz-ē-ˌbäd-ē\ *n* : MEDDLER

busy·work \-ˌwərk\ *n* : work that appears productive but only keeps one occupied

[1]**but** \(ˈ)bət\ *conj* **1** : except for the fact ⟨would have protested ~ that he was afraid⟩ **2** : as to the following, namely ⟨there's no doubt ~ he's the guilty one⟩ **3** : without the concomitant that ⟨never rains ~ it pours⟩ **4** : on the contrary ⟨not one, ~ two job offers⟩ **5** : yet nevertheless ⟨would like to go, ~ I can't⟩; *also* : while on the contrary ⟨would like to go ~ he is busy⟩ **6** : yet also ⟨came home sadder ~ wiser⟩ ⟨poor ~ proud⟩

[2]**but** *prep* : other than : EXCEPT ⟨there's no one here ~ me⟩

bu·tane \ˈbyü-ˌtān\ *n* : either of two gaseous hydrocarbons used as a fuel

[1]**butch·er** \ˈbu̇ch-ər\ *n* [ME *bocher*, fr. OF *bouchier*, fr. *bouc* he-goat] **1** : one who slaughters animals or dresses their flesh; *also* : a dealer in meat **2** : one that kills brutally or needlessly — **butch·ery** \-(ə-)rē\ *n*

[2]**butcher** *vb* **butch·ered; butch·er·ing** \-(ə-)riŋ\ **1** : to slaughter and dress for meat ⟨~ hogs⟩ **2** : to kill barbarously

but·ler \ˈbət-lər\ *n* [ME *buteler*, fr. OF *bouteillier* bottle bearer, fr. *bouteille* bottle] : the chief male servant of a household

[1]**butt** \ˈbət\ *vb* : to strike with the head or horns

[2]**butt** *n* : a blow or thrust with the head or horns

[3]**butt** *n* : a large cask

[4]**butt** *n* **1** : TARGET **2** : an object of abuse or ridicule

[5]**butt** *n* : a large, thicker, or bottom end of something

[6]**butt** *vb* **1** : ABUT **2** : to place or join edge to edge without overlapping

butte \ˈbyüt\ *n* : an isolated steep-sided hill

[1]**but·ter** \ˈbət-ər\ *n* [ME, fr. OE *butere*, fr. L *butyrum* butter, fr. Gk *boutyron*, fr. *bous* cow + *tyros* cheese] **1** : a solid edible emulsion of fat obtained from cream by churning **2** : a substance resembling butter — **but·tery** *adj*

[2]**butter** *vb* : to spread with butter

but·ter–and–eggs \ˌbət-ə-rə-ˈnegz\ *n sing or pl* : a common perennial herb related to the snapdragon that has showy yellow and orange flowers

but·ter·cup \ˈbət-ər-ˌkəp\ *n* : any of a genus of herbs usu. having yellow flowers with five petals and sepals

but·ter·fat \-ˌfat\ *n* : the natural fat of milk and chief constituent of butter

but·ter·fin·gered \-ˌfiŋ-gərd\ *adj* : likely to let things fall or slip through the fingers — **but·ter·fin·gers** \-gərz\ *n sing or pl*

but·ter·fly \-ˌflī\ *n* : any of a group of slender day-flying insects with four broad wings covered with bright-colored scales

but·ter·milk \-ˌmilk\ *n* : the liquid remaining after butter is churned

but·ter·nut \-ˌnət\ *n* : the edible oily nut of an American tree related to the walnut; *also* : this tree

but·ter·scotch \-ˌskäch\ *n* : a candy made from brown sugar, corn syrup, and water; *also* : the flavor of such candy

but·tock \ˈbət-ək\ *n* **1** : the back of a hip that forms one of the fleshy parts on which a person sits **2** *pl* : the seat of the body : RUMP

[1]**but·ton** \ˈbət-ᵊn\ *n* **1** : a small knob secured to an article (as of clothing) and used as a fastener by passing it through a buttonhole or loop **2** : something that resembles a button **3** : PUSH BUTTON

[2]**button** *vb* **but·toned; but·ton·ing** \ˈbət-(ᵊ-)niŋ\ : to close or fasten with buttons

[1]**but·ton·hole** \ˈbət-ᵊn-ˌhōl\ *n* : a slit or loop for a button to pass through

[2]**buttonhole** *vb* : to detain in conversation by or as if by holding on to the outer garments of

[1]**but·tress** \ˈbət-rəs\ *n* **1** : a projecting structure to support a wall **2** : PROP, SUPPORT

[2]**buttress** *vb* : PROP, SUPPORT

bu·tut \bu̇-ˈtüt\ *n* — see *dalasi* at MONEY table

bux·om \ˈbək-səm\ *adj* : healthily plump; *esp* : full-bosomed

[1]**buy** \ˈbī\ *vb* **bought** \ˈbȯt\; **buy·ing** : to obtain for a price : PURCHASE; *also* : BRIBE — **buy·er** *n*

[2]**buy** *n* **1** : PURCHASE 1, 2 **2** : an exceptional value

[1]**buzz** \ˈbəz\ *vb* **1** : to make a buzz **2** : to fly low over in an airplane

[2]**buzz** *n* : a low humming sound (as of bees in flight)

buz·zard \ˈbəz-ərd\ *n* : any of various usu. large birds of prey and esp. the turkey vulture

buzz·er \ˈbəz-ər\ *n* : a device that signals with a buzzing sound

buzz saw *n* : CIRCULAR SAW

BV *abbr* Blessed Virgin

BWI *abbr* British West Indies

bx *abbr* box

BX *abbr* base exchange

[1]**by** \(ˈ)bī, bə\ *prep* **1** : NEAR ⟨stood ~ the window⟩ **2** : through or through the medium of : VIA ⟨left ~ the door⟩ **3** : PAST ⟨drove ~ the house⟩ **4** : DURING, AT ⟨studied ~ night⟩ **5** : no later than ⟨get here ~ 3 p.m.⟩ **6** : through the means or direct agency of ⟨got it ~ fraud⟩ ⟨was seen ~ the others⟩ **7** : in conformity with : ACCORDING TO ⟨did it ~ the book⟩ **8** : with respect to ⟨an electrician ~ trade⟩ **9** : to the amount or extent of ⟨won ~ a nose⟩ ⟨overpaid ~ $3⟩ **10** — used to express relationship in multiplication, in division, and in measurements ⟨divide *a* ~ *b*⟩ ⟨multiply ~ 6⟩ ⟨15 feet ~ 20 feet⟩

[2]**by** \ˈbī\ *adv* **1** : near at hand; *also* : IN ⟨stopped ~ to chat⟩ **2** : PAST **3** : ASIDE, APART

bye \ˈbī\ *n* : a position of a participant in a tournament who has no opponent after pairs are drawn and advances to the next round without playing

by–elec·tion *also* **bye–election** \ˈbī-ə-ˌlek-shən\ *n* : a special election held between regular elections in order to fill a vacancy

by·gone \ˈbī-ˌgȯn\ *adj* : gone by : PAST — **bygone** *n*

by·law *or* **bye·law** \ˈbī-ˌlȯ\ *n* : a rule adopted by an organization for managing its internal affairs

by–line \ˈbī-ˌlīn\ *n* : a line at the beginning of a newspaper story or magazine article giving the writer's name

BYO *abbr* bring your own

BYOB *abbr* bring your own booze; bring your own bottle

[1]**by·pass** \ˈbī-ˌpas\ *n* : a passage to one side or around a blocked or congested area

[2]**bypass** *vb* : to avoid by means of a bypass

by·path \-ˌpath, -ˌpȧth\ *n* : BYWAY

by·play \ˈbī-ˌplā\ *n* : action engaged in at the side of a stage while the main action proceeds

by–prod·uct \-ˌpräd-(ˌ)əkt\ *n* : a product or result produced in addition to the main product or result

by·stand·er \-ˌstan-dər\ *n* : one present but not participating **syn** onlooker, witness, spectator, eyewitness

byte \ˈbīt\ *n* : a group of bits that a computer processes as a unit ⟨an 8-bit ~⟩

by the way *adv* : in passing : INCIDENTALLY

by·way \ˈbī-ˌwā\ *n* **1** : a little-traveled side road **2** : a secondary aspect

by·word \-ˌwərd\ *n* **1** : PROVERB **2** : an object of scorn

C

[1]**c** \ˈsē\ *n, pl* **c's** *or* **cs** \ˈsēz\ *often cap* **1** : the 3d letter of the English alphabet **2** : a grade rating a student's work as fair

[2]**c** *abbr, often cap* **1** calorie **2** carat **3** Celsius **4** cent **5** centigrade **6** centimeter **7** century **8** chapter **9** circa **10** cocaine **11** copyright

C *symbol* carbon

ca *abbr* circa

Ca *symbol* calcium

CA *abbr* **1** California **2** chartered accountant **3** chief accountant **4** chronological age

cab \ˈkab\ *n* **1** : a light closed horse-drawn carriage **2** : TAXICAB **3** : the covered compartment for the engineer and controls of a locomotive; *also* : a similar compartment (as on a truck)

CAB *abbr* Civil Aeronautics Board

ca·bal \kə-ˈbal\ *n* [F *cabale,* fr. ML *cabbala* cabala, fr. Heb *quabbālāh*, lit., received (lore)] : a secret group of plotters or political conspirators

ca·ba·la \ˈkab-ə-lə, kə-ˈbäl-ə\ *n, often cap* **1** : a medieval Jewish mysticism marked by belief in creation through emanation and a cipher method of interpreting scriptures **2** : esoteric doctrine or beliefs

ca·bana \kə-ˈban-(y)ə\ *n* : a shelter at a beach or swimming pool

cab·a·ret \ˌkab-ə-ˈrā\ *n* : NIGHTCLUB

cab·bage \ˈkab-ij\ *n* [ME *caboche,* fr. OF head] : a vegetable related to the turnip with a dense head of leaves

cab·bie *or* **cab·by** \ˈkab-ē\ *n, pl* **cabbies** : a driver of a cab

cab·in \ˈkab-ən\ *n* **1** : a private room on a ship; *also* : a compartment below deck on a small boat for passengers or crew **2** : an aircraft or spacecraft compartment for passengers, crew, or cargo **3** : a small simple one-story house
cabin boy *n* : a boy acting as servant on a ship
cabin class *n* : a class of accommodations on a passenger ship superior to tourist class and inferior to first class
cabin cruiser *n* : CRUISER 3
cab·i·net \ˈkab-(ə-)nət\ *n* **1** : a case or cupboard for holding or displaying articles (as jewels, specimens, or documents) **2** : an upright case housing a radio or television receiver **3** : the advisory council of a head of state (as a president or sovereign)
cab·i·net·mak·er \-ˌmā-kər\ *n* : a woodworker who makes fine furniture — **cab·i·net·mak·ing** \-ˌmā-kiŋ\ *n*
cab·i·net·work \-ˌwərk\ *n* : the finished work of a cabinetmaker
[1]**ca·ble** \ˈkā-bəl\ *n* **1** : a very strong rope, wire, or chain **2** : a bundle of insulated wires usu. twisted around a central core **3** : CABLEGRAM **4** : CABLE TELEVISION
[2]**cable** *vb* **ca·bled; ca·bling** \ˈkā-b(ə-)liŋ\ : to telegraph by cable
cable car *n* : a vehicle moved by an endless cable
ca·ble·gram \ˈkā-bəl-ˌgram\ *n* : a message sent by a submarine telegraph cable
cable television *n* : a system of television reception in which signals from distant stations are sent by cable to the receivers of paying subscribers
cab·o·chon \ˈkab-ə-ˌshän\ *n* : a gem or bead cut in convex form and highly polished but not given facets; *also* : this style of cutting — **cabochon** *adv*
ca·boose \kə-ˈbüs\ *n* : a car usu. at the rear of a freight train for the use of the train crew and railroad workers
cab·ri·o·let \ˌkab-rē-ə-ˈlā\ *n* [F] **1** : a light 2-wheeled one-horse carriage **2** : a convertible coupe
cab·stand \ˈkab-ˌstand\ *n* : a place for cabs to park while waiting for passengers
ca·cao \kə-ˈkaů, -ˈkā-ō\ *n, pl* **cacaos** [Sp] : a So. American tree whose seeds **(cacao beans)** are the source of cocoa and chocolate; *also* : its dried fatty seeds
cac·cia·to·re \ˌkäch-ə-ˈtōr-ē\ *adj* [It] : cooked with tomatoes and herbs ⟨veal ~⟩
[1]**cache** \ˈkash\ *n* [F] : a hiding place esp. for preserving provisions; *also* : something hidden or stored in a cache
[2]**cache** *vb* **cached; cach·ing** : to place or store in a cache
ca·chet \ka-ˈshā\ *n* [F] **1** : a seal used esp. as a mark of official approval **2** : a feature or quality conferring prestige; *also* : PRESTIGE **3** : a usu. flour paste capsule containing medicine **4** : a design, inscription, or advertisement printed or stamped on mail
cack·le \ˈkak-əl\ *vb* **cack·led; cack·ling** \-(ə-)liŋ\ **1** : to make the sharp broken cry characteristic of a hen **2** : to laugh or chatter noisily — **cackle** *n* — **cack·ler** \-(ə-)lər\ *n*
ca·coph·o·ny \ka-ˈkäf-ə-nē\ *n, pl* **-nies** : harsh or discordant sound — **ca·coph·o·nous** \-nəs\ *adj*
cac·tus \ˈkak-təs\ *n, pl* **cac·ti** \-ˌtī\ *also* **cac·tus·es** *or* **cactus** : any of a large family of drought-resistant flowering plants with fleshy usu. jointed stems and with leaves replaced by scales or prickles
cad \ˈkad\ *n* : a man who does not behave like a gentleman esp. toward women — **cad·dish** \-ish\ *adj* — **cad·dish·ly** *adv* — **cad·dish·ness** *n*
ca·dav·er \kə-ˈdav-ər\ *n* : a dead body : CORPSE
ca·dav·er·ous \kə-ˈdav-(ə-)rəs\ *adj* : suggesting a corpse esp. in gauntness or pallor **syn** wasted, emaciated, gaunt — **ca·dav·er·ous·ly** *adv*
cad·die *or* **cad·dy** \ˈkad-ē\ *n, pl* **caddies** [F *cadet* military cadet] : one that assists a golfer esp. by carrying his clubs — **caddie** *or* **caddy** *vb*
cad·dy \ˈkad-ē\ *n, pl* **caddies** [Malay *kati* a unit of weight] : a small box, can, or chest; *esp* : one to keep tea in
ca·dence \ˈkād-ᵊns\ *n* : the measure or beat of a rhythmical flow : RHYTHM — **ca·denced** \-ᵊnst\ *adj*
ca·den·za \kə-ˈden-zə\ *n* [It] : a brilliant sometimes improvised passage usu. toward the close of a musical composition
ca·det \kə-ˈdet\ *n* [F, fr. F dial. *capdet* chief, fr. L *capitellum*, fr. L *caput* head] **1** : a younger son or brother **2** : a student in a service academy
Ca·dette scout \kə-ˌdet-\ *n* : a Girl Scout between the ages of 12 and 14
cadge \ˈkaj\ *vb* **cadged; cadg·ing** : SPONGE, BEG — **cadg·er** *n*
cad·mi·um \ˈkad-mē-əm\ *n* : a bluish white metallic chemical element used in protective platings—see ELEMENT table
cad·re \ˈkad-rē\ *n* [F] **1** : FRAMEWORK **2** : a nucleus esp. of trained personnel capable of assuming control and training others **3** : a group of indoctrinated leaders active in promoting the interests of a revolutionary party
ca·du·ceus \kə-ˈd(y)ü-sē-əs, -shəs\ *n, pl* **-cei** \-sē-ˌī\ [L] **1** : the staff of a herald; *esp* : a representation of a staff with two entwined snakes and two wings at the top **2** : an insignia bearing a caduceus and symbolizing a physician
cae·cum *var of* CECUM
Cae·sar \ˈsē-zər\ *n* **1** : any of the Roman emperors succeeding Augustus Caesar — used as a title **2** *often not cap* : a powerful ruler : AUTOCRAT, DICTATOR; *also* : the civil or temporal power
caesarean *or* **caesarian** *var of* CESAREAN
cae·sura \si-ˈz(h)ůr-ə\ *n, pl* **-suras** *or* **-su·rae** \-ˈz(h)ůr-(ˌ)ē\ : a break in the flow of sound usu. in the middle of a line of verse
ca·fé \ka-ˈfā, kə-\ *n* [F, lit., coffee] **1** : RESTAURANT **2** : BARROOM **3** : NIGHTCLUB
ca·fé au lait \(ˌ)ka-ˌfā-ō-ˈlā\ *n* : coffee with hot milk in about equal parts
caf·e·te·ria \ˌkaf-ə-ˈtir-ē-ə\ *n* [AmerSp *cafetería* retail coffee store, fr. Sp *café* coffee] : a restaurant in which the customers serve themselves or are served at a counter
caf·feine \ka-ˈfēn, ˈka-ˌfēn\ *n* : a stimulating alkaloid found esp. in coffee and tea
caf·tan \kaf-ˈtan, ˈkaf-ˌtan\ *n* [Russ *kaftan*, fr. Turk, fr. Per *qaftān*] : an ankle-length garment with long sleeves worn in countries of the eastern Mediterranean
[1]**cage** \ˈkāj\ *n* **1** : an openwork enclosure for confining an animal **2** : something resembling a cage
[2]**cage** *vb* **caged; cag·ing** : to put or keep in or as if in a cage
ca·gey *also* **ca·gy** \ˈkā-jē\ *adj* **ca·gi·er; -est** : wary of being trapped or deceived : SHREWD — **ca·gi·ly** \ˈkā-jə-lē\ *adv* — **ca·gi·ness** \-jē-nəs\ *n*
CAGS *abbr* Certificate of Advanced Graduate Study
ca·hoot \kə-ˈhüt\ *n* : PARTNERSHIP, LEAGUE — usu. used in pl. ⟨officials in ~*s* with the underworld⟩
cai·man \kā-ˈman, kī-; ˈkā-mən\ *n* : any of several Central and So. American relatives of the crocodiles
cairn \ˈkaərn\ *n* : a heap of stones serving as a memorial or a landmark
cais·son \ˈkā-ˌsän, ˈkās-ᵊn\ *n* **1** : a usu. 2-wheeled vehicle for artillery ammunition **2** : a watertight chamber used in underwater construction work or as a foundation
caisson disease *n* : [3]BEND 3
cai·tiff \ˈkāt-əf\ *adj* [ME *caitif*, fr. OF, captive, vile, fr. L *captivus* captive] : being base, cowardly, or despicable — **caitiff** *n*
ca·jole \kə-ˈjōl\ *vb* **ca·joled; ca·jol·ing** [F *cajoler*] : to persuade or coax esp. with flattery or false promises : WHEEDLE — **ca·jole·ment** *n* — **ca·jol·ery** \-ˈjōl-(ə-)rē\ *n*
Ca·jun \ˈkā-jən\ *n* : a Louisianian descended from French-speaking immigrants from Acadia (Nova Scotia)
[1]**cake** \ˈkāk\ *n* **1** : a food made from batter that may be

fried or baked into a usu. small flat shape **2** : a sweet baked food made from batter or dough usu. containing a leaven (as baking powder) **3** : a substance hardened or molded into a solid mass ⟨a ~ of soap⟩

²cake *vb* **caked; cak·ing 1** : ENCRUST **2** : to form or harden into a cake

cake·walk \ˈkāk-ˌwȯk\ *n* **1** : a stage dance typically involving a high prance with backward tilt **2** : a one-sided contest

cal *abbr* **1** calendar **2** caliber

Cal *abbr* **1** California **2** calorie

cal·a·bash \ˈkal-ə-ˌbash\ *n* : the fruit of a gourd; *also* : a utensil made from its shell

cal·a·boose \ˈkal-ə-ˌbüs\ *n* [Sp *calabozo* dungeon] *dial* : JAIL

ca·la·di·um \kə-ˈlād-ē-əm\ *n* : any of a genus of tropical American ornamental plants related to the arums

cal·a·mari \ˌkäl-ə-ˈmär-ē\ *n* [It] : squid used as food

cal·a·mine \ˈkal-ə-ˌmīn\ *n* : a lotion of oxides of zinc and iron

ca·lam·i·ty \kə-ˈlam-ət-ē\ *n, pl* **-ties 1** : great distress or misfortune **2** : an event causing great harm or loss and affliction : DISASTER — **ca·lam·i·tous** \-ət-əs\ *adj* — **ca·lam·i·tous·ly** *adv* — **ca·lam·i·tous·ness** *n*

calc *abbr* calculate; calculated

cal·car·e·ous \kal-ˈkar-ē-əs\ *adj* : containing calcium or calcium carbonate; *also* : resembling calcium carbonate in hardness

cal·cif·er·ous \kal-ˈsif-(ə-)rəs\ *adj* : producing or containing calcium carbonate

cal·ci·fy \ˈkal-sə-ˌfī\ *vb* **-fied; -fy·ing** : to make or become calcareous — **cal·ci·fi·ca·tion** \ˌkal-sə-fə-ˈkā-shən\ *n*

cal·ci·mine \ˈkal-sə-ˌmīn\ *n* : a thin water paint used esp. on plastered surfaces — **calcimine** *vb*

cal·cine \kal-ˈsīn\ *vb* **cal·cined; cal·cin·ing** : to heat to a high temperature but without fusing to drive off volatile matter and often to reduce to powder — **cal·ci·na·tion** \ˌkal-sə-ˈnā-shən\ *n*

cal·cite \ˈkal-ˌsīt\ *n* : a crystalline mineral consisting of calcium carbonate — **cal·cit·ic** \kal-ˈsit-ik\ *adj*

cal·ci·um \ˈkal-sē-əm\ *n* : a silver-white soft metallic chemical element occurring only in combination — see ELEMENT table

calcium carbonate *n* : a substance found in nature as limestone and marble and in plant ashes, bones, and shells

cal·cu·late \ˈkal-kyə-ˌlāt\ *vb* **-lat·ed; -lat·ing** [L *calculare*, fr. *calculus* small stone, pebble used in reckoning] **1** : to determine by mathematical processes : COMPUTE **2** : to reckon by exercise of practical judgment : ESTIMATE **3** : to design or adapt for a purpose **4** : COUNT, RELY — **cal·cu·la·ble** \-lə-bəl\ *adj* — **cal·cu·la·tor** \-ˌlāt-ər\ *n*

cal·cu·lat·ed \-ˌlāt-əd\ *adj* : undertaken after estimating the probability of success or failure ⟨a ~ risk⟩

cal·cu·lat·ing \-ˌlāt-iŋ\ *adj* : marked by shrewd consideration esp. of self-interest — **cal·cu·lat·ing·ly** *adv*

cal·cu·la·tion \ˌkal-kyə-ˈlā-shən\ *n* **1** : the process or an act of calculating **2** : the result of an act of calculating **3** : studied care : CAUTION

cal·cu·lus \ˈkal-kyə-ləs\ *n, pl* **-li** \-ˌlī\ *also* **-lus·es** [L, pebble (used in reckoning)] **1** : a method of computation or calculation in a special notation (as of logic) **2** : a branch of higher mathematics concerned esp. with rates of change and the finding of lengths, areas, and volumes **3** : a concretion usu. of mineral salts esp. in hollow organs or ducts

cal·de·ra \kal-ˈder-ə, kȯl-, -ˈdir-\ *n* [Sp, lit., caldron] : a large crater usu. formed by the collapse of a volcanic cone

cal·dron \ˈkȯl-drən\ *n* : a large kettle

¹cal·en·dar \ˈkal-ən-dər\ *n* **1** : an arrangement of time into days, weeks, months, and years; *also* : a sheet or folder containing such an arrangement for a period **2** : an orderly list

²calendar *vb* **-dared; -dar·ing** \-d(ə-)riŋ\ : to enter in a calendar

¹cal·en·der \ˈkal-ən-dər\ *vb* : to press (as cloth or paper) between rollers or plates so as to make smooth or glossy or to thin into sheets

²calender *n* : a machine for calendering

ca·lends \ˈkal-əndz, ˈkāl-\ *n sing or pl* : the first day of the ancient Roman month

ca·len·du·la \kə-ˈlen-jə-lə\ *n* : any of a genus of yellow-flowered herbs related to the daisies

¹calf \ˈkaf, ˈkȧf\ *n, pl* **calves** \ˈkavz, ˈkȧvz\ **1** : the young of the domestic cow; *also* : the young of various other large mammals (as the elephant or whale) **2** : CALFSKIN

²calf *n, pl* **calves** \ˈkavz, ˈkȧvz\ : the fleshy back of the leg below the knee

calf·skin \ˈkaf-ˌskin, ˈkȧf-\ *n* : leather made of the skin of a calf

cal·i·ber *or* **cal·i·bre** \ˈkal-ə-bər\ *n* [MF *calibre*, fr. It *calibro*, fr. Ar *qālib* shoemaker's last] **1** : the diameter of a projectile **2** : the diameter of the bore of a gun **3** : degree of excellence or importance

cal·i·brate \ˈkal-ə-ˌbrāt\ *vb* **-brat·ed; -brat·ing 1** : to measure the caliber of **2** : to determine, correct, or put the measuring marks on ⟨~ a thermometer⟩ — **cal·i·bra·tion** \ˌkal-ə-ˈbrā-shən\ *n*

cal·i·co \ˈkal-i-ˌkō\ *n, pl* **-coes** *or* **-cos** : cotton cloth; *esp* : a cheap cotton printed fabric — **calico** *adj*

Calif *abbr* California

Cal·i·for·nia poppy \ˌkal-ə-ˈfȯr-nyə-\ *n* : a widely cultivated herb with pale yellow to red flowers that is related to the poppies

cal·i·for·ni·um \ˌkal-ə-ˈfȯr-nē-əm\ *n* : an artificially prepared radioactive chemical element—see ELEMENT table

cal·i·per *or* **cal·li·per** \ˈkal-ə-pər\ *n* **1** : an instrument with two adjustable legs used to measure the thickness of objects or distances between surfaces — usu. used in pl. ⟨a pair of ~*s*⟩ **2** : a device consisting of two plates lined with a frictional material that press against the sides of a rotating wheel or disk in certain brake systems

ca·liph *or* **ca·lif** \ˈkā-ləf, ˈkal-əf\ *n* : a successor of Muhammad as head of Islam — used as a title — **ca·liph·ate** \-ˌāt, -ət\ *n*

cal·is·then·ics \ˌkal-əs-ˈthen-iks\ *n sing or pl* [Gk *kalos* beautiful + *sthenos* strength] : bodily exercises without apparatus or with light hand apparatus — **cal·is·then·ic** *adj*

calk \ˈkȯk\ *var of* CAULK

¹call \ˈkȯl\ *vb* **1** : SHOUT, CRY; *also* : to utter a characteristic cry **2** : to utter in a loud clear voice **3** : to announce authoritatively **4** : SUMMON **5** : to make a request or demand ⟨~ for an investigation⟩ **6** : to get or try to get in communication by telephone **7** : to demand payment of (a loan); *also* : to demand surrender of (as a bond issue) for redemption **8** : to make a brief visit **9** : to speak of or address by name : give a name to **10** : to estimate or consider for practical purposes ⟨~ it ten miles⟩ **11** : to halt because of unsuitable conditions **12** : to temporarily transfer control of computer processing to (as a section of a computer program) — **call·er** *n*

²call *n* **1** : SHOUT **2** : the cry of an animal (as a bird) **3** : a request or a command to come or assemble : INVITATION, SUMMONS **4** : DEMAND, CLAIM; *also* : REQUEST **5** : a brief usu. formal visit **6** : an act of calling on the telephone **7** : a temporary transfer of control of computer processing to a particular set of instructions

cal·la lily \ˈkal-ə-\ *n* : a plant whose flowers form a fleshy yellow spike surrounded by a lilylike usu. white leaf

call·back \ˈkȯl-ˌbak\ *n* : a recall by a manufacturer of a product to correct a defect

call–board \-ˌbōrd\ *n* : a board for posting notices (as of rehearsal calls)

call down *vb* : REPRIMAND

call girl *n* : a prostitute with whom appointments are made by phone

cal·lig·ra·phy \kə-ˈlig-rə-fē\ *n* : beautiful or elegant handwriting; *also* : the art of producing such writing — **cal·lig·ra·pher** \-fər\ *n*

call in *vb* **1** : to order to return or be returned **2** : to summon to one's aid **3** : to report by telephone

call·ing \ˈkȯ-liŋ\ *n* **1** : a strong inner impulse toward a particular course of action **2** : the activity in which one customarily engages as an occupation

cal·li·ope \kə-ˈlī-ə-(ˌ)pē, ˈkal-ē-ˌōp\ *n* [fr. *Calliope*, chief of the Muses, fr. L, fr. Gk *Kalliopē*] : a musical instrument consisting of a series of whistles played by keys arranged as in an organ

call number *n* : a combination of characters assigned to a library book to indicate its place on a shelf

call off *vb* : CANCEL

cal·los·i·ty \ka-ˈläs-ət-ē, kə-\ *n, pl* **-ties** **1** : the quality or state of being callous **2** : CALLUS 1

[1]**cal·lous** \ˈkal-əs\ *adj* **1** : being thickened and usu. hardened ⟨~ skin⟩ **2** : hardened in feeling — **cal·lous·ly** *adv* — **cal·lous·ness** *n*

[2]**callous** *vb* : to make callous

cal·low \ˈkal-ō\ *adj* [ME *calu* bald, fr. OE] : lacking adult sophistication : IMMATURE — **cal·low·ness** *n*

call–up \ˈkȯl-ˌəp\ *n* : an order to report for active military service

call up \(ˈ)kȯl-ˈəp\ *vb* : to summon for active military duty

[1]**cal·lus** \ˈkal-əs\ *n* **1** : a callous area on skin or bark **2** : tissue that is converted into bone in the healing of a bone fracture

[2]**callus** *vb* : to form a callus

[1]**calm** \ˈkäm, ˈkalm\ *adj* : marked by calm : STILL, PLACID, SERENE — **calm·ly** *adv* — **calm·ness** *n*

[2]**calm** *vb* : to make or become calm

[3]**calm** *n* **1** : a period or a condition of freedom from storms, high winds, or rough water **2** : complete or almost complete absence of wind **3** : a state of tranquillity

cal·o·mel \ˈkal-ə-məl, -ˌmel\ *n* : a chloride of mercury used esp. as a purgative and fungicide

ca·lor·ic \kə-ˈlȯr-ik\ *adj* **1** : of or relating to heat **2** : of or relating to calories

cal·o·rie *also* **cal·o·ry** \ˈkal-(ə-)rē\ *n, pl* **-ries** : a unit for measuring heat; *esp* : one for measuring the value of foods for producing heat and energy in the human body equivalent to the amount of heat required to raise the temperature of one kilogram of water one degree Celsius

cal·o·rif·ic \ˌkal-ə-ˈrif-ik\ *adj* : CALORIC

cal·o·rim·e·ter \ˌkal-ə-ˈrim-ət-ər\ *n* : an apparatus for measuring quantities of heat — **cal·o·rim·e·try** \ˌkal-ə-ˈrim-ə-trē\ *n*

cal·u·met \ˈkal-yə-ˌmet, -mət\ *n* : an American Indian ceremonial pipe

ca·lum·ni·ate \kə-ˈləm-nē-ˌāt\ *vb* **-at·ed; -at·ing** : to accuse falsely and maliciously : SLANDER **syn** defame, malign, libel, slander, traduce — **ca·lum·ni·a·tion** \-ˌləm-nē-ˈā-shən\ *n* — **ca·lum·ni·a·tor** \-ˈləm-nē-ˌāt-ər\ *n*

cal·um·ny \ˈkal-əm-nē\ *n, pl* **-nies** : false and malicious accusation — **ca·lum·ni·ous** \kə-ˈləm-nē-əs\ *adj*

calve \ˈkav, ˈkȧv\ *vb* **calved; calv·ing** : to give birth to a calf

calves *pl of* CALF

Cal·vin·ism \ˈkal-və-ˌniz-əm\ *n* : the theological system of John Calvin and his followers — **Cal·vin·ist** \-və-nəst\ *n or adj* — **Cal·vin·is·tic** \ˌkal-və-ˈnis-tik\ *adj*

ca·lyp·so \kə-ˈlip-sō\ *n, pl* **-sos** : a style of music originating in the British West Indies and having lyrics that usu. satirize local personalities and events

ca·lyx \ˈkā-liks, ˈkal-iks\ *n, pl* **ca·lyx·es** *or* **ca·ly·ces** \ˈkā-lə-ˌsēz, ˈkal-ə-\ : the outside usu. green or leaflike part of a flower consisting of sepals

cam \ˈkam\ *n* : a rotating or sliding projection (as on a wheel) in a mechanical linkage by which rotary motion is transformed into linear motion or vice versa

ca·ma·ra·de·rie \ˌkam-(ə-)ˈrad-ə-rē, ˌkäm-(ə-)ˈräd-\ *n* [F] : friendly feeling and goodwill among comrades

cam·bi·um \ˈkam-bē-əm\ *n, pl* **-bi·ums** *or* **-bia** \-bē-ə\ : a thin cellular layer between xylem and phloem of most higher plants from which new tissues develop — **cam·bi·al** \-bē-əl\ *adj*

Cam·bri·an *adj* : of, relating to, or being the earliest period of the Paleozoic era — **Cambrian** *n*

cam·bric \ˈkām-brik\ *n* : a fine thin white linen or cotton fabric

came *past of* COME

cam·el \ˈkam-əl\ *n* : either of two large hoofed cud-chewing mammals used esp. in desert regions of Asia and Africa for carrying burdens and for riding

camel hair *also* **camel's hair** *n* **1** : the hair of a camel or a substitute for it **2** : cloth made of camel hair or of camel hair and wool

ca·mel·lia \kə-ˈmēl-yə\ *n* : any of several shrubs or trees related to the tea plant and grown in warm regions and greenhouses for their showy roselike flowers

Cam·em·bert \ˈkam-əm-ˌbeər\ *n* : a soft surface-ripened cheese with a grayish rind and yellow interior

cam·eo \ˈkam-ē-ˌō\ *n, pl* **-eos** **1** : a gem carved in relief; *also* : a small medallion with a profiled head in relief **2** : a brief appearance by a well-known actor in a play or movie

cam·era \ˈkam-(ə-)rə\ *n* : a closed lightproof box with a lens through which the image of an object is recorded on a light-sensitive material; *also* : an electronic device that forms an image and converts it into an electrical signal (as for television broadcast) — **cam·era·man** \ˈkam-(ə-)rə-ˌman, -mən\ *n*

Cam·er·oo·ni·an \ˌkam-ə-ˈrü-nē-ən\ *n* : a native or inhabitant of the Republic of Cameroon or the Cameroons region — **Cameroonian** *adj*

cam·i·sole \ˈkam-ə-ˌsōl\ *n* : a short sleeveless undergarment for women

camomile *var of* CHAMOMILE

cam·ou·flage \ˈkam-ə-ˌfläzh, -ˌfläj\ *n* [F] **1** : the disguising of military equipment with paint, nets, or foliage; *also* : the disguise itself **2** : a deceptive expedient — **camouflage** *vb*

[1]**camp** \ˈkamp\ *n* **1** : a place where tents or buildings are erected for usu. temporary shelter **2** : a collection of tents or other shelters **3** : a body of persons encamped — **camp·ground** \-ˌgraůnd\ *n* — **camp·site** \-ˌsīt\ *n*

[2]**camp** *vb* **1** : to make or occupy a camp **2** : to live in a camp or outdoors

[3]**camp** *n* **1** : exaggerated effeminate mannerisms **2** : something so outrageous or in such bad taste as to be considered amusing — **camp** *adj* — **camp·i·ly** \ˈkam-pə-lē\ *adv* — **camp·i·ness** \-pē-nəs\ *n* — **campy** \ˈkam-pē\ *adj*

[4]**camp** *vb* : to engage in camp : exhibit the qualities of camp

cam·paign \kam-ˈpān\ *n* **1** : a series of military operations forming one distinct stage in a war **2** : a series of activities designed to bring about a particular result ⟨advertising ~⟩ — **campaign** *vb* — **cam·paign·er** *n*

cam·pa·ni·le \ˌkam-pə-ˈnē-lē\ *n, pl* **-ni·les** *or* **-ni·li** \-ˈnē-lē\ : a usu. freestanding bell tower

cam·pa·nol·o·gy \ˌkam-pə-ˈnäl-ə-jē\ *n* : the art of bell ringing — **cam·pa·nol·o·gist** \-jəst\ *n*

camp·er \ˈkam-pər\ *n* **1** : one that camps **2** : a portable dwelling (as a specially equipped vehicle) for use during casual travel and camping

Camp Fire Girl *n* : a member of a national organization of girls from 7 to 18

camp follower *n* **1** : a civilian (as a prostitute) who follows a military unit to attend or exploit its personnel **2** : a follower of a group who is not an adherent; *esp* : a politician who joins a movement solely for personal gain

cam·phor \ˈkam(p)-fər\ *n* : a gummy volatile fragrant compound obtained from an evergreen Asian tree **(camphor tree)** and used esp. in medicine

camp meeting *n* : a series of evangelistic meetings usu. held outdoors

camp·o·ree \ˌkam-pə-ˈrē\ *n* : a gathering of Boy Scouts or Girl Scouts from a given geographic area

cam·pus \ˈkam-pəs\ *n* [L, plain] : the grounds and buildings of a college or school; *also* : a central grassy part of the grounds

cam·shaft \ˈkam-ˌshaft\ *n* : a shaft to which a cam is fastened

[1]**can** \kən, (ˈ)kan\ *vb, past* **could** \kəd, (ˈ)ku̇d\; *pres sing & pl* **can 1** : be able to **2** : may perhaps ⟨~ he still be alive⟩ **3** : be permitted by conscience or feeling to ⟨you ~ hardly blame him⟩ **4** : have permission or liberty to ⟨you ~ go now⟩

[2]**can** \ˈkan\ *n* **1** : a typically cylindrical metal container or receptacle ⟨garbage ~⟩ ⟨coffee ~⟩ **2** : JAIL

[3]**can** \ˈkan\ *vb* **canned; can·ning 1** : to put in a can : preserve by sealing in airtight cans or jars **2** *slang* : to discharge from employment **3** *slang* : to put a stop or an end to **4** : to record on discs or tape — **can·ner** *n*

Can *or* **Canad** *abbr* Canada; Canadian

Can·a·da goose \ˈkan-əd-ə-\ *n* : a common wild goose of No. America

Ca·na·di·an \kə-ˈnād-ē-ən\ *n* : a native or inhabitant of Canada — **Canadian** *adj*

ca·naille \kə-ˈnī, -ˈnāl\ *n* [F, fr. It *canaglia*, fr. *cane* dog] : RABBLE, RIFFRAFF

ca·nal \kə-ˈnal\ *n* **1** : a tubular passage in the body : DUCT **2** : an artificial waterway (as for boats or irrigation)

can·a·lize \ˈkan-ᵊl-ˌīz\ *vb* **-lized; -liz·ing 1** : to provide with a canal or make into or like a channel **2** : to provide with an outlet; *esp* : to direct into preferred channels — **ca·nal·iza·tion** \ˌkan-ᵊl-ə-ˈzā-shən\ *n*

can·a·pé \ˈkan-ə-pē, -ˌpā\ *n* [F, lit., sofa, fr. ML *canopeum, canapeum* mosquito net] : a piece of bread or toast or a cracker topped with a savory food

ca·nard \kə-ˈnärd\ *n* : a false or unfounded report or story

ca·nary \kə-ˈner-ē\ *n, pl* **ca·nar·ies** [fr. the *Canary* islands] **1** : a usu. sweet wine similar to Madeira **2** : a usu. yellow or greenish finch often kept in a cage **3** : a bright yellow

ca·nas·ta \kə-ˈnas-tə\ *n* [Sp, lit., basket] : rummy played with two full decks of cards plus four jokers

canc *abbr* canceled

can·can \ˈkan-ˌkan\ *n* : a woman's dance of French origin characterized by high kicking

[1]**can·cel** \ˈkan-səl\ *vb* **-celed** *or* **-celled; -cel·ing** *or* **-cel·ling** \-s(ə-)liŋ\ [ME *cancellen*, fr. MF *canceller*, fr. L *cancellare* to make like a lattice, fr. *cancer* lattice] **1** : to destroy the force or validity of : ANNUL **2** : to match in force or effect : OFFSET **3** : to cross out : DELETE **4** : to remove (a common divisor) from a numerator and denominator; *also* : to remove (equivalents) on opposite sides of an equation or account **5** : to mark (a postage stamp or check) so that it cannot be reused **6** : to neutralize each other's strength or effect — **can·cel·la·tion** \ˌkan-sə-ˈlā-shən\ *n* — **can·cel·er** *or* **can·cel·ler** \ˈkan(t)-s(ə-)lər\ *n*

[2]**cancel** *n* **1** : CANCELLATION **2** : a deleted part

can·cer \ˈkan-sər\ *n* [L, lit., crab] **1** *cap* : a zodiacal constellation between Gemini and Leo usu. pictured as a crab **2** *cap* : the 4th sign of the zodiac in astrology; *also* : one born under this sign **3** : a malignant tumor that tends to spread in the body **4** : a malignant evil that corrodes slowly and fatally — **can·cer·ous** \ˈkans-(ə-)rəs\ *adj* — **can·cer·ous·ly** *adv*

can·de·la·bra \ˌkan-də-ˈläb-rə, -ˈlab-\ *n* : an ornamental branched candlestick or lamp with several lights

can·de·la·brum \-rəm\ *n, pl* **-bra** \-rə\ *also* **-brums** : CANDELABRA

can·des·cent \kan-ˈdes-ᵊnt\ *adj* : glowing or dazzling esp. from great heat — **can·des·cence** \-ᵊns\ *n*

can·did \ˈkan-dəd\ *adj* **1** : FRANK, STRAIGHTFORWARD **2** : relating to photography of subjects acting naturally or spontaneously without being posed — **can·did·ly** *adv* — **can·did·ness** *n*

can·di·da·cy \ˈkan-(d)əd-ə-sē\ *n, pl* **-cies** : the state of being a candidate

can·di·date \ˈkan-(d)ə-ˌdāt, -(d)əd-ət\ *n* [L *candidatus*, fr. *candidatus* clothed in white, fr. *candidus* white; fr. the white toga worn by candidates in ancient Rome] : one who seeks or is proposed for an office, honor, or membership

can·di·da·ture \ˈkan-(d)əd-ə-ˌchu̇r\ *n, chiefly Brit* : CANDIDACY

can·died \ˈkan-dēd\ *adj* : preserved in or encrusted with sugar

[1]**can·dle** \ˈkan-dᵊl\ *n* : a usu. slender mass of tallow or wax molded around a wick and burned to give light

[2]**candle** *vb* **can·dled; can·dling** \ˈkan-(d)liŋ, -dᵊl-iŋ\ : to examine (as eggs) by holding between the eye and a light — **can·dler** \-d(ᵊ-)lər\ *n*

can·dle·light \ˈkan-dᵊl-(l)īt\ *n* **1** : the light of a candle; *also* : any soft artificial light **2** : the time when candles are lit : TWILIGHT

Can·dle·mas \ˈkan-dᵊl-məs\ *n* : February 2 observed as a church festival in commemoration of the presentation of Christ in the temple

can·dle·pin \-ˌpin\ *n* : a slender bowling pin tapering toward top and bottom used in a bowling game **(candlepins)** with a smaller ball than that used in tenpins

can·dle·stick \-ˌstik\ *n* : a holder with a socket for a candle

can·dle·wick \-ˌwik\ *n* : a soft cotton yarn; *also* : embroidery made with this yarn usu. in tufts

can·dor \ˈkan-dər\ *n* : FRANKNESS, OUTSPOKENNESS

C and W *abbr* country and western

[1]**can·dy** \ˈkan-dē\ *n, pl* **candies** : a confection made from sugar often with flavoring and filling

[2]**candy** *vb* **can·died; can·dy·ing 1** : to encrust in sugar often by cooking in a syrup **2** : to make attractive : SWEETEN **3** : to crystallize or become crystallized into sugar

candy strip·er \-ˌstrī-pər\ *n* : a teenage volunteer nurse's aide

[1]**cane** \ˈkān\ *n* **1** : a slender hollow or pithy stem (as of a reed or bramble) **2** : a tall woody grass or reed (as sugarcane) **3** : a walking stick; *also* : a rod for flogging

[2]**cane** *vb* **caned; can·ing 1** : to beat with a cane **2** : to weave or make with cane — **can·er** *n*

cane·brake \ˈkān-ˌbrāk\ *n* : a thicket of cane

[1]**ca·nine** \ˈkā-ˌnīn\ *n* [L *caninus*, fr. *canis* dog] **1** : a pointed tooth between the outer incisor and the first premolar **2** : DOG

[2]**canine** *adj* : of or relating to dogs or to the family to which they belong

can·is·ter \ˈkan-ə-stər\ *n* **1** : a small box for holding a dry product (as tea) **2** : a perforated box containing material to absorb or filter a harmful substance in the air

\ə\abut \ᵊ\kitten \ər\further \a\ash \ā\ace \ä\cot, cart \au̇\out \ch\chin \e\bet \ē\easy \g\go \i\hit \ī\ice \j\job \ŋ\sing \ō\go \ȯ\law \ȯi\boy \th\thin \th\the \ü\loot \u̇\foot \y\yet \zh\vision *see also* Pronunciation Symbols page

can·ker \ˈkaŋ-kər\ *n* : a spreading sore that eats into tissue — **can·ker·ous** \ˈkaŋ-k(ə-)rəs\ *adj*

can·ker·worm \-ˌwərm\ *n* : either of two moths and esp. their larvae that are pests of forest and shade trees

can·na \ˈkan-ə\ *n* : any of a genus of tropical herbs with large leaves and racemes of bright-colored flowers

can·na·bis \ˈkan-ə-bəs\ *n* : any of the psychoactive preparations (as marijuana) or chemicals (as THC) derived from hemp; *also* : HEMP

canned \ˈkand\ *adj* : prepared in standardized form for general use or wide distribution

can·nery \ˈkan-(ə-)rē\ *n, pl* **-ner·ies** : a factory for the canning of foods

can·ni·bal \ˈkan-ə-bəl\ *n* [NL *Canibalis* a member of a Caribbean Indian people, fr. Sp *Caníbal,* fr. a native word *Caniba* or *Carib*] : one that eats the flesh of its own kind — **can·ni·bal·ism** \ˈkan-ə-bə-ˌliz-əm\ *n* — **can·ni·bal·is·tic** \ˌkan-ə-bə-ˈlis-tik\ *adj*

can·ni·bal·ize \ˈkan-ə-bə-ˌlīz\ *vb* **-ized; -iz·ing 1** : to take usable parts from (as an inoperative machine) to construct or repair another machine **2** : to practice cannibalism

can·non \ˈkan-ən\ *n, pl* **cannons** *or* **cannon** [MF *canon,* fr. It *cannone,* lit., large tube, fr. *canna* reed, tube, fr. L, cane, reed] **1** : an artillery piece supported on a carriage or mount **2** : a large-caliber automatic gun on an aircraft

cannon 1

can·non·ade \ˌkan-ə-ˈnād\ *n* : a heavy fire of artillery — **cannonade** *vb*

can·non·ball \ˈkan-ən-ˌbȯl\ *n* : a usu. round solid missile for firing from a cannon

can·non·eer \ˌkan-ə-ˈniər\ *n* : an artillery gunner

can·not \ˈkan-ˌät; kə-ˈnät\ : can not — **cannot but** : to be unable to do otherwise than

can·nu·la \ˈkan-yə-lə\ *n, pl* **-las** *or* **-lae** \-ˌlē\ : a small tube for insertion into a body cavity or into a duct or vessel

can·ny \ˈkan-ē\ *adj* **can·ni·er; -est** : PRUDENT, SHREWD — **can·ni·ly** \ˈkan-ᵊl-ē\ *adv* — **can·ni·ness** \ˈkan-ē-nəs\ *n*

ca·noe \kə-ˈnü\ *n* : a light narrow boat with sharp ends and curved sides that is usu. propelled by paddles — **canoe** *vb* — **ca·noe·ist** *n*

[1]**can·on** \ˈkan-ən\ *n* **1** : a regulation decreed by a church council; *also* : a provision of canon law **2** : an official or authoritative list (as of the saints or the books of the Bible) **3** : an accepted principle ⟨the ~*s* of good taste⟩

[2]**canon** *n* : a clergyman on the staff of a cathedral

ca·ñon \ˈkan-yən\ *var of* CANYON

ca·non·i·cal \kə-ˈnän-i-kəl\ *adj* **1** : of, relating to, or forming a canon **2** : conforming to a general rule or acceptable procedure : ORTHODOX **3** : of or relating to a clergyman who is a canon — **ca·non·i·cal·ly** \-k(ə-)lē\ *adv*

ca·non·i·cals \-kəlz\ *n pl* : the vestments prescribed by canon for an officiating clergyman

can·on·ize \ˈkan-ə-ˌnīz\ *vb* **can·on·ized** \-ˌnīzd\; **can·on·iz·ing 1** : to declare an officially recognized saint **2** : GLORIFY, EXALT — **can·on·iza·tion** \ˌkan-ə-nə-ˈzā-shən\ *n*

canon law *n* : the law governing a church

canon regular *n, pl* **canons regular** : a member of one of several Roman Catholic religious institutes of regular priests living in community

can·o·py \ˈkan-ə-pē\ *n, pl* **-pies** [ME *canope,* fr. ML *canopeum* mosquito net, fr. L *conopeum,* fr. Gk *kōnōpion,* fr. *kōnōps* mosquito] : an overhanging cover, shelter, or shade — **canopy** *vb*

[1]**cant** \ˈkant\ *n* **1** : an oblique or slanting surface **2** : TILT, SLANT

[2]**cant** *vb* : to give a slant to

[3]**cant** *vb* **1** : to beg in a whining manner **2** : to talk hypocritically

[4]**cant** *n* **1** : the special idiom of a profession or trade : JARGON **2** : insincere speech; *esp* : insincerely pious words or statements

Cant *abbr* Canticle of Canticles

can·ta·bi·le \kän-ˈtäb-ə-ˌlā\ *adv or adj* [It] : in a singing manner — used as a direction in music

can·ta·loupe *also* **can·te·loupe** \ˈkant-ᵊl-ˌōp\ *n* : MUSKMELON; *esp* : one with orange flesh and rough skin

can·tan·ker·ous \kan-ˈtaŋ-k(ə-)rəs\ *adj* : ILL-NATURED, QUARRELSOME — **can·tan·ker·ous·ly** *adv* — **can·tan·ker·ous·ness** *n*

can·ta·ta \kən-ˈtät-ə\ *n* [It] : a choral composition usu. accompanied by organ, piano, or orchestra

can·teen \kan-ˈtēn\ *n* [F *cantine* bottle case, canteen (store), fr. It *cantina* wine cellar, fr. *canto* corner] **1** : a flask for carrying liquids **2** : a place of recreation and entertainment for military personnel **3** : a small cafeteria or counter at which snacks are served

can·ter \ˈkant-ər\ *n* : a horse's 3-beat gait resembling but smoother and slower than a gallop — **canter** *vb*

Can·ter·bury bell \ˌkant-ə(r)-ˌber-ē-\ *n* : any of several plants related to the bluebell that are cultivated for their showy flowers

can·ti·cle \ˈkant-i-kəl\ *n* : SONG; *esp* : any of several liturgical songs taken from the Bible

Canticle of Canticles *n* — see BIBLE table

[1]**can·ti·le·ver** \ˈkant-ᵊl-ˌē-vər\ *n* : a projecting beam or structure supported only at one end; *also* : either of a pair of such structures projecting toward each other so that when joined they form a bridge

[2]**cantilever** *vb* **1** : to project as a cantilever **2** : to build as a cantilever **3** : to support by a cantilever ⟨a ~*ed* shelf⟩

can·tle \ˈkant-ᵊl\ *n* : the upwardly projecting rear part of a saddle

can·to \ˈkan-ˌtō\ *n, pl* **cantos** [It, fr. L *cantus* song] : one of the major divisions of a long poem

can·ton \ˈkant-ᵊn, ˈkan-ˌtän\ *n* : a small territorial division of a country; *esp* : one of the political divisions of Switzerland — **can·ton·al** \ˈkant-ᵊn-əl, kan-ˈtän-ᵊl\ *adj*

can·ton·ment \kan-ˈtōn-mənt, -ˈtän-\ *n* : usu. temporary quarters for troops

can·tor \ˈkant-ər\ *n* : a synagogue official who sings liturgical music and leads the congregation in prayer

can·vas *also* **can·vass** \ˈkan-vəs\ *n* **1** : a strong cloth formerly much used for making tents and sails **2** : a set of sails **3** : a group of tents **4** : a piece of cloth prepared as a surface to receive oil paint; *also* : an oil painting **5** : the canvas-covered floor of a boxing or wrestling ring

can·vas·back \ˈkan-vəs-ˌbak\ *n* : a No. American wild duck with red head and gray back

[1]**can·vass** *also* **can·vas** \ˈkan-vəs\ *vb* : to go through (a district) or to go to (persons) to solicit votes or orders for goods or to determine public opinion or sentiment — **can·vass·er** *n*

[2]**canvass** *n* : an act of canvassing (as the solicitation of votes or survey of public opinion)

can·yon \ˈkan-yən\ *n* : a deep narrow valley with high steep sides

caou·tchouc \ˈkau̇-ˌchu̇k, -ˌchük\ *n* : RUBBER 3

[1]**cap** \ˈkap\ *n* **1** : a covering for the head esp. with a visor and no brim; *also* : something resembling such a covering **2** : a container holding an explosive charge **3** : an upper limit (as on expenditures)

[2]**cap** *vb* **capped; cap·ping 1** : to provide or protect with a cap **2** : to form a cap over : CROWN **3** : OUTDO, SURPASS **4** : CLIMAX

[3]**cap** *abbr* **1** capacity **2** capital **3** capitalize; capitalized
CAP *abbr* Civil Air Patrol
ca·pa·ble \ˈkā-pə-bəl\ *adj* **:** having ability, capacity, or power to do something **:** ABLE, COMPETENT — **ca·pa·bil·i·ty** \ˌkā-pə-ˈbil-ət-ē\ *n* — **ca·pa·bly** \ˈkā-pə-blē\ *adv*
ca·pa·cious \kə-ˈpā-shəs\ *adj* **:** able to contain much — **ca·pa·cious·ly** *adv* — **ca·pa·cious·ness** *n*
ca·pac·i·tance \kə-ˈpas-ət-əns\ *n* **:** the property of an electric nonconductor that permits the storage of energy
ca·pac·i·tor \kə-ˈpas-ət-ər\ *n* **:** an electronic circuit device for temporary storage of electrical energy
[1]**ca·pac·i·ty** \kə-ˈpas-ət-ē\ *n, pl* **-ties 1 :** legal qualification or fitness **2 :** the ability to contain, receive, or accommodate **3 :** extent of space **:** VOLUME **4 :** ABILITY **5 :** position or character assigned or assumed
[2]**capacity** *adj* **:** equaling maximum capacity ⟨a ~ crowd⟩
cap–a–pie *or* **cap–à–pie** \ˌkap-ə-ˈpē\ *adv* [MF] **:** from head to foot **:** at all points
ca·par·i·son \kə-ˈpar-ə-sən\ *n* **1 :** an ornamental covering for a horse **2 :** TRAPPINGS, ADORNMENT — **caparison** *vb*
[1]**cape** \ˈkāp\ *n* **1 :** a point of land jutting out into water **2** *usu cap* **:** CAPE COD COTTAGE
[2]**cape** *n* **:** a sleeveless garment hanging from the neck over the shoulders
Cape Cod cottage \ˌkāp-ˌkäd-\ *n* **:** a compact rectangular dwelling of one or one-and-a-half stories usu. with a steep gable roof
[1]**ca·per** \ˈkā-pər\ *n* **:** the flower bud or young berry of a Mediterranean shrub pickled for use as a relish; *also* **:** this shrub
[2]**caper** *vb* **ca·pered; ca·per·ing** \-p(ə-)riŋ\ **:** to leap about in a playful manner **:** PRANCE
[3]**caper** *n* **1 :** a frolicsome leap **2 :** a capricious escapade **3 :** an illegal or questionable act
cape·skin \ˈkāp-ˌskin\ *n* **:** a light flexible leather made from sheepskins
Cape Verd·ian \-ˈvərd-ē-ən\ *n* **:** a native or inhabitant of the Republic of Cape Verde
cap·ful \ˈkap-ˌfu̇l\ *n* **:** as much as a cap will hold
cap·il·lar·i·ty \ˌkap-ə-ˈlar-ət-ē\ *n, pl* **-ties :** the action by which the surface of a liquid where it is in contact with a solid (as in a slender tube) is raised or lowered depending on the relative attraction of the molecules of the liquid for each other and for those of the solid
[1]**cap·il·lary** \ˈkap-ə-ˌler-ē\ *adj* **1 :** resembling a hair **2 :** having a very small bore ⟨~ tube⟩ **3 :** of or relating to capillaries or to capillarity
[2]**capillary** *n, pl* **-lar·ies :** any of the tiny thin-walled blood vessels that carry blood between the smallest arteries and their corresponding veins
[1]**cap·i·tal** \ˈkap-ət-ᵊl\ *adj* **1 :** conforming to the series A, B, C rather than a, b, c ⟨~ letters⟩ ⟨~ G⟩ **2 :** punishable by death ⟨a ~ crime⟩ **3 :** most serious ⟨a ~ error⟩ **4 :** first in importance or position **:** CHIEF; *also* **:** being the seat of government ⟨the ~ city⟩ **5 :** of or relating to capital ⟨~ expenditures⟩; *esp* **:** relating to or being assets that add to the long-term net worth of a corporation **6 :** FIRST-RATE, EXCELLENT
[2]**capital** *n* **1 :** accumulated wealth esp. as used to produce more wealth **2 :** the total face value of shares of stock issued by a company **3 :** capitalists considered as a group **4 :** ADVANTAGE, GAIN **5 :** a letter larger than the ordinary small letter and often different in form **6 :** the capital city of a state or country; *also* **:** a city preeminent in some activity ⟨the fashion ~ of the world⟩
[3]**capital** *n* **:** the top part or piece of an architectural column
capital gain *n* **:** the increase in value of an asset (as stock or real estate) between the time it is bought and the time it is sold
capital goods *n pl* **:** machinery, tools, factories, and commodities used in the production of goods
cap·i·tal·ism \ˈkap-ət-ᵊl-ˌiz-əm\ *n* **:** an economic system characterized by private or corporate ownership of capital goods and by prices, production, and distribution of goods that are determined mainly in a free market
[1]**cap·i·tal·ist** \-əst\ *n* **1 :** a person who has capital esp. invested in business **2 :** a person of great wealth **:** PLUTOCRAT **3 :** a believer in capitalism
[2]**capitalist** *or* **cap·i·tal·is·tic** \ˌkap-ət-ᵊl-ˈis-tik\ *adj* **1 :** owning capital **2 :** practicing or advocating capitalism **3 :** marked by capitalism — **cap·i·tal·is·ti·cal·ly** \-ti-k(ə-)lē\ *adv*
cap·i·tal·iza·tion \ˌkap-ət-ᵊl-ə-ˈzā-shən\ *n* **1 :** the act or process of capitalizing **2 :** the total amount of money used as capital in a business
cap·i·tal·ize \ˈkap-ət-ᵊl-ˌīz\ *vb* **-ized; -iz·ing 1 :** to write or print with an initial capital or in capitals **2 :** to convert into or use as capital **3 :** to supply capital for **4 :** to gain by turning something to advantage **:** PROFIT
cap·i·tal·ly \ˈkap-ət-ᵊl-ē\ *adv* **:** ADMIRABLY, EXCELLENTLY
cap·i·ta·tion \ˌkap-ə-ˈtā-shən\ *n* **:** a direct uniform tax levied on each person
cap·i·tol \ˈkap-ət-ᵊl\ *n* **:** the building in which a legislature holds its sessions
ca·pit·u·late \kə-ˈpich-ə-ˌlāt\ *vb* **-lat·ed; -lat·ing 1 :** to surrender esp. on conditions agreed upon **2 :** to cease resisting **:** ACQUIESCE **syn** submit, yield, succumb, cave, defer — **ca·pit·u·la·tion** \-ˌpich-ə-ˈlā-shən\ *n*
ca·pon \ˈkā-ˌpän, -pən\ *n* **:** a castrated male chicken
cap·puc·ci·no \ˌkap-ə-ˈchē-nō, ˌkäp-\ *n* [It, lit., Capuchin; fr. the likeness of its color to that of a Capuchin's habit] **:** espresso mixed with foamy hot milk or cream and often flavored with cinnamon
ca·pric·cio \kə-ˈprē-ch(ē-ˌ)ō\ *n, pl* **-cios :** an instrumental piece in free form usu. lively in tempo and brilliant in style
ca·price \kə-ˈprēs\ *n* [F, fr. It *capriccio,* lit., head with hair standing on end, shudder, fr. *capo* head + *riccio* hedgehog] **1 :** a sudden whim or fancy **2 :** an inclination to change one's mind impulsively **3 :** CAPRICCIO — **ca·pri·cious** \kə-ˈprish-əs\ *adj* — **ca·pri·cious·ly** *adv* — **ca·pri·cious·ness** *n*
Cap·ri·corn \ˈkap-ri-ˌkȯrn\ *n* **1 :** a zodiacal constellation between Sagittarius and Aquarius usu. pictured as a goat **2 :** the 10th sign of the zodiac in astrology; *also* **:** one born under this sign
cap·ri·ole \ˈkap-rē-ˌōl\ *n* **:** [3]CAPER 1; *esp* **:** an upward leap of a horse with a backward kick at the height of the leap — **capriole** *vb*
caps *abbr* **1** capitals **2** capsule
cap·si·cum \ˈkap-si-kəm\ *n* **:** PEPPER 2
cap·size \ˈkap-ˌsīz, kap-ˈsīz\ *vb* **cap·sized; cap·siz·ing :** UPSET, OVERTURN
cap·stan \ˈkap-stən, -ˌstan\ *n* **1 :** a machine for moving or raising heavy weights that consists of a vertical drum which can be rotated and around which cable is turned **2 :** a rotating shaft that drives recorder tape
cap·su·lar \ˈkap-sə-lər\ *adj* **:** of, relating to, or resembling a capsule
cap·su·lat·ed \-ˌlāt-əd\ *adj* **:** enclosed in a capsule
[1]**cap·sule** \ˈkap-səl, -sül\ *n* **1 :** an enveloping cover (as of a bodily joint) ⟨a spore ~⟩; *esp* **:** an edible shell enclosing medicine or vitamins to be swallowed **2 :** a dry fruit made of two or more united carpels that splits open when ripe **3 :** a small pressurized compartment for a pilot or astronaut
[2]**capsule** *adj* **1 :** very brief **2 :** very compact
Capt *abbr* captain
[1]**cap·tain** \ˈkap-tən\ *n* **1 :** a commander of a body of troops **2 :** a commissioned officer in the army, air force, or marine corps ranking next below a major **3 :** an officer

in charge of a ship; *esp* : a commissioned officer in the navy ranking next below a rear admiral or a commodore **4** : a leader of a side or team **5** : a dominant figure — **cap·tain·cy** *n*

[2]**captain** *vb* : to be captain of : LEAD

cap·tion \ˈkap-shən\ *n* **1** : a heading esp. of an article or document : TITLE **2** : the explanatory matter accompanying an illustration **3** : a motion-picture subtitle — **cap·tion** *vb*

cap·tious \ˈkap-shəs\ *adj* : marked by an inclination to find fault — **cap·tious·ly** *adv* — **cap·tious·ness** *n*

cap·ti·vate \ˈkap-tə-ˌvāt\ *vb* **-vat·ed; -vat·ing** : to attract and hold irresistibly by some special charm or art — **cap·ti·va·tion** \ˌkap-tə-ˈvā-shən\ *n* — **cap·ti·va·tor** \ˈkap-tə-ˌvāt-ər\ *n*

cap·tive \ˈkap-tiv\ *adj* **1** : made prisoner esp. in war **2** : kept within bounds : CONFINED **3** : held under control — **captive** *n* — **cap·tiv·i·ty** \kap-ˈtiv-ət-ē\ *n*

cap·tor \ˈkap-tər\ *n* : one that captures

[1]**cap·ture** \ˈkap-chər\ *n* **1** : the act of capturing **2** : one that has been captured

[2]**capture** *vb* **cap·tured; cap·tur·ing** **1** : to take captive : WIN, GAIN **2** : to preserve in a relatively permanent form

Ca·pu·chin \ˈkap-yə-shən\ *n* : a member of an austere branch of the order of St. Francis of Assisi engaged in missionary work and preaching

car \ˈkär\ *n* **1** : a vehicle moving on wheels **2** : the compartment of an elevator **3** : the part of a balloon or airship that carries passengers or equipment

ca·ra·bao \ˌkar-ə-ˈbaů\ *n, pl* **-bao** *or* **-baos** : a water buffalo esp. in the Philippines

car·a·bi·neer *or* **car·a·bi·nier** \ˌkar-ə-bə-ˈniər\ *n* : a soldier armed with a carbine

car·a·cole \ˈkar-ə-ˌkōl\ *n* : a half turn to right or left executed by a mounted horse — **caracole** *vb*

ca·rafe \kə-ˈraf, -ˈräf\ *n* : a bottle with a flaring lip used esp. to hold wine

car·a·mel \ˈkar-ə-məl, ˈkär-məl\ *n* **1** : an amorphous substance obtained by heating sugar and used for flavoring and coloring **2** : a firm chewy candy

car·a·pace \ˈkar-ə-ˌpās\ *n* : a protective case or shell on the back of some animals (as turtles or crabs)

[1]**carat** *var of* KARAT

[2]**car·at** \ˈkar-ət\ *n* : a unit of weight for precious stones equal to 200 milligrams

car·a·van \ˈkar-ə-ˌvan\ *n* **1** : a group of travelers journeying together through desert or hostile regions **2** : a group of vehicles traveling in a file

car·a·van·sa·ry \ˌkar-ə-ˈvan-sə-rē\ *or* **car·a·van·se·rai** \-sə-ˌrī\ *n, pl* **-ries** *or* **-rais** *or* **-rai** [Per *kārwānsarāī*, fr. *kārwān* caravan + *sarāī* palace, inn] **1** : an inn in eastern countries where caravans rest at night **2** : HOTEL, INN

car·a·vel \ˈkar-ə-ˌvel\ *n* : a small 15th and 16th century ship with a broad bow, high narrow poop, and usu. three masts

car·a·way \ˈkar-ə-ˌwā\ *n* : an aromatic herb related to the carrot with fruits (**caraway seed**) used in seasoning and medicine; *also* : its fruit

car·bide \ˈkär-ˌbīd\ *n* : a compound of carbon with another element

car·bine \ˈkär-ˌbēn, -ˌbīn\ *n* : a short-barreled lightweight rifle

car·bo·hy·drate \ˌkär-bō-ˈhī-ˌdrāt, -drət\ *n* : any of various compounds composed of carbon, hydrogen, and oxygen (as sugars and starches)

car·bol·ic acid \ˌkär-ˌbäl-ik-\ *n* : PHENOL

car·bon \ˈkär-bən\ *n* **1** : a nonmetallic chemical element occurring in nature as diamond and graphite and as a constituent of coal, petroleum, and limestone — see ELEMENT table **2** : a sheet of carbon paper; *also* : CARBON COPY 1

car·bo·na·ceous \ˌkär-bə-ˈnā-shəs\ *adj* : relating to, containing, or composed of carbon

[1]**car·bon·ate** \ˈkär-bə-ˌnāt, -nət\ *n* : a salt or ester of carbonic acid

[2]**car·bon·ate** \-ˌnāt\ *vb* **-at·ed; -at·ing** : to impregnate with carbon dioxide ⟨a *carbonated* beverage⟩ — **car·bon·ation** \ˌkär-bə-ˈnā-shən\ *n*

carbon black *n* : any of various black substances consisting chiefly of carbon used esp. as pigments

carbon copy *n* **1** : a copy made by carbon paper **2** : DUPLICATE

carbon dating *n* : the determination of the age of old material (as an archaeological specimen) by means of the content of carbon 14

carbon dioxide *n* : a heavy colorless gas that does not support combustion and is formed in animal respiration and in the combustion and decomposition of organic substances

carbon 14 *n* : a heavy radioactive form of carbon used in dating archaeological and geological materials

car·bon·ic acid \kär-ˌbän-ik-\ *n* : a weak acid that decomposes readily into water and carbon dioxide

car·bon·if·er·ous \ˌkär-bə-ˈnif-(ə-)rəs\ *adj* **1** : producing or containing carbon or coal **2** *cap* : of, relating to, or being the period of the Paleozoic era between the Devonian and the Permian — **Carboniferous** *n*

carbon monoxide *n* : a colorless odorless very poisonous gas formed by the incomplete burning of carbon

carbon paper *n* : a thin paper coated with a pigment and used for making copies

carbon tet·ra·chlo·ride \-ˌte-trə-ˈklōr-ˌīd\ *n* : a colorless nonflammable toxic liquid used esp. as a solvent

carbon 12 *n* : the most abundant isotope of carbon having a nucleus of 6 protons and 6 neutrons and used as a reference in the determination of other atomic masses

car·boy \ˈkär-ˌbȯi\ *n* [Per *qarāba*, fr. Ar *qarrābah* demijohn] : a large container for liquids

car·bun·cle \ˈkär-ˌbəŋ-kəl\ *n* : a painful inflammation of the skin and underlying tissue that discharges pus from several openings — **car·bun·cu·lar** \kär-ˈbəŋ-kyə-lər\ *adj*

car·bu·re·tor \ˈkär-b(y)ə-ˌrāt-ər\ *n* : an apparatus for supplying an internal-combustion engine with an explosive mixture of vaporized fuel and air

car·cass \ˈkär-kəs\ *n* : a dead body; *esp* : one of an animal dressed for food

car·cin·o·gen \kär-ˈsin-ə-jən\ *n* : an agent causing or inciting cancer — **car·ci·no·gen·ic** \ˌkärs-ᵊn-ō-ˈjen-ik\ *adj* — **car·ci·no·ge·nic·i·ty** \-jə-ˈnis-ət-ē\ *n*

car·ci·no·ma \ˌkärs-ᵊn-ˈō-mə\ *n, pl* **-mas** *or* **-ma·ta** \-mət-ə\ : a malignant tumor of epithelial origin — **car·ci·no·ma·tous** \-ˈō-mət-əs\ *adj*

[1]**card** \ˈkärd\ *vb* : to comb with a card : cleanse and untangle before spinning — **card·er** *n*

[2]**card** *n* : an instrument for combing fibers (as wool or cotton)

[3]**card** *n* **1** : PLAYING CARD **2** *pl* : a game played with playing cards; *also* : card playing **3** : a usu. clownishly amusing person : WAG **4** : a flat stiff usu. small piece of paper, cardboard, or plastic **5** : PROGRAM; *esp* : a sports program

[4]**card** *vb* **1** : to list or schedule on a card **2** : SCORE

[5]**card** *abbr* cardinal

car·da·mom \ˈkärd-ə-məm\ *n* : the aromatic capsular fruit of an East Indian herb related to the ginger whose seeds are used as a condiment and in medicine; *also* : this plant

card·board \ˈkärd-ˌbōrd\ *n* : PAPERBOARD

card–car·ry·ing \ˈkärd-ˌkar-ē-iŋ\ *adv* : being a regularly enrolled member of an organized group and esp. of the Communist party and not merely a sympathizer with its ideals and programs

card catalog *n* : a catalog (as of books) in which the entries are arranged systematically on cards

car·di·ac \ˈkärd-ē-ˌak\ *adj* **1** : of, relating to, or located near the heart **2** : of, relating to, or affected with heart disease

car·di·gan \ˈkärd-i-gən\ *n* : a sweater or jacket usu. without a collar and with a full-length opening in the front

1**car·di·nal** \ˈkärd-(ᵊ-)nəl\ *n* [ME, fr. OF, fr. LL *cardinalis,* fr. L *cardo* hinge] **1** : an ecclesiastical official of the Roman Catholic Church ranking next below the pope **2** : a crested No. American finch that is nearly completely red in the male

2**cardinal** *adj* : of basic importance : CHIEF, MAIN, PRIMARY — **car·di·nal·ly** \-ē\ *adv*

car·di·nal·ate \-ət, -ˌāt\ *n* : the office, rank, or dignity of a cardinal

cardinal flower *n* : a No. American plant that bears a spike of brilliant red flowers

cardinal number *n* : a number (as 1, 5, 82, 357) that is used in simple counting and answers the question "how many?"

cardinal point *n* : one of the four principal compass points north, south, east, and west

car·di·ol·o·gy \ˌkärd-ē-ˈäl-ə-jē\ *n* : the study of the heart and its action and diseases — **car·di·ol·o·gist** \-ˈäl-ə-jəst\ *n*

car·dio·pul·mo·nary resuscitation \ˈkärd-ē-ō-ˈpu̇l-mə-ˌner-ē-\ *n* : a procedure to restore normal breathing after cardiac arrest that includes the clearance of air passages to the lungs, heart massage by the exertion of pressure on the chest, and the use of drugs

car·dio·vas·cu·lar \ˌkärd-ē-ō-ˈvas-kyə-lər\ *adj* : of or relating to the heart and blood vessels

card·sharp·er \ˈkärd-ˌshär-pər\ *or* **card·sharp** \-ˌshärp\ *n* : a cheater at cards

1**care** \ˈkeər\ *n* **1** : a heavy sense of responsibility : WORRY, ANXIETY **2** : watchful attention : HEED **3** : CHARGE, SUPERVISION **4** : a person or thing that is an object of anxiety or solicitude

2**care** *vb* **cared; car·ing 1** : to feel anxiety **2** : to feel interest **3** : to give care **4** : to have a liking, fondness, taste, or inclination **5** : to be concerned about ⟨~ what happens⟩

CARE *abbr* Cooperative for American Relief to Everywhere

ca·reen \kə-ˈrēn\ *vb* **1** : to cause (a boat) to lean over on one side **2** : to sway from side to side

1**ca·reer** \kə-ˈriər\ *n* [MF *carrière,* fr. Old Provençal *carriera* street, fr. ML *carraria* road for vehicles, fr. L *carrus* car] **1** : a course of action or events; *esp* : a person's progress in his or her chosen occupation **2** : an occupation or profession followed as a life's work

2**career** *vb* : to go at top speed esp. in a headlong manner

care·free \ˈkeər-ˌfrē\ *adj* : free from care or worry

care·ful \-fəl\ *adj* **care·ful·ler; care·ful·lest 1** : using or taking care : VIGILANT **2** : marked by solicitude, caution, or prudence — **care·ful·ly** \-ē\ *adv* — **care·ful·ness** *n*

care·less \-ləs\ *adj* **1** : free from care : UNTROUBLED **2** : UNCONCERNED, INDIFFERENT **3** : not taking care **4** : not showing or receiving care — **care·less·ly** *adv* — **care·less·ness** *n*

1**ca·ress** \kə-ˈres\ *n* : a tender or loving touch or embrace

2**caress** *vb* : to touch or stroke tenderly or lovingly — **ca·ress·er** *n*

car·et \ˈkar-ət\ *n* [L, is missing, fr. *carēre* to be lacking] : a mark ‸ used to indicate the place where something is to be inserted

care·tak·er \ˈkeər-ˌtā-kər\ *n* **1** : one in charge usu. as occupant in place of an absent owner **2** : one temporarily fulfilling the functions of an office

care·worn \-ˌwōərn\ *adj* : showing the effects of grief or anxiety

car·fare \ˈkär-ˌfaər\ *n* : passenger fare (as on a streetcar or bus)

car·go \ˈkär-gō\ *n, pl* **cargoes** *or* **cargos** : the goods carried in a ship, airplane, or vehicle : FREIGHT

car·hop \ˈkär-ˌhäp\ *n* : one who serves customers at a drive-in restaurant

Ca·rib·be·an \ˌkar-ə-ˈbē-ən, kə-ˈrib-ē-ən\ *adj* : of or relating to the eastern and southern West Indies or the Caribbean sea

car·i·bou \ˈkar-ə-ˌbü\ *n, pl* **caribou** *or* **caribous** : any of several large deer of northern No. America and Siberia with palmate antlers in both sexes that are grouped with the reindeer in one species

car·i·ca·ture \ˈkar-i-kə-ˌchu̇r\ *n* **1** : distorted representation to produce a ridiculous effect **2** : a representation esp. in literature or art having the qualities of caricature — **caricature** *vb* — **car·i·ca·tur·ist** \-ˌchu̇r-əst\ *n*

car·ies \ˈkar-ēz\ *n, pl* **caries** : tooth decay

car·il·lon \ˈkar-ə-ˌlän\ *n* : a set of tuned bells sounded by hammers controlled by a keyboard

car·il·lon·neur \ˌkar-ə-lə-ˈnər\ *n* [F] : a carillon player

car·i·ous \ˈkar-ē-əs\ *adj* : affected with caries

car·load \ˈkär-ˈlōd, -ˌlōd\ *n* : a load that fills a car

car·mi·na·tive \kär-ˈmin-ət-iv\ *adj* : expelling gas from the alimentary canal — **carminative** *n*

car·mine \ˈkär-mən, -ˌmīn\ *n* : a vivid red

car·nage \ˈkär-nij\ *n* : great destruction of life : SLAUGHTER

car·nal \ˈkärn-ᵊl\ *adj* **1** : of or relating to the body **2** : SENSUAL — **car·nal·i·ty** \kär-ˈnal-ət-ē\ *n* — **car·nal·ly** \ˈkärn-ᵊl-ē\ *adv*

car·na·tion \kär-ˈnā-shən\ *n* : a cultivated pink of any of numerous usu. double-flowered varieties derived from an Old World species

car·nau·ba wax \kär-ˈnȯ-bə-, ˌkär-nə-ˈü-bə-\ *n* : a brittle yellowish wax from a Brazilian palm that is used esp. in polishes

car·ne·lian \kär-ˈnēl-yən\ *n* : a hard tough reddish quartz used as a gem

car·ni·val \ˈkär-nə-vəl\ *n* [It *carnevale,* fr. *carnelevare,* lit., removal of meat] **1** : a season of merrymaking just before Lent **2** : a boisterous merrymaking **3** : a traveling enterprise offering amusements **4** : an organized program of entertainment

car·niv·o·ra \kär-ˈniv-ə-rə\ *n pl* : carnivorous mammals

car·ni·vore \ˈkär-nə-ˌvōr\ *n* : a flesh-eating animal; *esp* : any of an order of mammals (as dogs, cats, bears, minks, and seals) feeding mostly on animal flesh

car·niv·o·rous \kär-ˈniv-(ə-)rəs\ *adj* **1** : feeding on animal tissues **2** : of or relating to the carnivores — **car·niv·o·rous·ly** *adv* — **car·niv·o·rous·ness** *n*

car·ny *or* **car·ney** *or* **car·nie** \ˈkär-nē\ *n, pl* **carnies** *or* **carneys 1** : CARNIVAL 3 **2** : one who works with a carnival

car·ol \ˈkar-əl\ *n* : a song of joy, praise, or devotion — **carol** *vb* — **car·ol·er** *or* **car·ol·ler** \-ə-lər\ *n*

car·om \ˈkar-əm\ *n* **1** : a shot in billiards in which the cue ball strikes two other balls **2** : a rebounding esp. at an angle — **carom** *vb*

car·o·tene \ˈkar-ə-ˌtēn\ *n* : any of several orange to red pigments formed esp. in plants and used as a source of vitamin A

ca·rot·id \kə-ˈrät-əd\ *adj* : of, relating to, or being the chief artery or pair of arteries that pass up the neck and supply the head — **carotid** *n*

ca·rous·al \kə-ˈrau̇-zəl\ *n* : CAROUSE

ca·rouse \kə-ˈrau̇z\ *n* [MF *carrousse,* fr. *carous,* adv., all out (in *boire carous* to empty the cup), fr. G *garaus*] : a drunken revel — **carouse** *vb* — **ca·rous·er** *n*

car·ou·sel \ˌkar-ə-ˈsel, ˈkar-ə-ˌsel\ *n* : MERRY-GO-ROUND

[1]**carp** \ˈkärp\ *vb* : to find fault : CAVIL, COMPLAIN — **carp·er** *n*

[2]**carp** *n, pl* **carp** *or* **carps** : a long-lived freshwater fish of sluggish waters often raised for food

[1]**car·pal** \ˈkär-pəl\ *adj* : relating to the wrist or the bones of the wrist

[2]**carpal** *n* : a carpal element or bone

car·pe di·em \ˌkär-pē-ˈdē-ˌem, -ˈdī-\ *n* [L, enjoy the day] : enjoyment of the present without concern for the future

car·pel \ˈkär-pəl\ *n* : one of the highly modified leaves that together form the ovary of a flower of a seed plant

car·pen·ter \ˈkär-pən-tər\ *n* : one who builds or repairs wooden structures — **carpenter** *vb* — **car·pen·try** \-trē\ *n*

car·pet \ˈkär-pət\ *n* : a heavy fabric used esp. as a floor covering — **carpet** *vb*

car·pet·bag \-ˌbag\ *n* : a traveling bag common in the 19th century

car·pet·bag·ger \-ˌbag-ər\ *n* : a Northerner in the South after the American Civil War usu. seeking private gain under the reconstruction governments

car·pet·ing \ˌkär-pət-iŋ\ *n* : material for carpets; *also* : CARPETS

car pool *n* : an arrangement by a group of automobile drivers who take turns driving their own cars and carrying the others as passengers — **car·pool** \-ˌpül\ *vb*

car·port \ˈkär-ˌpōrt\ *n* : an open-sided automobile shelter

car·pus \ˈkär-pəs\ *n* : the wrist or its bones

car·ra·geen·an *or* **car·ra·geen·in** \ˌkar-ə-ˈgē-nən\ *n* : a colloid extracted esp. from a dark purple branching seaweed and used in foods esp. to stabilize and thicken them

car·rel \ˈkar-əl\ *n* : a table with bookshelves often partitioned or enclosed for individual study in a library

car·riage \ˈkar-ij\ *n* **1** : the act of carrying **2** : manner of holding the body **3** : a wheeled vehicle **4** *Brit* : a railway passenger coach **5** : a movable part of a machine for supporting some other moving part

carriage trade *n* : trade from well-to-do or upper-class people

car·ri·er \ˈkar-ē-ər\ *n* **1** : one that carries **2** : a person or organization in the transportation business **3** : one who carries germs of a disease in his or her system but is immune to the disease **4** : one who has a gene for a trait or condition that is not expressed in his or her system **5** : an electromagnetic wave whose amplitude or frequency is varied in order to convey a radio or television signal

carrier pigeon *n* : a pigeon used esp. to carry messages

car·ri·on \ˈkar-ē-ən\ *n* : dead and decaying flesh

car·rot \ˈkar-ət\ *n* : the elongated orange-red root of a common garden plant that is eaten as a vegetable; *also* : this plant

car·rou·sel *var of* CAROUSEL

[1]**car·ry** \ˈkar-ē\ *vb* **car·ried; car·ry·ing** **1** : to move while supporting : TRANSPORT, CONVEY, TAKE **2** : to influence by mental or emotional appeal **3** : to get possession or control of : CAPTURE, WIN **4** : to transfer from one place (as a column) to another ⟨~ a number in addition⟩ **5** : to have or wear on one's person; *also* : to bear within one **6** : INVOLVE, IMPLY **7** : to hold or bear (oneself) in a specified way **8** : to keep in stock for sale **9** : to sustain the weight or burden of : SUPPORT **10** : to prolong in space, time, or degree **11** : to keep on one's books as a debtor **12** : to succeed in (an election) **13** : to win adoption (as in a legislature) **14** : PUBLISH, PRINT **15** : to reach or penetrate to a distance

[2]**carry** *n* **1** : an act or method of carrying ⟨fireman's ~⟩ **2** : PORTAGE **3** : the range of a gun or projectile or of a struck or thrown ball

car·ry·all \ˈkar-ē-ˌȯl\ *n* **1** : a light covered carriage for four or more persons **2** : a capacious bag or case

carry away *vb* : to arouse to a high and often excessive degree of emotion

carrying charge *n* : a charge added to the price of merchandise sold on the installment plan

car·ry·on \ˈkar-ē-ˌȯn, -ˌän\ *n* : a piece of luggage suitable for being carried aboard an airplane by a passenger — **car·ry–on** \ˈkar-ē-ˌȯn, -ˌän\ *adj*

carry on \ˌkar-ē-ˈȯn, -ˈän\ *vb* **1** : CONDUCT, MANAGE **2** : to behave in a foolish, excited, or improper manner **3** : to continue in spite of hindrance or discouragement

carry out *vb* **1** : to put into execution **2** : to bring to a successful conclusion

car·sick \ˈkär-ˌsik\ *adj* : affected with motion sickness esp. in an automobile — **car sickness** *n*

[1]**cart** \ˈkärt\ *n* **1** : a heavy 2-wheeled wagon **2** : a small wheeled vehicle

[2]**cart** *vb* : to convey in or as if in a cart — **cart·er** *n*

cart·age \ˈkärt-ij\ *n* : the act of or rate charged for carting

carte blanche \ˈkärt-ˈblä^{n}sh\ *n, pl* **cartes blanches** \ˈkärt-ˈblä^{n}sh(-əz)\ [F, lit., blank document] : full discretionary power

car·tel \kär-ˈtel\ *n* : a combination of independent business enterprises designed to limit competition **syn** pool, syndicate, monopoly, trust

car·ti·lage \ˈkärt-^{ə}l-ij\ *n* : an elastic tissue composing most of the skeleton of embryonic and very young vertebrates and later mostly turning into bone in higher vertebrates — **car·ti·lag·i·nous** \ˌkärt-^{ə}l-ˈaj-ə-nəs\ *adj*

car·tog·ra·phy \kär-ˈtäg-rə-fē\ *n* : the making of maps — **car·tog·ra·pher** \-fər\ *n*

car·ton \ˈkärt-^{ə}n\ *n* : a cardboard box or container

car·toon \kär-ˈtün\ *n* **1** : a preparatory sketch (as for a painting) **2** : a drawing intended as humor, caricature, or satire **3** : COMIC STRIP — **cartoon** *vb* — **car·toon·ist** *n*

car·tridge \ˈkär-trij\ *n* **1** : a tube containing a complete charge for a firearm **2** : a container of material for insertion into an apparatus **3** : a case containing photographic film **4** : a small case containing a needle and transducer that attaches to the tone arm of a phonograph **5** : a case containing a magnetic tape or disk **6** : a case for holding integrated circuits containing a computer program ⟨a video-game ~⟩

cart·wheel \ˈkärt-ˌhwēl\ *n* **1** : a large coin (as a silver dollar) **2** : a lateral handspring with arms and legs extended

carve \kärv\ *vb* **carved; carv·ing** **1** : to cut with care or precision : shape by cutting **2** : to cut into pieces or slices **3** : to slice and serve meat at table — **carv·er** *n*

cary·at·id \ˌkar-ē-ˈat-əd\ *n, pl* **-ids** *or* **-i·des** \-ə-ˌdēz\ : a sculptured draped female figure used as an architectural column

ca·sa·ba \kə-ˈsäb-ə\ *n* : any of several muskmelons with a yellow rind and sweet flesh

[1]**cas·cade** \kas-ˈkād\ *n* **1** : a steep usu. small waterfall **2** : something arranged in a series or succession of stages so that each stage derives from or acts upon the product of the preceding

[2]**cas·cade** *vb* **cas·cad·ed; cas·cad·ing** : to fall, pass, or connect in or as if in a cascade

cas·cara \kas-ˈkar-ə\ *n* : the dried bark of a small Pacific coastal tree of the U.S. and southern Canada used as a laxative; *also* : this tree

[1]**case** \ˈkās\ *n* **1** : a particular instance or situation **2** : an inflectional form of a noun, pronoun, or adjective indicating its grammatical relation to other words; *also* : such a relation whether indicated by inflection or not **3** : what actually exists or happens : FACT **4** : a suit or action in law : CAUSE **5** : a convincing argument **6** : an instance of disease or injury; *also* : PATIENT **7** : IN-

STANCE, EXAMPLE — **in case 1** : IF **2** : as a precaution **3** : as a precaution against the event that — **in case of** : in the event of

[2]**case** *n* **1** : a box or container for holding something; *also* : a box with its contents **2** : an outer covering **3** : a divided tray for holding printing type **4** : CASING 2

[3]**case** *vb* **cased; cas·ing 1** : to enclose in or cover with a case **2** : to inspect esp. with intent to rob

ca·sein \kā-ˈsēn, ˈkā-sē-ən\ *n* : any of several phosphorus-containing proteins occurring in or produced from milk

case·ment \ˈkās-mənt\ *n* : a window sash that opens like a door; *also* : a window having such a sash

case·work \-ˌwərk\ *n* : social work that involves the individual person or family — **case·work·er** *n*

[1]**cash** \ˈkash\ *n* [MF or It; MF *casse* money box, fr. It *cassa*, fr. L *capsa* chest] **1** : ready money **2** : money or its equivalent paid at the time of purchase or delivery

[2]**cash** *vb* : to pay or obtain cash for

ca·shew \ˈkash-ü, kə-ˈshü\ *n* : an edible kidney-shaped nut of a tropical American tree related to the sumacs; *also* : the tree

[1]**ca·shier** \ka-ˈshiər\ *vb* : to dismiss from service; *esp* : to dismiss in disgrace

[2]**cash·ier** \ka-ˈshiər\ *n* **1** : a bank official responsible for moneys received and paid out **2** : one who receives and records payments

cashier's check *n* : a check drawn by a bank upon its own funds and signed by its cashier

cash in *vb* **1** : to convert into cash ⟨*cash in* bonds⟩ **2** : to settle accounts and withdraw from a gambling game or business deal **3** : to obtain financial profit or advantage

cash·mere \ˈkazh-ˌmiər, ˈkash-\ *n* : fine wool from the undercoat of an Indian goat (**cashmere goat**) or a yarn spun of this; *also* : a soft twilled fabric orig. woven from this yarn

cash register *n* : a business machine that indicates each sale and often records the money received

cas·ing \ˈkā-siŋ\ *n* **1** : something that encases **2** : the frame of a door or window

ca·si·no \kə-ˈsē-nō\ *n, pl* **-nos** [It, fr. *casa* house] **1** : a building or room for social amusements; *esp* : one used for gambling **2** *also* **cas·si·no** : a card game in which players win cards by matching those on the table

cask \ˈkask\ *n* [MF *casque* helmet, fr. Sp *casco* potsherd, skull, helmet, fr. *cascar* to break] : a barrel-shaped container usu. for liquids; *also* : the quantity held by such a container

cas·ket \ˈkas-kət\ *n* **1** : a small box (as for jewels) **2** : COFFIN

casque \ˈkask\ *n* : HELMET

cas·sa·va \kə-ˈsäv-ə\ *n* : any of several tropical spurges with rootstocks yielding a nutritious starch from which tapioca is prepared; *also* : the rootstock or its starch

cas·se·role \ˈkas-ə-ˌrōl, ˈkaz-\ *n* **1** : a dish in which food may be baked and served **2** : a dish cooked and served in a casserole

cas·sette *also* **ca·sette** \kə-ˈset\ *n* **1** : a lightproof container for photographic plates or film **2** : a plastic case containing magnetic tape

cas·sia \ˈkash-ə\ *n* **1** : a coarse cinnamon bark **2** : any of various East Indian leguminous herbs, shrubs, and trees of which several yield senna

cas·sit·er·ite \kə-ˈsit-ə-ˌrīt\ *n* : a dark mineral that is the chief tin ore

cas·sock \ˈkas-ək\ *n* : an ankle-length garment worn esp. by Roman Catholic and Anglican clergy

cas·so·wary \ˈkas-ə-ˌwer-ē\ *n, pl* **-war·ies** : any of several large birds closely related to the emu

[1]**cast** \ˈkast\ *vb* **cast; cast·ing 1** : THROW, FLING **2** : DIRECT ⟨~ a glance⟩ **3** : to deposit (a ballot) formally **4** : to throw off, out, or away : DISCARD, SHED **5** : COMPUTE; *esp* : to add up **6** : to assign the parts of (a play) to actors; *also* : to assign to a role or part **7** : to shape (a substance) by pouring in liquid or plastic form into a mold and letting harden without pressure **8** : to make (as a knot or stitch) by looping or catching up

[2]**cast** *n* **1** : THROW, FLING **2** : a throw of dice **3** : the group of actors to whom parts in a play are assigned **4** : something formed in or as if in a mold; *also* : a rigid surgical dressing (as for protecting and supporting a fractured bone) **5** : TINGE, HUE **6** : APPEARANCE, LOOK **7** : something thrown out or off, shed, or expelled ⟨worm ~*s*⟩

cas·ta·net \ˌkas-tə-ˈnet\ *n* [Sp *castañeta*, fr. *castaña* chestnut, fr. L *castanea*] : a rhythm instrument consisting of two small wooden, ivory, or plastic shells held in the hand and clicked together

cast·away \ˈkas-tə-ˌwā\ *adj* **1** : thrown away : REJECTED **2** : cast adrift or ashore as a survivor of a shipwreck — **castaway** *n*

caste \ˈkast\ *n* [Port *casta*, lit., race, lineage, fr. fem. of *casto* pure, chaste, fr. L *castus*] **1** : one of the hereditary social classes in Hinduism **2** : a division of a society based on wealth, inherited rank, or occupation **3** : social position : PRESTIGE **4** : a system of rigid social stratification

cas·tel·lat·ed \ˈkas-tə-ˌlāt-əd\ *adj* : having battlements like a castle

cast·er \ˈkas-tər\ *n* **1** *or* **cas·tor** : a small container to hold salt or pepper at the table **2** : a small wheel that turns freely and is used to support and move furniture, trucks, and machines

cas·ti·gate \ˈkas-tə-ˌgāt\ *vb* **-gat·ed; -gat·ing** : to punish or criticize severely — **cas·ti·ga·tion** \ˌkas-tə-ˈgā-shən\ *n* — **cas·ti·ga·tor** \ˈkas-tə-ˌgāt-ər\ *n*

cast·ing \ˈkas-tiŋ\ *n* **1** : CAST 7 **2** : something cast in a mold

casting vote *n* : a deciding vote cast by a presiding officer to break a tie

cast iron *n* : a hard brittle alloy of iron, carbon, and silicon cast in a mold

cas·tle \ˈkas-əl\ *n* **1** : a large fortified building or set of buildings **2** : a large or imposing house **3** : [3]ROOK

castle in the air : an impracticable project

cast–off \ˈkas-ˌtȯf\ *adj* : thrown away or aside : DISCARDED — **cast·off** *n*

cas·tor oil \ˌkas-tər-\ *n* : a thick yellowish oil extracted from the poisonous seeds of an herb (**castor–oil plant**) and used as a lubricant and cathartic

cas·trate \ˈkas-ˌtrāt\ *vb* **cas·trat·ed; cas·trat·ing** : to deprive of sex glands and esp. testes — **cas·trat·er** *or* **cas·tra·tor** \-ər\ *n* — **cas·tra·tion** \ka-ˈstrā-shən\ *n*

ca·su·al \ˈkazh-(ə-w)əl\ *adj* **1** : resulting from or occurring by chance **2** : OCCASIONAL, INCIDENTAL **3** : OFFHAND, NONCHALANT **4** : designed for informal use ⟨~ clothing⟩ — **ca·su·al·ly** \-ē\ *adv* — **ca·su·al·ness** *n*

ca·su·al·ty \ˈkazh-(ə-w)əl-tē\ *n, pl* **-ties 1** : serious or fatal accident **2** : a military person lost through death, injury, sickness, or capture or through being missing in action **3** : a person or thing injured, lost, or destroyed

ca·su·ist·ry \ˈkazh-ə-wə-strē\ *n, pl* **-ries** : adroit and esp. false or misleading argument or reasoning usu. about morals — **ca·su·ist** \-wəst\ *n* — **ca·su·is·tic** \ˌkazh-ə-ˈwis-tik\ *or* **ca·su·is·ti·cal** \-ti-kəl\ *adj*

ca·sus bel·li \ˌkäs-əs-ˈbel-ˌē, ˌkā-səs-ˈbel-ˌī\ *n, pl* **ca·sus belli** \ˌkäs-ˌüs-, ˌkā-ˌsüs-\ [NL, occasion of war] : a cause or pretext for a declaration of war

[1]**cat** \ˈkat\ *n* **1** : a common domestic mammal long kept by human beings as a pet or for catching rats and mice **2** : any of various animals (as the lion, lynx, or leopard) of

the same family as the domestic cat **3** : a spiteful woman **4** : CAT-O'-NINE-TAILS **5** *slang* : GUY

[2]**cat** *abbr* catalog

CAT *abbr* computerized axial tomography

ca·tab·o·lism \kə-ˈtab-ə-ˌliz-əm\ *n* : destructive metabolism involving the release of energy and resulting in the breakdown of complex materials — **cat·a·bol·ic** \ˌkat-ə-ˈbäl-ik\ *adj*

cat·a·clysm \ˈkat-ə-ˌkliz-əm\ *n* : a violent change or upheaval — **cat·a·clys·mal** \ˌkat-ə-ˈkliz-məl\ *or* **cat·a·clys·mic** \-ˈkliz-mik\ *adj*

cat·a·comb \ˈkat-ə-ˌkōm\ *n* : an underground burial place with galleries and recesses for tombs

cat·a·falque \ˈkat-ə-ˌfalk, -ˌfȯ(l)k\ *n* : an ornamental structure sometimes used in solemn funerals to hold the body

cat·a·lep·sy \ˈkat-ᵊl-ˌep-sē\ *n, pl* **-sies** : a trancelike nervous condition characterized esp. by loss of voluntary motion — **cat·a·lep·tic** \ˌkat-ᵊl-ˈep-tik\ *adj or n*

[1]**cat·a·log** *or* **cat·a·logue** \ˈkat-ᵊl-ˌȯg\ *n* **1** : LIST, REGISTER **2** : a systematic list of items with descriptive details; *also* : a book containing such a list

[2]**catalog** *or* **catalogue** *vb* **-loged** *or* **-logued; -log·ing** *or* **-logu·ing 1** : to make a catalog of **2** : to enter in a catalog — **cat·a·log·er** *or* **cat·a·logu·er** *n*

ca·tal·pa \kə-ˈtal-pə\ *n* : a broad-leaved tree with showy flowers and long slim pods

ca·tal·y·sis \kə-ˈtal-ə-səs\ *n, pl* **-y·ses** \-ˌsēz\ : the change and esp. increase in the rate of a chemical reaction brought about by a substance (**cat·a·lyst** \ˈkat-ᵊl-əst\) that is itself unchanged at the end of the reaction — **cat·a·lyt·ic** \ˌkat-ᵊl-ˈit-ik\ *adj* — **cat·a·lyt·i·cal·ly** \-i-k(ə-)lē\ *adv*

catalytic converter *n* : an automobile exhaust-system component in which a catalyst changes harmful gases into mostly harmless products

cat·a·lyze \ˈkat-ᵊl-ˌīz\ *vb* **-lyzed; -lyz·ing** : to bring about the catalysis of (a chemical reaction)

cat·a·ma·ran \ˌkat-ə-mə-ˈran\ *n* [Tamil (a language of southern India) *kaṭṭumaram,* fr. *kaṭṭu* to tie + *maram* tree] : a boat with twin hulls

cat·a·mount \ˈkat-ə-ˌmau̇nt\ *n* : COUGAR; *also* : LYNX

cat·a·pult \ˈkat-ə-ˌpəlt, -ˌpu̇lt\ *n* **1** : an ancient military machine for hurling missiles (as stones and arrows) **2** : a device for launching an airplane (as from an aircraft carrier) — **catapult** *vb*

cat·a·ract \ˈkat-ə-ˌrakt\ *n* **1** : a cloudiness of the lens of the eye obstructing vision **2** : a large waterfall; *also* : steep rapids in a river

ca·tarrh \kə-ˈtär\ *n* : inflammation of a mucous membrane esp. of the nose and throat — **ca·tarrh·al** \-əl\ *adj*

ca·tas·tro·phe \kə-ˈtas-trə(ˌ)fē\ *n* [Gk *katastrophē,* fr. *katastrephein* to overturn, fr. *kata-* down + *strephein* to turn] **1** : a great disaster or misfortune **2** : utter failure — **cat·a·stroph·ic** \ˌkat-ə-ˈsträf-ik\ *adj* — **cat·a·stroph·i·cal·ly** \-i-k(ə-)lē\ *adv*

cata·ton·ic \ˌkat-ə-ˈtän-ik\ *adj* : of, relating to, or marked by schizophrenia characterized esp. by stupor, negativism, rigidity, purposeless excitement, and abnormal posturing — **catatonic** *n*

cat·bird \ˈkat-ˌbərd\ *n* : an American songbird with a catlike mewing call

cat·boat \ˈkat-ˌbōt\ *n* : a single-masted sailboat with a single large sail extended by a long boom

cat·call \-ˌkȯl\ *n* : a sound like the cry of a cat; *also* : a noise made to express disapproval — **catcall** *vb*

[1]**catch** \ˈkach, ˈkech\ *vb* **caught** \ˈkȯt\; **catch·ing 1** : to capture esp. after pursuit **2** : TRAP **3** : to discover esp. unexpectedly : SURPRISE, DETECT **4** : to become suddenly aware of **5** : to take hold of : SNATCH ⟨~ at a straw⟩ **6** : INTERCEPT **7** : to get entangled **8** : to become affected with or by ⟨~ fire⟩ ⟨~ cold⟩ **9** : to seize and hold firmly; *also* : FASTEN **10** : OVERTAKE **11** : to be in time for ⟨~ a train⟩ **12** : to take in and retain **13** : to look at or listen to

[2]**catch** *n* **1** : something caught **2** : the act of catching; *also* : a game consisting of throwing and catching a ball **3** : something that catches or checks or holds immovable ⟨a door ~⟩ **4** : one worth catching esp. as a mate **5** : FRAGMENT, SNATCH **6** : a concealed difficulty or complication

catch·all \-ˌȯl\ *n* : something to hold a variety of odds and ends

catch-as-catch-can \ˌkach-əz-ˌkach-ˈkan, ˌkech-əz-ˌkech-\ *adj* : using any means available

catch·er \ˈkach-ər, ˈkech-\ *n* : one that catches; *esp* : a player stationed behind home plate in baseball

catch·ing \-iŋ\ *adj* **1** : INFECTIOUS, CONTAGIOUS **2** : ALLURING, CATCHY

catch·ment \ˈkach-mənt, ˈkech-\ *n* **1** : the action of catching water **2** : something that catches water

catch on *vb* **1** : UNDERSTAND **2** : to become popular

catch·pen·ny \-ˌpen-ē\ *adj* : designed esp. to get small sums of money from the ignorant ⟨a ~ plan⟩

catch-22 \-ˌtwent-ē-ˈtü\ *n, pl* **catch-22's** *or* **catch-22s** *often cap C* [fr. *Catch-22,* a paradoxical rule found in the novel *Catch-22* (1961) by Joseph Heller] : a problematic situation for which the only solution is denied by a circumstance inherent in the problem or by a rule; *also* : the circumstance or rule that denies a solution

catch·up \ˈkech-əp, ˈkach-\ *var of* CATSUP

catch up *vb* : to travel or work fast enough to overtake or complete

catch·word \ˈkach-ˌwərd, ˈkech-\ *n* **1** : GUIDE WORD **2** : a word or expression representative of a party, school, or point of view

catchy \ˈkach-ē, ˈkech-\ *adj* **catch·i·er; -est 1** : likely to attract attention **2** : easily remembered ⟨~ music⟩ **3** : TRICKY

cat·e·chism \ˈkat-ə-ˌkiz-əm\ *n* : a summary or test (as of religious doctrine) usu. in the form of questions and answers — **cat·e·chist** \-ˌkist\ *n* — **cat·e·chize** \ˌkīz\ *vb*

cat·e·chu·men \ˌkat-ə-ˈkyü-mən\ *n* : a religious convert receiving training before baptism

cat·e·gor·i·cal \ˌkat-ə-ˈgȯr-i-kəl\ *adj* **1** : ABSOLUTE, UNQUALIFIED **2** : of, relating to, or constituting a category — **cat·e·gor·i·cal·ly** \-i-k(ə-)lē\ *adv*

cat·e·go·rize \ˈkat-i-gə-ˌrīz\ *vb* **-rized; riz·ing** : to put into a category : CLASSIFY — **cat·e·go·ri·za·tion** \ˌkat-i-gə-rə-ˈzā-shən\ *n*

cat·e·go·ry \ˈkat-ə-ˌgōr-ē\ *n, pl* **-ries** : a division used in classification; *also* : CLASS, GROUP, KIND

ca·ter \ˈkāt-ər\ *vb* **1** : to provide a supply of food **2** : to supply what is wanted — **ca·ter·er** *n*

cat·er·cor·ner \ˌkat-ē-ˈkȯr-nər, ˌkat-ə-, ˌkit-ē-\ *or* **cat·er-cor·nered** *adv or adj* [obs. *cater* (four-spot of cards or dice) + E *corner*] : in a diagonal or oblique position

cat·er·pil·lar \ˈkat-ə(r)-ˌpil-ər\ *n* [ME *catyrpel,* fr. OF *catepelose,* lit., hairy cat] : a wormlike often hairy insect larva esp. of a butterfly or moth

cat·er·waul \ˈkat-ər-ˌwȯl\ *vb* : to make a harsh cry — **caterwaul** *n*

cat·fish \ˈkat-ˌfish\ *n* : any of several big-headed stout-bodied fishes with slender tactile processes around the mouth

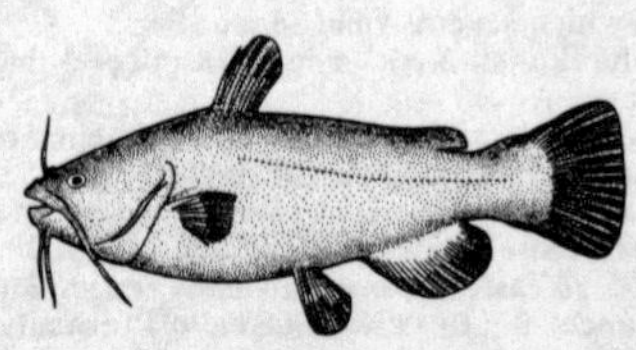

catfish

cat·gut \-ˌgət\ *n* : a tough cord made usu. from sheep intestines

ca·thar·sis \kə-ˈthär-səs\ *n, pl* **ca·thar·ses** \-ˌsēz\ **1** : an act of purging or purification **2** : elimination of a psychological problem by bringing it to consciousness and affording it expression

ca·thar·tic \kə-ˈthärt-ik\ *adj or n* : PURGATIVE

ca·the·dral \kə-ˈthē-drəl\ *n* : the principal church of a diocese

cath·e·ter \ˈkath-ət-ər\ *n* : a tube for insertion into a bodily passage or cavity esp. for injecting or drawing off material

cath·ode \ˈkath-ˌōd\ *n* **1** : the negative electrode of an electrolytic cell **2** : the positive terminal of a battery **3** : the electron-emitting electrode of an electron tube — **ca·thod·ic** \ka-ˈthäd-ik\ *or* **cath·od·al** \ˈkath-ˌōd-ᵊl\ *adj*

cathode–ray tube *n* : a vacuum tube in which a beam of electrons is projected on a fluorescent screen and produces a luminous spot

cath·o·lic \ˈkath-(ə-)lik\ *adj* **1** : GENERAL, UNIVERSAL **2** *cap* : of or relating to Catholics and esp. Roman Catholics

Cath·o·lic \ˈkath-(ə-)lik\ *n* : a member of a church claiming historical continuity from the ancient undivided Christian church; *esp* : a member of the Roman Catholic Church — **Ca·thol·i·cism** \kə-ˈthäl-ə-ˌsiz-əm\ *n*

cath·o·lic·i·ty \ˌkath-ə-ˈlis-ət-ē\ *n, pl* **-ties 1** *cap* : the character of being in conformity with a Catholic church **2** : liberality of sentiments or views **3** : comprehensive range

cat·ion \ˈkat-ˌī-ən\ *n* : the ion in an electrolyte that migrates to the cathode; *also* : a positively charged ion

cat·kin \ˈkat-kən\ *n* : a long flower cluster (as of a willow) bearing crowded flowers and prominent bracts

cat·like \-ˌlīk\ *adj* : resembling a cat or its behavior; *esp* : STEALTHY

cat·nap \-ˌnap\ *n* : a very short light nap — **catnap** *vb*

cat·nip \-ˌnip\ *n* : an aromatic mint that is esp. attractive to cats

cat–o'–nine–tails \ˌkat-ə-ˈnīn-ˌtālz\ *n, pl* **cat–o'–nine–tails** : a whip made of usu. nine knotted cords fastened to a handle

CAT scan \ˈkat-, ˈsē-ˈā-ˈtē-\ *n* [computerized *a*xial *t*omography] : an image made by computed tomography

CAT scanner *n* : a medical instrument consisting of integrated X-ray and computing equipment that is used to make CAT scans

cat's cradle *n* : a game played with a string looped on the fingers in such a way as to resemble a small cradle

cat's–eye \ˈkats-ˌī\ *n, pl* **cat's–eyes** : any of various iridescent gems

cat's–paw \-ˌpȯ\ *n, pl* **cat's–paws** : a person used by another as a tool

cat·sup \ˈkech-əp, ˈkach-; ˈkat-səp\ *n* [Malay *kĕchap* spiced fish sauce] : a seasoned tomato puree

cat·tail \ˈkat-ˌtāl\ *n* : a tall reedlike marsh plant with furry brown spikes of tiny flowers

cat·tle \ˈkat-ᵊl\ *n pl* : LIVESTOCK; *esp* : domestic bovines (as cows, bulls, or calves) — **cat·tle·man** \-mən, -ˌman\ *n*

cat·ty \ˈkat-ē\ *adj* **cat·ti·er, -est** : slyly spiteful — **cat·ti·ly** \ˈkat-ᵊl-e\ *adv* — **cat·ti·ness** \-ē-nəs\ *n*

cat·ty–cor·ner *or* **cat·ty–cor·nered** *var of* CATERCORNER

CATV *abbr* community antenna television

cat·walk \ˈkat-ˌwȯk\ *n* : a narrow walk (as along a bridge)

Cau·ca·sian \kȯ-ˈkā-zhən, -ˈkazh-ən\ *adj* : of or relating to the white race of mankind — **Caucasian** *n* — **Cau·ca·soid** \ˈkȯ-kə-ˌsȯid\ *adj or n*

cau·cus \ˈkȯ-kəs\ *n* : a meeting of a group of persons belonging to the same political party or faction usu. to decide upon policies and candidates — **caucus** *vb*

cau·dal \ˈkȯd-ᵊl\ *adj* : of, relating to, or located near the tail or the hind end of the body — **cau·dal·ly** \-ē\ *adv*

cau·di·llo \kau̇-ˈt͟hē-(y)ō, -ˈt͟hēl-yō\ *n, pl* **-llos** : a Spanish or Latin-American military dictator

caught \ˈkȯt\ *past and past part of* CATCH

caul \ˈkȯl\ *n* : the inner fetal membrane of higher vertebrates esp. when covering the head at birth

cauldron *var of* CALDRON

cau·li·flow·er \ˈkȯ-li-ˌflau̇(-ə)r\ *n* [It *cavolfiore*, fr. *cavolo* cabbage (fr. L *caulis* stem, cabbage) + *fiore* flower] : a garden plant closely related to cabbage and grown for its compact edible head of undeveloped flowers; *also* : this head

cauliflower ear *n* : an ear deformed from injury and excessive growth of scar tissue

[1]**caulk** \ˈkȯk\ *vb* [ME *caulken*, fr. OF *cauquer* to trample, fr. L *calcare*, fr. *calx* heel] : to make the seams of (a boat) watertight by filling with waterproofing material; *also* : to make tight against leakage ⟨~ a pipe joint⟩ — **caulk·er** *n*

[2]**caulk** *also* **caulk·ing** \ˈkȯ-kiŋ\ *n* : material used to caulk

cau·ri \ˈkau̇-rē\ *n, pl* **cauris** — see *syli* at MONEY table

caus·al \ˈkȯ-zəl\ *adj* **1** : expressing or indicating cause **2** : relating to or acting as a cause — **cau·sal·i·ty** \kȯ-ˈzal-ət-ē\ *n* — **caus·al·ly** \ˈkȯ-zə-lē\ *adv*

cau·sa·tion \kȯ-ˈzā-shən\ *n* **1** : the act or process of causing **2** : the means by which an effect is produced

[1]**cause** \ˈkȯz\ *n* **1** : REASON, MOTIVE **2** : something that brings about a result; *esp* : a person or thing that is the agent of bringing something about **3** : a suit or action in court : CASE **4** : a question or matter to be decided **5** : a principle or movement earnestly supported — **cause·less** *adj*

[2]**cause** *vb* **caused; caus·ing** : to be the cause or occasion of — **caus·ative** \ˈkȯ-zət-iv\ *adj* — **caus·er** *n*

cause cé·lè·bre \ˌkōz-sā-ˈlebrᵊ, ˌkȯz-\ *n, pl* **causes célèbres** *same*\ [F, lit., celebrated case] **1** : a legal case that excites widespread interest **2** : a notorious incident or episode

cau·se·rie \ˌkōz-(ə-)ˈrē\ *n* [F] **1** : an informal conversation : CHAT **2** : a short informal composition

cause·way \ˈkȯz-ˌwā\ *n* : a raised way or road across wet ground or water

[1]**caus·tic** \ˈkȯ-stik\ *adj* **1** : CORROSIVE **2** : SHARP, INCISIVE ⟨~ wit⟩

[2]**caustic** *n* **1** : a substance that burns or destroys organic tissue by chemical action **2** : SODIUM HYDROXIDE

cau·ter·ize \ˈkȯt-ə-ˌrīz\ *vb* **-ized; iz·ing** : to burn or sear usu. to prevent infection or bleeding — **cau·ter·iza·tion** \ˌkȯt-ə-rə-ˈzā-shən\ *n*

[1]**cau·tion** \ˈkȯ-shən\ *n* **1** : ADMONITION, WARNING **2** : prudent forethought to minimize risk : WARINESS **3** : one that arouses astonishment — **cau·tion·ary** \-shə-ˌner-ē\ *adj*

[2]**caution** *vb* **cau·tioned; cau·tion·ing** \ˈkȯ-sh(ə-)niŋ\ : to advise caution to : WARN

cau·tious \ˈkȯ-shəs\ *adj* : marked by or given to caution : CAREFUL — **cau·tious·ly** *adv* — **cau·tious·ness** *n*

cav *abbr* **1** cavalry **2** cavity

cav·al·cade \ˌkav-əl-ˈkād\ *n* **1** : a procession of riders or carriages; *also* : a procession of vehicles **2** : a dramatic sequence or procession

[1]**cav·a·lier** \ˌkav-ə-ˈliər\ *n* [MF, fr. It *cavaliere*, fr. Old Provençal *cavalier*, fr. LL *caballarius* groom, fr. L *caballus* horse] **1** : a mounted soldier : KNIGHT **2** *cap* : an adherent of Charles I of England **3** : a debonair person

[2]**cavalier** *adj* **1** : gay and easy in manner : DEBONAIR **2** : DISDAINFUL, HAUGHTY — **cav·a·lier·ly** *adv*

cav·al·ry \ˈkav-əl-rē\ *n, pl* **-ries** : troops mounted on

---

horseback or moving in motor vehicles — **cav·al·ry·man** \-mən, -ˌman\ *n*

[1]**cave** \ˈkāv\ *n* : a natural underground chamber with an opening to the surface

[2]**cave** *vb* **caved; cav·ing 1** : to collapse or cause to collapse **2** : to cease to resist : SUBMIT — usu. used with *in*

ca·ve·at \ˈkav-ē-ˌat, -ˌät; ˈkäv-ē-ˌät\ *n* [L, let him beware] : WARNING

caveat emp·tor \-ˈemp-tər, -ˌtȯr\ *n* [NL, let the buyer beware] : a warning principle in trading that buyers should be alert to see that they get the quantity and quality paid for

cave–in \ˈkā-ˌvin\ *n* **1** : the action of caving in **2** : a place where earth has caved in

cave·man \ˈkāv-ˌman\ *n* **1** : a cave dweller esp. of the Stone Age **2** : one who acts with rough or violent directness esp. toward women

cav·ern \ˈkav-ərn\ *n* : a cave often of large or unknown size — **cav·ern·ous** *adj* — **cav·ern·ous·ly** *adv*

cav·i·ar *or* **cav·i·are** \ˈkav-ē-ˌär, ˈkäv-\ *n* : the salted roe of a large fish (as sturgeon) used as an appetizer

cav·il \ˈkav-əl\ *vb* **-iled** *or* **-illed; il·ing** *or* **il·ling** \-(ə-)liŋ\ : to find fault without good reason : make frivolous objections — **cavil** *n* — **cav·il·er** *or* **cav·il·ler** *n*

cav·ing \ˈkā-viŋ\ *n* : the sport of exploring caves : SPELUNKING

cav·i·ta·tion \ˌkav-ə-ˈtā-shən\ *n* : the formation of partial vacuums in a liquid by a swiftly moving solid body (as a propeller) or by high-frequency sound waves; *also* : a cavity so formed

cav·i·ty \ˈkav-ət-ē\ *n, pl* **-ties 1** : an unfilled space within a mass : a hollow place **2** : an area of decay in a tooth

ca·vort \kə-ˈvȯrt\ *vb* : PRANCE, CAPER

ca·vy \ˈkā-vē\ *n, pl* **cavies** : GUINEA PIG

caw \ˈkȯ\ *vb* : to utter the harsh call of the crow or a similar cry — **caw** *n*

cay \ˈkē, ˈkā\ *n* : [4]KEY

cay·enne pepper \ˌkī-ˌen-, ˌkā-\ *n* : a condiment consisting of ground dried fruits or seeds of a hot pepper

cay·man *var of* CAIMAN

Ca·yu·ga \kā-ˈü-gə, kī-\ *n, pl* **Cayuga** *or* **Cayugas** : a member of an American Indian people of New York

Cay·use \ˈkī-ˌ(y)üs, kī-ˈ(y)üs\ *n* **1** *pl* **Cayuse** *or* **Cayuses** : a member of an American Indian people of Oregon and Washington **2** *pl cayuses, not cap, West* : a native range horse of the western U.S.

Cb *symbol* columbium

CB \ˈsē-ˈbē\ *n* : CITIZENS BAND

CBC *abbr* Canadian Broadcasting Corporation

CBD *abbr* cash before delivery

CBS *abbr* Columbia Broadcasting System

CBW *abbr* chemical and biological warfare

cc *abbr* cubic centimeter

CC *abbr* **1** carbon copy **2** community college **3** country club

CCC *abbr* Civilian Conservation Corps

CCD \ˈsē-ˈsē-ˈdē\ *n* : CHARGE-COUPLED DEVICE

CCTV *abbr* closed-circuit television

CCU *abbr* **1** cardiac care unit **2** coronary care unit **3** critical care unit

ccw *abbr* counterclockwise

cd *abbr* cord

Cd *symbol* cadmium

CD *abbr* **1** certificate of deposit **2** Civil Defense

CDR *abbr* commander

CDT *abbr* central daylight (saving) time

Ce *symbol* cerium

CE *abbr* **1** chemical engineer **2** civil engineer **3** Corps of Engineers

cease \ˈsēs\ *vb* **ceased; ceas·ing** : to come or bring to an end : STOP

cease–fire \ˈsēs-ˈfī(ə)r\ *n* : a suspension of active hostilities

cease·less \ˈsēs-ləs\ *adj* : being without pause or stop : CONTINUOUS — **cease·less·ly** *adv* — **cease·less·ness** *n*

ce·cum \ˈsē-kəm\ *n, pl* **ce·ca** \-kə\ : the blind pouch at the beginning of the large intestine into which the small intestine opens — **ce·cal** \-kəl\ *adj*

ce·dar \ˈsēd-ər\ *n* : any of a genus of trees related to the pines that are noted for their fragrant durable wood; *also* : this wood

cede \ˈsēd\ *vb* **ced·ed; ced·ing 1** : to yield or give up esp. by treaty **2** : ASSIGN, TRANSFER — **ced·er** *n*

ce·di \ˈsād-ē\ *n* — see MONEY table

ce·dil·la \si-ˈdil-ə\ *n* : a mark placed under the letter *c* (as ç) to show that the *c* is to be pronounced like *s*

ceil·ing \ˈsē-liŋ\ *n* **1** : the overhead inside lining of a room **2** : the height above the ground of the base of the lowest layer of clouds when over half of the sky is obscured **3** : the greatest height at which an airplane can operate efficiently **4** : a prescribed upper limit ⟨price ~⟩

cel·an·dine \ˈsel-ən-ˌdīn, -ˌdēn\ *n* : a yellow-flowered herb related to the poppies

cel·e·brate \ˈsel-ə-ˌbrāt\ *vb* **-brat·ed; -brat·ing 1** : to perform (as a sacrament) with appropriate rites **2** : to honor (as a holiday) by solemn ceremonies or by refraining from ordinary business **3** : to observe a notable occasion with festivities **4** : EXTOL — **cel·e·brant** \-brənt\ *n* — **cel·e·bra·tion** \ˌsel-ə-ˈbrā-shən\ *n* — **cel·e·bra·tor** \ˈsel-ə-brāt-ər\ *n*

cel·e·brat·ed \-əd\ *adj* : widely known and often referred to **syn** distinguished, renowned, noted, famous, illustrious, notorious

ce·leb·ri·ty \sə-ˈleb-rət-ē\ *n, pl* **-ties 1** : the state of being celebrated : RENOWN **2** : a celebrated person

ce·ler·i·ty \sə-ˈler-ət-ē\ *n* : SPEED, RAPIDITY

cel·ery \ˈsel-(ə-)rē\ *n, pl* **-er·ies** : a European herb related to the carrot and widely grown for the crisp edible stems of its leaves

celery cabbage *n* : CHINESE CABBAGE

ce·les·ta \sə-ˈles-tə\ *or* **ce·leste** \sə-ˈlest\ *n* : a keyboard instrument with hammers that strike steel plates

ce·les·tial \sə-ˈles-chəl\ *adj* **1** : HEAVENLY, DIVINE **2** : of or relating to the sky — **ce·les·tial·ly** \-ē\ *adv*

celestial navigation *n* : navigation by observation of the positions of celestial bodies

celestial sphere *n* : an imaginary sphere of infinite radius against which the celestial bodies appear to be projected

cel·i·ba·cy \ˈsel-ə-bə-sē\ *n* **1** : the state of being unmarried; *esp* : abstention by vow from marriage **2** : CHASTITY

cel·i·bate \ˈsel-ə-bət\ *n* : one who lives in celibacy — **celibate** *adj*

cell \ˈsel\ *n* **1** : a small room (as in a convent or prison) usu. for one person; *also* : a small compartment, cavity, or bounded space **2** : a tiny mass of protoplasm that contains a nucleus, is enclosed by a membrane, and forms the fundamental unit of living matter **3** : a container holding an electrolyte either for generating electricity or for use in electrolysis **4** : a single unit in a device for converting radiant energy into electrical energy

cel·lar \ˈsel-ər\ *n* **1** : BASEMENT 1 **2** : the lowest position (as in an athletic league) **3** : a stock of wines

cel·lar·age \ˈsel-ə-rij\ *n* : cellar space esp. for storage

cel·lar·ette *or* **cel·lar·et** \ˌsel-ə-ˈret\ *n* : a case or cabinet for a few bottles of wine or liquor

cel·lo \ˈchel-ō\ *n, pl* **cellos** : a bass member of the violin family tuned an octave below the viola — **cel·list** \-əst\ *n*

cel·lo·phane \ˈsel-ə-ˌfān\ *n* : a thin transparent material made from cellulose and used as a wrapping

cel·lu·lar \ˈsel-yə-lər\ *adj* : of, relating to, or consisting of cells

cel·lu·lite \ˈsel-yə-ˌlīt\ *n* : lumpy fat in the thighs, hips, and buttocks of some women

cel·lu·lose \-ˌlōs\ *n* : a complex carbohydrate of the cell walls of plants used esp. in making paper or rayon — **cel·lu·los·ic** \ˌsel-yə-ˈlō-sik\ *adj or n*

Cel·sius \ˈsel-sē-əs\ *adj* : relating to or having a scale for measuring temperature on which the interval between the triple point and the boiling point of water is divided into 99.99 degrees with 0.01° being the triple point and 100.00° the boiling point

Celt \ˈselt, ˈkelt\ *n* : a member of any of a group of peoples (as the Irish or Welsh) of western Europe — **Celt·ic** *adj*

cem·ba·lo \ˈchem-bə-ˌlō\ *n, pl* **-ba·li** \-ˌlē\ *or* **-balos** [It] : HARPSICHORD

[1]**ce·ment** \si-ˈment\ *n* **1** : a powder that is produced from a burned mixture chiefly of clay and limestone and that is used in mortar and concrete; *also* : CONCRETE **2** : a binding element or agency **3** : CEMENTUM; *also* : a substance for filling cavities in teeth

[2]**cement** *vb* **1** : to unite by or as if by cement **2** : to cover with concrete — **ce·ment·er** *n*

ce·men·tum \si-ˈment-əm\ *n* : a specialized external bony layer of the part of a tooth normally within the gum

cem·e·tery \ˈsem-ə-ˌter-ē\ *n, pl* **-ter·ies** [ME *cimitery*, fr. MF *cimitere*, fr. LL *coemeterium*, fr. Gk *koimētērion* sleeping chamber, burial place, fr. *koiman* to put to sleep] : a burial ground : GRAVEYARD

cen·o·bite \ˈsen-ə-ˌbīt\ *n* : a member of a religious group living together in a monastic community — **cen·o·bit·ic** \ˌsen-ə-ˈbit-ik\ *adj*

ceno·taph \ˈsen-ə-ˌtaf\ *n* [F *cénotaphe*, fr. L *cenotaphium*, fr. Gk *kenotaphion*, fr. *kenos* empty + *taphos* tomb] : a tomb or a monument erected in honor of a person whose body is elsewhere

Ce·no·zo·ic \ˌsē-nə-ˈzō-ik, ˌsen-ə-\ *adj* [deriv. of Gk *kainos* new, recent] : of, relating to, or being the most recent of the five eras of geologic history extending from about 70 million years ago to the present — **Cenozoic** *n*

cen·ser \ˈsen-sər\ *n* : a vessel for burning incense (as in a religious ritual)

[1]**cen·sor** \ˈsen-sər\ *n* **1** : one of two early Roman magistrates whose duties included taking the census **2** : an official who inspects printed matter or sometimes motion pictures with power to suppress anything objectionable — **cen·so·ri·al** \sen-ˈsōr-ē-əl\ *adj*

[2]**censor** *vb* : to subject to censorship

cen·so·ri·ous \sen-ˈsōr-ē-əs\ *adj* : marked by or given to censure : CRITICAL — **cen·so·ri·ous·ly** *adv* — **cen·so·ri·ous·ness** *n*

cen·sor·ship \ˈsen-sər-ˌship\ *n* **1** : the action of a censor esp. in stopping the transmission or publication of matter considered objectionable **2** : the office of a Roman censor

[1]**cen·sure** \ˈsen-chər\ *n* **1** : the act of blaming or condemning sternly **2** : an official reprimand

[2]**censure** *vb* **cen·sured; cen·sur·ing** \ˈsench-(ə-)riŋ\ : to find fault with and criticize as blameworthy — **cen·sur·able** *adj*

cen·sus \ˈsen-səs\ *n* **1** : a periodic governmental count of population **2** : COUNT, TALLY

[1]**cent** \ˈsent\ *n* [MF, hundred, fr. L *centum*] **1** : a monetary unit equal to 1/100 of a basic unit of value — see *birr, dollar, gulden, leone, lilangeni, rand, rupee, shilling* at MONEY table **2** : a coin, token, or note representing one cent

[2]**cent** *abbr* **1** centigrade **2** central **3** century

cen·taur \ˈsen-ˌtȯr\ *n* : any of a race of creatures in Greek mythology half man and half horse

[1]**cen·ta·vo** \sen-ˈtäv-(ˌ)ō\ *n, pl* **-vos** — see *colon, cordoba, lempira, peso, quetzal, sucre* at MONEY table

[2]**cen·ta·vo** \-ˈtäv-(ˌ)ü, -(ˌ)ō\ *n, pl* **-vos** — see *dobra, escudo, metical* at MONEY table

cen·te·nar·i·an \ˌsent-ᵊn-ˈer-ē-ən\ *n* : a person who is 100 or more years old

cen·te·na·ry \sen-ˈten-ə-rē, ˈsent-ᵊn-ˌer-ē\ *n, pl* **-ries** : CENTENNIAL — **cen- tenary** *adj*

cen·ten·ni·al \sen-ˈten-ē-əl\ *n* : a 100th anniversary or its celebration — **centennial** *adj*

[1]**cen·ter** \ˈsent-ər\ *n* **1** : the point that is equally distant from all points on the circumference of a circle or surface of a sphere; *also* : MIDDLE 1 **2** : the point about which an activity concentrates or from which something originates **3** : a region of concentrated population **4** : a middle part **5** *often cap* : political figures holding moderate views esp. between those of conservatives and liberals **6** : a player occupying a middle position (as in football or basketball)

[2]**center** *vb* **1** : to place or fix at or around a center or central area **2** : to gather to a center : CONCENTRATE **3** : to have a center : FOCUS

cen·ter·board \ˈsent-ər-ˌbōrd\ *n* : a retractable keel used esp. in sailboats

cen·ter·piece \ˈsent-ər-ˌpēs\ *n* **1** : an object in a central position; *esp* : an adornment in the center of a table **2** : one that is of central importance or interest

cen·tes·i·mal \sen-ˈtes-ə-məl\ *adj* : marked by or relating to division into hundredths

[1]**cen·tes·i·mo** \chen-ˈtez-ə-ˌmō\ *n, pl* **-mi** \-(ˌ)mē\ — see *lira* at MONEY table

[2]**cen·tes·i·mo** \sen-ˈtes-ə-ˌmō\ *n, pl* **-mos** — see *balboa, peso* at MONEY table

cen·ti·grade \ˈsent-ə-ˌgrād, ˈsänt-\ *adj* : relating to, conforming to, or having a thermometer scale on which the interval between the freezing and boiling points of water is divided into 100 degrees with 0° representing the freezing point and 100° the boiling point ⟨10° ~⟩

cen·ti·gram \-ˌgram\ *n* — see METRIC SYSTEM table

cen·ti·li·ter \ˈsent-i-ˌlēt-ər\ *n* — see METRIC SYSTEM table

cen·time \ˈsän-ˌtēm\ *n* — see *dinar, dirham, franc, gourde* at MONEY table

cen·ti·me·ter \ˈsent-ə-ˌmēt-ər, ˈsänt-\ *n* — see METRIC SYSTEM table

centimeter–gram–second *adj* : CGS

cen·ti·mo \ˈsent-ə-ˌmō\ *n, pl* **-mos** — see *bolivar, colon, ekuele, guarani, peseta* at MONEY table

cen·ti·pede \ˈsent-ə-ˌpēd\ *n* [L *centipeda*, fr. *centi-* hundred + *pes* foot] : any of a class of long flattened segmented arthropods with one pair of legs on each segment except the first which has a pair of poison fangs

[1]**cen·tral** \ˈsen-trəl\ *adj* **1** : constituting a center **2** : ESSENTIAL, PRINCIPAL **3** : situated at, in, or near the center **4** : centrally placed and superseding separate units ⟨~ heating⟩ — **cen·tral·ly** \-ē\ *adv*

[2]**central** *n* **1** : a telephone exchange or an operator handling calls there **2** : a central controlling office

cen·tral·ize \ˈsen-trə-ˌlīz\ *vb* **-ized; -iz·ing** : to bring to a central point or under central control — **cen·tral·iza·tion** \ˌsen-trə-lə-ˈzā-shən\ *n* — **cen·tral·iz·er** \ˈsen-trə-ˌlī-zər\ *n*

central nervous system *n* : the part of the nervous system which integrates nervous function and activity and which in vertebrates consists of the brain and spinal cord

cen·tre *chiefly Brit var of* CENTER

cen·trif·u·gal \sen-ˈtrif-yə-gəl, -ˈtrif-i-gəl\ *adj* [NL *centrifugus*, fr. *centr-* center + *fugere* to flee] **1** : proceeding or acting in a direction away from a center or axis **2** : using or acting by centrifugal force

centrifugal force *n* : the force that tends to impel a thing or parts of a thing outward from a center of rotation

cen·tri·fuge \ˈsen-trə-ˌfyüj\ *n* : a machine using centrifugal force (as for separating substances of different densities or for removing moisture)

cen·trip·e·tal \sen-ˈtrip-ət-ᵊl\ *adj* [NL *centripetus,* fr. *centr-* center + L *petere* seek] : proceeding or acting in a direction toward a center or axis

centripetal force *n* : the force needed to keep an object revolving about a point moving in a circular path

cen·trist \ˈsen-trəst\ *n* **1** *often cap* : a member of a center party **2** : one who holds moderate views

cen·tu·ri·on \sen-ˈt(y)u̇r-ē-ən\ *n* : an officer commanding a Roman century

cen·tu·ry \ˈsench-(ə-)rē\ *n, pl* **-ries 1** : a subdivision of a Roman legion **2** : a group or sequence of 100 like things **3** : a period of 100 years

century plant *n* : a Mexican agave maturing and flowering only once in many years and then dying

CEO *abbr* chief executive officer

ce·phal·ic \sə-ˈfal-ik\ *adj* **1** : of or relating to the head **2** : directed toward or situated on or in or near the head

ce·ram·ic \sə-ˈram-ik\ *n* **1** *pl* : the art or process of making articles from a nonmetallic mineral (as clay) by firing **2** : a product produced by ceramics — **ceramic** *adj*

ce·ra·mist \sə-ˈram-əst\ *or* **ce·ram·i·cist** \sə-ˈram-ə-səst\ *n* : one who engages in ceramics

[1]**ce·re·al** \ˈsir-ē-əl\ *adj* [L *cerealis,* fr. *Ceres,* the Roman goddess of agriculture] : relating to grain or to the plants that produce it; *also* : made of grain

[2]**cereal** *n* **1** : a grass (as wheat) yielding grain suitable for food; *also* : its grain **2** : grain of a cereal prepared for use as a breakfast food

cer·e·bel·lum \ˌser-ə-ˈbel-əm\ *n, pl* **-bellums** *or* **-bel·la** \-ˈbel-ə\ [ML, fr. L, dim. of *cerebrum*] : a part of the brain that projects over the medulla and is concerned esp. with coordination of muscular action and with bodily balance — **cer·e·bel·lar** \-ˈbel-ər\ *adj*

ce·re·bral cortex \sə-ˌrē-brəl-, ˌser-ə-\ *n* : the surface layer of gray matter of the cerebrum that functions chiefly in coordination of higher nervous activity

cerebral palsy *n* : a disorder caused by brain damage usu. before or during birth and marked esp. by defective muscle control

cer·e·brate \ˈser-ə-ˌbrāt\ *vb* **-brat·ed; -brat·ing** : THINK — **cer·e·bra·tion** \ˌser-ə-ˈbrā-shən\ *n*

ce·re·brum \sə-ˈrē-brəm, ˈser-ə-\ *n, pl* **-brums** *or* **-bra** \-brə\ [L] : the enlarged front and upper part of the brain that contains the higher nervous centers — **ce·re·bral** \sə-ˈrē-brəl, ˈser-ə-\ *adj* — **ce·re·bral·ly** \-ē\ *adv*

cere·cloth \ˈsiər-ˌklȯth\ *n* : cloth treated with melted wax or gummy matter and formerly used esp. for wrapping a dead body

cere·ment \ˈser-ə-mənt, ˈsiər-mənt\ *n* : a shroud for the dead

[1]**cer·e·mo·ni·al** \ˌser-ə-ˈmō-nē-əl\ *adj* : of, relating to, or forming a ceremony — **cer·e·mo·ni·al·ly** \-ē\ *adv*

[2]**ceremonial** *n* : a ceremonial act or system : RITUAL, FORM

cer·e·mo·ni·ous \ˌser-ə-ˈmō-nē-əs\ *adj* **1** : devoted to forms and ceremony **2** : CEREMONIAL **3** : according to formal usage or procedure **4** : marked by ceremony — **cer·e·mo·ni·ous·ly** *adv* — **cer·e·mo·ni·ous·ness** *n*

cer·e·mo·ny \ˈser-ə-ˌmō-nē\ *n, pl* **-nies 1** : a formal act or series of acts prescribed by law, ritual, or convention **2** : a conventional act of politeness **3** : a mere outward form **4** : FORMALITY

ce·re·us \ˈsir-ē-əs\ *n* : any of various cacti of the western U.S. and tropical America

ce·rise \sə-ˈrēs\ *n* [F, lit., cherry] : a moderate red

ce·ri·um \ˈsir-ē-əm\ *n* : a malleable metallic chemical element used esp. in alloys—see ELEMENT table

cer·met \ˈsər-ˌmet\ *n* : a strong alloy of a heat-resistant compound and a metal used esp. for turbine blades

cert *abbr* certificate; certification; certified; certify

[1]**cer·tain** \ˈsərt-ᵊn\ *adj* **1** : FIXED, SETTLED **2** : proved to be true **3** : of a specific but unspecified character ⟨~ people in authority⟩ **4** : DEPENDABLE, RELIABLE **5** : INDISPUTABLE, UNDENIABLE **6** : assured in mind or action — **cer·tain·ly** *adv*

[2]**certain** *pron* : certain ones

cer·tain·ty \-tē\ *n, pl* **-ties 1** : something that is certain **2** : the quality or state of being certain

cer·tif·i·cate \sər-ˈtif-i-kət\ *n* **1** : a document testifying to the truth of a fact **2** : a document testifying that one has fulfilled certain requirements (as of a course or school) **3** : a document evidencing ownership or debt

cer·ti·fi·ca·tion \ˌsərt-ə-fə-ˈkā-shən\ *n* **1** : the act of certifying : the state of being certified **2** : a certified statement

certified milk *n* : milk produced in dair- ies that operate under the rules and regulations of an authorized medical milk commission

certified public accountant *n* : an accountant who has met the requirements of a state law and has been granted a state certificate

cer·ti·fy \ˈsərt-ə-ˌfī\ *vb* **-fied; -fy·ing 1** : VERIFY, CONFIRM **2** : to endorse officially **3** : to guarantee (a bank check) as good by a statement to that effect stamped on its face **4** : to provide with a usu. professional certificate or license **syn** accredit, approve, sanction, endorse — **cer·ti·fi·able** \-ˌfī-ə-bəl\ *adj* — **cer·ti·fi·ably** \-blē\ *adv* — **cer·ti·fi·er** *n*

cer·ti·tude \ˈsərt-ə-ˌt(y)üd\ *n* : the state of being or feeling certain

ce·ru·le·an \sə-ˈrü-lē-ən\ *adj* : AZURE

ce·ru·men \sə-ˈrü-mən\ *n* : EARWAX

cer·vi·cal \ˈsər-vi-kəl\ *adj* : of or relating to a neck or cervix

cer·vix \ˈsər-viks\ *n, pl* **cer·vi·ces** \-və-ˌsēz\ *or* **cer·vix·es 1** : NECK; *esp* : the back part of the neck **2** : a constricted portion of an organ or part; *esp* : the narrow outer end of the uterus

ce·sar·e·an *also* **ce·sar·i·an** \si-ˈzar-ē-ən, -ˈzer-\ *n* : CESAREAN SECTION — **cesarean** *also* **cesarian** *adj*

cesarean section *also* **cesarian section** *n* [fr. the legend that Julius Caesar was born this way] : surgical incision of the walls of the abdomen and uterus for delivery of offspring

ce·si·um \ˈsē-zē-əm\ *n* : a silver-white soft ductile chemical element — see ELEMENT table

ces·sa·tion \se-ˈsā-shən\ *n* : a temporary or final ceasing (as of action)

ces·sion \ˈsesh-ən\ *n* : a yielding (as of rights) to another

cess·pool \ˈses-ˌpül\ *n* : an underground pit or tank for receiving household sewage

cf *abbr* [L *confer*] compare

Cf *symbol* californium

CF *abbr* cystic fibrosis

cg *or* **cgm** *abbr* centigram

CG *abbr* **1** coast guard **2** commanding general

cgs \ˈsē-ˈjē-ˈes\ *adj, often cap C&G&S* : of, relating to, or being a system of units based on the centimeter as the unit of length, the gram as the unit of weight, and the second as the unit of time

ch *abbr* **1** chain **2** champion **3** chapter **4** church

CH *abbr* **1** clearinghouse **2** courthouse **3** customhouse

Cha·blis \ˈshab-ˌlē; sha-ˈblē\ *n, pl* **Cha·blis** \-ˌlēz, -ˈblēz\ **1** : a dry sharp white Burgundy wine **2** : a white California wine that is a blend of several grapes

cha–cha \ˈchä-ˌchä\ *n* : a fast rhythmic ballroom dance of Latin American origin

Chad·ian \ˈchad-ē-ən\ *n* : a native or inhabitant of Chad — **Chadian** *adj*

chafe \ˈchāf\ *vb* **chafed; chaf·ing 1** : IRRITATE, VEX **2** : FRET **3** : to warm by rubbing **4** : to rub so as to wear away; *also* : to make sore by rubbing

cha·fer \ˈchā-fər\ *n* **:** any of various large beetles

[1]**chaff** \ˈchaf\ *n* **1 :** debris (as husks) separated from grain in threshing **2 :** something comparatively worthless — **chaffy** \-ē\ *adj*

[2]**chaff** *n* **:** light jesting talk **:** BANTER

[3]**chaff** *vb* **:** to tease in a good-natured manner

chaf·fer \ˈchaf-ər\ *vb* **:** BARGAIN, HAGGLE — **chaf·fer·er** *n*

chaf·finch \ˈchaf-ˌinch\ *n* **:** a European finch with a cheerful song

chaf·ing dish \ˈchā-fiŋ-\ *n* **:** a utensil for cooking food at the table

[1]**cha·grin** \shə-ˈgrin\ *n* **:** mental uneasiness or annoyance caused by failure, disappointment, or humiliation

[2]**chagrin** *vb* **cha·grined** \-ˈgrind\; **cha·grin·ing** \-ˈgrin-iŋ\ **:** to cause to feel chagrin

[1]**chain** \ˈchān\ *n* **1 :** a flexible series of connected links **2 :** a chainlike surveying instrument; *also* **:** a unit of length equal to 66 feet (about 20 meters) **3 :** a series of things linked together **syn** train, string, sequence, succession, series

[2]**chain** *vb* **:** to fasten, bind, or connect with a chain; *also* **:** FETTER

chain gang *n* **:** a gang of convicts chained together

chain letter *n* **:** a letter sent to several persons with a request that each send copies to an equal number of persons

chain mail *n* **:** flexible armor of interlocking metal rings

chain reaction *n* **1 :** a series of events in which each event initiates the succeeding one **2 :** a chemical or nuclear reaction yielding products that cause further reactions of the same kind

chain saw *n* **:** a portable power saw that has teeth linked together to form an endless chain

chain–smoke \ˈchān-ˈsmōk\ *vb* **:** to smoke esp. cigarettes continuously

chain store *n* **:** any of numerous stores under the same ownership that sell the same lines of goods

[1]**chair** \ˈcheər\ *n* **1 :** a seat with a back for one person **2 :** ELECTRIC CHAIR **3 :** an official seat; *also* **:** an office or position of authority or dignity **4 :** CHAIRMAN

[2]**chair** *vb* **:** to act as chairman of

chair lift *n* **:** a motor-driven conveyor for skiers consisting of seats hung from a moving cable

chair·man \ˈcheər-mən\ *n* **:** the presiding officer of a meeting or of a committee — **chair·man·ship** *n*

chair·wom·an \-ˌwu̇m-ən\ *n* **:** a woman who acts as chairman

chaise \ˈshāz\ *n* **1 :** a 2-wheeled carriage with a folding top **2 :** a light carriage or pleasure cart

chaise longue \ˈshāz-ˈlȯŋ\ *n, pl* **chaise longues** \-ˈlȯŋ(z)\ [F *chaise longue,* lit., long chair] **:** a long couch-like chair

chaise lounge \-ˈlau̇nj\ *n* **:** CHAISE LONGUE

chal·ced·o·ny \kal-ˈsed-ᵊn-ē\ *n, pl* **-nies :** a translucent pale blue or gray quartz

chal·co·py·rite \ˌkal-kə-ˈpī-ˌrīt\ *n* **:** a yellow mineral constituting an important ore of copper

cha·let \sha-ˈlā\ *n* **1 :** a herdsman's cabin in the Swiss mountains **2 :** a building in the style of a Swiss cottage with a wide roof overhang

chal·ice \ˈchal-əs\ *n* **:** a drinking cup; *esp* **:** the eucharistic cup

[1]**chalk** \ˈchȯk\ *n* **1 :** a soft limestone **2 :** chalk or chalky material esp. when used as a crayon — **chalky** *adj*

[2]**chalk** *vb* **1 :** to rub or mark with chalk **2 :** to record with or as if with chalk — usu. used with *up*

chalk·board \ˈchȯk-ˌbōrd\ *n* **:** BLACKBOARD

chalk up *vb* **1 :** ASCRIBE, CREDIT **2 :** ATTAIN, ACHIEVE

[1]**chal·lenge** \ˈchal-ənj\ *vb* **chal·lenged; chal·leng·ing** [ME *chalengen* to accuse, fr. OF *chalengier,* fr. L *calumniari* to accuse falsely, fr. *calumnia* calumny] **1 :** to order to halt and prove identity **2 :** to take exception to **:** DISPUTE **3 :** to issue an invitation to compete against one esp. in single combat **:** DARE, DEFY — **chal·leng·er** *n*

[2]**challenge** *n* **1 :** a summons to a duel **2 :** an invitation to compete in a sport **3 :** a calling into question **4 :** an exception taken to a juror **5 :** a sentry's command to halt and prove identity **6 :** a stimulating or interesting task or problem

chal·lis \ˈshal-ē\ *n, pl* **chal·lises** \-ēz\ **:** a lightweight clothing fabric of wool, cotton, or synthetic yarns

cham \ˈkam\ *var of* KHAN

cham·ber \ˈchām-bər\ *n* **1 :** ROOM; *esp* **:** BEDROOM **2 :** an enclosed space or compartment **3 :** a hall for meetings of a legislative body **4 :** a judge's consultation room — usu. used in pl. **5 :** a legislative or judicial body; *also* **:** a council for a business purpose **6 :** the part of a firearm that holds the cartridge or powder charge during firing — **cham·bered** \-bərd\ *adj*

cham·ber·lain \ˈchām-bər-lən\ *n* **1 :** a chief officer in the household of a king or nobleman **2 :** TREASURER

cham·ber·maid \-ˌmād\ *n* **:** a maid who takes care of bedrooms

chamber music *n* **:** music intended for performance by a few musicians before a small audience

chamber of commerce : an association of businesspeople for promoting commercial and industrial interests in the community

cham·bray \ˈsham-ˌbrā\ *n* **:** a lightweight clothing fabric of white and colored threads

cha·me·leon \kə-ˈmēl-yən\ *n* [ME *camelion,* fr. MF, fr. L *chamaeleon,* fr. Gk *chamaileōn,* fr. *chamai* on the ground + *leōn* lion] **:** a small lizard whose skin changes color esp. according to its surroundings

[1]**cham·fer** \ˈcham-fər\ *n* **:** a beveled edge

[2]**chamfer** *vb* **1 :** to cut a furrow in (as a column) **:** GROOVE **2 :** to make a chamfer on **:** BEVEL

cham·ois \ˈsham-ē\ *n, pl* **cham·ois** \-ē(z)\ **1 :** a small goatlike antelope of Europe and the Caucasus region of the U.S.S.R. **2** *also* **cham·my** \-ē\ **:** a soft leather made esp. from the skin of the sheep or goat **3 :** a cotton fabric made in imitation of chamois leather

cham·o·mile \ˈkam-ə-ˌmīl, -ˌmēl\ *n* **:** any of a genus of strong-scented herbs related to the daisies and having flower heads that yield a bitter medicinal substance

[1]**champ** \ˈchamp, ˈchämp\ *vb* **1 :** to chew noisily **2 :** to show impatience of delay or restraint

[2]**champ** \ˈchamp\ *n* **:** CHAMPION

cham·pagne \sham-ˈpān\ *n* **:** a white effervescent wine

cham·paign \sham-ˈpān\ *n* **:** a stretch of flat open country

[1]**cham·pi·on** \ˈcham-pē-ən\ *n* **1 :** a militant advocate or defender **2 :** one that wins first prize or place in a contest **3 :** one that is acknowledged to be better than all others

[2]**champion** *vb* **:** to protect or fight for as a champion **syn** back, advocate, uphold, support

cham·pi·on·ship \-ˌship\ *n* **1 :** the position or title of a champion **2 :** the act of championing **:** DEFENSE **3 :** a contest held to determine a champion

[1]**chance** \ˈchans\ *n* **1 :** something that happens without apparent cause **2 :** the unpredictable element in existence **:** LUCK, FORTUNE **3 :** OPPORTUNITY **4 :** the likelihood of a particular outcome in an uncertain situation **:** PROBABILITY **5 :** RISK **6 :** a raffle ticket — **chance** *adj* — **by chance :** in the haphazard course of events

[2]**chance** *vb* **chanced; chanc·ing 1 :** to take place by chance **:** HAPPEN **2 :** to come casually and unexpectedly — used with *upon* **3 :** to leave to chance **4 :** to accept the risk of

chan·cel \ˈchan-səl\ *n* **:** the part of a church including the altar and choir

chan·cel·lery *or* **chan·cel·lory** \ˈchan- s(ə-)lə-rē\ *n, pl* **-ler·ies** *or* **-lor·ies 1 :** the position or office of a chancellor **2**

: the building or room where a chancellor works **3** : the office or staff of an embassy or consulate

chan·cel·lor \ˈchan-s(ə-)lər\ *n* **1** : a high state official in various countries **2** : the head of a university **3** : a judge in the equity court in various states of the U.S. **4** : the chief minister of state in some European countries — **chan·cel·lor·ship** *n*

chan·cery \ˈchans-(ə-)rē\ *n, pl* **-cer·ies** **1** : any of various courts of equity in the U.S. and Britain **2** : a record office for public or diplomatic archives **3** : a chancellor's court or office **4** : the office of an embassy

chan·cre \ˈshaŋ-kər\ *n* [F, fr. L *cancer*] : a primary sore or ulcer at the site of entry of an infective agent (as of syphilis)

chan·croid \ˈchaŋ-ˌkrȯid\ *n* : a sexually transmitted disease caused by a bacterium and characterized by chancres that differ from those of syphilis in lacking hardened margins

chancy \ˈchan-sē\ *adj* **chanc·i·er; -est** **1** *Scot* : AUSPICIOUS **2** : RISKY

chan·de·lier \ˌshan-də-ˈliər\ *n* : a branched lighting fixture suspended from a ceiling

chan·dler \ˈchan-dlər\ *n* [ME *chandeler* a maker or seller of candles, fr. MF *chandelier,* fr. OF, fr. *chandelle* candle, fr. L *candela*] : a dealer in provisions and supplies of a specified kind ⟨ship's ∼⟩ — **chan·dlery** *n*

[1]**change** \ˈchānj\ *vb* **changed; chang·ing** **1** : to make or become different : ALTER **2** : to replace with another **3** : EXCHANGE **4** : to give or receive an equivalent sum in notes or coins of usu. smaller denominations or of another currency **5** : to put fresh clothes or covering on ⟨∼ a bed⟩ **6** : to put on different clothes — **change·able** *adj* — **chang·er** *n*

[2]**change** *n* **1** : the act, process, or result of changing **2** : a fresh set of clothes to replace those being worn **3** : money given in exchange for other money of higher denomination **4** : surplus money returned to a person who offers payment exceeding the sum due **5** : coins esp. of small denominations — **change·ful** *adj* — **change·less** *adj*

change·ling \ˈchānj-liŋ\ *n* : a child secretly exchanged for another in infancy

change of life : MENOPAUSE

change·over \ˈchānj-ˌō-vər\ *n* : CONVERSION, TRANSITION

change ringing *n* : the art or practice of ringing a set of tuned bells in continually varying order

[1]**chan·nel** \ˈchan-^{ə}l\ *n* **1** : the bed of a stream **2** : the deeper part of a waterway **3** : STRAIT **4** : a means of passage or transmission **5** : a range of frequencies of sufficient width for a single radio or television transmission **6** : a usu. tubular enclosed passage : CONDUIT **7** : a long gutter, groove, or furrow

[2]**channel** *vb* **-neled** *or* **-nelled; -nel·ing** *or* **-nel·ling** **1** : to make a channel in **2** : to direct into or through a channel

chan·nel·ize \ˈchan-^{ə}l-ˌīz\ *vb* **-ized; -iz·ing** : CHANNEL — **chan·nel·iza·tion** \ˌchan-^{ə}l-ə-ˈzā-shən\ *n*

chan·son \shä^{n}-sō^{n}\ *n, pl* **chan·sons** \-sō^{n}(z)\ : SONG; *esp* : a cabaret song

[1]**chant** \ˈchant\ *vb* **1** : SING; *esp* : to sing a chant **2** : to sing or speak in the manner of a chant **3** : to celebrate or praise in song — **chant·er** *n*

[2]**chant** *n* **1** : a repetitive melody in which several words are sung to one tone : SONG; *esp* : a liturgical melody **2** : a manner of singing or speaking in musical monotones

chan·teuse \shä^{n}-ˈtə(r)z, shan-ˈtüz\ *n, pl* **chan·teuses** \-ˈtə(r)z(-əz), -ˈtüz(-əz)\ [F] : a female concert or nightclub singer

chan·tey *or* **chan·ty** \ˈshant-ē, ˈchant-\ *n, pl* **chanteys** *or* **chanties** : a song sung by sailors in rhythm with their work

chan·ti·cleer \ˌchant-ə-ˈkliər, ˌshant-\ *n* : ROOSTER

Cha·nu·kah \ˈk̲än-ə-kə, ˈhän-\ *var of* HANUKKAH

cha·os \ˈkā-ˌäs\ *n* **1** *often cap* : the confused unorganized state existing before the creation of distinct forms **2** : complete disorder **syn** confusion, jumble, snarl, muddle, disarray — **cha·ot·ic** \kā-ˈät-ik\ *adj* — **cha·ot·i·cal·ly** \-i-k(ə-)lē\ *adv*

[1]**chap** \ˈchap\ *vb* **chapped; chap·ping** : to dry and crack open usu. from wind and cold ⟨*chapped* lips⟩

[2]**chap** *n* : a jaw with its fleshy covering — usu. used in pl.

[3]**chap** *n* : FELLOW

[4]**chap** *abbr* chapter

chap·ar·ral \ˌshap-ə-ˈral\ *n* **1** : a dense impenetrable thicket of shrubs or dwarf trees **2** : an ecological community of southern California comprised of shrubby plants

chap·book \ˈchap-ˌbu̇k\ *n* : a small book of ballads, tales, or tracts

cha·peau \sha-ˈpō\ *n, pl* **cha·peaus** \-ˈpōz\ *or* **cha·peaux** \-ˈpō(z)\ [MF] : HAT

cha·pel \ˈchap-əl\ *n* [ME, fr. OF *chapele,* fr. ML *cappella,* fr. LL *cappa* cloak; fr. the cloak of St. Martin of Tours preserved as a sacred relic in a chapel built for that purpose] **1** : a private or subordinate place of worship **2** : an assembly at an educational institution usu. including devotional exercises **3** : a place of worship used by a Christian group other than the established church

[1]**chap·er·on** *or* **chap·er·one** \ˈshap-ə-ˌrōn\ *n* [F *chaperon,* lit., hood, fr. MF, head covering, fr. *chape*] **1** : a person (as a matron) who accompanies young unmarried women in public for propriety **2** : an older person who accompanies young people at a social gathering to ensure proper behavior

[2]**chaperon** *or* **chaperone** *vb* **-oned; -on·ing** **1** : ESCORT, GUIDE **2** : to act as a chaperon to or for — **chap·er·on·age** \-ˌrō-nij\ *n*

chap·fall·en \ˈchap-ˌfȯ-lən, ˈchäp-\ *adj* **1** : having the lower jaw hanging loosely **2** : DEJECTED, DEPRESSED

chap·lain \ˈchap-lən\ *n* **1** : a clergyman officially attached to a special group (as the army) **2** : a person chosen to conduct religious exercises (as for a club) — **chap·lain·cy** \-sē\ *n*

chap·let \ˈchap-lət\ *n* **1** : a wreath for the head **2** : a string of beads : NECKLACE

chap·man \ˈchap-mən\ *n, Brit* : an itinerant dealer : PEDDLER

chaps \ˈshaps, ˈchaps\ *n pl* [fr. MexSp *chaparreras*] : leather leggings resembling trousers without a seat that are worn esp. by western ranch hands

chap·ter \ˈchap-tər\ *n* **1** : a main division of a book **2** : a body of canons (as of a cathedral) **3** : a local branch of a society or fraternity

[1]**char** \ˈchär\ *n, pl* **char** *or* **chars** : any of a genus of trouts (as the common brook trout) with small scales

[2]**char** *vb* **charred; char·ring** **1** : to burn to charcoal **2** : SCORCH **3** : to burn to a cinder

[3]**char** *vb* **charred; char·ring** : to work as a cleaning woman

char·a·banc \ˈshar-ə-baŋ\ *n, Brit* : a sight-seeing motor coach

char·ac·ter \ˈkar-ik-tər\ *n* [ME *caracter,* fr. MF *caractère,* fr. L *character* mark, distinctive quality, fr. Gk *charaktēr,* fr. *charassein* to scratch, engrave] **1** : a graphic symbol (as a letter) used in writing or printing **2** : a symbol that represents information; *also* : a representation of such a character that may be accepted by a computer **3** : a distinguishing feature : ATTRIBUTE **4** : the complex of mental and ethical traits marking a person or a group **5** : a person marked by conspicuous often peculiar traits **6** : one of the persons in a novel or play **7** : REPUTATION **8** : moral excellence

[1]**char·ac·ter·is·tic** \ˌkar-ik-tə-ˈris-tik\ *n* : a distinguishing trait, quality, or property

[2]**characteristic** *adj* : serving to mark individual character **syn** individual, peculiar, distinctive — **char·ac·ter·is·ti·cal·ly** \-ti-k(ə-)lē\ *adv*

char·ac·ter·ize \ˈkar-ik-tə-ˌrīz\ *vb* **-ized; -iz·ing** **1** : to describe the character of **2** : to be a characteristic of — **char·ac·ter·iza·tion** \ˌkar-ik-t(ə-)rə-ˈzā-shən\ *n*

cha·rades \shə-ˈrādz\ *n sing or pl* : a guessing game in which contestants act out the syllables of a word to be guessed

char·coal \ˈchär-ˌkōl\ *n* **1** : a porous carbon prepared from vegetable or animal substances **2** : a piece of fine charcoal used in drawing; *also* : a drawing made with charcoal

chard \ˈchärd\ *n* : a beet lacking the enlarged root but having leaves and stalks often cooked as a vegetable

char·don·nay \ˌshard-ᵊn-ˈā\ *n, often cap* [F] : a dry white wine of Chablis type

¹**charge** \ˈchärj\ *vb* **charged; charg·ing 1** : to load or fill to capacity **2** : to give an electric charge to; *also* : to restore the activity of (a storage battery) by means of an electric current **3** : to impose a task or responsibility on **4** : COMMAND, ORDER **5** : ACCUSE **6** : to rush against : rush forward in assault **7** : to make liable for payment; *also* : to record a debt or liability against **8** : to fix as a price — **charge·able** *adj*

²**charge** *n* **1** : a quantity (as of fuel or ammunition) required to fill something to capacity **2** : a store or accumulation of force **3** : an excess or deficiency of electrons in a body **4** : THRILL, KICK **5** : a task or duty imposed **6** : CARE, RESPONSIBILITY **7** : one given into another's care **8** : instructions from a judge to a jury **9** : COST, EXPENSE, PRICE; *also* : a debit to an account **10** : ACCUSATION, INDICTMENT **11** : ATTACK, ASSAULT

charge–coupled device *n* : a semiconductor device used esp. as an optical sensor

char·gé d'af·faires \shär-ˌzhād-ə-ˈfaər\ *n, pl* **chargés d'affaires** \-ˌzhā(z)d-ə-\ [F] : a diplomat who substitutes for an ambassador or minister

¹**char·ger** \ˈchär-jər\ *n* : a large platter

²**charg·er** *n* **1** : a device or a workman that charges something **2** : WAR-HORSE

char·i·ot \ˈchar-ē-ət\ *n* : a 2-wheeled vehicle of ancient times used in war and in races and processions — **char·i·o·teer** \ˌchar-ē-ə-ˈtiər\ *n*

cha·ris·ma \kə-ˈriz-mə\ *also* **char·ism** \ˈkar-ˌiz-əm\ *n, pl* **cha·ris·ma·ta** \kə-ˈriz-mət-ə\ *also* **charisms** : a personal quality of leadership arousing popular loyalty or enthusiasm — **char·is·mat·ic** \ˌkar-əz-ˈmat-ik\ *adj*

char·i·ta·ble \ˈchar-ət-ə-bəl\ *adj* **1** : liberal in giving to needy people **2** : merciful or lenient in judging others **syn** benevolent, philanthropic, altruistic, humanitarian — **char·i·ta·ble·ness** *n* — **char·i·ta·bly** \-blē\ *adv*

char·i·ty \ˈchar-ət-ē\ *n, pl* **-ties 1** : goodwill toward or love of humanity **2** : an act or feeling of generosity **3** : the giving of aid to the poor; *also* : ALMS **4** : an institution engaged in relief of the poor **5** : leniency in judging others **syn** mercy, clemency, lenity

char·la·tan \ˈshär-lə-tən\ *n* : a person pretending to knowledge or ability that he lacks : QUACK

Charles·ton \ˈchärl-stən\ *n* : a lively ballroom dance in which the knees are twisted in and out and the heels are swung sharply outward on each step

char·ley horse \ˈchär-lē-ˌhȯrs\ *n* : pain and stiffness from muscular strain in an arm or leg

¹**charm** \ˈchärm\ *n* [ME *charme,* fr. OF, fr. L *carmen* song, fr. *canere* to sing] **1** : an act or expression believed to have magic power **2** : something worn about the person to ward off evil or bring good fortune : AMULET **3** : a trait that fascinates or allures **4** : physical grace or attraction **5** : a small ornament worn on a bracelet or chain

²**charm** *vb* **1** : to affect by or as if by a magic spell **2** : to protect by or as if by charms **3** : FASCINATE, ENCHANT **syn** allure, captivate, bewitch, attract — **charm·er** \ˈchär-mər\ *n*

charm·ing \ˈchär-miŋ\ *adj* : extremely pleasing or delightful — **charm·ing·ly** *adv*

char·nel house \ˈchärn-ᵊl-\ *n* : a building or chamber in which bodies or bones are deposited

¹**chart** \ˈchärt\ *n* **1** : MAP **2** : a sheet giving information in the form of a table, list, or diagram; *also* : GRAPH

²**chart** *vb* **1** : to make a chart of **2** : PLAN

¹**char·ter** \ˈchärt-ər\ *n* **1** : an official document granting rights or privileges (as to a colony, town, or college) from a sovereign or a governing body **2** : CONSTITUTION **3** : a written instrument from a society creating a branch **4** : a mercantile lease of a ship

²**charter** *vb* **1** : to grant a charter to **2** *Brit* : CERTIFY ⟨~*ed* engineer⟩ **3** : to hire, rent, or lease for temporary use — **char·ter·er** *n*

charter member *n* : an original member of an organization

char·treuse \shär-ˈtrüz, -ˈtrüs\ *n* : a variable color averaging a brilliant yellow green

char·wom·an \ˈchär-ˌwu̇m-ən\ *n* : a cleaning woman esp. in large buildings

chary \ˈchar-ē\ *adj* **chari·er; -est** [ME, sorrowful, dear, fr. OE *cearig* sorrowful, fr. *caru* sorrow] **1** : CAUTIOUS, CIRCUMSPECT **2** : SPARING — **char·i·ly** \ˈchar-ə-lē\ *adv*

¹**chase** \ˈchās\ *n* **1** : PURSUIT; *also* : HUNTING **2** : QUARRY **3** : a tract of unenclosed land used as a game preserve

²**chase** *vb* **chased; chas·ing 1** : to follow rapidly : PURSUE **2** : HUNT **3** : to seek out ⟨*chasing* down clues⟩ **4** : to cause to depart or flee : drive away **5** : RUSH, HASTEN

³**chase** *vb* **chased; chas·ing** : to decorate (a metal surface) by embossing or engraving

⁴**chase** *n* : FURROW, GROOVE

chas·er \ˈchā-sər\ *n* **1** : one that chases **2** : a mild drink (as beer) taken after hard liquor

chasm \ˈkaz-əm\ *n* : GORGE 2

chas·sis \ˈshas-ē, ˈchas-ē\ *n, pl* **chas·sis** \-ēz\ : a supporting framework (as for the body of an automobile or the parts of a radio set)

chaste \ˈchāst\ *adj* **chast·er; chast·est 1** : innocent of unlawful sexual intercourse : VIRTUOUS, PURE **2** : CELIBATE **3** : pure in thought : MODEST **4** : severe or simple in design — **chaste·ly** *adv* — **chaste·ness** *n*

chas·ten \ˈchās-ᵊn\ *vb* **chas·tened; chas·ten·ing** \ˈchās-(ᵊ-)niŋ\ : to correct through punishment or suffering : DISCIPLINE; *also* : PURIFY — **chas·ten·er** *n*

chas·tise \chas-ˈtīz\ *vb* **chas·tised; chas·tis·ing** [ME *chastisen,* alter. of *chasten*] **1** : to punish esp. bodily **2** : to censure severely : CASTIGATE — **chas·tise·ment** \-mənt, ˈchas-təz-\ *n*

chas·ti·ty \ˈchas-tət-ē\ *n* : the quality or state of being chaste; *esp* : sexual purity

cha·su·ble \ˈchaz-ə-bəl, ˈchas-\ *n* : the outer vestment of the celebrant at the Eucharist

chat \ˈchat\ *n* : light familiar informal talk — **chat** *vb*

châ·teau \sha-ˈtō\ *n, pl* **châ·teaus** \-ˈtōz\ *or* **châ·teaux** \-ˈtō(z)\ [F, fr. L *castellum* castle, dim. of *castra* camp] **1** : a feudal castle in France **2** : a large country house **3** : a French vineyard estate

chat·e·laine \ˈshat-ᵊl-ˌān\ *n* **1** : the mistress of a chateau **2** : a clasp or hook for a watch, purse, or keys

chat·tel \ˈchat-ᵊl\ *n* **1** : an item of tangible property other than real estate **2** : SLAVE, BONDMAN

chat·ter \ˈchat-ər\ *vb* **1** : to utter speechlike but meaningless sounds **2** : to talk idly, incessantly, or fast **3** : to click repeatedly or uncontrollably — **chatter** *n* — **chat·ter·er** *n*

chat·ter·box \ˈchat-ər-ˌbäks\ *n* : one who talks incessantly

chat·ty \ˈchat-ē\ *adj* **chat·ti·er; -est** : TALKATIVE — **chat·ti·ly** \ˈchat-ᵊl-ē\ *adv* — **chat·ti·ness** \-ē-nəs\ *n*

[1]**chauf·feur** \ˈshō-fər, shō-ˈfər\ *n* [F, lit., stoker, fr. *chauffer* to heat] : a person employed to drive an automobile

[2]**chauffeur** *vb* **chauf·feured; chauf·feur·ing** \ˈshō-f(ə-)riŋ, shō-ˈfər-iŋ\ **1** : to do the work of a chauffeur **2** : to transport in the manner of a chauffeur

chaunt \ˈchónt, ˈchänt\ *var of* CHANT

chau·vin·ism \ˈshō-və-ˌniz-əm\ *n* [F *chauvinisme,* fr. Nicolas *Chauvin,* soldier of excessive patriotism and devotion to Napoleon] **1** : excessive or blind patriotism **2** : an attitude of superiority toward members of the opposite sex — **chau·vin·ist** \-və-nəst\ *n or adj* — **chau·vin·is·tic** \ˌshō-və-ˈnis-tik\ *adj* — **chau·vin·is·ti·cal·ly** \-ti-k(ə-)lē\ *adv*

cheap \ˈchēp\ *adj* **1** : INEXPENSIVE **2** : costing little effort to obtain **3** : worth little : SHODDY, TAWDRY **4** : worthy of scorn **5** : STINGY — **cheap** *adv* — **cheap·ly** *adv* — **cheap·ness** *n*

cheap·en \ˈchē-pən\ *vb* **cheap·ened; cheap·en·ing** \ˈchēp-(ə-)niŋ\ **1** : to make or become cheap or cheaper in price or value **2** : to make tawdry

cheap·skate \ˈchēp-ˌskāt\ *n* : a niggardly person; *esp* : one seeking to avoid his or her share of costs

[1]**cheat** \ˈchēt\ *vb* **1** : to deprive of something through fraud or deceit **2** : to practice fraud or trickery **3** : to violate rules (as of a game) dishonestly — **cheat·er** *n*

[2]**cheat** *n* **1** : the act of deceiving : FRAUD, DECEPTION **2** : one that cheats : a dishonest person

[1]**check** \ˈchek\ *n* **1** : a sudden stoppage of progress **2** : a sudden pause or break **3** : something that stops or restrains **4** : a standard for testing or evaluation **5** : EXAMINATION, INVESTIGATION **6** : the act of testing or verifying **7** : a written order to a bank to pay money **8** : a ticket or token showing ownership or identity **9** : a slip indicating an amount due **10** : a pattern in squares; *also* : a fabric in such a pattern **11** : a mark typically ✓ placed beside an item to show that it has been noted **12** : CRACK, SPLIT

[2]**check** *vb* **1** : to slow down or stop : BRAKE **2** : to restrain the action or force of : CURB **3** : to compare with a source, original, or authority : VERIFY **4** : to inspect or test for satisfactory condition **5** : to mark with a check as examined **6** : to consign for shipment for one holding a passenger ticket **7** : to mark into squares **8** : to leave or accept for safekeeping in a checkroom **9** : to correspond point by point : TALLY **10** : CRACK, SPLIT

check·book \ˈchek-ˌbu̇k\ *n* : a book containing blank checks

[1]**check·er** \ˈchek-ər\ *n* : a piece in the game of checkers

[2]**checker** *vb* **check·ered; check·er·ing** \ˈchek-(ə-)riŋ\ **1** : to variegate with different colors or shades **2** : to vary with contrasting elements ⟨a ~*ed* career⟩ **3** : to mark into squares

[3]**checker** *n* : one that checks; *esp* : one who checks out purchases in a supermarket

check·er·ber·ry \ˈchek-ə(r)-ˌber-ē\ *n* : WINTERGREEN 1; *also* : the spicy red fruit of this plant

check·er·board \-ə(r)-ˌbōrd\ *n* : a board of 64 squares of alternate colors used in various games

check·ers \ˈchek-ərz\ *n* : a game for two played on a checkerboard with each player having 12 pieces

check in *vb* : to report one's presence or arrival (as at a hotel)

check·list \ˈchek-ˌlist\ *n* : a list of items that may easily be referred to

check·mate \ˈchek-ˌmāt\ *vb* [ME *chekmaten,* fr. *chekmate,* interj. used to announce checkmate, fr. MF *eschec mat,* fr. Ar *shāh māt,* fr. Per, lit., the king is left unable to escape] **1** : to thwart completely : DEFEAT, FRUSTRATE **2** : to attack (an opponent's king) in chess so that escape is impossible — **checkmate** *n*

check·off \ˈchek-ˌóf\ *n* : the deduction of union dues from a worker's paycheck by the employer

check·out \ˈchek-ˌau̇t\ *n* **1** : the action or an instance of checking out **2** : a counter at which checking out is done **3** : the process of examining and testing something as to readiness for intended use **4** : the process of familiarizing oneself with the operation of a mechanical thing (as an airplane)

check out \-ˈau̇t\ *vb* **1** : to settle one's account (as at a hotel) and leave **2** : to total or have totaled the cost of purchases in a store and to make or receive payment for them

check·point \ˈchek-ˌpóint\ *n* : a point at which a check is performed

check·room \-ˌrüm, -ˌru̇m\ *n* : a room at which baggage, parcels, or clothing is checked

check·up \-ˌəp\ *n* : EXAMINATION; *esp* : a general physical examination

ched·dar \ˈched-ər\ *n, often cap* : a hard mild to sharp white or yellow cheese of smooth texture

cheek \ˈchēk\ *n* **1** : the fleshy side part of the face **2** : IMPUDENCE, BOLDNESS, AUDACITY **3** : BUTTOCK 1

cheek·bone \ˈchēk-ˈbōn, -ˌbōn\ *n* : the bone or bony ridge below the eye

cheeky \ˈchē-kē\ *adj* **cheek·i·er; -est** : IMPUDENT, SAUCY — **cheek·i·ly** \ˈchē-kə-lē\ *adv* — **cheek·i·ness** \-kē-nəs\ *n*

cheep \ˈchēp\ *vb* : to utter faint shrill sounds : PEEP — **cheep** *n*

[1]**cheer** \ˈchiər\ *n* [ME *chere* face, cheer, fr. OF, face] **1** : state of mind or heart : SPIRIT **2** : ANIMATION, GAIETY **3** : hospitable entertainment : WELCOME **4** : food and drink for a feast **5** : something that gladdens **6** : a shout of applause or encouragement

[2]**cheer** *vb* **1** : to give hope or courage to : COMFORT **2** : to make glad **3** : to urge on esp. by shouts **4** : to applaud with shouts **5** : to grow or be cheerful — usu. used with *up* — **cheer·er** *n*

cheer·ful \ˈchiər-fəl\ *adj* **1** : having or showing good spirits **2** : conducive to good spirits : pleasant and bright — **cheer·ful·ly** \-ē\ *adv* — **cheer·ful·ness** *n*

cheer·lead·er \ˈchiər-ˌlēd-ər\ *n* : a person who directs organized cheering esp. at a sports event

cheer·less \ˈchiər-ləs\ *adj* : BLEAK, DISPIRITING — **cheer·less·ly** *adv* — **cheer·less·ness** *n*

cheery \ˈchi(ə)r-ē\ *adj* **cheer·i·er; -est** : LIVELY, BRIGHT, GAY — **cheer·i·ly** \ˈchir-ə-lē\ *adv* — **cheer·i·ness** \-ē-nəs\ *n*

cheese \ˈchēz\ *n* : the curd of milk usu. pressed into cakes and cured for use as food

cheese·burg·er \ˈchēz-ˌbər-gər\ *n* : a hamburger containing a slice of cheese

cheese·cake \-ˌkāk\ *n* **1** : a dessert consisting of a creamy filling usu. containing cheese baked in a shell **2** : photographs of attractive usu. scantily clad women

cheese·cloth \-ˌklóth\ *n* : a lightweight coarse cotton gauze

cheese·par·ing \-ˌpa(ə)r-iŋ\ *n* : miserly or petty economizing — **cheeseparing** *adj*

cheesy \ˈchē-zē\ *adj* **chees·i·er; -est** **1** : resembling, suggesting, or containing cheese **2** *slang* : CHEAP 3

chee·tah \ˈchēt-ə\ *n* [Hindu *cītā,* fr. Skt *citrakāya* tiger, fr. *citra* bright + *kāya* body] : a large long-legged spotted swift-moving African and formerly Asian cat

cheetah

chef \ˈshef\ *n* **1** : a cook who manages the kitchen (as of a restaurant) **2** : COOK

chef d'oeu·vre \shā-dœvr$^{\vartheta}$\ *n, pl* **chefs d'oeuvre** \-dœvr$^{\vartheta}$\ : MASTERPIECE
chem *abbr* chemical; chemist; chemistry
[1]**chem·i·cal** \ˈkem-i-kəl\ *adj* **1** : of, relating to, used in, or produced by chemistry **2** : acting or operated or produced by chemicals — **chem·i·cal·ly** \-i-k(ə-)lē\ *adv*
[2]**chemical** *n* : a substance obtained by a chemical process or used for producing a chemical effect
chemical engineering *n* : engineering dealing with the industrial application of chemistry
chemical warfare *n* : warfare using incendiary mixtures, smokes, or irritant, burning, or asphyxiating gases
che·mise \shə-ˈmēz\ *n* **1** : a woman's one-piece undergarment **2** : a loose straight-hanging dress
chem·ist \ˈkem-əst\ *n* **1** : one trained in chemistry **2** *Brit* : PHARMACIST
chem·is·try \ˈkem-ə-strē\ *n, pl* **-tries 1** : the science that deals with the composition, structure, and properties of substances and of the changes they undergo **2** : chemical composition or properties ⟨the ~ of gasoline⟩ **3** : a strong mutual attraction
che·mo·ther·a·py \ˌkē-mō-ˈther-ə-pē\ *n* : the use of chemicals in the treatment or control of disease — **che·mo·ther·a·peu·tic** \-ˌther-ə-ˈpyüt-ik\ *adj*
che·nille \shə-ˈnēl\ *n* [F, lit., caterpillar, fr. L *canicula,* dim. of *canis* dog] : a fabric with a deep fuzzy pile often used for bedspreads and rugs
cheque \ˈchek\ *chiefly Brit var of* [1]CHECK 7
cher·ish \ˈcher-ish\ *vb* **1** : to hold dear : treat with care and affection **2** : to keep deeply in mind
Cher·o·kee \ˈcher-ə-(ˌ)kē\ *n, pl* **Cherokee** *or* **Cherokees** : a member of an American Indian people orig. of Tennessee and No. Carolina; *also* : their language
che·root \shə-ˈrüt\ *n* : a cigar cut square at both ends
cher·ry \ˈcher-ē\ *n, pl* **cherries** [ME *chery,* fr. OF *cherise* (taken as a plural), fr. LL *ceresia,* fr. L *cerasus* cherry tree, fr. Gk *kerasos*] **1** : the small fleshy pale yellow to deep blackish red fruit of a tree related to the roses; *also* : the tree or its wood **2** : a variable color averaging a moderate red
chert \ˈchərt, ˈchat\ *n* : a rock resembling flint and consisting essentially of fine crystalline quartz or fibrous chalcedony — **cherty** \-ē\ *adj*
cher·ub \ˈcher-əb\ *n* **1** *pl* **cher·u·bim** \ˈcher-(y)ə-ˌbim\ : an angel of the 2d highest rank **2** *pl* **cherubs** : a chubby rosy person — **che·ru·bic** \chə-ˈrü-bik\ *adj*
chess \ˈches\ *n* : a game for two played on a board of 64 squares of alternate colors with each player having 16 pieces — **chess·board** \-ˌbōrd\ *n* — **chess·man** \-ˌman, -mən\ *n*
chest \ˈchest\ *n* **1** : a box, case, or boxlike receptacle for storage or shipping **2** : the part of the body enclosed by the ribs and sternum
ches·ter·field \ˈches-tər-ˌfēld\ *n* : an overcoat with a velvet collar
chest·nut \ˈches-(ˌ)nət\ *n* **1** : the edible nut of any of a genus of trees related to the beech and oaks; *also* : this tree **2** : a grayish to reddish brown **3** : an old joke or story
chet·rum \ˈchet-rəm\ *n, pl* **chetrums** *or* **chetrum** — see *ngultrum* at MONEY table
che·val glass \shə-ˈval-\ *n* : a full-length mirror that may be tilted in a frame
che·va·lier \ˌshev-ə-ˈliər, shə-ˈval-ˌyā\ *n* : a member of one of various orders of knighthood or of merit
chev·i·ot \ˈshev-ē-ət\ *n, often cap* **1** : a twilled fabric with a rough nap **2** : a sturdy soft-finished cotton fabric
chev·ron \ˈshev-rən\ *n* : a sleeve badge of one or more V-shaped or inverted V-shaped stripes worn to indicate rank or service (as in the armed forces)
[1]**chew** \ˈchü\ *vb* : to crush or grind with the teeth — **chew·able** *adj* — **chew·er** *n*
[2]**chew** *n* **1** : an act of chewing **2** : something for chewing
chewy \ˈchü-ē\ *adj* : requiring chewing ⟨~ candy⟩
Chey·enne \shī-ˈan, -ˈen\ *n, pl* **Cheyenne** *or* **Cheyennes** [CanF, fr. Dakota *Shaiyena,* fr. *shaia* to speak unintelligibly] : a member of an American Indian people of the western plains of the U.S.; *also* : their language
chg *abbr* **1** change **2** charge
Chi·an·ti \kē-ˈänt-ē, -ˈant-\ *n* : a dry usu. red wine
chiao \ˈtyaů\ *n, pl* **chiao** : a monetary unit of the People's Republic of China equal to 1/10 yuan
chiar·oscu·ro \kē-ˌär-ə-ˈsk(y)ůr-ō\ *n, pl* **-ros** [It, fr. *chiaro* clear, light + *oscuro* obscure, dark] **1** : pictorial representation in terms of light and shade without regard to color **2** : the arrangement or treatment of light and dark parts in a pictorial work of art
[1]**chic** \ˈshēk\ *n* : STYLISHNESS
[2]**chic** *adj* : cleverly stylish : SMART; *also* : currently fashionable
chi·cane \shik-ˈān\ *n* : CHICANERY
chi·ca·nery \-ˈān-(ə-)rē\ *n, pl* **-ner·ies** : TRICKERY, DECEPTION
Chi·ca·no \chi-ˈkän-ō\ *n, pl* **-nos** : an American of Mexican descent — **Chicano** *adj*
chi·chi \ˈshē-(ˌ)shē, ˈchē-(ˌ)chē\ *adj* [F] **1** : SHOWY, FRILLY **2** : ARTY, PRECIOUS **3** : CHIC — **chichi** *n*
chick \ˈchik\ *n* **1** : a young chicken; *also* : a young bird **2** : a young woman
chick·a·dee \ˈchik-ə-(ˌ)dē\ *n* : any of several small grayish American birds with black or brown caps
Chick·a·saw \ˈchik-ə-ˌsȯ\ *n, pl* **Chickasaw** *or* **Chickasaws** : a member of an American Indian people of Mississippi and Alabama
[1]**chick·en** \ˈchik-ən\ *n* **1** : a common domestic fowl esp. when young; *also* : its flesh used as food **2** : COWARD
[2]**chicken** *adj* **1** *slang* : COWARDLY **2** *slang* : insistent on petty esp. military discipline
chicken feed *n, slang* : an insignificant sum of money
chick·en·heart·ed \ˌchik-ən-ˈhärt-əd\ *adj* : TIMID, COWARDLY
chicken out *vb* : to lose one's courage
chicken pox *n* : an acute contagious virus disease esp. of children characterized by a low fever and vesicles
chick–pea \ˈchik-ˌpē\ *n* : an Asian leguminous herb cultivated for its short pods with one or two edible seeds; *also* : its seed
chick·weed \ˈchik-ˌwēd\ *n* : any of several low-growing small-leaved weeds related to the pinks
chi·cle \ˈchik-əl\ *n* : a gum from the latex of a tropical evergreen tree used as the chief ingredient of chewing gum
chic·o·ry \ˈchik-(ə-)rē\ *n, pl* **-ries** : a usu. blue-flowered herb related to the daisies and grown for its root and for use in salads; *also* : its dried ground root used for flavoring or adulterating coffee
chide \ˈchīd\ *vb* **chid** \ˈchid\ *or* **chid·ed** \ˈchīd-əd\; **chid** *or* **chid·den** \ˈchid-$^{\vartheta}$n\ *or* **chided; chid·ing** \ˈchīd-iŋ\ : to speak disapprovingly to **syn** reproach, reprove, reprimand, admonish, scold, rebuke
[1]**chief** \ˈchēf\ *adj* **1** : highest in rank **2** : most eminent or important **syn** principal, main, leading, major — **chief·ly** *adv*
[2]**chief** *n* **1** : the leader of a body or organization : HEAD **2** : the principal or most valuable part — **chief·dom** *n*
chief master sergeant *n* : a noncommissioned officer of the highest rank in the air force
chief of staff 1 : the ranking officer of a staff in the armed forces **2** : the ranking office of the army or air force
chief of state : the formal head of a national state as distinguished from the head of the government

chief petty officer *n* : an enlisted man in the navy ranking next below a senior chief petty officer
chief·tain \ˈchēf-tən\ *n* : a chief esp. of a band, tribe, or clan — **chief·tain·cy** \-sē\ *n* — **chief·tain·ship** *n*
chief warrant officer *n* : a warrant officer of senior rank
chif·fon \shif-ˈän, ˈshif-ˌ\ *n* [F, lit., rag, fr. *chiffe* old rag] : a sheer fabric esp. of silk
chif·fo·nier \ˌshif-ə-ˈniər\ *n* : a high narrow chest of drawers
chig·ger \ˈchig-ər\ *n* : a bloodsucking larval mite that irritates the skin
chi·gnon \ˈshēn-ˌyän\ *n* [F] : a knot of hair worn at the back of the head
Chi·hua·hua \chə-ˈwä-ˌwä\ *n* : a very small large-eared dog of a breed that originated in Mexico
chil·blain \ˈchil-ˌblān\ *n* : a sore or inflamed swelling (as on the feet or hands) caused by exposure to cold
child \ˈchīld\ *n, pl* **chil·dren** \ˈchil-drən\ **1** : an unborn or recently born person **2** : a young person between the periods of infancy and youth **3** : a male or female offspring : SON, DAUGHTER **4** : one strongly influenced by another or by a place or state of affairs — **child·ish** *adj* — **child·ish·ly** *adv* — **child·ish·ness** *n* — **child·less** *adj* — **child·less·ness** *n* — **child·like** *adj*
child·bear·ing \ˈchīld-ˌbar-iŋ\ *n* : CHILDBIRTH — **childbearing** *adj*
child·birth \-ˌbərth\ *n* : the act or process of giving birth to offspring
child·hood \-ˌhu̇d\ *n* : the state or time of being a child
child·proof \-ˌprüf\ *adj* : made to prevent tampering by children
child's play *n* : a simple task or act
Chil·ean \ˈchil-ē-ən, chə-ˈlā-ən\ *n* : a native or inhabitant of Chile — **Chilean** *adj*
chili *or* **chile** *or* **chil·li** \ˈchil-ē\ *n, pl* **chil·ies** *or* **chil·es** *or* **chil·lies 1** : a pungent pepper related to the tomato **2** : a thick sauce of meat and chilies **3** : CHILI CON CARNE
chili con car·ne \ˌchil-ē-ˌkän-ˈkär-nē, -kən-\ *n* [Sp *chile con carne* chili with meat] : a spiced stew of ground beef and chilies or chili powder usu. with beans
chili powder *n* : a seasoning made of ground hot peppers and other spices
[1]**chill** \ˈchil\ *n* **1** : a feeling of coldness accompanied by shivering **2** : moderate coldness **3** : a check to enthusiasm or warmth of feeling
[2]**chill** *adj* **1** : moderately cold **2** : COLD, RAW **3** : DISTANT, FORMAL ⟨a ~ reception⟩ **4** : DEPRESSING, DISPIRITING
[3]**chill** *vb* **1** : to make or become cold or chilly **2** : to make cool esp. without freezing **3** : to harden the surface of (as metal) by sudden cooling — **chill·er** *n*
chilly \ˈchil-ē\ *adj* **chill·i·er; -est 1** : noticeably cold **2** : unpleasantly affected by cold **3** : lacking warmth of feeling — **chill·i·ness** *n*
[1]**chime** \ˈchīm\ *n* **1** : a set of bells musically tuned **2** : the sound of a set of bells — usu. used in pl. **3** : a musical sound suggesting bells
[2]**chime** *vb* **chimed; chim·ing 1** : to make bell-like sounds **2** : to indicate (as the time of day) by chiming **3** : to be or act in accord : be in harmony
chime in *vb* : to break into or join in a conversation
chi·me·ra *or* **chi·mae·ra** \kī-ˈmir-ə, kə-\ *n* [L *chimaera*, fr. Gk *chimaira* she-goat, chimera] **1** : an imaginary monster made up of incongruous parts **2** : a frightful or foolish fancy
chi·me·ri·cal \-ˈmer-i-kəl\ *also* **chi·me·ric** \-ik\ *adj* **1** : FANTASTIC, IMAGINARY **2** : inclined to fantastic schemes
chim·ney \ˈchim-nē\ *n, pl* **chimneys 1** : a vertical structure extending above the roof of a building for carrying off smoke **2** : a glass tube around a lamp flame
chimp \ˈchimp, ˈshimp\ *n* : CHIMPANZEE
chim·pan·zee \ˌchim-ˌpan-ˈzē, ˌshim-, -pən-; chim-ˈpan-zē, shim-\ *n* : an African manlike ape
[1]**chin** \ˈchin\ *n* : the part of the face below the lower lip including the prominence of the lower jaw — **chin·less** *adj*
[2]**chin** *vb* **chinned; chin·ning** : to raise (oneself) while hanging by the hands until the chin is level with the support
chi·na \ˈchī-nə\ *n* : porcelain ware; *also* : domestic pottery in general
Chi·na·town \-ˌtau̇n\ *n* : the Chinese quarter of a city
chinch bug \ˈchinch-\ *n* : a small black and white bug destructive to cereal grasses
chin·chil·la \chin-ˈchil-ə\ *n* **1** : a small So. American rodent with soft pearl-gray fur; *also* : its fur **2** : a heavy long-napped woolen cloth
chine \ˈchīn\ *n* **1** : BACKBONE, SPINE; *also* : a cut of meat including the backbone or part of it **2** : RIDGE, CREST
Chi·nese \chī-ˈnēz, -ˈnēs\ *n, pl* **Chinese 1** : a native or inhabitant of China **2** : any of a group of related languages of China — **Chinese** *adj*
Chinese cabbage *n* **1** : BOK CHOY **2** : a Chinese vegetable related to the cabbage that forms tight elongate cylindrical heads of pale green to cream-colored leaves
Chinese checkers *n* : a game in which each player in turn transfers a set of marbles from a home point to the opposite point of a pitted 6-pointed star
Chinese gooseberry *n* : a subtropical vine that bears kiwifruit; *also* : KIWIFRUIT
Chinese lantern *n* : a collapsible translucent cover for a light
[1]**chink** \ˈchiŋk\ *n* : a small crack or fissure
[2]**chink** *vb* : to fill the chinks of : stop up
[3]**chink** *n* : a slight sharp metallic sound
[4]**chink** *vb* : to make a slight sharp metallic sound
chi·no \ˈchē-nō\ *n, pl* **chinos 1** : a usu. khaki cotton twill **2** *pl* : an article of clothing made of chino
Chi·nook \shə-ˈnu̇k, chə-, -ˈnük\ *n, pl* **Chinook** *or* **Chinooks** : a member of an American Indian people of Oregon
chintz \ˈchints\ *n* : a usu. glazed printed cotton cloth
chintzy \ˈchint-sē\ *adj* **chintz·i·er; -est 1** : decorated with or as if with chintz **2** : GAUDY, CHEAP
chin–up \ˈchin-ˌəp\ *n* : the act of chinning oneself
[1]**chip** \ˈchip\ *n* **1** : a small usu. thin and flat piece (as of wood) cut or broken off **2** : a thin crisp morsel of food **3** : a counter used in games (as poker) **4** *pl, slang* : MONEY **5** : a flaw left after a chip is removed **6** : a very small slice of silicon containing electronic circuits
[2]**chip** *vb* **chipped; chip·ping 1** : to cut or break chips from **2** : to break off in small pieces at the edges **3** : to play a chip shot
chip in *vb* : CONTRIBUTE
chip·munk \ˈchip-ˌməŋk\ *n* : any of various ground-dwelling squirrels found in No. America into Mexico and in Asia
chipped beef \ˈchip(t)-\ *n* : smoked dried beef sliced thin
[1]**chip·per** \ˈchip-ər\ *n* : one that chips
[2]**chipper** *adj* : LIVELY, CHEERFUL
Chip·pe·wa \ˈchip-ə-ˌwȯ, -ˌwä, -ˌwā, -wə\ *n, pl* **Chippewa** *or* **Chippewas** : OJIBWA
chip shot *n* : a short usu. low shot to the green in golf
chi·rog·ra·phy \kī-ˈräg-rə-fē\ *n* : HANDWRITING, PENMANSHIP — **chi·ro·graph·ic** \ˌkī-rə-ˈgraf-ik\ *adj*
chi·rop·o·dy \kə-ˈräp-əd-ē, shə-\ *n* : PODIATRY — **chi·rop·o·dist** \-əd-əst\ *n*
chi·ro·prac·tic \ˈkī-rə-ˌprak-tik\ *n* : a system of therapy based esp. on manipulation of body structures — **chi·ro·prac·tor** \-tər\ *n*
chirp \ˈchərp\ *n* : a short sharp sound characteristic of a small bird or cricket — **chirp** *vb*
[1]**chis·el** \ˈchiz-əl\ *n* : a metal tool with a cutting edge at the end of a blade used in chipping away and shaping wood, stone, or metal
[2]**chisel** *vb* **-eled** *or* **-elled; -el·ing** *or* **-el·ling** \ˈchiz-(ə-)liŋ\ **1** : to work with or as if with a chisel **2** : to obtain by

shrewd often unfair methods; *also* : CHEAT — **chis·el·er** \-(ə-)lər\ *n*

[1]**chit** \ˈchit\ *n* [ME *chitte* kitten, cub] **1** : CHILD **2** : a pert young woman

[2]**chit** *n* [Hindi *ciṭṭhī* letter, note] : a signed voucher for a small debt

chit·chat \ˈchit-ˌchat\ *n* : casual or trifling conversation

chi·tin \ˈkīt-ᵊn\ *n* : a sugar polymer that forms part of the hard outer integument esp. of insects — **chi·tin·ous** *adj*

chit·ter·lings *or* **chit·lins** \ˈchit-lənz\ *n pl* : the intestines of hogs esp. prepared as food

chi·val·ric \shə-ˈval-rik\ *adj* : relating to chivalry : CHIVALROUS

chiv·al·rous \ˈshiv-əl-rəs\ *adj* **1** : of or relating to chivalry **2** : marked by honor, courtesy, and generosity **3** : marked by especial courtesy to women — **chiv·al·rous·ly** *adv* — **chiv·al·rous·ness** *n*

chiv·al·ry \ˈshiv-əl-rē\ *n, pl* **-ries** **1** : a body of knights **2** : the system or practices of knighthood **3** : the spirit or character of the ideal knight

chive \ˈchīv\ *n* : an herb related to the onion that has leaves used for flavoring

chlo·ral hydrate \ˌklōr-əl-\ *n* : a white crystalline compound used as a hypnotic and sedative

chlor·dane \ˈklȯr-ˌdān\ *also* **chlor·dan** \-ˌdan\ *n* : a viscous liquid insecticide

chlo·ride \ˈklōr-ˌīd\ *n* : a compound of chlorine with another element or group

chlo·ri·nate \ˈklōr-ə-ˌnāt\ *vb* **-nat·ed; -nat·ing** : to treat or cause to combine with chlorine or a chlorine-containing compound — **chlo·ri·na·tion** \ˌklōr-ə-ˈnā-shən\ *n* — **chlo·ri·na·tor** \ˈklōr-ə-ˌnāt-ər\ *n*

chlo·rine \ˈklōr-ˌēn\ *n* : a nonmetallic chemical element that is found alone as a heavy strong-smelling greenish yellow irritating gas and is used as a bleach, oxidizing agent, and disinfectant — see ELEMENT table

chlo·rite \ˈklōr-ˌīt\ *n* : a usu. green mineral found with and resembling mica

chlo·ro·flu·o·ro·car·bon \ˌklōr-ə-ˈflōr-ə-ˌkär-bən, -ˈflu̇r-\ *n* : a gaseous compound that contains carbon, chlorine, fluorine, and sometimes hydrogen and is used esp. as a solvent, a refrigerant, and an aerosol propellant

[1]**chlo·ro·form** \ˈklōr-ə-ˌfȯrm\ *n* : a colorless heavy fluid with etherlike odor used as a solvent and anesthetic

[2]**chloroform** *vb* : to treat with chloroform to produce anesthesia or death

chlo·ro·phyll \-ˌfil\ *n* : the green coloring matter of plants that functions in photosynthesis

chm *abbr* chairman

chock \ˈchäk\ *n* : a wedge for steadying something or for blocking the movement of a wheel — **chock** *vb*

chock·a·block \ˈchäk-ə-ˌbläk\ *adj* : very full : CROWDED

chock–full \ˈchək-ˈfu̇l, ˈchäk-\ *adj* : full to the limit : CRAMMED

choc·o·late \ˈchäk-(ə-)lət, ˈchȯk-\ *n* [Sp, fr. Nahuatl (an Indian language of southern Mexico) *xocoatl*] **1** : a food prepared from ground roasted cacao beans; *also* : a drink prepared from this **2** : a candy made of or with a coating of chocolate **3** : a dark brown color

Choc·taw \ˈchäk-ˌtȯ\ *n, pl* **Choctaw** *or* **Choctaws** : a member of an American Indian people of Mississippi, Alabama, and Louisiana; *also* : their language

[1]**choice** \ˈchȯis\ *n* **1** : the act of choosing : SELECTION **2** : the power or opportunity of choosing : OPTION **3** : the best part **4** : a person or thing selected **5** : a variety offered for selection

[2]**choice** *adj* **choic·er; choic·est** **1** : worthy of being chosen **2** : selected with care **3** : of high quality

choir \ˈkwī(-ə)r\ *n* **1** : an organized company of singers esp. in a church **2** : the part of a church occupied by the singers

choir·boy \ˈkwī(-ə)r-ˌbȯi\ *n* : a boy member of a church choir

choir·mas·ter \-ˌmas-tər\ *n* : the director of a choir (as in a church)

[1]**choke** \ˈchōk\ *vb* **choked; chok·ing** **1** : to hinder breathing (as by obstructing the windpipe) : STRANGLE **2** : to check the growth or action of **3** : CLOG, OBSTRUCT **4** : to decrease or shut off the air intake of the carburetor of a gasoline engine to make the fuel mixture richer **5** : to perform badly in a critical situation

[2]**choke** *n* **1** : the act of choking **2** : a narrowing in size toward the muzzle in the bore of a gun **3** : a valve for choking a gasoline engine

chok·er \ˈchō-kər\ *n* : something (as a necklace) worn tightly around the neck

cho·ler \ˈkäl-ər, ˈkō-lər\ *n* : a tendency toward anger : IRASCIBILITY

chol·era \ˈkäl-ə-rə\ *n* : a disease marked by severe vomiting and dysentery; *esp* : an often fatal epidemic disease (**Asiatic cholera**) chiefly of southeastern Asia caused by a bacillus

cho·ler·ic \ˈkäl-ə-rik, kə-ˈler-ik\ *adj* **1** : IRASCIBLE **2** : ANGRY, IRATE

cho·les·ter·ol \kə-ˈles-tə-ˌrȯl\ *n* : a physiologically important waxy substance found in animal tissues and implicated experimentally in arteriosclerosis

chomp \ˈchämp, ˈchȯmp\ *vb* : to chew or bite on something heavily

choose \ˈchüz\ *vb* **chose** \chōz\; **cho·sen** \ˈchōz-ᵊn\; **choos·ing** \chü-ziŋ\ **1** : to select esp. after consideration **2** : DECIDE **3** : to think proper : see fit : PLEASE — **choos·er** *n*

choosy *or* **choos·ey** \ˈchü-zē\ *adj* **choos·i·er; -est** : very particular in making choices

[1]**chop** \ˈchäp\ *vb* **chopped; chop·ping** **1** : to cut by repeated blows **2** : to cut into small pieces : MINCE **3** : to strike (a ball) with a short quick downward stroke

[2]**chop** *n* **1** : a sharp downward blow or stroke **2** : a small cut of meat often including part of a rib **3** : a short abrupt motion (as of a wave)

[3]**chop** *n* **1** : an official seal or stamp **2** : a mark on goods to indicate quality or kind; *also* : QUALITY, GRADE

chop·house \ˈchäp-ˌhau̇s\ *n* : RESTAURANT

chop·per \ˈchäp-ər\ *n* **1** : one that chops **2** : HELICOPTER

chop·pi·ness \ˈchäp-ē-nəs\ *n* : the quality or state of being choppy

[1]**chop·py** \ˈchäp-ē\ *adj* **chop·pi·er; -est** : CHANGEABLE, VARIABLE ⟨a ~ wind⟩

[2]**choppy** *adj* **chop·pi·er; -est** **1** : rough with small waves **2** : JERKY, DISCONNECTED — **chop·pi·ly** \ˈchäp-ə-lē\ *adv*

chops \ˈchäps\ *n pl* : the fleshy covering of the jaws

chop·stick \ˈchäp-ˌstik\ *n* : one of a pair of sticks used chiefly in oriental countries for lifting food to the mouth

chop su·ey \chäp-ˈsü-ē\ *n, pl* **chop sueys** : a dish made typically of bean sprouts, bamboo shoots, celery, onions, mushrooms, and meat or fish and served with rice

cho·ral \ˈkōr-əl\ *adj* : of, relating to, or sung by a choir or chorus or in chorus — **cho·ral·ly** \-ē\ *adv*

cho·rale \kə-ˈral, -ˈräl\ *n* **1** : a hymn or psalm sung in church; *also* : a hymn tune or a harmonization of a traditional melody **2** : CHORUS, CHOIR

[1]**chord** \ˈkȯrd\ *n* [alter. of ME *cord*, short for *accord*] : three or more musical tones sounded simultaneously

[2]**chord** *n* **1** : CORD, STRING; *esp* : a cordlike anatomical structure **2** : a straight line joining two points on a curve

chore \ˈchōr\ *n* **1** *pl* : the daily light work of a household or farm **2** : a routine task or job **3** : a difficult or disagreeable task

cho·rea \kə-ˈrē-ə\ *n* : a nervous disorder marked by spasmodic uncontrolled movements

---

cho·re·og·ra·phy \ˌkōr-ē-ˈäg-rə-fē\ *n, pl* **-phies** : the art of dancing or of arranging dances and esp. ballets — **cho·reo·graph** \ˈkōr-ē-ə-ˌgraf\ *vb* — **cho·re·og·ra·pher** \ˌkōr-ē-ˈäg-rə-fər\ *n* — **cho·reo·graph·ic** \ˌkōr-ē-ə-ˈgraf-ik\ *adj* — **cho·reo·graph·i·cal·ly** \-i-k(ə-)lē\ *adv*
cho·ris·ter \ˈkōr-ə-stər\ *n* : a singer in a choir
chor·tle \ˈchört-ᵊl\ *vb* **chor·tled; chor·tling** \ˈchört-(ᵊ-)liŋ\ : to laugh or chuckle esp. in satisfaction or exultation — **chortle** *n*
¹**chorus** \ˈkōr-əs\ *n* **1** : an organized company of singers : CHOIR **2** : a group of dancers and usu. singers (as in a musical comedy) **3** : a part of a song repeated at intervals **4** : a composition to be sung by a chorus; *also* : group singing **5** : sounds uttered by a number of persons or animals together
²**chorus** *vb* : to sing or utter in chorus
chose *past of* CHOOSE
cho·sen \ˈchōz-ᵊn\ *adj* : selected or marked for special favor or privilege
¹**chow** \ˈchau̇\ *n* : FOOD
²**chow** *n* : CHOW CHOW
chow·chow \ˈchau̇-ˌchau̇\ *n* : chopped mixed pickles in mustard sauce
chow chow \ˈchau̇-ˌchau̇\ *n* : any of a breed of thick-coated straight-legged muscular dogs with a blue-black tongue and a short tail curled close to the back
chow·der \ˈchau̇d-ər\ *n* : a soup or stew made from seafood or vegetables and containing milk or tomatoes
chow mein \ˈchau̇-ˈmān\ *n* : a seasoned stew of shredded or diced meat, mushrooms, and vegetables that is usu. served with fried noodles
chrism \ˈkriz-əm\ *n* : consecrated oil used esp. in baptism and confirmation
Christ \ˈkrīst\ *n* [L *Christus,* fr. Gk *Christos,* lit., anointed, trans. of Heb *māshīah*] : Jesus esp. as the Messiah — **Christ·like** *adj* — **Christ·ly** *adj*
chris·ten \ˈkris-ᵊn\ *vb* **chris·tened; chris·ten·ing** \ˈkris-(ᵊ-)niŋ\ **1** : BAPTIZE **2** : to name at baptism **3** : to name or dedicate (as a ship) by a ceremony suggestive of baptism — **chris·ten·ing** *n*
Chris·ten·dom \ˈkris-ᵊn-dəm\ *n* **1** : the entire body of Christians **2** : the part of the world in which Christianity prevails
¹**Chris·tian** \ˈkris-chən\ *n* : an adherent of Christianity
²**Christian** *adj* **1** : of or relating to Christianity **2** : based on or conforming with Christianity **3** : of or relating to a Christian **4** : professing Christianity
chris·ti·an·ia \ˌkris-chē-ˈan-ē-ə, ˌkris-tē-\ *n* : CHRISTIE
Chris·ti·an·i·ty \ˌkris-chē-ˈan-ət-ē\ *n* : the religion derived from Jesus Christ, based on the Bible as sacred scripture, and professed by Christians
Chris·tian·ize \ˈkris-chə-ˌnīz\ *vb* **-ized; -iz·ing** : to make Christian
Christian name *n* : GIVEN NAME
Christian Science *n* : a religion and system of healing founded by Mary Baker Eddy and taught by the Church of Christ, Scientist — **Christian Scientist** *n*
chris·tie *or* **chris·ty** \ˈkris-tē\ *n, pl* **christies** : a skiing turn made by shifting body weight forward and skidding into a turn with parallel skis
Christ·mas \ˈkris-məs\ *n* : December 25 celebrated as a church festival in commemoration of the birth of Christ and observed as a legal holiday
Christmas club *n* : a savings account in which regular deposits are made to provide money for Christmas shopping
Christ·mas·tide \ˈkris-mə-ˌstīd\ *n* : the season of Christmas
chro·mat·ic \krō-ˈmat-ik\ *adj* **1** : of or relating to color **2** : proceeding by half steps of the musical scale — **chro·mat·i·cism** \-ˈmat-ə-ˌsiz-əm\ *n*
chro·mato·graph \krō-ˈmat-ə-ˌgraf\ *n* : an instrument used in chromatography
chro·ma·tog·ra·phy \ˌkrō-mə-ˈtäg-rə-fē\ *n* : the separation of a complex mixture into its component compounds as a result of the different rates at which the compounds travel through or over a stationary substance due to differing affinities for the substance — **chro·mato·graph·ic** \krō-ˌmat-ə-ˈgraf-ik\ *adj* — **chro·mato·graph·i·cal·ly** \-i-k(ə-)lē\ *adv*
chrome \ˈkrōm\ *n* **1** : CHROMIUM **2** : a chromium pigment **3** : something plated with an alloy of chromium
chro·mi·um \ˈkrō-mē-əm\ *n* : a bluish white metallic element used esp. in alloys and chrome plating — see ELEMENT table
chro·mo·some \ˈkrō-mə-ˌsōm, -ˌzōm\ *n* : one of the usu. elongated bodies in a cell nucleus that contains most or all of the DNA or RNA comprising the genes — **chro·mo·som·al** \ˌkrō-mə-ˈsō-məl, -ˈzō-\ *adj*
chro·mo·sphere \ˈkrō-mə-ˌsfiər\ *n* : the lower atmosphere of a star (as the sun)
chron *abbr* **1** chronicle **2** chronological; chronology
Chron *abbr* Chronicles
chron·ic \ˈkrän-ik\ *adj* : marked by long duration or frequent recurrence ⟨a ~ disease⟩; *also* : HABITUAL ⟨a ~ grumbler⟩ — **chron·i·cal·ly** \-i-k(ə-)lē\ *adv*
¹**chron·i·cle** \ˈkrän-i-kəl\ *n* : HISTORY, NARRATIVE
²**chronicle** *vb* **-cled; -cling** \-k(ə-)liŋ\ : to record in or as if in a chronicle — **chron·i·cler** \-k(ə-)lər\ *n*
Chronicles *n* — see BIBLE table
chro·no·graph \ˈkrän-ə-ˌgraf\ *n* : an instrument for measuring and recording time intervals with accuracy — **chro·no·graph·ic** \ˌkrän-ə-ˈgraf-ik\ *adj* — **chro·nog·ra·phy** \krə-ˈnäg-rə-fē\ *n*
chro·nol·o·gy \krə-ˈnäl-ə-jē\ *n, pl* **-gies** **1** : the science that deals with measuring time and dating events **2** : a chronological list or table **3** : arrangement of events in the order of their occurrence — **chron·o·log·i·cal** \ˌkrän-ᵊl-ˈäj-i-kəl\ *adj* — **chron·o·log·i·cal·ly** \-i-k(ə-)lē\ *adv* — **chro·nol·o·gist** \krə-ˈnäl-ə-jəst\ *n*
chro·nom·e·ter \krə-ˈnäm-ət-ər\ *n* : a very accurate timepiece
chrys·a·lid \ˈkris-ə-ləd\ *n* : CHRYSALIS
chrys·a·lis \ˈkris-ə-ləs\ *n, pl* **chry·sal·i·des** \kris-ˈal-ə-ˌdēz\ *or* **chrys·a·lis·es** : an insect pupa in a firm case without a cocoon
chry·san·the·mum \kris-ˈan-thə-məm\ *n* [L, fr. Gk *chrysanthemon,* fr. *chrysos* gold + *anthemon* flower] : any of a genus of plants related to the daisies including some grown for their showy flowers or for medicinal products or insecticides; *also* : a flower of a chrysanthemum
chrys·o·lite \ˈkris-ə-ˌlīt\ *n* : OLIVINE
chub \ˈchəb\ *n, pl* **chub** *or* **chubs** : any of various small freshwater fishes related to the carp
chub·by \ˈchəb-ē\ *adj* **chub·bi·er; -est** : PLUMP — **chub·bi·ness** *n*
¹**chuck** \ˈchək\ *vb* **1** : to give a pat or tap **2** : to toss or throw with a short motion of the arms **3** : DISCARD; *also* : EJECT **4** : to have done with
²**chuck** *n* **1** : a light pat under the chin **2** : TOSS
³**chuck** *n* **1** : a cut of beef including most of the neck and the parts around the shoulder blade and the first three ribs **2** : a device for holding work or a tool in a machine (as a lathe)
chuck·hole \ˈchək-ˌhōl\ *n* : POTHOLE
chuck·le \ˈchək-əl\ *vb* **chuck·led; chuck·ling** \-(ə-)liŋ\ : to laugh in a quiet hardly audible manner — **chuckle** *n*
chuck wagon *n* : a wagon equipped with a stove and food supplies
¹**chug** \ˈchəg\ *n* : a dull explosive sound made by or as if by a laboring engine
²**chug** *vb* **chugged; chug·ging** : to move or go with chugs
chuk·ka \ˈchək-ə\ *n* : a short usu. ankle-length leather boot with two pairs of eyelets
chuk·ker *or* **chuk·kar** \ˈchək-ər\ *or* **chuk·ka** \-ə\ *n* : a playing period of a polo game

[1]**chum** \ˈchəm\ *n* : an intimate friend
[2]**chum** *vb* **chummed; chum·ming 1** : to room together **2** : to be a close friend
chum·my \ˈchəm-ē\ *adj* **chum·mi·er; -est** : INTIMATE, SOCIABLE — **chum·mi·ly** \ˈchəm-ə-lē\ *adv* — **chum·mi·ness** \-ē-nəs\ *n*
chump \ˈchəmp\ *n* : FOOL, BLOCKHEAD
chunk \ˈchəŋk\ *n* **1** : a short thick piece **2** : a sizable amount
chunky \ˈchəŋ-kē\ *adj* **chunk·i·er; -est 1** : STOCKY **2** : containing chunks
church \ˈchərch\ *n* [OE *cirice,* fr. LGk *kyriakon,* short for *kyriakon dōma,* lit., the Lord's house, fr. Gk *Kyrios* Lord + *dōma* house] **1** : a building esp. for Christian public worship **2** : the whole body of Christians **3** : DENOMINATION **4** : CONGREGATION **5** : public divine worship
church·go·er \ˈchərch-ˌgō(-ə)r\ *n* : one who habitually attends church — **church·go·ing** \-ˌgō-iŋ\ *adj or n*
church·less \ˈchərch-ləs\ *adj* : not affiliated with a church
church·man \ˈchərch-mən\ *n* **1** : CLERGYMAN **2** : a member of a church
church·war·den \ˈchərch-ˌwȯrd-ᵊn\ *n* : WARDEN 5
church·yard \-ˌyärd\ *n* : a yard that belongs to a church and is often used as a burial ground
churl \ˈchərl\ *n* **1** : a medieval peasant **2** : RUSTIC **3** : a rude ill-bred person — **churl·ish** *adj* — **churl·ish·ly** *adv* — **churl·ish·ness** *n*
[1]**churn** \ˈchərn\ *n* : a container in which milk or cream is violently stirred in making butter
[2]**churn** *vb* **1** : to stir in a churn; *also* : to make (butter) by such stirring **2** : to shake around violently
churn out *vb* : to produce mechanically and in large quantity
chute \ˈshüt\ *n* **1** : an inclined surface, trough, or passage down or through which something may pass ⟨a coal ~⟩ ⟨a mail ~⟩ **2** : PARACHUTE
chut·ney \ˈchət-nē\ *n, pl* **chutneys** : a condiment of acid fruits with raisins, dates, and onions
chutz·pah \ˈhu̇t-spə, ˈk̲u̇t-, -(ˌ)spä\ *n* : supreme self-confidence
CIA *abbr* Central Intelligence Agency
cía *abbr* [Sp *compañía*] company
ciao \ˈchau̇\ *interj* [It, fr. It dial., alter. of *schiavo* (I am your) slave, fr. ML *sclavus*] — used to express greeting or farewell
ci·ca·da \sə-ˈkād-ə\ *n* : any of a family of stout-bodied insects related to the aphids and having wide blunt heads and large transparent wings
ci·ca·trix \ˈsik-ə-ˌtriks\ *n, pl* **ci·ca·tri·ces** \ˌsik-ə-ˈtrī-ˌsēz\ [L] : a scar resulting from formation and contraction of fibrous tissue in a flesh wound
ci·ce·ro·ne \ˌsis-ə-ˈrō-nē, ˌchē-chə-\ *n, pl* **-ni** \-(ˌ)nē\ : a guide who conducts sightseers
CID *abbr* Criminal Investigation Department
ci·der \ˈsīd-ər\ *n* : juice pressed from fruit (as apples) and used as a beverage, vinegar, or flavoring
cie *abbr* [F *compagnie*] company
ci·gar \sig-ˈär\ *n* : a roll of tobacco for smoking
cig·a·rette \ˌsig-ə-ˈret, ˈsig-ə-ˌret\ *n* [F, dim. of *cigare* cigar] : a slender roll of cut tobacco enclosed in paper for smoking
cig·a·ril·lo \ˌsig-ə-ˈril-ō, -ˈrē-ō\ *n, pl* **-los** [Sp] **1** : a very small cigar **2** : a cigarette wrapped in tobacco rather than paper
ci·lan·tro \si-ˈlän-trō, -ˈlan-\ *n* : leaves of coriander used as a flavoring or garnish
cil·i·ate \ˈsil-ē-ˌāt\ *n* : any of a group of protozoans characterized by cilia
cil·i·um \ˈsil-ē-əm\ *n, pl* **-ia** \-ē-ə\ **1** : a minute short hairlike process; *esp* : one of a cell **2** : EYELASH
C in C *abbr* commander in chief
cinch \ˈsinch\ *n* **1** : a girth for holding a saddle or a pack in place **2** : a sure or an easy thing — **cinch** *vb*
cin·cho·na \siŋ-ˈkō-nə\ *n* : any of a genus of So. American trees; *also* : the bitter quinine-containing bark of a cinchona
cinc·ture \ˈsiŋk-chər\ *n* : BELT, GIRDLE
cin·der \ˈsin-dər\ *n* **1** : SLAG **2** *pl* : ASHES **3** : a hot piece of partly burned wood or coal **4** : a fragment of lava from an erupting volcano — **cinder** *vb* — **cin·dery** *adj*
cinder block *n* : a building block made of cement and coal cinders
cin·e·ma \ˈsin-ə-mə\ *n* **1** : a motion-picture theater **2** : MOVIES — **cin·e·mat·ic** \ˌsin-ə-ˈmat-ik\ *adj*
cin·e·ma·theque \ˌsin-ə-mə-ˈtek\ *n* : a small movie house specializing in avant-garde films
cin·e·ma·tog·ra·phy \ˌsin-ə-mə-ˈtäg- rə-fē\ *n* : motion-picture photography — **cin·e·ma·tog·ra·pher** \-fər\ *n* — **cin·e·mat·o·graph·ic** \-ˌmat-ə-ˈgraf-ik\ *adj*
cin·er·ar·i·um \ˌsin-ə-ˈrer-ē-əm\ *n, pl* **-ia** \-ē-ə\ : a place to receive the ashes of the cremated dead — **cin·er·ary** \ˈsin-ə-ˌrer-ē\ *adj*
cin·na·bar \ˈsin-ə-ˌbär\ *n* : a red mineral that is the only important ore of mercury
cin·na·mon \ˈsin-ə-mən\ *n* : a spice consisting of the highly aromatic bark of any of several trees related to the true laurel; *also* : a tree that yields cinnamon
cinque·foil \ˈsiŋk-ˌfȯil, ˈsaŋk-\ *n* : any of a genus of plants related to the roses with leaves having five lobes
[1]**ci·pher** \ˈsī-fər\ *n* [ME, fr. MF *cifre,* fr. ML *cifra,* fr. Ar *ṣifr* empty, zero] **1** : ZERO, NAUGHT **2** : a method of secret writing
[2]**cipher** *vb* **ci·phered; ci·pher·ing** \-f(ə-)riŋ\ : to compute arithmetically
cir *or* **circ** *abbr* circular
cir·ca \ˈsər-kə\ *prep* : ABOUT ⟨~ 1600⟩
cir·ca·di·an \ˌsər-ˈkad-ē-ən, ˌsər-kə-ˈdī-ən\ *adj* : being, having, characterized by, or occurring in approximately 24-hour intervals (as of biological activity)
[1]**cir·cle** \ˈsər-kəl\ *n* **1** : a closed curve every point of which is equally distant from a fixed point within it **2** : something in the form of a circle **3** : an area of action or influence **4** : CYCLE **5** : a group bound by a common tie
[2]**circle** *vb* **cir·cled; cir·cling** \-k(ə-)liŋ\ **1** : to enclose in a circle **2** : to move or revolve around; *also* : to move in a circle
cir·clet \ˈsər-klət\ *n* : a small circle; *esp* : a circular ornament
cir·cuit \ˈsər-kət\ *n* **1** : a boundary around an enclosed space **2** : a moving or revolving around (as in an orbit) **3** : a regular tour (as by a judge) around an assigned territory **4** : the complete path of an electric current **5** : LEAGUE; *also* : a chain of theaters — **cir·cuit·al** \-kət-ᵊl\ *adj*
circuit breaker *n* : a switch that automatically interrupts an electric circuit under an abnormal condition
circuit court *n* : a court that sits at two or more places within one judicial district
cir·cu·itous \ˌsər-ˈkyü-ət-əs\ *adj* **1** : not being forthright or direct in language or action **2** : having a circular or winding course
cir·cuit·ry \ˈsər-kə-trē\ *n, pl* **-ries** : the plan or the components of an electric circuit
cir·cu·ity \ˌsər-ˈkyü-ət-ē\ *n, pl* **-ities** : INDIRECTION
[1]**cir·cu·lar** \ˈsər-kyə-lər\ *adj* **1** : having the form of a circle : ROUND **2** : moving in or around a circle **3** : CIRCUITOUS **4** : sent around to a number of persons ⟨a ~ letter⟩ — **cir·cu·lar·i·ty** \ˌsər-kyə-ˈlar-ət-ē\ *n*

\ə\abut \ᵊ\kitten \ər\further \a\ash \ā\ace \ä\cot, cart \au̇\out \ch\chin \e\bet \ē\easy \g\go \i\hit \ī\ice \j\job \ŋ\sing \ō\go \ȯ\law \ȯi\boy \th\thin \th̲\the \ü\loot \u̇\foot \y\yet \zh\vision *see also* Pronunciation Symbols page

[2]**circular** *n* : a paper (as an advertising leaflet) intended for wide distribution
cir·cu·lar·ize \ˈsər-kyə-lə-ˌrīz\ *vb* **-ized; -iz·ing 1** : to send circulars to **2** : to poll by questionnaire
circular saw *n* : a power saw with a round cutting blade
cir·cu·late \ˈsər-kyə-ˌlāt\ *vb* **-lat·ed; -lat·ing 1** : to move or cause to move in a circle, circuit, or orbit **2** : to pass from place to place or from person to person — **cir·cu·la·tion** \ˌsər-kyə-ˈlā-shən\ *n*
cir·cu·la·to·ry \ˈsər-kyə-lə-ˌtōr-ē\ *adj* : of or relating to circulation or the circulatory system
circulatory system *n* : the system of blood, blood vessels, lymphatic vessels, and heart concerned with the circulation of the blood and lymph
cir·cum·am·bu·late \ˌsər-kəm-ˈam-byə-ˌlāt\ *vb* **-lat·ed; -lat·ing** : to circle on foot esp. ritualistically
cir·cum·cise \ˈsər-kəm-ˌsīz\ *vb* **-cised; -cis·ing** : to cut off the foreskin of — **cir·cum·ci·sion** \ˌsər-kəm-ˈsizh-ən\ *n*
cir·cum·fer·ence \sər-ˈkəm-f(ə-)rəns\ *n* **1** : the perimeter of a circle **2** : the external boundary or surface of a figure or object
cir·cum·flex \ˈsər-kəm-ˌfleks\ *n* : the mark ˆ over a vowel
cir·cum·lo·cu·tion \ˌsər-kəm-lō-ˈkyü-shən\ *n* : the use of unnecessary words in expressing an idea
cir·cum·lu·nar \-ˈlü-nər\ *adj* : revolving about or surrounding the moon
cir·cum·nav·i·gate \-ˈnav-ə-ˌgāt\ *vb* : to go completely around esp. by water — **cir·cum·nav·i·ga·tion** \-ˌnav-ə-ˈgā-shən\ *n*
cir·cum·po·lar \-ˈpō-lər\ *adj* **1** : continually visible above the horizon ⟨a ~ star⟩ **2** : surrounding or found near a terrestrial pole
cir·cum·scribe \ˈsər-kəm-ˌskrīb\ *vb* **1** : to limit narrowly the range or activity of **2** : to draw a line around — **cir·cum·scrip·tion** \ˌsər-kəm-ˈskrip-shən\ *n*
cir·cum·spect \ˈsər-kəm-ˌspekt\ *adj* : careful to consider all circumstances and consequences : PRUDENT — **cir·cum·spec·tion** \ˌsər-kəm-ˈspek-shən\ *n*
cir·cum·stance \ˈsər-kəm-ˌstans\ *n* **1** : a fact or event that must be considered along with another fact or event **2** : surrounding conditions **3** *pl* : situation with regard to wealth **4** : CEREMONY **5** : CHANCE, FATE
cir·cum·stan·tial \ˌsər-kəm-ˈstan-chəl\ *adj* **1** : consisting of or depending on circumstances **2** : INCIDENTAL **3** : containing full details — **cir·cum·stan·tial·ly** \-ē\ *adv*
cir·cum·vent \ˌsər-kəm-ˈvent\ *vb* : to check or defeat esp. by stratagem
cir·cus \ˈsər-kəs\ *n* **1** : a usu. traveling show that features feats of physical skill and daring, wild animal acts, and performances by clowns **2** : a circus performance; *also* : the equipment, livestock, and personnel of a circus
cirque \ˈsərk\ *n* : a deep steep-walled mountain basin shaped like half a bowl
cir·rho·sis \sə-ˈrō-səs\ *n, pl* **-rho·ses** \-ˌsēz\ [NL, fr. Gk *kirrhos* orange-colored] : fibrosis esp. of the liver — **cir·rhot·ic** \-ˈrät-ik\ *adj or n*
cir·rus \ˈsir-əs\ *n, pl* **cir·ri** \ˈsir-ˌī\ : a wispy white cloud usu. of minute ice crystals at high altitudes
cis·lu·nar \(ˈ)sis-ˈlü-nər\ *adj* : lying between the earth and the moon or the moon's orbit
cis·tern \ˈsis-tərn\ *n* : an often underground tank for storing water
cit *abbr* **1** citation; cited **2** citizen
cit·a·del \ˈsit-əd-ᵊl, -ə-ˌdel\ *n* **1** : a fortress commanding a city **2** : STRONGHOLD
ci·ta·tion \sī-ˈtā-shən\ *n* **1** : an official summons to appear (as before a court) **2** : QUOTATION **3** : a formal statement of the achievements of a person; *also* : a specific reference in a military dispatch to meritorious performance of duty
cite \ˈsīt\ *vb* **cit·ed; cit·ing 1** : to summon to appear before a court **2** : QUOTE **3** : to refer to esp. in commendation or praise
citi·fied \ˈsit-i-ˌfīd\ *adj* : of, relating to, or characterized by an urban style of living
cit·i·zen \ˈsit-ə-zən\ *n* **1** : an inhabitant of a city or town **2** : a person who owes allegiance to a government and is entitled to government protection — **cit·i·zen·ship** *n*
cit·i·zen·ry \-rē\ *n, pl* **-ries** : a whole body of citizens
citizens band *n* : a range of radio frequencies set aside for private radio communications
cit·ric acid \ˌsit-rik-\ *n* : a sour organic acid obtained from lemon and lime juices or by fermentation of sugars and used as a flavoring
cit·ron \ˈsit-rən\ *n* **1** : the oval lemonlike fruit of an Asian citrus tree **2** : a small hard-fleshed watermelon used esp. in pickles and preserves
cit·ro·nel·la \ˌsit-rə-ˈnel-ə\ *n* : an oil obtained from a grass of southern Asia and used in perfumes and as an insect repellent
cit·rus \ˈsit-rəs\ *n, pl* **citrus** *or* **cit·rus·es** : any of a genus of often thorny evergreen trees or shrubs grown in warm regions for their fruits (as the orange, lemon, lime, and grapefruit)
city \ˈsit-ē\ *n, pl* **cit·ies** [ME *citie* large or small town, fr. OF *cité* capital city, fr. ML *civitas*, fr. L, citizenship, state, city of Rome, fr. *civis* citizen] **1** : an inhabited place larger or more important than a town **2** : a municipality in the U.S. governed under a charter granted by the state; *also* : an incorporated municipal unit of the highest class in Canada
city manager *n* : an official employed by an elected council to direct the administration of a city government
city–state \ˈsit-ē-ˈstāt, -ˌstāt\ *n* : an autonomous state consisting of a city and surrounding territory
civ *abbr* civil; civilian
civ·et \ˈsiv-ət\ *n* : a yellowish strong-smelling substance obtained from a catlike mammal **(civet cat)** of Africa or Asia and used in making perfumes
civic \ˈsiv-ik\ *adj* : of or relating to a city, citizenship, or civil affairs
civ·ics \-iks\ *n* : a social science dealing with the rights and duties of citizens
civ·il \ˈsiv-əl\ *adj* **1** : of or relating to citizens or to the state as a political body **2** : COURTEOUS, POLITE **3** : of or relating to legal proceedings in connection with private rights and obligations ⟨the ~ code⟩ **4** : of or relating to the general population : not military or ecclesiastical
civil defense *n* : the protective measures and emergency relief activities conducted by civilians in case of hostile attack, sabotage, or natural disaster
civil disobedience *n* : refusal to obey governmental commands esp. as a nonviolent means of protest
civil engineer *n* : an engineer whose training or occupation is in the designing and construction chiefly of public works (as roads or harbors) — **civil engineering** *n*
ci·vil·ian \sə-ˈvil-yən\ *n* : a person not on active duty in a military, police, or fire-fighting force
ci·vil·i·ty \sə-ˈvil-ət-ē\ *n, pl* **-ties 1** : POLITENESS, COURTESY **2** : a polite act or expression
civ·i·li·za·tion \ˌsiv-ə-lə-ˈzā-shən\ *n* **1** : a relatively high level of cultural and technological development **2** : the culture characteristic of a time or place
civ·i·lize \ˈsiv-ə-ˌlīz\ *vb* **-lized; -liz·ing 1** : to raise from a primitive state to an advanced and ordered stage of cultural development **2** : REFINE — **civ·i·lized** *adj*
civil liberty *n* : freedom from arbitrary governmental interference specifically by denial of governmental power — usu. used in pl.
civ·il·ly \ˈsiv-ə(l)-lē\ *adv* **1** : in terms of civil rights, matters, or law ⟨~ dead⟩ **2** : in a civil manner : POLITELY
civil rights *n pl* : the nonpolitical rights of a citizen; *esp* : those guaranteed by the 13th and 14th amendments to the Constitution and by acts of Congress
civil servant *n* : a member of a civil service

civil service *n* : the administrative service of a government

civil war *n* : a war between opposing groups of citizens of the same country

civ·vies \ˈsiv-ēz\ *n pl* : civilian clothes as distinguished from a military uniform

CJ *abbr* chief justice

ck *abbr* 1 cask 2 check

cl *abbr* 1 centiliter 2 class

Cl *symbol* chlorine

[1]**clack** \ˈklak\ *vb* **1** : CHATTER, PRATTLE **2** : to make or cause to make a clatter

[2]**clack** *n* **1** : rapid continuous talk : CHATTER **2** : a sound of clacking ⟨the ~ of a typewriter⟩

clad \ˈklad\ *adj* **1** : CLOTHED, COVERED **2** : being or consisting of coins made of outer layers of one metal bonded to a core of a different metal ⟨~ coinage⟩

[1]**claim** \ˈklām\ *vb* **1** : to ask for as one's own; *also* : to take as the rightful owner **2** : to call for : REQUIRE **3** : to state as a fact : MAINTAIN

[2]**claim** *n* **1** : a demand for something due **2** : a right to something usu. in another's possession **3** : an assertion open to challenge **4** : something claimed

claim·ant \ˈklā-mənt\ *n* : a person making a claim

clair·voy·ant \klar-ˈvȯi-ənt\ *adj* [F, fr. *clair* clear + *voyant* seeing] **1** : unusually perceptive **2** : having the power of discerning objects not present to the senses — **clair·voy·ance** \-əns\ *n* — **clairvoyant** *n*

clam \ˈklam\ *n* **1** : any of numerous bivalve mollusks including many that are edible **2** : DOLLAR

clam·bake \-ˌbāk\ *n* : a party or gathering (as at the seashore) at which food is cooked usu. on heated rocks covered by seaweed

clam·ber \ˈklam-bər\ *vb* **clam·bered; clam·ber·ing** \ˈklam-b(ə-)riŋ, ˈklam-(ə-)riŋ\ : to climb awkwardly (as by scrambling)

clam·my \ˈklam-ē\ *adj* **clam·mi·er; -est** : being damp, soft, sticky, and usu. cool — **clam·mi·ness** *n*

[1]**clam·or** \ˈklam-ər\ *n* **1** : a noisy shouting **2** : a loud continuous noise **3** : vigorous protest or demand — **clam·or·ous** *adj*

[2]**clamor** *vb* **clam·ored; clam·or·ing** \ˈklam-(ə-)riŋ\ : to make a clamor

[1]**clamp** \ˈklamp\ *n* : a device that holds or presses parts together firmly

[2]**clamp** *vb* : to fasten with or as if with a clamp

clamp down \(ˈ)klamp-ˈdau̇n\ *vb* : to impose restrictions : become repressive — **clamp·down** \ˈklamp-ˌdau̇n\ *n*

clam·shell \ˈklam-ˌshel\ *n* : a bucket or grapple (as on a dredge) having two hinged jaws

clam up *vb* : to become silent

clan \ˈklan\ *n* [ME, fr. ScGael *clann* offspring, clan, fr. Old Irish *cland* plant, offspring, fr. L *planta* plant] : a group (as in the Scottish Highlands) made up of households whose heads claim descent from a common ancestor — **clan·nish** *adj* — **clan·nish·ness** *n*

clan·des·tine \klan-ˈdes-tən\ *adj* : held in or conducted with secrecy

clang \ˈklaŋ\ *n* : a loud metallic ringing sound — **clang** *vb*

clan·gor \ˈklaŋ-(g)ər\ *n* : a resounding clang or medley of clangs

clank \ˈklaŋk\ *n* : a sharp brief metallic ringing sound — **clank** *vb*

[1]**clap** \ˈklap\ *vb* **clapped; clap·ping** **1** : to strike noisily **2** : APPLAUD

[2]**clap** *n* **1** : a loud noisy crash **2** : the noise made by clapping the hands

[3]**clap** *n* : GONORRHEA

clap·board \ˈklab-ərd; ˈkla(p)-ˌbōrd\ *n* : a narrow board thicker at one edge than the other used for siding — **clap·board** *vb*

clap·per \ˈklap-ər\ *n* : one that makes a clapping sound; *esp* : the tongue of a bell

clap·trap \ˈklap-ˌtrap\ *n* : pretentious nonsense

claque \ˈklak\ *n* [F, fr. *claquer* to clap] **1** : a group hired to applaud at a performance **2** : a group of self-seeking flatterers

clar·et \ˈklar-ət\ *n* [ME, fr. MF (*vin*) *claret* clear wine] : a dry red wine

clar·i·fy \ˈklar-ə-ˌfī\ *vb* **-fied; -fy·ing** : to make or become clear — **clar·i·fi·ca·tion** \ˌklar-ə-fə-ˈkā-shən\ *n*

clar·i·net \ˌklar-ə-ˈnet\ *n* : a single-reed woodwind instrument in the form of a cylindrical tube with moderately flaring end — **clar·i·net·ist** *or* **clar·i·net·tist** \-əst\ *n*

clarinet

clar·i·on \ˈklar-ē-ən\ *adj* : brilliantly clear ⟨a ~ call⟩

clar·i·ty \ˈklar-ət-ē\ *n* : CLEARNESS

[1]**clash** \ˈklash\ *vb* **1** : to make or cause to make a clash **2** : CONFLICT, COLLIDE

[2]**clash** *n* **1** : a noisy usu. metallic sound of collision **2** : a hostile encounter; *also* : a conflict of opinion

[1]**clasp** \ˈklasp\ *n* **1** : a device (as a hook) for holding objects or parts together **2** : EMBRACE, GRASP

[2]**clasp** *vb* **1** : to fasten with a clasp **2** : EMBRACE **3** : GRASP

[1]**class** \ˈklas\ *n* **1** : a group of students meeting regularly in a course; *also* : a group graduating together **2** : a course of instruction; *also* : the period when such a course is taught **3** : social rank; *also* : high quality **4** : a group of the same general status or nature; *esp* : a major category in biological classification that is above the order and below the phylum **5** : a division or rating based on grade or quality — **class·less** *adj*

[2]**class** *vb* : CLASSIFY

class action *n* : a legal action undertaken in behalf of the plaintiffs and all others having an identical interest in the alleged wrong

[1]**clas·sic** \ˈklas-ik\ *adj* **1** : serving as a standard of excellence; *also* : TRADITIONAL **2** : CLASSICAL 2 **3** : notable esp. as the best example **4** : AUTHENTIC

[2]**classic** *n* **1** : a work of enduring excellence and esp. of ancient Greece or Rome; *also* : its author **2** : a traditional event

clas·si·cal \ˈklas-i-kəl\ *adj* **1** : CLASSIC **2** : of or relating to the ancient Greek and Roman classics **3** : of or relating to a form or system of primary significance before modern times ⟨~ economics⟩ **4** : concerned with a general study of the arts and sciences — **clas·si·cal·ly** \-k(ə-)lē\ *adv*

clas·si·cism \ˈklas-ə-ˌsiz-əm\ *n* **1** : the principles or style of the literature or art of ancient Greece and Rome **2** : adherence to traditional standards believed to be universally valid — **clas·si·cist** \-səst\ *n*

clas·si·fied \ˈklas-ə-ˌfīd\ *adj* : withheld from general circulation for reasons of national security

clas·si·fy \ˈklas-ə-ˌfī\ *vb* **-fied; -fy·ing** : to arrange in or assign to classes — **clas·si·fi·able** *adj* — **clas·si·fi·ca·tion** \ˌklas-ə-fə-ˈkā-shən\ *n*

class·mate \ˈklas-ˌmāt\ *n* : a member of the same class (as in a college)

class·room \-ˌrüm-, -ˌru̇m\ *n* : a room (as in a school) in which classes meet

classy \ˈklas-ē\ *adj* **class·i·er; -est** : ELEGANT, STYLISH

clat·ter \ˈklat-ər\ *n* : a rattling sound ⟨the ~ of dishes⟩ — **clatter** *vb*

clause \ˈklȯz\ *n* **1** : a group of words having its own

subject and predicate but forming only part of a compound or complex sentence **2** : a separate part of an article or document
claus·tro·pho·bia \ˌklȯ-strə-ˈfō-bē-ə\ *n* : abnormal dread of being in closed or narrow spaces — **claus·tro·pho·bic** \-bik\ *adj*
clav·i·chord \ˈklav-ə-ˌkȯrd\ *n* : an early keyboard instrument in use before the piano
clav·i·cle \ˈklav-i-kəl\ *n* [F *clavicule,* fr. NL *clavicula,* fr. L, dim. of L *clavis* key] : COLLARBONE
cla·vier \klə-ˈviər; ˈklā-vē-ər\ *n* **1** : the keyboard of a musical instrument **2** : an early keyboard instrument
[1]**claw** \ˈklȯ\ *n* **1** : a sharp usu. curved nail on the toe of an animal **2** : a sharp curved process (as on the foot of an insect); *also* : a pincerlike organ at the end of a limb of some arthropods (as a lobster) — **clawed** \ˈklȯd\ *adj*
[2]**claw** *vb* : to rake, seize, or dig with or as if with claws
clay \ˈklā\ *n* **1** : an earthy material that is plastic when moist but hard when fired and is used in making pottery; *also* : finely divided soil consisting largely of such clay **2** : EARTH, MUD **3** : a plastic substance used for modeling **4** : the mortal human body — **clay·ey** \ˈklā-ē\ *adj*
clay·more \ˈklā-ˌmōr\ *n* : a large 2-edged sword formerly used by Scottish Highlanders
clay pigeon *n* : a saucer-shaped target thrown from a trap in trapshooting
[1]**clean** \ˈklēn\ *adj* **1** : free from dirt or disease **2** : PURE; *also* : HONORABLE **3** : THOROUGH ⟨made a ~ sweep⟩ **4** : TRIM ⟨a ship with ~ lines⟩; *also* : EVEN **5** : habitually neat — **clean** *adv* — **clean·ly** \ˈklēn-lē\ *adv* — **clean·ness** \ˈklēn-nəs\ *n*
[2]**clean** *vb* : to make or become clean — **clean·er** *n*
clean–cut \ˈklēn-ˈkət\ *adj* **1** : cut so that the surface or edge is smooth and even **2** : sharply defined or outlined **3** : giving an effect of wholesomeness
clean·ly \ˈklen-lē\ *adj* **clean·li·er; -est 1** : careful to keep clean **2** : habitually kept clean — **clean·li·ness** *n*
clean room \ˈklēn-ˌrüm, -ˌru̇m\ *n* : an uncontaminated room maintained for the manufacture or assembly of objects (as precision parts)
cleanse \ˈklenz\ *vb* **cleansed; cleans·ing** : to make clean — **cleans·er** *n*
[1]**clean·up** \ˈklēn-ˌəp\ *n* **1** : an act or instance of cleaning **2** : a very large profit
[2]**cleanup** *adj* : being 4th in the batting order of a baseball team
clean up \(ˈ)klēn-ˈəp\ *vb* : to make a spectacular business profit
[1]**clear** \ˈkliər\ *adj* **1** : BRIGHT, LUMINOUS; *also* : UNTROUBLED, SERENE **2** : CLOUDLESS **3** : CLEAN, PURE; *also* : TRANSPARENT **4** : easily heard, seen, or understood **5** : capable of sharp discernment; *also* : free from doubt **6** : INNOCENT **7** : free from restriction, obstruction, or entanglement — **clear** *adv* — **clear·ly** *adv* — **clear·ness** *n*
[2]**clear** *vb* **1** : to make or become clear **2** : to go away : DISPERSE **3** : to free from accusation or blame; *also* : to certify as trustworthy **4** : EXPLAIN **5** : to get free from obstruction **6** : SETTLE **7** : NET **8** : to get rid of : REMOVE **9** : to jump or go by without touching; *also* : PASS
[3]**clear** *n* : a clear space or part
clear·ance \ˈklir-əns\ *n* **1** : an act or process of clearing **2** : the distance by which one object clears another
clear–cut \ˈkliər-ˈkət\ *adj* **1** : sharply outlined **2** : DEFINITE, UNEQUIVOCAL
clear·head·ed \-ˈhed-əd\ *adj* : having a clear understanding : PERCEPTIVE
clear·ing \ˈkli(ə)r-iŋ\ *n* **1** : a tract of land cleared of wood and brush **2** : the passage of checks and claims through a clearinghouse
clear·ing·house \-ˌhau̇s\ *n* : an institution maintained by banks for making an exchange of checks and claims held by each bank against other banks
cleat \ˈklēt\ *n* : a piece of wood or metal fastened on or projecting from something to give strength, provide a grip, or prevent slipping
cleav·age \ˈklē-vij\ *n* **1** : a splitting apart : SPLIT **2** : the depression between a woman's breasts esp. when exposed by a low-cut dress
[1]**cleave** \ˈklēv\ *vb* **cleaved** \ˈklēvd\ *or* **clove** \ˈklōv\; **cleaved; cleav·ing** : ADHERE, CLING
[2]**cleave** *vb* **cleaved** \ˈklēvd\ *also* **cleft** \ˈkleft\ *or* **clove** \ˈklōv\; **cleaved** *also* **cleft** *or* **clo·ven** \ˈklō-vən\; **cleav·ing 1** : to divide by force : split asunder **2** : DIVIDE
cleav·er \ˈklē-vər\ *n* : a heavy chopping knife for cutting meat
clef \ˈklef\ *n* : a sign placed on the staff in music to show what pitch is represented by each line and space
cleft \ˈkleft\ *n* : FISSURE, CRACK
cleft palate *n* : a split in the roof of the mouth that appears as a birth defect
clem·a·tis \ˈklem-ət-əs; kli-ˈmat-əs\ *n* : a vine related to the buttercups that has showy usu. white or purple flowers
clem·en·cy \ˈklem-ən-sē\ *n, pl* **-cies 1** : disposition to be merciful **2** : mildness of weather
clem·ent \-ənt\ *adj* **1** : MERCIFUL, LENIENT **2** : TEMPERATE, MILD
clench \ˈklench\ *vb* **1** : CLINCH 1 **2** : to hold fast **3** : to set or close tightly
clere·sto·ry \ˈkliər-ˌstōr-ē\ *n* : an outside wall of a room or building that rises above an adjoining roof and contains windows
cler·gy \ˈklər-jē\ *n* : a body of religious officials authorized to conduct services
cler·gy·man \-ji-mən\ *n* : a member of the clergy
cler·ic \ˈkler-ik\ *n* : CLERGYMAN
cler·i·cal \ˈkler-i-kəl\ *adj* **1** : of or relating to the clergy or a clergyman **2** : of or relating to a clerk
cler·i·cal·ism \ˈkler-i-kə-ˌliz-əm\ *n* : a policy of maintaining or increasing the power of a religious hierarchy
clerk \ˈklərk, *Brit* ˈklärk\ *n* **1** : CLERIC **2** : an official responsible for correspondence, records, and accounts; *also* : a person employed to perform general office work **3** : a store salesman — **clerk** *vb* — **clerk·ship** *n*
clev·er \ˈklev-ər\ *adj* **1** : showing skill or resourcefulness **2** : marked by wit or ingenuity — **clev·er·ly** *adv* — **clev·er·ness** *n*
clev·is \ˈklev-əs\ *n* : a U-shaped shackle used for attaching or suspending parts
[1]**clew** \ˈklü\ *n* **1** : CLUE **2** : a metal loop on a lower corner of a sail for holding ropes
[2]**clew** *vb* : to haul (a sail) up or down by ropes through the clews
cli·ché \kli-ˈshā\ *n* [F] : a trite phrase or expression — **cli·chéd** \-ˈshād\ *adj*
[1]**click** \ˈklik\ *vb* **1** : to make or cause to make a click **2** : to fit or work together smoothly
[2]**click** *n* : a slight sharp noise
cli·ent \ˈklī-ənt\ *n* **1** : DEPENDENT **2** : a person who engages the professional services of another; *also* : PATRON, CUSTOMER
cli·en·tele \ˌklī-ən-ˈtel, ˌklē-ən-\ *n* : a body of clients and esp. customers
cliff \ˈklif\ *n* : a high steep face of rock
cliff–hang·er \-ˌhaŋ-ər\ *n* **1** : an adventure serial or melodrama usu. presented in installments each of which ends in suspense **2** : a contest whose outcome is in doubt up to the very end
cli·mac·ter·ic \klī-ˈmak-t(ə-)rik\ *n* **1** : a major turning point or critical stage **2** : MENOPAUSE; *also* : a corresponding period in the male
cli·mate \ˈklī-mət\ *n* [ME *climat,* fr. MF, fr. LL *clima,* fr. Gk *klima* inclination, latitude, climate, fr. *klinein* to lean] **1** : a region having specific climatic conditions **2** : the average weather conditions at a place over a period

of years **3** : the prevailing set of conditions (as temperature and humidity) indoors **4** : a prevailing atmosphere or environment ⟨the ~ of opinion⟩ — **cli·mat·ic** \klī-ˈmat-ik\ *adj* — **cli·mat·i·cal·ly** \-i-k(ə-)lē\ *adv*

cli·ma·tol·o·gy \ˌklī-mə-ˈtäl-ə-jē\ *n* : the science that deals with climates — **cli·ma·to·log·i·cal** \ˌklī-mət-ᵊl-ˈäj-i-kəl\ *adj* — **cli·ma·to·log·i·cal·ly** \-k(ə-)lē\ *adv* — **cli·ma·tol·o·gist** \-mə-ˈtäl-ə-jəst\ *n*

[1]**cli·max** \ˈklī-ˌmaks\ *n* [L, fr. Gk *klimax* ladder, fr. *klinein* to lean] **1** : a series of ideas or statements so arranged that they increase in force and power from the first to the last; *also* : the last member of such a series **2** : the highest point **3** : ORGASM — **cli·mac·tic** \klī-ˈmak-tik\ *adj*

[2]**climax** *vb* : to come or bring to a climax

[1]**climb** \ˈklīm\ *vb* **1** : to rise to a higher point **2** : to go up or down esp. by use of hands and feet; *also* : to ascend in growing — **climb·er** *n*

[2]**climb** *n* **1** : a place where climbing is necessary **2** : the act of climbing : ascent by climbing

clime \ˈklīm\ *n* : CLIMATE

[1]**clinch** \ˈklinch\ *vb* **1** : to turn over or flatten the end of something sticking out ⟨~ a nail⟩; *also* : to fasten by clinching **2** : to make final : SETTLE **3** : to hold fast or firmly

[2]**clinch** *n* **1** : a fastening by means of a clinched nail, rivet, or bolt **2** : an act or instance of clinching in boxing

clinch·er \ˈklin-chər\ *n* : one that clinches; *esp* : a decisive fact, argument, act, or remark

cling \ˈkliŋ\ *vb* **clung** \ˈkləŋ\; **cling·ing** **1** : to adhere as if glued; *also* : to hold or hold on tightly **2** : to have a strong emotional attachment

cling·stone \ˈkliŋ-ˌstōn\ *n* : any of various fruits (as some peaches) whose flesh adheres strongly to the pit

clin·ic \ˈklin-ik\ *n* **1** : medical instruction featuring the examination and discussion of actual cases **2** : a group meeting for teaching a certain skill and working on individual problems ⟨a reading ~⟩ **3** : a facility (as of a hospital) for diagnosis and treatment of outpatients

clin·i·cal \ˈklin-i-kəl\ *adj* **1** : of, relating to, or typical of a clinic; *esp* : involving direct observation of the patient **2** : scientifically dispassionate — **clin·i·cal·ly** \-k(ə-)lē\ *adv*

cli·ni·cian \klin-ˈish-ən\ *n* : one qualified in the clinical practice of medicine, psychiatry, or psychology as distinguished from one specializing in laboratory or research techniques

[1]**clink** \ˈkliŋk\ *vb* : to make or cause to make a sharp short metallic sound

[2]**clink** *n* : a clinking sound

clin·ker \ˈkliŋ-kər\ *n* : stony matter fused by fire (as in a furnace from impurities in coal) : SLAG

[1]**clip** \ˈklip\ *vb* **clipped; clip·ping** : to fasten with a clip

[2]**clip** *n* **1** : a device that grips, clasps, or hooks **2** : a cartridge holder for a rifle

[3]**clip** *vb* **clipped; clip·ping** **1** : to cut or cut off with shears **2** : CURTAIL, DIMINISH **3** : HIT, PUNCH **4** : to illegally block (an opponent) in football

[4]**clip** *n* **1** : a 2-bladed instrument for cutting esp. the nails **2** : a sharp blow **3** : a rapid pace

clip·board \ˈklip-ˌbōrd\ *n* : a small writing board with a spring clip at the top for holding papers

clip joint *n, slang* : an establishment (as a nightclub) that makes a practice of defrauding its customers

clip·per \ˈklip-ər\ *n* **1** : an implement for clipping esp. the hair or nails — usu. used in pl. **2** : a fast sailing ship

clip·ping \ˈklip-iŋ\ *n* : a piece clipped from something (as a newspaper)

clique \ˈklēk, ˈklik\ *n* [F] : a small exclusive group of people : COTERIE — **cliqu·ey** \ˈklēk-ē, ˈklik-\ *adj* — **cliqu·ish** \-ish\ *adj*

cli·to·ris \ˈklit-ə-rəs\ *n, pl* **cli·to·ri·des** \kli-ˈtȯr-ə-ˌdēz\ : a small organ at the anterior or ventral part of the vulva homologous to the penis — **cli·to·ral** \-rəl\ *adj*

clk *abbr* clerk

clo *abbr* clothing

[1]**cloak** \ˈklōk\ *n* **1** : a loose outer garment **2** : something that conceals

[2]**cloak** *vb* : to cover or hide with a cloak

cloak–and–dag·ger *adj* : involving or suggestive of espionage

clob·ber \ˈkläb-ər\ *vb* **clob·bered; clob·ber·ing** \-(ə-)riŋ\ **1** : to pound mercilessly; *also* : to hit with force : SMASH **2** : to defeat overwhelmingly

cloche \ˈklōsh\ *n* [F, lit., bell] : a woman's small hat that somewhat resembles a helmet

[1]**clock** \ˈkläk\ *n* : a timepiece not intended to be carried on the person

[2]**clock** *vb* **1** : to time (a person or a performance) by a timing device **2** : to register (as speed) on a mechanical recording device — **clock·er** *n*

[3]**clock** *n* : an ornamental figure on a stocking or sock

clock·wise \ˈkläk-ˌwīz\ *adv* : in the direction in which the hands of a clock move — **clockwise** *adj*

clock·work \-ˌwərk\ *n* : machinery containing a set of small cogwheels

clod \ˈkläd\ *n* **1** : a lump esp. of earth or clay **2** : a dull or insensitive person

clod·hop·per \-ˌhäp-ər\ *n* **1** : an uncouth rustic **2** : a large heavy shoe

[1]**clog** \ˈkläg\ *n* **1** : a weight so attached as to impede motion **2** : a thick-soled shoe

[2]**clog** *vb* **clogged; clog·ging** **1** : to impede with a clog : HINDER **2** : to obstruct passage through **3** : to become filled with extraneous matter

cloi·son·né \ˌklȯiz-ᵊn-ˈā\ *adj* : a colored decoration made of enamels poured into the divided areas in a design outlined with wire or metal strips

[1]**clois·ter** \ˈklȯi-stər\ *n* [ME *cloistre,* fr. OF, fr. ML *claustrum,* fr. L, bar, bolt, fr. *claudere* to close] **1** : a monastic establishment **2** : a covered usu. colonnaded passage on the side of a court — **clois·tral** \-strəl\ *adj*

[2]**cloister** *vb* : to shut away from the world

clone \ˈklōn\ *n* [Gk *klōn* twig] **1** : the offspring produced asexually from an individual (as a plant increased by grafting) **2** : an individual grown from a single body cell of its parent and genetically identical to the parent **3** : one that appears to be a copy of an original form — **clon·al** \ˈklōn-ᵊl\ *adj* — **clone** *vb*

clop \ˈkläp\ *n* : a sound made by or as if by a hoof or wooden shoe against pavement — **clop** *vb*

[1]**close** \ˈklōz\ *vb* **closed; clos·ing** **1** : to bar passage through : SHUT **2** : to suspend the operations (as of a school) **3** : END, TERMINATE **4** : to bring together the parts or edges of; *also* : to fill up **5** : GRAPPLE ⟨~ with the enemy⟩ **6** : to enter into an agreement — **clos·able** *or* **close·able** *adj*

[2]**close** \ˈklōz\ *n* : CONCLUSION, END

[3]**close** \ˈklōs\ *adj* **clos·er; clos·est** **1** : having no openings **2** : narrowly restricting or restricted **3** : limited to a privileged class **4** : SECLUDED; *also* : SECRETIVE **5** : RIGOROUS **6** : SULTRY, STUFFY **7** : STINGY **8** : having little space between items or units **9** : fitting tightly; *also* : SHORT ⟨~ haircut⟩ **10** : NEAR **11** : INTIMATE ⟨~ friends⟩ **12** : ACCURATE **13** : decided by a narrow margin ⟨a ~ game⟩ — **close** *adv* — **close·ly** *adv* — **close·ness** *n*

closed circuit *n* : television installation in which the signal is transmitted by wire to a limited number of receivers

closed shop *n* : an establishment having only members of a labor union on the payroll

close·fist·ed \ˈklōs-ˈfis-təd\ *adj* : STINGY

close–knit \-ˈnit\ *adj* : closely bound together by social, cultural, economic, or political ties

close·mouthed \-ˈmau̇thd, -ˈmau̇tht\ *adj* : cautious in speaking
close·out \ˈklōz-ˌau̇t\ *n* : a sale of a business's entire stock at low prices
close out \ˈklōz-ˈau̇t\ *vb* **1** : to dispose of by a closeout **2** : to dispose of a business : sell out
[1]**clos·et** \ˈkläz-ət, ˈklȯz-\ *n* **1** : a small room for privacy **2** : a small compartment for household utensils or clothing **3** : WATER CLOSET
[2]**closet** *vb* : to take into a private room for an interview
close–up \ˈklōs-ˌəp\ *n* **1** : a photograph or movie shot taken at close range **2** : an intimate view or examination of something
clo·sure \ˈklō-zhər\ *n* **1** : an act of closing : the condition of being closed **2** : something that closes **3** : CLOTURE
clot \ˈklät\ *n* : a mass formed by a portion of liquid (as blood or cream) thickening and sticking together — **clot** *vb*
cloth \ˈklȯth\ *n, pl* **cloths** \ˈklȯthz, ˈklȯths\ **1** : a pliable fabric made usu. by weaving or knitting natural or synthetic fibers and filaments **2** : TABLECLOTH **3** : distinctive dress of the clergy; *also* : CLERGY
clothe \ˈklōth\ *vb* **clothed** *or* **clad** \ˈklad\; **cloth·ing** **1** : DRESS **2** : to express by suitably significant language
clothes \ˈklō(th)z\ *n pl* **1** : CLOTHING **2** : BEDCLOTHES
clothes·horse \-ˌhȯrs\ *n* **1** : a frame on which to hang clothes **2** : a conspicuously dressy person
clothes moth *n* : a small pale insect whose larvae eat wool, fur, and feathers
clothes·pin \ˈklō(th)z-ˌpin\ *n* : a device for fastening clothes on a line
clothes·press \-ˌpres\ *n* : a receptacle for clothes
cloth·ier \ˈklōth-yər, ˈklō-thē-ər\ *n* : a maker or seller of clothing
cloth·ing \ˈklō-thiŋ\ *n* : garments in general
clo·ture \ˈklō-chər\ *n* : the closing or limitation (as by calling for a vote) of debate in a legislative body
[1]**cloud** \ˈklau̇d\ *n* [ME, rock, cloud, fr. OE *clūd* rock, hill] **1** : a visible mass of water or ice particles usu. high in the air **2** : a usu. visible mass of minute airborne particles; *also* : a mass of obscuring matter in interstellar space **3** : CROWD, SWARM ⟨a ~ of mosquitoes⟩ **4** : something having a dark or threatening aspect — **cloud·i·ness** \-ē-nəs\ *n* — **cloud·less** *adj* — **cloudy** *adj*
[2]**cloud** *vb* **1** : to darken or hide with or as if with a cloud **2** : OBSCURE **3** : TAINT, SULLY
cloud·burst \-ˌbərst\ *n* : a sudden heavy rainfall
cloud·let \-lət\ *n* : a small cloud
cloud nine *n* : a feeling of extreme well-being or elation — usu. used with *on*
[1]**clout** \ˈklau̇t\ *n* **1** : a blow esp. with the hand **2** : PULL, INFLUENCE
[2]**clout** *vb* : to hit forcefully
[1]**clove** \ˈklōv\ *n* : one of the small bulbs that grows at the base of the scales of a large bulb ⟨a ~ of garlic⟩
[2]**clove** *past of* CLEAVE
[3]**clove** *n* [ME *clowe*, fr. OF *clou* (*de girofle*), lit., nail of clove, fr. L *clavus* nail] : the dried flower bud of an East Indian tree used esp. as a spice
clo·ven \ˈklō-vən\ *past part of* CLEAVE
cloven foot *n* : a foot (as of a sheep) with the front part divided into two parts — **cloven–foot·ed** \-ˈfu̇t-əd\ *adj*
cloven hoof *n* : CLOVEN FOOT — **cloven–hoofed** \-ˈhu̇ft, -ˈhu̇vd\ *adj*
clo·ver \ˈklō-vər\ *n* : any of a genus of leguminous herbs with usu. 3-parted leaves and dense flower heads
clo·ver·leaf \-ˌlēf\ *n, pl* **cloverleafs** \-ˌlēfs\ *or* **clo·ver·leaves** \-ˌlēvz\ : a road plan passing one highway over another and routing turning traffic without left turns or direct crossings
[1]**clown** \ˈklau̇n\ *n* **1** : BOOR **2** : a fool or comedian in an entertainment (as a circus) — **clown·ish** *adj* — **clown·ish·ly** *adv* — **clown·ish·ness** *n*
[2]**clown** *vb* : to act like a clown
cloy \ˈklȯi\ *vb* : to disgust or nauseate with excess of something orig. pleasing — **cloy·ing·ly** \-iŋ-lē\ *adv*
clr *abbr* clear
[1]**club** \ˈkləb\ *n* **1** : a heavy wooden stick or staff used as a weapon; *also* : BAT **2** : any of a suit of playing cards marked with a black figure resembling a clover leaf **3** : a group of persons associated for a common purpose; *also* : the meeting place of such a group
[2]**club** *vb* **clubbed; club·bing** **1** : to strike with a club **2** : to unite or combine for a common cause
club·foot \ˈkləb-ˈfu̇t\ *n* : a misshapen foot twisted out of position from birth — **club·foot·ed** \-ˈfu̇t-əd\ *adj*
club·house \ˈkləb-ˌhau̇s\ *n* **1** : a house occupied by a club **2** : locker rooms used by an athletic team
club sandwich *n* : a sandwich of three slices of bread with two layers of meat and lettuce, tomato, and mayonnaise
club soda *n* : SODA WATER 1
club steak *n* : a small steak cut from the end of the short loin
cluck \ˈklək\ *n* : the call of a hen esp. to her chicks — **cluck** *vb*
[1]**clue** \ˈklü\ *n* : something that guides through an intricate procedure or maze; *esp* : a piece of evidence leading to the solution of a problem
[2]**clue** *vb* **clued; clue·ing** *or* **clu·ing** : to provide with a clue; *also* : to give information to ⟨~ me in⟩
[1]**clump** \ˈkləmp\ *n* **1** : a group of things clustered together **2** : a heavy tramping sound
[2]**clump** *vb* : to tread clumsily and noisily
clum·sy \ˈkləm-zē\ *adj* **clum·si·er; -est** **1** : lacking dexterity, nimbleness, or grace **2** : not tactful or subtle — **clum·si·ly** \ˈkləm-zə-lē\ *adv* — **clum·si·ness** \-zē-nəs\ *n*
clung *past and past part of* CLING
[1]**clus·ter** \ˈkləs-tər\ *n* : GROUP, BUNCH
[2]**cluster** *vb* **clus·tered; clus·ter·ing** \-t(ə-)riŋ\ : to grow or gather in a cluster
[1]**clutch** \ˈkləch\ *vb* : to grasp with or as if with the hand
[2]**clutch** *n* **1** : the claws or a hand in the act of grasping; *also* : CONTROL, POWER **2** : a device for gripping an object **3** : a coupling used to connect and disconnect a driving and a driven part of a mechanism; *also* : a lever or pedal operating such a coupling **4** : a crucial situation
[3]**clutch** *adj* : made, done, or successful in a crucial situation
[4]**clutch** *n* **1** : a nest or batch of eggs; *also* : a brood of chicks **2** : GROUP, BUNCH
[1]**clut·ter** \ˈklət-ər\ *vb* : to fill or cover with a disorderly scattering of things
[2]**clutter** *n* : a crowded mass
cm *abbr* centimeter
Cm *symbol* curium
CM *abbr* [Commonwealth of the Northern Mariana Islands] Northern Mariana Islands
cmdr *abbr* commander
cml *abbr* commercial
CMSgt *abbr* chief master sergeant
CNO *abbr* chief of naval operations
CNS *abbr* central nervous system
co *abbr* **1** company **2** county
Co *symbol* cobalt
CO *abbr* **1** Colorado **2** commanding officer **3** conscientious objector
c/o *abbr* care of
[1]**coach** \ˈkōch\ *n* **1** : a large closed 4-wheeled carriage with an elevated outside front seat for the driver **2** : a railroad passenger car esp. for day travel **3** : BUS **4** : a private tutor; *also* : one who instructs or trains a team of performers
[2]**coach** *vb* **1** : to go in a horse-drawn coach **2** : to instruct, direct, or prompt as a coach — **coach·er** *n*
coach·man \-mən\ *n* : a man whose business is driving a coach or carriage

co·ad·ju·tor \ˌkō-ə-ˈjüt-ər, kō-ˈaj-ət-ər\ *n* : ASSISTANT; *esp* : an assistant bishop having the right of succession
co·ag·u·lant \kō-ˈag-yə-lənt\ *n* : something that produces coagulation
co·ag·u·late \kō-ˈag-yə-ˌlāt\ *vb* **-lat·ed; -lat·ing** : CLOT — **co·ag·u·la·tion** \kō-ˌag-yə-ˈlā-shən\ *n*
[1]**coal** \ˈkōl\ *n* **1** : EMBER **2** : a black solid combustible mineral used as fuel
[2]**coal** *vb* **1** : to supply with coal **2** : to take in coal
co·alesce \ˌkō-ə-ˈles\ *vb* **co·alesced; co·alesc·ing** : to grow together; *also* : FUSE **syn** merge, blend, mingle, mix — **co·ales·cence** \-ˈles-ᵊns\ *n*
coal·field \ˈkōl-ˌfēld\ *n* : a region where deposits of coal occur
coal gas *n* : gas from coal; *esp* : gas distilled from bituminous coal and used for heating
co·ali·tion \ˌkō-ə-ˈlish-ən\ *n* : UNION; *esp* : a temporary union for a common purpose — **co·ali·tion·ist** *n*
coal oil *n* : KEROSENE
coal tar *n* : tar distilled from bituminous coal and used in dyes and drugs
co–an·chor \ˈkō-ˈaŋ-kər\ *n* : a newscaster who shares the duties of head broadcaster
coarse \ˈkōrs\ *adj* **coars·er; coars·est 1** : of ordinary or inferior quality **2** : composed of large parts or particles ⟨~ sand⟩ **3** : CRUDE ⟨~ manners⟩ **4** : ROUGH, HARSH — **coarse·ly** *adv* — **coarse·ness** *n*
coars·en \ˈkōrs-ᵊn\ *vb* **coars·ened; coars·en·ing** \ˈkōrs-(ᵊ-)niŋ\ : to make or become coarse
[1]**coast** \ˈkōst\ *n* [ME *cost*, fr. MF *coste*, fr. L *costa* rib, side] **1** : SEASHORE **2** : a slide down a slope — **coast·al** *adj*
[2]**coast** *vb* **1** : to sail along the shore **2** : to move (as downhill on a sled or as on a bicycle while not pedaling) without effort
coast·er *n* **1** : one that coasts **2** : a shallow container or a plate or mat to protect a surface
coaster brake *n* : a brake in the hub of the rear wheel of a bicycle
coast guard *n* : a military force employed in guarding or patrolling a coast — **coast·guards·man** \ˈkōst-ˌgärdz-mən\ *n*
coast·line \ˈkōst-ˌlīn\ *n* : the outline or shape of a coast
[1]**coat** \ˈkōt\ *n* **1** : an outer garment for the upper part of the body **2** : an external growth (as of fur or feathers) on an animal **3** : a covering layer
[2]**coat** *vb* : to cover usu. with a finishing or protective coat
coat·ing \ˈkōt-iŋ\ *n* : COAT, COVERING
coat of arms : the heraldic bearings (as of a person) usu. depicted on an escutcheon
coat of mail : a garment of metal scales or rings worn as armor
co·au·thor \ˈkō-ˈȯ-thər\ *n* : a joint or associate author — **coauthor** *vb*
coax \ˈkōks\ *vb* : WHEEDLE; *also* : to gain by gentle urging or flattery
co·ax·i·al \ˈkō-ˈak-sē-əl\ *adj* : having coincident axes — **co·ax·i·al·ly** \-ē\ *adv*
coaxial cable *n* : a cable that consists of a tube of electrically conducting material surrounding a central conductor
cob \ˈkäb\ *n* **1** : a male swan **2** : CORN-COB **3** : a short-legged stocky horse
co·balt \ˈkō-ˌbȯlt\ *n* [G *kobalt*, alter. of *kobold*, lit., goblin, fr. its occurrence in silver ore, believed to be due to goblins] : a tough shiny silver-white magnetic metallic chemical element found with iron and nickel — see ELEMENT table
cobalt chloride *n* : a chloride of cobalt; *esp* : one that is blue when dry, turns deep pink in the presence of moisture, and is used to indicate humidity
cob·ble \ˈkäb-əl\ *vb* **cob·bled; cob·bling** \-(ə-)liŋ\ : to make or put together roughly or hastily
cob·bler \ˈkäb-lər\ *n* **1** : a mender or maker of shoes **2** : a deep-dish fruit pie with a thick crust
cob·ble·stone \ˈkäb-əl-ˌstōn\ *n* : a naturally rounded stone larger than a pebble and smaller than a boulder
co·bra \ˈkō-brə\ *n* : any of several venomous snakes of Asia and Africa that when excited expand the skin of the neck into a broad hood
cob·web \ˈkäb-ˌweb\ *n* [ME *coppeweb*, fr. *coppe* spider, fr. OE ātor*coppe*] **1** : SPIDERWEB; *also* : a thread spun by a spider or insect larva **2** : something flimsy or entangling
co·caine \kō-ˈkān, ˈkō-ˌkān\ *n* : a drug that is obtained from the leaves of a So. American shrub (**co·ca** \ˈkō-kə\), can result in severe psychological dependence, and is sometimes used as a local anesthetic
coc·cus \ˈkäk-əs\ *n, pl* **coc·ci** \ˈkäk-ˌ(s)ī\ : a spherical bacterium
coc·cyx \ˈkäk-siks\ *n, pl* **coc·cy·ges** \ˈkäk-sə-ˌjēz\ *also* **coc·cyx·es** \ˈkäk-sik-səz\ : the end of the spinal column beyond the sacrum esp. in man
co·chi·neal \ˈkäch-ə-ˌnēl\ *n* : a red dye made from the dried bodies of females of a tropical American insect **(cochineal insect)**
co·chlea \ˈkō-klē-ə, ˈkäk-lē-\ *n, pl* **co·chle·as** *or* **co·chle·ae** \-(k)lē-ˌē, -ˌī\ : the usu. spiral part of the inner ear containing nerve endings which carry information about sound to the brain — **co·chle·ar** \-lē-ər\ *adj*
[1]**cock** \ˈkäk\ *n* **1** : the adult male of a bird and esp. of the common domestic chicken **2** : VALVE, FAUCET **3** : LEADER **4** : the hammer of a firearm; *also* : the position of the hammer when ready for firing
[2]**cock** *vb* **1** : to draw back the hammer of a firearm **2** : to set or draw back in readiness for some action ⟨~ your arm to throw⟩ **3** : to turn or tilt usu. to one side
[3]**cock** *n* : a small pile (as of hay)
cock·ade \kä-ˈkād\ *n* : an ornament worn on the hat as a badge
cock·a·tiel \ˌkäk-ə-ˈtēl\ *n* : a small crested parrot often kept as a cage bird
cock·a·too \ˈkäk-ə-ˌtü\ *n, pl* **-toos** [D *kaketoe*, fr. Malay *kakatua*] : a large crested brilliantly colored Australian parrot
cock·a·trice \ˈkäk-ə-trəs, -ˌtrīs\ *n* : a legendary serpent with a deadly glance
cock·crow \ˈkäk-ˌkrō\ *n* : DAWN
cocked hat \ˈkäkt-\ *n* : a hat with the brim turned up on two or three sides
cock·er·el \ˈkäk-(ə-)rəl\ *n* : a young male domestic chicken
cock·er spaniel \ˌkäk-ər-\ *n* [*cocking* (woodcock hunting)] : any of a breed of small spaniels with long ears, square muzzle, and silky coat
cockeyed \ˈkäk-ˈīd\ *adj* **1** : turned or tilted to one side **2** : slightly crazy : FOOLISH
cock·fight \-ˌfīt\ *n* : a contest of gamecocks usu. fitted with metal spurs
[1]**cock·le** \ˈkäk-əl\ *n* : any of several weedy plants related to the pinks
[2]**cockle** *n* : a bivalve mollusk with a heart-shaped shell
cock·le·shell \-ˌshel\ *n* **1** : the shell of a cockle **2** : a light flimsy boat
cock·ney \ˈkäk-nē\ *n, pl* **cockneys** [ME *cokeney*, lit., cocks' egg, fr. *cok* cock + *ey* egg, fr. OE *ǣg*] : a native of London and esp. of the East End of London; *also* : the dialect of a cockney
cock·pit \ˈkäk-ˌpit\ *n* **1** : a pit for cockfights **2** : an open space in the deck from which a small boat is steered **3** : a space in an aircraft fuselage for the pilot

cock·roach \ˈkäk-ˌrōch\ *n* : any of an order of active nocturnal insects including some which infest houses and ships

cock·sure \ˈkäk-ˈshu̇r\ *adj* **1** : perfectly sure : CERTAIN **2** : COCKY

cock·tail \ˈkäk-ˌtāl\ *n* **1** : an iced drink made of liquor and flavoring ingredients **2** : an appetizer (as tomato juice) served as a first course of a meal

cocky \ˈkäk-ē\ *adj* **cock·i·er; -est** : marked by overconfidence : PERT, CONCEITED — **cock·i·ly** \ˈkäk-ə-lē\ *adv* — **cock·i·ness** \-ē-nəs\ *n*

co·coa \ˈkō-kō\ *n* **1** : CACAO **2** : chocolate deprived of some of its fat and powdered; *also* : a drink made of this heated with water or milk

co·co·nut \ˈkō-kə-(ˌ)nət\ *n* : a large edible nut produced by a tall tropical palm (**coconut palm**)

co·coon \kə-ˈkün\ *n* : a case usu. of silk which an insect larva forms and in which it passes the pupal stage

cod \ˈkäd\ *n, pl* **cod** *also* **cods** : a soft-finned large-mouthed food fish of the No. Atlantic

COD *abbr* **1** cash on delivery **2** collect on delivery

co·da \ˈkōd-ə\ *n* : a closing section in a musical composition that is formally distinct from the main structure

cod·dle \ˈkäd-ᵊl\ *vb* **cod·dled; cod·dling** \ˈkäd-(ᵊ-)liŋ\ **1** : to cook slowly in water below the boiling point **2** : PAMPER

¹**code** \ˈkōd\ *n* **1** : a systematic statement of a body of law **2** : a system of principles or rules ⟨moral ~⟩ **3** : a system of signals **4** : a system of symbols (as in secret communication) with special meanings **5** : GENETIC CODE

²**code** *vb* **cod·ed; cod·ing** : to put into the form or symbols of a code

co·deine \ˈkō-ˌdēn, ˈkōd-ē-ən\ *n* : a narcotic drug obtained from opium and used esp. in cough remedies

co·dex \ˈkō-ˌdeks\ *n, pl* **co·di·ces** \ˈkōd-ə-ˌsēz, ˈkäd-\ : a manuscript book (as of the Scriptures or classics)

cod·fish \ˈkäd-ˌfish\ *n* : COD

cod·ger \ˈkäj-ər\ *n* : an odd or cranky fellow

cod·i·cil \ˈkäd-ə-səl, -ˌsil\ *n* : a legal instrument modifying an earlier will

cod·i·fy \ˈkäd-ə-ˌfī, ˈkōd-\ *vb* **-fied; -fy·ing** : to arrange in a systematic form — **cod·i·fi·ca·tion** \ˌkäd-ə-fə-ˈkā-shən, ˌkōd-\ *n*

cod·ling \ˈkäd-liŋ\ *n* **1** : a young cod **2** : HAKE

co·ed \ˈkō-ˌed\ *n* : a female student in a coeducational institution — **coed** *adj*

co·ed·u·ca·tion \ˌkō-ˌej-ə-ˈkā-shən\ *n* : the education of male and female students at the same institution — **co·ed·u·ca·tion·al** \-sh(ə-)nəl\ *adj* — **co·ed·u·ca·tion·al·ly** \-ē\ *adv*

co·ef·fi·cient \ˌkō-ə-ˈfish-ənt\ *n* **1** : a constant factor as distinguished from a variable in a mathematical term **2** : a number that serves as a measure of some property (as of a substance or device)

coel·en·ter·ate \si-ˈlent-ə-ˌrāt, -rət\ *n* : any of a phylum of radially symmetrical invertebrate animals including the corals, sea anemones, and jellyfishes

co·equal \kō-ˈē-kwəl\ *adj* : equal with another — **coequal** *n* — **co·equal·i·ty** \ˌkō-ē-ˈkwäl-ət-ē\ *n* — **co·equal·ly** \kō-ˈē-kwə-lē\ *adv*

co·erce \kō-ˈərs\ *vb* **co·erced; co·erc·ing** **1** : RESTRAIN, REPRESS **2** : COMPEL **3** : ENFORCE — **co·er·cion** \-ˈər-zhən, -shən\ *n* — **co·er·cive** \-ˈər-siv\ *adj*

co·eval \kō-ˈē-vəl\ *adj* : of the same age — **coeval** *n*

co·ex·ist \ˌkō-ig-ˈzist\ *vb* **1** : to exist together or at the same time **2** : to live in peace with each other — **co·ex·is·tence** \-ˈzis-təns\ *n*

co·ex·ten·sive \ˌkō-ik-ˈsten-siv\ *adj* : having the same scope or extent in space or time

C of C *abbr* Chamber of Commerce

cof·fee \ˈkȯ-fē\ *n* [It & Turk; It *caffè*, fr. Turk *kahve*, fr. Ar *qahwa*] : a drink made from the roasted and ground seeds of a fruit of a tropical shrub or tree; *also* : these seeds (**coffee beans**) or a plant producing them

cof·fee·house \-ˌhau̇s\ *n* : a place where refreshments (as coffee) are sold

coffee klatch \-ˌklach\ *n* : KAFFEE-KLATSCH

cof·fee·pot \-ˌpät\ *n* : a pot for brewing or serving coffee

coffee shop *n* : a small restaurant

coffee table *n* : a low table customarily placed in front of a sofa

cof·fer \ˈkȯ-fər\ *n* : a chest or box used esp. for valuables

cof·fer·dam \-ˌdam\ *n* : a watertight enclosure from which water is pumped to expose the bottom of a body of water and permit construction

cof·fin \ˈkȯ-fən\ *n* : a box or chest for a corpse to be buried in

C of S *abbr* chief of staff

¹**cog** \ˈkäg\ *n* : a tooth on the rim of a wheel or gear — **cogged** \ˈkägd\ *adj*

²**cog** *abbr* cognate

co·gen·e·ra·tion \ˌkō-ˌjen-ə-ˈrā-shən\ *n* : the simultaneous generation of electricity and heat from the same fuel

co·gent \ˈkō-jənt\ *adj* : having power to compel or constrain : CONVINCING — **co·gen·cy** \-jən-sē\ *n*

cog·i·tate \ˈkäj-ə-ˌtāt\ *vb* **-tat·ed; -tat·ing** : THINK, PONDER — **cog·i·ta·tion** \ˌkäj-ə-ˈtā-shən\ *n* — **cog·i·ta·tive** \ˈkäj-ə-ˌtāt-iv\ *adj*

co·gnac \ˈkōn-ˌyak\ *n* : a French brandy

cog·nate \ˈkäg-ˌnāt\ *adj* **1** : of the same or similar nature **2** : RELATED; *esp* : related by descent from the same ancestral language — **cognate** *n*

cog·ni·tive \ˈkäg-nət-iv\ *adj* : of, relating to, or being conscious mental activity (as thinking, remembering, or learning) — **cog·ni·tion** \käg-ˈni-shən\ *n*

cog·ni·zance \ˈkäg-nə-zəns\ *n* **1** : apprehension by the mind : AWARENESS **2** : NOTICE, HEED — **cog·ni·zant** \ˈkäg-nə-zənt\ *adj*

cog·no·men \käg-ˈnō-mən, ˈkäg-nə-\ *n, pl* **cognomens** *or* **cog·no·mi·na** \käg-ˈnäm-ə-nə, -ˈnō-mə-\ : NAME; *esp* : NICKNAME

co·gno·scen·te \ˌkän-yə-ˈshent-ē\ *n, pl* **-scen·ti** \-ē\ [obs. It] : CONNOISSEUR

cog·wheel \ˈkäg-ˌhwēl\ *n* : a wheel with cogs or teeth

co·hab·it \kō-ˈhab-ət\ *vb* : to live together as husband and wife — **co·hab·i·ta·tion** \-ˌhab-ə-ˈtā-shən\ *n*

co·here \kō-ˈhiər\ *vb* **co·hered; co·her·ing** : to stick together

co·her·ent \kō-ˈhir-ənt\ *adj* **1** : having the quality of cohering **2** : logically consistent — **co·her·ence** \-əns\ *n* — **co·her·ent·ly** *adv*

co·he·sion \kō-ˈhē-zhən\ *n* **1** : a sticking together **2** : molecular attraction by which the particles of a body are united — **co·he·sive** \-siv\ *adj* — **co·he·sive·ly** *adv* — **co·he·sive·ness** *n*

co·ho \ˈkō-ˌhō\ *n, pl* **cohos** *or* **coho** : a rather small salmon with light-colored flesh

co·hort \ˈkō-ˌhȯrt\ *n* **1** : a group of warriors or followers **2** : COMPANION, ACCOMPLICE

coif \ˈkȯif; *2 usu* ˈkwäf\ *n* **1** : a close-fitting hat **2** : COIFFURE

coif·feur \kwä-ˈfər\ *n* [F] : HAIRDRESSER

coif·feuse \kwä-ˈfə(r)z, -ˈf(y)üz\ *n* : a female hairdresser

coif·fure \kwä-ˈfyu̇r\ *n* : a manner of arranging the hair

¹**coil** \ˈkȯil\ *vb* : to wind in a spiral shape

²**coil** *n* : a series of rings or loops (as of coiled rope, wire, or pipe) : RING, LOOP

¹**coin** \ˈkȯin\ *n* [ME, fr. MF, wedge, corner, fr. L *cuneus* wedge] **1** : a piece of metal issued by government authority as money **2** : metal money

²**coin** *vb* **1** : to make (a coin) esp. by stamping : MINT **2** : CREATE, INVENT ⟨~ a phrase⟩ — **coin·er** *n*

coin·age \ˈkȯi-nij\ *n* **1** : the act or process of coining **2** : COINS

co·in·cide \ˌkō-ən-ˈsīd, ˈkō-ən-ˌsīd\ *vb* **-cid·ed; -cid·ing** **1**

: to occupy the same place in space or time **2** : to correspond or agree exactly

co·in·ci·dence \kō-ˈin-səd-əns\ *n* **1** : exact agreement **2** : occurrence together apparently without reason; *also* : an event that so occurs

co·in·ci·dent \-səd-ənt\ *adj* **1** : of similar nature **2** : occupying the same space or time — **co·in·ci·den·tal** \kō-ˌin-sə-ˈdent-ᵊl\ *adj*

co·itus \ˈkō-ət-əs\ *n* [L, fr. pp. of *coire* to come together] : SEXUAL INTERCOURSE — **co·ital** \-ət-ᵊl\ *adj*

[1]**coke** \ˈkōk\ *n* : a hard gray porous fuel made by heating soft coal to drive off most of its volatile material

[2]**coke** *n* : COCAINE

col *abbr* **1** colonial; colony **2** column

Col *abbr* **1** colonel **2** Colorado **3** Colossians

COL *abbr* **1** colonel **2** cost of living

co·la \ˈkō-lə\ *n* : a carbonated soft drink usu. containing sugar, caffeine, caramel, and special flavoring

col·an·der \ˈkəl-ən-dər, ˈkäl-\ *n* : a perforated utensil for draining food

[1]**cold** \ˈkōld\ *adj* **1** : having a low or decidedly subnormal temperature **2** : lacking warmth of feeling **3** : suffering or uncomfortable from lack of warmth — **cold·ly** *adv* — **cold·ness** \ˈkōl(d)-nəs\ *n* — **in cold blood** : with premeditation : DELIBERATELY

[2]**cold** *n* **1** : a condition marked by low temperature; *also* : cold weather **2** : a chilly feeling **3** : a bodily disorder popularly associated with chilling; *esp* : COMMON COLD

[3]**cold** *adv* : TOTALLY, FINALLY

cold–blood·ed \ˈkōld-ˈbləd-əd\ *adj* **1** : lacking normal human feelings **2** : having a body temperature not internally regulated but close to that of the environment **3** : sensitive to cold

cold duck *n* : a blend of sparkling burgundy and champagne

cold feet *n pl* : doubt or fear that prevents action

cold shoulder *n* : cold or unsympathetic behavior — **cold–shoul·der** *vb*

cold sore *n* : a group of blisters appearing in or about the mouth in the oral form of herpes simplex

cold sweat *n* : concurrent perspiration and chill usu. associated with fear, pain, or shock

cold turkey *n* : abrupt complete cessation of the use of an addictive drug

cold war *n* : a conflict characterized by the use of means short of sustained overt military action

cole·slaw \ˈkōl-ˌslȯ\ *n* [D *koolsla*, fr. *kool* cabbage + *sla* salad] : a salad made of raw cabbage

col·ic \ˈkäl-ik\ *n* : sharp sudden abdominal pain — **col·icky** \ˈkäl-i-kē\ *adj*

col·i·se·um \ˌkäl-ə-ˈsē-əm\ *n* : a large structure esp. for athletic contests

coll *abbr* college

col·lab·o·rate \kə-ˈlab-ə-ˌrāt\ *vb* **-rat·ed; -rat·ing** **1** : to work jointly with others (as in writing a book) **2** : to cooperate with an enemy force occupying one's country — **col·lab·o·ra·tion** \-ˌlab-ə-ˈrā-shən\ *n* — **col·lab·o·ra·tor** \-ˈlab-ə-ˌrāt-ər\ *n*

col·lage \kə-ˈläzh\ *n* [F, gluing] : an artistic composition of fragments (as of printed matter) pasted on a picture surface

[1]**col·lapse** \kə-ˈlaps\ *vb* **col·lapsed; col·laps·ing** **1** : to shink together abruptly **2** : DISINTEGRATE; *also* : to fall in : give way **3** : to break down physically or mentally; *esp* : to fall helpless or unconscious **4** : to fold down compactly — **col·laps·ible** *adj*

[2]**collapse** *n* : BREAKDOWN

[1]**col·lar** \ˈkäl-ər\ *n* **1** : a band, strip, or chain worn around the neck or the neckline of a garment **2** : something resembling a collar — **col·lar·less** *adj*

[2]**collar** *vb* : to seize by the collar; *also* : CAPTURE, GRAB

col·lar·bone \-ˌbōn\ *n* : the bone of the shoulder that joins the breastbone and the shoulder blade

col·lard \ˈkäl-ərd\ *n* : a stalked smooth-leaved kale — usu. used in pl.

col·late \kə-ˈlāt; ˈkäl-ˌāt, ˈkōl-\ *vb* **col·lat·ed; col·lat·ing** **1** : to compare (as two texts) carefully and critically **2** : to assemble in proper order

[1]**col·lat·er·al** \kə-ˈlat-(ə-)rəl\ *adj* **1** : associated but of secondary importance **2** : descended from the same ancestors but not in the same line **3** : PARALLEL **4** : of, relating to, or being collateral used as security; *also* : secured by collateral

[2]**collateral** *n* : property (as stocks) used as security for the repayment of a loan

col·la·tion \kə-ˈlā-shən, kä-, kō-\ *n* **1** : a light meal **2** : the act, process, or result of collating

col·league \ˈkäl-ˌēg\ *n* : an associate esp. in a profession

[1]**col·lect** \ˈkäl-ikt, -ˌekt\ *n* : a short prayer comprising an invocation, petition, and conclusion

[2]**col·lect** \kə-ˈlekt\ *vb* **1** : to bring or come together into one body or place : ASSEMBLE **2** : to gather from numerous sources ⟨~ stamps⟩ **3** : to gain control of ⟨~ his thoughts⟩ **4** : to receive payment of — **col·lect·ible** *or* **col·lect·able** *adj or n* — **col·lec·tion** \-ˈlek-shən\ *n* — **col·lec·tor** \-ˈlek-tər\ *n*

[3]**col·lect** \kə-ˈlekt\ *adv or adj* : to be paid for by the receiver

col·lect·ed \kə-ˈlek-təd\ *adj* : SELF-POSSESSED, CALM

[1]**col·lec·tive** \kə-ˈlek-tiv\ *adj* **1** : of, relating to, or denoting a group of individuals considered as a whole **2** : formed by collecting **3** : involving all members of a group as distinct from its individuals **4** : shared or assumed by all members of the group — **col·lec·tive·ly** *adv*

[2]**collective** *n* **1** : GROUP **2** : a cooperative unit or organization

collective bargaining *n* : negotiation between an employer and union representatives

col·lec·tiv·ism \kə-ˈlek-ti-ˌviz-əm\ *n* : a political or economic theory advocating collective control esp. over production and distribution

col·lec·tiv·ize \-ˌvīz\ *vb* **-ized; -iz·ing** : to organize under collective control

col·leen \kä-ˈlēn, ˈkäl-ˌēn\ *n* : an Irish girl

col·lege \ˈkäl-ij\ *n* [ME, fr. MF, fr. L *collegium* society, fr. *collega* colleague, fr. *com-* with + *legare* to appoint] **1** : a building used for an educational or religious purpose **2** : an institution of higher learning granting a bachelor's degree; *also* : an institution offering instruction esp. in a vocational or technical field ⟨barber ~⟩ **3** : an organized body of persons having common interests or duties ⟨~ of cardinals⟩ — **col·le·giate** \kə-ˈlē-jət\ *adj*

col·le·gi·al·i·ty \kə-ˌlē-jē-ˈal-ət-ē\ *n* : the relationship of colleagues

col·le·gian \kə-ˈlē-jən\ *n* : a college student

col·le·gi·um \kə-ˈleg-ē-əm, -ˈläg-\ *n, pl* **-gia** \-ē-ə\ *or* **-giums** : a governing group in which each member has approximately equal power

col·lide \kə-ˈlīd\ *vb* **col·lid·ed; col·lid·ing** **1** : to come together with solid impact **2** : to come into conflict : CLASH — **col·li·sion** \-ˈlizh-ən\ *n*

col·lie \ˈkäl-ē\ *n* : a large dog of a breed with rough-coated and smooth-coated varieties developed in Scotland for herding sheep

col·lier \ˈkäl-yər\ *n* **1** : a coal miner **2** : a ship for carrying coal

col·liery \ˈkäl-yə-rē\ *n, pl* **-lier·ies** : a coal mine and its associated buildings

col·li·mate \ˈkäl-ə-ˌmāt\ *vb* **-mat·ed; -mat·ing** : to make (as rays of light) parallel

col·lo·ca·tion \ˌkäl-ə-ˈkā-shən\ *n* **1** : a placing together or side by side; *also* : the result of such placing **2** : a noticeable arrangement or conjoining of linguistic elements (as words)
col·lo·di·on \kə-ˈlōd-ē-ən\ *n* : a sticky substance that hardens in the air and is used to cover wounds and coat photographic films
col·loid \ˈkäl-ˌȯid\ *n* : a substance in the form of submicroscopic particles that when in solution or suspension do not settle out; *also* : such a substance together with the medium in which it is dispersed — **col·loi·dal** \kə-ˈlȯid-ᵊl\ *adj*
colloq *abbr* colloquial
col·lo·qui·al \kə-ˈlō-kwē-əl\ *adj* : of, relating to, or characteristic of conversation and esp. of familiar and informal conversation
col·lo·qui·al·ism \-ˈlō-kwē-ə-ˌliz-əm\ *n* : a colloquial expression
col·lo·qui·um \kə-ˈlō-kwē-əm\ *n, pl* **-qui·ums** *or* **-quia** \-kwē-ə\ : CONFERENCE, SEMINAR
col·lo·quy \ˈkäl-ə-kwē\ *n, pl* **-quies** : a usu. formal conversation or conference
col·lu·sion \kə-ˈlü-zhən\ *n* : secret agreement or cooperation for an illegal or deceitful purpose — **col·lu·sive** \-ˈlü-siv\ *adj*
Colo *abbr* Colorado
co·logne \kə-ˈlōn\ *n* [*Cologne*, Germany] : a perfumed liquid consisting of alcohol and aromatic oils — **co·logned** \-ˈlōnd\ *adj*
[1]**co·lon** \ˈkō-lən\ *n, pl* **colons** *or* **co·la** \-lə\ : the part of the large intestine extending from the cecum to the rectum — **co·lon·ic** \kō-ˈlän-ik\ *adj*
[2]**colon** *n, pl* **colons** : a punctuation mark : used esp. to direct attention to following matter
[3]**co·lon** \kə-ˈlōn\ *n, pl* **co·lo·nes** \-ˈlō-ˌnās\ — see MONEY table
col·o·nel \ˈkərn-ᵊl\ *n* [alter. of *coronel*, fr. MF, fr. It *colonnello* column of soldiers, colonel, fr. L *columna*] : a commissioned officer (as in the army) ranking next below a brigadier general
[1]**co·lo·nial** \kə-ˈlō-nē-əl, -nyəl\ *adj* **1** : of, relating to, or characteristic of a colony; *also* : possessing or composed of colonies **2** *often cap* : of or relating to the original 13 colonies forming the U.S.
[2]**colonial** *n* : a member or inhabitant of a colony
co·lo·nial·ism \-ˌiz-əm\ *n* : control by one power over a dependent area or people; *also* : a policy advocating or based on such control — **co·lo·nial·ist** \-əst\ *n or adj*
col·o·nist \ˈkäl-ə-nəst\ *n* **1** : COLONIAL **2** : one who takes part in founding a colony
col·o·nize \ˈkäl-ə-ˌnīz\ *vb* **-nized; -niz·ing 1** : to establish a colony in or on **2** : to settle in a colony — **col·o·ni·za·tion** \ˌkäl-ə-nə-ˈzā-shən\ *n* — **col·o·niz·er** *n*
col·on·nade \ˌkäl-ə-ˈnād\ *n* : an evenly spaced row of columns usu. supporting the base of the roof structure
col·o·ny \ˈkäl-ə-nē\ *n, pl* **-nies 1** : a body of people living in a new territory; *also* : the territory inhabited by these people **2** : a localized population of organisms ⟨a ∼ of bees⟩ **3** : a group with common interests situated in close association ⟨a writers' ∼⟩; *also* : the area occupied by such a group
col·o·phon \ˈkäl-ə-fən, -ˌfän\ *n* **1** : an inscription placed at the end of a book with facts relative to its production **2** : a distinctive symbol used by a printer or publisher
[1]**col·or** \ˈkəl-ər\ *n* **1** : a phenomenon of light (as red or blue) or visual perception that enables one to differentiate otherwise identical objects; *also* : a hue as contrasted with black, white, or gray **2** : APPEARANCE **3** : complexion tint **4** *pl* : FLAG; *also* : military service ⟨a call to the ∼*s*⟩ **5** : VIVIDNESS, INTEREST — **col·or·ful** *adj* — **col·or·less** *adj*
[2]**color** *vb* **col·ored; col·or·ing** \ˈkəl-(ə-)riŋ\ **1** : to give color to; *also* : to change the color of **2** : BLUSH
Col·o·ra·do potato beetle \ˌkäl-ə-ˈrad-ō-, -ˈräd-\ *n* : a black-and-yellow striped beetle that feeds on the leaves of the potato
col·or·ation \ˌkəl-ə-ˈrā-shən\ *n* : use or arrangement of colors
col·or·a·tu·ra \ˌkəl-ə-rə-ˈt(y)u̇r-ə\ *n* **1** : elaborate ornamentation in vocal music **2** : a soprano specializing in coloratura
col·or–blind \ˈkəl-ər-ˌblīnd\ *adj* : partially or totally unable to distinguish one or more chromatic colors — **color blindness** *n*
[1]**col·ored** \ˈkəl-ərd\ *adj* **1** : having color **2** : SLANTED, BIASED **3** : of a race other than the white; *esp* : NEGRO
[2]**colored** *n, pl* **colored** *or* **coloreds** *often cap* : a colored person
col·or·fast \ˈkəl-ər-ˌfast\ *adj* : having color that does not fade or run — **col·or·fast·ness** *n*
co·los·sal \kə-ˈläs-əl\ *adj* : of very great size or degree
Co·los·sians \kə-ˈläsh-ənz\ *n* — see BIBLE table
co·los·sus \kə-ˈläs-əs\ *n, pl* **co·los·sus·es** \-ˈläs-ə-səz\ *or* **co·los·si** \-ˈläs-ˌī\ [L] : a gigantic statue; *also* : something of great size or scope
col·por·teur \ˈkäl-ˌpōrt-ər\ *n* [F] : a peddler of religious books
colt \ˈkōlt\ *n* : FOAL; *also* : a young male horse, ass, or zebra — **colt·ish** *adj*
col·um·bine \ˈkäl-əm-ˌbīn\ *n* [ME, fr. ML *columbina*, fr. L, fem. of *columbinus* dovelike, fr. *columba* dove] : any of a genus of plants with showy spurred flowers that are related to the buttercups
co·lum·bi·um \kə-ˈləm-bē-əm\ *n* : NIOBIUM
Columbus Day \kə-ˈləm-bəs-\ *n* : the 2d Monday in October or formerly October 12 observed as a legal holiday in many states in commemoration of the landing of Columbus
col·umn \ˈkäl-əm\ *n* **1** : one of two or more vertical sections of a printed page; *also* : a special department (as in a newspaper) **2** : a supporting pillar; *also* : something resembling such a column ⟨a ∼ of water⟩ **3** : a long row (as of soldiers) — **co·lum·nar** \kə-ˈləm-nər\ *adj*
col·um·nist \ˈkäl-əm-(n)əst\ *n* : one who writes a newspaper or magazine column
com *or* **comm** *abbr* **1** command; commander **2** commerce; commercial **3** commission; commissioner **4** committee **5** common **6** commonwealth
co·ma \ˈkō-mə\ *n* : a state of deep unconsciousness caused by disease, injury, or poison — **co·ma·tose** \ˈkō-mə-ˌtōs, ˈkäm-ə-\ *adj*
Co·man·che \kə-ˈman-chē\ *n, pl* **Comanche** *or* **Comanches** : a member of an American Indian people ranging from Wyoming and Nebraska south into New Mexico and Texas
[1]**comb** \ˈkōm\ *n* **1** : a toothed instrument for arranging the hair or for separating and cleaning textile fibers **2** : a fleshy crest on the head of a fowl **3** : HONEYCOMB — **comb** *vb* — **combed** \ˈkōmd\ *adj*
[2]**comb** *abbr* combination; combining
com·bat \kəm-ˈbat, ˈkäm-ˌbat\ *vb* **-bat·ed** *or* **-bat·ted; -bat·ing** *or* **-bat·ting 1** : FIGHT, CONTEND **2** : to struggle or work against : OPPOSE — **com·bat** \ˈkäm-ˌbat\ *n* — **com·bat·ant** \kəm-ˈbat-ᵊnt, ˈkäm-bət-ənt\ *n* — **com·bat·ive** \kəm-ˈbat-iv\ *adj*
combat fatigue *n* : a traumatic neurotic or psychotic reaction occurring under conditions (as wartime combat) that cause intense stress
comb·er \ˈkō-mər\ *n* **1** : one that combs **2** : a long curling wave of the sea
com·bi·na·tion \ˌkäm-bə-ˈnā-shən\ *n* **1** : a result or product of combining **2** : a sequence of letters or numbers chosen in setting a lock **3** : the act or process of combining; *also* : the quality or state of being combined
[1]**com·bine** \kəm-ˈbīn\ *vb* **com·bined; com·bin·ing** : to become one : UNITE

[2]com·bine \ˈkäm-ˌbīn\ *n* **1** : COMBINATION; *esp* : one made to secure business or political advantage **2** : a machine that harvests and threshes grain while moving over the field

comb·ings \ˈkō-miŋz\ *n pl* : loose hairs or fibers removed by a comb

combining form *n* : a linguistic form that occurs only in compounds or derivatives

com·bo \ˈkäm-bō\ *n, pl* **combos** : a small jazz or dance band

com·bus·ti·ble \kəm-ˈbəs-tə-bəl\ *adj* : capable of being burned — **com·bus·ti·bil·i·ty** \-ˌbəs-tə-ˈbil-ət-ē\ *n* — **combustible** *n*

com·bus·tion \kəm-ˈbəs-chən\ *n* **1** : an act or instance of burning **2** : slow oxidation (as in the animal body)

comdg *abbr* commanding

comdr *abbr* commander

comdt *abbr* commandant

come \(ˈ)kəm\ *vb* **came** \ˈkām\; **come; com·ing** \ˈkəm-iŋ\ **1** : APPROACH **2** : ARRIVE **3** : to reach the point of being or becoming ⟨~ to a boil⟩ **4** : AMOUNT ⟨the bill *came* to $10⟩ **5** : to take place **6** : ORIGINATE, ARISE **7** : to be available **8** : REACH, EXTEND **9** : to experience orgasm — **come across** : to meet or find by chance — **come to pass** : HAPPEN — **come upon** : to come across

come·back \ˈkəm-ˌbak\ *n* **1** : RETORT **2** : RECOVERY — **come back** \(ˌ)kəm-ˈbak\ *vb*

co·me·di·an \kə-ˈmēd-ē-ən\ *n* **1** : an actor in comedy **2** : an amusing person **3** : an entertainer specializing in comedy

co·me·di·enne \-ˌmēd-ē-ˈen\ *n* : a woman who is a comedian

come·down \ˈkəm-ˌdau̇n\ *n* : a descent in rank or dignity

com·e·dy \ˈkäm-əd-ē\ *n, pl* **-dies** [ME, fr. MF *comedie,* fr. L *comoedia,* fr. Gk *kōmōidia,* fr. *kōmos* revel + *aeidein* to sing] **1** : a light amusing play with a happy ending **2** : a literary work treating a comic theme or written in a comic style **3** : humorous entertainment

come·ly \ˈkəm-lē\ *adj* **come·li·er; -est** : good-looking : HANDSOME — **come·li·ness** *n*

come off *vb* : SUCCEED

come–on \ˈkəm-ˌȯn, -ˌän\ *n* : INDUCEMENT, LURE

come out *vb* **1** : to come into public view **2** : to declare oneself **3** : TURN OUT 5 ⟨everything *came out* all right⟩ — **come out with** : SAY 1

com·er \ˈkəm-ər\ *n* : a promising beginner

[1]**co·mes·ti·ble** \kə-ˈmes-tə-bəl\ *adj* : EDIBLE

[2]**comestible** *n* : FOOD — usu. used in pl.

com·et \ˈkäm-ət\ *n* [ME *comete,* fr. OE *cometa,* fr. L, fr. Gk *komētēs,* lit., long-haired, fr. *komē* hair] : a small bright celestial body that develops a cloudy tail when near the sun

come to *vb* : to regain consciousness

come·up·pance \kə-ˈməp-əns\ *n* : a deserved rebuke or penalty

com·fit \ˈkəm-fət\ *n* : a candied fruit or nut

[1]**com·fort** \ˈkəm-fərt\ *n* **1** : CONSOLATION **2** : freedom from pain, trouble, or anxiety; *also* : something that gives such freedom — **com·fort·less** *adj*

[2]**comfort** *vb* **1** : to give strength and hope to **2** : CONSOLE

com·fort·able \ˈkəm(f)t-ə-bəl, ˈkəm-fərt-\ *adj* **1** : providing comfort **2** : more than adequate **3** : feeling at ease — **com·fort·ably** \-blē\ *adv*

com·fort·er \ˈkəm-fə(r)t-ər\ *n* **1** : one that comforts **2** : QUILT

com·fy \ˈkəm-fē\ *adj* : COMFORTABLE

[1]**com·ic** \ˈkäm-ik\ *adj* **1** : relating to comedy or comic strips **2** : provoking laughter or amusement **syn** laughable, funny, farcical — **com·i·cal** *adj*

[2]**comic** *n* **1** : COMEDIAN **2** : COMIC BOOK

comic book *n* : a magazine containing sequences of comic strips

comic strip *n* : a group of cartoons in narrative sequence

coming \ˈkəm-iŋ\ *adj* **1** : APPROACHING, NEXT **2** : gaining importance

co·mi·ty \ˈkäm-ət-ē, ˈkō-mət-\ *n, pl* **-ties** : friendly civility : COURTESY

coml *abbr* commercial

comm *abbr* — see COM

com·ma \ˈkäm-ə\ *n* : a punctuation mark , used esp. as a mark of separation within the sentence

[1]**com·mand** \kə-ˈmand\ *vb* **1** : to direct authoritatively : ORDER **2** : DOMINATE, CONTROL, GOVERN **3** : to overlook from a strategic position

[2]**command** *n* **1** : the act of commanding **2** : ability to control : MASTERY **3** : an order given **4** : an electrical signal that actuates a device (as a computer); *also* : the activation of a device by means of such a signal **5** : a body of troops under a commander; *also* : an area or position that one commands **6** : a position of highest authority

com·man·dant \ˈkäm-ən-ˌdant, -ˌdänt\ *n* : an officer in command

com·man·deer \ˌkäm-ən-ˈdiər\ *vb* : to take possession of by force

com·mand·er \kə-ˈman-dər\ *n* **1** : LEADER, CHIEF; *esp* : an officer commanding an army or subdivision of an army **2** : a commissioned officer in the navy ranking next below a captain

commander in chief : one who holds supreme command of the armed forces

com·mand·ment \kə-ˈman(d)-mənt\ *n* : COMMAND, ORDER; *esp* : any of the Ten Commandments

command module *n* : a space vehicle module designed to carry the crew and reentry equipment

com·man·do \kə-ˈman-dō\ *n, pl* **-dos** *or* **-does** [Afrikaans *kommando,* fr. Dutch *commando* command] : a member of a military unit trained for surprise raids

command sergeant major *n* : a noncommissioned officer in the army ranking above a first sergeant

com·mem·o·rate \kə-ˈmem-ə-ˌrāt\ *vb* **-rat·ed; -rat·ing 1** : to call or recall to mind **2** : to serve as a memorial of — **com·mem·o·ra·tion** \-ˌmem-ə-ˈrā-shən\ *n*

com·mem·o·ra·tive \kə-ˈmem-(ə-)rət-iv, -ˈmem-ə-ˌrāt-iv\ *adj* : intended to commemorate an event

com·mence \kə-ˈmens\ *vb* **com·menced; com·menc·ing** : BEGIN, START

com·mence·ment \-mənt\ *n* **1** : the act or time of a beginning **2** : the graduation exercises of a school or college

com·mend \kə-ˈmend\ *vb* **1** : to commit to one's care **2** : RECOMMEND **3** : PRAISE — **com·mend·able** \-ˈmen-də-bəl\ *adj* — **com·mend·ably** \-blē\ *adv* — **com·men·da·tion** \ˌkäm-ən-ˈdā-shən, -ˌen-\ *n*

com·men·su·ra·ble \kə-ˈmens-(ə-)rə-bəl\ *adj* : having a common measure; *esp* : divisible by a common unit an integral number of times

com·men·su·rate \kə-ˈmens(-ə)-rət, -ˈmench(-ə)-\ *adj* : equal in measure or extent; *also* : PROPORTIONAL, CORRESPONDING ⟨a job ~ with her abilities⟩

com·ment \ˈkäm-ˌent\ *n* **1** : an expression of opinion **2** : an explanatory, illustrative, or critical note or observation : REMARK — **comment** *vb*

com·men·tary \ˈkäm-ən-ˌter-ē\ *n, pl* **-tar·ies** : a systematic series of comments

com·men·ta·tor \-ˌtāt-ər\ *n* : one who comments; *esp* : one who gives talks on news events on radio or television

com·merce \ˈkäm-(ˌ)ərs\ *n* : the buying and selling of commodities : TRADE

[1]**com·mer·cial** \kə-ˈmər-shəl\ *adj* : having to do with com-

merce; *also* : designed for profit or for mass appeal — **com·mer·cial·ly** \-ē\ *adv*

[2]**commercial** *n* : an advertisement broadcast on radio or television

com·mer·cial·ism \kə-ˈmər-shə-ˌliz-əm\ *n* **1** : a spirit, method, or practice characteristic of business **2** : excessive emphasis on profit

com·mer·cial·ize \-ˌlīz\ *vb* **-ized; -iz·ing 1** : to manage on a business basis for profit **2** : to exploit for profit

com·mi·na·tion \ˌkäm-ə-ˈnā-shən\ *n* : DENUNCIATION — **com·mi·na·to·ry** \ˈkäm-ə-nə-ˌtōr-ē\ *adj*

com·min·gle \kə-ˈmiŋ-gəl\ *vb* : MINGLE, BLEND

com·mis·er·ate \kə-ˈmiz-ə-ˌrāt\ *vb* **-at·ed; -at·ing** : to feel or express pity : SYMPATHIZE — **com·mis·er·a·tion** \-ˌmiz-ə-ˈrā-shən\ *n*

com·mis·sar \ˈkäm-ə-ˌsär\ *n* [Russ] : a Communist party official assigned to a military unit to teach and enforce party principles and policy

com·mis·sar·i·at \ˌkäm-ə-ˈser-ē-ət\ *n* **1** : a system for supplying troops with food **2** : a department headed by a commissar

com·mis·sary \ˈkäm-ə-ˌser-ē\ *n, pl* **-sar·ies** : a store for equipment and provisions esp. for military personnel

[1]**com·mis·sion** \kə-ˈmish-ən\ *n* **1** : a warrant granting certain powers and imposing certain duties **2** : a certificate conferring military rank and authority **3** : authority to act as agent for another; *also* : something to be done by an agent **4** : a body of persons charged with performing a duty **5** : the doing of some act; *also* : the thing done **6** : the allowance made to an agent for transacting business for another

[2]**commission** *vb* **-mis·sioned; -mis·sion·ing** \-ˈmish-(ə-)niŋ\ **1** : to give a commission to **2** : to order to be made **3** : to put (a ship) into a state of readiness for service

commissioned officer *n* : an officer of the armed forces holding rank by virtue of a commission from the president

com·mis·sion·er \kə-ˈmish-(ə-)nər\ *n* **1** : a member of a commission **2** : an official in charge of a department of public service **3** : the administrative head of a professional sport — **com·mis·sion·er·ship** *n*

com·mit \kə-ˈmit\ *vb* **com·mit·ted; com·mit·ting 1** : to put into charge or trust : ENTRUST **2** : to put in a prison or mental institution **3** : TRANSFER, CONSIGN **4** : PERPETRATE ⟨~ a crime⟩ **5** : to pledge or assign to some particular course or use — **com·mit·ment** *n* — **com·mit·tal** *n*

com·mit·tee \kə-ˈmit-ē\ *n* : a body of persons selected to consider and act or report on some matter — **com·mit·tee·man** \-mən\ *n* — **com·mit·tee·wom·an** \-ˌwu̇m-ən\ *n*

commo *abbr* commodore

com·mode \kə-ˈmōd\ *n* [F, fr. *commode,* adj., suitable, convenient, fr. L *commodus,* fr. *com-* with + *modus* measure] **1** : a movable washstand with cupboard underneath **2** : TOILET 3

com·mo·di·ous \kə-ˈmōd-ē-əs\ *adj* : comfortably spacious : ROOMY

com·mod·i·ty \kə-ˈmäd-ət-ē\ *n, pl* **-ties 1** : a product of agriculture or mining **2** : an article of commerce ⟨wheat and soybeans are traded as *commodities*⟩

com·mo·dore \ˈkäm-ə-ˌdōr\ *n* **1** : a commissioned officer in the navy ranking next below a rear admiral **2** : an officer commanding a group of merchant ships; *also* : the chief officer of a yacht club

[1]**com·mon** \ˈkäm-ən\ *adj* **1** : belonging to or serving the community : PUBLIC **2** : shared by a number in a group **3** : widely or generally known, found, or observed : FAMILIAR ⟨~ knowledge⟩ **4** : VERNACULAR 3 ⟨~ names⟩ **5** : not above the average esp. in social status **syn** universal, general, generic — **com·mon·ly** *adv*

[2]**common** *n* **1** *pl* : the common people **2** *pl* : a dining hall **3** *pl, cap* : the lower house of the British and Canadian parliaments **4** : a piece of land held in common by a community — **in common** : shared together

com·mon·al·ty \ˈkäm-ən-ᵊl-tē\ *n, pl* **-ties** : the common people

common cold *n* : a contagious respiratory disease caused by a virus and characterized by a sore, swollen, and inflamed nose and throat, usu. by much mucus, and by coughing and sneezing

common denominator *n* **1** : a common multiple of the denominators of a number of fractions **2** : a common trait or theme

common divisor *n* : a number or expression that divides two or more numbers or expressions without remainder

com·mon·er \ˈkäm-ə-nər\ *n* : one of the common people : one having no rank of nobility

common fraction *n* : a fraction in which the numerator and denominator are both integers and are separated by a horizontal or slanted line

common law *n* : a group of legal practices and traditions based on judges' decisions and social customs and usu. having the same force as laws passed by legislative bodies

common logarithm *n* : a logarithm whose base is 10

common market *n* : an economic unit formed to remove trade barriers among members

common multiple *n* : a multiple of each of two or more numbers or expressions

[1]**com·mon·place** \ˈkäm-ən-ˌplās\ *n* : something that is ordinary or trite

[2]**commonplace** *adj* : ORDINARY

common sense *n* : ordinary good sense and judgment

com·mon·weal \ˈkäm-ən-ˌwēl\ *n* **1** *archaic* : COMMONWEALTH **2** : the general welfare

com·mon·wealth \-ˌwelth\ *n* **1** : the body of people politically organized into a state **2** : STATE; *also* : an association or federation of autonomous states

com·mo·tion \kə-ˈmō-shən\ *n* **1** : DISTURBANCE, UPRISING **2** : AGITATION

com·mu·nal \kə-ˈmyün-ᵊl, ˈkäm-yən-ᵊl\ *adj* **1** : of or relating to a commune or community **2** : marked by collective ownership and use of property **3** : shared or used in common

[1]**com·mune** \kə-ˈmyün\ *vb* **communed; com·mun·ing** : to communicate intimately

[2]**com·mune** \ˈkäm-ˌyün; kə-ˈmyün\ *n* **1** : the smallest administrative district in some European countries **2** : a community organized on a communal basis

com·mu·ni·ca·ble \kə-ˈmyü-ni-kə-bəl\ *adj* : capable of being communicated ⟨~ diseases⟩ — **com·mu·ni·ca·bil·i·ty** \-ˌmyü-ni-kə-ˈbil-ət-ē\ *n*

com·mu·ni·cant \-ˈmyü-ni-kənt\ *n* **1** : a church member entitled to receive Communion **2** : one that communicates; *esp* : INFORMANT

com·mu·ni·cate \kə-ˈmyü-nə-ˌkāt\ *vb* **-cat·ed; -cat·ing 1** : to make known **2** : TRANSMIT, IMPART **3** : to receive Communion **4** : to be in communication **5** : JOIN, CONNECT

com·mu·ni·ca·tion \kə-ˌmyü-nə-ˈkā-shən\ *n* **1** : an act of transmitting **2** : MESSAGE **3** : exchange of information or opinions **4** : a means of communicating — **com·mu·ni·ca·tive** \kə-ˈmyü-nə-ˌkāt-iv, -ni-kət-iv\ *adj*

com·mu·nion \kə-ˈmyü-nyən\ *n* **1** : a sharing of something with others **2** *cap* : a Christian sacrament in which bread and wine are partaken of as a commemoration of the death of Christ; *also* : the act of receiving the sacrament **3** : intimate fellowship or rapport **4** : a body of Christians having a common faith and discipline

com·mu·ni·qué \kə-ˈmyü-nə-ˌkā, -ˌmyü-nə-ˈkā\ *n* : BULLETIN 1

com·mu·nism \ˈkäm-yə-ˌniz-əm\ *n* **1** : social organization in which goods are held in common **2** : a theory of social organization advocating common ownership of means of production and a distribution of products of industry based on need **3** *cap* : a political doctrine based on revolutionary Marxian socialism that is the official ideology of the U.S.S.R. and some other countries; *also* : a system of government in which one party controls state-owned means of production — **com·mu·nist** \-nəst\ *n or adj, often cap* — **com·mu·nis·tic** \ˌkäm-yə-ˈnis-tik\ *adj, often cap*

com·mu·ni·ty \kə-ˈmyü-nət-ē\ *n, pl* **-ties 1** : a body of people living in the same place under the same laws; *also* : a natural population of plants and animals that interact ecologically and live in one place (as a pond) **2** : society at large **3** : joint ownership **4** : SIMILARITY, LIKENESS

community college *n* : a nonresidential 2-year college that is usu. government-supported

community property *n* : property held jointly by husband and wife

com·mu·ta·tion \ˌkäm-yə-ˈtā-shən\ *n* : substitution of one form of payment or penalty for another

com·mu·ta·tive \ˈkäm-yə-ˌtāt-iv, kə-ˈmyüt-ət-\ *adj* : of, relating to, having, or being the property that a given mathematical operation and set have when the result obtained using any two numbers of the set with the operation does not differ with the order in which the numbers are used ⟨addition of the real numbers is ~⟩ — **com·mu·ta·tiv·i·ty** \kə-ˌmyüt-ə-ˈtiv-ət-ē, ˌkäm-yə-tə-\ *n*

com·mu·ta·tor \ˈkäm-yə-ˌtāt-ər\ *n* : a device (as on a generator or motor) for changing the direction of electric current

¹com·mute \kə-ˈmyüt\ *vb* **com·mut·ed; com·mut·ing 1** : EXCHANGE **2** : to substitute a less severe penalty for (one more severe) **3** : to travel back and forth regularly — **com·mut·er** *n*

²commute *n* : a trip made in commuting

comp *abbr* **1** comparative **2** compiled; compiler **3** composition **4** compound

¹com·pact \kəm-ˈpakt, (ˈ)käm-\ *adj* **1** : SOLID, DENSE **2** : BRIEF, SUCCINCT **3** : occupying a small volume by efficient use of space ⟨~ camera⟩ — **com·pact·ly** *adv* — **com·pact·ness** *n*

²compact *vb* : to pack together

³com·pact \ˈkäm-ˌpakt\ *n* **1** : a small case for cosmetics **2** : a small automobile

⁴com·pact \ˈkäm-ˌpakt\ *n* : AGREEMENT, COVENANT

compact disc *n* : a small plastic optical disc usu. containing recorded music

¹com·pan·ion \kəm-ˈpan-yən\ *n* [OF *compagnon,* fr. LL *companion-, companio,* lit., one who shares bread, fr. L *com-* together + *panis* bread] **1** : an intimate friend or associate : COMRADE **2** : one that is closely connected with something similar — **com·pan·ion·able** *adj* — **com·pan·ion·ship** *n*

²companion *n* : COMPANIONWAY

com·pan·ion·way \-ˌwā\ *n* : a ship's stairway from one deck to another

com·pa·ny \ˈkəmp-(ə-)nē\ *n, pl* **-nies 1** : association with others : FELLOWSHIP; *also* : COMPANIONS **2** : GUESTS **3** : a group of persons or things **4** : an infantry unit consisting of two or more platoons and normally commanded by a captain **5** : a group of musical or dramatic performers **6** : the officers and crew of a ship **7** : an association of persons for carrying on a business **syn** party, band, troop, troupe, corps, outfit

com·pa·ra·ble \ˈkäm-p(ə-)rə-bəl\ *adj* : capable of being compared **syn** parallel, similar, like, alike, corresponding — **com·pa·ra·bil·i·ty** \ˌkäm-p(ə-)rə-ˈbil-ət-ē\ *n*

¹com·par·a·tive \kəm-ˈpar-ət-iv\ *adj* **1** : of, relating to, or constituting the degree of grammatical comparison that denotes increase in quality, quantity, or relation **2** : RELATIVE ⟨a ~ stranger⟩ — **com·par·a·tive·ly** *adv*

²comparative *n* : the comparative degree or a comparative form in a language

¹com·pare \kəm-ˈpaər\ *vb* **com·pared; com·par·ing 1** : to represent as like something : LIKEN **2** : to examine for likenesses and differences **3** : to inflect or modify (an adjective or adverb) according to the degrees of comparison

²compare *n* : the possibility of comparing ⟨beauty beyond ~⟩

com·par·i·son \-ˈpar-ə-sən\ *n* **1** : the act of comparing : relative estimate **2** : change in the form of an adjective or adverb to show different levels of quality, quantity, or relation

com·part·ment \kəm-ˈpärt-mənt\ *n* **1** : a separate division **2** : a section of an enclosed space : ROOM

com·part·men·tal·ize \kəm-ˌpärt-ˈment-ᵊl-ˌīz\ *vb* **-ized; -iz·ing** : to separate into compartments

¹com·pass \ˈkəm-pəs, ˈkäm-\ *vb* [ME *compassen,* fr. OF *compasser* to measure, fr. (assumed) VL *compassare* to pace off, fr. L *com-* + *passus* pace] **1** : CONTRIVE, PLOT **2** : to make a circuit of; *also* : SURROUND **3** : BRING ABOUT, ACHIEVE

²compass *n* **1** : BOUNDARY, CIRCUMFERENCE **2** : an enclosed space **3** : RANGE, SCOPE **4** : a device for determining direction by means of a magnetic needle swinging freely and pointing to the magnetic north; *also* : a nonmagnetic device that indicates direction **5** : an instrument for drawing circles or transferring measurements consisting of two legs joined by a pivot

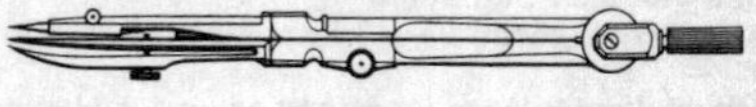

compass 5

com·pas·sion \kəm-ˈpash-ən\ *n* : sympathetic feeling : PITY, MERCY — **com·pas·sion·ate** \-(ə-)nət\ *adj*

com·pat·i·ble \kəm-ˈpat-ə-bəl\ *adj* : able to exist or act together harmoniously ⟨~ colors⟩ ⟨~ drugs⟩ **syn** consonant, congenial, sympathetic — **com·pat·i·bil·i·ty** \-ˌpat-ə-ˈbil-ət-ē\ *n*

com·pa·tri·ot \kəm-ˈpā-trē-ət, -trē-ˌät\ *n* : a fellow countryman

com·peer \ˈkäm-ˌpiər\ *n* : EQUAL, PEER

com·pel \kəm-ˈpel\ *vb* **com·pelled; com·pel·ling** : to drive or urge with force : CONSTRAIN

com·pen·di·um \kəm-ˈpen-dē-əm\ *n, pl* **-di·ums** *or* **-dia** \-dē-ə\ **1** : a brief summary of a larger work or of a field of knowledge **2** : COLLECTION

com·pen·sate \ˈkäm-pən-ˌsāt\ *vb* **-sat·ed; -sat·ing 1** : to be equivalent to in value or effect : make up for **2** : PAY, REMUNERATE **syn** balance, offset, counterbalance, counterpoise — **com·pen·sa·tion** \ˌkäm-pən-ˈsā-shən\ *n* — **com·pen·sa·to·ry** \kəm-ˈpen-sə-ˌtōr-ē\ *adj*

com·pete \kəm-ˈpēt\ *vb* **com·pet·ed; com·pet·ing** : CONTEND, VIE

com·pe·tence \ˈkäm-pət-əns\ *n* **1** : adequate means for subsistence **2** : FITNESS, ABILITY

com·pe·ten·cy \-pət-ən-sē\ *n, pl* **-cies** : COMPETENCE

com·pe·tent \-pət-ənt\ *adj* : CAPABLE, FIT, QUALIFIED

com·pe·ti·tion \ˌkäm-pə-ˈtish-ən\ *n* **1** : the act of competing : RIVALRY **2** : CONTEST, MATCH; *also* : one's competitors — **com·pet·i·tive** \kəm-ˈpet-ət-iv\ *adj* — **com·pet·i·tive·ly** *adv* — **com·pet·i·tive·ness** *n*

com·pet·i·tor \kəm-ˈpet-ət-ər\ *n* : one that competes : RIVAL

com·pile \kəm-ˈpīl\ *vb* **com·piled; com·pil·ing** [ME *compilen,* fr. MF *compiler,* fr. L *compilare* to plunder] **1** : to collect and edit into a volume **2** : to compose out of materials from other documents **3** : to translate (a computer program) with a compiler **4** : to build up gradually ⟨~ a record of four wins and two losses⟩ — **com·pi·la·tion** \ˌkäm-pə-ˈlā-shən\ *n*

com·pil·er \kəm-ˈpī-lər\ *n* **1** : one that compiles **2** : a computer program that translates another program written in a programming language into machine language

com·pla·cence \kəm-ˈplās-ᵊns\ *n* : SATISFACTION; *esp* : SELF-SATISFACTION — **com·pla·cent** \-ᵊnt\ *adj* — **com·pla·cent·ly** *adv*

com·pla·cen·cy \-ᵊn-sē\ *n, pl* **-cies** : COMPLACENCE

com·plain \kəm-ˈplān\ *vb* **1** : to express grief, pain, or discontent **2** : to make a formal accusation — **com·plain·ant** *n* — **com·plain·er** *n*

com·plaint \kəm-ˈplānt\ *n* **1** : expression of grief, pain, or dissatisfaction **2** : a bodily ailment or disease **3** : a formal accusation against a person

com·plai·sance \kəm-ˈplās-ᵊns, ˌkäm-plā-ˈzans\ *n* [F] : disposition to please — **com·plai·sant** \-ᵊnt, -ˈzant\ *adj*

com·pleat \kəm-ˈplēt\ *adj* : PROFICIENT

com·plect·ed \kəm-ˈplek-təd\ *adj* : having a specified facial complexion ⟨dark-*complected*⟩

¹**com·ple·ment** \ˈkäm-plə-mənt\ *n* **1** : a quantity needed to make a thing complete **2** : full quantity, number, or amount **3** : an added word by which a predicate is made complete **4** : a substance in blood that combines with antibodies to destroy antigens — **com·ple·men·ta·ry** \ˌkäm-plə-ˈmen-t(ə-)rē\ *adj*

²**com·ple·ment** \-ˌment\ *vb* : to be complementary to : fill out

¹**com·plete** \kəm-ˈplēt\ *adj* **com·plet·er; -est** **1** : having no part lacking **2** : brought to an end **3** : fully realized : THOROUGH — **com·plete·ly** *adv* — **com·plete·ness** *n* — **com·ple·tion** \-ˈplē-shən\ *n*

²**complete** *vb* **com·plet·ed; com·plet·ing** **1** : FINISH, CONCLUDE **2** : to make whole or perfect

¹**com·plex** \ˈkäm-ˌpleks\ *n* : something made up of or involving an often intricate combination of elements; *esp* : a system of repressed desires, memories, and ideas that exert a dominant influence on the personality and behavior ⟨a guilt ~⟩

²**com·plex** \käm-ˈpleks, kəm-ˈpleks, ˈkäm-ˌpleks\ *adj* **1** : composed of two or more parts **2** : consisting of a main clause and one or more subordinate clauses ⟨~ sentence⟩ **3** : COMPLICATED, INTRICATE — **com·plex·i·ty** \kəm-ˈplek-sət-ē, käm-\ *n*

complex fraction *n* : a fraction with a fraction or mixed number in the numerator or denominator or both

com·plex·ion \kəm-ˈplek-shən\ *n* **1** : the hue or appearance of the skin esp. of the face **2** : general appearance — **com·plex·ioned** \-shənd\ *adj*

complex number *n* : a number (as $3 + 4\sqrt{-1}$) formed by adding a real number to the product of a real number and the square root of minus one

com·pli·ance \kəm-ˈplī-əns\ *n* **1** : the act of complying to a demand or proposal **2** : a disposition to yield — **com·pli·ant** \-ənt\ *adj*

com·pli·cate \ˈkäm-plə-ˌkāt\ *vb* **-cat·ed; -cat·ing** : to make or become complex or intricate — **com·pli·ca·tion** \ˌkäm-plə-ˈkā-shən\ *n*

com·pli·cat·ed \ˈkäm-plə-ˌkāt-əd\ *adj* **1** : consisting of parts intricately combined **2** : difficult to analyze, understand, or explain — **com·pli·cat·ed·ly** *adv*

com·plic·i·ty \kəm-ˈplis-ət-ē\ *n, pl* **-ties** : the state of being an accomplice

¹**com·pli·ment** \ˈkäm-plə-ment\ *n* **1** : an expression of approval or courtesy; *esp* : a flattering remark **2** *pl* : best wishes : REGARDS

²**com·pli·ment** \-ˌment\ *vb* : to pay a compliment to

com·pli·men·ta·ry \ˌkäm-plə-ˈmen-t(ə-)rē\ *adj* **1** : containing or expressing a compliment **2** : given free as a courtesy ⟨~ ticket⟩

com·ply \kəm-ˈplī\ *vb* **com·plied; com·ply·ing** : ACQUIESCE, YIELD

¹**com·po·nent** \kəm-ˈpō-nənt, ˈkäm-ˌpō-\ *n* : a component part **syn** ingredient, element, factor, constituent

²**component** *adj* : serving to form a part of : CONSTITUENT

com·port \kəm-ˈpōrt\ *vb* **1** : AGREE, ACCORD **2** : CONDUCT **syn** behave, acquit, deport

com·port·ment \-mənt\ *n* : BEHAVIOR, BEARING

com·pose \kəm-ˈpōz\ *vb* **com·posed; com·pos·ing** **1** : to form by putting together : FASHION **2** : to produce (as pages of type) by composition **3** : ADJUST, ARRANGE **4** : CALM, QUIET **5** : to practice composition ⟨~ music⟩ — **com·posed** \-ˈpōzd\ *adj* — **com·pos·er** *n*

composing stick *n* : a hand-held compositor's tray with an adjustable slide for setting type

¹**com·pos·ite** \käm-ˈpäz-ət, kəm-\ *adj* **1** : made up of distinct parts or elements **2** : of, relating to, or being a large family of flowering plants (as the daisy) that bear many small flowers united into compact heads resembling single flowers

²**composite** *n* **1** : something composite **2** : a plant of the composite family **syn** blend, compound, mixture, amalgamation

com·po·si·tion \ˌkäm-pə-ˈzish-ən\ *n* **1** : the act or process of composing; *esp* : arrangement of elements in artistic form **2** : the arrangement or production of type for printing **3** : MAKEUP, CONSTITUTION **4** : a product of mixing various elements or ingredients **5** : a literary, musical, or artistic product; *esp* : ESSAY

com·pos·i·tor \kəm-ˈpäz-ət-ər\ *n* : one who sets type

com·post \ˈkäm-ˌpōst\ *n* : a fertilizing material consisting largely of decayed organic matter

com·po·sure \kəm-ˈpō-zhər\ *n* : CALMNESS, SELF-POSSESSION

com·pote \ˈkäm-ˌpōt\ *n* **1** : fruits cooked in syrup **2** : a bowl (as of glass) usu. with a base and stem from which compotes, fruits, nuts, or sweets are served

¹**com·pound** \(ˈ)käm-ˈpau̇nd, kəm-\ *vb* [ME *compounen*, fr. MF *compondre*, fr. L *componere*, fr. *com-* together + *ponere* to put] **1** : COMBINE **2** : to form by combining parts ⟨~ a medicine⟩ **3** : SETTLE ⟨~ a dispute⟩ **4** : to increase (as interest) by an amount that itself increases; *also* : to add to **5** : to forbear prosecution of (an offense) in return for some reward

²**com·pound** \ˈkäm-ˌpau̇nd\ *adj* **1** : made up of two or more parts **2** : composed of united similar parts esp. of a kind usu. separate ⟨a ~ plant ovary⟩ **3** : formed by the combination of two or more otherwise independent elements ⟨~ sentence⟩

³**com·pound** \ˈkäm-ˌpau̇nd\ *n* **1** : a word consisting of parts that are words **2** : something formed from a union of elements or parts; *esp* : a distinct substance formed by the union of two or more chemical elements **syn** mixture, composite, blend, admixture, alloy

⁴**com·pound** \ˈkäm-ˌpau̇nd\ *n* [by folk etymology fr. Malay *kampong* group of buildings, village] : an enclosure containing buildings

compound interest *n* : interest computed on the sum of an original principal and accrued interest

com·pre·hend \ˌkäm-pri-ˈhend\ *vb* **1** : UNDERSTAND **2** : INCLUDE — **com·pre·hen·si·ble** \-ˈhen-sə-bəl\ *adj* — **com·pre·hen·sion** \-ˈhen-chən\ *n* — **com·pre·hen·sive** \-siv\ *adj*

¹**com·press** \kəm-ˈpres\ *vb* : to squeeze together : CONDENSE **syn** constrict, contract, shrink — **com·pressed** *adj* — **com·pres·sion** \-ˈpresh-ən\ *n* — **com·pres·sor** \-ˈpres-ər\ *n*

²**com·press** \ˈkäm-ˌpres\ *n* : a soft often wet or medicated pad used to press upon an injured bodily part

compressed air *n* : air under pressure greater than that of the atmosphere

com·prise \kəm-ˈprīz\ *vb* **com·prised; com·pris·ing** **1** : INCLUDE, CONTAIN **2** : to be made up of **3** : COMPOSE, CONSTITUTE

¹**com·pro·mise** \ˈkäm-prə-ˌmīz\ *n* : a settlement of differences reached by mutual concessions; *also* : the agreement thus made

[2]compromise *vb* **-mised; -mis·ing** 1 : to settle by compromise 2 : to endanger the reputation of

comp·trol·ler \kən-ˈtrō-lər, ˈkämp-ˌtrō-\ *n* : an official who audits and supervises expenditures and accounts

com·pul·sion \kəm-ˈpəl-shən\ *n* 1 : COERCION 2 : an irresistible impulse **syn** constraint, force, violence, duress — **com·pul·sive** \-siv\ *adj* — **com·pul·so·ry** \-ˈpəls-(ə-)rē\ *adj*

com·punc·tion \kəm-ˈpəŋk-shən\ *n* : anxiety arising from guilt : REMORSE

com·pute \kəm-ˈpyüt\ *vb* **com·put·ed; com·put·ing** : CALCULATE, RECKON — **com·pu·ta·tion** \ˌkäm-pyu̇-ˈtā-shən\ *n* — **com·pu·ta·tion·al** *adj*

computed tomography *n* : radiography in which a three-dimensional image of a body structure is constructed by computer from a series of plane cross-sectional images made along an axis

com·put·er \kəm-ˈpyüt-ər\ *n* : a programmable electronic device that can store, retrieve, and process data

com·put·er·ize \kəm-ˈpyüt-ə-ˌrīz\ *vb* **-ized; -iz·ing** 1 : to carry out, control, or produce by means of a computer 2 : to provide with computers 3 : to store in a computer; *also* : put into a form that a computer can use — **com·put·er·iza·tion** \-ˌpyüt-ə-rə-ˈzā-shən\ *n*

computerized axial tomography *n* : COMPUTED TOMOGRAPHY

com·rade \ˈkäm-ˌrad, -rəd\ *n* [MF *comarade* group sleeping in one room, roommate, companion, fr. Sp *camarada*, fr. *cámara* room, fr. LL *camera*] : COMPANION, ASSOCIATE — **com·rade·ly** *adj* — **com·rade·ship** *n*

[1]**con** \ˈkän\ *vb* **conned; con·ning** 1 : MEMORIZE 2 : STUDY

[2]**con** *adv* : in opposition : AGAINST

[3]**con** *n* : an opposing argument, person, or position

[4]**con** *vb* **conned; con·ning** 1 : SWINDLE 2 : PERSUADE, CAJOLE

[5]**con** *n* : CONVICT

con brio \kän-ˈbrē-ō, kōn-\ *adv* : with spirit : VIGOROUSLY — used as a direction in music

conc *abbr* concentrated

con·cat·e·na·tion \(ˌ)kän-ˌkat-ə-ˈnā-shən\ *n* : a series connected like links in a chain — **con·cat·e·nate** \kän-ˈkat-ə-ˌnāt\ *vb*

con·cave \(ˈ)kän-ˈkāv\ *adj* : curved or rounded inward like the inside of a bowl — **con·cav·i·ty** \kän-ˈkav-ət-ē\ *n*

con·ceal \kən-ˈsēl\ *vb* : to place out of sight : HIDE — **con·ceal·ment** *n*

con·cede \kən-ˈsēd\ *vb* **con·ced·ed; con·ced·ing** 1 : to admit to be true 2 : GRANT, YIELD **syn** allow, acknowledge, admit, avow, confess

con·ceit \kən-ˈsēt\ *n* 1 : excessively high opinion of oneself, one's appearance, or ability : VANITY 2 : an elaborate or strained metaphor — **con·ceit·ed** \-əd\ *adj*

con·ceive \kən-ˈsēv\ *vb* **con·ceived; con·ceiv·ing** 1 : to become pregnant 2 : to form an idea of : THINK, IMAGINE — **con·ceiv·able** \-ˈsē-və-bəl\ *adj* — **con·ceiv·ably** \-blē\ *adv*

con·cel·e·brant \kən-ˈsel-ə-brənt\ *n* : one of two or more members of the clergy celebrating the Eucharist or Mass together

[1]**con·cen·trate** \ˈkän-sən-ˌtrāt\ *vb* **-trat·ed; -trat·ing** 1 : to gather into one body, mass, or force 2 : to make less dilute 3 : to fix one's powers, efforts, or attentions on one thing

[2]**concentrate** *n* : something concentrated

con·cen·tra·tion \ˌkän-sən-ˈtrā-shən\ *n* 1 : the act or process of concentrating : the state of being concentrated; *esp* : direction of attention on a single object 2 : the relative content of a component : STRENGTH

concentration camp *n* : a camp where persons (as prisoners of war or political prisoners) are confined

con·cen·tric \kən-ˈsen-trik\ *adj* 1 : having a common center ⟨~ circles⟩ 2 : COAXIAL

con·cept \ˈkän-ˌsept\ *n* : THOUGHT, NOTION, IDEA — **con·cep·tu·al** \kən-ˈsep-chə(-wə)l\ *adj*

con·cep·tion \kən-ˈsep-shən\ *n* 1 : the act of conceiving or being conceived 2 : the power to form ideas or concepts 3 : IDEA, CONCEPT 4 : the originating of something

con·cep·tu·al·ize \-ˈsep-chə(-wə)-ˌlīz\ *vb* **-ized; -iz·ing** : to form a conception of

[1]**con·cern** \kən-ˈsərn\ *vb* 1 : to relate to 2 : to be the business of : INVOLVE 3 : ENGAGE, OCCUPY

[2]**concern** *n* 1 : INTEREST, ANXIETY 2 : AFFAIR, MATTER 3 : a business organization **syn** care, worry, anxiety, disquiet, unease

con·cerned \-ˈsərnd\ *adj* : ANXIOUS, TROUBLED

con·cern·ing \-ˈsər-niŋ\ *prep* : relating to : REGARDING

con·cern·ment \kən-ˈsərn-mənt\ *n* 1 : something in which one is concerned 2 : IMPORTANCE, CONSEQUENCE

[1]**con·cert** \ˈkän-(ˌ)sərt\ *n* 1 : agreement in a plan or design 2 : a concerted action 3 : a public performance of several musical compositions

[2]**con·cert** \kən-ˈsərt\ *vb* : to plan together

con·cert·ed \kən-ˈsərt-əd\ *adj* : mutually agreed on; *also* : performed in unison

con·cer·ti·na \ˌkän-sər-ˈtē-nə\ *n* : an instrument of the accordion family

con·cert·mas·ter \ˈkän-sərt-ˌmas-tər\ *or* **con·cert·meis·ter** \-ˌmī-stər\ *n* : the leader of the first violins of an orchestra and assistant to the conductor

con·cer·to \kən-ˈchert-ō\ *n, pl* **-ti** \-(ˌ)ē\ *or* **-tos** [It] : a piece for one or more solo instruments and orchestra in three movements

con·ces·sion \kən-ˈsesh-ən\ *n* 1 : an act of conceding or yielding 2 : something yielded 3 : a grant by a government of land or of a right to use it 4 : a grant of a portion of premises for some specific purpose — **con·ces·sion·ary** \-ˈsesh-ə-ˌner-ē\ *adj*

con·ces·sion·aire \kən-ˌsesh-ə-ˈna(ə)r, -ˈne(ə)r\ *n* : one that owns or operates a concession

conch \ˈkäŋk, ˈkänch\ *n, pl* **conchs** \ˈkäŋks\ *or* **conch·es** \ˈkän-chəz\ : a large spiral-shelled marine gastropod mollusk; *also* : its shell

con·cierge \kōⁿ-ˈsyerzh\ *n, pl* **con·cierges** \-ˈsyerzh(-əz)\ [F, fr. L *conservus* fellow slave, fr. *com-* with + *servus* slave] 1 : a resident in an apartment building who performs services for the tenants 2 : a usu. multilingual hotel staff member

con·cil·i·ate \kən-ˈsil-ē-ˌāt\ *vb* **-at·ed; -at·ing** 1 : to bring into agreement : RECONCILE 2 : to gain the goodwill of — **con·cil·i·a·tion** \-ˌsil-ē-ˈā-shən\ *n* — **con·cil·ia·to·ry** \-ˈsil-yə-ˌtōr-ē, -ˈsil-ē-ə-\ *adj*

con·cise \kən-ˈsīs\ *adj* : expressing much in few words : TERSE, SUCCINCT — **con·cise·ly** *adv* — **con·cise·ness** *n*

con·clave \ˈkän-ˌklāv\ *n* [ML, fr. L, room that can be locked, fr. *com-* together + *clavis* key] : a private gathering; *also* : CONVENTION

con·clude \kən-ˈklüd\ *vb* **con·clud·ed; con·clud·ing** 1 : to bring to a close : END 2 : DECIDE, JUDGE 3 : to bring about as a result **syn** close, finish, terminate, complete, halt, end

con·clu·sion \kən-ˈklü-zhən\ *n* 1 : the logical consequence of a reasoning process 2 : TERMINATION, END 3 : OUTCOME, RESULT — **con·clu·sive** \-siv\ *adj* — **con·clu·sive·ly** *adv*

con·coct \kən-ˈkäkt, kän-\ *vb* 1 : to prepare by combining diverse ingredients 2 : DEVISE ⟨~ a scheme⟩ — **con·coc·tion** \-ˈkäk-shən\ *n*

con·com·i·tant \-ˈkäm-ət-ənt\ *adj* : ACCOMPANYING, ATTENDING — **concomitant** *n*

con·cord \ˈkän-ˌkȯrd, ˈkäŋ-\ *n* : AGREEMENT, HARMONY

con·cor·dance \kən-ˈkȯrd-ᵊns\ *n* 1 : an alphabetical index of words in a book or in an author's works with the passages in which they occur 2 : AGREEMENT

con·cor·dant \-ᵊnt\ *adj* : HARMONIOUS, AGREEING
con·cor·dat \kən-ˈkȯr-ˌdat\ *n* : AGREEMENT, COVENANT
con·course \ˈkän-ˌkōrs\ *n* **1** : a flocking together of people : GATHERING **2** : an open space or hall (as in a bus terminal) where crowds gather
con·cres·cence \kən-ˈkres-ᵊns\ *n* : a growing together — **con·cres·cent** \-ᵊnt\ *adj*
[1]**con·crete** \kän-ˈkrēt, ˈkän-ˌkrēt\ *adj* **1** : naming a real thing or class of things : not abstract **2** : not theoretical : ACTUAL **3** : made of or relating to concrete
[2]**con·crete** \ˈkän-ˌkrēt, kän-ˈkrēt\ *vb* **con·cret·ed; con·cret·ing 1** : SOLIDIFY **2** : to cover with concrete
[3]**con·crete** \ˈkän-ˌkrēt, kän-ˈkrēt\ *n* : a hard building material made by mixing cement, sand, and gravel with water
con·cre·tion \kän-ˈkrē-shən\ *n* : a hard mass esp. when formed abnormally in the body
con·cu·bine \ˈkäŋ-kyů-ˌbīn\ *n* [ME, fr. MF, fr. L *concubina*, fr. *com-* with + *cubare* to lie] : a woman who is not legally a wife but lives with a man and has a recognized position in his household — **con·cu·bi·nage** \kän-ˈkyü-bə-nij\ *n*
con·cu·pis·cence \kän-ˈkyü-pə-səns\ *n* : ardent sexual desire : LUST
con·cur \kən-ˈkər\ *vb* **con·curred; con·cur·ring 1** : to act together **2** : AGREE **3** : COINCIDE **syn** unite, combine, cooperate, band, join
con·cur·rence \-ˈkər-əns\ *n* **1** : agreement in action or opinion **2** : CONJUNCTION, COINCIDENCE
con·cur·rent \-ˈkər-ənt\ *adj* **1** : happening or operating at the same time **2** : joint and equal in authority
con·cus·sion \kən-ˈkəsh-ən\ *n* **1** : AGITATION, SHAKING **2** : a sharp sudden blow or collision; *also* : bodily injury (as to the brain) resulting from a sudden jar
con·demn \kən-ˈdem\ *vb* **1** : to declare to be wrong **2** : to convict of guilt **3** : to sentence judically **4** : to pronounce unfit for use ⟨~ a building⟩ **5** : to declare forfeited or taken for public use **syn** denounce, censure, blame, criticize, reprehend — **con·dem·na·tion** \ˌkän-ˌdem-ˈnā-shən\ *n* — **con·dem·na·to·ry** \kən-ˈdem-nə-ˌtōr-ē\ *adj*
con·den·sate \ˈkän-dən-ˌsāt, kən-ˈden-\ *n* : a product of condensation
con·dense \kən-ˈdens\ *vb* **con·densed; con·dens·ing 1** : to make or become more compact or dense : CONCENTRATE **2** : to change from vapor to liquid **syn** contract, shrink, compress, constrict — **con·den·sa·tion** \ˌkän-ˌden-ˈsā-shən, -dən-\ *n*
con·dens·er \kən-ˈden-sər\ *n* **1** : one that condenses **2** : CAPACITOR
con·de·scend \ˌkän-di-ˈsend\ *vb* : to assume an air of superiority **syn** stoop, deign — **con·de·scend·ing·ly** \-ˈsen-diŋ-lē\ *adv* — **con·de·scen·sion** \-ˈsen-chən\ *n*
con·dign \kən-ˈdīn, ˈkän-ˌdīn\ *adj* : DESERVED, APPROPRIATE ⟨~ punishment⟩
con·di·ment \ˈkän-də-mənt\ *n* : something used to make food savory; *esp* : a pungent seasoning (as pepper)
[1]**con·di·tion** \kən-ˈdish-ən\ *n* **1** : something essential to the occurrence of some other thing **2** : state of being **3** : station in life : social rank **4** : state in respect to fitness (as for action or use); *esp* : state of health **5** *pl* : state of affairs : CIRCUMSTANCES
[2]**condition** *vb* **-di·tioned; -di·tion·ing 1** : to put into proper condition for action or use **2** : to adapt, modify, or mold to respond in a particular way **3** : to modify so that an act or response previously associated with one stimulus becomes associated with another
con·di·tion·al \kən-ˈdish-(ə-)nəl\ *adj* : containing, implying, or depending on a condition — **con·di·tion·al·ly** \-ē\ *adv*
con·di·tioned *adj* : determined or established by conditioning
con·dole \kən-ˈdōl\ *vb* **con·doled; con·dol·ing** : to express sympathetic sorrow — **con·do·lence** \kən-ˈdō-ləns, ˈkän-də-\ *n*
con·dom \ˈkän-dəm, ˈkən-\ *n* : a usu. membranous or rubber sheath worn over the penis to prevent pregnancy or the transmission of sexually transmitted disease during sexual intercourse
con·do·min·i·um \ˌkän-də-ˈmin-ē-əm\ *n, pl* **-ums 1** : joint sovereignty (as by two or more nations) **2** : a politically dependent territory under condominium **3** : individual ownership of a unit (as an apartment) in a multiunit structure; *also* : a unit so owned
con·done \kən-ˈdōn\ *vb* **con·doned; con·don·ing** : to overlook or forgive (an offense) by treating the offender as if he had done nothing wrong **syn** excuse, pardon, forgive, remit — **con·do·na·tion** \ˌkän-də-ˈnā-shən\ *n*
con·dor \ˈkän-dər, -ˌdȯr\ *n* [Sp *cóndor*, fr. Quechua (a So. American Indian language) *kúntur*] : a very large American vulture of the high Andes; *also* : a related nearly extinct vulture of southern California now resident only in captivity
con·duce \kən-ˈd(y)üs\ *vb* **con·duced; con·duc·ing** : to lead or contribute to a result — **con·du·cive** *adj*
[1]**con·duct** \ˈkän-(ˌ)dəkt\ *n* **1** : MANAGEMENT, DIRECTION **2** : BEHAVIOR
[2]**con·duct** \kən-ˈdəkt\ *vb* **1** : GUIDE, ESCORT **2** : MANAGE, DIRECT **3** : to act as a medium for conveying **4** : BEHAVE, BEAR — **con·duc·tion** \-ˈdək-shən\ *n*
con·duc·tance \kən-ˈdək-təns\ *n* : the readiness with which a conductor transmits an electric current
con·duc·tive \kən-ˈdək-tiv\ *adj* : having the power to conduct (as heat or electricity) — **con·duc·tiv·i·ty** \ˌkän-ˌdək-ˈtiv-ət-ē\ *n*
con·duc·tor \kən-ˈdək-tər\ *n* **1** : one that conducts **2** : a collector of fares in a public conveyance **3** : the leader of a musical ensemble
con·duit \ˈkän-ˌd(y)ü-ət, -d(w)ət\ *n* **1** : a channel for conveying fluid **2** : a tube or trough for protecting electric wires or cables **3** : a means of transmitting or distributing
con·dyle \ˈkän-ˌdīl, -dᵊl\ *n* : an articular prominence of a bone — **con·dy·lar** \-də-lər\ *adj*
cone \ˈkōn\ *n* **1** : the scaly fruit of trees of the pine family **2** : a solid figure formed by rotating a right triangle about one of its legs **3** : a solid figure that slopes evenly to a point from a usu. circular base **4** : something shaped like a cone
Con·es·to·ga \ˌkän-ə-ˈstō-gə\ *n* : a broad-wheeled covered wagon formerly used for transporting freight across the prairies
co·ney \ˈkō-nē\ *n, pl* **coneys 1** : a rabbit or its fur **2** : PIKA
conf *abbr* conference
con·fab \ˈkän-ˌfab, kən-ˈfab\ *n* : CONFABULATION
con·fab·u·la·tion \kən-ˌfab-yə-ˈlā-shən\ *n* : CHAT; *also* : CONFERENCE
con·fec·tion \kən-ˈfek-shən\ *n* : a fancy dish or sweet; *also* : CANDY
con·fec·tion·er \-sh(ə-)nər\ *n* : a maker of or dealer in confections (as candies)
con·fec·tion·ery \-shə-ˌner-ē\ *n, pl* **-er·ies 1** : sweet foods **2** : a confectioner's place of business
Confed *abbr* Confederate
con·fed·er·a·cy \kən-ˈfed-(ə-)rə-sē\ *n, pl* **-cies 1** : LEAGUE, ALLIANCE **2** *cap* : the 11 southern states that seceded from the U.S. in 1860 and 1861
[1]**con·fed·er·ate** \kən-ˈfed-(ə-)rət\ *adj* **1** : united in a league : ALLIED **2** *cap* : of or relating to the Confederacy
[2]**confederate** *n* **1** : ALLY, ACCOMPLICE **2** *cap* : an adherent of the Confederacy
[3]**con·fed·er·ate** \-ˈfed-ə-ˌrāt\ *vb* **-at·ed; -at·ing** : to unite in a confederacy or a conspiracy
con·fed·er·a·tion \kən-ˌfed-ə-ˈrā-shən\ *n* **1** : an act of confederating : ALLIANCE **2** : LEAGUE
con·fer \kən-ˈfər\ *vb* **con·ferred; con·fer·ring 1** : GRANT,

BESTOW **2** : to exchange views : CONSULT — **con·fer·ee** \ˌkän-fə-ˈrē\ *n*

con·fer·ence \ˈkän-f(ə-)rəns\ *n* : an interchange of views; *also* : a meeting for this purpose

con·fess \kən-ˈfes\ *vb* **1** : to acknowledge or disclose one's misdeed, fault, or sin **2** : to acknowledge one's sins to God or to a priest **3** : to receive the confession of (a penitent) **syn** admit, own, avow, concede, grant

con·fessed·ly \-ˈfes-əd-lē\ *adv* : by confession : ADMITTEDLY

con·fes·sion \-ˈfesh-ən\ *n* **1** : an act of confessing (as in the sacrament of penance) **2** : an acknowledgment of guilt **3** : a formal statement of religious beliefs **4** : a religious body having a common creed — **con·fes·sion·al** *adj*

con·fes·sion·al \-ˈfesh-(ə-)nəl\ *n* : a place where a priest hears confessions

con·fes·sor \kən-ˈfes-ər, *2 also* ˈkän-ˌfes-\ *n* **1** : one that confesses **2** : a priest who hears confessions

con·fet·ti \kən-ˈfet-ē\ *n* [It, pl. of *confetto* sweetmeat, fr. ML *confectum*, fr. L *conficere* to prepare] : bits of colored paper or ribbon for throwing about in celebration

con·fi·dant \ˈkän-fə-ˌdant, -ˌdänt\ *n* : one to whom secrets are confided

con·fide \kən-ˈfīd\ *vb* **con·fid·ed; con·fid·ing** **1** : to have or show faith : TRUST ⟨~ in a friend⟩ **2** : to tell confidentially ⟨~ a secret⟩ **3** : ENTRUST

[1]**con·fi·dence** \ˈkän-fəd-əns\ *n* **1** : TRUST, RELIANCE **2** : SELF-ASSURANCE, BOLDNESS **3** : a state of trust or intimacy — **con·fi·dent** \-fəd-ənt\ *adj* — **con·fi·dent·ly** *adv*

[2]**confidence** *adj* : of or relating to swindling by false promises

con·fi·den·tial \ˌkän-fə-ˈden-chəl\ *adj* **1** : SECRET, PRIVATE **2** : enjoying or treated with confidence ⟨~ clerk⟩ — **con·fi·den·tial·ly** \-ē\ *adv*

con·fig·u·ra·tion \kən-ˌfig-yə-ˈrā-shən\ *n* : structural arrangement of parts : SHAPE

con·fine \kən-ˈfīn\ *vb* **con·fined; con·fin·ing** **1** : to restrict to a particular place or situation **2** : IMPRISON **3** : to keep within limits : RESTRAIN — **con·fine·ment** *n* — **con·fin·er** *n*

con·fines \ˈkän-ˌfīnz\ *n pl* : BOUNDS, BORDERS

con·firm \kən-ˈfərm\ *vb* **1** : to make firm or firmer **2** : RATIFY **3** : to administer the rite of confirmation to **4** : VERIFY, CORROBORATE — **con·fir·ma·to·ry** \-ˈfər-mə-ˌtōr-ē\ *adj* — **con·firmed** *adj*

con·fir·ma·tion \ˌkän-fər-ˈmā-shən\ *n* **1** : a religious ceremony admitting a person to full membership in a church or synagogue **2** : an act of ratifying or corroborating; *also* : PROOF

con·fis·cate \ˈkän-fə-ˌskāt\ *vb* **-cat·ed; -cat·ing** [L *confiscare*, fr. *com-* with + *fiscus* treasury] : to take possession of by or as if by public authority — **con·fis·ca·tion** \ˌkän-fə-ˈskā-shən\ *n* — **con·fis·ca·to·ry** \kən-ˈfis-kə-ˌtōr-ē\ *adj*

con·fla·gra·tion \ˌkän-flə-ˈgrā-shən\ *n* : FIRE; *esp* : a large disastrous fire

[1]**con·flict** \ˈkän-ˌflikt\ *n* **1** : WAR **2** : a clash between hostile or opposing elements or ideas

[2]**con·flict** \kən-ˈflikt\ *vb* : to show antagonism or irreconcilability : CLASH

con·flu·ence \ˈkän-ˌflü-əns, kən-ˈflü-\ *n* **1** : a coming together at one point **2** : the meeting or place of meeting of two or more streams — **con·flu·ent** \-ənt\ *adj*

con·flux \ˈkän-ˌfləks\ *n* : CONFLUENCE

con·fo·cal \kän-ˈfō-kəl\ *adj* : having the same foci — **con·fo·cal·ly** \-ē\ *adv*

con·form \kən-ˈfȯrm\ *vb* **1** : to make or be like : AGREE **2** : to obey customs or standards — **con·form·able** *adj*

con·for·mance \kən-ˈfȯr-məns\ *n* : CONFORMITY

con·for·ma·tion \ˌkän-fȯr-ˈmā-shən\ *n* : arrangement and congruity of parts

con·for·mi·ty \kən-ˈfȯr-mət-ē\ *n, pl* **-ties** **1** : HARMONY, AGREEMENT **2** : COMPLIANCE, OBEDIENCE

con·found \kən-ˈfau̇nd, kän-\ *vb* **1** : to throw into disorder or confusion : DISMAY **2** : to mix up : CONFUSE **syn** bewilder, puzzle, perplex, befog

con·fra·ter·ni·ty \ˌkän-frə-ˈtər-nət-ē\ *n* : a society devoted to a religious or charitable cause

con·frere \ˈkän-ˌfreər, ˈkōⁿ-\ *n* : COLLEAGUE, COMRADE

con·front \kən-ˈfrənt\ *vb* **1** : to face esp. in challenge : OPPOSE **2** : to cause to face or meet — **con·fron·ta·tion** \ˌkän-frən-ˈtā-shən\ *n*

Con·fu·cian·ism \kən-ˈfyü-shən-ˌiz-əm\ *n* : a religion growing out of the teachings of the Chinese philosopher Confucius — **Con·fu·cian** *n or adj*

con·fuse \kən-ˈfyüz\ *vb* **con·fused; con·fus·ing** **1** : to make mentally unclear or uncertain; *also* : to disturb the composure of **2** : to mix up : JUMBLE **syn** muddle, befuddle, addle, fluster — **con·fus·ed·ly** \-ˈfyü-zəd-lē\ *adv*

con·fu·sion \-ˈfyü-zhən\ *n* **1** : DISORDER, JUMBLE **2** : turmoil or uncertainty of mind

con·fute \kən-ˈfyüt\ *vb* **con·fut·ed; con·fut·ing** : to overwhelm by argument : REFUTE — **con·fu·ta·tion** \ˌkän-fyu̇-ˈtā-shən\ *n*

cong *abbr* congress; congressional

con·ga \ˈkäŋ-gə\ *n* : a Cuban dance of African origin performed by a group usu. in single file

con·geal \kən-ˈjēl\ *vb* **1** : FREEZE **2** : to make or become hard or thick

con·ge·ner \ˈkän-jə-nər\ *n* : one related to another; *esp* : one of the same taxonomic genus as another plant or animal — **con·ge·ner·ic** \ˌkän-jə-ˈner-ik\ *adj*

con·ge·nial \kən-ˈjē-nyəl\ *adj* **1** : KINDRED, SYMPATHETIC **2** : suited to one's taste or nature : AGREEABLE — **con·ge·ni·al·i·ty** \-ˌjē-nē-ˈal-ət-ē\ *n* — **con·ge·nial·ly** \-ˈjē-nyə-lē\ *adv*

con·gen·i·tal \kən-ˈjen-ə-tᵊl\ *adj* : existing at or dating from birth but usu. not hereditary **syn** inborn, innate, natural

con·ger eel \ˌkän-gər-\ *n* : a large edible marine eel

con·ge·ries \ˈkän-jə-(ˌ)rēz\ *n, pl* **congeries** *same*\ : AGGREGATION, COLLECTION

con·gest \kən-ˈjest\ *vb* **1** : to cause excessive fullness of the blood vessels of (as a lung) **2** : to obstruct by overcrowding — **con·ges·tion** \-ˈjes-chən\ *n* — **con·ges·tive** \-ˈjes-tiv\ *adj*

[1]**con·glom·er·ate** \kən-ˈgläm-(ə-)rət\ *adj* [L *conglomerare* to roll together, fr. *com-* together + *glomerare* to wind into a ball, fr. *glomer-*, *glomus* ball] : made up of parts from various sources

[2]**con·glom·er·ate** \-ə-ˌrāt\ *vb* **-at·ed; -at·ing** : to form into a ball or mass — **con·glom·er·a·tion** \-ˌgläm-ə-ˈrā-shən\ *n*

[3]**con·glom·er·ate** \-(ə-)rət\ *n* **1** : a mass formed of fragments from various sources; *esp* : a rock composed of fragments varying from pebbles to boulders held together by a cementing material **2** : a widely diversified corporation

con·grat·u·late \kən-ˈgrach-ə-ˌlāt\ *vb* **-lat·ed; -lat·ing** : to express sympathetic pleasure to on account of success or good fortune : FELICITATE — **con·grat·u·la·tion** \-ˌgrach-ə-ˈlā-shən\ *n* — **con·grat·u·la·to·ry** \-ˈgrach-ə-lə-ˌtōr-ē\ *adj*

con·gre·gate \ˈkäŋ-gri-ˌgāt\ *vb* **-gat·ed; -gat·ing** [ME *congregaten*, fr. L *congregare*, fr. *com-* together + *greg-*, *grex* flock] : ASSEMBLE

con·gre·ga·tion \ˌkäŋ-gri-ˈgā-shən\ *n* **1** : an assembly of persons met esp. for worship; *also* : a group that habitually so meets **2** : a company or order of religious per-

\ə\abut \ᵊ\kitten \ər\further \a\ash \ā\ace \ä\cot, cart \au̇\out \ch\chin \e\bet \ē\easy \g\go \i\hit \ī\ice \j\job \ŋ\sing \ō\go \ȯ\law \ȯi\boy \th\thin \th\the \ü\loot \u̇\foot \y\yet \zh\vision *see also* Pronunciation Symbols page

sons under a common rule **3** : the act or an instance of congregating

con·gre·ga·tion·al \-sh(ə-)nəl\ *adj* **1** : of or relating to a congregation **2** *cap* : observing the faith and practice of certain Protestant churches which recognize the independence of each congregation in church matters — **con·gre·ga·tion·al·ism** \-ˌiz-əm\ *n, often cap* — **con·gre·ga·tion·al·ist** \-əst\ *n, often cap*

con·gress \ˈkäŋ-grəs\ *n* **1** : an assembly esp. of delegates for discussion and usu. action on some question **2** : the body of senators and representatives constituting a nation's legislature — **con·gres·sio·nal** \kən-ˈgresh-(ə-)nəl\ *adj*

con·gress·man \ˈkäŋ-grəs-mən\ *n* : a member of a congress

con·gress·wom·an \-ˌwu̇m-ən\ *n* : a female member of a congress

con·gru·ence \kən-ˈgrü-əns, ˈkäŋ-grə-wəns\ *n* : the quality of according or coinciding : CONGRUITY — **con·gru·ent** \kən-ˈgrü-ənt, ˈkäŋ-grə-wənt\ *adj*

con·gru·en·cy \-ən-sē, -wən-\ *n, pl* **-cies** : CONGRUENCE

con·gru·ity \kən-ˈgrü-ət-ē, kän-\ *n, pl* **-ities** : correspondence between things — **con·gru·ous** \ˈkäŋ-grə-wəs\ *adj*

con·ic \ˈkän-ik\ *adj* **1** : of or relating to a cone **2** : CONICAL

con·i·cal \ˈkän-i-kəl\ *adj* : resembling a cone esp. in shape

co·ni·fer \ˈkän-ə-fər, ˈkōn-\ *n* : any of an order of shrubs or trees (as the pines) that usu. are evergreen and bear cones — **co·nif·er·ous** \kō-ˈnif-(ə-)rəs\ *adj*

conj *abbr* conjunction

con·jec·ture \kən-ˈjek-chər\ *n* : GUESS, SURMISE — **con·jec·tur·al** \-chə-rəl\ *adj* — **conjecture** *vb*

con·join \kən-ˈjȯin\ *vb* : to join together — **con·joint** \-ˈjȯint\ *adj*

con·ju·gal \ˈkän-ji-gəl, kən-ˈjü-\ *adj* : of or relating to marriage : MATRIMONIAL

[1]**con·ju·gate** \ˈkän-ji-gət, -jə-ˌgāt\ *adj* **1** : united esp. in pairs : COUPLED **2** : of kindred origin and meaning ⟨*sing* and *song* are ~⟩

[2]**con·ju·gate** \-jə-ˌgāt\ *vb* **-gat·ed; -gat·ing 1** : INFLECT ⟨~ a verb⟩ **2** : to join together : COUPLE

con·ju·ga·tion \ˌkän-jə-ˈgā-shən\ *n* **1** : a schematic arrangement of the inflectional forms of a verb **2** : the act of conjugating : the state of being conjugated

con·junct \kən-ˈjəŋkt, kän-\ *adj* : JOINED, UNITED

con·junc·tion \kən-ˈjəŋk-shən\ *n* **1** : UNION, COMBINATION **2** : occurrence at the same time **3** : a word that joins together sentences, clauses, phrases, or words

con·junc·ti·va \ˌkän-ˌjəŋk-ˈtī-və\ *n, pl* **-vas** *or* **-vae** \-(ˌ)vē\ : the mucous membrane lining the inner surface of the eyelids and continuing over the forepart of the eyeball

con·junc·tive \kən-ˈjəŋk-tiv\ *adj* **1** : CONNECTIVE **2** : CONJUNCT **3** : being or functioning like a conjunction

con·junc·ti·vi·tis \kən-ˌjəŋk-ti-ˈvīt-əs\ *n* : inflammation of the conjunctiva

con·junc·ture \kən-ˈjəŋk-chər\ *n* **1** : CONJUNCTION, UNION **2** : a combination of circumstances or events esp. producing a crisis

con·jure \ˈkän-jər, ˈkən- *for 1, 2;* kən-ˈju̇r *for 3*\ *vb* **con·jured; con·jur·ing** \ˈkänj-(ə-)riŋ, ˈkənj-; kən-ˈju̇(ə)r-iŋ\ **1** : to implore earnestly or solemnly **2** : to practice magic; *esp* : to summon (as a devil) by sorcery **3** : to practice sleight of hand — **con·ju·ra·tion** \ˌkän-ju̇-ˈrā-shən, ˌkən-\ *n* — **con·jur·er** *or* **con·ju·ror** \ˈkän-jər-ər, ˈkən-\ *n*

conk \ˈkäŋk\ *vb* : BREAK DOWN; *esp* : STALL ⟨the motor ~*ed* out⟩

Conn *abbr* Connecticut

con·nect \kə-ˈnekt\ *vb* **1** : JOIN, LINK **2** : to associate in one's mind — **con·nec·tor** *n*

con·nec·tion \kə-ˈnek-shən\ *n* **1** : JUNCTION, UNION **2** : logical relationship : COHERENCE; *esp* : relation of a word to other words in a sentence **3** : family relationship **4** : BOND, LINK **5** : a person related by blood or marriage **6** : relationship in social affairs or in business **7** : an association of persons; *esp* : a religious denomination

[1]**con·nec·tive** \kə-ˈnek-tiv\ *adj* : connecting or functioning in connecting — **con·nec·tiv·i·ty** \ˌkä-ˌnek-ˈtiv-ət-ē\ *n*

[2]**connective** *n* : a word (as a conjunction) that connects words or word groups

con·nip·tion \kə-ˈnip-shən\ *n* : a fit of rage, hysteria, or alarm

con·nive \kə-ˈnīv\ *vb* **con·nived; con·niv·ing** [F or L; F *conniver,* fr. L *conivēre* to close the eyes, connive] **1** : to pretend ignorance of something one ought to oppose as wrong **2** : to cooperate secretly : give secret aid — **con·niv·ance** *n*

con·nois·seur \ˌkän-ə-ˈsər\ *n* : a critical judge in matters of art or taste

con·no·ta·tion \ˌkän-ə-ˈtā-shən\ *n* : a meaning in addition to or apart from the thing explicitly named or described by a word

con·no·ta·tive \ˈkän-ə-ˌtāt-iv, kə-ˈnōt-ət-\ *adj* **1** : connoting or tending to connote **2** : relating to connotation

con·note \kə-ˈnōt\ *vb* **con·not·ed; con·not·ing** : to suggest or mean along with or in addition to the explicit meaning

con·nu·bi·al \kə-ˈn(y)ü-bē-əl\ *adj* : of or relating to marriage : CONJUGAL

con·quer \ˈkäŋ-kər\ *vb* **con·quered; con·quer·ing** \-k(ə-)riŋ\ **1** : to gain by force of arms : WIN **2** : to get the better of : OVERCOME **syn** defeat, subjugate, subdue, overthrow, vanquish — **con·quer·or** \-kər-ər\ *n*

con·quest \ˈkän-ˌkwest, ˈkäŋ-\ *n* **1** : an act of conquering : VICTORY **2** : something conquered

con·quis·ta·dor \kȯŋ-ˈkēs-tə-ˌdȯr, kän-ˈk(w)is-\ *n, pl* **con·quis·ta·do·res** \-ˌkēs-tə-ˈdȯr-ēz, -ˌk(w)is-\ *or* **con·quis·ta·dors** : CONQUEROR; *esp* : a leader in the Spanish conquest of America and esp. of Mexico and Peru in the 16th century

cons *abbr* consonant

con·san·guin·i·ty \ˌkän-ˌsan-ˈgwin-ət-ē, -ˌsaŋ-\ *n, pl* **-ties** : blood relationship — **con·san·guin·e·ous** \-ˈgwin-ē-əs\ *adj*

con·science \ˈkän-chəns\ *n* : consciousness of the moral right and wrong of one's own acts or motives — **con·science·less** *adj*

con·sci·en·tious \ˌkän-chē-ˈen-chəs\ *adj* : guided by one's own sense of right and wrong **syn** scrupulous, honorable, honest, upright, just — **con·sci·en·tious·ly** *adv*

conscientious objector *n* : one who refuses to serve in the armed forces or to bear arms on moral or religious grounds

con·scious \ˈkän-chəs\ *adj* **1** : AWARE **2** : known or felt by one's inner self **3** : mentally awake or alert : not asleep or unconscious **4** : INTENTIONAL — **con·scious·ly** *adv* — **con·scious·ness** *n*

con·script \kən-ˈskript\ *vb* : to enroll by compulsion for military or naval service — **con·script** \ˈkän-ˌskript\ *n* — **con·scrip·tion** \kən-ˈskrip-shən\ *n*

con·se·crate \ˈkän-sə-ˌkrāt\ *vb* **-crat·ed; -crat·ing 1** : to induct (as a bishop) into an office with a religious rite **2** : to make or declare sacred ⟨~ a church⟩ **3** : to devote solemnly to a purpose — **con·se·cra·tion** \ˌkän-sə-ˈkrā-shən\ *n*

con·sec·u·tive \kən-ˈsek-(y)ət-iv\ *adj* : following in regular order : SUCCESSIVE — **con·sec·u·tive·ly** *adv*

con·sen·su·al \kən-ˈsench-(ə-)wel, -ˈsen-shəl\ *adj* : involving or based on mutual consent

con·sen·sus \kən-ˈsen-səs\ *n* **1** : agreement in opinion, testimony, or belief **2** : collective opinion

[1]**con·sent** \kən-ˈsent\ *vb* : to give assent or approval

[2]**consent** *n* : approval or acceptance of something done or proposed by another

con·se·quence \ˈkän-sə-ˌkwens\ *n* **1** : RESULT **2** : IMPORTANCE **syn** effect, outcome, aftermath, upshot

con·se·quent \-kwənt, -ˌkwent\ *adj* : following as a result or effect

con·se·quen·tial \ˌkän-sə-ˈkwen-chəl\ *adj* **1** : having significant consequences **2** : showing self-importance

con·se·quent·ly \ˈkän-sə-ˌkwent-lē, -kwənt-\ *adv* : as a result : ACCORDINGLY

con·ser·van·cy \kən-ˈsər-vən-sē\ *n, pl* **-cies** : an organization or area designated to conserve and protect natural resources

con·ser·va·tion \ˌkän-sər-ˈvā-shən\ *n* : PRESERVATION; *esp* : planned management of natural resources

con·ser·va·tion·ist \-sh(ə-)nəst\ *n* : a person who advocates conservation esp. of natural resources

con·ser·va·tism \kən-ˈsər-və-ˌtiz-əm\ *n* : disposition to keep to established ways : opposition to change

[1]**con·ser·va·tive** \kən-ˈsər-vət-iv\ *adj* **1** : PRESERVATIVE **2** : disposed to maintain existing views, conditions, or institutions **3** : MODERATE, CAUTIOUS — **con·ser·va·tive·ly** *adv*

[2]**conservative** *n* : a person who is conservative esp. in politics

con·ser·va·tor \kən-ˈsər-vət-ər, ˈkän-sər-ˌvāt-\ *n* **1** : PROTECTOR, GUARDIAN **2** : one named by a court to protect the interests of an incompetent (as a child)

con·ser·va·to·ry \kən-ˈsər-və-ˌtōr-ē\ *n, pl* **-ries** **1** : GREENHOUSE **2** : a place of instruction in one of the fine arts (as music)

[1]**con·serve** \kən-ˈsərv\ *vb* **con·served; con·serv·ing** : to keep from losing or wasting : PRESERVE

[2]**con·serve** \ˈkän-ˌsərv\ *n* **1** : CONFECTION; *esp* : a candied fruit **2** : PRESERVE; *esp* : one prepared from a mixture of fruits

con·sid·er \kən-ˈsid-ər\ *vb* **-ered; -er·ing** \-(ə-)riŋ\ [ME *consideren,* fr. MF *considerer,* fr. L *considerare,* lit., to observe the stars, fr. *sider-, sidus* star] **1** : THINK, PONDER **2** : HEED, REGARD **3** : JUDGE, BELIEVE — **con·sid·ered** *adj*

con·sid·er·able \-ˈsid-ər(-ə)-bəl, -ˈsid-rə-bəl\ *adj* **1** : IMPORTANT **2** : large in extent, amount, or degree — **con·sid·er·ably** \-blē\ *adv*

con·sid·er·ate \kən-ˈsid-(ə-)rət\ *adj* : observant of the rights and feelings of others **syn** thoughtful, attentive

con·sid·er·ation \kən-ˌsid-ə-ˈrā-shən\ *n* **1** : careful thought : DELIBERATION **2** : a matter taken into account **3** : thoughtful attention **4** : JUDGMENT, OPINION **5** : RECOMPENSE

con·sid·er·ing \-(ə-)riŋ\ *prep* : in view of : taking into account

con·sign \kən-ˈsīn\ *vb* **1** : ENTRUST, COMMIT **2** : to deliver formally **3** : to send (goods) to an agent for sale — **con·sign·ee** \ˌkän-sə-ˈnē, -ˌsī-; kən-ˌsī-\ *n* — **con·sign·or** \ˌkän-sə-ˈnȯr, -ˌsī-; kən-ˌsī-\ *n*

con·sign·ment \kən-ˈsīn-mənt\ *n* : something consigned esp. in a single shipment

con·sist \kən-ˈsist\ *vb* **1** : to be inherent : LIE — used with *in* **2** : to be composed or made up

con·sis·tence \kən-ˈsis-təns\ *n* : CONSISTENCY

con·sis·ten·cy \-tən-sē\ *n, pl* **-cies** **1** : COHESIVENESS, FIRMNESS **2** : agreement or harmony in parts or of different things **3** : UNIFORMITY ⟨~ of behavior⟩ — **con·sis·tent** \-tənt\ *adj* — **con·sis·tent·ly** *adv*

con·sis·to·ry \kən-ˈsis-t(ə-)rē\ *n, pl* **-ries** : a solemn assembly (as of Roman Catholic cardinals)

consol *abbr* consolidated

[1]**con·sole** \ˈkän-ˌsōl\ *n* **1** : the desk-like part of an organ at which the organist sits **2** : a panel or cabinet for the controls of an electronic or mechanical device **3** : a cabinet for a radio or television set resting directly on the floor **4** : a small storage cabinet between bucket seats in an automobile

[2]**con·sole** \kən-ˈsōl\ *vb* **con·soled; con·sol·ing** : to soothe the grief of : COMFORT, SOLACE — **con·so·la·tion** \ˌkän-sə-ˈlā-shən\ *n* — **con·so·la·to·ry** \kən-ˈsōl-ə-ˌtōr-ē, -ˈsäl-\ *adj*

con·sol·i·date \kən-ˈsäl-ə-ˌdāt\ *vb* **-dat·ed; -dat·ing** **1** : to unite or become united into one whole : COMBINE **2** : to make firm or secure **3** : to form into a compact mass — **con·sol·i·da·tion** \-ˌsäl-ə-ˈdā-shən\ *n*

con·som·mé \ˌkän-sə-ˈmā\ *n* [F] : a clear soup made from well-seasoned meat broth

con·so·nance \ˈkän-s(ə-)nəns\ *n* **1** : AGREEMENT, HARMONY **2** : repetition of consonants esp. as an alternative to rhyme in verse

[1]**con·so·nant** \-s(ə-)nənt\ *adj* : having consonance, harmony, or agreement **syn** consistent, compatible, congruous, congenial, sympathetic, agreeable

[2]**consonant** *n* **1** : a speech sound (as \p\, \g\, \n\, \l\, \s\, \r\) characterized by constriction or closure at one or more points in the breath channel **2** : a letter other than *a, e, i, o,* and *u* — **con·so·nan·tal** \ˌkän-sə-ˈnant-ᵊl\ *adj*

[1]**con·sort** \ˈkän-ˌsȯrt\ *n* **1** : a ship accompanying another **2** : SPOUSE, MATE

[2]**con·sort** \kən-ˈsȯrt\ *vb* **1** : to keep company **2** : ACCORD, HARMONIZE

con·sor·tium \kən-ˈsȯrt-ē-əm, -ˈsȯr-sh(ē-)əm\ *n, pl* **-sor·tia** \-ˈsȯrt-ē-ə, -ˈsȯr-sh(ē-)ə\ [L, fellowship] : an international business or banking agreement or combination

con·spec·tus \kən-ˈspek-təs\ *n* **1** : a brief survey or summary **2** : OUTLINE, SYNOPSIS

con·spic·u·ous \kən-ˈspik-yə-wəs\ *adj* : attracting attention : PROMINENT, STRIKING **syn** noticeable, remarkable, outstanding — **con·spic·u·ous·ly** *adv*

con·spir·a·cy \kən-ˈspir-ə-sē\ *n, pl* **-cies** : an agreement among conspirators : PLOT

con·spire \kən-ˈspī(ə)r\ *vb* **conspired; con·spir·ing** : to plan secretly an unlawful act : PLOT — **con·spir·a·tor** \-ˈspir-ət-ər\ *n*

const *abbr* **1** constant **2** constitution; constitutional

con·sta·ble \ˈkän-stə-bəl, ˈkən-\ *n* [ME *conestable,* fr. OF, fr. LL *comes stabuli,* lit., officer of the stable] : a public officer responsible for keeping the peace

con·stab·u·lary \kən-ˈstab-yə-, ˌler-ē\ *n, pl* **-lar·ies** **1** : the police of a particular district or country **2** : a police force organized like the military

con·stan·cy \ˈkän-stən-sē\ *n, pl* **-cies** **1** : firmness of mind **2** : STABILITY

[1]**con·stant** \-stənt\ *adj* **1** : STEADFAST, FAITHFUL **2** : FIXED, UNCHANGING **3** : continually recurring : REGULAR — **con·stant·ly** *adv*

[2]**constant** *n* : something unchanging

con·stel·la·tion \ˌkän-stə-ˈlā-shən\ *n* : any of 88 groups of stars forming patterns

con·ster·na·tion \ˌkän-stər-ˈnā-shən\ *n* : amazed dismay and confusion

con·sti·pa·tion \ˌkän-stə-ˈpā-shən\ *n* : abnormally difficult or infrequent bowel movements — **con·sti·pate** \ˈkän-stə-ˌpāt\ *vb*

con·stit·u·en·cy \kən-ˈstich-ə-wən-sē\ *n, pl* **-cies** : a body of constituents; *also* : an electoral district

[1]**con·stit·u·ent** \-wənt\ *n* **1** : one entitled to vote for a representative for a district **2** : a component part

[2]**constituent** *adj* **1** : COMPONENT **2** : having power to create a government or frame or revise a constitution

con·sti·tute \ˈkän-stə-ˌt(y)üt\ *vb* **-tut·ed; -tut·ing** **1** : to appoint to an office or duty **2** : SET UP, ESTABLISH ⟨~ a law⟩ **3** : MAKE UP, COMPOSE

con·sti·tu·tion \ˌkän-stə-ˈt(y)ü-shən\ *n* **1** : an established law or custom **2** : the physical makeup of the individual **3** : the structure, composition, or makeup of something ⟨~ of the sun⟩ **4** : the basic law in a politically organized body; *also* : a document containing such law

[1]**con·sti·tu·tion·al** \-sh(ə-)nəl\ *adj* **1** : of or relating to the constitution of body or mind **2** : of or relating to the

---

\ə\abut \ᵊ\kitten \ər\further \a\ash \ā\ace \ä\cot, cart \au̇\out \ch\chin \e\bet \ē\easy \g\go \i\hit \ī\ice \j\job \ŋ\sing \ō\go \ȯ\law \ȯi\boy \th\thin \th\the \ü\loot \u̇\foot \y\yet \zh\vision *see also* Pronunciation Symbols page

constitution of a state or society — **con·sti·tu·tion·al·ly** \-ē\ *adv*

[2]**constitutional** *n* : an exercise (as a walk) taken for one's health

con·sti·tu·tion·al·i·ty \-ˌt(y)ü-shə-ˈnal-ət-ē\ *n* : the condition of being in accordance with the constitution of a state or society

con·sti·tu·tive \ˈkän-stə-ˌt(y)üt-iv, kən-ˈstich-ət-iv\ *adj* : CONSTITUENT, ESSENTIAL

constr *abbr* construction

con·strain \kən-ˈstrān\ *vb* **1** : COMPEL, FORCE **2** : CONFINE **3** : RESTRAIN

con·straint \-ˈstrānt\ *n* **1** : COMPULSION; *also* : RESTRAINT **2** : unnaturalness of manner produced by a repression of one's natural feelings

con·strict \kən-ˈstrikt\ *vb* : to draw together : SQUEEZE — **con·stric·tion** \-ˈstrik-shən\ *n* — **con·stric·tive** \-ˈstrik-tiv\ *adj*

con·stric·tor \kən-ˈstrikt-ər\ *n* : a snake that suffocates its prey by crushing in its coils

con·struct \kən-ˈstrəkt\ *vb* : BUILD, MAKE — **con·struc·tor** \-ˈstrək-tər\ *n*

con·struc·tion \kən-ˈstrək-shən\ *n* **1** : INTERPRETATION **2** : the art, process, or manner of building; *also* : something built : STRUCTURE **3** : syntactical arrangement of words in a sentence — **con·struc·tive** \-tiv\ *adj*

con·struc·tion·ist \-sh(ə-)nəst\ *n* : one who construes a legal document (as the U.S. Constitution) in a specific way ⟨a strict ~⟩

con·strue \kən-ˈstrü\ *vb* **con·strued; con·stru·ing** **1** : to explain the mutual relations of words in a sentence; *also* : TRANSLATE **2** : EXPLAIN, INTERPRET — **con·stru·able** *adj*

con·sub·stan·ti·a·tion \ˌkän-səb-ˌstan-chē-ˈā-shən\ *n* : the actual substantial presence and combination of the body of Christ with the eucharistic bread and wine

con·sul \ˈkän-səl\ *n* **1** : a chief magistrate of the Roman republic **2** : an official appointed by a government to reside in a foreign country to care for the commercial interests of that government's citizens — **con·sul·ar** \-sə-lər\ *adj* — **con·sul·ate** \-lət\ *n* — **con·sul·ship** *n*

con·sult \kən-ˈsəlt\ *vb* **1** : to ask the advice or opinion of **2** : CONFER — **con·sul·tant** \-ᵊnt\ *n* — **con·sul·ta·tion** \ˌkän-səl-ˈtā-shən\ *n*

con·sume \kən-ˈsüm\ *vb* **con·sumed; con·sum·ing** **1** : DESTROY ⟨*consumed* by fire⟩ **2** : to spend wastefully **3** : to eat up : DEVOUR **4** : to absorb the attention of : ENGROSS — **con·sum·able** *adj* — **con·sum·er** *n*

con·sum·er·ism \kən-ˈsü-mə-ˌriz-əm\ *n* : the promotion of consumers' interests (as against false advertising)

[1]**con·sum·mate** \kən-ˈsəm-ət\ *adj* : COMPLETE, PERFECT **syn** finished, accomplished

[2]**con·sum·mate** \ˈkän-sə-ˌmāt\ *vb* **-mat·ed; -mat·ing** : to make complete : FINISH, ACHIEVE — **con·sum·ma·tion** \ˌkän-sə-ˈmā-shən\ *n*

con·sump·tion \kən-ˈsəmp-shən\ *n* **1** : progressive bodily wasting away; *also* : TUBERCULOSIS **2** : the act of consuming or using up **3** : the use of economic goods

[1]**con·sump·tive** \-ˈsəmp-tiv\ *adj* **1** : tending to consume **2** : relating to or affected with consumption

[2]**consumptive** *n* : a person who has consumption

cont *abbr* **1** containing **2** contents **3** continent; continental **4** continued **5** control

[1]**con·tact** \ˈkän-ˌtakt\ *n* **1** : a touching or meeting of bodies **2** : ASSOCIATION, RELATIONSHIP; *also* : CONNECTION, COMMUNICATION **3** : CONTACT LENS

[2]**contact** *vb* **1** : to come or bring into contact : TOUCH **2** : to get in communication with

contact lens *n* : a thin lens fitting over the cornea

con·ta·gion \kən-ˈtā-jən\ *n* **1** : the passing of disease by contact **2** : a contagious disease; *also* : its causative agent **3** : transmission of an influence on the mind or emotions

con·ta·gious \-jəs\ *adj* **1** : communicable by contact; *also* : relating to contagion or to contagious diseases **2** : exciting similar emotion or conduct in others

con·tain \kən-ˈtān\ *vb* **1** : RESTRAIN **2** : to have within : HOLD **3** : COMPRISE, INCLUDE — **con·tain·ment** *n*

con·tain·er \kən-ˈtā-nər\ *n* : RECEPTACLE; *esp* : one for shipment of goods

con·tain·er·ship \-nər-ˌship\ *n* : a ship esp. designed or equipped for carrying very large containers of cargo

con·tam·i·nant \kən-ˈtam-ə-nənt\ *n* : something that contaminates

con·tam·i·nate \kən-ˈtam-ə-ˌnāt\ *vb* **-nat·ed; -nat·ing** : to soil, stain, or infect by contact or association — **con·tam·i·na·tion** \-ˌtam-ə-ˈnā-shən\ *n*

contd *abbr* continued

con·temn \kən-ˈtem\ *vb* : to view or treat with contempt

con·tem·plate \ˈkänt-əm-ˌplāt\ *vb* **-plat·ed; -plat·ing** [L *contemplari*, fr. *templum* space marked out for observation of auguries] **1** : to view or consider with continued attention **2** : INTEND — **con·tem·pla·tion** \ˌkänt-əm-ˈplā-shən\ *n* — **con·tem·pla·tive** \kən-ˈtem-plət-iv; ˈkänt-əm-ˌplāt-\ *adj*

con·tem·po·ra·ne·ous \kən-ˌtem-pə-ˈrā-nē-əs\ *adj* : CONTEMPORARY

con·tem·po·rary \kən-ˈtem-pə-ˌrer-ē\ *adj* **1** : occurring or existing at the same time **2** : marked by characteristics of the present period — **contemporary** *n*

con·tempt \kən-ˈtempt\ *n* **1** : the act of despising : the state of mind of one who despises : DISDAIN **2** : the state of being despised **3** : disobedience to or open disrespect of a court or legislature

con·tempt·ible \kən-ˈtemp-tə-bəl\ *adj* : deserving contempt : DESPICABLE — **con·tempt·ibly** \-blē\ *adv*

con·temp·tu·ous \-ˈtemp-chə(-wə)s\ *adj* : feeling or expressing contempt — **con·temp·tu·ous·ly** *adv*

con·tend \kən-ˈtend\ *vb* **1** : to strive against rivals or difficulties; *also* : ARGUE, DEBATE **2** : MAINTAIN, ASSERT — **con·tend·er** *n*

[1]**con·tent** \kən-ˈtent\ *adj* : SATISFIED

[2]**content** *vb* : SATISFY; *esp* : to limit (oneself) in requirements or actions

[3]**content** *n* : CONTENTMENT

[4]**con·tent** \ˈkän-ˌtent\ *n* **1** : something contained ⟨~*s* of a room⟩ ⟨~*s* of a bottle⟩ **2** : subject matter or topics treated (as in a book) **3** : MEANING, SIGNIFICANCE **4** : the amount of material contained

con·tent·ed \kən-ˈtent-əd\ *adj* : SATISFIED — **con·tent·ed·ly** *adv* — **con·tent·ed·ness** *n*

con·ten·tion \kən-ˈten-chən\ *n* **1** : CONTEST, STRIFE **2** : an idea or point for which a person argues — **con·ten·tious** \-chəs\ *adj*

con·tent·ment \kən-ˈtent-mənt\ *n* : ease of mind : SATISFACTION

con·ter·mi·nous \kən-ˈtər-mə-nəs, kän-\ *adj* : having the same or a common boundary — **con·ter·mi·nous·ly** *adv*

[1]**con·test** \kən-ˈtest\ *vb* **1** : to engage in strife : FIGHT **2** : CHALLENGE, DISPUTE — **con·tes·tant** \-ˈtes-tənt\ *n*

[2]**con·test** \ˈkän-ˌtest\ *n* : STRUGGLE, COMPETITION

con·text \ˈkän-ˌtekst\ *n* [ME, weaving together of words, fr. L *contextus* coherence, fr. *contexere* to weave together] : the part of a discourse surrounding a word or group of words that helps to explain the meaning of the word or word group; *also* : the circumstances surrounding an act or event

con·tig·u·ous \kən-ˈtig-yə-wəs\ *adj* : being in contact : TOUCHING; *also* : NEXT, ADJOINING — **con·ti·gu·i·ty** \ˌkänt-ə-ˈgyü-ət-ē\ *n*

con·ti·nence \ˈkänt-ᵊn-əns\ *n* **1** : SELF-RESTRAINT; *esp* : voluntary refraining from sexual intercourse **2** : the ability to retain urine or feces voluntarily within the body — **con·ti·nent** \-ᵊn-ənt\ *adj*

con·ti·nent \ˈkänt-(ᵊ-)nənt\ *n* **1** : one of the great divisions of land on the globe **2** *cap* : the continent of Europe

[1]**con·ti·nen·tal** \ˌkänt-ᵊn-ˈent-ᵊl\ *adj* **1** : of or relating to a

continent; *esp, often cap* : of or relating to the continent of Europe **2** *often cap* : of or relating to the colonies later forming the U.S.

[2]**continental** *n* **1** *often cap* : a soldier in the Continental army **2** : EUROPEAN

continental shelf *n* : a shallow submarine plain forming a border to a continent

continental slope *n* : a usu. steep slope from a continental shelf to the ocean floor

con·tin·gen·cy \kən-ˈtin-jən-sē\ *n, pl* **-cies** : a chance or possible event

[1]**con·tin·gent** \-jənt\ *adj* **1** : liable but not certain to happen : POSSIBLE **2** : happening by chance : not planned **3** : dependent on something that may or may not occur **4** : CONDITIONAL **syn** accidental, casual, incidental, odd

[2]**contingent** *n* : a quota (as of troops) supplied from an area or group

con·tin·u·al \kən-ˈtin-yə(-wə)l\ *adj* **1** : CONTINUOUS, UNBROKEN **2** : steadily recurring — **con·tin·u·al·ly** \-ē\ *adv*

con·tin·u·ance \-yə-wəns\ *n* **1** : unbroken succession **2** : a continuing in a state or course of action : DURATION **3** : adjournment of legal proceedings

con·tin·u·a·tion \kən-ˌtin-yə-ˈwā-shən\ *n* **1** : extension or prolongation of a state or activity **2** : resumption after an interruption; *also* : something that carries on after a pause or break

con·tin·ue \kən-ˈtin-yü\ *vb* **-tin·ued; -tinu·ing 1** : PERSEVERE **2** : ENDURE, LAST **3** : to remain in a place or condition : ABIDE, STAY **4** : to resume (as a story) after an intermission **5** : EXTEND; *also* : to persist in **6** : to allow to remain **7** : to keep (a legal case) on the calendar or undecided

con·ti·nu·ity \ˌkänt-ən-ˈ(y)ü-ət-ē\ *n, pl* **-ities 1** : the condition of being continuous **2** : something that has or provides continuity

con·tin·u·ous \kən-ˈtin-yə-wəs\ *adj* : continuing without interruption : UNBROKEN — **con·tin·u·ous·ly** *adv*

con·tin·u·um \-yə-wəm\ *n, pl* **-ua** \-yə-wə\ *also* **-u·ums** : something that is the same throughout or consists of a series of variations or of a sequence of things in regular order

con·tort \kən-ˈtȯrt\ *vb* : to twist out of shape — **con·tor·tion** \-ˈtȯr-shən\ *n*

con·tor·tion·ist \-ˈtȯr-sh(ə-)nəst\ *n* : an acrobat able to twist the body into unusual postures

con·tour \ˈkän-ˌtu̇r\ *n* [F, fr. It *contorno* fr. *contornare* to round off, sketch in outline, fr. L *com-* together + *tornare* to turn in a lathe, fr. *tornus* lathe] **1** : OUTLINE **2** : SHAPE, FORM — often used in pl. ⟨the ∼*s* of a statue⟩

contr *abbr* contract; contraction

con·tra·band \ˈkän-trə-ˌband\ *n* : goods legally prohibited in trade; *also* : smuggled goods

con·tra·cep·tion \ˌkän-trə-ˈsep-shən\ *n* : intentional prevention of conception and pregnancy — **con·tra·cep·tive** \-ˈsep-tive\ *adj or n*

[1]**con·tract** \ˈkän-ˌtrakt\ *n* **1** : a binding agreement : COVENANT **2** : an undertaking to win a specified number of tricks in contract bridge — **con·trac·tu·al** \kən-ˈtrak-chə(-wə)l\ *adj* — **con·trac·tu·al·ly** \-ē\ *adv*

[2]**con·tract** \kən-ˈtrakt, *1 usu* ˈkän-ˌtrakt\ *vb* **1** : to become affected with ⟨∼ a disease⟩ **2** : to establish or undertake by contract **3** : SHRINK, LESSEN; *esp* : to draw together esp. so as to shorten ⟨∼ a muscle⟩ **4** : to shorten (a word) by omitting letters or sounds in the middle — **con·trac·tion** \kən-ˈtrak-shən\ *n* — **con·trac·tor** \ˈkän-ˌtrak-tər, kən-ˈtrak-\ *n*

con·trac·tile \kən-ˈtrak-tᵊl\ *adj* : able to contract — **con·trac·til·i·ty** \ˌkän-ˌtrak-ˈtil-ət-ē\ *n*

con·tra·dict \ˌkän-trə-ˈdikt\ *vb* : to state the contrary of : deny the truth of — **con·tra·dic·tion** \-ˈdik-shən\ *n* — **con·tra·dic·to·ry** \-ˈdik-t(ə-)rē\ *adj*

con·tra·dis·tinc·tion \ˌkän-trə-dis-ˈtiŋk-shən\ *n* : distinction by contrast

con·trail \ˈkän-ˌtrāl\ *n* : streaks of condensed water vapor created in the air by an airplane or rocket at high altitudes

con·tral·to \kən-ˈtral-tō\ *n, pl* **-tos** : the lowest female voice; *also* : a singer having such a voice

con·trap·tion \kən-ˈtrap-shən\ *n* : CONTRIVANCE, DEVICE

con·tra·pun·tal \ˌkän-trə-ˈpənt-ᵊl\ *adj* : of or relating to counterpoint

con·tra·ri·ety \ˌkän-trə-ˈrī-ət-ē\ *n, pl* **-eties** : the state of being contrary : DISAGREEMENT, INCONSISTENCY

con·trari·wise \ˈkän-ˌtrer-ē-ˌwīz, kən-ˈtrer-\ *adv* **1** : on the contrary **2** : VICE VERSA

con·trary \ˈkän-ˌtrer-ē; *4 often* kən-ˈtre(ə)r-ē\ *adj* **1** : opposite in nature or position **2** : COUNTER, OPPOSED **3** : UNFAVORABLE **4** : unwilling to accept control or advice — **con·trari·ly** \-ˌtrer-ə-lē, -ˈtrer-\ *adv* — **con·trary** *n* ˈkän-ˌtrer-ē, *adv like adj*\ *n or adv*

[1]**con·trast** \kən-ˈtrast\ *vb* [F *contraster,* fr. MF, to oppose, resist, fr. (assumed) VL *contrastare,* fr. L *contra-* against + *stare* to stand] **1** : to show differences when compared **2** : to compare in such a way as to show differences

[2]**con·trast** \ˈkän-ˌtrast\ *n* **1** : diversity of adjacent parts in color, emotion, tone, or brightness ⟨the ∼ of a photograph⟩ **2** : unlikeness as shown when things are compared : DIFFERENCE

con·tra·vene \ˌkän-trə-ˈvēn\ *vb* **-vened; -ven·ing 1** : to go or act contrary to ⟨∼ a law⟩ **2** : CONTRADICT

con·tre·temps \ˈkän-trə-ˌtäⁿ, kōⁿ-trə-täⁿ\ *n, pl* **con·tre·temps** \-ˌtäⁿ(z)\ : an inopportune embarrassing occurrence

contrib *abbr* contribution; contributor

con·trib·ute \kən-ˈtrib-yət\ *vb* **-ut·ed; -ut·ing** : to give along with others (as to a fund) : supply or furnish a share to : HELP, ASSIST — **con·tri·bu·tion** \ˌkän-trə-ˈbyü-shən\ *n* — **con·trib·u·tor** \kən-ˈtrib-yət-ər\ *n* — **con·trib·u·to·ry** \-yə-ˌtōr-ē\ *adj*

con·trite \ˈkän-ˌtrīt, kən-ˈtrīt\ *adj* : PENITENT, REPENTANT — **con·tri·tion** \kən-ˈtrish-ən\ *n*

con·triv·ance \kən-ˈtrī-vəns\ *n* **1** : a mechanical device : APPLIANCE **2** : SCHEME, PLAN

con·trive \kən-ˈtrīv\ *vb* **con·trived; con·triv·ing 1** : PLAN, DEVISE **2** : FRAME, MAKE **3** : to bring about with difficulty — **con·triv·er** *n*

[1]**con·trol** \kən-ˈtrōl\ *vb* **con·trolled; con·trol·ling 1** : to exercise restraining or directing influence over : REGULATE **2** : DOMINATE, RULE

[2]**control** *n* **1** : power to direct or regulate **2** : RESERVE, RESTRAINT **3** : a device for regulating a mechanism

con·trol·ler \kən-ˈtrō-lər, ˈkän-ˌtrō-lər\ *n* **1** : COMPTROLLER **2** : one that controls

con·tro·ver·sy \ˈkän-trə-ˌvər-sē\ *n, pl* **-sies** : a clash of opposing views : DISPUTE — **con·tro·ver·sial** \ˌkän-trə-ˌvər-shəl, -sē-əl\ *adj*

con·tro·vert \ˈkän-trə-ˌvərt, ˌkän-trə-ˈvərt\ *vb* : DENY, CONTRADICT — **con·tro·vert·ible** *adj*

con·tu·ma·cious \ˌkän-t(y)ə-ˈmā-shəs\ *adj* : stubbornly resisting or disobeying authority **syn** rebellious, insubordinate, seditious — **con·tu·ma·cy** \kən-ˈt(y)ü-mə-sē, ˈkän-t(y)ə-\ *n* — **con·tu·ma·cious·ly** *adv*

con·tu·me·ly \kən-ˈt(y)ü-mə-lē, ˈkän-t(y)ə-ˌmē-lē\ *n, pl* **-lies** : contemptuous treatment : INSULT

con·tu·sion \kən-ˈt(y)ü-zhən\ *n* : BRUISE — **con·tuse** \-ˈt(y)üz\ *vb*

co·nun·drum \kə-ˈnən-drəm\ *n* : RIDDLE

con·ur·ba·tion \ˌkän-(ˌ)ər-ˈbā-shən\ *n* : a continuous network of urban communities

conv *abbr* 1 convention 2 convertible

con·va·lesce \ˌkän-və-ˈles\ *vb* **-lesced; -lesc·ing** : to recover health gradually — **con·va·les·cence** \-ˈles-ᵊns\ *n* — **con·va·les·cent** \-ᵊnt\ *adj or n*

con·vec·tion \kən-ˈvek-shən\ *n* : circulatory motion in a fluid due to warmer portions rising and cooler denser portions sinking; *also* : the transfer of heat by such motion — **con·vec·tion·al** \-ˈvek-sh(ə-)nəl\ *adj* — **con·vec·tive** \-ˈvek-tiv\ *adj*

convection oven *n* : an oven with a fan that circulates hot air uniformly and continuously around the food

con·vene \kən-ˈvēn\ *vb* **con·vened; con·ven·ing** : ASSEMBLE, MEET

con·ve·nience \kən-ˈvē-nyəns\ *n* 1 : SUITABLENESS 2 : a laborsaving device 3 : a suitable time 4 : personal comfort : EASE

con·ve·nient \-nyənt\ *adj* 1 : suited to one's comfort or ease 2 : placed near at hand — **con·ve·nient·ly** *adv*

con·vent \ˈkän-vənt, -ˌvent\ *n* [ME *covent,* fr. OF, fr. ML *conventus,* fr. L, assembly, fr. *convenire* come together] : a local community or house of a religious order esp. of nuns — **con·ven·tu·al** \kən-ˈven-chə-wəl, kän-\ *adj*

con·ven·ti·cle \kən-ˈvent-i-kəl\ *n* : MEETING; *esp* : a secret meeting for worship

con·ven·tion \kən-ˈven-chən\ *n* 1 : an agreement esp. between states on a matter of common concern 2 : MEETING, ASSEMBLY 3 : an assembly of delegates convened for some purpose 4 : generally accepted custom, practice, or belief

con·ven·tion·al \-ˈvench-(ə-)nəl\ *adj* 1 : sanctioned by general custom 2 : COMMONPLACE, ORDINARY **syn** formal, ceremonial, solemn — **con·ven·tion·al·i·ty** \-ˌven-chə-ˈnal-ət-ē\ *n* — **con·ven·tion·al·ize** \-ˈvench-(ə-)nə-ˌlīz\ *vb* — **con·ven·tion·al·ly** \-ˈvench-(ə-)nəl-ē\ *adv*

con·verge \kən-ˈvərj\ *vb* **con·verged; con·verg·ing** : to approach one common center or single point — **con·ver·gence** \kən-ˈvər-jəns\ *or* **con·ver·gen·cy** \-jən-sē\ *n* — **con·ver·gent** \-jənt\ *adj*

con·ver·sant \kən-ˈvərs-ᵊnt\ *adj* : having knowledge and experience

con·ver·sa·tion \ˌkän-vər-ˈsā-shən\ *n* : an informal talking together — **con·ver·sa·tion·al** \-sh(ə-)nəl\ *adj*

¹**con·verse** \ˈkän-ˌvərs\ *n* : CONVERSATION

²**con·verse** \kən-ˈvərs\ *vb* **con·versed; con·vers·ing** : to engage in conversation

³**con·verse** \ˈkän-ˌvərs\ *n* : a statement related to another statement by having its hypothesis and conclusion or its subject and predicate reversed or interchanged

⁴**con·verse** \kən-ˈvərs, ˈkän-ˌvers\ *adj* : reversed in order or relation — **con·verse·ly** *adv*

con·ver·sion \kən-ˈvər-zhən\ *n* 1 : a change in nature or form 2 : an experience associated with a decisive adoption of religion

¹**con·vert** \kən-ˈvərt\ *vb* 1 : to turn from one belief or party to another 2 : TRANSFORM, CHANGE 3 : MISAPPROPRIATE 4 : EXCHANGE — **con·vert·er** *or* **con·ver·tor** \-ər\ *n* — **con·vert·ible** *adj*

²**con·vert** \ˈkän-ˌvərt\ *n* : one who has undergone religious conversion

con·vert·ible \kən-ˈvərt-ə-bəl\ *n* : an automobile with a top that may be lowered or removed

con·vex \kän-ˈveks, ˈkän-ˌveks\ *adj* : curved or rounded like the exterior of a sphere or circle — **con·vex·i·ty** \kən-ˈvek-sət-ē, kän-\ *n*

con·vey \kən-ˈvā\ *vb* 1 : CARRY, TRANSPORT 2 : TRANSMIT, TRANSFER — **con·vey·er** *or* **con·vey·or** \-ər\ *n*

con·vey·ance \-ˈvā-əns\ *n* 1 : the act of conveying 2 : a legal paper transferring ownership of property 3 : VEHICLE

¹**con·vict** \kən-ˈvikt\ *vb* : to prove or find guilty

²**con·vict** \ˈkän-ˌvikt\ *n* : a person serving a prison sentence

con·vic·tion \kən-ˈvik-shən\ *n* 1 : the act of convicting esp. in a court 2 : the state of being convinced : strong belief

con·vince \kən-ˈvins\ *vb* **con·vinced; con·vinc·ing** : to bring by demonstration or argument to a sure belief — **con·vinc·ing** *adj* — **con·vinc·ing·ly** *adv*

con·viv·ial \kən-ˈviv-yəl, -ˈviv-ē-əl\ *adj* [LL *convivialis,* fr. L *convivium* banquet, fr. *com-* together + *vivere* to live] : enjoying companionship and the pleasures of feasting and drinking : JOVIAL, FESTIVE — **con·viv·i·al·i·ty** \-ˌviv-ē-ˈal-ət-ē\ *n* — **con·viv·ial·ly** \-ˈviv-yə-lē, -ˈviv-ē-ə-lē\ *adv*

con·vo·ca·tion \ˌkän-və-ˈkā-shən\ *n* 1 : a ceremonial assembly (as of clergymen) 2 : the act of convoking

con·voke \kən-ˈvōk\ *vb* **con·voked; con·vok·ing** : to call together to a meeting

con·vo·lut·ed \ˈkän-və-ˌlüt-əd\ *adj* 1 : folded in curved or tortuous windings 2 : INVOLVED, INTRICATE

con·vo·lu·tion \ˌkän-və-ˈlü-shən\ *n* : a tortuous or sinuous structure; *esp* : one of the ridges of the brain

¹**con·voy** \ˈkän-ˌvȯi, kən-ˈvȯi\ *vb* : to accompany for protection

²**con·voy** \ˈkän-ˌvȯi\ *n* 1 : one that convoys; *esp* : a protective escort for ships, persons, or goods 2 : the act of convoying 3 : a group of moving vehicles

con·vulse \kən-ˈvəls\ *vb* **con·vulsed; con·vuls·ing** : to agitate violently

con·vul·sion \kən-ˈvəl-shən\ *n* 1 : an abnormal and violent involuntary contraction or series of contractions of muscle 2 : a violent disturbance — **con·vul·sive** \-ˈvəl-siv\ *adj* — **con·vul·sive·ly** *adv*

cony *var of* CONEY

coo \ˈkü\ *n* : a soft low sound made by doves or pigeons; *also* : a sound like this — **coo** *vb*

¹**cook** \ˈku̇k\ *n* : one who prepares food for eating

²**cook** *vb* 1 : to prepare food for eating 2 : to subject to heat or fire — **cook·er** *n* — **cook·ware** \-ˌwaər\ *n*

cook·book \-ˌbu̇k\ *n* : a book of cooking directions and recipes

cook·ery \ˈku̇k-(ə-)rē\ *n, pl* **-er·ies** : the art or practice of cooking

cook·ie *or* **cooky** \ˈku̇k-ē\ *n, pl* **cook·ies** : a small sweet flat cake

cook·out \ˈku̇k-ˌau̇t\ *n* : an outing at which a meal is cooked and served in the open

¹**cool** \ˈkül\ *adj* 1 : moderately cold 2 : not excited : CALM 3 : not ardent 4 : IMPUDENT 5 : protecting from heat 6 *slang* : very good 7 : employing understatement **syn** unflappable, composed, collected, unruffled, nonchalant — **cool·ly** \ˈkül-(l)ē\ *adv* — **cool·ness** *n*

²**cool** *vb* : to make or become cool

³**cool** *n* 1 : a cool time or place 2 : INDIFFERENCE; *also* : SELF-ASSURANCE, COMPOSURE ⟨kept his ~⟩

cool·ant \ˈkü-lənt\ *n* : a usu. fluid cooling agent

cool·er \ˈkü-lər\ *n* 1 : a container for keeping food or drink cool 2 : JAIL, PRISON 3 : a tall iced drink

coo·lie \ˈkü-lē\ *n* [Hindi *kulī*] : an unskilled laborer usu. in or from the Far East

coon \ˈkün\ *n* : RACCOON

coon·hound \-ˌhau̇nd\ *n* : a sporting dog trained to hunt raccoons

coon·skin \-ˌskin\ *n* : the pelt of a raccoon; *also* : something (as a cap) made of this

¹**coop** \ˈküp, ˈku̇p\ *n* : a small enclosure or building usu. for poultry

²**coop** *vb* : to confine in or as if in a coop

co–op \ˈkō-ˌäp\ *n* : COOPERATIVE

coo·per \ˈkü-pər, ˈku̇p-ər\ *n* : one who makes or repairs barrels or casks — **cooper** *vb* — **coo·per·age** \ˈkü-p(ə-)rij, ˈku̇p-(ə-)\ *n*

co·op·er·ate \kō-ˈäp-ə-ˌrāt\ *vb* : to act jointly with another or others — **co·op·er·a·tion** \-ˌäp-ə-ˈrā-shən\ *n* — **co·op·er·a·tor** \-ˈäp-ə-ˌrāt-ər\ *n*

[1]**co·op·er·a·tive** \kō-ˈäp-(ə-)rət-iv, -ˈäp-ə-ˌrāt-\ *adj* **1** : willing to work with others **2** : of or relating to an association formed to enable its members to buy or sell to better advantage by eliminating middlemen's profits
[2]**cooperative** *n* : a cooperative association
co–opt \kō-ˈäpt\ *vb* **1** : to choose or elect as a colleague **2** : ABSORB, ASSIMILATE; *also* : TAKE OVER
[1]**co·or·di·nate** \kō-ˈȯrd-(ᵊ-)nət\ *adj* **1** : equal in rank or order **2** : of equal rank in a compound sentence ⟨~ clause⟩ **3** : joining words or word groups of the same rank
[2]**coordinate** *n* **1** : one of a set of numbers used in specifying the location of a point on a surface or in space **2** *pl* : articles (as of clothing) designed to be used together and to attain their effect through pleasing contrast
[3]**co·or·di·nate** \kō-ˈȯrd-ᵊn-ˌāt\ *vb* **-nat·ed; -nat·ing 1** : to make or become coordinate **2** : to work or act together harmoniously — **co·or·di·na·tion** \-ˌȯrd-ᵊn-ˈā-shən\ *n* — **co·or·di·na·tor** \-ˈȯrd-ᵊn-ˌāt-ər\ *n*
coot \ˈküt\ *n* **1** : a dark-colored ducklike bird related to the rails **2** : any of several No. American sea ducks **3** : a harmless simple person
coo·tie \ˈküt-ē\ *n* : a body louse
cop \ˈkäp\ *n* : POLICEMAN
co·part·ner \ˈkō-ˈpärt-nər\ *n* : PARTNER
[1]**cope** \ˈkōp\ *n* : a long cloaklike ecclesiastical vestment
[2]**cope** *vb* **coped; cop·ing** : to struggle to overcome problems or difficulties
copi·er \ˈkäp-ē-ər\ *n* : one that copies; *esp* : a machine for making copies
co·pi·lot \ˈkō-ˌpī-lət\ *n* : an assistant pilot of an aircraft or spacecraft
cop·ing \ˈkō-piŋ\ *n* : the top layer of a wall
co·pi·ous \ˈkō-pē-əs\ *adj* : LAVISH, ABUNDANT — **co·pi·ous·ly** *adv* — **co·pi·ous·ness** *n*
cop–out \ˈkäp-ˌau̇t\ *n* : an excuse for copping out; *also* : an act of copping out
cop out \(ˈ)käp-ˈau̇t\ *vb* : to back out (as of an unwanted responsibility)
cop·per \ˈkäp-ər\ *n* **1** : a malleable reddish metallic chemical element that is one of the best conductors of heat and electricity — see ELEMENT table **2** : a coin or token made of copper — **cop·pery** *adj*
cop·per·head \ˈkäp-ər-ˌhed\ *n* : a largely coppery brown venomous snake esp. of the eastern and central U.S.
cop·pice \ˈkäp-əs\ *n* : THICKET
co·pra \ˈkō-prə\ *n* : dried coconut meat yielding coconut oil
copse \ˈkäps\ *n* : THICKET
cop·ter \ˈkäp-tər\ *n* : HELICOPTER
cop·u·la \ˈkäp-yə-lə\ *n* : LINKING VERB — **cop·u·la·tive** \-ˌlāt-iv\ *adj*
cop·u·late \ˈkäp-yə-ˌlāt\ *vb* **-lat·ed; -lat·ing** : to engage in sexual intercourse — **cop·u·la·tion** \ˌkäp-yə-ˈlā-shən\ *n* — **cop·u·la·to·ry** \ˈkäp-yə-lə-ˌtōr-ē\ *adj*
[1]**copy** \ˈkäp-ē\ *n, pl* **cop·ies 1** : an imitation or reproduction of an original work **2** : material to be set in type **syn** duplicate, reproduction, facsimile, replica
[2]**copy** *vb* **cop·ied; copy·ing 1** : to make a copy of **2** : IMITATE — **copy·ist** *n*
copy·book \ˈkäp-ē-ˌbu̇k\ *n* : a book containing copies esp. of penmanship for learners to imitate
copy·boy \-ˌbȯi\ *n* : one who carries copy and runs errands (as in a newspaper office)
copy·cat \-ˌkat\ *n* : a slavish imitator
copy·desk \-ˌdesk\ *n* : the desk at which newspaper copy is edited
copy editor *n* : one who edits newspaper copy and writes headlines; *also* : one who reads and corrects manuscript copy in a publishing house
copy·read·er \-ˌrēd-ər\ *n* : COPY EDITOR
[1]**copy·right** \-ˌrīt\ *n* : the sole right to reproduce, publish, and sell a literary or artistic work
[2]**copyright** *vb* : to secure a copyright on
copy·writ·er \ˈkäp-ē-ˌrīt-ər\ *n* : a writer of advertising copy
co·quet *or* **co·quette** \kō-ˈket\ *vb* **co·quet·ted; co·quet·ting** : FLIRT — **co·quet·ry** \ˈkō-kə-trē, kō-ˈke-trē\ *n*
co·quette \kō-ˈket\ *n* [F, fem. of *coquet*, dim. of *coq* cock] : FLIRT — **co·quett·ish** *adj*
cor *abbr* corner
Cor *abbr* Corinthians
cor·a·cle \ˈkȯr-ə-kəl\ *n* [W *corwgl*] : a boat made of hoops covered with horsehide or canvas
cor·al \ˈkȯr-əl\ *n* **1** : a stony or horny material that forms the skeleton of colonies of tiny sea polyps and includes a red form used in jewelry; *also* : a coral-forming polyp or polyp colony **2** : a deep pink color — **coral** *adj*
coral snake *n* : any of several venomous chiefly tropical New World snakes brilliantly banded in red, black, and yellow or white
cor·bel \ˈkȯr-bəl\ *n* : a bracket-shaped architectural member that projects from a wall and supports a weight
[1]**cord** \ˈkȯrd\ *n* **1** : a usu. heavy string consisting of several strands woven or twisted together **2** : a long slender anatomical structure (as a tendon or nerve) **3** : a small flexible insulated electrical cable used to connect an appliance with a receptacle **4** : a cubic measure used esp. for firewood and equal to a stack 4×4×8 feet (about 3.6 cubic meters) **5** : a rib or ridge on cloth
[2]**cord** *vb* **1** : to tie or furnish with a cord **2** : to pile (wood) in cords
cord·age \ˈkȯrd-ij\ *n* : ROPES, CORDS; *esp* : ropes in the rigging of a ship
[1]**cor·dial** \ˈkȯr-jəl\ *n* **1** : a stimulating medicine or drink **2** : LIQUEUR
[2]**cordial** *adj* [ME, fr. ML *cordialis*, fr. L *cord-*, *cor* heart] : warmly receptive or welcoming : HEARTFELT, HEARTY — **cor·di·al·i·ty** \ˌkȯr-jē-ˈal-ət-ē, kȯr-ˈjal-; kȯrd-ˈyal-\ *n* — **cor·dial·ly** \ˈkȯr-jə-lē\ *adv*
cor·dil·le·ra \ˌkȯrd-ᵊl-ˈ(y)er-ə\ *n* [Sp] : a group of mountain ranges — **cor·dil·le·ran** *adj*
cord·less \ˈkȯrd-ləs\ *adj* : having no cord; *esp* : powered by a battery ⟨~ tools⟩
cor·do·ba \ˈkȯrd-ə-bə, -ə-və\ *n* — see MONEY table
cor·don \ˈkȯrd-ᵊn\ *n* **1** : an ornamental cord or ribbon **2** : an encircling line composed of individual units — **cordon** *vb*
cor·do·van \ˈkȯrd-ə-vən\ *n* : a soft fine-grained leather
cor·du·roy \ˈkȯrd-ə-ˌrȯi\ *n, pl* **-roys** : a heavy ribbed fabric; *also, pl* : trousers of this material
cord·wain·er \ˈkȯrd-ˌwā-nər\ *n* : SHOEMAKER
[1]**core** \ˈkōr\ *n* **1** : the central usu. inedible part of some fruits (as the apple); *also* : an inmost part of something **2** : GIST, ESSENCE
[2]**core** *vb* **cored; cor·ing** : to take out the core of — **cor·er** *n*
CORE \ˈkōr\ *abbr* Congress of Racial Equality
co·re·spon·dent \ˌkō-ri-ˈspän-dənt\ *n* : a person named as guilty of adultery with the defendant in a divorce suit
co·ri·an·der \ˈkōr-ē-ˌan-dər\ *n* : an herb related to the carrot; *also* : its aromatic dried fruit used as a flavoring
Cor·in·thi·ans \kə-ˈrin-thē-ənz\ *n* — see BIBLE table
[1]**cork** \ˈkȯrk\ *n* **1** : the tough elastic bark of a European oak (**cork oak**) used esp. for stoppers and insulation; *also* : a stopper of this **2** : a tissue of a woody plant making up most of the bark — **corky** *adj*
[2]**cork** *vb* : to furnish with or stop up with cork or a cork
cork·screw \ˈkȯrk-ˌskrü\ *n* : a device for drawing corks from bottles
corm \ˈkȯrm\ *n* : a solid bulblike underground part of a stem (as of the crocus or gladiolus)
cor·mo·rant \ˈkȯrm-(ə-)rənt, ˈkȯr-mə-ˌrant\ *n* [ME *cor-*

meraunt, fr. MF *cormorant,* fr. OF *cormareng,* fr. *corp* raven + *marenc* of the sea, fr. L *marinus*] : a dark seabird used in the Orient to catch fish

¹**corn** \ˈkȯrn\ *n* **1** : the seeds of a cereal grass and esp. of the chief cereal crop of a region (as wheat in Britain and Indian corn in the U.S.); *also* : a cereal grass **2** : sweet corn served as a vegetable

²**corn** *vb* : to salt (as beef) in brine and preservatives

³**corn** *n* : a local hardening and thickening of skin (as on a toe)

corn bread *n* : bread made with cornmeal

corn·cob \-ˌkäb\ *n* : the woody core on which the kernels of Indian corn are arranged

corn·crib \-ˌkrib\ *n* : a crib for storing ears of Indian corn

cor·nea \ˈkȯr-nē-ə\ *n* : the transparent part of the coat of the eyeball covering the iris and the pupil — **cor·ne·al** *adj*

corn earworm *n* : a moth whose larva is esp. destructive to Indian corn

¹**cor·ner** \ˈkȯ-nər\ *n* [ME, fr. OF *cornere,* fr. *corne* horn, corner, fr. L *cornu* horn, point] **1** : the point or angle formed by the meeting of lines, edges, or sides **2** : the place where two streets come together **3** : a quiet secluded place **4** : a position from which retreat or escape is impossible **5** : control of enough of the available supply (as of a commodity) to permit manipulation of the price

²**cor·ner** *vb* **cor·nered; cor·ner·ing** \ˈkȯrn-(ə-)riŋ\ **1** : to drive into a corner **2** : to get a corner on ⟨~ the wheat market⟩ **3** : to turn a corner

cor·ner·stone \ˈkȯr-nər-ˌstōn\ *n* **1** : a stone forming part of a corner in a wall; *esp* : such a stone laid with special ceremonies **2** : something of basic importance

cor·net \kȯr-ˈnet\ *n* : a brass band instrument resembling the trumpet

corn flour *n, Brit* : CORNSTARCH

corn·flow·er \ˈkȯrn-ˌflau̇(-ə)r\ *n* : BACHELOR'S BUTTON

cor·nice \ˈkȯr-nəs\ *n* : the horizontal projecting part crowning the wall of a building

corn·meal \ˈkȯrn-ˈmēl, -ˌmēl\ *n* : meal ground from corn

corn·row \ˈkȯrn-ˌrō\ *vb* : to braid (sections of hair) flat to the scalp in rows — **cornrow** *n*

corn·stalk \ˈkȯrn-ˌstȯk\ *n* : a stalk of Indian corn

corn·starch \-ˌstärch\ *n* : a starch made from corn and used in cookery as a thickening agent

corn syrup *n* : a syrup obtained by partial hydrolysis of cornstarch

cor·nu·co·pia \ˌkȯr-n(y)ə-ˈkō-pē-ə\ *n* [LL, fr. L *cornu copiae* horn of plenty] : a horn-shaped container filled with fruits and grain emblematic of abundance

corny \ˈkȯr-nē\ *adj* **corn·i·er; -est** : tiresomely simple or sentimental

co·rol·la \kə-ˈräl-ə, -ˈrōl-\ *n* : the petals of a flower

cor·ol·lary \ˈkȯr-ə-ˌler-ē\ *n, pl* **-lar·ies** **1** : a deduction from a proposition already proved true **2** : CONSEQUENCE, RESULT

co·ro·na \kə-ˈrō-nə\ *n* **1** : a colored ring surrounding the sun or moon; *esp* : a shining ring around the sun seen during eclipses **2** : a faint glow adjacent to the surface of a conductor at high voltage — **co·ro·nal** \ˈkȯr-ən-ᵊl, kə-ˈrōn-ᵊl\ *adj*

cor·o·nal \ˈkȯr-ən-ᵊl\ *n* : a circlet for the head

¹**cor·o·nary** \ˈkȯr-ə-ˌner-ē\ *adj* : of or relating to the heart or its blood vessels

²**coronary** *n, pl* **-nar·ies** **1** : a coronary blood vessel **2** : CORONARY THROMBOSIS

coronary thrombosis *n* : the blocking by a thrombus of one of the arteries supplying the heart tissues

cor·o·na·tion \ˌkȯr-ə-ˈnā-shən\ *n* : the act or ceremony of crowning a monarch

cor·o·ner \ˈkȯr-ə-nər\ *n* : a public official whose chief duty is to investigate the causes of deaths possibly not due to natural causes

cor·o·net \ˌkȯr-ə-ˈnet\ *n* **1** : a small crown indicating rank lower than sovereignty **2** : an ornamental band worn around the temples

corp *abbr* **1** corporal **2** corporation

¹**cor·po·ral** \ˈkȯr-p(ə-)rəl\ *adj* : of or relating to the body ⟨~ punishment⟩

²**corporal** *n* : a noncommissioned officer (as in the army) ranking next below a sergeant

cor·po·rate \ˈkȯr-p(ə-)rət\ *adj* **1** : INCORPORATED; *also* : belonging to an incorporated body **2** : combined into one body

cor·po·ra·tion \ˌkȯr-pə-ˈrā-shən\ *n* **1** : the municipal authorities of a town or city **2** : a legal creation authorized to act with the rights and liabilities of a person ⟨a business ~⟩

cor·po·re·al \kȯr-ˈpōr-ē-əl\ *adj* **1** : PHYSICAL, MATERIAL **2** *archaic* : BODILY — **cor·po·re·al·i·ty** \(ˌ)kȯr-ˌpōr-ē-ˈal-ət-ē\ *n* — **cor·po·re·al·ly** \-ē-ə-lē\ *adv*

corps \ˈkōr\ *n, pl* **corps** \ˈkōrz\ [F, fr. L *corpus* body] **1** : an organized subdivision of a country's military forces **2** : a group acting under common direction

corpse \ˈkȯrps\ *n* : a dead body

corps·man \ˈkōr(z)-mən\ *n* : an enlisted man trained to give first aid

cor·pu·lence \ˈkȯr-pyə-ləns\ *or* **cor·pu·len·cy** \-lən-sē\ *n* : excessive fatness — **cor·pu·lent** \-lənt\ *adj*

cor·pus \ˈkȯr-pəs\ *n, pl* **cor·po·ra** \-pə-rə\ [ME, fr. L] **1** : BODY; *esp* : CORPSE **2** : a body of writings or works

cor·pus·cle \ˈkȯr-(ˌ)pəs-əl\ *n* **1** : a minute particle **2** : a living cell (as in blood or cartilage) not aggregated into continuous tissues — **cor·pus·cu·lar** \kȯr-ˈpəs-kyə-lər\ *adj*

cor·pus de·lic·ti \ˌkȯr-pəs-di-ˈlik-ˌtī, -tē\ *n, pl* **corpora delicti** [NL, lit., body of the crime] : the substantial fact establishing that a crime has been committed; *also* : the body of a victim of murder

corr *abbr* **1** correct; corrected; correction **2** correspondence; correspondent; corresponding

cor·ral \kə-ˈral\ *n* [Sp] : an enclosure for confining or capturing animals; *also* : an enclosure for defense — **corral** *vb*

¹**cor·rect** \kə-ˈrekt\ *vb* **1** : to make right **2** : REPROVE, CHASTISE — **cor·rect·able** \-ˈrek-tə-bəl\ *adj* — **cor·rec·tion** \-ˈrek-shən\ *n* — **cor·rec·tion·al** \-ˈrek-sh(ə-)nəl\ *adj* — **cor·rec·tive** \-ˈrek-tiv\ *adj*

²**correct** *adj* **1** : conforming to a conventional standard **2** : agreeing with fact or truth — **cor·rect·ly** \kə-ˈrek-(t)lē\ *adv* — **cor·rect·ness** \-ˈrek(t)-nəs\ *n*

cor·re·late \ˈkȯr-ə-ˌlāt\ *vb* **-lat·ed; -lat·ing** : to connect in a systematic way : establish the mutual relations of — **cor·re·late** \-lət, -ˌlāt\ *n* — **cor·re·la·tion** \ˌkȯr-ə-ˈlā-shən\ *n*

cor·rel·a·tive \kə-ˈrel-ət-iv\ *adj* **1** : reciprocally related **2** : regularly used together (as *either* and *or*) — **correlative** *n*

cor·re·spond \ˌkȯr-ə-ˈspänd\ *vb* **1** : to be in agreement : SUIT, MATCH **2** : to communicate by letter — **cor·re·spond·ing·ly** \-ˈspän-diŋ-lē\ *adv*

cor·re·spon·dence \-ˈspän-dəns\ *n* **1** : agreement between particular things **2** : communication by letters; *also* : the letters exchanged

¹**cor·re·spon·dent** \-ˈspän-dənt\ *adj* **1** : SIMILAR **2** : FITTING, CONFORMING

²**correspondent** *n* **1** : something that corresponds **2** : a person with whom one communicates by letter **3** : a person employed to contribute news regularly from a place

cor·ri·dor \ˈkȯr-əd-ər, -ə-ˌdȯr\ *n* **1** : a passageway into which compartments or rooms open (as in a hotel or school) **2** : a narrow strip of land esp. through foreign-held territory **3** : a densely populated strip of land including two or more major cities

cor·ri·gen·dum \ˌkȯr-ə-ˈjen-dəm\ *n, pl* **-da** \-də\ [L] : an error in a printed work discovered after printing and shown with its correction on a separate sheet

cor·ri·gi·ble \ˈkȯr-ə-jə-bəl\ *adj* : CORRECTABLE

cor·rob·o·rate \kə-ˈräb-ə-ˌrāt\ *vb* **-rat·ed; -rat·ing** [L *corroborare*, fr. *robur* strength] : to support with evidence : CONFIRM — **cor·rob·o·ra·tion** \-ˌräb-ə-ˈrā-shən\ *n* — **cor·rob·o·ra·tive** \-ˈräb-ə-ˌrāt-iv, -ˈräb-(ə-)rət-\ *adj* — **cor·rob·o·ra·to·ry** \-ˈräb-(ə-)rə-ˌtōr-ē\ *adj*

cor·rode \kə-ˈrōd\ *vb* **cor·rod·ed; cor·rod·ing** : to eat or be eaten away gradually (as by chemical action) — **cor·ro·sion** \-ˈrō-zhən\ *n* — **cor·ro·sive** \-ˈrō-siv\ *adj or n*

cor·ru·gate \ˈkȯr-ə-ˌgāt\ *vb* **-gat·ed; -gat·ing** : to form into wrinkles or ridges and grooves — **cor·ru·gat·ed** *adj* — **cor·ru·ga·tion** \ˌkȯr-ə-ˈgā-shən\ *n*

[1]**cor·rupt** \kə-ˈrəpt\ *vb* **1** : to make evil : DEPRAVE; *esp* : BRIBE **2** : ROT, SPOIL — **cor·rupt·ible** *adj* — **cor·rup·tion** \-ˈrəp-shən\ *n*

[2]**corrupt** *adj* : DEPRAVED, DEBASED

corruption of blood : a bar on a person from inheriting, retaining, or transmitting any estate, rank, or title

cor·sage \kȯr-ˈsäzh, -ˈsäj\ *n* [F, bust, bodice, fr. OF, bust, fr. *cors* body, fr. L *corpus*] **1** : the waist or bodice of a dress **2** : a bouquet to be worn or carried

cor·sair \ˈkȯr-ˌsaər\ *n* : PIRATE

cor·set \ˈkȯr-sət\ *n* : a stiffened undergarment worn for support or to give shape to the waist and hips

cor·tege *also* **cor·tège** \kȯr-ˈtezh, ˈkȯr-ˌtezh\ *n* [F] : PROCESSION; *esp* : a funeral procession

cor·tex \ˈkȯr-ˌteks\ *n, pl* **cor·ti·ces** \ˈkȯrt-ə-ˌsēz\ *or* **cor·tex·es** : an outer or covering layer of an organism or one of its parts ⟨the adrenal ~⟩ ⟨~ of a plant stem⟩; *esp* : the outer layer of gray matter of the brain — **cor·ti·cal** \ˈkȯrt-i-kəl\ *adj*

cor·ti·sone \ˈkȯrt-ə-ˌsōn, -ˌzōn\ *n* : an adrenal hormone used in treating rheumatoid arthritis

co·run·dum \kə-ˈrən-dəm\ *n* : a very hard aluminum-containing mineral used as an abrasive or in some crystalline forms as a gem

cor·us·cate \ˈkȯr-ə-ˌskāt\ *vb* **-cat·ed; -cat·ing** : FLASH, SPARKLE — **cor·us·ca·tion** \ˌkȯr-ə-ˈskā-shən\ *n*

cor·vette \kȯr-ˈvet\ *n* **1** : a naval sailing ship smaller than a frigate **2** : an armed escort ship smaller than a destroyer

co·ry·za \kə-ˈrī-zə\ *n* : an inflammatory disorder of the upper respiratory tract; *esp* : COMMON COLD

COS *abbr* **1** cash on shipment **2** chief of staff

co·sig·na·to·ry \kō-ˈsig-nə-ˌtōr-ē\ *n* : a joint signer

co·sign·er \ˈkō-ˌsī-nər\ *n* : COSIGNATORY; *esp* : a joint signer of a promissory note

[1]**cos·met·ic** \käz-ˈmet-ik\ *n* : a cosmetic preparation

[2]**cosmetic** *adj* [Gk *kosmētikos* skilled in adornment, fr. *kosmein* to arrange, adorn, fr. *kosmos* order, ornament, universe] **1** : intended to beautify the hair or complexion **2** : SUPERFICIAL

cos·me·tol·o·gist \ˌkäz-mə-ˈtäl-ə-jəst\ *n* : one who gives beauty treatments — **cos·me·tol·o·gy** \-jē\ *n*

cos·mic \ˈkäz-mik\ *also* **cos·mi·cal** \-mi-kəl\ *adj* **1** : of or relating to the cosmos **2** : VAST, GRAND — **cos·mi·cal·ly** \-mi-k(ə-)lē\ *adv*

cosmic ray *n* : a stream of very penetrating atomic nuclei that enter the earth's atmosphere from outer space

cos·mog·o·ny \käz-ˈmäg-ə-nē\ *n, pl* **-nies** : the origin or creation of the world or universe

cos·mol·o·gy \käz-ˈmäl-ə-jē\ *n, pl* **-gies** : a branch of astronomy dealing with the origin and structure of the universe — **cos·mo·log·i·cal** \ˌkäz-mə-ˈläj-i-kəl\ *adj* — **cos·mol·o·gist** \käz-ˈmäl-ə-jəst\ *n*

cos·mo·naut \ˈkäz-mə-ˌnȯt\ *n* : a Soviet astronaut

cos·mo·pol·i·tan \ˌkäz-mə-ˈpäl-ət-ᵊn\ *adj* : belonging to all the world : not local **syn** universal, global, catholic — **cosmopolitan** *n*

cos·mos \ˈkäz-məs, 1 *also* -ˌmōs, -ˌmäs\ *n* **1** : UNIVERSE **2** : a tall garden herb related to the daisies

co·spon·sor \ˈkō-ˌspän-sər, -ˈspän-\ *n* : a joint sponsor — **cosponsor** *vb*

cos·sack \ˈkäs-ˌak, -ək\ *n* [Russ *kazak* & Ukrainian *kozak*, fr. Turk *kazak* free person] : a member of a group of frontiersmen of southern Russia organized as cavalry in the czarist army

[1]**cost** \ˈkȯst\ *n* **1** : the amount paid or charged for something : PRICE **2** : the loss or penalty incurred in gaining something **3** *pl* : expenses incurred in a law suit

[2]**cost** *vb* **cost; cost·ing** **1** : to require a specified amount in payment **2** : to cause to pay, suffer, or lose

co–star \ˈkō-ˌstär\ *n* : one of two leading players in a motion picture or play — **co–star** *vb*

cos·tive \ˈkäs-tiv\ *adj* : affected with or causing constipation

cost·ly \ˈkȯst-lē\ *adj* **cost·li·er; -est** : of great cost or value : not cheap **syn** dear, valuable, expensive — **cost·li·ness** *n*

cos·tume \ˈkäs-ˌt(y)üm\ *n* **1** : CLOTHES, ATTIRE; *also* : a suit or dress characteristic of a period or country **2** : special or fancy dress (as for wearing on the stage) — **cos·tum·er** \ˈkäs-ˌt(y)ü-mər\ *n* — **cos·tu·mi·er** \käs-ˈt(y)ü-mē-ər\ *n, chiefly Brit*

costume jewelry *n* : inexpensive jewelry

co·sy \ˈkō-zē\ *var of* COZY

[1]**cot** \ˈkät\ *n* : a small house : COTTAGE

[2]**cot** *n* : a small often collapsible bed

cote \ˈkōt, ˈkät\ *n* : a small shed or coop (as for sheep or doves)

co·te·rie \ˈkōt-ə-ˌrē, ˌkōt-ə-ˈrē\ *n* [F] : an intimate often exclusive group of persons with a common interest

co·ter·mi·nous \-mə-nəs\ *adj* : having the same scope or duration

co·til·lion \kō-ˈtil-yən, kə-\ *n* **1** : a complicated formal dance with frequent changing of partners **2** : a formal ball

cot·tage \ˈkät-ij\ *n* : a small house — **cot·tag·er** *n*

cottage cheese *n* : a soft uncured cheese made from soured skim milk

cot·ter *or* **cot·tar** \ˈkät-ər\ *n* : a farm laborer occupying a cottage and often a small holding

cotter pin *n* : a metal strip bent into a pin whose ends can be spread apart after insertion through a hole or slot

cot·ton \ˈkät-ᵊn\ *n* [ME *coton*, fr. MF, fr. Ar *quṭn*] **1** : a soft fibrous usu. white substance composed of hairs attached to the seeds of a plant related to the mallow; *also* : this plant **2** : thread or cloth made of cotton — **cot·tony** *adj*

cotton candy *n* : a candy made of spun sugar

cot·ton·mouth \ˈkät-ᵊn-ˌmau̇th\ *n* : WATER MOCCASIN

cot·ton·seed \-ˌsēd\ *n* : the seed of the cotton plant yielding a protein-rich meal and a fixed oil **(cottonseed oil)** used esp. in cooking

cot·ton·tail \-ˌtāl\ *n* : an American rabbit with a white-tufted tail

cot·ton·wood \-ˌwu̇d\ *n* : a poplar with cottony hair on its seed

cot·y·le·don \ˌkät-ᵊl-ˈēd-ᵊn\ *n* : the first leaf or one of the first pair or whorl of leaves developed by a seed plant

[1]**couch** \ˈkau̇ch\ *vb* **1** : to lie or place on a couch **2** : to phrase in a certain manner

[2]**couch** *n* : a piece of furniture (as a bed or sofa) that one can sit or lie on

couch·ant \ˈkau̇-chənt\ *adj* : lying down with the head raised ⟨coat of arms with lion ~⟩

cou·gar \ˈkü-gər, -ˌgär\ *n, pl* **cougars** *also* **cougar** [F *couguar*, fr. NL *cuguacuarana*, modif. of Tupi (a Brazilian Indian language) *suasuarana*, lit., false deer, fr. *suasú* deer + *rana* false] : a large tawny wild American cat

cougar

cough \ˈkȯf\ *vb* : to force air from the lungs with short sharp noises; *also* : to expel by coughing — **cough** *n*

could \kəd, (ˈ)ku̇d\ *past of* CAN — used as an auxiliary in the past or as a polite or less forceful alternative to *can* in the present

cou·lee \ˈkü-lē\ *n* **1** : a small stream **2** : a dry streambed **3** : GULLY

cou·lomb \ˈkü-ˌläm, -ˌlōm\ *n* : a unit of electric charge equal to the electricity transferred by a current of one ampere in one second

coun·cil \ˈkau̇n-səl\ *n* **1** : ASSEMBLY, MEETING **2** : an official body of lawmakers ⟨a city ~⟩ — **coun·cil·lor** *or* **coun·cil·or** \-s(ə-)lər\ *n* — **coun·cil·man** \-səl-mən\ *n* — **coun·cil·wom·an** \-ˌwu̇m-ən\ *n*

[1]**coun·sel** \ˈkau̇n-səl\ *n* **1** : ADVICE **2** : a plan of action **3** : deliberation together **4** *pl* **counsel** : LAWYER

[2]**counsel** *vb* **-seled** *or* **-selled; -sel·ing** *or* **-sel·ling** \-s(ə-)liŋ\ **1** : ADVISE, RECOMMEND **2** : CONSULT

coun·sel·or *or* **coun·sel·lor** \ˈkau̇n-s(ə-)lər\ *n* **1** : ADVISER **2** : LAWYER

[1]**count** \ˈkau̇nt\ *vb* [ME *counten*, fr. MF *compter*, fr. L *computare*, fr. *com-* with + *putare* to consider] **1** : to name or indicate one by one in order to find the total number **2** : to recite numbers in order **3** : CONSIDER, ACCOUNT **4** : RELY ⟨you can ~ on him⟩ **5** : to be of value or account — **count·able** *adj*

[2]**count** *n* **1** : the act of counting; *also* : the total obtained by counting **2** : a particular charge in an indictment or legal declaration

[3]**count** *n* [MF *comte*, fr. LL *comes*, fr. L, companion, one of the imperial court, fr. *com-* with + *ire* to go] : a European nobleman whose rank corresponds to that of a British earl

count·down \ˈkau̇nt-ˌdau̇n\ *n* : a backward counting in fixed units (as seconds) to indicate the time remaining before an event (as the launching of a rocket) — **count down** \-ˈdau̇n\ *vb*

[1]**coun·te·nance** \ˈkau̇nt-(ᵊ-)nəns\ *n* **1** : the human face esp. as an indicator of mood or character **2** : FAVOR, APPROVAL

[2]**countenance** *vb* **-nanced; -nanc·ing** : SANCTION, TOLERATE

[1]**count·er** \ˈkau̇nt-ər\ *n* **1** : a piece (as of metal or ivory) used in reckoning or in games **2** : a level surface over which business is transacted, food is served, or work is conducted

[2]**coun·ter** *vb* : to act in opposition to

[3]**count·er** *n* : a device for recording a number or amount

[4]**coun·ter** *adv* : in an opposite direction : CONTRARY

[5]**coun·ter** *n* **1** : OPPOSITE, CONTRARY **2** : an answering or offsetting force or blow

[6]**coun·ter** *adj* : CONTRARY, OPPOSITE

coun·ter·act \ˌkau̇nt-ər-ˈakt\ *vb* : to lessen the force of : OFFSET — **coun·ter·ac·tive** \-ˈak-tiv\ *adj*

coun·ter·at·tack \ˈkau̇nt-ər-ə-ˌtak\ *n* : an attack made to oppose an enemy's attack — **counterattack** *vb*

[1]**coun·ter·bal·ance** \ˈkau̇nt-ər-ˌbal-əns\ *n* : a weight or influence that balances another

[2]**counterbalance** \ˌkau̇nt-ər-ˈbal-əns\ *vb* : to oppose with equal weight or influence

coun·ter·claim \ˈkau̇nt-ər-ˌklām\ *n* : an opposing claim esp. in law

coun·ter·clock·wise \ˌkau̇nt-ər-ˈkläk-ˌwīz\ *adv* : in a direction opposite to that in which the hands of a clock rotate — **counterclockwise** *adj*

coun·ter·cul·ture \ˈkau̇nt-ər-ˌkəl-chər\ *n* : a culture esp. of the young with values and mores that run counter to those of established society

coun·ter·es·pi·o·nage \ˌkau̇nt-ər-ˈes-pē-ə-ˌnäzh, -nij\ *n* : activities intended to discover and defeat enemy espionage

[1]**coun·ter·feit** \ˈkau̇nt-ər-ˌfit\ *vb* **1** : to copy or imitate in order to deceive **2** : PRETEND, FEIGN — **coun·ter·feit·er** *n*

[2]**counterfeit** *adj* : SHAM, SPURIOUS; *also* : FORGED

[3]**counterfeit** *n* : something counterfeit : FORGERY **syn** fraud, sham, fake, imposture, deceit, deception

coun·ter·in·sur·gen·cy \ˌkau̇nt-ər-in-ˈsər-jən-sē\ *n* : military activity designed to deal with insurgents

coun·ter·in·tel·li·gence \ˌkau̇nt-ər-in-ˈtel-ə-jəns\ *n* : organized activities of an intelligence service designed to counter the activities of an enemy's intelligence service

count·er·man \ˈkau̇nt-ər-ˌman, -mən\ *n* : one who tends a counter

coun·ter·mand \ˈkau̇nt-ər-ˌmand\ *vb* : to withdraw (an order already given) by a contrary order

coun·ter·mea·sure \-ˌmezh-ər\ *n* : an action undertaken to counter another

coun·ter·of·fen·sive \-ə-ˌfen-siv\ *n* : a large-scale counterattack

coun·ter·pane \ˈkau̇nt-ər-ˌpān\ *n* : BEDSPREAD

coun·ter·part \-ˌpärt\ *n* : a person or thing very closely like or corresponding to another person or thing

coun·ter·point \-ˌpȯint\ *n* : music in which one melody is accompanied by one or more other melodies all woven into a harmonious whole

coun·ter·poise \-ˌpȯiz\ *n* : COUNTERBALANCE

coun·ter·rev·o·lu·tion \ˌkau̇nt-ə(r)-ˌrev-ə-ˈlü-shən\ *n* : a revolution opposed to a current or earlier one — **coun·ter·rev·o·lu·tion·ary** \-shə-ˌner-ē\ *adj or n*

coun·ter·sign \ˈkau̇nt-ər-ˌsīn\ *n* **1** : a confirmatory signature added to a writing already signed by another person **2** : a secret signal that must be given by a person who wishes to pass a guard — **countersign** *vb*

coun·ter·sink \ˈkau̇nt-ər-ˌsiŋk\ *vb* **-sunk** \-ˌsəŋk\; **-sink·ing 1** : to form a funnel-shaped enlargement at the outer end of a drilled hole **2** : to set the head of (as a screw) at or below the surface — **countersink** *n*

coun·ter·spy \-ˌspī\ *n* : a spy engaged in counterespionage

coun·ter·ten·or \-ˌten-ər\ *n* : a tenor with an unusually high range

coun·ter·vail \ˌkau̇nt-ər-ˈvāl\ *vb* : COUNTERACT

coun·ter·weight \ˈkau̇nt-ər-ˌwāt\ *n* : COUNTERBALANCE

count·ess \ˈkau̇nt-əs\ *n* **1** : the wife or widow of a count or an earl **2** : a woman holding the rank of a count or an earl in her own right

count·ing·house \ˈkau̇nt-iŋ-ˌhau̇s\ *n* : a building or office for keeping books and conducting business

count·less \ˈkau̇nt-ləs\ *adj* : INNUMERABLE

coun·tri·fied *also* **coun·try·fied** \ˈkən-tri-ˌfīd\ *adj* **1** : RURAL, RUSTIC **2** : UNSOPHISTICATED **3** : played or sung in the manner of country music

[1]**coun·try** \ˈkən-trē\ *n, pl* **countries** [ME *contree*, fr. OF *contrée*, fr. ML *contrata*, fr. L *contra* against, on the opposite side] **1** : REGION, DISTRICT **2** : FATHERLAND **3** : a nation or its territory **4** : rural regions as opposed to towns and cities

[2]**country** *adj* **1** : RURAL **2** : of or relating to country music ⟨a ~ singer⟩

country and western *n* : COUNTRY MUSIC

country club *n* : a suburban club for social life and recreation; *esp* : one having a golf course

coun·try–dance \ˈkən-trē-ˌdans\ *n* : an English dance in which partners face each other esp. in rows
coun·try·man \ˈkən-trē-mən, *2 often* -ˌman\ *n* **1** : an inhabitant of a certain country **2** : COMPATRIOT **3** : one raised in the country : RUSTIC
country music *n* : music derived from or imitating the folk style of the southern U.S. or of the Western cowboy
coun·try·side \ˈkən-trē-ˌsīd\ *n* : a rural area or its people
coun·ty \ˈkaụnt-ē\ *n, pl* **counties** **1** : the domain of a count **2** : a territorial division of a country or state for purposes of local government
coup \ˈkü\ *n, pl* **coups** \ˈküz\ [F, blow, stroke] **1** : a brilliant sudden stroke or stratagem **2** : COUP D'ÉTAT
coup de grace \ˌküd-ə-ˈgräs\ *n, pl* **coups de grace** \ˌküd-ə-\ [F *coup de grâce,* lit., stroke of mercy] : a deathblow or final decisive stroke or event
coup d'état \ˌküd-ə-ˈtä\ *n, pl* **coups d'état** \ˌküd-ə-ˈtä(z)\ [F, lit., stroke of state] : a sudden violent overthrow of a government by a small group
cou·pé *or* **coupe** \kü-ˈpā, *2 often* ˈküp\ *n* [F *coupé,* fr. *couper* to cut] **1** : a closed carriage for two persons inside with an outside seat for the driver in front **2** *usu* *coupe* : a 2-door automobile with an enclosed body
[1]**cou·ple** \ˈkəp-əl\ *vb* **cou·pled; cou·pling** \-(ə-)liŋ\ : to link together
[2]**couple** *n* **1** : two persons closely associated; *esp* : a man and a woman married or otherwise paired **2** : PAIR **3** : BOND, TIE **4** : an indefinite small number : FEW ⟨a ~ of days ago⟩
cou·plet \ˈkəp-lət\ *n* : two successive rhyming lines of verse
cou·pling \ˈkəp-liŋ (*usual for 2*), -ə-liŋ\ *n* **1** : CONNECTION **2** : a device for connecting two parts or things
cou·pon \ˈk(y)ü-ˌpän\ *n* **1** : a statement attached to a bond showing interest due and designed to be cut off and presented for payment **2** : a certificate given to a purchaser of goods and redeemable in merchandise, cash, or services; *also* : a similar ticket or form surrendered for other purposes ⟨a ration ~⟩ **3** : a part of an advertisement to be cut off to use as an order blank or inquiry form or to obtain a discount on merchandise
cour·age \ˈkər-ij\ *n* : ability to conquer fear or depair : BRAVERY, VALOR — **cou·ra·geous** \kə-ˈrā-jəs\ *adj* — **cou·ra·geous·ly** *adv*
cou·ri·er \ˈkụr-ē-ər, ˈkər-ē-\ *n* : one who bears messages or information esp. for the diplomatic or military services
[1]**course** \ˈkōrs\ *n* **1** : PROGRESS, PASSAGE; *also* : direction of progress **2** : the ground or path over which something moves **3** : method of procedure : CONDUCT, BEHAVIOR **4** : an ordered series of acts or proceedings : sequence of events **5** : a series of instruction periods dealing with a subject **6** : the series of studies leading to graduation from a school or college **7** : the part of a meal served at one time — **of course** : as might be expected
[2]**course** *vb* **coursed; cours·ing** **1** : to hunt with dogs ⟨~ a rabbit⟩ **2** : to run or go speedily
cours·er \ˈkōr-sər\ *n* : a swift or spirited horse
[1]**court** \ˈkōrt\ *n* **1** : the residence of a sovereign or similar dignitary **2** : a sovereign and his officials and advisers as a governing power **3** : an assembly of the retinue of a sovereign **4** : an open space enclosed by a building or buildings **5** : a space walled or marked off for playing a game (as tennis or basketball) **6** : the place where justice is administered; *also* : a judicial body or a meeting of a judicial body **7** : HOMAGE, COURTSHIP
[2]**court** *vb* **1** : to try to gain the favor of **2** : WOO **3** : ATTRACT, TEMPT
cour·te·ous \ˈkərt-ē-əs\ *adj* : marked by respect for others : CIVIL, POLITE — **cour·te·ous·ly** *adv*
cour·te·san \ˈkōrt-ə-zən, ˈkərt-\ *n* : PROSTITUTE
cour·te·sy \ˈkərt-ə-sē\ *n, pl* **-sies** **1** : courteous behavior : POLITENESS **2** : a favor courteously performed
court·house \ˈkōrt-ˌhaụs\ *n* : a building in which courts of law are held or county offices are located
court·ier \ˈkōrt-ē-ər, ˈkōrt-yər\ *n* : a person in attendance at a royal court
court·ly \ˈkōrt-lē\ *adj* **court·li·er; -est** : REFINED, ELEGANT, POLITE **syn** gallant, gracious — **court·li·ness** *n*
court–mar·tial \ˈkōrt-ˌmär-shəl\ *n, pl* **courts–martial** : a military or naval court for trial of offenses against military or naval law; *also* : a trial by this court — **court–martial** *vb*
court·room \-ˌrüm, -ˌrụm\ *n* : a room in which a court of law is held
court·ship \-ˌship\ *n* : the act of courting : WOOING
court·yard \-ˌyärd\ *n* : an enclosure next to a building
cous·in \ˈkəz-ᵊn\ *n* [ME *cosin,* fr. OF, fr. L *consobrinus,* fr. *com-* with + *sobrinus* cousin on the mother's side, fr. *soror* sister] : a child of one's uncle or aunt
cou·ture \kü-ˈtụr, -ˈtu̇er\ *n* [F] : the business of designing fashionable custom-made women's clothing; *also* : the designers and establishments engaged in this business
cou·tu·ri·er \kü-ˈtụr-ē-ər, -ē-ˌā\ *n* [F, dressmaker] : the owner of an establishment engaged in couture
cove \ˈkōv\ *n* **1** : a trough for lights at the upper part of a wall **2** : a small sheltered inlet or bay
co·ven \ˈkəv-ən\ *n* : an assembly or band of witches
cov·e·nant \ˈkəv-(ə-)nənt\ *n* : a formal binding agreement : COMPACT — **cov·e·nant** \ˈkəv-(ə-)nənt, -ə-ˌnant\ *vb*
[1]**cov·er** \ˈkəv-ər\ *vb* **cov·ered; cov·er·ing** \ˈkəv-(ə-)riŋ\ **1** : to bring or hold within range of a firearm **2** : PROTECT, SHIELD **3** : HIDE, CONCEAL **4** : to place something over or upon **5** : INCLUDE, COMPRISE **6** : to have as one's field of activity ⟨one salesman ~*s* the state⟩ **7** : to buy (stocks) in order to have them for delivery on a previous short sale
[2]**cover** *n* **1** : something that protects or shelters **2** : LID, TOP **3** : CASE, BINDING **4** : TABLECLOTH **5** : a cloth used on a bed **6** : SCREEN, DISGUISE **7** : an envelope or wrapper for mail
cov·er·age \ˈkəv-(ə-)rij\ *n* **1** : the act or fact of covering **2** : the total group covered : SCOPE
cov·er·all \ˈkəv-ər-ˌȯl\ *n* : a one-piece outer garment worn to protect one's clothes — usu. used in pl.
cover charge *n* : a charge made by a restaurant or nightclub in addition to the charge for food and drink
cover crop *n* : a crop planted to prevent soil erosion and to provide humus
cov·er·let \ˈkəv-ər-lət\ *n* : BEDSPREAD
[1]**co·vert** \ˈkō-(ˌ)vərt, ˈkəv-ərt\ *adj* **1** : HIDDEN, SECRET **2** : SHELTERED — **co·vert·ly** *adv*
[2]**co·vert** \ˈkəv-ərt, ˈkō-vərt\ *n* **1** : a secret or sheltered place; *esp* : a thicket sheltering game **2** : a feather covering the bases of the quills of the wings and tail of a bird **3** : a firm durable twilled cloth usu. of mixed-color yarns
cov·er–up \ˈkəv-ər-ˌəp\ *n* **1** : a device for masking or concealing **2** : a usu. concerted effort to keep an illegal or unethical act or situation from being made public
cov·et \ˈkəv-ət\ *vb* : to desire enviously (what belongs to another) — **cov·et·ous** *adj* — **cov·et·ous·ness** *n*
cov·ey \ˈkəv-ē\ *n, pl* **coveys** [ME, fr. MF *covee,* fr. OF, fr. *cover* to sit on, brood over, fr. L *cubare* to lie] **1** : a bird with her brood of young **2** : a small flock (as of quail)
[1]**cow** \ˈkaụ\ *n* **1** : the mature female of cattle or of an animal (as the moose) of which the male is called *bull* **2** : any domestic bovine animal irrespective of sex or age
[2]**cow** *vb* : INTIMIDATE, DAUNT, OVERAWE
cow·ard \ˈkaụ(-ə)rd\ *n* [ME, fr. OF *coart,* fr. *coe* tail, fr. L *cauda*] : one who lacks courage or shows shameful

fear or timidity — **coward** *adj* — **cow·ard·ice** \-əs\ *n* — **cow·ard·ly** *adv or adj*

cow·bird \ˈkaů-ˌbərd\ *n* : a small No. American bird that lays its eggs in the nests of other birds

cow·boy \-ˌbȯi\ *n* : one (as a mounted ranch hand) who tends cattle or horses

cow·er \ˈkaů(-ə)r\ *vb* : to shrink or crouch down from fear or cold : QUAIL

cow·girl \ˈkaů-ˌgərl\ *n* : a girl or woman who tends cattle or horses

cow·hand \ˈkaů-ˌhand\ *n* : COWBOY

cow·hide \-ˌhīd\ *n* **1** : the hide of a cow; *also* : leather made from it **2** : a coarse whip of braided rawhide

cowl \ˈkaůl\ *n* **1** : a monk's hood **2** : the top part of the front of the body of an automobile to which the windshield is attached

cow·lick \ˈkaů-ˌlik\ *n* : a turned-up tuft of hair that resists control

cowl·ing \ˈkaů-liŋ\ *n* : a usu. metal covering for the engine or another part of an airplane

cow·man \ˈkaů-mən, -ˌman\ *n* : COWBOY; *also* : a cattle owner or rancher

co·work·er \ˈkō-ˌwər-kər\ *n* : a fellow worker

cow·poke \ˈkaů-ˌpōk\ *n* : COWBOY

cow pony *n* : a strong and agile horse trained for herding cattle

cow·pox \ˈkaů-ˌpäks\ *n* : a mild disease of the cow that when communicated to man protects against smallpox

cow·punch·er \-ˌpən-chər\ *n* : COWBOY

cow·slip \ˈkaů-ˌslip\ *n* **1** : a yellow-flowered European primrose **2** : MARSH MARIGOLD

cox·comb \ˈkäks-ˌkōm\ *n* : a conceited foolish person : FOP

cox·swain \ˈkäk-sən, -ˌswān\ *n* : the steersman of a ship's boat or a racing shell

coy \ˈkȯi\ *adj* [ME, quiet, shy, fr. MF *coi* calm, fr. L *quietus* quiet] : BASHFUL, SHY; *esp* : pretending shyness — **coy·ly** *adv* — **coy·ness** *n*

coy·ote \kī-ˌōt, kī-ˈōt-ē\ *n, pl* **coyotes** *or* **coyote** : a mammal of No. America related to the domestic dog and the wolves

coy·pu \ˈkȯi-pü\ *n* : NUTRIA 2

coz·en \ˈkəz-ᵊn\ *vb* [obs. It *cozzonare*, fr. It *cozzone* horse trader, fr. L *cocio* trader] : CHEAT, DEFRAUD — **coz·en·age** \-ij\ *n*

[1]**co·zy** \ˈkō-zē\ *adj* **co·zi·er; -est** : SNUG, COMFORTABLE — **co·zi·ly** \ˈkō-zə-lē\ *adv* — **co·zi·ness** \-zē-nəs\ *n*

[2]**cozy** *n, pl* **cozies** : a padded covering for a vessel (as a teapot) to keep the contents hot

cp *abbr* **1** compare **2** coupon

CP *abbr* **1** chemically pure **2** command post **3** communist party

CPA *abbr* certified public accountant

cpd *abbr* compound

CPI *abbr* consumer price index

Cpl *abbr* corporal

CPO *abbr* chief petty officer

CPOM *abbr* master chief petty officer

CPOS *abbr* senior chief petty officer

CPR *abbr* cardiopulmonary resuscitation

CPT *abbr* captain

CQ *abbr* charge of quarters

cr *abbr* credit; creditor

Cr *symbol* chromium

[1]**crab** \ˈkrab\ *n* : any of various crustaceans with a short broad shell and small abdomen

[2]**crab** *n* : an ill-natured person

crab apple *n* : a small often highly colored sour apple; *also* : a tree that produces crab apples

crab·bed \ˈkrab-əd\ *adj* **1** : MOROSE, PEEVISH **2** : CRAMPED, IRREGULAR

crab·by \ˈkrab-ē\ *adj* **crab·bi·er; -est** : CROSS, ILL-NATURED

crab·grass \ˈkrab-ˌgras\ *n* : a weedy grass with creeping or sprawling stems that root freely at the nodes

crab louse *n* : a louse infesting the pubic region in man

[1]**crack** \ˈkrak\ *vb* **1** : to break with a sharp sudden sound **2** : to break with or without completely separating into parts **3** : to fail in tone or become harsh ⟨her voice ~*ed*⟩ **4** : to subject (as a petroleum oil) to heat for breaking down into lighter products (as gasoline)

[2]**crack** *n* **1** : a sudden sharp noise **2** : a witty or sharp remark **3** : a narrow break or opening : FISSURE **4** : a sharp blow **5** : ATTEMPT, TRY **6** : highly purified cocaine in the form of small chips used for smoking

[3]**crack** *adj* : extremely proficient

crack·down \ˈkrak-ˌdaůn\ *n* : an act or instance of taking positive disciplinary action ⟨a ~ on gambling⟩ — **crack down** \-ˈdaůn\ *vb*

crack·er \ˈkrak-ər\ *n* **1** : FIRECRACKER **2** : a dry thin crispy baked bread product made of flour and water

crack·er·jack \-ˌjak\ *n* : something very excellent — **crackerjack** *adj*

crack·le \ˈkrak-əl\ *vb* **crack·led; crack·ling** \-(ə-)liŋ\ **1** : to make small sharp snapping noises **2** : to develop fine cracks in a surface — **crackle** *n* — **crack·ly** \-(ə-)lē\ *adj*

crack·pot \ˈkrak-ˌpät\ *n* : an eccentric person

crack–up \ˈkrak-ˌəp\ *n* : CRASH, WRECK; *also* : BREAKDOWN

[1]**cra·dle** \ˈkrād-ᵊl\ *n* **1** : a baby's bed or cot **2** : INFANCY ⟨from ~ to the grave⟩ **3** : a place of origin **4** : a framework or support (as for a telephone receiver)

[2]**cradle** *vb* **cra·dled; cra·dling** \ˈkrād-(ᵊ-)liŋ\ **1** : to place in or as if in a cradle **2** : NURSE, REAR

cra·dle·song \ˈkrād-ᵊl-ˌsȯŋ\ *n* : LULLABY

craft \ˈkraft\ *n* **1** : ART, SKILL; *also* : an occupation requiring special skill **2** : CUNNING, GUILE **3** *pl usu* **craft** : a boat esp. of small size; *also* : AIRCRAFT, SPACECRAFT

crafts·man \ˈkrafts-mən\ *n* : a skilled artisan — **crafts·man·ship** *n*

crafty \ˈkraf-tē\ *adj* **craft·i·er; -est** : CUNNING, DECEITFUL, SUBTLE — **craft·i·ly** \ˈkraf-tə-lē\ *adv* — **craft·i·ness** \-tē-nəs\ *n*

crag \ˈkrag\ *n* : a steep rugged cliff or rock — **crag·gy** \-ē\ *adj*

cram \ˈkram\ *vb* **crammed; cram·ming** **1** : to pack in tight : JAM **2** : to eat greedily **3** : to study rapidly under pressure for an examination

[1]**cramp** \ˈkramp\ *n* **1** : a sudden painful contraction of muscle **2** : sharp abdominal pain — usu. used in pl.

[2]**cramp** *vb* **1** : to affect with a cramp or cramps **2** : to restrain from free action : HAMPER **3** : to turn (the front wheels) sharply to the side

cran·ber·ry \ˈkran-ˌber-ē, -b(ə-)rē\ *n* : the red acid berry of any of several trailing plants related to the heaths; *also* : one of these plants

[1]**crane** \ˈkrān\ *n* **1** : any of a family of tall wading birds related to the rails; *also* : any of several herons **2** : a machine for lifting and carrying heavy objects

[2]**crane** *vb* **craned; cran·ing** : to stretch one's neck to see better

crane fly *n* : any of numerous long-legged slender two-winged flies that resemble large mosquitoes but do not bite

cranial nerve *n* : any of the nerves that arise in pairs from the lower surface of the brain and pass through openings in the skull to the periphery of the body

cra·ni·um \ˈkrā-nē-əm\ *n, pl* **-ni·ums** *or* **-nia** \-nē-ə\ : SKULL; *esp* : the part enclosing the brain — **cra·ni·al** \-əl\ *adj*

[1]**crank** \ˈkraŋk\ *n* **1** : a bent part of an axle or shaft or an arm at right angles to the end of a shaft by which circular motion is imparted to or received from it **2** : an eccentric person **3** : a bad-tempered person : GROUCH

[2]**crank** *vb* : to start or operate by turning a crank

crank·case \ˈkraŋk-ˌkās\ *n* : the housing of a crankshaft

crank out *vb* : to produce in a mechanical manner
crank·shaft \ˈkraŋk-ˌshaft\ *n* : a shaft turning or driven by a crank
cranky \ˈkraŋ-kē\ *adj* **crank·i·er; -est** **1** : IRRITABLE **2** : operating uncertainly or imperfectly
cran·ny \ˈkran-ē\ *n, pl* **crannies** : CREVICE, CHINK
crape \ˈkrāp\ *n* : CREPE; *esp* : black crepe used in mourning
craps \ˈkraps\ *n* : a gambling game played with two dice
crap·shoot·er \ˈkrap-ˌshüt-ər\ *n* : a person who plays craps
[1]**crash** \ˈkrash\ *vb* **1** : to break noisily : SMASH **2** : to damage an airplane in landing **3** : to enter or attend without invitation or without paying ⟨~ a party⟩
[2]**crash** *n* **1** : a loud sound (as of things smashing) **2** : an instance of crashing ⟨a plane ~⟩; *also* : COLLISION **3** : a sudden failure (as of a business)
[3]**crash** *adj* : marked by concerted effort over the shortest possible time
[4]**crash** *n* : coarse linen fabric used for towels and draperies
crash–land \ˈkrash-ˈland\ *vb* : to land an aircraft or spacecraft under emergency conditions usu. with damage to the craft — **crash landing** *n*
crass \ˈkras\ *adj* : STUPID, GROSS — **crass·ly** *adv*
crate \ˈkrāt\ *n* : a container often of wooden slats — **crate** *vb*
cra·ter \ˈkrāt-ər\ *n* [L, mixing bowl, crater, fr. Gk *kratēr,* fr. *kerannynai* to mix] **1** : the depression around the opening of a volcano **2** : a depression formed by the impact of a meteorite or by the explosion of a bomb or shell
cra·vat \krə-ˈvat\ *n* : NECKTIE
crave \ˈkrāv\ *vb* **craved; crav·ing** **1** : to ask for earnestly : BEG **2** : to long for : DESIRE
cra·ven \ˈkrā-vən\ *adj* : COWARDLY — **craven** *n*
crav·ing \ˈkrā-viŋ\ *n* : an urgent or abnormal desire
craw·fish \ˈkrȯ-ˌfish\ *n* **1** : CRAYFISH 1 **2** : SPINY LOBSTER
[1]**crawl** \ˈkrȯl\ *vb* **1** : to move slowly by drawing the body along the ground **2** : to advance feebly, cautiously, or slowly **3** : to be swarming with or feel as if swarming with creeping things ⟨a place *~ing* with ants⟩ ⟨her flesh *~ed*⟩
[2]**crawl** *n* **1** : a very slow pace **2** : a prone speed swimming stroke
cray·fish \ˈkrā-ˌfish\ *n* **1** : any of numerous freshwater crustaceans usu. much smaller than the related lobsters **2** : SPINY LOBSTER
cray·on \ˈkrā-ˌän, -ən\ *n* : a stick of chalk or wax used for writing, drawing, or coloring; *also* : a drawing made with such material — **crayon** *vb*
[1]**craze** \ˈkrāz\ *vb* **crazed; craz·ing** [ME *crasen* to crush, craze] : to make or become insane
[2]**craze** *n* : FAD, MANIA
cra·zy \ˈkrā-zē\ *adj* **cra·zi·er; -est** **1** : mentally disordered : INSANE **2** : wildly impractical; *also* : ERRATIC — **cra·zi·ly** \ˈkrā-zə-lē\ *adv* — **cra·zi·ness** \-zē-nəs\ *n*
CRC *abbr* Civil Rights Commission
creak \ˈkrēk\ *vb* : to make a prolonged squeaking or grating sound — **creak** *n* — **creaky** *adj*
[1]**cream** \ˈkrēm\ *n* **1** : the yellowish fat-rich part of milk **2** : a thick smooth sauce, confection, or cosmetic **3** : the choicest part **4** : a pale yellow color — **creamy** *adj*
[2]**cream** *vb* **1** : to prepare with a cream sauce **2** : to beat or blend into creamy consistency **3** : to defeat decisively
cream cheese *n* : a cheese made from whole milk enriched with cream
cream·ery \ˈkrēm-(ə-)rē\ *n, pl* **-er·ies** : an establishment where butter and cheese are made or milk and cream are prepared for sale
crease \ˈkrēs\ *n* : a mark or line made by or as if by folding — **crease** *vb*
cre·ate \krē-ˈāt\ *vb* **cre·at·ed; cre·at·ing** : to bring into being : cause to exist : MAKE, PRODUCE — **cre·ative** \-ˈāt-iv\ *adj* — **cre·ativ·i·ty** \ˌkre-(ˌ)ā-ˈtiv-ət-ē, ˌkrē-ə-\ *n*
cre·ation \krē-ˈā-shən\ *n* **1** : the act of creating or producing ⟨~ of the world⟩ **2** : something that is created **3** : all created things : WORLD
cre·ation·ism \krē-ˈā-shə-ˌniz-əm\ *n* : a doctrine or theory holding that matter, the various forms of life, and the world were created by God out of nothing — **cre·ation·ist** \-shə-nəst\ *n or adj*
cre·ator \krē-ˈāt-ər\ *n* **1** : one that creates : MAKER, AUTHOR **2** *cap* : GOD 1
crea·ture \ˈkrē-chər\ *n* : a lower animal; *also* : a human being
crèche \ˈkresh\ *n* [F, manger, crib] : a representation of the Nativity scene
cre·dence \ˈkrēd-ᵊns\ *n* : BELIEF
cre·den·tial \kri-ˈden-chəl\ *n* : something that gives a basis for credit or confidence
cre·den·za \kri-ˈden-zə\ *n* [It, lit., belief, confidence] : a sideboard, buffet, or bookcase usu. without legs
cred·i·ble \ˈkred-ə-bəl\ *adj* : TRUSTWORTHY, BELIEVABLE — **cred·i·bil·i·ty** \ˌkred-ə-ˈbil-ət-ē\ *n*
[1]**cred·it** \ˈkred-ət\ *vb* **1** : BELIEVE **2** : to give credit to
[2]**credit** *n* [MF, fr. It *credito,* fr. L *creditum* something entrusted to another, loan, fr. *credere* to believe, entrust] **1** : the balance (as in a bank) in a person's favor **2** : time given for payment for goods sold on trust **3** : an accounting entry of payment received **4** : BELIEF, FAITH **5** : financial trustworthiness **6** : ESTEEM **7** : a source of honor or distinction **8** : a unit of academic work
cred·it·able \ˈkred-ət-ə-bəl\ *adj* : worthy of esteem or praise — **cred·it·ably** \-blē\ *adv*
credit card *n* : a card authorizing purchases on credit
cred·i·tor \ˈkred-ət-ər\ *n* : a person to whom money is owed
cre·do \ˈkrēd-ō, ˈkrād-\ *n, pl* **credos** [ME, fr. L, I believe] : CREED
cred·u·lous \ˈkrej-ə-ləs\ *adj* : inclined to believe esp. on slight evidence — **cre·du·li·ty** \kri-ˈd(y)ü-lət-ē\ *n*
Cree \ˈkrē\ *n, pl* **Cree** *or* **Crees** : a member of an American Indian people of Manitoba and Saskatchewan
creed \ˈkrēd\ *n* [ME *crede,* fr. OE *crēda,* fr. L *credo* I believe, first word of the Apostles' and Nicene Creeds] : a statement of the essential beliefs of a religious faith
creek \ˈkrēk, ˈkrik\ *n* **1** *chiefly Brit* : a small inlet **2** : a stream smaller than a river and larger than a brook
Creek \ˈkrēk\ *n* : a member of an American Indian people of Alabama, Georgia, and Florida
creel \ˈkrēl\ *n* : a wicker basket esp. for carrying fish
creep \ˈkrēp\ *vb* **crept** \ˈkrept\; **creep·ing** **1** : CRAWL **2** : to grow over a surface like ivy **3** : to feel as though insects were crawling on the skin — **creep** *n* — **creep·er** *n*
creep·ing \ˈkrē-piŋ\ *adj* : developing or advancing by imperceptible degrees
creepy \ˈkrē-pē\ *adj* **creep·i·er; -est** : having or producing a nervous shivery fear
cre·mate \ˈkrē-ˌmāt\ *vb* **cre·mat·ed; cre·mat·ing** : to reduce (a dead body) to ashes with fire — **cre·ma·tion** \kri-ˈmā-shən\ *n*
cre·ma·to·ry \ˈkrē-mə-ˌtōr-ē, ˈkrem-ə-\ *n, pl* **-ries** : a furnace for cremating; *also* : a structure containing such a furnace
crème \ˈkrem, ˈkrēm\ *n, pl* **crèmes** \ˈkrem(z), ˈkrēmz\ [F, lit., cream] : a sweet liqueur
cren·el·lat·ed *or* **cren·el·at·ed** \ˈkren-ᵊl-ˌāt-əd\ *adj* : having battlements ⟨a ~ tower⟩ — **cren·el·la·tion** \ˌkren-ᵊl-ˈā-shən\ *n*
Cre·ole \ˈkrē-ˌōl\ *n* : a descendant of early French or

Spanish settlers of the U.S. Gulf states preserving their speech and culture; *also* : a person of mixed French or Spanish and Negro descent speaking a dialect of French or Spanish

cre·o·sote \ˈkrē-ə-ˌsōt\ *n* : an oily liquid obtained by distillation of coal tar and used in preserving wood

crepe *or* **crêpe** \ˈkrāp\ *n* : a light crinkled fabric of any of various fibers

crepe su·zette \ˌkrāp-sü-ˈzet\ *n, pl* **crepes suzette** \ˌkrāp(s)-sü-ˈzet\ *or* **crepe suzettes** \ˌkrāp-sü-ˈzets\ : a thin folded or rolled pancake in a hot orange-butter sauce that is sprinkled with a liqueur and set ablaze for serving

cre·pus·cu·lar \kri-ˈpəs-kyə-lər\ *adj* **1** : of, relating to, or resembling twilight **2** : active in the twilight ⟨~ insects⟩

cre·scen·do \krə-ˈshen-dō\ *adv or adj* [It] : increasing in loudness — used as a direction in music — **crescendo** *n*

cres·cent \ˈkres-ᵊnt\ *n* [ME *cressant,* fr. MF *creissant,* fr. *creistre* to grow, increase, fr. L *crescere*] : the moon at any stage between new moon and first quarter and between last quarter and new moon; *also* : something shaped like the figure of the crescent moon with a convex and a concave edge — **cres·cen·tic** \kre-ˈsent-ik, krə-\ *adj*

cress \ˈkres\ *n* : any of several salad plants related to the mustards

[1]**crest** \ˈkrest\ *n* **1** : a tuft or process on the head of an animal (as a bird) **2** : a heraldic device **3** : an upper part, edge, or limit ⟨the ~ of a hill⟩ — **crest·ed** \ˈkres-təd\ *adj* — **crest·less** *adj*

[2]**crest** *vb* **1** : CROWN **2** : to reach the crest of **3** : to rise to a crest

crest·fall·en \ˈkrest-ˌfö-lən\ *adj* : DISPIRITED, DEJECTED

Cre·ta·ceous \kri-ˈtā-shəs\ *adj* : of, relating to, or being the latest period of the Mesozoic era — **Cretaceous** *n*

cre·tin \ˈkrēt-ᵊn\ *n* [F *crétin,* fr. F dial. *cretin* Christian, human being, kind of idiot found in the Alps, fr. L *christianus* Christian] **1** : one affected with cretinism **2** : a stupid person

cre·tin·ism \-ˌiz-əm\ *n* : a usu. congenital abnormal condition characterized by physical stunting and mental deficiency

cre·tonne \ˈkrē-ˌtän\ *n* : a strong unglazed cotton cloth for curtains and upholstery

cre·vasse \kri-ˈvas\ *n* : a deep fissure esp. in a glacier

crev·ice \ˈkrev-əs\ *n* : a narrow fissure

[1]**crew** \ˈkrü\ *chiefly Brit past of* CROW

[2]**crew** \ˈkrü\ *n* [ME *crue,* lit., reinforcement, fr. MF *creue* increase, fr. *creistre* to grow, fr. L *crescere*] **1** : a body of people trained to work together for certain purposes **2** : a group of people who operate a ship, train, aircraft, or spacecraft **3** : the rowers and coxswain of a racing shell; *also* : the sport of rowing engaged in by a crew — **crew·man** \-mən\ *n*

crew cut *n* : a very short bristly haircut

crew·el \ˈkrü-əl\ *n* : slackly twisted worsted yarn used for embroidery — **crew·el·work** \-ˌwərk\ *n*

[1]**crib** \ˈkrib\ *n* **1** : a manger for feeding animals **2** : a small bedstead for a child **3** : a building or bin for storage (as of grain) **4** : a translation prepared to aid a student in preparing a lesson

[2]**crib** *vb* **cribbed; crib·bing** **1** : to put in a crib **2** : STEAL, PLAGIARIZE — **crib·ber** *n*

crib·bage \ˈkrib-ij\ *n* : a card game usu. played by two players and scored on a board (**cribbage board**)

crib death *n* : SUDDEN INFANT DEATH SYNDROME

crick \ˈkrik\ *n* : a painful spasm of muscles (as of the neck)

[1]**crick·et** \ˈkrik-ət\ *n* : any of various leaping insects related to the grasshoppers and noted for the chirping noises of the male

[2]**cricket** *n* : a game played with a bat and ball by two teams on a field centering upon two wickets each defended by a batsman

cri·er \ˈkrī(-ə)r\ *n* : one who calls out proclamations and announcements

crime \ˈkrīm\ *n* : a serious offense against the public law

[1]**crim·i·nal** \ˈkrim-ən-ᵊl\ *adj* **1** : involving or being a crime **2** : relating to crime or its punishment — **crim·i·nal·i·ty** \ˌkrim-ə-ˈnal-ət-ē\ *n* — **crim·i·nal·ly** \ˈkrim-ən-ᵊl-ē\ *adv*

[2]**criminal** *n* : one who has committed a crime

crim·i·nol·o·gy \ˌkrim-ə-ˈnäl-ə-jē\ *n* : the scientific study of crime and criminals — **crim·i·nol·o·gist** \ˌkrim-ə-ˈnäl-ə-jəst\ *n*

[1]**crimp** \ˈkrimp\ *vb* : to cause to become crinkled, wavy, or bent

[2]**crimp** *n* : something (as a curl in hair) produced by or as if by crimping

[1]**crim·son** \ˈkrim-zən\ *n* : a deep purplish red — **crimson** *adj*

[2]**crimson** *vb* : to make or become crimson

cringe \ˈkrinj\ *vb* **cringed; cring·ing** : to shrink in fear : WINCE, COWER

crin·kle \ˈkriŋ-kəl\ *vb* **crin·kled; crin·kling** \-k(ə-)liŋ\ : to turn or wind in many short bends or curves; *also* : WRINKLE, RIPPLE — **crinkle** *n* — **crin·kly** \-k(ə-)lē\ *adj*

crin·o·line \ˈkrin-ᵊl-ən\ *n* **1** : an open-weave cloth used for stiffening and lining **2** : a full stiff skirt or underskirt made of crinoline

[1]**crip·ple** \ˈkrip-əl\ *n* : a lame or disabled person

[2]**cripple** *vb* **crip·pled; crip·pling** \-(ə-)liŋ\ **1** : to make lame **2** : to make useless or imperfect

cri·sis \ˈkrī-səs\ *n, pl* **cri·ses** \ˈkrī-ˌsēz\ [L, fr. Gk *krisis,* lit., decision, fr. *krinein* to decide] **1** : the turning point for better or worse in an acute disease or fever **2** : a decisive or critical moment

crisp \ˈkrisp\ *adj* **1** : CURLY, WAVY **2** : BRITTLE **3** : FIRM, FRESH ⟨~ lettuce⟩ **4** : being sharp and clear **5** : LIVELY, SPARKLING **6** : FROSTY, SNAPPY; *also* : BRACING — **crisp** *vb* — **crisp·ly** *adv* — **crisp·ness** *n* — **crispy** *adj*

[1]**criss·cross** \ˈkris-ˌkrȯs\ *vb* **1** : to mark with crossed lines **2** : to go or pass back and forth

[2]**crisscross** *adj* : marked or characterized by crisscrossing — **crisscross** *adv*

[3]**crisscross** *n* : a pattern formed by crossed lines

crit *abbr* critical; criticism

cri·te·ri·on \krī-ˈtir-ē-ən\ *n, pl* **-ria** \-ē-ə\ : a standard on which a judgment may be based

crit·ic \ˈkrit-ik\ *n* **1** : a person who judges literary or artistic works **2** : one inclined to find fault

crit·i·cal \ˈkrit-i-kəl\ *adj* **1** : inclined to criticize **2** : relating to criticism or critics **3** : requiring careful judgment **4** : being or relating to a condition or disease involving danger of death **5** : being a crisis **6** : UNCERTAIN — **crit·i·cal·ly** \-i-k(ə-)lē\ *adv*

crit·i·cism \ˈkrit-ə-ˌsiz-əm\ *n* **1** : the act of criticizing; *esp* : CENSURE **2** : a judgment or review **3** : the art of judging works of literature or art

crit·i·cize \ˈkrit-ə-ˌsīz\ *vb* **-cized; -ciz·ing** **1** : to judge as a critic : EVALUATE **2** : to find fault : express criticism **syn** blame, censure, condemn

cri·tique \krə-ˈtēk\ *n* : a critical estimate or discussion

crit·ter \ˈkrit-ər\ *n* : CREATURE

croak \ˈkrōk\ *n* : a hoarse harsh cry (as of a frog) — **croak** *vb*

cro·chet \krō-ˈshā\ *n* [F, hook, crochet, fr. MF, dim. of *croche* hook] : needlework done with a single thread and hooked needle — **crochet** *vb*

crock \ˈkräk\ *n* : a thick earthenware pot or jar

crock·ery \ˈkräk-(ə-)rē\ *n* : EARTHENWARE

croc·o·dile \ˈkräk-ə-ˌdīl\ *n* [ME & L; ME *cocodrille,* fr. OF, fr. ML *cocodrillus,* alter. of L *crocodilus,* fr. Gk *krokodilos* lizard, crocodile, fr. *krokē* pebble + *drillos* worm] : any of several thick-skinned long-bodied reptiles of tropical and subtropical waters

cro·cus \ˈkrō-kəs\ *n, pl* **cro·cus·es** *also* **crocus** *or* **cro·ci** \-ˌkī\ : any of a large genus of low herbs related to the irises and having brightly colored flowers borne singly in early spring

crois·sant \k(rə-ˌ)wä-ˈsä^{n}\ *n, pl* **croissants** \-ˈsä^{n}(z)\ : a rich crescent-shaped roll

crone \ˈkrōn\ *n* : WITCH 2

cro·ny \ˈkrō-nē\ *n, pl* **cronies** : a close friend esp. of long standing

[1]**crook** \ˈkru̇k\ *vb* : to curve or bend sharply

[2]**crook** *n* **1** : a bent or curved implement **2** : SWINDLER, THIEF **3** : a bent or curved part; *also* : BEND, CURVE

crook·ed \ˈkru̇k-əd\ *adj* **1** : having a crook : BENT, CURVED **2** : DISHONEST — **crook·ed·ly** *adv* — **crook·ed·ness** *n*

croon \ˈkrün\ *vb* : to sing or hum in a gentle murmuring voice — **croon·er** *n*

[1]**crop** \ˈkräp\ *n* **1** : the handle of a whip; *also* : a short riding whip **2** : a pouch in the throat of many birds and insects where food is received **3** : something that can be harvested; *also* : the yield at harvest

[2]**crop** *vb* **cropped; crop·ping 1** : to remove the tips of : cut off short; *also* : TRIM **2** : to feed on by cropping **3** : to devote (land) to crops **4** : to appear unexpectedly

crop·land \-ˌland\ *n* : land devoted to the production of plant crops

crop·per \ˈkräp-ər\ *n* : a raiser of crops; *esp* : SHARECROPPER

cro·quet \krō-ˈkā\ *n* : a game in which mallets are used to drive wooden balls through a series of wickets set out on a lawn

cro·quette \krō-ˈket\ *n* [F] : a small often rounded mass of minced meat, fish, or vegetables fried in deep fat

cro·sier \ˈkrō-zhər\ *n* : a staff carried by bishops and abbots

[1]**cross** \ˈkrȯs\ *n* **1** : a structure consisting of an upright beam and a crossbar used esp. by the ancient Romans for execution **2** : a figure of the cross on which Christ was crucified used as a Christian symbol **3** : a hybridizing of unlike individuals or strains; *also* : a product of this **4** : a punch delivered with a circular motion over an opponent's lead

[2]**cross** *vb* **1** : to lie or place across; *also* : INTERSECT **2** : to cancel by marking a cross on or by lining through **3** : THWART, OBSTRUCT **4** : to go or extend across : TRAVERSE **5** : HYBRIDIZE **6** : to meet and pass on the way

[3]**cross** *adj* **1** : lying across **2** : CONTRARY, OPPOSED **3** : marked by bad temper **4** : HYBRID — **cross·ly** *adv*

cross·bar \ˈkrȯs-ˌbär\ *n* : a transverse bar or piece

cross·bones \-ˌbōnz\ *n pl* : two leg or arm bones placed or depicted crosswise

cross·bow \-ˌbō\ *n* : a short bow mounted crosswise at the end of a wooden stock that shoots short arrows

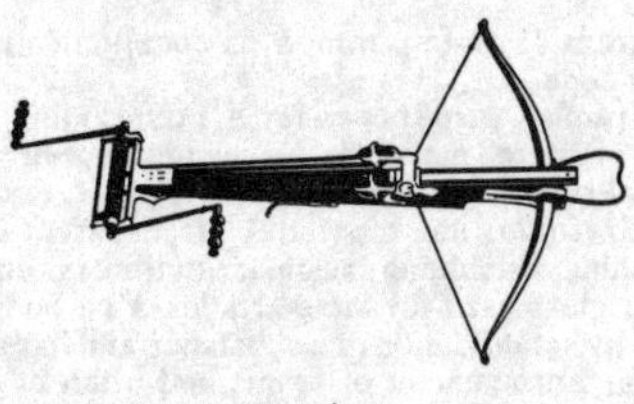

crossbow

cross·breed \ˈkrȯs-ˌbrēd, -ˈbrēd\ *vb* **-bred** \-ˈbred\; **-breed·ing** : HYBRIDIZE

cross–coun·try \-ˈkən-trē\ *adj* **1** : extending or moving across a country **2** : proceeding over the countryside (as fields and woods) rather than by roads **3** : of or relating to racing or skiing over the countryside instead of over a track or run — **cross–country** *adv*

cross·cur·rent \-ˈkər-ənt\ *n* **1** : a current running counter to another **2** : a conflicting tendency — usu. used in pl.

[1]**cross·cut** \-ˌkət\ *vb* : to cut or saw crosswise esp. of the grain of wood

[2]**crosscut** *adj* **1** : made or used for crosscutting ⟨a ~ saw⟩ **2** : cut across the grain

[3]**crosscut** *n* : something that cuts through transversely

cross–ex·am·ine \ˌkrȯs-ig-ˈzam-ən\ *vb* : to examine with questions to check the answers to previous questions — **cross–ex·am·i·na·tion** \-ˌzam-ə-ˈnā-shən\ *n*

cross–eyed \ˈkrȯs-ˌīd\ *adj* : having one or both eyes turned inward toward the nose

cross–fer·til·iza·tion \-ˌfərt-ᵊl-ə-ˈzā-shən\ *n* **1** : fertilization between sex cells produced by separate individuals or sometimes by individuals of different kinds; *also* : CROSS-POLLINATION **2** : a broadening or productive interchange (as between cultures) — **cross–fer·til·ize** \-ˈfərt-ᵊl-ˌīz\ *vb*

cross fire *n* **1** : crossing lines of fire in combat **2** : rapid or angry interchange

cross hair *n* : one of the fine wires or threads in the eyepiece of an optical instrument used as a reference line

cross·hatch \ˈkrȯs-ˌhach\ *vb* : to mark with a series of parallel lines that cross esp. obliquely — **cross–hatch·ing** *n*

cross·ing \ˈkrȯ-siŋ\ *n* **1** : a place or structure for crossing something (as a street or river) **2** : a point of intersection (as of a street and a railroad track)

cross·over \ˈkrȯs-ˌō-vər\ *n* **1** : CROSSING **2** : a member of one political party who votes in the primary of the other party

cross·piece \ˈkrȯs-ˌpēs\ *n* : a crosswise member

cross–pol·li·na·tion \ˌkrȯs-ˌpäl-ə-ˈnā- shən\ *n* : transfer of pollen from one flower to the stigma of another — **cross–pol·li·nate** \ˈkrȯs-ˈpäl-ə-ˌnāt\ *vb*

cross–pur·pose \ˈkrȯs-ˈpər-pəs\ *n* : a purpose contrary to another purpose ⟨working at ~*s*⟩

cross–ques·tion \-ˈkwes-chən\ *vb* : CROSS-EXAMINE

cross–re·fer \ˌkrȯs-ri-ˈfər\ *vb* : to refer by a notation or direction from one place to another (as in a book or list) — **cross–ref·er·ence** \ˈkrȯs-ˈref-(ə-)rəns\ *n*

cross·road \ˈkrȯs-ˌrōd\ *n* **1** : a road that crosses a main road or runs between main roads **2** : a place where roads meet — usu. used in pl. **3** : a crucial point where a decision must be made

cross section *n* **1** : a section cut across something; *also* : a representation made by or as if by such cutting **2** : a number of persons or things selected from a group that show the general nature of the whole group — **cross–sec·tion·al** *adj*

cross·walk \ˈkrȯs-ˌwȯk\ *n* : a specially marked path for pedestrians crossing a street

cross·ways \-ˌwāz\ *adv* : CROSSWISE

cross·wise \-ˌwīz\ *adv* : so as to cross something : ACROSS — **crosswise** *adj*

cross·word \ˌkrȯs-ˌwərd\ *n* : a puzzle in which words are fitted into a pattern of numbered squares in answer to clues

crotch \ˈkräch\ *n* : an angle formed by the parting of two legs, branches, or members

crotch·et \ˈkräch-ət\ *n* : an odd notion : WHIM — **crotch·ety** *adj*

crouch \ˈkrau̇ch\ *vb* **1** : to stoop or bend low **2** : CRINGE, COWER — **crouch** *n*

croup \ˈkrüp\ *n* : laryngitis esp. of infants marked by a hoarse ringing cough and difficult breathing — **croupy** *adj*

crou·pi·er \ˈkrü-pē-ər, -pē-ˌā\ *n* [F, lit., rider on the rump

\ə\abut \ᵊ\kitten \ər\further \a\ash \ā\ace \ä\cot, cart \au̇\out \ch\chin \e\bet \ē\easy \g\go \i\hit \ī\ice \j\job \ŋ\sing \ō\go \ȯ\law \ȯi\boy \th\thin \th\the \ü\loot \u̇\foot \y\yet \zh\vision *see also* Pronunciation Symbols page

of a horse, fr. *croupe* rump] : an employee of a gambling casino who collects and pays bets at a gaming table

crou·ton \ˈkrü-ˌtän\ *n* [F *croûton*, dim. of *croûte* crust] : a small cube of bread toasted or fried crisp

[1]**crow** \ˈkrō\ *n* **1** : any of various large glossy black birds related to the jays **2** *cap* : a member of an American Indian people of the region between the Platte and Yellowstone rivers; *also* : the language of the Crow people

[2]**crow** *vb* **1** : to make the loud shrill sound characteristic of the cock **2** : to utter a sound expressive of pleasure **3** : EXULT, GLOAT; *also* : BRAG, BOAST

[3]**crow** *n* : the cry of the cock

crow·bar \ˈkrō-ˌbär\ *n* : a metal bar usu. wedge-shaped at the end for use as a pry or lever

[1]**crowd** \ˈkrau̇d\ *vb* **1** : to press close **2** : to collect in numbers : THRONG **3** : CRAM, STUFF

[2]**crowd** *n* : a large number of people gathered together at random : THRONG

[1]**crown** \ˈkrau̇n\ *n* **1** : a mark of victory or honor; *esp* : the title of a champion in a sport **2** : a royal headdress **3** : the top of the head **4** : the highest part (as of a tree or tooth) **5** *often cap* : sovereign power; *also* : MONARCH **6** : a formerly used British silver coin — **crowned** \ˈkrau̇nd\ *adj*

[2]**crown** *vb* **1** : to place a crown on **2** : HONOR **3** : TOP, SURMOUNT **4** : to fit (a tooth) with an artificial crown

crown vetch *n* : a European leguminous herb with umbels of pink-and-white flowers and sharp-angled pods

crow's–foot \ˈkrōz-ˌfu̇t\ *n, pl* **crow's–feet** \-ˌfēt\ : any of the wrinkles around the outer corners of the eyes — usu. used in pl.

crow's nest *n* : a partly enclosed platform high on a ship's mast for use as a lookout

CRT *abbr* cathode-ray tube

cru·cial \ˈkrü-shəl\ *adj* : DECISIVE; *also* : IMPORTANT, SIGNIFICANT

cru·ci·ble \ˈkrü-sə-bəl\ *n* : a heat-resistant container in which material can be subjected to great heat

cru·ci·fix \ˈkrü-sə-ˌfiks\ *n* : a representation of Christ on the cross

cru·ci·fix·ion \ˌkrü-sə-ˈfik-shən\ *n* : the act of crucifying; *esp, cap* : the crucifying of Christ

cru·ci·form \ˈkrü-sə-ˌfȯrm\ *adj* : cross-shaped

cru·ci·fy \ˈkrü-sə-ˌfī\ *vb* **-fied; -fy·ing 1** : to put to death by nailing or binding the hands and feet to a cross **2** : MORTIFY 1 **3** : TORTURE, PERSECUTE

[1]**crude** \ˈkrüd\ *adj* **crud·er; crud·est 1** : not refined : RAW ⟨~ oil⟩ ⟨~ statistics⟩ **2** : lacking grace, taste, tact, or polish : RUDE — **crude·ly** *adv* — **cru·di·ty** \ˈkrüd-ət-ē\ *n*

[2]**crude** *n* : unrefined petroleum

cru·el \ˈkrü-əl\ *adj* **cru·el·er** *or* **cru·el·ler; cru·el·est** *or* **cru·el·lest** : causing pain and suffering to others : MERCILESS — **cru·el·ly** \-ē\ *adv* — **cru·el·ty** \-tē\ *n*

cru·et \ˈkrü-ət\ *n* : a small usu. glass bottle for vinegar, oil, or sauce

cruise \ˈkrüz\ *vb* **cruised; cruis·ing** [D *kruisen* to make a cross, cruise, fr. L *crux* cross] **1** : to sail about touching at a series of ports **2** : to travel for enjoyment **3** : to travel about the streets at random **4** : to travel at the most efficient operating speed ⟨the *cruising* speed of an airplane⟩ — **cruise** *n*

cruis·er \ˈkrü-zər\ *n* **1** : SQUAD CAR **2** : a large fast moderately armored and gunned warship **3** : a motorboat equipped for living aboard

crul·ler \ˈkrəl-ər\ *n* **1** : a small sweet cake in the form of a twisted strip fried in deep fat **2** *North & Midland* : an unraised doughnut

[1]**crumb** \ˈkrəm\ *n* : a small fragment

[2]**crumb** *vb* **1** : to break into crumbs **2** : to cover with crumbs

crum·ble \ˈkrəm-bəl\ *vb* **crum·bled; crum·bling** \-b(ə-)liŋ\ : to break into small pieces : DISINTEGRATE — **crum·bly** \-b(ə-)lē\ *adj*

crum·my *or* **crumby** \ˈkrəm-ē\ *adj* **crum·mi·er** *or* **crumb·i·er; -est 1** : MISERABLE, FILTHY **2** : CHEAP, WORTHLESS

crum·pet \ˈkrəm-pət\ *n* : a small round unsweetened bread cooked on a griddle

crum·ple \ˈkrəm-pəl\ *vb* **crum·pled; crum·pling** \-p(ə-)liŋ\ **1** : to crush together : RUMPLE **2** : COLLAPSE

[1]**crunch** \ˈkrənch\ *vb* : to chew with a grinding noise; *also* : to grind or press with a crushing noise

[2]**crunch** *n* **1** : an act of or a sound made by crunching **2** : a tight or critical situation — **crunchy** *adj*

cru·sade \krü-ˈsād\ *n* **1** *cap* : any of the expeditions in the 11th, 12th, and 13th centuries undertaken by Christian countries to take the Holy Land from the Muslims **2** : a reforming enterprise undertaken with zeal — **crusade** *vb* — **cru·sad·er** *n*

cruse \ˈkrüz, ˈkrüs\ *n* : a jar for water or oil

[1]**crush** \ˈkrəsh\ *vb* **1** : to squeeze out of shape **2** : HUG, EMBRACE **3** : to grind or pound to small bits **4** : OVERWHELM, SUPPRESS

[2]**crush** *n* **1** : an act of crushing **2** : a violent crowding **3** : INFATUATION

crust \ˈkrəst\ *n* **1** : the outside part of bread; *also* : a piece of old dry bread **2** : the cover of a pie **3** : a hard surface layer — **crust·al** *adj*

crus·ta·cean \ˌkrəs-ˈtā-shən\ *n* : any of a large class of mostly aquatic arthropods (as lobsters or crabs) having a firm crustlike shell

crusty *adj* **crust·i·er; -est 1** : having or being a crust **2** : CROSS, GRUMPY

crutch \ˈkrəch\ *n* : a supporting device; *esp* : a support fitting under the armpit for use by the disabled in walking

crux \ˈkrəks, ˈkru̇ks\ *n, pl* **crux·es 1** : a puzzling or difficult problem **2** : a crucial point

cru·za·do \krü-ˈzäd-ō\ *n* — see MONEY table

[1]**cry** \ˈkrī\ *vb* **cried; cry·ing 1** : to call out : SHOUT **2** : WEEP **3** : to proclaim publicly; *also* : to advertise wares by calling out

[2]**cry** *n, pl* **cries 1** : a loud outcry **2** : APPEAL, ENTREATY **3** : a fit of weeping **4** : the characteristic sound uttered by an animal

cry·ba·by \ˈkrī-ˌbā-bē\ *n* : one who cries easily or often

cryo·gen·ic \ˌkrī-ə-ˈjen-ik\ *adj* : of or relating to the production of very low temperatures; *also* : involving the use of a very low temperature — **cryo·gen·i·cal·ly** \-i-k(ə-)lē\ *adv*

cryo·gen·ics \-iks\ *n* : a branch of physics that relates to the production and effects of very low temperatures

cryo·lite \ˈkrī-ə-ˌlīt\ *n* : a usu. white mineral used in making aluminum

crypt \ˈkript\ *n* : a chamber wholly or partly underground

cryp·tic \ˈkrip-tik\ *adj* : meant to be puzzling or mysterious

cryp·to·gram \ˈkrip-tə-ˌgram\ *n* : a communication in cipher or code

cryp·tog·ra·phy \krip-ˈtäg-rə-fē\ *n* : the coding and decoding of secret messages — **cryp·tog·ra·pher** \-fər\ *n*

crys·tal \ˈkris-tᵊl\ *n* [ME *cristal*, fr. OF, fr. L *crystallum*, fr. Gk *krystallos* ice, crystal] **1** : transparent quartz **2** : something resembling crystal (as in transparency); *esp* : a clear glass used for table articles **3** : a body that is formed by solidification of a substance and has a regular repeating arrangement of atoms and often of external plane faces ⟨a snow ~⟩ ⟨a salt ~⟩ **4** : the transparent cover of a watch dial — **crys·tal·line** \-tə-lən\ *adj*

crys·tal·lize \ˈkris-tə-ˌlīz\ *vb* **-lized; -liz·ing 1** : to assume or cause to assume a crystalline form **2** : to take or cause to take a fixed and definite form — **crys·tal·li·za·tion** \ˌkris-tə-lə-ˈzā-shən\ *n*

crys·tal·log·ra·phy \ˌkris-tə-ˈläg-rə-fē\ *n* : the science dealing with the forms and structures of crystals — **crys·tal·log·ra·pher** \-fər\ *n*

cs *abbr* case; cases

Cs *symbol* cesium

CS *abbr* **1** civil service **2** county seat

C/S *abbr* cycles per second

CSA *abbr* Confederate States of America

CSM *abbr* command sergeant major

CST *abbr* central standard time

ct *abbr* **1** carat **2** cent **3** count **4** county **5** court

CT *abbr* **1** central time **2** Connecticut

ctg *or* **ctge** *abbr* cartage

ctn *abbr* carton

ctr *abbr* **1** center **2** counter

cu *abbr* cubic

Cu *symbol* [L *cuprum*] copper

cub \ˈkəb\ *n* **:** a young individual of some animals (as a fox, bear, or lion)

Cu·ban \ˈkyü-bən\ *n* **:** a native or inhabitant of Cuba — **Cuban** *adj*

cub·by·hole \ˈkəb-ē-ˌhōl\ *n* **:** a snug place (as for storing things)

[1]**cube** \ˈkyüb\ *n* **1 :** a solid having 6 equal square sides **2 :** the product obtained by taking a number 3 times as a factor ⟨27 is the ~ of 3⟩

[2]**cube** *vb* **cubed; cub·ing 1 :** to raise to the third power **2 :** to form into a cube **3 :** to cut into cubes

cube root *n* **:** a number whose cube is a given number

cu·bic \ˈkyü-bik\ *also* **cu·bi·cal** *adj* **1 :** having the form of a cube **2 :** having length, width, and height **3 :** being the volume of a cube whose edge is a specified unit

cu·bi·cle \ˈkyü-bi-kəl\ *n* **:** a small separate space (as for sleeping or studying)

cubic measure *n* **:** a unit (as cubic inch) for measuring volume — see METRIC SYSTEM table, WEIGHT table

cub·ism \ˈkyü-ˌbiz-əm\ *n* **:** a style of art characterized by the abstraction of natural forms into fragmented geometric shapes

cu·bit \ˈkyü-bət\ *n* **:** an ancient unit of length equal to about 18 inches (46 centimeters)

Cub Scout *n* **:** a member of the program of the Boy Scouts of America for boys 8–10 years of age

cuck·old \ˈkək-əld, ˈku̇k-\ *n* **:** a man whose wife is unfaithful

[1]**cuck·oo** \ˈkük-ü, ˈku̇k-\ *n, pl* **cuckoos :** a largely grayish brown European bird that lays its eggs in the nests of other birds for them to hatch

[2]**cuckoo** *adj* **:** SILLY, FOOLISH

cu·cum·ber \ˈkyü-(ˌ)kəm-bər\ *n* **:** the long fleshy many-seeded fruit of a vine of the gourd family that is grown as a garden vegetable; *also* **:** this vine

cud \ˈkəd\ *n* **:** food brought up into the mouth by ruminating animals (as cows) from the first stomach to be chewed again

cud·dle \ˈkəd-ᵊl\ *vb* **cud·dled; cud·dling** \ˈkəd-(ᵊ-)liŋ\ **:** to lie close

cud·gel \ˈkəj-əl\ *n* **:** a short heavy club — **cudgel** *vb*

[1]**cue** \ˈkyü\ *n* **1 :** a word, phrase, or action in a play serving as a signal for the next actor to speak or act **2 :** HINT — **cue** *vb*

[2]**cue** *n* **:** a tapered rod for striking the balls in billiards or pool

cue ball *n* **:** the ball a player strikes with a cue in billiards or pool

[1]**cuff** \ˈkəf\ *n* **1 :** a part (as of a sleeve or glove) encircling the wrist **2 :** the folded hem of a trouser leg

[2]**cuff** *vb* **:** to strike esp. with the open hand **:** SLAP

[3]**cuff** *n* **:** a blow with the hand esp. when open

cui·sine \kwi-ˈzēn\ *n* **:** manner of cooking; *also* **:** the food so prepared

cuke \ˈkyük\ *n* **:** CUCUMBER

cul–de–sac \ˌkəl-di-ˈsak, ˌku̇l-\ *n, pl* **culs–de–sac** \ˌkəl(z)-, ˌku̇l(z)-\ *also* **cul–de–sacs** \ˌkəl-də-ˈsaks, ˌku̇l-\ [F, lit., bottom of the bag] **:** a street or passage closed at one end

cu·li·nary \ˈkəl-ə-ˌner-ē, ˈkyü-lə-\ *adj* **:** of or relating to cookery

[1]**cull** \ˈkəl\ *vb* **:** to pick out from a group **:** CHOOSE

[2]**cull** *n* **:** something rejected from a group or lot as worthless or inferior

cul·mi·nate \ˈkəl-mə-ˌnāt\ *vb* **-nat·ed; -nat·ing :** to reach the highest point — **cul·mi·na·tion** \ˌkəl-mə-ˈnā-shən\ *n*

cu·lotte \ˈk(y)ü-ˌlät, k(y)ü-ˈlät\ *n* [F, breeches, fr. dim. of *cul* backside] **:** a divided skirt; *also* **:** a garment having a divided skirt — often used in pl.

cul·pa·ble \ˈkəl-pə-bəl\ *adj* **:** deserving blame — **cul·pa·bil·i·ty** \ˌkəl-pə-ˈbil-ət-ē\ *n*

cul·prit \ˈkəl-prət\ *n* [Anglo-French (the French of medieval England) *cul.* (abbr. of *culpable* guilty) + *prest, prit* ready (i.e. to prove it), fr. L *praestus*] **:** one accused or guilty of a crime

cult \ˈkəlt\ *n* **1 :** formal religious veneration **2 :** a religious system; *also* **:** its adherents **3 :** faddish devotion; *also* **:** a group of persons showing such devotion — **cult·ist** *n*

cul·ti·vate \ˈkəl-tə-ˌvāt\ *vb* **-vat·ed; -vat·ing 1 :** to prepare for the raising of crops **2 :** to foster the growth of ⟨~ vegetables⟩ **3 :** REFINE, IMPROVE **4 :** ENCOURAGE, FURTHER — **cul·ti·va·ble** \-və-bəl\ *adj* — **cul·ti·vat·able** \-ˌvāt-ə-bəl\ *adj* — **cul·ti·va·tion** \ˌkəl-tə-ˈvā-shən\ *n* — **cul·ti·va·tor** \ˈkəl-tə-ˌvāt-ər\ *n*

cul·ture \ˈkəl-chər\ *n* **1 :** TILLAGE, CULTIVATION; *also* **:** the growing of a particular crop ⟨grape ~⟩ **2 :** the act of developing by education and training **3 :** refinement of intellectual and artistic taste **4 :** a particular form or stage of civilization; *also* **:** a society characterized by such a culture — **cul·tur·al** \ˈkəlch(-ə)-rəl\ *adj* — **cul·tur·al·ly** \-ē\ *adv* — **cul·tured** \ˈkəl-chərd\ *adj*

cul·vert \ˈkəl-vərt\ *n* **:** a drain crossing under a road or railroad

cum *abbr* cumulative

cum·ber \ˈkəm-bər\ *vb* **cum·bered; cum·ber·ing** \-b(ə-)riŋ\ **:** to weigh down **:** BURDEN

cum·ber·some \ˈkəm-bər-səm\ *adj* **:** hard to handle or manage because of size or weight

cum·brous \ˈkəm-brəs\ *adj* **:** CUMBERSOME

cum·mer·bund \ˈkəm-ər-ˌbənd\ *n* [Hindi *kamarband,* fr. Per, fr. *kamar* waist + *band*] **:** a broad sash worn as a waistband

cu·mu·la·tive \ˈkyü-myə-lət-iv, -ˌlāt-\ *adj* **:** increasing in force or value by successive additions

cu·mu·lo·nim·bus \ˌkyü-myə-lō-ˈnim-bəs\ *n* **:** an anvil-shaped cumulus cloud extending to great heights

cu·mu·lus \ˈkyü-myə-ləs\ *n, pl* **-li** \-ˌlī, -ˌlē\ **:** a massive cloud having a flat base and rounded outlines

cu·ne·i·form \kyu̇-ˈnē-ə-ˌfȯrm\ *adj* **1 :** wedge-shaped **2 :** composed of wedge-shaped characters ⟨~ alphabet⟩

cun·ner \ˈkən-ər\ *n* **:** a small American food fish of the New England coast

cun·ni·lin·gus \ˌkən-i-ˈliŋ-gəs\ *also* **cun·ni·linc·tus** \-ˈliŋk-təs\ *n* **:** oral stimulation of the vulva or clitoris

[1]**cun·ning** \ˈkən-iŋ\ *adj* **1 :** SKILLFUL, DEXTEROUS **2 :** marked by wiliness and trickery **3 :** CUTE — **cun·ning·ly** *adv*

[2]**cunning** *n* **1 :** SKILL **2 :** CRAFTINESS, SLYNESS

[1]**cup** \ˈkəp\ *n* **1 :** a small bowl-shaped drinking vessel **2 :** the contents of a cup **3 :** communion wine **4 :** something resembling a cup **:** a small bowl or hollow — **cup·ful** *n*

[2]**cup** *vb* **cupped; cup·ping :** to curve into the shape of a cup

cup·bear·er \ˈkəp-ˌbar-ər\ *n* **:** one who has the duty of filling and serving cups of wine

cup·board \ˈkəb-ərd\ *n* **:** a small storage closet

cup·cake \ˈkəp-ˌkāk\ *n* : a small cake baked in a cuplike mold
Cu·pid \ˈkyü-pəd\ *n* : a winged naked figure of an infant often with a bow and arrow that represents the god Cupid
cu·pid·i·ty \kyu̇-ˈpid-ət-ē\ *n, pl* **-ties** : excessive desire for money : AVARICE
cu·po·la \ˈkyü-pə-lə, -ˌlō\ *n* : a small structure on top of a roof or building
cu·prite \ˈk(y)ü-ˌprīt\ *n* : a mineral that is an ore of copper
[1]**cur** \ˈkər\ *n* : a mongrel dog
[2]**cur** *abbr* **1** currency **2** current
cu·rate \ˈkyu̇r-ət\ *n* **1** : a clergyman in charge of a parish **2** : a clergyman who assists a rector or vicar — **cu·ra·cy** \-ə-sē\ *n*
cu·ra·tive \ˈkyu̇r-ət-iv\ *adj* : relating to or used in the cure of diseases — **curative** *n*
cu·ra·tor \kyu̇-ˈrāt-ər\ *n* : CUSTODIAN; *esp* : one in charge of a place of exhibit (as a museum or zoo)
[1]**curb** \ˈkərb\ *n* **1** : a bit that exerts pressure on a horse's jaws **2** : CHECK, RESTRAINT **3** : a raised edging (as of stone or concrete) along a paved street
[2]**curb** *vb* : to hold in or back : RESTRAIN
curb·ing \ˈkər-biŋ\ *n* **1** : the material for a curb **2** : CURB
curd \ˈkərd\ *n* : the thick protein-rich part of coagulated milk
cur·dle \ˈkərd-ᵊl\ *vb* **cur·dled; cur·dling** \ˈkərd-(ᵊ-)liŋ\ : to form curds; *also* : SPOIL, SOUR
[1]**cure** \ˈkyu̇r\ *n* **1** : spiritual care **2** : recovery or relief from disease **3** : a curative agent : REMEDY **4** : a course or period of treatment
[2]**cure** *vb* **cured; cur·ing 1** : to restore to health : HEAL, REMEDY **2** : to process for storage or use ⟨∼ bacon⟩; *also* : to become cured — **cur·able** *adj*
cu·ré \kyu̇-ˈrā\ *n* [F] : a parish priest
cure–all \ˈkyu̇r-ˌȯl\ *n* : a remedy for all ills : PANACEA
cu·ret·tage \ˌkyu̇r-ə-ˈtäzh\ *n* : a surgical scraping and cleaning by means of a scoop, loop, or ring
cur·few \ˈkər-ˌfyü\ *n* [ME, fr. MF *covrefeu,* signal given to bank the hearth fire, curfew, fr. *covrir* to cover + *feu* fire, fr. L *focus* hearth] : a regulation that specified persons (as children) be off the streets at a set hour of the evening; *also* : the sounding of a signal (as a bell) at this hour
cu·ria \ˈk(y)u̇r-ē-ə\ *n, pl* **cu·ri·ae** \ˈkyu̇r-ē-ˌē, ˈku̇r-ē-ˌī\ *often cap* : the body of congregations, tribunals, and offices through which the pope governs the Roman Catholic Church
cu·rie \ˈkyu̇r-ē\ *n* : a unit of radioactivity equal to 37 billion disintegrations per second
cu·rio \ˈkyu̇r-ē-ˌō\ *n, pl* **cu·ri·os** : an object or article valued because it is strange or rare
cu·ri·ous \ˈkyu̇r-ē-əs\ *adj* **1** : having a desire to investigate and learn **2** : STRANGE, UNUSUAL, ODD — **cu·ri·os·i·ty** \ˌkyu̇r-ē-ˈäs-ət-ē\ *n* — **cu·ri·ous·ly** *adv*
cu·ri·um \ˈkyu̇r-ē-əm\ *n* : a metallic radioactive element produced artificially—see ELEMENT table
[1]**curl** \ˈkərl\ *vb* **1** : to form into ringlets **2** : CURVE, COIL — **curl·er** *n*
[2]**curl** *n* **1** : a lock of hair that coils : RINGLET **2** : something having a spiral or twisted form — **curly** *adj*
cur·lew \ˈkərl-(y)ü\ *n, pl* **curlews** *or* **curlew** : any of various long-legged brownish birds that have a down-curved bill and are related to the woodcocks
curli·cue \ˈkər-li-ˌkyü\ *n* : a fancifully curved or spiral figure
cur·rant \ˈkər-ənt\ *n* **1** : a small seedless raisin **2** : the acid berry of a shrub related to the gooseberry; *also* : this plant
cur·ren·cy \ˈkər-ən-sē\ *n, pl* **-cies 1** : general use or acceptance **2** : something that is in circulation as a medium of exchange : MONEY
[1]**cur·rent** \ˈkər-ənt\ *adj* **1** : occurring in or belonging to the present **2** : used as a medium of exchange **3** : generally accepted or practiced
[2]**current** *n* **1** : the part of a body of fluid moving continuously in a certain direction; *also* : the swiftest part of a stream **2** : a flow of electric charge; *also* : the rate of such flow
cur·ric·u·lum \kə-ˈrik-yə-ləm\ *n, pl* **-la** \-lə\ *also* **-lums** [L, racecourse, fr. *currere* to run] : a course of study offered by a school or one of its divisions
[1]**cur·ry** \ˈkər-ē\ *vb* **cur·ried; cur·ry·ing 1** : to clean the coat of (a horse) with a currycomb **2** : to treat (tanned leather) esp. by incorporating oil or grease — **curry fa·vor** \-ˈfā-vər\ : to seek to gain favor by flattery or attention
[2]**cur·ry** \ˈkər-ē\ *n, pl* **curries** : a powder of blended spices used in cooking; *also* : a food seasoned with curry
cur·ry·comb \-ˌkōm\ *n* : a comb used esp. to curry horses — **currycomb** *vb*
[1]**curse** \ˈkərs\ *n* **1** : a prayer for harm to come upon one **2** : something that is cursed **3** : something that comes as if in response to a curse : SCOURGE
[2]**curse** *vb* **cursed; curs·ing 1** : to call on divine power to send injury upon **2** : BLASPHEME **3** : AFFLICT **syn** execrate, damn, anathematize, objurgate
cur·sive \ˈkər-siv\ *adj* : written or formed with the strokes of the letters joined together and the angles rounded
cur·sor \ˈkər-sər\ *n* : a bright figure (as a pointer) on a computer screen to indicate a character to be revised or a position where data is to be entered
cur·so·ry \ˈkərs-(ə-)rē\ *adj* : hastily and often superficially done : HASTY — **cur·so·ri·ly** \-rə-lē\ *adj*
curt \ˈkərt\ *adj* : rudely short or abrupt — **curt·ly** *adv*
cur·tail \(ˌ)kər-ˈtāl\ *vb* : to cut off the end of : SHORTEN — **cur·tail·ment** *n*
cur·tain \ˈkərt-ᵊn\ *n* **1** : a hanging screen that can be drawn back esp. at a window **2** : the screen between the stage and auditorium of a theater — **curtain** *vb*
curt·sy *or* **curt·sey** \ˈkərt-sē\ *n, pl* **curtsies** *or* **curtseys** : a courteous bow made by women chiefly by bending the knees — **curtsy** *or* **curtsey** *vb*
cur·va·ceous *also* **cur·va·cious** \ˌkər-ˈvā-shəs\ *adj* : having a well-proportioned feminine figure marked by pronounced curves
cur·va·ture \ˈkər-və-ˌchu̇r\ *n* : a measure or amount of curving : BEND
[1]**curve** \ˈkərv\ *vb* **curved; curv·ing** : to bend from a straight line or course
[2]**curve** *n* **1** : a line esp. when curved **2** : something that bends or curves without angles ⟨a ∼ in the road⟩ **3** : a ball thrown so that it swerves from a normal course
cur·vet \(ˌ)kər-ˈvet\ *n* : a prancing leap of a horse — **curvet** *vb*
[1]**cush·ion** \ˈku̇sh-ən\ *n* **1** : a soft pillow or pad to rest on or against **2** : the springy pad inside the rim of a billiard table **3** : something soft that prevents discomfort or protects against injury
[2]**cushion** *vb* **cush·ioned; cush·ion·ing** \-(ə-)niŋ\ **1** : to provide (as a seat) with a cushion **2** : to soften or lessen the force or shock of
cusp \ˈkəsp\ *n* : a pointed end or part (as of a tooth)
cus·pid \ˈkəs-pəd\ *n* : a canine tooth
cus·pi·dor \ˈkəs-pə-ˌdȯr\ *n* : SPITTOON
cus·tard \ˈkəs-tərd\ *n* : a sweetened mixture of milk and eggs baked, boiled, or frozen
cus·to·di·al \ˌkəs-ˈtōd-ē-əl\ *adj* : marked by watching and protecting rather than seeking to cure ⟨∼ care⟩
cus·to·di·an \ˌkəs-ˈtōd-ē-ən\ *n* : one who has custody (as of a building)
cus·to·dy \ˈkəs-təd-ē\ *n, pl* **-dies** : immediate care or charge
[1]**cus·tom** \ˈkəs-təm\ *n* **1** : habitual course of action : recog-

nized usage 2 *pl* : taxes levied on imports 3 : business patronage

[2]**custom** *adj* 1 : made to personal order 2 : doing work only on order

cus·tom·ary \ˈkəs-tə-ˌmer-ē\ *adj* 1 : based on or established by custom ⟨~ rent⟩ 2 : commonly practiced or observed : HABITUAL — **cus·tom·ar·i·ly** \ˌkəs-tə-ˈmer-ə-lē\ *adv*

cus·tom–built \ˌkəs-təm-ˈbilt\ *adj* : built to individual order

cus·tom·er \ˈkəs-tə-mər\ *n* : BUYER, PURCHASER; *esp* : a regular or frequent buyer

cus·tom·house \ˈkəs-təm-ˌhau̇s\ *n* : the building where customs are paid

cus·tom·ize \ˈkəs-tə-ˌmīz\ *vb* **-ized; -iz·ing** : to build, fit, or alter according to individual specifications

cus·tom–made \ˌkəs-təm-ˈ(m)ād\ *adj* : made to individual order

[1]**cut** \ˈkət\ *vb* **cut; cut·ting** 1 : to penetrate or divide with a sharp edge : CLEAVE, GASH; *also* : to experience the growth of (a tooth) through the gum 2 : to hurt the feelings of 3 : to strike sharply 4 : SHORTEN, REDUCE 5 : to remove by severing or paring 6 : INTERSECT, CROSS 7 : to divide into parts 8 : to go quickly or change direction abruptly 9 : to cause to stop

[2]**cut** *n* 1 : a customary segment of a meat carcass 2 : SHARE 3 : something made by cutting : GASH, CLEFT 4 : an excavated channel or roadway 5 : BAND 4 6 : a sharp stroke or blow 7 : REDUCTION ⟨~ in wages⟩ 8 : the shape or manner in which a thing is cut

cut–and–dried \ˌkət-ᵊn-ˈdrīd\ *also* **cut–and–dry** \-ˈdrī\ *adj* : according to a plan, set procedure, or formula

cu·ta·ne·ous \kyu̇-ˈtā-nē-əs\ *adj* : of, relating to, or affecting the skin

cut·back \ˈkət-ˌbak\ *n* 1 : something cut back 2 : REDUCTION

cute \ˈkyüt\ *adj* **cut·er; cut·est** [short for *acute*] 1 : CLEVER, SHREWD 2 : daintily attractive : PRETTY

cu·ti·cle \ˈkyüt-i-kəl\ *n* 1 : an outer layer (as of skin) 2 : dead or horny epidermis esp. around a fingernail — **cu·tic·u·lar** \kyu̇-ˈtik-yə-lər\ *adj*

cut in \ˌkət-ˈin\ *vb* 1 : to thrust oneself between others 2 : to interrupt a dancing couple and take one as one's partner

cut·lass \ˈkət-ləs\ *n* : a short heavy curved sword

cut·ler \ˈkət-lər\ *n* : one who makes, deals in, or repairs cutlery

cut·lery \ˈkət-lə-rē\ *n* : edged or cutting tools; *esp* : implements for cutting and eating food

cut·let \ˈkət-lət\ *n* : a slice of meat (as veal) for broiling or frying

cut·off \ˈkət-ˌȯf\ *n* 1 : the channel formed when a stream cuts through the neck of an oxbow; *also* : SHORTCUT 2 : a device for cutting off 3 *pl* : shorts orig. made from jeans with the legs cut off at the knees or higher

cut·out \ˈkət-ˌau̇t\ *n* : something cut out or prepared for cutting out from something else ⟨a page of animal ~*s*⟩

cut out \ˌkət-ˈau̇t\ *vb* 1 : to be all that one can handle ⟨had her work *cut out* for her⟩ 2 : DISCONNECT 3 : to cease operating ⟨the engine *cut out*⟩ 4 : ELIMINATE ⟨*cut out* unnecessary expense⟩

cut–rate \ˈkət-ˈrāt\ *adj* : relating to or dealing in goods sold at reduced rates

cut·ter \ˈkət-ər\ *n* 1 : a tool or a machine for cutting 2 : a ship's boat for carrying stores and passengers 3 : a small armed boat in government service 4 : a light sleigh

[1]**cut·throat** \ˈkət-ˌthrōt\ *n* : MURDERER

[2]**cutthroat** *adj* 1 : MURDEROUS, CRUEL 2 : MERCILESS, RUTHLESS ⟨~ competition⟩

cutthroat trout *n* : a large American trout with a red mark under the jaw

[1]**cut·ting** \ˈkət-iŋ\ *n* : a piece of a plant able to grow into a new plant

[2]**cutting** *adj* 1 : SHARP, EDGED 2 : marked by piercing cold 3 : likely to hurt the feelings : SARCASTIC

cut·tle·fish \ˈkət-ᵊl-ˌfish\ *n* : a 10-armed mollusk related to the squid with an internal shell (**cut·tle·bone** \-ˌbōn\) composed of calcium compounds

cut·up \ˈkət-ˌəp\ *n* : one that clowns or acts boisterously — **cut up** \ˌkət-ˈəp\ *vb*

cut·worm \-ˌwərm\ *n* : any of various smooth-bodied moth larvae that feed on plants at night

cw *abbr* clockwise

CWO *abbr* 1 cash with order 2 chief warrant officer

cwt *abbr* hundredweight

-cy \sē\ *n suffix* 1 : action : practice ⟨mendican*cy*⟩ 2 : rank : office ⟨chaplain*cy*⟩ 3 : body : class ⟨magistra*cy*⟩ 4 : state : quality ⟨accura*cy*⟩

cy·an \ˈsī-ˌan, -ən\ *n* : a greenish blue color

cy·a·nide \ˈsī-ə-ˌnīd, -nəd\ *n* : a poisonous compound of carbon and nitrogen with either sodium or potassium

cy·ber·net·ics \ˌsī-bər-ˈnet-iks\ *n* : the science of communication and control theory that is concerned esp. with the comparative study of automatic control systems — **cy·ber·net·ic** *adj*

cyc *or* **cycl** *abbr* cyclopedia

cy·cla·men \ˈsī-klə-mən\ *n* : any of a genus of plants related to the primroses and grown for their showy nodding flowers

[1]**cy·cle** \ˈsī-kəl\ *n* 1 : a period of time occupied by a series of events that repeat themselves regularly and in the same order 2 : a recurring round of operations or events 3 : one complete occurrence of a periodic process (as a vibration or current alternation) 4 : a circular or spiral arrangement 5 : a long period of time : AGE 6 : BICYCLE 7 : MOTORCYCLE — **cy·clic** \ˈsī-klik, ˈsik-lik\ *or* **cy·cli·cal** \ˈsī-kli-kəl, ˈsik-li-\ *adj* — **cy·cli·cal·ly** \-k(ə-)lē\ *also* **cy·clic·ly** \ˈsī-kli-klē, ˈsik-li-\ *adv*

[2]**cy·cle** \ˈsī-kəl\ *vb* **cy·cled; cy·cling** \ˈsī-k(ə-)liŋ, ˈsik(-ə)-\ : to ride a cycle

cy·clist \ˈsī-k(ə-)ləst\ *n* : one who rides a cycle

cy·clone \ˈsī-ˌklōn\ *n* 1 : a storm or system of winds that rotates about a center of low atmospheric pressure and advances at 20 to 30 miles an hour (about 30 to 50 kilometers per hour) 2 : TORNADO — **cy·clon·ic** \sī-ˈklän-ik\ *adj*

cy·clo·pe·dia *or* **cy·clo·pae·dia** \ˌsī-klə-ˈpēd-ē-ə\ *n* : ENCYCLOPEDIA

cy·clo·tron \ˈsī-klə-ˌträn\ *n* : a device for giving high speed to charged particles by magnetic and electric fields

cyg·net \ˈsig-nət\ *n* : a young swan

cyl *abbr* cylinder

cyl·in·der \ˈsil-ən-dər\ *n* : the solid figure formed by turning a rectangle about one side as an axis; *also* : a body or space of this form ⟨an engine ~⟩ ⟨a bullet in the ~ of a revolver⟩ — **cy·lin·dri·cal** \sə-ˈlin-dri-kəl\ *adj*

cym·bal \ˈsim-bəl\ *n* : one of a pair of concave brass plates clashed together

cyme \ˈsīm\ *n* : an inflorescence of several flowers each on a stem with the first-opening central flower on the main stem and later-opening flowers developing from lateral buds

cyn·ic \ˈsin-ik\ *n* [MF or L, MF *cynique*, fr. L *cynicus*, fr. Gk *kynikos*, lit., like a dog, fr. *kyōn* dog] : one who attributes all actions to selfish motives — **cyn·i·cal** \-i-kəl\ *adj* — **cyn·i·cal·ly** \-k(ə-)lē\ *adv* — **cyn·i·cism** \ˈsin-ə-ˌsiz-əm\ *n*

cy·no·sure \ˈsī-nə-ˌshu̇r, ˈsin-ə-\ *n* [MF & L; MF, Ursa

Minor, guide, fr. L *cynosura* Ursa Minor, fr. Gk *kynosoura*, fr. *kynos oura* dog's tail] : a center of attraction

CYO *abbr* Catholic Youth Organization

cy·press \ˈsī-prəs\ *n* **1** : any of a genus of scaly-leaved evergreen trees related to the pines **2** : either of two large swamp trees of the southern U.S. with hard red wood **3** : the wood of a cypress

cyst \ˈsist\ *n* : an abnormal closed bodily sac usu. containing liquid — **cys·tic** \ˈsis-tik\ *adj*

cystic fibrosis *n* : a common hereditary disease marked esp. by deficiency of pancreatic enzymes and by respiratory symptoms

cy·tol·o·gy \sī-ˈtäl-ə-jē\ *n* : a branch of biology dealing with cells — **cy·to·log·i·cal** \ˌsīt-ᵊl-ˈäj-i-kəl\ *or* **cy·to·log·ic** \-ˈäj-ik\ *adj* — **cy·tol·o·gist** \sī-ˈtäl-ə-jəst\ *n*

cy·to·plasm \ˈsīt-ə-ˌplaz-əm\ *n* : the protoplasm of a cell that lies external to the nucleus — **cy·to·plas·mic** \ˌsīt-ə-ˈplaz-mik\ *adj*

cy·to·sine \ˈsīt-ə-ˌsēn\ *n* : a chemical base that is a pyrimidine coding genetic information in DNA and RNA

CZ *abbr* Canal Zone

czar \ˈzär\ *n* : the ruler of Russia until 1917; *also* : one having great authority — **czar·ist** *n or adj*

cza·ri·na \zä-ˈrē-nə\ *n* : the wife of a czar

Czech \ˈchek\ *n* **1** : a native or inhabitant of Czechoslovakia **2** : the language of the Czechs — **Czech** *adj*

Czecho·slo·vak \ˌchek-ə-ˈslō-ˌväk, -ˌvak\ *or* **Czecho·slo·va·ki·an** \-slō-ˈväk-ē-ən, -ˈvak-\ *adj* : of, relating to, or characteristic of Czechoslovakia or its people — **Czechoslovak** *or* **Czechoslovakian** *n*

D

[1]d \ˈdē\ *n, pl* **d's** *or* **ds** \ˈdēz\ *often cap* **1** : the 4th letter of the English alphabet **2** : a grade rating a student's work as poor

[2]d *abbr, often cap* **1** date **2** daughter **3** day **4** dead **5** deceased **6** degree **7** [L *denarius*] penny; pence **8** depart; departure **9** diameter

D *symbol* deuterium

DA *abbr* **1** deposit account **2** district attorney **3** don't answer

[1]dab \ˈdab\ *n* **1** : a sudden blow or thrust : POKE; *also* : PECK **2** : a gentle touch or stroke : PAT

[2]dab *vb* **dabbed; dab·bing** **1** : to strike or touch gently : PAT **2** : to apply lightly or irregularly : DAUB

[3]dab *n* **1** : DAUB **2** : a small amount

dab·ble \ˈdab-əl\ *vb* **dab·bled; dab·bling** \-(ə-)liŋ\ **1** : to wet by splashing : SPATTER **2** : to paddle or play in or as if in water **3** : to work or concern oneself without serious effort

dace \ˈdās\ *n, pl* **dace** : any of various small No. American freshwater fishes related to the carp

da·cha \ˈdäch-ə\ *n* [Russ, lit., gift; fr. its frequently being the gift of a ruler] : a Russian country house

dachs·hund \ˈdäks-ˌhu̇nt\ *n, pl* **dachshunds** [G, fr. *dachs* badger + *hund* dog] : a small dog of a breed of German origin with a long body, short legs, and long drooping ears

dac·tyl \ˈdak-tᵊl\ *n* [ME *dactile*, fr. L *dactylus*, fr. Gk *daktylos*, lit., finger; fr. the fact that the three syllables have the first one longest like the joints of the finger] : a metrical foot of one accented syllable followed by two unaccented syllables — **dac·tyl·ic** \dak-ˈtil-ik\ *adj or n*

dad \ˈdad\ *n* : FATHER

Da·da \ˈdäd-(ˌ)ä\ *n* : a movement in art and literature based on deliberate irrationality and negation of traditional artistic values — **da·da·ism** \-ˌiz-əm\ *n, often cap* — **da·da·ist** \-ˌist\ *n or adj, often cap*

dad·dy \ˈdad-ē\ *n, pl* **daddies** : FATHER

dad·dy long·legs \ˌdad-ē-ˈlȯŋ-ˌlegz\ *n, pl* **daddy longlegs** : any of various arachnids resembling the true spiders but having small rounded bodies and long slender legs

dae·mon *var of* DEMON

daf·fo·dil \ˈdaf-ə-ˌdil\ *n* : any of a genus of bulbous herbs with usu. large flowers having a trumpetlike center

daf·fy \ˈdaf-ē\ *adj* **daf·fi·er; -est** : DAFT

daft \ˈdaft\ *adj* : FOOLISH; *also* : INSANE — **daft·ness** *n*

dag *abbr* dekagram

dag·ger \ˈdag-ər\ *n* **1** : a sharp pointed knife for stabbing **2** : a character † used as a reference mark or to indicate a death date

da·guerre·o·type \də-ˈger-(ē-)ə-ˌtīp\ *n* : an early photograph produced on a silver or a silver-covered copper plate

dahl·ia \ˈdal-yə, ˈdäl-\ *n* : any of a genus of tuberous herbs related to the daisies and having showy flowers

[1]dai·ly \ˈdā-lē\ *adj* **1** : occurring, done, or used every day or every weekday **2** : of or relating to every day ⟨~ visitors⟩ **3** : computed in terms of one day ⟨~ wages⟩ — **daily** *adv*

[2]daily *n, pl* **dailies** : a newspaper published every weekday

daily double *n* : a system of betting on races in which the bettor must pick the winners of two stipulated races in order to win

[1]dain·ty \ˈdānt-ē\ *n, pl* **dainties** [ME *deinte*, fr. OF *deintié*, fr. L *dignitas* dignity, worth] : something delicious or pleasing to the taste : DELICACY

[2]dainty *adj* **dain·ti·er; -est** **1** : pleasing to the taste **2** : delicately pretty **3** : having or showing delicate taste; *also* : FASTIDIOUS — **dain·ti·ly** \ˈdānt-ᵊl-ē\ *adv* — **dain·ti·ness** \-ē-nəs\ *n*

dai·qui·ri \ˈdī-kə-rē, ˈdak-ə-rē\ *n* [*Daiquirí*, Cuba] : a cocktail made of rum, lime juice, and sugar

dairy \ˈde(ə)r-ē\ *n, pl* **dair·ies** [ME *deyerie*, fr. *deye* dairymaid, fr. OE *dǣge* kneader of bread] **1** : CREAMERY **2** : a farm specializing in milk production

dairy·ing \ˈder-ē-iŋ\ *n* : the business of operating a dairy

dairy·maid \-ˌmād\ *n* : a woman employed in a dairy

dairy·man \-mən, -ˌman\ *n* : a person who operates a dairy farm or works in a dairy

da·is \ˈdā-əs\ *n* : a raised platform usu. above the floor of a hall or large room

dai·sy \ˈdā-zē\ *n, pl* **daisies** [ME *dayeseye*, fr. OE *dægesēage*, fr. *dæg* day + *ēage* eye] : any of numerous composite plants having flower heads in which the marginal flowers resemble petals

daisy wheel *n* : a printing element for an electric typewriter or computer printer that consists of a disk having spokes with type on the end

Da·ko·ta \də-ˈkōt-ə\ *n, pl* **Dakotas** *also* **Dakota** : a member of an American Indian people of the northern Mississippi valley; *also* : their language

dal *abbr* dekaliter

da·la·si \dä-ˈläs-ē\ *n, pl* **dalasi** *or* **dalasis** — see MONEY table

dale \ˈdāl\ *n* : VALLEY

dal·ly \ˈdal-ē\ *vb* **dal·lied; dal·ly·ing** **1** : to act playfully;

esp : to play amorously **2** : to waste time **3** : LINGER, DAWDLE — **dal·li·ance** \-əns\ *n*

dal·ma·tian \dal-ˈmā-shən\ *n, often cap* : any of a breed of medium-sized dogs having a white short-haired coat with black or brown spots

[1]**dam** \ˈdam\ *n* : a female parent — used esp. of a domestic animal

[2]**dam** *n* : a barrier (as across a stream) to prevent the flow of water — **dam** *vb*

[3]**dam** *abbr* dekameter

[1]**dam·age** \ˈdam-ij\ *n* **1** : loss or harm due to injury to persons, property, or reputation **2** *pl* : compensation in money imposed by law for loss or injury ⟨bring a suit for ∼*s*⟩

[2]**damage** *vb* **dam·aged; dam·ag·ing** : to cause damage to

dam·a·scene \ˈdam-ə-ˌsēn\ *vb* **-scened; -scen·ing** : to ornament (as iron or steel) with wavy patterns or with inlaid work of precious metals

dam·ask \ˈdam-əsk\ *n* **1** : a firm lustrous reversible figured fabric used for household linen **2** : a tough steel having decorative wavy lines

dame \ˈdām\ *n* **1** : a woman of rank, station, or authority **2** : an elderly woman **3** : WOMAN

damn \ˈdam\ *vb* **damned; damn·ing** \ˈdam-iŋ\ [ME *dampnen,* fr. OF *dampner,* fr. L *damnare,* fr. *damnum* damage, loss, fine] **1** : to condemn esp. to hell **2** : CURSE — **damned** *adj*

dam·na·ble \ˈdam-nə-bəl\ *adj* **1** : liable to or deserving punishment **2** : DETESTABLE ⟨∼ weather⟩ — **dam·na·bly** \-blē\ *adv*

dam·na·tion \dam-ˈnā-shən\ *n* **1** : the act of damning **2** : the state of being damned

[1]**damp** \ˈdamp\ *n* **1** : a noxious gas **2** : MOISTURE

[2]**damp** *vb* : DAMPEN

[3]**damp** *adj* : MOIST — **damp·ness** *n*

damp·en \ˈdam-pən\ *vb* **damp·ened; damp·en·ing** \ˈdamp-(ə-)niŋ\ **1** : to check or diminish in activity or vigor **2** : to make or become damp

damp·er \ˈdam-pər\ *n* : one that damps; *esp* : a valve or movable plate (as in the flue of a stove, furnace, or fireplace) to regulate the draft

dam·sel \ˈdam-zəl\ *n* : GIRL, MAIDEN

dam·sel·fly \-ˌflī\ *n* : any of a group of insects that are closely related to the dragonflies but fold their wings above the body when at rest

dam·son \ˈdam-zən\ *n* : a plum with acid purple fruit; *also* : its fruit

Dan *abbr* Daniel

[1]**dance** \ˈdans\ *vb* **danced; danc·ing** **1** : to glide, step, or move through a set series of movements usu. to music **2** : to move quickly up and down or about **3** : to perform or take part in as a dancer — **danc·er** *n*

[2]**dance** *n* **1** : an act or instance of dancing **2** : a social gathering for dancing **3** : a piece of music (as a waltz) by which dancing may be guided **4** : the art of dancing

D & C *abbr* dilation and curettage

dan·de·li·on \ˈdan-d^{ə}l-ˌī-ən\ *n* [MF *dent de lion,* lit., lion's tooth] : any of a genus of common yellow-flowered composite herbs

dan·der \ˈdan-dər\ *n* : ANGER, TEMPER

dan·di·fy \ˈdan-di-ˌfī\ *vb* **-fied; -fy·ing** : to cause to resemble a dandy

dan·dle \ˈdan-d^{ə}l\ *vb* **dan·dled; dan·dling** : to move up and down in one's arms or on one's knee in affectionate play

dan·druff \ˈdan-drəf\ *n* : a whitish scurf on the scalp that comes off in small scales

[1]**dan·dy** \ˈdan-dē\ *n, pl* **dandies** **1** : a man unduly attentive to dress **2** : something excellent in its class

[2]**dandy** *adj* **dan·di·er; -est** : very good : FIRST-RATE

Dane \ˈdān\ *n* : a native or inhabitant of Denmark

dan·ger \ˈdān-jər\ *n* **1** : exposure or liability to injury, harm, or evil **2** : something that may cause injury or harm **syn** peril, hazard, risk, jeopardy

dan·ger·ous \ˈdānj-(ə-)rəs\ *adj* **1** : HAZARDOUS, PERILOUS **2** : able or likely to inflict injury — **dan·ger·ous·ly** *adv*

dan·gle \ˈdaŋ-gəl\ *vb* **dan·gled; dan·gling** \-g(ə-)liŋ\ **1** : to hang loosely esp. with a swinging motion : SWING **2** : to be a hanger-on or dependent **3** : to be left without proper grammatical connection in a sentence **4** : to keep hanging uncertainly

Dan·iel \ˈdan-yəl\ *n* — see BIBLE table

Dan·ish \ˈdā-nish\ *n* : the language of the Danes — **Danish** *adj*

Danish pastry *n* : a pastry made of a rich yeast-raised dough

dank \ˈdaŋk\ *adj* : disagreeably wet or moist : DAMP

dan·seuse \dä^{n}-ˈsə(r)z, dän-ˈsüz\ *n* [F] : a female ballet dancer

dap·per \ˈdap-ər\ *adj* **1** : SPRUCE, TRIM **2** : being alert and lively in movement and manners : JAUNTY

dap·ple \ˈdap-əl\ *vb* **dap·pled; dap·pling** : to mark with different-colored spots

DAR *abbr* Daughters of the American Revolution

[1]**dare** \ˈdaər\ *vb* **dared; dar·ing** **1** : to have sufficient courage : be bold enough to **2** : CHALLENGE **3** : to confront boldly

[2]**dare** *n* : an act or instance of daring : CHALLENGE

dare·dev·il \-ˌdev-əl\ *n* : a recklessly bold person

dar·ing \ˈda(ə)r-iŋ\ *n* : venturesome boldness — **daring** *adj* — **dar·ing·ly** *adv*

[1]**dark** \ˈdärk\ *adj* **1** : being without light or without much light **2** : not light in color ⟨a ∼ suit⟩ **3** : GLOOMY **4** : being without knowledge and culture ⟨the *Dark* Ages⟩ **5** : SECRETIVE — **dark·ly** *adv* — **dark·ness** *n*

[2]**dark** *n* **1** : absence of light : DARKNESS; *esp* : NIGHT **2** : a dark or deep color — **in the dark** **1** : in secrecy **2** : in ignorance

dark adaptation *n* : the process by which the eye adapts to seeing in weak light — **dark–adapt·ed** \ˌdär-kə-ˈdap-təd\ *adj*

dark·en \ˈdär-kən\ *vb* **dark·ened; dark·en·ing** \ˈdärk-(ə-)niŋ\ **1** : to make or grow dark or darker **2** : DIM **3** : BESMIRCH, TARNISH **4** : to make or become gloomy or forbidding

dark horse *n* : a contestant or a political figure whose abilities and chances as a contender are not known

dark·ling \ˈdär-kliŋ\ *adj* **1** : DARK ⟨a ∼ plain⟩ **2** : MYSTERIOUS

dark·room \ˈdärk-ˌrüm, -ˌrům\ *n* : a room which is protected from light and in which photographic plates and film are developed

dark·some \ˈdärk-səm\ *adj* : DARK

[1]**dar·ling** \ˈdär-liŋ\ *n* **1** : a dearly loved person **2** : FAVORITE

[2]**darling** *adj* **1** : dearly loved : FAVORITE **2** : very pleasing : CHARMING

darn \ˈdärn\ *vb* : to mend with interlacing stitches — **darn·er** *n*

darning needle *n* **1** : a needle for darning **2** : DRAGONFLY

[1]**dart** \ˈdärt\ *n* **1** : a small missile with a point on one end and feathers on the other; *also, pl* : a game in which darts are thrown at a target **2** : something causing a sudden pain **3** : a stitched tapering fold in a garment **4** : a quick movement

[2]**dart** *vb* **1** : to throw with a sudden movement **2** : to thrust or move suddenly or rapidly

dart·er \ˈdärt-ər\ *n* : any of numerous small American freshwater fishes related to the perches

Dar·win·ism \ˈdär-wə-ˌniz-əm\ *n* : a theory of the origin and perpetuation of new species of plants and animals through the action of natural selection on chance variations — **Dar·win·ist** \-nəst\ *n or adj*

\ə\abut \$^{ə}$\kitten \ər\further \a\ash \ā\ace \ä\cot, cart \au̇\out \ch\chin \e\bet \ē\easy \g\go \i\hit \ī\ice \j\job \ŋ\sing \ō\go \ȯ\law \ȯi\boy \th\thin \th̲\the \ü\loot \u̇\foot \y\yet \zh\vision *see also* Pronunciation Symbols page

[1]**dash** \ˈdash\ *vb* **1** : to knock, hurl, or thrust violently **2** : SMASH **3** : SPLASH, SPATTER **4** : RUIN **5** : DEPRESS, SADDEN **6** : to perform or finish hastily **7** : to move with sudden speed

[2]**dash** *n* **1** : a sudden burst or splash **2** : a stroke of a pen **3** : a punctuation mark — that is used esp. to indicate a break in the thought or structure of a sentence **4** : a small addition ⟨add a ~ of salt⟩ **5** : flashy showiness **6** : animation in style and action **7** : a sudden rush or attempt ⟨made a ~ for the door⟩ **8** : a short foot race

dash·board \-ˌbōrd\ *n* : an instrument panel below the windshield in an automobile or aircraft

dash·er \ˈdash-ər\ *n* : a device (as in a churn) that agitates or stirs up something

da·shi·ki \də-ˈshē-kē\ *or* **dai·shi·ki** \dī-\ *n* [modif. of Yoruba (an African language) *danshiki*] : a usu. brightly colored loose-fitting pullover garment

dash·ing \ˈdash-iŋ\ *adj* **1** : marked by vigorous action **2** : marked by smartness esp. in dress and manners

das·tard \ˈdas-tərd\ *n* : COWARD; *esp* : one who sneakingly commits malicious acts — **das·tard·ly** *adj*

dat *abbr* dative

da·ta \ˈdāt-ə, ˈdat-\ *n sing or pl* : factual information (as measurements or statistics) used as a basis for reasoning, discussion, or calculation

data processing *n* : the action or process of supplying a computer with information and having the computer use it to produce a desired result

[1]**date** \ˈdāt\ *n* [ME, fr. OF, deriv. of L *dactylus*, fr. Gk *daktylos*, lit., finger] : the edible fruit of a tall Old World palm; *also* : this palm

[2]**date** *n* [ME, fr. MF, fr. LL *data*, fr. *data* (as in *data Romae* given at Rome), fr. L *dare* to give] **1** : the day, month, or year of an event **2** : a statement giving the time of execution or making (as of a coin or check) **3** : the period to which something belongs **4** : APPOINTMENT; *esp* : a social engagement between two persons of opposite sex **5** : a person of the opposite sex with whom one has a social engagement — **to date** : up to the present moment

[3]**date** *vb* **dat·ed; dat·ing** **1** : to record the date of or on **2** : to determine, mark, or reveal the date, age, or period of **3** : to make or have a date with **4** : ORIGINATE ⟨~*s* from ancient times⟩ **5** : EXTEND ⟨*dating* back to childhood⟩ **6** : to show qualities typical of a past period

dat·ed \ˈdāt-əd\ *adj* **1** : provided with a date **2** : OLD-FASHIONED

date·less \ˈdāt-ləs\ *adj* **1** : ENDLESS **2** : having no date **3** : too ancient to be dated **4** : TIMELESS

date·line \ˈdāt-ˌlīn\ *n* : a line in a publication giving the date and place of composition or issue — **dateline** *vb*

da·tive \ˈdāt-iv\ *adj* : of, relating to, or constituting a grammatical case marking typically the indirect object of a verb — **dative** *n*

da·tum \ˈdāt-əm, ˈdat-, ˈdät-\ *n, pl* **da·ta** \-ə\ *or* **datums** : a single piece of data : FACT

dau *abbr* daughter

[1]**daub** \ˈdȯb\ *vb* **1** : to cover with soft adhesive matter **2** : SMEAR, SMUDGE **3** : to paint crudely — **daub·er** *n*

[2]**daub** *n* **1** : something daubed on : SMEAR **2** : a crude picture

daugh·ter \ˈdȯt-ər\ *n* **1** : a female offspring esp. of human beings **2** : a human female having a specified ancestor or belonging to a group of common ancestry

daugh·ter–in–law \ˈdȯt-ə-rən-ˌlȯ, -ərn-ˌlȯ\ *n, pl* **daughters–in–law** \-ər-zən-\ : the wife of one's son

daunt \ˈdȯnt\ *vb* [ME *daunten*, fr. OF *danter*, alter. of *donter*, fr. L *domitare* to tame] : to lessen the courage of : INTIMIDATE, OVERWHELM

daunt·less \-ləs\ *adj* : FEARLESS, UNDAUNTED

dau·phin \ˈdȯ-fən\ *n, often cap* : the eldest son of a king of France

DAV *abbr* Disabled American Veterans

dav·en·port \ˈdav-ən-ˌpōrt\ *n* : a large upholstered sofa

da·vit \ˈdā-vət, ˈdav-ət\ *n* : either of a pair of small cranes used esp. on ships for raising and lowering small boats

daw·dle \ˈdȯd-ᵊl\ *vb* **daw·dled; daw·dling** \ˈdȯd-(ᵊ-)liŋ\ **1** : to spend time wastefully or idly **2** : LOITER — **daw·dler** \ˈdȯd-(ᵊ-)lər\ *n*

[1]**dawn** \ˈdȯn\ *vb* **1** : to begin to grow light as the sun rises **2** : to begin to appear or develop **3** : to begin to be understood ⟨the solution ~*ed* on him⟩

[2]**dawn** *n* **1** : the first appearance of light in the morning **2** : a first appearance : BEGINNING ⟨the ~ of a new era⟩

day \ˈdā\ *n* **1** : the period of light between one night and the next; *also* : DAYLIGHT **2** : the period of the earth's rotation on its axis **3** : a period of 24 hours beginning at midnight **4** : a specified day or date ⟨wedding ~⟩ **5** : a specified time or period : AGE ⟨in olden ~*s*⟩ **6** : the conflict or contention of the day **7** : the time set apart by usage or law for work ⟨the 8-hour ~⟩

day·bed \ˈdā-ˌbed\ *n* : a couch that can be converted into a bed

day·book \-ˌbu̇k\ *n* : DIARY, JOURNAL

day·break \-ˌbrāk\ *n* : DAWN

day–care \ˈdā-ˌkeər\ *adj* : relating to or providing supervision and facilities for preschool children during the day

day·dream \ˈdā-ˌdrēm\ *n* : a pleasant reverie — **daydream** *vb*

day·light \ˈdā-ˌlīt\ *n* **1** : the light of day **2** : DAYTIME **3** : DAWN **4** : understanding of something that has been obscure **5** *pl* : CONSCIOUSNESS; *also* : WITS

daylight saving time *n* : time usu. one hour ahead of standard time

Day of Atonement : YOM KIPPUR

day school *n* : a private school without boarding facilities

day student *n* : a student who attends regular classes at a college or preparatory school but does not live there

day·time \ˈdā-ˌtīm\ *n* : the period of daylight

daze \ˈdāz\ *vb* **dazed; daz·ing** **1** : to stupefy esp. by a blow **2** : DAZZLE — **daze** *n*

daz·zle \ˈdaz-əl\ *vb* **daz·zled; daz·zling** \-(ə-)liŋ\ **1** : to overpower with light **2** : to impress greatly or confound with brilliance — **dazzle** *n*

db *or* **dB** *abbr* decibel

d/b/a *abbr* doing business as

dbl *abbr* double

DC *abbr* **1** [It *da capo*] from the beginning **2** direct current **3** District of Columbia **4** doctor of chiropractic

DD *abbr* **1** days after date **2** demand draft **3** dishonorable discharge **4** doctor of divinity

D day *n* [*D*, abbr. for *day*] : a day set for launching an operation (as an invasion)

DDS *abbr* **1** doctor of dental science **2** doctor of dental surgery

DDT \ˌdē-(ˌ)dē-ˈtē\ *n* : a persistent insecticide poisonous to many higher animals

DE *abbr* Delaware

dea·con \ˈdē-kən\ *n* [ME *dekene*, fr. OE *dēacon*, fr. LL *diaconus*, fr. Gk *diakonos*, lit., servant] : a subordinate officer in a Christian church

dea·con·ess \ˈdē-kə-nəs\ *n* : a woman chosen to assist in the church ministry

de·ac·ti·vate \dē-ˈak-tə-ˌvāt\ *vb* : to make inactive or ineffective

[1]**dead** \ˈded\ *adj* **1** : LIFELESS **2** : DEATHLIKE, DEADLY ⟨in a ~ faint⟩ **3** : NUMB **4** : very tired **5** : UNRESPONSIVE **6** : EXTINGUISHED ⟨~ coals⟩ **7** : INANIMATE, INERT **8** : no longer active or functioning : EXHAUSTED, EXTINCT ⟨a ~ battery⟩ ⟨a ~ volcano⟩ **9** : lacking power, significance, or effect ⟨a ~ custom⟩ **10** : OBSOLETE ⟨a ~ language⟩ **11** : lacking in gaiety or animation ⟨a ~ party⟩ **12** : QUIET, IDLE, UNPRODUCTIVE ⟨~ capital⟩ **13** : lacking elasticity ⟨a ~ tennis ball⟩ **14** : not circulating : STAGNANT ⟨~ air⟩ **15** : lacking warmth, vigor, or taste ⟨~ wine⟩ **16** : absolute-

ly uniform ⟨~ level⟩ **17** : UNERRING, EXACT ⟨a ~ shot⟩ **18** : ABRUPT ⟨a ~ stop⟩ **19** : COMPLETE ⟨a ~ loss⟩

²dead *n, pl* **dead** **1** : one that is dead — usu. used collectively ⟨the living and the ~⟩ **2** : the time of greatest quiet ⟨the ~ of the night⟩

³dead *adv* **1** : UTTERLY ⟨~ right⟩ **2** : in a sudden and complete manner ⟨stopped ~⟩ **3** : DIRECTLY ⟨~ ahead⟩

dead·beat \-ˌbēt\ *n* : one who persistently fails to pay his debts or his way

dead·en \ˈded-ᵊn\ *vb* **dead·ened; dead·en·ing** \ˈded-(ᵊ-)niŋ\ **1** : to impair in force, activity, or sensation : BLUNT ⟨~ pain⟩ **2** : to lessen the luster or spirit of **3** : to make (as a wall) soundproof

dead end *n* **1** : an end (as of a street) without an exit **2** : a position, situation, or course of action that leads to nothing further — **dead–end** \ˌded-ˌend\ *adj*

dead heat *n* : a contest in which two or more contestants tie (as by crossing the finish line simultaneously)

dead letter *n* **1** : something that has lost its force or authority without being formally abolished **2** : a letter that cannot be delivered or returned

dead·line \ˈded-ˌlīn\ *n* : a date or time before which something must be done

dead·lock \ˈded-ˌläk\ *n* : a stoppage of action because neither faction in a struggle will give in — **deadlock** *vb*

¹dead·ly \ˈded-lē\ *adj* **dead·li·er; -est** **1** : likely to cause or capable of causing death **2** : HOSTILE, IMPLACABLE **3** : very accurate : UNERRING **4** : tending to deprive of force or vitality ⟨a ~ habit⟩ **5** : suggestive of death **6** : very great : EXTREME — **dead·li·ness** *n*

²deadly *adv* **1** : suggesting death ⟨~ pale⟩ **2** : EXTREMELY ⟨~ dull⟩

deadly sin *n* : one of seven sins of pride, covetousness, lust, anger, gluttony, envy, and sloth held to be fatal to spiritual progress

dead·pan \ˈded-ˌpan\ *adj* : marked by an impassive manner or expression — **deadpan** *vb*

dead reckoning *n* : the determination of the position of a ship or aircraft solely from the record of the direction and distance of its course

dead·weight \ˈded-ˈwāt\ *n* **1** : the unrelieved weight of an inert mass **2** : a ship's load including the weight of cargo, fuel, crew, and passengers

dead·wood \-ˌwu̇d\ *n* **1** : wood dead on the tree **2** : useless personnel or material

deaf \ˈdef\ *adj* **1** : unable to hear **2** : unwilling to hear or listen ⟨~ to all suggestions⟩ — **deaf·ness** *n*

deaf·en \ˈdef-ən\ *vb* **deaf·ened; deaf·en·ing** \-(ə-)niŋ\ : to make deaf

deaf–mute \ˈdef-ˌmyüt\ *n* : a deaf person who cannot speak

¹deal \ˈdēl\ *n* **1** : a usu. large or indefinite quantity or degree ⟨a great ~ of support⟩ **2** : the act or right of distributing cards to players in a card game; *also* : HAND

²deal *vb* **dealt** \ˈdelt\; **deal·ing** \ˈdē-liŋ\ **1** : DISTRIBUTE; *esp* : to distribute playing cards to players in a game **2** : ADMINISTER, DELIVER ⟨*dealt* him a blow⟩ **3** : to concern itself : TREAT ⟨the book ~*s* with crime⟩ **4** : to take action in regard to something ⟨~ with offenders⟩ **5** : TRADE; *also* : to sell or distribute something as a business ⟨~ in used cars⟩ — **deal·er** *n*

³deal *n* **1** : BARGAINING, NEGOTIATION; *also* : TRANSACTION **2** : treatment received ⟨a raw ~⟩

⁴deal *n* : wood or a board of fir or pine

deal·er·ship \ˈdē-lər-ˌship\ *n* : an authorized sales agency

deal·ing \ˈdē-liŋ\ *n* **1** *pl* : friendly or business transactions **2** : a way of acting or of doing business

dean \ˈdēn\ *n* [ME *deen,* fr. MF *deien,* fr. LL *decanus,* lit., chief of ten, fr. L *decem* ten] **1** : a clergyman who is head of a group of canons or of joint pastors of a church **2** : the head of a division, faculty, college, or school of a university **3** : a college or secondary school administrator in charge of counseling and disciplining students **4** : the senior member of a group ⟨the ~ of a diplomatic corps⟩ — **dean·ship** *n*

dean·ery \ˈdēn-(ə-)rē\ *n, pl* **-er·ies** : the office, jurisdiction, or official residence of a clerical dean

¹dear \ˈdiər\ *adj* **1** : highly valued : PRECIOUS **2** : AFFECTIONATE, FOND **3** : EXPENSIVE **4** : HEARTFELT — **dear·ly** *adv* — **dear·ness** *n*

²dear *n* : a loved one : DARLING

Dear John \-ˈjän\ *n* : a letter (as to a soldier) in which a woman breaks off a marital or romantic relationship

dearth \ˈdərth\ *n* : SCARCITY, FAMINE

death \ˈdeth\ *n* **1** : the end of life **2** : the cause of loss of life **3** : the state of being dead **4** : DESTRUCTION, EXTINCTION **5** : SLAUGHTER — **death·like** *adj*

death·bed \ˈdeth-ˈbed\ *n* **1** : the bed in which a person dies **2** : the last hours of life

death·blow \ˈdeth-ˈblō\ *n* : a destructive or killing stroke or event

death·less \ˈdeth-ləs\ *adj* : IMMORTAL, IMPERISHABLE ⟨~ fame⟩

death·ly \ˈdeth-lē\ *adj* **1** : FATAL **2** : of, relating to, or suggestive of death ⟨a ~ pallor⟩ — **deathly** *adv*

death rattle *n* : a sound produced by air passing through mucus in the lungs and air passages of a dying person

death's–head \ˈdeths-ˌhed\ *n* : a human skull emblematic of death

death·watch \ˈdeth-ˌwäch\ *n* : a vigil kept over the dead or dying

deb \ˈdeb\ *n* : DEBUTANTE

de·ba·cle \di-ˈbäk-əl, -ˈbak-əl\ *n* [F *débâcle*] : DISASTER, FAILURE, ROUT ⟨stock market ~⟩

de·bar \di-ˈbär\ *vb* : to bar from having or doing something : PRECLUDE

de·bark \di-ˈbärk\ *vb* : DISEMBARK — **de·bar·ka·tion** \ˌdē-ˌbär-ˈkā-shən\ *n*

de·base \di-ˈbās\ *vb* : to lower in character, quality, or value **syn** degrade, corrupt, deprave — **de·base·ment** *n*

de·bate \di-ˈbāt\ *vb* **de·bat·ed; de·bat·ing** **1** : to discuss or examine a question by presenting and considering arguments on both sides **2** : to take part in a debate — **de·bat·able** *adj* — **debate** *n* — **de·bat·er** *n*

de·bauch \di-ˈbȯch\ *vb* : SEDUCE, CORRUPT — **de·bauch·ery** \-(ə-)rē\ *n*

de·ben·ture \di-ˈben-chər\ *n* : a certificate of indebtedness; *esp* : a bond secured only by the general assets of the issuing government or company

de·bil·i·tate \di-ˈbil-ə-ˌtāt\ *vb* **-tat·ed; -tat·ing** : to impair the health or strength of

de·bil·i·ty \di-ˈbil-ət-ē\ *n, pl* **-ties** : an infirm or weakened state

¹deb·it \ˈdeb-ət\ *vb* : to enter as a debit : charge with or as a debit

²debit *n* **1** : an entry in an account showing money paid out or owed **2** : a disadvantageous or unfavorable quality or character

deb·o·nair \ˌdeb-ə-ˈnaər\ *adj* [ME *debonere,* fr. OF *debonaire,* fr. *de bon aire* of good family or nature] : gaily and gracefully charming : LIGHTHEARTED

de·bouch \di-ˈbau̇ch, -ˈbüsh\ *vb* [F *déboucher,* fr. *dé-* out of + *bouche* mouth] : to come out into an open area

de·brief \di-ˈbrēf\ *vb* : to question (as a pilot back from a mission) in order to obtain useful information

de·bris \də-ˈbrē, dā-; ˈdā-ˌbrē\ *n, pl* **debris** \-ˈbrēz, -ˌbrēz\ **1** : the remains of something broken down or destroyed : RUINS **2** : an accumulation of fragments of rock

debt \ˈdet\ *n* **1** : SIN, TRESPASS **2** : a condition of owing; *esp* : the state of owing money in amounts greater than one can pay **3** : something owed : OBLIGATION

debt·or \ˈdet-ər\ *n* **1** : one guilty of neglect or violation of duty **2** : one that owes a debt

de·bunk \dē-ˈbəŋk\ *vb* : to expose the sham or falseness of ⟨~ a rumor⟩

de·but \ˈdā-ˌbyü, dā-ˈbyü\ *n* **1** : a first appearance **2** : a formal entrance into society

deb·u·tante \ˈdeb-yu̇-ˌtänt\ *n* : a young woman making her formal entrance into society

dec *abbr* **1** deceased **2** decrease

Dec *abbr* December

de·cade \ˈdek-ˌād, -əd; de-ˈkād\ *n* : a period of 10 years

dec·a·dence \ˈdek-əd-əns, di-ˈkād-ᵊns\ *n* : DETERIORATION, DECLINE — **dec·a·dent** \ˈdek-əd-ənt, di-ˈkād-ᵊnt\ *adj or n*

deca·gon \ˈdek-ə-ˌgän\ *n* : a plane polygon of 10 angles and 10 sides

de·cal \ˈdē-ˌkal\ *n* : a picture, design, or label made to be transferred (as to glass) from specially prepared paper

de·cal·co·ma·nia \di-ˌkal-kə-ˈmā-nē-ə\ *n* [F *décalcomanie,* fr. *décalquer* to copy by tracing (fr. *calquer* to trace, fr. It *calcare,* lit., to trample, fr. L) + *manie* mania, fr. LL *mania*] : DECAL

Deca·logue \ˈdek-ə-ˌlȯg\ *n* : the ten commandments of God given to Moses on Mount Sinai

de·camp \di-ˈkamp\ *vb* **1** : to break up a camp **2** : to depart suddenly

de·cant \di-ˈkant\ *vb* : to pour (liquor) gently

de·cant·er \di-ˈkant-ər\ *n* : an ornamental glass bottle for serving wine

de·cap·i·tate \di-ˈkap-ə-ˌtāt\ *vb* **-tat·ed; -tat·ing** : BEHEAD — **de·cap·i·ta·tion** \-ˌkap-ə-ˈtā-shən\ *n*

deca·syl·lab·ic \ˌdek-ə-sə-ˈlab-ik\ *adj* : having or composed of verses having 10 syllables — **decasyllabic** *n*

de·cath·lon \di-ˈkath-lən, -ˌlän\ *n* : an athletic contest in which each competitor participates in each of a series of 10 track-and-field events

de·cay \di-ˈkā\ *vb* **1** : to decline from a sound or prosperous condition **2** : to cause or undergo decomposition ⟨radium ~*s* slowly⟩; *esp* : to break down while spoiling : ROT — **decay** *n*

decd *abbr* deceased

de·cease \di-ˈsēs\ *n* : DEATH

[1]**de·ceased** \-ˈsēst\ *adj* : no longer living; *esp* : recently dead

[2]**deceased** *n, pl* **deceased** : a dead person

de·ce·dent \di-ˈsēd-ᵊnt\ *n* : a deceased person

de·ceit \di-ˈsēt\ *n* **1** : DECEPTION **2** : TRICK **3** : DECEITFULNESS

de·ceit·ful \-fəl\ *adj* **1** : practicing or tending to practice deceit **2** : MISLEADING, DECEPTIVE ⟨a ~ answer⟩ — **de·ceit·ful·ly** *adv* — **de·ceit·ful·ness** *n*

de·ceive \di-ˈsēv\ *vb* **de·ceived; de·ceiv·ing** **1** : to cause to believe an untruth **2** : to use or practice deceit — **de·ceiv·er** *n*

de·cel·er·ate \dē-ˈsel-ə-ˌrāt\ *vb* **-at·ed; -at·ing** : to slow down

De·cem·ber \di-ˈsem-bər\ *n* [ME *Decembre,* fr. OF, fr. L *December* (tenth month), fr. *decem* ten] : the 12th month of the year having 31 days

de·cen·cy \ˈdēs-ᵊn-sē\ *n, pl* **-cies** **1** : PROPRIETY **2** : conformity to standards of taste, propriety, or quality **3** : standard of propriety — usu. used in pl.

de·cen·ni·al \di-ˈsen-ē-əl\ *adj* **1** : consisting of 10 years **2** : happening every 10 years ⟨~ census⟩

de·cent \ˈdēs-ᵊnt\ *adj* **1** : conforming to standards of propriety, good taste, or morality **2** : modestly clothed **3** : free from immodesty or obscenity **4** : ADEQUATE ⟨~ housing⟩ — **de·cent·ly** *adv*

de·cen·tral·iza·tion \dē-ˌsen-trə-lə-ˈzā-shən\ *n* **1** : the distribution of powers from a central authority to regional and local authorities **2** : the redistribution of population and industry from urban centers to outlying areas — **de·cen·tral·ize** \-ˈsen-trə-ˌlīz\ *vb*

de·cep·tion \di-ˈsep-shən\ *n* **1** : the act of deceiving **2** : the fact or condition of being deceived **3** : FRAUD, TRICK — **de·cep·tive** \-ˈsep-tiv\ *adj* — **de·cep·tive·ly** *adv*

deci·bel \ˈdes-ə-ˌbel, -bəl\ *n* : a unit for measuring the relative loudness of sounds

de·cide \di-ˈsīd\ *vb* **de·cid·ed; de·cid·ing** [ME *deciden,* fr. MF *decider,* fr. L *decidere,* lit., to cut off, fr. *caedere* to cut] **1** : to arrive at a solution that ends uncertainty or dispute about **2** : to bring to a definitive end ⟨one blow *decided* the fight⟩ **3** : to induce to come to a choice **4** : to make a choice or judgment

de·cid·ed \di-ˈsīd-əd\ *adj* **1** : CLEAR, UNMISTAKABLE **2** : FIRM, DETERMINED — **de·cid·ed·ly** *adv*

de·cid·u·ous \di-ˈsij-ə-wəs\ *adj* **1** : falling off usu. at the end of a period of growth or function ⟨~ leaves⟩ ⟨a ~ tooth⟩ **2** : having deciduous parts ⟨~ trees⟩

deci·gram \ˈdes-ə-ˌgram\ *n* — see METRIC SYSTEM table

deci·li·ter \ˈdes-ə-ˌlēt-ər\ *n* — see METRIC SYSTEM table

[1]**dec·i·mal** \ˈdes-ə-məl\ *adj* : based on the number 10 : reckoning by tens

[2]**decimal** *n* : any number expressed in base 10; *esp* : DECIMAL FRACTION

decimal fraction *n* : a fraction (as .25 = 25/100 or .025 = 25/1000) or mixed number (as 3.025 = 3 25/1000) in which the denominator is a power of 10 usu. expressed by use of the decimal point

decimal point *n* : the dot at the left of a decimal fraction (as .678) less than one or between the parts of a mixed number (as 3.678) composed of a whole number and a decimal fraction

dec·i·mate \ˈdes-ə-ˌmāt\ *vb* **-mat·ed; -mat·ing** **1** : to take or destroy the 10th part of **2** : to destroy a large part of

dec·i·me·ter \ˈdes-ə-ˌmēt-ər\ *n* — see METRIC SYSTEM table

de·ci·pher \di-ˈsī-fər\ *vb* **1** : to translate from secret writing (as code) **2** : to make out the meaning of despite indistinctness — **de·ci·pher·able** *adj*

de·ci·sion \di-ˈsizh-ən\ *n* **1** : the act or result of deciding **2** : promptness and firmness in deciding : DETERMINATION

de·ci·sive \-ˈsī-siv\ *adj* **1** : having the power to decide ⟨the ~ vote⟩ **2** : RESOLUTE, DETERMINED **3** : CONCLUSIVE ⟨a ~ victory⟩ — **de·ci·sive·ly** *adv* — **de·ci·sive·ness** *n*

[1]**deck** \ˈdek\ *n* **1** : a floorlike platform of a ship; *also* : something resembling the deck of a ship **2** : a pack of playing cards

[2]**deck** *vb* **1** : ARRAY **2** : DECORATE **3** : to furnish with a deck **4** : KNOCK DOWN, FLOOR

deck·hand \ˈdek-ˌhand\ *n* : a sailor who performs manual duties

deck·le edge \ˌdek-əl-\ *n* : the rough untrimmed edge of paper — **deck·le–edged** \ˌdek-ə-ˈlejd\ *adj*

de·claim \di-ˈklām\ *vb* : to speak or deliver in the manner of a formal speech — **dec·la·ma·tion** \ˌdek-lə-ˈmā-shən\ *n* — **de·clam·a·to·ry** \di-ˈklam-ə-ˌtōr-ē\ *adj*

de·clar·a·tive \di-ˈklar-ət-iv\ *adj* : making a declaration ⟨~ sentence⟩

de·clare \di-ˈklaər\ *vb* **de·clared; de·clar·ing** **1** : to make known formally or explicitly : ANNOUNCE ⟨~ war⟩ **2** : to state emphatically : AFFIRM **3** : to make a full statement of — **dec·la·ra·tion** \ˌdek-lə-ˈrā-shən\ *n* — **de·clar·a·to·ry** \di-ˈklar-ə-ˌtōr-ē\ *adj* — **de·clar·er** *n*

de·clas·si·fy \dē-ˈklas-ə-ˌfī\ *vb* : to remove or reduce the security classification of

de·clen·sion \di-ˈklen-chən\ *n* **1** : the inflectional forms of a noun, pronoun, or adjective **2** : DECLINE, DETERIORATION **3** : DESCENT, SLOPE

[1]**de·cline** \di-ˈklīn\ *vb* **de·clined; de·clin·ing** **1** : to slope downward : DESCEND **2** : DROOP **3** : RECEDE **4** : WANE **5** : to withhold consent; *also* : REFUSE, REJECT **6** : INFLECT 2 ⟨~ a noun⟩ — **de·clin·able** *adj* — **dec·li·na·tion** \ˌdek-lə-ˈnā-shən\ *n*

[2]**decline** *n* **1** : a gradual sinking and wasting away **2** : a change to a lower state or level **3** : the time when some-

thing is approaching its end **4** : a descending slope **5** : a wasting disease; *esp* : pulmonary tuberculosis

de·cliv·i·ty \di-ˈkliv-ət-ē\ *n, pl* **-ties** : a steep downward slope

de·code \dē-ˈkōd\ *vb* : to convert (a coded message) into ordinary language — **de·cod·er** *n*

dé·col·le·té \dā-ˌkäl-ə-ˈtā\ *adj* [F] **1** : wearing a strapless or low-necked gown **2** : having a low-cut neckline

de·com·mis·sion \ˌdē-kə-ˈmish-ən\ *vb* : to take out of commission

de·com·pose \ˌdē-kəm-ˈpōz\ *vb* **1** : to separate into constituent parts **2** : to break down in decay : ROT — **de·com·po·si·tion** \dē-ˌkäm-pə-ˈzish-ən\ *n*

de·com·press \ˌdē-kəm-ˈpres\ *vb* : to release (as a diver) from pressure or compression — **de·com·pres·sion** \-ˈpresh-ən\ *n*

de·con·ges·tant \ˌdē-kən-ˈjes-tənt\ *n* : an agent that relieves congestion (as of mucous membranes)

de·con·tam·i·nate \ˌdē-kən-ˈtam-ə-ˌnāt\ *vb* : to rid of contamination (as radioactive material) — **de·con·tam·i·na·tion** \-ˌtam-ə-ˈnā-shən\ *n*

de·con·trol \ˌdē-kən-ˈtrōl\ *vb* : to end control of ⟨~ prices⟩

de·cor *or* **dé·cor** \dā-ˈkȯr, ˈdā-ˌkȯr\ *n* : DECORATION; *esp* : the arrangement of accessories in interior decoration

dec·o·rate \ˈdek-ə-ˌrāt\ *vb* **-rat·ed; -rat·ing 1** : to make more attractive by adding something beautiful or becoming : ADORN, EMBELLISH **2** : to award a mark of honor (as a medal) to

dec·o·ra·tion \ˌdek-ə-ˈrā-shən\ *n* **1** : the act or process of decorating **2** : ORNAMENT **3** : a badge of honor

dec·o·ra·tive \ˈdek-(ə-)rət-iv\ *adj* : ORNAMENTAL

dec·o·ra·tor \ˈdek-ə-ˌrāt-ər\ *n* : one that decorates; *esp* : a person who designs or executes the interiors of buildings and their furnishings

dec·o·rous \ˈdek-ə-rəs, di-ˈkōr-əs\ *adj* : PROPER, SEEMLY, CORRECT

de·co·rum \di-ˈkōr-əm\ *n* [L] **1** : conformity to accepted standards of conduct **2** : ORDERLINESS, PROPRIETY

[1]**de·coy** \ˈdē-ˌkȯi, di-ˈkȯi\ *n* : something that lures or entices; *esp* : an artificial bird used to attract live birds within shot

[2]**de·coy** \di-ˈkȯi, ˈdē-ˌkȯi\ *vb* : to lure by or as if by a decoy : ENTICE

[1]**de·crease** \di-ˈkrēs\ *vb* **de·creased; de·creas·ing** : to grow or cause to grow less : DIMINISH

[2]**de·crease** \ˈdē-ˌkrēs\ *n* **1** : the process of decreasing **2** : REDUCTION

[1]**de·cree** \di-ˈkrē\ *n* **1** : ORDER, EDICT **2** : a judicial decision

[2]**decree** *vb* **de·creed; de·cree·ing 1** : COMMAND **2** : to determine or order judicially

dec·re·ment \ˈdek-rə-mənt\ *n* **1** : gradual decrease **2** : the quantity lost by diminution or waste

de·crep·it \di-ˈkrep-ət\ *adj* : broken down with age : WORN-OUT — **de·crep·i·tude** \-ə-ˌt(y)üd\ *n*

de·cre·scen·do \ˌdā-krə-ˈshen-dō\ *adv or adj* : with a decrease in volume — used as a direction in music

de·crim·i·nal·ize \dē-ˈkrim-ən-ᵊl-ˌīz\ *vb* : to remove or reduce the criminal status of

de·cry \di-ˈkrī\ *vb* **1** : to belittle publicly **2** : to find fault with : CONDEMN

ded·i·cate \ˈded-i-ˌkāt\ *vb* **-cat·ed; -cat·ing 1** : to devote to the worship of a divine being esp. with sacred rites **2** : to set apart for a definite purpose **3** : to inscribe or address as a compliment — **ded·i·ca·tion** \ˌded-i-ˈkā-shən\ *n* — **ded·i·ca·to·ry** \ˈded-i-kə-ˌtōr-ē\ *adj*

de·duce \di-ˈd(y)üs\ *vb* **de·duced; de·duc·ing 1** : to derive by reasoning : INFER **2** : to trace the course of ⟨~ their lineage⟩ — **de·duc·ible** *adj*

de·duct \di-ˈdəkt\ *vb* : SUBTRACT — **de·duct·ible** *adj*

de·duc·tion \di-ˈdək-shən\ *n* **1** : SUBTRACTION **2** : something that is or may be subtracted : ABATEMENT **3** : the deriving of a conclusion by reasoning : the conclusion so reached — **de·duc·tive** \-ˈdək-tiv\ *adj*

[1]**deed** \ˈdēd\ *n* **1** : something done **2** : FEAT, EXPLOIT **3** : a document containing some legal transfer, bargain, or contract

[2]**deed** *vb* : to convey or transfer by deed

dee·jay \ˈdē-ˈjā\ *n* : DISC JOCKEY

deem \ˈdēm\ *vb* : THINK, JUDGE

de–em·pha·size \dē-ˈem-fə-ˌsīz\ *vb* : to refrain from emphasizing — **de–em·pha·sis** \-fə-səs\ *n*

[1]**deep** \ˈdēp\ *adj* **1** : extending far down, back, within, or outward **2** : having a specified extension downward or backward **3** : difficult to understand; *also* : MYSTERIOUS, OBSCURE ⟨a ~ dark secret⟩ **4** : WISE **5** : ENGROSSED, INVOLVED ⟨~ in thought⟩ **6** : INTENSE, PROFOUND ⟨~ sleep⟩ **7** : dark and rich in color ⟨a ~ red⟩ **8** : having a low musical pitch or range ⟨a ~ voice⟩ **9** : situated well within **10** : covered, enclosed, or filled often to a specified degree — **deep·ly** *adv*

[2]**deep** *adv* **1** : DEEPLY **2** : far on : LATE ⟨~ in the night⟩

[3]**deep** *n* **1** : an extremely deep place or part; *esp* : OCEAN **2** : the middle or most intense part ⟨the ~ of winter⟩

deep·en \ˈdē-pən\ *vb* **deep·ened; deep·en·ing** \ˈdēp-(ə-)niŋ\ : to make or become deep or deeper

deep–freeze \ˈdēp-ˈfrēz\ *vb* **-froze** \-ˈfrōz\; **-fro·zen** \-ˈfrōz-ᵊn\ : QUICK-FREEZE

deep–root·ed \-ˈrüt-əd, -ˈru̇t-\ *adj* : deeply implanted or established

deep–sea \ˌdēp-ˌsē\ *adj* : of, relating to, or occurring in the deeper parts of the sea ⟨~ fishing⟩

deep–seat·ed \ˈdēp-ˈsēt-əd\ *adj* **1** : situated far below the surface **2** : firmly established ⟨~ convictions⟩

deer \ˈdiər\ *n, pl* **deer** [ME, deer, animal, fr. OE *dēor* beast] : any of a family of ruminant mammals with cloven hoofs and usu. antlers esp. in the males

deer

deer·fly \-ˌflī\ *n* : any of numerous small horseflies

deer·skin \-ˌskin\ *n* : leather made from the skin of a deer; *also* : a garment of such leather

de–es·ca·late \dē-ˈes-kə-ˌlāt\ *vb* : to decrease in extent, volume, or scope : REDUCE ⟨~ the war⟩ — **de–es·ca·la·tion** \dē-ˌes-kə-ˈlā-shən\ *n*

def *abbr* **1** defendant **2** definite **3** definition

de·face \di-ˈfās\ *vb* : to destroy or mar the face or surface of — **de·face·ment** *n*

de fac·to \di-ˈfak-tō, dā-\ *adj or adv* **1** : actually existing ⟨*de facto* segregation⟩ **2** : actually exercising power ⟨*de facto* government⟩

de·fal·ca·tion \ˌdē-ˌfal-ˈkā-shən, ˌdē-ˌfȯl-; ˌdef-əl-\ *n* : EMBEZZLEMENT

de·fame \di-ˈfām\ *vb* **de·famed; de·fam·ing** : to injure or destroy the reputation of by libel or slander — **def·a·ma-**

tion \ˌdef-ə-ˈmā-shən\ *n* — **de·fam·a·to·ry** \di-ˈfam-ə-ˌtōr-ē\ *adj*

de·fault \di-ˈfölt\ *n* **1** : failure to do something required by duty or law ⟨the defendant failed to appear and was held in ~⟩ **2** : failure to compete in or to finish an appointed contest ⟨lose a race by ~⟩ — **default** *vb* — **de·fault·er** *n*

[1]**de·feat** \di-ˈfēt\ *vb* **1** : FRUSTRATE, NULLIFY **2** : to win victory over : BEAT

[2]**defeat** *n* **1** : FRUSTRATION **2** : an overthrow of an army in battle **3** : loss of a contest

de·feat·ism \-ˌiz-əm,\ *n* : acceptance of or resignation to defeat — **de·feat·ist** \-əst\ *n or adj*

def·e·cate \ˈdef-i-ˌkāt\ *vb* **-cat·ed; -cat·ing 1** : to free from impurity or corruption : REFINE **2** : to discharge feces from the bowels — **def·e·ca·tion** \ˌdef-i-ˈkā-shən\ *n*

[1]**de·fect** \ˈdē-ˌfekt, di-ˈfekt\ *n* : BLEMISH, FAULT, IMPERFECTION

[2]**de·fect** \di-ˈfekt\ *vb* : to desert a cause or party esp. in order to espouse another — **de·fec·tion** \-ˈfek-shən\ *n* — **de·fec·tor** \-ˈfek-tər\ *n*

de·fec·tive \di-ˈfek-tiv\ *adj* : FAULTY, DEFICIENT — **defective** *n*

de·fend \di-ˈfend\ *vb* [ME *defenden*, fr. OF *defendre*, fr. L *defendere*, fr. *de-* from + *-fendere* to strike] **1** : to repel danger or attack from **2** : to act as attorney for **3** : to oppose the claim of another in a lawsuit : CONTEST **4** : to maintain against opposition ⟨~ an idea⟩ — **de·fend·er** *n*

de·fen·dant \di-ˈfen-dənt\ *n* : a person required to make answer in a legal action or suit

de·fense *or* **de·fence** \di-ˈfens\ *n* **1** : the act of defending : resistance against attack **2** : means, method, or capability of defending **3** : an argument in support **4** : the answer made by the defendant in a legal action **5** : a defending party, group, or team — **de·fense·less** *adj* — **de·fen·si·ble** *adj*

defense mechanism *n* : an often unconscious mental process (as repression or sublimation) that assists in reaching compromise solutions to personal problems

[1]**de·fen·sive** \di-ˈfen-siv\ *adj* **1** : serving or intended to defend or protect **2** : of or relating to the attempt to keep an opponent from scoring (as in a game) — **de·fen·sive·ly** *adv* — **de·fen·sive·ness** *n*

[2]**defensive** *n* : a defensive position

[1]**de·fer** \di-ˈfər\ *vb* **de·ferred; de·fer·ring** [ME *deferren, differren*, fr. MF *differer*, fr. L *differre* to postpone, be different] : POSTPONE, PUT OFF

[2]**defer** *vb* **deferred; deferring** [ME *deferren, differren*, fr. MF *deferer, defferer*, fr. LL *deferre*, fr. L, to bring down, bring, fr. *ferre* to carry] : to submit or yield to the opinion or wishes of another

def·er·ence \ˈdef-(ə-)rəns\ *n* : courteous, respectful, or ingratiating regard for another's wishes — **def·er·en·tial** \ˌdef-ə-ˈren-chəl\ *adj*

de·fer·ment \di-ˈfər-mənt\ *n* : the act of delaying; *esp* : official postponement of military service

de·fi·ance \di-ˈfī-əns\ *n* **1** : CHALLENGE **2** : a tendency to resist : contempt of opposition

de·fi·ant \-ənt\ *adj* : full of defiance ⟨a ~ gesture⟩ — **de·fi·ant·ly** *adv*

de·fi·bril·la·tor \dē-ˈfib-rə-ˌlāt-ər, -ˈfīb-\ *n* : an electronic device used to restore the rhythm of a fibrillating heart by applying an electric shock to it — **de·fi·bril·late** \-ˌlāt\ *vb* — **de·fi·bril·la·tion** \dē-ˌfib-rə-ˈlā-shən, -ˌfīb-\ *n*

deficiency disease *n* : a disease (as scurvy or beriberi) caused by a lack of essential dietary elements and esp. a vitamin or mineral

de·fi·cient \di-ˈfish-ənt\ *adj* : lacking in something necessary (as for completeness or health) : DEFECTIVE — **de·fi·cien·cy** \-ˈfish-ən-sē\ *n*

def·i·cit \ˈdef-ə-sət\ *n* : a deficiency in amount; *esp* : an excess of expenditures over revenue

[1]**de·file** \di-ˈfīl\ *vb* **de·filed; de·fil·ing 1** : to make filthy **2** : CORRUPT **3** : to violate the chastity of **4** : to violate the sanctity of : DESECRATE **5** : DISHONOR — **de·file·ment** *n*

[2]**de·file** \di-ˈfīl, ˈdē-ˌfīl\ *n* : a narrow passage or gorge

de·fine \di-ˈfīn\ *vb* **de·fined; de·fin·ing 1** : to set forth the meaning of ⟨~ a word⟩ **2** : to fix or mark the limits of **3** : to clarify in outline or character — **de·fin·able** *adj* — **de·fin·er** *n*

def·i·nite \ˈdef-(ə-)nət\ *adj* **1** : having distinct limits : FIXED **2** : clear in meaning **3** : typically designating an identified or immediately identifiable person or thing — **def·i·nite·ly** *adv* — **def·i·nite·ness** *n*

def·i·ni·tion \ˌdef-ə-ˈnish-ən\ *n* **1** : an act of determining or settling **2** : a statement of the meaning of a word or word group; *also* : the action or process of stating such a meaning **3** : the action or the power of making definite and clear : CLARITY, DISTINCTNESS

de·fin·i·tive \di-ˈfin-ət-iv\ *adj* **1** : DECISIVE, CONCLUSIVE **2** : being authoritative and apparently exhaustive **3** : serving to define or specify precisely

de·flate \di-ˈflāt\ *vb* **de·flat·ed; de·flat·ing 1** : to release air or gas from **2** : to cause to contract from an abnormally high level : reduce from a state of inflation **3** : to become deflated

de·fla·tion \-ˈflā-shən\ *n* **1** : an act or instance of deflating : the state of being deflated **2** : reduction in the volume of available money or credit resulting in a decline of the general price level

de·flect \di-ˈflekt\ *vb* : to turn aside — **de·flec·tion** \-ˈflek-shən\ *n*

de·flo·ra·tion \ˌdef-lə-ˈrā-shən\ *n* : rupture of the hymen

de·flow·er \dē-ˈflau̇(-ə)r\ *vb* : to deprive of virginity : RAVISH

de·fog \dē-ˈfög, -ˈfäg\ *vb* : to remove fog or condensed moisture from — **de·fog·ger** *n*

de·fo·li·ant \dē-ˈfō-lē-ənt\ *n* : a chemical spray or dust applied to plants to cause the leaves to drop off prematurely

de·fo·li·ate \-lē-ˌāt\ *vb* : to deprive of leaves esp. prematurely — **de·fo·li·a·tion** \dē-ˌfō-lē-ˈā-shən\ *n* — **de·fo·li·a·tor** \dē-ˈfō-lē-ˌāt-ər\ *n*

de·for·es·ta·tion \dē-ˌfȯr-ə-ˈstā-shən\ *n* : the action or process of clearing an area of forests; *also* : the state of having been cleared of forests — **de·for·est** \(ˈ)dē-ˈfȯr-əst, -ˈfär-\ *vb*

de·form \di-ˈfȯrm\ *vb* **1** : DISFIGURE, DEFACE **2** : to make or become misshapen or changed in shape — **de·for·ma·tion** \ˌdē-ˌfȯr-ˈmā-shən, ˌdef-ər-\ *n*

de·for·mi·ty \di-ˈfȯr-mət-ē\ *n, pl* **-ties 1** : the state of being deformed **2** : a physical blemish or distortion

de·fraud \di-ˈfrȯd\ *vb* : CHEAT

de·fray \di-ˈfrā\ *vb* : to provide for the payment of : PAY — **de·fray·al** *n*

de·frost \di-ˈfrȯst\ *vb* **1** : to thaw out **2** : to free from ice — **de·frost·er** *n*

deft \ˈdeft\ *adj* : quick and neat in action — **deft·ly** *adv* — **deft·ness** *n*

de·funct \di-ˈfəŋkt\ *adj* : DEAD, EXTINCT ⟨a ~ organization⟩

de·fuse \dē-ˈfyüz\ *vb* **1** : to remove the fuse from (as a bomb) **2** : to make less harmful, potent, or tense

de·fy \di-ˈfī\ *vb* **de·fied; de·fy·ing** [ME *defyen* to renounce faith in, challenge, fr. OF *defier*, fr. *de-* from + *fier* to entrust, fr. L *fidere* to trust] **1** : CHALLENGE, DARE **2** : to refuse boldly to obey or to yield to : DISREGARD ⟨~ the law⟩ **3** : WITHSTAND, BAFFLE ⟨a scene that *defies* description⟩

deg *abbr* degree

de·gas \dē-ˈgas\ *vb* : to remove gas from

de·gen·er·a·cy \di-ˈjen-(ə-)rə-sē\ *n, pl* **-cies 1** : the state of being degenerate **2** : the process of becoming degenerate

[1]**de·gen·er·ate** \di-ˈjen-(ə-)rət\ *adj* : fallen or deteriorated from a former, higher, or normal condition — **de·gen·er-**

a·cy \-rə-sē\ *n* — **de·gen·er·a·tion** \-ˌjen-ə-ˈrā-shən\ *n* — **de·gen·er·a·tive** \-ˈjen-ə-ˌrāt-iv\ *adj*

[2]**de·gen·er·ate** \di-ˈjen-ə-ˌrāt\ *vb* : to undergo deterioration (as in morality, intelligence, structure, or function)

[3]**de·gen·er·ate** \-(ə-)rət\ *n* : a degenerate person; *esp* : a sexual pervert

de·grad·able \di-ˈgrād-ə-bəl\ *adj* : capable of being chemically degraded ⟨~ detergents⟩

de·grade \di-ˈgrād\ *vb* **1** : to reduce from a higher to a lower rank or degree **2** : DEBASE, CORRUPT — **deg·ra·da·tion** \ˌdeg-rə-ˈdā-shən\ *n*

de·gree \di-ˈgrē\ *n* [ME, fr. OF *degré*, fr. (assumed) VL *degradus*, fr. L *gradus* step, grade] **1** : a step in a series **2** : the extent, intensity, or scope of something esp. as measured by a graded series **3** : one of the forms or sets of forms used in the comparison of an adjective or adverb **4** : a rank or grade of official, ecclesiastical, or social position; *also* : the civil condition of a person **5** : a title conferred upon students by a college, university, or professional school upon completion of a unified program of study **6** : a unit of measure for angles and arcs that for angles is equal to an angle with its vertex at the center of a circle and its sides cutting off 1/360 of the circumference and that for an arc of a circle is equal to 1/360 of the circumference **7** : a line or space of the musical staff; *also* : a note or tone of a musical scale

de·horn \dē-ˈhorn\ *vb* : to deprive of horns

de·hu·man·ize \dē-ˈhyü-mə-ˌnīz\ *vb* : to divest of human qualities or personality — **de·hu·man·iza·tion** \ˌdē-ˌhyü-mə-nə-ˈzā-shən\ *n*

de·hu·mid·i·fy \ˌdē-hyü-ˈmid-ə-ˌfī\ *vb* : to remove moisture from (as the air) — **de·hu·mid·i·fi·er** \-ˈmid-ə-ˌfī(-ə)r\ *n*

de·hy·drate \dē-ˈhī-ˌdrāt\ *vb* : to remove water from ⟨*dehydrated* by fever⟩ ⟨~ fruits⟩; *also* : to lose liquid — **de·hy·dra·tion** \ˌdē-hī-ˈdrā-shən\ *n*

de·hy·dro·ge·nate \ˌdē-hī-ˈdräj-ə-ˌnāt\ *vb* : to remove hydrogen from — **de·hy·dro·ge·na·tion** \ˌdē-hī-ˌdräj-ə-ˈnā-shən\ *n*

de·ice \dē-ˈīs\ *vb* : to keep free or rid of ice — **de·ic·er** *n*

de·i·fy \ˈdē-ə-ˌfī\ *vb* **-fied; -fy·ing 1** : to make a god of **2** : WORSHIP, GLORIFY — **de·i·fi·ca·tion** \ˌdē-ə-fə-ˈkā-shən\ *n*

deign \ˈdān\ *vb* [ME *deignen*, fr. OF *deignier*, fr. L *dignare, dignari*, fr. *dignus* worthy] : CONDESCEND

de·ion·ize \dē-ˈī-ə-ˌnīz\ *vb* : to remove ions from

de·ism \ˈdē-ˌiz-əm\ *n, often cap* : a system of thought advocating natural religion based on human reason rather than revelation — **de·ist** \ˈdē-əst\ *n, often cap* — **de·is·tic** \dē-ˈis-tik\ *adj*

de·i·ty \ˈdē-ət-ē\ *n, pl* **-ties 1** : DIVINITY 2 **2** *cap* : GOD 1 **3** : a god or goddess

de·ject·ed \di-ˈjek-təd\ *adj* : low in spirits : SAD — **de·ject·ed·ly** *adv*

de·jec·tion \di-ˈjek-shən\ *n* : lowness of spirits : DEPRESSION

de ju·re \dē-ˈju̇r-ē\ *adv or adj* : existing or exercising power by legal right ⟨*de jure* government⟩

deka·gram \ˈdek-ə-ˌgram\ *n* — see METRIC SYSTEM table

deka·li·ter \-ˌlēt-ər\ *n* — see METRIC SYSTEM table

deka·me·ter \-ˌmēt-ər\ *n* — see METRIC SYSTEM table

del *abbr* delegate; delegation

Del *abbr* Delaware

Del·a·ware \ˈdel-ə-ˌwaər\ *n, pl* **Delaware** *or* **Delawares** : a member of an American Indian people orig. of the Delaware valley; *also* : their language

[1]**de·lay** \di-ˈlā\ *n* **1** : the act of delaying : the state of being delayed **2** : the time for which something is delayed

[2]**delay** *vb* **1** : POSTPONE, PUT OFF **2** : to stop, detain, or hinder for a time **3** : to move or act slowly

de·lec·ta·ble \di-ˈlek-tə-bəl\ *adj* **1** : highly pleasing : DELIGHTFUL **2** : DELICIOUS

de·lec·ta·tion \ˌdē-ˌlek-ˈtā-shən\ *n* : DELIGHT, PLEASURE, DIVERSION

[1]**del·e·gate** \ˈdel-i-gət, -ˌgāt\ *n* **1** : DEPUTY, REPRESENTATIVE **2** : a member of the lower house of the legislature of Maryland, Virginia, or West Virginia

[2]**del·e·gate** \-ˌgāt\ *vb* **-gat·ed; -gat·ing 1** : to entrust to another ⟨*delegated* his authority⟩ **2** : to appoint as one's delegate

del·e·ga·tion \ˌdel-i-ˈgā-shən\ *n* **1** : the act of delegating **2** : one or more persons chosen to represent others

de·lete \di-ˈlēt\ *vb* **de·let·ed; de·let·ing** [L *delēre* to wipe out, destroy] : to eliminate esp. by blotting out, cutting out, or erasing — **de·le·tion** \-ˈlē-shən\ *n*

del·e·te·ri·ous \ˌdel-ə-ˈtir-ē-əs\ *adj* : HARMFUL, NOXIOUS

delft \ˈdelft\ *n* **1** : a Dutch pottery with an opaque white glaze and predominantly blue decoration **2** : glazed pottery esp. when blue and white

delft·ware \-ˌwaər\ *n* : DELFT

deli \ˈdel-ē\ *n, pl* **del·is** : DELICATESSEN

[1]**de·lib·er·ate** \di-ˈlib-ə-ˌrāt\ *vb* **-at·ed; -at·ing** : to consider carefully — **de·lib·er·a·tion** \-ˌlib-ə-ˈrā-shən\ *n*

[2]**de·lib·er·ate** \di-ˈlib-(ə-)rət\ *adj* [L *deliberare* to weigh in mind, ponder, fr. *libra* scale, pound] **1** : determined after careful thought **2** : done or said intentionally **3** : UNHURRIED, SLOW — **de·lib·er·ate·ly** *adv* — **de·lib·er·ate·ness** *n*

de·lib·er·a·tive \-ˈlib-ə-ˌrāt-iv, -ˈlib(-ə)-rət-\ *adj* : of, relating to, or marked by deliberation ⟨~ assembly⟩ — **de·lib·er·a·tive·ly** *adv*

del·i·ca·cy \ˈdel-i-kə-sē\ *n, pl* **-cies 1** : something pleasing to eat because it is rare or luxurious **2** : FINENESS, DAINTINESS; *also* : FRAILTY **3** : nicety or expressiveness of touch **4** : precise perception and discrimination : SENSITIVITY **5** : sensibility in feeling or conduct; *also* : SQUEAMISHNESS **6** : the quality or state of requiring delicate handling

del·i·cate \ˈdel-i-kət\ *adj* **1** : pleasing to the senses of taste or smell esp. in a mild or subtle way **2** : marked by daintiness or charm : EXQUISITE **3** : FASTIDIOUS, SQUEAMISH, SCRUPULOUS **4** : easily damaged : FRAGILE; *also* : SICKLY **5** : requiring skill or tact **6** : marked by care, skill, or tact **7** : marked by minute precision : very sensitive — **del·i·cate·ly** *adv*

del·i·ca·tes·sen \ˌdel-i-kə-ˈtes-ᵊn\ *n pl* [G, pl. of *delicatesse* delicacy, fr. F *délicatesse*] **1** : ready-to-eat food products (as cooked meats and prepared salads) **2** *sing, pl* **delicatessens** : a store where delicatessen are sold

de·li·cious \di-ˈlish-əs\ *adj* : affording great pleasure : DELIGHTFUL; *esp* : very pleasing to the taste or smell — **de·li·cious·ly** *adv*

[1]**de·light** \di-ˈlīt\ *n* **1** : great pleasure or satisfaction : JOY **2** : something that gives great pleasure — **de·light·ful** \-fəl\ *adj* — **de·light·ful·ly** \-ē\ *adv*

[2]**delight** *vb* **1** : to take great pleasure **2** : to satisfy greatly : PLEASE

de·light·ed \-əd\ *adj* : highly pleased : GRATIFIED — **de·light·ed·ly** *adv*

de·lim·it \di-ˈlim-ət\ *vb* : to fix the limits of : BOUND

de·lin·eate \di-ˈlin-ē-ˌāt\ *vb* **-eat·ed; -eat·ing 1** : SKETCH, PORTRAY **2** : to picture in words : DESCRIBE — **de·lin·ea·tion** \-ˌlin-ē-ˈā-shən\ *n*

de·lin·quen·cy \di-ˈliŋ-kwən-sē\ *n, pl* **-cies** : the quality or state of being delinquent

[1]**de·lin·quent** \-kwənt\ *n* : a delinquent person

[2]**delinquent** *adj* **1** : offending by neglect or violation of duty or of law **2** : being overdue in payment

del·i·quesce \ˌdel-i-ˈkwes\ *vb* **-quesced; -quesc·ing** : MELT,

DISSOLVE; *esp* : to become liquid by absorbing moisture from the air — **del·i·ques·cent** \-ˈkwes-ᵊnt\ *adj*
de·lir·i·um \di-ˈlir-ē-əm\ *n* [L, fr. *delirare* to be crazy, fr. *de-* from + *lira* furrow] : mental disturbance marked by confusion, disordered speech, and hallucinations; *also* : violent excitement — **de·lir·i·ous** \-ē-əs\ *adj* — **de·lir·i·ous·ly** *adv*
delirium tre·mens \-ˈtrē-mənz, -ˈtrem-ənz\ *n* : a violent delirium with tremors that is induced by excessive and prolonged use of alcoholic liquors
de·liv·er \di-ˈliv-ər\ *vb* **-ered; -er·ing** \-(ə-)riŋ\ **1** : to set free : SAVE **2** : CONVEY, TRANSFER ⟨~ a letter⟩ **3** : to assist in giving birth or at the birth of **4** : UTTER, COMMUNICATE **5** : to send to an intended target or destination — **de·liv·er·ance** *n* — **de·liv·er·er** *n*
de·liv·ery \di-ˈliv-(ə-)rē\ *n, pl* **-er·ies** : the act of delivering something; *also* : something delivered
dell \ˈdel\ *n* : a small secluded valley
de·louse \dē-ˈlau̇s\ *vb* : to remove lice from
del·phin·i·um \del-ˈfin-ē-əm\ *n* : any of a genus of mostly perennial herbs related to the buttercups with tall branching spikes of irregular flowers
del·ta \ˈdel-tə\ *n* [Gk, fr. *delta,* fourth letter of the Gk alphabet, Δ, which an alluvial delta resembles in shape] : triangular silt-formed land at the mouth of a river — **del·ta·ic** \del-ˈtā-ik\ *adj*
de·lude \di-ˈlüd\ *vb* **de·lud·ed; de·lud·ing** : MISLEAD, DECEIVE, TRICK
[1]**del·uge** \ˈdel-yüj\ *n* **1** : a flooding of land by water **2** : a drenching rain **3** : a great amount or number ⟨a ~ of Christmas mail⟩
[2]**deluge** *vb* **del·uged; del·ug·ing 1** : INUNDATE, FLOOD **2** : to overwhelm as if with a deluge
de·lu·sion \di-ˈlü-zhən\ *n* : a deluding or being deluded; *esp* : a persistent belief in something false typical of some mental disorders — **de·lu·sion·al** \-ˈlüzh-(ə-)nəl\ *adj* — **de·lu·sive** \-ˈlü-siv\ *adj*
de·luxe \di-ˈlu̇ks, -ˈləks, -ˈlüks\ *adj* : notably luxurious or elegant
delve \ˈdelv\ *vb* **delved; delv·ing 1** : DIG **2** : to seek laboriously for information
dely *abbr* delivery
Dem *abbr* Democrat; Democratic
de·mag·ne·tize \dē-ˈmag-nə-ˌtīz\ *vb* : to cause to lose magnetic properties — **de·mag·ne·ti·za·tion** \dē-ˌmag-nət-ə-ˈzā-shən\ *n*
dem·a·gogue *or* **dem·a·gog** \ˈdem-ə-ˌgäg\ *n* [Gk *dēmagōgos,* fr. *dēmos* people + *agōgos* leading, fr. *agein* to lead] : a person who appeals to the emotions and prejudices of people esp. in order to gain political power — **dem·a·gogu·ery** \-ˌgäg-(ə-)rē\ *n* — **dem·a·gogy** \-ˌgäg-ē, -ˌgäj-ē\ *n*
[1]**de·mand** \di-ˈmand\ *n* **1** : an act of demanding or asking esp. with authority; *also* : something claimed as due **2** : the ability and desire to buy goods or services; *also* : the quantity of goods wanted at a stated price **3** : a seeking or being sought after : urgent need **4** : a pressing need or requirement
[2]**demand** *vb* **1** : to ask for with authority : claim as due **2** : to ask earnestly or in the manner of a command **3** : REQUIRE, NEED ⟨an illness that ~*s* care⟩
de·mar·cate \di-ˈmär-ˌkāt, ˈdē-ˌmär-\ *vb* **-cat·ed; -cat·ing 1** : to mark the limits of **2** : SEPARATE — **de·mar·ca·tion** \ˌdē-ˌmär-ˈkā-shən\ *n*
de·marche \dā-ˈmärsh\ *n* : a course of action : MANEUVER
[1]**de·mean** \di-ˈmēn\ *vb* **de·meaned; de·mean·ing** : to behave or conduct (oneself) usu. in a proper manner
[2]**demean** *vb* **de·meaned; de·mean·ing** : DEGRADE, DEBASE
de·mean·or \di-ˈmē-nər\ *n* : CONDUCT, BEARING
de·ment·ed \di-ˈment-əd\ *adj* : MAD, INSANE — **de·ment·ed·ly** *adv*
de·men·tia \di-ˈmen-chə\ *n* **1** : mental deterioration **2** : INSANITY
de·mer·it \di-ˈmer-ət\ *n* **1** : FAULT **2** : a mark placed against a person's record for some fault or offense
de·mesne \di-ˈmān, -ˈmēn\ *n* **1** : REALM **2** : manorial land actually possessed by the lord and not held by free tenants **3** : ESTATE **4** : REGION
demi·god \ˈdem-i-ˌgäd\ *n* : a mythological being with more power than a mortal but less than a god
demi·john \ˈdem-i-ˌjän\ *n* [F *dame-jeanne,* lit., Lady Jane] : a large glass or pottery bottle enclosed in wickerwork
de·mil·i·ta·rize \dē-ˈmil-ə-tə-ˌrīz\ *vb* : to strip of military forces, weapons, or fortifications — **de·mil·i·tar·iza·tion** \dē-ˌmil-ə-t(ə-)rə-ˈzā-shən\ *n*
demi·mon·daine \ˌdem-i-ˌmän-ˈdān\ *n* : a woman of the demimonde
demi·monde \ˈdem-i-ˌmänd\ *n* [F *demi-monde,* fr. *demi-* half + *monde* world] **1** : a class of women on the fringes of respectable society supported by wealthy lovers **2** : a group engaged in activity of doubtful legality or propriety
de·min·er·al·ize \dē-ˈmin-(ə-)rə-ˌlīz\ *vb* : to remove the mineral matter from
de·mise \di-ˈmīz\ *n* **1** : LEASE **2** : transfer of sovereignty to a successor ⟨~ of the crown⟩ **3** : DEATH **4** : loss of status
demi·tasse \ˈdem-i-ˌtas\ *n* [F *demi-tasse,* fr. *demi-* half + *tasse* cup, fr. MF, fr. Ar *ṭass,* fr. Per *tast*] : a small cup of black coffee; *also* : the cup used to serve it
de·mo·bi·lize \di-ˈmō-bə-ˌlīz, dē-\ *vb* **1** : to discharge from military service **2** : to change from a state of war to a state of peace — **de·mo·bi·li·za·tion** \di-ˌmō-bə-lə-ˈzā-shən, dē-\ *n*
de·moc·ra·cy \di-ˈmäk-rə-sē\ *n, pl* **-cies 1** : government by the people; *esp* : rule of the majority **2** : a government in which the supreme power is held by the people **3** : a political unit that has a democratic government **4** *cap* : the principles and policies of the Democratic party in the U.S. **5** : the common people esp. when constituting the source of political authority **6** : the absence of hereditary or arbitrary class distinctions or privileges
dem·o·crat \ˈdem-ə-ˌkrat\ *n* **1** : one who believes in or practices democracy **2** *cap* : a member of the Democratic party of the U.S.
dem·o·crat·ic \ˌdem-ə-ˈkrat-ik\ *adj* **1** : of, relating to, or favoring democracy **2** *often cap* : of or relating to one of the two major political parties in the U.S. associated in modern times with policies of broad social reform and internationalism **3** : relating to or appealing to the common people ⟨~ art⟩ **4** : not snobbish
de·moc·ra·tize \di-ˈmäk-rə-ˌtīz\ *vb* **-tized; -tiz·ing** : to make democratic
dé·mo·dé \ˌdā-mō-ˈdā\ *adj* [F] : no longer fashionable : OUT-OF-DATE
de·mo·graph·ics \ˌdem-ə-ˈgraf-iks, ˌdēm-\ *n pl* : the statistical characteristics of human populations
de·mog·ra·phy \di-ˈmäg-rə-fē\ *n* : the statistical study of human populations and esp. their size and distribution and the number of births and deaths — **de·mog·ra·pher** \-fər\ *n* — **de·mo·graph·ic** \ˌdem-ə-ˈgraf-ik, ˌdēm-\ *adj* — **de·mo·graph·i·cal·ly** \-i-k(ə-)lē\ *adv*
dem·oi·selle \ˌdem-(w)ə-ˈzel\ *n* [F] : a young woman
de·mol·ish \di-ˈmäl-ish\ *vb* **1** : to destroy by breaking apart : RAZE **2** : SMASH **3** : to put an end to
de·mo·li·tion \ˌdem-ə-ˈlish-ən, ˌdē-mə-\ *n* : the act of demolishing; *esp* : destruction by means of explosives
de·mon *or* **dae·mon** \ˈdē-mən\ *n* **1** : an evil spirit : DEVIL **2** *usu daemon* : an attendant power or spirit **3** : one that has unusual drive or effectiveness
de·mon·e·tize \dē-ˈmän-ə-ˌtīz, -ˈmən-\ *vb* : to stop using as money or as a monetary standard ⟨~ silver⟩ — **de·mon·e·ti·za·tion** \dē-ˌmän-ət-ə-ˈzā-shən, -ˌmən-\ *n*
de·mo·ni·ac \di-ˈmō-nē-ˌak\ *also* **de·mo·ni·a·cal** \ˌdē-mə-ˈnī-ə-kəl\ *adj* **1** : possessed or influenced by a demon **2** : DEVILISH, FIENDISH

de·mon·ic \di-ˈmän-ik\ *also* **de·mon·i·cal** \-i-kəl\ *adj* : DEMONIAC 2

de·mon·ol·o·gy \ˌdē-mə-ˈnäl-ə-jē\ *n* **1** : the study of demons **2** : belief in demons

de·mon·stra·ble \di-ˈmän-strə-bəl\ *adj* **1** : capable of being demonstrated or proved **2** : APPARENT, EVIDENT

dem·on·strate \ˈdem-ən-ˌstrāt\ *vb* **-strat·ed; -strat·ing** **1** : to show clearly **2** : to prove or make clear by reasoning or evidence **3** : to explain esp. with many examples **4** : to show publicly ⟨~ a new car⟩ **5** : to make a public display (as of feelings or military force) ⟨~ in protest⟩ — **dem·on·stra·tion** \ˌdem-ən-ˈstrā-shən\ *n* — **dem·on·stra·tor** \ˈdem-ən-ˌstrāt-ər\ *n*

[1]**de·mon·stra·tive** \di-ˈmän-strət-iv\ *adj* **1** : domonstrating as real or true **2** : characterized by demonstration **3** : pointing out the one referred to and distinguishing it from others of the same class ⟨~ pronoun⟩ ⟨~ adjective⟩ **4** : marked by display of feeling : EFFUSIVE — **de·mon·stra·tive·ly** *adv* — **de·mon·stra·tive·ness** *n*

[2]**demonstrative** *n* : a demonstrative word and esp. a pronoun

de·mor·al·ize \di-ˈmȯr-ə-ˌlīz\ *vb* **1** : to corrupt in morals **2** : to weaken in discipline or spirit : DISORGANIZE — **de·mor·al·iza·tion** \di-ˌmȯr-ə-lə-ˈzā-shən\ *n*

de·mote \di-ˈmōt\ *vb* **de·mot·ed; de·mot·ing** : to reduce to a lower grade or rank — **de·mo·tion** \-ˈmō-shən\ *n*

de·mot·ic \di-ˈmät-ik\ *adj* : of or relating to the people ⟨~ Greek⟩

[1]**de·mul·cent** \di-ˈməl-sənt\ *adj* : SOOTHING

[2]**demulcent** *n* : a usu. mucilaginous or oily substance used to soothe or protect an irritated mucous membrane

de·mur \di-ˈmər\ *vb* **de·murred; de·mur·ring** [ME *demeoren* to linger, fr. OF *demorer,* fr. L *demorari,* fr. *morari* to linger, fr. *mora* delay] : to take exception : OBJECT — **de·mur** *n*

de·mure \di-ˈmyu̇r\ *adj* **1** : quietly modest : DECOROUS **2** : affectedly modest, reserved, or serious : PRIM — **de·mure·ly** *adv*

de·mur·rage \di-ˈmər-ij\ *n* : the detention of a ship by the shipper or receiver beyond the time allowed for loading, unloading, or sailing; *also* : a charge for detaining a ship, freight car, or truck for such a delay

de·mur·rer \di-ˈmər-ər\ *n* : a claim by the defendant in a legal action that the plaintiff does not have sufficient grounds to proceed

den \ˈden\ *n* **1** : a shelter or resting place of a wild animal **2** : a hiding place (as for thieves) **3** : a dirty wretched place in which people live or gather ⟨~*s* of misery⟩ **4** : a cozy private little room

Den *abbr* Denmark

de·na·ture \dē-ˈnā-chər\ *vb* **de·na·tured; de·na·tur·ing** \-ˈnāch-(ə-)riŋ\ : to remove the natural qualities of; *esp* : to make (alcohol) unfit for drinking

den·drol·o·gy \den-ˈdräl-ə-jē\ *n* : the study of trees — **den·drol·o·gist** \-ə-jəst\ *n*

den·gue \ˈdeŋ-gē, -ˌgā\ *n* [Sp] : an acute infectious disease characterized by headache, severe joint pain, and rash

de·ni·al \di-ˈnī(-ə)l\ *n* **1** : rejection of a request **2** : refusal to admit the truth of a statement or charge; *also* : assertion that something alleged is false **3** : DISAVOWAL **4** : restriction on one's own activity or desires

de·nier \ˈden-yər\ *n* : a unit of fineness for silk, rayon, or nylon yarn

den·i·grate \ˈden-i-ˌgrāt\ *vb* **-grat·ed; -grat·ing** [L *denigrare,* fr. *nigrare* to blacken, fr. *niger* black] : to cast aspersions on : DEFAME

den·im \ˈden-əm\ *n* [F *(serge) de Nîmes* serge of Nîmes, France] **1** : a firm durable twilled usu. cotton fabric woven with colored warp and white filling threads **2** *pl* : overalls or trousers of usu. blue denim

den·i·zen \ˈden-ə-zən\ *n* : INHABITANT

de·nom·i·nate \di-ˈnäm-ə-ˌnāt\ *vb* : to give a name to : DESIGNATE

de·nom·i·nate number \di-ˌnäm-ə-nət-\ *n* : a number (as 7 in *7 feet*) that specifies a quantity in terms of a unit of measurement

de·nom·i·na·tion \di-ˌnäm-ə-ˈnā-shən\ *n* **1** : an act of denominating **2** : a value or size of a series of related values (as of money) **3** : NAME, DESIGNATION; *esp* : a general name for a class of things **4** : a religious body comprising a number of local congregations having similar beliefs — **de·nom·i·na·tion·al** \-sh(ə-)nəl\ *adj*

de·nom·i·na·tor \di-ˈnäm-ə-ˌnāt-ər\ *n* : the part of a fraction that is below the line

de·no·ta·tive \ˈdē-nō-ˌtāt-iv, di-ˈnōt-ət-iv\ *adj* **1** : denoting or tending to denote **2** : relating to denotation

de·note \di-ˈnōt\ *vb* **1** : to mark out plainly : INDICATE **2** : to make known **3** : MEAN, NAME — **de·no·ta·tion** \ˌdē-nō-ˈtā-shən\ *n*

de·noue·ment \ˌdā-ˌnü-ˈmäⁿ\ *n* [F *dénouement,* lit., untying, fr. MF *desnouement,* fr. *desnouer* to untie, fr. OF *desnoer,* fr. *noer* to tie, fr. L *nodare,* fr. *nodus* knot] : the final outcome of the dramatic complications in a literary work

de·nounce \di-ˈnau̇ns\ *vb* **de·nounced; de·nounc·ing** **1** : to point out as deserving blame or punishment **2** : to inform against : ACCUSE **3** : to announce formally the termination of (as a treaty) — **de·nounce·ment** *n*

de no·vo \di-ˈnō-vō\ *adv* [L] : ANEW, AGAIN

dense \ˈdens\ *adj* **dens·er; dens·est** **1** : marked by compactness or crowding together of parts : THICK ⟨a ~ forest⟩ ⟨a ~ fog⟩ **2** : DULL, STUPID — **dense·ly** *adv* — **dense·ness** *n*

den·si·ty \ˈden-sət-ē\ *n, pl* **-ties** **1** : the quality or state of being dense **2** : the quantity of something per unit volume, unit area, or unit length

dent \ˈdent\ *n* **1** : a small depressed place made by a blow or by pressure **2** : an impression or effect made usu. against resistance **3** : initial progress — **dent** *vb*

den·tal \ˈdent-ᵊl\ *adj* : of or relating to the teeth or dentistry — **den·tal·ly** \-ē\ *adv*

dental floss *n* : a thread used to clean between the teeth

dental hygienist *n* : one who is licensed in the cleaning and examining of teeth

den·tate \ˈden-ˌtāt\ *adj* : having pointed projections : NOTCHED

den·ti·frice \ˈdent-ə-frəs\ *n* [MF, fr. L *dentifricium,* fr. *dent-, dens* tooth + *fricare* to rub] : a powder, paste, or liquid for cleaning the teeth

den·tin \ˈdent-ᵊn\ *or* **den·tine** \ˈden-ˌtēn, den-ˈtēn\ *n* : a calcareous material like bone but harder and denser that composes the principal mass of a tooth — **den·tin·al** \den-ˈtēn-ᵊl, ˈdent-ᵊn-əl\ *adj*

den·tist \ˈdent-əst\ *n* : one who is licensed in the care, treatment, and replacement of teeth — **den·tist·ry** *n*

den·ti·tion \den-ˈtish-ən\ *n* : the character of a set of teeth esp. with regard to number, kind, and arrangement; *also* : TEETH

den·ture \ˈden-chər\ *n* : an artificial replacement for teeth

de·nude \di-ˈn(y)üd\ *vb* **de·nud·ed; de·nud·ing** : to strip the covering from — **de·nu·da·tion** \dē-(ˌ)n(y)ü-ˈdā-shən\ *n*

de·nun·ci·a·tion \di-ˌnən-sē-ˈā-shən\ *n* : the act of denouncing; *esp* : a public accusation

de·ny \di-ˈnī\ *vb* **de·nied; de·ny·ing** **1** : to declare untrue **2** : to refuse to recognize or acknowledge : DISAVOW **3** : to refuse to grant ⟨~ a request⟩ **4** : to reject as false ⟨~ a theory⟩

de·o·dar \ˈdē-ə-ˌdär\ *also* **de·o·da·ra** \ˌdē-ə-ˈdär-ə\ *n* [Hindi *deodār*, fr. Skt *devadāru*, lit., timber of the gods, fr. *deva* god + *dāru* wood] : an East Indian cedar

de·odor·ant \dē-ˈōd-ə-rənt\ *n* : a preparation that destroys or masks unpleasant odors

de·odor·ize \dē-ˈōd-ə-ˌrīz\ *vb* : to eliminate the offensive odor of

de·ox·i·dize \dē-ˈäk-sə-ˌdīz\ *vb* : to remove oxygen from

de·oxy·ri·bo·nu·cle·ic acid \dē-ˈäk-si-ˌrī-bō-n(y)u̇-ˌklē-ik-\ *n* : DNA

de·oxy·ri·bose \dē-ˌäk-si-ˈrī-ˌbōs\ *n* : a sugar with five carbon and four oxygen atoms in each molecule that is part of DNA

dep *abbr* **1** depart; departure **2** deposit **3** deputy

de·part \di-ˈpärt\ *vb* **1** : to go away : go away from : LEAVE **2** : DIE **3** : to turn aside : DEVIATE

de·part·ment \di-ˈpärt-mənt\ *n* **1** : a distinct sphere : PROVINCE **2** : a functional or territorial division (as of a government, business, or college) — **de·part·men·tal** \di-ˌpärt-ˈment-ᵊl, ˌdē-\ *adj*

department store *n* : a store selling a wide variety of goods arranged in several departments

de·par·ture \di-ˈpär-chər\ *n* **1** : the act of going away **2** : a starting out (as on a journey) **3** : DIVERGENCE

de·pend \di-ˈpend\ *vb* **1** : to be determined by or based on some action or condition ⟨our success ~*s* on his cooperation⟩ **2** : TRUST, RELY ⟨you can ~ on me⟩ **3** : to be dependent esp. for financial support **4** : to hang down ⟨a vine ~*ing* from a tree⟩

de·pend·able \di-ˈpen-də-bəl\ *adj* : TRUSTWORTHY, RELIABLE — **de·pend·abil·i·ty** \-ˌpen-də-ˈbil-ət-ē\ *n*

de·pen·dence *also* **de·pen·dance** \di-ˈpen-dəns\ *n* **1** : the quality or state of being dependent; *esp* : the quality or state of being influenced by or subject to another **2** : RELIANCE, TRUST **3** : something on which one relies **4** : drug addiction; *also* : HABITUATION 2

de·pen·den·cy \-dən-sē\ *n, pl* **-cies** **1** : DEPENDENCE **2** : a territory under the jurisdiction of a nation but not formally annexed by it

¹de·pen·dent \di-ˈpen-dənt\ *adj* **1** : hanging down **2** : determined or conditioned by another; *also* : affected with drug dependence **3** : relying on another for support **4** : subject to another's jurisdiction **5** : SUBORDINATE 4

²dependent *also* **de·pen·dant** \-dənt\ *n* : one that is dependent; *esp* : a person who relies on another for support

de·pict \di-ˈpikt\ *vb* **1** : to represent by a picture **2** : to describe in words — **de·pic·tion** \-ˈpik-shən\ *n*

de·pil·a·to·ry \di-ˈpil-ə-ˌtōr-ē\ *n, pl* **-ries** : an agent for removing hair, wool, or bristles

de·plane \dē-ˈplān\ *vb* : to get out of an airplane

de·plete \di-ˈplēt\ *vb* **de·plet·ed; de·plet·ing** : to exhaust esp. of strength or resources — **de·ple·tion** \-ˈplē-shən\ *n*

de·plor·able \di-ˈplōr-ə-bəl\ *adj* **1** : LAMENTABLE **2** : WRETCHED — **de·plor·ably** \-blē\ *adv*

de·plore \-ˈplōr\ *vb* **de·plored; de·plor·ing** **1** : to feel or express grief for **2** : to regret strongly **3** : to consider unfortunate or deserving of disapproval

de·ploy \di-ˈplȯi\ *vb* : to spread out (as troops or ships) in order for battle — **de·ploy·ment** \-mənt\ *n*

de·po·nent \di-ˈpō-nənt\ *n* : one who gives evidence esp. in writing

de·pop·u·late \dē-ˈpäp-yə-ˌlāt\ *vb* : to reduce greatly the population of by destroying or driving away the inhabitants — **de·pop·u·la·tion** \dē-ˌpäp-yə-ˈlā-shən\ *n*

de·port \di-ˈpōrt\ *vb* **1** : CONDUCT, BEHAVE **2** : BANISH, EXILE — **de·por·ta·tion** \ˌdē-ˌpōr-ˈtā-shən\ *n*

de·port·ment \di-ˈpōrt-mənt\ *n* : BEHAVIOR, BEARING

de·pose \di-ˈpōz\ *vb* **de·posed; de·pos·ing** **1** : to remove from high office (as of king) **2** : to testify under oath or by affidavit

¹de·pos·it \di-ˈpäz-ət\ *vb* **de·pos·it·ed** \-ˈpäz-ət-əd\; **de·pos·it·ing** **1** : to place for safekeeping or as a pledge; *esp* : to put money in a bank **2** : to lay down : PUT **3** : to let fall or sink ⟨sand and silt ~*ed* by a flood⟩ — **de·pos·i·tor** \-ˈpäz-ət-ər\ *n*

²deposit *n* **1** : the state of being deposited ⟨money on ~⟩ **2** : something placed for safekeeping; *esp* : money deposited in a bank **3** : money given as a pledge **4** : an act of depositing **5** : something laid or thrown down ⟨a ~ of silt by a river⟩ **6** : an accumulation of mineral matter (as ore, oil, or gas) in nature

de·po·si·tion \ˌdep-ə-ˈzish-ən, ˌdē-pə-\ *n* **1** : an act of removing from a position of authority **2** : TESTIMONY **3** : the process of depositing **4** : DEPOSIT

de·pos·i·to·ry \di-ˈpäz-ə-ˌtōr-ē\ *n, pl* **-ries** : a place where something is deposited esp. for safekeeping

de·pot *1, 2 usu* ˈdep-ō, *3 usu* ˈdēp-\ *n* **1** : STOREHOUSE **2** : a place where military supplies are kept or where troops are assembled and trained **3** : a building for railroad or bus passengers : STATION

depr *abbr* depreciation

de·prave \di-ˈprāv\ *vb* **de·praved; de·prav·ing** [ME *depraven*, fr. MF *depraver*, fr. L *depravare* to pervert, fr. *pravus* crooked, bad] : CORRUPT, PERVERT — **de·praved** *adj* — **de·prav·i·ty** \-ˈprav-ət-ē\ *n*

dep·re·cate \ˈdep-ri-ˌkāt\ *vb* **-cat·ed; -cat·ing** [L *deprecari* to avert by prayer, fr. *precari* to pray] **1** : to express disapproval of **2** : DEPRECIATE — **dep·re·ca·tion** \ˌdep-ri-ˈkā-shən\ *n*

dep·re·ca·to·ry \ˈdep-ri-kə-ˌtōr-ē\ *adj* **1** : expressing deprecation : APOLOGETIC **2** : serving to deprecate

de·pre·ci·ate \di-ˈprē-shē-ˌāt\ *vb* **-at·ed; -at·ing** [LL *depretiare*, fr. L *pretium* price] **1** : to lessen in price or value **2** : UNDERVALUE, BELITTLE, DISPARAGE — **de·pre·ci·a·tion** \-ˌprē-shē-ˈā-shən\ *n*

dep·re·da·tion \ˌdep-rə-ˈdā-shən\ *n* : a laying waste or plundering — **dep·re·date** \ˈdep-rə-ˌdāt\ *vb*

de·press \di-ˈpres\ *vb* **1** : to press down : cause to sink to a lower position **2** : to lessen the activity or force of **3** : SADDEN, DISCOURAGE **4** : to lessen in price or value — **de·pres·sor** \di-ˈpres-ər\ *n*

de·pres·sant \di-ˈpres-ᵊnt\ *n* : one that depresses; *esp* : an agent that reduces bodily functional activity — **depressant** *adj*

de·pressed \di-ˈprest\ *adj* **1** : low in spirits; *also* : affected with emotional depression **2** : suffering from economic depression

de·pres·sion \di-ˈpresh-ən\ *n* **1** : an act of depressing : a state of being depressed **2** : a pressing down : LOWERING **3** : a state of feeling sad **4** : an emotional disorder marked esp. by sadness, inactivity, difficulty in thinking and concentration, and feelings of dejection **5** : a depressed area or part **6** : a period of low general economic activity with widespread unemployment

¹de·pres·sive \di-ˈpres-iv\ *adj* **1** : tending to depress **2** : characterized or affected by psychological depression

²depressive *n* : one who is psychologically depressed

de·pri·va·tion \ˌdep-rə-ˈvā-shən\ *n* : an act or instance of depriving : LOSS; *also* : PRIVATION

de·prive \di-ˈprīv\ *vb* **de·prived; de·priv·ing** **1** : to take something away from ⟨~ a king of his power⟩ **2** : to stop from having something

dept *abbr* department

depth \ˈdepth\ *n, pl* **depths** \ˈdep(th)s\ **1** : something that is deep; *esp* : the deep part of a body of water **2** : a part that is far from the outside or surface ⟨the ~*s* of the woods⟩ **3** : ABYSS **4** : the middle or innermost part ⟨the ~ of winter⟩ **5** : an extreme state (as of misery); *also* : the worst part ⟨the ~*s* of despair⟩ **6** : the perpendicular distance downward from a surface; *also* : the distance from front to back **7** : the quality of being deep **8** : the degree of intensity

depth charge *n* : an explosive device for use underwater esp. against submarines

dep·u·ta·tion \ˌdep-yə-ˈtā-shən\ *n* **1** : the act of appointing a deputy **2** : DELEGATION

de·pute \di-ˈpyüt\ *vb* **de·put·ed; de·put·ing** : DELEGATE

dep·u·tize \ˈdep-yə-ˌtīz\ *vb* **-tized; -tiz·ing** : to appoint as deputy

dep·u·ty \ˈdep-yət-ē\ *n, pl* **-ties 1** : a person appointed to act for or in place of another **2** : an assistant empowered to act as a substitute in the absence of his superior **3** : a member of a lower house of a legislative assembly

der *or* **deriv** *abbr* derivation; derivative

de·rail \di-ˈrāl\ *vb* : to cause to run off the rails — **de·rail·ment** *n*

de·rail·leur \di-ˈrā-lər\ *n* [F *dérailleur*] : a device for shifting gears on a bicycle by moving the chain from one set of exposed gears to another

de·range \di-ˈrānj\ *vb* **de·ranged; de·rang·ing 1** : DISARRANGE, UPSET **2** : to make insane — **de·range·ment** *n*

der·by \ˈdər-bē, *Brit* ˈdär-\ *n, pl* **derbies 1** : a horse race usu. for three-year-olds held annually **2** : a race or contest open to all **3** : a man's stiff felt hat with dome-shaped crown and narrow brim

[1]**der·e·lict** \ˈder-ə-ˌlikt\ *adj* **1** : abandoned by the owner or occupant ⟨a ~ ship⟩ **2** : NEGLIGENT ⟨~ in his duty⟩

[2]**derelict** *n* **1** : something voluntarily abandoned; *esp* : a ship abandoned on the high seas **2** : a destitute homeless social misfit : VAGRANT, BUM

der·e·lic·tion \ˌder-ə-ˈlik-shən\ *n* **1** : the act of abandoning : the state of being abandoned **2** : a failure in duty

de·ride \di-ˈrīd\ *vb* **de·rid·ed; de·rid·ing** [L *deridēre*, fr. *ridēre* to laugh] : to laugh at scornfully : make fun of : RIDICULE — **de·ri·sion** \-ˈrizh-ən\ *n* — **de·ri·sive** \-ˈrī-siv\ *adj* — **de·ri·sive·ly** *adv* — **de·ri·so·ry** \-ˈrī-sə-rē\ *adj*

de ri·gueur \də-rē-ˈgər\ *adj* [F] : prescribed or required by fashion, etiquette, or custom

der·i·va·tion \ˌder-ə-ˈvā-shən\ *n* **1** : the formation of a word from an earlier word or root; *also* : an act of ascertaining or stating the derivation of a word **2** : ETYMOLOGY **3** : SOURCE, ORIGIN; *also* : DESCENT **4** : an act or process of deriving

[1]**de·riv·a·tive** \di-ˈriv-ət-iv\ *n* **1** : a word formed by derivation **2** : something derived

[2]**derivative** *adj* : derived from something else

de·rive \di-ˈrīv\ *vb* **de·rived; de·riv·ing** [ME *deriven*, fr. MF *deriver*, fr. L *derivare*, fr. *de-* from + *rivus* stream] **1** : to receive or obtain from a source **2** : to obtain from a parent substance **3** : INFER, DEDUCE **4** : to trace the origin, descent, or derivation of **5** : to come from a certain source

der·mal \ˈdər-məl\ *adj* : of or relating to the skin

der·ma·ti·tis \ˌdər-mə-ˈtīt-əs\ *n* : skin inflammation

der·ma·tol·o·gy \-ˈtäl-ə-jē\ *n* : a branch of science dealing with the skin and its disorders — **der·ma·tol·o·gist** \-jəst\ *n*

der·mis \ˈdər-məs\ *n* : the sensitive vascular inner layer of the skin

der·o·gate \ˈder-ə-ˌgāt\ *vb* **-gat·ed; -gat·ing 1** : to cause to seem inferior : DISPARAGE **2** : DETRACT — **der·o·ga·tion** \ˌder-ə-ˈgā-shən\ *n*

de·rog·a·to·ry \di-ˈräg-ə-ˌtōr-ē\ *adj* : intended to lower the reputation of a person or thing : DISPARAGING

der·rick \ˈder-ik\ *n* [obs. *derrick* hangman, gallows, fr. *Derick*, name of 17th cent. E hangman] **1** : a hoisting apparatus : CRANE **2** : a framework over a drill hole (as for oil) supporting machinery

der·ri·ere *or* **der·ri·ère** \ˌder-ē-ˈeər\ *n* : BUTTOCKS

der·ring–do \ˌder-iŋ-ˈdü\ *n* : daring action : DARING

der·rin·ger \ˈder-ən-jər\ *n* : a short-barreled pocket pistol

der·vish \ˈdər-vish\ *n* [Turk *derviş*, lit., beggar, fr. Per *darvēsh*] : a member of a Muslim religious order noted for devotional exercises (as bodily movements leading to a trance)

de·sal·i·nate \dē-ˈsal-ə-ˌnāt\ *vb* **-nat·ed; -nat·ing** : DESALT — **de·sal·i·na·tion** \-ˌsal-ə-ˈnā-shən\ *n*

de·sal·i·nize \dē-ˈsal-ə-ˌnīz\ *vb* **-nized; -niz·ing** : DESALT — **de·sal·i·ni·za·tion** \-ˌsal-ə-nə-ˈzā-shən\ *n*

de·salt \dē-ˈsȯlt\ *vb* : to remove salt from ⟨~ seawater⟩ — **de·salt·er** *n*

des·cant \ˈdes-ˌkant\ *vb* **1** : to sing or play part music : SING **2** : to discourse or write at length

de·scend \di-ˈsend\ *vb* **1** : to pass from a higher to a lower place or level : pass, move, or climb down or down along **2** : DERIVE ⟨~*ed* from royalty⟩ **3** : to pass by inheritance or transmission **4** : to incline, lead, or extend downward **5** : to swoop down in a sudden attack

[1]**de·scen·dant** *or* **de·scen·dent** \di-ˈsen-dənt\ *adj* **1** : DESCENDING **2** : proceeding from an ancestor or source

[2]**descendant** *or* **descendent** *n* **1** : one descended from another or from a common stock **2** : one deriving directly from a precursor or prototype

de·scent \di-ˈsent\ *n* **1** : ANCESTRY, BIRTH, LINEAGE **2** : the act or process of descending **3** : SLOPE **4** : a descending way (as a downgrade) **5** : a sudden hostile raid or assault **6** : a downward step (as in station or value) : DECLINE

de·scribe \di-ˈskrīb\ *vb* **de·scribed; de·scrib·ing 1** : to represent or give an account of in words **2** : to trace the outline of — **de·scrib·able** *adj*

de·scrip·tion \di-ˈskrip-shən\ *n* **1** : an account of something; *esp* : an account that presents a picture to a person who reads or hears it **2** : KIND, SORT — **de·scrip·tive** \-ˈskrip-tiv\ *adj*

de·scry \di-ˈskrī\ *vb* **de·scried; de·scry·ing 1** : to catch sight of **2** : to discover by observation or investigation

des·e·crate \ˈdes-i-ˌkrāt\ *vb* **-crat·ed; -crat·ing** : PROFANE — **des·e·cra·tion** \ˌdes-i-ˈkrā-shən\ *n*

de·seg·re·gate \dē-ˈseg-ri-ˌgāt\ *vb* : to eliminate segregation in; *esp* : to free of any law, provision, or practice requiring isolation of the members of a particular race in separate units — **de·seg·re·ga·tion** \dē-ˌseg-ri-ˈgā-shən\ *n*

de·sen·si·tize \dē-ˈsen-sə-ˌtīz\ *vb* : to make (a sensitized or hypersensitive individual) insensitive or nonreactive to a sensitizing agent — **de·sen·si·ti·za·tion** \dē-ˌsen-sət-ə-ˈzā-shən\ *n*

[1]**des·ert** \ˈdez-ərt\ *n* : a dry barren region incapable of supporting a population without an artificial water supply

[2]**des·ert** \ˈdez-ərt\ *adj* : of, relating to, or resembling a desert; *esp* : being barren and without life ⟨a ~ island⟩

[3]**de·sert** \di-ˈzərt\ *n* **1** : worthiness of reward or punishment **2** : a just reward or punishment

[4]**de·sert** \di-ˈzərt\ *vb* **1** : to withdraw from **2** : FORSAKE — **de·sert·er** *n* — **de·ser·tion** \-ˈzər-shən\ *n*

de·serve \di-ˈzərv\ *vb* **de·served; de·serv·ing** : to be worthy of : MERIT — **de·serv·ing** *adj*

de·serv·ed·ly \-ˈzər-vəd-lē\ *adv* : according to merit : JUSTLY

des·ic·cate \ˈdes-i-ˌkāt\ *vb* **-cat·ed; -cat·ing** : DRY, DEHYDRATE — **des·ic·ca·tor** \ˈdes-i-ˌkāt-ər\ *n*

de·sid·er·a·tum \di-ˌsid-ə-ˈrät-əm, -ˌzid-, -ˈrāt-\ *n, pl* **-ta** \-ə\ [L] : something desired as essential or needed

[1]**de·sign** \di-ˈzīn\ *vb* **1** : to conceive and plan out in the mind **2** : INTEND **3** : to devise for a specific function or end **4** : to make a pattern or sketch of **5** : to conceive and draw the plans for ⟨~ an airplane⟩

[2]**design** *n* **1** : a particular purpose : deliberate planning **2** : a mental project or scheme : PLAN **3** : a secret project or scheme : PLOT **4** *pl* : aggressive or evil intent — used with *on* or *against* **5** : a preliminary sketch or plan : DELINEATION **6** : an underlying scheme that governs functioning, developing, or unfolding : MOTIF **7** : the arrangement of elements or details in a product or a

work of art **8** : a decorative pattern **9** : the art of executing designs

[1]des·ig·nate \ˈdez-ig-ˌnāt, -nət\ *adj* : chosen for an office but not yet installed ⟨ambassador ~⟩

[2]des·ig·nate \-ˌnāt\ *vb* **-nat·ed; -nat·ing 1** : to appoint or choose by name for a special purpose **2** : to mark or point out : INDICATE; *also* : SPECIFY, STIPULATE **3** : to call by a name or title — **des·ig·na·tion** \ˌdez-ig-ˈnā-shən\ *n*

designated hitter *n* : a baseball player designated at the start of the game to bat in place of the pitcher without causing the pitcher to be removed from the game

de·sign·er \di-ˈzī-nər\ *n* **1** : one who creates plans for a project or structure **2** : one who designs and manufactures high-fashion clothing — **designer** *adj*

de·sign·ing \di-ˈzī-niŋ\ *adj* : CRAFTY, SCHEMING

de·sir·able \di-ˈzī-rə-bəl\ *adj* **1** : PLEASING, ATTRACTIVE ⟨a ~ woman⟩ **2** : ADVISABLE ⟨~ legislation⟩ — **de·sir·abil·i·ty** \-ˌzī-rə-ˈbil-ət-ē\ *n*

[1]de·sire \di-ˈzī(ə)r\ *vb* **de·sired; de·sir·ing** [ME *desiren,* fr. OF *desirer,* fr. L *desiderare,* fr. *sider-, sidus* star] **1** : to long, hope, or wish for : COVET **2** : REQUEST

[2]desire *n* **1** : a strong wish : LONGING, CRAVING **2** : an expressed wish : REQUEST **3** : something desired

de·sir·ous \di-ˈzīr-əs\ *adj* : eagerly wishing : DESIRING

de·sist \di-ˈzist, -ˈsist\ *vb* : to cease to proceed or act

desk \ˈdesk\ *n* [ME *deske,* fr. ML *desca,* fr. It *desco* table, fr. L *discus* dish, disc] **1** : a table, frame, or case esp. for writing and reading **2** : a counter, stand, or booth at which a person performs duties **3** : a specialized division of an organization (as a newspaper) ⟨city ~⟩

[1]des·o·late \ˈdes-ə-lət, ˈdez-\ *adj* **1** : DESERTED, ABANDONED **2** : FORSAKEN, LONELY **3** : DILAPIDATED **4** : BARREN, LIFELESS **5** : CHEERLESS, GLOOMY — **des·o·late·ly** *adv*

[2]des·o·late \-ˌlāt\ *vb* **-lat·ed; -lat·ing** : to make desolate : lay waste : make wretched

des·o·la·tion \ˌdes-ə-ˈlā-shən, ˌdez-\ *n* **1** : the action of desolating **2** : GRIEF, SADNESS **3** : LONELINESS **4** : DEVASTATION, RUIN **5** : barren wasteland

des·oxy·ri·bo·nu·cle·ic acid \de-ˌzäk-sē-ˈrī-bō-n(y)ü-ˌklē-ik-\ *n* : DNA

[1]de·spair \di-ˈspaər\ *vb* : to lose all hope or confidence — **de·spair·ing** *adj* — **de·spair·ing·ly** *adv*

[2]despair *n* **1** : utter loss of hope **2** : a cause of hopelessness

des·patch \dis-ˈpach\ *var of* DISPATCH

des·per·a·do \ˌdes-pə-ˈräd-ō, -ˈräd-\ *n, pl* **-does** *or* **-dos** : a bold or reckless criminal

des·per·ate \ˈdes-p(ə-)rət\ *adj* **1** : being beyond or almost beyond hope : causing despair **2** : RASH **3** : extremely intense — **des·per·ate·ly** *adv*

des·per·a·tion \ˌdes-pə-ˈrā-shən\ *n* **1** : a loss of hope and surrender to despair **2** : a state of hopelessness leading to rashness

de·spi·ca·ble \di-ˈspik-ə-bəl, ˈdes-pik-\ *adj* : deserving to be despised — **de·spi·ca·bly** \-blē\ *adv*

de·spise \di-ˈspīz\ *vb* **de·spised; de·spis·ing 1** : to look down on with contempt or aversion : DISDAIN, DETEST **2** : to regard as negligible, worthless, or distasteful

de·spite \di-ˈspīt\ *prep* : in spite of

de·spoil \di-ˈspȯil\ *vb* : to strip of belongings, possessions, or value — **de·spoil·er** *n* — **de·spoil·ment** *n*

de·spo·li·a·tion \di-ˌspō-lē-ˈā-shən\ *n* : the act of plundering : the state of being despoiled

[1]de·spond \di-ˈspänd\ *vb* : to become discouraged or disheartened

[2]despond *n* : DESPONDENCY

de·spon·den·cy \-ˈspän-dən-sē\ *n* : DEJECTION, HOPELESSNESS — **de·spon·dent** \-dənt\ *adj*

des·pot \ˈdes-pət, -ˌpät\ *n* [MF *despote,* fr. Gk *despotēs* master] **1** : a ruler with absolute power and authority : AUTOCRAT, TYRANT **2** : a person exercising power abusively, oppressively, or tyrannously — **des·pot·ic** \des-ˈpät-ik\ *adj* — **des·po·tism** \ˈdes-pə-ˌtiz-əm\ *n*

des·sert \di-ˈzərt\ *n* : a course of sweet food, fruit, or cheese served at the close of a meal

des·ti·na·tion \ˌdes-tə-ˈnā-shən\ *n* **1** : a purpose for which something is destined **2** : an act of appointing, setting aside for a purpose, or predetermining **3** : a place to which one is journeying or to which something is sent

des·tine \ˈdes-tən\ *vb* **des·tined; des·tin·ing 1** : to settle in advance **2** : to designate, assign, or dedicate in advance **3** : to be bound or directed ⟨freight *destined* for English ports⟩

des·ti·ny \ˈdes-tə-nē\ *n, pl* **-nies 1** : something to which a person or thing is destined : FATE, FORTUNE **2** : a predetermined course of events

des·ti·tute \ˈdes-tə-ˌt(y)üt\ *adj* **1** : lacking something needed or desirable **2** : extremely poor — **des·ti·tu·tion** \ˌdes-tə-ˈt(y)ü-shən\ *n*

de·stroy \di-ˈstrȯi\ *vb* **1** : to put an end to : RUIN **2** : KILL

de·stroy·er \di-ˈstrȯi(-ə)r\ *n* **1** : one that destroys **2** : a small speedy warship

[1]de·struct \di-ˈstrəkt\ *vb* : DESTROY

[2]destruct *n* : the deliberate destruction of a rocket after launching

de·struc·ti·ble \di-ˈstrək-tə-bəl\ *adj* : capable of being destroyed — **de·struc·ti·bil·i·ty** \di-ˌstrək-tə-ˈbil-ət-ē\ *n*

de·struc·tion \di-ˈstrək-shən\ *n* **1** : RUIN **2** : the action or process of destroying something **3** : a destroying agency

de·struc·tive \di-ˈstrək-tiv\ *adj* **1** : causing destruction : RUINOUS **2** : designed or tending to destroy — **de·struc·tive·ly** *adv* — **de·struc·tive·ness** *n*

de·struc·tor \di-ˈstrək-tər\ *n* : a furnace for burning refuse : INCINERATOR

de·sue·tude \ˈdes-wi-ˌt(y)üd\ *n* : DISUSE

des·ul·to·ry \ˈdes-əl-ˌtōr-ē\ *adj* : passing aimlessly from one thing or subject to another : DISCONNECTED

det *abbr* **1** detached; detachment **2** detail

de·tach \di-ˈtach\ *vb* **1** : to separate esp. from a larger mass **2** : DISENGAGE, WITHDRAW — **de·tach·able** *adj*

de·tached \di-ˈtacht\ *adj* **1** : not joined or connected : SEPARATE **2** : ALOOF, IMPARTIAL ⟨a ~ attitude⟩

de·tach·ment \di-ˈtach-mənt\ *n* **1** : SEPARATION **2** : the dispatching of a body of troops or part of a fleet from the main body for special service; *also* : the portion so dispatched **3** : a small permanent military unit different in composition from normal units **4** : indifference to worldly concerns : ALOOFNESS, UNWORLDLINESS **5** : IMPARTIALITY

[1]de·tail \di-ˈtāl, ˈdē-ˌtāl\ *n* [F *détail,* fr. OF *detail* slice, piece, fr. *detaillier* to cut in pieces, fr. *taillier* to cut] **1** : a dealing with something item by item ⟨go into ~⟩; *also* : ITEM, PARTICULAR ⟨the ~*s* of a story⟩ **2** : selection (as of soldiers) for special duty; *also* : the persons thus selected

[2]detail *vb* **1** : to report in detail **2** : ENUMERATE, SPECIFY **3** : to select for some special duty

de·tain \di-ˈtān\ *vb* **1** : to hold in or as if in custody **2** : STOP, DELAY

de·tect \di-ˈtekt\ *vb* : to discover the nature, existence, presence, or fact of — **de·tect·able** *adj* — **de·tec·tion** \-ˈtek-shən\ *n* — **de·tec·tor** \-tər\ *n*

[1]de·tec·tive \di-ˈtek-tiv\ *adj* **1** : fitted or used for detection ⟨a ~ device for coal gas⟩ **2** : of or relating to detectives

[2]detective *n* : a person employed or engaged in detecting lawbreakers or getting information that is not readily accessible

dé·tente \dā-ˈtänt\ *n* [F] : a relaxation of strained relations or tensions (as between nations)

de·ten·tion \di-ˈten-chən\ *n* **1** : the act or fact of detaining : CONFINEMENT; *esp* : a period of temporary custody prior to disposition by a court **2** : a forced delay

de·ter \di-ˈtər\ *vb* **de·terred; de·ter·ring** [L *deterrēre,* fr.

terrēre to frighten] **1** : to turn aside, discourage, or prevent from acting (as by fear) **2** : INHIBIT

de·ter·gent \di-ˈtər-jənt\ *n* : a cleansing agent; *esp* : a chemical product similar to soap in its cleaning ability

de·te·ri·o·rate \di-ˈtir-ē-ə-ˌrāt\ *vb* **-rat·ed; -rat·ing** : to make or grow worse : DEGENERATE — **de·te·ri·o·ra·tion** \-ˌtir-ē-ə-ˈrā-shən\ *n*

de·ter·min·able \-ˈtər-mə-nə-bəl\ *adj* : capable of being determined; *esp* : ASCERTAINABLE

de·ter·mi·nant \-mə-nənt\ *n* **1** : something that determines or conditions **2** : a hereditary factor : GENE

de·ter·mi·nate \di-ˈtər-mə-nət\ *adj* **1** : having fixed limits : DEFINITE **2** : definitely settled — **de·ter·mi·na·cy** \-nə-sē\ *n* — **de·ter·mi·nate·ness** *n*

de·ter·mi·na·tion \di-ˌtər-mə-ˈnā-shən\ *n* **1** : the act of coming to a decision; *also* : the decision or conclusion reached **2** : the act of fixing the extent, position, or character of something **3** : accurate measurement (as of length or volume) **4** : firm or fixed purpose

de·ter·mine \di-ˈtər-mən\ *vb* **-mined; -min·ing** \-ˈtərm-(ə-)niŋ\ **1** : to fix conclusively or authoritatively **2** : to come to a decision : SETTLE, RESOLVE **3** : to fix the form or character of beforehand : ORDAIN; *also* : REGULATE **4** : to find out the limits, nature, dimensions, or scope of ⟨~ a position at sea⟩ **5** : to be the cause of or reason for : DECIDE

de·ter·mined \-ˈtər-mənd\ *adj* **1** : DECIDED, RESOLVED **2** : FIRM, RESOLUTE — **de·ter·mined·ly** \-mən-dlē, -mə-nəd-lē\ *adv* — **de·ter·mined·ness** \-mən(d)-nəs\ *n*

de·ter·min·ism \di-ˈtər-mə-ˌniz-əm\ *n* : a doctrine that acts of the will, natural events, or social changes are determined by preceding events or natural causes — **de·ter·min·ist** \-nəst\ *n or adj*

de·ter·rence \di-ˈtər-əns\ *n* : the act, process, or capacity of deterring

de·ter·rent \-ənt\ *adj* **1** : serving to deter **2** : relating to deterrence — **deterrent** *n*

de·test \di-ˈtest\ *vb* [ME *detesten*, fr. L *detestari*, lit., to curse while calling a deity to witness, fr. *de-* from + *testari* to call to witness] : LOATHE, HATE — **de·test·able** *adj* — **de·tes·ta·tion** \ˌdē-ˌtes-ˈtā-shən\ *n*

de·throne \di-ˈthrōn\ *vb* : to remove from a throne : DEPOSE — **de·throne·ment** *n*

det·o·nate \ˈdet-ᵊn-ˌāt, ˈdet-ə-ˌnāt\ *vb* **-nat·ed; -nat·ing** : to explode or cause to explode with violence — **det·o·na·tion** \ˌdet-ᵊn-ˈā-shən, ˌdet-ə-ˈnā-\ *n*

det·o·na·tor \ˈdet-ᵊn-ˌāt-ər, -ə-ˌnāt-\ *n* : a device for detonating a high explosive

[1]**de·tour** \ˈdē-ˌtu̇r\ *n* : a roundabout way temporarily replacing part of a route

[2]**detour** *vb* : to go by detour

de·tox·i·fy \dē-ˈtäk-sə-ˌfī\ *vb* **-fied; -fy·ing** **1** : to remove a poison or toxin or the effect of such from **2** : to free (as a drug user or alcoholic) from an intoxicating or addictive substance or from dependence on it — **de·tox·i·fi·ca·tion** \dē-ˌtäk-sə-fə-ˈkā-shən\ *n*

de·tract \di-ˈtrakt\ *vb* **1** : to take away : WITHDRAW, SUBTRACT **2** : DISTRACT — **de·trac·tion** \-ˈtrak-shən\ *n* — **de·trac·tor** \-ˈtrak-tər\ *n*

de·train \dē-ˈtrān\ *vb* : to leave or cause to leave a railroad train

det·ri·ment \ˈde-trə-mənt\ *n* : injury or damage or its cause : HURT — **det·ri·men·tal** \ˌde-trə-ˈment-ᵊl\ *adj* — **det·ri·men·tal·ly** \-ē\ *adv*

de·tri·tus \di-ˈtrīt-əs\ *n, pl* **de·tri·tus** : fragments resulting from disintegration (as of rocks) : DEBRIS

deuce \ˈd(y)üs\ *n* **1** : a two in cards or dice **2** : a tie in tennis with both sides at 40 **3** : DEVIL — used chiefly as a mild oath

Deut *abbr* Deuteronomy

deu·te·ri·um \d(y)ü-ˈtir-ē-əm\ *n* : the isotope of hydrogen that is of twice the mass of ordinary hydrogen

Deu·ter·on·o·my \ˌd(y)üt-ə-ˈrän-ə-mē\ *n* — see BIBLE table

deut·sche mark \ˌdȯi-chə-ˈmärk\ *n* — see MONEY table

dev *abbr* deviation

de·val·ue \dē-ˈval-yü\ *vb* : to reduce the international exchange value of ⟨~ a currency⟩ — **de·val·u·a·tion** \dē-ˌval-yə-ˈwā-shən\ *n*

dev·as·tate \ˈdev-ə-ˌstāt\ *vb* **-tat·ed; -tat·ing** **1** : to bring to ruin : lay waste **2** : to reduce to chaos, disorder, or helplessness — **dev·as·ta·tion** \ˌdev-ə-ˈstā-shən\ *n*

de·vel·op \di-ˈvel-əp\ *vb* **1** : to unfold gradually or in detail **2** : to place (exposed photographic material) in chemicals in order to make the image visible **3** : to bring out the possibilities of **4** : to make more available or usable ⟨~ natural resources⟩ **5** : to acquire gradually ⟨~ a taste for olives⟩ **6** : to go through a natural process of growth and differentiation : EVOLVE **7** : to become apparent — **de·vel·op·er** *n* — **de·vel·op·ment** *n* — **de·vel·op·men·tal** \-ˌvel-əp-ˈment-ᵊl\ *adj*

de·vi·ant \ˈdē-vē-ənt\ *adj* : deviating esp. from some accepted norm (as of behavior) — **de·vi·ance** \-əns\ *n* — **de·vi·an·cy** \-ən-sē\ *n* — **deviant** *n*

de·vi·ate \ˈdē-vē-ˌāt\ *vb* **-at·ed; -at·ing** [LL *deviare*, fr. L *de-* from + *via* way] : to turn aside from a course, standard, principle, or topic — **de·vi·ate** \-vē-ət, -vē-ˌāt\ *n* — **de·vi·a·tion** \ˌdē-vē-ˈā-shən\ *n*

de·vice \di-ˈvīs\ *n* **1** : SCHEME, STRATAGEM **2** : a piece of equipment or a mechanism for a special purpose **3** : DESIRE, INCLINATION ⟨left to his own ~*s*⟩ **4** : an emblematic design

[1]**dev·il** \ˈdev-əl\ *n* [ME *devel*, fr. OE *dēofol*, fr. LL *diabolus*, fr. Gk *diabolos*, lit., slanderer, fr. *diaballein* to throw across, slander, fr. *dia-* across + *ballein* to throw] **1** *often cap* : the personal supreme spirit of evil **2** : DEMON **3** : a wicked person **4** : a reckless or dashing person **5** : FELLOW ⟨poor ~⟩ ⟨lucky ~⟩

[2]**devil** *vb* **-iled** *or* **-illed; -il·ing** *or* **-il·ling** \ˈdev-(ə-)liŋ\ **1** : to chop fine and season highly ⟨~*ed* eggs⟩ **2** : TEASE, ANNOY

dev·il·ish \ˈdev-(ə-)lish\ *adj* **1** : resembling or befitting a devil **2** : EXTREME, EXCESSIVE — **dev·il·ish·ly** *adv* — **dev·il·ish·ness** *n*

dev·il·ment \ˈdev-əl-mənt, -ˌment\ *n* : MISCHIEF

dev·il·ry \-rē\ *or* **dev·il·try** \-trē\ *n, pl* **-il·ries** *or* **-il·tries** **1** : action performed with the help of the devil **2** : reckless mischievousness

de·vi·ous \ˈdē-vē-əs\ *adj* **1** : deviating from a straight line : ROUNDABOUT **2** : ERRING **3** : TRICKY

[1]**de·vise** \di-ˈvīz\ *vb* **de·vised; de·vis·ing** **1** : INVENT **2** : PLOT **3** : to give (real estate) by will

[2]**devise** *n* **1** : a disposing of real property by will **2** : a will or clause of a will disposing of real property **3** : property given by will

de·vi·tal·ize \dē-ˈvīt-ᵊl-ˌīz\ *vb* : to deprive of life or vitality

de·void \di-ˈvȯid\ *adj* : entirely lacking : DESTITUTE ⟨a book ~ of interest⟩

de·voir \dəv-ˈwär\ *n* **1** : DUTY **2** : a formal act of civility or respect

de·volve \di-ˈvälv\ *vb* **de·volved; de·volv·ing** : to pass from one person to another by succession or transmission — **dev·o·lu·tion** \ˌdev-ə-ˈlü-shən, ˌdē-və-\ *n*

De·vo·ni·an \di-ˈvō-nē-ən\ *adj* : of, relating to, or being the period of the Paleozoic era between the Silurian and the Mississippian — **Devonian** *n*

de·vote \di-ˈvōt\ *vb* **de·vot·ed; de·vot·ing** **1** : to set apart for a special purpose : DEDICATE **2** : to give up to wholly or chiefly

de·vot·ed \-ˈvōt-əd\ *adj* : characterized by loyalty and devotion

dev·o·tee \ˌdev-ə-ˈtē, -ˈtā\ *n* : an ardent follower, sup-

porter, or enthusiast (as of a religion, art form, or sport)
de·vo·tion \di-ˈvō-shən\ *n* **1** : religious fervor **2** : an act of prayer or private worship — usu. used in pl. **3** : a religious exercise for private use **4** : the act of devoting or quality of being devoted ⟨~ to music⟩ **5** : strong love or affection — **de·vo·tion·al** \-sh(ə-)nəl\ *adj*
de·vour \di-ˈvau̇(ə)r\ *vb* **1** : to eat up greedily or ravenously **2** : WASTE, ANNIHILATE **3** : to take in eagerly by the senses or mind ⟨~ a book⟩ — **de·vour·er** *n*
de·vout \di-ˈvau̇t\ *adj* **1** : devoted to religion : PIOUS **2** : expressing devotion or piety **3** : EARNEST, SINCERE — **de·vout·ly** *adv* — **de·vout·ness** *n*
dew \ˈd(y)ü\ *n* : moisture that condenses on the surfaces of cool bodies at night — **dewy** *adj*
DEW *abbr* distant early warning
dew·ber·ry \ˈd(y)ü-ˌber-ē\ *n* : any of several sweet edible berries related to and resembling blackberries
dew·claw \-ˌklȯ\ *n* : a digit on the foot of a mammal that does not reach the ground; *also* : its claw or hoof
dew·drop \-ˌdräp\ *n* : a drop of dew
dew·lap \-ˌlap\ *n* : loose skin hanging under the neck of various animals (as a bovine)
dew point *n* : the temperature at which the moisture in the air begins to condense
dex·ter·i·ty \dek-ˈster-ət-ē\ *n, pl* **-ties** **1** : mental skill or quickness **2** : readiness and grace in physical activity; *esp* : skill and ease in using the hands
dex·ter·ous *or* **dex·trous** \ˈdek-strəs\ *adj* **1** : CLEVER **2** : done with skillfulness **3** : skillful and competent with the hands — **dex·ter·ous·ly** *adv*
dex·trose \ˈdek-ˌstrōs\ *n* : the naturally occurring form of glucose found in plants and blood
DFC *abbr* Distinguished Flying Cross
DFM *abbr* Distinguished Flying Medal
dg *abbr* decigram
DG *abbr* **1** [LL *Dei gratia*] by the grace of God **2** director general
DH *abbr* designated hitter
dhow \ˈdau̇\ *n* : an Arab sailing ship usu. having a long overhang forward and a high poop
DI *abbr* drill instructor
dia *abbr* diameter
di·a·be·tes \ˌdī-ə-ˈbēt-ēz, -ˈbēt-əs\ *n* : an abnormal state marked by passage of excessive amounts of urine; *esp* : one (**diabetes mel·li·tus** \-ˈmel-ət-əs\) in which insulin is deficient and the urine and blood contain excess sugar — **di·a·bet·ic** \-ˈbet-ik\ *adj or n*
di·a·bol·ic \ˌdī-ə-ˈbäl-ik\ *or* **di·a·bol·i·cal** \-i-kəl\ *adj* : DEVILISH, FIENDISH — **di·a·bol·i·cal·ly** \-k(ə-)lē\ *adv*
di·a·crit·ic \ˌdī-ə-ˈkrit-ik\ *n* : a mark accompanying a letter and indicating a sound value different from that of the same letter when unmarked — **di·a·crit·i·cal** \-ˈkrit-i-kəl\ *adj*
di·a·dem \ˈdī-ə-ˌdem\ *n* : CROWN; *esp* : a band worn on or around the head as a badge of royalty
di·aer·e·sis \dī-ˈer-ə-səs\ *n, pl* **-e·ses** \-ˌsēz\ : a mark ¨ placed over a vowel to show that it is pronounced in a separate syllable (as in *naïve*)
diag *abbr* **1** diagonal **2** diagram
di·ag·no·sis \ˌdī-ig-ˈnō-səs, -əg-\ *n, pl* **-no·ses** \-ˌsēz\ : the art or act of identifying a disease from its signs and symptoms; *also* : the decision reached by diagnosis — **di·ag·nose** \ˈdī-ig-ˌnōs, -əg-\ *vb* — **di·ag·nos·tic** \ˌdī-ig-ˈnäs-tik, -əg-\ *adj* — **di·ag·nos·ti·cian** \-ˌnäs-ˈtish-ən\ *n*
[1]**di·ag·o·nal** \dī-ˈag-(ə-)nəl\ *adj* **1** : extending from one corner to the opposite corner in a 4-sided figure **2** : running in a slanting direction ⟨~ stripes⟩ **3** : having slanting markings or parts ⟨a ~ weave⟩ — **di·ag·o·nal·ly** \-ē\ *adv*
[2]**diagonal** *n* **1** : a diagonal line **2** : a diagonal direction **3** : a diagonal row, arrangement, or pattern
[1]**di·a·gram** \ˈdī-ə-ˌgram\ *n* : a drawing, sketch, plan, or chart that makes something easier to understand — **di·a·gram·mat·ic** \ˌdī-ə-grə-ˈmat-ik\ *adj* — **di·a·gram·mat·i·cal·ly** \-i-k(ə-)lē\ *adv*
[2]**diagram** *vb* **-gramed** \-ˌgramd\ *or* **-grammed; -gram·ing** \-ˌgram-iŋ\ *or* **-gram·ming** : to represent by a diagram
[1]**di·al** \ˈdī(-ə)l\ *n* [ME, fr. L *dies* day] **1** : the face of a sundial **2** : the face of a timepiece **3** : a plate or face with a pointer and numbers that indicate something ⟨the ~ of a gauge⟩ **4** : a disk with a knob or slots that is turned for making connections (as on a telephone) or for regulating operation (as of a radio)
[2]**dial** *vb* **di·aled** *or* **di·alled; di·al·ing** *or* **di·al·ling** **1** : to manipulate a dial so as to operate or select **2** : to make a telephone call or connection
[3]**dial** *abbr* dialect
di·a·lect \ˈdī-ə-ˌlekt\ *n* : a regional variety of a language
di·a·lec·tic \ˌdī-ə-ˈlek-tik\ *n* : the process or art of reasoning correctly
di·a·logue *also* **di·a·log** \ˈdī-ə-ˌlȯg\ *n* **1** : a conversation between two or more persons **2** : the parts of a literary or dramatic composition that represent conversation
di·al·y·sis \dī-ˈal-ə-səs\ *n, pl* **-y·ses** \-ˌsēz\ : the separation of substances from solution by means of their unequal diffusion through semipermeable membranes
diam *abbr* diameter
di·am·e·ter \dī-ˈam-ət-ər\ *n* [ME *diametre,* fr. MF, fr. L *diametros,* fr. Gk, fr. *dia-* through + *metron* measure] **1** : a straight line passing through the center of a figure or body; *esp* : a straight line that passes through the center of a circle and divides it in half **2** : the length of a diameter
di·a·met·ric \ˌdī-ə-ˈme-trik\ *or* **di·a·met·ri·cal** \-tri-kəl\ *adj* **1** : of, relating to, or constituting a diameter **2** : completely opposed or opposite — **di·a·met·ri·cal·ly** \-tri-k(ə-)lē\ *adv*
di·a·mond \ˈdī-(ə-)mənd\ *n* **1** : a hard brilliant mineral that consists of crystalline carbon and is used as a gem **2** : a flat figure having four equal sides, two acute angles, and two obtuse angles **3** : any of a suit of playing cards marked with a red diamond **4** : INFIELD; *also* : the entire playing field in baseball
di·a·mond·back rattlesnake \ˈdī-(ə-)mən(d)-ˌbak-\ *n* : a large and very deadly rattlesnake
di·an·thus \dī-ˈan-thəs\ *n* : [1]PINK 1
di·a·pa·son \ˌdī-ə-ˈpāz-ᵊn, -ˈpās-\ *n* **1** : an organ stop covering the range of the organ **2** : the range of notes sounded by a voice or instrument
[1]**di·a·per** \ˈdī(-ə)-pər\ *n* **1** : a cotton or linen fabric woven in a simple geometric pattern **2** : a piece of folded cloth drawn up between the legs of a baby and fastened about the waist
[2]**diaper** *vb* **di·a·pered; di·a·per·ing** \-p(ə-)riŋ\ **1** : to ornament with diaper designs **2** : to put a diaper on
di·aph·a·nous \dī-ˈaf-ə-nəs\ *adj* : so fine of texture as to be transparent
di·a·pho·ret·ic \ˌdī-ə-fə-ˈret-ik\ *adj* : having the power to increase perspiration — **diaphoretic** *n*
di·a·phragm \ˈdī-ə-ˌfram\ *n* **1** : a sheet of muscle between the chest and abdominal cavities of a mammal **2** : a vibrating disk (as in a telephone receiver) **3** : a cup-shaped device usu. of thin rubber fitted over the uterine cervix to act as a mechanical contraceptive barrier — **di·a·phrag·mat·ic** \ˌdī-ə-frə(g)-ˈmat-ik, -ˌfrag-\ *adj*
di·a·rist \ˈdī-ə-rəst\ *n* : one who keeps a diary
di·ar·rhea *or* **di·ar·rhoea** \ˌdī-ə-ˈrē-ə\ *n* : abnormally frequent and watery bowel movements
di·a·ry \ˈdī-(ə-)rē\ *n, pl* **-ries** : a daily record esp. of personal experiences and observations; *also* : a book for keeping such private notes and records
di·as·to·le \dī-ˈas-tə-(ˌ)lē\ *n* : the stretching of the cavities of the heart during which they fill with blood — **di·a·stol·ic** \ˌdī-ə-ˈstäl-ik\ *adj*
di·as·tro·phism \dī-ˈas-trə-ˌfiz-əm\ *n* : the process of deformation of the earth's crust by which major relief

features are formed — **di·a·stroph·ic** \ˌdī-ə-ˈsträf-ik\ *adj*

dia·ther·my \ˈdī-ə-ˌthər-mē\ *n* : the generation of heat in tissue by electric currents for medical or surgical purposes

di·a·tom \ˈdī-ə-ˌtäm\ *n* : any of a class of planktonic one-celled or colonial algae with skeletons of silica

di·atom·ic \ˌdī-ə-ˈtäm-ik\ *adj* : having two atoms in the molecule

di·at·o·mite \dī-ˈat-ə-ˌmīt\ *n* : a light crumbly siliceous material derived chiefly from diatom remains and used esp. as a filter

di·a·tribe \ˈdī-ə-ˌtrīb\ *n* : a bitter or violent attack in speech or writing

dib·ble \ˈdib-əl\ *n* : a pointed hand tool for making holes (as for planting bulbs) in the ground — **dibble** *vb*

[1]**dice** \ˈdīs\ *n, pl* **dice** : DIE 1

[2]**dice** *vb* **diced; dic·ing 1** : to cut into small cubes ⟨~ carrots⟩ **2** : to play games with dice

di·chot·o·my \dī-ˈkät-ə-mē\ *n, pl* **-mies** : a division or the process of dividing into two esp. mutually exclusive or contradictory groups — **di·chot·o·mous** \-məs\ *adj*

dick·er \ˈdik-ər\ *vb* **dick·ered; dick·er·ing** \ˈdik-(ə-)riŋ\ : BARGAIN, HAGGLE

dick·ey *or* **dicky** \ˈdik-ē\ *n, pl* **dickeys** *or* **dick·ies** : a small fabric insert worn to fill in the neckline

di·cot·y·le·don \ˌdī-ˌkät-ᵊl-ˈēd-ᵊn\ *n* : any of a group of seed plants having an embryo with two cotyledons — **di·cot·y·le·don·ous** *adj*

dict *abbr* dictionary

[1]**dic·tate** \ˈdik-ˌtāt\ *vb* **dic·tat·ed; dic·tat·ing 1** : to speak or read for a person to transcribe or for a machine to record **2** : COMMAND, ORDER — **dic·ta·tion** \dik-ˈtā-shən\ *n*

[2]**dic·tate** \ˈdik-ˌtāt\ *n* : an authoritative rule, prescription, or injunction : COMMAND ⟨the ~*s* of conscience⟩

dic·ta·tor \ˈdik-ˌtāt-ər\ *n* **1** : a person ruling absolutely and often brutally and oppressively **2** : one that dictates

dic·ta·to·ri·al \ˌdik-tə-ˈtōr-ē-əl\ *adj* : of, relating to, or characteristic of a dictator or a dictatorship

dic·ta·tor·ship \dik-ˈtāt-ər-ˌship, ˈdik-ˌtāt-\ *n* **1** : the office or term of office of a dictator **2** : autocratic rule, control, or leadership **3** : a government or country in which absolute power is held by a dictator or a small clique

dic·tion \ˈdik-shən\ *n* **1** : choice of words esp. with regard to correctness, clearness, or effectiveness : WORDING **2** : ENUNCIATION

dic·tio·nary \ˈdik-shə-ˌner-ē\ *n, pl* **-nar·ies** : a reference book containing words usu. alphabetically arranged along with information about their forms, pronunciations, functions, etymologies, meanings, and syntactical and idiomatic uses

dic·tum \ˈdik-təm\ *n, pl* **dic·ta** \-tə\ *also* **dictums** : a formal authoritative statement : PRONOUNCEMENT

did *past of* DO

di·dac·tic \dī-ˈdak-tik\ *adj* **1** : intended primarily to instruct; *esp* : intended to teach a moral lesson **2** : making moral observations

di·do \ˈdīd-ō\ *n, pl* **didoes** *or* **didos** : a foolish or mischievous act

[1]**die** \ˈdī\ *vb* **died; dy·ing** \ˈdī-iŋ\ **1** : to stop living : EXPIRE **2** : to pass out of existence ⟨a *dying* race⟩ **3** : to disappear or subside gradually ⟨the wind *died* down⟩ **4** : to long keenly ⟨*dying* to go⟩ **5** : STOP ⟨the motor *died*⟩

[2]**die** \ˈdī\ *n, pl* **dice** \ˈdīs\ *or* **dies** \ˈdīz\ **1** *pl dice* : a small cube marked on each face with one to six spots and used usu. in pairs in various games and gambling **2** *pl dies* : a device used in shaping or stamping an object or material

die·hard \ˈdī-ˌhärd\ *n* : one who resists against hopeless odds

diel·drin \ˈdē(ə)l-drən\ *n* : a persistent chlorinated hydrocarbon insecticide

die·sel \ˈdē-zəl, -səl\ *n* **1** : DIESEL ENGINE **2** : a vehicle driven by a diesel engine

diesel engine *n* : an internal-combustion engine in whose cylinders air is compressed to a temperature sufficiently high to ignite the fuel

die·sel·ing \ˈdēz-(ə-)liŋ\ *n* : an instance of an internal-combustion engine continuing to operate after the ignition has been turned off

[1]**di·et** \ˈdī-ət\ *n* [ME *diete,* fr. OF, fr. L *diaeta* prescribed diet, fr. Gk *diaita,* lit., manner of living] **1** : the food and drink regularly consumed (as by a person or group) : FARE **2** : an allowance of food prescribed with reference to a particular state (as ill health) — **di·etary** \ˈdī-ə-ˌter-ē\ *adj or n*

[2]**diet** *vb* : to eat or cause to eat less or according to a prescribed rule — **di·et·er** *n*

di·etet·ics \ˌdī-ə-ˈtet-iks\ *n sing or pl* : the science or art of applying the principles of nutrition to diet — **di·etet·ic** *adj*

di·eti·tian *or* **di·eti·cian** \ˌdī-ə-ˈtish-ən\ *n* : a specialist in dietetics

dif *or* **diff** *abbr* difference

dif·fer \ˈdif-ər\ *vb* **dif·fered; dif·fer·ing** \-(ə-)riŋ\ **1** : to be unlike **2** : DISAGREE

dif·fer·ence \ˈdif-(ə-)rəns, ˈdif-ərns\ *n* **1** : UNLIKENESS ⟨~ in their looks⟩ **2** : distinction or discrimination in preference **3** : DISAGREEMENT, DISSENSION; *also* : an instance or cause of disagreement ⟨unable to settle their ~*s*⟩ **4** : the amount by which one number or quantity differs from another

dif·fer·ent \ˈdif-(ə-)rənt, ˈdif-ərnt\ *adj* **1** : UNLIKE, DISSIMILAR **2** : not the same ⟨~ age groups⟩ ⟨seen at ~ times⟩ ⟨try a ~ book⟩ **3** : UNUSUAL, SPECIAL — **dif·fer·ent·ly** *adv*

[1]**dif·fer·en·tial** \ˌdif-ə-ˈren-chəl\ *adj* : showing, creating, or relating to a difference

[2]**differential** *n* **1** : the amount or degree by which things differ **2** : DIFFERENTIAL GEAR

differential gear *n* : an arrangement of gears in an automobile that allows one wheel to go faster than another (as in rounding curves)

dif·fer·en·ti·ate \ˌdif-ə-ˈren-chē-ˌāt\ *vb* **-at·ed; -at·ing 1** : to make or become different **2** : to recognize or state the difference ⟨~ between two plants⟩ — **dif·fer·en·ti·a·tion** \-ˌren-chē-ˈā-shən\ *n*

dif·fi·cult \ˈdif-i-(ˌ)kəlt\ *adj* **1** : hard to do or make **2** : hard to understand or deal with ⟨~ reading⟩ ⟨a ~ child⟩

dif·fi·cul·ty \-(ˌ)kəl-tē\ *n, pl* **-ties 1** : difficult nature ⟨the ~ of a task⟩ **2** : DISAGREEMENT ⟨settled their *difficulties*⟩ **3** : OBSTACLE ⟨overcome *difficulties*⟩ **4** : TROUBLE ⟨in financial *difficulties*⟩ **syn** hardship, rigor, vicissitude

dif·fi·dent \ˈdif-əd-ənt\ *adj* **1** : lacking confidence : TIMID **2** : RESERVED, UNASSERTIVE — **dif·fi·dence** \-əns\ *n* — **dif·fi·dent·ly** *adv*

dif·frac·tion \dif-ˈrak-shən\ *n* : the bending or spreading of a light beam esp. when passing through narrow slits or when reflecting from a ruled surface

[1]**dif·fuse** \dif-ˈyüs\ *adj* **1** : VERBOSE, WORDY ⟨~ writing⟩ **2** : not concentrated : SCATTERED ⟨~ light⟩

[2]**dif·fuse** \dif-ˈyüz\ *vb* **dif·fused; dif·fus·ing** : to pour out or spread widely — **dif·fu·sion** \-ˈyü-zhən\ *n*

[1]**dig** \ˈdig\ *vb* **dug** \ˈdəg\; **dig·ging 1** : to turn up the soil (as with a spade) **2** : to hollow out or form by removing earth ⟨~ a hole⟩ **3** : to uncover or seek by turning up earth ⟨~ potatoes⟩ **4** : DISCOVER ⟨~ up information⟩ **5** : POKE, THRUST ⟨~ a person in the ribs⟩ **6** : to work hard **7** : NOTICE, APPRECIATE; *also* : LIKE, ADMIRE

[2]**dig** *n* **1** : THRUST, POKE **2** : a cutting remark : GIBE

[3]**dig** *abbr* digest

---

¹di·gest \ˈdī-ˌjest\ *n* : a summation or condensation of a body of information or of a literary work

²di·gest \dī-ˈjest, də-\ *vb* **1** : to think over and arrange in the mind **2** : to convert (food) into simpler forms that can be absorbed by the body **3** : to compress into a short summary — **di·gest·ibil·i·ty** \-ˌjes-tə-ˈbil-ət-ē\ *n* — **di·gest·ible** *adj* — **di·ges·tion** \-ˈjes-chən\ *n* — **di·ges·tive** \-ˈjes-tiv\ *adj*

dig in *vb* **1** : to dig defensive trenches **2** : to go resolutely to work **3** : to begin eating

dig·it \ˈdij-ət\ *n* [ME, fr. L *digitus* finger, toe] **1** : any of the Arabic numerals 1 to 9 and usu. the symbol 0 **2** : FINGER, TOE

dig·i·tal \ˈdij-ət-ᵊl\ *adj* **1** : of, relating to, or done with a finger or toe **2** : of, relating to, or using calculation directly with digits rather than through measurable physical quantities ⟨a ~ computer⟩ **3** : providing a readout in numerical digits ⟨a ~ watch⟩ — **dig·i·tal·ly** \-ē\ *adv*

dig·i·tal·is \ˌdij-ə-ˈtal-əs\ *n* : a drug from the common foxglove that is a powerful heart stimulant; *also* : FOXGLOVE

dig·ni·fied \ˈdig-nə-ˌfīd\ *adj* : showing or expressing dignity

dig·ni·fy \-ˌfī\ *vb* **-fied; -fy·ing** : to give dignity or distinction to : HONOR

dig·ni·tary \ˈdig-nə-ˌter-ē\ *n, pl* **-tar·ies** : a person of high position or honor

dig·ni·ty \ˈdig-nət-ē\ *n, pl* **-ties** **1** : the quality or state of being worthy, honored, or esteemed : true worth : EXCELLENCE **2** : high rank, office, or position **3** : formal reserve of manner or language

di·graph \ˈdī-ˌgraf\ *n* : a group of two successive letters whose phonetic value is a single sound (as *ea* in *bread*)

di·gress \dī-ˈgres, də-\ *vb* : to turn aside esp. from the main subject in writing or speaking — **di·gres·sion** \-ˈgresh-ən\ *n* — **di·gres·sive** \-ˈgres-iv\ *adj*

dike \ˈdīk\ *n* : a bank of earth to control water : LEVEE

dil *abbr* dilute

di·lap·i·dat·ed \də-ˈlap-ə-ˌdāt-əd\ *adj* : fallen into partial ruin or decay — **di·lap·i·da·tion** \-ˌlap-ə-ˈdā-shən\ *n*

di·late \dī-ˈlāt, ˈdī-ˌlāt\ *vb* **di·lat·ed; di·lat·ing** : SWELL, DISTEND, EXPAND — **dil·a·ta·tion** \ˌdil-ə-ˈtā-shən\ *n* — **di·la·tion** \dī-ˈlā-shən\ *n*

dil·a·to·ry \ˈdil-ə-ˌtōr-ē\ *adj* **1** : DELAYING **2** : TARDY, SLOW

di·lem·ma \də-ˈlem-ə\ *n* : a choice between equally unsatisfactory alternatives

dil·et·tante \ˌdil-ə-ˈtänt(-ē), -ˈtant(-ē)\ *n, pl* **-tantes** *or* **-tan·ti** \-ˈtänt-ē, -ˈtant-ē\ [It, fr. *dilettare* to delight, fr. L *dilectare*] : a person having a superficial interest in an art or a branch of knowledge

dil·i·gent \ˈdil-ə-jənt\ *adj* : characterized by steady, earnest, and energetic application and effort : PAINSTAKING — **dil·i·gence** \-jəns\ *n* — **dil·i·gent·ly** *adv*

dill \ˈdil\ *n* : an herb related to the carrot with aromatic leaves and seeds used in pickles

dil·ly \ˈdil-ē\ *n, pl* **dil·lies** : one that is remarkable or outstanding

dil·ly·dal·ly \ˈdil-ē-ˌdal-ē\ *vb* : to waste time by loitering or delay

¹di·lute \dī-ˈlüt, də-\ *vb* **di·lut·ed; di·lut·ing** : to lessen the consistency or strength of by mixing with something else — **di·lu·tion** \-ˈlü-shən\ *n*

²dilute *adj* : DILUTED, WEAK

¹dim \ˈdim\ *adj* **dim·mer; dim·mest** **1** : LUSTERLESS, DULL **2** : not bright or distinct : OBSCURE, FAINT **3** : not seeing or understanding clearly — **dim·ly** *adv* — **dim·ness** *n*

²dim *vb* **dimmed; dim·ming** **1** : to make or become dim or lusterless **2** : to reduce the light from (headlights) by switching to the low beam

³dim *abbr* **1** dimension **2** diminished **3** diminutive

dime \ˈdīm\ *n* [ME, tenth part, tithe, fr. MF, fr. L *decima*, fr. fem. of *decimus* tenth, fr. *decem* ten] : a U.S. coin worth 1/10 dollar

di·men·sion \də-ˈmen-chən, dī-\ *n* **1** : measurement of extension (as in length, height, or breadth) **2** : EXTENT, SCOPE, PROPORTIONS — usu. used in pl. — **di·men·sion·al** \-ˈmench-(ə-)nəl\ *adj* — **di·men·sion·al·i·ty** \-ˌmen-chə-ˈnal-ət-ē\ *n*

di·min·ish \də-ˈmin-ish\ *vb* **1** : to make less or cause to appear less **2** : BELITTLE **3** : DWINDLE **4** : TAPER — **dim·i·nu·tion** \ˌdim-ə-ˈn(y)ü-shən\ *n*

di·min·u·en·do \də-ˌmin-(y)ə-ˈwen-dō\ *adv or adj* : DECRESCENDO

¹di·min·u·tive \də-ˈmin-yət-iv\ *n* **1** : a diminutive word or affix **2** : a diminutive individual

²diminutive *adj* **1** : indicating small size and sometimes the state or quality of being lovable, pitiable, or contemptible ⟨the ~ suffixes *-ette* and *-ling*⟩ **2** : extremely small : TINY

dim·i·ty \ˈdim-ət-ē\ *n, pl* **-ties** : a thin usu. corded cotton fabric

dim·mer \ˈdim-ər\ *n* : a device for controlling the amount of light from an electric lighting unit

di·mor·phic \(ˈ)dī-ˈmȯr-fik\ *adj* : occurring in two distinct forms — **di·mor·phism** \-ˌfiz-əm\ *n*

¹dim·ple \ˈdim-pəl\ *n* : a small depression esp. in the cheek or chin

²dimple *vb* **dim·pled; dim·pling** : to form dimples (as in smiling)

din \ˈdin\ *n* : a loud confused mixture of noises

di·nar \di-ˈnär\ *n* **1** — see MONEY table **2** — see *rial* at MONEY table

dine \ˈdīn\ *vb* **dined; din·ing** [ME *dinen*, fr. OF *diner*, fr. (assumed) VL *disjejunare* to break one's fast, deriv. of L *jejunus* fasting] **1** : to eat dinner **2** : to give a dinner to : FEED

din·er \ˈdī-nər\ *n* **1** : one that dines **2** : a railroad dining car **3** : a restaurant usu. resembling a dining car

di·nette \dī-ˈnet\ *n* : an alcove or small room used for dining

din·ghy \ˈdiŋ-ē\ *n, pl* **dinghies** **1** : a small rowboat **2** : LIFE RAFT

din·gle \ˈdiŋ-gəl\ *n* : a small wooded valley

din·go \ˈdiŋ-gō\ *n, pl* **dingoes** : a reddish brown wild dog of Australia

dingo

din·gus \ˈdiŋ-(g)əs\ *n* : DOODAD

din·gy \ˈdin-jē\ *adj* **din·gi·er; -est** **1** : DARK, DULL **2** : not fresh or clean : GRIMY — **din·gi·ness** *n*

din·ky \ˈdiŋ-kē\ *adj* **din·ki·er; -est** : SMALL, INSIGNIFICANT

din·ner \ˈdin-ər\ *n* : the main meal of the day; *also* : a formal banquet

din·ner·ware \ˈdin-ər-ˌwaər\ *n* : china, glassware, or tableware used in table service

di·no·fla·gel·late \ˌdī-nō-ˈflaj-ə-lət, -ˌlāt\ *n* : any of an order of planktonic plantlike flagellates of which some cause red tide

di·no·saur \ˈdī-nə-ˌsȯr\ *n* [fr. Gk *deinos* terrible + *sauros* lizard] : any of a group of extinct long-tailed reptiles often of huge size

dint \ˈdint\ *n* **1** : FORCE ⟨reached the top by ~ of sheer grit⟩ **2** : DENT

di·o·cese \ˈdī-ə-səs, -ˌsēz, -ˌsēs\ *n, pl* **-ces·es** \-sə-səz, -ˌsē-zəz, -ˌsē-səz, -ə-ˌsēz\ : the territorial jurisdiction of a bishop — **di·oc·e·san** \dī-ˈäs-ə-sən, ˌdī-ə-ˈsēz-ᵊn\ *adj or n*

di·ode \ˈdī-ˌōd\ *n* **1** : an electron tube having a cathode and anode **2** : a semiconductor device that functions as a rectifier

di·ox·in \dī-ˈäk-sən\ *n* : a hydrocarbon that occurs esp. as a persistent toxic impurity in herbicides (as Agent Orange)

[1]dip \ˈdip\ *vb* **dipped; dip·ping 1** : to plunge temporarily or partially under the surface (as of a liquid) **2** : to thrust in a way to suggest immersion **3** : to scoop up or out : LADLE **4** : to lower and then raise quickly ⟨~ a flag in salute⟩ **5** : to drop or slope down esp. suddenly ⟨the moon *dipped* below the crest⟩ **6** : to decrease moderately and usu. temporarily ⟨prices *dipped*⟩ **7** : to reach inside or as if inside or below a surface ⟨*dipped* into their savings⟩ **8** : to delve casually into something; *esp* : to read superficially ⟨~ into a book⟩

[2]dip *n* **1** : an act of dipping; *esp* : a short swim **2** : inclination downward : DROP **3** : something obtained by or used in dipping **4** : a sauce or soft mixture into which food may be dipped **5** : a liquid into which something may be dipped (as for cleansing or coloring)

diph·the·ria \dif-ˈthir-ē-ə, dip-\ *n* : an acute contagious bacterial disease marked by fever and by coating of the air passages with a membrane that interferes with breathing

diph·thong \ˈdif-ˌthȯŋ, ˈdip-\ *n* : two vowel sounds joined in one syllable to form one speech sound (as *ou* in *out*)

dip·loid \ˈdip-ˌlȯid\ *adj* : having the basic chromosome number doubled — **diploid** *n*

di·plo·ma \də-ˈplō-mə\ *n, pl* **diplomas** : an official record of graduation from or of a degree conferred by a school

di·plo·ma·cy \də-ˈplō-mə-sē\ *n* **1** : the art and practice of conducting negotiations between nations **2** : TACT

dip·lo·mat \ˈdip-lə-ˌmat\ *n* : one employed or skilled in diplomacy — **dip·lo·mat·ic** \ˌdip-lə-ˈmat-ik\ *adj*

di·plo·ma·tist \də-ˈplō-mət-əst\ *n* : DIPLOMAT

dip·per \ˈdip-ər\ *n* **1** : any of a genus of birds that are related to the thrushes and are skilled in diving **2** : something (as a ladle or scoop) that dips or is used for dipping **3** *cap* : the seven bright stars of Ursa Major arranged in a form resembling a dipper **4** *cap* : the seven bright stars of Ursa Minor arranged in a form resembling a dipper with the North Star forming the outer end of the handle

dip·so·ma·nia \ˌdip-sə-ˈmā-nē-ə\ *n* : an uncontrollable craving for alcoholic liquors — **dip·so·ma·ni·ac** \-nē-ˌak\ *n*

dip·stick \ˈdip-ˌstik\ *n* : a graduated rod for indicating depth

dip·ter·ous \ˈdip-tə-rəs\ *adj* : of, relating to, or being a two-winged fly — **dip·ter·an** \-rən\ *adj or n*

dir *abbr* director

dire \ˈdī(ə)r\ *adj* **dir·er; dir·est 1** : very horrible : DREADFUL **2** : warning of disaster **3** : EXTREME

[1]di·rect \də-ˈrekt, dī-\ *vb* **1** : ADDRESS ⟨~ a letter⟩; *also* : to impart orally : AIM ⟨~ a remark to the gallery⟩ **2** : to regulate the activities or course of : guide the supervision, organizing, or performance of **3** : to cause to turn, move, or point or to follow a certain course **4** : to point, extend, or project in a specified line or course **5** : to request or instruct with authority **6** : to show or point out the way

[2]direct *adj* **1** : stemming immediately from a source, cause, or reason ⟨~ result⟩ **2** : being or passing in a straight line of descent : LINEAL ⟨~ ancestor⟩ **3** : leading from one point to another in time or space without turn or stop : STRAIGHT **4** : NATURAL, STRAIGHTFORWARD ⟨a ~ manner⟩ **5** : operating without an intervening agency or step ⟨~ action⟩ **6** : effected by the action of the people or the electorate and not by representatives ⟨~ legislation⟩ **7** : consisting of or reproducing the exact words of a speaker ⟨~ discourse⟩ — **direct** *adv* — **di·rect·ly** \də-ˈrek-(t)lē, dī-\ *adv* — **di·rect·ness** \-ˈrek(t)-nəs\ *n*

direct current *n* : an electric current flowing in one direction only

di·rec·tion \də-ˈrek-shən, dī-\ *n* **1** : MANAGEMENT, GUIDANCE **2** : COMMAND, ORDER, INSTRUCTION **3** : the course or line along which something moves, lies, or points **4** : TENDENCY, TREND — **di·rec·tion·al** \-sh(ə-)nəl\ *adj*

di·rec·tive \də-ˈrek-tiv, dī-\ *n* : a general instruction as to procedure

di·rec·tor \də-ˈrek-tər, dī-\ *n* **1** : one that directs : MANAGER, SUPERVISOR, CONDUCTOR **2** : one of a group of persons who direct the affairs of an organized body — **di·rec·tor·ship** *n*

di·rec·tor·ate \də-ˈrek-t(ə-)rət, dī-\ *n* **1** : the office or position of director **2** : a board of directors; *also* : membership on such a board **3** : an executive staff

di·rec·to·ry \-t(ə-)rē\ *n, pl* **-ries** : an alphabetical or classified list of names and addresses

dire·ful \ˈdī(ə)r-fəl\ *adj* : producing dire effects

dirge \ˈdərj\ *n* : a song of lamentation; *also* : a slow mournful piece of music

dir·ham \ˈdir-həm\ *n* **1** — see MONEY table **2** — see *dinar, riyal* at MONEY table

di·ri·gi·ble \ˈdir-ə-jə-bəl, də-ˈrij-ə-\ *n* : AIRSHIP

dirk \ˈdərk\ *n* : DAGGER 1

dirndl \ˈdərn-dᵊl\ *n* [short for G *dirndlkleid,* fr. G dial. *dirndl* girl + G *kleid* dress] : a full skirt with a tight waistband

dirt \ˈdərt\ *n* **1** : a filthy or soiling substance (as mud, dust, or grime) **2** : loose or packed earth : SOIL **3** : moral uncleanness **4** : scandalous gossip **5** : embarrassing or incriminating information

[1]dirty \ˈdərt-ē\ *adj* **dirt·i·er; -est 1** : SOILED, FILTHY **2** : INDECENT, SMUTTY ⟨~ talk⟩ **3** : BASE, UNFAIR ⟨a ~ trick⟩ **4** : STORMY, FOGGY ⟨~ weather⟩ **5** : not clear in color : DULL ⟨a ~ red⟩ — **dirt·i·ness** \ˈdərt-ē-nəs\ *n* — **dirty** *adv*

[2]dirty *vb* **dirt·ied; dirty·ing** : to make or become dirty

dis·able \dis-ˈā-bəl\ *vb* **dis·abled; dis·abling** \-b(ə-)liŋ\ **1** : to disqualify legally **2** : to make unable to perform by or as if by illness, injury, or malfunction — **dis·abil·i·ty** \ˌdis-ə-ˈbil-ət-ē\ *n*

dis·abuse \ˌdis-ə-ˈbyüz\ *vb* : to free from error or fallacy

di·sac·cha·ride \dī-ˈsak-ə-ˌrīd\ *n* : a sugar that yields two molecules of simple sugar upon hydrolysis

dis·ad·van·tage \ˌdis-əd-ˈvant-ij\ *n* **1** : loss or damage esp. to reputation or finances **2** : an unfavorable, inferior, or prejudicial condition; *also* : HANDICAP — **dis·ad·van·ta·geous** \dis-ˌad-ˌvan-ˈtā-jəs, -vən-\ *adj*

dis·af·fect \ˌdis-ə-ˈfect\ *vb* : to alienate the affection or loyalty of : cause discontent in ⟨the troops were ~*ed*⟩ — **dis·af·fec·tion** \-ˈfek-shən\ *n*

dis·agree \ˌdis-ə-ˈgrē\ *vb* **1** : to fail to agree **2** : to differ in opinion **3** : to have an unpleasant effect ⟨fried foods ~ with her⟩ — **dis·agree·ment** *n*

dis·agree·able \-ə-bəl\ *adj* **1** : causing discomfort : UNPLEASANT, OFFENSIVE **2** : ILL-TEMPERED, PEEVISH — **dis·agree·able·ness** *n* — **dis·agree·ably** \-blē\ *adv*

dis·al·low \ˌdis-ə-ˈlau̇\ *vb* : to refuse to admit or recognize : REJECT ⟨~ a claim⟩ — **dis·al·low·ance** *n*

dis·ap·pear \ˌdis-ə-ˈpiər\ *vb* **1** : to pass out of sight **2** : to cease to be : become lost — **dis·ap·pear·ance** *n*

dis·ap·point \ˌdis-ə-ˈpȯint\ *vb* : to fail to fulfill the expectation or hope of — **dis·ap·point·ment** *n*

dis·ap·pro·ba·tion \dis-ˌap-rə-ˈbā-shən\ *n* : DISAPPROVAL

dis·ap·prov·al \ˌdis-ə-ˈprü-vəl\ *n* : adverse judgment : CENSURE

dis·ap·prove \-ˈprüv\ *vb* **1** : CONDEMN **2** : to feel or express disapproval ⟨~*s* of smoking⟩ **3** : REJECT

dis·arm \dis-ˈärm\ *vb* **1** : to take arms or weapons from **2** : to reduce the size and strength of the armed forces of a country **3** : to make harmless, peaceable, or friendly : win over ⟨a ~*ing* smile⟩ — **dis·ar·ma·ment** \-ˈär-mə-mənt\ *n*

dis·ar·range \ˌdis-ə-ˈrānj\ *vb* : to disturb the arrangement or order of — **dis·ar·range·ment** *n*

dis·ar·ray \-ˈrā\ *n* **1** : DISORDER, CONFUSION **2** : disorderly or careless dress

dis·as·sem·ble \ˌdis-ə-ˈsem-bəl\ *vb* : to take apart

dis·as·so·ci·ate \-ˈsō-s(h)ē-ˌāt\ *vb* : to detach from association

di·sas·ter \diz-ˈas-tər, dis-\ *n* [MF *desastre,* fr. It *disastro,* fr. *astro* star, fr. L *astrum*] : a sudden or great misfortune — **di·sas·trous** \-ˈas-trəs\ *adj* — **di·sas·trous·ly** *adv*

dis·avow \ˌdis-ə-ˈvaů\ *vb* : to deny responsibility for : REPUDIATE — **dis·avow·al** \-ˈvaů(-ə)l\ *n*

dis·band \dis-ˈband\ *vb* : to break up the organization of : DISPERSE

dis·bar \dis-ˈbär\ *vb* : to expel from the legal profession — **dis·bar·ment** *n*

dis·be·lieve \ˌdis-bə-ˈlēv\ *vb* **1** : to hold not to be true or real ⟨*disbelieved* his testimony⟩ **2** : to withhold or reject belief — **dis·be·lief** \-ˈlēf\ *n* — **dis·be·liev·er** *n*

dis·bur·den \dis-ˈbərd-ᵊn\ *vb* : to rid of a burden

dis·burse \dis-ˈbərs\ *vb* **dis·bursed; dis·burs·ing** : to pay out : EXPEND — **dis·burse·ment** *n*

¹disc *var of* DISK

²disc *abbr* discount

dis·card \dis-ˈkärd, ˈdis-ˌkärd\ *vb* **1** : to let go a playing card from one's hand; *also* : to play (a card) from a suit other than a trump but different from the one led **2** : to get rid of as unwanted — **dis·card** \ˈdis-ˌkärd\ *n*

disc brake *n* : a brake that operates by the friction of a pair of plates pressing against the sides of a rotating disc

dis·cern \dis-ˈərn, diz-\ *vb* **1** : to detect with the eyes : DISTINGUISH **2** : DISCRIMINATE **3** : to come to know or recognize mentally — **dis·cern·ible** *adj* — **dis·cern·ment** *n*

dis·cern·ing \-iŋ\ *adj* : revealing insight and understanding

¹dis·charge \dis-ˈchärj, ˈdis-ˌchärj\ *vb* **1** : to relieve of a charge, load, or burden : UNLOAD; *esp* : to remove the electrical energy from ⟨~ a storage battery⟩ **2** : SHOOT ⟨~ a gun⟩ ⟨~ an arrow⟩ **3** : to set free ⟨~ a prisoner⟩ **4** : to dismiss from service or employment ⟨~ a soldier⟩ **5** : to let go or let off ⟨~ passengers⟩ **6** : to give forth fluid ⟨the river ~*s* into the ocean⟩ **7** : to get rid of by paying or doing ⟨~ a debt⟩

²dis·charge \ˈdis-ˌchärj, dis-ˈchärj\ *n* **1** : the act of discharging, unloading, or releasing **2** : something that discharges; *esp* : a certification of release or payment **3** : a firing off (as of a gun) **4** : a flowing out (as of blood from a wound); *also* : something that is emitted ⟨a purulent ~⟩ **5** : release or dismissal esp. from an office or employment; *also* : complete separation from military service **6** : a flow of electricity (as through a gas)

dis·ci·ple \dis-ˈī-pəl\ *n* **1** : one who accepts and helps to spread the teachings of another; *also* : a convinced adherent **2** *cap* : a member of the Disciples of Christ

dis·ci·pli·nar·i·an \ˌdis-ə-plə-ˈner-ē-ən\ *n* : one who enforces order

dis·ci·plin·ary \ˈdis-ə-plə-ˌner-ē\ *adj* : of or relating to discipline; *also* : CORRECTIVE ⟨take ~ action⟩

¹dis·ci·pline \ˈdis-ə-plən\ *n* **1** : PUNISHMENT **2** : a field of study : SUBJECT **3** : training that corrects, molds, or perfects **4** : control gained by obedience or training : orderly conduct **5** : a system of rules governing conduct

²discipline *vb* **-plined; -plin·ing** **1** : PUNISH **2** : to train or develop by instruction and exercise esp. in self-control **3** : to bring under control ⟨~ troops⟩; *also* : to impose order upon

disc jockey *n* : a person who conducts a radio show of popular recorded music

dis·claim \dis-ˈklām\ *vb* : to deny having a connection with or responsibility for : DISAVOW — **dis·claim·er** *n*

dis·close \dis-ˈklōz\ *vb* : to expose to view — **dis·clo·sure** \-ˈklō-zhər\ *n*

dis·co \ˈdis-kō\ *n, pl* **discos** **1** : DISCOTHEQUE **2** : popular dance music characterized by hypnotic rhythm, repetitive lyrics, and electronically produced sounds

dis·col·or \dis-ˈkəl-ər\ *vb* : to alter or change in hue or color : STAIN — **dis·col·or·ation** \dis-ˌkəl-ə-ˈrā-shən\ *n*

dis·com·bob·u·late \ˌdis-kəm-ˈbäb-(y)ə-ˌlāt\ *vb* **-lat·ed; -lat·ing** : UPSET, CONFUSE

dis·com·fit \dis-ˈkəm-fət, *esp South* ˌdis-kəm-ˈfit\ *vb* : UPSET, FRUSTRATE — **dis·com·fi·ture** \dis-ˈkəm-fə-ˌchůr\ *n*

¹dis·com·fort \dis-ˈkəm-fərt\ *vb* : to make uncomfortable or uneasy

²discomfort *n* : lack of comfort : uneasiness of mind or body : DISTRESS

dis·com·mode \ˌdis-kə-ˈmōd\ *vb* **-mod·ed; -mod·ing** : INCONVENIENCE, TROUBLE

dis·com·pose \-kəm-ˈpōz\ *vb* **1** : AGITATE **2** : DISARRANGE — **dis·com·po·sure** \-ˈpō-zhər\ *n*

dis·con·cert \ˌdis-kən-ˈsərt\ *vb* : CONFUSE, UPSET

dis·con·nect \ˌdis-kə-ˈnekt\ *vb* : to undo the connection of — **dis·con·nec·tion** \-ˈnek-shən\ *n*

dis·con·nect·ed \-əd\ *adj* : not connected : RAMBLING, INCOHERENT — **dis·con·nect·ed·ly** *adv*

dis·con·so·late \dis-ˈkän-sə-lət\ *adj* **1** : CHEERLESS **2** : hopelessly sad — **dis·con·so·late·ly** *adv*

dis·con·tent \ˌdis-kən-ˈtent\ *n* : uneasiness of mind : DISSATISFACTION — **dis·con·tent·ed** *adj*

dis·con·tin·ue \ˌdis-kən-ˈtin-yü\ *vb* **1** : to break the continuity of : cease to operate, use, or take **2** : END — **dis·con·tin·u·ance** \-yə-wəns\ *n* — **dis·con·ti·nu·i·ty** \dis-ˌkänt-ᵊn-ˈ(y)ü-ət-ē\ *n* — **dis·con·tin·u·ous** \ˌdis-kən-ˈtin-yə-wəs\ *adj*

dis·cord \ˈdis-ˌkȯrd\ *n* **1** : lack of agreement or harmony : DISSENSION, CONFLICT **2** : a harsh combination of musical sounds **3** : a harsh or unpleasant sound — **dis·cor·dant** \dis-ˈkȯrd-ᵊnt\ *adj* — **dis·cor·dant·ly** *adv*

dis·co·theque \ˈdis-kə-ˌtek\ *n* : a nightclub for dancing to live or recorded music

¹dis·count \ˈdis-ˌkaůnt\ *n* **1** : a reduction made from a regular or list price **2** : a deduction of interest in advance when lending money

²dis·count \ˈdis-ˌkaůnt, dis-ˈkaůnt\ *vb* **1** : to deduct from the amount of a bill, debt, or charge usu. for cash or prompt payment; *also* : to sell or offer for sale at a discount **2** : to lend money after deducting the discount ⟨~ a note⟩ **3** : DISREGARD; *also* : MINIMIZE **4** : to make allowance for bias or exaggeration; *also* : DISBELIEVE **5** : to take into account (as a future event) in present calculations — **dis·count·able** *adj* — **dis·count·er** *n*

dis·coun·te·nance \dis-ˈkaůnt-(ᵊ-)nəns\ *vb* **1** : EMBARRASS, DISCONCERT **2** : to look with disfavor on

dis·cour·age \dis-ˈkər-ij\ *vb* **-aged; -ag·ing** **1** : to deprive of courage or confidence : DISHEARTEN **2** : to hinder by inspiring fear of consequences : DETER **3** : to attempt to dissuade — **dis·cour·age·ment** *n* — **dis·cour·ag·ing·ly** \-ij-iŋ-lē\ *adv*

¹dis·course \ˈdis-ˌkōrs\ *n* [ME *discours,* fr. ML & LL *discursus;* ML, argument, fr. LL, conversation, fr. L, act of running about, fr. *discurrere* to run about, fr. *currere* to run] **1** : CONVERSATION **2** : formal and usu. extended expression of thought on a subject

²dis·course \dis-ˈkōrs\ *vb* **dis·coursed; dis·cours·ing** **1** : to express oneself in esp. oral discourse **2** : TALK, CONVERSE

dis·cour·te·ous \dis-ˈkərt-ē-əs\ *adj* : lacking courtesy : UNCIVIL, RUDE — **dis·cour·te·ous·ly** *adv*

dis·cour·te·sy \-ˈkərt-ə-sē\ *n* : RUDENESS; *also* : a rude act
dis·cov·er \dis-ˈkəv-ər\ *vb* **1** : to make known or visible **2** : to obtain sight or knowledge of for the first time : FIND — **dis·cov·er·er** *n*
dis·cov·ery \dis-ˈkəv-(e-)rē\ *n, pl* **-er·ies** **1** : the act or process of discovering **2** : something discovered **3** : the disclosure usu. before a civil trial of pertinent facts or documents
[1]**dis·cred·it** \dis-ˈkred-ət\ *vb* **1** : DISBELIEVE **2** : to cause disbelief in the accuracy or authority of **3** : DISGRACE — **dis·cred·it·able** *adj*
[2]**discredit** *n* **1** : loss of reputation **2** : lack or loss of belief or confidence
dis·creet \dis-ˈkrēt\ *adj* : showing good judgment; *esp* : capable of observing prudent silence — **dis·creet·ly** *adv*
dis·crep·an·cy \dis-ˈkrep-ən-sē\ *n, pl* **-cies** **1** : DIFFERENCE, DISAGREEMENT **2** : an instance of being discrepant
dis·crep·ant \-ənt\ *adj* [L *discrepans*, prp. of *discrepare* to sound discordantly, fr. *crepare* to rattle, creak] : being at variance : DISAGREEING
dis·crete \dis-ˈkrēt, ˈdis-ˌkrēt\ *adj* **1** : individually distinct **2** : NONCONTINUOUS
dis·cre·tion \dis-ˈkresh-ən\ *n* **1** : the quality of being discreet : PRUDENCE **2** : individual choice or judgment **3** : power of free decision or latitude of choice — **dis·cre·tion·ary** *adj*
dis·crim·i·nate \dis-ˈkrim-ə-ˌnāt\ *vb* **-nat·ed; -nat·ing** **1** : DISTINGUISH, DIFFERENTIATE **2** : to make a distinction in favor of or against one person or thing as compared with others — **dis·crim·i·na·tion** \-ˌkrim-ə-ˈnā-shən\ *n*
dis·crim·i·nat·ing \-ˌnāt-iŋ\ *adj* : marked by discrimination; *esp* : DISCERNING, JUDICIOUS
dis·crim·i·na·to·ry \dis-ˈkrim-ə-nə-ˌtōr-ē\ *adj* : marked by esp. unjust discrimination ⟨~ treatment⟩
dis·cur·sive \dis-ˈkər-siv\ *adj* : passing from one topic to another : RAMBLING — **dis·cur·sive·ly** *adv* — **dis·cur·sive·ness** *n*
dis·cus \ˈdis-kəs\ *n, pl* **dis·cus·es** : a disk that is hurled for distance in a track-and-field contest
dis·cuss \dis-ˈkəs\ *vb* [ME *discussen*, fr. L *discutere*, fr. *dis-* apart + *quatere* to shake] **1** : to argue or consider carefully by presenting the various sides **2** : to talk about — **dis·cus·sion** \-ˈkəsh-ən\ *n*
dis·cus·sant \dis-ˈkəs-ᵊnt\ *n* : one who takes part in a formal discussion
[1]**dis·dain** \dis-ˈdān\ *n* : CONTEMPT, SCORN — **dis·dain·ful** \-fəl\ *adj* — **dis·dain·ful·ly** \-ē\ *adv*
[2]**disdain** *vb* **1** : to look upon with scorn **2** : to reject or refrain from because of disdain
dis·ease \diz-ˈēz\ *n* : an abnormal bodily condition that impairs functioning and can usu. be recognized by signs and symptoms : SICKNESS — **dis·eased** \-ˈēzd\ *adj*
dis·em·bark \ˌdis-əm-ˈbärk\ *vb* : to go or put ashore from a ship — **dis·em·bar·ka·tion** \dis-ˌem-ˌbär-ˈkā-shən\ *n*
dis·em·body \ˌdis-əm-ˈbäd-ē\ *vb* : to deprive of bodily existence
dis·em·bow·el \-ˈbau̇(-ə)l\ *vb* : EVISCERATE 1 — **dis·em·bow·el·ment** *n*
dis·en·chant \ˌdis-ᵊn-ˈchant\ *vb* : DISILLUSION — **dis·en·chant·ment** *n*
dis·en·cum·ber \ˌdis-ᵊn-ˈkəm-bər\ *vb* : to free from something that burdens
dis·en·fran·chise \ˌdis-ᵊn-ˈfran-ˌchīz\ *vb* : DISFRANCHISE — **dis·en·fran·chise·ment** *n*
dis·en·gage \ˌdis-ᵊn-ˈgāj\ *vb* : RELEASE, EXTRICATE, DISENTANGLE — **dis·en·gage·ment** *n*
dis·en·tan·gle \ˌdis-ᵊn-ˈtaŋ-gəl\ *vb* : to free from entanglement : UNRAVEL
dis·equi·lib·ri·um \dis-ˌē-kwə-ˈlib-rē-əm\ *n* : loss or lack of equilibrium
dis·es·tab·lish \ˌdis-ə-ˈstab-lish\ *vb* : to end the establishment of; *esp* : to deprive of the status of an established church — **dis·es·tab·lish·ment** *n*
dis·es·teem \ˌdis-ə-ˈstēm\ *n* : lack of esteem : DISFAVOR, DISREPUTE
di·seuse \dē-ˈzə(r)z, -ˈzüz\ *n, pl* **diseuses** \-ˈzə(r)z(-əz), -ˈzüz(-əz)\ [F] : a skilled and usu. professional woman reciter
dis·fa·vor \dis-ˈfā-vər\ *n* **1** : DISAPPROVAL, DISLIKE **2** : the state or fact of being no longer favored
dis·fig·ure \dis-ˈfig-yər\ *vb* : to spoil the appearance of ⟨*disfigured* by a scar⟩ — **dis·fig·ure·ment** *n*
dis·fran·chise \dis-ˈfran-ˌchīz\ *vb* : to deprive of a franchise, a legal right, or a privilege; *esp* : to deprive of the right to vote — **dis·fran·chise·ment** *n*
dis·gorge \-ˈgȯrj\ *vb* : VOMIT; *also* : to discharge forcefully or confusedly
[1]**dis·grace** \dis-ˈgrās\ *vb* : to bring reproach or shame to
[2]**disgrace** *n* **1** : SHAME, DISHONOR; *also* : a cause of shame **2** : the condition of being out of favor : loss of respect — **dis·grace·ful** \-fəl\ *adj* — **dis·grace·ful·ly** \-ē\ *adv*
dis·grun·tle \dis-ˈgrənt-ᵊl\ *vb* **dis·grun·tled; dis·grun·tling** : to put in bad humor
[1]**dis·guise** \dis-ˈgīz\ *vb* **dis·guised; dis·guis·ing** **1** : to change the appearance of to conceal the identity or to resemble another **2** : HIDE, CONCEAL
[2]**disguise** *n* **1** : clothing put on to conceal one's identity or counterfeit another's **2** : an outward appearance that hides what something really is
[1]**dis·gust** \dis-ˈgəst\ *n* : AVERSION, REPUGNANCE
[2]**disgust** *vb* : to provoke to loathing, repugnance, or aversion : be offensive to — **dis·gust·ed·ly** *adv* — **dis·gust·ing·ly** \-ˈgəs-tiŋ-lē\ *adv*
[1]**dish** \ˈdish\ *n* [ME, fr. OE *disc* plate, fr. L *discus* quoit, disk, dish, fr. Gk *diskos*, fr. *dikein* to throw] **1** : a vessel used for serving food **2** : the food served in a dish ⟨a ~ of berries⟩ **3** : food prepared in a particular way **4** : something resembling a dish esp. in being shallow and concave
[2]**dish** *vb* **1** : to put into a dish **2** : to make concave like a dish
dis·ha·bille \ˌdis-ə-ˈbēl\ *n* [F *déshabillé*] : the state of being dressed in a casual or careless manner
dis·har·mo·ny \dis-ˈhär-mə-nē\ *n* : lack of harmony — **dis·har·mo·ni·ous** \ˌdis-(ˌ)här-ˈmō-nē-əs\ *adj*
dish·cloth \ˈdish-ˌklȯth\ *n* : a cloth for washing dishes
dis·heart·en \dis-ˈhärt-ᵊn\ *vb* : DISCOURAGE, DEJECT
dished \ˈdisht\ *adj* : CONCAVE
di·shev·el \dish-ˈev-əl\ *vb* **-shev·eled** *or* **-shev·elled; -shev·el·ing** *or* **-shev·el·ling** [ME *discheveled*, fr. MF *deschevelé*, fr. *descheveler* to disarrange the hair, fr. *chevel* hair, fr. L *capillus*] : to let hang or fall loosely in disorder : DISARRAY — **di·shev·eled** *or* **di·shev·elled** *adj*
dis·hon·est \dis-ˈän-əst\ *adj* : not honest : UNTRUSTWORTHY, DECEITFUL — **dis·hon·est·ly** *adv* — **dis·hon·es·ty** \-ə-stē\ *n*
[1]**dis·hon·or** \dis-ˈän-ər\ *vb* **1** : DISGRACE **2** : to refuse to accept or pay ⟨~ a check⟩
[2]**dishonor** *n* **1** : lack or loss of honor **2** : SHAME, DISGRACE **3** : something dishonorable : a cause of disgrace **4** : the act of dishonoring a negotiable instrument when presented for payment — **dis·hon·or·able** \-ˈän-(ə-)rə-bəl, -ˈän-ər-bəl\ *adj* — **dis·hon·or·ably** \-blē\ *adv*
dish out *vb* : to give freely
dish·rag \ˈdish-ˌrag\ *n* : DISHCLOTH
dish·wash·er \-ˌwȯsh-ər, -ˌwäsh-\ *n* : a person or machine that washes dishes
dish·wa·ter \-ˌwȯt-ər, -ˌwät-\ *n* : water in which dishes have been or are to be washed
dis·il·lu·sion \ˌdis-ə-ˈlü-zhən\ *vb* **-sioned; -sion·ing** \-ˈlüzh-

(ə-)niŋ\ : to free from mistaken beliefs or foolish hopes — **dis·il·lu·sion·ment** *n*

dis·in·cli·na·tion \dis-ˌin-klə-ˈnā-shən\ *n* : a feeling of unwillingness or aversion : DISTASTE

dis·in·cline \ˌdis-ᵊn-ˈklīn\ *vb* : to make or be unwilling

dis·in·fect \ˌdis-ᵊn-ˈfekt\ *vb* : to cleanse of infection-causing germs — **dis·in·fec·tant** \-ˈfek-tənt\ *n* — **dis·in·fec·tion** \-ˈfek-shən\ *n*

dis·in·gen·u·ous \-ˈjen-yə-wəs\ *adj* : lacking in candor : not frank or naive

dis·in·her·it \ˌdis-ᵊn-ˈher-ət\ *vb* : to deprive of the right to inherit

dis·in·te·grate \dis-ˈint-ə-ˌgrāt\ *vb* **1** : to break or decompose into constituent parts or small particles **2** : to destroy the unity or integrity of — **dis·in·te·gra·tion** \dis-ˌint-ə-ˈgrā-shən\ *n*

dis·in·ter \ˌdis-ᵊn-ˈtər\ *vb* **1** : to take from the grave or tomb **2** : UNEARTH

dis·in·ter·est·ed \dis-ˈin-t(ə-)rəs-təd, -tə-ˌres-\ *adj* **1** : not interested **2** : free from selfish motive or interest : UNBIASED — **dis·in·ter·est·ed·ness** *n*

dis·join \dis-ˈjöin\ *vb* : SEPARATE

dis·joint \dis-ˈjoint\ *vb* : to separate the parts of : DISCONNECT; *also* : to separate at the joints

dis·joint·ed \-əd\ *adj* **1** : DISCONNECTED; *esp* : INCOHERENT **2** : separated at or as if at the joint

disk *or* **disc** \ˈdisk\ *n* **1** : something round and flat; *esp* : a flat rounded anatomical structure (as the central part of the flower head of a composite plant or a pad of cartilage between vertebrae) **2** *usu disc* : a phonograph record **3** : a round flat plate coated with a magnetic substance on which data for a computer is stored

¹dis·like \dis-ˈlīk\ *n* : a feeling of distaste or disapproval

²dislike *vb* : to regard with dislike : DISAPPROVE

dis·lo·cate \ˈdis-lō-ˌkāt, dis-ˈlō-\ *vb* **1** : to put out of place; *esp* : to displace (a bone or joint) from normal connections ⟨~ a shoulder⟩ **2** : DISRUPT — **dis·lo·ca·tion** \ˌdis-(ˌ)lō-ˈkā-shən\ *n*

dis·lodge \dis-ˈläj\ *vb* : to force out of a place esp. of rest, hiding, or defense

dis·loy·al \dis-ˈlȯi(-ə)l\ *adj* : lacking in loyalty — **dis·loy·al·ty** *n*

dis·mal \ˈdiz-məl\ *adj* [ME, fr. *dismal*, n., days marked as unlucky in medieval calendars, fr. ML *dies mali*, lit., evil days] **1** : showing or causing gloom or depression **2** : lacking interest or merit — **dis·mal·ly** \-ē\ *adv*

dis·man·tle \dis-ˈmant-ᵊl\ *vb* **-tled; -tling** \-ˈmant-(ə-)liŋ\ **1** : to take apart **2** : to strip of furniture and equipment — **dis·man·tle·ment** *n*

dis·may \dis-ˈmā\ *vb* : to cause to lose courage or resolution from alarm or fear : DAUNT — **dismay** *n* — **dis·may·ing·ly** \-iŋ-lē\ *adv*

dis·mem·ber \dis-ˈmem-bər\ *vb* **-bered; -ber·ing** \-b(ə-)riŋ\ **1** : to cut off or separate the limbs or parts of **2** : to break up or tear into pieces — **dis·mem·ber·ment** *n*

dis·miss \dis-ˈmis\ *vb* **1** : to send away **2** : to send or remove from office, service, or employment **3** : to put aside or out of mind **4** : to refuse further judicial hearing or consideration to ⟨the judge ~*ed* the charge⟩ — **dis·miss·al** *n*

dis·mount \dis-ˈmau̇nt\ *vb* **1** : to get down from something (as a horse or bicycle) **2** : UNHORSE **3** : DISASSEMBLE

dis·obe·di·ence \ˌdis-ə-ˈbēd-ē-əns\ *n* : neglect or refusal to obey — **dis·obe·di·ent** \-ənt\ *adj*

dis·obey \ˌdis-ə-ˈbā\ *vb* : to fail to obey : be disobedient

dis·oblige \ˌdis-ə-ˈblīj\ *vb* **1** : to go counter to the wishes of **2** : INCONVENIENCE

¹dis·or·der \dis-ˈȯrd-ər\ *vb* **1** : to disturb the order of **2** : to cause disorder in ⟨a ~*ed* digestion⟩

²disorder *n* **1** : lack of order : CONFUSION **2** : breach of the peace or public order : TUMULT **3** : an abnormal state of body or mind : AILMENT

dis·or·der·ly \-lē\ *adj* **1** : offensive to public order or decency; *also* : guilty of disorderly conduct **2** : marked by disorder : DISARRANGED ⟨a ~ desk⟩ — **dis·or·der·li·ness** *n*

dis·or·ga·nize \dis-ˈȯr-gə-ˌnīz\ *vb* : to break up the regular system of : throw into disorder — **dis·or·ga·ni·za·tion** \dis-ˌȯrg-(ə-)nə-ˈzā-shən\ *n*

dis·ori·ent \dis-ˈōr-ē-ˌent\ *vb* : to cause to be confused or lost — **dis·ori·en·ta·tion** \dis-ˌōr-ē-ən-ˈtā-shən\ *n*

dis·own \dis-ˈōn\ *vb* : REPUDIATE, RENOUNCE, DISCLAIM

dis·par·age \dis-ˈpar-ij\ *vb* **-aged; -ag·ing** [ME *disparagen* to degrade by marriage below one's class, disparage, fr. MF *desparagier* to marry below one's class, fr. OF, fr. *parage* extraction, lineage, fr. *per* peer] **1** : to lower in rank or reputation : DEGRADE **2** : BELITTLE — **dis·par·age·ment** *n* — **dis·par·ag·ing·ly** \-ij-iŋ-lē\ *adv*

dis·pa·rate \ˈdis-p(ə-)rət, dis-ˈpar-ət\ *adj* : distinct in quality or character — **dis·par·i·ty** \dis-ˈpar-ət-ē\ *n*

dis·pas·sion·ate \dis-ˈpash-(ə-)nət\ *adj* : not influenced by strong feeling : CALM, IMPARTIAL — **dis·pas·sion** \-ən\ *n* — **dis·pas·sion·ate·ly** *adv*

¹dis·patch \dis-ˈpach\ *vb* **1** : to send off or away with promptness or speed esp. on official business **2** : to put to death **3** : to attend to rapidly or efficiently — **dis·patch·er** *n*

²dispatch *n* **1** : the act of dispatching; *esp* : SHIPMENT **2** : the act of putting to death **3** : MESSAGE **4** : a news item sent in by a correspondent to a newspaper **5** : promptness and efficiency in performing a task

dis·pel \dis-ˈpel\ *vb* **dis·pelled; dis·pel·ling** : to drive away by scattering : DISSIPATE

dis·pens·able \dis-ˈpen-sə-bəl\ *adj* : capable of being dispensed with

dis·pen·sa·ry \dis-ˈpens-(ə-)rē\ *n, pl* **-ries** : a place where medicine or medical or dental aid is dispensed

dis·pen·sa·tion \ˌdis-pən-ˈsā-shən\ *n* **1** : a system of rules for ordering affairs **2** : a particular arrangement or provision esp. of nature **3** : an exemption from a rule or from a vow or oath **4** : the act of dispensing **5** : something dispensed or distributed

dis·pense \dis-ˈpens\ *vb* **dis·pensed; dis·pens·ing 1** : to portion out **2** : ADMINISTER ⟨~ justice⟩ **3** : EXEMPT **4** : to make up and give out (remedies) — **dis·pens·er** *n* — **dispense with 1** : SUSPEND **2** : to do without

dis·perse \dis-ˈpərs\ *vb* **dis·persed; dis·pers·ing** : to break up and scatter about : SPREAD — **dis·per·sal** \-ˈpər-səl\ *n* — **dis·per·sion** \-ˈpər-zhən\ *n*

dispir·it \dis-ˈpir-ət\ *vb* : DEPRESS, DISCOURAGE, DISHEARTEN

dis·place \dis-ˈplās\ *vb* **1** : to remove from the usual or proper place; *esp* : to expel or force to flee from home or native land ⟨*displaced* persons⟩ **2** : to move out of position ⟨water *displaced* by a floating object⟩ **3** : to take the place of : REPLACE

dis·place·ment \dis-ˈplās-mənt\ *n* **1** : the act of displacing : the state of being displaced **2** : the volume or weight of a fluid displaced by a floating body (as a ship) **3** : the difference between the initial position of an object and a later position

¹dis·play \dis-ˈplā\ *vb* : to present to view

²display *n* **1** : a displaying of something **2** : an electronic device (as a cathode-ray tube) that gives information in visual form; *also* : the visual information

dis·please \dis-ˈplēz\ *vb* **1** : to arouse the disapproval and dislike of **2** : to be offensive to : give displeasure

dis·plea·sure \dis-ˈplezh-ər\ *n* : a feeling of dislike and irritation

dis·port \dis-ˈpōrt\ *vb* **1** : DIVERT, AMUSE **2** : FROLIC **3** : DISPLAY

dis·pos·able \dis-ˈpō-zə-bəl\ *adj* **1** : remaining after deduction of taxes ⟨~ income⟩ **2** : designed to be used once and then thrown away ⟨~ diapers⟩ — **disposable** *n*

dis·pos·al \dis-ˈpō-zəl\ *n* **1** : CONTROL, COMMAND **2** : an orderly arrangement **3** : a getting rid of **4** : MANAGE-

MENT, ADMINISTRATION **5** : the transfer of something into new hands

dis·pose \dis-ˈpōz\ *vb* **dis·posed; dis·pos·ing 1** : to give a tendency to : INCLINE ⟨*disposed* to accept⟩ **2** : to put in place : ARRANGE ⟨troops *disposed* for withdrawal⟩ **3** : SETTLE — **dis·pos·er** *n* — **dispose of 1** : to transfer to the control of another **2** : to get rid of **3** : to deal with conclusively

dis·po·si·tion \ˌdis-pə-ˈzish-ən\ *n* **1** : the act or power of disposing : DISPOSAL ⟨funds at their ~⟩ **2** : RELINQUISHMENT **3** : ARRANGEMENT **4** : TENDENCY, INCLINATION **5** : natural attitude toward things ⟨a cheerful ~⟩

dis·pos·sess \ˌdis-pə-ˈzes\ *vb* : to put out of possession or occupancy — **dis·pos·ses·sion** \-ˈzesh-ən\ *n*

dis·praise \dis-ˈprāz\ *vb* : DISPARAGE — **dispraise** *n*

dis·pro·por·tion \ˌdis-prə-ˈpōr-shən\ *n* : lack of proportion, symmetry, or proper relation — **dis·pro·por·tion·ate** \-sh(ə-)nət\ *adj*

dis·prove \dis-ˈprüv\ *vb* : to prove to be false — **dis·proof** \-ˈprüf\ *n*

dis·pu·tant \dis-ˈpyüt-ᵊnt, ˈdis-pyət-ənt\ *n* : one that is engaged in a dispute

dis·pu·ta·tion \ˌdis-pyə-ˈtā-shən\ *n* **1** : DEBATE **2** : an oral defense of an academic thesis

dis·pu·ta·tious \-shəs\ *adj* : inclined to dispute : ARGUMENTATIVE

¹dis·pute \dis-ˈpyüt\ *vb* **dis·put·ed; dis·put·ing 1** : ARGUE, DEBATE **2** : WRANGLE **3** : to deny the truth or rightness of **4** : to struggle against or over : CONTEST — **dis·put·able** \dis-ˈpyüt-ə-bəl, ˈdis-pyət-ə-bəl\ *adj* — **dis·put·er** \dis-ˈpyüt-ər\ *n*

²dis·pute *n* **1** : DEBATE **2** : QUARREL

dis·qual·i·fy \dis-ˈkwäl-ə-ˌfī\ *vb* : to make or declare unfit or not qualified — **dis·qual·i·fi·ca·tion** \-ˌkwäl-ə-fə-ˈkā-shən\ *n*

¹dis·qui·et \dis-ˈkwī-ət\ *vb* : to make uneasy or restless : DISTURB

²disquiet *n* : lack of peace or tranquillity : ANXIETY

dis·qui·etude \dis-ˈkwī-ə-ˌt(y)üd\ *n* : AGITATION, ANXIETY

dis·qui·si·tion \ˌdis-kwə-ˈzish-ən\ *n* : a formal inquiry or discussion

¹dis·re·gard \ˌdis-ri-ˈgärd\ *vb* : to pay no attention to : treat as unworthy of notice or regard

²disregard *n* : the act of disregarding : the state of being disregarded : NEGLECT — **dis·re·gard·ful** *adj*

dis·re·pair \ˌdis-ri-ˈpaər\ *n* : the state of being in need of repair

dis·rep·u·ta·ble \dis-ˈrep-yət-ə-bəl\ *adj* : not reputable : DISCREDITABLE; *esp* : having a bad reputation

dis·re·pute \ˌdis-ri-ˈpyüt\ *n* : loss or lack of reputation : low esteem

dis·re·spect \ˌdis-ri-ˈspekt\ *n* : DISCOURTESY — **dis·re·spect·ful** *adj*

dis·robe \dis-ˈrōb\ *vb* : UNDRESS

dis·rupt \dis-ˈrəpt\ *vb* **1** : to break apart **2** : to throw into disorder — **dis·rup·tion** \-ˈrəp-shən\ *n* — **dis·rup·tive** \-ˈrəp-tiv\ *adj*

dis·sat·is·fac·tion \dis-ˌat-əs-ˈfak-shən\ *n* : DISCONTENT

dis·sat·is·fy \dis-ˈat-əs-ˌfī\ *vb* : to fail to satisfy : DISPLEASE — **dis·sat·is·fied** *adj*

dis·sect \dis-ˈekt\ *vb* **1** : to divide into parts esp. for examination and study **2** : ANALYZE — **dis·sec·tion** \-ˈek-shən\ *n*

dis·sect·ed *adj* : cut deeply into narrow lobes ⟨a ~ leaf⟩

dis·sem·ble \dis-ˈem-bəl\ *vb* **-bled; -bling** \-b(ə-)liŋ\ **1** : to hide under or put on a false appearance : conceal facts, intentions, or feelings under some pretense **2** : SIMULATE — **dis·sem·bler** \-b(ə-)lər\ *n*

dis·sem·i·nate \dis-ˈem-ə-ˌnāt\ *vb* **-nat·ed; -nat·ing** : to spread abroad as if sowing seed ⟨~ ideas⟩ — **dis·sem·i·na·tion** \-ˌem-ə-ˈnā-shən\ *n*

dis·sen·sion \dis-ˈen-chən\ *n* : disagreement in opinion : DISCORD

¹dis·sent \dis-ˈent\ *vb* **1** : to withhold assent **2** : to differ in opinion

²dissent *n* **1** : difference of opinion; *esp* : religious nonconformity **2** : a written statement in which a justice disagrees with the opinion of the majority — **dis·sen·tient** \-ˈen-chənt\ *adj or n*

dis·sent·er \dis-ˈent-ər\ *n* **1** : one that dissents **2** *cap* : an English Nonconformist

dis·ser·ta·tion \ˌdis-ər-ˈtā-shən\ *n* : an extended usu. written treatment of a subject; *esp* : one submitted for a doctorate

dis·ser·vice \dis-ˈər-vəs\ *n* : INJURY, HARM, MISCHIEF

dis·sev·er \dis-ˈev-ər\ *vb* : SEPARATE, DISUNITE

dis·si·dent \ˈdis-əd-ənt\ *adj* [L *dissidens*, prp. of *dissidēre* to sit apart, disagree, fr. *dis-* apart + *sedēre* to sit] : disagreeing with an opinion or a group — **dis·si·dence** \-əns\ *n* — **dissident** *n*

dis·sim·i·lar \dis-ˈim-ə-lər\ *adj* : UNLIKE — **dis·sim·i·lar·i·ty** \dis-ˌim-ə-ˈlar-ət-ē\ *n*

dis·sim·u·late \dis-ˈim-yə-ˌlāt\ *vb* : to hide under a false appearance : DISSEMBLE — **dis·sim·u·la·tion** \dis-ˌim-yə-ˈlā-shən\ *n*

dis·si·pate \ˈdis-ə-ˌpāt\ *vb* **-pat·ed; -pat·ing 1** : to break up and drive off : DISPERSE, SCATTER ⟨~ a crowd⟩ **2** : DISPEL, DISSOLVE ⟨the breeze *dissipated* the fog⟩ **3** : SQUANDER **4** : to break up and vanish **5** : to be dissolute; *esp* : to drink alcoholic beverages to excess — **dis·si·pat·ed** *adj* — **dis·si·pa·tion** \dis-ə-ˈpā-shən\ *n*

dis·so·ci·ate \dis-ˈō-s(h)ē-ˌāt\ *vb* **-at·ed; -at·ing** : DISCONNECT, DISUNITE — **dis·so·ci·a·tion** \dis-ˌō-s(h)ē-ˈā-shən\ *n*

dis·so·lute \ˈdis-ə-ˌlüt\ *adj* : loose in morals or conduct — **dis·so·lute·ly** *adv* — **dis·so·lute·ness** *n*

dis·so·lu·tion \ˌdis-ə-ˈlü-shən\ *n* **1** : the action or process of dissolving **2** : separation of a thing into its parts **3** : DECAY; *also* : DEATH **4** : the termination or breaking up of an assembly or a partnership

dis·solve \diz-ˈälv\ *vb* **1** : to separate into component parts **2** : to pass or cause to pass into solution ⟨sugar ~*s* in water⟩ **3** : TERMINATE, DISPERSE ⟨~ parliament⟩ **4** : to waste or fade away ⟨his courage *dissolved*⟩ **5** : to be overcome emotionally ⟨~ in tears⟩ **6** : to resolve itself as if by dissolution

dis·so·nance \ˈdis-ə-nəns\ *n* : DISCORD — **dis·so·nant** \-nənt\ *adj*

dis·suade \dis-ˈwād\ *vb* **dis·suad·ed; dis·suad·ing** : to advise against a course of action : persuade or try to persuade not to do something — **dis·sua·sion** \-ˈwā-zhən\ *n* — **dis·sua·sive** \-ˈwā-siv\ *adj*

dist *abbr* **1** distance **2** district

¹dis·taff \ˈdis-ˌtaf\ *n, pl* **distaffs** \-ˌtafs, -ˌtavz\ **1** : a staff for holding the flax, tow, or wool in spinning **2** : a woman's work or domain **3** : the female branch or side of a family

²distaff *adj* : MATERNAL, FEMALE

dis·tal \ˈdis-tᵊl\ *adj* **1** : away from the point of attachment or origin **2** : of, relating to, or being the surface of a tooth that faces the back of the mouth — **dis·tal·ly** \-ē\ *adv*

¹dis·tance \ˈdis-təns\ *n* **1** : measure of separation in space or time **2** : EXPANSE **3** : the full length ⟨go the ~⟩ **4** : spatial remoteness **5** : COLDNESS, RESERVE **6** : DIFFERENCE, DISPARITY **7** : a distant point

²distance *vb* **dis·tanced; dis·tanc·ing** : to leave far behind : OUTSTRIP

dis·tant \ˈdis-tənt\ *adj* **1** : separate in space : AWAY **2** : FAR-OFF **3** : far apart **4** : not close in relationship ⟨a ~ cousin⟩ **5** : different in kind **6** : RESERVED, ALOOF, COLD

⟨~ politeness⟩ 7 : coming from or going to a distance — **dis·tant·ly** *adv* — **dis·tant·ness** *n*

dis·taste \dis-ˈtāst\ *n* : DISINCLINATION, DISLIKE — **dis·taste·ful** *adj*

dis·tem·per \dis-ˈtem-pər\ *n* : a bodily disorder usu. of a domestic animal; *esp* : a contagious often fatal virus disease of dogs

dis·tend \dis-ˈtend\ *vb* : EXPAND, SWELL — **dis·ten·si·ble** \-ˈten-sə-bəl\ *adj* — **dis·ten·sion** *or* **dis·ten·tion** \-chən\ *n*

dis·tich \ˈdis-(ˌ)tik\ *n* : a strophic unit of two lines

dis·till *also* **dis·til** \dis-ˈtil\ *vb* **dis·tilled; dis·till·ing 1** : to fall or let fall drop by drop **2** : to obtain or purify by distillation — **dis·till·er** *n* — **dis·till·ery** \-(ə-)rē\ *n*

dis·til·late \ˈdis-tə-ˌlāt, -lət\ *n* : a liquid product condensed from vapor during distillation

dis·til·la·tion \ˌdis-tə-ˈlā-shən\ *n* : the driving off of gas or vapor from liquids or solids by heat and then condensing to a liquid product

dis·tinct \dis-ˈtiŋkt\ *adj* **1** : SEPARATE, INDIVIDUAL **2** : presenting a clear unmistakable impression — **dis·tinct·ly** *adv* — **dis·tinct·ness** *n*

dis·tinc·tion \dis-ˈtiŋk-shən\ *n* **1** : the act of distinguishing a difference **2** : DIFFERENCE **3** : a distinguishing quality or mark **4** : special honor or recognition

dis·tinc·tive \dis-ˈtiŋk-tiv\ *adj* **1** : clearly marking a person or a thing as different from others **2** : having or giving style or distinction — **dis·tinc·tive·ly** *adv* — **dis·tinc·tive·ness** *n*

dis·tin·guish \dis-ˈtiŋ-gwish\ *vb* [MF *distinguer,* fr. L *distinguere,* lit., to separate by pricking] **1** : to recognize by some mark or characteristic **2** : to hear or see clearly : DISCERN **3** : to make distinctions ⟨~ between right and wrong⟩ **4** : to set apart : mark as different — **dis·tin·guish·able** *adj*

dis·tin·guished \-gwisht\ *adj* **1** : marked by eminence or excellence **2** : befitting an eminent person

dis·tort \dis-ˈtȯrt\ *vb* **1** : to twist out of the true meaning **2** : to twist out of a natural, normal, or original shape or condition — **dis·tor·tion** \-ˈtȯr-shən\ *n*

distr *abbr* distribute; distribution

dis·tract \dis-ˈtrakt\ *vb* **1** : to draw (the attention or mind) to a different object : DIVERT **2** : to stir up or confuse with conflicting emotions or motives : HARASS — **dis·trac·tion** \-ˈtrak-shən\ *n*

dis·trait \di-ˈstrā\ *adj* [F, fr. L *distractus*] : ABSENTMINDED, DISTRAUGHT

dis·traught \dis-ˈtrȯt\ *adj* : PERPLEXED, CONFUSED; *also* : CRAZED

1dis·tress \dis-ˈtres\ *n* **1** : suffering of body or mind : PAIN, ANGUISH **2** : TROUBLE, MISFORTUNE **3** : a condition of danger or desperate need — **dis·tress·ful** *adj*

2distress *vb* **1** : to subject to great strain or difficulties **2** : UPSET

dis·trib·ute \dis-ˈtrib-yət\ *vb* **-ut·ed; -ut·ing 1** : to divide among several or many : APPORTION **2** : to spread out : SCATTER; *also* : DELIVER **3** : CLASSIFY — **dis·tri·bu·tion** \ˌdis-trə-ˈbyü-shən\ *n*

dis·trib·u·tive \dis-ˈtrib-yət-iv\ *adj* **1** : of or relating to distribution **2** : being or concerned with a mathematical operation (as multiplication in $a(b + c) = ab + ac$) that produces the same result when operating on a whole mathematical expression as when operating on each part and collecting the results — **dis·trib·u·tive·ly** *adv*

dis·trib·u·tor \dis-ˈtrib-yət-ər\ *n* **1** : one that distributes **2** : an agent or agency for marketing goods **3** : a device for directing current to the spark plugs of an engine

dis·trict \ˈdis-(ˌ)trikt\ *n* **1** : a fixed territorial division (as for administrative or electoral purposes) **2** : an area, region, or section with a distinguishing character

district attorney *n* : the prosecuting attorney of a judicial district

1dis·trust \dis-ˈtrəst\ *vb* : to feel no confidence in : SUSPECT

2distrust *n* : a lack of trust or confidence : SUSPICION, WARINESS — **dis·trust·ful** \-fəl\ *adj* — **dis·trust·ful·ly** \-ē\ *adv*

dis·turb \dis-ˈtərb\ *vb* **1** : to interfere with : INTERRUPT **2** : to alter the position or arrangement of **3** : to destroy the tranquillity or composure of : make uneasy **4** : to throw into disorder **5** : INCONVENIENCE — **dis·tur·bance** \-ˈtər-bəns\ *n* — **dis·turb·er** *n*

dis·turbed \-ˈtərbd\ *adj* : showing symptoms of mental or emotional illness

dis·unite \ˌdis-yü-ˈnīt\ *vb* : DIVIDE, SEPARATE

dis·uni·ty \dis-ˈyü-nət-ē\ *n* : lack of unity; *esp* : DISSENSION

dis·use \-ˈyüs\ *n* : a cessation of use or practice

1ditch \ˈdich\ *n* : a long narrow channel or trench dug in the earth

2ditch *vb* **1** : to enclose with a ditch; *also* : to dig a ditch in **2** : to get rid of : DISCARD **3** : to make a forced landing of an airplane on water

dith·er \ˈdith-ər\ *n* : a highly nervous, excited, or agitated state

dit·to \ˈdit-ō\ *n, pl* **dittos** [It dial., pp. of It *dire* to say, fr. L *dicere*] **1** : the same or more of the same : ANOTHER — used to avoid repeating a word ⟨lost: one book (new); ~ (old)⟩ **2** : a mark composed of a pair of inverted commas or apostrophes used as a symbol for the word *ditto*

dit·ty \ˈdit-ē\ *n, pl* **ditties** : a short simple song

di·uret·ic \ˌdī-(y)ə-ˈret-ik\ *adj* : tending to increase urine flow — **diuretic** *n*

di·ur·nal \dī-ˈərn-ᵊl\ *adj* **1** : DAILY **2** : of, relating to, or occurring in the daytime

div *abbr* **1** divided **2** dividend **3** division **4** divorced

di·va \ˈdē-və\ *n, pl* **divas** *or* **di·ve** \-ˌvā\ [It, lit., goddess, fr. L, fem. of *divus* divine, god] : PRIMA DONNA

di·va·gate \ˈdī-və-ˌgāt\ *vb* **-gat·ed; -gat·ing** : to wander about or stray from a course or subject : DIVERGE — **di·va·ga·tion** \ˌdī-və-ˈgā-shən\ *n*

di·van \ˈdī-ˌvan, di-ˈvan\ *n* : COUCH, SOFA

1dive \ˈdīv\ *vb* **dived** \ˈdīvd\ *or* **dove** \ˈdōv\; **dived; div·ing 1** : to plunge into water headfirst **2** : SUBMERGE **3** : to descend or fall precipitously **4** : to descend in an airplane at a steep angle **5** : to plunge into some matter or activity **6** : DART, LUNGE — **div·er** *n*

2dive *n* **1** : the act or an instance of diving **2** : a sharp decline **3** : a disreputable bar or place of amusement

di·verge \də-ˈvərj, dī-\ *vb* **di·verged; di·verg·ing 1** : to move or extend in different directions from a common point : draw apart **2** : to differ in character, form, or opinion **3** : DEVIATE **4** : DEFLECT — **di·ver·gence** \-ˈvər-jəns\ *n* — **di·ver·gent** \-jənt\ *adj*

di·vers \ˈdī-vərz\ *adj* : VARIOUS

di·verse \dī-ˈvərs, də-, ˈdī-ˌvərs\ *adj* **1** : UNLIKE **2** : composed of distinct forms or qualities ⟨the ~ nature of man⟩ — **di·verse·ly** *adv*

di·ver·si·fy \də-ˈvər-sə-ˌfī, dī-\ *vb* **-fied; -fy·ing** : to make different or various in form or quality — **di·ver·si·fi·ca·tion** \-ˌvər-sə-fə-ˈkā-shən\ *n*

di·ver·sion \də-ˈvər-zhən, dī-\ *n* **1** : a turning aside from a course, activity, or use : DEVIATION **2** : something that diverts or amuses : PASTIME

di·ver·si·ty \də-ˈvər-sət-ē, dī-\ *n, pl* **-ties 1** : the condition of being different : VARIETY **2** : an instance or a point of difference

di·vert \də-ˈvərt, dī-\ *vb* **1** : to turn from a course or purpose : DEFLECT **2** : DISTRACT **3** : ENTERTAIN, AMUSE

di·vest \dī-ˈvest, də-\ *vb* **1** : to strip esp. of clothing, ornament, or equipment **2** : to deprive or dispossess esp. of property, authority, or rights

1di·vide \də-ˈvīd\ *vb* **di·vid·ed; di·vid·ing 1** : SEPARATE; *also* : CLASSIFY **2** : CLEAVE, PART **3** : DISTRIBUTE, APPORTION **4** : to possess or make use of in common : share in **5** : to cause to be separate, distinct, or apart from one another **6** : to separate into opposing sides or parties **7** : to mark divisions on **8** : to subject to or use in mathematical division **9** : to branch out

[2]**divide** *n* : WATERSHED 1

div·i·dend \ˈdiv-ə-ˌdend\ *n* **1** : an individual share of something distributed **2** : BONUS **3** : a number to be divided by another **4** : a sum or fund to be divided or distributed

di·vid·er \də-ˈvīd-ər\ *n* **1** : one that divides (as a partition) ⟨room ~⟩ **2** *pl* : COMPASS 5

div·i·na·tion \ˌdiv-ə-ˈnā-shən\ *n* **1** : the art or practice of using omens or magic powers to foretell the future **2** : unusual insight or intuitive perception

[1]**di·vine** \də-ˈvīn\ *adj* **di·vin·er; -est** **1** : of, relating to, or being God or a god **2** : supremely good : SUPERB; *also* : HEAVENLY — **di·vine·ly** *adv*

[2]**divine** *n* **1** : CLERGYMAN **2** : THEOLOGIAN

[3]**divine** *vb* **di·vined; di·vin·ing** **1** : INFER, CONJECTURE **2** : PROPHESY **3** : DOWSE — **di·vin·er** *n*

di·vin·ing rod \də-ˈvī-niŋ-\ *n* : a forked rod believed to reveal the presence of water or minerals by dipping downward when held over a vein

di·vin·i·ty \də-ˈvin-ət-ē\ *n, pl* **-ties** **1** : THEOLOGY **2** : the quality or state of being divine **3** : a divine being; *esp* : GOD 1

di·vis·i·ble \də-ˈviz-ə-bəl\ *adj* : capable of being divided — **di·vis·i·bil·i·ty** \-ˈbil-ət-ē\ *n*

di·vi·sion \də-ˈvizh-ən\ *n* **1** : DISTRIBUTION, SEPARATION **2** : one of the parts or groupings into which a whole is divided **3** : DISAGREEMENT, DISUNITY **4** : something that divides or separates **5** : the mathematical operation of finding how many times one number or quantity is contained in another **6** : a large self-contained military unit **7** : an administrative or operating unit of a governmental, business, or educational organization — **di·vi·sion·al** \-ˈvizh-(ə-)nəl\ *adj*

di·vi·sive \də-ˈvī-siv, -ˈviz-iv\ *adj* : creating disunity or dissension — **di·vi·sive·ly** *adv* — **di·vi·sive·ness** *n*

di·vi·sor \də-ˈvī-zər\ *n* : the number by which a dividend is divided

di·vorce \də-ˈvōrs\ *n* **1** : a complete legal breaking up of a marriage **2** : SEPARATION, SEVERANCE — **divorce** *vb* — **di·vorce·ment** *n*

di·vor·cé \də-ˌvōr-ˈsā\ *n* [F] : a divorced man

di·vor·cée \də-ˌvōr-ˈsā, -ˈsē\ *n* : a divorced woman

div·ot \ˈdiv-ət\ *n* : a piece of turf dug from a golf fairway in making a stroke

di·vulge \də-ˈvəlj, dī-\ *vb* **di·vulged; di·vulg·ing** : REVEAL, DISCLOSE

Dix·ie·land \ˈdik-sē-ˌland\ *n* : lively jazz music in a style developed in New Orleans

diz·zy \ˈdiz-ē\ *adj* **diz·zi·er; -est** [ME *disy*, fr. OE *dysig* stupid] **1** : having a sensation of whirling : GIDDY **2** : causing or caused by giddiness — **diz·zi·ly** \ˈdiz-ə-lē\ *adv* — **diz·zi·ness** \-ē-nəs\ *n*

DJ *abbr* disc jockey

dk *abbr* **1** dark **2** deck **3** dock

dl *abbr* deciliter

DLitt *or* **DLit** *abbr* [L *doctor litterarum*] doctor of letters; doctor of literature

DLO *abbr* dead letter office

dm *abbr* decimeter

DMD *abbr* [NL *dentariae medicinae doctor*] doctor of dental medicine

DMZ *abbr* demilitarized zone

dn *abbr* down

DNA \ˌdē-ˌen-ˈā\ *n* : any of various nucleic acids usu. of cell nuclei that are the molecular basis of heredity in many organisms

[1]**do** \(ˈ)dü\ *vb* **did** \(ˈ)did\; **done** \ˈdən\; **do·ing** \ˈdü-iŋ\; **does** \(ˈ)dəz\ **1** : to bring to pass : ACCOMPLISH **2** : ACT, BEHAVE ⟨~ as I say⟩ **3** : to be active or busy ⟨up and ~*ing*⟩ **4** : HAPPEN ⟨what's ~*ing*?⟩ **5** : to work at ⟨he *does* tailoring⟩ **6** : PREPARE ⟨*did* his homework⟩ **7** : to put in order (as by cleaning or arranging) ⟨~ the dishes⟩ **8** : DECORATE ⟨*did* the hall in blue⟩ **9** : GET ALONG ⟨he *does* well⟩ **10** : CARRY ON, MANAGE **11** : to feel or function better ⟨could ~ with some food⟩ **12** : RENDER ⟨sleep will ~ you good⟩ **13** : FINISH ⟨when he had *done*⟩ **14** : EXERT ⟨*did* my best⟩ **15** : PRODUCE ⟨*did* a poem⟩ **16** : to play the part of **17** : CHEAT ⟨*did* him out of his share⟩ **18** : TRAVERSE, TOUR **19** : TRAVEL **20** : to serve out in prison **21** : to serve the needs or purpose of : SUIT **22** : to be fitting or proper **23** — used as an auxiliary verb (1) before the subject in an interrogative sentence ⟨*does* he work?⟩ and after some adverbs ⟨never *did* he say so⟩, (2) in a negative statement ⟨I *don't* know⟩, (3) for emphasis ⟨he *does* know⟩, and (4) as a substitute for a preceding predicate ⟨he works harder than I ~⟩ — **do away with** **1** : to put an end to **2** : DESTROY, KILL — **do by** : to act toward in a specified way : TREAT ⟨*did* right *by* her⟩ — **do for** : to bring about the death or ruin of — **do one's thing** : to do what is personally satisfying

[2]**do** *abbr* ditto

DOA *abbr* dead on arrival

DOB *abbr* date of birth

dob·bin \ˈdäb-ən\ *n* [*Dobbin*, nickname for *Robert*] **1** : a farm horse **2** : a quiet plodding horse

Do·ber·man pin·scher \ˌdō-bər-mən-ˈpin-chər\ *n* : a short-haired medium-sized dog of a breed of German origin

do·bra \ˈdō-brə\ *n* — see MONEY table

dob·son·fly \ˈdäb-sən-ˌflī\ *n* : a large-eyed winged insect with long slender mandibles in the male and a large carnivorous aquatic larva

[1]**doc** \ˈdäk\ *n* : DOCTOR

[2]**doc** *abbr* document

do·cent \ˈdōs-ᵊnt, dō(t)-ˈsent\ *n* [obs. G (now *dozent*), deriv. of L *docēre* to teach] : TEACHER, LECTURER

doc·ile \ˈdäs-əl\ *adj* [L *docilis*, fr. *docēre* to teach] : easily taught, led, or managed : TRACTABLE — **do·cil·i·ty** \dä-ˈsil-ət-ē\ *n*

[1]**dock** \ˈdäk\ *n* : any of a genus of coarse weedy herbs related to buckwheat

[2]**dock** *vb* **1** : to cut off the end of : cut short **2** : to take away a part of : deduct from ⟨~ a man's wages⟩

[3]**dock** *n* **1** : an artificial basin to receive ships **2** : a slip between two piers to receive ships **3** : a wharf or platform for loading or unloading materials

[4]**dock** *vb* **1** : to bring or come into dock **2** : to join (as two spacecraft) mechanically in space

[5]**dock** *n* : the place in a court where a prisoner stands or sits during trial

dock·age \ˈdäk-ij\ *n* : the provision or use of a dock; *also* : the charge for using a dock

dock·et \ˈdäk-ət\ *n* **1** : a formal abridged record of the proceedings in a legal action; *also* : a register of such records **2** : a list of legal causes to be tried **3** : a calendar of matters to be acted on : AGENDA **4** : a label attached to a document containing identification or directions — **docket** *vb*

dock·hand \ˈdäk-ˌhand\ *n* : LONGSHOREMAN

dock·work·er \-ˌwər-kər\ *n* : LONGSHOREMAN

dock·yard \-ˌyärd\ *n* : SHIPYARD

[1]**doc·tor** \ˈdäk-tər\ *n* [ME *doctour* teacher, doctor, fr. MF & ML; MF, fr. ML *doctor*, fr. L, teacher, fr. *docēre* to teach] **1** : a person holding one of the highest academic degrees (as a PhD) conferred by a university **2** : one skilled in healing arts; *esp* : an academically and legally qualified physician, surgeon, dentist, or veterinarian **3** : a person who restores or repairs things — **doc·tor·al** \-t(ə-)rəl\ *adj*

[2]**doctor** *vb* **doc·tored; doc·tor·ing** \-t(ə-)riŋ\ **1** : to give medical treatment to **2** : to practice medicine **3** : REPAIR

4 : to adapt or modify for a desired end **5** : to alter deceptively

doc·tor·ate \ˈdäk-t(ə-)rət\ *n* : the degree, title, or rank of a doctor

doc·tri·naire \ˌdäk-trə-ˈnaər\ *n* [F] : one who attempts to put an abstract theory into effect without regard to practical difficulties — **doctrinaire** *adj*

doc·trine \ˈdäk-trən\ *n* **1** : something that is taught **2** : DOGMA, TENET — **doc·tri·nal** \-trən-ᵊl\ *adj*

docu·dra·ma \ˈdäk-yə-ˌdräm-ə, -ˌdram-ə\ *n* : a television or motion-picture drama that deals with historical events

doc·u·ment \ˈdäk-yə-mənt\ *n* : a paper that furnishes information, proof, or support of something else — **doc·u·ment** \-ˌment\ *vb* — **doc·u·men·ta·tion** \ˌdäk-yə-mən-ˈtā-shən\ *n*

doc·u·men·ta·ry \ˌdäk-yə-ˈment-(ə-)rē\ *adj* **1** : consisting of documents; *also* : being in writing ⟨~ proof⟩ **2** : giving a factual presentation in artistic form ⟨a ~ movie⟩ — **documentary** *n*

DOD *abbr* Department of Defense

[1]**dod·der** \ˈdäd-ər\ *n* : any of a genus of leafless elongated wiry parasitic herbs deficient in chlorophyll

[2]**dodder** *vb* **dod·dered; dod·der·ing** \ˈdäd-(ə-)riŋ\ **1** : to tremble or shake usu. from age **2** : to progress feebly and unsteadily

[1]**dodge** \ˈdäj\ *vb* **dodged; dodg·ing 1** : to move suddenly aside; *also* : to avoid or evade by so doing **2** : to avoid by trickery or evasion

[2]**dodge** *n* **1** : an act of evading by sudden bodily movement **2** : an artful device to evade, deceive, or trick **3** : EXPEDIENT

do·do \ˈdōd-ō\ *n, pl* **dodoes** *or* **dodos** [Port *doudo,* fr. *doudo* silly, stupid] **1** : a heavy flightless extinct bird related to the pigeons but larger than a turkey and formerly found on the island of Mauritius **2** : one hopelessly behind the times; *also* : a stupid person

doe \ˈdō\ *n, pl* **does** *or* **doe** : an adult female deer; *also* : the female of a mammal of which the male is called buck — **doe·skin** \-ˌskin\ *n*

DOE *abbr* Department of Energy

do·er \ˈdü-ər\ *n* : one that does

does *pres 3d sing of* DO, *pl of* DOE

doff \ˈdäf\ *vb* [ME *doffen,* fr. *don* to do + *of* off] **1** : to take off (the hat) in greeting or as a sign of respect **2** : to rid oneself of

[1]**dog** \ˈdȯg\ *n* **1** : a flesh-eating domestic mammal related to the wolves; *esp* : a male of this animal **2** : a worthless person **3** : FELLOW, CHAP ⟨you lucky ~⟩ **4** : a mechanical device for holding something **5** : uncharacteristic or affected stylishness or dignity ⟨put on the ~⟩ **6** *pl* : RUIN ⟨gone to the ~*s*⟩

[2]**dog** *vb* **dogged; dog·ging 1** : to hunt or track like a hound **2** : to worry as if by pursuit with dogs : HOUND

dog·bane \ˈdȯg-ˌbān\ *n* : any of a genus of mostly poisonous herbs with milky juice and often showy flowers

dog·cart \-ˌkärt\ *n* : a light one-horse carriage with two seats back to back

dog·catch·er \-ˌkach-ər, -ˌkech-\ *n* : a community official assigned to catch and dispose of stray dogs

dog–ear \ˈdȯg-ˌiər\ *n* : the turned-down corner of a leaf of a book — **dog–eared** \-ˌiərd\ *adj*

dog·fight \ˈdȯg-ˌfīt\ *n* : a fight between two or more fighter planes usu. at close quarters

dog·fish \-ˌfish\ *n* : any of various small sharks

dog·ged \ˈdȯg-əd\ *adj* : stubbornly determined : TENACIOUS — **dog·ged·ly** *adv* — **dog·ged·ness** *n*

dog·ger·el \ˈdȯg-(ə-)rəl\ *n* : verse that is loosely styled and irregular in measure esp. for comic effect

dog·gie bag *or* **doggy bag** \ˈdȯg-ē-\ *n* : a bag provided by a restaurant to a customer for carrying home leftover food

[1]**dog·gy** *or* **dog·gie** \ˈdȯg-ē\ *n, pl* **doggies** : a small dog

[2]**dog·gy** *adj* **dog·gi·er; -est** : of or resembling a dog ⟨a ~ odor⟩

dog·house \ˈdȯg-ˌhau̇s\ *n* : a shelter for a dog — **in the doghouse** : in a state of disfavor

do·gie \ˈdō-gē\ *n, chiefly West* : a motherless calf in a range herd

dog·leg \ˈdȯg-ˌleg\ *n* : a sharp bend or angle (as in a road) — **dogleg** *vb*

dog·ma \ˈdȯg-mə\ *n* **1** : a tenet or code of tenets **2** : a doctrine or body of doctrines formally proclaimed by a church

dog·ma·tism \ˈdȯg-mə-ˌtiz-əm\ *n* : positiveness in stating matters of opinion esp. when unwarranted or arrogant — **dog·mat·ic** \dȯg-ˈmat-ik\ *adj* — **dog·mat·i·cal·ly** \-i-k(ə-)lē\ *adv*

dog·tooth violet \ˈdȯg-ˌtüth-\ *n* : any of a genus of wild spring-flowering bulbous herbs related to the lilies

dog·trot \ˈdȯg-ˌträt\ *n* : a gentle trot — **dogtrot** *vb*

dog·wood \ˈdȯg-ˌwu̇d\ *n* : any of a genus of trees and shrubs having heads of small flowers often with showy bracts

doi·ly \ˈdȯi-lē\ *n, pl* **doilies** : a small often decorative mat

do in *vb* **1** : RUIN **2** : KILL **3** : TIRE, EXHAUST **4** : CHEAT

do·ings \ˈdü-iŋz\ *n pl* : ACTS, DEEDS, EVENTS

do–it–your·self \ˌdü-ə-chər-ˈself\ *adj* : of, relating to, or designed for use by or as if by an amateur or hobbyist — **do–it–your·self·er** \-ˈsel-fər\ *n*

dol *abbr* dollar

dol·drums \ˈdōl-drəmz, ˈdäl-\ *n pl* **1** : a spell of listlessness or despondency **2** : a part of the ocean near the equator abounding in calms **3** : a state of inactivity, stagnation, or slump ⟨business is in the ~⟩

[1]**dole** \ˈdōl\ *n* **1** : a distribution esp. of food, money, or clothing to the needy; *also* : something so distributed **2** : a grant of government funds to the unemployed

[2]**dole** *vb* **doled; dol·ing 1** : to give or distribute as a charity **2** : to give in small portions : PARCEL ⟨~ out food⟩

dole·ful \ˈdōl-fəl\ *adj* : full of grief : SAD — **dole·ful·ly** \-ē\ *adv*

doll \ˈdäl, ˈdȯl\ *n* **1** : a small figure of a human being used esp. as a child's plaything **2** : a pretty woman **3** : an attractive person

dol·lar \ˈdäl-ər\ *n* [Dutch or LG *daler,* fr. G *taler,* short for *joachimstaler,* fr. Sankt *Joachimsthal,* Bohemia, where talers were first made] **1** : any of various basic monetary units (as in the U.S. and Canada) — see MONEY table **2** : a coin, note, or token representing one dollar

dol·lop \ˈdäl-əp\ *n* : LUMP, BLOB

doll up *vb* **1** : to dress elegantly or extravagantly **2** : to make more attractive

dol·ly \ˈdäl-ē\ *n, pl* **dollies** : a small wheeled truck used in moving heavy loads; *esp* : a wheeled platform for a television or movie camera

dol·men \ˈdōl-mən, ˈdäl-\ *n* : a prehistoric monument consisting of two or more upright stones supporting a horizontal stone slab

do·lo·mite \ˈdō-lə-ˌmīt, ˈdäl-ə-\ *n* : a mineral found in broad layers as a compact limestone

do·lor \ˈdō-lər, ˈdäl-ər\ *n* : mental suffering or anguish : SORROW — **do·lor·ous** *adj* — **do·lor·ous·ly** *adv* — **do·lor·ous·ness** *n*

dol·phin \ˈdäl-fən\ *n* **1** : any of various small toothed whales with the snout more or less elongated into a beak **2** : either of two active food fishes of tropical and temperate seas

dolt \ˈdōlt\ *n* : a stupid fellow — **dolt·ish** *adj*

dom *abbr* **1** domestic **2** dominant **3** dominion

-dom \dəm\ *n suffix* **1** : dignity : office ⟨duke*dom*⟩ **2** : realm : jurisdiction ⟨king*dom*⟩ **3** : state or fact of being ⟨free*dom*⟩ **4** : those having a (specified) office, occupation, interest, or character ⟨official*dom*⟩

do·main \dō-ˈmān, də-\ *n* **1** : complete and absolute own-

dolphin 1

ership of land **2** : land completely owned **3** : a territory over which dominion is exercised **4** : a sphere of influence or action ⟨the ~ of science⟩

dome \ˈdōm\ *n* **1** : a large hemispherical roof or ceiling **2** : a structure or natural formation that resembles the dome of a building

¹do·mes·tic \də-ˈmes-tik\ *adj* **1** : living near or about the habitations of humans **2** : TAME, DOMESTICATED **3** : relating and limited to one's own country or the country under consideration **4** : of or relating to the household or the family **5** : devoted to home duties and pleasures **6** : INDIGENOUS — **do·mes·ti·cal·ly** \-ti-k(ə-)lē\ *adv*

²domestic *n* : a household servant

do·mes·ti·cate \də-ˈmes-ti-ˌkāt\ *vb* **-cat·ed; -cat·ing** : to adapt to life in association with and to the use of human beings — **do·mes·ti·ca·tion** \-ˌmes-ti-ˈkā-shən\ *n*

do·mes·tic·i·ty \ˌdō-ˌmes-ˈtis-ət-ē, də-\ *n, pl* **-ties 1** : the quality or state of being domestic or domesticated **2** : domestic activities or life

do·mi·cile \ˈdäm-ə-ˌsīl, ˈdō-mə-; ˈdäm-ə-səl\ *n* : a dwelling place : HOME — **domicile** *vb* — **dom·i·cil·i·ary** \ˌdäm-ə-ˈsil-ē-ˌer-ē, ˌdō-mə-\ *adj*

dom·i·nance \ˈdäm-ə-nəns\ *n* **1** : AUTHORITY, CONTROL **2** : the property of a genetic dominant that prevents expression of a genetic recessive

¹dom·i·nant \ˈdäm-ə-nənt\ *adj* **1** : controlling or prevailing over all others **2** : overlooking from a high elevation **3** : producing or being a bodily characteristic that is expressed when a contrasting recessive gene or trait is present

²dominant *n* : a dominant gene or a character which it controls

dom·i·nate \ˈdäm-ə-ˌnāt\ *vb* **-nat·ed; -nat·ing 1** : RULE, CONTROL **2** : to have a commanding position or controlling power over **3** : to rise high above in a position suggesting power to dominate

dom·i·na·tion \ˌdäm-ə-ˈnā-shən\ *n* **1** : supremacy or preeminence over another **2** : exercise of mastery or preponderant influence

dom·i·neer \ˌdäm-ə-ˈniər\ *vb* **1** : to rule in an arrogant manner **2** : to be overbearing

do·mi·nie *1 oftenest* ˈdäm-ə-nē, *2 oftenest* ˈdō-mə-\ *n* **1** *chiefly Scot* : SCHOOLMASTER **2** : CLERGYMAN

do·min·ion \də-ˈmin-yən\ *n* **1** : DOMAIN **2** : supreme authority : SOVEREIGNTY **3** *often cap* : a self-governing nation of the Commonwealth

dom·i·no \ˈdäm-ə-ˌnō\ *n, pl* **-noes** *or* **-nos 1** : a long loose hooded cloak usu. worn with a half mask as a masquerade costume **2** : a flat rectangular block used as a piece in a game **(dominoes)**

¹don \ˈdän\ *vb* **donned; don·ning** [*do* + *on*] : to put on (as clothes)

²don *n* [Sp, fr. L *dominus* lord, master] **1** : a Spanish nobleman or gentleman — used as a title prefixed to the Christian name **2** : a head, tutor, or fellow in an English university

do·ña \ˈdō-nyə\ *n* : a Spanish woman of rank — used as a title prefixed to the Christian name

do·nate \ˈdō-ˌnāt\ *vb* **do·nat·ed; do·nat·ing 1** : to make a gift of : CONTRIBUTE **2** : to make a donation

do·na·tion \dō-ˈnā-shən\ *n* **1** : the action of making a gift esp. to a charity **2** : a free contribution : GIFT

¹done \ˈdən\ *past part of* DO

²done *adj* **1** : doomed to failure, defeat, or death **2** : gone by : OVER ⟨when day is ~⟩ **3** : cooked sufficiently **4** : conformable to social convention

dong \ˈdȯŋ, ˈdäŋ\ *n* — see MONEY table

don·key \ˈdäŋ-kē, ˈdəŋ-\ *n, pl* **donkeys 1** : a domestic mammal classified with the asses **2** : a stupid or obstinate person

don·ny·brook \ˈdän-ē-ˌbru̇k\ *n, often cap* [*Donnybrook* Fair, annual Irish event once known for its brawls] : an uproarious brawl

do·nor \ˈdō-nər\ *n* : one that gives, donates, or presents

donut *var of* DOUGHNUT

doo·dad \ˈdü-ˌdad\ *n* : a small article whose common name is unknown or forgotten

doo·dle \ˈdüd-ᵊl\ *vb* **doo·dled; doo·dling** \ˈdüd-(ᵊ-)liŋ\ : to draw or scribble aimlessly while occupied with something else — **doodle** *n* — **doo·dler** \ˈdüd-(ᵊ-)lər\ *n*

doom \ˈdüm\ *n* **1** : JUDGMENT, SENTENCE; *esp* : a judicial condemnation or sentence **2** : DESTINY, FATE **3** : RUIN, DEATH — **doom** *vb*

dooms·day \ˈdümz-ˌdā\ *n* : JUDGMENT DAY

door \ˈdōr\ *n* **1** : a barrier by which an entry is closed and opened; *also* : a similar part of a piece of furniture **2** : DOORWAY **3** : a means of access

door·jamb \-ˌjam\ *n* : an upright piece forming the side of a door opening

door·keep·er \-ˌkē-pər\ *n* : one who tends a door

door·knob \-ˌnäb\ *n* : a knob that when turned releases a door latch

door·man \-ˌman, -mən\ *n* : one who tends a door and assists people by calling taxis and helping them in and out of cars

door·mat \-ˌmat\ *n* : a mat placed before or inside a door for wiping dirt from the shoes

door·plate \-ˌplāt\ *n* : a nameplate on a door

door·step \-ˌstep\ *n* : a step or series of steps before an outer door

door·way \-ˌwā\ *n* **1** : the opening that a door closes **2** : a means of gaining access

door·yard \-ˌyärd\ *n* : a yard outside the door of a house

do·pa \ˈdō-pə\ *n* : a form of an amino acid that is used esp. in the treatment of Parkinson's disease

¹dope \ˈdōp\ *n* **1** : a preparation for giving a desired quality **2** : a drug preparation esp. when narcotic or addictive and used illegally **3** : a stupid person **4** : INFORMATION

²dope *vb* **doped; dop·ing 1** : to treat with dope; *esp* : to give a narcotic to **2** : FIGURE OUT — usu. used with *out*

dop·ey *also* **dopy** \ˈdō-pē\ *adj* **dop·i·er; -est 1** : dulled by alcohol or a narcotic **2** : SLUGGISH **3** : STUPID

dorm \ˈdȯrm\ *n* : DORMITORY

dor·mant \ˈdȯr-mənt\ *adj* : INACTIVE; *esp* : not actively growing or functioning ⟨~ buds⟩ — **dor·man·cy** \-mən-sē\ *n*

dor·mer \ˈdȯr-mər\ *n* [MF *dormeor* dormitory, fr. L *dormitorium*, fr. *dormire* to sleep] : a window built upright in a sloping roof

dor·mi·to·ry \ˈdȯr-mə-ˌtōr-ē\ *n, pl* **-ries 1** : a room for sleeping; *esp* : a large room containing a number of beds **2** : a residence hall providing sleeping rooms

dor·mouse \ˈdȯr-ˌmau̇s\ *n* : any of numerous Old World squirrellike rodents

dor·sal \ˈdȯr-səl\ *adj* : of, relating to, or located near or on the surface of the body that in man is the back but in most other animals is the upper surface — **dor·sal·ly** \-ē\ *adv*

do·ry \ˈdōr-ē\ *n, pl* **dories** : a flat-bottomed boat with high flaring sides and a sharp bow

DOS *abbr* disk operating system

[1]**dose** \ˈdōs\ *n* [F, fr. LL *dosis,* fr. Gk, lit., act of giving, fr. *didonai* to give] **1** : a measured quantity (as of medicine) to be taken or administered at one time **2** : the quantity of radiation administered or absorbed — **dos·age** \ˈdō-sij\ *n*

[2]**dose** *vb* **dosed; dos·ing 1** : to give in doses **2** : to give medicine to

do·sim·e·ter \dō-ˈsim-ət-ər\ *n* : a device for measuring doses of X rays or of radioactivity — **do·sim·e·try** \-ə-trē\ *n*

dos·sier \ˈdȯs-ˌyā, ˈdȯs-ē-ˌā\ *n* [F, bundle of documents labeled on the back, dossier, fr. *dos* back, fr. L *dorsum*] : a file of papers containing a detailed report or detailed information

[1]**dot** \ˈdät\ *n* **1** : a small spot : SPECK **2** : a small round mark **3** : a precise point esp. in time ⟨be here on the ~⟩

[2]**dot** *vb* **dot·ted; dot·ting 1** : to mark with a dot ⟨~ an *i*⟩ **2** : to cover with or as if with dots

DOT *abbr* Department of Transportation

dot·age \ˈdōt-ij\ *n* : feebleness of mind esp. in old age : SENILITY

dot·ard \-ərd\ *n* : a person in dotage

dote \ˈdōt\ *vb* **dot·ed; dot·ing 1** : to be feebleminded esp. from old age **2** : to be lavish or excessive in one's attention, affection, or fondness ⟨*doted* on her niece⟩

dot matrix *n* : a rectangular arrangement of dots from which alphanumeric characters can be formed (as by a computer printer)

Dou·ay Version \dü-ˈā-\ *n* : an English translation of the Vulgate used by Roman Catholics

[1]**dou·ble** \ˈdəb-əl\ *adj* **1** : TWOFOLD, DUAL **2** : consisting of two members or parts **3** : being twice as great or as many **4** : folded in two **5** : having more than one whorl of petals ⟨~ roses⟩

[2]**double** *vb* **dou·bled; dou·bling** \ˈdəb-(ə-)liŋ\ **1** : to make, be, or become twice as great or as many **2** : to make a call in bridge that increases the trick values and penalties of (an opponent's bid) **3** : FOLD **4** : CLENCH **5** : to be or cause to be bent over **6** : to take the place of another **7** : to hit a double **8** : to turn sharply and suddenly; *esp* : to turn back on one's course

[3]**double** *adv* **1** : DOUBLY **2** : two together ⟨sleep ~⟩

[4]**double** *n* **1** : something twice another in size, strength, speed, quantity, or value **2** : a hit in baseball that enables the batter to reach second base **3** : COUNTERPART, DUPLICATE; *esp* : a person who closely resembles another **4** : UNDERSTUDY, SUBSTITUTE **5** : a sharp turn : REVERSAL **6** : FOLD **7** : a combined bet placed on two different contests **8** *pl* : a game between two pairs of players **9** : an act of doubling in a card game

double bond *n* : a chemical bond in which two atoms in a molecule share two pairs of electrons

double cross *n* : an act of betraying or cheating esp. an associate — **dou·ble–cross** \ˌdəb-əl-ˈkrȯs\ *vb* — **dou·ble–cross·er** *n*

dou·ble–deal·ing \-ˈdē-liŋ\ *n* : DUPLICITY — **dou·ble–deal·er** \-ˈdē-lər\ *n* — **double–dealing** *adj*

dou·ble–deck·er \-ˈdek-ər\ *n* : something having two decks, levels, or layers

dou·ble–dig·it \ˌdəb-əl-ˈdij-ət\ *adj* : amounting to 10 percent or more

dou·ble en·ten·dre \ˌdüb(-ə)-ˌläⁿ-ˈtäⁿdrᵊ, ˌdəb-ə-\ *n, pl* **double entendres** \-ˈtäⁿdrᵊ, -ˈtäⁿd-rəz\ [obs. F, lit., double meaning] : a word or expression capable of two interpretations one of which is usu. risqué

dou·ble·head·er \ˌdəb-əl-ˈhed-ər\ *n* : two games played consecutively on the same day

double helix *n* : a helix or spiral consisting of two strands (as of DNA) in the surface of a cylinder which coil around its axis

dou·ble–joint·ed \-ˈjȯint-əd\ *adj* : having a joint that permits an exceptional degree of freedom of motion of the parts joined

double play *n* : a play in baseball by which two players are put out

double pneumonia *n* : pneumonia involving both lungs

dou·blet \ˈdəb-lət\ *n* **1** : a man's close-fitting jacket worn in Europe esp. in the 16th century **2** : one of two similar or identical things

dou·ble take \ˈdəb-əl-ˌtāk\ *n* : a delayed reaction to a surprising or significant situation after an initial failure to notice anything unusual

dou·ble–talk \-ˌtȯk\ *n* : language that appears to be meaningful but in fact is a mixture of sense and nonsense

double up *vb* : to share accommodations designed for one

dou·bloon \ˌdəb-ˈlün\ *n* : a former gold coin of Spain and Spanish America

dou·bly \ˈdəb-lē\ *adv* **1** : in a twofold manner **2** : to twice the degree

[1]**doubt** \ˈdau̇t\ *vb* **1** : to be uncertain about **2** : to lack confidence in : DISTRUST, FEAR **3** : to consider unlikely — **doubt·able** *adj* — **doubt·er** *n*

[2]**doubt** *n* **1** : uncertainty of belief or opinion **2** : a condition causing uncertainty, hesitation, or suspense ⟨the outcome was in ~⟩ **3** : DISTRUST **4** : an inclination not to believe or accept

doubt·ful \ˈdau̇t-fəl\ *adj* **1** : QUESTIONABLE **2** : UNDECIDED — **doubt·ful·ly** \-ē\ *adv*

[1]**doubt·less** \ˈdau̇t-ləs\ *adv* **1** : without doubt **2** : PROBABLY

[2]**doubtless** *adj* : free from doubt

douche \ˈdüsh\ *n* [F] **1** : a jet of fluid (as water) directed against a part or into a cavity of the body; *also* : a cleansing with a douche **2** : a device for giving douches — **douche** *vb*

dough \ˈdō\ *n* **1** : a mixture that consists of flour or meal and a liquid (as milk or water) and is stiff enough to knead or roll **2** : something resembling dough esp. in consistency **3** : MONEY — **doughy** \ˈdō-ē\ *adj*

dough·boy \-ˌbȯi\ *n* : an American infantryman esp. in World War I

dough·nut \-(ˌ)nət\ *n* : a small usu. ring-shaped cake fried in fat

dough·ty \ˈdau̇t-ē\ *adj* **dough·ti·er; -est** : ABLE, STRONG, VALIANT

Doug·las fir \ˌdəg-ləs-\ *n* : a tall evergreen timber tree of the western U.S.

do up *vb* **1** : to prepare (as by cleaning) for use **2** : to wrap up

dour \ˈdau̇(ə)r, ˈdu̇r\ *adj* [ME, fr. L *durus* hard] **1** : STERN, HARSH **2** : GLOOMY, SULLEN

douse \ˈdau̇s, ˈdau̇z\ *vb* **doused; dous·ing 1** : to plunge into water **2** : DRENCH **3** : EXTINGUISH

[1]**dove** \ˈdəv\ *n* **1** : any of numerous pigeons; *esp* : a small wild pigeon **2** : an advocate of peace or of a peaceful policy — **dove·cote** \-ˌkōt, -ˌkät\ *also* **dove·cot** \-ˌkät\ *n* — **dov·ish** \ˈdəv-ish\ *adj*

[2]**dove** \ˈdōv\ *past of* DIVE

[1]**dove·tail** \ˈdəv-ˌtāl\ *n* : something that resembles a dove's tail; *esp* : a flaring tenon and a mortise into which it fits tightly

[2]**dovetail** *vb* **1** : to join (as timbers) by means of dovetails **2** : to fit skillfully together to form a whole ⟨our plans ~ perfectly⟩

dow·a·ger \ˈdau̇-i-jər\ *n* **1** : a widow owning property or a title from her deceased husband **2** : a dignified elderly woman

dowdy \ˈdau̇d-ē\ *adj* **dowd·i·er; -est** : lacking neatness and charm : SHABBY, UNTIDY; *also* : lacking smartness

dow·el \ˈdau̇(-ə)l\ *n* : a pin used for fastening together two pieces (as of board) — **dowel** *vb*

[1]**dow·er** \ˈdau̇(-ə)r\ *n* **1** : the part of a deceased husband's real estate which the law gives for life to his widow **2** : DOWRY

[2]**dower** *vb* : to supply with a dower or dowry : ENDOW

dow·itch·er \ˈdau̇-i-chər\ *n, pl* **dowitchers** : any of several long-billed wading birds related to the sandpipers

[1]**down** \ˈdau̇n\ *n* : a rolling usu. treeless upland with sparse soil — usu. used in pl.

[2]**down** *adv* **1** : toward or in a lower physical position **2** : to a lying or sitting position **3** : toward or to the ground, floor, or bottom **4** : as a down payment ⟨paid $5 ~⟩ **5** : on paper ⟨put ~ what he says⟩ **6** : in a direction that is the opposite of up **7** : SOUTH **8** : to or in a lower or worse condition or status **9** : from a past time **10** : to or in a state of less activity **11** : into defeat ⟨voted the motion ~⟩

[3]**down** *prep* : down in, on, along, or through : toward the bottom of

[4]**down** *vb* **1** : to go or cause to go or come down **2** : DEFEAT **3** : to cause (a football) to be out of play

[5]**down** *adj* **1** : occupying a low position; *esp* : lying on the ground **2** : directed or going downward **3** : being in a state of reduced or low activity **4** : DEPRESSED, DEJECTED **5** : SICK ⟨~ with a cold⟩ **6** : FINISHED, DONE

[6]**down** *n* **1** : a low or falling period (as in activity, emotional life, or fortunes) **2** : one of a series of attempts to advance a football

[7]**down** *n* **1** : a covering of soft fluffy feathers; *also* : such feathers **2** : a downlike covering or material

down·beat \ˈdau̇n-ˌbēt\ *n* : the downward stroke of a conductor indicating the principally accented note of a measure of music

down·cast \-ˌkast\ *adj* **1** : DEJECTED **2** : directed down ⟨a ~ glance⟩

down·draft \-ˌdraft\ *n* : a downward current of gas (as air in a chimney)

down·er \ˈdau̇-nər\ *n* **1** : a depressant drug; *esp* : BARBITURATE **2** : a depressing experience or situation

down·fall \ˈdau̇n-ˌfȯl\ *n* **1** : a sudden fall (as from high rank) **2** : a fall (as of rain) esp. when sudden or heavy **3** : something that causes a downfall — **down·fall·en** \-ˌfȯ-lən\ *adj*

[1]**down·grade** \ˈdau̇n-ˌgrād\ *n* **1** : a downward grade or slope (as of a road) **2** : a decline toward a worse condition

[2]**downgrade** *vb* : to lower in grade, rank, position, or status

down·heart·ed \-ˈhärt-əd\ *adj* : DEJECTED

down·hill \ˈdau̇n-ˈhil\ *adv* : toward the bottom of a hill — **downhill** \-ˌhil\ *adj*

down·load \ˈdau̇n-ˌlōd\ *vb* : to transfer (as data) from one computer to another device

down payment *n* : a part of the full price paid at the time of purchase or delivery with the balance to be paid later

down·pour \ˈdau̇n-ˌpōr\ *n* : a heavy rain

down·range \-ˈrānj\ *adv or adj* : toward the target area of a firing range

[1]**down·right** \-ˌrīt\ *adv* : THOROUGHLY

[2]**downright** *adj* **1** : ABSOLUTE, UTTER ⟨a ~ lie⟩ **2** : PLAIN, BLUNT ⟨a ~ man⟩

down·shift \-ˌshift\ *vb* : to shift an automotive vehicle into a lower gear

down·size \-ˌsīz\ *vb* : to design or produce in smaller size

Down's syndrome *or* **Down syndrome** \ˈdau̇n(z)-\ *n* : a birth defect characterized by mental deficiency, slanting eyes, a broad short skull, broad hands with short fingers, and the presence of an extra chromosome

down·stage \ˈdau̇n-ˈstāj\ *adv or adj* : toward or at the front of a theatrical stage

down·stairs \ˈdau̇n-ˈstaərz\ *adv* : on or to a lower floor and esp. the main or ground floor — **downstairs** *adj or n*

down·stream \ˈdau̇n-ˈstrēm\ *adv or adj* : in the direction of flow of a stream

down·stroke \-ˌstrōk\ *n* : a stroke made in a downward direction

down·swing \-ˌswiŋ\ *n* **1** : a swing downward **2** : DOWNTURN

down–to–earth \ˌdau̇n-tə-ˈ(w)ərth\ *adj* : PRACTICAL, REALISTIC

down·town \ˈdau̇n-ˌtau̇n\ *n* : the main business district of a town or city — **downtown** \ˌdau̇n-ˌtau̇n\ *adj or adv*

down·trod·den \ˈdau̇n-ˈträd-ᵊn\ *adj* : suffering oppression

down·turn \-ˌtərn\ *n* : a turning downward esp. in business activity

[1]**down·ward** \ˈdau̇n-wərd\ *or* **down·wards** \-wərdz\ *adv* **1** : from a higher to a lower place or condition **2** : from an earlier time **3** : from an ancestor or predecessor

[2]**downward** *adj* : directed toward or situated in a lower place or condition

down·wind \ˈdau̇n-ˈwind\ *adv or adj* : in the direction toward which the wind is blowing

downy \ˈdau̇-nē\ *adj* **down·i·er; -est** : resembling or covered with down

downy mildew *n* : any of various parasitic fungi producing whitish masses esp. on the underside of plant leaves; *also* : a plant disease caused by downy mildew

downy woodpecker *n* : a small black-and-white woodpecker of No. America

dow·ry \ˈdau̇(ə)r-ē\ *n, pl* **dowries** : the property that a woman brings to her husband in marriage

dowse \ˈdau̇z\ *vb* **dowsed; dows·ing** : to use a divining rod esp. to find water — **dows·er** *n*

dox·ol·o·gy \däk-ˈsäl-ə-jē\ *n, pl* **-gies** : a usu. short hymn of praise to God

doy·en \ˈdȯi-ən, ˈdwä-ˌyaⁿ(n)\ *n* : the senior or most experienced person in a group

doy·enne \dȯi-ˈ(y)en, dwä-ˈyen\ *n* : a woman who is a doyen

doz *abbr* dozen

doze \ˈdōz\ *vb* **dozed; doz·ing** : to sleep lightly — **doze** *n*

doz·en \ˈdəz-ᵊn\ *n, pl* **dozens** *or* **dozen** [ME *dozeine*, fr. OF *dozaine*, fr. *doze* twelve, fr. L *duodecim*, fr. *duo* two + *decem* ten] : a group of twelve — **doz·enth** \-ᵊnth\ *adj*

[1]**DP** \ˈdē-ˈpē\ *n, pl* **DP's** *or* **DPs** : a displaced person

[2]**DP** *abbr* **1** data processing **2** double play

dpt *abbr* department

DPT *abbr* diphtheria-pertussis-tetanus (vaccines)

dr *abbr* **1** debtor **2** dram **3** drive **4** drum

Dr *abbr* doctor

DR *abbr* **1** dead reckoning **2** dining room

drab \ˈdrab\ *adj* **drab·ber; drab·best** **1** : being of a light olive-brown color **2** : DULL, MONOTONOUS, CHEERLESS — **drab·ness** *n*

drach·ma \ˈdrak-mə\ *n, pl* **drach·mas** *or* **drach·mai** \-ˌmī\ *or* **drach·mae** \-(ˌ)mē\ — see MONEY table

dra·co·ni·an \drā-ˈkō-nē-ən, drə-\ *adj, often cap* : HARSH, CRUEL

[1]**draft** \ˈdraft, ˈdraft\ *n* **1** : the act of drawing or hauling **2** : the act or an instance of drinking or inhaling; *also* : the portion drunk or inhaled in one such act **3** : DOSE, POTION **4** : the force required to pull an implement **5** : DELINEATION, PLAN, DESIGN; *also* : a preliminary sketch, outline, or version ⟨a rough ~ of a speech⟩ **6** : the act of drawing (as from a cask); *also* : a portion of liquid so drawn **7** : the depth of water a ship draws esp. when loaded **8** : the selection of a person esp. for compulsory military service; *also* : the persons so selected **9** : an order for the payment of money drawn by one person or bank on another **10** : a heavy demand : STRAIN **11** : a current of

air; *also* : a device to regulate air supply (as to a fire) — **on draft** : ready to be drawn from a receptacle ⟨beer *on draft*⟩

²**draft** *adj* **1** : used or adapted for drawing loads ⟨~ animals⟩ **2** : being or having been on draft ⟨~ beer⟩ **3** : constituting a preliminary sketch, outline, or version

³**draft** *vb* **1** : to select usu. on a compulsory basis; *esp* : to conscript for military service **2** : to draw the preliminary sketch, version, or plan of **3** : COMPOSE, PREPARE **4** : to draw off or away — **draft·ee** \draf-ˈtē, dráf-\ *n*

drafts·man \ˈdraft-smən, ˈdráft-\ *n* : one who draws plans (as for buildings or machinery)

drafty \ˈdraf-tē, ˈdráf-\ *adj* **draft·i·er; -est** : exposed to a draft

¹**drag** \ˈdrag\ *n* **1** : something (as a harrow, grapnel, sledge, or clog) that is dragged along over a surface **2** : the act or an instance of dragging **3** : something that hinders progress **4** : STREET ⟨the main ~⟩ **5** : woman's dress worn by a man **6** : something boring ⟨the party was a ~⟩

²**drag** *vb* **dragged; drag·ging 1** : HAUL **2** : to move with painful slowness or difficulty **3** : to force into or out of some situation, condition, or course of action **4** : to pass (time) in pain or tedium **5** : PROTRACT ⟨~ a story out⟩ **6** : to hang or lag behind **7** : to trail along on the ground **8** : to explore, search, or fish with a drag **9** : DRAW, PUFF ⟨~ on a cigarette⟩ — **drag·ger** *n*

drag·net \-ˌnet\ *n* **1** : NET, TRAWL **2** : a network of planned actions for pursuing and catching ⟨a police ~⟩

drag·o·man \ˈdrag-ə-mən\ *n, pl* **-mans** *or* **-men** \-mən\ : an interpreter employed esp. in the Near East

drag·on \ˈdrag-ən\ *n* [ME, fr. OF, fr. L *dracon-, draco* serpent, dragon, fr. Gk *drakōn* serpent] : a fabulous animal usu. represented as a huge winged scaly serpent with a crested head and large claws

drag·on·fly \-ˌflī\ *n* : any of a group of large harmless 4-winged insects

¹**dra·goon** \drə-ˈgün, dra-\ *n* [F *dragon* dragon, dragoon, fr. MF] : a heavily armed mounted soldier

²**dragoon** *vb* : to force or attempt to force into submission by violent measures

drag race *n* : an acceleration contest between vehicles

drag strip *n* : a site for drag races

¹**drain** \ˈdrān\ *vb* **1** : to draw off or flow off gradually or completely **2** : to exhaust physically or emotionally **3** : to make or become gradually dry or empty **4** : to carry away the surface water of : discharge surface or surplus water **5** : EMPTY, EXHAUST — **drain·er** *n*

²**drain** *n* **1** : a means (as a channel or sewer) of draining **2** : the act of draining **3** : DEPLETION **4** : BURDEN, STRAIN ⟨a ~ on his savings⟩

drain·age \-ij\ *n* **1** : the act or process of draining; *also* : something that is drained off **2** : a means for draining : DRAIN, SEWER **3** : an area drained

drain·pipe \ˈdrān-ˌpīp\ *n* : a pipe for drainage

drake \ˈdrāk\ *n* : a male duck

dram \ˈdram\ *n* **1** — see WEIGHT table **2** : FLUIDRAM **3** : a small drink

dra·ma \ˈdräm-ə, ˈdram-\ *n* [LL, fr. Gk, deed, drama, fr. *dran* to do, act] **1** : a literary composition designed for theatrical presentation **2** : dramatic art, literature, or affairs **3** : a series of events involving conflicting forces — **dra·mat·ic** \drə-ˈmat-ik\ *adj* — **dra·mat·i·cal·ly** \-i-k(ə-)lē\ *adv* — **dram·a·tist** \ˈdram-ət-əst, ˈdräm-\ *n*

dra·ma·tize \ˈdram-ə-ˌtīz, ˈdräm-\ *vb* **-tized; -tiz·ing 1** : to adapt for or be suitable for theatrical presentation **2** : to present or represent in a dramatic manner — **dram·a·ti·za·tion** \ˌdram-ət-ə-ˈzā-shən, ˌdräm-\ *n*

drank *past and past part of* DRINK

¹**drape** \ˈdrāp\ *n* **1** : CURTAIN **2** : arrangement in or of folds **3** : the cut or hang of clothing

²**drape** *vb* **draped; drap·ing 1** : to cover or adorn with or as if with folds of cloth **2** : to cause to hang or stretch out loosely or carelessly **3** : to arrange or become arranged in flowing lines or folds

drap·er \ˈdrā-pər\ *n, chiefly Brit* : a dealer in cloth and sometimes in clothing and dry goods

drap·ery \ˈdrā-p(ə-)rē\ *n, pl* **-er·ies 1** *Brit* : DRY GOODS **2** : a decorative fabric esp. when hung loosely and in folds : HANGINGS **3** : the draping or arranging of materials

dras·tic \ˈdras-tik\ *adj* : HARSH, RIGOROUS, SEVERE ⟨~ punishment⟩ — **dras·ti·cal·ly** \-ti-k(ə-)lē\ *adv*

draught \ˈdráft\ , **draughty** \ˈdráf-tē\ *chiefly Brit var of* DRAFT, DRAFTY

draughts \ˈdráfts\ *n, Brit* : CHECKERS

¹**draw** \ˈdrȯ\ *vb* **drew** \ˈdrü\; **drawn** \ˈdrȯn\; **draw·ing 1** : HAUL, DRAG **2** : to cause to go in a certain direction ⟨*drew* him aside⟩ **3** : to move or go steadily or gradually ⟨night ~*s* near⟩ **4** : ATTRACT, ENTICE **5** : PROVOKE, ROUSE ⟨*drew* enemy fire⟩ **6** : INHALE ⟨~ a deep breath⟩ **7** : to bring or pull out **8** : to force out from cover or possession ⟨~ trumps⟩ **9** : to extract the essence from ⟨~ tea⟩ **10** : EVISCERATE **11** : to require (a specified depth) to float in **12** : ACCUMULATE, GAIN ⟨~*ing* interest⟩ **13** : to take money from a place of deposit : WITHDRAW **14** : to receive regularly from a source ⟨~ a salary⟩ **15** : to take (cards) from a stack or the dealer **16** : to receive or take at random ⟨~ a winning number⟩ **17** : to bend (a bow) by pulling back the string **18** : WRINKLE, SHRINK **19** : to change shape by or as if by pulling or stretching ⟨a face *drawn* with sorrow⟩ **20** : to leave (a contest) undecided : TIE **21** : DELINEATE, SKETCH **22** : to write out in due form : DRAFT ⟨~ up a will⟩ **23** : FORMULATE ⟨~ comparisons⟩ **24** : DEDUCE **25** : to spread or elongate (metal) by hammering or by pulling through dies **26** : to produce or allow a draft or current of air ⟨the furnace ~*s* well⟩ **27** : to swell out in a wind ⟨all sails ~*ing*⟩

²**draw** *n* **1** : the act, process, or result of drawing **2** : a lot or chance drawn at random **3** : a contest left undecided or deadlocked : TIE **4** : ATTRACTION

draw·back \ˈdrȯ-ˌbak\ *n* : HINDRANCE, HANDICAP

draw·bridge \-ˌbrij\ *n* : a bridge made to be drawn up, down, or aside

draw·er \ˈdrȯ(-ə)r\ *n* **1** : one that draws **2** *pl* : an undergarment for the lower part of the body **3** : a sliding boxlike compartment (as in a table or desk)

draw·ing \ˈdrȯ(-)iŋ\ *n* **1** : an act or instance of drawing; *esp* : an occasion when something is decided by drawing lots **2** : the act or art of making a figure, plan, or sketch by means of lines **3** : a representation made by drawing : SKETCH

drawing card *n* : one that attracts attention or patronage

drawing room *n* : a formal reception room

drawl \ˈdrȯl\ *vb* : to speak or utter slowly with vowels greatly prolonged — **drawl** *n*

draw on *vb* : APPROACH ⟨night *draws on*⟩

draw out *vb* **1** : PROLONG **2** : to cause to speak freely

draw·string \ˈdrȯ-ˌstriŋ\ *n* : a string, cord, or tape for use in closing a bag or controlling fullness in garments or curtains

draw up *vb* **1** : to prepare a draft or version of **2** : to pull oneself erect **3** : to bring or come to a stop

dray \ˈdrā\ *n* : a strong low cart for carrying heavy loads

dray

¹**dread** \ˈdred\ *vb* **1** : to fear greatly **2** : to feel extreme reluctance to meet or face

²**dread** *n* : great fear esp. of some harm to come

[3]**dread** *adj* **1** : causing great fear or anxiety **2** : inspiring awe

dread·ful \ˈdred-fəl\ *adj* **1** : inspiring dread or awe : FRIGHTENING **2** : extremely distasteful, unpleasant, or shocking — **dread·ful·ly** \-ē\ *adv*

dread·locks \ˈdred-ˌläks\ *n pl* : long braids of hair over the entire head

dread·nought \ˈdred-ˌnȯt\ *n* : a battleship armed with big guns of the same caliber

[1]**dream** \ˈdrēm\ *n* [ME *dreem,* fr. OE *drēam* noise, joy] **1** : a series of thoughts, images, or emotions occurring during sleep **2** : a dreamlike vision : DAYDREAM, REVERIE **3** : something notable for its beauty, excellence, or enjoyable quality **4** : IDEAL — **dream·like** *adj* — **dreamy** *adj*

[2]**dream** \ˈdrēm\ *vb* **dreamed** \ˈdremt, ˈdrēmd\ *or* **dreamt** \ˈdremt\; **dream·ing 1** : to have a dream of **2** : to indulge in daydreams or fantasies : pass (time) in reverie or inaction **3** : IMAGINE — **dream·er** *n*

dream·land \ˈdrēm-ˌland\ *n* : an unreal delightful country that exists in imagination or in dreams

dream up *vb* : INVENT, CONCOCT

dream·world \-ˌwərld\ *n* : a world of illusion or fantasy

drear \ˈdriər\ *adj* : DREARY

drea·ry \ˈdri(ə)r-ē\ *adj* **drea·ri·er; -est** [ME *drery,* fr. OE *drēorig* sad, bloody, fr. *drēor* gore] **1** : DOLEFUL, SAD **2** : DISMAL, GLOOMY — **drea·ri·ly** \ˈdrir-ə-lē\ *adv*

[1]**dredge** \ˈdrej\ *vb* **dredged; dredg·ing** : to gather or search with or as if with a dredge — **dredg·er** *n*

[2]**dredge** *n* : a machine or barge for removing earth or silt

[3]**dredge** *vb* **dredged; dredg·ing** : to coat (food) by sprinkling (as with flour)

dregs \ˈdregz\ *n pl* **1** : SEDIMENT 1 **2** : the most undesirable part ⟨the ~ of humanity⟩

drench \ˈdrench\ *vb* : to wet through

[1]**dress** \ˈdres\ *vb* **1** : to make or set straight : ALIGN **2** : to prepare for use; *esp* : BUTCHER **3** : TRIM, EMBELLISH ⟨~ a store window⟩ **4** : to put clothes on : CLOTHE; *also* : to put on or wear formal or fancy clothes **5** : to apply dressings or medicine to **6** : to arrange (the hair) by combing, brushing, or curling **7** : to apply fertilizer to **8** : SMOOTH, FINISH ⟨~ leather⟩

[2]**dress** *n* **1** : APPAREL, CLOTHING **2** : FROCK, GOWN — **dress·mak·er** \-ˌmā-kər\ *n* — **dress·mak·ing** \-ˌmā-kiŋ\ *n*

[3]**dress** *adj* : suitable for a formal occasion; *also* : requiring formal dress

dres·sage \drə-ˈsäzh\ *n* [F] : the execution by a trained horse of complex movements in response to barely perceptible signals from its rider

dress down *vb* : to scold severely

[1]**dress·er** \ˈdres-ər\ *n* : a chest of drawers or bureau with a mirror

[2]**dresser** *n* : one that dresses

dress·ing \-iŋ\ *n* **1** : the act or process of one who dresses **2** : a sauce for adding to a dish (as a salad) **3** : a seasoned mixture usu. used as a stuffing (as for poultry) **4** : material used to cover an injury

dressing gown *n* : a loose robe worn esp. while dressing or resting

dressy \ˈdres-ē\ *adj* **dress·i·er; -est 1** : showy in dress **2** : STYLISH, SMART

drew *past of* DRAW

[1]**drib·ble** \ˈdrib-əl\ *vb* **drib·bled; drib·bling** \-(ə-)liŋ\ **1** : to fall or flow in drops : TRICKLE **2** : DROOL **3** : to propel by successive slight taps or bounces

[2]**dribble** *n* **1** : a small trickling stream or flow **2** : a drizzling shower **3** : the dribbling of a ball or puck

drib·let \ˈdrib-lət\ *n* **1** : a trifling amount **2** : a drop of liquid

dri·er *also* **dry·er** \ˈdrī(-ə)r\ *n* **1** : a substance dissolved in paints, varnishes, or inks to speed drying **2** *usu dryer* : a device for drying

[1]**drift** \ˈdrift\ *n* **1** : the motion or course of something drifting **2** : a mass of matter (as snow or sand) blown up by wind **3** : earth, gravel, and rock deposited by a glacier or by running water **4** : a general underlying design or tendency : MEANING

[2]**drift** *vb* **1** : to float or be driven along by or as if by a current of water or air **2** : to pile up under the force of the wind or water

drift·er \ˈdrif-tər\ *n* : a person without aim, ambition, or initiative

drift·wood \ˈdrift-ˌwu̇d\ *n* : wood drifted or floated by water

[1]**drill** \ˈdril\ *n* **1** : a boring tool **2** : the training of soldiers in marching and the manual of arms **3** : strict training and instruction in a subject

[2]**drill** *vb* **1** : to instruct and exercise by repetition **2** : to train in or practice military drill **3** : to bore with a drill — **drill·er** *n*

[3]**drill** *n* **1** : a shallow furrow or trench in which seed is sown **2** : an agricultural implement for making furrows and dropping seed into them

[4]**drill** *n* : a firm cotton fabric in twill weave

drill·mas·ter \ˈdril-ˌmas-tər\ *n* : one who drills; *esp* : an instructor in military drill

drill press *n* : an upright drilling machine in which the drill is pressed to the work usu. by a hand lever

drily *var of* DRYLY

[1]**drink** \ˈdriŋk\ *vb* **drank** \ˈdraŋk\; **drunk** \ˈdrəŋk\ *or* **drank; drink·ing 1** : to swallow liquid : IMBIBE **2** : ABSORB **3** : to take in through the senses ⟨~ in the beautiful scenery⟩ **4** : to give or join in a toast **5** : to drink alcoholic beverages esp. to excess — **drink·able** *adj* — **drink·er** *n*

[2]**drink** *n* **1** : BEVERAGE **2** : alcoholic liquor **3** : a draft or portion of liquid **4** : excessive consumption of alcoholic beverages

[1]**drip** \ˈdrip\ *vb* **dripped; drip·ping 1** : to fall or let fall in drops **2** : to let fall drops of moisture or liquid ⟨a *dripping* faucet⟩ **3** : to overflow with or as if with moisture

[2]**drip** *n* **1** : a falling in drops **2** : liquid that falls, overflows, or is extruded in drops **3** : the sound made by or as if by falling drops

[1]**drive** \ˈdrīv\ *vb* **drove** \ˈdrōv\; **driv·en** \ˈdriv-ən\; **driv·ing 1** : to urge, push, or force onward **2** : to direct the movement or course of **3** : to convey in a vehicle **4** : to set or keep in motion or operation **5** : to carry through strongly ⟨~ a bargain⟩ **6** : FORCE, COMPEL ⟨*driven* by hunger to steal⟩ **7** : to project, inject, or impress forcefully ⟨*drove* the lesson home⟩ **8** : to bring into a specified condition ⟨the noise ~*s* me crazy⟩ **9** : to produce by opening a way ⟨~ a well⟩ **10** : to rush and press with violence ⟨a *driving* rain⟩ **11** : to propel an object of play (as a golf ball) by a hard blow — **driv·er** *n*

[2]**drive** *n* **1** : a trip in a carriage or automobile **2** : a driving together of animals (as for capture or slaughter) **3** : the guiding of logs downstream to a mill **4** : the act of driving a ball; *also* : the flight of a ball **5** : DRIVEWAY **6** : a public road for driving (as in a park) **7** : an offensive or aggressive move : a military attack **8** : an intensive campaign ⟨membership ~⟩ **9** : the state of being hurried and under pressure **10** : NEED, LONGING **11** : dynamic quality **12** : the apparatus by which motion is imparted to a machine **13** : a device for reading and writing on magnetic media (as magnetic tape or disks)

drive–in \ˈdrī-ˌvin\ *adj* : accommodating patrons while they remain in their automobiles — **drive–in** *n*

[1]**driv·el** \ˈdriv-əl\ *vb* **-eled** *or* **-elled; -el·ing** *or* **-el·ling** \-(ə-)liŋ\ **1** : DROOL, SLAVER **2** : to talk or utter stupidly, carelessly, or in an infantile way — **driv·el·er** \-(ə-)lər\ *n*

[2]**drivel** *n* : NONSENSE
drive shaft *n* : a shaft that transmits mechanical power
drive·way \ˈdrīv-ˌwā\ *n* : a short private road leading from the street to a house, garage, or parking lot
[1]**driz·zle** \ˈdriz-əl\ *n* : a fine misty rain
[2]**drizzle** *vb* **driz·zled; driz·zling** \-(ə-)liŋ\ : to rain in very small drops
drogue \ˈdrōg\ *n* : a small parachute for slowing down or stabilizing something (as an astronaut's capsule)
droll \ˈdrōl\ *adj* [F *drôle,* fr. *drôle* scamp, fr. MF *drolle,* fr. Middle Dutch, imp] : having a humorous, whimsical, or odd quality ⟨a ~ expression⟩ — **droll·ery** \-(ə-)rē\ *n* — **drol·ly** \ˈdrō(l)-lē\ *adv*
drom·e·dary \ˈdräm-ə-ˌder-ē\ *n, pl* **-dar·ies** [ME *dromedarie,* fr. MF *dromedaire,* fr. LL *dromedarius,* fr. L *dromad-, dromas,* fr. Gk, running] : CAMEL; *esp* : a domesticated one-humped camel of western Asia and northern Africa
[1]**drone** \ˈdrōn\ *n* **1** : a male honeybee **2** : one that lives on the labors of others : PARASITE **3** : a pilotless aircraft or ship controlled by radio
[2]**drone** *vb* **droned; dron·ing** : to sound with a low dull monotonous murmuring sound : speak monotonously
[3]**drone** *n* : a deep monotonous sound
drool \ˈdrül\ *vb* **1** : to let liquid flow from the mouth **2** : to talk foolishly
droop \ˈdrüp\ *vb* **1** : to hang or incline downward **2** : to sink gradually **3** : LANGUISH — **droop** *n*
[1]**drop** \ˈdräp\ *n* **1** : the quantity of fluid that falls in one spherical mass **2** *pl* : a dose of medicine measured by drops **3** : a small quantity of drink **4** : the smallest practical unit of liquid measure **5** : something (as a pendant or a small round candy) that resembles a liquid drop **6** : FALL **7** : a decline in quantity or quality **8** : a descent by parachute **9** : the distance through which something drops **10** : a slot into which something is to be dropped **11** : something that drops or has dropped
[2]**drop** *vb* **dropped; drop·ping 1** : to fall or let fall in drops **2** : to let fall : LOWER ⟨~ a glove⟩ ⟨*dropped* his voice⟩ **3** : SEND ⟨~ me a note⟩ **4** : to let go : DISMISS ⟨~ the subject⟩ **5** : to knock down : cause to fall **6** : to go lower : become less ⟨prices *dropped*⟩ **7** : to come or go unexpectedly or informally ⟨~ in to call⟩ **8** : to pass from one state into a less active one ⟨~ off to sleep⟩ **9** : to move downward or with a current **10** : QUIT ⟨*dropped* out of the race⟩ — **drop back** : to move toward the rear — **drop behind** : to fail to keep up
drop·kick \-ˈkik\ *n* : a kick made by dropping a ball to the ground and kicking it at the moment it starts to rebound — **drop–kick** *vb*
drop·let \ˈdräp-lət\ *n* : a tiny drop
drop–off \ˈdräp-ˌȯf\ *n* **1** : a steep or perpendicular descent **2** : a marked decline ⟨a ~ in attendance⟩
drop off \dräp-ˈȯf\ *vb* : to fall asleep
drop out \dräp-ˈau̇t\ *vb* : to withdraw from participation or membership; *esp* : to leave school before graduation — **drop·out** \ˈdräp-ˌau̇t\ *n*
drop·per \ˈdräp-ər\ *n* **1** : one that drops **2** : a short glass tube with a rubber bulb used to measure out liquids by drops
drop·pings *n pl* : DUNG
drop·sy \ˈdräp-sē\ *n* [ME *dropesie,* short for *ydropesie,* fr. OF, fr. L *hydropisis,* fr. Gk *hydrōps,* fr. *hydōr* water] : EDEMA — **drop·si·cal** \-si-kəl\ *adj*
dross \ˈdräs\ *n* **1** : the scum that forms on the surface of a molten metal **2** : waste matter : REFUSE
drought *also* **drouth** \ˈdrau̇t(h)\ *n* : a long spell of dry weather
[1]**drove** \ˈdrōv\ *n* **1** : a group of animals driven or moving in a body **2** : a crowd of people moving or acting together
[2]**drove** *past of* DRIVE
drov·er \ˈdrō-vər\ *n* : one that drives domestic animals usu. to market
drown \ˈdrau̇n\ *vb* **drowned** \ˈdrau̇nd\; **drown·ing 1** : to suffocate by submersion esp. in water **2** : to become drowned **3** : to cover with water **4** : OVERCOME, OVERPOWER
drowse \ˈdrau̇z\ *vb* **drowsed; drows·ing** : DOZE — **drowse** *n*
drowsy \ˈdrau̇-zē\ *adj* **drows·i·er; -est 1** : ready to fall asleep **2** : making one sleepy — **drows·i·ly** \ˈdrau̇-zə-lē\ *adv* — **drows·i·ness** \-zē-nəs\ *n*
drub \ˈdrəb\ *vb* **drubbed; drub·bing 1** : to beat severely : PUMMEL, THRASH **2** : to defeat decisively
drudge \ˈdrəj\ *vb* **drudged; drudg·ing** : to do hard, menial, or monotonous work — **drudge** *n* — **drudg·ery** \-(ə-)rē\ *n*
[1]**drug** \ˈdrəg\ *n* **1** : a substance used as or in medicine **2** : a substance (as heroin or marijuana) affecting bodily activities often in a harmful way and taken for other than medical reasons
[2]**drug** *vb* **drugged; drug·ging** : to affect with drugs; *esp* : to stupefy with a narcotic
drug·gist \ˈdrəg-əst\ *n* : a dealer in drugs and medicines; *also* : PHARMACIST
drug·store \ˈdrəg-ˌstōr\ *n* : a retail shop where medicines and miscellaneous articles are sold
dru·id \ˈdrü-əd\ *n, often cap* : one of an ancient Celtic priesthood of Gaul, Britain, and Ireland appearing in legends as magicians and wizards
[1]**drum** \ˈdrəm\ *n* **1** : a percussion instrument usu. consisting of a hollow cylinder with a skin or plastic head stretched over one or both ends that is beaten with the hands or with a stick **2** : the sound of a drum; *also* : a similar sound **3** : a drum-shaped object
[2]**drum** *vb* **drummed; drum·ming 1** : to beat a drum **2** : to sound rhythmically : THROB, BEAT **3** : to summon or assemble by or as if by beating a drum **4** : EXPEL ⟨*drummed* out of camp⟩ **5** : to drive or force by steady effort ⟨~ a lesson into his head⟩ **6** : to strike or tap repeatedly so as to produce rhythmic sounds
drum·beat \ˈdrəm-ˌbēt\ *n* : a stroke on a drum or its sound
drum·lin \ˈdrəm-lən\ *n* : an oval hill of glacial drift
drum major *n* : the leader of a marching band
drum ma·jor·ette \ˌdrəm-ˌmā-jə-ˈret\ *n* : a girl or woman who leads a marching band; *also* : a baton twirler who accompanies a marching band
drum·mer \ˈdrəm-ər\ *n* **1** : one that plays a drum **2** : a traveling salesman
drum·stick \-ˌstik\ *n* **1** : a stick for beating a drum **2** : the lower segment of a fowl's leg
drum up *vb* **1** : to bring about by persistent effort ⟨*drum up* business⟩ **2** : INVENT, ORIGINATE
[1]**drunk** *past part of* DRINK
[2]**drunk** \ˈdrəŋk\ *adj* **1** : having the faculties impaired by alcohol **2** : dominated by an intense feeling ⟨~ with power⟩ **3** : of, relating to, or caused by intoxication
[3]**drunk** *n* **1** : a period of excessive drinking **2** : a drunken person : DRUNKARD
drunk·ard \ˈdrəŋ-kərd\ *n* : one who is habitually drunk
drunk·en \ˈdrəŋ-kən\ *adj* **1** : DRUNK **2** : given to habitual excessive use of alcohol **3** : of, relating to, or resulting from intoxication **4** : unsteady or lurching as if from intoxication — **drunk·en·ly** *adv* — **drunk·en·ness** \-kən-nəs\ *n*
drupe \ˈdrüp\ *n* : a partly fleshy one-seeded fruit (as a plum or cherry) that remains closed at maturity
[1]**dry** \ˈdrī\ *adj* **dri·er** \ˈdrī(-ə)r\; **dri·est** \ˈdrī-əst\ **1** : free or freed from water or liquid **2** : characterized by loss or lack of water or moisture **3** : lacking freshness : WITHERED; *also* : low in or deprived of succulence ⟨~ fruits⟩ **4** : not being in or under water ⟨~ land⟩ **5** : THIRSTY **6** : marked by the absence of alcoholic beverages **7** : no

longer liquid or sticky ⟨the ink is ∼⟩ **8** : containing or employing no liquid **9** : not giving milk ⟨a ∼ cow⟩ **10** : lacking natural lubrication ⟨a ∼ cough⟩ **11** : solid as opposed to liquid ⟨∼ groceries⟩ **12** : SEVERE **13** : not productive : BARREN **14** : marked by a matter-of-fact, ironic, or terse manner of expression ⟨∼ humor⟩ **15** : UNINTERESTING, WEARISOME **16** : not sweet ⟨∼ wine⟩ **17** : relating to, favoring, or practicing prohibition of alcoholic beverages — **dry·ly** *adv* — **dry·ness** *n*

[2]**dry** *vb* **dried; dry·ing** : to make or become dry

[3]**dry** *n, pl* **drys** : PROHIBITIONIST

dry·ad \ˈdrī-əd, -ˌad\ *n* : WOOD NYMPH

dry cell *n* : a battery whose contents are not spillable

dry–clean \ˈdrī-ˌklēn\ *vb* : to clean (fabrics) chiefly with solvents (as naphtha) other than water — **dry cleaning** *n*

dry dock \ˈdrī-ˌdäk\ *n* : a dock that can be kept dry during ship construction or repair

dry·er *var of* DRIER

dry farm·ing *n* : farming without irrigation in areas of limited rainfall — **dry–farm** *vb* — **dry farm·er** *n*

dry goods \ˈdrī-ˌgu̇dz\ *n pl* : cloth goods (as fabrics, ribbon, and ready-to-wear clothing)

dry ice *n* : solid carbon dioxide used chiefly as a refrigerant

dry measure *n* : a series of units of capacity for dry commodities — see METRIC SYSTEM table, WEIGHT table

dry run *n* : REHEARSAL, TRIAL

dry·wall \ˈdrī-ˌwȯl\ *n* : PLASTERBOARD

DSC *abbr* **1** Distinguished Service Cross **2** doctor of surgical chiropody

DSM *abbr* Distinguished Service Medal

DSO *abbr* Distinguished Service Order

DST *abbr* daylight saving time

DTP *abbr* diphtheria, tetanus, pertussis (vaccines)

d.t.'s \(ˈ)dē-ˈtēz\ *n pl, often cap D&T* : DELIRIUM TREMENS

du·al \ˈd(y)ü-əl\ *adj* **1** : TWOFOLD, DOUBLE **2** : having a double character or nature — **du·al·ism** \-ə-ˌliz-əm\ *n* — **du·al·i·ty** \d(y)ü-ˈal-ət-ē\ *n*

[1]**dub** \ˈdəb\ *vb* **dubbed; dub·bing 1** : to confer knighthood upon **2** : NAME, NICKNAME

[2]**dub** *n* : a clumsy person : DUFFER

[3]**dub** *vb* **dubbed; dub·bing** : to add (sound effects) to a motion picture or to a radio or television production

du·bi·ety \d(y)u̇-ˈbī-ət-ē\ *n, pl* **-eties 1** : UNCERTAINTY **2** : a matter of doubt

du·bi·ous \ˈd(y)ü-bē-əs\ *adj* **1** : occasioning doubt : UNCERTAIN **2** : feeling doubt : UNDECIDED **3** : QUESTIONABLE — **du·bi·ous·ly** *adv* — **du·bi·ous·ness** *n*

du·cal \ˈd(y)ü-kəl\ *adj* : of or relating to a duke or dukedom

duc·at \ˈdək-ət\ *n* : a gold coin formerly used in various European countries

duch·ess \ˈdəch-əs\ *n* **1** : the wife or widow of a duke **2** : a woman holding the rank of duke in her own right

duchy \ˈdəch-ē\ *n, pl* **duch·ies** : the territory of a duke or duchess : DUKEDOM

[1]**duck** \ˈdək\ *n, pl* **ducks** : any of various swimming birds related to but smaller than geese and swans

[2]**duck** *vb* **1** : to thrust or plunge under water **2** : to lower the head or body suddenly **3** : BOW, BOB **4** : DODGE **5** : to evade a duty, question, or responsibility ⟨∼ the issue⟩

[3]**duck** *n* **1** : a durable closely woven usu. cotton fabric **2** *pl* : clothes made of duck

duck·bill \ˈdək-ˌbil\ *n* : PLATYPUS

duck·ling \ˈdək-liŋ\ *n* : a young duck

duck·pin \-ˌpin\ *n* **1** : a small bowling pin shorter and wider in the middle than a tenpin **2** *pl but sing in constr* : a bowling game using duckpins

duct \ˈdəkt\ *n* : a tube or canal for conveying a bodily fluid; *also* : a pipe or tube for electrical conductors — **duct·less** \ˈdək-tləs\ *adj*

duc·tile \ˈdək-tᵊl\ *adj* **1** : capable of being drawn out (as into wire) or hammered thin **2** : DOCILE — **duc·til·i·ty** \ˌdək-ˈtil-ət-ē\ *n*

ductless gland *n* : an endocrine gland

dud \ˈdəd\ *n* **1** : one that fails completely **2** : a missile that fails to explode

dude \ˈd(y)üd\ *n* **1** : FOP, DANDY **2** : a city person; *esp* : an Easterner in the West

dude ranch *n* : a vacation resort offering activities (as horseback riding) typical of western ranches

dud·geon \ˈdəj-ən\ *n* : ill humor : RESENTMENT ⟨in high ∼⟩

duds \ˈdədz\ *n pl* : CLOTHES

[1]**due** \ˈd(y)ü\ *adj* [ME, fr. MF *deu,* pp. of *devoir* to owe, fr. L *debēre*] **1** : owed or owing as a debt **2** : owed or owing as a right **3** : APPROPRIATE, FITTING **4** : SUFFICIENT, ADEQUATE **5** : REGULAR, LAWFUL ⟨∼ process of law⟩ **6** : ATTRIBUTABLE, ASCRIBABLE ⟨∼ to negligence⟩ **7** : PAYABLE ⟨a bill ∼ today⟩ **8** : required or expected to happen ⟨∼ to arrive soon⟩

[2]**due** *n* **1** : something that rightfully belongs to one ⟨give to each his ∼⟩ **2** : something owed : DEBT **3** *pl* : FEES, CHARGES

[3]**due** *adv* : DIRECTLY, EXACTLY ⟨∼ north⟩

du·el \ˈd(y)ü-əl\ *n* : a combat between two persons; *esp* : one fought with weapons in the presence of witnesses — **duel** *vb* — **du·el·ist** *n*

du·en·de \dü-ˈen-dā\ *n* [Sp dial., charm, fr. Sp, ghost, goblin, fr. *duen de casa,* prob. fr. *dueño de casa* owner of a house] : the power to attract through personal magnetism and charm

du·en·na \d(y)ü-ˈen-ə\ *n* **1** : an elderly woman in charge of the younger ladies in a Spanish or Portuguese family **2** : CHAPERON

du·et \d(y)ü-ˈet\ *n* : a musical composition for two performers

due to *prep* : BECAUSE OF

duf·fel bag \ˈdəf-əl-\ *n* : a large cylindrical bag for personal belongings

duf·fer \ˈdəf-ər\ *n* : an incompetent or clumsy person

dug *past and past part of* DIG

dug·out \ˈdəg-ˌau̇t\ *n* **1** : a boat made by hollowing out a log **2** : a shelter dug in the ground **3** : a low shelter facing a baseball diamond that contains the players' bench

DUI *abbr* driving under the influence

duke \ˈd(y)ük\ *n* **1** : a sovereign ruler of a continental European duchy **2** : a nobleman of the highest rank; *esp* : a member of the highest grade of the British peerage **3** *slang* : FIST 1 — usu. used in pl. — **duke·dom** *n*

dul·cet \ˈdəl-sət\ *adj* **1** : sweet to the ear **2** : AGREEABLE, SOOTHING

dul·ci·mer \ˈdəl-sə-mər\ *n* **1** : a wire-stringed instrument of trapezoidal shape played with light hammers held in the hands **2** *or* **dul·ci·more** \-ˌmōr, -ˌmȯr\ : an American folk instrument with three or four strings held on the lap and played by plucking or strumming

[1]**dull** \ˈdəl\ *adj* **1** : mentally slow : STUPID **2** : slow in perception or sensibility **3** : LISTLESS **4** : slow in action : SLUGGISH ⟨a ∼ market⟩ **5** : BLUNT **6** : lacking brilliance or luster **7** : DIM, INDISTINCT **8** : not resonant or ringing **9** : low in saturation and lightness ⟨∼ color⟩ **10** : TEDIOUS, UNINTERESTING **11** : CLOUDY, OVERCAST — **dull·ness** *or* **dul·ness** *n* — **dul·ly** \ˈdəl-(l)ē\ *adv*

[2]**dull** *vb* : to make or become dull

dull·ard \ˈdəl-ərd\ *n* : a stupid person

du·ly \ˈd(y)ü-lē\ *adv* : in a due manner, time, or degree

du·ma \ˈdü-mə\ *n* : the principal legislative assembly in czarist Russia

---

dumb \ˈdəm\ *adj* **1** : lacking the power of speech **2** : SILENT **3** : STUPID — **dumb·ly** *adv*
dumb·bell \ˈdəm-ˌbel\ *n* **1** : a bar with weights at the end used for gymnastic exercises **2** : one who is stupid
dumb·found *or* **dum·found** \ˌdəm-ˈfau̇nd\ *vb* : ASTONISH, AMAZE
dumb·wait·er \ˈdəm-ˈwāt-ər\ *n* : a small elevator for conveying food and dishes or small goods from one story of a building to another
dum·dum \ˈdəm-ˌdəm\ *n* : a bullet (as one with a hollow point) that expands more than usual upon hitting an object
dum·my \ˈdəm-ē\ *n, pl* **dummies 1** : a dumb person **2** : the exposed hand in bridge played by the declarer in addition to his own hand; *also* : a bridge player whose hand is a dummy **3** : an imitation of something used as a substitute **4** : one seeming to act for itself but really acting for another **5** : a pattern arrangement of matter to be reproduced esp. by printing
[1]**dump** \ˈdəmp\ *vb* : to let fall in a mass : UNLOAD ⟨∼ coal⟩
[2]**dump** *n* **1** : a place for dumping something (as refuse) **2** : a reserve supply; *esp* : one of military materials ⟨an ammunition ∼⟩ **3** : a slovenly or dilapidated place
dump·ing \-iŋ\ *n* : the selling of goods in quantity at below market price esp. in international trade
dump·ling \ˈdəm-pliŋ\ *n* **1** : a small mass of boiled or steamed dough **2** : a dessert of fruit baked in biscuit dough
dumps \ˈdəmps\ *n pl* : a dull gloomy state of mind : low spirits ⟨in the ∼⟩
dump truck *n* : a truck for transporting and dumping loose materials
dumpy \ˈdəm-pē\ *adj* **dump·i·er; -est** : short and thick in build
[1]**dun** \ˈdən\ *n* : a slightly brownish dark gray
[2]**dun** *vb* **dunned; dun·ning 1** : to make persistent demands for payment **2** : PLAGUE, PESTER — **dun** *n*
dunce \ˈdəns\ *n* [John *Duns* Scotus, whose once accepted writings were ridiculed in the 16th cent.] : a dull-witted and stupid person
dun·der·head \ˈdən-dər-ˌhed\ *n* : DUNCE, BLOCKHEAD
dune \ˈd(y)ün\ *n* : a hill or ridge of sand piled up by the wind
dune buggy *n* : a motor vehicle with oversize tires for use on sand
[1]**dung** \ˈdəŋ\ *n* : MANURE
[2]**dung** *vb* : to dress (land) with dung
dun·ga·ree \ˌdəŋ-gə-ˈrē\ *n* **1** : a heavy coarse cotton twill; *esp* : blue denim **2** *pl* : clothes made of blue denim
dun·geon \ˈdən-jən\ *n* [ME *donjon*, fr. MF, fr. (assumed) ML *dominion-*, *dominio*, fr. L *dominus* lord] : a dark prison commonly underground
dung·hill \ˈdəŋ-ˌhil\ *n* : a manure pile
dunk \ˈdəŋk\ *vb* **1** : to dip or submerge temporarily in liquid **2** : to submerge oneself in water
duo \ˈd(y)ü-(ˌ)ō\ *n, pl* **du·os 1** : DUET **2** : PAIR
duo·dec·i·mal \ˌd(y)ü-ə-ˈdes-ə-məl\ *adj* : of, relating to, or being a system of numbers with a base of 12
du·o·de·num \ˌd(y)ü-ə-ˈdē-nəm, d(y)u̇-ˈäd-ᵊn-əm\ *n, pl* **-de·na** \-ˈdē-nə, -ᵊn-ə\ *or* **-denums** : the part of the small intestine extending from the stomach to the jejunum — **du·o·de·nal** \-ˈdēn-ᵊl, -ᵊn-əl\ *adj*
dup *abbr* **1** duplex **2** duplicate
[1]**dupe** \ˈd(y)üp\ *n* : one who is easily deceived or cheated : FOOL
[2]**dupe** *vb* **duped; dup·ing** : to make a dupe of : DECEIVE, FOOL
du·ple \ˈd(y)ü-pəl\ *adj* : having two beats or a multiple of two beats to the measure ⟨∼ time⟩
[1]**du·plex** \ˈd(y)ü-ˌpleks\ *adj* : DOUBLE
[2]**duplex** *n* : something duplex; *esp* : a 2-family house
[1]**du·pli·cate** \ˈd(y)ü-pli-kət\ *adj* **1** : consisting of or existing in two corresponding or identical parts or examples **2** : being the same as another
[2]**du·pli·cate** \ˈd(y)ü-pli-ˌkāt\ *vb* **-cat·ed; -cat·ing 1** : to make double or twofold **2** : to make an exact copy of — **du·pli·ca·tion** \ˌd(y)ü-pli-ˈkā-shən\ *n*
[3]**du·pli·cate** \-kət\ *n* : a thing that exactly resembles another in appearance, pattern, or content : COPY
du·pli·ca·tor \ˈd(y)ü-pli-ˌkāt-ər\ *n* : COPIER
du·plic·i·ty \d(y)u̇-ˈplis-ət-ē\ *n, pl* **-ties** : deception by pretending to feel and act one way while acting another
du·ra·ble \ˈd(y)u̇r-ə-bəl\ *adj* : able to exist for a long time without significant deterioration ⟨∼ clothing⟩ — **du·ra·bil·i·ty** \ˌd(y)u̇r-ə-ˈbil-ət-ē\ *n*
durable press *n* : PERMANENT PRESS
du·rance \ˈd(y)u̇r-əns\ *n* : IMPRISONMENT
du·ra·tion \d(y)u̇-ˈrā-shən\ *n* : the time during which something exists or lasts
du·ress \d(y)u̇-ˈres\ *n* : compulsion by threat ⟨confession made under ∼⟩
dur·ing \ˌd(y)u̇r-iŋ\ *prep* **1** : THROUGHOUT ⟨swims every day ∼ the summer⟩ **2** : at some point in ⟨broke in ∼ the night⟩
dusk \ˈdəsk\ *n* **1** : the darker part of twilight esp. at night **2** : partial darkness
dusky \ˈdəs-kē\ *adj* **dusk·i·er; -est 1** : somewhat dark in color **2** : SHADOWY — **dusk·i·ness** *n*
[1]**dust** \ˈdəst\ *n* **1** : particles of powdery matter **2** : the particles into which something disintegrates **3** : something worthless **4** : the surface of the ground — **dust·less** *adj* — **dusty** *adj*
[2]**dust** *vb* **1** : to make free of or remove dust **2** : to sprinkle with fine particles **3** : to sprinkle in the form of dust
dust bowl *n* : a region suffering from long droughts and dust storms
dust devil *n* : a small whirlwind containing sand or dust
dust·er \ˈdəs-tər\ *n* **1** : one that removes dust **2** : a dress-length housecoat **3** : one that scatters fine particles; *esp* : a device for applying insecticides to crops
dust·pan \ˈdəst-ˌpan\ *n* : a shovel-shaped pan for sweepings
dust storm *n* : a violent wind carrying dust across a dry region
dutch \ˈdəch\ *adv, often cap* : with each person paying his or her own way ⟨go ∼⟩
Dutch \ˈdəch\ *n* **1 Dutch** *pl* : the people of the Netherlands **2** : the language of the Netherlands — **Dutch** *adj* — **Dutch·man** \-mən\ *n*
Dutch elm disease *n* : a fungous disease of elms characterized by yellowing of the foliage, defoliation, and death
Dutch treat *n* : an entertainment (as a meal) for which each person pays his or her own way
du·te·ous \ˈd(y)üt-ē-əs\ *adj* : DUTIFUL, OBEDIENT
du·ti·able \ˈd(y)üt-ē-ə-bəl\ *adj* : subject to a duty ⟨∼ imports⟩
du·ti·ful \ˈd(y)üt-i-fəl\ *adj* **1** : motivated by a sense of duty ⟨a ∼ son⟩ **2** : coming from or showing a sense of duty ⟨∼ affection⟩ — **du·ti·ful·ly** \-f(ə-)lē\ *adv* — **du·ti·ful·ness** *n*
du·ty \ˈd(y)üt-ē\ *n, pl* **duties 1** : conduct or action required by one's occupation or position **2** : assigned service or business; *esp* : active military service **3** : a moral or legal obligation **4** : TAX **5** : the service required (as of a machine) : USE ⟨a heavy-*duty* tire⟩
DV *abbr* **1** [L *Deo volente*] God willing **2** Douay Version
DVM *abbr* doctor of veterinary medicine
[1]**dwarf** \ˈdwȯrf\ *n, pl* **dwarfs** \ˈdwȯ(ə)rfs\ *or* **dwarves** \ˈdwȯrvz\ : one that is much below normal size — **dwarf·ish** *adj*
[2]**dwarf** *vb* **1** : to restrict the growth or development of : STUNT **2** : to cause to appear smaller ⟨people *dwarfed* by tall trees⟩
dwell \ˈdwel\ *vb* **dwelt** \ˈdwelt\ *or* **dwelled** \ˈdweld, ˈdwelt\; **dwell·ing** [ME *dwellen*, fr. OE *dwellan* to go

astray, hinder] **1** : ABIDE, REMAIN **2** : RESIDE, EXIST **3** : to keep the attention directed **4** : to write or speak at length or insistently — **dwell·er** *n*

dwell·ing \ˈdwel-iŋ\ *n* : RESIDENCE

DWI *abbr* driving while intoxicated

dwin·dle \ˈdwin-dᵊl\ *vb* **dwin·dled; dwin·dling** \ˈdwin-d(ᵊ-)liŋ\ : to make or become steadily less : DIMINISH

dwt *abbr* pennyweight

Dy *symbol* dysprosium

dyb·buk \ˈdib-ək\ *n, pl* **dyb·bu·kim** \ˌdib-ú-ˈkēm\ *also* **dybbuks** : a wandering soul believed in Jewish folklore to enter and possess a person

[1]**dye** \ˈdī\ *n* **1** : color produced by dyeing **2** : material used for coloring or staining

[2]**dye** *vb* **dyed; dye·ing** **1** : to impart a new color to esp. by impregnating with a dye **2** : to take up or impart color in dyeing

dye·stuff \ˈdī-ˌstəf\ *n* : DYE 2

dying *pres part of* DIE

dyke *var of* DIKE

dy·nam·ic \dī-ˈnam-ik\ *also* **dy·nam·i·cal** \-i-kəl\ *adj* : of or relating to physical force producing motion : ENERGETIC, FORCEFUL

[1]**dy·na·mite** \ˈdī-nə-ˌmīt\ *n* : an explosive made of nitroglycerin absorbed in a porous material; *also* : a blasting explosive made without nitroglycerin

[2]**dynamite** *vb* **-mit·ed; -mit·ing** : to blow up with dynamite

dy·na·mo \ˈdī-nə-ˌmō\ *n, pl* **-mos** : an electrical generator

dy·na·mom·e·ter \ˌdī-nə-ˈmäm-ət-ər\ *n* : an instrument for measuring mechanical power (as of an engine)

dy·nas·ty \ˈdī-nəs-tē, -ˌnas-\ *n, pl* **-ties** **1** : a succession of rulers of the same family **2** : a powerful group or family that maintains its position for a long time — **dy·nas·tic** \dī-ˈnas-tik\ *adj*

dys·en·tery \ˈdis-ᵊn-ˌter-ē\ *n, pl* **-ter·ies** : a disorder marked by diarrhea with blood and mucus in the feces

dys·lex·ia \dis-ˈlek-sē-ə\ *n* : a disturbance of the ability to read — **dys·lex·ic** \-sik\ *adj or n*

dys·pep·sia \dis-ˈpep-shə, -sē-ə\ *n* : INDIGESTION — **dys·pep·tic** \-ˈpep-tik\ *adj or n*

dys·pro·si·um \dis-ˈprō-zē-əm\ *n* : a metallic chemical element that forms highly magnetic compounds — see ELEMENT table

dys·tro·phy \ˈdis-trə-fē\ *n, pl* **-phies** : any of several disorders involving atrophy of muscular tissue; *esp* : MUSCULAR DYSTROPHY

dz *abbr* dozen

E

[1]**e** \ˈē\ *n, pl* **e's** *or* **es** \ˈēz\ *often cap* **1** : the 5th letter of the English alphabet **2** : the base of the system of natural logarithms having the approximate value 2.71828 **3** : a grade rating a student's work as poor or failing

[2]**e** *abbr, often cap* **1** east; eastern **2** error **3** excellent

E *symbol* einsteinium

ea *abbr* each

[1]**each** \ˈēch\ *adj* : being one of the class named ⟨∼ man⟩

[2]**each** *pron* : every individual one

[3]**each** *adv* : APIECE ⟨cost five cents ∼⟩

each other *pron* : each of two or more in reciprocal action or relation ⟨looked at *each other*⟩

ea·ger \ˈē-gər\ *adj* : marked by urgent or enthusiastic desire or interest ⟨∼ to learn⟩ **syn** avid, anxious, ardent, keen — **ea·ger·ly** *adv* — **ea·ger·ness** *n*

ea·gle \ˈē-gəl\ *n* **1** : a large bird of prey related to the hawks **2** : a score of two under par on a hole in golf

ea·glet \ˈē-glət\ *n* : a young eagle

-ean — see -AN

E and OE *abbr* errors and omissions excepted

[1]**ear** \ˈiər\ *n* **1** : the organ of hearing; *also* : the outer part of this in a vertebrate **2** : something resembling a mammal's ear in shape, position, or function **3** : an ability to understand and appreciate something heard ⟨a good ∼ for music⟩ **4** : sympathetic attention

[2]**ear** *n* : the fruiting spike of a cereal (as wheat)

ear·ache \-ˌāk\ *n* : an ache or pain in the ear

ear·drum \-ˌdrəm\ *n* : a thin membrane that receives and transmits sound waves in the ear

eared \ˈiərd\ *adj* : having ears — used esp. in combination ⟨a long-*eared* dog⟩

earl \ˈərl\ *n* [ME *erl,* fr. OE *eorl* warrior, nobleman] : a member of the British peerage ranking below a marquess and above a viscount — **earl·dom** \-dəm\ *n*

ear·lobe \ˈiər-ˌlōb\ *n* : the pendent part of the ear

[1]**ear·ly** \ˈər-lē\ *adv* **ear·li·er; -est** : at an early time (as in a period or series)

[2]**early** *adj* **ear·li·er; -est** **1** : of, relating to, or occurring near the beginning **2** : ANCIENT, PRIMITIVE **3** : occurring before the usual time ⟨an ∼ breakfast⟩; *also* : occurring in the near future

[1]**ear·mark** \ˈiər-ˌmärk\ *n* : an identification mark (as on the ear of an animal)

[2]**earmark** *vb* : to designate for a specific purpose

ear·muff \-ˌməf\ *n* : one of a pair of ear coverings worn as protection against cold

earn \ˈərn\ *vb* **1** : to receive as a return for service **2** : DESERVE, MERIT **syn** gain, secure, get, obtain, acquire, win

[1]**ear·nest** \ˈər-nəst\ *n* : an intensely serious state of mind ⟨spoke in ∼⟩

[2]**earnest** *adj* **1** : seriously intent and sober ⟨an ∼ face⟩ ⟨an ∼ attempt⟩ **2** : GRAVE, IMPORTANT **syn** solemn, sedate, staid, sober — **ear·nest·ly** *adv* — **ear·nest·ness** \-nəs(t)-nəs\ *n*

[3]**earnest** *n* **1** : something of value given by a buyer to a seller to bind a bargain **2** : PLEDGE

earn·ings \ˈər-niŋz\ *n pl* **1** : something (as wages) earned **2** : the balance of revenue after deduction of costs and expenses

ear·phone \ˈiər-ˌfōn\ *n* : a device that reproduces sound and is worn over or in the ear

ear·plug \-ˌpləg\ *n* : a protective device for insertion into the opening of the ear

ear·ring \-ˌriŋ\ *n* : an ornament for the earlobe

ear·shot \-ˌshät\ *n* : range of hearing

ear·split·ting \-ˌsplit-iŋ\ *adj* : intolerably loud or shrill

earth \ˈərth\ *n* **1** : SOIL, DIRT **2** : LAND, GROUND **3** : the planet inhabited by man : WORLD

earth·en \ˈər-thən\ *adj* : made of earth or baked clay

earth·en·ware \-ˌwaər\ *n* : slightly porous opaque pottery fired at low heat

earth·ling \ˈərth-liŋ\ *n* : an inhabitant of the earth

---

earth·ly \ˈərth-lē\ *adj* : having to do with the earth esp. as distinguished from heaven — **earth·li·ness** *n*

earth·quake \-ˌkwāk\ *n* : a shaking or trembling of a portion of the earth

earth science *n* : any of the sciences (as geology or meteorology) that deal with the earth or one of its parts

earth·shak·ing \ˈərth-ˌshā-kiŋ\ *adj* : of fundamental importance

earth·ward \-wərd\ *or* **earth·wards** \-wərdz\ *adv* : toward the earth

earth·work \ˈərth-ˌwərk\ *n* : an embankment or fortification of earth

earth·worm \-ˌwərm\ *n* : a long segmented worm found in damp soil

earthy \ˈər-thē\ *adj* **earth·i·er; -est** **1** : consisting of or resembling soil **2** : PRACTICAL **3** : COARSE, GROSS — **earth·i·ness** \ˈər-thē-nəs\ *n*

ear·wax \ˈier-ˌwaks\ *n* : the yellow waxy secretion from the ear

ear·wig \-ˌwig\ *n* : any of numerous insects with slender many-jointed antennae and a pair of appendages resembling forceps at the end of the body

¹ease \ˈēz\ *n* **1** : comfort of body or mind **2** : naturalness of manner **3** : freedom from difficulty or effort **syn** relaxation, rest, repose, comfort, leisure

²ease *vb* **eased; eas·ing** **1** : to relieve from distress **2** : to lessen the pressure or tension of **3** : to make or become less difficult ⟨~ credit⟩

ea·sel \ˈē-zəl\ *n* [Dutch, lit., ass] : a frame to hold a painter's canvas or a picture

¹east \ˈēst\ *adv* : to or toward the east

²east *adj* **1** : situated toward or at the east **2** : coming from the east

³east *n* **1** : the general direction of sunrise **2** : the compass point directly opposite to west **3** *cap* : regions or countries east of a specified or implied point — **east·er·ly** \ˈē-stər-lē\ *adv or adj* — **east·ward** *adv or adj* — **east·wards** *adv*

Eas·ter \ˈē-stər\ *n* : a church feast observed on a Sunday in March or April in commemoration of Christ's resurrection

east·ern \ˈē-stərn\ *adj* **1** *often cap* : of, relating to, or characteristic of a region designated East **2** *cap* : of, relating to, or being the Christian churches originating in the Church of the Eastern Roman Empire **3** : lying toward or coming from the east — **East·ern·er** *n*

easy \ˈē-zē\ *adj* **eas·i·er; -est** **1** : marked by ease ⟨an ~ life⟩; *esp* : not causing distress or difficulty ⟨~ tasks⟩ **2** : MILD, LENIENT ⟨be ~ on him⟩ **3** : GRADUAL ⟨an ~ slope⟩ **4** : free from pain, trouble, or worry ⟨rest ~⟩ **5** : LEISURELY ⟨an ~ pace⟩ **6** : NATURAL ⟨an ~ manner⟩ **7** : COMFORTABLE ⟨an ~ chair⟩ **syn** facile, simple, effortless — **eas·i·ly** \ˈēz-(ə-)lē\ *adv* — **eas·i·ness** \-ē-nəs\ *n*

easy·go·ing \ˌē-zē-ˈgō-iŋ\ *adj* : taking life easy : CAREFREE

eat \ˈēt\ *vb* **ate** \ˈāt\; **eat·en** \ˈēt-ᵊn\; **eat·ing** **1** : to take in as food : take food **2** : to use up : DEVOUR **3** : CORRODE — **eat·able** *adj or n* — **eat·er** *n*

eat·ery \ˈēt-ə-rē\ *n, pl* **-er·ies** : LUNCHEONETTE, RESTAURANT

eaves \ˈēvz\ *n pl* : the overhanging lower edge of a roof

eaves·drop \ˈēvz-ˌdräp\ *vb* : to listen secretly — **eaves·drop·per** *n*

¹ebb \ˈeb\ *n* **1** : the flowing back of water brought in by the tide **2** : a point or state of decline

²ebb *vb* **1** : to recede from the flood state **2** : DECLINE ⟨as his fortunes ~*ed*⟩

EBCDIC \ˈep-sə-ˌdik\ *n* [*e*xtended *b*inary *c*oded *d*ecimal *i*nterchange *c*ode] : a computer code for representing alphanumeric information

¹eb·o·ny \ˈeb-ə-nē\ *n, pl* **-nies** : a hard heavy wood of Old World tropical trees **(ebony trees)** related to the persimmon

²ebony *adj* **1** : made of or resembling ebony **2** : BLACK, DARK

ebul·lient \i-ˈbu̇l-yənt, -ˈbəl-\ *adj* **1** : BOILING, AGITATED **2** : EXUBERANT — **ebul·lience** \-yəns\ *n*

ec·cen·tric \ik-ˈsen-trik\ *adj* **1** : deviating from a usual or accepted pattern **2** : deviating from a circular path ⟨~ orbits⟩ **3** : set with axis or support off center ⟨an ~ cam⟩; *also* : being off center **syn** erratic, queer, singular, curious, odd — **eccentric** *n* — **ec·cen·tri·cal·ly** \-tri-k(ə-)lē\ *adv* — **ec·cen·tric·i·ty** \ˌek-ˌsen-ˈtris-ət-ē\ *n*

Eccles *abbr* Ecclesiastes

Ec·cle·si·as·tes \ik-ˌlē-zē-ˈas-tēz\ — see BIBLE table

ec·cle·si·as·tic \ik-ˌlē-zē-ˈas-tik\ *n* : CLERGYMAN

ec·cle·si·as·ti·cal \-ti-kəl\ *or* **ec·cle·si·as·tic** \-tik\ *adj* : of or relating to a church esp. as an institution ⟨~ art⟩ — **ec·cle·si·as·ti·cal·ly** \-ti-k(ə-)lē\ *adv*

Ec·cle·si·as·ti·cus \ik-ˌlē-zē-ˈas-ti-kəs\ *n* — see BIBLE table

Ecclus *abbr* Ecclesiasticus

ECG *abbr* electrocardiogram

ech·e·lon \ˈesh-ə-ˌlän\ *n* [F *échelon*, lit., rung of a ladder] **1** : a steplike arrangement (as of troops or airplanes) **2** : a level (as of authority or responsibility) within an organization

echi·no·derm \i-ˈkī-nə-ˌdərm\ *n* : any of a phylum of marine animals (as starfishes and sea urchins) having similar body parts (as the arms of a starfish) arranged around a central axis and often having a calcium-containing outer skeleton

echo \ˈek-ō\ *n, pl* **ech·oes** : repetition of a sound caused by a reflection of the sound waves; *also* : the reflection of a radar signal by an object — **echo** *vb*

echo·lo·ca·tion \ˌek-o-lō-ˈkā-shən\ *n* : a process for locating distant or invisible objects by means of sound waves reflected back to the sender (as a bat or submarine) by the objects

éclair \ā-ˈklaər\ *n* [F, lit., lightning] : an oblong shell of light pastry with whipped cream or custard filling

éclat \ā-ˈklä\ *n* [F] **1** : a dazzling effect or success **2** : ACCLAIM

eclec·tic \e-ˈklek-tik, i-\ *adj* : selecting or made up of what seems best of varied sources — **eclectic** *n*

¹eclipse \i-ˈklips\ *n* **1** : the total or partial obscuring of one heavenly body by another; *also* : a passing into the shadow of a heavenly body **2** : a falling into obscurity, decline, or disgrace

²eclipse *vb* **eclipsed; eclips·ing** : to cause an eclipse of

eclip·tic \i-ˈklip-tik\ *n* : the great circle of the celestial sphere that is the apparent path of the sun

ec·logue \ˈek-ˌlóg, -ˌläg\ *n* : a pastoral poem

ECM *abbr* European Common Market

ecol *abbr* ecological; ecology

ecol·o·gy \i-ˈkäl-ə-jē, e-\ *n, pl* **-gies** [G *ökologie*, fr. Gk *oikos* house] **1** : a branch of science concerned with the relationships between organisms and their environment **2** : the pattern of relations between organisms and their environment — **eco·log·i·cal** \ˌē-kə-ˈläj-i-kəl, ˌek-ə-\ *also* **eco·log·ic** \-ik\ *adj* — **eco·log·i·cal·ly** \-i-k(ə-)lē\ *adv* — **ecol·o·gist** \i-ˈkäl-ə-jəst, e-\ *n*

econ *abbr* economics; economist; economy

eco·nom·ic \ˌek-ə-ˈnäm-ik, ˌē-kə-\ *adj* : of or relating to the satisfaction of material needs of humans

eco·nom·i·cal \-ˈnäm-i-kəl\ *adj* **1** : THRIFTY **2** : operating with little waste or at a saving **syn** frugal, sparing, provident, thrifty — **ec·o·nom·i·cal·ly** \-k(ə-)lē\ *adv*

eco·nom·ics \ˌek-ə-ˈnäm-iks, ˌē-kə-\ *n* : a branch of knowledge dealing with the production, distribution, and consumption of goods and services — **econ·o·mist** \i-ˈkän-ə-məst\ *n*

econ·o·mize \i-ˈkän-ə-ˌmīz\ *vb* **-mized; -miz·ing** : to practice economy : be frugal

¹econ·o·my \i-ˈkän-ə-mē\ *n, pl* **-mies** [MF *yconomie*, fr. ML *oeconomia*, fr. Gk *oikonomia*, fr. *oikonomos* household manager, fr. *oikos* house + *nemein* to manage] **1** : thrifty management or use of resources; *also* : an instance of this **2** : manner of arrangement or functioning : ORGANIZATION **3** : an economic system ⟨a money ~⟩

²economy *adj* : ECONOMICAL ⟨~ cars⟩

eco·sys·tem \ˈē-kō-ˌsis-təm, ˈek-ō-\ *n* : the complex of an ecological community and its environment functioning as a unit in nature

ecru \ˈek-rü, ˈā-krü\ *n* [F *écru* unbleached] : BEIGE

ec·sta·sy \ˈek-stə-sē\ *n, pl* **-sies** : extreme and usu. rapturous emotional excitement — **ec·stat·ic** \ek-ˈstat-ik, ik-ˈstat-\ *adj* — **ec·stat·i·cal·ly** \-i-k(ə-)lē\ *adv*

Ecua *abbr* Ecuador

ec·u·men·i·cal \ˌek-yə-ˈmen-i-kəl\ *adj* : general in extent or influence; *esp* : promoting or tending toward worldwide Christian unity — **ec·u·men·i·cal·ly** \-k(ə-)lē\ *adv*

ec·ze·ma \ig-ˈzē-mə, ˈeg-zə-mə, ˈek-sə-\ *n* : an itching skin inflammation with crusted lesions — **ec·zem·a·tous** \ig-ˈzem-ət-əs\ *adj*

ed *abbr* **1** edited; edition; editor **2** education

¹-ed \d *after a vowel or* b, g, j, l, m, n, ŋ, r, t͟h, v, z, zh; əd, id *after* d, t; t *after other sounds*\ *vb suffix or adj suffix* **1** — used to form the past participle of regular weak verbs ⟨end*ed*⟩ ⟨fad*ed*⟩ ⟨tri*ed*⟩ ⟨patt*ed*⟩ **2** — used to form adjectives of identical meaning from Latin-derived adjectives ending in *-ate* ⟨pinnat*ed*⟩ **3** : having : characterized by ⟨cultur*ed*⟩ ⟨two-legg*ed*⟩; *also* : having the characteristics of ⟨bigot*ed*⟩

²-ed *vb suffix* — used to form the past tense of regular weak verbs ⟨judg*ed*⟩ ⟨deni*ed*⟩ ⟨dropp*ed*⟩

Edam \ˈēd-əm, ˈē-ˌdam\ *n* : a yellow Dutch pressed cheese made in balls

ed·dy \ˈed-ē\ *n, pl* **eddies** : WHIRLPOOL — **eddy** *vb*

edel·weiss \ˈād-ᵊl-ˌwīs, -ˌvīs\ *n* [G, fr. *edel* noble + *weiss* white] : a small perennial woolly herb that is related to the thistles and grows high in the Alps

ede·ma \i-ˈdē-mə\ *n* : abnormal accumulation of watery fluid in connective tissue or in a serous cavity; *also* : a condition marked by such accumulation — **edem·a·tous** \-ˈdem-ət-əs\ *adj*

Eden \ˈēd-ᵊn\ *n* : PARADISE 2

¹edge \ˈej\ *n* **1** : the cutting side of a blade **2** : power to cut or penetrate : SHARPNESS **3** : the line where something begins or ends; *also* : the area adjoining such an edge **4** : ADVANTAGE — **edged** \ˈejd\ *adj*

²edge *vb* **edged; edg·ing 1** : to give or form an edge **2** : to move or force gradually ⟨~ into a crowd⟩ — **edg·er** *n*

edge·ways \ˈej-ˌwāz\ *adv* : SIDEWAYS

edg·ing \ˈej-iŋ\ *n* : something that forms an edge or border ⟨a lace ~⟩

edgy \ˈej-ē\ *adj* **edg·i·er; -est 1** : SHARP ⟨an ~ tone⟩ **2** : TENSE, NERVOUS — **edg·i·ness** \ˈej-ē-nəs\ *n*

ed·i·ble \ˈed-ə-bəl\ *adj* : fit or safe to be eaten — **ed·i·bil·i·ty** \ˌed-ə-ˈbil-ət-ē\ *n* — **edible** *n*

edict \ˈē-ˌdikt\ *n* : DECREE

ed·i·fi·ca·tion \ˌed-ə-fə-ˈkā-shən\ *n* : instruction and improvement esp. in morality — **ed·i·fy** \ˈed-ə-ˌfī\ *vb*

ed·i·fice \ˈed-ə-fəs\ *n* : a usu. large building

ed·it \ˈed-ət\ *vb* **1** : to revise and prepare for publication **2** : to direct the publication and policies of (as a newspaper) — **ed·i·tor** \ˈed-ət-ər\ *n* — **ed·i·tor·ship** *n*

edi·tion \i-ˈdish-ən\ *n* **1** : the form in which a text is published **2** : the total number of copies (as of a book) published at one time **3** : VERSION

¹ed·i·to·ri·al \ˌed-ə-ˈtōr-ē-əl\ *adj* **1** : of, relating to, or functioning as an editor **2** : being an editorial; *also* : expressing opinion — **ed·i·to·ri·al·ly** \-ē\ *adv*

²editorial *n* : an article (as in a newspaper) giving the views of a publisher; *also* : an expression of opinion resembling an editorial ⟨a television ~⟩

ed·i·to·ri·al·ize \ˌed-ə-ˈtōr-ē-ə-ˌlīz\ *vb* **-ized; -iz·ing 1** : to express an opinion in an editorial **2** : to introduce opinions into factual reporting **3** : to express an opinion — **ed·i·to·ri·al·iza·tion** \-ˌtōr-ē-ə-lə-ˈzā-shən\ *n* — **ed·i·to·ri·al·iz·er** *n*

EDP *abbr* electronic data processing

EDT *abbr* Eastern daylight (saving) time

educ *abbr* education; educational

ed·u·ca·ble \ˈej-ə-kə-bəl\ *adj* : capable of being educated

ed·u·cate \ˈej-ə-ˌkāt\ *vb* **-cat·ed; -cat·ing 1** : to provide with schooling **2** : to develop mentally and morally **syn** train, discipline, school, instruct, teach — **ed·u·ca·tor** \-ˌkāt-ər\ *n*

ed·u·ca·tion \ˌej-ə-ˈkā-shən\ *n* **1** : the action or process of educating or being educated **2** : a field of knowledge dealing with technical aspects of teaching — **ed·u·ca·tion·al** \-sh(ə-)nəl\ *adj*

educational television *n* : PUBLIC TELEVISION

educe \i-ˈd(y)üs\ *vb* **educed; educ·ing 1** : ELICIT, EVOKE **2** : DEDUCE **syn** extract, evince, extort

EE *abbr* electrical engineer

EEC *abbr* European Economic Community

EEG *abbr* **1** electroencephalogram **2** electroencephalograph

eel \ˈēl\ *n* : any of numerous snakelike fishes with a smooth slimy skin

eel

EEO *abbr* equal employment opportunity

ee·rie *also* **ee·ry** \ˈi(ə)r-ē\ *adj* **ee·ri·er; -est** : WEIRD, UNCANNY — **ee·ri·ly** \ˈir-ə-lē\ *adv*

eff *abbr* efficiency

ef·face \i-ˈfās, e-\ *vb* **ef·faced; ef·fac·ing** : to obliterate or obscure by or as if by rubbing out **syn** erase, delete, annul, cancel, expunge — **ef·face·able** *adj* — **ef·face·ment** *n*

¹ef·fect \i-ˈfekt\ *n* **1** : RESULT **2** : MEANING, INTENT **3** : APPEARANCE **4** : FULFILLMENT **5** : INFLUENCE **6** *pl* : GOODS, POSSESSIONS **7** : the quality or state of being operative : OPERATION **syn** consequence, outcome, upshot, aftermath, result, issue

²effect *vb* **1** : ACCOMPLISH ⟨~ repairs⟩ **2** : to put into effect ⟨~ changes⟩

ef·fec·tive \i-ˈfek-tiv\ *adj* **1** : producing a decisive or desired effect **2** : IMPRESSIVE, STRIKING **3** : ready for service or action **4** : being in effect — **ef·fec·tive·ly** *adv* — **ef·fec·tive·ness** *n*

ef·fec·tu·al \i-ˈfek-chə(-wə)l\ *adj* : producing an intended effect : ADEQUATE — **ef·fec·tu·al·ly** \-ē\ *adv*

ef·fec·tu·ate \i-ˈfek-chə-ˌwāt\ *vb* **-at·ed; -at·ing** : BRING ABOUT, EFFECT

ef·fem·i·nate \ə-ˈfem-ə-nət\ *adj* : marked by qualities more typical of and suitable to women than men; : UNMANLY — **ef·fem·i·na·cy** \-nə-sē\ *n*

ef·fen·di \e-ˈfen-dē\ *n* [Turk *efendi* master, fr. NGk *aphentēs*, alter. of Gk *authentēs*] : a man of property, authority, or education in an eastern Mediterranean country

ef·fer·ent \ˈef-ə-rənt\ *adj* : bearing or conducting outward from a more central part ⟨~ nerves⟩

ef·fer·vesce \ˌef-ər-ˈves\ *vb* **-vesced; -vesc·ing** : to bubble and hiss as gas escapes; *also* : to be exhilarated —

ef·fer·ves·cence \-ˈves-ᵊns\ *n* — **ef·fer·ves·cent** \-ᵊnt\ *adj* — **ef·fer·ves·cent·ly** *adv*

ef·fete \e-ˈfēt\ *adj* : worn out : EXHAUSTED; *also* : DECADENT

ef·fi·ca·cious \ˌef-ə-ˈkā-shəs\ *adj* : producing an intended effect ⟨~ remedies⟩ **syn** effectual, effective, efficient — **ef·fi·ca·cy** \ˈef-i-kə-sē\ *n*

ef·fi·cient \i-ˈfish-ənt\ *adj* : productive of desired effects esp. without loss or waste : COMPETENT — **ef·fi·cien·cy** \-ən-sē\ *n* — **ef·fi·cient·ly** *adv*

ef·fi·gy \ˈef-ə-jē\ *n, pl* **-gies** : IMAGE; *esp* : a crude figure of a hated person

ef·flo·resce \ˌef-lə-ˈres\ *vb* **-resced; -resc·ing** : to burst forth : BLOOM

ef·flo·res·cence \-ˈres-ᵊns\ *n* **1** : the period or state of flowering **2** : the action or process of developing **3** : fullness of manifestation : CULMINATION — **ef·flo·res·cent** \-ᵊnt\ *adj*

ef·flu·ence \ˈef-ˌlü-əns\ *n* **1** : something that flows out **2** : an action or process of flowing out — **ef·flu·ent** \-ənt\ *adj or n*

ef·flu·vi·um \e-ˈflü-vē-əm\ *n, pl* **-via** \-vē-ə\ *or* **-vi·ums** [L outflow] **1** : a usu. unpleasant emanation **2** : a by-product usu. in the form of waste

ef·fort \ˈef-ərt\ *n* **1** : EXERTION, ENDEAVOR; *also* : a product of effort **2** : active or applied force — **ef·fort·less** *adj* — **ef·fort·less·ly** *adv*

ef·fron·tery \i-ˈfrənt-ə-rē\ *n, pl* **-ter·ies** : shameless boldness : IMPUDENCE **syn** temerity, audacity, brass, gall, nerve

ef·ful·gence \i-ˈfu̇l-jəns, -ˈfəl-\ *n* : radiant splendor : BRILLIANCE — **ef·ful·gent** \-jənt\ *adj*

ef·fu·sion \i-ˈfyü-zhən, e-\ *n* : a gushing forth; *also* : unrestrained utterance — **ef·fuse** \-ˈfyüz, e-\ *vb* — **ef·fu·sive** \i-ˈfyü-siv, e-\ *adj*

eft \ˈeft\ *n* : NEWT

EFT *or* **EFTS** *abbr* electronic funds transfer (system)

e.g. \f(ə-)rig-ˈzam-pəl, (ˈ)ē-ˈjē\ *abbr* [L *exempli gratia*] for example

Eg *abbr* Egypt; Egyptian

egal·i·tar·i·an·ism \i-ˌgal-ə-ˈter-ē- ə-ˌniz-əm\ *n* : a belief in human equality esp. in social, political, and economic affairs — **egal·i·tar·i·an** *adj or n*

¹egg \ˈeg\ *vb* [ME *eggen*, fr. ON *eggja;* akin to OE *ecg* edge] : to urge to action

²egg *n* [ME *egge*, fr. ON *egg;* akin to OE *ǣg* egg, L *ovum*] **1** : a rounded usu. hard-shelled reproductive body esp. of birds and reptiles from which the young hatches; *also* : the egg of domestic poultry as an article of food ⟨allergic to ~*s*⟩ **2** : a germ cell produced by a female

egg·beat·er \ˈeg-ˌbēt-ər\ *n* : a hand-operated kitchen utensil for beating, stirring, or whipping

egg cell *n* : EGG 2

egg·head \-ˌhed\ *n* : INTELLECTUAL, HIGHBROW

egg·nog \-ˌnäg\ *n* : a drink consisting of eggs beaten up with sugar, milk or cream, and often alcoholic liquor

egg·plant \-ˌplant\ *n* : the edible usu. large and purplish fruit of a plant related to the potato; *also* : the plant

egg roll *n* : a thin egg-dough casing filled with minced vegetables and often bits of meat and usu. fried in deep fat

egg·shell \ˈeg-ˌshel\ *n* : the hard exterior covering of an egg

egis \ˈē-jəs\ *var of* AEGIS

eg·lan·tine \ˈeg-lən-ˌtīn, -ˌtēn\ *n* : SWEETBRIER

ego \ˈē-gō\ *n, pl* **egos** [L, I] **1** : the self as distinguished from others **2** : the one of the three divisions of the psyche in psychoanalytic theory that serves as the organized conscious mediator between the person and reality

ego·cen·tric \ˌē-gō-ˈsen-trik\ *adj* : concerned or overly concerned with the self; *esp* : SELF-CENTERED

ego·ism \ˈē-gə-ˌwiz-əm\ *n* **1** : a doctrine holding self-interest to be the motive or the valid end of action **2** : excessive concern for oneself usu. without exaggerated feelings of self-importance — **ego·ist** \-wəst\ *n* — **ego·is·tic** \ˌē-gə-ˈwis-tik\ *adj* — **ego·is·ti·cal·ly** \-ē\ *adv*

ego·tism \ˈē-gə-ˌtiz-əm\ *n* **1** : the practice of talking about oneself too much **2** : an exaggerated sense of self-importance : CONCEIT — **ego·tist** \-təst\ *n* — **ego·tis·tic** \ˌē-gə-ˈtis-tik\ *or* **ego·tis·ti·cal** \-ti-kəl\ *adj* — **ego·tis·ti·cal·ly** \-ē\ *adv*

ego trip *n* : an act that enhances and satisfies one's ego

egre·gious \i-ˈgrē-jəs\ *adj* [L *egregius* outstanding from the herd, fr. *ex, e* out of + *greg-, grex* flock, herd] : notably bad : FLAGRANT — **egre·gious·ly** *adv* — **egre·gious·ness** *n*

egress \ˈē-ˌgres\ *n* : a way out : EXIT

egret \ˈē-grət, i-ˈgret\ *n* : any of various herons that bear long plumes during the breeding season

Egyp·tian \i-ˈjip-shən\ *n* **1** : a native or inhabitant of Egypt **2** : the language of the ancient Egyptians from earliest times to about the 3d century A.D. — **Egyptian** *adj*

EHF *abbr* extremely high frequency

ei·der \ˈīd-ər\ *n* : any of several northern sea ducks that yield a soft down

ei·der·down \-ˌdau̇n\ *n* : the down of the eider **2** : a quilt filled with eiderdown

ei·do·lon \ī-ˈdō-lən\ *n, pl* **-lons** *or* **-la** \-lə\ **1** : an insubstantial image : PHANTOM **2** : IDEAL

eight \ˈāt\ *n* **1** : one more than seven **2** : the 8th in a set or series **3** : something having eight units; *esp* : an 8-cylinder engine or automobile — **eight** *adj or pron* — **eighth** \ˈātth\ *adj or adv or n*

eight ball *n* : a black pool ball numbered 8 — **behind the eight ball** : in a highly disadvantageous position or baffling situation

eigh·teen \ˈā(t)-ˈtēn\ *n* : one more than 17 — **eighteen** *adj or pron* — **eigh·teenth** \-ˈtēnth\ *adj or n*

eighty \ˈāt-ē\ *n, pl* **eight·ies** : eight times 10 — **eight·i·eth** \ˈāt-ē-əth\ *adj or n* — **eighty** *adj or pron*

ein·stei·ni·um \īn-ˈstī-nē-əm\ *n* : an artificially produced radioactive element — see ELEMENT table

¹ei·ther \ˈē-t͟hər, ˈī-\ *adj* **1** : being the one and the other of two : EACH ⟨trees on ~ side⟩ **2** : being the one or the other of two ⟨take ~ road⟩

²either *pron* : the one or the other

³either *conj* — used as a function word before the first of two or more words or word groups of which the last is preceded by *or* to indicate that they represent alternatives ⟨a statement is ~ true or false⟩

ejac·u·late \i-ˈjak-yə-ˌlāt\ *vb* **-lat·ed; -lat·ing 1** : to eject a fluid (as semen) **2** : to utter suddenly : EXCLAIM — **ejac·u·la·tion** \-ˌjak-yə-ˈlā-shən\ *n* — **ejac·u·la·to·ry** \-ˈjak-yə-lə-ˌtōr-ē\ *adj*

eject \i-ˈjekt\ *vb* : to drive or throw out or off **syn** expel, oust, evict, dismiss — **ejec·tion** \-ˈjek-shən\ *n*

ejection seat *n* : an emergency escape seat for propelling an occupant out of an airplane

eke \ˈēk\ *vb* **eked; ek·ing** : to gain, supplement, or extend usu. with effort — usu. used with *out* ⟨~ out a living⟩

EKG *abbr* [G *elektrokardiogramm*] **1** : electrocardiogram **2** : electrocardiograph

ekue·le \ā-ˈkwā-(ˌ)lā\ *n, pl* **ekuele** — see MONEY table

el *abbr* elevation

¹elab·o·rate \i-ˈlab-(ə-)rət\ *adj* **1** : planned or carried out with care and in detail **2** : being complex and usu. ornate — **elab·o·rate·ly** *adv* — **elab·o·rate·ness** *n*

²elab·o·rate \i-ˈlab-ə-ˌrāt\ *vb* **-rat·ed; -rat·ing 1** : to build up from simpler ingredients **2** : to work out in detail : develop fully — **elab·o·ra·tion** \-ˌlab-ə-ˈrā-shən\ *n*

élan \ā-ˈläⁿ\ *n* [F] : ARDOR, SPIRIT

eland \ˈē-lənd, -ˌland\ *n, pl* **eland** *also* **elands** [Afrikaans, elk] : either of two large African antelopes with spirally twisted horns

elapse \i-ˈlaps\ *vb* **elapsed; elaps·ing** : to slip by : PASS
¹elas·tic \i-ˈlas-tik\ *adj* **1** : SPRINGY **2** : FLEXIBLE, PLIABLE **3** : ADAPTABLE **syn** resilient, supple, stretch — **elas·tic·i·ty** \-ˌlas-ˈtis-ət-ē, ˌē-ˌlas-\ *n*
²elastic *n* **1** : elastic material **2** : a rubber band
elate \i-ˈlāt\ *vb* **elat·ed; elat·ing** : to fill with joy — **ela·tion** \-ˈlā-shən\ *n*
¹el·bow \ˈel-ˌbō\ *n* **1** : the joint of the arm; *also* : the outer curve of the bent arm **2** : a bend or joint resembling an elbow in shape
²elbow *vb* : to push aside with the elbow; *also* : to make one's way by elbowing
el·bow·room \ˈel-ˌbō-ˌrüm, -ˌru̇m\ *n* **1** : room for moving the elbows freely **2** : enough space for work or operation
¹el·der \ˈel-dər\ *n* : ELDERBERRY 2
²elder *adj* **1** : OLDER **2** : EARLIER, FORMER **3** : of higher rank : SENIOR
³elder *n* **1** : an older individual : SENIOR **2** : one having authority by reason of age and experience **3** : a church officer
el·der·ber·ry \ˈel-də(r)-ˌber-ē\ *n* **1** : the edible black or red fruit of a shrub or tree related to the honeysuckle and bearing flat clusters of small white or pink flowers **2** : a tree or shrub bearing elderberries
el·der·ly \ˈel-dər-lē\ *adj* **1** : rather old; *esp* : past middle age **2** : of, relating to, or characteristic of later life
el·dest \ˈel-dəst\ *adj* : of the greatest age
El Do·ra·do \ˌel-də-ˈräd-ō, -ˈrād-\ *n* [Sp, lit., the gilded one] : a place of vast riches or abundance
elec *abbr* electric; electrical; electricity
¹elect \i-ˈlekt\ *adj* **1** : CHOSEN, SELECT **2** : elected but not yet installed in office ⟨the president-*elect*⟩
²elect *n, pl* **elect 1** : a selected person **2** *pl* : a select or exclusive group
³elect *vb* **1** : to select by vote (as for office or membership) **2** : CHOOSE, PICK **syn** prefer, select
elec·tion \i-ˈlek-shən\ *n* **1** : an act or process of electing **2** : the fact of being elected
elec·tion·eer \i-ˌlek-shə-ˈniər\ *vb* : to work for the election of a candidate or party
¹elec·tive \i-ˈlek-tiv\ *adj* **1** : chosen or filled by election **2** : permitting a choice : OPTIONAL
²elective *n* : an elective course or subject of study
elec·tor \i-ˈlek-tər\ *n* **1** : one qualified to vote in an election **2** : one elected to an electoral college — **elec·tor·al** \i-ˈlek-t(ə-)rəl\ *adj*
electoral college *n* : a body of electors who elect the president and vice president of the U.S.
elec·tor·ate \i-ˈlek-t(ə-)rət\ *n* : a body of persons entitled to vote
elec·tric \i-ˈlek-trik\ *or* **elec·tri·cal** \-tri-kəl\ *adj* [NL *electricus* produced from amber by friction, electric, fr. ML, of amber, fr. L *electrum* amber, fr. Gk *ēlektron*] **1** : of, relating to, operated by, or produced by electricity **2** : ELECTRIFYING, THRILLING — **elec·tri·cal·ly** \-k(ə-)lē\ *adv*
electrical storm *n* : THUNDERSTORM
electric chair *n* : a chair used in legal electrocution
electric eye *n* : PHOTOELECTRIC CELL
elec·tri·cian \i-ˌlek-ˈtrish-ən\ *n* : one who installs, operates, or repairs electrical equipment
elec·tric·i·ty \i-ˌlek-ˈtris-(ə-)tē\ *n, pl* **-ties 1** : a form of energy that occurs in nature and is observable in natural phenomena (as lightning) and that can be produced by friction, chemical reaction, or mechanical effort **2** : electric current
elec·tri·fy \i-ˈlek-trə-ˌfī\ *vb* **-fied; -fy·ing 1** : to charge with electricity **2** : to equip for use of electric power **3** : THRILL — **elec·tri·fi·ca·tion** \-ˌlek-trə-fə-ˈkā-shən\ *n*
elec·tro·car·dio·gram \i-ˌlek-trō-ˈkärd-ē-ə-ˌgram\ *n* : the tracing made by an electrocardiograph
elec·tro·car·dio·graph \-ˌgraf\ *n* : an instrument for recording the changes of electrical potential occurring during the heartbeat — **elec·tro·car·dio·graph·ic** \-ˌkärd-ē-ə-ˈgraf-ik\ *adj* — **elec·tro·car·di·og·ra·phy** \-ē-ˈäg-rə-fē\ *n*
elec·tro·chem·is·try \-ˈkem-ə-strē\ *n* : a branch of chemistry that deals with the relation of electricity to chemical changes — **elec·tro·chem·i·cal** \-ˈkem-i-kəl\ *adj*
elec·tro·cute \i-ˈlek-trə-ˌkyüt\ *vb* **-cut·ed; -cut·ing** : to kill by an electric shock; *esp* : to kill (a criminal) in this way — **elec·tro·cu·tion** \-ˌlek-trə-ˈkyü-shən\ *n*
elec·trode \i-ˈlek-ˌtrōd\ *n* : a conductor used to establish electrical contact with a nonmetallic part of a circuit
elec·tro·en·ceph·a·lo·gram \i-ˌlek-trō-in-ˈsef-ə-lə-ˌgram\ *n* : the tracing of the electrical activity of the brain that is made by an electroencephalograph
elec·tro·en·ceph·a·lo·graph \-ˌgraf\ *n* : an apparatus for detecting and recording the electrical activity of the brain — **elec·tro·en·ceph·a·lo·graph·ic** \-ˌsef-ə-lə-ˈgraf-ik\ *adj* — **elec·tro·en·ceph·a·log·ra·phy** \-ˈläg-rə-fē\ *n*
elec·trol·o·gist \i-ˌlek-ˈträl-ə-jəst\ *n* : one that uses electrical means to remove hair, warts, moles, and birthmarks from the body
elec·trol·y·sis \i-ˌlek-ˈträl-ə-səs\ *n* **1** : the production of chemical changes by passage of an electric current through an electrolyte **2** : the destruction of hair roots with an electric current — **elec·tro·lyt·ic** \-trə-ˈlit-ik\ *adj*
elec·tro·lyte \i-ˈlek-trə-ˌlīt\ *n* : a nonmetallic electric conductor in which current is carried by the movement of ions; *also* : a substance whose solution or molten form is such a conductor
elec·tro·mag·net \i-ˌlek-trō-ˈmag-nət\ *n* : a core of magnetic material surrounded by a coil of wire through which an electric current is passed to magnetize the core
elec·tro·mag·net·ic \-mag-ˈnet-ik\ *adj* : of, relating to, or produced by electromagnetism
electromagnetic radiation *n* : a series of electromagnetic waves
electromagnetic wave *n* : a wave (as a radio wave, an X ray, or a wave of visible light) that consists of associated electric and magnetic effects and that travels at the speed of light
elec·tro·mag·ne·tism \i-ˌlek-trō-ˈmag-nə-ˌtiz-əm\ *n* **1** : magnetism developed by a current of electricity **2** : physics dealing with the relations between electricity and magnetism
elec·tro·mo·tive force \i-ˌlek-trə-ˌmōt-iv-\ *n* : the work per unit charge required to carry a positive charge around a closed path in an electric field
elec·tron \i-ˈlek-ˌträn\ *n* : a negatively charged elementary particle that forms the part of an atom outside the nucleus
elec·tron·ic \i-ˌlek-ˈträn-ik\ *adj* : of or relating to electrons or electronics — **elec·tron·i·cal·ly** \-i-k(ə-)lē\ *adv*
electronic mail *n* : messages sent and received electronically
elec·tron·ics \i-ˌlek-ˈträn-iks\ *n* **1** : the physics of electrons and their utilization **2** : electronic devices or equipment
electron microscope *n* : an instrument in which a focused beam of electrons is used to produce an enlarged image of a minute object on a fluorescent screen or photographic plate
electron tube *n* : a device in which electrical conduction by electrons takes place within a container and which is used for the controlled flow of electrons
elec·tro·pho·re·sis \i-ˌlek-trə-fə-ˈrē-səs\ *n* : the movement

of suspended particles through a fluid by an electromotive force — **elec·tro·pho·ret·ic** \-ˈrēt-ik\ *adj*

elec·tro·plate \i-ˈlek-trə-ˌplāt\ *vb* : to coat (as with metal) by electrolysis

elec·tro·pos·i·tive \i-ˌlek-trō-ˈpäz-ət-iv\ *adj* : having a tendency to give up electrons

elec·tro·shock therapy \-trō-ˌshäk-\ *n* : the treatment of mental disorder by the induction of coma with an electric current

elec·tro·stat·ics \i-ˌlek-trə-ˈstat-iks\ *n* : physics dealing with the interactions of stationary electric charges

el·ee·mos·y·nary \ˌel-i-ˈmäs-ᵊn-ˌer-ē\ *adj* : CHARITABLE

el·e·gance \ˈel-i-gəns\ *n* **1** : refined gracefulness; *also* : tasteful richness (as of design) **2** : something marked by elegance — **el·e·gant** \-gənt\ *adj* — **el·e·gant·ly** *adv*

el·e·gy \ˈel-ə-jē\ *n, pl* **-gies** : a poem expressing grief for one who is dead; *also* : a reflective poem usu. melancholy in tone — **ele·gi·ac** \ˌel-ə-ˈjī-ək, -ˌak\ *adj*

elem *abbr* elementary

el·e·ment \ˈel-ə-mənt\ *n* **1** *pl* : weather conditions; *esp* : severe weather ⟨boards exposed to the ∼*s*⟩ **2** : natural environment ⟨in her ∼⟩ **3** : a constituent part **4** *pl* : the simplest principles (as of an art or science) : RUDIMENTS **5** : a basic member of a mathematical set **6** : a substance not separable by ordinary chemical means into substances different from itself **syn** component, ingredient, factor, constituent — **el·e·men·tal** \ˌel-ə-ˈment-ᵊl\ *adj*

CHEMICAL ELEMENTS

ELEMENT	SYMBOL	ATOMIC NUMBER	ATOMIC WEIGHT (C = 12)
actinium	Ac	89	227.0278
aluminum	Al	13	26.98154
americium	Am	95	
antimony	Sb	51	121.75
argon	Ar	18	39.948
arsenic	As	33	74.9216
astatine	At	85	
barium	Ba	56	137.33
berkelium	Bk	97	
beryllium	Be	4	9.01218
bismuth	Bi	83	208.9804
boron	B	5	10.81
bromine	Br	35	79.904
cadmium	Cd	48	112.41
calcium	Ca	20	40.08
californium	Cf	98	
carbon	C	6	12.011
cerium	Ce	58	140.12
cesium	Cs	55	132.9054
chlorine	Cl	17	35.453
chromium	Cr	24	51.996
cobalt	Co	27	58.9332
copper	Cu	29	63.546
curium	Cm	96	
dysprosium	Dy	66	162.50
einsteinium	Es	99	
erbium	Er	68	167.26
europium	Eu	63	151.96
fermium	Fm	100	
fluorine	F	9	18.998403
francium	Fr	87	
gadolinium	Gd	64	157.25
gallium	Ga	31	69.72
germanium	Ge	32	72.59
gold	Au	79	196.9665
hafnium	Hf	72	178.49
helium	He	2	4.00260
holmium	Ho	67	164.9304
hydrogen	H	1	1.0079
indium	In	49	114.82
iodine	I	53	126.9045
iridium	Ir	77	192.22
iron	Fe	26	55.847
krypton	Kr	36	83.80
lanthanum	La	57	138.9055
lawrencium	Lr	103	
lead	Pb	82	207.2
lithium	Li	3	6.941
lutetium	Lu	71	174.967
magnesium	Mg	12	24.305
manganese	Mn	25	54.9380
mendelevium	Md	101	
mercury	Hg	80	200.59
molybdenum	Mo	42	95.94
neodymium	Nd	60	144.24
neon	Ne	10	20.179
neptunium	Np	93	237.0482
nickel	Ni	28	58.69
niobium	Nb	41	92.9064
nitrogen	N	7	14.0067
nobelium	No	102	
osmium	Os	76	190.2
oxygen	O	8	15.9994
palladium	Pd	46	106.42
phosphorus	P	15	30.97376
platinum	Pt	78	195.08
plutonium	Pu	94	
polonium	Po	84	
potassium	K	19	39.0983
praseodymium	Pr	59	140.9077
promethium	Pm	61	
protactinium	Pa	91	231.0359
radium	Ra	88	226.0254
radon	Rn	86	
rhenium	Re	75	186.207
rhodium	Rh	45	102.9055
rubidium	Rb	37	85.4678
ruthenium	Ru	44	101.07
samarium	Sm	62	150.36
scandium	Sc	21	44.9559
selenium	Se	34	78.96
silicon	Si	14	28.0855
silver	Ag	47	107.868
sodium	Na	11	22.98977
strontium	Sr	38	87.62
sulfur	S	16	32.06
tantalum	Ta	73	180.9479
technetium	Tc	43	
tellurium	Te	52	127.60
terbium	Tb	65	158.9254
thallium	Tl	81	204.383
thorium	Th	90	232.0381
thulium	Tm	69	168.9342
tin	Sn	50	118.69
titanium	Ti	22	47.88
tungsten	W	74	183.85
unnilhexium	Unh	106	
unnilpentium	Unp	105	
unnilquadium	Unq	104	
uranium	U	92	238.0289
vanadium	V	23	50.9415
xenon	Xe	54	131.29
ytterbium	Yb	70	173.04
yttrium	Y	39	88.9059
zinc	Zn	30	65.38
zirconium	Zr	40	91.22

el·e·men·ta·ry \ˌel-ə-ˈmen-t(ə-)rē\ *adj* : SIMPLE, RUDIMENTARY; *also* : of, relating to, or teaching the basic subjects of education

elementary particle *n* : a subatomic particle (as the electron or photon) of matter and energy that does not appear to be made up of other smaller particles

elementary school *n* : a school usu. including the first six or the first eight grades

el·e·phant \ˈel-ə-fənt\ *n* : any of a family of huge thickset nearly hairless mammals that have the snout lengthened into a trunk and two long curving pointed tusks which furnish ivory

elephant: *1* African, *2* Indian

el·e·phan·ti·a·sis \ˌel-ə-fən-ˈtī-ə-səs\ *n, pl* **-a·ses** \-ˌsēz\ : enlargement and thickening of tissues in response esp. to infection by minute parasitic worms

el·e·phan·tine \ˌel-ə-ˈfan-ˌtēn, -ˌtīn, ˈel-ə-fən-\ *adj* **1** : of great size or strength **2** : CLUMSY, PONDEROUS

elev *abbr* elevation

el·e·vate \ˈel-ə-ˌvāt\ *vb* **-vat·ed; -vat·ing 1** : to lift up : RAISE **2** : EXALT, ENNOBLE **3** : ELATE

el·e·va·tion \ˌel-ə-ˈvā-shən\ *n* **1** : the height to which something is raised (as above sea level) **2** : a lifting up **3** : something (as a hill or swelling) that is elevated **syn** altitude, height

el·e·va·tor \ˈel-ə-ˌvāt-ər\ *n* **1** : a cage or platform for conveying something from one level to another **2** : a building for storing and discharging grain **3** : a movable surface on an airplane to produce motion up or down

elev·en \i-ˈlev-ən\ *n* **1** : one more than 10 **2** : the 11th in a set or series **3** : something having 11 units; *esp* : a football team — **eleven** *adj or pron* — **elev·enth** \-ənth\ *adj or n*

elf \ˈelf\ *n, pl* **elves** \ˈelvz\ : a mischievous fairy — **elf·in** \ˈel-fən\ *adj* — **elf·ish** \ˈel-fish\ *adj*

ELF *abbr* extremely low frequency

elic·it \i-ˈlis-ət\ *vb* : to draw out or forth **syn** evoke, educe, extract, extort

elide \i-ˈlīd\ *vb* **elid·ed; elid·ing** : to suppress or alter by elision

el·i·gi·ble \ˈel-ə-jə-bəl\ *adj* : qualified to participate or to be chosen — **el·i·gi·bil·i·ty** \ˌel-ə-jə-ˈbil-ət-ē\ *n* — **eligible** *n*

elim·i·nate \i-ˈlim-ə-ˌnāt\ *vb* **-nat·ed; -nat·ing** [L *eliminatus,* pp. of *eliminare,* fr. *limen* threshold] **1** : EXCLUDE, EXPEL; *esp* : to pass (wastes) from the body **2** : to leave out : IGNORE — **elim·i·na·tion** \-ˌlim-ə-ˈnā-shən\ *n*

eli·sion \i-ˈlizh-ən\ *n* : the omission of a final or initial sound or a word; *esp* : the omission of an unstressed vowel or syllable in a verse to achieve a uniform rhythm

elite \ā-ˈlēt\ *n* [F *élite*] **1** : the choice part; *also* : a superior group **2** : a typewriter type providing 12 characters to the inch

elit·ism \-ˈlēt-ˌiz-əm\ *n* : leadership or rule by an elite; *also* : advocacy of such elitism

elix·ir \i-ˈlik-sər\ *n* [ME, fr. ML, fr. Ar *al-iksīr* the elixir, fr. *al* the + *iksīr* elixir] **1** : a substance held capable of prolonging life indefinitely; *also* : PANACEA **2** : a sweetened alcoholic medicinal solution

Eliz·a·be·than \i-ˌliz-ə-ˈbē-thən\ *adj* : of, relating to, or characteristic of Elizabeth I of England or her times

elk \ˈelk\ *n, pl* **elks 1** : the largest existing deer of Europe and Asia related to the American moose and having broad spreading antlers **2** : a large North American deer with curved antlers having many branches

¹ell \ˈel\ *n* : a unit of length; *esp* : a former English cloth measure of 45 inches (1.1 meters)

²ell *n* : an extension at right angles to a building **syn** wing, annex, arm

el·lipse \i-ˈlips, e-\ *n* : a closed curve of oval shape

el·lip·sis \i-ˈlip-səs, e-\ *n, pl* **el·lip·ses** \-ˌsēz\ **1** : omission from an expression of a word clearly implied **2** : marks (as . . . or ***) to show omission

el·lip·soid \i-ˈlip-ˌsȯid, e-\ *n* : a surface all plane sections of which are circles or ellipses — **ellipsoid** *or* **el·lip·soi·dal** \-ˌlip-ˈsȯid-ᵊl\ *adj*

el·lip·tic \i-ˈlip-tik, e-\ *or* **el·lip·ti·cal** \-ti-kəl\ *adj* **1** : of, relating to, or shaped like an ellipse **2** : of, relating to, or marked by ellipsis — **el·lip·ti·cal·ly** \-ti-k(ə-)lē\ *adv*

elm \ˈelm\ *n* : any of a genus of large graceful trees that have toothed leaves and nearly circular one-seeded winged fruits and are often grown as shade trees; *also* : the wood of an elm

el·o·cu·tion \ˌel-ə-ˈkyü-shən\ *n* : the art of effective public speaking — **el·o·cu·tion·ist** \-sh(ə-)nəst\ *n*

elon·gate \i-ˈlȯŋ-ˌgāt\ *vb* **-gat·ed; -gat·ing** : to make or grow longer **syn** extend, lengthen, prolong, protract — **elon·ga·tion** \(ˌ)ē-ˌlȯŋ-ˈgā-shən\ *n*

elope \i-ˈlōp\ *vb* **eloped; elop·ing** : to run away esp. to be married — **elope·ment** *n*

el·o·quent \ˈel-ə-kwənt\ *adj* **1** : having or showing clear and forceful expression **2** : clearly showing some feeling or meaning — **el·o·quence** \-kwəns\ *n* — **el·o·quent·ly** *adv*

¹else \ˈels\ *adv* **1** : in a different manner or place or at a different time ⟨where ~ can we meet⟩ **2** : OTHERWISE ⟨obey or ~ you'll be sorry⟩

²else *adj* : OTHER; *esp* : being in addition ⟨what ~ do you want⟩

else·where \-ˌhweər\ *adv* : in or to another place

elu·ci·date \i-ˈlü-sə-ˌdāt\ *vb* **-dat·ed; -dat·ing** : to make clear usu. by explanation **syn** clarify, explain, illuminate — **elu·ci·da·tion** \-ˌlü-sə-ˈdā-shən\ *n*

elude \ē-ˈlüd\ *vb* **elud·ed; elud·ing 1** : EVADE **2** : to escape the notice of

elu·sive \ē-ˈlü-siv\ *adj* : tending to elude : EVASIVE — **elu·sive·ly** *adv* — **elu·sive·ness** *n*

el·ver \ˈel-vər\ *n* [alter. of *eelfare* (migration of eels)] : a young eel

elves *pl of* ELF

Ely·si·um \i-ˈliz(h)-ē-əm\ *n, pl* **-si·ums** *or* **-sia** \-ē-ə\ : PARADISE 2 — **Ely·sian** \-ˈlizh-ən\ *adj*

em \ˈem\ *n* : a length approximately the width of the letter *M*

EM *abbr* **1** electromagnetic **2** electron microscope **3** enlisted man

ema·ci·ate \i-ˈmā-shē-ˌāt\ *vb* **-at·ed; -at·ing** : to become or cause to become very thin — **ema·ci·a·tion** \-ˌmā-s(h)ē-ˈā-shən\ *n*

emalangeni *pl of* LILANGENI

em·a·nate \ˈem-ə-ˌnāt\ *vb* **-nat·ed; -nat·ing** : to come out from a source **syn** proceed, spring, rise, arise, originate — **em·a·na·tion** \ˌem-ə-ˈnā-shən\ *n*

eman·ci·pate \i-ˈman-sə-ˌpāt\ *vb* **-pat·ed; -pat·ing** : to set free **syn** liberate, release, deliver, discharge — **eman·ci·pa·tion** \-ˌman-sə-ˈpā-shən\ *n* — **eman·ci·pa·tor** \-ˈman-sə-ˌpāt-ər\ *n*

emas·cu·late \i-ˈmas-kyə-ˌlāt\ *vb* **-lat·ed; -lat·ing** : CASTRATE, GELD; *also* : WEAKEN — **emas·cu·la·tion** \-ˌmas-kyə-ˈlā-shən\ *n*

em·balm \im-ˈbäm, -ˈbälm\ *vb* : to treat (a corpse) with preservative preparations — **em·balm·er** *n*

em·bank \im-ˈbaŋk\ *vb* : to enclose or confine by an embankment

em·bank·ment \-mənt\ *n* : a raised structure (as of earth) to hold back water or carry a roadway

em·bar·go \im-ˈbär-gō\ *n, pl* **-goes** [Sp, fr. *embargar* to bar] : a prohibition on commerce — **embargo** *vb*

em·bark \im-ˈbärk\ *vb* **1** : to put or go on board a ship or airplane **2** : to make a start — **em·bar·ka·tion** \ˌem-ˌbär-ˈkā-shən\ *n*

em·bar·rass \im-ˈbar-əs\ *vb* **1** : CONFUSE, DISCONCERT **2** : to involve in financial difficulties **3** : HINDER, IMPEDE — **em·bar·rass·ing·ly** *adv* — **em·bar·rass·ment** *n*

em·bas·sy \ˈem-bə-sē\ *n, pl* **-sies 1** : the function, position, or mission of an ambassador **2** : a group of representatives headed by an ambassador **3** : the official residence and offices of an ambassador

em·bat·tle \im-ˈbat-ᵊl\ *vb* **-tled; -tling** \-ˈbat-(ᵊ-)liŋ\ : to arrange in order for battle

em·bat·tled *adj* **1** : engaged in battle, conflict, or controversy **2** : being a site of battle, conflict, or controversy **3** : characterized by conflict or controversy

em·bed \im-ˈbed\ *vb* **em·bed·ded; em·bed·ding** : to enclose closely in a surrounding mass

em·bel·lish \im-ˈbel-ish\ *vb* **1** : ADORN, DECORATE **2** : to add ornamental details to **syn** beautify, deck, bedeck, garnish, ornament, dress — **em·bel·lish·ment** *n*

em·ber \ˈem-bər\ *n* **1** : a glowing or smoldering fragment from a fire **2** *pl* : smoldering remains of a fire

em·bez·zle \im-ˈbez-əl\ *vb* **-zled; -zling** \-(ə-)liŋ\ : to steal (as money) by falsifying records — **em·bez·zle·ment** *n* — **em·bez·zler** \-(ə-)lər\ *n*

em·bit·ter \im-ˈbit-ər\ *vb* **1** : to make bitter **2** : to arouse bitter feelings in

em·bla·zon \-ˈblāz-ᵊn\ *vb* **1** : to adorn with heraldic devices **2** : to display conspicuously

em·blem \ˈem-bləm\ *n* : something (as an object or picture) suggesting another object or an idea : SYMBOL — **em·blem·at·ic** \ˌem-blə-ˈmat-ik\ *also* **em·blem·at·i·cal** \-i-kəl\ *adj*

em·body \im-ˈbäd-ē\ *vb* **em·bod·ied; em·body·ing 1** : INCARNATE **2** : to express in definite form **3** : to incorporate into a system or body **syn** combine, incorporate, integrate — **em·bodi·ment** \-ˈbäd-i-mənt\ *n*

em·bold·en \im-ˈbōl-dən\ *vb* : to inspire with courage

em·bo·lism \ˈem-bə-ˌliz-əm\ *n* : the obstruction of a blood vessel by a foreign or abnormal particle

em·bon·point \äⁿ-bōⁿ-pwaⁿ\ *n* [F] : plumpness of person : STOUTNESS

em·boss \im-ˈbäs, -ˈbȯs\ *vb* : to ornament with raised work

em·bou·chure \ˌäm-bü-ˈshu̇r\ *n* [F, deriv. of *bouche* mouth] : the position and use of the lips in producing a musical tone on a wind instrument

em·bow·er \im-ˈbau̇-(-ə)r\ *vb* : to shelter or enclose in a bower

[1]**em·brace** \im-ˈbrās\ *vb* **em·braced; em·brac·ing 1** : to clasp in the arms; *also* : CHERISH, LOVE **2** : ENCIRCLE **3** : TAKE UP, ADOPT; *also* : WELCOME **4** : INCLUDE **5** : to participate in an embrace **syn** comprehend, involve, encompass, embody

[2]**embrace** *n* : an encircling with the arms

em·bra·sure \im-ˈbrā-zhər\ *n* **1** : a recess of a door or window **2** : an opening in a wall through which a cannon is fired

em·bro·ca·tion \ˌem-brə-ˈkā-shən\ *n* : LINIMENT

em·broi·der \im-ˈbrȯid-ər\ *vb* **-dered; -der·ing** \-(ə-)riŋ\ **1** : to ornament with or do needlework **2** : to elaborate with exaggerated detail

em·broi·dery \im-ˈbrȯid-(ə-)rē\ *n, pl* **-der·ies 1** : the forming of decorative designs with needlework **2** : something embroidered

em·broil \im-ˈbrȯil\ *vb* **1** : to throw into confusion or strife **2** : to involve in conflict or difficulties — **em·broil·ment** *n*

em·bryo \ˈem-brē-ˌō\ *n, pl* **embryos** : a living thing in its earliest stages of development — **em·bry·on·ic** \ˌem-brē-ˈän-ik\ *adj*

em·bry·ol·o·gy \ˌem-brē-ˈäl-ə-jē\ *n* : a branch of biology dealing with embryos and their development — **em·bry·o·log·i·cal** \-i-kəl\ *adj* — **em·bry·ol·o·gist** \-brē-ˈäl-ə-jəst\ *n*

em·cee \ˈem-ˈsē\ *n* : MASTER OF CEREMONIES — **emcee** *vb*

emend \ē-ˈmend\ *vb* : to correct usu. by altering the text of **syn** rectify, revise, amend — **emen·da·tion** \ˌē-ˌmen-ˈdā-shən\ *n*

emer *abbr* emeritus

[1]**em·er·ald** \ˈem-(ə-)rəld\ *n* : a green beryl prized as a gem

[2]**emerald** *adj* : brightly or richly green

emerge \i-ˈmərj\ *vb* **emerged; emerg·ing** : to rise, come forth, or come out into view **syn** appear, loom, show — **emer·gence** \-ˈmər-jəns\ *n* — **emer·gent** \-jənt\ *adj*

emer·gen·cy \i-ˈmər-jən-sē\ *n, pl* **-cies** : an unforeseen event or condition requiring prompt action **syn** exigency, contingency, crisis, juncture

emer·i·ta \i-ˈmer-ət-ə\ *adj* : EMERITUS — used of a woman

emer·i·tus \i-ˈmer-ət-əs\ *adj* [L] : retired from active duty ⟨professor ~⟩

em·ery \ˈem-(ə-)rē\ *n, pl* **em·er·ies** : a dark granular corundum used esp. for grinding and polishing

emet·ic \i-ˈmet-ik\ *n* : an agent that induces vomiting — **emetic** *adj*

emf *abbr* electromotive force

em·i·grate \ˈem-ə-ˌgrāt\ *vb* **-grat·ed; -grat·ing** : to leave a place (as a country) to settle elsewhere — **em·i·grant** \-i-grənt\ *n* — **em·i·gra·tion** \ˌem-ə-ˈgrā-shən\ *n*

émi·gré *also* **emi·gré** \ˈem-i-ˌgrā, ˌem-i-ˈgrā\ *n* [F] : a person who emigrates esp. because of political conditions

em·i·nence \ˈem-ə-nəns\ *n* **1** : high rank or position; *also* : a person of high rank or attainments **2** : a lofty place

em·i·nent \ˈem-ə-nənt\ *adj* **1** : CONSPICUOUS, EVIDENT **2** : DISTINGUISHED, PROMINENT ⟨~ men⟩ — **em·i·nent·ly** *adv*

eminent domain *n* : a right of a government to take private property for public use

emir \i-ˈmiər, ā-\ *n* [Ar *amīr* commander] : a native ruler in parts of Africa and Asia — **emir·ate** \ˈem-ər-ət\ *n*

em·is·sary \ˈem-ə-ˌser-ē\ *n, pl* **-sar·ies** : AGENT; *esp* : a secret agent

emit \ē-ˈmit\ *vb* **emit·ted; emit·ting 1** : to give off or out ⟨~ light⟩; *also* : EJECT **2** : EXPRESS, UTTER — **emis·sion** \-ˈmish-ən\ *n* — **emit·ter** *n*

emol·lient \i-ˈmäl-yənt\ *adj* : making soft or supple; *also* : soothing esp. to the skin or mucous membrane — **emol·lient** *n*

emol·u·ment \i-ˈmäl-yə-mənt\ *n* [ME, fr. L *emolumentum,* lit., miller's fee, fr. *emolere* to grind up] : the product (as salary or fees) of an employment

emote \i-ˈmōt\ *vb* **emot·ed; emot·ing** : to give expression to emotion in or as if in a play

emo·tion \i-ˈmō-shən\ *n* : a usu. intense feeling (as of love, hate, or despair) — **emo·tion·al** \-sh(ə-)nəl\ *adj* — **emo·tion·al·ly** \-ē\ *adv*

emp *abbr* emperor; empress

em·pa·thy \ˈem-pə-thē\ *n* : the capacity for experiencing as one's own the feelings of another — **em·path·ic** \em-ˈpath-ik\ *adj*

em·pen·nage \ˌäm-pə-ˈnäzh, ˌem-\ *n* [F] : the tail assembly of an airplane

em·per·or \ˈem-pər-ər\ *n* : the sovereign ruler of an empire

em·pha·sis \ˈem-fə-səs\ *n, pl* **-pha·ses** \-ˌsēz\ : particular stress or prominence given (as to a phrase in speaking or to a phase of action)

em·pha·size \-ˌsīz\ *vb* **-sized; -siz·ing** : to place emphasis on : STRESS

em·phat·ic \im-ˈfat-ik, em-\ *adj* : uttered with emphasis : STRESSED — **em·phat·i·cal·ly** \-ˈfat-i-k(ə-)lē\ *adv*

em·phy·se·ma \ˌem-fə-ˈzē-mə, -ˈsē-\ *n* : a condition marked esp. by abnormal expansion of the air spaces of the lungs and often by impairment of heart action

em·pire \ˈem-ˌpī(ə)r\ *n* **1** : a large state or a group of states under a single sovereign who is usu. an emperor **2** : imperial sovereignty or dominion

em·pir·i·cal \im-ˈpir-i-kəl\ *also* **em·pir·ic** \-ik\ *adj* : based on observation; *also* : subject to verification by observation or experiment ⟨~ laws⟩ — **em·pir·i·cal·ly** \-i-k(ə-)lē\ *adv*

em·pir·i·cism \im-ˈpir-ə-ˌsiz-əm, em-\ *n* : the practice of relying on observation and experiment esp. in the natural sciences — **em·pir·i·cist** \-səst\ *n*

em·place·ment \im-ˈplās-mənt\ *n* **1** : a prepared position for weapons or military equipment **2** : PLACEMENT

[1]**em·ploy** \im-ˈplȯi\ *vb* **1** : to make use of **2** : to use the services of **3** : OCCUPY, DEVOTE — **em·ploy·er** *n*

[2]**employ** *n* : EMPLOYMENT

em·ploy·ee *or* **em·ploye** \im-ˌplȯi-ˈē, ˌem-; im-ˈplȯi-ˌē, em-\ *n* : a person who works for another

em·ploy·ment \im-ˈplȯi-mənt\ *n* **1** : OCCUPATION, ACTIVITY **2** : the act of employing : the condition of being employed

em·po·ri·um \im-ˈpōr-ē-əm, em-\ *n, pl* **-ri·ums** *also* **-ria** \-ē-ə\ [L, fr. Gk *emporion,* fr. *emporos* traveler, trader] : a commercial center; *esp* : a store carrying varied articles

em·pow·er \im-ˈpau̇(-ə)r\ *vb* : AUTHORIZE

em·press \ˈem-prəs\ *n* **1** : the wife or widow of an emperor **2** : a woman holding an imperial title

[1]**emp·ty** \ˈemp-tē\ *adj* **emp·ti·er; -est 1** : containing nothing **2** : UNOCCUPIED, UNINHABITED **3** : lacking value, force, sense, or purpose **syn** vacant, blank, void, stark, vacuous — **emp·ti·ness** \-tē-nəs\ *n*

[2]**empty** *vb* **emp·tied; emp·ty·ing 1** : to make or become empty **2** : to discharge contents; *also* : to transfer by emptying

[3]**empty** *n, pl* **empties** : an empty container or vehicle

emp·ty–hand·ed \ˌemp-tē-ˈhan-dəd\ *adj* **1** : having nothing in the hands **2** : having acquired or gained nothing

em·py·re·an \ˌem-ˌpī-ˈrē-ən, -pə-\ *n* : the highest heaven; *also* : FIRMAMENT

EMT \ˈē-ˈem-ˈtē\ *n* [*e*mergency *m*edical *t*echnician] : a person trained and certified to provide basic medical services before and during transportation to a hospital

[1]**emu** \ˈē-myü\ *n* : a swift-running flightless Australian bird smaller than the related ostrich

[2]**emu** *abbr* electromagnetic unit

em·u·late \ˈem-yə-ˌlāt\ *vb* **-lat·ed; -lat·ing** : to strive to equal or excel — **em·u·la·tion** \ˌem-yə-ˈlā-shən\ *n* — **em·u·lous** \ˈem-yə-ləs\ *adj*

emul·si·fi·er \i-ˈməl-sə-ˌfī(-ə)r\ *n* : something promoting the formation and stabilizing of an emulsion

emul·si·fy \-ˌfī\ *vb* **-fied; -fy·ing** : to convert (as an oil) into an emulsion — **emul·si·fi·ca·tion** \i-ˌməl-sə-fə-ˈkā-shən\ *n*

emul·sion \i-ˈməl-shən\ *n* **1** : a mixture of mutually insoluble liquids in which one is dispersed in droplets throughout the other ⟨an ~ of oil in water⟩ **2** : a light-sensitive coating on photographic film or paper

en \ˈen\ *n* : a length approximately half the width of the letter *M*

[1]**-en** \ən, ᵊn\ *also* **-n** \n\ *adj suffix* : made of : consisting of ⟨earth*en*⟩

[2]**-en** *vb suffix* **1** : become or cause to be ⟨sharp*en*⟩ **2** : cause or come to have ⟨length*en*⟩

en·able \in-ˈā-bəl\ *vb* **en·abled; en·abling** \-b(ə-)liŋ\ **1** : to make able or feasible **2** : to give legal power, capacity, or sanction to

en·act \in-ˈakt\ *vb* **1** : to make into law **2** : to act out — **en·act·ment** *n*

enam·el \in-ˈam-əl\ *n* **1** : a glasslike substance used for coating the surface of metal or pottery **2** : the hard outer layer of a tooth **3** : a usu. glossy paint that forms a hard coat — **enamel** *vb*

enam·el·ware \-ˌwaər\ *n* : metal utensils coated with enamel

en·am·or \in-ˈam-ər\ *vb* **-ored; -or·ing** \-(ə-)riŋ\ : to inflame with love

en·am·our *chiefly Brit var of* ENAMOR

en bloc \äⁿ-ˈbläk\ *adv or adj* : as a whole : in a mass

enc *or* **encl** *abbr* enclosure

en·camp \in-ˈkamp\ *vb* : to make camp — **en·camp·ment** *n*

en·cap·su·late \in-ˈkap-sə-ˌlāt\ *vb* **-lat·ed; -lat·ing 1** : to encase or become encased in a capsule **2** : to condense (as a report) into a few words — **en·cap·su·la·tion** \-ˌkap-sə-ˈlā-shən\ *n*

en·case \in-ˈkās\ *vb* : to enclose in or as if in a case

-ence \əns, ᵊns\ *n suffix* **1** : action or process ⟨emerg*ence*⟩ : instance of an action or process ⟨refer*ence*⟩ **2** : quality or state ⟨depend*ence*⟩

en·ceinte \äⁿn-ˈsant\ *adj* : PREGNANT

en·ceph·a·li·tis \in-ˌsef-ə-ˈlīt-əs\ *n, pl* **-lit·i·des** \-ˈlit-ə-ˌdēz\ : inflammation of the brain — **en·ceph·a·lit·ic** \-ˈlit-ik\ *adj*

en·ceph·a·lo·my·eli·tis \in-ˌsef-ə-lō-ˌmī-ə-ˈlīt-əs\ *n* : concurrent inflammation of the brain and spinal cord

en·chain \in-ˈchān\ *vb* : FETTER, CHAIN

en·chant \in-ˈchant\ *vb* **1** : BEWITCH **2** : ENRAPTURE, FASCINATE — **en·chant·er** *n* — **en·chant·ing·ly** *adv* — **en·chant·ment** *n* — **en·chant·ress** \-ˈchan-trəs\ *n*

en·chi·la·da \ˌen-chə-ˈläd-ə\ *n* : a tortilla rolled with meat filling and served with chili-seasoned sauce

en·ci·pher \in-ˈsī-fər, en-\ *vb* : ENCODE

en·cir·cle \in-ˈsər-kəl\ *vb* : to pass completely around : SURROUND — **en·cir·cle·ment** *n*

en·clave \ˈen-ˌklāv; ˈän-ˌklāv\ *n* : a territorial or culturally distinct unit enclosed within foreign territory

en·close \in-ˈklōz\ *vb* **1** : to shut up or in; *esp* : to surround with a fence **2** : to include along with something else in a parcel or envelope ⟨~ a check⟩ — **en·clo·sure** \in-ˈklō-zhər\ *n*

en·code \in-ˈkōd, en-\ *vb* : to convert (a message) into code

en·co·mi·um \en-ˈkō-mē-əm\ *n, pl* **-mi·ums** *or* **-mia** \-mē-ə\ [L] : high or glowing praise

en·com·pass \in-ˈkəm-pəs\ *vb* **1** : ENCIRCLE **2** : ENVELOP, INCLUDE

[1]**en·core** \ˈän-ˌkōr\ *n* : a demand for repetition or reappearance; *also* : a further performance (as of a singer) in response to such a demand

[2]**encore** *vb* **en·cored; en·cor·ing** : to request an encore from

[1]**en·coun·ter** \in-ˈkau̇nt-ər\ *n* **1** : a hostile meeting; *esp* : COMBAT **2** : a chance meeting

[2]**encounter** *vb* **1** : to meet as an enemy : FIGHT **2** : to meet usu. unexpectedly

en·cour·age \in-ˈkər-ij\ *vb* **-aged; -ag·ing 1** : to inspire with courage and hope **2** : STIMULATE, INCITE **3** : FOSTER — **en·cour·age·ment** *n* — **en·cour·ag·ing·ly** *adv*

en·croach \in-ˈkrōch\ *vb* [ME *encrochen* to seize, fr. MF *encrochier,* fr. OF, fr. *croche* hook] : to enter or force oneself gradually upon another's property or rights — **en·croach·ment** *n*

en·crust \in-ˈkrəst\ *vb* : to provide with or form a crust

encrustation *var of* INCRUSTATION

en·cum·ber \in-ˈkəm-bər\ *vb* **-bered; -ber·ing** \-b(ə-)riŋ\ **1** : to weigh down : BURDEN **2** : to hinder the function or activity of — **en·cum·brance** \-brəns\ *n*

ency *or* **encyc** *abbr* encyclopedia

-en·cy \ən-sē, ᵊn-\ *n suffix* : quality or state ⟨despond*ency*⟩

[1]**en·cyc·li·cal** \in-ˈsik-li-kəl, en-\ *adj* : addressed to all the individuals of a group

[2]**encyclical** *n* : an encyclical letter; *esp* : a papal letter to the bishops of the church

en·cy·clo·pe·dia *also* **en·cy·clo·pae·dia** \in-ˌsī-klə-ˈpēd-ē-ə\ *n* [ML *encyclopaedia* course of general education, fr. Gk *enkyklios paideia* general education] : a work treating the various branches of learning — **en·cy·clo·pe·dic** \-ˈpēd-ik\ *adj*

en·cyst \in-ˈsist, en-\ *vb* : to form or become enclosed in a cyst — **en·cyst·ment** *n*

[1]**end** \ˈend\ *n* **1** : the part of an area that lies at the boundary; *also* : a point which marks the extent or limit of something or at which something ceases to exist **2** : a ceasing of a course (as of action or activity); *also* : DEATH **3** : the ultimate state; *also* : RESULT, ISSUE **4** : REMNANT **5** : PURPOSE, OBJECTIVE **6** : a player stationed at the extremity of a line (as in football) **7** : a share, operation, or aspect of an undertaking

[2]**end** *vb* **1** : to bring or come to an end **2** : DESTROY; *also* : DIE **3** : to form or be at the end of **syn** close, conclude, terminate, finish, complete

en·dan·ger \in-ˈdān-jər\ *vb* **-gered; -ger·ing** \-ˈdānj-(ə-)riŋ\ : to bring into danger

en·dan·gered \-jərd\ *adj* : threatened with extinction ⟨~ species⟩

en·dear \in-ˈdiər\ *vb* : to cause to become an object of affection

en·dear·ment \-mənt\ *n* : a sign of affection : CARESS

en·deav·or \in-ˈdev-ər\ *vb* **-ored; -or·ing** \-(ə-)riŋ\ : TRY, ATTEMPT — **endeavor** *n*

en·dem·ic \en-ˈdem-ik, in-\ *adj* : restricted or peculiar to a particular place ⟨~ plants⟩ ⟨an ~ disease⟩ — **endemic** *n*

end·ing \ˈen-diŋ\ *n* : something that forms an end; *esp* : SUFFIX

en·dive \ˈen-ˌdīv\ *n* **1** : an herb related to chicory and grown as a salad plant **2** : the blanched shoot of chicory

end·less \ˈend-ləs\ *adj* **1** : having no end : ETERNAL **2** : united at the ends : CONTINUOUS ⟨an ~ belt⟩ **syn** interminable, everlasting, unceasing, ceaseless, unending — **end·less·ly** *adv*

end·most \ˈend-ˌmōst\ *adj* : situated at the very end

end·note \-ˌnōt\ *n* : a note placed at the end of the text (as of an article, chapter, or book)

en·do·crine \ˈen-də-krən, -ˌkrīn, -ˌkrēn\ *adj* : producing secretions that are distributed by way of the bloodstream ⟨~ glands⟩ — **endocrine** *n* — **en·do·cri·nol·o·gist** \ˌen-də-kri-ˈnäl-ə-jəst\ *n* — **en·do·cri·nol·o·gy** \-jē\ *n*

en·dog·e·nous \en-ˈdäj-ə-nəs\ *adj* : caused or produced by factors inside the organism or system ⟨~ psychic depression⟩ — **en·dog·e·nous·ly** *adv*

en·dorse \in-ˈdȯrs\ *vb* **en·dorsed; en·dors·ing** **1** : to sign one's name on the back of (as a check) for some purpose **2** : APPROVE, SANCTION **syn** accredit, certify — **en·dorse·ment** *n*

en·do·scope \ˈen-də-ˌskōp\ *n* : an instrument with which the interior of a hollow organ (as the rectum) may be visualized — **en·do·scop·ic** \ˌen-də-ˈskäp-ik\ *adj* — **en·dos·co·py** \en-ˈdäs-kə-pē\ *n*

en·do·ther·mic \ˌen-də-ˈthər-mik\ *also* **en·do·ther·mal** \-məl\ *adj* : characterized by or formed with absorption of heat

en·dow \in-ˈdau̇\ *vb* **1** : to furnish with funds for support ⟨~ a school⟩ **2** : to furnish with something freely or naturally — **en·dow·ment** *n*

end run *n* : a football play in which the ballcarrier attempts to run wide around the end

en·due \in-ˈd(y)ü\ *vb* **en·dued; en·du·ing** : to provide with some quality or power

en·dur·ance \in-ˈd(y)u̇r-əns\ *n* **1** : DURATION **2** : the ability to withstand hardship or stress : FORTITUDE

en·dure \in-ˈd(y)u̇r\ *vb* **en·dured; en·dur·ing** **1** : LAST, PERSIST **2** : to suffer firmly or patiently : BEAR **3** : TOLERATE **syn** continue, abide, persist — **en·dur·able** *adj*

end·ways \ˈend-ˌwāz\ *adv or adj* **1** : with the end forward **2** : LENGTHWISE **3** : on end

end·wise \-ˌwīz\ *adv or adj* : ENDWAYS

ENE *abbr* east-northeast

en·e·ma \ˈen-ə-mə\ *n, pl* **enemas** *also* **ene·ma·ta** \ˌen-ə-ˈmät-ə, ˈen-ə-mə-tə\ : injection of liquid into the rectum; *also* : material so injected

en·e·my \ˈen-ə-mē\ *n, pl* **-mies** : one that attacks or tries to harm another : FOE; *esp* : a military opponent

en·er·get·ic \ˌen-ər-ˈjet-ik\ *adj* : marked by energy : ACTIVE, VIGOROUS **syn** strenuous, lusty, dynamic, vital — **en·er·get·i·cal·ly** \-i-k(ə-)lē\ *adv*

en·er·gize \ˈen-ər-ˌjīz\ *vb* **-gized; -giz·ing** : to give energy to

en·er·giz·er \-ˌjī-zər\ *n* : ANTIDEPRESSANT

en·er·gy \ˈen-ər-jē\ *n, pl* **-gies** **1** : vigorous action : EFFORT **2** : capacity for action **3** : capacity for performing work **4** : usable power (as heat or electricity); *also* : the resources for producing such power **syn** strength, might, vigor

energy level *n* : one of the stable states of constant energy that may be assumed by a physical system (as the electrons in an atom)

en·er·vate \ˈen-ər-ˌvāt\ *vb* **-vat·ed; -vat·ing** : to lessen the strength or vigor of : weaken in mind or body — **en·er·va·tion** \ˌen-ər-ˈvā-shən\ *n*

en·fee·ble \in-ˈfē-bəl\ *vb* **-bled; -bling** \-b(ə-)liŋ\ : to make feeble **syn** weaken, debilitate, sap, undermine, cripple — **en·fee·ble·ment** *n*

en·fi·lade \ˈen-fə-ˌlād, -ˌläd\ *n* : gunfire directed along the length of an enemy battle line

en·fold \in-ˈfōld\ *vb* **1** : ENVELOP **2** : EMBRACE

en·force \in-ˈfōrs\ *vb* **1** : COMPEL ⟨~ obedience by threats⟩ **2** : to execute effectively ⟨~ the law⟩ — **en·force·able** *adj* — **en·force·ment** *n*

en·fran·chise \in-ˈfran-ˌchīz\ *vb* **-chised; -chis·ing** **1** : to set free (as from slavery) **2** : to admit to citizenship; *also* : to grant the vote to — **en·fran·chise·ment** \-ˌchīz-mənt, -chəz-\ *n*

eng *abbr* engine; engineer; engineering

Eng *abbr* England; English

en·gage \in-ˈgāj\ *vb* **en·gaged; en·gag·ing** **1** : PLEDGE; *esp* : to bind by a pledge to marry **2** : EMPLOY, HIRE **3** : to attract and hold esp. by interesting ⟨*engaged* his friend's attention⟩; *also* : to cause to participate **4** : to commence or take part in a venture **5** : to bring or enter into conflict **6** : to connect or interlock with : MESH; *also* : to cause to mesh

en·gage·ment \in-ˈgāj-mənt\ *n* **1** : APPOINTMENT **2** : EMPLOYMENT **3** : a mutual promise to marry **4** : a hostile encounter

en·gag·ing *adj* : ATTRACTIVE — **en·gag·ing·ly** *adv*

en·gen·der \in-ˈjen-dər\ *vb* **-dered; -der·ing** \-d(ə-)riŋ\ **1** : BEGET **2** : BRING ABOUT, CREATE **syn** generate, breed, occasion, produce

en·gine \ˈen-jən\ *n* [ME *engin*, fr. OF, fr. L *ingenium* natural disposition, talent] **1** : a mechanical device **2** : a machine for converting energy into mechanical motion **3** : LOCOMOTIVE

[1]**en·gi·neer** \ˌen-jə-ˈniər\ *n* **1** : a member of a military group devoted to engineering work **2** : a designer or builder of engines **3** : one trained in engineering **4** : one that operates an engine

[2]**engineer** *vb* : to lay out or manage as an engineer **syn** guide, pilot, lead, steer

en·gi·neer·ing \-iŋ\ *n* : the practical applications of scientific and mathematical principles

En·glish \ˈiŋ-glish\ *n* **1** : the language of England, the U.S., and many areas now or formerly under British rule **2 English** *pl* : the people of England — **English** *adj* — **En·glish·man** \-mən\ *n* — **En·glish·wom·an** \-ˌwu̇m-ən\ *n*

English horn *n* : a woodwind instrument longer than and having a range lower than the oboe

English setter *n* : any of a breed of bird dogs with a flat silky coat of white with flecks or patches of black or brown

English sparrow *n* : HOUSE SPARROW

English system *n* : a system of weights and measures in which the foot is the principal unit of length and the pound is the principal unit of weight

engr *abbr* 1 engineer 2 engraved

en·gram \ˈen-ˌgram\ *n* : a hypothetical change in neural tissue postulated in order to account for persistence of memory

en·grave \in-ˈgrāv\ *vb* **en·graved; en·grav·ing** 1 : to produce (as letters or lines) by incising a surface 2 : to incise (as stone or metal) to produce a representation (as of letters or figures) esp. that may be printed from 3 : PHOTOENGRAVE — **en·grav·er** *n*

en·grav·ing \in-ˈgrā-viŋ\ *n* 1 : the art of one who engraves 2 : an engraved plate; *also* : a print made from it

en·gross \in-ˈgrōs\ *vb* : to take up the whole interest or attention of **syn** monopolize, absorb, consume

en·gulf \in-ˈgəlf\ *vb* : to flow over and enclose

en·hance \in-ˈhans\ *vb* **en·hanced; en·hanc·ing** : to make greater (as in value or desirability) **syn** heighten, intensify, magnify — **en·hance·ment** *n*

enig·ma \i-ˈnig-mə\ *n* [L *aenigma,* fr. Gk *ainigma,* fr. *ainissesthai* to speak in riddles, fr. *ainos* fable] : something obscure or hard to understand : PUZZLE

enig·mat·ic \ˌen-ig-ˈmat-ik\ *adj* : resembling an enigma **syn** obscure, cryptic, mystifying — **en·ig·mat·i·cal·ly** \-i-k(ə-)lē\ *adv*

en·isle \in-ˈīl\ *vb* : ISOLATE

en·jamb·ment \in-ˈjam-mənt\ *or* **en·jambe·ment** *same, or* ä^{n}-zhä^{n}b-(ə-)mä^{n}\ *n* [F *enjambement*] : the running over of a sentence from one verse or couplet into another so that closely related words fall in different lines

en·join \in-ˈjȯin\ *vb* 1 : COMMAND, ORDER 2 : FORBID **syn** direct, bid, charge, command, instruct

en·joy \in-ˈjȯi\ *vb* 1 : to have for one's benefit or use ⟨~ good health⟩ 2 : to take pleasure or satisfaction in ⟨~*ed* the concert⟩ **syn** like, love, relish, fancy — **en·joy·able** *adj* — **en·joy·ment** *n*

enl *abbr* 1 enlarged 2 enlisted

en·large \in-ˈlärj\ *vb* **en·larged; en·larg·ing** 1 : to make or grow larger 2 : ELABORATE **syn** increase, augment, multiply, expand — **en·large·ment** *n*

en·light·en \in-ˈlīt-ᵊn\ *vb* **-ened; -en·ing** \-ˈlīt-(ᵊ-)niŋ\ 1 : INSTRUCT, INFORM 2 : to give spiritual insight to **syn** illuminate, edify — **en·light·en·ment** *n*

en·list \in-ˈlist\ *vb* 1 : to engage for service in the armed forces 2 : to secure the aid or support of — **en·list·ee** \-ˌlis-ˈtē\ *n* — **en·list·ment** \-ˈlis(t)-mənt\ *n*

en·list·ed \in-ˈlis-təd\ *adj* : of, relating to, or forming the part of a military force below commissioned or warrant officers

en·liv·en \in-ˈlī-vən\ *vb* : to give life, action, or spirit to : ANIMATE

en masse \ä^{n}-ˈmas\ *adv* [F] : in a body : as a whole

en·mesh \in-ˈmesh\ *vb* : to catch or entangle in or as if in meshes

en·mi·ty \ˈen-mət-ē\ *n, pl* **-ties** : ILL WILL; *esp* : mutual hatred **syn** hostility, antipathy, animosity, rancor, antagonism

en·no·ble \in-ˈō-bəl\ *vb* **-bled; -bling** \-b(ə-)liŋ\ : ELEVATE, EXALT; *esp* : to raise to noble rank — **en·no·ble·ment** *n*

en·nui \ˈän-ˈwē\ *n* [F] : BOREDOM

enor·mi·ty \i-ˈnȯr-mət-ē\ *n, pl* **-ties** 1 : a grave offense against order, right, or decency 2 : great wickedness 3 : IMMENSITY

enor·mous \i-ˈnȯr-məs\ *adj* [L *enormis,* fr. *e, ex* out of + *norma* rule] 1 : exceedingly wicked 2 : great in size, number, or degree : HUGE **syn** immense, vast, gigantic, colossal, mammoth, elephantine

[1]**enough** \i-ˈnəf\ *adj* : SUFFICIENT **syn** adequate, satisfactory, sufficing

[2]**enough** *adv* 1 : SUFFICIENTLY 2 : FULLY, QUITE 3 : TOLERABLY

[3]**enough** *pron* : a sufficient number, quantity, or amount

en·plane \in-ˈplān\ *vb* : to board an airplane

en·quire \in-ˈkwī(ə)r\, **en·qui·ry** \ˈin-ˌkwī(ə)r-ē, in-ˈkwī(ə)r-; ˈin-kwə-rē, ˈiŋ-\ *var of* INQUIRE, INQUIRY

en·rage \in-ˈrāj\ *vb* : to fill with rage

en·rap·ture \in-ˈrap-chər\ *vb* **en·rap·tured; en·rap·tur·ing** : DELIGHT

en·rich \in-ˈrich\ *vb* 1 : to make rich or richer 2 : ORNAMENT, ADORN — **en·rich·ment** *n*

en·roll *or* **en·rol** \in-ˈrōl\ *vb* **en·rolled; en·roll·ing** 1 : to enter or register on a roll or list 2 : to offer (oneself) for enrolling — **en·roll·ment** *n*

en route \än-ˈrüt, en-\ *adv or adj* : on or along the way

ENS *abbr* ensign

en·sconce \in-ˈskäns\ *vb* **en·sconced; en·sconc·ing** 1 : SHELTER, CONCEAL 2 : to settle snugly or securely **syn** secrete, hide, cache, stash

en·sem·ble \än-ˈsäm-bəl\ *n* [F, fr. *ensemble* together, fr. L *insimul* at the same time] 1 : SET, WHOLE 2 : integrated music of two or more parts 3 : a complete costume of harmonizing garments 4 : a group of persons (as musicians) acting together to produce a particular effect or end

en·sheathe \in-ˈshēth\ *vb* : to cover with or as if with a sheath

en·shrine \in-ˈshrīn\ *vb* 1 : to enclose in or as if in a shrine 2 : to cherish as sacred

en·shroud \in-ˈshraủd\ *vb* : SHROUD, OBSCURE

en·sign \ˈen-sən, *1 also* ˈen-ˌsīn\ *n* 1 : FLAG; *also* : BADGE, EMBLEM 2 : a commissioned officer in the navy ranking next below a lieutenant junior grade

en·si·lage \ˈen-sə-lij\ *n* : the process of converting feed crops into silage; *also* : SILAGE

en·sile \en-ˈsīl\ *vb* **en·siled; en·sil·ing** : to prepare and store (fodder) for silage

en·slave \in-ˈslāv\ *vb* : to make a slave of — **en·slave·ment** *n*

en·snare \in-ˈsnaər\ *vb* : SNARE, TRAP **syn** entrap, bag, catch, capture

en·sue \in-ˈsü\ *vb* **en·sued; en·su·ing** : to follow as a consequence or in time : RESULT

en·sure \in-ˈshủr\ *vb* **en·sured; en·sur·ing** : INSURE, GUARANTEE **syn** assure, secure

en·tail \in-ˈtāl\ *vb* 1 : to limit the inheritance of (property) to the owner's lineal descendants or to a class thereof 2 : to include or involve as a necessary step or result — **en·tail·ment** *n*

en·tan·gle \in-ˈtaŋ-gəl\ *vb* : TANGLE, CONFUSE — **en·tan·gle·ment** *n*

en·tente \än-ˈtänt\ *n* [F agreement, understanding] : an understanding providing for joint action; *also* : parties linked by such an entente

en·ter \ˈent-ər\ *vb* **en·tered; en·ter·ing** \ˈent-ə-riŋ, ˈen-triŋ\ 1 : to go or come in or into 2 : to become a member of : JOIN ⟨~ the ministry⟩ 3 : BEGIN 4 : to take part in : CONTRIBUTE 5 : to go into or upon and take possession 6 : to set down (as in a list) : REGISTER 7 : to place (a complaint) before a court; *also* : to put on record ⟨~*ed* his objections⟩

en·ter·i·tis \ˌent-ə-ˈrīt-əs\ *n* : intestinal inflammation; *also* : a disease marked by this

en·ter·prise \ˈent-ər-ˌprīz\ *n* 1 : UNDERTAKING, PROJECT 2 : readiness for daring action : INITIATIVE 3 : a business organization

en·ter·pris·ing \-ˌprī-ziŋ\ *adj* : bold and vigorous in action : ENERGETIC

en·ter·tain \ˌent-ər-ˈtān\ *vb* 1 : to treat or receive as a guest 2 : AMUSE, DIVERT 3 : to hold in mind **syn** harbor, shelter, lodge, house, billet — **en·ter·tain·er** *n* — **en·ter·tain·ment** *n*

en·thrall *or* **en·thral** \in-ˈthrȯl\ *vb* **en·thralled; en·thrall·ing** 1 : to hold spellbound 2 : ENSLAVE

en·throne \in-ˈthrōn\ *vb* 1 : to seat on or as if on a throne 2 : EXALT

en·thuse \in-ˈth(y)üz\ *vb* **en·thused; en·thus·ing** 1 : to make enthusiastic 2 : to show enthusiasm

en·thu·si·asm \in-ˈth(y)ü-zē-ˌaz-əm\ *n* [Gk *enthousiasmos*, fr. *enthousiazein* to be inspired, fr. *entheos* inspired, fr. *theos* god] 1 : strong warmth of feeling : keen interest : FERVOR 2 : a cause of fervor — **en·thu·si·ast** \-ˌast, -əst\ *n* — **en·thu·si·as·tic** \in-ˌth(y)ü-zē-ˈas-tik\ *adj* — **en·thu·si·as·ti·cal·ly** \-ti-k(ə-)lē\ *adv*

en·tice \in-ˈtīs\ *vb* **en·ticed; en·tic·ing** : ALLURE, TEMPT — **en·tice·ment** *n*

en·tire \in-ˈtī(ə)r\ *adj* : COMPLETE, WHOLE **syn** sound, perfect, intact, undamaged — **en·tire·ly** *adv*

en·tire·ty \in-ˈtī-rət-ē, -ˈtī(-ə)rt-ē\ *n, pl* **-ties** 1 : COMPLETENESS 2 : WHOLE, TOTALITY

en·ti·tle \in-ˈtīt-ᵊl\ *vb* **en·ti·tled; en·ti·tling** \-ˈtīt-(ᵊ-)liŋ\ 1 : NAME, DESIGNATE 2 : to give a right or claim to

en·ti·tle·ment \in-ˈtīt-ᵊl-mənt\ *n* : a government program providing benefits to members of a specified group

en·ti·ty \ˈent-ət-ē\ *n, pl* **-ties** 1 : EXISTENCE, BEING 2 : something with separate and real existence

en·tomb \in-ˈtüm\ *vb* : to place in a tomb : BURY — **en·tomb·ment** \-ˈtüm-mənt\ *n*

en·to·mol·o·gy \ˌent-ə-ˈmäl-ə-jē\ *n* : a branch of zoology that deals with insects — **en·to·mo·log·i·cal** \-mə-ˈläj-i-kəl\ *adj* — **en·to·mol·o·gist** \ˌent-ə-ˈmäl-ə-jəst\ *n*

en·tou·rage \ˌän-tü-ˈräzh\ *n* [F] : RETINUE

en·tr'acte \ˈäⁿn-ˌtrakt\ *n* [F] 1 : something (as a dance) performed between two acts of a play 2 : the interval between two acts of a play

en·trails \ˈen-ˌtrālz\ *n pl* : VISCERA; *esp* : INTESTINES

en·train \in-ˈtrān\ *vb* : to put or go aboard a railroad train

[1]**en·trance** \ˈen-trəns\ *n* 1 : a means or place of entry 2 : the act of entering 3 : permission or right to enter

[2]**en·trance** \in-ˈtrans\ *vb* **en·tranced; en·tranc·ing** : CHARM, DELIGHT

en·trant \ˈen-trənt\ *n* : one that enters esp. as a competitor

en·trap \in-ˈtrap\ *vb* : ENSNARE, TRAP — **en·trap·ment** *n*

en·treat \in-ˈtrēt\ *vb* : to ask earnestly or urgently : BESEECH **syn** beg, implore, plead, supplicate — **en·treaty** \-ˈtrēt-ē\ *n*

en·trée *or* **en·tree** \ˈän-ˌtrā\ *n* [F *entrée*] 1 : the principal dish of the meal in the U.S. 2 : ENTRANCE **syn** entry, access, admission, admittance

en·trench \in-ˈtrench\ *vb* 1 : to surround with a trench; *also* : to establish in a strong defensive position ⟨~*ed* customs⟩ 2 : ENCROACH, TRESPASS — **en·trench·ment** *n*

en·tre·pre·neur \ˌän-trə-prə-ˈnər\ *n* [F, fr. OF, fr. *entreprendre* to undertake] : one who organizes and assumes the risk of a business or enterprise

en·tro·py \ˈen-trə-pē\ *n, pl* **-pies** 1 : a measure of the unavailable energy of a closed thermodynamic system 2 : an ultimate state of inert uniformity

en·trust \in-ˈtrəst\ *vb* 1 : to commit something to as a trust 2 : to commit to another with confidence **syn** confide, consign, relegate, commend

en·try \ˈen-trē\ *n, pl* **entries** 1 : ENTRANCE 1, 2; *also* : VESTIBULE 2 2 : an entering in a record; *also* : an item so entered 3 : a headword with its definition or identification; *also* : VOCABULARY ENTRY 4 : one entered in a contest

en·twine \in-ˈtwīn\ *vb* : to twine together or around

enu·mer·ate \i-ˈn(y)ü-mə-ˌrāt\ *vb* **-at·ed; -at·ing** 1 : to determine the number of : COUNT 2 : LIST — **enu·mer·a·tion** \-ˌn(y)ü-mə-ˈrā-shən\ *n*

enun·ci·ate \ē-ˈnən-sē-ˌāt\ *vb* **-at·ed; -at·ing** 1 : to state definitely; *also* : ANNOUNCE, PROCLAIM 2 : PRONOUNCE, ARTICULATE — **enun·ci·a·tion** \-ˌnən-sē-ˈā-shən\ *n*

en·ure·sis \ˌen-yu̇-ˈrē-səs\ *n* : involuntary discharge of urine : BED-WETTING

env *abbr* envelope

en·vel·op \in-ˈvel-əp\ *vb* : to enclose completely with or as if with a covering — **en·vel·op·ment** *n*

en·ve·lope \ˈen-və-ˌlōp, ˈän-\ *n* 1 : a usu. paper container for a letter 2 : WRAPPER, COVERING 3 : the bag containing the gas in a balloon or airship

en·ven·om \in-ˈven-əm\ *vb* 1 : to poison with venom 2 : EMBITTER

en·vi·able \ˈen-vē-ə-bəl\ *adj* : highly desirable — **en·vi·ably** \-blē\ *adv*

en·vi·ous \ˈen-vē-əs\ *adj* : feeling or showing envy — **en·vi·ous·ly** *adv* — **en·vi·ous·ness** *n*

en·vi·ron·ment \in-ˈvī-rən-mənt\ *n* 1 : SURROUNDINGS 2 : the whole complex of factors (as soil, climate, and living things) that influence the form and the ability to survive of a plant or animal or ecological community — **en·vi·ron·men·tal** \-ˌvī-rən-ˈment-ᵊl\ *adj*

en·vi·ron·men·tal·ist \-ᵊl-əst\ *n* : a person concerned about the quality of the human environment

en·vi·rons \in-ˈvī-rənz\ *n pl* 1 : SUBURBS 2 : SURROUNDINGS; *also* : VICINITY

en·vis·age \in-ˈviz-ij\ *vb* **-aged; -ag·ing** : to have a mental picture of

en·voy \ˈen-ˌvȯi, ˈän-\ *n* 1 : a diplomatic agent 2 : REPRESENTATIVE, MESSENGER

[1]**en·vy** \ˈen-vē\ *n, pl* **envies** [ME *envie*, fr. OF, fr. L *invidia*, fr. *invidus* envious, fr. *invidēre* to look askance at, envy, fr. *vidēre* to see] : grudging desire for or discontent at the sight of another's excellence or advantages; *also* : an object of envy

[2]**envy** *vb* **en·vied; en·vy·ing** : to feel envy toward or on account of

en·zyme \ˈen-ˌzīm\ *n* : any of various complex proteins produced by living cells that induce or accelerate chemical reactions (as in the digestion of food) at body temperatures without being permanently altered — **en·zy·mat·ic** \ˌen-zə-ˈmat-ik\ *adj*

Eo·cene \ˈē-ə-ˌsēn\ *adj* : of, relating to, or being the epoch of the Tertiary between the Paleocene and the Oligocene — **Eocene** *n*

eo·lian \ē-ˈō-lē-ən\ *adj* : borne, deposited, or produced by the wind

EOM *abbr* end of month

eon \ˈē-ən, ˈē-ˌän\ *var of* AEON

EP *abbr* European plan

EPA *abbr* Environmental Protection Agency

ep·au·let *also* **ep·au·lette** \ˌep-ə-ˈlet\ *n* [F *épaulette*, dim. of *épaule* shoulder] : a shoulder ornament esp. on a uniform

épée \ˈep-ˌā, ā-ˈpā\ *n* [F] : a fencing or dueling sword

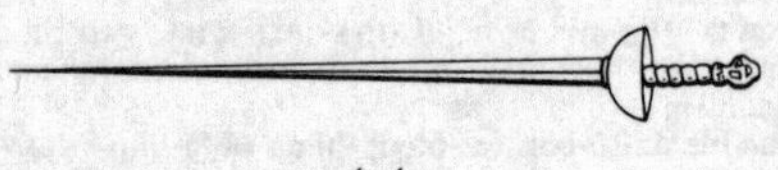

épée

Eph *or* **Ephes** *abbr* Ephesians

ephed·rine \i-ˈfed-rən\ *n* : a drug used in relieving hay fever, asthma, and nasal congestion

ephem·er·al \i-ˈfem(-ə)-rəl\ *adj* [Gk *ephēmeros* lasting a day, daily, fr. *hēmera* day] : SHORT-LIVED, TRANSITORY **syn** passing, fleeting, transient, evanescent

Ephe·sians \i-ˈfē-zhənz\ *n* — see BIBLE table

ep·ic \ˈep-ik\ *n* : a long poem in elevated style narrating the deeds of a hero — **epic** *adj*

epi·cen·ter \ˈep-i-ˌsent-ər\ *n* : the point on the earth's surface directly above the point of origin of an earthquake

ep·i·cure \ˈep-i-ˌkyu̇r\ *n* : a person with sensitive and discriminating tastes esp. in food and wine

ep·i·cu·re·an \ˌep-i-kyu̇-ˈrē-ən, -ˈkyu̇r-ē-\ *n* : EPICURE — **epicurean** *adj*

[1]**ep·i·dem·ic** \ˌep-ə-ˈdem-ik\ *adj* : affecting many persons at one time ⟨~ disease⟩; *also* : excessively prevalent

[2]**epidemic** *n* : an epidemic outbreak esp. of disease

epi·der·mis \ˌep-ə-ˈdər-məs\ *n* : an outer layer esp. of skin — **epi·der·mal** \-məl\ *adj*

epi·glot·tis \-ˈglät-əs\ *n* : a thin plate of flexible tissue protecting the tracheal opening during swallowing

ep·i·gram \ˈep-ə-ˌgram\ *n* : a short witty poem or saying — **ep·i·gram·mat·ic** \ˌep-ə-grə-ˈmat-ik\ *adj*

ep·i·lep·sy \ˈep-ə-ˌlep-sē\ *n, pl* **-sies** : a disorder typically marked by disturbed electrical rhythms of the central nervous system, by attacks of convulsions, and by loss of consciousness — **ep·i·lep·tic** \ˌep-ə-ˈlep-tik\ *adj or n*

ep·i·logue *or* **ep·i·log** \ˈep-ə-ˌlȯg, -ˌläg\ *n* : a speech addressed to the spectators by an actor at the end of a play

epi·neph·rine *also* **epi·neph·rin** \ˌep-ə-ˈnef-rən\ *n* : an adrenal hormone used medicinally esp. as a heart stimulant, a muscle relaxant, and a vasoconstrictor

Epiph·a·ny \i-ˈpif-ə-nē\ *n, pl* **-nies** : January 6 observed as a church festival in commemoration of the coming of the Magi to Jesus at Bethlehem

epis·co·pa·cy \i-ˈpis-kə-pə-sē\ *n, pl* **-cies 1** : government of a church by bishops **2** : EPISCOPATE

epis·co·pal \i-ˈpis-kə-pəl\ *adj* **1** : of or relating to a bishop or episcopacy **2** *cap* : or or relating to the Protestant Episcopal Church

Epis·co·pa·lian \i-ˌpis-kə-ˈpāl-yən\ *n* : a member of the Protestant Episcopal Church

epis·co·pate \i-ˈpis-kə-pət, -ˌpāt\ *n* **1** : the rank, office, or term of a bishop **2** : a body of bishops

ep·i·sode \ˈep-ə-ˌsōd, -ˌzōd\ *n* [Gk *epeisodion*, fr. *epeisodios* coming in besides, fr. *eisodios* coming in, fr. *eis* into + *hodos* road, journey] **1** : a unit of action in a dramatic or literary work **2** : an incident in a course of events : OCCURRENCE ⟨a feverish ~⟩ — **ep·i·sod·ic** \ˌep-ə-ˈsäd-ik, -ˈzäd-\ *adj*

epis·tle \i-ˈpis-əl\ *n* **1** *cap* : one of the letters of the New Testament **2** : LETTER — **epis·to·lary** \i-ˈpis-tə-ˌler-ē\ *adj*

ep·i·taph \ˈep-ə-ˌtaf\ *n* : an inscription in memory of a dead person

ep·i·tha·la·mi·um \ˌep-ə-thə-ˈlā-mē-əm\ *or* **ep·i·tha·la·mi·on** \-mē-ən\ *n pl* **-mi·ums** *or* **-mia** \-mē-ə\ : a song or poem in honor of a bride and bridegroom

ep·i·the·li·um \ˌep-ə-ˈthē-lē-əm\ *n, pl* **-lia** \-lē-ə\ : a cellular membrane covering a bodily surface or lining a cavity — **ep·i·the·li·al** \-lē-əl\ *adj*

ep·i·thet \ˈep-ə-ˌthet, -thət\ *n* : a characterizing and often abusive word or phrase

epit·o·me \i-ˈpit-ə-mē\ *n* **1** : ABSTRACT, SUMMARY **2** : EMBODIMENT — **epit·o·mize** \-ˌmīz\ *vb*

ep·och \ˈep-ək, ˈep-ˌäk\ *n* : a usu. extended period : ERA, AGE — **ep·och·al** \ˈep-ə-kəl, ˈep-ˌäk-əl\ *adj*

ep·oxy \i-ˈpäk-sē\ *vb* **ep·ox·ied** *or* **ep·oxyed; ep·oxy·ing** : to glue with epoxy resin

epoxy resin *n* : a synthetic resin used in coatings and adhesives

Ep·som salts \ˈep-səm-\ *n* : a bitter colorless or white magnesium salt with cathartic properties

eq *abbr* **1** equal **2** equation

equa·ble \ˈek-wə-bəl, ˈē-kwə-\ *adj* : UNIFORM, EVEN; *esp* : free from unpleasant extremes — **eq·ua·bil·i·ty** \ˌek-wə-ˈbil-ət-ē, ˌē-kwə-\ *n* — **eq·ua·bly** \ˈek-wə-blē, ˈē-kwə-\ *adv*

[1]**equal** \ˈē-kwəl\ *adj* **1** : of the same measure, quantity, value, quality, number, or degree as another **2** : IMPARTIAL **3** : free from extremes **4** : able to cope with a situation or task **syn** same, identical, equivalent, tantamount — **equal·i·ty** \i-ˈkwäl-ət-ē\ *n* — **equal·ly** \ˈē-kwə-lē\ *adv*

[2]**equal** *vb* **equaled** *or* **equalled; equal·ing** *or* **equal·ling** : to be or become equal to : MATCH

[3]**equal** *n* : one that is equal; *esp* : a person of like rank, abilities, or age

equal·ize \ˈē-kwə-ˌlīz\ *vb* **-ized; -iz·ing** : to make equal, uniform, or constant — **equal·iza·tion** \ˌē-kwə-lə-ˈzā-shən\ *n* — **equal·iz·er** \ˈē-kwə-ˌlī-zər\ *n*

equa·nim·i·ty \ˌē-kwə-ˈnim-ət-ē, ˌek-wə-\ *n, pl* **-ties** : COMPOSURE

equate \i-ˈkwāt\ *vb* **equat·ed; equat·ing** : to make, treat, or regard as equal or comparable

equa·tion \i-ˈkwā-zhən, -shən\ *n* **1** : an act of equating : the state of being equated **2** : a usu. formal statement of equivalence (as between mathematical or logical expressions) with the relation typically symbolized by the sign =

equa·tor \i-ˈkwāt-ər\ *n* : an imaginary circle around the earth that is everywhere equally distant from the two poles — **equa·to·ri·al** \ˌē-kwə-ˈtōr- ē-əl, ˌek-wə-\ *adj*

equer·ry \ˈek-wə-rē, i-ˈkwer-ē\ *n, pl* **-ries 1** : an officer in charge of the horses of a prince or nobleman **2** : a personal attendant of a member of the British royal family

[1]**eques·tri·an** \i-ˈkwes-trē-ən\ *adj* **1** : of or relating to horses, horsemen, or horsemanship **2** : representing a person on horseback

[2]**equestrian** *n* : one that rides on horseback

eques·tri·enne \i-ˌkwes-trē-ˈen\ *n* : a female rider on horseback

equi·dis·tant \ˌē-kwə-ˈdis-tənt\ *adj* : equally distant

equi·lat·er·al \ˌē-kwə-ˈlat-(ə-)rəl\ *adj* : having all sides or faces equal ⟨~ triangles⟩

equi·lib·ri·um \ˌē-kwə-ˈlib-rē-əm, ˌek-wə-\ *n, pl* **-ri·ums** *or* **-ria** \-rē-ə\ : a state of balance between opposing forces or actions **syn** poise, balance, equipoise

equine \ˈē-ˌkwīn, ˈek-ˌwīn\ *adj* [L *equinus*, fr. *equus* horse] : of or relating to the horse — **equine** *n*

equi·nox \ˈē-kwə-ˌnäks, ˈek-wə-\ *n* : either of the two times each year when the sun appears directly overhead at the equator and day and night are everywhere of equal length that occur about March 21 and September 23 — **equi·noc·tial** \ˌē-kwə-ˈnäk-shəl, ˌek-wə-\ *adj*

equip \i-ˈkwip\ *vb* **equipped; equip·ping** : to supply with needed resources

eq·ui·page \ˈek-wə-pij\ *n* : a horse-drawn carriage usu. with its attendant servants

equip·ment \i-ˈkwip-mənt\ *n* **1** : things used in equipping : SUPPLIES, OUTFIT **2** : the equipping of a person or thing : the state of being equipped

equi·poise \ˈek-wə-ˌpȯiz, ˈē-kwə-\ *n* **1** : BALANCE, EQUILIBRIUM **2** : COUNTERBALANCE

eq·ui·ta·ble \ˈek-wət-ə-bəl\ *adj* : JUST, FAIR — **eq·ui·ta·bly** \-blē\ *adv*

eq·ui·ta·tion \ˌek-wə-ˈtā-shən\ *n* : the act or art of riding on horseback

eq·ui·ty \ˈek-wət-ē\ *n, pl* **-ties 1** : JUSTNESS, IMPARTIALITY **2** : value of a property or of an interest in it in excess of claims against it

equiv *abbr* equivalent

equiv·a·lent \i-ˈkwiv(-ə)-lənt\ *adj* : EQUAL; *also* : virtually identical **syn** same, tantamount — **equiv·a·lence** \-ləns\ *n* — **equivalent** *n*

equiv·o·cal \i-ˈkwiv-ə-kəl\ *adj* **1** : AMBIGUOUS **2** : UNCERTAIN **3** : SUSPICIOUS, DUBIOUS ⟨~ behavior⟩ **syn** obscure, dark, vague, enigmatic — **equiv·o·cal·ly** \-ē\ *adv*

equiv·o·cate \i-ˈkwiv-ə-ˌkāt\ *vb* **-cat·ed; -cat·ing 1** : to use misleading language **2** : to avoid giving a definite answer — **equiv·o·ca·tion** \-ˌkwiv-ə-ˈkā-shən\ *n*

[1]**-er** \ər\ *adj suffix or adv suffix* — used to form the comparative degree of adjectives and adverbs of one syllable ⟨hott*er*⟩ ⟨dri*er*⟩ and of some adjectives and adverbs of two syllables ⟨complet*er*⟩ and sometimes of longer ones

[2]**-er** \ər\ *also* **-ier** \ē-ər, yər\ *or* **-yer** \yər\ *n suffix* **1** : a person occupationally connected with ⟨hatt*er*⟩ ⟨law*yer*⟩ **2** : a person or thing belonging to or associated with ⟨old-tim*er*⟩ **3** : a native of : resident of ⟨New York*er*⟩ **4** : one that has ⟨double-deck*er*⟩ **5** : one that produces or yields ⟨pork*er*⟩ **6** : one that does or performs (a specified action) ⟨report*er*⟩ **7** : one that is a suitable object of (a specified action) ⟨broil*er*⟩ **8** : one that is ⟨foreign*er*⟩

Er *symbol* erbium

ER *abbr* emergency room

era \ˈir-ə, ˈer-ə, ˈē-rə\ *n* [LL *aera*, fr. L, counters, pl. of *aes* copper, money] **1** : a chronological order or system of notation reckoned from a given date as basis **2** : a period typified by some special feature **3** : any of the five major divisions of geologic time **syn** age, epoch, period, time

ERA *abbr* Equal Rights Amendment

erad·i·cate \i-ˈrad-ə-ˌkāt\ *vb* **-cat·ed; -cat·ing** [L *eradicatus*, pp. of *eradicare*, fr. *e-* out + *radix* root] : UPROOT, ELIMINATE **syn** exterminate, annihilate, abolish, extinguish — **erad·i·ca·ble** \-ˈrad-i-kə-bəl\ *adj*

erase \i-ˈrās\ *vb* **erased; eras·ing** : to rub or scratch out (as written words); *also* : OBLITERATE **syn** cancel, efface, delete, expunge — **eras·er** \i-ˈrā-sər\ *n* — **era·sure** \-shər\ *n*

er·bi·um \ˈər-bē-əm\ *n* : a rare metallic element — see ELEMENT table

[1]**ere** \(ˌ)eər\ *prep* : BEFORE

[2]**ere** *conj* : BEFORE

[1]**erect** \i-ˈrekt\ *adj* **1** : not leaning or lying down : UPRIGHT **2** : being in a state of physiological erection

[2]**erect** *vb* **1** : BUILD **2** : to fix or set in an upright position **3** : SET UP; *also* : ESTABLISH, DEVELOP

erec·tile \i-ˈrek-tᵊl, -ˌtīl\ *adj* : capable of becoming erect ⟨~ tissue⟩ ⟨~ feathers of a bird⟩

erec·tion \i-ˈrek-shən\ *n* **1** : the turgid state of a previously flaccid bodily part when it becomes dilated with blood **2** : CONSTRUCTION

ere·long \eər-ˈlȯŋ\ *adv* : before long

er·e·mite \ˈer-ə-ˌmīt\ *n* : HERMIT

er·go \ˈer-gō, ˈər-\ *adv* [L] : THEREFORE

er·got \ˈər-gət, -ˌgät\ *n* **1** : a disease of rye and other cereals caused by a fungus; *also* : this fungus **2** : a medicinal compound or preparation derived from an ergot fungus

Erie \ˈi(ə)r-ē\ *n* : a member of an American Indian people of the Lake Erie region; *also* : their language

er·mine \ˈər-mən\ *n, pl* **ermines 1** : any of several weasels with winter fur mostly white; *also* : the white fur of an ermine **2** : a rank or office whose official robe is ornamented with ermine

ermine 1

erode \i-ˈrōd\ *vb* **erod·ed; erod·ing** : to diminish or destroy by degrees; *esp* : to gradually eat into or wear away ⟨soil *eroded* by wind and water⟩ — **erod·ible** \-ˈrōd-ə-bəl\ *adj*

erog·e·nous \i-ˈräj-ə-nəs\ *adj* **1** : sexually sensitive ⟨~ zones⟩ **2** : of, relating to, or arousing sexual feelings

ero·sion \i-ˈrō-zhən\ *n* : the process or state of being eroded — **ero·sion·al** \-ˈrōzh-(ə-)nəl\ *adj* — **ero·sion·al·ly** \-ē\ *adv*

ero·sive \i-ˈrō-siv\ *adj* : tending to erode — **ero·sive·ness** *n*

erot·ic \i-ˈrät-ik\ *adj* : relating to or dealing with sexual love : AMATORY — **erot·i·cal·ly** \-i-k(ə-)lē\ *adv* — **erot·i·cism** \i-ˈrät-ə-ˌsiz-əm\ *n*

err \ˈər, ˈer\ *vb* : to be or do wrong

er·rand \ˈer-ənd\ *n* : a short trip taken to do something; *also* : the object or purpose of such a trip

er·rant \ˈer-ənt\ *adj* **1** : WANDERING **2** : straying outside proper bounds **3** : deviating from an accepted pattern or standard

er·ra·ta \e-ˈrät-ə\ *n* : a list of corrigenda

er·rat·ic \ir-ˈat-ik\ *adj* **1** : IRREGULAR, CAPRICIOUS **2** : ECCENTRIC, UNUSUAL — **er·rat·i·cal·ly** \-i-k(ə-)lē\ *adv*

er·ra·tum \e-ˈrät-əm\ *n, pl* **-ta** \-ə\ : CORRIGENDUM

er·ro·ne·ous \ir-ˈō-nē-əs, e-ˈrō-\ *adj* : INCORRECT — **er·ro·ne·ous·ly** *adv*

er·ror \ˈer-ər\ *n* **1** : a usu. ignorant or unintentional deviating from accuracy or truth ⟨made an ~ in adding⟩ **2** : a defensive misplay in baseball **3** : the state of one that errs ⟨to be in ~⟩ **4** : a product of mistake ⟨a typographical ~⟩ — **er·ror·less** *adj*

er·satz \ˈer-ˌzäts\ *adj* [G] : SUBSTITUTE, SYNTHETIC ⟨~ flour⟩

erst \ˈərst\ *adv, archaic* : ERSTWHILE

[1]**erst·while** \-ˌhwīl\ *adv* : in the past : FORMERLY

[2]**erstwhile** *adj* : FORMER, PREVIOUS

er·u·di·tion \ˌer-(y)ə-ˈdish-ən\ *n* : LEARNING, SCHOLARSHIP — **er·u·dite** \ˈer-(y)ə-ˌdīt\ *adj*

erupt \i-ˈrəpt\ *vb* **1** : to burst forth or cause to burst forth : EXPLODE **2** : to break through a surface ⟨teeth ~*ing* through the gum⟩ **3** : to break out with or as if with a skin rash — **erup·tion** \-ˈrəp-shən\ *n* — **erup·tive** \-tiv\ *adj*

-ery \(ə-)rē\ *n suffix* **1** : qualities collectively : character : -NESS ⟨snobb*ery*⟩ **2** : art : practice ⟨cook*ery*⟩ **3** : place of doing, keeping, producing, or selling (the thing specified) ⟨fish*ery*⟩ ⟨bak*ery*⟩ **4** : collection : aggregate ⟨fin*ery*⟩

ery·sip·e·las \ˌer-ə-ˈsip-(ə-)ləs, ˌir-\ *n* : an acute bacterial disease marked by fever and severe skin inflammation

er·y·the·ma \ˌer-ə-ˈthē-mə\ *n* : abnormal redness of the skin due to capillary congestion (as in inflammation)

eryth·ro·cyte \i-ˈrith-rə-ˌsīt\ *n* : RED BLOOD CELL

Es *symbol* einsteinium

[1]**-es** \əz, iz *after* s, z, sh, ch; z *after* v *or a vowel*\ *n pl suffix* — used to form the plural of most nouns that end in *s* ⟨glass*es*⟩, *z* ⟨fuzz*es*⟩, *sh* ⟨bush*es*⟩, *ch* ⟨peach*es*⟩, or a final *y* that changes to *i* ⟨lad*ies*⟩ and of some nouns ending in *f* that changes to *v* ⟨loav*es*⟩

[2]**-es** *adv suffix* : [2]-s

[3]**-es** *vb suffix* — used to form the third person singular present of most verbs that end in *s* ⟨bless*es*⟩, *z* ⟨fizz*es*⟩, *sh* ⟨hush*es*⟩, *ch* ⟨catch*es*⟩, or a final *y* that changes to *i* ⟨def*ies*⟩

es·ca·late \ˈes-kə-ˌlāt\ *vb* **-lat·ed; -lat·ing** : to increase in extent, volume, number, intensity, or scope — **es·ca·la·tion** \ˌes-kə-ˈlā-shən\ *n*

es·ca·la·tor \ˈes-kə-ˌlāt-ər\ *n* : a power-driven set of stairs

es·cal·lop \is-ˈkäl-əp, -ˈkal-\ *var of* SCALLOP

es·ca·pade \ˈes-kə-ˌpād\ *n* [F, action of escaping] : a mischievous adventure : PRANK

[1]**es·cape** \is-ˈkāp\ *vb* **es·caped; es·cap·ing** [ME *escapen*, fr. OF *escaper*, fr. (assumed) VL *excappare*, fr. L *ex-* out + LL *cappa* head covering, cloak] **1** : to get free or away **2** : to avoid a threatening evil **3** : to miss or succeed in averting ⟨~ injury⟩ **4** : ELUDE ⟨his name ~*s* me⟩ **5** : to be produced or uttered involuntarily by ⟨let a sob ~ him⟩

[2]**escape** *n* **1** : flight from or avoidance of something unpleasant **2** : LEAKAGE **3** : a means of escape

[3]**escape** *adj* : providing a means or way of escape

es·cap·ee \is-ˌkā-ˈpē, ˌes-(ˌ)kā-\ *n* : one that has escaped esp. from prison

escape velocity *n* : the minimum velocity needed by a body (as a rocket) to escape from the gravitational field of a celestial body (as the earth)

es·cap·ism \is-ˈkā-ˌpiz-əm\ *n* : diversion of the mind to imaginative activity as an escape from routine — **es·cap·ist** \-pəst\ *adj or n*

es·ca·role \ˈes-kə-ˌrōl\ *n* : ENDIVE 1

es·carp·ment \is-ˈkärp-mənt\ *n* **1** : a steep slope in front of a fortification **2** : a long cliff

es·chew \is-ˈchü\ *vb* : SHUN, AVOID

[1]**es·cort** \ˈes-ˌkȯrt\ *n* : one (as a person or warship) accompanying another esp. as a protection or courtesy

[2]**es·cort** \is-ˈkȯrt, es-\ *vb* : to accompany as an escort

es·crow \ˈes-ˌkrō\ *n* : something (as a deed or a sum of money) delivered by one person to another to be delivered to a third party only upon the fulfillment of a condition; *also* : a fund or deposit serving as an escrow

es·cu·do \is-ˈküd-ō\ *n, pl* **-dos** — see MONEY table

es·cutch·eon \is-ˈkəch-ən\ *n* : the usu. shield-shaped surface on which a coat of arms is shown

Esd *abbr* Esdras

Es·dras \ˈez-drəs\ *n* — see BIBLE table

ESE *abbr* east-southeast

Es·ki·mo \ˈes-kə-ˌmō\ *n* **1** : a member of a group of peoples of northern Canada, Greenland, Alaska, and eastern Siberia **2** : the language of the Eskimo people

Eskimo dog *n* : a sled dog of American origin

ESL *abbr* English as a second language

esoph·a·gus \i-ˈsäf-ə-gəs\ *n, pl* **-gi** \-ˌgī, -ˌjī\ : a muscular tube that leads from the cavity behind the mouth to the stomach — **esoph·a·geal** \-ˌsäf-ə-ˈjē-əl\ *adj*

es·o·ter·ic \ˌes-ə-ˈter-ik\ *adj* **1** : designed for or understood only by the specially initiated **2** : PRIVATE, SECRET

esp *abbr* especially

ESP \ˌē-ˌes-ˈpē\ *n* : extrasensory perception

es·pa·drille \ˈes-pə-ˌdril\ *n* [F] : a flat sandal usu. having a fabric upper and a flexible sole

es·pal·ier \is-ˈpal-yər, -ˌyā\ *n* : a plant (as a fruit tree) trained to grow flat against a support — **espalier** *vb*

es·pe·cial \is-ˈpesh-əl\ *adj* : SPECIAL, PARTICULAR — **es·pe·cial·ly** \-ˈpesh-(ə-)lē\ *adv*

Es·pe·ran·to \ˌes-pə-ˈrant-ō, -ˈrän-tō\ *n* : an artificial international language based as far as possible on words common to the chief European languages

es·pi·o·nage \ˈes-pē-ə-ˌnäzh, -nij\ *n* [F *espionnage*] : the practice of spying

es·pla·nade \ˈes-plə-ˌnäd\ *n* : a level open stretch or area; *esp* : one for walking or driving along a shore

es·pous·al \is-ˈpaů-zəl\ *n* **1** : BETROTHAL; *also* : WEDDING **2** : a taking up (as of a cause) as a supporter — **es·pouse** \-ˈpaůz\ *vb*

espres·so \e-ˈspres-ō\ *n, pl* **-sos** [It (*caffè*) *espresso,* lit., pressed out coffee] : coffee brewed by forcing steam through finely ground darkly roasted coffee beans

es·prit \is-ˈprē\ *n* : sprightly wit

es·prit de corps \is-ˌprēd-ə-ˈkōr\ *n* [F] : the common spirit existing in the members of a group

es·py \is-ˈpī\ *vb* **es·pied; es·py·ing** : to catch sight of **syn** behold, see, view, descry

Esq *or* **Esqr** *abbr* esquire

es·quire \ˈes-ˌkwī(ə)r\ *n* [ME, fr. MF *esquier* squire, fr. LL *scutarius,* fr. L *scutum* shield] **1** : a man of the English gentry ranking next below a knight **2** : a candidate for knighthood serving as attendant to a knight **3** — used as a title of courtesy

-ess \əs, ˌes\ *n suffix* : female ⟨author*ess*⟩

[1]**es·say** \e-ˈsā, ˈes-ˌā\ *vb* : ATTEMPT, TRY

[2]**es·say** *n* **1** \ˈes-ˌā, e-ˈsā\ : ATTEMPT **2** \ˈes-ˌā\ : a literary composition usu. dealing with a subject from a limited or personal point of view — **es·say·ist** \ˈes-ˌā-əst\ *n*

es·sence \ˈes-ᵊns\ *n* **1** : fundamental nature or quality **2** : a substance distilled or extracted from another substance (as a plant or drug) and having the special qualities of the original substance ⟨~ of peppermint⟩ **3** : PERFUME

[1]**es·sen·tial** \i-ˈsen-chəl\ *adj* **1** : containing or constituting an essence ⟨free speech is an ~ right of citizenship⟩ ⟨~ oils⟩ **2** : of the utmost importance : INDISPENSABLE **syn** imperative, necessary, necessitous — **es·sen·tial·ly** \-ē\ *adv*

[2]**essential** *n* : something essential

est *abbr* **1** established **2** estimate; estimated

EST *abbr* eastern standard time

[1]**-est** \əst, ist\ *adj suffix or adv suffix* — used to form the superlative degree of adjectives and adverbs of one syllable ⟨fatt*est*⟩ ⟨lat*est*⟩, of some adjectives and adverbs of two syllables ⟨luck*iest*⟩ ⟨often*est*⟩, and less often of longer ones ⟨beggarl*iest*⟩

[2]**-est** \əst, ist\ *or* **-st** \st\ *vb suffix* — used to form the archaic second person singular of English verbs (with *thou*) ⟨gett*est*⟩ ⟨did*st*⟩

es·tab·lish \is-ˈtab-lish\ *vb* **1** : to make firm or stable **2** : ORDAIN **3** : FOUND ⟨~ a settlement⟩; *also* : EFFECT **4** : to put on a firm basis : SET UP ⟨~ a son in business⟩ **5** : to gain acceptance or recognition of (as a claim or fact) ⟨~*ed* his right to help⟩; *also* : PROVE

es·tab·lish·ment \-mənt\ *n* **1** : something established **2** : a place of residence or business with its furnishings and staff **3** : an established ruling or controlling group ⟨the literary ~⟩ **4** : the act or state of establishing or being established

es·tate \is-ˈtāt\ *n* **1** : STATE, CONDITION; *also* : social standing : STATUS **2** : a social or political class ⟨the three ~*s* of nobility, clergy, and commons⟩ **3** : a person's possessions : FORTUNE **4** : a landed property

[1]**es·teem** \is-ˈtēm\ *n* : high regard

[2]**esteem** *vb* **1** : REGARD **2** : to set a high value on **syn** respect, admire, revere

es·ter \ˈes-tər\ *n* : an often fragrant organic compound formed by the reaction of an acid and an alcohol

Esth *abbr* Esther

Es·ther \ˈes-tər\ *n* — see BIBLE table

esthete, esthetic, esthetics *var of* AESTHETE, AESTHETIC, AESTHETICS

es·ti·ma·ble \ˈes-tə-mə-bəl\ *adj* : worthy of esteem

[1]**es·ti·mate** \ˈes-tə-ˌmāt\ *vb* **-mat·ed; -mat·ing 1** : to give or form an approximation (as of value, size, or cost) **2** : JUDGE, CONCLUDE **syn** evaluate, value, rate, appraise, assay, assess — **es·ti·ma·tor** \-ˌmā-tər\ *n*

[2]**es·ti·mate** \ˈes-tə-mət\ *n* **1** : OPINION, JUDGMENT **2** : a rough or approximate calculation **3** : a statement of the cost of work to be done

es·ti·ma·tion \ˌes-tə-ˈmā-shən\ *n* **1** : JUDGMENT, OPINION **2** : ESTIMATE **3** : ESTEEM, HONOR

es·ti·vate \ˈes-tə-ˌvāt\ *vb* **-vat·ed; -vat·ing** : to pass the summer in an inactive or resting state — **es·ti·va·tion** \ˌes-tə-ˈvā-shən\ *n*

Es·to·nian \e-ˈstō-nē-ən\ *n* : a native or inhabitant of Estonia

es·trange \is-ˈtrānj\ *vb* **es·tranged; es·trang·ing** : to alienate the affections or confidence of — **es·trange·ment** *n*

es·tro·gen \ˈes-trə-jən\ *n* : a substance (as a sex hormone) that tends to cause estrus and the development of secondary sex characteristics in the female — **es·tro·gen·ic** \ˌes-trə-ˈjen-ik\ *adj*

estrous cycle *n* : the cycle of changes in the endocrine and reproductive systems of a female mammal from the beginning of one period of estrus to the beginning of the next

es·trus \ˈes-trəs\ *n* : a periodic state of sexual excitability during which the female of most mammals is willing to mate with the male and is capable of becoming pregnant : HEAT — **es·trous** \-trəs\ *adj*

es·tu·ary \ˈes-chə-ˌwer-ē\ *n, pl* **-ar·ies** : an arm of the sea at the mouth of a river

ET *abbr* eastern time

ETA *abbr* estimated time of arrival

et al \et-ˈal\ *abbr* [L *et alii* (masc.), *et aliae* (fem.), or *et alia* (neut.)] and others

etc \ən-ˈsō-ˌfōrth, et-ˈset-ə-rə, -ˈse-trə\ *abbr* et cetera

et cet·era \et-ˈset-ə-rə, -ˈse-trə\ [L] and others esp. of the same kind

etch \ˈech\ *vb* [Dutch *etsen,* fr G *ätzen,* lit., to feed] **1** : to make lines on (as metal) usu. by the action of acid; *also* : to produce (as a design) by etching **2** : to delineate clearly — **etch·er** *n*

etch·ing \-iŋ\ *n* **1** : the act, process, or art of etching **2** : a design produced on or print made from an etched plate

ETD *abbr* estimated time of departure

eter·nal \i-ˈtərn-ᵊl\ *adj* : EVERLASTING, PERPETUAL — **eter·nal·ly** \-ē\ *adv*

eter·ni·ty \i-ˈtər-nət-ē\ *n, pl* **-ties 1** : infinite duration **2** : IMMORTALITY

¹-eth \əth, ith\ *or* **-th** \th\ *vb suffix* — used to form the archaic third person singular present of verbs ⟨go*eth*⟩ ⟨do*th*⟩

²-eth — see ²-TH

eth·ane \ˈeth-ˌān\ *n* : a colorless odorless gaseous hydrocarbon found in natural gas and used esp. as a fuel

eth·a·nol \ˈeth-ə-ˌnȯl\ *n* : ALCOHOL 1

ether \ˈē-thər\ *n* **1** : the upper regions of space; *also* : the gaseous element formerly held to fill these regions **2** : a light flammable liquid used as an anesthetic and solvent

ethe·re·al \i-ˈthir-ē-əl\ *adj* **1** : CELESTIAL, HEAVENLY **2** : exceptionally delicate AIRY, DAINTY — **ethe·re·al·ly** \-ē\ *adv* — **ethe·re·al·ness** *n*

eth·i·cal \ˈeth-i-kəl\ *adj* **1** : of or relating to ethics **2** : conforming to accepted and esp. professional standards of conduct **syn** virtuous, moral, principled — **eth·i·cal·ly** \-i-k(ə-)lē\ *adv*

eth·ics \ˈeth-iks\ *n sing or pl* **1** : a discipline dealing with good and evil and with moral duty **2** : moral principles or practice

Ethi·o·pi·an \ˌē-thē-ˈō-pē-ən\ *n* : a native or inhabitant of Ethiopia — **Ethiopian** *adj*

¹eth·nic \ˈeth-nik\ *n* : a member of a minority ethnic group who retains its customs, language, or social views

²ethnic *adj* : of or relating to races or large groups of people classed according to common traits and customs — **eth·ni·cal·ly** \-ni-k(ə-)lē\ *adv*

eth·nol·o·gy \eth-ˈnäl-ə-jē\ *n* : a science dealing with the races of man, their origin, distribution, characteristics, and relations — **eth·no·log·i·cal** \ˌeth-nə-ˈläj-i-kəl\ *adj* — **eth·nol·o·gist** \eth-ˈnäl-ə-jəst\ *n*

ethol·o·gy \ē-ˈthäl-ə-jē\ *n* : the scientific and objective study of animal behavior — **etho·log·i·cal** \ˌē-thə-ˈläj-i-kəl, ˌeth-ə-\ *adj* — **ethol·o·gist** \ē-ˈthäl-ə-jəst\ *n*

ethos \ˈē-ˌthäs\ *n* : the distinguishing character, sentiment, moral nature, or guiding beliefs of a person, group, or institution

ethyl alcohol *n* : ALCOHOL 1

eth·yl·ene \ˈeth-ə-ˌlēn\ *n* : a colorless flammable gas found in coal gas or obtained from petroleum

eti·ol·o·gy \ˌēt-ē-ˈäl-ə-jē\ *n* **1** : CAUSE, ORIGIN; *esp* : the causes of a disease or abnormal condition **2** : a branch of medicine concerned with the causes and origins of diseases — **eti·o·log·ic** \ˌēt-ē-ə-ˈläj-ik\ *or* **eti·o·log·i·cal** \-i-kəl\ *adj*

et·i·quette \ˈet-i-kət, -ˌket\ *n* [F *étiquette,* lit., ticket] : the forms prescribed by custom or authority to be observed in social, official, or professional life **syn** propriety, decorum, decency, dignity

Etrus·can \i-ˈtrəs-kən\ *n* **1** : the language of the Etruscans **2** : an inhabitant of ancient Etruria — **Etruscan** *adj*

et seq *abbr* [L *et sequens*] and the following one; [L *et sequentes* (masc. & fem. pl.) or *et sequentia* (neut. pl.)] and the following ones

-ette \ˈet, ˌet, ət, it\ *n suffix* **1** : little one ⟨din*ette*⟩ **2** : female ⟨major*ette*⟩

étude \ˈā-ˌt(y)üd\ *n* [F, lit., study] : a musical composition for practice to develop technical skill

ety *abbr* etymology

et·y·mol·o·gy \ˌet-ə-ˈmäl-ə-jē\ *n, pl* **-gies 1** : the history of a linguistic form (as a word) shown by tracing its development and relationships **2** : a branch of linguistics dealing with etymologies — **et·y·mo·log·i·cal** \-mə-ˈläj-i-kəl\ *adj* — **et·y·mol·o·gist** \-ˈmäl-ə-jəst\ *n*

Eu *symbol* europium

eu·ca·lyp·tus \ˌyü-kə-ˈlip-təs\ *n, pl* **-ti** \-ˌtī\ *or* **-tus·es** : any of a genus of mostly Australian evergreen trees widely grown for shade or their wood, oils, resins, and gums

Eu·cha·rist \ˈyü-k(ə-)rəst\ *n* : COMMUNION 2 — **eu·cha·ris·tic** \ˌyü-kə-ˈris-tik\ *adj, often cap*

¹eu·chre \ˈyü-kər\ *n* : a card game in which the side naming the trump must take three of five tricks to win

²euchre *vb* **eu·chred; eu·chring** \-k(ə-)riŋ\ : CHEAT, TRICK

eu·clid·e·an *also* **eu·clid·i·an** \yu̇-ˈklid-ē-ən\ *adj, often cap* : of or relating to the geometry of Euclid or a geometry based on similar axioms

eu·gen·ics \yu̇-ˈjen-iks\ *n* : a science dealing with the improvement (as by selective breeding) of hereditary qualities esp. of human beings — **eu·gen·ic** \-ik\ *adj*

eu·lo·gy \ˈyü-lə-jē\ *n, pl* **-gies 1** : a speech in praise of some person or thing **2** : high praise — **eu·lo·gis·tic** \ˌyü-lə-ˈjis-tik\ *adj* — **eu·lo·gize** \ˈyü-lə-ˌjīz\ *vb*

eu·nuch \ˈyü-nək\ *n* : a castrated man

eu·phe·mism \ˈyü-fə-ˌmiz-əm\ *n* [Gk *euphēmismos,* fr. *euphēmos* auspicious, sounding good, fr. *eu-* good + *phēmē* speech] : the substitution of a mild or pleasant expression for one offensive or unpleasant; *also* : the expression substituted — **eu·phe·mis·tic** \ˌyü-fə-ˈmis-tik\ *adj*

eu·pho·ni·ous \yu̇-ˈfō-nē-əs\ *adj* : pleasing to the ear

eu·pho·ny \ˈyü-fə-nē\ *n, pl* **-nies** : the effect produced by words so combined as to please the ear

eu·pho·ria \yu̇-ˈfōr-ē-ə\ *n* : a marked feeling of well-being or elation — **eu·phor·ic** \-ˈfȯr-ik\ *adj*

Eur *abbr* Europe; European

Eur·asian \yu̇-ˈrā-zhən, -shən\ *adj* **1** : of mixed European and Asian origin **2** : of or relating to Europe and Asia — **Eurasian** *n*

eu·re·ka \yu̇-ˈrē-kə\ *interj* [Gk *heurēka* I have found, fr. *heuriskein* to find; fr. the exclamation attributed to Archimedes on discovering a method for determining the purity of gold] — used to express triumph on a discovery

Eu·ro·bond \ˈyu̇r-ō-ˌbänd\ *n* : a bond of a U.S. corporation that is sold outside the U.S. but that is valued and paid for in dollars and yields interest in dollars

Eu·ro·cur·ren·cy \ˌyu̇r-ō-ˈkər-ən-sē, -ˈkə-rən-\ *n* : moneys (as of the U.S. and Japan) held outside their countries of origin and used in the money markets of Europe

Eu·ro·dol·lar \ˈyu̇r-ō-ˌdäl-ər\ *n* : a U.S. dollar held (as by a bank) outside the U.S. and esp. in Europe

Eu·ro·pe·an \ˌyu̇r-ə-ˈpē-ən\ *n* : a native or inhabitant of Europe — **European** *adj*

European plan *n* : a hotel plan whereby the daily rates cover only the cost of the room

eu·ro·pi·um \yu̇-ˈrō-pē-əm\ *n* : a metallic chemical element — see ELEMENT table

eu·sta·chian tube \yu̇-ˈstā-shən-\ *n, often cap E* : a tube connecting the inner cavity of the ear with the throat and equalizing air pressure on both sides of the eardrum

eu·tha·na·sia \ˌyü-thə-ˈnā-zh(ē-)ə\ *n* [Gk, easy death, fr. *eu-* good + *thanatos* death] : MERCY KILLING
eu·tro·phi·ca·tion \yu̇-ˌtrō-fə-ˈkā-shən\ *n* : the process by which a body of water becomes rich in dissolved nutrients (as phosphates) and often shallow with a seasonal deficiency in dissolved oxygen — **eu·tro·phic** \yu̇-ˈtrō-fik\ *adj*
EVA *abbr* extravehicular activity
evac·u·ate \i-ˈvak-yə-ˌwāt\ *vb* **-at·ed; -at·ing 1** : EMPTY **2** : to discharge wastes from the body **3** : to remove or withdraw from : VACATE — **evac·u·a·tion** \-ˌvak-yə-ˈwā-shən\ *n*
evac·u·ee \i-ˌvak-yə-ˈwē\ *n* : an evacuated person
evade \i-ˈvād\ *vb* **evad·ed; evad·ing** : to manage to avoid esp. by dexterity or slyness : ELUDE, ESCAPE
eval·u·ate \i-ˈval-yə-ˌwāt\ *vb* **-at·ed; -at·ing** : APPRAISE, VALUE — **eval·u·a·tion** \-ˌval-yə-ˈwā-shən\ *n*
ev·a·nes·cent \ˌev-ə-ˈnes-ᵊnt\ *adj* : tending to vanish like vapor **syn** passing, transient, transitory, momentary — **ev·a·nes·cence** \-ᵊns\ *n*
evan·gel·i·cal \ˌē-ˌvan-ˈjel-i-kəl, ˌev-ən-\ *adj* [LL *evangelium* gospel, fr. Gk *evangelion,* fr. *eu-* good + *angelos* messenger] **1** : of or relating to the Christian gospel esp. as presented in the four Gospels **2** : of or relating to certain Protestant churches emphasizing the authority of Scripture and the importance of preaching as contrasted with ritual **3** : ZEALOUS ⟨~ fervor⟩ — **Evangelical** *n* — **Evan·gel·i·cal·ism** \-kə-ˌliz-əm\ *n* — **evan·gel·i·cal·ly** \-k(ə-)lē\ *adv*
evan·ge·lism \i-ˈvan-jə-ˌliz-əm\ *n* **1** : the winning or revival of personal commitments to Christ **2** : militant or crusading zeal — **evan·ge·lis·tic** \-ˌvan-jə-ˈlis-tik\ *adj* — **evan·ge·lis·ti·cal·ly** \-ti-k(ə-)lē\ *adv*
evan·ge·list \i-ˈvan-jə-ləst\ *n* **1** *often cap* : the writer of any of the four Gospels **2** : one who evangelizes; *esp* : a preacher who conducts revival services
evan·ge·lize \i-ˈvan-jə-ˌlīz\ *vb* **-lized; -liz·ing 1** : to preach the gospel **2** : to convert to Christianity
evap *abbr* evaporate
evap·o·rate \i-ˈvap-ə-ˌrāt\ *vb* **-rat·ed; -rat·ing 1** : to pass off or cause to pass off in vapor **2** : to disappear quickly **3** : to drive out the moisture from (as by heat) — **evap·o·ra·tion** \-ˌvap-ə-ˈrā-shən\ *n* — **evap·o·ra·tor** \-ˌrāt-ər\ *n*
evap·o·rite \i-ˈvap-ə-ˌrīt\ *n* : a sedimentary rock that originates by the evaporation of seawater in an enclosed basin
eva·sion \i-ˈvā-zhən\ *n* **1** : an act or instance of evading **2** : a means of evading; *esp* : an equivocal statement used in evading — **eva·sive** \i-ˈvā-siv\ *adj* — **eva·sive·ness** *n*
eve \ˈēv\ *n* **1** : EVENING **2** : the period just before some important event
[1]**even** \ˈē-vən\ *adj* **1** : LEVEL, FLAT **2** : REGULAR, SMOOTH **3** : EQUAL, FAIR **4** : BALANCED; *also* : fully revenged **5** : divisible by two **6** : EXACT **syn** stable, uniform, steady, constant — **even·ly** *adv* — **even·ness** \-vən-nəs\ *n*
[2]**even** *adv* **1** : EXACTLY, PRECISELY **2** : FULLY, QUITE **3** : at the very time **4** — used as an intensive to stress identity ⟨~ we know that⟩ **5** — used as an intensive to stress the comparative degree ⟨did ~ better⟩
[3]**even** *vb* **evened; even·ing** \ˈēv-(ə-)niŋ\ : to make or become even
even·hand·ed \ˌē-vən-ˈhan-dəd\ *adj* : FAIR, IMPARTIAL
eve·ning \ˈēv-niŋ\ *n* : the end of the day and early part of the night
evening primrose *n* : a coarse biennial herb with yellow flowers that open in the evening
evening star *n* : a bright planet seen esp. in the western sky at or after sunset
even·song \ˈē-vən-ˌsȯŋ\ *n, often cap* **1** : VESPERS **2** : evening prayer esp. when sung
event \i-ˈvent\ *n* [MF or L; MF, fr. L *eventus,* fr. *evenire* to happen, fr. *venire* to come] **1** : OCCURRENCE **2** : a noteworthy happening **3** : CONTINGENCY ⟨in the ~ of rain⟩ **4** : a contest in a program of sports — **event·ful** *adj*
even·tide \ˈē-vən-ˌtīd\ *n* : EVENING
even·tu·al \i-ˈvench-(ə-w)əl\ *adj* : coming at some later time : ULTIMATE — **even·tu·al·ly** \-ē\ *adv*
even·tu·al·i·ty \i-ˌven-chə-ˈwal-ət-ē\ *n, pl* **-ties** : a possible event or outcome
even·tu·ate \i-ˈven-chə-ˌwāt\ *vb* **-at·ed; -at·ing** : to result finally
ev·er \ˈev-ər\ *adv* **1** : ALWAYS **2** : at any time **3** : in any way : AT ALL
ev·er·bloom·ing \ˌev-ər-ˈblü-miŋ\ *adj* : blooming more or less continuously throughout the growing season
ev·er·glade \ˈev-ər-ˌglād\ *n* : a low-lying tract of swampy or marshy land
ev·er·green \-ˌgrēn\ *adj* : having foliage that remains green ⟨coniferous trees are mostly ~⟩ — **evergreen** *n*
[1]**ev·er·last·ing** \ˌev-ər-ˈlas-tiŋ\ *adj* **1** : enduring forever : ETERNAL **2** : keeping form or color for a long time when dried ⟨~ flowers⟩ — **ev·er·last·ing·ly** *adv*
[2]**everlasting** *n* **1** : ETERNITY ⟨from ~⟩ **2** : a plant with everlasting flowers; *also* : its flower
ev·er·more \ˌev-ər-ˈmōr\ *adv* : FOREVER
ev·ery \ˈev-rē\ *adj* **1** : being each one of a group **2** : all possible ⟨given ~ chance⟩; *also* : COMPLETE ⟨have ~ confidence⟩
ev·ery·body \ˈev-ri-ˌbäd-ē, -bəd-\ *pron* : every person
ev·ery·day \ˈev-rē-ˌdā\ *adj* : used or fit for daily use : ORDINARY
ev·ery·one \-(ˌ)wən\ *pron* : EVERYBODY
ev·ery·thing \ˈev-rē-ˌthiŋ\ *pron* : all that exists; *also* : all that is relevant
ev·ery·where \ˈev-rē-ˌhweər\ *adv* : in every place or part
evg *abbr* evening
evict \i-ˈvikt\ *vb* : to put (a person) out from a property by legal process; *also* : EXPEL **syn** eject, oust, dismiss — **evic·tion** \-ˈvik-shən\ *n*
ev·i·dence \ˈev-əd-əns\ *n* **1** : an outward sign **2** : PROOF, TESTIMONY; *esp* : matter submitted in court to determine the truth of alleged facts
ev·i·dent \ˈev-əd-ənt\ *adj* : clear to the vision and understanding **syn** manifest, distinct, obvious, apparent, plain — **ev·i·dent·ly** \ˈev-əd-ənt-lē, -ə-ˌdent-\ *adv*
[1]**evil** \ˈē-vəl\ *adj* **evil·er** *or* **evil·ler; evil·est** *or* **evil·lest 1** : WICKED **2** : causing or threatening distress or harm : PERNICIOUS — **evil·ly** *adv*
[2]**evil** *n* **1** : a source of sorrow or distress : CALAMITY **2** : the fact of suffering, misfortune, and wrongdoing — **evil·do·er** \ˌē-vəl-ˈdü-ər\ *n*
evil–mind·ed \ˌē-vəl-ˈmīn-dəd\ *adj* : having an evil disposition or evil thoughts
evince \i-ˈvins\ *vb* **evinced; evinc·ing** : SHOW, REVEAL
evis·cer·ate \i-ˈvis-ə-ˌrāt\ *vb* **-at·ed; -at·ing 1** : to remove the entrails of **2** : to deprive of vital content or force — **evis·cer·a·tion** \-ˌvis-ə-ˈrā-shən\ *n*
evoke \i-ˈvōk\ *vb* **evoked; evok·ing** : to call forth or up — **evo·ca·tion** \ˌē-vō-ˈkā-shən, ˌev-ə-\ *n* — **evoc·a·tive** \i-ˈväk-ət-iv\ *adj*
evo·lu·tion \ˌev-ə-ˈlü-shən\ *n* **1** : a process of change in a particular direction **2** : one of a series of prescribed movements (as in a dance or military exercise) **3** : a theory that the various kinds of plants and animals are descended from other kinds that lived in earlier times and that the differences are due to inherited changes that took place over many generations — **evo·lu·tion·ary** \-shə-ˌner-ē\ *adj* — **evo·lu·tion·ist** \-sh(ə-)nəst\ *n*
evolve \i-ˈvälv\ *vb* **evolved; evolv·ing** [L *evolvere* to unroll] : to develop by or as if by evolution
EW *abbr* enlisted woman

ewe \ˈyü\ *n* : a female sheep
ew·er \ˈyü-ər\ *n* : a vase-shaped jug
[1]**ex** \(ˌ)eks\ *prep* [L] : out of : FROM
[2]**ex** \ˈeks\ *n* : a former spouse
[3]**ex** *abbr* **1** example **2** express **3** extra
Ex *abbr* Exodus
ex- \e *also occurs in this prefix where only* i *is shown below (as in "express") and* ks *sometimes occurs where only* gz *is shown (as in "exact")*\ *prefix* **1** : out of : outside **2** : former ⟨*ex*-president⟩
ex·ac·er·bate \ig-ˈzas-ər-ˌbāt\ *vb* **-bat·ed; -bat·ing** : to make more violent, bitter, or severe — **ex·ac·er·ba·tion** \-ˌzas-ər-ˈbā-shən\ *n*
[1]**ex·act** \ig-ˈzakt\ *vb* **1** : to compel to furnish **2** : to call for as suitable or necessary — **ex·ac·tion** \-ˈzak-shən\ *n*
[2]**exact** *adj* : precisely accurate or correct **syn** right, precise, proper, nice — **ex·act·ly** \-zak-(t)lē\ *adv* — **ex·act·ness** \-ˈzak(t)-nəs\ *n*
ex·act·ing \ig-ˈzak-tiŋ\ *adj* **1** : greatly demanding ⟨an ~ taskmaster⟩ **2** : requiring close attention and precision
ex·ac·ti·tude \ig-ˈzak-tə-ˌt(y)üd\ *n* : the quality or state of being exact
ex·ag·ger·ate \ig-ˈzaj-ə-ˌrāt\ *vb* **-at·ed; -at·ing** [L *exaggeratus*, pp. of *exaggerare*, lit., to heap up, fr. *agger* heap] : to enlarge (as a statement) beyond bounds : OVERSTATE — **ex·ag·ger·at·ed·ly** *adv* — **ex·ag·ger·a·tion** \-ˌzaj-ə-ˈrā-shən\ *n* — **ex·ag·ger·a·tor** \-ˈzaj-ə-rāt-ər\ *n*
ex·alt \ig-ˈzȯlt\ *vb* **1** : to raise up esp. in rank, power, or dignity **2** : GLORIFY **3** : to elate the mind or spirits — **ex·al·ta·tion** \ˌeg-ˌzȯl-ˈtā-shən, ˌek-ˌsȯl-\ *n*
ex·am \ig-ˈzam\ *n* : EXAMINATION
ex·am·ine \ig-ˈzam-ən\ *vb* **ex·am·ined; ex·am·in·ing** \-(ə-)niŋ\ **1** : to inspect closely **2** : QUESTION; *esp* : to test by questioning **syn** interrogate, query, quiz, catechize — **ex·am·i·na·tion** \-ˌzam-ə-ˈnā-shən\ *n*
ex·am·ple \ig-ˈzam-pəl\ *n* **1** : something forming a model to be followed or avoided **2** : a representative sample **3** : a problem to be solved in order to show the application of some rule
ex·as·per·ate \ig-ˈzas-pə-ˌrāt\ *vb* **-at·ed; -at·ing** : VEX, IRRITATE — **ex·as·per·a·tion** \ig-ˌzas-pə-ˈrā-shən\ *n*
exc *abbr* **1** excellent **2** except
ex·ca·vate \ˈek-skə-ˌvāt\ *vb* **-vat·ed; -vat·ing** **1** : to hollow out; *also* : to form by hollowing out **2** : to dig out and remove (as earth) **3** : to reveal to view by digging away a covering — **ex·ca·va·tion** \ˌek-skə-ˈvā-shən\ *n* — **ex·ca·va·tor** \ˈek-skə-ˌvāt-ər\ *n*
ex·ceed \ik-ˈsēd\ *vb* **1** : to go or be beyond the limit of **2** : SURPASS
ex·ceed·ing·ly \-iŋ-lē\ *or* **ex·ceed·ing** *adv* : EXTREMELY, VERY
ex·cel \ik-ˈsel\ *vb* **ex·celled; ex·cel·ling** : SURPASS, OUTDO
ex·cel·lence \ˈek-s(ə-)ləns\ *n* **1** : the quality of being excellent **2** : an excellent or valuable quality : VIRTUE **3** : EXCELLENCY 2
ex·cel·len·cy \-s(ə-)lən-sē\ *n, pl* **-cies** **1** : EXCELLENCE **2** — used as a title of honor
ex·cel·lent \ˈek-s(ə-)lənt\ *adj* : very good of its kind : FIRST-CLASS — **ex·cel·lent·ly** *adv*
ex·cel·si·or \ik-ˈsel-sē-ər\ *n* : fine curled wood shavings used esp. for packing fragile items
[1]**ex·cept** \ik-ˈsept\ *also* **ex·cept·ing** \-ˈsep-tiŋ\ *prep* **1** : not including ⟨daily ~ Sundays⟩ **2** : other than : BUT ⟨saw no one ~ him⟩
[2]**except** *vb* **1** : to take or leave out **2** : OBJECT
[3]**except** *also* **excepting** *conj* : ONLY ⟨I'd go, ~ it's too far⟩
ex·cep·tion \ik-ˈsep-shən\ *n* **1** : the act of excepting **2** : something excepted **3** : OBJECTION
ex·cep·tion·able \ik-ˈsep-sh(ə-)nə-bəl\ *adj* : OBJECTIONABLE
ex·cep·tion·al \ik-ˈsep-sh(ə-)nəl\ *adj* **1** : UNUSUAL **2** : SUPERIOR — **ex·cep·tion·al·ly** \-ˈsep-sh(ə-)nə-lē\ *adv*
ex·cerpt \ˈek-ˌsərpt, ˈeg-ˌzərpt\ *n* : a passage selected or copied : EXTRACT — **excerpt** \ek-ˈsərpt, eg-ˈzərpt; ˈek-ˌsərpt, ˈeg-ˌzərpt\ *vb*
ex·cess \ik-ˈses, ˈek-ˌses\ *n* **1** : SUPERFLUITY, SURPLUS **2** : the amount by which one quantity exceeds another **3** : INTEMPERANCE — **excess** *adj* — **ex·ces·sive** \ik-ˈses-iv\ *adj* — **ex·ces·sive·ly** *adv*
exch *abbr* exchange; exchanged
[1]**ex·change** \iks-ˈchānj, ˈeks-ˌchānj\ *n* **1** : the giving or taking of one thing in return for another : TRADE **2** : a substituting of one thing for another **3** : interchange of valuables and esp. of bills of exchange or money of different countries **4** : a place where things and services are exchanged; *esp* : a marketplace for securities **5** : a central office in which telephone lines are connected for communication
[2]**exchange** *vb* **ex·changed; ex·chang·ing** : to transfer in return for some equivalent : BARTER, SWAP — **ex·change·able** \iks-ˈchān-jə-bəl\ *adj*
ex·che·quer \ˈeks-ˌchek-ər\ *n* [ME *escheker*, fr. OF *eschequier* chessboard, counting table] : TREASURY; *esp* : a national treasury
ex·cise \ˈek-ˌsīz, -ˌsīs\ *n* : a tax on the manufacture, sale, or consumption of goods within a country
ex·ci·sion \-ˈsizh-ən\ *n* : removal by or as if by cutting out esp. by surgical means — **ex·cise** \ik-ˈsīz\ *vb*
ex·cit·able \ik-ˈsīt-ə-bəl\ *adj* : easily excited — **ex·cit·abil·i·ty** \-ˌsīt-ə-ˈbil-ət-ē\ *n*
ex·cite \ik-ˈsīt\ *vb* **ex·cit·ed; ex·cit·ing** **1** : to stir up the emotions of : ROUSE **2** : to increase the activity of : STIMULATE **syn** provoke, stimulate, pique, quicken — **ex·ci·ta·tion** \ˌek-ˌsī-ˈtā-shən, ˌek-sə-\ *n* — **ex·cit·ed·ly** *adv*
ex·cite·ment \ik-ˈsīt-mənt\ *n* : AGITATION, STIR
ex·claim \iks-ˈklām\ *vb* : to cry out, speak, or utter sharply or vehemently — **ex·cla·ma·tion** \ˌeks-klə-ˈmā-shən\ *n* — **ex·clam·a·to·ry** \iks-ˈklam-ə-ˌtōr-ē\ *adj*
exclamation point *n* : a punctuation mark ! used esp. after an interjection or exclamation
ex·clude \iks-ˈklüd\ *vb* **ex·clud·ed; ex·clud·ing** **1** : to shut out (as from using or participating) : BAR **2** : to put out : EXPEL — **ex·clu·sion** \-ˈklü-zhən\ *n*
ex·clu·sive \iks-ˈklü-siv\ *adj* **1** : reserved for particular persons **2** : snobbishly aloof; *also* : STYLISH **3** : SOLE ⟨~ rights⟩; *also* : UNDIVIDED **syn** chic, modish, smart, swank, fashionable — **ex·clu·sive·ly** *adv* — **ex·clu·sive·ness** *n*
exclusive of *prep* : not taking into account
ex·cog·i·tate \ek-ˈskäj-ə-ˌtāt\ *vb* : to think out : DEVISE
ex·com·mu·ni·cate \ˌek-skə-ˈmyü-nə-ˌkāt\ *vb* : to cut off officially from communion with the church — **ex·com·mu·ni·ca·tion** \-ˌmyü-nə-ˈkā-shən\ *n*
ex·co·ri·ate \ek-ˈskōr-ē-ˌāt\ *vb* **-at·ed; -at·ing** : to criticize severely — **ex·co·ri·a·tion** \(ˌ)ek-ˌskōr-ē-ˈā-shən\ *n*
ex·cre·ment \ˈek-skrə-mənt\ *n* : waste discharged from the body and esp. from the alimentary canal — **ex·cre·men·tal** \ˌek-skrə-ˈment-ᵊl\ *adj*
ex·cres·cence \ik-ˈskres-ᵊns\ *n* : OUTGROWTH; *esp* : an abnormal outgrowth (as a wart) — **ex·cres·cent** \-ᵊnt\ *adj*
ex·cre·ta \ik-ˈskrēt-ə\ *n pl* : waste matter separated or eliminated from an organism
ex·crete \ik-ˈskrēt\ *vb* **ex·cret·ed; ex·cret·ing** : to separate and eliminate wastes from the body esp. in urine — **ex·cre·tion** \-ˈskrē-shən\ *n* — **ex·cre·to·ry** \ˈek-skrə-ˌtōr-ē\ *adj*
ex·cru·ci·at·ing \ik-ˈskrü-shē-ˌāt-iŋ\ *adj* [L *excruciare*, fr. *cruciare* to crucify, fr. *crux* cross] : intensely painful or distressing **syn** agonizing, harrowing, torturous — **ex·cru·ci·at·ing·ly** *adv*
ex·cul·pate \ˈek-(ˌ)skəl-ˌpāt\ *vb* **-pat·ed; -pat·ing** : to clear from alleged fault or guilt **syn** absolve, exonerate, acquit, vindicate, clear
ex·cur·sion \ik-ˈskər-zhən\ *n* **1** : EXPEDITION; *esp* : a pleasure trip **2** : DIGRESSION — **ex·cur·sion·ist** \-ˈskərzh-(ə-)nəst\ *n*

ex·cur·sive \-ˈskər-siv\ *adj* : constituting or characterized by digression

[1]**ex·cuse** \ik-ˈskyüz\ *vb* **ex·cused; ex·cus·ing** [ME *excusen,* fr. OF *excuser,* fr. L *excusare,* fr. *causa* cause, explanation] **1** : to offer excuse for **2** : PARDON **3** : to release from an obligation **4** : JUSTIFY — **ex·cus·able** *adj*

[2]**excuse** \ik-ˈskyüs\ *n* **1** : an act of excusing **2** : grounds for being excused : JUSTIFICATION **3** : something that excuses or is a reason for excusing

exec *abbr* executive

ex·e·cra·ble \ˈek-si-krə-bəl\ *adj* **1** : DETESTABLE **2** : very bad ⟨~ spelling⟩

ex·e·crate \ˈek-sə-ˌkrāt\ *vb* **-crat·ed; -crat·ing** [L *exsecratus,* pp. of *exsecrari* to put under a curse, fr. *ex-* out of + *sacer* sacred] : to denounce as evil or detestable; *also* : DETEST — **ex·e·cra·tion** \ˌek-sə-ˈkrā-shən\ *n*

ex·e·cute \ˈek-si-ˌkyüt\ *vb* **-cut·ed; -cut·ing** **1** : to carry to completion : PERFORM **2** : to do what is called for by (as a law) **3** : to put to death in accordance with a legal sentence **4** : to produce in accordance with a plan or design **5** : to do what is needed to give legal force to (as a deed) — **ex·e·cu·tion** \ˌek-si-ˈkyü-shən\ *n* — **ex·e·cu·tion·er** \-sh(ə-)nər\ *n*

[1]**ex·ec·u·tive** \ig-ˈzek-(y)ət-iv\ *adj* **1** : designed for or related to carrying out plans or purposes **2** : of or relating to the enforcement of laws and the conduct of affairs

[2]**executive** *n* **1** : the branch of government with executive duties **2** : one having administrative or managerial responsibility

ex·ec·u·tor \ig-ˈzek-(y)ət-ər\ *n* : the person named in a will to carry out its provisions

ex·ec·u·trix \ig-ˈzek-(y)ə-ˌtriks\ *n, pl* **ex·ec·u·tri·ces** \-ˌzek-(y)ə-ˈtrī-ˌsēz\ *or* **ex·ec·u·trix·es** \-ˈzek-(y)ə-ˌtrik-səz\ : a woman who is an executor

ex·e·ge·sis \ˌek-sə-ˈjē-səs\ *n, pl* **-ge·ses** \-ˈjē-ˌsēz\ : explanation or critical interpretation of a text

ex·e·gete \ˈek-sə-ˌjēt\ *n* : one who practices exegesis

ex·em·plar \ig-ˈzem-ˌplär, -plər\ *n* **1** : one that serves as a model or pattern; *esp* : an ideal model **2** : a typical instance or example

ex·em·pla·ry \ig-ˈzem-plə-rē\ *adj* : serving as a pattern; *also* : COMMENDABLE

ex·em·pli·fy \ig-ˈzem-plə-ˌfī\ *vb* **-fied; -fy·ing** : to illustrate by example : serve as an example of — **ex·em·pli·fi·ca·tion** \-ˌzem-plə-fə-ˈkā-shən\ *n*

[1]**ex·empt** \ig-ˈzempt\ *adj* : free from some liability to which others are subject

[2]**exempt** *vb* : to make exempt : EXCUSE — **ex·emp·tion** \ig-ˈzemp-shən\ *n*

[1]**ex·er·cise** \ˈek-sər-ˌsīz\ *n* **1** : EMPLOYMENT, USE ⟨~ of authority⟩ **2** : exertion made for the sake of training **3** : a task or problem done to develop skill **4** *pl* : a public exhibition or ceremony

[2]**exercise** *vb* **-cised; -cis·ing** **1** : EXERT ⟨~ control⟩ **2** : to train by or engage in exercise **3** : WORRY, DISTRESS — **ex·er·cis·er** *n*

ex·ert \ig-ˈzərt\ *vb* : to bring or put into action ⟨~ influence⟩ ⟨~*ed* himself⟩ — **ex·er·tion** \-ˈzər-shən\ *n*

ex·hale \eks-ˈhāl\ *vb* **ex·haled; ex·hal·ing** **1** : to breathe out **2** : to give or pass off in the form of vapor — **ex·ha·la·tion** \ˌeks-(h)ə-ˈlā-shən\ *n*

[1]**ex·haust** \ig-ˈzȯst\ *vb* **1** : to use up wholly **2** : to tire or wear out **3** : to draw out completely (as air from a jar); *also* : EMPTY **4** : to develop (a subject) completely

[2]**exhaust** *n* **1** : the escape of used vapor or gas from an engine; *also* : the gas that escapes **2** : a system of pipes through which exhaust escapes

ex·haus·tion \ig-ˈzȯs-chən\ *n* : extreme weariness : FATIGUE

ex·haus·tive \ig-ˈzȯ-stiv\ *adj* : covering all possibilities : THOROUGH

[1]**ex·hib·it** \ig-ˈzib-ət\ *vb* **1** : to display esp. publicly **2** : to present to a court in legal form **syn** display, show, parade, flaunt — **ex·hi·bi·tion** \ek-sə-ˈbish-ən\ *n* — **ex·hib·i·tor** \ig-ˈzib-ət-ər\ *n*

[2]**exhibit** *n* **1** : an act or instance of exhibiting; *also* : something exhibited **2** : something produced and identified in court for use as evidence

ex·hi·bi·tion·ism \ˌek-sə-ˈbish-ə-ˌniz-əm\ *n* : the act or practice of so behaving as to attract undue attention sometimes by indecent exposure — **ex·hi·bi·tion·ist** \-ˈbish-(ə-)nəst\ *n or adj*

ex·hil·a·rate \ig-ˈzil-ə-ˌrāt\ *vb* **-rat·ed; -rat·ing** : ENLIVEN, STIMULATE — **ex·hil·a·ra·tion** \-ˌzil-ə-ˈrā-shən\ *n*

ex·hort \ig-ˈzȯrt\ *vb* : to urge, advise, or warn earnestly — **ex·hor·ta·tion** \ˌeks-ˌȯr-tā-shən, ˌegz-, -ər-\ *n*

ex·hume \igz-ˈ(y)üm, iks-ˈ(h)yüm\ *vb* **ex·humed; ex·hum·ing** [F or ML; F *exhumer,* fr. ML *exhumare,* fr. L *ex* out of + *humus* earth] : DISINTER — **ex·hu·ma·tion** \ˌeks-(h)yü-ˈmā-shən, ˌegz-(y)ü-\ *n*

ex·i·gen·cy \ˈek-sə-jən-sē, ig-ˈzij-ən-\ *n, pl* **-cies** **1** : urgent need **2** *pl* : REQUIREMENTS — **ex·i·gent** \ˈek-sə-jənt\ *adj*

ex·ig·u·ous \ig-ˈzig-yə-wəs\ *adj* : scanty in amount — **ex·i·gu·i·ty** \ˌeg-zi-ˈgyü-ət-ē\ *n*

[1]**ex·ile** \ˈeg-ˌzīl, ˈek-ˌsīl\ *n* **1** : BANISHMENT **2** : a person driven from his native place

[2]**exile** *vb* **ex·iled; ex·il·ing** : BANISH, EXPEL **syn** expatriate, deport, ostracize

ex·ist \ig-ˈzist\ *vb* **1** : to have being **2** : to continue to be : LIVE

ex·is·tence \ig-ˈzis-təns\ *n* **1** : continuance in living **2** : actual occurrence **3** : something existing — **ex·is·tent** \-tənt\ *adj*

ex·is·ten·tial \ˌeg-zis-ˈten-chəl, ˌek-sis-\ *adj* **1** : of or relating to existence **2** : EMPIRICAL **3** : having being in time and space **4** : of or relating to existentialism or existentialists

ex·is·ten·tial·ism \ˌeg-zis-ˈten-chə-ˌliz-əm\ *n* : a philosophy centered upon the analysis of existence and stressing the freedom, responsibility, and usu. the isolation of the individual — **ex·is·ten·tial·ist** \-ləst\ *adj or n*

ex·it \ˈeg-zət, ˈek-sət\ *n* **1** : a departure from a stage **2** : a going out or away; *also* : DEATH **3** : a way out of an enclosed space **4** : a point of departure from an expressway — **exit** *vb*

exo·bi·ol·o·gy \ˌek-sō-bī-ˈäl-ə-jē\ *n* : biology concerned with life originating or existing outside the earth or its atmosphere — **exo·bi·ol·o·gist** \-bī-ˈäl-ə-jəst\ *n*

exo·crine gland \ˈek-sə-krən-, -ˌkrīn-, -ˌkrēn-\ *n* : a gland (as a sweat gland or a kidney) that releases a secretion externally by means of a canal or duct

Exod *abbr* Exodus

ex·o·dus \ˈek-səd-əs\ *n* : a mass departure : EMIGRATION

Ex·o·dus *n* — see BIBLE table

ex of·fi·cio \ˌek-sə-ˈfish-ē-ˌō\ *adv or adj* : by virtue of or because of an office ⟨*ex officio* chairman⟩

ex·og·e·nous \ek-ˈsäj-ə-nəs\ *adj* : caused or produced by factors outside the organism or system — **ex·og·e·nous·ly** *adv*

ex·on·er·ate \ig-ˈzän-ə-ˌrāt\ *vb* **-at·ed; -at·ing** [ME *exoneraten,* fr. L *exonerare* to unburden, fr. *ex-* out + *onus* load] : to free from blame **syn** acquit, absolve, exculpate, vindicate — **ex·on·er·a·tion** \-ˌzän-ə-ˈrā-shən\ *n*

ex·or·bi·tant \ig-ˈzȯr-bət-ənt\ *adj* : exceeding what is usual or proper

ex·or·cise \ˈek-ˌsȯr-ˌsīz, -sər-\ *vb* **-cised; -cis·ing** **1** : to get rid of by or as if by solemn command **2** : to free of an evil spirit — **ex·or·cism** \-ˌsiz-əm\ *n* — **ex·or·cist** \-ˌsist\ *n*

exo·sphere \ˈek-sō-ˌsfiər\ *n* : the outermost region of the atmosphere

exo·ther·mic \ˌek-sō-ˈthər-mik\ *adj* : characterized by or formed with evolution of heat

ex·ot·ic \ig-ˈzät-ik\ *adj* : FOREIGN, STRANGE — **exotic** *n* — **ex·ot·i·cal·ly** \-i-k(ə-)lē\ *adv* — **ex·ot·i·cism** \-ˈzät-ə-ˌsiz-əm\ *n*

exp *abbr* **1** expense **2** experiment **3** export **4** express

ex·pand \ik-ˈspand\ *vb* **1** : to open up : UNFOLD **2** : ENLARGE **3** : to develop in detail **syn** amplify, swell, distend, inflate, dilate — **ex·pand·er** *n*

ex·panse \ik-ˈspans\ *n* : a broad extent (as of land or sea)

ex·pan·sion \ik-ˈspan-chən\ *n* **1** : the act or process of expanding **2** : the quality or state of being expanded **3** : an expanded part or thing

ex·pan·sive \ik-ˈspan-siv\ *adj* **1** : tending to expand or to cause expansion **2** : warmly benevolent or emotional **3** : of large extent or scope — **ex·pan·sive·ly** *adv* — **ex·pan·sive·ness** *n*

ex par·te \eks-ˈpärt-ē\ *adv or adj* [ML] : from a one-sided point of view

ex·pa·ti·ate \ek-ˈspā-shē-ˌāt\ *vb* **-at·ed; -at·ing** : to talk or write at length — **ex·pa·ti·a·tion** \ek-ˌspā-shē-ˈā-shən\ *n*

[1]**ex·pa·tri·ate** \ek-ˈspā-trē-ˌāt\ *vb* **-at·ed; -at·ing** : EXILE — **ex·pa·tri·a·tion** \ek-ˌspā-trē-ˈā-shən\ *n*

[2]**ex·pa·tri·ate** \ek-ˈspā-trē-ˌāt, -trē-ət\ *adj* : living in a foreign country — **expatriate** *n*

ex·pect \ik-ˈspekt\ *vb* **1** : SUPPOSE, THINK **2** : to look forward to : ANTICIPATE **3** : to consider reasonable, due, or necessary **4** : to consider to be obliged

ex·pec·tan·cy \-ˈspek-tən-sē\ *n, pl* **-cies 1** : EXPECTATION **2** : the expected amount (as of years of life)

ex·pec·tant \-tənt\ *adj* : EXPECTING; *esp* : expecting the birth of a child — **ex·pec·tant·ly** *adv*

ex·pec·ta·tion \ˌek-ˌspek-ˈtā-shən\ *n* **1** : the act or state of expecting **2** : prospect of good or bad fortune — usu. used in pl. **3** : something expected

ex·pec·to·rant \ik-ˈspek-t(ə-)rənt\ *n* : an agent that promotes the discharge or expulsion of mucus from the respiratory tract — **expectorant** *adj*

ex·pec·to·rate \-tə-ˌrāt\ *vb* **-rat·ed; -rat·ing** : SPIT — **ex·pec·to·ra·tion** \-ˌspek-tə-ˈrā-shən\ *n*

ex·pe·di·ence \ik-ˈspēd-ē-əns\ *n* : EXPEDIENCY

ex·pe·di·en·cy \-ən-sē\ *n, pl* **-cies 1** : fitness to some end **2** : use of expedient means and methods; *also* : something expedient

[1]**ex·pe·di·ent** \ik-ˈspēd-ē-ənt\ *adj* [ME, fr. MF or L; MF, fr. L *expediens* prp. of *expedire* to extricate, arrange, be advantageous, fr. *ex-* out + *ped-*, *pes* foot] **1** : adapted for achieving a particular end **2** : marked by concern with what is advantageous; *esp* : governed by self-interest

[2]**expedient** *n* : something expedient; *esp* : a temporary means to an end

ex·pe·dite \ˈek-spə-ˌdīt\ *vb* **-dit·ed; -dit·ing** : to carry out promptly; *also* : to speed up

ex·pe·dit·er \-ˌdīt-ər\ *n* : one that expedites; *esp* : one employed to ensure efficient movement of goods or supplies in a business

ex·pe·di·tion \ˌek-spə-ˈdish-ən\ *n* **1** : a journey for a particular purpose; *also* : the persons making it **2** : efficient promptness

ex·pe·di·tion·ary \-ˈdish-ə-ˌner-ē\ *adj* : of, relating to, or constituting an expedition; *also* : sent on military service abroad

ex·pe·di·tious \ˌek-spə-ˈdish-əs\ *adj* : marked by or acting with prompt efficiency **syn** swift, fast, rapid, speedy

ex·pel \ik-ˈspel\ *vb* **ex·pelled; ex·pel·ling** : to drive or force out : EJECT

ex·pend \ik-ˈspend\ *vb* **1** : to pay out : SPEND **2** : UTILIZE; *also* : USE UP — **ex·pend·able** *adj*

ex·pen·di·ture \ik-ˈspen-di-chər, -də-ˌchu̇r\ *n* **1** : the act or process of expending **2** : something expended

ex·pense \ik-ˈspens\ *n* **1** : EXPENDITURE **2** : COST **3** : a cause of expenditure **4** : SACRIFICE

ex·pen·sive \ik-ˈspen-siv\ *adj* : COSTLY, DEAR — **ex·pen·sive·ly** *adv*

[1]**ex·pe·ri·ence** \ik-ˈspir-ē-əns\ *n* **1** : observation or practice resulting in or tending toward knowledge; *also* : the resulting state of enhanced comprehension and efficiency **2** : a state of being affected from without (as by events); *also* : an affecting event ⟨a startling ~⟩ **3** : something or the totality experienced (as by a person or community)

[2]**experience** *vb* **-enced; -enc·ing 1** : FIND OUT, DISCOVER **2** : to know as an experience : SUFFER, UNDERGO

ex·pe·ri·enced \-ənst\ *adj* : made capable by repeated experience

[1]**ex·per·i·ment** \ik-ˈsper-ə-mənt\ *n* : a controlled procedure carried out to discover, test, or demonstrate something; *also* : the process of testing — **ex·per·i·men·tal** \-ˌsper-ə-ˈment-ᵊl\ *adj*

[2]**ex·per·i·ment** \-ˌment\ *vb* : to make experiments — **ex·per·i·men·ta·tion** \ik-ˌsper-ə-mən-ˈtā-shən\ *n* — **ex·per·i·men·ter** \-ˈsper-ə-ˌment-ər\ *n*

[1]**ex·pert** \ˈek-ˌspərt\ *adj* : showing special skill or knowledge — **ex·pert·ly** *adv* — **ex·pert·ness** *n*

[2]**ex·pert** \ˈek-ˌspərt\ *n* : an expert person : SPECIALIST

ex·per·tise \ˌek-(ˌ)spər-ˈtēz\ *n* : the skill of an expert

ex·pi·ate \ˈek-spē-ˌāt\ *vb* **-at·ed; -at·ing** : to make amends : ATONE — **ex·pi·a·tion** \ˌek-spē-ˈā-shən\ *n*

ex·pi·a·to·ry \ˈek-spē-ə-ˌtōr-ē\ *adj* : serving to expiate

ex·pire \ik-ˈspī(ə)r, ek-\ *vb* **ex·pired; ex·pir·ing 1** : to breathe one's last breath : DIE **2** : to come to an end **3** : to breathe out from or as if from the lungs — **ex·pi·ra·tion** \ˌek-spə-ˈrā-shən\ *n*

ex·plain \ik-ˈsplān\ *vb* [ME *explanen*, fr. L *explanare*, lit., to make level, fr. *planus* level, flat] **1** : to make clear **2** : to give the reason for — **ex·pla·na·tion** \ˌek-splə-ˈnā-shən\ *n* — **ex·plan·a·to·ry** \ik-ˈsplan-ə-ˌtōr-ē\ *adj*

ex·ple·tive \ˈek-splət-iv\ *n* : a usu. profane exclamation

ex·pli·ca·ble \ek-ˈsplik-ə-bəl, ˈek-(ˌ)splik-\ *adj* : capable of being explained

ex·pli·cate \ˈek-splə-ˌkāt\ *vb* **-cat·ed; -cat·ing** : to give a detailed explanation of

ex·plic·it \ik-ˈsplis-ət\ *adj* : clearly and precisely expressed — **ex·plic·it·ly** *adv* — **ex·plic·it·ness** *n*

ex·plode \ik-ˈsplōd\ *vb* **ex·plod·ed; ex·plod·ing** [L *explodere* to drive off the stage by clapping, fr. *ex-* out + *plaudere* to clap] **1** : DISCREDIT ⟨~ a belief⟩ **2** : to burst or cause to burst violently and noisily ⟨~ a bomb⟩ ⟨the boiler *exploded*⟩ **3** : to undergo a rapid chemical or nuclear reaction with production of heat and violent expansion of gas ⟨~ dynamite⟩ **4** : to give forth a sudden strong and noisy outburst of emotion ⟨~ with rage⟩

ex·plod·ed \-əd\ *adj* : showing the parts separated but in correct relationship to each other ⟨an ~ view of a carburetor⟩

[1]**ex·ploit** \ˈek-ˌsplȯit\ *n* : DEED; *esp* : a notable or heroic act

[2]**ex·ploit** \ik-ˈsplȯit\ *vb* **1** : to put to productive use ⟨~ resources⟩; *also* : UTILIZE **2** : to use unfairly for one's own advantage — **ex·ploi·ta·tion** \ˌek-ˌsplȯi-ˈtā-shən\ *n*

ex·plore \ik-ˈsplōr\ *vb* **ex·plored; ex·plor·ing 1** : to look into or travel over thoroughly **2** : to examine carefully ⟨~ a wound⟩ — **ex·plo·ra·tion** \ˌek-splə-ˈrā-shən\ *n* — **ex·plor·ato·ry** \ik-ˈsplōr-ə-ˌtōr-ē\ *adj* — **ex·plor·er** *n*

ex·plo·sion \ik-ˈsplō-zhən\ *n* : the act or an instance of exploding

ex·plo·sive \ik-ˈsplō-siv\ *adj* **1** : relating to or able to cause explosion **2** : tending to explode — **explosive** *n* — **ex·plo·sive·ly** *adv*

ex·po \ˈek-ˌspō\ *n, pl* **expos** : EXPOSITION 2

ex·po·nent \ik-ˈspō-nənt, ˈek-ˌspō-\ *n* **1** : a symbol written above and to the right of a mathematical expression to signify how many times it is to be used as a factor ⟨in

a^3 the ∼ *3* indicates that *a* is to be used three times in the product *a·a·a*⟩ **2** : INTERPRETER, EXPOUNDER **3** : ADVOCATE, CHAMPION — **ex·po·nen·tial** \ˌek-spə-ˈnen-chəl\ *adj* — **ex·po·nen·tial·ly** \-ē\ *adv*

ex·po·nen·ti·a·tion \ˌek-spə-ˌnen-chē-ˈā-shen\ *n* : the mathematical operation of raising a quantity to a power

[1]ex·port \ek-ˈspōrt, ˈek-ˌspōrt\ *vb* : to send (as merchandise) to foreign countries — **ex·por·ta·tion** \ˌek-ˌspōr-ˈtā-shən, -spər-\ *n* — **ex·port·er** \ek-ˈspōrt-ər, ˈek-ˌspōrt-\ *n*

[2]ex·port \ˈek-ˌspōrt\ *n* **1** : something exported esp. for trade **2** : an act or the business of exporting

ex·pose \ik-ˈspōz\ *vb* **ex·posed; ex·pos·ing 1** : to deprive of shelter or protection **2** : to submit or subject to an action or influence; *esp* : to subject (as photographic film) to radiant energy (as light) **3** : to display esp. for sale **4** : to bring to light : DISCLOSE

ex·po·sé *or* **ex·po·se** \ˌek-spō-ˈzā\ *n* : an exposure of something discreditable

ex·po·si·tion \ˌek-spə-ˈzish-ən\ *n* **1** : a setting forth of the meaning or purpose (as of a writing); *also* : discourse designed to convey information **2** : a public exhibition

ex·pos·i·tor \ik-ˈspäz-ət-ər\ *n* : one who explains : COMMENTATOR

ex post fac·to \ˌek-ˈspōst-ˌfak-tō\ *adv or adj* : after the fact

ex·pos·tu·late \ik-ˈspäs-chə-ˌlāt\ *vb* : to reason earnestly with a person esp. in dissuading : REMONSTRATE — **ex·pos·tu·la·tion** \-ˌspäs-chə-ˈlā-shən\ *n*

ex·po·sure \ik-ˈspō-zhər\ *n* **1** : the fact or condition of being exposed **2** : the act or an instance of exposing **3** : the length of time for which a film is exposed **4** : a section of a photographic film for one picture

ex·pound \ik-ˈspau̇nd\ *vb* **1** : STATE **2** : INTERPRET, EXPLAIN — **ex·pound·er** *n*

[1]ex·press \ik-ˈspres\ *adj* **1** : EXPLICIT; *also* : EXACT, PRECISE **2** : SPECIFIC ⟨his ∼ purpose⟩ **3** : traveling at high speed and esp. with few stops ⟨∼ train⟩; *also* : adapted to high speed use ⟨∼ roads⟩ — **ex·press·ly** *adv*

[2]express *adv* : by express ⟨ship it ∼⟩

[3]express *n* **1** : a system for the prompt transportation of goods; *also* : a company operating such a service or the shipments so transported **2** : an express vehicle

[4]express *vb* **1** : to make known : SHOW, STATE ⟨∼ regret⟩; *also* : SYMBOLIZE **2** : to squeeze out : extract by pressing **3** : to send by express

ex·pres·sion \ik-ˈspresh-ən\ *n* **1** : UTTERANCE **2** : something that represents or symbolizes : SIGN; *esp* : a mathematical symbol or combination of signs and symbols representing a quantity or operation **3** : a significant word or phrase; *also* : manner of expressing (as in writing or music) **4** : facial aspect or vocal intonation indicative of feeling — **ex·pres·sion·less** *adj*

ex·pres·sion·ism \ik-ˈspresh-ə-ˌniz-əm\ *n* : a theory or practice in art of seeking to depict the artist's subjective responses to objects and events — **ex·pres·sion·ist** \-ˈspresh-(ə-)nəst\ *n or adj* — **ex·pres·sion·is·tic** \-ˌspresh-ə-ˈnis-tik\ *adj*

ex·pres·sive \ik-ˈspres-iv\ *adj* **1** : of or relating to expression **2** : serving to express — **ex·pres·sive·ly** *adv* — **ex·pres·sive·ness** *n*

ex·press·way \ik-ˈspres-ˌwā\ *n* : a divided superhighway with limited access

ex·pro·pri·ate \ek-ˈsprō-prē-ˌāt\ *vb* **-at·ed; -at·ing** : to deprive of possession or the right to own — **ex·pro·pri·a·tion** \(ˌ)ek-ˌsprō-prē-ˈā-shən\ *n*

expt *abbr* experiment

ex·pul·sion \ik-ˈspəl-shən\ *n* : an expelling or being expelled : EJECTION

ex·punge \ik-ˈspənj\ *vb* **ex·punged; ex·pung·ing** [L *expungere* to mark for deletion by dots, fr. *ex-* out + *pungere* to prick] : OBLITERATE, ERASE

ex·pur·gate \ˈek-spər-ˌgāt\ *vb* **-gat·ed; -gat·ing** : to clear (as a book) of objectionable passages — **ex·pur·ga·tion** \ˌek-spər-ˈgā-shən\ *n*

ex·qui·site \ek-ˈskwiz-ət, ˈek-(ˌ)skwiz-\ *adj* [ME *exquisit*, fr. L *exquisitus*, fr. pp. of *exquirere* to search out, fr. *quaerere* to seek] **1** : excellent in form or workmanship **2** : keenly appreciative **3** : pleasingly beautiful or delicate **4** : INTENSE

ext *abbr* **1** extension **2** exterior **3** external **4** extra **5** extract

ex·tant \ˈek-stənt; ek-ˈstant\ *adj* : EXISTENT; *esp* : not lost or destroyed

ex·tem·po·ra·ne·ous \ek-ˌstem-pə-ˈrā-nē-əs\ *adj* : not planned beforehand : IMPROMPTU — **ex·tem·po·ra·ne·ous·ly** *adv*

ex·tem·po·rary \ik-ˈstem-pə-ˌrer-ē\ *adj* : EXTEMPORANEOUS

ex·tem·po·re \ik-ˈstem-pə-(ˌ)rē\ *adv* : EXTEMPORANEOUSLY

ex·tem·po·rize \ik-ˈstem-pə-ˌrīz\ *vb* **-rized; -riz·ing** : to do something extemporaneously

ex·tend \ik-ˈstend\ *vb* **1** : to spread or stretch forth or out (as in reaching or straightening) **2** : to exert or cause to exert to full capacity **3** : PROFFER ⟨∼ credit⟩ **4** : PROLONG ⟨∼ a note⟩ **5** : to make greater or broader ⟨∼ knowledge⟩ ⟨∼ a business⟩ **6** : to stretch out or reach across a distance, space, or time **syn** lengthen, elongate, protract — **ex·tend·able** *or* **ex·tend·ible** \-ˈsten-də-bəl\ *adj*

ex·ten·sion \ik-ˈsten-chən\ *n* **1** : an extending or being extended **2** : educational programs (as correspondence courses) that reach beyond the campus of a school **3** : an additional part ⟨∼ on a house⟩

ex·ten·sive \ik-ˈsten-siv\ *adj* : of considerable extent : FAR-REACHING, BROAD — **ex·ten·sive·ly** *adv*

ex·tent \ik-ˈstent\ *n* **1** : the size, length, or bulk of something ⟨a property of large ∼⟩ **2** : the degree or measure of something ⟨the ∼ of his guilt⟩

ex·ten·u·ate \ik-ˈsten-yə-ˌwāt\ *vb* **-at·ed; -at·ing** : to lessen the seriousness of — **ex·ten·u·a·tion** \-ˌsten-yə-ˈwā-shən\ *n*

[1]ex·te·ri·or \ek-ˈstir-ē-ər\ *adj* **1** : EXTERNAL **2** : suitable for use on an outside surface ⟨∼ paint⟩

[2]exterior *n* : an exterior part or surface

ex·ter·mi·nate \ik-ˈstər-mə-ˌnāt\ *vb* **-nat·ed; -nat·ing** : to get rid of completely **syn** extirpate, eradicate, abolish, annihilate — **ex·ter·mi·na·tion** \-ˈstər-mə-ˈnā-shən\ *n*

ex·ter·mi·na·tor \ik-ˈstər-mə-ˌnāt-ər\ *n* : one that exterminates; *esp* : a person whose occupation is destroying household vermin with chemicals

[1]ex·ter·nal \ek-ˈstərn-ᵊl\ *adj* **1** : outwardly perceivable; *also* : SUPERFICIAL **2** : of, relating to, or located on the outside or an outer part **3** : arising or acting from without; *also* : FOREIGN ⟨∼ affairs⟩ — **ex·ter·nal·ly** \-ē\ *adv*

[2]external *n* : an external feature

ex·tinct \ik-ˈstiŋkt\ *adj* **1** : EXTINGUISHED ⟨with hope ∼⟩; *also* : no longer active (as a volcano) **2** : no longer existing (as a kind of plant or animal) or in use (as a language) — **ex·tinc·tion** \ik-ˈstiŋk-shən\ *n*

ex·tin·guish \ik-ˈstiŋ-gwish\ *vb* : to put out (as a fire); *also* : to bring to an end (as by destroying) — **ex·tin·guish·able** *adj* — **ex·tin·guish·er** *n*

ex·tir·pate \ˈek-stər-ˌpāt\ *vb* **-pat·ed; -pat·ing** [L *exstirpatus*, pp. *exstirpare*, fr. *ex-* out + *stirps* trunk, root] **1** : UPROOT **2** : to destroy completely **syn** exterminate, eradicate, abolish, annihilate — **ex·tir·pa·tion** \ˌek-stər-ˈpā-shən\ *n*

ex·tol *also* **ex·toll** \ik-ˈstōl\ *vb* **ex·tolled; ex·tol·ling** : to praise highly : GLORIFY **syn** laud, eulogize

ex·tort \ik-ˈstȯrt\ *vb* [L *extortus*, pp. of *extorquēre* to wrench out, extort, fr. *ex-* out + *torquēre* to twist] : to obtain by force or improper pressure ⟨~ a bribe⟩ — **ex·tor·tion** \-ˈstȯr-shən\ *n* — **ex·tor·tion·er** *n* — **ex·tor·tion·ist** *n*

ex·tor·tion·ate \ik-ˈstȯr-sh(ə-)nət\ *adj* : EXCESSIVE, EXORBITANT — **ex·tor·tion·ate·ly** *adv*

¹ex·tra \ˈek-strə\ *adj* **1** : ADDITIONAL **2** : SUPERIOR **syn** spare, surplus, superfluous

²extra *n* **1** : something (as a charge) added **2** : a special edition of a newspaper **3** : an additional worker or performer (as in a group scene)

³extra *adv* : beyond what is usual

¹ex·tract \ik-ˈstrakt, *esp for 3* ˈek-ˌstrakt\ *vb* **1** : to draw out; *esp* : to pull out forcibly ⟨~ a tooth⟩ **2** : to withdraw (as a juice or a constituent) by a physical or chemical process **3** : to select for citation : QUOTE — **ex·tract·able** *adj* — **ex·trac·tion** \-ˈstrak-shən\ *n* — **ex·trac·tor** \-tər\ *n*

²ex·tract \ˈek-ˌstrakt\ *n* **1** : EXCERPT, CITATION **2** : a product (as a juice or concentrate) obtained by extracting

ex·tra·cur·ric·u·lar \ˌek-strə-kə-ˈrik-yə-lər\ *adj* : lying outside the regular curriculum; *esp* : of or relating to school-connected activities (as sports) carrying no academic credit

ex·tra·dite \ˈek-strə-ˌdīt\ *vb* **-dit·ed; -dit·ing** : to obtain by or deliver up to extradiction

ex·tra·di·tion \ˌek-strə-ˈdish-ən\ *n* : surrendering an alleged criminal to a different jurisdiction for trial

ex·tra·mar·i·tal \ˌek-strə-ˈmar-ət-ᵊl\ *adj* : of or relating to sexual intercourse by a married person with someone other than his or her spouse

ex·tra·mu·ral \-ˈmyu̇r-əl\ *adj* : existing or functioning beyond the bounds of an organized unit

ex·tra·ne·ous \ek-ˈstrā-nē-əs\ *adj* **1** : coming from without ⟨~ moisture⟩ **2** : not intrinsic ⟨~ incidents in a story⟩; *also* : IRRELEVANT ⟨~ digressions⟩ — **ex·tra·ne·ous·ly** *adv*

ex·traor·di·nary \ik-ˈstrȯrd-ᵊn-ˌer-ē, ˌek-strə-ˈȯrd-\ *adj* **1** : notably unusual or exceptional **2** : employed on special service — **ex·traor·di·nari·ly** \ik-ˌstrȯrd-ᵊn-ˈer-ə-lē, ˌek-strə-ˌȯrd-\ *adv*

ex·trap·o·late \ik-ˈstrap-ə-ˌlāt\ *vb* **-lat·ed; -lat·ing** : to infer (unknown data) from known data — **ex·trap·o·la·tion** \-ˌstrap-ə-ˈlā-shən\ *n*

ex·tra·sen·so·ry \ˌek-strə-ˈsens-(ə-)rē\ *adj* : not acting or occurring through the known senses ⟨~ perception⟩

ex·tra·ter·res·tri·al \-tə-ˈres-trē-əl\ *adj* : originating or existing outside the earth or its atmosphere ⟨~ life⟩ — **extraterrestrial** *n*

ex·tra·ter·ri·to·ri·al \-ˌter-ə-ˈtōr-ē-əl\ *adj* : existing or taking place outside the territorial limits of a jurisdiction

ex·tra·ter·ri·to·ri·al·i·ty \-ˌtōr-ē-ˈal-ət-ē\ *n* : exemption from the application or jurisdiction of local law or tribunals ⟨diplomats enjoy ~⟩

ex·trav·a·gant \ik-ˈstrav-i-gənt\ *adj* **1** : EXCESSIVE ⟨~ claims⟩ **2** : unduly lavish : WASTEFUL **3** : too costly **syn** immoderate, exorbitant, extreme, inordinate, undue — **ex·trav·a·gance** \-gəns\ *n* — **ex·trav·a·gant·ly** *adv*

ex·trav·a·gan·za \ik-ˌstrav-ə-ˈgan-zə\ *n* **1** : a literary or musical work marked by extreme freedom of style and structure **2** : a spectacular show

ex·tra·ve·hic·u·lar \ˌek-strə-vē-ˈhik-yə-lər\ *adj* : taking place outside a vehicle (as a spacecraft) ⟨~ activity⟩

¹ex·treme \ik-ˈstrēm\ *adj* **1** : very great or intense ⟨~ cold⟩ **2** : very severe or drastic ⟨~ measures⟩ **3** : going to great lengths or beyond normal limits ⟨politically ~⟩ **4** : most remote ⟨the ~ end⟩ **5** : UTMOST; *also* : MAXIMUM ⟨an ~ effort⟩ — **ex·treme·ly** *adv*

²extreme *n* **1** : something located at one end or the other of a range or series **2** : EXTREMITY 4

extremely high frequency *n* : a radio frequency in the highest range of the radio frequency spectrum

ex·trem·ism \ik-ˈstrē-ˌmiz-əm\ *n* : the quality or state of being extreme; *esp* : advocacy of extreme political measures : RADICALISM — **ex·trem·ist** \-məst\ *n or adj*

ex·trem·i·ty \ik-ˈstrem-ət-ē\ *n, pl* **-ties 1** : the most remote part or point **2** : a limb of the body; *esp* : a human hand or foot **3** : the greatest need or danger **4** : the utmost degree; *also* : a drastic or desperate measure

ex·tri·cate \ˈek-strə-ˌkāt\ *vb* **-cat·ed; -cat·ing** [L *extricatus,* pp. of *extricare,* fr. *ex-* out + *tricae* trifles, perplexities] : to free from an entanglement or difficulty **syn** disentangle, untangle, disencumber — **ex·tri·ca·ble** \ik-ˈstrik-ə-bəl, ek-; ˈek-(ˌ)strik-\ *adj* — **ex·tri·ca·tion** \ˌek-strə-ˈkā-shən\ *n*

ex·trin·sic \ek-ˈstrin-zik, -sik\ *adj* **1** : not forming part of or belonging to a thing **2** : EXTERNAL — **ex·trin·si·cal·ly** \-zi-k(ə-)lē, -si-\ *adv*

ex·tro·vert *or* **ex·tra·vert** \ˈek-strə-ˌvərt\ *n* : a person who is interested only or mostly in things outside the self — **ex·tro·ver·sion** *or* **ex·tra·ver·sion** \ˌek-strə-ˈvər-zhən\ *n* — **ex·tro·vert·ed** *or* **ex·tra·vert·ed** *adj*

ex·trude \ik-ˈstrüd\ *vb* **ex·trud·ed; ex·trud·ing 1** : to force, press, or push out **2** : to shape (as plastic) by forcing through a die — **ex·tru·sion** \-ˈstrü-zhən\ *n* — **ex·trud·er** *n*

ex·tru·sive \ik-ˈstrü-siv\ *adj* : relating to or formed by geological extrusion from the earth in a molten state or as volcanic ash

ex·u·ber·ant \ig-ˈzü-b(ə-)rənt\ *adj* **1** : joyously unrestrained **2** : PROFUSE — **ex·u·ber·ance** \-b(ə-)rəns\ *n* — **ex·u·ber·ant·ly** *adv*

ex·ude \ig-ˈzüd\ *vb* **ex·ud·ed; ex·ud·ing** [L *exsudare,* fr. *ex-* out + *sudare* to sweat] **1** : to discharge slowly through pores or cuts : OOZE **2** : to give off or out conspicuously or abundantly ⟨~*s* charm⟩ — **ex·u·date** \ˈek-s(y)u̇-ˌdāt\ *n* — **ex·u·da·tion** \ˌek-s(y)u̇-ˈdā-shən\ *n*

ex·ult \ig-ˈzəlt\ *vb* : to rejoice in triumph : GLORY — **ex·ul·tant** \-ˈzəlt-ᵊnt\ *adj* — **ex·ul·tant·ly** *adv* — **ex·ul·ta·tion** \ˌek-(ˌ)səl-ˈtā-shən, ˌeg-(ˌ)zəl-\ *n*

ex·urb \ˈek-ˌsərb, ˈeg-ˌzərb\ *n* : a region outside a city and its suburbs inhabited chiefly by well-to-do families — **ex·ur·bia** \ek-ˈsər-bē-ə, eg-ˈzer-\ *n*

ex·ur·ban·ite \ek-ˈsər-bə-ˌnīt; eg-ˈzər-\ *n* : one who lives in an exurb

-ey — see -Y

¹eye \ˈī\ *n* **1** : an organ of sight typically consisting of a globular structure in a socket of the skull with thin movable covers bordered with hairs **2** : VISION, PERCEPTION; *also* : faculty of discrimination ⟨a good ~ for bargains⟩ **3** : POINT OF VIEW, JUDGMENT — often used in pl. ⟨an offender in the ~*s* of the law⟩ **4** : something suggesting an eye ⟨the ~ of a needle⟩; *esp* : an undeveloped bud (as on a potato) — **eyed** \ˈīd\ *adj*

²eye *vb* **eyed; eye·ing** *or* **ey·ing** : to look at : WATCH

eye·ball \ˈī-ˌbȯl\ *n* : the globular capsule of the vertebrate eye

eye·brow \ī-ˌbrau̇\ *n* : the bony arch forming the upper edge of the eye socket; *also* : the hair growing on this

eye·drop·per \ˈī-ˌdräp-ər\ *n* : DROPPER 2

eye·glass \ˈī-ˌglas\ *n* **1** : a lens variously mounted for personal use as an aid to vision **2** *pl* : GLASSES, SPECTACLES

eye·lash \ˈī-ˌlash\ *n* **1** : the fringe of hair edging the eyelid — usu. used in pl. **2** : a single hair of the eyelashes

eye·let \ˈī-lət\ *n* **1** : a small reinforced hole in material intended for ornament or for passage of something (as a cord or lace) **2** : a typically metal ring for reinforcing an eyelet : GROMMET

eye·lid \ˈī-ˌlid\ *n* : either of the movable lids of skin and muscle that can be closed over the eyeball

eye·lin·er \ˈī-ˌlī-nər\ *n* : makeup used to emphasize the contour of the eyes

eye–open·er \ˈī-ˌōp(-ə)-nər\ *n* : something startling or surprising — **eye–open·ing** \-niŋ\ *adj*

eye·piece \ˈī-ˌpēs\ *n* : the lens or combination of lenses at the eye end of an optical instrument
eye shadow *n* : a colored cosmetic applied to the eyelids to accent the eyes
eye·sight \ˈī-ˌsīt\ *n* : SIGHT, VISION
eye·sore \ˈī-ˌsōr\ *n* : something offensive to view
eye·strain \ˈī-ˌstrān\ *n* : weariness or a strained state of the eye
eye·tooth \ˈī-ˈtüth\ *n* : a canine tooth of the upper jaw
eye·wash \ˈī-ˌwȯsh, -ˌwäsh\ *n* **1** : an eye lotion **2** : misleading or deceptive statements, actions, or procedures
eye·wit·ness \ˈī-ˈwit-nəs\ *n* : a person who actually sees something happen
ey·rie \ˈī(ə)r-ē, *or like* AERIE\ *var of* AERIE
ey·rir \ˈā-ˌriər\ *n, pl* **au·rar** \ˈau̇-ˌrär\ — see *krona* at MONEY table
Ez *or* **Ezr** *abbr* Ezra
Ezech *abbr* Ezechiel
Eze·chiel \i-ˈzē-kyəl\ *n* — see BIBLE table
Ezek *abbr* Ezekiel
Eze·kiel \i-ˈzē-kyəl\ *n* — see BIBLE table
Ez·ra \ˈez-rə\ *n* — see BIBLE table

F

¹f \ˈef\ *n, pl* **f's** *or* **fs** \ˈefs\ *often cap* **1** : the 6th letter of the English alphabet **2** : a grade rating a student's work as failing
²f *abbr, often cap* **1** Fahrenheit **2** false **3** family **4** farad **5** female **6** feminine **7** forte **8** French **9** frequency
³f *symbol* **1** focal length **2** the relative aperture of a photographic lens — often written *f*/ **3** function
F *symbol* fluorine
FAA *abbr* Federal Aviation Agency
Fa·bi·an \ˈfā-bē-ən\ *adj* : of, relating to, or being a society of socialists organized in England in 1884 to spread socialist principles gradually — **Fabian** *n* — **Fa·bi·an·ism** *n*
fa·ble \ˈfā-bəl\ *n* **1** : a legendary story of supernatural happenings **2** : a narration intended to teach a lesson; *esp* : one in which animals speak and act like people **3** : FALSEHOOD
fa·bled \ˈfā-bəld\ *adj* **1** : FICTITIOUS **2** : told or celebrated in fable
fab·ric \ˈfab-rik\ *n* [MF *fabrique,* fr. L *fabrica* workshop, structure] **1** : STRUCTURE, FRAMEWORK ⟨the ~ of society⟩ **2** : CLOTH; *also* : a material that resembles cloth
fab·ri·cate \ˈfab-ri-ˌkāt\ *vb* **-cat·ed; -cat·ing 1** : CONSTRUCT, MANUFACTURE **2** : INVENT, CREATE **3** : to make up for the sake of deception — **fab·ri·ca·tion** \ˌfab-ri-ˈkā-shən\ *n*
fab·u·lous \ˈfab-yə-ləs\ *adj* **1** : resembling a fable : LEGENDARY **2** : told in or based on fable **3** : INCREDIBLE, MARVELOUS — **fab·u·lous·ly** *adv*
fac *abbr* **1** facsimile **2** faculty
fa·cade *also* **fa·çade** \fə-ˈsäd\ *n* [F *façade,* fr. It *facciata,* fr. *faccia* face] **1** : the principal face or front of a building **2** : a false, superficial, or artificial appearance ⟨a ~ of composure⟩
¹face \ˈfās\ *n* **1** : the front part of the head **2** : PRESENCE ⟨in the ~ of danger⟩ **3** : facial expression : LOOK ⟨put a sad ~ on⟩ **4** : GRIMACE ⟨made a ~⟩ **5** : outward appearance ⟨looks easy on the ~ of it⟩ **6** : BOLDNESS **7** : DIGNITY, PRESTIGE ⟨afraid to lose ~⟩ **8** : the surface of something; *esp* : the front or principal surface — **faced** \ˈfāst\ *adj* — **face·less** *adj* — **face·less·ness** *n*
²face *vb* **faced; fac·ing 1** : to confront brazenly **2** : to line near the edge esp. with a different material; *also* : to cover the front or surface of ⟨~ a building with marble⟩ **3** : to bring face to face ⟨*faced* him with proof⟩ **4** : to stand or sit with the face toward ⟨~ the sun⟩ **5** : to front on ⟨a house *facing* the park⟩ **6** : to oppose firmly ⟨*faced* up to his foe⟩ **7** : to turn the face or body in a specified direction
face·down \ˈfās-ˈdau̇n\ *adv* : with the face downward
face–lift·ing \-ˌlif-tiŋ\ *n* **1** : a plastic operation for removal of facial defects (as wrinkles or sagging) usu. associated with aging **2** : MODERNIZATION
face–off \ˈfās-ˌȯf\ *n* **1** : a method of putting a puck in play in ice hockey by dropping it between two opposing players each of whom attempts to control it **2** : CONFRONTATION
fac·et \ˈfas-ət\ *n* [F *facette,* dim. of *face*] **1** : one of the small plane surfaces of a cut gem **2** : ASPECT, PHASE
fa·ce·tious \fə-ˈsē-shəs\ *adj* **1** : FLIPPANT **2** : JOCULAR, JOCOSE — **fa·ce·tious·ly** *adv* — **fa·ce·tious·ness** *n*
¹fa·cial \ˈfā-shəl\ *adj* : of or relating to the face
²facial *n* : a facial treatment
fac·ile \ˈfas-əl\ *adj* **1** : easily accomplished, handled, or attained **2** : SUPERFICIAL **3** : readily manifested and often insincere ⟨~ prose⟩ **4** : READY, FLUENT ⟨a ~ writer⟩
fa·cil·i·tate \fə-ˈsil-ə-ˌtāt\ *vb* **-tat·ed; -tat·ing** : to make easier
fa·cil·i·ty \fə-ˈsil-ət-ē\ *n, pl* **-ties 1** : the quality of being easily performed **2** : ease in performance : APTITUDE **3** : PLIANCY **4** : something that makes easier an action, operation, or course of conduct **5** : something (as a hospital) built or installed for a particular purpose
fac·ing \ˈfā-siŋ\ *n* **1** : a lining at the edge esp. of a garment **2** *pl* : the collar, cuffs, and trimmings of a uniform coat **3** : an ornamental or protective layer **4** : material for facing
fac·sim·i·le \fak-ˈsim-ə-lē\ *n* [L *fac simile* make similar] **1** : an exact copy **2** : the transmitting of printed matter or pictures by wire or radio for reproduction
fact \ˈfakt\ *n* **1** : DEED; *esp* : CRIME ⟨accessory after the ~⟩ **2** : the quality of being actual **3** : something that exists or occurs : EVENT; *also* : a piece of information about such a fact
fac·tion \ˈfak-shən\ *n* : a group or combination (as in a government) acting together within and usu. against a larger body : CLIQUE — **fac·tion·al·ism** \-sh(ə-)nə-ˌliz-əm\ *n*
fac·tious \ˈfak-shəs\ *adj* **1** : of, relating to, or caused by faction **2** : inclined to faction or the formation of factions : causing dissension
fac·ti·tious \fak-ˈtish-əs\ *adj* : ARTIFICIAL, SHAM ⟨a ~ display of grief⟩
¹fac·tor \ˈfak-tər\ *n* **1** : AGENT **2** : something that actively contributes to a result **3** : GENE **4** : any of the numbers or symbols in mathematics that when multiplied together form a product; *esp* : any of the integers that divide a given integer without a remainder
²factor *vb* **fac·tored; fac·tor·ing** \-t(ə-)riŋ\ **1** : to work as a factor **2** : to find the mathematical factors of and esp. the prime mathematical factors of
¹fac·to·ri·al \fak-ˈtōr-ē-əl\ *adj* : of, relating to, or being a factor

[2]factorial *n* : the product of all the positive integers from one to a given integer

fac·to·ry \ˈfak-t(ə-)rē\ *n, pl* **-ries** **1** : a trading post where resident factors trade **2** : a building or group of buildings used for manufacturing

fac·to·tum \fak-ˈtōt-əm\ *n* [NL, lit., do everything, fr. L *fac* do + *totum* everything] : an employee with numerous varied duties

facts of life : the physiological processes and behavior involved in sex and reproduction

fac·tu·al \ˈfak-chə(-wə)l\ *adj* : of or relating to facts; *also* : based on fact — **fac·tu·al·ly** \-ē\ *adv*

fac·ul·ty \ˈfak-əl-tē\ *n, pl* **-ties** **1** : ability to act or do : POWER; *also* : natural aptitude **2** : one of the powers of the mind or body ⟨the ~ of hearing⟩ **3** : the teachers in a school or college or one of its divisions

fad \ˈfad\ *n* : a practice or interest followed for a time with exaggerated zeal : CRAZE — **fad·dish** *adj* — **fad·dist** *n*

fade \ˈfād\ *vb* **fad·ed; fad·ing** **1** : WITHER **2** : to lose or cause to lose freshness or brilliance of color **3** : VANISH **4** : to grow dim or faint

FADM *abbr* fleet admiral

fae·cal, fae·ces *var of* FECAL, FECES

fa·er·ie *also* **fa·ery** \ˈfā-rē, ˈfa(ə)r-ē\ *n, pl* **fa·er·ies** **1** : FAIRYLAND **2** : FAIRY

[1]fag \ˈfag\ *vb* **fagged; fag·ging** **1** : DRUDGE **2** : to act as a fag **3** : TIRE, EXHAUST

[2]fag *n* **1** : an English public-school boy who acts as servant to another **2** : MENIAL, DRUDGE

[3]fag *n* : CIGARETTE

fag end *n* **1** : the last part or coarser end of a web of cloth **2** : the untwisted end of a rope **3** : REMNANT **4** : the extreme end

fag·ot *or* **fag·got** \ˈfag-ət\ *n* : a bundle of sticks or twigs esp. as used for fuel

fag·ot·ing *or* **fag·got·ing** *n* : an embroidery produced by tying threads in hourglass-shaped clusters

Fah *or* **Fahr** *abbr* Fahrenheit

Fahr·en·heit \ˈfar-ən-ˌhīt\ *adj* : relating to, conforming to, or having a thermometer scale with the boiling point of water at 212 degrees and the freezing point at 32 degrees above zero

fa·ience *or* **fa·ïence** \fā-ˈäns\ *n* [F] : earthenware decorated with opaque colored glazes

[1]fail \ˈfāl\ *vb* **1** : to become feeble; *esp* : to decline in health **2** : to die away **3** : to stop functioning **4** : to fall short ⟨~*ed* in his duty⟩ **5** : to be or become absent or inadequate **6** : to be unsuccessful **7** : to become bankrupt **8** : DISAPPOINT, DESERT **9** : NEGLECT

[2]fail *n* : FAILURE ⟨without ~⟩

[1]fail·ing \ˈfā-liŋ\ *n* : WEAKNESS, SHORTCOMING

[2]failing *prep* : in the absence or lack of

faille \ˈfīl\ *n* : a somewhat shiny closely woven ribbed silk, rayon, or cotton fabric

fail–safe \ˈfāl-ˌsāf\ *adj* **1** : incorporating a counteractive feature for a possible source of failure **2** : having no chance of failure

fail·ure \ˈfāl-yər\ *n* **1** : a failing to do or perform **2** : a state of inability to perform a normal function adequately ⟨heart ~⟩ **3** : a fracturing under or yielding to stress **4** : a lack of success **5** : BANKRUPTCY **6** : DEFICIENCY **7** : DETERIORATION, BREAKDOWN **8** : one that has failed

[1]fain \ˈfān\ *adj, archaic* **1** : GLAD **2** : INCLINED **3** : OBLIGED

[2]fain *adv, archaic* **1** : WILLINGLY **2** : RATHER

[1]faint \ˈfānt\ *adj* [ME *faint, feint,* fr. OF, fr. *faindre, feindre* to feign, shirk] **1** : COWARDLY, SPIRITLESS **2** : weak, dizzy, and likely to faint **3** : lacking vigor or strength : FEEBLE ⟨~ praise⟩ **4** : INDISTINCT, DIM — **faint·ly** *adv* — **faint·ness** *n*

[2]faint *vb* : to lose consciousness

[3]faint *n* : the action of fainting; *also* : the resulting condition

faint·heart·ed \ˈfānt-ˈhärt-əd\ *adj* : lacking courage : TIMID

[1]fair \ˈfaər\ *adj* **1** : attractive in appearance : BEAUTIFUL **2** : superficially pleasing : SPECIOUS **3** : CLEAN, PURE **4** : CLEAR, LEGIBLE **5** : not stormy or cloudy ⟨~ weather⟩ **6** : JUST **7** : conforming with the rules : ALLOWED; *also* : being within the foul lines ⟨~ ball⟩ **8** : open to legitimate pursuit or attack ⟨~ game⟩ **9** : PROMISING, LIKELY ⟨a ~ chance of winning⟩ **10** : favorable to a ship's course ⟨a ~ wind⟩ **11** : light in coloring : BLOND **12** : ADEQUATE — **fair·ness** *n*

[2]fair *adv* : FAIRLY

[3]fair *n* **1** : a gathering of buyers and sellers at a stated time and place for trade **2** : a competitive exhibition (as of farm products) **3** : a sale of assorted articles usu. for a charitable purpose

fair·ground \-ˌgraủnd\ *n* : an area where outdoor fairs, circuses, or exhibitions are held

fair·ing \ˈfa(ə)r-iŋ\ *n* : a structure for producing a smooth outline and reducing drag (as on an airplane)

fair·ly \ˈfa(ə)r-lē\ *adv* **1** : HANDSOMELY, FAVORABLY ⟨~ situated⟩ **2** : QUITE, COMPLETELY **3** : in a fair manner : JUSTLY **4** : MODERATELY, TOLERABLY ⟨a ~ easy job⟩

fair–spo·ken \ˈfaər-ˈspō-kən\ *adj* : pleasant and courteous in speech

fair–trade \-ˈtrād\ *adj* : of, relating to, or being an agreement between a producer and a seller that branded merchandise will be sold at or above a specified price ⟨~ items⟩ — **fair–trade** *vb*

fair·way \-ˌwā\ *n* : the mowed part of a golf course between tee and green

fairy \ˈfa(ə)r-ē\ *n, pl* **fai·ries** [ME *fairie* fairyland, fairy people, fr. OF *faerie,* fr. *feie, fee* fairy, fr. L *Fata,* goddess of fate, fr. *fatum* fate] : an imaginary being of folklore and romance usu. having diminutive human form and magic powers

fairy·land \-ˌland\ *n* **1** : the land of fairies **2** : a beautiful or charming place

fairy tale *n* **1** : a simple children's story about fairies **2** : FIB

fait ac·com·pli \ˈfāt-ˌak-ˌōⁿ-ˈplē\ *n, pl* **faits accomplis** *same, or* -ˈplēz\ [F, accomplished fact] : a thing accomplished and presumably irreversible

faith \ˈfāth\ *n, pl* **faiths** \ˈfāths, ˈfāt͟hz\ [deriv. of L *fides*] **1** : allegiance to duty or a person : LOYALTY **2** : belief and trust in God **3** : complete trust **4** : a system of religious beliefs — **faith·ful** \-fəl\ *adj* — **faith·ful·ly** \-ē\ *adv* — **faith·ful·ness** *n*

faith·less \ˈfāth-ləs\ *adj* **1** : DISLOYAL **2** : not to be relied on : UNTRUSTWORTHY — **faith·less·ly** *adv* — **faith·less·ness** *n*

[1]fake \ˈfāk\ *adj* : COUNTERFEIT, SHAM

[2]fake *vb* **faked; fak·ing** **1** : to treat so as to falsify **2** : COUNTERFEIT **3** : PRETEND, SIMULATE — **fak·er** *n*

[3]fake *n* **1** : IMITATION, FRAUD, COUNTERFEIT **2** : IMPOSTOR

fa·kir \fə-ˈkiər\ *n* [Ar *faqīr,* lit., poor man] **1** : a Muslim mendicant : DERVISH **2** : a wandering Hindu holy man who performs tricks

fal·chion \ˈfȯl-chən\ *n* : a broad-bladed slightly curved medieval sword

fal·con \ˈfal-kən, ˈfȯ(l)-\ *n* **1** : a hawk trained for use in falconry **2** : any of various swift long-winged dark-eyed hawks having a beak adapted to snapping the spine of prey

fal·con·ry \ˈfal-kən-rē, ˈfȯl-, ˈfȯ-\ *n* **1** : the art of training hawks to hunt in cooperation with a person **2** : the sport of hunting with hawks — **fal·con·er** \-ər\ *n*

[1]fall \ˈfȯl\ *vb* **fell** \ˈfel\; **fall·en** \ˈfȯ-lən\; **fall·ing** **1** : to descend freely by the force of gravity **2** : to hang freely **3** : to come as if by descending ⟨darkness *fell*⟩ **4** : to become uttered **5** : to lower or become lowered : DROP ⟨her eyes *fell*⟩ **6** : to leave an erect position suddenly and involuntarily **7** : STUMBLE, STRAY **8** : to drop down wounded or dead : die in battle **9** : to become captured or defeated **10** : to suffer ruin or failure **11** : to commit an immoral act **12** : to move or extend in a downward direction **13** : SUBSIDE, ABATE **14** : to decline in quality, activity, quantity, or value **15** : to assume a look of shame or dejection ⟨her face *fell*⟩ **16** : to occur at a certain time **17** : to come by chance **18** : DEVOLVE **19** : to have the proper place or station ⟨the accent ~*s* on the first syllable⟩ **20** : to come within the scope of something **21** : to pass from one condition to another ⟨*fell* ill⟩ **22** : to set about heartily or actively ⟨~ to work⟩ — **fall flat** : to produce no response or result — **fall for 1** : to fall in love with **2** : to become a victim of — **fall foul 1** : to have a collision **2** : to have a quarrel : CLASH — **fall from grace** : BACKSLIDE — **fall into line** : to comply with a certain course of action — **fall over oneself** *or* **fall over backward** : to display excessive eagerness — **fall short 1** : to be deficient **2** : to fail to attain

[2]**fall** *n* **1** : the act of falling **2** : a falling out, off, or away : DROPPING **3** : AUTUMN **4** : a thing or quantity that falls ⟨a light ~ of snow⟩ **5** : COLLAPSE, DOWNFALL **6** : the surrender or capture of a besieged place **7** : departure from virtue or goodness **8** : SLOPE **9** : WATERFALL — usu. used in pl. **10** : a decrease in size, quantity, degree, or value ⟨a ~ in price⟩ **11** : the distance which something falls **12** : an act of forcing a wrestler's shoulders to the mat; *also* : a bout of wrestling

fal·la·cious \fə-ˈlā-shəs\ *adj* **1** : embodying a fallacy ⟨a ~ argument⟩ **2** : MISLEADING, DECEPTIVE

fal·la·cy \ˈfal-ə-sē\ *n, pl* **-cies 1** : a false or mistaken idea **2** : an often plausible argument using false or illogical reasoning

fall back \ˈfȯl-ˈbak\ *vb* : RETREAT, RECEDE

fall guy *n* **1** : one that is easily duped **2** : SCAPEGOAT

fal·li·ble \ˈfal-ə-bəl\ *adj* **1** : liable to be erroneous **2** : capable of making a mistake

fall·ing–out \ˌfȯ-liŋ-ˈau̇t\ *n, pl* **fallings–out** *or* **falling–outs** : QUARREL

falling star *n* : METEOR

fal·lo·pi·an tube \fə-ˌlō-pē-ən-\ *n, often cap F* : either of the pair of anatomical tubes that carry the egg from the ovary to the uterus

fall·out \ˈfȯl-ˌau̇t\ *n* **1** : the often radioactive particles that result from a nuclear explosion and descend through the air **2** : an incidental result : BY-PRODUCT

fall out \(ˈ)fȯl-ˈau̇t\ *vb* : QUARREL

fal·low \ˈfal-ō\ *n* **1** : land for crops allowed to lie idle during the growing season **2** : the tilling of land without sowing it for a season — **fal·low** *vb* — **fallow** *adj*

false \ˈfȯls\ *adj* **fals·er; fals·est 1** : not genuine : ARTIFICIAL **2** : intentionally untrue **3** : adjusted or made so as to deceive ⟨~ scales⟩ **4** : tending to mislead : DECEPTIVE ⟨~ promises⟩ **5** : not true ⟨~ concepts⟩ **6** : not faithful or loyal : TREACHEROUS **7** : not essential or permanent ⟨~ front⟩ **8** : inaccurate in pitch **9** : based on mistaken ideas — **false·ly** *adv* — **false·ness** *n* — **fal·si·ty** \ˈfȯl-sət-ē\ *n*

false·hood \ˈfȯls-ˌhu̇d\ *n* **1** : LIE **2** : absence of truth or accuracy **3** : the practice of lying

fal·set·to \fȯl-ˈset-ō\ *n, pl* **-tos** [It, fr. dim. of *falso* false] : an artificially high voice; *esp* : an artificial singing voice that overlaps and extends above the range of the full voice esp. of a tenor

fal·si·fy \ˈfȯl-sə-ˌfī\ *vb* **-fied; -fy·ing 1** : to make false : change so as to deceive **2** : LIE **3** : MISREPRESENT **4** : to prove to be false — **fal·si·fi·ca·tion** \ˌfȯl-sə-fə-ˈkā-shən\ *n*

fal·ter \ˈfȯl-tər\ *vb* **fal·tered; fal·ter·ing** \-t(ə-)riŋ\ **1** : to move unsteadily : STUMBLE, TOTTER **2** : to hesitate in speech : STAMMER **3** : to hesitate in purpose or action : WAVER, FLINCH — **fal·ter·ing·ly** \-t(ə-)riŋ-lē\ *adv*

fam *abbr* **1** familiar **2** family

fame \ˈfām\ *n* : public reputation : RENOWN — **famed** \ˈfāmd\ *adj*

fa·mil·ial \fə-ˈmil-yəl\ *adj* **1** : of, relating to, or characteristic of a family **2** : tending to occur in more members of a family than expected by chance alone ⟨a ~ disorder⟩

[1]**fa·mil·iar** \fə-ˈmil-yər\ *n* **1** : COMPANION **2** : a spirit held to attend and serve or guard a person **3** : one who frequents a place

[2]**familiar** *adj* **1** : closely acquainted : INTIMATE **2** : of or relating to a family **3** : INFORMAL **4** : FORWARD, PRESUMPTUOUS **5** : frequently seen or experienced **6** : of everyday occurrence — **fa·mil·iar·ly** *adv*

fa·mil·iar·i·ty \fə-ˌmil-ˈyar-ət-ē, -ˌmil-ē-ˈ(y)ar-\ *n, pl* **-ties 1** : close friendship : INTIMACY **2** : INFORMALITY **3** : an unduly bold or forward act or expression : IMPROPRIETY **4** : close acquaintance with something

fa·mil·iar·ize \fə-ˈmil-yə-ˌrīz\ *vb* **-ized; -iz·ing 1** : to make known or familiar **2** : to make thoroughly acquainted : ACCUSTOM

fam·i·ly \ˈfam-(ə-)lē\ *n, pl* **-lies** [ME *familie*, fr. L *familia* household] **1** : a group of persons of common ancestry : CLAN **2** : a group of individuals living under one roof and under one head : HOUSEHOLD **3** : a group of things having common characteristics; *esp* : a group of related plants or animals ranking in biological classification above a genus and below an order **4** : a social group composed of parents and their children

family planning *n* : planning intended to determine the number and spacing of one's children through effective methods of birth control

family tree *n* : GENEALOGY; *also* : a genealogical diagram

fam·ine \ˈfam-ən\ *n* **1** : an extreme scarcity of food **2** : a great shortage

fam·ish \ˈfam-ish\ *vb* **1** : STARVE **2** : to suffer for lack of something necessary

fa·mous \ˈfā-məs\ *adj* **1** : widely known **2** : honored for achievement **3** : EXCELLENT, FIRST-RATE **syn** renowned, celebrated, noted, notorious, distinguished, eminent, illustrious

fa·mous·ly *adv* : SPLENDIDLY, EXCELLENTLY

[1]**fan** \ˈfan\ *n* : a device (as a hand-waved triangular piece or a mechanism with blades) for producing a current of air

[2]**fan** *vb* **fanned; fan·ning 1** : to drive away the chaff from grain by winnowing **2** : to move (air) with or as if with a fan **3** : to direct a current of air upon ⟨~ a fire⟩ **4** : to stir up to activity : STIMULATE **5** : to spread like a fan **6** : to strike out in baseball

[3]**fan** *n* : an enthusiastic follower or admirer

fa·nat·ic \fə-ˈnat-ik\ *or* **fa·nat·i·cal** \-i-kəl\ *adj* [L *fanaticus* inspired by a deity, frenzied, fr. *fanum* temple] : marked by excessive enthusiasm and often intense uncritical devotion — **fanatic** *n* — **fa·nat·i·cism** \fə-ˈnat-ə-ˌsiz-əm\ *n*

fan·ci·er \ˈfan-sē-ər\ *n* : a person who breeds or grows some kind of animal or plant for points of excellence

fan·ci·ful \ˈfan-si-fəl\ *adj* **1** : full of fancy : guided by fancy : WHIMSICAL **2** : coming from the fancy rather than from the reason **3** : curiously made or shaped — **fan·ci·ful·ly** \-f(ə-)lē\ *adv*

[1]**fan·cy** \ˈfan-sē\ *n, pl* **fancies** [ME *fantasie, fantsy* fantasy, fancy, fr. MF *fantasie*, fr. L *phantasia*, fr. Gk, appearance, imagination] **1** : LIKING, INCLINATION; *also* : LOVE **2** : NOTION, IDEA, WHIM ⟨a passing ~⟩ **3** : IMAGINATION **4** : TASTE, JUDGMENT

[2]**fancy** *vb* **fan·cied; fan·cy·ing 1** : LIKE **2** : IMAGINE **3** : to believe without evidence **4** : to believe without being certain

[3]**fancy** *adj* **fan·ci·er; -est 1** : WHIMSICAL **2** : not plain : ORNA-

MENTAL **3** : of particular excellence **4** : bred esp. for a showy appearance **5** : above the usual price or the real value : EXTRAVAGANT **6** : executed with technical skill and superior grace — **fan·ci·ly** \ˈfan-sə-lē\ *adv*

fancy dress *n* : a costume (as for a masquerade) chosen to suit a fancy

fan·cy–free \ˈfan-sē-ˌfrē\ *adj* : not centering the attention on any one person or thing; *esp* : not in love

fan·cy·work \ˈfan-sē-ˌwərk\ *n* : ornamental needlework (as embroidery)

fan·dan·go \fan-ˈdaŋ-gō\ *n, pl* **-gos** : a lively Spanish or Spanish-American dance

fane \ˈfān\ *n* : TEMPLE

fan·fare \ˈfan-ˌfaər\ *n* **1** : a flourish of trumpets **2** : a showy display

fang \ˈfaŋ\ *n* : a long sharp tooth; *esp* : a grooved or hollow tooth of a venomous snake

fan–jet \ˈfan-ˌjet\ *n* **1** : a jet engine having a fan in its forward end that draws in extra air whose compression and expulsion provide extra thrust **2** : an airplane powered by a fan-jet

fan·light \ˈfan-ˌlīt\ *n* : a semicircular window with radiating bars like the ribs of a fan set over a door or window

fan·tail \ˈfan-ˌtāl\ *n* **1** : a fan-shaped tail or end **2** : an overhang at the stern of a ship

fan·ta·sia \fan-ˈtā-zhə, -z(h)ē-ə; ˌfant-ə-ˈzē-ə\ *also* **fan·ta·sie** \ˌfant-ə-ˈzē ˌfänt-\ *n* : a musical composition free and fanciful in form

fan·ta·size \ˈfant-ə-ˌsīz\ *vb* **-sized; -siz·ing** : IMAGINE, DAYDREAM

fan·tas·tic \fan-ˈtas-tik\ *also* **fan·tas·ti·cal** \-ti-kəl\ *adj* **1** : IMAGINARY, UNREAL, UNREALISTIC **2** : conceived by unrestrained fancy : GROTESQUE **3** : exceedingly or unbelievably great **4** : ECCENTRIC — **fan·tas·ti·cal·ly** \-ti-k(ə-)lē\ *adv*

fan·ta·sy \ˈfant-ə-sē\ *n, pl* **-sies** **1** : IMAGINATION, FANCY **2** : a product of the imagination : ILLUSION **3** : FANTASIA — **fantasy** *vb*

[1]**far** \ˈfär\ *adv* **far·ther** \-t͟hər\ *or* **fur·ther** \ˈfər-\; **far·thest** *or* **fur·thest** \-t͟həst\ **1** : at or to a considerable distance in space or time ⟨~ from home⟩ **2** : by a broad interval : WIDELY, MUCH ⟨~ better⟩ **3** : to or at a definite distance, point, or degree ⟨as ~ as I know⟩ **4** : to an advanced point or extent ⟨go ~ in his field⟩ — **by far** : GREATLY — **far and away** : DECIDEDLY — **so far** : until now

[2]**far** *adj* **farther** *or* **further; farthest** *or* **furthest** **1** : remote in space or time : DISTANT **2** : DIFFERENT ⟨a ~ cry from former methods⟩ **3** : LONG ⟨a ~ journey⟩ **4** : being the more distant of two ⟨on the ~ side of the lake⟩

far·ad \ˈfar-ˌad, -əd\ *n* : a unit of capacitance equal to the capacitance of a capacitor having a potential difference of one volt between its plates when it is charged with one coulomb of electricity

far·away \ˌfär-ə-ˌwā\ *adj* **1** : DISTANT, REMOTE **2** : DREAMY

farce \ˈfärs\ *n* **1** : a broadly satirical comedy with an improbable plot **2** : the humor characteristic of farce or pretense **3** : a ridiculous action, display, or pretense — **far·ci·cal** \ˈfär-si-kəl\ *adj*

[1]**fare** \ˈfaər\ *vb* **fared; far·ing** **1** : GO, TRAVEL **2** : GET ALONG, SUCCEED **3** : EAT, DINE

[2]**fare** *n* **1** : the price charged to transport a person **2** : a person paying a fare : PASSENGER **3** : range of food : DIET; *also* : material provided for use, consumption, or enjoyment

[1]**fare·well** \faər-ˈwel\ *vb imper* : get along well — used interjectionally to or by one departing

[2]**farewell** *n* **1** : a wish of well-being at parting : GOOD-BYE **2** : LEAVE-TAKING

[3]**fare·well** \ˌfaər-ˌwel\ *adj* : PARTING, FINAL ⟨a ~ concert⟩

far·fetched \ˈfär-ˈfecht\ *adj* : not easily or naturally deduced or introduced : IMPROBABLE

far–flung \-ˈfləŋ\ *adj* : widely spread or distributed

fa·ri·na \fə-ˈrē-nə\ *n* [L, meal, flour] : a fine meal (as of wheat) used in puddings or as a breakfast cereal

far·i·na·ceous \ˌfar-ə-ˈnā-shəs\ *adj* **1** : containing or rich in starch **2** : having a mealy texture or surface

[1]**farm** \ˈfärm\ *n* [ME *ferme* rent, lease, fr. OF, lease, fr. *fermer* to fix, make a contract, fr. L *firmare* to make firm, fr. *firmus* firm] **1** : a tract of land used for raising crops or livestock **2** : a minor-league subsidiary of a major-league baseball team

[2]**farm** *vb* : to use (land) as a farm ⟨~*ed* 200 acres⟩; *also* : to raise crops or livestock esp. as a business — **farm·er** *n*

farm·hand \ˈfärm-ˌhand\ *n* : a farm laborer

farm·house \-ˌhau̇s\ *n* : a dwelling on a farm

farm·ing \ˈfär-miŋ\ *n* : the practice of agriculture

farm·land \ˈfärm-ˌland\ *n* : land used or suitable for farming

farm out *vb* : to turn over (as a task) to another

farm·stead \ˈfärm-ˌsted\ *also* **farm·stead·ing** \-iŋ\ *n* : the buildings and adjacent service areas of a farm

farm·yard \-ˌyärd\ *n* : space around or enclosed by farm buildings

far–off \ˈfär-ˈȯf\ *adj* : remote in time or space : DISTANT

fa·rouche \fə-ˈrüsh\ *adj* [F] **1** : marked by shyness and lack of polish **2** : WILD

far–out \ˈfär-ˈau̇t\ *adj* : very unconventional : EXTREME ⟨~ clothes⟩

far·ra·go \fə-ˈräg-ō, -ˈrā-gō\ *n, pl* **-goes** [L, mixed fodder] : a confused collection : MIXTURE

far–reach·ing \ˈfär-ˈrē-chiŋ\ *adj* : having a wide range or effect

far·ri·er \ˈfar-ē-ər\ *n* : one that shoes horses

[1]**far·row** \ˈfar-ō\ *vb* : to give birth to a farrow

[2]**farrow** *n* : a litter of pigs

far·seeing \ˈfär-ˈsē-iŋ\ *adj* : FARSIGHTED

far·sight·ed \ˈfär-ˈsīt-əd\ *adj* **1** : seeing or able to see to a great distance **2** : JUDICIOUS, WISE, SHREWD **3** : affected with an eye condition in which the image comes into focus behind the retina — **far·sight·ed·ness** *n*

[1]**far·ther** \ˈfär-t͟hər\ *adv* **1** : at or to a greater distance or more advanced point **2** : more completely

[2]**farther** *adj* **1** : more distant **2** : ADDITIONAL

far·ther·most \-ˌmōst\ *adj* : most distant

[1]**far·thest** \ˈfär-t͟həst\ *adj* : most distant

[2]**farthest** *adv* **1** : to or at the greatest distance : REMOTEST **2** : to the most advanced point **3** : by the greatest degree or extent : MOST

far·thing \ˈfär-t͟hiŋ\ *n* : a former British monetary unit equal to ¼ of a penny; *also* : a coin representing this unit

far·thin·gale \ˈfär-t͟hən-ˌgāl, -t͟hiŋ-\ *n* [modif. of MF *verdugale*, fr. Sp *verdugado*, fr. *verdugo* young shoot of a tree, fr. *verde* green, fr. L *viridis*] : a support (as of hoops) worn esp. in the 16th century to swell out a skirt

fas·ci·cle \ˈfas-i-kəl\ *n* **1** : a small bundle or cluster (as of flowers or roots) **2** : one of the divisions of a book published in parts — **fas·ci·cled** \-kəld\ *adj*

fas·ci·nate \ˈfas-ᵊn-ˌāt\ *vb* **-nat·ed; -nat·ing** [L *fascinare*, fr. *fascinum* witchcraft] **1** : to transfix and hold spellbound by an irresistible power **2** : ALLURE **3** : to be irresistibly attractive — **fas·ci·na·tion** \ˌfas-ᵊn-ˈā-shən\ *n*

fas·cism \ˈfash-ˌiz-əm\ *n, often cap* : a political philosophy, movement, or regime that exalts nation and often race and stands for a centralized autocratic government headed by a dictatorial leader, severe economic and social regimentation, and forcible suppression of opposition — **fas·cist** \-əst\ *n or adj, often cap* — **fas·cis·tic** \fa-ˈshis-tik\ *adj, often cap*

[1]**fash·ion** \ˈfash-ən\ *n* **1** : the make or form of something **2** : MANNER, WAY **3** : a prevailing custom, usage, or style **4** : the prevailing style (as in dress) **syn** mode, vogue, rage, trend

[2]**fashion** *vb* **fash·ioned; fash·ion·ing** \ˈfash-(ə-)niŋ\ **1** : MOLD, CONSTRUCT **2** : FIT, ADAPT

fash·ion·able \ˈfash-(ə-)nə-bəl\ *adj* **1** : dressing or behaving according to fashion : STYLISH **2** : of or relating to the world of fashion ⟨~ resorts⟩ — **fash·ion·ably** \-blē\ *adv*

[1]**fast** \ˈfast\ *adj* **1** : firmly fixed **2** : tightly shut **3** : adhering firmly **4** : STUCK **5** : STAUNCH ⟨~ friends⟩ **6** : characterized by quick motion, operation, or effect ⟨a ~ trip⟩ ⟨a ~ track⟩ **7** : indicating ahead of the correct time ⟨the clock is ~⟩ **8** : not easily disturbed : SOUND ⟨a ~ sleep⟩ **9** : permanently dyed; *also* : being proof against fading ⟨colors ~ to sunlight⟩ **10** : DISSIPATED, WILD **11** : sexually promiscuous **syn** rapid, swift, fleet, quick, speedy, hasty

[2]**fast** *adv* **1** : in a firm or fixed manner ⟨stuck ~ in the mud⟩ **2** : SOUNDLY, DEEPLY ⟨~ asleep⟩ **3** : SWIFTLY **4** : RECKLESSLY

[3]**fast** *vb* **1** : to abstain from food **2** : to eat sparingly or abstain from some foods

[4]**fast** *n* **1** : the act or practice of fasting **2** : a time of fasting

fast·back \ˈfas(t)-ˌbak\ *n* : an automobile having a roof with a long slope to the rear

fast·ball \ˈfas(t)-ˌbȯl\ *n* : a baseball pitch thrown at full speed

fas·ten \ˈfas-ᵊn\ *vb* **fas·tened; fas·ten·ing** \ˈfas-(ᵊ-)niŋ\ **1** : to attach or join by or as if by pinning, tying, or nailing **2** : to make fast : fix securely **3** : to fix or set steadily ⟨~*ed* his eyes on her⟩ **4** : to become fixed or joined — **fas·ten·er** \ˈfas-(ə-)nər\ *n*

fas·ten·ing \ˈfas-(ᵊ-)niŋ\ *n* : something that fastens : FASTENER

fast–food \ˌfas(t)-ˈfüd\ *adj* : specializing in food that is prepared and served quickly ⟨a ~ restaurant⟩

fas·tid·i·ous \fas-ˈtid-ē-əs\ *adj* **1** : overly difficult to please **2** : showing or demanding excessive delicacy or care — **fas·tid·i·ous·ly** *adv* — **fas·tid·i·ous·ness** *n*

fast·ness \ˈfas(t)-nəs\ *n* **1** : the quality or state of being fast **2** : a fortified or secure place : STRONGHOLD

fast–talk \ˈfas(t)-ˈtȯk\ *vb* : to influence by persuasive and usu. deceptive talk

[1]**fat** \ˈfat\ *adj* **fat·ter; fat·test 1** : FLESHY, PLUMP **2** : OILY, GREASY **3** : well filled out : BIG **4** : well stocked : ABUNDANT **5** : PROFITABLE — **fat·ness** *n*

[2]**fat** *n* **1** : animal tissue rich in greasy or oily matter **2** : any of numerous energy-rich esters that occur naturally in animal fats and in plants and are soluble in organic solvents (as ether) but not in water **3** : the best or richest portion ⟨lived on the ~ of the land⟩ **4** : OBESITY **5** : excess matter

fa·tal \ˈfāt-ᵊl\ *adj* **1** : FATEFUL **2** : MORTAL, DEADLY, DISASTROUS — **fa·tal·ly** \-ē\ *adv*

fa·tal·ism \-ˌiz-əm\ *n* : the belief that events are determined by fate — **fa·tal·ist** \-əst\ *n* — **fa·tal·is·tic** \ˌfāt-ᵊl-ˈis-tik\ *adj*

fa·tal·i·ty \fā-ˈtal-ət-ē, fə-\ *n, pl* **-ties 1** : DEADLINESS **2** : the quality or state of being destined for disaster **3** : FATE **4** : death resulting from a disaster or accident

fat·back \ˈfat-ˌbak\ *n* : a fatty strip from the back of the hog usu. cured by salting and drying

fat cat *n* **1** : a wealthy contributor to a political campaign **2** : a wealthy privileged person

fate \ˈfāt\ *n* [ME, fr. MF or L; fr. L *fatum,* lit., what has been spoken, fr. *fari* to speak] **1** : the cause beyond man's control that is held to determine events : DESTINY **2** : LOT, FORTUNE **3** : DISASTER; *esp* : DEATH **4** : END, OUTCOME **5** *cap, pl* : the three goddesses of classical mythology who determine the course of human life

fat·ed \ˈfā-təd\ *adj* : decreed, controlled, or marked by fate

fate·ful \ˈfāt-fəl\ *adj* **1** : OMINOUS, PROPHETIC **2** : IMPORTANT, DECISIVE **3** : DEADLY, DESTRUCTIVE **4** : determined by fate — **fate·ful·ly** \-ē\ *adv*

fath *abbr* fathom

fat·head \ˈfat-ˌhed\ *n* : a stupid person — **fat·head·ed** \-ˈhed-əd\ *adj*

fa·ther \ˈfäth-ər\ *n* **1** : a male parent **2** *cap* : God esp. as the first person of the Trinity **3** : FOREFATHER **4** : one deserving the respect and love given to a father **5** *often cap* : an early Christian writer accepted by the church as an authoritative witness to its teaching and practice **6** : ORIGINATOR ⟨the ~ of modern radio⟩; *also* : SOURCE **7** : PRIEST — used esp. as a title **8** : one of the leading men ⟨city ~*s*⟩ — **fa·ther·hood** \-ˌhu̇d\ *n* — **fa·ther·less** *adj* — **fa·ther·ly** *adj*

[2]**father** *vb* **1** : BEGET **2** : to be the founder, producer, or author of **3** : to treat or care for as a father

father–in–law \ˈfäth-(ə-)rən-ˌlȯ\ *n, pl* **fa·thers–in–law** \-ər-zən-\ : the father of one's husband or wife

fa·ther·land \ˈfäth-ər-ˌland\ *n* **1** : one's native land **2** : the native land of one's ancestors

[1]**fath·om** \ˈfath-əm\ *n* [ME *fadme,* fr. OE *fæthm* outstretched arms, fathom] : a unit of length equal to 6 feet (about 1.8 meters) used esp. for measuring the depth of water

[2]**fathom** *vb* **1** : to measure by a sounding line **2** : PROBE **3** : to penetrate and come to understand — **fath·om·able** \ˈfath-ə-mə-bəl\ *adj*

fath·om·less \ˈfath-əm-ləs\ *adj* : incapable of being fathomed

[1]**fa·tigue** \fə-ˈtēg\ *n* [F] **1** : manual or menial work performed by military personnel **2** *pl* : the uniform or work clothing worn on fatigue and in the field **3** : weariness from labor or use **4** : the tendency of a material to break under repeated stress

[2]**fatigue** *vb* **fa·tigued; fa·tigu·ing** : WEARY, TIRE

fat·ten \ˈfat-ᵊn\ *vb* : to make or grow fat

[1]**fat·ty** \ˈfat-ē\ *adj* **fat·ti·er; -est 1** : containing fat esp. in unusual amounts **2** : GREASY

[2]**fatty** *n, pl* **fatties** : a fat person

fatty acid *n* : any of numerous acids that contain only carbon, hydrogen, and oxygen and that occur naturally in fats and various oils

fa·tu·ity \fə-ˈt(y)ü-ət-ē\ *n, pl* **-ities** : FOOLISHNESS, STUPIDITY

fat·u·ous \ˈfach-(ə-)wəs\ *adj* : FOOLISH, INANE, SILLY — **fat·u·ous·ly** *adv*

fau·bourg \fō-ˈbu̇r\ *n* **1** : SUBURB; *esp* : a suburb of a French city **2** : a city quarter

fau·ces \ˈfȯ-ˌsēz\ *n pl* [L, throat] : the narrow passage located between the soft palate and the base of the tongue that joins the mouth to the pharynx

fau·cet \ˈfȯs-ət, ˈfäs-\ *n* : a fixture for drawing off a liquid (as from a pipe)

[1]**fault** \ˈfȯlt\ *n* **1** : a weakness in character : FAILING **2** : IMPERFECTION, IMPAIRMENT **3** : an error esp. in service in a net or racket game **4** : MISDEMEANOR; *also* : MISTAKE **5** : responsibility for something wrong **6** : a fracture in the earth's crust accompanied by a displacement of one side relative to the other — **fault·i·ly** \ˈfȯl-tə-lē\ *adv* — **fault·less** *adj* — **fault·less·ly** *adv* — **faulty** *adj*

[2]**fault** *vb* **1** : to commit a fault : ERR **2** : to fracture so as to produce a geologic fault **3** : to find a fault in

fault·find·er \ˈfȯlt-ˌfīn-dər\ *n* : a person who tends to find fault or complain — **fault·find·ing** \-diŋ\ *n or adj*

faun \ˈfȯn\ *n* : a Roman god of fields and herds represented as part goat and part man

fau·na \ˈfȯn-ə\ *n, pl* **faunas** *also* **fau·nae** \-ˌē, -ˌī\ [LL *Fauna,* sister of Faunus (the Roman god of animals)] : animals or animal life esp. of a region, period, or environment — **fau·nal** \-ᵊl\ *adj*

fau·vism \ˈfō-ˌviz-əm\ *n, often cap* : a movement in

painting characterized by vivid colors, free treatment of form, and a vibrant and decorative effect — **fau·vist** \-vəst\ *n, often cap*

faux pas \ˈfō-ˈpä\ *n, pl* **faux pas** \-ˈpä(z)\ [F, lit., false step] : BLUNDER; *esp* : a social blunder

[1]**fa·vor** \ˈfā-vər\ *n* **1** : friendly regard shown toward another esp. by a superior **2** : APPROVAL **3** : PARTIALITY **4** : POPULARITY **5** : gracious kindness; *also* : an act of such kindness **6** *pl* : effort in one's behalf : ATTENTION **7** : a token of love (as a ribbon) usu. worn conspicuously **8** : a small gift or decorative item given out at a party **9** : a special privilege **10** *archaic* : LETTER **11** : BEHALF, INTEREST

[2]**favor** *vb* **fa·vored; fa·vor·ing** \ˈfāv-(ə-)riŋ\ **1** : to regard or treat with favor **2** : OBLIGE **3** : ENDOW ⟨~*ed* by nature⟩ **4** : to treat gently or carefully : SPARE ⟨~ a lame leg⟩ **5** : PREFER **6** : SUPPORT, SUSTAIN **7** : FACILITATE ⟨darkness ~*s* attack⟩ **8** : RESEMBLE ⟨he ~*s* his father⟩

fa·vor·able \ˈfāv-(ə-)rə-bəl\ *adj* **1** : APPROVING **2** : HELPFUL, PROMISING, ADVANTAGEOUS ⟨~ weather⟩ — **fa·vor·ably** \-blē\ *adv*

fa·vor·ite \ˈfāv-(ə-)rət\ *n* **1** : a person or a thing that is favored above others **2** : a competitor regarded as most likely to win — **favorite** *adj*

favorite son *n* : a candidate supported by the delegates of his state at a presidential nominating convention

fa·vor·it·ism \ˈfāv-(ə-)rət-ˌiz-əm\ *n* : PARTIALITY, BIAS

fa·vour *chiefly Brit var of* FAVOR

[1]**fawn** \ˈfȯn, ˈfän\ *n* **1** : a young deer **2** : a variable color averaging a light grayish brown

[2]**fawn** *vb* **1** : to show affection ⟨a dog ~*ing* on its master⟩ **2** : to court favor by a cringing or flattering manner

fax \ˈfaks\ *n* : FACSIMILE 2

fay \ˈfā\ *n* : FAIRY, ELF — **fay** *adj*

faze \ˈfāz\ *vb* **fazed; faz·ing** : to disturb the composure or courage of : DAUNT

FBI *abbr* Federal Bureau of Investigation

FCC *abbr* Federal Communications Commission

FD *abbr* fire department

FDA *abbr* Food and Drug Administration

FDIC *abbr* Federal Deposit Insurance Corporation

Fe *symbol* [L *ferrum*] iron

fe·al·ty \ˈfē(-ə)l-tē\ *n, pl* **-ties** : LOYALTY, ALLEGIANCE

[1]**fear** \ˈfi(ə)r\ *vb* **1** : to have a reverent awe of ⟨~ God⟩ **2** : to be afraid of : have fear **3** : to be apprehensive

[2]**fear** *n* **1** : an unpleasant often strong emotion caused by expectation or awareness of danger; *also* : an instance of or a state marked by this emotion **2** : anxious concern : SOLICITUDE **3** : profound reverence esp. toward God **syn** dread, fright, alarm, panic, terror, trepidation

fear·ful \-fəl\ *adj* **1** : causing fear **2** : filled with fear **3** : showing or caused by fear **4** : extremely bad, intense, or large — **fear·ful·ly** \-ē\ *adv*

fear·less \-ləs\ *adj* : free from fear : BRAVE — **fear·less·ly** *adv* — **fear·less·ness** *n*

fear·some \-səm\ *adj* **1** : causing fear **2** : TIMID

fea·si·ble \ˈfē-zə-bəl\ *adj* **1** : capable of being done or carried out ⟨a ~ plan⟩ **2** : SUITABLE **3** : REASONABLE, LIKELY — **fea·si·bil·i·ty** \ˌfē-zə-ˈbil-ət-ē\ *n* — **fea·si·bly** \ˈfē-zə-blē\ *adv*

[1]**feast** \ˈfēst\ *n* **1** : an elaborate meal : BANQUET **2** : FESTIVAL 1

[2]**feast** *vb* **1** : to take part in a feast; *also* : to give a feast for **2** : to enjoy some unusual pleasure or delight **3** : DELIGHT, GRATIFY

feat \ˈfēt\ *n* : DEED, EXPLOIT, ACHIEVEMENT; *esp* : an act notable for courage, skill, endurance, or ingenuity

[1]**feath·er** \ˈfet͟h-ər\ *n* **1** : one of the light horny outgrowths that form the external covering of the body of a bird **2** : PLUME **3** : PLUMAGE **4** : KIND, NATURE ⟨birds of a ~⟩ **5** : ATTIRE, DRESS ⟨in full ~⟩ **6** : CONDITION, MOOD ⟨in fine ~⟩ — **feath·ered** \-ərd\ *adj* — **feath·er·less** *adj* — **feath·ery** *adj* — **a feather in one's cap** : a mark of distinction : HONOR

[2]**feather** *vb* **1** : to furnish with a feather ⟨~ an arrow⟩ **2** : to cover, clothe, line, or adorn with feathers — **feather one's nest** : to provide for oneself esp. while in a position of trust

feath·er·bed·ding \ˈfet͟h-ər-ˌbed-iŋ\ *n* : the requiring of an employer usu. under a union rule or safety statute to employ more workers than are needed

feath·er·edge \-ˌej\ *n* : a very thin sharp edge; *esp* : one that is easily broken or bent over

feath·er·weight \-ˌwāt\ *n* : one that is very light in weight; *esp* : a boxer weighing more than 118 but not over 126 pounds

[1]**fea·ture** \ˈfē-chər\ *n* **1** : the shape or appearance of the face or its parts **2** : a part of the face : LINEAMENT **3** : a prominent part or characteristic **4** : a special attraction (as in a motion picture or newspaper) **5** : something offered to the public or advertised as particularly attractive — **fea·ture·less** *adj*

[2]**feature** *vb* **1** : to picture in the mind : IMAGINE **2** : to give special prominence to ⟨~ a story in a newspaper⟩ **3** : to play an important part

feaze \ˈfēz, ˈfāz\ *var of* FAZE

Feb *abbr* February

feb·ri·fuge \ˈfeb-rə-ˌfyüj\ *n* : a medicine for relieving fever — **febrifuge** *adj*

fe·brile \ˈfeb-rəl, -ˌrīl; ˈfēb-\ *adj* : FEVERISH

Feb·ru·ary \ˈfeb-(y)ə-ˌwer-ē, ˈfeb-rə-\ *n* [ME *Februarie*, fr. L *Februarius*, fr. *Februa*, pl., feast of purification] : the second month of the year having 28 and in leap years 29 days

fe·ces \ˈfē-ˌsēz\ *n pl* : bodily waste discharged from the intestine — **fe·cal** \-kəl\ *adj*

feck·less \ˈfek-ləs\ *adj* **1** : WEAK, INEFFECTIVE **2** : WORTHLESS, IRRESPONSIBLE

fe·cund \ˈfek-ənd, ˈfēk-\ *adj* : FRUITFUL, PROLIFIC — **fe·cun·di·ty** \fi-ˈkən-dət-ē, fe-\ *n*

fe·cun·date \ˈfek-ən-ˌdāt, ˈfē-kən-\ *vb* **-dat·ed; -dat·ing** **1** : to make fecund **2** : IMPREGNATE — **fe·cun·da·tion** \ˌfek-ən-ˈdā-shən, ˌfē-kən-\ *n*

fed *abbr* federal; federation

fed·er·al \ˈfed(-ə)-rəl\ *adj* **1** : formed by a compact between political units that surrender individual sovereignty to a central authority but retain certain limited powers **2** : of or constituting a form of government in which power is distributed between a central authority and constituent territorial units **3** : of or relating to the central government of a federation **4** *cap* : FEDERALIST **5** *often cap* : of, relating to, or loyal to the federal government or the Union armies of the U.S. in the American Civil War — **fed·er·al·ly** \-ē\ *adv*

Federal *n* : a supporter of the U.S. government in the Civil War; *esp* : a soldier in the federal armies

federal district *n* : a district (as the District of Columbia) set apart as the seat of the central government of a federation

fed·er·al·ism \ˈfed(-ə)-rə-ˌliz-əm\ *n* **1** *often cap* : the distribution of power in an organization (as a government) between a central authority and the constituent units **2** : support or advocacy of federalism **3** *cap* : the principles of the Federalists

fed·er·al·ist \-ləst\ *n* **1** : an advocate of federalism **2** *often cap* : an advocate of a federal union between the American colonies after the Revolution and of adoption of the U.S. Constitution **3** *cap* : a member of a major political party in the early years of the U.S. favoring a strong centralized national government — **federalist** *adj, often cap*

fed·er·al·ize \ˈfed(-ə)-rə-ˌlīz\ *vb* **-ized; -iz·ing** **1** : to unite in or under a federal system **2** : to bring under the jurisdiction of a federal government

fed·er·ate \ˈfed-ə-ˌrāt\ *vb* **-at·ed; -at·ing** : to join in a federation

fed·er·a·tion \ˌfed-ə-ˈrā-shən\ *n* **1** : the act of federating; *esp* : the forming of a federal union **2** : a federal government **3** : a union of organizations

fedn *abbr* federation

fe·do·ra \fi-ˈdōr-ə\ *n* : a low soft felt hat with the crown creased lengthwise

fed up *adj* : satiated, tired, or disgusted beyond endurance

fee \ˈfē\ *n* **1** : an estate in land held from a feudal lord **2** : an inherited or heritable estate in land **3** : a fixed charge; *also* : a charge for a professional service **4** : TIP

fee·ble \ˈfē-bəl\ *adj* **fee·bler** \-b(ə-)lər\; **fee·blest** \-b(ə-)ləst\ [ME *feble,* fr. OF, fr. L *flebilis* lamentable, wretched, fr. *flēre* to weep] **1** : DECREPIT, FRAIL **2** : INEFFECTIVE, INADEQUATE ⟨a ~ protest⟩ — **fee·ble·ness** *n* — **fee·bly** \-blē\ *adv*

fee·ble·mind·ed \ˌfē-bəl-ˈmīn-dəd\ *adj* : lacking normal intelligence — **fee·ble·mind·ed·ness** *n*

[1]**feed** \ˈfēd\ *vb* **fed** \ˈfed\; **feed·ing** **1** : to give food to; *also* : to give as food **2** : EAT 1; *also* : PREY **3** : to furnish what is necessary to the growth or function of — **feed·er** *n*

[2]**feed** *n* **1** : a usu. large meal **2** : food for livestock **3** : material supplied (as to a furnace) **4** : a mechanism for feeding material to a machine

feed·back \ˈfēd-ˌbak\ *n* **1** : the return to the input of a part of the output of a machine, system, or process **2** : response esp. to one in authority about an activity or policy

feed·lot \ˈfēd-ˌlät\ *n* : land on which cattle are fattened for market

feed·stuff \-ˌstəf\ *n* : [2]FEED 2

[1]**feel** \ˈfēl\ *vb* **felt** \ˈfelt\; **feel·ing** **1** : to perceive or examine through physical contact : TOUCH, HANDLE **2** : EXPERIENCE; *also* : to suffer from **3** : to ascertain by cautious trial ⟨~ out public sentiment⟩ **4** : to be aware of **5** : to be conscious of an inward impression, state of mind, or physical condition **6** : BELIEVE, THINK **7** : to search for something with the fingers : GROPE **8** : to seem esp. to the touch **9** : to have sympathy or pity

[2]**feel** *n* **1** : the sense of touch **2** : SENSATION, FEELING **3** : the quality of a thing as imparted through touch

feel·er \ˈfē-lər\ *n* **1** : one that feels; *esp* : a tactile organ (as on the head of an insect) **2** : a proposal or remark made to find out the views of other people

[1]**feel·ing** \ˈfē-liŋ\ *n* **1** : the sense of touch; *also* : a sensation perceived by this **2** : a state of mind ⟨a ~ of loneliness⟩ **3** *pl* : general emotional condition : SENSIBILITIES ⟨hurt their ~*s*⟩ **4** : OPINION, BELIEF, SENTIMENT **5** : capacity to respond emotionally

[2]**feeling** *adj* **1** : SENSITIVE; *esp* : easily moved emotionally **2** : expressing emotion or sensitivity — **feel·ing·ly** *adv*

feet *pl of* FOOT

feign \ˈfān\ *vb* **1** : to give a false appearance of : SHAM ⟨~ illness⟩ **2** : to assert as if true : PRETEND

feint \ˈfānt\ *n* : something feigned; *esp* : a mock blow or attack intended to distract attention from the real point of attack — **feint** *vb*

feld·spar \ˈfel(d)-ˌspär\ *n* : any of a group of crystalline minerals consisting of silicates of aluminum with either potassium, sodium, calcium, or barium

fe·lic·i·tate \fi-ˈlis-ə-ˌtāt\ *vb* **-tat·ed; -tat·ing** : CONGRATULATE — **fe·lic·i·ta·tion** \-ˌlis-ə-ˈtā-shən\ *n*

fe·lic·i·tous \fi-ˈlis-ət-əs\ *adj* **1** : suitably expressed : APT **2** : PLEASANT, DELIGHTFUL — **fe·lic·i·tous·ly** *adv*

fe·lic·i·ty \fi-ˈlis-ət-ē\ *n, pl* **-ties** **1** : the quality or state of being happy; *esp* : great happiness **2** : something that causes happiness **3** : a pleasing manner or quality esp. in art or language : APTNESS **4** : an apt expression

fe·line \ˈfē-ˌlīn\ *adj* [L *felinus,* fr. *felis* cat] **1** : of or relating to cats or their kin **2** : SLY, TREACHEROUS **3** : STEALTHY — **feline** *n*

[1]**fell** \ˈfel\ *n* : SKIN, HIDE, PELT

[2]**fell** *vb* **1** : to cut, beat, or knock down ⟨~ trees⟩; *also* : KILL **2** : to sew (a seam) by folding one raw edge under the other

[3]**fell** *past of* FALL

[4]**fell** *adj* : CRUEL, FIERCE; *also* : DEADLY

fel·lah \ˈfel-ə, fə-ˈlä\ *n, pl* **fel·la·hin** *or* **fel·la·heen** \ˌfel-ə-ˈhēn\ : a peasant or agricultural laborer in Arab countries (as Egypt or Syria)

fel·la·tio \fə-ˈlā-shē-ˌō\ *also* **fel·la·tion** \-ˈlā-shən\ *n* [deriv. of L *fellare* to suck] : oral stimulation of the penis

fel·low \ˈfel-ō\ *n* [ME *felawe,* fr. OE *fēolaga,* fr. ON *fēlagi,* fr. *fēlag* partnership, fr. *fē* cattle, money + *lag* act of laying] **1** : COMRADE, ASSOCIATE **2** : EQUAL, PEER **3** : one of a pair : MATE **4** : a member of an incorporated literary or scientific society **5** : MAN, BOY **6** : BOYFRIEND **7** : a person granted a stipend for advanced study

fel·low·man \ˌfel-ō-ˈman\ *n* : a kindred human being

fel·low·ship \ˈfel-ō-ˌship\ *n* **1** : the condition of friendly relationship existing among persons : COMRADESHIP **2** : a community of interest or feeling **3** : a group with similar interests **4** : the position of a fellow (as of a university) **5** : the stipend granted a fellow

fellow traveler *n* : a person who sympathizes with and often furthers the ideals and program of an organized group (as the Communist party) without joining it or regularly participating in its activities

fel·on \ˈfel-ən\ *n* **1** : one who has committed a felony **2** : WHITLOW

fel·o·ny \ˈfel-ə-nē\ *n, pl* **-nies** : a serious crime punishable by a heavy sentence — **fe·lo·ni·ous** \fə-ˈlō-nē-əs\ *adj*

[1]**felt** \ˈfelt\ *n* **1** : a cloth made of wool and fur often mixed with natural or synthetic fibers **2** : a material resembling felt

[2]**felt** *past and past part of* FEEL

fem *abbr* **1** female **2** feminine

fe·male \ˈfē-ˌmāl\ *adj* [ME, alter. of *femel,* deriv. of ML *femella,* fr. L, girl, dim. of *femina* woman] : of, relating to, or being the sex that bears young; *also* : PISTILLATE **syn** feminine, womanly, womanlike, womanish, effeminate — **female** *n*

[1]**fem·i·nine** \ˈfem-ə-nən\ *adj* **1** : of the female sex; *also* : characteristic of or appropriate or peculiar to women **2** : of, relating to, or constituting the gender that includes most words or grammatical forms referring to females — **fem·i·nin·i·ty** \ˌfem-ə-ˈnin-ət-ē\ *n*

[2]**feminine** *n* : a noun, pronoun, adjective, or inflectional form or class of the feminine gender; *also* : the feminine gender

fem·i·nism \ˈfem-ə-ˌniz-əm\ *n* **1** : the theory of the political, economic, and social equality of the sexes **2** : organized activity on behalf of women's rights and interests — **fem·i·nist** \-nəst\ *n or adj*

femme fa·tale \ˌfem-fə-ˈtal\ *n, pl* **femmes fa·tales** \-ˈtal(z)\ [F, lit., disastrous woman] : a seductive woman : SIREN

fe·mur \ˈfē-mər\ *n, pl* **fe·murs** *or* **fem·o·ra** \ˈfem-(ə-)rə\ : the long bone of the thigh — **fem·o·ral** \ˈfem-(ə-)rəl\ *adj*

[1]**fen** \ˈfen\ *n* : low swampy land

[2]**fen** \ˈfən\ *n, pl* **fen** — see *yuan* at MONEY table

[1]**fence** \ˈfens\ *n* [ME *fens,* short for *defens* defense] **1** : a barrier (as of wood or wire) to prevent escape or entry or to mark a boundary **2** : a person who receives stolen goods; *also* : a place where stolen goods are disposed of — **on the fence** : in a position of neutrality or indecision

[2]**fence** *vb* **fenced; fenc·ing** **1** : to enclose with a fence **2** : to keep in or out with a fence **3** : to practice fencing **4** : to use tactics of attack and defense esp. in debate — **fenc·er** *n*

\ə\abut \ᵊ\kitten \ər\further \a\ash \ā\ace \ä\cot, cart \au̇\out \ch\chin \e\bet \ē\easy \g\go \i\hit \ī\ice \j\job \ŋ\sing \ō\go \ȯ\law \ȯi\boy \th\thin \t͟h\the \ü\loot \u̇\foot \y\yet \zh\vision *see also* Pronunciation Symbols page

fenc·ing \ˈfen-siŋ\ *n* **1** : the art or practice of attack and defense with the foil, épée, or saber **2** : the fences of a property or region **3** : material used for building fences

fend \ˈfend\ *vb* **1** : to keep or ward off : REPEL **2** : SHIFT ⟨~ for himself⟩

fend·er \ˈfen-dər\ *n* : a protective device (as a guard over the wheel of an automobile or as a screen before a fire)

fen·es·tra·tion \ˌfen-ə-ˈstrā-shən\ *n* : the arrangement and design of windows and doors in a building

Fe·ni·an \ˈfē-nē-ən\ *n* : a member of a secret 19th century Irish and Irish-American organization dedicated to the overthrow of British rule in Ireland

fen·nel \ˈfen-ᵊl\ *n* : a garden plant related to the carrot and grown for its aromatic foliage and seeds

FEPC *abbr* Fair Employment Practices Commission

fe·ral \ˈfir-əl, ˈfer-\ *adj* **1** : SAVAGE **2** : WILD 1 **3** : having escaped from domestication and become wild

fer–de–lance \ˈferd-ᵊl-ˈans\ *n, pl* **fer–de–lance** [F, lit., lance iron, spearhead] : a large venomous pit viper of Central and So. America

[1]**fer·ment** \fər-ˈment\ *vb* **1** : to cause or undergo fermentation **2** : to be or cause to be in a state of agitation or intense activity

[2]**fer·ment** \ˈfər-ˌment\ *n* **1** : a living organism (as a yeast) causing fermentation by its enzymes; *also* : ENZYME **2** : AGITATION, TUMULT

fer·men·ta·tion \ˌfər-mən-ˈtā-shən, -ˌmen-\ *n* **1** : chemical decomposition of an organic substance (as in the souring of milk or the formation of alcohol from sugar) in the absence of oxygen by enzymatic action often with formation of gas **2** : AGITATION, UNREST

fer·mi·um \ˈfer-mē-əm, ˈfər-\ *n* : an artificially produced radioactive metallic chemical element — see ELEMENT table

fern \ˈfərn\ *n* : any of an order of vascular plants resembling seed plants in having root, stem, and leaflike fronds but reproducing by spores instead of by flowers and seeds

fern·ery \ˈfərn-(ə-)rē\ *n, pl* **-er·ies** **1** : a place for growing ferns **2** : a collection of growing ferns

fe·ro·cious \fə-ˈrō-shəs\ *adj* **1** : FIERCE, SAVAGE **2** : extremely intense ⟨~ heat⟩ — **fe·ro·cious·ly** *adv* — **fe·ro·cious·ness** *n*

fe·roc·i·ty \fə-ˈräs-ət-ē\ *n* : the quality or state of being ferocious

[1]**fer·ret** \ˈfer-ət\ *n* : a partially domesticated usu. white European mammal related to the weasels and used esp. for hunting rodents

[2]**ferret** *vb* **1** : to hunt game with ferrets **2** : to drive out of a hiding place **3** : to find and bring to light by searching ⟨~ out the truth⟩

fer·ric \ˈfer-ik\ *adj* : of, relating to, or containing iron

ferric oxide *n* : an oxide of iron that is found in nature as hematite and as rust and that is used as a pigment and for polishing

Fer·ris wheel \ˈfer-əs-\ *n* : an amusement device consisting of a large upright power-driven wheel carrying seats that remain horizontal around its rim

fer·ro·mag·net·ic \ˌfer-ō-mag-ˈnet-ik\ *adj* : of or relating to substances that are easily magnetized

fer·rous \ˈfer-əs\ *adj* : of, relating to, or containing iron

fer·rule \ˈfer-əl\ *n* : a metal ring or cap around a slender wooden shaft to prevent splitting

[1]**fer·ry** \ˈfer-ē\ *vb* **fer·ried; fer·ry·ing** [ME *ferien*, fr. OE *ferian* to carry, convey] **1** : to carry by boat over a body of water **2** : to cross by a ferry **3** : to convey from one place to another

[2]**ferry** *n, pl* **ferries** **1** : a place where persons or things are ferried **2** : FERRYBOAT

fer·ry·boat \ˈfer-ē-ˌbōt\ *n* : a boat used in ferrying

fer·tile \ˈfərt-ᵊl\ *adj* **1** : producing plentifully : PRODUCTIVE ⟨~ soils⟩ **2** : capable of developing or reproducing ⟨~ eggs⟩ ⟨a ~ family⟩ **syn** fruitful, prolific, fecund, productive — **fer·til·i·ty** \(ˌ)fər-ˈtil-ət-ē\ *n*

fer·til·ize \ˈfərt-ᵊl-ˌīz\ *vb* **-ized; -iz·ing** **1** : to unite with in the process of fertilization ⟨one sperm ~*s* each egg⟩ **2** : to apply fertilizer to — **fer·til·iza·tion** \ˌfərt-ᵊl-ə-ˈzā-shən\ *n*

fer·til·iz·er \-ˌī-zər\ *n* : material (as manure or a chemical mixture) for enriching land

fer·ule \ˈfer-əl\ *also* **fer·u·la** \ˈfer-(y)ə-lə\ *n* : a rod or ruler used to punish children

fer·ven·cy \ˈfər-vən-sē\ *n, pl* **-cies** : FERVOR

fer·vent \ˈfər-vənt\ *adj* **1** : very hot : GLOWING **2** : marked by great intensity of feeling — **fer·vent·ly** *adv*

fer·vid \-vəd\ *adj* **1** : very hot **2** : ARDENT, ZEALOUS — **fer·vid·ly** *adv*

fer·vor \ˈfər-vər\ *n* **1** : intense heat **2** : intensity of feeling or expression

fes·tal \ˈfest-ᵊl\ *adj* : FESTIVE

[1]**fes·ter** \ˈfes-tər\ *n* : a pus-filled sore

[2]**fester** *vb* **fes·tered; fes·ter·ing** \-t(ə-)riŋ\ **1** : to form pus **2** : PUTREFY, ROT **3** : RANKLE

fes·ti·val \ˈfes-tə-vəl\ *n* **1** : a time of celebration marked by special observances; *esp* : an occasion marked with religious ceremonies **2** : a periodic season or program of cultural events or entertainment ⟨a dance ~⟩

fes·tive \ˈfes-tiv\ *adj* **1** : of, relating to, or suitable for a feast or festival **2** : JOYFUL, GAY — **fes·tive·ly** *adv*

fes·tiv·i·ty \fes-ˈtiv-ət-ē\ *n, pl* **-ties** **1** : FESTIVAL 1 **2** : the quality or state of being festive **3** : festive activity

[1]**fes·toon** \fes-ˈtün\ *n* [F *feston*, fr. It *festone*, fr. *festa* festival] **1** : a decorative chain or strip hanging between two points **2** : a carved, molded, or painted ornament representing a decorative chain

[2]**festoon** *vb* **1** : to hang or form festoons on **2** : to shape into festoons

fe·tal \ˈfēt-ᵊl\ *adj* : of, relating to, or being a fetus

fetal position *n* : a resting position with body curved, legs bent and drawn toward the chest, head bowed forward, and arms tucked in in the manner of the fetus in the womb that is assumed in some forms of psychic disorder

fetch \ˈfech\ *vb* **1** : to go or come after and bring or take back ⟨teach a dog to ~ a stick⟩ **2** : to cause to come : bring out ⟨~*ed* tears from the eyes⟩ **3** : to sell for **4** : to give by striking ⟨~ him a blow⟩

fetch·ing \ˈfech-iŋ\ *adj* : ATTRACTIVE, PLEASING — **fetch·ing·ly** *adv*

[1]**fete** *or* **fête** \ˈfāt, ˈfet\ *n* [F *fête*, fr. OF *feste*] **1** : FESTIVAL **2** : a large elaborate entertainment or party

[2]**fete** *or* **fête** *vb* **fet·ed** *or* **fêt·ed; fet·ing** *or* **fêt·ing** **1** : to honor or commemorate with a fete **2** : to pay high honor to

fet·id \ˈfet-əd\ *adj* : having an offensive smell : STINKING

fe·tish *also* **fe·tich** \ˈfet-ish, ˈfēt-\ *n* [F & Pg; F *fétiche*, fr. Pg *feitiço*, fr. *feitiço* artificial, false, fr. L *facticius* factitious] **1** : an object (as an idol or image) believed to have magical powers (as in curing disease) **2** : an object of unreasoning devotion or concern **3** : an object whose real or fantasied presence is psychologically necessary for sexual gratification

fe·tish·ism \-ish-ˌiz-əm\ *n* : belief in, devotion to, or pathological attachment to fetishes — **fe·tish·ist** \-ish-əst\ *n* — **fe·tish·is·tic** \ˌfet-ish-ˈis-tik, ˌfēt-\ *adj*

fet·lock \ˈfet-ˌläk\ *n* : a projection on the back of a horse's leg above the hoof; *also* : a tuft of hair on this

fet·ter \ˈfet-ər\ *n* **1** : a chain or shackle for the feet **2** : something that confines : RESTRAINT — **fetter** *vb*

fet·tle \ˈfet-ᵊl\ *n* : a state of fitness or order : CONDITION ⟨in fine ~⟩

fe·tus \ˈfēt-əs\ *n* : an unborn or unhatched vertebrate esp. after its basic structure is laid down; *esp* : a developing human being in the uterus from usu. three months after pregnancy occurs to birth

feud \ˈfyüd\ *n* : a prolonged quarrel; *esp* : a lasting conflict between families or clans marked by violent attacks undertaken for revenge — **feud** *vb*

feu·dal \ˈfyüd-ᵊl\ *adj* **1** : of, relating to, or having the characteristics of a medieval fee **2** : of, relating to, or characteristic of feudalism

feu·dal·ism \ˈfyüd-ᵊl-ˌiz-əm\ *n* : a system of political organization prevailing in medieval Europe in which a vassal renders service to a lord and receives protection and land in return; *also* : a similar political or social system — **feu·dal·is·tic** \ˌfyüd-ᵊl-ˈis-tik\ *adj*

¹feu·da·to·ry \ˈfyüd-ə-ˌtōr-ē\ *adj* : owing feudal allegiance

²feudatory *n, pl* **-ries 1** : a person who holds lands by feudal law or usage **2** : FIEF

fe·ver \ˈfē-vər\ *n* **1** : a rise in body temperature above the normal; *also* : a disease of which this is a chief symptom **2** : a state of heightened emotion or activity **3** : CRAZE — **fe·ver·ish** *adj* — **fe·ver·ish·ly** *adv*

¹few \ˈfyü\ *pron* : not many : a small number

²few *adj* **1** : consisting of or amounting to a small number **2** : not many but some ⟨caught a ~ fish⟩ — **few·ness** *n*

³few *n* **1** : a small number of units or individuals ⟨a ~ of them⟩ **2** : a special limited number ⟨among the ~⟩

few·er \ˈfyü-ər\ *pron* : a smaller number of persons or things

fey \ˈfā\ *adj* **1** *chiefly Scot* : fated to die; *also* : marked by a foreboding of death or calamity **2** : able to see into the future : VISIONARY **3** : marked by an otherworldly air or attitude **4** : CRAZY, TOUCHED

fez \ˈfez\ *n, pl* **fez·zes** *also* **fez·es** : a round red felt hat that has a flat top and a tassel but no brim

ff *abbr* **1** folios **2** [*f*ollowing] and the following ones **3** fortissimo

FHA *abbr* Federal Housing Administration

fi·an·cé \ˌfē-ˌän-ˈsā\ *n* [F, fr. MF, fr. *fiancer* to promise, betroth, fr. OF *fiancier*, fr. *fiance* promise, trust, fr. *fier* to trust, fr. L *fidere*] : a man engaged to be married

fi·an·cée \ˌfē-ˌän-ˈsā\ *n* : a woman engaged to be married

fi·as·co \fē-ˈas-kō\ *n, pl* **-coes** [F] : a complete failure

fi·at \ˈfē-ət, -ˌat, -ˌät; ˈfī-ət, -ˌat\ *n* [L, let it be done] : an authoritative and often arbitrary order or decree

fiat money *n* : paper currency backed only by the authority of the government and not by metal

¹fib \ˈfib\ *n* : a trivial or childish lie

²fib *vb* **fibbed; fib·bing** : to tell a fib — **fib·ber** *n*

fi·ber *or* **fi·bre** \ˈfī-bər\ *n* **1** : a threadlike substance or structure (as a muscle cell or fine root); *esp* : a natural (as wool or flax) or artificial (as rayon) filament capable of being spun or woven **2** : ROUGHAGE **3** : an element that gives texture or substance **4** : basic toughness : STRENGTH — **fi·brous** \-brəs\ *adj*

fi·ber·board \-ˌbōrd\ *n* : a material made by compressing fibers (as of wood) into stiff sheets

fi·ber·fill \-ˌfil\ *n* : man-made fibers used as a filling material (as for cushions)

fi·ber·glass \-ˌglas\ *n* : glass in fibrous form used in making various products (as yarn and insulation)

fiber optics *n* **1** *pl* : thin transparent fibers of glass or plastic that are enclosed by a less refractive material and that transmit light by internal reflection; *also* : a bundle of such fibers used in an instrument **2** : the technique of the use of fiber optics — **fiber–optic** *adj*

fi·bril \ˈfīb-rəl, ˈfib-\ *n* : a small fiber

fi·bril·la·tion \ˌfib-rə-ˈlā-shən, ˌfīb-\ *n* : rapid irregular contractions of muscle fibers (as of the heart) — **fib·ril·late** \ˈfib-rə-ˌlāt, ˈfīb-\ *vb*

fi·brin \ˈfī-brən\ *n* : a white insoluble fibrous protein formed from fibrinogen in the clotting of blood

fi·brin·o·gen \fī-ˈbrin-ə-jən\ *n* : a globulin produced in the liver, present esp. in blood plasma, and converted into fibrin during clotting of blood

fi·broid \ˈfīb-ròid, ˈfib-\ *adj* : resembling, forming, or consisting of fibrous tissue ⟨~ tumors⟩

fi·bro·sis \fī-ˈbrō-səs\ *n* : a condition marked by abnormal increase of fiber-containing tissue

fib·u·la \ˈfib-yə-lə\ *n, pl* **-lae** \-lē, -ˌlī\ *or* **-las** : the outer and usu. the smaller of the two bones of the hind limb below the knee — **fib·u·lar** \-lər\ *adj*

FICA *abbr* Federal Insurance Contributions Act

fiche \ˈfēsh, ˈfish\ *n, pl* **fiche** : MICROFICHE

fi·chu \ˈfish-ü\ *n* [F] : a woman's light triangular scarf draped over the shoulders and fastened in front

fick·le \ˈfik-əl\ *adj* : not firm or steadfast in disposition or character : INCONSTANT — **fick·le·ness** *n*

fic·tion \ˈfik-shən\ *n* **1** : something (as a story) invented by the imagination **2** : fictitious literature (as novels) — **fic·tion·al** \-sh(ə-)nəl\ *adj* — **fic·tion·al·ly** \-ē\ *adv*

fic·ti·tious \fik-ˈtish-əs\ *adj* **1** : of, relating to, or characteristic of fiction : IMAGINARY **2** : FEIGNED **syn** chimerical, fanciful, fantastic, unreal

¹fid·dle \ˈfid-ᵊl\ *n* : VIOLIN

²fiddle *vb* **fid·dled; fid·dling** \ˈfid-(ᵊ-)liŋ\ **1** : to play on a fiddle **2** : to move the hands or fingers restlessly **3** : PUTTER **4** : MEDDLE, TAMPER — **fid·dler** \ˈfid-(ᵊ-)lər\ *n*

fiddler crab *n* : a burrowing crab with one claw much enlarged in the male

fid·dle·stick \ˈfid-ᵊl-ˌstik\ *n* **1** *archaic* : a violin bow **2** *pl* : NONSENSE — used as an interjection

fi·del·i·ty \fə-ˈdel-ət-ē, fī-\ *n, pl* **-ties 1** : the quality or state of being faithful **2** : ACCURACY ⟨~ of a news report⟩ ⟨~ in sound reproduction⟩ **syn** allegiance, loyalty, devotion, fealty

¹fidg·et \ˈfij-ət\ *n* **1** *pl* : uneasiness or restlessness as shown by nervous movements **2** : one that fidgets — **fidg·ety** *adj*

²fidget *vb* : to move or cause to move or act restlessly or nervously

fi·du·cia·ry \fə-ˈd(y)ü-shē-ˌer-ē, -shə-rē\ *adj* **1** : involving a confidence or trust **2** : held or holding in trust for another ⟨~ accounts⟩ — **fiduciary** *n*

fie \ˈfī\ *interj* — used to express disgust or disapproval

fief \ˈfēf\ *n* : a feudal estate : FEE

¹field \ˈfēld\ *n* **1** : open country **2** : a piece of cleared land for cultivation or pasture **3** : a piece of land yielding some special product **4** : the place where a battle is fought; *also* : BATTLE **5** : an area, division, or sphere of activity ⟨the ~ of science⟩ ⟨salesmen in the ~⟩ **6** : an area for military exercises **7** : an area for sports **8** : a background on which something is drawn or projected ⟨a flag with white stars on a ~ of blue⟩ **9** : a region or space in which a given effect (as magnetism) exists — **field** *adj*

²field *vb* **1** : to handle a batted or thrown baseball while on defense **2** : to put into the field **3** : to answer satisfactorily ⟨~ a tough question⟩ — **field·er** *n*

field day *n* **1** : a day devoted to outdoor sports and athletic competition **2** : a time of extraordinary pleasure or opportunity

field event *n* : a track-and-field event (as weight-throwing) other than a race

field glass *n* : a hand-held binocular telescope — usu. used in pl.

field hockey *n* : a field game played between two teams of 11 players each whose object is to knock a ball into the opponent's goal with a curved stick

field marshal *n* : an officer (as in the British army) of the highest rank

field–test \-ˌtest\ *vb* : to test (as a new product) in a natural environment — **field test** *n*

fiend \ˈfēnd\ *n* **1** : DEVIL 1 **2** : DEMON **3** : an extemely wicked or cruel person **4** : a person excessively devot-

---

\ə\abut \ᵊ\kitten \ər\further \a\ash \ā\ace \ä\cot, cart \aù\out \ch\chin \e\bet \ē\easy \g\go \i\hit \ī\ice \j\job \ŋ\sing \ō\go \ò\law \òi\boy \th\thin \th\the \ü\loot \ù\foot \y\yet \zh\vision *see also* Pronunciation Symbols page

ed to a pursuit 5 : ADDICT ⟨dope ~⟩ — **fiend·ish** *adj* — **fiend·ish·ly** *adv*

fierce \ˈfirs\ *adj* **fierc·er; fierc·est** 1 : violently hostile or aggressive in temperament 2 : PUGNACIOUS 3 : INTENSE 4 : furiously active or determined 5 : wild or menacing in appearance **syn** ferocious, barbarous, savage, cruel — **fierce·ly** *adv* — **fierce·ness** *n*

fi·ery \ˈfī(-ə)-rē\ *adj* **fi·er·i·er; -est** 1 : consisting of fire 2 : BURNING, BLAZING 3 : FLAMMABLE 4 : hot like a fire : INFLAMED, FEVERISH 5 : RED 6 : full of emotion or spirit 7 : IRRITABLE — **fi·eri·ness** \ˈfī(-ə)-rē-nəs\ *n*

fi·es·ta \fē-ˈes-tə\ *n* [Sp] : FESTIVAL

fife \ˈfīf\ *n* [G *pfeife* pipe, fife] : a small shrill flutelike musical instrument

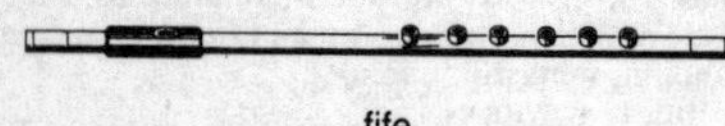

fife

FIFO *abbr* first in, first out

fif·teen \fif-ˈtēn\ *n* : one more than 14 — **fifteen** *adj or pron* — **fif·teenth** \-ˈtēnth\ *adj or n*

fifth \ˈfifth\ *n* 1 : one that is number five in a countable series 2 : one of five equal parts of something 3 : a unit of measure for liquor equal to ⅕ U.S. gallon (about 0.75 liter) — **fifth** *adj or adv*

fifth column *n* : a group of secret supporters of a nation's enemy that engage in espionage or sabotage within the country — **fifth col·um·nist** \-ˈkäl-əm-(n)əst\ *n*

fifth wheel *n* : one that is unnecessary and often burdensome

fif·ty \ˈfif-tē\ *n, pl* **fifties** : five times 10 — **fif·ti·eth** \-tē-əth\ *adj or n* — **fifty** *adj or pron*

fif·ty–fif·ty \ˌfif-tē-ˈfif-tē\ *adj* 1 : shared equally ⟨a ~ proposition⟩ 2 : half favorable and half unfavorable

[1]**fig** \ˈfig\ *n* : a usu. pear-shaped edible fruit of warm regions; *also* : a tree related to the mulberry that bears this fruit

[2]**fig** *abbr* 1 figurative; figuratively 2 figure

[1]**fight** \ˈfīt\ *vb* **fought** \ˈfȯt\; **fight·ing** 1 : to contend against another in battle or physical combat 2 : BOX 3 : to put forth a determined effort 4 : STRUGGLE, CONTEND 5 : to attempt to prevent the success or effectiveness of 6 : WAGE 7 : to gain by struggle

[2]**fight** *n* 1 : a hostile encounter : BATTLE 2 : a boxing match 3 : a verbal disagreement 4 : a struggle for a goal or an objective 5 : strength or disposition for fighting ⟨full of ~⟩

fight·er \-ər\ *n* 1 : one that fights; *esp* : WARRIOR 2 : BOXER 3 : a fast maneuverable airplane armed for destroying enemy aircraft

fig·ment \ˈfig-mənt\ *n* : something imagined or made up

fig·u·ra·tion \ˌfig-(y)ə-ˈrā-shən\ *n* 1 : FORM, OUTLINE 2 : an act or instance of representation in figures and shapes

fig·u·ra·tive \ˈfig-(y)ə-rət-iv\ *adj* 1 : EMBLEMATIC 2 : SYMBOLIC, METAPHORICAL ⟨~ language⟩ 3 : characterized by figures of speech — **fig·u·ra·tive·ly** *adv*

[1]**fig·ure** \ˈfig-yər\ *n* 1 : NUMERAL 2 *pl* : arithmetical calculations 3 : a written or printed character 4 : PRICE, AMOUNT 5 : SHAPE, FORM, OUTLINE 6 : the graphic representation of a form and esp. of a person 7 : a diagram or pictorial illustration of textual matter 8 : a combination of points, lines, or surfaces in geometry ⟨a circle is a closed plane ~⟩ 9 : PATTERN, DESIGN 10 : appearance made or impression produced ⟨they cut quite a ~⟩ 11 : a series of movements (as in a dance) 12 : PERSONAGE

[2]**figure** *vb* **fig·ured; fig·ur·ing** \ˈfig-yə-riŋ\ 1 : to represent by or as if by a figure or outline : PORTRAY 2 : to decorate with a pattern 3 : to indicate or represent by numerals 4 : REGARD, CONSIDER 5 : to be or appear important or conspicuous 6 : COMPUTE, CALCULATE

fig·ure·head \ˈfig-(y)ər-ˌhed\ *n* 1 : a figure on the bow of a ship 2 : a head or chief in name only

figure of speech : a form of expression (as a simile or metaphor) that uses words in other than a plain or literal way

figure out *vb* 1 : FIND OUT, DISCOVER 2 : SOLVE

fig·u·rine \ˌfig-(y)ə-ˈrēn\ *n* : a small carved or molded figure

Fi·ji·an \ˈfē-ˌjē-ən, fi-ˈjē-ən\ *n* : a native or inhabitant of the Pacific island country of Fiji — **Fijian** *adj*

fil·a·ment \ˈfil-ə-mənt\ *n* : a fine thread or threadlike object, part, or process — **fil·a·men·tous** \ˌfil-ə-ˈment-əs\ *adj*

fil·bert \ˈfil-bərt\ *n* : the sweet thick-shelled nut of either of two European hazels; *also* : a shrub or small tree bearing filberts

filch \ˈfilch\ *vb* : to steal furtively

[1]**file** \ˈfīl\ *n* : a usu. steel tool with a ridged or toothed surface used esp. for smoothing a hard substance

[2]**file** *vb* **filed; fil·ing** : to rub, smooth, or cut away with a file

[3]**file** *vb* **filed; fil·ing** [ME *filen*, fr. MF *filer* to string documents on a string or wire, fr. *fil* thread, fr. L *filum*] 1 : to arrange in order 2 : to enter or record officially or as prescribed by law ⟨~ a lawsuit⟩ 3 : to send (copy) to a newspaper

[4]**file** *n* 1 : a device (as a folder or cabinet) by means of which papers may be kept in order 2 : a collection of papers or publications usu. arranged or classified

[5]**file** *n* : a row of persons, animals, or things arranged one behind the other

[6]**file** *vb* **filed; fil·ing** : to march or proceed in file

fi·let mi·gnon \ˌfil-(ˌ)ā-mēn-ˈyōⁿ, fi-ˌlā-\ *n, pl* **filets mignons** \-(ˌ)ā-mēn-ˈyōⁿz, -ˌlā-\ [F, lit., dainty fillet] : a fillet of beef cut from the thick end of a beef tenderloin

fil·ial \ˈfil-ē-əl, ˈfil-yəl\ *adj* : of, relating to, or befitting a son or daughter

fil·i·bus·ter \ˈfil-ə-ˌbəs-tər\ *n* [Sp *filibustero*, lit., freebooter] 1 : a military adventurer; *esp* : an American engaged in fomenting 19th century Latin American uprisings 2 : the use of delaying tactics (as extremely long speeches) esp. in a legislative assembly; *also* : an instance of this practice — **filibuster** *vb* — **fil·i·bus·ter·er** *n*

fil·i·gree \ˈfil-ə-ˌgrē\ *n* [F *filigrane*] : ornamental openwork (as of fine wire)

fil·ing \ˈfī-liŋ\ *n* 1 : the act of one who files 2 : a small piece scraped off by a file ⟨iron ~*s*⟩

Fil·i·pi·no \ˌfil-ə-ˈpē-nō\ *n, pl* **Filipinos** : a native or inhabitant of the Philippines — **Filipino** *adj*

[1]**fill** \ˈfil\ *vb* 1 : to make or become full 2 : to stop up : PLUG ⟨~ a cavity⟩ 3 : FEED, SATIATE 4 : SATISFY, FULFILL ⟨~ all requirements⟩ 5 : to occupy fully 6 : to spread through ⟨laughter ~*ed* the room⟩ 7 : OCCUPY ⟨~ the office of president⟩ 8 : to put a person in ⟨~ a vacancy⟩ 9 : to supply as directed ⟨~ a prescription⟩

[2]**fill** *n* 1 : a full supply; *esp* : a quantity that satisfies or satiates 2 : material used esp. for filling a low place

[1]**fill·er** \ˈfil-ər\ *n* 1 : one that fills 2 : a substance added to another substance (as to increase bulk or weight) 3 : a material used for filling cracks and pores in wood before painting

[2]**fil·ler** \ˈfil-ˌeər\ *n, pl* **fillers** *or* **filler** — see *forint* at MONEY table

[1]**fil·let** \ˈfil-ət, *in sense 2* fi-ˈlā, ˈfil-(ˌ)ā\ *also* **fi·let** \fi-ˈlā, ˈfil-(ˌ)ā\ *n* [ME *filet*, fr. MF, dim. of *fil* thread] 1 : a narrow band, strip, or ribbon 2 : a piece or slice of boneless meat or fish; *esp* : the tenderloin of beef

[2]**fil·let** \ˈfil-ət, *in sense 2 also* fi-ˈlā, ˈfil-(ˌ)ā\ *vb* 1 : to bind or adorn with or as if with a fillet 2 : to cut into fillets

fill in \(ˈ)fil-ˈin\ *vb* 1 : to provide necessary or recent information 2 : to serve as a temporary substitute

fill·ing \ˈfil-iŋ\ *n* 1 : material used to fill something ⟨a ~

for a tooth⟩ **2** : the yarn interlacing the warp in a fabric **3** : a food mixture used to fill pastry or sandwiches

filling station *n* : SERVICE STATION

fil·lip \ˈfil-əp\ *n* **1** : a blow or gesture made by a flick or snap of the finger across the thumb **2** : something that serves to arouse or stimulate — **fillip** *vb*

fil·ly \ˈfil-ē\ *n, pl* **fillies** : a young female horse usu. less than four years old

1film \ˈfilm\ *n* **1** : a thin skin or membrane **2** : a thin coating or layer **3** : a flexible strip of chemically treated material used in taking pictures **4** : MOTION PICTURE — **filmy** *adj*

2film *vb* **1** : to cover with a film **2** : to make a motion picture of

film·dom \ˈfilm-dəm\ *n* : the motion-picture industry

film·og·ra·phy \fil-ˈmäg-rə-fē\ *n, pl* **-phies** : a list or catalog of motion pictures relating usu. to a particular actor or director

film·strip \ˈfilm-ˌstrip\ *n* : a strip of film bearing images to be projected on a screen as still pictures

fils \ˈfils\ *n, pl* **fils** — see *dinar, dirham, rial* at MONEY table

1fil·ter \ˈfil-tər\ *n* **1** : a porous material through which a fluid is passed to separate out matter in suspension; *also* : a device containing such material **2** : a device for suppressing waves of certain frequencies; *esp* : one (as for a camera) that absorbs light of certain colors

2filter *vb* **fil·tered; fil·ter·ing** \-t(ə-)riŋ\ **1** : to remove by means of a filter **2** : to pass through a filter — **fil·ter·able** *also* **fil·tra·ble** \-t(ə-)rə-bəl\ *adj* — **fil·tra·tion** \fil-ˈtrā-shən\ *n*

filter bed *n* : a bed of sand or gravel for filtering water or sewage

filth \ˈfilth\ *n* [ME, fr. OE *fȳlth*, fr. *fūl* foul] **1** : foul matter; *esp* : loathsome dirt or refuse **2** : moral corruption **3** : OBSCENITY — **filth·i·ness** \ˈfil-thē-nəs\ *n* — **filthy** \ˈfil-thē\ *adj*

fil·trate \ˈfil-ˌtrāt\ *n* : material that has passed through a filter

1fin \ˈfin\ *n* **1** : one of the thin external processes by which an aquatic animal (as a fish) moves through water **2** : a fin-shaped part (as on an airplane) **3** : FLIPPER 2 — **finned** \ˈfind\ *adj*

2fin *abbr* **1** finance; financial **2** finish

fi·na·gle \fə-ˈnā-gəl\ *vb* **-gled; -gling** \-g(ə-)liŋ\ **1** : to obtain by indirect or dishonest means : WANGLE **2** : to use devious dishonest methods to achieve one's ends — **fi·na·gler** \-g(ə-)lər\ *n*

1fi·nal \ˈfīn-ᵊl\ *adj* **1** : not to be altered or undone **2** : ULTIMATE **3** : relating to or occurring at the end or conclusion — **fi·nal·i·ty** \fī-ˈnal-ət-ē, fə-\ *n* — **fi·nal·ly** \ˈfīn-(ᵊ-)lē\ *adv*

2final *n* **1** : a deciding match, game, or trial — usu. used in pl. **2** : the last examination in a course — usu. used in pl.

fi·na·le \fə-ˈnal-ē, fi-ˈnäl-\ *n* : the close or end of something; *esp* : the last section of a musical composition

fi·nal·ist \ˈfīn-ᵊl-əst\ *n* : a contestant in the finals of a competition

fi·nal·ize \ˈfīn-ᵊl-ˌīz\ *vb* **-ized; -iz·ing** : to put in final or finished form

1fi·nance \fə-ˈnans, ˈfī-ˌnans\ *n* [ME, payment, ransom, fr. MF, fr. *finer* to end, pay, fr. *fin* end, fr. L *finis* boundary, end] **1** *pl* : money resources available esp. to a government or business **2** : management of money affairs

2finance *vb* **fi·nanced; fi·nanc·ing** **1** : to raise or provide funds for **2** : to furnish with necessary funds **3** : to sell or supply on credit

finance company *n* : a company that makes usu. small short-term loans usu. to individuals

fi·nan·cial \fə-ˈnan-chəl, fī-\ *adj* : having to do with finance or financiers ⟨in ~ circles⟩ — **fi·nan·cial·ly** \-ˈnanch-(ə-)lē\ *adv*

fi·nan·cier \ˌfin-ən-ˈsiər, ˌfī-ˌnan-\ *n* **1** : a person skilled in managing public moneys **2** : a person who invests large sums of money

finch \ˈfinch\ *n* : any of numerous songbirds (as sparrows, linnets, or buntings) with strong conical bills

1find \ˈfīnd\ *vb* **found** \ˈfaůnd\; **find·ing** **1** : to meet with either by chance or by searching or study : ENCOUNTER, DISCOVER **2** : to obtain by effort or management ⟨~ time to read⟩ **3** : to arrive at : REACH ⟨the bullet *found* its mark⟩ **4** : EXPERIENCE, DETECT, PERCEIVE, FEEL **5** : to gain or regain the use of ⟨*found* his voice again⟩ **6** : PROVIDE, SUPPLY **7** : to settle upon and make a statement about ⟨~ a verdict⟩

2find *n* **1** : an act or instance of finding **2** : something found; *esp* : a valuable item of discovery

find·er \ˈfīn-dər\ *n* : one that finds; *esp* : a device on a camera showing the view being photographed

fin de siè·cle \ˌfa^{n}-də-sē-ˈeklᵊ\ *adj* [F, end of century] : of, relating to, or characteristic of the close of the 19th century

find·ing \ˈfīn-diŋ\ *n* **1** : the act of finding **2** : FIND 2 **3** : the result of a judicial proceeding or inquiry

find out *vb* : to learn by study, observation, or search : DISCOVER

1fine \ˈfīn\ *n* : money exacted as a penalty for an offense

2fine *vb* **fined; fin·ing** : to impose a fine on : punish by a fine

3fine *adj* **fin·er; fin·est** **1** : free from impurity **2** : very thin in gauge or texture **3** : not coarse **4** : SUBTLE, SENSITIVE ⟨a ~ distinction⟩ **5** : superior in quality, conception, or appearance **6** : ELEGANT, REFINED — **fine·ly** *adv* — **fine·ness** \ˈfīn-nəs\ *n*

4fine *adv* : FINELY

fine art *n* : art (as painting, sculpture, or music) concerned primarily with the creation of beautiful objects — usu. used in pl.

fin·ery \ˈfīn-(ə-)rē\ *n, pl* **-er·ies** : ORNAMENT, DECORATION; *esp* : showy clothing and jewels

fine·spun \ˈfīn-ˈspən\ *adj* : developed with extremely or excessively fine delicacy or detail

fi·nesse \fə-ˈnes\ *n* **1** : refinement or delicacy of workmanship, structure, or texture **2** : CUNNING, SUBTLETY — **finesse** *vb*

fine–tune \ˈfīn-ˈtün\ *vb* : to adjust so as to bring to the highest level of performance or effectiveness

fin·fish \ˈfin-ˌfish\ *n* : FISH 2

1fin·ger \ˈfiŋ-gər\ *n* **1** : any of the five divisions at the end of the hand; *esp* : one other than the thumb **2** : something that resembles or does the work of a finger **3** : a part of a glove into which a finger is inserted

2finger *vb* **fin·gered; fin·ger·ing** \-g(ə-)riŋ\ **1** : to perform with the fingers or with a certain fingering **2** : to mark the notes of a piece of music as a guide in playing **3** : to touch or feel with the fingers : HANDLE **4** : to point out

fin·ger·board \ˈfiŋ-gər-ˌbōrd\ *n* : the part of a stringed instrument against which the fingers press the strings to vary the pitch

finger bowl *n* : a basin to hold water for rinsing the fingers at table

fin·ger·ing \ˈfiŋ-g(ə-)riŋ\ *n* **1** : handling or touching with the fingers **2** : the act or method of using the fingers in playing an instrument **3** : the marking of the method of fingering

fin·ger·ling \ˈfiŋ-gər-liŋ\ *n* : a small fish

fin·ger·nail \ˈfiŋ-gər-ˌnāl\ *n* : the nail of a finger

fin·ger·print \-ˌprint\ *n* : the pattern of marks made by

---

pressing the tip of a finger or thumb on a surface; *esp* : an ink impression of such a pattern taken for the purpose of identification — **fingerprint** *vb*

fin·ger·tip \-ˌtip\ *n* : the tip of a finger

fin·i·al \ˈfin-ē-əl\ *n* : an ornamental projection or end (as on a spire)

fin·ick·ing \ˈfin-i-kiŋ\ *adj* : FINICKY

fin·icky \ˈfin-i-kē\ *adj* : excessively particular in taste or standards

fi·nis \ˈfin-əs\ *n* : END, CONCLUSION

[1]**fin·ish** \ˈfin-ish\ *vb* **1** : TERMINATE **2** : to use or dispose of entirely **3** : to bring to completion : ACCOMPLISH; *also* : PERFECT **4** : to put a final coat or surface on **5** : to come to the end of a course or undertaking — **fin·ish·er** *n*

[2]**finish** *n* **1** : END, CONCLUSION **2** : something that completes or perfects **3** : the final treatment or coating of a surface

fi·nite \ˈfī-ˌnīt\ *adj* **1** : having definite or definable limits **2** : having a limited nature or existence **3** : being neither infinite nor infinitesimal

fink \ˈfiŋk\ *n* **1** : a contemptible person **2** : STRIKEBREAKER **3** : INFORMER

Finn \ˈfin\ *n* : a native or inhabitant of Finland

fin·nan had·die \ˌfin-ən-ˈhad-ē\ *n* : smoked haddock

[1]**Finn·ish** \ˈfin-ish\ *adj* : of or relating to Finland, the Finns, or Finnish

[2]**Finnish** *n* : the language of Finland

fin·ny \ˈfin-ē\ *adj* **1** : having or characterized by fins **2** : relating to or being fish

fiord *var of* FJORD

fir \ˈfər\ *n* : an erect evergreen tree related to the pines; *also* : its light soft wood

[1]**fire** \ˈfī(ə)r\ *n* **1** : the light or heat and esp. the flame of something burning **2** : ENTHUSIASM, ZEAL **3** : fuel that is burning (as in a stove or fireplace) **4** : destructive burning of something (as a house) **5** : the discharge of firearms — **fire·less** *adj*

[2]**fire** *vb* **fired; fir·ing 1** : KINDLE, IGNITE ⟨~ a house⟩ **2** : STIR, ENLIVEN ⟨~ the imagination⟩ **3** : to dismiss from employment **4** : SHOOT ⟨~ a gun⟩ ⟨~ an arrow⟩ **5** : BAKE ⟨*firing* pottery in a kiln⟩ **6** : to apply fire or fuel to something ⟨~ a furnace⟩

fire ant *n* : either of two small fiercely stinging South American ants that are pests in the southeastern U.S. esp. in fields used to grow crops

fire·arm \ˈfī(ə)r-ˌärm\ *n* : a weapon (as a rifle or pistol) from which a shot is discharged by an explosion of gunpowder

fire·ball \ˈfī(ə)r-ˌbȯl\ *n* **1** : a ball of fire **2** : a very bright meteor **3** : the highly luminous cloud of vapor and dust created by a nuclear explosion **4** : a highly energetic person

fire·boat \ˈfī(ə)r-ˌbōt\ *n* : a boat equipped for fighting fires

fire·bomb \-ˌbäm\ *n* : an incendiary bomb — **firebomb** *vb*

fire·box \-ˌbäks\ *n* **1** : a chamber (as of a furnace) that contains a fire **2** : a box containing a fire alarm

fire·brand \-ˌbrand\ *n* **1** : a piece of burning wood **2** : a person who creates unrest or strife : AGITATOR

fire·break \-ˌbrāk\ *n* : a barrier of cleared or plowed land intended to check a forest or grass fire

fire·brick \-ˌbrik\ *n* : a brick capable of withstanding great heat and used for lining furnaces or fireplaces

fire·bug \ˈfī(ə)r-ˌbəg\ *n* : a person who deliberately sets destructive fires

fire·clay \-ˌklā\ *n* : clay capable of withstanding high temperatures and used esp. for firebrick and crucibles

fire·crack·er \ˈfī(ə)r-ˌkrak-ər\ *n* : a paper tube containing an explosive and a fuse and usu. set off for amusement

fire·damp \-ˌdamp\ *n* : a combustible mine gas that consists chiefly of methane

fire engine *n* : a motor vehicle with equipment for extinguishing fires

fire escape *n* : a stairway or ladder for escape from a burning building

fire·fly \ˈfī(ə)r-ˌflī\ *n* : any of various small night-flying beetles that produce flashes of light for courtship purposes

fire·house \ˈfī(ə)r-ˌhau̇s\ *n* : FIRE STATION

fire irons *n pl* : tools for tending a fire esp. in a fireplace

fire·man \-mən\ *n* **1** : a member of a company organized to put out fires **2** : STOKER

fire·place \ˈfī(ə)r-ˌplās\ *n* **1** : a framed opening made in a chimney to hold an open fire : HEARTH **2** : an outdoor structure of brick or stone for an open fire

fire·plug \-ˌpləg\ *n* : HYDRANT

fire·pow·er \-ˌpau̇(-ə)r\ *n* : the ability to deliver gunfire or warheads on a target

[1]**fire·proof** \-ˈprüf\ *adj* : proof against or resistant to fire

[2]**fireproof** *vb* : to make fireproof

fire screen *n* : a protecting wire screen before a fireplace

[1]**fire·side** \ˈfī(ə)r-ˌsīd\ *n* **1** : a place near the fire or hearth **2** : HOME

[2]**fireside** *adj* : having an informal or intimate quality

fire station *n* : a building housing fire engines and usu. firemen

fire tower *n* : a tower (as in a forest) from which a watch for fires is kept

fire·trap \ˈfī(ə)r-ˌtrap\ *n* : a building or place apt to catch on fire or difficult to escape from in case of fire

fire truck *n* : FIRE ENGINE

fire·wa·ter \ˈfī(ə)r-ˌwȯt-ər, -ˌwät-\ *n* : intoxicating liquor

fire·wood \-ˌwu̇d\ *n* : wood cut for fuel

fire·work \-ˌwərk\ *n* : a device designed to produce a display of light, noise, and smoke by the burning of explosive or flammable materials

firing line *n* **1** : a line from which fire is delivered against a target **2** : the forefront of an activity

[1]**firm** \ˈfərm\ *adj* **1** : securely fixed in place **2** : SOLID, VIGOROUS ⟨a ~ handshake⟩ **3** : having a solid or compact texture ⟨~ flesh⟩ **4** : not subject to change of fluctuation : STEADY ⟨~ prices⟩ **5** : STEADFAST **6** : indicating firmness or resolution ⟨a ~ mouth⟩ — **firm·ly** *adv* — **firmness** *n*

[2]**firm** *vb* : to make or become firm

[3]**firm** *n* [G *firma,* fr. It, signature, deriv. of L *firmare* to make firm, confirm] **1** : the name under which a company transacts business **2** : a business partnership of two or more persons **3** : a business enterprise

fir·ma·ment \ˈfər-mə-mənt\ *n* : the arch of the sky : HEAVENS

firm·ware \ˈfirm-ˌwaər\ *n* : computer programs contained permanently in a hardware device (as read-only memory)

[1]**first** \ˈfərst\ *adj* : preceding all others as in time, order, or importance

[2]**first** *adv* **1** : before any other **2** : for the first time **3** : in preference to something else

[3]**first** *n* **1** : number one in a countable series **2** : something that is first **3** : the lowest forward gear in an automotive vehicle

first aid *n* : emergency care or treatment given an injured or ill person

first·born \ˈfərs(t)-ˈbȯrn\ *adj* : ELDEST — **firstborn** *n*

first class *n* : the best or highest group in a classification — **first–class** *adj or adv*

first·hand \ˈfərst-ˈhand\ *adj* : coming directly from the original source ⟨~ knowledge⟩ — **firsthand** *adv*

first lady *n, often cap F&L* : the wife or hostess of the chief executive of a political unit (as a country)

first lieutenant *n* : a commissioned officer (as in the army) ranking next below a captain

first·ling \ˈfərst-liŋ\ *n* : one that comes or is produced first

first·ly \-lē\ *adv* : in the first place : FIRST

first–rate \-ˈrāt\ *adj* : of the first order of size, importance, or quality — **first–rate** *adv*

first sergeant *n* **1** : a noncommissioned officer serving as the chief assistant to the commander of a military unit (as a company) **2** : a rank in the army below a command sergeant major and in the marine corps below a sergeant major

first–string \ˈfərs(t)-ˈstriŋ\ *adj* : being a regular as distinguished from a substitute

firth \ˈfərth\ *n* [ME, fr. ON *fjörthr*] : a narrow arm of the sea

fis·cal \ˈfis-kəl\ *adj* [L *fiscalis,* fr. *fiscus* basket, treasury] **1** : of or relating to taxation, public revenues, or public debt **2** : of or relating to financial matters

[1]**fish** \ˈfish\ *n, pl* **fish** *or* **fish·es** **1** : a water-dwelling animal — usu. used in combination ⟨star*fish*⟩ ⟨shell*fish*⟩ **2** : any of numerous cold-blooded water-breathing vertebrates with fins, gills, and usu. scales **3** : the flesh of fish used as food

[2]**fish** *vb* **1** : to attempt to catch fish **2** : to seek something by roundabout means ⟨~ for praise⟩ **3** : to search for something underwater **4** : to engage in a search by groping **5** : to draw forth

fish–and–chips \ˌfish-ən-ˈchips\ *n pl* : fried fish and french fried potatoes

fish·bowl \ˈfish-ˌbōl\ *n* **1** : a bowl for the keeping of live fish **2** : a place or condition that affords no privacy

fish·er \ˈfish-ər\ *n* **1** : one that fishes **2** : a large dark brown No. American arboreal carnivorous mammal related to the weasels

fish·er·man \-mən\ *n* : a person engaged in fishing; *also* : a fishing boat

fish·ery \ˈfish-(ə-)rē\ *n, pl* **-er·ies** : the business of catching fish; *also* : a place for catching fish

fish·hook \ˈfish-ˌhu̇k\ *n* : a usu. barbed hook for catching fish

fish·ing \ˈfish-iŋ\ *n* : the business or sport of catching fish

fish ladder *n* : an arrangement of pools by which fish can pass around a dam

fish protein concentrate *n* : flour made of pulverized dried fish

fish·wife \ˈfish-ˌwīf\ *n* **1** : a woman who sells fish **2** : a vulgar abusive woman

fishy \ˈfish-ē\ *adj* **fish·i·er; -est** **1** : of or resembling fish **2** : QUESTIONABLE

fis·sion \ˈfish-ən, ˈfizh-\ *n* [L *fissio,* fr. *fissus,* pp. of *findere* to split] **1** : a cleaving into parts **2** : a method of reproduction in which a living cell or body divides into two or more parts each of which grows into a whole new individual **3** : the splitting of an atomic nucleus resulting in the release of large amounts of energy — **fis·sion·able** \ˈfish-(ə-)nə-bəl, ˈfizh-\ *adj*

fis·sure \ˈfish-ər\ *n* : a narrow opening or crack

fist \ˈfist\ *n* **1** : the hand with fingers doubled into the palm **2** : INDEX 6

fist·ful \-ˌfu̇l\ *n* : HANDFUL

fist·i·cuffs \ˈfis-ti-ˌkəfs\ *n pl* : a fight with usu. bare fists

fis·tu·la \ˈfis-chə-lə\ *n, pl* **-las** *or* **-lae** : an abnormal passage leading from an abscess or hollow organ — **fis·tu·lous** \-ləs\ *adj*

[1]**fit** \ˈfit\ *adj* **fit·ter; fit·test** **1** : adapted to a purpose : APPROPRIATE **2** : PROPER, RIGHT, BECOMING **3** : PREPARED, READY **4** : physically and mentally sound — **fit·ly** *adv* — **fit·ness** *n*

[2]**fit** *n* **1** : a sudden violent attack (as of bodily disorder) **2** : a sudden outburst (as of laughter)

[3]**fit** *vb* **fit·ted** *also* **fit; fit·ting** **1** : to be suitable for or to : BEFIT **2** : to be correctly adjusted to or shaped for **3** : to insert or adjust until correctly in place **4** : to make a place or room for **5** : to be in agreement or accord with **6** : PREPARE **7** : ADJUST **8** : SUPPLY, EQUIP **9** : BELONG — **fit·ter** *n*

[4]**fit** *n* : the fact, condition, or manner of fitting or being fitted

fit·ful \ˈfit-fəl\ *adj* : not regular : INTERMITTENT ⟨~ sleep⟩ — **fit·ful·ly** \-ē\ *adv*

[1]**fit·ting** \ˈfit-iŋ\ *adj* : APPROPRIATE, SUITABLE — **fit·ting·ly** *adv*

[2]**fitting** *n* **1** : the action or act of one that fits; *esp* : a trying on of clothes being made or altered **2** : a small often standardized part ⟨a plumbing ~⟩

five \ˈfīv\ *n* **1** : one more that four **2** : the 5th in a set or series **3** : something having five units; *esp* : a basketball team — **five** *adj or pron*

[1]**fix** \ˈfiks\ *vb* **1** : to make firm, stable, or fast **2** : to give a permanent or final form to ⟨~ a photographic film⟩ **3** : AFFIX, ATTACH **4** : to hold or direct steadily ⟨~*es* his eyes on the horizon⟩ **5** : ESTABLISH ⟨~ a date⟩ **6** : ASSIGN ⟨~ blame⟩ **7** : to set in order : ADJUST **8** : PREPARE **9** : to make whole or sound again **10** : to get even with **11** : to influence by improper or illegal methods ⟨~ a horse race⟩ — **fix·er** *n*

[2]**fix** *n* **1** : PREDICAMENT **2** : a determination of position (as of a ship) **3** : an accurate determination or understanding **4** : an act of improper influence (as bribery) **5** : a shot of a narcotic **6** : something that fixes or restores

fix·a·tion \fik-ˈsā-shən\ *n* : an obsessive or unhealthy preoccupation or attachment — **fix·ate** \ˈfik-ˌsāt\ *vb*

fix·a·tive \ˈfik-sət-iv\ *n* : something (as a varnish for crayon drawings) that stabilizes or sets

fixed \ˈfikst\ *adj* **1** : securely placed or fastened : STATIONARY **2** : not volatile **3** : SETTLED, FINAL **4** : INTENT, CONCENTRATED ⟨a ~ stare⟩ **5** : supplied with a definite amount of something needed (as money) — **fixed·ly** \ˈfik-səd-lē\ *adv* — **fixed·ness** \-nəs\ *n*

fixed star *n* : a star so distant that its motion can be measured only by very precise observations over long periods

fix·i·ty \ˈfik-sət-ē\ *n, pl* **-ties** : the quality or state of being fixed or stable

fix·ture \ˈfiks-chər\ *n* : something firmly attached as a permanent part of some other thing ⟨an electrical ~⟩

[1]**fizz** \ˈfiz\ *vb* : to make a hissing or sputtering sound

[2]**fizz** *n* : an effervescent beverage

[1]**fiz·zle** \ˈfiz-əl\ *vb* **fiz·zled; fiz·zling** \-(ə-)liŋ\ **1** : FIZZ **2** : to fail after a good start

[2]**fizzle** *n* : FAILURE

fjord \fē-ˈȯrd\ *n* : a narrow inlet of the sea between cliffs or steep slopes

fl *abbr* **1** [L *floruit*] flourished **2** fluid

FL *or* **Fla** *abbr* Florida

flab \ˈflab\ *n* : soft flabby body tissue

flab·ber·gast \ˈflab-ər-ˌgast\ *vb* : ASTOUND

flab·by \ˈflab-ē\ *adj* **flab·bi·er; -est** : lacking firmness and substance : FLACCID ⟨~ muscles⟩ — **flab·bi·ness** \ˈflab-ē-nəs\ *n*

flac·cid \ˈflak-səd, ˈflas-əd\ *adj* : deficient in firmness ⟨~ plant stems⟩

fla·con \ˈflak-ən\ *n* : a small usu. ornamental bottle with a tight cap

[1]**flag** \ˈflag\ *n* : any of various irises; *esp* : a wild iris

[2]**flag** *n* **1** : a usu. rectangular piece of fabric of distinctive design that is used as a symbol (as of a nation) or as a signaling device **2** : something used like a flag to signal or attract attention **3** : one of the cross strokes of a musical note less that a quarter note in value

[3]**flag** *vb* **flagged; flag·ging** **1** : to signal with or as if with a flag; *esp* : to signal to stop ⟨~ a taxi⟩ **2** : to put a flag on

[4]**flag** *vb* **flagged; flag·ging** **1** : to be loose, yielding, or limp : DROOP **2** : to become unsteady, feeble, or spiritless ⟨his

interest *flagged*⟩ **3** : to decline in interest or attraction ⟨the topic *flagged*⟩

[5]**flag** *n* : a hard flat stone suitable for paving

flag·el·late \ˈflaj-ə-ˌlāt\ *vb* **-lat·ed; -lat·ing** : to punish by whipping — **flag·el·la·tion** \ˌflaj-ə-ˈlā-shən\ *n*

fla·gel·lum \flə-ˈjel-əm\ *n, pl* **-la** \-ə\ *also* **-lums** : a tapering process that projects singly or in groups from a cell and is the primary organ of motion of many microorganisms — **fla·gel·lar** \-ˈjel-ər\ *adj*

fla·geo·let \ˌflaj-ə-ˈlet, -ˈlā\ *n* [F] : a small woodwind instrument belonging to the flute class

fla·gi·tious \flə-ˈjish-əs\ *adj* : grossly wicked : VILLAINOUS

flag·on \ˈflag-ən\ *n* : a container for liquids usu. with a handle, spout, and lid

flag·pole \ˈflag-ˌpōl\ *n* : a pole to raise a flag on

fla·grant \ˈflā-grənt\ *adj* [L *flagrans,* prp. of *flagrare* to burn] : conspicuously bad — **fla·grant·ly** *adv*

fla·gran·te de·lic·to \flə-ˌgrant-ē-di-ˈlik- tō\ *adv* [ML, lit., while the crime is blazing] : in the very act of committing a misdeed

flag·ship \ˈflag-ˌship\ *n* **1** : the ship that carries the commander of a fleet or subdivision thereof and flies his flag **2** : the most important one of a group ⟨a ~ store⟩

flag·staff \-ˌstaf\ *n* : FLAGPOLE

flag·stone \-ˌstōn\ *n* : [5]FLAG

[1]**flail** \ˈflāl\ *n* : a tool for threshing grain by hand

[2]**flail** *vb* **1** : to beat with or as if with a flail **2** : to move as if swinging a flail

flair \ˈflaər\ *n* [F, lit., sense of smell, fr. OF, odor, fr. *flairier* to give off an odor, fr. LL *flagrare,* fr. L *fragrare*] **1** : discriminating sense **2** : natural aptitude : BENT ⟨a ~ for acting⟩

flak \ˈflak\ *n, pl* **flak** [G, fr. *fl*ieger*a*bwehr*k*anonen, fr. *flieger* flyer + *abwehr* defense + *kanonen* cannons] : antiaircraft guns or bursting shells fired from them

[1]**flake** \ˈflāk\ *n* **1** : a small loose mass or bit **2** : a thin flattened piece or layer : CHIP — **flaky** *adj*

[2]**flake** *vb* **flaked; flak·ing** : to form or separate into flakes

flam·beau \ˈflam-ˌbō\ *n, pl* **flambeaux** \-ˌbōz\ *or* **flambeaus** [F, fr. MF, fr. *flambe* flame] : a flaming torch

flam·boy·ant \flam-ˈbȯi-ənt\ *adj* : FLORID, SHOWY — **flam·boy·ance** \-əns\ *n* — **flam·boy·an·cy** \-ən-sē\ *n* — **flam·boy·ant·ly** *adv*

flame \ˈflām\ *n* **1** : the glowing gaseous part of a fire **2** : a state of blazing combustion **3** : a flamelike condition **4** : burning zeal or passion **5** : BRILLIANCE **6** : SWEETHEART — **flame** *vb* — **flam·ing** \ˈflā-miŋ\ *adj*

fla·men·co \flə-ˈmeŋ-kō\ *n, pl* **-cos** [Sp, Flemish, like a Gypsy, fr. Dutch *Vlaminc* Fleming] : a vigorous rhythmic dance style of the Spanish Gypsies

flame·throw·er \ˈflām-ˌthrō(-ə)r\ *n* : a device that expels from a nozzle a burning stream of liquid or semiliquid fuel under pressure

fla·min·go \flə-ˈmiŋ-gō\ *n, pl* **-gos** *also* **-goes** : any of several long-legged long-necked tropical water birds with scarlet wings and a broad bill bent downward

flam·ma·ble \ˈflam-ə-bəl\ *adj* : easily ignited and quick-burning — **flam·ma·bil·i·ty** *n* — **flammable** *n*

flange \ˈflanj\ *n* : a rim used for strengthening or guiding something or for attachment to another object

[1]**flank** \ˈflaŋk\ *n* **1** : the fleshy part of the side between the ribs and the hip; *also* : the side of a quadruped **2** : SIDE **3** : the right or left of a formation

[2]**flank** *vb* **1** : to attack or threaten the flank of **2** : to be situated on the side of : BORDER

flank·er \ˈflaŋ-kər\ *n* : a football player stationed wide of the formation slightly behind the line of scrimmage as a pass receiver

flan·nel \ˈflan-ᵊl\ *n* **1** : a soft twilled wool or worsted fabric with a napped surface **2** : a stout cotton fabric napped on one side **3** *pl* : flannel underwear or trousers

flan·nel·ette \ˌflan-ᵊl-ˈet\ *n* : a lightweight cotton flannel

[1]**flap** \ˈflap\ *n* **1** : a stroke with something broad : SLAP **2** : something broad, limber, or flat and usu. thin that hangs loose ⟨the ~ of a pocket⟩ **3** : the motion or sound of something broad and limber as it swings to and fro **4** : a state of excitement or confusion

[2]**flap** *vb* **flapped; flap·ping 1** : to beat with something broad and flat **2** : FLING **3** : to move (as wings) with a beating motion **4** : to sway loosely usu. with a noise of striking

flap·jack \-ˌjak\ *n* : PANCAKE

flap·per \ˈflap-ər\ *n* **1** : one that flaps **2** : a young woman of the 1920s who showed freedom from conventions (as in conduct)

[1]**flare** \ˈflaər\ *vb* **flared; flar·ing 1** : to flame with a sudden unsteady light **2** : to become suddenly excited or angry ⟨~ up⟩ **3** : to spread outward

[2]**flare** *n* **1** : an unsteady glaring light **2** : a blaze of light used to signal or illuminate; *also* : a device for producing such a blaze

flare–up \-ˌəp\ *n* : a sudden outburst or intensification

[1]**flash** \ˈflash\ *vb* **1** : to break forth in or like a sudden flame **2** : to appear or pass suddenly or with great speed **3** : to send out in or as if in flashes ⟨~ a message⟩ **4** : to make a sudden display (as of brilliance or feeling) **5** : to gleam or glow intermittently **6** : to fill by a sudden rush of water **7** : to expose to view very briefly ⟨~ a badge⟩ **syn** glance, glint, sparkle, twinkle — **flash·er** *n*

[2]**flash** *n* **1** : a sudden burst of light **2** : a movement of a flag or light in signaling **3** : a sudden and brilliant burst (as of wit) **4** : a brief time **5** : SHOW, DISPLAY; *esp* : ostentatious display **6** : one that attracts notice; *esp* : an outstanding athlete **7** : GLIMPSE, LOOK **8** : a first brief news report **9** : a device for producing a brief and very bright flash of light for taking photographs **10** : a quick-spreading flame or momentary intense outburst of radiant heat

[3]**flash** *adj* **1** : of sudden origin and short duration ⟨a ~ fire⟩ **2** : involving brief exposure to an intense agent (as heat or cold) ⟨~ freezing of food⟩

flash·back \ˈflash-ˌbak\ *n* : introduction into the chronological sequence of events (as in a literary or theatrical work) of an event of earlier occurrence

flash·bulb \-ˌbəlb\ *n* : an electric light bulb in which metal foil or wire is burned to produce a brief and very bright flash of light for taking photographs

flash card *n* : a card bearing words, numbers, or pictures briefly displayed usu. by a teacher as a learning aid

flash·cube \ˈflash-ˌkyüb\ *n* : a cubical device incorporating four flashbulbs

flash·gun \-ˌgən\ *n* : a device for holding and operating a flashbulb

flash·ing \ˈflash-iŋ\ *n* : sheet metal used in waterproofing roof valleys or the angle between a chimney and a roof

flash·light \ˈflash-ˌlīt\ *n* : a small battery-operated portable electric light

flash point *n* : the lowest temperature at which vapors above a volatile combustible substance ignite in air when exposed to flame

flashy \ˈflash-ē\ *adj* **flash·i·er; -est 1** : momentarily dazzling **2** : BRIGHT **3** : SHOWY — **flash·i·ly** \ˈflash-ə-lē\ *adv* — **flash·i·ness** \-ē-nəs\ *n*

flask \ˈflask\ *n* : a flattened bottle-shaped container ⟨a whiskey ~⟩

[1]**flat** \ˈflat\ *n* **1** : a level surface of land : PLAIN **2** : a flat part or surface **3** : a musical tone one half step lower than a specified tone; *also* : a character ♭ on the musical staff indicating a flat **4** : something flat **5** : an apartment on one floor **6** : a deflated tire

[2]**flat** *adj* **flat·ter; flat·test 1** : having a smooth, level, or even surface **2** : spread out along a surface; *also* : being or characterized by a horizontal line **3** : having a broad smooth surface and little thickness **4** : DOWNRIGHT, POSITIVE ⟨a ~ refusal⟩ **5** : FIXED, UNCHANGING ⟨charge a ~

rate⟩ **6** : EXACT, PRECISE ⟨in four minutes ~⟩ **7** : DULL, UNINTERESTING ⟨a ~ story⟩; *also* : INSIPID ⟨a ~ taste⟩ **8** : DEFLATED **9** : lower that the true pitch; *also* : lower by a half step ⟨a ~ note⟩ **10** : free from gloss — **flat·ly** *adv* — **flat·ness** *n*

³flat *adv* **1** : FLATLY **2** : COMPLETELY ⟨~ broke⟩ **3** : below the true musical pitch

⁴flat *vb* **flat·ted; flat·ting 1** : FLATTEN **2** : to lower in pitch esp. by a half step **3** : to sing or play below the true pitch

flat·bed \ˈflat-ˌbed\ *n* : a truck or trailer with a body in the form of a platform or shallow box

flat·boat \-ˌbōt\ *n* : a flat-bottomed boat used esp. for carrying bulky freight

flat·car \-ˌkär\ *n* : a railroad freight car without sides or roof

flat·fish \-ˌfish\ *n* : any of a group of flattened bony sea fishes with both eyes on the upper side

flat·foot \-ˌfu̇t, -ˈfu̇t\ *n, pl* **flat·feet** \-ˌfēt, -ˈfēt\ : a condition in which the arch of the foot is flattened so that the entire sole rests upon the ground — **flat–foot·ed** \-ˈfu̇t-əd\ *adj*

Flat·head \-ˌhed\ *n, pl* **Flatheads** *or* **Flathead** : a member of an American Indian people of Montana

flat·iron \-ˌī(-ə)rn\ *n* : IRON 3

flat·land \-ˌland\ *n* : land lacking significant variation in elevation

flat out \-ˈau̇t\ *adv* **1** : BLUNTLY, DIRECTLY **2** : at top speed

flat·ten \ˈflat-ᵊn\ *vb* **flat·tened; flat·ten·ing** \ˈflat-(ᵊ-)niŋ\ : to make or become flat

flat·ter \ˈflat-ər\ *vb* [ME *flateren,* fr. OF *flater* to lick, flatter] **1** : to praise too much or without sincerity **2** : to represent too favorably ⟨the picture ~*s* her⟩ **3** : to judge (oneself) favorably or too favorably — **flat·ter·er** *n*

flat·tery \ˈflat-ə-rē\ *n, pl* **-ter·ies** : flattering speech or attentions : insincere or excessive praise

flat·top \ˈflat-ˌtäp\ *n* **1** : AIRCRAFT CARRIER **2** : CREW CUT

flat·u·lent \ˈflach-ə-lənt\ *adj* **1** : full of gas ⟨a ~ stomach⟩ **2** : TURGID ⟨~ oratory⟩ — **flat·u·lence** \-ləns\ *n*

fla·tus \ˈflāt-əs\ *n* : gas formed in the intestine or stomach

flat·ware \ˈflat-ˌwaər\ *n* : eating and serving utensils (as forks, spoons, and knives)

flat·worm \-ˌwərm\ *n* : any of a phylum of flattened mostly parasitic segmented worms (as trematodes and tapeworms)

flaunt \ˈflȯnt\ *vb* **1** : to display oneself to public notice **2** : to wave or flutter showily **3** : to display ostentatiously or impudently : PARADE — **flaunt** *n*

flau·tist \ˈflȯt-əst, ˈflau̇t-\ *n* [It *flautista*] : FLUTIST

¹fla·vor \ˈflā-vər\ *n* **1** : the quality of something that affects the sense of taste or of taste and smell; *also* : the resulting sensation **2** : a substance that adds flavor **3** : characteristic or predominant quality — **fla·vor·ful** *adj* — **fla·vor·less** *adj* — **fla·vor·some** *adj*

²flavor *vb* **fla·vored; fla·vor·ing** \ˈflāv-(ə-)riŋ\ : to give or add flavor to

fla·vor·ing *n* : FLAVOR 2

fla·vour *chiefly Brit var of* FLAVOR

flaw \ˈflȯ\ *n* : a small often hidden defect — **flaw·less** *adj*

flax \ˈflaks\ *n* : a fiber that is the source of linen; *also* : a blue-flowered plant grown for this fiber and its oily seeds

flax·en \ˈflak-sən\ *adj* **1** : made of flax **2** : resembling flax esp. in pale soft straw color

flay \ˈflā\ *vb* **1** : to strip off the skin or surface of **2** : to criticize harshly

flea \ˈflē\ *n* : any of an order of small wingless leaping bloodsucking insects

flea·bane \-ˌbān\ *n* : any of various plants of the daisy family once believed to drive away fleas

flea–bit·ten \-ˌbit-ᵊn\ *adj* : bitten by or infested with fleas

flea market *n* : a usu. open-air market for secondhand articles and antiques

¹fleck \ˈflek\ *vb* : STREAK, SPOT

²fleck *n* **1** : SPOT, MARK **2** : FLAKE, PARTICLE

fledg·ling \ˈflej-liŋ\ *n* **1** : a young bird with flight feathers newly developed **2** : an immature or inexperienced person

flee \ˈflē\ *vb* **fled** \ˈfled\; **flee·ing 1** : to run away often from danger or evil **2** : to run away from **3** : VANISH

¹fleece \ˈflēs\ *n* **1** : the woolly coat of an animal and esp. a sheep **2** : a soft or woolly covering — **fleecy** *adj*

²fleece *vb* **fleeced; fleec·ing 1** : to strip of money or property by fraud or extortion **2** : SHEAR

fleer \ˈfliər\ *vb* : to laugh or grimace in a coarse manner : SNEER

¹fleet \ˈflēt\ *vb* : to pass rapidly

²fleet *n* [ME *flete,* fr. OE *flēot* ship, fr. *flēotan* to float] **1** : a group of warships under one command **2** : a group of ships or vehicles (as trucks or airplanes) under one management

³fleet *adj* **1** : SWIFT, NIMBLE **2** : not enduring : FLEETING — **fleet·ness** *n*

fleet admiral *n* : a commissioned officer of the highest rank in the navy

fleet·ing \ˈflēt-iŋ\ *adj* : passing swiftly

Flem·ing \ˈflem-iŋ\ *n* : a member of a Germanic people inhabiting chiefly northern Belgium

Flem·ish \ˈflem-ish\ *n* **1** : the Germanic language of the Flemings **2 Flemish** *pl* : FLEMINGS — **Flemish** *adj*

flesh \ˈflesh\ *n* **1** : the soft parts of an animal's body; *esp* : muscular tissue **2** : MEAT **3** : the physical being of man as distinguished from the soul **4** : human beings; *also* : living beings **5** : STOCK, KINDRED **6** : fleshy plant tissue (as fruit pulp) — **fleshed** \ˈflesht\ *adj*

flesh fly *n* : a two-winged fly whose maggots feed on flesh

flesh·ly \ˈflesh-lē\ *adj* **1** : CORPOREAL, BODILY **2** : CARNAL, SENSUAL **3** : not spiritual : WORLDLY

flesh·pot \ˈflesh-ˌpät\ *n* **1** *pl* : bodily comfort : LUXURY **2** : a place of lascivious entertainment — usu. used in pl.

fleshy \ˈflesh-ē\ *adj* **flesh·i·er; -est 1** : consisting of or resembling animal flesh **2** : PLUMP, FAT

flew *past of* FLY

flex \ˈfleks\ *vb* : to bend esp. repeatedly

flex·i·ble \ˈflek-sə-bəl\ *adj* **1** : capable of being flexed : PLIANT **2** : yielding to influence : TRACTABLE **3** : readily changed or changing : ADAPTABLE **syn** elastic, supple, resilient, springy — **flex·i·bil·i·ty** \ˌflek-sə-ˈbil-ət-ē\ *n*

flex·ure \ˈflex-shər\ *n* : TURN, FOLD, BEND

flib·ber·ti·gib·bet \ˌflib-ərt-ē-ˈjib-ət\ *n* : a silly flighty person

¹flick \ˈflik\ *n* **1** : a light sharp jerky stroke or movement **2** : a sound produced by a flick **3** : FLICKER

²flick *vb* **1** : to strike lightly with a quick sharp motion **2** : FLUTTER, DART, FLIT

¹flick·er \ˈflik-ər\ *vb* **flick·ered; flick·er·ing** \-(ə-)riŋ\ **1** : to move irregularly or unsteadily : FLUTTER **2** : to burn fitfully or with a fluctuating light ⟨a ~*ing* candle⟩

²flicker *n* **1** : an act of flickering **2** : a sudden brief movement ⟨a ~ of an eyelid⟩ **3** : a momentary stirring ⟨a ~ of interest⟩ **4** : a slight indication : HINT **5** : a wavering light

³flicker *n* : a large insect-eating North American woodpecker with yellow or red on the underside of the wings and tail

flied *past of* FLY

fli·er \ˈflī(-ə)r\ *n* **1** : one that flies; *esp* : PILOT **2** : a reckless or speculative undertaking **3** : an advertising circular for mass distribution

¹flight \ˈflīt\ *n* **1** : an act or instance of flying **2** : the ability to fly **3** : a passing through the air or through space **4** : the distance covered in a flight **5** : swift movement **6**

: a trip made by or in an airplane or spacecraft **7** : a group of similar individuals (as birds or airplanes) flying as a unit **8** : a passing (as of the imagination) beyond ordinary limits **9** : a series of stairs from one landing to another — **flight·less** *adj*

[2]**flight** *n* : an act or instance of running away

flight bag *n* **1** : a lightweight traveling bag with zippered outside pockets **2** : a small canvas satchel

flight line *n* : a parking and servicing area for airplanes

flighty \ˈflīt-ē\ *adj* **flight·i·er; -est 1** : easily upset : VOLATILE **2** : easily excited : SKITTISH **3** : IRRESPONSIBLE, SILLY

flim·flam \ˈflim-ˌflam\ *n* : DECEPTION, FRAUD

flim·sy \ˈflim-zē\ *adj* **flim·si·er; -est 1** : lacking strength or substance **2** : of inferior materials and workmanship **3** : having little worth or plausibility ⟨a ~ excuse⟩ — **flim·si·ly** \ˈflim-zə-lē\ *adv* — **flim·si·ness** \-zē-nəs\ *n*

flinch \ˈflinch\ *vb* [MF *flenchir* to bend] : to shrink from or as if from physical pain : WINCE

[1]**fling** \ˈfliŋ\ *vb* **flung** \ˈfləŋ\; **fling·ing** \ˈfliŋ-iŋ\ **1** : to move hastily, brusquely, or violently ⟨*flung* out of the room⟩ **2** : to kick or plunge vigorously **3** : to throw with force or recklessness : HURL; *also* : to cast as if by throwing **4** : to put suddenly into a state or condition

[2]**fling** *n* **1** : an act or instance of flinging **2** : a casual try : ATTEMPT **3** : a period of self-indulgence

flint \ˈflint\ *n* **1** : a hard quartz that produces a spark when struck by steel **2** : an alloy used for producing a spark in lighters — **flinty** *adj*

flint glass *n* : heavy glass containing an oxide of lead that is used for optical structures (as lenses)

flint·lock \ˈflint-ˌläk\ *n* **1** : a lock for a firearm using a flint to ignite the charge **2** : a firearm fitted with a flintlock

[1]**flip** \ˈflip\ *vb* **flipped; flip·ping 1** : to turn by tossing ⟨~ a coin⟩ **2** : to turn over; *also* : to leaf through **3** : FLICK, JERK ⟨~ a light switch⟩ **4** : to lose self-control — **flip** *n*

[2]**flip** *adj* : FLIPPANT, IMPERTINENT

flip·pant \ˈflip-ənt\ *adj* : lacking proper respect or seriousness — **flip·pan·cy** \ˈflip-ən-sē\ *n*

flip·per \ˈflip-ər\ *n* **1** : a broad flat limb (as of a seal) adapted for swimming **2** : a paddlelike shoe used in skin diving

flip side *n* : the reverse and usu. less popular side of a phonograph record

[1]**flirt** \ˈflərt\ *vb* **1** : to move erratically : FLIT **2** : to behave amorously without serious intent **3** : to show casual interest ⟨~*ed* with the idea of quitting⟩ — **flir·ta·tion** \ˌflər-ˈtā-shən\ *n* — **flir·ta·tious** \-shəs\ *adj*

[2]**flirt** *n* **1** : an act or instance of flirting **2** : a person who flirts

flit \ˈflit\ *vb* **flit·ted; flit·ting** : to pass or move quickly or abruptly from place to place : DART

flitch \ˈflich\ *n* : a side of pork cured and smoked as bacon

fliv·ver \ˈfliv-ər\ *n* : a small cheap usu. old automobile

[1]**float** \ˈflōt\ *n* **1** : something (as a raft) that floats **2** : a cork buoying up the baited end of a fishing line **3** : a hollow ball that floats at the end of a lever in a cistern or tank and regulates the level of the liquid **4** : a vehicle with a platform to carry an exhibit **5** : a soft drink with ice cream floating in it

[2]**float** *vb* **1** : to rest on the surface of or be suspended in a fluid **2** : to move gently on or through a fluid **3** : to cause to float **4** : to wander esp. without a permanent home ⟨the ~*ing* population⟩ **5** : FLOOD **6** : to offer (securities) in order to finance an enterprise **7** : to finance by floating an issue of stocks or bonds **8** : to arrange for ⟨~ a loan⟩ — **float·er** *n*

[1]**flock** \ˈfläk\ *n* **1** : a group of birds or mammals assembled or herded together **2** : a group of people under the guidance of a leader; *esp* : CONGREGATION **3** : a large number

[2]**flock** *vb* : to gather or move in a flock

floe \ˈflō\ *n* : a flat mass of floating ice

flog \ˈfläg\ *vb* **flogged; flog·ging** : to beat severely with a rod or whip : LASH — **flog·ger** *n*

[1]**flood** \ˈfləd\ *n* **1** : a great flow of water over the land **2** : the flowing in of the tide **3** : an overwhelming volume

[2]**flood** *vb* **1** : to cover or become filled with a flood **2** : to fill abundantly or excessively; *esp* : to supply (a carburetor) with too much fuel **3** : to pour forth in a flood

flood·gate \ˈfləd-ˌgāt\ *n* : a gate for controlling a body of water : SLUICE

flood·light \-ˌlīt\ *n* : a lamp that throws a broad beam of light; *also* : the beam itself — **floodlight** *vb*

flood·plain \-ˌplān\ *n* : a plain that may be submerged by floodwaters

flood tide *n* **1** : a rising tide **2** : an overwhelming quantity **3** : a high point : PEAK

flood·wa·ter \ˈfləd-ˌwȯt-ər, -ˌwät-\ *n* : the water of a flood

[1]**floor** \ˈflōr\ *n* **1** : the bottom of a room on which one stands **2** : a ground surface **3** : a story of a building **4** : a main level space (as in a legislative chamber) distinguished from a platform or gallery **5** : AUDIENCE **6** : the right to speak from one's place in an assembly **7** : a lower limit ⟨put a ~ under wheat prices⟩ — **floor·ing** \-iŋ\ *n*

[2]**floor** *vb* **1** : to furnish with a floor **2** : to knock down **3** : SHOCK, OVERWHELM **4** : DEFEAT

floor·board \-ˌbōrd\ *n* **1** : a board in a floor **2** : the floor of an automobile

floor leader *n* : a member of a legislative body who has charge of a party's organization and strategy on the floor

floor show *n* : a series of acts presented in a nightclub

floor·walk·er \ˈflōr-ˌwȯ-kər\ *n* : a person employed in a retail store to oversee the sales force and aid customers

floo·zy *or* **floo·zie** \ˈflü-zē\ *n, pl* **floozies** : a tawdry or immoral woman

flop \ˈfläp\ *vb* **flopped; flop·ping 1** : FLAP **2** : to throw oneself down heavily, clumsily, or in a relaxed manner ⟨*flopped* into a chair⟩ **3** : FAIL — **flop** *n*

flop·house \ˈfläp-ˌhaủs\ *n* : a cheap hotel

flop·py \ˈfläp-ē\ *adj* **flop·pi·er; -est** : tending to flop; *esp* : soft and flexible

floppy disk *n* : a small flexible disk with a magnetic coating on which computer data can be stored

flo·ra \ˈflōr-ə\ *n, pl* **floras** *also* **flo·rae** \-ˌē, -ˌī\ [L *Flora*, Roman goddess of flowers] : plants or plant life esp. of a region or period

flo·ral \ˈflōr-əl\ *adj* : of or relating to flowers or a flora

flo·res·cence \flō-ˈres-ᵊns, flə-\ *n* : a state or period of being in bloom or flourishing — **flo·res·cent** \-ᵊnt\ *adj*

flor·id \ˈflȯr-əd\ *adj* **1** : excessively flowery in style : ORNATE ⟨~ writing⟩ **2** : tinged with red : RUDDY

flo·rin \ˈflȯr-ən\ *n* **1** : an old gold coin first struck at Florence in 1252 **2** : a gold coin of a European country patterned after the Florentine florin **3** : a modern silver coin in the Netherlands and in Great Britain **4** : GULDEN

flo·rist \ˈflōr-əst\ *n* : one who deals in flowers

[1]**floss** \ˈfläs\ *n* **1** : waste or short silk fibers that cannot be reeled **2** : soft thread of silk or mercerized cotton used for embroidery; *also* : DENTAL FLOSS **3** : a lightweight wool knitting yarn **4** : a fluffy filamentous mass esp. of plant fiber ⟨milkweed ~⟩

[2]**floss** *vb* : to use dental floss on (one's teeth)

flossy \ˈfläs-ē\ *adj* **floss·i·er; -est 1** : of, relating to, or having the characteristics of floss; *also* : DOWNY **2** : STYLISH, GLAMOROUS

flo·ta·tion \flō-ˈtā-shən\ *n* : the process or an instance of floating

flo·til·la \flō-ˈtil-ə\ *n* [Sp, dim. of *flota* fleet] : FLEET 1; *esp* : a fleet of small ships

flot·sam \ˈflät-səm\ *n* : floating wreckage of a ship or its cargo

[1]**flounce** \ˈflaủns\ *vb* **flounced; flounc·ing 1** : to move with

exaggerated jerky motions **2 :** to go with sudden determination

[2]**flounce** *n* **:** an act or instance of flouncing

[3]**flounce** *n* **:** a strip of fabric attached by one edge (as to a skirt)

[1]**floun·der** \ˈflau̇n-dər\ *n, pl* **flounder** *or* **flounders :** FLATFISH; *esp* **:** one important as food

[2]**flounder** *vb* **floun·dered; floun·der·ing** \-d(ə-)riŋ\ **1 :** to struggle to move or obtain footing **2 :** to proceed clumsily ⟨~*ed* through his speech⟩

[1]**flour** \ˈflau̇(ə)r\ *n* **:** finely ground and sifted meal of a grain (as wheat); *also* **:** a fine soft powder — **floury** *adj*

[2]**flour** *vb* **:** to coat with or as if with flour

[1]**flour·ish** \ˈflər-ish\ *vb* **1 :** THRIVE, PROSPER **2 :** to be in a state of activity or production ⟨~*ed* about 1850⟩ **3 :** to reach a height of development or influence **4 :** to make bold and sweeping gestures **5 :** BRANDISH

[2]**flourish** *n* **1 :** a florid embellishment or passage ⟨a ~ of drums⟩ **2 :** WAVE ⟨with a ~ of his cane⟩ **3 :** a dramatic action ⟨introduced her with a ~⟩

[1]**flout** \ˈflau̇t\ *vb* **1 :** SCORN **2 :** to indulge in scornful behavior **:** MOCK

[2]**flout** *n* **:** INSULT, MOCKERY

[1]**flow** \ˈflō\ *vb* **1 :** to issue or move in a stream **2 :** RISE ⟨the tide ebbs and ~*s*⟩ **3 :** ABOUND **4 :** to proceed smoothly and readily **5 :** to have a smooth continuity **6 :** to hang loose and billowing **7 :** COME, ARISE **8 :** MENSTRUATE

[2]**flow** *n* **1 :** an act of flowing **2 :** FLOOD 1, 2 **3 :** a smooth uninterrupted movement **4 :** STREAM; *also* **:** a mass of material that has flowed when molten **5 :** the quantity that flows in a certain time **6 :** MENSTRUATION **7 :** YIELD, PRODUCTION **8 :** a continuous flow of energy

flow·chart \ˈflō-ˌchärt\ *n* **:** a symbolic diagram showing step-by-step progression through a procedure

flow diagram *n* **:** FLOWCHART

[1]**flow·er** \ˈflau̇(-ə)r\ *n* **1 :** a plant branch modified for seed production and bearing leaves specialized into floral organs (as petals) **2 :** a plant cultivated or outstanding for its blossoms **3 :** the best part or example **4 :** the finest most vigorous period **5 :** a state of blooming or flourishing — **flow·ered** \ˈflau̇(-ə)rd\ *adj* — **flow·er·less** *adj*

[2]**flower** *vb* **1 :** to produce flowers **:** BLOOM **2 :** DEVELOP; *also* **:** FLOURISH

flower girl *n* **:** a little girl who carries flowers at a wedding

flower head *n* **:** a very short compact flower cluster suggesting a single flower

flow·er·pot \ˈflau̇(-ə)r-ˌpät\ *n* **:** a pot in which to grow plants

flow·ery \ˈflau̇(-ə)r-ē\ *adj* **1 :** full of or covered with flowers **2 :** full of fine words or phrases — **flow·er·i·ness** *n*

flown \ˈflōn\ *past part of* FLY

fl oz *abbr* fluidounce

flu \ˈflü\ *n* **1 :** INFLUENZA **2 :** any of several minor virus ailments usu. with respiratory symptoms

flub \ˈfləb\ *vb* **flubbed; flub·bing :** BOTCH, BLUNDER — **flub** *n*

fluc·tu·ate \ˈflək-chə-ˌwāt\ *vb* **-at·ed; -at·ing 1 :** to move up and down or back and forth **2 :** WAVER, VACILLATE — **fluc·tu·a·tion** \ˌflək-chə-ˈwā-shən\ *n*

flue \ˈflü\ *n* **:** a passage (as in a chimney) for directing a current (as of smoke or gases)

flu·ent \ˈflü-ənt\ *adj* **1 :** capable of flowing **:** FLUID **2 :** ready or facile in speech ⟨~ in French⟩ **3 :** effortlessly smooth and rapid ⟨~ speech⟩ — **flu·en·cy** \-ən-sē\ *n* — **flu·ent·ly** *adv*

[1]**fluff** \ˈfləf\ *n* **1 :** NAP, DOWN ⟨~ from a pillow⟩ **2 :** something fluffy **3 :** something inconsequential **4 :** BLUNDER; *esp* **:** an actor's lapse of memory

[2]**fluff** *vb* **1 :** to make or become fluffy ⟨~ up a pillow⟩ **2 :** to make a mistake

fluffy \ˈfləf-ē\ *adj* **fluff·i·er; -est 1 :** having, covered with, or resembling fluff or down **2 :** being light and soft or airy ⟨a ~ omelet⟩ **3 :** FATUOUS, SILLY

[1]**flu·id** \ˈflü-əd\ *adj* **1 :** capable of flowing like a liquid or gas **2 :** likely to change or move **3 :** showing a smooth easy style ⟨~ movements⟩ **4 :** available for a different use; *esp* **:** easily converted into cash ⟨~ assets⟩ — **flu·id·i·ty** \flü-ˈid-ət-ē\ *n*

[2]**fluid** *n* **:** a substance tending to flow or take the shape of its container ⟨liquids and gases are ~*s*⟩

flu·id·ounce \ˌflü-əd-ˈau̇ns\ *n* — see WEIGHT table

flu·idram \ˌflü-ə(d)-ˈdram\ *n* — see WEIGHT table

[1]**fluke** \ˈflük\ *n* **:** any of various trematode flatworms

[2]**fluke** *n* **1 :** the part of an anchor that fastens in the ground **2 :** a barbed head (as of a harpoon) **3 :** a lobe of a whale's tail

[3]**fluke** *n* **:** a stroke of luck ⟨won by a ~⟩

flume \ˈflüm\ *n* **1 :** an inclined channel for carrying water (as for power) **2 :** a ravine or gorge with a stream running through it

flung *past and past part of* FLING

flunk \ˈfləŋk\ *vb* **:** to fail esp. in an examination or course

flun·ky *or* **flun·key** \ˈfləŋ-kē\ *n, pl* **flunkies** *or* **flunkeys 1 :** a liveried servant; *also* **:** one performing menial duties **2 :** YES-MAN

flu·o·res·cence \ˌflu̇(-ə)r-ˈes-ᵊns\ *n* **:** emission of radiation usu. as visible light during exposure to radiation from some other source; *also* **:** the emitted radiation — **flu·o·resce** \-ˈes\ *vb* — **flu·o·res·cent** \-ˈes-ᵊnt\ *adj*

fluorescent lamp *n* **:** a tubular electric lamp in which light is produced by the action of ultraviolet light on a fluorescent material that coats the inner surface of the lamp

flu·o·ri·date \ˈflu̇r-ə-ˌdāt\ *vb* **-dat·ed; -dat·ing :** to add a fluoride to (as drinking water) to reduce tooth decay — **flu·o·ri·da·tion** \ˌflu̇r-ə-ˈdā-shən\ *n*

flu·o·ride \ˈflu̇(-ə)r-ˌīd\ *n* **:** a compound of fluorine with another chemical element or group

flu·o·ri·nate \ˈflu̇r-ə-ˌnāt\ *vb* **-nat·ed; -nat·ing :** to treat or cause to combine with fluorine or a compound of fluorine — **flu·o·ri·na·tion** \ˌflu̇r-ə-ˈnā-shən\ *n*

flu·o·rine \ˈflu̇(-ə)r-ˌēn, -ən\ *n* **:** a pale yellowish flammable irritating toxic gaseous chemical element — see ELEMENT table

flu·o·rite \ˈflu̇(-ə)r-ˌīt\ *n* **:** a mineral that consists of a fluoride of calcium used as a flux and in making glass

flu·o·ro·car·bon \ˌflu̇(-ə)r-ō-ˈkär-bən\ *n* **:** a compound containing fluorine and carbon used chiefly as a lubricant, refrigerant, or nonstick-coating material

flu·o·ro·scope \ˈflu̇r-ə-ˌskōp\ *n* **:** an instrument for observing the internal structure of an opaque object (as the living body) by means of X rays — **flu·o·ro·scop·ic** \ˌflu̇r-ə-ˈskäp-ik\ *adj* — **flu·o·ros·co·py** \-pē\ *n*

flu·o·ro·sis \ˌflu̇r-ˈō-səs\ *n* **:** an abnormal condition (as spotting of the tooth enamel) caused by fluorine or its compounds

flur·ry \ˈflər-ē\ *n, pl* **flurries 1 :** a gust of wind **2 :** a brief light snowfall **3 :** COMMOTION, BUSTLE **4 :** a brief outburst of activity ⟨a ~ of trading⟩ — **flurry** *vb*

[1]**flush** \ˈfləsh\ *vb* **:** to cause (a bird) to take wing suddenly

[2]**flush** *n* **:** a hand of cards all of the same suit

[3]**flush** *n* **1 :** a sudden flow (as of water) **2 :** a surge esp. of emotion ⟨a ~ of triumph⟩ **3 :** a tinge of red **:** BLUSH **4 :** a fresh and vigorous state ⟨in the ~ of youth⟩ **5 :** a passing sensation of extreme heat

[4]**flush** *vb* **1 :** to flow and spread suddenly and freely **2 :** to glow brightly **3 :** BLUSH **4 :** to wash out with a rush of fluid **5 :** INFLAME, EXCITE **6 :** to cause to blush

[5]**flush** *adj* **1 :** full of life and vigor **2 :** of a ruddy healthy

color **3** : filled to overflowing **4** : AFFLUENT **5** : readily available : ABUNDANT **6** : having an unbroken or even surface **7** : directly abutting : immediately adjacent **8** : set even with the left edge of the type page or column

[6]**flush** *adv* **1** : in a flush manner **2** : SQUARELY ⟨a blow ~ on the chin⟩

[7]**flush** *vb* : to make flush

flus·ter \ˈfləs-tər\ *vb* : to put into a state of agitated confusion : UPSET — **fluster** *n*

flute \ˈflüt\ *n* **1** : a hollow pipelike musical instrument **2** : a grooved pleat **3** : CHANNEL, GROOVE — **flute** *vb* — **flut·ed** *adj*

flute 1

flut·ing \ˈflüt-iŋ\ *n* : fluted decoration

flut·ist \ˈflüt-əst\ *n* : a flute player

[1]**flut·ter** \ˈflət-ər\ *vb* [ME *floteren* to float, flutter, fr. OE *floterian*, fr. *flotian* to float] **1** : to flap the wings rapidly **2** : to move with quick wavering or flapping motions **3** : to vibrate in irregular spasms **4** : to move about or behave in an agitated aimless manner — **flut·tery** \-ə-rē\ *adj*

[2]**flutter** *n* **1** : an act of fluttering **2** : a state of nervous confusion **3** : FLURRY, COMMOTION

[1]**flux** \ˈfləks\ *n* **1** : an act of flowing **2** : a state of continuous change **3** : a substance used to aid in fusing metals

[2]**flux** *vb* : FUSE

[1]**fly** \ˈflī\ *vb* **flew** \ˈflü\; **flown** \ˈflōn\; **fly·ing** **1** : to move in or pass through the air with wings **2** : to move through the air or before the wind **3** : to float or cause to float, wave, or soar in the air **4** : FLEE **5** : to fade and disappear : VANISH **6** : to move or pass swiftly **7** : to become expended or dissipated rapidly **8** : to pursue or attack in flight **9** : to operate or travel in an aircraft or spacecraft **10** : to journey over by flying **11** : AVOID, SHUN **12** : to transport by flying

[2]**fly** *n, pl* **flies** **1** : the action or process of flying : FLIGHT **2** *pl* : the space over a theater stage **3** : a garment closing concealed by a fold of cloth extending over the fastener **4** : the outer canvas of a tent with a double top **5** : the length of an extended flag from its staff or support **6** : a baseball hit high into the air — **on the fly** : while still in the air

[3]**fly** *vi* **flied; fly·ing** : to hit a fly in baseball

[4]**fly** *n, pl* **flies** **1** : a winged insect — usu. used in combination ⟨butter*fly*⟩ **2** : TWO-WINGED FLY; *esp* : one (as a housefly) that is large and stout-bodied **3** : a fishhook dressed to suggest an insect

fly·able \ˈflī-ə-bəl\ *adj* : suitable for flying or being flown

fly ball *n* : [2]FLY 6

fly·blown \ˈflī-ˌblōn\ *adj* : not pure : TAINTED, CORRUPT

fly·by \ˈflī-ˌbī\ *n, pl* **flybys** **1** : a usu. low-altitude flight past a designated point by an aircraft **2** : a flight of a spacecraft past a heavenly body (as Jupiter) close enough to obtain scientific data; *also* : a spacecraft that makes a flyby

fly–by–night \ˈflī-bə-ˌnīt\ *adj* **1** : seeking a quick profit usu. by shady acts **2** : TRANSITORY, PASSING

fly casting *n* : the act or practice of throwing the lure in angling with artificial flies

fly·catch·er \ˈflī-ˌkach-ər, -ˌkech-\ *n* : a small bird that feeds on insects caught in flight

fly·er *var of* FLIER

flying boat *n* : a seaplane with a hull designed for floating

flying buttress *n* : a projecting arched structure to support a wall or building

flying fish *n* : any of numerous fishes with long fins suggesting wings that enable them to glide some distance through the air

flying saucer *n* : an unidentified flying object reported to be saucer-shaped or disk-shaped

flying squirrel *n* : any of several No. American squirrels with folds of skin connecting the forelegs and hind legs that enable them to make long gliding leaps

fly·leaf \ˈflī-ˌlēf\ *n* : a blank leaf at the beginning or end of a book

fly·pa·per \-ˌpā-pər\ *n* : paper poisoned or coated with a sticky substance for killing or catching flies

fly·speck \-ˌspek\ *n* **1** : a speck of fly dung **2** : something small and insignificant — **flyspeck** *vb*

fly·way \-ˌwā\ *n* : an established air route of migratory birds

fly·wheel \-ˌhwēl\ *n* : a heavy wheel for regulating the speed of machinery

fm *abbr* fathom

Fm *symbol* fermium

FM \ˈef-ˈem\ *n* : a broadcasting system using frequency modulation; *also* : a radio receiver of such a system — **FM** *adj*

fn *abbr* footnote

fo *or* **fol** *abbr* folio

FO *abbr* foreign office

foal \ˈfōl\ *n* : the young of a horse or related animal; *esp* : one under one year — **foal** *vb*

[1]**foam** \ˈfōm\ *n* **1** : a mass of bubbles formed on the surface of a liquid : FROTH, SPUME **2** : material (as rubber) in a lightweight cellular form — **foamy** *adj*

[2]**foam** *vb* : to form foam : FROTH

fob \ˈfäb\ *n* **1** : a short strap, ribbon, or chain attached esp. to a pocket watch **2** : a small ornament worn on a fob

FOB *abbr* free on board

fob off *vb* **1** : to put off with a trick, excuse, or inferior substitute **2** : to pass or offer as genuine **3** : to put aside

FOC *abbr* free of charge

focal length *n* : the distance of a focus from a lens or concave mirror

fo'·c'sle *var of* FORECASTLE

[1]**fo·cus** \ˈfō-kəs\ *n, pl* **fo·ci** \-ˌsī\ *also* **fo·cus·es** [L, *hearth*] **1** : a point at which rays (as of light, heat, or sound) meet or diverge or appear to diverge; *esp* : the point at which an image is formed by a mirror, lens, or optical system **2** : FOCAL LENGTH **3** : adjustment (as of eyes or eyeglasses) that gives clear vision **4** : central point : CENTER — **fo·cal** \ˈfō-kəl\ *adj* — **fo·cal·ly** \-ē\ *adv*

[2]**focus** *vb* **-cused** *also* **-cussed; -cus·ing** *also* **cus·sing** **1** : to bring or come to a focus ⟨~ rays of light⟩ **2** : CENTER ⟨~ attention on a problem⟩ **3** : to adjust the focus of

fod·der \ˈfäd-ər\ *n* : coarse dry food (as cornstalks) for livestock

foe \ˈfō\ *n* [ME *fo*, fr. OE *fāh*, fr. *fāh* hostile] : ENEMY

FOE *abbr* Fraternal Order of Eagles

foehn *or* **föhn** \ˈfə(r)n, ˈfœn, ˈfān\ *n* [G föhn] : a warm dry wind blowing down a mountainside

foe·man \ˈfō-mən\ *n* : FOE

foe·tal, foe·tus *chiefly Brit var of* FETAL, FETUS

[1]**fog** \ˈfòg, ˈfäg\ *n* **1** : fine particles of water suspended in the lower atmosphere **2** : mental confusion — **fog·gy** *adj*

[2]**fog** *vb* **fogged; fog·ging** : to obscure or become obscured with or as if with fog

fog·horn \-ˌhòrn\ *n* : a horn sounded in a fog to give warning

fo·gy *also* **fo·gey** \ˈfō-gē\ *n, pl* **fogies** *also* **fogeys** : a person with old-fashioned ideas ⟨he's an old ~⟩

foi·ble \ˈfȯi-bəl\ *n* : a minor failing or weakness in character or behavior

[1]**foil** \ˈfȯil\ *vb* [ME *foilen* to trample, full cloth, fr. MF *fouler*] **1** : to prevent from attaining an end : DEFEAT **2** : to bring to naught : THWART

[2]**foil** *n* : a fencing weapon with a light flexible blade tapering to a blunt point

[3]**foil** *n* [ME, leaf, fr. MF *foille, foil,* fr. L *folium*] **1** : a very thin sheet of metal **2** : one that serves as a contrast to another

foist \ˈfȯist\ *vb* : to pass off (something false or worthless) as genuine

[1]**fold** \ˈfōld\ *n* **1** : an enclosure for sheep **2** : a group of people with a common faith, belief, or interest

[2]**fold** *vb* : to house (sheep) in a fold

[3]**fold** *vb* **1** : to lay one part over or against another part **2** : to clasp together **3** : EMBRACE **4** : to bend (as a layer of rock) into folds **5** : to incorporate into a mixture by overturning repeatedly without stirring or beating **6** : to become doubled or pleated **7** : FAIL, COLLAPSE

[4]**fold** *n* **1** : a doubling or folding over **2** : a part doubled or laid over another part

fold·away \ˌfōl-də-ˌwā\ *adj* : designed to fold out of the way or out of sight

fold·er \ˈfōl-dər\ *n* **1** : one that folds **2** : a folded printed circular **3** : a folded cover or large envelope for loose papers

fol·de·rol \ˈfäl-də-ˌräl\ *n* **1** : a useless trifle **2** : NONSENSE

fold·out \ˈfōld-ˌau̇t\ *n* : a folded leaf (as in a magazine) larger in some dimensions than the page

fo·liage \ˈfō-l(ē-)ij\ *n* : a mass of leaves (as of a plant or forest)

fo·li·at·ed \ˈfō-lē-ˌāt-əd\ *adj* : separable into layers

fo·lio \ˈfō-lē-ˌō\ *n, pl* **fo·li·os** **1** : a leaf of a book; *also* : a page number **2** : the size of a piece of paper cut two from a sheet **3** : a book printed on folio pages

[1]**folk** \ˈfōk\ *n, pl* **folk** *or* **folks** **1** : a group of people forming a tribe or nation; *also* : the largest number or most characteristic part of such a group **2** *pl* : PEOPLE, PERSONS ⟨country ~⟩ ⟨old ~*s*⟩ **3** *folks pl* : the persons of one's own family

[2]**folk** *adj* : of, relating to, or originating among the common people ⟨~ music⟩

folk·lore \-ˌlōr\ *n* : customs, beliefs, stories, and sayings of a people handed down from generation to generation — **folk·lor·ist** \-əst\ *n*

folk mass *n* : a mass in which traditional liturgical music is replaced by folk music

folk·sing·er \ˈfōk-ˌsiŋ-ər\ *n* : a singer of folk songs — **folk·sing·ing** \-ˌsiŋ-iŋ\ *n*

folksy \ˈfōk-sē\ *adj* **folks·i·er; -est** **1** : SOCIABLE, FRIENDLY **2** : informal, casual, or familiar in manner or style

folk·way \ˈfōk-ˌwā\ *n* : a way of thinking, feeling, or acting common to a given group of people; *esp* : a traditional social custom

fol·li·cle \ˈfäl-i-kəl\ *n* **1** : a small anatomical cavity or gland ⟨a hair ~⟩ **2** : a small fluid-filled cavity in the ovary of a mammal enclosing a developing egg

fol·low \ˈfäl-ō\ *vb* **1** : to go or come after **2** : PURSUE **3** : OBEY **4** : to proceed along **5** : to engage in as a way of life ⟨~ the sea⟩ ⟨~ a profession⟩ **6** : to come after in order or rank or natural sequence **7** : to keep one's attention fixed on **8** : to result from **syn** succeed, ensue, supervene — **fol·low·er** *n* — **follow suit** **1** : to play a card of the same suit as the card led **2** : to follow an example set

[1]**fol·low·ing** \ˈfäl-ə-wiŋ\ *adj* **1** : next after : SUCCEEDING **2** : that immediately follows

[2]**following** *n* : a group of followers, adherents, or partisans

[3]**following** *prep* : subsequent to : AFTER

follow–up \ˈfäl-ə-ˌwəp\ *n* : a system or instance of pursuing an initial effort by supplementary action

fol·ly \ˈfäl-ē\ *n, pl* **follies** [ME *folie,* fr. OF, fr. *fol* fool] **1** : lack of good sense **2** : a foolish act or idea : FOOLISHNESS **3** : an excessively costly or unprofitable undertaking

fo·ment \fō-ˈment\ *vb* : to stir up : INSTIGATE

fo·men·ta·tion \ˌfō-mən-ˈtā-shən, -ˌmen-\ *n* **1** : a hot moist material (as a damp cloth) applied to the body to ease pain **2** : the act of fomenting : INSTIGATION

fond \ˈfänd\ *adj* [ME, fr. *fonne* fool] **1** : FOOLISH, SILLY ⟨~ pride⟩ **2** : prizing highly : DESIROUS ⟨~ of praise⟩ **3** : strongly attracted or predisposed ⟨~ of music⟩ **4** : foolishly tender : INDULGENT; *also* : LOVING, AFFECTIONATE **5** : CHERISHED, DEAR ⟨his ~*est* hopes⟩ — **fond·ly** \ˈfän-(d)lē\ *adv* — **fond·ness** \ˈfän(d)-nəs\ *n*

fon·dant \ˈfän-dənt\ *n* : a creamy preparation of sugar used as a basis for candies or icings

fon·dle \ˈfän-dᵊl\ *vb* **fon·dled; fon·dling** \-(d)liŋ, -dᵊl-iŋ\ : to touch or handle lovingly : CARESS, PET

fon·due *also* **fon·du** \fän-ˈd(y)ü\ *n* [F] : a preparation of melted cheese usu. flavored with wine or brandy

[1]**font** \ˈfänt\ *n* **1** : a receptacle for baptismal or holy water **2** : FOUNTAIN, SOURCE

[2]**font** *n* : an assortment of printing type of one size and style

food \ˈfüd\ *n* **1** : material taken into an organism and used for growth, repair, and vital processes and as a source of energy; *also* : organic material produced by green plants and used by them as food **2** : solid nutritive material as distinguished from drink **3** : something that nourishes, sustains, or supplies ⟨~ for thought⟩

food chain *n* : a hierarchical arrangement of organisms in an ecological community such that each uses the next usu. lower member as a food source

food poisoning *n* : a digestive illness caused by bacteria or by chemicals in food

food·stuff \ˈfüd-ˌstəf\ *n* : something with food value; *esp* : a specific nutrient (as fat or protein)

food web *n* : the interacting food chains of an ecological community

[1]**fool** \ˈfül\ *n* [ME, fr. OF *fol,* fr. LL *follis,* fr. L, bellows, bag] **1** : a person who lacks sense or judgment **2** : JESTER **3** : DUPE **4** : IDIOT

[2]**fool** *vb* **1** : to spend time idly or aimlessly **2** : to meddle or tamper thoughtlessly or ignorantly **3** : JOKE **4** : DECEIVE **5** : FRITTER ⟨~*ed* away his time⟩

fool·ery \ˈfül-(ə-)rē\ *n, pl* **-er·ies** **1** : the habit of fooling : the behavior of a fool **2** : a foolish act : HORSEPLAY

fool·har·dy \ˈfül-ˌhärd-ē\ *adj* : foolishly daring : RASH — **fool·har·di·ness** \-ˌhärd-ē-nəs\ *n*

fool·ish \ˈfü-lish\ *adj* **1** : showing or arising from folly or lack of judgment **2** : ABSURD, RIDICULOUS **3** : ABASHED — **fool·ish·ly** *adv* — **fool·ish·ness** *n*

fool·proof \ˈfül-ˌprüf\ *adj* : so simple or reliable as to leave no opportunity for error, misuse, or failure

fools·cap \ˈfül-ˌskap\ *n* [fr. the watermark of a fool's cap formerly applied to such paper] : a size of paper typically 16 × 13 inches

[1]**foot** \ˈfu̇t\ *n, pl* **feet** \ˈfēt\ *also* **foot** **1** : the terminal part of a leg on which one stands **2** — see WEIGHT table **3** : a group of syllables forming the basic unit of verse meter **4** : something resembling an animal's foot in position or use **5** *foot pl, chiefly Brit* : INFANTRY **6** : the lowest part : BOTTOM **7** : the part at the opposite end from the head **8** : the part (as of a stocking) that covers the foot

[2]**foot** *vb* **1** : DANCE **2** : to go on foot **3** : to add up **4** : to pay or provide for paying

foot·age \ˈfu̇t-ij\ *n* : length expressed in feet
foot·ball \ˈfu̇t-ˌbȯl\ *n* **1** : any of several games played by two teams on a rectangular field with goalposts at each end; *esp* : one in which the ball is in possession of one team at a time and is advanced by running or passing **2** : the ball used in football
foot·board \-ˌbōrd\ *n* **1** : a narrow platform on which to stand or brace the feet **2** : a board forming the foot of a bed
foot·bridge \-ˌbrij\ *n* : a bridge for pedestrians
foot·ed \ˈfu̇t-əd\ *adj* : having a foot or feet of a specified kind or number ⟨flat-*footed*⟩ ⟨four-*footed*⟩
-foot·er \ˈfu̇t-ər\ *comb form* : one that is a specified number of feet in height, length, or breadth ⟨a six-*footer*⟩
foot·fall \ˈfu̇t-ˌfȯl\ *n* : the sound of a footstep
foot·hill \-ˌhil\ *n* : a hill at the foot of higher hills or mountains
foot·hold \-ˌhōld\ *n* **1** : a hold for the feet : FOOTING **2** : a position usable as a base for further advance
foot·ing \ˈfu̇t-iŋ\ *n* **1** : the placing of one's feet in a stable position **2** : the act of moving on foot **3** : a place or space for standing : FOOTHOLD **4** : position with respect to one another : STATUS **5** : BASIS **6** : the sum of a column of figures
foot·less \ˈfu̇t-ləs\ *adj* **1** : having no feet **2** : INEPT
foot·lights \-ˌlīts\ *n pl* **1** : a row of lights along the front of a stage floor **2** : the stage as a profession
foo·tling \ˈfüt-liŋ\ *adj* **1** : INEPT **2** : TRIVIAL
foot·lock·er \ˈfu̇t-ˌläk-ər\ *n* : a small trunk designed to be placed at the foot of a bed (as in a barracks)
foot·loose \-ˌlüs\ *adj* : having no ties : FREE, UNTRAMMELED
foot·man \-mən\ *n* : a male servant who attends a carriage, waits on table, admits visitors, and runs errands
foot·note \-ˌnōt\ *n* **1** : a note of reference, explanation, or comment placed usu. at the bottom of a page **2** : COMMENTARY
foot·pad \-ˌpad\ *n* : a round somewhat flat foot on the leg of a spacecraft for distributing weight to minimize sinking into a surface
foot·path \ˈfu̇t-ˌpath, -ˌpȧth\ *n* : a narrow path for pedestrians
foot·print \-ˌprint\ *n* : an impression of the foot
foot·race \-ˌrās\ *n* : a race run on foot
foot·rest \-ˌrest\ *n* : a support for the feet
foot·sore \-ˌsōr\ *adj* : having sore or tender feet (as from much walking)
foot·step \-ˌstep\ *n* **1** : the mark of the foot : TRACK **2** : TREAD **3** : distance covered by a step : PACE **4** : a step on which to ascend or descend **5** : a way of life, conduct, or action
foot·stool \-ˌstül\ *n* : a low stool to support the feet
foot·wear \-ˌwaər\ *n* : apparel (as shoes or boots) for the feet
foot·work \-ˌwərk\ *n* : the management of the feet (as in boxing)
fop \ˈfäp\ *n* : DANDY 1 — **fop·pery** \-(ə-)rē\ *n* — **fop·pish** *adj*
[1]**for** \fər, (ˈ)fȯr\ *prep* **1** : as a preparation toward ⟨dress ~ dinner⟩ **2** : toward the purpose or goal of ⟨need time ~ study⟩ ⟨money ~ a trip⟩ **3** : so as to reach or attain ⟨run ~ cover⟩ **4** : as being ⟨took him ~ a fool⟩ **5** : because of ⟨cry ~ joy⟩ **6** — used to indicate a recipient ⟨a letter ~ you⟩ **7** : in support of ⟨fought ~ his country⟩ **8** : directed at : AFFECTING ⟨a cure ~ what ails you⟩ **9** — used with a noun or pronoun followed by an infinitive to form the equivalent of a noun clause ⟨~ you to go would be silly⟩ **10** : in exchange as equal to : so as to return the value of ⟨a lot of trouble ~ nothing⟩ ⟨pay $10 ~ a hat⟩ **11** : CONCERNING ⟨a stickler ~ detail⟩ **12** : CONSIDERING ⟨tall ~ his age⟩ **13** : through the period of ⟨served ~ three years⟩ **14** : in honor of
[2]**for** *conj* : BECAUSE
[3]**for** *abbr* **1** foreign **2** forestry
fora *pl of* FORUM
[1]**for·age** \ˈfȯr-ij\ *n* **1** : food for animals esp. when taken by browsing or grazing **2** : a search for provisions
[2]**forage** *vb* **for·aged; for·ag·ing 1** : to collect forage from **2** : to wander in search of provisions **3** : to get by foraging **4** : to make a search : RUMMAGE
for·ay \ˈfȯr-ˌā\ *vb* : to raid esp. in search of plunder : PILLAGE — **foray** *n*
[1]**for·bear** \fȯr-ˈbaər\ *vb* **-bore** \-ˈbōr\; **-borne** \-ˈbōrn\; **-bear·ing 1** : to refrain from : ABSTAIN **2** : to be patient — **for·bear·ance** \-ˈbar-əns\ *n*
[2]**forbear** *var of* FOREBEAR
for·bid \fər-ˈbid\ *vb* **-bade** \-ˈbad, -ˈbād\ *or* **-bad** \-ˈbad\; **-bid·den** \-ˈbid-ᵊn\; **-bid·ding 1** : to command against : PROHIBIT **2** : HINDER, PREVENT **syn** enjoin, interdict, inhibit, ban
for·bid·ding \-iŋ\ *adj* : DISAGREEABLE, REPELLENT
forbode *var of* FOREBODE
[1]**force** \ˈfōrs\ *n* **1** : strength or energy esp. of an exceptional degree : active power **2** : capacity to persuade or convince **3** : military strength; *also, pl* : the whole military strength (as of a nation) **4** : a body (as of persons or ships) available for a particular purpose **5** : VIOLENCE, COMPULSION **6** : an influence (as a push or pull) that causes motion or a change of motion — **force·ful** \-fəl\ *adj* — **force·ful·ly** \-ē\ *adv* — **in force 1** : in great numbers **2** : VALID, OPERATIVE
[2]**force** *vb* **forced; forc·ing 1** : COMPEL, COERCE **2** : to cause through necessity ⟨*forced* to admit defeat⟩ **3** : to press, attain to, or effect against resistance or inertia ⟨~ your way through⟩ **4** : to raise or accelerate to the utmost ⟨~ the pace⟩ **5** : to produce with unnatural or unwilling effort ⟨*forced* laughter⟩ **6** : to hasten (as in growth) by artificial means
for·ceps \ˈfȯr-səps\ *n, pl* **forceps** [L] : a hand-held instrument for grasping, holding, or pulling objects esp. for delicate operations (as by a surgeon)
forc·ible \ˈfōr-sə-bəl\ *adj* **1** : obtained or done by force **2** : showing force or energy : POWERFUL — **forc·i·bly** \-blē\ *adv*
[1]**ford** \ˈfōrd\ *n* : a place where a stream may be crossed by wading
[2]**ford** *vb* : to cross (a body of water) by wading
[1]**fore** \ˈfōr\ *adv* : in, toward, or adjacent to the front : FORWARD
[2]**fore** *adj* : being or coming before in time, order, or space
[3]**fore** *n* : something that occupies a front position
[4]**fore** *interj* — used by a golfer to warn anyone within range of the probable line of flight of his ball
fore-and-aft \ˌfōr-ə-ˈnaft\ *adj* : lying, running, or acting along the length of a structure (as a ship)
[1]**fore·arm** \ˈfōr-ˈärm\ *vb* : to arm in advance : PREPARE
[2]**fore·arm** \ˈfōr-ˌärm\ *n* : the part of the arm between the elbow and the wrist
fore·bear *or* **for·bear** \-ˌbaər\ *n* : ANCESTOR, FOREFATHER
fore·bode *also* **for·bode** \fōr-ˈbōd, fȯr-\ *vb* **1** : to have a premonition esp. of misfortune **2** : FORETELL, PREDICT **syn** augur, bode, foreshadow, portend, promise — **fore·bod·ing** *n*
fore·cast \ˈfōr-ˌkast\ *vb* **-cast** *also* **-cast·ed; -cast·ing 1** : PREDICT, CALCULATE ⟨~ weather conditions⟩ **2** : to indicate as likely to occur — **forecast** *n* — **fore·cast·er** *n*
fore·cas·tle \ˈfōk-səl\ *n* **1** : the forward part of the upper deck of a ship **2** : the living area for the crew in the forward part of a ship
fore·close \fōr-ˈklōz\ *vb* **1** : to shut out : PRECLUDE **2** : to take legal measures to terminate a mortgage and take possession of the mortgaged property
fore·clo·sure \-ˈklō-zhər\ *n* : the act of foreclosing; *esp* : the legal procedure of foreclosing a mortgage
fore·doom \fōr-ˈdüm\ *vb* : to doom beforehand

fore·fa·ther \ˈfōr-ˌfäth-ər\ *n* **1** : ANCESTOR **2** : a person of an earlier period and common heritage
forefend *var of* FORFEND
fore·fin·ger \-ˌfiŋ-gər\ *n* : the finger next to the thumb
fore·foot \-ˌfu̇t\ *n* : either of the front feet of a quadruped
fore·front \-ˌfrənt\ *n* : the foremost part or place : VANGUARD
fore·gath·er *var of* FORGATHER
[1]**fore·go** \fōr-ˈgō\ *vb* **-went** \-ˈwent\; **-gone** \-ˈgȯn\; **-go·ing** \-ˈgō-iŋ\ : PRECEDE
[2]**forego** *var of* FORGO
fore·go·ing \-ˈgō-iŋ\ *adj* : PRECEDING
fore·gone \ˌfōr-ˌgȯn\ *adj* : determined in advance ⟨a ~ conclusion⟩
fore·ground \ˈfōr-ˌgrau̇nd\ *n* **1** : the part of a scene or representation that appears nearest to and in front of the spectator **2** : a position of prominence
fore·hand \-ˌhand\ *n* : a stroke (as in tennis) made with the palm of the hand turned in the direction in which the hand is moving; *also* : the side on which such a stroke is made — **forehand** *adj*
fore·hand·ed \-ˈhan-dəd\ *adj* : mindful of the future : THRIFTY, PRUDENT
fore·head \ˈfȯr-əd, ˈfōr-ˌhed\ *n* : the part of the face above the eyes
for·eign \ˈfȯr-ən\ *adj* [ME *forein*, fr. OF, fr. LL *foranus* on the outside, fr. L *foris* outside] **1** : situated outside a place or country and esp. one's own country **2** : born in, belonging to, or characteristic of some place or country other than the one under consideration ⟨~ language⟩ **3** : not connected or pertinent **4** : related to or dealing with other nations ⟨~ affairs⟩ **5** : occurring in an abnormal situation in the living body ⟨a ~ body in the eye⟩
for·eign·er \ˈfȯr-ə-nər\ *n* : a person belonging to or owing allegiance to a foreign country
foreign minister *n* : a governmental minister for foreign affairs
fore·know \fōr-ˈnō\ *vb* **-knew** \-ˈn(y)ü\; **-known** \-ˈnōn\; **-know·ing** : to have previous knowledge of — **fore·knowl·edge** \-ˈnäl-ij\ *n*
fore·la·dy \ˈfōr-ˌlād-ē\ *n* : a woman who acts as a foreman
fore·leg \-ˌleg\ *n* : a front leg
fore·limb \-ˌlim\ *n* : either of an anterior pair of limbs (as wings, arms, or fins)
fore·lock \-ˌläk\ *n* : a lock of hair growing from the front part of the head
fore·man \ˈfōr-mən\ *n* **1** : a spokesperson of a jury **2** : a person in charge of a group of workers
fore·mast \-ˌmast\ *n* : the mast nearest the bow of a ship
fore·most \-ˌmōst\ *adj* : first in time, place, or order : most important : PREEMINENT — **foremost** *adv*
fore·name \-ˌnām\ *n* : a first name
fore·named \-ˌnāmd\ *adj* : previously named : AFORESAID
fore·noon \-ˌnün\ *n* : MORNING
[1]**fo·ren·sic** \fə-ˈren-sik\ *adj* [L *forensis* public, forensic, fr. *forum* forum] : belonging to, used in, or suitable to courts of law or to public speaking or debate
[2]**forensic** *n* **1** : an argumentative exercise **2** *pl* : the art or study of argumentative discourse
fore·or·dain \ˌfōr-ȯr-ˈdān\ *vb* : to ordain or decree beforehand : PREDESTINE
fore·part \ˈfōr-ˌpärt\ *n* **1** : the anterior part of something **2** : the earlier part of a period of time
fore·quar·ter \-ˌkwȯrt-ər\ *n* : the front half of a lateral half of the body or carcass of a quadruped ⟨a ~ of beef⟩
fore·run·ner \ˈfōr-ˌrən-ər\ *n* **1** : one that goes before to give notice of the approach of others : HARBINGER **2** : PREDECESSOR, ANCESTOR **syn** precursor, herald
fore·sail \ˈfōr-ˌsāl, -səl\ *n* : the largest sail on the foremast of a square-rigged ship or schooner
fore·see \fōr-ˈsē\ *vb* **-saw** \-ˈsȯ\; **-seen** \-ˈsēn\; **-see·ing** : to see or realize beforehand : EXPECT **syn** foreknow, divine, apprehend, anticipate — **fore·see·able** *adj*
fore·shad·ow \-ˈshad-ō\ *vb* : to give a hint or suggestion of beforehand
fore·short·en \fōr-ˈshȯrt-ᵊn\ *vb* : to shorten (a detail) in a drawing or painting so that it appears to have depth
fore·sight \ˈfōr-ˌsīt\ *n* **1** : the act or power of foreseeing **2** : an act of looking forward; *also* : a view forward **3** : care or provision for the future : PRUDENCE — **fore·sight·ed** \-əd\ *adj* — **fore·sight·ed·ness** *n*
fore·skin \-ˌskin\ *n* : a fold of skin enclosing the end of the penis
for·est \ˈfȯr-əst\ *n* [ME, fr. OF, fr. ML *forestis*, fr. L *foris* outside] : a large thick growth of trees and underbrush — **for·est·ed** \ˈfȯr-ə-stəd\ *adj* — **for·est·land** \ˈfȯr-əst-ˌland\ *n*
fore·stall \fōr-ˈstȯl, fȯr-\ *vb* **1** : to keep out, hinder, or prevent by measures taken in advance **2** : ANTICIPATE
forest ranger *n* : a person in charge of the management and protection of a portion of a forest
for·est·ry \ˈfȯr-ə-strē\ *n* : the science of growing and caring for forests — **for·est·er** \ˈfȯr-ə-stər\ *n*
foreswear *var of* FORSWEAR
[1]**fore·taste** \ˈfōr-ˌtāst\ *n* : an advance indication, warning, or notion
[2]**fore·taste** \fōr-ˈtāst\ *vb* : to taste beforehand : ANTICIPATE
fore·tell \fōr-ˈtel\ *vb* **-told** \-ˈtōld\; **-tell·ing** : to tell of beforehand : PREDICT **syn** forecast, prophesy, prognosticate
fore·thought \ˈfōr-ˌthȯt\ *n* **1** : PREMEDITATION **2** : consideration for the future
fore·to·ken \fōr-ˈtō-kən\ *vb* **-kened; -ken·ing** \-ˈtōk-(ə-)niŋ\ : to indicate in advance
fore·top \ˈfōr-ˌtäp\ *n* : a platform near the top of a ship's foremast
for·ev·er \fȯr-ˈev-ər\ *adv* **1** : for a limitless time **2** : at all times : ALWAYS
for·ev·er·more \-ˌev-ər-ˈmōr\ *adv* : FOREVER
fore·warn \fōr-ˈwȯrn\ *vb* : to warn beforehand
forewent *past of* FOREGO
fore·wing \ˈfōr-ˌwiŋ\ *n* : either of the anterior wings of a 4-winged insect
fore·wom·an \ˈfōr-ˌwu̇m-ən\ *n* : FORELADY
fore·word \-ˌwərd\ *n* : PREFACE
[1]**for·feit** \ˈfȯr-fət\ *n* **1** : something forfeited : PENALTY, FINE **2** : FORFEITURE **3** : something deposited and then redeemed on payment of a fine **4** *pl* : a game in which forfeits are exacted
[2]**forfeit** *vb* : to lose or lose the right to by some error, offense, or crime
for·fei·ture \ˈfȯr-fə-ˌchu̇r\ *n* **1** : the act of forfeiting **2** : something forfeited : PENALTY
for·fend \fȯr-ˈfend\ *vb* **1** : PREVENT **2** : PROTECT, PRESERVE
for·gath·er *or* **fore·gath·er** \fȯr-ˈgath-ər, fōr-, -ˈgeth-\ *vb* **1** : to come together : ASSEMBLE **2** : to meet someone usu. by chance
[1]**forge** \ˈfōrj\ *n* [ME, fr. OF, fr. L *fabrica*, fr. *faber* smith] : a furnace or shop with its furnace where metal is heated and worked
[2]**forge** *vb* **forged; forg·ing** **1** : to form (metal) by heating and hammering **2** : FASHION, SHAPE ⟨~ an agreement⟩ **3** : to make or imitate falsely esp. with intent to defraud ⟨~ a signature⟩ — **forg·er** *n* — **forg·ery** \ˈfōrj-(ə-)rē\ *n*
[3]**forge** *vb* **forged; forg·ing** : to move ahead steadily but gradually
for·get \fər-ˈget\ *vb* **-got** \-ˈgät\; **-got·ten** \-ˈgät-ᵊn\ *or* **-got; -get·ting** **1** : to be unable to think of or recall **2** : to fail to become mindful of at the proper time **3** : NEGLECT, DISREGARD — **for·get·ful** \-ˈget-fəl\ *adj* — **for·get·ful·ly** \-ē\ *adv*

for·get–me–not \fər-ˈget-mē-ˌnät\ *n* : any of a genus of small herbs having bright-blue or white flowers usu. arranged in a curving spike

forg·ing \ˈfōr-jiŋ\ *n* : a piece of forged work

for·give \fər-ˈgiv\ *vb* **-gave** \-ˈgāv\; **-giv·en** \-ˈgiv-ən\; **-giv·ing** **1** : PARDON, ABSOLVE **2** : to give up resentment of **3** : to grant relief from payment of — **for·giv·able** *adj* — **for·give·ness** *n*

for·giv·ing \-iŋ\ *adj* **1** : showing forgiveness : inclined or ready to forgive **2** : allowing room for error or weakness

for·go *or* **fore·go** \fȯr-ˈgō, fōr-\ *vb* **-went** \-ˈwent\; **-gone** \-ˈgȯn\; **-go·ing** \-ˈgō-iŋ\ : to abstain from : GIVE UP, RENOUNCE

fo·rint \ˈfȯr-int\ *n, pl* **forints** *also* **forint** — see MONEY table

[1]**fork** \ˈfȯrk\ *n* **1** : an implement with two or more prongs for taking up (as in eating), piercing, pitching, or digging **2** : a forked part, tool, or piece of equipment **3** : a dividing into branches or a place where something branches; *also* : a branch of such a fork

[2]**fork** *vb* **1** : to divide into two or more branches **2** : to give the form of a fork to ⟨∼*ing* her fingers⟩ **3** : to raise or pitch with a fork ⟨∼ hay⟩

forked \ˈfȯrkt, ˈfȯr-kəd\ *adj* : having a fork : shaped like a fork ⟨∼ lightning⟩

fork·lift \ˈfōrk-ˌlift\ *n* : a machine for hoisting heavy objects by means of steel fingers inserted under the load

for·lorn \fər-ˈlȯrn\ *adj* **1** : sad and lonely because of isolation or desertion **2** : WRETCHED **3** : nearly hopeless — **for·lorn·ly** *adv*

forlorn hope *n* [modif. of Dutch *verloren hoop,* lit., lost band] **1** : a body of men selected to perform a perilous service **2** : a desperate or extremely difficult enterprise

[1]**form** \ˈfȯrm\ *n* **1** : SHAPE, STRUCTURE **2** : a body esp. of a person : FIGURE **3** : the essential nature of a thing **4** : established manner of doing or saying something **5** : FORMULA **6** : a document with blank spaces for insertion of information ⟨tax ∼⟩ **7** : CEREMONY, CONVENTIONALITY **8** : manner of performing according to recognized standards **9** : a long seat : BENCH **10** : a model of the human figure used for displaying clothes **11** : MOLD ⟨a ∼ for concrete⟩ **12** : type or plates in a frame ready for printing **13** : MODE, KIND, VARIETY ⟨coal is a ∼ of carbon⟩ **14** : orderly method of arrangement; *also* : a particular kind or instance of such arrangement ⟨the sonnet ∼ in poetry⟩ **15** : the structural element, plan, or design of a work of art **16** : a bounded surface or volume **17** : a grade in a British secondary school or in some American private schools **18** : RACING FORM **19** : known ability to perform; *also* : condition (as of an athlete) suitable for performing **20** : one of the ways in which a word is changed to show difference in use ⟨the plural ∼ of a noun⟩

[2]**form** *vb* **1** : to give form or shape to : FASHION, MAKE **2** : TRAIN, INSTRUCT **3** : DEVELOP, ACQUIRE ⟨∼ a habit⟩ **4** : CONSTITUTE, COMPOSE **5** : to arrange in order ⟨∼ a battle line⟩ **6** : to take form : ARISE ⟨clouds are ∼*ing*⟩ **7** : to take a definite form, shape, or arrangement

[1]**for·mal** \ˈfȯr-məl\ *adj* **1** : based on conventional forms and rules; *also* : being or requiring elegant dress and manners ⟨a ∼ reception⟩ **2** : done in due or lawful form ⟨a ∼ contract⟩ **3** : CEREMONIOUS, PRIM ⟨a ∼ manner⟩ **4** : NOMINAL — **for·mal·ly** \-ē\ *adv*

[2]**formal** *n* : something (as a social event) formal in character

form·al·de·hyde \fȯr-ˈmal-də-ˌhīd\ *n* : a colorless pungent gas used in water solution as a preservative and disinfectant

for·mal·ism \ˈfȯr-mə-ˌliz-əm\ *n* : strict adherence to set forms

for·mal·i·ty \fȯr-ˈmal-ət-ē\ *n, pl* **-ties** **1** : the quality or state of being formal **2** : compliance with formal or conventional rules **3** : an established form that is required or conventional

for·mal·ize \ˈfȯr-mə-ˌlīz\ *vb* **-ized; -iz·ing** **1** : to give a certain or definite form to **2** : to make formal; *also* : to give formal status or approval to

[1]**for·mat** \ˈfȯr-ˌmat\ *n* **1** : the general composition or style of a publication **2** : the general plan or arrangement of something

[2]**format** *vb* **for·mat·ted; for·mat·ting** : to produce (as a book, printed matter, or data) in a particular form

for·ma·tion \fȯr-ˈmā-shən\ *n* **1** : a giving form to something : DEVELOPMENT **2** : something that is formed **3** : STRUCTURE, SHAPE **4** : an arrangement of persons, ships, or airplanes

for·ma·tive \ˈfȯr-mət-iv\ *adj* **1** : giving or capable of giving form : CONSTRUCTIVE **2** : of, relating to, or characterized by important growth or formation ⟨a child's ∼ years⟩

for·mer \ˈfȯr-mər\ *adj* **1** : PREVIOUS, EARLIER **2** : FOREGOING **3** : being first mentioned or in order of two things

for·mer·ly \-lē\ *adv* : in time past : HERETOFORE, PREVIOUSLY

form·fit·ting \ˈfȯrm-ˌfit-iŋ\ *adj* : conforming to the outline of the body

for·mi·da·ble \ˈfȯr-məd-ə-bəl, fȯr-ˈmid-\ *adj* **1** : exciting fear, dread, or awe **2** : imposing serious difficulties — **for·mi·da·bly** \-blē\ *adv*

form·less \ˈfȯrm-ləs\ *adj* : having no definite shape or form

form letter *n* **1** : a letter on a frequently recurring topic that can be sent to different people at different times **2** : a letter sent out in many printed copies to a large number of people

for·mu·la \ˈfȯr-myə-lə\ *n, pl* **-las** *or* **-lae** \-ˌlē, -ˌlī\ **1** : a set form of words for ceremonial use **2** : RECIPE, PRESCRIPTION **3** : a milk mixture or substitute for a baby **4** : a group of symbols or figures joined to express information concisely **5** : a prescribed or set form or method

for·mu·late \-ˌlāt\ *vb* **-lat·ed; -lat·ing** **1** : to express in a formula **2** : to state definitely and clearly **3** : to prepare according to a formula — **for·mu·la·tion** \ˌfȯr-myə-ˈlā-shən\ *n*

for·ni·ca·tion \ˌfȯr-nə-ˈkā-shən\ *n* : human sexual intercourse other than between a man and his wife — **for·ni·cate** \ˈfȯr-nə-ˌkāt\ *vb* — **for·ni·ca·tor** \-ˌkāt-ər\ *n*

for·sake \fər-ˈsāk\ *vb* **for·sook** \-ˈsu̇k\; **for·sak·en** \-ˈsā-kən\; **for·sak·ing** [ME *forsaken,* fr. OE *forsacan,* fr. *sacan* to dispute] **1** : GIVE UP, RENOUNCE **2** : to quit or leave entirely : ABANDON

for·sooth \fər-ˈsüth\ *adv* : in truth : INDEED

for·swear *or* **fore·swear** \fȯr-ˈswaər\ *vb* **-swore** \-ˈswōr\; **-sworn** \-ˈswōrn\; **-swear·ing** **1** : to renounce earnestly or under oath **2** : to deny under oath **3** : to swear falsely : commit perjury

for·syth·ia \fər-ˈsith-ē-ə\ *n* : any of a genus of shrubs related to the olive and having yellow bell-shaped flowers appearing before the leaves in early spring

fort \ˈfōrt\ *n* [ME *forte,* fr. MF *fort,* fr. *fort* strong, fr. L *fortis*] **1** : a fortified place **2** : a permanent army post

[1]**forte** \ˈfōrt, ˈfȯr-ˌtā\ *n* [F *fort,* fr. *fort,* adj., strong] : something in which a person excels

[2]**for·te** \ˈfȯr-ˌtā\ *adv or adj* [It, fr. *forte* strong] : LOUDLY, POWERFULLY — used as a direction in music

forth \ˈfōrth\ *adv* **1** : FORWARD, ONWARD ⟨from that day ∼⟩ **2** : out into view ⟨put ∼ leaves⟩

forth·com·ing \fōrth-ˈkəm-iŋ\ *adj* : coming or available soon ⟨the ∼ holidays⟩ ⟨the funds will be ∼⟩

forth·right \ˈfōrth-ˌrīt\ *adj* : free from ambiguity or evasiveness : going straight to the point ⟨a ∼ answer⟩ — **forth·right·ly** *adv* — **forth·right·ness** *n*

forth·with \fōrth-ˈwith, -ˈwith\ *adv* : IMMEDIATELY

for·ti·fy \ˈfȯrt-ə-ˌfī\ *vb* **-fied; -fy·ing** **1** : to strengthen by military defenses **2** : to give physical strength or endurance to **3** : ENCOURAGE **4** : ENRICH ⟨∼ bread with vitamins⟩ — **for·ti·fi·ca·tion** \ˌfȯrt-ə-fə-ˈkā-shən\ *n*

for·tis·si·mo \för-ˈtis-ə-ˌmō\ *adv or adj* : very loud — used as a direction in music

for·ti·tude \ˈfört-ə-ˌt(y)üd\ *n* : strength of mind that enables a person to meet danger or bear pain or adversity with courage **syn** grit, backbone, pluck, guts

fort·night \ˈfört-ˌnīt\ *n* [ME *fourtenight,* fr. *fourtene night* fourteen nights] : two weeks — **fort·night·ly** \-lē\ *adj or adv*

for·tress \ˈför-trəs\ *n* : FORT 1

for·tu·itous \för-ˈt(y)ü-ət-əs\ *adj* **1** : happening by chance **2** : FORTUNATE

for·tu·ity \-ət-ē\ *n, pl* **-ities** **1** : the quality or state of being fortuitous **2** : a chance event or occurrence

for·tu·nate \ˈförch-(ə-)nət\ *adj* **1** : coming by good luck **2** : LUCKY — **for·tu·nate·ly** *adv*

for·tune \ˈför-chən\ *n* **1** : an apparent cause of something that happens to one suddenly and unexpectedly : CHANCE, LUCK **2** : what happens to a person : good or bad luck **3** : FATE, DESTINY **4** : RICHES, WEALTH

fortune hunter *n* : a person who seeks wealth esp. by marriage

for·tune–tell·er \-ˌtel-ər\ *n* : a person who professes to tell future events — **for·tune–tell·ing** \-iŋ\ *n or adj*

for·ty \ˈfört-ē\ *n, pl* **forties** : four times 10 — **for·ti·eth** \ˈfört-ē-əth\ *adj or n* — **forty** *adj or pron*

for·ty–five \ˌfört-ē-ˈfīv\ *n* **1** : a .45 caliber handgun — usu. written .45 **2** : a phonograph record designed to be played at 45 revolutions per minute

for·ty–nin·er \ˌfört-ē-ˈnī-nər\ *n* : a person in the rush to California for gold in 1849

forty winks *n sing or pl* : a short sleep

fo·rum \ˈfōr-əm\ *n, pl* **forums** *also* **fo·ra** \-ə\ [L] **1** : the marketplace or central meeting place of an ancient Roman city **2** : a medium (as a publication) of open discussion **3** : COURT **4** : a public assembly, lecture, or program involving audience or panel discussion

¹for·ward \ˈför-wərd\ *adj* **1** : being near or at or belonging to the front **2** : EAGER, READY **3** : BRASH, BOLD **4** : notably advanced or developed : PRECOCIOUS **5** : moving, tending, or leading toward a position in front ⟨a ~ movement⟩ **6** : EXTREME, RADICAL **7** : of, relating to, or getting ready for the future — **for·ward·ness** *n*

²forward *adv* : to or toward what is before or in front

³forward *n* : a player stationed near the front of his team (as in hockey) or in the corner (as in basketball)

⁴forward *vb* **1** : to help onward : ADVANCE **2** : to send forward : TRANSMIT **3** : to send or ship onward

for·ward·er \-wərd-ər\ *n* : one that forwards; *esp* : an agent who forwards goods — **for·ward·ing** \-iŋ\ *n*

for·wards \ˈför-wərdz\ *adv* : FORWARD

¹fos·sil \ˈfäs-əl\ *adj* [L *fossilis* dug up, fr. *fossus,* pp. of *fodere* to dig] **1** : being or resembling a fossil ⟨~ plants⟩ **2** : of or relating to fossil fuels

²fossil *n* **1** : a trace or impression or the remains of a plant or animal preserved in the earth's crust from past ages **2** : a person whose ideas are out-of-date — **fos·sil·ize** *vb*

fossil fuel *n* : a fuel (as coal or oil) that is formed in the earth from plant or animal remains

¹fos·ter \ˈfös-tər\ *adj* [ME, fr. OE *fōstor-,* fr. *fōstor* food, feeding] : affording, receiving, or sharing nourishment or parental care though not related by blood or legal ties ⟨~ parent⟩ ⟨~ child⟩

²foster *vb* **fos·tered; fos·ter·ing** \-t(ə-)riŋ\ **1** : to give parental care to : NURTURE **2** : to promote the growth or development of : ENCOURAGE

fos·ter·ling \-tər-liŋ\ *n* : a foster child

Fou·cault pendulum \ˌfü-ˈkō-\ *n* : a device that consists of a heavy weight hung by a long wire and that swings in a constant direction which appears to change showing that the earth rotates

fought *past and past part of* FIGHT

¹foul \ˈfau̇l\ *adj* **1** : offensive to the senses : LOATHSOME; *also* : clogged with dirt **2** : ODIOUS, DETESTABLE **3** : OBSCENE, ABUSIVE **4** : DISAGREEABLE, STORMY ⟨~ weather⟩ **5** : TREACHEROUS, DISHONORABLE, UNFAIR **6** : marking the bounds of a playing field ⟨~ lines⟩; *also* : being outside the foul line ⟨~ ball⟩ ⟨~ territory⟩ **7** : containing marked-up corrections **8** : ENTANGLED — **foul·ly** \-ē\ *adv* — **foul·ness** *n*

²foul *n* **1** : an entanglement or collision in fishing or sailing **2** : an infraction of the rules in a game or sport; *also* : a baseball hit outside the foul line

³foul *vb* **1** : to make or become foul or filthy **2** : to make or hit a foul **3** : to entangle or become entangled **4** : OBSTRUCT, BLOCK : **5** : to collide with

⁴foul *adv* : in a foul manner

fou·lard \fü-ˈlärd\ *n* : a lightweight silk of plain or twill weave usu. decorated with a printed pattern

foul·mouthed \ˈfau̇l-ˈmau̇t͟hd, -ˈmau̇tht\ *adj* : given to the use of obscene, profane, or abusive language

foul play *n* : VIOLENCE; *esp* : MURDER

foul–up \ˈfau̇l-ˌəp\ *n* **1** : a state of being fouled up **2** : a mechanical difficulty

foul up \(ˈ)fau̇l-ˈəp\ *vb* **1** : to spoil by mistakes or poor judgment **2** : to make a mistake : BUNGLE

¹found \ˈfau̇nd\ *past and past part of* FIND

²found *vb* **1** : to take the first steps in building ⟨~ a colony⟩ **2** : to set or ground on something solid : BASE **3** : to establish and often to provide for the future maintenance of ⟨~ a college⟩ — **found·er** *n*

³found *vb* : to melt (metal) and pour into a mold — **found·er** *n*

foun·da·tion \fau̇n-ˈdā-shən\ *n* **1** : the act of founding **2** : a basis upon which something stands or is supported ⟨suspicions without ~⟩ **3** : funds given for the permanent support of an institution : ENDOWMENT; *also* : an institution so endowed **4** : supporting structure : BASE **5** : CORSET — **foun·da·tion·al** \-sh(ə-)nəl\ *adj*

foun·der \ˈfau̇n-dər\ *vb* **foun·dered; foun·der·ing** \-d(ə-)riŋ\ **1** : to make or become lame ⟨~ a horse⟩ **2** : COLLAPSE **3** : SINK ⟨a ~*ing* ship⟩ **4** : FAIL

found·ling \ˈfau̇n-(d)liŋ\ *n* : an infant found after its unknown parents have abandoned it

found·ry \ˈfau̇n-drē\ *n, pl* **foundries** : a building or works where metal is cast

fount \ˈfau̇nt\ *n* : SOURCE, FOUNTAIN

foun·tain \ˈfau̇nt-ᵊn\ *n* **1** : a spring of water **2** : SOURCE **3** : an artificial jet of water **4** : a container for liquid that can be drawn off as needed

foun·tain·head \-ˌhed\ *n* : SOURCE

fountain pen *n* : a pen with a reservoir that feeds the writing point with ink

four \ˈfōr\ *n* **1** : one more than three **2** : the 4th in a set or series **3** : something having four units — **four** *adj or pron*

four·flush \-ˌfləsh\ *vb* : to make a false claim : BLUFF — **four–flush·er** \-ər\ *n*

four·fold \-ˌfōld, -ˈfōld\ *adj* **1** : being four times as great or as many **2** : having four units or members — **four·fold** \-ˈfōld\ *adv*

4–H \ˈfōr-ˈāch\ *adj* : of or relating to a program set up by the U.S. Department of Agriculture to help young people become productive citizens — **4–H'·er** \-ər\ *n*

Four Hundred *or* **400** *n* : the exclusive social set of a community — used with *the*

four–in–hand \ˈfōr-ən-ˌhand\ *n* **1** : a necktie tied in a slipknot with long ends overlapping vertically in front **2** : a team of four horses driven by one person; *also* : a vehicle drawn by such a team

four–o'clock \ˈfōr-ə-ˌkläk\ *n* : a garden plant with fra-

grant yellow, red, or white flowers without petals that open late in the afternoon
four–post·er \ˈfōr-ˈpō-stər\ *n* : a bed with tall corner posts orig. designed to support curtains or a canopy
four·score \ˈfōr-ˈskōr\ *adj* : being four times twenty : EIGHTY
four·some \ˈfōr-səm\ *n* **1** : a group of four persons or things **2** : a golf match between two pairs of partners
four·square \-ˈskwaər\ *adj* **1** : SQUARE **2** : marked by boldness and conviction; *also* : FORTHRIGHT — **foursquare** *adv*
four·teen \ˈfōr-ˈtēn\ *n* : one more than 13 — **fourteen** *adj or pron* — **four·teenth** \-ˈtēnth\ *adj or n*
fourth \ˈfōrth\ *n* **1** : one that is number four in a countable series **2** : one of four equal parts of something — **fourth** *adj or adv*
fourth estate *n, often cap F&E* : the public press
4WD *abbr* four-wheel drive
four–wheel \ˌfōr-ˌhwēl\ *or* **four·wheeled** \-ˌhwēld\ *adj* : acting on or by means of four wheels of an automotive vehicle
[1]**fowl** \ˈfau̇l\ *n, pl* **fowl** *or* **fowls** **1** : BIRD **2** : a cock or hen of the domestic chicken; *also* : the flesh of these used as food
[2]**fowl** *vb* : to hunt wildfowl
[1]**fox** \ˈfäks\ *n, pl* **fox·es** *also* **fox** **1** : any of various flesh-eating mammals related to the wolves but smaller and with shorter legs and a more pointed muzzle; *also* : the fur of a fox **2** : a clever crafty person **3** *cap* : a member of an American Indian people formerly living in Wisconsin
[2]**fox** *vb* : TRICK, OUTWIT
foxed \ˈfäkst\ *adj* : discolored with yellowish brown stains
fox·glove \ˈfäks-ˌgləv\ *n* : a plant related to the snapdragons and grown for its showy spikes of dotted white or purple tubular flowers and as a source of digitalis
fox·hole \-ˌhōl\ *n* : a pit dug for protection against enemy fire
fox·hound \-ˌhau̇nd\ *n* : any of various large swift powerful hounds used in hunting foxes
fox terrier *n* : a small lively terrier that occurs in varieties with smooth dense coats or with harsh wiry coats

fox terrier

fox–trot \ˈfäks-ˌträt\ *n* **1** : a short broken slow trotting gait **2** : a ballroom dance in duple time
foxy \ˈfäk-sē\ *adj* **fox·i·er; -est** **1** : resembling or suggestive of a fox **2** : WILY; *also* : CLEVER
foy·er \ˈfȯi-ər, ˈfȯi-ˌ(y)ā\ *n* [F, lit., fireplace, fr. ML *focarius*, fr. L *focus* hearth] : LOBBY; *also* : an entrance hallway
FPC *abbr* fish protein concentrate
fpm *abbr* feet per minute
FPO *abbr* fleet post office
fps *abbr* feet per second
fr *abbr* **1** father **2** franc **3** friar **4** from
[1]**Fr** *abbr* French
[2]**Fr** *symbol* francium
fra·cas \ˈfrāk-əs, ˈfrak-\ *n, pl* **fra·cas·es** \-ə-səz\ [F, din, row, fr. It *fracasso*, fr. *fracassare* to shatter] : BRAWL

frac·tion \ˈfrak-shən\ *n* **1** : a number (as ½ or ¾) indicating one or more equal parts or the division of one number by another; *also* : a number (as 3.323) consisting of a whole number and a decimal **2** : FRAGMENT **3** : PORTION — **frac·tion·al** \-sh(ə-)nəl\ *adj* — **frac·tion·al·ly** \-ē\ *adv*
frac·tious \ˈfrak-shəs\ *adj* **1** : tending to be troublesome : hard to handle or control **2** : QUARRELSOME, IRRITABLE
frac·ture \ˈfrak-chər\ *n* **1** : a breaking of something and esp. a bone **2** : CRACK, CLEFT — **fracture** *vb*
frag·ile \ˈfraj-əl, -ˌīl\ *adj* : easily broken : DELICATE — **fra·gil·i·ty** \frə-ˈjil-ət-ē\ *n*
[1]**frag·ment** \ˈfrag-mənt\ *n* : a part broken off, detached, or incomplete
[2]**frag·ment** \-ˌment\ *vb* : to break into fragments — **frag·men·ta·tion** \ˌfrag-mən-ˈtā-shən, -ˌmən-\ *n*
frag·men·tary \ˈfrag-mən-ˌter-ē\ *adj* : made up of fragments : INCOMPLETE
fra·grant \ˈfrā-grənt\ *adj* : sweet or agreeable in smell — **fra·grance** \-grəns\ *n* — **fra·grant·ly** *adv*
frail \ˈfrāl\ *adj* **1** : morally or physically weak **2** : FRAGILE, DELICATE
frail·ty \ˈfrā(-ə)l-tē\ *n, pl* **frailties** **1** : the quality or state of being frail **2** : a fault due to weakness
[1]**frame** \ˈfrām\ *vb* **framed; fram·ing** **1** : PLAN, CONTRIVE **2** : FORMULATE **3** : SHAPE, CONSTRUCT **4** : DRAW UP ⟨~ a constitution⟩ **5** : to fit or adjust for a purpose : ARRANGE **6** : to provide with or enclose in a frame **7** : to make appear guilty — **fram·er** *n*
[2]**frame** *n* **1** : something made of parts fitted and joined together **2** : the physical makeup of the body **3** : an arrangement of structural parts that gives form or support **4** : a supporting or enclosing border or open case (as for a window or picture) **5** : a particular state or disposition (as of mind) : MOOD **6** : one picture of a series (as on a length of motion-picture film or of television images) **7** : FRAME-UP
[3]**frame** *adj* : having a wood frame
frame–up \ˈfrām-ˌəp\ *n* : a scheme to cause an innocent person to be accused of a crime; *also* : the action resulting from such a scheme
frame·work \-ˌwərk\ *n* : a basic supporting part or structure
franc \ˈfraŋk\ *n* — see MONEY table
fran·chise \ˈfran-ˌchīz\ *n* [ME, fr. OF, fr. *franchir* to free, fr. *franc* free] **1** : a special privilege granted to an individual or group ⟨a ~ to operate a ferry⟩ **2** : a constitutional or statutory right or privilege; *esp* : the right to vote
fran·chi·see \ˌfran-ˌchī-ˈzē, -chə-\ *n* : one who is granted a marketing franchise
fran·chis·er \ˈfran-ˌchī-zər\ *n* **1** : FRANCHISEE **2** : FRANCHISOR
fran·chi·sor \ˌfran-ˌchī-ˈzȯr, -chə-\ *n* : one that grants a marketing franchise
fran·ci·um \ˈfran-sē-əm\ *n* : a radioactive metallic chemical element — see ELEMENT table
Fran·co–Amer·i·can \ˌfraŋ-kō-ə-ˈmer-ə-kən\ *n* : an American of French or esp. French-Canadian descent — **Franco–American** *adj*
fran·gi·ble \ˈfran-jə-bəl\ *adj* : BREAKABLE — **fran·gi·bil·i·ty** \ˌfran-jə-ˈbil-ət-ē\ *n*
[1]**frank** \ˈfraŋk\ *adj* : marked by free, forthright, and sincere expression — **frank·ly** *adv* — **frank·ness** *n*
[2]**frank** *vb* : to mark (a piece of mail) with an official signature or sign indicating that it can be mailed free; *also* : to mail in this manner
[3]**frank** *n* **1** : a signature, mark, or stamp on a piece of mail indicating that it can be mailed free **2** : the privilege of sending mail free of charge
Fran·ken·stein \ˈfraŋ-kən-ˌstīn\ *n* **1** : a creation that ruins its originator **2** : a monster in the shape of a man
frank·furt·er *or* **frank·fort·er** \ˈfraŋk-fə(r)t-ər, -ˌfərt-\ *or*

frank·furt *or* **frank·fort** \-fərt\ *n* : a seasoned sausage (as of beef or beef and pork)

frank·in·cense \ˈfraŋ-kən-ˌsens\ *n* : a fragrant resin burned as incense

fran·tic \ˈfrant-ik\ *adj* : wildly excited — **fran·ti·cal·ly** \-i-k(ə-)lē\ *adv* — **fran·tic·ly** \-i-klē\ *adv*

frap·pé \fra-ˈpā\ *or* **frappe** \ˈfrap, fra-ˈpā\ [F *frappé,* fr. pp. of *frapper* to strike, chill] *n* **1** : an iced or frozen mixture or drink **2** : a thick milk shake — **frap·pé** *or* **frap·pe** \fra-ˈpā\ *adj*

fra·ter·nal \frə-ˈtərn-ᵊl\ *adj* **1** : of, relating to, or involving brothers **2** : of, relating to, or being a fraternity or society **3** : FRIENDLY, BROTHERLY — **fra·ter·nal·ly** \-ē\ *adv*

fra·ter·ni·ty \frə-ˈtər-nət-ē\ *n, pl* **-ties** **1** : a social, honorary, or professional organization; *esp* : a social club of male college students **2** : BROTHERLINESS, BROTHERHOOD **3** : men of the same class, profession, or tastes

frat·er·nize \ˈfrat-ər-ˌnīz\ *vb* **-nized; -niz·ing** **1** : to mingle as friends **2** : to associate on intimate terms with citizens or troops of a hostile nation — **frat·er·ni·za·tion** \ˌfrat-ər-nə-ˈzā-shən\ *n*

frat·ri·cide \ˈfra-trə-ˌsīd\ *n* **1** : one that kills his brother or sister **2** : the act of a fratricide — **frat·ri·cid·al** \ˌfra-trə-ˈsīd-ᵊl\ *adj*

fraud \ˈfrȯd\ *n* **1** : DECEIT, TRICKERY **2** : TRICK **3** : IMPOSTOR, CHEAT

fraud·u·lent \ˈfrȯ-jə-lənt\ *adj* : characterized by, based on, or done by fraud : DECEITFUL — **fraud·u·lent·ly** *adv*

fraught \ˈfrȯt\ *adj* : full of or accompanied by something specified ⟨~ with danger⟩

[1]**fray** \ˈfrā\ *n* : BRAWL, FIGHT; *also* : DISPUTE

[2]**fray** *vb* **1** : to wear (as an edge of cloth) by rubbing **2** : to separate the threads at the edge of **3** : STRAIN, IRRITATE ⟨~*ed* nerves⟩

fraz·zle \ˈfraz-əl\ *vb* **fraz·zled; fraz·zling** \ˈfraz-(ə-)liŋ\ **1** : FRAY **2** : to put in a state of extreme physical or nervous fatigue — **frazzle** *n*

[1]**freak** \ˈfrēk\ *n* **1** : WHIM, CAPRICE **2** : a strange, abnormal, or unusual person or thing **3** : a person who uses an illicit drug **4** : an ardent enthusiast — **freak·ish** *adj*

[2]**freak** *vb* **1** : to experience or appear to experience the effects (as hallucinations) of taking illicit drugs — often used with *out* **2** : to disturb one's calmness of mind : UPSET — often used with *out* — **freak–out** \ˈfrēk-ˌau̇t\ *n*

freck·le \ˈfrek-əl\ *n* : a brownish spot on the skin — **freckle** *vb*

[1]**free** \ˈfrē\ *adj* **fre·er; fre·est** **1** : having liberty **2** : not controlled by others : INDEPENDENT; *also* : not allowing slavery **3** : made or done voluntarily : SPONTANEOUS **4** : released or not suffering from something unpleasant **5** : not subject to a duty, tax, or other charge **6** : not obstructed : CLEAR **7** : not being used or occupied **8** : not fastened **9** : LAVISH **10** : OPEN, FRANK **11** : given without charge **12** : not literal or exact **13** : not restricted by conventional forms — **free·ly** *adv*

[2]**free** *vb* **freed; free·ing** **1** : to set free **2** : RELIEVE, RID **3** : DISENTANGLE, CLEAR **syn** release, liberate, discharge, emancipate, loose

[3]**free** *adv* **1** : FREELY **2** : without charge

free·bie *or* **free·bee** \ˈfrē-bē\ *n* : something given without charge

free·board \ˈfrē-ˌbōrd\ *n* : the vertical distance between the waterline and the upper edge of the side of a boat

free·boo·ter \ˈfrē-ˌbüt-ər\ *n* [D *vrijbuiter,* fr. *vrijbuit* plunder, fr. *vrij* free + *buit* booty] : PLUNDERER, PIRATE

free·born \-ˈbȯrn\ *adj* **1** : not born in vassalage or slavery **2** : of, relating to, or befitting one that is freeborn

freed·man \ˈfrēd-mən, -ˌman\ *n* : a man freed from slavery

free·dom \ˈfrēd-əm\ *n* **1** : the quality or state of being free : INDEPENDENCE **2** : EXEMPTION, RELEASE **3** : EASE, FACILITY **4** : FRANKNESS **5** : unrestricted use **6** : a political right; *also* : FRANCHISE, PRIVILEGE

free–for–all \ˈfrē-fə-ˌrȯl\ *n* : a competition or fight open to all comers and usu. with no rules : BRAWL — **free–for–all** *adj*

free·hand \ˈfrē-ˌhand\ *adj* : done without mechanical aids or devices

free·hold \ˌfrē-ˌhōld\ *n* : ownership of an estate for life usu. with the right to bequeath it to one's heirs; *also* : an estate thus owned — **free·hold·er** *n*

free lance *n* : one who pursues a profession (as writing) without long-term contractual commitments to any one employer — **free–lance** *adj or vb*

free–living \ˈfrē-ˈliv-iŋ\ *adj* : being neither parasitic nor symbiotic ⟨~ organisms⟩

free·load \ˈfrē-ˌlōd\ *vb* : to impose upon another's generosity or hospitality — **free·load·er** *n*

free love *n* : the practice of living openly with one of the opposite sex without marriage

free·man \ˈfrē-mən, -ˌman\ *n* **1** : one who has civil or political liberty **2** : one having the full rights of a citizen

Free·ma·son \-ˌmās-ᵊn\ *n* : a member of a secret fraternal society called Free and Accepted Masons — **Free·ma·son·ry** \-rē\ *n*

free·stand·ing \ˈfrē-ˈstan-diŋ\ *adj* : standing alone or on its own foundation

free·stone \ˈfrē-ˌstōn\ *n* **1** : a stone that may be cut freely without splitting **2** : a fruit stone to which the flesh does not cling; *also* : a fruit (as a peach or cherry) having such a stone

free·think·er \-ˈthiŋ-kər\ *n* : one who forms opinions on the basis of reason independently of authority; *esp* : one who doubts or denies religious dogma — **free·think·ing** *n or adj*

free trade *n* : trade between nations without restrictions (as high taxes on imports)

free verse *n* : verse whose meter is irregular or whose rhythm is not metrical

free·way \ˈfrē-ˌwā\ *n* : an expressway with fully controlled access

free·wheel \-ˈhwēl\ *vb* : to move, live, or drift along freely or irresponsibly

free·will \ˌfrē-ˌwil\ *adj* : VOLUNTARY

free will *n* : voluntary choice or decision

[1]**freeze** \ˈfrēz\ *vb* **froze** \ˈfrōz\; **fro·zen** \ˈfrōz-ᵊn\; **freez·ing** **1** : to harden or cause to harden into a solid (as ice) by loss of heat **2** : to chill or become chilled with cold **3** : to become coldly formal in manner; *also* : to act toward in a stiff and formal way **4** : to damage by frost **5** : to adhere solidly by freezing **6** : to cause to grip tightly or remain in immovable contact **7** : to become clogged with ice **8** : to become fixed or motionless **9** : to fix at a certain stage or level

[2]**freeze** *n* **1** : a state of weather marked by low temperature **2** : an act or instance of freezing ⟨a price ~⟩ **3** : the state of being frozen

freeze–dry \ˈfrēz-ˌdrī\ *vb* : to dry in a frozen state under vacuum esp. for preservation — **freeze–dried** *adj*

freez·er \ˈfrē-zər\ *n* : a compartment, device, or room for freezing food or keeping it frozen

[1]**freight** \ˈfrāt\ *n* **1** : payment for carrying goods **2** : CARGO **3** : BURDEN **4** : the carrying of goods by a common carrier **5** : a train that carries freight

[2]**freight** *vb* **1** : to load with goods for transportation **2** : BURDEN, CHARGE **3** : to ship or transport by freight

freight·er \ˈfrāt-ər\ *n* : a ship or airplane used chiefly to carry freight

French \ˈfrench\ *n* **1** : the language of France **2 French** *pl*

\ə\abut \ᵊ\kitten \ər\further \a\ash \ā\ace \ä\cot, cart \au̇\out \ch\chin \e\bet \ē\easy \g\go \i\hit \ī\ice \j\job \ŋ\sing \ō\go \ȯ\law \ȯi\boy \th\thin \t͟h\the \ü\loot \u̇\foot \y\yet \zh\vision *see also* Pronunciation Symbols page

: the people of France — **French** *adj* — **French·man** \-mən\ *n* — **French·wom·an** \-ˌwu̇m-ən\ *n*

french fry *vb, often cap 1st F* : to fry (as strips of potato) in deep fat until brown — **french fry** *n, often cap 1st F*

French horn *n* : a curved brass instrument with a funnel-shaped mouthpiece and a flaring bell

fre·net·ic \fri-ˈnet-ik\ *adj* : FRENZIED, FRANTIC — **fre·net·i·cal·ly** \-i-k(ə-)lē\ *adv*

fren·zy \ˈfren-zē\ *n, pl* **frenzies** : temporary madness or a violently agitated state — **fren·zied** \-zēd\ *adj*

freq *abbr* frequency, frequent, frequently

fre·quen·cy \ˈfrē-kwən-sē\ *n, pl* **-cies 1** : the fact or condition of occurring frequently **2** : rate of occurrence **3** : the number of cycles per second of an alternating current **4** : the number of waves (as of sound or electromagnetic energy) that pass a fixed point each second

frequency modulation *n* : variation of the frequency of a carrier wave according to another signal; *also* : a broadcasting system using such modulation

¹fre·quent \ˈfrē-kwənt\ *adj* **1** : happening often or at short intervals **2** : HABITUAL — **fre·quent·ly** *adv*

²fre·quent \frē-ˈkwent, ˈfrē-kwənt\ *vb* : to associate with, be in, or resort to habitually — **fre·quent·er** *n*

fres·co \ˈfres-kō\ *n, pl* **frescoes** [It, fr. *fresco* fresh] : the art of painting on fresh plaster; *also* : a painting done by this method

fresh \ˈfresh\ *adj* **1** : not salt ⟨~ water⟩ **2** : PURE, INVIGORATING **3** : fairly strong : BRISK ⟨~ breeze⟩ **4** : not altered by processing (as freezing or canning) **5** : VIGOROUS, REFRESHED **6** : not stale, sour, or decayed ⟨~ bread⟩ **7** : not faded **8** : not worn or rumpled **9** : experienced, made, or received newly or anew **10** : ADDITIONAL, ANOTHER ⟨made a ~ start⟩ **11** : ORIGINAL, VIVID **12** : INEXPERIENCED **13** : newly come or arrived ⟨~ from school⟩ **14** : IMPUDENT — **fresh·ly** *adv* — **fresh·ness** *n*

fresh·en \ˈfresh-ən\ *vb* **fresh·ened; fresh·en·ing** \-(ə-)niŋ\ : to make, grow, or become fresh

fresh·et \ˈfresh-ət\ *n* : an overflowing of a stream (as by heavy rains)

fresh·man \ˈfresh-mən\ *n* **1** : BEGINNER, NEWCOMER **2** : a 1st-year student

fresh·wa·ter \ˈfresh-ˌwȯt-ər, -ˌwät-\ *adj* : of, relating to, or living in fresh water

¹fret \ˈfret\ *vb* **fret·ted; fret·ting** [ME *freten* to devour, fret, fr. OE *fretan* to devour] **1** : to become irritated : WORRY, VEX **2** : WEAR, CORRODE; *also* : FRAY **3** : RUB, CHAFE **4** : to make by wearing away **5** : GRATE ⟨the siren *fretted* at their nerves⟩ **6** : AGITATE, RIPPLE

²fret *n* : an irritated or worried state ⟨in a ~⟩

³fret *n* : ornamental work esp. of straight lines in symmetrical patterns

⁴fret *n* : one of a series of ridges across the fingerboard of a stringed musical instrument — **fret·ted** *adj*

fret·ful \ˈfret-fəl\ *adj* : IRRITABLE — **fret·ful·ly** \-ē\ *adv* — **fret·ful·ness** *n*

fret·saw \-ˌsȯ\ *n* : a narrow-bladed saw used for cutting curved outlines

fret·work \-ˌwərk\ *n* **1** : decoration consisting of frets **2** : ornamental openwork or work in relief

Fri *abbr* Friday

fri·a·ble \ˈfrī-ə-bəl\ *adj* : easily pulverized ⟨~ soil⟩

fri·ar \ˈfrī(-ə)r\ *n* [ME *frere, fryer,* fr. OF *frere,* lit., brother, fr. L *frater*] : a member of a mendicant religious order

fri·ary \ˈfrī(-ə)r-ē\ *n, pl* **-ar·ies** : a monastery of friars

¹fric·as·see \ˈfrik-ə-ˌsē, ˌfrik-ə-ˈsē\ *n* : a dish made of meat (as chicken or veal) cut into pieces and stewed in a gravy

²fricassee *vb* **-seed; -see·ing** : to cook as a fricassee

fric·tion \ˈfrik-shən\ *n* **1** : the rubbing of one body against another **2** : the force that resists motion between bodies in contact **3** : clash in opinions between persons or groups : DISAGREEMENT — **fric·tion·al** *adj*

friction tape *n* : a usu. cloth tape impregnated with insulating material and an adhesive and used esp. to protect and insulate electrical conductors

Fri·day \ˈfrīd-ē\ *n* : the sixth day of the week

fried·cake \ˈfrīd-ˌkāk\ *n* : DOUGHNUT, CRULLER

friend \ˈfrend\ *n* **1** : a person attached to another by respect or affection **2** : ACQUAINTANCE **3** : one who is not hostile **4** : one who supports or favors something ⟨a ~ of art⟩ **5** *cap* : a member of the Society of Friends : QUAKER — **friend·less** \ˈfren-(d)ləs\ *adj* — **friend·li·ness** \ˈfren-(d)lē-nəs\ *n* — **friend·ly** *adj* — **friend·ship** \ˈfren(d)-ˌship\ *n*

frieze \ˈfrēz\ *n* : an ornamental often sculptured band extending around something (as a building or room)

frig·ate \ˈfrig-ət\ *n* **1** : a square-rigged warship **2** : a warship smaller than a destroyer used for escort and patrol duties

fright \ˈfrīt\ *n* **1** : sudden terror : ALARM **2** : something that is ugly or shocking

fright·en \ˈfrīt-ᵊn\ *vb* **fright·ened; fright·en·ing** \ˈfrīt-(ᵊ-)niŋ\ **1** : to make afraid **2** : to drive away or out by frightening **3** : to become frightened — **fright·en·ing·ly** *adv*

fright·ful \ˈfrīt-fəl\ *adj* **1** : TERRIFYING **2** : STARTLING **3** : EXTREME ⟨~ thirst⟩ — **fright·ful·ly** \-ē\ *adv* — **fright·ful·ness** *n*

frig·id \ˈfrij-əd\ *adj* **1** : intensely cold **2** : lacking warmth or ardor : INDIFFERENT **3** : abnormally averse to or unable to achieve orgasm during sexual intercourse — used esp. of women — **fri·gid·i·ty** \frij-ˈid-ət-ē\ *n*

frigid zone *n* : the area or region between the arctic circle and the north pole or between the antarctic circle and the south pole

frill \ˈfril\ *n* **1** : a gathered, pleated, or ruffled edging **2** : an ornamental addition : something unessential — **frilly** \-ē\ *adj*

fringe \ˈfrinj\ *n* **1** : an ornamental border consisting of short threads or strips hanging from an edge or band **2** : something that resembles a fringe : BORDER **3** : something on the margin of an activity, process, or subject matter — **fringe** *vb*

fringe benefit *n* **1** : an employment benefit paid for by an employer without affecting basic wage rates **2** : any additional benefit

frip·pery \ˈfrip-(ə-)rē\ *n, pl* **-per·ies** [MF *friperie*] **1** : cheap showy finery **2** : pretentious display

frisk \ˈfrisk\ *vb* **1** : to leap, skip, or dance in a lively or playfuly way : GAMBOL **2** : to search (a person) esp. for concealed weapons by running the hand rapidly over the clothing

frisky \ˈfris-kē\ *adj* **frisk·i·er; -est** : FROLICSOME — **frisk·i·ly** \ˈfris-kə-lē\ *adv* — **frisk·i·ness** \-kē-nəs\ *n*

¹frit·ter \ˈfrit-ər\ *n* : a small lump of fried batter often containing fruit or meat

²fritter *vb* **1** : to reduce or waste piecemeal **2** : to break into small fragments

fritz \ˈfrits\ *n* : a state of disorder or disrepair — used in the phrase *on the fritz*

friv·o·lous \ˈfriv-(ə-)ləs\ *adj* **1** : of little importance : TRIVIAL **2** : lacking in seriousness — **fri·vol·i·ty** \friv-ˈäl-ət-ē\ *n* — **friv·o·lous·ly** *adv*

frizz \ˈfriz\ *vb* : to curl in small tight curls — **frizz** *n* — **frizzy** *adj*

¹friz·zle \ˈfriz-əl\ *vb* **friz·zled; friz·zling** \-(ə-)liŋ\ : FRIZZ, CURL — **frizzle** *n*

²frizzle *vb* **friz·zled; friz·zling 1** : to fry until crisp and curled **2** : to cook with a sizzling noise

fro \ˈfrō\ *adv* : BACK, AWAY — used in the phrase *to and fro*

frock \ˈfräk\ *n* **1** : an outer garment worn by monks and friars **2** : an outer garment worn esp. by men **3** : a woman's or girl's dress

frock coat *n* : a man's usu. double-breasted coat with knee-length skirts

frog \ˈfrȯg, ˈfräg\ *n* **1** : any of various largely aquatic smooth-skinned tailless leaping amphibians **2** : an ornamental braiding for fastening the front of a garment by a loop through which a button passes **3** : a condition in the throat causing hoarseness **4** : a small holder (as of metal, glass, or plastic) with perforations or spikes that is placed in a bowl or vase to keep cut flowers in position

frog·man \ˈfrȯg-ˌman, ˈfräg-, -mən\ *n* : a swimmer equipped to work underwater for long periods of time

[1]**frol·ic** \ˈfräl-ik\ *vb* **frol·icked; frol·ick·ing 1** : to make merry **2** : to play about happily : ROMP

[2]**frolic** *n* **1** : a playful or mischievous action **2** : FUN, MERRIMENT — **frol·ic·some** \-səm\ *adj*

from \(ˈ)frəm, ˈfräm\ *prep* **1** — used to show a starting point ⟨a letter ~ home⟩ **2** — used to show removal or separation ⟨subtract 3 ~ 9⟩ **3** — used to show a material, source, or cause ⟨suffering ~ a cold⟩

frond \ˈfränd\ *n* : a usu. large divided leaf esp. of a fern or palm tree

[1]**front** \ˈfrənt\ *n* **1** : FOREHEAD; *also* : the whole face **2** : external and often feigned appearance **3** : a region of active fighting; *also* : a sphere of activity **4** : a political coalition **5** : the side of a building containing the main entrance **6** : the forward part or surface **7** : FRONTAGE **8** : a boundary between two dissimilar air masses **9** : a position directly before or ahead of something else **10** : a person, group, or thing used to mask the identity or true character or activity of the actual controlling agent

[2]**front** *vb* **1** : FACE **2** : to serve as a front **3** : CONFRONT

front·age \ˈfrənt-ij\ *n* **1** : a piece of land that fronts something (as on a river or road) **2** : the front side of a building **3** : the extent or measure of a frontage

front·al \ˈfrənt-ᵊl\ *adj* **1** : of, relating to, or next to the forehead **2** : of, relating to, or directed at the front ⟨a ~ attack⟩ — **fron·tal·ly** \-ᵊl-ē\ *adv*

fron·tier \ˌfrən-ˈtiər\ *n* **1** : a border between two countries **2** : a region that forms the margin of settled territory **3** : the outer limits of knowledge or achievement ⟨the ~*s* of science⟩ — **fron·tiers·man** \-ˈtiərz-mən\ *n*

fron·tis·piece \ˈfrənt-ə-ˌspēs\ *n* : an illustration preceding and usu. facing the title page of a book

front man *n* : a person serving as a front or figurehead

front·ward \ˈfrənt-wərd\ *or* **front·wards** \-wərdz\ *adv or adj* : toward the front

[1]**frost** \ˈfrȯst\ *n* **1** : freezing temperature **2** : a covering of tiny ice crystals on a cold surface — **frosty** *adj*

[2]**frost** *vb* **1** : to cover with frost **2** : to put icing on (as a cake) **3** : to produce a slightly roughened surface on (as glass) **4** : to injure or kill by frost

[1]**frost·bite** \ˈfrȯs(t)-ˌbīt\ *vb* **-bit** \-ˌbit\; **-bit·ten** \-ˌbit-ᵊn\; **-bit·ing** \-ˌbīt-iŋ\ : to injure by frost or frostbite

[2]**frostbite** *n* : the freezing or the local effect of a partial freezing of some part of the body

frost heave *n* : an upthrust of pavement caused by freezing of moist soil

frost·ing \ˈfrȯ-stiŋ\ *n* **1** : ICING **2** : dull finish on metal or glass

froth \ˈfrȯth\ *n, pl* **froths** \ˈfrȯths, ˈfrȯt͟hz\ **1** : bubbles formed in or on a liquid **2** : something light or frivolous — **frothy** *adj*

frou·frou \ˈfrü-frü\ *n* [F] **1** : a rustling esp. of a woman's skirts **2** : frilly ornamentation esp. in women's clothing

fro·ward \ˈfrō-(w)ərd\ *adj* : DISOBEDIENT, WILLFUL

frown \ˈfrau̇n\ *vb* **1** : to wrinkle the forehead (as in anger, displeasure, or thought) : SCOWL **2** : to look with disapproval **3** : to express with a frown — **frown** *n*

frow·sy *or* **frow·zy** \ˈfrau̇-zē\ *adj* **frow·si·er** *or* **frow·zi·er; -est** : having a slovenly or uncared-for appearance

froze *past of* FREEZE

fro·zen \ˈfrōz-ᵊn\ *adj* **1** : treated, affected, or crusted over by freezing **2** : subject to long and severe cold **3** : expressing or characterized by cold unfriendliness **4** : incapable of being changed, moved, or undone : FIXED ⟨~ wages⟩ **5** : not available for present use ⟨~ capital⟩

FRS *abbr* Federal Reserve System

frt *abbr* freight

fruc·ti·fy \ˈfrək-tə-ˌfī, ˈfru̇k-\ *vb* **-fied; -fy·ing 1** : to bear fruit **2** : to make fruitful or productive

fru·gal \ˈfrü-gəl\ *adj* : ECONOMICAL, THRIFTY — **fru·gal·i·ty** \frü-ˈgal-ət-ē\ *n* — **fru·gal·ly** \ˈfrü-gə-lē\ *adv*

[1]**fruit** \ˈfrüt\ *n* [ME, fr. OF, fr. L *fructus* fruit, use, fr. *frui* to enjoy, have the use of] **1** : a usu. useful product of plant growth; *esp* : a usu. edible and sweet reproductive body (as a strawberry or apple) of a seed plant **2** : a product of fertilization in a plant; *esp* : the ripe ovary of a seed plant with its contents and appendages **3** : CONSEQUENCE, RESULT — **fruit·ed** \-əd\ *adj*

[2]**fruit** *vb* : to bear or cause to bear fruit

fruit·cake \ˈfrüt-ˌkāk\ *n* : a rich cake containing nuts, dried or candied fruits, and spices

fruit fly *n* : any of various small two-winged flies whose larvae feed on fruit or decaying vegetable matter

fruit·ful \ˈfrüt-fəl\ *adj* **1** : yielding or producing fruit **2** : very productive ⟨a ~ soil⟩; *also* : bringing results ⟨a ~ idea⟩ — **fruit·ful·ly** \-fə-lē\ *adv* — **fruit·ful·ness** *n*

fru·ition \frü-ˈish-ən\ *n* **1** : ENJOYMENT **2** : the state of bearing fruit **3** : REALIZATION, ACCOMPLISHMENT

fruit·less \ˈfrüt-ləs\ *adj* **1** : not bearing fruit **2** : producing no good results : UNSUCCESSFUL ⟨a ~ attempt⟩ — **fruit·less·ly** *adv*

fruity \ˈfrüt-ē\ *adj* **fruit·i·er; -est** : resembling a fruit esp. in flavor

frumpy \ˈfrəm-pē\ *adj* **frump·i·er; -est** : DRAB, DOWDY

frus·trate \ˈfrəs-ˌtrāt\ *vb* **frus·trat·ed; frus·trat·ing 1** : to balk in an endeavor : BLOCK **2** : to bring to nothing **3** : to fill with dissatisfaction due to unresolved problems or unfulfilled needs — **frus·trat·ing·ly** \-iŋ-lē\ *adv* — **frus·tra·tion** \ˌfrəs-ˈtrā-shən\ *n*

frus·tum \ˈfrəs-təm\ *n, pl* **frustums** *or* **frus·ta** \-tə\ : the part of a cone or pyramid formed by cutting off the top by a plane parallel to the base

frwy *abbr* freeway

[1]**fry** \ˈfrī\ *vb* **fried; fry·ing 1** : to cook in a pan or on a griddle over a fire esp. with the use of fat **2** : to undergo frying

[2]**fry** *n, pl* **fries 1** : a dish of something fried **2** : a social gathering where fried food is eaten

[3]**fry** *n, pl* **fry 1** : recently hatched fishes; *also* : very small adult fishes **2** : members of a group or class ⟨small ~⟩

fry·er \ˈfrī(-ə)r\ *n* **1** : something (as a young chicken) suitable for frying **2** : a deep utensil for frying foods

FSLIC *abbr* Federal Savings and Loan Insurance Corporation

ft *abbr* **1** feet; foot **2** fort

FTC *abbr* Federal Trade Commission

fuch·sia \ˈfyü-shə\ *n* **1** : any of a genus of shrubs related to the evening primrose and grown for their showy nodding often red or purple flowers **2** : a vivid reddish purple

fud·dle \ˈfəd-ᵊl\ *vb* **fud·dled; fud·dling** : MUDDLE, CONFUSE

fud·dy–dud·dy \ˈfəd-ē-ˌdəd-ē\ *n, pl* **-dies** : a person who is old-fashioned, pompous, unimaginative, or fussy

[1]**fudge** \ˈfəj\ *vb* **fudged; fudg·ing 1** : to cheat or exaggerate by blurring or overstepping a boundary **2** : to avoid coming to grips with something

[2]**fudge** *n* **1** : NONSENSE **2** : a soft creamy candy of milk, sugar, butter, and flavoring

[1]**fu·el** \ˈfyü-əl\ *n* : a substance (as coal) used to produce

heat or power by combustion; *also* : a substance from which nuclear energy can be liberated

²fuel *vb* **-eled** *or* **-elled; -el·ing** *or* **-el·ling** : to provide with or take in fuel

fuel cell *n* : a device that continuously changes the chemical energy of a fuel directly into electrical energy

¹fu·gi·tive \ˈfyü-jət-iv\ *n* **1** : one who flees or tries to escape **2** : something elusive or hard to find

²fugitive *adj* **1** : running away or trying to escape **2** : likely to vanish suddenly : not fixed or lasting

fugue \ˈfyüg\ *n* **1** : a musical composition in which different parts successively repeat the theme **2** : a disturbed state of consciousness characterized by acts that are not recalled upon recovery

füh·rer *or* **fueh·rer** \ˈfyu̇r-ər, ˈfir-\ *n* : LEADER — used chiefly of the leader of the German Nazis

¹-ful \fəl\ *adj suffix, sometimes* **-ful·ler;** *sometimes* **-ful·lest** **1** : full of ⟨event*ful*⟩ **2** : characterized by ⟨peace*ful*⟩ **3** : having the qualities of ⟨master*ful*⟩ **4** : tending, given, or liable to ⟨mourn*ful*⟩

²-ful \ˌfu̇l\ *n suffix* : number or quantity that fills or would fill ⟨room*ful*⟩

ful·crum \ˈfu̇l-krəm, ˈfəl-\ *n, pl* **ful·crums** *or* **ful·cra** \-krə\ [LL, fr. L, bedpost] : the support on which a lever turns

ful·fill *or* **ful·fil** \fu̇l-ˈfil\ *vb* **ful·filled; ful·fill·ing** **1** : to put into effect **2** : to bring to an end **3** : SATISFY — **ful·fill·ment** *n*

¹full \ˈfu̇l\ *adj* **1** : FILLED **2** : complete esp. in detail, number, or duration **3** : having all the distinguishing characteristics ⟨a ~ member⟩ **4** : MAXIMUM **5** : rounded in outline ⟨a ~ figure⟩ **6** : possessing or containing an abundance ⟨~ of wrinkles⟩ **7** : having an abundance of material ⟨a ~ skirt⟩ **8** : satisfied esp. with food or drink **9** : having volume or depth of sound **10** : completely occupied with a thought or plan — **full·ness** *also* **ful·ness** \ˈfu̇l-nəs\ *n*

²full *adv* **1** : VERY, EXTREMELY **2** : ENTIRELY **3** : STRAIGHT, SQUARELY ⟨hit him ~ in the face⟩

³full *n* **1** : the utmost extent **2** : the highest or fullest state or degree **3** : the requisite or complete amount

⁴full *vb* : to shrink and thicken (woolen cloth) by moistening, heating, and pressing — **full·er** *n*

full·back \ˈfu̇l-ˌbak\ *n* : a football back stationed between the halfbacks

full–blood·ed \ˈfu̇l-ˈbləd-əd\ *adj* : of unmixed ancestry : PUREBRED

full–blown \-ˈblōn\ *adj* **1** : being at the height of bloom **2** : fully mature or developed

full–bod·ied \-ˈbäd-ēd\ *adj* : marked by richness and fullness

full dress *n* : the style of dress worn for ceremonial or formal occasions

full–fledged \ˈfu̇l-ˈflejd\ *adj* **1** : fully developed **2** : having full plumage

full house *n* : a poker hand containing three of a kind and a pair

full moon *n* : the moon with its whole disk illuminated

full–scale \ˈfu̇l-ˈskāl\ *adj* **1** : identical to an original in proportion and size ⟨~ drawing⟩ **2** : involving full use of available resources ⟨a ~ revolt⟩

full tilt *adv* : at high speed

full–time \ˈfu̇l-ˈtīm\ *adj or adv* : involving or working a full or regular schedule

ful·ly \ˈfu̇l-ē\ *adv* **1** : in a full manner or degree : COMPLETELY **2** : at least

ful·mi·nate \ˈfu̇l-mə-ˌnāt, ˈfəl-\ *vb* **-nat·ed; -nat·ing** [ME *fulminaten,* fr. ML *fulminare,* fr. L, to flash with lightning, strike with lightning, fr. *fulmen* lightning] **1** : to utter or send out censure or invective : condemn severely **2** : EXPLODE — **ful·mi·na·tion** \ˌfu̇l-mə-ˈnā-shən, ˌfəl-\ *n*

ful·some \ˈfu̇l-səm\ *adj* **1** : COPIOUS, ABUNDANT ⟨~ detail⟩ **2** : OFFENSIVE, DISGUSTING **3** : excessively flattering ⟨~ praise⟩

fu·ma·role \ˈfyü-mə-ˌrōl\ *n* : a hole in a volcanic region from which hot gases issue

fum·ble \ˈfəm-bəl\ *vb* **fum·bled; fum·bling** \-b(ə-)liŋ\ **1** : to grope about clumsily **2** : to fail to hold, catch, or handle properly — **fumble** *n*

¹fume \ˈfyüm\ *n* : a usu. irritating smoke, vapor, or gas

²fume *vb* **fumed; fum·ing** **1** : to treat with fumes **2** : to give off fumes **3** : to express anger or annoyance

fu·mi·gant \ˈfyü-mi-gənt\ *n* : a substance used for fumigation

fu·mi·gate \ˈfyü-mə-ˌgāt\ *vb* **-gat·ed; -gat·ing** : to treat with fumes to disinfect or destroy pests — **fu·mi·ga·tion** \ˌfyü-mə-ˈgā-shən\ *n* — **fu·mi·ga·tor** \ˈfyü-mə-ˌgāt-ər\ *n*

fun \ˈfən\ *n* [E dial. *fun* to hoax] **1** : something that provides amusement or enjoyment **2** : ENJOYMENT

¹func·tion \ˈfəŋk-shən\ *n* **1** : OCCUPATION **2** : special purpose **3** : the particular purpose for which a person or thing is specially fitted or used or for which a thing exists ⟨the ~ of a knife is cutting⟩; *also* : the natural or proper action of a bodily part in a living thing ⟨the ~ of the heart⟩ **4** : a formal ceremony or social affair **5** : the mathematical relationship that assigns to each element of a set one and only one element of the same or another set **6** : a variable (as a quality, trait, or measurement) that depends on and varies with another ⟨height is a ~ of age in children⟩ — **func·tion·al** \-sh(ə-)nəl\ *adj* — **func·tion·al·ly** \-ē\ *adv* — **func·tion·less** *adj*

²function *vb* **func·tioned; func·tion·ing** \-sh(ə-)niŋ\ **1** : SERVE **2** : OPERATE, WORK

func·tion·ary \ˈfəŋk-shə-ˌner-ē\ *n, pl* **-ar·ies** : one who performs a certain function; *esp* : OFFICIAL

function word *n* : a word (as a preposition, auxiliary verb, or conjunction) expressing the grammatical relationship between other words

¹fund \ˈfənd\ *n* [L *fundus* bottom, piece of landed property] **1** : STORE, SUPPLY **2** : a sum of money or resources intended for a special purpose **3** *pl* : available money **4** : an organization administering a special fund

²fund *vb* **1** : to provide funds for **2** : to convert (a short-term obligation) into a long-term interest-bearing debt

fun·da·men·tal \ˌfən-də-ˈment-ᵊl\ *adj* **1** : serving as an origin : PRIMARY **2** : BASIC, ESSENTIAL **3** : RADICAL ⟨~ change⟩ **4** : of central importance : PRINCIPAL — **fundamental** *n* — **fun·da·men·tal·ly** \-ē\ *adv*

fun·da·men·tal·ism \-ˌiz-əm\ *n, often cap* : a Protestant religious movement emphasizing the literal infallibility of the Bible — **fun·da·men·tal·ist** \-əst\ *adj or n*

¹fu·ner·al \ˈfyün-(ə-)rəl\ *adj* **1** : of, relating to, or constituting a funeral **2** : FUNEREAL 2

²funeral *n* : the ceremonies held for a dead person usu. before burial

fu·ner·ary \ˈfyü-nə-ˌrer-ē\ *adj* : of, used for, or associated with burial

fu·ne·re·al \fyü-ˈnir-ē-əl\ *adj* **1** : of or relating to a funeral **2** : suggesting a funeral

fun·gi·cide \ˈfən-jə-ˌsīd, ˈfəŋ-gə-\ *n* : an agent that kills or checks the growth of fungi — **fun·gi·cid·al** \ˌfən-jə-ˈsīd-ᵊl, ˌfəŋ-gə-\ *adj*

fun·gus \ˈfəŋ-gəs\ *n, pl* **fun·gi** \ˈfən-ˌjī, ˈfəŋ-ˌgī\ *also* **fun·gus·es** \ˈfəŋ-gə-səz\ : any of a large group of lower plants that lack chlorophyll and include molds, mildews, mushrooms, and yeasts — **fun·gal** \-gəl\ *adj* — **fun·gous** \-gəs\ *adj*

fu·nic·u·lar \fyu̇-ˈnik-yə-lər, fə-\ *n* : a cable railway ascending a mountain

funk \ˈfəŋk\ *n* : a depressed state of mind

funky \ˈfəŋ-kē\ *adj* **funk·i·er; -est** **1** : having an earthy, unsophisticated style and feeling; *esp* : having the style and feeling of blues **2** : odd or quaint in appearance or style

[1]**fun·nel** \ˈfən-ᵊl\ *n* **1** : a cone-shaped utensil with a tube used for catching and directing a downward flow (as of liquid) **2** : FLUE, SMOKESTACK

[2]**funnel** *vb* **-neled** *also* **-nelled; -nel·ing** *also* **-nel·ling 1** : to pass through or as if through a funnel **2** : to move to a central point or into a central channel

[1]**fun·ny** \ˈfən-ē\ *adj* **fun·ni·er; -est 1** : AMUSING **2** : FACETIOUS **3** : QUEER, ODD **4** : UNDERHANDED

[2]**funny** *n, pl* **funnies** : a comic strip or a comic section (as of a newspaper)

funny bone *n* : a place at the back of the elbow where a blow compresses a nerve and causes a painful tingling sensation

[1]**fur** \ˈfər\ *n* **1** : an article of clothing made of or with fur **2** : the hairy coat of a mammal esp. when fine, soft, and thick; *also* : this coat dressed for human use — **fur** *adj* — **furred** \ˈfərd\ *adj*

[2]**fur** *abbr* furlong

fur·be·low \ˈfər-bə-ˌlō\ *n* **1** : FLOUNCE, RUFFLE **2** : showy trimming

fur·bish \ˈfər-bish\ *vb* **1** : to make lustrous : POLISH **2** : to give a new look to : RENOVATE

fu·ri·ous \ˈfyu̇r-ē-əs\ *adj* **1** : FIERCE, ANGRY, VIOLENT **2** : BOISTEROUS **3** : INTENSE — **fu·ri·ous·ly** *adv*

furl \ˈfərl\ *vb* **1** : to wrap or roll (as a sail or a flag) close to or around something **2** : to curl in furls — **furl** *n*

fur·long \ˈfər-ˌlȯŋ\ *n* [ME, fr. OE *furlang,* fr. *furh* furrow + *lang* long] : a unit of length equal to 220 yards (about 201 meters)

fur·lough \ˈfər-lō\ *n* [Dutch *verlof,* lit., permission] : a leave of absence from duty granted esp. to a soldier — **furlough** *vb*

fur·nace \ˈfər-nəs\ *n* : an enclosed structure in which heat is produced

fur·nish \ˈfər-nish\ *vb* **1** : to provide with what is needed : EQUIP **2** : SUPPLY, GIVE

fur·nish·ings \-iŋs\ *n pl* **1** : articles or accessories of dress **2** : FURNITURE

fur·ni·ture \ˈfər-ni-chər\ *n* : equipment that is necessary, useful, or desirable; *esp* : movable articles (as chairs, tables, or beds) for a room

fu·ror \ˈfyu̇r-ˌȯr\ *n* **1** : ANGER, RAGE **2** : a contagious excitement; *esp* : a fashionable craze **3** : UPROAR

fu·rore \-ˌōr\ *n* [It] : FUROR 2, 3

fur·ri·er \ˈfər-ē-ər\ *n* : one who prepares or deals in fur

fur·ring \ˈfər-iŋ\ *n* : wood or metal strips applied to a wall or ceiling to form a level surface or an air space

fur·row \ˈfər-ō\ *n* **1** : a trench in the earth made by or as if by a plow **2** : a narrow groove or wrinkle — **furrow** *vb*

fur·ry \ˈfər-ē\ *adj* **fur·ri·er; -est 1** : resembling or consisting of fur **2** : covered with fur

[1]**fur·ther** \ˈfər-t͟hər\ *adv* **1** : [1]FARTHER 1 **2** : in addition : MOREOVER **3** : to a greater extent or degree

[2]**further** *vb* **fur·thered; fur·ther·ing** \ˈfərt͟h-(ə-)riŋ\ : to help forward — **fur·ther·ance** \ˈfərt͟h-(ə-)rəns\ *n*

[3]**further** *adj* **1** : [2]FARTHER 1 **2** : ADDITIONAL

fur·ther·more \ˈfər-t͟hə(r)-ˌmōr\ *adv* : in addition to what precedes : BESIDES

fur·ther·most \-t͟hər-ˌmōst\ *adj* : most distant : FARTHEST

fur·thest \ˈfər-t͟həst\ *adv or adj* : FARTHEST

fur·tive \ˈfərt-iv\ *adj* [F or L; F *furtif,* fr. L *furtivus,* fr. *furtum* theft, fr. *fur* thief] : done by stealth : SLY — **fur·tive·ly** *adv* — **fur·tive·ness** *n*

fu·ry \ˈfyu̇r-ē\ *n, pl* **furies 1** : violent anger : RAGE **2** : extreme fierceness or violence **3** : FRENZY

furze \ˈfərz\ *n* : GORSE

[1]**fuse** \ˈfyüz\ *n* **1** : a cord or cable that is set afire to ignite an explosive charge **2** *usu* **fuze** : a mechanical or electrical device for setting off the explosive charge of a projectile, bomb, or torpedo

[2]**fuse** *or* **fuze** \ˈfyüz\ *vb* **fused** *or* **fuzed; fus·ing** *or* **fuz·ing** : to equip with a fuse

[3]**fuse** *vb* **fused; fus·ing 1** : MELT **2** : to unite by or as if by melting together — **fus·ible** *adj*

[4]**fuse** *n* : an electrical safety device having a metal wire or strip that melts and interrupts the circuit when the current becomes too strong

fu·se·lage \ˈfyü-sə-ˌläzh, -zə-\ *n* : the central body portion of an airplane that holds the crew, passengers, and cargo

fu·sil·lade \ˈfyü-sə-ˌläd, -ˌlād\ *n* : a number of shots fired simultaneously or in rapid succession

fu·sion \ˈfyü-zhən\ *n* **1** : the act or process of melting or making plastic by heat **2** : union by or as if by melting **3** : the union of light atomic nuclei to form heavier nuclei with the release of huge quantities of energy

[1]**fuss** \ˈfəs\ *n* **1** : needless bustle or excitement : COMMOTION **2** : effusive praise **3** : a state of agitation **4** : OBJECTION, PROTEST **5** : DISPUTE

[2]**fuss** *vb* : to make a fuss

fuss·bud·get \ˈfəs-ˌbəj-ət\ *n* : one who fusses about trifles

fussy \ˈfəs-ē\ *adj* **fuss·i·er; -est 1** : IRRITABLE **2** : requiring or giving close attention to details **3** : revealing a sometimes extreme concern for niceties : FASTIDIOUS ⟨not ~ about food⟩ — **fuss·i·ly** \ˈfəs-ə-lē\ *adv* — **fuss·i·ness** \-ē-nəs\ *n*

fus·tian \ˈfəs-chən\ *n* **1** : a strong cotton and linen cloth **2** : pretentious writing or speech

fus·ty \ˈfəs-tē\ *adj* **fus·ti·er; -est** [ME, fr. *fust* wine cask, fr. MF, club, cask, fr. L *fustis*] **1** : MUSTY **2** : OLD-FASHIONED

fut *abbr* future

fu·tile \ˈfyüt-ᵊl, ˈfyü-ˌtīl\ *adj* **1** : USELESS, VAIN **2** : FRIVOLOUS, TRIVIAL — **fu·til·i·ty** \fyü-ˈtil-ət-ē\ *n*

[1]**fu·ture** \ˈfyü-chər\ *adj* **1** : of, relating to, or constituting a verb tense that expresses time yet to come **2** : coming after the present

[2]**future** *n* **1** : time that is to come **2** : what is going to happen **3** : an expectation of advancement or progressive development **4** : the future tense; *also* : a verb form in it

fu·tur·ism \ˈfyü-chə-ˌriz-əm\ *n* : a modern movement in art, music, and literature that tries esp. to express the energy and activity of mechanical processes — **fu·tur·ist** \ˈfyüch-(ə-)rəst\ *n*

fu·tur·is·tic \ˌfyü-chə-ˈris-tik\ *adj* : of or relating to the future or to futurism; *also* : very modern

fu·tu·ri·ty \fyu̇-ˈt(y)u̇r-ət-ē\ *n, pl* **-ties 1** : FUTURE **2** : the quality or state of being future **3** *pl* : future events or prospects

fuze *var of* FUSE

fuzz \ˈfəz\ *n* : fine light particles or fibers (as of down or fluff)

fuzzy \ˈfəz-ē\ *adj* **fuzz·i·er; -est 1** : having or resembling fuzz **2** : INDISTINCT — **fuzz·i·ness** \ˈfəz-ē-nəs\ *n*

fwd *abbr* forward

FWD *abbr* front-wheel drive

FY *abbr* fiscal year

-fy \ˌfī\ *vb suffix* : make : form into ⟨dandi*fy*⟩

FYI *abbr* for your information

G

[1]**g** \ˈjē\ *n, pl* **g's** *or* **gs** \ˈjēz\ *often cap* **1** : the 7th letter of the English alphabet **2** : a unit of force equal to the force exerted by gravity on a body at rest and used to indicate the force to which a body is subjected when accelerated **3** *slang* : a sum of $1000

[2]**g** *abbr, often cap* **1** game **2** gauge **3** good **4** gram **5** gravity

ga *abbr* gauge

[1]**Ga** *abbr* Georgia

[2]**Ga** *symbol* gallium

GA *abbr* **1** general assembly **2** general average **3** general of the army **4** Georgia

gab \ˈgab\ *vb* **gabbed; gab·bing** : to talk in a rapid or thoughtless manner : CHATTER — **gab** *n*

gab·ar·dine \ˈgab-ər-ˌdēn\ *n* **1** : GABERDINE 1, 2 **2** : a firm durable twilled fabric having diagonal ribs and made of various fibers; *also* : a garment of gabardine

gab·ble \ˈgab-əl\ *vb* **gab·bled; gab·bling** \-(ə-)liŋ\ : JABBER, BABBLE

gab·by \ˈgab-ē\ *adj* **gab·bi·er; -est** : TALKATIVE, GARRULOUS

gab·er·dine \ˈgab-ər-ˌdēn\ *n* **1** : a long coat or smock worn chiefly by Jews in medieval times **2** : an English laborer's smock **3** : GABARDINE

gab·fest \ˈgab-ˌfest\ *n* **1** : an informal gathering for general talk **2** : an extended conversation

ga·ble \ˈgā-bəl\ *n* : the triangular part of the end of a building formed by the sides of the roof sloping from the ridgepole down to the eaves — **ga·bled** \-bəld\ *adj*

gable

gad \ˈgad\ *vb* **gad·ded; gad·ding** : to be on the go to little purpose — usu. used with *about* — **gad·der** *n*

gad·about \ˈgad-ə-ˌbau̇t\ *n* : a person who flits about in social activity

gad·fly \ˈgad-ˌflī\ *n* **1** : a fly that bites or harasses livestock **2** : a usu. intentionally annoying and persistently critical person

gad·get \ˈgaj-ət\ *n* : DEVICE, CONTRIVANCE — **gad·ge·teer** \ˌgaj-ə-ˈtiər\ *n* — **gad·get·ry** \ˈgaj-ə-trē\ *n*

gad·o·lin·i·um \ˌgad-ᵊl-ˈin-ē-əm\ *n* : a magnetic metallic chemical element — see ELEMENT table

[1]**Gael** \ˈgāl\ *n* : a Celtic inhabitant of Ireland or Scotland

[2]**Gael** *abbr* Gaelic

Gael·ic \ˈgā-lik\ *adj* : of or relating to the Gaels or their languages — **Gaelic** *n*

gaff \ˈgaf\ *n* **1** : a spear used in taking fish or turtles; *also* : a metal hook for holding or lifting heavy fish **2** : the spar supporting the top of a fore-and-aft sail **3** : rough treatment : ABUSE — **gaff** *vb*

gaffe \ˈgaf\ *n* : a social blunder

gaf·fer \ˈgaf-ər\ *n* : an old man

[1]**gag** \ˈgag\ *vb* **gagged; gag·ging 1** : to prevent from speaking or crying out by stopping up the mouth **2** : to prevent from speaking freely **3** : to retch or cause to retch **4** : OBSTRUCT, CHOKE **5** : BALK **6** : to make quips

[2]**gag** *n* **1** : something thrust into the mouth esp. to prevent speech or outcry **2** : an official check or restraint on free speech **3** : a laugh-provoking remark or act **4** : PRANK, TRICK

[1]**gage** \ˈgāj\ *n* **1** : a token of defiance; *esp* : a glove or cap cast on the ground as a pledge of combat **2** : SECURITY

[2]**gage** *var of* GAUGE

gag·gle \ˈgag-əl\ *n* [ME *gagyll,* fr. *gagelen* to cackle] **1** : a flock of geese **2** : GROUP, CLUSTER

gai·ety \ˈgā-ət-ē\ *n, pl* **-eties 1** : MERRYMAKING **2** : MERRIMENT **3** : FINERY

gai·ly \ˈgā-lē\ *adv* : in a gay manner

[1]**gain** \ˈgān\ *n* **1** : PROFIT **2** : ACQUISITION, ACCUMULATION **3** : INCREASE

[2]**gain** *vb* **1** : to get possession of : EARN **2** : WIN ⟨~ a victory⟩ **3** : ACHIEVE ⟨~ strength⟩ **4** : to arrive at **5** : PERSUADE **6** : to increase in ⟨~ momentum⟩ **7** : to run fast ⟨the watch ~*s* a minute a day⟩ **8** : PROFIT **9** : INCREASE **10** : to improve in health — **gain·er** *n*

gain·ful \ˈgān-fəl\ *adj* : PROFITABLE — **gain·ful·ly** \-ē\ *adv*

gain·say \gān-ˈsā\ *vb* **-said** \-ˈsād, -ˈsed\; **-say·ing** \-ˈsā-iŋ\; **-says** \-ˈsāz, -ˈsez\ [ME *gainsayen,* fr. *gain-* against + *-sayen* to say] **1** : DENY, DISPUTE **2** : to speak against — **gain·say·er** *n*

gait \ˈgāt\ *n* : manner of moving on foot; *also* : a particular pattern or style of such moving — **gait·ed** \-əd\ *adj*

gai·ter \ˈgāt-ər\ *n* **1** : a leg covering reaching from the instep to ankle, mid-calf, or knee **2** : an ankle-high shoe with elastic gores in the sides **3** : an overshoe with a fabric upper

[1]**gal** \ˈgal\ *n* : GIRL

[2]**gal** *abbr* gallon

Gal *abbr* Galatians

ga·la \ˈgā-lə, ˈgal-ə, ˈgäl-ə\ *n* : a gay celebration : FESTIVITY — **gala** *adj*

ga·lac·tose \gə-ˈlak-ˌtōs\ *n* : a sugar less soluble and less sweet than glucose

Ga·la·tians \gə-ˈlā-shənz\ *n* — see BIBLE table

gal·axy \ˈgal-ək-sē\ *n, pl* **-ax·ies** [ME *galaxie, galaxias,* fr. LL *galaxias,* fr. Gk, fr. *galakt-, gala* milk] **1** *often cap* : MILKY WAY GALAXY — used with *the* **2** : a very large group of stars **3** : an assemblage of brilliant or famous persons or things — **ga·lac·tic** \gə-ˈlak-tik\ *adj*

gale \ˈgāl\ *n* **1** : a strong wind **2** : an emotional outburst (as of laughter)

ga·le·na \gə-ˈlē-nə\ *n* : a lustrous bluish gray mineral that consists of the sulfide of lead and is the chief ore of lead

[1]**gall** \ˈgȯl\ *n* **1** : BILE **2** : something bitter to endure **3** : RANCOR **4** : IMPUDENCE

[2]**gall** *n* : a sore on the skin caused by chafing

[3]**gall** *vb* **1** : CHAFE; *esp* : to become sore or worn by rubbing **2** : VEX, HARASS

[4]**gall** *n* : a swelling of plant tissue caused by parasites (as fungi or mites)

[1]**gal·lant** \gə-ˈlant, gə-ˈlänt, ˈgal-ənt\ *n* **1** : a young man of fashion **2** : a man who shows a marked fondness for the company of women and who is esp. attentive to them **3** : SUITOR

[2]**gal·lant** \ˈgal-ənt *(usual for 2, 3, 4);* gə-ˈlant, gə-ˈlänt *(usual for 5)*\ *adj* **1** : showy in dress or bearing : SMART **2** : SPLENDID, STATELY **3** : SPIRITED, BRAVE **4** : CHIVALROUS, NOBLE **5** : polite and attentive to women — **gal·lant·ly** *adv*

gal·lant·ry \ˈgal-ən-trē\ *n, pl* **-ries 1** *archaic* : gallant appearance **2** : an act of marked courtesy **3** : courteous attention to a woman **4** : conspicuous bravery

gall·blad·der \ˈgȯl-ˌblad-ər\ *n* : a membranous muscular sac attached to the liver in which bile is stored

gal·le·on \ˈgal-ē-ən\ *n* : a large square-rigged sailing ship formerly used esp. by the Spanish

gal·le·ria \ˌgal-ə-ˈrē-ə\ *n* [It] : a roofed and usu. glass-enclosed promenade or court

gal·lery \ˈgal(-ə)-rē\ *n, pl* **-ler·ies 1 :** an outdoor balcony; *also* **:** PORCH, VERANDA **2 :** a long narrow room or hall; *esp* **:** one with windows along one side **3 :** a narrow passage (as one made underground by a miner or through wood by an insect) **4 :** a room where works of art are exhibited; *also* **:** an organization dealing in works of art **5 :** a balcony in a theater, auditorium, or church; *esp* **:** the highest one in a theater **6 :** a body of spectators (as at a tennis match) **7 :** a photographer's studio — **gal·ler·ied** \-rēd\ *adj*

gal·ley \ˈgal-ē\ *n, pl* **galleys 1 :** a long low ship propelled esp. by oars and formerly used esp. in the Mediterranean sea **2 :** the kitchen esp. of a boat or airplane **3 :** a tray to hold printer's type that has been set; *also* **:** proof from type in such a tray

Gal·lic \ˈgal-ik\ *adj* **:** of or relating to Gaul or France

gal·li·mau·fry \ˌgal-ə-ˈmȯ-frē\ *n, pl* **-fries** [MF *galimafree* hash] **:** HODGEPODGE

gal·li·nule \ˈgal-ə-ˌn(y)ü(ə)l\ *n* **:** any of several aquatic birds related to the rails

gal·li·um \ˈgal-ē-əm\ *n* **:** a rare bluish white metallic chemical element — see ELEMENT table

gal·li·vant \ˈgal-ə-ˌvant\ *vb* **:** to go roaming about for pleasure

gal·lon \ˈgal-ən\ *n* — see WEIGHT table

[1]**gal·lop** \gal-əp\ *vb* **1 :** to go or cause to go at a gallop **2 :** to run fast — **gal·lop·er** *n*

[2]**gallop** *n* **1 :** a springing gait of a quadruped; *esp* **:** a fast 3-beat gait of a horse **2 :** a ride or run at a gallop

gal·lows \ˈgal-ōz\ *n, pl* **gallows** *or* **gal·lows·es :** a frame usu. of two upright posts and a crosspiece from which criminals are hanged

gall·stone \ˈgȯl-ˌstōn\ *n* **:** an abnormal concretion occurring in the gallbladder or bile passages

gal·lus·es \ˈgal-ə-səz\ *n pl, chiefly dial* **:** SUSPENDERS

ga·lore \gə-ˈlōr\ *adj* [IrGael *go leor* enough] **:** ABUNDANT, PLENTIFUL

ga·losh \gə-ˈläsh\ *n* **:** a high overshoe

galv *abbr* galvanized

gal·va·nize \ˈgal-və-ˌnīz\ *vb* **-nized; -niz·ing 1 :** to stimulate as if by an electric shock **2 :** to coat (iron or steel) with zinc — **gal·va·ni·za·tion** \ˌgal-və-nə-ˈzā-shən\ *n* — **gal·va·niz·er** \ˈgal-və-ˌnī-zər\ *n*

gal·va·nom·e·ter \ˌgal-və-ˈnäm-ət-ər\ *n* **:** an instrument for detecting or measuring a small electric current

Gam·bi·an \ˈgam-bē-ən\ *n* **:** a native or inhabitant of Gambia — **Gambian** *adj*

gam·bit \ˈgam-bət\ *n* [It *gambetto*, lit., act of tripping someone, fr. *gamba* leg] **1 :** a chess opening in which a player risks one or more minor pieces to gain an advantage in position **2 :** a calculated move **:** STRATAGEM

[1]**gam·ble** \ˈgam-bəl\ *vb* **gam·bled; gam·bling** \-b(ə-)liŋ\ **1 :** to play a game for money or other stakes **2 :** SPECULATE, BET, WAGER **3 :** VENTURE, HAZARD — **gam·bler** \-blər\ *n*

[2]**gamble** *n* **:** a risky undertaking

gam·bol \ˈgam-bəl\ *vb* **-boled** *or* **-bolled; -bol·ing** *or* **-bol·ling** \-b(ə-)liŋ\ **:** to skip about in play **:** FRISK — **gambol** *n*

gam·brel roof \ˌgam-brəl-\ *n* **:** a roof with a lower steeper slope and an upper flatter one on each side

[1]**game** \ˈgām\ *n* **1 :** AMUSEMENT, DIVERSION **2 :** SPORT, FUN **3 :** SCHEME, PROJECT **4 :** a line of work **:** PROFESSION **5 :** CONTEST **6 :** animals hunted for sport or food; *also* **:** the flesh of a game animal

[2]**game** *vb* **gamed; gam·ing :** to play for a stake **:** GAMBLE

[3]**game** *adj* **:** PLUCKY — **game·ly** *adv* — **game·ness** *n*

[4]**game** *adj* **:** LAME ⟨a ~ leg⟩

game·cock \ˈgām-ˌkäk\ *n* **:** a rooster trained for fighting

game fish *n* **:** SPORT FISH

game·keep·er \ˈgām-ˌkē-pər\ *n* **:** a person in charge of the breeding and protection of game animals or birds on a private preserve

game·some \ˈgām-səm\ *adj* **:** MERRY

game·ster \ˈgām-stər\ *n* **:** GAMBLER

gam·ete \ˈgam-ˌēt\ *n* **:** a matured germ cell — **ga·met·ic** \gə-ˈmet-ik\ *adj*

game theory *n* **:** the analysis of a situation involving conflicting interests (as in business) in terms of gains and losses among opposing players

gam·in \ˈgam-ən\ *n* [F] **1 :** a boy who hangs out on the streets **2 :** GAMINE 2

ga·mine \ga-ˈmēn\ *n* **1 :** a girl who hangs out on the streets **2 :** a small playfully mischievous girl

gam·ma globulin \ˈgam-ə-\ *n* **:** a blood protein fraction rich in antibodies; *also* **:** a solution of this from human blood donors that is given to provide immunity against some infectious diseases (as measles)

gamma rays *n pl* **:** very penetrating radiation similar to X rays but of shorter wavelength

gam·mer \ˈgam-ər\ *n, archaic* **:** an old woman

gam·mon \ˈgam-ən\ *n, chiefly Brit* **:** a cured ham or side of bacon

gam·ut \ˈgam-ət\ *n* [ML *gamma*, lowest note of a medieval scale (fr. LL, 3d letter of the Greek alphabet) + *ut*, lowest of each series of six tones in the scale] **:** an entire range or series

gamy *or* **gam·ey** \ˈgā-mē\ *adj* **gam·i·er; -est 1 :** GAME, PLUCKY **2 :** having the flavor of game esp. when slightly tainted ⟨~ meat⟩ **3 :** SCANDALOUS; *also* **:** DISREPUTABLE — **gam·i·ness** \-mē-nəs\ *n*

[1]**gan·der** \ˈgan-dər\ *n* **:** a male goose

[2]**gander** *n* **:** LOOK, GLANCE

[1]**gang** \ˈgaŋ\ *n* **1 :** a set of implements or devices arranged to operate together **2 :** a group of persons working or associated together; *esp* **:** a group of criminals or young delinquents

[2]**gang** *vb* **1 :** to attack in a gang — usu. used with *up* **2 :** to form into or move or act as a gang

gang·land \ˈgaŋ-ˌland\ *n* **:** the world of organized crime

gan·gling \ˈgaŋ-gliŋ\ *adj* **:** LANKY, SPINDLING

gan·gli·on \ˈgaŋ-glē-ən\ *n, pl* **-glia** \-glē-ə\ *also* **-gli·ons :** a mass of nerve cells outside the central nervous system; *also* **:** NUCLEUS 3 — **gan·gli·on·ic** \ˌgaŋ-glē-ˈän-ik\ *adj*

gang·plank \ˈgaŋ-ˌplaŋk\ *n* **:** a movable bridge from a ship to the shore

gang·plow \-ˌplau̇\ *n* **:** a plow that turns two or more furrows at one time

gan·grene \ˈgaŋ-ˌgrēn, gaŋ-ˈgrēn\ *n* **:** the death of soft tissues in a local area of the body due to loss of the blood supply — **gangrene** *vb* — **gan·gre·nous** \ˈgaŋ-grə-nəs\ *adj*

gang·ster \ˈgaŋ-stər\ *n* **:** a member of a gang of criminals **:** RACKETEER

gang·way \ˈgaŋ-ˌwā\ *n* **1 :** a passage into, through, or out of an enclosed place **2 :** GANGPLANK

gan·net \ˈgan-ət\ *n, pl* **gannets** *also* **gannet :** any of several large fish-eating usu. white and black marine birds that breed on offshore islands

gant·let \ˈgȯnt-lət\ *var of* GAUNTLET

gan·try \ˈgan-trē\ *n, pl* **gantries :** a frame structure on side supports over or around something

GAO *abbr* General Accounting Office

gaol \ˈjāl\ **, gaol·er** \ˈjā-lər\ *chiefly Brit var of* JAIL, JAILER

gap \ˈgap\ *n* **1 :** BREACH, CLEFT **2 :** a mountain pass **3 :** a blank space **4 :** a wide difference in character or attitude

gape \ˈgāp, ˈgap\ *vb* **gaped; gap·ing 1 :** to open the mouth wide **2 :** to open or part widely **3 :** to stare with mouth open **4 :** YAWN — **gape** *n*

[1]**gar** \ˈgär\ *n* **:** any of several fishes that have a long body resembling that of a pike and long narrow jaws

---

\ə\abut \ᵊ\kitten \ər\further \a\ash \ā\ace \ä\cot, cart \au̇\out \ch\chin \e\bet \ē\easy \g\go \i\hit \ī\ice \j\job \ŋ\sing \ō\go \ȯ\law \ȯi\boy \th\thin \t͟h\the \ü\loot \u̇\foot \y\yet \zh\vision *see also* Pronunciation Symbols page

[2]**gar** *abbr* garage
GAR *abbr* Grand Army of the Republic
[1]**ga·rage** \gə-ˈräzh, -ˈräj\ *n* [F] **:** a building for housing or repairing automobiles
[2]**garage** *vb* **ga·raged; ga·rag·ing :** to keep or put in a garage
garage sale *n* **:** a sale of used household articles held on one's own premises
garb \ˈgärb\ *n* **1 :** style of dress **2 :** outward form **:** APPEARANCE **— garb** *vb*
gar·bage \ˈgär-bij\ *n* **1 :** food waste **2 :** unwanted or useless material
gar·ble \ˈgär-bəl\ *vb* **gar·bled; gar·bling** \-b(ə-)liŋ\ [ME *garbelen,* fr. It *garbellare* to sift, fr. Ar *ghirbāl* sieve] **:** to distort the meaning or sound of ⟨~ a story⟩ ⟨~ words⟩
gar·çon \gär-ˈsōⁿ\ *n, pl* **garçons** \-ˈsōⁿ(z)\ [F, boy, waiter] **:** WAITER
[1]**gar·den** \ˈgärd-ᵊn\ *n* **1 :** a plot for growing fruits, flowers, or vegetables **2 :** a public recreation area; *esp* **:** one for displaying plants or animals
[2]**garden** *vb* **gar·dened; gar·den·ing** \ˈgärd-(ᵊ-)niŋ\ **:** to develop or work in a garden **— gar·den·er** \ˈgärd-(ᵊ-)nər\ *n*
gar·de·nia \gär-ˈdē-nyə\ *n* [NL, genus name, fr. Alexander *Garden* †1791 Scot. naturalist] **:** the fragrant white or yellow flower of any of a genus of trees or shrubs of the madder family; *also* **:** one of these trees
garden–variety *adj* **:** COMMONPLACE, ORDINARY
gar·fish \ˈgär-ˌfish\ *n* **:** GAR
gar·gan·tuan \gär-ˈganch-(ə-)wən\ *adj, often cap* **:** of tremendous size or volume
gar·gle \ˈgär-gəl\ *vb* **gar·gled; gar·gling** \-g(ə-)liŋ\ **:** to rinse the throat with liquid agitated by air forced through it from the lungs **— gargle** *n*
gar·goyle \ˈgär-ˌgȯil\ *n* **1 :** a waterspout in the form of a grotesque human or animal figure projecting from the roof or eaves of a building **2 :** a grotesquely carved figure
gar·ish \ˈga(ə)r-ish\ *adj* **:** FLASHY, GLARING, SHOWY, GAUDY
[1]**gar·land** \ˈgär-lənd\ *n* **:** a wreath or rope of leaves or flowers
[2]**garland** *vb* **:** to form into or deck with a garland
gar·lic \ˈgär-lik\ *n* [ME *garlek,* fr. OE *gārlēac,* fr. *gār* spear + *lēac* leek] **:** an herb related to the lilies and grown for its pungent bulbs used in cooking; *also* **:** its bulb **— gar·licky** \-li-kē\ *adj*
gar·ment \ˈgär-mənt\ *n* **:** an article of clothing
gar·ner \ˈgär-nər\ *vb* **gar·nered; gar·ner·ing** \ˈgärn-(ə-)riŋ\ **1 :** to gather into storage **2 :** to acquire by effort **3 :** ACCUMULATE, COLLECT
gar·net \ˈgär-nət\ *n* [ME *grenat,* fr. MF, fr. *grenat,* adj., red like a pomegranate, fr. *(pomme) grenate* pomegranate] **:** a transparent deep red mineral sometimes used as a gem
gar·nish \ˈgär-nish\ *vb* **1 :** DECORATE, EMBELLISH **2 :** to add decorative or savory touches to (food) **— garnish** *n*
gar·nish·ee \ˌgär-nə-ˈshē\ *vb* **-eed; -ee·ing 1 :** to serve with a garnishment **2 :** to take (as a debtor's wages) by legal authority
gar·nish·ment \ˈgär-nish-mənt\ *n* **1 :** GARNISH **2 :** a legal warning to the holder of property of a debtor to give it to a creditor; *also* **:** the attachment of such property to satisfy a creditor
gar·ni·ture \-ni-chər, -nə-ˌchu̇(ə)r\ *n* **:** EMBELLISHMENT, TRIMMING
gar·ret \ˈgar-ət\ *n* [ME *garette* watchtower, fr. MF *garite*] **:** the part of a house just under the roof **:** ATTIC
gar·ri·son \ˈgar-ə-sən\ *n* **1 :** a military post; *esp* **:** a permanent military installation **2 :** the troops stationed at a garrison **— garrison** *vb*
garrison state *n* **:** a state organized on a primarily military basis
gar·rote *or* **ga·rotte** \gə-ˈrät, -ˈrōt\ *n* [Sp *garrote*] **1 :** a method of execution by strangling with an iron collar; *also* **:** the iron collar used **2 :** strangulation esp. for the purpose of robbery; *also* **:** an implement for this purpose **— garrote** *or* **garotte** *vb*
gar·ru·lous \ˈgar-ə-ləs\ *adj* **:** CHATTERING, TALKATIVE, WORDY **— gar·ru·li·ty** \gə-ˈrü-lət-ē\ *n* **— gar·ru·lous·ly** \ˈgar-ə-ləs-lē\ *adv* **— gar·ru·lous·ness** *n*
gar·ter \ˈgärt-ər\ *n* **:** a band or strap worn to hold up a stocking or sock
garter snake *n* **:** any of numerous harmless American snakes with longitudinal stripes on the back
[1]**gas** \ˈgas\ *n, pl* **gas·es** *also* **gas·ses** [NL, alter. of L *chaos* space, chaos] **1 :** a fluid (as hydrogen or air) that tends to expand indefinitely **2 :** a gas or mixture of gases used as a fuel or anesthetic **3 :** a substance that can be used to produce a poisonous, asphyxiating, or irritant atmosphere **4 :** GASOLINE **— gas·eous** \-ē-əs, ˈgash-əs\ *adj*
[2]**gas** *vb* **gassed; gas·sing 1 :** to treat with gas; *also* **:** to poison with gas **2 :** to fill with gasoline
gash \ˈgash\ *n* **:** a deep long cut **— gash** *vb*
gas·ket \ˈgas-kət\ *n* **:** material (as rubber or metal) used to prevent a joint from leaking
gas·light \ˈgas-ˌlīt\ *n* **1 :** light made by burning illuminating gas **2 :** a gas flame; *also* **:** a gas lighting fixture
gas mask *n* **:** a mask connected to a chemical air filter and used to protect the face and lungs against poison gases
gas·o·line *also* **gas·o·lene** \ˈgas-ə-ˌlēn, ˌgas-ə-ˈlēn\ *n* **:** a flammable liquid made esp. by blending products from natural gas and petroleum and used as a motor fuel
gasp \ˈgasp\ *vb* **1 :** to catch the breath with emotion (as shock) **2 :** to breathe laboriously **:** PANT **3 :** to utter in a gasping manner **— gasp** *n*
gas·tric \ˈgas-trik\ *adj* **:** of, relating to, or located near the stomach
gastric juice *n* **:** the acid digestive secretion of the stomach
gas·tri·tis \gas-ˈtrīt-əs\ *n* **:** inflammatory disorder of the stomach
gas·tro·en·ter·ol·o·gy \ˌgas-trō-ˌent-ə-ˈräl-ə-jē\ *n* **:** a branch of medicine dealing with the alimentary canal **— gas·tro·en·ter·ol·o·gist** \-jəst\ *n*
gas·tro·in·tes·ti·nal \ˌgas-trō-in-ˈtes-tən-ᵊl\ *adj* **:** of, relating to, affecting, or including both stomach and intestine
gas·tron·o·my \gas-ˈträn-ə-mē\ *n* [F *gastronomie,* fr. Gk *Gastronomia,* title of a 4th cent. B.C. poem, fr. *gastēr* belly] **:** the art of good eating **— gas·tro·nom·ic** \ˌgas-trə-ˈnäm-ik\ *also* **gas·tro·nom·i·cal** \-i-kəl\ *adj*
gas·tro·pod \ˈgas-trə-ˌpäd\ *n* **:** any of a large class of mollusks (as snails, whelks, and slugs) with a muscular foot and a spiral shell or none
gas·works \ˈgas-ˌwərks\ *n pl* **:** a plant for manufacturing gas
gate \ˈgāt\ *n* **1 :** an opening for passage in a wall or fence **2 :** a city or castle entrance often with defensive structures **3 :** the frame or door that closes a gate **4 :** a device (as a valve) for controlling the passage of a fluid or signal **5 :** the total admission receipts or the number of people at an event
gate–crash·er \ˈgāt-ˌkrash-ər\ *n* **:** one who enters without paying admission or attends without invitation
gate·keep·er \-ˌkē-pər\ *n* **:** a person who tends or guards a gate
gate·post \ˈgāt-ˌpōst\ *n* **:** the post to which a gate is hung or the one against which it closes
gate·way \-ˌwā\ *n* **1 :** an opening for a gate **2 :** a means of entrance or exit
[1]**gath·er** \ˈgath-ər\ *vb* **gath·ered; gath·er·ing** \-(ə-)riŋ\ **1 :** to bring together **:** COLLECT **2 :** PICK, HARVEST **3 :** to pick up little by little **4 :** to gain or win by gradual increase **:** ACCUMULATE ⟨~ speed⟩ **5 :** to summon up ⟨~ courage to dive⟩ **6 :** to draw about or close to something **7 :** to pull (fabric) along a line of stitching into puckers **8 :** GUESS, DEDUCE, INFER **9 :** ASSEMBLE **10 :** to swell out and

fill with pus **11** : GROW, INCREASE — **gath·er·er** *n* — **gath·er·ing** *n*

²**gather** *n* : a puckering in cloth made by gathering

GATT *abbr* General Agreement on Tariffs and Trade

gauche \ˈgōsh\ *adj* [F, lit., left] : lacking social experience or grace

gau·che·rie \ˌgōsh-(ə-)ˈrē\ *n* : a tactless or awkward action

gau·cho \ˈgau̇-chō\ *n, pl* **gauchos** : a cowboy of the So. American pampas

gaud \ˈgȯd\ *n* : ORNAMENT, TRINKET

gaudy \ˈgȯd-ē\ *adj* **gaud·i·er; -est** : ostentatiously or tastelessly ornamented **syn** garish, flashy, glaring, tawdry — **gaud·i·ly** \ˈgȯd-ᵊl-ē\ *adv* — **gaud·i·ness** \-ē-nəs\ *n*

¹**gauge** *or* **gage** \ˈgāj\ *n* **1** : measurement according to some standard or system **2** : DIMENSIONS, SIZE **3** *usu gage* : an instrument for measuring, testing, or registering

²**gauge** *or* **gage** *vb* **gauged** *or* **gaged; gaug·ing** *or* **gag·ing 1** : MEASURE **2** : to determine the capacity or contents of **3** : ESTIMATE, JUDGE

gaunt \ˈgȯnt\ *adj* **1** : being thin and angular (as from hunger or suffering) **2** : BARREN, DESOLATE — **gaunt·ness** *n*

¹**gaunt·let** \ˈgȯnt-lət\ *n* **1** : a protective glove **2** : a challenge to combat **3** : a dress glove extending above the wrist

²**gauntlet** *n* **1** : a double file of men armed with weapons (as clubs) with which to strike at an individual who is made to run between them **2** : ORDEAL

gauze \ˈgȯz\ *n* : a very thin often transparent fabric used esp. for draperies and surgical dressings — **gauzy** *adj*

gave *past of* GIVE

gav·el \ˈgav-əl\ *n* : the mallet of a presiding officer or auctioneer

ga·votte \gə-ˈvät\ *n* : a dance of French peasant origin marked by the raising rather than sliding of the feet

gawk \ˈgȯk\ *vb* : to gape or stare stupidly

gawky \ˈgȯ-kē\ *adj* **gawk·i·er; -est** : AWKWARD, CLUMSY

gay \ˈgā\ *adj* **1** : MERRY **2** : BRIGHT, LIVELY **3** : brilliant in color **4** : given to social pleasures; *also* : LICENTIOUS **5** : HOMOSEXUAL

gay·ety, gay·ly *var of* GAIETY, GAILY

gaz *abbr* gazette

gaze \ˈgāz\ *vb* **gazed; gaz·ing** : to fix the eyes in a steady intent look — **gaze** *n* — **gaz·er** *n*

ga·ze·bo \gə-ˈzā-bō, -ˈzē-\ *n, pl* **-bos 1** : BELVEDERE **2** : a freestanding roofed structure usu. open on the sides

ga·zelle \gə-ˈzel\ *n, pl* **gazelles** *also* **gazelle** : any of several small swift graceful antelopes

¹**ga·zette** \gə-ˈzet\ *n* **1** : NEWSPAPER **2** : an official journal

²**gazette** *vb* **ga·zett·ed; ga·zett·ing** *chiefly Brit* : to announce or publish in a gazette

gaz·et·teer \ˌgaz-ə-ˈtiər\ *n* : a geographical dictionary

GB *abbr* Great Britain

GCA *abbr* ground-controlled approach

gd *abbr* good

Gd *symbol* gadolinium

GDR *abbr* German Democratic Republic

Ge *symbol* germanium

gear \ˈgiər\ *n* **1** : CLOTHING **2** : movable property : GOODS **3** : EQUIPMENT ⟨fishing ~⟩ ⟨photographic ~⟩ **4** : a mechanism that performs a specific function ⟨steering ~⟩ **5** : a toothed wheel that interlocks with another toothed wheel or shaft for transmitting motion **6** : working adjustment of gears ⟨in ~⟩ **7** : an adjustment of transmission gears (as of an automobile or bicycle) that determines speed and direction of travel — **gear** *vb* — **gear·ing** \-iŋ\ *n*

gear·box \ˈgiər-ˌbäks\ *n* : TRANSMISSION 3

gear·shift \-ˌshift\ *n* : a mechanism by which transmission gears are shifted

gear wheel *n* : COGWHEEL

GED *abbr* general equivalency diploma

geese *pl of* GOOSE

gee·zer \ˈgē-zər\ *n* : an odd or eccentric man

Gei·ger counter \ˈgī-gər-\ *or* **Gei·ger–Mül·ler counter** \-ˈmyül-ər-, -ˈmil-, -ˈməl-\ *n* : an electronic instrument for detecting the presence of cosmic rays or radioactive substances

gei·sha \ˈgā-shə, ˈgē-\ *n, pl* **geisha** *or* **geishas** [Jp, fr. *gei* art + *-sha* person] : a Japanese girl who is trained to provide entertaining company for men

gel \ˈjel\ *n* : a solid jellylike colloid (as gelatin dessert) — **gel** *vb*

gel·a·tin *also* **gel·a·tine** \ˈjel-ət-ᵊn\ *n* : glutinous material and esp. protein obtained from animal tissues by boiling and used as a food, in dyeing, and in photography; *also* : an edible jelly formed with gelatin — **ge·lat·i·nous** \jə-ˈlat-(ᵊ-)nəs\ *adj*

geld \ˈgeld\ *vb* : CASTRATE

geld·ing \ˈgel-diŋ\ *n* : a gelded individual; *esp* : a castrated male horse

gel·id \ˈjel-əd\ *adj* : extremely cold

gem \ˈjem\ *n* **1** : JEWEL **2** : a usu. valuable stone cut and polished for ornament **3** : something valued for beauty or perfection

Gem·i·ni \ˈjem-ə-(ˌ)nē, -ˌnī; ˈgem-ə-ˌnē\ *n* **1** : a zodiacal constellation between Taurus and Cancer usu. pictured as twins sitting together **2** : the 3d sign of the zodiac in astrology; *also* : one born under this sign

gem·ol·o·gy *or* **gem·mol·o·gy** \je-ˈmäl-ə-jē, jə-\ *n* : the science of gems — **gem·olog·i·cal** *or* **gem·mo·log·i·cal** \ˌjem-ə-ˈläj-i-kəl\ *adj* — **gem·ol·o·gist** *or* **gem·mol·o·gist** \-jəst\ *n*

gem·stone \ˈjem-ˌstōn\ *n* : a mineral or petrified material that when cut and polished can be used in jewelry

gen *abbr* **1** general **2** genitive

Gen *abbr* Genesis

Gen AF *abbr* general of the air force

gen·darme \ˈzhän-ˌdärm, ˈjän-\ *n* [F, intended as sing. of *gensdarmes*, pl. of *gent d'armes*, lit., armed people] : one of a body of soldiers esp. in France serving as an armed police force

gen·dar·mer·ie *or* **gen·dar·mery** \jän-ˈdärm-ə-rē, zhän-\ *n, pl* **-mer·ies** : a body of gendarmes

gen·der \ˈjen-dər\ *n* **1** : SEX 1 **2** : any of two or more divisions within a grammatical class that determine agreement with and selection of other words or grammatical forms

gene \ˈjēn\ *n* : a part of DNA or sometimes RNA that contains chemical information needed to make a particular protein (as an enzyme) controlling or influencing an inherited bodily trait or activity (as eye color) or that influences or controls the activity of another gene or genes — **gen·ic** \ˈjē-nik, ˈjen-\ *adj*

ge·ne·al·o·gy \ˌjē-nē-ˈäl-ə-jē, -ˈal-\ *n, pl* **-gies** : PEDIGREE, LINEAGE; *also* : the study of family pedigrees — **ge·ne·a·log·i·cal** \ˌjē-nē-ə-ˈläj-i-kəl, ˌjen-ē-\ *adj* — **ge·ne·a·log·i·cal·ly** \-k(ə-)lē\ *adv* — **ge·ne·al·o·gist** \ˌjē-nē-ˈäl-ə-jəst, ˌjen-ē-; -ˈal-\ *n*

genera *pl of* GENUS

¹**gen·er·al** \ˈjen-(ə-)rəl\ *adj* **1** : of or relating to the whole : not local **2** : taken as a whole **3** : relating to or covering all instances ⟨a ~ conclusion⟩ **4** : not limited in meaning : not specific ⟨a ~ outline⟩ **5** : common to many ⟨a ~ custom⟩ **6** : not special or specialized **7** : holding superior rank ⟨inspector ~⟩ — **gen·er·al·ly** \-ē\ *adv*

²**general** *n* **1** : something that involves or is applicable to the whole **2** : a commissioned officer ranking next below a general of the army or a general of the air force **3**

: a commissioned officer of the highest rank in the marine corps — **in general** : for the most part

general assembly *n* **1** : a legislative assembly; *esp* : a U.S. state legislature **2** *cap G&A* : the supreme deliberative body of the United Nations

gen·er·a·lis·si·mo \ˌjen-(ə-)rə-ˈlis- ə-ˌmō\ *n, pl* **-mos** [It, fr. *generale* general] : COMMANDER IN CHIEF

gen·er·al·i·ty \ˌjen-ə-ˈral-ət-ē\ *n, pl* **-ties 1** : the quality or state of being general **2** : GENERALIZATION 2 **3** : a vague or inadequate statement **4** : the greatest part : BULK

gen·er·al·iza·tion \ˌjen-(ə-)rə-lə-ˈzā- shən\ *n* **1** : the act or process of generalizing **2** : a general statement, law, principle, or proposition

gen·er·al·ize \ˈjen-(ə-)rə-ˌlīz\ *vb* **-ized; -iz·ing 1** : to make general **2** : to draw general conclusions from **3** : to reach a general conclusion esp. on the basis of particular instances **4** : to extend throughout the body

general of the air force : a commissioned officer of the highest rank in the air force

general of the army : a commissioned officer of the highest rank in the army

general practitioner *n* : a physician or veterinarian who does not limit his practice to a specialty

gen·er·al·ship \ˈjen-(ə-)rəl-ˌship\ *n* **1** : office or tenure of office of a general **2** : military skill as a high commander **3** : LEADERSHIP

general store *n* : a retail store that carries a wide variety of goods but is not divided into departments

gen·er·ate \ˈjen-ə-ˌrāt\ *vb* **-at·ed; -at·ing** : to bring into existence : PRODUCE

gen·er·a·tion \ˌjen-ə-ˈrā-shən\ *n* **1** : a body of living beings constituting a single step in the line of descent from an ancestor; *also* : the average period between generations **2** : PRODUCTION ⟨~ of electric current⟩

gen·er·a·tive \ˈjen-(ə-)rət-iv, ˈjen-ə-ˌrāt-iv\ *adj* : having the power or function of generating, originating, producing, or reproducing ⟨~ organs⟩

gen·er·a·tor \ˈjen-ə-ˌrāt-ər\ *n* : one that generates; *esp* : a machine by which mechanical energy is changed into electrical energy

ge·ner·ic \jə-ˈner-ik\ *adj* **1** : not specific : GENERAL **2** : not protected by a trademark ⟨a ~ drug⟩ **3** : of or relating to a genus — **generic** *n*

gen·er·ous \ˈjen-(ə-)rəs\ *adj* **1** : free in giving or sharing **2** : HIGH-MINDED, NOBLE **3** : ABUNDANT, AMPLE, COPIOUS — **gen·er·os·i·ty** \ˌjen-ə-ˈräs-ət-ē\ *n* — **gen·er·ous·ly** \ˈjen-(ə-)rəs-lē\ *adv* — **gen·er·ous·ness** *n*

gen·e·sis \ˈjen-ə-səs\ *n, pl* **-e·ses** \-ˌsēz\ : the origin or coming into existence of something

Gen·e·sis \ˈjen-ə-səs\ *n* — see BIBLE table

gene–splic·ing \-ˌsplī-siŋ\ *n* : the technique by which recombinant DNA is produced and made to function in an organism

ge·net·ic \jə-ˈnet-ik\ *adj* : of or relating to the origin, development, or causes of something; *also* : of or relating to genetics — **ge·net·i·cal·ly** \-i-k(ə-)lē\ *adv*

genetic code *n* : the chemical code that is the basis of genetic inheritance and consists of triplets of three linked chemical groups which specify particular kinds of amino acids used to make proteins or which start or stop the process of making proteins

genetic engineering *n* : the directed alteration of genetic material by intervention in genetic processes; *esp* : GENE-SPLICING

ge·net·ics \jə-ˈnet-iks\ *n* : a branch of biology dealing with heredity and variation — **ge·net·i·cist** \-ˈnet-ə-səst\ *n*

ge·nial \ˈjē-nyəl\ *adj* **1** : favorable to growth or comfort ⟨~ sunshine⟩ **2** : CHEERFUL, KINDLY ⟨a ~ host⟩ — **ge·nial·i·ty** \ˌjē-nē-ˈal-ət-ē, jēn-ˈyal-\ *n* — **ge·nial·ly** \ˈjē-nyə-lē\ *adv*

-gen·ic \ˈjen-ik\ *adj comb form* **1** : producing : forming **2** : produced by : formed from **3** : suitable for production or reproduction by (such) a medium

ge·nie \ˈjē-nē\ *n, pl* **ge·nies** *also* **ge·nii** \ˈjē-nē-ˌī\ [F *génie*, fr. Ar *jinnīy*] : a supernatural spirit that often takes human form

gen·i·tal \ˈjen-ə-tᵊl\ *adj* **1** : concerned with reproduction ⟨~ organs⟩ **2** : of, relating to, or characterized by the stage of psychosexual development in which oral and anal impulses are subordinated to adaptive interpersonal mechanisms — **gen·i·tal·ly** \-tə-lē\ *adv*

gen·i·ta·lia \ˌjen-ə-ˈtāl-yə\ *n pl* : reproductive organs; *esp* : the external genital organs — **gen·i·ta·lic** \-ˈtal-ik, -ˈtāl-\ *adj*

gen·i·tals \ˈjen-ə-tᵊlz\ *n pl* : GENITALIA

gen·i·tive \ˈjen-ət-iv\ *adj* : of, relating to, or constituting a grammatical case marking typically a relationship of possessor or source — **genitive** *n*

gen·i·to·uri·nary \ˌjen-ə-tō-ˈyu̇r-ə-ˌner-ē\ *adj* : of or relating to the genital and urinary organs or functions

ge·nius \ˈjē-nyəs\ *n, pl* **ge·nius·es** *or* **ge·nii** \-nē-ˌī\ [L, tutelary spirit, fondness for social enjoyment, fr. *gignere* to beget] **1** *pl genii* : an attendant spirit of a person or place; *also* : a person who influences another for good or evil **2** : a strong leaning or inclination **3** : a peculiar or distinctive character or spirit (as of a nation or a language) **4** *pl usu genii* : SPIRIT, GENIE **5** : a single strongly marked capacity or aptitude **6** : extraordinary intellectual power; *also* : a person having such power

genl *abbr* general

geno·cide \ˈjen-ə-ˌsīd\ *n* : the deliberate and systematic destruction of a racial, political, or cultural group

-g·e·nous \j-ə-nəs\ *adj comb form* **1** : producing : yielding **2** : having (such) an origin

genre \ˈzhän-rə, ˈzhäⁿ-; ˈzhäⁿ(-ə)r\ *n* **1** : a distinctive type or category esp. of literary composition **2** : a style of painting in which everyday subjects are treated realistically

gens \ˈjenz, ˈgens\ *n, pl* **gen·tes** \ˈjen-ˌtēz, ˈgen-ˌtās\ : a Roman clan embracing the families of the same stock in the male line

gent *n* : GENTLEMAN

gen·teel \jen-ˈtēl\ *adj* **1** : ARISTOCRATIC **2** : ELEGANT, STYLISH **3** : POLITE, REFINED **4** : maintaining the appearance of superior or middle-class social status **5** : marked by false delicacy, prudery, or affectation

gen·tian \ˈjen-chən\ *n* : any of numerous herbs with opposite leaves and showy usu. blue flowers in the fall

gen·tile \ˈjen-ˌtīl\ *n* [LL *gentilis* heathen, pagan, lit., belonging to the nations, fr. L *gent-, gens* family, clan, nation] **1** *often cap* : a person who is not Jewish **2** : HEATHEN, PAGAN — **gentile** *adj, often cap*

gen·til·i·ty \jen-ˈtil-ət-ē\ *n, pl* **-ties 1** : good birth and family **2** : the qualities characteristic of a well-bred person **3** : good manners **4** : maintenance of the appearance of superior or middle-class social status

[1]**gen·tle** \ˈjent-ᵊl\ *adj* **gen·tler** \ˈjent-(ᵊ-)lər\; **gen·tlest** \ˈjent-(ᵊ-)ləst\ **1** : belonging to a family of high social station **2** : of, relating to, or characteristic of a gentleman **3** : KIND, AMIABLE **4** : TRACTABLE, DOCILE **5** : not harsh, stern, or violent **6** : SOFT, DELICATE **7** : MODERATE — **gen·tly** \ˈjent-lē\ *adv*

[2]**gentle** *vb* **gen·tled; gen·tling** \ˈjent-(ᵊ-)liŋ\ **1** : to make mild, docile, soft, or moderate **2** : MOLLIFY, PLACATE

gen·tle·folk \ˈjent-ᵊl-ˌfōk\ *also* **gen·tle·folks** \-ˌfōks\ *n* : persons of good family and breeding

gen·tle·man \ˈjent-ᵊl-mən\ *n* **1** : a man of good family **2** : a well-bred man **3** : MAN — used in pl. as a form of address — **gen·tle·man·ly** *adj*

gen·tle·wom·an \ˈjent-ᵊl-ˌwu̇m-ən\ *n* **1** : a woman of good family **2** : a woman attending a lady of rank **3** : a woman with very good manners : LADY

gen·tri·fi·ca·tion \ˌjen-trə-fə-ˈkā-shən\ *n* : the immigration of middle-class people into a run-down or recently renewed city area — **gen·tri·fy** \ˈjen-trə-fī\ *vb*

gen·try \ˈjen-trē\ *n, pl* **gentries 1** : people of good birth, breeding, and education : ARISTOCRACY **2** : the class of English people between the nobility and the yeomanry **3** : PEOPLE; *esp* : persons of a designated class

gen·u·flect \ˈjen-yə-ˌflekt\ *vb* : to bend the knee esp. in worship — **gen·u·flec·tion** \ˌjen-yə-ˈflek-shən\ *n*

gen·u·ine \ˈjen-yə-wən\ *adj* **1** : AUTHENTIC, REAL **2** : SINCERE, HONEST — **gen·u·ine·ly** *adv* — **gen·u·ine·ness** \-wən-(n)əs\ *n*

ge·nus \ˈjē-nəs\ *n, pl* **gen·era** \ˈjen-ə-rə\ [L, birth, race, kind] : a category of biological classification that ranks between the family and the species and contains related species

geo·cen·tric \ˌjē-ō-ˈsen-trik\ *adj* **1** : relating to or measured from the earth's center **2** : having or relating to the earth as a center

geo·chem·is·try \-ˈkem-ə-strē\ *n* : a branch of geology that deals with the chemical composition of and chemical changes in the earth — **geo·chem·i·cal** \-ˈkem-i-kəl\ *adj* — **geo·chem·ist** \-ˈkem-əst\ *n*

ge·ode \ˈjē-ˌōd\ *n* : a nodule of stone having a cavity lined with mineral matter

1**geo·de·sic** \ˌjē-ə-ˈdes-ik\ *adj* : made of a framework of light straight-sided polygons in tension ⟨a ~ dome⟩

2**geodesic** *n* : the shortest line between two points on a surface

ge·od·e·sy \jē-ˈäd-ə-sē\ *n* : a branch of applied mathematics that determines the exact positions of points and the figures and areas of large portions of the earth's surface, the shape and size of the earth, and the variations of terrestrial gravity and magnetism — **geo·det·ic** \ˌjē-ə-ˈdet-ik\ *adj*

geodetic survey *n* : a survey of a large land area in which corrections are made for the curving of the earth's surface

geog *abbr* geographic; geographical; geography

ge·og·ra·phy \jē-ˈäg-rə-fē\ *n, pl* **-phies 1** : a science that deals with the natural features of the earth and the climate, products, and inhabitants **2** : the natural features of a region — **ge·og·ra·pher** \-fər\ *n* — **geo·graph·ic** \ˌjē-ə-ˈgraf-ik\ *or* **geo·graph·i·cal** \-i-kəl\ *adj* — **geo·graph·i·cal·ly** \-i-k(ə-)lē\ *adv*

geol *abbr* geologic; geological; geology

ge·ol·o·gy \jē-ˈäl-ə-jē\ *n, pl* **-gies 1** : a science that deals with the history of the earth and its life esp. as recorded in rocks; *also* : a study of the solid matter of a celestial body (as the moon) **2** : the geologic features of an area — **ge·o·log·ic** \ˌjē-ə-ˈläj-ik\ *or* **ge·o·log·i·cal** \-i-kəl\ *adj* — **geo·log·i·cal·ly** \-i-k(ə-)lē\ *adv* — **ge·ol·o·gist** \jē-ˈäl-ə-jəst\ *n*

geom *abbr* geometric; geometrical; geometry

geo·mag·net·ic \ˌjē-ō-mag-ˈnet-ik\ *adj* : of or relating to the magnetism of the earth — **geo·mag·ne·tism** \-ˈmag-nə-ˌtiz-əm\ *n*

geometric mean *n* : the *n*th root of the product of *n* numbers; *esp* : a number that is the second term of three consecutive terms of a geometric progression ⟨the *geometric mean* of 9 and 4 is 6⟩

geometric progression *n* : a progression (as 1, ½, ¼) in which the ratio of a term to its predecessor is always the same

ge·om·e·try \jē-ˈäm-ə-trē\ *n, pl* **-tries** : a branch of mathematics dealing with the relations, properties, and measurements of solids, surfaces, lines, points, and angles — **ge·om·e·ter** \ˈäm-ət-ər\ *n* — **ge·o·met·ric** \ˌjē-ə-ˈme-trik\ *or* **ge·o·met·ri·cal** \-tri-kəl\ *adj*

geo·phys·ics \ˌjē-ə-ˈfiz-iks\ *n* : the physics of the earth — **geo·phys·i·cal** \-i-kəl\ *adj* — **geo·phys·i·cist** \-ˈfiz-ə-səst\ *n*

geo·pol·i·tics \-ˈpäl-ə-ˌtiks\ *n* : a combination of political and geographic factors relating to a state

geo·ther·mal \-ˈthər-məl\ *also* **geo·ther·mic** \-mik\ *adj* : of, relating to, or using the heat of the earth's interior

ger *abbr* gerund

Ger *abbr* German; Germany

ge·ra·ni·um \jə-ˈrā-nē-əm\ *n* [L, fr. Gk *geranion,* fr. *geranos* crane] **1** : any of a genus of herbs with usu. deeply cut leaves and pink, purple, or white flowers followed by long slender dry fruits **2** : any of a genus of herbs of the same family as the geraniums that have clusters of scarlet, pink, or white flowers with the sepals joined at the base into a hollow tube closed at one end

ger·bil *also* **ger·bile** \ˈjər-bəl\ *n* : any of numerous Old World burrowing desert rodents with long hind legs

ge·ri·at·ric \ˌjer-ē-ˈa-trik\ *adj* : of or relating to aging, the aged, or geriatrics

ge·ri·at·rics \-triks\ *n* : a branch of medicine dealing with the problems and diseases of old age and aging

germ \ˈjərm\ *n* **1** : a bit of living matter capable of growth and development (as into an organism) **2** : SOURCE, RUDIMENTS **3** : MICROORGANISM; *esp* : one causing disease

Ger·man \ˈjər-mən\ *n* **1** : a native or inhabitant of Germany **2** : the language of Germany, Austria, and parts of Switzerland — **German** *adj* — **Ger·man·ic** \jər-ˈman-ik\ *adj*

ger·mane \jər-ˈmān\ *adj* [ME *germain,* lit., having the same parents, fr. MF] : RELEVANT, PERTINENT

ger·ma·ni·um \jər-ˈmā-nē-əm\ *n* : a grayish white hard chemical element used as a semiconductor — see ELEMENT table

German measles *n sing or pl* : an acute contagious virus disease milder than typical measles but damaging to the fetus when occurring early in pregnancy

German shepherd *n* : an intelligent responsive working dog often used in police work and as a guide dog for the blind

germ cell *n* : an egg or sperm or one of their antecedent cells

ger·mi·cide \ˈjər-mə-ˌsīd\ *n* : an agent that destroys germs — **ger·mi·cid·al** \ˌjər-mə-ˈsīd-ᵊl\ *adj*

ger·mi·nal \ˈjərm-(ə-)nəl\ *adj* : of or relating to a germ or germ cell; *also* : EMBRYONIC

ger·mi·nate \ˈjər-mə-ˌnāt\ *vb* **-nat·ed; -nat·ing 1** : to begin to develop : SPROUT **2** : to come into being : EVOLVE — **ger·mi·na·tion** \ˌjər-mə-ˈnā-shən\ *n*

ger·on·tol·o·gy \ˌjer-ən-ˈtäl-ə-jē\ *n* : a scientific study of aging and the problems of the aged — **ge·ron·to·log·i·cal** \jə-ˌränt-ᵊl-ˈäj-i-kəl\ *adj* — **ger·on·tol·o·gist** \ˌjer-ən-ˈtäl-ə-jəst\ *n*

ger·ry·man·der \ˈjer-ē-ˌman-dər\ *vb* **-man·dered; -man·der·ing** \-d(ə-)riŋ\ : to divide into election districts so as to give one political party an advantage — **gerrymander** *n*

ger·und \ˈjer-ənd\ *n* : a word having the characteristics of both verb and noun

ge·sta·po \gə-ˈstäp-ō\ *n, pl* **-pos** [G, fr. *Ge*heime *Sta*ats*po*lizei, lit., secret state police] : a secret-police organization operating esp. against suspected political criminals

ges·ta·tion \je-ˈstā-shən\ *n* : PREGNANCY, INCUBATION — **ges·tate** \ˈjes-ˌtāt\ *vb*

ges·tic·u·late \je-ˈstik-yə-ˌlāt\ *vb* **-lat·ed; -lat·ing** : to make gestures esp. when speaking — **ges·tic·u·la·tion** \-ˌstik-yə-ˈlā-shən\ *n*

ges·ture \ˈjes-chər\ *n* **1** : a movement usu. of the body or limbs that expresses or emphasizes an idea, sentiment, or attitude **2** : something said or done by way of formality or courtesy, as a symbol or token, or for its effect on the attitudes of others — **ges·tur·al** \-chə-rəl\ *adj* — **gesture** *vb*

ge·sund·heit \gə-ˈzu̇nt-ˌhīt\ *interj* [G, lit., health] — used to wish good health esp. to one who has just sneezed

1**get** \ˈget\ *vb* **got** \ˈgät\; **got** *or* **got·ten** \ˈgät-ᵊn\; **get·ting 1**

: to gain possession of (as by receiving, acquiring, earning, buying, or winning) : PROCURE, OBTAIN, FETCH **2** : to succeed in coming or going ⟨*got* home early⟩ **3** : to cause to come or go ⟨*got* the car to the station⟩ **4** : BEGET **5** : to cause to be in a certain condition or position ⟨don't ~ wet⟩ **6** : BECOME ⟨~ sick⟩ **7** : PREPARE **8** : SEIZE **9** : to move emotionally; *also* : IRRITATE **10** : BAFFLE, PUZZLE **11** : HIT **12** : KILL **13** : to be subjected to ⟨~ the measles⟩ **14** : to receive as punishment **15** : to find out by calculation **16** : HEAR; *also* : UNDERSTAND **17** : PERSUADE, INDUCE **18** : HAVE ⟨he's *got* no money⟩ **19** : to have as an obligation or necessity ⟨he has *got* to come⟩ **20** : to establish communication with **21** : to be able : CONTRIVE, MANAGE **22** : to leave at once

[2]**get** \ˈget\ *n* : OFFSPRING, PROGENY

get along *vb* **1** : GET BY **2** : to be on friendly terms

get·away \ˈget-ə-ˌwā\ *n* **1** : START **2** : ESCAPE

get by *vb* : to meet one's needs

get–to·geth·er \ˈget-tə-ˌgeth-ər\ *n* : an informal social gathering

get·up \ˈget-ˌəp\ *n* **1** : general composition or structure **2** : OUTFIT, COSTUME

gew·gaw \ˈg(y)ü-ˌgȯ\ *n* : a showy trifle : BAUBLE, TRINKET

gey·ser \ˈgī-zər\ *n* [Icelandic *geysir* gusher] : a spring that intermittently shoots up hot water and steam

Gha·na·ian \gä-ˈnā-(y)ən\ *n* : a native or inhabitant of Ghana — **Ghanaian** *adj*

ghast·ly \ˈgast-lē\ *adj* **ghast·li·er; -est 1** : HORRIBLE, SHOCKING **2** : resembling a ghost : DEATHLIKE, PALE **syn** gruesome, grim, lurid, grisly, macabre

ghat \ˈgȯt\ *n* [Hindi] : a broad flight of steps that is situated on an Indian riverbank and provides access to the water

gher·kin \ˈgər-kən\ *n* : a small young cucumber used to make pickles; *also* : a small prickly fruit of a vine related to the cucumber used for the same purpose

ghet·to \ˈget-ō\ *n, pl* **ghettos** *or* **ghettoes** : a quarter of a city in which members of a minority group live because of social, legal, or economic pressure

[1]**ghost** \ˈgōst\ *n* **1** : the seat of life : SOUL **2** : a disembodied soul; *esp* : the soul of a dead person believed to be an inhabitant of the unseen world or to appear in bodily form to living people **3** : SPIRIT, DEMON **4** : a faint trace ⟨a ~ of a smile⟩ **5** : a false image in a photographic negative or on a television screen — **ghost·ly** *adv*

[2]**ghost** *vb* : GHOSTWRITE

ghost·write \-ˌrīt\ *vb* **-wrote** \-ˌrōt\; **-writ·ten** \-ˌrit-ᵊn\ : to write for and in the name of another — **ghost·writ·er** *n*

ghoul \ˈgül\ *n* [Ar *ghūl*] : a legendary evil being that robs graves and feeds on corpses — **ghoul·ish** *adj*

GHQ *abbr* general headquarters

gi *abbr* gill

[1]**GI** \(ˈ)jē-ˈī\ *adj* [*g*alvanized *i*ron; fr. abbr. used in listing such articles as garbage cans, but taken as abbr. for *government issue*] **1** : provided by an official U.S. military supply department ⟨~ shoes⟩ **2** : of, relating to, or characteristic of U.S. military personnel **3** : conforming to military regulations or customs ⟨a ~ haircut⟩

[2]**GI** *n, pl* **GI's** *or* **GIs** \-ˈīz\ : a member or former member of the U.S. armed forces; *esp* : an enlisted man

[3]**GI** *abbr* **1** galvanized iron **2** gastrointestinal **3** general issue **4** government issue

gi·ant \ˈjī-ənt\ *n* **1** : a huge legendary manlike being of great strength **2** : a living being or thing of extraordinary size or powers — **giant** *adj*

gi·ant·ess \-əs\ *n* : a female giant

gib·ber \ˈjib-ər\ *vb* **gib·bered; gib·ber·ing** \-(ə-)riŋ\ : to speak rapidly, inarticulately, and often foolishly

gib·ber·ish \ˈjib-(ə-)rish\ *n* : unintelligible or confused speech or language

[1]**gib·bet** \ˈjib-ət\ *n* : GALLOWS

[2]**gibbet** *vb* **1** : to hang on a gibbet **2** : to expose to public scorn **3** : to execute by hanging

gib·bon \ˈgib-ən\ *n* : any of several tailless apes of southeastern Asia and the East Indies

gib·bous \ˈjib-əs, ˈgib-\ *adj* **1** : convexly rounded in form : PROTUBERANT **2** : seen with more than half but not all of the apparent disk illuminated ⟨~ moon⟩ **3** : having a hump : HUMPBACKED

gibe \ˈjīb\ *vb* **gibed; gib·ing** : to utter taunting words : SNEER — **gibe** *n*

gib·lets \ˈjib-ləts\ *n pl* : the edible viscera of a fowl

Gib·son \ˈgib-sən\ *n* : a martini with a small onion

gid·dy \ˈgid-ē\ *adj* **gid·di·er; -est 1** : DIZZY **2** : causing dizziness **3** : not serious : FRIVOLOUS, SILLY — **gid·di·ness** \ˈgid-ē-nəs\ *n*

gift \ˈgift\ *n* **1** : a special ability : TALENT **2** : something given : PRESENT **3** : the act or power of giving

gift·ed \ˈgif-təd\ *adj* : TALENTED

[1]**gig** \ˈgig\ *n* **1** : a long light ship's boat **2** : a light 2-wheeled one-horse carriage

[2]**gig** *n* : a pronged spear for catching fish — **gig** *vb*

[3]**gig** *n* : JOB; *esp* : an entertainer's engagement for a specified time

[4]**gig** *n* : a military demerit — **gig** *vb*

gi·gan·tic \jī-ˈgant-ik\ *adj* : resembling a giant : IMMENSE, HUGE

gig·gle \ˈgig-əl\ *vb* **gig·gled; gig·gling** \-(ə-)liŋ\ : to laugh with repeated short catches of the breath — **giggle** *n* — **gig·gly** \-(ə-)lē\ *adj*

GIGO *abbr* garbage in, garbage out

gig·o·lo \ˈjig-ə-ˌlō\ *n, pl* **-los 1** : a man supported by a woman usu. in return for his attentions **2** : a professional dancing partner or male escort

Gi·la monster \ˌhē-lə-\ *n* : a large orange and black venomous lizard of the southwestern U.S.

Gila monster

[1]**gild** \ˈgild\ *vb* **gild·ed** \ˈgil-dəd\ *or* **gilt** \ˈgilt\; **gild·ing 1** : to overlay with or as if with a thin covering of gold **2** : to give an attractive but often deceptive outward appearance to — **gild·ing** *n*

[2]**gild** *var of* GUILD

[1]**gill** \ˈjil\ *n* — see WEIGHT table

[2]**gill** \ˈgil\ *n* : an organ (as of a fish) for obtaining oxygen from water

[1]**gilt** \ˈgilt\ *adj* : of the color of gold

[2]**gilt** *n* : gold or a substance resembling gold laid on the surface of an object

[3]**gilt** *n* : a young female swine

gim·crack \ˈjim-ˌkrak\ *n* : a showy object of little use or value

gim·let \ˈgim-lət\ *n* : a small tool with screw point and cross handle for boring

gim·mick \ˈgim-ik\ *n* **1** : CONTRIVANCE, GADGET **2** : an important feature that is not immediately apparent : CATCH **3** : a new and ingenious scheme — **gim·micky** \-i-kē\ *adj*

gim·mick·ry \ˈgim-i-krē\ *n, pl* **-ries** : an array of or the use of gimmicks

gimpy \ˈgim-pē\ *adj* : CRIPPLED, LAME

[1]**gin** \ˈjin\ *n* [ME *gin*, modif. of OF *engin*] **1** : TRAP, SNARE **2** : a machine to separate seeds from cotton — **gin** *vb*

[2]**gin** \ˈjin\ *n* [by shortening & alter. fr. *geneva*] : a liquor distilled from a grain mash and flavored with juniper berries

gin·ger \ˈjin-jər\ *n* : the pungent aromatic rootstock of a tropical plant used esp. as a spice and in medicine; *also* : the spice or the plant

ginger ale *n* : a carbonated soft drink flavored with ginger

gin·ger·bread \ˈjin-jər-ˌbred\ *n* **1** : a cake made with molasses and flavored with ginger **2** : tawdry, gaudy, or superfluous ornament

gin·ger·ly \ˈjin-jər-lē\ *adj* : very cautious or careful — **gingerly** *adv*

gin·ger·snap \-ˌsnap\ *n* : a thin brittle molasses cookie flavored with ginger

ging·ham \ˈgiŋ-əm\ *n* : a clothing fabric usu. of yarn-dyed cotton in plain weave

gin·gi·vi·tis \ˌjin-jə-ˈvīt-əs\ *n* : inflammation of the gums

gink·go *also* **ging·ko** \ˈgiŋ-(ˌ)kō\ *n, pl* **ginkgoes** *or* **ginkgos** : a tree of eastern China with fan-shaped leaves often grown as a shade tree

gin·seng \ˈjin-ˌseŋ\ *n* : an aromatic root of a Chinese or No. American herb used esp. in Oriental medicine; *also* : one of these herbs

Gipsy *var of* GYPSY

gi·raffe \jə-ˈraf\ *n, pl* **giraffes** [It *giraffa,* fr. Ar *zirāfah*] : an African ruminant mammal with an extraordinarily long neck

gird \ˈgərd\ *vb* **gird·ed** \ˈgərd-əd\ *or* **girt** \ˈgərt\; **gird·ing** **1** : to encircle or fasten with or as if with a belt : GIRDLE ⟨~ on a sword⟩ **2** : to clothe or invest esp. with power or authority **3** : PREPARE, BRACE

gird·er \ˈgərd-ər\ *n* : a horizontal main supporting beam

gir·dle \ˈgərd-ᵊl\ *n* **1** : something (as a belt or sash) that encircles or confines **2** : a woman's supporting undergarment that extends from the waist to below the hips — **girdle** *vb*

girl \ˈgərl\ *n* **1** : a female child **2** : a typically young woman **3** : a female servant or employee **4** : SWEETHEART — **girl·hood** \-ˌhu̇d\ *n* — **girl·ish** *adj*

girl Friday *n* : a female assistant (as in an office) entrusted with a wide variety of tasks

girlfriend *n* **1** : a female friend **2** : a frequent or regular female companion of a boy or man

Girl Scout *n* : a member of the Girl Scouts of the United States of America

girth \ˈgərth\ *n* **1** : a band around an animal by which something (as a saddle) may be fastened on its back **2** : a measure around something

gist \ˈjist\ *n* [MF, it lies, fr. *gesir* to lie, fr. L *jacēre*] : the main point of a matter

¹give \ˈgiv\ *vb* **gave** \ˈgāv\; **giv·en** \ˈgiv-ən\; **giv·ing** **1** : to make a present of **2** : to bestow by formal action **3** : to accord or yield to another **4** : to put into the possession or keeping of another **5** : PROFFER **6** : DELIVER; *esp* : to deliver in exchange **7** : PAY **8** : to present in public performance or to view **9** : PROVIDE **10** : ATTRIBUTE **11** : to make, form, or yield as a product or result ⟨cows ~ milk⟩ **12** : to deliver by some bodily action ⟨*gave* me a push⟩ **13** : UTTER, PRONOUNCE **14** : DEVOTE **15** : to cause to have or receive **16** : CONTRIBUTE, DONATE **17** : to yield to force, strain, or pressure

²give *n* **1** : capacity or tendency to yield to force or strain **2** : the quality or state of being springy

give-and-take \ˌgiv-ən-ˈtāk\ *n* : an exchange (as of remarks or ideas) esp. on fair or equal terms

give·away \ˈgiv-ə-ˌwā\ *n* **1** : an unintentional revelation or betrayal **2** : something given away free; *esp* : PREMIUM

give in *vb* : SUBMIT, SURRENDER

giv·en \ˈgiv-ən\ *adj* **1** : DISPOSED, INCLINED ⟨~ to swearing⟩ **2** : SPECIFIED, FIXED ⟨at a ~ time⟩ **3** : granted as true : ASSUMED

given name *n* : a name that precedes one's surname

give out *vb* **1** : EMIT **2** : to become exhausted : COLLAPSE **3** : BREAK DOWN

give up *vb* **1** : SURRENDER **2** : to abandon (oneself) to a feeling, influence, or activity **3** : QUIT

giz·mo *or* **gis·mo** \ˈgiz-mō\ *n, pl* **gizmos** *or* **gismos** : GADGET

giz·zard \ˈgiz-ərd\ *n* : a muscular usu. horny-lined enlargement of the alimentary canal of a bird used for churning and grinding up food

gla·brous \ˈglā-brəs\ *adj* : SMOOTH; *esp* : having a surface without hairs or projections ⟨a ~ leaf⟩

gla·cial \ˈglā-shəl\ *adj* **1** : extremely cold **2** : of or relating to glaciers **3** : being or relating to a past period of time when a large part of the earth was covered by glaciers **4** *cap* : PLEISTOCENE — **gla·cial·ly** \-ē\ *adv*

gla·ci·ate \ˈglā-shē-ˌāt\ *vb* **-at·ed; -at·ing** **1** : to subject to glacial action **2** : to produce glacial effects in or on — **gla·ci·a·tion** \ˌglā-s(h)ē-ˈā-shən\ *n*

gla·cier \ˈglā-shər\ *n* : a large body of ice moving slowly down a slope or spreading outward on a land surface

¹glad \ˈglad\ *adj* **glad·der; glad·dest** **1** : experiencing pleasure, joy, or delight **2** : PLEASED **3** : very willing **4** : PLEASANT, JOYFUL **5** : CHEERFUL — **glad·ly** *adv* — **glad·ness** *n*

²glad *n* : GLADIOLUS

glad·den \ˈglad-ᵊn\ *vb* : to make glad

glade \ˈglād\ *n* : a grassy open space surrounded by woods

glad·i·a·tor \ˈglad-ē-ˌāt-ər\ *n* **1** : a person engaged in a fight to the death for public entertainment in ancient Rome **2** : a person engaging in a fierce fight or controversy — **glad·i·a·to·ri·al** \ˌglad-ē-ə-ˈtōr-ē-əl\ *adj*

glad·i·o·lus \ˌglad-ē-ˈō-ləs\ *n, pl* **-li** \-(ˌ)lē, -ˌlī\ [L, fr. dim. of *gladius* sword] : any of a genus of chiefly African plants related to the irises and having erect sword-shaped leaves and stalks of brilliantly colored flowers

glad·some \ˈglad-səm\ *adj* : giving or showing joy : CHEERFUL

glad·stone \ˈglad-ˌstōn\ *n, often cap* : a traveling bag with flexible sides on a rigid frame that opens flat into two compartments

glam·or·ize *also* **glam·our·ize** \ˈglam-ə-ˌrīz\ *vb* **-ized; -iz·ing** : to make or look upon as glamorous

glam·our *or* **glam·or** \ˈglam-ər\ *n* [Sc *glamour,* alter. of E *grammar;* fr. the popular association of erudition with occult practices] : an exciting and often illusory and romantic attractiveness; *esp* : alluring personal attraction — **glam·or·ous** *also* **glam·our·ous** \-(ə-)rəs\ *adj*

¹glance \ˈglans\ *vb* **glanced; glanc·ing** **1** : to strike and fly off to one side **2** : GLEAM **3** : to give a quick look

²glance *n* **1** : a quick intermittent flash or gleam **2** : a glancing impact or blow **3** : a quick look

gland \ˈgland\ *n* : a cell or group of cells that prepares and secretes a substance (as saliva or sweat) for further use in or discharge from the body — **glan·du·lar** \ˈglan-jə-lər\ *adj*

glans \ˈglanz\ *n, pl* **glan·des** \ˈglan-ˌdēz\ [L, lit., acorn] : a conical vascular body forming the extremity of the penis or clitoris

¹glare \ˈglaər\ *vb* **glared; glar·ing** **1** : to shine with a harsh dazzling light **2** : to stare fiercely or angrily — **glar·ing** \ˈgla(ə)r-iŋ\ *adj* — **glar·ing·ly** *adv*

²glare *n* **1** : a harsh dazzling light **2** : an angry or fierce stare

glass \ˈglas\ *n* **1** : a hard brittle usu. transparent or translucent substance made by melting sand and other materials and cooling to hardness **2** : something made of glass **3** *pl* : a pair of lenses used to correct defects of vision : SPECTACLES **4** : the quantity held by a glass — **glass** *adj* — **glass·ful** \-ˌfu̇l\ *n* — **glass·ware** \-ˌwaər\ *n* — **glassy** *adj*

glass·blow·ing \-ˌblō-iŋ\ *n* : the art of shaping a mass of glass that has been softened by heat by blowing air into it through a tube — **glass·blow·er** \-ˌblō(-ə)r\ *n*

glau·co·ma \glau̇-ˈkō-mə, glȯ-\ *n* : a disease of the eye marked by increased pressure within the eyeball resulting in damage to the retina and gradual loss of vision

[1]**glaze** \ˈglāz\ *vb* **glazed; glaz·ing 1** : to furnish (as a window frame) with glass **2** : to apply glaze to

[2]**glaze** *n* : a glassy coating or surface

gla·zier \ˈglā-zhər\ *n* : a person who sets glass in window frames

[1]**gleam** \ˈglēm\ *n* **1** : a transient subdued or partly obscured light **2** : GLINT **3** : a faint trace ⟨a ~ of hope⟩

[2]**gleam** *vb* **1** : to shine with subdued light or moderate brightness **2** : to appear briefly or faintly

glean \ˈglēn\ *vb* **1** : to gather grain left by reapers **2** : to collect little by little or with patient effort — **glean·able** *adj* — **glean·er** *n*

glean·ings \ˈglē-niŋz\ *n pl* : things acquired by gleaning

glee \ˈglē\ *n* [ME, fr. OE *glēo* entertainment, music] **1** : JOY, HILARITY **2** : an unaccompanied song for three or more solo usu. male voices — **glee·ful** *adj*

glee club *n* : a chorus organized for singing usu. short choral pieces

glen \ˈglen\ *n* : a secluded narrow valley

glen·gar·ry \glen-ˈgar-ē\ *n, pl* **-ries** *often cap* : a woolen cap of Scottish origin

glib \ˈglib\ *adj* **glib·ber; glib·best** : speaking or spoken with careless ease — **glib·ly** *adv*

glide \ˈglīd\ *vb* **glid·ed; glid·ing 1** : to move smoothly and effortlessly **2** : to descend gradually without engine power ⟨~ in an airplane⟩ — **glide** *n*

glid·er \ˈglīd-ər\ *n* **1** : one that glides **2** : an aircraft resembling an airplane but having no engine **3** : a porch seat suspended from an upright framework by short chains or straps

[1]**glim·mer** \ˈglim-ər\ *vb* **glim·mered; glim·mer·ing** \-(ə-)riŋ\ : to shine faintly or unsteadily

[2]**glimmer** *n* **1** : a faint unsteady light **2** : INKLING **3** : a small amount : BIT

[1]**glimpse** \ˈglimps\ *vb* **glimpsed; glimps·ing** : to take a brief look : see momentarily or incompletely

[2]**glimpse** *n* **1** : a faint idea : GLIMMER **2** : a short hurried look

glint \ˈglint\ *vb* **1** : to shine by reflection : SPARKLE, GLITTER, GLEAM **2** : to appear briefly or faintly — **glint** *n*

glis·san·do \gli-ˈsän-(ˌ)dō\ *n, pl* **-di** \-(ˌ)dē\ *or* **-dos** : a rapid sliding up or down the musical scale

[1]**glis·ten** \ˈglis-ᵊn\ *vb* **glis·tened; glis·ten·ing** \ˈglis-(ᵊ-)niŋ\ : to shine by reflection with a soft luster or sparkle

[2]**glisten** *n* : GLITTER, SPARKLE

glis·ter \ˈglis-tər\ *vb* : GLITTER

glitch \ˈglich\ *n* : MALFUNCTION; *also* : SNAG 2

[1]**glit·ter** \ˈglit-ər\ *vb* **1** : to shine with brilliant or metallic luster : SPARKLE **2** : to shine with strong emotion : FLASH ⟨eyes ~*ing* in anger⟩ **3** : to be brilliantly attractive esp. in a superficial way

[2]**glitter** *n* **1** : sparkling brilliancy, showiness, or attractiveness **2** : small glittering objects used for ornamentation — **glit·tery** \ˈglit-ə-rē\ *adj*

gloam·ing \ˈglō-miŋ\ *n* : TWILIGHT, DUSK

gloat \ˈglōt\ *vb* : to think about something with great and often malicious delight

glob \ˈgläb\ *n* **1** : a small drop **2** : a large rounded mass

glob·al \ˈglō-bəl\ *adj* **1** : WORLDWIDE **2** : COMPREHENSIVE, GENERAL — **glob·al·ly** \-ē\ *adv*

globe \ˈglōb\ *n* **1** : BALL, SPHERE **2** : EARTH; *also* : a spherical representation of the earth

globe–trot·ter \-ˌträt-ər\ *n* : one that travels widely — **globe–trot·ting** \-ˌträt-iŋ\ *n or adj*

glob·u·lar \ˈgläb-yə-lər\ *adj* : having the shape of a globe or globule

glob·ule \ˈgläb-yül\ *n* : a tiny globe or ball

glob·u·lin \ˈgläb-yə-lən\ *n* : any of a class of simple proteins insoluble in pure water but soluble in dilute salt solutions that occur widely in plant and animal tissues

glock·en·spiel \ˈgläk-ən-ˌs(h)pēl\ *n* [G, fr. *glocke* bell + *spiel* play] : a percussion musical instrument consisting of a series of metal bars played with two hammers

gloom \ˈglüm\ *n* **1** : partial or total darkness **2** : lowness of spirits : DEJECTION **3** : an atmosphere of despondency — **gloom·i·ly** \ˈglü-mə-lē\ *adv* — **gloom·i·ness** \-mē-nəs\ *n* — **gloomy** \ˈglü-mē\ *adj*

glop \ˈgläp\ *n* : a messy mass or mixture

glo·ri·fy \ˈglōr-ə-ˌfī\ *vb* **-fied; -fy·ing 1** : to raise to heavenly glory **2** : to light up brilliantly **3** : EXTOL **4** : to give glory to (as in worship) — **glo·ri·fi·ca·tion** \ˌglōr-ə-fə-ˈkā-shən\ *n*

glo·ri·ous \ˈglōr-ē-əs\ *adj* **1** : possessing or deserving glory : PRAISEWORTHY **2** : conferring glory **3** : RESPLENDENT, MAGNIFICENT **4** : DELIGHTFUL, WONDERFUL — **glo·ri·ous·ly** *adv*

[1]**glo·ry** \ˈglōr-ē\ *n, pl* **glories 1** : RENOWN **2** : honor and praise rendered in worship **3** : something that secures praise or renown **4** : a distinguishing quality or asset **5** : RESPLENDENCE, MAGNIFICENCE **6** : heavenly bliss **7** : a height of prosperity or achievement

[2]**glory** *vb* **glo·ried; glo·ry·ing** : to rejoice proudly : EXULT

[1]**gloss** \ˈgläs, ˈglȯs\ *n* **1** : LUSTER, SHEEN, BRIGHTNESS **2** : outward show — **glossy** *adj*

[2]**gloss** *vb* **1** : to give a deceptive appearance to **2** : to deal with too lightly or not at all ⟨~ over inadequacies⟩

[3]**gloss** *n* [ME *glose*, fr. OF, fr. L *glossa* unusual word requiring explanation, fr. Gk *glōssa, glōtta* tongue, language, unusual word] **1** : an explanatory note (as in the margin of a text) **2** : GLOSSARY **3** : an interlinear translation **4** : a continuous commentary accompanying a text

[4]**gloss** *vb* : to furnish glosses for

glos·sa·ry \ˈgläs-(ə-)rē, ˈglȯs-\ *n, pl* **-ries** : a collection of difficult or specialized terms with their meanings — **glos·sar·i·al** \glä-ˈsar-ē-əl, glȯ-\ *adj*

glos·so·la·lia \ˌgläs-ə-ˈlā-lē-ə, ˌglȯs-\ *n* [Gk *glōssa* tongue, language + *lalia* chatter, fr. *lalein* to chatter, talk] : TONGUE 6

[1]**glossy** \ˈgläs-ē, ˈglȯs-\ *adj* **gloss·i·er; -est** : having a surface luster or brightness — **gloss·i·ly** \-ə-lē\ *adv* — **gloss·i·ness** \-ē-nəs\ *n*

[2]**glossy** *n, pl* **gloss·ies** : a photograph printed on smooth shiny paper

glot·tis \ˈglät-əs\ *n, pl* **glot·tis·es** *or* **glot·ti·des** \-ə-ˌdēz\ : the slitlike opening between the vocal cords in the larynx — **glot·tal** \-ᵊl\ *adj*

glove \ˈgləv\ *n* **1** : a covering for the hand having separate sections for each finger **2** : a padded leather covering for the hand for use in a sport

[1]**glow** \ˈglō\ *vb* **1** : to shine with or as if with intense heat **2** : to have a rich warm usu. ruddy color : FLUSH, BLUSH **3** : to feel hot **4** : to show exuberance or elation ⟨~ with pride⟩

[2]**glow** *n* **1** : brightness or warmth of color; *esp* : REDNESS **2** : warmth of feeling or emotion **3** : a sensation of warmth **4** : light such as is emitted from a heated substance

glow·er \ˈglau̇(-ə)r\ *vb* : to stare angrily : SCOWL — **glower** *n*

glow·worm \ˈglō-ˌwərm\ *n* : any of various insect larvae or adults that give off light

glox·in·ia \gläk-ˈsin-ē-ə\ *n* : any of a genus of Brazilian herbs related to the African violets; *esp* : one with showy bell-shaped or slipper-shaped flowers

gloze \ˈglōz\ *vb* **glozed; gloz·ing** : to make appear right or acceptable

glu·cose \ˈglü-ˌkōs\ *n* **1** : a sugar known in three different forms; *esp* : DEXTROSE **2** : a sweet light-colored syrup made from cornstarch

glue \ˈglü\ *n* : a jellylike protein substance made from animal materials and used for sticking things together;

also : any of various other strong adhesives — **glue** *vb* — **glu·ey** \ˈglü-ē\ *adj*

glum \ˈgləm\ *adj* **glum·mer; glum·mest 1** : MOROSE, SULLEN **2** : DREARY, GLOOMY

[1]**glut** \ˈglət\ *vb* **glut·ted; glut·ting 1** : to fill esp. with food to satiety : SATIATE **2** : OVERSUPPLY

[2]**glut** *n* : an excessive supply

glu·ten \ˈglüt-ᵊn\ *n* : a gluey protein substance that causes dough to be sticky

glu·ti·nous \ˈglüt-(ᵊ-)nəs\ *adj* : STICKY

glut·ton \ˈglət-ᵊn\ *n* : one that eats to excess — **glut·ton·ous** \ˈglət-(ᵊ-)nəs\ *adj* — **glut·tony** \ˈglət-(ᵊ-)nē\ *n*

glyc·er·in *or* **glyc·er·ine** \ˈglis-(ə-)rən\ *n* : GLYCEROL

glyc·er·ol \ˈglis-ə-ˌrȯl, -ˌrōl\ *n* : a sweet colorless syrupy liquid obtained from fats or synthesized and used as a solvent, moistener, and lubricant

gly·co·gen \ˈglī-kə-jən\ *n* : a white tasteless substance that is the chief storage carbohydrate of animals

gm *abbr* gram

GM *abbr* **1** general manager **2** guided missile

G–man \ˈjē-ˌman\ *n* : a special agent of the Federal Bureau of Investigation

GMT *abbr* Greenwich mean time

gnarled \ˈnär-əld\ *adj* **1** : KNOTTY **2** : GLOOMY, SULLEN

gnash \ˈnash\ *vb* : to grind (as teeth) together

gnat \ˈnat\ *n* : any of various small usu. biting two-winged flies

gnaw \ˈnȯ\ *vb* **1** : to consume, wear away, or make by persistent biting or nibbling **2** : to affect as if by gnawing — **gnaw·er** \ˈnȯ(-ə)r\ *n*

gneiss \ˈnīs\ *n* : a layered granitelike rock

gnome \ˈnōm\ *n* : a dwarf of folklore who lives inside the earth and guards precious ore or treasure — **gnom·ish** \ˈnō-mish\ *adj*

GNP *abbr* gross national product

gnu \ˈnü\ *n, pl* **gnu** *or* **gnus** : any of several large African antelopes with an oxlike head and horns and a horselike mane and tail

[1]**go** \ˈgō\ *vb* **went** \ˈwent\; **gone** \ˈgȯn, ˈgän\; **go·ing** \ˈgō-iŋ\; **goes** \ˈgōz\ **1** : to move on a course : PROCEED ⟨~ slow⟩ **2** : LEAVE, DEPART **3** : to take a certain course or follow a certain procedure **4** : EXTEND, RUN ⟨his land ~*es* to the river⟩; *also* : LEAD ⟨that door ~*es* to the cellar⟩ **5** : to be habitually in a certain state ⟨~*es* armed after dark⟩ **6** : to become lost, consumed, or spent; *also* : DIE **7** : ELAPSE, PASS **8** : to pass by sale ⟨*went* for a good price⟩ **9** : to become impaired or weakened **10** : to give way under force or pressure : BREAK **11** : HAPPEN ⟨what's ~*ing* on⟩ **12** : to be in general or on an average ⟨cheap, as yachts ~⟩ **13** : to become esp. as the result of a contest ⟨the decision *went* against him⟩ **14** : to put or subject oneself ⟨~ to great expense⟩ **15** : RESORT ⟨*went* to court to recover damages⟩ **16** : to begin or maintain an action or motion ⟨here ~*es*⟩ **17** : to function properly ⟨the clock doesn't ~⟩ **18** : to have currency : CIRCULATE ⟨the report ~*es*⟩ **19** : to be or act in accordance ⟨a good rule to ~ by⟩ **20** : to come to be applied **21** : to pass by award, assignment, or lot **22** : to contribute to a result ⟨qualities that ~ to make a hero⟩ **23** : to be about, intending, or expecting something ⟨is ~*ing* to leave town⟩ **24** : to arrive at a certain state or condition ⟨~ to sleep⟩ **25** : to come to be ⟨the tire *went* flat⟩ **26** : to be capable of being sung or played ⟨the tune ~*es* like this⟩ **27** : to be suitable or becoming : HARMONIZE **28** : to be capable of passing, extending, or being contained or inserted ⟨this coat will ~ in the trunk⟩ **29** : to have a usual or proper place or position : BELONG ⟨these books ~ on the top shelf⟩ **30** : to be capable of being divided ⟨3 ~*es* into 6 twice⟩ **31** : to have a tendency ⟨that ~*es* to show that he is honest⟩ **32** : to be acceptable, satisfactory, or adequate **33** : to proceed along or according to : FOLLOW **34** : TRAVERSE **35** : BET, BID ⟨willing to ~ $50⟩ **36** : to assume the function or obligation of ⟨~ bail for a friend⟩ **37** : to participate to the extent of ⟨~ halves⟩ **38** : WEIGH **39** : ENDURE, TOLERATE **40** : AFFORD ⟨can't ~ the price⟩ — **go at 1** : ATTACK, ATTEMPT **2** : UNDERTAKE — **go back on 1** : ABANDON **2** : BETRAY **3** : FAIL — **go by the board** : to be discarded — **go down the line** : to give wholehearted support — **go for 1** : to pass for or serve as **2** : to try to secure **3** : FAVOR — **go one better** : OUTDO, SURPASS — **go over 1** : EXAMINE **2** : REPEAT **3** : STUDY, REVIEW — **go places** : to be on the way to success — **go to bat for** : DEFEND, CHAMPION — **go to town 1** : to work or act efficiently **2** : to be very successful

[2]**go** \ˈgō\ *n, pl* **goes 1** : the act or manner of going **2** : the height of fashion ⟨boots are all the ~⟩ **3** : a turn of affairs : OCCURRENCE **4** : ENERGY, VIGOR **5** : ATTEMPT, TRY **6** : a spell of activity — **no go** : USELESS, HOPELESS — **on the go** : constantly active

[3]**go** *adj* : functioning properly

GO *abbr* general order

goad \ˈgōd\ *n* [ME *gode,* fr. OE *gād* spear, goad] **1** : a pointed rod used to urge on an animal **2** : something that urges : SPUR — **goad** *vb*

go–ahead \ˈgō-ə-ˌhed\ *n* : authority to proceed

goal \ˈgōl\ *n* **1** : the mark set as limit to a race; *also* : an area to be reached safely in children's games **2** : AIM, PURPOSE **3** : an area or object toward which play is directed in order to score; *also* : a successful attempt to score

goal·ie \ˈgō-lē\ *n* : GOALKEEPER

goal·keep·er \ˈgōl-ˌkē-pər\ *n* : a player who defends the goal in various games

goal·post \ˈgōl-ˌpōst\ *n* : one of the two vertical posts with a crossbar that constitute the goal (as in soccer)

goat \ˈgōt\ *n, pl* **goats** *or* **goat** : any of various hollow-horned ruminant mammals related to the sheep that have backward-curving horns, a short tail, and usu. straight hair

goa·tee \gō-ˈtē\ *n* : a small trim pointed or tufted beard on a man's chin

goat·herd \ˈgōt-ˌhərd\ *n* : one who tends goats

goat·skin \-ˌskin\ *n* : the skin of a goat or a leather made from it

[1]**gob** \ˈgäb\ *n* : LUMP, MASS

[2]**gob** *n* : SAILOR

gob·bet \ˈgäb-ət\ *n* : LUMP, MASS

[1]**gob·ble** \ˈgäb-əl\ *vb* **gob·bled; gob·bling** \-(ə-)liŋ\ **1** : to swallow or eat greedily **2** : to take eagerly : GRAB

[2]**gobble** *vb* **gob·bled; gob·bling** \-(ə-)liŋ\ : to make the natural guttural noise of a male turkey

gob·ble·dy·gook *or* **gob·ble·de·gook** \ˈgäb-əl-dē-ˌgu̇k, -ˌgük\ *n* : generally unintelligible jargon

gob·bler \ˈgäb-lər\ *n* : a male turkey

go–be·tween \ˈgō-bə-ˌtwēn\ *n* : an intermediate agent : BROKER

gob·let \ˈgäb-lət\ *n* : a drinking glass with a foot and stem

gob·lin \ˈgäb-lən\ *n* : an ugly or grotesque sprite that is mischievous and sometimes evil and malicious

god \ˈgäd, ˈgȯd\ *n* **1** *cap* : the supreme reality; *esp* : the Being worshiped as the creator and ruler of the universe **2** : a being or object believed to have supernatural attributes and powers and to require worship **3** : a person or thing of supreme value

god·child \-ˌchīld\ *n* : a person for whom one stands as sponsor at baptism

god·daugh·ter \-ˌdȯt-ər\ *n* : a female godchild

god·dess \ˈgäd-əs\ *n* **1** : a female god **2** : a woman whose charm or beauty arouses adoration

god·fa·ther \ˈgäd-ˌfäth-ər, ˈgȯd-\ *n* : a man who sponsors a person at baptism
god·head \-ˌhed\ *n* **1** : divine nature or essence **2** *cap* : GOD 1; *also* : the nature of God esp. as existing in three persons
god·hood \-ˌhu̇d\ *n* : DIVINITY
god·less \ˈgäd-ləs, ˈgȯd-\ *adj* : not acknowledging a deity or divine law — **god·less·ness** *n*
god·like \-ˌlīk\ *adj* : resembling or having the qualities of God or a god
god·ly \-lē\ *adj* **god·li·er; -est 1** : DIVINE **2** : PIOUS, DEVOUT — **god·li·ness** \-lē-nəs\ *n*
god·moth·er \-ˌməth-ər\ *n* : a woman who sponsors a person at baptism
god·par·ent \-ˌpar-ənt\ *n* : a sponsor at baptism
god·send \-ˌsend\ *n* : a desirable or needed thing that comes unexpectedly
god·son \-ˌsən\ *n* : a male godchild
go·fer \ˈgō-fər\ *n* [alter. of *go for*] : an employee whose duties include running errands
go–get·ter \ˈgō-ˈget-ər\ *n* : an aggressively enterprising person — **go–get·ting** \-ˌget-iŋ\ *adj or n*
gog·gle \ˈgäg-əl\ *vb* **gog·gled; gog·gling** \-(ə-)liŋ\ : to stare with wide or protuberant eyes
gog·gles \ˈgäg-əlz\ *n pl* : protective glasses set in a flexible frame that fits snugly against the face
go–go \ˈgō-ˌgō\ *adj* [*a-go-go*] **1** : related to, being, or employed to entertain in a discotheque ⟨~ dancers⟩ **2** : aggressively enterprising and energetic
go·ings–on \ˌgō-iŋz-ˈȯn, -ˈän\ *n pl* : ACTIONS, EVENTS
goi·ter \ˈgȯit-ər\ *n* : an abnormally enlarged thyroid gland visible as a swelling at the base of the neck — **goi·trous** \-(ə-)rəs\ *adj*
goi·tre *chiefly Brit var of* GOITER
gold \ˈgōld\ *n* **1** : a malleable yellow metallic chemical element used esp. for coins and jewelry — see ELEMENT table **2** : gold coins; *also* : MONEY **3** : a yellow color
gold·brick \-ˌbrik\ *n* : a person (as a soldier) who shirks assigned work — **goldbrick** *vb*
Gold Coast *n* : an exclusive residential district
gold digger *n* : a woman who uses feminine charm to extract money or gifts from men
gold·en \ˈgōl-dən\ *adj* **1** : made of or relating to gold **2** : having the color of gold; *also* : BLOND **3** : SHINING, LUSTROUS **4** : SUPERB **5** : FLOURISHING, PROSPEROUS **6** : radiantly youthful and vigorous **7** : FAVORABLE, ADVANTAGEOUS ⟨a ~ opportunity⟩ **8** : MELLOW, RESONANT
gold·en–ag·er \ˈgōl-dən-ˈā-jər\ *n* : an elderly and often retired person usu. engaging in club activities
golden hamster *n* : a small tawny hamster often kept as a pet
gold·en·rod \ˈgōl-dən-ˌräd\ *n* : any of numerous plants related to the daisies but having tall slender stalks with many tiny usu. yellow flower heads
gold·field \ˈgōld-ˌfēld\ *n* : a gold-mining district
gold·finch \-ˌfinch\ *n* **1** : a small largely red, black, and yellow European finch often kept in a cage **2** : any of several small American finches of which the males usu. become bright yellow and black in summer
gold·fish \-ˌfish\ *n* : a small usu. yellow or golden carp often kept as an aquarium fish
gold·smith \ˈgōld-ˌsmith\ *n* : one who makes or deals in articles of gold
golf \ˈgälf, ˈgȯlf\ *n* : a game played with a small ball and various clubs on a course having 9 or 18 holes — **golf** *vb* — **golf·er** *n*
-gon \ˌgän\ *n comb form* : figure having (so many) angles ⟨hexa*gon*⟩
go·nad \ˈgō-ˌnad\ *n* : a sperm- or egg-producing gland : OVARY, TESTIS — **go·nad·al** \gō-ˈnad-ᵊl\ *adj*
go·nad·o·trop·ic \gō-ˌnad-ə-ˈträp-ik\ *or* **go·nad·o·tro·phic** \-ˈtrō-fik,-ˈträf-ik\ *adj* : acting on or stimulating the gonads ⟨~ hormones⟩
go·nad·o·tro·pin \-ˈtrō-pən\ *or* **go·nad·o·tro·phin** \-fən\ *n* : a gonadotropic hormone
gon·do·la \ˈgän-də-lə (*usual for 1*), gän-ˈdō-\ *n* **1** : a long narrow boat used on the canals of Venice **2** : a railroad car with no top used for hauling loose freight (as coal) **3** : an enclosure attached to the underside of an airship or balloon **4** : an enclosed car suspended from a cable and used esp. for transporting skiers
gon·do·lier \ˌgän-də-ˈliər\ *n* : one who propels a gondola
gone \ˈgȯn\ *adj* **1** : DEAD **2** : LOST, RUINED **3** : SINKING, WEAK **4** : INVOLVED, ABSORBED **5** : INFATUATED **6** : PREGNANT **7** : PAST
gon·er \ˈgȯn-ər\ *n* : one whose case is hopeless
gon·fa·lon \ˈgän-fə-ˌlän\ *n* : a flag that hangs from a crosspiece or frame
gong \ˈgäŋ, ˈgȯŋ\ *n* : a metallic disk that produces a resounding tone when struck
gono·coc·cus \ˌgän-ə-ˈkäk-əs\ *n, pl* **-coc·ci** \-ˈkäk-ˌ(s)ī, -ˈkäk-(ˌ)(s)ē\ : a pus-producing bacterium that causes gonorrhea — **gono·coc·cal** \-ˈkäk-əl\ *or* **gono·coc·cic** \-ˈkäk-(s)ik\ *adj*
gon·or·rhea \ˌgän-ə-ˈrē-ə\ *n* : a contagious sexually transmitted inflammation of the genital tract caused by a bacterium — **gon·or·rhe·al** \-ˈrē-əl\ *adj*
goo \ˈgü\ *n* **1** : a viscid or sticky substance **2** : sentimental tripe — **goo·ey** \-ē\ *adj*
goo·ber \ˈgü-bər, ˈgu̇b-ər\ *n, South & Midland* : PEANUT
[1]**good** \ˈgu̇d\ *adj* **bet·ter** \ˈbet-ər\; **best** \ˈbest\ **1** : of a favorable character or tendency **2** : BOUNTIFUL, FERTILE **3** : COMELY, ATTRACTIVE **4** : SUITABLE, FIT **5** : SOUND, WHOLE **6** : AGREEABLE, PLEASANT **7** : SALUTARY, WHOLESOME **8** : CONSIDERABLE, AMPLE **9** : FULL **10** : WELL-FOUNDED **11** : TRUE ⟨holds ~ for everybody⟩ **12** : recognized or valid esp. in law **13** : ADEQUATE, SATISFACTORY **14** : conforming to a standard **15** : DISCRIMINATING **16** : COMMENDABLE, VIRTUOUS **17** : KIND **18** : UPPER-CLASS **19** : COMPETENT **20** : LOYAL — **good–heart·ed** \-ˈhärt-əd\ *adj* **13** : ADEQUATE, SATISFACTORY — **good·ish** *adj* — **good–look·ing** \ˈgu̇d-ˈlu̇k-iŋ\ *adj* — **good–na·tured** \-ˈnā-chərd\ *adj* — **good–tem·pered** \-ˈtem-pərd\ *adj*
[2]**good** *n* **1** : something good **2** : GOODNESS **3** : BENEFIT, WELFARE ⟨for the ~ of mankind⟩ **4** : something that has economic utility **5** *pl* : personal property **6** *pl* : CLOTH **7** *pl* : WARES, COMMODITIES **8** : good persons ⟨the ~ die young⟩ **9** *pl* : proof of wrongdoing — **for good** : FOREVER, PERMANENTLY — **to the good** : in a position of net gain or profit ⟨$10 *to the good*⟩
[3]**good** *adv* : WELL
good–bye *or* **good–by** \gu̇d-ˈbī, gə(d)-\ *n* : a concluding remark at parting
good–for–noth·ing \ˈgu̇d-fər-ˌnəth-iŋ\ *n* : an idle worthless person
Good Friday *n* : the Friday before Easter observed as the anniversary of the crucifixion of Christ
good·ly \ˈgu̇d-lē\ *adj* **good·li·er; -est 1** : of pleasing appearance **2** : LARGE, CONSIDERABLE
good·man \ˈgu̇d-mən\ *n, archaic* : MR.
good·ness \ˈgu̇d-nəs\ *n* : EXCELLENCE, VIRTUE
good·wife \ˈgu̇d-ˌwīf\ *n, archaic* : MRS.
good·will \ˈgu̇d-ˈwil\ *n* **1** : BENEVOLENCE **2** : the value of the trade a business has built up over time **3** : cheerful consent **4** : willing effort
goody \ˈgu̇d-ē\ *n, pl* **good·ies** : something that is good esp. to eat
goody–goody \ˌgu̇d-ē-ˈgu̇d-ē\ *adj* : affectedly good — **goody–goody** *n*
goof \ˈgüf\ *vb* **1** : BLUNDER **2** : to spend time idly or foolishly — often used with *off* — **goof** *n*
goof·ball \ˈgüf-ˌbȯl\ *n* **1** *slang* : a barbiturate sleeping pill **2** *slang* : a goofy person
go off *vb* **1** : EXPLODE **2** : to follow a course ⟨the party *went off* well⟩

goof–off \ˈgüf-ˌȯf\ *n* : one who evades work or responsibility

goofy \ˈgü-fē\ *adj* **goof·i·er; -est** : CRAZY, SILLY — **goof·i·ness** \ˈgü-fē-nəs\ *n*

goon \ˈgün\ *n* : a man hired to terrorize or kill opponents

go on *vb* **1** : to continue in a course of action **2** : to take place : HAPPEN

goose \ˈgüs\ *n, pl* **geese** \ˈgēs\ **1** : any of numerous long-necked web-footed birds related to the swans and ducks; *esp* : a female goose as distinguished from a gander **2** : a foolish person **3** *pl* **goos·es** : a tailor's smoothing iron

goose·ber·ry \ˈgüs-ˌber-ē, ˈgüz-, -b(ə-)rē\ *n* : the acid berry of any of several shrubs related to the currant and used esp. in jams and pies

goose·flesh \ˈgüs-ˌflesh\ *n* : a roughening of the skin caused usu. by cold or fear

goose pimples *n pl* : GOOSEFLESH

go out *vb* **1** : to become extinguished **2** : to become a candidate ⟨*went out* for the football team⟩

go over *vb* : SUCCEED

GOP *abbr* Grand Old Party (Republican)

go·pher \ˈgō-fər\ *n* **1** : a burrowing American land tortoise **2** : any of several No. American burrowing rodents with large cheek pouches opening beside the mouth **3** : any of numerous small ground squirrels of the prairie region of No. America

[1]**gore** \ˈgōr\ *n* : BLOOD

[2]**gore** *n* : a tapering or triangular piece (as of cloth in a skirt)

[3]**gore** *vb* **gored; gor·ing** : to pierce or wound with something pointed

[1]**gorge** \ˈgȯrj\ *n* **1** : THROAT **2** : a narrow ravine **3** : a mass of matter that chokes up a passage

[2]**gorge** *vb* **gorged; gorg·ing** : to eat greedily : stuff to capacity : GLUT

gor·geous \ˈgȯr-jəs\ *adj* [ME *gorgayse,* fr. MF *gorgias* elegant] : resplendently beautiful

Gor·gon·zo·la \ˌgȯr-gən-ˈzō-lə\ *n* : a blue cheese of Italian origin

go·ril·la \gə-ˈril-ə\ *n* [fr. Gk *Gorillai,* an African tribe of hairy women] : an African manlike ape related to but much larger than the chimpanzee

gor·man·dize \ˈgȯr-mən-ˌdīz\ *vb* **-dized; -diz·ing** : to eat ravenously — **gor·man·diz·er** *n*

gorp \ˈgȯrp\ *n* : a snack consisting of high-calorie food (as raisins and nuts)

gorse \ˈgȯrs\ *n* : a prickly mostly leafless evergreen Old World shrub of the legume family that bears yellow flowers

gory \ˈgōr-ē\ *adj* **gor·i·er; -est 1** : BLOODSTAINED **2** : HORRIBLE, SENSATIONAL

gos·hawk \ˈgäs-ˌhȯk\ *n* : any of several long-tailed hawks with short rounded wings

gos·ling \ˈgäz-liŋ, ˈgȯz-\ *n* : a young goose

[1]**gos·pel** \ˈgäs-pəl\ *n* [ME, fr. OE *gōdspel,* fr. *gōd* good + *spell* tale] **1** : the teachings of Christ and the apostles **2** *cap* : any of the first four books of the New Testament **3** : something accepted as infallible truth

[2]**gospel** *adj* **1** : of, relating to, or emphasizing the gospel **2** : relating to or being American religious songs associated with evangelism

gos·sa·mer \ˈgäs-ə-mər, ˈgäz(-ə)-mər\ *n* [ME *gossomer,* fr. *gos* goose + *somer* summer] **1** : a film of cobwebs floating in the air **2** : something light, delicate, or tenuous

[1]**gos·sip** \ˈgäs-əp\ *n* **1** : a person who habitually reveals personal or sensational facts **2** : rumor or report of an intimate nature **3** : an informal conversation — **gos·sipy** *adj*

[2]**gossip** *vb* : to spread gossip

got *past and past part of* GET

Goth \ˈgäth\ *n* : a member of a Germanic race that early in the Christian era overran the Roman Empire

[1]**Goth·ic** \ˈgäth-ik\ *adj* **1** : of or relating to the Goths **2** : of or relating to a style of architecture prevalent in western Europe from the middle 12th to the earth 16th century

[2]**Gothic** *n* **1** : the Germanic language of the Goths **2** : the Gothic architectural style or decoration

gotten *past part of* GET

Gou·da \ˈgüd-ə\ *n* : a mild Dutch milk cheese shaped in balls

[1]**gouge** \ˈgau̇j\ *n* **1** : a rounded troughlike chisel **2** : a hole or groove made with or as if with a gouge

[2]**gouge** *vb* **gouged; goug·ing 1** : to cut holes or grooves in with or as if with a gouge **2** : DEFRAUD, CHEAT

gou·lash \ˈgü-ˌläsh, -ˌlash\ *n* [Hungarian *gulyás*] : a stew made with meat, assorted vegetables, and paprika

go under *vb* : to be overwhelmed, defeated, or destroyed : FAIL

gourd \ˈgōrd, ˈgu̇rd\ *n* **1** : any of a family of tendril-bearing vines including the cucumber, squash, and melon **2** : the fruit of a gourd; *esp* : any of various inedible hard-shelled fruits used esp. for ornament or implements

gourde \ˈgu̇rd\ *n* — see MONEY table

gour·mand \ˈgu̇r-ˌmänd\ *n* **1** : one who is excessively fond of eating and drinking **2** : GOURMET

gour·met \ˈgu̇r-ˌmā, gu̇r-ˈmā\ *n* [F, fr. MF, fr. *gromet* boy servant, vintner's assistant] : a connoisseur in eating and drinking

gout \ˈgau̇t\ *n* : a disease marked by painful inflammation and swelling of the joints — **gouty** *adj*

gov *abbr* **1** government **2** governor

gov·ern \ˈgəv-ərn\ *vb* **1** : to control and direct the making and administration of policy in : RULE **2** : CONTROL, DIRECT, INFLUENCE **3** : DETERMINE, REGULATE **4** : RESTRAIN — **gov·er·nance** \ˈgəv-ər-nəns\ *n*

gov·ern·ess \ˈgəv-ər-nəs\ *n* : a woman who teaches and trains a child esp. in a private home

gov·ern·ment \ˈgəv-ər(n)-mənt\ *n* **1** : authoritative direction or control : RULE **2** : the making of policy **3** : the organization or agency through which a political unit exercises authority **4** : the complex of institutions, laws, and customs through which a political unit is governed **5** : the governing body — **gov·ern·men·tal** \ˌgəv-ər(n)-ˈment-ᵊl\ *adj*

gov·er·nor \ˈgəv(-ə)-nər, ˈgəv-ər-nər\ *n* **1** : one that governs; *esp* : a ruler, chief executive, or head of a political unit (as a state) **2** : an attachment to a machine for automatic control of speed — **gov·er·nor·ship** *n*

govt *abbr* government

gown \ˈgau̇n\ *n* **1** : a loose flowing outer garment **2** : an official robe worn esp. by a judge, clergyman, or teacher **3** : a woman's dress ⟨evening ∼*s*⟩ **4** : a loose robe — **gown** *vb*

gp *abbr* group

GP *abbr* general practitioner

GPO *abbr* **1** general post office **2** Government Printing Office

GQ *abbr* general quarters

gr *abbr* **1** grade **2** grain **3** gram **4** gravity **5** gross

grab \ˈgrab\ *vb* **grabbed; grab·bing** : to take hastily : SNATCH — **grab** *n*

[1]**grace** \ˈgrās\ *n* **1** : help given man by God (as in overcoming temptation) **2** : freedom from sin through divine grace **3** : a virtue coming from God **4** : a short prayer at a meal **5** : a temporary respite (as from the payment of a debt) **6** : APPROVAL, ACCEPTANCE ⟨in his good ∼*s*⟩ **7** : CHARM **8** : ATTRACTIVENESS, BEAUTY **9** : fitness or pro-

---

\ə\abut \ᵊ\kitten \ər\further \a\ash \ā\ace \ä\cot, cart \au̇\out \ch\chin \e\bet \ē\easy \g\go \i\hit \ī\ice \j\job \ŋ\sing \ō\go \ȯ\law \ȯi\boy \th\thin \t͟h\the \ü\loot \u̇\foot \y\yet \zh\vision *see also* Pronunciation Symbols page

portion of line or expression **10** : ease of movement **11** : a musical trill or ornament **12** — used as a title for a duke, a duchess, or an archbishop — **grace·ful** \-fəl\ *adj* — **grace·ful·ly** \-ē\ *adv* — **grace·ful·ness** *n* — **grace·less** *adj*

²grace *vb* **graced; grac·ing 1** : HONOR **2** : ADORN, EMBELLISH

gra·cious \ˈgrā-shəs\ *adj* **1** : marked by kindness and courtesy **2** : GRACEFUL **3** : characterized by charm and good taste **4** : MERCIFUL — **gra·cious·ly** *adv* — **gra·cious·ness** *n*

grack·le \ˈgrak-əl\ *n* **1** : an Old World starling **2** : an American blackbird with glossy iridescent plumage

grad *abbr* graduate

gra·da·tion \grā-ˈdā-shən, grə-\ *n* **1** : a series forming successive stages **2** : a step, degree, or stage in a series **3** : an advance by regular degrees **4** : the act or process of grading

¹grade \ˈgrād\ *vb* **grad·ed; grad·ing 1** : to arrange in grades : SORT **2** : to make level or evenly sloping ⟨~ a highway⟩ **3** : to give a grade to ⟨~ a pupil in history⟩ **4** : to assign to a grade

²grade *n* **1** : a degree or stage in a series, order, or ranking **2** : a position in a scale of rank, quality, or order **3** : a class of persons or things of the same rank or quality **4** : a division of the school course representing one year's work; *also* : the pupils in such a division **5** *pl* : the elementary school system **6** : a mark or rating esp. of accomplishment in school **7** : the degree of slope (as of a road); *also* : SLOPE

grad·er \ˈgrād-ər\ *n* : a machine for leveling earth

grade school *n* : ELEMENTARY SCHOOL

gra·di·ent \ˈgrād-ē-ənt\ *n* : SLOPE, GRADE

grad·u·al \ˈgraj-(ə-w)əl\ *adj* : proceeding or changing by steps or degrees — **grad·u·al·ly** \-ē\ *adv*

grad·u·al·ism \-ˌiz-əm\ *n* : the policy of approaching a desired end gradually

¹grad·u·ate \ˈgraj-(ə-)wət, -ə-ˌwāt\ *n* **1** : a holder of an academic degree or diploma **2** : a graduated container for measuring contents

²graduate *adj* **1** : holding an academic degree or diploma **2** : of or relating to studies beyond the first or bachelor's degree ⟨~ school⟩

³grad·u·ate \ˈgraj-ə-ˌwāt\ *vb* **-at·ed; -at·ing 1** : to grant or receive an academic degree or diploma **2** : to admit to a particular standing or grade **3** : to divide into grades, classes, or intervals ⟨*graduated* thermometer⟩

grad·u·a·tion \ˌgraj-ə-ˈwā-shən\ *n* **1** : a mark that graduates something **2** : an act or process of graduating **3** : COMMENCEMENT 2

graf·fi·to \grə-ˈfēt-ō, grə-\ *n, pl* **-ti** \-(ˌ)ē\ : an inscription or drawing made on a public surface (as a wall)

¹graft \ˈgraft\ *n* **1** : a grafted plant; *also* : the point of union in this **2** : material (as skin) used in grafting **3** : the getting of money or advantage dishonestly; *also* : the money or advantage so gained

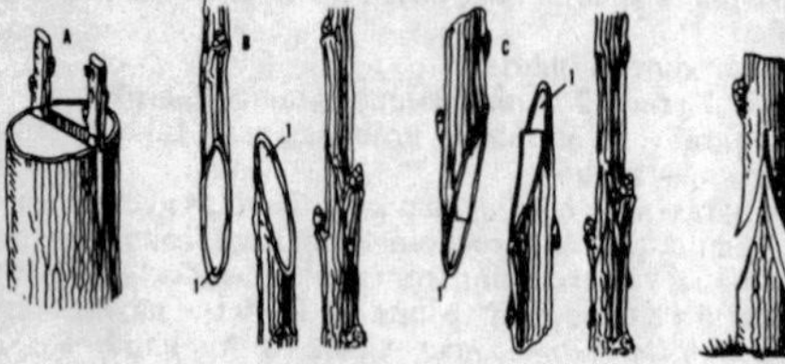

graft 1: *A* cleft, *B* splice, *C* whip, *D* saddle, *1* cambium

²graft *vb* **1** : to insert a shoot from one plant into another so that they join and grow; *also* : to join one thing to another as in plant grafting ⟨~ skin over a burn⟩ **2** : to get (as money) dishonestly — **graft·er** *n*

gra·ham cracker \ˈgrā-əm-, ˈgram-\ *n* : a slightly sweet cracker made chiefly of whole wheat flour

Grail \ˈgrāl\ *n* : the cup or platter used according to medieval legend by Christ at the Last Supper and thereafter the object of knightly quests

grain \ˈgrān\ *n* **1** : a seed or fruit of a cereal grass **2** : seeds or fruits of various food plants and esp. cereal grasses; *also* : a plant producing grain **3** : a small hard particle **4** : a unit of weight based on the weight of a grain of wheat — see WEIGHT table **5** : TEXTURE; *also* : the arrangement of fibers in wood **6** : natural disposition — **grained** \ˈgrānd\ *adj*

grain alcohol *n* : ALCOHOL 1

grain·field \ˈgrān-ˌfēld\ *n* : a field where grain is grown

grainy \ˈgrā-nē\ *adj* **grain·i·er; -est 1** : resembling or having some characteristic of grain : not smooth or fine **2** *of a photograph* : appearing to be composed of grain-like particles

¹gram \ˈgram\ *n* [F *gramme,* fr. LL *gramma,* a small weight, fr. Gk *gramma* letter, writing, a small weight, fr. *graphein* to write] : a metric unit of mass and weight equal to 1/1000 kilogram and nearly equal to one cubic centimeter of water at its maximum density — see METRIC SYSTEM table

²gram *abbr* grammar; grammatical

-gram \ˌgram\ *n comb form* : drawing : writing : record ⟨tele*gram*⟩

gram·mar \ˈgram-ər\ *n* **1** : the study of the classes of words, their inflections, and their functions and relations in the sentence **2** : a study of what is to be preferred and what avoided in inflection and syntax; *also* : speech or writing evaluated according to its conformity to the principles of grammar — **gram·mar·i·an** \grə-ˈmer-ē-ən, -ˈmar-\ *n* — **gram·mat·i·cal** \-ˈmat-i-kəl\ *adj* — **gram·mat·i·cal·ly** \-k(ə-)lē\ *adv*

grammar school *n* **1** : a secondary school emphasizing Latin and Greek in preparation for college; *also* : a British college preparatory school **2** : a school intermediate between the primary grades and high school **3** : ELEMENTARY SCHOOL

gramme \ˈgram\ *chiefly Brit var of* GRAM

gram·o·phone \ˈgram-ə-ˌfōn\ *n* : PHONOGRAPH

gra·na·ry \ˈgrān-(ə-)rē, ˈgran-\ *n, pl* **-ries 1** : a storehouse for grain **2** : a region producing grain in abundance

¹grand \ˈgrand\ *adj* **1** : higher in rank or importance : FOREMOST, CHIEF **2** : great in size **3** : INCLUSIVE, COMPLETE ⟨a ~ total⟩ **4** : MAGNIFICENT, SPLENDID **5** : showing wealth or high social standing **6** : IMPRESSIVE, STATELY **7** : very good : FINE — **grand·ly** \ˈgran-(d)lē\ *adv* — **grand·ness** \ˈgran(d)-nəs\ *n*

²grand *n, slang* : a thousand dollars

gran·dam \ˈgran-ˌdam, -dəm\ *or* **gran·dame** \-ˌdām, -dəm\ *n* : an old woman

grand·child \ˈgran(d)-ˌchīld\ *n* : a child of one's son or daughter

grand·daugh·ter \ˈgran-ˌdȯt-ər\ *n* : a daughter of one's son or daughter

grande dame \ˈgrän-ˈdäm\ *n, pl* **grandes dames** : a usu. elderly woman of great prestige or ability

gran·dee \gran-ˈdē\ *n* : a high-ranking Spanish or Portuguese nobleman

gran·deur \ˈgran-jər\ *n* **1** : the quality or state of being grand : MAGNIFICENCE **2** : something that is grand

grand·fa·ther \ˈgran(d)-ˌfäth-ər\ *n* : the father of one's father or mother; *also* : ANCESTOR

grandfather clock *n* : a tall clock standing directly on the floor

gran·dil·o·quence \gran-ˈdil-ə-kwəns\ *n* : pompous eloquence — **gran·dil·o·quent** \-kwənt\ *adj*

gran·di·ose \ˈgran-dē-ˌōs, ˌgran-dē-ˈōs\ *adj* : IMPRESSIVE,

IMPOSING; *also* : affectedly splendid — **gran·di·ose·ly** *adv* — **gran·di·os·i·ty** \ˌgran-dē-ˈäs-ət-ē\ *n*
grand jury *n* : a jury that examines accusations of crime against persons and makes formal charges on which persons are later tried
grand mal \ˈgrän(d)-ˌmäl; ˈgran(d)-ˌmal\ *n* [F, lit., great illness] : severe epilepsy
grand·moth·er \ˈgran(d)-ˌməth-ər\ *n* : the mother of one's father or mother; *also* : a female ancestor
grand·par·ent \-ˌpar-ənt\ *n* : a parent of one's father or mother
grand piano *n* : a piano with horizontal frame and strings
grand prix \ˈgräⁿ-ˈprē\ *n, pl* **grand prix** \-ˈprē(z)\ *often cap G&P* : a long-distance auto race over a road course
grand slam *n* **1** : a total victory or success **2** : a home run hit with three runners on base
grand·son \ˈgran(d)-ˌsən\ *n* : a son of one's son or daughter
grand·stand \-ˌstand\ *n* : a usu. roofed stand for spectators at a racecourse or stadium
grange \ˈgrānj\ *n* **1** : a farm or farmhouse with its various buildings **2** *cap* : one of the lodges of a national association originally made up of farmers; *also* : the association itself — **grang·er** \ˈgrān-jər\ *n*
gran·ite \ˈgran-ət\ *n* : a hard igneous rock that takes a polish and is used for building — **gra·nit·ic** \gra-ˈnit-ik\ *adj*
gran·ite·ware \-ˌwaər\ *n* : enameled ironware
gra·no·la \grə-ˈnō-lə\ *n* : a mixture of rolled oats and usu. raisins and nuts eaten esp. for breakfast
[1]**grant** \ˈgrant\ *vb* **1** : to consent to : ALLOW, PERMIT **2** : GIVE, BESTOW **3** : to admit as true — **grant·er** \-ər\ *n* — **grant·or** \ˈgrant-ər, -ˌȯr\ *n*
[2]**grant** *n* **1** : the act of granting **2** : something granted; *esp* : a gift for a particular purpose ⟨a ~ for study abroad⟩ **3** : a transfer of property by deed or writing; *also* : the instrument by which such a transfer is made **4** : the property transferred by grant
grant·ee \grant-ˈē\ *n* : one to whom a grant is made
grants·man·ship \ˈgrants-mən-ˌship\ *n* : the art of obtaining grants (as for research) — **grants·man** *n*
gran·u·lar \ˈgran-yə-lər\ *adj* : consisting of or appearing to consist of granules — **gran·u·lar·i·ty** \ˌgran-yə-ˈlar-ət-ē\ *n*
gran·u·late \ˈgran-yə-ˌlāt\ *vb* **-lat·ed; -lat·ing** : to form into grains or crystals — **gran·u·la·tion** \ˌgran-yə-ˈlā-shən\ *n*
gran·ule \ˈgran-yül\ *n* : a small grain or particle
grape \ˈgrāp\ *n* [ME, fr. OF *crape, grape* hook, grape stalk, bunch of grapes, grape] **1** : a smooth-skinned juicy edible greenish white, deep red, or purple berry that is the chief source of wine **2** : any of numerous woody vines widely grown for their bunches of grapes
grape·fruit \ˈgrāp-ˌfrüt\ *n* : a large edible yellow-skinned citrus fruit; *also* : a tree bearing grapefruit
grape hyacinth *n* : any of several small bulbous spring-flowering herbs with racemes of usu. blue flowers that are related to the lilies
grape·shot \ˈgrāp-ˌshät\ *n* : a cluster of small iron balls formerly fired at people from short range by a cannon
grape·vine \ˈgrāp-ˌvīn\ *n* **1** : GRAPE 2 **2** : RUMOR; *also* : an informal means of circulating information or gossip
graph \ˈgraf\ *n* : a diagram that usu. by means of dots and lines shows relationships between things — **graph** *vb*
-graph \ˌgraf\ *n comb form* **1** : something written ⟨auto*graph*⟩ **2** : instrument for making or transmitting records ⟨seismo*graph*⟩
graph·ic \ˈgraf-ik\ *also* **graph·i·cal** \-i-kəl\ *adj* **1** : being written, drawn, or engraved **2** : vividly described **3** : of or relating to the arts **(graphic arts)** of representation, decoration, and printing on flat surfaces — **graph·i·cal·ly** \-i-k(ə-)lē\ *adv* — **graph·ics** \-iks\ *n*
graphics tablet *n* : a computer input device for entering graphics information by drawing or tracing
graph·ite \ˈgraf-ˌīt\ *n* [G *graphit*, fr. Gk *graphein* to write] : soft carbon used esp. for lead pencils and lubricants
grap·nel \ˈgrap-nᵊl\ *n* : a small anchor with two or more claws used esp. in dragging or grappling operations
[1]**grap·ple** \ˈgrap-əl\ *n* [MF *grappelle*, dim. of *grape* hook] **1** : GRAPNEL **2** : the act of grappling
[2]**grapple** *vb* **grap·pled; grap·pling** \ˈgrap-(ə-)liŋ\ **1** : to seize or hold with or as if with a hooked implement **2** : to come to grips with : WRESTLE **3** : COPE ⟨~ with a problem⟩
[1]**grasp** \ˈgrasp\ *vb* **1** : to make the motion of seizing **2** : to take or seize firmly **3** : to enclose and hold with the fingers or arms **4** : COMPREHEND
[2]**grasp** *n* **1** : HANDLE **2** : EMBRACE **3** : HOLD, CONTROL **4** : the reach of the arms **5** : the power of seizing and holding **6** : COMPREHENSION
grasp·ing \-iŋ\ *adj* : GREEDY, AVARICIOUS
grass \ˈgras\ *n* **1** : herbage for grazing animals **2** : any of a large family of plants (as wheat, bamboo, or sugarcane) with jointed stems and narrow leaves **3** : grass-covered land **4** : MARIJUANA — **grassy** *adj*
grass·hop·per \-ˌhäp-ər\ *n* : any of numerous leaping plant-eating insects
grass·land \-ˌland\ *n* : land covered naturally or under cultivation with grasses and low-growing herbs
grass roots *n pl* : society at the local level as distinguished from the centers of political leadership
[1]**grate** \ˈgrāt\ *vb* **grat·ed; grat·ing** **1** : to pulverize by rubbing against something rough **2** : to grind or rub against with a rasping noise **3** : IRRITATE — **grat·er** *n* — **grat·ing·ly** \ˈgrāt-iŋ-lē\ *adv*
[2]**grate** *n* **1** : a framework with bars across it (as in a window) **2** : a frame of iron bars for holding fuel while it is burning
grate·ful \ˈgrāt-fəl\ *adj* **1** : THANKFUL, APPRECIATIVE; *also* : expressing gratitude **2** : PLEASING — **grate·ful·ly** \-ē\ *adv* — **grate·ful·ness** *n*
grat·i·fy \ˈgrat-ə-ˌfī\ *vb* **-fied; -fy·ing** : to afford pleasure to — **grat·i·fi·ca·tion** \ˌgrat-ə-fə-ˈkā-shən\ *n*
grat·ing \ˈgrāt-iŋ\ *n* : GRATE
gra·tis \ˈgrat-əs, ˈgrāt-\ *adv or adj* : without charge or recompense : FREE
grat·i·tude \ˈgrat-ə-ˌt(y)üd\ *n* : THANKFULNESS
gra·tu·itous \grə-ˈt(y)ü-ət-əs\ *adj* **1** : done or provided without recompense : FREE **2** : UNWARRANTED
gra·tu·ity \-ət-ē\ *n, pl* **-ities** : TIP
gra·va·men \grə-ˈvā-mən\ *n, pl* **-va·mens** *or* **-vam·i·na** \-ˈvam-ə-nə\ [LL burden] : the basic or significant part of a grievance or complaint
[1]**grave** \ˈgrāv\ *vb* **graved; grav·en** \ˈgrā-vən\ *or* **graved; grav·ing** : SCULPTURE, ENGRAVE
[2]**grave** *n* : an excavation in the earth as a place of burial; *also* : TOMB
[3]**grave** \ˈgrāv; *5 also* ˈgräv\ *adj* **1** : IMPORTANT **2** : threatening great harm or danger **3** : DIGNIFIED, SOLEMN **4** : drab in color : SOMBER **5** : of, marked by, or being an accent mark having the form ` — **grave·ly** *adv* — **grave·ness** *n*
grav·el \ˈgrav-əl\ *n* : pebbles and small pieces of rock larger than grains of sand — **grav·el·ly** \-ē\ *adj*
grave·stone \ˈgrāv-ˌstōn\ *n* : a burial monument
grave·yard \-ˌyärd\ *n* : CEMETERY
grav·id \ˈgrav-əd\ *adj* [L *gravidus*, fr. *gravis* heavy] : PREGNANT
gra·vi·me·ter \gra-ˈvim-ət-ər, ˈgrav-ə-ˌmēt-\ *n* : a device for measuring variations in a gravitational field
grav·i·tate \ˈgrav-ə-ˌtāt\ *vb* **-tat·ed; -tat·ing** : to move or tend to move toward something
grav·i·ta·tion \ˌgrav-ə-ˈtā-shən\ *n* **1** : a natural force of

---

\ə\abut \ᵊ\kitten \ər\further \a\ash \ā\ace \ä\cot, cart \au̇\out \ch\chin \e\bet \ē\easy \g\go \i\hit \ī\ice \j\job \ŋ\sing \ō\go \ȯ\law \ȯi\boy \th\thin \th\the \ü\loot \u̇\foot \y\yet \zh\vision *see also* Pronunciation Symbols page

attraction that tends to draw bodies together **2** : the action or process of gravitating — **grav·i·ta·tion·al** \-sh(ə-)nəl\ *adj* — **grav·i·ta·tion·al·ly** \-ē\ *adv* — **grav·i·ta·tive** \ˈgrav-ə-ˌtāt-iv\ *adj*

grav·i·ty \ˈgrav-ət-ē\ *n, pl* **-ties 1** : IMPORTANCE; *esp* : SERIOUSNESS **2** : [2]MASS 5 **3** : the gravitational attraction of the mass of a celestial object (as earth) for bodies close to it; *also* : GRAVITATION 1

gra·vure \grə-ˈvyu̇r\ *n* [F] : PHOTOGRAVURE

gra·vy \ˈgrā-vē\ *n, pl* **gravies 1** : a sauce made from the thickened and seasoned juices of cooked meat **2** : unearned or illicit gain : GRAFT

[1]**gray** \ˈgrā\ *adj* **1** : of the color gray; *also* : dull in color **2** : having gray hair **3** : CHEERLESS, DISMAL **4** : intermediate in position or character — **gray·ish** *adj* — **gray·ness** *n*

[2]**gray** *n* **1** : something of a gray color **2** : a neutral color ranging between black and white

[3]**gray** *vb* : to make or become gray

gray·beard \ˈgrā-ˌbiərd\ *n* : an old man

gray birch *n* : a small No. American birch with many lateral branches, grayish white bark, and soft wood

gray·ling \ˈgrā-liŋ\ *n, pl* **grayling** *also* **graylings** : any of several slender freshwater food and sport fishes related to the trouts

gray matter *n* **1** : the grayish part of nervous tissue consisting mostly of nerve cell bodies **2** : INTELLIGENCE

[1]**graze** \ˈgrāz\ *vb* **grazed; graz·ing 1** : to feed on herbage or pasture **2** : to feed (livestock) on grass or pasture — **graz·er** *n*

[2]**graze** *vb* **grazed; graz·ing 1** : to touch lightly in passing **2** : SCRATCH, ABRADE

[1]**grease** \ˈgrēs\ *n* **1** : rendered animal fat **2** : oily material **3** : a thick lubricant — **greasy** \ˈgrē-sē, -zē\ *adj*

[2]**grease** \ˈgrēs, ˈgrēz\ *vb* **greased; greas·ing** : to smear or lubricate with grease

grease·paint \ˈgrēs-ˌpānt\ *n* : theater makeup

great \ˈgrāt\ *adj* **1** : large in size : BIG **2** : ELABORATE, AMPLE **3** : large in number : NUMEROUS **4** : being beyond the average : MIGHTY, INTENSE ⟨a ~ weight⟩ ⟨in ~ pain⟩ **5** : EMINENT, GRAND **6** : long continued ⟨a ~ while⟩ **7** : MAIN, PRINCIPAL **8** : more distant in a family relationship by one generation ⟨a *great*-grandfather⟩ **9** : markedly superior in character, quality, or skill ⟨~ at bridge⟩ **10** : EXCELLENT, FINE ⟨had a ~ time⟩ — **great·ly** *adv* — **great·ness** *n*

great circle *n* : a circle on the surface of a sphere that has the same center as the sphere; *esp* : one on the surface of the earth an arc of which is the shortest travel distance between two points

great·coat \ˈgrāt-ˌkōt\ *n* : a heavy overcoat

Great Dane *n* : any of a breed of tall massive powerful smooth-coated dogs

great·heart·ed \ˈgrāt-ˈhärt-əd\ *adj* **1** : COURAGEOUS **2** : MAGNANIMOUS

great power *n, often cap G&P* : one of the nations that figure most decisively in international affairs

great white shark *n* : WHITE SHARK

grebe \ˈgrēb\ *n* : any of a family of lobe-toed diving birds related to the loons

Gre·cian \ˈgrē-shən\ *adj* : GREEK

greed \ˈgrēd\ *n* : acquisitive or selfish desire beyond reason — **greed·i·ly** \ˈgrēd-ᵊl-ē\ *adv* — **greed·i·ness** \-ē-nəs\ *n* — **greedy** \ˈgrēd-ē\ *adj*

[1]**Greek** \ˈgrēk\ *n* **1** : a native or inhabitant of Greece **2** : the ancient or modern language of Greece

[2]**Greek** *adj* **1** : of, relating to, or characteristic of Greece, the Greeks, or Greek **2** : ORTHODOX 3

[1]**green** \ˈgrēn\ *adj* **1** : of the color green **2** : covered with verdure; *also* : consisting of green plants or of the leafy parts of plants ⟨a ~ salad⟩ **3** : UNRIPE; *also* : IMMATURE **4** : having a sickly appearance **5** : not fully processed or treated ⟨~ liquor⟩ ⟨~ hides⟩ **6** : INEXPERIENCED; *also* : NAIVE — **green·ish** *adj* — **green·ness** \ˈgrēn-nəs\ *n*

[2]**green** *vb* : to make or become green

[3]**green** *n* **1** : a color between blue and yellow in the spectrum : the color of growing fresh grass or of the emerald **2** : something of a green color **3** *pl* : leafy parts of plants **4** : a grassy plot; *esp* : a smooth grassy area around the hole into which the ball must be played in golf

green·back \ˈgrēn-ˌbak\ *n* : a U.S. legal-tender note

green bean *n* : a kidney bean that is used as a snap bean when the pods are colored green

green·belt \ˈgrēn-ˌbelt\ *n* : a belt of parkways or farmlands that encircles a community

green·ery \ˈgrēn-(ə-)rē\ *n, pl* **-er·ies** : green foliage or plants

green–eyed \ˈgrēn-ˈīd\ *adj* : JEALOUS

green·gro·cer \ˈgrēn-ˌgrō-sər\ *n* : a retailer of fresh vegetables and fruit

green·horn \-ˌhȯrn\ *n* : an inexperienced person; *esp* : one easily tricked or cheated

green·house \-ˌhau̇s\ *n* : a glass structure for the growing of tender plants

green manure *n* : an herbaceous crop (as clover) plowed under when green to enrich the soil

green onion *n* : a young onion pulled before the bulb has enlarged and used esp. in salads

green pepper *n* : SWEET PEPPER

green·room \ˈgrēn-ˌrüm, -ˌru̇m\ *n* : a room in a theater or concert hall where actors or musicians relax before, between, or after appearances

green·sward \-ˌswȯrd\ *n* : turf that is green with growing grass

green thumb *n* : an unusual ability to make plants grow

Green·wich mean time \ˈgrin-ij-, ˈgren-, -ich-\ *n* [*Greenwich*, England] : GREENWICH TIME

Greenwich time *n* : the time of the meridian of Greenwich used as the basis of worldwide standard time

green·wood \ˈgrēn-ˌwu̇d\ *n* : a forest green with foliage

greet \ˈgrēt\ *vb* **1** : to address with expressions of kind wishes **2** : to meet or react to in a specified manner **3** : to be perceived by — **greet·er** *n*

greet·ing \-iŋ\ *n* **1** : a salutation on meeting **2** *pl* : best wishes : REGARDS

greeting card *n* : a card that bears a message usu. sent on a special occasion

gre·gar·i·ous \gri-ˈgar-ē-əs\ *adj* [L *gregarius* of a flock or herd, fr. *greg-, grex* flock, herd] **1** : SOCIAL, COMPANIONABLE **2** : tending to flock together — **gre·gar·i·ous·ly** *adv* — **gre·gar·i·ous·ness** *n*

grem·lin \ˈgrem-lən\ *n* : a small gnome held to be responsible for malfunction of equipment esp. in aircraft

gre·nade \grə-ˈnād\ *n* [MF, pomegranate, fr. LL *granata*, fr. L *granatus* seedy, fr. *granum* grain] : a small bomb that is thrown by hand or launched (as by a rifle)

gren·a·dier \ˌgren-ə-ˈdiər\ *n* : a member of a European regiment formerly armed with grenades

gren·a·dine \ˌgren-ə-ˈdēn, ˈgren-ə-ˌdēn\ *n* : a syrup flavored with pomegranates and used in mixed drinks

grew *past of* GROW

grey *var of* GRAY

grey·hound \ˈgrā-ˌhau̇nd\ *n* : a tall slender dog noted for speed and keen sight

grid \ˈgrid\ *n* **1** : GRATE **2** : a metal plate used as a conductor in a storage battery **3** : an element in an electron tube consisting of a mesh of fine wire **4** : GRIDIRON 2; *also* : FOOTBALL

grid·dle \ˈgrid-ᵊl\ *n* : a flat usu. metal surface for cooking food

griddle cake *n* : PANCAKE

grid·iron \ˈgrid-ˌī(-ə)rn\ *n* **1** : a grate (as of parallel bars) for broiling food **2** : something resembling a gridiron in appearance; *esp* : a football field

grid·lock \ˈgrid-ˌläk\ *n* : a traffic jam in which an intersection is so blocked that no vehicular movement is possible

grief \ˈgrēf\ *n* **1 :** emotional suffering caused by or as if by bereavement; *also* **:** a cause of such suffering **2 :** MISHAP **3 :** DISASTER

griev·ance \ˈgrē-vəns\ *n* **1 :** a cause of distress affording reason for complaint or resistance **2 :** COMPLAINT

grieve \ˈgrēv\ *vb* **grieved; griev·ing** [ME *greven,* fr. OF *grever,* fr. L *gravare* to burden, fr. *gravis* heavy, grave] **1 :** to cause grief or sorrow to **:** DISTRESS **2 :** to feel grief **:** SORROW

griev·ous \ˈgrē-vəs\ *adj* **1 :** OPPRESSIVE, ONEROUS **2 :** causing suffering, grief, or sorrow **:** SEVERE ⟨a ~ wound⟩ **3 :** SERIOUS, GRAVE — **griev·ous·ly** *adv*

[1]**grill** \ˈgril\ *vb* **1 :** to broil on a grill; *also* **:** to fry or toast on a griddle **2 :** to question intensely

[2]**grill** *n* **1 :** a cooking utensil of parallel bars on which food is grilled **2 :** an informal restaurant

grille *or* **grill** \ˈgril\ *n* **:** a grating that forms a barrier or screen

grill·work \ˈgril-ˌwərk\ *n* **:** work constituting or resembling a grille

grim \ˈgrim\ *adj* **grim·mer; grim·mest 1 :** CRUEL, FIERCE **2 :** harsh and forbidding in appearance **3 :** RELENTLESS **4 :** ghastly or repellent in character — **grim·ly** *adv* — **grim·ness** *n*

gri·mace \ˈgrim-əs, grim-ˈās\ *n* **:** a facial expression usu. of disgust or disapproval — **grimace** *vb*

grime \ˈgrīm\ *n* **:** soot, smut, or dirt adhering to or embedded in a surface; *also* **:** accumulated dirtiness and disorder — **grimy** *adj*

grin \ˈgrin\ *vb* **grinned; grin·ning :** to draw back the lips so as to show the teeth esp. in amusement — **grin** *n*

[1]**grind** \ˈgrīnd\ *vb* **ground** \ˈgraůnd\; **grind·ing 1 :** to reduce to small particles **2 :** to wear down, polish, or sharpen by friction **3 :** to press with a grating noise **:** GRIT ⟨~ the teeth⟩ **4 :** OPPRESS **5 :** to operate or produce by turning a crank **6 :** DRUDGE; *esp* **:** to study hard **7 :** to move with difficulty or friction ⟨gears ~*ing*⟩

[2]**grind** *n* **1 :** monotonous labor or routine; *esp* **:** intensive study **2 :** one who works or studies excessively

grind·er \ˈgrīn-dər\ *n* **1 :** MOLAR **2** *pl* **:** TEETH **3 :** one that grinds **4 :** SUBMARINE 2

grind·stone \ˈgrīn-ˌstōn\ *n* **:** a flat circular stone of natural sandstone that revolves on an axle and is used for grinding, shaping, or smoothing

[1]**grip** \ˈgrip\ *vb* **gripped; grip·ping 1 :** to seize or hold firmly **2 :** to hold strongly the interest of

[2]**grip** *n* **1 :** GRASP; *also* **:** strength in gripping **2 :** a firm tenacious hold **3 :** UNDERSTANDING **4 :** a device for grasping and holding **5 :** TRAVELING BAG

gripe \ˈgrīp\ *vb* **griped; grip·ing 1 :** SEIZE, GRIP **2 :** IRRITATE, VEX **3 :** to cause or experience spasmodic pains in the bowels **4 :** COMPLAIN — **gripe** *n*

grippe \ˈgrip\ *n* **:** INFLUENZA

gris–gris \ˈgrē-ˌgrē\ *n, pl* **gris–gris** \-ˌgrēz\ [F] **:** an amulet or incantation used chiefly by people of African Negro ancestry

gris·ly \ˈgriz-lē\ *adj* **gris·li·er; -est :** HORRIBLE, GRUESOME

grist \ˈgrist\ *n* **:** grain to be ground or already ground

gris·tle \ˈgris-əl\ *n* **:** CARTILAGE — **gris·tly** \-(ə-)lē\ *adj*

grist·mill \ˈgrist-ˌmil\ *n* **:** a mill for grinding grain

[1]**grit** \ˈgrit\ *n* **1 :** a hard sharp granule (as of sand); *also* **:** material composed of such granules **2 :** unyielding courage — **grit·ty** *adj*

[2]**grit** *vb* **grit·ted; grit·ting :** GRIND, GRATE

grits \ˈgrits\ *n pl* **:** coarsely ground hulled grain ⟨hominy ~⟩

griz·zled \ˈgriz-əld\ *adj* **:** streaked or mixed with gray

griz·zly \ˈgriz-lē\ *adj* **griz·zli·er; -est :** GRIZZLED

grizzly bear *n* **:** a large pale-coated bear of western No. America

gro *abbr* gross

groan \ˈgrōn\ *vb* **1 :** MOAN **2 :** to make a harsh sound under sudden or prolonged strain ⟨the chair ~*ed* under his weight⟩ — **groan** *n*

groat \ˈgrōt\ *n* **:** an old British coin worth four pennies

gro·cer \ˈgrō-sər\ *n* [ME, fr. MF *grossier* wholesaler, fr. *gros* coarse, wholesale, fr. L *grossus* coarse] **:** a dealer esp. in staple foodstuffs — **gro·cery** \ˈgrōs-(ə-)rē\ *n*

grog \ˈgräg\ *n* [*Old Grog,* nickname of Edward Vernon †1757 Eng. admiral responsible for diluting the sailors' rum] **:** alcoholic liquor; *esp* **:** liquor (as rum) mixed with water

grog·gy \ˈgräg-ē\ *adj* **grog·gi·er; -est :** weak and unsteady on the feet or in action — **grog·gi·ly** \ˈgräg-ə-lē\ *adv* — **grog·gi·ness** \-ē-nəs\ *n*

groin \ˈgrȯin\ *n* **1 :** the fold marking the juncture of the abdomen and thigh; *also* **:** the region of this fold **2 :** the curved line or rib on a ceiling along which two vaults meet

grom·met \ˈgräm-ət, ˈgrəm-\ *n* **1 :** a ring of rope **2 :** an eyelet of firm material to strengthen or protect an opening

[1]**groom** \ˈgrüm, ˈgrům\ *n* **1 :** a male servant; *esp* **:** one in charge of horses **2 :** BRIDEGROOM

[2]**groom** *vb* **1 :** to attend to the cleaning of (an animal) **2 :** to make neat, attractive, or acceptable **:** POLISH

grooms·man \ˈgrümz-mən, ˈgrůmz-\ *n* **:** a male friend who attends a bridegroom at his wedding

groove \ˈgrüv\ *n* **1 :** a long narrow channel **2 :** a fixed routine — **groove** *vb*

groovy \ˈgrü-vē\ *adj* **groov·i·er; -est :** very good **:** EXCELLENT

grope \ˈgrōp\ *vb* **groped; grop·ing 1 :** to feel about blindly or uncertainly in search ⟨~ for the right word⟩ **2 :** to feel one's way by groping

gros·beak \ˈgrōs-ˌbēk\ *n* **:** any of several finches of Europe or America with large stout conical bills

gro·schen \ˈgrō-shən\ *n, pl* **groschen** — see *schilling* at MONEY table

gros·grain \ˈgrō-ˌgrān\ *n* [F *gros grain* coarse texture] **:** a silk or rayon fabric with crosswise cotton ribs

[1]**gross** \ˈgrōs\ *adj* **1 :** glaringly noticeable **2 :** OUT-AND-OUT, UTTER **3 :** BIG, BULKY; *esp* **:** excessively fat **4 :** excessively luxuriant **:** RANK **5 :** GENERAL, BROAD **6 :** consisting of an overall total exclusive of deductions ⟨~ earnings⟩ **7 :** EARTHY, CARNAL ⟨~ pleasures⟩ **8 :** lacking knowledge or culture **:** UNREFINED **9 :** OBSCENE — **gross·ly** *adv* — **gross·ness** *n*

[2]**gross** *n* **:** an overall total exclusive of deductions — **gross** *vb*

[3]**gross** *n, pl* **gross :** a total of 12 dozen things ⟨a ~ of pencils⟩

gross national product *n* **:** the total value of the goods and services produced in a nation during a year

gro·szy \ˈgrȯ-shē\ *n, pl* **groszy** — see *zloty* at MONEY table

grot \ˈgrät\ *n* **:** GROTTO

gro·tesque \grō-ˈtesk\ *adj* **1 :** FANCIFUL, BIZARRE **2 :** absurdly incongruous **3 :** ECCENTRIC — **gro·tesque·ly** *adv*

grot·to \ˈgrät-ō\ *n, pl* **grottoes** *also* **grottos 1 :** CAVE **2 :** an artificial cavelike structure

grouch \ˈgraůch\ *n* **1 :** a fit of bad temper **2 :** an habitually irritable or complaining person — **grouch** *vb* — **grouchy** *adj*

[1]**ground** \ˈgraůnd\ *n* **1 :** the bottom of a body of water **2** *pl* **:** sediment at the bottom of a liquid **:** DREGS, LEES **3 :** a basis for belief, action, or argument **4 :** BACKGROUND **5 :** FOUNDATION **6 :** the surface of the earth; *also* **:** SOIL **7 :** an area with a particular use ⟨fishing ~*s*⟩ **8** *pl* **:** the area about and belonging to a building **9 :** a conductor that

---

makes electrical connection with the earth — **groundless** \ˈgrau̇n-(d)ləs\ *adj*

²**ground** *vb* **1** : to bring to or place on the ground **2** : to provide a reason or justification for **3** : to instruct in fundamental principles **4** : to connect electrically with a ground **5** : to restrict to the ground **6** : to run aground

³**ground** *past and past part of* GRIND

ground ball *n* : a batted baseball that rolls or bounces along the ground

ground cover *n* : low plants that grow over and cover the soil; *also* : a plant suitable for this use

ground·er \ˈgrau̇n-dər\ *n* : GROUND BALL

ground glass *n* : glass with a light-diffusing surface produced by etching or abrading

ground·hog \ˈgrau̇nd-ˌhȯg, -ˌhäg\ *n* : WOODCHUCK

ground·ling \ˈgrau̇nd-liŋ\ *n* **1** : a spectator in the cheaper part of a theater **2** : a person of inferior judgment or taste

ground rule *n* **1** : a sports rule adopted to modify play on a particular field, court, or course **2** : a rule of procedure

ground squirrel *n* : any of various burrowing rodents that are related to the squirrels and live in colonies in open areas

ground swell *n* **1** : a broad deep ocean swell caused by an often distant gale or earthquake **2** : a rapid spontaneous growth (as of political opinion)

ground·wa·ter \ˈgrau̇nd-ˌwȯt-ər, -ˌwät-\ *n* : water within the earth that supplies wells and springs

ground·work \-ˌwərk\ *n* : FOUNDATION, BASIS

ground zero *n* : the point above, below, or at which a nuclear explosion occurs

¹**group** \ˈgrüp\ *n* **1** : a number of individuals related by a common factor (as physical association, community of interests, or blood) **2** : a combination of atoms commonly found together in a molecule ⟨a methyl ~⟩

²**group** *vb* : to associate in groups : CLUSTER, AGGREGATE

grou·per \ˈgrü-pər\ *n, pl* **groupers** *also* **grouper** : any of numerous large solitary bottom fishes of warm seas

group·ie \ˈgrü-pē\ *n* : a fan of a rock group who usu. follows the group around on concert tours

group therapy *n* : therapy in the presence of a therapist in which several patients discuss their personal problems

¹**grouse** \ˈgrau̇s\ *n, pl* **grouse** *or* **grouses** : any of numerous plump-bodied ground-dwelling game birds related to but usu. less brightly colored than the pheasants

²**grouse** *vb* **groused; grous·ing** : COMPLAIN, GRUMBLE

grout \ˈgrau̇t\ *n* : material (as mortar) used for filling spaces — **grout** *vb*

grove \ˈgrōv\ *n* : a small wood usu. without underbrush

grov·el \ˈgräv-əl, ˈgrəv-\ *vb* **-eled** *or* **-elled; -el·ing** *or* **-el·ling** \-(ə-)liŋ\ **1** : to creep or lie with the body prostrate in fear or humility **2** : to abase oneself

grow \ˈgrō\ *vb* **grew** \ˈgrü\; **grown** \ˈgrōn\; **grow·ing 1** : to spring up and come to maturity **2** : to be able to grow : THRIVE **3** : to take on some relation through or as if through growth ⟨tree limbs *grown* together⟩ **4** : INCREASE, EXPAND **5** : RESULT, ORIGINATE **6** : to come into existence : ARISE **7** : BECOME **8** : to have an increasing influence **9** : to cause to grow — **grow·er** \ˈgrō(-ə)r\ *n*

growl \ˈgrau̇l\ *vb* **1** : RUMBLE **2** : to utter a deep throaty threatening sound **3** : GRUMBLE — **growl** *n*

grown-up \ˈgrōn-ˌəp\ *adj* : not childish : ADULT — **grown-up** *n*

growth \ˈgrōth\ *n* **1** : stage or condition attained in growing **2** : a process of growing esp. through progressive development or increase **3** : a result or product of growing ⟨a fine ~ of hair⟩; *also* : an abnormal mass of tissue (as a tumor)

¹**grub** \ˈgrəb\ *vb* **grubbed; grub·bing 1** : to clear or root out by digging **2** : to dig in the ground usu. for a hidden object **3** : RUMMAGE

²**grub** *n* **1** : a soft thick wormlike larva ⟨beetle ~*s*⟩ **2** : DRUDGE; *also* : a slovenly person **3** : FOOD

grub·by \ˈgrəb-ē\ *adj* **grub·bi·er; -est** : DIRTY, SLOVENLY — **grub·bi·ness** \ˈgrəb-ē-nəs\ *n*

grub·stake \ˈgrəb-ˌstāk\ *n* : supplies or funds furnished a mining prospector in return for a share in his finds

¹**grudge** \ˈgrəj\ *vb* **grudged; grudg·ing** : to be reluctant to give : BEGRUDGE

²**grudge** *n* : a feeling of deep-seated resentment or ill will

gru·el \ˈgrü-əl\ *n* : a thin porridge

gru·el·ing *or* **gru·el·ling** \-ə-liŋ\ *adj* : requiring extreme effort : EXHAUSTING

grue·some \ˈgrü-səm\ *adj* [fr. earlier *growsome,* fr. E dial. *grow, grue* to shiver] : inspiring horror or repulsion : GRISLY

gruff \ˈgrəf\ *adj* **1** : rough in speech or manner **2** : being deep and harsh : HOARSE — **gruff·ly** *adv*

grum·ble \ˈgrəm-bəl\ *vb* **grum·bled; grum·bling** \-b(ə-)liŋ\ **1** : to mutter in discontent **2** : GROWL, RUMBLE — **grum·bler** \-b(ə-)lər\ *n*

grumpy \ˈgrəm-pē\ *adj* **grump·i·er; -est** : moodily cross : SURLY — **grump·i·ly** \ˈgrəm-pə-lē\ *adv* — **grump·i·ness** \-pē-nəs\ *n*

grun·gy \ˈgrən-jē\ *adj* **grun·gi·er; -est** : shabby or dirty in character or condition

grun·ion \ˈgrən-yən\ *n* : a fish of the California coast which comes inshore to spawn at nearly full moon

grunt \ˈgrənt\ *n* : a deep throaty sound (as that of a hog) — **grunt** *vb*

GSA *abbr* **1** General Services Administration **2** Girl Scouts of America

G suit *n* [gravity *suit*] : an astronaut's or aviator's suit designed to counteract the physiological effects of acceleration

gt *abbr* great

Gt Brit *abbr* Great Britain

gtd *abbr* guaranteed

GU *abbr* Guam

gua·ca·mo·le \ˌgwäk-ə-ˈmō-lē\ *n* [AmerSp] : mashed and seasoned avocado

gua·nine \ˈgwän-ˌēn\ *n* : a purine base that codes genetic information in the molecular chain of DNA or RNA

gua·no \ˈgwän-ō\ *n* [Sp, fr. Quechua (a South American Indian language) *huanu* dung] : a substance composed chiefly of the excrement of seabirds and used as a fertilizer

gua·ra·ni \ˌgwär-ə-ˈnē\ *n, pl* **guaranies** *also* **guaranis** — see MONEY table

¹**guar·an·tee** \ˌgar-ən-ˈtē\ *n* **1** : GUARANTOR **2** : GUARANTY 1 **3** : an agreement by which one person undertakes to secure another in the possession or enjoyment of something **4** : an assurance of the quality of or of the length of use to be expected from a product offered for sale **5** : GUARANTY 3

²**guarantee** *vb* **-teed; -tee·ing 1** : to undertake to answer for the debt, failure to perform, or faulty performance of (another) **2** : to undertake an obligation to establish, perform, or continue **3** : to give security to

guar·an·tor \ˌgar-ən-ˈtȯr\ *n* : one who gives a guarantee

¹**guar·an·ty** \ˈgar-ən-tē\ *n, pl* **-ties 1** : an undertaking to answer for another's failure to pay a debt or perform a duty **2** : GUARANTEE 3 **3** : PLEDGE, SECURITY **4** : GUARANTOR

²**guaranty** *vb* **-tied; -ty·ing** : GUARANTEE

¹**guard** \ˈgärd\ *n* **1** : one assigned to protect or oversee another **2** : a man or a body of men on sentinel duty **3** *pl* : troops attached to the person of the sovereign **4** : a defensive position (as in boxing) **5** : the act or duty of protecting or defending **6** : PROTECTION **7** : a football lineman playing between center and tackle; *also* : a basketball player stationed toward the rear **8** : a protective or safety device — **on guard** : WATCHFUL, ALERT

²guard *vb* **1** : PROTECT, DEFEND **2** : to watch over **3** : to be on guard

guard·house \ˈgärd-ˌhau̇s\ *n* **1** : a building occupied by a guard or used as a headquarters by soldiers on guard duty **2** : a military jail

guard·ian \ˈgärd-ē-ən\ *n* **1** : CUSTODIAN **2** : one who has the care of the person or property of another — **guard·ian·ship** *n*

guard·room \ˈgärd-ˌrüm\ *n* **1** : a room used by a military guard while on duty **2** : a room where military prisoners are confined

guards·man \ˈgärdz-mən\ *n* : a member of a military body called *guard* or *guards*

gua·va \ˈgwäv-ə\ *n* : the sweet yellow acid fruit of a shrubby tropical American tree of the myrtle family used esp. for making jam and jelly; *also* : the tree

gu·ber·na·to·ri·al \ˌgüb-ə(r)-nə-ˈtōr-ē-əl\ *adj* : of or relating to a governor

guer·don \ˈgərd-ᵊn\ *n* [ME, fr. MF, fr. Old High German *widarlōn,* fr. *widar* back + *lōn* reward] : REWARD, RECOMPENSE

guern·sey \ˈgərn-zē\ *n, pl* **guernseys** *often cap* : any of a breed of fawn and white dairy cattle that produce rich yellowish milk

guer·ril·la *or* **gue·ril·la** \gə-ˈril-ə\ *n* [Sp *guerrilla,* fr. dim. of *guerra* war, of Gmc origin] : one who engages in irregular warfare esp. as a member of an independent unit

guess \ˈges\ *vb* **1** : to form an opinion from little or no evidence **2** : to conjecture correctly about : DISCOVER **3** : BELIEVE, SUPPOSE — **guess** *n*

guest \ˈgest\ *n* **1** : a person to whom hospitality (as of a house or a club) is extended **2** : a patron of a commercial establishment (as a hotel or restaurant) **3** : a person not a regular member of a cast who appears on a program

guf·faw \gə-ˈfȯ\ *n* : a loud burst of laughter — **guf·faw** \(ˌ)gə-ˈfȯ\ *vb*

guid·ance \ˈgīd-ᵊns\ *n* **1** : the act or process of guiding **2** : ADVICE, DIRECTION

¹guide \ˈgīd\ *n* **1** : one who leads or directs another on a course **2** : one who shows and explains points of interest **3** : something that provides guiding information; *also* : SIGNPOST **4** : a device to direct the motion of something

²guide *vb* **guid·ed; guid·ing 1** : CONDUCT **2** : MANAGE, DIRECT **3** : to superintend the training of — **guid·able** \ˈgīd-ə-bəl\ *adj*

guide·book \ˈgīd-ˌbu̇k\ *n* : a book of information for travelers

guided missile *n* : a missile whose course may be altered during flight

guide·line \ˈgīd-ˌlīn\ *n* : an indication or outline of policy or conduct

guide word *n* : a term at the head of a page of an alphabetical reference work that indicates the alphabetically first or last word on that page

gui·don \ˈgīd-ˌän, -ᵊn\ *n* : a small flag (as of a military unit)

guild \ˈgild\ *n* : an association of people with common aims and interests; *esp* : a medieval association of merchants or craftsmen — **guild·hall** \-ˌhȯl\ *n*

guil·der \ˈgil-dər\ *n* : GULDEN

guile \ˈgīl\ *n* : deceitful cunning : DUPLICITY — **guile·ful** *adj* — **guile·less** \ˈgīl-ləs\ *adj* — **guile·less·ness** *n*

guil·lo·tine \ˈgil-ə-ˌtēn, ˌgē-(y)ə-ˈtēn\ *n* : a machine for beheading persons — **guillotine** *vb*

guilt \ˈgilt\ *n* **1** : the fact of having committed an offense esp. against the law **2** : BLAMEWORTHINESS **3** : a feeling of responsibility for wrongdoing — **guilt·less** *adj*

guilty \ˈgil-tē\ *adj* **guilt·i·er; -est 1** : having committed a breach of conduct **2** : suggesting or involving guilt **3** : aware of or suffering from guilt — **guilt·i·ly** \ˈgil-tə-lē\ *adv* — **guilt·i·ness** \-tē-nəs\ *n*

guin·ea \ˈgin-ē\ *n* **1** : a British gold coin no longer issued worth 21 shillings **2** : a unit of value equal to 21 shillings

guinea fowl *n* : a gray and white spotted West African bird related to the pheasants and widely raised for food; *also* : any of several related birds

guinea hen *n* : a female guinea fowl; *also* : GUINEA FOWL

guinea pig *n* : a small stocky short-eared and nearly tailless So. American rodent

guise \ˈgīz\ *n* **1** : a form or style of dress : COSTUME **2** : external appearance : SEMBLANCE

gui·tar \gi-ˈtär\ *n* : a musical instrument with usu. six strings plucked with a pick or with the fingers

gulch \ˈgəlch\ *n* : RAVINE

gul·den \ˈgül-dən, ˈgu̇l-\ *n, pl* **guldens** *or* **gulden** — see MONEY table

gulf \ˈgəlf\ *n* [ME *goulf,* fr. MF *golfe,* fr. It *golfo,* fr. LL *colpus,* fr. Gk *kolpos* bosom, gulf] **1** : an extension of an ocean or a sea into the land **2** : ABYSS, CHASM **3** : a wide separation

¹gull \ˈgəl\ *n* : any of numerous mostly white or gray long-winged web-footed seabirds

¹gull

²gull *vb* : to make a dupe of : DECEIVE — **gull·ible** *adj*

³gull *n* : DUPE

gul·let \ˈgəl-ət\ *n* : ESOPHAGUS; *also* : THROAT

gul·ly \ˈgəl-ē\ *n, pl* **gullies** : a trench worn in the earth by running water after rains

gulp \ˈgəlp\ *vb* **1** : to swallow hurriedly or greedily **2** : SUPPRESS ⟨~ down a sob⟩ **3** : to catch the breath as if in taking a long drink — **gulp** *n*

¹gum \ˈgəm\ *n* : the tissue along the jaws that surrounds the necks of the teeth

²gum *n* **1** : a sticky plant exudate; *esp* : one that hardens on drying and is soluble in or swells in water and that includes substances used as emulsifiers, adhesives, and thickeners and in inks **2** : a sticky substance **3** : a preparation usu. of a plant gum sweetened and flavored and used for chewing — **gum·my** *adj*

gum arabic *n* : a water-soluble gum obtained from several acacias and used esp. in adhesives, in confectionery, and in pharmacy

gum·bo \ˈgəm-bō\ *n* [AmerF *gombo,* of Bantu origin] : a rich thick soup usu. thickened with okra

gum·drop \ˈgəm-ˌdräp\ *n* : a candy made usu. from corn syrup with gelatin and coated with sugar crystals

gump·tion \ˈgəmp-shən\ *n* **1** : shrewd common sense **2** : ENTERPRISE, INITIATIVE

gum·shoe \ˈgəm-ˌshü\ *n* : DETECTIVE — **gumshoe** *vb*

¹gun \ˈgən\ *n* **1** : CANNON **2** : a portable firearm **3** : a discharge of a gun **4** : something suggesting a gun in shape or function **5** : THROTTLE

²gun *vb* **gunned; gun·ning 1** : to hunt with a gun **2** : SHOOT

3 : to open up the throttle of so as to increase speed
gun·boat \ˈgən-ˌbōt\ *n* : a small lightly armed ship for use in shallow waters
gun·fight \-ˌfīt\ *n* : a duel with guns — **gun·fight·er** \-ər\ *n*
gun·fire \-ˌfī(ə)r\ *n* : the firing of guns
gung ho \ˈgəŋ-ˈhō\ *adj* [*Gung ho!,* motto (interpreted as meaning "work together") of certain U.S. marine raiders in World War II, fr. Chin *kung*¹-*ho*², short for *chung*¹-*kuo*² *kung*¹-*yeh*⁴ *ho*²-*tso*⁴ *she*⁴ Chinese Industrial Cooperatives Society] : extremely zealous
gun·lock \ˈgən-ˌläk\ *n* : a device on a firearm by which the charge is ignited
gun·man \-mən\ *n* : a man armed with a gun; *esp* : an armed bandit or gangster
gun·ner \ˈgən-ər\ *n* **1** : a soldier or airman who operates or aims a gun **2** : one who hunts with a gun
gun·nery \ˈgən-(ə-)rē\ *n* : the use of guns; *esp* : the science of the flight of projectiles and effective use of guns
gunnery sergeant *n* : a noncommissioned officer in the marine corps ranking next below a first sergeant
gun·ny \ˈgən-ē\ *n* : coarse jute or hemp material for making sacks
gun·ny·sack \-ˌsak\ *n* : a sack made of gunny
gun·point \-ˌpȯint\ *n* : the muzzle of a gun — **at gunpoint** : under a threat of death by being shot
gun·pow·der \-ˌpau̇d-ər\ *n* : an explosive powder used in guns and blasting
gun·shot \ˈgən-ˌshät\ *n* **1** : shot fired from a gun **2** : the range of a gun ⟨within ~⟩
gun–shy \-ˌshī\ *adj* **1** : afraid of a loud noise **2** : markedly distrustful
gun·sling·er \-ˌsliŋ-ər\ *n* : a gunman esp. in the old West
gun·smith \-ˌsmith\ *n* : one who designs, makes, or repairs firearms
gun·wale *also* **gun·nel** \ˈgən-ᵊl\ *n* : the upper edge of a ship's or boat's side
gup·py \ˈgəp-ē\ *n, pl* **guppies** [after R.J.L. *Guppy* †1916 Trinidadian naturalist] : a tiny brightly colored tropical fish
gur·gle \ˈgər-gəl\ *vb* **gur·gled; gur·gling** \-g(ə-)liŋ\ : to make a sound like that of a flowing and gently splashing liquid — **gurgle** *n*
Gur·kha \ˈgu̇r-kə, ˈgər-\ *n* : a soldier from Nepal in the British or Indian army
gur·ney \ˈgər-nē\ *n, pl* **gurneys** : a wheeled cot or stretcher
gu·ru \ˈgu̇r-ü, gə-ˈrü\ *n, pl* **gurus** [Hindi] **1** : a personal religious and spiritual teacher in Hinduism **2** : a teacher in matters of fundamental concern
gush \ˈgəsh\ *vb* **1** : to issue or pour forth copiously or violently : SPOUT **2** : to make an effusive display of affection or enthusiasm
gush·er \ˈgəsh-ər\ *n* : one that gushes; *esp* : an oil well with a large natural flow
gushy \ˈgəsh-ē\ *adj* **gush·i·er; -est** : marked by effusive sentimentality
gus·set \ˈgəs-ət\ *n* [ME, piece of armor covering the joints in a suit of armor, fr. MF *gousset*] : a triangular insert (as in a seam of a sleeve) to give width or strength — **gusset** *vb*
gus·sy up \ˌgəs-ē-\ *vb* : to dress up
¹**gust** \ˈgəst\ *n* **1** : a sudden brief rush of wind **2** : a sudden outburst : SURGE — **gusty** *adj*
²**gust** *vb* : to blow in gusts
gus·ta·to·ry \ˈgəs-tə-ˌtōr-ē\ *adj* : of, relating to, or being the sense or sensation of taste
gus·to \ˈgəs-tō\ *n, pl* **gustoes** : RELISH, ZEST
¹**gut** \ˈgət\ *n* **1** *pl* : BOWELS, ENTRAILS **2** : the alimentary canal or a part of it (as the intestine); *also* : BELLY, ABDOMEN **3** *pl* : the inner essential parts **4** *pl* : COURAGE, STAMINA
²**gut** *vb* **gut·ted; gut·ting** **1** : EVISCERATE **2** : to destroy the inside of
gutsy \ˈgət-sē\ *adj* **guts·i·er; -est** : aggressively tough : COURAGEOUS
gut·ter \ˈgət-ər\ *n* : a channel or low area for carrying off rainwater
gut·ter·snipe \-ˌsnīp\ *n* : a street urchin
gut·tur·al \ˈgət-ə-rəl\ *adj* **1** : sounded in the throat **2** : being or marked by an utterance that is strange, unpleasant, or disagreeable — **guttural** *n*
gut·ty \ˈgət-ē\ *adj* **gut·ti·er; -est** **1** : GUTSY **2** : having a vigorous challenging quality
¹**guy** \ˈgī\ *n* : a rope, chain, or rod attached to something as a brace or guide
²**guy** *vb* : to steady or reinforce with a guy
³**guy** *n* : MAN, FELLOW
⁴**guy** *vb* : to make fun of : RIDICULE
Guy·a·nese \ˌgī-ə-ˈnēz\ *n, pl* **Guyanese** : a native or inhabitant of Guyana — **Guyanese** *adj*
guz·zle \ˈgəz-əl\ *vb* **guz·zled; guz·zling** \-(ə-)liŋ\ : to drink greedily
gym \ˈjim\ *n* : GYMNASIUM
gym·kha·na \jim-ˈkän-ə\ *n* : a meet featuring sports contests; *esp* : a contest of automobile-driving skill
gym·na·si·um *for 1* jim-ˈnā-zē-əm, -zhəm, *for 2* gim-ˈnä-zē-əm\ *n, pl* **-na·si·ums** *or* **-na·sia** \-ˈnā-zē-ə, -ˈnā-zhə; -ˈnä-zē-ə\ [L, exercise ground, school, fr. Gk *gymnasion,* fr. *gymnazein* to exercise naked, fr. *gymnos* naked] **1** : a room or building for indoor sports activities **2** : a German secondary school that prepares students for the university
gym·nas·tics \jim-ˈnas-tiks\ *n* : physical exercises performed in or adapted to performance in a gymnasium — **gym·nast** \ˈjim-ˌnast\ *n* — **gym·nas·tic** *adj*
gym·no·sperm \ˈjim-nə-ˌspərm\ *n* : any of a class or subdivision of woody vascular seed plants (as conifers) that produce naked seeds not enclosed in an ovary
gyn *or* **gynecol** *abbr* gynecology
gy·ne·col·o·gy \ˌgīn-ə-ˈkäl-ə-jē, ˌjin-\ *n* : a branch of medicine dealing with the diseases and hygiene of women — **gy·ne·co·log·ic** \ˌgīn-i-kə-ˈläj-ik, ˌjin-\ *or* **gy·ne·co·log·i·cal** \-i-kəl\ *adj* — **gy·ne·col·o·gist** \ˌgīn-ə-ˈkäl-ə-jəst, ˌjin-\ *n*
gyp \ˈjip\ *n* **1** : CHEAT, SWINDLER **2** : FRAUD, SWINDLE — **gyp** *vb*
gyp·sum \ˈjip-səm\ *n* : a calcium-containing mineral used in making plaster of paris
Gyp·sy \ˈjip-sē\ *n, pl* **Gypsies** [by shortening & alter. fr. *Egyptian*] : one of a dark Caucasian race coming orig. from India and living chiefly in Europe and the U.S.; *also* : the language of the Gypsies
gypsy moth *n* : an Old World moth that was introduced into the U.S. where its caterpillar is a destructive defoliator of many trees
gy·rate \ˈjī-ˌrāt\ *vb* **gy·rat·ed; gy·rat·ing** **1** : to revolve around a point or axis **2** : to oscillate with or as if with a circular or spiral motion — **gy·ra·tion** \jī-ˈrā-shən\ *n*
gyr·fal·con \ˈjər-ˌfal-kən, -ˌfȯ(l)-\ *n* : an arctic falcon that is the largest of all falcons and occurs in several forms
gy·ro \ˈjī-rō\ *n, pl* **gyros** **1** : GYROSCOPE **2** : GYROCOMPASS
gy·ro·com·pass \-ˌkəm-pəs, -ˌkäm-\ *n* : a compass in which the axis of a spinning gyroscope points to the north
gy·ro·scope \-ˌskōp\ *n* : a wheel or disk mounted to spin rapidly about an axis that is free to turn in various directions
Gy Sgt *abbr* gunnery sergeant
gyve \ˈjīv, ˈgīv\ *n* : FETTER — **gyve** *vb*

H

[1]**h** \ˈāch\ *n, pl* **h's** *or* **hs** \ˈā-chəz\ *often cap* : the 8th letter of the English alphabet

[2]**h** *abbr, often cap* **1** hard; hardness **2** heroin **3** hit **4** husband

H *symbol* hydrogen

ha *abbr* hectare

Hab *abbr* Habacuc; Habakkuk

Ha·ba·cuc \ˈhab-ə-ˌkək, hə-ˈbak-ək\ *n* — see BIBLE table

Ha·bak·kuk \ˈhab-ə-ˌkək, hə-ˈbak-ək\ *n* — see BIBLE table

ha·ba·ne·ra \ˌ(h)äb-ə-ˈner-ə\ *n* [Sp *(danza) habanera,* lit., dance of Havana] : a Cuban dance in slow time; *also* : the music for this dance

ha·be·as cor·pus \ˈhā-bē-əs-ˈkȯr-pəs\ *n* [ME, fr. ML, lit., you should have the body (the opening words of the writ)] : a writ issued to bring a party before a court

hab·er·dash·er \ˈhab-ə(r)-ˌdash-ər\ *n* : a dealer in men's clothing and accessories

hab·er·dash·ery \-ˌdash-(ə-)rē\ *n, pl* **-er·ies** **1** : goods sold by a haberdasher **2** : a haberdasher's shop

ha·bil·i·ment \hə-ˈbil-ə-mənt\ *n* **1** *pl* : TRAPPINGS, EQUIPMENT **2** : DRESS; *esp* : the dress characteristic of an occupation or occasion — usu. used in pl.

hab·it \ˈhab-ət\ *n* **1** : DRESS, GARB **2** : BEARING, CONDUCT **3** : PHYSIQUE **4** : mental makeup **5** : a usual manner of behavior : CUSTOM **6** : a behavior pattern acquired by frequent repetition **7** : ADDICTION **8** : mode of growth or occurrence

hab·it·able \ˈhab-ət-ə-bəl\ *adj* : capable of being lived in — **hab·it·abil·i·ty** \ˌhab-ət-ə-ˈbil-ət-ē\ *n*

ha·bi·tant \ˈhab-ət-ənt\ *n* : INHABITANT, RESIDENT

hab·i·tat \ˈhab-ə-ˌtat\ *n* [L, it inhabits] : the place or kind of place where a plant or animal naturally occurs

hab·i·ta·tion \ˌhab-ə-ˈtā-shən\ *n* **1** : OCCUPANCY **2** : a dwelling place : RESIDENCE **3** : SETTLEMENT

hab·it–form·ing \ˈhab-ət-ˌfȯr-miŋ\ *adj* : inducing the formation of an addiction

ha·bit·u·al \hə-ˈbich-(ə-w)əl\ *adj* **1** : CUSTOMARY **2** : doing, practicing, or acting by force of habit **3** : inherent in an individual — **ha·bit·u·al·ly** \-ē\ *adv* — **ha·bit·u·al·ness** *n*

ha·bit·u·ate \hə-ˈbich-ə-ˌwāt\ *vb* **-at·ed; -at·ing** **1** : ACCUSTOM **2** : to cause habituation

ha·bit·u·a·tion \hə-ˌbich-ə-ˈwā-shən\ *n* **1** : the process of making habitual **2** : psychological dependence on a drug after a period of use

ha·bi·tué \hə-ˈbich-ə-ˌwā\ *n* [F] : one who frequents a place or class of places

ha·ci·en·da \ˌ(h)äs-ē-ˌen-də\ *n* **1** : a large estate in a Spanish-speaking country **2** : the main building of a farm or ranch

[1]**hack** \ˈhak\ *vb* **1** : to cut with repeated irregular blows : CHOP **2** : to cough in a short dry manner **3** : to manage successfully — **hack·er** *n*

[2]**hack** *n* **1** : an implement for hacking **2** : a short dry cough **3** : a hacking blow

[3]**hack** *n* **1** : a horse hired or used for varied work **2** : a horse worn out in service **3** : a light easy often 3-gaited saddle horse **4** : HACKNEY 2, TAXICAB **5** : a writer who works mainly for hire **6** : one who serves a cause merely for reward — **hack** *adj*

[4]**hack** *vb* : to operate a taxicab

hack·ie \ˈhak-ē\ *n* : a taxicab driver

hack·le \ˈhak-əl\ *n* **1** : one of the long feathers on the neck or back of a bird **2** *pl* : hairs (as on a dog's neck) that can be erected **3** *pl* : TEMPER, DANDER

hack·man \ˈhak-mən\ *n* : HACKIE

[1]**hack·ney** \ˈhak-nē\ *n, pl* **hackneys** **1** : a horse for riding or driving **2** : a carriage or automobile kept for hire

[2]**hackney** *vb* : to make trite

hack·neyed \ˈhak-nēd\ *adj* : lacking in freshness or originality

hack·saw \ˈhak-ˌsȯ\ *n* : a fine-tooth saw in a frame for cutting metal

hack·work \-ˌwərk\ *n* : work done on order usu. according to a formula

had *past and past part of* HAVE

had·dock \ˈhad-ək\ *n, pl* **haddock** *also* **haddocks** : an Atlantic food fish usu. smaller than the related cod

Ha·des \ˈhād-(ˌ)ēz\ *n* **1** : the abode of the dead in Greek mythology **2** *often not cap* : HELL

haf·ni·um \ˈhaf-nē-əm\ *n* : a gray metallic chemical element — see ELEMENT table

haft \ˈhaft\ *n* : the handle of a weapon or tool

hag \ˈhag\ *n* **1** : an ugly, slatternly, or evil-looking old woman **2** : WITCH 2

Hag *abbr* Haggai

Hag·gai \ˈhag-ē-ˌī, ˈhag-ˌī\ *n* — see BIBLE table

hag·gard \ˈhag-ərd\ *adj* : having a worn or emaciated appearance **syn** careworn, wasted, drawn — **hag·gard·ly** *adv*

hag·gis \ˈhag-əs\ *n* : a traditionally Scottish dish made of the heart, liver, and lungs of a sheep or a calf minced with suet, onions, oatmeal, and seasonings

hag·gle \ˈhag-əl\ *vb* **hag·gled; hag·gling** \-(ə-)liŋ\ : to argue in bargaining — **hag·gler** \-(ə-)lər\ *n*

ha·gi·og·ra·phy \ˌhag-ē-ˈäg-rə-fē, ˌhā-jē-\ *n* **1** : biography of saints or venerated persons **2** : idealizing or idolizing biography — **ha·gi·og·ra·pher** \-fər\ *n*

hai·ku \ˈhī-(ˌ)kü\ *n, pl* **haiku** : an unrhymed Japanese verse form of three lines containing usu. 5, 7, and 5 syllables respectively; *also* : a poem in this form

[1]**hail** \ˈhāl\ *n* **1** : precipitation in the form of small lumps of ice **2** : something that gives the effect of falling hail

[2]**hail** *vb* **1** : to precipitate hail **2** : to hurl forcibly

[3]**hail** *interj* [ME, fr. ON *heill,* fr. *heill* healthy] — used to express acclamation

[4]**hail** *vb* **1** : SALUTE, GREET **2** : SUMMON

[5]**hail** *n* **1** : an expression of greeting, approval, or praise **2** : hearing distance

Hail Mary *n* : a salutation and prayer to the Virgin Mary

hail·stone \ˈhāl-ˌstōn\ *n* : a pellet of hail

hail·storm \-ˌstȯrm\ *n* : a storm accompanied by hail

hair \ˈhaər\ *n* : a threadlike outgrowth esp. of the skin of a mammal; *also* : a covering (as of the head) consisting of such hairs — **haired** \ˈhaərd\ *adj* — **hair·less** *adj*

hair·breadth \-ˌbredth\ *or* **hairs·breadth** \ˈhaərz-\ *n* : a very small distance or margin

hair·brush \-ˌbrəsh\ *n* : a brush for the hair

hair·cloth \-ˌklȯth\ *n* : a stiff wiry fabric used esp. for upholstery

hair·cut \-ˌkət\ *n* : the act, process, or style of cutting and shaping the hair

hair·do \-ˌdü\ *n, pl* **hairdos** : a way of dressing the hair

hair·dress·er \-ˌdres-ər\ *n* : one who dresses or cuts hair — **hair·dress·ing** *n*

hair·line \-ˈlīn\ *n* **1** : a very slender line **2** : the outline of the hair on the head

hair·piece \-ˌpēs\ *n* **1** : TOUPEE **2** : supplementary hair (as a switch) used in some women's hairdos

hair·pin \-ˌpin\ *n* **1** : a U-shaped pin to hold the hair in place **2** : a sharp U-shaped turn in a road — **hairpin** *adj*

hair–rais·ing \ˈhaər-ˌrā-ziŋ\ *adj* : causing terror or astonishment

hair·split·ter \-ˌsplit-ər\ *n* : a person who makes unnecessarily fine distinctions in reasoning or argument — **hair·split·ting** \-ˌsplit-iŋ\ *adj or n*

hair·style \-ˌstīl\ *n* : a way of wearing the hair

hair·styl·ist \-ˌstī-ləst\ *n* : HAIRDRESSER —**hair·styl·ing** \-ˌstī-liŋ\ *n*

hair–trigger *adj* : immediately responsive to the slightest stimulus

hairy \ˈha(ə)r-ē\ *adj* **hair·i·er; -est** : covered with or as if with hair — **hair·i·ness** \ˈhar-ē-nəs\ *n*

hairy woodpecker *n* : a common No. American woodpecker with a white back that is larger than the similarly marked downy woodpecker

hajj \ˈhaj\ *n* : the Islamic religious pilgrimage to Mecca

hajji \ˈhaj-ē\ *n* : one who has made a pilgrimage to Mecca — often used as a title

hake \ˈhāk\ *n* : a marine food fish related to the cod

ha·la·la \hə-ˈläl-ə\ *n, pl* **halala** *or* **halalas** — see *riyal* at MONEY table

hal·berd \ˈhal-bərd, ˈhȯl-\ *or* **hal·bert** \-bərt\ *n* : a weapon esp. of the 15th and 16th centuries consisting of a battle-ax and pike on a long handle

hal·cy·on \ˈhal-sē-ən\ *adj* [Gk *halkyōn*, a mythical bird believed to nest at sea and to calm the waves] : CALM, PEACEFUL

1hale \ˈhāl\ *adj* : free from defect, disease, or infirmity **syn** healthy, sound, robust, well

2hale *vb* **haled; hal·ing 1** : HAUL, PULL **2** : to compel to go ⟨*haled* him into court⟩

ha·ler \ˈhäl-ər\ *n, pl* **ha·le·ru** \ˈhäl-ə-ˌrü\ — see *koruna* at MONEY table

1half \ˈhaf, ˈhȧf\ *n, pl* **halves** \ˈhavz, ˈhȧvz\ **1** : one of two equal parts into which something is divisible **2** : one of a pair

2half *adj* **1** : being one of two equal parts **2** : amounting to nearly half **3** : PARTIAL, IMPERFECT — **half** *adv*

half–and–half \ˌhaf-ən-ˈhaf, ˌhȧf-ən-ˈhȧf\ *n* : something that is half one thing and half another

half·back \ˈhaf-ˌbak, ˈhȧf-\ *n* **1** : a football back stationed on or near the flank **2** : a player stationed immediately behind the forward line

half–baked \-ˈbākt\ *adj* **1** : not thoroughly baked **2** : poorly planned; *also* : lacking common sense

half boot *n* : a boot with a top reaching above the ankle

half–breed \ˈhaf-ˌbrēd, ˈhȧf-\ *n* : the offspring of parents of different races — **half–breed** *adj*

half brother *n* : a brother by one parent only

half–caste \ˈhaf-ˌkast, ˈhȧf-\ *n* : one of mixed racial descent — **half–caste** *adj*

half–dol·lar \-ˈdäl-ər\ *n* **1** : a coin representing one half of a dollar **2** : the sum of fifty cents

half·heart·ed \-ˈhärt-əd\ *adj* : lacking spirit or interest — **half·heart·ed·ly** *adv* — **half·heart·ed·ness** *n*

half–life \-ˌlīf\ *n* : the time required for half of something (as atoms or a drug) to undergo a process

half–mast \-ˈmast\ *n* : a point some distance but not necessarily halfway down below the top of a mast or staff or the peak of a gaff ⟨flags hanging at ~⟩

half note *n* : a musical note equal in time to ½ of a whole note

half·pen·ny \ˈhāp-(ə-)nē\ *n, pl* **half·pence** \ˈhā-pəns\ *or* **halfpennies** : a formerly used British coin representing one half of a penny

half–pint \ˈhaf-ˌpīnt, ˈhȧf-\ *adj* : of less than average size — **half–pint** *n*

half sister *n* : a sister by one parent only

half sole *n* : a shoe sole extending from the shank forward — **half–sole** *vb*

half–staff \ˈhaf-ˈstaf, ˈhȧf-\ *n* : HALF-MAST

half step *n* : the pitch interval between any two adjacent keys on a keyboard instrument

half·time \ˈhaf-ˌtīm, ˈhȧf-\ *n* : an intermission between halves of a game

half–track \-ˌtrak\ *n* **1** : an endless chain-track drive system that propels a vehicle supported in front by a pair of wheels **2** : a motor vehicle propelled by half-tracks; *esp* : such a vehicle lightly armored for military use

half–truth \-ˌtrüth\ *n* : a statement that is only partially true; *esp* : one that deliberately mixes truth and falsehood

half·way \-ˈwā\ *adj* **1** : midway between two points **2** : PARTIAL — **halfway** *adv*

half–wit \ˈhaf-ˌwit, ˈhȧf-\ *n* : a foolish or imbecilic person — **half–wit·ted** \-ˈwit-əd\ *adj*

hal·i·but \ˈhal-ə-bət\ *n, pl* **halibut** *also* **halibuts** [ME *halybutte*, fr. *haly, holy* holy + *butte* flatfish, fr. its being eaten on holy days] : a large edible marine flatfish

ha·lite \ˈhal-ˌīt, ˈhā-ˌlīt\ *n* : ROCK SALT

hal·i·to·sis \ˌhal-ə-ˈtō-səs\ *n* : a condition of having fetid breath

hall \ˈhȯl\ *n* **1** : the residence of a medieval king or noble; *also* : the house of a landed proprietor **2** : a large public building **3** : a college or university building **4** : LOBBY; *also* : CORRIDOR **5** : AUDITORIUM

hal·le·lu·jah \ˌhal-ə-ˈlü-yə\ *interj* [Heb *hallĕlūyāh* praise (ye) the Lord] — used to express praise, joy, or thanks

hall·mark \ˈhȯl-ˌmärk\ *n* **1** : a mark put on an article to indicate origin, purity, or genuineness **2** : a distinguishing characteristic

hal·low \ˈhal-ō\ *vb* **1** : CONSECRATE **2** : REVERE — **hal·lowed** \-ōd, -ə-wəd\ *adj*

Hal·low·een \ˌhal-ə-ˈwēn, ˌhäl-\ *n* : the evening of October 31 observed esp. by children in merrymaking and masquerading

hal·lu·ci·nate \hə-ˈlüs-ᵊn-ˌāt\ *vb* **-nat·ed; -nat·ing** : to perceive or experience as an hallucination

hal·lu·ci·na·tion \hə-ˌlüs-ᵊn-ˈā-shən\ *n* : perception of objects or events with no existence in reality due usu. to use of drugs or to disorder of the nervous system; *also* : something so perceived **syn** delusion, illusion, mirage — **hal·lu·ci·na·to·ry** \-ᵊn-ə-ˌtōr-ē\ *adj*

hal·lu·ci·no·gen \hə-ˈlüs-ᵊn-ə-jən\ *n* : a substance that induces hallucinations — **hal·lu·ci·no·gen·ic** \-ˌlüs-ᵊn-ə-ˈjen-ik\ *adj or n*

hall·way \ˈhȯl-ˌwā\ *n* **1** : an entrance hall **2** : CORRIDOR

ha·lo \ˈhā-lō\ *n, pl* **halos** *or* **haloes** [L *halos*, fr. Gk *halōs* threshing floor, disk, halo] **1** : a circle of light appearing to surround a shining body (as the sun) **2** : the aura of glory surrounding an idealized person or thing

1halt \ˈhȯlt\ *adj* : LAME

2halt *n* : STOP

3halt *vb* **1** : to stop marching or traveling **2** : DISCONTINUE, END

1hal·ter \ˈhȯl-tər\ *n* **1** : a rope or strap for leading or tying an animal; *also* : HEADSTALL **2** : NOOSE **3** : a brief blouse held in place by straps around the neck and across the back

2halter *vb* **hal·tered; hal·ter·ing** \-t(ə-)riŋ\ **1** : to catch with or as if with a halter; *also* : to put a halter on (as a horse) **2** : IMPEDE, RESTRAIN

halt·ing \ˈhȯl-tiŋ\ *adj* : UNCERTAIN, FALTERING — **halt·ing·ly** *adv*

halve \ˈhav, ˈhȧv\ *vb* **halved; halv·ing 1** : to divide into two equal parts **2** : to reduce to one half

halv·ers \ˈhav-ərz, ˈhȧv-\ *n pl* : half shares

halves *pl of* HALF

hal·yard \ˈhal-yərd\ *n* : a rope or tackle for hoisting and lowering something (as sails)

1ham \ˈham\ *n* **1** : a buttock with its associated thigh **2** : a cut of meat and esp. pork from this region **3** : a showy performer **4** : an operator of an amateur radio station — **ham** *adj*

2ham *vb* **hammed; ham·ming** : to overplay a part : OVERACT

ham·burg·er \ˈham-ˌbər-gər\ *or* **ham·burg** \-ˌbərg\ *n* [G *Hamburger* of Hamburg, West Germany] **1** : ground beef **2** : a sandwich consisting of a ground-beef patty in a round roll

ham·let \ˈham-lət\ *n* : a small village

[1]**ham·mer** \ˈham-ər\ *n* **1** : a hand tool used for pounding; *also* : something resembling a hammer in form or function **2** : the part of a gun whose striking action causes explosion of the charge **3** : a metal sphere with a flexible wire handle that is hurled for distance in a track-and-field event **(hammer throw)** **4** : ACCELERATOR 2

[2]**hammer** *vb* **ham·mered; ham·mer·ing** \ˈham-(ə-)riŋ\ **1** : to beat, drive, or shape with repeated blows of a hammer : POUND **2** : to produce or bring about as if by repeated blows

ham·mer·head \ˈham-ər-ˌhed\ *n* **1** : the striking part of a hammer **2** : any of various medium-sized sharks with eyes at the ends of lateral extensions of the flattened head

hammerhead 2

ham·mer·lock \-ˌläk\ *n* : a wrestling hold in which an opponent's arm is held bent behind his back

ham·mer·toe \-ˈtō\ *n* : a deformed toe with the 2d and 3d joints permanently flexed

[1]**ham·mock** \ˈham-ək\ *n* [Sp *hamaca,* of AmerInd origin] : a swinging couch hung by cords at each end

[2]**hammock** *n* : a fertile elevated area of the southern U.S. and esp. Florida with hardwood vegetation and soil rich in humus

[1]**ham·per** \ˈham-pər\ *vb* **ham·pered; ham·per·ing** \-p(ə-)riŋ\ : IMPEDE **syn** trammel, clog, fetter, shackle

[2]**hamper** *n* : a large basket

ham·ster \ˈham-stər\ *n* [G, fr. OHG *hamustro,* of Slavic origin] : a stocky short-tailed Old World rodent with large cheek pouches

[1]**ham·string** \ˈham-ˌstriŋ\ *vb* **-strung** \-ˌstrəŋ\; **-string·ing** \-ˌstriŋ-iŋ\ **1** : to cripple by cutting the leg tendons **2** : to make ineffective or powerless

[2]**hamstring** *n* : any of several muscles at the back of the thigh or tendons at the back of the knee

[1]**hand** \ˈhand\ *n* **1** : the end of a front limb when modified (as in humans) for grasping **2** : personal possession — usu. used in pl; *also* : CONTROL **3** : SIDE 5 **4** : a pledge esp. of betrothal **5** : HANDWRITING **6** : SKILL, ABILITY; *also* : a significant part **7** : ASSISTANCE; *also* : PARTICIPATION **8** : an outburst of applause **9** : a single round in a card game; *also* : the cards held by a player after a deal **10** : WORKER, EMPLOYEE; *also* : a member of a ship's crew — **hand·less** \ˈhan-(d)ləs\ *adj* — **at hand** : near in time or place

[2]**hand** *vb* **1** : to lead, guide, or assist with the hand **2** : to give, pass, or transmit with the hand

hand·bag \ˈhan(d)-ˌbag\ *n* : a bag for carrying small personal articles and money

hand·ball \-ˌbȯl\ *n* : a game played by striking a small rubber ball against a wall with the hand

hand·bar·row \-ˌbar-ō\ *n* : a flat rectangular frame with handles at both ends that is carried by two persons

hand·bill \-ˌbil\ *n* : a small printed sheet for distribution by hand

hand·book \-ˌbu̇k\ *n* : a concise reference book : MANUAL

hand·car \ˈhan(d)-ˌkär\ *n* : a small 4-wheeled railroad car propelled by hand or by a small motor

hand·clasp \-ˌklasp\ *n* : HANDSHAKE

hand·craft \-ˌkraft\ *vb* : to fashion by manual skill

[1]**hand·cuff** \-ˌkəf\ *n* : a metal fastening that can be locked around a wrist and is usu. connected with another such fastening

[2]**handcuff** *vb* : MANACLE

hand·ful \ˌhan(d)-ˌfu̇l\ *n, pl* **hand·fuls** \-ˌfu̇lz\ *also* **hands·ful** \ˈhan(d)z-ˌfu̇l\ **1** : as much or as many as the hand will grasp **2** : a small number ⟨a ~ of people⟩ **3** : as much as one can manage

hand·gun \-ˌgən\ *n* : a firearm held and fired with one hand

[1]**hand·i·cap** \ˈhan-di-ˌkap\ *n* [obs. E *handicap* (a game in which forfeits were held in a cap), fr. *hand in cap*] **1** : a contest in which an artificial advantage is given or disadvantage imposed on a contestant to equalize chances of winning; *also* : the advantage given or disadvantage imposed **2** : a disadvantage that makes achievement difficult

[2]**handicap** *vb* **-capped; -cap·ping** **1** : to give a handicap to **2** : to put at a disadvantage

hand·i·capped *adj* : having a physical or mental disability that limits activity

hand·i·cap·per \-ˌkap-ər\ *n* : one who predicts the winners in a horse race usu. for a publication

hand·i·craft \ˈhan-di-ˌkraft\ *n* **1** : manual skill **2** : an occupation requiring manual skill **3** : the articles fashioned by those engaged in handicraft — **hand·i·craft·er** *n* — **hand·i·crafts·man** \-ˌkrafts-mən\ *n*

hand in glove *or* **hand and glove** *adv* : in an extremely close relationship

hand·i·work \ˈhan-di-ˌwərk\ *n* : work done personally

hand·ker·chief \ˈhaŋ-kər-chəf, -ˌchēf\ *n, pl* **-chiefs** \-chəfs, -ˌchēfs\ *also* **-chieves** \-ˌchēvz\ : a small piece of cloth used for various personal purposes (as the wiping of the face)

[1]**han·dle** \ˈhan-dᵊl\ *n* : a part (as of a tool) designed to be grasped by the hand — **han·dled** \-dᵊld\ *adj* — **off the handle** : into a state of sudden and violent anger

[2]**handle** *vb* **han·dled; han·dling** \ˈhan-dliŋ\ **1** : to touch, hold, or manage with the hands **2** : to have responsibility for **3** : to deal or trade in **4** : to behave in a certain way when managed or directed ⟨a car that ~s well⟩ — **han·dler** \ˈhan-dlər\ *n*

han·dle·bar \-dᵊl-ˌbär\ *n* : a straight or bent bar with a handle at each end (as for steering a bicycle) — usu. used in pl.

hand·made \ˈhan(d)-ˈmād\ *adj* : made by hand or a hand process

hand·maid·en \-ˌmād-ᵊn\ *or* **hand·maid** \-ˌmād\ *n* : a female attendant

hand–me–down \-me-ˌdau̇n\ *adj* : used by one person after being used by another ⟨~ clothes⟩ — **hand–me–down** *n*

hand·out \ˈhand-ˌau̇t\ *n* **1** : a portion (as of food) given to a beggar **2** : a piece of printed information for free distribution; *also* : a prepared statement released to the press

hand·pick \ˈhan(d)-ˈpik\ *vb* : to select personally ⟨a ~*ed* candidate⟩

hand·rail \ˈhand-ˌrāl\ *n* : a narrow rail for grasping as a support

hand·saw \ˈhan(d)-ˌsȯ\ *n* : a saw usu. operated with one hand

hands down \ˈhan(d)z-ˈdau̇n\ *adv* **1** : with little effort **2** : without question

---

\ə\abut \ᵊ\kitten \ər\further \a\ash \ā\ace \ä\cot, cart \au̇\out \ch\chin \e\bet \ē\easy \g\go \i\hit \ī\ice \j\job \ŋ\sing \ō\go \ȯ\law \ȯi\boy \th\thin \t͟h\the \ü\loot \u̇\foot \y\yet \zh\vision *see also* Pronunciation Symbols page

hand·sel \ˈhan-səl\ *n* **1** : a gift made as a token of good luck **2** : a first installment : earnest money
hand·set \ˈhan(d)-ˌset\ *n* : a combined telephone transmitter and receiver mounted on a handle
hand·shake \-ˌshāk\ *n* : a clasping of right hands by two people
hand·some \ˈhan-səm\ *adj* [ME *handsom* easy to manipulate] **1** : SIZABLE, AMPLE **2** : GENEROUS, LIBERAL **3** : pleasing and usu. impressive in appearance **syn** beautiful, lovely, pretty, comely, fair — **hand·some·ly** *adv* — **hand·some·ness** *n*
hands–on \ˈhan(d)-ˈzȯn, -ˈzän\ *adj* : being or providing direct practical experience in the operation of something
hand·spring \-ˌspriŋ\ *n* : an acrobatic feat in which the body turns forward or backward in a full circle from a standing position and lands first on the hands and then on the feet
hand·stand \-ˌstand\ *n* : an act of supporting the body on the hands with the trunk and legs balanced in the air
hand–to–hand \ˌhan-tə-ˌhand\ *adj* : being at very close quarters — **hand to hand** *adv*
hand–to–mouth \-ˌmau̇th\ *adj* : having or providing nothing to spare
hand·wo·ven \ˈhand-ˌwō-vən\ *adj* : produced on a hand-operated loom
hand·writ·ing \-ˌrīt-iŋ\ *n* : writing done by hand; *also* : the form of writing peculiar to a person — **hand·writ·ten** \-ˌrit-ᵊn\ *adj*
handy \ˈhan-dē\ *adj* **hand·i·er; -est** **1** : conveniently near **2** : easily used **3** : DEXTEROUS — **hand·i·ly** \ˈhan-də-lē\ *adv* — **hand·i·ness** \-dē-nəs\ *n*
handy·man \-ˌman\ *n* **1** : one who does odd jobs **2** : one competent in a variety of small skills or repair work
[1]**hang** \ˈhaŋ\ *vb* **hung** \ˈhəŋ\ *also* **hanged** \ˈhaŋd\; **hang·ing** \ˈhaŋ-iŋ\ **1** : to fasten or remain fastened to an elevated point without support from below; *also* : to fasten or be fastened so as to allow free motion on the point of suspension ⟨~ a door⟩ **2** : to put or come to death by suspension (as from a gallows) **3** : DROOP ⟨*hung* his head in shame⟩ **4** : to fasten to a wall ⟨~ wallpaper⟩ **5** : to prevent (a jury) from coming to a decision **6** : to display (pictures) in a gallery **7** : to remain stationary in the air **8** : to be imminent **9** : DEPEND **10** : to take hold for support **11** : to be burdensome **12** : to undergo delay **13** : to incline downward; *also* : to fit or fall from the figure in easy lines **14** : to be raptly attentive **15** : LINGER, LOITER — **hang·er** *n*
[2]**hang** *n* **1** : the manner in which a thing hangs **2** : peculiar and significant meaning **3** : KNACK
han·gar \ˈhaŋ-ər\ *n* [F] : a covered and usu. enclosed area for housing and repairing aircraft
hang·dog \ˈhaŋ-ˌdȯg\ *adj* **1** : ASHAMED, GUILTY **2** : ABJECT, COWED
hang·er–on \ˈhaŋ-ər-ˈȯn, -ˈän\ *n, pl* **hangers–on** : one who hangs around a person or place esp. for personal gain
hang in *vb* : to persist tenaciously
hang·ing \ˈhaŋ-iŋ\ *n* **1** : an execution by strangling or snapping the neck by a suspended noose **2** : something hung — **hanging** *adj*
hang·man \-mən\ *n* : a public executioner
hang·nail \-ˌnāl\ *n* : a bit of skin hanging loose at the side or base of a fingernail
hang on *vb* **1** : HANG IN **2** : to keep a telephone connection open
hang·out \ˈhaŋ-ˌau̇t\ *n* : a favorite or usual place of resort
hang·over \-ˌō-vər\ *n* **1** : something that remains from what is past **2** : disagreeable physical effects following heavy drinking
hang–up \ˈhaŋ-ˌəp\ *n* : a source of mental or emotional difficulty
hang up \(ˈ)haŋ-ˈəp\ *vb* **1** : to place on a hook or hanger **2** : to end a telephone conversation by replacing the receiver on the cradle **3** : to keep delayed or suspended
hank \ˈhaŋk\ *n* : COIL, LOOP
han·ker \ˈhaŋ-kər\ *vb* **han·kered; han·ker·ing** \-k(ə-)riŋ\ : to desire strongly or persistently : LONG — **han·ker·ing** *n*
han·kie *or* **han·ky** \ˈhaŋ-kē\ *n, pl* **hankies** : HANDKERCHIEF
han·ky–pan·ky \ˌhaŋ-kē-ˈpaŋ-kē\ *n* : questionable or underhanded activity
han·sel *var of* HANDSEL
han·som \ˈhan-səm\ *n* : a 2-wheeled covered carriage with the driver's seat elevated at the rear
Ha·nuk·kah \ˈḵän-ə-kə, ˈhän-\ *n* [Heb *ḥănukkāh* dedication] : an 8-day Jewish holiday commemorating the rededication of the Temple of Jerusalem after its defilement by Antiochus of Syria
hap \ˈhap\ *n* **1** : HAPPENING **2** : CHANCE, FORTUNE
[1]**hap·haz·ard** \hap-ˈhaz-ərd\ *n* : CHANCE
[2]**haphazard** *adj* : marked by lack of plan or order : AIMLESS — **hap·haz·ard·ly** *adv* — **hap·haz·ard·ness** *n*
hap·less \ˈhap-ləs\ *adj* : UNFORTUNATE — **hap·less·ly** *adv* — **hap·less·ness** *n*
hap·loid \ˈhap-ˌlȯid\ *adj* : having the number of chromosomes characteristic of gametic cells — **haploid** *n*
hap·ly \ˈhap-lē\ *adv* : by chance
hap·pen \ˈhap-ən\ *vb* **hap·pened; hap·pen·ing** \ˈhap-(ə-)niŋ\ **1** : to occur by chance **2** : to take place **3** : CHANCE 2
hap·pen·ing \ˈhap-(ə-)niŋ\ *n* **1** : OCCURRENCE **2** : an event that is especially interesting, entertaining, or important
hap·pi·ly \ˈhap-ə-lē\ *adv* **1** : LUCKILY **2** : in a happy manner or state ⟨lived ~ ever after⟩ **3** : APTLY, SUCCESSFULLY
hap·pi·ness \ˈhap-i-nəs\ *n* **1** : a state of well-being and contentment; *also* : a pleasurable satisfaction **2** : APTNESS
hap·py \ˈhap-ē\ *adj* **hap·pi·er; -est** **1** : FORTUNATE **2** : APT, FELICITOUS **3** : enjoying well-being and contentment **4** : PLEASANT; *also* : PLEASED, GRATIFIED **syn** glad, cheerful, lighthearted, joyful, joyous
hap·py–go–lucky \ˌhap-ē-gō-ˈlək-ē\ *adj* : CAREFREE
happy hour *n* : a period of time when the price of drinks at a bar is reduced
hara–kiri \ˌhar-ə-ˈkir-ē, ˌher-ē-ˈker-ē\ *n* [Jp *harakiri,* fr. *hara* belly + *kiri* cutting] : suicide by disembowelment
ha·rangue \hə-ˈraŋ\ *n* **1** : a bombastic ranting speech **2** : LECTURE — **harangue** *vb* — **ha·rangu·er** \-ˈraŋ-ər\ *n*
ha·rass \hə-ˈras, ˈhar-əs\ *vb* [F *harasser,* fr. MF, fr. *harer* to set a dog on, fr. OF *hare,* interj. used to incite dogs] **1** : to worry and impede by repeated raids **2** : EXHAUST, FATIGUE **3** : to annoy continually **syn** harry, plague, pester, tease, bedevil — **ha·rass·ment** *n*
har·bin·ger \ˈhär-bən-jər\ *n* : one that announces or foreshadows what is coming : PRECURSOR; *also* : PORTENT
[1]**har·bor** \ˈhär-bər\ *n* **1** : a place of security and comfort **2** : a part of a body of water protected and deep enough to furnish anchorage : PORT
[2]**harbor** *vb* **har·bored; har·bor·ing** \-b(ə-)riŋ\ **1** : to give or take refuge : SHELTER **2** : to be the home or habitat of; *also* : LIVE **3** : to hold a thought or feeling ⟨~ a grudge⟩
har·bor·age \-bə-rij\ *n* : HARBOR
har·bour *chiefly Brit var of* HARBOR
hard \ˈhärd\ *adj* **1** : not easily penetrated **2** : high in alcoholic content; *also* : containing salts that prevent lathering with soap ⟨~ water⟩ **3** : stable in value ⟨~ currency⟩ **4** : physically fit; *also* : free from flaw **5** : FIRM, DEFINITE ⟨~ agreement⟩; *also* : based on clear fact ⟨~ evidence⟩ **6** : CLOSE, SEARCHING ⟨~ look⟩ **7** : REALISTIC ⟨good ~ sense⟩ **8** : OBDURATE, UNFEELING ⟨~ heart⟩ **9** : difficult to bear ⟨~ times⟩; *also* : HARSH, SEVERE **10** : RESENTFUL ⟨~ feelings⟩ **11** : STRICT, UNRELENTING ⟨~ bargain⟩ **12** : INCLEMENT ⟨~ winter⟩ **13** : intense in force or manner ⟨~ blow⟩ **14** : ARDUOUS, STRENUOUS ⟨~ work⟩ **15** : sounding as in *arcing* and *geese* respectively — used of *c* and *g* **16** : TROUBLESOME ⟨~ problem⟩

17 : having difficulty in doing something ⟨~ of hearing⟩ 18 : addictive and gravely detrimental to health ⟨~ drugs⟩ — **hard** *adv* — **hard·ness** *n*

hard–and–fast \ˌhärd-ᵊn-ˈfast\ *adj* : rigidly binding : STRICT ⟨a ~ rule⟩

hard·back \ˈhärd-ˌbak\ *n* : a book bound in hard covers

hard·ball \-ˌbȯl\ *n* **1** : BASEBALL **2** : forceful uncompromising methods

hard–bit·ten \-ˈbit-ᵊn\ *adj* : SEASONED, TOUGH ⟨~ campaigners⟩

hard·board \-ˌbōrd\ *n* : a very dense fiberboard

hard–boiled \-ˈbȯild\ *adj* **1** : boiled until both white and yolk have solidified **2** : lacking sentiment : CALLOUS; *also* : HARDHEADED

hard·bound \-ˌbau̇nd\ *adj* : HARDCOVER

hard copy *n* : copy produced on paper in normal-size type

hard–core \ˈhärd-ˈkōr\ *adj* **1** : extremely resistant to solution or improvement **2** : being the most determined or dedicated members of a specified group **3** : containing explicit depictions of sex acts — **hard core** *n*

hard·cov·er \-ˈkəv-ər\ *adj* : having rigid boards on the sides covered in cloth or paper ⟨~ books⟩

hard·en \ˈhärd-ᵊn\ *vb* **hard·ened; hard·en·ing** \ˈhärd-(ᵊ-)niŋ\ **1** : to make or become hard or harder **2** : to confirm or become confirmed in disposition or action — **hard·en·er** *n*

hard·hack \ˈhärd-ˌhak\ *n* : an American spirea with rusty hairy leaves and dense clusters of pink or white flowers

hard hat *n* **1** : a protective hat worn esp. by construction workers **2** : a construction worker

hard·head·ed \ˈhärd-ˈhed-əd\ *adj* **1** : STUBBORN, WILLFUL **2** : SOBER, REALISTIC — **hard·head·ed·ly** *adv* — **hard·head·ed·ness** *n*

hard–heart·ed \-ˈhärt-əd\ *adj* : PITILESS, CRUEL — **hard–heart·ed·ly** *adv* — **hard–heart·ed·ness** *n*

har·di·hood \ˈhärd-ē-ˌhu̇d\ *n* **1** : resolute courage and fortitude **2** : VIGOR, ROBUSTNESS

hard–line \ˈhärd-ˈlīn\ *adj* : advocating or involving a persistently firm course of action — **hard–lin·er** \-ˈlī-nər\ *n*

hard·ly \ˈhärd-lē\ *adv* **1** : with force **2** : SEVERELY **3** : with difficulty **4** : only just : BARELY **5** : certainly not

hard palate *n* : the bony anterior part of the palate forming the roof of the mouth

hard·pan \ˈhärd-ˌpan\ *n* : a compact often clayey layer in soil that is impenetrable by roots

hard–pressed \-ˈprest\ *adj* : HARD PUT; *esp* : being under financial strain

hard put *adj* **1** : barely able **2** : faced with difficulty or perplexity

hard rock *n* : rock music marked by a heavy beat, high amplification, and usu. frenzied performances

hard–shell \ˈhärd-ˌshel\ *adj* : CONFIRMED, UNCOMPROMISING ⟨a ~ conservative⟩

hard·ship \-ˌship\ *n* **1** : SUFFERING, PRIVATION **2** : something that causes suffering or privation

hard·stand \-ˌstand\ *n* : a hard-surfaced area for parking an airplane

hard–sur·face \-ˈsər-fəs\ *vb* : to provide (as a road) with a paved surface

hard·tack \-ˌtak\ *n* : a hard biscuit made of flour and water without salt

hard·top \-ˌtäp\ *n* : an automobile resembling a convertible but having a rigid top

hard·ware \-ˌwaər\ *n* **1** : ware (as cutlery or tools) made of metal **2** : the physical components (as electronic devices) of a vehicle (as a spacecraft) or an apparatus (as a computer)

[1]**hard·wood** \ˈhärd-ˌwu̇d\ *n* : the wood of a broad-leaved usu. deciduous tree as distinguished from that of a conifer; *also* : such a tree

[2]**hardwood** *adj* **1** : having or made of hardwood ⟨~ floors⟩ **2** : consisting of mature woody tissue ⟨~ cuttings⟩

hard·work·ing \-ˈwər-kiŋ\ *adj* : INDUSTRIOUS

har·dy \ˈhärd-ē\ *adj* **har·di·er; -est** **1** : BOLD, BRAVE **2** : AUDACIOUS, BRAZEN **3** : ROBUST; *also* : able to withstand adverse conditions (as of weather) ⟨~ shrubs⟩ — **har·di·ly** \ˈhärd-ə-lē\ *adv* — **har·di·ness** \-ē-nəs\ *n*

hare \ˈhaər\ *n, pl* **hare** *or* **hares** : a swift timid long-eared mammal distinguished from the related rabbit by being open-eyed and furry at birth

hare·bell \-ˌbel\ *n* : a slender herb with blue bell-shaped flowers

hare·brained \-ˈbrānd\ *adj* : FLIGHTY, FOOLISH

hare·lip \-ˈlip\ *n* : a deformity in which the upper lip is vertically split — **hare·lipped** \-ˈlipt\ *adj*

ha·rem \ˈhar-əm\ *n* [Ar *ḥarīm,* lit., something forbidden & *ḥaram,* lit., sanctuary] **1** : a house or part of a house allotted to women in a Muslim household **2** : the women and servants occupying a harem **3** : a group of females associated with one male

hark \ˈhärk\ *vb* : LISTEN

harken *var of* HEARKEN

har·le·quin \ˈhär-li-k(w)ən\ *n* **1** *cap* : a character (as in comedy) with a shaved head, masked face, variegated tights, and wooden sword **2** : CLOWN 2

har·lot \ˈhär-lət\ *n* : PROSTITUTE

[1]**harm** \ˈhärm\ *n* **1** : physical or mental damage : INJURY **2** : MISCHIEF, HURT — **harm·ful** \-fəl\ *adj* — **harm·ful·ly** \-ē\ *adv* — **harm·ful·ness** *n* — **harm·less** *adj* — **harm·less·ly** *adv* — **harm·less·ness** *n*

[2]**harm** *vb* : to cause harm to : INJURE

[1]**har·mon·ic** \här-ˈmän-ik\ *adj* **1** : of or relating to musical harmony or harmonics **2** : pleasing to the ear — **har·mon·i·cal·ly** \-i-k(ə-)lē\ *adv*

[2]**harmonic** *n* : a musical overtone

har·mon·i·ca \här-ˈmän-i-kə\ *n* : a small wind instrument played by breathing through metallic reeds

har·mo·ni·ous \här-ˈmō-nē-əs\ *adj* **1** : musically concordant **2** : CONGRUOUS **3** : marked by accord in sentiment or action — **har·mo·ni·ous·ly** *adv* — **har·mo·ni·ous·ness** *n*

har·mo·ni·um \här-ˈmō-nē-əm\ *n* : a keyboard wind instrument in which the wind acts on a set of metal reeds

har·mo·nize \ˈhär-mə-ˌnīz\ *vb* **-nized; -niz·ing** **1** : to play or sing in harmony **2** : to be in harmony **3** : to bring into consonance or accord — **har·mo·ni·za·tion** \ˌhär-mə-nə-ˈzā-shən\ *n*

har·mo·ny \ˈhär-mə-nē\ *n, pl* **-nies** **1** : musical agreement of sounds; *esp* : the combination of tones into chords and progressions of chords **2** : a pleasing arrangement of parts; *also* : ACCORD **3** : internal calm

[1]**har·ness** \ˈhär-nəs\ *n* **1** : the gear other than a yoke of a draft animal **2** : something that resembles a harness

[2]**harness** *vb* **1** : to put a harness on; *also* : YOKE **2** : UTILIZE

[1]**harp** \ˈhärp\ *n* : a musical instrument consisting of a triangular frame set with strings plucked by the fingers — **harp·ist** *n*

[2]**harp** *vb* **1** : to play on a harp **2** : to dwell on a subject tiresomely — **harp·er** *n*

har·poon \här-ˈpün\ *n* : a barbed spear used esp. in hunting large fish or whales — **harpoon** *vb* — **har·poon·er** *n*

harp·si·chord \ˈhärp-si-ˌkȯrd\ *n* : a keyboard instrument producing tones by the plucking of its strings with quills or with leather or plastic points

har·py \ˈhär-pē\ *n, pl* **harpies** [L *Harpyia,* a mythical predatory monster having a woman's head and a vulture's body, fr. Gk] **1** : a predatory person : LEECH **2** : a shrewish woman

har·ri·dan \ˈhar-əd-ᵊn\ *n* : a scolding woman

[1]**har·ri·er** \ˈhar-ē-ər\ *n* **1** : a small hound used esp. in hunting rabbits **2** : a runner on a cross-country team

[2]**harrier** *n* : a slender long-legged hawk

[1]**har·row** \ˈhar-ō\ *n* : a cultivating tool that has spikes, spring teeth, or disks and is used esp. to pulverize and smooth the soil

[2]**harrow** *vb* **1** : to cultivate with a harrow **2** : TORMENT, VEX

har·ry \ˈhar-ē\ *vb* **har·ried; har·ry·ing 1** : RAID, PILLAGE **2** : to torment by or as if by constant attack **syn** worry, annoy, plague, pester

harsh \ˈhärsh\ *adj* **1** : disagreeably rough **2** : causing discomfort or pain **3** : unduly exacting : SEVERE — **harsh·ly** *adv* — **harsh·ness** *n*

hart \ˈhärt\ *n* : STAG

har·um–scar·um \ˌhar-əm-ˈskar-əm\ *adj* : RECKLESS, IRRESPONSIBLE

[1]**har·vest** \ˈhär-vəst\ *n* **1** : the season for gathering in crops; *also* : the act of gathering in a crop **2** : a mature crop **3** : the product or reward of exertion

[2]**harvest** *vb* : to gather in a crop : REAP — **har·vest·er** *n*

has *pres 3d sing of* HAVE

has–been \ˈhaz-ˌbin\ *n* : one that has passed the peak of ability, power, effectiveness, or popularity

[1]**hash** \ˈhash\ *vb* [F *hacher,* fr. OF *hachier,* fr. *hache* battle-ax] **1** : to chop into small pieces **2** : to talk about

[2]**hash** *n* **1** : chopped meat mixed with potatoes and browned **2** : HODGEPODGE, JUMBLE

[3]**hash** *n* : HASHISH

hash browns *n pl* : boiled potatoes that have been diced, mixed with chopped onions and shortening, and fried

hash·ish \ˈhash-ˌēsh, ha-ˈshēsh\ [Ar] *n* : an intoxicating preparation of resin from the hemp plant

hasp \ˈhasp\ *n* : a fastener (as for a door) consisting of a hinged metal strap that fits over a staple and is secured by a pin or padlock

has·sle \ˈhas-əl\ *n* **1** : WRANGLE; *also* : FIGHT **2** : an annoying or troublesome concern — **hassle** *vb*

has·sock \ˈhas-ək\ *n* [ME, sedge, fr. OE *hassuc*] : a cushion that serves as a seat or leg rest; *also* : a cushion to kneel on in prayer

haste \ˈhāst\ *n* **1** : rapidity of motion or action : SPEED **2** : rash or headlong action **3** : excessive eagerness — **hast·i·ly** \ˈhā-stə-lē\ *adv* — **hast·i·ness** \-stē-nəs\ *n* — **hasty** \ˈhā-stē\ *adj*

has·ten \ˈhās-ᵊn\ *vb* **has·tened; has·ten·ing** \ˈhās-(ᵊ-)niŋ\ **1** : to urge on **2** : to move or act quickly : HURRY **syn** speed, accelerate, quicken

hat \ˈhat\ *n* : a covering for the head usu. having a shaped crown and brim

hat·box \ˈhat-ˌbäks\ *n* : a round piece of luggage esp. for carrying hats

[1]**hatch** \ˈhach\ *n* **1** : a small door or opening **2** : a door or cover for access down into a compartment of a ship

[2]**hatch** *vb* **1** : to produce by incubation; *also* : INCUBATE **2** : to emerge from an egg or pupa; *also* : to give forth young **3** : ORIGINATE — **hatch·ery** \-(ə-)rē\ *n*

hatch·back \ˈhach-ˌbak\ *n* **1** : a back on an automobile having an upward-opening hatch **2** : an automobile having a hatchback

hatch·et \ˈhach-ət\ *n* **1** : a short-handled ax with a hammerlike part opposite the blade **2** : TOMAHAWK

hatchet man *n* : a person hired for murder, coercion, or unscrupulous attack

hatch·ing \ˈhach-iŋ\ *n* : the engraving or drawing of fine lines in close proximity chiefly to give an effect of shading; *also* : the pattern so created

hatch·way \ˈhach-ˌwā\ *n* : an opening having a hatch

[1]**hate** \ˈhāt\ *n* **1** : intense hostility and aversion **2** : an object of hatred — **hate·ful** \-fəl\ *adj* — **hate·ful·ly** \-ē\ *adv* — **hate·ful·ness** *n*

[2]**hate** *vb* **hat·ed; hat·ing 1** : to express or feel extreme enmity **2** : to find distasteful **syn** detest, abhor, abominate, loathe — **hat·er** *n*

ha·tred \ˈhā-trəd\ *n* : HATE; *also* : prejudiced hostility or animosity

hat·ter \ˈhat-ər\ *n* : one that makes, sells, or cleans and repairs hats

hau·berk \ˈhȯ-bərk\ *n* : a coat of mail

haugh·ty \ˈhȯt-ē\ *adj* **haugh·ti·er; -est** [obs. *haught,* fr. ME *haute,* fr. MF *haut,* lit., high, fr. L *altus*] : disdainfully proud **syn** insolent, lordly, overbearing, arrogant — **haugh·ti·ly** \ˈhȯt-ə-lē\ *adv* — **haugh·ti·ness** \-e-nəs\ *n*

[1]**haul** \ˈhȯl\ *vb* **1** : to exert traction on : DRAW, PULL **2** : to furnish transportation : CART — **haul·er** *n*

[2]**haul** *n* **1** : PULL, TUG **2** : the result of an effort to collect : TAKE **3** : the distance over which a load is transported; *also* : LOAD

haul·age \-ij\ *n* **1** : the act or process of hauling **2** : a charge for hauling

haunch \ˈhȯnch\ *n* **1** : [1]HIP 1 **2** : HINDQUARTER 2 — usu. used in pl. **3** : HINDQUARTER 1

[1]**haunt** \ˈhȯnt\ *vb* **1** : to visit often : FREQUENT **2** : to recur constantly and spontaneously to; *also* : to reappear continually in **3** : to visit or inhabit as a ghost — **haunt·er** *n* — **haunt·ing·ly** \-iŋ-lē\ *adv*

[2]**haunt** \ˈhȯnt, *2 is usu* ˈhant\ *n* **1** : a place habitually frequented **2** *chiefly dial* : GHOST

haut·bois *or* **haut·boy** \ˈ(h)ō-ˌbȯi\ *n, pl* **hautbois** \-ˌbȯiz\ *or* **hautboys** : OBOE

haute cou·ture \ˌōt-kü-ˈtü(ə)r\ *n* [F] : the establishments or designers that create fashions for women; *also* : the fashions created

haute cui·sine \-kwi-ˈzēn\ *n* : artful or elaborate cuisine

hau·teur \hȯ-ˈtər, (h)ō-\ *n* : HAUGHTINESS

[1]**have** \(ˈ)hav, (h)əv, v; *in sense 2 before "to" usu* ˈhaf\ *vb* **had** \(ˈ)had, (h)əd\; **hav·ing** \ˈhav-iŋ\; **has** \(ˈ)haz, (h)əz, *in sense 2 before "to" usu* ˈhas\ **1** : to hold in possession; *also* : to hold in one's use, service, or regard **2** : to be compelled or forced to **3** : to stand in relationship to ⟨*has* many enemies⟩ **4** : OBTAIN; *also* : RECEIVE, ACCEPT **5** : to be marked by **6** : SHOW; *also* : USE, EXERCISE **7** : EXPERIENCE; *also* : TAKE ⟨~ a look⟩ **8** : to entertain in the mind **9** : to cause to **10** : ALLOW **11** : to be competent in **12** : to hold in a disadvantageous position; *also* : TRICK **13** : BEGET **14** : to partake of **15** — used as an auxiliary with the past participle to form the present perfect, past perfect, or future perfect — **have at** : ATTACK — **have coming** : DESERVE — **have done with** : to be finished with — **have had it** : to have endured all one will permit or can stand — **have to do with 1** : to deal with **2** : to have in the way of connection or relation with or effect on

[2]**have** \ˈhav\ *n* : one that has material wealth

ha·ven \ˈhā-vən\ *n* **1** : HARBOR, PORT **2** : a place of safety **3** : a place offering favorable conditions ⟨a tourist's ~⟩

have–not \ˈhav-ˌnät, -ˈnät\ *n* : one that is poor in material wealth

hav·er·sack \ˈhav-ər-ˌsak\ *n* [F *havresac,* fr. G *habersack* bag for oats] : a bag similar to a knapsack but worn over one shoulder

hav·oc \ˈhav-ək\ *n* **1** : wide and general destruction **2** : great confusion and disorder

haw \ˈhȯ\ *n* : a hawthorn berry; *also* : HAWTHORN

Ha·wai·ian \hə-ˈwä-yən, -ˈwī-(y)ən\ *n* : the Polynesian language of Hawaii

[1]**hawk** \ˈhȯk\ *n* **1** : any of numerous mostly small or medium-sized day-flying birds of prey (as a falcon or kite) **2** : a supporter of a war or a warlike policy — **hawk·ish** *adj*

[2]**hawk** *vb* : to offer goods for sale by calling out in the street — **hawk·er** *n*

hawk·weed \ˈhȯk-ˌwēd\ *n* : any of several plants related to the daisies usu. having red or orange flower heads

haw·ser \ˈhȯ-zər\ *n* : a large rope for towing, mooring, or securing a ship

haw·thorn \ˈhȯ-ˌthȯrn\ *n* : a spiny shrub or tree related to the apple and having white or pink fragrant flowers

[1]**hay** \ˈhā\ *n* **1** : herbage (as grass) mowed and cured for

fodder 2 : REWARD 3 *slang* : BED ⟨hit the ~⟩ 4 : a small amount of money

²**hay** *vb* : to cut, cure, and store for hay

hay·cock \ˈhā-ˌkäk\ *n* : a small conical pile of hay

hay fever *n* : an acute allergic catarrh

hay·fork \ˈhā-ˌfȯrk\ *n* : a fork for loading or unloading hay

hay·loft \-ˌlȯft\ *n* : a loft for hay

hay·mow \-ˌmau̇\ *n* : a mow of or for hay

hay·rick \-ˌrik\ *n* : a large sometimes thatched outdoor stack of hay

hay·seed \-ˌsēd\ *n, pl* **hayseed** *or* **hayseeds 1** : clinging bits of straw or chaff from hay **2** : BUMPKIN, YOKEL

hay·stack \-ˌstak\ *n* : a stack of hay

hay·wire \-ˌwī(ə)r\ *adj* : being out of order or control : CRAZY

¹**haz·ard** \ˈhaz-ərd\ *n* [ME, a dice game, fr. MF *hasard,* fr. Ar *az-zahr* the die] **1** : a source of danger **2** : CHANCE; *also* : ACCIDENT **3** : an obstacle on a golf course — **haz·ard·ous** *adj*

²**hazard** *vb* : VENTURE, RISK

¹**haze** \ˈhāz\ *n* **1** : fine dust, smoke, or light vapor causing lack of transparency in the air **2** : vagueness of mind or perception

²**haze** *vb* **hazed; haz·ing** : to harass by abusive and humiliating tricks

ha·zel \ˈhā-zəl\ *n* **1** : any of a genus of shrubs or small trees related to the birches and bearing edible nuts (**ha·zel·nuts** \-ˌnəts\) **2** : a light brown color

hazy \ˈhā-zē\ *adj* **haz·i·er; -est 1** : obscured or darkened by haze **2** : VAGUE, INDEFINITE — **haz·i·ly** \ˈhā-zə-lē\ *adv* — **haz·i·ness** \-zē-nəs\ *n*

Hb *abbr* hemoglobin

HBM *abbr* Her Britannic Majesty; His Britannic Majesty

H–bomb \ˈāch-ˌbäm\ *n* : HYDROGEN BOMB

HC *abbr* **1** Holy Communion **2** House of Commons

hd *abbr* head

HD *abbr* heavy-duty

hdbk *abbr* handbook

hdkf *abbr* handkerchief

hdwe *abbr* hardware

he \(ˈ)hē, ē\ *pron* **1** : that male one **2** : a or the person ⟨~ who hesitates is lost⟩

He *symbol* helium

HE *abbr* **1** Her Excellency **2** His Eminence **3** His Excellency

¹**head** \ˈhed\ *n* **1** : the front or upper part of the body containing the brain, the chief sense organs, and the mouth **2** : MIND; *also* : natural aptitude **3** : POISE **4** : the obverse of a coin **5** : INDIVIDUAL; *also, pl* **head** : one of a number (as of cattle) **6** : the end that is upper or higher or opposite the foot; *also* : either end of something (as a drum) whose two ends need not be distinguished **7** : DIRECTOR, LEADER; *also* : a leading element (as of a procession) **8** : a projecting part; *also* : the striking part of a weapon **9** : the place of leadership or honor **10** : a separate part or topic **11** : the foam on a fermenting or effervescing liquid **12** : CRISIS — **head·ed** \-əd\ *adj* — **head·less** *adj*

²**head** *adj* : PRINCIPAL, CHIEF

³**head** *vb* **1** : to cut back the upper growth of **2** : to provide with or form a head; *also* : to form the head of **3** : LEAD, CONDUCT **4** : to get in front of esp. so as to stop; *also* : SURPASS **5** : to put or stand at the head **6** : to point or proceed in a certain direction **7** : ORIGINATE

head·ache \-ˌāk\ *n* **1** : pain in the head **2** : a baffling situation or problem

head·band \-ˌband\ *n* : a band worn on or around the head

head·board \-ˌbōrd\ *n* : a board forming the head (as of a bed)

head cold *n* : a common cold centered in the nasal passages and adjacent mucous tissues

head·dress \ˈhed-ˌdres\ *n* : an often elaborate covering for the head

headdress

head·first \-ˈfərst\ *adv* : HEADLONG — **headfirst** *adj*

head·gear \-ˌgiər\ *n* : a covering or protective device for the head

head–hunt·ing \-ˌhənt-iŋ\ *n* : the act or custom of seeking out and decapitating enemies and preserving their heads as trophies — **head·hunt·er** \-ər\ *n*

head·ing \ˈhed-iŋ\ *n* **1** : the compass direction in which the longitudinal axis of a ship or airplane points **2** : something that forms or serves as a head

head·land \ˈhed-lənd, -ˌland\ *n* : PROMONTORY

head·light \-ˌlīt\ *n* : a light with a reflector and special lens mounted on the front of a vehicle

head·line \-ˌlīn\ *n* : a head of a newspaper story or article usu. printed in large type

head·lock \-ˌläk\ *n* : a wrestling hold in which one encircles his opponent's head with one arm

¹**head·long** \-ˈlȯŋ\ *adv* **1** : with the head foremost **2** : RECKLESSLY **3** : without delay

²**head·long** \-ˌlȯŋ\ *adj* **1** : PRECIPITATE, RASH **2** : plunging with the head foremost

head·man \ˈhed-ˈman, -ˌman\ *n* : one who is a leader : CHIEF

head·mas·ter \-ˌmas-tər\ *n* : a man heading the staff of a private school

head·mis·tress \-ˌmis-trəs\ *n* : a woman head of a private school

head–on \ˈhed-ˈȯn, -ˈän\ *adj* : having the front facing in the direction of initial contact or line of sight ⟨~ collision⟩ — **head–on** *adv*

head·phone \-ˌfōn\ *n* : an earphone held on by a band over the head

head·piece \-ˌpēs\ *n* **1** : a covering for the head **2** : an ornament esp. at the beginning of a chapter

head·pin \-ˌpin\ *n* : a bowling pin that stands foremost in the arrangement of pins

head·quar·ters \-ˌkwȯrt-ərz\ *n sing or pl* **1** : a place from which a commander exercises command **2** : the administrative center of an enterprise

head·rest \-ˌrest\ *n* **1** : a support for the head **2** : a pad at the top of the back of an automobile seat

head·room \ˈhed-ˌrüm, -ˌru̇m\ *n* : vertical space in which to stand, sit, or move

head·set \-ˌset\ *n* : a pair of headphones

head·ship \-ˌship\ *n* : the position, office, or dignity of a head

heads·man \ˈhedz-mən\ *n* : EXECUTIONER

head·stall \ˈhed-ˌstȯl\ *n* : an arrangement of straps or rope encircling the head of an animal and forming part of a bridle or halter

head·stone \-ˌstōn\ *n* : a memorial stone at the head of a grave

head·strong \-ˌstrȯŋ\ *adj* **1** : not easily restrained **2** : di-

---

\ə\abut \ᵊ\kitten \ər\further \a\ash \ā\ace \ä\cot, cart \au̇\out \ch\chin \e\bet \ē\easy \g\go \i\hit \ī\ice \j\job \ŋ\sing \ō\go \ȯ\law \ȯi\boy \th\thin \th\the \ü\loot \u̇\foot \y\yet \zh\vision *see also* Pronunciation Symbols page

rected by ungovernable will **syn** unruly, intractable, willful, pertinacious, refractory, stubborn

head·wait·er \-ˈwāt-ər\ *n* : the head of the dining-room staff of a restaurant or hotel

head·wa·ter \-ˌwȯt-ər, -ˌwät-\ *n* : the source of a stream — usu. used in pl.

head·way \-ˌwā\ *n* : forward motion; *also* : PROGRESS

head wind *n* : a wind blowing in a direction opposite to a course esp. of a ship or aircraft

head·word \ˈhed-ˌwərd\ *n* **1** : a word or term placed at the beginning **2** : a word qualified by a modifier

head·work \-ˌwərk\ *n* : mental work or effort : THINKING

heady \ˈhed-ē\ *adj* **head·i·er; -est 1** : WILLFUL, RASH; *also* : IMPETUOUS **2** : INTOXICATING **3** : SHREWD

heal \ˈhēl\ *vb* **1** : to make or become sound or whole; *also* : to restore to health **2** : CURE, REMEDY — **heal·er** *n*

health \ˈhelth\ *n* **1** : sound physical or mental condition; *also* : overall condition of the body ⟨in poor ~⟩ **2** : WELL-BEING **3** : a toast to someone's health or prosperity

health·ful \ˈhelth-fəl\ *adj* **1** : beneficial to health **2** : HEALTHY — **health·ful·ly** \-ē\ *adv* — **health·ful·ness** *n*

healthy \ˈhel-thē\ *adj* **health·i·er; -est 1** : enjoying or typical of good health : WELL **2** : evincing or conducive to health **3** : PROSPEROUS; *also* : CONSIDERABLE — **health·i·ly** \ˈhel-thə-lē\ *adv* — **health·i·ness** \-thē-nəs\ *n*

[1]heap \ˈhēp\ *n* : PILE; *also* : LOT

[2]heap *vb* **1** : to throw or lay in a heap **2** : to give in large quantities; *also* : to fill more than full

hear \ˈhiər\ *vb* **heard** \ˈhərd\; **hear·ing** \ˈhi(ə)r-iŋ\ **1** : to perceive by the ear **2** : HEED; *also* : ATTEND **3** : to give a legal hearing to or take testimony from **4** : LEARN — **hear·er** \ˈhir-ər\ *n*

hear·ing *n* **1** : the process, function, or power of perceiving sound; *esp* : the special sense by which noises and tones are received as stimuli **2** : EARSHOT **3** : opportunity to be heard **4** : a listening to arguments (as in a court); *also* : a session in which witnesses are heard (as by a legislative committee)

hear·ken \ˈhär-kən\ *vb* : to give attention : LISTEN **syn** hear, hark, heed

hear·say \ˈhiər-ˌsā\ *n* : RUMOR

hearse \ˈhərs\ *n* [ME *herse*, fr. MF *herce* harrow, frame for holding candles] : a vehicle for carrying the dead to the grave

heart \ˈhärt\ *n* **1** : a hollow muscular organ that by rhythmic contraction keeps up the circulation of the blood in the body; *also* : something resembling a heart in shape **2** : any of a suit of playing cards marked with a red figure of a heart; *also, pl* : a card game in which the object is to avoid taking tricks containing hearts **3** : the whole personality; *also* : the emotional or moral as distinguished from the intellectual nature **4** : COURAGE **5** : one's innermost being **6** : CENTER; *also* : the essential part **7** : the younger central part of a compact leafy cluster (as of lettuce) — **heart·ed** \-əd\ *adj* — **by heart** : by rote or from memory

heart·ache \-ˌāk\ *n* : anguish of mind

heart attack *n* : an acute episode of heart disease due to insufficient blood supply to the heart muscle itself

heart·beat \ˈhärt-ˌbēt\ *n* : one complete pulsation of the heart

heart·break \-ˌbrāk\ *n* : crushing grief

heart·break·ing \-ˌbrā-kiŋ\ *adj* : causing extreme sorrow or distress — **heart·break·er** \-ˌbrā-kər\ *n*

heart·bro·ken \-ˌbrō-kən\ *adj* : overcome by sorrow

heart·burn \-ˌbərn\ *n* : a burning distress behind the lower sternum usu. due to spasm of the esophagus or upper stomach

heart disease *n* : an abnormal organic condition of the heart or of the heart and circulation

heart·en \ˈhärt-ᵊn\ *vb* **heart·ened; heart·en·ing** \ˈhärt-(ᵊ-)niŋ\ : ENCOURAGE

heart·felt \ˈhärt-ˌfelt\ *adj* : deeply felt : SINCERE

hearth \ˈhärth\ *n* **1** : an area (as of brick) in front of a fireplace; *also* : the floor of a fireplace **2** : HOME

hearth·stone \-ˌstōn\ *n* **1** : a stone forming a hearth **2** : HOME

heart·less \ˈhärt-ləs\ *adj* : CRUEL

heart·rend·ing \-ˌren-diŋ\ *adj* : HEARTBREAKING

heart·sick \-ˌsik\ *adj* : very despondent — **heart·sick·ness** *n*

heart·strings \-ˌstriŋz\ *n pl* : the deepest emotions or affections

heart·throb \-ˌthräb\ *n* **1** : the throb of a heart **2** : sentimental emotion **3** : SWEETHEART

heart–to–heart \ˌhärt-tə-ˌhärt\ *adj* : SINCERE, FRANK ⟨a ~ talk⟩

heart·warm·ing \ˈhärt-ˌwȯr-miŋ\ *adj* : inspiring sympathetic feeling

heart·wood \-ˌwu̇d\ *n* : the older harder nonliving central portion of wood

[1]hearty \ˈhärt-ē\ *adj* **heart·i·er; -est 1** : THOROUGHGOING; *also* : JOVIAL **2** : vigorously healthy **3** : ABUNDANT; *also* : NOURISHING **syn** sincere, wholehearted, unfeigned, heartfelt — **heart·i·ly** \ˈhärt-ə-lē\ *adv* — **heart·i·ness** \-ē-nəs\ *n*

[2]hearty *n, pl* **heart·ies** : COMRADE; *also* : SAILOR

[1]heat \ˈhēt\ *vb* **1** : to make or become warm or hot **2** : EXCITE — **heat·ed·ly** \-əd-lē\ *adv* — **heat·er** *n*

[2]heat *n* **1** : a condition of being hot : WARMTH **2** : a form of energy that causes a body to rise in temperature, to fuse, to evaporate, or to expand **3** : high temperature **4** : intensity of feeling; *also* : sexual excitement esp. in a female mammal **5** : pungency of flavor **6** : a single continuous effort; *also* : a preliminary race for eliminating less competent contenders **7** : PRESSURE, COERCION; *also* : ABUSE, CRITICISM — **heat·less** *adj*

heat engine *n* : a mechanism for converting heat energy into mechanical energy

heat exchanger *n* : a device (as an automobile radiator) for transferring heat from one fluid to another without allowing them to mix

heat exhaustion *n* : a condition marked by weakness, nausea, dizziness, and profuse sweating that results from physical exertion in a hot environment

heath \ˈhēth\ *n* **1** : any of a large family of often evergreen shrubby plants (as a blueberry or heather) of wet acid soils **2** : a tract of wasteland — **heathy** *adj*

hea·then \ˈhē-t͟hən\ *n, pl* **heathens** *or* **heathen 1** : an unconverted member of a people or nation that does not acknowledge the God of the Bible **2** : an uncivilized or irreligious person — **heathen** *adj* — **hea·then·dom** *n* — **hea·then·ish** *adj* — **hea·then·ism** *n*

heath·er \ˈhet͟h-ər\ *n* : a northern evergreen heath with usu. lavender flowers — **heath·ery** *adj*

heat lightning *n* : flashes of light without thunder ascribed to distant lightning reflected by high clouds

heat·stroke \ˈhēt-ˌstrōk\ *n* : a disorder marked esp. by high body temperature without sweating and by collapse that follows prolonged exposure to excessive heat

[1]heave \ˈhēv\ *vb* **heaved** *or* **hove** \ˈhōv\; **heav·ing 1** : to rise or lift upward **2** : THROW **3** : to rise and fall rhythmically; *also* : PANT **4** : RETCH **5** : PULL, PUSH — **heav·er** *n*

[2]heave *n* **1** : an effort to lift or raise **2** : THROW, CAST **3** : an upward motion **4** *pl* : a chronic lung disease of horses marked by difficult breathing and persistent cough

heav·en \ˈhev-ən\ *n* **1** : FIRMAMENT — usu. used in pl. **2** *often cap* : the abode of the Deity and of the blessed dead; *also* : a spiritual state of everlasting communion with God **3** *cap* : GOD 1 **4** : a place of supreme happiness — **heav·en·ly** *adj* — **heav·en·ward** *adv or adj*

[1]heavy \ˈhev-ē\ *adj* **heavi·er; -est 1** : having great weight **2** : hard to bear **3** : SERIOUS **4** : DEEP, PROFOUND **5** : burdened with something oppressive; *also* : PREGNANT **6** : SLUGGISH **7** : DRAB; *also* : DOLEFUL **8** : DROWSY **9** : greater than the average of its kind or class **10** : digested with difficulty; *also* : not properly raised or leavened **11** : producing goods (as steel) used in the production of other goods **12** : heavily armed or armored — **heav·i·ly** \ˈhev-ə-lē\ *adv* — **heavi·ness** \-ē-nəs\ *n*

²**heavy** *n, pl* **heav·ies** : a theatrical role representing a dignified or imposing person; *also* : a villain esp. in a story or a play

heavy–du·ty \ˌhev-ē-ˈd(y)üt-ē\ *adj* : able to withstand unusual strain

heavy–hand·ed \-ˈhan-dəd\ *adj* **1** : CLUMSY, UNGRACEFUL **2** : OPPRESSIVE, HARSH

heavy·heart·ed \-ˈhärt-əd\ *adj* : SADDENED, DESPONDENT

heavy metal *n* : highly amplified electronic rock with elements of the fantastic

heavy·set \ˌhev-ē-ˈset\ *adj* : stocky and compact in build

heavy water *n* : water enriched in deuterium

heavy·weight \ˈhev-ē-ˌwāt\ *n* : one above average in weight; *esp* : a boxer weighing over 175 pounds

Heb *abbr* Hebrews

He·bra·ism \ˈhē-brā-ˌiz-əm\ *n* : the thought, spirit, or practice characteristic of the Hebrews — **He·bra·ic** \hi-ˈbrā-ik\ *adj*

He·bra·ist \ˈhē-ˌbrā-əst\ *n* : a specialist in Hebrew and Hebraic studies

He·brew \ˈhē-brü\ *n* **1** : the language of the Hebrews **2** : a member of or descendant from a group of Semitic peoples; *esp* : ISRAELITE — **Hebrew** *adj*

He·brews \ˈhē-(ˌ)brüz\ *n* — see BIBLE table

hec·a·tomb \ˈhek-ə-ˌtōm\ *n* : an ancient Greek and Roman sacrifice of 100 oxen or cattle

heck·le \ˈhek-əl\ *vb* **heck·led; heck·ling** \-(ə-)liŋ\ : to harass with questions or gibes : BADGER — **heck·ler** \-(ə-)lər\ *n*

hect·are \ˈhek-ˌtaər\ *n* — see METRIC SYSTEM table

hec·tic \ˈhek-tik\ *adj* **1** : being hot and flushed **2** : filled with excitement or confusion — **hec·ti·cal·ly** \-ti-k(ə-)lē\ *adv*

hec·to·gram \ˈhek-tə-ˌgram\ *n* — see METRIC SYSTEM table

hec·to·li·ter \ˈhek-tə-ˌlēt-ər\ *n* — see METRIC SYSTEM table

hec·to·me·ter \ˈhek-tə-ˌmēt-ər, hek-ˈtäm-ət-ər\ *n* — see METRIC SYSTEM table

hec·tor \ˈhek-tər\ *vb* **hec·tored; hec·tor·ing** \-t(ə-)riŋ\ **1** : SWAGGER **2** : to intimidate by bluster or personal pressure

¹**hedge** \ˈhej\ *n* **1** : a fence or boundary formed of shrubs or small trees **2** : BARRIER **3** : a means of protection (as against financial loss)

²**hedge** *vb* **hedged; hedg·ing 1** : ENCIRCLE **2** : HINDER **3** : to protect oneself financially by a counterbalancing transaction **4** : to evade the risk of commitment — **hedg·er** *n*

hedge·hog \-ˌhȯg, -ˌhäg\ *n* : a small Old World insect-eating mammal covered with spines; *also* : PORCUPINE

hedge·hop \-ˌhäp\ *vb* : to fly an airplane very close to the ground

hedge·row \-ˌrō\ *n* : a row of shrubs or trees bounding or separating fields

he·do·nism \ˈhēd-ᵊn-ˌiz-əm\ *n* [Gk *hēdonē* pleasure] : the doctrine that pleasure is the chief good in life; *also* : a way of life based on this — **he·do·nist** \-ᵊn-əst\ *n* — **he·do·nis·tic** \ˌhēd-ᵊn-ˈis-tik\ *adj*

¹**heed** \ˈhēd\ *vb* : to pay attention

²**heed** *n* : ATTENTION, NOTICE — **heed·ful** \-fəl\ *adj* — **heed·ful·ly** \-ē\ *adv* — **heed·ful·ness** *n* — **heed·less** *adj* — **heed·less·ly** *adv* — **heed·less·ness** *n*

¹**heel** \ˈhēl\ *n* **1** : the hind part of the foot **2** : one of the crusty ends of a loaf of bread **3** : a solid attachment forming the back of the sole of a shoe **4** : a rear, low, or bottom part **5** : a contemptible person — **heel·less** \ˈhēl-ləs\ *adj*

²**heel** *vb* : to tilt to one side : LIST

¹**heft** \ˈheft\ *n* : WEIGHT, HEAVINESS

²**heft** *vb* : to test the weight of by lifting

hefty \ˈhef-tē\ *adj* **heft·i·er; -est 1** : marked by bigness, bulk, and usu. strength **2** : impressively large

he·ge·mo·ny \hi-ˈjem-ə-nē\ *n* : preponderant influence or authority esp. of one nation over others

he·gi·ra \hi-ˈjī-rə\ *n* [the *Hegira,* flight of Muhammad from Mecca in A.D. 622, fr. ML, fr. Ar *hijrah,* lit., flight] : a journey esp. when undertaken to seek refuge away from a dangerous or undesirable environment

heif·er \ˈhef-ər\ *n* : a young cow; *esp* : one that has not had a calf

height \ˈhīt, ˈhītth\ *n* **1** : the highest part or point **2** : the distance from the bottom to the top of something standing upright **3** : ALTITUDE

height·en \ˈhīt-ᵊn\ *vb* **height·ened; height·en·ing** \ˈhīt-(ᵊ-)niŋ\ **1** : to increase in amount or degree : AUGMENT **2** : to make or become high or higher **syn** enhance, intensify, aggravate, magnify

Heim·lich maneuver \ˈhīm-lik-\ *n* [Henry J. *Heimlich* *b*1920 Am. surgeon] : the manual application of sudden upward pressure on the upper abdomen of a choking victim to force a foreign object from the windpipe

hei·nous \ˈhā-nəs\ *adj* [ME, fr. MF *haineus,* fr. *haine* hate, fr. *hair* to hate] : hatefully or shockingly evil — **hei·nous·ly** *adv* — **hei·nous·ness** *n*

heir \ˈaər\ *n* : one who inherits or is entitled to inherit property, rank, title, or office — **heir·ship** *n*

heir apparent *n, pl* **heirs apparent** : an heir whose right to succeed (as to a title) cannot be taken away if he or she survives the present holder

heir·ess \ˈar-əs\ *n* : a female heir esp. to great wealth

heir·loom \ˈaər-ˌlüm\ *n* **1** : a piece of personal property that descends by inheritance **2** : something handed on from one generation to another

heir presumptive *n, pl* **heirs presumptive** : an heir whose present right to inherit could be lost through the birth of a nearer relative

heist \ˈhīst\ *vb, slang* : to commit armed robbery on; *also* : STEAL — **heist** *n, slang*

held *past and past part of* HOLD

he·li·cal \ˈhel-i-kəl, ˈhē-li-\ *adj* : SPIRAL

he·li·coid \ˈhel-ə-ˌkȯid, ˈhē-lə-\ *or* **he·li·coi·dal** \ˌhel-ə-ˈkȯid-ᵊl, ˌhē-lə-\ *adj* : forming or arranged in a spiral

he·li·cop·ter \ˈhel-ə-ˌkäp-tər, ˈhē-lə-\ *n* [F *hélicoptère,* fr. Gk *helix* spiral + *pteron* wing] : an aircraft that is supported in the air by one or more rotors revolving on substantially vertical axes

he·lio·cen·tric \ˌhē-lē-ō-ˈsen-trik\ *adj* : having or relating to the sun as center

he·lio·trope \ˈhēl-yə-ˌtrōp\ *n* [L *heliotropium,* fr. Gk *hēliotropion,* fr. *hēlio-* sun + *tropos* turn; fr. its flowers' turning toward the sun] : a hairy-leaved garden herb related to the forget-me-not that has clusters of small fragrant white or purple flowers

he·li·port \ˈhel-ə-ˌpōrt\ *n* : a landing and takeoff place for a helicopter

he·li·um \ˈhē-lē-əm\ *n* [NL, fr. Gk *hēlios* sun; so called from the fact that its existence in the sun's atmosphere was inferred before it was identified on the earth] : a very light nonflammable gaseous chemical element occurring in various natural gases — see ELEMENT table

he·lix \ˈhē-liks\ *n, pl* **he·li·ces** \ˈhel-ə-ˌsēz, ˈhē-lə-\ *also* **he·lix·es** \ˈhē-lik-səz\ : something spiral in form

hell \ˈhel\ *n* **1** : a nether world in which the dead continue to exist **2** : the realm of the devil in which the damned suffer everlasting punishment **3** : a place or state of torment or destruction — **hell·ish** *adj*

hell–bent \-ˌbent\ *adj* : stubbornly determined

hell·cat \-ˌkat\ *n* **1** : WITCH 2 **2** : TORMENTOR; *esp* : SHREW 2

hel·le·bore \ˈhel-ə-ˌbōr\ *n* **1** : a plant related to the buttercup; *also* : its roots used formerly in medicine **2** : a poisonous plant related to the lilies; *also* : its dried roots used in medicine and insecticides

Hel·lene \ˈhel-ˌēn\ *n* : GREEK

Hel·le·nism \ˈhel-ə-ˌniz-əm\ *n* : a body of humanistic and classical ideals associated with ancient Greece — **Hel·len·ic** \he-ˈlen-ik\ *adj* — **Hel·le·nist** \ˈhel-ə-nəst\ *n*

Hel·le·nis·tic \ˌhel-ə-ˈnis-tik\ *adj* : of or relating to Greek history, culture, or art after Alexander the Great

hell–for–leather *adv* : at full speed

hell·gram·mite \ˈhel-grə-ˌmīt\ *n* : an aquatic insect larva that is used as bait in fishing

hell·hole \ˈhel-ˌhōl\ *n* : a place of extreme misery or squalor

hel·lion \ˈhel-yən\ *n* : a troublesome or mischievous person

hel·lo \hə-ˈlō, he-\ *n, pl* **hellos** : an expression of greeting — used interjectionally

helm \ˈhelm\ *n* **1** : a lever or wheel for steering a ship **2** : a position of control

hel·met \ˈhel-mət\ *n* : a protective covering for the head

helms·man \ˈhelmz-mən\ *n* : the person at the helm : STEERSMAN

hel·ot \ˈhel-ət\ *n* : SLAVE, SERF

[1]**help** \ˈhelp\ *vb* **1** : AID, ASSIST **2** : REMEDY, RELIEVE **3** : to be of use; *also* : PROMOTE **4** : to change for the better **5** : to refrain from; *also* : PREVENT **6** : to serve with food or drink — **help·er** *n*

[2]**help** *n* **1** : AID, ASSISTANCE; *also* : a source of aid **2** : REMEDY, RELIEF **3** : one who assists another **4** : the services of a paid worker — **help·ful** \-fəl\ *adj* — **help·ful·ly** \-ē\ *adv* — **help·ful·ness** *n* — **help·less** *adj* — **help·less·ly** *adv* — **help·less·ness** *n*

help·ing \ˈhel-piŋ\ *n* : a portion of food ⟨asked for a second ~ of potatoes⟩

help·mate \ˈhelp-ˌmāt\ *n* **1** : HELPER **2** : WIFE

help·meet \-ˌmēt\ *n* : HELPMATE

hel·ter–skel·ter \ˌhel-tər-ˈskel-tər\ *adv* **1** : in headlong disorder **2** : HAPHAZARDLY

helve \ˈhelv\ *n* : a handle of a tool or weapon

Hel·ve·tian \hel-ˈvē-shən\ *adj* : SWISS — **Helvetian** *n*

[1]**hem** \ˈhem\ *n* **1** : a border of an article (as of cloth) doubled back and stitched down **2** : RIM, MARGIN

[2]**hem** *vb* **hemmed; hem·ming 1** : to make a hem in sewing; *also* : BORDER, EDGE **2** : to surround restrictively

he–man \ˈhē-ˌman\ *n* : a strong virile man

he·ma·tite \ˈhē-mə-ˌtīt\ *n* : a mineral that consists of an oxide of iron and that constitutes an important iron ore

he·ma·tol·o·gy \ˌhē-mə-ˈtäl-ə-jē\ *n* : a branch of biology that deals with the blood and blood-forming organs — **he·ma·to·log·ic** \-mət-ᵊl-ˈäj-ik\ *also* **he·ma·to·log·i·cal** \-i-kəl\ *adj* — **he·ma·tol·o·gist** \-ˈtäl-ə-jəst\ *n*

heme \ˈhēm\ *n* : the deep red iron-containing part of hemoglobin

hemi·sphere \ˈhem-ə-ˌsfiər\ *n* **1** : one of the halves of the earth as divided by the equator into northern and southern parts (**northern hemisphere, southern hemisphere**) or by a meridian into two parts so that one half (**eastern hemisphere**) to the east of the Atlantic ocean includes Europe, Asia, and Africa and the half (**western hemisphere**) to the west includes No. and So. America and surrounding waters **2** : either of two half spheres formed by a plane through the sphere's center — **hemi·spher·ic** \ˌhem-ə-ˈsfiər-ik, -ˈsfer-\ *or* **hemi·spher·i·cal** \-ˈsfir-i-kəl, -ˈsfer-\ *adj*

hem·line \ˈhem-ˌlīn\ *n* : the line formed by the lower edge of a dress, skirt, or coat

hem·lock \ˈhem-ˌläk\ *n* **1** : any of several poisonous herbs related to the carrot **2** : an evergreen tree related to the pines; *also* : its soft light wood

he·mo·glo·bin \ˈhē-mə-ˌglō-bən\ *n* : an iron-containing compound found in red blood cells that carries oxygen from the lungs to the body tissues

he·mo·phil·ia \ˌhē-mə-ˈfil-ē-ə\ *n* : a usu. hereditary tendency to severe prolonged bleeding — **he·mo·phil·i·ac** \-ē-ˌak\ *adj or n* — **he·mo·phil·ic** \-ˈfil-ik\ *n or adj*

hem·or·rhage \ˈhem-(ə-)rij\ *n* : a large discharge of blood from the blood vessels — **hemorrhage** *vb* — **hem·or·rhag·ic** \ˌhem-ə-ˈraj-ik\ *adj*

hem·or·rhoid \ˈhem-(ə-)ˌrȯid\ *n* : a swollen mass of dilated veins situated at or just within the anus — usu. used in pl.

hemp \ˈhemp\ *n* : a tall widely grown Asian herb related to the mulberry that is the source of a tough fiber used in cordage and of marijuana and hashish from its flowers and leaves — **hemp·en** \ˈhem-pən\ *adj*

hem·stitch \ˈhem-ˌstich\ *vb* : to embroider (fabric) by drawing out parallel threads and stitching the exposed threads in groups to form designs

hen \ˈhen\ *n* : a female chicken esp. over a year old; *also* : a female bird

hence \ˈhens\ *adv* **1** : AWAY **2** : from this time **3** : CONSEQUENTLY **4** : from this source or origin

hence·forth \-ˌfōrth\ *adv* : from this point on

hence·for·ward \hens-ˈfȯr-wərd\ *adv* : HENCEFORTH

hench·man \ˈhench-mən\ *n* [ME *hengestman* groom, fr. *hengest* stallion] : a trusted follower or supporter

hen·na \ˈhen-ə\ *n* **1** : an Old World tropical shrub with fragrant white flowers; *also* : a reddish brown dye obtained from its leaves and used esp. for the hair **2** : the color of henna dye

hen·peck \ˈhen-ˌpek\ *vb* : to nag and boss one's husband

hep \ˈhep\ *var of* HIP

hep·a·rin \ˈhep-ə-rən\ *n* : a compound found esp. in liver that slows the clotting of blood and is used medically

he·pat·ic \hi-ˈpat-ik\ *adj* : of, relating to, or associated with the liver

he·pat·i·ca \hi-ˈpat-i-kə\ *n* : any of a genus of herbs related to the buttercups that have lobed leaves and delicate flowers

hep·a·ti·tis \ˌhep-ə-ˈtīt-əs\ *n, pl* **-tit·i·des** \-ˈtit-ə-ˌdēz\ : inflammation of the liver; *also* : an acute virus disease of which this is a feature

hep·tam·e·ter \hep-ˈtam-ət-ər\ *n* : a line of verse containing seven metrical feet

[1]**her** \(h)ər, ˌhər\ *adj* : of or relating to her or herself

[2]**her** \ər, (ˈ)hər\ *pron, objective case of* SHE

[1]**her·ald** \ˈher-əld\ *n* **1** : an official crier or messenger **2** : HARBINGER **3** : ANNOUNCER, SPOKESMAN

[2]**herald** *vb* **1** : to give notice of **2** : HAIL, GREET; *also* : PUBLICIZE

he·ral·dic \he-ˈral-dik, hə-\ *adj* : of or relating to heralds or heraldry

her·ald·ry \ˈher-əl-drē\ *n, pl* **-ries 1** : the practice of devising and granting armorial insignia and of tracing a person's family to find out its coat of arms **2** : COAT OF ARMS **3** : PAGEANTRY

herb \ˈ(h)ərb\ *n* **1** : a seed plant that lacks woody tissue and dies to the ground at the end of a growing season **2** : a plant or plant part valued for medicinal or savory qualities — **her·ba·ceous** \ˌ(h)ər-ˈbā-shəs\ *adj*

herb·age \ˈ(h)ər-bij\ *n* : green plants esp. when used or fit for grazing

herb·al·ist \ˈ(h)ər-bə-ləst\ *n* **1** : one that collects, grows, or deals in herbs **2** : one who practices healing by the use of herbs

her·bar·i·um \ˌ(h)ər-ˈbar-ē-əm\ *n, pl* **-ia** \-ē-ə\ **1** : a collection of dried plant specimens **2** : a place that houses an herbarium

her·bi·cide \ˈ(h)ər-bə-ˌsīd\ *n* : an agent used to destroy unwanted plants — **her·bi·cid·al** \ˌ(h)ər-bə-ˈsīd-ᵊl\ *adj*

her·biv·o·rous \ˌ(h)ər-ˈbiv-ə-rəs\ *adj* : feeding on plants — **her·bi·vore** \ˈ(h)ər-bə-ˌvōr\ *n*

her·cu·le·an \ˌhər-kyə-ˈlē-ən, ˌhər-ˈkyü-lē-\ *adj, often cap* : of extraordinary power, size, or difficulty

[1]**herd** \ˈhərd\ *n* **1** : a group of animals of one kind kept or living together **2** : a group of people with a common bond **3** : MOB

[2]**herd** *vb* : to assemble or move in a herd — **herd·er** *n*

herds·man \ˈhərdz-mən\ *n* : one who manages, breeds, or tends livestock

[1]**here** \ˈhiər\ *adv* **1** : in or at this place; *also* : NOW **2** : at or in this point, particular, or case **3** : in the present life or state **4** : HITHER

[2]**here** *n* : this place ⟨get away from ~⟩

here·abouts \ˈhir-ə-ˌbau̇ts\ *or* **here·about** \-ˌbau̇t\ *adv* : in this vicinity : about or near this place

[1]**here·af·ter** \hir-ˈaf-tər\ *adv* **1** : after this in sequence or in time **2** : in some future time or state

[2]**hereafter** *n, often cap* **1** : FUTURE **2** : an existence beyond earthly life

here·by \hiər-ˈbī\ *adv* : by means of this

he·red·i·tary \hə-ˈred-ə-ˌter-ē\ *adj* **1** : genetically passed or passable from parent to offspring **2** : passing by inheritance; *also* : having title or possession through inheritance **3** : of a kind established by tradition

he·red·i·ty \-ət-ē\ *n* : the qualities and potentialities genetically derived from one's ancestors; *also* : the passing of these from ancestor to descendant

Her·e·ford \ˈhər-fərd\ *n* : any of an English breed of hardy red beef cattle with white faces and markings

here·in \hir-ˈin\ *adv* : in this

here·of \-ˈəv, -ˈäv\ *adv* : of this

here·on \-ˈȯn, -ˈän\ *adv* : on this

her·e·sy \ˈher-ə-sē\ *n, pl* **-sies** [ME *heresie*, fr. OF, fr. LL *haeresis*, fr. LGk *hairesis*, fr. Gk, action of taking, choice, sect, fr. *hairein* to take] **1** : adherence to a religious opinion contrary to church dogma **2** : an opinion or doctrine contrary to church dogma **3** : dissent from a dominant theory, opinion, or practice — **her·e·tic** \-ˌtik\ *n* — **he·ret·i·cal** \hə-ˈret-i-kəl\ *adj*

here·to \hir-ˈtü\ *adv* : to this document

here·to·fore \ˈhirt-ə-ˌfōr\ *adv* : up to this time

here·un·der \hir-ˈən-dər\ *adv* : under this or according to this writing

here·un·to \hir-ˈən-tü\ *adv* : to this

here·upon \ˈhir-ə-ˌpȯn, -ˌpän\ *adv* : on this or immediately after this

here·with \ˈhiər-ˈwith, -ˈwith\ *adv* **1** : with this **2** : HEREBY

her·i·ta·ble \ˈher-ət-ə-bəl\ *adj* : capable of being inherited

her·i·tage \ˈher-ət-ij\ *n* **1** : property that descends to an heir **2** : LEGACY **3** : BIRTHRIGHT

her·maph·ro·dite \(ˌ)hər-ˈmaf-rə-ˌdīt\ *n* : an animal or plant having both male and female reproductive organs — **hermaphrodite** *adj* — **her·maph·ro·dit·ic** \(ˌ)hər-ˌmaf-rə-ˈdit-ik\ *adj*

her·met·ic \hər-ˈmet-ik\ *also* **her·met·i·cal** \-i-kəl\ *adj* : tightly sealed : AIRTIGHT — **her·met·i·cal·ly** \-i-k(ə-)lē\ *adv*

her·mit \ˈhər-mət\ *n* [ME *eremite*, fr. OF, fr. LL *eremita*, fr. Gk *erēmitēs*, adj., living in the desert, fr. *erēmia* desert, fr. *erēmos* lonely] : one who lives in solitude esp. for religious reasons

her·mit·age \-ij\ *n* **1** : the dwelling of a hermit **2** : a secluded dwelling

her·nia \ˈhər-nē-ə\ *n, pl* **-ni·as** *or* **-ni·ae** \-nē-ˌē, -nē-ˌī\ : a protruding of a bodily part (as a loop of intestine) into a pouch of the weakened wall of a cavity in which it is normally enclosed; *also* : the protruded mass — **her·ni·ate** \-nē-ˌāt\ *vb* — **her·ni·a·tion** \ˌhər-nē-ˈā-shən\ *n*

he·ro \ˈhē-rō\ *n, pl* **heroes** **1** : a mythological or legendary figure of great strength or ability **2** : a man admired for his achievements and qualities **3** : the chief male character in a literary or dramatic work **4** *pl usu* **heros** : SUBMARINE **2** — **he·ro·ic** \hi-ˈrō-ik\ *adj* — **he·ro·i·cal·ly** \-i-k(ə-)lē\ *adv*

heroic couplet *n* : a rhyming couplet in iambic pentameter

he·ro·ics \hi-ˈrō-iks\ *n pl* : heroic or showy behavior

her·o·in \ˈher-ə-wən\ *n* : an illicit addictive narcotic drug made from morphine

her·o·ine \ˈher-ə-wən\ *n* **1** : a woman admired for her achievements and qualities **2** : the chief female character in a literary or dramatic work

her·o·ism \ˈher-ə-ˌwiz-əm\ *n* **1** : heroic conduct **2** : the qualities of a hero **syn** valor, prowess, gallantry

her·on \ˈher-ən\ *n, pl* **herons** *also* **heron** : a long-legged long-billed wading bird with soft plumage

her·pes \ˈhər-pēz\ *n* : any of several virus diseases characterized by the formation of blisters on the skin or mucous membranes

herpes sim·plex \-ˈsim-ˌpleks\ *n* : either of two forms of herpes marked in one by watery blisters above the waist (as on the mouth and lips) and in the other on the genitalia

herpes zos·ter \-ˈzäs-tər\ *n* : SHINGLES

her·pe·tol·o·gy \ˌhər-pə-ˈtäl-ə-jē\ *n* : a branch of zoology dealing with reptiles and amphibians — **her·pe·tol·o·gist** \ˌhər-pə-ˈtäl-ə-jəst\ *n*

her·ring \ˈher-iŋ\ *n, pl* **herring** *or* **herrings** : a soft-finned narrow-bodied food fish of the north Atlantic; *also* : any of various similar or related fishes

her·ring·bone \ˈher-iŋ-ˌbōn\ *n* : a pattern made up of rows of parallel lines with adjacent rows slanting in reverse directions; *also* : a twilled fabric with this pattern

hers \ˈhərz\ *pron* : one or the ones belonging to her

her·self \(h)ər-ˈself\ *pron* : SHE, HER — used reflexively, for emphasis, or in absolute constructions

hertz \ˈhərts, ˈherts\ *n, pl* **hertz** : a unit of frequency equal to one cycle per second

hes·i·tant \ˈhez-ə-tənt\ *adj* : tending to hesitate — **hes·i·tance** \-tən(t)s\ *n* — **hes·i·tan·cy** \-tən-sē\ *n* — **hes·i·tant·ly** *adv*

hes·i·tate \ˈhez-ə-ˌtāt\ *vb* **-tat·ed; -tat·ing** **1** : to hold back (as in doubt) **2** : PAUSE **syn** waver, vacillate, falter, shilly-shally — **hes·i·ta·tion** \ˌhez-ə-ˈtā-shən\ *n*

het·ero·dox \ˈhet-(ə-)rə-ˌdäks\ *adj* **1** : differing from an acknowledged standard **2** : holding unorthodox opinions — **het·er·o·doxy** \-ˌdäk-sē\ *n*

het·er·o·ge·neous \ˌhet-(ə-)rə-ˈjē-nē-əs, -nyəs\ *adj* : consisting of dissimilar ingredients or constituents : MIXED — **het·er·o·ge·ne·ity** \-jə-ˈnē-ət-ē\ *n* — **het·er·o·ge·neous·ly** *adv* — **het·er·o·ge·neous·ness** *n*

het·ero·sex·u·al \ˌhet-ə-rō-ˈsek-sh(ə-w)əl\ *adj* : tending to direct sexual desire toward the opposite sex; *also* : of or relating to different sexes — **heterosexual** *n* — **het·ero·sex·u·al·i·ty** \-ˌsek-shə-ˈwal-ət-ē\ *n*

hew \ˈhyü\ *vb* **hewed; hewed** *or* **hewn** \ˈhyün\; **hew·ing** **1** : to cut or fell with blows (as of an ax) **2** : to give shape to with or as if with an ax **3** : to conform strictly — **hew·er** *n*

HEW *abbr* Department of Health, Education, and Welfare

[1]**hex** \ˈheks\ *vb* **1** : to practice witchcraft **2** : JINX

[2]**hex** *n* : SPELL, JINX

[3]**hex** *abbr* hexagon; hexagonal

hexa·gon \ˈhek-sə-ˌgän\ *n* : a polygon having six angles and six sides — **hex·ag·o·nal** \hek-ˈsag-ən-ᵊl\ *adj*

hex·am·e·ter \hek-ˈsam-ət-ər\ *n* : a line of verse containing six metrical feet

hey·day \ˈhā-ˌdā\ *n* : a period of greatest strength, vigor, or prosperity

hf *abbr* half

Hf *symbol* hafnium

HF *abbr* high frequency

hg *abbr* hectogram

Hg *symbol* [NL *hydrargyrum*, lit., water silver] mercury

hgt *abbr* height

hgwy *abbr* highway

HH *abbr* **1** Her Highness; His Highness **2** His Holiness

HHS *abbr* Department of Health and Human Services

HI *abbr* **1** Hawaii **2** humidity index

hi·a·tus \hī-ˈāt-əs\ *n* [L, fr. *hiatus*, pp. of *hiare* to yawn] **1** : a break in an object : GAP **2** : a lapse in continuity

hi·ba·chi \hi-ˈbäch-ē\ *n* [Jp] : a charcoal brazier

hi·ber·nate \ˈhī-bər-ˌnāt\ *vb* **-nat·ed; -nat·ing** : to pass the winter in a torpid or resting state — **hi·ber·na·tion** \ˌhī-bər-ˈnā-shən\ *n* — **hi·ber·na·tor** \ˈhī-bər-ˌnāt-ər\ *n*

hi·bis·cus \hī-ˈbis-kəs, hə-\ *n* : any of a genus of herbs, shrubs, and trees related to the mallows and noted for large showy flowers

hic·cup *also* **hic·cough** \ˈhik-(ˌ)əp\ *n* : a spasmodic breathing movement checked by sudden closing of the glottis accompanied by a peculiar sound; *also* : this sound — **hiccup** *vb*

hick \ˈhik\ *n* [*Hick*, nickname for *Richard*] : an awkward provincial person — **hick** *adj*

hick·o·ry \ˈhik-(ə-)rē\ *n, pl* **-ries** : any of a genus of No. American hardwood trees related to the walnuts; *also* : the wood of a hickory — **hickory** *adj*

hi·dal·go \hid-ˈal-gō\ *n, pl* **-gos** *often cap* [Sp, fr. earlier *fijo dalgo*, lit., son of something, son of property] : a member of the lower nobility of Spain

hidden tax *n* **1** : a tax ultimately paid by someone other than the person on whom it is formally levied **2** : an economic injustice that reduces one's income or buying power

[1]**hide** \ˈhīd\ *vb* **hid** \ˈhid\; **hid·den** \ˈhid-ᵊn\ *or* **hid; hid·ing** \ˈhīd-iŋ\ **1** : to put or remain out of sight **2** : to conceal for shelter or protection; *also* : to seek protection **3** : to keep secret **4** : to turn away in shame or anger

[2]**hide** *n* : the skin of an animal

hide–and–seek \ˌhīd-ᵊn-ˈsēk\ *n* : a children's game in which everyone hides from one player who tries to find them

hide·away \ˈhīd-ə-ˌwā\ *n* : HIDEOUT

hide·bound \-ˌbau̇nd\ *adj* : obstinately conservative

hid·eous \ˈhid-ē-əs\ *adj* [ME *hidous*, fr. OF, fr. *hisde*, *hide* terror] **1** : offensive to one of the senses : UGLY **2** : morally offensive : SHOCKING — **hid·eous·ly** *adv* — **hid·eous·ness** *n*

hide·out \ˈhīd-ˌau̇t\ *n* : a place of refuge or concealment

hie \ˈhī\ *vb* **hied; hy·ing** *or* **hie·ing** : HASTEN

hi·er·ar·chy \ˈhī-(ə-)ˌrär-kē\ *n, pl* **-chies** **1** : a ruling body of clergy organized into ranks **2** : persons or things arranged in a graded series — **hi·er·ar·chi·cal** \ˌhī-ə-ˈrär-ki-kəl\ *adj* — **hi·er·ar·chi·cal·ly** \-k(ə-)lē\ *adv*

hi·er·o·glyph·ic \ˌhī-(ə-)rə-ˈglif-ik\ *n* [MF *hieroglyphique*, adj., deriv. of Gk *hieroglyphikos*, fr. *hieros* sacred + *glyphein* to carve] **1** : a character in a system of picture writing (as of the ancient Egyptians) **2** : a symbol or sign difficult to decipher

hi–fi \ˈhī-ˈfī\ *n* **1** : HIGH FIDELITY **2** : equipment for reproduction of sound with high fidelity

hig·gle·dy–pig·gle·dy \ˌhig-əl-dē-ˈpig-əl-dē\ *adv* : in confusion

[1]**high** \ˈhī\ *adj* **1** : ELEVATED; *also* : TALL **2** : advanced toward fullness or culmination; *also* : slightly tainted **3** : long past **4** : SHRILL, SHARP **5** : far from the equator ⟨~ latitudes⟩ **6** : exalted in character **7** : of greater degree, size, or amount than average **8** : of relatively great importance **9** : FORCIBLE, STRONG ⟨~ winds⟩ **10** : BOASTFUL, ARROGANT **11** : showing elation or excitement **12** : COSTLY, DEAR **13** : advanced esp. in complexity ⟨~*er* mathematics⟩ **14** : INTOXICATED; *also* : excited or stupefied by or as if by a drug (as heroin) — **high·ly** *adv*

[2]**high** *adv* **1** : at or to a high place or degree **2** : LUXURIOUSLY ⟨living ~⟩

[3]**high** *n* **1** : an elevated place **2** : a high point or level **3** : the arrangement of gears in an automobile that gives the highest speed **4** : an excited or stupefied state produced by or as if by a drug

high·ball \ˈhī-ˌbȯl\ *n* : a usu. tall drink of liquor mixed with water or a carbonated beverage

high beam *n* : the long-range focus of a vehicle headlight

high·born \ˈhī-ˈbȯrn\ *adj* : of noble birth

high·boy \-ˌbȯi\ *n* : a high chest of drawers mounted on a base with legs

high·bred \-ˈbred\ *adj* : coming from superior stock

high·brow \-ˌbrau̇\ *n* : a person of superior learning or culture — **highbrow** *adj*

high·er–up \ˌhī-ər-ˈəp\ *n* : a superior officer of official

high·fa·lu·tin \ˌhī-fə-ˈlüt-ᵊn\ *adj* : PRETENTIOUS, POMPOUS

high fashion *n* **1** : HIGH STYLE **2** : HAUTE COUTURE

high fidelity *n* : the reproduction of sound or image with a high degree of faithfulness to the original

high five *n* : a slapping of upraised right hands by two people (as in celebration) — **high–five** *vb*

high–flown \ˈhī-ˈflōn\ *adj* **1** : EXALTED **2** : BOMBASTIC

high frequency *n* : a radio frequency between 3 and 30 megahertz

high gear *n* **1** : HIGH 3 **2** : a state of intense or maximum activity

high–hand·ed \ˈhī-ˈhan-dəd\ *adj* : OVERBEARING — **high–hand·ed·ly** *adv* — **high–hand·ed·ness** *n*

high–hat \-ˈhat\ *adj* : SUPERCILIOUS, SNOBBISH — **high–hat** *vb*

high·land \-lənd\ *n* : elevated or mountainous land

high·land·er \-lən-dər\ *n* **1** : an inhabitant of a highland **2** *cap* : an inhabitant of the Scottish Highlands

[1]**high·light** \-ˌlīt\ *n* : an event or detail of major importance

[2]**highlight** *vb* **1** : EMPHASIZE **2** : to constitute a highlight of

high–mind·ed \-ˈmīn-dəd\ *adj* : marked by elevated principles and feelings — **high–mind·ed·ness** *n*

high·ness \ˈhī-nəs\ *n* **1** : the quality or state of being high **2** — used as a title (as for kings)

high–pres·sure \-ˈpresh-ər\ *adj* : using or involving aggressive and insistent sales techniques

high–rise \-ˈrīz\ *adj* : having several stories and being equipped with elevators ⟨~ apartments⟩; *also* : of or relating to high-rise buildings

high·road \-ˌrōd\ *n* : HIGHWAY

high school *n* : a school usu. including grades 9 to 12 or 10 to 12

high sea *n* : the open sea outside territorial waters — usu. used in pl.

high–sound·ing \ˈhī-ˈsau̇n-diŋ\ *adj* : POMPOUS, IMPOSING

high–spir·it·ed \-ˈspir-ət-əd\ *adj* : characterized by a bold or lofty spirit

high–strung \-ˈstrəŋ\ *adj* : having an extremely nervous or sensitive temperament

high style *n* : the newest in fashion or design usu. adopted by a limited number of people

high·tail \ˈhī-ˌtāl\ *vb* : to retreat at full speed

high tech \-ˈtek\ *n* : HIGH TECHNOLOGY

high technology *n* : technology involving the use of advanced devices or techniques

high–ten·sion \ˈhī-ˈten-chən\ *adj* : having, using, or relating to high voltage

high–test \-ˈtest\ *adj* : having a high octane number

high–toned \-ˈtōnd\ *adj* **1** : high in social, moral, or intellectual quality **2** : PRETENTIOUS, POMPOUS

high·way \ˈhī-ˌwā\ *n* : a main direct road

high·way·man \-mən\ *n* : a person who robs travelers on a road

hi·jack *or* **high–jack** \ˈhī-ˌjak\ *vb* : to steal esp. by stopping a vehicle on the highway; *also* : to commandeer a flying airplane — **hijack** *n* — **hi·jack·er** *n*

[1]**hike** \ˈhīk\ *vb* **hiked; hik·ing 1 :** to move or raise with a sudden motion **2 :** to take a long walk — **hik·er** *n*

[2]**hike** *n* **1 :** a long walk **2 :** RISE, INCREASE

hi·lar·i·ous \hil-ˈar-ē-əs, hī-ˈlar-\ *adj* **:** marked by or providing boisterous merriment — **hi·lar·i·ous·ly** *adv* — **hi·lar·i·ty** \-ət-ē\ *n*

hill \ˈhil\ *n* **1 :** a usu. rounded elevation of land **2 :** a little heap or mound (as of earth) — **hilly** *adj*

hill·bil·ly \ˈhil-ˌbil-ē\ *n, pl* **-lies :** a person from a backwoods area

hill·ock \ˈhil-ək\ *n* **:** a small hill

hill·side \-ˌsīd\ *n* **:** the part of a hill between the summit and the foot

hill·top \-ˌtäp\ *n* **:** the top of a hill

hilt \ˈhilt\ *n* **:** a handle esp. of a sword or dagger

him \im, (ˈ)him\ *pron, objective case of* HE

Hi·ma·la·yan \ˌhim-ə-ˈlā-ən, him-ˈäl-yən\ *adj* **:** of, relating to, or characteristic of the Himalaya mountains or the people living there

him·self \(h)im-ˈself\ *pron* **:** HE, HIM — used reflexively, for emphasis, or in absolute constructions

[1]**hind** \ˈhīnd\ *n, pl* **hinds** *also* **hind :** a female deer **:** DOE

[2]**hind** *adj* **:** REAR

[1]**hin·der** \ˈhin-dər\ *vb* **hin·dered; hin·der·ing** \-d(ə-)riŋ\ **1 :** to impede the progress of **2 :** to hold back **syn** obstruct, block, bar, impede

[2]**hind·er** \ˈhīn-dər\ *adj* **:** HIND

Hin·di \ˈhin-dē\ *n* **:** a literary and official language of northern India

hind·most \ˈhīn(d)-ˌmōst\ *adj* **:** farthest to the rear

hind·quar·ter \-ˌkwȯrt-ər\ *n* **1 :** one side of the back half of the carcass of a quadruped **2** *pl* **:** the part of the body of a quadruped behind the junction of hind limbs and trunk

hin·drance \ˈhin-drəns\ *n* **1 :** the state of being hindered; *also* **:** the action of hindering **2 :** IMPEDIMENT

hind·sight \ˈhīn(d)-ˌsīt\ *n* **:** understanding of an event after it has happened

Hin·du·ism \ˈhin-dü-ˌiz-əm\ *n* **:** a body of religious beliefs and practices native to India — **Hin·du** *n or adj*

hind wing *n* **:** either of the posterior wings of a 4-winged insect

[1]**hinge** \ˈhinj\ *n* **:** a jointed piece on which one piece (as a door, gate, or lid) turns or swings on another

[2]**hinge** *vb* **hinged; hing·ing 1 :** to attach by or furnish with hinges **2 :** to be contingent on a single consideration

hint \ˈhint\ *n* **1 :** an indirect or summary suggestion **2 :** CLUE **3 :** a very small amount — **hint** *vb*

hin·ter·land \ˈhint-ər-ˌland\ *n* **1 :** a region behind a coast **2 :** a region remote from cities

[1]**hip** \ˈhip\ *n* **:** the fruit of a rose

[2]**hip** *n* **1 :** the part of the body on either side below the waist consisting of the side of the pelvis and the upper thigh **2 :** the joint between pelvis and femur

[3]**hip** *also* **hep** *adj* **hip·per; hip·pest :** keenly aware of or interested in the newest developments

[4]**hip** *vb* **hipped; hip·ping :** TELL, INFORM

hip·bone \-ˈbōn, -ˌbōn\ *n* **:** the large flaring bone that makes a lateral half of the pelvis in mammals

hip joint *n* **:** the articulation between the femur and the hipbone

hipped \ˈhipt\ *adj* **:** having hips esp. of a specified kind ⟨broad-*hipped*⟩

hip·pie *or* **hip·py** \ˈhip-ē\ *n, pl* **hippies :** a usu. young person who rejects established mores, advocates nonviolence, and often uses psychedelic drugs or marijuana; *also* **:** a long-haired unconventionally dressed young person

hip·po·drome \ˈhip-ə-ˌdrōm\ *n* **:** an arena for equestrian performances

hip·po·pot·a·mus \ˌhip-ə-ˈpät-ə-məs\ *n, pl* **-mus·es** *or* **-mi** \-ˌmī\ [L, fr. Gk *hippopotamos,* fr. *hippos* horse + *potamos* river] **:** a large thick-skinned African river animal related to the swine

hippopotamus

[1]**hire** \ˈhī(ə)r\ *n* **1 :** payment for labor or personal services **:** WAGES **2 :** EMPLOYMENT

[2]**hire** *vb* **hired; hir·ing 1 :** to employ for pay **2 :** to engage the temporary use of for pay

hire·ling \ˈhī(ə)r-liŋ\ *n* **:** a hired person; *esp* **:** one whose motives are mercenary

hir·sute \ˈhər-ˌsüt, ˈhiər-\ *adj* **:** HAIRY

[1]**his** \(h)iz, ˌhiz\ *adj* **:** of or relating to him or himself

[2]**his** \ˈhiz\ *pron* **:** one or the ones belonging to him

His·pan·ic \his-ˈpan-ik\ *adj* **:** of or relating to the people, speech, or culture of Spain or Latin America

hiss \ˈhis\ *vb* **:** to make a sharp sibilant sound; *also* **:** to express disapproval of by hissing — **hiss** *n*

hist *abbr* historian; historical; history

his·ta·mine \ˈhis-tə-ˌmēn, -mən\ *n* **:** a chemical compound widespread in animal tissues and playing a major role in allergic reactions

his·to·gram \ˈhis-tə-ˌgram\ *n* **:** representation of statistical data by means of rectangles whose widths represent class intervals and whose heights represent corresponding frequencies

his·to·ri·an \his-ˈtōr-ē-ən\ *n* **:** a student or writer of history

his·to·ric·i·ty \ˌhis-tə-ˈris-ət-ē\ *n* **:** historical actuality

his·to·ri·og·ra·pher \his-ˌtōr-ē-ˈäg-rə-fər\ *n* **:** HISTORIAN

his·to·ry \ˈhis-t(ə-)rē\ *n, pl* **-ries** [L *historia,* fr. Gk, inquiry, history, fr. *histōr, istōr* knowing, learned] **1 :** a chronological record of significant events often with an explanation of their causes **2 :** a branch of knowledge that records and explains past events **3 :** events that form the subject matter of history — **his·tor·ic** \his-ˈtȯr-ik\ *adj* — **his·tor·i·cal** \-i-kəl\ *adj* — **his·tor·i·cal·ly** \-k(ə-)lē\ *adv*

his·tri·on·ic \ˌhis-trē-ˈän-ik\ *adj* [LL *histrionicus,* fr. L *histrio* actor] **1 :** deliberately affected **2 :** of or relating to actors or the theater — **his·tri·on·i·cal·ly** \-i-k(ə-)lē\ *adv*

his·tri·on·ics \-iks\ *n pl* **1 :** theatrical performances **2 :** deliberate display of emotion for effect

[1]**hit** \ˈhit\ *vb* **hit; hit·ting 1 :** to reach with a blow **:** STRIKE **2 :** to make or bring into contact **:** COLLIDE **3 :** to affect detrimentally **4 :** to make a request of **5 :** to come upon **6 :** to accord with **:** SUIT **7 :** REACH, ATTAIN **8 :** to indulge in often to excess — **hit·ter** *n*

[2]**hit** *n* **1 :** BLOW; *also* **:** COLLISION **2 :** something highly successful **3 :** a stroke in an athletic contest; *esp* **:** BASE HIT **4 :** a dose of an illegal drug **5 :** a murder committed by a gangster

[1]**hitch** \ˈhich\ *vb* **1 :** to move by jerks **2 :** to catch or fasten esp. by a hook or knot **3 :** HITCHHIKE

[2]**hitch** *n* **1 :** JERK, PULL **2 :** a sudden halt **3 :** a connection between something towed and its mover **4 :** KNOT

hitch·hike \ˈhich-ˌhīk\ *vb* **:** to travel by securing free rides from passing vehicles — **hitch·hik·er** *n*

[1]**hith·er** \ˈhith-ər\ *adv* : to this place
[2]**hither** *adj* : being on the near or adjacent side
hith·er·to \-ˌtü\ *adv* : up to this time
HIV *n* [*h*uman *i*mmunodeficiency *v*irus] : AIDS VIRUS
hive \ˈhīv\ *n* **1** : a container for housing honeybees **2** : a colony of bees **3** : a place swarming with busy occupants — **hive** *vb*
hives \ˈhīvz\ *n sing or pl* : an allergic disorder marked by the presence of itching wheals
HJ *abbr* [L *hic jacet*] here lies — used in epitaphs
hl *abbr* hectoliter
HL *abbr* House of Lords
hm *abbr* hectometer
HM *abbr* **1** Her Majesty; Her Majesty's **2** His Majesty; His Majesty's
HMS *abbr* Her Majesty's ship; His Majesty's ship
Ho *symbol* holmium
hoa·gie *also* **hoa·gy** \ˈhō-gē\ *n, pl* **hoagies** : SUBMARINE 2
hoard \ˈhōrd\ *n* : a hidden accumulation — **hoard** *vb* — **hoard·er** *n*
hoar·frost \ˈhōr-ˌfrȯst\ *n* : FROST 2
hoarse \ˈhōrs\ *adj* **hoars·er; hoars·est 1** : rough and harsh in sound **2** : having a grating voice — **hoarse·ly** *adv* — **hoarse·ness** *n*
hoary \ˈhōr-ē\ *adj* **hoar·i·er; -est 1** : gray or white with age **2** : ANCIENT — **hoar·i·ness** *n*
hoax \ˈhōks\ *n* : an act intended to trick or dupe; *also* : something accepted or established by fraud — **hoax** *vb* — **hoax·er** *n*
hob \ˈhäb\ *n* : MISCHIEF, TROUBLE
[1]**hob·ble** \ˈhäb-əl\ *vb* **hob·bled, hob·bling** \-(ə-)liŋ\ **1** : to limp along; *also* : to make lame **2** : FETTER
[2]**hobble** *n* **1** : a hobbling movement **2** : something used to hobble an animal
hob·by \ˈhäb-ē\ *n, pl* **hobbies** : a pursuit or interest engaged in for relaxation — **hob·by·ist** \-ē-əst\ *n*
hob·by·horse \ˈhäb-ē-ˌhȯrs\ *n* **1** : a stick with a horse's head on which children pretend to ride **2** : a toy horse mounted on rockers **3** : a favorite topic to which one constantly reverts
hob·gob·lin \ˈhäb-ˌgäb-lən\ *n* **1** : a mischievous goblin **2** : BOGEY 1
hob·nail \-ˌnāl\ *n* : a short large-headed nail for studding shoe soles — **hob·nailed** \-ˌnāld\ *adj*
hob·nob \-ˌnäb\ *vb* **hob·nobbed; hob·nob·bing** : to associate familiarly
ho·bo \ˈhō-bō\ *n, pl* **hoboes** *also* **hobos** : TRAMP 2
[1]**hock** \ˈhäk\ *n* : a joint or region in the hind limb of a quadruped just above the foot and corresponding to the human ankle
[2]**hock** *n* [D *hok* pen, prison] : PAWN; *also* : DEBT 2 — **hock** *vb*
hock·ey \ˈhäk-ē\ *n* **1** : FIELD HOCKEY **2** : ICE HOCKEY
ho·cus–po·cus \ˌhō-kəs-ˈpō-kəs\ *n* **1** : SLEIGHT OF HAND **2** : nonsense or sham used to conceal deception
hod \ˈhäd\ *n* **1** : a long-handled tray or trough for carrying a load esp. of mortar or bricks **2** : a coal scuttle
hodge·podge \ˈhäj-ˌpäj\ *n* : a heterogeneous mixture
hoe \ˈhō\ *n* : a long-handled implement with a thin flat blade used esp. for cultivating, weeding, or loosening the earth around plants — **hoe** *vb*
hoe·cake \ˈhō-ˌkāk\ *n* : a small cornmeal cake
hoe·down \-ˌdau̇n\ *n* **1** : SQUARE DANCE **2** : a gathering featuring hoedowns
[1]**hog** \ˈhȯg, ˈhäg\ *n, pl* **hogs** *also* **hog 1** : a domestic swine esp. when grown **2** : a selfish, gluttonous, or filthy person — **hog·gish** *adj*
[2]**hog** *vb* **hogged; hog·ging** : to take or hold selfishly
ho·gan \ˈhō-ˌgän\ *n* : an earth-covered dwelling of the Navaho Indians
hog·back \ˈhȯg-ˌbak, ˈhäg-\ *n* : a ridge with a sharp summit and steep sides
hog·nose snake \ˌhȯg-ˌnōz-, ˌhäg-\ *or* **hog·nosed snake** \-ˌnōz(d)-\ *n* : any of several rather small harmless stout-bodied No. American snakes with an upturned snout that play dead when their threatening display is ineffective
hogs·head \ˈhȯgz-ˌhed, ˈhägz-\ *n* **1** : a large cask or barrel; *esp* : one holding from 63 to 140 gallons **2** : a liquid measure equal to 63 U.S. gallons
hog–tie \ˈhȯg-ˌtī, ˈhäg-\ *vb* **1** : to tie together the feet of ⟨~ a calf⟩ **2** : to make helpless
hog·wash \-ˌwȯsh, -ˌwäsh\ *n* **1** : SWILL 1, SLOP 2 **2** : NONSENSE, BALONEY
hog–wild \-ˈwīld\ *adj* : lacking in restraint
hoi pol·loi \ˌhȯi-pə-ˈlȯi\ *n pl* [Gk, the many] : the general populace
[1]**hoist** \ˈhȯist\ *vb* : RAISE, LIFT
[2]**hoist** *n* **1** : LIFT **2** : an apparatus for hoisting
hoke \ˈhōk\ *vb* **hoked; hok·ing** : FAKE — usu. used with *up*
ho·kum \ˈhō-kəm\ *n* : NONSENSE
[1]**hold** \ˈhōld\ *vb* **held** \ˈheld\; **hold·ing 1** : POSSESS; *also* : KEEP **2** : RESTRAIN **3** : to have a grasp on **4** : to remain or keep in a particular situation or position **5** : SUSTAIN; *also* : RESERVE **6** : BEAR, COMPORT **7** : to maintain in being or action : PERSIST **8** : CONTAIN, ACCOMMODATE **9** : HARBOR, ENTERTAIN; *also* : CONSIDER, REGARD **10** : to carry on by concerted action; *also* : CONVOKE **11** : to occupy esp. by appointment or election **12** : to be valid **13** : HALT, PAUSE — **hold·er** *n* — **hold forth** : to speak at length — **hold to** : to adhere to : MAINTAIN — **hold with** : to agree with or approve of
[2]**hold** *n* **1** : STRONGHOLD **2** : CONFINEMENT; *also* : PRISON **3** : the act or manner of holding : GRIP **4** : a restraining, dominating, or controlling influence **5** : something that may be grasped as a support **6** : an order or indication that something is to be reserved or delayed
[3]**hold** *n* **1** : the interior of a ship below decks; *esp* : a ship's cargo deck **2** : an airplane's cargo compartment
hold·ing \ˈhōl-diŋ\ *n* **1** : land or other property owned **2** : a ruling of a court esp. on an issue of law
holding pattern *n* : a course flown by an aircraft waiting to land
hold out \(ˈ)hōl-ˈdau̇t\ *vb* **1** : to continue to fight or work **2** : to refuse to come to an agreement — **hold·out** \ˈhōl-ˌdau̇t\ *n*
hold·over \ˈhōl-ˌdō-vər\ *n* : a person who continues in office
hold·up \ˈhōl-ˌdəp\ *n* **1** : DELAY **2** : robbery at the point of a gun
hole \ˈhōl\ *n* **1** : an opening into or through something **2** : a hollow place (as a pit or cave) **3** : DEN, BURROW **4** : a unit of play from tee to cup in golf **5** : a wretched or dingy place **6** : an awkward position — **hole** *vb*
hol·i·day \ˈhäl-ə-ˌdā\ *n* [ME, fr. OE *hāligdæg*, fr. *hālig* holy + *dæg* day] **1** : a day observed in Judaism with commemorative ceremonies **2** : a day of freedom from work; *esp* : one in commemoration of an event **3** : VACATION — **holiday** *vb*
ho·li·ness \ˈhō-lē-nəs\ *n* **1** : the quality or state of being holy **2** — used as a title for various high religious officials
hol·ler \ˈhäl-ər\ *vb* **hol·lered; hol·ler·ing** \-(ə-)riŋ\ : to cry out : SHOUT — **holler** *n*
[1]**hol·low** \ˈhäl-ō\ *adj* **hol·low·er** \ˈhäl-ə-wər\; **hol·low·est** \-ə-wəst\ **1** : CONCAVE, SUNKEN **2** : having a cavity within **3** : MUFFLED ⟨a ~ sound⟩ **4** : lacking in real value, sincerity, or substance; *also* : FALSE — **hol·low·ness** *n*
[2]**hollow** *n* **1** : a surface depression **2** : CAVITY, HOLE
[3]**hollow** *vb* : to make or become hollow
hol·low·ware *or* **hol·lo·ware** \ˈhäl-ə-ˌwaər\ *n* : vessels (as bowls or cups) that have a significant depth and volume
hol·ly \ˈhäl-ē\ *n, pl* **hollies** : a tree or shrub with usu. evergreen glossy spiny-margined leaves and red berries
hol·ly·hock \-ˌhäk, -ˌhȯk\ *n* [ME *holihoc*, fr. *holi* holy +

hoc mallow] : a tall perennial herb related to the mallows that is widely grown for its showy flowers

hol·mi·um \ˈhōl-mē-əm\ *n* : a metallic chemical element — see ELEMENT table

ho·lo·caust \ˈhäl-ə-ˌkȯst, ˈhō-lə-, ˈhȯ-lə-\ *n* **1** : a thorough destruction esp. by fire **2** *often cap* : the killing of European Jews by the Nazis during World War II

Ho·lo·cene \ˈhō-lə-ˌsēn\ *adj* : RECENT 3 — **Holocene** *n*

ho·lo·gram \ˈhō-lə-ˌgram, ˈhäl-ə-\ *n* : a three-dimensional picture made by reflected laser light on a photographic film without the use of a camera

ho·lo·graph \ˈhō-lə-ˌgraf, ˈhäl-ə-\ *n* : a document wholly in the handwriting of its author

ho·log·ra·phy \hō-ˈläg-rə-fē\ *n* : the process of making or using a hologram — **ho·lo·graph·ic** \ˌhō-lə-ˈgraf-ik, ˌhäl-ə-\ *adj*

hol·stein \ˈhōl-ˌstēn, -ˌstīn\ *n* : any of a breed of large black-and-white dairy cattle that produce large quantities of comparatively low-fat milk

hol·stein–frie·sian \-ˈfrē-zhən\ *n* : HOLSTEIN

hol·ster \ˈhōl-stər\ *n* [Dutch] : a usu. leather case for a firearm

ho·ly \ˈhō-lē\ *adj* **ho·li·er; -est 1** : worthy of absolute devotion **2** : SACRED **3** : having a divine quality **syn** hallowed, blessed, sacred, sanctified, consecrated

Holy Spirit *n* : the active presence of God in human life constituting the third person of the Trinity

ho·ly·stone \ˈhō-lē-ˌstōn\ *n* : a soft sandstone used to scrub a ship's decks — **holy·stone** *vb*

hom·age \ˈ(h)äm-ij\ *n* [ME, fr. OF *hommage*, fr. *homme* man, vassal, fr. L *homo* man] : reverential regard

hom·bre \ˈäm-brē, ˈəm-, -ˌbrā\ *n* : GUY, FELLOW

hom·burg \ˈhäm-ˌbərg\ *n* [*Homburg*, Germany] : a man's felt hat with a stiff curled brim and a high crown creased lengthwise

[1]**home** \ˈhōm\ *n* **1** : one's residence; *also* : HOUSE **2** : the social unit formed by a family living together **3** : a congenial environment; *also* : HABITAT **4** : a place of origin **5** : the objective in various games — **home·less** *adj*

[2]**home** *vb* **homed; hom·ing 1** : to go or return home **2** : to proceed to or toward a source of radiated energy used as a guide

home·body \ˈhōm-ˌbäd-ē\ *n* : one whose life centers in the home

home·bred \-ˈbred\ *adj* : produced at home : INDIGENOUS

home·com·ing \-ˌkəm-iŋ\ *n* **1** : a return home **2** : the return of a group of people esp. on a special occasion to a place formerly frequented

home computer *n* : a small inexpensive microcomputer

home economics *n* : the theory and practice of homemaking

home·grown \ˈhōm-ˈgrōn\ *adj* **1** : grown domestically ⟨~ corn⟩ **2** : LOCAL, INDIGENOUS

home·land \-ˌland\ *n* **1** : native land **2** : an area set aside to be a state for a people of a particular national, cultural, or racial origin

home·ly \ˈhōm-lē\ *adj* **home·li·er; -est 1** : FAMILIAR **2** : unaffectedly natural **3** : lacking beauty or proportion — **home·li·ness** *n*

home·made \ˈhōm-ˌ(m)ād\ *adj* : made in the home, on the premises, or by one's own efforts

home·mak·er \-ˌmā-kər\ *n* : one who manages a household esp. as a wife and mother — **home·mak·ing** \-kiŋ\ *n*

ho·me·op·a·thy \ˌhō-mē-ˈäp-ə-thē\ *n* : a system of medical practice that treats disease esp. with minute doses of a remedy that would in healthy persons produce symptoms of the disease treated — **ho·meo·path** \ˈhō-mē-ə-ˌpath\ *n* — **ho·meo·path·ic** \ˌhō-mē-ə-ˈpath-ik\ *adj*

ho·meo·sta·sis \ˌhō-mē-ō-ˈstā-səs\ *n* : a tendency toward a stable state of equilibrium between interrelated physiological, psychological, or social factors characteristic of an individual or group — **ho·meo·stat·ic** \-ˈstat-ik\ *adj*

home plate *n* : a slab at the apex of a baseball diamond that a base runner must touch in order to score

hom·er \ˈhō-mər\ *n* : HOME RUN — **homer** *vb*

home·room \ˈhōm-ˌrüm, -ˌru̇m\ *n* : a classroom where pupils report at the beginning of each school day

home run *n* : a hit in baseball that enables the batter to make a circuit of the bases and score a run

home·sick \ˈhōm-ˌsik\ *adj* : longing for home and family while absent from them — **home·sick·ness** *n*

home·spun \-ˌspən\ *adj* **1** : spun or made at home; *also* : made of a loosely woven usu. woolen or linen fabric **2** : SIMPLE, HOMELY

[1]**home·stead** \ˈhōmˌsted\ *n* : the home and land occupied by a family

[2]**homestead** *vb* : to acquire or settle on public land — **home·stead·er** \-ˌsted-ər\ *n*

home·stretch \ˈhōm-ˈstrech\ *n* **1** : the part of a racecourse between the last curve and the winning post **2** : a final stage (as of a project)

[1]**home·ward** \ˈhōm-wərd\ *or* **home·wards** \-wərdz\ *adv* : in the direction of home

[2]**homeward** *adj* : being or going in the direction of home

home·work \ˈhōm-ˌwərk\ *n* **1** : an assignment given a student to be completed outside the classroom **2** : preparatory reading or research

hom·ey \ˈhō-mē\ *adj* **hom·i·er; -est** : intimate or homelike

ho·mi·cide \ˈhäm-ə-ˌsīd, ˈhō-mə-\ *n* [L *homicida* manslayer & *homicidium* manslaughter; both fr. *homo* man + *caedere* to cut, kill] **1** : a person who kills another **2** : a killing of one human being by another — **hom·i·cid·al** \ˌhäm-ə-ˈsīd-ᵊl\ *adj*

hom·i·ly \ˈhäm-ə-lē\ *n, pl* **-lies** : SERMON — **hom·i·let·ic** \ˌhäm-ə-ˈlet-ik\ *adj*

homing pigeon *n* : a racing pigeon trained to return home

hom·i·ny \ˈhäm-ə-nē\ *n* : hulled corn with the germ removed

ho·mo \ˈhō-mō\ *n, pl* **homos** : any of the genus of primate mammals that includes all surviving and various extinct human beings

ho·mo·ge·neous \ˌhō-mə-ˈjē-nē-əs, -nyəs\ *adj* : of the same or a similar kind; *also* : of uniform structure — **ho·mo·ge·ne·i·ty** \-jə-ˈnē-ət-ē\ *n* — **ho·mo·ge·neous·ly** *adv* — **ho·mo·ge·nous·ness** *n*

ho·mog·e·nize \hō-ˈmäj-ə-ˌnīz, hə-\ *vb* **-nized; -niz·ing 1** : to make homogeneous **2** : to reduce the particles in (as milk or paint) to uniform size and distribute them evenly throughout the liquid — **ho·mog·e·ni·za·tion** \-ˌmäj-ə-nə-ˈzā-shən\ *n* — **ho·mog·e·niz·er** *n*

ho·mo·graph \ˈhäm-ə-ˌgraf, ˈhō-mə-\ *n* : one of two or more words spelled alike but different in origin or meaning or pronunciation ⟨the noun *conduct* and the verb *conduct* are ~*s*⟩

ho·mol·o·gy \hō-ˈmäl-ə-jē, hə-\ *n, pl* **-gies 1** : structural likeness between corresponding parts of different plants or animals due to evolution from a common ancestor **2** : structural likeness between different parts of the same individual — **ho·mol·o·gous** \-ˈmäl-ə-gəs\ *adj*

hom·onym \ˈhäm-ə-ˌnim, ˈhō-mə-\ *n* **1** : HOMOPHONE, HOMOGRAPH **2** : one of two or more words spelled and pronounced alike but different in meaning ⟨*pool* of water and *pool* the game are ~*s*⟩

ho·mo·phone \ˈhäm-ə-ˌfōn, ˈhō-mə-\ *n* : one of two or more words (as *to, too, two*) pronounced alike but different in meaning or derivation or spelling

Ho·mo sa·pi·ens \ˌhō-mō-ˈsā-pē-ənz, -ˈsap-ē-\ *n* : the totality of human beings : MANKIND 1

ho·mo·sex·u·al \ˌhō-mō-ˈsek-sh(ə-w)əl\ *adj* : of, relating to, or exhibiting sexual desire toward another of the same sex — **homosexual** *n* — **ho·mo·sex·u·al·i·ty** \-ˌsek-shə-ˈwal-ət-ē\ *n*

hon *abbr* honor; honorable; honorary

hone \ˈhōn\ *n* : a fine-grit stone for sharpening a cutting implement — **hone** *vb* — **hon·er** *n*

hon·est \ˈän-əst\ *adj* **1** : free from deception : TRUTHFUL; *also* : GENUINE, REAL **2** : REPUTABLE **3** : CREDITABLE **4** : marked by integrity **5** : FRANK **syn** upright, just, conscientious, honorable — **hon·est·ly** *adv* — **hon·esty** \-ə-stē\ *n*

hon·ey \ˈhən-ē\ *n, pl* **honeys** : a sweet sticky substance made by bees (**hon·ey·bees** \-ˌbēz\) from the nectar of flowers

[1]**hon·ey·comb** \-ˌkōm\ *n* : a mass of 6-sided wax cells built by honeybees; *also* : something of similar structure or appearance

[2]**honeycomb** *vb* : to make or become full of cavities like a honeycomb

hon·ey·dew \-ˌd(y)ü\ *n* : a sweetish deposit secreted on plants by aphids, scale insects, or fungi

honeydew melon *n* : a smooth-skinned muskmelon with sweet green flesh

honey locust *n* : a tall usu. spiny No. American leguminous tree with hard durable wood and long twisted pods

hon·ey·moon \ˈhən-ē-ˌmün\ *n* **1** : a holiday taken by a newly married couple **2** : a period of harmony esp. just after marriage — **honeymoon** *vb*

hon·ey·suck·le \ˈhən-ē-ˌsək-əl\ *n* : any of various shrubs, vines, or herbs with tube-shaped flowers rich in nectar

honk \ˈhäŋk, ˈhȯŋk\ *n* : the cry of a goose; *also* : a similar sound (as of a horn) — **honk** *vb* — **honk·er** *n*

hon·ky–tonk \ˈhäŋ-kē-ˌtäŋk, ˈhȯŋ-kē-ˌtȯŋk\ *n* : a tawdry nightclub or dance hall

[1]**hon·or** \ˈän-ər\ *n* **1** : good name : REPUTATION; *also* : outward respect **2** : PRIVILEGE **3** : a person of superior standing — used esp. as a title **4** : one who brings respect or fame **5** : an evidence or symbol of distinction **6** : CHASTITY, PURITY **7** : INTEGRITY **syn** homage, reverence, deference, obeisance

[2]**honor** *vb* **hon·ored; hon·or·ing** \-(ə-)riŋ\ **1** : to regard or treat with honor **2** : to confer honor on **3** : to fulfill the terms of; *also* : to accept as payment — **hon·or·er** \ˈän-ər-ər\ *n*

hon·or·able \ˈän-(ə-)rə-bəl\ *adj* **1** : deserving of honor **2** : accompanied with marks of honor **3** : of great renown **4** : doing credit to the possessor **5** : characterized by integrity — **hon·or·able·ness** *n* — **hon·or·ably** \-blē\ *adv*

hon·o·rar·i·um \ˌän-ə-ˈrer-ē-əm\ *n, pl* **-ia** \-ē-ə\ *also* **-i·ums** : a reward usu. for services on which custom or propriety forbids a price to be set

hon·or·ary \ˈän-ə-ˌrer-ē\ *adj* **1** : having or conferring distinction **2** : conferred in recognition of achievement without the usual prerequisites ⟨~ degree⟩ **3** : UNPAID, VOLUNTARY — **hon·or·ari·ly** \ˌän-ə-ˈrer-ə-lē\ *adv*

hon·or·if·ic \ˌän-ə-ˈrif-ik\ *adj* : conferring or conveying honor ⟨~ titles⟩

hon·our \ˈän-ər\ *chiefly Brit var of* HONOR

[1]**hood** \ˈhu̇d\ *n* **1** : a covering for the head and neck and sometimes the face **2** : an ornamental fold (as at the back of an ecclesiastical vestment) **3** : a cover for parts of mechanisms; *esp* : the metal covering over an automobile engine — **hood·ed** \-əd\ *adj*

[2]**hood** \ˈhu̇d, ˈhüd\ *n* : HOODLUM

-hood \ˌhu̇d\ *n suffix* **1** : state : condition : quality : character ⟨boy*hood*⟩ ⟨hardi*hood*⟩ **2** : instance of a (specified) state or quality ⟨false*hood*⟩ **3** : individuals sharing a (specified) state or character ⟨brother*hood*⟩

hood·lum \ˈhüd-ləm, ˈhu̇d-\ *n* **1** : THUG **2** : a young ruffian

hoo·doo \ˈhüd-ü\ *n, pl* **hoodoos** **1** : VOODOO **2** : something that brings bad luck — **hoodoo** *vb*

hood·wink \ˈhu̇d-ˌwiŋk\ *vb* : to deceive by false appearance

hoo·ey \ˈhü-ē\ *n* : NONSENSE

hoof \ˈhu̇f, ˈhüf\ *n, pl* **hooves** \ˈhu̇vz, ˈhüvz\ *or* **hoofs** : a horny covering that protects the ends of the toes of ungulate mammals (as horses or cattle); *also* : a hoofed foot — **hoofed** \ˈhu̇ft, ˈhüft\ *adj*

[1]**hook** \ˈhu̇k\ *n* **1** : a curved or bent device for catching, holding, or pulling **2** : something curved or bent like a hook **3** : a flight of a ball (as in golf) that curves in a direction opposite to the dominant hand of the player propelling it **4** : a short punch delivered with a circular motion and with the elbow bent and rigid

[2]**hook** *vb* **1** : CURVE, CROOK **2** : to seize or make fast with a hook **3** : STEAL **4** : to work as a prostitute

hoo·kah \ˈhu̇k-ə, ˈhü-kə\ *n* [Ar *huqqah* bottle of a water pipe] : a pipe for smoking that has a long flexible tube whereby the smoke is cooled by passing through water

hook·er \ˈhu̇k-ər\ *n* **1** : one that hooks **2** : PROSTITUTE

hook·up \ˈhu̇k-ˌəp\ *n* : an assemblage (as of apparatus or circuits) used for a specific purpose (as in radio)

hook·worm \ˈhu̇k-ˌwərm\ *n* : a parasitic intestinal nematode worm having hooks or plates around the mouth

hoo·li·gan \ˈhü-li-gən\ *n* : RUFFIAN, HOODLUM

hoop \ˈhu̇p, ˈhüp\ *n* **1** : a circular strip used esp. for holding together the staves of a barrel **2** : a circular figure or object : RING **3** : a circle or flexible material for expanding a woman's skirt

hoop·la \ˈhüp-ˌlä, ˈhu̇p-ˌlä\ *n* [F *houp-là*, interj.] **1** : TO-DO; *also* : BALLYHOO **2** : bewildering language

hoose·gow \ˈhüs-ˌgau̇\ *n* [Sp *juzgado* panel of judges, courtroom] *slang* : JAIL

hoot \ˈhüt\ *vb* **1** : to shout or laugh usu. in contempt **2** : to make the natural throat noise of an owl — **hoot** *n* — **hoot·er** *n*

[1]**hop** \ˈhäp\ *vb* **hopped; hop·ping** **1** : to move by quick springy leaps **2** : to make a quick trip **3** : to ride on esp. surreptitiously and without authorization

[2]**hop** *n* **1** : a short brisk leap esp. on one leg **2** : DANCE **3** : a short trip by air

[3]**hop** *n* : a vine related to the mulberry whose ripe dried pistillate catkins are used in medicine and in flavoring malt liquors; *also* : its pistillate catkin

[4]**hop** *vb* **hopped; hop·ping** : to increase the power of ⟨~ up an engine⟩

[1]**hope** \ˈhōp\ *vb* **hoped; hop·ing** : to desire with expectation of fulfillment

[2]**hope** *n* **1** : TRUST, RELIANCE **2** : desire accompanied by expectation of fulfillment; *also* : something hoped for **3** : one that gives promise for the future — **hope·ful** \-fəl\ *adj* — **hope·ful·ly** \-ē\ *adv* — **hope·ful·ness** *n* — **hope·less** *adj* — **hope·less·ly** *adv* — **hope·less·ness** *n*

HOPE *abbr* Health Opportunity for People Everywhere

Ho·pi \ˈhō-pē\ *n, pl* **Hopi** *also* **Hopis** [Hopi *Hópi*, lit., good, peaceful] : a member of an American Indian people of Arizona; *also* : the language of the Hopi people

hop·per \ˈhäp-ər\ *n* **1** : a usu. immature hopping insect **2** : a usu. funnel-shaped container for delivering material (as grain) **3** : a freight car with hinged doors in a sloping bottom **4** : a box into which a bill to be considered by a legislative body is dropped **5** : a tank holding a liquid and having a device for releasing its contents through a pipe

hop·scotch \ˈhäp-ˌskäch\ *n* : a child's game in which a player tosses an object (as a stone) consecutively into areas of a figure outlined on the ground and hops through the figure and back to regain the object

hor *abbr* horizontal

horde \ˈhōrd\ *n* : THRONG, SWARM

hore·hound \ˈhōr-ˌhau̇nd\ *n* [ME *horhoune*, fr. OE *hārhūne*, fr. *hār* hoary + *hūne* horehound] : an aromatic bitter mint with downy leaves used esp. in candy or as an extract in cold and cough remedies

ho·ri·zon \hə-ˈrīz-ᵊn\ *n* [Gk *horizont-*, *horizōn*, fr. prp. of *horizein* to bound, fr. *horos* limit, boundary] **1** : the line marking the apparent junction of earth and sky **2** : range of outlook or experience

hor·i·zon·tal \ˌhȯr-ə-ˈzänt-ᵊl\ *adj* : parallel to the horizon : LEVEL — **horizontal** *n* — **hor·i·zon·tal·ly** \-ē\ *adv*

hor·mon·al \hȯr-ˈmōn-ᵊl\ *adj* : of, relating to, or resembling a hormone

hor·mone \ˈhȯr-ˌmōn\ *n* [Gk *hormōn,* prp. of *horman* to stir up, fr. *hormē* impulse, assault] : a product of living cells that circulates in body fluids and has a specific effect on some other cells; *esp* : the secretion of an endocrine gland

horn \ˈhȯrn\ *n* **1** : one of the hard projections of bone or keratin on the head of many hoofed animals **2** : something resembling or suggesting a horn **3** : a brass wind instrument **4** : a usu. electrical device that makes a noise ⟨automobile ~⟩ — **horned** \ˈhȯrnd\ *adj* — **horn·less** *adj* — **horny** *adj*

horn·book \ˈhȯrn-ˌbu̇k\ *n* **1** : a child's primer consisting of a sheet of parchment or paper protected by a sheet of transparent horn **2** : a rudimentary treatise

horned toad *n* : any of several small harmless insect-eating lizards with spines on the head resembling horns and spiny scales on the body

hor·net \ˈhȯr-nət\ *n* : any of the larger social wasps

horn in *vb* : to participate without invitation : INTRUDE

horn·pipe \ˈhȯrn-ˌpīp\ *n* : a lively folk dance of the British Isles

ho·rol·o·gy \hə-ˈräl-ə-jē\ *n* : the science of measuring time or constructing time-indicating instruments — **hor·o·log·ic** \ˌhȯr-ə-ˈläj-ik\ *adj* — **ho·rol·o·gist** \hə-ˈräl-ə-jəst\ *n*

horo·scope \ˈhȯr-ə-ˌskōp\ *n* [MF, fr. L *horoscopus,* fr. Gk *hōroskopos,* fr. *hōra* hour + *skopein* to look at] **1** : a diagram of the relative positions of planets and signs of the zodiac at a particular time for use by astrologers to foretell events of a person's life **2** : an astrological forecast

hor·ren·dous \hȯ-ˈren-dəs\ *adj* : DREADFUL, HORRIBLE

hor·ri·ble \ˈhȯr-ə-bəl\ *adj* **1** : marked by or conducive to horror **2** : highly disagreeable — **hor·ri·ble·ness** *n* — **hor·ri·bly** \-blē\ *adv*

hor·rid \ˈhȯr-əd\ *adj* **1** : HIDEOUS **2** : REPULSIVE — **hor·rid·ly** *adv*

hor·ri·fy \ˈhȯr-ə-ˌfī\ *vb* **-fied; -fy·ing** : to cause to feel horror **syn** appall, daunt, dismay

hor·ror \ˈhȯr-ər\ *n* **1** : painful and intense fear, dread, or dismay **2** : intense repugnance **3** : something that horrifies

hors de com·bat \ˌȯrd-ə-kōⁿ-ˈbä\ *adv or adj* : in a disabled condition

hors d'oeuvre \ȯr-ˈdərv\ *n, pl* **hors d'oeuvres** *also* **hors d'oeuvre** \-ˈdərv(z)\ [F *hors-d'oeuvre,* lit., outside of work] : any of various savory foods usu. served as appetizers

horse \ˈhȯrs\ *n, pl* **hors·es** *also* **horse 1** : a large solid-hoofed herbivorous mammal domesticated as a draft and saddle animal **2** : a supporting framework usu. with legs — **horse·less** *adj*

¹horse·back \ˈhȯrs-ˌbak\ *adv* : on horseback

²horseback *n* : the back of a horse

horse chestnut *n* : a large Asian tree with palmate leaves, erect conical clusters of showy flowers, and large glossy brown seeds enclosed in a prickly bur

horse·flesh \ˈhȯrs-ˌflesh\ *n* : horses for riding, driving, or racing

horse·fly \-ˌflī\ *n* : any of a group of large two-winged flies with bloodsucking females

horse·hair \-ˌhaər\ *n* **1** : the hair of a horse esp. from the mane or tail **2** : cloth made from horsehair

horse·hide \-ˌhīd\ *n* **1** : the dressed or raw hide of a horse **2** : the ball used in baseball

horse latitudes *n pl* : either of two calm regions near 30°N and 30°S latitude

horse·laugh \ˈhȯrs-ˌlaf, -ˌläf\ *n* : a loud boisterous laugh

horse·man \-mən\ *n* **1** : one who rides horseback; *also* : one skilled in managing horses **2** : a breeder or raiser of horses — **horse·man·ship** *n*

horse·play \-ˌplā\ *n* : rough boisterous play

horse·play·er \-ər\ *n* : a bettor on horse races

horse·pow·er \ˈhȯrs-ˌpau̇(-ə)r\ *n* : a unit of power equal in the U.S. to 746 watts

horse·rad·ish \-ˌrad-ish\ *n* : a tall white-flowered herb related to the mustards whose pungent root is used as a condiment

horse·shoe \ˈhȯrs(h)-ˌshü\ *n* **1** : a protective metal plate fitted to the rim of a horse's hoof **2** *pl* : a game in which horseshoes are pitched at a fixed object — **horse·sho·er** \-ˌshü-ər\ *n*

horseshoe crab *n* : any of several marine arthropods with a broad crescent-shaped combined head and thorax

horse·tail \ˈhȯrs-ˌtāl\ *n* : any of a genus of perennial flowerless plants related to the ferns

horse·whip \-ˌhwip\ *vb* : to flog with a whip made to be used on a horse

horse·wom·an \-ˌwu̇m-ən\ *n* : a woman skilled in riding horseback or in caring for or managing horses; *also* : a woman who breeds or raises horses

hors·ey *or* **horsy** \ˈhȯr-sē\ *adj* **hors·i·er; -est 1** : of, relating to, or suggesting a horse **2** : having to do with horses or horse racing

hort *abbr* horticultural; horticulture

hor·ta·tive \ˈhȯrt-ət-iv\ *adj* : giving exhortation

hor·ta·to·ry \ˈhȯrt-ə-ˌtōr-ē\ *adj* : HORTATIVE

hor·ti·cul·ture \ˈhȯrt-ə-ˌkəl-chər\ *n* : the science and art of growing fruits, vegetables, flowers, and ornamental plants — **hor·ti·cul·tur·al** \ˌhȯrt-ə-ˈkəlch(-ə)-rəl\ *adj* — **hor·ti·cul·tur·ist** \-rəst\ *n*

Hos *abbr* Hosea

ho·san·na \hō-ˈzan-ə, -ˈzän-\ *interj* [Gk *hōsanna,* fr. Heb *hōshīʽāh-nnā* pray, save (us)!] — used as a cry of acclamation and adoration

¹hose \ˈhōz\ *n, pl* **hose** *or* **hos·es 1** *pl* **hose** : STOCKING, SOCK; *also* : a close-fitting garment covering the legs and waist **2** : a flexible tube for conveying fluids (as from a faucet)

²hose *vb* **hosed; hos·ing** : to spray, water, or wash with a hose

Ho·sea \hō-ˈzā-ə, -ˈzē-\ *n* — see BIBLE table

ho·siery \ˈhōzh(-ə)-rē, ˈhōz(-ə)-\ *n* : STOCKINGS, SOCKS

hosp *abbr* hospital

hos·pice \ˈhäs-pəs\ *n* **1** : a lodging for travelers or for young persons or the underprivileged **2** : a facility or program supplying a caring environment for those with fatal illnesses

hos·pi·ta·ble \hä-ˈspit-ə-bəl, ˈhäs-(ˌ)pit-\ *adj* **1** : given to generous and cordial reception of guests **2** : readily receptive — **hos·pi·ta·bly** \-blē\ *adv*

hos·pi·tal \ˈhäs-ˌpit-ᵊl\ *n* [ME, fr. OF, fr. ML *hospitale,* fr. LL, hospice, fr. L, guest room, fr. *hospit-, hospes* guest, host, fr. *hostis* stranger, enemy] : an institution where the sick or injured receive medical or surgical care

hos·pi·tal·i·ty \ˌhäs-pə-ˈtal-ət-ē\ *n, pl* **-ties** : hospitable treatment, reception, or disposition

hos·pi·tal·ize \ˈhäs-ˌpit-ᵊl-ˌīz\ *vb* **-ized; -iz·ing** : to place in a hospital for care and treatment — **hos·pi·tal·iza·tion** \ˌhäs-ˌpit-ᵊl-ə-ˈzā-shən\ *n*

¹host \ˈhōst\ *n* [ME, fr. OF, fr. LL *hostis,* fr. L, stranger, enemy] **1** : ARMY **2** : MULTITUDE

²host *n* [ME *hoste* host, guest, fr. OF, fr. L *hospit-, hospes*] **1** : one who receives or entertains guests **2** : an animal or plant on or in which a parasite lives — **host** *vb*

---

[3]**host** *n, often cap* [deriv. of L *hostia* sacrifice] : the eucharistic bread

hos·tage \ˈhäs-tij\ *n* : a person kept as a pledge pending the fulfillment of an agreement

hos·tel \ˈhäs-tᵊl\ *n* [ME, fr. OF, fr. LL *hospitale* hospice] **1** : INN **2** : a supervised lodging for youth — **hos·tel·er** *n*

hos·tel·ry \-rē\ *n, pl* **-ries** : INN, HOTEL

host·ess \ˈhō-stəs\ *n* : a woman who acts as host

hos·tile \ˈhäs-tᵊl, -ˌtīl\ *adj* : marked by usu. overt antagonism : UNFRIENDLY — **hostile** *n* — **hos·tile·ly** \-ē\ *adv*

hos·til·i·ty \hä-ˈstil-ət-ē\ *n, pl* **-ties** **1** : an unfriendly state or action **2** *pl* : overt acts of war

hos·tler \ˈ(h)äs-lər\ *n* : one who takes care of horses or mules

hot \ˈhät\ *adj* **hot·ter; hot·test** **1** : marked by a high temperature or an uncomfortable degree of body heat **2** : giving a sensation of heat or of burning **3** : ARDENT, FIERY **4** : LUSTFUL **5** : EAGER **6** : newly made or received **7** : PUNGENT **8** : unusually lucky or favorable ⟨~ dice⟩ **9** : recently and illegally obtained ⟨~ jewels⟩ — **hot** *adv* — **hot·ly** *adv* — **hot·ness** *n*

hot·bed \-ˌbed\ *n* **1** : a glass-covered bed of soil heated (as by fermenting manure) and used esp. for raising seedlings **2** : an environment that favors rapid growth or development

hot–blood·ed \-ˈbləd-əd\ *adj* : easily roused or excited

hot·box \-ˌbäks\ *n* : a journal bearing (as of a railroad car) overheated by friction

hot·cake \-ˌkāk\ *n* : PANCAKE

hot dog \ˈhät-ˌdȯg\ *n* : a cooked frankfurter usu. served in a long split roll

ho·tel \hō-ˈtel\ *n* [F *hôtel*, fr. OF *hostel*, fr. LL *hospitale* hospice] : a building where lodging and usu. meals, entertainment, and various personal services are provided for the public

hot flash *n* : a sudden brief flushing and sensation of heat caused by dilation of skin capillaries usu. associated with menopausal endocrine imbalance

hot·head·ed \ˈhät-ˈhed-əd\ *adj* : FIERY, IMPETUOUS — **hot·head** \-ˌhed\ *n* — **hot·head·ed·ly** *adv* — **hot·head·ed·ness** *n*

hot·house \-ˌhau̇s\ *n* : a heated glass-enclosed house for raising plants

hot line *n* : a telephone line for emergency use (as between governments or to a counseling service)

hot plate *n* : a simple portable appliance for heating or for cooking

hot potato *n* : an embarrassing or controversial issue

hot rod *n* : an automobile modified for high speed and fast acceleration — **hot–rod·der** \ˈhät-ˈräd-ər\ *n*

hots \ˈhäts\ *n pl* : strong sexual desire — usu. used with *the*

hot seat *n* : a position of anxiety or embarrassment

hot·shot \ˈhät-ˌshät\ *n* : a showily skillful person

hot tub *n* : a large wooden tub of hot water for soaking and socializing

hot–wire \ˈhät-ˌwī(ə)r\ *vb* : to start (an automobile) by short-circuiting the ignition system

[1]**hound** \ˈhau̇nd\ *n* **1** : : a long-eared hunting dog that follows its prey by scent **2** : FAN, ADDICT

[2]**hound** *vb* : to pursue relentlessly

hour \ˈau̇(ə)r\ *n* **1** : the 24th part of a day **2** : the time of day **3** : a particular or customary time **4** : a class session — **hour·ly** *adv or adj*

hour·glass \ˈau̇(ə)r-ˌglas\ *n* : a glass vessel for measuring time in which sand, water, or mercury runs from an upper compartment to a lower compartment in an hour

hou·ri \ˈhu̇r-ē\ *n* [F, fr. Per *hūrī*, fr. Ar *ḥūrīyah*] : one of the beautiful maidens of the Muslim paradise

[1]**house** \ˈhau̇s\ *n, pl* **hous·es** \ˈhau̇-zəz\ **1** : a building for human habitation **2** : a shelter for an animal **3** : a building in which something is stored **4** : HOUSEHOLD; *also* : FAMILY **5** : a residence for a religious community or for students; *also* : those in residence **6** : a legislative body **7** : a place of business or entertainment **8** : a business organization **9** : the audience in a theater or concert hall — **house·ful** *n*

[2]**house** \ˈhau̇z\ *vb* **housed; hous·ing** **1** : to provide with or take shelter : LODGE **2** : STORE

house·boat \ˈhau̇s-ˌbōt\ *n* : a roomy pleasure boat fitted for use as a dwelling or for leisurely cruising

house·boy \-ˌbȯi\ *n* : a boy or man hired to act as a household servant

house·break \-ˌbrāk\ *vb* **-broke; -bro·ken; -break·ing** : to train in excretory habits acceptable in indoor living

house·break·ing \-ˌbrā-kiŋ\ *n* : the act of breaking into a dwelling with the intent of committing a felony

house·clean \-ˌklēn\ *vb* : to clean a house and its furniture — **house·clean·ing** *n*

house·coat \ˈhau̇s-ˌkōt\ *n* : a woman's often long-skirted informal garment for wear around the house

house·fly \-ˌflī\ *n* : a two-winged fly that is common about human habitations and acts as a vector of diseases (as typhoid fever)

[1]**house·hold** \ˈhau̇s-ˌhōld\ *n* : those who dwell as a family under the same roof — **house·hold·er** *n*

[2]**household** *adj* **1** : DOMESTIC **2** : FAMILIAR, COMMON ⟨a ~ name⟩

house·keep·er \-ˌkē-pər\ *n* : a woman employed to take care of a house — **house·keep·ing** \-piŋ\ *n*

house·lights \-ˌlīts\ *n pl* : the lights that illuminate the parts of a theater occupied by the audience

house·maid \-ˌmād\ *n* : a female servant employed to do housework

house·moth·er \-ˌmət͟h-ər\ *n* : a woman acting as hostess, chaperon, and often housekeeper in a residence for young people

house·plant \ˈhau̇s-ˌplant\ *n* : a plant grown or kept indoors

house sparrow *n* : a sparrow native to Europe and parts of Asia that has been widely introduced elsewhere

house·top \ˈhau̇s-ˌtäp\ *n* : ROOF

house·wares \-ˌwaərz\ *n pl* : small articles of household equipment

house·warm·ing \-ˌwȯr-miŋ\ *n* : a party to celebrate the taking possession of a house or premises

house·wife \ˈhau̇s-ˌwīf\ *n* : a married woman in charge of a household — **house·wife·ly** \-lē\ *adj* — **house·wif·ery** \-ˌwīf-(ə-)rē\ *n*

house·work \ˈhau̇s-ˌwərk\ *n* : the work of housekeeping

[1]**hous·ing** \ˈhau̇-ziŋ\ *n* **1** : SHELTER; *also* : dwellings provided for people **2** : something that covers or protects

[2]**housing** *n* **1** : CAPARISON 1 **2** *pl* : decorative trappings and harness

hove *past and past part of* HEAVE

hov·el \ˈhəv-əl, ˈhäv-\ *n* : a small, wretched, and often dirty house : HUT

hov·er \ˈhəv-ər, ˈhäv-\ *vb* **hov·ered; hov·er·ing** \-(ə-)riŋ\ **1** : FLUTTER; *also* : to move to and fro **2** : to be in an uncertain state

[1]**how** \(ˈ)hau̇\ *adv* **1** : in what way or manner ⟨~ was it done⟩ **2** : with what meaning ⟨~ do we interpret such behavior⟩ **3** : for what reason ⟨~ could you have done such a thing⟩ **4** : to what extent or degree ⟨~ deep is it⟩ **5** : in what state or condition ⟨~ are you⟩ — **how about** : what do you say to or think of ⟨*how about* coming with me⟩ — **how come** : why is it that

[2]**how** *conj* **1** : in what manner or condition ⟨remember ~ they fought⟩ **2** : HOWEVER ⟨do it ~ you like⟩

[1]**how·be·it** \hau̇-ˈbē-ət\ *adv* : NEVERTHELESS

[2]**howbeit** *conj* : ALTHOUGH

how·dah \ˈhau̇d-ə\ *n* [Hindi *hauda*] : a seat or covered pavilion on the back of an elephant or camel

[1]**how·ev·er** \hau̇-ˈev-ər\ *conj* : in whatever manner

[2]**however** *adv* **1** : to whatever degree; *also* : in whatever manner **2** : in spite of that

how·it·zer \ˈhau̇-ət-sər\ *n* : a short cannon that shoots shells at a high angle of fire
howl \ˈhau̇l\ *vb* **1** : to emit a loud long doleful sound characteristic of dogs **2** : to cry loudly — **howl** *n*
howl·er \ˈhau̇-lər\ *n* **1** : one that howls **2** : a humorous and ridiculous blunder
howl·ing \ˈhau̇-liŋ\ *adj* **1** : DESOLATE, WILD **2** : very great ⟨a ~ success⟩
how·so·ev·er \ˌhau̇-sə-ˈwev-ər\ *adv* : HOWEVER 1
hoy·den \ˈhȯid-ᵊn\ *n* : a girl or woman of saucy, boisterous, or carefree behavior
HP *abbr* **1** high pressure **2** horsepower
HPF *abbr* highest possible frequency
HQ *abbr* headquarters
hr *abbr* **1** here **2** hour
HR *abbr* House of Representatives
HRH *abbr* Her Royal Highness; His Royal Highness
hrzn *abbr* horizon
HS *abbr* high school
HST *abbr* Hawaiian standard time
ht *abbr* height
HT *abbr* high-tension
hua·ra·che \wə-ˈräch-ē\ *n* [MexSp] : a sandal with an upper made of interwoven leather thongs
hub \ˈhəb\ *n* **1** : the central part of a wheel, propeller, or fan **2** : a center of activity
hub·bub \ˈhəb-əb\ *n* : UPROAR; *also* : TURMOIL
hub·cap \ˈhəb-ˌkap\ *n* : a removable metal cap over the end of an axle
hu·bris \ˈhyü-brəs\ *n* : exaggerated pride or self-confidence
huck·le·ber·ry \ˈhək-əl-ˌber-ē\ *n* **1** : an American shrub related to the blueberry; *also* : its edible dark blue berry **2** : BLUEBERRY
huck·ster \ˈhək-stər\ *n* : PEDDLER, HAWKER
HUD *abbr* Department of Housing and Urban Development
[1]**hud·dle** \ˈhəd-ᵊl\ *vb* **hud·dled; hud·dling** \ˈhəd-(ᵊ-)liŋ\ **1** : to crowd together **2** : CONFER
[2]**huddle** *n* **1** : a closely packed group **2** : MEETING, CONFERENCE
hue \ˈhyü\ *n* **1** : a color as distinct from white, gray, and black; *also* : gradation of color **2** : the attribute of colors that permits them to be classed as red, yellow, green, blue, or an intermediate color — **hued** \ˈhyüd\ *adj*
hue and cry *n* : a clamor of pursuit or protest
huff \ˈhəf\ *n* : a fit of anger or pique — **huffy** *adj*
hug \ˈhəg\ *vb* **hugged; hug·ging 1** : EMBRACE **2** : to stay close to ⟨the road ~*s* the river⟩ — **hug** *n*
huge \ˈhyüj\ *adj* **hug·er; hug·est** : very large or extensive — **huge·ly** *adv* — **huge·ness** *n*
hug·ger–mug·ger \ˈhəg-ər-ˌməg-ər\ *n* **1** : SECRECY **2** : CONFUSION, MUDDLE
Hu·gue·not \ˈhyü-gə-ˌnät\ *n* : a French Protestant in the 16th and 17th centuries
hu·la \ˈhü-lə\ *n* : a sinuous Polynesian dance usu. accompanied by chants
hulk \ˈhəlk\ *n* **1** : a heavy clumsy ship **2** : an old ship unfit for service **3** : a bulky or unwieldy person or thing
hulk·ing \ˈhəl-kiŋ\ *adj* : BURLY, MASSIVE
[1]**hull** \ˈhəl\ *n* **1** : the outer covering of a fruit or seed **2** : the frame or body esp. of a ship
[2]**hull** *vb* : to remove the hulls of — **hull·er** *n*
hul·la·ba·loo \ˈhəl-ə-bə-ˌlü\ *n, pl* **-loos** : a confused noise : UPROAR
hum \ˈhəm\ *vb* **hummed; hum·ming 1** : to utter a sound like that of the speech sound \m\ prolonged **2** : DRONE **3** : to be busily active **4** : to sing with closed lips — **hum** *n* — **hum·mer** *n*
hu·man \ˈ(h)yü-mən\ *adj* **1** : of, relating to, being, or characteristic of man **2** : having human form or attributes — **human** *n* — **hu·man·ly** *adv* — **hu·man·ness** \-mən-nəs\ *n*
hu·mane \(h)yü-ˈmān\ *adj* **1** : marked by compassion, sympathy, or consideration for others **2** : HUMANISTIC — **hu·mane·ly** *adv* — **hu·mane·ness** \-ˈmān-nəs\ *n*
human immunodeficiency virus *n* : AIDS VIRUS
hu·man·ism \ˈ(h)yü-mə-ˌniz-əm\ *n* **1** : devotion to the humanities; *also* : the revival of classical letters characteristic of the Renaissance **2** : a doctrine or way of life centered on human interests or values — **hu·man·ist** \-nəst\ *n or adj* — **hu·man·is·tic** \ˌ(h)yü-mə-ˈnis-tik\ *adj*
hu·man·i·tar·i·an \(h)yü-ˌman-ə-ˈter-ē-ən\ *n* : one who practices philanthropy — **humanitarian** *adj* — **hu·man·i·tar·i·an·ism** *n*
hu·man·i·ty \(h)yü-ˈman-ət-ē\ *n, pl* **-ties 1** : the quality or state of being human or humane **2** *pl* : the branches of learning dealing with human concerns (as philosophy) as opposed to natural processes (as physics) **3** : MANKIND 1
hu·man·ize \ˈ(h)yü-mə-ˌnīz\ *vb* **-ized; -iz·ing** : to make human or humane — **hu·man·iza·tion** \ˌ(h)yü-mə-nə-ˈzā-shən\ *n*
hu·man·kind \ˈ(h)yü-mən-ˌkīnd\ *n* : MANKIND 1
hu·man·oid \ˈ(h)yü-mə-ˌnȯid\ *adj* : having human form or characteristics — **humanoid** *n*
[1]**hum·ble** \ˈ(h)əm-bəl\ *adj* **hum·bler** \-b(ə-)lər\; **hum·blest** \-b(ə-)ləst\ [ME, fr. OF, fr. L *humilis* low, humble, fr. *humus* earth] **1** : not proud or haughty **2** : not pretentious : UNASSUMING **3** : INSIGNIFICANT **syn** meek, modest, lowly, unassuming — **hum·ble·ness** *n* — **hum·bly** \-blē\ *adv*
[2]**humble** *vb* **hum·bled; hum·bling** \-b(ə-)liŋ\ **1** : to make humble **2** : to destroy the power or prestige of — **hum·bler** \-b(ə-)lər\ *n*
[1]**hum·bug** \ˈhəm-ˌbəg\ *n* **1** : HOAX, FRAUD **2** : NONSENSE
[2]**humbug** *vb* **hum·bugged; hum·bug·ging** : DECEIVE
hum·ding·er \ˈhəm-ˈdiŋ-ər\ *n* : a person or thing of striking excellence
hum·drum \ˈhəm-ˌdrəm\ *adj* : MONOTONOUS, DULL
hu·mer·us \ˈhyüm-(ə-)rəs\ *n, pl* **hu·meri** \ˈhyü-mə-ˌrī, -ˌrē\ : the long bone extending from elbow to shoulder
hu·mid \ˈ(h)yü-məd\ *adj* : containing or characterized by perceptible moisture : DAMP — **hu·mid·ly** *adv*
hu·mid·i·fy \hyü-ˈmid-ə-ˌfī\ *vb* **-fied; -fy·ing** : to make humid — **hu·mid·i·fi·ca·tion** \-ˌmid-ə-fə-ˈkā-shən\ *n* — **hu·mid·i·fi·er** \-ˈmid-ə-ˌfī(-ə)r\ *n*
hu·mid·i·ty \(h)yü-ˈmid-ət-ē\ *n, pl* **-ties** : the amount of atmospheric moisture
hu·mi·dor \ˈ(h)yü-mə-ˌdȯr\ *n* : a case usu. for storing cigars in which the air is kept properly humidified
hu·mil·i·ate \(h)yü-ˈmil-ē-ˌāt\ *vb* **-at·ed; -at·ing** : to injure the self-respect of : MORTIFY — **hu·mil·i·at·ing·ly** \-ˌāt-iŋ-lē\ *adv* — **hu·mil·i·a·tion** \-ˌmil-ē-ˈā-shən\ *n*
hu·mil·i·ty \(h)yü-ˈmil-ət-ē\ *n* : the quality or state of being humble
hum·ming·bird \ˈhəm-iŋ-ˌbərd\ *n* : a tiny American bird related to the swifts
hum·mock \ˈhəm-ək\ *n* : a rounded mound : KNOLL
hu·mon·gous \hyü-ˈməŋ-gəs, -ˈmäŋ-\ *adj* [prob. alter. of *huge* + *monstrous*] *slang* : extremely large
[1]**hu·mor** \ˈ(h)yü-mər\ *n* **1** : TEMPERAMENT **2** : MOOD **3** : WHIM **4** : a quality that appeals to a sense of the ludicrous or incongruous; *also* : a keen perception of the ludicrous or incongruous **5** : comical or amusing entertainment — **hu·mor·ist** \ˈ(h)yüm-(ə-)rəst\ *n* — **hu·mor·less** \ˈ(h)yü-mər-ləs\ *adj* — **hu·mor·less·ly** *adv* — **hu·mor·less·ness** *n* — **hu·mor·ous** \ˈ(h)yüm-(ə-)rəs\ *adj* — **hu·mor·ous·ly** *adv* — **hu·mor·ous·ness** *n*

---

²humor *vb* **hu·mored; hu·mor·ing** \ˈ(h)yüm-(ə-)riŋ\ : to comply with the wishes or mood of

hu·mour *chiefly Brit var of* HUMOR

hump \ˈhəmp\ *n* **1** : a rounded protuberance (as on the back of a camel) **2** : a difficult phase ⟨over the ~⟩

hump·back \-ˌbak; *1 also* -ˈbak\ *n* **1** : HUNCHBACK **2** : HUMPBACK WHALE — **hump·backed** *adj*

humpback whale *n* : a large whalebone whale having very long flippers

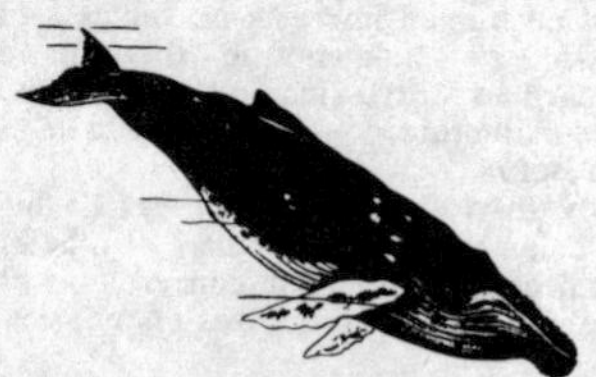

humpback whale

hu·mus \ˈ(h)yü-məs\ *n* : the dark organic part of soil formed from decaying matter

Hun \ˈhən\ *n* : a member of an Asian people that invaded Europe in the 5th century A.D.

¹hunch \ˈhənch\ *vb* **1** : to thrust oneself forward **2** : to assume or cause to assume a bent or crooked posture

²hunch *n* **1** : PUSH **2** : a strong intuitive feeling as to how something will turn out

hunch·back \ˈhənch-ˌbak\ *n* : a back with a hump; *also* : a person with a crooked back — **hunch·backed** *adj*

hun·dred \ˈhən-drəd\ *n, pl* **hundreds** *or* **hundred** : 10 times 10 — **hundred** *adj* — **hun·dredth** \-drədth\ *adj or n*

hun·dred·weight \-ˌwāt\ *n, pl* **hundredweight** *or* **hundredweights** — see WEIGHT table

hung *past and past part of* HANG

Hung *abbr* Hungarian; Hungary

Hun·gar·i·an \ˌhəŋ-ˈger-ē-ən\ *n* **1** : a native or inhabitant of Hungary **2** : the language of Hungary — **Hungarian** *adj*

hun·ger \ˈhəŋ-gər\ *n* **1** : a craving or urgent need for food **2** : a strong desire — **hunger** *vb* — **hun·gri·ly** \-grə-lē\ *adv* — **hun·gry** *adj*

hung over *adj* : having a hangover

hung up *adj* **1** : DELAYED **2** : ENTHUSIASTIC; *also* : PREOCCUPIED

hunk \ˈhəŋk\ *n* **1** : a large piece **2** : an attractive well-built man

hun·ker \ˈhəŋ-kər\ *vb* **hun·kered; hun·ker·ing** \-k(ə-)riŋ\ : CROUCH, SQUAT — usu. used with *down*

hun·kers \ˈhəŋ-kərz\ *n pl* : HAUNCHES

hun·ky–do·ry \ˌhəŋ-kē-ˈdōr-ē\ *adj* : quite satisfactory : FINE

¹hunt \ˈhənt\ *vb* **1** : to pursue for food or in sport; *also* : to take part in a hunt **2** : to try to find : SEEK **3** : to drive or chase esp. by harrying **4** : to traverse in search of prey — **hunt·er** *n*

²hunt *n* : an act, practice, or instance of hunting

hunt·ress \ˈhən-trəs\ *n* : a woman who hunts

hunts·man \ˈhənts-mən\ *n* **1** : HUNTER **2** : one who manages a hunt and looks after the hounds

hur·dle \ˈhərd-ᵊl\ *n* **1** : an artificial barrier to leap over in a race **2** : OBSTACLE — **hurdle** *vb* — **hur·dler** \ˈhərd-(ᵊ-)lər\ *n*

hur·dy–gur·dy \ˌhərd-ē-ˈgərd-ē, ˈhərd-ē-ˌgərd-ē\ *n, pl* **-gur·dies** : a musical instrument in which the sound is produced by turning a crank

hurl \ˈhərl\ *vb* **1** : to move or cause to move vigorously **2** : to throw down with violence **3** : FLING; *also* : PITCH — **hurl** *n* — **hurl·er** *n*

hur·ly–bur·ly \ˌhər-lē-ˈbər-lē\ *n* : UPROAR, TUMULT

Hu·ron \ˈhyůr-ən, ˈhyůr-ˌän\ *n, pl* **Hurons** *or* **Huron** : a member of an American Indian people orig. of the St. Lawrence valley

hur·rah \hů-ˈrȯ, -ˈrä\ *also* **hur·ray** \hů-ˈrā\ *interj* — used to express joy, approval, or encouragement

hur·ri·cane \ˈhər-ə-ˌkān\ *n* [Sp *huracán,* of AmerInd origin] : a tropical cyclone that has winds of 74 miles per hour (117 kilometers per hour) or greater and is usu. accompanied by rain, thunder, and lightning

¹hur·ry \ˈhər-ē\ *vb* **hur·ried; hur·ry·ing** **1** : to carry or cause to go with haste **2** : to impel to a greater speed **3** : to move or act with haste — **hur·ried·ly** *adv* — **hur·ried·ness** *n*

²hurry *n* : extreme haste or eagerness

¹hurt \ˈhərt\ *vb* **hurt; hurt·ing** **1** : to feel or cause to feel pain **2** : to do harm to : DAMAGE **3** : OFFEND **4** : HAMPER

²hurt *n* **1** : a bodily injury or wound **2** : SUFFERING **3** : HARM, WRONG — **hurt·ful** *adj*

hur·tle \ˈhərt-ᵊl\ *vb* **hur·tled; hur·tling** \ˈhərt-(ᵊ-)liŋ\ **1** : to move with a rushing sound **2** : : HURL, FLING

¹hus·band \ˈhəz-bənd\ *n* [ME *husbonde,* fr. OE *hūsbonda* master of a house, fr. ON *hūsbōndi,* fr. *hūs* house + *bōndi* householder] : a married man

²husband *vb* : to manage prudently

hus·band·man \ˈhəz-bən(d)-mən\ *n* : FARMER

hus·band·ry \ˈhəz-bən-drē\ *n* **1** : the control or judicious use of resources **2** : AGRICULTURE

¹hush \ˈhəsh\ *vb* **1** : to make or become quiet or calm **2** : SUPPRESS

²hush *n* : SILENCE, QUIET

hush–hush \ˈhəsh-ˌhəsh\ *adj* : SECRET, CONFIDENTIAL

¹husk \ˈhəsk\ *n* **1** : a usu. thin dry outer covering of a seed or fruit **2** : an outer layer : SHELL

²husk *vb* : to strip the husk from — **husk·er** *n*

¹hus·ky \ˈhəs-kē\ *adj* **hus·ki·er; -est** : HOARSE — **hus·ki·ly** \ˈhəs-kə-lē\ *adv* — **hus·ki·ness** \-kē-nəs\ *n*

²husky *adj* **1** : BURLY, ROBUST **2** : LARGE

³husky *n, pl* **huskies** : a heavy-coated working dog of the New World arctic

hus·sar \(ˌ)hə-ˈzär\ *n* [Hung *huszár* hussar, (obs.) highway robber, fr. Serb *husar* pirate, fr. ML *cursarius,* fr. *cursus* course] : a member of any of various European cavalry units

hus·sy \ˈhəz-ē, ˈhəs-\ *n, pl* **hussies** [alter. of *housewife*] **1** : a lewd or brazen woman **2** : a pert or mischievous girl

hus·tings \ˈhəs-tiŋz\ *n pl* : a place where political campaign speeches are made; *also* : the proceedings in an election campaign

hus·tle \ˈhəs-əl\ *vb* **hus·tled; hus·tling** \ˈhəs-(ə-)liŋ\ **1** : JOSTLE, SHOVE **2** : HASTEN, HURRY **3** : to work energetically — **hustle** *n* — **hus·tler** \ˈhəs-lər\ *n*

hut \ˈhət\ *n* : a small and often temporary dwelling : SHACK

hutch \ˈhəch\ *n* **1** : a chest or compartment for storage **2** : a low cupboard usu. surmounted with open shelves **3** : a pen or coop for an animal **4** : HUT, SHACK

huz·zah *or* **huz·za** \(ˌ)hə-ˈzä\ *n* : a cheer of acclaim — often used interjectionally to express joy or approbation

HV *abbr* **1** high velocity **2** high voltage

hvy *abbr* heavy

HW *abbr* hot water

hwy *abbr* highway

hy·a·cinth \ˈhī-ə-(ˌ)sinth\ *n* : a bulbous herb related to the lilies and widely grown for its spikes of fragrant bell-shaped flowers

hy·ae·na *var of* HYENA

hy·brid \ˈhī-brəd\ *n* **1** : an offspring of genetically differing parents (as members of different breeds or species) **2** : one of mixed origin or composition — **hybrid** *adj* — **hy·brid·iza·tion** \ˌhī-brəd-ə-ˈzā-shən\ *n* — **hy·brid·ize** \ˈhī-brəd-ˌīz\ *vb* — **hy·brid·iz·er** \-ˌīz-ər\ *n*

hy·dra \ˈhī-drə\ *n* : any of numerous small tubular freshwater polyps having at one end a mouth surrounded by tentacles

hy·dran·gea \hī-ˈdrān-jə\ *n* : any of a genus of shrubs related to the currants and grown for their large clusters of white or tinted flowers

hy·drant \ˈhī-drənt\ *n* : a pipe with a valve and spout at which water may be drawn from a main pipe

hy·drate \ˈhī-ˌdrāt\ *n* : a compound formed by union of water with some other substance — **hydrate** *vb*

hy·drau·lic \hī-ˈdrȯ-lik\ *adj* **1** : operated, moved, or effected by means of water **2** : of or relating to hydraulics **3** : operated by the resistance offered or the pressure transmitted when a quantity of liquid is forced through a small orifice or through a tube **4** : hardening or setting under water

hy·drau·lics \hī-ˈdrȯ-liks\ *n* : a science that deals with practical applications of liquids in motion

hydro \ˈhī-drō\ *adj* : HYDROELECTRIC

hy·dro·car·bon \ˌhī-drə-ˈkär-bən\ *n* : an organic compound (as acetylene) containing only carbon and hydrogen

hy·dro·ceph·a·lus \ˌhī-drō-ˈsef-ə-ləs\ *n* : abnormal increase in the amount of fluid in the cranial cavity accompanied by expansion of the ventricles, enlargement of the skull, and atrophy of the brain

hy·dro·chlo·ric acid \ˌhī-drə-ˌklōr-ik-\ *n* : a sharp-smelling corrosive acid used in the laboratory and in industry and present in dilute form in gastric juice

hy·dro·dy·nam·ics \ˌhī-drō-dī-ˈnam-iks\ *n* : a science that deals with the motion of fluids and the forces acting on moving bodies immersed in fluids — **hy·dro·dy·nam·ic** *adj*

hy·dro·elec·tric \ˌhī-drō-i-ˈlek-trik\ *adj* : of, relating to, or used in the production of electricity by waterpower — **hy·dro·elec·tric·i·ty** \-ˌlek-ˈtris-ət-ē\ *n*

hy·dro·flu·or·ic acid \ˌhī-drō-flu̇-ˌȯr-ik-\ *n* : a weak poisonous acid used esp. in finishing and etching glass

hy·dro·foil \ˈhī-drə-ˌfȯil\ *n* : a boat that has fins attached to the bottom by struts for lifting the hull clear of the water to allow faster speeds

hy·dro·gen \ˈhī-drə-jən\ *n* [F *hydrogène*, fr. Gk *hydōr* water + *-genēs* born, fr. the fact that water is generated by its combustion] : a gaseous colorless odorless highly flammable chemical element that is the lightest of the elements — see ELEMENT table — **hy·drog·e·nous** \hī-ˈdräj-ə-nəs\ *adj*

hy·dro·ge·nate \hī-ˈdräj-ə-ˌnāt, hī-drə-jə-\ *vb* **-nat·ed; -nat·ing** : to combine or treat with hydrogen; *esp* : to add hydrogen to the molecule of — **hy·dro·ge·na·tion** \hī-ˌdräj-ə-ˈnā-shən, ˌhī-drə-jə-\ *n*

hydrogen bomb *n* : a bomb whose violent explosive power is due to the sudden release of atomic energy resulting from the union of light nuclei (as of hydrogen atoms)

hydrogen peroxide *n* : an unstable compound of hydrogen and oxygen used as an oxidizing and bleaching agent, an antiseptic, and a propellant

hy·drog·ra·phy \hī-ˈdräg-rə-fē\ *n* : the description and study of bodies of water — **hy·drog·ra·pher** \-fər\ *n* — **hy·dro·graph·ic** \ˌhī-drə-ˈgraf-ik\ *adj*

hy·drol·o·gy \hī-ˈdräl-ə-jē\ *n* : a science dealing with the properties, distribution, and circulation of water — **hy·dro·log·ic** \ˌhī-drə-ˈläj-ik\ *or* **hy·dro·log·i·cal** \-i-kəl\ *adj* — **hy·drol·o·gist** \hī-ˈdräl-ə-jəst\ *n*

hy·dro·ly·sis \hī-ˈdräl-ə-səs\ *n* : a chemical decomposition involving the addition of the elements of water

hy·drom·e·ter \hī-ˈdräm-ət-ər\ *n* : a floating instrument for determining specific gravities of liquids and hence the strength (as of alcoholic liquors)

hy·dro·pho·bia \ˌhī-drə-ˈfō-bē-ə\ *n* [LL, fr. Gk, fr. *hydōr* water + *phobos* fear] : RABIES

hy·dro·phone \ˈhī-drə-ˌfōn\ *n* : an underwater listening device

¹hy·dro·plane \ˈhī-drə-ˌplān\ *n* **1** : a speedboat usu. with a stepped bottom so that the hull is raised wholly or partly out of the water **2** : SEAPLANE

²hydroplane *vb* : to skid on a wet road due to loss of contact between the tires and road

hy·dro·pon·ics \ˌhī-drə-ˈpän-iks\ *n* : the growing of plants in nutrient solutions — **hy·dro·pon·ic** *adj*

hy·dro·pow·er \ˈhī-drə-ˌpau̇(-ə)r\ *n* : hydroelectric power

hy·dro·sphere \ˈhī-drə-ˌsfiər\ *n* : the water (as vapor or lakes) of the earth

hy·dro·stat·ic \ˌhī-drə-ˈstat-ik\ *adj* : of or relating to fluids at rest or to the pressures they exert or transmit

hy·dro·ther·a·py \ˌhī-drə-ˈther-ə-pē\ *n* : the external application of water in the treatment of disease or disability

hy·dro·ther·mal \ˌhī-drə-ˈthər-məl\ *adj* : of or relating to hot water

hy·drous \ˈhī-drəs\ *adj* : containing water

hy·drox·ide \hī-ˈdräk-ˌsīd\ *n* **1** : a negatively charged ion consisting of one atom of oxygen and one atom of hydrogen **2** : a compound of hydroxide with an element or group

hy·e·na \hī-ˈē-nə\ *n* [L *hyaena*, fr. Gk *hyaina*, fr. *hys* hog] : a large nocturnal carnivorous mammal of Asia and Africa

hy·giene \ˈhī-ˌjēn\ *n* **1** : a science dealing with the establishment and maintenance of health **2** : conditions or practices conducive to health — **hy·gien·ic** \ˌhī-jē-ˈen-ik, hī-ˈjen-, hī-ˈjēn-\ *adj* — **hy·gien·i·cal·ly** \-i-k(ə-)lē\ *adv* — **hy·gien·ist** \hī-ˈjēn-əst, ˈhī-ˌjēn-, hī-ˈjen-\ *n*

hy·grom·e·ter \hī-ˈgräm-ət-ər\ *n* : any of several instruments for measuring the humidity of the atmosphere

hy·gro·scop·ic \ˌhī-grə-ˈskäp-ik\ *adj* : readily taking up and retaining moisture

hying *pres part of* HIE

hy·men \ˈhī-mən\ *n* : a fold of mucous membrane partly or wholly closing the orifice of the vagina

hy·me·ne·al \ˌhī-mə-ˈnē-əl\ *adj* : NUPTIAL

hymn \ˈhim\ *n* : a song of praise esp. to God — **hymn** *vb* — **hym·nal** \ˈhim-nəl\ *n*

hyp *abbr* hypothesis; hypothetical

hype \ˈhīp\ *n* **1** *slang* : HYPODERMIC **2** *slang* : DECEPTION, PUT-ON

hy·per \ˈhī-pər\ *adj* : EXCITABLE, HIGH-STRUNG

hy·per·acid·i·ty \ˌhī-pə-rə-ˈsid-ət-ē\ *n* : the condition of containing excessive acid esp. in the stomach — **hy·per·ac·id** \-pə-ˈras-əd\ *adj*

hy·per·ac·tive \ˌhī-pə-ˈrak-tiv\ *adj* : excessively or pathologically active — **hy·per·ac·tiv·i·ty** \-ˌrak-ˈtiv-ət-ē\ *n*

hy·per·bar·ic \ˌhī-pər-ˈbar-ik\ *adj* : of, relating to, or utilizing greater than normal pressure esp. of oxygen

hy·per·bo·la \hī-ˈpər-bə-lə\ *n, pl* **-las** *or* **-lae** \-(ˌ)lē\ : a curve formed by the intersection of a double right circular cone with a plane that cuts both halves of the cone — **hy·per·bol·ic** \ˌhī-pər-ˈbäl-ik\ *adj*

hy·per·bo·le \hī-ˈpər-bə-(ˌ)lē\ *n* : extravagant exaggeration used as a figure of speech

hy·per·crit·i·cal \ˌhī-pər-ˈkrit-i-kəl\ *adj* : excessively critical — **hy·per·crit·i·cal·ly** \-k(ə-)lē\ *adv*

hy·per·sen·si·tive \-ˈsen-sət-iv\ *adj* **1** : excessively or abnormally sensitive **2** : abnormally susceptible physiologically to a specific agent (as a drug or antigen) — **hy·per·sen·si·tive·ness** *n* — **hy·per·sen·si·tiv·i·ty** \-ˌsen-sə-ˈtiv-ət-ē\ *n*

hy·per·ten·sion \ˈhī-pər-ˌten-chən\ *n* : high blood pressure — **hy·per·ten·sive** \ˌhī-pər-ˈten-siv\ *adj or n*

hy·per·thy·roid·ism \ˌhī-pər-ˈthī-ˌrȯid-ˌiz-əm\ *n* : excessive functional activity of the thyroid gland; *also* : the resulting bodily condition — **hy·per·thy·roid** \-ˈthī-ˌrȯid\ *adj*

hy·per·tro·phy \hī-ˈpər-trə-fē\ *n, pl* **-phies** : excessive growth or development of a body part — **hy·per·tro·phic** \ˌhī-pər-ˈtrō-fik\ *adj* — **hypertrophy** *vb*

hy·phen \ˈhī-fən\ *n* : a punctuation mark - used to divide or to compound words or word elements — **hyphen** *vb*

hy·phen·ate \ˈhī-fə-ˌnāt\ *vb* **-at·ed; -at·ing** : to connect or divide with a hyphen — **hy·phen·ation** \ˌhī-fə-ˈnā-shən\ *n*

hyp·no·sis \hip-ˈnō-səs\ *n, pl* **-no·ses** \-ˌsēz\ : an induced state that resembles sleep and in which the subject is responsive to suggestions of the inducer (**hyp·no·tist** \ˈhip-nə-təst\) — **hyp·no·tism** \ˈhip-nə-ˌtiz-əm\ *n* — **hyp·no·tiz·able** \ˈhip-nə-ˌtī-zə-bəl\ *adj* — **hyp·no·tize** \-ˌtīz\ *vb*

[1]**hyp·not·ic** \hip-ˈnät-ik\ *adj* **1** : inducing sleep : SOPORIFIC **2** : of or relating to hypnosis or hypnotism — **hyp·not·i·cal·ly** \-i-k(ə-)lē\ *adv*

[2]**hypnotic** *n* : a sleep-inducing drug

[1]**hy·po** \ˈhī-pō\ *n, pl* **hypos** [short for *hyposulfite*] : SODIUM THIOSULFATE

[2]**hypo** *n, pl* **hypos** : HYPODERMIC

hy·po·cen·ter \ˈhī-pə-ˌsent-ər\ *n* : EPICENTER

hy·po·chon·dria \ˌhī-pə-ˈkän-drē-ə\ *n* [NL, fr. LL, pl., upper abdomen (formerly regarded as the seat of hypochondria), fr. Gk, lit., the parts under the cartilage (of the breastbone), fr. *hypo-* under + *chondros* cartilage] : depression of mind usu. centered on imaginary physical ailments — **hy·po·chon·dri·ac** \-drē-ˌak\ *adj or n*

hy·poc·ri·sy \hip-ˈäk-rə-sē\ *n, pl* **-sies** : a feigning to be what one is not or to believe what one does not; *esp* : the false assumption of an appearance of virtue or religion — **hyp·o·crite** \ˈhip-ə-ˌkrit\ *n* — **hyp·o·crit·i·cal** \ˌhip-ə-ˈkrit-i-kəl\ *adj* — **hyp·o·crit·i·cal·ly** \-k(ə-)lē\ *adv*

[1]**hy·po·der·mic** \ˌhī-pə-ˈdər-mik\ *adj* : adapted for use in or administered by injection beneath the skin ⟨~ injection⟩ ⟨~ syringe⟩

[2]**hypodermic** *n* : a small syringe with a hollow needle for injecting material into or through the skin; *also* : an injection made with this

hypodermic needle *n* **1** : NEEDLE 3 **2** : a hypodermic syringe complete with needle

hy·po·gly·ce·mia \ˌhī-pō-glī-ˈsē-mē-ə\ *n* : abnormal decrease of sugar in the blood — **hy·po·gly·ce·mic** \-mik\ *adj*

hy·pot·e·nuse \hī-ˈpät-ᵊn-ˌ(y)üs, -ˌ(y)üz\ *n* : the side of a triangle having a right angle that is opposite the right angle

hy·poth·e·sis \hī-ˈpäth-ə-səs\ *n, pl* **-e·ses** \-ˌsēz\ : an assumption made esp. in order to test its logical or empirical consequences — **hy·po·thet·i·cal** \ˌhī-pə-ˈthet-i-kəl\ *adj* — **hy·po·thet·i·cal·ly** \-k(ə-)lē\ *adv*

hy·poth·e·size \-ˌsīz\ *vb* **-sized; -siz·ing** : to adopt as a hypothesis

hy·po·thy·roid·ism \ˌhī-pō-ˈthī-ˌrȯid-ˌiz-əm\ *n* : deficient activity of the thyroid gland; *also* : a resultant lowered metabolic rate and general loss of vigor — **hy·po·thy·roid** *adj*

hys·sop \ˈhis-əp\ *n* : a European mint used in medicine

hys·ter·ec·to·my \ˌhis-tə-ˈrek-tə-mē\ *n, pl* **-mies** : surgical removal of the uterus

hys·te·ria \his-ˈter-ē-ə, -ˈtir-\ *n* [NL, fr. E *hysteric*, adj., fr. L *hystericus*, fr. Gk *hysterikos*, fr. *hystera* womb; fr. the former notion that hysteric women were suffering from disturbances of the womb] **1** : a nervous disorder marked esp. by defective emotional control **2** : uncontrollable fear or emotion — **hys·ter·i·cal** \-ˈter-i-kəl\ *also* **hys·ter·ic** \-ik\ *adj* — **hys·ter·i·cal·ly** \-k(ə-)lē\ *adv*

hys·ter·ics \-ˈter-iks\ *n, pl* a fit of uncontrollable laughter or crying

Hz *abbr* hertz

I

[1]**i** \ˈī\ *n, pl* **i's** *or* **is** \ˈīz\ *often cap* : the 9th letter of the English alphabet

[2]**i** *abbr, often cap* island; isle

[1]**I** \(ˈ)ī, ə\ *pron* : the one speaking or writing

[2]**I** *abbr* interstate highway

[3]**I** *symbol* iodine

Ia *or* **IA** *abbr* Iowa

iamb \ˈī-ˌam\ *or* **iam·bus** \ī-ˈam-bəs\ *n, pl* **iambs** \ˈī-ˌamz\ *or* **iam·bus·es** : a metrical foot of one unaccented syllable followed by one accented syllable — **iam·bic** \ī-ˈam-bik\ *adj or n*

-ian — see -AN

-i·at·ric \ē-ˈa-trik\ *also* **-i·at·ri·cal** \-tri-kəl\ *adj comb form* : of or relating to (such) medical treatment or healing

-i·at·rics \ē-ˈa-triks\ *n pl comb form* : medical treatment

ib *or* **ibid** *abbr* ibidem

ibex \ˈī-ˌbeks\ *n, pl* **ibex** *or* **ibex·es** [L] : an Old World wild goat with large curved horns

ibi·dem \ˈib-ə-ˌdem, ib-ˈīd-əm\ *adv* [L] : in the same place

ibis \ˈī-bəs\ *n, pl* **ibis** *or* **ibis·es** [L, fr. Gk, fr. Egypt *hyb*] : any of several wading birds related to the herons but having a downwardly curved bill

-ible — see -ABLE

[1]**-ic** \ik\ *adj suffix* **1** : of, relating to, or having the form of : being ⟨panoram*ic*⟩ **2** : related to, derived from, or containing ⟨alcohol*ic*⟩ **3** : in the manner of : like that of : characteristic of **4** : associated or dealing with : utilizing ⟨electron*ic*⟩ **5** : characterized by : exhibiting ⟨nostalg*ic*⟩ : affected with ⟨allerg*ic*⟩ **6** : caused by **7** : tending to produce

[2]**-ic** *n suffix* : one having the character or nature of : one belonging to or associated with : one exhibiting or affected by : one that produces

-i·cal \i-kəl\ *adj suffix* : -IC ⟨symmetr*ical*⟩ ⟨geolog*ical*⟩ — **-i·cal·ly** \i-k(ə-)lē\ *adv suffix*

ICBM \ˌī-ˌsē-(ˌ)bē-ˈem\ *n, pl* **ICBM's** *or* **ICBMs** \-ˈemz\ : an intercontinental ballistic missile

ICC *abbr* Interstate Commerce Commission

[1]**ice** \ˈīs\ *n* **1** : frozen water **2** : a state of coldness (as from formality or reserve) **3** : a substance resembling ice **4** : a frozen dessert; *esp* : one containing no milk or cream

[2]**ice** *vb* **iced; ic·ing 1** : FREEZE **2** : CHILL **3** : to cover with or as if with icing

ice age *n* : a time of widespread glaciation

ice bag *n* : a waterproof bag to hold ice for local application of cold to the body

ice·berg \ˈīs-ˌbərg\ *n* : a large floating mass of ice broken off from a glacier

iceberg lettuce *n* : any of various crisp light green lettuces that when mature have the leaves arranged in a compact head resembling a cabbage

ice·boat \ˈīs-ˌbōt\ *n* **1** : a boatlike frame on runners propelled on ice usu. by sails **2** : ICEBREAKER 2

ice·bound \-ˌbau̇nd\ *adj* : surrounded or obstructed by ice

ice·box \-ˌbäks\ *n* : REFRIGERATOR

ice·break·er \-ˌbrā-kər\ *n* : a ship equipped to make a channel through ice

ice cap *n* : a glacier forming on relatively level land and flowing outward from its center

ice cream *n* : a frozen food containing sweetened or flavored cream or butterfat

ice hockey *n* : a game in which two teams of ice-skating players try to shoot a puck into the opponent's goal

ice·house \ˈīs-ˌhau̇s\ *n* : a building in which ice is made or stored

Ice·land·er \-ˌlan-dər, -lən-\ *n* : a native or inhabitant of Iceland

[1]**ice·lan·dic** \īs-ˈlan-dik\ *adj* : of, relating to, or characteristic of Iceland, the Icelanders, or their language

[2]**Icelandic** *n* : the language of Iceland

ice·man \ˈīs-ˌman\ *n* : one who sells or delivers ice

ice milk *n* : a sweetened frozen food made of skim milk

ice pick *n* : a hand tool ending in a spike for chipping ice

ice–skate \ˈīs-ˌskāt\ *vb* : to skate on ice — **ice skater** *n*

ice storm *n* : a storm in which falling rain freezes on contact

ice water *n* : chilled or iced water esp. for drinking

ich·thy·ol·o·gy \ˌik-thē-ˈäl-ə-jē\ *n* : a branch of zoology dealing with fishes — **ich·thy·ol·o·gist** \-jəst\ *n*

ici·cle \ˈī-ˌsik-əl\ *n* : a hanging mass of ice formed by the freezing of dripping water

ic·ing \ˈī-siŋ\ *n* : a sweet usu. creamy mixture used to coat baked goods

ICJ *abbr* International Court of Justice

icky \ˈik-ē\ *adj* **ick·i·er; -est** : OFFENSIVE, DISTASTEFUL

icon \ˈī-ˌkän\ *n* : IMAGE; *esp* : a religious image painted on a wood panel

icon·o·clasm \ī-ˈkän-ə-ˌklaz-əm\ *n* : the doctrine, practice, or attitude of an iconoclast

icon·o·clast \-ˌklast\ *n* [ML *iconoclastes,* fr. MGk *eikonoklastēs,* lit., image destroyer, fr. Gk *eikōn* image + *klan* to break] **1** : one who destroys religious images or opposes their veneration **2** : one who attacks cherished beliefs or institutions

-ics \iks\ *n sing or pl suffix* **1** : study : knowledge : skill : practice ⟨linguist*ics*⟩ ⟨electron*ics*⟩ **2** : characteristic actions or activities ⟨acrobat*ics*⟩ **3** : characteristic qualities, operations, or phenomena ⟨mechan*ics*⟩

ic·tus \ˈik-təs\ *n* : the recurring stress or beat in a rhythmic or metrical series of sounds

ICU *abbr* intensive care unit

icy \ˈī-sē\ *adj* **ic·i·er; -est** **1** : covered with, abounding in, or consisting of ice **2** : intensely cold **3** : being cold and unfriendly — **ic·i·ly** \ˈī-sə-lē\ *adv* — **ic·i·ness** \-sē-nəs\ *n*

[1]**id** \ˈid\ *n* [L, it] : the part of the psyche in psychoanalytic theory that is completely unconscious and is the source of psychic energy derived from instinctual needs and drives

[2]**id** *abbr* idem

ID *abbr* **1** Idaho **2** identification

idea \ī-ˈdē-ə\ *n* **1** : a plan for action : DESIGN, PROJECT **2** : something imagined or pictured in the mind **3** : a central meaning or purpose **syn** concept, conception, notion, impression

[1]**ide·al** \ī-ˈdē(-ə)l\ *adj* **1** : existing only in the mind : IMAGINARY; *also* : lacking practicality **2** : of or relating to an ideal or to perfection : PERFECT

[2]**ideal** *n* **1** : a standard of excellence **2** : one regarded as a model worthy of imitation **3** : GOAL

ide·al·ism \ī-ˈdē-(ə-)ˌliz-əm\ *n* **1** : the practice of forming or living according to ideals **2** : the tendency to see things as they should be — **ide·al·ist** \-(ə-)ləst\ *n* — **ide·al·is·tic** \ī-ˌdē-(ə-)ˈlis-tik\ *adj* — **ide·al·is·ti·cal·ly** \-tik(ə-)lē\ *adv*

ide·al·ize \ī-ˈdē-(ə-)ˌlīz\ *vb* **-ized; -iz·ing** : to think of or represent as ideal — **ide·al·iza·tion** \-ˌdē-(ə-)lə-ˈzā-shən\ *n*

ide·al·ly \ī-ˈdē-(ə-)lē\ *adv* **1** : in idea or imagination : MENTALLY **2** : in agreement with an ideal : PERFECTLY

ide·ation \ˌīd-ē-ˈā-shən\ *n* : the capacity for or process of forming ideas — **ide·ate** \ˈīd-ē-ˌāt\ *vb* — **ide·ation·al** \ˌīd-ē-ˈā-sh(ə-)nəl\ *adj*

idem \ˈīd-ˌem, ˈēd-, ˈid-\ *pron* [L, same] : something previously mentioned

iden·ti·cal \ī-ˈdent-i-kəl\ *adj* **1** : being the same **2** : exactly or essentially alike **syn** equivalent, equal, tantamount

iden·ti·fi·ca·tion \ī-ˌdent-ə-fə-ˈkā-shən\ *n* **1** : an act of identifying : the state of being identified **2** : evidence of identity **3** : an unconscious psychological process by which an individual models thoughts, feelings, and actions after another person or an object

iden·ti·fy \ī-ˈdent-ə-ˌfī\ *vb* **-fied; -fy·ing** **1** : to regard as identical **2** : ASSOCIATE **3** : to establish the identity of **4** : to practice psychological identification — **iden·ti·fi·able** \-ˌfī-ə-bəl\ *adj* — **iden·ti·fi·ably** \-blē\ *adv* — **iden·ti·fi·er** \-ˌfī(-ə)r\ *n*

iden·ti·ty \ī-ˈdent-ət-ē\ *n, pl* **-ties** **1** : sameness of essential character **2** : INDIVIDUALITY **3** : the fact of being the same person or thing as claimed

identity crisis *n* : psychological conflict esp. in adolescence involving confusion about one's social role and one's personality

ideo·gram \ˈīd-ē-ə-ˌgram, ˈid-\ *n* **1** : a picture or symbol used in a system of writing to represent a thing or an idea **2** : a character or symbol used in a system of writing to represent an entire word

ide·ol·o·gy \ˌīd-ē-ˈäl-ə-jē, ˌid-\ *also* **ide·al·o·gy** \-ˈäl-ə-jē, -ˈal-\ *n, pl* **-gies** **1** : the body of ideas characteristic of a particular individual, group, or culture **2** : the assertions, theories, and aims that constitute a political, social, and economic program — **ide·o·log·i·cal** \ˌīd-ē-ə-ˈläj-i-kəl, ˌid-\ *adj* — **ide·ol·o·gist** \-ē-ˈäl-ə-jəst\ *n*

ides \ˈīdz\ *n sing or pl* : the 15th day of March, May, July, or October or the 13th day of any other month in the ancient Roman calendar

id·i·o·cy \ˈid-ē-ə-sē\ *n, pl* **-cies** **1** : extreme mental deficiency **2** : something notably stupid or foolish

id·i·om \ˈid-ē-əm\ *n* **1** : the language peculiar to a person or group **2** : the characteristic form or structure of a language **3** : an expression that cannot be understood from the meanings of its separate words (as *give way*) — **id·i·om·at·ic** \ˌid-ē-ə-ˈmat-ik\ *adj* — **id·i·om·at·i·cal·ly** \-i-k(ə-)lē\ *adv*

id·io·path·ic \ˌid-ē-ə-ˈpath-ik\ *adj* : arising spontaneously or from an obscure or unknown cause ⟨an ~ disease⟩

id·io·syn·cra·sy \ˌid-ē-ə-ˈsiŋ-krə-sē\ *n, pl* **-sies** : personal peculiarity — **id·io·syn·crat·ic** \ˌid-ē-ō-sin-ˈkrat-ik\ *adj* — **id·io·syn·crat·i·cal·ly** \-ˈkrat-i-k(ə-)lē\ *adv*

id·i·ot \ˈid-ē-ət\ *n* [ME, fr. L *idiota* ignorant person, fr. Gk *idiōtēs* one in a private station, ignorant person, fr. *idios* one's own, private] **1** : a feebleminded person **2** : a silly or foolish person — **id·i·ot·ic** \ˌid-ē-ˈät-ik\ *adj* — **id·i·ot·i·cal·ly** \-i-k(ə-)lē\ *adv*

[1]**idle** \ˈīd-ᵊl\ *adj* **idler** \ˈīd-(ə-)lər\; **idlest** \ˈīd-(ə-)ləst\ **1** : GROUNDLESS, WORTHLESS, USELESS ⟨~ rumor⟩ ⟨~ talk⟩ **2** : not occupied or employed : INACTIVE **3** : LAZY ⟨~ fellows⟩ — **idle·ness** *n* — **idly** \ˈīd-lē\ *adv*

[2]**idle** *vb* **idled; idling** \ˈīd-(ᵊ-)liŋ\ **1** : to spend time doing nothing **2** : to make idle **3** : to run without being connected so that power is not used for useful work — **idler** \ˈīd-(ᵊ-)lər\ *n*

idol \ˈīd-ᵊl\ *n* **1** : an image worshiped as a god **2** : a false god **3** : an object of passionate devotion

idol·a·ter \ī-ˈdäl-ət-ər\ *n* : a worshiper of idols

idol·a·try \-ə-trē\ *n, pl* **-tries** **1** : the worship of a physical

\ə\abut \ᵊ\kitten \ər\further \a\ash \ā\ace \ä\cot, cart \au̇\out \ch\chin \e\bet \ē\easy \g\go \i\hit \ī\ice \j\job \ŋ\sing \ō\go \ȯ\law \ȯi\boy \th\thin \th\the \ü\loot \u̇\foot \y\yet \zh\vision *see also* Pronunciation Symbols page

object as a god **2** : immoderate devotion — **idol·a·trous** \-trəs\ *adj*

idol·ize \ˈīd-ᵊl-ˌīz\ *vb* **-ized; -iz·ing** : to make an idol of — **idol·iza·tion** \ˌīd-ᵊl-ə-ˈzā-shən\ *n*

idyll *or* **idyl** \ˈīd-ᵊl\ *n* **1** : a simple descriptive or narrative composition; *esp* : a poem about country life **2** : a fit subject for an idyll — **idyl·lic** \ī-ˈdil-ik\ *adj*

i.e. \t͟hat-ˈiz, (ˈ)ī-ˈē\ *abbr* [L *id est* that is]

IE *abbr* **1** Indo-European **2** industrial engineer

-ier — see -ER

if \(ˌ)if, əf\ *conj* **1** : in the event that ⟨~ he stays, I leave⟩ **2** : WHETHER ⟨ask ~ he left⟩ **3** — used as a function word to introduce an exclamation expressing a wish ⟨~ it would only rain⟩ **4** : even though ⟨an interesting ~ untenable argument⟩

IF *abbr* intermediate freqency

if·fy \ˈif-ē\ *adj* : full of contingencies or unknown conditions

-i·fy \ə-ˌfī\ *vb suffix* : -FY

IG *abbr* inspector general

ig·loo \ˈig-lü\ *n, pl* **igloos** [Eskimo *iglu* house] : an Eskimo house or hut often made of snow blocks and in the shape of a dome

ig·ne·ous \ˈig-nē-əs\ *adj* **1** : FIERY **2** : formed by solidification of molten rock

ig·nite \ig-ˈnīt\ *vb* **ig·nit·ed; ig·nit·ing** : to set afire or catch fire — **ig·nit·able** \-ˈnīt-ə-bəl\ *n*

ig·ni·tion \ig-ˈnish-ən\ *n* **1** : a setting on fire **2** : the process or means (as an electric spark) of igniting the fuel mixture in an engine

ig·no·ble \ig-ˈnō-bəl\ *adj* **1** : of low birth : PLEBEIAN **2** : not honorable : BASE, MEAN — **ig·no·bly** \-blē\ *adv*

ig·no·min·i·ous \ˌig-nə-ˈmin-ē-əs\ *adj* **1** : DISHONORABLE **2** : DESPICABLE **3** : HUMILIATING, DEGRADING — **ig·no·min·i·ous·ly** *adv* — **ig·no·mi·ny** \ˈig-nə-ˌmin-ē, ig-ˈnäm-ə-nē\ *n*

ig·no·ra·mus \ˌig-nə-ˈrā-məs\ *n* [*Ignoramus*, ignorant lawyer in *Ignoramus* (1615), play by George Ruggle] : an utterly ignorant person : DUNCE

ig·no·rance \ˈig-nə-rəns\ *n* : the state of being ignorant : lack of knowledge

ig·no·rant \ˈig-nə-rənt\ *adj* **1** : lacking knowledge : UNEDUCATED **2** : resulting from or showing lack of knowledge or intelligence **3** : UNAWARE, UNINFORMED — **ig·no·rant·ly** *adv*

ig·nore \ig-ˈnōr\ *vb* **ig·nored; ig·nor·ing** : to refuse to take notice of **syn** overlook, slight, neglect

igua·na \i-ˈgwän-ə\ *n* : a large edible tropical American lizard

IGY *abbr* International Geophysical Year

IHP *abbr* indicated horsepower

IHS \ˌī-ˌā-ˈches\ [LL, part transliteration of Gk ΙΗΣ, abbreviation for ΙΗΣΟΥΣ *Iēsous* Jesus] — used as a Christian symbol and monogram for Jesus

ikon *var of* ICON

IL *abbr* Illinois

il·e·itis \ˌil-ē-ˈīt-əs\ *n* : inflammation of the ileum

il·e·um \ˈil-ē-əm\ *n, pl* **il·ea** \-ē-ə\ : the part of the small intestine between the jejunum and the large intestine — **il·e·al** \-ē-əl\ *adj*

il·i·ac \ˈil-ē-ˌak\ *adj* : of, relating to, or located near the ilium

il·i·um \ˈil-ē-əm\ *n* : the upper one of the three bones making up either side of the pelvis

ilk \ˈilk\ *n* : SORT, FAMILY

¹ill \ˈil\ *adj* **worse** \ˈwərs\; **worst** \ˈwərst\ **1** : not normal or sound ⟨~ health⟩; *also* : suffering ill health : SICK **2** : BAD, UNLUCKY ⟨~ omen⟩ **3** : not right or proper ⟨~ manners⟩ **4** : UNFRIENDLY, HOSTILE ⟨~ feeling⟩ **5** : HARSH, CRUEL ⟨~ treatment⟩

²ill *adv* **worse; worst 1** : with displeasure **2** : in a harsh manner **3** : HARDLY, SCARCELY ⟨can ~ afford it⟩ **4** : BADLY, UNLUCKILY **5** : in a faulty way

³ill *n* **1** : EVIL **2** : MISFORTUNE, DISTRESS **3** : AILMENT, SICKNESS; *also* : TROUBLE

⁴ill *abbr* illustrated; illustration; illustrator

Ill *abbr* Illinois

ill–ad·vised \ˌil-əd-ˈvīzd\ *adj* : not well counseled ⟨~ efforts⟩ — **ill–ad·vis·ed·ly** \-ˈvī-zəd-lē\ *adv*

ill–bred \-ˈbred\ *adj* : badly brought up : IMPOLITE

il·le·gal \il-ˈ(l)ē-gəl\ *adj* : not lawful; *also* : not sanctioned by official rules — **il·le·gal·i·ty** \ˌil-i-ˈgal-ət-ē\ *n* — **il·le·gal·ly** \il-ˈ(l)ē-gə-lē\ *adv*

il·leg·i·ble \il-ˈ(l)ej-ə-bəl\ *adj* : not legible — **il·leg·i·bil·i·ty** \il-ˌ(l)ej-ə-ˈbil-ət-ē\ *n* — **il·leg·i·bly** \il-ˈ(l)ej-ə-blē\ *adv*

il·le·git·i·mate \ˌil-i-ˈjit-ə-mət\ *adj* **1** : born of unmarried parents **2** : ILLOGICAL **3** : ILLEGAL — **il·le·git·i·ma·cy** \-ˈjit-ə-mə-sē\ *n* — **il·le·git·i·mate·ly** \-ˈjit-ə-mət-lē\ *adv*

ill–fat·ed \ˈil-ˈfāt-əd\ *adj* : having or destined to an evil fate : UNFORTUNATE

ill–fa·vored \-ˈfā-vərd\ *adj* : UGLY, UNATTRACTIVE

ill–got·ten \-ˈgät-ᵊn\ *adj* : acquired by evil means ⟨~ gains⟩

ill–hu·mored \-ˈ(h)yü-mərd\ *adj* : SURLY, IRRITABLE

il·lib·er·al \il-ˈ(l)ib-(ə-)rəl\ *adj* : not liberal : NARROW, BIGOTED

il·lic·it \il-ˈ(l)is-ət\ *adj* : not permitted : UNLAWFUL — **il·lic·it·ly** *adv*

il·lim·it·able \il-ˈ(l)im-ət-ə-bəl\ *adj* : BOUNDLESS, MEASURELESS — **il·lim·it·ably** \-blē\ *adv*

Il·li·nois \ˌil-ə-ˈnȯi *also* -ˈnȯiz\ *n, pl* **Illinois** : a member of an American Indian people of Illinois, Iowa, and Wisconsin

il·lit·er·ate \il-ˈ(l)it-(ə-)rət\ *adj* **1** : having little or no education; *esp* : unable to read or write **2** : showing a lack of familiarity with the fundamentals of a particular field of knowledge — **il·lit·er·a·cy** \-ˈ(l)it-(ə-)rə-sē\ *n* — **illiterate** *n*

ill–man·nered \ˈil-ˈman-ərd\ *adj* : marked by bad manners : RUDE

ill–na·tured \-ˈnā-chərd\ *adj* : CROSS, SURLY — **ill–na·tured·ly** *adv*

ill·ness \ˈil-nəs\ *n* : SICKNESS

il·log·i·cal \il-ˈ(l)äj-i-kəl\ *adj* : not according to good reasoning; *also* : SENSELESS — **il·log·i·cal·ly** \-i-k(ə-)lē\ *adv*

ill–starred \ˈil-ˈstärd\ *adj* : ILL-FATED, UNLUCKY

ill–tem·pered \-ˈtem-pərd\ *adj* : ILL-NATURED, QUARRELSOME

ill–treat \-ˈtrēt\ *vb* : to treat cruelly or improperly : MALTREAT — **ill–treat·ment** \-mənt\ *n*

il·lume \il-ˈüm\ *vb* **il·lumed; il·lum·ing** : ILLUMINATE

il·lu·mi·nate \il-ˈü-mə-ˌnāt\ *vb* **-nat·ed; -nat·ing 1** : to supply or brighten with light : light up **2** : to make clear : ELUCIDATE **3** : to decorate (as a manuscript) with designs or pictures in gold or colors — **il·lu·mi·nat·ing·ly** \-ˌnāt-iŋ-lē\ *adv* — **il·lu·mi·na·tion** \-ˌü-mə-ˈnā-shən\ *n* — **il·lu·mi·na·tor** \-ˈü-mə-ˌnāt-ər\ *n*

il·lu·mine \il-ˈü-mən\ *vb* **-mined; -min·ing** : ILLUMINATE

ill–us·age \ˈil-ˈyü-sij, -zij\ *n* : harsh, unkind, or abusive treatment

ill–use \-ˈyüz\ *vb* : MALTREAT, ABUSE

il·lu·sion \il-ˈü-zhən\ *n* [ME, fr. MF, fr. LL *illusio*, fr. L, action of mocking, fr. *illudere* to mock at, fr. *ludere* to play, mock] **1** : a mistaken idea : MISAPPREHENSION, MIS-

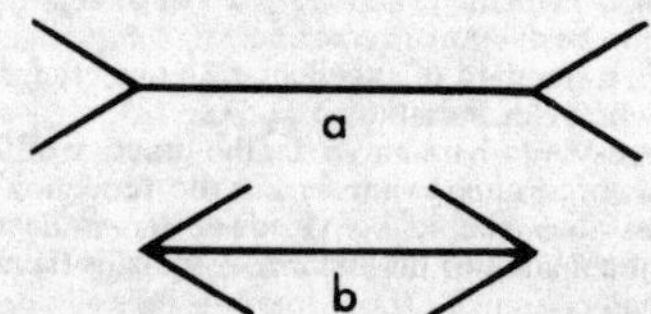

illusion 2: *a* equals *b* in length

CONCEPTION, FANCY **2** : a misleading visual image : HALLUCINATION

il·lu·sion·ist \il-ˈüzh-(ə-)nəst\ *n* : one that produces illusions; *esp* : a sleight-of-hand performer

il·lu·sive \il-ˈü-siv\ *adj* : ILLUSORY

il·lu·so·ry \il-ˈüs-(ə-)rē, -ˈüz-\ *adj* : based on or producing illusion

illust *or* **illus** *abbr* illustrated; illustration

il·lus·trate \ˈil-əs-ˌtrāt\ *vb* **-trat·ed; -trat·ing** [L *illustrare*, fr. *lustrare* to purify, make bright] **1** : to explain by use of examples : CLARIFY; *also* : DEMONSTRATE **2** : to provide with pictures or figures that explain or decorate **3** : to serve to explain or decorate — **il·lus·tra·tor** \ˈil-əs-ˌtrāt-ər\ *n*

il·lus·tra·tion \ˌil-əs-ˈtrā-shən\ *n* **1** : the act of illustrating : the condition of being illustrated **2** : an example or instance that helps make something clear **3** : a picture or diagram that explains or decorates

il·lus·tra·tive \il-ˈəs-trət-iv\ *adj* : serving, tending, or designed to illustrate — **il·lus·tra·tive·ly** *adv*

il·lus·tri·ous \il-ˈəs-trē-əs\ *adj* : notably outstanding because of rank or achievement : EMINENT — **il·lus·tri·ous·ness** *n*

ill will *n* : unfriendly feeling

ILS *abbr* instrument landing system

[1]**im·age** \ˈim-ij\ *n* **1** : a likeness or imitation of a person or thing; *esp* : STATUE **2** : a picture of an object formed by a device (as a mirror or lens) **3** : a person strikingly like another person ⟨he is the ~ of his father⟩ **4** : a mental picture or conception : IMPRESSION, IDEA, CONCEPT **5** : a vivid representation or description

[2]**image** *vb* **im·aged; im·ag·ing** **1** : to call up a mental picture of **2** : to describe or portray in words **3** : to create a representation of **4** : REFLECT, MIRROR **5** : to make appear : PROJECT

im·ag·ery \ˈim-ij-(ə-)rē\ *n* **1** : IMAGES; *also* : the art of making images **2** : figurative language **3** : mental images; *esp* : the products of imagination

imag·in·able \im-ˈaj-(ə-)nə-bəl\ *adj* : capable of being imagined : CONCEIVABLE — **imag·in·ably** \-blē\ *adv*

imag·i·nary \im-ˈaj-ə-ˌner-ē\ *adj* **1** : existing only in the imagination **2** : containing or relating to the imaginary unit

imaginary number *n* : a complex number (as $2 + 3i$) whose imaginary part is not zero

imaginary part *n* : the part of a complex number (as $3i$ in $2 + 3i$) that has the imaginary unit as a factor

imaginary unit *n* : the positive square root of minus 1 : $+\sqrt{-1}$

imag·i·na·tion \im-ˌaj-ə-ˈnā-shən\ *n* **1** : the act or power of forming a mental image of something not present to the senses or not previously known or experienced **2** : creative ability **3** : RESOURCEFULNESS **4** : a mental image : a creation of the mind — **imag·i·na·tive** \im-ˈaj-(ə-)nət-iv, -ə-ˌnāt-iv\ *adj* — **imag·i·na·tive·ly** *adv*

imag·ine \im-ˈaj-ən\ *vb* **imag·ined; imag·in·ing** \-ˈaj-(ə-)niŋ\ **1** : to form a mental picture of something not present **2** : THINK, GUESS ⟨I ~ it will rain⟩

im·ag·ism \ˈim-ij-ˌiz-əm\ *n*, *often cap* : a movement in poetry advocating free verse and the expression of ideas and emotions through clear precise images — **im·ag·ist** \-ij-əst\ *n*

ima·go \im-ˈā-gō, -ˈäg-ō\ *n*, *pl* **imagoes** *or* **ima·gi·nes** \-ˈā-gə-ˌnēz, -ˈäg-ə-\ [L, image] : an insect in its final adult stage — **ima·gi·nal** \im-ˈā-gən-ᵊl, -ˈäg-ən-\ *adj*

im·bal·ance \(ˈ)im-ˈbal-əns\ *n* : lack of balance : the state of being out of equilibrium or out of proportion

im·be·cile \ˈim-bə-səl, -ˌsil\ *n* **1** : a feebleminded person; *esp* : one capable of performing routine personal care under supervision **2** : FOOL, IDIOT — **imbecile** *or* **im·be·cil·ic** \ˌim-bə-ˈsil-ik\ *adj* — **im·be·cil·i·ty** \ˌim-bə-ˈsil-ət-ē\ *n*

imbed *var of* EMBED

im·bibe \im-ˈbīb\ *vb* **im·bibed; im·bib·ing** **1** : to receive and retain in the mind **2** : DRINK **3** : to drink in : ABSORB — **im·bib·er** *n*

im·bi·bi·tion \ˌim-bə-ˈbish-ən\ *n* : the act or action of imbibing; *esp* : the taking up of fluid by a colloidal system resulting in swelling

im·bri·ca·tion \ˌim-brə-ˈkā-shən\ *n* **1** : an overlapping of edges (as of tiles) **2** : a pattern showing imbrication — **im·bri·cate** \ˈim-bri-kət\ *adj*

im·bro·glio \im-ˈbrōl-yō\ *n*, *pl* **-glios** [It, fr. *imbrogliare* to entangle] **1** : a confused mass **2** : a difficult or embarrassing situation; *also* : a serious or embarrassing misunderstanding

im·brue \im-ˈbrü\ *vb* **im·brued; im·bru·ing** : DRENCH, STAIN ⟨a nation *imbrued* with the blood of executed men⟩

im·bue \-ˈbyü\ *vb* **im·bued; im·bu·ing** **1** : to permeate or influence as if by dyeing **2** : to tinge or dye deeply

IMF *abbr* International Monetary Fund

imit *abbr* imitative

im·i·ta·ble \ˈim-ət-ə-bəl\ *adj* : capable or worthy of being imitated or copied

im·i·tate \ˈim-ə-ˌtāt\ *vb* **-tat·ed; -tat·ing** **1** : to follow as a model : COPY **2** : RESEMBLE **3** : REPRODUCE **4** : MIMIC, COUNTERFEIT — **im·i·ta·tor** \-ˌtāt-ər\ *n*

im·i·ta·tion \ˌim-ə-ˈtā-shən\ *n* **1** : an act of imitating **2** : COPY, COUNTERFEIT **3** : a literary work that reproduces the style of another author — **imitation** *adj*

im·i·ta·tive \ˈim-ə-ˌtāt-iv\ *adj* **1** : marked by imitation **2** : exhibiting mimicry **3** : inclined to imitate or copy **4** : COUNTERFEIT

im·mac·u·late \im-ˈak-yə-lət\ *adj* **1** : being without stain or blemish : PURE **2** : spotlessly clean ⟨~ linen⟩ — **im·mac·u·late·ly** *adv*

im·ma·nent \ˈim-ə-nənt\ *adj* : having existence only in the mind — **im·ma·nence** \-nəns\ *n* — **im·ma·nen·cy** \-nən-sē\ *n*

im·ma·te·ri·al \ˌim-ə-ˈtir-ē-əl\ *adj* **1** : not consisting of matter : SPIRITUAL **2** : UNIMPORTANT, TRIFLING — **im·ma·te·ri·al·i·ty** \-ˌtir-ē-ˈal-ət-ē\ *n*

im·ma·ture \ˌim-ə-ˈt(y)u̇r\ *adj* : lacking complete development : not yet mature — **im·ma·tu·rity** \-ˈt(y)u̇r-ət-ē\ *n*

im·mea·sur·able \(ˈ)im-ˈezh-(ə-)rə-bəl\ *adj* : not capable of being measured : indefinitely extensive : ILLIMITABLE — **im·mea·sur·ably** \-blē\ *adv*

im·me·di·a·cy \im-ˈēd-ē-ə-sē\ *n*, *pl* **-cies** **1** : the quality or state of being immediate **2** : URGENCY **3** : something that is of immediate importance

im·me·di·ate \im-ˈēd-ē-ət\ *adj* **1** : acting directly and alone : DIRECT ⟨the ~ cause of death⟩ **2** : being next in line or relation ⟨members of the ~ family attended⟩ **3** : not distant : CLOSE **4** : made or done at once ⟨an ~ response⟩ **5** : near to or related to the present time ⟨the ~ future⟩ — **im·me·di·ate·ly** *adv*

im·me·mo·ri·al \ˌim-ə-ˈmōr-ē-əl\ *adj* : extending beyond the reach of memory, record, or tradition

im·mense \im-ˈens\ *adj* [MF, fr. L *immensus* immeasurable, fr. *mensus*, pp. of *metiri* to measure] **1** : very great in size or degree : VAST, HUGE **2** : EXCELLENT — **im·mense·ly** *adv* — **im·men·si·ty** \-ˈen-sət-ē\ *n*

im·merse \im-ˈərs\ *vb* **im·mersed; im·mers·ing** **1** : to plunge or dip esp. into a fluid **2** : ENGROSS, ABSORB **3** : to baptize by immersing — **im·mer·sion** \im-ˈər-zhən\ *n*

im·mi·grant \ˈim-i-grənt\ *n* **1** : a person who immigrates **2** : a plant or animal that becomes established where it did not previously occur

im·mi·grate \ˈim-ə-ˌgrāt\ *vb* **-grat·ed; -grat·ing** : to come into a foreign country and take up residence — **im·mi·gra·tion** \ˌim-ə-ˈgrā-shən\ *n*

im·mi·nent \ˈim-ə-nənt\ *adj* : ready to take place; *esp* : hanging threateningly over one's head — **im·mi·nence** \-nəns\ *n* — **im·mi·nent·ly** *adv*

im·mis·ci·ble \(ˈ)im-ˈis-ə-bəl\ *adj* : incapable of mixing — **im·mis·ci·bil·i·ty** \(ˌ)im-ˌis-ə-ˈbil-ət-ē\ *n*

im·mo·bile \(ˈ)im-ˈō-bəl\ *adj* : incapable of being moved : IMMOVABLE, FIXED — **im·mo·bil·i·ty** \ˌim-ō-ˈbil-ət-ē\ *n*

im·mo·bi·lize \im-ˈō-bə-ˌlīz\ *vb* : to make immobile — **im·mo·bi·li·za·tion** \im-ˌō-bə-lə-ˈzā-shən\ *n*

im·mod·er·ate \(ˈ)im-ˈäd-(ə-)rət\ *adj* : lacking in moderation : EXCESSIVE — **im·mod·er·a·cy** \-(ə-)rə-sē\ *n* — **im·mod·er·ate·ly** *adv*

im·mod·est \(ˈ)im-ˈäd-əst\ *adj* : not modest : BRAZEN, INDECENT ⟨an ~ dress⟩ ⟨~ conduct⟩ — **im·mod·est·ly** *adv* — **im·mod·es·ty** \-ə-stē\ *n*

im·mo·late \ˈim-ə-ˌlāt\ *vb* **-lat·ed; -lat·ing** [L *immolare*, fr. *mola* grits; fr. the custom of sprinkling victims with sacrificial meal] : to offer in sacrifice; *esp* : to kill as a sacrificial victim — **im·mo·la·tion** \ˌim-ə-ˈlā-shən\ *n*

im·mor·al \(ˈ)im-ˈȯr-əl\ *adj* : not moral : WICKED — **im·mor·al·ly** \-ē\ *adv*

im·mo·ral·i·ty \ˌim-ȯ-ˈral-ət-ē, ˌim-ə-ˈral-\ *n* **1** : WICKEDNESS; *esp* : UNCHASTITY **2** : an immoral act or practice

¹im·mor·tal \(ˈ)im-ˈȯrt-ᵊl\ *adj* **1** : not mortal : exempt from death ⟨~ gods⟩ **2** : exempt from oblivion ⟨those ~ words⟩ — **im·mor·tal·ly** \-ē\ *adv*

²immortal *n* **1** : one exempt from death **2** *pl, often cap* : the gods in Greek and Roman mythology **3** : a person whose fame is lasting ⟨an ~ of baseball⟩

im·mor·tal·i·ty \ˌim-ˌȯr-ˈtal-ət-ē\ *n* : the quality or state of being immortal; *esp* : unending existence

im·mor·tal·ize \im-ˈȯrt-ᵊl-ˌīz\ *vb* **-ized; -iz·ing** : to make immortal

im·mov·able \(ˈ)im-ˈü-və-bəl\ *adj* **1** : firmly fixed, settled, or fastened : FAST, STATIONARY ⟨~ mountains⟩ **2** : STEADFAST, UNYIELDING **3** : IMPASSIVE — **im·mov·abil·ity** \(ˌ)im-ˌü-və-ˈbil-ət-ē\ *n* — **im·mov·ably** \-blē\ *adv*

im·mune \im-ˈyün\ *adj* **1** : EXEMPT **2** : having a special capacity for resistance (as to a disease) — **im·mu·ni·ty** \im-ˈyü-nət-ē\ *n*

immune response *n* : a response of the body to an antigen resulting in the formation of antibodies and cells capable of reacting with the antigen and rendering it harmless

im·mu·nize \ˈim-yə-ˌnīz\ *vb* **-nized; -niz·ing** : to make immune — **im·mu·ni·za·tion** \ˌim-yə-nə-ˈzā-shən\ *n*

im·mu·no·de·fi·cien·cy \ˌim-yə-nō-di-ˈfish-ən-sē\ *n* : inability to produce the normal number of antibodies or immunologically sensitized cells esp. in response to specific antigens — **im·mu·no·de·fi·cient** \-ənt\ *adj*

im·mu·no·glob·u·lin \ˌim-yə-nō-ˈgläb-yə-lən\ *n* : any of a group of vertebrate serum proteins that include all known antibodies

im·mu·nol·o·gy \ˌim-yə-ˈnäl-ə-jē\ *n* : a science that deals with the phenomena and causes of immunity — **im·mu·no·log·ic** \-yən-ᵊl-ˈäj-ik\ *or* **im·mu·no·log·i·cal** \-i-kəl\ *adj* — **im·mu·no·log·i·cal·ly** \-i-k(ə-)lē\ *adv* — **im·mu·nol·o·gist** \ˌim-yə-ˈnäl-ə-jəst\ *n*

im·mu·no·sup·pres·sion \ˌim-yə-nō-sə-ˈpresh-ən\ *n* : suppression (as by drugs) of natural immune responses — **im·mu·no·sup·press** \-sə-ˈpres\ *vb* — **im·mu·no·sup·pres·sant** \-sə-ˈpres-ᵊnt\ *n or adj* — **im·mu·no·sup·pres·sive** \-sə-ˈpres-iv\ *adj*

im·mure \im-ˈyu̇(ə)r\ *vb* **im·mured; im·mur·ing** **1** : to enclose within or as if within walls **2** : to build into a wall; *esp* : to entomb in a wall

im·mu·ta·ble \(ˈ)im-ˈyüt-ə-bəl\ *adj* : UNCHANGEABLE, UNCHANGING — **im·mu·ta·bil·i·ty** \(ˌ)im-ˌyüt-ə-ˈbil-ət-ē\ *n* — **im·mu·ta·bly** \(ˈ)im-ˈyüt-ə-blē\ *adv*

¹imp \ˈimp\ *n* **1** : a small demon : FIEND **2** : a mischievous child

²imp *abbr* **1** imperative **2** imperfect **3** imperial **4** import; imported

¹im·pact \im-ˈpakt\ *vb* **1** : to press together **2** : to have an impact on

²im·pact \ˈim-ˌpakt\ *n* **1** : a forceful contact, collision, or onset; *also* : the impetus communicated in or as if in a collision **2** : EFFECT

im·pact·ed \im-ˈpak-təd\ *adj* : wedged between the jawbone and another tooth

im·pair \im-ˈpaər\ *vb* : to diminish in quantity, value, excellence, or strength : DAMAGE, LESSEN — **im·pair·ment** *n*

im·pa·la \im-ˈpal-ə\ *n* : a large brownish African antelope that in the male has slender lyre-shaped horns

im·pale \im-ˈpāl\ *vb* **im·paled; im·pal·ing** : to pierce with or as if with something pointed — **im·pale·ment** *n*

im·pal·pa·ble \(ˈ)im-ˈpal-pə-bəl\ *adj* **1** : unable to be felt by touch : INTANGIBLE **2** : not easily seen or understood — **im·pal·pa·bly** \(ˌ)im-ˈpal-pə-blē\ *adv*

im·pan·el \im-ˈpan-ᵊl\ *vb* : to enter in or on a panel : ENROLL ⟨~ a jury⟩

im·part \im-ˈpärt\ *vb* **1** : to give from one's store or abundance ⟨the sun ~*s* warmth⟩ **2** : to make known

im·par·tial \(ˈ)im-ˈpär-shəl\ *adj* : not partial : UNBIASED, JUST — **im·par·tial·i·ty** \(ˌ)im-ˌpär-shē-ˈal-ət-ē, -ˌpär-ˈshal-\ *n* — **im·par·tial·ly** \(ˈ)im-ˈpärsh-(ə-)lē\ *adv*

im·pass·able \(ˈ)im-ˈpas-ə-bəl\ *adj* : incapable of being passed, traversed, or circulated ⟨~ roads⟩ — **im·pass·ably** \(ˈ)im-ˈpas-ə-blē\ *adv*

im·passe \ˈim-ˌpas\ *n* **1** : an impassable road or way **2** : a predicament from which there is no obvious escape

im·pas·si·ble \(ˈ)im-ˈpas-ə-bəl\ *adj* : UNFEELING, IMPASSIVE

im·pas·sioned \im-ˈpash-ənd\ *adj* : filled with passion or zeal : showing great warmth or intensity of feeling **syn** passionate, ardent, fervent, fervid

im·pas·sive \(ˈ)im-ˈpas-iv\ *adj* : showing no signs of feeling, emotion, or interest : EXPRESSIONLESS, INDIFFERENT **syn** stoic, phlegmatic, apathetic, stolid — **im·pas·sive·ly** *adv* — **im·pas·siv·i·ty** \ˌim-ˌpas-ˈiv-ət-ē\ *n*

im·pas·to \im-ˈpas-tō, -ˈpäs-\ *n* : the thick application of a pigment to a canvas or panel in painting; *also* : the body of pigment so applied

im·pa·tience \(ˈ)im-ˈpā-shən(t)s\ *n* **1** : restlessness of spirit esp. under irritation, delay, or opposition **2** : restless or eager desire or longing

im·pa·tiens \im-ˈpā-shənz, -shəns\ *n* : any of a genus of watery-juiced annual herbs with spurred flowers and seed capsules that readily split open

im·pa·tient \(ˈ)im-ˈpā-shənt\ *adj* **1** : not patient : restless or short of temper esp. under irritation, delay, or opposition **2** : INTOLERANT ⟨~ of poverty⟩ **3** : prompted or marked by impatience **4** : ANXIOUS — **im·pa·tient·ly** *adv*

im·peach \im-ˈpēch\ *vb* [ME *empechen*, fr. MF *empeechier* to hinder, fr. LL *impedicare* to fetter, fr. L *pedica* fetter, fr. *ped-, pes* foot] **1** : to charge (a public official) before an authorized tribunal with misbehavior in office **2** : to challenge the credibility or validity of — **im·peach·ment** *n*

im·pec·ca·ble \(ˈ)im-ˈpek-ə-bəl\ *adj* **1** : not capable of sinning or wrongdoing **2** : FAULTLESS, FLAWLESS, IRREPROACHABLE ⟨a man of ~ character⟩ — **im·pec·ca·bil·i·ty** \(ˌ)im-ˌpek-ə-ˈbil-ət-ē\ *n* — **im·pec·ca·bly** \(ˈ)im-ˈpek-ə-blē\ *adv*

im·pe·cu·nious \ˌim-pi-ˈkyü-nyəs, -nē-əs\ *adj* : having little or no money — **im·pe·cu·nious·ness** *n*

im·ped·ance \im-ˈpēd-ᵊns\ *n* : the opposition in an electrical circuit to the flow of an alternating current

im·pede \im-ˈpēd\ *vb* **im·ped·ed; im·ped·ing** [L *impedire*, fr. *ped-, pes* foot] : to interfere with the progress of

im·ped·i·ment \im-ˈped-ə-mənt\ *n* : OBSTRUCTION, BLOCK; *esp* : a speech defect

im·ped·i·men·ta \im-ˌped-ə-ˈment-ə\ *n pl* : things that impede

im·pel \im-ˈpel\ *vb* **im·pelled; im·pel·ling** : to urge or drive forward or on : FORCE; *also* : PROPEL

im·pel·ler *also* **im·pel·lor** \im-ˈpel-ər\ *n* : ROTOR

im·pend \im-ˈpend\ *vb* **1** : to hover or hang over threateningly : MENACE **2** : to be about to occur

im·pen·e·tra·ble \(ˈ)im-ˈpen-ə-trə-bəl\ *adj* **1** : incapable of being penetrated or pierced ⟨an ~ jungle⟩ **2** : incapable of being comprehended : INSCRUTABLE ⟨an ~ mystery⟩ — **im·pen·e·tra·bil·i·ty** \(ˌ)im-ˌpen-ə-trə-ˈbil-ət-ē\ *n* — **im·pen·e·tra·bly** \(ˈ)im-ˈpen-ə-trə-blē\ *adv*

im·pen·i·tent \(ˈ)im-ˈpen-ə-tənt\ *adj* : not penitent : not repenting of sin — **im·pen·i·tence** \-təns\ *n*

im·per·a·tive \im-ˈper-ət-iv\ *adj* **1** : expressing a command, request, or encouragement ⟨~ sentence⟩ **2** : having power to restrain, control, or direct **3** : NECESSARY — **imperative** *n* — **im·per·a·tive·ly** *adv*

im·per·cep·ti·ble \ˌim-pər-ˈsep-tə-bəl\ *adj* : not perceptible by the senses or by the mind ⟨~ changes⟩ — **im·per·cep·ti·bly** \-ˈsep-tə-blē\ *adv*

im·per·cep·tive \ˌim-pər-ˈsep-tiv\ *adj* : not perceptive

imperf *abbr* **1** imperfect **2** imperforate

[1]**im·per·fect** \(ˈ)im-ˈpər-fikt\ *adj* **1** : not perfect : DEFECTIVE, INCOMPLETE **2** : of, relating to, or being a verb tense used to designate a continuing state or an incomplete action esp. in the past — **im·per·fect·ly** *adv*

[2]**imperfect** *n* : the imperfect tense; *also* : a verb form in it

im·per·fec·tion \ˌim-pər-ˈfek-shən\ *n* : the quality or state of being imperfect; *also* : DEFICIENCY, FAULT, BLEMISH

im·per·fo·rate \im-ˈpər-fə-rət\ *adj* : lacking perforations or tiny slits ⟨~ postage stamps⟩

[1]**im·pe·ri·al** \im-ˈpir-ē-əl\ *adj* **1** : of, relating to, or befitting an empire or an emperor; *also* : of or relating to the United Kingdom or to the Commonwealth or British Empire **2** : ROYAL, SOVEREIGN; *also* : REGAL, IMPERIOUS **3** : of unusual size or excellence

[2]**imperial** *n* : a pointed beard growing below the lower lip

im·pe·ri·al·ism \im-ˈpir-ē-ə-ˌliz-əm\ *n* : the policy of seeking to extend the power, dominion, or territories of a nation — **im·pe·ri·al·ist** \-ləst\ *n or adj* — **im·pe·ri·al·is·tic** \-ˌpir-ē-ə-ˈlis-tik\ *adj* — **im·pe·ri·al·is·ti·cal·ly** \-ti-k(ə-)lē\ *adv*

im·per·il \im-ˈper-əl\ *vb* **-iled** *or* **-illed; -il·ing** *or* **-il·ling** : ENDANGER

im·pe·ri·ous \im-ˈpir-ē-əs\ *adj* **1** : COMMANDING, LORDLY **2** : ARROGANT, DOMINEERING **3** : IMPERATIVE, URGENT — **im·pe·ri·ous·ly** *adv*

im·per·ish·able \(ˈ)im-ˈper-ish-ə-bəl\ *adj* : not perishable or subject to decay

im·per·ma·nent \(ˈ)im-ˈpər-mə-nənt\ *adj* : not permanent : TRANSIENT — **im·per·ma·nent·ly** *adv*

im·per·me·able \(ˈ)im-ˈpər-mē-ə-bəl\ *adj* : not permitting passage (as of a fluid) through its substance

im·per·mis·si·ble \ˌim-pər-ˈmis-ə-bəl\ *adj* : not permissible

im·per·son·al \(ˈ)im-ˈpərs-(ᵊ-)nəl\ *adj* **1** : not referring to any particular person or thing **2** : not involving human emotions — **im·per·son·al·i·ty** \(ˌ)im-ˌpərs-ᵊn-ˈal-ət-ē\ *n* — **im·per·son·al·ly** \-ē\ *adv*

im·per·son·ate \im-ˈpərs-ᵊn-ˌāt\ *vb* **-at·ed; -at·ing** : to assume or act the character of — **im·per·son·ation** \-ˌpərs-ᵊn-ˈā-shən\ *n* — **im·per·son·ator** \-ˈpərs-ᵊn-ˌāt-ər\ *n*

im·per·ti·nent \(ˈ)im-ˈpərt-ᵊn-ənt\ *adj* **1** : IRRELEVANT **2** : not restrained within due or proper bounds : RUDE, INSOLENT, SAUCY — **im·per·ti·nence** \-ᵊn-əns\ *n* — **im·per·ti·nent·ly** *adv*

im·per·turb·able \ˌim-pər-ˈtər-bə-bəl\ *adj* : marked by extreme calm, impassivity, and steadiness : SERENE

im·per·vi·ous \(ˈ)im-ˈpər-vē-əs\ *adj* **1** : incapable of being penetrated (as by moisture) **2** : not capable of being affected or disturbed ⟨~ to criticism⟩

im·pe·ti·go \ˌim-pə-ˈtē-gō, -ˈtī-\ *n* : a contagious skin disease characterized by vesicles, pustules, and yellowish crusts

im·pet·u·ous \im-ˈpech-(ə-)wəs\ *adj* **1** : marked by impulsive vehemence ⟨~ temper⟩ **2** : marked by force and violence ⟨with ~ speed⟩ — **im·pet·u·os·i·ty** \(ˌ)im-ˌpech-ə-ˈwäs-ət-ē\ *n* — **im·pet·u·ous·ly** *adv*

im·pe·tus \ˈim-pət-əs\ *n* [L, assault, impetus, fr. *impetere* to attack, fr. *petere* to go to, seek] **1** : a driving force : IMPULSE **2** : INCENTIVE **3** : MOMENTUM

im·pi·ety \(ˈ)im-ˈpī-ət-ē\ *n, pl* **-eties** **1** : the quality or state of being impious **2** : an impious act

im·pinge \im-ˈpinj\ *vb* **im·pinged; im·ping·ing** **1** : to strike or dash esp. with a sharp collision **2** : ENCROACH, INFRINGE — **im·pinge·ment** \-ˈpinj-mənt\ *n*

im·pi·ous \ˈim-pē-əs, (ˈ)im-ˈpī-\ *adj* : not pious : IRREVERENT, PROFANE

imp·ish \ˈim-pish\ *adj* : of, relating to, or befitting an imp; *esp* : MISCHIEVOUS — **imp·ish·ly** *adv* — **imp·ish·ness** *n*

im·pla·ca·ble \(ˈ)im-ˈplak-ə-bəl, -ˈplā-kə-\ *adj* : not capable of being appeased, pacified, mitigated, or changed ⟨an ~ enemy⟩ — **im·pla·ca·bil·i·ty** \(ˌ)im-ˌplak-ə-ˈbil-ət-ē, -ˌplā-kə-\ *n* — **im·pla·ca·bly** \(ˈ)im-ˈplak-ə-blē\ *adv*

im·plant \im-ˈplant\ *vb* **1** : to set firmly or deeply **2** : to fix in the mind or spirit **3** : to insert in a living site — **im·plant** \ˈim-ˌplant\ *n* — **im·plan·ta·tion** \ˌim-ˌplan-ˈtā-shən\ *n*

im·plau·si·ble \(ˈ)im-ˈplȯ-zə-bəl\ *adj* : not plausible — **im·plau·si·bil·i·ty** \(ˌ)im-ˌplȯ-zə-ˈbil-ət-ē\ *n* — **im·plau·si·bly** \(ˈ)im-ˈplȯ-zə-blē\ *adv*

[1]**im·ple·ment** \ˈim-plə-mənt\ *n* [ME, fr. LL *implementum* action of filling up, fr. L *implēre* to fill up] : TOOL, UTENSIL, INSTRUMENT

[2]**im·ple·ment** \-ˌment\ *vb* **1** : to carry out; *esp* : to put into practice **2** : to provide implements for — **im·ple·men·ta·tion** \ˌim-plə-mən-ˈtā-shən\ *n*

im·pli·cate \ˈim-plə-ˌkāt\ *vb* **-cat·ed; -cat·ing** **1** : IMPLY **2** : INVOLVE — **im·pli·ca·tion** \ˌim-plə-ˈkā-shən\ *n*

im·plic·it \im-ˈplis-ət\ *adj* **1** : understood though not directly stated or expressed : IMPLIED; *also* : POTENTIAL **2** : COMPLETE, UNQUESTIONING, ABSOLUTE ⟨~ faith⟩ — **im·plic·it·ly** *adv*

im·plode \im-ˈplōd\ *vb* **im·plod·ed; im·plod·ing** : to burst or collapse inward — **im·plo·sion** \-ˈplō-zhən\ *n* — **im·plo·sive** \-ˈplō-siv\ *adj*

im·plore \im-ˈplōr\ *vb* **im·plored; im·plor·ing** : BESEECH, ENTREAT **syn** supplicate, beg, importune, plead

im·ply \im-ˈplī\ *vb* **im·plied; im·ply·ing** **1** : to involve or indicate by inference, association, or necessary consequence rather than by direct statement ⟨war *implies* fighting⟩ **2** : to express indirectly : hint at : SUGGEST

im·po·lite \ˌim-pə-ˈlīt\ *adj* : not polite : RUDE, DISCOURTEOUS

im·pol·i·tic \(ˈ)im-ˈpäl-ə-ˌtik\ *adj* : not politic : RASH

im·pon·der·a·ble \(ˈ)im-ˈpän-d(ə-)rə-bəl\ *adj* : incapable of being weighed or evaluated with exactness — **imponderable** *n*

[1]**im·port** \im-ˈpōrt\ *vb* **1** : MEAN, SIGNIFY **2** : to bring (as merchandise) into a place or country from a foreign or external source — **im·port·er** *n*

[2]**im·port** \ˈim-ˌpōrt\ *n* **1** : IMPORTANCE, SIGNIFICANCE **2** : MEANING, SIGNIFICATION **3** : something (as merchandise) brought in from another country

im·por·tance \im-ˈpȯrt-ᵊns\ *n* : the quality or state of being important : MOMENT, SIGNIFICANCE **syn** consequence, import, weight

im·por·tant \im-ˈpȯrt-ᵊnt\ *adj* **1** : marked by importance : SIGNIFICANT **2** : giving an impression of importance — **im·por·tant·ly** *adv*

im·por·ta·tion \ˌim-ˌpōr-ˈtā-shən, -pər-\ *n* **1** : the act or practice of importing **2** : something imported

im·por·tu·nate \im-ˈpȯrch-(ə-)nət\ *adj* **1** : troublesomely urgent **2** : BURDENSOME, TROUBLESOME

im·por·tune \ˌim-pər-ˈt(y)ün, im-ˈpȯr-chən\ *vb* **-tuned; -tun·ing** : to urge or beg with troublesome persistence — **im·por·tu·ni·ty** \-ˌim-pər-ˈt(y)ü-nət-ē\ *n*

im·pose \im-ˈpōz\ *vb* **im·posed; im·pos·ing 1** : to establish or apply by authority ⟨~ a tax⟩; *also* : INFLICT ⟨*imposed* himself as leader⟩ **2** : to make public or offer for sale with intent to deceive ⟨~ fake antiques on buyers⟩ **3** : OBTRUDE ⟨*imposed* herself upon others⟩ **4** : to take unwarranted advantage of something ⟨~ on her good nature⟩ — **im·po·si·tion** \ˌim-pə-ˈzish-ən\ *n*

im·pos·ing \im-ˈpō-ziŋ\ *adj* : impressive because of size, bearing, dignity, or grandeur — **im·pos·ing·ly** *adv*

im·pos·si·ble \(ˈ)im-ˈpäs-ə-bəl\ *adj* **1** : incapable of being or of occurring **2** : felt to be too difficult **3** : extremely undesirable : UNACCEPTABLE — **im·pos·si·bil·i·ty** \(ˌ)im-ˌpäs-ə-ˈbil-ət-ē\ *n* — **im·pos·si·bly** \(ˈ)im-ˈpäs-ə-blē\ *adv*

[1]**im·post** \ˈim-ˌpōst\ *n* : TAX, DUTY

[2]**impost** *n* : a block, capital, or molding from which an arch springs

im·pos·tor *or* **im·pos·ter** \im-ˈpäs-tər\ *n* : one that assumes an identity or title not his own in order to deceive

im·pos·ture \im-ˈpäs-chər\ *n* : DECEPTION; *esp* : fraudulent impersonation

im·po·tent \ˈim-pət-ənt\ *adj* **1** : lacking in power or strength : HELPLESS **2** : unable to copulate; *also* : STERILE — **im·po·tence** \-pət-əns\ *n* — **im·po·ten·cy** \-ən-sē\ *n* — **im·po·tent·ly** *adv*

im·pound \im-ˈpau̇nd\ *vb* **1** : CONFINE, ENCLOSE ⟨~ stray dogs⟩ **2** : to seize and hold in legal custody **3** : to collect in a reservoir ⟨~ water⟩ — **im·pound·ment** \-ˈpau̇n(d)-mənt\ *n*

im·pov·er·ish \im-ˈpäv-(ə-)rish\ *vb* : to make poor; *also* : to deprive of strength, richness, or fertility — **im·pov·er·ish·ment** *n*

im·prac·ti·ca·ble \(ˈ)im-ˈprak-ti-kə-bəl\ *adj* : not practicable : incapable of being put into practice or use

im·prac·ti·cal \(ˈ)im-ˈprak-ti-kəl\ *adj* **1** : not practical **2** : IMPRACTICABLE

im·pre·cate \ˈim-pri-ˌkāt\ *vb* **-cat·ed; -cat·ing** : CURSE — **im·pre·ca·tion** \ˌim-pri-ˈkā-shən\ *n*

im·pre·cise \ˌim-pri-ˈsīs\ *adj* : not precise — **im·pre·cise·ly** *adv* — **im·pre·cise·ness** *n* — **im·pre·ci·sion** \-ˈsizh-ən\ *n*

im·preg·na·ble \im-ˈpreg-nə-bəl\ *adj* : able to resist attack : UNCONQUERABLE, UNASSAILABLE — **im·preg·na·bil·i·ty** \(ˌ)im-ˌpreg-nə-ˈbil-ət-ē\ *n*

im·preg·nate \im-ˈpreg-ˌnāt\ *vb* **-nat·ed; -nat·ing 1** : to fertilize or make pregnant **2** : to fill or soak with some other substance — **im·preg·na·tion** \ˌim-ˌpreg-ˈnā-shən\ *n*

im·pre·sa·rio \ˌim-prə-ˈsär-ē-ˌō\ *n, pl* **-ri·os** [It, fr. *impresa* undertaking, fr. *imprendere* to undertake] **1** : the manager or conductor of an opera or concert company **2** : one who puts on an entertainment **3** : MANAGER, PRODUCER

[1]**im·press** \im-ˈpres\ *vb* **1** : to apply with or produce (as a mark) by pressure : IMPRINT **2** : to press, stamp, or print in or upon **3** : to produce a vivid impression of **4** : to affect esp. forcibly or deeply — **im·press·ible** *adj*

[2]**im·press** \ˈim-ˌpres\ *n* **1** : a characteristic or distinctive mark : STAMP **2** : IMPRESSION, EFFECT **3** : a mark made by pressure : IMPRINT **4** : an image of something formed by or as if by pressure; *esp* : SEAL **5** : a product of pressure or influence

[3]**im·press** \im-ˈpres\ *vb* **1** : to force into naval service **2** : to get the aid or services of by forcible argument or persuasion — **im·press·ment** *n*

im·pres·sion \im-ˈpresh-ən\ *n* **1** : a stamp, form, or figure made by impressing : IMPRINT **2** : an esp. marked influence or effect on feeling, sense, or mind **3** : a characteristic trait or feature resulting from influence : IMPRESS **4** : a single print or copy (as from type or from an engraved plate or book) **5** : all the copies of a publication (as a book) printed for one issue : PRINTING **6** : a usu. vague notion, recollection, belief, or opinion **7** : an imitation in caricature of a noted personality as a form of entertainment

im·pres·sion·able \im-ˈpresh-(ə-)nə-bəl\ *adj* : capable of being easily impressed : easily molded or influenced

im·pres·sion·ism \im-ˈpresh-ə-ˌniz-əm\ *n* **1** *often cap* : a theory or practice in modern art of depicting the natural appearances of objects by dabs or strokes of primary unmixed colors in order to simulate actual reflected light **2** : the depiction of scene, emotion, or character by details intended to achieve a vividness or effectiveness esp. by evoking subjective and sensory impressions — **im·pres·sion·is·tic** \(ˌ)im-ˌpresh-ə-ˈnis-tik\ *adj*

im·pres·sion·ist \im-ˈpresh-(ə-)nəst\ *n* **1** *often cap* : a painter who practices impressionism **2** : an entertainer who does impressions

im·pres·sive \im-ˈpres-iv\ *adj* : making or tending to make a marked impression ⟨an ~ speech⟩ — **im·pres·sive·ly** *adv* — **im·pres·sive·ness** *n*

im·pri·ma·tur \ˌim-prə-ˈmä-ˌtu̇(ə)r\ *n* [NL, let it be printed] **1** : a license to print or publish; *also* : official approval of a publication by a censor **2** : SANCTION, APPROVAL

[1]**im·print** \im-ˈprint, ˈim-ˌprint\ *vb* **1** : to stamp or mark by or as if by pressure : IMPRESS **2** : to fix firmly (as on the memory)

[2]**im·print** \ˈim-ˌprint\ *n* **1** : something imprinted or printed : IMPRESS **2** : a publisher's name printed at the foot of a title page **3** : an indelible distinguishing effect or influence

im·pris·on \im-ˈpriz-ᵊn\ *vb* : to put in or as if in prison : CONFINE — **im·pris·on·ment** \im-ˈpriz-ən-mənt\ *n*

im·prob·a·ble \(ˈ)im-ˈpräb-ə-bəl\ *adj* : unlikely to be true or to occur — **im·prob·a·bil·i·ty** \(ˌ)im-ˌpräb-ə-ˈbil- ət-ē\ *n* — **im·prob·a·bly** \(ˈ)im-ˈpräb-ə-blē\ *adv*

im·promp·tu \im-ˈprämp-t(y)ü\ *adj* [F, fr. *impromptu* extemporaneously, fr. L *in promptu* in readiness] **1** : made or done on or as if on the spur of the moment **2** : EXTEMPORANEOUS, UNREHEARSED — **impromptu** *adv or n*

im·prop·er \(ˈ)im-ˈpräp-ər\ *adj* **1** : not proper, fit, or suitable **2** : INCORRECT, INACCURATE **3** : not in accord with propriety, modesty, or good manners — **im·prop·er·ly** *adv*

improper fraction *n* : a fraction whose numerator is equal to or larger than the denominator

im·pro·pri·ety \ˌim-prə-ˈprī-ət-ē\ *n, pl* **-eties 1** : the quality or state of being improper **2** : an improper act or remark; *esp* : an unacceptable use of a word or of language

im·prove \im-ˈprüv\ *vb* **im·proved; im·prov·ing 1** : INCREASE, AUGMENT ⟨education *improved* his chances⟩ **2** : to enhance or increase in value or quality ⟨~ farmlands by cultivation⟩ **3** : to grow or become better ⟨~ in health⟩ **4** : to make good use of ⟨~ the time by reading⟩ — **im·prov·able** \-ˈprü-və-bəl\ *adj*

im·prove·ment \im-ˈprüv-mənt\ *n* **1** : the act or process of improving **2** : increased value or excellence of something **3** : something that adds to the value or appearance of a thing

im·prov·i·dent \(ˈ)im-ˈpräv-əd-ənt\ *adj* : not providing for the future — **im·prov·i·dence** \-əns\ *n*

im·pro·vise \ˈim-prə-ˌvīz\ *vb* **-vised; -vis·ing** [F *improviser*, fr. It *improvvisare*, fr. *improvviso* sudden, fr. L *improvisus*, lit., unforeseen] **1** : to compose, recite, play, or sing on the spur of the moment : EXTEMPORIZE ⟨~ on the piano⟩ **2** : to make, invent, or arrange offhand

⟨~ a sail out of shirts⟩ — **im·pro·vi·sa·tion** \im-ˌpräv-ə-ˈzā- shən, ˌim-prə-və-\ *n* — **im·pro·vis·er** *or* **im·pro·vi·sor** \ˌim-prə-ˈvī-zər, ˈim-prə-ˌvī-\ *n*

im·pru·dent \(ˈ)im-ˈprüd-ᵊnt\ *adj* : not prudent : lacking discretion — **im·pru·dence** \-ᵊns\ *n*

im·pu·dent \ˈim-pyəd-ənt\ *adj* : marked by contemptuous boldness or disregard of others — **im·pu·dence** \-əns\ *n* — **im·pu·dent·ly** *adv*

im·pugn \im-ˈpyün\ *vb* [ME, deriv. of L *inpugnare,* deriv. of *pugnare* to fight] : to attack by words or arguments : oppose or attack as false ⟨~ the motives of an opponent⟩

im·puis·sance \im-ˈpwis-ᵊns, -ˈpyü-ə-səns\ *n* [ME, fr. MF] : the quality or state of being powerless : WEAKNESS

im·pulse \ˈim-ˌpəls\ *n* **1** : a force that starts a body into motion; *also* : the motion produced by such a force **2** : an arousing of the mind and spirit to action; *also* : a wave of nervous excitation **3** : a natural tendency

im·pul·sion \im-ˈpəl-shən\ *n* **1** : the act of impelling : the state of being impelled **2** : a force that impels **3** : IMPETUS **4** : a sudden inclination

im·pul·sive \im-ˈpəl-siv\ *adj* **1** : having the power of or actually driving or impelling **2** : acting or prone to act on impulse ⟨~ buying⟩ — **im·pul·sive·ly** *adv* — **im·pul·sive·ness** *n*

im·pu·ni·ty \im-ˈpyü-nət-ē\ *n* [MF or L; MF *impunité,* fr. L *impunitas,* fr. *impune* without punishment, fr. *poena* pain, punishment] : exemption from punishment, harm, or loss

im·pure \(ˈ)im-ˈpyu̇r\ *adj* **1** : not pure : UNCHASTE, OBSCENE **2** : DIRTY, FOUL **3** : ADULTERATED, MIXED — **im·pu·ri·ty** \-ˈpyu̇r-ət-ē\ *n*

im·pute \im-ˈpyüt\ *vb* **im·put·ed; im·put·ing** **1** : to lay the responsibility or blame for often falsely or unjustly : CHARGE **2** : to credit to a person or a cause : ATTRIBUTE — **im·put·able** \-ˈpyüt-ə-bəl\ *adj* — **im·pu·ta·tion** \ˌim-pyə-ˈtā-shən\ *n*

¹in \(ˈ)in, ən, ᵊn\ *prep* **1** — used to indicate physical surroundings ⟨swim ~ the lake⟩ **2** : INTO 1 ⟨ran ~ the house⟩ **3** : DURING ⟨~ the summer⟩ **4** : WITH ⟨written ~ pencil⟩ **5** — used to indicate one's situation or state of being ⟨~ luck⟩ ⟨~ love⟩ **6** — used to indicate manner or purpose ⟨~ a hurry⟩ ⟨said ~ reply⟩ **7** : INTO 2 ⟨broke ~ pieces⟩

²in \ˈin\ *adv* **1** : to or toward the inside ⟨come ~⟩ : to or toward some destination or place ⟨flew ~ from the South⟩ **2** : at close quarters : NEAR ⟨the enemy closed ~⟩ **3** : into the midst of something ⟨mix ~ the flour⟩ **4** : to or at its proper place ⟨fit a piece ~⟩ **5** : WITHIN ⟨locked ~⟩ **6** : in vogue or season; *also* : at hand **7** : in a completed or terminated state

³in \ˈin\ *adj* **1** : located inside or within **2** : that is in position, connection, operation, or power ⟨the ~ party⟩ **3** : directed inward : INCOMING ⟨the ~ train⟩ **4** : keenly aware of and responsive to what is new and smart ⟨the ~ crowd⟩; *also* : extremely fashionable ⟨the ~ thing to do⟩

⁴in \ˈin\ *n* **1** : one who is in office or power or on the inside **2** : INFLUENCE, PULL ⟨he has an ~ with the owner⟩

⁵in *abbr* **1** inch **2** inlet

In *symbol* indium

IN *abbr* Indiana

in- \(ˈ)in, ˌin\ *prefix* **1** : not : NON-, UN- **2** : opposite of : contrary to

inacceptable
inaccessibility
inaccessible
inaccuracy
inaccurate
inaction
inactive
inactivity
inadmissibility
inadmissible
inadvisability
inadvisable
inapplicable
inapposite
inappreciative
inapproachable
inappropriate
inapt
inartistic
inattentive
inaudible
inaudibly
inauspicious
incautious
incomprehension
inconceivable
inconclusive
inconsistency
inconsistent
incoordination
indecipherable
indefensible
indemonstrable
indestructible
indeterminable
indiscernible
indistinguishable
inedible
ineducable
inefficacious
inefficacy
inelastic
inelasticity
inequitable
inequity
ineradicable
inexpedient
inexpensive
inexpressive
inextinguishable
infeasible
inharmonious
inhospitable
injudicious
inoffensive
insanitary
insensitive
insensitivity
insignificance
insignificant
insuppressible
insusceptible

in·abil·i·ty \ˌin-ə-ˈbil-ət-ē\ *n* : the quality or state of being unable

in ab·sen·tia \ˌin-ab-ˈsen-ch(ē-)ə\ *adv* : in one's absence

in·ac·ti·vate \(ˈ)in-ˈak-tə-ˌvāt\ *vb* : to make inactive — **in·ac·ti·va·tion** \(ˌ)in-ˌak-tə-ˈvā-shən\ *n*

in·ad·e·quate \(ˈ)in-ˈad-i-kwət\ *adj* : not adequate : INSUFFICIENT — **in·ad·e·qua·cy** \-kwə-sē\ *n* — **in·ad·e·quate·ly** *adv* — **in·ad·e·quate·ness** *n*

in·ad·ver·tent \ˌin-əd-ˈvərt-ᵊnt\ *adj* **1** : HEEDLESS, INATTENTIVE **2** : UNINTENTIONAL — **in·ad·ver·tence** \-ᵊns\ *n* — **in·ad·ver·ten·cy** \-ᵊn-sē\ *n* — **in·ad·ver·tent·ly** *adv*

in·alien·able \(ˈ)in-ˈāl-yə-nə-bəl, -ˈā-lē-ə-nə-\ *adj* : incapable of being alienated, surrendered, or transferred ⟨~ rights⟩ — **in·alien·abil·i·ty** \(ˌ)in-ˌāl-yə-nə-ˈbil-ət-ē, -ˌā-lē-ə-nə-\ *n* — **in·alien·ably** \(ˈ)in-ˈāl-yə-nə-blē, -ˈā-lē-ə-nə-\ *adv*

in·amo·ra·ta \in-ˌam-ə-ˈrät-ə\ *n* : a woman with whom one is in love

inane \in-ˈān\ *adj* **inan·er; -est** : EMPTY, INSUBSTANTIAL; *also* : SHALLOW, SILLY — **inan·i·ty** \in-ˈan-ət-ē\ *n*

in·an·i·mate \(ˈ)in-ˈan-ə-mət\ *adj* : not animate or animated : lacking the qualities of living things — **in·an·i·mate·ly** *adv* — **in·an·i·mate·ness** *n*

in·ap·pre·cia·ble \ˌin-ə-ˈprē-shə-bəl\ *adj* : too small to be perceived — **in·ap·pre·cia·bly** \-blē\ *adv*

in·ap·ti·tude \(ˈ)in-ˈap-tə-ˌt(y)üd\ *n* : lack of aptitude

in·ar·tic·u·late \ˌin-är-ˈtik-yə-lət\ *adj* **1** : not understandable as spoken words **2** : MUTE **3** : incapable of being expressed by speech; *also* : UNSPOKEN **4** : not having the power of distinct utterance or effective expression — **in·ar·tic·u·late·ly** *adv*

in·as·much as \ˌin-əz-ˌməch-əz\ *conj* : seeing that : SINCE

in·at·ten·tion \ˌin-ə-ˈten-chən\ *n* : failure to pay attention : DISREGARD

¹in·au·gu·ral \in-ˈȯ-gyə-rəl, -g(ə-)rəl\ *adj* **1** : of or relating to an inauguration **2** : marking a beginning

²inaugural *n* **1** : an inaugural address **2** : INAUGURATION

in·au·gu·rate \in-ˈȯ-g(y)ə-ˌrāt\ *vb* **-rat·ed; -rat·ing** **1** : to introduce into an office with suitable ceremonies : INSTALL **2** : to dedicate ceremoniously **3** : BEGIN, INITIATE — **in·au·gu·ra·tion** \-ˌȯ-g(y)ə-ˈrā-shən\ *n*

in·board \ˈin-ˌbōrd\ *adv* **1** : inside the hull of a ship **2** : close or closest to the center line of a ship or aircraft — **inboard** *adj*

in·born \ˈin-ˈbȯrn\ *adj* : present from birth rather than acquired : NATURAL **syn** innate, congenital, native

in·bound \ˈin-ˌbau̇nd\ *adj* : inward bound ⟨~ traffic⟩
in·bred \ˈin-ˈbred\ *adj* **1** : INBORN, INNATE **2** : subjected to or produced by inbreeding
in·breed·ing \ˈin-ˌbrēd-iŋ\ *n* **1** : the interbreeding of closely related individuals esp. to preserve and fix desirable characters of and to eliminate unfavorable characters from a stock **2** : confinement to a narrow range or a local or limited field of choice — **in·breed** \-ˈbrēd\ *vb*
inc *abbr* **1** incomplete **2** incorporated **3** increase
In·ca \ˈiŋ-kə\ *n* [Sp, fr. Quechua (a So. American Indian language) *inka* king, prince] **1** : a noble or a member of the ruling family of an Indian empire of Peru, Bolivia, and Ecuador until the Spanish conquest **2** : a member of any people under Inca influence
in·cal·cu·la·ble \(ˈ)in-ˈkal-kyə-lə-bəl\ *adj* : not capable of being calculated; *esp* : too large or numerous to be calculated — **in·cal·cu·la·bly** \-blē\ *adv*
in·can·des·cent \ˌin-kən-ˈdes-ᵊnt\ *adj* **1** : glowing with heat **2** : SHINING, BRILLIANT — **in·can·des·cence** \-ᵊns\ *n*
incandescent lamp *n* : a lamp in which an electrically heated filament emits light
in·can·ta·tion \ˌin-ˌkan-ˈtā-shən\ *n* : a use of spells or verbal charms spoken or sung as a part of a ritual of magic; *also* : a formula of words used in or as if in such a ritual
in·ca·pa·ble \(ˈ)in-ˈkā-pə-bəl\ *adj* : lacking ability or qualification for a particular purpose; *also* : UNQUALIFIED — **in·ca·pa·bil·i·ty** \(ˌ)in-ˌkā-pə-ˈbil-ət-ē\ *n*
in·ca·pac·i·tate \ˌin-kə-ˈpas-ə-ˌtāt\ *vb* **-tat·ed; -tat·ing** : to make incapable or unfit : DISQUALIFY, DISABLE
in·ca·pac·i·ty \ˌin-kə-ˈpas-ət-ē\ *n, pl* **-ties** : the quality or state of being incapable
in·car·cer·ate \in-ˈkär-sə-ˌrāt\ *vb* **-at·ed; -at·ing** : IMPRISON, CONFINE — **in·car·cer·a·tion** \(ˌ)in-ˌkär-sə-ˈrā-shən\ *n*
in·car·na·dine \in-ˈkär-nə-ˌdīn, -ˌdēn\ *vb* **-dined; -din·ing** : REDDEN
in·car·nate \in-ˈkär-nət, -ˌnāt\ *adj* **1** : having bodily and esp. human form and substance **2** : PERSONIFIED — **in·car·nate** \-ˌnāt\ *vb*
in·car·na·tion \ˌin-ˌkär-ˈnā-shən\ *n* **1** : the embodiment of a deity or spirit in an earthly form **2** *cap* : the union of divine and human natures in Jesus Christ **3** : a person showing a trait or typical character to a marked degree **4** : the act of incarnating : the state of being incarnate
incase *var of* ENCASE
in·cen·di·ary \in-ˈsen-dē-ˌer-ē\ *adj* **1** : of or relating to a deliberate burning of property **2** : tending to excite or inflame **3** : designed to kindle fires ⟨an ~ bomb⟩ — **incendiary** *n*
¹in·cense \ˈin-ˌsens\ *n* **1** : material used to produce a fragrant odor when burned **2** : the perfume or smoke from some spices and gums when burned
²in·cense \in-ˈsens\ *vb* **in·censed; in·cens·ing** : to make extremely angry
in·cen·tive \in-ˈsent-iv\ *n* [ME, fr. LL *incentivum*, fr. *incentivus* stimulating, fr. L, setting the tune, fr. *incinere* to set the tune, fr. *canere* to sing] : something that incites or is likely to incite to determination or action
in·cep·tion \in-ˈsep-shən\ *n* : BEGINNING, COMMENCEMENT
in·cer·ti·tude \(ˈ)in-ˈsərt-ə-ˌt(y)üd\ *n* **1** : UNCERTAINTY, DOUBT, INDECISION **2** : INSECURITY, INSTABILITY
in·ces·sant \(ˈ)in-ˈses-ᵊnt\ *adj* : continuing or flowing without interruption ⟨~ rains⟩ — **in·ces·sant·ly** *adv*
in·cest \ˈin-ˌsest\ *n* [ME, fr. L *incestum*, fr. *incestus* impure, fr. *castus* pure] : sexual intercourse between persons so closely related that marriage is illegal — **in·ces·tu·ous** \in-ˈses-chə-wəs\ *adj*
¹inch \ˈinch\ *n* [ME, fr. OE *ynce*, fr. L *uncia* twelfth part, inch, ounce] — see WEIGHT table
²inch *vb* : to move by small degrees
in·cho·ate \in-ˈkō-ət, ˈin-kə-ˌwāt\ *adj* [L *inchoatus*, pp. of *inchoare*, lit., to hitch up, fr. *cohum* strap fastening a plow beam to the yoke] : being only partly in existence or operation : INCOMPLETE, INCIPIENT
inch·worm \ˈinch-ˌwərm\ *n* : LOOPER
in·ci·dence \ˈin-səd-əns\ *n* : rate of occurrence or effect
¹in·ci·dent \ˈin-səd-ənt\ *n* **1** : OCCURRENCE, HAPPENING **2** : an action likely to lead to grave consequences esp. in diplomatic matters
²incident *adj* **1** : occurring or likely to occur esp. in connection with some other happening **2** : falling or striking on something ⟨~ light rays⟩
¹in·ci·den·tal \ˌin-sə-ˈdent-ᵊl\ *adj* **1** : subordinate, nonessential, or attendant in position or significance ⟨~ expenses⟩ **2** : CASUAL, CHANCE — **in·ci·den·tal·ly** \-ē\ *adv*
²incidental *n* **1** *pl* : minor items (as of expense) that are not individually accounted for **2** : something that is incidental
in·cin·er·ate \in-ˈsin-ə-ˌrāt\ *vb* **-at·ed; -at·ing** : to burn to ashes
in·cin·er·a·tor \in-ˈsin-ə-ˌrāt-ər\ *n* : a furnace for burning waste
in·cip·i·ent \in-ˈsip-ē-ənt\ *adj* : beginning to be or become apparent
in·cise \in-ˈsīz\ *vb* **in·cised; in·cis·ing** : to cut into : CARVE, ENGRAVE
in·ci·sion \in-ˈsizh-ən\ *n* : CUT, GASH; *esp* : a surgical wound
in·ci·sive \in-ˈsī-siv\ *adj* : impressively direct and decisive — **in·ci·sive·ly** *adv*
in·ci·sor \in-ˈsī-zər\ *n* : a tooth for cutting; *esp* : one of the cutting teeth in front of the canines of a mammal
in·cite \in-ˈsīt\ *vb* **in·cit·ed; in·cit·ing** : to arouse to action : stir up — **in·cite·ment** *n*
in·ci·vil·i·ty \ˌin-sə-ˈvil-ət-ē\ *n* **1** : DISCOURTESY, RUDENESS **2** : a rude or discourteous act
incl *abbr* including; inclusive
in·clem·ent \(ˈ)in-ˈklem-ənt\ *adj* : SEVERE, STORMY ⟨~ weather⟩ — **in·clem·en·cy** \-ən-sē\ *n*
in·cli·na·tion \ˌin-klə-ˈnā-shən\ *n* **1** : PROPENSITY, BENT; *esp* : LIKING **2** : BOW, NOD ⟨an ~ of the head⟩ **3** : a tilting of something **4** : SLANT, SLOPE
¹in·cline \in-ˈklīn\ *vb* **in·clined; in·clin·ing** **1** : BOW, BEND **2** : to be drawn toward an opinion or course of action **3** : to deviate from the vertical or horizontal : SLOPE **4** : INFLUENCE, PERSUADE
²in·cline \ˈin-ˌklīn\ *n* : SLOPE
inclose, inclosure *var of* ENCLOSE, ENCLOSURE
in·clude \in-ˈklüd\ *vb* **in·clud·ed; in·clud·ing** : to take in or comprise as a part of a whole ⟨the price ~s tax⟩ — **in·clu·sion** \in-ˈklü-zhən\ *n* — **in·clu·sive** \-ˈklü-siv\ *adj*
incog *abbr* incognito
¹in·cog·ni·to \ˌin-ˌkäg-ˈnēt-ō, in-ˈkäg-nə-ˌtō\ *adv or adj* [It, fr. L *incognitus* unknown, fr. *cognoscere* to know] : with one's identity concealed
²incognito *n, pl* **-tos** **1** : one appearing or living incognito **2** : the state or disguise of an incognito
in·co·her·ent \ˌin-kō-ˈhir-ənt, -ˈher-\ *adj* **1** : not sticking closely or compactly together : LOOSE **2** : not clearly or logically connected : RAMBLING — **in·co·her·ence** \-əns\ *n* — **in·co·her·ent·ly** *adv*
in·com·bus·ti·ble \ˌin-kəm-ˈbəs-tə-bəl\ *adj* : incapable of being burned — **incombustible** *n*
in·come \ˈin-ˌkəm\ *n* : a gain usu. measured in money that derives from labor, business, or property
income tax \ˌin-(ˌ)kəm-\ *n* : a tax on the net income of an individual or business concern
in·com·ing \ˈin-ˌkəm-iŋ\ *adj* : coming in ⟨the ~ tide⟩ ⟨~ freshmen⟩
in·com·men·su·rate \ˌin-kə-ˈmens-(ə-)rət, -ˈmench-(ə-)rət\ *adj* : not commensurate; *esp* : INADEQUATE
in·com·mode \ˌin-kə-ˈmōd\ *vb* **-mod·ed; -mod·ing** : INCONVENIENCE, DISTURB
in·com·mu·ni·ca·ble \ˌin-kə-ˈmyü-ni-kə-bəl\ *adj* : not

communicable : not capable of being communicated or imparted; *also* : UNCOMMUNICATIVE

in·com·mu·ni·ca·do \ˌin-kə-ˌmyü-nə-ˈkäd-ō\ *adv or adj* : without means of communication; *also* : in solitary confinement ⟨a prisoner held ~⟩

in·com·pa·ra·ble \(ˈ)in-ˈkäm-p(ə-)rə-bəl\ *adj* **1** : eminent beyond comparison : MATCHLESS **2** : not suitable for comparison

in·com·pat·i·ble \ˌin-kəm-ˈpat-ə-bəl\ *adj* : incapable of or unsuitable for association or use together ⟨~ colors⟩ ⟨temperamentally ~⟩ — **in·com·pat·i·bil·i·ty** \ˌin-kəm-ˌpat-ə-ˈbil-ət-ē\ *n*

in·com·pe·tent \(ˈ)in-ˈkäm-pət-ənt\ *adj* **1** : not legally qualified **2** : not competent : lacking sufficient knowledge, skill, or ability — **in·com·pe·tence** \-pət-əns\ *n* — **in·com·pe·ten·cy** \-ən-sē\ *n* — **incompetent** *n*

in·com·plete \ˌin-kəm-ˈplēt\ *adj* : lacking a part or parts : UNFINISHED, IMPERFECT — **in·com·plete·ly** *adv* — **in·com·plete·ness** *n*

in·com·pre·hen·si·ble \ˌin-ˌkäm-prē-ˈhen-sə-bəl\ *adj* : impossible to comprehend : UNINTELLIGIBLE

in·com·press·ible \ˌin-kəm-ˈpres-ə-bəl\ *adj* : not capable of or resistant to compression

in·con·gru·ent \ˌin-kən-ˈgrü-ənt, (ˈ)in-ˈkäŋ-grə-wənt\ *adj* : not congruent

in·con·gru·ous \(ˈ)in-ˈkäŋ-grə-wəs\ *adj* : not consistent with or suitable to the surroundings or associations — **in·con·gru·i·ty** \ˌin-kən-ˈgrü-ət-ē, -ˌkän-\ *n* — **in·con·gru·ous·ly** \(ˈ)in-ˈkäŋ-grə-wəs-lē\ *adv*

in·con·se·quen·tial \ˌin-ˌkän-sə-ˈkwen-chəl\ *adj* **1** : ILLOGICAL; *also* : IRRELEVANT **2** : of no significance : UNIMPORTANT — **in·con·se·quence** \(ˈ)in-ˈkän-sə-ˌkwens\ *n* — **in·con·se·quen·tial·ly** \ˌin-ˌkän-sə-ˈkwench-(ə-)lē\ *adv*

in·con·sid·er·able \ˌin-kən-ˈsid-ər-(ə-)bəl, -ˈsid-rə-bəl\ *adj* : SLIGHT, TRIVIAL

in·con·sid·er·ate \ˌin-kən-ˈsid-(ə-)rət\ *adj* : HEEDLESS, THOUGHTLESS; *esp* : not respecting the rights or feelings of others — **in·con·sid·er·ate·ly** *adv* — **in·con·sid·er·ate·ness** *n*

in·con·sol·able \ˌin-kən-ˈsō-lə-bəl\ *adj* : incapable of being consoled — **in·con·sol·ably** \-blē\ *adv*

in·con·spic·u·ous \ˌin-kən-ˈspik-yə-wəs\ *adj* : not readily noticeable — **in·con·spic·u·ous·ly** *adv*

in·con·stant \(ˈ)in-ˈkän-stənt\ *adj* : not constant : CHANGEABLE **syn** fickle, capricious, mercurial, unstable, volatile — **in·con·stan·cy** \-stən-sē\ *n* — **in·con·stant·ly** *adv*

in·con·test·able \ˌin-kən-ˈtes-tə-bəl\ *adj* : not contestable : INDISPUTABLE — **in·con·test·ably** \-ˈtes-tə-blē\ *adv*

in·con·ti·nent \(ˈ)in-ˈkänt-ᵊn-ənt\ *adj* **1** : lacking self-restraint **2** : unable to retain a bodily discharge (as urine) voluntarily — **in·con·ti·nence** \-ᵊn-əns\ *n*

in·con·tro·vert·ible \ˌin-ˌkän-trə-ˈvərt-ə-bəl\ *adj* : not open to question : INDISPUTABLE ⟨~ evidence⟩ — **in·con·tro·vert·ibly** \-blē\ *adv*

¹in·con·ve·nience \ˌin-kən-ˈvē-nyəns\ *n* **1** : something that is inconvenient **2** : the quality or state of being inconvenient

²inconvenience *vb* : to subject to inconvenience

in·con·ve·nient \ˌin-kən-ˈvē-nyənt\ *adj* : not convenient : causing trouble or annoyance : INOPPORTUNE — **in·con·ve·nient·ly** *adv*

in·cor·po·rate \in-ˈkȯr-pə-ˌrāt\ *vb* **-rat·ed; -rat·ing 1** : to unite closely or so as to form one body : BLEND **2** : to form, form into, or become a corporation **3** : to give material form to : EMBODY — **in·cor·po·ra·tion** \-ˌkȯr-pə-ˈrā-shən\ *n*

in·cor·po·re·al \ˌin-kȯr-ˈpōr-ē-əl\ *adj* : having no material body or form

in·cor·rect \ˌin-kə-ˈrekt\ *adj* **1** : INACCURATE, FAULTY **2** : not true : WRONG **3** : UNBECOMING, IMPROPER — **in·cor·rect·ly** \-ˈrek-(t)lē\ *adv* — **in·cor·rect·ness** \-ˈrek(t)-nəs\ *n*

in·cor·ri·gi·ble \(ˈ)in-ˈkȯr-ə-jə-bəl\ *adj* : incapable of being corrected, amended, or reformed — **in·cor·ri·gi·bil·i·ty** \(ˌ)in-ˌkȯr-ə-jə-ˈbil-ət-ē\ *n* — **in·cor·ri·gi·bly** \(ˈ)in-ˈkȯr-ə-jə-blē\ *adv*

in·cor·rupt·ible \ˌin-kə-ˈrəp-tə-bəl\ *adj* **1** : not subject to decay or dissolution **2** : incapable of being bribed or morally corrupted — **in·cor·rupt·ibil·i·ty** \-ˌrəp-tə-ˈbil-ət-ē\ *n* — **in·cor·rupt·ibly** \-ˈrəp-tə-blē\ *adv*

incr *abbr* increase; increased

¹in·crease \in-ˈkrēs, ˈin-ˌkrēs\ *vb* **in·creased; in·creas·ing 1** : to become greater : GROW **2** : to multiply by the production of young ⟨rabbits ~ rapidly⟩ **3** : to make greater — **in·creas·ing·ly** \-ˈkrē-siŋ-lē\ *adv*

²in·crease \ˈin-ˌkrēs, in-ˈkrēs\ *n* **1** : addition or enlargement in size, extent, or quantity : GROWTH **2** : something (as offspring, produce, or profit) that is added

in·cred·i·ble \(ˈ)in-ˈkred-ə-bəl\ *adj* : too extraordinary and improbable to be believed; *also* : hard to believe — **in·cred·ibil·i·ty** \(ˌ)in-ˌkred-ə-ˈbil-ət-ē\ *n* — **in·cred·i·bly** \(ˈ)in-ˈkred-ə-blē\ *adv*

in·cred·u·lous \(ˈ)in-ˈkrej-ə-ləs\ *adj* **1** : SKEPTICAL **2** : expressing disbelief — **in·cre·du·li·ty** \ˌin-kri-ˈd(y)ü-lət-ē\ *n* — **in·cred·u·lous·ly** *adv*

in·cre·ment \ˈiŋ-krə-mənt, ˈin-\ *n* **1** : the action or process of increasing esp. in quantity or value : ENLARGEMENT; *also* : QUANTITY **2** : something gained or added; *esp* : one of a series of regular consecutive additions — **in·cre·men·tal** \ˌiŋ-krə-ˈment-ᵊl, ˌin-\ *adj* — **in·cre·men·tal·ly** \-ᵊl-ē\ *adv*

in·crim·i·nate \in-ˈkrim-ə-ˌnāt\ *vb* **-nat·ed; -nat·ing** : to charge with or prove involvement in a crime or fault : ACCUSE — **in·crim·i·na·tion** \-ˌkrim-ə-ˈnā-shən\ *n* — **in·crim·i·na·to·ry** \-ˈkrim-(ə-)nə-ˌtōr-ē\ *adj*

incrust *var of* ENCRUST

in·crus·ta·tion \ˌin-ˌkrəs-ˈtā-shən\ *n* **1** : the act of encrusting : the state of being encrusted **2** : CRUST; *also* : something resembling a crust ⟨~ of habits⟩

in·cu·bate \ˈiŋ-kyə-ˌbāt, ˈin-\ *vb* **-bat·ed; -bat·ing** : to sit on eggs to hatch them; *also* : to keep (as eggs) under conditions favorable for development — **in·cu·ba·tion** \ˌiŋ-kyə-ˈbā-shən, ˌin-\ *n*

in·cu·ba·tor \ˈiŋ-kyə-ˌbāt-ər, ˈin-\ *n* : one that incubates; *esp* : an apparatus providing suitable conditions (as of warmth and moisture) for incubating something

in·cu·bus \ˈiŋ-kyə-bəs, ˈin-\ *n, pl* **-bi** \-ˌbī, -ˌbē\ *also* **-bus·es** [ME, fr. LL, fr. L *incubare* to lie on] **1** : a spirit supposed to work evil on persons in their sleep **2** : NIGHTMARE **3** : one that oppresses like a nightmare

in·cul·cate \in-ˈkəl-ˌkāt, ˈin-(ˌ)kəl-\ *vb* **-cat·ed; -cat·ing** [L *inculcare,* lit., to tread on, fr. *calcare* to trample, fr. *calx* heel] : to teach and impress by frequent repetitions or admonitions — **in·cul·ca·tion** \ˌin-(ˌ)kəl-ˈkā-shən\ *n*

in·cul·pa·ble \(ˈ)in-ˈkəl-pə-bəl\ *adj* : free from guilt : BLAMELESS

in·cul·pate \in-ˈkəl-ˌpāt, ˈin-(ˌ)kəl-\ *vb* **-pat·ed; -pat·ing** : to involve or implicate in guilt : INCRIMINATE

in·cum·ben·cy \in-ˈkəm-bən-sē\ *n, pl* **-cies 1** : something that is incumbent **2** : the quality of state of being incumbent **3** : the office or period of office of an incumbent

¹in·cum·bent \in-ˈkəm-bənt\ *n* : the holder of an office or position

²incumbent *adj* **1** : imposed as a duty **2** : occupying a specified office **3** : lying or resting on something else

incumber *var of* ENCUMBER

in·cu·nab·u·lum \ˌin-kyə-ˈnab-yə-ləm, iŋ-\ *n, pl* **-la** \-lə\ [NL, fr. L *incunabula,* pl., swaddling clothes, cradle, fr. *cunae* cradle] : a book printed before 1501

in·cur \in-ˈkər\ *vb* **in·curred; in·cur·ring 1** : to meet with (as an inconvenience) **2** : to become liable or subject to : bring down upon oneself

in·cur·able \(ˈ)in-ˈkyu̇r-ə-bəl\ *adj* : not subject to cure — **in·cur·abil·i·ty** \(ˌ)in-ˌkyu̇r-ə-ˈbil-ət-ē\ *n* — **incurable** *n* — **in·cur·ably** \(ˈ)in-ˈkyu̇r-ə-blē\ *adv*

in·cu·ri·ous \(ˈ)in-ˈkyu̇r-ē-əs\ *adj* : not curious or inquisitive

in·cur·sion \in-ˈkər-zhən\ *n* : a sudden usu. temporary invasion : RAID

in·cus \ˈiŋ-kəs\ *n, pl* **in·cu·des** \iŋ-ˈkyüd-(ˌ)ēz\ [NL, fr. L, anvil] : the middle of a chain of three small bones in the ear of a mammal

ind *abbr* **1** independent **2** index **3** industrial; industry

Ind *abbr* **1** Indian **2** Indiana

in·debt·ed \in-ˈdet-əd\ *adj* **1** : owing money **2** : owing gratitude or recognition to another — **in·debt·ed·ness** *n*

in·de·cent \(ˈ)in-ˈdēs-ᵊnt\ *adj* : not decent : UNBECOMING, UNSEEMLY; *also* : morally offensive — **in·de·cen·cy** \-ᵊn-sē\ *n* — **in·de·cent·ly** *adv*

in·de·ci·sion \ˌin-di-ˈsizh-ən\ *n* : a wavering between two or more possible courses of action : IRRESOLUTION

in·de·ci·sive \ˌin-di-ˈsī-siv\ *adj* **1** : not decisive : INCONCLUSIVE **2** : marked by or prone to indecision **3** : INDEFINITE — **in·de·ci·sive·ly** *adv* — **in·de·ci·sive·ness** *n*

in·de·co·rous \(ˈ)in-ˈdek-(ə-)rəs; ˌin-di-ˈkōr-əs\ *adj* : not decorous **syn** improper, unseemly, indecent, unbecoming, indelicate — **in·de·co·rous·ly** *adv* — **in·de·co·rous·ness** *n*

in·deed \in-ˈdēd\ *adv* **1** : without any question : TRULY — often used interjectionally to express irony, disbelief, or surprise **2** : in reality **3** : all things considered

indef *abbr* indefinite

in·de·fat·i·ga·ble \ˌin-di-ˈfat-i-gə-bəl\ *adj* : UNTIRING — **in·de·fat·i·ga·bly** \-blē\ *adv*

in·de·fea·si·ble \-ˈfē-zə-bəl\ *adj* : not capable of or not liable to being annulled, made void, or forfeited — **in·de·fea·si·bly** \-ˈfē-zə-blē\ *adv*

in·de·fin·able \-ˈfī-nə-bəl\ *adj* : incapable of being precisely described or analyzed

in·def·i·nite \(ˈ)in-ˈdef-(ə-)nət\ *adj* **1** : not defining or identifying ⟨*an* is an ~ article⟩ **2** : not precise : VAGUE **3** : having no fixed limit or amount — **in·def·i·nite·ly** *adv* — **in·def·i·nite·ness** *n*

in·del·i·ble \in-ˈdel-ə-bəl\ *adj* [ML *indelibilis,* fr. L *indelebilis,* fr. *delēre* to delete, destroy] **1** : not capable of being removed or erased ⟨~ impression⟩ **2** : making marks that cannot easily be removed ⟨an ~ pencil⟩ — **in·del·i·bly** \in-ˈdel-ə-blē\ *adv*

in·del·i·cate \(ˈ)in-ˈdel-i-kət\ *adj* : not delicate; *esp* : IMPROPER, COARSE, TACTLESS **syn** indecent, unseemly, indecorous, unbecoming — **in·del·i·ca·cy** \in-ˈdel-ə-kə-sē\ *n*

in·dem·ni·fy \in-ˈdem-nə-ˌfī\ *vb* **-fied; -fy·ing** [L *indemnis* unharmed, fr. *in-* not + *damnum* damage] **1** : to secure against hurt, loss, or damage **2** : to make compensation to for some loss or damage — **in·dem·ni·fi·ca·tion** \-ˌdem-nə-fə-ˈkā-shən\ *n*

in·dem·ni·ty \in-ˈdem-nət-ē\ *n, pl* **-ties 1** : security against hurt, loss, or damage; *also* : exemption from incurred penalties or liabilities **2** : something that indemnifies

¹in·dent \in-ˈdent\ *vb* [ME *indenten,* fr. MF *endenter,* fr. OF, fr. *dent* tooth, fr. L *dent-, dens*] **1** : INDENTURE **2** : to make a toothlike cut on the edge of **3** : to space in (as the first line of a paragraph) from the margin

²indent *vb* **1** : to force inward so as to form a depression : IMPRESS ⟨~ a pattern in metal⟩ **2** : to form a dent in

in·den·ta·tion \ˌin-ˌden-ˈtā-shən\ *n* **1** : NOTCH; *also* : a usu. deep recess (as in a coastline) **2** : the action of indenting : the condition of being indented **3** : DENT **4** : INDENTION 2

in·den·tion \in-ˈden-chən\ *n* **1** : the action of indenting : the condition of being indented **2** : the blank space produced by indenting

¹in·den·ture \in-ˈden-chər\ *n* **1** : a written certificate or agreement; *esp* : a contract binding one person (as an apprentice) to work for another for a given period of time — usu. used in pl. **2** : INDENTATION 1 **3** : DENT

²indenture *vb* **in·den·tured; in·den·tur·ing** : to bind (as an apprentice) by indentures

in·de·pen·dence \ˌin-də-ˈpen-dəns\ *n* : the quality or state of being independent : FREEDOM

Independence Day *n* : July 4 observed as a legal holiday in commemoration of the adoption of the Declaration of Independence in 1776

in·de·pen·dent \ˌin-də-ˈpen-dənt\ *adj* **1** : SELF-GOVERNING; *also* : not affiliated with a larger controlling unit **2** : not requiring or relying on something else or somebody else ⟨an ~ conclusion⟩ ⟨an ~ source of income⟩ **3** : not easily influenced : showing self-reliance ⟨an ~ mind⟩ **4** : not committed to a political party ⟨an ~ voter⟩ **5** : refusing or disliking to look to others for help ⟨too ~ to accept charity⟩ **6** : MAIN ⟨an ~ clause⟩ — **independent** *n* — **in·de·pen·dent·ly** *adv*

in·de·scrib·able \ˌin-di-ˈskrī-bə-bəl\ *adj* **1** : that cannot be described ⟨an ~ sensation⟩ **2** : being too intense or great for description — **in·de·scrib·ably** \-blē\ *adv*

in·de·ter·mi·nate \ˌin-di-ˈtərm-(ə-)nət\ *adj* **1** : VAGUE; *also* : not known in advance **2** : not limited in advance; *also* : not leading to a definite end or result — **in·de·ter·mi·na·cy** \-(ə-)nə-sē\ *n* — **in·de·ter·mi·nate·ly** *adv*

¹in·dex \ˈin-ˌdeks\ *n, pl* **in·dex·es** *or* **in·di·ces** \-də-ˌsēz\ **1** : POINTER, INDICATOR **2** : SIGN, TOKEN ⟨an ~ of character⟩ **3** : a guide for facilitating references; *esp* : an alphabetical list of items (as topics or names) treated in a printed work with the page number where each item may be found **4** : a list of restricted or prohibited material ⟨an ~ of forbidden books⟩ **5** *pl usu indices* : a number or symbol or expression (as an exponent) associated with another to indicate a mathematical operation or use or position in an arrangement or expansion **6** : a character ☞ used to direct attention (as to a note) **7** : INDEX NUMBER

²index *vb* **1** : to provide with or put into an index **2** : to serve as an index of **3** : to regulate by indexation

in·dex·ation \ˌin-ˌdek-ˈsā-shən\ *n* : a system of economic control in which a body of variables (as wages and interest) rise or fall at the same rate as an index of the cost of living

index finger *n* : FOREFINGER

in·dex·ing *n* : INDEXATION

index number *n* : a number used to indicate change in magnitude (as of cost) as compared with the magnitude at some specified time usu. taken as 100

index of refraction : the ratio of the velocity of radiation in the first of two media to its velocity in the second

in·dia ink \ˌin-dē-ə-\ *n, often cap 1st I* **1** : a black solid pigment used in drawing **2** : a fluid made from india ink

In·di·an \ˈin-dē-ən\ *n* **1** : a native or inhabitant of the subcontinent of India **2** : AMERICAN INDIAN — **Indian** *adj*

Indian corn *n* : a tall widely grown American cereal grass bearing seeds on long ears; *also* : its ears or seeds

Indian meal *n* : CORNMEAL

Indian paintbrush *n* : any of a genus of herbaceous plants with brightly colored bracts that are related to the snapdragon

Indian pipe *n* : a waxy white leafless saprophytic herb of Asia and the U.S.

Indian summer *n* : a period of mild weather in late autumn or early winter

In·dia paper \ˌin-dē-ə-\ *n* **1** : a thin absorbent paper used esp. for taking impressions (as of steel engravings) **2** : a thin tough opaque printing paper

indic *abbr* indicative

in·di·cate \ˈin-də-ˌkāt\ *vb* **-cat·ed; -cat·ing 1** : to point out or to **2** : to state briefly : show indirectly : SUGGEST — **in·di·ca·tion** \ˌin-də-ˈkā-shən\ *n* — **in·di·ca·tor** \ˈin-də-ˌkāt-ər\ *n*

[1]in·dic·a·tive \in-ˈdik-ət-iv\ *adj* **1** : of, relating to, or being a verb form that represents an act or state as a fact ⟨~ mood⟩ **2** : serving to indicate ⟨actions ~ of fear⟩

[2]indicative *n* **1** : the indicative mood of a language **2** : a form in the indicative mood

in·di·cia \in-ˈdish-(ē-)ə\ *n pl* **1** : distinctive marks **2** : postal markings often imprinted on mail or mailing labels

in·dict \in-ˈdīt\ *vb* **1** : to charge with an offense **2** : to charge with a crime by the finding of a grand jury — **in·dict·able** *adj* — **in·dict·ment** *n*

in·dif·fer·ent \in-ˈdif-ərnt, -ˈdif-(ə-)rənt\ *adj* **1** : UNBIASED, UNPREJUDICED **2** : of no importance one way or the other **3** : marked by no special liking for or dislike of something **4** : being neither excessive nor defective **5** : PASSABLE, MEDIOCRE **6** : being neither right nor wrong — **in·dif·fer·ence** \in-ˈdif-ərns, -ˈdif-(ə-)rəns\ *n* — **in·dif·fer·ent·ly** *adv*

in·dig·e·nous \in-ˈdij-ə-nəs\ *adj* : produced, growing, or living naturally in a particular region

in·di·gent \ˈin-di-jənt\ *adj* : IMPOVERISHED, NEEDY — **in·di·gence** \-jəns\ *n*

in·di·gest·ible \ˌin-dī-ˈjes-tə-bəl, -də-\ *adj* : not readily digested

in·di·ges·tion \-ˈjes-chən\ *n* : inadequate or difficult digestion : DYSPEPSIA

in·dig·nant \in-ˈdig-nənt\ *adj* : filled with or marked by indignation — **in·dig·nant·ly** *adv*

in·dig·na·tion \ˌin-dig-ˈnā-shən\ *n* : anger aroused by something unjust, unworthy, or mean

in·dig·ni·ty \in-ˈdig-nət-ē\ *n, pl* **-ties** : an offense against personal dignity or self-respect; *also* : humiliating treatment

in·di·go \ˈin-di-ˌgō\ *n, pl* **-gos** *or* **-goes** [It dial., fr. L *indicum,* fr. Gk *indikon,* fr. *indikos* Indic, fr. *Indos* India] **1** : a blue dye obtained from plants or synthesized **2** : a color between blue and violet

indigo bunting *n* : a common small finch of the eastern U.S. of which the male is largely indigo-blue

indigo snake *n* : a large harmless blue-black snake of the southern U.S.

in·di·rect \ˌin-də-ˈrekt, -dī-\ *adj* **1** : not straight ⟨an ~ route⟩ **2** : not straightforward and open ⟨~ methods⟩ **3** : not having a plainly seen connection ⟨an ~ cause⟩ **4** : not directly to the point ⟨an ~ answer⟩ — **in·di·rec·tion** \-ˈrek-shən\ *n* — **in·di·rect·ly** \-ˈrek-(t)lē\ *adv* — **in·di·rect·ness** \-ˈrek(t)-nəs\ *n*

in·dis·creet \ˌin-dis-ˈkrēt\ *adj* : not discreet : IMPRUDENT — **in·dis·cre·tion** \-dis-ˈkresh-ən\ *n*

in·dis·crim·i·nate \ˌin-dis-ˈkrim-ə-nət\ *adj* **1** : not marked by discrimination or careful distinction **2** : HAPHAZARD, RANDOM **3** : UNRESTRAINED **4** : JUMBLED, CONFUSED — **in·dis·crim·i·nate·ly** *adv*

in·dis·pens·able \ˌin-dis-ˈpen-sə-bəl\ *adj* : absolutely essential : REQUISITE — **in·dis·pens·abil·i·ty** \-ˌpen-sə-ˈbil-ət-ē\ *n* — **indispensable** *n* — **in·dis·pens·ably** \-ˈpen-sə-blē\ *adv*

in·dis·posed \-ˈpōzd\ *adj* **1** : slightly ill **2** : AVERSE — **in·dis·po·si·tion** \(ˌ)in-ˌdis-pə-ˈzish-ən\ *n*

in·dis·put·able \ˌin-dis-ˈpyüt-ə-bəl, (ˈ)in-ˌdis-pyət-\ *adj* : not disputable : UNQUESTIONABLE ⟨~ proof⟩ — **in·dis·put·ably** \-blē\ *adv*

in·dis·sol·u·ble \ˌin-dis-ˈäl-yə-bəl\ *adj* : not capable of being dissolved, undone, or broken : PERMANENT

in·dis·tinct \ˌin-dis-ˈtiŋkt\ *adj* **1** : not sharply outlined or separable : BLURRED, FAINT, DIM **2** : not readily distinguishable : UNCERTAIN — **in·dis·tinct·ly** *adv* — **in·dis·tinct·ness** *n*

in·dite \in-ˈdīt\ *vb* **in·dit·ed; in·dit·ing** : COMPOSE ⟨~ a poem⟩; *also* : to put in writing ⟨~ a letter⟩

in·di·um \ˈin-dē-əm\ *n* : a malleable silvery metallic chemical element — see ELEMENT table

indiv *abbr* individual

[1]in·di·vid·u·al \ˌin-də-ˈvij-(ə-w)əl\ *adj* **1** : of, relating to, or used by an individual ⟨~ traits⟩ **2** : being an individual : existing as an indivisible whole **3** : intended for one person ⟨an ~ serving⟩ **4** : SEPARATE ⟨~ copies⟩ **5** : having marked individuality ⟨an ~ style⟩ — **in·di·vid·u·al·ly** \-ē\ *adv*

[2]individual *n* **1** : a single member of a category : a particular person, animal, or thing **2** : PERSON ⟨a disagreeable ~⟩

in·di·vid·u·al·ism \ˌin-də-ˈvij-ə(-wə)-ˌliz-əm\ *n* **1** : EGOISM **2** : a doctrine that the interests of the individual are primary **3** : a doctrine holding that the individual has political or economic rights with which the state must not interfere

in·di·vid·u·al·ist \-ləst\ *n* **1** : one that pursues a markedly independent course in thought or action **2** : one that advocates or practices individualism — **individualist** *or* **in·di·vid·u·al·is·tic** \-ˌvij-ə(-wə)-ˈlis-tik\ *adj*

in·di·vid·u·al·i·ty \-ˌvij-ə-ˈwal-ət-ē\ *n, pl* **-ties** **1** : the sum of qualities that characterize and distinguish an individual from all others; *also* : PERSONALITY **2** : INDIVIDUAL, PERSON **3** : separate or distinct existence

in·di·vid·u·al·ize \-ˈvij-ə(-wə)-ˌlīz\ *vb* **-ized; -iz·ing** **1** : to make individual in character **2** : to treat or notice individually : PARTICULARIZE **3** : to adapt to the needs of an individual

in·di·vid·u·ate \ˌin-də-ˈvij-ə-ˌwāt\ *vb* **-at·ed; -at·ing** : to give individuality to : form into an individual — **in·di·vid·u·a·tion** \-ˌvij-ə-ˈwā-shən\ *n*

in·di·vis·i·ble \ˌin-də-ˈviz-ə-bəl\ *adj* : not divisible — **in·di·vis·i·bil·i·ty** \-ˌviz-ə-ˈbil-ət-ē\ *n* — **in·di·vis·i·bly** \-ˈviz-ə-blē\ *adv*

in·doc·tri·nate \in-ˈdäk-trə-ˌnāt\ *vb* **-nat·ed; -nat·ing** **1** : to instruct esp. in fundamentals or rudiments : TEACH **2** : to teach the beliefs and doctrines of a particular group — **in·doc·tri·na·tion** \(ˌ)in-ˌdäk-trə-ˈnā-shən\ *n*

In·do–Eu·ro·pe·an \ˌin-dō-ˌyür-ə-ˈpē-ən\ *adj* : of, relating to, or constituting a family of languages comprising those spoken in most of Europe and in the parts of the world colonized by Europeans since 1500 and also in Persia, the subcontinent of India, and some other parts of Asia

in·do·lent \ˈin-də-lənt\ *adj* [LL *indolens* insensitive to pain, fr. L *dolēre* to feel pain] **1** : slow to develop or heal ⟨~ ulcers⟩ **2** : LAZY — **in·do·lence** \-ləns\ *n*

in·dom·i·ta·ble \in-ˈdäm-ət-ə-bəl\ *adj* : UNCONQUERABLE ⟨~ courage⟩ — **in·dom·i·ta·bly** \-blē\ *adv*

In·do·ne·sian \ˌin-də-ˈnē-zhən\ *n* : a native or inhabitant of the Republic of Indonesia — **Indonesian** *adj*

in·door \ˌin-ˌdōr\ *adj* **1** : of or relating to the inside of a building **2** : living, located, or carried on within a building

in·doors \in-ˈdōrz\ *adv* : in or into a building

indorse *var of* ENDORSE

in·du·bi·ta·ble \(ˈ)in-ˈd(y)ü-bət-ə-bəl\ *adj* : UNQUESTIONABLE — **in·du·bi·ta·bly** \-blē\ *adv*

in·duce \in-ˈd(y)üs\ *vb* **in·duced; in·duc·ing** **1** : PERSUADE, INFLUENCE **2** : BRING ABOUT ⟨illness *induced* by overwork⟩ **3** : to produce (as an electric current) by induction **4** : to determine by induction; *esp* : to infer from particulars — **in·duc·er** *n*

in·duce·ment \in-ˈd(y)üs-mənt\ *n* **1** : something that induces : MOTIVE **2** : the act or process of inducing

in·duct \in-ˈdəkt\ *vb* **1** : to place in office **2** : to admit as a member **3** : to enroll for military training or service

in·duc·tance \in-ˈdək-təns\ *n* : a property of an electric circuit by which a varying current produces an electromotive force in that circuit or in a nearby circuit

---

in·duct·ee \(ˌ)in-ˌdək-ˈtē\ *n* : a person inducted into military service

in·duc·tion \in-ˈdək-shən\ *n* **1** : INSTALLATION; *also* : INITIATION **2** : the formality by which a civilian is inducted into military service **3** : inference of a generalized conclusion from particular instances; *also* : a conclusion so reached **4** : the act of causing or bringing on or about **5** : the process by which an electric current, an electric charge, or magnetism is produced in a body by the proximity of an electric or magnetic field

in·duc·tive \in-ˈdək-tiv\ *adj* : of, relating to, or employing induction

indue *var of* ENDUE

in·dulge \in-ˈdəlj\ *vb* **in·dulged; in·dulg·ing 1** : to give free rein to : GRATIFY ⟨~ a taste for exotic dishes⟩ **2** : to yield to the desire of ⟨~ a sick child⟩ **3** : to gratify one's taste or desire for ⟨~ in alcohol⟩

in·dul·gence \in-ˈdəl-jəns\ *n* **1** : remission of temporal punishment due in Roman Catholic doctrine for sins whose eternal punishment has been remitted by reception of the sacrifice of penance **2** : the act of indulging : the state of being indulgent **3** : an indulgent act **4** : the thing indulged in **5** : SELF-INDULGENCE — **in·dul·gent** \-jənt\ *adj* — **in·dul·gent·ly** *adv*

[1]**in·du·rate** \ˈin-d(y)ə-rət\ *adj* : physically or morally hardened

[2]**in·du·rate** \ˈin-d(y)ə-ˌrāt\ *vb* **-rat·ed; -rat·ing 1** : to make unfeeling, stubborn, or obdurate **2** : to make hardy : INURE **3** : to make hard **4** : to grow hard : HARDEN — **in·du·ra·tion** \ˌin-d(y)ə-ˈrā-shən\ *n*

in·dus·tri·al \in-ˈdəs-trē-əl\ *adj* : of, relating to, or having to do with industry — **in·dus·tri·al·ly** \-ē\ *adv*

in·dus·tri·al·ist \-ə-ləst\ *n* : a person owning or engaged in the management of an industry : MANUFACTURER

in·dus·tri·al·ize \in-ˈdəs-trē-ə-ˌlīz\ *vb* **-ized; -iz·ing** : to make or become industrial — **in·dus·tri·al·iza·tion** \-ˌdəs-trē-ə-lə-ˈzā-shən\ *n*

in·dus·tri·ous \in-ˈdəs-trē-əs\ *adj* : DILIGENT, BUSY — **in·dus·tri·ous·ly** *adv* — **in·dus·tri·ous·ness** *n*

in·dus·try \ˈin-(ˌ)dəs-trē\ *n, pl* **-tries 1** : DILIGENCE **2** : a department or branch of a craft, art, business, or manufacture; *esp* : one that employs a large personnel and capital **3** : a distinct group of productive enterprises **4** : manufacturing activity as a whole

in·dwell \(ˈ)in-ˈdwel\ *vb* : to exist within as an activating spirit, force, or principle

[1]**ine·bri·ate** \in-ˈē-brē-ˌāt\ *vb* **-at·ed; -at·ing** : to make drunk : INTOXICATE — **ine·bri·a·tion** \-ˌē-brē-ˈā-shən\ *n*

[2]**ine·bri·ate** \-ət\ *n* : one that is drunk; *esp* : an habitual drunkard

in·ef·fa·ble \(ˈ)in-ˈef-ə-bəl\ *adj* **1** : incapable of being expressed in words : INDESCRIBABLE ⟨~ joy⟩ **2** : UNSPEAKABLE ⟨~ disgust⟩ **3** : not to be uttered : TABOO ⟨the ~ name of Jehovah⟩ — **in·ef·fa·bly** \-blē\ *adv*

in·ef·face·able \ˌin-ə-ˈfā-sə-bəl\ *adj* : not effaceable : INERADICABLE

in·ef·fec·tive \ˌin-ə-ˈfek-tiv\ *adj* **1** : not effective : INEFFECTUAL **2** : INCAPABLE — **in·ef·fec·tive·ly** *adv*

in·ef·fec·tu·al \ˌin-ə-ˈfek-chə(-wə)l\ *adj* : not producing the proper or usual effect — **in·ef·fec·tu·al·ly** \-ē\ *adv*

in·ef·fi·cient \ˌin-ə-ˈfish-ənt\ *adj* **1** : not producing the effect intended or desired **2** : INCAPABLE, INCOMPETENT — **in·ef·fi·cien·cy** \-ˈfish-ən-sē\ *n* — **in·ef·fi·cient·ly** *adv*

in·el·e·gant \(ˈ)in-ˈel-i-gənt\ *adj* : lacking in refinement, grace, or good taste — **in·el·e·gance** \-gəns\ *n*

in·el·i·gi·ble \(ˈ)in-ˈel-ə-jə-bəl\ *adj* : not qualified to be chosen for an office — **in·el·i·gi·bil·i·ty** \(ˌ)in-ˌel-ə-jə-ˈbil-ət-ē\ *n* — **ineligible** *n*

in·eluc·ta·ble \ˌin-i-ˈlək-tə-bəl\ *adj* : not to be avoided, changed, or resisted

in·ept \in-ˈept\ *adj* **1** : lacking in fitness or aptitude : UNFIT **2** : FOOLISH **3** : being out of place : INAPPROPRIATE **4** : generally incompetent : BUNGLING — **in·ep·ti·tude** \in-ˈep-tə-ˌt(y)üd\ *n* — **in·ept·ly** *adv* — **in·ept·ness** *n*

in·equal·i·ty \ˌin-i-ˈkwäl-ət-ē\ *n* **1** : the quality of being unequal or uneven; *esp* : UNEVENNESS, DISPARITY, CHANGEABLENESS **2** : an instance of being unequal

in·er·rant \(ˈ)in-ˈer-ənt\ *adj* : INFALLIBLE

in·ert \in-ˈərt\ *adj* [L *inert-, iners* unskilled, idle, fr. *art-, ars* skill] **1** : powerless to move itself **2** : SLUGGISH **3** : lacking in active properties ⟨chemically ~⟩ — **in·ert·ly** *adv* — **in·ert·ness** *n*

in·er·tia \in-ˈər-sh(ē-)ə\ *n* **1** : a property of matter whereby it remains at rest or continues in uniform motion unless acted upon by some outside force **2** : INERTNESS, SLUGGISHNESS — **in·er·tial** \-shəl\ *adj*

in·es·cap·able \ˌin-ə-ˈskā-pə-bəl\ *adj* : incapable of being escaped : INEVITABLE — **in·es·cap·ably** \-blē\ *adv*

in·es·ti·ma·ble \(ˈ)in-ˈes-tə-mə-bəl\ *adj* **1** : incapable of being estimated or computed ⟨~ errors⟩ **2** : too valuable or excellent to be fully appreciated — **in·es·ti·ma·bly** \-blē\ *adv*

in·ev·i·ta·ble \in-ˈev-ət-ə-bəl\ *adj* : incapable of being avoided or evaded : bound to happen — **in·ev·i·ta·bil·i·ty** \(ˌ)in-ˌev-ət-ə-ˈbil-ət-ē\ *n* — **in·ev·i·ta·bly** \in-ˈev-ət-ə-blē\ *adv*

in·ex·act \ˌin-ig-ˈzakt\ *adj* **1** : not precisely correct or true : INACCURATE **2** : not rigorous and careful — **in·ex·act·ly** \-ˈzak-(t)lē\ *adv*

in·ex·cus·able \ˌin-ik-ˈskyü-zə-bəl\ *adj* : being without excuse or justification — **in·ex·cus·ably** \-blē\ *adv*

in·ex·haust·ible \ˌin-ig-ˈzȯ-stə-bəl\ *adj* **1** : incapable of being used up ⟨an ~ supply⟩ **2** : UNTIRING — **in·ex·haust·ibly** \-blē\ *adv*

in·ex·o·ra·ble \(ˈ)in-ˈeks-(ə-)rə-bəl\ *adj* : not to be moved by entreaty : RELENTLESS — **in·ex·o·ra·bly** *adv*

in·ex·pe·ri·ence \ˌin-ik-ˈspir-ē-əns\ *n* : lack of experience or of knowledge or proficiency gained by experience — **in·ex·pe·ri·enced** \-ənst\ *adj*

in·ex·pert \(ˈ)in-ˈek-ˌspərt\ *adj* : not expert : UNSKILLED — **in·ex·pert·ly** *adv*

in·ex·pi·a·ble \(ˈ)in-ˈek-spē-ə-bəl\ *adj* : not capable of being atoned for

in·ex·pli·ca·ble \ˌin-ik-ˈsplik-ə-bəl, (ˈ)in-ˈek-(ˌ)splik-\ *adj* : incapable of being explained or accounted for — **in·ex·pli·ca·bly** \-blē\ *adv*

in·ex·press·ible \-ˈspres-ə-bəl\ *adj* : not capable of being expressed — **in·ex·press·ibly** \-blē\ *adv*

in ex·tre·mis \ˌin-ik-ˈstrā-məs, -ˈstrē-\ *adv* : in extreme circumstances; *esp* : at the point of death

in·ex·tri·ca·ble \ˌin-ik-ˈstrik-ə-bəl, (ˈ)in-ˈek-(ˌ)strik-\ *adj* **1** : forming a maze or tangle from which it is impossible to get free **2** : incapable of being disentangled or untied : UNSOLVABLE — **in·ex·tri·ca·bly** \-blē\ *adv*

inf *abbr* **1** infantry **2** infinitive

in·fal·li·ble \(ˈ)in-ˈfal-ə-bəl\ *adj* **1** : incapable of error : UNERRING **2** : SURE, CERTAIN ⟨an ~ remedy⟩ — **in·fal·li·bil·i·ty** \(ˌ)in-ˌfal-ə-ˈbil-ət-ē\ *n* — **in·fal·li·bly** \(ˈ)in-ˈfal-ə-blē\ *adv*

in·fa·mous \ˈin-fə-məs\ *adj* **1** : having a reputation of the worst kind **2** : DISGRACEFUL — **in·fa·mous·ly** *adv*

in·fa·my \-mē\ *n, pl* **-mies 1** : evil reputation brought about by something grossly criminal, shocking, or brutal **2** : an extreme and publicly known criminal or evil act **3** : the state of being infamous

in·fan·cy \ˈin-fən-sē\ *n, pl* **-cies 1** : early childhood **2** : a beginning or early period of existence

in·fant \ˈin-fənt\ *n* [ME *enfaunt,* fr. MF *enfant,* fr. L *infant-, infans,* incapable of speech, young, fr. *fant-, fans,* prp. of *fari* to speak] : BABY; *also* : a person who is a legal minor

in·fan·ti·cide \in-ˈfant-ə-ˌsīd\ *n* : the killing of an infant; *also* : one who kills an infant

in·fan·tile \ˈin-fən-ˌtīl, -tᵊl, -ˌtēl\ *adj* : of or relating to infants; *also* : CHILDISH

infantile paralysis *n* : POLIOMYELITIS

in·fan·try \ˈin-fən-trē\ *n, pl* **-tries** [MF & It; MF *infanterie,* fr. It *infanteria,* fr. *infante* boy, foot soldier] : soldiers trained, armed, and equipped for service on foot — **in·fan·try·man** \-mən\ *n*

in·farct \ˈin-ˌfärkt\ *n* [L *infarctus,* pp. of *infarcire* to stuff] : an area of dead tissue (as of the heart wall) caused by blocking of local blood circulation — **in·farction** \in-ˈfärk-shən\ *n*

in·fat·u·ate \in-ˈfach-ə-ˌwāt\ *vb* **-at·ed; -at·ing** : to inspire with a foolish or extravagant love or admiration — **in·fat·u·a·tion** \-ˌfach-ə-ˈwā-shən\ *n*

in·fect \in-ˈfekt\ *vb* **1** : to contaminate with disease-producing matter **2** : to communicate a germ or disease to **3** : to cause to share one's feelings

in·fec·tion \in-ˈfek-shən\ *n* **1** : an act of infecting : the state of being infected **2** : a communicable disease; *also* : an infective agent (as a germ) — **in·fec·tious** \-shəs\ *adj* — **in·fec·tive** \-ˈfek-tiv\ *adj*

in·fe·lic·i·tous \ˌin-fi-ˈlis-ət-əs\ *adj* : not apt in application or expression — **in·fe·lic·i·ty** \-ət-ē\ *n*

in·fer \in-ˈfər\ *vb* **in·ferred; in·fer·ring** **1** : to derive as a conclusion from facts or premises **2** : GUESS, SURMISE **3** : to lead to as a conclusion or consequence **4** : HINT, SUGGEST **syn** deduce, conclude, judge, gather — **in·fer·ence** \ˈin-f(ə-)rəns\ *n* — **in·fer·en·tial** \ˌin-fə-ˈren-chəl\ *adj*

in·fe·ri·or \in-ˈfir-ē-ər\ *adj* **1** : situated lower down **2** : of low or lower degree or rank **3** : of little or less importance, value, or merit — **inferior** *n* — **in·fe·ri·or·i·ty** \(ˌ)in-ˌfir-ē-ˈȯr-ət-ē\ *n*

in·fer·nal \in-ˈfərn-ᵊl\ *adj* **1** : of or relating to hell ⟨~ fires⟩ **2** : HELLISH, FIENDISH ⟨~ schemes⟩ **3** : DAMNABLE, DAMNED — **in·fer·nal·ly** \-ē\ *adv*

in·fer·no \in-ˈfər-nō\ *n, pl* **-nos** [It, hell, fr. LL *infernus* hell, fr. L, lower] : a place or a state that resembles or suggests hell

in·fer·tile \(ˈ)in-ˈfərt-ᵊl\ *adj* : not fertile or productive : BARREN — **in·fer·til·i·ty** \ˌin-fər-ˈtil-ət-ē\ *n*

in·fest \in-ˈfest\ *vb* : to trouble by spreading or swarming in or over; *also* : to live in or on as a parasite — **in·fes·ta·tion** \ˌin-ˌfes-ˈtā-shən\ *n*

in·fi·del \ˈin-fəd-ᵊl, -fə-ˌdel\ *n* **1** : one who is not a Christian or opposes Christianity **2** : an unbeliever esp. with respect to a particular religion

in·fi·del·i·ty \ˌin-fə-ˈdel-ət-ē, -fī-\ *n, pl* **-ties** **1** : lack of belief in a religion **2** : UNFAITHFULNESS, DISLOYALTY

in·field \ˈin-ˌfēld\ *n* : the part of a baseball field inside the baselines — **in·field·er** *n*

in·fight·ing \ˈin-ˌfīt-iŋ\ *n* **1** : fighting or boxing at close quarters **2** : dissension or rivalry among members of a group

in·fil·trate \in-ˈfil-ˌtrāt, ˈin-(ˌ)fil-\ *vb* **-trat·ed; -trat·ing** **1** : to enter or filter into or through something **2** : to pass into or through by or as if by filtering or permeating — **in·fil·tra·tion** \ˌin-(ˌ)fil-ˈtrā-shən\ *n*

in·fi·nite \ˈin-fə-nət\ *adj* **1** : LIMITLESS, BOUNDLESS, ENDLESS ⟨~ space⟩ ⟨~ wisdom⟩ ⟨~ patience⟩ **2** : VAST, IMMENSE; *also* : INEXHAUSTIBLE ⟨~ wealth⟩ **3** : greater than any preassigned finite value however large ⟨~ number of positive integers⟩; *also* : extending to infinity ⟨~ plane surface⟩ — **infinite** *n* — **in·fi·nite·ly** *adv*

in·fin·i·tes·i·mal \(ˌ)in-ˌfin-ə-ˈtes-ə-məl\ *adj* : immeasurably or incalculably small : very minute — **in·fin·i·tes·i·mal·ly** \-ē\ *adv*

in·fin·i·tive \in-ˈfin-ət-iv\ *n* : a verb form having the characteristics of both verb and noun and in English usu. being used with *to*

in·fin·i·tude \in-ˈfin-ə-ˌt(y)üd\ *n* **1** : the quality or state of being infinite **2** : something that is infinite esp. in extent

in·fin·i·ty \in-ˈfin-ət-ē\ *n, pl* **-ties** **1** : the quality of being infinite **2** : unlimited extent of time, space, or quantity : BOUNDLESSNESS **3** : an indefinitely great number or amount

in·firm \in-ˈfərm\ *adj* **1** : deficient in vitality; *esp* : feeble from age **2** : not solid or stable : INSECURE

in·fir·ma·ry \in-ˈfərm-(ə-)rē\ *n, pl* **-ries** : a place for the care of the infirm or sick

in·fir·mi·ty \in-ˈfər-mət-ē\ *n, pl* **-ties** **1** : FEEBLENESS **2** : DISEASE, AILMENT **3** : a personal failing : FOIBLE

infl *abbr* influenced

in·flame \in-ˈflām\ *vb* **in·flamed; in·flam·ing** **1** : KINDLE **2** : to excite to excessive or uncontrollable action or feeling; *also* : INTENSIFY **3** : to affect or become affected with inflammation

in·flam·ma·ble \in-ˈflam-ə-bəl\ *adj* **1** : FLAMMABLE **2** : easily inflamed, excited, or angered : IRASCIBLE

in·flam·ma·tion \ˌin-flə-ˈmā-shən\ *n* : a bodily response to injury in which an affected area becomes red, hot, and painful and congested with blood

in·flam·ma·to·ry \in-ˈflam-ə-ˌtōr-ē\ *adj* **1** : tending to excite the senses or to arouse anger, disorder, or tumult : SEDITIOUS **2** : causing or accompanied by inflammation ⟨an ~ disease⟩

in·flate \in-ˈflāt\ *vb* **in·flat·ed; in·flat·ing** **1** : to swell with air or gas ⟨~ a balloon⟩ **2** : to puff up : ELATE ⟨*inflated* with pride⟩ **3** : to expand or increase abnormally ⟨~ prices⟩ — **in·flat·able** *adj*

in·fla·tion \in-ˈflā-shən\ *n* **1** : an act of inflating : the state of being inflated **2** : empty pretentiousness : POMPOSITY **3** : an abnormal increase in the volume of money and credit resulting in a substantial and continuing rise in the general price level

in·fla·tion·ary \-shə-ˌner-ē\ *adj* : of, characterized by, or productive of inflation

in·flect \in-ˈflekt\ *vb* **1** : to turn from a direct line or course : CURVE **2** : to vary a word by inflection **3** : to change or vary the pitch of the voice

in·flec·tion \in-ˈflek-shən\ *n* **1** : the act or result of curving or bending **2** : a change in pitch or loudness of the voice **3** : the change of form that words undergo to mark case, gender, number, tense, person, mood, or voice — **in·flec·tion·al** \-sh(ə-)nəl\ *adj*

in·flex·i·ble \(ˈ)in-ˈflek-sə-bəl\ *adj* **1** : UNYIELDING **2** : RIGID **3** : UNALTERABLE — **in·flex·i·bil·i·ty** \(ˌ)in-ˌflek-sə-ˈbil-ət-ē\ *n* — **in·flex·i·bly** \(ˈ)in-ˈflek-sə-blē\ *adv*

in·flex·ion \in-ˈflek-shən\ *chiefly Brit var of* INFLECTION

in·flict \in-ˈflikt\ *vb* : IMPOSE, AFFLICT; *also* : to give or deliver by or as if by striking — **in·flic·tion** \-ˈflik-shən\ *n*

in·flo·res·cence \ˌin-flə-ˈres-ᵊns\ *n* : the manner of development and arrangement of flowers on a stem; *also* : a flowering stem with its appendages : a flower cluster

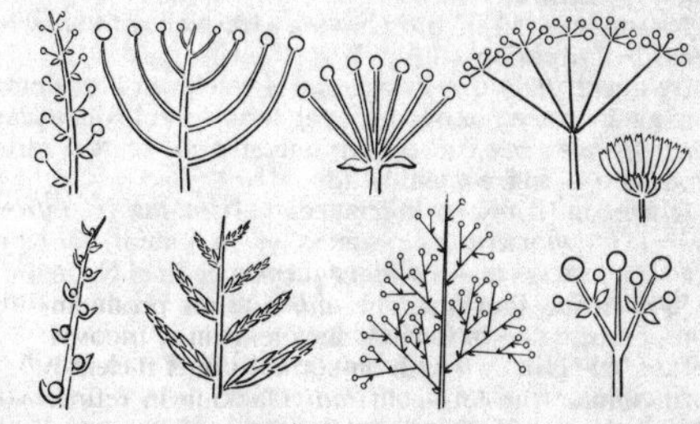

inflorescence

in·flow \ˈin-ˌflō\ *n* : a flowing in

[1]in·flu·ence \ˈin-ˌflü-əns\ *n* **1** : the act or power of producing an effect without apparent force or direct authority **2** : the power or capacity of causing an effect in indirect or intangible ways ⟨under the ~ of liquor⟩ **3** : a person or thing that exerts influence — **in·flu·en·tial** \ˌin-flü-ˈen-chəl\ *adj*

[2]influence *vb* **-enced; -enc·ing 1** : to affect or alter by influence : SWAY **2** : to have an effect on the condition or development of : MODIFY

in·flu·en·za \ˌin-flü-ˈen-zə\ *n* [It, lit., influence, fr. ML *influentia;* fr. the belief that epidemics were due to the influence of the stars] : an acute and very contagious virus disease marked by fever, prostration, aches and pains, and respiratory inflammation; *also* : any of various feverish usu. virus diseases typically with respiratory symptoms

in·flux \ˈin-ˌfləks\ *n* : a coming in

in·fo \ˈin-(ˌ)fō\ *n* : INFORMATION

in·fold \in-ˈfōld\ *vb* **1** : ENFOLD **2** : to fold inward or toward one another

in·form \in-ˈfórm\ *vb* **1** : to communicate knowledge to : TELL **2** : to give information or knowledge **3** : to act as an informer **syn** acquaint, apprise, advise, notify

in·for·mal \(ˈ)in-ˈfór-məl\ *adj* **1** : conducted or carried out without formality or ceremony ⟨an ~ party⟩ **2** : characteristic of or appropriate to ordinary, casual, or familiar use ⟨~ clothes⟩ — **in·for·mal·i·ty** \ˌin-fór-ˈmal-ət-ē, -fər-\ *n* — **in·for·mal·ly** \(ˈ)in-ˈfór-mə-lē\ *adv*

in·for·mant \in-ˈfór-mənt\ *n* : one who gives information : INFORMER

in·for·ma·tion \ˌin-fər-ˈmā-shən\ *n* **1** : the communication or reception of knowledge or intelligence **2** : knowledge obtained from investigation, study, or instruction : FACTS, DATA — **in·for·ma·tion·al** \-sh(ə-)nəl\ *adj*

in·for·ma·tive \in-ˈfór-mət-iv\ *adj* : imparting knowledge : INSTRUCTIVE

in·formed \in-ˈfórmd\ *adj* : EDUCATED, KNOWLEDGEABLE

informed consent *n* : consent to a medical procedure by a subject who understands what is involved

in·form·er \-ˈfór-mər\ *n* : one that informs; *esp* : a person who secretly provides information about the activities of another

in·frac·tion \in-ˈfrak-shən\ *n* [deriv. of L *infractus,* pp. of *infringere* to break off] : the act of infringing : VIOLATION

in·fra dig \ˌin-frə-ˈdig\ *adj* [short for L *infra dignitatem*] : being beneath one's dignity

in·fra·red \ˌin-frə-ˈred\ *adj* : being, relating to, or using radiation having wavelengths longer than those of red light — **infrared** *n*

in·fra·son·ic \-ˈsän-ik\ *adj* : having a frequency too low to hear ⟨~ vibration⟩

in·fre·quent \(ˈ)in-ˈfrē-kwənt\ *adj* **1** : seldom happening : RARE **2** : placed or occurring at considerable distances or intervals : OCCASIONAL **syn** uncommon, scarce, rare, sporadic — **in·fre·quent·ly** *adv*

in·fringe \in-ˈfrinj\ *vb* **in·fringed; in·fring·ing** [L *infringere*] **1** : VIOLATE, TRANSGRESS ⟨~ a patent⟩ **2** : ENCROACH, TRESPASS — **in·fringe·ment** *n*

in·fu·ri·ate \in-ˈfyu̇r-ē-ˌāt\ *vb* **-at·ed; -at·ing** : to make furious : ENRAGE — **in·fu·ri·at·ing·ly** \-ˌāt-iŋ-lē\ *adv*

in·fuse \in-ˈfyüz\ *vb* **in·fused; in·fus·ing 1** : to instill a principle or quality in : INTRODUCE **2** : INSPIRE, ANIMATE **3** : to steep (as tea) without boiling — **in·fu·sion** \-ˈfyü-zhən\ *n*

in·fus·ible \(ˈ)in-ˈfyü-zə-bəl\ *adj* : very difficult or impossible to fuse

[1]-ing \iŋ\ *vb suffix or adj suffix* — used to form the present participle ⟨sail*ing*⟩ and sometimes to form an adjective resembling a present participle but not derived from a verb ⟨swashbuckl*ing*⟩

[2]-ing *n suffix* : one of a (specified) kind

[3]-ing *n suffix* **1** : action or process ⟨sleep*ing*⟩ : instance of an action or process ⟨a meet*ing*⟩ **2** : product or result of an action or process ⟨an engrav*ing*⟩ ⟨earn*ings*⟩ **3** : something used in an action or process ⟨a bed cover*ing*⟩ **4** : something connected with, consisting of, or used in making (a specified thing) ⟨scaffold*ing*⟩ **5** : something related to (a specified concept) ⟨off*ing*⟩

in·gath·er·ing \ˈin-ˌgath-(ə-)riŋ\ *n* **1** : COLLECTION, HARVEST **2** : ASSEMBLY

in·ge·nious \in-ˈjēn-yəs\ *adj* **1** : marked by special aptitude at discovering, inventing, or contriving **2** : marked by originality, resourcefulness, and cleverness in conception or execution — **in·ge·nious·ly** *adv* — **in·ge·nious·ness** *n*

in·ge·nue *or* **in·gé·nue** \ˈan-jə-ˌnü, ˈän-; ˈaⁿ-zhə-\ *n* : a naive girl or young woman; *esp* : an actress representing such a person

in·ge·nu·ity \ˌin-jə-ˈn(y)ü-ət-ē\ *n, pl* **-ities** : skill or cleverness in planning or inventing : INVENTIVENESS

in·gen·u·ous \in-ˈjen-yə-wəs\ *adj* [L *ingenuus* native, freeborn, fr. *gignere* to beget] **1** : STRAIGHTFORWARD, FRANK **2** : NAIVE — **in·gen·u·ous·ly** *adv* — **in·gen·u·ous·ness** *n*

in·gest \in-ˈjest\ *vb* : to take in for or as if for digestion : ABSORB — **in·ges·tion** \-ˈjes-chən\ *n*

in·gle·nook \-ˌnu̇k\ *n* **1** : a corner by the fire or chimney **2** : a high-backed wooden settee placed close to a fireplace

in·glo·ri·ous \(ˈ)in-ˈglōr-ē-əs\ *adj* **1** : SHAMEFUL **2** : not glorious : lacking fame or honor — **in·glo·ri·ous·ly** *adv*

in·got \ˈiŋ-gət\ *n* : a mass of metal cast in a form convenient for storage or transportation

[1]in·grain \(ˈ)in-ˈgrān\ *vb* : to work indelibly into the natural texture or mental or moral constitution : IMBUE — **in·grained** *adj*

[2]in·grain \ˌin-ˌgrān\ *adj* **1** : made of fiber that is dyed before being spun into yarn **2** : made of yarn that is dyed before being woven or knitted **3** : INNATE — **ingrain** \ˈin-ˌgrān\ *n*

in·grate \ˈin-ˌgrāt\ *n* : an ungrateful person

in·gra·ti·ate \in-ˈgrā-shē-ˌāt\ *vb* **-at·ed; -at·ing** : to gain favor by deliberate effort

in·gra·ti·at·ing *adj* **1** : capable of winning favor : PLEASING ⟨an ~ smile⟩ **2** : FLATTERING ⟨an ~ manner⟩

in·grat·i·tude \(ˈ)in-ˈgrat-ə-ˌt(y)üd\ *n* : lack of gratitude : UNGRATEFULNESS

in·gre·di·ent \in-ˈgrēd-ē-ənt\ *n* : one of the substances that make up a mixture or compound : CONSTITUENT

in·gress \ˈin-ˌgres\ *n* : ENTRANCE, ACCESS

in·grow·ing \ˈin-ˌgrō-iŋ\ *adj* : growing or tending inward

in·grown \-ˌgrōn\ *adj* : grown in; *esp* : having the free tip or edge embedded in the flesh ⟨~ toenail⟩

in·gui·nal \ˈiŋ-gwən-ᵊl\ *adj* : of, relating to, or situated in the region of the groin

in·hab·it \in-ˈhab-ət\ *vb* : to live or dwell in — **in·hab·it·able** *adj*

in·hab·it·ant \in-ˈhab-ət-ənt\ *n* : a permanent resident in a place

in·hal·ant \in-ˈhā-lənt\ *n* : something (as a medicine) that is inhaled

in·ha·la·tor \ˈin-(h)ə-ˌlāt-ər\ *n* : a device that provides a mixture of carbon dioxide and oxygen for breathing

in·hale \in-ˈhāl\ *vb* **in·haled; in·hal·ing** : to draw in by breathing : draw air into the lungs — **in·ha·la·tion** \ˌin-(h)ə-ˈlā-shən\ *n*

in·hal·er \in-ˈhā-lər\ *n* : a device by means of which medicinal material is inhaled

in·here \in-ˈhiər\ *vb* **in·hered; in·her·ing** : to be inherent : BELONG

in·her·ent \in-ˈhir-ənt, -ˈher-\ *adj* : established as an essential part of something : INTRINSIC — **in·her·ent·ly** *adv*

in·her·it \in-ˈher-ət\ *vb* : to receive esp. from one's ances-

tors — **in·her·it·able** \-ə-bəl\ *adj* — **in·her·i·tance** \-ət-əns\ *n* — **in·her·i·tor** \-ət-ər\ *n*
in·hib·it \in-ˈhib-ət\ *vb* **1** : PROHIBIT, FORBID **2** : to hold in check : RESTRAIN
in·hi·bi·tion \ˌin-(h)ə-ˈbish-ən\ *n* **1** : PROHIBITION, RESTRAINT **2** : a usu. inner check on free activity, expression, or functioning
in–house \ˌin-ˌhau̇s, ˈin-ˈhau̇s\ *adj* : existing, originating, or carried on within a group or organization
in·hu·man \(ˈ)in-ˈ(h)yü-mən\ *adj* **1** : lacking pity or kindness : CRUEL, SAVAGE **2** : COLD, IMPERSONAL **3** : not worthy of or conforming to the needs of human beings **4** : of or suggesting a nonhuman class of beings — **in·hu·man·ly** *adv*
in·hu·mane \ˌin-(h)yü-ˈmān\ *adj* : not humane : INHUMAN 1
in·hu·man·i·ty \-ˈman-ət-ē\ *n, pl* **-ities** **1** : the quality or state of being cruel or barbarous **2** : a cruel or barbarous act
in·hu·ma·tion \ˌin-hyü-ˈmā-shən\ *n* : BURIAL
in·im·i·cal \in-ˈim-i-kəl\ *adj* **1** : being adverse often by reason of hostility **2** : HOSTILE, UNFRIENDLY — **in·im·i·cal·ly** \-ē\ *adv*
in·im·i·ta·ble \(ˈ)in-ˈim-ət-ə-bəl\ *adj* : not capable of being imitated
in·iq·ui·ty \in-ˈik-wət-ē\ *n, pl* **-ties** [ME *iniquite*, fr. MF *iniquité*, fr. L *iniquitas*, fr. *iniquus* uneven, fr. *aequus* equal] **1** : WICKEDNESS **2** : a wicked act — **in·iq·ui·tous** \-wət-əs\ *adj*
¹**ini·tial** \in-ˈish-əl\ *adj* **1** : of or relating to the beginning : INCIPIENT **2** : FIRST — **ini·tial·ly** \-ē\ *adv*
²**initial** *n* : the first letter of a word or name
³**initial** *vb* **-tialed** *or* **-tialled; -tial·ing** *or* **-tial·ling** \-ˈish-(ə-)liŋ\ : to affix an initial to
¹**ini·ti·ate** \in-ˈish-ē-ˌāt\ *vb* **-at·ed; -at·ing** **1** : START, BEGIN **2** : to induct into membership by or as if by special ceremonies **3** : to instruct in the first principles of something — **ini·ti·a·tion** \-ˌish-ē-ˈā-shən\ *n*
²**ini·tiate** \in-ˈish-(ē-)ət\ *n* **1** : a person who is undergoing or has passed an initation **2** : a person who is instructed or adept in some special field
ini·tia·tive \in-ˈish-ət-iv\ *n* **1** : an introductory step **2** : self-reliant enterprise **3** : a process by which laws may be introduced or enacted directly by vote of the people
ini·tia·to·ry \in-ˈish-(ē-)ə-ˌtōr-ē\ *adj* **1** : INTRODUCTORY **2** : tending or serving to initiate ⟨~ rites⟩
in·ject \in-ˈjekt\ *vb* **1** : to force into something ⟨~ serum with a needle⟩ **2** : to introduce into some situation or subject ⟨~ a note of suspicion⟩ — **in·jec·tion** \-ˈjek-shən\ *n*
in·junc·tion \in-ˈjəŋk-shən\ *n* **1** : ORDER, ADMONITION **2** : a court writ whereby one is required to do or to refrain from doing a specified act
in·jure \ˈin-jər\ *vb* **in·jured; in·jur·ing** \ˈinj-(ə-)riŋ\ : WRONG, DAMAGE, HURT **syn** harm, impair, mar, spoil
in·ju·ry \ˈinj-(ə-)rē\ *n, pl* **-ries** **1** : an act that damages or hurts : WRONG **2** : hurt, damage, or loss sustained — **in·ju·ri·ous** \in-ˈju̇r-ē-əs\ *adj*
in·jus·tice \(ˈ)in-ˈjəs-təs\ *n* **1** : violation of a person's rights : UNFAIRNESS, WRONG **2** : an unjust act or deed
¹**ink** \ˈiŋk\ *n* [ME *enke*, fr. OF, fr. LL *encaustum*, fr. L *encaustus* burned in, fr. Gk *enkaustos*, verbal of *enkaiein* to burn in] : a usu. liquid and colored material for writing and printing — **inky** *adj*
²**ink** *vb* : to put ink on; *esp* : SIGN
ink·blot test \-ˌblät-\ *n* : any of several psychological tests based on the interpretation of irregular figures
ink·horn \ˈiŋk-ˌhȯrn\ *n* : a small bottle (as of horn) for holding ink
in·kling \ˈiŋ-kliŋ\ *n* **1** : HINT, INTIMATION **2** : a vague idea
ink·stand \ˈiŋk-ˌstand\ *n* : INKWELL; *also* : a pen and ink stand
ink·well \-ˌwel\ *n* : a container for ink

in·laid \ˈin-ˈlād\ *adj* : decorated with material set into a surface
¹**in·land** \ˈin-ˌland, -lənd\ *n* : the interior of a country
²**inland** *adj* **1** *chiefly Brit* : not foreign : DOMESTIC ⟨~ revenue⟩ **2** : of or relating to the interior of a country
³**inland** *adv* : into or toward the interior
in–law \ˈin-ˌlȯ\ *n* : a relative by marriage
¹**in·lay** \(ˈ)in-ˈlā, ˈin-ˌlā\ *vb* **in·laid** \-ˈlād\; **in·lay·ing** : to set (one material into another) by way of decoration
²**in·lay** \ˈin-ˌlā\ *n* **1** : inlaid work **2** : a shaped filling cemented into a tooth
in·let \ˈin-ˌlet, -lət\ *n* **1** : a bay in the shore of a sea, lake, or river **2** : a narrow strip of water running into the land
in·mate \ˈin-ˌmāt\ *n* : a person who lives in the same house or institution with another; *esp* : a person confined to an institution (as a hospital or prison)
in me·di·as res \in-ˌmād-ē-əs-ˈrās\ *adv* [L, lit., into the midst of things] : in or into the middle of a narrative or plot
in me·mo·ri·am \ˌin-mə-ˈmōr-ē-əm\ *prep* : in memory of
in·most \ˈin-ˌmōst\ *adj* : deepest within : INNERMOST
inn \ˈin\ *n* : HOTEL, TAVERN
in·nards \ˈin-ərdz\ *n pl* **1** : the internal organs of a man or animal; *esp* : VISCERA **2** : the internal parts of a structure or mechanism
in·nate \in-ˈāt\ *adj* **1** : existing in, belonging to, or determined by factors present in an individual from birth : NATIVE **2** : belonging to the essential nature of something : INHERENT — **in·nate·ly** *adv*
in·ner \ˈin-ər\ *adj* **1** : situated farther in ⟨the ~ bark⟩ **2** : near a center esp. of influence ⟨the ~ circle⟩ **3** : of or relating to the mind or spirit
in·ner–di·rect·ed \ˌin-ər-də-ˈrek-təd, -(ˌ)dī-\ *adj* : directed in thought and action by one's own scale of values as opposed to external norms
inner ear *n* : the part of the ear that consists of a complex membranous labyrinth located in a cavity in the temporal bone and contains sense organs of hearing and of awareness of position in space
in·ner·most \ˈin-ər-ˌmōst\ *adj* : farthest inward : INMOST
in·ner·sole \ˈin-ər-ˌsōl\ *n* : INSOLE
in·ner·spring \ˌin-ər-ˌspriŋ\ *adj* : having coil springs inside a padded casing
inner tube *n* : TUBE 5
in·ning \ˈin-iŋ\ *n* : a baseball team's turn at bat; *also* : a division of a baseball game consisting of a turn at bat for each team
in·nings \ˈin-iŋz\ *n sing or pl* : a division of a cricket match
inn·keep·er \ˈin-ˈkē-pər\ *n* **1** : the landlord of an inn **2** : a hotel manager
in·no·cence \ˈin-ə-səns\ *n* **1** : BLAMELESSNESS; *also* : freedom from legal guilt **2** : GUILELESSNESS, SIMPLICITY; *also* : IGNORANCE
in·no·cent \-sənt\ *adj* [ME, fr. MF, fr. L *innocens*, fr. *nocens*, wicked, fr. *nocēre* to harm] **1** : free from guilt or sin : BLAMELESS **2** : harmless in effect or intention; *also* : CANDID **3** : free from legal guilt or fault : LAWFUL **4** : INGENUOUS **5** : DESTITUTE — **innocent** *n* — **in·no·cent·ly** *adv*
in·noc·u·ous \in-ˈäk-yə-wəs\ *adj* **1** : HARMLESS **2** : INOFFENSIVE, INSIPID
in·nom·i·nate \in-ˈäm-ə-nət\ *adj* : having no name; *also* : ANONYMOUS
in·no·vate \ˈin-ə-ˌvāt\ *vb* **-vat·ed; -vat·ing** : to introduce as or as if new : make changes — **in·no·va·tive** \-ˌvāt-iv\ *adj* — **in·no·va·tor** \-ˌvāt-ər\ *n*

in·no·va·tion \ˌin-ə-ˈvā-shən\ *n* **1** : the introduction of something new **2** : a new idea, method, or device

in·nu·en·do \ˌin-yə-ˈwen-dō\ *n, pl* **-dos** *or* **-does** [L, by hinting, fr. *innuere* to hint, fr. *nuere* to nod] : HINT, INSINUATION; *esp* : a veiled reflection on character or reputation

in·nu·mer·a·ble \in-ˈ(y)üm(-ə)-rə-bəl\ *adj* : too many to be numbered

in·oc·u·late \in-ˈäk-yə-ˌlāt\ *vb* **-lat·ed; -lat·ing** [ME *inoculaten* to insert a bud in a plant, fr. L *inoculare*, fr. *oculus* eye, bud] : to introduce something into; *esp* : to treat with a serum or antibody to prevent or cure a disease — **in·oc·u·la·tion** \-ˌäk-yə-ˈlā-shən\ *n*

in·op·er·a·ble \(ˈ)in-ˈäp-(ə-)rə-bəl\ *adj* **1** : not suitable for surgery **2** : not operable

in·op·er·a·tive \-ˈäp-(ə-)rət-iv, -ˈäp-ə-ˌrāt-\ *adj* : not functioning

in·op·por·tune \(ˌ)in-ˌäp-ər-ˈt(y)ün\ *adj* : happening or coming at the wrong time — **in·op·por·tune·ly** *adv*

in·or·di·nate \in-ˈȯrd-(ᵊ-)nət\ *adj* **1** : UNREGULATED, DISORDERLY **2** : EXTRAORDINARY, IMMODERATE ⟨an ~ curiosity⟩ — **in·or·di·nate·ly** *adv*

in·or·gan·ic \ˌin-ˌȯr-ˈgan-ik\ *adj* : being or composed of matter of other than plant or animal origin : MINERAL

in·pa·tient \ˈin-ˌpā-shənt\ *n* : a hospital patient who receives lodging and food as well as treatment

in·put \ˈin-ˌpu̇t\ *n* **1** : something put in **2** : power or energy put into a machine or system **3** : information fed into a data processing system or computer **4** : ADVICE, OPINION — **input** *vb*

in·quest \ˈin-ˌkwest\ *n* **1** : an official inquiry or examination esp. before a jury **2** : INQUIRY, INVESTIGATION

in·qui·etude \(ˈ)in-ˈkwī-ə-ˌt(y)üd\ *n* : UNEASINESS, RESTLESSNESS

in·quire \in-ˈkwī(ə)r\ *vb* **in·quired; in·quir·ing** **1** : to ask about : ASK **2** : INVESTIGATE, EXAMINE — **in·quir·er** *n* — **in·quir·ing·ly** *adv*

in·qui·ry \ˈin-ˌkwī(ə)r-ē, in-ˈkwī(ə)r-ē; ˈin-kwə-rē, ˈiŋ-\ *n, pl* **-ries** **1** : a request for information; *also* : a search for truth or knowledge **2** : a systematic investigation of a matter of public interest

in·qui·si·tion \ˌin-kwə-ˈzish-ən, ˌiŋ-\ *n* **1** : a judicial or official inquiry usu. before a jury **2** *cap* : a former Roman Catholic tribunal for the discovery and punishment of heretics **3** : a severe questioning — **in·quis·i·tor** \in-ˈkwiz-ət-ər\ *n* — **in·quis·i·to·ri·al** \-ˌkwiz-ə-ˈtōr-ē-əl\ *adj*

in·quis·i·tive \in-ˈkwiz-ət-iv\ *adj* **1** : given to examination or investigation ⟨an ~ mind⟩ **2** : unduly curious — **in·quis·i·tive·ly** *adv* — **in·quis·i·tive·ness** *n*

in re \in-ˈrā, -ˈrē\ *prep* : in the matter of

INRI *abbr* [L *Iesus Nazarenus Rex Iudaeorum*] Jesus of Nazareth, King of the Jews

in·road \ˈin-ˌrōd\ *n* **1** : INVASION, RAID **2** : ENCROACHMENT

in·rush \ˈin-ˌrəsh\ *n* : a crowding or flooding in

ins *abbr* **1** inches **2** insurance

INS *abbr* Immigration and Naturalization Service

in·sa·lu·bri·ous \ˌin-sə-ˈlü-brē-əs\ *adj* : UNWHOLESOME, NOXIOUS

ins and outs *n pl* : characteristic peculiarities : RAMIFICATIONS

in·sane \(ˈ)in-ˈsān\ *adj* **1** : not mentally sound : MAD; *also* : used by or for the insane **2** : FOOLISH, WILD — **in·sane·ly** *adv* — **in·san·i·ty** \in-ˈsan-ət-ē\ *n*

in·sa·tia·ble \(ˈ)in-ˈsā-shə-bəl\ *adj* : incapable of being satisfied

in·sa·tiate \(ˈ)in-ˈsā-sh(ē-)ət\ *adj* : INSATIABLE

in·scribe \in-ˈskrīb\ *vb* **1** : to write, engrave, or print esp. as a lasting record **2** : ENROLL **3** : to write, engrave, or print characters upon **4** : to dedicate to someone **5** : to stamp deeply or impress esp. on the memory **6** : to draw within a figure so as to touch in as many places as possible — **in·scrip·tion** \-ˈskrip-shən\ *n*

in·scru·ta·ble \in-ˈskrüt-ə-bəl\ *adj* : not readily comprehensible : MYSTERIOUS ⟨an ~ smile⟩ — **in·scru·ta·bly** \-blē\ *adv*

in·seam \ˈin-ˌsēm\ *n* : the seam on the inside of the leg of a pair of pants; *also* : the length of this seam

in·sect \ˈin-ˌsekt\ *n* [L *insectum*, fr. *insectus*, pp. of *insecare* to cut into, fr. *secare* to cut] : any of a major group of small usu. winged animals (as flies, bees, beetles, and moths) with three pairs of legs

in·sec·ti·cide \in-ˈsek-tə-ˌsīd\ *n* : a preparation for destroying insects — **in·sec·ti·cid·al** \(ˌ)in-ˌsek-tə-ˈsīd-ᵊl\ *adj*

in·sec·tiv·o·rous \ˌin-ˌsek-ˈtiv-(ə-)rəs\ *adj* : depending on insects as food

in·se·cure \ˌin-si-ˈkyu̇r\ *adj* **1** : UNCERTAIN **2** : UNPROTECTED, UNSAFE **3** : LOOSE, SHAKY **4** : INFIRM **5** : beset by fear or anxiety — **in·se·cure·ly** *adv* — **in·se·cu·ri·ty** \-ˈkyu̇r-ət-ē\ *n*

in·sem·i·nate \in-ˈsem-ə-ˌnāt\ *vb* **-nat·ed; -nat·ing** : to introduce semen into the genital tract of (a female) — **in·sem·i·na·tion** \-ˌsem-ə-ˈnā-shən\ *n*

in·sen·sate \(ˈ)in-ˈsen-ˌsāt, -sət\ *adj* **1** : INANIMATE **2** : lacking sense or understanding; *also* : FOOLISH **3** : BRUTAL, INHUMAN ⟨~ rage⟩

in·sen·si·ble \(ˌ)in-ˈsen-sə-bəl\ *adj* **1** : IMPERCEPTIBLE; *also* : SLIGHT, GRADUAL **2** : INANIMATE **3** : UNCONSCIOUS **4** : lacking sensory perception or ability to react ⟨~ to pain⟩ ⟨~ from cold⟩ **5** : APATHETIC, INDIFFERENT; *also* : UNAWARE ⟨~ of their danger⟩ **6** : MEANINGLESS **7** : lacking delicacy or refinement — **in·sen·si·bil·i·ty** \(ˌ)in-ˌsen-sə-ˈbil-ət-ē\ *n* — **in·sen·si·bly** \(ˈ)in-ˈsen-sə-blē\ *adv*

in·sen·tient \(ˈ)in-ˈsen-ch(ē-)ənt\ *adj* : lacking perception, consciousness, or animation — **in·sen·tience** \-ch(ē-)əns\ *n*

in·sep·a·ra·ble \(ˈ)in-ˈsep-(ə-)rə-bəl\ *adj* : incapable of being separated or disjoined — **in·sep·a·ra·bil·i·ty** \(ˌ)in-ˌsep-(ə-)rə-ˈbil-ət-ē\ *n* — **inseparable** *n* — **in·sep·a·ra·bly** \(ˈ)in-ˈsep-(ə-)rə-blē\ *adv*

¹in·sert \in-ˈsərt\ *vb* **1** : to put or thrust in ⟨~ a key in a lock⟩ ⟨~ a comma⟩ **2** : INTERPOLATE **3** : to set in (as a piece of fabric) and make fast

²in·sert \ˈin-ˌsərt\ *n* : something that is inserted or is for insertion; *esp* : written or printed material inserted (as between the leaves of a book)

in·ser·tion \in-ˈsər-shən\ *n* **1** : something that is inserted **2** : the act or process of inserting

in·set \ˈin-ˌset\ *vb* **inset** *or* **in·set·ted; in·set·ting** : to set in : INSERT — **inset** *n*

¹in·shore \ˈin-ˈshōr\ *adj* **1** : situated or carried on near shore **2** : moving toward shore

²inshore *adv* : to or toward shore

¹in·side \in-ˈsīd, ˈin-ˌsīd\ *n* **1** : an inner side or surface : INTERIOR **2** : inward nature, thoughts, or feeling **3** *pl* : VISCERA, ENTRAILS **4** : a position of power or confidence — **inside** *adj*

²inside *prep* **1** : in or into the inside of **2** : before the end of ⟨~ an hour⟩

³inside *adv* **1** : on the inner side **2** : in or into the interior

inside of *prep* : INSIDE

in·sid·er \in-ˈsīd-ər\ *n* : a person who is in a position of power or has access to confidential information

in·sid·i·ous \in-ˈsid-ē-əs\ *adj* [L *insidiosus*, fr. *insidiae* ambush, fr. *insidēre* to sit in, sit on, fr. *sedēre* to sit] **1** : SLY, TREACHEROUS **2** : SEDUCTIVE **3** : having a gradual and cumulative effect : SUBTLE — **in·sid·i·ous·ly** *adv* — **in·sid·i·ous·ness** *n*

in·sight \ˈin-ˌsīt\ *n* : the power or act of seeing into a situation : UNDERSTANDING, PENETRATION; *also* : INTUITION — **in·sight·ful** \ˈin-ˌsīt-fəl, in-ˈsīt-\ *adj*

in·sig·nia \in-ˈsig-nē-ə\ *or* **in·sig·ne** \-(ˌ)nē\ *n, pl* **-nia** *or* **-ni·as** : a distinguishing mark esp. of authority, office, or honor : BADGE, EMBLEM

in·sin·cere \ˌin-sin-ˈsiər\ *adj* : not sincere : HYPOCRITICAL — **in·sin·cere·ly** *adv* — **in·sin·cer·i·ty** \-ˈser-ət-ē\ *n*

in·sin·u·ate \in-ˈsin-yə-ˌwāt\ *vb* **-at·ed; -at·ing** [L *insinuare,* fr. *sinuare* to bend, curve, fr. *sinus* curve] **1** : to introduce gradually or in a subtle, indirect, or artful way **2** : to imply in a subtle or devious way — **in·sin·u·a·tion** \(ˌ)in-ˌsin-yə-ˈwā-shən\ *n*

in·sin·u·at·ing *adj* **1** : tending gradually to cause doubt, distrust, or change of outlook **2** : winning favor and confidence by imperceptible degrees

in·sip·id \in-ˈsip-əd\ *adj* **1** : lacking savor **2** : DULL, UNINTERESTING — **in·si·pid·i·ty** \ˌin-sə-ˈpid-ət-ē\ *n*

in·sist \in-ˈsist\ *vb* [MF or L; MF *insister,* fr. L *insistere* to stand upon, persist, fr. *sistere* to stand] : to take a resolute stand

in·sis·tence \in-ˈsis-təns\ *n* : the act of insisting; *also* : an insistent attitude or quality : URGENCY

in·sis·tent \in-ˈsis-tənt\ *adj* : disposed to insist — **in·sis·tent·ly** *adv*

in si·tu \in-ˈsī-tü\ *adv or adj* [L, in position] : in the natural or original position

insofar as \ˌin-sə-ˌfär-əz\ *conj* : to the extent or degree that

insol *abbr* insoluble

in·so·la·tion \ˌin-(ˌ)sō-ˈlā-shən\ *n* : solar radiation that has been received

in·sole \ˈin-ˌsōl\ *n* **1** : an inside sole of a shoe **2** : a loose thin strip placed inside a shoe for warmth or comfort

in·so·lent \ˈin-sə-lənt\ *adj* : contemptuous, rude, disrespectful, or brutal in behavior or language : OVERBEARING, BOLD — **in·so·lence** \-ləns\ *n*

in·sol·u·ble \(ˈ)in-ˈsäl-yə-bəl\ *adj* **1** : having or admitting of no solution or explanation **2** : difficult or impossible to dissolve — **in·sol·u·bil·i·ty** \(ˌ)in-ˌsäl-yə-ˈbil-ət-ē\ *n*

in·solv·able \(ˈ)in-ˈsäl-və-bəl\ *adj* : not capable of being solved

in·sol·vent \(ˈ)in-ˈsäl-vənt\ *adj* **1** : unable to pay one's debts **2** : insufficient to pay all debts charged against it ⟨an ~ estate⟩ **3** : IMPOVERISHED, DEFICIENT — **in·sol·ven·cy** \-vən-sē\ *n*

in·som·nia \in-ˈsäm-nē-ə\ *n* : prolonged and usu. abnormal sleeplessness

in·so·much as \ˌin-sə-ˌməch-əz\ *conj* : INASMUCH AS

insomuch that *conj* : to such a degree that : SO

in·sou·ci·ance \in-ˈsü-sē-əns, aⁿ-süs-yäⁿs\ *n* [F] : lighthearted unconcern — **in·sou·ci·ant** \in-ˈsü-sē-ənt, aⁿ-süs-yäⁿ\ *adj*

insp *abbr* inspector

in·spect \in-ˈspekt\ *vb* : to view closely and critically : EXAMINE — **in·spec·tion** \-ˈspek-shən\ *n* — **in·spec·tor** \-tər\ *n*

in·spi·ra·tion \ˌin-spə-ˈrā-shən\ *n* **1** : INHALATION **2** : the act or power of moving the intellect or emotions **3** : the quality or state of being inspired; *also* : something that is inspired **4** : an inspiring agent or influence — **in·spi·ra·tion·al** \-sh(ə-)nəl\ *adj*

in·spire \in-ˈspī(ə)r\ *vb* **in·spired; in·spir·ing 1** : INHALE **2** : to influence, move, or guide by divine or supernatural inspiration **3** : exert an animating, enlivening, or exalting influence upon **4** : AFFECT **5** : to communicate to an agent supernaturally; *also* : CREATE **6** : to bring about; *also* : INCITE **7** : to spread by indirect means — **in·spir·er** *n*

in·spir·it \in-ˈspir-ət\ *vb* : ANIMATE, HEARTEN

inst *abbr* **1** instant **2** institute; institution; institutional

in·sta·bil·i·ty \ˌin-stə-ˈbil-ət-ē\ *n* : lack of firmness or steadiness

in·stall *or* **in·stal** \in-ˈstȯl\ *vb* **in·stalled; in·stall·ing 1** : to place formally in office : induct into an office, rank, or order **2** : to establish in an indicated place, condition, or status **3** : to set up for use or service — **in·stal·la·tion** \ˌin-stə-ˈlā-shən\ *n*

¹in·stall·ment *or* **in·stal·ment** \in-ˈstȯl-mənt\ *n* : INSTALLATION

²installment *also* **instalment** *n* **1** : one of the parts into which a debt or sum is divided for payment **2** : one of several parts presented at intervals

¹in·stance \ˈin-stəns\ *n* **1** : INSTIGATION, REQUEST ⟨entered the contest at the ~ of friends⟩ **2** : EXAMPLE ⟨an ~ of heroism⟩ ⟨for ~⟩ **3** : an event or step that is part of a process or series **syn** case, illustration, sample, specimen

²instance *vb* **in·stanced; in·stanc·ing** : to mention as a case or example

¹in·stant \ˈin-stənt\ *n* **1** : MOMENT ⟨the ~ we met⟩ **2** : the present or current month ⟨your letter of the 10th ~⟩

²instant *adj* **1** : URGENT **2** : PRESENT, CURRENT **3** : IMMEDIATE ⟨~ relief⟩ **4** : partially prepared by the manufacturer to make final preparation easy ⟨~ cake mix⟩; *also* : immediately soluble in water ⟨~ coffee⟩

in·stan·ta·neous \ˌin-stən-ˈtā-nē-əs\ *adj* : done or occurring in an instant or without delay — **in·stan·ta·neous·ly** *adv*

in·stan·ter \in-ˈstant-ər\ *adv* : at once

in·stan·ti·ate \in-ˈstan-chē-ˌāt\ *vb* **-at·ed; -at·ing** : to represent by a concrete example — **in·stan·ti·a·tion** \-ˌstan-chē-ˈā-shən\ *n*

in·stant·ly \ˈin-stənt-lē\ *adv* : at once : IMMEDIATELY

in·state \in-ˈstāt\ *vb* : to establish in a rank or office : INSTALL

in·stead \in-ˈsted\ *adv* **1** : as a substitute or equivalent **2** : as an alternative : RATHER

instead of \in-ˌsted-ə(v), -ˌstid-\ *prep* : as a substitute for or alternative to

in·step \ˈin-ˌstep\ *n* : the arched part of the human foot in front of the ankle joint

in·sti·gate \ˈin-stə-ˌgāt\ *vb* **-gat·ed; -gat·ing** : to goad or urge forward : PROVOKE, INCITE ⟨~ a revolt⟩ — **in·sti·ga·tion** \ˌin-stə-ˈgā-shən\ *n* — **in·sti·ga·tor** \ˈin-stə-ˌgāt-ər\ *n*

in·still *also* **in·stil** \in-ˈstil\ *vb* **in·stilled; in·still·ing 1** : to cause to enter drop by drop **2** : to impart gradually

¹in·stinct \ˈin-ˌstiŋkt\ *n* **1** : a natural aptitude **2** : a largely inheritable and unalterable tendency of an organism to make a complex and specific response to environmental stimuli without involving reason; *also* : behavior originating below the conscious level — **in·stinc·tive** \in-ˈstiŋk-tiv\ *adj* — **in·stinc·tive·ly** *adv*

²in·stinct \in-ˈstiŋkt, ˈin-ˌstiŋkt\ *adj* : IMBUED, INFUSED

in·stinc·tu·al \in-ˈstiŋ(k)-chə(-wə)l\ *adj* : of, relating to, or based on instinct

¹in·sti·tute \ˈin-stə-ˌt(y)üt\ *vb* **-tut·ed; -tut·ing 1** : to establish in a position or office **2** : to originate and get established : ORGANIZE **3** : INAUGURATE, INITIATE

²institute *n* **1** : an elementary principle recognized as authoritative; *also, pl* : a collection of such principles and precepts **2** : an organization for the promotion of a cause : ASSOCIATION **3** : an educational institution **4** : a meeting for instruction or a brief course of such meetings

in·sti·tu·tion \ˌin-stə-ˈt(y)ü-shən\ *n* **1** : an act of originating, setting up, or founding **2** : an established practice, law, or custom **3** : a society or corporation esp. of a public character ⟨a charitable ~⟩; *also* : the building which houses it — **in·sti·tu·tion·al** \-ˈt(y)ü-sh(ə-)nəl\ *adj* — **in·sti·tu·tion·al·ize** \-ˌīz\ *vb* — **in·sti·tu·tion·al·ly** \-ē\ *adv*

instr *abbr* **1** instructor **2** instrument; instrumental

in·struct \in-ˈstrəkt\ *vb* [ME *instructen,* fr. L *instructus,* pp. of *instruere,* fr. *struere* to build] **1** : TEACH **2** : INFORM **3** : to give directions or commands to

in·struc·tion \in-ˈstrək-shən\ *n* **1** : LESSON, PRECEPT **2** : COMMAND, ORDER **3** *pl* : DIRECTIONS **4** : the action, practice, or profession of a teacher — **in·struc·tion·al** \-sh(ə-)nəl\ *adj*

in·struc·tive \in-ˈstrək-tiv\ *adj* : carrying a lesson : ENLIGHTENING

in·struc·tor \in-ˈstrək-tər\ *n* : one that instructs; *esp* : a college teacher below professorial rank — **in·struc·tor·ship** *n*

¹in·stru·ment \ˈin-strə-mənt\ *n* **1** : a device used to produce music **2** : a means by which something is done **3** : TOOL, UTENSIL **4** : a legal document (as a deed) **5** : a device used in navigating an airplane

²in·stru·ment \-ˌment\ *vb* : to equip with instruments

in·stru·men·tal \ˌin-strə-ˈment-ᵊl\ *adj* **1** : acting as an agent or means **2** : of, relating to, or done with an instrument **3** : relating to, composed for, or performed on a musical instrument

in·stru·men·tal·ist \-əst\ *n* : a player on a musical instrument

in·stru·men·tal·i·ty \ˌin-strə-mən-ˈtal-ət-ē, -ˌmen-\ *n, pl* **-ties** **1** : the quality or state of being instrumental **2** : MEANS, AGENCY

in·stru·men·ta·tion \ˌin-strə-mən-ˈtā-shən, -ˌmen-\ *n* **1** : the arrangement or composition of music for instruments (as for an orchestra) **2** : the use or application of instruments

instrument flying *n* : airplane navigation by instruments only

instrument panel *n* : DASHBOARD

in·sub·or·di·nate \ˌin-sə-ˈbȯrd-(ᵊ-)nət\ *adj* : disobedient to authority — **in·sub·or·di·na·tion** \-ˌbȯrd-ᵊn-ˈā-shən\ *n*

in·sub·stan·tial \ˌin-səb-ˈstan-chəl\ *adj* **1** : lacking substance or reality **2** : lacking firmness or solidity

in·suf·fer·able \(ˈ)in-ˈsəf-(ə-)rə-bəl\ *adj* : not to be endured : INTOLERABLE ⟨an ~ bore⟩ — **in·suf·fer·ably** \-blē\ *adv*

in·suf·fi·cient \ˌin-sə-ˈfish-ənt\ *adj* : not sufficient; *also* : INCOMPETENT — **in·suf·fi·cien·cy** \-ˈfish-ən-sē\ *n* — **in·suf·fi·cient·ly** *adv*

in·su·lar \ˈins-(y)ə-lər, ˈin-shə-lər\ *adj* **1** : of, relating to, or forming an island **2** : ISOLATED, DETACHED **3** : of or relating to island people **4** : NARROW, PREJUDICED — **in·su·lar·i·ty** \ˌins-(y)ə-ˈlar-ət-ē, ˌin-shə-ˈlar-\ *n*

in·su·late \ˈin-sə-ˌlāt\ *vb* **-lat·ed; -lat·ing** [L *insula* island] : ISOLATE; *esp* : to separate a conductor of electricity, heat, or sound from other conducting bodies by means of a nonconductor — **in·su·la·tion** \ˌin-sə-ˈlā-shən\ *n* — **in·su·la·tor** \ˈin-sə-ˌlāt-ər\ *n*

in·su·lin \ˈin-s(ə-)lən\ *n* : a pancreatic hormone essential for bodily use of sugars and used in the control of diabetes mellitus

insulin shock *n* : hypoglycemia associated with the presence of excessive insulin in the system

¹in·sult \in-ˈsəlt\ *vb* [MF or L; MF *insulter,* fr. L *insultare,* lit., to spring upon, fr. *saltare* to leap] : to treat with insolence or contempt : AFFRONT — **in·sult·ing·ly** \-iŋ-lē\ *adv*

²in·sult \ˈin-ˌsəlt\ *n* : a gross indignity

in·su·per·a·ble \(ˈ)in-ˈsü-p(ə-)rə-bəl\ *adj* : incapable of being surmounted, overcome, or passed over — **in·su·per·a·bly** \-blē\ *adv*

in·sup·port·able \ˌin-sə-ˈpōrt-ə-bəl\ *adj* **1** : UNENDURABLE **2** : UNJUSTIFIABLE

in·sur·able \in-ˈshu̇r-ə-bəl\ *adj* : capable of being or proper to be insured

in·sur·ance \in-ˈshu̇r-əns\ *n* **1** : the business of insuring persons or property **2** : coverage by contract whereby one party agrees to indemnify or guarantee another against loss by a specified contingent event or peril **3** : the state of being insured; *also* : means of insuring **4** : the sum for which something is insured

in·sure \in-ˈshu̇r\ *vb* **in·sured; in·sur·ing** **1** : to provide or obtain insurance on or for : UNDERWRITE **2** : to make certain : ENSURE

in·sured \in-ˈshu̇rd\ *n* : a person whose life or property is insured

in·sur·er \in-ˈshu̇r-ər\ *n* : one that insures; *esp* : a company issuing insurance

in·sur·gent \in-ˈsər-jənt\ *n* **1** : a person who revolts against civil authority or an established government : REBEL **2** : one who acts contrary to the policies and decisions of his political party — **in·sur·gence** \-jəns\ *n* — **in·sur·gen·cy** \-jən-sē\ *n* — **in·sur·gent** *adj*

in·sur·mount·able \ˌin-sər-ˈmau̇nt-ə-bəl\ *adj* : INSUPERABLE — **in·sur·mount·ably** \-blē\ *adv*

in·sur·rec·tion \ˌin-sə-ˈrek-shən\ *n* : an act or instance of revolting against civil authority or an established government — **in·sur·rec·tion·ist** *n*

int *abbr* **1** interest **2** interior **3** intermediate **4** internal **5** international **6** intransitive

in·tact \in-ˈtakt\ *adj* : untouched esp. by anything that harms or diminishes

in·ta·glio \in-ˈtal-yō\ *n, pl* **-glios** [It] : an engraving cut deeply into the surface of a hard material

in·take \ˈin-ˌtāk\ *n* **1** : an opening through which fluid enters **2** : the act of taking in **3** : the amount taken in

in·tan·gi·ble \(ˈ)in-ˈtan-jə-bəl\ *adj* **1** : incapable of being touched : not tangible : IMPALPABLE **2** : impossible to define or determine with certainty or precision : VAGUE — **intangible** *n* — **in·tan·gi·bly** \-blē\ *adv*

in·te·ger \ˈint-i-jər\ *n* [L, adj., whole, entire] : a number (as 1, 2, 3, 12, 432) that is not a fraction and does not include a fraction, is the negative of such a number, or is 0

in·te·gral \ˈint-i-grəl\ *adj* **1** : essential to completeness : CONSTITUENT **2** : formed as a unit with another part **3** : composed of parts that make up a whole **4** : ENTIRE

in·te·grate \ˈint-ə-ˌgrāt\ *vb* **-grat·ed; -grat·ing** **1** : to form, coordinate, or blend into a functioning or unified whole : UNITE **2** : to incorporate into a larger unit **3** : to end the segregation of and bring into common and equal membership in society or an organization; *also* : DESEGREGATE — **in·te·gra·tion** \ˌint-ə-ˈgrā-shən\ *n*

integrated circuit *n* : a group of tiny electronic components and their connections in or on a small slice of material (as silicon)

in·teg·ri·ty \in-ˈteg-rət-ē\ *n* **1** : SOUNDNESS **2** : adherence to a code of values : utter sincerity, honesty, and candor **3** : COMPLETENESS

in·teg·u·ment \in-ˈteg-yə-mənt\ *n* : a covering layer (as a skin or cuticle) of an organism

in·tel·lect \ˈint-ᵊl-ˌekt\ *n* **1** : the power of knowing : the capacity for knowledge **2** : the capacity for rational or intelligent thought esp. when highly developed **3** : a person with great intellectual powers

in·tel·lec·tu·al \ˌint-ᵊl-ˈek-ch(ə-w)əl\ *adj* **1** : of, relating to, or performed by the intellect : RATIONAL **2** : given to study, reflection, and speculation **3** : engaged in activity requiring the creative use of the intellect — **intellectual** *n* — **in·tel·lec·tu·al·ly** \-ē\ *adv*

in·tel·lec·tu·al·ism \-chə(-wə)-ˌliz-əm\ *n* : devotion to the exercise of intellect or to intellectual pursuits

in·tel·li·gence \in-ˈtel-ə-jəns\ *n* **1** : ability to learn and understand or to deal with new or trying situations **2** : relative intellectual capacity **3** : INFORMATION, NEWS **4** : an agency engaged in obtaining information esp. concerning an enemy or possible enemy; *also* : the information so gained

intelligence quotient *n* : a number expressing the intelligence of a person determined by dividing the person's mental age by his or her chronological age and multiplying by 100

in·tel·li·gent \in-ˈtel-ə-jənt\ *adj* : having or showing intelligence or intellect — **in·tel·li·gent·ly** *adv*

in·tel·li·gen·tsia \in-ˌtel-ə-ˈjent-sē-ə, -ˈgent-\ *n* [Russ *intelligentsiya,* fr. L *intelligentia* intelligence] : intellectual people as a group : the educated class

in·tel·li·gi·ble \in-ˈtel-ə-jə-bəl\ *adj* : capable of being understood or comprehended — **in·tel·li·gi·bil·i·ty** \-ˌtel-ə-jə-ˈbil-ət-ē\ *n* — **in·tel·li·gi·bly** \-ˈtel-ə-jə-blē\ *adv*

in·tem·per·ance \(ˈ)in-ˈtem-p(ə-)rəns\ *n* : lack of moderation; *esp* : habitual or excessive drinking of intoxicants — **in·tem·per·ate** \-p(ə-)rət\ *adj* — **in·tem·per·ate·ness** *n*

in·tend \in-ˈtend\ *vb* [ME *entenden, intenden,* fr. MF *entendre* to purpose, fr. L *indendere* to stretch out, to purpose, fr. *tendere* to stretch] **1** : to have in mind as a purpose or aim **2** : to design for a specified use or future

in·ten·dant \in-ˈten-dənt\ *n* : a governor or similar administrative official esp. under the French, Spanish, or Portuguese monarchies

¹in·tend·ed \-ˈten-dəd\ *adj* **1** : expected to be such in the future; *esp* : BETROTHED **2** : INTENTIONAL

²intended *n* : an affianced person

in·tense \in-ˈtens\ *adj* **1** : existing in an extreme degree **2** : very large : CONSIDERABLE **3** : strained or straining to the utmost **4** : feeling deeply; *also* : deeply felt — **in·tense·ly** *adv*

in·ten·si·fy \in-ˈten-sə-ˌfī\ *vb* **-fied; -fy·ing 1** : to make or become intense or more intensive **2** : to make more acute : SHARPEN **syn** aggravate, heighten, enhance, magnify — **in·ten·si·fi·ca·tion** \-ˌten-sə-fə-ˈkā-shən\ *n*

in·ten·si·ty \in-ˈten-sət-ē\ *n, pl* **-ties 1** : the quality or state of being intense **2** : degree of strength, energy, or force

¹in·ten·sive \in-ˈten-siv\ *adj* **1** : involving or marked by special effort **2** : serving to give emphasis — **in·ten·sive·ly** *adv*

²intensive *n* : an intensive word, particle, or prefix

intensive care *adj* : having special medical facilities, services, and equipment to meet the needs of gravely ill patients — **intensive care** *n*

¹in·tent \in-ˈtent\ *n* **1** : PURPOSE, AIM **2** : the state of mind with which an act is done : VOLITION **3** : MEANING, SIGNIFICANCE

²intent *adj* **1** : directed with keen or eager attention ⟨an ~ gaze⟩ **2** : ENGROSSED; *also* : DETERMINED — **in·tent·ly** *adv* — **in·tent·ness** *n*

in·ten·tion \in-ˈten-chən\ *n* **1** : a determination to act in a certain way **2** : PURPOSE, AIM, END **syn** intent, design, object, objective, goal

in·ten·tion·al \in-ˈtench-(ə-)nəl\ *adj* : done by intention or design : INTENDED — **in·ten·tion·al·ly** *adv*

in·ter \in-ˈtər\ *vb* **in·terred; in·ter·ring** [ME *enteren,* fr. OF *enterrer,* fr. L *in* in + *terra* earth] : BURY

in·ter·ac·tion \ˌint-ər-ˈak-shən\ *n* : mutual or reciprocal action or influence — **in·ter·act** \-ˈakt\ *vb*

in·ter·ac·tive \-ˈak-tiv\ *adj* **1** : mutually or reciprocally active **2** : allowing two-way electronic communications (as between a person and a computer) — **in·ter·ac·tive·ly** *adv*

in·ter alia \ˌint-ər-ˈā-lē-ə, -ˈäl-ē-\ *adv* : among other things

in·ter·atom·ic \ˌint-ər-ə-ˈtäm-ik\ *adj* : existing or acting between atoms

in·ter·breed \-ˈbrēd\ *vb* **-bred** \-ˈbred\; **-breed·ing** : to breed together

in·ter·ca·la·ry \in-ˈtər-kə-ˌler-ē\ *adj* **1** : INTERCALATED ⟨February 29 is an ~ day⟩ **2** : INTERPOLATED

in·ter·ca·late \-ˌlāt\ *vb* **-lat·ed; -lat·ing 1** : to insert (as a day) in a calendar **2** : to insert between or among existing elements or layers — **in·ter·ca·la·tion** \-ˌtər-kə-ˈlā-shən\ *n*

in·ter·cede \ˌint-ər-ˈsēd\ *vb* **-ced·ed; -ced·ing** : to act between parties with a view to reconciling differences

¹in·ter·cept \ˌint-ər-ˈsept\ *vb* **1** : to stop or interrupt the progress or course of **2** : to include (as part of a curve or solid) between two points, curves, or surfaces **3** : to gain possession of (an opponent's pass in football) — **in·ter·cep·tion** \-ˈsep-shən\ *n*

²in·ter·cept \ˈint-ər-ˌsept\ *n* : INTERCEPTION; *esp* : the interception of a target by an interceptor or missile

in·ter·cep·tor \ˌint-ər-ˈsep-tər\ *n* : a fighter plane or missile designed for defense against attacking bombers or missiles

in·ter·ces·sion \ˌint-ər-ˈsesh-ən\ *n* **1** : MEDIATION **2** : prayer or petition in favor of another — **in·ter·ces·sor** \-ˈses-ər\ *n* — **in·ter·ces·so·ry** \-ˈses-(ə-)rē\ *adj*

¹in·ter·change \ˌint-ər-ˈchānj\ *vb* **1** : to put each in the place of the other **2** : EXCHANGE **3** : to change places mutually — **in·ter·change·able** \-ˈchān-jə-bəl\ *adj* — **in·ter·change·ably** \-blē\ *adv*

²in·ter·change \ˈint-ər-ˌchānj\ *n* **1** : EXCHANGE **2** : a highway junction that by separated levels permits passage between highways without crossing traffic streams

in·ter·col·le·giate \ˌint-ər-kə-ˈlē-j(ē-)ət\ *adj* : existing or carried on between colleges

in·ter·com \ˈint-ər-ˌkäm\ *n* : INTERCOMMUNICATION SYSTEM

in·ter·com·mun·i·ca·tion system \ˌint-ər-kə-ˌmyü-nə-ˈkā-shən-\ *n* : a two-way communication system with microphone and loudspeaker at each station for localized use

in·ter·con·ti·nen·tal \-ˌkänt-ᵊn-ˈent-ᵊl\ *adj* **1** : extending among or carried on between continents ⟨~ trade⟩ **2** : capable of traveling between continents ⟨~ ballistic missiles⟩

in·ter·course \ˈint-ər-ˌkōrs\ *n* **1** : connection or dealings between persons or nations **2** : physical sexual contact between individuals that involves the genitalia of at least one person ⟨oral ~⟩ ⟨heterosexual ~⟩; *esp* : SEXUAL INTERCOURSE

in·ter·de·nom·i·na·tion·al \ˌint-ər-di-ˌnäm-ə-ˈnā-sh(ə-)nəl\ *adj* : involving different denominations

in·ter·de·part·men·tal \ˌint-ər-di-ˌpärt-ˈment-ᵊl, -ˌdē-\ *adj* : carried on between or involving different departments (as of a college)

in·ter·de·pen·dent \ˌint-ər-di-ˈpen-dənt\ *adj* : dependent upon one another — **in·ter·de·pen·dence** \-dəns\ *n*

in·ter·dict \ˌint-ər-ˈdikt\ *vb* **1** : to prohibit by decree **2** : to destroy, cut, or damage (as an enemy line of supply) — **in·ter·dic·tion** \-ˈdik-shən\ *n*

in·ter·dis·ci·plin·ary \-ˈdis-ə-plə-ˌner-ē\ *adj* : involving two or more academic, scientific, or artistic disciplines

¹in·ter·est \ˈin-t(ə-)rəst, -tə-ˌrest\ *n* **1** : right, title, or legal share in something **2** : a charge for borrowed money that is generally a percentage of the amount borrowed : the return received by capital on its investment **3** : WELFARE, BENEFIT; *also* : SELF-INTEREST **4** *pl* : a group financially interested in an industry or enterprise **5** : CURIOSITY, CONCERN **6** : readiness to be concerned with or moved by an object or class of objects **7** : a quality in a thing that arouses interest

²interest *vb* **1** : to persuade to participate or engage **2** : to engage the attention of

in·ter·est·ing *adj* : holding the attention — **in·ter·est·ing·ly** *adv*

in·ter·face \ˈint-ər-ˌfās\ *n* **1** : a surface forming a common boundary of two bodies, spaces, or phases ⟨an oil-water ~⟩ **2** : the place at which two independent systems meet and act on or communicate with each other ⟨the man-machine ~⟩ **3** : the means by which interaction or communication is effected at an interface — **in·ter·fa·cial** \ˌint-ər-ˈfā-shəl\ *adj*

in·ter·faith \ˌint-ər-ˈfāth\ *adj* : involving persons of different religious faiths

in·ter·fere \ˌint-ə(r)-ˈfiər\ *vb* **-fered; -fer·ing** [MF *(s')entreferir* to strike one another, fr. OF, fr. *entre* between, among + *ferir* to strike, fr. L *ferire*] **1** : to come in collision or be in opposition : CLASH **2** : to enter into the affairs of others **3** : to affect one another

in·ter·fer·ence \-ˈfir-əns\ *n* **1** : the act or process of interfering **2** : something that interferes : OBSTRUCTION **3** : the mutual effect on meeting of two waves resulting in areas of increased and decreased amplitude **4** : the blocking of an opponent in football to make way for the ballcarrier **5** : the illegal hindering of an opponent in sports

in·ter·fer·om·e·ter \ˌint-ə(r)-fə-ˈräm-ət-ər\ *n* : a device that uses the interference of waves for making precise measurements — **in·ter·fer·om·e·try** \-fə-ˈräm-ə-trē\ *n*

in·ter·fer·on \ˌint-ər-ˈfiər-ˌän\ *n* : an antiviral protein of low molecular weight produced usu. by animal cells in response to a virus, a parasite in the cell, or a chemical

in·ter·fuse \ˌint-ər-ˈfyüz\ *vb* **1** : to combine by fusing : BLEND **2** : INFUSE

in·ter·ga·lac·tic \ˌint-ər-gə-ˈlak-tik\ *adj* : relating to or situated in the spaces between galaxies

in·ter·gla·cial \-ˈglā-shəl\ *adj* : occurring between successive glaciations

in·ter·gov·ern·men·tal \-ˌgəv-ər(n)-ˈment-ᵊl\ *adj* : existing or occurring between two governments or levels of government

in·ter·im \ˈin-tə-rəm\ *n* [L, adv., meanwhile, fr. *inter* between] : a time intervening : INTERVAL — **interim** *adj*

[1]**in·te·ri·or** \in-ˈtir-ē-ər\ *adj* **1** : lying, occurring, or functioning within the limiting boundaries : INSIDE, INNER **2** : remote from the surface, border, or shore : INLAND

[2]**interior** *n* **1** : INSIDE **2** : the inland part (as of a country) **3** : the internal affairs of a state or nation **4** : a scene or view of the interior of a building

interior decoration *n* : INTERIOR DESIGN — **interior decorator** *n*

interior design *n* : the art or practice of planning and supervising the design and execution of architectural interiors and their furnishings — **interior designer** *n*

interj *abbr* interjection

in·ter·ject \ˌint-ər-ˈjekt\ *vb* : to throw in between or among other things

in·ter·jec·tion \ˌint-ər-ˈjek-shən\ *n* : an exclamatory word (as *ouch*) — **in·ter·jec·tion·al·ly** \-sh(ə-)nəl-ē\ *adv*

in·ter·lace \ˌint-ər-ˈlās\ *vb* **1** : to unite by or as if by lacing together : INTERWEAVE **2** : INTERSPERSE

in·ter·lard \ˌint-ər-ˈlärd\ *vb* : to insert or introduce at intervals : INTERSPERSE

in·ter·leave \ˌint-ər-ˈlēv\ *vb* **-leaved; -leav·ing** : to arrange in alternate layers

[1]**in·ter·line** \ˌint-ər-ˈlīn\ *vb* : to insert between lines already written or printed

[2]**interline** *vb* : to provide (as a coat) with an interlining

in·ter·lin·ear \ˌint-ər-ˈlin-ē-ər\ *adj* : inserted between lines already written or printed ⟨an ~ translation of a text⟩

in·ter·lin·ing \ˈint-ər-ˌlī-niŋ\ *n* : a lining (as of a coat) between the ordinary lining and the outside fabric

in·ter·link \ˌint-ər-ˈliŋk\ *vb* : to link together

in·ter·lock \ˌint-ər-ˈläk\ *vb* **1** : to engage or interlace together : lock together : UNITE **2** : to connect in such a way that action of one part affects action of another part — **in·ter·lock** \ˈint-ər-ˌläk\ *n*

in·ter·loc·u·tor \ˌint-ər-ˈläk-yət-ər\ *n* : one who takes part in dialogue or conversation

in·ter·loc·u·to·ry \-yə-ˌtōr-ē\ *adj* : pronounced during the progress of a legal action and having only provisional force ⟨an ~ decree⟩

in·ter·lope \ˌint-ər-ˈlōp\ *vb* **-loped; -lop·ing** **1** : to encroach on the rights (as in trade) of others **2** : INTRUDE, INTERFERE — **in·ter·lop·er** *n*

in·ter·lude \ˈint-ər-ˌlüd\ *n* **1** : a usu. short simple play or dramatic entertainment **2** : an intervening period, space, or event **3** : a short piece of music inserted between the parts of a longer composition or a religious service

in·ter·mar·riage \ˌint-ər-ˈmar-ij\ *n* : marriage between members of different groups; *also* : marriage within one's own group

in·ter·mar·ry \-ˈmar-ē\ *vb* **1** : to marry each other **2** : to marry within a group **3** : to become connected by intermarriage

in·ter·med·dle \ˌint-ər-ˈmed-ᵊl\ *vb* : MEDDLE, INTERFERE

[1]**in·ter·me·di·ary** \ˌint-ər-ˈmēd-ē-ˌer-ē\ *adj* **1** : INTERMEDIATE **2** : acting as a mediator

[2]**intermediary** *n, pl* **-ar·ies** : MEDIATOR, GO-BETWEEN

[1]**in·ter·me·di·ate** \ˌint-ər-ˈmēd-ē-ət\ *adj* : being or occurring at the middle place or degree or between extremes

[2]**intermediate** *n* **1** : an intermediate term, object, or class **2** : INTERMEDIARY

intermediate school *n* **1** : JUNIOR HIGH SCHOOL **2** : a school usu. comprising grades 4–6

in·ter·ment \in-ˈtər-mənt\ *n* : BURIAL

in·ter·mez·zo \ˌint-ər-ˈmet-sō, -ˈmed-zō\ *n, pl* **-zi** \-sē, -zē\ *or* **-zos** [It, deriv. of L *intermedius* intermediate] : a short movement connecting major sections of an extended musical work (as a symphony); *also* : a short independent instrumental composition

in·ter·mi·na·ble \(ˈ)in-ˈtərm-(ə-)nə-bəl\ *adj* : ENDLESS; *esp* : wearisomely protracted — **in·ter·mi·na·bly** \-blē\ *adv*

in·ter·min·gle \ˌint-ər-ˈmiŋ-gəl\ *vb* : to mingle or mix together

in·ter·mis·sion \ˌint-ər-ˈmish-ən\ *n* **1** : INTERRUPTION, BREAK **2** : a temporary halt esp. in a public performance

in·ter·mit \-ˈmit\ *vb* **-mit·ted; -mit·ting** : DISCONTINUE; *also* : to be intermittent

in·ter·mit·tent \-ˈmit-ᵊnt\ *adj* : coming and going at intervals **syn** recurrent, periodic, alternate — **in·ter·mit·tent·ly** *adv*

in·ter·mix \ˌint-ər-ˈmiks\ *vb* : to mix together : INTERMINGLE — **in·ter·mix·ture** \-ˈmiks-chər\ *n*

in·ter·mo·lec·u·lar \-mə-ˈlek-yə-lər\ *adj* : existing or acting between molecules

in·ter·mon·tane \ˌint-ər-ˈmän-ˌtān\ *or* **in·ter·mont** \ˈint-ər-ˌmänt\ *adj* : situated between mountains

[1]**in·tern** \ˈin-ˌtərn, in-ˈtərn\ *vb* : to confine or impound esp. during a war — **in·tern·ee** \(ˌ)in-ˌtər-ˈnē\ *n* — **in·tern·ment** \in-ˈtərn-mənt\ *n*

[2]**in·tern** *or* **in·terne** \ˈin-ˌtərn\ *n* : an advanced student or recent graduate (as in medicine) gaining supervised practical experience — **in·tern·ship** *n*

[3]**in·tern** \ˈin-ˌtərn\ *vb* : to act as an intern

in·ter·nal \in-ˈtərn-ᵊl\ *adj* **1** : INWARD, INTERIOR **2** : having to do with or situated in the inside of the body ⟨~ pain⟩ **3** : of or relating to the domestic affairs of a country or state ⟨~ revenue⟩ **4** : of, relating to, or existing within the mind **5** : INTRINSIC, INHERENT — **in·ter·nal·ly** \-ē\ *adv*

internal–combustion engine *n* : a heat engine in which the combustion that generates the heat takes place inside the engine proper

internal medicine *n* : a branch of medicine that deals with the diagnosis and treatment of nonsurgical diseases

[1]**in·ter·na·tion·al** \ˌint-ər-ˈnash-(ə-)nəl\ *adj* **1** : common to or affecting two or more nations ⟨~ trade⟩ **2** : of, relating to, or constituting a group having members in two or more nations — **in·ter·na·tion·al·ly** \-ē\ *adv*

[2]**international** *n* : one that is international; *esp* : an organization of international scope

in·ter·na·tion·al·ism \-ˈnash-(ə-)nəl-ˌiz-əm\ *n* : a policy of political and economic cooperation among nations; *also* : an attitude favoring such a policy

in·ter·na·tion·al·ize \ˌint-ər-ˈnash-(ə-)nəl-ˌīz\ *vb* : to make international; *esp* : to place under international control

in·ter·ne·cine \ˌint-ər-ˈnes-ˌēn, -ˈnē-ˌsīn\ *adj* [L *internecinus*, fr. *internecare* to destroy, kill, fr. *necare* to kill, fr. *nec-*, *nex* violent death] **1** : DEADLY; *esp* : mutually destructive **2** : of, relating to, or involving conflict within a group ⟨~ feuds⟩

in·ter·nist \ˈin-ˌtər-nəst\ *n* : a specialist in internal medicine esp. as distinguished from a surgeon

in·ter·node \ˈint-ər-ˌnōd\ *n* : an interval or part between two nodes (as of a stem)

in·ter·nun·cio \ˌint-ər-ˈnən-sē-ˌō, -ˈnu̇n-\ *n* [It *internunzio*] : a papal legate of lower rank than a nuncio

in·ter·of·fice \-ˈöf-əs\ *adj* : functioning or communicating between the offices of an organization

in·ter·per·son·al \-ˈpərs-(ᵊ-)nəl\ *adj* : being, relating to, or involving relations between persons — **in·ter·per·son·al·ly** \-ē\ *adv*

in·ter·plan·e·tary \ˌint-ər-ˈplan-ə-ˌter-ē\ *adj* : existing, carried on, or operating between planets ⟨~ space⟩

in·ter·play \ˈint-ər-ˌplā\ *n* : INTERACTION

in·ter·po·late \in-ˈtər-pə-ˌlāt\ *vb* **-lat·ed; -lat·ing 1** : to change (as a text) by inserting new or foreign matter **2** : to insert (as words) into a text or into a conversation **3** : to estimate values of (a function) between two known values — **in·ter·po·la·tion** \-ˌtər-pə-ˈlā-shən\ *n*

in·ter·pose \ˌint-ər-ˈpōz\ *vb* **-posed; -pos·ing 1** : to place between **2** : to thrust in : INTRUDE, INTERRUPT **3** : to inject between parts of a conversation or argument **4** : to be or come between **syn** interfere, intercede, intermediate, intervene — **in·ter·po·si·tion** \-pə-ˈzish-ən\ *n*

in·ter·pret \in-ˈtər-prət\ *vb* **1** : to explain the meaning of; *also* : to act as an interpreter : TRANSLATE **2** : to understand according to individual belief, judgment, or interest **3** : to represent artistically — **in·ter·pret·er** *n* — **in·ter·pre·tive** \-ˈtər-prət-iv\ *adj*

in·ter·pre·ta·tion \in-ˌtər-prə-ˈtā-shən\ *n* **1** : EXPLANATION **2** : an instance of artistic interpretation in performance or adaptation — **in·ter·pre·ta·tive** \-ˈtər-prə-ˌtāt-iv\ *adj*

in·ter·ra·cial \-ˈrā-shəl\ *adj* : of, involving, or designed for members of different races

in·ter·reg·num \ˌint-ə-ˈreg-nəm\ *n, pl* **-nums** *or* **-na** \-nə\ **1** : the time during which a throne is vacant between two successive reigns or regimes **2** : a pause in a continuous series

in·ter·re·late \ˌint-ə(r)-ri-ˈlāt\ *vb* : to bring into or have a mutual relationship — **in·ter·re·lat·ed·ness** \-lāt-əd-nəs\ *n* — **in·ter·re·la·tion** \-ˈlā-shən\ *n* — **in·ter·re·la·tion·ship** *n*

interrog *abbr* interrogative

in·ter·ro·gate \in-ˈter-ə-ˌgāt\ *vb* **-gat·ed; -gat·ing** : to question esp. formally and systematically : ASK — **in·ter·ro·ga·tion** \-ˌter-ə-ˈgā-shən\ *n* — **in·ter·ro·ga·tor** \-ˈter-ə-ˌgāt-ər\ *n*

in·ter·rog·a·tive \ˌint-ə-ˈräg-ət-iv\ *adj* : asking a question ⟨~ sentence⟩ — **interrogative** *n*

in·ter·rog·a·to·ry \ˌint-ə-ˈräg-ə-ˌtōr-ē\ *adj* : INTERROGATIVE

in·ter·rupt \ˌint-ə-ˈrəpt\ *vb* **1** : to stop or hinder by breaking in **2** : to break the uniformity or continuity of **3** : to break in with questions or remarks while another is speaking — **in·ter·rupt·er** *n* — **in·ter·rup·tion** \-ˈrəp-shən\ *n* — **in·ter·rup·tive** \-ˈrəp-tiv\ *adv*

in·ter·scho·las·tic \ˌint-ər-skə-ˈlas-tik\ *adj* : existing or carried on between schools

in·ter·sect \ˌint-ər-ˈsekt\ *vb* : to cut or divide by passing through : cut across : meet and cross : OVERLAP — **in·ter·sec·tion** \-ˈsek-shən\ *n*

in·ter·sperse \ˌint-ər-ˈspərs\ *vb* **-spersed; -spers·ing 1** : to place something at intervals in or among **2** : to insert at intervals among other things — **in·ter·sper·sion** \-ˈspər-zhən\ *n*

[1]**in·ter·state** \ˌint-ər-ˈstāt\ *adj* : relating to, including, or connecting two or more states esp. of the U.S.

[2]**in·ter·state** \ˈint-ər-ˌstāt\ *n* : an interstate highway

in·ter·stel·lar \ˌint-ər-ˈstel-ər\ *adj* : located or taking place among the stars

in·ter·stice \in-ˈtər-stəs\ *n, pl* **-stic·es** \-stə-ˌsēz, -stə-səz\ : a space that intervenes between things : CHINK — **in·ter·sti·tial** \ˌint-ər-ˈstish-əl\ *adj*

in·ter·tid·al \ˌint-ər-ˈtīd-ᵊl\ *adj* : of, relating to, or being the area that is above low-tide mark but exposed to tidal flooding

in·ter·twine \-ˈtwīn\ *vb* : to twine or cause to twine about one another : INTERLACE

in·ter·twist \-ˈtwist\ *vb* : INTERTWINE

in·ter·ur·ban \-ˈər-bən\ *adj* : going between cities or towns

in·ter·val \ˈint-ər-vəl\ *n* [ME *intervalle,* fr. MF, fr. L *intervallum* space between ramparts, interval, fr. *inter-* between + *vallum* rampart] **1** : a space of time between events or states : PAUSE **2** : a space between objects, units, or states **3** : the difference in pitch between two tones

in·ter·vene \ˌint-ər-ˈvēn\ *vb* **-vened; -ven·ing 1** : to occur, fall, or come between points of time or between events **2** : to enter or appear as an unrelated feature or circumstance ⟨rain *intervened* and we postponed the trip⟩ **3** : to come in or between in order to stop, settle, or modify ⟨~ in a quarrel⟩ **4** : to occur or lie between two things — **in·ter·ven·tion** \-ˈven-chən\ *n*

in·ter·ven·tion·ism \-ˈven-chə-ˌniz-əm\ *n* : interference by one country in the political affairs of another — **in·ter·ven·tion·ist** \-ˈvench-(ə-)nəst\ *n or adj*

in·ter·view \ˈint-ər-ˌvyü\ *n* **1** : a formal consultation **2** : a meeting at which a writer or reporter obtains information from a person; *also* : the recorded or written account of such a meeting — **interview** *vb* — **in·ter·view·er** *n*

in·ter·vo·cal·ic \ˌint-ər-vō-ˈkal-ik\ *adj* : immediately preceded and immediately followed by a vowel

in·ter·weave \ˌint-ər-ˈwēv\ *vb* **-wove** \-ˈwōv\ *also* **-weaved; -wo·ven** \-ˈwō-vən\ *also* **-weaved; -weav·ing** : to weave or blend together : INTERTWINE, INTERMINGLE — **in·ter·wo·ven** \-ˈwō-vən\ *adj*

in·tes·tate \in-ˈtes-ˌtāt, -tət\ *adj* **1** : having made no valid will ⟨died ~⟩ **2** : not disposed of by will ⟨~ estate⟩

in·tes·tine \in-ˈtes-tən\ *n* : the tubular part of the alimentary canal that extends from stomach to anus and consists of a long narrow upper part (**small intestine**) followed by a broader shorter lower part (**large intestine**) — **in·tes·ti·nal** \-tən-ᵊl\ *adj*

in·ti \ˈint-ē\ *n* — see MONEY table

[1]**in·ti·mate** \ˈint-ə-ˌmāt\ *vb* **-mat·ed; -mat·ing 1** : ANNOUNCE, NOTIFY **2** : to communicate indirectly : HINT — **in·ti·ma·tion** \ˌint-ə-mā-shən\ *n*

[2]**in·ti·mate** \ˈint-ə-mət\ *adj* **1** : INTRINSIC; *also* : INNERMOST **2** : marked by very close association, contact, or familiarity **3** : marked by a warm friendship **4** : suggesting informal warmth or privacy **5** : of a very personal or private nature — **in·ti·ma·cy** \ˈint-ə-mə-sē\ *n* — **in·ti·mate·ly** *adv*

[3]**in·ti·mate** \ˈint-ə-mət\ *n* : an intimate friend, associate, or confidant

in·tim·i·date \in-ˈtim-ə-ˌdāt\ *vb* **-dat·ed; -dat·ing** : to make timid or fearful : FRIGHTEN; *esp* : to compel or deter by or as if by threats **syn** cow, bulldoze, bully, browbeat — **in·tim·i·da·tion** \-ˌtim-ə-ˈdā-shən\ *n*

intl *or* **intnl** *abbr* international

in·to \ˌin-tə, ˈin-tü\ *prep* **1** : to the inside of ⟨ran ~ the house⟩ **2** : to the state, condition, or form of ⟨got ~ trouble⟩ **3** : AGAINST ⟨ran ~ a wall⟩

in·tol·er·a·ble \(ˈ)in-ˈtäl-(ə-)rə-bəl\ *adj* **1** : UNBEARABLE **2** : EXCESSIVE — **in·tol·er·a·bly** \-blē\ *adv*

in·tol·er·ant \(ˈ)in-ˈtäl-ə-rənt\ *adj* **1** : unable to endure **2** : unwilling to endure **3** : unwilling to grant equality, freedom, or other social rights : BIGOTED — **in·tol·er·ance** \-rəns\ *n*

in·to·na·tion \ˌin-tə-ˈnā-shən\ *n* **1** : the act of intoning and esp. of chanting **2** : something that is intoned **3** : the manner of singing, playing, or uttering tones **4** : the rise and fall in pitch of the voice in speech

in·tone \in-ˈtōn\ *vb* **in·toned; in·ton·ing** : to utter in musical or prolonged tones : CHANT

in to·to \in-ˈtōt-ō\ *adv* [L, on the whole] : TOTALLY, ENTIRELY

in·tox·i·cant \in-ˈtäk-si-kənt\ *n* : something that intoxicates; *esp* : an alcoholic drink — **intoxicant** *adj*

in·tox·i·cate \-sə-ˌkāt\ *vb* **-cat·ed; -cat·ing** [ML *intoxicare*, fr. L *toxicum* poison] **1** : to make drunk **2** : to excite or elate greatly — **in·tox·i·ca·tion** \-ˌtäk-sə-ˈkā-shən\ *n*

in·trac·ta·ble \(ˈ)in-ˈtrak-tə-bəl\ *adj* : not easily controlled : OBSTINATE

in·tra·mo·lec·u·lar \ˌin-trə-mə-ˈlek-yə-lər\ *adj* : exciting or acting within a molecule

in·tra·mu·ral \-ˈmyu̇r-əl\ *adj* : being or occurring within the walls or limits (as of a city or college) ⟨~ sports⟩

in·tra·mus·cu·lar \-ˈməs-kyə-lər\ *adj* : situated within or administered by entering a muscle — **in·tra·mus·cu·lar·ly** *adv*

intrans *abbr* intransitive

in·tran·si·geance \in-ˈtrans-ə-jəns, -ˈtranz-\ *n* : INTRANSIGENCE

in·tran·si·gence \-jəns\ *n* : the quality or state of being intransigent

in·tran·si·gent \-jənt\ *adj* : UNCOMPROMISING; *also* : IRRECONCILABLE — **intransigent** *n*

in·tran·si·tive \(ˈ)in-ˈtrans-ət-iv, -ˈtranz-\ *adj* : not transitive; *esp* : not having or containing an object ⟨an ~ verb⟩ — **in·tran·si·tive·ly** *adv* — **in·tran·si·tive·ness** *n*

in·tra·state \ˌin-trə-ˈstāt\ *adj* : existing or occurring within a state

in·tra·uter·ine device \-ˈyüt-ə-rən-, -ˌrīn\ *n* : a device (as a spiral of plastic or a ring of stainless steel) inserted and left in the uterus to prevent pregnancy

in·tra·ve·nous \ˌin-trə-ˈvē-nəs\ *adj* : being within or entering by way of the veins — **in·tra·ve·nous·ly** *adv*

intrench *var of* ENTRENCH

in·trep·id \in-ˈtrep-əd\ *adj* : characterized by resolute fearlessness, fortitude, and endurance — **in·tre·pid·i·ty** \ˌin-trə-ˈpid-ət-ē\ *n*

in·tri·cate \ˈin-tri-kət\ *adj* [ME, fr. L *intricatus*, pp. of *intricare* to entangle, fr. *tricae* trifles, impediments] **1** : having many complexly interrelated parts : COMPLICATED **2** : difficult to follow, understand, or solve — **in·tri·ca·cy** \-tri-kə-sē\ *n* — **in·tri·cate·ly** *adv*

¹**in·trigue** \in-ˈtrēg\ *vb* **in·trigued; in·trigu·ing 1** : to accomplish by intrigue **2** : to carry on an intrigue; *esp* : PLOT, SCHEME **3** : to arouse the interest, desire, or curiosity of — **in·trigu·ing·ly** \-iŋ-lē\ *adv*

²**in·trigue** \ˈin-ˌtrēg, in-ˈtrēg\ *n* **1** : a secret scheme : MACHINATION **2** : a clandestine love affair

in·trin·sic \in-ˈtrin-zik, -sik\ *adj* : belonging to the essential nature or constitution of a thing — **in·trin·si·cal·ly** \-zi-k(ə-)lē, -si-\ *adv*

introd *abbr* introduction

in·tro·duce \ˌin-trə-ˈd(y)üs\ *vb* **-duced; -duc·ing 1** : to lead or bring in esp. for the first time **2** : to bring into practice or use **3** : to cause to be acquainted **4** : to present for discussion **5** : to put in **syn** insinuate, interpolate, interpose, interject — **in·tro·duc·tion** \-dək-shən\ *n* — **in·tro·duc·to·ry** \-ˈdək-t(ə-)rē\ *adj*

in·troit \ˈin-ˌtrō-ət, -ˌtrȯit\ *n* **1** *often cap* : the first part of the traditional proper of the Mass **2** : a piece of music sung or played at the beginning of a worship service

in·tro·mit \ˌin-trə-ˈmit\ *vb* **-mit·ted; -mit·ting** : to send or put in : INSERT — **in·tro·mis·sion** \-ˈmish-ən\ *n*

in·tro·spec·tion \-ˈspek-shən\ *n* : a reflective looking inward : an examination of one's own thoughts or feelings — **in·tro·spect** \ˌin-trə-ˈspekt\ *vb* — **in·tro·spec·tive** \-ˈspek-tiv\ *adj* — **in·tro·spec·tive·ly** *adv*

in·tro·vert \ˈin-trə-ˌvərt\ *n* : a person more interested in his own mental life than in the world about him — **in·tro·ver·sion** \ˌin-trə-ˈvər-zhən\ *n* — **introvert** *adj* — **in·tro·vert·ed** \ˈin-trə-ˌvərt-əd\ *adj*

in·trude \in-ˈtrüd\ *vb* **in·trud·ed; in·trud·ing 1** : to thrust, enter, or force in or upon **2** : ENCROACH, TRESPASS — **in·trud·er** *n* — **in·tru·sion** \-ˈtrü-zhən\ *n* — **in·tru·sive** \-ˈtrü-siv\ *adj* — **in·tru·sive·ness** *n*

intrust *var of* ENTRUST

in·tu·it \in-ˈt(y)ü-ət\ *vb* : to apprehend by intuition

in·tu·ition \ˌin-t(y)u̇-ˈish-ən\ *n* **1** : the power or faculty of knowing things without conscious reasoning **2** : quick and ready insight — **in·tu·i·tive** \in-ˈt(y)ü-ət-iv\ *adj* — **in·tu·i·tive·ly** *adv*

in·tu·mes·cence \ˌin-t(y)u̇-ˈmes-ᵊns\ *n* **1** : the state of being or the action of becoming swollen **2** : something swollen or enlarged — **in·tu·mesce** \-ˈmes\ *vb* — **in·tu·mes·cent** \-ᵊnt\ *adj*

In·u·it \ˈin-(y)ə-wət\ *n* [Aleut *inuit*, pl. of *inuk* person] **1** : a member of the Eskimo people of America **2** : the language of the Inuit people

in·un·date \ˈin-ən-ˌdāt\ *vb* **-dat·ed; -dat·ing** : to cover with or as if with a flood : OVERFLOW — **in·un·da·tion** \ˌin-ən-ˈdā-shən\ *n*

in·ure \in-ˈ(y)u̇r\ *vb* **in·ured; in·ur·ing** [ME *enuren*, fr. *en-* in + *ure*, n., use, custom, fr. MF *uevre* work, practice, fr. L *opera* work] **1** : to accustom to accept something undesirable **2** : to become of advantage : ACCRUE

inv *abbr* **1** inventor **2** invoice

in vac·uo \in-ˈvak-yə-ˌwō\ *adv* [L] : in a vacuum

in·vade \in-ˈvād\ *vb* **in·vad·ed; in·vad·ing 1** : to enter for conquest or plunder **2** : to encroach upon **3** : to spread through and usu. harm ⟨germs ~ the tissues⟩ — **in·vad·er** *n*

¹**in·val·id** \(ˈ)in-ˈval-əd\ *adj* : being without foundation or force in fact, reason, or law — **in·va·lid·i·ty** \ˌin-və-ˈlid-ət-ē\ *n* — **in·val·id·ly** *adv*

²**in·va·lid** \ˈin-və-ləd\ *adj* : defective in health : SICKLY

³**invalid** \ˈin-və-ləd\ *n* : a person in usu. chronic ill health — **in·va·lid·ism** \-ˌiz-əm\ *n*

⁴**in·va·lid** \ˈin-və-ləd, -ˌlid\ *vb* **1** : to remove from active duty by reason of sickness or disability **2** : to make sickly or disabled

in·val·i·date \(ˈ)in-ˈval-ə-ˌdāt\ *vb* : to make invalid; *esp* : to weaken or make valueless

in·valu·able \(ˈ)in-ˈval-yə(-wə)-bəl\ *adj* : valuable beyond estimation

in·vari·able \(ˈ)in-ˈver-ē-ə-bəl\ *adj* : not changing or capable of change : CONSTANT — **in·vari·ably** \-blē\ *adv*

in·va·sion \in-ˈvā-zhən\ *n* : an act or instance of invading; *esp* : entry of an army into a country for conquest

in·vec·tive \in-ˈvek-tiv\ *n* **1** : an abusive expression or speech **2** : abusive language — **invective** *adj*

in·veigh \in-ˈvā\ : to protest or complain bitterly or vehemently : RAIL

in·vei·gle \in-ˈvā-gəl, -ˈvē-\ *vb* **in·vei·gled; in·vei·gling** \-g(ə-)liŋ\ [modif. of MF *aveugler* to blind, hoodwink] **1** : to win over by flattery : ENTICE **2** : to acquire by ingenuity or flattery

in·vent \in-ˈvent\ *vb* **1** : to think up **2** : to create or produce for the first time — **in·ven·tor** \-ˈvent-ər\ *n*

in·ven·tion \in-ˈven-chən\ *n* **1** : INVENTIVENESS **2** : a creation of the imagination; *esp* : a false conception **3** : a device, contrivance, or process originated after study and experiment **4** : the act or process of inventing

in·ven·tive \in-ˈvent-iv\ *adj* **1** : CREATIVE, INGENIOUS ⟨an ~ composer⟩ **2** : characterized by invention ⟨an ~ turn of mind⟩ — **in·ven·tive·ness** *n*

in·ven·to·ry \ˈin-vən-ˌtōr-ē\ *n, pl* **-ries 1** : an itemized list of current goods or assets **2** : SURVEY, SUMMARY **3**

: STOCK, SUPPLY **4** : the act or process of taking an inventory — **inventory** *vb*
in·verse \(ˈ)in-ˈvərs, ˈin-ˌvərs\ *adj* : opposite in order, nature, or effect : REVERSED — **in·verse·ly** *adv*
in·ver·sion \in-ˈvər-zhən\ *n* **1** : a reversal of position, order, or relationship; *esp* : an increase of temperature with altitude through a layer of air **2** : the act or process of inverting
in·vert \in-ˈvərt\ *vb* **1** : to reverse in position, order, or relationship **2** : to turn upside down or inside out **3** : to turn inward
[1]**in·ver·te·brate** \(ˈ)in-ˈvərt-ə-brət, -ˌbrāt\ *adj* : lacking a backbone; *also* : of or relating to invertebrates
[2]**invertebrate** *n* : an invertebrate animal
[1]**in·vest** \in-ˈvest\ *vb* **1** : to install formally in an office or honor **2** : to furnish with power or authority : VEST **3** : to cover completely : ENVELOP **4** : CLOTHE, ADORN **5** : BESIEGE **6** : to endow with a quality or characteristic
[2]**invest** *vb* **1** : to commit money in order to earn a financial return **2** : to expend for future benefits or advantages **3** : to make an investment — **in·ves·tor** \-ˈves-tər\ *n*
in·ves·ti·gate \in-ˈves-tə-ˌgāt\ *vb* **-gat·ed; -gat·ing** [L *investigare* to track, investigate, fr. *vestigium* footprint, track] : to study by close examination and systematic inquiry — **in·ves·ti·ga·tion** \-ˌves-tə-ˈgā-shən\ *n* — **in·ves·ti·ga·tor** \-ˈves-tə-ˌgāt-ər\ *n*
in·ves·ti·ture \in-ˈves-tə-ˌchu̇r, -chər\ *n* **1** : the act of ratifying or establishing in office : CONFIRMATION **2** : something that covers or adorns
[1]**in·vest·ment** \in-ˈves(t)-mənt\ *n* **1** : an outer layer : ENVELOPE **2** : INVESTITURE 1 **3** : BLOCKADE, SIEGE
[2]**investment** *n* : the outlay of money for income or profit; *also* : the sum invested or the property purchased
in·vet·er·ate \in-ˈvet-(ə-)rət\ *adj* **1** : firmly established by age or long persistence **2** : confirmed in a habit — **in·vet·er·a·cy** \-(ə-)rə-sē\ *n*
in·vi·a·ble \(ˈ)in-ˈvī-ə-bəl\ *adj* : incapable of surviving
in·vid·i·ous \in-ˈvid-ē-əs\ *adj* **1** : tending to cause discontent, animosity, or envy **2** : ENVIOUS **3** : INJURIOUS — **in·vid·i·ous·ly** *adv*
in·vig·o·rate \in-ˈvig-ə-ˌrāt\ *vb* **-rat·ed; -rat·ing** : to give life and energy to : ANIMATE — **in·vig·o·ra·tion** \-ˌvig-ə-ˈrā-shən\ *n*
in·vin·ci·ble \(ˈ)in-ˈvin-sə-bəl\ *adj* : incapable of being conquered, overcome, or subdued — **in·vin·ci·bil·i·ty** \(ˌ)in-ˌvin-sə-ˈbil-ət-ē\ *n* — **in·vin·ci·bly** \(ˈ)in-ˈvin-sə-blē\ *adv*
in·vi·o·la·ble \(ˈ)in-ˈvī-ə-lə-bəl\ *adj* **1** : safe from violation or profanation **2** : UNASSAILABLE — **in·vi·o·la·bil·i·ty** \(ˌ)in-ˌvī-ə-lə-ˈbil-ət-ē\ *n*
in·vi·o·late \(ˈ)in-ˈvī-ə-lət\ *adj* : not violated or profaned : PURE
in·vis·i·ble \(ˈ)in-ˈviz-ə-bəl\ *adj* **1** : incapable of being seen ⟨~ to the naked eye⟩ **2** : HIDDEN **3** : IMPERCEPTIBLE, INCONSPICUOUS — **in·vis·i·bil·i·ty** \(ˌ)in-ˌviz-ə-ˈbil-ət-ē\ *n* — **in·vis·i·bly** \(ˈ)in-ˈviz-ə-blē\ *adv*
in·vi·ta·tion·al \ˌin-və-ˈtā-sh(ə-)nəl\ *adj* : limited to invited participants
in·vite \in-ˈvīt\ *vb* **in·vit·ed; in·vit·ing** **1** : ENTICE, TEMPT **2** : to increase the likelihood of **3** : to request the presence or participation of : ASK **4** : to request formally **5** : ENCOURAGE — **in·vi·ta·tion** \ˌin-və-ˈtā-shən\ *n*
in·vit·ing \in-ˈvīt-iŋ\ *adj* : ATTRACTIVE, TEMPTING
in·vo·ca·tion \ˌin-və-ˈkā-shən\ *n* **1** : SUPPLICATION; *esp* : a prayer at the beginning of a service **2** : a formula for conjuring : INCANTATION
[1]**in·voice** \ˈin-ˌvȯis\ *n* [modif. of MF *envois*, pl. of *envoi* message] **1** : an itemized list of goods shipped usu. specifying the price and the terms of sale : BILL **2** : a consignment of merchandise
[2]**invoice** *vb* **in·voiced; in·voic·ing** : to make an invoice for : BILL
in·voke \in-ˈvōk\ *vb* **in·voked; in·vok·ing** **1** : to petition for help or support **2** : to appeal to or cite as authority ⟨~ a law⟩ **3** : to call forth by incantation : CONJURE ⟨~ spirits⟩ **4** : to make an earnest request for : SOLICIT **5** : to put into effect or operation **6** : to bring about : CAUSE
in·vo·lu·cre \ˈin-və-ˌlü-kər\ *n* : one or more whorls of bracts below and close to a flower or fruit
in·vol·un·tary \(ˈ)in-ˈväl-ən-ˌter-ē\ *adj* **1** : done contrary to or without choice **2** : COMPULSORY **3** : not subject to control by the will ⟨~ muscles⟩ — **in·vol·un·tari·ly** \(ˌ)in-ˌväl-ən-ˈter-ə-lē\ *adv*
in·vo·lute \ˈin-və-ˌlüt\ *adj* **1** : curled spirally and usu. closely ⟨~ shell⟩ **2** : INVOLVED, INTRICATE
in·vo·lu·tion \ˌin-və-ˈlü-shən\ *n* **1** : the act or an instance of enfolding or entangling **2** : COMPLEXITY, INTRICACY
in·volve \in-ˈvälv\ *vb* **in·volved; in·volv·ing** **1** : to draw in as a participant **2** : ENVELOP **3** : to relate closely : CONNECT **4** : to have as part of itself : INCLUDE **5** : ENTAIL, IMPLY **6** : to have an effect on — **in·volve·ment** *n*
in·volved \-ˈvälvd\ *adj* : INTRICATE, COMPLEX ⟨an ~ assassination plot⟩
in·vul·ner·a·ble \(ˈ)in-ˈvəl-nə-rə-bəl\ *adj* **1** : incapable of being wounded, injured, or damaged **2** : immune to or proof against attack — **in·vul·ner·a·bil·i·ty** \(ˌ)in-ˌvəl-nə-rə-ˈbil-ət-ē\ *n* — **in·vul·ner·a·bly** \(ˈ)in-ˈvəl-nə-rə-blē\ *adv*
[1]**in·ward** \ˈin-wərd\ *adj* **1** : situated on the inside **2** : MENTAL; *also* : SPIRITUAL **3** : directed toward the interior
[2]**inward** *or* **in·wards** \-wərdz\ *adv* **1** : toward the inside, center, or interior **2** : toward the inner being
in·ward·ly \ˈin-wərd-lē\ *adv* **1** : MENTALLY, SPIRITUALLY **2** : INTERNALLY ⟨bled ~⟩ **3** : to oneself ⟨cursed ~⟩ **4** : toward the center or interior
IOC *abbr* International Olympic Committee
io·dide \ˈī-ə-ˌdīd\ *n* : a compound of iodine with another element or group
io·dine \ˈī-ə-ˌdīn, -əd-ᵊn\ *n* : a nonmetallic chemical element used in medicine and photography — see ELEMENT table
io·dize \ˈī-ə-ˌdīz\ *vb* **io·dized; io·diz·ing** : to treat with iodine or an iodide
ion \ˈī-ən, ˈī-ˌän\ *n* [Gk, neut. of *iōn*, prp. of *ienai* to go; so called because in electrolysis it goes to one of the two poles] : an electrically charged particle or group of atoms — **ion·ic** \ī-ˈän-ik\ *adj*
ion·ize \ˈī-ə-ˌnīz\ *vb* **ion·ized; ion·iz·ing** **1** : to convert wholly or partly into ions **2** : to become ionized — **ion·iz·able** \-ˌnī-zə-bəl\ *adj* — **ion·iza·tion** \ˌī-ə-nə-ˈzā-shən\ *n* — **ion·iz·er** \ˈī-ə-ˌnī-zər\ *n*
ion·o·sphere \ī-ˈän-ə-ˌsfiər\ *n* : the part of the earth's atmosphere beginning at an altitude of about 30 miles and extending outward 300 miles or more that contains free electrically charged particles — **ion·o·spher·ic** \ī-ˌän-ə-ˈsfi(ə)r-ik, -ˈsfer-\ *adj*
IOOF *abbr* Independent Order of Odd Fellows
io·ta \ī-ˈōt-ə\ *n* [L, fr. Gk *iōta*, the 9th letter of the Greek alphabet] : a very small quantity : JOT
IOU \ˌī-(ˌ)ō-ˈyü\ *n* : an acknowledgement of a debt
IP *abbr* innings pitched
ip·e·cac \ˈip-i-ˌkak\ *n* [Pg *ipecacuanha*] **1** : the dried rhizome and roots of ipecac used esp. as the source of an emetic **2** : a tropical So. American creeping plant related to the madder
ip·so fac·to \ˌip-sō-ˈfak-tō\ *adv* [NL, lit., by the fact itself] : by the very nature of the case
iq *abbr* [L *idem quod*] the same as
IQ \ˈī-ˈkyü\ *n* : INTELLIGENCE QUOTIENT
[1]**Ir** *abbr* Irish
[2]**Ir** *symbol* iridium

IR *abbr* **1** information retrieval **2** internal revenue
IRA *abbr* **1** individual retirement account **2** Irish Republican Army
Ira·ni·an \ir-ˈā-nē-ən *also* -ˈä-\ *n* : a native or inhabitant of Iran — **Iranian** *adj*
Iraqi \i-ˈräk-ē, -ˈrak-\ *n* : a native or inhabitant of Iraq — **Iraqi** *adj*
iras·ci·ble \ir-ˈas-ə-bəl, ī-ˈras-\ *adj* : marked by hot temper and easily provoked anger **syn** choleric, testy, touchy, cranky, cross — **iras·ci·bil·i·ty** \-ˌas-ə-ˈbil-ət-ē, -ˌras-\ *n*
irate \ī-ˈrāt\ *adj* **1** : roused to ire **2** : arising from anger ⟨~ words⟩ — **irate·ly** *adv*
IRBM *abbr* intermediate range ballistic missile
ire \ˈī(ə)r\ *n* : ANGER, WRATH — **ire·ful** *adj*
Ire *abbr* Ireland
ire·nic \ī-ˈren-ik\ *adj* : conducive to or operating toward peace or conciliation
ir·i·des·cence \ˌir-ə-ˈdes-ᵊns\ *n* : a rainbowlike play of colors — **ir·i·des·cent** \-ᵊnt\ *adj*
irid·i·um \ir-ˈid-ē-əm\ *n* : a hard brittle very heavy metallic chemical element used in alloys — see ELEMENT table
iris \ˈī-rəs\ *n, pl* **iris·es** *or* **iri·des** \ˈī-rə-ˌdēz, ˈir-ə-\ [ME, fr. L *iris* rainbow, iris plant, fr. Gk, rainbow, iris plant, iris of the eye] **1** : the colored part around the pupil of the eye **2** : any of a large genus of plants with linear basal leaves and large showy flowers
Irish \ˈī-rish\ *n* **1 Irish** *pl* : the people of Ireland **2** : the Celtic language of Ireland — **Irish** *adj* — **Irish·man** \-mən\ *n* — **Irish·wom·an** \-ˌwu̇m-ən\ *n*
Irish bull *n* : an incongruous statement (as "it was hereditary in his family to have no children")
Irish coffee *n* : hot sugared coffee with Irish whiskey and whipped cream
Irish moss *n* : the dried and bleached plants of two red algae; *also* : either of these two red algae
Irish setter *n* : any of a breed of bird dogs with a mahogany-red coat
irk \ˈərk\ *vb* : to make weary, irritated, or bored : ANNOY
irk·some \ˈərk-səm\ *adj* : tending to irk : ANNOYING — **irk·some·ly** *adv*
¹iron \ˈī(-ə)rn\ *n* **1** : a heavy magnetic metallic chemical element that rusts easily, can be readily shaped, and is vital to biological processes — see ELEMENT table **2** : something made of metal and esp. iron; *also* : something (as handcuffs) used to bind or restrain ⟨put them in ~*s*⟩ **3** : a household device with a flat base that is heated and used for pressing cloth **4** : STRENGTH, HARDNESS
²iron *vb* **1** : to press or smooth with or as if with a heated flatiron **2** : to remove (as wrinkles) by ironing — **iron·er** *n*
iron·bound \ˈī(-ə)rn-ˈbau̇nd\ *adj* **1** : HARSH, RUGGED ⟨~ coast⟩ **2** : STERN, RIGOROUS ⟨~ traditions⟩
¹iron·clad \-ˈklad\ *adj* **1** : sheathed in iron armor **2** : so firm or secure as to be unbreakable
²iron·clad \-ˌklad\ *n* : an armored naval vessel
iron curtain *n* : a political, military, and ideological barrier that cuts off and isolates an area; *esp* : one between an area under Soviet control and other areas
iron·ic \ī-ˈrän-ik\ *or* **iron·i·cal** \-i-kəl\ *adj* **1** : of, relating to, or marked by irony **2** : given to irony — **iron·i·cal·ly** \-i-k(ə-)lē\ *adv*
iron·ing \ˈī(-ə)r-niŋ\ *n* : clothes ironed or to be ironed
iron lung *n* : a device for artificial respiration (as in polio) that encloses the chest or body in a chamber in which changes of pressure force air into and out of the lungs
iron out *vb* : to remove or lessen difficulties in or extremes of
iron oxide *n* : FERRIC OXIDE
iron·stone \ˈī(-ə)rn-ˌstōn\ *n* **1** : a hard iron-rich sedimentary rock **2** : a hard heavy durable pottery developed in England in the 19th century
iron·ware \-ˌwaər\ *n* : articles made of iron
iron·weed \-ˌwēd\ *n* : any of several weedy American plants related to the daisy that have terminal heads of red or purple tubular flowers
iron·wood \-ˌwu̇d\ *n* : a tree or shrub with exceptionally hard wood; *also* : its wood
iron·work \-ˌwərk\ *n* **1** : work in iron **2** *pl* : a mill or building where iron or steel is smelted or heavy iron or steel products are made — **iron·work·er** *n*
iro·ny \ˈī-rə-nē\ *n, pl* **-nies** [L *ironia*, fr. Gk *eirōnia*, fr. *eirōn* dissembler] **1** : the use of words to express the opposite of what one really means **2** : incongruity between the actual result of a sequence of events and the expected result
Ir·o·quois \ˈir-ə-ˌkwȯi\ *n, pl* **Iroquois** \-ˌkwȯi(z)\ [F, fr. Algonquin (a No. American Indian dialect) *Irinakhoiw*, lit., real adders] **1** *pl* : an American Indian confederacy of New York that consisted of the Cayuga, Mohawk, Oneida, Onondaga, and Seneca and later included the Tuscarora **2** : a member of any of the Iroquois peoples
ir·ra·di·ate \ir-ˈād-ē-ˌāt\ *vb* **-at·ed; -at·ing 1** : ILLUMINATE **2** : ENLIGHTEN **3** : to treat by exposure to radiation **4** : RADIATE — **ir·ra·di·a·tion** \-ˌād-ē-ˈā-shən\ *n*
¹ir·ra·tio·nal \(ˈ)ir-ˈash-(ə-)nəl\ *adj* **1** : incapable of reasoning ⟨~ beasts⟩; *also* : defective in mental power ⟨~ with fever⟩ **2** : not based on reason ⟨~ fears⟩ **3** : relating to, consisting of, or being one or more irrational numbers — **ir·ra·tio·nal·i·ty** \(ˌ)ir-ˌash-ə-ˈnal-ət-ē\ *n* — **ir·ra·tio·nal·ly** \(ˈ)ir-ˈash-(ə-)nə-lē\ *adv*
²irrational *n* : IRRATIONAL NUMBER
irrational number *n* : a real number that cannot be expressed as the quotient of two integers
ir·rec·on·cil·able \(ˌ)ir-ˌek-ən-ˈsī-lə-bəl, (ˈ)ir-ˈek-ən-ˌsī-\ *adj* : impossible to reconcile, adjust, or harmonize — **ir·rec·on·cil·abil·i·ty** \(ˌ)ir-ˌek-ən-ˌsī-lə-ˈbil-ət-ē\ *n*
ir·re·cov·er·able \ˌir-i-ˈkəv-(ə-)rə-bəl\ *adj* : not capable of being recovered or rectified : IRREPARABLE — **ir·re·cov·er·ably** \-blē\ *adv*
ir·re·deem·able \ˌir-i-ˈdē-mə-bəl\ *adj* **1** : not redeemable; *esp* : not terminable by payment of the principal ⟨an ~ bond⟩ **2** : not convertible into gold or silver at the will of the holder **3** : being beyond remedy : HOPELESS
ir·re·den·tism \-ˈden-ˌtiz-əm\ *n* : a principle or policy directed toward the incorporation of a territory historically or ethnically part of another into that other — **ir·re·den·tist** \-ˈdent-əst\ *n or adj*
ir·re·duc·ible \ˌir-i-ˈd(y)ü-sə-bəl\ *adj* : not reducible — **ir·re·duc·ibly** \-ˈd(y)ü-sə-blē\ *adv*
ir·re·fra·ga·ble \(ˈ)ir-ˈ(r)ef-rə-gə-bəl\ *adj* : IRREFUTABLE
ir·re·fut·able \ˌir-i-ˈfyüt-ə-bəl, (ˈ)ir-ˈ(r)ef-yət-\ *adj* : impossible to refute
irreg *abbr* irregular
ir·reg·u·lar \(ˈ)ir-ˈeg-yə-lər\ *adj* **1** : not regular : not natural or uniform **2** : not conforming to the normal or usual manner of inflection ⟨~ verbs⟩ **3** : not belonging to a regular or organized army organization ⟨~ troops⟩ — **irregular** *n* — **ir·reg·u·lar·i·ty** \(ˌ)ir-ˌeg-yə-ˈlar-ət-ē\ *n* — **ir·reg·u·lar·ly** \(ˈ)ir-ˈeg-yə-lər-lē\ *adv*
ir·rel·e·vant \(ˈ)ir-ˈel-ə-vənt\ *adj* : not relevant — **ir·rel·e·vance** \-vəns\ *n*
ir·re·li·gious \ˌir-i-ˈlij-əs\ *adj* : lacking religious emotions, doctrines, or practices
ir·re·me·di·a·ble \ˌir-i-ˈmēd-ē-ə-bəl\ *adj* : impossible to remedy or correct : INCURABLE
ir·re·mov·able \-ˈmü-və-bəl\ *adj* : not removable
ir·rep·a·ra·ble \(ˈ)ir-ˈep-(ə-)rə-bəl\ *adj* : impossible to make good, undo, repair, or remedy ⟨~ damage⟩
ir·re·place·able \ˌir-i-ˈplā-sə-bəl\ *adj* : not replaceable
ir·re·press·ible \-ˈpres-ə-bəl\ *adj* : impossible to repress or control
ir·re·proach·able \-ˈprō-chə-bəl\ *adj* : not reproachable : BLAMELESS

ir·re·sist·ible \ˌir-i-ˈzis-tə-bəl\ *adj* : impossible to successfully resist — **ir·re·sist·ibly** \-blē\ *adv*

ir·res·o·lute \(ˈ)ir-ˈez-ə-ˌlüt\ *adj* : uncertain how to act or proceed : VACILLATING — **ir·res·o·lute·ly** \-ˌlüt-lē; (ˌ)ir-ˌez-ə-ˈlüt\ *adv* — **ir·res·o·lu·tion** \(ˌ)ir-ˌez-ə-ˈlü-shən\ *n*

ir·re·spec·tive of \ˌir-i-ˈspek-tiv-\ *prep* : without regard to

ir·re·spon·si·ble \-ˈspän-sə-bəl\ *adj* : not responsible — **ir·re·spon·si·bil·i·ty** \-ˌspän-sə-ˈbil-ət-ē\ *n* — **ir·re·spon·si·bly** \-ˈspän-sə-blē\ *adv*

ir·re·triev·able \ˌir-i-ˈtrē-və-bəl\ *adj* : not retrievable : IRRECOVERABLE

ir·rev·er·ence \(ˈ)ir-ˈev-(ə-)rəns\ *n* **1** : lack of reverence **2** : an irreverent act or utterance — **ir·rev·er·ent** \-(ə-)rənt\ *adj*

ir·re·vers·ible \ˌir-i-ˈvər-sə-bəl\ *adj* : incapable of being reversed

ir·re·vo·ca·ble \(ˈ)ir-ˈev-ə-kə-bəl\ *adj* : incapable of being revoked or recalled — **ir·re·vo·ca·bly** \-blē\ *adv*

ir·ri·gate \ˈir-ə-ˌgāt\ *vb* **-gat·ed; -gat·ing** : to supply (as land) with water by artificial means; *also* : to flush with liquid — **ir·ri·ga·tion** \ˌir-ə-ˈgā-shən\ *n*

ir·ri·ta·ble \ˈir-ət-ə-bəl\ *adj* : capable of being irritated; *esp* : readily or easily irritated — **ir·ri·ta·bil·i·ty** \ˌir-ət-ə-ˈbil-ət-ē\ *n* — **ir·ri·ta·bly** \ˈir-ət-ə-blē\ *adv*

ir·ri·tate \ˈir-ə-ˌtāt\ *vb* **-tat·ed; -tat·ing 1** : to excite to anger : EXASPERATE **2** : to act as a stimulus toward : STIMULATE; *also* : to make sore or inflamed — **ir·ri·tant** \ˈir-ə-tənt\ *adj or n* — **ir·ri·tat·ing·ly** \-ˌtāt-iŋ-lē\ *adv* — **ir·ri·ta·tion** \ˌir-ə-ˈtā-shən\ *n*

ir·rupt \(ˈ)ir-ˈəpt\ *vb* **1** : to rush in forcibly or violently **2** : to increase suddenly in numbers ⟨rabbits ~ in cycles⟩ — **ir·rup·tion** \-ˈəp-shən\ *n*

IRS *abbr* Internal Revenue Service

is *pres 3d sing of* BE

Isa *or* **Is** *abbr* Isaiah

Isa·iah \ī-ˈzā-ə\ *n* — see BIBLE table

Isa·ias \ī-ˈzā-əs\ *n* — see BIBLE table

ISBN *abbr* International Standard Book Number

-ish \ish\ *adj suffix* **1** : of, relating to, or being ⟨Finn*ish*⟩ **2** : characteristic of ⟨boy*ish*⟩ ⟨mul*ish*⟩ **3** : having a touch or trace of : somewhat ⟨purpl*ish*⟩ **4** : having the approximate age of ⟨forty*ish*⟩ **5** : being or occurring at the approximate time of ⟨eight*ish*⟩

isin·glass \ˈīz-ᵊn-ˌglas, ˈī-ziŋ-\ *n* **1** : a gelatin obtained from various fish **2** : MICA

isl *abbr* island

Is·lam \is-ˈläm, iz-, -ˈlam, ˈis-ˌ, ˈiz-ˌ\ *n* [Ar *islām* submission (to the will of God)] : the religious faith of Muslims; *also* : the civilization built on this faith — **Is·lam·ic** \is-ˈläm-ik, iz-, -ˈlam-\ *adj*

is·land \ˈī-lənd\ *n* **1** : a body of land surrounded by water and smaller than a continent **2** : something resembling an island in its isolation

is·land·er \ˈī-lən-dər\ *n* : a native or inhabitant of an island

isle \ˈīl\ *n* : ISLAND; *esp* : a small island

is·let \ˈī-lət\ *n* : a small island

ism \ˈiz-əm\ *n* : a distinctive doctrine, cause, or theory

-ism \ˌiz-əm\ *n suffix* **1** : act : practice : process ⟨critic*ism*⟩ **2** : manner of action or behavior characteristic of a (specified) person or thing **3** : state : condition : property ⟨barbarian*ism*⟩ **4** : abnormal state or condition resulting from excess of a (specified) thing or marked by resemblance to (such) a person or thing ⟨alcohol*ism*⟩ ⟨mongol*ism*⟩ **5** : doctrine : theory : cult ⟨Buddh*ism*⟩ **6** : adherence to a set of principles ⟨stoic*ism*⟩ **7** : characteristic or peculiar feature or trait ⟨colloquial*ism*⟩

iso·bar \ˈī-sə-ˌbär\ *n* : a line on a map connecting places of equal barometric pressure — **iso·bar·ic** \ˌī-sə-ˈbär-ik, -ˈbar-\ *adj*

iso·late \ˈī-sə-ˌlāt, ˈis-ə-\ *vb* **-lat·ed; -lat·ing** [fr. *isolated* set apart, fr. F *isolé*, fr. It *isolato*, fr. *isola* island, fr. L *insula*] : to place or keep by itself : separate from others — **iso·la·tion** \ˌī-sə-ˈlā-shən, ˌis-ə-\ *n*

iso·lat·ed *adj* **1** : occurring alone or once : UNIQUE **2** : SPORADIC

iso·la·tion·ism \ˌī-sə-ˈlā-shə-ˌniz-əm, ˌis-ə-\ *n* : a policy of national isolation by abstention from international political and economic relations — **iso·la·tion·ist** \-sh(ə-)nəst\ *n or adj*

iso·mer \ˈī-sə-mər\ *n* : any of two or more chemical compounds that contain the same numbers of atoms of the same elements but differ in structural arrangement and properties — **iso·mer·ic** \ˌī-sə-ˈmer-ik\ *adj* — **isom·er·ism** \ī-ˈsäm-ə-ˌriz-əm\ *n*

iso·met·rics \ˌī-sə-ˈme-triks\ *n sing or pl* : exercise involving contraction of muscles taking place against resistance but without significant shortening of muscle fibers — **isometric** *adj*

iso·prene \ˈī-sə-ˌprēn\ *n* : a hydrocarbon used esp. in making synthetic rubber

isos·ce·les \ī-ˈsäs-ə-ˌlēz\ *adj* : having two equal sides ⟨an ~ triangle⟩

isos·ta·sy \ī-ˈsäs-tə-sē\ *n* : general equilibrium in the earth's crust maintained by the gravity-induced flow of deep rock material — **iso·stat·ic** \ˌī-sə-ˈstat-ik\ *adj* — **iso·stat·i·cal·ly** \-i-k(ə-)lē\ *adv*

iso·therm \ˈī-sə-ˌthərm\ *n* : a line on a map connecting points having the same temperature

iso·ther·mal \ˌī-sə-ˈthər-məl\ *adj* : of, relating to, or marked by equality of temperature

iso·ton·ic \ˌī-sə-ˈtän-ik\ *adj* : having the same or equal osmotic pressure ⟨a salt solution ~ with red blood cells⟩

iso·tope \ˈī-sə-ˌtōp\ *n* [Gk *isos* equal + *topos* place] : any of the forms of a chemical element that differ chiefly in the number of neutrons in an atom — **iso·to·pic** \ˌī-sə-ˈtäp-ik, -ˈtō-pik\ *adj* — **iso·to·pi·cal·ly** \-ˈtäp-i-k(ə-)lē, -ˈtō-pi-\ *adv*

Isr \abbr\ Israel; Israeli

Is·rae·li \iz-ˈrā-lē\ *n, pl* **Israelis** *also* **Israeli** : a native or inhabitant of Israel — **Israeli** *adj*

Is·ra·el·ite \ˈiz-rē-ə-ˌlīt\ *n* : a member of the Hebrew people descended from Jacob

is·su·ance \ˈish-ə-wəns\ *n* : the act of issuing or giving out esp. officially

¹is·sue \ˈish-ü\ *n* **1** *pl* : proceeds from a source of revenue (as an estate) **2** : the action of going, coming, or flowing out : EGRESS, EMERGENCE **3** : EXIT, OUTLET, VENT **4** : OFFSPRING, PROGENY **5** : OUTCOME, RESULT **6** : a point of debate or controversy; *also* : the point at which an unsettled matter is ready for a decision **7** : a discharge (as of blood) from the body **8** : something coming forth from a specified source **9** : the act of officially giving out or printing : PUBLICATION; *also* : the quantity of things given out at one time

²issue *vb* **is·sued; is·su·ing 1** : to go, come, or flow out **2** : to come forth or cause to come forth : EMERGE, DISCHARGE, EMIT **3** : ACCRUE **4** : to descend from a specified parent or ancestor **5** : to result in **6** : to put forth or distribute officially **7** : PUBLISH **8** : EMANATE, RESULT — **is·su·er** *n*

¹-ist \əst\ *n suffix* **1** : one that performs a (specified) action ⟨cycl*ist*⟩ : one that makes or produces ⟨novel*ist*⟩ **2** : one that plays a (specified) musical instrument ⟨harp*ist*⟩ **3** : one that operates a (specified) mechanical instrument or contrivance ⟨automobil*ist*⟩ **4** : one that specializes in a (specified) art or science or skill ⟨geolog*ist*⟩ **5** : one that adheres to or advocates a (specified) doctrine or system or code of behavior ⟨social*ist*⟩ or that of a (specified) individual ⟨Darwin*ist*⟩

²-ist *adj suffix* : -ISTIC

isth·mi·an \ˈis-mē-ən\ *adj* : of, relating to, or situated in or near an isthmus

isth·mus \ˈis-məs\ *n* : a narrow strip of land connecting two larger portions of land

-is·tic \ˈis-tik\ *or* **-is·ti·cal** \ˈis-ti-kəl\ *adj suffix* : of, relating to, or characteristic of ⟨altru*istic*⟩

ISV *abbr* International Scientific Vocabulary

¹it \(ˈ)it, ət\ *pron* **1** : that one — used of a lifeless thing, a plant, a person or animal, or an abstract entity ⟨~'s a big building⟩ ⟨~'s a shade tree⟩ ⟨who is ~⟩ ⟨beauty is everywhere and ~ is a source of joy⟩ **2** — used as an anticipatory subject or object ⟨~'s good to see you⟩

²it \ˈit\ *n* : the player in a game who performs a function (as trying to catch others in a game of tag) essential to the nature of the game

It *abbr* Italian; Italy

ital *abbr* italic; italicized

Ital *abbr* Italian

Ital·ian \ə-ˈtal-yən, i-\ *n* **1** : a native or inhabitant of Italy **2** : the language of Italy — **Italian** *adj*

Italian sandwich *n* : SUBMARINE 2

ital·ic \i-ˈtal-ik, ī-\ *adj* : relating to type in which the letters slope up toward the right (as in *"italic"*) — **italic** *n*

ital·i·cize \i-ˈtal-ə-ˌsīz, ī-\ *vb* **-cized; -ciz·ing** : to print in italics

itch \ˈich\ *n* **1** : an uneasy irritating skin sensation related to pain **2** : a skin disorder accompanied by an itch **3** : a persistent desire — **itch** *vb* — **itchy** *adj*

-ite \ˌīt\ *n suffix* **1** : native : resident ⟨Brooklyn*ite*⟩ **2** : descendant ⟨Ishmael*ite*⟩ **3** : adherent : follower ⟨Lenin*ite*⟩ **4** : product ⟨metabol*ite*⟩ **5** : mineral : rock ⟨quartz*ite*⟩

item \ˈīt-əm\ *n* [L, likewise, also] **1** : a separate particular in a list, account, or series : ARTICLE **2** : a separate piece of news (as in a newspaper)

item·ize \ˈīt-ə-ˌmīz\ *vb* **-ized; -iz·ing** : to set down in detail : LIST — **item·iza·tion** \ˌīt-ə-mə-ˈzā-shən\ *n*

it·er·ate \ˈit-ə-ˌrāt\ *vb* **-at·ed; -at·ing** : REITERATE, REPEAT

it·er·a·tion \ˌit-ə-ˈrā-shən\ *n* : REPETITION; *esp* : a computational process in which a series of operations is repeated a number of times

itin·er·ant \ī-ˈtin-ə-rənt, ə-\ *adj* : traveling from place to place; *esp* : covering a circuit ⟨an ~ preacher⟩

itin·er·ary \ī-ˈtin-ə-ˌrer-ē, ə-\ *n, pl* **-ar·ies** **1** : the route of a journey or the proposed outline of one **2** : a travel diary **3** : GUIDEBOOK

its \(ˌ)its, əts\ *adj* : of or relating to it or itself

it·self \it-ˈself, ət-\ *pron* : that identical one — used reflexively, for emphasis, or in absolute constructions

-ity \ət-ē\ *n suffix* : quality : state : degree ⟨alkalin*ity*⟩

IUD \ˌī-ˌyü-ˈdē\ *n* : INTRAUTERINE DEVICE

IV *abbr* intravenous; intravenously

-ive \iv\ *adj suffix* : that performs or tends toward an (indicated) action ⟨correct*ive*⟩

ivo·ry \ˈīv-(ə-)rē\ *n, pl* **-ries** [ME *ivorie,* fr. OF *ivoire,* fr. L *eboreus* of ivory, fr. *ebur* ivory] **1** : the hard creamy-white material composing elephants' tusks **2** : a variable door averaging a pale yellow **3** : something made of ivory or of a similar substance

ivory tower *n* **1** : an impractical lack of concern with urgent problems **2** : a place of learning

ivy \ˈī-vē\ *n, pl* **ivies** : a trailing woody vine with evergreen leaves and small black berries

IWW *abbr* Industrial Workers of the World

-ize \ˌīz\ *vb suffix* **1** : cause to be or conform to or resemble ⟨American*ize*⟩ : cause to be formed into ⟨union*ize*⟩ **2** : subject to a (specified) action ⟨satir*ize*⟩ **3** : saturate, treat, or combine with ⟨macadam*ize*⟩ **4** : treat like ⟨idol*ize*⟩ **5** : become : become like ⟨crystall*ize*⟩ **6** : be productive in or of : engage in a (specified) activity ⟨philosoph*ize*⟩ **7** : adopt or spread the manner of activity or the teaching of ⟨Christian*ize*⟩

J

¹j \ˈjā\ *n, pl* **j's** *or* **js** \ˈjāz\ *often cap* : the 10th letter of the English alphabet

²j *abbr, often cap* **1** jack **2** journal **3** judge **4** justice

¹jab \ˈjab\ *vb* **jabbed; jab·bing** : to thrust quickly or abruptly : POKE

²jab *n* : a usu. short straight punch

jab·ber \ˈjab-ər\ *vb* **jab·bered; jab·ber·ing** \ˈjab-(ə-)riŋ\ : to talk rapidly, indistinctly, or unintelligibly : CHATTER — **jabber** *n*

jab·ber·wocky \ˈjab-ər-ˌwäk-ē\ *n* : meaningless speech or writing

ja·bot \zha-ˈbō, ˈjab-ˌō\ *n* : a ruffle worn down the front of a dress or shirt

jac·a·ran·da \ˌjak-ə-ˈran-də\ *n* : any of a genus of pinnate-leaved tropical American trees with clusters of showy blue flowers

ja·cinth \ˈjās-ᵊnth\ *n* : HYACINTH

¹jack \ˈjak\ *n* **1** : a mechanical device; *esp* : one used to raise a heavy body a short distance **2** : a male donkey **3** : a small target ball in lawn bowling **4** : a small national flag flown by a ship **5** : a small 6-pointed metal object used in a game (**jacks**) **6** : a playing card bearing the figure of a soldier or servant **7** : a socket into which a plug is inserted for connecting electric circuits

²jack *vb* **1** : to raise by means of a jack **2** : INCREASE ⟨~ up prices⟩

jack·al \ˈjak-əl, -ˌȯl\ *n* [Turk *çakal,* fr. Per *shagāl,* fr. Skt *sṛgāla*] : an Old World wild dog smaller than the related wolves

jack·a·napes \ˈjak-ə-ˌnāps\ *n* **1** : MONKEY, APE **2** : an impudent or conceited person

jack·ass \-ˌas\ *n* **1** : a male ass; *also* : DONKEY **2** : a stupid person : FOOL

jack·boot \-ˌbüt\ *n* **1** : a heavy military boot of glossy black leather extending above the knee **2** : a military boot reaching to the calf and having no laces

jack·daw \ˈjak-ˌdȯ\ *n* : a black and gray Eurasian crowlike bird

jack·et \ˈjak-ət\ *n* [ME *jaket,* fr. MF *jaquet,* dim. of *jaque* short jacket, fr. *jacque* peasant, fr. the name *Jacques* James] **1** : a garment for the upper body usu. having a front opening, collar, and sleeves **2** : an outer covering or casing ⟨a book ~⟩

Jack Frost *n* : frost or frosty weather personified

jack·ham·mer \ˈjak-ˌham-ər\ *n* : a pneumatic percussion tool for drilling rock or breaking pavement

jack–in–the–box \ˈjak-ən-t͟hə-ˌbäks\ *n, pl* **jack–in–the–box·es** *or* **jacks–in–the–box** : a toy consisting of a small box out of which a figure springs when the lid is raised

jack–in–the–pul·pit \ˌjak-ən-t͟hə-ˈpu̇l-ˌpit, -pət, -ˈpəl-\ *n, pl* **jack–in–the–pulpits** *or* **jacks–in–the–pulpit** : an American spring-flowering woodland herb having an upright club-shaped spadix arched over by a green and purple spathe

[1]**jack·knife** \ˈjak-ˌnīf\ *n* **1** : a large pocketknife **2** : a dive in which the diver bends from the waist and touches his ankles before straightening out

[2]**jackknife** *vb* : to fold like a jackknife ⟨the trailer truck *jackknifed*⟩

jack·leg \ˈjak-ˌleg\ *adj* **1** : lacking skill or training **2** : MAKESHIFT

jack–of–all–trades \ˌjak-əv-ˌȯl-ˈtrādz\ *n, pl* **jacks–of–all–trades** : one who is able to do passable work at various tasks

jack–o'–lan·tern \ˈjak-ə-ˌlant-ərn\ *n* : a lantern made of a pumpkin cut to look like a human face

jack·pot \ˈjak-ˌpät\ *n* **1** : a large sum of money formed by the accumulation of stakes from previous play (as in poker) **2** : an impressive and often unexpected success or reward

jack·rab·bit \-ˌrab-ət\ *n* : a large hare of western No. America with very long hind legs

jack·screw \-ˌskrü\ *n* : a screw-operated jack

jack·straw \-ˌstrȯ\ *n* **1** : a straw or a thin strip used in the game of jackstraws **2** *pl* : a game in which jackstraws are let fall in a heap and each player in turn tries to remove them one at a time without disturbing the rest

jack–tar \-ˈtär\ *n, often cap* : SAILOR

Ja·cob's ladder \ˌjā-kəbz-\ *n* : any of several perennial herbs related to phlox that have pinnate leaves and bright blue or white bell-shaped flowers

jac·quard \ˈjak-ˌärd\ *n, often cap* : a fabric of intricate variegated weave or pattern

[1]**jade** \ˈjād\ *n* **1** : a broken-down, vicious, or worthless horse **2** : a disreputable woman

[2]**jade** *vb* **jad·ed; jad·ing 1** : to wear out by overwork or abuse **2** : to become weary **syn** exhaust, fatigue, tire

[3]**jade** *n* [F, fr. obs. Sp (*piedra de la*) *ijada,* lit., loin stone; fr. the belief that jade cures renal colic] : a usu. green gemstone that takes a high polish

jad·ed \ˈjād-əd\ *adj* : dulled by a surfeit or excess

[1]**jag** \ˈjag\ *n* : a sharp projecting part

[2]**jag** *n* : SPREE

jag·ged \ˈjag-əd\ *adj* : sharply notched

jag·uar \ˈjag(-yə)-ˌwär\ *n* : a black-spotted tropical American cat that is larger and stockier than the Old World leopard

jaguar

jai alai \ˈhī-ˌlī\ *n* [Sp, fr. Basque, fr. *jai* festival + *alai* merry] : a court game played by usu. two or four players with a ball and a curved wicker basket strapped to the right wrist

[1]**jail** \ˈjāl\ *n* [ME *jaiole,* fr. OF, fr. LL *caveola,* dim. of L *cavea* cage] : PRISON; *esp* : one for persons held in lawful custody

[2]**jail** *vb* : to confine in a jail

jail·bird \-ˌbərd\ *n* : an habitual criminal

jail·break \-ˌbrāk\ *n* : a forcible escape from jail

jail·er *or* **jail·or** \ˈjā-lər\ *n* : a keeper of a jail

jal·ap \ˈjal-əp, ˈjäl-\ *n* : a purgative drug from the root of a Mexican plant related to the morning glory; *also* : this root or plant

ja·la·pe·ño \ˌhäl-ə-ˈpān-(ˌ)yō\ *n* : a Mexican hot pepper

ja·lopy \jə-ˈläp-ē\ *n, pl* **ja·lop·ies** : a dilapidated automobile

jal·ou·sie \ˈjal-ə-sē\ *n* [F, lit., jealousy] : a blind, window, or door with adjustable horizontal slats or louvers

[1]**jam** \ˈjam\ *vb* **jammed; jam·ming 1** : to press into a close or tight position **2** : to cause to become wedged so as to be unworkable; *also* : to make or become unworkable through the jamming of a movable part **3** : to push forcibly ⟨~ on the brakes⟩ **4** : CRUSH, BRUISE **5** : to make unintelligible by sending out interfering signals or messages **6** : to take part in a jam session

[2]**jam** *n* **1** : a crowded mass that impedes or blocks ⟨traffic ~⟩ **2** : a difficult state of affairs

[3]**jam** *n* : a food made by boiling fruit and sugar to a thick consistency

Jam *abbr* Jamaica

jamb \ˈjam\ *n* [ME *jambe,* fr. MF, lit., leg] : an upright piece forming the side of an opening (as of a door)

jam·ba·laya \ˌjəm-bə-ˈlī-ə\ *n* [LaF] : rice cooked with ham, sausage, chicken, shrimp, or oysters and seasoned with herbs

jam·bo·ree \ˌjam-bə-ˈrē\ *n* : a large festive gathering

James \ˈjāmz\ *n* — see BIBLE table

jam–pack \ˈjam-ˈpak\ *vb* : to pack tightly or to excess

jam session *n* : an impromptu performance by jazz musicians

Jan *abbr* January

jan·gle \ˈjaŋ-gəl\ *vb* **jan·gled; jan·gling** \-g(ə-)liŋ\ : to make a harsh or discordant sound — **jangle** *n*

jan·i·tor \ˈjan-ət-ər\ *n* [L, fr. *janua* door] : a person who has the care of a building — **jan·i·to·ri·al** \ˌjan-ə-ˈtōr-ē-əl\ *adj*

Jan·u·ary \ˈjan-yə-ˌwer-ē\ *n* [ME *Januarie,* fr. L *Januarius,* first month of the ancient Roman year, fr. *Janus,* two-faced god of gates and beginnings] : the 1st month of the year having 31 days

[1]**ja·pan** \jə-ˈpan\ *n* : a varnish giving a hard brilliant finish

[2]**japan** *vb* **ja·panned; ja·pan·ning** : to cover with a coat of japan

Jap·a·nese \ˌjap-ə-ˈnēz, -ˈnēs\ *n, pl* **Japanese 1** : a native or inhabitant of Japan **2** : the language of Japan — **Japanese** *adj*

Japanese beetle *n* : a small metallic green and brown beetle introduced from Japan that is a pest on the roots of grasses as a grub and on foliage and fruits as an adult

[1]**jape** \ˈjāp\ *vb* **japed; jap·ing 1** : JOKE **2** : MOCK

[2]**jape** *n* : JEST, GIBE

[1]**jar** \ˈjär\ *vb* **jarred; jar·ring 1** : to make a harsh or discordant sound **2** : to have a harsh or disagreeable effect **3** : VIBRATE, SHAKE

[2]**jar** *n* **1** : a harsh discordant sound **2** : QUARREL, DISPUTE **3** : JOLT **4** : a painful effect : SHOCK

[3]**jar** *n* : a broad-mouthed container usu. of glass or earthenware

jar·di·niere \ˌjärd-ᵊn-ˈiər\ *n* : an ornamental stand or pot for plants or flowers

jar·gon \ˈjär-gən, -ˌgän\ *n* **1** : confused unintelligible language **2** : the special vocabulary of a particular group or activity **3** : obscure and often pretentious language

Jas *abbr* James

jas·mine \ˈjaz-mən\ *n* [F *jasmin,* fr. Ar *yāsamīn*] : any of various climbing shrubs with fragrant flowers

jas·per \ˈjas-pər\ *n* : a red, yellow, or brown opaque quartz

jaun·dice \ˈjȯn-dəs\ *n* : yellowish discoloration of skin, tissues, and body fluids by bile pigments; *also* : a disorder marked by jaundice

jaun·diced \-dəst\ *adj* **1** : affected with or as if with jaundice **2** : exhibiting envy, distaste, or hostility

jaunt \ˈjȯnt\ *n* : a short trip usu. for pleasure

jaun·ty \ˈjȯnt-ē\ *adj* **jaun·ti·er; -est** : sprightly in manner or appearance : LIVELY — **jaun·ti·ly** \ˈjȯnt-ᵊl-ē\ *adv* — **jaun·ti·ness** \-ē-nəs\ *n*

Ja·va·nese \ˌjav-ə-ˈnēz, ˌjäv-, -ˈnēs\ *n* : a native or inhabitant of the Indonesian island of Java

jav·e·lin \ˈjav-(ə-)lən\ *n* **1** : a light spear **2** : a slender shaft thrown for distance in a track-and-field contest

[1]**jaw** \ˈjȯ\ *n* **1** : either of the bony or cartilaginous structures that support the soft tissues enclosing the mouth and that usu. bear teeth **2** : the parts forming the walls of the mouth and serving to open and close it — usu. used in pl. **3** : one of a pair of movable parts for holding or crushing something — **jaw·bone** \-ˈbōn, -ˌbōn\ *n* — **jawed** \ˈjȯd\ *adj*

[2]**jaw** *vb* : to talk abusively, indignantly, or at length

jaw·break·er \-ˌbrā-kər\ *n* **1** : a word difficult to pronounce **2** : a round hard candy

jay \ˈjā\ *n* : any of various noisy brightly colored birds smaller than the related crows

jay·bird \ˈjā-ˌbərd\ *n* : JAY

jay·gee \ˈjā-ˈjē\ *n* : LIEUTENANT JUNIOR GRADE

jay·vee \ˈjā-ˈvē\ *n* **1** : JUNIOR VARSITY **2** : a member of a junior varsity team

jay·walk \ˈjā-ˌwȯk\ *vb* : to cross a street carelessly without regard for traffic regulations — **jay·walk·er** *n*

[1]**jazz** \ˈjaz\ *n* **1** : American music characterized by improvisation, syncopated rhythms, and contrapuntal ensemble playing **2** : empty talk **3** : similar but unspecified things : STUFF

[2]**jazz** *vb* : ENLIVEN ⟨~ things up⟩

jazzy \ˈjaz-ē\ *adj* **jazz·i·er; -est 1** : having the characteristics of jazz **2** : marked by unrestraint, animation, or flashiness

JCS *abbr* joint chiefs of staff

jct *abbr* junction

JD *abbr* **1** [L *juris doctor*] doctor of jurisprudence; doctor of law **2** [L *jurum doctor*] doctor of laws **3** justice department **4** juvenile delinquent

jeal·ous \ˈjel-əs\ *adj* **1** : demanding complete devotion **2** : suspicious of a rival or of one believed to enjoy an advantage **3** : VIGILANT — **jeal·ous·ly** *adv* — **jeal·ou·sy** \-ə-sē\ *n*

jeans \ˈjēnz\ *n pl* [short for *jean fustian,* fr. ME *Gene* Genoa] : pants made of durable twilled cotton cloth

jeep \ˈjēp\ *n* [alter. of *gee pee,* fr. *g*eneral-*p*urpose] : a small four-wheel drive general-purpose motor vehicle used by the U.S. army in World War II

[1]**jeer** \ˈjiər\ *vb* : to speak or cry out in derision : MOCK

[2]**jeer** *n* : TAUNT

Je·ho·vah \ji-ˈhō-və\ *n* : GOD 1

je·hu \ˈjē-h(y)ü\ *n* : a driver of a coach or cab

je·june \ji-ˈjün\ *adj* : lacking interest or significance : DULL

je·ju·num \ji-ˈjü-nəm\ *n* [L] : the section of the small intestine between the duodenum and the ileum — **je·ju·nal** \-ˈjün-ᵊl\ *adj*

jell \ˈjel\ *vb* **1** : to come to the consistency of jelly **2** : to take shape

jel·ly \ˈjel-ē\ *n, pl* **jellies 1** : a food with a soft elastic consistency due usu. to the presence of gelatin or pectin; *esp* : a fruit product made by boiling sugar and the juice of a fruit **2** : a substance resembling jelly — **jelly** *vb*

jelly bean *n* : a bean-shaped candy

jel·ly·fish \ˈjel-ē-ˌfish\ *n* : an invertebrate sea animal with a saucer-shaped jellylike body

jen·net \ˈjen-ət\ *n* **1** : a small Spanish horse **2** : a female donkey

jen·ny \ˈjen-ē\ *n, pl* **jennies** : a female bird or donkey

je·on \jə-ˈȯn\ *n, pl* **jeon** — see *won* at MONEY table

jeop·ar·dy \ˈjep-ərd-ē\ *n* [ME *jeopardie,* fr. OF *jeu parti* alternative, lit., divided game] : exposure to death, loss, or injury **syn** peril, hazard, risk, danger — **jeop·ar·dize** \-ər-ˌdīz\ *vb*

Jer *abbr* Jeremiah; Jeremias

jer·e·mi·ad \ˌjer-ə-ˈmī-əd, -ˌad\ *n* : a prolonged lamentation or complaint

Jer·e·mi·ah \ˌjer-ə-ˈmī-ə\ *n* — see BIBLE table

Jer·e·mi·as \ˌjer-ə-ˈmī-əs\ *n* — see BIBLE table

[1]**jerk** \ˈjərk\ *n* **1** : a short quick pull or twist : TWITCH **2** : a stupid, foolish, or eccentric person — **jerk·i·ly** \ˈjər-kə-lē\ *adv* — **jerky** \ˈjər-kē\ *adj*

[2]**jerk** *vb* **1** : to give a sharp quick push, pull, or twist **2** : to move in short abrupt motions

jer·kin \ˈjər-kən\ *n* : a close-fitting usu. sleeveless jacket

jerk·wa·ter \ˈjərk-ˌwȯt-ər, -ˌwät-\ *adj* [fr. *jerkwater* (rural train); fr. the fact that it took on water carried in buckets from the source of supply] : of minor importance : INSIGNIFICANT ⟨~ towns⟩

jer·ry–built \ˈjer-ē-ˌbilt\ *adj* : built cheaply and flimsily

jer·sey \ˈjər-zē\ *n, pl* **jerseys** [*Jersey,* one of the Channel islands] **1** : a plain weft-knitted fabric **2** : a close fitting knitted shirt **3** : any of a breed of small usu. fawn-colored dairy cattle

jess \ˈjes\ *n* : a leg strap by which a captive bird of prey may be controlled

jes·sa·mine \ˈjes-ə-mən\ *var of* JASMINE

jest \ˈjest\ *n* **1** : an act intended to provoke laughter **2** : a witty remark **3** : a frivolous mood ⟨spoken in ~⟩ — **jest** *vb*

jest·er \ˈjes-tər\ *n* : a retainer formerly kept to provide casual entertainment

[1]**jet** \ˈjet\ *n* : a velvet-black coal that takes a good polish and is used for jewelry

[2]**jet** *vb* **jet·ted; jet·ting** : to spout or emit in a stream

[3]**jet** *n* **1** : a forceful rush (as of liquid or gas) through a narrow opening; *also* : a nozzle for a jet of fluid **2** : a jet-propelled airplane

[4]**jet** *vb* **jet·ted; jet·ting** : to travel by jet

jet lag *n* : a condition that is marked esp. by fatigue and irritability and occurs following a long flight through several time zones

jet·lin·er \ˈjet-ˌlī-nər\ *n* : a jet-propelled airliner

jet·port \ˈjet-ˌpōrt\ *n* : an airport designed to handle jets

jet–propelled \ˌjet-prə-ˈpeld\ *adj* : driven by an engine (**jet engine**) that produces propulsion (**jet propulsion**) by the rearward discharge of a jet of fluid (as heated air and exhaust gases)

jet·sam \ˈjet-səm\ *n* : jettisoned goods; *esp* : such goods washed ashore

jet set *n* : an international group of wealthy people who frequent fashionable resorts

jet stream *n* : a long narrow high-altitude current of high-speed winds blowing generally from the west

jet·ti·son \ˈjet-ə-sən\ *vb* **1** : to throw (goods) overboard to lighten a ship or aircraft in distress **2** : DISCARD — **jettison** *n*

jet·ty \ˈjet-ē\ *n, pl* **jetties 1** : a pier built to influence the current or to protect a harbor **2** : a landing wharf

jeu d'es·prit \zhœ-des-prē\ *n, pl* **jeux d'esprit** *same*\ [F, lit., play of the mind] : a witty comment or composition

Jew \ˈjü\ *n* **1** : ISRAELITE **2** : one whose religion is Judaism — **Jew·ish** *adj*

[1]**jew·el** \ˈjü-əl\ *n* [ME *juel,* fr. OF, dim. of *jeu* game, play, fr. L *jocus* game, joke] **1** : an ornament of precious metal **2** : GEMSTONE, GEM

[2]**jewel** *vb* **-eled** *or* **-elled; -el·ing** *or* **-el·ling** : to adorn or equip with jewels

jew·el·er *or* **jew·el·ler** \ˈjü-ə-lər\ *n* : a person who makes or deals in jewelry and related articles

jew·el·ry \ˈjü-əl-rē\ *n* : JEWELS; *esp* : objects of precious metal set with gems and worn for personal adornment

jew·el·weed \-ˌwēd\ *n* : IMPATIENS

Jew·ry \ˈju̇(ə)r-ē, ˈjü-rē\ *n* : the Jewish people
jg *abbr* junior grade
[1]**jib** \ˈjib\ *n* : a triangular sail set on a line running from the bow to the mast
[2]**jib** *vb* **jibbed; jib·bing** : to refuse to proceed further
jibe \ˈjīb\ *vb* **jibed; jib·ing** : to be in accord : AGREE
jif·fy \ˈjif-ē\ *n, pl* **jiffies** : MOMENT, INSTANT ⟨I'll be ready in a ~⟩
[1]**jig** \ˈjig\ *n* **1** : a lively dance in triple rhythm **2** : TRICK, GAME ⟨the ~ is up⟩ **3** : a device used to hold work during manufacture or assembly
[2]**jig** *vb* **jigged; jig·ging** : to dance a jig
jig·ger \ˈjig-ər\ *n* : a measure usu. holding 1½ ounces used in mixing drinks
jig·gle \ˈjig-əl\ *vb* **jig·gled; jig·gling** \-(ə-)liŋ\ : to move with quick little jerks — **jiggle** *n*
jig·saw \ˈjig-ˌsȯ\ *n* : a machine saw with a narrow vertically reciprocating blade for cutting curved lines
jigsaw puzzle *n* : a puzzle consisting of small irregularly cut pieces to be fitted together to form a picture
ji·had \ji-ˈhäd, -ˈhad\ *n* **1** : a Muslim holy war **2** : CRUSADE 2
[1]**jilt** \ˈjilt\ *vb* : to drop (one's lover) unfeelingly
[2]**jilt** *n* : one who jilts a lover
jim crow \ˈjim-ˈkrō\ *n, often cap J&C* : discrimination against blacks esp. by legal enforcement or traditional sanctions — **jim crow** *adj, often cap J&C* — **jim crow·ism** *n, often cap J&C*
jim–dan·dy \ˈjim-ˈdan-dē\ *n* : something excellent of its kind
jim·mies \ˈjim-ēz\ *n pl* : tiny rod-shaped bits of usu. chocolate-flavored candy often sprinkled on ice cream
[1]**jim·my** \ˈjim-ē\ *n, pl* **jimmies** : a small crowbar
[2]**jimmy** *vb* **jim·mied; jim·my·ing** : to force open with a jimmy
jim·son·weed \ˈjim-sən-ˌwēd\ *n, often cap* : a coarse poisonous weed that is related to the potato and tomato and has large trumpet-shaped white or violet flowers
[1]**jin·gle** \ˈjiŋ-gəl\ *vb* **jin·gled; jin·gling** \-g(ə-)liŋ\ : to make a light clinking or tinkling sound
[2]**jingle** *n* **1** : a light clinking or tinkling sound **2** : a short verse or song with catchy repetition
jin·go·ism \ˈjiŋ-gō-ˌiz-əm\ *n* : extreme chauvinism or nationalism marked esp. by a belligerent foreign policy — **jin·go·ist** \-əst\ *n* — **jin·go·is·tic** \ˌjiŋ-gō-ˈis-tik\ *adj*
jin·rik·i·sha \jin-ˈrik-ˌshȯ\ *n* : RICKSHA
[1]**jinx** \ˈjiŋks\ *n* : one that brings bad luck
[2]**jinx** *vb* : to foredoom to failure or misfortune
jit·ney \ˈjit-nē\ *n, pl* **jitneys** : a small bus that serves a regular route according to a flexible schedule
jit·ter·bug \ˈjit-ər-ˌbəg\ *n* : a dance in which couples two-step, balance, and twirl vigorously in standardized patterns — **jitterbug** *vb*
jit·ters \ˈjit-ərz\ *n pl* : extreme nervousness — **jit·tery** \-ə-rē\ *adj*
[1]**jive** \ˈjīv\ *n* **1** : swing music or dancing performed to it **2** : glib, deceptive, or foolish talk **3** : the jargon of jazz enthusiasts
[2]**jive** *vb* **jived; jiv·ing 1** : KID, TEASE; *also* : DECEIVE, SWINDLE **2** : to dance to or play jive
Jn *or* **Jno** *abbr* John
Jo *abbr* Joel
[1]**job** \ˈjäb\ *n* **1** : a piece of work **2** : something that has to be done : DUTY **3** : a regular remunerative position — **job·less** *adj*
[2]**job** *vb* **jobbed; job·bing 1** : to do occasional pieces of work for hire **2** : to hire or let by the job
Job \ˈjōb\ *n* — see BIBLE table
job action *n* : a protest action by workers to force compliance with demands
job·ber \ˈjäb-ər\ *n* **1** : a person who buys goods and then sells them to other dealers : MIDDLEMAN **2** : a person who does work by the job
job·hold·er \ˈjäb-ˌhōl-dər\ *n* : one having a regular job
jock \ˈjäk\ *n* [*jockstrap*] : ATHLETE; *esp* : a college athlete
[1]**jock·ey** \ˈjäk-ē\ *n, pl* **jockeys** : one who rides a horse esp. as a professional in a race
[2]**jockey** *vb* **jock·eyed; jock·ey·ing** : to maneuver or manipulate by adroit or devious means
jock·strap \ˈjäk-ˌstrap\ *n* [E slang *jock* (penis)] : ATHLETIC SUPPORTER
jo·cose \jō-ˈkōs\ *adj* : MERRY, HUMOROUS **syn** jocular, facetious, witty
joc·u·lar \ˈjäk-yə-lər\ *adj* : marked by jesting : PLAYFUL — **joc·u·lar·i·ty** \ˌjäk-yə-ˈlar-ət-ē\ *n*
jo·cund \ˈjäk-ənd\ *adj* : marked by mirth or cheerfulness
jodh·pur \ˈjäd-pər\ *n* **1** *pl* : riding breeches loose above the knee and tight-fitting below **2** : an ankle-high boot fastened with a strap
Jo·el \ˈjō-əl\ *n* — see BIBLE table
[1]**jog** \ˈjäg\ *vb* **jogged; jog·ging 1** : to give a slight shake or push to **2** : to go at a slow monotonous pace **3** : to run or ride at a slow trot — **jog·ger** *n*
[2]**jog** *n* **1** : a slight shake **2** : a jogging movement or pace
[3]**jog** *n* **1** : a projecting or retreating part of a line or surface **2** : a brief abrupt change in direction
jog·gle \ˈjäg-əl\ *vb* **jog·gled; jog·gling** \-(ə-)liŋ\ : to shake slightly — **joggle** *n*
john \ˈjän\ *n* **1** : TOILET **2** : a prostitute's client
John \ˈjän\ *n* — see BIBLE table
john·ny \ˈjän-ē\ *n, pl* **johnnies** : a short gown opening in the back that is worn by hospital patients
John·ny–jump–up \ˌjän-ē-ˈjəm-ˌpəp\ *n* : any of various small-flowered cultivated pansies
joie de vi·vre \ˌzhwäd-ə-ˈvēvrᵊ\ *n* [F] : keen enjoyment of life
join \ˈjȯin\ *vb* **1** : to come or bring together so as to form a unit **2** : to come or bring into close association **3** : to become a member of ⟨~ a church⟩ **4** : ADJOIN **5** : to take part in a collective activity
join·er \ˈjȯi-nər\ *n* **1** : a worker who constructs articles by joining pieces of wood **2** : a gregarious person who joins many organizations
[1]**joint** \ˈjȯint\ *n* **1** : the point of contact between bones of an animal skeleton with the parts that surround and support it **2** : a cut of meat suitable for roasting **3** : a place where two things or parts are connected **4** : ESTABLISHMENT; *esp* : a shabby or disreputable establishment **5** : a marijuana cigarette
[2]**joint** *adj* **1** : UNITED **2** : common to two or more — **joint·ly** *adv*
[3]**joint** *vb* **1** : to unite by or provide with a joint **2** : to separate the joints of
joist \ˈjȯist\ *n* : any of the small beams ranged parallel from wall to wall in a building to support the floor or ceiling
[1]**joke** \ˈjōk\ *n* : something said or done to provoke laughter; *esp* : a brief narrative with a humorous climax
[2]**joke** *vb* **joked; jok·ing** : to make jokes — **jok·ing·ly** \ˈjō-kiŋ-lē\ *adv*
jok·er \ˈjō-kər\ *n* **1** : a person who jokes **2** : an extra card used in some card games **3** : a misleading part of an agreement that works to one party's disadvantage
jol·li·fi·ca·tion \ˌjäl-i-fə-ˈkā-shən\ *n* : a festive celebration
jol·li·ty \ˈjäl-ət-ē\ *n, pl* **-ties** : GAIETY, MERRIMENT
jol·ly \ˈjäl-ē\ *adj* **jol·li·er; -est** : full of high spirits : MERRY
[1]**jolt** \ˈjōlt\ *vb* **1** : to give a quick hard knock or blow to **2** : to move with a sudden jerky motion — **jolt·er** *n*
[2]**jolt** *n* **1** : an abrupt jerky blow or movement **2** : a sudden shock
Jo·nah \ˈjō-nə\ *n* — see BIBLE table

Jo·nas \ˈjō-nəs\ *n* — see BIBLE table

jon·gleur \zhōⁿ-ˈglər\ *n* : an itinerant medieval minstrel

jon·quil \ˈjän-kwəl\ *n* [F *jonquille*, fr. Sp *junquillo*, dim. of *junco* reed, fr. L *juncus*] : a narcissus with fragrant clustered white or yellow flowers

josh \ˈjäsh\ *vb* : TEASE, JOKE

Josh *abbr* Joshua

Josh·ua \ˈjäsh-(ə-)wə\ *n* — see BIBLE table

Joshua tree *n* : a tall branched yucca of the southwestern U.S.

jos·tle \ˈjäs-əl\ *vb* **jos·tled; jos·tling** \-(ə-)liŋ\ **1** : to come in contact or into collision **2** : to make one's way by pushing and shoving

Jos·ue \ˈjäsh-ə-ˌwē\ *n* — see BIBLE table

[1]**jot** \ˈjät\ *n* : the least bit : IOTA

[2]**jot** *vb* **jot·ted; jot·ting** : to write briefly and hurriedly

jot·ting \ˈjät-iŋ\ *n* : a brief note

joule \ˈjül\ *n* : a unit of work or energy equal to the work done by a force of one newton acting through a distance of one meter

jounce \ˈjau̇ns\ *vb* **jounced; jounc·ing** : JOLT — **jounce** *n*

jour *abbr* **1** journal **2** journeyman

jour·nal \ˈjərn-ᵊl\ *n* [ME, service book containing the day hours, fr. MF, fr. *journal* daily, fr. L *diurnalis*, fr. *dies* day] **1** : a brief account of daily events **2** : a record of proceedings (as of a legislative body) **3** : a periodical (as a newspaper) dealing esp. with current events **4** : the part of a rotating axle or spindle that turns in a bearing

jour·nal·ese \ˌjərn-ᵊl-ˈēz, -ˈēs\ *n* : a style of writing held to be characteristic of newspapers

jour·nal·ism \ˈjərn-ᵊl-ˌiz-əm\ *n* **1** : the business of writing for, editing, or publishing periodicals (as newspapers) **2** : writing designed for or characteristic of newspapers — **jour·nal·ist** \-əst\ *n* — **jour·nal·is·tic** \ˌjərn-ᵊl-ˈis-tik\ *adj*

[1]**jour·ney** \ˈjər-nē\ *n, pl* **journeys** [ME, fr. OF *journee* day's journey, fr. *jour* day] : travel from one place to another

[2]**journey** *vb* **jour·neyed; jour·ney·ing** : to go on a journey : TRAVEL

jour·ney·man \-mən\ *n* **1** : a worker who has learned a trade and works for another person **2** : an experienced reliable worker

[1]**joust** \ˈjau̇st\ *n* : a combat on horseback between two knights with lances esp. as part of a tournament

[2]**joust** *vb* : to engage in a joust

jo·vial \ˈjō-vē-əl\ *adj* : marked by good humor — **jo·vi·al·i·ty** \ˌjō-vē-ˈal-ət-ē\ *n* — **jo·vi·al·ly** \ˈjō-vē-ə-lē\ *adv*

[1]**jowl** \ˈjau̇l\ *n* **1** : the lower jaw **2** : CHEEK

[2]**jowl** *n* : loose flesh about the lower jaw or throat

[1]**joy** \ˈjȯi\ *n* [ME, fr. OF *joie*, fr. L *gaudia*] **1** : a feeling of happiness that comes from success, good fortune, or a sense of well-being **2** : a source of happiness **syn** bliss, delight, enjoyment, pleasure — **joy·less** *adj*

[2]**joy** *vb* : REJOICE

joy·ful \-fəl\ *adj* : experiencing, causing, or showing joy — **joy·ful·ly** \-ē\ *adv*

joy·ous \ˈjȯi-əs\ *adj* : JOYFUL — **joy·ous·ly** *adv* — **joy·ous·ness** *n*

joy·ride \-ˌrīd\ *n* : a ride for pleasure often marked by reckless driving — **joy·rid·er** *n* — **joy·rid·ing** *n*

JP *abbr* **1** jet propulsion **2** justice of the peace

Jr *abbr* junior

JRC *abbr* Junior Red Cross

jt *or* **jnt** *abbr* joint

ju·bi·lant \ˈjü-bə-lənt\ *adj* [L *jubilans*, prp. of *jubilare* to rejoice] : EXULTANT — **ju·bi·lant·ly** *adv*

ju·bi·la·tion \ˌjü-bə-ˈlā-shən\ *n* : EXULTATION

ju·bi·lee \ˈjü-bə-ˌlē\ *n* [ME, fr. MF & LL; MF *jubilé*, fr. LL *jubilaeus*, fr. LGk *iōbēlaios*, fr. Heb *yōbhēl* ram's horn, trumpet, jubilee] **1** : a 50th anniversary **2** : a season or occasion of celebration

Jud *abbr* Judith

Ju·da·ic \jü-ˈdā-ik\ *also* **Ju·da·ical** \-ˈdā-ə-kəl\ *adj* : of, relating to, or characteristic of Jews or Judaism

Ju·da·ism \ˈjüd-ə-ˌiz-əm\ *n* : a religion developed among the ancient Hebrews and marked by belief in one God and by the moral and ceremonial laws of the Old Testament and the rabinic tradition

Ju·das tree \ˈjüd-əs-\ *n* : a Eurasian leguminous tree with purplish rosy flowers

Jude \ˈjüd\ *n* — see BIBLE table

Judg *abbr* Judges

[1]**judge** \ˈjəj\ *vb* **judged; judg·ing** **1** : to form an authoritative opinion **2** : to decide as a judge : TRY **3** : to form an estimate or evaluation about something : THINK **syn** conclude, deduce, gather, infer

[2]**judge** *n* **1** : a public official authorized to decide questions brought before a court **2** : UMPIRE **3** : one who gives an authoritative opinion : CRITIC — **judge·ship** *n*

Judges *n* — see BIBLE table

judg·ment *or* **judge·ment** \ˈjəj-mənt\ *n* **1** : a decision or opinion given after judging; *esp* : a formal decision given by a court **2** *cap* : the final judging of mankind by God **3** : the process of forming an opinion by discerning and comparing **4** : the capacity for judging : DISCERNMENT

Judgment Day *n* : the day of the final judging of all human beings by God

ju·di·ca·ture \ˈjüd-i-kə-ˌchu̇r\ *n* **1** : the administration of justice **2** : JUDICIARY 1

ju·di·cial \ju̇-ˈdish-əl\ *adj* **1** : of or relating to the administration of justice or the judiciary **2** : ordered or enforced by a court **3** : CRITICAL — **ju·di·cial·ly** \-ē\ *adv*

ju·di·cia·ry \ju̇-ˈdish-ē-ˌer-ē, -ˈdish-ə-rē\ *n* **1** : a system of courts of law; *also* : the judges of these courts **2** : a branch of government in which judicial power is vested — **judiciary** *adj*

ju·di·cious \ju̇-ˈdish-əs\ *adj* : having, exercising, or characterized by sound judgment **syn** prudent, sage, sane, sensible, wise — **ju·di·cious·ly** *adv*

Ju·dith \ˈjüd-əth\ *n* — see BIBLE table

ju·do \ˈjüd-ō\ *n* [Jp, lit., gentleness art] : a sport derived from jujitsu that emphasizes the use of quick movement and leverage to throw an opponent — **ju·do·ist** *n*

[1]**jug** \ˈjəg\ *n* **1** : a large deep container with a narrow mouth and a handle **2** : JAIL, PRISON

[2]**jug** *vb* **jugged; jug·ging** : JAIL, IMPRISON

jug·ger·naut \ˈjəg-ər-ˌnȯt\ *n* [Hindi *Jagannāth*, title of Vishnu (a Hindu god), lit., lord of the world] : a massive inexorable force or object that crushes everything in its path

jug·gle \ˈjəg-əl\ *vb* **jug·gled; jug·gling** \-(ə-)liŋ\ **1** : to keep several objects in motion in the air at the same time **2** : to manipulate esp. in order to achieve a desired and often fraudulent end — **jug·gler** \ˈjəg-lər\ *n*

jug·u·lar \ˈjəg-yə-lər\ *adj* : of, relating to, or situated in or on the throat or neck ⟨the ~ veins⟩

juice \ˈjüs\ *n* **1** : the extractable fluid contents of cells or tissues **2** *pl* : the natural fluids of an animal body **3** : a medium (as electricity) that supplies power

juic·er \ˈjü-sər\ *n* : an appliance for extracting juice (as from fruit)

juice up *vb* : to give life, energy, or spirit to

juicy \ˈjü-sē\ *adj* **juic·i·er; -est** **1** : SUCCULENT **2** : rich in interest; *also* : RACY — **juic·i·ly** \ˈjü-sə-lē\ *adv* — **juic·i·ness** \-sē-nəs\ *n*

ju·jit·su *or* **ju·jut·su** \jü-ˈjit-sü\ *n* [Jp *jūjutsu*, fr. *jū* weakness, gentleness + *jutsu* art, skill] : an art of fighting employing holds, throws, and paralyzing blows

ju·jube \ˈjü-ˌjüb, ˈjü-ju̇-ˌbē\ *n* : a fruit-flavored gumdrop or lozenge

juke·box \ˈjük-ˌbäks\ *n* : a coin-operated automatic record player

Jul *abbr* July

ju·lep \ˈjü-ləp\ *n* [ME sweetened water, fr. MF, fr. Ar *julāb*, fr. Per *gulāb*, fr. *gul* rose + *āb* water] : a drink made of bourbon, sugar, and mint served over crushed ice in a tall glass

Ju·ly \jü-ˈlī\ *n* [ME *Julie*, fr. OE *Julius*, fr. L, fr. Gaius *Julius* Caesar] : the 7th month of the year having 31 days

[1]**jum·ble** \ˈjəm-bəl\ *vb* **jum·bled; jum·bling** \-b(ə-)liŋ\ : to mix in a confused mass

[2]**jumble** *n* : a disorderly mass or pile

jum·bo \ˈjəm-bō\ *n, pl* **jumbos** [*Jumbo*, a huge elephant exhibited by P.T. Barnum] : a very large specimen of its kind — **jumbo** *adj*

[1]**jump** \ˈjəmp\ *vb* **1** : to spring into the air : leap over **2** : to give a start **3** : to rise or increase suddenly or sharply **4** : to make a sudden attack **5** : ANTICIPATE ⟨~ the gun⟩ **6** : to leave hurriedly and often furtively ⟨~ town⟩ **7** : to act or move before (as a signal)

[2]**jump** *n* **1** : a spring into the air; *esp* : one made for height or distance in a track meet **2** : a sharp sudden increase **3** : an initial advantage

[1]**jump·er** \ˈjəm-pər\ *n* : one that jumps

[2]**jumper** *n* **1** : a loose blouse **2** : a sleeveless one-piece dress worn usu. with a blouse **3** *pl* : a child's sleeveless coverall

jumping bean *n* : a seed of any of several Mexican shrubs that tumbles about because of the movements of the larva of a small moth inside it

jumping–off place \ˌjəm-piŋ-ˈȯf-\ *n* **1** : a remote or isolated place **2** : a place from which an enterprise is launched

jump·suit \ˈjəmp-ˌsüt\ *n* **1** : a uniform worn by parachutists in jumping **2** : a one-piece garment consisting of a blouse or shirt with attached trousers or shorts

jumpy \ˈjəm-pē\ *adj* **jump·i·er; -est** : NERVOUS, JITTERY

[1]**jun** \ˈjən\ *n, pl* **jun** — see *won* at MONEY table

[2]**jun** *abbr* junior

Jun *abbr* June

junc *abbr* junction

jun·co \ˈjəŋ-kō\ *n, pl* **juncos** *or* **juncoes** : any of several small common pink-billed American finches that are largely gray with conspicuous white feathers in the tail

junc·tion \ˈjəŋk-shən\ *n* **1** : an act of joining **2** : a place or point of meeting ⟨a railroad ~⟩

junc·ture \ˈjeŋk-chər\ *n* **1** : JOINT, CONNECTION **2** : UNION **3** : a critical time or state of affairs

June \ˈjün\ *n* [ME, fr. L *Junius*] : the 6th month of the year having 30 days

jun·gle \ˈjəŋ-gəl\ *n* **1** : a thick tangled mass of tropical vegetation; *also* : a tract overgrown with vegetation **2** : a place of ruthless struggle for survival

[1]**ju·nior** \ˈjü-nyər\ *adj* **1** : YOUNGER **2** : lower in rank **3** : of or relating to juniors

[2]**junior** *n* **1** : a person who is younger or of lower rank than another **2** : a student in his next-to-last year (as at a college)

junior college *n* : a school that offers studies corresponding to those of the 1st two years of college

junior high school *n* : a school usu. including grades 7-9

junior varsity *n* : a team whose members lack the experience or qualifications required for the varsity

ju·ni·per \ˈjü-nə-pər\ *n* : any of various evergreen shrubs or trees related to the pines

[1]**junk** \ˈjəŋk\ *n* **1** : old iron, glass, paper, or waste; *also* : discarded articles **2** : a shoddy product **3** *slang* : NARCOTICS; *esp* : HEROIN — **junky** *adj*

[2]**junk** *vb* : DISCARD, SCRAP

[3]**junk** *n* : a ship of Chinese waters with a high poop and overhanging stem

junk·er \ˈjəŋ-kər\ *n* : something (as an old automobile) ready for scrapping

Jun·ker \ˈyüŋ-kər\ *n* [G] : a member of the Prussian landed aristocracy

jun·ket \ˈjəŋ-kət\ *n* **1** : a dessert of sweetened flavored milk set by rennet as a pudding **2** : a trip made by an official at public expense

[3]junk

junk food *n* : food that is high in calories but low in nutritional content

junk·ie *or* **junky** \ˈjəŋ-kē\ *n, pl* **junkies 1** *slang* : a narcotics peddler or addict **2** : one that derives inordinate pleasure from or is dependent on something ⟨sugar ~⟩

jun·ta \ˈhün-tə, ˈjənt-ə, ˈhən-tə\ *n* [Sp, fr. *junto* joined, fr. L *jungere* to join] : a group of persons controlling a government esp. after a revolutionary seizure of power

Ju·pi·ter \ˈjü-pət-ər\ *n* : the largest of the planets and the one 5th in order of distance from the sun

Ju·ras·sic \jü-ˈras-ik\ *adj* : of, relating to, or being the period of the Mesozoic era between the Triassic and the Cretaceous — **Jurassic** *n*

ju·rid·i·cal \jü-ˈrid-i-kəl\ *or* **ju·rid·ic** \-ik\ *adj* **1** : of or relating to the administration of justice **2** : LEGAL — **ju·rid·i·cal·ly** \-i-k(ə-)lē\ *adv*

ju·ris·dic·tion \ˌjür-əs-ˈdik-shən\ *n* **1** : the power, right, or authority to interpret and apply the law **2** : the authority of a sovereign power **3** : the limits or territory within which authority may be exercised — **ju·ris·dic·tion·al** \-sh(ə-)nəl\ *adj*

ju·ris·pru·dence \-ˈprüd-ᵊns\ *n* **1** : a system of laws **2** : the science or philosophy of law

ju·rist \ˈjür-əst\ *n* : one having a thorough knowledge of law

ju·ris·tic \jü-ˈris-tik\ *adj* **1** : of or relating to a jurist or jurisprudence **2** : of, relating to, or recognized in law

ju·ror \ˈjür-ər\ *n* : a member of a jury

[1]**ju·ry** \ˈjür-ē\ *n, pl* **juries 1** : a body of persons sworn to inquire into a matter submitted to them and to give their verdict **2** : a committee for judging and awarding prizes (as at a contest)

[2]**jury** *adj* : improvised for temporary use esp. in an emergency ⟨a ~ mast⟩

jury–rig \ˈjür-ē-ˌrig\ *vb* : to erect, construct, or arrange in a makeshift fashion

[1]**just** \ˈjəst\ *adj* **1** : having a basis in or conforming to fact or reason : REASONABLE ⟨~ comment⟩ **2** : CORRECT, PROPER ⟨~ proportions⟩ **3** : morally or legally right ⟨a ~ title⟩ **4** : DESERVED, MERITED ⟨~ punishment⟩ **syn** upright, honorable, conscientious, honest — **just·ly** *adv* — **just·ness** *n*

[2]**just** \(ˌ)jəst, (ˌ)jist\ *adv* **1** : EXACTLY ⟨~ right⟩ **2** : very recently ⟨has ~ left⟩ **3** : BARELY ⟨lives ~ outside the city⟩ **4** : DIRECTLY ⟨~ across the street⟩ **5** : ONLY ⟨~ a note⟩ **6** : VERY

jus·tice \ˈjəs-təs\ *n* **1** : the administration of what is just (as by assigning merited rewards or punishments) **2** : JUDGE **3** : the administration of law **4** : FAIRNESS; *also* : RIGHTEOUSNESS

justice of the peace : a local magistrate empowered chiefly to try minor cases, to administer oaths, and to perform marriages

jus·ti·fy \ˈjəs-tə-ˌfī\ *vb* **-fied; -fy·ing 1** : to prove to be just, right, or reasonable **2** : to pronounce free from guilt or blame **3** : to adjust or arrange spaces in a line of printed text so the margins are even — **jus·ti·fi·able** *adj* — **jus·ti·fi·ca·tion** \ˌjəs-tə-fə-ˈkā-shən\ *n*

jut \ˈjət\ *vb* **jut·ted; jut·ting** : PROJECT, PROTRUDE

jute \ˈjüt\ *n* : a strong glossy fiber from a tropical herb used esp. for making sacks and twine

juv *abbr* juvenile

[1]**ju·ve·nile** \ˈjü-və-ˌnīl, -vən-ᵊl\ *adj* **1** : showing incomplete development **2** : of, relating to, or characteristic of children or young people

[2]**juvenile** *n* **1** : a young person **2** : a young lower animal (as a fish or a bird) **3** : an actor or actress who plays youthful parts

jux·ta·pose \ˈjək-stə-ˌpōz\ *vb* **-posed; -pos·ing** : to place side by side — **jux·ta·po·si·tion** \ˌjək-stə-pə-ˈzish-ən\ *n*

JV *abbr* junior varsity

K

[1]**k** \ˈkā\ *n, pl* **k's** *or* **ks** \ˈkāz\ *often cap* : the 11th letter of the English alphabet

[2]**k** *abbr* **1** karat **2** kilogram **3** kitchen **4** knit **5** kosher

[1]**K** *abbr* Kelvin

[2]**K** *symbol* **1** [NL *kalium*] potassium **2** strikeout

ka·bob \ˈkā-ˌbäb, kə-ˈbäb\ *n* : cubes of meat cooked with vegetables usu. on a skewer

Ka·bu·ki \kə-ˈbü-kē\ *n* : traditional Japanese popular drama with highly stylized singing and dancing

kad·dish \ˈkäd-ish\ *n, often cap* : a Jewish prayer recited in the daily synagogue ritual and by mourners at public services after the death of a close relative

kaf·fee·klatsch \ˈkȯf-ē-ˌklach, ˈkäf-\ *n, often cap* [G] : an informal social gathering for coffee and talk

kai·ser \ˈkī-zər\ *n* : EMPEROR; *esp* : the ruler of Germany from 1871 to 1918

kale \ˈkāl\ *n* : a hardy cabbage with curled leaves that do not form a head

ka·lei·do·scope \kə-ˈlīd-ə-ˌskōp\ *n* : an instrument containing loose bits of colored glass between two flat plates and two plane mirrors so placed that changes of position of the bits of glass are reflected in an endless variety of patterns — **ka·lei·do·scop·ic** \-ˌlīd-ə-ˈskäp-ik\ *adj* — **ka·lei·do·scop·i·cal·ly** \-i-k(ə-)lē\ *adv*

ka·ma·ai·na \ˌkäm-ə-ˈī-nə\ *n* [Hawaiian *kama'āina,* fr. *kama* child + *'āina* land] : one who has lived in Hawaii for a long time

kame \ˈkām\ *n* [Sc, lit., comb] : a short ridge or mound of material deposited by glacial meltwater

ka·mi·ka·ze \ˌkäm-i-ˈkäz-ē\ *n* [Jp, lit., divine wind] : a member of a corps of Japanese pilots assigned to make a suicidal crash on a target; *also* : an airplane flown in such an attack

Kan *or* **Kans** *abbr* Kansas

kan·ga·roo \ˌkaŋ-gə-ˈrü\ *n, pl* **-roos** : any of several large leaping marsupial mammals of Australia with powerful hind legs and a long thick tail

kangaroo court *n* : a court or an illegal self-appointed tribunal characterized by irresponsible, perverted, or irregular procedures

ka·olin \ˈkā-ə-lən\ *n* : a fine usu. white clay used in ceramics and refractories and in medicine in the treatment of diarrhea

ka·pok \ˈkā-ˌpäk\ *n* : silky fiber from the seeds of a tropical tree used esp. as a filling (as for life preservers)

Kap·o·si's sar·co·ma \ˈkap-ə-sēz-sär-ˈkō-mə\ *n* : a serious disease now usu. associated with AIDS that affects esp. the skin and mucous membranes and is characterized usu. by the formation of pink to reddish-brown or bluish plaques

ka·put *also* **ka·putt** \kä-ˈpu̇t, kə-, -ˈpüt\ *adj* [G, fr. F *capot* not having made a trick at piquet] **1** : utterly defeated or destroyed **2** : made useless or unable to function

kar·a·kul \ˈkar-ə-kəl\ *n* : the dark tightly curled pelt of the newborn lamb of an Asian sheep

kar·at \ˈkar-ət\ *n* : a unit for expressing proportion of gold in an alloy equal to 1/24 part of pure gold

ka·ra·te \kə-ˈrät-ē\ *n* [Jp, lit., empty hand] : an art of self-defense in which an attacker is disabled by crippling kicks and punches

kar·ma \ˈkär-mə\ *n, often cap* [Skt] : the force generated by a person's actions held in Hinduism and Buddhism to perpetuate transmigration and to determine his destiny in his next existence — **kar·mic** \-mik\ *adj, often cap*

karst \ˈkärst\ *n* [G] : an irregular limestone region with sinks, underground streams, and caverns

ka·ty·did \ˈkāt-ē-ˌdid\ *n* : any of several large green tree-dwelling American grasshoppers

kay·ak \ˈkī-ˌak\ *n* : an Eskimo canoe made of a skin-covered frame with a small opening and propelled by a double-bladed paddle; *also* : a similar portable boat

kayo \(ˈ)kā-ˈō, ˈkā-ō\ *n* : KNOCKOUT — **kayo** *vb*

ka·zoo \kə-ˈzü\ *n, pl* **kazoos** : a toy musical instrument consisting of a tube with a membrane sealing one end and a side hole to sing or hum into

KB *abbr* kilobyte

kc *abbr* kilocycle

KC *abbr* **1** Kansas City **2** King's Counsel **3** Knights of Columbus

kc/s *abbr* kilocycles per second

KD *abbr* knocked down

ke·bab *or* **ke·bob** \kə-ˈbäb\ *var of* KABOB

[1]**kedge** \ˈkej\ *vb* **kedged; kedg·ing** : to move a ship by hauling on a line attached to a small anchor dropped at the distance and in the direction desired

[2]**kedge** *n* : a small anchor

keel \ˈkēl\ *n* **1** : a timber or plate running lengthwise along the center of the bottom of a ship **2** : something (as a bird's breastbone) like a ship's keel in form or use — **keeled** \ˈkēld\ *adj*

keel·boat \ˈkēl-ˌbōt\ *n* : a shallow covered keeled riverboat for freight that is usu. rowed, poled, or towed

keel·haul \-ˌhȯl\ *vb* : to haul under the keel of a ship as punishment

keel over *vb* **1** : OVERTURN, CAPSIZE **2** : FAINT, SWOON

keel·son \ˈkel-sən, ˈkēl-\ *n* : a reinforcing structure above and fastened to a ship's keel

[1]**keen** \ˈkēn\ *adj* **1** : SHARP ⟨a ~ knife⟩ **2** : SEVERE ⟨a ~ wind⟩ **3** : ENTHUSIASTIC ⟨~ about swimming⟩ **4** : mentally alert ⟨a ~ mind⟩ **5** : STRONG, ACUTE ⟨~ eyesight⟩ **6** : WONDERFUL, EXCELLENT — **keen·ly** *adv* — **keen·ness** \ˈkēn-nəs\ *n*

[2]**keen** *n* : a lamentation for the dead uttered in a loud wailing voice or in a wordless cry — **keen** *vb*

[1]**keep** \ˈkēp\ *vb* **kept** \ˈkept\; **keep·ing 1** : FULFILL, OBSERVE ⟨~ a promise⟩ ⟨~ a holiday⟩ **2** : GUARD ⟨~ us from

harm⟩; *also* : to take care of ⟨~ a neighbor's children⟩ **3** : MAINTAIN ⟨~ silence⟩ **4** : to have in one's service or at one's disposal ⟨~ a horse⟩ **5** : to preserve a record in ⟨~ a diary⟩ **6** : to have in stock for sale **7** : to retain in one's possession ⟨~ what you find⟩ **8** : to carry on (as a business) : CONDUCT **9** : HOLD, DETAIN ⟨~ him in jail⟩ **10** : to refrain from revealing ⟨~ a secret⟩ **11** : to continue in good condition ⟨meat will ~ in a freezer⟩ **12** : ABSTAIN, REFRAIN — **keep·er** *n*

²**keep** *n* **1** : FORTRESS **2** : the means or provisions by which one is kept — **for keeps 1** : with the provision that one keeps what he wins ⟨play marbles *for keeps*⟩ **2** : PERMANENTLY

keep·ing \ˈkē-piŋ\ *n* : CONFORMITY ⟨in ~ with good taste⟩

keep·sake \ˈkēp-ˌsāk\ *n* : MEMENTO

keep up *vb* **1** : to persevere in **2** : MAINTAIN, SUSTAIN **3** : to keep informed **4** : to continue without interruption

keg \ˈkeg\ *n* : a small cask or barrel

keg·ler \ˈkeg-lər\ *n* : ¹BOWLER

kelp \ˈkelp\ *n* : any of various coarse brown seaweeds; *also* : a mass of these or their ashes often used as fertilizer

Kelt \ˈkelt\ *var of* CELT

kel·vin \ˈkel-vən\ *n* : a unit of temperature equal to 1/273.16 of the Kelvin scale temperature of the triple point of water and equal to the Celsius degree in size

Kelvin *adj* : relating to, conforming to, or being a temperature scale according to which absolute zero is 0 K, the equivalent of —273.15°C

ken \ˈken\ *n* **1** : range of vision : SIGHT **2** : range of understanding

ken·nel \ˈken-ᵊl\ *n* : a shelter for a dog or cat; *also* : an establishment for the breeding or boarding of dogs or cats — **kennel** *vb*

ke·no \ˈkē-nō\ *n* : a game resembling bingo

Ken·tucky bluegrass \kən-ˌtək-ē-\ *n* : a valuable pasture and meadow grass of both Europe and America

Ke·ogh plan \ˈkē-(ˌ)ō-\ *n* [Eugene James *Keogh b*1907 Am. politician] : an individual retirement account for the self-employed

ke·pi \ˈkā-pē, ˈkep-ē\ *n* [F] : a military cap with a round flat top sloping toward the front and a visor

ker·a·tin \ˈker-ət-ᵊn\ *n* : any of various sulfur-containing fibrous proteins that form the chemical basis of hair and horny tissues — **ke·ra·ti·nous** \kə-ˈrat-ᵊn-əs, ˌker-ə-ˈtī-nəs\ *adj*

kerb \ˈkərb\ *n, Brit* : CURB

ker·chief \ˈkər-chəf, -ˌchēf\ *n, pl* **kerchiefs** \-chəfs, -ˌchēfs\ *also* **kerchieves** \-ˌchēvz\ [ME *courchef,* fr. OF *cuevrechief,* fr. *covrir* to cover + *chief* head] **1** : a square of cloth worn by women esp. as a head covering **2** : HANDKERCHIEF

kerf \ˈkərf\ *n* : a slit or notch made by a saw or cutting torch

ker·nel \ˈkərn-ᵊl\ *n* **1** : the inner softer part of a seed, fruit stone, or nut **2** : a whole seed of a cereal **3** : a central or essential part : CORE

ker·o·sene *or* **ker·o·sine** \ˈker-ə-ˌsēn, ˌker-ə-ˈsēn, ˈkar-, ˌkar-\ *n* : a thin oil produced from petroleum and used for a fuel and as a solvent

ketch \ˈkech\ *n* : a large fore-and-aft rigged boat with two masts

ketch·up *var of* CATSUP

ket·tle \ˈket-ᵊl\ *n* : a metallic vessel for boiling liquids

ket·tle·drum \-ˌdrəm\ *n* : a brass or copper drum with parchment stretched across the top

¹**key** \ˈkē\ *n* **1** : a usu. metal instrument by which the bolt of a lock is turned; *also* : a device having the form or function of a key **2** : a means of gaining or preventing entrance, possession, or control **3** : EXPLANATION, SOLUTION **4** : one of the levers pressed by a finger in operating or playing an instrument **5** : a leading individual or principle **6** : a system of seven tones based on their relationship to a tonic; *also* : the tone or pitch of a voice **7** : a small switch for opening or closing an electric circuit

²**key** *vb* **1** : SECURE, FASTEN **2** : to regulate the musical pitch of **3** : to bring into harmony or conformity **4** : to make nervous — usu. used with *up*

³**key** *adj* : BASIC, CENTRAL ⟨~ issues⟩

⁴**key** *n* : a low island or reef (as off the southern coast of Florida)

⁵**key** *n, slang* : a kilogram esp. of marijuana or heroin

key·board \-ˌbōrd\ *n* **1** : a row of keys (as on a piano) **2** : an assemblage of keys for operating a machine

key club *n* : a private club serving liquor and providing entertainment

key·hole \ˈkē-ˌhōl\ *n* : a hole for receiving a key

¹**key·note** \-ˌnōt\ *n* **1** : the first and harmonically fundamental tone of a scale **2** : the central fact, idea, or mood

²**keynote** *vb* **1** : to set the keynote of **2** : to deliver the major address (as at a convention) — **key·not·er** *n*

key·punch \ˈkē-ˌpənch\ *n* : a machine with a keyboard used to cut holes or notches in punch cards — **keypunch** *vb* — **key·punch·er** *n*

key·stone \ˈkē-ˌstōn\ *n* : the wedge-shaped piece at the crown of an arch that locks the other pieces in place

key word *n* : a word that is a key; *esp* : a word exemplifying the meaning or value of a letter or symbol

kg *abbr* kilogram

KGB *abbr* [Russ *Komitet Gosudarstvennoi Bezopasnosti*] (Soviet) State Security Committee

kha·ki \ˈkak-ē, ˈkäk-\ *n* [Hindi *khaki* dust-colored, fr. *khāk* dust, fr. Per] **1** : a light yellowish brown **2** : a khaki-colored cloth; *also* : a military uniform of this cloth

khan \ˈkän, ˈkan\ *n* : a Mongol leader; *esp* : a successor of Genghis Khan

khe·dive \kə-ˈdēv\ *n* : a ruler of Egypt from 1867 to 1914 governing as a viceroy of the sultan of Turkey

khoum \ˈküm\ *n* — see *ouguiya* at MONEY table

kHz *abbr* kilohertz

KIA *abbr* killed in action

kib·ble \ˈkib-əl\ *vb* **kib·bled; kib·bling** : to grind coarsely — **kibble** *n*

kib·butz \kib-ˈu̇ts, -ˈüts\ *n, pl* **kib·but·zim** \-ˌu̇t-ˈsēm, -ˌüt-\ [NHeb *qibbūṣ*] : a collective farm or settlement in Israel

ki·bitz·er \ˈkib-ət-sər, kə-ˈbit-\ *n* [Yiddish] : one who looks on and usu. offers unwanted advice esp. at a card game — **kib·itz** \ˈkib-əts\ *vb*

ki·bosh \ˈkī-ˌbäsh\ *n* : something that serves as a check or stop ⟨put the ~ on his plan⟩

¹**kick** \ˈkik\ *vb* **1** : to strike out or hit with the foot; *also* : to score by kicking a ball **2** : to object strongly **3** : to recoil when fired — **kick·er** *n*

²**kick** *n* **1** : a blow or thrust with the foot; *esp* : a propelling of a ball with the foot **2** : the recoil of a gun **3** : a feeling or expression of objection **4** : stimulating effect esp. of pleasure

kick·back \ˈkik-ˌbak\ *n* **1** : a sharp violent reaction **2** : a secret return of a part of a sum received

kick in *vb* **1** : CONTRIBUTE **2** *slang* : DIE

kick·off \ˈkik-ˌȯf\ *n* **1** : a kick that puts the ball in play (as in football) **2** : COMMENCEMENT

kick off *vb* **1** : to start or resume play with a placekick **2** : to begin proceedings **3** *slang* : DIE

kick over *vb* : to begin or cause to begin to fire — used of an internal-combustion engine

kick·shaw \ˈkik-ˌshȯ\ *n* [fr. F *quelque chose* something] **1** : DELICACY **2** : BAUBLE
kick·stand \ˈkik-ˌstand\ *n* : a swiveling metal bar attached to a 2-wheeled vehicle for holding it up when not in use
kicky \ˈkik-ē\ *adj* : providing a kick or thrill : EXCITING
[1]**kid** \ˈkid\ *n* **1** : a young goat **2** : the flesh, fur, or skin of a young goat; *also* : something (as leather) made of kid **3** : CHILD, YOUNGSTER — **kid·dish** \ˈkid-ish\ *adj*
[2]**kid** *vb* **kid·ded; kid·ding 1** : FOOL **2** : TEASE — **kid·der** *n* — **kid·ding·ly** \ˈkid-iŋ-lē\ *adv*
kid·nap \ˈkid-ˌnap\ *vb* **-napped** *or* **-naped** \-ˌnapt\; **-nap·ping** *or* **-nap·ing** : to hold or carry a person away by unlawful force or by fraud and against his will — **kid·nap·per** *or* **kid·nap·er** *n*
kid·ney \ˈkid-nē\ *n, pl* **kidneys 1** : either of a pair of organs lying near the backbone that excrete waste products of the body in the form of urine **2** : TEMPERAMENT; *also* : SORT
kidney bean *n* **1** : an edible seed of the common cultivated bean; *esp* : one that is large and dark red **2** : a plant bearing kidney beans
kid·skin \ˈkid-ˌskin\ *n* : the skin of a young goat used for leather
kiel·ba·sa \k(y)el-ˈbäs-ə, kil-\ *n, pl* **-basas** *also* **-ba·sy** \-ˈbäs-ē\ : a smoked sausage of Polish origin
kie·sel·guhr *or* **kie·sel·gur** \ˈkē-zəl-ˌgu̇r\ *n* : loose or porous diatomite
[1]**kill** \ˈkil\ *vb* **1** : to deprive of life **2** : to put an end to ⟨~ competition⟩; *also* : DEFEAT ⟨~ a proposed amendment⟩ **3** : USE UP ⟨~ time⟩ **4** : to mark for omission **syn** slay, murder, assassinate, execute — **kill·er** *n*
[2]**kill** *n* **1** : an act of killing **2** : an animal or animals killed (as in a hunt); *also* : an aircraft, ship, or vehicle destroyed by military action
kill·deer \ˈkil-ˌdiər\ *n, pl* **killdeers** *or* **killdeer** [imit.] : a plover of temperate No. America with a plaintive penetrating cry
kill·ing \ˈkil-iŋ\ *n* : a sudden notable gain or profit
kill·joy \ˈkil-ˌjȯi\ *n* : one who spoils the pleasures of others
kiln \ˈkil(n)\ *n* : a heated enclosure (as an oven) for processing a substance by burning, firing, or drying — **kiln** *vb*
ki·lo \ˈkē-lō\ *n, pl* **kilos** : KILOGRAM
ki·lo·byte \ˈkil-ə-ˌbīt, ˈkē-lə-\ *n* : 1024 bytes
kilo·cy·cle \ˈkil-ə-ˌsī-kəl\ *n* : KILOHERTZ
ki·lo·gram \ˈkē-lə-ˌgram, ˈkil-ə-\ *n* : the basic metric unit of mass and weight — see METRIC SYSTEM table
ki·lo·hertz \ˈkil-ə-ˌhərts, ˈkē-lə-, -ˌherts\ *n* : 1000 hertz
kilo·li·ter \ˈkil-ə-ˌlēt-ər\ *n* — see METRIC SYSTEM table
ki·lo·me·ter \kil-ˈäm-ət-ər, ˈkil-ə-ˌmēt-\ *n* — see METRIC SYSTEM table
ki·lo·ton \ˈkil-ə-ˌtən, ˈkē-lō-\ *n* **1** : 1000 tons **2** : an explosive force equivalent to that of 1000 tons of TNT
ki·lo·volt \-ˌvōlt\ *n* : 1000 volts
kilo·watt \ˈkil-ə-ˌwät\ *n* : 1000 watts
kilowatt–hour *n* : a unit of energy equal to that expended by one kilowatt in one hour
kilt \ˈkilt\ *n* : a knee-length pleated skirt usu. of tartan worn by men in Scotland
kil·ter \ˈkil-tər\ *n* : proper condition ⟨out of ~⟩
ki·mo·no \kə-ˈmō-nə\ *n, pl* **-nos 1** : a loose robe with wide sleeves traditionally worn with a wide sash as an outer garment by the Japanese **2** : a loose dressing gown or jacket
kin \ˈkin\ *n* **1** : an individual's relatives **2** : KINSMAN
ki·na \ˈkē-nə\ *n* — see MONEY table
[1]**kind** \ˈkīnd\ *n* **1** : essential quality or character **2** : a group united by common traits or interests : CATEGORY; *also* : VARIETY **3** : goods or commodities as distinguished from money
[2]**kind** *adj* **1** : of a sympathetic, forbearing, or pleasant nature ⟨~ friends⟩ **2** : arising from sympathy or forbearance ⟨~ deeds⟩ **syn** benevolent, benign, benignant, kindly — **kind·ness** \ˈkīn(d)-nəs\ *n*
kin·der·gar·ten \ˈkin-dər-ˌgärt-ᵊn\ *n* [Ger, lit., children's garden] : a school or class for children usu. from four to six years old
kin·der·gart·ner \-ˌgärt-nər\ *n* **1** : a kindergarten pupil **2** : a kindergarten teacher
kind·heart·ed \ˈkīnd-ˈhärt-əd\ *adj* : marked by a sympathetic nature
kin·dle \ˈkin-dᵊl\ *vb* **kin·dled; kin·dling** \-(d)liŋ, -dᵊl-iŋ\ **1** : to set on fire : start burning **2** : to stir up : AROUSE **3** : ILLUMINATE, GLOW
kin·dling \ˈkin-(d)liŋ, ˈkin-lən\ *n* : easily combustible material for starting a fire
[1]**kind·ly** \ˈkīn-dlē\ *adj* **kind·li·er; -est 1** : of an agreeable or beneficial nature **2** : of a sympathetic or generous nature ⟨~ men⟩ — **kind·li·ness** *n*
[2]**kindly** *adv* **1** : READILY ⟨does not take ~ to criticism⟩ **2** : SYMPATHETICALLY **3** : COURTEOUSLY, OBLIGINGLY
kind of \ˌkīn-də(v)\ *adv* : to a moderate degree ⟨it's *kind of* late to begin⟩
[1]**kin·dred** \ˈkin-drəd\ *n* **1** : a group of related individuals **2** : one's relatives
[2]**kindred** *adj* : of a like nature or character
kine \ˈkīn\ *archaic pl of* cow
ki·ne·mat·ics \ˌkin-ə-ˈmat-iks\ *n* : a science that deals with motion apart from considerations of mass and force — **ki·ne·mat·ic** \-ik\ *or* **ki·ne·mat·i·cal** \-i-kəl\ *adj*
kin·e·scope \ˈkin-ə-ˌskōp\ *n* **1** : PICTURE TUBE **2** : a moving picture made from the image on a picture tube
kin·es·the·sia \ˌkin-əs-ˈthē-zh(ē-)ə\ *or* **kin·es·the·sis** \-ˈthē-səs\ *n, pl* **-the·sias** *or* **-the·ses** \-ˌsēz\ : a sense mediated by nervous elements in muscles, tendons, and joints and stimulated by bodily movements and tensions; *also* : sensory experience derived from this source — **kin·es·thet·ic** \-ˈthet-ik\ *adj*
ki·net·ic \kə-ˈnet-ik\ *adj* : of or relating to the motion of material bodies and the forces and energy (**kinetic energy**) associated with them
ki·net·ics \kə-ˈnet-iks\ *n sing or pl* : a science that deals with the effects of forces upon the motions of material bodies or with changes in a physical or chemical system
kin·folk \ˈkin-ˌfōk\ *or* **kinfolks** *n pl* : RELATIVES
king \ˈkiŋ\ *n* **1** : a male sovereign **2** : a chief among competitors ⟨home-run ~⟩ **3** : the principal piece in the game of chess **4** : a playing card bearing the figure of a king **5** : a checker that has been crowned — **king·less** *adj* — **king·ly** *adj* — **king·ship** *n*
king·bolt \-ˌbōlt\ *n* : a vertical bolt by which the forward axle and wheels of a vehicle are connected to the other parts
king crab *n* **1** : HORSESHOE CRAB **2** : any of several very large crabs
king·dom \ˈkiŋ-dəm\ *n* **1** : a country whose head is a king or queen **2** : a realm or region in which something or someone is dominant ⟨a cattle ~⟩ **3** : one of the three primary divisions of lifeless material, plants, and animals into which natural objects are grouped
king·fish·er \-ˌfish-ər\ *n* : a bright-colored crested bird that feeds chiefly on fish
king·pin \ˈkiŋ-ˌpin\ *n* **1** : any of several bowling pins **2** : the leader in a group or undertaking **3** : KINGBOLT
Kings *n* — see BIBLE table
king–size \ˈkiŋ-ˌsīz\ *or* **king–sized** \-ˌsīzd\ *adj* **1** : longer than the regular or standard size **2** : unusually large **3** : having dimensions of about 76 by 80 inches ⟨a ~ bed⟩; *also* : of a size that fits a king-size bed
kink \ˈkiŋk\ *n* **1** : a short tight twist or curl **2** : a mental peculiarity : QUIRK **3** : CRAMP ⟨a ~ in the back⟩ **4** : an imperfection likely to cause difficulties in operation — **kinky** *adj*
kin·ship \ˈkin-ˌship\ *n* : RELATIONSHIP

kins·man \ˈkinz-mən\ *n* : RELATIVE; *esp* : a male relative
kins·wom·an \-ˌwu̇m-ən\ *n* : a female relative
ki·osk \ˈkē-ˌäsk\ *n* : a small structure with one or more open sides
Ki·o·wa \ˈkī-ə-ˌwȯ, -ˌwä, -ˌwā\ *n, pl* **Kiowa** *or* **Kiowas** : a member of an American Indian people of Colorado, Kansas, New Mexico, Oklahoma, and Texas
[1]**kip** \ˈkip\ *n* : the undressed hide of a young or small animal
[2]**kip** \ˈkip, ˈgip\ *n, pl* **kip** *or* **kips** — see MONEY table
kip·per \ˈkip-ər\ *n* : a fish (as a herring) preserved by salting and drying or smoking — **kipper** *vb*
kirk \ˈkərk, ˈkirk\ *n, chiefly Scot* : CHURCH
kir·tle \ˈkərt-ᵊl\ *n* : a long gown or dress worn by women
kis·met \ˈkiz-ˌmet, -mət\ *n, often cap* [Turk, fr. Ar *qismah* portion, lot] : FATE
[1]**kiss** \ˈkis\ *vb* **1** : to touch or caress with the lips as a mark of affection or greeting **2** : to touch gently or lightly
[2]**kiss** *n* **1** : a caress with the lips **2** : a gentle touch or contact **3** : a bite-size candy
kiss·er \ˈkis-ər\ *n* **1** : one that kisses **2** *slang* : MOUTH **3** *slang* : FACE
kit \ˈkit\ *n* **1** : a set of articles for personal use; *also* : a set of tools or implements or of parts to be assembled **2** : a container (as a case) for a kit
kitch·en \ˈkich-ən\ *n* **1** : a room with cooking facilities **2** : the personnel that prepares, cooks, and serves food
kitch·en·ette \ˌkich-ə-ˈnet\ *n* : a small kitchen or an alcove containing cooking facilities
kitchen police *n* **1** : KP **2** : the work of KPs
kitch·en·ware \ˈkich-ən-ˌwaər\ *n* : utensils and appliances for use in a kitchen
kite \ˈkīt\ *n* **1** : any of various hawks with deeply forked tails **2** : a light frame covered with paper or cloth and designed to be flown in the air at the end of a long string
kith \ˈkith\ *n* [ME, fr. OE *cȳthth*, fr. *cūth* known] : familiar friends, neighbors, or relatives ⟨~ and kin⟩
kitsch \ˈkich\ *n* [G] : shoddy or cheap artistic or literary material
kit·ten \ˈkit-ᵊn\ *n* : a young cat — **kit·ten·ish** *adj*
[1]**kit·ty** \ˈkit-ē\ *n, pl* **kitties** : CAT; *esp* : KITTEN
[2]**kitty** *n, pl* **kitties** : a fund in a poker game made up of contributions from each pot; *also* : POOL
kit·ty–cor·ner *or* **kit·ty–cor·nered** *var of* CATERCORNER
ki·wi \ˈkē-(ˌ)wē\ *n* : a flightless New Zealand bird
ki·wi·fruit \-ˌfrüt\ *n* : a brownish hairy egg-shaped fruit with sweet bright green flesh and small edible black seeds
KJV *abbr* King James Version
KKK *abbr* Ku Klux Klan
kl *abbr* kiloliter
klatch *or* **klatsch** \ˈklach\ *n* [G *klatsch* gossip] : a gathering marked by informal conversation
klep·to·ma·nia \ˌklep-tə-ˈmā-nē-ə\ *n* : a persistent neurotic impulse to steal esp. without economic motive — **klep·to·ma·ni·ac** \-nē-ˌak\ *n*
klieg light *or* **kleig light** \ˈklēg-\ *n* : a very bright lamp used in making motion pictures
km *abbr* kilometer
kn *abbr* knot
knack \ˈnak\ *n* **1** : a clever way of doing something **2** : natural aptitude
knap·sack \ˈnap-ˌsak\ *n* : a usu. canvas or leather bag or case strapped on the back and used esp. for carrying supplies (as on a hike)
knave \ˈnāv\ *n* **1** : ROGUE **2** : JACK 6 — **knav·ery** \ˈnāv-(ə-)rē\ *n* — **knav·ish** \ˈnā-vish\ *adj*
knead \ˈnēd\ *vb* : to work and press into a mass with the hands; *also* : MASSAGE — **knead·er** *n*
knee \ˈnē\ *n* : the joint in the middle part of the leg — **kneed** \ˈnēd\ *adj*
knee·cap \ˈnē-ˌkap\ *n* : a thick flat movable bone forming the front of the knee
knee·hole \-ˌhōl\ *n* : a space (as under a desk) for the knees
kneel \ˈnēl\ *vb* **knelt** \ˈnelt\ *or* **kneeled; kneel·ing** : to bend the knee : fall or rest on the knees
[1]**knell** \ˈnel\ *vb* **1** : to ring esp. for a death or disaster **2** : to summon, announce, or proclaim by a knell
[2]**knell** *n* **1** : a stroke of a bell esp. when tolled (as for a funeral) **2** : an indication of the end or failure of something
knew *past of* KNOW
knick·ers \ˈnik-ərz\ *n pl* : loose-fitting short pants gathered at the knee
knick·knack \ˈnik-ˌnak\ *n* : a small trivial article intended for ornament
[1]**knife** \ˈnīf\ *n, pl* **knives** \ˈnīvz\ **1** : a cutting instrument consisting of a sharp blade fastened to a handle **2** : a sharp cutting tool in a machine
[2]**knife** *vb* **knifed; knif·ing** : to stab, slash, or wound with a knife
[1]**knight** \ˈnīt\ *n* **1** : a mounted warrior of feudal times serving a king **2** : a man honored by a sovereign for merit and in Great Britain ranking below a baronet **3** : a man devoted to the service of a lady **4** : a member of an order or society **5** : a chess piece having a move of two squares to a square of the opposite color — **knight·ly** *adj*
[2]**knight** *vb* : to make a knight of
knight·hood \ˈnīt-ˌhu̇d\ *n* **1** : the rank, dignity, or profession of a knight **2** : CHIVALRY **3** : knights as a class or body
knish \kə-ˈnish\ *n* [Yiddish] : a small round or square of dough stuffed with a filling (as of meat or fruit) and baked or fried
[1]**knit** \ˈnit\ *vb* **knit** *or* **knit·ted; knit·ting 1** : to link firmly or closely **2** : WRINKLE ⟨~ her brows⟩ **3** : to form a fabric by interlacing yarn or thread in connected loops with needles **4** : to grow together — **knit·ter** *n*
[2]**knit** *n* **1** : a basic knitting stitch **2** : a knitted garment or fabric
knit·wear \-ˌwaər\ *n* : knitted clothing
knob \ˈnäb\ *n* **1** : a rounded protuberance; *also* : a small rounded ornament or handle **2** : a rounded usu. isolated hill — **knobbed** \ˈnäbd\ *adj* — **knob·by** \ˈnäb-ē\ *adj*
[1]**knock** \ˈnäk\ *vb* **1** : to strike with a sharp blow **2** : BUMP, COLLIDE **3** : to make a pounding noise; *esp* : to have engine knock **4** : to find fault with
[2]**knock** *n* **1** : a sharp blow **2** : a pounding noise; *esp* : one caused by abnormal ignition in an engine
knock·down \ˈnäk-ˌdau̇n\ *n* **1** : the action of knocking down **2** : something (as a blow) that knocks down **3** : something that can be easily assembled or disassembled
knock down \-ˈdau̇n\ *vb* **1** : to strike to the ground with or as if with as sharp blow **2** : to take apart : DISASSEMBLE **3** : to receive an income or salary : EARN **4** : to make a reduction in
knock·er \ˈnäk-ər\ *n* : one that knocks; *esp* : a device hinged to a door for use in knocking
knock–knee \ˈnäk-ˈnē, -ˌnē\ *n* : a condition in which the legs curve inward at the knees — **knock–kneed** \-ˈnēd\ *adj*
knock off *vb* **1** : to stop doing something **2** : to do quickly, carelessly, or routinely **3** : to deduct from a price **4** : KILL **5** : ROB
knock·out \ˈnäk-ˌau̇t\ *n* **1** : a blow that fells and immobilizes an opponent (as in boxing) **2** : something sensationally striking or attractive
knock out \-ˈau̇t\ *vb* **1** : to defeat by a knockout **2** : to

\ə\abut \ᵊ\kitten \ər\further \a\ash \ā\ace \ä\cot, cart \au̇\out \ch\chin \e\bet \ē\easy \g\go \i\hit \ī\ice \j\job \ŋ\sing \ō\go \ȯ\law \ȯi\boy \th\thin \t͟h\the \ü\loot \u̇\foot \y\yet \zh\vision *see also* Pronunciation Symbols page

make unconscious or inoperative **3** : to tire out : EXHAUST
knock·wurst *or* **knack·wurst** \ˈnäk-ˌwərst, -ˌvu̇(r)st\ *n* : a short thick heavily seasoned sausage
knoll \ˈnōl\ *n* : a small round hill
¹knot \ˈnät\ *n* **1** : an interlacing (as of string or ribbon) that forms a lump or knob **2** : PROBLEM **3** : a bond of union; *esp* : the marriage bond **4** : a protuberant lump or swelling in tissue; *also* : the base of a woody branch enclosed in the stem from which it arises **5** : GROUP, CLUSTER **6** : an ornamental bow of ribbon **7** : one nautical mile per hour; *also* : one nautical mile — **knot·ty** *adj*
²knot *vb* **knot·ted; knot·ting 1** : to tie in or with a knot **2** : ENTANGLE
knot·hole \-ˌhōl\ *n* : a hole in a board or tree trunk where a knot has come out
knout \ˈnau̇t, ˈnüt\ *n* : a whip used for flogging
know \ˈnō\ *vb* **knew** \ˈn(y)ü\; **known** \ˈnōn\; **know·ing 1** : to perceive directly : have understanding or direct cognition of; *also* : to recognize the nature of **2** : to be acquainted or familiar with **3** : to be aware of the truth of **4** : to have a practical understanding of — **know·able** *adj* — **know·er** *n* — **in the know** : possessing confidential information
know–how \ˈnō-ˌhau̇\ *n* : knowledge of how to do something smoothly and efficiently
know·ing \ˈnō-iŋ\ *adj* **1** : having or reflecting knowledge, intelligence, or information **2** : shrewdly and keenly alert **3** : DELIBERATE, INTENTIONAL **syn** intelligent, clever, bright, smart — **know·ing·ly** *adv*
knowl·edge \ˈnäl-ij\ *n* **1** : understanding gained by actual experience ⟨a ~ of carpentry⟩ **2** : range of information ⟨within my ~⟩ **3** : clear perception of truth **4** : something learned and kept in the mind
knowl·edge·able \-ə-bəl\ *adj* : having or showing knowledge or intelligence
knuck·le \ˈnək-əl\ *n* : the rounded knob at a joint and esp. at a finger joint
knuck·le·bone \ˈnək-əl-ˌbōn\ *n* : one of the bones forming a knuckle
knuckle down *vb* : to apply oneself earnestly
knuckle under *vb* : SUBMIT, SURRENDER
knurl \ˈnərl\ *n* **1** : KNOB **2** : one of a series of small ridges on a metal surface to aid in gripping — **knurled** \ˈnərld\ *adj*
¹KO \(ˈ)kā-ˈō, ˈkā-ō\ *n* : KNOCKOUT
²KO *vb* **KO'd** \kā-ˈōd, ˈkā-ōd\; **KO'·ing** \-ˈō-iŋ, -ō-\ : to knock out in boxing
ko·ala \kō-ˈäl-ə\ *n* : a gray furry Australian marsupial with large hairy ears that feeds on eucalyptus leaves
ko·bo \ˈkō-(ˌ)bō\ *n, pl* **kobo** — see *naira* at MONEY table
K of C *abbr* Knights of Columbus
kohl·ra·bi \kōl-ˈräb-ē\ *n, pl* **-bies** [G, fr. It *cavolo rapa*, lit., cabbage turnip] : a cabbage that forms no head but has a swollen fleshy edible stem
ko·lin·sky \kə-ˈlin-skē\ *n, pl* **-skies** : the fur of various Asian minks
kook \ˈkük\ *n* : SCREWBALL 2
kooky *also* **kook·ie** \ˈkü-kē\ *adj* **kook·i·er; -est** : having the characteristics of a kook — **kook·i·ness** *n*
ko·peck *or* **ko·pek** \ˈkō-ˌpek\ *n* — see *ruble* at MONEY table
Ko·ran \kə-ˈran, -ˈrän\ *n* [Ar *qur'ān*] : a book of sacred writings accepted by Muslims as revelations made to Muhammad by Allah
Ko·re·an \kə-ˈrē-ən\ *n* : a native or inhabitant of Korea — **Korean** *adj*
ko·ru·na \ˈkȯr-ə-ˌnä\ *n, pl* **ko·ru·ny** \-ə-nē\ *or* **korunas** *or* **ko·rum** \ˈkȯr-əm\ — see MONEY table
ko·sher \ˈkō-shər\ *adj* [Yiddish, fr. Heb *kāshēr* fit, proper] : ritually fit for use according to Jewish law; *also* : selling or serving such food
kow·tow \kau̇-ˈtau̇, ˈkau̇-ˌtau̇\ *vb* [Chin *k'o¹ t'ou²*, fr. *k'o¹* to bump + *t'ou²* head] **1** : to show obsequious deference **2** : to kneel and touch the forehead to the ground as a sign of homage or deep respect
KP \(ˈ)kā-ˈpē\ *n* **1** : enlisted persons detailed to help the cooks in a military mess **2** : the work of KPs
kph *abbr* kilometers per hour
Kr *symbol* krypton
kraal \ˈkräl, ˈkrȯl\ *n* **1** : a village of southern African natives **2** : an enclosure for domestic animals in southern Africa
kraut \ˈkrau̇t\ *n* : SAUERKRAUT
Krem·lin \ˈkrem-lən\ *n* : the Russian government
Krem·lin·ol·o·gist \ˌkrem-lə-ˈnäl-ə-jəst\ *n* : a specialist in the policies and practices of the Soviet government
¹kro·na \ˈkrō-nə\ *n, pl* **kro·nor** \-ˌnȯr\ [Sw] — see MONEY table
²kro·na \ˈkrō-nə\ *n, pl* **kro·nur** \-nər\ [Icel] — see MONEY table
kro·ne \ˈkrō-nə\ *n, pl* **kro·ner** \-nər\ — see MONEY table
Kru·ger·rand \ˈkrü-gə(r)-ˌrand, -ˌränd\ *n* : a 1-ounce gold coin of the Republic of South Africa equal in bullion value to 25 rand and having an official price of 31 rand
kryp·ton \ˈkrip-ˌtän\ *n* : a gaseous chemical element that occurs in small quantities in air and is used in electric lamps — see ELEMENT table
KS *abbr* Kansas
kt *abbr* **1** karat **2** knight
ku·do \ˈk(y)üd-ō\ *n, pl* **kudos** [fr. *kudos* (taken as pl.)] **1** : AWARD, HONOR **2** : COMPLIMENT, PRAISE
ku·dos \ˈk(y)ü-ˌdäs\ *n* : fame and renown resulting from achievement
kud·zu \ˈku̇d-zü\ *n* [Jp *kuzu*] : a creeping vine widely grown for hay and forage and for erosion control
ku·lak \k(y)ü-ˈlak\ *n* [Russ, lit., fist] **1** : a wealthy peasant farmer in 19th century Russia **2** : a farmer characterized by Communists as too wealthy
kum·quat \ˈkəm-ˌkwät\ *n* [Chin *kam kwat*, fr. *kam* gold + *kwat* orange] : a small citrus fruit with sweet spongy rind and acid pulp
kung fu \ˌkəŋ-ˈfü, ˌkuŋ-\ *n* : a Chinese art of self-defense resembling karate
ku·rus \kə-ˈrüsh\ *n, pl* **kurus** — see *lira* at MONEY table
kv *abbr* kilovolt
kw *abbr* kilowatt
kwa·cha \ˈkwäch-ə\ *n, pl* **kwacha** — see MONEY table
kwan·za \ˈkwän-zə\ *n, pl* **kwanzas** *or* **kwanza** — see MONEY table
kwash·i·or·kor \ˌkwäsh-ē-ˈȯr-kȯr, -ȯr-ˈkȯr\ *n* : a disease of young children resulting from deficient intake of protein
kwhr *or* **kwh** *abbr* kilowatt-hour
Ky *or* **KY** *abbr* Kentucky
kyat \ˈchät\ *n* — see MONEY table

L

[1]**l** \ˈel\ *n, pl* **l's** *or* **ls** \ˈelz\ *often cap* : the 12th letter of the English alphabet

[2]**l** *abbr, often cap* **1** lake **2** large **3** left **4** [L *libra*] pound **5** line **6** liter

[1]**La** *abbr* Louisiana

[2]**La** *symbol* lanthanum

LA *abbr* **1** law agent **2** Los Angeles **3** Louisiana

lab \ˈlab\ *n* : LABORATORY

Lab *abbr* Labrador

[1]**la·bel** \ˈlā-bəl\ *n* **1** : a slip attached to something for identification or description **2** : a descriptive or identifying word or phrase **3** : BRAND 3

[2]**label** *vb* **-beled** *or* **-belled; -bel·ing** *or* **-bel·ling** \-b(ə-)liŋ\ **1** : to affix a label to **2** : to describe or name with a label

la·bi·al \ˈlā-bē-əl\ *adj* : of or relating to the lips or labia

la·bia ma·jo·ra \ˌlā-bē-ə-mə-ˈjōr-ə\ *n pl* : the outer fatty folds of the vulva

labia mi·no·ra \-mə-ˈnōr-ə\ *n pl* : the inner highly vascular folds of the vulva

la·bile \ˈlā-ˌbīl, -bəl\ *adj* **1** : UNSTABLE **2** : ADAPTABLE

la·bi·um \ˈlā-bē-əm\ *n, pl* **la·bia** \-ə\ [NL, fr. L, lip] : any of the folds at the margin of the vulva

[1]**la·bor** \ˈlā-bər\ *n* **1** : physical or mental effort; *also* : human activity that provides the goods or services in an economy **2** : the physical activities involved in parturition **3** : TASK **4** : those who do manual labor or work for wages; *also* : labor unions or their officials

[2]**labor** *vb* **la·bored; la·bor·ing** \-b(ə-)riŋ\ **1** : WORK **2** : to move with great effort **3** : to be in the labor of giving birth **4** : to suffer from some disadvantage or distress ⟨∼ under a delusion⟩ **5** : to treat or work out laboriously — **la·bor·er** *n*

lab·o·ra·to·ry \ˈlab-(ə-)rə-ˌtōr-ē\ *n, pl* **-ries** : a place equipped for making scientific experiments or tests

Labor Day *n* : the 1st Monday in September observed as a legal holiday in recognition of the working people

la·bored \ˈlā-bərd\ *adj* : not freely or easily done ⟨∼ breathing⟩

la·bo·ri·ous \lə-ˈbōr-ē-əs\ *adj* **1** : INDUSTRIOUS **2** : requiring great effort — **la·bo·ri·ous·ly** *adv*

la·bor·sav·ing \ˈlā-bər-ˌsā-viŋ\ *adj* : designed to replace or decrease labor

la·bour *chiefly Brit var of* LABOR

lab·ra·dor·ite \ˈlab-rə-ˌdȯr-ˌīt\ *n* : a feldspar showing a play of several colors

Lab·ra·dor retriever \ˈlab-rə-ˌdȯr-\ *n* : a strongly built retriever having a short dense black, yellow, or chocolate coat

la·bur·num \lə-ˈbər-nəm\ *n* : a leguminous shrub or tree with hanging clusters of yellow flowers

lab·y·rinth \ˈlab-ə-ˌrinth\ *n* : a place constructed of or filled with confusing intricate passageways : MAZE — **lab·y·rin·thine** \ˌlab-ə-ˈrin-thən\ *adj*

lac \ˈlak\ *n* : a resinous substance secreted by a scale insect and used in the manufacture of shellac and lacquers

[1]**lace** \ˈlās\ *vb* **laced; lac·ing 1** : TIE **2** : to adorn with lace **3** : INTERTWINE **4** : BEAT, LASH **5** : to give zest or savor to

[2]**lace** *n* [ME, fr. OF *laz,* fr. L *laqueus* snare, noose] **1** : a cord or string used for drawing together two edges **2** : an ornamental braid **3** : a fine openwork usu. figured fabric made of thread — **lacy** \ˈlā-sē\ *adj*

lac·er·ate \ˈlas-ə-ˌrāt\ *vb* **-at·ed; -at·ing** : to tear roughly — **lac·er·a·tion** \ˌlas-ə-ˈrā-shən\ *n*

lace·wing \ˈlās-ˌwiŋ\ *n* : any of various insects with delicate wing veins, long antennae, and brilliant eyes

lach·ry·mose \ˈlak-rə-ˌmōs\ *adj* **1** : TEARFUL **2** : MOURNFUL

[1]**lack** \ˈlak\ *vb* **1** : to be wanting or missing **2** : to be deficient in

[2]**lack** *n* : the fact or state of being wanting or deficient : NEED

lack·a·dai·si·cal \ˌlak-ə-ˈdā-zi-kəl\ *adj* : lacking life, spirit, or zest — **lack·a·dai·si·cal·ly** \-k(ə-)lē\ *adv*

lack·ey \ˈlak-ē\ *n, pl* **lackeys 1** : a liveried retainer **2** : TOADY

lack·lus·ter \ˈlak-ˌləs-tər\ *adj* : DULL

la·con·ic \lə-ˈkän-ik\ *adj* [L *laconicus* Spartan, fr. Gk *lakōnikos;* fr. the Spartan reputation for terseness of speech] : sparing of words : TERSE — **la·con·i·cal·ly** \-i-k(ə-)lē\ *adv*

lac·quer \ˈlak-ər\ *n* : a clear or colored usu. glossy and quick-drying surface coating that contains natural or synthetic substances — **lacquer** *vb*

lac·ri·mal *also* **lach·ry·mal** \ˈlak-rə-məl\ *adj* : of, relating to, or being the glands that produce tears

lac·ri·ma·tion \ˌlak-rə-ˈmā-shən\ *n* : secretion of tears

la·crosse \lə-ˈkrȯs\ *n* [CanF *la crosse,* lit., the crosier] : a game played on a field by two teams with a hard ball and long-handled rackets

lac·tate \ˈlak-ˌtāt\ *vb* **lac·tat·ed; lac·tat·ing** : to secrete milk — **lac·ta·tion** \lak-ˈtā-shən\ *n*

lac·tic \ˈlak-tik\ *adj* **1** : of or relating to milk **2** : formed in the souring of milk

lactic acid *n* : a syrupy acid present in blood and muscle tissue, produced by bacterial fermentation of carbohydrates, and used in food and medicine

lac·tose \ˈlak-ˌtōs\ *n* : a sugar present in milk

la·cu·na \lə-ˈk(y)ü-nə\ *n, pl* **la·cu·nae** \-nē\ *or* **la·cu·nas** [L, pool, pit, gap, fr. *lacus* lake] : a blank space or missing part : GAP

lad \ˈlad\ *n* : YOUTH; *also* : FELLOW

lad·der \ˈlad-ər\ *n* : a device for climbing that consists of two parallel sidepieces joined at intervals by crosspieces

lad·die \ˈlad-ē\ *n* : a young lad

lad·en \ˈlād-ᵊn\ *adj* : LOADED, BURDENED

lad·ing \ˈlād-iŋ\ *n* : CARGO, FREIGHT

la·dle \ˈlād-ᵊl\ *n* : a deep-bowled long-handled spoon used in taking up and conveying liquids — **ladle** *vb*

la·dy \ˈlād-ē\ *n, pl* **ladies** [ME, fr. OE *hlǣfdīge,* fr. *hlāf* bread + *-dīge* (akin to *dǣge* kneader of bread)] **1** : a woman of property, rank, or authority; *also* : a woman of superior social position or of refinement **2** : WOMAN **3** : WIFE

lady beetle *n* : LADYBUG

la·dy·bird \ˈlād-ē-ˌbərd\ *n* : LADYBUG

la·dy·bug \-ˌbəg\ *n* : any of various small nearly hemispherical and usu. brightly colored beetles that feed mostly on other insects

la·dy·fin·ger \ˈlād-ē-ˌfiŋ-gər\ *n* : a small finger-shaped sponge cake

la·dy–in–wait·ing \ˌlād-ē-in-ˈwāt-iŋ\ *n, pl* **ladies–in–waiting** : a lady appointed to attend or wait on a queen or princess

la·dy·like \ˈlād-ē-ˌlīk\ *adj* : WELL-BRED

la·dy·love \-ˌləv\ *n* : SWEETHEART

la·dy·ship \ˈlād-ē-ˌship\ *n* : the condition of being a lady : rank of lady

lady's slipper \ˈlād-ē(z)-ˌslip-ər\ *n* : any of several No. American orchids with slipper-shaped flowers

[1]lag \ˈlag\ *n* **1** : a slowing up or falling behind; *also* : the amount by which one lags **2** : INTERVAL
[2]lag *vb* **lagged; lag·ging** **1** : to fail to keep up : stay behind **2** : to slacken gradually **syn** dawdle, dally, tarry, loiter
la·ger \ˈläg-ər\ *n* : a light-colored usu. dry beer
[1]lag·gard \ˈlag-ərd\ *adj* : DILATORY, SLOW — **lag·gard·ly** *adv or adj* — **lag·gard·ness** *n*
[2]laggard *n* : one that lags or lingers
la·gniappe \ˈlan-ˌyap\ *n* : something given free esp. with a purchase
la·goon \lə-ˈgün\ *n* : a shallow sound, channel, or pond near or communicating with a larger body of water
laid *past and past part of* LAY
laid–back \ˈlād-ˈbak\ *adj* : having a relaxed style or character ⟨~ music⟩
lain *past part of* [1]LIE
lair \ˈlaər\ *n* : the resting or living place of a wild animal : DEN
laird \ˈlaərd\ *n, Scot* : a landed proprietor
lais·sez–faire \ˌles-ˌā-ˈfar\ *n* [F *laissez faire* let do] : a doctrine opposing governmental interference in economic affairs beyond that necessary to maintain peace and property rights
la·ity \ˈlā-ət-ē\ *n* **1** : the people of a religious faith who are not members of its clergy **2** : the mass of people who are of a particular field
lake \ˈlāk\ *n* : an inland body of standing water of considerable size; *also* : a pool of liquid (as lava or pitch)
[1]lam \ˈlam\ *vb* **lammed; lam·ming** : to flee hastily — **lam** *n*
[2]lam *abbr* laminated
Lam *abbr* Lamentations
la·ma \ˈläm-ə\ *n* : a Buddhist monk of Tibet or Mongolia
la·ma·sery \ˈläm-ə-ˌser-ē\ *n, pl* **-ser·ies** : a monastery for lamas
[1]lamb \ˈlam\ *n* **1** : a young sheep; *also* : its flesh used as food **2** : an innocent or gentle person
[2]lamb *vb* : to bring forth a lamb
lam·baste *or* **lam·bast** \lam-ˈbāst, -ˈbast\ *vb* **1** : BEAT **2** : EXCORIATE
lam·bent \ˈlam-bənt\ *adj* [L *lambens*, prp. of *lambere* to lick] **1** : FLICKERING **2** : softly radiant ⟨~ eyes⟩ **3** : marked by lightness or brilliance ⟨~ humor⟩ — **lam·ben·cy** \-bən-sē\ *n* — **lam·bent·ly** *adv*
lamb·skin \ˈlam-ˌskin\ *n* : a lamb's skin or a small fine-grade sheepskin or the leather made from either
[1]lame \ˈlām\ *adj* **lam·er; lam·est** **1** : having a body part and usu. a limb so disabled as to impair freedom of movement; *also* : marked by stiffness and soreness **2** : lacking substance : WEAK — **lame·ly** *adv* — **lame·ness** *n*
[2]lame *vb* **lamed; lam·ing** : to make lame : CRIPPLE
la·mé \lä-ˈmā, la-\ *n* [F] : a brocaded clothing fabric with tinsel filling threads (as of gold or silver)
lame·brain \ˈlām-ˌbrān\ *n* : a stupid person
lame duck *n* : an elected official continuing to hold office between an election and the inauguration of a successor
[1]la·ment \lə-ˈment\ *vb* **1** : to mourn aloud : WAIL **2** : to express sorrow for : BEWAIL — **lam·en·ta·ble** \ˈlam-ən-tə-bəl, lə-ˈment-ə-\ *adj* — **lam·en·ta·bly** \-blē\ *adv* — **lam·en·ta·tion** \ˌlam-ən-ˈtā-shən\ *n*
[2]lament *n* **1** : a crying out in grief : WAIL **2** : DIRGE, ELEGY
Lamentations *n* — see BIBLE table
la·mia \ˈlā-mē-ə\ *n* : a female demon
lam·i·na \ˈlam-ə-nə\ *n, pl* **-nae** \-ˌnē\ *or* **-nas** : a thin plate or scale
lam·i·nar \ˈlam-ə-nər\ *adj* : arranged in or consisting of laminae
lam·i·nat·ed \-ˌnāt-əd\ *adj* : consisting of laminae; *esp* : composed of layers of firmly united material — **lam·i·nate** \-ˌnāt\ *vb* — **lam·i·nate** \-nət\ *n or adj* — **lam·i·na·tion** \ˌlam-ə-ˈnā-shən\ *n*
lamp \ˈlamp\ *n* **1** : a vessel with a wick for burning a flammable liquid (as oil) to produce light **2** : a device for producing light or heat
lamp·black \-ˌblak\ *n* : black soot made by incomplete burning of carbonaceous matter and used esp. as a pigment
lamp·light·er \-ˌlīt-ər\ *n* : a person employed to light gas streetlights
lam·poon \lam-ˈpün\ *n* : SATIRE; *esp* : one that is harsh and usu. directed against an individual — **lampoon** *vb*
lam·prey \ˈlam-prē\ *n, pl* **lampreys** : an eellike aquatic vertebrate animal with sucking mouth and no jaws

lamprey

la·nai \lə-ˈnī\ *n* [Hawaiian] : a porch furnished for use as a living room
[1]lance \ˈlans\ *n* **1** : a spear carried by mounted soldiers **2** : any of various sharp-pointed implements; *esp* : LANCET
[2]lance *vb* **lanced; lanc·ing** : to pierce or open with a lance ⟨~ a boil⟩
lance corporal *n* : an enlisted man in the marine corps ranking above a private first class and below a corporal
lanc·er \ˈlan-sər\ *n* : a cavalryman of a unit formerly armed with lances
lan·cet \ˈlan-sət\ *n* : a sharp-pointed and usu. 2-edged surgical instrument
[1]land \ˈland\ *n* **1** : the solid part of the surface of the earth; *also* : a part of the earth's surface ⟨fenced ~⟩ ⟨marshy ~⟩ **2** : NATION **3** : REALM, DOMAIN — **land·less** *adj*
[2]land *vb* **1** : DISEMBARK; *also* : to touch at a place on shore **2** : to alight or cause to alight on a surface **3** : to bring to or arrive at a destination **4** : to catch with a hook and bring in ⟨~ a fish⟩; *also* : GAIN, SECURE ⟨~ a job⟩
lan·dau \ˈlan-ˌdau̇\ *n* **1** : a 4-wheeled carriage with a top divided into two sections that can be lowered, thrown back, or removed **2** : an automobile with a folding top over the rear passenger compartment
land·ed \ˈlan-dəd\ *adj* : having an estate in land ⟨~ gentry⟩
land·er \ˈlan-dər\ *n* : a space vehicle designed to land on a celestial body
land·fall \ˈlan(d)-ˌfȯl\ *n* : a sighting or making of land (as after a voyage); *also* : the land first sighted
land·fill \-ˌfil\ *n* : a low-lying area on which trash and garbage is buried between layers of earth
land·form \-ˌfȯrm\ *n* : a natural feature of a land surface
land·hold·er \ˈland-ˌhōl-dər\ *n* : a holder or owner of land — **land·hold·ing** \-diŋ\ *adj or n*
land·ing \ˈlan-diŋ\ *n* **1** : the action of one that lands **2** : a place for discharging or taking on passengers and cargo **3** : a level part of a staircase
landing gear *n* : the part that supports the weight of an airplane or spacecraft
land·la·dy \ˈland-ˌlād-ē\ *n* : a woman who is a landlord
land·locked \-ˌläkt\ *adj* **1** : enclosed or nearly enclosed by land ⟨a ~ country⟩ **2** : confined to fresh water by some barrier ⟨~ salmon⟩
land·lord \-ˌlȯrd\ *n* **1** : the owner of property leased or rented to another **2** : a person who rents lodgings : INNKEEPER
land·lub·ber \-ˌləb-ər\ *n* : one who knows little of the sea or seamanship
land·mark \ˈlan(d)-ˌmärk\ *n* **1** : an object that marks a course or boundary or serves as a guide **2** : an event that marks a turning point **3** : a structure of unusual historical and usu. aesthetic interest
land·mass \-ˌmas\ *n* : a large area of land
land·own·er \ˈland-ˌō-nər\ *n* : an owner of land

[1]**land·scape** \ˈlan(d)-ˌskāp\ *n* **1** : a picture of natural inland scenery **2** : a portion of land that can be seen in one glance

[2]**landscape** *vb* **land·scaped; land·scap·ing** : to improve the natural beauties of a tract of land by grading, clearing, or decorative planting

land·slide \ˈlan(d)-ˌslīd\ *n* **1** : the slipping down of a mass of rocks or earth on a steep slope; *also* : the mass of material that slides **2** : an overwhelming victory esp. in a political contest

lands·man \ˈlan(d)z-mən\ *n* : a person who lives or works on land

land·ward \ˈland-wərd\ *adv or adj* : to or toward the land

lane \ˈlān\ *n* **1** : a narrow passageway (as between fences) **2** : a relatively narrow way or track ⟨traffic ~⟩

lang *abbr* language

lan·guage \ˈlaŋ-gwij\ *n* [ME, fr. OF, fr. *langue* tongue, language, fr. L *lingua*] **1** : the words, their pronunciation, and the methods of combining them used and understood by a considerable community **2** : form or style of verbal expression **3** : a system of signs and symbols and rules for using them that is used to carry information

lan·guid \ˈlaŋ-gwəd\ *adj* **1** : WEAK **2** : sluggish in character or disposition : LISTLESS **3** : SLOW — **lan·guid·ly** *adv* — **lan·guid·ness** *n*

lan·guish \ˈlaŋ-gwish\ *vb* **1** : to become languid **2** : to become dispirited : PINE **3** : to appeal for sympathy by assuming an expression of grief

lan·guor \ˈlaŋ-(g)ər\ *n* **1** : a languid feeling **2** : SLUGGISHNESS **syn** lethargy, lassitude, torpidity, torpor — **lan·guor·ous** *adj* — **lan·guor·ous·ly** *adv*

lank \ˈlaŋk\ *adj* **1** : not well filled out **2** : hanging straight and limp

lanky \ˈlaŋ-kē\ *adj* **lank·i·er; -est** : ungracefully tall and thin

lan·o·lin \ˈlan-ᵊl-ən\ *n* : the fatty coating of sheep's wool esp. when refined for use in ointments and cosmetics

lan·ta·na \lan-ˈtän-ə\ *n* : any of a genus of tropical shrubs related to the vervains with heads of small bright flowers

lan·tern \ˈlant-ərn\ *n* **1** : a usu. portable light with a protective covering **2** : the chamber in a lighthouse containing the light **3** : a projector for slides

lan·tha·num \ˈlan-thə-nəm\ *n* : a soft malleable metallic chemical element — see ELEMENT table

lan·yard \ˈlan-yərd\ *n* : a piece of rope for fastening something in ships; *also* : any of various cords

[1]**lap** \ˈlap\ *n* **1** : a loose panel of a garment **2** : the clothing that lies on the knees, thighs, and lower part of the trunk when one sits; *also* : the front part of the lower trunk and thighs of a seated person **3** : an environment of nurture ⟨the ~ of luxury⟩ **4** : CHARGE, CONTROL ⟨in the ~ of the gods⟩

[2]**lap** *vb* **lapped; lap·ping 1** : FOLD **2** : WRAP **3** : to lay over or near so as to partly cover

[3]**lap** *n* **1** : the amount by which an object overlaps another; *also* : the part of an object that overlaps another **2** : a smoothing and polishing tool **3** : one circuit around a racecourse **4** : one complete turn (as of a rope around a drum)

[4]**lap** *vb* **lapped; lap·ping 1** : to scoop up food or drink with the tip of the tongue; *also* : DEVOUR — usu. used with *up* **2** : to splash gently ⟨*lapping* waves⟩

[5]**lap** *n* **1** : an act or instance of lapping **2** : a gentle splashing sound

lap·board \ˈlap-ˌbōrd\ *n* : a board used on the lap as a table or desk

lap·dog \-ˌdȯg\ *n* : a small dog that may be held in the lap

la·pel \lə-ˈpel\ *n* : the fold of the front of a coat that is usu. a continuation of the collar

[1]**lap·i·dary** \ˈlap-ə-ˌder-ē\ *n, pl* **-dar·ies** : one who cuts, polishes, and engraves precious stones

[2]**lapidary** *adj* **1** : of, relating to, or suitable for engraved inscriptions **2** : of or relating to precious stones or the art of cutting them

lap·in \ˈlap-ən\ *n* : rabbit fur usu. sheared and dyed

la·pis la·zu·li \ˌlap-əs-ˈlaz(h)-ə-lē\ *n* : a usu. blue semiprecious stone often having sparkling bits of pyrite

Lapp \ˈlap\ *n* : a member of a people of northern Scandinavia, Finland, and the Kola peninsula of Russia

lap·pet \ˈlap-ət\ *n* : a fold or flap on a garment

[1]**lapse** \ˈlaps\ *n* [L *lapsus*, fr. *labi* to slip] **1** : a slight error **2** : a fall from a higher to a lower state **3** : the termination of a right or privilege through failure to meet requirements **4** : a passage of time; *also* : INTERVAL

[2]**lapse** *vb* **lapsed; laps·ing 1** : to commit apostasy **2** : to sink or slip gradually : SUBSIDE **3** : CEASE

lap·wing \ˈlap-ˌwiŋ\ *n* : an Old World crested plover

lar·board \ˈlär-bərd\ *n* : [5]PORT

lar·ce·ny \ˈlärs(-ᵊ)-nē\ *n, pl* **-nies** [ME, fr. MF *larcin* theft, fr. L *latrocinium* robbery, fr. *latro* mercenary soldier] : THEFT — **lar·ce·nous** \-nəs\ *adj*

larch \ˈlärch\ *n* : a conical tree related to the pines that sheds its needles in the fall

[1]**lard** \ˈlärd\ *vb* **1** : to insert strips of usu. pork fat into (meat) before cooking; *also* : GREASE **2** *obs* : ENRICH

[2]**lard** *n* : a soft white fat obtained by rendering fatty tissue of the hog

lar·der \ˈlärd-ər\ *n* : a place where foods (as meat) are kept

lar·es and pe·na·tes \ˌlar-ēz-ən-pə-ˈnāt-ēz\ *n pl* **1** : household gods **2** : personal or household effects

large \ˈlärj\ *adj* **larg·er; larg·est 1** : having more than usual power, capacity, or scope **2** : exceeding most other things of like kind in quantity or size **syn** big, great, oversize — **large·ness** *n* — **at large 1** : UNCONFINED **2** : as a whole

large·ly \ˈlärj-lē\ *adv* : to a large extent

lar·gess *or* **lar·gesse** \lär-ˈzhes, -ˈjes\ *n* **1** : liberal giving **2** : a generous gift

[1]**lar·go** \ˈlär-gō\ *adv or adj* [It, slow, broad, fr. L *largus* abundant] : in a very slow and stately manner — used as a direction in music

[2]**largo** *n, pl* **largos** : a largo movement

lar·i·at \ˈlar-ē-ət\ *n* [AmerSp *la reata* the lasso, fr. Sp *la* the + AmerSp *reata* lasso, fr. Sp *reatar* to tie again] : a long rope used to catch or tether livestock

[1]**lark** \ˈlärk\ *n* : any of various small songbirds; *esp* : SKYLARK

[2]**lark** *n* : something done solely for fun or adventure : ESCAPADE

[3]**lark** *vb* : to engage in harmless fun or mischief — usu. used with *about*

lark·spur \ˈlärk-ˌspər\ *n* : any of various mostly annual delphiniums

lar·va \ˈlär-və\ *n, pl* **lar·vae** \-(ˌ)vē\ *also* **larvas** [L, specter, mask] : the wingless often wormlike form in which insects hatch from the egg; *also* : any young animal (as a tadpole) that is fundamentally unlike its parent — **lar·val** \-vəl\ *adj*

lar·yn·gi·tis \ˌlar-ən-ˈjīt-əs\ *n* : inflammation of the larynx

lar·ynx \ˈlar-iŋks\ *n, pl* **la·ryn·ges** \lə-ˈrin-ˌjēz\ *or* **lar·ynx·es** : the upper part of the trachea containing the vocal cords — **la·ryn·ge·al** \ˌlar-ən-ˈjē-əl, lə-ˈrin-jē-əl\ *adj*

la·sa·gna \lə-ˈzän-yə\ *n* [It] : boiled broad flat noodles baked with a sauce usu. of tomatoes, cheese, and meat

las·car \ˈlas-kər\ *n* : an Indian sailor

las·civ·i·ous \lə-ˈsiv-ē-əs\ *adj* : LEWD, LUSTFUL — **las·civ·i·ous·ness** *n*

la·ser \ˈlā-zər\ *n* [*l*ight *a*mplification by *s*timulated

---

\ə\abut \ᵊ\kitten \ər\further \a\ash \ā\ace \ä\cot, cart \au̇\out \ch\chin \e\bet \ē\easy \g\go \i\hit \ī\ice \j\job \ŋ\sing \ō\go \ȯ\law \ȯi\boy \th\thin \t͟h\the \ü\loot \u̇\foot \y\yet \zh\vision *see also* Pronunciation Symbols page

*e*mission of *r*adiation] : a device that produces an intense monochromatic beam of light

[1]**lash** \ˈlash\ *vb* **1** : to move vigorously **2** : WHIP **3** : to attack verbally

[2]**lash** *n* **1** : a stroke esp. with a whip **2** : a stinging rebuke **3** : EYELASH

[3]**lash** *vb* : to bind with a rope, cord, or chain

lass \ˈlas\ *n* : GIRL

lass·ie \ˈlas-ē\ *n* : LASS

las·si·tude \ˈlas-ə-ˌt(y)üd\ *n* **1** : WEARINESS, FATIGUE **2** : LANGUOR

las·so \ˈlas-ō, la-ˈsü\ *n, pl* **lassos** *or* **lassoes** [Sp *lazo*] : a rope or long leather thong with a noose used for catching livestock — **lasso** *vb*

[1]**last** \ˈlast\ *vb* **1** : to continue in existence or operation **2** : to remain valid, valuable, or important : ENDURE **3** : to be enough for the needs of

[2]**last** *n* : a foot-shaped form on which a shoe is shaped or repaired

[3]**last** *vb* : to shape with a last

[4]**last** *adj* **1** : following all the rest : FINAL **2** : next before the present **3** : least likely ⟨the ~ thing he wants⟩ **4** : CONCLUSIVE; *also* : SUPREME — **last·ly** *adv*

[5]**last** *adv* **1** : at the end **2** : most recently **3** : in conclusion

[6]**last** *n* : something that is last — **at last** : FINALLY

Last Supper *n* : the supper eaten by Jesus and his disciples on the night of his betrayal

lat *abbr* latitude

Lat *abbr* Latin

lat·a·kia \ˌlat-ə-ˈkē-ə\ *n* : an aromatic Turkish smoking tobacco

[1]**latch** \ˈlach\ *vb* : to catch or get hold

[2]**latch** *n* : a catch that holds a door or gate closed

[3]**latch** *vb* : CATCH, FASTEN

latch·et \ˈlach-ət\ *n* : a strap, thong, or lace for fastening a shoe or sandal

latch·key \ˈlach-ˌkē\ *n* : a key for opening a door latch esp. from the outside

latch·string \-ˌstriŋ\ *n* : a string on a latch that may be left hanging outside the door for raising the latch

[1]**late** \ˈlāt\ *adj* **lat·er; lat·est 1** : coming or remaining after the due, usual, or proper time : TARDY **2** : far advanced toward the close or end **3** : recently deceased ⟨her ~ husband⟩ **4** : made, appearing, or happening just previous to the present : RECENT — **late·ly** *adv* — **late·ness** *n*

[2]**late** *adv* **lat·er; lat·est 1** : after the usual or proper time; *also* : at or to an advanced point in time **2** : RECENTLY

late·com·er \ˈlāt-ˌkəm-ər\ *n* : one who arrives late

la·teen \lə-ˈtēn\ *adj* : relating to or being a triangular sail extended by a long spar slung to a low mast

la·tent \ˈlāt-ᵊnt\ *adj* : present but not visible or active **syn** dormant, quiescent, potential — **la·ten·cy** \-ᵊn-sē\ *n*

[1]**lat·er·al** \ˈlat-(ə-)rəl\ *adj* : situated on, directed toward, or coming from the side — **lat·er·al·ly** \-ē\ *adv*

[2]**lateral** *n* **1** : a lateral passage (as a drainage ditch) **2** : a football pass thrown parallel to the line of scrimmage or away from the opponent's goal

la·tex \ˈlā-ˌteks\ *n, pl* **la·ti·ces** \ˈlāt-ə-ˌsēz, ˈlat-\ *or* **la·tex·es 1** : a milky plant juice esp. of members of the milkweed group ⟨rubber is made from a ~⟩ **2** : a water emulsion of a synthetic rubber or plastic used esp. as a paint

lath \ˈlath, ˈlath\ *n, pl* **laths** *or* **lath** : a thin narrow strip of wood used esp. as a base for plaster; *also* : a building material in sheets used for the same purpose — **lath·ing** \-iŋ\ *n*

lathe \ˈlāth\ *n* : a machine in which a piece of material is held and turned while being shaped by a tool

[1]**lath·er** \ˈlath-ər\ *n* **1** : a foam or froth formed when a detergent is agitated in water; *also* : foam from profuse sweating (as by a horse) **2** : DITHER

[2]**lather** *vb* **lath·ered; lath·er·ing** \-(ə-)riŋ\ : to spread lather over; *also* : to form a lather

Lat·in \ˈlat-ᵊn\ *n* **1** : the language of ancient Rome **2** : a member of any of the peoples whose languages derive from Latin — **Latin** *adj*

Latin American *n* : a native or inhabitant of any of the countries of No., Central, or So. America whose official language is Spanish or Portuguese — **Latin–American** *adj*

La·ti·no \lə-ˈtē-nō\ *n, pl* **-nos** : a native or inhabitant of Latin America; *also* : a person of Latin-American origin living in the U.S.

lat·i·tude \ˈlat-ə-ˌt(y)üd\ *n* **1** : angular distance north or south from the earth's equator measured in degrees **2** : a region marked by its latitude **3** : freedom of action or choice

lat·i·tu·di·nar·i·an \ˌlat-ə-ˌt(y)üd-ᵊn-ˈer-ē-ən\ *n* : a person who is broad and liberal in religious belief and conduct

la·trine \lə-ˈtrēn\ *n* : TOILET

lat·ter \ˈlat-ər\ *adj* **1** : more recent; *also* : FINAL **2** : of, relating to, or being the second of two things referred to — **lat·ter·ly** *adv*

lat·ter–day *adj* **1** : of present or recent times **2** : of a later or subsequent time

Latter–day Saint *n* : a member of a religious body founded by Joseph Smith in 1830 and accepting the Book of Mormon as divine revelation : MORMON

lat·tice \ˈlat-əs\ *n* **1** : a framework of crossed wood or metal strips; *also* : a window, door, or gate having a lattice **2** : a regular geometrical arrangement

lat·tice·work \-ˌwərk\ *n* : LATTICE; *also* : work made of lattices

[1]**laud** \ˈlȯd\ *n* : PRAISE, ACCLAIM

[2]**laud** *vb* : PRAISE, EXTOL — **laud·able** *adj* — **laud·ably** *adv*

lau·da·num \ˈlȯd-(ᵊ-)nəm\ *n* : OPIATE; *esp* : a tincture of opium

lau·da·to·ry \ˈlȯd-ə-ˌtōr-ē\ *adj* : of, relating to, or expressive of praise

[1]**laugh** \ˈlaf, ˈlàf\ *vb* : to show mirth, joy, or scorn with a smile and chuckle or explosive sound; *also* : to become amused or derisive — **laugh·able** *adj* — **laugh·ing·ly** \-iŋ-lē\ *adv*

[2]**laugh** *n* **1** : the act of laughing **2** : JOKE; *also* : JEER

laugh·ing·stock \ˈlaf-iŋ-ˌstäk, ˈlàf-\ *n* : an object of ridicule

laugh·ter \ˈlaf-tər, ˈlàf-\ *n* : the action or sound of laughing

[1]**launch** \ˈlȯnch\ *vb* [ME *launchen,* fr. OF *lancher,* fr. LL *lanceare* to wield a lance] **1** : THROW, HURL; *also* : to send off ⟨~ a rocket⟩ **2** : to set afloat **3** : to set in operation : START

[2]**launch** *n* : an act or instance of launching

[3]**launch** *n* : a small open or half-decked motorboat

launch·er \ˈlȯn-chər\ *n* **1** : one that launches **2** : a device for firing a grenade from a rifle **3** : a device for launching a rocket or rocket shell

launch·pad \ˈlȯnch-ˌpad\ *n* : a platform from which a rocket is launched

laun·der \ˈlȯn-dər\ *vb* **laun·dered; laun·der·ing** \-d(ə-)riŋ\ : to wash or wash and iron clothing and household linens — **laun·der·er** *n* — **laun·dress** \-drəs\ *n*

laun·dry \ˈlȯn-drē\ *n, pl* **laundries** [fr. obs. *launder* launderer, fr. MF *lavandier,* fr. ML *lavandarius,* fr. L *lavandus* needing to be washed, fr. *lavare* to wash] **1** : a place where laundering is done **2** : clothes or linens that have been or are to be laundered — **laun·dry·man** \-mən\ *n* — **laun·dry·wom·an** \-wu̇m-ən\ *n*

lau·re·ate \ˈlȯr-ē-ət\ *n* : the recipient of honor for achievement in an art or science — **lau·re·ate·ship** *n*

lau·rel \ˈlȯ-rəl\ *n* **1** : any of several trees or shrubs related to the sassafras and cinnamon; *esp* : a small evergreen tree of southern Europe **2** : MOUNTAIN LAUREL **3** : a crown of laurel : HONOR, DISTINCTION — usu. used in pl.

lav *abbr* lavatory

la·va \ˈläv-ə, ˈlav-\ *n* [It] **:** melted rock coming from a volcano; *also* **:** such rock solidified
la·vage \lə-ˈväzh\ *n* [F] **:** WASHING; *esp* **:** the washing out (as of an organ) for medicinal reasons
la·va·liere *or* **la·val·liere** \ˌläv-ə-ˈliər\ *n* [F *lavallière* necktie with a large bow] **:** a pendant on a fine chain that is worn as a necklace
lav·a·to·ry \ˈlav-ə-ˌtōr-ē\ *n, pl* **-ries 1 :** a fixed washbowl with running water and drainpipe **2 :** BATHROOM
lave \ˈlāv\ *vb* **laved; lav·ing :** WASH
lav·en·der \ˈlav-ən-dər\ *n* **1 :** a European mint or its dried leaves and flowers used to perfume clothing and bed linen **2 :** a pale purple
[1]**lav·ish** \ˈlav-ish\ *adj* [ME *lavas* abundance, fr. MF *lavasse* downpour, fr. *laver* to wash] **1 :** expending or bestowing profusely **2 :** expended or produced in abundance — **lav·ish·ly** *adv*
[2]**lavish** *vb* **:** to expend or give freely
law \ˈlȯ\ *n* **1 :** a rule of conduct or action established by custom or laid down and enforced by a governing authority; *also* **:** the whole body of such rules **2 :** the control brought about by enforcing rules **3** *cap* **:** the revelation of the divine will set forth in the Old Testament; *also* **:** the first part of the Jewish scriptures **4 :** a rule or principle of construction or procedure **5 :** the science that deals with laws and their interpretation and application **6 :** the profession of a lawyer **7 :** a rule or principle stating something that always works in the same way under the same conditions
law·break·er \ˈlȯ-ˌbrā-kər\ *n* **:** one who violates the law
law·ful \ˈlȯ-fəl\ *adj* **1 :** permitted by law **2 :** RIGHTFUL — **law·ful·ly** \-ē\ *adv*
law·giv·er \-ˌgiv-ər\ *n* **:** LEGISLATOR
law·less \ˈlȯ-ləs\ *adj* **1 :** having no laws **2 :** UNRULY, DISORDERLY ⟨a ~ mob⟩ — **law·less·ness** *n*
law·mak·er \-ˌmā-kər\ *n* **:** LEGISLATOR
law·man \ˈlȯ-mən\ *n* **:** a law enforcement official (as a sheriff or marshal)
[1]**lawn** \ˈlȯn\ *n* **:** ground (as around a house) covered with closely mowed grass
[2]**lawn** *n* **:** a fine sheer linen or cotton fabric
law·ren·ci·um \lȯ-ˈren-sē-əm\ *n* **:** a short-lived radioactive element — see ELEMENT table
law·suit \ˈlȯ-ˌsüt\ *n* **:** a suit in law
law·yer \ˈlȯ-yər\ *n* **:** one who conducts lawsuits for clients or advises as to legal rights and obligations in other matters
lax \ˈlaks\ *adj* **1 :** not strict ⟨~ discipline⟩ **2 :** not tense or rigid **syn** remiss, negligent, neglectful, delinquent, derelict — **lax·i·ty** \ˈlak-sət-ē\ *n* — **lax·ly** *adv*
[1]**lax·a·tive** \ˈlak-sət-iv\ *adj* **:** relieving constipation
[2]**laxative** *n* **:** a usu. mild laxative drug
[1]**lay** \ˈlā\ *vb* **laid** \ˈlād\; **lay·ing 1 :** to beat or strike down **2 :** to put on or against a surface **:** PLACE **3 :** to produce and deposit eggs **4 :** SETTLE; *also* **:** ALLAY **5 :** SPREAD **6 :** PREPARE, CONTRIVE **7 :** WAGER **8 :** to impose esp. as a duty or burden **9 :** to set in order or position **10 :** to bring to a specified condition **11 :** to put forward **:** SUBMIT
[2]**lay** *n* **:** the way in which something lies or is laid in relation to something else
[3]**lay** *past of* [1]LIE
[4]**lay** *n* **1 :** a simple narrative poem **2 :** SONG
[5]**lay** *adj* **:** of or relating to the laity
lay·away \ˈlā-ə-ˌwā\ *n* **:** a purchasing agreement by which a retailer agrees to hold merchandise secured by a deposit until the price is paid in full by the customer
lay·er \ˈlā-ər\ *n* **1 :** one that lays **2 :** one thickness, course, or fold laid or lying over or under another
lay·ette \lā-ˈet\ *n* [F, fr. MF, dim. of *laye* box] **:** an outfit of clothing and equipment for a newborn infant
lay·man \ˈlā-mən\ *n* **:** a member of the laity
lay·off \ˈlā-ˌȯf\ *n* **1 :** the act of dismissing an employee temporarily **2 :** a period of inactivity
lay·out \ˈlā-ˌau̇t\ *n* **1 :** ARRANGEMENT **2 :** SET, OUTFIT
lay·wom·an \ˈlā-ˌwu̇m-ən\ *n* **:** a woman who is a member of the laity
la·zar \ˈlaz-ər, ˈlā-zər\ *n* **:** LEPER
laze \ˈlāz\ *vb* **lazed; laz·ing :** to pass time in idleness or relaxation
la·zy \ˈlā-zē\ *adj* **la·zi·er; -est 1 :** disliking activity or exertion **2 :** SLUGGISH — **la·zi·ly** \ˈlā-zə-lē\ *adv* — **la·zi·ness** \-zē-nəs\ *n*
la·zy·bones \ˈlā-zē-ˌbōnz\ *n* **:** a lazy person
lazy Su·san \ˌlā-zē-ˈsüz-ᵊn\ *n* **:** a revolving tray placed on a dining table
lb *abbr* [L *libra*] pound
lc *abbr* lowercase
LC *abbr* Library of Congress
[1]**LCD** \ˈel-ˈsē-ˈdē\ *n* [*l*iquid *c*rystal *d*isplay] **:** a display (as of the time in a watch) that consists of segments of a liquid crystal whose reflectivity varies with the voltage applied to them
[2]**LCD** *abbr* least common denominator; lowest common denominator
LCDR *abbr* lieutenant commander
LCM *abbr* least common multiple; lowest common multiple
LCpl *abbr* lance corporal
ld *abbr* **1** load **2** lord
LD *abbr* lethal dose
LDC *abbr* less developed country
ldg *abbr* **1** landing **2** loading
LDS *abbr* Latter-day Saints
lea \ˈlē, ˈlā\ *n* **:** PASTURE, MEADOW
leach \ˈlēch\ *vb* **:** to pass a liquid (as water) through to carry off the soluble components; *also* **:** to dissolve out by such means ⟨~ alkali from ashes⟩
[1]**lead** \ˈlēd\ *vb* **led** \ˈled\; **lead·ing 1 :** to guide on a way; *also* **:** to run in a specified direction **2 :** LIVE ⟨~ a quiet life⟩ **3 :** to direct the operations, activity, or performance of ⟨~ an orchestra⟩ **4 :** to go at the head of **:** be first ⟨~ a parade⟩ **5 :** to begin play with; *also* **:** BEGIN, OPEN **6 :** to tend toward a definite result ⟨study *~ing* to a degree⟩ — **lead·er** *n* — **lead·er·less** *adj* — **lead·er·ship** *n*
[2]**lead** \ˈlēd\ *n* **1 :** a position at the front; *also* **:** a margin by which one leads **2 :** the privilege of leading in cards; *also* **:** the card or suit led **3 :** EXAMPLE **4 :** one that leads **5 :** a principal role (as in a play); *also* **:** one who plays such a role **6 :** INDICATION, CLUE **7 :** an insulated electrical conductor
[3]**lead** \ˈled\ *n* **1 :** a heavy bluish white chemical element that is easily bent and shaped — see ELEMENT table **2 :** an article made of lead; *esp* **:** a weight for sounding at sea **3 :** a thin strip of metal used to separate lines of type in printing **4 :** a thin stick of marking substance in or for a pencil
[4]**lead** \ˈled\ *vb* **1 :** to cover, line, or weight with lead **2 :** to fix (glass) in position with lead **3 :** to treat or mix with lead or a lead compound
lead·en \ˈled-ᵊn\ *adj* **1 :** made of lead; *also* **:** of the color of lead **2 :** SLUGGISH, DULL
lead off \(ˈ)lēd-ˈȯf\ *vb* **:** OPEN, BEGIN; *esp* **:** to bat first in an inning — **lead·off** \ˈlēd-ˌȯf\ *adj*
lead poisoning *n* **:** chronic intoxication produced by the absorption of lead into the system
[1]**leaf** \ˈlēf\ *n, pl* **leaves** \ˈlēvz\ **1 :** a usu. flat and green outgrowth of a plant stem that is a unit of foliage and functions esp. in photosynthesis; *also* **:** FOLIAGE **2**

: something that is suggestive of a leaf — **leaf·less** *adj* — **leafy** *adj*

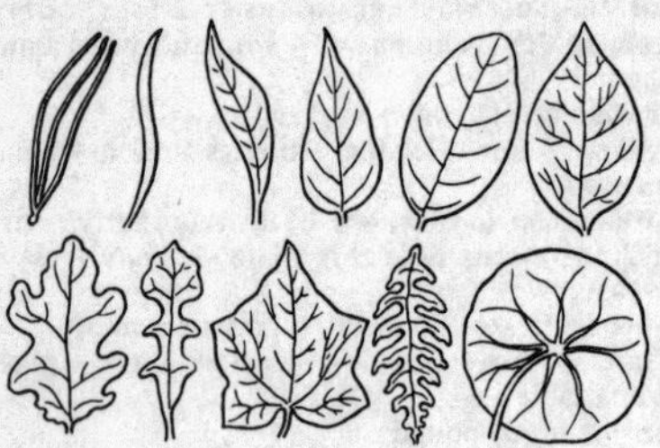

leaf 1

[2]**leaf** *vb* **1** : to produce leaves **2** : to turn the pages of a book

leaf·age \ˈlē-fij\ *n* : FOLIAGE

leafed \ˈlēft\ *adj* : LEAVED

leaf·hop·per \ˈlēf-ˌhäp-ər\ *n* : any of numerous small leaping insects related to the cicadas that suck the juices of plants

leaf·let \ˈlēf-lət\ *n* **1** : a division of a compound leaf **2** : PAMPHLET, FOLDER

leaf mold *n* : a compost or layer composed chiefly of decayed vegetable matter

leaf·stalk \ˈlēf-ˌstȯk\ *n* : PETIOLE

[1]**league** \ˈlēg\ *n* : a measure of distance equal to about three miles

[2]**league** *n* **1** : an association or alliance for a common purpose **2** : CLASS, CATEGORY — **league** *vb*

leagu·er \ˈlē-gər\ *n* : a member of a league

[1]**leak** \ˈlēk\ *vb* **1** : to enter or escape through a leak **2** : to let a substance in or out through an opening **3** : to become or make known

[2]**leak** *n* **1** : a crack or hole that accidentally admits a fluid or light or lets it escape; *also* : something that secretly or accidentally permits the admission or escape of something else **2** : LEAKAGE — **leaky** *adj*

leak·age \ˈlē-kij\ *n* **1** : the act of leaking **2** : the thing or amount that leaks

leal \ˈlēl\ *adj, chiefly Scot* : LOYAL

[1]**lean** \ˈlēn\ *vb* **1** : to bend from a vertical position : INCLINE **2** : to cast one's weight to one side for support **3** : to rely on for support **4** : to incline in opinion, taste, or desire — **lean** *n*

[2]**lean** *adj* **1** : lacking or deficient in flesh and esp. in fat **2** : lacking richness or productiveness **3** : low in fuel content — **lean·ness** \ˈlēn-nəs\ *n*

lean–to \ˈlēn-ˌtü\ *n, pl* **lean–tos** \-ˌtüz\ : a wing or extension of a building having a roof of only one slope; *also* : a rough shed or shelter with a similar roof

[1]**leap** \ˈlēp\ *vb* **leapt** \ˈlēpt, ˈlept\ *or* **leaped; leap·ing** : to spring free from a surface or over an obstacle : JUMP

[2]**leap** *n* : JUMP

leap·frog \ˈlēp-ˌfrȯg, -ˌfräg\ *n* : a game in which one player bends down and another vaults over him — **leapfrog** *vb*

leap year *n* : a year containing 366 days with February 29 as the extra day

learn \ˈlərn\ *vb* **learned** \ˈlərnd, ˈlərnt\; **learn·ing** **1** : to gain knowledge, understanding, or skill by study or experience; *also* : MEMORIZE **2** : to find out : ASCERTAIN — **learn·er** *n*

learn·ed \ˈlər-nəd\ *adj* : SCHOLARLY, ERUDITE

learn·ing \ˈlər-niŋ\ *n* : KNOWLEDGE, ERUDITION

learnt \ˈlərnt\ *chiefly Brit past & past part of* LEARN

[1]**lease** \ˈlēs\ *n* : a contract transferring real estate for a term of years or at will usu. for a specified rent

[2]**lease** *vb* **leased; leas·ing** **1** : to grant by lease **2** : to hold under a lease **syn** let, charter, hire, rent

lease·hold \ˈlēs-ˌhōld\ *n* **1** : a tenure by lease **2** : land held by lease — **lease·hold·er** *n*

leash \ˈlēsh\ *n* [ME *lees, leshe,* fr. OF *laisse,* fr. *laissier* to let go, fr. L *laxare* to loosen, fr. *laxus* slack] : a line for leading or restraining an animal — **leash** *vb*

[1]**least** \ˈlēst\ *adj* **1** : lowest in importance or position **2** : smallest in size or degree **3** : SLIGHTEST

[2]**least** *n* : one that is least

[3]**least** *adv* : in the smallest or lowest degree

least common denominator *n* : the least common multiple of two or more denominators

least common multiple *n* : the smallest common multiple of two or more numbers

least·wise \ˈlēst-ˌwīz\ *adv* : at least

leath·er \ˈleth-ər\ *n* : animal skin dressed for use — **leath·ern** \-ərn\ *adj* — **leath·ery** *adj*

leath·er·neck \-ˌnek\ *n* : MARINE

[1]**leave** \ˈlēv\ *vb* **left** \ˈleft\; **leav·ing** **1** : to allow or cause to remain behind; *also* : DELIVER **2** : to have as a remainder **3** : BEQUEATH **4** : to let stay without interference **5** : to go away : depart from **6** : to give up : ABANDON

[2]**leave** *n* **1** : PERMISSION; *also* : authorized absence from duty **2** : DEPARTURE

[3]**leave** *vb* **leaved; leav·ing** : LEAF

leaved \ˈlēvd\ *adj* : having leaves

[1]**leav·en** \ˈlev-ən\ *n* **1** : a substance (as yeast) used to produce fermentation (as in dough) **2** : something that modifies or lightens a mass or aggregate

[2]**leaven** *vb* **leav·ened; leav·en·ing** \ˈlev-(ə-)niŋ\ : to raise (dough) with a leaven; *also* : to permeate with a modifying or vivifying element

leav·en·ing \ˈlev-(ə-)niŋ\ *n* : LEAVEN

leaves *pl of* LEAF

leave–tak·ing \ˈlēv-ˌtā-kiŋ\ *n* : DEPARTURE, FAREWELL

leav·ings \ˈlē-viŋz\ *n pl* : REMNANT, RESIDUE

lech·ery \ˈlech-ə-rē\ *n* : inordinate indulgence in sexual activity — **lech·er** \ˈlech-ər\ *n* — **lech·er·ous** *adj* — **lech·er·ous·ness** *n*

lec·i·thin \ˈles-ə-thən\ *n* : any of several waxy phosphorus-containing substances that are common in animals and plants, form colloidal solutions in water, and have emulsifying and wetting properties

lect *abbr* lecture; lecturer

lec·tern \ˈlek-tərn\ *n* : a desk to support a book in a convenient position for a standing reader

lec·tor \-tər\ *n* : one whose chief duty is to read the lessons in a church service

lec·ture \ˈlek-chər\ *n* **1** : a discourse given before an audience or a class esp. for instruction **2** : REPRIMAND — **lec·ture** *vb* — **lec·tur·er** *n* — **lec·ture·ship** *n*

led *past and past part of* LEAD

LED \ˌel-ˌē-ˈdē\ *n* [*l*ight-*e*mitting *d*iode] : a semiconductor diode that emits light when a voltage is applied to it and is used esp. for electronic displays

le·der·ho·sen \ˈlād-ər-ˌhōz-ᵊn\ *n pl* : leather shorts often with suspenders worn esp. in Bavaria

ledge \ˈlej\ *n* [ME *legge* bar of a gate] **1** : a shelflike projection from a top or an edge **2** : REEF

led·ger \ˈlej-ər\ *n* : a book containing accounts to which debits and credits are transferred in final form

lee \ˈlē\ *n* **1** : a protecting shelter **2** : the side (as of a ship) that is sheltered from the wind — **lee** *adj*

leech \ˈlēch\ *n* [ME *leche* physician, fr. OE *lǣce*] **1** : any of various segmented usu. freshwater worms related to the earthworms; *esp* : one formerly used by physicians to draw blood **2** : a hanger-on who seeks gain

leek \ˈlēk\ *n* : an onionlike herb grown for its mildly pungent leaves and stalk

leer \ˈliər\ *n* : a suggestive, knowing, or malicious look — **leer** *vb*

leery \ˈli(ə)r-ē\ *adj* : SUSPICIOUS, WARY

lees \ˈlēz\ *n pl* : DREGS

[1]**lee·ward** \ˈlē-wərd, ˈlü-ərd\ *n* : the lee side

[2]**leeward** *adj* : situated away from the wind

lee·way \ˈlē-ˌwā\ *n* **1** : lateral movement of a ship when under way **2** : an allowable margin of freedom or variation

[1]**left** \ˈleft\ *adj* [ME, fr. OE, weak; fr. the left hand's being the weaker in most individuals] **1** : of, relating to, or being the side of the body in which the heart is mostly located; *also* : located nearer to this side than to the right **2** *often cap* : of, adhering to, or constituted by the political Left — **left** *adv*

[2]**left** *n* **1** : the left hand; *also* : the side or part that is on or toward the left side **2** *cap* : those professing political views marked by desire to reform the established order and usu. to give greater freedom to the common man

[3]**left** *past and past part of* LEAVE

left–hand *adj* **1** : LEFT-HANDED **2** : situated on the left

left–hand·ed \ˈleft-ˈhan-dəd\ *adj* **1** : using the left hand habitually or better than the right **2** : designed for or done with the left hand **3** : INSINCERE, BACKHANDED **4** : COUNTERCLOCKWISE — **left–handed** *adv*

left·ism \ˈlef-ˌtiz-əm\ *n* **1** : the principles and views of the Left; *also* : the movement embodying these principles **2** : advocacy of or adherence to the doctrines of the Left — **left·ist** \-təst\ *n or adj*

left·over \ˈleft-ˌō-vər\ *n* : an unused or unconsumed residue

[1]**leg** \ˈleg\ *n* **1** : a limb of an animal used esp. for supporting the body and in walking; *esp* : the part of the vertebrate leg between knee and foot **2** : something resembling or analogous to an animal leg ⟨table ~⟩ **3** : the part of an article of clothing that covers the leg **4** : a portion of a trip — **legged** \ˈleg-əd\ *adj* — **leg·less** *adj*

[2]**leg** *vb* **legged; leg·ging** : to use the legs in walking or esp. in running

[3]**leg** *abbr* **1** legal **2** legislative; legislature

leg·a·cy \ˈleg-ə-sē\ *n, pl* **-cies** : INHERITANCE, BEQUEST; *also* : something that has come from an ancestor or predecessor or the past

le·gal \ˈlē-gəl\ *adj* **1** : of or relating to law or lawyers **2** : LAWFUL; *also* : STATUTORY **3** : enforced in courts of law — **le·gal·i·ty** \li-ˈgal-ət-ē\ *n* — **le·gal·ize** \ˈlē-gə-ˌlīz\ *vb* — **le·gal·ly** \-gə-lē\ *adv*

le·gal·ism \ˈlē-gə-ˌliz-əm\ *n* : strict, literal, or excessive conformity to the law or to a religious or moral code — **le·gal·is·tic** \ˌlē-gə-ˈlis-tik\ *adj*

leg·ate \ˈleg-ət\ *n* : an official representative; *esp* : AMBASSADOR

leg·a·tee \ˌleg-ə-ˈtē\ *n* : a person to whom a legacy is bequeathed

le·ga·tion \li-ˈgā-shən\ *n* **1** : a diplomatic mission headed by a minister **2** : the official residence and office of a minister to a foreign government

le·ga·to \li-ˈgät-ō\ *adv or adj* [It, lit., tied] : in a smooth and connected manner — used as a direction in music

leg·end \ˈlej-ənd\ *n* [ME *legende,* fr. MF & ML; MF *legende,* fr. ML *legenda,* fr. L *legere* to gather, select, read] **1** : a story coming down from the past; *esp* : one popularly accepted as historical though not verifiable **2** : an inscription on an object; *also* : CAPTION **3** : an explanatory list of the symbols on a map or chart

leg·end·ary \ˈlej-ən-ˌder-ē\ *adj* : of, relating to, or characteristic of a legend

leg·er·de·main \ˌlej-ərd-ə-ˈmān\ *n* [ME, fr. MF *leger de main* light of hand] : SLEIGHT OF HAND

leg·ging *or* **leg·gin** \ˈleg-ən, -iŋ\ *n* : a covering for the leg

leg·gy \ˈleg-ē\ *adj* **leg·gi·er; -est 1** : having unusually long legs **2** : having attractive legs **3** : SPINDLY — used of a plant

leg·horn \ˈleg-ˌ(h)ȯrn, ˈleg-ərn\ *n* **1** : a fine plaited straw; *also* : a hat made of this straw **2** : any of a Mediterranean breed of small hardy fowls

leg·i·ble \ˈlej-ə-bəl\ *adj* : capable of being read : CLEAR — **leg·i·bil·i·ty** \ˌlej-ə-ˈbil-ət-ē\ *n* — **leg·i·bly** \ˈlej-ə-blē\ *adv*

[1]**le·gion** \ˈlē-jən\ *n* **1** : a unit of the Roman army comprising 3000 to 6000 soldiers **2** : MULTITUDE **3** : an association of ex-servicemen — **le·gion·ary** \-ˌer-ē\ *n* — **le·gion·naire** \ˌlē-jən-ˈaər\ *n*

[2]**legion** *adj* : MANY, NUMEROUS

Le·gion·naires' disease *also* **Le·gion·naire's disease** \ˌlē-jə-ˈnerz-\ *n* [so called fr. its first recognized occurrence during the 1976 American Legion convention] : a pneumonia that is caused by a bacterium and affects one or more lobes of the lung

legis *abbr* legislation; legislative; legislature

leg·is·late \ˈlej-ə-ˌslāt\ *vb* **-lat·ed; -lat·ing** : to make or enact laws; *also* : to bring about by legislation — **leg·is·la·tor** \-ˌslāt-ər\ *n*

leg·is·la·tion \ˌlej-ə-ˈslā-shən\ *n* **1** : the action of legislating **2** : laws made by a legislative body

leg·is·la·tive \ˈlej-ə-ˌslāt-iv\ *adj* **1** : having the power of legislating **2** : of or relating to a legislature

leg·is·la·ture \ˈlej-ə-ˌslā-chər\ *n* : an organized body of persons having the authority to make laws

le·git \li-ˈjit\ *adj, slang* : LEGITIMATE

le·git·i·mate \li-ˈjit-ə-mət\ *adj* **1** : lawfully begotten **2** : GENUINE **3** : LAWFUL **4** : conforming to recognized principles or accepted rules or standards — **le·git·i·ma·cy** \-mə-sē\ *n* — **le·git·i·mate·ly** *adv*

le·git·i·mize \li-ˈjit-ə-ˌmīz\ *vb* **-mized; -miz·ing** : LEGITIMATE

leg·man \ˈleg-ˌman\ *n* **1** : a reporter assigned usu. to gather information **2** : an assistant who gathers information and runs errands

le·gume \ˈleg-ˌyüm, li-ˈgyüm\ *n* [F] **1** : any of a large group of plants having fruits that are dry pods and split when ripe and including important food and forage plants (as beans and clover) **2** : the part of a legume used as food; *also* : VEGETABLE 2 — **le·gu·mi·nous** \li-ˈgyü-mə-nəs\ *adj*

[1]**lei** \ˈlā(-ˌē)\ *n* : a wreath or necklace usu. of flowers

[2]**lei** \ˈlā\ *pl of* LEU

lei·sure \ˈlēzh-ər, ˈlezh-, ˈlāzh-\ *n* **1** : time free from work or duties **2** : EASE; *also* : CONVENIENCE **syn** relaxation, rest, repose — **lei·sure·ly** *adj*

leit·mo·tiv *or* **leit·mo·tif** \ˈlīt-mō-ˌtēf\ *n* [G *leitmotiv,* fr. *leiten* to lead + *motiv* motive] : a dominant recurring theme

lek \ˈlek\ *n, pl* **leks** *or* **le·ke** *also* **lek** *or* **le·ku** — see MONEY table

lem·ming \ˈlem-iŋ\ *n* [Norw] : any of several short-tailed northern rodents

lem·on \ˈlem-ən\ *n* **1** : an acid yellow usu. nearly oblong citrus fruit; *also* : a citrus tree that bears lemons **2** : something unsatisfactory or defective (as an automobile) : DUD — **lem·ony** *adj*

lem·on·ade \ˌlem-ə-ˈnād\ *n* : a beverage of lemon juice, sugar, and water

lem·pi·ra \lem-ˈpir-ə\ *n* — see MONEY table

le·mur \ˈlē-mər\ *n* : any of numerous arboreal mammals largely of Madagascar usu. with a muzzle like a fox, large eyes, very soft woolly fur, and a long furry tail

lend \ˈlend\ *vb* **lent** \ˈlent\; **lend·ing 1** : to give for temporary use on condition that the same or its equivalent be returned **2** : AFFORD, FURNISH **3** : ACCOMMODATE — **lend·er** *n*

lend–lease \-ˈlēs\ *n* : the transfer of goods and services to an ally to aid in a common cause with payment being made by a return of the items or their use in the common cause or by a similar transfer of other goods and services

length \ˈleŋth\ *n* **1** : the longer or longest dimension of an object; *also* : a measured distance **2** : duration or extent in time or space **3** : the length of something taken as a unit of measure ⟨the horse won by a ~⟩ **4** : PIECE; *esp* : one in a series of pieces designed to be joined

length·en \ˈleŋ-thən\ *vb* **length·ened; length·en·ing** \ˈleŋth-(ə-)niŋ\ : to make or become longer **syn** extend, elongate, prolong, protract

length·wise \-ˌwīz\ *adv* : in the direction of the length — **lengthwise** *adj*

lengthy \ˈleŋ-thē\ *adj* **length·i·er; -est** **1** : protracted excessively **2** : EXTENDED, LONG

le·nient \ˈlē-nē-ənt, -nyənt\ *adj* : of mild and tolerant disposition or effect **syn** indulgent, forbearing, merciful, tolerant — **le·ni·en·cy** \ˈlē-nē-ən-sē, -nyən-sē\ *n* — **le·ni·ent·ly** *adv*

len·i·tive \ˈlen-ət-iv\ *adj* : alleviating pain or acrimony

len·i·ty \ˈlen-ət-ē\ *n* : LENIENCY, MILDNESS

lens \ˈlenz\ *n* [L *lent-, lens* lentil; so called fr. the shape of a convex lens] **1** : a curved piece of glass or plastic used singly or combined in an optical instrument for forming an image; *also* : a device for focusing radiation other than light **2** : a transparent body in the eye that focuses light rays on receptors at the back of the eye

Lent \ˈlent\ *n* : a 40-day period of penitence and fasting observed from Ash Wednesday to Easter by many churches — **Lent·en** \-ᵊn\ *adj*

len·til \ˈlent-ᵊl\ *n* : an Old World legume grown for its flat edible seeds and for fodder; *also* : its seed

Leo \ˈlē-ō\ *n* [L, lit., lion] : the 5th sign of the zodiac in astrology

le·one \lē-ˈōn\ *n, pl* **leones** *or* **leone** — see MONEY table

le·o·nine \ˈlē-ə-ˌnīn\ *adj* : of, relating to, or resembling a lion

leop·ard \ˈlep-ərd\ *n* : a large strong usu. tawny and black-spotted cat of southern Asia and Africa

le·o·tard \ˈlē-ə-ˌtärd\ *n* : a close-fitting garment worn esp. by dancers and people doing exercises

lep·er \ˈlep-ər\ *n* **1** : a person affected with leprosy **2** : OUTCAST

lep·re·chaun \ˈlep-rə-ˌkän\ *n* : a mischievous elf of Irish folklore

lep·ro·sy \ˈlep-rə-sē\ *n* : a chronic bacterial disease marked esp. by slow-growing swellings with deformity and loss of sensation of affected parts — **lep·rous** \-rəs\ *adj*

lep·ton \lep-ˈtän\ *n, pl* **lep·ta** \-ˈtä\ — see *drachma* at MONEY table

les·bi·an \ˈlez-bē-ən\ *n, often cap* [fr. the reputed homosexual group associated with the poet Sappho of Lesbos] : a female homosexual — **lesbian** *adj* — **les·bi·an·ism** \-ˌiz-əm\ *n*

lèse ma·jes·té *or* **lese maj·es·ty** \ˈlēz-ˈmaj-ə-stē\ *n* [MF *lese majesté*, fr. L *laesa majestas*, lit., injured majesty] : an offense violating the dignity of a sovereign

le·sion \ˈlē-zhən\ *n* : an abnormal structural change in the body due to injury or disease

[1]**less** \ˈles\ *adj* **1** : FEWER ⟨~ than six⟩ **2** : of lower rank, degree, or importance **3** : SMALLER; *also* : more limited in quantity

[2]**less** *adv* : to a lesser extent or degree

[3]**less** *prep* : diminished by : MINUS

[4]**less** *n, pl* **less** **1** : a smaller portion **2** : something of less importance

-less \ləs\ *adj suffix* **1** : destitute of : not having ⟨child*less*⟩ **2** : unable to be acted on or to act (in a specified way) ⟨daunt*less*⟩

les·see \le-ˈsē\ *n* : a tenant under a lease

less·en \ˈles-ᵊn\ *vb* **less·ened; less·en·ing** \ˈles-(ᵊ-)niŋ\ : to make or become less **syn** decrease, diminish, dwindle, abate

less·er \ˈles-ər\ *adj* : of less size, quality, or significance

les·son \ˈles-ᵊn\ *n* **1** : a passage from sacred writings read in a service of worship **2** : a reading or exercise to be studied by a pupil; *also* : something learned **3** : a period of instruction **4** : an instructive example

les·sor \ˈles-ˌȯr, le-ˈsȯr\ *n* : one who conveys property by a lease

lest \ˌlest\ *conj* : for fear that

[1]**let** \ˈlet\ *n* [ME *lette*, fr. *letten* to delay, hinder, fr. OE *lettan*] **1** : HINDRANCE, OBSTACLE **2** : a shot or point in racket games that does not count

[2]**let** *vb* **let; let·ting** [ME *leten*, fr. OE *lǣtan*] **1** : to cause to : MAKE ⟨~ it be known⟩ **2** : RENT, LEASE; *also* : to assign esp. after bids **3** : ALLOW, PERMIT ⟨~ me go⟩

-let \lət\ *n suffix* **1** : small one ⟨book*let*⟩ **2** : article worn on ⟨wrist*let*⟩

let·down \ˈlet-ˌdau̇n\ *n* **1** : DISAPPOINTMENT **2** : a slackening of effort **3** : the descent of an aircraft to the beginning of a landing approach

le·thal \ˈlē-thəl\ *adj* : DEADLY, FATAL — **le·thal·ly** \-ē\ *adv*

leth·ar·gy \ˈleth-ər-jē\ *n* **1** : abnormal drowsiness **2** : the quality or state of being lazy or indifferent **syn** languor, lassitude, torpidity, torpidness — **le·thar·gic** \li-ˈthär-jik\ *adj*

let on *vb* **1** : REVEAL, ADMIT **2** : PRETEND

[1]**let·ter** \ˈlet-ər\ *n* **1** : a symbol that stands for a speech sound and constitutes a unit of an alphabet **2** : a written or printed communication **3** *pl* : LITERATURE; *also* : LEARNING **4** : the literal meaning ⟨the ~ of the law⟩ **5** : a single piece of type

[2]**letter** *vb* : to mark with letters : INSCRIBE — **let·ter·er** *n*

let·ter·head \ˈlet-ər-ˌhed\ *n* : stationery with a printed or engraved heading; *also* : the heading itself

let·ter–per·fect \ˌlet-ər-ˈpər-fikt\ *adj* : correct to the smallest detail

let·ter·press \ˈlet-ər-ˌpres\ *n* **1** : printing done directly by impressing the paper on an inked raised surface **2** *chiefly Brit* : TEXT

letters of marque \-ˈmärk\ : written authority granted to a private person by a government to seize the subjects of a foreign state or their goods; *esp* : a license granted to a private person to fit out an armed ship to plunder the enemy

letters patent *n pl* : a written grant from a government to a person in a form readily open for inspection by all

let·tuce \ˈlet-əs\ *n* [ME *letuse*, fr. OF *laitues*, pl. of *laitue*, fr. L *lactuca*, fr. *lac* milk; fr. its milky juice] : a garden plant with crisp leaves used esp. in salads

let·up \ˈlet-ˌəp\ *n* : a lessening of effort

leu \ˈleu̇\ *n, pl* **lei** \ˈlā\ — see MONEY table

leu·ke·mia \lü-ˈkē-mē-ə\ *n* : a cancerous disease in which white blood cells increase greatly — **leu·ke·mic** \-mik\ *adj or n*

leu·ko·cyte *also* **leu·co·cyte** \ˈlü-kə-ˌsīt\ *n* : WHITE BLOOD CELL

lev \ˈlef\ *n, pl* **le·va** \ˈlev-ə\ — see MONEY table

Lev *or* **Levit** *abbr* Leviticus

[1]**le·vee** \ˈlev-ē; lə-ˈvē, -ˈvā\ *n* [F *lever* act of arising] : a reception held by a person of distinction

[2]**lev·ee** \ˈlev-ē\ *n* : an embankment to prevent or confine flooding (as by a river); *also* : a river landing place

[1]**lev·el** \ˈlev-əl\ *n* **1** : a device for establishing a horizontal line or plane **2** : horizontal condition **3** : a horizontal position, line, or surface often taken as an index of altitude; *also* : a flat area of ground **4** : height, position, rank, or size in a scale

[2]**level** *vb* **-eled** *or* **-elled; -el·ing** *or* **-el·ling** \-(ə-)liŋ\ **1** : to make flat or level; *also* : to come to a level **2** : AIM, DIRECT **3** : EQUALIZE **4** : RAZE — **lev·el·er** *n*

[3]**level** *adj* **1** : having a flat even surface **2** : HORIZONTAL **3** : of the same height or rank; *also* : UNIFORM **4** : steady and cool in judgment — **lev·el·ly** \ˈlev-əl-(l)ē\ *adv* — **lev·el·ness** *n*

lev·el·head·ed \ˌlev-əl-ˈhed-əd\ *adj* : having sound judgment : SENSIBLE

le·ver \ˈlev-ər, ˈlē-vər\ *n* **1** : a bar used for prying or dislodging something; *also* : a means for achieving one's purpose **2** : a rigid piece turning about an axis and used for transmitting and changing force and motion

le·ver·age \ˈlev-(ə-)rij, ˈlēv-\ *n* : the action or mechanical effect of a lever

le·vi·a·than \li-ˈvī-ə-thən\ *n* **1** : a large sea animal **2** : something very large or formidable of its kind

lev·i·tate \ˈlev-ə-ˌtāt\ *vb* **-tat·ed; -tat·ing** : to rise or cause to rise in the air in seeming defiance of gravitation — **lev·i·ta·tion** \ˌlev-ə-ˈtā-shən\ *n*

Le·vit·i·cus \li-ˈvit-ə-kəs\ *n* — see BIBLE table

lev·i·ty \ˈlev-ət-ē\ *n* : lack of earnestness **syn** lightness, flippancy, frivolity

[1]**levy** \ˈlev-ē\ *n, pl* **lev·ies** **1** : the imposition or collection of an assessment; *also* : an amount levied **2** : the enlistment of men for military service; *also* : troops raised by levy

[2]**levy** *vb* **lev·ied; levy·ing** **1** : to impose or collect by legal authority **2** : to enlist for military service **3** : WAGE ⟨~ war⟩ **4** : to seize property in satisfaction of a legal claim

lewd \ˈlüd\ *adj* [ME *lewed* vulgar, fr. OE *lǣwede* lay, ignorant] **1** : sexually unchaste **2** : OBSCENE, SALACIOUS — **lewd·ly** *adv* — **lewd·ness** *n*

lex·i·cog·ra·phy \ˌlek-sə-ˈkäg-rə-fē\ *n* **1** : the editing or making of a dictionary **2** : the principles and practices of dictionary making — **lex·i·cog·ra·pher** \-fər\ *n* — **lex·i·co·graph·i·cal** \-kō-ˈgraf-i-kəl\ *or* **lex·i·co·graph·ic** \-ik\ *adj*

lex·i·con \ˈlek-sə-ˌkän\ *n, pl* **lex·i·ca** \-si-kə\ *or* **lexicons** : DICTIONARY

LF *abbr* low frequency

lg *abbr* **1** large **2** long

LH *abbr* **1** left hand **2** lower half

li *abbr* link

Li *symbol* lithium

LI *abbr* Long Island

li·a·bil·i·ty \ˌlī-ə-ˈbil-ət-ē\ *n, pl* **-ties** **1** : the quality or state of being liable **2** *pl* : DEBTS **3** : DISADVANTAGE

li·a·ble \ˈlī-ə-bəl\ *adj* **1** : legally obligated : RESPONSIBLE **2** : LIKELY, APT ⟨~ to fall⟩ **3** : SUSCEPTIBLE

li·ai·son \ˈlē-ə-ˌzän, lē-ˈā-\ *n* [F] **1** : a close bond : INTERRELATIONSHIP **2** : an illicit sexual relationship **3** : communication for mutual understanding (as between parts of an armed force)

li·ar \ˈlī-ər\ *n* : a person who lies

[1]**lib** \ˈlib\ *n* : LIBERATION

[2]**lib** *abbr* **1** liberal **2** librarian; library

li·ba·tion \lī-ˈbā-shən\ *n* **1** : an act of pouring a liquid as a sacrifice (as to a god); *also* : the liquid poured **2** : DRINK — **li·ba·tion·ary** *adj*

[1]**li·bel** \ˈlī-bəl\ *n* [ME, written declaration, fr. MF, fr. L *libellus,* dim. of *liber* book] **1** : a spoken or written statement or a representation that gives an unjustly unfavorable impression of a person or thing **2** : the action or crime of publishing a libel — **li·bel·ous** *or* **li·bel·lous** \-bə-ləs\ *adj*

[2]**libel** *vb* **-beled** *or* **-belled; -bel·ing** *or* **-bel·ling** : to make or publish a libel — **li·bel·er** *n* — **li·bel·ist** *n*

[1]**lib·er·al** \ˈlib(-ə)-rəl\ *adj* [ME, fr. MF, fr. L *liberalis* suitable for a freeman, generous, fr. *liber* free] **1** : of, relating to, or based on the liberal arts **2** : GENEROUS, BOUNTIFUL **3** : not literal **4** : not narrow in opinion or judgment : TOLERANT; *also* : not orthodox **5** : not conservative — **lib·er·al·i·ty** \ˌlib-ə-ˈral-ət-ē\ *n* — **lib·er·al·ize** \ˈlib-(ə-)rə-ˌlīz\ *vb* — **lib·er·al·ly** \-rə-lē\ *adv*

[2]**liberal** *n* : a person who holds liberal views

liberal arts *n pl* : the studies (as language, philosophy, history, literature, or abstract science) in a college or university intended to provide chiefly general knowledge and to develop the general intellectual capacities

lib·er·al·ism \ˈlib(-ə)-rə-ˌliz-əm\ *n* : liberal principles and theories

lib·er·ate \ˈlib-ə-ˌrāt\ *vb* **-at·ed; -at·ing** **1** : to free from bondage or restraint; *also* : to raise to equal rights and status **2** : to free (as a gas) from combination — **lib·er·a·tion** \ˌlib-ə-ˈrā-shən\ *n* — **lib·er·a·tor** \ˈlib-ə-ˌrāt-ər\ *n*

lib·er·at·ed *adj* : freed from or opposed to traditional social and sexual attitudes or roles ⟨a ~ woman⟩

lib·er·tar·i·an \ˌlib-ər-ˈter-ē-ən\ *n* **1** : an advocate of the doctrine of free will **2** : one who upholds the principles of liberty

lib·er·tine \ˈlib-ər-ˌtēn\ *n* : one who leads a dissolute life

lib·er·ty \ˈlib-ərt-ē\ *n, pl* **-ties** **1** : FREEDOM **2** : an action going beyond normal limits; *esp* : FAMILIARITY **3** : a short leave from naval duty

li·bid·i·nous \lə-ˈbid-ᵊn-əs\ *adj* **1** : LASCIVIOUS **2** : LIBIDINAL

li·bi·do \lə-ˈbēd-ō, -ˈbīd-\ *n, pl* **-dos** [NL, fr. L, desire, lust] : psychic energy derived from basic biological urges; *also* : sexual drive — **li·bid·i·nal** \lə-ˈbid-ᵊn-əl\ *adj*

Li·bra \ˈlē-brə\ *n* [L, lit., scales] : the 7th sign of the zodiac in astrology

li·brar·i·an \lī-ˈbrer-ē-ən\ *n* : a specialist in the management of a library

li·brary \ˈlī-ˌbrer-ē\ *n, pl* **-brar·ies** **1** : a place in which books and related materials are kept for use but not for sale **2** : a collection of books

li·bret·to \lə-ˈbret-ō\ *n, pl* **-tos** *or* **-ti** \-ē\ [It, dim. of *libro* book, fr. L *liber*] : the text of a work (as an opera) for the musical theater — **li·bret·tist** \-əst\ *n*

Lib·y·an \ˈlib-ē-ən\ *n* : a native or inhabitant of Libya — **Libyan** *adj*

lice *pl of* LOUSE

li·cense *or* **li·cence** \ˈlīs-ᵊns\ *n* **1** : permission to act; *esp* : legal permission to engage in an activity **2** : a document, plate, or tag evidencing a license granted **3** : freedom used irresponsibly — **license** *vb*

licensed practical nurse *n* : a specially trained person who is licensed (as by a state) to provide routine care for the sick

li·cens·ee \ˌlīs-ᵊn-ˈsē\ *n* : a licensed person

li·cen·te \lə-ˈsent-ē\ *n, pl* **licente** *or* **li·cen·ti** \-ē\ — see *loti* at MONEY table

li·cen·ti·ate \lī-ˈsen-chē-ət\ *n* : one licensed to practice a profession

li·cen·tious \lī-ˈsen-chəs\ *adj* : LEWD, LASCIVIOUS — **li·cen·tious·ly** *adv* — **li·cen·tious·ness** *n*

li·chee *var of* LITCHI

li·chen \ˈlī-kən\ *n* : any of various complex lower plants made up of an alga and a fungus growing as a unit on a solid surface — **li·chen·ous** *adj*

lichen

lic·it \ˈlis-ət\ *adj* : LAWFUL

[1]**lick** \ˈlik\ *vb* **1** : to draw the tongue over; *also* : to flicker over like a tongue **2** : THRASH; *also* : DEFEAT

[2]**lick** *n* **1** : a stroke of the tongue **2** : a small amount **3** : a hasty careless effort **4** : BLOW **5** : a natural deposit of salt that animals lick

lick·e·ty–split \ˌlik-ət-ē-ˈsplit\ *adv* : at great speed

lick·spit·tle \ˈlik-ˌspit-ᵊl\ *n* : a fawning subordinate : TOADY

lic·o·rice \ˈlik(-ə)-rish, -rəs\ *n* [ME *licorice,* fr. OF, fr. LL *liquiritia,* alter. of L *glycyrrhiza,* fr. Gk *glykyrrhiza,* fr. *glykys* sweet + *rhiza* root] **1** : the dried root of a European leguminous plant; *also* : an extract from it used esp. as a flavoring and in medicine **2** : a confection flavored with licorice **3** : a plant yielding licorice

lid \ˈlid\ *n* **1** : a movable cover **2** : EYELID **3** : a force that represses — **lid·ded** \ˈlid-əd\ *adj*

li·do \ˈlēd-ō\ *n, pl* **lidos** : a fashionable beach resort

[1]**lie** \ˈlī\ *vb* **lay** \ˈlā\; **lain** \ˈlān\; **ly·ing** \ˈlī-iŋ\ **1** : to be in, stay at rest in, or assume a horizontal position; *also* : to be in a helpless or defenseless state **2** : EXTEND **3** : to occupy a certain relative position **4** : to have an effect esp. through mere presence

[2]**lie** *n* : the position in which something lies

[3]**lie** *vb* **lied; ly·ing** \ˈlī-iŋ\ : to tell a lie

[4]**lie** *n* : an untrue statement made with intent to deceive

lied \ˈlēt\ *n, pl* **lie·der** \ˈlēd-ər\ [G] : a German song esp. of the 19th century

lief \ˈlēv, ˈlēf\ *adv* : GLADLY, WILLINGLY

[1]**liege** \ˈlēj\ *adj* [ME, fr. OF, fr. LL *laeticus,* fr. *laetus* serf] : LOYAL, FAITHFUL

[2]**liege** *n* **1** : VASSAL **2** : a feudal superior

lien \ˈlēn, ˈlē-ən\ *n* : a legal claim on the property of another for the satisfaction of a debt or the fulfillment of a duty

lieu \ˈlü\ *n, archaic* : PLACE, STEAD — **in lieu of** : in the place of

lieut *abbr* lieutenant

lieu·ten·ant \lü-ˈten-ənt\ *n* [ME, fr. MF, fr. *lieu* place + *tenant* holding, fr. *tenir* to hold, fr. L *tenēre*] **1** : a representative of another in the performance of duty **2** : FIRST LIEUTENANT; *also* : SECOND LIEUTENANT **3** : a commissioned officer in the navy ranking next below a lieutenant commander — **lieu·ten·an·cy** \-ən-sē\ *n*

lieutenant colonel *n* : a commissioned officer (as in the army) ranking next below a colonel

lieutenant commander *n* : a commissioned officer in the navy ranking next below a commander

lieutenant general *n* : a commissioned officer (as in the army) ranking next below a general

lieutenant governor *n* : a deputy or subordinate governor

lieutenant junior grade *n, pl* **lieutenants junior grade** : a commissioned officer in the navy ranking next below a lieutenant

life \ˈlīf\ *n, pl* **lives** \ˈlīvz\ **1** : the quality that distinguishes a vital and functional being from a dead body or inanimate matter; *also* : a state of an organism characterized esp. by capacity for metabolism, growth, reaction to stimuli, and reproduction **2** : the physical and mental experiences of an individual **3** : BIOGRAPHY **4** : the period of existence **5** : manner of living **6** : PERSON **7** : ANIMATION, SPIRIT; *also* : LIVELINESS **8** : animate activity ⟨signs of ~⟩ **9** : one providing interest and vigor — **life·less** *adj* — **life·like** *adj*

life·blood \ˈlīf-ˈbləd, -ˌbləd\ *n* : a basic source of strength and vitality

life·boat \-ˌbōt\ *n* : a sturdy boat designed for use in saving lives at sea

life·guard \-ˌgärd\ *n* : a usu. expert swimmer employed to safeguard bathers

life·line \-ˌlīn\ *n* **1** : a line to which persons may cling for safety **2** : a trade route or means of communication considered indispensable

life·long \-ˌlȯŋ\ *adj* : continuing through life

life preserver *n* : a device designed to save a person from drowning by providing buoyancy in water

lif·er \ˈlī-fər\ *n* **1** : a person sentenced to life imprisonment **2** : a person who makes a career in the armed forces

life raft *n* : a raft for use by people forced into the water

life·sav·ing \ˈlīf-ˌsā-viŋ\ *n* : the skill or practice of saving or protecting lives esp. of drowning persons — **life·sav·er** \-ˌsā-vər\ *n*

life science *n* : a branch of science (as biology, medicine, anthropology, or sociology) that deals with living organisms and life processes — usu. used in pl

life·time \-ˌtīm\ *n* : the duration of an individual's existence

life·work \-ˈwərk\ *n* : the entire or principal work of one's lifetime; *also* : a work extending over a lifetime

LIFO *abbr* last in, first out

[1]**lift** \ˈlift\ *vb* **1** : RAISE, ELEVATE; *also* : RISE, ASCEND **2** : to put an end to : STOP **3** : to pay off ⟨~ a mortgage⟩

[2]**lift** *n* **1** : LOAD **2** : the action or an instance of lifting **3** : HELP; *also* : a ride along one's way **4** : RISE, ADVANCE **5** *chiefly Brit* : ELEVATOR **6** : an elevation of the spirits **7** : the upward force that is developed by a moving airfoil and that opposes the pull of gravity

lift–off \ˈlif-ˌtȯf\ *n* : a vertical takeoff (as by a rocket)

lift truck *n* : a small truck for lifting and transporting loads

lig·a·ment \ˈlig-ə-mənt\ *n* : a band of tough tissue that holds bones together

li·gate \ˈlī-ˌgāt\ *vb* **li·gat·ed; li·gat·ing** : to tie with a ligature — **li·ga·tion** \lī-ˈgā-shən\ *n*

lig·a·ture \ˈlig-ə-ˌchu̇r, -chər\ *n* **1** : something that binds or ties; *also* : a thread used in surgery esp. for tying blood vessels **2** : a printed or written character consisting of two or more letters or characters (as *æ*) united

[1]**light** \ˈlīt\ *n* **1** : something that makes vision possible : electromagnetic radiation visible to the human eye; *also* : BRIGHTNESS **2** : DAYLIGHT **3** : a source of light (as a candle) **4** : ENLIGHTENMENT; *also* : TRUTH **5** : public knowledge **6** : a particular aspect or appearance presented to view ⟨now saw the matter in a different ~⟩ **7** : WINDOW **8** *pl* : STANDARDS ⟨according to his ~*s*⟩ **9** : CELEBRITY **10** : LIGHTHOUSE, BEACON; *also* : a traffic signal **11** : a flame for lighting something

[2]**light** *adj* **1** : BRIGHT **2** : PALE ⟨~ blue⟩ — **light·ness** *n*

[3]**light** *vb* **light·ed** *or* **lit** \ˈlit\; **light·ing 1** : to make or become light **2** : to cause to burn : BURN **3** : to conduct with a light **4** : ILLUMINATE

[4]**light** *adj* **1** : not heavy **2** : not serious ⟨~ reading⟩ **3** : SCANTY ⟨~ rain⟩ **4** : GENTLE ⟨a ~ blow⟩ **5** : easily endurable ⟨~ cold⟩ ; *also* : requiring little effort ⟨~ exercise⟩ **6** : SWIFT, NIMBLE **7** : FRIVOLOUS **8** : DIZZY **9** : producing goods for direct consumption by the consumer ⟨~ industry⟩ — **light·ly** *adv* — **light·ness** *n*

[5]**light** *adv* **1** : LIGHTLY **2** : with little baggage ⟨travel ~⟩

[6]**light** *vb* **light·ed** *or* **lit** \ˈlit\; **light·ing 1** : SETTLE, ALIGHT **2** : to fall unexpectedly **3** : HAPPEN

light adaptation *n* : the whole process by which the eye adapts to seeing in strong light — **light–adapt·ed** \ˈlīt-ə-ˌdap-təd\ *adj*

light–emitting diode *n* : LED

[1]**light·en** \ˈlīt-ᵊn\ *vb* **light·ened; light·en·ing** \ˈlīt-(ᵊ-)niŋ\ **1** : ILLUMINATE, BRIGHTEN **2** : to give out flashes of lightning

[2]**lighten** *vb* **light·ened; light·en·ing** \ˈlīt-(ᵊ-)niŋ\ **1** : to relieve of a burden **2** : GLADDEN **3** : to become lighter

[1]**ligh·ter** \ˈlīt-ər\ *n* : a barge used esp. in loading or unloading ships

[2]**light·er** \ˈlīt-ər\ *n* : a device for lighting ⟨a cigarette ~⟩

light·face \ˈlīt-ˌfās\ *n* : a type having light thin lines — **light·faced** \-ˈfāst\ *adj*

light–head·ed \ˈlīt-ˈhed-əd\ *adj* **1** : feeling confused or dizzy **2** : lacking maturity or seriousness

light·heart·ed \-ˈhärt-əd\ *adj* : free from worry — **light·heart·ed·ly** *adv* — **light·heart·ed·ness** *n*

light·house \-ˌhau̇s\ *n* : a structure with a powerful light for guiding mariners

light meter *n* : a small portable device for measuring

illumination; *esp* : a device for indicating correct photographic exposure

[1]**light·ning** \ˈlīt-niŋ\ *n* : the flashing of light produced by a discharge of atmospheric electricity from one cloud to another or between a cloud and the earth; *also* : the discharge itself

[2]**lightning** *adj* : extremely fast

lightning bug *n* : FIREFLY

lightning rod *n* : a grounded metallic rod set up on a structure to protect it from lightning

light out *vb* : to leave in a hurry

light·proof \ˈlīt-ˈprüf\ *adj* : impenetrable by light

lights \ˈlīts\ *n pl* : the lungs esp. of a slaughtered animal

light·ship \ˈlīt-ˌship\ *n* : a ship with a powerful light moored at a place dangerous to navigation

light show *n* : a kaleidoscopic display (as of colored lights) imitating the effects of psychedelic drugs

light·some \ˈlīt-səm\ *adj* **1** : free from care **2** : NIMBLE

[1]**light·weight** \ˈlīt-ˌwāt\ *n* : one of less than average weight; *esp* : a boxer weighing more than 126 but not over 135 pounds

[2]**lightweight** *adj* **1** : INCONSEQUENTIAL **2** : of less than average weight

light–year \ˈlīt-ˌyiər\ *n* **1** : an astronomical unit of distance equal to the distance that light travels in one year or about 5,878,000,000,000 miles **2** : an extremely long distance esp. as a measure of progress

lig·ne·ous \ˈlig-nē-əs\ *adj* : WOODY

lig·ni·fy \ˈlig-nə-ˌfī\ *vb* **-fied; -fy·ing** : to convert into or become wood or woody tissue — **lig·ni·fi·ca·tion** \ˌlig-nə-fə-ˈkā-shən\ *n*

lig·nite \ˈlig-ˌnīt\ *n* : brownish black soft coal esp. of a slightly woody texture

[1]**like** \ˈlīk\ *vb* **liked; lik·ing 1** : ENJOY ⟨~*s* baseball⟩ **2** : WANT **3** : CHOOSE ⟨does as she ~*s*⟩ — **lik·able** *or* **like·able** \ˈlī-kə-bəl\ *adj*

[2]**like** *n* : PREFERENCE

[3]**like** *adj* : SIMILAR **syn** alike, analogous, comparable, parallel, uniform

[4]**like** *prep* **1** : similar or similarly to **2** : typical of **3** : inclined to ⟨looks ~ rain⟩ **4** : such as ⟨a subject ~ physics⟩

[5]**like** *n* : COUNTERPART

[6]**like** *conj* : in the same way that

-like \ˌlīk\ *adj comb form* : resembling or characteristic of ⟨lady*like* behavior⟩ ⟨a life*like* statue⟩

like·li·hood \ˈlī-klē-ˌhu̇d\ *n* : PROBABILITY

[1]**like·ly** \ˈlī-klē\ *adj* **like·li·er; -est 1** : PROBABLE **2** : BELIEVABLE **3** : PROMISING ⟨a ~ place to fish⟩

[2]**likely** *adv* : in all probability

lik·en \ˈlī-kən\ *vb* **lik·ened; lik·en·ing** \ˈlīk-(ə-)niŋ\ : COMPARE

like·ness \ˈlīk-nəs\ *n* **1** : COPY, PORTRAIT **2** : APPEARANCE, GUISE **3** : RESEMBLANCE

like·wise \-ˌwīz\ *adv* **1** : in like manner **2** : in addition : ALSO

lik·ing \ˈlī-kiŋ\ *n* : favorable regard; *also* : TASTE

li·ku·ta \li-ˈküt-ə\ *n, pl* **ma·ku·ta** \mä-\ — see MONEY table

li·lac \ˈlī-lək, -ˌlak, -ˌläk\ *n* [obs. F (now *lilas*), fr. Ar *līlak*, fr. Per *nīlak* bluish, fr. *nīl* blue, fr. Skt *nīla* dark blue] **1** : a shrub with large clusters of fragrant grayish pink, purple, or white flowers **2** : a moderate purple

lil·an·ge·ni \ˌlil-ən-ˈgen-ē\ *n, pl* **em·a·lan·ge·ni** \ˌem-ə-lən-ˈgen-ē\ — see MONEY table

lil·li·pu·tian \ˌlil-ə-ˈpyü-shən\ *adj, often cap* **1** : SMALL, MINIATURE **2** : PETTY

lilt \ˈlilt\ *n* **1** : a cheerful lively song or tune **2** : a rhythmical swing, flow, or cadence

lily \ˈlil-ē\ *n, pl* **lil·ies** : any of numerous tall bulbous herbs with leafy stems and usu. funnel-shaped flowers; *also* : any of various related plants (as the onion, amaryllis, or iris)

lily of the valley : a low perennial herb of the lily family that produces a raceme of fragrant nodding bell-shaped white flowers

li·ma bean \ˌlī-mə-\ *n* : any of various bushy or tall-growing beans that have flat edible usu. pale green or whitish seeds; *also* : the seed of a lima bean

limb \ˈlim\ *n* **1** : one of the projecting paired appendages (as legs, arms, or wings) that an animal uses esp. in moving or grasping **2** : a large branch of a tree : BOUGH — **limb·less** *adj*

[1]**lim·ber** \ˈlim-bər\ *adj* **1** : FLEXIBLE, SUPPLE **2** : LITHE, NIMBLE

[2]**limber** *vb* **lim·bered; lim·ber·ing** \-b(ə-)riŋ\ : to make or become limber

[1]**lim·bo** \ˈlim-bō\ *n, pl* **limbos** [ME, fr. ML, abl. of *limbus* limbo, fr. L, border] **1** *often cap* : an abode of souls barred from heaven through no fault of their own **2** : a place or state of confinement or oblivion

[2]**limbo** *n, pl* **limbos** [native name in West Indies] : a West Indian acrobatic dance orig. for men

Lim·burg·er \ˈlim-ˌbər-gər\ *n* : a creamy semisoft surface-ripened cheese with a pungent odor and strong flavor

[1]**lime** \ˈlīm\ *n* : a caustic infusible white substance that consists of calcium and oxygen, is obtained by heating limestone or shells until they crumble to powder, and is used in making cement and in fertilizer — **limy** \ˈlī-mē\ *adj*

[2]**lime** *n* : a small lemonlike greenish yellow citrus fruit with juicy acid pulp

lime·ade \ˌlīm-ˈād\ *n* : a beverage of lime juice, sugar, and water

lime·light \ˈlīm-ˌlīt\ *n* **1** : a device in which flame is directed against a cylinder of lime formerly used in the theater to cast a strong white light on the stage **2** : the center of public attention

lim·er·ick \ˈlim-(ə-)rik\ *n* : a light or humorous poem of 5 lines

lime·stone \ˈlīm-ˌstōn\ *n* : a rock that is formed by accumulation of organic remains (as shells), is used in building, and yields lime when burned

[1]**lim·it** \ˈlim-ət\ *vb* **1** : to set limits to **2** : to reduce in quantity or extent — **lim·i·ta·tion** \ˌlim-ə-ˈtā-shən\ *n*

[2]**limit** *n* **1** : BOUNDARY; *also, pl* : BOUNDS **2** : something that restrains or confines; *also* : the utmost extent **3** : a prescribed maximum or minimum — **lim·it·less** *adj*

lim·it·ed \ˈlim-ət-əd\ *adj* **1** : confined within limits **2** : offering superior and faster service and transportation

limn \ˈlim\ *vb* **limned; limn·ing** \lim-(n)iŋ\ **1** : DRAW; *also* : PAINT **2** : DELINEATE **3** : DESCRIBE

li·mo·nite \ˈlī-mə-ˌnīt\ *n* : a ferric oxide that is a major ore of iron — **li·mo·nit·ic** \ˌlī-mə-ˈnit-ik\ *adj*

lim·ou·sine \ˈlim-ə-ˌzēn, ˌlim-ə-ˈzēn\ *n* [F] **1** : a large luxurious often chauffeur-driven sedan **2** : a large vehicle for transporting passengers to and from an airport

[1]**limp** \ˈlimp\ *vb* : to walk lamely; *also* : to proceed with difficulty

[2]**limp** *n* : a limping movement or gait

[3]**limp** *adj* **1** : having no defined shape; *also* : not stiff or rigid **2** : lacking in strength or firmness — **limp·ly** *adv* — **limp·ness** *n*

lim·pet \ˈlim-pət\ *n* : a sea mollusk with a conical shell that clings to rocks or timbers

lim·pid \ˈlim-pəd\ *adj* [F or L; F *limpide*, fr. L *limpidus*, fr. *lympha*, *limpa* water] : CLEAR, TRANSPARENT

lin *abbr* **1** lineal **2** linear

lin·age \ˈlī-nij\ *n* : the number of lines of written or printed matter

---

\ə\abut \ᵊ\kitten \ər\further \a\ash \ā\ace \ä\cot, cart \au̇\out \ch\chin \e\bet \ē\easy \g\go \i\hit \ī\ice \j\job \ŋ\sing \ō\go \ȯ\law \ȯi\boy \th\thin \t͟h\the \ü\loot \u̇\foot \y\yet \zh\vision *see also* Pronunciation Symbols page

linch·pin \ˈlinch-ˌpin\ *n* : a locking pin inserted crosswise (as through the end of an axle)

lin·den \ˈlin-dən\ *n* : any of a genus of trees with large heart-shaped leaves and clustered yellowish flowers rich in nectar

¹line \ˈlīn\ *vb* **lined; lin·ing** : to cover the inner surface of

²line *n* **1** : CORD, ROPE, WIRE; *also* : a length of material used in measuring and leveling **2** : pipes for conveying a fluid ⟨a gas ~⟩ **3** : a horizontal row of written or printed characters; *also* : VERSE **4** : NOTE **5** : the words making up a part in a drama — usu. used in pl. **6** : something distinct, long, and narrow; *also* : ROUTE **7** : a state of agreement **8** : a course of conduct, action, or thought; *also* : OCCUPATION **9** : LIMIT **10** : an arrangement of persons or objects of one kind in an orderly series ⟨a ~ of trees⟩ ⟨waiting in ~⟩ **11** : a transportation system **12** : the football players who are stationed on the line of scrimmage **13** : a long narrow mark; *also* : EQUATOR **14** : a geometric element that is the path of a moving point **15** : CONTOUR **16** : a general plan **17** : an indication based on insight or investigation

³line *vb* **lined; lin·ing 1** : to mark with a line **2** : to place or form a line along **3** : ALIGN

lin·eage \ˈlin-ē-ij\ *n* : lineal descent from a common progenitor; *also* : FAMILY

lin·eal \ˈlin-ē-əl\ *adj* **1** : LINEAR **2** : consisting of or being in a direct line of ancestry; *also* : HEREDITARY

lin·ea·ment \ˈlin-ē-ə-mənt\ *n* : an outline, feature, or contour of a body and esp. of a face — usu. used in pl.

lin·ear \ˈlin-ē-ər\ *adj* **1** : of, relating to, or consisting of a line : STRAIGHT **2** : composed of simply drawn lines with little attempt at pictorial representation ⟨~ script⟩ **3** : being long and uniformly narrow

line·back·er \ˈlīn-ˌbak-ər\ *n* : a defensive football player who lines up immediately behind the line of scrimmage

line drive *n* : a baseball hit in a nearly straight line not far above the ground

line·man \ˈlīn-mən\ *n* **1** : one who sets up or repairs communication or power lines **2** : a player in the line in football

lin·en \ˈlin-ən\ *n* **1** : cloth made of flax; *also* : thread or yarn spun from flax **2** : clothing or household articles made of linen cloth or similar fabric

line of scrimmage : an imaginary line in football parallel to the goal lines and tangent to the nose of the ball laid on the ground before a scrimmage

¹lin·er \ˈlī-nər\ *n* : a ship or airplane of a regular transportation line

²liner *n* : one that lines or is used as a lining

line score *n* : a score of a baseball game giving the runs, hits, and errors made by each team

lines·man \ˈlīnz-mən\ *n* **1** : LINEMAN **2** : an official who assists a referee

line·up \ˈlīn-ˌəp\ *n* **1** : a list of players taking part in a game (as of baseball) **2** : a line of persons arranged esp. for identification by police

ling \ˈliŋ\ *n* : any of several fishes related to the cod

lin·ger \ˈliŋ-gər\ *vb* **lin·gered; lin·ger·ing** \-g(ə-)riŋ\ : TARRY; *also* : PROCRASTINATE

lin·ge·rie \ˌlän-jə-ˈrā, ˌlaⁿ-zhə-, -ˈrē\ *n* [F, fr. MF, fr. *linge* linen, fr. L *lineus* made of linen, fr. *linum* flax, linen] : women's intimate apparel

lin·go \ˈliŋ-gō\ *n, pl* **lingoes** : usu. strange or incomprehensible language

lin·gua fran·ca \ˌliŋ-gwə-ˈfraŋ-kə\ *n, pl* **lingua francas** *or* **lin·guae fran·cae** \-gwē-ˈfraŋ-ˌkē\ [It] **1** : a common language that consists of Italian mixed with French, Spanish, Greek, and Arabic and is spoken in Mediterranean ports **2** : any of various languages used as common or commercial tongues among speakers of different languages

lin·gual \ˈliŋ-gwəl\ *adj* : of, relating to, or produced by the tongue

lin·guist \ˈliŋ-gwəst\ *n* **1** : a person skilled in languages **2** : one who specializes in linguistics

lin·guis·tics \liŋ-ˈgwis-tiks\ *n* : the study of human speech including the units, nature, structure, and development of language or a language — **lin·guis·tic** *adj*

lin·i·ment \ˈlin-ə-mənt\ *n* : a liquid preparation rubbed on the skin esp. to relieve pain

lin·ing \ˈlī-niŋ\ *n* : material used to line esp. an inner surface

link \ˈliŋk\ *n* **1** : a connecting structure; *esp* : a single ring of a chain **2** : BOND, TIE — **link** *vb*

link·age \ˈliŋ-kij\ *n* **1** : the manner or style of being united **2** : the quality or state of being linked **3** : a system of links

linking verb *n* : a word or expression (as a form of *be, become, feel,* or *seem*) that links a subject with its predicate

links \ˈliŋks\ *n pl* : a golf course

link·up \ˈliŋk-ˌəp\ *n* **1** : MEETING **2** : something that serves as a linking device or factor

lin·net \ˈlin-ət\ *n* : an Old World finch

li·no·leum \lə-ˈnō-lē-əm\ *n* [L *linum* flax + *oleum* oil] : a floor covering with a canvas back and a surface of hardened linseed oil and a filler (as cork dust)

lin·seed \ˈlin-ˌsēd\ *n* : the seeds of flax yielding a yellowish oil **(linseed oil)** used esp. in paints and linoleum

lin·sey–wool·sey \ˌlin-zē-ˈwu̇l-zē\ *n* : a coarse sturdy fabric of wool and linen or cotton

lint \ˈlint\ *n* **1** : linen made into a soft fleecy substance for use in surgical dressings **2** : fine ravels, fluff, or loose short fibers from yarn or fabrics **3** : the fibers that surround cotton seeds and form the cotton staple

lin·tel \ˈlint-ᵊl\ *n* : a horizontal piece across the top of an opening (as of a door) that carries the weight of the structure above it

li·on \ˈlī-ən\ *n, pl* **lions** : a large flesh-eating cat of Africa and southern Asia with a shaggy mane in the male

li·on·ess \ˈlī-ə-nəs\ *n* : a female lion

li·on·heart·ed \ˌlī-ən-ˈhärt-əd\ *adj* : COURAGEOUS, BRAVE

li·on·ize \ˈlī-ə-ˌnīz\ *vb* **-ized; iz·ing** : to treat as an object of great interest or importance — **li·on·iza·tion** \lī-ə-nə-ˈzā-shən\ *n*

lip \ˈlip\ *n* **1** : either of the two fleshy folds that surround the mouth; *also* : a part or projection suggesting such a lip **2** : the edge of a hollow vessel or cavity — **lipped** \ˈlipt\ *adj*

lip·read·ing \ˈlip-ˌrēd-iŋ\ *n* : the interpreting of a speaker's words without hearing the voice by watching lip and facial movements

lip service *n* : avowal of allegiance that goes no further than verbal expression

lip·stick \ˈlip-ˌstik\ *n* : a waxy solid colored cosmetic in stick form for the lips

liq *abbr* **1** liquid **2** liquor

liq·ue·fy *also* **liq·ui·fy** \ˈlik-wə-ˌfī\ *vb* **-fied; -fy·ing** : to make or become liquid — **liq·ue·fac·tion** \ˌlik-wə-ˈfak-shən\ *n* — **liq·ue·fi·able** \-ˌfī-ə-bəl\ *adj* — **liq·ue·fi·er** \-ˌfī(-ə)r\ *n*

li·queur \li-ˈkər\ *n* [F] : a distilled alcoholic liquor flavored with aromatic susbtances and usu. sweetened

¹liq·uid \ˈlik-wəd\ *adj* **1** : flowing freely like water **2** : neither solid nor gaseous **3** : shining and clear ⟨large ~ eyes⟩ **4** : smooth and musical in tone; *also* : smooth and unconstrained in movement **5** : consisting of or capable of ready conversion into cash ⟨~ assets⟩ — **li·quid·i·ty** \lik-ˈwid-ət-ē\ *n*

²liquid *n* : a liquid substance

liq·ui·date \ˈlik-wə-ˌdāt\ *vb* **-dat·ed; -dat·ing 1** : to pay off ⟨~ a debt⟩ **2** : to settle the accounts and distribute the assets of (as a business) **3** : to get rid of; *esp* : KILL — **liq·ui·da·tion** \ˌlik-wə-ˈdā-shən\ *n*

liquid crystal *n* : an organic liquid that resembles a crystal in having ordered molecular arrays

liquid crystal display *n* : LCD
liquid measure *n* : a unit or series of units for measuring liquid capacity — see METRIC SYSTEM table, WEIGHT table
li·quor \ˈlik-ər\ *n* : a liquid substance; *esp* : a distilled alcoholic beverage
li·ra \ˈlir-ə, ˈlē-rə\ *n* — see MONEY table
lisle \ˈlīl\ *n* : a smooth tightly twisted thread usu. made of long-staple cotton
lisp \ˈlisp\ *vb* : to pronounce \s\ and \z\ imperfectly esp. by giving them the sounds of \th\ and \th\; *also* : to speak childishly — **lisp** *n*
lis·some *also* **lis·som** \ˈlis-əm\ *adj* : LITHE; *also* : NIMBLE
[1]**list** \ˈlist\ *vb, archaic* : PLEASE; *also* : WISH
[2]**list** *vb, archaic* : LISTEN
[3]**list** *n* **1** : a simple series of words or numerals; *also* : an official roster **2** : CATALOG, CHECKLIST
[4]**list** *vb* : to make a list of; *also* : to include on a list
[5]**list** *vb* : TILT
[6]**list** *n* : a leaning to one side : TILT
lis·ten \ˈlis-ᵊn\ *vb* **lis·tened; lis·ten·ing** \ˈlis-(ᵊ-)niŋ\ **1** : to pay attention in order to hear **2** : HEED — **lis·ten·er** \ˈlis-(ᵊ-)nər\ *n*
lis·ten·er·ship \ˈlis-(ᵊ-)nər-ˌship\ *n* : the audience for a radio program or record album
list·ing \ˈlis-tiŋ\ *n* **1** : an act or instance of making or including in a list **2** : something that is listed
list·less \ˈlist-ləs\ *adj* : LANGUID, SPIRITLESS — **list·less·ly** *adv* — **list·less·ness** *n*
list price *n* : the price of an item as published in a catalog, price list, or advertisement but subject to discounts
lists \ˈlists\ *n pl* : an arena for combat (as jousting)
[1]**lit** \ˈlit\ *past and past part of* LIGHT
[2]**lit** *abbr* **1** liter **2** literal; literally **3** literary **4** literature
lit·a·ny \ˈlit-ᵊn-ē\ *n, pl* **-nies** [ME *letanie,* fr. OF, fr. LL *litania,* fr. LGk *litaneia,* fr. Gk, entreaty, fr. *litanos* entreating] : a prayer consisting of a series of supplications and responses said alternately by a leader and a group
li·tchi \ˈlī-chē, ˈlē-\ *n* [Chin (Peking dialect) *li⁴ chih¹*] **1** : an oval fruit with a hard scaly outer covering, a small hard seed, and edible flesh **2** : a tree bearing litchis
li·ter \ˈlēt-ər\ *n* — see METRIC SYSTEM table
lit·er·al \ˈlit-(ə-)rəl\ *adj* **1** : adhering to fact or to the ordinary or usual meaning (as of a word) **2** : UNADORNED; *also* : PROSAIC **3** : VERBATIM
lit·er·al·ism \ˈlit-(ə-)rə-ˌliz-əm\ *n* **1** : adherence to the explicit substance (as of an idea) **2** : fidelity to observable fact — **lit·er·al·is·tic** \ˌlit-(ə-)rə-ˈlis-tik\ *adj*
lit·er·al·ly \ˈlit-ər-(ə-)lē, ˈli-trə-lē\ *adv* **1** : ACTUALLY ⟨was ~ insane⟩ **2** : VIRTUALLY ⟨~ poured out new ideas⟩
lit·er·ary \ˈlit-ə-ˌrer-ē\ *adj* **1** : of or relating to literature **2** : versed in literature : WELL-READ
lit·er·ate \ˈlit-(ə-)rət\ *adj* **1** : EDUCATED; *also* : able to read and write **2** : LITERARY; *also* : POLISHED, LUCID — **lit·er·a·cy** \ˈlit-(ə-)rə-sē\ *n*
li·te·ra·ti \ˌlit-ə-ˈrät-ē\ *n pl* **1** : the educated class **2** : persons interested in literature or the arts
lit·er·a·tim \ˌlit-ə-ˈrāt-əm, -ˈrät-\ *adv or adj* : letter for letter
lit·er·a·ture \ˈlit-(ə-)rə-ˌchu̇r, -chər\ *n* **1** : the production of written works having excellence of form or expression and dealing with ideas of permanent interest **2** : the written works produced in a particular language, country, or age
lithe \ˈlīth, ˈlīth\ *adj* **1** : SUPPLE, RESILIENT **2** : characterized by effortless grace
lithe·some \ˈlīth-səm, ˈlīth-\ *adj* : LISSOME
lith·i·um \ˈlith-ē-əm\ *n* : a light silver-white chemical element — see ELEMENT table
li·thog·ra·phy \lith-ˈäg-rə-fē\ *n* : the process of printing from a plane surface (as a smooth stone or metal plate) on which the image to be printed is ink-receptive and the blank area ink-repellent — **lith·o·graph** \ˈlith-ə-ˌgraf\ *vb* — **lithograph** *n* — **li·thog·ra·pher** \lith-ˈäg-rə-fər, ˈlith-ə-ˌgraf-ər\ *n* — **lith·o·graph·ic** \ˌlith-ə-ˈgraf-ik\ *adj* — **lith·o·graph·i·cal·ly** \-i-k(ə-)lē\ *adv*
li·thol·o·gy \lith-ˈäl-ə-jē\ *n, pl* **-gies** : the study of rocks — **lith·o·log·ic** \ˌlith-ə-ˈläj-ik\ *adj*
lith·o·sphere \ˈlith-ə-ˌsfiər\ *n* : the outer part of the solid earth
Lith·u·a·nian \ˌlith-(y)ə-ˈwā-nē-ən\ *n* **1** : a native or inhabitant of Lithuania **2** : the language of the Lithuanians — **Lithuanian** *adj*
lit·i·gant \ˈlit-i-gənt\ *n* : a party to a lawsuit
lit·i·gate \ˈlit-ə-ˌgāt\ *vb* **-gat·ed; -gat·ing** : to carry on a legal contest by judicial process; *also* : to contest at law — **lit·i·ga·tion** \ˌlit-ə-ˈgā-shən\ *n*
li·ti·gious \lə-ˈtij-əs\ *adj* **1** : CONTENTIOUS **2** : prone to engage in lawsuits **3** : of or relating to litigation — **li·ti·gious·ness** *n*
lit·mus \ˈlit-məs\ *n* : a coloring matter from lichens that turns red in acid solutions and blue in alkaline
litmus test *n* : a test in which a single factor (as an attitude) is decisive
Litt D *or* **Lit D** *abbr* [ML *litterarum doctor*] : doctor of letters; doctor of literature
[1]**lit·ter** \ˈlit-ər\ *n* [ME, fr. OF *litiere,* fr. *lit* bed, fr. L *lectus*] **1** : a covered and curtained couch with shafts used to carry a single passenger; *also* : a device (as a stretcher) for carrying a sick or injured person **2** : material used as bedding for animals; *also* : the uppermost layer of organic debris on the forest floor **3** : the offspring of an animal at one birth **4** : RUBBISH
[2]**litter** *vb* **1** : to give birth to young **2** : to strew with litter
lit·ter·a·teur \ˌlit-ə-rə-ˈtər\ *n* [F] : a literary person; *esp* : a professional writer
lit·ter·bug \ˈlit-ər-ˌbəg\ *n* : one who litters a public area
[1]**lit·tle** \ˈlit-ᵊl\ *adj* **lit·tler** \ˈlit-(ᵊ-)lər\ *or* **less** \ˈles\ *or* **less·er** \ˈles-ər\; **lit·tlest** \ˈlit-(ᵊ-)ləst\ *or* **least** \ˈlēst\ **1** : not big **2** : not important **3** : not much **4** : NARROW, MEAN — **lit·tle·ness** *n*
[2]**little** *adv* **less** \ˈles\; **least** \ˈlēst\ **1** : SLIGHTLY; *also* : not at all **2** : INFREQUENTLY
[3]**little** *n* **1** : a small amount or quantity **2** : a short time or distance
Little Dipper *n* : DIPPER 4
little theater *n* : a small theater for low-cost usu. experimental drama designed for a limited audience
lit·to·ral \ˈlit-ə-rəl; ˌlit-ə-ˈral\ *adj* : of, relating to, or growing on or near a shore esp. of the sea — **littoral** *n*
lit·ur·gy \ˈlit-ər-jē\ *n, pl* **-gies** : a rite or body of rites prescribed for public worship — **li·tur·gi·cal** \lə-ˈtər-ji-kəl\ *adj* — **li·tur·gi·cal·ly** \-k(ə-)lē\ *adv* — **lit·ur·gist** \ˈlit-ər-jəst\ *n*
liv·able *also* **live·able** \ˈliv-ə-bəl\ *adj* **1** : suitable for living in or with **2** : ENDURABLE — **liv·a·bil·i·ty** \ˌliv-ə-ˈbil-ət-ē\ *n*
[1]**live** \ˈliv\ *vb* **lived; liv·ing** **1** : to be or continue alive **2** : SUBSIST **3** : RESIDE **4** : to conduct one's life **5** : to remain in human memory or record
[2]**live** \ˈlīv\ *adj* **1** : having life **2** : BURNING, GLOWING ⟨a ~ cigar⟩ **3** : connected to electric power ⟨a ~ wire⟩ **4** : UNEXPLODED ⟨a ~ bomb⟩ **5** : of continuing interest ⟨a ~ issue⟩ **6** : of or involving the actual presence of real people ⟨~ audience⟩; *also* : broadcast directly at the time of production ⟨a ~ radio program⟩ **7** : being in play ⟨a ~ ball⟩
lived–in \ˈlivd-ˌin\ *adj* : of or suggesting long-term human habitation or use
live down *vb* : to live so as to wipe out the memory or effects of

live in \(ˈ)liv-ˈin\ *vb* : to live in one's place of employment — used of a servant — **live–in** \ˌliv-ˌin\ *adj*
live·li·hood \ˈlīv-lē-ˌhu̇d\ *n* : means of support or subsistence
live·long \ˌliv-ˌlȯŋ\ *adj* [ME *lef long*, fr. *lef* dear + *long* long] : WHOLE, ENTIRE ⟨the ~ day⟩
live·ly \ˈlīv-lē\ *adj* **live·li·er; -est 1** : full of life **2** : KEEN, VIVID ⟨~ interest⟩ **3** : ANIMATED ⟨~ debate⟩ **4** : showing activity or vigor ⟨a ~ manner⟩ **5** : quick to rebound ⟨a ~ ball⟩ **syn** vivacious, sprightly, gay, animated, spirited — **live·li·ness** *n*
liv·en \ˈlī-vən\ *vb* **liv·ened; liv·en·ing** \ˈlīv-(ə-)niŋ\ : ENLIVEN
[1]**liv·er** \ˈliv-ər\ *n* : a large glandular organ of vertebrates that secretes bile and is a center of metabolic activity — **liv·ered** \ˈliv-ərd\ *adj*
[2]**liver** *n* : one that lives esp. in a specified way ⟨a fast ~⟩
liv·er·ish \ˈliv-(ə-)rish\ *adj* **1** : resembling liver esp. in color **2** : BILIOUS **3** : MELANCHOLY
liv·er·wort \ˈliv-ər-ˌwərt\ *n* : any of various plants resembling the related mosses
liv·er·wurst \-ˌwərst, -ˌwu̇(r)st\ *n* [part trans. of G *leberwurst*, fr. *leber* liver + *wurst* sausage] : a sausage consisting chiefly of liver
liv·ery \ˈliv-(ə-)rē\ *n, pl* **-er·ies 1** : a special uniform worn by the servants of a wealthy household; *also* : distinctive dress **2** : the feeding, care, and stabling of horses for pay; *also* : the keeping of horses and vehicles for hire — **liv·er·ied** \-rēd\ *adj*
liv·ery·man \-mən\ *n* : the keeper of a livery stable
lives *pl of* LIFE
live·stock \ˈlīv-ˌstäk\ *n* : farm animals kept for use and profit
live wire *n* : an alert active aggressive person
liv·id \ˈliv-əd\ *adj* [F *livide*, fr. L *lividus*, fr. *livēre* to be blue] **1** : discolored by bruising **2** : ASHEN, PALLID **3** : REDDISH **4** : ENRAGED
[1]**liv·ing** \ˈliv-iŋ\ *adj* **1** : having life **2** : NATURAL **3** : full of life and vigor; *also* : VIVID
[2]**living** *n* **1** : the condition of being alive; *also* : manner of life **2** : LIVELIHOOD
living room *n* : a room in a residence used for the common social activities of the occupants
living wage *n* : a wage sufficient to provide the necessities and comforts held to comprise an acceptable standard of living
liz·ard \ˈliz-ərd\ *n* : a 4-legged scaly reptile with a long tapering tail

lizard

Lk *abbr* Luke
ll *abbr* lines
lla·ma \ˈläm-ə\ *n* [Sp] : any of several wild or domesticated So. American mammals related to the camel but smaller and without a hump
lla·no \ˈlän-ō\ *n, pl* **llanos** : an open grassy plain esp. of Latin America
LLD *abbr* [NL *legum doctor*] doctor of laws
LNG *abbr* liquefied natural gas
[1]**load** \ˈlōd\ *n* **1** : PACK; *also* : CARGO **2** : a mass of weight supported by something **3** : something that burdens the mind or spirits **4** : a large quantity — usu. used in pl. **5** : a standard, expected, or authorized burden
[2]**load** *vb* **1** : to put a load in or on; *also* : to receive a load **2** : BURDEN **3** : to increase the weight of by adding something **4** : to supply abundantly **5** : to put a charge in (as a firearm)
load·ed \ˈlōd-əd\ *adj* **1** *slang* : DRUNK **2** : having a large amount of money
load·stone *var of* LODESTONE
[1]**loaf** \ˈlōf\ *n, pl* **loaves** \ˈlōvz\ : a shaped or molded mass esp. of bread
[2]**loaf** *vb* : to spend time in idleness : LOUNGE — **loaf·er** *n*
loam \ˈlōm, ˈlüm\ *n* : SOIL; *esp* : a loose soil of mixed clay, sand, and silt — **loamy** *adj*
[1]**loan** \ˈlōn\ *n* **1** : money lent at interest; *also* : something lent for the borrower's temporary use **2** : the grant of temporary use
[2]**loan** *vb* : LEND
loan shark *n* : a person who lends money at excessive rates of interest — **loan·shark·ing** \ˈlōn-ˌshär-kiŋ\ *n*
loan·word \ˈlōn-ˌwərd\ *n* : a word taken from another language and at least partly naturalized
loath \ˈlōth, ˈlōth\ *also* **loathe** \lōth, lōth\ *adj* : RELUCTANT
loathe \ˈlōth\ *vb* **loathed; loath·ing** : to dislike greatly **syn** abominate, abhor, detest, hate
loath·ing \ˈlō-thiŋ\ *n* : extreme disgust
loath·some \ˈlōth-səm, ˈlōth-\ *adj* : exciting loathing : REPULSIVE
lob \ˈläb\ *vb* **lobbed; lob·bing** : to throw, hit, or propel something in a high arc — **lob** *n*
[1]**lob·by** \ˈläb-ē\ *n, pl* **lobbies 1** : a corridor or hall used esp. as a passageway or waiting room **2** : a group of persons engaged in lobbying
[2]**lobby** *vb* **lob·bied; lob·by·ing** : to try to influence public officials and esp. legislators — **lob·by·ist** *n*
lobe \ˈlōb\ *n* : a curved or rounded projection or division — **lo·bar** \ˈlō-bər\ *adj* — **lobed** \ˈlōbd\ *adj*
lo·bot·o·my \lō-ˈbät-ə-mē\ *n, pl* **-mies** : severance of nerve fibers by incision into the brain for the relief of some mental disorders
lob·ster \ˈläb-stər\ *n* [ME, fr. OE *loppestre*, fr. *loppe* spider] : an edible marine crustacean with two large pincerlike claws and four other pairs of legs; *also* : SPINY LOBSTER
lob·ule \ˈläb-yül\ *n* : a small lobe; *also* : a subdivision of a lobe — **lob·u·lar** \ˈläb-yə-lər\ *adj*
[1]**lo·cal** \ˈlō-kəl\ *adj* **1** : of, relating to, or occupying a particular place **2** : serving a particular limited district; *also* : making all stops ⟨a ~ train⟩ **3** : affecting a small part of the body ⟨~ infection⟩ — **lo·cal·ly** \-ē\ *adv*
[2]**local** *n* : one that is local
lo·cale \lō-ˈkal\ *n* : a place that is the setting for a particular event
lo·cal·i·ty \lō-ˈkal-ət-ē\ *n, pl* **-ties** : a particular spot, situation, or location
lo·cal·ize \ˈlō-kə-ˌlīz\ *vb* **-ized; -iz·ing** : to fix in or confine to a definite place or locality — **lo·cal·iza·tion** \ˌlō-kə-lə-ˈzā-shən\ *n*
lo·cate \ˈlō-ˌkāt, lō-ˈkāt\ *vb* **lo·cat·ed; lo·cat·ing 1** : STATION, SETTLE **2** : to determine the site of **3** : to find or fix the place of in a sequence
lo·ca·tion \lō-ˈkā-shən\ *n* **1** : SITUATION, PLACE **2** : the process of locating **3** : a place outside a studio where a motion picture is filmed
loc cit *abbr* [L *loco citato*] in the place cited
loch \ˈläk, ˈläk\ *n, Scot* : LAKE; *also* : a bay or arm of the sea esp. when nearly landlocked
[1]**lock** \ˈläk\ *n* : a tuft, strand, or ringlet of hair; *also* : a cohering bunch (as of wool or flax)
[2]**lock** *n* **1** : a fastening in which a bolt is operated **2** : the mechanism of a firearm by which the charge is exploded **3** : an enclosure (as in a canal) used in raising or lowering boats from level to level **4** : a wrestling hold
[3]**lock** *vb* **1** : to fasten the lock of; *also* : to make fast with a lock **2** : to confine or exclude by means of a lock **3** : INTERLOCK
lock·er \ˈläk-ər\ *n* **1** : a drawer, cupboard, or compart-

ment for individual storage use **2** : an insulated compartment for storing frozen food

lock·et \ˈläk-ət\ *n* : a small usu. metal case for a memento worn suspended from a chain or necklace

lock·jaw \ˈläk-ˌjȯ\ *n* : TETANUS

lock·nut \-ˌnət\ *n* **1** : a nut screwed tight on another to prevent it from slacking back **2** : a nut designed to lock itself when screwed tight

lock·out \ˈläk-ˌau̇t\ *n* : the suspension of work by an employer during a labor dispute in order to make employees accept the terms being offered

lock·smith \ˈläk-ˌsmith\ *n* : one who makes or repairs locks

lock·step \ˈläk-ˌstep\ *n* : a mode of marching in step by a body of men moving in a very close single file

lock·up \ˈläk-ˌəp\ *n* : JAIL

lo·co \ˈlō-kō\ *adj, slang* [Sp] : CRAZY, FRENZIED

lo·co·mo·tion \ˌlō-kə-ˈmō-shən\ *n* **1** : the act or power of moving from place to place **2** : TRAVEL

[1]**lo·co·mo·tive** \ˌlō-kə-ˈmōt-iv\ *adj* : of or relating to locomotion or a locomotive

[2]**locomotive** *n* : a self-propelled vehicle used to move railroad cars

lo·co·mo·tor \ˌlō-kə-ˈmōt-ər\ *adj* : of or relating to locomotion or organs used in locomotion

lo·co·weed \ˈlō-kō-ˌwēd\ *n* : any of several leguminous plants of western No. America that are poisonous to livestock

lo·cus \ˈlō-kəs\ *n, pl* **lo·ci** \ˈlō-ˌsī\ [L] **1** : PLACE, LOCALITY **2** : the set of all points whose location is determined by stated conditions

lo·cust \ˈlō-kəst\ *n* **1** : a usu. destructive migratory grasshopper **2** : CICADA **3** : any of various leguminous trees with hard wood

lo·cu·tion \lō-ˈkyü-shən\ *n* : a particular form of expression; *also* : PHRASEOLOGY

lode \ˈlōd\ *n* : an ore deposit

lode·star \ˈlōd-ˌstär\ *n* [ME *lode sterre,* fr. *lode* course, fr. OE *lād*] : a guiding star; *esp* : NORTH STAR

lode·stone \-ˌstōn\ *n* : an iron-containing rock with magnetic properties

[1]**lodge** \ˈläj\ *vb* **lodged; lodg·ing 1** : to provide quarters for; *also* : to settle in a place **2** : CONTAIN **3** : to come to a rest and remain **4** : to deposit for safekeeping **5** : to vest (as authority) in an agent **6** : FILE ⟨~ a complaint⟩

[2]**lodge** *n* **1** : a house set apart for residence in a special season or by an employee on an estate; *also* : INN **2** : the meeting place of a branch of a fraternal organization; *also* : the members of such a branch **3** : a den or lair esp. of gregarious animals

lodg·er \ˈläj-ər\ *n* : a person who occupies a rented room in another's house

lodg·ing \ˈläj-iŋ\ *n* **1** : DWELLING **2** : a room or suite of rooms in another's house rented as a dwelling place — usu. used in pl.

lodg·ment *or* **lodge·ment** \ˈläj-mənt\ *n* **1** : a lodging place **2** : the act or manner of lodging **3** : DEPOSIT

loess \ˈles, ˈlə(r)s, ˈlō-əs\ *n* : a usu. yellowish brown loamy deposit believed to be chiefly deposited by the wind

[1]**loft** \ˈlȯft\ *n* [ME, fr. OE, fr. ON *lopt* air] **1** : ATTIC **2** : GALLERY ⟨organ ~⟩ **3** : an upper floor (as in a warehouse or barn) esp. when not partitioned **4** : the thickness of a fabric or insulated material (as of a sleeping bag)

[2]**loft** *vb* : to strike or throw a ball so that it rises high in the air

lofty \ˈlȯf-tē\ *adj* **loft·i·er; -est 1** : NOBLE; *also* : SUPERIOR **2** : extremely proud **3** : HIGH, TALL — **loft·i·ly** \ˈlȯf-tə-lē\ *adv* — **loft·i·ness** \-tē-nəs\ *n*

[1]**log** \ˈlȯg, ˈläg\ *n* **1** : a bulky piece of unshaped timber **2** : an apparatus for measuring a ship's speed **3** : the daily record of a ship's progress; *also* : a regularly kept record of performance (as of an airplane)

[2]**log** *vb* **logged; log·ging 1** : to cut trees for lumber **2** : to enter in a log **3** : to sail a ship or fly an airplane for (an indicated distance or period of time) **4** : to have (an indicated record) to one's credit : ACHIEVE — **log·ger** \ˈlȯg-ər, ˈläg-\ *n*

[3]**log** *n* : LOGARITHM

lo·gan·ber·ry \ˈlō-gən-ˌber-ē\ *n* : a red-fruited upright-growing dewberry; *also* : its fruit

log·a·rithm \ˈlȯg-ə-ˌrit͟h-əm, ˈläg-\ *n* : the exponent that indicates the power to which a base number is raised to produce a given number ⟨the ~ of 100 to the base number of 10 is 2⟩ — **log·a·rith·mic** \ˌlȯg-ə-ˈrit͟h-mik, ˌläg-\ *adj*

loge \ˈlōzh\ *n* **1** : a small compartment; *also* : a box in a theater **2** : a small partitioned area; *also* : the forward section of a theater mezzanine

log·ger·head \ˈlȯg-ər-ˌhed, ˈläg-\ *n* : a large sea turtle of the warmer parts of the Atlantic — **at loggerheads** : in a state of quarrelsome disagreement

log·gia \ˈlō-jē-ə, ˈlȯ-jä\ *n, pl* **loggias** \ˈlō-jē-əz, ˈlȯ-jäz\ : a roofed open gallery

log·ic \ˈläj-ik\ *n* **1** : a science that deals with the rules and tests of sound thinking and proof by reasoning **2** : sound reasoning **3** : the fundamental principles and the connection of circuit elements for arithmetical computation in a computer — **log·i·cal** \-i-kəl\ *adj* — **log·i·cal·ly** \-i-k(ə-)lē\ *adv* — **lo·gi·cian** \lō-ˈjish-ən\ *n*

lo·gis·tics \lō-ˈjis-tiks\ *n sing or pl* : the procurement, maintenance, and transportation of matériel, facilities, and personnel — **lo·gis·tic** *adj*

log·jam \ˈlȯg-ˌjam, ˈläg-\ *n* **1** : a deadlocked jumble of logs in a watercourse **2** : DEADLOCK

logo \ˈlȯg-ō, ˈläg-\ *n, pl* **log·os** \-ōz\ : LOGOTYPE

logo·type \ˈlȯg-ə-ˌtīp, ˈläg-\ *n* : an identifying symbol (as for advertising)

log·roll·ing \-ˌrō-liŋ\ *n* : the trading of votes by legislators to secure favorable action on projects of individual interest

lo·gy \ˈlō-gē\ *also* **log·gy** \ˈlȯg-ē, ˈläg-\ *adj* **lo·gi·er; -est** : deficient in vitality : SLUGGISH

loin \ˈlȯin\ *n* **1** : the part of the body on each side of the spinal column and between the hip and the lower ribs; *also* : a cut of meat from this part of an animal **2** *pl* : the upper and lower abdominal regions and the region about the hips

loin·cloth \-ˌklȯth\ *n* : a cloth worn about the loins often as the sole article of clothing in warm climates

loi·ter \ˈlȯit-ər\ *vb* **1** : LINGER **2** : to hang around idly **syn** dawdle, dally, procrastinate, lag, tarry — **loi·ter·er** *n*

loll \ˈläl\ *vb* **1** : DROOP, DANGLE **2** : LOUNGE

lol·li·pop *or* **lol·ly·pop** \ˈläl-i-ˌpäp\ *n* : a lump of hard candy on a stick

lol·ly·gag \ˈläl-ē-ˌgag\ *vb* **-gagged; -gag·ging** : DAWDLE

Lond *abbr* London

lone \ˈlōn\ *adj* **1** : SOLITARY ⟨a ~ sentinel⟩ **2** : SOLE, ONLY ⟨the ~ theater in town⟩ **3** : ISOLATED ⟨a ~ tree⟩

lone·ly \ˈlōn-lē\ *adj* **lone·li·er; -est 1** : being without company **2** : UNFREQUENTED ⟨a ~ spot⟩ **3** : LONESOME — **lone·li·ness** *n*

lon·er \ˈlō-nər\ *n* : one that avoids others

lone·some \ˈlōn-səm\ *adj* **1** : sad from lack of companionship **2** : REMOTE; *also* : SOLITARY — **lone·some·ly** *adv* — **lone·some·ness** *n*

[1]**long** \ˈlȯŋ\ *adj* **lon·ger** \ˈlȯŋ-gər\; **lon·gest** \ˈlȯŋ-gəst\ **1** : extending for a considerable distance; *also* : TALL, ELONGATED **2** : having a specified length **3** : extending over a

considerable time; *also* : TEDIOUS **4** : containing many items in a series **5** : being a syllable or speech sound of relatively great duration **6** : extending far into the future **7** : well furnished with something — used with *on*

[2]**long** *adv* : for or during a long time

[3]**long** *n* : a long period of time

[4]**long** *vb* **longed; long·ing** \ˈlȯŋ-iŋ\ : to feel a strong desire or wish **syn** yearn, hanker, pine, hunger, thirst

[5]**long** *abbr* longitude

long·boat \ˈlȯŋ-ˌbōt\ *n* : the largest boat carried by a merchant sailing ship

long·bow \-ˌbō\ *n* : a wooden bow drawn by hand and usu. 5 to 6 feet long

lon·gev·i·ty \län-ˈjev-ət-ē\ *n* [LL *longaevitas*, fr. L *longaevus* long-lived, fr. *longus* long + *aevum* age] : a long duration of individual life; *also* : length of life

long·hair \ˈlȯŋ-ˌhaər\ *n* **1** : a lover of classical music **2** : HIPPIE **3** : a domestic cat having long outer fur

long·hand \-ˌhand\ *n* : HANDWRITING

long·horn \-ˌhȯrn\ *n* : any of the cattle with long horns formerly common in the southwestern U.S.

long hundredweight *n* — see WEIGHT table

long·ing \ˈlȯŋ-iŋ\ *n* : an eager desire esp. for something unattainable — **long·ing·ly** *adv*

lon·gi·tude \ˈlän-jə-ˌt(y)üd\ *n* : angular distance expressed usu. in degrees east or west from the meridian that runs between the north and south poles and passes through Greenwich, England

lon·gi·tu·di·nal \ˌlän-jə-ˈt(y)üd-(ə-)nəl\ *adj* **1** : extending lengthwise **2** : of or relating to length — **lon·gi·tu·di·nal·ly** \-ē\ *adv*

long·shore·man \ˈlȯŋ-ˈshōr-mən\ *n* : a laborer at a wharf who loads and unloads cargo

long–suf·fer·ing \-ˈsəf(-ə)-riŋ\ *n* : long and patient endurance of offense

long–term \ˈlȯŋ-ˈtərm\ *adj* **1** : extending over or involving a long period of time **2** : constituting a financial obligation based on a term usu. of more than 10 years ⟨a ~ mortgage⟩

long·time \ˌlȯŋ-ˌtīm\ *adj* : of long duration ⟨~ friends⟩

long ton *n* — see WEIGHT table

lon·gueur \lōⁿ-gœr\ *n*, *pl* **longueurs** \-gœr(z)\ [F, lit., length] : a dull tedious passage or section

long–wind·ed \ˈlȯŋ-ˈwin-dəd\ *adj* : tediously long in speaking or writing

loo·fah \ˈlü-fə\ *n* : a sponge consisting of the fibrous skeleton of a gourd

[1]**look** \ˈlu̇k\ *vb* **1** : to exercise the power of vision : SEE **2** : EXPECT **3** : to have an appearance that befits ⟨~*s* the part⟩ **4** : SEEM ⟨~*s* thin⟩ **5** : to direct one's attention : HEED **6** : POINT, FACE **7** : to show a tendency — **look after** : to take care of — **look for** : EXPECT

[2]**look** *n* **1** : the action of looking : GLANCE **2** : EXPRESSION; *also* : physical appearance **3** : ASPECT

look down \(ˈ)lu̇k-ˈdau̇n\ *vb* : DESPISE — used with *on* or *upon*

looking glass *n* : MIRROR

look·out \ˈlu̇k-ˌau̇t\ *n* **1** : a person assigned to watch (as on a ship) **2** : a careful watch **3** : VIEW **4** : a matter of concern

look up \(ˈ)lu̇k-ˈəp\ *vb* **1** : IMPROVE ⟨business is *looking up*⟩ **2** : to search for in or as if in a reference work **3** : to seek out esp. for a brief visit

[1]**loom** \ˈlüm\ *n* : a frame or machine for weaving together threads or yarns into cloth

[2]**loom** *vb* **1** : to come into sight in an unnaturally large, indistinct, or distorted form **2** : to appear in an impressively exaggerated form

loon \ˈlün\ *n* : a web-footed black-and-white fish-eating diving bird

loo·ny *or* **loo·ney** \ˈlü-nē\ *adj* **loo·ni·er; -est** : CRAZY, FOOLISH

loony bin *n* : an insane asylum

loop \ˈlüp\ *n* **1** : a fold or doubling of a line through which another line or hook can be passed; *also* : a loop-shaped figure or course ⟨a ~ in a river⟩ **2** : a circular airplane maneuver involving flying upside down **3** : a ring-shaped intrauterine device **4** : a piece of film whose ends are spliced together to project continuously — **loop** *vb*

loop·er \ˈlü-pər\ *n* : any of numerous rather small hairless moth caterpillars that move with a looping movement

loop·hole \ˈlüp-ˌhōl\ *n* **1** : a small opening in a wall through which firearms may be discharged **2** : a means of escape; *esp* : an ambiguity or omission that allows one to evade the intent of a law or contract

[1]**loose** \ˈlüs\ *adj* **loos·er; loos·est 1** : not rigidly fastened **2** : free from restraint or obligation **3** : not dense or compact in structure **4** : not chaste : LEWD **5** : SLACK **6** : not precise or exact — **loose·ly** *adv* — **loose·ness** *n*

[2]**loose** *vb* **loosed; loos·ing 1** : RELEASE **2** : UNTIE **3** : DETACH **4** : DISCHARGE **5** : RELAX, SLACKEN

[3]**loose** *adv* : LOOSELY

loos·en \ˈlüs-ᵊn\ *vb* **loos·ened; loos·en·ing** \ˈlüs-(ᵊ-)niŋ\ **1** : FREE **2** : to make or become loose **3** : to relax the severity of

loot \ˈlüt\ *n* [Hindi *lūṭ*, fr. Skt *luṇṭati* he robs] : goods taken in war or by robbery : PLUNDER — **loot** *vb* — **loot·er** *n*

[1]**lop** \ˈläp\ *vb* **lopped; lop·ping** : to cut branches or twigs from : TRIM; *also* : to cut off

[2]**lop** *vb* **lopped; lop·ping** : to hang downward; *also* : to flop or sway loosely

lope \ˈlōp\ *n* : an easy bounding gait — **lope** *vb*

lop·sid·ed \ˈläp-ˈsīd-əd\ *adj* **1** : leaning to one side **2** : UNSYMMETRICAL — **lop·sid·ed·ly** *adv* — **lop·sid·ed·ness** *n*

lo·qua·cious \lō-ˈkwā-shəs\ *adj* : excessively talkative — **lo·quac·i·ty** \-ˈkwas-ət-ē\ *n*

[1]**lord** \ˈlȯrd\ *n* [ME *loverd, lord*, fr. OE *hlāford*, fr. *hlāf* loaf + *weard* keeper] **1** : one having power and authority over others; *esp* : a person from whom a feudal fee or estate is held **2** : a man of rank or high position; *esp* : a British nobleman **3** *pl*, *cap* : the upper house of the British parliament **4** : a person of great power in some field

[2]**lord** *vb* : to act like a lord; *esp* : to put on airs — usu. used with *it*

lord chancellor *n*, *pl* **lords chancellor** : a British officer of state who presides over the House of Lords, serves as head of the British judiciary, and is usu. a leading member of the cabinet

lord·ly \-lē\ *adj* **lord·li·er; -est 1** : DIGNIFIED; *also* : NOBLE **2** : HAUGHTY

lord·ship \-ˌship\ *n* **1** : the rank or dignity of a lord — used as a title **2** : the authority or territory of a lord

Lord's Supper *n* : COMMUNION

lore \ˈlōr\ *n* : KNOWLEDGE; *esp* : traditional knowledge or belief

lor·gnette \lȯrn-ˈyet\ *n* [F, fr. *lorgner* to take a sidelong look at, fr. MF, fr. *lorgne* cross-eyed] : a pair of eyeglasses or opera glasses with a handle

lorn \ˈlȯrn\ *adj* : FORSAKEN, DESOLATE

lor·ry \ˈlȯr-ē\ *n*, *pl* **lorries 1** : a large low horse-drawn wagon without sides **2** *Brit* : MOTORTRUCK

lose \ˈlüz\ *vb* **lost** \ˈlȯst\; **los·ing** \ˈlü-ziŋ\ **1** : DESTROY **2** : to miss from a customary place : MISLAY **3** : to suffer deprivation of **4** : to fail to use : WASTE **5** : to fail to win or obtain ⟨~ the game⟩ **6** : to fail to keep or maintain ⟨~ his balance⟩ **7** : to wander from ⟨~ his way⟩ **8** : to get rid of ⟨~ weight⟩ — **los·er** *n*

loss \ˈlȯs\ *n* **1** : the harm resulting from losing **2** : something that is lost **3** *pl* : killed, wounded, or captured soldiers **4** : failure to win **5** : an amount by which the cost exceeds the selling price **6** : decrease in amount or degree **7** : RUIN

loss leader *n* : an article sold at a loss in order to draw customers

lost \ˈlȯst\ *adj* **1** : not used, won, or claimed **2** : no longer possessed or known **3** : ruined or destroyed physically or morally **4** : DENIED; *also* : HARDENED **5** : unable to find the way; *also* : HELPLESS **6** : ABSORBED, RAPT

lot \ˈlät\ *n* **1** : an object used in deciding something by chance; *also* : the use of lots to decide something **2** : SHARE, PORTION; *also* : FORTUNE, FATE **3** : a plot of land **4** : a group of individuals : SET **5** : a considerable quantity

loth \ˈlōth, ˈlōth\ *var of* LOATH

lo·ti \ˈlōt-ē\ *n, pl* **ma·lo·ti** \mə-ˈlōt-ē\ — see MONEY table

lo·tion \ˈlō-shən\ *n* : a liquid preparation for cosmetic and external medicinal use

lot·tery \ˈlät-ə-rē\ *n, pl* **-ter·ies** **1** : a drawing of lots in which prizes are given to the winning names or numbers **2** : a matter determined by chance

lo·tus \ˈlōt-əs\ *n* **1** : a fruit held in Greek legend to cause dreamy content and forgetfulness **2** : a water lily used in ancient Egyptian and Hindu art and religious symbolism **3** : any of several forage plants related to the clovers

loud \ˈlau̇d\ *adj* **1** : marked by intensity or volume of sound **2** : CLAMOROUS, NOISY **3** : obtrusive or offensive in color or pattern ⟨a ~ suit⟩ — **loud** *adv* — **loud·ly** *adv* — **loud·ness** *n*

loud·mouthed \-ˈmau̇thd, -ˈmau̇tht\ *adj* : given to loud offensive talk

loud·speak·er \ˈlau̇d-ˈspē-kər\ *n* : a device that changes electrical signals into sound

[1]**lounge** \ˈlau̇nj\ *vb* **lounged; loung·ing** : to act or move lazily or listlessly

[2]**lounge** *n* **1** : a room with comfortable furniture; *also* : a room (as in a theater) with lounging, smoking, and toilet facilities **2** : a long couch

lour \ˈlau̇(-ə)r\, **loury** \ˈlau̇(ə)r-ē\ *var of* LOWER, LOWERY

louse \ˈlau̇s\ *n, pl* **lice** \ˈlīs\ **1** : a small wingless insect parasitic on warm-blooded animals **2** : a plant pest (as an aphid) **3** : a contemptible person

lousy \ˈlau̇-zē\ *adj* **lous·i·er; -est** **1** : infested with lice **2** : POOR, INFERIOR **3** : amply supplied ⟨~ with money⟩ — **lous·i·ly** \ˈlau̇-zə-lē\ *adv* — **lous·i·ness** \-zē-nəs\ *n*

lout \ˈlau̇t\ *n* : a stupid awkward fellow — **lout·ish** *adj* — **lout·ish·ly** *adv*

lou·ver *or* **lou·vre** \ˈlü-vər\ *n* **1** : an opening having parallel slanted slats to allow flow of air but to exclude rain or sun or to provide privacy; *also* : a slat in such an opening **2** : a device with movable slats for controlling the flow of air or light

[1]**love** \ˈləv\ *n* **1** : strong affection **2** : warm attachment ⟨~ of the sea⟩ **3** : attraction based on sexual desire **4** : a beloved person **5** : a score of zero in tennis — **love·less** *adj*

[2]**love** *vb* **loved; lov·ing** **1** : CHERISH **2** : to feel a passion, devotion, or tenderness for **3** : CARESS **4** : to take pleasure in ⟨~s to play bridge⟩ — **lov·able** \ˈləv-ə-bəl\ *adj* — **lov·er** *n*

love·bird \ˈləv-ˌbərd\ *n* : any of various small usu. gray or green parrots that seemingly show great affection for their mates

love·lorn \-ˌlȯrn\ *adj* : deprived of love or of a lover

love·ly \ˈləv-lē\ *adj* **love·li·er; -est** : BEAUTIFUL — **love·li·ness** *n*

love·mak·ing \-ˌmā-kiŋ\ *n* **1** : COURTSHIP **2** : sexual activity; *esp* : COPULATION

love·sick \-ˌsik\ *adj* **1** : YEARNING **2** : expressing a lover's longing — **love·sick·ness** *n*

lov·ing \ˈləv-iŋ\ *adj* : AFFECTIONATE — **lov·ing·ly** *adv*

[1]**low** \ˈlō\ *vb* : MOO

[2]**low** *n* : MOO

[3]**low** *adj* **low·er** \ˈlō(-ə)r\; **low·est** \ˈlō-əst\ **1** : not high or tall ⟨~ wall⟩; *also* : DÉCOLLETÉ **2** : situated or passing below the normal level or surface ⟨~ ground⟩ ; *also* : marking a nadir **3** : STRICKEN, PROSTRATE **4** : not loud ⟨~ voice⟩ **5** : being near the equator **6** : humble in status **7** : WEAK; *also* : DEPRESSED **8** : less than usual **9** : falling short of a standard **10** : UNFAVORABLE — **low** *adv* — **low·ness** *n*

[4]**low** *n* **1** : something that is low **2** : a region of low barometric pressure **3** : the arrangement of gears in an automobile transmission that gives the slowest speed and greatest power

low beam *n* : the short-range focus of a vehicle headlight

low blow *n* : an unprincipled attack

low·brow \ˈlō-ˌbrau̇\ *n* : a person without intellectual interests or culture

low·down \ˈlō-ˌdau̇n\ *n* : pertinent and esp. guarded information

low–down \ˈlō-dau̇n\ *adj* **1** : MEAN, CONTEMPTIBLE **2** : deeply emotional

low–end \-ˌend\ *adj* : of, relating to, or being the lowest-priced merchandise in a manufacturer's line

[1]**low·er** \ˈlau̇(-ə)r\ *vb* **1** : FROWN **2** : to become dark, gloomy, and threatening

[2]**low·er** \ˈlō(-ə)r\ *adj* **1** : relatively low (as in rank) **2** : constituting the popular and more representative branch of a bicameral legislative body **3** : situated beneath the earth's surface

[3]**low·er** \ˈlō(-ə)r\ *vb* **1** : DROP; *also* : DIMINISH **2** : to let descend by its own weight; *also* : to reduce the height of **3** : to reduce in value, number, or amount **4** : DEGRADE; *also* : HUMBLE

low·er·case \ˌlō(-ə)r-ˈkās\ *adj* : being a letter that belongs to or conforms to the series a, b, c, etc., rather than A, B, C, etc. — **lowercase** *n*

lower class *n* : a social class occupying a position below the middle class and having the lowest status in a society — **lower–class** \-ˈklas\ *adj*

low·er·most \ˈlō(-ə)r-ˌmōst\ *adj* : LOWEST

low·ery \ˈlau̇-(ə-)rē\ *adj* : GLOOMY, LOWERING

lowest common denominator *n* **1** : LEAST COMMON DENOMINATOR **2** : something acceptable to the greatest number of people

lowest common multiple *n* : LEAST COMMON MULTIPLE

low frequency *n* : a frequency of a radio wave in the range between 30 and 300 kilohertz

low–key \ˈlō-ˈkē\ *also* **low–keyed** \-ˈkēd\ *adj* : of low intensity : restrained

low·land \ˈlō-lənd, -ˌland\ *n* : low and usu. level country

low·life \ˈlō-ˌlīf\ *n, pl* **low·lifes** \-ˌlīfs\ *also* **low·lives** \-ˌlīvz\ : a person of low social status or moral character

low·ly \ˈlō-lē\ *adj* **low·li·er; -est** **1** : HUMBLE, MEEK **2** : ranking low in some hierarchy — **low·li·ness** *n*

low–rise \ˈlō-ˈrīz\ *adj* : being one or two stories and not equipped with elevators ⟨a ~ building⟩

[1]**lox** \ˈläks\ *n* : liquid oxygen

[2]**lox** *n, pl* **lox** *or* **lox·es** : smoked salmon

loy·al \ˈlȯi(-ə)l\ *adj* [MF, fr. OF *leial, leel,* fr. L *legalis* legal] **1** : faithful in allegiance to one's government **2** : faithful esp. to a cause or ideal : CONSTANT — **loy·al·ly** \ˈlȯi-ə-lē\ *adv* — **loy·al·ty** \ˈlȯi(-ə)l-tē\ *n*

loy·al·ist \ˈlȯi-ə-ləst\ *n* : one who is or remains loyal to a political party, government, or sovereign

loz·enge \ˈläz-ᵊnj\ *n* **1** : a diamond-shaped figure **2** : a small flat often medicated candy

LP *abbr* low pressure

LPG *abbr* liquefied petroleum gas

LPN \ˈel-ˈpē-ˈen\ *n* : LICENSED PRACTICAL NURSE

LSD \ˌel-ˌes-ˈdē\ *n* [*lys*ergic acid *d*iethylamide] : a crys-

---

\ə\abut \ᵊ\kitten \ər\further \a\ash \ā\ace \ä\cot, cart \au̇\out \ch\chin \e\bet \ē\easy \g\go \i\hit \ī\ice \j\job \ŋ\sing \ō\go \ȯ\law \ȯi\boy \th\thin \th\the \ü\loot \u̇\foot \y\yet \zh\vision *see also* Pronunciation Symbols page

talline compound that causes psychotic symptoms similar to those of schizophrenia
lt *abbr* light
Lt *abbr* lieutenant
LT *abbr* long ton
LTC *or* **Lt Col** *abbr* lieutenant colonel
Lt Comdr *abbr* lieutenant commander
ltd *abbr* limited
LTG *or* **Lt Gen** *abbr* lieutenant general
LTJG *abbr* lieutenant, junior grade
ltr *abbr* letter
Lu *symbol* lutetium
lu·au \ˈlü-ˌau̇\ *n* : a Hawaiian feast
lub *abbr* lubricant; lubricating
lub·ber \ˈləb-ər\ *n* **1** : LOUT **2** : an unskilled seaman — **lub·ber·ly** *adj*
lube \ˈlüb\ *n* : lubricant; *also* : an application of a lubricant
lu·bri·cant \ˈlü-bri-kənt\ *n* : a material (as grease) capable of reducing friction when applied between moving parts
lu·bri·cate \ˈlü-brə-ˌkāt\ *vb* **-cat·ed; -cat·ing** : to apply a lubricant to — **lu·bri·ca·tion** \ˌlü-brə-ˈkā-shən\ *n* — **lu·bri·ca·tor** \ˈlü-brə-ˌkāt-ər\ *n*
lu·bri·cious \lü-ˈbrish-əs\ *or* **lu·bri·cous** \ˈlü-bri-kəs\ *adj* **1** : SMOOTH, SLIPPERY **2** : LECHEROUS; *also* : SALACIOUS — **lu·bric·i·ty** \lü-ˈbris-ət-ē\ *n*
lu·cent \ˈlüs-ᵊnt\ *adj* **1** : LUMINOUS **2** : CLEAR, LUCID
lu·cerne \lü-ˈsərn\ *n, chiefly Brit* : ALFALFA
lu·cid \ˈlü-səd\ *adj* **1** : SHINING **2** : clear-minded **3** : easily understood — **lu·cid·i·ty** \lü-ˈsid-ət-ē\ *n* — **lu·cid·ly** *adv* — **lu·cid·ness** *n*
Lu·ci·fer \ˈlü-sə-fər\ *n* [ME, the morning star, a fallen rebel archangel, the Devil, fr. OE, fr. L, the morning star, fr. *lucifer* light-bearing] : DEVIL, SATAN
[1]**luck** \ˈlək\ *n* **1** : CHANCE, FORTUNE **2** : good fortune — **luck·less** *adj*
[2]**luck** *vb* **1** : to prosper or succeed esp. through chance or good fortune **2** : to come upon something desirable by chance — usu. used with *out, on, onto,* or *into*
lucky \ˈlək-ē\ *adj* **luck·i·er; -est 1** : favored by luck : FORTUNATE **2** : FORTUITOUS **3** : seeming to bring good luck — **luck·i·ly** \ˈlək-ə-lē\ *adv* — **luck·i·ness** \-ē-nəs\ *n*
lu·cra·tive \ˈlü-krət-iv\ *adj* : PROFITABLE — **lu·cra·tive·ly** *adv* — **lu·cra·tive·ness** *n*
lu·cre \ˈlü-kər\ *n* [ME, fr. L *lucrum*] : PROFIT; *also* : MONEY
lu·cu·bra·tion \ˌlü-k(y)ə-ˈbrā-shən\ *n* : laborious study : MEDITATION
lu·di·crous \ˈlüd-ə-krəs\ *adj* : LAUGHABLE, RIDICULOUS — **lu·di·crous·ly** *adv* — **lu·di·crous·ness** *n*
luff \ˈləf\ *vb* : to sail a ship closer to the wind — **luff** *n*
[1]**lug** \ˈləg\ *vb* **lugged; lug·ging 1** : DRAG, PULL **2** : to carry laboriously
[2]**lug** *n* **1** : a projecting piece (as for fastening, support, or traction) **2** : a heavy nut used with a bolt
lug·gage \ˈləg-ij\ *n* **1** : BAGGAGE **2** : containers (as suitcases) for carrying personal belongings
lu·gu·bri·ous \lu̇-ˈgü-brē-əs\ *adj* : mournful often to an exaggerated degree — **lu·gu·bri·ous·ly** *adv* — **lu·gu·bri·ous·ness** *n*
Luke \ˈlük\ *n* — see BIBLE table
luke·warm \ˈlük-ˈwȯrm\ *adj* **1** : moderately warm : TEPID **2** : not enthusiastic — **luke·warm·ly** *adv*
[1]**lull** \ˈləl\ *vb* **1** : SOOTHE, CALM **2** : to cause to relax vigilance
[2]**lull** *n* **1** : a temporary calm (as during a storm) **2** : a temporary drop in activity
lul·la·by \ˈləl-ə-ˌbī\ *n, pl* **-bies** : a song to lull children to sleep
lum·ba·go \ˌləm-ˈbā-gō\ *n* : rheumatic pain in the lower back and loins
lum·bar \ˈləm-bər, -ˌbär\ *adj* : of, relating to, or constituting the loins or the vertebrae between the thoracic vertebrae and sacrum ⟨~ region⟩
[1]**lum·ber** \ˈləm-bər\ *vb* **lum·bered; lum·ber·ing** \-b(ə-)riŋ\ : to move heavily or clumsily
[2]**lumber** *n* **1** : surplus or disused articles that are stored away **2** : timber esp. when dressed for use
[3]**lumber** *vb* **lum·bered; lum·ber·ing** \-b(ə-)riŋ\ : to cut logs; *also* : to saw logs into lumber — **lum·ber·man** \-mən\ *n*
lum·ber·jack \-ˌjak\ *n* : LOGGER
lum·ber·yard \-ˌyärd\ *n* : a place where lumber is kept for sale
lu·mi·nary \ˈlü-mə-ˌner-ē\ *n, pl* **-nar·ies 1** : a very famous person **2** : a source of light; *esp* : a celestial body
lu·mi·nes·cence \-ˈnes-ᵊns\ *n* : the low-temperature emission of light (as by a chemical or physiological process) — **lu·mi·nes·cent** \-ᵊnt\ *adj*
lu·mi·nous \ˈlü-mə-nəs\ *adj* **1** : emitting light; *also* : LIGHTED **2** : CLEAR, INTELLIGIBLE — **lu·mi·nance** \-nəns\ *n* — **lu·mi·nos·i·ty** \ˌlü-mə-ˈnäs-ət-ē\ *n* — **lu·mi·nous·ly** *adv*
lum·mox \ˈləm-əks\ *n* : a clumsy person
[1]**lump** \ˈləmp\ *n* **1** : a piece or mass of irregular shape **2** : AGGREGATE, TOTALITY **3** : a usu. abnormal swelling — **lump·ish** *adj* — **lumpy** *adj*
[2]**lump** *vb* **1** : to leap together in a lump **2** : to form into lumps
[3]**lump** *adj* : not divided into parts ⟨a ~ sum⟩
lu·na·cy \ˈlü-nə-sē\ *n, pl* **-cies 1** : INSANITY **2** : extreme folly
lu·nar \ˈlü-nər\ *adj* : of or relating to the moon
lu·na·tic \ˈlü-nə-ˌtik\ *adj* [ME *lunatik*, fr. LL *lunaticus*, fr. L *luna*; fr. the belief that lunacy fluctuated with the phases of the moon] **1** : INSANE; *also* : used for insane persons **2** : extremely foolish — **lunatic** *n*
[1]**lunch** \ˈlənch\ *n* **1** : a light meal usu. eaten in the middle of the day **2** : the food prepared for a lunch
[2]**lunch** *vb* : to eat lunch
lun·cheon \ˈlən-chən\ *n* : a usu. formal lunch
lun·cheon·ette \ˌlən-chə-ˈnet\ *n* : a small restaurant serving light lunches
lunch·room \ˈlənch-ˌrüm, -ˌru̇m\ *n* **1** : LUNCHEONETTE **2** : a room (as in a school) where lunches are sold and eaten or lunches brought from home may be eaten
lu·nette \lü-ˈnet\ *n* : something shaped like a crescent
lung \ˈləŋ\ *n* **1** : one of the usu. paired baglike breathing organs in the chest of an air-breathing vertebrate **2** : a mechanical device for introducing fresh air into and removing stale air from the lungs — **lunged** \ˈləŋd\ *adj*
lunge \ˈlənj\ *n* **1** : a sudden thrust or pass (as with a sword) **2** : a sudden forward stride or leap — **lunge** *vb*
lu·pine \ˈlü-pən\ *n* : any of a genus of leguminous plants with long upright clusters of pealike flowers
lu·pus \ˈlü-pəs\ *n* [ML, fr. L *wolf*] : any of several diseases (as systemic lupus erythematosus) characterized by skin lesions
lupus er·y·the·ma·to·sus \-ˌer-ə-ˌthē-mə-ˈtō-səs\ *n* : a disorder characterized by skin inflammation; *esp* : SYSTEMIC LUPUS ERYTHEMATOSUS
lurch \ˈlərch\ *n* : a sudden swaying or tipping movement — **lurch** *vb*
[1]**lure** \ˈlu̇r\ *n* **1** : ENTICEMENT; *also* : APPEAL **2** : an artificial bait for catching fish
[2]**lure** *vb* **lured; lur·ing** : to draw on with a promise of pleasure or gain
lu·rid \ˈlu̇r-əd\ *adj* **1** : LIVID **2** : shining with the red glow of fire seen through smoke or cloud **3** : GRUESOME; *also* : SENSATIONAL **syn** ghastly, grisly, grim, horrible, macabre — **lu·rid·ly** *adv*
lurk \ˈlərk\ *vb* **1** : to move furtively : SNEAK **2** : to lie concealed
lus·cious \ˈləsh-əs\ *adj* **1** : having a pleasingly sweet taste or smell **2** : sensually appealing — **lus·cious·ly** *adv* — **lus·cious·ness** *n*

[1]lush \ˈləsh\ *adj* : having or covered with abundant growth ⟨~ pastures⟩

[2]lush *n* : an habitual heavy drinker

lust \ˈləst\ *n* **1** : sexual desire often to an intense or unrestrained degree **2** : an intense longing — **lust** *vb* — **lust·ful** *adj*

lus·ter *or* **lus·tre** \ˈləs-tər\ *n* **1** : a shine or sheen esp. from reflected light **2** : BRIGHTNESS, GLITTER **3** : GLORY, SPLENDOR — **lus·ter·less** *adj* — **lus·trous** \-trəs\ *adj*

lus·tral \ˈləs-trəl\ *adj* : PURIFICATORY

lusty \ˈləs-tē\ *adj* **lust·i·er; -est** : full of vitality : ROBUST — **lust·i·ly** \ˈləs-tə-lē\ *adv* — **lust·i·ness** \-tē-nəs\ *n*

lute \ˈlüt\ *n* : a stringed musical instrument with a large pear-shaped body and a fretted fingerboard — **lu·te·nist** *or* **lu·ta·nist** \ˈlüt-ᵊn-əst\ *n*

lu·te·tium *also* **lu·te·cium** \lü-ˈtē-sh(ē-)əm\ *n* : a rare metallic chemical element — see ELEMENT table

Lu·ther·an \ˈlü-th(ə-)rən\ *n* : a member of a Protestant denomination adhering to the doctrines of Martin Luther — **Lu·ther·an·ism** \-ˌiz-əm\ *n*

lux·u·ri·ant \ˌləg-ˈzhůr-ē-ənt, ˌlək-ˈshůr-\ *adj* **1** : yielding or growing abundantly : LUSH, PRODUCTIVE **2** : abundantly rich and varied; *also* : FLORID — **lux·u·ri·ance** \-ē-əns\ *n* — **lux·u·ri·ant·ly** *adv*

lux·u·ri·ate \-ē-ˌāt\ *vb* **-at·ed; -at·ing 1** : to grow profusely **2** : REVEL

lux·u·ry \ˈləksh-(ə-)rē, ˈləgzh-\ *n, pl* **-ries 1** : great ease and comfort **2** : something desirable but costly or hard to get **3** : something adding to pleasure or comfort but not absolutely necessary — **lux·u·ri·ous** \ˌləg-ˈzhůr-ē-əs, ˌlək-ˈshůr-\ *adj* — **lux·u·ri·ous·ly** *adv*

lv *abbr* leave

lwei \lə-ˈwā\ *n, pl* **lwei** — see *kwanza* at MONEY table

LWV *abbr* League of Women Voters

[1]-ly \lē\ *adj suffix* **1** : like in appearance, manner, or nature ⟨queen*ly*⟩ **2** : characterized by regular recurrence in (specified) units of time : every ⟨hour*ly*⟩

[2]-ly \lē\ (*corresponding adjectives may end in* əl, *as* "double"); *-ically is* i-k(ə-)lē\ *adv suffix* **1** : in a (specified) manner ⟨slow*ly*⟩ **2** : from a (specified) point of view ⟨grammatical*ly*⟩

ly·ce·um \lī-ˈsē-əm, ˈlī-sē-\ *n* **1** : a hall for public lectures **2** : an association providing public lectures, concerts, and entertainments

lye \ˈlī\ *n* : a white crystalline corrosive alkaline substance used in making rayon and soap

ly·ing \ˈlī-iŋ\ *adj* : UNTRUTHFUL, FALSE

ly·ing–in \ˌlī-iŋ-ˈin\ *n, pl* **lyings–in** *or* **lying–ins** : the state during and consequent to childbirth : CONFINEMENT

lymph \ˈlimf\ *n* [L *lympha,* water goddess, water, fr. Gk *nymphē* nymph] : a pale liquid consisting chiefly of blood plasma and white blood cells, circulating in thin-walled tubes (**lymphatic vessels**), and bathing the body tissues — **lym·phat·ic** \lim-ˈfat-ik\ *adj*

lymph·ade·nop·a·thy \ˌlim-ˌfad-ᵊn-ˈäp-ə-thē\ *n, pl* **-thies** : abnormal enlargement of the lymph nodes

lymph node *n* : one of the rounded masses of lymphoid tissue surrounded by a capsule

lym·pho·cyte \ˈlim-fə-ˌsīt\ *n* : any of the weakly motile leukocytes produced in lymphoid tissue that are the typical cells in lymph and include the cellular mediators (as a B cell or a T cell) of immunity

lym·phoid \ˈlim-ˌföid\ *adj* **1** : of, relating to, or constituting the tissue characteristic of the lymph nodes **2** : of, relating to, or resembling lymph

lynch \ˈlinch\ *vb* : to put to death by mob action without legal sanction or due process of law — **lynch·er** *n*

lynx \ˈliŋks\ *n, pl* **lynx** *or* **lynx·es** : a wildcat with a short tail, long legs, and usu. tufted ears

lyre \ˈlī(ə)r\ *n* : a stringed musical instrument of the harp class used by the ancient Greeks

[1]lyr·ic \ˈlir-ik\ *n* **1** : a lyric poem **2** *pl* : the words of a popular song — **lyr·i·cal** \-i-kəl\ *adj*

[2]lyric *adj* **1** : suitable for singing : MELODIC **2** : expressing direct and usu. intense personal emotion

ly·ser·gic acid di·eth·yl·am·ide \lə-ˌsər-jik . . . ˌdī-ˌeth-ə-ˈlam-ˌīd, lī-, -ˈlam-əd\ *n* : LSD

LZ *abbr* landing zone

M

[1]m \ˈem\ *n, pl* **m's** *or* **ms** \ˈemz\ *often cap* : the 13th letter of the English alphabet

[2]m *abbr, often cap* **1** Mach **2** male **3** married **4** masculine **5** medium **6** [L *meridies*] noon **7** meter **8** mile **9** [L *mille*] thousand **10** minute **11** month **12** moon

ma \ˈmä, ˈmȯ\ *n* : MOTHER

MA *abbr* **1** [ML *magister artium*] master of arts **2** Massachusetts **3** mental age

ma'am \ˈmam, *after* "*yes*" *often* əm\ *n* : MADAM

Mac *or* **Macc** *abbr* Maccabees

ma·ca·bre \mə-ˈkäb(-rə), -ˈkäb-ər\ *adj* [F] **1** : having death as a subject **2** : GRUESOME **3** : HORRIBLE

mac·ad·am \mə-ˈkad-əm\ *n* **1** : a roadway or pavement of small closely packed broken stone **2** : the broken stone used in macadamizing — **mac·ad·am·ize** \-ˌīz\ *vb*

ma·caque \mə-ˈkak, -ˈkäk\ *n* : any of several short-tailed Asian and East Indian monkeys

mac·a·ro·ni \ˌmak-ə-ˈrō-nē\ *n* **1** : a food made chiefly of wheat flour dried in the form of usu. slender tubes **2** *pl* **-nis** *or* **-nies** : FOP, DANDY

mac·a·roon \ˌmak-ə-ˈrün\ *n* : a small cookie made chiefly of egg whites, sugar, and ground almonds or coconut

ma·caw \mə-ˈkȯ\ *n* : a large long-tailed parrot of Central and So. America

Mac·ca·bees \ˈmak-ə-ˌbēz\ *n* — see BIBLE table

Mc·Coy \mə-ˈkȯi\ *n* [alter. of *Mackay* (in the phrase *the real Mackay* the true chief of the Mackay clan, a position often disputed)] : something that is neither imitation nor substitute ⟨the real ~⟩

[1]mace \ˈmās\ *n* **1** : a heavy often spiked club used as a weapon esp. in the Middle Ages **2** : an ornamental staff carried as a symbol of authority

[1]mace 2

[2]mace *n* : a spice from the fibrous coating of the nutmeg

mac·er·ate \ˈmas-ə-ˌrāt\ *vb* **-at·ed; -at·ing 1** : to cause to waste away **2** : to soften by steeping or soaking so as to separate the parts — **mac·er·a·tion** \ˌmas-ə-ˈrā-shən\ *n*

mach *abbr* machine; machinery; machinist

Mach \ˈmäk\ *n* : MACH NUMBER

Mach·a·bees \ˈmak-ə-ˌbēz\ *n* — see BIBLE table

ma·chete \mə-ˈshet-ē\ *n* : a large heavy knife used for cutting sugarcane and underbrush and as a weapon

Ma·chi·a·vel·lian \ˌmak-ē-ə-ˈvel-ē-ən\ *adj* [Niccolo *Machiavelli*, †1527 Ital. political philosopher] : characterized by cunning, duplicity, and bad faith — **Ma·chi·a·vel·lian·ism** *n*

mach·i·na·tion \ˌmak-ə-ˈnā-shən, ˌmash-ə-\ *n* : an act of planning esp. to do harm; *esp* : PLOT — **mach·i·nate** \ˈmak-ə-ˌnāt, ˈmash-\ *vb*

[1]**ma·chine** \mə-ˈshēn\ *n* **1** : CONVEYANCE, VEHICLE; *esp* : AUTOMOBILE **2** : a combination of mechanical parts that transmit forces, motion, and energy to do some desired work ⟨a sewing ~⟩ **3** : an instrument (as a pulley or lever) for transmitting or modifying force or motion **4** : an electrical, electronic, or mechanical device for performing a task ⟨a calculating ~⟩ **5** : a highly organized political group under the leadership of a boss or small clique

[2]**machine** *vb* **ma·chined; ma·chin·ing** : to shape or finish by machine-operated tools — **ma·chin·able** \-ˈshē-nə-bəl\ *adj*

machine gun *n* : an automatic gun capable of rapid continuous firing — **machine–gun** *vb* — **machine gunner** *n*

machine language *n* : the set of symbolic instruction codes usu. in binary form that is used to represent operations and data in a machine (as a computer)

machine–readable *adj* : directly usable by a computer

ma·chin·ery \mə-ˈshēn-(ə-)rē\ *n, pl* **-er·ies 1** : MACHINES; *also* : the working parts of a machine **2** : the means by which something is done

ma·chin·ist \mə-ˈshē-nəst\ *n* : a person who makes or works on machines

ma·chis·mo \mä-ˈchēz-(ˌ)mō, -ˈchiz-\ *n* : a strong or exaggerated pride in one's masculinity

Mach number \ˈmäk-\ *n* : a number representing the ratio of the speed of a body to the speed of sound in the surrounding atmosphere ⟨a *Mach number* of 2 indicates a speed that is twice the speed of sound⟩

ma·cho \ˈmä-chō\ *adj* [Sp, male, fr. L *masculus*] : characterized by machismo

mack·er·el \ˈmak-(ə-)rəl\ *n, pl* **mackerel** *or* **mackerels** : a No. Atlantic food fish greenish above and silvery below

mack·i·naw \ˈmak-ə-ˌnȯ\ *n* : a short heavy plaid coat

mack·in·tosh *also* **mac·in·tosh** \ˈmak-ən-ˌtäsh\ *n* **1** *chiefly Brit* : RAINCOAT **2** : a lightweight waterproof fabric

mac·ra·mé *also* **mac·ra·me** \ˈmak-rə-ˌmā\ *n* [deriv. of Ar *miqramah* embroidered veil] : a coarse lace or fringe made by knotting threads or cords in a geometrical pattern

mac·ro \ˈmak-(ˌ)rō\ *adj* : very large; *also* : involving large quantities or being on a large scale

mac·ro·bi·ot·ic \ˌmak-rō-bī-ˈät-ik, -bē-\ *adj* : relating to or being a very restricted diet (as one containing chiefly whole grains)

mac·ro·cosm \ˈmak-rə-ˌkäz-əm\ *n* : the great world : UNIVERSE

ma·cron \ˈmāk-ˌrän, ˈmak-\ *n* : a mark ¯ placed over a vowel (as in \māk\) to show that the vowel is long

mac·ro·scop·ic \ˌmak-rə-ˈskäp-ik\ *adj* : visible to the naked eye — **mac·ro·scop·i·cal·ly** \-i-k(ə-)lē\ *adv*

mad \ˈmad\ *adj* **mad·der; mad·dest 1** : disordered in mind : INSANE **2** : being rash and foolish **3** : FURIOUS, ENRAGED **4** : carried away by enthusiasm **5** : RABID **6** : marked by wild gaiety and merriment **7** : FRANTIC — **mad·ly** *adv* — **mad·ness** *n*

Mad·a·gas·can \ˌmad-ə-ˈgas-kən\ *n* : a native or inhabitant of Madagascar

mad·am \ˈmad-əm\ *n* **1** *pl* **mes·dames** \mā-ˈdäm\ — used as a form of polite address to a woman **2** *pl* **madams** : the female head of a house of prostitution

ma·dame \mə-ˈdam, *before a surname also* ˌmad-əm\ *n, pl* **mes·dames** \mā-ˈdäm\ : MISTRESS — used as a title for a woman not of English-speaking nationality

mad·cap \ˈmad-ˌkap\ *adj* : WILD, RECKLESS — **madcap** *n*

mad·den \ˈmad-ᵊn\ *vb* **mad·dened; mad·den·ing** \ˈmad-(ᵊ-)niŋ\ : to make mad — **mad·den·ing·ly** *adv*

mad·der \ˈmad-ər\ *n* : a Eurasian plant with yellow flowers and fleshy red roots; *also* : its root or a dye prepared from it

made *past and past part of* MAKE

Ma·dei·ra \mə-ˈdir-ə\ *n* : an amber-colored dessert wine

ma·de·moi·selle \ˌmad-(ə-)m(w)ə-ˈzel, mam-ˈzel\ *n, pl* **ma·de·moi·selles** \-ˈzelz\ *or* **mes·de·moi·selles** \ˌmād-(ə-)m(w)e-ˈzel\ : an unmarried girl or woman — used as a title for an unmarried woman not of English-speaking and esp. of French nationality

made–up \ˈmād-ˈəp\ *adj* **1** : marked by the use of makeup **2** : fancifully conceived or falsely devised

mad·house \ˈmad-ˌhau̇s\ *n* **1** : a place for the detention and care of the insane **2** : a place of great uproar

mad·man \ˈmad-ˌman, -mən\ *n* : LUNATIC

ma·don·na \mə-ˈdän-ə\ *n* : a representation (as a picture or statue) of the Virgin Mary

ma·dras \ˈmad-rəs; ˌmə-ˈdras, -ˈdräs\ *n* [*Madras*, India] : a fine usu. cotton fabric with various designs (as plaid)

mad·ri·gal \ˈmad-ri-gəl\ *n* [It *madrigale*] : a somewhat elaborate part-song esp. of the 16th century; *also* : a love poem suitable for a musical setting

mad·wom·an \ˈmad-ˌwu̇m-ən\ *n* : a woman who is insane

mael·strom \ˈmāl-strəm\ *n* : a violent whirlpool

mae·stro \ˈmī-strō\ *n, pl* **maestros** *or* **mae·stri** \-ˌstrē\ [It] : a master in an art; *esp* : an eminent composer, conductor, or teacher of music

Ma·fia \ˈmäf-ē-ə\ *n* [It] **1** : a secret society of political terrorists **2** : a secret criminal organization

ma·fi·o·so \ˌmäf-ē-ˈō-(ˌ)sō\ *n, pl* **-si** \-(ˌ)sē,\ : a member of the Mafia

[1]**mag** *abbr* **1** magnetism **2** magneto **3** magnitude

[2]**mag** \ˈmag\ *n* : MAGAZINE

mag·a·zine \ˈmag-ə-ˌzēn\ *n* **1** : a storehouse esp. for military supplies **2** : a place for keeping gunpowder in a fort or ship **3** : a publication usu. containing stories, articles, or poems and issued periodically **4** : a container in a gun for holding cartridges; *also* : a chamber (as on a camera) for film

ma·gen·ta \mə-ˈjent-ə\ *n* : a deep purplish red

mag·got \ˈmag-ət\ *n* : the legless wormlike larva of a two-winged fly — **mag·goty** *adj*

ma·gi \ˈmā-jī\ *n pl, often cap* : the three wise men from the East who paid homage to the infant Jesus

mag·ic \ˈmaj-ik\ *n* **1** : the art of persons who claim to be able to do things by the help of supernatural powers or by their own knowledge of nature's secrets **2** : an extraordinary power or influence seemingly from a supernatural force **3** : SLEIGHT OF HAND — **magic** *adj* — **mag·i·cal** \-i-kəl\ *adj* — **mag·i·cal·ly** \-i-k(ə-)lē\ *adv*

ma·gi·cian \mə-ˈjish-ən\ *n* : one skilled in magic

mag·is·te·ri·al \ˌmaj-ə-ˈstir-ē-əl\ *adj* **1** : AUTHORITATIVE **2** : of or relating to a magistrate or his office or duties

ma·gis·tral \ˈmaj-ə-strəl\ *adj* : AUTHORITATIVE

mag·is·trate \ˈmaj-ə-ˌstrāt\ *n* : an official entrusted with administration of the laws — **mag·is·tra·cy** \-strə-sē\ *n*

mag·ma \ˈmag-mə\ *n* : molten rock material within the earth — **mag·mat·ic** \mag-ˈmat-ik\ *adj*

mag·nan·i·mous \mag-ˈnan-ə-məs\ *adj* **1** : showing or suggesting a lofty and courageous spirit **2** : NOBLE, GENEROUS — **mag·na·nim·i·ty** \ˌmag-nə-ˈnim-ət-ē\ *n* — **mag·nan·i·mous·ly** *adv* — **mag·nan·i·mous·ness** *n*

mag·nate \ˈmag-ˌnāt\ *n* : a person of rank, influence, or distinction

mag·ne·sia \mag-ˈnē-shə, -zhə\ *n* [NL, fr. *magnes carneus*, a white earth, lit., flesh magnet] : a light white substance that is an oxide of magnesium and is used as a laxative

mag·ne·sium \mag-ˈnē-zē-əm, -zhəm\ *n* : a silver-white

light and easily worked metallic chemical element — see ELEMENT table
mag·net \ˈmag-nət\ *n* **1** : LODESTONE **2** : a body that is able to attract iron **3** : something that attracts
mag·net·ic \mag-ˈnet-ik\ *adj* **1** : of or relating to a magnet or magnetism **2** : magnetized or capable of being magnetized **3** : having an unusual ability to attract ⟨a ~ leader⟩ — **mag·net·i·cal·ly** \-i-k(ə-)lē\ *adv*
magnetic disk *n* : DISK 3
magnetic north *n* : the northerly direction in the earth's magnetic field indicated by the north-seeking pole of a horizontal magnetic needle
magnetic tape *n* : a ribbon coated with a magnetic material on which information (as sound) may be stored
mag·ne·tism \ˈmag-nə-ˌtiz-əm\ *n* **1** : the power to attract as possessed by a magnet **2** : the science that deals with magnetic phenomena **3** : an ability to attract
mag·ne·tite \ˈmag-nə-ˌtīt\ *n* : a black mineral that is an important iron ore
mag·ne·tize \ˈmag-nə-ˌtīz\ *vb* **-tized; -tiz·ing 1** : to induce magnetic properties in **2** : to attract like a magnet : CHARM — **mag·ne·tiz·able** *adj* — **mag·ne·ti·za·tion** \ˌmag-nət-ə-ˈzā-shən\ *n* — **mag·ne·tiz·er** *n*
mag·ne·to \mag-ˈnēt-ō\ *n, pl* **-tos** : a generator used to produce sparks in an internal-combustion engine
mag·ne·tom·e·ter \ˌmag-nə-ˈtäm-ət-ər\ *n* : an instrument for measuring the strength of a magnetic field
mag·ne·to·sphere \mag-ˈnēt-ə-ˌsfiər, -ˈnet-\ *n* : a region of the upper atmosphere that extends out for thousands of miles and in which charged particles are trapped by the earth's magnetic field — **mag·ne·to·spher·ic** \-ˌnēt-ə-ˈsfiər-ik, -ˈsfer-\ *adj*
mag·nif·i·cent \mag-ˈnif-ə-sənt\ *adj* **1** : characterized by grandeur or beauty : SPLENDID **2** : EXALTED, NOBLE **syn** imposing, stately, noble, grand, majestic — **mag·nif·i·cence** \-səns\ *n* — **mag·nif·i·cent·ly** *adv*
mag·nif·i·co \mag-ˈnif-i-ˌkō\ *n, pl* **-coes** *or* **-cos 1** : a nobleman of Venice **2** : a person of high position
mag·ni·fy \ˈmag-nə-ˌfī\ *vb* **-fied; -fy·ing 1** : EXTOL, LAUD; *also* : to cause to be held in greater esteem **2** : INTENSIFY; *also* : EXAGGERATE **3** : to enlarge in fact or in appearance ⟨a microscope *magnifies* an object⟩ — **mag·ni·fi·ca·tion** \ˌmag-nə-fə-ˈkā-shən\ *n* — **mag·ni·fi·er** \ˈmag-nə-ˌfī(-ə)r\ *n*
mag·nil·o·quent \mag-ˈnil-ə-kwənt\ *adj* : characterized by an exalted and often bombastic style or manner — **mag·nil·o·quence** \-kwəns\ *n*
mag·ni·tude \ˈmag-nə-ˌt(y)üd\ *n* **1** : greatness of size or extent **2** : SIZE **3** : QUANTITY **4** : a number representing the brightness of a celestial body
mag·no·lia \mag-ˈnōl-yə\ *n* : any of several spring-flowering shrubs and trees with large often fragrant flowers
mag·num opus \ˌmag-nəm-ˈō-pəs\ *n* [L] : the greatest achievement of an artist or writer
mag·pie \ˈmag-ˌpī\ *n* : a long-tailed black-and-white bird related to the jays
Mag·yar \ˈmag-ˌyär, ˈmäg-; ˈmäj-ˌär\ *n* : a member of the dominant people of Hungary — **Magyar** *adj*
ma·ha·ra·ja *or* **ma·ha·ra·jah** \ˌmä-hə-ˈräj-ə\ *n* : a Hindu prince ranking above a raja
ma·ha·ra·ni *or* **ma·ha·ra·nee** \-ˈrän-ē\ *n* : the wife of a maharaja; *also* : a Hindu princess ranking above a rani
ma·ha·ri·shi \ˌmä-hə-ˈrē-shē\ *n* : a Hindu teacher of mystical knowledge
ma·hat·ma \mə-ˈhät-mə, -ˈhat-\ *n* [Skt *mahātman,* fr. *mahātman* great-souled, fr. *mahat* great + *ātman* soul] : a person revered for high-mindedness, wisdom, and selflessness
Ma·hi·can \mə-ˈhē-kən\ *n, pl* **Mahican** *or* **Mahicans** : a member of an American Indian people of the upper Hudson river valley
ma·hog·a·ny \mə-ˈhäg-ə-nē\ *n, pl* **-nies** : any of various tropical trees with reddish wood used in furniture; *esp* : an American evergreen tree or its durable lustrous reddish brown wood
ma·hout \mə-ˈhaùt\ *n* [Hindi *mahāut*] : a keeper and driver of an elephant
maid \ˈmād\ *n* **1** : an unmarried girl or young woman **2** : a female servant
[1]**maid·en** \ˈmād-ᵊn\ *n* : MAID 1 — **maid·en·ly** *adj*
[2]**maiden** *adj* **1** : UNMARRIED; *also* : VIRGIN **2** : of, relating to, or befitting a maiden **3** : FIRST ⟨~ voyage⟩
maid·en·hair \-ˌhaər\ *n* : a fern with delicate feathery fronds
maid·en·head \ˈmād-ᵊn-ˌhed\ *n* **1** : VIRGINITY **2** : HYMEN
maid·en·hood \-ˌhùd\ *n* : the condition or time of being a maiden
maid–in–wait·ing \ˌmād-ᵊn-ˈwāt-iŋ\ *n, pl* **maids–in–wait·ing** \ˌmād-zən-\ : a young woman appointed to attend a queen or princess
maid of honor : a bride's principal unmarried wedding attendant
maid·ser·vant \ˈmād-ˌsər-vənt\ *n* : a female servant
[1]**mail** \ˈmāl\ *n* [ME *male,* fr. OF] **1** : something sent or carried in the postal system **2** : a nation's postal system — often used in pl.
[2]**mail** *vb* : to send by mail
[3]**mail** *n* [ME *maille,* fr. MF, fr. L *macula* spot, mesh] : armor made of metal links or plates
mail·box \-ˌbäks\ *n* **1** : a public box for the collection of mail **2** : a private box for the delivery of mail
mail·man \-ˌman\ *n* : a man who delivers mail
maim \ˈmām\ *vb* : to mutilate, disfigure, or wound seriously : CRIPPLE
[1]**main** \ˈmān\ *n* **1** : FORCE ⟨with might and ~⟩ **2** : MAINLAND; *also* : HIGH SEA **3** : the chief part **4** : a principal pipe, duct, or circuit of a utility system
[2]**main** *adj* **1** : CHIEF, PRINCIPAL **2** : fully exerted ⟨~ force⟩ **3** : expressing the chief predication in a complex sentence ⟨the ~ clause⟩ — **main·ly** *adv*
main·frame \ˈmān-ˌfrām\ *n* : a large fast computer
main·land \ˈmān-ˌland, -lənd\ *n* : a continuous body of land constituting the chief part of a country or continent
main·line \ˈmān-ˈlīn\ *vb, slang* : to inject a narcotic drug into a vein
main line *n* : a principal highway or railroad line
main·mast \ˈmān-ˌmast, -məst\ *n* : the principal mast on a sailing ship
main·sail \ˈmān-ˌsāl, -səl\ *n* : the largest sail on the mainmast
main·spring \-ˌspriŋ\ *n* **1** : the chief spring in a mechanism (as of a watch) **2** : the chief motive, agent, or cause
main·stay \-ˌstā\ *n* **1** : a stay running from the head of the mainmast to the foot of the foremast **2** : a chief support
main·stream \-ˌstrēm\ *n* : a prevailing current or direction of activity or influence — **mainstream** *adj*
main·tain \mān-ˈtān\ *vb* [ME *mainteinen,* fr. OF *maintenir,* fr. ML *manutenēre,* fr. L *manu tenēre* to hold in the hand] **1** : to keep in an existing state (as of repair) **2** : to sustain against opposition or danger **3** : to continue in : CARRY ON **4** : to provide for : SUPPORT **5** : ASSERT — **main·tain·abil·i·ty** \-ˌtā-nə-ˈbil-ət-ē\ *n* — **main·tain·able** \-ˈtā-nə-bəl\ *adj* — **main·te·nance** \ˈmānt-(ᵊ-)nəns\ *n*
main·top \ˈmān-ˌtäp\ *n* : a platform at the head of the mainmast of a square-rigged ship
mai·son·ette \ˌmāz-ᵊn-ˈet\ *n* **1** : a small house **2** : an apartment often on two floors
maî·tre d' *or* **mai·tre d'** \ˌmā-trə-ˈdē, ˌme-\ *n, pl* **maître d's** *or* **maitre d's** \-ˈdēz\ : MAÎTRE D'HÔTEL

maî·tre d'hô·tel \ˌmā-trə-dō-ˈtel, ˌme-\ *n, pl* **maîtres d'hôtel** *same*\ [F, lit., master of house] **1** : MAJORDOMO **2** : the head of a dining-room staff (as of a hotel)
maize \ˈmāz\ *n* : INDIAN CORN
Maj *abbr* major
maj·es·ty \ˈmaj-ə-stē\ *n, pl* **-ties 1** : sovereign power, authority, or dignity; *also* : the person of a sovereign — used as a title **2** : GRANDEUR, SPLENDOR — **ma·jes·tic** \mə-ˈjes-tik\ *adj* — **ma·jes·ti·cal·ly** \-ti-k(ə-)lē\ *adv*
Maj Gen *abbr* Major General
ma·jol·i·ca \mə-ˈjäl-i-kə\ *also* **ma·iol·i·ca** \-ˈyäl-\ *n* : any of several faiences; *esp* : an Italian tin-glazed pottery
[1]**ma·jor** \ˈmā-jər\ *adj* **1** : greater in number, extent, or importance ⟨a ~ poet⟩ **2** : notable or conspicuous in effect or scope ⟨a ~ improvement⟩ **3** : SERIOUS ⟨a ~ illness⟩ **4** : having half steps between the 3d and 4th and the 7th and 8th degrees ⟨~ scale⟩; *also* : based on a major scale ⟨~ key⟩ ⟨~ chord⟩
[2]**major** *n* **1** : a commissioned officer (as in the army) ranking next below a lieutenant colonel **2** : a subject of academic study chosen as a field of specialization; *also* : a student specializing in such a field
[3]**major** *vb* **ma·jored; ma·jor·ing** \ˈmāj-(ə-)riŋ\ : to pursue an academic major
ma·jor·do·mo \ˌmā-jər-ˈdō-mō\ *n, pl* **-mos** [Sp *mayordomo* or obs. It *maiordomo,* fr. ML *major domus,* lit., chief of the house] **1** : a head steward **2** : BUTLER
majorette *n* : DRUM MAJORETTE
major general *n* : a commissioned officer (as in the army) ranking next below a lieutenant general
ma·jor·i·ty \mə-ˈjȯr-ət-ē\ *n, pl* **-ties 1** : the age at which full civil rights are accorded; *also* : the status of one who has attained this age **2** : a number greater than half of a total; *also* : the excess of this greater number over the remainder **3** : the military rank of a major
major–medical *adj* : of, relating to, or being a form of insurance designed to pay all or part of the medical bills of major illnesses usu. after deduction of a fixed initial sum
ma·jus·cule \ˈmaj-əs-ˌkyül, mə-ˈjəs-\ *n* : a large letter (as a capital)
[1]**make** \ˈmāk\ *vb* **made** \ˈmād\; **mak·ing 1** : to cause to exist, occur, or appear; *also* : DESTINE ⟨was *made* to be an actor⟩ **2** : FASHION ⟨~ a dress⟩; *also* : COMPOSE **3** : to formulate in the mind ⟨~ plans⟩ **4** : CONSTITUTE ⟨house *made* of stone⟩ **5** : to compute to be **6** : to set in order : PREPARE ⟨~ a bed⟩ **7** : to cause to be or become; *also* : APPOINT **8** : ENACT; *also* : EXECUTE ⟨~ a will⟩ **9** : CONCLUDE ⟨didn't know what to ~ of it⟩ **10** : to carry out : PERFORM ⟨~ a speech⟩ **11** : COMPEL **12** : to assure the success of ⟨anyone he likes is *made*⟩ **13** : to amount to in significance ⟨~*s* no difference⟩ **14** : to be capable of developing or being fashioned into **15** : REACH, ATTAIN; *also* : GAIN **16** : to start out : GO **17** : to have weight or effect ⟨courtesy ~*s* for safer driving⟩ **syn** form, shape, fabricate, manufacture — **mak·er** *n* — **make believe** : PRETEND — **make do** : to manage with the means at hand — **make fun of** : RIDICULE, MOCK — **make good 1** : INDEMNIFY ⟨*make good* the loss⟩; *also* : to carry out successfully ⟨*make good* his promise⟩ **2** : SUCCEED — **make way 1** : to give room for passing, entering, or occupying **2** : to make progress
[2]**make** *n* **1** : the manner or style of construction; *also* : BRAND 3 **2** : MAKEUP **3** : the action of manufacturing — **on the make** : in search of wealth, social status, or sexual adventure
[1]**make–be·lieve** \ˈmāk-bə-ˌlēv\ *n* : a pretending to believe : PRETENSE
[2]**make–believe** *adj* : IMAGINED, PRETENDED
make–do \-ˌdü\ *adj* : MAKESHIFT
make out *vb* **1** : to draw up in writing ⟨*make out* a shopping list⟩ **2** : to find or grasp the meaning of ⟨how do you *make* that *out*⟩ **3** : to pretend to be true **4** : DISCERN ⟨*make out* a form in the fog⟩ **5** : GET ALONG, FARE ⟨*make out* well in business⟩ **6** : to engage in amorous kissing and caressing
make over *vb* : REMAKE, REMODEL
make·shift \ˈmāk-ˌshift\ *n* : a temporary expedient — **makeshift** *adj*
make·up \-ˌəp\ *n* **1** : the way in which something is put together; *also* : physical, mental, and moral constitution **2** : cosmetics esp. for the face; *also* : materials (as wigs and cosmetics) used in costuming (as for a play)
make up \(ˈ)māk-ˈəp\ *vb* **1** : FORM, COMPOSE **2** : to compensate for a deficiency **3** : SETTLE ⟨*made up* my mind⟩ **4** : INVENT, IMPROVISE **5** : to become reconciled **6** : to put on makeup
make–work \ˈmāk-ˌwərk\ *n* : assigned busywork
mak·ings \ˈmā-kiŋz\ *n pl* : the material from which something is made
makuta *pl of* LIKUTA
Mal *abbr* Malachi
Mal·a·chi \ˈmal-ə-ˌkī\ *n* — see BIBLE table
Mal·a·chi·as \ˌmal-ə-ˈkī-əs\ *n* — see BIBLE table
mal·a·chite \ˈmal-ə-ˌkīt\ *n* : a mineral that is a green carbonate of copper used for making ornamental objects
mal·adapt·ed \ˌmal-ə-ˈdap-təd\ *adj* : poorly suited to a particular use, purpose, or situation
mal·ad·just·ed \ˌmal-ə-ˈjəs-təd\ *adj* : poorly or inadequately adjusted (as to one's environment) — **mal·ad·just·ment** \-ˈjəs(t)-mənt\ *n*
mal·adroit \ˌmal-ə-ˈdrȯit\ *adj* : not adroit : INEPT
mal·a·dy \ˈmal-əd-ē\ *n, pl* **-dies** : a disease or disorder of body or mind
mal·aise \mə-ˈlāz, ma-\ *n* [F] : a vague feeling of bodily or mental disorder
mal·a·mute \ˈmal-ə-ˌmyüt\ *n* : a dog often used to draw sleds esp. in northern No. America
mal·a·prop·ism \ˈmal-ə-ˌpräp-ˌiz-əm\ *n* : a usu. humorous misuse of a word
mal·ap·ro·pos \ˌmal-ˌap-rə-ˈpō, mal-ˈap-rə-ˌpō\ *adv* : in an inappropriate or inopportune way — **malapropos** *adj*
ma·lar·ia \mə-ˈler-ē-ə\ *n* [It, fr. *mala aria* bad air] : a disease marked by recurring chills and fever and caused by a parasite carried by a mosquito — **ma·lar·i·al** \-əl\ *adj*
ma·lar·key \mə-ˈlär-kē\ *n* : insincere or foolish talk
mal·a·thi·on \ˌmal-ə-ˈthī-ən, -ˌän\ *n* : an insecticide with a relatively low toxicity for mammals
Ma·la·wi·an \mə-ˈlä-wē-ən\ *n* : a native or inhabitant of Malawi — **Malawian** *adj*
Ma·lay \mə-ˈlā, ˈmā-ˌlā\ *n* **1** : a member of a people of the Malay peninsula and archipelago **2** : the language of the Malays — **Malay** *adj* — **Ma·lay·an** \mə-ˈlā-ən, ˈmā-ˌlā-\ *n or adj*
Ma·lay·sian \mə-ˈlā-zhən, -shən\ *n* : a native or inhabitant of Malaysia — **Malaysian** *adj*
mal·con·tent \ˌmal-kən-ˈtent\ *adj* : marked by a dissatisfaction with the existing state of affairs : DISCONTENTED — **malcontent** *n*
mal de mer \ˌmal-də-ˈmeər\ *n* : SEASICKNESS
[1]**male** \ˈmāl\ *adj* **1** : of, relating to, or being the sex that begets young; *also* : STAMINATE **2** : MASCULINE — **maleness** *n*
[2]**male** *n* : a male individual
male·dic·tion \ˌmal-ə-ˈdik-shən\ *n* : CURSE, EXECRATION
male·fac·tor \ˈmal-ə-ˌfak-tər\ *n* : EVILDOER; *esp* : one who commits an offense against the law — **mal·e·fac·tion** \ˌmal-ə-ˈfak-shən\ *n*
ma·lef·ic \mə-ˈlef-ik\ *adj* **1** : BALEFUL **2** : MALICIOUS
ma·lef·i·cent \-ə-sənt\ *adj* : working or productive of harm or evil
ma·lev·o·lent \mə-ˈlev-ə-lənt\ *adj* : having, showing, or arising from ill will, spite, or hatred **syn** malignant, malign, malicious, spiteful — **ma·lev·o·lence** \-ləns\ *n*

mal·fea·sance \mal-ˈfēz-ᵊns\ *n* : wrongful conduct esp. by a public official

mal·for·ma·tion \ˌmal-fȯr-ˈmā-shən\ *n* : an irregular or faulty formation or structure — **mal·formed** \mal-ˈfȯrmd\ *adj*

mal·func·tion \mal-ˈfəŋk-shən\ *vb* : to fail to operate in the normal or usual manner — **malfunction** *n*

Ma·li·an \ˈmäl-ē-ən\ *n* : a native or inhabitant of Mali — **Malian** *adj*

mal·ice \ˈmal-əs\ *n* : ILL WILL — **ma·li·cious** \mə-ˈlish-əs\ *adj* — **ma·li·cious·ly** *adv*

¹**ma·lign** \mə-ˈlīn\ *adj* **1** : evil in nature, influence, or effect ⟨hindered by ~ influences⟩; *also* : MALIGNANT 2 **2** : moved by ill will toward others

²**malign** *vb* : to speak evil of : DEFAME

ma·lig·nant \mə-ˈlig-nənt\ *adj* **1** : INJURIOUS, MALIGN **2** : tending or likely to cause death : VIRULENT — **ma·lig·nan·cy** \-nən-sē\ *n* — **ma·lig·nant·ly** *adv* — **ma·lig·ni·ty** \-nət-ē\ *n*

ma·lin·ger \mə-ˈliŋ-gər\ *vb* **-gered; -ger·ing** \-g(ə-)riŋ\ [F *malingre* sickly] : to pretend illness so as to avoid duty — **ma·lin·ger·er** *n*

mal·i·son \ˈmal-ə-sən, -zən\ *n* : CURSE

mall \ˈmȯl, ˈmal\ *n* **1** : a shaded walk : PROMENADE **2** : an urban shopping area featuring a variety of shops surrounding a concourse **3** : a usu. large enclosed suburban shopping area containing various shops

mal·lard \ˈmal-ərd\ *n, pl* **mallard** *or* **mallards** : a common wild duck that is the ancestor of domestic ducks

mal·lea·ble \ˈmal-ē-ə-bəl\ *adj* **1** : capable of being extended or shaped by beating with a hammer or by the pressure of rollers **2** : ADAPTABLE, PLIABLE **syn** plastic, pliant, ductile, supple — **mal·le·a·bil·i·ty** \ˌmal-ē-ə-ˈbil-ət-ē\ *n*

mal·let \ˈmal-ət\ *n* **1** : a tool with a large head for driving another tool or for striking a surface without marring it **2** : a hammerlike implement for striking a ball (as in polo or croquet)

mal·le·us \ˈmal-ē-əs\ *n, pl* **mal·lei** \-ē-ˌī, -ē-ˌē\ [NL, fr. L, hammer] : the outermost of the three small bones of the mammalian ear

mal·low \ˈmal-ō\ *n* : any of several tall herbs with lobed leaves and 5-petaled white, yellow, rose, or purplish flowers

malm·sey \ˈmä(l)m-zē\ *n, often cap* : the sweetest variety of Madeira wine

mal·nour·ished \mal-ˈnər-isht\ *adj* : poorly nourished

mal·nu·tri·tion \ˌmal-n(y)ü-ˈtrish-ən\ *n* : faulty and esp. inadequate nutrition

mal·oc·clu·sion \ˌmal-ə-ˈklü-zhən\ *n* : faulty coming together of teeth in biting

mal·odor·ous \mal-ˈōd-ə-rəs\ *adj* : ill-smelling — **mal·odor·ous·ly** *adv* — **mal·odor·ous·ness** *n*

ma·lo·ti \mə-ˈlōt-ē\ *pl of* LOTI

mal·prac·tice \mal-ˈprak-təs\ *n* : a dereliction of professional duty or a failure of professional skill that results in injury, loss, or damage

malt \ˈmȯlt\ *n* **1** : grain and esp. barley steeped in water until it has sprouted and used in brewing and distilling **2** : liquor made with malt — **malty** *adj*

malted milk \ˌmȯl-təd-\ *n* : a powder prepared from dried milk and an extract from malt; *also* : a beverage of this powder in milk or other liquid

Mal·thu·sian \mal-ˈth(y)ü-zhən\ *adj* : of or relating to Malthus or his theory that population unless checked (as by war) tends to increase faster than its means of subsistence — **Malthusian** *n* — **Mal·thu·sian·ism** \-zhə-ˌniz-əm\ *n*

malt·ose \ˈmȯl-ˌtōs\ *n* : a sugar formed esp. from starch by the action of enzymes and used in brewing and distilling

mal·treat \mal-ˈtrēt\ *vb* : to treat cruelly or roughly : ABUSE — **mal·treat·ment** *n*

ma·ma *or* **mam·ma** \ˈmäm-ə\ *n* : MOTHER

mam·bo \ˈmäm-bō\ *n, pl* **mambos** : a dance of Cuban origin related to the rumba — **mambo** *vb*

mam·mal \ˈmam-əl\ *n* : any of the group of vertebrate animals that includes man and all others which nourish their young with milk — **mam·ma·li·an** \mə-ˈmā-lē-ən, ma-\ *adj or n*

mam·ma·ry \ˈmam-ə-rē\ *adj* : of, relating to, or being the glands (**mammary glands**) that in female mammals secrete milk

mam·mo·gram \ˈmam-ə-ˌgram\ *n* : a photograph of the breasts made by X rays

mam·mog·ra·phy \ma-ˈmäg-rə-fē\ *n, pl* **-phies** : X-ray examination of the breasts (as for early detection of cancer)

mam·mon \ˈmam-ən\ *n, often cap* : material wealth having a debasing influence

¹**mam·moth** \ˈmam-əth\ *n* : any of various large hairy extinct elephants

²**mammoth** *adj* : of very great size : GIGANTIC **syn** colossal, enormous, immense, vast, elephantine

¹**man** \ˈman\ *n, pl* **men** \ˈmen\ **1** : a human being; *esp* : an adult male **2** : MANKIND **3** : one possessing in high degree the qualities considered distinctive of manhood; *also* : HUSBAND **4** : an adult male servant or employee **5** : one of the pieces with which various games (as chess) are played **6** *often cap* : white society or people

²**man** *vb* **manned; man·ning** **1** : to supply with men ⟨~ a fleet⟩ **2** : FORTIFY, BRACE

³**man** *abbr* manual

Man *abbr* Manitoba

man–about–town \ˌman-ə-ˌbau̇t-ˈtau̇n\ *n, pl* **men–about–town** \ˌmen-\ : a worldly and socially active man

man·a·cle \ˈman-i-kəl\ *n* **1** : a shackle for the hand or wrist **2** : something used as a restraint

man·age \ˈman-ij\ *vb* **man·aged; man·ag·ing** **1** : HANDLE, CONTROL; *also* : to direct or carry on business or affairs **2** : to make and keep submissive **3** : to treat with care : HUSBAND **4** : to achieve one's purpose : CONTRIVE — **man·age·abil·i·ty** \ˌman-ij-ə-ˈbil-ət-ē\ *n* — **man·age·able** \ˈman-ij-ə-bəl\ *adj* — **man·age·able·ness** *n* — **man·age·ably** \-blē\ *adv*

man·age·ment \ˈman-ij-mənt\ *n* **1** : the act or art of managing : CONTROL **2** : judicious use of means to accomplish an end **3** : executive ability **4** : the group of those who manage or direct an enterprise

man·ag·er \ˈman-ij-ər\ *n* : one that manages — **man·a·ge·ri·al** \ˌman-ə-ˈjir-ē-əl\ *adj*

ma·ña·na \mən-ˈyän-ə\ [Sp., lit., tomorrow] *n* : an indefinite time in the future

man–at–arms \ˌman-ət-ˈärmz\ *n, pl* **men–at–arms** \ˌmen-\ : SOLDIER; *esp* : one who is heavily armed and mounted

Man·chu·ri·an \man-ˈchu̇r-ē-ən\ *n* : a native or inhabitant of Manchuria, China — **Manchurian** *adj*

man·ci·ple \ˈman-sə-pəl\ *n* : a steward or purveyor esp. for a college or monastery

man·da·mus \man-ˈdā-məs\ *n* [L, we enjoin, fr. *mandare*] : a writ issued by a superior court commanding that an official act or duty be performed

man·da·rin \ˈman-də-rən\ *n* **1** : a public official of high rank under the Chinese Empire **2** *cap* : the chief dialect of China **3** : a reddish orange to yellow loose-skinned citrus fruit; *also* : a tree that bears mandarins

man·date \ˈman-ˌdāt\ *n* **1** : an authoritative command **2** : an authorization to act given to a representative **3** : a commission granted by the League of Nations to a member nation for governing conquered territory; *also* : a territory so governed

man·da·to·ry \ˈman-də-ˌtōr-ē\ *adj* **1** : containing or constituting a command : OBLIGATORY **2** : of or relating to a League of Nations mandate

man·di·ble \ˈman-də-bəl\ *n* **1** : JAW; *esp* : a lower jaw **2** : either segment of a bird's bill — **man·dib·u·lar** \man-ˈdib-yə-lər\ *adj*

man·do·lin \ˈman-də-ˈlin, ˈman-dᵊl-ən\ *n* : a stringed musical instrument with a pear-shaped body and a fretted neck

man·drag·o·ra \man-ˈdrag-ə-rə\ *n* : MANDRAKE 1

man·drake \ˈman-ˌdrāk\ *n* **1** : an Old World herb of the nightshade family or its large forked root superstitiously credited with human and medicinal attributes **2** : MAYAPPLE

man·drel *also* **man·dril** \ˈman-drəl\ *n* **1** : an axle or spindle inserted into a hole in a piece of work to support it during machining **2** : a metal bar used as a core around which material may be cast, shaped, or molded

man·drill \ˈman-drəl\ *n* : a large fierce gregarious baboon of western Africa

mane \ˈmān\ *n* : long heavy hair growing about the neck of some mammals (as a horse) — **maned** \ˈmānd\ *adj*

man–eat·er \ˈman-ˌēt-ər\ *n* : one (as a shark or cannibal) that has or is thought to have an appetite for human flesh — **man–eat·ing** \-ˌēt-iŋ\ *adj*

ma·nège \ma-ˈnezh, mə-\ *n* : the art of horsemanship or of training horses

ma·nes \ˈmän-ˌās, ˈmā-ˌnēz\ *n pl, often cap* : the spirits of the dead and gods of the lower world in ancient Roman belief

ma·neu·ver \mə-ˈn(y)ü-vər\ *n* [F *manœuvre,* fr. OF *maneuvre* work done by hand, fr. ML *manuopera,* fr. L *manu operare* to work by hand] **1** : a military or naval movement; *also* : an armed forces training exercise — often used in pl. **2** : a procedure involving expert physical movement **3** : an evasive movement or shift of tactics; *also* : an action taken to gain a tactical end — **maneuver** *vb* — **ma·neu·ver·abil·i·ty** \-ˌn(y)üv-(ə-)rə-ˈbil-ət-ē\ *n*

man Fri·day \ˈman-ˈfrīd-ē\ *n* : an efficient and devoted aide or employee

man·ful \ˈman-fəl\ *adj* : having or showing courage and resolution — **man·ful·ly** \-ē\ *adv*

man·ga·nese \ˈmaŋ-gə-ˌnēz, -ˌnēs\ *n* : a grayish white metallic chemical element resembling iron but not magnetic — see ELEMENT table

mange \ˈmānj\ *n* : a contagious itchy skin disease esp. of domestic animals — **mangy** \ˈmān-jē\ *adj*

man·ger \ˈmān-jər\ *n* : a trough or open box for livestock feed or fodder

[1]**man·gle** \ˈmaŋ-gəl\ *vb* **man·gled; man·gling** \-g(ə-)liŋ\ **1** : to cut, bruise, or hack with repeated blows **2** : to spoil or injure in making or performing — **man·gler** \-g(ə-)lər\ *n*

[2]**mangle** *n* : a machine for ironing laundry by passing it between heated rollers

man·go \ˈmaŋ-gō\ *n, pl* **mangoes** *also* **mangos** [Pg *manga*] : a yellowish red tropical fruit with juicy slightly acid pulp; *also* : an evergreen tree related to the sumacs that bears this fruit

man·grove \ˈman-ˌgrōv\ *n* : a tropical maritime tree that sends out many prop roots and forms dense thickets important in coastal land building

man·han·dle \ˈman-ˌhan-dᵊl\ *vb* : to handle roughly

man·hat·tan \man-ˈhat-ᵊn\ *n, often cap* : a cocktail made of whiskey and vermouth

man·hole \ˈman-ˌhōl\ *n* : a hole through which a person may go esp. to gain access to an underground or enclosed structure

man·hood \-ˌhu̇d\ *n* **1** : the condition of being an adult male **2** : manly qualities : COURAGE **3** : MEN ⟨the nation's ~⟩

man–hour \-ˈau̇(-ə)r\ *n* : a unit of one hour's work by one person

man·hunt \-ˌhənt\ *n* : an organized hunt for a person and esp. for one charged with a crime

ma·nia \ˈmā-nē-ə, -nyə\ *n* **1** : insanity esp. when marked by extreme excitement **2** : excessive enthusiasm

ma·ni·ac \ˈmā-nē-ˌak\ *n* : LUNATIC, MADMAN

ma·ni·a·cal \mə-ˈnī-ə-kəl\ *also* **ma·ni·ac** \ˈmā-nē-ak\ *adj* **1** : affected with or suggestive of madness **2** : FRANTIC

man·ic \ˈman-ik\ *adj* : affected with, relating to, or resembling mania — **manic** *n*

man·ic–de·pres·sive \ˌman-ik-di-ˈpres-iv\ *adj* : characterized by mania, by psychotic depression, or by alternating mania and depression — **manic–depressive** *n*

[1]**man·i·cure** \ˈman-ə-ˌkyu̇ər\ *n* **1** : MANICURIST **2** : a treatment for the care of the hands and nails

[2]**manicure** *vb* **-cured; -cur·ing 1** : to do manicure work on **2** : to trim closely and evenly

man·i·cur·ist \-ˌkyu̇r-əst\ *n* : a person who gives manicure treatments

[1]**man·i·fest** \ˈman-ə-ˌfest\ *adj* [ME, fr. MF or L; MF *manifeste,* fr. L *manifestus,* lit., hit by the hand, fr. *manus* hand + *-festus* (akin to L in*festus* hostile)] **1** : readily perceived by the senses and esp. by the sight **2** : easily understood : OBVIOUS — **man·i·fest·ly** *adv*

[2]**manifest** *vb* : to make evident or certain by showing or displaying **syn** evidence, evince, demonstrate, exhibit

[3]**manifest** *n* : a list of passengers or an invoice of cargo for a ship or plane

man·i·fes·ta·tion \ˌman-ə-fə-ˈstā-shən\ *n* : DISPLAY, DEMONSTRATION

man·i·fes·to \ˌman-ə-ˈfes-tō\ *n, pl* **-tos** *or* **-toes** : a public declaration of intentions, motives, or views

[1]**man·i·fold** \ˈman-ə-ˌfōld\ *adj* **1** : marked by diversity or variety **2** : consisting of or operating many of one kind combined

[2]**manifold** *n* : a pipe fitting with several lateral outlets for connecting it with other pipes

[3]**manifold** *vb* **1** : to make a number of copies of (as a letter) **2** : MULTIPLY

man·i·kin *or* **man·ni·kin** \ˈman-i-kən\ *n* **1** : MANNEQUIN **2** : a little man : DWARF, PYGMY

Ma·nila hemp \mə-ˌnil-ə-\ *n* : a tough fiber from a Philippine banana plant used esp. for cordage

manila paper \mə-ˌnil-ə-\ *n, often cap M* : a tough brownish paper made orig. from Manila hemp

man·i·oc \ˈman-ē-ˌäk\ *n* : CASSAVA

ma·nip·u·late \mə-ˈnip-yə-ˌlāt\ *vb* **-lat·ed; -lat·ing** [fr. *manipulation,* fr. F, fr. *manipule* handful, fr. L *manipulus*] **1** : to treat or operate manually or mechanically esp. with skill **2** : to manage or use skillfully **3** : to influence esp. with intent to deceive — **ma·nip·u·la·tion** \mə-nip-yə-ˈlā-shən\ *n* — **ma·nip·u·la·tive** \-ˈnip-yə-ˌlāt-iv\ *adj* — **ma·nip·u·la·tor** \-ˌlāt-ər\ *n*

man·kind *n* **1** \ˈman-ˈkīnd\ : the human race **2** \-ˌkīnd\ : men as distinguished from women

[1]**man·ly** \ˈman-lē\ *adj* **man·li·er; -est** : having qualities appropriate to or generally associated with a man : BOLD, RESOLUTE — **man·li·ness** *n*

[2]**manly** *adv* : in a manly manner

man–made \ˈman-ˈmād\ *adj* : made by man rather than nature ⟨~ systems⟩; *esp* : SYNTHETIC ⟨~ fibers⟩

man·na \ˈman-ə\ *n* **1** : food miraculously supplied to the Israelites in the wilderness **2** : something of value that comes unexpectedly : WINDFALL

manned \ˈmand\ *adj* : carrying or performed by a person ⟨~ spaceflight⟩

man·ne·quin \ˈman-i-kən\ *n* **1** : a form representing the human figure used esp. for displaying clothes **2** : a person employed to model clothing

man·ner \ˈman-ər\ *n* **1** : KIND, SORT **2** : a way of acting or proceeding ⟨worked in a brisk ~⟩; *also* : normal behavior ⟨spoke bluntly as was his ~⟩ **3** : a method of artistic execution **4** *pl* : social conduct; *also* : BEARING **5** *pl* : BEHAVIOR ⟨taught the child good ~*s*⟩

man·nered \ˈman-ərd\ *adj* **1** : having manners of a specified kind ⟨well-*mannered*⟩ **2** : having an artificial character ⟨a highly ~ style⟩

man·ner·ism \ˈman-ə-ˌriz-əm\ *n* **1** : ARTIFICIALITY, PRECIOSITY **2** : a peculiarity of action, bearing, or treatment **syn** pose, air, affectation

man·ner·ly \ˈman-ər-lē\ *adj* : showing good manners : POLITE — **man·ner·li·ness** *n*

man·nish \ˈman-ish\ *adj* **1** : resembling or suggesting a man rather than a woman **2** : generally associated with or characteristic of a man — **man·nish·ly** *adv* — **man·nish·ness** *n*

ma·noeu·vre \mə-ˈn(y)ü-vər\ *chiefly Brit var of* MANEUVER

man–of–war \ˌman-ə(v)-ˈwȯr\ *n, pl* **men–of–war** \ˌmen-\ : WARSHIP

ma·nom·e·ter \mə-ˈnäm-ət-ər\ *n* : an instrument for measuring the pressure of gases — **mano·met·ric** \ˌman-ə-ˈme-trik\ *adj*

man·or \ˈman-ər\ *n* **1** : the house or hall of an estate; *also* : a landed estate **2** : an English estate of a feudal lord — **ma·no·ri·al** \mə-ˈnōr-ē-əl\ *adj* — **ma·no·ri·al·ism** \-ə-ˌliz-əm\ *n*

man power *n* **1** : power available from or supplied by the physical effort of human beings **2** *usu* **man·pow·er** : the total supply of persons available and fitted for service

man·qué \mäⁿ-ˈkā\ *adj* [F, fr. pp. of *manquer* to lack, fail] : short of or frustrated in the fulfillment of one's aspirations or talents ⟨a poet ~⟩

man·sard \ˈman-ˌsärd, -sərd\ *n* : a roof having two slopes on all sides with the lower slope steeper than the upper one

manse \ˈmans\ *n* : the residence esp. of a Presbyterian clergyman

man·ser·vant \ˈman-ˌsər-vənt\ *n, pl* **men·ser·vants** \ˈmen-ˌsər-vənts\ : a male servant

man·sion \ˈman-chən\ *n* : a large imposing residence; *also* : a separate apartment in a large structure

man–size \ˈman-ˌsīz\ *or* **man–sized** \-ˌsīzd\ *adj* : suitable for or requiring a man

man·slaugh·ter \-ˌslȯt-ər\ *n* : the unlawful killing of a human being without express or implied malice

man·slay·er \-ˌslā-ər\ *n* : one who slays a man

man·ta \ˈmant-ə\ *n* : a square piece of cloth or blanket used in southwestern U.S. and Latin America as a cloak or shawl

man·teau \man-ˈtō\ *n* : a loose cloak, coat, or robe

man·tel \ˈmant-ᵊl\ *n* : a beam, stone, or arch serving as a lintel to support the masonry above a fireplace; *also* : a shelf above a fireplace

man·tel·piece \ˈmant-ᵊl-ˌpēs\ *n* : the shelf of a mantel

man·til·la \man-ˈtē-(y)ə, -ˈtil-ə\ *n* : a light scarf worn over the head and shoulders esp. by Spanish and Latin-American women

man·tis \ˈmant-əs\ *n, pl* **man·tis·es** *or* **man·tes** \ˈman-ˌtēz\ [NL, fr. Gk, lit., divener, prophet] : a large insect related to the grasshoppers that feeds on other insects which it holds in forelimbs folded as if in prayer

man·tis·sa \man-ˈtis-ə\ *n* : the decimal part of a logarithm

¹**man·tle** \ˈmant-ᵊl\ *n* **1** : a loose sleeveless garment worn over other clothes **2** : something that covers, enfolds, or envelopes **3** : a lacy sheath that gives light by incandescence when placed over a flame **4** : the portion of the earth lying between the crust and the core **5** : MANTEL

²**mantle** *vb* **man·tled; man·tling** \ˈmant-(ᵊ-)liŋ\ **1** : to cover with a mantle **2** : BLUSH

man·tra \ˈman-trə\ *n* : a Hindu or Buddhist mystical formula of incantation

¹**man·u·al** \ˈman-yə(-wə)l\ *adj* **1** : of, relating to, or involving the hands; *also* : worked by hand ⟨a ~ choke⟩ **2** : requiring or using physical skill and energy — **man·u·al·ly** \-ē\ *adv*

²**manual** *n* **1** : a small book; *esp* : HANDBOOK **2** : the prescribed movements in the handling of a military item and esp. a weapon during a drill or ceremony ⟨the ~ of arms⟩ **3** : a keyboard esp. of an organ

man·u·fac·to·ry \ˌman-(y)ə-ˈfak-t(ə-)rē\ *n* : FACTORY

¹**man·u·fac·ture** \ˌman-(y)ə-ˈfak-chər\ *n* [MF, fr. L *manu factus* made by hand] **1** : something made from raw materials **2** : the process of making wares by hand or by machinery; *also* : a productive industry using mechanical power and machinery

²**manufacture** *vb* **-tured; -tur·ing 1** : to make from raw materials by hand or by machinery; *also* : to engage in manufacture **2** : INVENT, FABRICATE; *also* : CREATE — **man·u·fac·tur·er** *n*

man·u·mit \ˌman-yə-ˈmit\ *vb* **-mit·ted; -mit·ting** : to free from slavery — **man·u·mis·sion** \-ˈmish-ən\ *n*

¹**ma·nure** \mə-ˈn(y)u̇r\ *vb* **ma·nured; ma·nur·ing** : to fertilize land with manure

²**manure** *n* : FERTILIZER; *esp* : refuse from stables and barnyards — **ma·nu·ri·al** \-ˈn(y)u̇r-ē-əl\ *adj*

man·u·script \ˈman-yə-ˌskript\ *n* [L *manu scriptus* written by hand] **1** : a written or typewritten composition or document **2** : writing as opposed to print

Manx \ˈmaŋks\ *n pl* : the people of the Isle of Man — **Manx** *adj*

¹**many** \ˈmen-ē\ *adj* **more** \ˈmōr\; **most** \ˈmōst\ : consisting of or amounting to a large but indefinite number

²**many** *pron* : a large number

³**many** *n* : a large but indefinite number

many·fold \ˌmen-ē-ˈfōld\ *adv* : by many times

many–sid·ed \-ˈsīd-əd\ *adj* **1** : having many sides or aspects **2** : VERSATILE

Mao·ism \ˈmau̇-ˌiz-əm\ *n* : the theory and practice of Communism developed in China chiefly by Mao Tse-tung — **Mao·ist** \ˈmau̇-əst\ *n or adj*

Mao·ri \ˈmau̇(ə)r-ē\ *n, pl* **Maori** *or* **Maoris** : a member of a Polynesian people native to New Zealand

¹**map** \ˈmap\ *n* [ML *mappa*, fr. L, napkin, towel] **1** : a representation usu. on a flat surface of the whole or part of an area **2** : a representation of the celestial sphere or part of it

²**map** *vb* **mapped; map·ping 1** : to make a map of **2** : to plan in detail ⟨~ out a program⟩ — **map·pa·ble** \ˈmap-ə-bəl\ *adj* — **map·per** *n*

ma·ple \ˈmā-pəl\ *n* : any of various trees or shrubs with 2-winged dry fruit and opposite leaves; *also* : the hard light-colored wood of a maple used esp. for floors and furniture

maple sugar *n* : sugar made by boiling maple syrup

maple syrup *n* : syrup made by concentrating the sap of maple trees and esp. the sugar maple

mar \ˈmär\ *vb* **marred; mar·ring** : to detract from the wholeness or perfection of : SPOIL **syn** injure, hurt, harm, damage, impair, blemish

Mar *abbr* March

ma·ra·ca \mə-ˈräk-ə, -ˈrak-\ *n* [Pg *maracá*] : a dried gourd or a rattle like a gourd that contains dried seeds or pebbles and is used as a percussion instrument

mar·a·schi·no \ˌmar-ə-ˈskē-nō, -ˈshē-\ *n, pl* **-nos** *often cap* [It] : a cherry preserved in a true or imitation sweet cherry liqueur

mar·a·thon \ˈmar-ə-ˌthän\ *n* [*Marathon*, Greece, site of a victory of Greeks over Persians in 490 B.C. the news of which was carried to Athens by a long-distance runner] **1** : a long-distance race esp. on foot **2** : an endurance contest

mar·a·thon·er \ˈmar-ə-ˌthän-ər\ *n* : one who takes part in a marathon — **mar·a·thon·ing** *n*
ma·raud \mə-ˈrȯd\ *vb* : to roam about and raid in search of plunder : PILLAGE — **ma·raud·er** *n*
mar·ble \ˈmär-bəl\ *n* **1** : a limestone that can be polished and used in fine building work **2** : something resembling marble (as in coldness) **3** : a small ball (as of glass) used in various games; *also, pl* : a children's game played with these small balls — **marble** *adj*
mar·bling \-b(ə-)liŋ\ *n* : an intermixture of fat through the lean of a cut of meat
mar·cel \mär-ˈsel\ *n* : a deep soft wave made in the hair by the use of a heated curling iron — **marcel** *vb*
[1]**march** \ˈmärch\ *n* : a border region : FRONTIER
[2]**march** *vb* **1** : to move along in or as if in military formation **2** : to walk in a direct purposeful manner; *also* : PROGRESS, ADVANCE **3** : TRAVERSE — **march·er** *n*
[3]**march** *n* **1** : the action of marching; *also* : the distance covered (as by a military unit) in a march **2** : a regular measured stride or rhythmic step used in marching **3** : forward movement **4** : a piece of music with marked rhythm suitable for marching to
March *n* [ME, fr. OF, fr. L *martius*, fr. *Mart-*, *Mars*, Roman god of war] : the third month of the year having 31 days
mar·chio·ness \ˈmär-shə-nəs\ *n* **1** : the wife or widow of a marquess **2** : a woman holding the rank of a marquess in her own right
march–past \ˈmärch-ˌpast\ *n* : a marching by esp. of troops in review
Mar·di Gras \ˈmärd-ē-ˌgrä\ *n* [F, lit., fat Tuesday] : the Tuesday before Ash Wednesday often observed with parades and merrymaking
[1]**mare** \ˈmaər\ *n* : a female of an animal of the horse group
[2]**ma·re** \ˈmär-(ˌ)ā\ *n, pl* **ma·ria** \ˈmär-ē-ə\ : any of several large dark areas on the surface of the moon or Mars
mar·ga·rine \ˈmärj-(ə-)rən, -ə-ˌrēn\ *n* : a food product made usu. from vegetable oils churned with skimmed milk and used as a substitute for butter
mar·gin \ˈmär-jən\ *n* **1** : the part of a page outside the main body of printed or written matter **2** : EDGE **3** : a spare amount, measure, or degree allowed for use if needed **4** : measure or degree of difference ⟨passed the bill by a ~ of one vote⟩ — **mar·gin·al** \-ᵊl\ *adj* — **mar·gin·al·ly** \-ē\ *adv*
mar·gi·na·lia \ˌmär-jə-ˈnā-lē-ə\ *n pl* : marginal notes
mar·grave \ˈmär-ˌgrāv\ *n* : the military governor esp. of a medieval German border province
mar·gue·rite \ˌmär-g(y)ə-ˈrēt\ *n* [F] : any of several daisies or chrysanthemums
ma·ri·a·chi \ˌmär-ē-ˈäch-ē\ *n* : a Mexican street band; *also* : a member of or the music of such a band
mari·gold \ˈmar-ə-ˌgōld, ˈmer-\ *n* : a garden plant related to the daisies with double yellow, orange, or reddish flower heads
mar·i·jua·na *also* **mar·i·hua·na** \ˌmar-ə-ˈ(h)wän-ə\ *n* [MexSp *marihuana*] : the dried leaves and flowering tops of the female hemp plant that are sometimes smoked for their intoxicating effect; *also* : HEMP
ma·rim·ba \mə-ˈrim-bə\ *n* : a xylophone of southern Africa and Central America; *also* : a modern version of it
ma·ri·na \mə-ˈrē-nə\ *n* : a dock or basin providing secure moorings for motorboats and yachts
mar·i·na·ra \ˌmar-ə-ˈnar-ə\ *adj* [It (*alla*) *marinara*, lit., in sailor style] : made with tomatoes, onions, garlic, and spices; *also* : served with marinara sauce
mar·i·nate \ˈmar-ə-ˌnāt\ *vb* **-nat·ed; -nat·ing** : to steep (as meat or fish) in a brine or pickle
[1]**ma·rine** \mə-ˈrēn\ *adj* **1** : of or relating to the sea or its navigation or commerce **2** : of or relating to marines
[2]**marine 1** : the mercantile and naval shipping of a country **2** : any of a class of soldiers serving on shipboard or with a naval force
mar·i·ner \ˈmar-ə-nər\ *n* : SAILOR
mar·i·o·nette \ˌmar-ē-ə-ˈnet, ˌmer-\ *n* : a puppet moved by strings or by hand
mar·i·tal \ˈmar-ət-ᵊl\ *adj* : of or relating to marriage : CONJUGAL **syn** matrimonial, connubial, nuptial
mar·i·time \ˈmar-ə-ˌtīm\ *adj* **1** : of, relating to, or bordering on the sea **2** : of or relating to navigation or commerce of the sea
mar·jo·ram \ˈmärj-(ə-)rəm\ *n* : a fragrant aromatic mint used esp. as a seasoning
[1]**mark** \ˈmärk\ *n* **1** : TARGET; *also* : GOAL, OBJECT **2** : something (as a line or fixed object) designed to record position; *also* : the starting line or position in a track event **3** : an object of abuse or ridicule **4** : the question under discussion **5** : NORM ⟨not up to the ~⟩ **6** : a visible sign : INDICATION; *also* : CHARACTERISTIC **7** : a written or printed symbol **8** : GRADE ⟨a ~ of B+⟩ **9** : IMPORTANCE, DISTINCTION **10** : a lasting impression ⟨made his ~ in the world⟩; *also* : a damaging impression left on a surface
[2]**mark** *vb* **1** : to set apart by a line or boundary **2** : to designate by a mark or make a mark on **3** : CHARACTERIZE ⟨the vehemence that ~*s* his speeches⟩; *also* : SIGNALIZE ⟨this year ~*s* the 50th anniversary⟩ **4** : to take notice of : OBSERVE — **mark·er** *n*
[3]**mark** *n* — see MONEY table
Mark \ˈmärk\ *n* — see BIBLE table
mark·down \ˈmärk-ˌdau̇n\ *n* **1** : a lowering of price **2** : the amount by which an original price is reduced
mark down \(ˈ)märk-ˈdau̇n\ *vb* : to put a lower price on
marked \ˈmärkt\ *adj* : NOTICEABLE — **mark·ed·ly** \ˈmär-kəd-lē\ *adv*
[1]**mar·ket** \ˈmär-kət\ *n* **1** : a meeting together of people for trade by purchase and sale; *also* : a public place where such a meeting is held **2** : the rate or price offered for a commodity or security **3** : a geographical area of demand for commodities; *also* : extent of demand **4** : a retail establishment usu. of a specific kind ⟨a meat ~⟩
[2]**market** *vb* : to go to a market to buy or sell; *also* : SELL — **mar·ket·able** *adj*
mar·ket·place \ˈmär-kət-ˌplās\ *n* **1** : an open square in a town where markets are held **2** : the world of trade or economic activity
mark·ka \ˈmär-ˌkä\ *n, pl* **mark·kaa** \ˈmär-ˌkä\ *or* **markkas** \-ˌkäz\ — see MONEY table
marks·man \ˈmärks-mən\ *n* : a person skillful at hitting a target — **marks·man·ship** *n*
mark·up \ˈmärk-ˌəp\ *n* **1** : a raising of price **2** : an amount added to the cost price of an article to determine the selling price
mark up \(ˈ)märk-ˈəp\ *vb* : to put a higher price on
marl \ˈmärl\ *n* : an earthy deposit rich in lime used as fertilizer — **marly** \ˈmär-lē\ *adj*
mar·lin \ˈmär-lən\ *n* : a large oceanic sport fish
mar·line·spike *also* **mar·lin·spike** \ˈmär-lən-ˌspīk\ *n* : a pointed iron tool used to separate strands of rope or wire (as in splicing)
mar·ma·lade \ˈmär-mə-ˌlād\ *n* : a clear jelly holding in suspension pieces of fruit and fruit rind
mar·mo·re·al \mär-ˈmōr-ē-əl\ *adj* : of, relating to, or resembling marble
mar·mo·set \ˈmär-mə-ˌset\ *n* : any of various small bushy-tailed tropical American monkeys
mar·mot \ˈmär-mət\ *n* : a stout short-legged burrowing No. American rodent
[1]**ma·roon** \mə-ˈrün\ *vb* **1** : to put ashore (as on a desolate island) and leave to one's fate **2** : to leave in isolation and without hope of escape
[2]**maroon** *n* : a dark red
mar·plot \ˈmär-ˌplät\ *n* : one who endangers the success of an enterprise by his meddling
mar·quee \mär-ˈkē\ *n* [modif. of F *marquise*, lit., mar-

marmot

chioness] **1** : a large tent set up (as for an outdoor party) **2** : a usu. metal and glass canopy over an entrance (as of a theater)

mar·quess \ˈmär-kwəs\ *n* **1** : a nobleman of hereditary rank in Europe and Japan **2** : a member of the British peerage ranking below a duke and above an earl

mar·que·try \ˈmär-kə-trē\ *n* : inlaid work of wood, shell, or ivory (as on a table or cabinet)

mar·quis \ˈmär-kwəs, mär-ˈkē\ *n* : MARQUESS

mar·quise \mär-ˈkēz\ *n, pl* **mar·quises** \-ˈkēz(-əz)\ : MARCHIONESS

mar·qui·sette \ˌmär-k(w)ə-ˈzet\ *n* : a sheer meshed fabric

mar·riage \ˈmar-ij\ *n* **1** : the state of being married **2** : a wedding ceremony and attendant festivities **3** : a close union — **mar·riage·able** *adj*

mar·row \ˈmar-ō\ *n* : a soft vascular tissue that fills the cavities of most bones

mar·row·bone \ˈmar-ə-ˌbōn, -ō-ˌbōn\ *n* : a bone (as a shinbone) rich in marrow

mar·ry \ˈmar-ē\ *vb* **mar·ried; mar·ry·ing** **1** : to join as husband and wife according to law or custom **2** : to take as husband or wife : WED **3** : to enter into a close union — **mar·ried** *adj or n*

Mars \ˈmärz\ *n* : the planet fourth from the sun conspicuous for its red appearance

marsh \ˈmärsh\ *n* : a tract of soft wet land — **marshy** *adj*

[1]**mar·shal** \ˈmär-shəl\ *n* **1** : a high official in a medieval household; *also* : a person in charge of the ceremonial aspects of a gathering **2** : a general officer of the highest military rank **3** : an administrative officer (as of a U.S. judicial district) having duties similar to a sheriff's **4** : the administrative head of a city police or fire department

[2]**marshal** *vb* **-shaled** *or* **-shalled; -shal·ing** *or* **-shal·ling** \ˈmärsh-(ə-)liŋ\ **1** : to arrange in order, rank, or position **2** : to lead with ceremony : USHER

marsh gas *n* : METHANE

marsh·mal·low \ˈmärsh-ˌmel-ō, -ˌmal-\ *n* : a light creamy confection made from corn syrup, sugar, albumen, and gelatin

marsh marigold *n* : a swamp herb related to the buttercups that has bright yellow flowers

mar·su·pi·al \mär-ˈsü-pē-əl\ *n* : any of a large group of mostly Australian primitive mammals that bear very immature young which are nourished in a pouch on the abdomen of the female — **marsupial** *adj*

mart \ˈmärt\ *n* : MARKET

mar·ten \ˈmärt-ᵊn\ *n, pl* **marten** *or* **martens** : a slender weasel-like mammal with fine gray or brown fur; *also* : this fur

mar·tial \ˈmär-shəl\ *adj* [L *martialis* of Mars, fr. *Mart-, Mars* Mars, Roman god of war] **1** : of, relating to, or suited for war or a warrior ⟨~ music⟩ **2** : of or relating to an army or military life **3** : WARLIKE

martial law *n* **1** : the law applied in occupied territory by the occupying military forces **2** : the established law of a country administered by military forces in an emergency when civilian law enforcement agencies are unable to maintain public order and safety

mar·tian \ˈmär-shən\ *adj, often cap* : of or relating to the planet Mars or its hypothetical inhabitants — **martian** *n, often cap*

mar·tin \ˈmärt-ᵊn\ *n* : any of several small swallows and flycatchers

mar·ti·net \ˌmärt-ᵊn-ˈet\ *n* : a strict disciplinarian

mar·tin·gale \ˈmärt-ᵊn-ˌgāl\ *n* : a strap connecting a horse's girth to the bit or reins so as to hold down its head

mar·ti·ni \mär-ˈtē-nē\ *n* : a cocktail made of gin or vodka and dry vermouth

[1]**mar·tyr** \ˈmärt-ər\ *n* [ME, fr. OE, fr. LL, fr. Gk *martyr-, martys,* lit., witness] **1** : a person who dies rather than renounce his religion; *also* : one who makes a great sacrifice for the sake of principle **2** : a great or constant sufferer

[2]**martyr** *vb* **1** : to put to death for adhering to a belief **2** : TORTURE

mar·tyr·dom \ˈmärt-ər-dəm\ *n* **1** : the suffering and death of a martyr **2** : TORTURE

[1]**mar·vel** \ˈmär-vəl\ *n* **1** : something that causes wonder or astonishment **2** : intense surprise or interest

[2]**marvel** *vb* **-veled** *or* **-velled; -vel·ing** *or* **-vel·ling** \ˈmärv-(ə-)liŋ\ : to feel surprise, wonder, or amazed curiosity

mar·vel·ous *or* **mar·vel·lous** \ˈmärv-(ə-)ləs\ *adj* **1** : causing wonder **2** : of the highest kind or quality : SPLENDID — **mar·vel·ous·ly** *adv* — **mar·vel·ous·ness** *n*

Marx·ism \ˈmärk-ˌsiz-əm\ *n* : the political, economic, and social principles and policies advocated by Karl Marx — **Marx·ist** \-səst\ *n or adj*

mar·zi·pan \ˈmärt-sə-ˌpän, -ˌpan; ˈmär-zə-ˌpan\ *n* [G] : a confection of almond paste, sugar, and egg whites

masc *abbr* masculine

mas·cara \mas-ˈkar-ə\ *n* : a cosmetic for coloring the eyelashes and eyebrows

mas·cot \ˈmas-ˌkät, -kət\ *n* [F *mascotte,* fr. Provençal *mascoto,* fr. *masco* witch, fr. ML *masca*] : a person, animal, or object believed to bring good luck

[1]**mas·cu·line** \ˈmas-kyə-lən\ *adj* **1** : MALE; *also* : MANLY **2** : of, relating to, or constituting the gender that includes most words or grammatical forms referring to males — **mas·cu·lin·i·ty** \ˌmas-kyə-ˈlin-ət-ē\ *n*

[2]**masculine** *n* **1** : a male person **2** : a noun, pronoun, adjective, or inflectional form or class of the masculine gender; *also* : the masculine gender

ma·ser \ˈmā-zər\ *n* [*m*icrowave *a*mplification by *s*timulated *e*mission of *r*adiation] : a device that utilizes the natural oscillation of atoms or molecules between energy levels for generating microwaves

[1]**mash** \ˈmash\ *n* **1** : crushed malt or grain steeped in hot water to make wort **2** : a mixture of ground feeds for livestock **3** : a soft pulpy mass

[2]**mash** *vb* **1** : to reduce to a soft pulpy state **2** : CRUSH, SMASH ⟨~ a finger⟩ — **mash·er** *n*

MASH *abbr* mobile army surgical hospital

[1]**mask** \ˈmask\ *n* **1** : a cover for the face usu. for disguise or protection **2** : MASQUE **3** : a figure of a head worn on the stage in antiquity **4** : a copy of a face made by means of a mold ⟨death ~⟩ **5** : something that conceals or disguises **6** : the face of an animal (as a fox)

[2]**mask** *vb* **1** : to conceal from view : DISGUISE **2** : to cover for protection

mask·er \ˈmas-kər\ *n* : a participant in a masquerade

mas·och·ism \ˈmas-ə-ˌkiz-əm, ˈmaz-\ *n* **1** : a sexual perversion characterized by pleasure in being subjected to pain and humiliation **2** : pleasure in being abused or dominated — **mas·och·ist** \-kəst\ *n* — **mas·och·is·tic** \ˌmas-ə-ˈkis-tik, ˌmaz-\ *adj*

ma·son \ˈmās-ᵊn\ *n* **1** : a skilled worker who builds with stone, brick, or concrete **2** *cap* : FREEMASON

Ma·son·ic \mə-ˈsän-ik\ *adj* : of or relating to Freemasons or Freemasonry

ma·son·ry \ˈmās-ᵊn-rē\ *n, pl* **-ries 1** : something constructed of materials used by masons **2** : the art, trade, or work of a mason **3** *cap* : FREEMASONRY

masque \ˈmask\ *n* **1** : MASQUERADE **2** : a short allegorical dramatic performance (as of the 17th century)

[1]**mas·quer·ade** \ˌmas-kə-ˈrād\ *n* **1** : a social gathering of persons wearing masks; *also* : a costume for wear at such a gathering **2** : DISGUISE

[2]**masquerade** *vb* **-ad·ed; -ad·ing 1** : to disguise oneself : POSE **2** : to take part in a masquerade — **mas·quer·ad·er** *n*

[1]**mass** \ˈmas\ *n* **1** *cap* : a sequence of prayers and ceremonies forming the eucharistic service of the Roman Catholic Church **2** *often cap* : a celebration of the Eucharist **3** : a musical setting for parts of the Mass

[2]**mass** *n* **1** : a quantity or aggregate of matter usu. of considerable size **2** : EXPANSE, BULK; *also* : MASSIVENESS **3** : the principal part **4** : AGGREGATE, WHOLE ⟨people in the ~⟩ **5** : the quantity of matter that a body possesses as evidenced by inertia **6** : a large quantity, amount, or number **7** : the great body of people — usu. used in pl. — **massy** *adj*

[3]**mass** *vb* : to form or collect into a mass

Mass *abbr* Massachusetts

mas·sa·cre \ˈmas-i-kər\ *n* **1** : the killing of many persons under cruel or atrocious circumstances **2** : a wholesale slaughter — **massacre** *vb*

[1]**mas·sage** \mə-ˈsäzh, -ˈsäj\ *n* : remedial or hygienic treatment of the body by manipulation (as rubbing and kneading)

[2]**massage** *vb* **mas·saged; mas·sag·ing 1** : to subject to massage **2** : to treat flatteringly; *also* : MANIPULATE ⟨~ data⟩

mas·seur \ma-ˈsər\ *n* : a man who practices massage

mas·seuse \-ˈsə(r)z, -ˈsüz\ *n* : a woman who practices massage

mas·sif \ma-ˈsēf\ *n* : a principal mountain mass

mas·sive \ˈmas-iv\ *adj* **1** : forming or consisting of a large mass **2** : large in structure, scope, or degree — **mas·sive·ly** *adv* — **mas·sive·ness** *n*

mass·less \ˈmas-ləs\ *adj* : having no mass ⟨~ particles⟩

mass medium *n, pl* **mass media** : a medium of communication (as the newspapers or television) that is designed to reach the mass of the people

mass–pro·duce \ˌmas-prə-ˈd(y)üs\ *vb* : to produce in quantity usu. by machinery — **mass production** *n*

[1]**mast** \ˈmast\ *n* **1** : a long pole or spar rising from the keel or deck of a ship and supporting the yards, booms, and rigging **2** : a vertical pole — **mast·ed** \ˈmas-təd\ *adj*

[2]**mast** *n* : nuts (as acorns) accumulated on the forest floor and often serving as food for hogs

[1]**mas·ter** \ˈmas-tər\ *n* **1** : a male teacher; *also* : a person holding an academic degree higher than a bachelor's but lower than a doctor's **2** : one highly skilled (as in an art or profession) **3** : one having authority or control **4** : VICTOR, SUPERIOR **5** : the commander of a merchant ship **6** : a youth or boy too young to be called *mister* — used as a title **7** : an original (as of a phonograph record) from which copies are made

[2]**master** *vb* **mas·tered; mas·ter·ing** \-t(ə-)riŋ\ **1** : OVERCOME, SUBDUE **2** : to become skilled or proficient in **3** : to produce a master record or tape of (as a musical performance)

master chief petty officer *n* : a petty officer of the highest rank in the navy

mas·ter·ful \ˈmas-tər-fəl\ *adj* **1** : inclined and usu. competent to act as a master **2** : having or reflecting the skill of a master ⟨did a ~ job of reporting⟩ — **mas·ter·ful·ly** \-ē\ *adv*

master gunnery sergeant *n* : a noncommissioned officer in the marine corps ranking above a master sergeant

master key *n* : a key designed to open several different locks

mas·ter·ly \ˈmas-tər-lē\ *adj* : indicating thorough knowledge or superior skill ⟨~ performance⟩

mas·ter·mind \-ˌmīnd\ *n* : a person who provides the directing or creative intelligence for a project — **mastermind** *vb*

master of ceremonies : a person who acts as host at a formal event or a program of entertainment

mas·ter·piece \ˈmas-tər-ˌpēs\ *n* : a work done with extraordinary skill

master plan *n* : an overall plan

master sergeant *n* **1** : a noncommissioned officer in the army ranking next below a sergeant major **2** : a noncommissioned officer in the air force ranking next below a senior master sergeant **3** : a noncommissioned officer in the marine corps ranking next below a master gunnery sergeant

mas·ter·stroke \ˈmas-tər-ˌstrōk\ *n* : a masterly performance or move

mas·ter·work \-ˌwərk\ *n* : MASTERPIECE

mas·tery \ˈmas-t(ə-)rē\ *n* **1** : DOMINION; *also* : SUPERIORITY **2** : possession or display of great skill or knowledge

mast·head \ˈmast-ˌhed\ *n* **1** : the top of a mast **2** : the printed matter in a newspaper giving the title and details of ownership and rates

mas·tic \ˈmas-tik\ *n* : a pasty material used as a protective coating or cement

mas·ti·cate \ˈmas-tə-ˌkāt\ *vb* **-cat·ed; -cat·ing** : CHEW — **mas·ti·ca·tion** \ˌmas-tə-ˈkā-shən\ *n*

mas·tiff \ˈmas-təf\ *n* : a large smooth-coated dog used esp. as a guard dog

mast·odon \ˈmas-tə-ˌdän\ *n* [NL, fr. Gk *mastos* breast + *odōn, odous* tooth] : a huge elephantlike extinct animal

mas·toid \ˈmas-ˌtȯid\ *n* : a bony prominence behind the ear — **mastoid** *adj*

mas·tur·ba·tion \ˌmas-tər-ˈbā-shən\ *n* : stimulation of the genital organs to a climax of excitement by contact (as manual) exclusive of sexual intercourse — **mas·tur·bate** \ˈmas-tər-ˌbāt\ *vb*

[1]**mat** \ˈmat\ *n* **1** : a piece of coarse woven or plaited fabric **2** : something made up of many intertwined strands **3** : a large thick pad used as a surface for wrestling and gymnastics

[2]**mat** *vb* **mat·ted; mat·ting** : to form into a tangled mass

[3]**mat** *or* **matt** *or* **matte** *adj* [F, fr. OF, defeated, fr. L *mattus* drunk] : not shiny : DULL

[4]**mat** *or* **matt** *or* **matte** *n* **1** : a border going around a picture between picture and frame or serving as the frame **2** : a dull finish

mat·a·dor \ˈmat-ə-ˌdȯr\ *n* [Sp, fr. *matar* to kill] : a bullfighter whose role is to kill the bull in a bullfight

[1]**match** \ˈmach\ *n* **1** : a person or thing equal or similar to another : COUNTERPART **2** : a pair of persons or objects that harmonize **3** : a contest or game between two or more individuals **4** : a marriage union; *also* : a prospective marriage partner — **match·less** *adj*

[2]**match** *vb* **1** : to meet as an antagonist; *also* : PIT ⟨~*ing* his strength against his enemy's⟩ **2** : to provide with a worthy competitor; *also* : to set in comparison with **3** : MARRY **4** : to combine suitably or congenially; *also* : ADAPT, SUIT **5** : to provide with a counterpart

[3]**match** *n* : a short slender piece of flammable material (as wood) tipped with a combustible mixture that ignites through friction

match·book \-ˌbu̇k\ *n* : a small folder containing rows of paper matches

match·lock \-ˌläk\ *n* : a musket with a slow-burning cord lowered over a hole in the breech to ignite the charge

match·mak·er \-ˌmā-kər\ *n* : one who arranges a match and esp. a marriage

match·wood \-ˌwu̇d\ *n* : small pieces of wood

[1]**mate** \ˈmāt\ *vb* **mat·ed; mat·ing** : CHECKMATE — **mate** *n*

[2]**mate** *n* **1** : ASSOCIATE, COMPANION; *also* : HELPER **2** : a deck officer on a merchant ship ranking below the captain **3** : one of a pair; *esp* : either member of a married couple or a breeding pair of animals

[3]**mate** *vb* **mat·ed; mat·ing 1** : to join or fit together : COUPLE **2** : to come or bring together as mates

ma·té *or* **ma·te** \ˈmä-ˌtā\ *n* : a tealike beverage used esp. in So. America

[1]**ma·te·ri·al** \mə-ˈtir-ē-əl\ *adj* **1** : PHYSICAL ⟨~ world⟩; *also* : BODILY ⟨~ needs⟩ **2** : of or relating to matter rather than form ⟨~ cause⟩; *also* : EMPIRICAL ⟨~ knowledge⟩ **3** : highly important : SIGNIFICANT **4** : of a physical or worldly nature ⟨~ progress⟩ — **ma·te·ri·al·ly** \-ē\ *adv*

[2]**material** *n* **1** : the elements or substance of which something is composed or made **2** : apparatus necessary for doing or making something

ma·te·ri·al·ism \mə-ˈtir-ē-ə-ˌliz-əm\ *n* **1** : a theory that everything can be explained as being or coming from matter **2** : a preoccupation with material rather than intellectual or spiritual things — **ma·te·ri·al·ist** \-ləst\ *n or adj* — **ma·te·ri·al·is·tic** \-ˌtir-ē-ə-ˈlis-tik\ *adj* — **ma·te·ri·al·is·ti·cal·ly** \-ti-k(ə-)lē\ *adv*

ma·te·ri·al·ize \mə-ˈtir-ē-ə-ˌlīz\ *vb* **-ized; -iz·ing 1** : to give material form to; *also* : to assume bodily form **2** : to make an often unexpected appearance — **ma·te·ri·al·iza·tion** \mə-ˌtir-ē-ə-lə-ˈzā-shən\ *n*

ma·té·ri·el *or* **ma·te·ri·el** \mə-ˌtir-ē-ˈel\ *n* [F *matériel*] : equipment, apparatus, and supplies used by an organization

ma·ter·nal \mə-ˈtərn-ᵊl\ *adj* **1** : MOTHERLY **2** : related through or inherited or derived from a mother — **ma·ter·nal·ly** \-ē\ *adv*

ma·ter·ni·ty \mə-ˈtər-nət-ē\ *n, pl* **-ties 1** : the quality or state of being a mother; *also* : MOTHERLINESS **2** : a hospital facility for the care of women before and during childbirth and for newborn babies — **maternity** *adj*

[1]**math** \ˈmath\ *n* : MATHEMATICS

[2]**math** *abbr* mathematical; mathematician

math·e·mat·ics \ˌmath-ə-ˈmat-iks\ *n pl* : the science of numbers and their operations and the relations between them and of space configurations and their structure and measurement — **math·e·mat·i·cal** \-ˈmat-i-kəl\ *adj* — **math·e·mat·i·cal·ly** \-i-k(ə-)lē\ *adv* — **math·e·ma·ti·cian** \ˌmath-ə-mə-ˈtish-ən\ *n*

mat·i·nee *or* **mat·i·née** \ˌmat-ᵊn-ˈā\ *n* [F *matinée*, lit., morning, fr. OF, fr. *matin* morning, fr. L *matutinum*, fr. neut. of *matutinus* of the morning, fr. *Matuta*, goddess of morning] : a musical or dramatic performance usu. in the afternoon

mat·ins \ˈmat-ᵊnz\ *n pl, often cap* **1** : special prayers said between midnight and 4 a.m. **2** : a morning service of liturgical prayer in Anglican churches

ma·tri·arch \ˈmā-trē-ˌärk\ *n* : a female who rules or dominates a family, group, or state — **ma·tri·ar·chal** \ˌmā-trē-ˈär-kəl\ *adj* — **ma·tri·ar·chy** \ˈmā-trē-ˌär-kē\ *n*

ma·tri·cide \ˈma-trə-ˌsīd, ˈmā-\ *n* **1** : the murder of a mother by her child **2** : one who kills his mother — **ma·tri·cid·al** \ˌma-trə-ˈsīd-ᵊl, ˌmā-\ *adj*

ma·tric·u·late \mə-ˈtrik-yə-ˌlāt\ *vb* **-lat·ed; -lat·ing** : to enroll as a member of a body and esp. of a college or university — **ma·tric·u·la·tion** \-ˌtrik-yə-ˈlā-shən\ *n*

mat·ri·mo·ny \ˈmat-rə-ˌmō-nē\ *n* [ME, fr. MF *matremoine*, fr. L *matrimonium*, fr. *mater* mother, matron] : MARRIAGE — **mat·ri·mo·nial** \ˌmat-rə-ˈmō-nē-əl\ *adj* —**mat·ri·mo·nial·ly** *adv*

ma·trix \ˈmā-triks\ *n, pl* **ma·tri·ces** \ˈmā-trə-ˌsēz, ˈma-\ *or* **ma·trix·es** \ˈmā-trik-səz\ **1** : something within which something else originates or develops **2** : a mold from which a relief surface (as a piece of type) is made

ma·tron \ˈmā-trən\ *n* **1** : a married woman usu. of dignified maturity or social distinction **2** : a woman supervisor (as in a school or police station) — **ma·tron·ly** *adj*

Matt *abbr* Matthew

[1]**mat·ter** \ˈmat-ər\ *n* **1** : a subject of interest or concern **2** *pl* : events or circumstances of a particular situation; *also* : elements that constitute material for treatment (as in writing) **3** : TROUBLE, DIFFICULTY ⟨what's the ~⟩ **4** : the substance of which a physical object is composed **5** : PUS **6** : an indefinite amount or quantity ⟨a ~ of a few days⟩ **7** : something written or printed **8** : MAIL

[2]**matter** *vb* : to be of importance : SIGNIFY

mat·ter–of–fact \ˌmat-ə-rə(v)-ˈfakt\ *adj* : adhering to or concerned with fact — **mat·ter–of–fact·ly** *adv* — **mat·ter–of–fact·ness** *n*

Mat·thew \ˈmath-yü\ *n* — see BIBLE table

mat·tins *often cap, chiefly Brit var of* MATINS

mat·tock \ˈmat-ək\ *n* : a digging and grubbing tool with features of an adz and an ax or pick

mat·tress \ˈma-trəs\ *n* **1** : a fabric case filled with resilient material used either alone as a bed or on a bedstead **2** : an inflatable airtight sack for use as a mattress

mat·u·rate \ˈmach-ə-ˌrāt\ *vb* **-rat·ed; -rat·ing** : MATURE

mat·u·ra·tion \ˌmach-ə-ˈrā-shən\ *n* **1** : the process of becoming mature **2** : the emergence of personal and behavioral characteristics through growth processes — **mat·u·ra·tion·al** \-sh(ə-)nəl\ *adj*

[1]**ma·ture** \mə-ˈt(y)u̇r\ *adj* **ma·tur·er; -est 1** : based on slow careful consideration **2** : having attained a final or desired state ⟨~ wine⟩ **3** : of or relating to a condition of full development **4** : due for payment ⟨a ~ loan⟩

[2]**mature** *vb* **ma·tured; ma·tur·ing** : to bring to maturity or completion

ma·tu·ri·ty \mə-ˈt(y)u̇r-ət-ē\ *n* : the quality or state of being mature; *esp* : full development

ma·tu·ti·nal \ˌmach-ü-ˈtīn-ᵊl; mə-ˈt(y)üt-(ᵊ-)nəl\ *adj* : of, relating to, or occurring in the morning : EARLY

mat·zo \ˈmät-sə\ *n, pl* **mat·zoth** \-ˌsōt(h), -sōs\ *or* **mat·zos** [Yiddish *matse*] : unleavened bread eaten esp. at the Passover

maud·lin \ˈmȯd-lən\ *adj* [alter. of Mary *Magdalene;* fr. the practice of depicting her as a weeping, penitent sinner] **1** : weakly and effusively sentimental **2** : drunk enough to be emotionally silly : FUDDLED

[1]**maul** \ˈmȯl\ *n* : a heavy hammer often with a wooden head used esp. for driving wedges or piles

[2]**maul** *vb* **1** : BEAT, BRUISE; *also* : MANGLE **2** : to handle roughly

maun·der \ˈmȯn-dər\ *vb* **maun·dered; maun·der·ing** \-d(ə-)riŋ\ **1** : to wander slowly and idly **2** : to speak indistinctly or disconnectedly

mau·so·le·um \ˌmȯ-sə-ˈlē-əm, ˌmȯ-zə-\ *n, pl* **-leums** *or* **-lea** \-ˈlē-ə\ [L, fr. Gk *mausōleion*, fr. *Mausōlos* Mausolus † *ab* 353 B.C. ruler of Caria whose tomb was one of the seven wonders of the ancient world] : a large tomb; *esp* : a usu. stone building for entombment of the dead above ground

mauve \ˈmōv, ˈmȯv\ *n* : a moderate purple, violet, or lilac color

ma·ven *or* **ma·vin** \ˈmā-vən\ *n* [Yiddish *meyvn*, fr. LHeb *mēbhīn*, fr. Heb *l'havin* to understand] : EXPERT

mav·er·ick \ˈmav-(ə-)rik\ *n* [Samuel A. *Maverick* † 1870 Am. pioneer who did not brand his calves] **1** : an unbranded range animal **2** : NONCONFORMIST

ma·vis \ˈmā-vəs\ *n* : an Old World thrush

maw \ˈmȯ\ *n* **1** : STOMACH; *also* : the crop of a bird **2** : the throat, gullet, or jaws usu. of a carnivore

mawk·ish \ˈmȯ-kish\ *adj* [ME *mawke* maggot, fr. ON *mathkr*] : sickly sentimental — **mawk·ish·ly** *adv* — **mawk·ish·ness** *n*

max *abbr* maximum

maxi \ˈmak-sē\ *n, pl* **max·is** : a long skirt, dress, or coat that usu. extends to the ankle
maxi- *comb form* **1** : extra long ⟨*maxi*-kilt⟩ **2** : extra large ⟨*maxi*-problems⟩
max·il·la \mak-ˈsil-ə\ *n, pl* **max·il·lae** \-ˈsil-(ˌ)ē\ *or* **maxillas** : JAW 1; *esp* : an upper jaw — **max·il·lary** \ˈmak-sə-ˌler-ē\ *adj*
max·im \ˈmak-səm\ *n* : a proverbial saying
max·i·mal \ˈmak-s(ə-)məl\ *adj* : MAXIMUM — **max·i·mal·ly** \-ē\ *adv*
max·i·mize \ˈmak-sə-ˌmīz\ *vb* **-mized; -miz·ing 1** : to increase to a maximum **2** : to make the most of
max·i·mum \ˈmak-s(ə-)məm\ *n, pl* **max·i·ma** \-sə-mə\ *or* **maximums** \-s(ə-)məmz\ **1** : the greatest quantity, value, or degree **2** : an upper limit allowed by authority **3** : the largest of a set of numbers — **maximum** *adj*
may \(ˈ)mā\ *verbal auxiliary, past* **might** \(ˈ)mīt\; *pres sing & pl* **may 1** : have permission or liberty to ⟨you ~ go now⟩ **2** : be in some degree likely to ⟨you ~ be right⟩ **3** — used as an auxiliary to express a wish, purpose, contingency, or concession
May \ˈmā\ *n* [ME, fr. OF *mai,* fr. L *Maius,* fr. *Maia,* Roman goddess] : the fifth month of the year having 31 days
Ma·ya \ˈmī-ə\ *n, pl* **Maya** *or* **Mayas** : a member of a group of peoples of the Yucatan peninsula and adjacent areas — **Ma·yan** \ˈmī-ən\ *adj*
may·ap·ple \ˈmā-ˌap-əl\ *n* : a No. American woodland herb related to the barberry that has a poisonous root, large leaf, and edible but insipid yellow fruit
may·be \ˈmā-bē, ˈmeb-ē\ *adv* : PERHAPS
May Day \ˈmā-ˌdā\ *n* : May 1 celebrated as a springtime festival and in some countries as Labor Day
may·flow·er \ˈmā-ˌflau̇(-ə)r\ *n* : any of several spring blooming herbs (as the trailing arbutus or anemone)
may·fly \ˈmā-flī\ *n* : any of an order of insects with an aquatic nymph and a short-lived fragile adult having membranous wings
may·hem \ˈmā-ˌhem, ˈmā-əm\ *n* **1** : willful and permanent crippling, mutilation, or disfigurement of a person **2** : needless or willful damage
may·on·naise \ˈmā-ə-ˌnāz\ *n* [F] : a dressing made of raw eggs or egg yolks, vegetable oil, and vinegar or lemon juice
may·or \ˈmā-ər\ *n* : an official elected to act as chief executive or nominal head of a city or borough — **may·or·al** \-əl\ *adj* — **may·or·al·ty** \-əl-tē\ *n*
may·pole \ˈmā-ˌpōl\ *n, often cap* : a tall flower-wreathed pole forming a center for May Day sports and dances
maze \ˈmāz\ *n* : a confusing intricate network of passages — **mazy** *adj*
ma·zur·ka \mə-ˈzər-kə\ *n* : a Polish dance in moderate triple measure
MB *abbr* Manitoba
MBA *abbr* master of business administration
mc *abbr* megacycle
[1]**MC** *n* : MASTER OF CEREMONIES
[2]**MC** *abbr* member of Congress
MCPO *abbr* master chief petty officer
[1]**Md** *abbr* Maryland
[2]**Md** *symbol* mendelevium
MD *abbr* **1** [NL *medicinae doctor*] doctor of medicine **2** Maryland **3** muscular dystrophy
mdnt *abbr* midnight
mdse *abbr* merchandise
MDT *abbr* mountain daylight (saving) time
me \(ˈ)mē\ *pron, objective case of* I
Me *abbr* Maine
ME *abbr* **1** Maine **2** mechanical engineer **3** medical examiner **4** Middle English
[1]**mead** \ˈmēd\ *n* : an alcoholic beverage brewed from water and honey, malt, and yeast
[2]**mead** *n, archaic* : MEADOW
mead·ow \ˈmed-ō\ *n* : land in or mainly in grass; *esp* : a tract of moist low-lying usu. level grassland — **mead·ow·land** \-ˌland\ *n* — **mead·owy** \ˈmed-ə-wē\ *adj*
mead·ow·lark \ˈmed-ō-ˌlärk\ *n* : any of several No. American songbirds that are largely brown and buff above and have a yellow breast marked with a black crescent
mead·ow·sweet \-ˌswēt\ *n* : a No. American native or naturalized spirea
mea·ger *or* **mea·gre** \ˈmē-gər\ *adj* **1** : THIN **2** : lacking richness, fertility, or strength : POOR **syn** scanty, scant, spare, sparse —**mea·ger·ly** *adv* — **mea·ger·ness** *n*
[1]**meal** \ˈmēl\ *n* **1** : the portion of food taken at one time : REPAST **2** : an act or the time of eating a meal
[2]**meal** *n* **1** : usu. coarsely ground seeds of a cereal (as Indian corn) **2** : a product resembling seed meal — **mealy** *adj*
meal·time \ˈmēl-ˌtīm\ *n* : the usual time at which a meal is served
mealy·bug \ˈmē-lē-ˌbəg\ *n* : any of numerous scale insects with a white powdery covering that are destructive pests esp. of fruit trees
mealy·mouthed \ˌmē-lē-ˈmau̇t͟hd, -ˈmau̇tht\ *adj* : not plain and straightforward : DEVIOUS
[1]**mean** \ˈmēn\ *adj* **1** : HUMBLE **2** : lacking power or acumen : ORDINARY **3** : SHABBY, CONTEMPTIBLE **4** : IGNOBLE, BASE **5** : STINGY **6** : pettily selfish or malicious — **mean·ly** *adv* — **mean·ness** \ˈmēn-nəs\ *n*
[2]**mean** \ˈmēn\ *vb* **meant** \ˈment\; **mean·ing** \ˈmē-niŋ\ **1** : to have in the mind as a purpose **2** : to serve to convey, show, or indicate : SIGNIFY **3** : to have importance to the degree of ⟨health ~*s* everything⟩ **4** : to direct to a particular individual
[3]**mean** *adj* **1** : occupying a middle position (as in space, order, or time) **2** : being a mean ⟨a ~ value⟩
[4]**mean** *n* **1** : a middle point between extremes **2** *pl* : something helpful in achieving a desired end **3** *pl* : material resources affording a secure life **4** : ARITHMETIC MEAN
[1]**me·an·der** \mē-ˈan-dər\ *n* [L *maeander,* fr. Gk *maiandros,* fr. *Maiandros* (now *Menderes*), river in Asia Minor] **1** : a turn or winding of a stream **2** : a winding course
[2]**meander** *vb* **-dered; -der·ing** \-d(ə-)riŋ\ **1** : to follow a winding course **2** : to wander aimlessly or casually
mean·ing \ˈmē-niŋ\ *n* **1** : the thing one intends to convey esp. by language; *also* : the thing that is thus conveyed **2** : PURPOSE **3** : SIGNIFICANCE **4** : CONNOTATION; *also* : DENOTATION — **mean·ing·ful** \-fəl\ *adj* — **mean·ing·ful·ly** \-ē\ *adv* — **mean·ing·less** *adj*
[1]**mean·time** \ˈmēn-ˌtīm\ *n* : the intervening time
[2]**meantime** *adv* : MEANWHILE
[1]**mean·while** \-ˌhwīl\ *n* : MEANTIME
[2]**meanwhile** *adv* : during the intervening time
meas *abbr* measure
mea·sles \ˈmē-zəlz\ *n pl* : an acute virus disease marked by fever and an eruption of distinct circular red spots
mea·sly \ˈmēz-(ə-)lē\ *adj* **mea·sli·er; -est** : contemptibly small or insignificant
[1]**mea·sure** \ˈmezh-ər, ˈmāzh-\ *n* **1** : an adequate or moderate portion; *also* : a suitable limit **2** : the dimensions, capacity, or amount of something ascertained by measuring; *also* : an instrument for measuring **3** : a unit of measurement; *also* : a system of such units ⟨metric ~⟩ **4** : the act or process of measuring **5** : rhythmic structure or movement **6** : the part of a musical staff between two adjacent bars **7** : CRITERION **8** : a means to an end **9** : a legislative bill — **mea·sure·less** *adj*
[2]**measure** *vb* **mea·sured; mea·sur·ing** \ˈmezh-(ə-)riŋ, ˈmāzh-\ **1** : to regulate esp. by a standard **2** : to apportion by measure **3** : to mark off by making measurements **4** : to ascertain the measurements of **5** : to bring into comparison or competition **6** : to serve as a means of measuring **7** : to have a specified measurement —

mea·sur·able \ˈmezh-(ə-)rə-bəl, ˈmāzh-\ *adj* — **mea·sur·ably** \-blē\ *adv* — **mea·sur·er** *n*

mea·sure·ment \ˈmezh-ər-mənt, ˈmāzh-\ *n* **1** : the act or process of measuring **2** : a figure, extent, or amount obtained by measuring

measure up *vb* **1** : to have necessary qualifications **2** : to equal esp. in ability

meat \ˈmēt\ *n* **1** : FOOD; *esp* : solid food as distinguished from drink **2** : animal and esp. mammal flesh considered as food **3** : the edible part inside a covering (as a shell or rind) — **meaty** *adj*

meat·ball \-ˌbȯl\ *n* : a small ball of chopped or ground meat

mec·ca \ˈmek-ə\ *n, often cap* [*Mecca,* Saudi Arabia, birthplace of Muhammad and holy city of Islam] : a center of activity sought as a goal by people sharing a common interest

mech *abbr* mechanical; mechanics

[1]**me·chan·ic** \mi-ˈkan-ik\ *adj* : of or relating to manual work or skill

[2]**mechanic** *n* **1** : a manual worker **2** : MACHINIST; *esp* : one who repairs machines

me·chan·i·cal \mi-ˈkan-i-kəl\ *adj* **1** : of or relating to machinery, to manual operations, or to mechanics **2** : done as if by a machine : AUTOMATIC **syn** instinctive, impulsive, spontaneous — **me·chan·i·cal·ly** \-k(ə-)lē\ *adv*

mechanical drawing *n* : drawing done with the aid of instruments

me·chan·ics \mi-ˈkan-iks\ *n sing or pl* **1** : a branch of physics that deals with energy and forces and their effect on bodies **2** : the practical application of mechanics (as to the operation of machines) **3** : mechanical or functional details

mech·a·nism \ˈmek-ə-ˌniz-əm\ *n* **1** : a piece of machinery; *also* : a process or technique for achieving a result **2** : mechanical operation or action **3** : the fundamental processes involved in or responsible for a natural phenomenon ⟨the visual ~⟩

mech·a·nis·tic \ˌmek-ə-ˈnis-tik\ *adj* : mechanically determined ⟨~ universe⟩ — **mech·a·nis·ti·cal·ly** \-ti-k(ə-)lē\ *adv*

mech·a·nize \ˈmek-ə-ˌnīz\ *vb* **-nized; -niz·ing 1** : to make mechanical **2** : to equip with machinery esp. in order to replace human or animal labor **3** : to equip with armed and armored motor vehicles — **mech·a·ni·za·tion** \ˌmek-ə-nə-ˈzā-shən\ *n* — **mech·a·niz·er** \ˈmek-ə-ˌnī-zər\ *n*

med *abbr* **1** medical; medicine **2** medieval **3** medium

MEd *abbr* master of education

med·al \ˈmed-ᵊl\ *n* [MF *medaille,* fr. OIt *medaglia* coin worth half a denarius, medal, fr. (assumed) VL *medalis* half, fr. LL *medialis* middle, fr. L *medius*] **1** : a small usu. metal object bearing a religious emblem or picture **2** : a piece of metal issued to commemorate a person or event or awarded for excellence or achievement

med·al·ist *or* **med·al·list** \ˈmed-ᵊl-əst\ *n* **1** : a designer or maker of medals **2** : a recipient of a medal

me·dal·lion \mə-ˈdal-yən\ *n* **1** : a large medal **2** : a tablet or panel bearing a portrait or an ornament

med·dle \ˈmed-ᵊl\ *vb* **med·dled; med·dling** \ˈmed-(ᵊ-)liŋ\ : to interfere without right or propriety — **med·dler** \ˈmed-(ᵊ-)lər\ *n*

med·dle·some \ˈmed-ᵊl-səm\ *adj* : inclined to meddle in the affairs of others

me·dia \ˈmēd-ē-ə\ *n, pl* **me·di·as** : MEDIUM 4

me·di·al \ˈmēd-ē-əl\ *adj* **1** : occurring in or extending toward the middle : MEDIAN **2** : MEAN, AVERAGE

[1]**me·di·an** \ˈmēd-ē-ən\ *n* **1** : a medial part **2** : a value in an ordered set of values below and above which there are an equal number of values

[2]**median** *adj* **1** : MEDIAL 1 **2** : relating to or constituting a statistical median

median strip *n* : a strip dividing a highway into lanes according to the direction of travel

[1]**me·di·ate** \ˈmēd-ē-ət\ *adj* **1** : occupying a middle or mediating position **2** : acting through a mediate agency — **me·di·ate·ly** *adv*

[2]**me·di·ate** \ˈmēd-ē-ˌāt\ *vb* **-at·ed; -at·ing** : to act as an intermediary (as in settling a dispute or promoting a chemical or physiological result or activity) **syn** intercede, intervene, interpose, interfere — **me·di·a·tion** \ˌmēd-ē-ˈā-shən\ *n* — **me·di·a·tor** \ˈmēd-ē-ˌāt-ər\ *n*

med·ic \ˈmed-ik\ *n* : one engaged in medical work; *esp* : CORPSMAN

med·i·ca·ble \ˈmed-i-kə-bəl\ *adj* : CURABLE, REMEDIABLE — **med·i·ca·bly** \-blē\ *adv*

med·ic·aid \ˈmed-i-ˌkād\ *n, often cap* : a program of financial assistance for medical care designed for those unable to afford regular medical service and financed jointly by the state and federal governments

med·i·cal \ˈmed-i-kəl\ *adj* : of or relating to the science or practice of medicine or the treatment of disease — **med·i·cal·ly** \-k(ə-)lē\ *adv*

medical examiner *n* : a public officer who makes postmortem examinations of bodies to find the cause of death

me·di·ca·ment \mi-ˈdik-ə-mənt, ˈmed-i-kə-\ *n* : a medicine or healing application

medi·care \ˈmed-i-ˌkeər\ *n, often cap* : a government program of financial assistance for medical care esp. for the aged

med·i·cate \ˈmed-ə-ˌkāt\ *vb* **-cat·ed; -cat·ing** : to treat with medicine — **med·i·ca·tion** \ˌmed-ə-ˈkā-shən\ *n*

me·dic·i·nal \mə-ˈdis-(ᵊ-)nəl\ *adj* : tending or used to cure disease or relieve pain — **me·dic·i·nal·ly** \-ē\ *adv*

med·i·cine \ˈmed-ə-sən\ *n* **1** : a substance or preparation used in treating disease **2** : a science or art dealing with the prevention or cure of disease

medicine ball *n* : a heavy stuffed leather ball used for conditioning exercises

medicine man *n* : a priestly healer or sorcerer esp. among the American Indians

med·i·co \ˈmed-i-ˌkō\ *n, pl* **-cos** : a medical practitioner or student

me·di·eval *or* **me·di·ae·val** \ˌmēd-ē-ˈē-vəl, ˌmed-, mē-ˈdē-vəl\ *adj* : of, relating to, or characteristic of the Middle Ages — **me·di·e·val·ism** \-ˌiz-əm\ *n* — **me·di·e·val·ist** \-əst\ *n*

me·di·o·cre \ˌmēd-ē-ˈō-kər\ *adj* [MF, fr. L *mediocris,* lit., halfway up a mountain, fr. *medius* middle + *ocris* stony mountain] : of moderate or low quality : ORDINARY — **me·di·oc·ri·ty** \-ˈäk-rət-ē\ *n*

med·i·tate \ˈmed-ə-ˌtāt\ *vb* **-tat·ed; -tat·ing 1** : to muse over : CONTEMPLATE, PONDER **2** : INTEND, PURPOSE — **med·i·ta·tion** \ˌmed-ə-ˈtā-shən\ *n* — **med·i·ta·tive** \ˈmed-ə-ˌtāt-iv\ *adj* — **med·i·ta·tive·ly** *adv*

Med·i·ter·ra·nean \ˌmed-ə-tə-ˈrā-nē-ən, -ˈrā-nyən\ *adj* : of or relating to the Mediterranean sea or to the lands or people around it

[1]**me·di·um** \ˈmēd-ē-əm\ *n, pl* **mediums** *or* **me·dia** \-ē-ə\ [L] **1** : something in a middle position; *also* : a middle position or degree **2** : a means of effecting or conveying something **3** : a surrounding or enveloping substance **4** : a channel or system of communication, information, or entertainment **5** : a mode of artistic expression **6** : an individual held to be a channel of communication between the earthly world and a world of spirits **7** : a condition in which something may function or flourish

[2]**medium** *adj* : intermediate in amount, quality, position, or degree

me·di·um·is·tic \ˌmēd-ē-ə-ˈmis-tik\ *adj* : of, relating to, or being a spiritualistic medium

med·ley \ˈmed-lē\ *n, pl* **medleys 1** : HODGEPODGE **2** : a musical composition made up esp. of a series of songs
me·dul·la \mə-ˈdəl-ə\ *n, pl* **-las** *or* **-lae** \-(ˌ)ē, -ˌī\ [L] : an inner or deep anatomical part; *also* : the posterior part (**medulla ob·lon·ga·ta** \-ˌäb-ˌlȯŋ-ˈgät-ə\) of the brain
meed \ˈmēd\ *n* **1** *archaic* : REWARD **2** : a fitting return
meek \ˈmēk\ *adj* **1** : characterized by patience and long-suffering **2** : deficient in spirit and courage **3** : MODERATE — **meek·ly** *adv* — **meek·ness** *n*
meer·schaum \ˈmiər-shəm, -ˌshȯm\ *n* [G, fr. *meer* sea + *schaum* foam] : a tobacco pipe made of a light white clayey mineral
[1]**meet** \ˈmēt\ *vb* **met** \ˈmet\; **meet·ing 1** : to come upon : FIND **2** : JOIN, INTERSECT **3** : to appear to the perception of **4** : OPPOSE, FIGHT **5** : to join in conversation or discussion; *also* : ASSEMBLE **6** : to conform to **7** : to pay fully **8** : to cope with **9** : to provide for **10** : to be introduced to
[2]**meet** *n* : an assembling esp. for a hunt or for competitive sports
[3]**meet** *adj* : SUITABLE, PROPER
meet·ing \ˈmēt-iŋ\ *n* **1** : an act of coming together : ASSEMBLY **2** : JUNCTION, INTERSECTION
meet·ing·house \-ˌhau̇s\ *n* : a building for public assembly and esp. for Protestant worship
mega·byte \ˈmeg-ə-ˌbīt\ *n* : a unit of computer storage capacity approximately equal to one million bytes
mega·cy·cle \-ˌsī-kəl\ *n* : MEGAHERTZ
mega·death \-ˌdeth\ *n* : one million deaths — used as a unit in reference to atomic warfare
mega·hertz \ˈmeg-ə-ˌhərts, -ˌheərts\ *n* : a unit of frequency equal to one million hertz
mega·lith \ˈmeg-ə-ˌlith\ *n* : one of the huge stones used in various prehistoric monuments — **mega·lith·ic** \ˌmeg-ə-ˈlith-ik\ *adj*
meg·a·lo·ma·nia \ˌmeg-ə-lō-ˈmā-nē-ə, -nyə\ *n* : a disorder of mind marked by feelings of personal omnipotence and grandeur — **meg·a·lo·ma·ni·ac** \-ˈmā-nē-ˌak\ *adj or n*
meg·a·lop·o·lis \ˌmeg-ə-ˈläp-ə-ləs\ *n* : a very large urban unit
mega·phone \ˈmeg-ə-ˌfōn\ *n* : a cone-shaped device used to intensify or direct the voice — **megaphone** *vb*
mega·ton \-ˌtən\ *n* : an explosive force equivalent to that of one million tons of TNT
mega·vi·ta·min \-ˌvīt-ə-mən\ *adj* : relating to or consisting of very large doses of vitamins — **mega·vi·ta·mins** *n pl*
mei·o·sis \mī-ˈō-səs\ *n* : the cellular process that results in the number of chromosomes in gamete-producing cells being reduced to one half — **mei·ot·ic** \mī-ˈät-ik\ *adj*
mel·an·cho·lia \ˌmel-ən-ˈkō-lē-ə\ *n* : a mental condition marked by extreme depression often with delusions
mel·an·chol·ic \ˌmel-ən-ˈkäl-ik\ *adj* **1** : DEPRESSED **2** : of or relating to melancholia
mel·an·choly \ˈmel-ən-ˌkäl-ē\ *n, pl* **-chol·ies** [ME *malencolie*, fr. MF *melancolie*, fr. LL *melancholia*, fr. Gk, fr. *melan-, melas* black + *cholē* bile; so called fr. the former belief that it was caused by an excess in the system of black bile, a substance supposedly secreted by the kidneys or spleen] : depression of spirits : DEJECTION, GLOOM — **melancholy** *adj*
Mel·a·ne·sian \ˌmel-ə-ˈnē-zhən\ *n* : a member of the dominant native group of the Pacific island grouping of Melanesia — **Melanesian** *adj*
mé·lange \mā-ˈläⁿzh, -ˈlänj\ *n* : a mixture esp. of incongruous elements
me·lan·ic \mə-ˈlan-ik\ *adj* **1** : having black pigment **2** : affected with or characterized by melanism — **melanic** *n*
mel·a·nin \ˈmel-ə-nən\ *n* : a dark brown or black animal or plant pigment
mel·a·nism \ˈmel-ə-ˌniz-əm\ *n* : an increased amount of black or nearly black pigmentation
mel·a·no·ma \ˌmel-ə-ˈnō-mə\ *n, pl* **-mas** *also* **-ma·ta** \-mət-ə\ : a usu. malignant tumor containing black pigment
[1]**meld** \ˈmeld\ *vb* : to show or announce for a score in a card game
[2]**meld** *n* : a card or combination of cards that is or can be melded
me·lee \ˈmā-ˌlā, mā-ˈlā\ *n* [F *mêlée*] : a confused struggle **syn** fracas, row, brawl, donnybrook
me·lio·rate \ˈmēl-yə-ˌrāt, ˈmē-lē-ə-\ *vb* **-rat·ed; -rat·ing** : to make or become better — **me·lio·ra·tion** \ˌmēl-yə-ˈrā-shən, ˌmē-lē-ə-\ *n* — **me·lio·ra·tive** \ˈmēl-yə-ˌrāt-iv, ˈmē-lē-ə-\ *adj*
mel·lif·lu·ous \me-ˈlif-lə-wəs, mə-\ *adj* [LL *mellifluus*, fr. L *mel* honey + *fluere* to flow] : sweetly flowing — **mel·lif·lu·ous·ly** *adv* — **mel·lif·lu·ous·ness** *n*
[1]**mel·low** \ˈmel-ō\ *adj* **1** : soft and sweet because of ripeness ⟨~ apple⟩; *also* : well aged and pleasingly mild ⟨~ wine⟩ **2** : made gentle by age or experience **3** : being rich and full but not garish or strident ⟨~ colors⟩ **4** : of soft loamy consistency ⟨~ soil⟩ — **mel·low·ness** *n*
[2]**mellow** *vb* : to make or become mellow
me·lo·de·on \mə-ˈlōd-ē-ən\ *n* : a small reed organ in which a suction bellows draws air inward through the reeds
me·lo·di·ous \mə-ˈlōd-ē-əs\ *adj* : pleasing to the ear — **me·lo·di·ous·ly** *adv* — **me·lo·di·ous·ness** *n*
melo·dra·ma \ˈmel-ə-ˌdräm-ə, -ˌdram-\ *n* : an extravagantly theatrical play in which action and plot predominate over characterization — **melo·dra·mat·ic** \ˌmel-ə-drə-ˈmat-ik\ *adj* — **melo·dra·ma·tist** \ˌmel-ə-ˈdram-ət-əst, -ˈdräm-\ *n*
mel·o·dy \ˈmel-əd-ē\ *n, pl* **-dies 1** : sweet or agreeable sound ⟨birds making ~⟩ **2** : a particular succession of notes : TUNE, AIR — **me·lod·ic** \mə-ˈläd-ik\ *adj* — **me·lod·i·cal·ly** \-i-k(ə-)lē\ *adv*
mel·on \ˈmel-ən\ *n* : any of certain fruits (as a muskmelon or watermelon) of the gourd family usu. eaten raw
[1]**melt** \ˈmelt\ *vb* **1** : to change from a solid to a liquid state usu. by heat **2** : DISSOLVE, DISINTEGRATE; *also* : to cause to disperse or disappear **3** : to make or become tender or gentle
[2]**melt** *n* : a melted substance
melt·down \ˈmelt-ˌdau̇n\ *n* : the melting of the core of a nuclear reactor
melt·wa·ter \ˈmelt-ˌwȯt-ər, -ˌwät-\ *n* : water derived from the melting of ice and snow
mem *abbr* **1** member **2** memoir **3** memorial
mem·ber \ˈmem-bər\ *n* **1** : a part (as an arm, leg, or branch) of a person, lower animal, or plant **2** : one of the individuals composing a group **3** : a constituent part of a whole
mem·ber·ship \-ˌship\ *n* **1** : the state or status of being a member **2** : the body of members
mem·brane \ˈmem-ˌbrān\ *n* : a thin pliable layer esp. of animal or plant tissue — **mem·bra·nous** \-brə-nəs\ *adj*
me·men·to \mə-ˈment-ō\ *n, pl* **-tos** *or* **-toes** [ME, fr. L remember] : something that serves to warn or remind : SOUVENIR
memo \ˈmem-ō\ *n, pl* **mem·os** : MEMORANDUM
mem·oir \ˈmem-ˌwär\ *n* **1** : MEMORANDUM **2** : AUTOBIOGRAPHY — usu. used in pl. **3** : an account of something noteworthy; *also, pl* : the record of the proceedings of a learned society
mem·o·ra·bil·ia \ˌmem-ə-rə-ˈbil-ē-ə, -ˈbil-yə\ *n pl* [L] : things worthy of remembrance; *also* : a record of such things
mem·o·ra·ble \ˈmem-(ə-)rə-bəl\ *adj* : worth remembering : NOTABLE — **mem·o·ra·bil·i·ty** \ˌmem-ə-rə-ˈbil-ət-ē\ *n* — **mem·o·ra·ble·ness** *n* — **mem·o·ra·bly** \-blē\ *adv*
mem·o·ran·dum \ˌmem-ə-ˈran-dəm\ *n, pl* **-dums** *or* **-da** \-də\ **1** : an informal record; *also* : a written reminder **2** : an informal written note
[1]**me·mo·ri·al** \mə-ˈmōr-ē-əl\ *adj* : serving to preserve remembrance
[2]**memorial** *n* **1** : something designed to keep remembrance

alive; *esp* : MONUMENT **2** : a statement of facts often accompanied with a petition — **me·mo·ri·al·ize** *vb*

Memorial Day *n* : the last Monday in May or formerly May 30 observed as a legal holiday in honor of those who died in war

mem·o·rize \ˈmem-ə-ˌrīz\ *vb* **-rized; -riz·ing** : to learn by heart — **mem·o·ri·za·tion** \ˌmem-(ə-)rə-ˈzā-shən\ *n* — **mem·o·riz·er** \ˈmem-ə-ˌrīz-ər\ *n*

mem·o·ry \ˈmem-(ə-)rē\ *n, pl* **-ries** **1** : the power or process of remembering **2** : the store of things remembered **3** : COMMEMORATION **4** : something remembered **5** : the time within which past events are remembered **6** : a device (as in a computer) in which information can be stored **syn** remembrance, recollection, reminiscence

men *pl of* MAN

[1]**men·ace** \ˈmen-əs\ *n* **1** : THREAT **2** : DANGER; *also* : NUISANCE

[2]**menace** *vb* **men·aced; men·ac·ing** **1** : THREATEN **2** : ENDANGER — **men·ac·ing·ly** *adv*

mé·nage \mā-ˈnäzh\ *n* [F] : HOUSEHOLD

me·nag·er·ie \mə-ˈnaj-(ə-)rē\ *n* : a collection of wild animals esp. for exhibition

[1]**mend** \ˈmend\ *vb* **1** : to improve in manners or morals **2** : to put into good shape : REPAIR **3** : to restore to health : HEAL — **mend·er** *n*

[2]**mend** *n* **1** : an act of mending **2** : a mended place

men·da·cious \men-ˈdā-shəs\ *adj* : given to deception or falsehood : UNTRUTHFUL **syn** dishonest, deceitful — **men·da·cious·ly** *adv* — **men·dac·i·ty** \-ˈdas-ət-ē\ *n*

men·de·le·vi·um \ˌmen-də-ˈlē-vē-əm, -ˈlā-\ *n* : a radioactive chemical element artificially produced — see ELEMENT table

men·di·cant \ˈmen-di-kənt\ *n* **1** : BEGGAR **2** *often cap* : FRIAR — **men·di·can·cy** \-kən-sē\ *n* — **mendicant** *adj*

men·folk \ˈmen-ˌfōk\ *or* **men·folks** \-ˌfōks\ *n pl* **1** : men in general **2** : the men of a family or community

men·ha·den \men-ˈhād-ᵊn, mən-\ *n, pl* **-den** *also* **-dens** : a marine fish related to the herring that is abundant along the Atlantic coast of the U.S.

[1]**me·nial** \ˈmē-nē-əl, -nyəl\ *adj* **1** : of or relating to servants **2** : HUMBLE; *also* : SERVILE — **me·ni·al·ly** \-ē\ *adv*

[2]**menial** *n* : a domestic servant

men·in·gi·tis \ˌmen-ən-ˈjīt-əs\ *n, pl* **-git·i·des** \-ˈjit-ə-ˌdēz\ : inflammation of the membranes enclosing the brain and spinal cord; *also* : a usu. bacterial disease marked by this

me·ninx \ˈmē-niŋks, ˈmen-iŋks\ *n, pl* **me·nin·ges** \mə-ˈnin-(ˌ)jēz\ : any of the three membranes that envelop the brain and spinal cord — **men·in·ge·al** \ˌmen-ən-ˈjē-əl\ *adj*

me·nis·cus \mə-ˈnis-kəs\ *n, pl* **me·nis·ci** \-ˈnis-ˌ(k)ī, -ˌkē\ *also* **me·nis·cus·es** **1** : CRESCENT **2** : the curved upper surface of a column of liquid

meno·pause \ˈmen-ə-ˌpȯz\ *n* : the period of natural cessation of menstruation — **meno·paus·al** \ˌmen-ə-ˈpȯ-zəl\ *adj*

men·ses \ˈmen-ˌsēz\ *n pl* : the menstrual flow

men·stru·a·tion \ˌmen-strə-ˈwā-shən, men-ˈstrā-\ *n* : a discharging of bloody matter at approximately monthly intervals from the uterus of breeding-age nonpregnant primate females — **men·stru·al** \ˈmen-strə(-wə)l\ *adj* — **men·stru·ate** \ˈmen-strə-ˌwāt, -ˌstrāt\ *vb*

men·su·ra·ble \ˈmens-(ə-)rə-bəl, ˈmench-(ə-)rə-\ *adj* : MEASURABLE

men·su·ra·tion \ˌmen-sə-ˈrā-shən, ˌmen-chə-\ *n* : MEASUREMENT

-ment \mənt\ *n suffix* **1** : concrete result, object, or agent of a (specified) action ⟨embank*ment*⟩ ⟨entangle*ment*⟩ **2** : concrete means or instrument of a (specified) action ⟨entertain*ment*⟩ **3** : action : process ⟨encircle*ment*⟩ ⟨develop*ment*⟩ **4** : place of a (specified) action ⟨encamp*ment*⟩ **5** : state : condition ⟨amaze*ment*⟩

men·tal \ˈment-ᵊl\ *adj* **1** : of or relating to the mind **2** : of, relating to, or affected with a disorder of the mind — **men·tal·ly** \-ē\ *adv*

mental age *n* : a measure used in psychological testing that expresses a person's mental attainment in terms of the number of years it takes the average child to reach the same level

mental deficiency *n* : failure in intellectual development that results in social incompetence and is considered to be the result of a defective central nervous system

men·tal·i·ty \men-ˈtal-ət-ē\ *n, pl* **-ties** **1** : mental power or capacity **2** : mode or way of thought

men·thol \ˈmen-ˌthȯl, -ˌthōl\ *n* : a white soothing substance from oil of peppermint — **men·tho·lat·ed** \-thə-ˌlāt-əd\ *adj*

[1]**men·tion** \ˈmen-chən\ *n* **1** : a brief or casual reference **2** : a formal citation for outstanding achievement

[2]**mention** *vb* **men·tioned; men·tion·ing** \ˈmench-(ə-)niŋ\ **1** : to refer to : CITE **2** : to cite for outstanding achievement — **not to mention** : AS WELL AS

men·tor \ˈmen-ˌtȯr, ˈment-ər\ *n* : a trusted counselor or guide; *also* : TUTOR, COACH

menu \ˈmen-yü, ˈmān-\ *n, pl* **menus** [F, fr. *menu* small, detailed, fr. L *minutus* minute (adj.)] : a list of the dishes available (as in a restaurant) for a meal; *also* : the dishes served

me·ow \mē-ˈaů\ *vb* : to make the characteristic cry of a cat — **meow** *n*

me·phit·ic \mə-ˈfit-ik\ *adj* : foul-smelling

mer *abbr* meridian

mer·can·tile \ˈmər-kən-ˌtēl, -ˌtīl\ *adj* : of or relating to merchants or trading

[1]**mer·ce·nary** \ˈmərs-ᵊn-ˌer-ē\ *n, pl* **-nar·ies** : one who serves merely for wages; *esp* : a soldier serving in a foreign army

[2]**mercenary** *adj* **1** : serving merely for pay or gain **2** : hired for service in a foreign army — **mer·ce·nari·ly** \ˌmərs-ᵊn-ˈer-ə-lē\ *adv* — **mer·ce·nari·ness** \ˈmərs-ᵊn-ˌer-ē-nəs\ *n*

mer·cer \ˈmər-sər\ *n* : a dealer in usu. expensive fabrics

mer·cer·ize \ˈmər-sə-ˌrīz\ *vb* **-ized; -iz·ing** : to treat cotton yarn or cloth with alkali so that it looks silky or takes a better dye

[1]**mer·chan·dise** \ˈmər-chən-ˌdīz, -ˌdīs\ *n* : the commodities or goods that are bought and sold in business

[2]**mer·chan·dise** \-ˌdīz\ *vb* **-dised; -dis·ing** : to buy and sell in business : TRADE — **mer·chan·dis·er** *n*

mer·chant \ˈmər-chənt\ *n* **1** : a buyer and seller of commodities for profit **2** : STOREKEEPER

mer·chant·able \ˈmər-chənt-ə-bəl\ *adj* : acceptable to buyers : MARKETABLE

mer·chant·man \ˈmər-chənt-mən\ *n* : a ship used in commerce

merchant marine *n* : the commercial ships of a nation

merchant ship *n* : MERCHANTMAN

mer·cu·ri·al \ˌmər-ˈkyůr-ē-əl\ *adj* **1** : unpredictably changeable **2** : MERCURIC — **mer·cu·ri·al·ly** \-ē\ *adv* — **mer·cu·ri·al·ness** *n*

mer·cu·ric \ˌmər-ˈkyůr-ik\ *adj* : of, relating to, or containing mercury

mercuric chloride *n* : a poisonous compound of mercury and chlorine used as an antiseptic and fungicide

mer·cu·ry \ˈmər-kyə-rē\ *n, pl* **-ries** **1** : a heavy silver-white liquid metallic chemical element used esp. in scientific instruments — see ELEMENT table **2** *cap* : the planet nearest the sun

mer·cy \ˈmər-sē\ *n, pl* **mercies** [ME, fr. OF *merci*, fr. ML *merces*, fr. L, price paid, wages, fr. *merc-*, *merx* merchandise] **1** : compassion shown to an offender; *also*

: imprisonment rather than death for first-degree murder **2** : a blessing resulting from divine favor or compassion; *also* : a fortunate circumstance **3** : compassion shown to victims of misfortune — **mer·ci·ful** \-si-fəl\ *adj* — **mer·ci·ful·ly** \-ē\ *adv* — **mer·ci·less** \-si-ləs\ *adj* — **mer·ci·less·ly** *adv* — **mercy** *adj*

mercy killing *n* : the act or practice of killing or permitting the death of hopelessly sick or injured persons or animals with as little pain as possible for reasons of mercy

¹mere \ˈmiər\ *n* : LAKE, POOL

²mere *adj* **mer·est 1** : being nothing more than : BARE **2** : not diluted : PURE — **mere·ly** *adv*

mer·e·tri·cious \ˌmer-ə-ˈtrish-əs\ *adj* [L *meretricius,* fr. *meretrix* prostitute, fr. *merēre* to earn] : tawdrily attractive; *also* : SPECIOUS — **mer·e·tri·cious·ly** *adv* — **mer·e·tri·cious·ness** *n*

mer·gan·ser \(ˌ)mər-ˈgan-sər\ *n* : any of various fish-eating ducks with a crested head and a slender bill hooked at the end and serrated along the margins

merge \ˈmərj\ *vb* **merged; merg·ing 1** : to blend gradually **2** : to combine, unite, or coalesce into one **syn** mingle, amalgamate, fuse, interfuse, intermingle

merg·er \ˈmər-jər\ *n* **1** : the act or process of merging **2** : absorption by a corporation of one or more others

me·rid·i·an \mə-ˈrid-ē-ən\ *n* [ME, fr. MF *meridien,* fr. *meridien* of noon, fr. L *meridianus,* fr. *meridies* noon, south, irreg. fr. *medius* mid + *dies* day] **1** : the highest point : CULMINATION **2** : one of the imaginary circles on the earth's surface passing through the north and south poles — **meridian** *adj*

me·ringue \mə-ˈraŋ\ *n* [F] : a dessert topping of baked beaten egg whites and powdered sugar

me·ri·no \mə-ˈrē-nō\ *n, pl* **-nos** [Sp] **1** : any of a breed of sheep noted for fine soft wool; *also* : its wool or fleece **2** : a fine soft fabric or yarn of wool or wool and cotton

¹mer·it \ˈmer-ət\ *n* **1** : laudable or blameworthy traits or actions **2** : a praiseworthy quality; *also* : character or conduct deserving reward or honor **3** *pl* : the intrinsic nature of a legal case; *also* : legal significance

²merit *vb* : EARN, DESERVE

mer·i·toc·ra·cy \ˌmer-ə-ˈtäk-rə-sē\ *n, pl* **-cies** : an educational system where-by the talented are chosen and moved ahead on the basis of their achievement; *also* : leadership by the talented

mer·i·to·ri·ous \ˌmer-ə-ˈtōr-ē-əs\ *adj* : deserving honor or esteem — **mer·i·to·ri·ous·ly** *adv* — **mer·i·to·ri·ous·ness** *n*

mer·maid \ˈmər-ˌmād\ *n* : a legendary sea creature with a woman's upper body and a fish's tail

mer·man \-ˌman, -mən\ *n* : a legendary sea creature with a man's upper body and a fish's tail

mer·ri·ment \ˈmer-i-mənt\ *n* **1** : HILARITY **2** : FESTIVITY

mer·ry \ˈmer-ē\ *adj* **mer·ri·er; -est 1** : full of gaiety or high spirits **2** : marked by festivity **3** : BRISK ⟨a ~ pace⟩ **syn** blithe, jocund, jovial, jolly, mirthful — **mer·ri·ly** \ˈmer-ə-lē\ *adv*

merry–go–round \ˈmer-ē-gō-ˌraund\ *n* **1** : a circular revolving platform with benches and figures of animals on which people sit for a ride **2** : a busy round of activities

mer·ry·mak·ing \ˈmer-ē-ˌmā-kiŋ\ *n* **1** : CONVIVIALITY **2** : a festive occasion — **mer·ry·mak·er** \-ˌmā-kər\ *n*

me·sa \ˈmā-sə\ *n* [Sp, lit., table, fr. L *mensa*] : a flat-topped hill with steep sides

més·al·liance \ˌmā-ˌzal-ˈyäⁿs, ˌmā-zə-ˈlī-əns\ *n, pl* **més·al·liances** \-ˈyäⁿs(-əz), -ˈlī-ən-səz\ [F] : a marriage with a person of inferior social position

mes·cal \me-ˈskal, mə-\ *n* **1** : a small cactus that is the source of a stimulant used esp. by Mexican Indians **2** : a usu. colorless liquor distilled from the leaves of an agave; *also* : AGAVE

mes·ca·line \ˈmes-kə-lən, -ˌlēn\ *n* : a hallucinatory alkaloid from the mescal cactus

mesdames *pl of* MADAM *or of* MADAME *or of* MRS.

mesdemoiselles *pl of* MADEMOISELLE

¹mesh \ˈmesh\ *n* **1** : one of the openings between the threads or cords of a net; *also* : one of the similar spaces in a network **2** : the fabric of a net **3** : NETWORK **4** : working contact (as of the teeth of gears) ⟨in ~⟩ — **meshed** \ˈmesht\ *adj*

²mesh *vb* **1** : to catch in or as if in a mesh **2** : to be in or come into mesh : ENGAGE **3** : to fit together properly

mesh·work \ˈmesh-ˌwərk\ *n* : NETWORK

me·si·al \ˈmē-zē-əl, -sē-\ *adj* : of, relating to, or being the surface of a tooth that is closest to the middle of the front of the jaw

mes·mer·ize \ˈmez-mə-ˌrīz\ *vb* **-ized; -iz·ing** : HYPNOTIZE — **mes·mer·ic** \mez-ˈmer-ik\ *adj* — **mes·mer·ism** \ˈmez-mə-ˌriz-əm\ *n*

Me·so·lith·ic \ˌmez-ə-ˈlith-ik\ *adj* : of, relating to, or being a transitional period of the Stone Age between the Paleolithic and the Neolithic periods

me·so·sphere \ˈmez-ə-ˌsfiər\ *n* : a layer of the atmosphere above the stratosphere

Me·so·zo·ic \ˌmez-ə-ˈzō-ik, ˌmēz-\ *adj* : of, relating to, or being the era of geologic history between the Paleozoic and the Cenozoic and extending from about 230 million years ago to about 70 million years ago — **Mesozoic** *n*

mes·quite \mə-ˈskēt, me-\ *n* : a thorny leguminous shrub of Mexico and the southwestern U.S. with sugar-rich pods important as fodder

¹mess \ˈmes\ *n* **1** : a quantity of food; *also* : enough food of a specified kind for a dish or meal ⟨a ~ of beans⟩ **2** : a group of persons who regularly eat together; *also* : a meal eaten by such a group **3** : a confused, dirty, or offensive state — **messy** *adj*

²mess *vb* **1** : to supply with meals; *also* : to take meals with a mess **2** : to make dirty or untidy; *also* : BUNGLE **3** : INTERFERE, MEDDLE **4** : PUTTER, TRIFLE

mes·sage \ˈmes-ij\ *n* : a communication sent by one person to another

messeigneurs *pl of* MONSEIGNEUR

mes·sen·ger \ˈmes-ᵊn-jər\ *n* : one who carries a message or does an errand

messenger RNA *n* : an RNA that carries the code for a particular protein from the nuclear DNA to a ribosome in the cytoplasm and acts as a template for the formation of that protein

Mes·si·ah \mə-ˈsī-ə\ *n* **1** : the expected king and deliverer of the Jews **2** : Jesus **3** *not cap* : a professed or accepted leader of a cause — **mes·si·an·ic** \ˌmes-ē-ˈan-ik\ *adj*

messieurs *pl of* MONSIEUR

mess·mate \ˈmes-ˌmāt\ *n* : a member of a group who eat regularly together

Messrs. \ˌmes-ərz\ *pl of* MR.

mes·ti·zo \me-ˈstē-zō\ *n, pl* **-zos** [Sp, fr. *mestizo* mixed, fr. LL *mixticius,* fr. L *mixtus,* pp. of *miscēre* to mix] : a person of mixed blood

¹met *past and past part of* MEET

²met *abbr* metropolitan

me·tab·o·lism \mə-ˈtab-ə-ˌliz-əm\ *n* : the sum of the processes in the building up and breaking down of the substance of plants and animals incidental to life; *also* : the processes by which a substance is handled in the body ⟨~ of sugar⟩ — **met·a·bol·ic** \ˌmet-ə-ˈbäl-ik\ *adj* — **me·tab·o·lize** \mə-ˈtab-ə-ˌlīz\ *vb*

me·tab·o·lite \-ˌlīt\ *n* **1** : a product of metabolism **2** : a substance essential to the metabolism of a particular organism

meta·car·pal \ˌmet-ə-ˈkär-pəl\ *n* : any of usu. five more or less elongated bones of the part of the hand or forefoot between the carpus and the bones of the digits — **metacarpal** *adj*

meta·car·pus \-ˈkär-pəs\ *n* : the part of the hand or forefoot that contains the metacarpals

met·al \ˈmet-ᵊl\ *n* **1** : any of various opaque, fusible, ductile, and typically lustrous substances; *esp* : one that is a chemical element **2** : METTLE; *also* : the material out of which a person or thing is made — **me·tal·lic** \mə-ˈtal-ik\ *adj* — **met·al·loid** \ˈmet-ᵊl-ˌȯid\ *n or adj*

met·al·lur·gy \ˈmet-ᵊl-ˌər-jē\ *n* : the science and technology of metals — **met·al·lur·gi·cal** \ˌmet-ᵊl-ˈər-ji-kəl\ *adj* — **met·al·lur·gist** \ˈmet-ᵊl-ˌər-jəst\ *n*

met·al·ware \ˈmet-ᵊl-ˌwaər\ *n* : metal utensils for household use

met·al·work \-ˌwərk\ *n* : work and esp. artistic work made of metal — **met·al·work·er** \-ˌwər-kər\ *n* — **met·al·work·ing** \-ˌwər-kiŋ\ *n*

meta·mor·phism \ˌmet-ə-ˈmȯr-ˌfiz-əm\ *n* : a change in the structure of rock; *esp* : a change to a more compact highly crystalline condition produced by pressure, heat, and water — **met·a·mor·phic** \-ˈmȯr-fik\ *adj*

meta·mor·pho·sis \ˌmet-ə-ˈmȯr-fə-səs\ *n, pl* **-pho·ses** \-ˌsēz\ **1** : a change of physical form, structure, or substance esp. by supernatural means; *also* : a striking alteration (as in appearance or character) **2** : a fundamental change in form and often habits of an animal accompanying the transformation of a larva into an adult — **met·a·mor·phose** \-ˌfōz, -ˌfōs\ *vb*

met·a·phor \ˈmet-ə-ˌfȯr\ *n* : a figure of speech in which a word denoting one subject or idea is used in place of another to suggest a likeness between them (as in "the ship plows the sea") — **met·a·phor·i·cal** \ˌmet-ə-ˈfȯr-i-kəl\ *adj*

meta·phys·ics \ˌmet-ə-ˈfiz-iks\ *n* [ML *Metaphysica*, title of Aristotle's treatise on the subject, fr. Gk *(ta) meta (ta) physika*, lit., the (works) after the physical (works); fr. its position in his collected works] : the part of philosophy concerned with the study of the ultimate causes and underlying nature of things — **meta·phys·i·cal** \-ˈfiz-i-kəl\ *adj* — **meta·phy·si·cian** \-fə-ˈzish-ən\ *n*

me·tas·ta·sis \mə-ˈtas-tə-səs\ *n, pl* **-ta·ses** \-ˌsēz\ : transfer of a health-impairing agency (as tumor cells) to a new site in the body; *also* : a secondary growth of a malignant tumor — **met·a·stat·ic** \ˌmet-ə-ˈstat-ik\ *adj*

meta·tar·sal \ˌmet-ə-ˈtär-səl\ *n* : any of the bones of the foot between the tarsus and the bones of the digits that in human beings include five more or less elongated bones — **metatarsal** *adj*

meta·tar·sus \-ˈtär-səs\ *n* : the part of the foot in man or of the hind foot in quadrupeds that contains the metatarsals

[1]**mete** \ˈmēt\ *vb* **met·ed; met·ing 1** *archaic* : MEASURE **2** : ALLOT

[2]**mete** *n* : BOUNDARY ⟨~*s* and bounds⟩

me·tem·psy·cho·sis \mə-ˌtem(p)-si-ˈkō-səs, ˌmet-əm-ˌsī-\ *n* : the passing of the soul at death into another body either human or animal

me·te·or \ˈmēt-ē-ər, -ē-ˌȯr\ *n* **1** : a usu. small particle of matter in the solar system observable only when it falls into the earth's atmosphere where friction causes it to glow **2** : the streak of light produced by passage of a meteor

me·te·or·ic \ˌmēt-ē-ˈȯr-ik\ *adj* **1** : of, relating to, or resembling a meteor **2** : transiently brilliant ⟨a ~ career⟩ — **me·te·or·i·cal·ly** \-i-k(ə-)lē\ *adv*

me·te·or·ite \ˈmēt-ē-ə-ˌrīt\ *n* : a meteor that reaches the surface of the earth

me·te·or·oid \ˈmēt-ē-ə-ˌrȯid\ *n* : a meteor in orbit around the sun

me·te·o·rol·o·gy \ˌmēt-ē-ə-ˈräl-ə-jē\ *n* : a science that deals with the atmosphere and its phenomena and esp. with weather and weather forecasting — **me·te·o·ro·log·ic** \ˌmēt-ē-ˌȯr-ə-ˈläj-ik\ *or* **me·te·o·ro·log·i·cal** \-ˈläj-i-kəl\ *adj* — **me·te·o·rol·o·gist** \ˌmēt-ē-ə-ˈräl-ə-jəst\ *n*

[1]**me·ter** \ˈmēt-ər\ *n* : rhythm in verse or music

[2]**met·er** \ˈmēt-ər\ *n* : the basic metric unit of length — see METRIC SYSTEM table

[3]**me·ter** \ˈmēt-ər\ *n* : a measuring and sometimes recording instrument

[4]**me·ter** *vb* **1** : to measure by means of a meter **2** : to print postal indicia on by means of a postage meter ⟨~*ed* mail⟩

meter–kilogram–second *adj* : MKS

meter maid *n* : a female member of a police department who is assigned to write tickets for parking violations

meth·a·done \ˈmeth-ə-ˌdōn\ *also* **meth·a·don** \-ˌdän\ *n* : a synthetic addictive narcotic drug used esp. as a substitute narcotic in the treatment of heroin addiction

meth·am·phet·amine \ˌmeth-am-ˈfet-ə-ˌmēn, ˌmeth-əm-, -mən\ *n* : a drug used in the form of its hydrochloride as a stimulant for the central nervous system and in the treatment of obesity

meth·ane \ˈmeth-ˌān\ *n* : a colorless odorless flammable gas produced by decomposition of organic matter (as in marshes) or from coal and used as a fuel

meth·a·nol \ˈmeth-ə-ˌnȯl, -ˌnōl\ *n* : a volatile flammable poisonous liquid alcohol that consists of carbon, hydrogen, and oxygen and that is used esp. as a solvent and as an antifreeze

meth·aqua·lone \me-ˈthak-wə-ˌlōn\ *n* : a sedative and hypnotic habit-forming drug that is not a barbiturate

meth·od \ˈmeth-əd\ *n* [MF *methode*, fr. L *methodus*, fr. Gk *methodos*, fr. *meta* with + *hodos* way] **1** : a procedure or process for achieving an end **2** : orderly arrangement : PLAN **syn** mode, manner, way, fashion, system — **me·thod·i·cal** \mə-ˈthäd-i-kəl\ *adj* — **me·thod·i·cal·ly** \-k(ə-)lē\ *adv* — **me·thod·i·cal·ness** *n*

Meth·od·ist \ˈmeth-əd-əst\ *n* : a member of a Protestant denomination adhering to the doctrines of John Wesley — **Meth·od·ism** \-ə-ˌdiz-əm\ *n*

meth·od·ize \ˈmeth-ə-ˌdīz\ *vb* **-ized; -iz·ing** : SYSTEMATIZE

meth·od·ol·o·gy \ˌmeth-ə-ˈdäl-ə-jē\ *n, pl* **-gies 1** : a body of methods and rules followed in a science or discipline **2** : the study of the principles or procedures of inquiry in a particular field

meth·yl \ˈmeth-əl\ *n* : a chemical group consisting of carbon and hydrogen

methyl alcohol *n* : METHANOL

meth·yl·mer·cury \ˌmeth-əl-ˈmər-kyə-rē\ *n* : any of various toxic compounds of mercury that tend to accumulate in animals esp. at the top of a food chain

met·i·cal \ˈmet-i-kəl\ *n* — see MONEY table

me·tic·u·lous \mə-ˈtik-yə-ləs\ *adj* [L *meticulosus* timid, fr. *metus* fear] : extremely careful in attending to details — **me·tic·u·lous·ly** *adv* — **me·tic·u·lous·ness** *n*

mé·tier \ˈme-ˌtyā, me-ˈtyā\ *n* : an area of activity in which one is expert or successful

me·tre \ˈmēt-ər\ *chiefly Brit var of* METER

met·ric \ˈme-trik\ *adj* **1** : of or relating to measurement; *esp* : of or relating to the metric system **2** : METRICAL 1

met·ri·cal \ˈme-tri-kəl\ *adj* **1** : of, relating to, or composed in meter **2** : METRIC 1 — **met·ri·cal·ly** \-tri-k(ə-)lē\ *adv*

met·ri·ca·tion \ˌme-tri-ˈkā-shən\ *n* : the act or process of converting into or expressing in the metric system

met·ri·cize \ˈme-trə-ˌsīz\ *vb* **-cized; -ciz·ing** : to change into or express in the metric system

metric system *n* : a decimal system of weights and measures based on the meter and on the kilogram ☞ see next page

metric ton *n* — see METRIC SYSTEM table

[1]**met·ro** \ˈme-trō\ *n, pl* **metros** : SUBWAY

[2]**metro** *adj* : of, relating to, or characteristic of a metropolis and sometimes including its suburbs

me·trol·o·gy \me-ˈträl-ə-jē\ *n* : the science of weights and measures or of measurement

METRIC SYSTEM[1]

LENGTH

unit	abbreviation	number of meters	approximate U.S. equivalent
kilometer	km	1,000	0.62 mile
hectometer	hm	100	109.36 yards
dekameter	dam	10	32.81 feet
meter	m	1	39.37 inches
decimeter	dm	0.1	3.94 inches
centimeter	cm	0.01	0.39 inch
millimeter	mm	0.001	0.039 inch

AREA

unit	abbreviation	number of square meters	approximate U.S. equivalent
square kilometer	sq km *or* km^2	1,000,000	0.3861 square mile
hectare	ha	10,000	2.47 acres
are	a	100	119.60 square yards
square centimeter	sq cm *or* cm^2	0.0001	0.155 square inch

VOLUME

unit	abbreviation	number of cubic meters	approximate U.S. equivalent
cubic meter	m^3	1	1.307 cubic yards
cubic decimeter	dm^3	0.10	61.023 cubic inches
cubic centimeter	cu cm *or* cm^3 *also* cc	0.000001	0.061 cubic inch

CAPACITY

unit	abbreviation	number of liters	approximate U.S. equivalent *cubic*	*dry*	*liquid*
kiloliter	kl	1,000	1.31 cubic yards		
hectoliter	hl	100	3.53 cubic feet	2.84 bushels	
dekaliter	dal	10	0.35 cubic foot	1.14 pecks	2.64 gallons
liter	l	1	61.02 cubic inches	0.908 quart	1.057 quarts
deciliter	dl	0.1	6.1 cubic inches	0.18 pint	0.21 pint
centiliter	cl	0.01	0.61 cubic inch		0.338 fluidounce
milliliter	ml	0.001	0.061 cubic inch		0.27 fluidram

MASS AND WEIGHT

unit	abbreviation	number of grams	approximate U.S. equivalent
metric ton	t	1,000,000	1.102 short tons
kilogram	kg	1,000	2.2046 pounds
hectogram	hg	100	3.527 ounces
dekagram	dag	10	0.353 ounce
gram	g	1	0.035 ounce
decigram	dg	0.10	1.543 grains
centigram	cg	0.01	0.154 grain
milligram	mg	0.001	0.015 grain

[1]For metric equivalents of U.S. units see Weights and Measures table

met·ro·nome \ˈme-trə-ˌnōm\ *n* **:** an instrument for marking exact time by a regularly repeated tick

me·trop·o·lis \mə-ˈträp-(ə-)ləs\ *n* [LL, fr. Gk *mētropolis*, fr. *mētēr* mother + *polis* city] **:** the chief or capital city of a country, state, or region — **met·ro·pol·i·tan** \ˌme-trə-ˈpäl-ət-ᵊn\ *adj*

met·tle \ˈmet-ᵊl\ *n* **1 :** quality of temperament **2 :** SPIRIT, COURAGE

met·tle·some \ˈmet-ᵊl-səm\ *adj* **:** full of mettle

MeV *abbr* million electron volts

mew \ˈmyü\ *vb* **:** CONFINE

mews \ˈmyüz\ *n pl, chiefly Brit* **:** stables usu. with living quarters built around a court; *also* **:** a narrow street with dwellings converted from stables

Mex *abbr* Mexican; Mexico

Mex·i·can \ˈmek-si-kən\ *n* **:** a native or inhabitant of Mexico — **Mexican** *adj*

mez·za·nine \ˈmez-ᵊn-ˌēn, ˌmez-ᵊn-ˈēn\ *n* **1 :** a low-ceilinged story between two main stories of a building **2 :** the lowest balcony in a theater; *also* **:** the first few rows of such a balcony

mez·zo–so·pra·no \ˌmet-sō-sə-ˈpran-ō, ˌme(d)z-\ *n* **:** a woman's voice having a range between that of the soprano and contralto; *also* **:** a singer having such a voice

MF *abbr* medium frequency

MFA *abbr* master of fine arts

mg *abbr* milligram

Mg *symbol* magnesium

MG *abbr* **1** machine gun **2** major general **3** military government

mgr *abbr* **1** manager **2** monseigneur **3** monsignor

mgt *or* **mgmt** *abbr* management

MGy Sgt *abbr* master gunnery sergeant

MHz *abbr* megahertz

mi *abbr* **1** mile; mileage **2** mill

MI *abbr* **1** Michigan **2** military intelligence

MIA \ˈem-ˈī-ˈā\ *n* [*m*issing *i*n *a*ction] **:** a member of the armed forces whose whereabouts following a combat mission are unknown

Mi·ami \mī-ˈam-ē, -ˈam-ə\ *n, pl* **Mi·ami** *or* **Mi·am·is :** a member of an American Indian people orig. of Wisconsin and Indiana

mi·as·ma \mī-ˈaz-mə, mē-\ *n, pl* **-mas** *also* **-ma·ta** \-mət-ə\

: an exhalation formerly held to cause disease : a noxious vapor — **mi·as·mic** \-mik\ *adj*
Mic *abbr* Micah
mi·ca \ˈmī-kə\ *n* [NL, fr. L, grain, crumb] : any of various minerals readily separable into thin transparent sheets
Mi·cah \ˈmī-kə\ *n* — see BIBLE table
mice *pl of* MOUSE
Mich *abbr* Michigan
Mi·che·as \ˈmī-kē-əs, mī-ˈkē-əs\ *n* — see BIBLE table
Mic·mac \ˈmik-ˌmak\ *n, pl* **Micmac** *or* **Micmacs** : a member of an American Indian people of eastern Canada
micr- *or* **micro-** *comb form* **1** : small : minute **2** : one millionth part of a specified unit ⟨*micro*second⟩
[1]**mi·cro** \ˈmī-krō\ *adj* **1** : very small; *esp* : MICROSCOPIC **2** : involving minute quantities or variations
[2]**micro** *n* : MICROCOMPUTER
mi·crobe \ˈmī-ˌkrōb\ *n* : MICROORGANISM; *esp* : one causing disease — **mi·cro·bi·al** \mī-ˈkrō-bē-əl\ *adj*
mi·cro·bi·ol·o·gy \ˌmī-krō-bī-ˈäl-ə-jē\ *n* : a branch of biology dealing esp. with microscopic forms of life — **mi·cro·bi·o·log·i·cal** \ˈmī-krō-ˌbī-ə-ˈläj-i-kəl\ *adj* — **mi·cro·bi·ol·o·gist** \ˌmī-krō-bī-ˈäl-ə-jəst\ *n*
mi·cro·bus \ˈmī-krō-ˌbəs\ *n* : a station wagon shaped like a bus
mi·cro·cap·sule \-ˌkap-səl, -sül\ *n* : a tiny capsule containing material (as a medicine) that is released when the capsule is broken, melted, or dissolved
mi·cro·chip \-ˌchip\ *n* : INTEGRATED CIRCUIT
mi·cro·cir·cuit \-ˌsər-kət\ *n* : a compact electronic circuit
mi·cro·com·put·er \-kəm-ˌpyüt-ər\ *n* : a very small computer
mi·cro·copy \-ˌkäp-ē\ *n* : a photographic copy (as of print) on a reduced scale — **microcopy** *vb*
mi·cro·cosm \ˈmī-krə-ˌkäz-əm\ *n* : an individual or community thought of as a miniature world or universe
mi·cro·elec·tron·ics \ˈmī-krō-i-ˌlek-ˈträn-iks\ *n* : a branch of electronics that deals with the miniaturization of electronic circuits and components — **mi·cro·elec·tron·ic** \-ik\ *adj*
mi·cro·en·cap·su·late \ˌmī-krō-in-ˈkap-sə-ˌlāt\ *vb* : to enclose in a microcapsule ⟨*microencapsulated* aspirin⟩ — **mi·cro·en·cap·su·la·tion** \-in-ˌkap-sə-ˈlā-shən\ *n*
mi·cro·fiche \ˈmī-krō-ˌfēsh, -ˌfish\ *n, pl* **-fiche** *or* **-fiches** \-ˌfēsh(-əz), -ˌfish(-əz)\ : a sheet of microfilm containing rows of images of pages of printed matter
mi·cro·film \-ˌfilm\ *n* : a film bearing a photographic record (as of print) on a reduced scale — **microfilm** *vb*
mi·cro·graph \ˈmī-krə-ˌgraf\ *n* : a graphic reproduction of the image of an object formed by a microscope — **micrograph** *vb*
mi·cro·me·te·or·ite \ˌmī-krō-ˈmēt-ē-ə-ˌrīt\ *n* **1** : a meteorite particle of very small size **2** : a very small particle in interplanetary space
mi·crom·e·ter \mī-ˈkräm-ət-ər\ *n* : an instrument used with a telescope or microscope for measuring minute distances
mi·cro·min·ia·ture \ˌmī-krō-ˈmin-ē-ə-ˌchu̇r, -ˈmin-i-ˌchu̇r, -chər\ *adj* : MICROMINIATURIZED
mi·cro·min·ia·tur·iza·tion \-ˌmin-ē-ə-ˌchu̇r-ə-ˈzā-shən, -ˌmin-i-ˌchu̇r-, -chər-\ *n* : the process of producing microminiaturized things
mi·cro·min·ia·tur·ized \-ˈmin-ē-ə-chə-ˌrīzd, -ˈmin-i-chə-\ *adj* : reduced to or produced in a very small size and esp. in a size smaller than one considered miniature
mi·cron \ˈmī-ˌkrän\ *n, pl* **microns** *also* **mi·cra** \-krə\ : one millionth of a meter
mi·cro·or·gan·ism \ˌmī-krō-ˈȯr-gə-ˌniz-əm\ *n* : a living being (as a bacterium) too tiny to be seen by the unaided eye
mi·cro·phone \ˈmī-krə-ˌfōn\ *n* : an instrument for converting sound waves into variations of an electric current for transmitting or recording sound
mi·cro·pho·to·graph \ˌmī-krə-ˈfōt-ə-ˌgraf\ *n* : PHOTOMICROGRAPH
mi·cro·pro·ces·sor \ˌmi-krō-ˈpräs-ˌes-ər\ *n* : a computer processor contained on a microchip
mi·cro·scope \ˈmī-krə-ˌskōp\ *n* : an instrument for making magnified images of minute objects usu. using light — **mi·cros·co·py** \mī-ˈkräs-kə-pē\ *n*
mi·cro·scop·ic \ˌmī-krə-ˈskäp-ik\ *or* **mi·cro·scop·i·cal** \-i-kəl\ *adj* **1** : of, relating to, or involving the use of the microscope **2** : too tiny to be seen without the use of a microscope : very small — **mi·cro·scop·i·cal·ly** \-i-k(ə-)lē\ *adv*
mi·cro·sec·ond \ˌmī-krō-ˈsek-ənd\ *n* : one millionth of a second
mi·cro·state \ˈmī-krō-ˌstāt\ *n* : a nation that is extremely small in area and population
mi·cro·sur·gery \ˌmī-krō-ˈsərj-(ə-)rē\ *n* : minute dissection or manipulation (as by a laser beam) of living structures (as cells) for surgical or experimental purposes — **mi·cro·sur·gi·cal** \-ˈsər-ji-kəl\ *adj*
mi·cro·wave \ˈmī-krə-ˌwāv\ *n* : a radio wave between one millimeter and one meter in wavelength
microwave oven *n* : an oven in which food is cooked by the heat produced from microwave penetration of the food
[1]**mid** \ˈmid\ *adj* : MIDDLE
[2]**mid** *abbr* middle
mid·air \ˈmid-ˈaər\ *n* : a point or region in the air well above the ground
mid·day \ˈmid-ˌdā, -ˈdā\ *n* : NOON
mid·den \ˈmid-ᵊn\ *n* : a refuse heap
[1]**mid·dle** \ˈmid-ᵊl\ *adj* **1** : equally distant from the extremes : MEDIAL, CENTRAL **2** : being at neither extreme : INTERMEDIATE **3** *cap* : constituting an intermediate period
[2]**middle** *n* **1** : a middle part, point, or position **2** : WAIST
middle age *n* : the period of life from about 40 to about 60 — **mid·dle–aged** \ˌmid-ᵊl-ˈājd\ *adj*
Middle Ages *n pl* : the period of European history from about A.D. 500 to about 1500
mid·dle·brow \ˈmid-ᵊl-ˌbrau̇\ *n* : a person who is moderately but not highly cultivated
middle class *n* : a social class holding a position between the upper class and the lower class — **middle–class** *adj*
middle ear *n* : a small membrane-lined cavity of the ear through which sound waves are transmitted by a chain of tiny bones
middle finger *n* : the midmost of the five digits of the hand
mid·dle·man \ˈmid-ᵊl-ˌman\ *n* : INTERMEDIARY; *esp* : one intermediate between the producer of goods and the retailer or consumer
middle–of–the–road *adj* : standing for or following a course of action midway between extremes; *esp* : being neither liberal nor conservative in politics — **mid·dle–of–the–road·er** \-ˈrōd-ər\ *n* — **midd·dle–of–the–road·ism** \-ˈrōd-ˌiz-əm\ *n*
middle school *n* : a school usu. including grades 5 to 8 or 6 to 8
mid·dle·weight \ˈmid-ᵊl-ˌwāt\ *n* : one of average weight; *esp* : a boxer weighing more than 147 but not over 160 pounds
mid·dling \ˈmid-liŋ, -lən\ *adj* **1** : of middle, medium, or moderate size, degree, or quality **2** : MEDIOCRE
mid·dy \ˈmid-ē\ *n, pl* **middies** : MIDSHIPMAN
midge \ˈmij\ *n* : a very small fly : GNAT
midg·et \ˈmij-ət\ *n* **1** : a very small person : DWARF **2** : something (as an animal) very small of its kind
midi \ˈmid-ē\ *n* : a calf-length dress, coat, or skirt

mid·land \ˈmid-lənd, -ˌland\ *n* : the interior or central region of a country

mid–life \ˈmid-ˈlīf\ *n* : MIDDLE AGE

mid·most \-ˌmōst\ *adj* : being in or near the exact middle — **midmost** *adv*

mid·night \-ˌnīt\ *n* : 12 o'clock at night

midnight sun *n* : the sun above the horizon at midnight in the arctic or antarctic summer

mid·point \ˈmid-ˌpȯint, -ˈpȯint\ *n* : a point at or near the center or middle

mid·riff \ˈmid-ˌrif\ *n* [ME *midrif,* fr. OE *midhrif,* fr. *midde* mid + *hrif* belly] **1** : DIAPHRAGM 1 **2** : the mid-region of the human torso

mid·ship·man \ˈmid-ˌship-mən, (ˈ)mid-ˈship-mən\ *n* : a student in a naval academy

mid·ships \-ˌships\ *adv* : AMIDSHIPS

midst \ˈmidst\ *n* **1** : the interior or central part or point **2** : a position of proximity to the members of a group ⟨in our ~⟩ **3** : the condition of being surrounded or beset — **midst** *prep*

mid·stream \ˈmid-ˈstrēm, -ˌstrēm\ *n* : the middle of a stream

mid·sum·mer \-ˈsəm-ər, -ˌsəm-\ *n* **1** : the middle of summer **2** : the summer solstice

mid·town \ˈmid-ˌtau̇n, -ˈtau̇n\ *n* : a central section of a city; *esp* : one situated between sections called *downtown* and *uptown* — **midtown** *adj*

[1]**mid·way** \ˈmid-ˌwā, -ˈwā\ *adv* : in the middle of the way or distance

[2]**mid·way** \-ˌwā\ *n* : an avenue (as at a carnival) for concessions and light amusements

mid·week \-ˌwēk\ *n* : the middle of the week — **mid·week·ly** \-ˌwē-klē, -ˈwē-\ *adj or adv*

mid·wife \ˈmid-ˌwīf\ *n* : a woman who helps other women in childbirth — **mid·wife·ry** \-ˌwī-f(ə-)rē\ *n*

mid·win·ter \ˈmid-ˈwint-ər, -ˌwint-\ *n* **1** : the middle of winter **2** : the winter solstice

mid·year \-ˌyiər\ *n* **1** : the middle of a year **2** : a midyear examination — **midyear** *adj*

mien \ˈmēn\ *n* **1** : air or bearing esp. as expressive of mood or personality : DEMEANOR **2** : APPEARANCE, ASPECT

miff \ˈmif\ *vb* : to put into an ill humor

[1]**might** \(ˈ)mīt\ *past of* MAY — used as an auxiliary to express permission or possibility in the past, a present condition contrary to fact, less probability or possibility than *may,* or as a polite alternative to *may, ought,* or *should*

[2]**might** \ˈmīt\ *n* : the power, authority, or resources of an individual or a group

mighty \ˈmīt-ē\ *adj* **might·i·er; -est 1** : very strong : POWERFUL **2** : GREAT, NOTABLE — **might·i·ly** \ˈmīt-ə-lē\ *adv* — **might·i·ness** \-ē-nəs\ *n* — **mighty** *adv*

mi·gnon·ette \ˌmin-yə-ˈnet\ *n* : a garden plant with spikes of tiny fragrant flowers

mi·graine \ˈmī-ˌgrān\ *n* [F, fr. LL *hemicrania* pain in one side of the head, fr. Gk *hēmikrania,* fr. *hēmi-* half + *kranion* cranium] : a condition marked by recurrent severe headache and often nausea

mi·grant \ˈmī-grənt\ *n* : one that migrates; *esp* : a person who moves in order to find work (as picking crops)

mi·grate \ˈmī-ˌgrāt\ *vb* **mi·grat·ed; mi·grat·ing 1** : to move from one country or place to another **2** : to pass usu. periodically from one region or climate to another for feeding or breeding — **mi·gra·tion** \mī-ˈgrā-shən\ *n* — **mi·gra·tion·al** \-sh(ə-)nəl\ *adj* — **mi·gra·to·ry** \ˈmī-grə-ˌtōr-ē\ *adj*

mi·ka·do \mə-ˈkäd-ō\ *n, pl* **-dos** : an emperor of Japan

mike \ˈmīk\ *n* : MICROPHONE

[1]**mil** \ˈmil\ *n* **1** : a unit of length equal to 1/1000 inch **2** — see *pound* at MONEY table

[2]**mil** *abbr* military

milch \ˈmilk, ˈmilch\ *adj* : giving milk ⟨~ cow⟩

mild \ˈmīld\ *adj* **1** : gentle in nature or behavior **2** : moderate in action or effect **3** : TEMPERATE **syn** easy, complaisant, amiable, lenient — **mild·ly** *adv* — **mild·ness** *n*

mil·dew \ˈmil-ˌd(y)ü\ *n* : a superficial usu. whitish growth produced on organic matter and on plants by a fungus; *also* : a fungus producing this growth — **mildew** *vb*

mile \ˈmīl\ *n* [ME, fr. OE *mīl,* fr. L *milia* miles, fr. *milia passuum,* lit., thousands of paces] **1** — see WEIGHT table **2** : NAUTICAL MILE

mile·age \ˈmī-lij\ *n* **1** : an allowance for traveling expenses at a certain rate per mile **2** : distance in miles traveled (as in a day) **3** : the amount of service yielded (as by a tire) expressed in terms of miles of travel **4** : the average number of miles a car will travel on a gallon of gasoline

mile·post \ˈmīl-ˌpōst\ *n* : a post indicating the distance in miles from a given point

mile·stone \ˈmīl-ˌstōn\ *n* **1** : a stone serving as a milepost **2** : a significant point in development

mi·lieu \mēl-ˈyə(r), -ˈyü\ *n, pl* **mi·lieus** *or* **mi·lieux** \-ˈyə(r)(z), -ˈyüz\ [F] : ENVIRONMENT, SETTING

mil·i·tant \ˈmil-ə-tənt\ *adj* **1** : engaged in warfare **2** : aggressively active esp. in a cause — **mil·i·tance** \-təns\ *n* — **mil·i·tan·cy** \-tən-sē\ *n* — **militant** *n* — **mil·i·tant·ly** *adv*

mil·i·ta·rism \ˈmil-ə-tə-ˌriz-əm\ *n* **1** : predominance of the military class or its ideals **2** : a policy of aggressive military preparedness — **mil·i·ta·rist** \-rəst\ *n* — **mil·i·ta·ris·tic** \ˌmil-ə-tə-ˈris-tik\ *adj*

mil·i·ta·rize \ˈmil-ə-tə-ˌrīz\ *vb* **-rized; -riz·ing 1** : to equip with military forces and defenses **2** : to give a military character to

[1]**mil·i·tary** \ˈmil-ə-ˌter-ē\ *adj* **1** : of or relating to soldiers, arms, war, or the army **2** : performed by armed forces; *also* : supported by armed force **syn** martial, warlike — **mil·i·tar·i·ly** \ˌmil-ə-ˈter-ə-lē\ *adv*

[2]**military** *n, pl* **military** *also* **mil·i·tar·ies 1** : the military, naval, and air forces of a nation **2** : military persons

mil·i·tate \ˈmil-ə-ˌtāt\ *vb* **-tat·ed; -tat·ing** : to have weight or effect

mi·li·tia \mə-ˈlish-ə\ *n* : a part of the organized armed forces of a country liable to call only in emergency — **mi·li·tia·man** \-mən\ *n*

[1]**milk** \ˈmilk\ *n* **1** : a nutritive usu. whitish fluid secreted by female mammals for feeding their young **2** : a milk-like liquid (as a plant juice) — **milk·i·ness** \-ē-nəs\ *n* — **milky** *adj*

[2]**milk** *vb* **1** : to draw off the milk of ⟨~ a cow⟩ **2** : to draw something from as if by milking — **milk·er** *n*

milk·maid \ˈmilk-ˌmād\ *n* : DAIRYMAID

milk·man \-ˌman, -mən\ *n* : a person who sells or delivers milk

milk of magnesia : a milk-white mixture of hydroxide of magnesium and water used as an antacid and laxative

milk shake *n* : a thoroughly blended drink made of milk, a flavoring syrup, and often ice cream

milk·sop \ˈmilk-ˌsäp\ *n* : an unmanly man

milk·weed \-ˌwēd\ *n* : any of a genus of coarse herbs with milky juice and clustered flowers

Milky Way *n* **1** : a broad irregular band of light that stretches across the sky and is caused by the light of a very great number of faint stars **2** : MILKY WAY GALAXY

Milky Way galaxy *n* : the galaxy of which the sun is a member and which includes the stars that comprise the Milky Way

[1]**mill** \ˈmil\ *n* **1** : a building with machinery for grinding grain into flour **2** : a machine used in processing (as by grinding, stamping, cutting, or finishing) raw material **3** : FACTORY

[2]**mill** *vb* **1** : to process in a mill **2** : to move in a circle or in an eddying mass

[3]**mill** *n* : one tenth of a cent

mill·age \ˈmil-ij\ *n* : a rate (as of taxation) expressed in mills
mill·dam \ˈmil-ˌdam\ *n* : a dam to make a millpond; *also* : MILLPOND
mil·len·ni·um \mə-ˈlen-ē-əm\ *n, pl* **-nia** \-ē-ə\ *or* **-niums 1** : a period of 1000 years; *also* : a 1000th anniversary or its celebration **2** : the 1000 years mentioned in Revelation 20 when holiness is to prevail and Christ is to reign on earth **3** : a period of great happiness or perfect government
mill·er \ˈmil-ər\ *n* **1** : one that operates a mill and esp. a flour mill **2** : any of various moths having powdery wings
mil·let \ˈmil-ət\ *n* : any of several small-seeded cereal and forage grasses cultivated for grain or hay; *also* : the grain of a millet
mil·li·am·pere \ˌmil-ē-ˈam-ˌpiər\ *n* : one thousandth of an ampere
mil·liard \ˈmil-ˌyärd, ˈmil-ē-ˌärd\ *n, Brit* : a thousand millions
mil·li·bar \ˈmil-ə-ˌbär\ *n* : a unit of atmospheric pressure
mil·li·gram \ˈmil-ə-ˌgram\ *n* — see METRIC SYSTEM table
mil·li·li·ter \-ˌlēt-ər\ *n* — see METRIC SYSTEM table
mil·lime \mə-ˈlēm\ *n* — see *dinar* at MONEY table
mil·li·me·ter \ˈmil-ə-ˌmēt-ər\ *n* — see METRIC SYSTEM table
mil·li·ner \ˈmil-ə-nər\ *n* [fr. *Milan,* Italy; fr. the importation of women's finery from Italy in the 16th century] : one who designs, makes, trims, or sells women's hats
mil·li·nery \ˈmil-ə-ˌner-ē\ *n* **1** : women's apparel for the head **2** : the business or work of a milliner
mill·ing \ˈmil-iŋ\ *n* : a corrugated edge on a coin
mil·lion \ˈmil-yən\ *n, pl* **millions** *or* **million** : a thousand thousands — **million** *adj* — **mil·lionth** \-yənth\ *adj or n*
mil·lion·aire \ˌmil-yə-ˈner, ˈmil-yə-ˌner\ *n* : one whose wealth is estimated at a million or more (as of dollars or pounds)
mil·li·pede \ˈmil-ə-ˌpēd\ *n* : any of a class of arthropods related to the centipedes and having a long segmented body with a hard covering, two pairs of legs on most segments, and no poison fangs
mil·li·sec·ond \ˈmil-ə-ˌsek-ənd\ *n* : one thousandth of a second
mil·li·volt \-ˌvōlt\ *n* : one thousandth of a volt
mill·pond \ˈmil-ˌpänd\ *n* : a pond made by damming a stream to produce a fall of water for operating a mill
mill·race \-ˌrās\ *n* : a canal in which water flows to and from a mill wheel
mill·stone \-ˌstōn\ *n* : either of two round flat stones used for grinding grain
mill·stream \-ˌstrēm\ *n* : a stream whose flow is used to run a mill; *also* : the stream in a millrace
mill wheel *n* : a waterwheel that drives a mill
mill·wright \ˈmil-ˌrīt\ *n* : one whose occupation is planning and building mills or setting up their machinery
milt \ˈmilt\ *n* : the male reproductive glands of fishes when filled with secretion; *also* : the secretion itself
mime \ˈmīm, ˈmēm\ *n* **1** : MIMIC **2** : the art of characterization or of narration by body movement; *also* : a performance of mime — **mime** *vb*
mim·eo·graph \ˈmim-ē-ə-ˌgraf\ *n* : a machine for making many copies by means of a stencil through which ink is pressed — **mimeograph** *vb*
mi·me·sis \mə-ˈmē-səs, mī-\ *n* : IMITATION, MIMICRY
mi·met·ic \-ˈmet-ik\ *adj* **1** : IMITATIVE **2** : relating to, characterized by, or exhibiting mimicry
[1]**mim·ic** \ˈmim-ik\ *n* : one that mimics
[2]**mimic** *vb* **mim·icked** \-ikt\; **mim·ick·ing 1** : to imitate closely **2** : to ridicule by imitation **3** : to resemble by biological mimicry
mim·ic·ry \ˈmim-i-krē\ *n, pl* **-ries 1** : an instance of mimicking **2** : a superficial resemblance of one organism to another or to natural objects among which it lives that gives it an advantage (as protection from predation)
mi·mo·sa \mə-ˈmō-sə, mī-, -zə\ *n* : any of various leguminous trees, shrubs, and herbs of warm regions with globular heads of small white or pink flowers
min *abbr* **1** minim **2** minimum **3** mining **4** minister **5** minor **6** minute
min·a·ret \ˌmin-ə-ˈret\ *n* [F, fr. Turk *minare,* fr. Ar *manārah* lighthouse] : a slender lofty tower attached to a mosque
mi·na·to·ry \ˈmin-ə-ˌtōr-ē, ˈmī-nə-\ *adj* : THREATENING, MENACING
mince \ˈmins\ *vb* **minced; minc·ing 1** : to cut into small pieces **2** : to restrain (words) within the bounds of decorum **3** : to walk in a prim affected manner — **minc·ing** *adj*
mince·meat \ˈmins-ˌmēt\ *n* : a finely chopped mixture esp. of raisins, apples, spices, and often meat used as a filling for a pie
mince pie *n* : a pie filled with mincemeat
[1]**mind** \ˈmīnd\ *n* **1** : MEMORY **2** : the part of an individual that feels, perceives, thinks, wills, and esp. reasons **3** : INTENTION, DESIRE **4** : normal mental condition **5** : OPINION, VIEW **6** : mental qualities of a person or group **7** : intellectual ability
[2]**mind** *vb* **1** *chiefly dial* : REMEMBER **2** : to attend to ⟨~ your own business⟩ **3** : HEED, OBEY **4** : to be concerned about : WORRY; *also* : DISLIKE **5** : to be careful or cautious **6** : to take charge of **7** : to regard with attention
mind–bend·ing \ˈmīn(d)-ˌben-diŋ\ *adj* : MIND-BLOWING
mind–blow·ing \-ˌblō-iŋ\ *adj* : PSYCHEDELIC; *also* : MIND-BOGGLING
mind–bog·gling \-ˌbäg-(ə-)liŋ\ *adj* : mentally or emotionally exciting
mind·ed \ˈmīn-dəd\ *adj* **1** : having a mind of a specified kind — usu. used in combination ⟨narrow-*minded*⟩ **2** : INCLINED, DISPOSED
mind·ful \ˈmīnd-fəl\ *adj* : bearing in mind : AWARE — **mind·ful·ly** \-ē\ *adv* — **mind·ful·ness** *n*
mind·less \ˈmīn-dləs\ *adj* **1** : destitute of mind or consciousness; *esp* : UNINTELLIGENT **2** : UNTHINKING, HEEDLESS — **mind·less·ly** *adv* — **mind·less·ness** *n*
[1]**mine** \ˈmīn\ *pron* : one or the ones belonging to me
[2]**mine** \ˈmīn\ *n* **1** : an excavation in the earth from which mineral substances are taken; *also* : an ore deposit **2** : a subterranean passage under an enemy position; *also* : an encased explosive for destroying enemy personnel, vehicles, or ships **3** : a rich source of supply
[3]**mine** \ˈmīn\ *vb* **mined; min·ing 1** : to dig a mine **2** : UNDERMINE **3** : to get ore from the earth **4** : to place military mines in — **min·er** *n*
mine·lay·er \ˈmīn-ˌlā-ər\ *n* : a naval vessel for laying underwater mines
min·er·al \ˈmin(-ə)-rəl\ *n* **1** : a solid homogeneous crystalline substance (as diamond, gold, or quartz) not of animal or vegetable origin **2** : any of various naturally occurring homogeneous substances (as coal, salt, water, or gas) obtained usu. from the ground **3** *pl, Brit* : MINERAL WATER — **mineral** *adj*
min·er·al·ize \ˈmin-(ə-)rə-ˌlīz\ *vb* **-ized; -iz·ing 1** : to transform (a metal) into an ore **2** : to impregnate or supply with minerals
min·er·al·o·gy \ˌmin-ə-ˈräl-ə-jē, -ˈral-\ *n* : a science dealing with minerals — **min·er·al·og·i·cal** \ˌmin(-ə)-rə-ˈläj-i-kəl\ *adj* — **min·er·al·o·gist** \ˌmin-ə-ˈräl-ə-jəst, -ˈral-\ *n*
mineral oil *n* : an oil of mineral origin; *esp* : a refined petroleum oil used as a laxative
mineral water *n* : water infused with mineral salts or gases
min·e·stro·ne \ˌmin-ə-ˈstrō-nē, -ˈstrōn\ *n* [It, fr. *minestra,*

fr. *minestrare* to serve, dish up, fr. L *ministrare*, fr. *minister* servant] : a rich thick vegetable soup

mine·sweep·er \ˈmīn-ˌswē-pər\ *n* : a warship designed for removing or neutralizing underwater mines

min·gle \ˈmiŋ-gəl\ *vb* **min·gled; min·gling** \-g(ə-)liŋ\ **1** : to bring or combine together : MIX **2** : CONCOCT

ming tree \ˈmiŋ-\ *n* : a dwarfed usu. evergreen tree grown in a pot; *also* : an artificial imitation of this made from plant materials

mini \ˈmin-ē\ *n, pl* **min·is** : something small of its kind — **mini** *adj*

mini- *comb form* : miniature : of small dimensions

min·ia·ture \ˈmin-ē-ə-ˌchu̇r, ˈmin-i-ˌchu̇r, -chər\ *n* [It *miniatura* art of illuminating a manuscript, fr. ML, fr. L *miniare* to color with red lead, fr. *minium* red lead] **1** : a copy on a much reduced scale; *also* : something small of its kind **2** : a small painting (as on ivory or metal) — **miniature** *adj* — **min·ia·tur·ist** \-ˌchu̇r-əst, -chər-\ *n*

min·ia·tur·ize \ˈmin-ē-ə-ˌchə-ˌrīz, ˈmin-i-\ *vb* **-ized; iz·ing** : to design or construct in small size — **min·ia·tur·iza·tion** \ˌmin-ē-ə-ˌchu̇r-ə-ˈzā-shən, ˌmin-i-, -chər-\ *n*

mini·bike \ˈmin-ē-ˌbīk\ *n* : a small one-passenger motorcycle

mini·bus \-ˌbəs\ *n* : a small bus

mini·com·put·er \-kəm-ˌpyüt-ər\ *n* : a computer intermediate between a mainframe and a microcomputer in size and speed

min·im \ˈmin-əm\ *n* — see WEIGHT table

min·i·mal \ˈmin-ə-məl\ *adj* **1** : relating to or being a minimum : LEAST **2** : of or relating to minimal art — **min·i·mal·ly** \-ē\ *adv*

minimal art *n* : an impersonal style of abstract art and esp. sculpture consisting primarily of simple geometric forms — **minimal artist** *n*

min·i·mal·ist \ˈmin-ə-mə-ləst\ *n* : MINIMAL ARTIST

min·i·mize \ˈmin-ə-ˌmīz\ *vb* **-mized; -miz·ing 1** : to reduce to a minimum **2** : to estimate at a minimum; *also* : BELITTLE **syn** depreciate, decry, disparage

min·i·mum \ˈmin-ə-məm\ *n, pl* **-ma** \-mə\ *or* **-mums 1** : the least quantity assignable, admissible, or possible **2** : the least of a set of numbers **3** : the lowest degree or amount of variation (as of temperature) reached or recorded — **minimum** *adj*

min·ion \ˈmin-yən\ *n* [MF *mignon* darling] **1** : a servile dependent **2** : one highly favored **3** : a subordinate official

min·is·cule \ˈmin-əs-ˌkyül\ *var of* MINUSCULE

mini·se·ries \ˈmin ē-ˌsir-ēz\ *n* : a motion picture made for television and presented in several parts

mini·skirt \-ˌskərt\ *n* : a skirt with the hemline several inches above the knee

mini·state \-ˌstāt\ *n* : MICROSTATE

¹min·is·ter \ˈmin-ə-stər\ *n* **1** : AGENT **2** : CLERGYMAN; *esp* : a Protestant clergyman **3** : a high officer of state who heads a division of governmental activities **4** : a diplomatic representative to a foreign state — **min·is·te·ri·al** \ˌmin-ə-ˈstir-ē-əl\ *adj*

²minister *vb* **min·is·tered; min·is·ter·ing** \-st(ə-)riŋ\ **1** : to perform the functions of a minister of religion **2** : to give aid — **min·is·tra·tion** \ˌmin-ə-ˈstrā-shən\ *n*

min·is·trant \ˈmin-ə-strənt\ *adj, archaic* : performing service as a minister — **ministrant** *n*

min·is·try \ˈmin-ə-strē\ *n, pl* **-tries 1** : MINISTRATION **2** : the office, duties, or functions of a minister; *also* : his period of service or office **3** : CLERGY **4** : AGENCY **5** *often cap* : the body of ministers governing a nation or state; *also* : a government department headed by a minister

mink \ˈmiŋk\ *n, pl* **mink** *or* **minks** : a slender mammal resembling the related weasels; *also* : its soft lustrous typically dark brown fur

Minn *abbr* Minnesota

min·ne·sing·er \ˈmin-i-ˌsiŋ-ər, ˈmin-ə-ˌziŋ-\ *n* [G, fr. Middle High German, fr. *minne* love + *singer*] : one of a class of German lyric poets and musicians of the 12th to the 14th centuries

mink

min·now \ˈmin-ō\ *n, pl* **minnows** *also* **minnow** : any of numerous small freshwater fishes

¹mi·nor \ˈmī-nər\ *adj* **1** : inferior in importance, size, or degree **2** : not having reached majority **3** : having the third, sixth, and sometimes the seventh degrees lowered by a half step ⟨~ scale⟩; *also* : based on a minor scale ⟨~ key⟩

²minor *n* **1** : a person who has not attained majority **2** : a subject of academic study chosen as a secondary field of specialization

³minor *vb* : to pursue an academic minor

mi·nor·i·ty \mə-ˈnȯr-ət-ē, mī-\ *n, pl* **-ties 1** : the period or state of being a minor **2** : the smaller in number of two groups; *esp* : a group having less than the number of votes necessary for control **3** : a part of a population differing from others (as in race or religion); *also* : a member of a minority

min·ster \ˈmin-stər\ *n* **1** : a church attached to a monastery **2** : a large or important church

min·strel \ˈmin-strəl\ *n* **1** : a medieval singer of verses; *also* : MUSICIAN, POET **2** : one of a group of performers in a program usu. of black American songs, jokes, and impersonations — **min·strel·sy** \-sē\ *n*

¹mint \ˈmint\ *n* **1** : a place where coins are made **2** : a vast sum — **mint** *vb* — **mint·age** \-ij\ *n* — **mint·er** *n*

²mint *adj* : unmarred as if fresh from a mint ⟨~ coins⟩

³mint *n* : any of a large family of square-stemmed herbs and shrubs; *esp* : one (as spearment) with fragrant aromatic foliage used in flavoring — **minty** *adj*

min·u·end \ˈmin-yə-ˌwend\ *n* : a number from which another is to be subtracted

min·u·et \ˌmin-yə-ˈwet\ *n* : a slow graceful dance

¹mi·nus \ˈmī-nəs\ *prep* **1** : diminished by : LESS ⟨7 ~ 3 equals 4⟩ **2** : LACKING, WITHOUT ⟨~ his hat⟩

²minus *n* : a negative quantity or quality

³minus *adj* **1** : requiring subtraction **2** : algebraically negative ⟨~ quantity⟩ **3** : having negative qualities

¹mi·nus·cule \ˈmin-əs-ˌkyül\ *n* : a lowercase letter

²minuscule *adj* : very small

minus sign *n* : a sign — used in mathematics to indicate subtraction or a negative quantity

¹min·ute \ˈmin-ət\ *n* **1** : the 60th part of an hour or of a degree **2** : a short space of time **3** *pl* : the official record of the proceedings of a meeting

²mi·nute \mī-ˈn(y)üt, mə-\ *adj* **mi·nut·er; -est 1** : very small **2** : of little importance : TRIFLING **3** : marked by close attention to details **syn** diminutive, tiny, miniature, wee — **mi·nute·ly** *adv* — **mi·nute·ness** *n*

min·ute·man \ˈmin-ət-ˌman\ *n* : a member of a group of armed men pledged to take the field at a minute's notice during and immediately before the American Revolution

mi·nu·tia \mə-ˈn(y)ü-sh(ē-)ə, mī-\ *n, pl* **-ti·ae** \-shē-ˌē\ [L] : a minute or minor detail — usu. used in pl.

minx \ˈmiŋks\ *n* : a pert girl

Mio·cene \ˈmī-ə-ˌsēn\ *adj* : of, relating to, or being the epoch of the Tertiary between the Oligocene and the Pliocene — **Miocene** *n*

mir·a·cle \ˈmir-i-kəl\ *n* **1** : an extraordinary event manifesting a supernatural work of God **2** : an unusual event, thing, or accomplishment : WONDER, MARVEL — **mi·rac·u·lous** \mə-ˈrak-yə-ləs\ *adj* — **mi·rac·u·lous·ly** *adv*

miracle drug *n* : a usu. newly discovered drug capable of producing a marked and favorable change in a patient's condition

mi·rage \mə-ˈräzh\ *n* **1** : an illusion visible at sea, in deserts, or above a hot pavement of some distant object often in distorted form as a result of atmospheric conditions **2** : something illusory and unattainable

¹mire \ˈmī(ə)r\ *n* : heavy and often deep mud or slush — **miry** *adj*

²mire *vb* **mired; mir·ing** : to stick or sink in or as if in mire

¹mir·ror \ˈmir-ər\ *n* **1** : a polished or smooth substance (as of glass) that forms images by reflection **2** : a true representation; *also* : MODEL

²mirror *vb* : to reflect in or as if in a mirror

mirth \ˈmərth\ *n* : gladness or gaiety accompanied with laughter **syn** glee, jollity, hilarity, merriment — **mirth·ful** \-fəl\ *adj* — **mirth·ful·ly** \-ē\ *adv* — **mirth·ful·ness** *n* — **mirth·less** *adj*

MIRV \ˈmərv\ *n* [*m*ultiple *i*ndependently targeted *r*eentry *v*ehicle] : an ICBM with multiple warheads that have different targets — **MIRV** *vb*

mis·ad·ven·ture \ˌmis-əd-ˈven-chər\ *n* : MISFORTUNE, MISHAP

mis·aligned \ˌmis-ə-ˈlīnd\ *adj* : not properly aligned — **mis·align·ment** \-ˈlīn-mənt\ *n*

mis·al·li·ance \ˌmis-ə-ˈlī-əns\ *n* : MÉSALLIANCE; *also* : a marriage between persons unsuited to each other

mis·al·lo·ca·tion \ˌmis-ˌal-ə-ˈkā-shən\ *n* : faulty or improper allocation

mis·an·thrope \ˈmis-ᵊn-ˌthrōp\ *n* : one who hates mankind — **mis·an·throp·ic** \ˌmis-ᵊn-ˈthräp-ik\ *adj* — **mis·an·throp·i·cal·ly** \-i-k(ə-)lē\ *adv* — **mis·an·thro·py** \mis-ˈan-thrə-pē\ *n*

mis·ap·ply \ˌmis-ə-ˈplī\ *vb* : to apply wrongly — **mis·ap·pli·ca·tion** \ˌmis-ˌap-lə-ˈkā-shən\ *n*

mis·ap·pre·hend \ˌmis-ˌap-ri-ˈhend\ *vb* : MISUNDERSTAND — **mis·ap·pre·hen·sion** \-ˈhen-chən\ *n*

mis·ap·pro·pri·ate \ˌmis-ə-ˈprō-prē-ˌāt\ *vb* : to appropriate wrongly; *esp* : to take dishonestly for one's own use — **mis·ap·pro·pri·a·tion** \-ˌprō-prē-ˈā-shən\ *n*

mis·be·got·ten \-bi-ˈgät-ᵊn\ *adj* : ILLEGITIMATE

mis·be·have \ˌmis-bi-ˈhāv\ *vb* : to behave improperly — **mis·be·hav·er** *n* — **mis·be·hav·ior** \-ˈhā-vyər\ *n*

mis·be·liev·er \-bə-ˈlē-vər\ *n* : one who holds a false or unorthodox belief

mis·brand \mis-ˈbrand\ *vb* : to brand falsely or in a misleading manner

misc *abbr* miscellaneous

mis·cal·cu·late \mis-ˈkal-kyə-ˌlāt\ *vb* : to calculate wrongly — **mis·cal·cu·la·tion** \ˌmis-ˌkal-kyə-ˈlā-shən\ *n*

mis·call \mis-ˈkȯl\ *vb* : MISNAME

mis·car·riage \-ˈkar-ij\ *n* **1** : a corrupt or incompetent administration ⟨~ of justice⟩ **2** : expulsion of a fetus before it is capable of independent life

mis·car·ry \-ˈkar-ē\ *vb* **1** : to give birth prematurely and esp. before the fetus is capable of living independently **2** : to go wrong; *also* : to be unsuccessful

mis·ce·ge·na·tion \mis-ˌej-ə-ˈnā-shən, ˌmis-i-jə-ˈnā-\ *n* [L *miscēre* to mix + *genus* race] : a mixture of races; *esp* : marriage or cohabitation between a white person and a member of another race

mis·cel·la·neous \ˌmis-ə-ˈlā-nē-əs\ *adj* **1** : consisting of diverse things or members; *also* : having various traits **2** : dealing with or interested in diverse subjects — **mis·cel·la·neous·ly** *adv* — **mis·cel·la·neous·ness** *n*

mis·cel·la·ny \ˈmis-ə-ˌlā-nē\ *n, pl* **-nies** **1** : a collection of writings on various subjects **2** : HODGEPODGE

mis·chance \mis-ˈchans\ *n* : bad luck; *also* : MISHAP

mis·chief \ˈmis-chəf\ *n* **1** : injury caused by a human agency **2** : a source of harm or irritation **3** : action that annoys; *also* : MISCHIEVOUSNESS

mis·chie·vous \ˈmis-chə-vəs\ *adj* **1** : HARMFUL, INJURIOUS **2** : causing annoyance or minor injury **3** : irresponsibly playful — **mis·chie·vous·ly** *adv* — **mis·chie·vous·ness** *n*

mis·ci·ble \ˈmis-ə-bəl\ *adj* : capable of being mixed or dissolved

mis·com·mu·ni·ca·tion \ˌmis-kə-ˌmyü-nə-ˈkā-shən\ *n* : failure to communicate clearly

mis·con·ceive \ˌmis-kən-ˈsēv\ *vb* : to interpret incorrectly — **mis·con·cep·tion** \-ˈsep-shən\ *n*

mis·con·duct \mis-ˈkän-(ˌ)dəkt\ *n* **1** : MISMANAGEMENT **2** : intentional wrongdoing **3** : improper behavior

mis·con·strue \ˌmis-kən-ˈstrü\ *vb* : MISINTERPRET — **mis·con·struc·tion** \-ˈstrək-shən\ *n*

mis·count \mis-ˈkau̇nt\ *vb* : to count incorrectly : MISCALCULATE

mis·cre·ant \ˈmis-krē-ənt\ *n* : one who behaves criminally or viciously — **miscreant** *adj*

mis·cue \mis-ˈkyü\ *n* : MISTAKE, ERROR — **miscue** *vb*

mis·deed \mis-ˈdēd\ *n* : a wrong deed

mis·de·mean·or \ˌmis-di-ˈmē-nər\ *n* **1** : a crime less serious than a felony **2** : MISDEED

mis·di·rect \ˌmis-də-ˈrekt, -dī-\ *vb* : to give a wrong direction to — **mis·di·rec·tion** \-ˈrek-shən\ *n*

mis·do·ing \mis-ˈdü-iŋ\ *n* : WRONGDOING — **mis·do·er** \-ˈdü-ər\ *n*

mise–en–scène \ˌmē-ˌzäⁿ-ˈsen, -ˈsān\ *n, pl* **mise–en–scènes** \-ˈsen(z), -ˈsān(z)\ [F] **1** : the arrangement of the scenery, property, and actors on a stage **2** : SETTING; *also* : ENVIRONMENT

mi·ser \ˈmī-zər\ *n* [L *miser* miserable] : a person who hoards his money — **mi·ser·li·ness** \-lē-nəs\ *n* — **mi·ser·ly** *adj*

mis·er·a·ble \ˈmiz-(ə-)rə-bəl, ˈmiz-ər-bəl\ *adj* **1** : wretchedly deficient; *also* : causing extreme discomfort **2** : extremely poor **3** : SHAMEFUL — **mis·er·a·ble·ness** *n* — **mis·er·a·bly** \-blē\ *adv*

mis·ery \ˈmiz-(ə-)rē\ *n, pl* **-er·ies** **1** : suffering and want caused by poverty or affliction **2** : a cause of suffering or discomfort **3** : emotional distress

mis·fea·sance \mis-ˈfēz-ᵊns\ *n* : the performance of a lawful action in an illegal or improper manner

mis·file \-ˈfīl\ *vb* : to file in an inappropriate place

mis·fire \-ˈfī(ə)r\ *vb* **1** : to fail to fire **2** : to miss an intended effect — **misfire** *n*

mis·fit \ˈmis-ˌfit, mis-ˈfit\ *n* **1** : an imperfect fit **2** : a person poorly adjusted to his environment

mis·for·tune \mis-ˈfȯr-chən\ *n* **1** : bad fortune : ill luck **2** : an unfortunate condition or event

mis·giv·ing \-ˈgiv-iŋ\ *n* : a feeling of doubt or suspicion esp. concerning a future event

mis·gov·ern \-ˈgəv-ərn\ *vb* : to govern badly — **mis·gov·ern·ment** \-ˈgəv-ər(n)-mənt\ *n*

mis·guid·ance \mis-ˈgīd-ᵊns\ *n* : faulty guidance — **mis·guide** \-ˈgīd\ *vb* — **mis·guid·ed·ly** \-ˈgīd-əd-lē\ *adv*

mis·han·dle \-ˈhan-dᵊl\ *vb* **1** : MALTREAT **2** : to manage wrongly

mis·hap \ˈmis-ˌhap\ *n* : an unfortunate accident

mish·mash \ˈmish-ˌmash, -ˌmäsh\ *n* : HODGEPODGE, JUMBLE

mis·in·form \ˌmis-ᵊn-ˈfȯrm\ *vb* : to give false or misleading information to — **mis·in·for·ma·tion** \ˌmis-ˌin-fər-ˈmā-shən\ *n*

mis·in·ter·pret \ˌmis-ᵊn-ˈtər-prət\ *vb* : to understand or explain wrongly — **mis·in·ter·pre·ta·tion** \-ˌtər-prə-ˈtā-shən\ *n*

mis·judge \mis-ˈjəj\ *vb* **1** : to estimate wrongly **2** : to have

---

an unjust opinion of — **mis·judg·ment** \mis-ˈjəj-mənt\ *n*
mis·la·bel \-ˈlā-bəl\ *vb* : to label incorrectly or falsely
mis·lay \mis-ˈlā\ *vb* **-laid** \-ˈlād\; **-lay·ing** : MISPLACE, LOSE
mis·lead \mis-ˈlēd\ *vb* **-led** \-ˈled\; **-lead·ing** : to lead in a wrong direction or into a mistaken action or belief — **mis·lead·ing·ly** *adv*
mis·like \-ˈlīk\ *vb* : DISLIKE — **mis·like** *n*
mis·man·age \-ˈman-ij\ *vb* : to manage badly — **mis·man·age·ment** *n*
mis·match \-ˈmach\ *vb* : to match unsuitably or badly — **mis·match** \mis-ˈmach, ˈmis-ˌmach\ *n*
mis·name \-ˈnām\ *vb* : to name incorrectly : MISCALL
mis·no·mer \mis-ˈnō-mər\ *n* : a wrong name or designation
mi·sog·y·nist \mə-ˈsäj-ə-nəst\ *n* : one who hates women — **mi·sog·y·nis·tic** \mə-ˌsäj-ə-ˈnis-tik\ *adj* — **mi·sog·y·ny** \mə-ˈsäj-ə-nē\ *n*
mis·ori·ent \mis-ˈōr-ē-ˌent\ *vb* : to orient improperly or incorrectly — **mis·ori·en·ta·tion** \mis-ˌōr-ē-ən-ˈtā-shən\ *n*
mis·place \-ˈplās\ *vb* **1** : to put in a wrong place; *also* : MISLAY **2** : to set on a wrong object ⟨~ trust⟩
mis·play \-ˈplā\ *n* : a wrong or unskillful play — **mis·play** \mis-ˈplā, ˈmis-ˌplā\ *vb*
mis·print \mis-ˈprint\ *vb* : to print incorrectly — **mis·print** \ˈmis-ˌprint, mis-ˈprint\ *n*
mis·pro·nounce \ˌmis-prə-ˈnau̇ns\ *vb* : to pronounce incorrectly — **mis·pro·nun·ci·a·tion** \-prə-ˌnən-sē-ˈā-shən\ *n*
mis·quote \mis-ˈkwōt\ *vb* : to quote incorrectly — **mis·quo·ta·tion** \ˌmis-kwō-ˈtā-shən\ *n*
mis·read \-ˈrēd\ *vb* **-read** \-ˈred\; **-read·ing** \-ˈrēd-iŋ\ : to read or interpret incorrectly
mis·rep·re·sent \ˌmis-ˌrep-ri-ˈzent\ *vb* : to represent falsely or unfairly — **mis·rep·re·sen·ta·tion** \-ˌzen-ˈtā-shən\ *n*
¹**mis·rule** \mis-ˈrül\ *vb* : MISGOVERN
²**mis·rule** *n* **1** : MISGOVERNMENT **2** : DISORDER
¹**miss** \ˈmis\ *vb* **1** : to fail to hit, reach, or contact **2** : to feel the absence of **3** : to fail to obtain **4** : AVOID ⟨just ~*ed* hitting the other car⟩ **5** : OMIT **6** : to fail to understand **7** : to fail to perform or attend; *also* : MISFIRE
²**miss** *n* **1** : a failure to hit or to attain a result **2** : MISFIRE
³**miss** *n* **1** *cap* — used as a title prefixed to the name of an unmarried woman or girl **2** : a young unmarried woman or girl
Miss *abbr* Mississippi
mis·sal \ˈmis-əl\ *n* : a book containing all that is said or sung at mass during the entire year
mis·send \mis-ˈsend\ *vb* : to send incorrectly ⟨*missent* mail⟩
mis·shap·en \-ˈshā-pən\ *adj* : badly shaped : having an ugly shape
mis·sile \ˈmis-əl\ *n* [L, fr. neut. of *missilis* capable of being thrown, fr. *mittere* to let go, send] : an object (as a stone, bullet, or rocket) thrown or projected usu. so as to strike a target
mis·sile·ry *also* **mis·sil·ry** \ˈmis-əl-rē\ *n* **1** : MISSILES **2** : the science of the making and use of guided missiles
miss·ing \ˈmis-iŋ\ *adj* : ABSENT; *also* : LOST
mis·sion \ˈmish-ən\ *n* **1** : a group of missionaries; *also* : a place where missionaries work **2** : a group of envoys to a foreign country; *also* : a team of specialists or cultural leaders sent to a foreign country **3** : TASK
¹**mis·sion·ary** \ˈmish-ə-ˌner-ē\ *adj* : of, relating to, or engaged in church missions
²**missionary** *n, pl* **-ar·ies** : a person commissioned by a church to propagate its faith or carry on humanitarian work
mis·sion·er \ˈmish-(ə-)nər\ *n* : MISSIONARY
Mis·sis·sip·pi·an \ˌmis-ə-ˈsip-ē-ən\ *adj* : of, relating to, or being the period of the Paleozoic era between the Devonian and the Pennsylvanian — **Mississippian** *n*
mis·sive \ˈmis-iv\ *n* : LETTER
mis·spell \mis-ˈspel\ *vb* : to spell incorrectly — **mis·spell·ing** *n*
mis·spend \mis-ˈspend\ *vb* **-spent** \-ˈspent\; **-spend·ing** : WASTE, SQUANDER ⟨a *misspent* youth⟩
mis·state \-ˈstāt\ *vb* : to state incorrectly — **mis·state·ment** *n*
mis·step \-ˈstep\ *n* **1** : a wrong step **2** : MISTAKE, BLUNDER
mist \ˈmist\ *n* **1** : water in the form of particles suspended or falling in the air **2** : something that dims or obscures
mis·tak·able \mə-ˈstā-kə-bəl\ *adj* : capable of being misunderstood or mistaken
mis·take \mə-ˈstāk\ *n* **1** : a misunderstanding of the meaning or implication of something **2** : a wrong action or statement : ERROR — **mistake** *vb*
mis·tak·en \-ˈstā-kən\ *adj* **1** : MISUNDERSTOOD **2** : having a wrong opinion or incorrect information **3** : ERRONEOUS — **mis·tak·en·ly** *adv*
mis·ter \ˈmis-tər\ *n* **1** *cap* — used sometimes instead of *Mr.* **2** : SIR — used without a name in addressing a man
mis·tle·toe \ˈmis-əl-ˌtō\ *n* : a parasitic green plant with yellowish flowers and waxy white berries that grows on trees
mis·tral \ˈmis-trəl, mi-ˈsträl\ *n* [F, fr. Provençal, fr. *mistral* masterful, fr. L *magistralis,* fr. *magister* master] : a strong cold dry northerly wind of southern Europe
mis·treat \mis-ˈtrēt\ *vb* : to treat badly : ABUSE — **mis·treat·ment** *n*
mis·tress \ˈmis-trəs\ *n* **1** : a woman who has power, authority, or ownership ⟨~ of the house⟩ **2** : a country or state having supremacy ⟨~ of the seas⟩ **3** : a woman with whom a man has sexual relations outside of marriage; *also, archaic* : SWEETHEART **4** — used archaically as a title prefixed to the name of a married or unmarried woman
mis·tri·al \ˈmis-ˌtrīl\ *n* : a trial that has no legal effect (as by reason of an error)
¹**mis·trust** \mis-ˈtrəst\ *n* : a lack of confidence : DISTRUST — **mis·trust·ful** \-fəl\ *adj* — **mis·trust·ful·ly** \-ē\ *adv* — **mis·trust·ful·ness** *n*
²**mistrust** *vb* : to have no trust or confidence in : SUSPECT
misty \ˈmis-tē\ *adj* **mist·i·er; -est** : obscured by or as if by mist : INDISTINCT — **mist·i·ly** \ˈmis-tə-lē\ *adv* — **mist·i·ness** \-tē-nəs\ *n*
mis·un·der·stand \ˌmis-ˌən-dər-ˈstand\ *vb* **-stood** \-ˈstu̇d\; **-stand·ing** **1** : to fail to understand **2** : to interpret incorrectly
mis·un·der·stand·ing \-ˈstan-diŋ\ *n* **1** : MISINTERPRETATION **2** : DISAGREEMENT, QUARREL
mis·us·age \mish-ˈü-sij, mis(h)-ˈyü-, -zij\ *n* **1** : bad treatment : ABUSE **2** : wrong or improper use
mis·use \mish-ˈüz, mis(h)-ˈyüz\ *vb* **1** : to use incorrectly **2** : ABUSE, MISTREAT — **mis·use** \-ˈyüs\ *n*
mite \ˈmīt\ *n* **1** : any of various tiny animals related to the spiders that often live and feed on animals or plants **2** : a small coin or sum of money **3** : a small amount : BIT
¹**mi·ter** *or* **mi·tre** \ˈmīt-ər\ *n* [ME *mitre,* fr. MF, fr. L *mitra* headband, turban, fr. Gk] **1** : a headdress worn by bishops and abbots **2** : a joint or corner made by cutting two pieces of wood at an angle and fitting the cut edges together
²**miter** *or* **mitre** *vb* **mi·tered** *or* **mi·tred; mi·ter·ing** *or* **mi·tring** \ˈmīt-ə-riŋ\ **1** : to match or fit together in a miter joint **2** : to bevel the ends of for making a miter joint
mit·i·gate \ˈmit-ə-ˌgāt\ *vb* **-gat·ed; -gat·ing** **1** : to make less harsh or hostile **2** : to make less severe or painful — **mit·i·ga·tion** \ˌmit-ə-ˈgā-shən\ *n* — **mit·i·ga·tive** \ˈmit-ə-ˌgāt-iv\ *adj*
mi·to·sis \mī-ˈtō-səs\ *n, pl* **-to·ses** \-ˌsēz\ : a process that takes place in the nucleus of a dividing cell and results in the formation of two new nuclei each having the same number of chromosomes as the parent nucleus; *also*

: cell division in which mitosis occurs — **mi·tot·ic** \-ˈtät-ik\ *adj*

mitt \ˈmit\ *n* : a baseball glove (as for a catcher)

mit·ten \ˈmit-ᵊn\ *n* : a covering for the hand having a separate section for the thumb only

[1]**mix** \ˈmiks\ *vb* **1** : to combine into one mass **2** : ASSOCIATE **3** : to form by mingling components **4** : to produce (a recording) by electronically combining sounds from different sources **5** : CROSSBREED **6** : CONFUSE ⟨~*es* up the facts⟩ **7** : to become involved **syn** blend, merge, coalesce, amalgamate, fuse — **mix·able** *adj* — **mix·er** *n*

[2]**mix** *n* : a product of mixing; *esp* : a commercially prepared mixture of food ingredients

mixed number *n* : a number (as 5⅔) composed of an integer and a fraction

mixed–up \ˈmikst-ˈəp\ *adj* : marked by bewilderment, perplexity, or disorder : CONFUSED

mixt *abbr* mixture

mix·ture \ˈmiks-chər\ *n* **1** : the act or process of mixing; *also* : the state of being mixed **2** : a product of mixing

mix–up \ˈmiks-ˌəp\ *n* : an instance of confusion ⟨a ~ about the train⟩

miz·zen *or* **miz·en** \ˈmiz-ᵊn\ *n* **1** : a fore-and-aft sail set on the mizzenmast **2** : MIZZENMAST — **mizzen** *or* **mizen** *adj*

miz·zen·mast \-ˌmast, -məst\ *n* : the mast aft or next aft of the mainmast

mk *abbr* **1** mark **2** markka

Mk *abbr* Mark

mks \ˈem-ˈkā-ˈes\ *adj, often cap M&K&S* : of, relating to, or being a system of units based on the meter, the kilogram, and the second

mktg *abbr* marketing

ml *abbr* milliliter

MLD *abbr* **1** median lethal dose **2** minimum lethal dose

Mlle *abbr* [F] mademoiselle

Mlles *abbr* [F] mesdemoiselles

mm *abbr* millimeter

MM *abbr* [F] messieurs

Mme *abbr* [F] madame

Mn *symbol* manganese

MN *abbr* Minnesota

mne·mon·ic \nə-ˈmän-ik\ *adj* : assisting or designed to assist memory

mo *abbr* month

[1]**Mo** *abbr* Missouri

[2]**Mo** *symbol* molybdenum

MO *abbr* **1** mail order **2** medical officer **3** Missouri **4** modus operandi **5** money order

moan \ˈmōn\ *n* : a low prolonged sound indicative of pain or grief — **moan** *vb*

moat \ˈmōt\ *n* : a deep wide usu. water-filled trench around a castle

[1]**mob** \ˈmäb\ *n* [L *mobile vulgus* vacillating crowd] **1** : MASSES, RABBLE **2** : a large disorderly crowd **3** : a criminal gang

[2]**mob** *vb* **mobbed; mob·bing 1** : to crowd around and attack or annoy **2** : to crowd into or around ⟨shoppers *mobbed* the stores⟩

[1]**mo·bile** \ˈmō-bəl, -ˌbīl, -ˌbēl\ *adj* **1** : capable of moving or being moved **2** : changeable in appearance, mood, or purpose; *also* : ADAPTABLE **3** : having the opportunity for or undergoing a shift in social status **4** : using vehicles for transportation ⟨~ warfare⟩ — **mo·bil·i·ty** \mō-ˈbil-ət-ē\ *n*

[2]**mo·bile** \ˈmō-ˌbēl\ *n* : a construction (as of wire and sheet metal) with parts that can be set in motion by air currents; *also* : a similar structure suspended so that it is moved by a current of air

mobile home *n* : a trailer used as a permanent dwelling

mo·bi·lize \ˈmō-bə-ˌlīz\ *vb* **-lized; -liz·ing 1** : to put into movement or circulation **2** : to assemble and make ready for action ⟨~ army reserves⟩ — **mo·bi·li·za·tion** \ˌmō-bə-lə-ˈzā-shən\ *n* — **mo·bi·liz·er** \ˈmō-bə-ˌlī-zər\ *n*

mob·ster \ˈmäb-stər\ *n* : a member of a criminal gang

moc·ca·sin \ˈmäk-ə-sən\ *n* **1** : a soft leather heelless shoe **2** : WATER MOCCASIN

[1]**mock** \ˈmäk, ˈmȯk\ *vb* **1** : to treat with contempt or ridicule **2** : DELUDE **3** : DEFY **4** : to mimic in sport or derision — **mock·er** *n* — **mock·ery** \-(ə-)rē\ *n* — **mock·ing·ly** *adv*

[2]**mock** *adj* : SHAM, PSEUDO

mock–he·ro·ic \ˌmäk-hi-ˈrō-ik, ˌmȯk-\ *adj* : ridiculing or burlesquing the heroic style, character, or action ⟨a ~ poem⟩

mock·ing·bird \ˈmäk-iŋ-ˌbərd, ˈmȯk-\ *n* : a songbird of the southern U.S. that mimics the calls of other birds

mock–up \ˈmäk-ˌəp, ˈmȯk-\ *n* : a full-sized structural model built for study, testing, or display ⟨a ~ of an airplane⟩

[1]**mod** \ˈmäd\ *adj* : MODERN; *esp* : bold, free, and unconventional in style, behavior, or dress

[2]**mod** *abbr* **1** moderate **2** modern

mode \ˈmōd\ *n* **1** : a particular form or variety of something; *also* : STYLE **2** : a manner of doing something **3** : the most frequent value of a set of data — **mod·al** \ˈmōd-ᵊl\ *adj*

[1]**mod·el** \ˈmäd-ᵊl\ *n* **1** : structural design **2** : a miniature representation; *also* : a pattern of something to be made **3** : an example for imitation or emulation **4** : one who poses for an artist; *also* : MANNEQUIN **5** : TYPE, DESIGN — **model** *adj*

[2]**model** *vb* **-eled** *or* **-elled; -el·ing** *or* **-el·ling** \-(ᵊ-)liŋ\ **1** : SHAPE, FASHION, CONSTRUCT **2** : to work as a fashion model

[3]**model** *adj* **1** : serving as or worthy of being a pattern ⟨a ~ student⟩ **2** : being a miniature representation of something ⟨a ~ airplane⟩

[1]**mod·er·ate** \ˈmäd-(ə-)rət\ *adj* **1** : avoiding extremes; *also* : TEMPERATE **2** : AVERAGE; *also* : MEDIOCRE **3** : limited in scope or effect **4** : not expensive — **moderate** *n* — **mod·er·ate·ly** *adv* — **mod·er·ate·ness** *n*

[2]**mod·er·ate** \ˈmäd-ə-ˌrāt\ *vb* **-at·ed; -at·ing 1** : to lessen the intensity of : TEMPER **2** : to act as a moderator — **mod·er·a·tion** \ˌmäd-ə-ˈrā-shən\ *n*

mod·er·a·tor \ˈmäd-ə-ˌrāt-ər\ *n* **1** : MEDIATOR **2** : one who presides over an assembly, meeting, or discussion

mod·ern \ˈmäd-ərn\ *adj* [LL *modernus,* fr. L *modo* just now, fr. *modus* measure] : of, relating to, or characteristic of the present or the immediate past : CONTEMPORARY — **modern** *n* — **mo·der·ni·ty** \mə-ˈdər-nət-ē\ *n* — **mod·ern·ly** \ˈmäd-ərn-lē\ *adv* — **mod·ern·ness** \-ərn-nəs\ *n*

mod·ern·ism \ˈmäd-ər-ˌniz-əm\ *n* : a practice, movement, or belief peculiar to modern times

mod·ern·ize \ˈmäd-ər-ˌnīz\ *vb* **-ized; -iz·ing** : to make or become modern — **mod·ern·iza·tion** \ˌmäd-ər-nə-ˈzā-shən\ *n* — **mod·ern·iz·er** \ˈmäd-ər-ˌnī-zər\ *n*

mod·est \ˈmäd-əst\ *adj* **1** : having a moderate estimate of oneself; *also* : DIFFIDENT **2** : observing the proprieties of dress and behavior **3** : limited in size, amount, or scope — **mod·est·ly** *adv* — **mod·es·ty** \-ə-stē\ *n*

mod·i·cum \ˈmäd-i-kəm\ *n* : a small amount

modif *abbr* modification

mod·i·fy \ˈmäd-ə-ˌfī\ *vb* **-fied; -fy·ing 1** : MODERATE **2** : to limit the meaning of esp. in a grammatical construction **3** : CHANGE, ALTER — **mod·i·fi·ca·tion** \ˌmäd-ə-fə-ˈkā-shən\ *n* — **mod·i·fi·er** \ˈmäd-ə-ˌfī(-ə)r\ *n*

mod·ish \ˈmōd-ish\ *adj* : FASHIONABLE, STYLISH — **mod·ish·ly** *adv* — **mod·ish·ness** *n*

mo·diste \mō-ˈdēst\ *n* : a maker of fashionable dresses

mod·u·lar \ˈmäj-ə-lər\ *adj* : constructed with standardized units

---

\ə\abut \ᵊ\kitten \ər\further \a\ash \ā\ace \ä\cot, cart \au̇\out \ch\chin \e\bet \ē\easy \g\go \i\hit \ī\ice \j\job \ŋ\sing \ō\go \ȯ\law \ȯi\boy \th\thin \t͟h\the \ü\loot \u̇\foot \y\yet \zh\vision *see also* Pronunciation Symbols page

mod·u·lar·ized \ˈmäj-ə-lə-ˌrīzd\ *adj* : containing or consisting of modules

mod·u·late \ˈmäj-ə-ˌlāt\ *vb* **-lat·ed; -lat·ing 1** : to tune to a key or pitch **2** : to keep in proper measure or proportion : TEMPER **3** : to vary the amplitude or frequency of a carrier wave for the transmission of intelligence (as in radio or television) — **mod·u·la·tion** \ˌmäj-ə-ˈlā-shən\ *n* — **mod·u·la·tor** \ˈmäj-ə-ˌlāt-ər\ *n* — **mod·u·la·to·ry** \-lə-ˌtōr-ē\ *adj*

mod·ule \ˈmäj-ül\ *n* **1** : any in a series of standardized units for use together **2** : an assembly of wired electronic parts for use with other such assemblies **3** : an independent unit that constitutes a part of the total structure of a space vehicle ⟨a propulsion ~⟩

mo·dus ope·ran·di \ˌmōd-əs-ˌäp-ə-ˈran-dē, -ˌdī\ *n, pl* **modi operandi** \ˈmō-ˌdē-ˌäp-, ˈmō-ˌdī-\ [NL] : a method of procedure

[1]**mo·gul** \ˈmō-gəl, mō-ˈgəl\ *n* [fr. *Mogul,* one of the Mongol conquerors of India or their descendants, fr. Per *Mughul* Mongol, fr. Mongolian *Mongol*] : an important person : magnate

[2]**mogul** \ˈmō-gəl\ *n* : a bump in a ski run

mo·hair \ˈmō-ˌhaər\ *n* [modif. of obs. It *mocaiarro,* fr. Ar *mukhayyar,* lit., choice] : a fabric or yarn made wholly or in part from the long silky hair of the Angora goat

Mo·ham·med·an *var of* MUHAMMADAN

Mo·hawk \ˈmō-ˌhòk\ *n, pl* **Mohawk** *or* **Mohawks** : a member of an American Indian people of the Mohawk river valley, New York; *also* : the language of the Mohawk people

Mo·he·gan \mō-ˈhē-gən, mə-\ *or* **Mo·hi·can** \-ˈhē-kən\ *n, pl* **Mohegan** *or* **Mohegans** *or* **Mohican** *or* **Mohicans** : a member of an American Indian people of southeastern Connecticut

Mo·hi·can \mō-ˈhē-kən, mə-\ *var of* MAHICAN

moi·ety \ˈmòi-ət-ē\ *n, pl* **-eties** : one of two equal or approximately equal parts

moil \ˈmòil\ *vb* : to work hard : DRUDGE — **moil** *n* — **moil·er** *n*

moi·ré \mò-ˈrā, mwä-\ *or* **moire** *same, or* ˈmòi(-ə)r, ˈmwär\ *n* : a fabric (as silk) having a watered appearance

moist \ˈmòist\ *adj* : slightly or moderately wet — **moist·ly** *adv* — **moist·ness** *n*

moist·en \ˈmòis-ᵊn\ *vb* **moist·ened; moist·en·ing** \ˈmòis-(ᵊ-)niŋ\ : to make or become moist — **moist·en·er** \ˈmòis-(ᵊ-)nər\ *n*

mois·ture \ˈmòis-chər\ *n* : the small amount of liquid that causes dampness

mol *abbr* molecular; molecule

mo·lar \ˈmō-lər\ *n* [L *molaris,* fr. *molaris* of a mill, fr. *mola* millstone] : one of the broad teeth adapted to grinding food and located in the back of the jaw — **molar** *adj*

mo·las·ses \mə-ˈlas-əz\ *n* : the thick brown syrup that is separated from raw sugar in sugar manufacture

[1]**mold** \ˈmōld\ *n* : crumbly soil rich in organic matter

[2]**mold** *n* **1** : distinctive nature or character **2** : the frame on or around which something is constructed **3** : a cavity in which something is shaped; *also* : an object so shaped **4** : MOLDING

[3]**mold** *vb* **1** : to shape in or as if in a mold **2** : to ornament with molding — **mold·er** *n*

[4]**mold** *n* : a surface growth of fungus on damp or decaying matter; *also* : a fungus that forms molds — **mold·i·ness** \ˈmōl-dē-nəs\ *n* — **moldy** *adj*

[5]**mold** *vb* : to become moldy

mold·board \ˈmōl(d)-ˌbōrd\ *n* : a curved iron plate attached above the plowshare to lift and turn the soil

mold·er \ˈmōl-dər\ *vb* **mold·ered; mold·er·ing** \-d(ə-)riŋ\ : to crumble into small pieces

mold·ing \ˈmōl-diŋ\ *n* **1** : an act or process of shaping in a mold; *also* : an object so shaped **2** : a decorative surface, plane, or curved strip

molding 2

[1]**mole** \ˈmōl\ *n* : a small often pigmented spot or protuberance on the skin

[2]**mole** *n* : a small burrowing mammal with tiny eyes, hidden ears, and soft fur

[3]**mole** *n* : a massive breakwater or jetty

mo·lec·u·lar biology \mə-ˈlək-yə-lər-\ *n* : a branch of biology dealing with the ultimate physical and chemical organization of living matter and esp. with the molecular basis of inheritance and protein synthesis — **molecular biologist** *n*

mol·e·cule \ˈmäl-i-ˌkyül\ *n* : the smallest particle of matter that is the same chemically as the whole mass — **mo·lec·u·lar** \mə-ˈlek-yə-lər\ *adj*

mole·hill \ˈmōl-ˌhil\ *n* : a little ridge of earth thrown up by a mole

mole·skin \-ˌskin\ *n* **1** : the skin of the mole used as fur **2** : a heavy durable cotton fabric for industrial, medical, or clothing use

mo·lest \mə-ˈlest\ *vb* **1** : ANNOY, DISTURB **2** : to make annoying sexual advances to — **mo·les·ta·tion** \ˌmōl-ˌes-ˈtā-shən\ *n* — **mo·lest·er** \mə-ˈles-tər\ *n*

moll \ˈmäl\ *n* : a gangster's girlfriend

mol·li·fy \ˈmäl-ə-ˌfī\ *vb* **-fied; -fy·ing 1** : to soothe in temper : APPEASE **2** : SOFTEN **3** : to reduce in intensity : ASSUAGE — **mol·li·fi·ca·tion** \ˌmäl-ə-fə-ˈkā-shən\ *n*

mol·lusk *or* **mol·lusc** \ˈmäl-əsk\ *n* : any of a large group of mostly shelled and aquatic invertebrate animals including snails, clams, and squids — **mol·lus·can** *also* **mol·lus·kan** \mə-ˈləs-kən\ *adj*

[1]**mol·ly·cod·dle** \ˈmäl-ē-ˌkäd-ᵊl\ *n* : a pampered man or boy

[2]**mollycoddle** *vb* **mol·ly·cod·dled; mol·ly·cod·dling** \-ˌkäd-(ᵊ-)liŋ\ : PAMPER

Mo·lo·tov cocktail \ˌmäl-ə-ˌtòf-, ˌmōl-\ *n* : a crude bomb made of a bottle filled usu. with gasoline and fitted with a wick or saturated rag and ignited usu. just prior to hurling

[1]**molt** \ˈmōlt\ *vb* : to shed hair, feathers, outer skin, or horns periodically with the parts being replaced by new growth — **molt·er** *n*

[2]**molt** *n* : the act or process of molting

mol·ten \ˈmōlt-ᵊn\ *adj* **1** : fused or liquefied by heat **2** : GLOWING

mo·ly \ˈmō-lē\ *n* : a mythical herb with black root, white flowers, and magic powers

mo·lyb·de·num \mə-ˈlib-də-nəm\ *n* : a metallic chemical element used in strengthening and hardening steel — see ELEMENT table

mom \ˈmäm, ˈməm\ *n* : MOTHER

mom–and–pop *adj* : being a small owner-operated business

mo·ment \ˈmō-mənt\ *n* **1** : a minute portion of time : INSTANT **2** : a time of excellence ⟨he has his ~*s*⟩ **3** : IMPORTANCE **syn** consequence, significance, weight, import

mo·men·tari·ly \ˌmō-mən-ˈter-ə-lē\ *adv* **1** : for a moment **2** : INSTANTLY **3** : at any moment : SOON

mo·men·tary \ˈmō-mən-ˌter-ē\ *adj* **1** : continuing only a moment; *also* : EPHEMERAL **2** : recurring at every moment — **mo·men·tar·i·ness** \ˈmō-mən-ˌter-ē-nəs\ *n*

mo·men·tous \mō-ˈment-əs\ *adj* : very important — **mo·men·tous·ly** *adv* — **mo·men·tous·ness** *n*

mo·men·tum \mō-ˈment-əm\ *n, pl* **mo·men·ta** \-ˈment-ə\ *or* **momentums** : a property that a moving body has due to its mass and motion; *also* : IMPETUS

mom·my \ˈmäm-ē, ˈməm-\ *n, pl* **mom·mies** : MOTHER
Mon *abbr* Monday
mon·arch \ˈmän-ərk, -ˌärk\ *n* **1** : a person who reigns over a kingdom or an empire **2** : one holding preeminent position or power — **mo·nar·chi·cal** \mə-ˈnär-ki-kəl\ *also* **mo·nar·chic** \-ˈnär-kik\ *adj*
monarch butterfly *n* : a large orange and black migratory American butterfly whose larva feeds on milkweed
mon·ar·chist \ˈmän-ər-kəst\ *n* : a believer in monarchical government — **mon·ar·chism** \-ˌkiz-əm\ *n*
mon·ar·chy \ˈmän-ər-kē\ *n, pl* **-chies** : a nation or state governed by a monarch
mon·as·tery \ˈmän-ə-ˌster-ē\ *n, pl* **-ter·ies** : a house for persons under religious vows (as monks)
mo·nas·tic \mə-ˈnas-tik\ *adj* : of or relating to monasteries or to monks or nuns — **monastic** *n* — **mo·nas·ti·cal·ly** \-ti-k(ə-)lē\ *adv*
mo·nas·ti·cism \mə-ˈnas-tə-ˌsiz-əm\ *n* : the monastic life, system, or condition
mon·au·ral \mä-ˈnȯr-əl\ *adj* : MONOPHONIC — **mon·au·ral·ly** \-ē\ *adv*
Mon·day \ˈmən-dē, -ˌdā\ *n* : the second day of the week
mon·e·tary \ˈmän-ə-ˌter-ē, ˈmən-\ *adj* : of or relating to money or to the mechanisms by which it is supplied and circulated in the economy
mon·ey \ˈmən-ē\ *n, pl* **moneys** *or* **mon·ies** \ˈmən-ēz\ **1** : something (as metal currency) accepted as a medium of exchange **2** : wealth reckoned in monetary terms **3** : the 1st, 2d, and 3d places in a horse or dog race

MONEY

NAME	SUBDIVISIONS	COUNTRY
afghani	100 puls	Afghanistan
austral		Argentina
baht *or* tical	100 satang	Thailand
balboa	100 centesimos	Panama
birr	100 cents	Ethiopia
bolivar	100 centimos	Venezuela
cedi	100 pesewas	Ghana
colon	100 centimos	Costa Rica
colon	100 centavos	El Salvador
cordoba	100 centavos	Nicaragua
cruzado		Brazil
dalasi	100 bututs	Gambia
deutsche mark	100 pfennigs	West Germany
dinar	100 centimes	Algeria
dinar	1000 fils	Bahrain
dinar	1000 fils	Iraq
dinar	1000 fils	Jordan
dinar	1000 fils	Kuwait
dinar	1000 dirhams	Libya
dinar	1000 fils	Southern Yemen (People's Democratic Republic of Yemen)
dinar	1000 millimes	Tunisia
dinar	100 paras	Yugoslavia
dirham	100 centimes	Morocco
dirham	1000 fils	United Arab Emirates
dobra	100 centavos	Sao Tome and Principe
dollar	100 cents	Australia
dollar	100 cents	Bahamas
dollar	100 cents	Barbados
dollar	100 cents	Belize
dollar	100 cents	Bermuda
dollar	100 sen	Brunei
dollar	100 cents	Canada
dollar *or* yuan	100 cents	China (Taiwan)
dollar	100 cents	Ethiopia
dollar	100 cents	Fiji
dollar	100 cents	Grenada
dollar	100 cents	Guyana
dollar	100 cents	Hong Kong
dollar	100 cents	Jamaica
dollar	100 cents	Liberia
dollar	100 cents	New Zealand
dollar	100 cents	St. Vincent and the Grenadines
dollar	100 cents	Singapore
dollar	100 cents	Trinidad and Tobago
dollar	100 cents	United States
dollar	100 cents	Zimbabwe
dong	100 xu	Vietnam
drachma	100 lepta	Greece
ekuele	100 centimos	Equatorial Guinea
escudo	100 centavos	Cape Verde
escudo	100 centavos	Portugal
escudo—see PESO, below		
florin—see GULDEN, below		
forint	100 filler	Hungary
franc	100 centimes	Belgium
franc	100 centimes	Benin
franc	100 centimes	Burkina Faso
franc	100 centimes	Burundi
franc	100 centimes	Cameroon
franc	100 centimes	Central African Republic
franc	100 centimes	Chad
franc	100 centimes	Congo
franc	100 centimes	Djibouti
franc	100 centimes	France
franc	100 centimes	Gabon
franc	100 centimes	Ivory Coast
franc	100 centimes	Luxembourg
franc	100 centimes	Madagascar
franc	100 centimes	Mali
franc	100 centimes	Niger
franc	100 centimes	Rwanda
franc	100 centimes	Senegal
franc	100 centimes *or* rappen	Switzerland
franc	100 centimes	Togo
gourde	100 centimes	Haiti
guarani	100 centimos	Paraguay
gulden *or* guilder *or* florin	100 cents	Netherlands
gulden *or* guilder *or* florin	100 cents	Suriname
inti		Peru
kina	100 toea	Papua New Guinea
kip	100 at	Laos
koruna	100 halers	Czechoslovakia
krona	100 aurar (*sing* eyrir)	Iceland
krona	100 ore	Sweden
krone	100 ore	Denmark
krone	100 ore	Norway
kwacha	100 tambala	Malawi
kwacha	100 ngwee	Zambia
kwanza	100 lwei	Angola
kyat	100 pyas	Burma
lek	100 qindarka	Albania
lempira	100 centavos	Honduras
leone	100 cents	Sierra Leone
leu	100 bani	Romania
lev	100 stotinki	Bulgaria

NAME	SUBDIVISIONS	COUNTRY
lilangeni (*pl* emalangeni)	100 cents	Swaziland
lira	100 centesimi	Italy
lira *or* pound	100 kurus *or* piasters	Turkey
lira—see POUND, below		
loti (*pl* maloti)	100 licente	Lesotho
mark *or* ostmark	100 pfennigs	East Germany
mark—see DEUTSCHE MARK, above		
markka	100 pennia	Finland
metical	100 centavos	Mozambique
naira	100 kobo	Nigeria
ngultrum	100 chetrums	Bhutan
ostmark—see MARK, above		
ouguiya	5 khoums	Mauritania
pa'anga	100 seniti	Tonga
pataca	100 avos	Macao
peseta	100 centimos	Spain
peso	100 centavos	Bolivia
peso	100 centavos	Chile
peso	100 centavos	Colombia
peso	100 centavos	Cuba
peso	100 centavos	Dominican Republic
peso	100 centavos	Guinea-Bissau
peso	100 centavos	Mexico
peso	100 sentimos *or* centavos	Philippines
peso	100 centesimos	Uruguay
pound	1000 mils	Cyprus
pound	100 piasters	Egypt
pound	100 pence	Ireland
pound	100 piasters	Lebanon
pound *or* lira	100 pence	Malta
pound	100 piasters	Sudan
pound	100 piasters	Syria
pound	100 pence	United Kingdom
pound—see LIRA, above		
pula	100 thebe	Botswana
quetzal	100 centavos	Guatemala
rand	100 cents	South Africa
rial	100 dinars	Iran
rial	1000 baizas	Oman
rial *or* riyal	100 fils	Yemen Arab Republic
riel	100 sen	Cambodia
ringgit	100 sen	Malaysia
riyal	100 dirhams	Qatar
riyal	20 qursh 100 halala	Saudi Arabia
riyal—see RIAL, above		
ruble	100 kopecks	U.S.S.R.
rupee	100 paise	India
rupee	100 cents	Mauritius
rupee	100 paisa	Nepal
rupee	100 paisa	Pakistan
rupee	100 cents	Seychelles
rupee	100 cents	Sri Lanka
rupiah	100 sen	Indonesia
schilling	100 groschen	Austria
shekel	100 agorot	Israel
shilingi—see SHILLING, below		
shilling	100 cents	Kenya
shilling	100 cents	Somalia
shilling *or* shilingi	100 senti *or* cents	Tanzania
shilling	100 cents	Uganda
sucre	100 centavos	Ecuador
syli	100 cauris	Guinea
taka	100 paisa	Bangladesh
tala	100 sene	Western Samoa
tical—see BAHT, above		
tugrik	100 mongo	Mongolia
vatu		Vanuatu
won	100 jun	North Korea
won	100 jeon	South Korea
yen	100 sen	Japan
yuan	100 fen	China (mainland)
yuan—see DOLLAR, above		
zaire	100 makuta (*sing.* likuta) 10,000 sengi	Zaire
zloty	100 groszy	Poland

mon·eyed \ˈmən-ēd\ *adj* **1** : having money : WEALTHY **2** : consisting in or derived from money

mon·ey·lend·er \ˈmən-ē-ˌlen-dər\ *n* : one whose business is lending money; *specif* : PAWNBROKER

money market *n* : the trade in short-term negotiable financial instruments

money of account : a denominator of value or basis of exchange used in keeping accounts

money order *n* : an order purchased at a post office, bank, or telegraph office directing another office to pay a sum of money to a party named on it

mon·ger \ˈməŋ-gər, ˈmäŋ-\ *n* **1** : DEALER **2** : one who tries to stir up or spread something

mon·go \ˈmäŋ-(ˌ)gō\ *n, pl* **mongo** — see *tugrik* at MONEY table

Mon·gol \ˈmäŋ-gəl, ˈmän-ˌgōl\ *n* : a person of Mongoloid racial stock and esp. of the chiefly pastoral Mongoloid peoples of Mongolia — **Mongol** *adj*

Mon·go·lian \män-ˈgōl-yən, mäŋ-, -ˈgō-lē-ən\ *n* **1** : a native or inhabitant of Mongolia **2** : a member of the Mongoloid racial stock — **Mongolian** *adj*

mon·gol·ism \ˈmäŋ-gə-ˌliz-əm\ *n* : DOWN'S SYNDROME

Mon·gol·oid \ˈmäŋ-gə-ˌlȯid\ *adj* **1** : of or relating to a major racial stock native to Asia that includes peoples of northern and eastern Asia, Malaysians, Eskimos, and often American Indians **2** *often not cap* : of, relating to, or affected with Down's syndrome — **Mongoloid** *n*

mon·goose \ˈmän-ˌgüs, ˈmäŋ-\ *n, pl* **mon·goos·es** *also* **mon·geese** \-ˌgēs\ : a small agile mammal of India that is related to the civet cats and feeds on snakes and rodents

mon·grel \ˈmäŋ-grəl, ˈməŋ-\ *n* : an offspring of parents of different breeds or uncertain ancestry

mo·nism \ˈmō-ˌniz-əm, ˈmän-iz-\ *n* : a view that reality is basically one — **mo·nist** \ˈmō-nəst, ˈmän-əst\ *n*

mo·ni·tion \mō-ˈnish-ən, mə-\ *n* : WARNING, CAUTION

¹**mon·i·tor** \ˈmän-ət-ər\ *n* **1** : a student appointed to assist a teacher **2** : one that monitors; *esp* : a video display screen (as for a computer)

²**monitor** *vb* **mon·i·tored; mon·i·tor·ing** \ˈmän-ət-ə-riŋ, ˈmän-ə-triŋ\ : to watch, check, or observe for a special purpose

mon·i·to·ry \ˈmän-ə-ˌtōr-ē\ *adj* : giving admonition : WARNING

¹**monk** \ˈməŋk\ *n* [ME, fr. OE *munuc*, fr. LL *monachus*, fr. LGk *monachos*, fr. Gk, adj., single, fr. *monos* single, alone] : a man belonging to a religious order and living in a monastery — **monk·ish** *adj*

²**monk** *n* : MONKEY

¹**mon·key** \ˈməŋ-kē\ *n, pl* **monkeys** : a primate mammal other than man; *esp* : one of the smaller, longer-tailed, and usu. more arboreal primates as contrasted with the apes

²**monkey** *vb* **mon·keyed; mon·key·ing 1** : FOOL, TRIFLE **2** : TAMPER

monkey bars *n pl* : a framework of bars on which children can play

mon·key·shine \ˈmən-kē-ˌshīn\ *n* : PRANK — usu. used in pl.

monkey wrench *n* : a wrench with one fixed and one adjustable jaw at right angles to a handle

monks·hood \ˈməŋks-ˌhu̇d\ *n* : any of a genus of poisonous plants related to the buttercups; *esp* : a tall Old World plant grown for its white or purplish flowers or as a source of drugs (as aconite)

[1]**mono** \ˈmän-ō\ *adj* : MONOPHONIC

[2]**mono** *n* : MONONUCLEOSIS

mono·chro·mat·ic \ˌmän-ə-krō-ˈmat-ik\ *adj* **1** : having or consisting of one color **2** : consisting of radiation (as light) of a single wavelength

mono·chrome \ˈmän-ə-ˌkrōm\ *adj* : characterized by the reproduction or transmission of visual images in tones of gray ⟨~ television⟩

mon·o·cle \ˈmän-i-kəl\ *n* : an eyeglass for one eye

mono·clo·nal \ˌmän-ə-ˈklō-nəl\ *adj* : produced by, being, or composed of cells derived from a single cell ⟨~ antibodies⟩

mono·cot·y·le·don \ˌmän-ə-ˌkät-ᵊl-ˈēd-ᵊn\ *n* : any of a subclass of seed plants having an embryo with a single cotyledon and usu. parallel-veined leaves — **mono·cot·y·le·don·ous** *adj*

mon·o·dy \ˈmän-əd-ē\ *n, pl* **-dies** : ELEGY, DIRGE — **mo·nod·ic** \mə-ˈnäd-ik\ *or* **mo·nod·i·cal** \-i-kəl\ *adj* — **mon·o·dist** \ˈmän-əd-əst\ *n*

mo·nog·a·my \mə-ˈnäg-ə-mē\ *n* : marriage with but one person at a time — **mo·nog·a·mist** \mə-ˈnäg-ə-məst\ *n* — **mo·nog·a·mous** \mə-ˈnäg-ə-məs\ *adj*

mono·gram \ˈmän-ə-ˌgram\ *n* : a sign of identity composed of the combined initials of a name — **monogram** *vb*

mono·graph \ˈmän-ə-ˌgraf\ *n* : a learned treatise on a small area of learning

mono·lin·gual \ˌmän-ə-ˈliŋ-gwəl\ *adj* : expressed in or knowing or using only one language

mono·lith \ˈmän-ᵊl-ˌith\ *n* **1** : a single great stone often in the form of a monument or column **2** : something large and powerful that acts as a single unified force — **mono·lith·ic** \ˌmän-ᵊl-ˈith-ik\ *adj*

mono·logue *also* **mono·log** \ˈmän-ᵊl-ˌȯg\ *n* : a dramatic soliloquy; *also* : a long speech monopolizing conversation — **mono·logu·ist** \-ˌȯg-əst\ *or* **mo·no·lo·gist** \mə-ˈnäl-ə-jəst; ˈmän-ᵊl-ˌȯg-əst\ *n*

mono·ma·nia \ˌmän-ə-ˈmā-nē-ə, -nyə\ *n* **1** : mental derangement involving a single idea or area of thought **2** : excessive concentration on a single object or idea — **mono·ma·ni·ac** \-nē-ˌak\ *n or adj*

mono·mer \ˈmän-ə-mər\ *n* : a simple chemical compound that can be polymerized

mono·nu·cle·o·sis \ˌmän-ō-ˌn(y)ü-klē-ˈō-səs\ *n* : an acute infectious disease characterized by fever, swelling of lymph glands, and increased numbers of lymph cells in the blood

mono·phon·ic \ˌmän-ə-ˈfän-ik\ *adj* : of or relating to sound transmission, recording, or reproduction by techniques that provide a single transmission path

mono·plane \ˈmän-ə-ˌplān\ *n* : an airplane with only one set of wings

mo·nop·o·ly \mə-ˈnäp-(ə-)lē\ *n, pl* **-lies** [L *monopolium,* fr. Gk *monopōlion,* fr. *monos* alone, single + *pōlein* to sell] **1** : exclusive ownership (as through command of supply) **2** : a commodity controlled by one party **3** : one that has a monopoly — **mo·nop·o·list** \-ləst\ *n* — **mo·nop·o·lis·tic** \mə-ˌnäp-ə-ˈlis-tik\ *adj* — **mo·nop·o·li·za·tion** \-lə-ˈzā-shən\ *n* — **mo·nop·o·lize** \mə-ˈnäp-ə-ˌlīz\ *vb*

mono·rail \ˈmän-ə-ˌrāl\ *n* : a single rail serving as a track for a wheeled vehicle; *also* : a vehicle traveling on such a track

mono·so·di·um glu·ta·mate \ˌmän-ə-ˌsōd-ē-əm-ˈglüt-ə-ˌmāt\ *n* : a crystalline salt used for seasoning foods

mono·syl·la·ble \ˈmän-ə-ˈsil-ə-bəl\ *n* : a word of one syllable — **mono·syl·lab·ic** \ˌmän-ə-sə-ˈlab-ik\ *adj* — **mono·syl·lab·i·cal·ly** \-i-k(ə-)lē\ *adv*

mono·the·ism \ˈmän-ə-(ˌ)thē-ˌiz-əm\ *n* : a doctrine or belief that there is only one deity — **mono·the·ist** \-ˌthē-əst\ *n*

mono·tone \ˈmän-ə-ˌtōn\ *n* : a succession of syllables, words, or sentences in one unvaried key or pitch

mo·not·o·nous \mə-ˈnät-ᵊn-əs\ *adj* **1** : uttered or sounded in one unvarying tone **2** : tediously uniform — **mo·not·o·nous·ly** *adv* — **mo·not·o·nous·ness** *n* — **mo·not·o·ny** \-ᵊn-ē\ *n*

mon·ox·ide \mə-ˈnäk-ˌsīd\ *n* : an oxide containing one atom of oxygen in the molecule

mon·sei·gneur \ˌmōⁿ-ˌsān-ˈyər\ *n, pl* **mes·sei·gneurs** \ˌmā-ˌsān-ˈyər(z)\ : a French dignitary — used as a title

mon·sieur \məs-ˈyə(r), *Fr* mə-ˈsyœ\ *n, pl* **mes·sieurs** \məs(h)-(ˈ)yə(r)(z), mās-; mə-ˈsi(ə)r(z)\ : a Frenchman of high rank or station — used as a title equivalent to *Mister*

mon·si·gnor \män-ˈsē-nyər\ *n, pl* **monsignors** *or* **mon·si·gno·ri** \ˌmän-ˌsēn-ˈyōr-ē\ [It *monsignore*] : a Roman Catholic prelate — used as a title

mon·soon \män-ˈsün\ *n* [obs. Dutch *monssoen,* fr. Pg *monção,* fr. Ar *mawsim* time, season] **1** : a periodic wind esp. in the Indian ocean and southern Asia **2** : the season of the southwest monsoon esp. in India **3** : rainfall associated with the monsoon

[1]**mon·ster** \ˈmän-stər\ *n* **1** : an abnormally developed plant or animal **2** : an animal of strange or terrifying shape; *also* : one unusually large of its kind **3** : an extremely ugly, wicked, or cruel person — **mon·stros·i·ty** \män-ˈsträs-ət-ē\ *n* — **mon·strous** \ˈmän-strəs\ *adj* — **mon·strous·ly** *adv*

[2]**monster** *adj* : very large : ENORMOUS

mon·strance \ˈmän-strəns\ *n* : a vessel in which the consecrated Host is exposed for the adoration of the faithful

Mont *abbr* Montana

mon·tage \män-ˈtäzh\ *n* [F] **1** : a composite photograph made by combining several separate pictures **2** : an artistic composition made up of several different kinds of items (as strips of newspaper, pictures, bits of wood) arranged together

month \ˈmənth\ *n, pl* **months** \ˈməns, ˈmənths\ [OE *mōnath,* fr. *mōna* moon] : one of the 12 parts into which the year is divided — **month·ly** *adv or adj or n*

month·long \ˈmənth-ˈlȯŋ\ *adj* : lasting a month

mon·u·ment \ˈmän-yə-mənt\ *n* **1** : a lasting reminder; *esp* : a structure erected in remembrance of a person or event **2** : a natural feature or area of special interest set aside by the government as public property

mon·u·men·tal \ˌmän-yə-ˈment-ᵊl\ *adj* **1** : of or relating to a monument **2** : MASSIVE; *also* : OUTSTANDING **3** : very great — **mon·u·men·tal·ly** \-ē\ *adv*

moo \ˈmü\ *vb* : to make the natural throat noise of a cow — **moo** *n*

[1]**mood** \ˈmüd\ *n* **1** : a conscious state of mind or predominant emotion : FEELING **2** : a prevailing attitude : DISPOSITION

[2]**mood** *n* : distinction of form of a verb to express whether its action or state is conceived as fact or in some other manner (as wish)

moody \ˈmüd-ē\ *adj* **mood·i·er; -est 1** : GLOOMY **2** : subject to moods : TEMPERAMENTAL — **mood·i·ly** \ˈmüd-ᵊl-ē\ *adv* — **mood·i·ness** \-ē-nəs\ *n*

[1]**moon** \ˈmün\ *n* **1** : the earth's natural satellite **2** : SATELLITE 2

[2]**moon** *vb* : to engage in idle reverie

moon·beam \ˈmün-ˌbēm\ *n* : a ray of light from the moon

[1]**moon·light** \-ˌlīt\ *n* : the light of the moon — **moon·lit** \-ˌlit\ *adj*

[2]**moonlight** *vb* **moon·light·ed; moon·light·ing** : to hold a

second job in addition to a regular one — **moon·light·er** *n*

moon·scape \-ˌskāp\ *n* : the surface of the moon as seen or as pictured

moon·shine \-ˌshīn\ *n* **1** : MOONLIGHT **2** : empty talk **3** : intoxicating liquor usu. illegally distilled

moon·stone \-ˌstōn\ *n* : a transparent or translucent feldspar of pearly luster used as a gem

moon·struck \-ˌstrək\ *adj* **1** : mentally unbalanced **2** : romantically sentimental

[1]**moor** \ˈmu̇r\ *n* : an area of open and usu. infertile and wet or peaty wasteland

[2]**moor** *vb* : to make fast with or as if with cables, lines, or anchors

Moor \ˈmu̇r\ *n* : one of a North African people of Arab and Berber ancestry that conquered Spain in the 8th century — **Moor·ish** *adj*

moor·ing \ˈmu̇r-iŋ\ *n* **1** : a place where or an object to which a craft can be made fast **2** : an established practice or stabilizing influence — usu. used in pl.

moor·land \-lənd, -ˌland\ *n* : land consisting of moors

moose \ˈmüs\ *n, pl* **moose** : a large heavy-antlered American deer; *also* : the European elk

[1]**moot** \ˈmüt\ *vb* : to bring up for debate or discussion; *also* : DEBATE

[2]**moot** *adj* **1** : open to question; *also* : DISPUTED **2** : having no practical significance

[1]**mop** \ˈmäp\ *n* : an implement made of absorbent material fastened to a handle and used esp. for cleaning floors

[2]**mop** *vb* **mopped; mop·ping** : to use a mop on : clean with a mop

mope \ˈmōp\ *vb* **moped; mop·ing 1** : to become dull, dejected, or listless **2** : DAWDLE

mop·pet \ˈmäp-ət\ *n* [obs. E *mop* fool, child] : CHILD

mop–up \ˈmäp-ˌəp\ *n* : a final clearance or disposal

mo·raine \mə-ˈrān\ *n* : an accumulation of earth and stones left by a glacier

[1]**mor·al** \ˈmȯr-əl\ *adj* **1** : of or relating to principles of right and wrong **2** : conforming to a standard of right behavior; *also* : capable of right and wrong action **3** : probable but not proved ⟨a ~ certainty⟩ **4** : having the effects of such on the mind, confidence, or will ⟨a ~ victory⟩ **syn** virtuous, righteous, noble, ethical, principled — **mor·al·ly** \-ē\ *adv*

[2]**moral** *n* **1** : the practical meaning (as of a story) **2** *pl* : moral practices or teachings

mo·rale \mə-ˈral\ *n* **1** : MORALITY **2** : the mental and emotional attitudes of an individual to the tasks at hand; *also* : ESPRIT DE CORPS

mor·al·ist \ˈmȯr-ə-ləst\ *n* **1** : a teacher or student of morals **2** : one concerned with regulating the morals of others — **mor·al·is·tic** \ˌmȯr-ə-ˈlis-tik\ *adj* — **mor·al·is·ti·cal·ly** \-ti-k(ə-)lē\ *adv*

mo·ral·i·ty \mə-ˈral-ət-ē\ *n, pl* **-ties** : moral conduct : VIRTUE

mor·al·ize \ˈmȯr-ə-ˌlīz\ *vb* **-ized; -iz·ing** : to make moral reflections — **mor·al·iza·tion** \ˌmȯr-ə-lə-ˈzā-shən\ *n* — **mor·al·iz·er** \ˈmȯr-ə-ˌlī-zər\ *n*

mo·rass \mə-ˈras\ *n* : SWAMP

mor·a·to·ri·um \ˌmȯr-ə-ˈtōr-ē-əm\ *n, pl* **-ri·ums** *or* **-ria** \-ē-ə\ [deriv. of L *mora* delay] : a suspension of activity

mo·ray \mə-ˈrā, ˈmȯr-ˌā\ *n* : any of numerous often brightly colored savage eels occurring in warm seas

mor·bid \ˈmȯr-bəd\ *adj* **1** : of, relating to, or typical of disease; *also* : DISEASED, SICKLY **2** : characterized by gloomy or unwholesome ideas or feelings **3** : GRISLY, GRUESOME ⟨~ details⟩ — **mor·bid·i·ty** \mȯr-ˈbid-ət-ē\ *n* — **mor·bid·ly** \ˈmȯr-bəd-lē\ *adv* — **mor·bid·ness** *n*

mor·dant \ˈmȯrd-ᵊnt\ *adj* **1** : INCISIVE **2** : BURNING, PUNGENT — **mor·dant·ly** *adv*

[1]**more** \ˈmōr\ *adj* **1** : GREATER **2** : ADDITIONAL

[2]**more** *adv* **1** : in addition ⟨a couple of times ~⟩ **2** : to a greater or higher degree

[3]**more** *n* **1** : a greater quantity, number, or amount ⟨the ~ the merrier⟩ **2** : an additional amount ⟨too full to eat ~⟩

[4]**more** *pron* : additional persons or things ⟨~ were found in the road⟩

mo·rel \mə-ˈrel\ *n* : any of several pitted edible fungi

more·over \mōr-ˈō-vər\ *adv* : in addition : FURTHER

mo·res \ˈmȯr-ˌāz\ *n pl* **1** : the fixed morally binding customs of a group **2** : HABITS, MANNERS

Mor·gan \ˈmȯr-gən\ *n* : any of an American breed of lightly built horses

morgue \ˈmȯrg\ *n* : a place where the bodies of dead persons are kept until released for burial

mor·i·bund \ˈmȯr-ə-(ˌ)bənd\ *adj* : being in a dying condition — **mor·i·bun·di·ty** \ˌmȯr-ə-ˈbən-dət-ē\ *n*

Mor·mon \ˈmȯr-mən\ *n* : a member of the Church of Jesus Christ of Latter-day Saints — **Mor·mon·ism** \-mə-ˌniz-əm\ *n*

morn \ˈmȯrn\ *n* : MORNING

morn·ing \ˈmȯr-niŋ\ *n* **1** : the early part of the day; *esp* : the time from the sunrise to noon **2** : BEGINNING

morning glory *n* : any of various twining plants related to the sweet potato that have often showy bell-shaped or funnel-shaped flowers

morning sickness *n* : nausea and vomiting that occur in the morning esp. during early pregnancy

morning star *n* : a bright planet (as Venus) seen in the eastern sky before or at sunrise

Mo·roc·can \mə-ˈräk-ən\ *n* : a native or inhabitant of Morocco

mo·roc·co \mə-ˈräk-ō\ *n* : a fine leather made of goatskins tanned with sumac

mo·ron \ˈmōr-ˌän\ *n* : a defective person having a potential mental age of between 8 and 12 years and capable of doing routine work under supervision; *also* : a stupid person — **mo·ron·ic** \mə-ˈrän-ik\ *adj* — **mo·ron·i·cal·ly** \-i-k(ə-)lē\ *adv*

mo·rose \mə-ˈrōs\ *adj* [L *morosus*, lit., capricious, fr. *mor-, mos* will] : having a sullen disposition; *also* : GLOOMY — **mo·rose·ly** *adv* — **mo·rose·ness** *n*

mor·pheme \ˈmȯr-ˌfēm\ *n* : a meaningful linguistic unit that contains no smaller meaningful parts — **mor·phe·mic** \mȯr-ˈfē-mik\ *adj*

mor·phia \ˈmȯr-fē-ə\ *n* : MORPHINE

mor·phine \ˈmȯr-ˌfēn\ *n* [F, fr. Gk *Morpheus* Greek god of dreams] : an addictive drug obtained from opium and used to ease pain or induce sleep

mor·phol·o·gy \mȯr-ˈfäl-ə-jē\ *n* **1** : a branch of biology dealing with the form and structure of organisms **2** : a study and description of word formation in a language — **mor·pho·log·i·cal** \ˌmȯr-fə-ˈläj-i-kəl\ *adj* — **mor·phol·o·gist** \mȯr-ˈfäl-ə-jəst\ *n*

mor·ris \ˈmȯr-əs\ *n* : a vigorous English dance performed traditionally by men wearing costumes and bells

mor·row \ˈmär-ō\ *n* : the next day

Morse code \ˈmȯrs-\ *n* : either of two codes consisting of dots and dashes or long and short sounds used for transmitting messages

mor·sel \ˈmȯr-səl\ *n* [ME, fr. OF, dim. of *mors* bite, fr. L *morsus*, fr. *mordēre* to bite] **1** : a small piece or quantity **2** : a tasty dish

mor·tal \ˈmȯrt-ᵊl\ *adj* **1** : causing death : FATAL; *also* : leading to eternal punishment ⟨~ sin⟩ **2** : subject to death ⟨~ man⟩ **3** : implacably hostile ⟨~ foe⟩ **4** : very great : EXTREME ⟨~ fear⟩ **5** : HUMAN ⟨~ limitations⟩ — **mortal** *n* — **mor·tal·i·ty** \mȯr-ˈtal-ət-ē\ *n* — **mor·tal·ly** \ˈmȯrt-ᵊl-ē\ *adv*

[1]**mor·tar** \ˈmȯrt-ər\ *n* **1** : a strong bowl in which substances are pounded or crushed with a pestle **2** : a short-barreled cannon used to fire shells at high angles

[2]**mortar** *n* : a plastic building material (as a mixture of cement, lime, or gypsum plaster with sand and water) that is spread between bricks or stones to bind them together as it hardens — **mortar** *vb*

mor·tar·board \ˈmȯrt-ər-ˌbōrd\ *n* **1** : a board or platform about three feet square for holding mortar **2** : an academic cap with a broad square top
mort·gage \ˈmȯr-gij\ *n* [ME *morgage*, fr. MF, fr. OF, fr. *mort* dead + *gage* gage] : a transfer of rights to a piece of property usu. as security for the payment of a loan or debt that becomes void when the debt is paid — **mortgage** *vb* — **mort·gag·ee** \ˌmȯr-gi-ˈjē\ *n* — **mort·ga·gor** \ˌmȯr-gi-ˈjȯr\ *n*
mor·ti·cian \mȯr-ˈtish-ən\ *n* [L *mort-*, *mors* death + E *-ician* (as in *physician*)] : UNDERTAKER
mor·ti·fy \ˈmȯrt-ə-ˌfī\ *vb* **-fied; -fy·ing 1** : to subdue (as the body) esp. by abstinence or self-inflicted pain **2** : HUMILIATE **3** : to become necrotic or gangrenous — **mor·ti·fi·ca·tion** \ˌmȯrt-ə-fə-ˈkā-shən\ *n*
mor·tise *also* **mor·tice** \ˈmȯrt-əs\ *n* : a hole cut in a piece of wood into which another piece fits to form a joint
mor·tu·ary \ˈmȯr-chə-ˌwer-ē\ *n, pl* **-ar·ies** : a place in which dead bodies are kept until burial
mos *abbr* months
mo·sa·ic \mō-ˈzā-ik\ *n* : a surface decoration made by inlaying small pieces (as of colored glass or stone) to form figures or patterns; *also* : a design made in mosaic
mo·sey \ˈmō-zē\ *vb* **mo·seyed; mo·sey·ing** : SAUNTER
Mos·lem \ˈmäz-ləm\ *var of* MUSLIM
mosque \ˈmäsk\ *n* : a building used for public worship by Muslims
mos·qui·to \mə-ˈskēt-ō\ *n, pl* **-toes** *also* **-tos** : a two-winged fly the female of which sucks the blood of man and lower animals
mosquito net *n* : a net or screen for keeping out mosquitoes
moss \ˈmȯs\ *n* : any of a large group of green plants without flowers but with small leafy stems growing in clumps — **mossy** *adj*
moss·back \ˈmȯs-ˌbak\ *n* : an extremely conservative person : FOGY
[1]**most** \ˈmōst\ *adj* **1** : the majority of ⟨~ people⟩ **2** : GREATEST ⟨the ~ ability⟩
[2]**most** *adv* **1** : to the greatest or highest degree ⟨~ beautiful⟩ **2** : to a very great degree ⟨a ~ careful driver⟩
[3]**most** *n* : the greatest amount ⟨the ~ he can do⟩
[4]**most** *pron* : the greatest number or part ⟨~ became discouraged⟩
-most \ˌmōst\ *adj suffix* : most ⟨inner*most*⟩
most·ly \ˈmōst-lē\ *adv* : MAINLY
mot \ˈmō\ *n, pl* **mots** \ˈmō(z)\ [F, word, saying, fr. L *muttum* grunt] : a witty saying
mote \ˈmōt\ *n* : a small particle
mo·tel \mō-ˈtel\ *n* [blend of *motor* and *hotel*] : a hotel in which the rooms are accessible from an outdoor parking area
mo·tet \mō-ˈtet\ *n* : a choral work on a sacred text for several voices usu. without instrumental accompaniment
moth \ˈmȯth\ *n, pl* **moths** \ˈmȯt͟hz, ˈmȯths\ : any of various insects belonging to the same order as the butterflies but usu. night-flying and with a stouter body and smaller wings; *esp* : CLOTHES MOTH
moth·ball \ˈmȯth-ˌbȯl\ *n* **1** : a ball (as of naphthalene) used to keep moths out of clothing **2** *pl* : protective storage ⟨ships put in ~*s* after the war⟩
[1]**moth·er** \ˈmət͟h-ər\ *n* **1** : a female parent **2** : the superior of a religious community of women **3** : SOURCE, ORIGIN — **moth·er·hood** \-ˌhu̇d\ *n* — **moth·er·less** *adj* — **moth·er·li·ness** \-lē-nəs\ *n* — **moth·er·ly** *adj*
[2]**mother** *vb* **moth·ered; moth·er·ing** \ˈmət͟h-(ə-)riŋ\ **1** : to give birth to; *also* : PRODUCE **2** : to protect like a mother
moth·er–in–law \ˈmət͟h-ə-rən-ˌlȯ, ˈmət͟h-ərn-ˌlȯ\ *n, pl* **mothers–in–law** \ˈmət͟h-ər-zən-\ : the mother of one's spouse
moth·er·land \ˈmət͟h-ər-ˌland\ *n* **1** : the land of origin of something **2** : the native land of one's ancestors
moth·er–of–pearl \ˌmət͟h-ə-rə(v)-ˈpərl\ *n* : the hard pearly matter forming the inner layer of a mollusk shell
mo·tif \mō-ˈtēf\ *n* [F, motive, motif] : a dominant idea or central theme (as in a work of art)
mo·tile \ˈmōt-ᵊl, ˈmō-ˌtīl\ *adj* : capable of spontaneous movement — **mo·til·i·ty** \mō-ˈtil-ət-ē\ *n*
[1]**mo·tion** \ˈmō-shən\ *n* **1** : a proposal for action (as by a deliberative body) **2** : an act, process, or instance of moving **3** *pl* : ACTIVITIES, MOVEMENTS — **mo·tion·less** *adj* — **mo·tion·less·ly** *adv* — **mo·tion·less·ness** *n*
[2]**motion** *vb* **mo·tioned; mo·tion·ing** \ˈmō-sh(ə-)niŋ\ : to direct or signal by a motion
motion picture *n* : a series of pictures thrown on a screen so rapidly that they produce a continuous picture in which persons and objects seem to move
motion sickness *n* : sickness induced by motion and characterized by nausea
mo·ti·vate \ˈmōt-ə-ˌvāt\ *vb* **-vat·ed; -vat·ing** : to provide with a motive : IMPEL — **mo·ti·va·tion** \ˌmōt-ə-ˈvā-shən\ *n*
[1]**mo·tive** \ˈmōt-iv, *2 also* mō-ˈtēv\ *n* **1** : something (as a need or desire) that causes a person to act **2** : a recurrent theme in a musical composition — **mo·tive·less** *adj*
[2]**mo·tive** \ˈmōt-iv\ *adj* **1** : moving to action **2** : of or relating to motion
mot·ley \ˈmät-lē\ *adj* **1** : variegated in color **2** : made up of diverse often incongruous elements **syn** heterogeneous, miscellaneous, assorted, mixed, varied
[1]**mo·tor** \ˈmōt-ər\ *n* **1** : one that imparts motion **2** : a machine that produces motion or power for doing work **3** : AUTOMOBILE
[2]**motor** *vb* : to travel or transport by automobile : DRIVE — **mo·tor·ist** *n*
mo·tor·bike \ˈmōt-ər-ˌbīk\ *n* : a small lightweight motorcycle
mo·tor·boat \-ˌbōt\ *n* : a boat propelled by a motor
mo·tor·cade \-ˌkād\ *n* : a procession of motor vehicles
mo·tor·car \-ˌkär\ *n* : AUTOMOBILE
motor court *n* : MOTEL
mo·tor·cy·cle \ˈmōt-ər-ˌsī-kəl\ *n* : a 2-wheeled automotive vehicle — **mo·tor·cy·clist** \-k(ə-)ləst\ *n*
motor home *n* : a motor vehicle built on a truck or bus chassis and equipped as a self-contained traveling home
mo·tor·ize \ˈmōt-ə-ˌrīz\ *vb* **-ized; -iz·ing 1** : to equip with a motor **2** : to equip with motor-driven vehicles
mo·tor·man \ˈmōt-ər-mən\ *n* : an operator of a motor-driven vehicle (as a streetcar or subway train)
motor scooter *n* : a low 2- or 3-wheeled automotive vehicle resembling a child's scooter but having a seat
mo·tor·truck \ˈmōt-ər-ˌtrək\ *n* : an automotive truck
motor vehicle *n* : an automotive vehicle (as an automobile) not operated on rails
mot·tle \ˈmät-ᵊl\ *vb* **mot·tled; mot·tling** \ˈmät-(ᵊ-)liŋ\ : to mark with spots of different color : BLOTCH
mot·to \ˈmät-ō\ *n, pl* **mottoes** *also* **mottos** [It, fr. L *muttum* grunt, fr. *muttire* to mutter] **1** : a sentence, phrase, or word inscribed on something to indicate its character or use **2** : a short expression of a guiding rule of conduct
moue \ˈmü\ *n* : a little grimace
mould \ˈmōld\ *var of* MOLD
moult \ˈmōlt\ *var of* MOLT
mound \ˈmau̇nd\ *n* **1** : an artificial bank or hill of earth or stones **2** : KNOLL
[1]**mount** \ˈmau̇nt\ *n* : a high hill
[2]**mount** *vb* **1** : to increase in amount or extent; *also* : RISE, ASCEND **2** : to get up on something; *esp* : to seat oneself on (as a horse) for riding **3** : to put in position ⟨~ artillery⟩ **4** : to set on something that elevates **5** : to

attach to a support **6** : to prepare esp. for examination or display : ARRANGE — **mount·able** *adj* — **mount·er** *n*

[3]**mount** *n* **1** : FRAME, SUPPORT **2** : a means of conveyance; *esp* : SADDLE HORSE

moun·tain \ˈmau̇nt-ᵊn\ *n* : a landmass higher than a hill — **moun·tain·ous** \-(ᵊ-)nəs\ *adj*

mountain ash *n* : any of various trees related to the roses that have pinnate leaves and red or orange-red fruits

moun·tain·eer \ˌmau̇nt-ᵊn-ˈiər\ *n* **1** : a native or inhabitant of a mountainous region **2** : one who climbs mountains for sport

mountain goat *n* : an antelope of mountainous northwestern No. America that resembles a goat

mountain laurel *n* : a No. American evergreen shrub of the heath family that has glossy leaves and clusters of rose-colored or white flowers

mountain lion *n* : COUGAR

moun·tain·side \ˈmau̇nt-ᵊn-ˌsīd\ *n* : the side of a mountain

moun·tain·top \-ˌtäp\ *n* : the summit of a mountain

moun·te·bank \ˈmau̇nt-i-ˌbaŋk\ *n* [It *montimbanco,* fr. *montare* to mount + *in* in, on + *banco, banca* bench] : QUACK, CHARLATAN

Mount·ie \ˈmau̇nt-ē\ *n* : a member of the Royal Canadian Mounted Police

mount·ing \ˈmau̇nt-iŋ\ *n* : something that serves as a frame or support

mourn \ˈmōrn\ *vb* : to feel or express grief or sorrow — **mourn·er** *n*

mourn·ful \-fəl\ *adj* : expressing, feeling, or causing sorrow — **mourn·ful·ly** \-ē\ *adv* — **mourn·ful·ness** *n*

mourn·ing \ˈmōr-niŋ\ *n* **1** : an outward sign (as black clothes) of grief for a person's death **2** : a period of time during which signs of grief are shown

mouse \ˈmau̇s\ *n, pl* **mice** \ˈmīs\ : any of various small rodents with pointed snout, long body, and slender tail

mous·er \ˈmau̇-zər\ *n* : a cat proficient at catching mice

mouse·trap \ˈmau̇s-ˌtrap\ *n* **1** : a trap for catching mice **2** : a stratagem that lures one to defeat or destruction — **mousetrap** *vb*

mousse \ˈmüs\ *n* [F, lit., froth] : a molded chilled dessert made with sweetened and flavored whipped cream or egg whites and gelatin

mous·tache \ˈməs-ˌtash, (ˌ)məs-ˈtash\ *var of* MUSTACHE

mousy *or* **mous·ey** \ˈmau̇-sē, -zē\ *adj* **mous·i·er; -est 1** : QUIET, STEALTHY **2** : TIMID — **mous·i·ness** \ˈmau̇-sē-nəs, -zē-\ *n*

[1]**mouth** \ˈmau̇th\ *n, pl* **mouths** \ˈmau̇t͟hz, ˈmau̇ths\ **1** : the opening through which an animal takes in food; *also* : the space between the mouth and the pharynx **2** : something resembling a mouth (as in affording entrance) — **mouthed** \ˈmau̇t͟hd, ˈmau̇tht\ *adj* — **mouth·ful** *n*

[2]**mouth** \ˈmau̇t͟h\ *vb* : SPEAK; *also* : DECLAIM

mouth·part \ˈmau̇th-ˌpärt\ *n* : a structure or appendage near the mouth (as of an insect) esp. when adapted for eating

mouth·piece \-ˌpēs\ *n* **1** : a part (as of a musical instrument) that goes in the mouth or to which the mouth is applied **2** : SPOKESMAN

mouth·wash \-ˌwȯsh, -ˌwäsh\ *n* : a usu. antiseptic liquid preparation for cleaning the mouth and teeth

mou·ton \ˈmü-ˌtän\ *n* : processed sheepskin that has been sheared or dyed to resemble beaver or seal

[1]**move** \ˈmüv\ *vb* **moved; mov·ing 1** : to change or cause to change position or posture : SHIFT **2** : to go or cause to go from one point to another : ADVANCE; *also* : DEPART **3** : to take or cause to take action : PROMPT **4** : to show marked activity **5** : to stir the emotions **6** : to make a formal request, application, or appeal **7** : to change one's residence **8** : EVACUATE 2 — **mov·able** *or* **move·able** \-ə-bəl\ *adj*

[2]**move** *n* **1** : an act of moving **2** : a calculated procedure : MANEUVER

move·ment \ˈmüv-mənt\ *n* **1** : the act or process of moving : MOVE **2** : TENDENCY, TREND; *also* : a series of organized activities working toward an objective **3** : the moving parts of a mechanism (as of a watch) **4** : RHYTHM **5** : a unit or division of an extended musical composition **6** : CADENCE **7** : an act of voiding the bowels; *also* : STOOL 4

mov·er \ˈmü-vər\ *n* : one that moves; *esp* : a person or company that moves the belongings of others from one home or place of business to another

mov·ie \ˈmü-vē\ *n* **1** : MOTION PICTURE **2** *pl* : a showing of a motion picture **3** *pl* : the motion-picture industry

[1]**mow** \ˈmau̇\ *n* : the part of a barn where hay or straw is stored

[2]**mow** \ˈmō\ *vb* **mowed; mowed** *or* **mown** \ˈmōn\; **mow·ing 1** : to cut (as grass) with a scythe or machine **2** : to cut the standing herbage of ⟨~ the lawn⟩ — **mow·er** *n*

Mo·zam·bi·can \ˌmō-zəm-ˈbē-kən\ *n* : a native or inhabitant of Mozambique

moz·za·rel·la \ˌmät-sə-ˈrel-ə\ *n* [It] : a moist white unsalted unripened mild cheese of a smooth rubbery texture

MP *abbr* **1** melting point **2** member of parliament **3** metropolitan police **4** military police; military policeman

mpg *abbr* miles per gallon

mph *abbr* miles per hour

Mr. \ˌmis-tər\ *n, pl* **Messrs.** \ˌmes-ərz\ — used as a conventional title of courtesy before a man's surname or his title of office

Mrs. \ˌmis-əz, -əs, *esp Southern* ˌmiz-əz, -əs, *or* (ˌ)miz, *or before given names* (ˌ)mis\ *n, pl* **Mes·dames** \mā-ˈdäm, -ˈdam\ — used as a conventional title of courtesy before a married woman's surname

Ms. \(ˈ)miz\ *n* — used instead of *Miss* or *Mrs.*

MS *abbr* **1** manuscript **2** master of science **3** military science **4** Mississippi **5** motor ship **6** multiple sclerosis

msec *abbr* millisecond

msg *abbr* message

MSG *abbr* **1** master sergeant **2** monosodium glutamate

msgr *abbr* **1** monseigneur **2** monsignor

MSgt *abbr* master sergeant

MSS *abbr* manuscripts

MST *abbr* mountain standard time

mt *abbr* mount; mountain

Mt *abbr* Matthew

MT *abbr* **1** metric ton **2** Montana **3** mountain time

mtg *abbr* **1** meeting **2** mortgage

mtge *abbr* mortgage

[1]**much** \ˈməch\ *adj* **more** \ˈmōr\; **most** \ˈmōst\ : great in quantity, amount, extent, or degree ⟨~ money⟩

[2]**much** *adv* **more; most 1** : to a great degree or extent ⟨~ happier⟩ **2** : APPROXIMATELY, NEARLY ⟨looks ~ as he did years ago⟩

[3]**much** *n* **1** : a great quantity, amount, extent, or degree **2** : something considerable or impressive

mu·ci·lage \ˈmyü-s(ə-)lij\ *n* : a watery sticky solution (as of a gum) used esp. as an adhesive — **mu·ci·lag·i·nous** \ˌmyü-sə-ˈlaj-ə-nəs\ *adj*

muck \ˈmək\ *n* **1** : soft moist barnyard manure **2** : FILTH, DIRT **3** : a dark richly organic soil; *also* : MUD, MIRE — **mucky** *adj*

muck·rak·er \-ˌrā-kər\ *n* : one who exposes publicly real or apparent misconduct of prominent individuals — **muck·rak·ing** \-ˌrā-kiŋ\ *n*

mu·cus \ˈmyü-kəs\ *n* : a slimy slippery protective secretion of membranes (**mucous membranes**) lining some body cavities — **mu·cous** \-kəs\ *adj*

mud \ˈməd\ *n* : soft wet earth : MIRE — **mud·di·ly** \ˈməd-ᵊl-ē\ *adv* — **mud·di·ness** \-ē-nəs\ *n* — **mud·dy** *adj or vb*

mud·dle \ˈməd-ᵊl\ *vb* **mud·dled; mud·dling** \ˈməd-(ᵊ-)liŋ\ **1** : to make muddy **2** : to confuse esp. with liquor **3** : to mix up or make a mess of **4** : to think or act in a confused way

mud·dle·head·ed \ˌməd-ᵊl-ˈhed-əd\ *adj* **1** : mentally confused **2** : INEPT

mud·guard \ˈməd-ˌgärd\ *n* : a guard over or a flap behind a wheel of a vehicle to catch or deflect mud

mud·room \ˈməd-ˌrüm, -ˌru̇m\ *n* : a room in a house for removing dirty or wet footwear and clothing

mud·sling·er \-ˌsliŋ-ər\ *n* : one who uses invective esp. against a political opponent — **mud·sling·ing** \-ˌsliŋ-iŋ\ *n*

Muen·ster \ˈmən-stər, ˈm(y)ün-, ˈmu̇n-\ *n* : a semisoft bland or sharp cheese

mu·ez·zin \m(y)ü-ˈez-ᵊn\ *n* : a Muslim crier who calls the hour of daily prayer

[1]**muff** \ˈməf\ *n* : a warm tubular covering for the hands

[2]**muff** *n* : a bungling performance; *esp* : a failure to hold a ball in attempting a catch — **muff** *vb*

muf·fin \ˈməf-ən\ *n* : a small soft biscuit baked in a small cup-shaped container

muf·fle \ˈməf-əl\ *vb* **muf·fled; muf·fling** \ˈməf-(ə-)liŋ\ **1** : to wrap up so as to conceal or protect **2** : to wrap or pad with something to dull the sound of **3** : to keep down : SUPPRESS

muf·fler \ˈməf-lər\ *n* **1** : a scarf worn around the neck **2** : a device to deaden noise

muf·ti \ˈməf-tē\ *n* : civilian clothes

[1]**mug** \ˈməg\ *n* : a usu. metal or earthenware cylindrical drinking cup

[2]**mug** *vb* **mugged; mug·ging 1** : to make faces esp. in order to attract the attention of an audience **2** : PHOTOGRAPH

[3]**mug** *vb* **mugged; mug·ging** : to assault usu. with intent to rob — **mug·ger** *n*

mug·gy \ˈməg-ē\ *adj* **mug·gi·er; -est** : being warm and humid — **mug·gi·ness** \ˈməg-ē-nəs\ *n*

mug·wump \ˈməg-ˌwəmp\ *n* [obs. slang *mugwump* (kingpin), fr. Natick (a No. American Indian dialect) *mugwomp* captain] : an independent in politics

Mu·ham·mad·an \mō-ˈham-əd-ən, -ˈhäm-; mü-\ *n* : MUSLIM — **Mu·ham·mad·an·ism** \-ˌiz-əm\ *n*

muk·luk \ˈmək-ˌlək\ *n* [Esk *muklok* large seal] **1** : an Eskimo boot of sealskin or reindeer skin **2** : a boot with a soft leather sole worn over several pairs of socks

mu·lat·to \m(y)u̇-ˈlat-ō, -ˈlät-\ *n, pl* **-toes** *or* **-tos** [Sp *mulato,* fr. *mulo* mule, fr. L *mulus;* so called because the mule is the offspring of parents of different species] : a first-generation offspring of a Negro and a white; *also* : a person of mixed Caucasian and Negro ancestry

mul·ber·ry \ˈməl-ˌber-ē\ *n* : a tree grown for its leaves that are used as food for silkworms or for its edible berrylike fruit; *also* : this fruit

mulch \ˈməlch\ *n* : a protective covering (as of straw or leaves) spread on the ground esp. to reduce evaporation or control weeds — **mulch** *vb*

[1]**mulct** \ˈməlkt\ *vb* **1** : FINE **2** : DEFRAUD

[2]**mulct** *n* : FINE, PENALTY

[1]**mule** \ˈmyül\ *n* **1** : a hybrid offspring of a male donkey and a female horse **2** : a very stubborn person — **mul·ish** \ˈmyü-lish\ *adj* — **mul·ish·ly** *adv* — **mu·lish·ness** *n*

[2]**mule** *n* : a slipper whose upper does not extend around the heel of the foot

mule deer *n* : a long-eared deer of western No. America

mu·le·teer \ˌmyü-lə-ˈtiər\ *n* : one who drives mules

[1]**mull** \ˈməl\ *vb* : PONDER, MEDITATE

[2]**mull** *vb* : to heat, sweeten, and flavor (as wine) with spices

mul·lein \ˈməl-ən\ *n* : a tall herb with coarse woolly leaves and flowers in spikes

mul·let \ˈməl-ət\ *n, pl* **mullet** *or* **mullets 1** : any of various largely gray marine food fishes **2** : any of various red or golden mostly tropical marine food fishes

mul·li·gan stew \ˌməl-i-gən-\ *n* : a stew made from whatever ingredients are available

mul·li·ga·taw·ny \ˌməl-i-gə-ˈtȯ-nē\ *n* : a soup usu. of chicken stock seasoned with curry

mul·lion \ˈməl-yən\ *n* : a vertical strip separating windowpanes

multi- *comb form* **1** : many : multiple ⟨*multi*unit⟩ **2** : many times over ⟨*multi*millionaire⟩

mul·ti·col·ored \ˌməl-ti-ˈkəl-ərd\ *adj* : having many colors

mul·ti·di·men·sion·al \-ti-də-ˈmench-nəl, -dī-; -ˌtī-də-\ *adj* : of, relating to, or having many dimensions ⟨a ~ problem⟩

mul·ti·fac·et·ed \-ˈfas-ət-əd\ *adj* : having several distinct facets

mul·ti·fam·i·ly \-ˈfam-(ə-)lē\ *adj* : designed for use by several families

mul·ti·far·i·ous \ˌməl-tə-ˈfar-ē-əs\ *adj* : having great variety : DIVERSE — **mul·ti·far·i·ous·ly** *adv*

mul·ti·flo·ra rose \ˌməl-tə-ˌflōr-ə-\ *n* : a vigorous thorny rose with clusters of small flowers

mul·ti·form \ˈməl-ti-ˌfȯrm\ *adj* : having many forms or appearances — **mul·ti·for·mi·ty** \ˌməl-ti-ˈfȯr-mət-ē\ *n*

mul·ti·lat·er·al \ˌməl-ti-ˈlat-ə-rəl, -ˌtī-, -ˈla-trəl\ *adj* : having many sides or participants ⟨~ treaty⟩

mul·ti·lev·el \-ˈlev-əl\ *adj* : having several levels

mul·ti·lin·gual \-ˈliŋ-gwəl\ *adj* : containing, expressed in, or able to use several languages — **mul·ti·lin·gual·ism** \-gwə-ˌliz-əm\ *n*

mul·ti·me·dia \-ˈmēd-ē-ə\ *adj* : using, involving, or encompassing several media ⟨a ~ advertising campaign⟩

mul·ti·mil·lion·aire \ˌməl-ti-ˌmil-yə-ˈnaər, -ˌtī-, -ˈmil-yə-ˌnaər\ *n* : a person worth several million dollars

mul·ti·na·tion·al \-ˈnash-(ə-)nəl\ *adj* **1** : of or relating to several nationalities ⟨a ~ society⟩ **2** : relating to or involving several nations **3** : having divisions in several countries

[1]**mul·ti·ple** \ˈməl-tə-pəl\ *adj* **1** : more than one; *also* : MANY **2** : VARIOUS, COMPLEX

[2]**multiple** *n* : the product of a quantity by an integer ⟨35 is a ~ of 7⟩

multiple–choice *adj* : having several answers given from which the correct one is to be chosen ⟨a ~ question⟩

multiple sclerosis *n* : a disease marked by patches of hardened tissue in the brain or spinal cord resulting in partial or complete paralysis and muscular twitching

mul·ti·pli·cand \ˌməl-tə-pli-ˈkand\ *n* : a number that is to be multiplied by another

mul·ti·pli·ca·tion \ˌməl-tə-plə-ˈkā-shən\ *n* **1** : INCREASE **2** : a short method of finding out what would be the result of adding a figure the number of times indicated by another figure

multiplication sign *n* **1** : TIMES SIGN **2** : a centered dot used to indicate multiplication

mul·ti·plic·i·ty \ˌməl-tə-ˈplis-ət-ē\ *n, pl* **-ties** : a great number or variety

mul·ti·pli·er \ˈməl-tə-ˌplī(-ə)r\ *n* : one that multiplies; *esp* : a number by which another number is multiplied

mul·ti·ply \ˈməl-tə-ˌplī\ *vb* **-plied; -ply·ing 1** : to increase in number (as by breeding) **2** : to find the product of by multiplication

mul·ti·pur·pose \ˌməl-ti-ˈpər-pəs, -ˌtī-\ *adj* : having or serving several purposes

mul·ti·ra·cial \-ˈrā-shəl\ *adj* : composed of, involving, or representing several races

mul·ti·sense \-ˌsen(t)s\ *adj* : having several meanings ⟨~ words⟩

mul·ti·stage \-ˌstāj\ *adj* : having successive operating stages ⟨~ rockets⟩

mul·ti·sto·ry \-ˌstōr-ē\ *adj* : having several stories ⟨~ buildings⟩

\ə\abut \ᵊ\kitten \ər\further \a\ash \ā\ace \ä\cot, cart \au̇\out \ch\chin \e\bet \ē\easy \g\go \i\hit \ī\ice \j\job \ŋ\sing \ō\go \ȯ\law \ȯi\boy \th\thin \t͟h\the \ü\loot \u̇\foot \y\yet \zh\vision *see also* Pronunciation Symbols page

mul·ti·tude \ˈməl-tə-ˌt(y)üd\ *n* : a great number — **mul·ti·tu·di·nous** \ˌməl-tə-ˈt(y)üd-(ᵊ-)nəs\ *adj*

mul·ti·unit \ˌməl-ti-ˈyü-nət, -ˌtī-\ *adj* : having several units

mul·ti·ver·si·ty \ˌməl-ti-ˈvər-s(ə-)tē\ *n, pl* **-ties** : a very large university with many divisions and diverse functions

mul·ti·vi·ta·min \-ˈvīt-ə-mən\ *adj* : containing several vitamins and esp. all known to be essential to health

[1]**mum** \ˈməm\ *adj* : SILENT

[2]**mum** *n* : CHRYSANTHEMUM

mum·ble \ˈməm-bəl\ *vb* **mum·bled; mum·bling** \-b(ə-)liŋ\ : to speak in a low indistinct manner — **mumble** *n* — **mum·bler** \-b(ə-)lər\ *n* — **mum·bly** \-b(ə-)lē\ *adj*

mum·ble·ty-peg *or* **mum·ble-the-peg** \ˈməm-bəl-(tē-)ˌpeg\ *n* : a game in which the players try to flip a knife from various positions so that the blade will stick into the ground

mum·bo jum·bo \ˌməm-bō-ˈjəm-bō\ *n* **1** : a complicated ritual with elaborate trappings **2** : confusing or meaningless talk : NONSENSE

mum·mer \ˈməm-ər\ *n* **1** : an actor esp. in a pantomime **2** : one who goes merrymaking in disguise during festivals — **mum·mery** *n*

mum·my \ˈməm-ē\ *n, pl* **mummies** [ME *mummie* powdered parts of a mummified body used as a drug, fr. MF *momie,* fr. ML *mumia* mummy, powdered mummy, fr. Ar *mūmiyah* bitumen, mummy, fr. Per *mūm* wax] : a body embalmed for burial in the manner of the ancient Egyptians — **mum·mi·fi·ca·tion** \ˌməm-i-fə-ˈkā-shən\ *n* — **mum·mi·fy** \ˈməm-i-ˌfī\ *vb*

mumps \ˈməmps\ *n sing or pl* [fr. pl. of obs. *mump* (grimace)] : a virus disease marked by fever and swelling esp. of the salivary glands

mun *or* **munic** *abbr* municipal

munch \ˈmənch\ *vb* : to chew with a crunching sound

munch·ies \ˈmən-chēz\ *n pl* **1** : hunger pangs **2** : light snack foods

mun·dane \ˌmən-ˈdān, ˈmən-ˌdān\ *adj* **1** : of or relating to the world **2** : concerned with the practical details of everyday life — **mun·dane·ly** *adv*

mu·nic·i·pal \myu̇-ˈnis-ə-pəl\ *adj* **1** : of, relating to, or characteristic of a municipality **2** : restricted to one locality — **mu·nic·i·pal·ly** \-ē\ *adv*

mu·nic·i·pal·i·ty \myu̇-ˌnis-ə-ˈpal-ət-ē\ *n, pl* **-ties** : an urban political unit with corporate status and usu. powers of self-government

mu·nif·i·cent \myu̇-ˈnif-ə-sənt\ *adj* : liberal in giving : GENEROUS — **mu·nif·i·cence** \-səns\ *n*

mu·ni·tions \myu̇-ˈnish-ənz\ *n pl* : military materiel; *esp* : AMMUNITION

[1]**mu·ral** \ˈmyu̇r-əl\ *adj* **1** : of or relating to a wall **2** : applied to and made part of a wall surface

[2]**mural** *n* : a mural painting — **mu·ral·ist** *n*

[1]**mur·der** \ˈmərd-ər\ *n* **1** : the crime of unlawfully killing a person esp. with malice aforethought **2** : something unusually difficult or dangerous

[2]**murder** *vb* **1** : to commit a murder; *also* : to kill brutally **2** : to put an end to **3** : to spoil by performing poorly ⟨~ a song⟩ — **mur·der·er** *n*

mur·der·ess \ˈmərd-ə-rəs\ *n* : a woman who murders

mur·der·ous \ˈmərd-ər-əs\ *adj* **1** : marked by or causing murder or bloodshed ⟨~ gunfire⟩ **2** : having or appearing to have the purpose of murder — **mur·der·ous·ly** *adv*

murk \ˈmərk\ *n* : DARKNESS, GLOOM — **murk·i·ly** \ˈmər-kə-lē\ *adv* — **murk·i·ness** \-kē-nəs\ *n* — **murky** *adj*

mur·mur \ˈmər-mər\ *n* **1** : a muttered complaint **2** : a low indistinct often continuous sound — **murmur** *vb* — **mur·mur·er** *n* — **mur·mur·ous** *adj*

mur·rain \ˈmər-ən\ *n* : PLAGUE

mus *abbr* **1** museum **2** music

mus·ca·tel \ˌməs-kə-ˈtel\ *n* : a sweet dessert wine

[1]**mus·cle** \ˈməs-əl\ *n* [MF, fr. L *musculus,* fr. dim. of *mus* mouse] **1** : body tissue consisting of long cells that contract when stimulated; *also* : an organ consisting of this tissue and functioning in moving a body part **2** : STRENGTH, BRAWN — **mus·cled** \ˈməs-əld\ *adj* — **mus·cu·lar** \ˈməs-kyə-lər\ *adj* — **mus·cu·lar·i·ty** \ˌməs-kyə-ˈlar-ət-ē\ *n*

[2]**muscle** *vb* **mus·cled; mus·cling** \ˈməs-(ə-)liŋ\ : to force one's way ⟨~ in on another racketeer⟩

mus·cle–bound \ˈməs-əl-ˌbau̇nd\ *adj* : having some of the muscles abnormally enlarged and lacking in elasticity (as from excessive athletic exercise)

muscular dystrophy *n* : a disease characterized by progressive wasting of muscles

mus·cu·la·ture \ˈməs-kyə-lə-ˌchu̇r\ *n* : the muscles of the body or its parts

[1]**muse** \ˈmyüz\ *vb* **mused; mus·ing** [ME *musen,* fr. MF *muser* to gape, idle, muse, fr. *muse* mouth of an animal, fr. ML *musus*] : to become absorbed in thought — **mus·ing·ly** *adv*

[2]**muse** *n* [fr. *Muse* any of the nine sister goddesses of learning and the arts in Greek mythology, fr. ME, fr. MF, fr. L *Musa,* fr. Gk *Mousa*] : a source of inspiration

mu·sette \myu̇-ˈzet\ *n* [F] : a small knapsack with a shoulder strap used esp. by soldiers for carrying provisions and personal belongings

musette bag *n* : MUSETTE

mu·se·um \myu̇-ˈzē-əm\ *n* : an institution devoted to the procurement, care, and display of objects of lasting interest or value

[1]**mush** \ˈməsh\ *n* **1** : cornmeal boiled in water **2** : sentimental drivel

[2]**mush** *vb* : to travel esp. over snow with a sled drawn by dogs

[1]**mush·room** \ˈməsh-ˌrüm, -ˌru̇m\ *n* : the fleshy usu. caplike spore-bearing organ of various fungi esp. when edible

[2]**mushroom** *vb* **1** : to grow rapidly **2** : to spread out : EXPAND

mushy \ˈməsh-ē\ *adj* **mush·i·er; -est 1** : soft like mush **2** : weakly sentimental

mu·sic \ˈmyü-zik\ *n* **1** : the science or art of combining tones into a composition having structure and continuity; *also* : vocal or instrumental sounds having rhythm, melody, or harmony **2** : an agreeable sound **3** : the unpleasant consequences of one's actions ⟨face the ~⟩

[1]**mu·si·cal** \ˈmyü-zi-kəl\ *adj* **1** : of or relating to music or musicians **2** : having the pleasing tonal qualities of music **3** : having an interest in or a talent for music — **mu·si·cal·ly** \-k(ə-)lē\ *adv*

[2]**musical** *n* : a film or theatrical production consisting of musical numbers and dialogue based on a unifying plot

mu·si·cale \ˌmyü-zi-ˈkal\ *n* : a usu. private social gathering featuring music

mu·si·cian \myu̇-ˈzish-ən\ *n* : a composer, conductor, or performer of music — **mu·si·cian·ly** *adj* — **mu·si·cian·ship** *n*

mu·si·col·o·gy \ˌmyü-zi-ˈkäl-ə-jē\ *n* : a study of music as a field of knowledge or research — **mu·si·co·log·i·cal** \-kə-ˈläj-i-kəl\ *adj* — **mu·si·col·o·gist** \-ˈkäl-ə-jəst\ *n*

musk \ˈməsk\ *n* : a substance obtained esp. from a small Asian deer (**musk deer**) and used as a perfume fixative — **musk·i·ness** \ˈməs-kē-nəs\ *n* — **musky** *adj*

mus·keg \ˈməs-ˌkeg\ *n* : BOG; *esp* : a mossy bog in northern No. America

mus·kel·lunge \ˈməs-kə-ˌlənj\ *n, pl* **muskellunge** : a large No. American pike prized as a sport fish

mus·ket \ˈməs-kət\ *n* [MF *mousquet,* fr. It *moschetto* arrow for a crossbow, musket, fr. dim. of *mosca* fly, fr. L *musca*] : a heavy large-caliber usu. muzzle-loading shoulder firearm — **mus·ke·teer** \ˌməs-kə-ˈtiər\ *n*

mus·ket·ry \ˈməs-kə-trē\ *n* **1** : MUSKETS **2** : MUSKETEERS **3** : musket fire

musk·mel·on \ˈməsk-ˌmel-ən\ *n* : a small round to oval

muskellunge

melon that has usu. a sweet edible green or orange flesh

musk–ox \ˈməsk-ˌäks\ *n* : a heavyset shaggy-coated wild ox of Greenland and the arctic tundra of northern No. America

musk·rat \ˈməs-ˌkrat\ *n, pl* **muskrat** *or* **muskrats** : a large No. American water rodent with webbed feet and dark brown fur; *also* : its fur

Mus·lim \ˈməz-ləm\ *n* : an adherent of the religion founded by the Arab prophet Muhammad

mus·lin \ˈməz-lən\ *n* : a plain-woven sheer to coarse cotton fabric

¹muss \ˈməs\ *n* : a state of disorder — **muss·i·ly** \ˈməs-ə-lē\ *adv* — **muss·i·ness** \-ē-nəs\ *n* — **mussy** *adj*

²muss *vb* : to make untidy : DISARRANGE

mus·sel \ˈməs-əl\ *n* **1** : a dark edible saltwater bivalve mollusk **2** : any of various freshwater bivalve mollusks of the central U.S. having shells with a pearly lining

¹must \(ˈ)məst\ *vb* — used as an auxiliary esp. to express a command, requirement, obligation, or necessity

²must \ˈməst\ *n* **1** : an imperative duty **2** : an indispensable item

mus·tache \ˈməs-ˌtash, (ˌ)məs-ˈtash\ *n* : the hair growing on the human upper lip

mus·tang \ˈməs-ˌtaŋ\ *n* [MexSp *mestengo,* fr. Sp, stray, fr. *mesteño* strayed, fr. *mesta* annual roundup of cattle that disposed of strays, fr. ML *(animalia) mixta* mixed animals] : a small hardy naturalized horse of the western plains of America

mus·tard \ˈməs-tərd\ *n* **1** : a pungent yellow powder obtained from the seeds of an herb related to the turnips and used as a condiment or in medicine **2** : the mustard plant; *also* : a closely related plant

mustard gas *n* : an irritant vesicant poisonous gas used in warfare

¹mus·ter \ˈməs-tər\ *vb* **mus·tered; mus·ter·ing** \-t(ə-)riŋ\ [ME *mustren* to show, muster, fr. OF *monstrer,* fr. L *monstrare* to show, fr. *monstrum* evil omen, monster] **1** : CONVENE, ASSEMBLE; *also* : to call the roll of **2** : ACCUMULATE **3** : to call forth : ROUSE **4** : to amount to : COMPRISE

²muster *n* **1** : an act of assembling (as for military inspection); *also* : critical examination **2** : an assembled group

muster out *vb* : to discharge from military service

musty \ˈməs-tē\ *adj* **mus·ti·er; -est** : MOLDY, STALE; *also* : tasting or smelling of damp or decay — **must·i·ly** \ˈməs-tə-lē\ *adv* — **must·i·ness** \-tē-nəs\ *n*

mu·ta·ble \ˈmyüt-ə-bəl\ *adj* **1** : prone to change : FICKLE **2** : liable to mutation : VARIABLE — **mu·ta·bil·i·ty** \ˌmyüt-ə-ˈbil-ət-ē\ *n*

mu·tant \ˈmyüt-ᵊnt\ *adj* : of, relating to, or produced by mutation — **mu·tant** *n*

mu·tate \ˈmyü-ˌtāt\ *vb* **mu·tat·ed; mu·tat·ing** : to undergo or cause to undergo mutation — **mu·ta·tive** \ˈmyü-ˌtāt-iv, ˈmyüt-ət-\ *adj*

mu·ta·tion \myü-ˈtā-shən\ *n* **1** : CHANGE **2** : a sudden and relatively permanent change in a hereditary character; *also* : the process of producing a mutation **3** : an individual or strain resulting from mutation — **mu·ta·tion·al** *adj*

¹mute \ˈmyüt\ *adj* **mut·er; mut·est 1** : unable to speak : DUMB **2** : SILENT — **mute·ly** *adv* — **mute·ness** *n*

²mute *n* **1** : a person who cannot or does not speak **2** : a device on a musical instrument that reduces, softens, or muffles the tone

³mute *vb* **mut·ed; mut·ing** : to muffle or reduce the sound of

mu·ti·late \ˈmyüt-ᵊl-ˌāt\ *vb* **-lat·ed; -lat·ing 1** : MAIM, CRIPPLE **2** : to cut up or alter radically so as to make imperfect — **mu·ti·la·tion** \ˌmyüt-ᵊl-ˈā-shən\ *n* — **mu·ti·la·tor** \ˈmyüt-ᵊl-ˌāt-ər\ *n*

mu·ti·ny \ˈmyüt-(ə-)nē\ *n, pl* **-nies** : willful refusal to obey constituted authority; *esp* : revolt against a superior officer — **mu·ti·neer** \ˌmyüt-ᵊn-ˈiər\ *n* — **mu·ti·nous** \ˈmyüt-ᵊn-əs\ *adj* — **mu·ti·nous·ly** *adv*

mutt \ˈmət\ *n* : MONGREL, CUR

mut·ter \ˈmət-ər\ *vb* **1** : to speak indistinctly or with a low voice and lips partly closed **2** : GRUMBLE — **mutter** *n*

mut·ton \ˈmət-ᵊn\ *n* [ME *motoun,* fr. OF *moton* ram] : the flesh of a mature sheep used for food — **mut·tony** *adj*

mut·ton·chops \ˈmət-ᵊn-ˌchäps\ *n pl* : whiskers on the side of the face that are narrow at the temple and broad and round by the lower jaws

mu·tu·al \ˈmyü-chə(-wə)l\ *adj* **1** : given and received in equal amount ⟨~ trust⟩ **2** : having the same feelings one for the other ⟨~ enemies⟩ **3** : COMMON, JOINT ⟨a ~ friend⟩ — **mu·tu·al·ly** \-ē\ *adv*

mutual fund *n* : an investment company that invests money of its shareholders in a usu. diversified group of securities of other corporations

muu·muu \ˈmü-ˌmü\ *n* : a loose dress of Hawaiian origin for informal wear

¹muz·zle \ˈməz-əl\ *n* **1** : the nose and jaws of an animal; *also* : a covering for the muzzle to prevent the animal from biting or eating **2** : the mouth of a gun

²muzzle *vb* **muz·zled; muz·zling** \-(ə-)liŋ\ **1** : to put a muzzle on **2** : to restrain from expression : GAG

mv *or* **mV** *abbr* millivolt

MV *abbr* motor vessel

MVP *abbr* most valuable player

MW *abbr* megawatt

my \(ˈ)mī, mə\ *adj* **1** : of or relating to me or myself **2** — used interjectionally esp. to express surprise

my·col·o·gy \mī-ˈkäl-ə-jē\ *n* : the study of fungi — **my·co·log·i·cal** \ˌmī-kə-ˈläj-i-kəl\ *adj* — **my·col·o·gist** \mī-ˈkäl-ə-jəst\ *n*

my·elo·ma \ˌmī-ə-ˈlō-mə\ *n, pl* **-mas** *or* **-ma·ta** \-mət-ə\ : a primary tumor of the bone marrow

my·nah *or* **my·na** \ˈmī-nə\ *n* : any of several Asian starlings; *esp* : a dark brown slightly crested bird sometimes taught to mimic speech

my·o·pia \mī-ˈō-pē-ə\ *n* : SHORTSIGHTEDNESS — **my·o·pic** \-ˈō-pik, -ˈäp-ik\ *adj* — **my·o·pi·cal·ly** \-(ə-)lē\ *adv*

¹myr·i·ad \ˈmir-ē-əd\ *n* [Gk *myriad-, myrias,* fr. *myrioi* countless, ten thousand] : an indefinitely large number

²myriad *adj* : consisting of a very great but indefinite number

myr·mi·don \ˈmər-mə-ˌdän\ *n* : a loyal follower; *esp* : one who executes orders without protest or pity

myrrh \ˈmər\ *n* : a fragrant aromatic plant gum used in perfumes and formerly for incense

myr·tle \ˈmərt-ᵊl\ *n* : an evergreen shrub of southern Europe with shiny leaves, fragrant flowers, and black berries; *also* : PERIWINKLE

my·self \mī-ˈself, mə-\ *pron* : I, ME — used reflexively, for emphasis, or in absolute constructions ⟨I hurt ~⟩ ⟨I ~ did it⟩ ⟨~ busy, I sent him instead⟩

mys·tery \ˈmis-t(ə-)rē\ *n, pl* **-ter·ies 1** : a religious truth known by revelation alone **2** : something not understood or beyond understanding **3** : enigmatic quality or character **4** : a work of fiction dealing with the solution of a mysterious crime — **mys·te·ri·ous** \mis-ˈtir-ē-əs\ *adj* — **mys·te·ri·ous·ly** *adv* — **mys·te·ri·ous·ness** *n*

[1]**mys·tic** \ˈmis-tik\ *adj* **1** : of or relating to mystics or mysticism **2** : MYSTERIOUS; *also* : MYSTIFYING

[2]**mystic** *n* : a person who experiences mystical union or direct communion with God or ultimate reality

mys·ti·cal \ˈmis-ti-kəl\ *adj* **1** : SPIRITUAL, SYMBOLIC **2** : of or relating to an intimate knowledge of or direct communion with God (as through contemplation or visions)

mys·ti·cism \ˈmis-tə-ˌsiz-əm\ *n* : the belief that direct knowledge of God or ultimate reality is attainable through immediate intuition or insight

mys·ti·fy \ˈmis-tə-ˌfī\ *vb* **-fied; -fy·ing 1** : to perplex the mind of **2** : to make mysterious — **mys·ti·fi·ca·tion** \ˌmis-tə-fə-ˈkā-shən\ *n*

mys·tique \mis-ˈtēk\ *n* [F] **1** : an air or attitude of mystery and reverence developing around something **2** : the special esoteric skill essential in a calling or activity

myth \ˈmith\ *n* **1** : a usu. legendary narrative that presents part of the beliefs of a people or explains a practice or natural phenomenon **2** : an imaginary or unverifiable person or thing — **myth·i·cal** \-i-kəl\ *adj*

my·thol·o·gy \mith-ˈäl-ə-jē\ *n, pl* **-gies** : a body of myths and esp. of those dealing with the gods and heroes of a people — **myth·o·log·i·cal** \ˌmith-ə-ˈläj-i-kəl\ *adj* — **my·thol·o·gist** \mith-ˈäl-ə-jəst\ *n*

N

[1]**n** \ˈen\ *n, pl* **n's** *or* **ns** \ˈenz\ *often cap* **1** : the 14th letter of the English alphabet **2** : an unspecified quantity

[2]**n** *abbr, often cap* **1** net **2** neuter **3** noon **4** normal **5** north; northern **6** note **7** noun **8** number

N *symbol* nitrogen

-n — see -EN

Na *symbol* [NL *natrium*] sodium

NA *abbr* **1** no account **2** North America **3** not applicable **4** not available

NAACP \ˌen-ˌdəb-əl-ˌā-ˌsē-ˈpē, ˌen-ˌā-ˌā-ˌsē-\ *abbr* National Association for the Advancement of Colored People

nab \ˈnab\ *vb* **nabbed; nab·bing** : SEIZE; *esp* : ARREST

na·bob \ˈnā-ˌbäb\ *n* [Hindi & Urdu *nawwāb,* fr. Ar *nuwwāb,* pl. of *nā'ib* governor] : a man of great wealth or prominence

na·celle \nə-ˈsel\ *n* : an enclosed shelter on an aircraft (as for an engine)

na·cre \ˈnā-kər\ *n* : MOTHER-OF-PEARL

na·dir \ˈnā-ˌdir, ˈnād-ər\ *n* [ME, fr. MF, fr. Ar *naẓīr* opposite] **1** : the point of the celestial sphere that is directly opposite the zenith and directly beneath the observer **2** : the lowest point

[1]**nag** \ˈnag\ *n* : HORSE; *esp* : an old or decrepit horse

[2]**nag** *vb* **nagged; nag·ging 1** : to find fault incessantly : COMPLAIN **2** : to irritate by constant scolding or urging **3** : to be a continuing source of annoyance ⟨a *nagging* toothache⟩

[3]**nag** *n* : one who nags habitually

Nah *abbr* Nahum

Na·huatl \ˈnä-ˌwät-ᵊl\ *n* : an American Indian language of southern Mexico

Na·hum \ˈnā-(h)əm\ *n* — see BIBLE table

na·iad \ˈnā-əd, ˈnī-, -ˌad\ *n, pl* **naiads** *or* **na·ia·des** \-ə-ˌdēz\ **1** : one of the nymphs in ancient mythology living in lakes, rivers, springs, and fountains **2** : an aquatic young of some insects (as a dragonfly)

na·ïf *or* **na·if** \nä-ˈēf\ *adj* : NAIVE

[1]**nail** \ˈnāl\ *n* **1** : a horny sheath protecting the end of each finger and toe in man and related primates **2** : a slender pointed fastener with a head designed to be pounded in

[2]**nail** *vb* : to fasten with or as if with a nail — **nail·er** *n*

nail down *vb* : to settle or establish clearly and unmistakably

nain·sook \ˈnān-ˌsu̇k\ *n* [Hindi *nainsukh,* fr. *nain* eye + *sukh* delight] : a soft lightweight muslin

nai·ra \ˈnī-rə\ *n* — see MONEY table

na·ive *or* **na·ïve** \nä-ˈēv\ *adj* **na·iv·er; -est** [F *naïve,* fem. of *naïf,* fr. OF, inborn, natural, fr. L *nativus* native] **1** : marked by unaffected simplicity : ARTLESS, INGENUOUS **2** : CREDULOUS — **na·ive·ly** *adv* — **na·ive·ness** *n*

na·ïve·té *also* **na·ive·té** *or* **na·ive·te** \ˌnä-ˌēv(-ə)-ˈtā, nä-ˈē-və-ˌtā\ *n* **1** : a naive remark or action **2** : the quality or state of being naive

na·ive·ty *also* **na·ïve·ty** \nä-ˈēv-(ə-)tē\ *n, pl* **-ties** : NAÏVETÉ

na·ked \ˈnā-kəd\ *adj* **1** : having no clothes on : NUDE **2** : UNSHEATHED ⟨a ~ sword⟩ **3** : lacking a usual or natural covering (as of foliage or feathers) **4** : PLAIN, UNADORNED ⟨the ~ truth⟩ **5** : not aided by artificial means ⟨seen by the ~ eye⟩ — **na·ked·ly** *adv* — **na·ked·ness** *n*

nam·by–pam·by \ˌnam-bē-ˈpam-bē\ *adj* **1** : INSIPID **2** : WEAK, INDECISIVE

[1]**name** \ˈnām\ *n* **1** : a word or words by which a person or thing is known **2** : a disparaging epithet ⟨call someone ~*s*⟩ **3** : REPUTATION; *esp* : distinguished reputation ⟨made a ~ for himself⟩ **4** : FAMILY, CLAN ⟨was a disgrace to his ~⟩ **5** : appearance as opposed to reality ⟨a friend in ~ only⟩

[2]**name** *vb* **named; nam·ing 1** : to give a name to : CALL **2** : to mention or identify by name **3** : NOMINATE, APPOINT **4** : to decide on : CHOOSE **5** : to speak about : MENTION ⟨~ a price⟩ — **name·able** *adj*

[3]**name** *adj* **1** : of, relating to, or bearing a name ⟨~ tag⟩ **2** : having an established reputation ⟨~ brands⟩

name day *n* : the church feast day of the saint after whom one is named

name·less \ˈnām-ləs\ *adj* **1** : having no name **2** : not marked with a name ⟨a ~ grave⟩ **3** : not known by name ⟨a ~ hero⟩ **4** : too distressing to be described ⟨~ fears⟩ — **name·less·ly** *adv*

name·ly \ˈnām-lē\ *adv* : that is to say : AS ⟨the cat family, ~, lions, tigers, and similar animals⟩

name·plate \-ˌplāt\ *n* : a plate or plaque bearing a name (as of a resident)

name·sake \-ˌsāk\ *n* : one that has the same name as another; *esp* : one named after another

nan·keen \nan-ˈkēn\ *n* : a durable brownish yellow cotton fabric orig. woven by hand in China

nan·ny goat \ˈnan-ē-\ *n* : a female domestic goat

nano·me·ter \ˈnan-ə-ˌmēt-ər\ *n* : one billionth of a meter

nano·sec·ond \-ˌsek-ənd\ *n* : one billionth of a second

[1]**nap** \ˈnap\ *vb* **napped; nap·ping 1** : to sleep briefly esp. during the day : DOZE **2** : to be off guard ⟨was caught *napping*⟩

[2]**nap** *n* : a short sleep esp. during the day

[3]**nap** *n* : a soft downy fibrous surface (as on yarn and cloth) — **nap·less** *adj*

na·palm \ˈnā-ˌpä(l)m\ *n* [*na*phthalene + *palm*itate salt of a fatty acid] **1** : a thickener used in jelling gasoline (as for incendiary bombs) **2** : fuel jelled with napalm

nape \ˈnāp, ˈnap\ *n* : the back of the neck

na·pery \ˈnā-p(ə-)rē\ *n* : household linen esp. for the table

naph·tha \ˈnaf-thə, ˈnap-\ *n* : any of various liquid hydrocarbon mixtures used chiefly as solvents

naph·tha·lene \-ˌlēn\ *n* **:** a crystalline substance obtained from coal tar used in organic synthesis and as a moth repellent

nap·kin \ˈnap-kən\ *n* **1 :** a piece of material (as cloth) used at table to wipe the lips or fingers and protect the clothes **2 :** a small cloth or towel

na·po·leon \nə-ˈpōl-yən, -ˈpō-lē-ən\ *n* **:** an oblong pastry with a filling of cream, custard, or jelly between layers of puff paste

Na·po·le·on·ic \nə-ˌpō-lē-ˈän-ik\ *adj* **:** of, relating to, or characteristic of Napoleon I or his family

narc \ˈnärk\ *n, slang* **:** one (as a government agent) who investigates narcotics violations

nar·cis·sism \ˈnär-sə-ˌsiz-əm\ *n* [G *narzissismus,* fr. *Narziss* Narcissus, fr. L *Narcissus,* fr. Gk *Narkissos,* beautiful youth of Greek mythology who fell in love with his own image] **1 :** undue dwelling on one's own self or attainments **2 :** love of or sexual desire for one's own body — **nar·cis·sist** \-səst\ *n or adj* — **nar·cis·sis·tic** \ˌnär-sə-ˈsis-tik\ *adj*

nar·cis·sus \när-ˈsis-əs\ *n, pl* **-cis·sus** *or* **-cis·sus·es** *or* **-cis·si** \-ˈsis-ˌī, -ē\ **:** DAFFODIL; *esp* **:** one with short-tubed flowers usu. borne separately

nar·co·sis \när-ˈkō-səs\ *n, pl* **-co·ses** \-ˌsēz\ **:** a state of stupor, unconsciousness, or arrested activity produced by the influence of chemicals (as narcotics)

nar·cot·ic \när-ˈkät-ik\ *n* [ME *narkotik,* fr. MF *narcotique,* fr. *narcotique,* adj., fr. ML *narcoticus,* fr. Gk *narkōtikos,* fr. *narkoun* to benumb, fr. *narkē* numbness] **:** a drug (as opium) that dulls the senses and induces sleep — **narcotic** *adj*

nar·co·tize \ˈnär-kə-ˌtīz\ *vb* **-tized; -tiz·ing 1 :** to treat with or subject to a narcotic; *also* **:** to put into a state of narcosis **2 :** to soothe to unconsciousness or unawareness

nard \ˈnärd\ *n* **:** a fragment ointment of the ancients

na·ris \ˈnar-əs\ *n, pl* **na·res** \ˈnar-(ˌ)ēz\ [L] **:** an opening of the nose **:** NOSTRIL

nark *var of* NARC

Nar·ra·gan·set \ˌnar-ə-ˈgan-sət\ *n, pl* **Narraganset** *or* **Narragansets :** a member of an American Indian people of Rhode Island

nar·rate \ˈnar-ˌāt\ *vb* **nar·rat·ed; nar·rat·ing :** to recite the details of (as a story) **:** RELATE, TELL — **nar·ra·tion** \na-ˈrā-shən\ *n* — **nar·ra·tor** \ˈnar-ˌāt-ər\ *n*

nar·ra·tive \ˈnar-ət-iv\ *n* **1 :** something that is narrated **:** STORY **2 :** the art or practice of narrating

¹nar·row \ˈnar-ō\ *adj* **1 :** of slender or less than standard width **2 :** limited in size or scope **:** RESTRICTED **3 :** not liberal in views **:** PREJUDICED **4 :** interpreted or interpreting strictly **5 :** CLOSE ⟨a ~ escape⟩ ; *also* **:** barely successful ⟨won by a ~ margin⟩ — **nar·row·ly** *adv* — **nar·row·ness** *n*

²narrow *n* **:** a narrow passage **:** STRAIT — usu. used in pl.

³narrow *vb* **:** to lessen in width or extent

nar·row–mind·ed \ˌnar-ō-ˈmīn-dəd\ *adj* **:** not liberal or broad-minded

nar·whal \ˈnär-ˌhwäl, ˈnär-wəl\ *n* **:** an arctic sea animal about 20 feet (6 meters) long that is related to the dolphin and in the male has a long twisted ivory tusk

narwhal

NAS *abbr* naval air station

NASA \ˈnas-ə\ *abbr* National Aeronautics and Space Administration

¹na·sal \ˈnā-zəl\ *n* **1 :** a nasal part **2 :** a nasal consonant or vowel

²nasal *adj* **1 :** of or relating to the nose **2 :** uttered through the nose — **na·sal·ly** \-ē\ *adv*

na·sal·ize \ˈnā-zə-ˌlīz\ *vb* **-ized; -iz·ing 1 :** to make nasal **2 :** to speak in a nasal manner — **na·sal·iza·tion** \ˌnā-zə-lə-ˈzā-shən\ *n*

na·scent \ˈnas-ᵊnt, ˈnās\ *adj* **:** coming into existence **:** beginning to grow or develop — **na·scence** \-ᵊns\ *n*

nas·tur·tium \nə-ˈstər-shəm, na-\ *n* **:** a watery-stemmed herb with showy spurred flowers and pungent seeds

nas·ty \ˈnas-tē\ *adj* **nas·ti·er; -est 1 :** FILTHY **2 :** INDECENT, OBSCENE **3 :** DISHONORABLE ⟨a ~ trick⟩ **4 :** HARMFUL, DANGEROUS ⟨took a ~ fall⟩ **5 :** DISAGREEABLE ⟨~ weather⟩ **6 :** MEAN, ILL-NATURED ⟨a ~ temper⟩ — **nas·ti·ly** \ˈnas-tə-lē\ *adv* — **nas·ti·ness** \-tē-nəs\ *n*

nat *abbr* **1** national **2** native **3** natural

na·tal \ˈnāt-ᵊl\ *adj* **1 :** NATIVE **2 :** of, relating to, or present at birth

na·tal·i·ty \nā-ˈtal-ət-ē, nə-\ *n, pl* **-ties :** BIRTHRATE

na·ta·to·ri·um \ˌnāt-ə-ˈtōr-ē-əm, ˌnat-\ *n* **:** a swimming pool esp. indoors

na·tion \ˈnā-shən\ *n* [ME *nacioun,* fr. MF *nation,* fr. L *nation-, natio* birth, race, nation, fr. *natus,* pp. of *nasci* to be born] **1 :** NATIONALITY 5; *also* **:** a politically organized nationality **2 :** a community of people composed of one or more nationalities with its own territory and government **3 :** the territory of a nation **4 :** a federation of tribes (as of American Indians) — **na·tion·hood** *n*

¹na·tion·al \ˈnash-(ə-)nəl\ *adj* **1 :** of or relating to a nation **2 :** comprising or characteristic of a nationality **3 :** FEDERAL 3 — **na·tion·al·ly** \-ē\ *adv*

²national *n* **1 :** one who is under the protection of a nation without regard to the more formal status of citizen or subject **2 :** an organization (as a labor union) having local units throughout a nation **3 :** a competition that is national in scope — usu. used in pl.

National Guard *n* **1 :** a militia force recruited by each state, equipped by the federal government, and jointly maintained subject to the call of either **2 :** a military force serving as a national constabulary and defense force

na·tion·al·ism \ˈnash-(ə-)nəl-ˌiz-əm\ *n* **:** devotion to national interests, unity, and independence

na·tion·al·ist \-əst\ *n* **1 :** an advocate of or believer in nationalism **2** *cap* **:** a member of a political party or group advocating national independence or strong national government — **nationalist** *adj, often cap* — **na·tion·al·is·tic** \ˌnash-(ə-)nəl-ˈis-tik\ *adj*

na·tion·al·i·ty \ˌnash-(ə-)ˈnal-ət-ē\ *n, pl* **-ties 1 :** national character **2 :** a legal relationship involving allegiance of an individual and his protection by the state **3 :** membership in a particular nation **4 :** political independence or existence as a separate nation **5 :** a people having a common origin, tradition, and language and capable of forming a state **6 :** an ethnic group within a larger unit (as a nation)

na·tion·al·ize \ˈnash-(ə-)nəl-ˌīz\ *vb* **-ized; -iz·ing 1 :** to make national **:** make a nation of **2 :** to remove from private ownership and place under government control — **na·tion·al·iza·tion** \ˌnash-(ə-)nəl-ə-ˈzā-shən\ *n*

national park *n* **:** an area of special scenic, historical, or scientific importance set aside and maintained by a national government esp. for recreation or study

national seashore *n* : a recreational area adjacent to a seacoast and maintained by the federal government

na·tion·wide \ˌnā-shən-ˈwīd\ *adj* : extending throughout a nation

[1]**na·tive** \ˈnāt-iv\ *adj* **1** : INBORN, NATURAL **2** : born in a particular place or country **3** : belonging to a person because of the place or circumstances of his birth ⟨his ~ language⟩ **4** : grown, produced, or originating in a particular place : INDIGENOUS

[2]**native** *n* : one that is native; *esp* : a person who belongs to a particular country by birth

Native American *n* : AMERICAN INDIAN

na·tiv·ism \ˈnāt-iv-ˌiz-əm\ *n* **1** : a policy of favoring native inhabitants over immigrants **2** : the revival or perpetuation of a native culture esp. in opposition to acculturation

Na·tiv·i·ty \nə-ˈtiv-ət-ē, nā-\ *n, pl* **-ties** **1** : the birth of Christ **2** *not cap* : the process or circumstances of being born : BIRTH

natl *abbr* national

NATO \ˈnāt-(ˌ)ō\ *abbr* North Atlantic Treaty Organization

nat·ty \ˈnat-ē\ *adj* **nat·ti·er; -est** : trimly neat and tidy : SMART — **nat·ti·ly** \ˈnat-ᵊl-ē\ *adv* — **nat·ti·ness** \-ē-nəs\ *n*

[1]**nat·u·ral** \ˈnach-(ə-)rəl\ *adj* **1** : determined by nature : INBORN, INNATE ⟨~ ability⟩ **2** : BORN ⟨a ~ fool⟩ **3** : ILLEGITIMATE **4** : HUMAN **5** : of or relating to nature **6** : not artificial **7** : being simple and sincere : not affected **8** : LIFELIKE **9** : having neither sharps nor flats in the key signature **syn** ingenuous, naive, unsophisticated, artless, guileless — **nat·u·ral·ness** *n*

[2]**natural** *n* **1** : IDIOT **2** : a character placed on a line or space of the musical staff to nullify the effect of a preceding sharp or flat **3** : one obviously suitable for a specific purpose **4** : AFRO

natural childbirth *n* : a system of managing childbirth in which the mother prepares to remain conscious and assist in delivery with little or no use of drugs

natural gas *n* : gas coming from the earth's crust through natural openings or bored wells; *esp* : a combustible mixture of hydrocarbons and esp. methane used chiefly as a fuel and raw material

natural history *n* **1** : a treatise on some aspect of nature **2** : the study of natural objects esp. from an amateur or popular point of view

nat·u·ral·ism \ˈnach-(ə-)rə-ˌliz-əm\ *n* **1** : action or thought based only on natural desires and instincts **2** : a doctrine that denies a supernatural explanation of the origin or development of the universe and holds that scientific laws account for all of nature **3** : realism in art and literature — **nat·u·ral·is·tic** \ˌnach-(ə-)rə-ˈlis-tik\ *adj*

nat·u·ral·ist \-ləst\ *n* **1** : one that advocates or practices naturalism **2** : a student of animals or plants esp. in the field

nat·u·ral·ize \-ˌlīz\ *vb* **-ized; -iz·ing** **1** : to become or cause to become established as if native ⟨~ new forage crops⟩ **2** : to confer the rights of a citizen on — **nat·u·ral·iza·tion** \ˌnach-(ə-)rə-lə-ˈzā-shən\ *n*

nat·u·ral·ly \ˈnach-(ə-)rə-lē, ˈnach-ər-lē\ *adv* **1** : by nature : by natural character or ability **2** : as might be expected **3** : without artificial aid; *also* : without affectation **4** : REALISTICALLY

natural science *n* : a science (as physics, chemistry, or biology) that deals with matter, energy, and their interrelations and transformations or with objectively measurable phenomena — **natural scientist** *n*

natural selection *n* : the natural process that results in the survival of individuals or groups best adjusted to the conditions under which they live

na·ture \ˈnā-chər\ *n* [ME, fr. MF, fr. L *natura*, fr. *natus*, pp. of *nasci* to be born] **1** : the inherent quality or basic constitution of a person or thing **2** : KIND, SORT **3** : DISPOSITION, TEMPERAMENT **4** : the physical universe **5** : one's natural instincts or way of life ⟨quirks of human ~⟩; *also* : primitive state ⟨a return to ~⟩ **6** : natural scenery or environment ⟨beauties of ~⟩

naught \ˈnȯt, ˈnät\ *n* **1** : NOTHING **2** : the arithmetical symbol 0 : ZERO

naugh·ty \ˈnȯt-ē, ˈnät-\ *adj* **naugh·ti·er; -est** **1** : guilty of disobedience or misbehavior **2** : lacking in taste or propriety — **naugh·ti·ly** \ˈnȯt-ᵊl-ē, ˈnät-\ *adv* — **naugh·ti·ness** \-ē-nəs\ *n*

nau·sea \ˈnȯ-zē-ə, ˈnȯ-shə\ *n* [L, seasickness, nausea, fr. Gk *nautia, nausia*, fr. *nautēs* sailor] **1** : sickness of the stomach with a desire to vomit **2** : extreme disgust

nau·se·ate \ˈnȯ-z(h)ē-ˌāt, -s(h)ē-\ *vb* **-at·ed; -at·ing** : to affect or become affected with nausea — **nau·se·at·ing·ly** \-ˌāt-iŋ-lē\ *adv*

nau·seous \ˈnȯ-shəs, -zē-əs\ *adj* **1** : causing nausea or disgust **2** : affected with nausea or disgust

naut *abbr* nautical

nau·ti·cal \ˈnȯt-i-kəl\ *adj* : of or relating to seamen, navigation, or ships — **nau·ti·cal·ly** \-k(ə-)lē\ *adv*

nautical mile *n* : a unit of distance equal to about 6076.115 feet

nau·ti·lus \ˈnȯt-ᵊl-əs\ *n, pl* **-lus·es** *or* **-li** \-ᵊl-ˌī, -ˌē\ : a sea mollusk related to the octopuses but having a spiral shell divided into chambers

nav *abbr* **1** naval **2** navigable; navigation

Na·va·ho *or* **Na·va·jo** \ˈnav-ə-ˌhō, ˈnäv-\ *n, pl* **Navaho** *or* **Navahos** *or* **Navajo** *or* **Navajos** : a member of an American Indian people of northern New Mexico and Arizona; *also* : their language

na·val \ˈnā-vəl\ *adj* : of, relating to, or possessing a navy

naval stores *n pl* : products (as pitch, turpentine, or rosin) obtained from resinous conifers (as pines)

nave \ˈnāv\ *n* [ML *navis*, fr. L, ship] : the central part of a church running lengthwise

na·vel \ˈnā-vəl\ *n* : a depression in the middle of the abdomen that marks the point of attachment of fetus and mother

navel orange *n* : a seedless orange having a pit at the blossom end where the fruit encloses a small secondary fruit

nav·i·ga·ble \ˈnav-i-gə-bəl\ *adj* **1** : capable of being navigated ⟨a ~ river⟩ **2** : capable of being steered ⟨a ~ balloon⟩ — **nav·i·ga·bil·i·ty** \ˌnav-i-gə-ˈbil-ət-ē\ *n*

nav·i·gate \ˈnav-ə-ˌgāt\ *vb* **-gat·ed; -gat·ing** **1** : to sail on or through ⟨~ the Atlantic ocean⟩ **2** : to steer or direct the course of a ship or aircraft **3** : MOVE; *esp* : WALK ⟨could hardly ~⟩ — **nav·i·ga·tion** \ˌnav-ə-ˈgā-shən\ *n* — **nav·i·ga·tor** \ˈnav-ə-ˌgāt-ər\ *n*

na·vy \ˈnā-vē\ *n, pl* **navies** **1** : FLEET; *also* : the warships belonging to a nation **2** *often cap* : a nation's organization for naval warfare

navy exchange *n* : a post exchange at a navy installation

navy yard *n* : a yard where naval vessels are built or repaired

[1]**nay** \ˈnā\ *adv* **1** : NO **2** : not merely this but also : not only so but ⟨the letter made him happy, ~, ecstatic⟩

[2]**nay** *n* : a negative vote; *also* : a person casting such a vote

nay·say·er \ˈnā-ˌsā-ər\ *n* : one who denies, refuses, or opposes something

Na·zi \ˈnät-sē, ˈnat-\ *n* [G, fr. *nationalsozialist*, lit., national socialist] : a member of a German fascist party controlling Germany from 1933 to 1945 under Adolf Hitler — **Nazi** *adj* — **Na·zism** \ˈnät-ˌsiz-əm, ˈnat-\ *or* **Na·zi·ism** \-sē-ˌiz-əm\ *n*

Nb *symbol* niobium

NB *abbr* **1** New Brunswick **2** nota bene

NBA *abbr* **1** National Basketball Association **2** National Boxing Association

NBC *abbr* National Broadcasting Company

NBS *abbr* National Bureau of Standards
NC *abbr* **1** no charge **2** North Carolina
NCAA *abbr* National Collegiate Athletic Association
NCE *abbr* New Catholic Edition
NCO \ˌen-ˌsē-ˈō\ *n* : NONCOMMISSIONED OFFICER
Nd *symbol* neodymium
ND *abbr* **1** no date **2** North Dakota
N Dak *abbr* North Dakota
Ne *symbol* neon
NE *abbr* **1** Nebraska **2** New England **3** northeast
Ne·an·der·thal \nē-ˈan-dər-ˌt(h)ȯl, nā-ˈän-dər-ˌtäl\ *adj* : of, relating to, or being an extinct primitive Old World man; *also* : crudely primitive (as in manner or conduct) — **Neanderthal** *n*
neap tide \ˈnēp-\ *n* : a tide of minimum range occurring at the first and third quarters of the moon
[1]**near** \ˈniər\ *adv* **1** : at, within, or to a short distance or time **2** : ALMOST
[2]**near** *prep* : close to
[3]**near** *adj* **1** : closely related or associated; *also* : INTIMATE **2** : not far away; *also* : being the closer or left-hand member of a pair **3** : barely avoided ⟨a ~ accident⟩ **4** : DIRECT, SHORT ⟨by the ~*est* route⟩ **5** : STINGY **6** : not real but very like ⟨~ silk⟩ — **near·ly** *adv* — **near·ness** *n*
[4]**near** *vb* : APPROACH
near beer *n* : any of various malt liquors low in alcohol
near·by \niər-ˈbī, ˈniər-ˌbī\ *adv or adj* : close at hand
near·sight·ed \ˈniər-ˈsīt-əd\ *adj* : seeing distinctly at short distances only : SHORTSIGHTED — **near·sight·ed·ly** *adv* — **near·sight·ed·ness** *n*
neat \ˈnēt\ *adj* [MF *net,* fr. L *nitidus* bright, neat, fr. *nitēre* to shine] **1** : being orderly and clean **2** : not mixed or diluted ⟨~ brandy⟩ **3** : marked by tasteful simplicity **4** : PRECISE, SYSTEMATIC **5** : SKILLFUL, ADROIT **6** : FINE, ADMIRABLE — **neat** *adv* — **neat·ly** *adv* — **neat·ness** *n*
neath \ˈnēth\ *prep, dial* : BENEATH
neat's–foot oil \ˈnēts-ˌfu̇t-\ *n* [*neat* (bovine)] : a pale yellow fatty oil made esp. from the bones of cattle and used chiefly as a leather dressing
neb \ˈneb\ *n* **1** : the beak of a bird or tortoise; *also* : NOSE, SNOUT **2** : NIB
Neb *or* **Nebr** *abbr* Nebraska
NEB *abbr* New English Bible
neb·u·la \ˈneb-yə-lə\ *n, pl* **-las** *or* **-lae** \-ˌlē, -ˌlī\ [NL, fr. L, mist, cloud] **1** : any of many vast cloudlike masses of gas or dust among the stars **2** : GALAXY — **neb·u·lar** \-lər\ *adj*
neb·u·lize \ˈneb-yə-ˌlīz\ *vb* **-lized; -liz·ing** : to reduce to a fine spray — **neb·u·liz·er** \-ˌlī-zər\ *n*
neb·u·los·i·ty \ˌneb-yə-ˈläs-ət-ē\ *n, pl* **-ties** **1** : the quality or state of being nebulous **2** : nebulous matter
neb·u·lous \ˈneb-yə-ləs\ *adj* **1** : of or relating to a nebula **2** : HAZY, INDISTINCT ⟨a ~ memory⟩
[1]**nec·es·sary** \ˈnes-ə-ˌser-ē\ *n, pl* **-saries** : an indispensable item
[2]**necessary** *adj* [ME *necessarie,* fr. L *necessarius,* fr. *necesse* necessary, fr. *ne-* not + *cedere* to withdraw] **1** : INEVITABLE, INESCAPABLE; *also* : CERTAIN **2** : PREDETERMINED **3** : COMPULSORY **4** : positively needed : INDISPENSABLE **syn** imperative, necessitous, essential — **nec·es·sar·i·ly** \ˌnes-ə-ˈser-ə-lē\ *adv*
ne·ces·si·tate \ni-ˈses-ə-ˌtāt\ *vb* **-tat·ed; -tat·ing** : to make necessary
ne·ces·si·tous \ni-ˈses-ət-əs\ *adj* **1** : NEEDY, IMPOVERISHED **2** : URGENT **3** : NECESSARY
ne·ces·si·ty \ni-ˈses-ət-ē\ *n, pl* **-ties** **1** : conditions that cannot be changed **2** : WANT, POVERTY **3** : something that is necessary **4** : very great need
[1]**neck** \ˈnek\ *n* **1** : the part of the body connecting the head and the trunk **2** : the part of a garment covering or near to the neck **3** : a relatively narrow part suggestive of a neck ⟨~ of a bottle⟩ ⟨~ of land⟩ **4** : a narrow margin esp. of victory ⟨won by a ~⟩ — **necked** \ˈnekt\ *adj*
[2]**neck** *vb* : to kiss and caress amorously
neck and neck *adv or adj* : very close (as in a race)
neck·er·chief \ˈnek-ər-chəf, -ˌchēf\ *n, pl* **-chiefs** \-chəfs, -ˌchēfs\ *also* **-chieves** \-ˌchēvz\ : a square of cloth worn folded about the neck like a scarf
neck·lace \ˈnek-ləs\ *n* : an ornamental chain or a string (as of jewels or beads) worn around the neck
neck·line \-ˌlīn\ *n* : the outline of the neck opening of a garment
neck·tie \-ˌtī\ *n* : a strip of cloth worn around the neck and tied in front
ne·crol·o·gy \nə-ˈkräl-ə-jē\ *n, pl* **-gies** **1** : a list of the recently dead **2** : OBITUARY
nec·ro·man·cy \ˈnek-rə-ˌman-sē\ *n* **1** : the art or practice of conjuring up the spirits of the dead for purposes of magically revealing the future **2** : MAGIC, SORCERY — **nec·ro·man·cer** \-sər\ *n*
ne·crop·o·lis \nə-ˈkräp-ə-ləs, ne-\ *n, pl* **-lis·es** *or* **-les** \-ˌlēz\ *or* **-leis** \-ˌlās\ *or* **-li** \-ˌlī, -ˌlē\ : CEMETERY; *esp* : a large elaborate cemetery of an ancient city
ne·cro·sis \nə-ˈkrō-səs, ne-\ *n, pl* **ne·cro·ses** \-ˌsēz\ : usu. local death of body tissue — **ne·crot·ic** \-ˈkrät-ik\ *adj*
nec·tar \ˈnek-tər\ *n* **1** : the drink of the Greek and Roman gods; *also* : any delicious drink **2** : a sweet plant secretion that is the raw material of honey
nec·tar·ine \ˌnek-tə-ˈrēn\ *n* : a smooth-skinned peach
née *or* **nee** \ˈnā\ *adj* [F, lit., born] — used to identify a woman by her maiden family name
[1]**need** \ˈnēd\ *n* **1** : OBLIGATION ⟨no ~ to hurry⟩ **2** : a lack of something requisite, desirable, or useful **3** : a condition requiring supply or relief ⟨when the ~ arises⟩ **4** : POVERTY **syn** necessity, exigency
[2]**need** *vb* **1** : to be in want **2** : to have cause or occasion for : REQUIRE ⟨he ~*s* advice⟩ **3** : to be under obligation or necessity ⟨we ~ to know the truth⟩
need·ful \ˈnēd-fəl\ *adj* : NECESSARY, REQUISITE
[1]**nee·dle** \ˈnēd-ᵊl\ *n* **1** : a slender pointed usu. steel implement used in sewing **2** : a slender rod (as for knitting, controlling a small opening, or transmitting vibrations to or from a recording) ⟨a phonograph ~⟩ **3** : a slender hollow instrument by which material is introduced into or withdrawn from the body **4** : a slender indicator on a dial **5** : a needle-shaped leaf (as of a pine)
[2]**needle** *vb* **nee·dled; nee·dling** \ˈnēd-(ᵊ-)liŋ\ : PROD, GOAD; *esp* : to incite to action by repeated gibes
nee·dle·point \ˈnēd-ᵊl-ˌpȯint\ *n* **1** : lace worked with a needle over a paper pattern **2** : embroidery done on canvas across counted threads — **needlepoint** *adj*
need·less \ˈnēd-ləs\ *adj* : UNNECESSARY — **need·less·ly** *adv* — **need·less·ness** *n*
nee·dle·wom·an \ˈnēd-ᵊl-ˌwu̇m-ən\ *n* : a woman who does needlework; *esp* : SEAMSTRESS
nee·dle·work \-ˌwərk\ *n* : work done with a needle; *esp* : work (as embroidery) other than plain sewing
needs \ˈnēdz\ *adv* : of necessity : NECESSARILY ⟨must ~ be recognized⟩
needy \ˈnēd-ē\ *adj* **need·i·er; -est** : being in want : POVERTY-STRICKEN
ne'er \ˈneər\ *adv* : NEVER
ne'er–do–well \ˈneər-du̇-ˌwel\ *n* : an idle worthless person — **ne'er–do–well** *adj*
ne·far·i·ous \ni-ˈfar-ē-əs\ *adj* [L *nefarius,* fr. *nefas* crime, fr. *ne-* not + *fas* right, divine law] : very wicked : EVIL — **ne·far·i·ous·ly** *adv*
neg *abbr* negative
ne·gate \ni-ˈgāt\ *vb* **ne·gat·ed; ne·gat·ing** **1** : to deny the existence or truth of **2** : to cause to be ineffective or invalid : NULLIFY

ne·ga·tion \ni-ˈgā-shən\ *n* **1** : the action or operation of negating or making negative **2** : a negative doctrine or statement

[1]**neg·a·tive** \ˈneg-ət-iv\ *adj* **1** : marked by denial, prohibition, or refusal ⟨a ~ reply⟩ **2** : not positive or constructive; *esp* : not affirming the presence of what is sought or suspected to be present ⟨a ~ test⟩ **3** : less than zero ⟨a ~ number⟩ **4** : being, relating to, or charged with electricity of which the electron is the elementary unit ⟨a ~ particle⟩ **5** : having the light and dark parts opposite to what they were in the original photographic subject — **neg·a·tive·ly** *adv*

[2]**negative** *n* **1** : a negative word or statement **2** : a negative vote or reply; *also* : REFUSAL **3** : something that is the opposite or negation of something else **4** : the side that votes or argues for the opposition (as in a debate) **5** : a negative photographic image on transparent material

[3]**negative** *vb* **-tived; -tiv·ing** **1** : to refuse to accept or approve **2** : to vote against **3** : DISPROVE

negative income tax *n* : a system of federal subsidy payments to families with incomes below a stipulated level

neg·a·tiv·ism \ˈneg-ət-iv-ˌiz-əm\ *n* : an attitude of skepticism and denial of nearly everything affirmed or suggested by others

[1]**ne·glect** \ni-ˈglekt\ *vb* [L *neglegere, neclegere,* fr. *nec-* not + *legere* to gather] **1** : DISREGARD **2** : to leave undone or unattended to esp. through carelessness **syn** omit, ignore, over-look, slight, forget, miss

[2]**neglect** *n* **1** : an act or instance of neglecting something **2** : the condition of being neglected — **ne·glect·ful** *adj*

neg·li·gee *also* **neg·li·gé** \ˌneg-lə-ˈzhā\ *n* : a woman's long flowing dressing gown

neg·li·gent \ˈneg-li-jənt\ *adj* : marked by neglect **syn** neglectful, remiss, delinquent, derelict — **neg·li·gence** \-jəns\ *n* — **neg·li·gent·ly** *adv*

neg·li·gi·ble \ˈneg-li-jə-bəl\ *adj* : so small as to be neglected or disregarded

ne·go·tiant \ni-ˈgō-sh(ē-)ənt\ *n* : NEGOTIATOR

ne·go·ti·ate \ni-ˈgō-shē-ˌāt\ *vb* **-at·ed; -at·ing** [L *negotiari* to carry on business, fr. *negotium* business, fr. *neg-* not + *otium* leisure] **1** : to confer with another so as to arrive at the settlement of some matter; *also* : to arrange for or bring about by such conferences ⟨~ a treaty⟩ **2** : to transfer to another by delivery or endorsement in return for equivalent value ⟨~ a check⟩ **3** : to get through, around, or over successfully ⟨~ a turn⟩ — **ne·go·tia·ble** \-sh(ē-)ə-bəl\ *adj* — **ne·go·ti·a·tion** \ni-ˌgō-s(h)ē-ˈā-shən\ *n* — **ne·go·ti·a·tor** \-ˈgō-shē-ˌāt-ər\ *n*

ne·gri·tude \ˈneg-rə-ˌt(y)üd, ˈnē-grə-\ *n* : a consciousness of and pride in one's African heritage

Ne·gro \ˈnē-grō\ *n, pl* **Negroes** [Sp or Pg, fr. *negro* black] : a member of the black race — **Negro** *adj* — **Ne·groid** \ˈnē-ˌgrȯid\ *n or adj, often not cap*

Neh *abbr* Nehemiah

Ne·he·mi·ah \ˌnē-(h)ə-ˈmī-ə\ *n* — see BIBLE table

NEI *abbr* not elsewhere included

neigh \ˈnā\ *n* : a loud prolonged cry of a horse — **neigh** *vb*

[1]**neigh·bor** \ˈnā-bər\ *n* **1** : one living or located near another **2** : FELLOWMAN

[2]**neighbor** *vb* **neigh·bored; neigh·bor·ing** \-b(ə-)riŋ\ : to be next to or near to : border on

neigh·bor·hood \ˈnā-bər-ˌhu̇d\ *n* **1** : NEARNESS **2** : a place or region near : VICINITY; *also* : a number or amount near ⟨costs in the ~ of $10⟩ **3** : the people living near one another **4** : a section lived in by neighbors and usu. having distinguishing characteristics

neigh·bor·ly \-lē\ *adj* : befitting congenial neighbors; *esp* : FRIENDLY — **neigh·bor·li·ness** *n*

[1]**nei·ther** \ˈnē-t͟hər, ˈnī-\ *pron* : neither one : not the one and not the other ⟨~ of the two⟩

[2]**neither** *conj* **1** : not either ⟨~ good nor bad⟩ **2** : NOR ⟨~ did I⟩

[3]**neither** *adj* : not either ⟨~ hand⟩

nel·son \ˈnel-sən\ *n* : a wrestling hold in which one applies leverage against an opponent's arm, neck, and head

nem·a·tode \ˈnem-ə-ˌtōd\ *n* : any of a group of elongated cylindrical worms parasitic in animals or plants or free-living in soil or water

nem·e·sis \ˈnem-ə-səs\ *n, pl* **-e·ses** \-ə-ˌsēz\ [L *Nemesis,* goddess of divine retribution, fr. Gk] **1** : one that inflicts retribution or vengeance **2** : a formidable and usu. victorious rival **3** : an act or effect of retribution; *also* : CURSE

neo·clas·sic \ˌnē-ō-ˈklas-ik\ *or* **neo·clas·si·cal** \-i-kəl\ *adj* : of or relating to a revival or adaptation of the classical style esp. in literature, art, or music

neo·co·lo·nial·ism \ˌnē-ō-kə-ˈlō-nyəl-ˌiz-əm, -ˈlō-nē-ə-ˌliz-əm\ *n* : the economic and political policies by which a nation indirectly maintains or extends its influence over other areas or peoples — **neo·co·lo·nial** *adj* — **neo·co·lo·nial·ist** \-əst\ *n or adj*

neo·con·ser·va·tive \-kən-ˈsər-vət-iv\ *n* : a former liberal espousing political conservatism — **neo·con·ser·va·tism** \-və-ˌtiz-əm\ *n* — **neoconservative** *adj*

neo·dym·i·um \ˌnē-ō-ˈdim-ē-əm\ *n* : a yellow metallic chemical element — see ELEMENT table

neo–im·pres·sion·ism \ˌnē-ō-im-ˈpresh-ə-ˌniz-əm\ *n, often cap N&I* : a late 19th century French art movement that attempted to make impressionism more precise and to use a pointillist painting technique

Neo·lith·ic \ˌnē-ə-ˈlith-ik\ *adj* : of or relating to the latest period of the Stone Age characterized by polished stone implements

ne·ol·o·gism \nē-ˈäl-ə-ˌjiz-əm\ *n* : a new word or expression

ne·on \ˈnē-ˌän\ *n* [Gk, neut. of *neos* new] **1** : a gaseous colorless chemical element used in electric lamps — see ELEMENT table **2** : a lamp in which a discharge through neon gives a reddish glow — **neon** *adj*

neo·na·tal \ˌnē-ō-ˈnāt-ᵊl\ *adj* : of, relating to, or affecting the newborn — **neo·na·tal·ly** \-ē\ *adv* — **ne·o·nate** \ˈnē-ō-ˌnāt\ *n*

neo·phyte \ˈnē-ə-ˌfīt\ *n* **1** : a new convert : PROSELYTE **2** : NOVICE **3** : BEGINNER

neo·plasm \ˈnē-ə-ˌplaz-əm\ *n* : TUMOR — **neo·plas·tic** \ˌnē-ə-ˈplas-tik\ *adj*

Ne·pali \nə-ˈpȯl-ē, -ˈpäl-\ *n, pl* **Nepali** : a native or inhabitant of Nepal

ne·pen·the \nə-ˈpen-thē\ *n* **1** : a potion used by the ancients to dull pain and sorrow **2** : something capable of making one forget grief or suffering

neph·ew \ˈnef-yü, *chiefly Brit* ˈnev-\ *n* : a son of one's brother, sister, brother-in-law, or sister-in-law

ne·phrit·ic \ni-ˈfrit-ik\ *adj* **1** : RENAL **2** : of, relating to, or affected with nephritis

ne·phri·tis \ni-ˈfrīt-əs\ *n, pl* **ne·phrit·i·des** \-ˈfrit-ə-ˌdēz\ : kidney inflammation

ne plus ul·tra \ˌnē-ˌpləs-ˈəl-trə\ *n* [NL, (go) no more beyond] : the highest point capable of being attained

nep·o·tism \ˈnep-ə-ˌtiz-əm\ *n* [F *népotisme,* fr. It *nepotismo,* fr. *nepote* nephew, fr. L *nepot-, nepos* grandson, nephew] : favoritism shown to a relative (as in the granting of jobs)

Nep·tune \ˈnep-ˌt(y)ün\ *n* : the 8th planet in order of distance from the sun — **Nep·tu·ni·an** \nep-ˈt(y)ü-nē-ən\ *adj*

nep·tu·ni·um \nep-ˈt(y)ü-nē-əm\ *n* : a short-lived radioactive chemical element artificially produced as a by-product in the production of plutonium — see ELEMENT table

Ne·re·id \ˈnir-ē-əd\ *n* : a sea nymph in Greek mythology

[1]**nerve** \ˈnərv\ *n* **1** : one of the strands of nervous tissue that carry nervous impulses between the brain and spinal cord and every part of the body **2** : power of endur-

ance or control : FORTITUDE; *also* : BOLDNESS, DARING **3** *pl* : NERVOUSNESS **4** : a vein of a leaf or insect wing — **nerved** \ˈnərvd\ *adj* — **nerve·less** *adj*

[2]**nerve** *vb* **nerved; nerv·ing** : to give strength or courage to

nerve cell *n* : NEURON; *also* : the nucleus-containing central part of a neuron exclusive of its processes

nerve gas *n* : a war gas damaging esp. to the nervous and respiratory systems

nerve–rack·ing *or* **nerve–wrack·ing** \ˈnərv-ˌrak-iŋ\ *adj* : extremely trying on the nerves

ner·vous \ˈnər-vəs\ *adj* **1** : FORCIBLE, SPIRITED **2** : of, relating to, or made up of nerve cells or nerves **3** : easily excited or annoyed : JUMPY **4** : TIMID, APPREHENSIVE ⟨a ~ smile⟩ **5** : UNEASY, UNSTEADY — **ner·vous·ly** *adv* — **ner·vous·ness** *n*

nervous breakdown *n* : an attack of mental or emotional disorder of sufficient severity to be incapacitating esp. when requiring hospitalization

nervous system *n* : a bodily system that in vertebrates is made up of the brain and spinal cord, nerves, ganglia, and parts of the sense organs and that receives and interprets stimuli and transmits impulses

nervy \ˈnər-vē\ *adj* **nerv·i·er; -est** **1** : showing calm courage **2** : marked by impudence or presumption ⟨a ~ salesman⟩ **3** : EXCITABLE, NERVOUS

-ness \nəs\ *n suffix* : state : condition : quality : degree ⟨good*ness*⟩

[1]**nest** \ˈnest\ *n* **1** : the shelter prepared by a bird for its eggs and young **2** : a place where eggs (as of insects or fish) are laid and hatched **3** : a place of rest, retreat, or lodging **4** : DEN, HANGOUT ⟨a ~ of theives⟩ **5** : the occupants of a nest **6** : a series of objects (as bowls or tables) fitting inside or under one another

[2]**nest** *vb* **1** : to build or occupy a nest **2** : to fit compactly together or within one another

nest egg *n* : a fund of money accumulated as a reserve

nes·tle \ˈnes-əl\ *vb* **nes·tled; nes·tling** \-(ə-)liŋ\ **1** : to settle snugly or comfortably **2** : to press closely and affectionately : CUDDLE **3** : to settle, shelter, or house as if in a nest

nest·ling \ˈnest-liŋ\ *n* : a bird too young to leave its nest

[1]**net** \ˈnet\ *n* **1** : a meshed fabric twisted, knotted, or woven together at regular intervals; *esp* : a device of net used esp. to catch birds, fish, or insects **2** : something made of net used esp. for protecting, confining, carrying, or dividing ⟨a tennis ~⟩ **3** : SNARE, TRAP

[2]**net** *vb* **net·ted; net·ting** **1** : to cover or enclose with or as if with a net **2** : to catch in or as if in a net

[3]**net** *adj* : free from all charges or deductions ⟨~ profit⟩ ⟨~ weight⟩

[4]**net** *vb* **net·ted; net·ting** to gain or produce as profit : CLEAR, YIELD ⟨his business *netted* $50,000 a year⟩

[5]**net** *n* : a net amount, profit, weight, or price

NET *abbr* National Educational Television

Neth *abbr* Netherlands

neth·er \ˈneth-ər\ *adj* : situated down or below ⟨the ~ regions of the earth⟩

Neth·er·land·er \ˈneth-ər-ˌland-ər\ *n* : a native or inhabitant of the Netherlands

neth·er·most \-ˌmōst\ *adj* : LOWEST

neth·er·world \-ˌwərld\ *n* **1** : the world of the dead **2** : UNDERWORLD

net·ting \ˈnet-iŋ\ *n* **1** : NETWORK **2** : the act or process of making a net or network **3** : the act, process, or right of fishing with a net

[1]**net·tle** \ˈnet-ᵊl\ *n* : any of various coarse herbs with stinging hairs

[2]**nettle** *vb* **net·tled; net·tling** : PROVOKE, VEX, IRRITATE

net·tle·some \ˈnet-ᵊl-səm\ *adj* : causing vexation : IRRITATING

net·work \ˈnet-ˌwərk\ *n* **1** : NET **2** : a system of elements (as lines or channels) that cross in the manner of the threads in a net **3** : a group or system of related or connected parts; *esp* : a chain of radio or television stations

net·work·ing \ˈnet-ˌwərk-iŋ\ *n* : the exchange of information or services among individuals, groups, or institutions

neu·ral \ˈn(y)u̇r-əl\ *adj* : of, relating to, or involving a nerve or the nervous system

neu·ral·gia \n(y)u̇-ˈral-jə\ *n* : acute pain that follows the course of a nerve — **neu·ral·gic** \-jik\ *adj*

neur·as·the·nia \ˌn(y)u̇r-əs-ˈthē-nē-ə\ *n* : an emotional and psychic disorder characterized esp. by easy susceptibility to fatigue and often by lack of motivation, feelings of inadequacy, and psychosomatic symptoms — **neur·as·then·ic** \-ˈthen-ik\ *adj or n*

neu·ri·tis \n(y)u̇-ˈrīt-əs\ *n, pl* **-rit·i·des** \-ˈrit-ə-ˌdēz\ *or* **-ri·tis·es** : inflammation of a nerve — **neu·rit·ic** \-ˈrit-ik\ *adj or n*

neu·rol·o·gy \n(y)u̇-ˈräl-ə-jē\ *n* : the scientific study of the nervous system — **neu·ro·log·i·cal** \ˌn(y)u̇r-ə-ˈläj-i-kəl\ *or* **neu·ro·log·ic** \-ik\ *adj* — **neu·ro·log·i·cal·ly** \-i-k(ə-)lē\ *adv* — **neu·rol·o·gist** \n(y)u̇-ˈräl-ə-jəst\ *n*

neu·ron \ˈn(y)ü-ˌrän\ *also* **neu·rone** \-ˌrōn\ *n* : a cell with specialized processes that is the fundamental functional unit of nervous tissue

neu·ro·sci·ence \ˌn(y)u̇r-ō-ˈsī-ən(t)s\ *n* : a branch of the life sciences that deals with the anatomy, physiology, biochemistry, or molecular biology of nerves and nervous tissue and esp. with their relation to behavior and learning — **neu·ro·sci·en·tist** \-ənt-əst\ *n*

neu·ro·sis \n(y)u̇-ˈrō-səs\ *n, pl* **-ro·ses** \-ˌsēz\ : a mental and emotional disorder that is less serious than a psychosis, is not characterized by disturbance of the use of language, and is accompanied by various bodily and mental disturbances (as visceral symptoms, anxieties, or phobias)

[1]**neu·rot·ic** \n(y)u̇-ˈrät-ik\ *adj* : of, relating to, being, or affected with a neurosis; *also* : NERVOUS — **neu·rot·i·cal·ly** \-i-k(ə-)lē\ *adv*

[2]**neurotic** *n* : an emotionally unstable or neurotic person

neut *abbr* neuter

[1]**neu·ter** \ˈn(y)üt-ər\ *adj* [ME *neutre*, fr. MF & L; MF *neutre*, fr. L *neuter*, lit., neither, fr. *ne-* not + *uter* which of two] **1** : of, relating to, or constituting the gender that includes most words or grammatical forms referring to things classed as neither masculine nor feminine **2** : having imperfectly developed or no sex organs

[2]**neuter** *n* **1** : a noun, pronoun, adjective, or inflectional form or class of the neuter gender; *also* : the neuter gender **2** : WORKER 2; *also* : a spayed or castrated animal

[1]**neu·tral** \ˈn(y)ü-trəl\ *n* **1** : one that is neutral **2** : a neutral color **3** : the position of machine gears in which power is not transmitted

[2]**neutral** *adj* **1** : not favoring either side in a quarrel, contest, or war **2** : of or relating to a neutral state or power **3** : MIDDLING, INDIFFERENT **4** : having no hue : GRAY; *also* : not decided in color **5** : neither acid nor basic ⟨a ~ solution⟩ **6** : not electrically charged

neu·tral·ism \ˈn(y)ü-trə-ˌliz-əm\ *n* : a policy or the advocacy of neutrality esp. in international affairs

neu·tral·i·ty \n(y)ü-ˈtral-ət-ē\ *n* : the quality or state of being neutral; *esp* : immunity from invasion or from use by belligerents

neu·tral·ize \ˈn(y)ü-trə-ˌlīz\ *vb* **-ized; -iz·ing** : to make neutral; *esp* : COUNTERACT — **neu·tral·iza·tion** \ˌn(y)ü-trə-lə-ˈzā-shən\ *n*

neu·tri·no \n(y)ü-ˈtrē-nō\ *n, pl* **-nos** : an uncharged elementary particle held to be massless

---

neu·tron \ˈn(y)ü-ˌträn\ *n* : an uncharged atomic particle that is nearly equal in mass to the proton and is present in all atomic nuclei except hydrogen
neutron bomb *n* : a nuclear bomb designed to produce lethal neutrons but less blast and fire damage than other nuclear bombs
Nev *abbr* Nevada
nev·er \ˈnev-ər\ *adv* **1** : not ever **2** : not in any degree, way, or condition
nev·er·more \ˌnev-ər-ˈmōr\ *adv* : never again
nev·er–nev·er land \ˌnev-ər-ˈnev-ər-\ *n* : an ideal or imaginary place
nev·er·the·less \ˌnev-ər-t͟hə-ˈles\ *adv* : in spite of that : HOWEVER
ne·vus \ˈnē-vəs\ *n, pl* **ne·vi** \-ˌvī\ : a usu. pigmented birthmark
[1]**new** \ˈn(y)ü\ *adj* **1** : not old : RECENT, MODERN **2** : recently discovered, recognized, or learned about ⟨~ drugs⟩ **3** : not formerly known or experienced : UNFAMILIAR **4** : different from the former **5** : not accustomed ⟨~ to the work⟩ **6** : beginning as a repetition of a previous act or thing ⟨a ~ year⟩ **7** : REFRESHED, REGENERATED ⟨rest made a ~ man of him⟩ **8** : being in a position or place for the first time ⟨a ~ member⟩ **9** *cap* : having been in use after medieval times : MODERN ⟨*New* Latin⟩ **syn** novel, modern, newfangled, fresh — **new·ish** *adj* — **new·ness** *n*
[2]**new** *adv* : NEWLY ⟨*new*-mown hay⟩
[1]**new·born** \-ˈbȯrn\ *adj* **1** : recently born **2** : born anew ⟨~ hope⟩
[2]**newborn** *n, pl* **newborn** *or* **newborns** : a newborn individual
new·com·er \ˈn(y)ü-ˌkəm-ər\ *n* **1** : one recently arrived **2** : BEGINNER
New Deal *n* : the legislative and administrative program of President F. D. Roosevelt to promote economic recovery and social reform during the 1930s — **New Deal·er** \-ˈdē-lər\ *n*
new·el \ˈn(y)ü-əl\ *n* [ME *nowell,* fr. MF *nouel* stone of a fruit, fr. LL *nucalis* like a nut, fr. L *nuc-, nux* nut] : a post about which the steps of a circular staircase wind; *also* : a post at the foot of a stairway or one at a landing
new·fan·gled \ˈn(y)ü-ˈfaŋ-gəld\ *adj* [ME, fr. *newefangel,* fr. *new* + OE *fangen,* pp. of *fōn* to take, seize] **1** : attracted to novelty **2** : of the newest style : NOVEL
new–fash·ioned \-ˈfash-ənd\ *adj* **1** : made in a new fashion or form **2** : UP-TO-DATE
new·found \-ˈfau̇nd\ *adj* : newly found
New Left *n* : a political movement originating in the 1960s that advocates radical change in prevailing political, social, and educational practices
new·ly \ˈn(y)ü-lē\ *adv* **1** : LATELY, RECENTLY **2** : ANEW, AFRESH
new·ly·wed \-ˌwed\ *n* : one recently married
new math *n* : mathematics based on the theory of sets
new mathematics *n* : NEW MATH
new moon *n* : the phase of the moon with its dark side toward the earth; *also* : the thin crescent moon seen for a few days after the new moon phase
news \ˈn(y)üz\ *n* **1** : a report of recent events : TIDINGS **2** : material reported in a newspaper or news periodical or on a newscast
news·boy \ˈn(y)üz-ˌbȯi\ *n* : one who delivers or sells newspapers
news·cast \-ˌkast\ *n* : a radio or television broadcast of news — **news·cast·er** \-ˌkas-tər\ *n*
news·let·ter \-ˌlet-ər\ *n* : a small newspaper containing news or information of interest chiefly to a special group
news·mag·a·zine \ˈn(y)üz-ˌmag-ə-ˌzēn\ *n* : a usu. weekly magazine devoted chiefly to summarizing and analyzing the news
news·man \-mən, -ˌman\ *n* : one who gathers, reports, or comments on the news
news·pa·per \-ˌpā-pər\ *n* : a paper that is published at regular intervals and contains news, articles of opinion, features, and advertising
news·pa·per·man \ˈn(y)üz-ˌpā-pər-ˌman\ *n* : one who owns or is employed by a newspaper
news·print \ˈn(y)üz-ˌprint\ *n* : cheap paper made chiefly from wood pulp and used mostly for newspapers
news·reel \-ˌrēl\ *n* : a short motion picture portraying current events
news·stand \-ˌstand\ *n* : a place where newspapers and periodicals are sold
news·week·ly \-ˌwēk-lē\ *n* : a weekly newspaper or newsmagazine
news·wor·thy \-ˌwər-t͟hē\ *adj* : sufficiently interesting to the general public to warrant reporting (as in a newspaper)
newsy \ˈn(y)ü-zē\ *adj* **news·i·er; -est** : filled with news; *esp* : CHATTY
newt \ˈn(y)üt\ *n* : any of various small salamanders living chiefly in the water
New Testament *n* : the second of the two chief divisions of the Bible — see BIBLE table
new·ton \ˈn(y)üt-ᵊn\ *n* : the unit of force in the metric system equal to the force required to impart an acceleration of one meter per second per second to a mass of one kilogram
new wave *n, often cap N&W* : a cinematic movement characterized by improvisation, abstraction, subjective symbolism, and often experimental photographic techniques
New World *n* : the western hemisphere; *esp* : the continental landmass of No. and So. America
New Year *n* : NEW YEAR'S DAY; *also* : the first days of the year
New Year's Day *n* : January 1 observed as a legal holiday
New Zea·land·er \n(y)ü-ˈzē-lən-dər\ *n* : a native or inhabitant of New Zealand
[1]**next** \ˈnekst\ *adj* : immediately preceding or following : NEAREST
[2]**next** *prep* : nearest or adjacent to
[3]**next** *adv* **1** : in the time, place, or order nearest or immediately succeeding **2** : on the first occasion to come
nex·us \ˈnek-səs\ *n, pl* **nex·us·es** \-sə-səz\ *or* **nex·us** \-səs, -ˌsüs\ : CONNECTION, LINK
Nez Percé \ˈnez-ˈpərs, *F* nā-per-sā\ *n* : a member of an American Indian people of Idaho, Washington, and Oregon
NF *abbr* Newfoundland
NFC *abbr* National Football Conference
NFL *abbr* National Football League
Nfld *abbr* Newfoundland
NG *abbr* **1** National Guard **2** no good
ngul·trum \eŋ-ˈgu̇l-trəm\ *n* — see MONEY table
ngwee \eŋ-ˈgwē\ *n, pl* **ngwee** — see *kwacha* at MONEY table
NH *abbr* New Hampshire
NHL *abbr* National Hockey League
Ni *symbol* nickel
ni·a·cin \ˈnī-ə-sən\ *n* : NICOTINIC ACID
nib \ˈnib\ *n* : POINT; *esp* : a pen point
[1]**nib·ble** \ˈnib-əl\ *vb* **nib·bled; nib·bling** \-(ə-)liŋ\ : to bite gently or bit by bit
[2]**nibble** *n* : a small or cautious bite
nice \ˈnīs\ *adj* **nic·er; nic·est** [ME, foolish, wanton, fr. OF, fr. L *nescius* ignorant, fr. *nescire* not to know] **1** : FASTIDIOUS, DISCRIMINATING **2** : marked by delicate discrimination or treatment **3** : PLEASING, AGREEABLE; *also* : well-executed **4** : WELL-BRED ⟨~ people⟩ **5** : VIRTUOUS, RESPECTABLE — **nice·ly** *adv* — **nice·ness** *n*
nice–nel·ly \ˈnīs-ˈnel-ē\ *adj, often cap 2d N* **1** : PRUDISH **2** : having the nature of or containing a euphemism — **nice nelly** *n, often cap 2d N* — **nice–nel·ly·ism** \-ˌiz-əm\ *n, often cap 2d N*

nice·ty \ˈnī-sət-ē\ *n, pl* **-ties** **1** : a dainty, delicate, or elegant thing ⟨enjoy the *niceties* of life⟩ **2** : a fine detail ⟨*niceties* of workmanship⟩ **3** : EXACTNESS, PRECISION, ACCURACY

niche \ˈnich\ *n* [F] **1** : a recess (as for a statue) in a wall **2** : a place, work, or use for which a person or thing is best fitted

¹nick \ˈnik\ *n* **1** : a small notch or groove **2** : the final critical moment ⟨in the ~ of time⟩

²nick *vb* : NOTCH, CHIP

¹nick·el \ˈnik-əl\ *n* **1** : a hard silver-white metallic chemical element capable of a high polish and used in alloys — see ELEMENT table **2** *also* **nick·le** : the U.S. 5-cent piece made of copper and nickel; *also* : the Canadian 5-cent piece

²nick·el *vb* **-eled** *or* **-elled; -el·ing** *or* **-el·ling** : to plate with nickel

nick·el·ode·on \ˌnik-ə-ˈlōd-ē-ən\ *n* **1** : an early movie theater charging an admission price of five cents **2** : a coin-operated musical device

nickel silver *n* : a silver-white alloy of copper, zinc, and nickel

nick·er \ˈnik-ər\ *vb* **nick·ered; nick·er·ing** : NEIGH, WHINNY

nick·name \ˈnik-ˌnām\ *n* [ME *nekename* additional name, alter. (resulting from incorrect division of *an ekename*) of *ekename*, fr. *eke* addition + *name*] **1** : a usu. descriptive name given instead of or in addition to the one belonging to a person, place, or thing **2** : a familiar form of a proper name — **nickname** *vb*

nic·o·tine \ˈnik-ə-ˌtēn\ *n* : a poisonous substance found in tobacco and used as an insecticide

nicotinic acid *n* : an organic acid of the vitamin B complex found in plants and animals and used against pellagra

niece \ˈnēs\ *n* : a daughter of one's brother, sister, brother-in-law, or sister-in-law

nif·ty \ˈnif-tē\ *adj* **nif·ti·er; -est** : very good : very attractive

Ni·ge·ri·an \nī-ˈjir-ē-ən\ *n* : a native or inhabitant of Nigeria — **Nigerian** *adj*

Ni·ge·rois \ˌnē-zhər-ˈwä\ *n, pl* **Nigerois** : a native or inhabitant of Niger

nig·gard \ˈnig-ərd\ *n* : a stingy person : MISER — **nig·gard·li·ness** \-lē-nəs\ *n* — **nig·gard·ly** *adj or adv*

nig·gling \ˈnig-(ə-)liŋ\ *adj* **1** : PETTY **2** : bothersome in a petty way

¹nigh \ˈnī\ *adv* **1** : near in place, time, or relationship **2** : NEARLY, ALMOST

²nigh *adj* : CLOSE, NEAR

³nigh *prep* : NEAR

night \ˈnīt\ *n* **1** : the period between dusk and dawn **2** : the darkness of night **3** : a period of misery or unhappiness **4** : NIGHTFALL — **night** *adj*

night blindness *n* : reduced visual capacity in faint light (as at night)

night·cap \ˈnīt-ˌkap\ *n* **1** : a cloth cap worn with nightclothes **2** : a usu. alcoholic drink taken at bedtime

night·clothes \-ˌklō(th)z\ *n pl* : garments worn in bed

night·club \-ˌkləb\ *n* : a place of entertainment open at night usu. serving food and liquor and providing music for dancing

night crawler *n* : EARTHWORM; *esp* : a large earthworm found on the soil surface at night

night·dress \ˈnīt-ˌdres\ *n* : NIGHTGOWN

night·fall \-ˌfȯl\ *n* : the coming of night

night·gown \-ˌgau̇n\ *n* : a loose garment designed for wear in bed

night·hawk \-ˌhȯk\ *n* : any of several birds related to and resembling the whippoorwill

night·in·gale \ˈnīt-ᵊn-ˌgāl, -iŋ-\ *n* [ME, fr. OE *nihtegale*, fr. *niht* night + *galan* to sing] : any of several Old World thrushes noted for the sweet nocturnal song of the male

nighthawk

night·life \ˈnīt-ˌlīf\ *n* : the activity of pleasure-seekers at night

night·ly \ˈnīt-lē\ *adj* **1** : happening, done, or produced by night or every night **2** : of or relating to the night or every night — **nightly** *adv*

night·mare \ˈnīt-ˌmar\ *n* : a frightening oppressive dream or state occurring during sleep — **nightmare** *adj* — **night·mar·ish** \-ˌmar-ish\ *adj*

night rider *n* : a member of a secret band who ride masked at night doing violence to punish or terrorize

night·shade \ˈnīt-ˌshād\ *n* : any of a large genus of woody or herbaceous plants having alternate leaves, flowers in clusters, and fruits that are berries and including poisonous forms (as belladonna) and important food plants (as potato, tomato, or eggplant)

night·shirt \-ˌshərt\ *n* : a nightgown esp. for a man or a boy

night soil *n* : human excrement collected for fertilizing the soil

night·stick \ˈnīt-ˌstik\ *n* : a policeman's club

night·time \-ˌtīm\ *n* : the time from dusk to dawn

night·walk·er \-ˌwȯ-kər\ *n* : a person who roves about at night esp. with criminal or immoral intent

ni·hil·ism \ˈnī-(h)ə-ˌliz-əm, ˈnē-\ *n* **1** : an attitude or doctrine that traditional values and beliefs are unfounded and that existence is senseless and useless **2** : ANARCHISM **3** : TERRORISM — **ni·hil·ist** \-ləst\ *n or adj* — **ni·hil·is·tic** \ˌnī-(h)ə-ˈlis-tik, ˌnē-\ *adj*

nil \ˈnil\ *n* : NOTHING, ZERO

nim·ble \ˈnim-bəl\ *adj* **nim·bler** \-b(ə-)lər\; **nim·blest** \-b(ə-)ləst\ [ME *nimel*, fr. OE *numol* holding much, fr. *niman* to take] **1** : quick and light in motion : AGILE ⟨a ~ dancer⟩ **2** : quick in understanding and learning : CLEVER ⟨a ~ mind⟩ — **nim·ble·ness** *n* — **nim·bly** \-blē\ *adv*

nim·bus \ˈnim-bəs\ *n, pl* **nim·bi** \-ˌbī, -bē\ *or* **nim·bus·es** **1** : a figure (as a disk) suggesting radiant light about the head of a drawn or sculptured divinity, saint, or sovereign **2** : a rain cloud that is of uniform grayness and extends over the entire sky

nim·rod \ˈnim-ˌräd\ *n* : HUNTER

nin·com·poop \ˈnin-kəm-ˌpüp\ *n* : FOOL, SIMPLETON

nine \ˈnīn\ *n* **1** : one more than eight **2** : the 9th in a set or series **3** : something having nine units; *esp* : a baseball team — **nine** *adj or pron* — **ninth** \ˈnīnth\ *adj or adv or n*

nine days' wonder *n* : something that creates a short-lived sensation

nine·pins \ˈnīn-ˌpinz\ *n* : tenpins played without the headpin

nine·teen \ˈnīn-ˈtēn\ *n* : one more than 18 — **nineteen** *adj or pron* — **nine·teenth** \-ˈtēnth\ *adj or n*

nine·ty \ˈnīnt-ē\ *n, pl* **nineties** : nine times 10 — **nine·ti·eth** \-ē-əth\ *adj or n* — **ninety** *adj or pron*

nin·ny \ˈnin-ē\ *n, pl* **ninnies** : FOOL

---

ni·o·bi·um \nī-ˈō-bē-əm\ *n* : a gray metallic chemical element used in alloys — see ELEMENT table

¹nip \ˈnip\ *vb* **nipped; nip·ping 1** : to catch hold of and squeeze tightly between two surfaces, edges, or points **2** : CLIP **3** : to destroy the growth, progress, or fulfillment of ⟨*nipped* in the bud⟩ **4** : to injure or make numb with cold : CHILL **5** : SNATCH, STEAL

²nip *n* **1** : a sharp stinging cold **2** : a biting or pungent flavor **3** : PINCH, BITE **4** : a small portion : BIT

³nip *n* : a small quantity of liquor : SIP

⁴nip *vb* **nipped; nip·ping** : to take liquor in nips : TIPPLE

nip and tuck \ˌnip-ən-ˈtək\ *adj or adv* : so close that the lead shifts rapidly from one contestant to another

nip·per \ˈnip-ər\ *n* **1** : one that nips **2** *pl* : PINCERS **3** : a small boy

nip·ple \ˈnip-əl\ *n* : the protuberance of a mammary gland through which milk is drawn off : TEAT; *also* : something resembling a nipple

nip·py \ˈnip-ē\ *adj* **nip·pi·er; -est 1** : PUNGENT, SHARP **2** : CHILLY

nir·va·na \nir-ˈvän-ə\ *n, often cap* [Skt *nirvāṇa*, lit., act of extinguishing, fr. *nis-* out + *vāti* it blows] **1** : the final freeing of a soul from all that enslaves it; *esp* : the supreme happiness that according to Buddhism comes when all passion, hatred, and delusion die out and the soul is released from the necessity of further purification **2** : OBLIVION; *also* : PARADISE

ni·sei \ˈnē-ˈsā\ *n, pl* **nisei** *also* **niseis** : a son or daughter of immigrant Japanese parents who is born and educated in America

ni·si \ˈnī-ˌsī\ *adj* [L, unless, fr. *ne-* not + *si* if] : taking effect at a specified time unless previously modified or voided ⟨a divorce decree ~⟩

nit \ˈnit\ *n* : the egg of a parasitic insect (as a louse); *also* : the young insect

ni·ter \ˈnīt-ər\ *n* **1** : POTASSIUM NITRATE **2** : SODIUM NITRATE

nit–pick·ing \ˈnit-ˌpik-iŋ\ *n* : minute and usu. unjustified criticism — **nit·pick·er** \-ər\ *n*

¹ni·trate \ˈnī-ˌtrāt, -trət\ *n* **1** : a salt or ester of nitric acid **2** : sodium nitrate or potassium nitrate used as a fertilizer

²ni·trate \-ˌtrāt\ *vb* **ni·trat·ed; ni·trat·ing** : to treat or combine with nitric acid or a nitrate — **ni·tra·tion** \nī-ˈtrā-shən\ *n*

ni·tric acid \ˌnī-trik-\ *n* : a corrosive liquid acid used in making dyes, explosives, and fertilizers

ni·tri·fi·ca·tion \ˌnī-trə-fə-ˈkā-shən\ *n* : the process of nitrifying; *esp* : the oxidation (as by bacteria) of ammonium salts to nitrites and then to nitrates

ni·tri·fy \ˈnī-trə-ˌfī\ *vb* **-fied; -fy·ing 1** : to combine with nitrogen or a nitrogen compound **2** : to subject to or produce by nitrification

ni·trite \ˈnī-ˌtrīt\ *n* : a salt of nitrous acid

ni·tro \ˈnī-trō\ *n, pl* **nitros** : any of various nitrated products; *esp* : NITROGLYCERIN

ni·tro·gen \ˈnī-trə-jən\ *n* : a tasteless odorless gaseous chemical element constituting 78 percent of the atmosphere by volume — see ELEMENT table — **ni·trog·e·nous** \nī-ˈträj-ə-nəs\ *adj*

ni·tro·glyc·er·in *or* **ni·tro·glyc·er·ine** \ˌnī-trə-ˈglis-(ə-)rən\ *n* : a heavy oily explosive liquid used in making dynamite and in medicine

ni·trous acid \ˌnī-trəs-\ *n* : an unstable nitrogen-containing acid known only in solution or in the form of its salts

nitrous oxide *n* : a colorless gas used esp. as an anesthetic in dentistry

nit·ty–grit·ty \ˈnit-ē-ˌgrit-ē, ˌnit-ē-ˈgrit-ē\ *n* : the actual state of things : what is ultimately essential and true

nit·wit \ˈnit-ˌwit\ *n* : a flighty stupid person

¹nix \ˈniks\ *n* : NOTHING

²nix *vb* : VETO, REJECT

³nix *adv* : NO

NJ *abbr* New Jersey

NL *abbr* National League

NLRB *abbr* National Labor Relations Board

NM *abbr* **1** nautical mile **2** New Mexico

N Mex *abbr* New Mexico

NNE *abbr* north-northeast

NNW *abbr* north-northwest

¹no \(ˈ)nō\ *adv* **1** — used to express the negative of an alternative ⟨shall we continue or ~⟩ **2** : in no respect or degree ⟨he is ~ better than the others⟩ **3** : not so ⟨~, I'm not ready⟩ **4** — used with adjective to imply a meaning opposite to the positive statement ⟨in ~ uncertain terms⟩ **5** — used to introduce a more emphatic or explicit statement ⟨has the right, ~, the duty to continue⟩ **6** — used as an interjection to express surprise or doubt ⟨~—you don't say⟩ **7** — used in combination with a verb to form a compound adjective ⟨*no*-bake pie⟩

²no *adj* **1** : not any; *also* : hardly any **2** : not a ⟨she's ~ expert⟩

³no \ˈnō\ *n, pl* **noes** *or* **nos** \ˈnōz\ **1** : REFUSAL, DENIAL **2** : a negative vote or decision; *also, pl* : persons voting in the negative

⁴no *abbr* **1** north; northern **2** [L *numero*, abl. of *numerus*] number

¹No *or* **Noh** \ˈnō\ *n, pl* **No** *or* **Noh** : classic Japanese dance-drama having a heroic theme, a chorus, and highly stylized action, costuming, and scenery

²No *symbol* nobelium

No·bel·ist \nō-ˈbel-əst\ *n* : a winner of a Nobel prize

no·bel·i·um \nō-ˈbel-ē-əm\ *n* : a radioactive chemical element produced artificially — see ELEMENT table

No·bel prize \(ˌ)nō-ˌbel-\ *n* : any of various annual prizes (as in peace, literature, or medicine) established by the will of Alfred Nobel for the encouragement of persons who work for the interests of humanity

no·bil·i·ty \nō-ˈbil-ət-ē\ *n* **1** : the quality or state of being noble ⟨~ of character⟩ **2** : nobles considered as forming a class

¹no·ble \ˈnō-bəl\ *adj* **no·bler** \-b(ə-)lər\; **no·blest** \-b(ə-)ləst\ [ME, fr. OF, fr. L *nobilis* knowable, well known, noble, fr. *noscere* to come to know] **1** : ILLUSTRIOUS; *also* : FAMOUS, NOTABLE **2** : of high birth, rank, or station : ARISTOCRATIC **3** : EXCELLENT **4** : STATELY, IMPOSING ⟨a ~ edifice⟩ **5** : of a magnanimous nature — **no·ble·ness** *n* — **no·bly** \-blē\ *adv*

²noble *n* : a person of noble rank or birth

no·ble·man \ˈnō-bəl-mən\ *n* : a member of the nobility : PEER

no·blesse oblige \nō-ˌbles-ə-ˈblēzh\ *n* : the obligation of honorable, generous, and responsible behavior associated with high rank or birth

¹no·body \ˈnō-ˌbäd-ē, -bəd-ē\ *pron* : no person

²nobody *n, pl* **no·bod·ies** : a person of no influence, importance, or worth

noc·tur·nal \näk-ˈtərn-ᵊl\ *adj* **1** : of, relating to, or occurring in the night **2** : active at night ⟨a ~ bird⟩

noc·turne \ˈnäk-ˌtərn\ *n* **1** : a dreamy pensive composition for the piano **2** : a work of art dealing with night

noc·u·ous \ˈnäk-yə-wəs\ *adj* : likely to cause injury : HARMFUL

nod \ˈnäd\ *vb* **nod·ded; nod·ding 1** : to bend the head downward or forward (as in bowing, going to sleep, or giving assent) **2** : to move up and down ⟨tulips *nodding* in the breeze⟩ **3** : to show by a nod of the head ⟨~ agreement⟩ **4** : to make a slip or error in a moment of abstraction — **nod** *n*

nod·dle \ˈnäd-ᵊl\ *n* : HEAD

nod·dy \ˈnäd-ē\ *n, pl* **noddies 1** : SIMPLETON **2** : a stout-bodied tropical tern

node \ˈnōd\ *n* : a thickened, swollen, or differentiated area (as of tissue); *esp* : the part of a stem from which a leaf arises — **nod·al** \-ᵊl\ *adj*

nod·ule \ˈnäj-ül\ *n* : a small lump or swelling — **nod·u·lar** \ˈnäj-ə-lər\ *adj*

no·el \nō-ˈel\ *n* [F *noël* Christmas, carol, fr. L *natalis* birthday] **1** : a Christmas carol **2** *cap* : the Christmas season
noes *pl of* NO
no–fault \ˈnō-ˈfȯlt\ *adj* **1** : of, relating to, or being a motor vehicle insurance plan under which an accident victim is compensated usu. up to a stipulated limit for actual losses by his own insurance company regardless of who is responsible **2** : of, relating to, or being a divorce law according to which neither party is held responsible for the breakup of the marriage
nog·gin \ˈnäg-ən\ *n* **1** : a small mug or cup; *also* : a small quantity of drink **2** : a person's head
no–good \ˌnō-ˌgu̇d\ *adj* : having no worth, use, or chance of success — **no–good** \ˈnō-ˌgu̇d\ *n*
Noh *var of* NO
no–hit·ter \(ˈ)nō-ˈhit-ər\ *n* : a baseball game or part of a game in which a pitcher allows the opposition no base hits
no·how \ˈnō-ˌhau̇\ *adv* : in no manner
[1]**noise** \ˈnȯiz\ *n* [ME, fr. OF, strife, quarrel, noise, fr. L *nausea* nausea] **1** : loud, confused, or senseless shouting or outcry **2** : SOUND; *esp* : one that lacks agreeable musical quality or is noticeably unpleasant **3** : unwanted electronic signal or disturbance — **noise·less** *adj* — **noise·less·ly** *adv*
[2]**noise** *vb* **noised; nois·ing** : to spread by rumor or report ⟨the story was *noised* abroad⟩
noise·mak·er \ˈnȯiz-ˌmā-kər\ *n* : one that makes noise; *esp* : a device used to make noise at parties
noise pollution *n* : environmental pollution consisting of annoying or harmful noise
noi·some \ˈnȯi-səm\ *adj* **1** : HARMFUL, UNWHOLESOME **2** : offensive to the senses (as smell) : DISGUSTING
noisy \ˈnȯi-zē\ *adj* **nois·i·er; -est 1** : making loud noises **2** : full of noises : LOUD — **nois·i·ly** \ˈnȯi-zə-lē\ *adv* — **nois·i·ness** \-zē-nəs\ *n*
nol·le pro·se·qui \ˌnäl-ē-ˈpräs-ə-ˌkwī\ *n* [L, to be unwilling to pursue] : an entry on the record of a legal action that the prosecutor or plaintiff will proceed no further in an action or suit or in some aspect of it
no·lo con·ten·de·re \ˌnō-lō-kən-ˈten-də-rē\ *n* [L, I do not wish to contend] : a plea in a criminal prosecution that subjects the defendant to conviction but does not admit guilt or preclude denying the charges in another proceeding
nol–pros \ˈnäl-ˈpräs\ *vb* **nol–prossed; nol–pros·ing** : to discontinue by entering a nolle prosequi
nom *abbr* nominative
no·mad \ˈnō-ˌmad\ *n* **1** : a member of a people with no fixed residence but wandering from place to place **2** : an individual who roams about aimlessly — **nomad** *adj* — **no·mad·ic** \nō-ˈmad-ik\ *adj*
no–man's–land \ˈnō-ˌmanz-ˌland\ *n* **1** : an area of unowned, unclaimed, or uninhabited land **2** : an unoccupied area between opposing troops
nom de guerre \ˌnäm-di-ˈgeər\ *n, pl* **noms de guerre** \ˌnäm(z)-di-\ [F, lit., war name] : PSEUDONYM
nom de plume \-ˈplüm\ *n, pl* **noms de plume** \ˌnäm(z)-di-\ [F *nom* name + *de* of + *plume* pen] : PSEUDONYM
no·men·cla·ture \ˈnō-mən-ˌklā-chər\ *n* **1** : NAME, DESIGNATION **2** : a system of names used in a science or art
nom·i·nal \ˈnäm-ən-ᵊl\ *adj* **1** : being something in name or form only ⟨~ head of a party⟩ **2** : TRIFLING ⟨a ~ price⟩ — **nom·i·nal·ly** \-ē\ *adv*
nom·i·nate \ˈnäm-ə-ˌnāt\ *vb* **-nat·ed; -nat·ing** : to choose as a candidate for election, appointment, or honor — **nom·i·na·tion** \ˌnäm-ə-ˈnā-shən\ *n*
nom·i·na·tive \ˈnäm-(ə-)nət-iv\ *adj* : of, relating to, or constituting a grammatical case marking typically the subject of a verb — **nominative** *n*
nom·i·nee \ˌnäm-ə-ˈnē\ *n* : a person nominated for an office, duty, or position

non- \(ˈ)nän, ˌnän\ *prefix* : not : reverse of : absence of

nonabrasive
nonabsorbent
nonacademic
nonacceptance
nonacid
nonactivated
nonadaptive
nonaddicting
nonadhesive
nonadjacent
nonadjustable
nonaggression
nonalcoholic
nonappearance
nonaromatic
nonathletic
nonattendance
nonbeliever
nonbelligerent
nonbreakable
nonburnable
noncancerous
noncandidate
noncellular
nonchargeable
nonclerical
noncoital
noncombat
noncombustible
noncommercial
noncommunicable
non-Communist
noncompeting
noncompetitive
noncompliance
noncomplying
nonconcurrence
nonconcurrent
nonconducting
nonconflicting
nonconformance
nonconforming
nonconstructive
noncontagious
noncontinuous
noncontributing
noncorroding
noncorrosive
noncrystalline
nondeductible
nondelivery
nondemocratic
nondenominational
nondepartmental
nondestructive
nondevelopment
nondiscrimination
nondiscriminitory
nondistinctive
nondistribution
nondivided
nondurable
noneconomic
noneducational
nonelastic
nonelection
nonelective
nonelectric
nonelectrical
nonemotional
nonenforceable
nonenforcement
nonessential
nonethical
nonexchangeable
nonexempt
nonexistence
nonexistent
nonexplosive
nonfarm
nonfatal
nonfattening
nonfederated
nonferrous
nonfiction
nonfictional
nonfilamentous
nonfilterable
nonflammable
nonflowering
nonfood
nonfreezing
nonfulfillment
nonfunctional
nongraded
nonhereditary
nonhomogeneous
nonhomologous
nonhuman
nonidentical
nonimportation
nonindustrial
noninfectious
noninflammable
nonintellectual
nonintercourse
noninterference
nonintoxicant
nonintoxicating
nonionizing
nonirritating
nonlegal
nonlife
nonlinear
nonliterary
nonliving
nonlogical
nonmagnetic
nonmalignant
nonmaterial
nonmember
nonmembership
nonmigratory
nonmilitary
nonmoral
nonmotile
nonmoving
nonnegotiable
nonobservance
nonoccurrence
nonofficial
nonoily
nonorthodox
nonparallel
nonparasitic
nonparticipant

nonparticipating
nonpathogenic
nonpaying
nonpayment
nonperformance
nonperishable
nonphysical
nonpoisonous
nonpolar
nonpolitical
nonporous
nonpregnant
nonproductive
nonprofessional
nonprotein
nonradioactive
nonrandom
nonreactive
nonreciprocal
nonrecognition
nonrecoverable
nonrecurrent
nonrecurring
nonrefillable
nonreligious
nonrenewable
nonresidential
nonrestricted
nonreturnable
nonreversible
nonruminant
nonsalable
nonscientific
nonscientist
nonseasonal
nonsectarian
nonsegregated
nonselective
non-self-governing
nonsexist
nonsexual
nonshrinkable
nonsinkable
nonskid
nonslip
nonsmoker
nonsmoking
nonsocial
nonspeaking
nonspecialist
nonspecialized
nonstaining
nonstriated
nonstriker
nonsubscriber
nonsuccess
nonsurgical
nontaxable
nonteaching
nontechnical
nontemporal
nontenured
nontheistic
nonthreatening
nontoxic
nontraditional
nontransferable
nontransparent
nontypical
nonuniform
nonuser
nonvascular
nonvenomous
nonviable
nonviolation
nonvisual
nonvocal
nonvolatile
nonvoter
nonvoting
nonworker
nonworking
nonzero

non·age \ˈnän-ij, ˈnō-nij\ *n* **1** : legal minority **2** : a period of youth **3** : IMMATURITY

no·na·ge·nar·i·an \ˌnō-nə-jə-ˈner-ē-ən, ˌnän-ə-\ *n* : a person who is in his nineties

non·aligned \ˌnän-ᵊl-ˈīnd\ *adj* : not allied with other nations

non·book \ˈnän-ˌbu̇k\ *n* : a book of little literary merit which is often a compilation (as of press clippings)

[1]**nonce** \ˈnäns\ *n* : the one, particular, or present occasion or purpose ⟨for the ~⟩

[2]**nonce** *adj* : occurring, used, or made only once or for a special occasion ⟨a ~ word⟩

non·cha·lant \ˌnän-shə-ˈlänt\ *adj* [F, fr. OF, fr. prp. of *nonchaloir* to disregard, fr. *non-* not + *chaloir* to concern, fr. L *calēre* to be warm] : giving an effect of unconcern or indifference — **non·cha·lance** \-ˈläns\ *n* — **non·cha·lant·ly** *adv*

non·com \ˈnän-ˌkäm\ *n* : NONCOMMISSIONED OFFICER

non·com·ba·tant \ˌnän-kəm-ˈbat-ᵊnt, nän-ˈkäm-bət-ənt\ *n* : a member (as a chaplain) of the armed forces whose duties do not include fighting; *also* : CIVILIAN — **noncombatant** *adj*

non·com·mis·sioned officer \ˌnän-kə-ˌmish-ənd-\ *n* : a subordinate officer in the armed forces appointed from enlisted personnel

non·com·mit·tal \ˌnän-kə-ˈmit-ᵊl\ *adj* : indicating neither consent nor dissent

non com·pos men·tis \ˌnän-ˌkäm-pəs-ˈment-əs\ *adj* : not of sound mind

non·con·duc·tor \ˌnän-kən-ˈdək-tər\ *n* : a substance that is a very poor conductor of heat, electricity, or sound

non·con·form·ist \-kən-ˈfȯr-məst\ *n* **1** *often cap* : a person who does not conform to an established church and esp. the Church of England **2** : a person who does not conform to a generally accepted pattern of thought or action — **non·con·for·mi·ty** \-ˈfȯr-mət-ē\ *n*

non·co·op·er·a·tion \ˌnän-kō-ˌäp-ə-ˈrā-shən\ *n* : failure or refusal to cooperate; *esp* : refusal through civil disobedience of a people to cooperate with the government of a country

non·cred·it \(ˈ)nän-ˈkred-ət\ *adj* : not offering credit toward a degree

non·dairy \ˈnän-ˈde(ə)r-ē\ *adj* : containing no milk or milk products

non·de·script \ˌnän-di-ˈskript\ *adj* : not belonging to any particular class or kind : not easily described

non·drink·er \-ˈdriŋ-kər\ *n* : one who abstains from alcoholic beverages

[1]**none** \ˈnən\ *pron* **1** : not any ⟨~ of them went⟩ **2** : not one ⟨~ of the family⟩ **3** : not any such thing or person ⟨half a loaf is better than ~⟩

[2]**none** *adj, archaic* : not any : NO

[3]**none** *adv* : by no means : not at all ⟨he got there ~ too soon⟩

non·en·ti·ty \ˌnän-ˈent-ət-ē\ *n* **1** : something that does not exist or exists only in the imagination **2** : one of no consequence or significance

nones \ˈnōnz\ *n sing or pl* : the 7th day of March, May, July, or October or the 5th day of any other month in the ancient Roman calendar

none·such \ˈnən-ˌsəch\ *n* : one without an equal — **nonesuch** *adj*

none·the·less \ˌnən-t͟hə-ˈles\ *adv* : NEVERTHELESS

non–eu·clid·e·an \ˌnän-yü-ˈklid-ē-ən\ *adj, often cap E* : not assuming or in accordance with all the postulates of Euclid's *Elements* ⟨~ geometry⟩

non·event \ˈnän-i-ˌvent\ *n* **1** : an event that fails to take place or to satisfy expectations **2** : a highly promoted event of little or no consequence

non·fat \-ˈfat\ *adj* : lacking fat solids : having fat solids removed ⟨~ milk⟩

non·gono·coc·cal \ˈnän-ˌgän-ə-ˈkäk-əl\ *adj* : not caused by the gonococcus

non·he·ro \-ˈhē-rō\ *n* : ANTIHERO

non·in·ter·ven·tion \ˌnän-ˌint-ər-ˈven-chən\ *n* : refusal or failure to intervene (as in the affairs of another state)

non·met·al \ˈnän-ˈmet-ᵊl\ *n* : a chemical element (as carbon, phosphorus, or oxygen) that lacks metallic properties — **non·me·tal·lic** \ˌnän-mə-ˈtal-ik\ *adj*

non·neg·a·tive \-ˈneg-ət-iv\ *adj* : not negative : being either positive or zero

non·ob·jec·tive \ˌnän-əb-ˈjek-tiv\ *adj* **1** : not objective **2** : representing no natural or actual object, figure, or scene ⟨~ art⟩

[1]**non·pa·reil** \ˌnän-pə-ˈrel\ *adj* : having no equal : PEERLESS

[2]**nonpareil** *n* **1** : an individual of unequaled excellence : PARAGON **2** : a small flat disk of chocolate covered with white sugar pellets

non·par·ti·san \ˈnän-ˈpärt-ə-zən\ *adj* : not partisan; *esp* : not influenced by political party spirit or interests

non·per·son \-ˈpərs-ᵊn\ *n* **1** : UNPERSON **2** : a person having no social or legal status

non·plus \ˈnän-ˈpləs\ *vb* **-plussed** *also* **-plused** \-ˈpləst\; **-plus·sing** *also* **-plus·ing** : PUZZLE, PERPLEX

non·pre·scrip·tion \ˌnän-pri-ˈskrip-shən\ *adj* : available for sale legally without a doctor's prescription

non·prof·it \ˈnän-ˈpräf-ət\ *adj* : not conducted or maintained for the purpose of making a profit

non·pro·lif·er·a·tion \ˌnän-prə-ˌlif-ə-ˈrā-shən\ *adj* : providing for the stoppage of proliferation (as of nuclear arms) ⟨a ~ treaty⟩

non·read·er \ˈnän-ˈrēd-ər\ *n* : one who does not read

non·rep·re·sen·ta·tion·al \ˌnän-ˌrep-ri-ˌzen-ˈtā-sh(ə-)nəl\ *adj* : NONOBJECTIVE 2

non·res·i·dent \ˈnän-ˈrez-əd-ənt\ *adj* : not living in a particular place — **non·res·i·dence** \-əd-əns\ *n* — **nonresident** *n*

non·re·sis·tance \ˌnän-ri-ˈzis-təns\ *n* : the principles or practice of passive submission to authority even when unjust or oppressive

non·re·stric·tive \-ri-ˈstrik-tiv\ *adj* **1** : not serving or tending to restrict **2** : not limiting the reference of the word or phrase modified ⟨a ~ clause⟩

non·rig·id \nän-ˈrij-əd\ *adj* : maintaining form by pressure of contained gas ⟨a ~ airship⟩

non·sched·uled \ˈnän-ˈskej-üld\ *adj* : licensed to carry passengers or freight by air without a regular schedule

non·sense \ˈnän-ˌsens, -səns\ *n* **1** : foolish or meaningless words or actions **2** : things of no importance or value : TRIFLES — **non·sen·si·cal** \nän-ˈsen-si-kəl\ *adj* — **non·sen·si·cal·ly** \-k(ə-)lē\ *adv*

non seq *abbr* non sequitur

non se·qui·tur \nän-ˈsek-wət-ər\ *n* [L, it does not follow] : an inference that does not follow from the premises

non·sked \ˈnän-ˈsked\ *n* : a nonscheduled airline or transport plane

non·stan·dard \ˌnän-ˈstan-dərd\ *adj* **1** : not standard **2** : not conforming to the usage characteristic of educated native speakers of a language

non·start·er \ˈnän-ˈstärt-ər\ *n* : one that does not start or gets off to a poor start

non·stick \-ˈstik\ *adj* : allowing easy removal of cooked food particles

non·stop \-ˈstäp\ *adj* : done or made without a stop — **nonstop** *adv*

non·sup·port \ˌnän-sə-ˈpōrt\ *n* : failure to support; *esp* : failure on the part of one under obligation to provide maintenance

non trop·po \ˈnän-ˈtrȯ-pō\ *adv or adj* [It] : not too much so : moderately so — used as a direction in music

non–U \ˈnän-ˈyü\ *adj* : not characteristic of the upper classes

non·union \-ˈyü-nyən\ *adj* **1** : not belonging to a trade union ⟨~ carpenters⟩ **2** : not recognizing or favoring trade unions or their members ⟨~ employers⟩

non·us·er \-ˈyü-zər\ *n* : one who does not make use of something (as drugs)

non·vi·o·lence \-ˈnän-ˈvī-ə-ləns\ *n* **1** : abstention from violence as a matter of principle **2** : avoidance of violence **3** : nonviolent political demonstrations — **non·vi·o·lent** \-lənt\ *adj*

non·white \ˌnän-ˈhwīt, -ˈwīt\ *adj* : a person whose features and esp. skin color are different from those of Caucasians of northwestern Europe — **nonwhite** *adj*

non·wo·ven \ˈnän-ˈwō-vən\ *adj* : made of fibers held together by interlocking or bonding (as by chemical or thermal means) — **nonwoven** *n*

noo·dle \ˈnüd-ᵊl\ *n* : a food paste made with egg and shaped typically in ribbon form

nook \ˈnu̇k\ *n* **1** : an interior angle or corner formed usu. by two walls ⟨a chimney ~⟩ **2** : a sheltered or hidden place ⟨a shady ~⟩

noon \ˈnün\ *n* : the middle of the day : 12 o'clock in the daytime — **noon** *adj*

noon·day \-ˌdā\ *n* : NOON, MIDDAY

no one *pron* : NOBODY

noon·tide \ˈnün-ˌtīd\ *n* : NOON

noon·time \-ˌtīm\ *n* : NOON

noose \ˈnüs\ *n* : a loop with a running knot (as in a lasso) that binds closer the more it is drawn

no–par \ˈno-ˈpär\ *or* **no–par–val·ue** *adj* : having no nominal value ⟨~ stock⟩

nope \ˈnōp\ *adv* : NO

nor \nər, (ˈ)nȯr\ *conj* : and not ⟨not for you ~ for me⟩ — used esp. to introduce and negate the second member and each later member of a series of items preceded by *neither* ⟨neither here ~ there⟩

Nor *abbr* Norway; Norwegian

Nor·dic \ˈnȯrd-ik\ *adj* **1** : of or relating to the Germanic peoples of northern Europe and esp. of Scandinavia **2** : of or relating to a physical type characterized by tall stature, long head, light skin and hair, and blue eyes — **Nordic** *n*

nor·epi·neph·rine \ˈnȯr-ˌep-ə-ˈnef-rən\ *n* [*nor*mal + *epinephrine*] : a nitrogen-containing compound that is the chemical means of transmission across synapses in parts of the sympathetic and central nervous systems

norm \ˈnȯrm\ *n* [L *norma,* lit., carpenter's square] : AVERAGE; *esp* : a set standard of development or achievement usu. derived from the average or median achievement of a large group

[1]**nor·mal** \ˈnȯr-məl\ *adj* **1** : REGULAR, STANDARD, NATURAL **2** : of average intelligence; *also* : sound in mind and body — **nor·mal·cy** \-sē\ *n* — **nor·mal·i·ty** \nȯr-ˈmal-ət-ē\ *n* — **nor·mal·ly** \ˈnȯr-mə-lē\ *adv*

[2]**normal** *n* **1** : one that is normal **2** : the usual condition, level, or quantity

nor·mal·ize \ˈnȯr-mə-ˌlīz\ *vb* **-ized; -iz·ing** : to make normal or average — **nor·mal·iza·tion** \ˌnȯr-mə-lə-ˈzā-shən\ *n*

normal school *n* : a usu. 2-year school for training chiefly elementary teachers

Nor·man \ˈnȯr-mən\ *n* **1** : a native or inhabitant of Normandy **2** : one of the 10th century Scandinavian conquerors of Normandy **3** : one of the Norman-French conquerors of England in 1066 — **Norman** *adj*

nor·ma·tive \ˈnȯr-mət-iv\ *adj* : of, relating to, or prescribing norms — **nor·ma·tive·ly** *adv* — **nor·ma·tive·ness** *n*

Norse \ˈnȯrs\ *n, pl* **Norse 1** *pl* : SCANDINAVIANS; *also* : NORWEGIANS **2** : NORWEGIAN; *also* : any of the western Scandinavian dialects or languages

Norse·man \-mən\ *n* : one of the ancient Scandinavians

[1]**north** \ˈnȯrth\ *adv* : to or toward the north

[2]**north** *adj* **1** : situated toward or at the north **2** : coming from the north

[3]**north** *n* **1** : the direction to the left of one facing east **2** : the compass point directly opposite to south **3** *cap* : regions or countries north of a specified or implied point — **north·er·ly** \ˈnȯr-t͟hər-lē\ *adv or adj* — **north·ern** \-ərn\ *adj* — **North·ern·er** \-ə(r)n-ər\ *n* — **north·ern·most** \-ərn-ˌmōst\ *adj* — **north·ward** \ˈnȯrth-wərd\ *adv or adj* — **north·wards** \-wərdz\ *adv*

north·east \nȯrth-ˈēst\ *n* **1** : the general direction between north and east **2** : the compass point midway between north and east **3** *cap* : regions or countries northeast of a specified or implied point — **northeast** *adj or adv* — **north·east·er·ly** \-ər-lē\ *adv or adj* — **north·east·ern** \-ərn\ *adj*

north·east·er \-ər\ *n* **1** : a strong northeast wind **2** : a storm with northeast winds

north·er \ˈnȯr-t͟hər\ *n* **1** : a strong north wind **2** : a storm with north winds

northern lights *n pl* : AURORA BOREALIS

north pole *n, often cap N&P* : the northernmost point of the earth

North Star *n* : the star toward which the northern end of the earth's axis points

north·west \nȯrth-ˈwest\ *n* **1** : the general direction between north and west **2** : the compass point midway between north and west **3** *cap* : regions or countries northwest of a specified or implied point — **northwest** *adj or adv* — **north·west·er·ly** \-ər-lē\ *adv or adj* — **north·west·ern** \-ərn\ *adj*

Norw *abbr* Norway; Norwegian

Nor·we·gian \nȯr-ˈwē-jən\ *n* **1** : a native or inhabitant of

Norway 2 : the language of Norway — **Norwegian** *adj*

nos *abbr* numbers

[1]**nose** \ˈnōz\ *n* **1** : the part of the face containing the nostrils and covering the front of the nasal cavity **2** : the organ or sense of smell **3** : something (as a point, edge, or projecting front part) that resembles a nose ⟨the ~ of a plane⟩ — **nosed** \ˈnōzd\ *adj*

[2]**nose** *vb* **nosed; nos·ing 1** : to detect by or as if by smell : SCENT **2** : to push or move with the nose **3** : to touch or rub with the nose : NUZZLE **4** : PRY **5** : to move ahead slowly ⟨the ship *nosed* into her berth⟩

nose·bleed \-ˌblēd\ *n* : a bleeding from the nose

nose cone *n* : a protective cone constituting the forward end of a rocket or missile

nose dive *n* **1** : a downward nose-first plunge (as of an airplane) **2** : a sudden extreme drop (as in prices)

nose·gay \ˈnōz-ˌgā\ *n* : a small bunch of flowers : POSY

nose out *vb* : to defeat by a narrow margin

nose·piece \-ˌpēs\ *n* **1** : a fitting at the lower end of a microscope tube to which the objectives are attached **2** : the bridge of a pair of eyeglasses

no–show \ˈnō-ˈshō\ *n* : a person who reserves space (as on an airplane or at a concert) but neither uses nor cancels the reservation

nos·tal·gia \nä-ˈstal-jə\ *n* [NL, fr. Gk *nostos* return home + *algos* pain, grief] **1** : HOMESICKNESS **2** : a wistful yearning for something past or irrecoverable — **nos·tal·gic** \-jik\ *adj*

nos·tril \ˈnäs-trəl\ *n* [ME *nosethirl,* fr. OE *nosthyrl,* fr. *nosu* nose + *thyrel* hole] : an external naris usu. with the adjoining nasal wall and passage

nos·trum \ˈnäs-trəm\ *n* [L, neut. of *noster* our, ours, fr. *nos* we] : a questionable medicine or remedy

nosy *or* **nos·ey** \ˈnō-zē\ *adj* **nos·i·er; -est** : INQUISITIVE, PRYING

not \(ˈ)nät\ *adv* **1** — used to make negative a group of words or a word ⟨the boys are ~ here⟩ **2** — used to stand for the negative of a preceding group of words ⟨sometimes hard to see and sometimes ~⟩

no·ta be·ne \ˌnōt-ə-ˈbē-nē, -ˈben-ē\ [L, mark well] — used to call attention to something important

no·ta·bil·i·ty \ˌnōt-ə-ˈbil-ət-ē\ *n, pl* **-ties 1** : the quality or state of being notable **2** : NOTABLE

[1]**no·ta·ble** \ˈnōt-ə-bəl\ *adj* **1** : NOTEWORTHY, REMARKABLE ⟨a ~ achievement⟩ **2** : DISTINGUISHED, PROMINENT ⟨two ~ politicians made speeches⟩

[2]**no·ta·ble** *n* : a person of note

no·ta·bly \ˈnōt-ə-blē\ *adv* **1** : in a notable manner **2** : ESPECIALLY, PARTICULARLY

no·tar·i·al \nō-ˈter-ē-əl\ *adj* : of, relating to, or done by a notary public

no·ta·rize \ˈnōt-ə-ˌrīz\ *vb* **-rized; -riz·ing** : to acknowledge or make legally authentic as a notary public

no·ta·ry public \ˌnōt-ə-rē-\ *n, pl* **notaries public** *or* **notary publics** : a public official who attests or certifies writings (as deeds) to make them legally authentic

no·ta·tion \nō-ˈtā-shən\ *n* **1** : ANNOTATION, NOTE **2** : the act, process, or method of representing data by marks, signs, figures, or characters; *also* : a system of symbols (as letters, numerals, or musical notes) used in such notation

[1]**notch** \ˈnäch\ *n* **1** : a V-shaped hollow in an edge or surface **2** : a narrow pass between two mountains

[2]**notch** *vb* **1** : to cut or make notches in **2** : to score or record by or as if by cutting a series of notches ⟨~*ed* 20 points for the team⟩

notch·back \ˈnäch-ˌbak\ *n* : an automobile with a trunk whose lid forms a distinct deck

[1]**note** \ˈnōt\ *vb* **not·ed; not·ing 1** : to notice or observe with care; *also* : to record or preserve in writing **2** : to make special mention of : REMARK

[2]**note** *n* **1** : a musical sound **2** : a cry, call, or sound esp. of a bird **3** : a special tone in a person's words or voice ⟨a ~ of fear⟩ **4** : a character in music used to indicate duration of a tone by its shape and pitch by its position on the staff **5** : a characteristic feature : MOOD, QUALITY ⟨a ~ of optimism⟩ **6** : MEMORANDUM **7** : a brief and informal record; *also* : a written or printed comment or explanation **8** : a written promise to pay a debt **9** : a piece of paper money **10** : a short informal letter **11** : a formal diplomatic or official communication **12** : DISTINCTION, REPUTATION ⟨an artist of ~⟩ **13** : OBSERVATION, NOTICE, HEED ⟨take ~ of the time⟩

note·book \ˈnōt-ˌbu̇k\ *n* : a book for notes or memoranda

not·ed \ˈnōt-əd\ *adj* : well known by reputation : EMINENT, CELEBRATED

note·wor·thy \-ˌwər-t͟hē\ *adj* : worthy of note : REMARKABLE

[1]**noth·ing** \ˈnəth-iŋ\ *pron* **1** : no thing ⟨leaves ~ to the imagination⟩ **2** : no part **3** : one of no interest, value, or importance ⟨she's ~ to me⟩

[2]**nothing** *adv* : not at all : in no degree

[3]**nothing** *n* **1** : something that does not exist **2** : ZERO **3** : a person or thing of little or no value or importance

[4]**nothing** *adj* : of no account : worthless

noth·ing·ness \-nəs\ *n* **1** : the quality or state of being nothing **2** : NONEXISTENCE; *also* : utter insignificance **3** : something insignificant or valueless

[1]**no·tice** \ˈnōt-əs\ *n* **1** : WARNING, ANNOUNCEMENT **2** : notification of the termination of an agreement or contract at a specified time **3** : ATTENTION, HEED ⟨bring the matter to my ~⟩ **4** : a written or printed announcement **5** : a short critical account or examination (as of a play) : REVIEW

[2]**notice** *vb* **no·ticed; no·tic·ing 1** : to make mention of : remark on : NOTE **2** : to take notice of : OBSERVE, MARK

no·tice·able \ˈnōt-ə-sə-bəl\ *adj* **1** : worthy of notice **2** : capable of being or likely to be noticed — **not·tice·ably** \-blē\ *adv*

no·ti·fy \ˈnōt-ə-ˌfī\ *vb* **-fied; -fy·ing 1** : to give notice of : report the occurrence of **2** : to give notice to — **no·ti·fi·ca·tion** \ˌnōt-ə-fə-ˈkā-shən\ *n*

no·tion \ˈnō-shən\ *n* **1** : IDEA, CONCEPTION ⟨have a ~ of what he means⟩ **2** : a belief held : OPINION, VIEW **3** : WHIM, FANCY ⟨a sudden ~ to go⟩ **4** *pl* : small useful articles (as pins, needles, or thread)

no·tion·al \ˈnō-sh(ə-)nəl\ *adj* **1** : existing in the mind only : IMAGINARY, UNREAL **2** : given to foolish or fanciful moods or ideas : WHIMSICAL

no·to·ri·ous \nō-ˈtōr-ē-əs\ *adj* : generally known and talked of; *esp* : widely and unfavorably known — **no·to·ri·ety** \ˌnōt-ə-ˈrī-ət-ē\ *n* — **no·to·ri·ous·ly** \nō-ˈtōr-ē-əs-lē\ *adv*

[1]**not·with·stand·ing** \ˌnät-with-ˈstan-diŋ, -wit͟h-\ *prep* : in spite of

[2]**notwithstanding** *adv* : NEVERTHELESS

[3]**notwithstanding** *conj* : ALTHOUGH

nou·gat \ˈnü-gət\ *n* [F, fr. Provençal, fr. Old Provençal *nogat,* fr. *noga* nut, fr. L *nuc-, nux*] : a confection of nuts or fruit pieces in a sugar paste

nought \ˈnȯt, ˈnät\ *var of* NAUGHT

noun \ˈnau̇n\ *n* : a word that is the name of a subject of discourse (as a person or place)

nour·ish \ˈnər-ish\ *vb* : to cause to grow and develop (as by care and feeding)

nour·ish·ing *adj* : giving nourishment

nour·ish·ment \ˈnər-ish-mənt\ *n* **1** : FOOD, NUTRIMENT **2** : the action or process of nourishing

nou·veau riche \ˌnü-ˌvō-ˈrēsh\ *n, pl* **nou·veaux riches** *same*\ [F] : a person newly rich : PARVENU

Nov *abbr* November

no·va \ˈnō-və\ *n, pl* **novas** *or* **no·vae** \-(ˌ)vē, -ˌvī\ [NL, fem. of L *novus* new] : a star that suddenly increases greatly in brightness and then within a few months or years grows dim again

[1]**nov·el** \ˈnäv-əl\ *adj* **1** : having no precedent : NEW **2** : STRANGE, UNUSUAL

²**novel** *n* : a long invented prose narrative dealing with human experience through a connected sequence of events — **nov·el·ist** \-(ə-)ləst\ *n*
nov·el·ette \ˌnäv-ə-ˈlet\ *n* : a brief novel or long short story
nov·el·ize \ˈnäv-ə-ˌlīz\ *vb* **-ized; -iz·ing** : to convert into the form of a novel — **nov·el·iza·tion** \ˌnäv-ə-lə-ˈzā-shən\ *n*
no·vel·la \nō-ˈvel-ə\ *n, pl* **novellas** *or* **no·vel·le** \-ˈvel-ē\ : NOVELETTE
nov·el·ty \ˈnäv-əl-tē\ *n, pl* **-ties 1** : something new or unusual **2** : NEWNESS **3** : a small manufactured article intended mainly for personal or household adornment — usu. used in pl.
No·vem·ber \nō-ˈvem-bər\ *n* [ME *Novembre,* fr. OF, fr. L *November* (ninth month), fr. *novem* nine] : the 11th month of the year having 30 days
no·ve·na \nō-ˈvē-nə\ *n* : a Roman Catholic nine days devotion
nov·ice \ˈnäv-əs\ *n* **1** : a new member of a religious order who is preparing to take the vows of religion **2** : one who is inexperienced or untrained
no·vi·tiate \nō-ˈvish-ət\ *n* **1** : the period or state of being a novice **2** : NOVICE **3** : a house where novices are trained
¹**now** \(ˈ)naù\ *adv* **1** : at the present time or moment **2** : in the time immediately before the present **3** : FORTHWITH **4** — used with the sense of present time weakened or lost (as to express command, introduce an important point, or indicate a transition) ⟨~ hear this⟩ **5** : SOMETIMES ⟨~ one and ~ another⟩ **6** : under the present circumstances **7** : at the time referred to
²**now** *conj* : in view of the fact ⟨~ that you're here, we'll start⟩
³**now** \ˈnaù\ *n* : the present time or moment : PRESENT
⁴**now** \ˈnaù\ *adj* **1** : of or relating to the present time ⟨the ~ president⟩ **2** : excitingly new ⟨~ clothes⟩; *also* : constantly aware of what is new ⟨~ people⟩
NOW *abbr* **1** National Organization for Women **2** negotiable order of withdrawal
now·a·days \ˈnaù-(ə-)ˌdāz\ *adv* : at the present time
no·way \ˈnō-ˌwā\ *or* **no·ways** \-ˌwāz\ *adv* : NOWISE
no·where \-ˌhweər\ *adv* : not anywhere — **no·where** *n*
nowhere near *adv* : not nearly
no·wise \ˈnō-ˌwīz\ *adv* : in no way
nox·ious \ˈnäk-shəs\ *adj* : harmful esp. to health or morals
noz·zle \ˈnäz-əl\ *n* : a short tube constricted in the middle or at one end and used (as on a hose) to speed up or direct a flow of fluid
np *abbr* **1** no pagination **2** no place (of publication)
Np *symbol* neptunium
NP *abbr* **1** notary public **2** noun phrase
NS *abbr* **1** not specified **2** Nova Scotia **3** nuclear ship
NSA *abbr* National Security Agency
NSC *abbr* National Security Council
NSF *abbr* **1** National Science Foundation **2** not sufficient funds
NSW *abbr* New South Wales
NT *abbr* **1** New Testament **2** Northern Territory **3** Northwest Territories
nth \ˈenth\ *adj* **1** : numbered with an unspecified or indefinitely large ordinal number **2** : EXTREME, UTMOST ⟨to the ~ degree⟩
NTP *abbr* normal temperature and pressure
nt wt *or* **n wt** *abbr* net weight
NU *abbr* name unknown
nu·ance \ˈn(y)ü-ˌäns, n(y)ü-ˈäns\ *n* [F] : a shade of difference : a delicate variation (as in tone or meaning)
nub \ˈnəb\ *n* **1** : KNOB, LUMP **2** : GIST, POINT ⟨the ~ of the story⟩
nub·bin \ˈnəb-ən\ *n* **1** : something (as an ear of Indian corn) that is small for its kind, stunted, undeveloped, or imperfect **2** : a small projecting bit
nub·ble \ˈnəb-əl\ *n* : a small knob or lump — **nub·bly** \-(ə-)lē\ *adj*
nu·bile \ˈn(y)ü-bəl, -ˌbīl\ *adj* : of marriageable condition or age ⟨~ girls⟩
nu·cle·ar \ˈn(y)ü-klē-ər\ *adj* **1** : of, relating to, or constituting a nucleus **2** : of, relating to, or using the atomic nucleus or energy derived from it
nu·cle·ate \ˈn(y)ü-klē-ˌāt\ *vb* **-at·ed; -at·ing** : to form, act as, or have a nucleus — **nu·cle·ation** \ˌn(y)ü-klē-ˈā-shən\ *n*
nu·cle·ic acid \n(y)ù-ˌklē-ik-, -ˌklā-\ *n* : any of various complex organic acids (as DNA) found esp. in cell nuclei
nu·cle·on \ˈn(y)ü-klē-ˌän\ *n* : a proton or a neutron esp. in the atomic nucleus — **nu·cle·on·ic** \ˌn(y)ü-klē-ˈän-ik\ *adj*
nu·cle·us \ˈn(y)ü-klē-əs\ *n, pl* **nu·clei** \-klē-ˌī\ *also* **nu·cle·us·es** [NL, fr. L, kernel, dim. of *nuc-, nux* nut] **1** : a central mass or part about which matter gathers or is collected : CORE **2** : a cell part that is characteristic of all living things except viruses, bacteria, and certain algae, that is necessary for heredity and for making proteins, that contains the chromosomes with their genes, and that is enclosed in a membrane **3** : a mass of gray matter or group of nerve cells in the central nervous system **4** : the central part of an atom that comprises nearly all of the atomic mass
nu·clide \ˈn(y)ü-ˌklīd\ *n* : a species of atom characterized by the constitution of its nucleus
¹**nude** \ˈn(y)üd\ *adj* **nud·er; nud·est** : BARE, NAKED, UNCLOTHED — **nu·di·ty** \ˈn(y)üd-ət-ē\ *n*
²**nude** *n* **1** : a nude human figure esp. as depicted in art **2** : the condition of being nude ⟨in the ~⟩
nudge \ˈnəj\ *vb* **nudged; nudg·ing** : to touch or push gently (as with the elbow) usu. in order to seek attention — **nudge** *n*
nud·ism \ˈn(y)üd-ˌiz-əm\ *n* : the practice of going nude esp. in mixed groups at specially secluded places — **nud·ist** \ˈn(y)üd-əst\ *n*
nu·ga·to·ry \ˈn(y)ü-gə-ˌtōr-ē\ *adj* **1** : INCONSEQUENTIAL, WORTHLESS **2** : having no force : INOPERATIVE
nug·get \ˈnəg-ət\ *n* : a lump of precious metal (as gold)
nui·sance \ˈn(y)üs-ᵊns\ *n* : an annoying or troublesome person or thing
nuisance tax *n* : an excise tax collected in small amounts directly from the consumer
null \ˈnəl\ *adj* **1** : having no legal or blinding force : INVALID, VOID **2** : amounting to nothing **2** : INSIGNIFICANT — **nul·li·ty** \ˈnəl-ət-ē\ *n*
null and void *adj* : having no force, binding power, or validity
nul·li·fy \ˈnəl-ə-ˌfī\ *vb* **-fied; -fy·ing** : to make null or valueless; *also* : ANNUL — **nul·li·fi·ca·tion** \ˌnəl-ə-fə-ˈkā-shən\ *n*
num *abbr* numeral
Num *or* **Numb** *abbr* Numbers
numb \ˈnəm\ *adj* : lacking sensation or emotion : BENUMBED — **numb** *vb* — **numb·ly** *adv* — **numb·ness** *n*
¹**num·ber** \ˈnəm-bər\ *n* **1** : the total of individuals or units taken together **2** : a group or aggregate not specif. enumerated ⟨a small ~ of tickets remain unsold⟩ **3** : the possibility of being counted ⟨the sands of the desert are without ~⟩ **4** : a distinction of word form to denote reference to one or more than one **5** : a unit belonging to a mathematical system and subject to its laws; *also, pl* : ARITHMETIC **6** : a symbol used to represent a mathematical number; *also* : such a number used to identify

TABLE OF NUMBERS

CARDINAL NUMBERS[1]

NAME[2]	SYMBOL Arabic	SYMBOL Roman[3]
zero *or* naught *or* cipher	0	
one	1	I
two	2	II
three	3	III
four	4	IV
five	5	V
six	6	VI
seven	7	VII
eight	8	VIII
nine	9	IX
ten	10	X
eleven	11	XI
twelve	12	XII
thirteen	13	XIII
fourteen	14	XIV
fifteen	15	XV
sixteen	16	XVI
seventeen	17	XVII
eighteen	18	XVIII
nineteen	19	XIX
twenty	20	XX
twenty-one	21	XXI
twenty-two	22	XXII
twenty-three	23	XXIII
twenty-four	24	XXIV
twenty-five	25	XXV
twenty-six	26	XXVI
twenty-seven	27	XXVII
twenty-eight	28	XXVIII
twenty-nine	29	XXIX
thirty	30	XXX
thirty-one *etc*	31	XXXI
forty	40	XL
fifty	50	L
sixty	60	LX
seventy	70	LXX
eighty	80	LXXX
ninety	90	XC
one hundred	100	C
one hundred one *or* one hundred and one *etc*	101	CI
two hundred	200	CC
three hundred	300	CCC
four hundred	400	CD
five hundred	500	D
six hundred	600	DC
seven hundred	700	DCC
eight hundred	800	DCCC
nine hundred	900	CM
one thousand *or* ten hundred *etc*	1,000	M
two thousand *etc*	2,000	MM
five thousand	5,000	$\overline{V}$
ten thousand	10,000	$\overline{X}$
one hundred thousand	100,000	$\overline{C}$
one million	1,000,000	$\overline{M}$

ORDINAL NUMBERS[4]

NAME[5]	SYMBOL
first	1st
second	2d *or* 2nd
third	3d *or* 3rd
fourth	4th
fifth	5th
sixth	6th
seventh	7th
eighth	8th
ninth	9th
tenth	10th
eleventh	11th
twelfth	12th
thirteenth	13th
fourteenth	14th
fifteenth	15th
sixteenth	16th
seventeenth	17th
eighteenth	18th
nineteenth	19th
twentieth	20th
twenty-first	21st
twenty-second	22d *or* 22nd
twenty-third	23d *or* 23rd
twenty-fourth	24th
twenty-fifth	25th
twenty-sixth	26th
twenty-seventh	27th
twenty-eighth	28th
twenty-ninth	29th
thirtieth	30th
thirty-first *etc*	31st
fortieth	40th
fiftieth	50th
sixtieth	60th
seventieth	70th
eightieth	80th
ninetieth	90th
hundredth *or* one hundredth	100th
hundred and first *or* one hundred and first *etc*	101st
two hundredth	200th
three hundredth	300th
four hundredth	400th
five hundredth	500th
six hundredth	600th
seven hundredth	700th
eight hundredth	800th
nine hundredth	900th
thousandth *or* one thousandth	1,000th
two thousandth *etc*	2,000th
five thousandth	5,000th
ten thousandth	10,000th
hundred thousandth *or* one hundred thousandth	100,000th
millionth *or* one millionth	1,000,000th

[1]The cardinal numbers are used in simple counting or in answer to "how many?" The words for these numbers may be used as nouns (I counted to *ten*), as pronouns (*ten* were found), or as adjectives (*ten* cows).

[2]In formal writing the numbers one to one hundred and in less formal writing the numbers one to nine are commonly written out, while larger numbers are given in numerals. A number occurring at the beginning of a sentence is usually written out. Except in very formal writing numerals are used for dates. Arabic numerals from 1,000 to 9,999 are often written without commas (1000; 9999). Year numbers are always written without commas (1783).

[3]The Roman numerals are written either in capitals or in lowercase letters.

[4]The ordinal numbers are used to show the order in which such items as names, objects, and periods of time are considered (the *twelfth* month; the *fourth* row of seats; the *18th* century).

[5]Each of the names of the ordinal numbers except *first* and *second* is used for one of the equal parts into which a whole may be divided (a *fourth;* a *sixth;* a *tenth*) and also as the denominator in fractions *(one fourth; three fifths)*. Fractions used as nouns are usually written as two words, but fractions used as adjectives are usually hyphenated (a *two-thirds* majority). When a two-word ordinal number is used as a noun to name a denominator, a hyphen is usually used to make sure that there is only one meaning (*six hundred ten-thousandths* means only 600/10,000 and not 610/1000). When fractions are written in numerals, the cardinal symbols are used (1/4, 3/5, 4/6).

or designate ⟨a phone ~⟩ **7** : one in a series ⟨the best ~ on the program⟩

[2]**number** *vb* **num·bered; num·ber·ing** \-b(ə-)riŋ\ **1** : COUNT, ENUMERATE **2** : to include with or be one of a group **3** : to restrict to a small or definite number **4** : to assign a number to **5** : to comprise in number : TOTAL

num·ber·less \-ləs\ *adj* : INNUMERABLE, COUNTLESS

Numbers *n* — see BIBLE table

nu·mer·al \ˈn(y)üm-(ə-)rəl\ *n* : a word or symbol representing a number — **numeral** *adj*

nu·mer·ate \ˈn(y)ü-mə-ˌrāt\ *vb* **-at·ed; -at·ing** : ENUMERATE

nu·mer·a·tor \ˈn(y)ü-mə-ˌrāt-ər\ *n* : the part of a fraction above the line

nu·mer·ic \n(y)u̇-ˈmer-ik\ *adj* : NUMERICAL; *esp* : denoting a number or a system of numbers

nu·mer·i·cal \n(y)u̇-ˈmer-i-kəl\ *adj* **1** : of or relating to numbers **2** : denoting a number or expressed in numbers — **nu·mer·i·cal·ly** \-k(ə-)lē\ *adv*

nu·mer·ol·o·gy \ˌn(y)ü-mə-ˈräl-ə-jē\ *n* : the study of the occult significance of numbers — **nu·mer·ol·o·gist** \-jəst\ *n*

nu·mer·ous \ˈn(y)üm-(ə-)rəs\ *adj* : consisting of, including, or relating to a great number : MANY

nu·mis·mat·ics \ˌn(y)ü-məz-ˈmat-iks\ *n* : the study or collection of monetary objects — **nu·mis·mat·ic** \-ik\ *adj* — **nu·mis·ma·tist** \n(y)ü-ˈmiz-mət-əst\ *n*

num·skull \ˈnəm-ˌskəl\ *n* : a stupid person : DUNCE

nun \ˈnən\ *n* : a woman belonging to a religious order; *esp* : one under solemn vows of poverty, chastity, and obedience

nun·cio \ˈnən-sē-ˌō, ˈnu̇n-\ *n, pl* **-ci·os** [It, fr. L *nuntius* messenger] : a permanent high-ranking papal representative to a civil government

nun·nery \ˈnən-ə-rē\ *n, pl* **-ner·ies** : a convent of nuns

[1]**nup·tial** \ˈnəp-shəl\ *adj* : of or relating to marriage or a wedding

[2]**nuptial** *n* : MARRIAGE, WEDDING — usu. used in pl.

[1]**nurse** \ˈnərs\ *n* [ME, fr. OF *nurice*, fr. LL *nutricia*, fr. L, fem. of *nutricius* nourishing] **1** : a girl or woman employed to take care of children **2** : a person trained to care for sick people

[2]**nurse** *vb* **nursed; nurs·ing 1** : SUCKLE **2** : to take charge of and watch over **3** : TEND ⟨~ an invalid⟩ **4** : to treat with special care ⟨~ a headache⟩ **5** : to hold in one's mind or consideration ⟨~ a grudge⟩ **6** : to act or serve as a nurse

nurse·maid \-ˌmād\ *n* : a girl or woman employed to look after children

nurs·ery \ˈnərs-(ə-)rē\ *n, pl* **-er·ies 1** : a room for children **2** : a place where children are temporarily cared for in their parents' absence **3** : a place where young plants are grown usu. for transplanting

nurs·ery·man \-mən\ *n* : a man who keeps or works in a plant nursery

nursery school *n* : a school for children under kindergarten age

nursing home *n* : a private establishment where care is provided for persons (as the chronically ill) who are unable to care for themselves

nurs·ling \ˈnərs-liŋ\ *n* **1** : one that is solicitously cared for **2** : a nursing child

[1]**nur·ture** \ˈnər-chər\ *n* **1** : TRAINING, UPBRINGING; *also* : the influences that modify the expression of an individual's heredity **2** : FOOD, NOURISHMENT

[2]**nurture** *vb* **nur·tured; nur·tur·ing 1** : to care for : FEED, NOURISH **2** : EDUCATE, TRAIN **3** : FOSTER

nut \ˈnət\ *n* **1** : a dry fruit or seed with a hard shell and a firm inner kernel; *also* : its kernel **2** : a metal block with a hole through it that is fastened to a bolt or screw by means of a screw thread within the hole **3** : the ridge on the upper end of the fingerboard in a stringed musical instrument over which the strings pass **4** : a foolish, eccentric, or crazy person **5** : ENTHUSIAST

nut·crack·er \-ˌkrak-ər\ *n* : an instrument for cracking nuts

nut·hatch \ˈnət-ˌhach\ *n* [ME *notehache*, fr. *note* nut + *hache* ax, fr. OF, battle-ax] : any of various small birds that creep on tree trunks in search of food and resemble titmice

nut·meg \ˈnət-ˌmeg, -ˌmāg\ *n* [ME *notemuge*, deriv. of Old Provençal *noz muscada*, fr. *noz* nut (fr. L *nuc-*, *nux*) + *muscada*, fem. of *muscat* musky] : the nutlike aromatic seed of a tropical tree that is ground for use as a spice; *also* : this spice

nut·pick \ˈnət-ˌpik\ *n* : a small sharp-pointed table implement for extracting the kernels from nuts

nu·tria \ˈn(y)ü-trē-ə\ *n* [Sp] **1** : the durable usu. light brown fur of a nutria **2** : a So. American aquatic rodent with webbed feet and dorsal mammary glands

[1]**nu·tri·ent** \ˈn(y)ü-trē-ənt\ *adj* : NOURISHING

[2]**nutrient** *n* : a nutritive substance or ingredient

nu·tri·ment \-trə-mənt\ *n* : NUTRIENT

nu·tri·tion \n(y)u̇-ˈtrish-ən\ *n* : the act or process of nourishing; *esp* : the processes by which an individual takes in and utilizes food material — **nu·tri·tion·al** \-ˈtrish-(ə-)nəl\ *adj* — **nu·tri·tious** \-ˈtrish-əs\ *adj* — **nu·tri·tive** \ˈn(y)ü-trət-iv\ *adj*

nuts \ˈnəts\ *adj* **1** : ENTHUSIASTIC, KEEN **2** : CRAZY, DEMENTED

nut·shell \ˈnət-ˌshel\ *n* : the shell of a nut — **in a nutshell** : in a few words ⟨that's the story *in a nutshell*⟩

nut·ty \ˈnət-ē\ *adj* **nut·ti·er; -est 1** : containing or suggesting nuts ⟨a ~ flavor⟩ **2** : mentally unbalanced

nuz·zle \ˈnəz-əl\ *vb* **nuz·zled; nuz·zling** \-(ə-)liŋ\ **1** : to root around, push, or touch with or as if with the nose **2** : NESTLE, SNUGGLE

NV *abbr* Nevada

NW *abbr* northwest

NWT *abbr* Northwest Territories

NY *abbr* New York

NYC *abbr* New York City

ny·lon \ˈnī-ˌlän\ *n* **1** : any of numberous strong tough elastic synthetic materials used esp. in textiles and plastics **2** *pl* : stockings made of nylon

nymph \ˈnimf\ *n* **1** : any of the lesser goddesses in ancient mythology represented as maidens living in the mountains, forests, meadows, and waters **2** : an immature insect; *esp* : one that resembles the adult but is smaller and less differentiated and usu. lacks wings

nym·pho·ma·nia \ˌnim-fə-ˈmā-nē-ə, -nyə\ *n* : excessive sexual desire by a female — **nym·pho·ma·ni·ac** \-nē-ˌak\ *n or adj*

NZ *abbr* New Zealand

O

[1]o \ˈō\ *n, pl* **o's** *or* **os** \ˈōz\ *often cap* : the 15th letter of the English alphabet
[2]o *abbr, often cap* 1 ocean 2 Ohio 3 ohm
[1]O \ˈō\ *var of* OH
[2]O *symbol* oxygen
o/a *abbr* on or about
oaf \ˈōf\ *n* : a stupid or awkward person — **oaf·ish** \ˈō-fish\ *adj*
oak \ˈōk\ *n, pl* **oaks** *or* **oak** : any of various trees or shrubs related to the beech and chestnut and having a rounded thin-shelled nut surrounded at the base by a hardened cup; *also* : the usu. tough hard durable wood of an oak — **oak·en** \ˈō-kən\ *adj*
oa·kum \ˈō-kəm\ *n* : loosely twisted hemp or jute fiber impregnated with tar and used esp. in caulking ships
oar \ˈōr\ *n* : a long pole with a broad blade at one end used for propelling or steering a boat
oar·lock \-ˌläk\ *n* : a U-shaped device for holding an oar in place
oars·man \ˈōrz-mən\ *n* : one who rows esp. in a racing crew
OAS *abbr* Organization of American States
oa·sis \ō-ˈā-səs\ *n, pl* **oa·ses** \-ˌsēz\ : a fertile or green area in an arid region
oat \ˈōt\ *n* : a cereal grass widely grown for its edible seed; *also* : this seed — **oat·en** \-ᵊn\ *adj*
oat·cake \ˈōt-ˌkāk\ *n* : a thin flat oatmeal cake
oath \ˈōth\ *n, pl* **oaths** \ˈōthz, ˈōths\ 1 : a solemn appeal to God to witness to the truth of a statement or the sacredness of a promise 2 : an irreverent or careless use of a sacred name
oat·meal \ˈōt-ˌmēl\ *n* 1 : meal made from oats 2 : porridge made from ground or rolled oats
Ob *or* **Obad** *abbr* Obadiah
Oba·di·ah \ˌō-bə-ˈdī-əh\ *n* — see BIBLE table
ob·bli·ga·to \ˌäb-lə-ˈgät-ō\ *n, pl* **-tos** *also* **-ti** \-ˈgät-ē\ [It] : an accompanying part usu. played by a solo instrument
ob·du·rate \ˈäb-d(y)ə-rət\ *adj* : stubbornly resistant : UNYIELDING **syn** inflexible, adamant, rigid, uncompromising — **ob·du·ra·cy** \-rə-sē\ *n*
obe·di·ent \ō-ˈbēd-ē-ənt\ *adj* : submissive to the restraint or command of authority **syn** docile, tractable, amenable, biddable — **obe·di·ence** \-əns\ *n* — **obe·di·ent·ly** *adv*
obei·sance \ō-ˈbās-əns, -ˈbēs-\ *n* : a bow made to show respect or submission; *also* : DEFERENCE, HOMAGE
obe·lisk \ˈäb-ə-ˌlisk\ *n* [MF *obelisque,* fr. L *obeliscus,* fr. Gk *obeliskos,* fr. dim. of *obelos* spit, pointed pillar] : a 4-sided pillar that tapers toward the top and ends in a pyramid
obese \ō-ˈbēs\ *adj* [L *obesus,* fr. pp. of *obedere* to eat up, fr. *ob-* against + *edere* to eat] : excessively fat — **obe·si·ty** \-ˈbē-sət-ē\ *n*
obey \ō-ˈbā\ *vb* **obeyed; obey·ing** 1 : to follow the commands or guidance of : behave obediently 2 : to comply with ⟨~ orders⟩
ob·fus·cate \ˈäb-fə-ˌskāt\ *vb* **-cat·ed; -cat·ing** 1 : to make dark or obscure 2 : CONFUSE — **ob·fus·ca·tion** \ˌäb-fəs-ˈkā-shən\ *n*
obi \ˈō-bē\ *n* : a broad sash worn with a Japanese kimono
obit \ō-ˈbit, ˈō-bət\ *n* : OBITUARY
obi·ter dic·tum \ˌō-bət-ər-ˈdik-təm\ *n, pl* **obiter dic·ta** \-tə\ [LL, lit., something said in passing] : an incidental remark or observation
obit·u·ary \ə-ˈbich-ə-ˌwer-ē\ *n, pl* **-ar·ies** : a notice of a person's death usu. with a short biographical account
obj *abbr* object; objective
[1]**ob·ject** \ˈäb-jikt\ *n* 1 : something that may be seen or felt; *also* : something that may be perceived or examined mentally 2 : something that arouses an emotional response (as of affection or pity) 3 : AIM, PURPOSE 4 : a word or word group denoting that on or toward which the action of a verb is directed; *also* : a noun or noun equivalent in a prepositional phrase
[2]**ob·ject** \əb-ˈjekt\ *vb* 1 : to offer in opposition 2 : to oppose something; *also* : DISAPPROVE **syn** protest, remonstrate, expostulate — **ob·jec·tor** \-ˈjek-tər\ *n*
ob·jec·ti·fy \əb-ˈjek-tə-ˌfī\ *vb* **-fied; -fy·ing** : to make objective
ob·jec·tion \əb-ˈjek-shən\ *n* 1 : the act of objecting 2 : a reason for or a feeling of disapproval
ob·jec·tion·able \əb-ˈjek-sh(ə-)nə-bəl\ *adj* : UNDESIRABLE, OFFENSIVE — **ob·jec·tion·ably** \-blē\ *adv*
[1]**ob·jec·tive** \əb-ˈjek-tiv\ *adj* 1 : of or relating to an object or end 2 : existing outside and independent of the mind 3 : of, relating to, or constituting a grammatical case marking typically the object of a verb or preposition 4 : treating or dealing with facts without distortion by personal feelings or prejudices — **ob·jec·tive·ly** *adv* — **ob·jec·tive·ness** *n* — **ob·jec·tiv·i·ty** \ˌäb-ˌjek-ˈtiv-ət-ē\ *n*
[2]**objective** *n* 1 : the lens (as in a microscope) nearest the object and forming an image of it 2 : an aim, goal, or end of action
ob·jet d'art \ˌȯb-ˌzhā-ˈdär\ *n, pl* **ob·jets d'art** *same*\ [F] : an article of artistic worth; *also* : CURIO
ob·jet trou·vé \ˈȯb-ˌzhā-trü-ˈvā\ *n, pl* **objets trouvés** *same*\ [F, lit., found object] : a found natural object (as a piece of driftwood) held to have aesthetic value; *also* : an artifact not orig. intended as art but displayed as a work of art
ob·jur·gate \ˈäb-jər-ˌgāt\ *vb* **-gat·ed; -gat·ing** : to denounce harshly — **ob·jur·ga·tion** \ˌäb-jər-ˈgā-shən\ *n*
obl *abbr* 1 oblique 2 oblong
ob·late \äb-ˈlāt\ *adj* : flattened or depressed at the poles ⟨an ~ spheroid⟩
ob·la·tion \ə-ˈblā-shən\ *n* : a religious offering
ob·li·gate \ˈäb-lə-ˌgāt\ *vb* **-gat·ed; -gat·ing** : to bind legally or morally; *also* : to bind by a favor
ob·li·ga·tion \ˌäb-lə-ˈgā-shən\ *n* 1 : an act of obligating oneself to a course of action 2 : something (as a promise or a contract) that binds one to a course of action 3 : INDEBTEDNESS; *also* : LIABILITY 4 : DUTY — **oblig·a·to·ry** \ə-ˈblig-ə-ˌtōr-ē, ˈäb-li-gə-\ *adj*
oblige \ə-ˈblīj\ *vb* **obliged; oblig·ing** 1 : FORCE, COMPEL 2 : to bind by a favor; *also* : to do a favor for or do something as a favor
oblig·ing \ə-ˈblī-jiŋ\ *adj* : willing to do favors — **oblig·ing·ly** *adv*
oblique \ō-ˈblēk *also* ō-ˈblīk\ *adj* 1 : neither perpendicular nor parallel : SLANTING 2 : not straightforward : INDIRECT — **oblique·ly** *adv* — **oblique·ness** *n* — **obliq·ui·ty** \-ˈblik-wət-ē\ *n*
oblit·er·ate \ə-ˈblit-ə-ˌrāt\ *vb* **-at·ed; -at·ing** [L *oblitterare,* fr. *ob* in the way of + *littera* letter] 1 : to make undecipherable by wiping out or covering over 2 : to remove from recognition or memory 3 : CANCEL — **oblit·er·a·tion** \-ˌblit-ə-ˈrā-shən\ *n*
obliv·i·on \ə-ˈbliv-ē-ən\ *n* 1 : the condition of being oblivious 2 : the condition or state of being forgotten
obliv·i·ous \-ē-əs\ *adj* 1 : lacking memory or mindful attention 2 : UNAWARE — **obliv·i·ous·ly** *adv* — **obliv·i·ous·ness** *n*
ob·long \ˈäb-ˌlȯŋ\ *adj* : deviating from a square, circular, or spherical form by elongation in one dimension ⟨the ~ fruit of a lemon tree⟩ — **oblong** *n*
ob·lo·quy \ˈäb-lə-kwē\ *n, pl* **-quies** 1 : strongly condemna-

tory utterance or language **2** : bad repute : DISGRACE **syn** dishonor, shame, infamy, disrepute, ignominy

ob·nox·ious \äb-ˈnäk-shəs, əb-\ *adj* : REPUGNANT, OFFENSIVE — **ob·nox·ious·ly** *adv* — **ob·nox·ious·ness** *n*

oboe \ˈō-bō\ *n* [It, fr. F *hautbois,* fr. *haut* high + *bois* wood] : a woodwind instrument shaped like a slender conical tube with holes and keys and a reed mouthpiece — **obo·ist** \ˈō-ˌbō-əst\ *n*

oboe

ob·scene \äb-ˈsēn, əb-\ *adj* **1** : REPULSIVE **2** : deeply offensive to morality or decency; *esp* : designed to incite to lust or depravity **syn** gross, vulgar, coarse, crude, indecent — **ob·scene·ly** *adv* — **ob·scen·i·ty** \-ˈsen-ət-ē\ *n*

ob·scu·ran·tism \äb-ˈskyu̇r-ən-ˌtiz-əm, ˌäb-skyu̇-ˈran-\ *n* **1** : opposition to the spread of knowledge **2** : deliberate vagueness or abstruseness — **ob·scu·ran·tist** \-ən-təst, -ˈrant-əst\ *n or adj*

¹ob·scure \äb-ˈskyu̇r, əb-\ *adj* **1** : DIM, GLOOMY **2** : not readily understood : VAGUE **3** : REMOTE; *also* : HUMBLE — **ob·scure·ly** *adv* — **ob·scu·ri·ty** \-ˈskyu̇r-ət-ē\ *n*

²obscure *vb* **ob·scured; ob·scur·ing 1** : to make dark, dim, or indistinct **2** : to conceal or hide by or as if by covering

ob·se·qui·ous \əb-ˈsē-kwē-əs\ *adj* : humbly or excessively attentive (as to a person in authority) : FAWNING, SYCOPHANTIC — **ob·se·qui·ous·ly** *adv* — **ob·se·qui·ous·ness** *n*

ob·se·quy \ˈäb-sə-kwē\ *n, pl* **-quies** : a funeral or burial rite — usu. used in pl.

ob·serv·able \əb-ˈzər-və-bəl\ *adj* **1** : necessarily or customarily observed **2** : NOTICEABLE

ob·ser·vance \əb-ˈzər-vəns\ *n* **1** : a customary practice or ceremony **2** : an act or instance of following a custom, rule, or law **3** : OBSERVATION

ob·ser·vant \-vənt\ *adj* **1** : WATCHFUL ⟨~ spectators⟩ **2** : KEEN, PERCEPTIVE **3** : MINDFUL ⟨~ of the amenities⟩

ob·ser·va·tion \ˌäb-sər-ˈvā-shən, -zər-\ *n* **1** : an act or the power of observing **2** : the gathering of information (as for scientific studies) by noting facts or occurrences **3** : a conclusion drawn from observing; *also* : REMARK, STATEMENT **4** : the fact of being observed

ob·ser·va·to·ry \əb-ˈzər-və-ˌtōr-ē\ *n, pl* **-ries** : a place or institution equipped for observation of natural phenomena (as in astronomy)

ob·serve \əb-ˈzərv\ *vb* **ob·served; ob·serv·ing 1** : to conform one's action or practice to **2** : CELEBRATE **3** : to make a scientific observation of **4** : to see or sense esp. through careful attention **5** : to come to realize esp. through consideration of noted facts **6** : REMARK — **ob·serv·er** *n*

ob·sess \əb-ˈses\ *vb* : to preoccupy intensely or abnormally

ob·ses·sion \äb-ˈsesh-ən, əb-\ *n* : a persistent disturbing preoccupation with an idea or feeling; *also* : an emotion or idea causing such a preoccupation — **ob·ses·sive** \-ˈses-iv\ *adj or n* — **ob·ses·sive·ly** *adv*

ob·sid·i·an \əb-ˈsid-ē-ən\ *n* : a dark natural glass formed by the cooling of molten lava

ob·so·les·cent \ˌäb-sə-ˈles-ᵊnt\ *adj* : going out of use : becoming obsolete — **ob·so·les·cence** \-ᵊns\ *n*

ob·so·lete \ˌäb-sə-ˈlēt, ˈäb-sə-ˌlēt\ *adj* : no longer in use; *also* : OLD-FASHIONED **syn** extinct, outworn, passé, superseded

ob·sta·cle \ˈäb-sti-kəl\ *n* : something that stands in the way or opposes

ob·stet·rics \əb-ˈstet-riks\ *n sing or pl* : a branch of medicine that deals with childbirth — **ob·stet·ric** \-rik\ *or* **ob·stet·ri·cal** \-ri-kəl\ *adj* — **ob·ste·tri·cian** \ˌäb-stə-ˈtrish-ən\ *n*

ob·sti·nate \ˈäb-stə-nət\ *adj* : fixed and unyielding (as in an opinion or course) despite reason or persuasion : STUBBORN — **ob·sti·na·cy** \-nə-sē\ *n* — **ob·sti·nate·ly** *adv*

ob·strep·er·ous \əb-ˈstrep-(ə-)rəs\ *adj* **1** : uncontrollably noisy **2** : stubbornly resistant to control : UNRULY — **ob·strep·er·ous·ness** *n*

ob·struct \əb-ˈstrəkt\ *vb* **1** : to block by an obstacle **2** : to impede the passage, action, or operation of **3** : to shut off from sight — **ob·struc·tive** \-ˈstrək-tiv\ *adj* — **ob·struc·tor** \-tər\ *n*

ob·struc·tion \əb-ˈstrək-shən\ *n* **1** : an act of obstructing : the state of being obstructed **2** : something that obstructs : HINDRANCE

ob·struc·tion·ist \-sh(ə-)nəst\ *n* : a person who hinders progress or business esp. in a legislative body — **ob·struc·tion·ism** \-shə-ˌniz-əm\ *n*

ob·tain \əb-ˈtān\ *vb* **1** : to gain or attain usu. by planning or effort **2** : to be generally recognized or established **syn** procure, secure, win, earn, acquire — **ob·tain·able** *adj*

ob·trude \əb-ˈtrüd\ *vb* **ob·trud·ed; ob·trud·ing 1** : to thrust out **2** : to thrust forward without warrant or request **3** : INTRUDE — **ob·tru·sion** \-ˈtrü-zhən\ *n* — **ob·tru·sive** \-ˈtrü-siv\ *adj* — **ob·tru·sive·ly** *adv* — **ob·tru·sive·ness** *n*

ob·tuse \äb-ˈt(y)üs, əb-\ *adj* **ob·tus·er; -est 1** : not sharp or quick of wit **2** : exceeding 90 degrees but less than 180 degrees ⟨~ angle⟩ **3** : not pointed or acute : BLUNT — **ob·tuse·ly** *adv* — **ob·tuse·ness** *n*

obv *abbr* obverse

¹ob·verse \äb-ˈvərs, ˈäb-ˌvərs\ *adj* **1** : facing the observer or opponent **2** : having the base narrower than the top **3** : being a counterpart or complement — **ob·verse·ly** *adv*

²ob·verse \ˈäb-ˌvərs, äb-ˈvərs\ *n* **1** : the side (as of a coin) bearing the principal design and lettering **2** : a front or principal surface **3** : a similar but contrasting element or condition

ob·vi·ate \ˈäb-vē-ˌāt\ *vb* **-at·ed; -at·ing** : to anticipate and prevent (as a situation) or make unnecessary (as an action) **syn** prevent, avert, forestall, forfend, preclude — **ob·vi·a·tion** \ˌäb-vē-ˈā-shən\ *n*

ob·vi·ous \ˈäb-vē-əs\ *adj* [L *obvius,* fr. *obviam* in the way, fr. *ob* in the way of + *viam,* acc. of *via* way] : easily found, seen, or understood : PLAIN **syn** evident, manifest, patent, clear — **ob·vi·ous·ly** *adv* — **ob·vi·ous·ness** *n*

OC *abbr* officer candidate

oc·a·ri·na \ˌäk-ə-ˈrē-nə\ *n* [It, fr. *oca* goose, fr. LL *auca,* deriv. of L *avis* bird] : a simple wind instrument with holes that may be opened or closed by the finger to vary the pitch

occas *abbr* occasionally

¹oc·ca·sion \ə-ˈkā-zhən\ *n* **1** : a favorable opportunity **2** : a direct or indirect cause **3** : the time of an event **4** : EXIGENCY **5** *pl* : AFFAIRS, BUSINESS **6** : a special event : CELEBRATION

²occasion *vb* **-sioned; -sion·ing** \-ˈkāzh-(ə-)niŋ\ : CAUSE

oc·ca·sion·al \ə-ˈkāzh-(ə-)nəl\ *adj* **1** : happening or met with now and then ⟨~ references to the war⟩ **2** : used or designed for a special occasion ⟨~ verse⟩ **syn** infrequent, rare, sporadic — **oc·ca·sion·al·ly** \-ē\ *adv*

oc·ci·den·tal \ˌäk-sə-ˈdent-ᵊl\ *adj, often cap* [fr. *Occident* West, fr. ME, fr. L *occident-, occidens,* fr. prp. of *occidere* to fall, set (of the sun)] : WESTERN — **Occidental** *n*

oc·clude \ə-ˈklüd\ *vb* **oc·clud·ed; oc·clud·ing 1** : OBSTRUCT **2** : to shut in or out **3** : to come together with opposing surfaces in contact — **oc·clu·sion** \-ˈklü-zhən\ *n* — **oc·clu·sive** \-ˈklü-siv\ *adj*

¹oc·cult \ə-ˈkəlt\ *adj* **1** : not revealed : SECRET **2** : AB-

STRUSE, MYSTERIOUS **3** : of or relating to supernatural agencies, their effects, or knowledge of them

²occult *n* : occult matters — used with *the*

oc·cult·ism \ə-ˈkəl-ˌtiz-əm\ *n* : occult theory or practice — **oc·cult·ist** \-təst\ *n*

oc·cu·pan·cy \ˈäk-yə-pən-sē\ *n, pl* **-cies 1** : the act of occupying : the state of being occupied **2** : an occupied building or part of a building

oc·cu·pant \-pənt\ *n* : one who occupies something; *esp* : RESIDENT

oc·cu·pa·tion \ˌäk-yə-ˈpā-shən\ *n* **1** : an activity in which one engages; *esp* : VOCATION **2** : the taking possession of property; *also* : the taking possession of an area by a foreign military force — **oc·cu·pa·tion·al** \-sh(ə-)nəl\ *adj* — **oc·cu·pa·tion·al·ly** \-ē\ *adv*

occupational therapy *n* : therapy by means of activity; *esp* : creative activity prescribed for its effect in promoting recovery or rehabilitation — **occupational therapist** *n*

oc·cu·py \ˈäk-yə-ˌpī\ *vb* **-pied; -py·ing 1** : to engage the attention or energies of **2** : to fill up (an extent in space or time) **3** : to take or hold possession of **4** : to reside in as owner or tenant — **oc·cu·pi·er** \-ˌpī(-ə)r\ *n*

oc·cur \ə-ˈkər\ *vb* **oc·curred; oc·cur·ring** \-ˈkər-iŋ\ **1** : to be found or met with : APPEAR **2** : HAPPEN **3** : to come to mind

oc·cur·rence \ə-ˈkər-əns\ *n* **1** : something that takes place **2** : the action or process of occurring

ocean \ˈō-shən\ *n* **1** : the whole body of salt water that covers nearly three fourths of the surface of the earth **2** : one of the large bodies of water into which the great ocean is divided — **oce·an·ic** \ˌō-shē-ˈan-ik\ *adj*

ocean·ar·i·um \ˌō-shə-ˈnar-ē-əm\ *n, pl* **-iums** *or* **-ia** \-ē-ə\ : a large marine aquarium

ocean·front \ˈō-shən-ˌfrənt\ *n* : a shore area on the ocean

ocean·go·ing \-ˌgō-iŋ\ *adj* : of, relating to, or suitable for travel on the ocean

ocean·og·ra·phy \ˌō-shə-ˈnäg-rə-fē\ *n* : a science dealing with the ocean and its phenomena — **ocean·og·ra·pher** \-fər\ *n* — **ocean·o·graph·ic** \-nə-ˈgraf-ik\ *adj*

ocean·ol·o·gy \ˌō-shə-ˈnäl-ə-jē\ *n* : OCEANOGRAPHY — **ocean·ol·o·gist** \-jəst\ *n*

oce·lot \ˈäs-ə-ˌlät, ˈō-sə-\ *n* : a medium-sized American wildcat ranging southward from Texas and having a tawny yellow or gray coat with black markings

ocher *or* **ochre** \ˈō-kər\ *n* : an earthy usu. red or yellow iron ore used as a pigment; *also* : the color esp. of yellow ocher

o'·clock \ə-ˈkläk\ *adv* : according to the clock

OCS *abbr* officer candidate school

oct *abbr* octavo

Oct *abbr* October

oc·ta·gon \ˈäk-tə-ˌgän\ *n* : a polygon of eight angles and eight sides — **oc·tag·o·nal** \äk-ˈtag-ən-ᵊl\ *adj*

oc·tane \ˈäk-ˌtān\ *n* **1** : any of several isomeric liquid hydrocarbons containing 8 carbon atoms per molecule **2** : OCTANE NUMBER

octane number *n* : a number that is used to measure the antiknock properties of gasoline and that increases as the likelihood of knocking decreases

oc·tave \ˈäk-tiv\ *n* **1** : a musical interval embracing eight degrees; *also* : a tone or note at this interval or the whole series of notes, tones, or keys within this interval **2** : a group of eight

oc·ta·vo \äk-ˈtā-vō, -ˈtäv-ō\ *n, pl* **-vos 1** : the size of a piece of paper cut eight from a sheet **2** : a book printed on octavo pages

oc·tet \äk-ˈtet\ *n* **1** : a musical composition for eight voices or eight instruments; *also* : the performers of such a composition **2** : a group or set of eight

Oc·to·ber \äk-ˈtō-bər\ *n* [ME *Octobre,* fr. OF, fr. L *October* (eighth month), fr. *octo* eight] : the 10th month of the year having 31 days

oc·to·ge·nar·i·an \ˌäk-tə-jə-ˈner-ē-ən\ *n* : a person who is in his eighties

oc·to·pus \ˈäk-tə-pəs\ *n, pl* **-pus·es** *or* **-pi** \-ˌpī\ : any of various sea mollusks with eight long arms furnished with two rows of suckers

oc·to·syl·lab·ic \ˌäk-tə-sə-ˈlab-ik\ *adj* : having or composed of verses having eight syllables — **octosyllabic** *n*

¹oc·u·lar \ˈäk-yə-lər\ *adj* **1** : VISUAL **2** : of or relating to the eye or the eyesight

²ocular *n* : EYEPIECE

oc·u·list \ˈäk-yə-ləst\ *n* **1** : OPHTHALMOLOGIST **2** : OPTOMETRIST

¹OD \(ˈ)ō-ˈdē\ *n* : an overdose of a narcotic

²OD *abbr* **1** doctor of optometry **2** [L *oculus dexter*] right eye **3** officer of the day **4** olive drab **5** overdraft **6** overdrawn

odd \ˈäd\ *adj* [ME *odde,* fr. ON *oddi* point of land, triangle, odd number] **1** : being only one of a pair or set ⟨an ~ shoe⟩ **2** : somewhat more than the number mentioned ⟨forty ~ years ago⟩ **3** : not divisible by two without leaving a remainder ⟨~ numbers⟩ **4** : additional to what is usual ⟨~ jobs⟩ **5** : STRANGE ⟨an ~ way of behaving⟩ — **odd·ly** *adv* — **odd·ness** *n*

odd·ball \ˈäd-ˌbȯl\ *n* : one that is eccentric

odd·i·ty \ˈäd-ət-ē\ *n, pl* **-ties 1** : one that is odd **2** : the quality or state of being odd

odd·ment \ˈäd-mənt\ *n* : something left over : REMNANT

odds \ˈädz\ *n pl* **1** : a difference by which one thing is favored over another **2** : DISAGREEMENT — usu. used with *at* **3** : an equalizing allowance made to one believed to have a smaller chance of winning

odds and ends *n pl* : miscellaneous things or matters

odds–on \ˈädz-ˈȯn, -ˈän\ *adj* : having a better than even chance to win

ode \ˈōd\ *n* : a lyric poem that expresses a noble feeling with dignity

odi·ous \ˈōd-ē-əs\ *adj* : causing or deserving hatred or repugnance — **odi·ous·ly** *adv* — **odi·ous·ness** *n*

odi·um \ˈōd-ē-əm\ *n* **1** : merited loathing : HATRED **2** : DISGRACE

odom·e·ter \ō-ˈdäm-ət-ər\ *n* [F *odomètre,* fr. Gk *hodometron,* fr. *hodos* way, road + *metron* measure] : an instrument for measuring distance traveled (as by a vehicle)

odor \ˈōd-ər\ *n* **1** : the quality of something that stimulates the sense of smell; *also* : a sensation resulting from such stimulation **2** : REPUTE, ESTIMATION — **odor·less** *adj* — **odor·ous** *adj*

od·ys·sey \ˈäd-ə-sē\ *n, pl* **-seys** [the *Odyssey,* epic poem attributed to Homer recounting the long wanderings of Odysseus] : a long wandering marked usu. by many changes of fortune

OED *abbr* Oxford English Dictionary

oe·di·pal \ˈed-ə-pəl, ˈēd-\ *adj, often cap* : of or relating to the Oedipus complex

Oe·di·pus complex \-pəs-\ *n* : the positive sexual feelings of a child toward the parent of the opposite sex that may be a source of adult personality disorder when unresolved

OEO *abbr* Office of Economic Opportunity

o'er \ˈō(ə)r\ *adv or prep* : OVER

OES *abbr* Order of the Eastern Star

oe·soph·a·gus *chiefly Brit var of* ESOPHAGUS

oeu·vre \œvrᵊ\ *n, pl* **oeuvres** *same*\ : a substantial body of work constituting the lifework of a writer, an artist, or a composer

of \(ˈ)əv, ˈäv\ *prep* **1** : FROM ⟨a man ~ the West⟩ **2** : having as a significant background or character element ⟨a man ~ noble birth⟩ ⟨a woman ~ ability⟩ **3** : owing to ⟨died ~ flu⟩ **4** : BY ⟨the plays ~ Shakespeare⟩ **5** : having as component parts or material, contents, or members ⟨a house ~ brick⟩ ⟨a glass ~ water⟩ ⟨a pack ~ fools⟩ **6** : belonging to or included by ⟨the front ~ the house⟩ ⟨a time ~ life⟩ ⟨one ~ you⟩ ⟨the best ~ his kind⟩ ⟨the son ~ a doctor⟩ 7 : ABOUT ⟨tales ~ the West⟩ 8 : connected with : OVER ⟨the king ~ England⟩ 9 : that is : signified as ⟨the city ~ Rome⟩ 10 — used to indicate apposition of the words it joins ⟨that fool ~ a husband⟩ 11 : as concerns : FOR ⟨love ~ country⟩ 12 — used to indicate the application of an adjective ⟨fond ~ candy⟩ 13 : BEFORE ⟨five minutes ~ ten⟩

OF *abbr* outfield

[1]**off** \ˈȯf\ *adv* **1** : from a place or position ⟨drove ~ in a new car⟩; *also* : ASIDE ⟨turned ~ into a side road⟩ **2** : at a distance in time or space ⟨stood ~ a few yards⟩ ⟨several years ~⟩ **3** : so as to be unattached or removed ⟨the lid blew ~⟩ **4** : to a state of discontinuance, exhaustion, or completion ⟨shut the radio ~⟩ **5** : away from regular work ⟨took time ~ for lunch⟩

[2]**off** \(ˈ)ȯf\ *prep* **1** : away from ⟨just ~ the highway⟩ ⟨take it ~ the table⟩ **2** : to seaward of ⟨sail ~ the Maine coast⟩ **3** : FROM ⟨borrowed a dollar ~ me⟩ **4** : at the expense of ⟨lives ~ his sister⟩ **5** : not now engaged in ⟨~ duty⟩ **6** : abstaining from ⟨~ liquor⟩ **7** : below the usual level of ⟨~ his game⟩

[3]**off** \(ˈ)ȯf\ *adj* **1** : more removed or distant **2** : started on the way **3** : not operating **4** : not correct **5** : REMOTE, SLIGHT **6** : INFERIOR **7** : provided for ⟨well ~⟩

[4]**off** *abbr* office; officer; official

of·fal \ˈȯ-fəl\ *n* : the waste or by-product of a process; *esp* : the viscera and trimmings of a butchered animal removed in dressing

off and on *adv* : with periodic cessation

[1]**off·beat** \ˈȯf-ˌbēt\ *n* : the unaccented part of a musical measure

[2]**offbeat** *adj* : ECCENTRIC, UNCONVENTIONAL

off–col·or \ˈȯf-ˈkəl-ər\ *or* **off–col·ored** \-ərd\ *adj* **1** : not having the right or standard color **2** : of doubtful propriety : RISQUÉ

of·fend \ə-ˈfend\ *vb* **1** : SIN, TRANSGRESS **2** : to cause discomfort or pain : HURT **3** : to cause dislike or vexation : ANNOY **syn** affront, insult, outrage — **of·fend·er** *n*

of·fense *or* **of·fence** \ə-ˈfens, *esp for 2 & 3* ˈäf-ˌens\ *n* **1** : something that outrages the senses **2** : ATTACK, ASSAULT **3** : the offensive team or members of a team playing offensive positions **4** : DISPLEASURE **5** : SIN, MISDEED **6** : an infraction of law : CRIME

[1]**of·fen·sive** \ə-ˈfen-siv *esp for 1 & 2* ˈäf-ˌen-\ *adj* **1** : AGGRESSIVE **2** : of or relating to an attempt to score in a game; *also* : of or relating to a team in possession of the ball or puck **3** : OBNOXIOUS **4** : INSULTING — **of·fen·sive·ly** *adv* — **of·fen·sive·ness** *n*

[2]**offensive** *n* : ATTACK

[1]**of·fer** \ˈȯf-ər\ *vb* **of·fered; of·fer·ing** \-(ə-)riŋ\ **1** : SACRIFICE **2** : to present for acceptance : TENDER; *also* : to propose as payment **3** : PROPOSE, SUGGEST; *also* : to declare one's readiness **4** : to try or begin to exert ⟨~ resistance⟩ **5** : to place on sale — **of·fer·ing** *n*

[2]**offer** *n* **1** : PROPOSAL **2** : BID **3** : TRY

of·fer·to·ry \ˈȯf-ə(r)-ˌtōr-ē\ *n, pl* **-ries** : the presentation of offerings at a church service; *also* : the musical accompaniment during it

off·hand \ˈȯf-ˈhand\ *adv or adj* : without previous thought or preparation

off–hour \-ˌau̇(-ə)r\ *n* : a period of time other than a rush hour; *also* : a period of time other than business hours

of·fice \ˈȯf-əs\ *n* **1** : a special duty or position; *esp* : a position of authority in government ⟨run for ~⟩ **2** : a prescribed form or service of worship; *also* : RITE **3** : an assigned or assumed duty or role **4** : a place where a business is transacted or a service is supplied

of·fice·hold·er \-ˌhōl-dər\ *n* : one holding a public office

of·fi·cer \ˈȯf-ə-sər\ *n* **1** : one charged with the enforcement of law **2** : one who holds an office of trust or authority **3** : one who holds a commission in the armed forces

[1]**of·fi·cial** \ə-ˈfish-əl\ *n* : OFFICER

[2]**official** *adj* **1** : of or relating to an office or to officers **2** : AUTHORIZED, AUTHORITATIVE **3** : befitting or characteristic of a person in office — **of·fi·cial·ly** \-ē\ *adv*

of·fi·cial·dom \ə-ˈfish-əl-dəm\ *n* : officials as a class

of·fi·cial·ism \ə-ˈfish-ə-ˌliz-əm\ *n* : lack of flexibility and initiative combined with excessive adherence to regulations

of·fi·ci·ant \ə-ˈfish-ē-ənt\ *n* : an officiating clergyman

of·fi·ci·ate \ə-ˈfish-ē-ˌāt\ *vb* **-at·ed; -at·ing 1** : to perform a ceremony, function, or duty **2** : to act in an official capacity

of·fi·cious \ə-ˈfish-əs\ *adj* : volunteering one's services where they are neither asked for nor needed — **of·fi·cious·ly** *adv* — **of·fi·cious·ness** *n*

off·ing \ˈȯf-iŋ\ *n* : the near or foreseeable future

off·ish \ˈȯf-ish\ *adj* : inclined to stand aloof

off–line \ˈȯf-ˈlīn\ *adj or adv* : not controlled directly by a computer

off of *prep* : OFF

off·print \ˈȯf-ˌprint\ *n* : a separately printed excerpt (as from a magazine)

off–sea·son \-ˌsēz-ᵊn\ *n* : a time of suspended or reduced activity

[1]**off·set** \-ˌset\ *n* **1** : a sharp bend (as in a pipe) by which one part is turned aside out of line **2** : a printing process in which an inked impression is first made on a rubber-blanketed cylinder and then transferred to the paper

[2]**off·set** *vb* **-set; -set·ting 1** : to place over against : BALANCE **2** : to compensate for **3** : to form an offset in (as a wall)

off·shoot \ˈȯf-ˌshüt\ *n* **1** : a collateral or derived branch, descendant, or member **2** : a branch of a main stem (as of a plant)

[1]**off·shore** \ˈȯf-ˈshōr\ *adv* : at a distance from the shore

[2]**off·shore** \ˈȯf-ˌshōr\ *adj* **1** : moving away from the shore **2** : situated off the shore but within waters under a country's control

off·side \-ˈsīd\ *adv or adj* : illegally in advance of the ball or puck

off·spring \-ˌspriŋ\ *n, pl* **offspring** *also* **offsprings** : PROGENY, YOUNG

off·stage \ˈȯf-ˈstāj, -ˌstāj\ *adv or adj* : off or away from the stage

off–the–record *adj* : given or made in confidence and not for publication

off–the–shelf *adj* : available as a stock item : not specially designed or made

off–white \ˈȯf-ˈhwīt\ *n* : a yellowish or grayish white

off year *n* **1** : a year in which no major election is held **2** : a year of diminished activity or production

oft \ˈȯft\ *adv* : OFTEN

of·ten \ˈȯf-(t)ən\ *adv* : many times : FREQUENTLY

of·ten·times \-ˌtīmz\ *or* **oft·times** \ˈȯf(t)-ˌtīmz\ *adv* : OFTEN

ogle \ˈō-gəl\ *vb* **ogled; ogling** \-(ə-)liŋ\ : to look at in a flirtatious way — **ogle** *n* — **ogler** \-(ə-)lər\ *n*

ogre \ˈō-gər\ *n* **1** : a monster of fairy tales and folklore that feeds on human beings **2** : a dreaded person or object

ogress \ˈō-g(ə-)rəs\ *n* : a female ogre

oh \(ˈ)ō\ *interj* **1** — used to express an emotion or in response to physical stimuli **2** — used in direct address

OH *abbr* Ohio

ohm \ˈōm\ *n* : a unit of electrical resistance equal to the resistance of a circuit in which a potential difference of one volt produces a current of one ampere — **ohm·ic** \ˈō-mik\ *adj*

ohm·me·ter \ˈō(m)-ˌmēt-ər\ *n* : an instrument for indicating resistance in ohms directly

[1]**oil** \ˈoil\ *n* [ME *oile,* fr. OF, fr. L *oleum* olive oil, fr. Gk *elaion,* fr. *elaia* olive] **1** : a fatty or greasy liquid substance obtained from plants, animals, or minerals and used for fuel, food, medicines, and manufacturing **2** : PETROLEUM **3** : artists' colors made with oil; *also* : a painting in such colors — **oil·i·ness** \ˈoi-lē-nəs\ *n* — **oily** \ˈoi-lē\ *adj*

[2]**oil** *vb* : to put oil in or on — **oil·er** *n*

oil·cloth \-ˌklȯth\ *n* : cloth treated with oil or paint and used for table and shelf coverings

oil shale *n* : a rock (as shale) from which oil can be recovered by distillation

oil·skin \ˈoil-ˌskin\ *n* **1** : an oiled waterproof cloth **2** : an oilskin raincoat **3** *pl* : an oilskin coat and trousers

oink \ˈoiŋk\ *n* : the natural noise of a hog — **oink** *vb*

oint·ment \ˈoint-mənt\ *n* : a medicinal or cosmetic preparation usu. with a fatty or greasy base for use on the skin

OJ *abbr* orange juice

Ojib·wa *or* **Ojib·way** \ō-ˈjib-ˌwā\ *n, pl* **Ojibwa** *or* **Ojibwas** *or* **Ojibway** *or* **Ojibways** : a member of an American Indian people orig. of Michigan

OJT *abbr* on-the-job training

[1]**OK** *or* **okay** \ō-ˈkā\ *adv or adj* : all right

[2]**OK** *or* **okay** *vb* **OK'd** *or* **okayed; OK'·ing** *or* **okay·ing** : APPROVE, AUTHORIZE — **OK** *or* **okay** *n*

[3]**OK** *abbr* Oklahoma

Okla *abbr* Oklahoma

okra \ˈō-krə, *Southern also* -krē\ *n* : a tall annual plant related to the hollyhocks that has edible green pods; *also* : these pods

[1]**old** \ˈōld\ *adj* **1** : ANCIENT; *also* : of long standing **2** *cap* : belonging to an early period ⟨*Old* Irish⟩ **3** : having existed for a specified period of time **4** : of or relating to a past era **5** : advanced in years **6** : showing the effects of age or use **7** : no longer in use — **old·ish** \ˈōl-dish\ *adj*

[2]**old** *n* : old or earlier time ⟨days of ~⟩

old·en \ˈōl-dən\ *adj* : of or relating to a bygone era

[1]**old–fash·ioned** \ˈōl(d)-ˈfash-ənd\ *adj* **1** : OUT-OF-DATE, ANTIQUATED **2** : CONSERVATIVE

[2]**old–fashioned** *n* : a cocktail usu. made with whiskey, bitters, sugar, a twist of lemon peel, and water or soda water

old guard *n, often cap O&G* : the conservative members of an organization

old hat *adj* **1** : OLD-FASHIONED **2** : STALE, TRITE

old·ie \ˈōl-dē\ *n* : something old; *esp* : a popular song from the past

old–line \ˈōl(d)-ˈlīn\ *adj* **1** : ORIGINAL, ESTABLISHED ⟨an ~ business⟩ **2** : adhering to old policies or practices

old maid *n* **1** : SPINSTER **2** : a prim fussy person — **old–maid·ish** \ˈōl(d)-ˈmād-ish\ *adj*

old man *n* **1** : HUSBAND **2** : FATHER

old·ster \ˈōl(d)-stər\ *n* : an old or elderly person

Old Testament *n* : the first of the two chief divisions of the Bible — see BIBLE table

old–time \ˌōl(d)-ˌtīm\ *adj* **1** : of, relating to, or characteristic of an earlier period **2** : of long standing

old–tim·er \ōl(d)-ˈtī-mər\ *n* VETERAN; *also* : OLDSTER

old–world \ˈōl(d)-ˈwərld\ *adj* : having old-fashioned charm

Old World *n* : the eastern hemisphere; *esp* : continental Europe

ole·ag·i·nous \ˌō-lē-ˈaj-ə-nəs\ *adj* : OILY

ole·an·der \ˈō-lē-ˌan-dər\ *n* : a poisonous evergreen shrub often grown for its fragrant red or white flowers

oleo \ˈō-lē-ˌō\ *n, pl* **oleos** : MARGARINE

oleo·mar·ga·rine \ˌō-lē-ō-ˈmärj-(ə-)rən, -ˈmärj-ə-ˌrēn\ *n* : MARGARINE

ol·fac·to·ry \äl-ˈfak-t(ə-)rē, ōl-\ *adj* : of or relating to the sense of smell

oli·gar·chy \ˈäl-ə-ˌgär-kē, ˈō-lə-\ *n, pl* **-chies** **1** : a government in which power is in the hands of a few **2** : a state having an oligarchy; *also* : the group holding power in such a state — **oli·garch** \-ˌgärk\ *n* — **oli·gar·chic** \ˌäl-ə-ˈgär-kik, ˌō-lə-\ *or* **oli·gar·chi·cal** \-ki-kəl\ *adj*

Oli·go·cene \ˈäl-i-gō-ˌsēn, ə-ˈlig-ə-ˌsēn\ *adj* : of, relating to, or being the epoch of the Tertiary between the Eocene and the Miocene — **Oligocene** *n*

olio \ˈō-lē-ˌō\ *n, pl* **oli·os** : HODGEPODGE, MEDLEY

ol·ive \ˈäl-iv, -əv\ *n* **1** : an Old World evergreen tree grown in warm regions for its fruit that is important as food and for its edible oil **(olive oil)** **2** : a dull yellow to yellowish green color

olive drab *n* **1** : a variable color averaging a grayish olive **2** : a wool or cotton fabric of an olive drab color; *also* : a uniform of this fabric

ol·iv·ine \ˈäl-ə-ˌvēn\ *n* : a usu. greenish mineral that is a complex silicate of magnesium and iron

Olym·pic Games \ə-ˈlim-pik-, ō-\ *n pl* : a modified revival of an ancient Greek festival held every four years and consisting of international athletic contests

om \ˈōm\ *n* : a mantra consisting of the sound "om" used in contemplating ultimate reality

Oma·ha \ˈō-mə-ˌhä, -ˌhȯ\ *n, pl* **Omaha** *or* **Omahas** : a member of an American Indian people of northeastern Nebraska

om·buds·man \ˈäm-ˌbu̇dz-mən, äm-ˈbu̇dz-\ *n, pl* **-men** \-mən\ **1** : a government official appointed to investigate complaints made by individuals against abuses or capricious acts of public officials **2** : one that investigates reported complaints (as from students or consumers)

om·elet *or* **om·elette** \ˈäm-(ə-)lət\ *n* [F *omelette,* alter. of MF *alumelle,* lit., knife blade, modif. of L *lamella,* dim. of *lamina* thin plate] : eggs beaten with milk or water, cooked without stirring until set, and folded over

omen \ˈō-mən\ *n* : an event or phenomenon believed to be a sign or warning of a future occurrence

om·i·nous \ˈäm-ə-nəs\ *adj* : foretelling evil : THREATENING — **om·i·nous·ly** *adv* — **om·i·nous·ness** *n*

omis·sion \ō-ˈmish-ən\ *n* **1** : something neglected or left undone **2** : the act of omitting : the state of being omitted

omit \ō-ˈmit\ *vb* **omit·ted; omit·ting** **1** : to leave out or leave unmentioned **2** : to fail to perform : NEGLECT

[1]**om·ni·bus** \ˈäm-ni-(ˌ)bəs\ *n* : BUS

[2]**omnibus** *adj* : of, relating to, or providing for many things at once ⟨an ~ bill⟩

om·nip·o·tent \äm-ˈnip-ət-ənt\ *adj* : having unlimited authority or influence : ALMIGHTY — **om·nip·o·tence** \-əns\ *n* — **om·nip·o·tent·ly** *adv*

om·ni·pres·ent \ˌäm-ni-ˈprez-ᵊnt\ *adj* : present in all places at all times — **om·ni·pres·ence** \-ᵊns\ *n*

om·ni·scient \äm-ˈnish-ənt\ *adj* : having infinite awareness, understanding, and insight — **om·ni·science** \-əns\ *n* — **om·ni·scient·ly** *adv*

om·ni·um–gath·er·um \ˌäm-nē-əm-ˈgath-ə-rəm\ *n, pl* **omnium–gatherums** : a miscellaneous collection

om·niv·o·rous \äm-ˈniv-(ə-)rəs\ *adj* : feeding on both animal and vegetable substances; *also* : AVID ⟨an ~ reader⟩ — **om·niv·o·rous·ly** *adv*

[1]**on** \(ˈ)ȯn, (ˈ)än\ *prep* **1** : in or to a position over and in contact with ⟨a book ~ the table⟩ ⟨jumped ~ his horse⟩ **2** : touching the surface of ⟨shadows ~ the wall⟩ **3** : AT, TO ⟨~ the right were the mountains⟩ **4** : IN, ABOARD ⟨went ~ the train⟩ **5** : during or at the time of ⟨came ~ Monday⟩ ⟨every hour ~ the hour⟩ **6** : through the agency of ⟨was cut ~ a tin can⟩ **7** : in a state or process of ⟨~ fire⟩ ⟨~ the wane⟩ **8** : connected with as a member or participant ⟨~ a committee⟩ ⟨~ tour⟩ **9** — used to indicate a basis, source, or standard of computation ⟨has it ~ good authority⟩ ⟨10 cents ~ the dollar⟩ **10** : with regard to ⟨a monopoly ~ wheat⟩ **11** : at or toward as an object ⟨crept up ~ her⟩ ⟨smiled ~ him⟩ **12** : ABOUT, CONCERNING ⟨a book ~ minerals⟩

²on \ˈȯn, ˈän\ *adv* **1** : in or into a position of contact with or attachment to a surface **2** : FORWARD **3** : into operation

³on \ˈȯn, ˈän\ *adj* : being in operation or in progress

ON *abbr* Ontario

¹once \ˈwəns\ *adv* **1** : one time only **2** : at any one time **3** : FORMERLY **4** : by one degree of relationship

²once *n* : one single time — **at once 1** : at the same time **2** : IMMEDIATELY

³once *adj* : FORMER

⁴once *conj* : AS SOON AS

once–over \-ˌō-vər\ *n* : a swift examination or survey

on·com·ing \ˈȯn-ˌkəm-iŋ, ˈän-\ *adj* : APPROACHING ⟨~ traffic⟩

¹one \ˈwən\ *adj* **1** : being a single unit or thing ⟨~ person went⟩ **2** : being one in particular ⟨early ~ morning⟩ **3** : being the same in kind or quality ⟨members of ~ race⟩; *also* : UNITED **4** : being not specified or fixed ⟨at ~ time or another⟩

²one *n* **1** : the number denoting unity **2** : the 1st in a set or series **3** : a single person or thing — **one·ness** \ˈwən-nəs\ *n*

³one *pron* **1** : a single member or specimen ⟨saw ~ of his friends⟩ **2** : a person in general ⟨~ never knows⟩ **3** — used in place of a first-person pronoun

Onei·da \ō-ˈnīd-ə\ *n, pl* **Oneida** *or* **Oneidas** : a member of an American Indian people orig. of New York

oner·ous \ˈän-ə-rəs, ˈō-nə-\ *adj* : imposing or constituting a burden : TROUBLESOME **syn** oppressive, exacting, burdensome, weighty

one·self \(ˌ)wən-ˈself\ *also* **one's self** \(ˌ)wən-, ˌwənz-\ *pron* : one's own self — usu. used reflexively or for emphasis

one–sid·ed \ˈwən-ˈsīd-əd\ *adj* **1** : having or occurring on one side only; *also* : having one side prominent or more developed **2** : UNEQUAL ⟨a ~ game⟩ **3** : PARTIAL ⟨a ~ attitude⟩

one·time \ˈwən-ˌtīm\ *adj* : FORMER

one–to–one \ˌwən-tə-ˈwən\ *adj* : pairing each element of a class uniquely with an element of another class

one up *adj* : being in a position of advantage ⟨was *one up* on the others⟩

one–way *adj* : moving, allowing movement, or functioning in only one direction ⟨~ streets⟩

on·go·ing \ˈȯn-ˌgō-iŋ, ˈän-\ *adj* : continuously moving forward

on·ion \ˈən-yən\ *n* : a plant related to the lilies and grown for its pungent edible bulb; *also* : this bulb

on·ion·skin \-ˌskin\ *n* : a thin strong translucent paper of very light weight

on–line *adj or adv* : controlled directly by a computer ⟨~ equipment⟩

on·look·er \ˈȯn-ˌlu̇k-ər, ˈän-\ *n* : SPECTATOR

¹on·ly \ˈōn-lē\ *adj* **1** : unquestionably the best **2** : SOLE

²only *adv* **1** : MERELY, JUST ⟨~ $2⟩ **2** : SOLELY ⟨known ~ to me⟩ **3** : at the very least ⟨was ~ too true⟩ **4** : as a final result ⟨will ~ make you sick⟩

³only *conj* : except that

on·o·mato·poe·ia \ˌän-ə-ˌmat-ə-ˈpē-(y)ə\ *n* **1** : formation of words in imitation of natural sounds (as *buzz* or *hiss*) **2** : the use of words whose sound suggests the sense — **on·o·mato·poe·ic** \-ˈpē-ik\ *or* **on·o·mato·po·et·ic** \-pō-ˈet-ik\ *adj* — **on·o·mato·poe·i·cal·ly** \-ˈpē-ə-k(ə-)lē\ *or* **on·o·mato·po·et·i·cal·ly** \-pō-ˈet-i-k(ə-)lē\ *adv*

On·on·da·ga \ˌän-ə(n)-ˈdȯ-gə\ *n, pl* **-ga** *or* **-gas** : a member of an American Indian people of New York and Canada

on·rush \ˈȯn-ˌrəsh, ˈän-\ *n* : a rushing onward — **on·rush·ing** \-iŋ\ *adj*

on·set \-ˌset\ *n* **1** : ATTACK **2** : BEGINNING

on·shore \-ˌshōr\ *adj* **1** : moving toward the shore **2** : situated on or near the shore — **on·shore** \-ˈshōr\ *adv*

on·slaught \ˈȯn-ˌslȯt, ˈän-\ *n* : a fierce attack

Ont *abbr* Ontario

on·to \ˌȯn-tə, ˌän-; ˈȯn-tü, ˈän-\ *prep* : to a position or point on

onus \ˈō-nəs\ *n* **1** : BURDEN **2** : OBLIGATION **3** : BLAME

¹on·ward \ˈȯn-wərd, ˈän-\ *also* **on·wards** \-wərdz\ *adv* : FORWARD

²onward *adj* : directed or moving onward : FORWARD

on·yx \ˈän-iks\ *n* [ME *onix*, fr. OF & L; OF, fr. L *onyx*, fr. Gk, lit., claw, nail] : a translucent chalcedony in parallel layers of different colors

oo·dles \ˈüd-ᵊlz\ *n pl* : a great quantity

oo·lite \ˈō-ə-ˌlīt\ *n* : a rock consisting of small round grains cemented together — **oo·lit·ic** \ˌō-ə-ˈlit-ik\ *adj*

¹ooze \ˈüz\ *n* **1** : a soft deposit (as of mud) on the bottom of a body of water **2** : soft wet ground : MUD — **oozy** \ˈü-zē\ *adj*

²ooze *n* : something that oozes

³ooze *vb* **oozed; ooz·ing 1** : to flow or leak out slowly or imperceptibly **2** : EXUDE

op *abbr* opus

OP *abbr* **1** observation post **2** out of print

opac·i·ty \ō-ˈpas-ət-ē\ *n, pl* **-ties 1** : the quality or state of being opaque **2** : obscurity of meaning **3** : mental dullness **4** : an opaque spot in a normally transparent structure

opal \ˈō-pəl\ *n* : a mineral with soft changeable colors that is used as a gem

opal·es·cent \ˌō-pə-ˈles-ᵊnt\ *adj* : IRIDESCENT — **opal·es·cence** \-ᵊns\ *n*

opaque \ō-ˈpāk\ *adj* **1** : not allowing radiant energy and esp. light to pass through **2** : not easily understood **3** : OBTUSE — **opaque·ly** *adv* — **opaque·ness** *n*

op art \ˈäp-\ *n* : OPTICAL ART — **op artist** *n*

op cit *abbr* [L *opere citato*] in the work cited

ope \ˈōp\ *vb* **oped; op·ing** *archaic* : OPEN

OPEC *abbr* Organization of Petroleum Exporting Countries

¹open \ˈō-pən\ *adj* **open·er** \ˈōp-(ə-)nər\; **open·est** \ˈōp-(ə-)nəst\ **1** : not shut or shut up ⟨an ~ door⟩ **2** : not secret or hidden; *also* : FRANK **3** : not enclosed or covered ⟨an ~ fire⟩; *also* : not protected **4** : free to be entered or used ⟨an ~ tournament⟩ **5** : easy to get through or see ⟨~ country⟩ **6** : spread out : EXTENDED **7** : not decided ⟨an ~ question⟩ **8** : readily accessible and cooperative; *also* : GENEROUS **9** : having components separated by a space in writing and printing ⟨the name *Spanish moss* is an ~ compound⟩ **10** : ready to operate ⟨stores are ~⟩ **11** : free from restraints or controls ⟨~ season⟩ — **open·ly** *adv* — **open·ness** \-pən-nəs\ *n*

²open \ˈō-pən\ *vb* **opened** \ˈō-pənd\; **open·ing** \ˈōp-(ə-)niŋ\ **1** : to change or move from a shut position; *also* : to make open by clearing away obstacles **2** : to make accessible **3** : to make openings in **4** : to make or become functional ⟨~ a store⟩ **5** : REVEAL; *also* : ENLIGHTEN **6** : BEGIN — **open·er** \ˈōp-(ə-)nər\ *n*

³open *n* **1** : OUTDOORS **2** : a contest or tournament open to all

open–air *adj* : OUTDOOR ⟨~ theaters⟩

open·hand·ed \ˌō-pən-ˈhan-dəd\ *adj* : GENEROUS

open–heart *adj* : of, relating to, or performed on a heart temporarily relieved of circulatory function and laid open for inspection and treatment

open–hearth *adj* : of, relating to, or being a process of making steel in a furnace that reflects the heat from the roof onto the material

open·ing \ˈōp-(ə-)niŋ\ *n* **1** : an act or instance of making or becoming open **2** : BEGINNING **3** : something that is open **4** : OCCASION; *also* : an opportunity for employment

open–mind·ed \ˌō-pən-ˈmīn-dəd\ *adj* : free from rigidly fixed preconceptions

open sentence *n* : a statement (as in mathematics) containing at least one blank or unknown so that when the blank is filled or a quantity substituted for the unknown the statement becomes a complete statement that is either true or false

open shop *n* : an establishment having members and nonmembers of a labor union on the payroll

open·work \ˈō-pən-ˌwərk\ *n* : work so made as to show openings through its substance ⟨a railing of wrought-iron ~⟩ — **open–worked** \-ˌwərkt\ *adj*

[1]**opera** *pl of* OPUS

[2]**op·era** \ˈäp-(ə-)rə\ *n* : a drama set to music — **op·er·at·ic** \ˌäp-ə-ˈrat-ik\ *adj*

op·er·a·ble \ˈäp-(ə-)rə-bəl\ *adj* **1** : fit, possible, or desirable to use **2** : likely to result in a favorable outcome upon surgical treatment

opera glasses *n pl* : small binoculars for use in a theater

op·er·ate \ˈäp-ə-ˌrāt\ *vb* **-at·ed; -at·ing 1** : to perform work : FUNCTION **2** : to produce an effect **3** : to put or keep in operation **4** : to perform an operation — **op·er·a·tor** \-ˌrāt-ər\ *n*

op·er·a·tion \ˌäp-ə-ˈrā-shən\ *n* **1** : a doing or performing of a practical work **2** : an exertion of power or influence; *also* : method or manner of functioning **3** : a surgical procedure **4** : a process of deriving one mathematical expression from others according to a rule **5** : a military action or mission — **op·er·a·tion·al** \-sh(ə-)nəl\ *adj*

[1]**op·er·a·tive** \ˈäp-(ə-)rət-iv, ˈäp-ə-ˌrāt-\ *adj* **1** : producing an appropriate effect **2** : OPERATING ⟨an ~ force⟩ **3** : having to do with physical operations; *also* : WORKING ⟨an ~ craftsman⟩ **4** : based on or consisting of an operation

[2]**operative** *n* : OPERATOR; *esp* : a secret agent

op·er·et·ta \ˌäp-ə-ˈret-ə\ *n* [It, dim. of *opera*] : a light musical-dramatic work with a romantic plot, spoken dialogue, and dancing scenes

oph·thal·mic \äf-ˈthal-mik, äp-\ *adj* : of, relating to, or located near the eye

oph·thal·mol·o·gy \ˌäf-ˌthal-ˈmäl-ə-jē, ˌäp-\ *n* : a branch of medicine dealing with the structure, functions, and diseases of the eye — **oph·thal·mol·o·gist** \-jəst\ *n*

oph·thal·mo·scope \äf-ˈthal-mə-ˌskōp, äp-\ *n* : an instrument with a mirror centrally perforated for use in viewing the interior of the eye

opi·ate \ˈō-pē-ət, -pē-ˌāt\ *n* : a preparation or derivative of opium; *also* : NARCOTIC — **opiate** *adj*

opine \ō-ˈpīn\ *vb* **opined; opin·ing** : to express an opinion : STATE

opin·ion \ə-ˈpin-yən\ *n* **1** : a belief stronger than impression and less strong than positive knowledge **2** : JUDGMENT **3** : a formal statement by an expert after careful study

opin·ion·at·ed \ə-ˈpin-yə-ˌnāt-əd\ *adj* : obstinately adhering to personal opinions

opi·um \ˈō-pē-əm\ *n* [ME, fr. L, fr. Gk *opion*, fr. dim. of *opos* sap] : an addictive narcotic drug that is the dried juice of a poppy

opos·sum \ə-ˈpäs-əm\ *n, pl* **opossums** *also* **opossum** [fr. *âpäsûm*, lit., white animal (in some American Indian language of Virginia)] : any of various American marsupial mammals; *esp* : a common omnivorous tree-dwelling animal of the eastern U.S.

opp *abbr* opposite

op·po·nent \ə-ˈpō-nənt\ *n* : one that opposes : ADVERSARY

op·por·tune \ˌäp-ər-ˈt(y)ün\ *adj* [ME, fr. MF *opportun*, fr. L *opportunus*, fr. *ob-* toward + *portus* port, harbor] : SUITABLE — **op·por·tune·ly** *adv*

op·por·tun·ism \ˌäp-ər-ˈt(y)ü-ˌniz-əm\ *n* : a taking advantage of opportunities or circumstances esp. with little regard for principles or ultimate consequences — **op·por·tun·ist** \-nəst\ *n* — **op·por·tu·nis·tic** \-t(y)ü-ˈnis-tik\ *adj*

opossum

op·por·tu·ni·ty \ˌäp-ər-ˈt(y)ü-nət-ē\ *n, pl* **-ties 1** : a favorable combination of circumstances, time, and place **2** : a chance for advancement or progress

op·pose \ə-ˈpōz\ *vb* **op·posed; op·pos·ing 1** : to place opposite or against something (as to provide resistance or contrast) **2** : to strive against : RESIST — **op·po·si·tion** \ˌäp-ə-ˈzish-ən\ *n*

[1]**op·po·site** \ˈäp-ə-zət\ *n* : one that is opposed or contrary

[2]**opposite** *adj* **1** : set over against something that is at the other end or side **2** : OPPOSED, HOSTILE; *also* : CONTRARY **3** : contrarily turned or moving — **op·po·site·ly** *adv* — **op·po·site·ness** *n*

[3]**opposite** *adv* : on opposite sides

[4]**opposite** *prep* : across from and usu. facing ⟨the house ~ ours⟩

op·press \ə-ˈpres\ *vb* **1** : to crush by abuse of power or authority **2** : to weigh down : BURDEN **syn** aggrieve, wrong, persecute — **op·pres·sive** \-ˈpres-iv\ *adj* — **op·pres·sive·ly** *adv* — **op·pres·sor** \-ˈpres-ər\ *n*

op·pres·sion \ə-ˈpresh-ən\ *n* **1** : unjust or cruel exercise of power or authority **2** : DEPRESSION

op·pro·bri·ous \ə-ˈprō-brē-əs\ *adj* : expressing or deserving opprobrium — **op·pro·bri·ous·ly** *adv*

op·pro·bri·um \-brē-əm\ *n* **1** : something that brings disgrace **2** : INFAMY

[1]**opt** \ˈäpt\ *vb* : to make a choice

[2]**opt** *abbr* **1** optical; optician; optics **2** optional

op·tic \ˈäp-tik\ *adj* : of or relating to vision or the eye

op·ti·cal \ˈäp-ti-kəl\ *adj* **1** : relating to optics **2** : OPTIC **3** : of, relating to, or using light **4** : of or relating to optical art

optical art *n* : nonobjective art characterized by the use of geometric patterns often for an illusory effect

optical disc *n* : a disc on which information has been recorded digitally and which is read using a laser

optical fiber *n* : a single fiber-optic strand

op·ti·cian \äp-ˈtish-ən\ *n* **1** : a maker of or dealer in optical items and instruments **2** : one that grinds lenses to prescription and dispenses spectacles

op·tics \ˈäp-tiks\ *n pl* : a science that deals with the nature and properties of light and the effects that it undergoes and produces

op·ti·mal \ˈäp-tə-məl\ *adj* : most desirable or satisfactory — **op·ti·mal·ly** \-ē\ *adv*

op·ti·mism \ˈäp-tə-ˌmiz-əm\ *n* [F *optimisme*, fr. L *optimum*, n., best, fr. neut. of *optimus* best] **1** : a doctrine that this world is the best possible world **2** : an inclination to anticipate the best possible outcome of actions or events — **op·ti·mist** \-məst\ *n* — **op·ti·mis·tic** \ˌäp-tə-ˈmis-tik\ *adj* — **op·ti·mis·ti·cal·ly** \-ti-k(ə-)lē\ *adv*

op·ti·mum \ˈäp-tə-məm\ *n, pl* **-ma** \-mə\ *also* **-mums** [L] : the amount or degree of something most favorable to an end; *also* : greatest degree attained under implied or specified conditions

op·tion \ˈäp-shən\ *n* **1** : the power or right to choose **2** : a right to buy or sell something at a specified price during

a specified period **3** : something offered for choice — **op·tion·al** \-sh(ə-)nəl\ *adj*
op·tom·e·try \äp-ˈtäm-ə-trē\ *n* : the art or profession of examining the eyes for defects of refraction and of prescribing lenses to correct these — **op·tom·e·trist** \-trəst\ *n*
opt out *vb* : to choose not to participate
op·u·lence \ˈäp-yə-ləns\ *n* **1** : WEALTH **2** : ABUNDANCE
op·u·lent \ˈäp-yə-lənt\ *adj* **1** : WEALTHY **2** : richly abundant
opus \ˈō-pəs\ *n, pl* **opera** \ˈō-pə-rə, ˈäp-ə-\ *also* **opus·es** \ˈō-pə-səz\ : WORK; *esp* : a musical composition
or \ər, (ˌ)ȯr\ *conj* — used as a function word to indicate an alternative ⟨sink ~ swim⟩
OR *abbr* **1** operating room **2** Oregon
-or \ər\ *n suffix* : one that does a (specified) thing ⟨calculat*or*⟩ ⟨elevat*or*⟩
or·a·cle \ˈȯr-ə-kəl\ *n* **1** : one held to give divinely inspired answers or revelations **2** : an authoritative or wise utterance; *also* : a person of great authority or wisdom — **orac·u·lar** \ȯ-ˈrak-yə-lər\ *adj*
[1]**oral** \ˈōr-əl, ˈȯr-\ *adj* **1** : SPOKEN **2** : of or relating to the mouth **3** : of, relating to, or characterized by the first stage of psychosexual development in which libidinal gratification is derived from intake (as of food), by sucking, and later by biting **4** : relating to or characterized by personality traits of passive dependency and aggressiveness — **oral·ly** \ˈōr-ə-lē, ˈȯr-\ *adv*
[2]**oral** *n* : an oral examination — usu. used in pl.
orang \ə-ˈraŋ\ *n* : ORANGUTAN
or·ange \ˈȯr-inj\ *n* **1** : a juicy citrus fruit with reddish yellow rind; *also* : the evergreen tree with fragrant white flowers that bears this fruit **2** : a color between red and yellow
or·ange·ade \ˌȯr-inj-ˈād\ *n* : a beverage of orange juice, sugar, and water
orange hawkweed *n* : a weedy herb related to the daisies with bright orange-red flower heads
or·ange·ry \ˈȯr-inj-(ə-)rē\ *n, pl* **-ries** : a protected place (as a greenhouse) for raising oranges in cool climates
orang·utan \ə-ˈraŋ-ə-ˌtaŋ, -ˌtan\ *n* [Malay *orang hutan*, fr. *orang* man + *hutan* forest] : a reddish brown manlike tree-living ape of Borneo and Sumatra
orate \ȯ-ˈrāt\ *vb* **orat·ed; orat·ing** : to speak in a declamatory manner
ora·tion \ə-ˈrā-shən\ *n* : an elaborate discourse delivered in a formal dignified manner
or·a·tor \ˈȯr-ət-ər\ *n* : one noted for skill and power as a public speaker
or·a·tor·i·cal \ˌȯr-ə-ˈtȯr-i-kəl\ *adj* : of, relating to, or characteristic of an orator or oratory
or·a·to·rio \ˌȯr-ə-ˈtōr-ē-ˌō\ *n, pl* **-rios** : a lengthy choral work usu. on a scriptural subject
[1]**or·a·to·ry** \ˈȯr-ə-ˌtōr-ē\ *n, pl* **-ries** : a private or institutional chapel
[2]**oratory** *n* : the art of speaking eloquently and effectively in public **syn** rhetoric, elocution
orb \ˈȯrb\ *n* : a spherical body; *esp* : a celestial body (as a planet)
or·bic·u·lar \ȯr-ˈbik-yə-lər\ *adj* : SPHERICAL
[1]**or·bit** \ˈȯr-bət\ *n* [L *orbita*, lit., track, rut] **1** : a path described by one body or object in its revolution about another **2** : range or sphere of activity — **or·bit·al** \-ᵊl\ *adj*
[2]**orbit** *vb* **1** : CIRCLE **2** : to send up and make revolve in an orbit ⟨~ a satellite⟩ — **or·bit·er** \-bət-ər\ *n*
orch *abbr* orchestra
or·chard \ˈȯr-chərd\ *n* : a place where fruit trees or nut trees are grown; *also* : the trees of such a place — **or·chard·ist** \-əst\ *n*
or·ches·tra \ˈȯr-kə-strə\ *n* [L, fr. Gk *orchēstra*, fr. *orcheisthai* to dance] **1** : a group of instrumentalists organized to perform ensemble music **2** : the front section of seats on the main floor of a theater — **or·ches·tral** \ȯr-ˈkes-trəl\ *adj*
or·ches·trate \ˈȯr-kə-ˌstrāt\ *vb* **-trat·ed; -trat·ing** : to compose or arrange for an orchestra — **or·ches·tra·tion** \ˌȯr-kə-ˈstrā-shən\ *n*
or·chid \ˈȯr-kəd\ *n* [irreg. from L *orchis*, fr. Gk, testicle] : any of numerous related plants having often showy flowers with three petals of which the middle one is enlarged into a lip; *also* : a flower of an orchid
ord *abbr* **1** order **2** ordnance
or·dain \ȯr-ˈdān\ *vb* **1** : to admit to the ministry or priesthood by the ritual of a church **2** : DECREE, ENACT; *also* : DESTINE
or·deal \ȯr-ˈdē(-ə)l, ˈȯr-ˌdē(-ə)l\ *n* : a severe trial or experience
[1]**or·der** \ˈȯrd-ər\ *vb* **or·dered; or·der·ing** \ˈȯrd-(ə-)riŋ\ **1** : ARRANGE, REGULATE **2** : COMMAND **3** : to place an order
[2]**order** *n* **1** : a group of people formally united; *also* : a badge or medal of such a group **2** : any of the several grades of the Christian ministry; *also, pl* : ORDINATION **3** : a rank, class, or special group of persons or things **4** : a category of biological classification ranking above the family and below the class **5** : ARRANGEMENT, SEQUENCE; *also* : the prevailing mode of things **6** : a customary mode of procedure; *also* : the rule of law or proper authority **7** : a specific rule, regulation, or authoritative direction **8** : a style of building; *also* : an architectural column forming the unit of a style **9** : condition esp. with regard to repair **10** : a written direction to pay money or to buy or sell goods; *also* : goods bought or sold
[1]**or·der·ly** \ˈȯrd-ər-lē\ *adj* **1** : arranged according to some order; *also* : NEAT, TIDY **2** : well behaved ⟨an ~ crowd⟩ **syn** methodical, systematic, regular — **or·der·li·ness** *n*
[2]**orderly** *n, pl* **-lies** **1** : a soldier who attends a superior officer **2** : a hospital attendant who does general work
[1]**or·di·nal** \ˈȯrd-(ᵊ-)nəl\ *n* : an ordinal number
[2]**ordinal** *adj* : indicating order or rank (as sixth) in a series
or·di·nance \ˈȯrd-(ᵊ-)nəns\ *n* : an authoritative decree or law; *esp* : a municipal regulation
or·di·nary \ˈȯrd-ᵊn-ˌer-ē\ *adj* **1** : to be expected : USUAL **2** : of common quality, rank, or ability; *also* : POOR, INFERIOR **syn** customary, routine, normal, everyday — **or·di·nar·i·ly** \ˌȯrd-ᵊn-ˈer-ə-lē\ *adv*
or·di·nate \ˈȯrd-(ᵊ-)nət, ˈȯrd-ᵊn-ˌāt\ *n* : the coordinate of a point in a plane coordinate system that is the distance of the point from the horizontal axis found by measuring along a line parallel to the vertical axis
or·di·na·tion \ˌȯrd-ᵊn-ˈā-shən\ *n* : the act or ceremony by which a person is ordained
ord·nance \ˈȯrd-nəns\ *n* **1** : military supplies (as weapons, ammunition, or vehicles) **2** : CANNON, ARTILLERY
Or·do·vi·cian \ˌȯrd-ə-ˈvish-ən\ *adj* : of, relating to, or being the period of the Paleozoic era between the Cambrian and the Silurian — **Ordovician** *n*
or·dure \ˈȯr-jər\ *n* : EXCREMENT
[1]**ore** \ˈōr\ *n* : a mineral mined to obtain a substance that it contains
[2]**ore** \ˈər-ə\ *n, pl* **ore** — see *krona, krone* at MONEY table
Oreg *or* **Ore** *abbr* Oregon
oreg·a·no \ə-ˈreg-ə-ˌnō\ *n* [AmerSp] : a bushy perennial mint used as a seasoning and a source of oil
org *abbr* organization; organized
or·gan \ˈȯr-gən\ *n* **1** : a musical instrument having sets of pipes sounded by compressed air and controlled by keyboards; *also* : an instrument in which the sounds of the pipe organ are approximated by electronic devices **2** : a differentiated animal or plant structure made up of

cells and tissues and performing some bodily function **3** : a means of performing a function or accomplishing an end **4** : PERIODICAL

or·gan·dy *also* **or·gan·die** \'ór-gən-dē\ *n, pl* **-dies** [F *organdi*] : a fine transparent muslin with a stiff finish

or·gan·ic \ór-'gan-ik\ *adj* **1** : of, relating to, or arising in a bodily organ **2** : ORGANIZED ⟨an ~ whole⟩ **3** : of, relating to, or derived from living things **4** : of, relating to, or containing carbon compounds **5** : of or relating to a branch of chemistry dealing with carbon compounds **6** : involving, producing, or dealing in foods produced without the use of laboratory-made fertilizers, growth substances, antibiotics, or pesticides ⟨~ gardeners⟩ — **or·gan·i·cal·ly** \-i-k(ə-)lē\ *adv*

or·gan·ism \'ór-gə-ˌniz-əm\ *n* : a living person, animal, or plant — **or·gan·is·mic** \ˌór-gə-'niz-mik\ *adj*

or·gan·ist \'ór-gə-nəst\ *n* : one who plays an organ

or·ga·ni·za·tion \ˌórg-(ə-)nə-'zā-shən\ *n* **1** : the act or process of organizing or of being organized; *also* : the condition or manner of being organized **2** : ASSOCIATION, SOCIETY **3** : MANAGEMENT — **or·ga·ni·za·tion·al** *adj*

or·ga·nize \'ór-gə-ˌnīz\ *vb* **-nized; -niz·ing** **1** : to develop an organic structure **2** : to arrange or form into a complete and functioning whole **3** : to set up an administrative structure for **4** : to arrange by systematic planning and united effort **5** : to join in a union; *also* : UNIONIZE **syn** institute, found, establish, constitute — **or·ga·niz·er** *n*

or·gano·chlo·rine \ór-ˌgan-ə-'klōr-ˌēn\ *adj* : of or relating to the chlorinated hydrocarbon pesticides (as DDT) — **organochlorine** *n*

or·gano·phos·phate \-'fäs-ˌfāt\ *n* : an organophosphorus pesticide — **organophosphate** *adj*

or·gano·phos·pho·rus \-'fäs-f(ə-)rəs\ *also* **or·gano·phos·pho·rous** \-fäs-'fōr-əs\ *adj* : of, relating to, or being a phosphorus-containing organic pesticide (as malathion)

or·gan·za \ór-'gan-zə\ *n* : a sheer dress fabric resembling organdy and usu. made of silk, rayon, or nylon

or·gasm \'ór-ˌgaz-əm\ *n* : a climax of sexual excitement

or·gi·as·tic \ˌór-jē-'as-tik\ *adj* : of, relating to, or marked by orgies

or·gu·lous \'ór-g(y)ə-ləs\ *adj* : PROUD

or·gy \'ór-jē\ *n, pl* **orgies** : a gathering marked by unrestrained indulgence (as in alcohol, drugs, or sexual practices)

ori·el \'ōr-ē-əl\ *n* : a window built out from a wall and usu. supported by a bracket

ori·ent \'ōr-ē-ˌent\ *vb* **1** : to set in a definite position esp. in relation to the points of the compass **2** : to acquaint with an existing situation or environment — **ori·en·ta·tion** \ˌōr-ē-ən-'tā-shən\ *n*

Orient *n* : EAST 3; *esp* : the countries of eastern Asia

ori·en·tal \ˌōr-ē-'ent-ᵊl\ *adj* [fr. *Orient* East, fr. ME, fr. MF, fr. L *orient-, oriens,* fr. prp. of *oriri* to rise] *often cap* : of or situated in the Orient — **Oriental** *n*

ori·en·tate \'ōr-ē-ən-ˌtāt\ *vb* **-tat·ed; -tat·ing** **1** : ORIENT **2** : to face east

or·i·fice \'ór-ə-fəs\ *n* : OPENING, MOUTH

ori·flamme \'ór-ə-ˌflam\ *n* : a brightly colored banner used as a standard or ensign in battle

orig *abbr* original; originally

ori·ga·mi \ˌór-ə-'gäm-ē\ *n* : the art or process of Japanese paper folding

or·i·gin \'ór-ə-jən\ *n* **1** : ANCESTRY **2** : rise, beginning, or derivation from a source; *also* : CAUSE **3** : the intersection of coordinate axes

[1]**orig·i·nal** \ə-'rij-(ə-)nəl\ *n* : something from which a copy, reproduction, or translation is made : PROTOTYPE

[2]**original** *adj* **1** : FIRST, INITIAL **2** : not copied from something else : FRESH **3** : INVENTIVE — **orig·i·nal·i·ty** \-ˌrij-ə-'nal-ət-ē\ *n* — **orig·i·nal·ly** \-'rij-ən-ᵊl-ē\ *adv*

orig·i·nate \ə-'rij-ə-ˌnāt\ *vb* **-nat·ed; -nat·ing** **1** : to give rise to : INITIATE **2** : to come into existence : BEGIN — **orig·i·na·tor** \-ˌnāt-ər\ *n*

ori·ole \'ōr-ē-ˌōl\ *n* [F *oriol,* fr. L *aureolus,* dim. of *aureus* golden, fr. *aurum* gold] : any of a family of New World birds of which the males are usually black and yellow or orange and the females chiefly greenish or yellowish

or·i·son \'ór-ə-sən\ *n* : PRAYER

or·mo·lu \'ór-mə-ˌlü\ *n* : a brass made to imitate gold and used for decorative purposes

[1]**or·na·ment** \'ór-nə-mənt\ *n* : something that lends grace or beauty — **or·na·men·tal** \ˌór-nə-'ment-ᵊl\ *adj*

[2]**or·na·ment** \-ˌment\ *vb* : to provide with ornament : ADORN — **or·na·men·ta·tion** \ˌór-nə-mən-'tā-shən\ *n*

or·nate \ór-'nāt\ *adj* : elaborately decorated — **or·nate·ly** *adv* — **or·nate·ness** *n*

or·nery \'órn-(ə-)rē, 'än-\ *adj* : having an irritable disposition

ornith *abbr* ornithology

or·ni·thol·o·gy \ˌór-nə-'thäl-ə-jē\ *n, pl* **-gies** : a branch of zoology dealing with birds — **or·ni·tho·log·i·cal** \-thə-'läj-i-kəl\ *adj* — **or·ni·thol·o·gist** \-'thäl-ə-jəst\ *n*

oro·tund \'ór-ə-ˌtənd\ *adj* **1** : SONOROUS **2** : POMPOUS

or·phan \'ór-fən\ *n* : a child deprived by death of one or usu. both parents — **orphan** *vb*

or·phan·age \'órf-(ə-)nij\ *n* : an institution for the care of orphans

or·ris \'ór-əs\ *n* : a European iris with a fragrant rootstock (**orrisroot**) used in perfume and sachets

orth·odon·tia \ˌór-thə-'dän-ch(ē-)ə\ *n* : ORTHODONTICS

or·tho·don·tics \ˌór-thə-'dänt-iks\ *n* : a branch of dentistry dealing with faulty tooth occlusion and its correction — **or·tho·don·tist** \-'dänt-əst\ *n*

or·tho·dox \'ór-thə-ˌdäks\ *adj* [MF or LL; MF *orthodoxe,* fr. LL *orthodoxus,* fr. LGk *orthodoxos,* fr. Gk *orthos* right + *doxa* opinion] **1** : conforming to established doctrine esp. in religion **2** : CONVENTIONAL **3** *cap* : of or relating to a Christian church originating in the church of the Eastern Roman Empire — **or·tho·doxy** \-ˌdäk-sē\ *n*

or·thog·ra·phy \ór-'thäg-rə-fē\ *n* : SPELLING — **or·tho·graph·ic** \ˌór-thə-'graf-ik\ *adj*

or·tho·pe·dics \ˌór-thə-'pēd-iks\ *n sing or pl* : the correction or prevention of skeletal deformities — **or·tho·pe·dic** \-ik\ *adj* — **or·tho·pe·dist** \-'pēd-əst\ *n*

or·to·lan \'órt-ᵊl-ən\ *n* : a European bunting valued as a table delicacy

-ory \ˌōr-ē, (ə-)rē\ *adj suffix* **1** : of, relating to, or characterized by **2** : serving for, producing, or maintaining

Os *symbol* osmium

OS *abbr* **1** [L *oculus sinister*] left eye **2** out of stock

Osage \ō-'sāj\ *n, pl* **Osag·es** *or* **Osage** : a member of an American Indian people orig. of Missouri

os·cil·late \'äs-ə-ˌlāt\ *vb* **-lat·ed; -lat·ing** **1** : to swing backward and forward like a pendulum **2** : to move or travel back and forth between two points **3** : VARY, FLUCTUATE — **os·cil·la·tion** \ˌäs-ə-'lā-shən\ *n* — **os·cil·la·tor** \'äs-ə-ˌlāt-ər\ *n* — **os·cil·la·to·ry** \ä-'sil-ə-ˌtōr-ē\ *adj*

os·cil·lo·scope \ä-'sil-ə-ˌskōp\ *n* : an instrument in which variations in current or voltage appear as a visible wave form on a fluorescent screen

os·cu·late \'äs-kyə-ˌlāt\ *vb* **-lat·ed; -lat·ing** : KISS — **os·cu·la·tion** \ˌäs-kyə-'lā-shən\ *n*

Osee \'ō-ˌzē, ō-'zā-ə\ *n* — see BIBLE table

OSHA *abbr* Occupational Safety and Health Administration

osier \'ō-zhər\ *n* : a willow tree with pliable twigs used esp. in making baskets and furniture; *also* : a twig from an osier

os·mi·um \'äz-mē-əm\ *n* : a heavy hard brittle metallic chemical element used in alloys — see ELEMENT table

os·mo·sis \äz-'mō-səs, äs-\ *n* : diffusion of a solvent through a partially permeable membrane into a solution of higher concentration that tends to equalize the concentrations of the solutions on either side of the membrane — **os·mot·ic** \-ˈmät-ik\ *adj*

os·prey \ˈäs-prē, -ˌprā\ *n, pl* **ospreys** : a large brown and white fish-eating hawk

os·si·fy \ˈäs-ə-ˌfī\ *vb* **-fied; -fy·ing** : to change into bone — **os·si·fi·ca·tion** \ˌäs-ə-fə-ˈkā-shən\ *n*

os·su·ary \ˈäsh-ə-ˌwer-ē, ˈäs-(y)ə-\ *n, pl* **-ar·ies** : a depository for the bones of the dead

os·ten·si·ble \ä-ˈsten-sə-bəl\ *adj* : shown outwardly : PROFESSED, APPARENT — **os·ten·si·bly** \-blē\ *adv*

os·ten·ta·tion \ˌäs-tən-ˈtā-shən\ *n* : pretentious or excessive display — **os·ten·ta·tious** \-shəs\ *adj* — **os·ten·ta·tious·ly** *adv*

os·teo·path \ˈäs-tē-ə-ˌpath\ *n* : a practitioner of osteopathy

os·te·op·a·thy \ˌäs-tē-ˈäp-ə-thē\ *n* : a system of healing that emphasizes manipulation (as of joints) but does not exclude other agencies (as the use of medicine and surgery) — **os·teo·path·ic** \ˌäs-tē-ə-ˈpath-ik\ *adj*

os·teo·po·ro·sis \ˌäs-tē-ō-pə-ˈrō-səs\ *n, pl* **-ro·ses** \-ˌsēz\ : a bodily disorder occurring esp. after age 45, characterized by fragile and porous bones, and caused by faulty nutrition and mineral metabolism

ostler *var of* HOSTLER

ost·mark \ˈōst-ˌmärk, ˈȯst-\ *n* — see MONEY table

os·tra·cize \ˈäs-trə-ˌsīz\ *vb* **-cized; -ciz·ing** [Gk *ostrakizein* to banish by voting with potsherds, fr. *ostrakon* shell, potsherd] : to exclude from a group by common consent — **os·tra·cism** \-ˌsiz-əm\ *n*

os·trich \ˈäs-trich, ˈȯs-\ *n* : a very large swift-footed flightless bird of Africa and Arabia

Os·we·go tea \ä-ˌswē-gō-\ *n* : a No. American mint with showy scarlet flowers

OT *abbr* **1** Old Testament **2** overtime

[1]**oth·er** \ˈəth-ər\ *adj* **1** : being the one left; *also* : being the ones distinct from those first mentioned **2** : ALTERNATE ⟨every ~ day⟩ **3** : DIFFERENT **4** : ADDITIONAL **5** : recently past ⟨the ~ night⟩

[2]**other** *pron* **1** : remaining one or ones ⟨one foot and then the ~⟩ **2** : a different or additional one ⟨something or ~⟩

oth·er·wise \-ˌwīz\ *adv* **1** : in a different way **2** : in different circumstances **3** : in other respects — **otherwise** *adj*

oth·er·world \-ˌwərld\ *n* : a world beyond death or beyond present reality

oth·er·world·ly \-ˌwərl-(d)lē\ *adj* : not worldly : concerned with spiritual, intellectual, or imaginative matters

oti·ose \ˈō-shē-ˌōs, ˈōt-ē-\ *adj* **1** : IDLE **2** : STERILE **3** : USELESS

oto·lar·yn·gol·o·gist \ˈōt-ō-ˌlar-ən-ˈgäl-ə-jəst\ *n* : a specialist in otorhinolaryngology — **oto·lar·yn·gol·o·gy** \-ə-jē\ *n*

oto·rhi·no·lar·yn·gol·o·gy \ˌōt-ō-ˌrī-nō-ˌlar-ən-ˈgäl-ə-jē\ *n* : a medical specialty concerned esp. with the ear, nose, and throat — **oto·rhi·no·lar·yn·gol·o·gist** \-jəst\ *n*

OTS *abbr* officers' training school

Ot·ta·wa \ˈät-ə-wə, -ˌwä, -ˌwȯ\ *n, pl* **Ottawas** *or* **Ottawa** : a member of an American Indian people of Michigan and southern Ontario

ot·ter \ˈät-ər\ *n, pl* **otters** *also* **otter** : a web-footed fish-eating mammal that is related to the weasels and has dark brown fur; *also* : its fur

otter

ot·to·man \ˈät-ə-mən\ *n* : an upholstered seat or couch; *also* : an overstuffed footstool

ou·bli·ette \ˌü-blē-ˈet\ *n* [F, fr. MF, fr. *oublier* to forget, fr. L *oblivisci*] : a dungeon with an opening at the top

ought \ˈȯt\ *verbal auxiliary* — used to express moral obligation, advisability, natural expectation, or logical consequence

ou·gui·ya \ü-ˈg(w)ē-(y)ə\ *n, pl* **ouguiya** — see MONEY table

ounce \ˈau̇ns\ *n* [ME, fr. MF *unce*, fr. L *uncia* twelfth part, ounce, fr. *unus* one] : a unit of avoirdupois, troy, and apothecaries' weight — see WEIGHT table

our \är, (ˈ)au̇(ə)r\ *adj* : of or relating to us or ourselves

ours \(ˈ)au̇(ə)rz, ärz\ *pron* : one or the ones belonging to us

our·selves \är-ˈselvz, au̇(ə)r-\ *pron* : our own selves — used reflexively, for emphasis, or in absolute constructions ⟨we pleased ~⟩ ⟨we'll do it ~⟩ ⟨~ tourists, we avoided other tourists⟩

-ous \əs\ *adj suffix* : full of : abounding in : having : possessing the qualities of ⟨clamor*ous*⟩ ⟨poison*ous*⟩

oust \ˈau̇st\ *vb* : to eject from or deprive of property or position : EXPEL **syn** evict, dismiss, banish, deport

oust·er \ˈau̇s-tər\ *n* : EXPULSION

[1]**out** \ˈau̇t\ *adv* **1** : in a direction away from the inside or center **2** : beyond control **3** : to extinction, exhaustion, or completion **4** : in or into the open **5** : so as to retire a batter or base runner; *also* : so as to be retired

[2]**out** *vb* : to become known ⟨the truth will ~⟩

[3]**out** *prep* **1** : out through ⟨looked ~ the window⟩ **2** : outward on or along ⟨drive ~ the river road⟩

[4]**out** *adj* **1** : situated outside or at a distance **2** : not in : ABSENT; *also* : not being in power **3** : not successful in reaching base **4** : not being in vogue or fashion : not up-to-date

[5]**out** *n* **1** : one who is out of office **2** : the retiring of a batter or base runner

out–and–out \ˌau̇t-ᵊn(d)-ˈau̇t\ *adj* : COMPLETE, THOROUGHGOING ⟨an ~ fraud⟩

out·bid \au̇t-ˈbid\ *vb* : to make a higher bid than

[1]**out·board** \ˈau̇t-ˌbōrd\ *adj* **1** : situated outboard **2** : having or using an outboard motor

[2]**outboard** *adv* **1** : outside a ship's hull : away from the long axis of a ship **2** : in a position closer to the wing tip of an airplane

outboard motor *n* : a small internal-combustion engine with propeller attached for mounting at the stern of a small boat

out·bound \ˈau̇t-ˌbau̇nd\ *adj* : outward bound ⟨~ traffic⟩

out·break \-ˌbrāk\ *n* **1** : a sudden or violent breaking out **2** : something (as an epidemic) that breaks out

out·build·ing \-ˌbil-diŋ\ *n* : a building separate from but accessory to a main house

out·burst \-ˌbərst\ *n* : ERUPTION; *esp* : a violent expression of feeling

out·cast \-ˌkast\ *n* : one who is cast out by society : PARIAH

out·class \au̇t-ˈklas\ *vb* : SURPASS

out·come \ˈau̇t-ˌkəm\ *n* : a final consequence : RESULT

out·crop \-ˌkräp\ *n* : a coming out of bedrock to the surface of the ground; *also* : the part of a rock formation that thus appears — **outcrop** *vb*

out·cry \-ˌkrī\ *n* : a loud cry : CLAMOR

out·dat·ed \au̇t-ˈdāt-əd\ *adj* : OUTMODED

out·dis·tance \-ˈdis-təns\ *vb* : to go far ahead of (as in a race) : OUTSTRIP

out·do \-ˈdü\ *vb* **-did** \-ˈdid\; **-done** \-ˈdən\; **-do·ing** \-ˈdü-iŋ\; **-does** \-ˈdəz\ : to go beyond in action or performance : EXCEL

out·door \ˌau̇t-ˌdōr\ *also* **out·doors** \-ˌdōrz\ *adj* **1** : of or relating to the outdoors **2** : performed outdoors **3** : not enclosed (as by a roof)

[1]out·doors \au̇t-ˈdōrz\ *adv* : in or into the open air

[2]outdoors *n* **1** : the open air **2** : the world away from human habitation

out·draw \au̇t-ˈdrȯ\ *vb* **-drew** \-ˈdrü\; **-drawn** \-ˈdrȯn\; **-draw·ing 1** : to attract a larger audience than **2** : to draw a handgun more quickly than

out·er \ˈau̇t-ər\ *adj* **1** : EXTERNAL **2** : situated farther out; *also* : being away from a center

out·er·most \-ˌmōst\ *adj* : farthest out

outer space *n* : SPACE 5; *esp* : the region beyond the solar system

out·face \au̇t-ˈfās\ *vb* **1** : to cause to waver or submit **2** : DEFY

out·field \ˈau̇t-ˌfēld\ *n* : the part of a baseball field beyond the infield and within the foul lines; *also* : players in the outfield — **out·field·er** \-ˌfēl-dər\ *n*

out·fight \au̇t-ˈfīt\ *vb* : to surpass in fighting : DEFEAT

[1]out·fit \ˈau̇t-ˌfit\ *n* **1** : the equipment or apparel for a special purpose or occasion **2** : GROUP

[2]outfit *vb* **out·fit·ted; out·fit·ting** : EQUIP — **out·fit·ter** *n*

out·flank \au̇t-ˈflaŋk\ *vb* : to get around the flank of (an opposing force)

out·flow \ˈau̇t-ˌflō\ *n* **1** : a flowing out **2** : something that flows out

out·fox \au̇t-ˈfäks\ *vb* : OUTWIT

out·gen·er·al \-ˈjen-(ə-)rəl\ *vb* : to surpass in generalship

out·go \ˈau̇t-ˌgō\ *n, pl* **outgoes** : EXPENDITURES, OUTLAY

out·go·ing \-ˌgō-iŋ\ *adj* **1** : going out ⟨~ tide⟩ **2** : retiring from a place or position **3** : FRIENDLY

out·grow \au̇t-ˈgrō\ *vb* **-grew** \-ˈgrü\; **-grown** \-ˈgrōn\; **-grow·ing 1** : to grow faster than **2** : to grow too large for

out·growth \ˈau̇t-ˌgrōth\ *n* : a product of growing out : OFFSHOOT; *also* : CONSEQUENCE

out·guess \au̇t-ˈges\ *vb* : OUTWIT

out·gun \-ˈgən\ *vb* : to surpass in firepower

out·house \ˈau̇t-ˌhau̇s\ *n* : OUTBUILDING; *esp* : an outdoor toilet

out·ing \ˈau̇t-iŋ\ *n* : a brief stay or trip in the open

out·land·ish \au̇t-ˈlan-dish\ *adj* **1** : of foreign appearance or manner; *also* : BIZARRE **2** : remote from civilization — **out·land·ish·ly** *adv*

out·last \-ˈlast\ *vb* : to last longer than

[1]out·law \ˈau̇t-ˌlȯ\ *n* **1** : a person excluded from the protection of the law **2** : a lawless person

[2]outlaw *vb* **1** : to deprive of the protection of the law **2** : to make illegal — **out·law·ry** \ˈau̇t-ˌlȯ(ə)r-ē\ *n*

out·lay \ˈau̇t-ˌlā\ *n* **1** : the act of spending **2** : EXPENDITURE

out·let \ˈau̇t-ˌlet, -lət\ *n* **1** : EXIT, VENT **2** : a means of release (as for an emotion) **3** : a market for a commodity **4** : a receptacle for the plug of an electrical device

[1]out·line \ˈau̇t-ˌlīn\ *n* **1** : a line marking the outer limits of an object or figure **2** : a drawing in which only contours are marked **3** : SUMMARY, SYNOPSIS **4** : PLAN

[2]outline *vb* **1** : to draw the outline of **2** : to indicate the chief features or parts of

out·live \au̇t-ˈliv\ *vb* : to live longer than **syn** outlast, survive

out·look \ˈau̇t-ˌlu̇k\ *n* **1** : a place offering a view; *also* : VIEW **2** : STANDPOINT **3** : the prospect for the future

out·ly·ing \-ˌlī-iŋ\ *adj* : distant from a center or main body

out·ma·neu·ver \ˌau̇t-mə-ˈn(y)ü-vər\ *vb* **1** : to defeat by more skillful maneuvering **2** : to surpass in maneuverability

out·mod·ed \au̇t-ˈmōd-əd\ *adj* **1** : being out of style **2** : no longer acceptable or approved

out·num·ber \-ˈnəm-bər\ *vb* : to exceed in number

out of *prep* **1** : out from within or behind ⟨walk *out of* the room⟩ ⟨look *out of* the window⟩ **2** : from a state of ⟨wake up *out of* a deep sleep⟩ **3** : beyond the limits of ⟨*out of* sight⟩ **4** : BECAUSE OF ⟨came *out of* curiosity⟩ **5** : FROM, WITH ⟨built it *out of* scrap⟩ **6** : in or into a state of loss or not having ⟨cheated him *out of* $5000⟩ ⟨we're *out of* matches⟩ **7** : from among ⟨one *out of* four⟩ — **out of it** : SQUARE, OLD-FASHIONED

out–of–bounds \ˌau̇t-ə(v)-ˈbau̇n(d)z\ *adv or adj* : outside the prescribed boundaries or limits

out–of–date \-ˈdāt\ *adj* : no longer in fashion or in use : OUTMODED

out–of–door \-ˈdōr\ *or* **out–of–doors** \-ˈdōrz\ *adj* : OUTDOOR

out–of–the–way \-t͟hə-ˈwā\ *adj* **1** : being off the beaten track **2** : UNUSUAL

out·pa·tient \ˈau̇t-ˌpā-shənt\ *n* : a person not an inmate of a hospital who visits it for diagnosis or treatment

out·per·form \ˌau̇t-pər-ˈfȯrm\ *vb* : to perform better than

out·play \au̇t-ˈplā\ *vb* : to play more skillfully than

out·point \-ˈpȯint\ *vb* : to win more points than

out·post \ˈau̇t-ˌpōst\ *n* **1** : a military detachment stationed at some distance from a main force to protect it from surprise attack; *also* : a military base established (as by treaty) in a foreign country **2** : an outlying or frontier settlement

out·pour·ing \-ˌpōr-iŋ\ *n* : something that pours out or is poured out

out·pull \au̇t-ˈpu̇l\ *vb* : OUTDRAW 1

[1]out·put \ˈau̇t-ˌpu̇t\ *n* **1** : the amount produced (as by a machine or factory) : PRODUCTION **2** : the information fed out by a computer

[2]output *vb* **out·put·ted** *or* **output; out·put·ting** : to produce as output

[1]out·rage \ˈau̇t-ˌrāj\ *n* [ME, fr. OF, excess, outrage, fr. *outre* beyond, in excess, fr. L *ultra*] **1** : a violent or shameful act **2** : INJURY, INSULT **3** : the anger or resentment aroused by an outrage

[2]outrage *vb* **out·raged; out·rag·ing 1** : RAPE **2** : to subject to violent injury or gross insult **3** : to arouse to extreme resentment

out·ra·geous \au̇t-ˈrā-jəs\ *adj* : extremely offensive, insulting, or shameful : SHOCKING — **out·ra·geous·ly** *adv*

out·rank \-ˈraŋk\ *vb* : to rank higher than

ou·tré \ü-ˈtrā\ *adj* [F] : violating convention or propriety : BIZARRE

[1]out·reach \au̇t-ˈrēch\ *vb* **1** : to surpass in reach **2** : to get the better of by trickery

[2]out·reach \ˈau̇t-ˌrēch\ *n* **1** : the act of reaching out **2** : the extent of reach **3** : the extending of services beyond usual limits

out·rid·er \-ˌrīd-ər\ *n* : a mounted attendant

out·rig·ger \-ˌrig-ər\ *n* **1** : a frame that extends from the side of a canoe or boat to prevent upsetting **2** : a craft equipped with an outrigger

outrigger 2

[1]out·right \(ˈ)au̇t-ˈrīt\ *adv* **1** : COMPLETELY **2** : INSTANTANEOUSLY

[2]outright *adj* **1** : being exactly what is stated ⟨~ lie⟩ **2** : given or made without reservation or encumbrance ⟨~ sale⟩

out·run \au̇t-ˈrən\ *vb* **-ran** \-ˈran\; **-run; -run·ning** : to run faster than; *also* : EXCEED

out·sell \-ˈsel\ *vb* **-sold** \-ˈsōld\; **-sell·ing** : to exceed in sales

out·set \ˈau̇t-ˌset\ *n* : BEGINNING, START

out·shine \au̇t-ˈshīn\ *vb* **-shone** \-ˈshōn\ *or* **-shined; -shin·ing 1** : to shine brighter than **2** : SURPASS

[1]**out·side** \au̇t-ˈsīd, ˈau̇t-ˌsīd\ *n* **1** : a place or region beyond an enclosure or boundary **2** : EXTERIOR **3** : the utmost limit or extent

[2]**outside** *adj* **1** : OUTER **2** : coming from without ⟨~ influences⟩ **3** : being apart from one's regular duties ⟨~ activities⟩ **4** : REMOTE ⟨an ~ chance⟩

[3]**outside** *adv* : on or to the outside

[4]**outside** *prep* **1** : on or to the outside of **2** : beyond the limits of **3** : EXCEPT

outside of *prep* **1** : OUTSIDE **2** : BESIDES

out·sid·er \au̇t-ˈsīd-ər\ *n* : one who does not belong to a group

out·size \ˈau̇t-ˌsīz\ *n* : an unusual size; *esp* : a size larger than the standard

out·skirts \-ˌskərts\ *n pl* : the outlying parts (as of a city) : BORDERS

out·smart \au̇t-ˈsmärt\ *vb* : OUTWIT

out·spend \-ˈspend\ *vb* **1** : to exceed the limits of in spending ⟨~*s* his income⟩ **2** : to surpass in spending

out·spo·ken \au̇t-ˈspō-kən\ *adj* : direct and open in speech or expression — **out·spo·ken·ness** \-kən-nəs\ *n*

out·spread \-ˈspred\ *vb* **-spread; -spread·ing** : to spread out : EXTEND

out·stand·ing \-ˈstan-diŋ\ *adj* **1** : PROJECTING **2** : UNPAID; *also* : UNRESOLVED **3** : publicly issued and sold **4** : CONSPICUOUS; *also* : DISTINGUISHED — **out·stand·ing·ly** *adv*

out·stay \-ˈstā\ *vb* **1** : OVERSTAY **2** : to surpass in endurance

out·stretched \-ˈstrecht\ *adj* : stretched out : EXTENDED

out·strip \-ˈstrip\ *vb* **1** : to go faster than **2** : EXCEL, SURPASS

out·vote \-ˈvōt\ *vb* : to defeat by a majority of votes

[1]**out·ward** \ˈau̇t-wərd\ *adj* **1** : moving or directed toward the outside **2** : showing outwardly

[2]**outward** *or* **out·wards** \-wərdz\ *adv* : toward the outside

out·ward·ly \-wərd-lē\ *adv* : on the outside : EXTERNALLY

out·wear \au̇t-ˈwaər\ *vb* **-wore** \-ˈwōr\; **-worn** \-ˈwōrn\; **-wear·ing** : to wear longer than : OUTLAST

out·weigh \-ˈwā\ *vb* : to exceed in weight, value, or importance

out·wit \-ˈwit\ *vb* : to get the better of by superior cleverness

[1]**out·work** \-ˈwərk\ *vb* : to outdo in working

[2]**out·work** \ˈau̇t-ˌwərk\ *n* : a minor defensive position outside a fortified area

out·worn \au̇t-ˈwōrn\ *adj* : OUTMODED

ou·zo \ˈü-(ˌ)zō, -(ˌ)zȯ\ *n* : a colorless anise-flavored unsweetened Greek liqueur

ova *pl of* OVUM

oval \ˈō-vəl\ *adj* [ML *ovalis*, fr. LL, of an egg, fr. L *ovum*] : egg-shaped; *also* : broadly elliptical — **oval** *n*

ova·ry \ˈōv-(ə-)rē\ *n, pl* **-ries** **1** : a usu. paired organ of a female animal in which eggs and often sex hormones are produced **2** : the part of a flower in which seeds are produced — **ovar·i·an** \ō-ˈvar-ē-ən, -ˈver-\ *adj*

ovate \ˈō-ˌvāt\ *adj* : egg-shaped

ova·tion \ō-ˈvā-shən\ *n* [L *ovation-, ovatio*, fr. *ovatus*, pp. of *ovare* to exult] : an enthusiastic popular tribute

ov·en \ˈəv-ən\ *n* : a chamber (as in a stove) for baking, heating, or drying

oven·bird \-ˌbərd\ *n* : a large American warbler that builds its dome-shaped nest on the ground

[1]**over** \ˈō-vər\ *adv* **1** : across a barrier or intervening space **2** : across the brim ⟨boil ~⟩ **3** : so as to bring the underside up **4** : out of a vertical position **5** : beyond some quantity, limit, or norm **6** : ABOVE **7** : at an end **8** : THROUGH; *also* : THOROUGHLY **9** : AGAIN

[2]**over** \ˌō-vər, ˈō-\ *prep* **1** : above in position, authority, or scope ⟨towered ~ her⟩ ⟨obeyed those ~ him⟩ ⟨the talk was ~ their heads⟩ **2** : more than ⟨paid ~ $100 for it⟩ **3** : ON, UPON ⟨a cape ~ his shoulders⟩ **4** : along the length of ⟨~ the road⟩ **5** : through the medium of : ON ⟨spoke ~ TV⟩ **6** : all through ⟨showed me ~ the house⟩ **7** : on or above so as to cross ⟨walk ~ the bridge⟩ ⟨jump ~ a ditch⟩ **8** : DURING ⟨~ the past 25 years⟩ **9** : on account of ⟨fought ~ a woman⟩

[3]**over** \ˈō-vər, ˌō-\ *adj* **1** : UPPER, HIGHER **2** : REMAINING **3** : ENDED

over- *prefix* **1** : so as to exceed or surpass **2** : excessive; excessively

overabundance
overabundant
overactive
overaggressive
overambitious
overanxious
overbid
overbold
overbuild
overburden
overbuy
overcapacity
overcapitalize
overcareful
overcautious
overcompensation
overconfidence
overconfident
overconscientious
overcook
overcritical
overcrowd
overdecorated
overdetermined
overdevelop
overdose
overdress
overeager
overeat
overemphasis
overemphasize
overenthusiastic
overestimate
overexcite
overexert
overexertion
overextend
overfatigued
overfeed
overfill
overgenerous
overgraze
overhasty
overheat
overindulge
overindulgence
overindulgent
overlarge
overlearn
overliberal
overload
overlong
overmodest
overnice
overoptimism
overoptimistic
overpay
overpopulated
overpopulation
overpraise
overprice
overproduce
overproduction
overprotect
overproud
overrate
overreact
overrefinement
overrepresented
overripe
oversell
oversensitive
oversensitiveness
oversimple
oversimplification
oversimplify
overspecialization
overspecialize
overspend
overstock
overstrict
oversubtle
oversupply
overtax
overtired
overtrain
overuse
overvalue
overzealous

over·act \ˌō-vər-ˈakt\ *vb* : to exaggerate in acting

[1]**over·age** \-ˈāj\ *adj* **1** : too old to be useful **2** : older than is normal for one's position, function, or grade

[2]**over·age** \ˈōv-(ə-)rij\ *n* : SURPLUS

over·all \ˌō-vər-ˈȯl\ *adj* : including everything ⟨~ expenses⟩

over·alls \ˈō-vər-ˌȯlz\ *n pl* : trousers of strong material usu. with a piece extending up to cover the chest

over·arm \-ˌärm\ *adj* : done with the arm raised above the shoulder

over·awe \ˌō-vər-ˈȯ\ *vb* : to restrain or subdue by awe

over·bal·ance \-ˈbal-əns\ *vb* **1** : OUTWEIGH **2** : to cause to lose balance

over·bear·ing \-ˈba(ə)r-iŋ\ *adj* : ARROGANT, DOMINEERING

over·blown \-ˈblōn\ *adj* **1** : PORTLY **2** : INFLATED, PRETENTIOUS

over·board \ˈō-vər-ˌbōrd\ *adv* **1** : over the side of a ship into the water **2** : to extremes of enthusiasm

[1]**over·cast** \ˈō-vər-ˌkast\ *adj* : clouded over : GLOOMY

[2]**over·cast** *n* : COVERING; *esp* : a covering of clouds

over·charge \ˌō-vər-ˈchärj\ *vb* **1** : to charge too much **2** : to fill or load too full — **over·charge** \ˈō-vər-ˌchärj\ *n*

over·coat \ˈō-vər-ˌkōt\ *n* : a warm coat worn over indoor clothing

over·come \ˌō-vər-ˈkəm\ *vb* **-came** \-ˈkām\; **-come; -com·ing 1** : CONQUER **2** : to make helpless or exhausted

over·do \ˌō-vər-ˈdü\ *vb* **-did** \-ˈdid\; **-done** \-ˈdən\; **-do·ing** \-ˈdü-iŋ\; **-does** \-ˈdəz\ **1** : to do too much; *also* : to tire oneself **2** : EXAGGERATE **3** : to cook too long

over·draft \ˈō-vər-ˌdraft, -ˌdraft\ *n* : an overdrawing of a bank account; *also* : the sum overdrawn

over·draw \ˌō-vər-ˈdrȯ\ *vb* **-drew** \-ˈdrü\; **-drawn** \-ˈdrȯn\; **-draw·ing 1** : to draw checks on a bank account for more than the balance **2** : EXAGGERATE

over·drive \ˈō-vər-ˌdrīv\ *n* : an automotive transmission gear that transmits to the drive shaft a speed greater than the engine speed

over·dub \ˌō-vər-ˈdəb\ *vb* : to transfer (recorded sound) onto an earlier recording for a combined effect — **over·dub** \ˈō-vər-ˌdəb\ *n*

over·due \-ˈd(y)ü\ *adj* **1** : unpaid when due; *also* : not appearing or presented on time **2** : more than ready

over·ex·pose \ˌō-vər-ik-ˈspōz\ *vb* : to expose (a photographic plate or film) for more time than is needed — **over·ex·po·sure** \-ˈspō-zhər\ *n*

[1]**over·flow** \-ˈflō\ *vb* **1** : INUNDATE; *also* : to pour forth in a flood **2** : to flow over the brim or top of

[2]**over·flow** \ˈō-vər-ˌflō\ *n* **1** : FLOOD; *also* : SURPLUS **2** : an outlet for surplus liquid

over·fly \ˌō-vər-ˈflī\ *vb* **-flew** \-ˈflü\; **-flown** \-ˈflōn\; **-fly·ing** : to fly over in an airplane or spacecraft — **over·flight** \ˈō-vər-ˌflīt\ *n*

over·grow \ˌō-vər-ˈgrō\ *vb* **-grew** \-ˈgrü\; **-grown** \-ˈgrōn\; **-grow·ing 1** : to grow over so as to cover **2** : OUTGROW **3** : to grow excessively

over·hand \ˈō-vər-ˌhand\ *adj* : made with the hand brought down from above — **overhand** *adv*

[1]**over·hang** \ˈō-vər-ˌhaŋ, ˌō-vər-ˈhaŋ\ *vb* **-hung** \-ˌhəŋ, -ˈhəŋ\; **-hang·ing 1** : to project over : jut out **2** : to hang over threateningly

[2]**over·hang** \ˈō-vər-ˌhaŋ\ *n* : a part (as of a roof) that overhangs

over·haul \ˌō-vər-ˈhȯl\ *vb* **1** : to examine thoroughly and make necessary repairs and adjustments **2** : OVERTAKE

[1]**over·head** \ˌō-vər-ˈhed\ *adv* : ALOFT

[2]**over·head** \ˈō-vər-ˌhed\ *adj* : operating or lying above ⟨~ door⟩

[3]**over·head** \ˈō-vər-ˌhed\ *n* : business expenses not chargeable to a particular part of the work

over·hear \ˌō-vər-ˈhiər\ *vb* **-heard** \-ˈhərd\; **-hear·ing** \-ˈhi(ə)r-iŋ\ : to hear without the speaker's knowledge or intention

over·joyed \ˌō-vər-ˈjȯid\ *adj* : filled with great joy

over·kill \ˈō-vər-ˌkil\ *n* **1** : a capacity for destruction of a target greatly exceeding that required **2** : a large excess

over·land \ˈō-vər-ˌland, -lənd\ *adv or adj* : by, on, or across land

over·lap \ˌō-vər-ˈlap\ *vb* **1** : to lap over **2** : to have something in common

over·lay \ˌō-vər-ˈlā\ *vb* **-laid** \-ˈlād\; **-lay·ing** : to lay or spread over or across — **over·lay** \ˈō-vər-ˌlā\ *n*

over·leap \ˌō-vər-ˈlēp\ *vb* **-leaped** *or* **-leapt** \-ˈlēpt, -ˈlept\; **-leap·ing** \-ˈlē-piŋ\ **1** : to leap over or across **2** : to defeat (oneself) by going too far

over·lie \ˌō-vər-ˈlī\ *vb* **-lay** \-ˈlā\; **-lain** \-ˈlān\; **-ly·ing** \-ˈlī-iŋ\ : to lie over or upon

[1]**over·look** \ˌō-vər-ˈlu̇k\ *vb* **1** : INSPECT **2** : to look down on from above **3** : to fail to see **4** : IGNORE; *also* : EXCUSE **5** : SUPERVISE

[2]**over·look** \ˈō-vər-ˌlu̇k\ *n* : a place from which to look down upon a scene below

over·lord \-ˌlȯrd\ *n* : a lord who has supremacy over other lords

over·ly \ˈō-vər-lē\ *adv* : EXCESSIVELY

over·mas·ter \ˌō-vər-ˈmas-tər\ *vb* : OVERPOWER, SUBDUE

over·match \-ˈmach\ *vb* : to be more than a match for : DEFEAT

over·much \-ˈməch\ *adj or adv* : too much

[1]**over·night** \-ˈnīt\ *adv* **1** : on or during the night **2** : SUDDENLY ⟨became famous ~⟩

[2]**overnight** *adj* : of, lasting, or staying the night ⟨~ guests⟩

over·pass \ˈō-vər-ˌpas\ *n* **1** : a crossing (as of two highways) at different levels by means of a bridge **2** : the upper level of an overpass

over·play \ˌō-vər-ˈplā\ *vb* **1** : EXAGGERATE; *also* : OVEREMPHASIZE **2** : to rely too much on the strength of

over·pow·er \-ˈpau̇(-ə)r\ *vb* **1** : to overcome by superior force **2** : OVERWHELM ⟨~*ed* by hunger⟩

over·print \-ˈprint\ *vb* : to print over with something additional — **over·print** \ˈō-vər-ˌprint\ *n*

over·qual·i·fied \-ˈkwäl-ə-ˌfīd\ *adj* : having more education, training, or experience than a job calls for

over·reach \ˌō-və(r)-ˈrēch\ *vb* **1** : to reach above or beyond **2** : to defeat (oneself) by too great an effort

over·ride \-ˈrīd\ *vb* **-rode** \-ˈrōd\; **-rid·den** \-ˈrid-ᵊn\; **-rid·ing** \-ˈrīd-iŋ\ **1** : to ride over or across **2** : to prevail over; *also* : to set aside

over·rule \-ˈrül\ *vb* **1** : to prevail over **2** : to rule against **3** : to set aside

[1]**over·run** \-ˈrən\ *vb* **-ran** \-ˈran\; **-run·ning 1** : to defeat and occupy the positions of **2** : OVERSPREAD; *also* : INFEST **3** : to go beyond **4** : to flow over

[2]**over·run** \ˈō-və(r)-ˌrən\ *n* **1** : an act or instance of overrunning; *esp* : an exceeding of estimated costs **2** : the amount by which something overruns

over·sea \ˌō-vər-ˈsē, ˈō-vər-ˌsē\ *adj or adv* : OVERSEAS

over·seas \ˌō-vər-ˈsēz, -ˌsēz\ *adv or adj* : beyond or across the sea : ABROAD

over·see \ˌō-vər-ˈsē\ *vb* **-saw** \-ˈsȯ\; **-seen** \-ˈsēn\; **-see·ing 1** : OVERLOOK **2** : INSPECT; *also* : SUPERVISE — **over·seer** \ˈō-vər-ˌsiər\ *n*

over·sexed \ˌō-vər-ˈsekst\ *adj* : exhibiting excessive sexual drive or interest

over·shad·ow \-ˈshad-ō\ *vb* **1** : DARKEN **2** : to exceed in importance

over·shoe \ˈō-vər-ˌshü\ *n* : a protective outer shoe; *esp* : GALOSH

over·shoot \ˌō-vər-ˌshüt\ *vb* **-shot** \-ˈshät\; **-shoot·ing 1** : to pass swiftly beyond **2** : to shoot over or beyond (as a target)

over·sight \ˈō-vər-ˌsīt\ *n* **1** : SUPERVISION **2** : an inadvertent omission or error

over·size \ˌō-vər-ˈsīz\ *or* **over·sized** \-ˈsīzd\ *adj* : of more than ordinary size

over·sleep \ˌō-vər-ˈslēp\ *vb* **-slept** \-ˈslept\; **-sleep·ing** : to sleep beyond the time for waking

over·spread \-ˈspred\ *vb* **-spread; -spread·ing** : to spread over or above

over·state \-ˈstāt\ *vb* : EXAGGERATE — **over·state·ment** *n*

over·stay \-ˈstā\ *vb* : to stay beyond the time or limits of

over·step \-ˈstep\ *vb* : EXCEED

over·sub·scribe \-səb-ˈskrīb\ *vb* : to subscribe for more of than is available, asked for, or offered for sale

overt \ō-ˈvərt, ˈō-ˌvərt\ *adj* [ME, fr. MF *ouvert, overt,* fr. pp. of *ouvrir* to open] : not secret

over·take \ˌō-vər-ˈtāk\ *vb* **-took** \-ˈtu̇k\; **-tak·en** \-ˈtā-kən\; **-tak·ing** : to catch up with; *also* : to catch up with and pass by

over·throw \ˌō-vər-ˈthrō\ *vb* **-threw** \-ˈthrü\; **-thrown** \-ˈthrōn\; **-throw·ing 1** : UPSET **2** : to bring down : DEFEAT ⟨~ a government⟩ **3** : to throw over or past — **over·throw** \ˈō-vər-ˌthrō\ *n*

over·time \ˈō-vər-ˌtīm\ *n* : time beyond a set limit; *esp* : working time in excess of a standard day or week — **overtime** *adv*
over·tone \-ˌtōn\ *n* **1** : one of the higher tones in a complex musical tone **2** : IMPLICATION, SUGGESTION
over·top \ˌō-vər-ˈtäp\ *vb* **1** : to tower above **2** : SURPASS
over·trick \ˈō-vər-ˌtrik\ *n* : a card trick won in excess of the number bid
over·ture \ˈō-vər-ˌchu̇r, -chər\ *n* [ME, lit., opening, fr. MF, fr. (assumed) VL *opertura*, alter. of L *apertura*] **1** : an opening offer **2** : an orchestral introduction to a musical dramatic work
over·turn \ˌō-vər-ˈtərn\ *vb* **1** : to turn over : UPSET **2** : OVERTHROW
over·view \ˈō-vər-ˌvyü\ *n* : a general survey : SUMMARY
over·ween·ing \ˌō-vər-ˈwē-niŋ\ *adj* **1** : ARROGANT **2** : IMMODERATE
over·weigh \-ˈwā\ *vb* **1** : to exceed in weight **2** : OPPRESS
over·weight \ˈō-vər-ˌwāt\ *n* **1** : weight above what is required or allowed **2** : bodily weight greater than normal for one's age, height, and build — **overweight** *adj*
over·whelm \ˌō-vər-ˈhwelm\ *vb* **1** : OVERTHROW **2** : SUBMERGE **3** : to overcome completely
over·whelm·ing *adj* : EXTREME, GREAT ⟨~ indifference⟩ — **over·whelm·ing·ly** *adv*
over·win·ter \-ˈwint-ər\ *vb* : to survive the winter
over·work \-ˈwərk\ *vb* **1** : to work or cause to work too hard or long **2** : to use too much — **overwork** *n*
over·wrought \ˌō-və(r)-ˈro̊t\ *adj* **1** : extremely excited **2** : elaborated to excess
ovi·duct \ˈō-və-ˌdəkt\ *n* : a tube that serves for the passage of eggs from an ovary
ovip·a·rous \ō-ˈvip-ə-rəs\ *adj* : reproducing by eggs that hatch outside the parent's body
ovoid \ˈō-ˌvȯid\ *or* **ovoi·dal** \ō-ˈvȯid-ᵊl\ *adj* : egg-shaped : OVAL
ovu·late \ˈäv-yə-ˌlāt, ˈōv-\ *vb* **-lat·ed; -lat·ing** : to produce eggs or discharge them from an ovary — **ovu·la·tion** \ˌäv-yə-ˈlā-shən, ˌōv-\ *n*
ovule \ˈäv-yül, ˈōv-\ *n* : any of the bodies in a plant ovary that after fertilization become seeds
ovum \ˈō-vəm\ *n, pl* **ova** \-və\ : EGG 2
ow \ˈau̇\ *interj* — used esp. to express sudden pain
owe \ˈō\ *vb* **owed; ow·ing** **1** : to be under obligation to pay or render **2** : to be indebted to or for; *also* : to be in debt
owing to *prep* : BECAUSE OF
owl \ˈau̇l\ *n* : a nocturnal bird of prey with large head and eyes and strong talons — **owl·ish** *adj* — **owl·ish·ly** *adv*
owl·et \ˈau̇-lət\ *n* : a young or small owl
¹own \ˈōn\ *adj* : belonging to oneself — used as an intensive after a possessive adjective ⟨his ~ car⟩
²own *vb* **1** : to have or hold as property **2** : ACKNOWLEDGE; *also* : CONFESS — **own·er** *n* — **own·er·ship** *n*
³own *pron* : one or ones belonging to oneself
ox \ˈäks\ *n, pl* **ox·en** \ˈäk-sən\ *also* **ox** : one of the common large domestic cattle kept for milk, draft, and meat; *esp* : an adult castrated male
ox·blood \ˈäks-ˌbləd\ *n* : a moderate reddish brown
ox·bow \ˈäks-ˌbō\ *n* **1** : a U-shaped collar worn by a draft ox **2** : a U-shaped bend in a river — **oxbow** *adj*

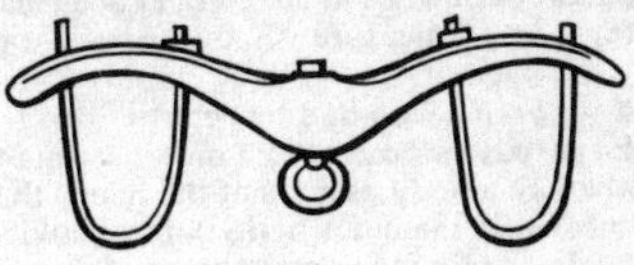

oxbow 1

ox·ford \ˈäks-fərd\ *n* : a low shoe laced or tied over the instep
ox·i·dant \ˈäk-səd-ənt\ *n* : OXIDIZING AGENT — **oxidant** *adj*
ox·i·da·tion \ˌäk-sə-ˈdā-shən\ *n* : the act or process of oxidizing; *also* : the condition of being oxidized — **ox·i·da·tive** \ˈäk-sə-ˌdāt-iv\ *adj*
ox·ide \ˈäk-ˌsīd\ *n* : a compound of oxygen with another element or group
ox·i·dize \ˈäk-sə-ˌdīz\ *vb* **-dized; -diz·ing** : to combine with oxygen ⟨iron rusts because it is *oxidized* by exposure to the air⟩ — **ox·i·diz·er** *n*
oxidizing agent *n* : a substance (as oxygen or nitric acid) that oxidizes by taking up electrons
oxy·acet·y·lene \ˌäk-sē-ə-ˈset-ᵊl-ən, -ᵊl-ˌēn\ *adj* : of, relating to, or utilizing a mixture of oxygen and acetylene
ox·y·gen \ˈäk-si-jən\ *n* [F *oxygène*, fr. Gk *oxys*, adj., acid, lit., sharp + *-genēs* born; so called because it was once thought to be an essential element of all acids] : a colorless odorless gaseous chemical element that is found in the air, is essential to life, and is involved in combustion — see ELEMENT table
ox·y·gen·ate \ˈäk-si-jə-ˌnāt\ *vb* **-at·ed; -at·ing** : to impregnate, combine, or supply with oxygen — **ox·y·gen·ation** \ˌäk-si-jə-ˈnā-shən\ *n*
oxygen tent *n* : a canopy which can be placed over a bedridden person and within which a flow of oxygen can be maintained
oys·ter \ˈȯi-stər\ *n* : any of various mollusks with an irregular 2-valved shell that live on stony bottoms in shallow seas and include edible shellfish and pearl producers — **oys·ter·ing** \ˈȯi-st(ə-)riŋ\ *n* — **oys·ter·man** \ˈȯi-stər-mən\ *n*
oz *abbr* [obs. It *onza* (now *oncia*)] ounce; ounces
ozone \ˈō-ˌzōn\ *n* **1** : a faintly blue form of oxygen that is produced by the silent discharge of electricity in air or oxygen and is used for disinfecting, deodorizing, and bleaching **2** : pure and refreshing air

P

¹p \ˈpē\ *n, pl* **p's** *or* **ps** \ˈpēz\ *often cap* : the 16th letter of the English alphabet
²p *abbr, often cap* **1** page **2** participle **3** past **4** pawn **5** pence; penny **6** per **7** petite **8** pint **9** pressure **10** purl
P *symbol* phosphorus
pa \ˈpä, ˈpȯ\ *n* : FATHER
¹Pa *abbr* Pennsylvania
²Pa *symbol* protactinium
PA *abbr* **1** Pennsylvania **2** per annum **3** physician's assistant **4** power of attorney **5** press agent **6** private account **7** professional association **8** public address **9** purchasing agent
pa·'an·ga \pä-ˈäŋ-(g)ə\ *n* — see MONEY table
pab·u·lum \ˈpab-yə-ləm\ *n* [L, food, fodder] : usu. soft digestible food

Pac *abbr* Pacific

PAC *abbr* political action committee

[1]**pace** \ˈpās\ *n* **1** : rate of movement or progress (as in walking or working) **2** : a step in walking; *also* : the length of such a step **3** : GAIT; *esp* : a horse's gait in which the legs on the same side move together

[2]**pace** *vb* **paced; pac·ing 1** : to go or cover at a pace or with slow steps **2** : to measure off by paces **3** : to set or regulate the pace of

[3]**pace** \ˈpā-sē\ *prep* : with due respect to

pace·mak·er \ˈpās-ˌmā-kər\ *n* **1** : one that sets the pace for another **2** : a body part (as of the heart) that serves to establish and maintain a rhythmic activity **3** : an electrical device for stimulating or steadying the heartbeat

pac·er \ˈpā-sər\ *n* **1** : a horse that paces **2** : PACEMAKER

pachy·derm \ˈpak-i-ˌdərm\ *n* [F *pachyderme,* fr. Gk *pachydermos* thick-skinned, fr. *pachys* thick + *derma* skin] : any of various thick-skinned hoofed mammals (as an elephant)

pach·ys·an·dra \ˌpak-i-ˈsan-drə\ *n* : any of a genus of low evergreen plants used as a ground cover

pa·cif·ic \pə-ˈsif-ik\ *adj* **1** : tending to lessen conflict **2** : CALM, PEACEFUL **3** *cap* : of or relating to the Pacific Ocean

pac·i·fi·er \ˈpas-ə-ˌfī(-ə)r\ *n* : one that pacifies; *esp* : a device for a baby to chew or suck on

pac·i·fism \ˈpas-ə-ˌfiz-əm\ *n* : opposition to war or violence as a means of settling disputes — **pac·i·fist** \-fəst\ *n or adj* — **pac·i·fis·tic** \ˌpas-ə-ˈfis-tik\ *adj*

pac·i·fy \ˈpas-ə-ˌfī\ *vb* **-fied; -fy·ing 1** : to allay anger or agitation in **2** : SETTLE; *also* : SUBDUE — **pac·i·fi·ca·tion** \ˌpas-ə-fə-ˈkā-shən\ *n*

[1]**pack** \ˈpak\ *n* **1** : a compact bundle; *also* : a flexible container for carrying a bundle esp. on the back **2** : a large amount : HEAP **3** : a set of playing cards **4** : a group or band of people or animals **5** : wet absorbent material for application to the body

[2]**pack** *vb* **1** : to stow goods in for transportation **2** : to fill in or surround so as to prevent passage of air, steam, or water **3** : to put into a protective container **4** : to load with a pack ⟨~ a mule⟩ **5** : to crowd in **6** : to make into a pack **7** : to cause to go without ceremony ⟨~ them off to school⟩ **8** : WEAR, CARRY ⟨~ a gun⟩

[3]**pack** *vb* : to make up fraudulently so as to secure a desired result ⟨~ a jury⟩

[1]**pack·age** \ˈpak-ij\ *n* **1** : BUNDLE, PARCEL **2** : a group of related things offered as a whole

[2]**package** *vb* **pack·aged; pack·ag·ing** : to make into or enclose in a package

package deal *n* : an offer containing several items all or none of which must be accepted

package store *n* : a store that sells alcoholic beverages in sealed containers for consumption off the premises

pack·er \ˈpak-ər\ *n* : one that packs; *esp* : a wholesale food dealer

pack·et \ˈpak-ət\ *n* **1** : a passenger boat carrying mail and cargo on a regular schedule **2** : a small bundle or package

pack·horse \ˈpak-ˌhȯrs\ *n* : a horse used to carry goods or supplies

pack·ing \ˈpak-iŋ\ *n* : material used to pack something

pack·ing·house \-ˌhau̇s\ *n* : an establishment for processing and packing food and esp. meat and its by-products

pack rat *n* : a bushy-tailed rodent of the Rocky Mountain area that hoards food and miscellaneous objects

pack·sad·dle \ˈpak-ˌsad-ᵊl\ *n* : a saddle for supporting packs on the back of an animal

pack·thread \-ˌthred\ *n* : strong thread for tying

pact \ˈpakt\ *n* : AGREEMENT, TREATY

[1]**pad** \ˈpad\ *n* **1** : a cushioning part or thing : CUSHION **2** : the cushioned part of the foot of some mammals **3** : the floating leaf of a water plant **4** : a writing tablet **5** : LAUNCHPAD **6** : living quarters; *also* : BED

[2]**pad** *vb* **pad·ded; pad·ding 1** : to furnish with a pad or padding **2** : to expand with needless or fraudulent matter

pad·ding \ˈpad-iŋ\ *n* : the material with which something is padded

[1]**pad·dle** \ˈpad-ᵊl\ *vb* **pad·dled; pad·dling** : to move the hands and feet about in shallow water

[2]**paddle** *n* **1** : an implement with a flat blade used in propelling and steering a small craft (as a canoe) **2** : an implement used for stirring, mixing, or beating **3** : a broad board on the outer rim of a waterwheel or a paddle wheel

[3]**paddle** *vb* **pad·dled; pad·dling** \ˈpad-(ᵊ-)liŋ\ **1** : to move on or through water by or as if by using a paddle **2** : to beat or stir with a paddle

paddle wheel *n* : a wheel with boards around its outer edge used to move a water craft

paddle wheeler *n* : a steam-driven vessel propelled by a paddle wheel

pad·dock \ˈpad-ək\ *n* : a usu. enclosed area for pasturing or exercising animals; *esp* : one where racehorses are saddled and paraded before a race

pad·dy \ˈpad-ē\ *n, pl* **paddies** : wet land where rice is grown

pad·dy wagon \ˈpad-ē-\ *n* : PATROL WAGON

pad·lock \ˈpad-ˌläk\ *n* : a removable lock with a curved piece that snaps into a catch — **padlock** *vb*

pa·dre \ˈpäd-rā\ *n* [Sp or It or Pg, lit., father, fr. L *pater*] **1** : PRIEST, CLERGYMAN **2** : a military chaplain

pae·an \ˈpē-ən\ *n* : an exultant song of praise or thanksgiving

pa·gan \ˈpā-gən\ *n* [ME, fr. LL *paganus,* fr. L, country dweller, fr. *pagus* country district] : HEATHEN — **pagan** *adj* — **pa·gan·ism** \-ˌiz-əm\ *n*

[1]**page** \ˈpāj\ *n* : ATTENDANT; *esp* : one employed to deliver messages

[2]**page** *vb* **paged; pag·ing** : to summon by repeatedly calling out the name of

[3]**page** *n* : a single leaf (as of a book); *also* : a single side of such a leaf

[4]**page** *vb* **paged; pag·ing** : to mark or number the pages of

pag·eant \ˈpaj-ənt\ *n* [ME *pagyn, padgeant,* lit., scene of a play, fr. ML *pagina,* fr. L, page] : an elaborate spectacle, show, or procession esp. with tableaux or floats — **pag·eant·ry** \-ən-trē\ *n*

page·boy \ˈpāj-ˌbȯi\ *n* [[1]*page*] : an often shoulder-length hairdo with the ends of the hair turned under in a smooth roll

pag·er \ˈpā-jər\ *n* : one that pages; *esp* : BEEPER

pag·i·nate \ˈpaj-ə-ˌnāt\ *vb* **-nat·ed; -nat·ing** : [4]PAGE

pag·i·na·tion \ˌpaj-ə-ˈnā-shən\ *n* **1** : the paging of written or printed matter **2** : the number and arrangement of pages (as of a book)

pa·go·da \pə-ˈgōd-ə\ *n* : a tower with roofs curving upward at the division of each of several stories ⟨Chinese ~⟩

paid *past and past part of* PAY

pail \ˈpāl\ *n* : a usu. cylindrical vessel with a handle — **pail·ful** \-ˌfu̇l\ *n*

[1]**pain** \ˈpān\ *n* **1** : PUNISHMENT, PENALTY **2** : suffering or distress of body or mind; *also* : a sensation marked by discomfort (as throbbing or aching) **3** *pl* : great care — **pain·ful** \-fəl\ *adj* — **pain·ful·ly** \-ē\ *adv* — **pain·less** *adj* — **pain·less·ly** *adv*

[2]**pain** *vb* : to cause or experience pain

pain·kill·er \ˈpān-ˌkil-ər\ *n* : something (as a drug) that relieves pain — **pain·kill·ing** \-iŋ\ *adj*

pains·tak·ing \ˈpān-ˌstā-kiŋ\ *adj* : taking pains : showing care — **pains·taking** *n* — **pains·tak·ing·ly** *adv*

[1]**paint** \ˈpānt\ *vb* **1** : to apply color, pigment, or paint to **2**

: to produce or portray in lines or colors on a surface; *also* : to practice the art of painting **3** : to decorate with colors **4** : to use cosmetics **5** : to describe vividly **6** : SWAB — **paint·er** *n*

[2]**paint** *n* **1** : something produced by painting **2** : MAKEUP **3** : a mixture of a pigment and a liquid that forms a thin adherent coating when spread on a surface; *also* : the dry pigment used in making this mixture **4** : an applied coating of paint

paint·brush \ˈpānt-ˌbrəsh\ *n* : a brush for applying paint

paint·ing \ˈpānt-iŋ\ *n* **1** : a work (as a picture) produced by painting **2** : the art or occupation of painting

[1]**pair** \ˈpaər\ *n, pl* **pairs** *also* **pair** [ME *paire,* fr. OF, fr. L *paria* equal things, fr. neut. pl. of *par* equal] **1** : two things of a kind designed for use together **2** : something made up of two corresponding pieces ⟨a ~ of trousers⟩ **3** : a set of two people or animals ⟨a carriage and ~⟩ ⟨a married ~⟩

[2]**pair** *vb* **1** : to arrange in pairs **2** : to form a pair : MATCH **3** : to become associated with another

pai·sa \pī-ˈsä\ *n, pl* **paisa** *or* **pai·se** \-ˈsā\ — see *rupee, taka* at MONEY table

pais·ley \ˈpāz-lē\ *adj, often cap* : decorated with colorful curved abstract figures ⟨a ~ shawl⟩

Pai·ute \ˈpī-ˌ(y)üt\ *n* : a member of an American Indian people orig. of Utah, Arizona, Nevada, and California

pa·ja·mas \pə-ˈjäm-əz, -ˈjam-\ *n pl* : a loose suit for sleeping or lounging

Pak·i·stani \ˌpak-i-ˈstan-ē, ˌpäk-i-ˈstän-ē\ *n* : a native or inhabitant of Pakistan — **Pakistani** *adj*

pal \ˈpal\ *n* : a close friend

pal·ace \ˈpal-əs\ *n* [ME *palais,* fr. OF, fr. L *palatium,* fr. *Palatium,* the Palatine Hill in Rome where the emperors' residences were built] **1** : the official residence of a sovereign **2** : MANSION

pal·a·din \ˈpal-əd-ən\ *n* : a knightly supporter of a medieval prince

pa·laes·tra \pə-ˈles-trə\ *n, pl* **-trae** \-(ˌ)trē\ : a school in ancient Greece or Rome for sports (as wrestling)

pa·lan·quin \ˌpal-ən-ˈkēn\ *n* : an enclosed couch for one person borne on the shoulders of men by means of poles

pal·at·able \ˈpal-ət-ə-bəl\ *adj* : agreeable to the taste **syn** appetizing, savory, tasty, toothsome

pal·a·tal \ˈpal-ət-ᵊl\ *adj* **1** : of or relating to the palate **2** : pronounced with the front of the tongue near or touching the hard palate ⟨the \y\ in *yeast* and the \sh\ in *she* are ~ sounds⟩

pal·a·tal·ize \ˈpal-ət-ᵊl-ˌīz\ *vb* **-ized; -iz·ing** : to pronounce as or change into a palatal sound — **pal·a·tal·iza·tion** \ˌpal-ət-ᵊl-ə-ˈzā-shən\ *n*

pal·ate \ˈpal-ət\ *n* **1** : the roof of the mouth consisting of an anterior bony part and a posterior membranous fold **2** : TASTE

pa·la·tial \pə-ˈlā-shəl\ *adj* **1** : of, relating to, or being a palace **2** : MAGNIFICENT

pa·lat·i·nate \pə-ˈlat-ᵊn-ət\ *n* : the territory of a palatine

[1]**pal·a·tine** \ˈpal-ə-ˌtīn\ *adj* **1** : of or relating to a palace : PALATIAL **2** : possessing royal privileges; *also* : of or relating to a palatine or a palatinate

[2]**palatine** *n* **1** : a high officer of an imperial palace **2** : a feudal lord having sovereign power within his domains

pa·la·ver \pə-ˈlav-ər, -ˈläv-\ *n* [Pg *palavra* word, speech, fr. LL *parabola* parable, speech] : a long parley : TALK — **palaver** *vb*

[1]**pale** \ˈpāl\ *adj* **pal·er; pal·est 1** : deficient in color : WAN ⟨~ face⟩ **2** : lacking in brightness : DIM ⟨~ star⟩ **3** : light in color or shade ⟨~ blue⟩ — **pale·ness** *n*

[2]**pale** *vb* **paled; pal·ing** : to make or become pale

[3]**pale** *vb* **paled; pal·ing** : to enclose with or as if with pales : FENCE

[4]**pale** *n* **1** : a stake or picket of a fence **2** : an enclosed place; *also* : a district or territory within certain bounds or under a particular jurisdiction **3** : LIMITS, BOUNDS ⟨conduct beyond the ~⟩

pale·face \ˈpāl-ˌfās\ *n* : a white person

Pa·leo·cene \ˈpā-lē-ə-ˌsēn\ *adj* : of, relating to, or being the earliest epoch of the Tertiary — **Paleocene** *n*

pa·le·og·ra·phy \ˌpā-lē-ˈäg-rə-fē\ *n* : the study of ancient writings and inscriptions — **pa·le·og·ra·pher** \-fər\ *n*

Pa·leo·lith·ic \ˌpā-lē-ə-ˈlith-ik\ *adj* : of or relating to an early period of the Stone Age characterized by rough or chipped stone implements

pa·le·on·tol·o·gy \ˌpā-lē-ˌän-ˈtäl-ə-jē\ *n* : a science dealing with the life of past geologic periods esp. as known from fossil remains — **pa·le·on·tol·o·gist** \-ˌän-ˈtäl-ə-jəst, -ən-\ *n*

Pa·leo·zo·ic \ˌpā-lē-ə-ˈzō-ik\ *adj* : of, relating to, or being the era of geologic history between the Proterozoic and Mesozoic and extending from about 620 million years ago to about 230 million years ago — **Paleozoic** *n*

pal·ette \ˈpal-ət\ *n* : a thin often oval board on which a painter lays and mixes colors; *also* : the colors on a palette

pal·frey \ˈpȯl-frē\ *n, pl* **palfreys** *archaic* : a saddle horse; *esp* : one suitable for a woman

pa·limp·sest \ˈpal-əmp-ˌsest\ *n* [L *palimpsestus,* fr. Gk *palimpsēstos* scraped again] : writing material (as a parchment) used after the erasure of earlier writing

pal·in·drome \ˈpal-ən-ˌdrōm\ *n* : a word, verse, or sentence (as 'Able was I ere I saw Elba') that reads the same backward or forward

pal·ing \ˈpā-liŋ\ *n* **1** : a fence of pales **2** : material for pales **3** : PALE, PICKET

pal·in·ode \ˈpal-ə-ˌnōd\ *n* : an ode or song of recantation or retraction

pal·i·sade \ˌpal-ə-ˈsād\ *n* **1** : a high fence of stakes esp. for defense **2** : a line of steep cliffs

[1]**pall** \ˈpȯl\ *vb* **1** : to lose in interest or attraction **2** : SATIATE, CLOY

[2]**pall** *n* **1** : a heavy cloth draped over a coffin **2** : something that produces a gloomy atmosphere

pal·la·di·um \pə-ˈlād-ē-əm\ *n* : a silver-white metallic chemical element used esp. as a catalyst and in alloys — see ELEMENT table

pall·bear·er \ˈpȯl-ˌbar-ər\ *n* : a person who attends the coffin at a funeral

[1]**pal·let** \ˈpal-ət\ *n* : a small, hard, or makeshift bed

[2]**pallet** *n* : a portable platform for transporting and storing materials

pal·li·ate \ˈpal-ē-ˌāt\ *vb* **-at·ed; -at·ing 1** : to ease without curing **2** : to cover by excuses and apologies — **pal·li·a·tion** \ˌpal-ē-ˈā-shən\ *n* — **pal·li·a·tive** \ˈpal-ē-ˌāt-iv\ *adj or n*

pal·lid \ˈpal-əd\ *adj* : PALE, WAN

pal·lor \ˈpal-ər\ *n* : PALENESS

[1]**palm** \ˈpäm, ˈpälm\ *n* [ME, fr. OE, fr. L *palma* palm of the hand, palm tree; fr. the resemblance of the tree's leaves to the outstretched hand] **1** : any of a family of mostly tropical trees, shrubs, or vines usu. with a tall unbranched stem topped by a crown of large leaves **2** : a symbol of victory; *also* : VICTORY

[2]**palm** *n* : the underpart of the hand between the fingers and the wrist

[3]**palm** *vb* **1** : to conceal in or with the hand ⟨~ a card⟩ **2** : to impose by fraud

pal·mate \ˈpal-ˌmāt, ˈpä(l)m-ˌāt\ *also* **pal·mat·ed** \-ˌmāt-əd, -ˌāt-\ *adj* : resembling a hand with the fingers spread

palm·er \ˈpäm-ər, ˈpäl-mər\ *n* : a person wearing two crossed palm leaves as a sign of having gone on a pilgrimage to the Holy Land

pal·met·to \pal-ˈmet-ō\ *n, pl* **-tos** *or* **-toes** : any of several usu. small palms with fan-shaped leaves

palm·ist·ry \ˈpäm-ə-strē, ˈpäl-mə-\ *n* : the practice of reading a person's character or future from the markings on the palms — **palm·ist** \ˈpäm-əst, ˈpäl-məst\ *n*

Palm Sunday *n* : the Sunday preceding Easter and commemorating Christ's triumphal entry into Jerusalem

palmy \ˈpäm-ē, ˈpäl-mē\ *adj* **palm·i·er; -est 1** : abounding in or bearing palms **2** : FLOURISHING, PROSPEROUS

pal·o·mi·no \ˌpal-ə-ˈmē-nō\ *n, pl* **-nos** [AmerSp, fr. Sp, like a dove, fr. L *palumbinus,* fr. *palumbes* wood pigeon] : a horse with a pale cream to golden coat and cream or white mane and tail

pal·pa·ble \ˈpal-pə-bəl\ *adj* **1** : capable of being touched or felt : TANGIBLE **2** : OBVIOUS, PLAIN **syn** perceptible, sensible, appreciable, tangible, detectable — **pal·pa·bly** \-blē\ *adv*

pal·pate \ˈpal-ˌpāt\ *vb* **pal·pat·ed; pal·pat·ing** : to examine by touch esp. medically — **pal·pa·tion** \pal-ˈpā-shən\ *n*

pal·pi·tate \ˈpal-pə-ˌtāt\ *vb* **-tat·ed; -tat·ing** : to beat strongly and irregularly : THROB, QUIVER — **pal·pi·ta·tion** \ˌpal-pə-ˈtā-shən\ *n*

pal·sy \ˈpȯl-zē\ *n, pl* **palsies 1** : PARALYSIS **2** : a condition marked by tremor — **pal·sied** \-zēd\ *adj*

pal·ter \ˈpȯl-tər\ *vb* **pal·tered; pal·ter·ing** \-t(ə-)riŋ\ **1** : to act insincerely : EQUIVOCATE **2** : HAGGLE

pal·try \ˈpȯl-trē\ *adj* **pal·tri·er; -est 1** : TRASHY ⟨a ~ pamphlet⟩ **2** : MEAN ⟨a ~ trick⟩ **3** : TRIVIAL ⟨~ excuses⟩ **4** : MEAGER, MEASLY ⟨a ~ sum⟩

pam *abbr* pamphlet

pam·pa \ˈpam-pə, ˈpäm-\ *n, pl* **pam·pas** \-pəz, -pəs\ : a grassy So. American plain

pam·per \ˈpam-pər\ *vb* **pam·pered; pam·per·ing** \-p(ə-)riŋ\ : to treat with excessive attention : INDULGE **syn** coddle, humor, baby, spoil

pam·phlet \ˈpam-flət\ *n* [ME *pamflet* unbound booklet, fr. *Pamphilus seu De Amore* Pamphilus or On Love, popular Latin love poem of the 12th cent.] : an unbound printed publication

pam·phle·teer \ˌpam-flə-ˈtir\ *n* : a writer of pamphlets attacking something or urging a cause

[1]**pan** \ˈpan\ *n* **1** : a usu. broad, shallow, and open container for domestic use; *also* : something resembling such a container **2** : a basin or depression in land **3** : HARDPAN

[2]**pan** *vb* **panned; pan·ning 1** : to wash earth or gravel in a pan in searching for gold **2** : to criticize severely ⟨a new play *panned* by the critics⟩

Pan *abbr* Panama

pan·a·cea \ˌpan-ə-ˈsē-ə\ *n* : a remedy for all ills or difficulties

pa·nache \pə-ˈnash, -ˈnäsh\ *n* [MF *pennache,* deriv. of LL *pinnaculum* small wing] **1** : an ornamental tuft (as of feathers) esp. on a helmet **2** : dash or flamboyance in style and action

pan·a·ma \ˈpan-ə-ˌmä, -ˌmȯ\ *n, often cap* : a handmade hat braided from strips of the leaves from a tropical American tree

pan·a·tela \ˌpan-ə-ˈtel-ə\ *n* [Sp, fr. AmerSp, a long thin biscuit, deriv. of L *panis* bread] : a long slender cigar with straight sides rounded off at the sealed end

pan·cake \ˈpan-ˌkāk\ *n* : a flat cake made of thin batter and fried on both sides

pan·chro·mat·ic \ˌpan-krō-ˈmat-ik\ *adj* : sensitive to light of all colors ⟨~ film⟩

pan·cre·as \ˈpaŋ-krē-əs, ˈpan-\ *n* : a large gland that produces insulin and discharges enzymes into the intestine — **pan·cre·at·ic** \ˌpaŋ-krē-ˈat-ik, ˌpan-\ *adj*

pan·da \ˈpan-də\ *n* **1** : a long-tailed Himalayan mammal related to and resembling the racoon **2** : a large black-and-white mammal of western China usu. classified with the bears

pan·dem·ic \pan-ˈdem-ik\ *n* : a widespread outbreak of disease — **pandemic** *adj*

pan·de·mo·ni·um \ˌpan-də-ˈmō-nē-əm\ *n* : a wild uproar : TUMULT

[1]**pan·der** \ˈpan-dər\ *n* **1** : a go-between in love intrigues **2** : PIMP **3** : someone who caters to or exploits others' desires or weaknesses

[2]**pander** *vb* **pan·dered; pan·der·ing** \-d(ə-)riŋ\ : to act as a pander

P and L *abbr* profit and loss

pan·dow·dy \pan-ˈdau̇d-ē\ *n, pl* **-dies** : a deep-dish apple dessert spiced, sweetened, and covered with a crust

pane \ˈpān\ *n* : a sheet of glass (as in a door or window)

pan·e·gy·ric \ˌpan-ə-ˈjir-ik\ *n* : a eulogistic oration or writing — **pan·e·gyr·ist** \-ˈjir-əst\ *n*

[1]**pan·el** \ˈpan-ᵊl\ *n* **1** : a list of persons appointed for special duty ⟨a jury ~⟩; *also* : a group of people taking part in a discussion or quiz program **2** : a section of something (as a wall or door) often sunk below the level of the frame; *also* : a flat piece of construction material **3** : a flat piece of wood on which a picture is painted **4** : a board mounting instruments or controls

[2]**panel** *vb* **-eled** *or* **-elled; -el·ing** *or* **-el·ling** : to decorate with panels

pan·el·ing \ˈpan-ᵊl-iŋ\ *n* : decorative panels

pan·el·ist \ˈpan-ᵊl-əst\ *n* : a member of a discussion or quiz panel

panel truck *n* : a small motortruck with a fully enclosed body

pang \ˈpaŋ\ *n* : a sudden sharp attack (as of pain)

[1]**pan·han·dle** \ˈpan-ˌhan-dᵊl\ *n* : a narrow projection of a larger territory (as a state)

[2]**panhandle** *vb* **-dled; -dling** \-ˌhan-d(ᵊ-)liŋ\ : to ask for money on the street — **pan·han·dler** \-d(ᵊ-)lər\ *n*

[1]**pan·ic** \ˈpan-ik\ *n* : a sudden overpowering fright **syn** terror, consternation, dismay, alarm, dread, fear — **pan·icky** \-i-kē\ *adj*

[2]**panic** *vb* **pan·icked** \-ikt\; **pan·ick·ing** : to affect or be affected with panic

pan·i·cle \ˈpan-i-kəl\ *n* : a compound loosely branched racemose flower cluster

pan·jan·drum \pan-ˈjan-drəm\ *n, pl* **-drums** *also* **-dra** \-drə\ : a powerful personage or pretentious official

pan·nier *also* **pan·ier** \ˈpan-yər\ *n* : a large basket esp. for bearing on the back

pan·o·ply \ˈpan-ə-plē\ *n, pl* **-plies 1** : a full suit of armor **2** : a protective covering **3** : an impressive array

pan·ora·ma \ˌpan-ə-ˈram-ə, -ˈräm-\ *n* **1** : a picture unrolled before one's eyes **2** : a complete view in every direction — **pan·oram·ic** \-ˈram-ik\ *adj*

pan out *vb* : TURN OUT; *esp* : SUCCEED

pan·sy \ˈpan-zē\ *n, pl* **pansies** [MF *pensée,* fr. *pensée* thought, fr. *penser* to think, fr. L *pensare* to ponder] : a low-growing garden herb related to the violet; *also* : its showy flower

[1]**pant** \ˈpant\ *vb* [ME *panten,* fr. MF *pantaisier,* fr. (assumed) VL *phantasiare* to have hallucinations, fr. Gk *phantasioun,* fr. *phantasia* appearance, imagination] **1** : to breathe in a labored manner **2** : YEARN **3** : THROB

[2]**pant** *n* : a panting breath or sound

[3]**pant** *n* **1** : an outer garment covering each leg separately and usu. extending from the waist to the ankle — usu. used in pl. **2** *pl* : PANTIE

pan·ta·loons \ˌpant-ᵊl-ˈünz\ *n pl* **1** : close-fitting trousers of the 19th century usu. having straps passing under the instep **2** : loose-fitting usu. shorter than ankle-length trousers

pan·the·ism \ˈpan-thē-ˌiz-əm\ *n* : a doctrine that equates God with the forces and laws of the universe — **pan·the·ist** \-əst\ *n* — **pan·the·is·tic** \ˌpan-thē-ˈis-tik\ *adj*

pan·the·on \ˈpan-thē-ˌän, -ən\ *n* **1** : a temple dedicated to all the gods **2** : a building serving as the burial place of or containing memorials to famous dead **3** : the gods of a people

pan·ther \ˈpan-thər\ *n, pl* **panthers** *also* **panther 1** : LEOP-

ARD; *esp* : one of a black form **2** : COUGAR **3** : JAGUAR
pant·ie *or* **panty** \ˈpant-ē\ *n, pl* **pant·ies** : a woman's or child's undergarment covering the lower trunk and made with closed crotch — usu. used in pl.
pan·to·mime \ˈpant-ə-ˌmīm\ *n* **1** : a play in which the actors use no words **2** : expression of something by bodily or facial movements only — **pantomime** *vb* — **pan·to·mim·ic** \ˌpant-ə-ˈmim-ik\ *adj*
pan·try \ˈpan-trē\ *n, pl* **pantries** : a storage room for food or dishes
pant·suit \ˈpant-ˌsüt\ *n* : a woman's outfit consisting usu. of a long jacket and pants of the same material
panty hose *n pl* : a one-piece undergarment for women consisting of hosiery combined with a panty
panty·waist \ˈpant-ē-ˌwāst\ *n* : SISSY
pap \ˈpap\ *n* : soft food for infants or invalids
pa·pa \ˈpäp-ə\ *n* : FATHER
pa·pa·cy \ˈpā-pə-sē\ *n, pl* **-cies** **1** : the office of pope **2** : a succession of popes **3** : the term of a pope's reign **4** *cap* : the system of government of the Roman Catholic Church
pa·pa·in \pə-ˈpā-ən, -ˈpī-ən\ *n* : an enzyme in the juice of unripe papayas that is used esp. as a meat tenderizer and in medicine
pa·pal \ˈpā-pəl\ *adj* : of or relating to the pope or to the Roman Catholic Church
pa·paw *n* **1** \pə-ˈpȯ\ : PAPAYA **2** \ˈpäp-ˌȯ\ : a No. American tree with yellow edible fruit; *also* : its fruit
pa·pa·ya \pə-ˈpī-ə\ *n* : a tropical American tree with large yellow black-seeded edible fruit; *also* : its fruit
pa·per \ˈpā-pər\ *n* [ME *papir*, fr. MF *papier*, fr. L *papyrus* papyrus, paper, fr. Gk *papyros* papyrus] **1** : a pliable substance made usu. of vegetable matter and used to write or print on, to wrap things in, or to cover walls; *also* : a single sheet of this substance **2** : a printed or written document **3** : NEWSPAPER **4** : WALLPAPER — **paper** *adj or vb* — **pa·pery** \ˈpā-p(ə-)rē\ *adj*
pa·per·back \-ˌbak\ *n* : a paper-covered book
pa·per·board \-ˌbōrd\ *n* : a material made from cellulose fiber (as wood pulp) like paper but usu. thicker
pa·per·hang·er \ˈpā-pər-ˌhaŋ-ər\ *n* : one that applies wallpaper — **pa·per·hang·ing** \-iŋ\ *n*
pa·per·weight \-ˌwāt\ *n* : an object used to hold down loose papers by its weight
pa·pier–mâ·ché \ˌpā-pər-mə-ˈshā, ˌpap-ˌyā-mə-, -ma-\ *n* [F, lit., chewed paper] : a molding material of wastepaper and additives (as glue) — **papier–mâché** *adj*
pa·pil·la \pə-ˈpil-ə\ *n, pl* **pa·pil·lae** \-ˈpil-(ˌ)ē, -ˌī\ [L, nipple] : a small projecting bodily part — **pap·il·lary** \ˈpap-ə-ˌler-ē, pə-ˈpil-ə-rē\ *adj*
pa·pil·lote \ˌpäp-ē-ˈ(y)ōt\ *n* [F] : a greased paper wrapper in which food is cooked
pa·poose \pa-ˈpüs, pə-\ *n* : a young child of No. American Indian parents
pa·pri·ka \pə-ˈprē-kə, pa-\ *n* [Hung] : a mild red spice made from the fruit of some sweet peppers
Pap smear \ˈpap-\ *n* : a method for the early detection of cancer
Pap test \ˈpap-\ *n* : PAP SMEAR
pap·ule \ˈpap-yül\ *n* : a small solid usu. conical lesion of the skin — **pap·u·lar** \-yə-lər\ *adj*
pa·py·rus \pə-ˈpī-rəs\ *n, pl* **pa·py·rus·es** *or* **pa·py·ri** \-(ˌ)rē, -ˌrī\ **1** : a tall grassy Egyptian sedge **2** : paper made from papyrus pith
[1]**par** \ˈpär\ *n* **1** : a stated value (as of a security) **2** : a common level : EQUALITY **3** : an accepted standard or normal condition **4** : the score standard set for each hole of a golf course — **par** *adj*
[2]**par** *abbr* **1** paragraph **2** parallel **3** parish
pa·ra \ˈpär-ə\ *n, pl* **paras** *or* **para** — see *dinar* at MONEY table
par·a·ble \ˈpar-ə-bəl\ *n* : a simple story told to illustrate a moral truth
pa·rab·o·la \pə-ˈrab-ə-lə\ *n* : a plane curve generated by a point moving so that its distance from a fixed point is equal to its distance from a fixed line : a curve formed by the intersection of a cone with a plane parallel to its side — **par·a·bol·ic** \ˌpar-ə-ˈbäl-ik\ *adj*
para·chute \ˈpar-ə-ˌshüt\ *n* : a device for slowing the descent of a person or object through the air that consists of a usu. hemispherical canopy beneath which the person or object is suspended — **parachute** *vb* — **par·a·chut·ist** \-ˌshüt-əst\ *n*
[1]**pa·rade** \pə-ˈrād\ *n* **1** : a pompous display : EXHIBITION ⟨a ~ of wealth⟩ **2** : MARCH, PROCESSION; *esp* : a ceremonial formation and march (as of troops) **3** : a place for strolling
[2]**parade** *vb* **pa·rad·ed; pa·rad·ing** **1** : to march in a parade **2** : PROMENADE **3** : SHOW OFF **4** : MASQUERADE
par·a·digm \ˈpar-ə-ˌdīm, -ˌdim\ *n* **1** : MODEL, PATTERN **2** : a systematic inflection of a verb or noun showing a complete conjugation or declension
par·a·dise \ˈpar-ə-ˌdīs, -ˌdīz\ *n* [ME *paradis*, fr. OF, fr. LL *paradisus*, fr. Gk *paradeisos*, lit., enclosed park, of Iranian origin] **1** : HEAVEN **2** : a place or state of bliss
par·a·di·si·a·cal \ˌpar-ə-də-ˈsī-ə-kəl\ *or* **par·a·dis·i·ac** \-ˈdiz-ē-ˌak, -ˈdis-\ *adj* : of, relating to, or resembling paradise
par·a·dox \ˈpar-ə-ˌdäks\ *n* : a statement that seems contrary to common sense and yet is perhaps true — **par·a·dox·i·cal** \ˌpar-ə-ˈdäk-si-kəl\ *adj* — **par·a·dox·i·cal·ly** \-k(ə-)lē\ *adv*
par·af·fin \ˈpar-ə-fən\ *n* : a waxy substance used esp. for making candles and sealing foods
par·a·gon \ˈpar-ə-ˌgän, -gən\ *n* : a model of perfection : PATTERN
[1]**para·graph** \ˈpar-ə-ˌgraf\ *n* : a subdivision of a written composition that deals with one point or gives the words of one speaker; *also* : a character (as ¶) marking the beginning of a paragraph
[2]**paragraph** *vb* : to divide into paragraphs
par·a·keet \ˈpar-ə-ˌkēt\ *n* : any of numerous usu. small slender parrots with a long graduated tail
para·le·gal \ˌpar-ə-ˈlē-gəl\ *adj* : of, relating to, or being a paraprofessional who assists a lawyer — **paralegal** *n*
Par·a·li·pom·e·non \ˌpar-ə-lə-ˈpäm-ə-ˌnän\ *n* — see BIBLE table
par·al·lax \ˈpar-ə-ˌlaks\ *n* : the difference in apparent direction of an object as seen from two different points
[1]**par·al·lel** \ˈpar-ə-ˌlel\ *adj* [L *parallelus*, fr. Gk *parallēlos*, fr. *para* beside + *allēlōn* of one another, fr. *allos* . . . *allos* one . . . another, fr. *allos* other] **1** : lying or moving in the same direction but always the same distance apart **2** : similar in essential parts : LIKE — **par·al·lel·ism** \-ˌiz-əm\ *n*
[2]**parallel** *n* **1** : a parallel line, curve, or surface **2** : one of the imaginary circles on the earth's surface that parallel the equator and mark the latitude **3** : something essentially similar to another **4** : LIKENESS, SIMILARITY
[3]**parallel** *vb* **1** : COMPARE **2** : to correspond to **3** : to extend in a parallel direction with
par·al·lel·o·gram \ˌpar-ə-ˈlel-ə-ˌgram\ *n* : a 4-sided geometrical figure with opposite sides equal and parallel
pa·ral·y·sis \pə-ˈral-ə-səs\ *n, pl* **-y·ses** \-ˌsēz\ : loss of function and esp. of feeling or the power of voluntary motion — **par·a·lyt·ic** \ˌpar-ə-ˈlit-ik\ *adj or n*
par·a·lyze \ˈpar-ə-ˌlīz\ *vb* **-lyzed; -lyz·ing** **1** : to affect with paralysis **2** : to make powerless or inactive — **par·a·lyz·ing·ly** \-ˌlī-ziŋ-lē\ *adv*
par·a·me·cium \ˌpar-ə-ˈmē-sh(ē-)əm, -sē-əm\ *n, pl* **-cia**

\-sh(ē-)ə, -sē-ə\ *also* **-ci·ums** : any of a genus of slipper-shaped protozoans that move by cilia

para·med·i·cal \ˌpar-ə-ˈmed-i-kəl\ *adj* : concerned with supplementing the work of trained medical professionals — **para·med·ic** \ˌpar-ə-ˈmed-ik\ *n*

pa·ram·e·ter \pə-ˈram-ət-ər\ *n* **1** : an arbitrary constant whose value characterizes a member of a system (as a family of curves) **2** : a physical property whose value determines the characteristics or behavior of a system **3** : a characteristic element : FACTOR — **para·met·ric** \ˌpar-ə-ˈme-trik\ *adj*

para·mil·i·tary \ˌpar-ə-ˈmil-ə-ˌter-ē\ *adj* : formed on a military pattern esp. as an auxiliary military force

par·a·mount \ˈpar-ə-ˌmau̇nt\ *adj* : superior to all others : SUPREME **syn** preponderant, predominant, dominant, chief, sovereign

par·amour \ˈpar-ə-ˌmu̇r\ *n* : an illicit lover

para·noia \ˌpar-ə-ˈnȯi-ə\ *n* : a psychosis marked by delusions and irrational suspicion usu. without hallucinations — **par·a·noid** \ˈpar-ə-ˌnȯid\ *adj or n*

par·a·pet \ˈpar-ə-pət, -ˌpet\ *n* **1** : a protecting rampart **2** : a low wall or railing (as at the edge of a bridge)

par·a·pher·na·lia \ˌpar-ə-fə(r)-ˈnāl-yə\ *n sing or pl* **1** : personal belongings **2** : EQUIPMENT, APPARATUS

para·phrase \ˈpar-ə-ˌfrāz\ *n* : a restatement of a text giving the meaning in different words — **paraphrase** *vb*

para·ple·gia \ˌpar-ə-ˈplē-j(ē-)ə\ *n* : paralysis of the lower trunk and legs — **para·ple·gic** \-jik\ *adj or n*

para·pro·fes·sion·al \-prə-ˈfesh-(ə-)nəl\ *n* : a trained aide who assists a professional

para·psy·chol·o·gy \ˌpar-ə-sī-ˈkäl-ə-jē\ *n* : a branch of study involving the investigation of telepathy and related subjects — **para·psy·chol·o·gist** \-jəst\ *n*

par·a·site \ˈpar-ə-ˌsīt\ *n* [MF, fr. L *parasitus*, fr. Gk *parasitos*, fr. *para-* beside + *sitos* grain, food] **1** : a plant or animal living in or on another organism usu. to its harm **2** : one depending on another and not making adequate return — **par·a·sit·ic** \ˌpar-ə-ˈsit-ik\ *adj* — **par·a·sit·ism** \ˈpar-ə-sə-ˌtiz-əm, -ˌsīt-ˌiz-\ *n* — **par·a·sit·ize** \-sə-ˌtīz\ *vb*

par·a·si·tol·o·gy \ˌpar-ə-sə-ˈtäl-ə-jē\ *n* : a branch of biology dealing with parasites and parasitism esp. among animals — **par·a·si·tol·o·gist** \-jəst\ *n*

para·sol \ˈpar-ə-ˌsȯl\ *n* [F, fr. It *parasole*, fr. *parare* to shield + *sole* sun, fr. L *sol*] : a lightweight umbrella used as a shield against the sun

para·sym·pa·thet·ic nervous system \ˌpar-ə-ˌsim-pə-ˈthet-ik-\ *n* : the part of the autonomic nervous system that tends to induce secretion, to increase the tone and contractility of smooth muscle, and to cause the dilatation of blood vessels

para·thi·on \ˌpar-ə-ˈthī-ən, -ˌän\ *n* : an extremely toxic insecticide

para·thy·roid \-ˈthī-ˌrȯid\ *n* : PARATHYROID GLAND — **parathyroid** *adj*

parathyroid gland *n* : any of usu. four small endocrine glands that are adjacent to or embedded in the thyroid gland and produce a hormone concerned with calcium metabolism

para·troop·er \ˈpar-ə-ˌtrü-pər\ *n* : a member of the paratroops

para·troops \-ˌtrüps\ *n pl* : troops trained to parachute from an airplane

para·ty·phoid \ˌpar-ə-ˈtī-ˌfȯid, -tī-ˈfȯid\ *n* : a food poisoning resembling typhoid fever

par·boil \ˈpär-ˌbȯil\ *vb* : to boil briefly

[1]**par·cel** \ˈpär-səl\ *n* **1** : a tract or plot of land **2** : COLLECTION, LOT **3** : a wrapped bundle : PACKAGE

[2]**parcel** *vb* **-celed** *or* **-celled; -cel·ing** *or* **-cel·ling** \ˈpär-s(ə-)liŋ\ : to divide into portions

parcel post *n* **1** : a mail service handling parcels **2** : packages handled by parcel post

parch \ˈpärch\ *vb* **1** : to toast under dry heat **2** : to shrivel with heat

parch·ment \ˈpärch-mənt\ *n* : the skin of an animal prepared for writing on; *also* : a writing on such material

pard \ˈpärd\ *n* : LEOPARD

[1]**par·don** \ˈpärd-ᵊn\ *n* : excuse of an offense without penalty; *esp* : an official release from legal punishment

[2]**pardon** *vb* **par·doned; par·don·ing** \ˈpärd-(ᵊ-)niŋ\ : to free from penalty : EXCUSE, FORGIVE — **par·don·able** \ˈpärd-(ᵊ-)nə-bəl\ *adj*

par·don·er \ˈpärd-(ᵊ-)nər\ *n* **1** : a medieval preacher delegated to raise money for religious works by soliciting offerings and granting indulgences **2** : one that pardons

pare \ˈpaər\ *vb* **pared; par·ing** **1** : to trim or shave off an outside part (as the skin or rind) of ⟨~ an apple⟩ **2** : to reduce as if by paring ⟨~ expenses⟩ — **par·er** *n*

par·e·go·ric \ˌpar-ə-ˈgȯr-ik\ *n* : an alcoholic preparation of opium and camphor

par·ent \ˈpar-ənt\ *n* **1** : one that begets or brings forth offspring : FATHER, MOTHER **2** : SOURCE, ORIGIN — **par·ent·age** \-ij\ *n* — **pa·ren·tal** \pə-ˈrent-ᵊl\ *adj* — **par·ent·hood** *n*

pa·ren·the·sis \pə-ˈren-thə-səs\ *n, pl* **-the·ses** \-ˌsēz\ **1** : a word, phrase, or sentence inserted in a passage to explain or modify the thought **2** : one of a pair of punctuation marks () used esp. to enclose parenthetic matter — **par·en·thet·ic** \ˌpar-ən-ˈthet-ik\ *or* **par·en·thet·i·cal** \-i-kəl\ *adj* — **par·en·thet·i·cal·ly** \-k(ə-)lē\ *adv*

pa·ren·the·size \pə-ˈren-thə-ˌsīz\ *vb* **-sized; -siz·ing** : to make a parenthesis of

par·ent·ing \ˈpar-ənt-iŋ, ˈper-\ *n* : the raising of a child by its parents

pa·re·sis \pə-ˈrē-səs, ˈpar-ə-\ *n, pl* **pa·re·ses** \-ˌsēz\ : a usu. incomplete paralysis; *also* : insanity caused by syphilitic alteration of the brain that leads to dementia and paralysis

par ex·cel·lence \ˌpär-ˌek-sə-ˈläⁿs\ *adj* [F, lit., by excellence] : being the best of a kind : PREEMINENT

par·fait \pär-ˈfā\ *n* [F, lit., something perfect, fr. *parfait* perfect, fr. L *perfectus*] **1** : a flavored custard containing whipped cream and a syrup frozen without stirring **2** : a cold dessert made of layers of fruit, syrup, ice cream, and whipped cream

pa·ri·ah \pə-ˈrī-ə\ *n* : OUTCAST

pa·ri·etal \pə-ˈrī-ət-ᵊl\ *adj* **1** : of, relating to, or forming the walls of an anatomical structure **2** : of or relating to college living or its regulation

pari–mu·tu·el \ˌpar-i-ˈmyü-chə(-wə)l\ *n* : a betting system in which winners share the total stakes minus a percentage for the management

par·ing \ˈpar-iŋ\ *n* : something pared off ⟨potato ~*s*⟩

pa·ri pas·su \ˌpar-i-ˈpas-ü\ *adv or adj* [L, with equal step] : at an equal rate or pace

Par·is green \ˌpar-əs-\ *n* : a poisonous bright green powder used as a pigment and as an insecticide

par·ish \ˈpar-ish\ *n* **1** : a church district in the care of one pastor; *also* : the residents of such an area **2** : a local church community **3** : a civil division of the state of Louisiana : COUNTY

pa·rish·io·ner \pə-ˈrish-(ə-)nər\ *n* : a member or resident of a parish

par·i·ty \ˈpar-ət-ē\ *n, pl* **-ties** : EQUALITY, EQUIVALENCE

[1]**park** \ˈpärk\ *n* **1** : a tract of ground kept as a game preserve or recreation area **2** : a level valley between mountain ranges **3** : a place where vehicles (as automobiles) are parked **4** : an enclosed stadium used esp. for ball games

[2]**park** *vb* **1** : to leave a vehicle temporarily (as in a parking lot or garage) **2** : to set and leave temporarily

par·ka \ˈpär-kə\ *n* : a very warm jacket with a hood

Par·kin·son's disease \ˈpär-kən-sənz-\ *n* : a chronic progressive nervous disease of later life that is marked by tremor and weakness of resting muscles and by a peculiar gait

Par·kin·son's Law *n* **1** : an observation in office organization: the number of subordinates increases at a fixed rate regardless of the amount of work produced **2** : an observation in office organization: work expands so as to fill the time available for its completion

park·way \ˈpärk-ˌwā\ *n* : a broad landscaped thoroughfare

par·lance \ˈpär-ləns\ *n* **1** : SPEECH **2** : manner of speaking ⟨military ~⟩

¹par·lay \ˈpär-ˌlā, -lē\ *vb* : to increase or change into something of much greater value

²parlay *n* : a series of bets in which the original stake plus its winnings are risked on successive wagers

par·ley \ˈpär-lē\ *n, pl* **parleys** : a conference usu. over matters in dispute : DISCUSSION — **parley** *vb*

par·lia·ment \ˈpär-lə-mənt\ *n* **1** : a formal governmental conference **2** *cap* : an assembly that constitutes the supreme legislative body of a country (as the United Kingdom) — **par·lia·men·ta·ry** \ˌpär-lə-ˈmen-t(ə-)rē\ *adj*

par·lia·men·tar·i·an \ˌpär-lə-ˌmen-ˈter-ē-ən\ *n* **1** *often cap* : an adherent of the parliament in opposition to the king during the English Civil War **2** : an expert in parliamentary procedure

par·lor \ˈpär-lər\ *n* **1** : a room for conversation or the reception of guests **2** : a place of business ⟨beauty ~⟩

par·lour \ˈpär-lər\ *chiefly Brit var of* PARLOR

par·lous \ˈpär-ləs\ *adj* : full of danger or risk : PRECARIOUS ⟨~ state of a country's finances⟩ — **par·lous·ly** *adv*

Par·me·san \ˈpär-mə-ˌzän, -ˌzan\ *n* : a hard dry cheese with a sharp flavor

par·mi·gia·na \ˌpär-mi-ˈjän-ə, ˌpär-mi-ˈzhän\ *or* **par·mi·gia·no** \-ˈjän-(ˌ)ō\ *adj* : made or covered with Parmesan cheese ⟨veal ~⟩

pa·ro·chi·al \pə-ˈrō-kē-əl\ *adj* **1** : of or relating to a church parish **2** : limited in scope : NARROW, PROVINCIAL — **pa·ro·chi·al·ism** \-ə-ˌliz-əm\ *n*

parochial school *n* : a school maintained by a religious body

par·o·dy \ˈpar-əd-ē\ *n, pl* **-dies** [L *parodia,* fr. Gk *parōidia,* fr. *para-* beside + *aidein* to sing] : a humorous or satirical imitation — **parody** *vb*

pa·role \pə-ˈrōl\ *n* : a conditional release of a prisoner before his sentence expires — **parole** *vb* — **pa·rol·ee** \-ˌrō-ˈlē, -ˈrō-ˌlē\ *n*

par·ox·ysm \ˈpar-ək-ˌsiz-əm, pə-ˈräk-\ *n* : a sudden sharp attack (as of pain or coughing) : SPASM **syn** convulsion, fit — **par·ox·ys·mal** \ˌpar-ək-ˈsiz-məl, pə-ˌräk-\ *adj*

par·quet \ˈpär-ˌkā, pär-ˈkā\ *n* [F] **1** : a flooring of parquetry **2** : the lower floor of a theater; *esp* : the forward part of the orchestra

par·que·try \ˈpär-kə-trē\ *n, pl* **-tries** : fine woodwork inlaid in patterns

par·ra·keet *var of* PARAKEET

par·ri·cide \ˈpar-ə-ˌsīd\ *n* **1** : one that murders his or her father, mother, or a close relative **2** : the act of a parricide

par·rot \ˈpar-ət\ *n* : any of numerous bright-colored tropical birds that have a stout hooked bill

parrot fever *n* : an infectious disease of birds that is marked by diarrhea and wasting and is transmissible to man

par·ry \ˈpar-ē\ *vb* **par·ried; par·ry·ing 1** : to ward off a weapon or blow **2** : to evade esp. by an adroit answer — **parry** *n*

parse \ˈpärs *also* ˈpärz\ *vb* **parsed; pars·ing** : to give a grammatical description of a word or a group of words

par·sec \ˈpär-ˌsek\ *n* : a unit of measure for interstellar space equal to 3.26 light-years or 19.2 trillion miles

par·si·mo·ny \ˈpär-sə-ˌmō-nē\ *n* : extreme or excessive frugality — **par·si·mo·ni·ous** \ˌpär-sə-ˈmō-nē-əs\ *adj* — **par·si·mo·ni·ous·ly** *adv*

pars·ley \ˈpär-slē\ *n* : a garden plant with finely divided leaves used as a seasoning or garnish

pars·nip \ˈpär-snəp\ *n* : a garden plant with a long edible root; *also* : this root

par·son \ˈpärs-ᵊn\ *n* [ME *persone,* fr. OF, fr. ML *persona,* lit., person, fr. L] : a usu. Protestant clergyman

par·son·age \ˈpärs-(ᵊ-)nij\ *n* : a house provided by a church for its pastor

¹part \ˈpärt\ *n* **1** : a division or portion of a whole **2** : the melody or score for a particular voice or instrument ⟨the alto ~⟩ **3** : a spare piece for a machine **4** : DUTY, FUNCTION **5** : one of the sides in a dispute ⟨took his friend's ~⟩ **6** : ROLE; *also* : an actor's lines in a play **7** *pl* : TALENTS, ABILITY **8** : the line where one's hair divides (as in combing)

²part *vb* **1** : to take leave of someone **2** : to divide or break into parts : SEPARATE **3** : to go away : DEPART; *also* : DIE **4** : to give up possession ⟨~*ed* with her jewels⟩ **5** : APPORTION, SHARE

³part *abbr* **1** participial; participle **2** particular

par·take \pär-ˈtāk, pər-\ *vb* **-took** \-ˈtu̇k\; **-tak·en** \-ˈtā-kən\; **-tak·ing 1** : to have a share or part **2** : to take a portion (as of food) — **par·tak·er** *n*

par·terre \pär-ˈteər\ *n* [F, fr. MF, fr. *par terre* on the ground] **1** : an ornamental arrangement of flower beds **2** : the part of a theater floor behind the orchestra

par·the·no·gen·e·sis \ˌpär-thə-nō-ˈjen-ə-səs\ *n* [NL, fr. Gk *parthenos* virgin + L *genesis* genesis] : development of a new individual from an unfertilized egg — **par·the·no·ge·net·ic** \-jə-ˈnet-ik\ *adj*

par·tial \ˈpär-shəl\ *adj* **1** : favoring one party over the other : BIASED **2** : markedly or foolishly fond — used with *to* **3** : not total or general : affecting a part only — **par·tial·i·ty** \ˌpärsh-(ē-)ˈal-ət-ē\ *n* — **par·tial·ly** \ˈpärsh-(ə-)lē\ *adv*

par·tic·i·pate \pər-ˈtis-ə-ˌpāt, pär-\ *vb* **-pat·ed; -pat·ing 1** : to take part in something ⟨~ in a game⟩ **2** : SHARE — **par·tic·i·pant** \-pənt\ *adj or n* — **par·tic·i·pa·tion** \-ˌtis-ə-ˈpā-shən\ *n* — **par·tic·i·pa·tor** \-ˈtis-ə-ˌpāt-ər\ *n* — **par·tic·i·pa·to·ry** \-ˈtis-ə-pə-ˌtōr-ē\ *adj*

par·ti·ci·ple \ˈpärt-ə-ˌsip-əl\ *n* : a word having the characteristics of both verb and adjective — **par·ti·cip·i·al** \ˌpärt-ə-ˈsip-ē-əl\ *adj*

par·ti·cle \ˈpärt-i-kəl\ *n* **1** : a very small bit of matter **2** : ELEMENTARY PARTICLE **3** : a unit of speech (as an article, preposition, or conjunction) expressing some general aspect of meaning or some connective or limiting relation

par·ti·cle·board \-ˌbōrd\ *n* : a board made of very small pieces of wood bonded together

par·ti–col·or \ˌpärt-ē-ˈkəl-ər\ *or* **par·ti–col·ored** \-ərd\ *adj* : showing different colors or tints; *esp* : having patches of two or more colors

¹par·tic·u·lar \pə(r)-ˈtik-yə-lər\ *adj* **1** : of or relating to a specific person or thing ⟨the laws of a ~ state⟩ **2** : DISTINCTIVE, SPECIAL ⟨the ~ point of his talk⟩ **3** : SEPARATE, INDIVIDUAL ⟨each ~ hair⟩ **4** : attentive to details : PRECISE **5** : hard to please : EXACTING **syn** single, sole, unique, lone, solitary — **par·tic·u·lar·i·ty** \-ˌtik-yə-ˈlar-ət-ē\ *n* — **par·tic·u·lar·ly** \-ˈtik-yə-lər-lē\ *adv*

²particular *n* : an individual fact or detail

par·tic·u·lar·ize \pə(r)-ˈtik-yə-lə-ˌrīz\ *vb* **-ized; -iz·ing 1** : to state in detail : SPECIFY **2** : to go into details

par·tic·u·late \pər-ˈtik-yə-lət, pär-, -ˌlāt\ *adj* : relating to or existing as minute separate particles

¹part·ing \ˈpärt-iŋ\ *n* **1** : SEPARATION, DIVISION **2** : the action of leaving one another ⟨lovers' ~⟩ **3** : a place of separation or divergence

[2]**parting** *adj* : given, taken, or performed at parting ⟨a ~ kiss⟩

par·ti·san *or* **par·ti·zan** \ˈpärt-ə-zən, -sən\ *n* **1** : one that takes the part of another : ADHERENT **2** : GUERRILLA — **partisan** *adj* — **par·ti·san·ship** *n*

par·tite \ˈpär-ˌtīt\ *adj* : divided into a usu. specified number of parts

par·ti·tion \pər-ˈtish-ən, pär-\ *n* **1** : DIVISION **2** : something that divides or separates; *esp* : an interior wall dividing one part of a house from another — **partition** *vb*

par·ti·tive \ˈpärt-ət-iv\ *adj* : of, relating to, or denoting a part ⟨a ~ construction⟩

part·ly \ˈpärt-lē\ *adv* : in part : in some measure or degree

part·ner \ˈpärt-nər\ *n* **1** : ASSOCIATE, COLLEAGUE **2** : either of two persons who dance together **3** : one who plays on the same team with another **4** : HUSBAND, WIFE **5** : one of two or more persons contractually associated as joint principals in a business — **part·ner·ship** *n*

part of speech : a traditional class of words distinguished according to the kind of idea denoted and the function performed in a sentence

par·tridge \ˈpär-trij\ *n, pl* **partridge** *or* **par·tridg·es** : any of various stout-bodied game birds

part–song \ˈpärt-ˌsȯŋ\ *n* : a song with two or more voice parts

part–time \-ˈtīm\ *adj or adv* : involving or working less than a full or regular schedule

par·tu·ri·tion \ˌpärt-ə-ˈrish-ən, ˌpär-chə-, ˌpär-tyu̇-\ *n* : CHILDBIRTH

part·way \ˈpärt-ˈwā\ *adv* : to some extent : PARTLY

par·ty \ˈpärt-ē\ *n, pl* **parties** **1** : a person or group taking one side of a question; *esp* : a group of persons organized for the purpose of directing the policies of a government **2** : a person or group concerned in an action or affair : PARTICIPANT **3** : a group of persons detailed for a common task **4** : a social gathering

par·ve·nu \ˈpär-və-ˌn(y)ü\ *n* [F, fr. pp. of *parvenir* to arrive, fr. L *pervenire*, fr. *per* through + *venire* to come] : one who has recently or suddenly risen to wealth or power and has not yet secured the social position associated with it

pas \ˈpä\ *n, pl* **pas** \ˈpä(z)\ *n* : a dance step or combination of steps

pas·cal \pas-ˈkal\ *n* : a unit of pressure in the metric system equal to one newton per square meter

pas·chal \ˈpas-kəl\ *adj* [deriv. of Heb *pesah* Passover] : of, relating to, appropriate for, or used during Passover or Easter ceremonies

pa·sha \ˈpäsh-ə, ˈpash-; pə-ˈshä\ *n* : a man (as formerly a governor in Turkey) of high rank

[1]**pass** \ˈpas\ *vb* **1** : MOVE, PROCEED **2** : to go away; *also* : DIE **3** : to move past, beyond, or over **4** : to allow to elapse : SPEND **5** : to go or make way through **6** : to go or allow to go unchallenged **7** : to undergo transfer **8** : to render a legal judgment **9** : OCCUR **10** : to secure the approval of (as a legislature) **11** : to go or cause to go through an inspection, test, or course of study successfully **12** : to be regarded **13** : CIRCULATE **14** : VOID **15** : to transfer the ball or puck to another player **16** : to decline to bid or bet on one's hand in a card game **17** : to permit to reach first base by a base on balls — **pass·er** *n*

[2]**pass** *n* : a gap in a mountain range

[3]**pass** *n* **1** : the act or an instance of passing **2** : REALIZATION, ACCOMPLISHMENT **3** : a state of affairs **4** : a written authorization to leave, enter, or move about freely **5** : a transfer of a ball or puck from one player to another **6** : BASE ON BALLS **7** : EFFORT, TRY **8** : a sexually inviting gesture or approach

[4]**pass** *abbr* **1** passenger **2** passive

pass·able \ˈpas-ə-bəl\ *adj* **1** : capable of being passed or traveled on **2** : just good enough : TOLERABLE — **pass·ably** \-blē\ *adv*

pas·sage \ˈpas-ij\ *n* **1** : the action or process of passing **2** : a means (as a road or corridor) of passing **3** : a voyage esp. by sea or air **4** : a right or permission to pass **5** : ENACTMENT **6** : a mutual act (as an exchange of blows) **7** : a usu. brief portion or section (as of a book)

pas·sage·way \-ˌwā\ *n* : a way that allows passage

pass·book \ˈpas-ˌbu̇k\ *n* : BANKBOOK

pas·sé \pa-ˈsā\ *adj* **1** : past one's prime **2** : not up-to-date : OUTMODED

pas·sel \ˈpas-əl\ *n* : a large number

pas·sen·ger \ˈpas-ᵊn-jər\ *n* : a traveler in a public or private conveyance

passe–par·tout \ˌpas-pər-ˈtü\ *n* [F] : something that passes or enables one to pass everywhere

pass·er·by \ˈpas-ər-ˌbī\ *n, pl* **pass·ers·by** \-ərz-\ : one who passes by

pas·ser·ine \ˈpas-ə-ˌrīn\ *adj* : of or relating to the large order of birds comprising singing birds that perch

pas·sim \ˈpas-əm\ *adv* [L, fr. *passus* scattered, fr. pp. of *pandere* to spread] : here and there : THROUGHOUT

pass·ing \ˈpas-iŋ\ *n* : the act of one that passes or causes to pass; *esp* : DEATH

pas·sion \ˈpash-ən\ *n* **1** *often cap* : the sufferings of Christ between the night of the Last Supper and his death **2** : strong feeling; *also pl* : the emotions as distinguished from reason **3** : RAGE, ANGER **4** : LOVE; *also* : an object of affection or enthusiasm **5** : sexual desire — **pas·sion·ate** \ˈpash-(ə-)nət\ *adj* — **pas·sion·ate·ly** *adv* — **pas·sion·less** *adj*

pas·sion·flow·er \ˈpash-ən-ˌflau̇(-ə)r\ *n* [trans. of L *flos passionis*; fr. the fancied resemblance of parts of the flower to the instruments of Christ's crucifixion] : any of a genus of chiefly tropical woody climbing vines or erect herbs with showy flowers and pulpy often edible berries

passion fruit *n* : the edible fruit of a passionflower

pas·sive \ˈpas-iv\ *adj* **1** : not active : acted upon **2** : asserting that the grammatical subject is subjected to or affected by the action represented by the verb ⟨~ voice⟩ **3** : making use of the sun's heat usu. without the aid of mechanical devices **4** : SUBMISSIVE, PATIENT — **passive** *n* — **pas·sive·ly** *adv* — **pas·siv·i·ty** \pa-ˈsiv-ət-ē\ *n*

pass·key \ˈpas-ˌkē\ *n* : a key for opening two or more locks

pass out *vb* : to lose consciousness

Pass·over \ˈpas-ˌō-vər\ *n* [fr. the exemption of the Israelites from the slaughter of the firstborn in Egypt (Exod 12:23–27)] : a Jewish holiday celebrated in March or April in commemoration of the Hebrews' liberation from slavery in Egypt

pass·port \ˈpas-ˌpōrt\ *n* : an official document issued by a country upon request to a citizen requesting protection during travel abroad

pass up *vb* : DECLINE, REJECT

pass·word \ˈpas-ˌwərd\ *n* **1** : a word or phrase that must be spoken by a person before he is allowed to pass a guard **2** : a sequence of characters required for access to a computer system

[1]**past** \ˈpast\ *adj* **1** : AGO ⟨10 years ~⟩ **2** : just gone or elapsed ⟨the ~ month⟩ **3** : having existed or taken place in a period before the present : BYGONE **4** : of, relating to, or constituting a verb tense that expresses time gone by

[2]**past** *prep or adv* : BEYOND

[3]**past** *n* **1** : time gone by **2** : something that happened or was done in a former time **3** : the past tense; *also* : a verb form in it **4** : a secret past life

pas·ta \ˈpäs-tə\ *n* [It] **1** : a paste in processed form (as spaghetti) or in the form of fresh dough (as ravioli) **2** : a dish of cooked pasta

[1]**paste** \ˈpāst\ *n* **1** : DOUGH **2** : a smooth food product made by evaporation or grinding ⟨almond ~⟩ **3** : a shaped dough (as spaghetti or ravioli) **4** : a preparation (as of

flour and water) for sticking things together **5** : a brilliant glass of high lead content used in imitation gems

[2]paste *vb* **past·ed; past·ing** : to cause to adhere by paste : STICK

paste·board \ˈpās(t)-ˌbōrd\ *n* : a stiff material made of sheets of paper pasted together; *also* : PAPERBOARD

[1]pas·tel \pas-ˈtel\ *n* **1** : a paste made of powdered pigment; *also* : a crayon of such paste **2** : a drawing in pastel **3** : a pale or light color

[2]pastel *adj* **1** : of or relating to a pastel **2** : pale and light in color

pas·tern \ˈpas-tərn\ *n* : the part of a horse's foot extending from the fetlock to the top of the hoof

pas·teur·i·za·tion \ˌpas-chə-rə-ˈzā-shən, ˌpas-tə-\ *n* : partial sterilization of a substance (as milk) by heat or radiation — **pas·teur·ize** \ˈpas-chə-ˌrīz, ˈpas-tə-\ *vb* — **pas·teur·iz·er** *n*

pas·tiche \pas-ˈtēsh\ *n* : a composition (as in literature or music) made up of selections from different works

pas·tille \pas-ˈtēl\ *n* **1** : a small mass of aromatic paste for fumigating or scenting the air of a room **2** : an aromatic or medicated lozenge

pas·time \ˈpas-ˌtīm\ *n* : DIVERSION

pas·tor \ˈpas-tər\ *n* [ME *pastour,* fr. OF, fr. L *pastor,* herdsman, fr. *pastus,* pp. of *pascere* to feed] : a clergyman serving a local church or parish — **pas·tor·ate** \-t(ə-)rət\ *n*

[1]pas·to·ral \ˈpas-t(ə-)rəl\ *adj* **1** : of or relating to shepherds or to rural life **2** : of or relating to spiritual guidance esp. of a congregation **3** : of or relating to the pastor of a church

[2]pastoral \ˈpas-t(ə-)rəl\ *n* : a literary work dealing with shepherds or rural life

pas·to·rale \ˌpas-tə-ˈräl, -ˈral\ *n* [It] : a musical composition having a pastoral theme

past participle *n* : a participle that typically expresses completed action, that is one of the principal parts of the verb, and that is used in the formation of perfect tenses in the active voice and of all tenses in the passive voice

pas·tra·mi *also* **pas·tro·mi** \pə-ˈsträm-ē\ *n* [Yiddish] : a highly seasoned smoked beef prepared esp. from shoulder cuts

pas·try \ˈpā-strē\ *n, pl* **pastries** : sweet baked goods made of dough or with a crust made of enriched dough

pas·tur·age \ˈpas-chə-rij\ *n* : PASTURE

[1]pas·ture \ˈpas-chər\ *n* **1** : plants (as grass) for the feeding of grazing livestock **2** : land or a plot of land used for grazing

[2]pasture *vb* **pas·tured; pas·tur·ing 1** : GRAZE **2** : to use as pasture

pasty \ˈpā-stē\ *adj* **past·i·er; -est** : resembling paste; *esp* : pallid and unhealthy in appearance

[1]pat \ˈpat\ *n* **1** : a light tap esp. with the hand or a flat instrument; *also* : the sound made by it **2** : something (as butter) shaped into a small flat usu. square individual portion

[2]pat *adv* : in a pat manner : APTLY, PERFECTLY

[3]pat *vb* **pat·ted; pat·ting 1** : to strike lightly with a flat instrument **2** : to flatten, smooth, or put into place or shape with a pat **3** : to tap gently or lovingly with the hand

[4]pat *adj* **1** : exactly suited to the occasion **2** : memorized exactly **3** : UNYIELDING

[5]pat *abbr* patent

pa·ta·ca \pə-ˈtäk-ə\ *n* — see MONEY table

[1]patch \ˈpach\ *n* **1** : a piece used to cover a torn or worn place; *also* : one worn on a garment as an ornament or insignia **2** : a small area distinct from that about it **3** : a shield worn over the socket of an injured or missing eye

[2]patch *vb* **1** : to mend or cover with a patch **2** : to make of fragments **3** : to repair usu. in hasty fashion

patch test *n* : a test for allergic sensitivity made by applying to the unbroken skin small pads soaked with the allergen to be tested

patch·work \ˈpach-ˌwərk\ *n* : something made of pieces of different materials, shapes, or colors

pate \ˈpāt\ *n* : HEAD; *esp* : the crown of the head

pâ·té \pä-ˈtā\ *n* [F] **1** : a meat or fish pie or patty **2** : a spread of finely mashed seasoned and spiced meat

pa·tel·la \pə-ˈtel-ə\ *n, pl* **-lae** \-ˈtel-(ˌ)ē, -ˌī\ *or* **-las** [L] : KNEECAP

pat·en \ˈpat-ᵊn\ *n* **1** : PLATE; *esp* : one of precious metal for the eucharistic bread **2** : a thin disk

[1]pa·tent *1 & 4 are* ˈpat-ᵊnt, *Brit also* ˈpāt-, *2 & 3 are* ˈpat-ᵊnt, ˈpāt-\ *adj* **1** : open to public inspection — used chiefly in the phrase *letters patent* **2** : free from obstruction **3** : EVIDENT, OBVIOUS **4** : protected by a patent **syn** manifest, distinct, apparent, palpable, plain, clear — **pat·ent·ly** *adv*

[2]pat·ent \ˈpat-ᵊnt, *Brit also* ˈpāt-\ *n* **1** : an official document conferring a right or privilege **2** : a document securing to an inventor for a term of years exclusive right to his invention **3** : something patented — **pat·en·tee** \ˌpat-ᵊn-ˈtē, *Brit also* ˌpāt-\ *n*

[3]pat·ent *vb* : to secure by patent

pa·ter·fa·mil·i·as \ˌpāt-ər-fə-ˈmil-ē-əs\ *n, pl* **pa·tres·fa·mil·i·as** \ˌpā-ˌtrēz-\ [L] : the father of a family : the male head of a household

pa·ter·nal \pə-ˈtərn-ᵊl\ *adj* **1** : FATHERLY **2** : related through or inherited or derived from a father — **pa·ter·nal·ly** \-ē\ *adv*

pa·ter·nal·ism \-ˌiz-əm\ *n* : a system under which an authority treats those under its control paternally (as by regulating their conduct and supplying their needs)

pa·ter·ni·ty \pə-ˈtər-nət-ē\ *n* **1** : FATHERHOOD **2** : descent from a father

[1]path \ˈpath, ˈpȧth\ *n, pl* **paths** \ˈpat͟hz, ˈpaths, ˈpȧt͟hz, ˈpȧths\ **1** : a trodden way **2** : ROUTE, COURSE — **path·less** *adj*

[2]path *or* **pathol** *abbr* pathology

pa·thet·ic \pə-ˈthet-ik\ *adj* : evoking tenderness, pity, or sorrow **syn** pitiful, piteous, pitiable, poor — **pa·thet·i·cal·ly** \-i-k(ə-)lē\ *adv*

path·find·er \ˈpath-ˌfīn-dər, ˈpȧth-\ *n* : one that discovers a way; *esp* : one that explores untraveled regions to mark out a new route

patho·gen \ˈpath-ə-jən\ *n* : a specific cause (as a bacterium or virus) of disease — **patho·gen·ic** \ˌpath-ə-ˈjen-ik\ *adj* — **patho·ge·nic·i·ty** \-jə-ˈnis-ət-ē\ *n*

pa·thol·o·gy \pə-ˈthäl-ə-jē\ *n, pl* **-gies 1** : the study of the essential nature of disease **2** : the abnormality of structure and function characteristic of a disease — **path·o·log·i·cal** \ˌpath-ə-ˈläj-i-kəl\ *adj* — **pa·thol·o·gist** \pə-ˈthäl-ə-jəst\ *n*

pa·thos \ˈpā-ˌthäs\ *n* : an element in experience or artistic representation evoking pity or compassion

path·way \ˈpath-ˌwā, ˈpȧth-\ *n* : PATH

pa·tience \ˈpā-shəns\ *n* **1** : the capacity, habit, or fact of being patient **2** *chiefly Brit* : SOLITAIRE 2

[1]pa·tient \ˈpā-shənt\ *adj* **1** : bearing pain or trials without complaint **2** : showing self-control : CALM **3** : STEADFAST, PERSEVERING — **pa·tient·ly** *adv*

[2]patient *n* : a person under medical care

pa·ti·na \ˈpat-ə-nə, pə-ˈtē-nə\ *n, pl* **pa·ti·nas** \-nəz\ *or* **pa·ti·nae** \ˈpat-ə-ˌnē, -ˌnī\ : a green film formed on copper and bronze by exposure to moist air

pa·tio \ˈpat-ē-ˌō, ˈpät-\ *n, pl* **pa·ti·os 1** : COURTYARD **2** : a paved recreation area near a house

pa·tois \ˈpa-ˌtwä\ *n, pl* **pa·tois** \-ˌtwäz\ [F] **1** : a dialect other than the standard dialect; *esp* : illiterate or provincial speech **2** : JARGON 2

pa·tri·arch \ˈpā-trē-ˌärk\ *n* **1** : a man revered as father or founder (as of a tribe) **2** : a venerable old man **3** : an ecclesiastical dignitary (as the bishop of an Eastern Orthodox see) — **pa·tri·ar·chal** \ˌpā-trē-ˈär-kəl\ *adj* — **pa·tri·arch·ate** \ˈpā-trē-ˌär-kət, -ˌkāt\ *n* — **pa·tri·ar·chy** \-ˌär-kē\ *n*

pa·tri·cian \pə-ˈtrish-ən\ *n* : a person of high birth : ARISTOCRAT — **patrician** *adj*

pat·ri·cide \ˈpa-trə-ˌsīd\ *n* **1** : one who murders his own father **2** : the murder of one's own father

pat·ri·mo·ny \ˈpa-trə-ˌmō-nē\ *n* : something (as an estate) inherited or derived esp. from one's father : HERITAGE — **pat·ri·mo·ni·al** \ˌpat-rə-ˈmō-nē-əl\ *adj*

pa·tri·ot \ˈpā-trē-ət, -ˌät\ *n* [MF *patriote*, fr. LL *patriota*, fr. Gk *patriōtēs*, fr. *patrios* of one's father, fr. *patr-*, *patēr* father] : one who loves his country — **pa·tri·ot·ic** \ˌpā-trē-ˈät-ik\ *adj* — **pa·tri·ot·i·cal·ly** \-i-k(ə-)lē\ *adv* — **pa·tri·o·tism** \ˈpā-trē-ə-ˌtiz-əm\ *n*

pa·tris·tic \pə-ˈtris-tik\ *adj* : of or relating to the church fathers or their writings

1**pa·trol** \pə-ˈtrōl\ *n* : the action of going the rounds (as of an area) for observation or the maintenance of security; *also* : a person or group performing such an action

2**patrol** *vb* **pa·trolled; pa·trol·ling** [F *patrouiller*, fr. MF, to tramp around in the mud, fr. *patte* paw] : to carry out a patrol

pa·trol·man \pə-ˈtrōl-mən\ *n* : a policeman assigned to a beat

patrol wagon *n* : an enclosed motortruck for carrying prisoners

pa·tron \ˈpā-trən\ *n* [ME, fr. MF, fr. ML & L; ML *patronus* patron saint, patron of a benefice, pattern, fr. L, defender, fr. *patr-*, *pater* father] **1** : a person chosen or named as special protector **2** : a wealthy or influential supporter ⟨~ of poets⟩; *also* : BENEFACTOR **3** : a regular client or customer **syn** sponsor, guarantor, angel, backer

pa·tron·ess \ˈpā-trə-nəs\ *n* : a woman who is a patron

pa·tron·age \ˈpa-trə-nij, ˈpā-\ *n* **1** : the support or influence of a patron **2** : the trade of customers **3** : control of appointment to government jobs

pa·tron·ize \ˈpā-trə-ˌnīz, ˈpa-\ *vb* **-ized; -iz·ing** **1** : to be a customer of **2** : to treat condescendingly

pat·ro·nym·ic \ˌpa-trə-ˈnim-ik\ *n* : a name derived from the name of one's father or paternal ancestor usu. by the addition of a prefix or suffix

pa·troon \pə-ˈtrün\ *n* : the proprietor of a manorial estate esp. in New York under Dutch rule

pat·sy \ˈpat-sē\ *n*, *pl* **pat·sies** : one who is duped or victimized

1**pat·ter** \ˈpat-ər\ *vb* : to talk glibly or mechanically **syn** chatter, prate, chat, prattle, babble

2**patter** *n* **1** : a specialized lingo **2** : extremely rapid talk ⟨a comedian's ~⟩

3**patter** *vb* : to strike, pat, or tap rapidly

4**patter** *n* : a quick succession of taps or pats ⟨the ~ of rain⟩

1**pattern** \ˈpat-ərn\ *n* [ME *patron*, fr. MF, fr. ML *patronus*, fr. L, defender, fr. *patr-*, *pater* father] **1** : an ideal model **2** : something used as a model for making things ⟨a dressmaker's ~⟩ **3** : SAMPLE **4** : an artistic design **5** : CONFIGURATION

2**pattern** *vb* : to form according to a pattern

pat·ty *also* **pat·tie** \ˈpat-ē\ *n*, *pl* **patties** **1** : a little pie **2** : a small flat cake esp. of chopped food

pau·ci·ty \ˈpȯ-sət-ē\ *n* : smallness of number or quantity

paunch \ˈpȯnch\ *n* : a usu. large belly : POTBELLY — **paunchy** *adj*

pau·per \ˈpȯ-pər\ *n* : a person without means of support except from charity — **pau·per·ism** \-pə-ˌriz-əm\ *n* — **pau·per·ize** \-pə-ˌrīz\ *vb*

1**pause** \ˈpȯz\ *n* **1** : a temporary stop; *also* : a period of inaction **2** : a brief suspension of the voice **3** : a sign ⌒ or ◡ above or below a musical note or rest to show it is to be prolonged **4** : a reason for pausing

2**pause** *vb* **paused; paus·ing** : to stop, rest, or linger for a time

pave \ˈpāv\ *vb* **paved; pav·ing** : to cover (as a road) with hard material in order to smooth or firm the surface

pave·ment \ˈpāv-mənt\ *n* **1** : a paved surface **2** : the material with which something is paved

pa·vil·ion \pə-ˈvil-yən\ *n* [ME *pavilon*, fr. OF *paveillon*, fr. L *papilion-*, *papilio* butterfly] **1** : a large tent **2** : a light structure (as in a park) used for entertainment or shelter

pav·ing \ˈpā-viŋ\ *n* : PAVEMENT

1**paw** \ˈpȯ\ *n* : the foot of a quadruped (as a dog or lion) having claws

2**paw** *vb* **1** : to feel or handle clumsily or rudely **2** : to touch or strike with a paw; *also* : to scrape with a hoof **3** : to flail about or grab for with the hands

pawl \ˈpȯl\ *n* : a pivoted tongue or sliding bolt designed to fall into notches on another machine part to permit motion in one direction only

1**pawn** \ˈpȯn\ *n* **1** : goods deposited as security for a loan; *also* : HOSTAGE **2** : the state of being pledged

2**pawn** *vb* : to deposit as a pledge

3**pawn** *n* [ME *pown*, fr. MF *poon*, fr. ML *pedon-*, *pedo* foot soldier, fr. LL, one with broad feet, fr. L *ped-*, *pes* foot] : a chessman of the least value

pawn·bro·ker \ˈpȯn-ˌbrō-kər\ *n* : one who loans money on goods pledged

Paw·nee \pȯ-ˈnē\ *n*, *pl* **Pawnee** *or* **Pawnees** : a member of an American Indian people orig. of Kansas and Nebraska

pawn·shop \ˈpȯn-ˌshäp\ *n* : a pawnbroker's place of business

paw·paw *var of* PAPAW

1**pay** \ˈpā\ *vb* **paid** \ˈpād\ *also in sense 7* **payed; pay·ing** [ME *payen*, fr. OF *paier*, fr. L *pacare* to pacify, fr. *pac-*, *pax* peace] **1** : to make due return to for goods or services **2** : to discharge indebtedness for : SETTLE ⟨~ a bill⟩ **3** : to give in forfeit ⟨~ the penalty⟩ **4** : REQUITE **5** : to give, offer, or make freely or as fitting ⟨~ attention⟩ **6** : to be profitable to : RETURN **7** : to make slack and allow to run out ⟨~ out a rope⟩ — **pay·able** *adj* — **pay·ee** \pā-ˈē\ *n* — **pay·er** *n*

2**pay** *n* **1** : the status of being paid by an employer : EMPLOY **2** : something paid; *esp* : WAGES

3**pay** *adj* **1** : containing something valuable (as gold) ⟨~ dirt⟩ **2** : equipped to receive a fee for use ⟨~ telephone⟩

pay·check \ˈpā-ˌchek\ *n* **1** : a check in payment of wages or salary **2** : WAGES, SALARY

pay·load \ˈpā-ˌlōd\ *n* : the load carried by a vehicle in addition to what is necessary for its operation

pay·mas·ter \-ˌmas-tər\ *n* : one who distributes the payroll

pay·ment \ˈpā-mənt\ *n* **1** : the act of paying **2** : something paid

pay·off \-ˌȯf\ *n* **1** : payment at the outcome of an enterprise ⟨a big ~ from an investment⟩ **2** : the climax of an incident or enterprise ⟨the ~ of a story⟩

pay·roll \ˈpā-ˌrōl\ *n* : a list of persons entitled to receive pay; *also* : the money to pay those on such a list

payt *abbr* payment

pay up *vb* : to pay what is due; *also* : to pay in full

Pb *symbol* [L *plumbum*] lead

PBX *abbr* private branch exchange

PC *abbr* **1** Peace Corps **2** percent; percentage **3** personal computer **4** postcard **5** [L *post cibum*] after meals **6** professional corporation

PCB \ˈpē-ˈsē-ˈbē\ *n* : POLYCHLORINATED BIPHENYL

PCP \ˈpē-ˈsē-ˈpē\ *n* : PHENCYCLIDINE

pct *abbr* percent; percentage

pd *abbr* paid
Pd *symbol* palladium
PD *abbr* **1** per diem **2** police department **3** potential difference
PDQ \ˈpē-ˈdē-ˈkyü\ *adv, often not cap* [abbr. of *pretty damned quick*] : IMMEDIATELY
PDT *abbr* Pacific daylight time
PE *abbr* **1** physical education **2** printer's error **3** professional engineer
pea \ˈpē\ *n, pl* **peas** *also* **pease** \ˈpēz\ **1** : the round edible protein-rich seed borne in the pod of a widely grown leguminous vine; *also* : this vine **2** : any of various plants resembling or related to the pea
peace \ˈpēs\ *n* **1** : a state of calm and quiet; *esp* : public security under law **2** : freedom from disturbing thoughts or emotions **3** : a state of concord (as between persons or governments); *also* : an agreement to end hostilities — **peace·able** \-ə-bəl\ *adj* — **peace·ably** \-blē\ *adv* — **peace·ful** \-fəl\ *adj* — **peace·ful·ly** \-ē\ *adv*
peace·keep·ing \ˈpēs-ˌkē-piŋ\ *n* : the preserving of peace; *esp* : international enforcement and supervision of a truce — **peace·keep·er** \-pər\ *n*
peace·mak·er \-ˌmā-kər\ *n* : one who settles an argument or stops a fight
peace·time \-ˌtīm\ *n* : a time when a nation is not at war
peach \ˈpēch\ *n* [ME *peche*, fr. MF (the fruit), fr. LL *persica*, fr. L *persicum*, fr. neut. of *persicus* Persian, fr. *Persia*] : a sweet juicy fruit of a low tree with pink blossoms; *also* : this tree
pea·cock \ˈpē-ˌkäk\ *n* : the male peafowl having long tail coverts which can be spread at will displaying brilliant colors
pea·fowl \-ˌfau̇l\ *n* : a very large domesticated Asian pheasant
pea·hen \-ˌhen\ *n* : the female peafowl
[1]**peak** \ˈpēk\ *n* **1** : a pointed or projecting part **2** : the top of a hill or mountain; *also* : MOUNTAIN **3** : the front projecting part of a cap **4** : the narrow part of a ship's bow or stern **5** : the highest level or greatest degree — **peak** *adj*
[2]**peak** *vb* : to bring to or reach a maximum
peak·ed \ˈpē-kəd\ *adj* : THIN, SICKLY
[1]**peal** \ˈpēl\ *n* **1** : the loud ringing of bells **2** : a set of tuned bells **3** : a loud sound or succession of sounds
[2]**peal** *vb* : to give out peals : RESOUND
pea·nut \ˈpē-(ˌ)nət\ *n* **1** : an annual herb related to the pea but having pods that ripen underground; *also* : this pod or one of the edible seeds it bears **2** *pl* : a very small amount
pear \ˈpaər\ *n* : the fleshy fruit of a tree related to the apple; *also* : this tree
pearl \ˈpərl\ *n* **1** : a small hard often lustrous body formed within the shell of some mollusks and used as a gem **2** : one that is choice or precious ⟨~*s* of wisdom⟩ **3** : a slightly bluish medium gray — **pearly** \ˈpər-lē\ *adj*
peas·ant \ˈpez-ᵊnt\ *n* **1** : any of a class of small landowners or laborers tilling the soil **2** : a person of low social or cultural status — **peas·ant·ry** \-ᵊn-trē\ *n*
pea·shoot·er \ˈpē-ˌshüt-ər\ *n* : a toy blowgun for shooting peas
peat \ˈpēt\ *n* : a dark substance formed by partial decay of plants (as mosses) in water — **peaty** *adj*
peat moss *n* : SPHAGNUM
[1]**peb·ble** \ˈpeb-əl\ *n* : a small usu. round stone — **peb·bly** \-(ə-)lē\ *adj*
[2]**pebble** *vb* **peb·bled; peb·bling** \-(ə-)liŋ\ : to produce a rough surface texture in ⟨~ leather⟩
pe·can \pi-ˈkän, -ˈkan\ *n* : a large American hickory tree bearing a smooth-shelled edible nut; *also* : this nut
pec·ca·dil·lo \ˌpek-ə-ˈdil-ō\ *n, pl* **-loes** *or* **-los** : a slight offense
pec·ca·ry \ˈpek-ə-rē\ *n, pl* **-ries** : an American chiefly tropical mammal resembling but smaller than the related pigs
pec·ca·vi \pe-ˈkä-ˌvē\ *n* [L, I have sinned, fr. *peccare* to sin] : an acknowledgment of sin
[1]**peck** \ˈpek\ *n* — see WEIGHT table
[2]**peck** *vb* **1** : to strike or pierce with or as if with the bill **2** : to make (as a hole) by pecking **3** : to pick up with or as if with the bill
[3]**peck** *n* **1** : an impression made by pecking **2** : a quick sharp stroke; *also* : KISS
pecking order *also* **peck order** *n* : a basic pattern of social organization within a flock of poultry in which each bird pecks another lower in the scale without fear of retaliation and submits to pecking by one of higher rank; *also* : a social hierarchy
pec·tin \ˈpek-tən\ *n* : any of various water-soluble plant substances that cause fruit jellies to set — **pec·tic** \-tik\ *adj*
pec·to·ral \ˈpek-t(ə-)rəl\ *adj* : of or relating to the breast or chest
pec·u·late \ˈpek-yə-ˌlāt\ *vb* **-lat·ed; -lat·ing** : EMBEZZLE — **pec·u·la·tion** \ˌpek-yə-ˈlā-shən\ *n*
pe·cu·liar \pi-ˈkyül-yər\ *adj* [ME *peculier*, fr. L *peculiaris* of private property, special, fr. *peculium* private property, fr. *pecus* cattle] **1** : belonging exclusively to one person or group **2** : CHARACTERISTIC, DISTINCTIVE **3** : QUEER, ODD **syn** idiosyncratic, eccentric, singular, strange, weird — **pe·cu·liar·i·ty** \-ˌkyül-ˈyar-ət-ē, -ē-ˈar-\ *n* — **pe·cu·liar·ly** \-ˈkyül-yər-lē\ *adv*
pe·cu·ni·ary \pi-ˈkyü-nē-ˌer-ē\ *adj* : of or relating to money : MONETARY
ped·a·gogue *also* **ped·a·gog** \ˈped-ə-ˌgäg\ *n* : TEACHER, SCHOOLMASTER
ped·a·go·gy \ˈped-ə-ˌgōj-ē, -ˌgäj-\ *n* : the art or profession of teaching; *esp* : EDUCATION 2 — **ped·a·gog·ic** \ˌped-ə-ˈgäj-ik, -ˈgōj-\ *or* **ped·a·gog·i·cal** \-i-kəl\ *adj*
[1]**pedal** \ˈped-ᵊl\ *n* : a lever worked by the foot
[2]**ped·al** *adj* : of or relating to the foot
[3]**ped·al** \ˈped-ᵊl\ *vb* **-aled** *also* **-alled; -al·ing** *also* **-al·ling** \-(ᵊ-)liŋ\ **1** : to use or work a pedal (as of a piano or bicycle) **2** : to ride a bicycle
ped·ant \ˈped-ᵊnt\ *n* **1** : a person who makes a display of his learning **2** : a formal uninspired teacher — **pe·dan·tic** \pi-ˈdant-ik\ *adj* — **ped·ant·ry** \ˈped-ᵊn-trē\ *n*
ped·dle \ˈped-ᵊl\ *vb* **ped·dled; ped·dling** \ˈped-(ᵊ-)liŋ\ : to sell or offer for sale from place to place — **ped·dler** *also* **ped·lar** \ˈped-lər\ *n*
ped·er·ast \ˈped-ə-ˌrast\ *n* [Gk *paiderastēs*, lit., lover of boys] : one that practices anal intercourse esp. with a boy — **ped·er·as·ty** \ˈped-ə-ˌras-tē\ *n*
ped·es·tal \ˈped-əs-tᵊl\ *n* **1** : the support or foot of something (as a column, statue, or vase) that is upright **2** : a position of high regard
[1]**pe·des·tri·an** \pə-ˈdes-trē-ən\ *adj* **1** : COMMONPLACE **2** : going on foot
[2]**pedestrian** *n* : WALKER
pe·di·at·rics \ˌpēd-ē-ˈa-triks\ *n* : a branch of medicine dealing with the care and diseases of children — **pe·di·at·ric** \-trik\ *adj* — **pe·di·a·tri·cian** \ˌpēd-ē-ə-ˈtrish-ən\ *n*
pedi·cab \ˈped-i-ˌkab\ *n* : a pedal-driven tricycle with seats for a driver and two passengers
ped·i·cure \ˈped-i-ˌkyu̇r\ *n* : care of the feet, toes, and nails; *also* : a single treatment of these parts — **ped·i·cur·ist** \-ˌkyu̇r-əst\ *n*
ped·i·gree \ˈped-ə-ˌgrē\ *n* [ME *pedegru*, fr. MF *pie de grue* crane's foot; fr. the shape made by the lines of genealogical chart] **1** : a record of a line of ancestors **2** : an ancestral line — **ped·i·greed** \-grēd\ *adj*

---

ped·i·ment \ˈped-ə-mənt\ *n* : a low triangular gablelike decoration (as over a door or window) on a building

pediment

pe·dom·e·ter \pi-ˈdäm-ət-ər\ *n* : an instrument that measures the distance one walks
pe·dun·cle \ˈpē-ˌdəŋ-kəl\ *n* : a narrow supporting stalk
peek \ˈpēk\ *vb* **1** : to look furtively **2** : to peer from a place of concealment **3** : GLANCE — **peek** *n*
[1]**peel** \ˈpēl\ *n* : a skin or rind esp. of a fruit
[2]**peel** *vb* [ME *pelen*, fr. MF *peler*, fr. L *pilare* to remove the hair from, fr. *pilus* hair] **1** : to strip the skin, bark, or rind from **2** : to strip off (as a coat); *also* : to come off **3** : to lose the skin, bark, or rind
peel·ing \ˈpē-liŋ\ *n* : a peeled-off piece or strip (as of skin or rind)
peen \ˈpēn\ *n* : the usu. hemispherical or wedge-shaped end of the head of a hammer opposite the face
[1]**peep** \ˈpēp\ *vb* : to utter a feeble shrill sound
[2]**peep** *n* : a feeble shrill sound
[3]**peep** *vb* **1** : to look slyly esp. through an aperture : PEEK **2** : to begin to emerge — **peep·er** *n*
[4]**peep** *n* **1** : a first faint appearance **2** : a brief or furtive look
peep·hole \ˈpēp-ˌhōl\ *n* : a hole to peep through
[1]**peer** \ˈpiər\ *n* **1** : one of equal standing with another : EQUAL **2** : NOBLE — **peer·age** \-ij\ *n*
[2]**peer** *vb* **1** : to look intently or curiously **2** : to come slightly into view
peer·ess \ˈpir-əs\ *n* : a woman who is a peer
peer·less \ˈpiər-ləs\ *adj* : having no equal : MATCHLESS **syn** supreme, unequalled, unparalleled, incomparable
[1]**peeve** \ˈpēv\ *vb* **peeved; peev·ing** : to make resentful : ANNOY
[2]**peeve** *n* **1** : a feeling or mood of resentment **2** : a particular grievance
pee·vish \ˈpē-vish\ *adj* : querulous in temperament : FRETFUL **syn** irritable, petulant, huffy — **pee·vish·ly** *adv* — **pee·vish·ness** *n*
pee·wee \ˈpē-(ˌ)wē\ *n* : one that is diminutive or tiny
[1]**peg** \ˈpeg\ *n* **1** : a small pointed piece (as of wood) used to pin down or fasten things or to fit into holes **2** : a projecting piece used as a support or boundary marker **3** : SUPPORT, PRETEXT **4** : STEP, DEGREE **5** : THROW
[2]**peg** *vb* **pegged; peg·ging 1** : to put a peg into : fasten, pin down, or attach with or as if with pegs **2** : to work hard and steadily : PLUG **3** : HUSTLE **4** : to mark by pegs **5** : to hold (as prices) at a set level or rate **6** : THROW
peg·ma·tite \ˈpeg-mə-ˌtīt\ *n* : a coarse variety of granite occurring in veins
PEI *abbr* Prince Edward Island
pei·gnoir \pān-ˈwär, pen-\ *n* [F, lit., garment worn while combing the hair, fr. MF, fr. *peigner* to comb the hair, fr. L *pectinare*, fr. *pectin-*, *pecten* comb] : NEGLIGEE
pe·jo·ra·tive \pi-ˈjȯr-ət-iv, ˈpej-(ə-)rət-\ *adj* : having a tendency to make or become worse : DISPARAGING
peke \ˈpēk\ *n, often cap* : PEKINGESE
Pe·king·ese *or* **Pe·kin·ese** \ˌpē-kən-ˈēz, -kiŋ-, -ˈēs\ *n, pl* **Pekingese** *or* **Pekinese** : a small short-legged long-haired Chinese dog
pe·koe \ˈpē-(ˌ)kō\ *n* : a black tea made from small-sized tea leaves esp. in India and Ceylon
pel·age \ˈpel-ij\ *n* : the hairy covering of a mammal
pe·lag·ic \pə-ˈlaj-ik\ *adj* : OCEANIC
pelf \ˈpelf\ *n* : MONEY, RICHES
pel·i·can \ˈpel-i-kən\ *n* : a large web-footed bird having a pouched lower bill used to scoop in fish
pel·la·gra \pə-ˈlag-rə, -ˈlāg-\ *n* : a chronic disease marked by skin and digestive disorders and nervous symptoms and caused by a faulty diet
pel·let \ˈpel-ət\ *n* **1** : a little ball (as of medicine) **2** : BULLET — **pel·let·al** \-ᵊl\ *adj* — **pel·let·ize** \-ˌīz\ *vb*
pell–mell \ˈpel-ˈmel\ *adv* **1** : in mingled confusion **2** : HEADLONG
pel·lu·cid \pə-ˈlü-səd\ *adj* : extremely clear : LIMPID, TRANSPARENT **syn** translucent, lucid, lucent
[1]**pelt** \ˈpelt\ *n* : a skin esp. of a fur-bearing animal
[2]**pelt** *vb* : to strike with a succession of blows or missiles
pel·vis \ˈpel-vəs\ *n, pl* **pel·vis·es** \-və-səz\ *or* **pel·ves** \-ˌvēz\ : a basin-shaped part of the vertebrate skeleton consisting chiefly of the two large bones of the hip — **pel·vic** \-vik\ *adj*
pem·mi·can *also* **pem·i·can** \ˈpem-i-kən\ *n* : dried meat pounded fine and mixed with melted fat
[1]**pen** \ˈpen\ *n* **1** : a small enclosure for animals **2** : a small place of confinement or storage
[2]**pen** *vb* **penned; pen·ning** : to shut in a pen : ENCLOSE
[3]**pen** *n* : an instrument with a split point to hold ink used for writing; *also* : a fluid-using writing instrument
[4]**pen** *vb* **penned; pen·ning** : WRITE
[5]**pen** *n* : PENITENTIARY
[6]**pen** *abbr* peninsula
PEN *abbr* International Association of Poets, Playwrights, Editors, Essayists and Novelists
pe·nal \ˈpēn-ᵊl\ *adj* : of or relating to punishment
pe·nal·ize \ˈpēn-ᵊl-ˌīz, ˈpen-\ *vb* **-ized; -iz·ing** : to put a penalty on
pen·al·ty \ˈpen-ᵊl-tē\ *n, pl* **-ties 1** : punishment for crime or offense **2** : something forfeited when a person fails to do something agreed to **3** : disadvantage, loss, or hardship due to some action
pen·ance \ˈpen-əns\ *n* **1** : an act performed to show sorrow or repentance for sin **2** : a sacrament (as in the Roman Catholic Church) consisting of repentance, confession, a penance, and absolution
Pe·na·tes \pə-ˈnāt-ēz\ *n pl* : the Roman gods of the household
pence \ˈpens\ *pl of* PENNY
pen·chant \ˈpen-chənt\ *n* [F, fr. prp. of *pencher* to incline, fr. (assumed) VL *pendicare*, fr. L *pendere* to weigh] : a strong inclination : LIKING **syn** leaning, propensity, predilection, predisposition
[1]**pen·cil** \ˈpen-səl\ *n* : a writing or drawing tool consisting of or having a slender cylinder of a solid marking substance
[2]**pencil** *vb* **-ciled** *or* **-cilled; -cil·ing** *or* **-cil·ling** \-s(ə-)liŋ\ : to paint, draw, or write with a pencil
pen·dant *also* **pen·dent** \ˈpen-dənt\ *n* : a hanging ornament (as an earring)
pen·dent *or* **pen·dant** \ˈpen-dənt\ *adj* : SUSPENDED, OVERHANGING
[1]**pend·ing** \ˈpen-diŋ\ *prep* **1** : DURING **2** : while awaiting
[2]**pending** *adj* **1** : not yet decided **2** : IMMINENT
pen·du·lous \ˈpen-jə-ləs, -də-\ *adj* : hanging loosely : DROOPING
pen·du·lum \-ləm\ *n* : a body that swings freely from a fixed point
pe·ne·plain *also* **pe·ne·plane** \ˈpēn-i-ˌplān\ *n* : a large almost flat land surface shaped by erosion
pen·e·trate \ˈpen-ə-ˌtrāt\ *vb* **-trat·ed; -trat·ing 1** : to enter into : PIERCE **2** : PERMEATE **3** : to see into : UNDERSTAND **4** : to affect deeply — **pen·e·tra·ble** \-trə-bəl\ *adj* — **pen·e·tra·tion** \ˌpen-ə-ˈtrā-shən\ *n* — **pen·e·tra·tive** \ˈpen-ə-ˌtrāt-iv\ *adj*
pen·e·trat·ing \-ˌtrāt-iŋ\ *adj* **1** : having the power of entering, piercing, or pervading ⟨a ~ shriek⟩ ⟨a ~ odor⟩ **2** : ACUTE, DISCERNING ⟨a ~ look⟩
pen·guin \ˈpen-gwən, ˈpeŋ-\ *n* : any of several erect short-legged flightless seabirds of the southern hemisphere

pen·hold·er \ˈpen-ˌhōl-dər\ *n* **:** a holder or handle for a pen

pen·i·cil·lin \ˌpen-ə-ˈsil-ən\ *n* **:** any of several antibiotics produced by a green mold and used against various bacteria

pen·in·su·la \pə-ˈnin-sə-lə\ *n* [L *paeninsula*, fr. *paene* almost + *insula* island] **:** a long narrow portion of land extending out into the water — **pen·in·su·lar** \-lər\ *adj*

pe·nis \ˈpē-nəs\ *n, pl* **pe·nes** \-ˌnēz\ *or* **pe·nis·es** [L, penis, tail] **:** a male organ of copulation that in the human male also functions as the channel by which urine leaves the body

[1]**pen·i·tent** \ˈpen-ə-tənt\ *adj* **:** feeling sorrow for sins or offenses **:** REPENTANT — **pen·i·tence** \-təns\ *n* — **pen·i·ten·tial** \ˌpen-ə-ˈten-chəl\ *adj*

[2]**penitent** *n* **:** a penitent person

[1]**pen·i·ten·tia·ry** \ˌpen-ə-ˈtench-(ə-)rē\ *n, pl* **-ries :** a state or federal prison

[2]**pen·i·ten·tia·ry** *adj* **:** of, relating to, or incurring confinement in a penitentiary

pen·knife \ˈpen-ˌnīf\ *n* **:** a small pocketknife

pen·light *or* **pen·lite** \ˈpen-ˌlīt\ *n* **:** a small flashlight resembling a fountain pen in size or shape

pen·man \ˈpen-mən\ *n* **1 :** COPYIST **2 :** one skilled in penmanship **3 :** AUTHOR

pen·man·ship \-ˌship\ *n* **:** the art or practice of writing with the pen

Penn *or* **Penna** *abbr* Pennsylvania

pen name *n* **:** an author's pseudonym

pen·nant \ˈpen-ənt\ *n* **1 :** a tapering flag used esp. for signaling **2 :** a flag symbolic of championship

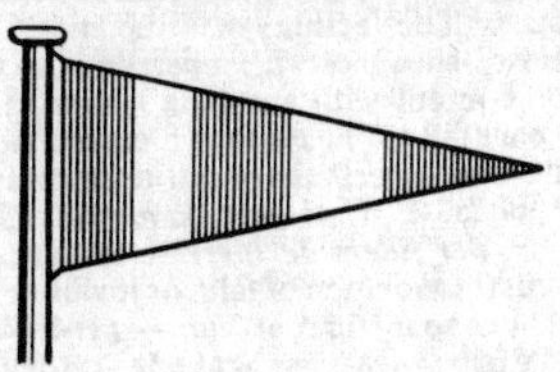

pennant

pen·ni \ˈpen-ē\ *n, pl* **pen·nia** \-ē-ə\ *or* **pen·nis** \-ēz\ — see *markka* at MONEY table

pen·non \ˈpen-ən\ *n* **1 :** a long narrow ribbonlike flag borne on a lance **2 :** WING

Penn·syl·va·nian \ˌpen-səl-ˈvā-nyən\ *adj* **:** of, relating to, or being the period of the Paleozoic era between the Mississippian and the Permian — **Pennsylvanian** *n*

pen·ny \ˈpen-ē\ *n, pl* **pennies** \-ēz\ *or* **pence** \ˈpens\ **1 :** a British monetary unit formerly equal to 1/12 shilling but now equal to 1/100 pound; *also* **:** a coin of this value — see *pound* at MONEY table **2** *pl* **pennies :** a cent of the U.S. or Canada — **pen·ni·less** \ˈpen-i-ləs\ *adj*

pen·ny–pinch·ing \ˈpen-ē-ˌpin-chiŋ\ *n* **:** FRUGALITY, PARSIMONY — **pen·ny–pinch·er** \-chər\ *n* — **penny–pinching** *adj*

pen·ny·roy·al \ˌpen-ē-ˈrói-əl, ˈpen-i-ˌrīl\ *n* **:** a hairy perennial mint with small pungently aromatic leaves

pen·ny·weight \ˈpen-ē-ˌwāt\ *n* — see WEIGHT table

pen·ny–wise \ˈpen-ē-ˌwīz\ *adj* **:** wise or prudent only in small matters

pe·nol·o·gy \pi-ˈnäl-ə-jē\ *n* **:** a branch of criminology dealing with prisons and the treatment of offenders

[1]**pen·sion** \ˈpen-chən\ *n* **:** a fixed sum paid regularly esp. to a person retired from service

[2]**pen·sion** \ˈpen-chən\ *vb* **pen·sioned; pen·sion·ing** \ˈpench-(ə-)niŋ\ **:** to pay a pension to — **pen·sion·er** *n*

pen·sive \ˈpen-siv\ *adj* **:** musingly, dreamily, or sadly thoughtful **syn** reflective, speculative, contemplative, meditative — **pen·sive·ly** *adv*

pen·stock \ˈpen-ˌstäk\ *n* **1 :** a sluice or gate for regulating a flow **2 :** a conduit for conducting water

pent \ˈpent\ *adj* **:** shut up **:** CONFINED

pen·ta·gon \ˈpent-ə-ˌgän\ *n* **:** a polygon of five angles and five sides — **pen·tag·o·nal** \pen-ˈtag-ən-ᵊl\ *adj*

pen·tam·e·ter \pen-ˈtam-ət-ər\ *n* **:** a line consisting of five metrical feet

Pen·te·cost \ˈpent-i-ˌkóst\ *n* **:** the 7th Sunday after Easter observed as a church festival commemorating the descent of the Holy Spirit on the apostles — **Pen·te·cos·tal** \ˌpent-i-ˈkäst-ᵊl\ *adj*

Pentecostal *n* **:** a member of a fundamentalist Christian religious body that stresses religious revivals — **Pen·te·cos·tal·ism** \ˌpent-i-ˈkäst-ᵊl-ˌiz-əm\ *n*

pent·house \ˈpent-ˌhaůs\ *n* [ME *pentis*, fr. MF *appentis*, prob. fr. ML *appenticium* appendage, fr. L *appendic-, appendix*] **1 :** a shed or sloping roof attached to a wall or building **2 :** an apartment built on the roof of a building

pen·ul·ti·mate \pi-ˈnəl-tə-mət\ *adj* **:** next to the last ⟨~ syllable⟩

pen·um·bra \pə-ˈnəm-brə\ *n, pl* **-brae** \-(ˌ)brē\ *or* **-bras :** the partial shadow surrounding a complete shadow (as in an eclipse)

pe·nu·ri·ous \pə-ˈn(y)ůr-ē-əs\ *adj* **1 :** marked by penury **2 :** MISERLY **syn** stingy, close, tightfisted, parsimonious

pen·u·ry \ˈpen-yə-rē\ *n* **:** extreme poverty

pe·on \ˈpē-ˌän, -ən\ *n, pl* **peons** *or* **pe·o·nes** \pā-ˈō-nēz\ **1 :** a member of the landless laboring class in Spanish America **2 :** one bound to service for payment of a debt — **pe·on·age** \-ə-nij\ *n*

pe·o·ny \ˈpē-ə-nē\ *n, pl* **-nies :** a garden plant with large usu. double red, pink, or white flowers; *also* **:** its flower

[1]**peo·ple** \ˈpē-pəl\ *n, pl* **people** [ME *peple*, fr. OF *peuple*, fr. L *populus*] **1** *pl* **:** human beings making up a group or linked by a common characteristic or interest **2** *pl* **:** human beings — often used in compounds instead of *persons* ⟨sales*people*⟩ **3** *pl* **:** the mass of persons in a community **:** POPULACE; *also* **:** ELECTORATE ⟨the ~'*s* choice⟩ **4** *pl* **peoples :** a body of persons (as a tribe, nation, or race) united by a common culture, sense of kinship, or political organization

[2]**people** *vb* **peo·pled; peo·pling** \-p(ə-)liŋ\ **:** to supply or fill with or as if with people

[1]**pep** \ˈpep\ *n* **:** brisk energy or initiative — **pep·py** *adj*

[2]**pep** *vb* **pepped; pep·ping :** to put pep into **:** STIMULATE

[1]**pep·per** \ˈpep-ər\ *n* **1 :** a pungent condiment from the berry (**pep·per·corn** \-ˌkórn\) of an East Indian climbing plant; *also* **:** this plant **2 :** a plant related to the tomato and widely grown for its hot or mild sweet fruit; *also* **:** this fruit

[2]**pepper** *vb* **pep·pered; pep·per·ing** \ˈpep-(ə-)riŋ\ **1 :** to sprinkle or season with or as if with pepper **2 :** to shower with missiles or rapid blows

pep·per·mint \-ˌmint, -mənt\ *n* **:** a pungent aromatic mint; *also* **:** candy flavored with its oil

pep·per·o·ni \ˌpep-ə-ˈrō-nē\ *n* **:** a highly seasoned beef and pork sausage

pep·pery \ˈpep-(ə-)rē\ *adj* **1 :** having the qualities of pepper **:** PUNGENT, HOT **2 :** having a hot temper **3 :** FIERY

pep·sin \ˈpep-sən\ *n* **:** an enzyme of the stomach that begins the digestion of proteins; *also* **:** a preparation of this used medicinally

pep·tic \ˈpep-tik\ *adj* **1 :** relating to or promoting digestion **2 :** resulting from the action of digestive juices ⟨a ~ ulcer⟩

Pe·quot \ˈpē-ˌkwät\ *n* **:** a member of an American Indian people of eastern Connecticut

---

\ə\abut \ᵊ\kitten \ər\further \a\ash \ā\ace \ä\cot, cart \aů\out \ch\chin \e\bet \ē\easy \g\go \i\hit \ī\ice \j\job \ŋ\sing \ō\go \ó\law \ói\boy \th\thin \t͟h\the \ü\loot \ů\foot \y\yet \zh\vision *see also* Pronunciation Symbols page

[1]**per** \(ˈ)pər\ *prep* **1** : by means of **2** : to or for each **3** : ACCORDING TO

[2]**per** *adv* : for each : APIECE

[3]**per** *abbr* **1** period **2** person

[1]**per·ad·ven·ture** \ˈpər-əd-ˌven-chər\ *adv, archaic* : PERHAPS

[2]**peradventure** *n* : DOUBT, CHANCE

per·am·bu·late \pə-ˈram-byə-ˌlāt\ *vb* **-lat·ed; -lat·ing** : to travel over esp. on foot — **per·am·bu·la·tion** \-ˌram-byə-ˈlā-shən\ *n*

per·am·bu·la·tor \pə-ˈram-byə-ˌlāt-ər\ *n, chiefly Brit* : a baby carriage

per an·num \(ˌ)pər-ˈan-əm\ *adv* [ML] : in or for each year : ANNUALLY

per·cale \(ˌ)pər-ˈkāl, ˈpər-ˌ; (ˌ)pər-ˈkal\ *n* : a fine woven cotton cloth

per cap·i·ta \(ˌ)pər-ˈkap-ət-ə\ *adv or adj* [ML, by heads] : by or for each person

per·ceive \pər-ˈsēv\ *vb* **per·ceived; per·ceiv·ing 1** : to attain awareness : REALIZE **2** : to become aware of through the senses — **per·ceiv·able** *adj*

[1]**per·cent** \pər-ˈsent\ *adv* [fr. *per* + L *centum* hundred] : in each hundred

[2]**percent** *n, pl* **percent** *or* **percents 1** : one part in a hundred : HUNDREDTH **2** : PERCENTAGE

per·cent·age \pər-ˈsent-ij\ *n* **1** : a part of a whole expressed in hundredths **2** : the result obtained by multiplying a number by a percent **3** : ADVANTAGE, PROFIT **4** : PROBABILITY; *also* : favorable odds

per·cen·tile \pər-ˈsen-ˌtīl\ *n* : a statistical measure expressing the standing of a score or grade in terms of the percentage of scores or grades falling with or below it

per·cept \ˈpər-ˌsept\ *n* : a sense impression of an object accompanied by an understanding of what it is

per·cep·ti·ble \pər-ˈsep-tə-bəl\ *adj* : capable of being perceived — **per·cep·ti·bly** \-blē\ *adv*

per·cep·tion \pər-ˈsep-shən\ *n* **1** : an act or result of perceiving **2** : awareness of environment through physical sensation **3** : ability to perceive : INSIGHT, COMPREHENSION **syn** penetration, discernment, discrimination

per·cep·tive \pər-ˈsep-tiv\ *adj* : of or relating to perception : having perception; *also* : DISCERNING — **per·cep·tive·ly** *adv*

per·cep·tu·al \-chə(-wə)l\ *adj* : of, relating to, or involving sensory stimulus as opposed to abstract concept — **per·cep·tu·al·ly** \-ē\ *adv*

[1]**perch** \ˈpərch\ *n* **1** : a roost for birds **2** : a high station or vantage point

[2]**perch** *vb* : ROOST

[3]**perch** *n, pl* **perch** *or* **perch·es** : either of two small freshwater spiny-finned food fishes; *also* : any of various fishes resembling or related to these

per·chance \pər-ˈchans\ *adv* : PERHAPS

per·cip·i·ent \pər-ˈsip-ē-ənt\ *adj* : capable of or characterized by perception — **per·cip·i·ence** \-əns\ *n*

per·co·late \ˈpər-kə-ˌlāt\ *vb* **-lat·ed; -lat·ing 1** : to trickle or filter through a permeable substance **2** : to filter hot water through to extract the essence ⟨~ coffee⟩ — **per·co·la·tor** \-ˌlāt-ər\ *n*

per con·tra \(ˌ)pər-ˈkän-trə\ *adv* [It, by the opposite side (of the ledger)] **1** : on the contrary **2** : by way of contrast

per·cus·sion \pər-ˈkəsh-ən\ *n* **1** : a sharp blow : IMPACT; *esp* : a blow upon a cap (**percussion cap**) filled with powder and designed to explode the charge in a firearm **2** : the beating or striking of a musical instrument; *also* : instruments sounded by striking, shaking, or scraping

per di·em \-ˈdē-əm, -ˈdī-\ *adv* [ML] : by the day — **per diem** *adj or n*

per·di·tion \pər-ˈdish-ən\ *n* [ME *perdicion,* fr. LL *perdition-, perditio,* fr. L *perdere* to destroy, fr. *per-* to destruction + *dare* to give] **1** : eternal damnation **2** : HELL

per·du·ra·ble \(ˌ)pər-ˈd(y)u̇r-ə-bəl\ *adj* : very durable — **per·du·ra·bil·i·ty** \-ˌd(y)u̇r-ə-ˈbil-ət-ē\ *n*

per·e·gri·na·tion \ˌper-ə-grə-ˈnā-shən\ *n* : a journeying about from place to place

pe·remp·to·ry \pə-ˈremp-t(ə-)rē\ *adj* **1** : barring a right of action or delay : FINAL **2** : expressive of urgency or command : IMPERATIVE **3** : marked by self-assurance : DECISIVE **syn** imperious, masterful, domineering, magisterial — **pe·remp·to·ri·ly** \-t(ə-)rə-lē\ *adv*

[1]**pe·ren·ni·al** \pə-ˈren-ē-əl\ *adj* **1** : present at all seasons of the year ⟨~ streams⟩ **2** : continuing to live from year to year ⟨~ plants⟩ **3** : recurring regularly : PERMANENT ⟨~ problems⟩ **syn** lasting, perpetual, enduring, everlasting — **pe·ren·ni·al·ly** \-ē\ *adv*

[2]**perennial** *n* : a plant that lives for an indefinite number of years

perf *abbr* **1** perfect **2** perforated

[1]**per·fect** \ˈpər-fikt\ *adj* **1** : being without fault or defect **2** : EXACT, PRECISE **3** : COMPLETE **4** : relating to or being a verb tense that expresses an action or state completed at the time of speaking or at a time spoken of **syn** whole, entire, intact — **per·fect·ly** \-fik-(t)lē\ *adv* — **per·fect·ness** \-fik(t)-nəs\ *n*

[2]**per·fect** \pər-ˈfekt\ *vb* : to make perfect

[3]**per·fect** \ˈpər-fikt\ *n* : the perfect tense; *also* : a verb form in it

per·fect·ible \pər-ˈfek-tə-bəl, ˈpər-fik-\ *adj* : capable of improvement or perfection — **per·fect·ibil·i·ty** \pər-ˌfek-tə-ˈbil-ət-ē, ˌpər-fik-\ *n*

per·fec·tion \pər-ˈfek-shən\ *n* **1** : the quality or state of being perfect **2** : the highest degree of excellence **3** : the act or process of perfecting **syn** virtue, merit, excellence

per·fec·tion·ist \-sh(ə-)nəst\ *n* : a person who will not accept or be content with anything less than perfection

per·fec·to \pər-ˈfek-tō\ *n, pl* **-tos** : a cigar that is thick in the middle and tapers almost to a point at each end

per·fi·dy \ˈpər-fəd-ē\ *n, pl* **-dies** [L *perfidia,* fr. *perfidus* faithless, fr. *per fidem decipere* to betray, lit., to deceive by trust] : violation of faith or loyalty : TREACHERY — **per·fid·i·ous** \pər-ˈfid-ē-əs\ *adj* — **per·fid·i·ous·ly** *adv*

per·fo·rate \ˈpər-fə-ˌrāt\ *vb* **-rat·ed; -rat·ing** : to bore through : PIERCE; *esp* : to make a line of holes in to facilitate separation **syn** puncture, punch, prick — **per·fo·ra·tion** \ˌpər-fə-ˈrā-shən\ *n*

per·force \pər-ˈfōrs\ *adv* : of necessity

per·form \pə(r)-ˈfȯrm\ *vb* **1** : FULFILL **2** : to carry out : ACCOMPLISH **3** : FUNCTION **4** : to do in a set manner **5** : to give a performance : PLAY **syn** execute, discharge, achieve — **per·form·er** *n*

per·for·mance \pər-ˈfȯr-ˌməns\ *n* **1** : the act or process of performing **2** : DEED, FEAT **3** : a public presentation

[1]**per·fume** \pər-ˈfyüm, ˈpər-ˌfyüm\ *n* **1** : a usu. pleasant odor : FRAGRANCE **2** : a preparation used for scenting

[2]**per·fume** \pər-ˈfyüm, ˈpər-ˌfyüm\ *vb* **per·fumed; per·fum·ing** : to treat with a perfume; *also* : SCENT

per·fum·ery \ˌpər-ˈfyüm-(ə-)rē\ *n, pl* **-er·ies** : PERFUMES

per·func·to·ry \pər-ˈfəŋk-t(ə-)rē\ *adj* : done merely as a duty — **per·func·to·ri·ly** \-t(ə-)rə-lē\ *adv*

per·go·la \ˈpər-gə-lə\ *n* [It] : a structure consisting of posts supporting an open roof in the form of a trellis

perh *abbr* perhaps

per·haps \pər-ˈ(h)aps, ˈpraps\ *adv* : possibly but not certainly

per·i·gee \ˈper-ə-ˌjē\ *n* [fr. *perigee* point in the orbit of a satellite of the earth when it is nearest the earth, fr. NL *perigeum,* fr. Gk *perigeion,* fr. *peri* around, near + *gē* earth] : the point at which an orbiting object is nearest the body (as the earth) being orbited

peri·he·lion \ˌper-ə-ˈhēl-yən\ *n, pl* **-he·lia** \-ˈhēl-yə\ : the point in the path of a celestial body (as a planet) that is nearest to the sun

per·il \ˈper-əl\ *n* : DANGER; *also* : a source of danger : RISK **syn** jeopardy, hazard — **per·il·ous** *adj* — **per·il·ous·ly** *adv*

peri·lune \ˈper-ə-ˌlün\ *n* : the point in a lunar orbit closest to the moon's surface
pe·rim·e·ter \pə-ˈrim-ət-ər\ *n* : the outer boundary of a body or figure; *also* : the length of a perimeter
[1]**pe·ri·od** \ˈpir-ē-əd\ *n* **1** : SENTENCE; *also* : the full pause closing the utterance of a sentence **2** : END, STOP **3** : a punctuation mark . used esp. to mark the end of a declarative sentence or an abbreviation **4** : an extent of time; *esp* : one regarded as a stage or division in a process or development **5** : a portion or division of time in which something comes to an end and is ready to begin again **6** : a single cyclic occurrence of menstruation **syn** epoch, era, age
[2]**period** *adj* : of or relating to a particular historical period ⟨~ furniture⟩
pe·ri·od·ic \ˌpir-ē-ˈäd-ik\ *adj* **1** : occurring at regular intervals of time **2** : happening repeatedly **3** : of or relating to a sentence that has no trailing elements following full grammatical statement of the essential idea
[1]**pe·ri·od·i·cal** \ˌpir-ē-ˈäd-i-kəl\ *adj* **1** : PERIODIC **2** : published at regular intervals **3** : of or relating to a periodical — **pe·ri·od·i·cal·ly** \-k(ə-)lē\ *adv*
[2]**periodical** *n* : a periodical publication
peri·odon·tal \ˌper-ē-ō-ˈdänt-ᵊl\ *adj* : surrounding or occurring about the teeth
per·i·pa·tet·ic \ˌper-ə-pə-ˈtet-ik\ *adj* : performed or performing while moving about : ITINERANT
pe·riph·er·al \pə-ˈrif-(ə-)rəl\ *n* : a device connected to a computer to provide communication or auxiliary functions
peripheral nervous system *n* : the part of the nervous system that is outside the central nervous system and comprises the spinal nerves, the cranial nerves except the one supplying the retina, and the autonomic nervous system
pe·riph·ery \pə-ˈrif-(ə-)rē\ *n, pl* **-er·ies 1** : the boundary of a rounded fgure **2** : outward bounds : border area — **pe·riph·er·al** \-(ə-)rəl\ *adj*
pe·riph·ra·sis \pə-ˈrif-rə-səs\ *n, pl* **-ra·ses** \-ˌsēz\ : CIRCUMLOCUTION
pe·rique \pə-ˈrēk\ *n* [LaF] : a strong-flavored Louisiana tobacco used in smoking mixtures
peri·scope \ˈper-ə-ˌskōp\ *n* : a tubular optical instrument enabling an observer to get an otherwise blocked field of view
per·ish \ˈper-ish\ *vb* : to become destroyed or ruined : DIE
per·ish·able \ˈper-ish-ə-bəl\ *adj* : easily spoiled ⟨~ foods⟩ — **perishable** *n*
peri·stal·sis \ˌper-ə-ˈstȯl-səs, -ˈstal-\ *n, pl* **-stal·ses** : waves of contraction passing along the intestine and forcing its contents onward — **per·i·stal·tic** \-ˈstȯl-tik, -ˈstal-\ *adj*
peri·style \ˈper-ə-ˌstīl\ *n* : a row of columns surrounding a building or court
peri·to·ne·um \ˌper-ət-ᵊn-ˈē-əm\ *n, pl* **-ne·ums** *or* **-nea** : the smooth transparent serous membrane that lines the cavity of the abdomen — **peri·to·ne·al** \-ˈē-əl\ *adj*
peri·to·ni·tis \ˌper-ət-ᵊn-ˈīt-əs\ *n* : inflammation of the membrane lining the cavity of the abdomen
peri·wig \ˈper-i-ˌwig\ *n* : WIG
[1]**per·i·win·kle** \ˈper-i-ˌwiŋ-kəl\ *n* : a usu. blue-flowered creeping plant cultivated as a ground cover
[2]**periwinkle** *n* : any of various small edible seashore snails
per·ju·ry \ˈpərj-(ə-)rē\ *n* : the voluntary violation of an oath to tell the truth : false swearing — **per·jure** \ˈpər-jər\ *vb* — **per·jur·er** *n*
[1]**perk** \ˈpərk\ *vb* **1** : to thrust (as the head) up impudently or jauntily **2** : to make trim or brisk : FRESHEN **3** : to regain vigor or spirit — **perky** *adj*
[2]**perk** *vb* : PERCOLATE
per·lite \ˈpər-ˌlīt\ *n* : volcanic glass that when expanded by heat forms a lightweight material used esp. in concrete and plaster and for potting plants
[1]**perm** \ˈpərm\ *n* : PERMANENT
[2]**perm** *vb* : to give (hair) a permanent
[3]**perm** *abbr* permanent
per·ma·frost \ˈpər-mə-ˌfrȯst\ *n* : a permanently frozen layer below the surface in frigid regions of a planet (as earth)
[1]**per·ma·nent** \ˈpər-mə-nənt\ *adj* : LASTING, STABLE — **per·ma·nence** \-nəns\ *n* — **per·ma·nen·cy** \-nən-sē\ *n* — **per·ma·nent·ly** *adv*
[2]**permanent** *n* : a long-lasting hair wave or straightening
permanent press *n* : the process of treating fabrics with chemicals (as resin) and heat for setting the shape and for aiding wrinkle resistance
per·me·able \ˈpər-mē-ə-bəl\ *adj* : having small openings that permit liquids or gases to seep through — **per·me·a·bil·i·ty** \ˌpər-mē-ə-ˈbil-ət-ē\ *n*
per·me·ate \ˈpər-mē-ˌāt\ *vb* **-at·ed; -at·ing 1** : PERVADE **2** : to seep through the pores of : PENETRATE — **per·me·ation** \ˌpər-mē-ˈā-shən\ *n*
Perm·ian \ˈpər-mē-ən\ *adj* : of, relating to, or being the latest period of the Paleozoic era — **Permian** *n*
per·mis·si·ble \pər-ˈmis-ə-bəl\ *adj* : that may be permitted : ALLOWABLE
per·mis·sion \pər-ˈmish-ən\ *n* : formal consent : AUTHORIZATION
per·mis·sive \pər-ˈmis-iv\ *adj* : granting permission; *esp* : INDULGENT — **per·mis·sive·ness** *n*
[1]**per·mit** \pər-ˈmit\ *vb* **per·mit·ted; per·mit·ting 1** : to consent to : ALLOW **2** : to make possible
[2]**per·mit** \ˈpər-ˌmit, pər-ˈmit\ *n* : a written permission : LICENSE
per·mu·ta·tion \ˌpər-myu̇-ˈtā-shən\ *n* **1** : TRANSFORMATION **2** : any one of the total number of changes in position or order possible among the units or members of a group ⟨~*s* of the alphabet⟩ **syn** innovation, mutation, vicissitude
per·ni·cious \pər-ˈnish-əs\ *adj* [MF *pernicieus*, fr. L *perniciosus*, fr. *pernicies* destruction, fr. *per-* through + *nec-*, *nex* violent death] : very destructive or injurious — **per·ni·cious·ly** *adv*
per·ora·tion \ˈper-ər-ˌā-shən, ˈpər-\ *n* : the concluding part of a speech
[1]**per·ox·ide** \pə-ˈräk-ˌsīd\ *n* : an oxide containing a large proportion of oxygen; *esp* : HYDROGEN PEROXIDE
[2]**peroxide** *vb* **-id·ed; -id·ing** : to bleach with hydrogen peroxide
perp *abbr* perpendicular
per·pen·dic·u·lar \ˌpər-pən-ˈdik-yə-lər\ *adj* **1** : standing at right angles to the plane of the horizon **2** : meeting another line at a right angle — **pependicular** *n* — **per·pen·dic·u·lar·i·ty** \-ˌdik-yə-ˈlar-ət-ē\ *n* — **per·pen·dic·u·lar·ly** *adv*
per·pe·trate \ˈpər-pə-ˌtrāt\ *vb* **-trat·ed; -trat·ing** : to be guilty of : COMMIT — **per·pe·tra·tion** \ˌpər-pə-ˈtrā-shən\ *n* — **per·pe·tra·tor** \ˈpər-pə-ˌtrāt-ər\ *n*
per·pet·u·al \pər-ˈpech-(ə-w)əl\ *adj* **1** : continuing forever : EVERLASTING **2** : occurring continually : CONSTANT ⟨~ annoyance⟩ **syn** ceaseless, unceasing, continual, continuous, incessant, unremitting — **per·pet·u·al·ly** \-ē\ *adv*
per·pet·u·ate \pər-ˈpech-ə-ˌwāt\ *vb* **-at·ed; -at·ing** : to make perpetual : cause to last indefinitely — **per·pet·u·a·tion** \-ˌpech-ə-ˈwā-shən\ *n*
per·pe·tu·ity \ˌpər-pə-ˈt(y)ü-ət-ē\ *n, pl* **-it·ies 1** : endless time : ETERNITY **2** : the quality or state of being perpetual
per·plex \pər-ˈpleks\ *vb* : to disturb mentally; *esp* : CONFUSE — **per·plex·i·ty** \-ət-ē\ *n*
per·plexed \-ˈplekst\ *adj* **1** : filled with uncertainty : PUZ-

ZLED **2** : full of difficulty : COMPLICATED — **per·plexed·ly** \-ˈplek-səd-lē\ *adv*

per·qui·site \ˈpər-kwə-zət\ *n* : a privilege or profit beyond regular pay

pers *abbr* person; personal

per se \(ˌ)pər-ˈsā\ *adv* [L] : by, of, or in itself : as such

per·se·cute \ˈpər-si-ˌkyüt\ *vb* **-cut·ed; -cut·ing** : to pursue in such a way as to injure or afflict : HARASS; *esp* : to cause to suffer because of belief **syn** oppress, wrong, aggrieve — **per·se·cu·tion** \ˌpər-si-ˈkyü-shən\ *n* — **per·se·cu·tor** \ˈpər-si-ˌkyüt-ər\ *n*

per·se·vere \ˌpər-sə-ˈviər\ *vb* **-vered; -ver·ing** : to persist (as in an undertaking) in spite of difficulties — **per·se·ver·ance** \-ˈvir-əns\ *n*

Per·sian \ˈpər-zhən\ *n* **1** : a native or inhabitant of ancient Persia **2** : a member of one of the peoples of modern Iran **3** : the language of the Persians

Persian cat *n* : a stocky round-headed domestic cat that has long and silky fur

Persian lamb *n* : a pelt that is obtained from lambs that are older than those yielding broadtail and that has very silky tightly curled fur

per·si·flage \ˈpər-si-ˌfläzh, ˈper-\ *n* [F, fr. *persifler* to banter, fr. *per-* thoroughly + *siffler* to whistle, hiss, boo, fr. L *sibilare*] : lightly jesting or mocking talk

per·sim·mon \pər-ˈsim-ən\ *n* : a tree related to the ebony; *also* : its edible orange-red plumlike fruit

per·sist \pər-ˈsist, -ˈzist\ *vb* **1** : to go on resolutely or stubbornly in spite of difficulties : PERSEVERE **2** : to continue to exist — **per·sis·tence** \-ˈsis-təns, -ˈzis-\ *n* — **per·sis·ten·cy** \-tən-sē\ *n* — **per·sis·tent** \-tənt\ *adj* — **per·sis·tent·ly** *adv*

per·snick·e·ty \pər-ˈsnik-ət-ē\ *adj* : fussy about small details

per·son \ˈpərs-ᵊn\ *n* [ME, fr. OF *persone*, fr. L *persona* actor's mask, character in a play, person, prob. fr. Etruscan *phersu* mask] **1** : a human being : INDIVIDUAL — used in combination esp. by those who prefer to avoid *man* in compounds applicable to both sexes ⟨chair*person*⟩ **2** : one of the three modes of being in the Godhead as understood by Trinitarians **3** : the body of a human being **4** : the individual personality of a human being : SELF **5** : reference of a segment of discourse to the speaker, to one spoken to, or to one spoken of esp. as indicated by certain pronouns

per·son·able \ˈpərs-(ᵊ-)nə-bəl\ *adj* : pleasing in person : ATTRACTIVE

per·son·age \ˈpərs-(ᵊ-)nij\ *n* : a person of rank, note, or distinction

¹**per·son·al** \ˈpərs-(ᵊ-)nəl\ *adj* **1** : of, relating to, or affecting a person : PRIVATE ⟨~ correspondence⟩ **2** : done in person ⟨a ~ inquiry⟩ **3** : relating to the person or body ⟨~ injuries⟩ **4** : relating to an individual esp. in an offensive way ⟨resented such ~ remarks⟩ **5** : of or relating to temporary or movable property as distinguished from real estate **6** : denoting grammatical person — **per·son·al·ly** \-ē\ *adv*

²**personal** *n* **1** : a short newspaper paragraph relating to a person or group or to personal matters **2** : a short personal or private communication in the classified ads section of a newspaper

personal computer *n* : MICROCOMPUTER

per·son·al·i·ty \ˌpərs-ᵊn-ˈal-ət-ē\ *n, pl* **-ties** **1** : an offensively personal remark ⟨indulges in *personalities*⟩ **2** : distinctive personal character **3** : distinction of personal and social traits; *also* : a person having such quality **syn** individuality, temperament, disposition, make-up

per·son·al·ize \ˈpərs-(ᵊ-)nə-ˌlīz\ *vb* **-ized; -iz·ing** : to make personal or individual; *esp* : to mark as belonging to a particular person

per·son·al·ty \ˈpərs-(ᵊ-)nəl-tē\ *n, pl* **-ties** : personal property

per·so·na non gra·ta \pər-ˌsō-nə-ˌnän-ˈgrat-ə, -ˈgrät-\ *adj* [L] : being personally unacceptable or unwelcome

per·son·ate \ˈpərs-ᵊn-ˌāt\ *vb* **-at·ed; -at·ing** : IMPERSONATE, REPRESENT

per·son·i·fy \pər-ˈsän-ə-ˌfī\ *vb* **-fied; -fy·ing** **1** : to think of or represent as a person **2** : to be the embodiment of : INCARNATE ⟨~ the law⟩ — **per·son·i·fi·ca·tion** \-ˌsän-ə-fə-ˈkā-shən\ *n*

per·son·nel \ˌpərs-ᵊn-ˈel\ *n* : a body of persons employed in a service or an organization

per·spec·tive \pər-ˈspek-tiv\ *n* **1** : the science of painting and drawing so that objects represented have apparent depth and distance **2** : the aspect in which a subject or its parts are mentally viewed; *esp* : a view of things (as objects or events) in their true relationship or relative importance

per·spi·cac·i·ty \ˌpər-spə-ˈkas-ət-ē\ *n* : acuteness of understanding or judgment — **per·spi·ca·cious** \-ˈkā-shəs\ *adj*

per·spic·u·ous \pər-ˈspik-yə-wəs\ *adj* : plain to the understanding — **per·spi·cu·i·ty** \ˌpər-spə-ˈkyü-ət-ē\ *n*

per·spire \pər-ˈspīr\ *vb* **per·spired; per·spir·ing** : SWEAT — **per·spi·ra·tion** \ˌpər-spə-ˈrā-shən\ *n*

per·suade \pər-ˈswād\ *vb* **per·suad·ed; per·suad·ing** : to move by argument or entreaty to a belief or course of action — **per·sua·sive** \-ˈswā-siv, -ziv\ *adj* — **per·sua·sive·ly** *adv* — **per·sua·sive·ness** *n*

per·sua·sion \pər-ˈswā-zhən\ *n* **1** : the act or process of persuading **2** : OPINION, BELIEF

¹**pert** \ˈpərt\ *adj* [ME, open, bold, pert, modif. of OF *apert*, fr. L *apertus* open, fr. pp. of *aperire* to open] **1** : saucily free and forward : IMPUDENT **2** : stylishly trim : JAUNTY **3** : LIVELY

²**pert** *abbr* pertaining

per·tain \pər-ˈtān\ *vb* **1** : to belong to as a part, quality, or function ⟨duties ~*ing* to the office⟩ **2** : to have reference : RELATE ⟨facts that ~ to the case⟩ **syn** bear, appertain, apply

per·ti·na·cious \ˌpərt-ᵊn-ˈā-shəs\ *adj* **1** : holding resolutely to an opinion or purpose **2** : obstinately persistent : TENACIOUS ⟨a ~ bill collector⟩ **syn** obstinate, dogged, mulish, headstrong, perverse — **per·ti·nac·i·ty** \-ˈas-ət-ē\ *n*

per·ti·nent \ˈpərt-ᵊn-ənt\ *adj* : relating to the matter under consideration **syn** relevant, germane, applicable, apropos — **per·ti·nence** \-əns\ *n*

per·turb \pər-ˈtərb\ *vb* : to disturb greatly esp. in mind : UPSET — **per·tur·ba·tion** \ˌpərt-ər-ˈbā-shən\ *n*

per·tus·sis *n* : WHOOPING COUGH

pe·ruke \pə-ˈrük\ *n* : WIG

pe·ruse \pə-ˈrüz\ *vb* **pe·rused; pe·rus·ing** : READ; *esp* : to read attentively — **pe·rus·al** \-ˈrü-zəl\ *n*

Pe·ru·vi·an \pə-ˈrü-vē-ən\ *n* : a native or inhabitant of Peru

per·vade \pər-ˈvād\ *vb* **per·vad·ed; per·vad·ing** : to spread through every part of : PERMEATE, PENETRATE — **per·va·sive** \-ˌvā-siv, -ziv\ *adj*

per·verse \pər-ˈvərs\ *adj* **1** : turned away from what is right or good : CORRUPT **2** : obstinate in opposing what is reasonable or accepted — **per·verse·ly** *adv* — **per·verse·ness** *n* — **per·ver·si·ty** \-ˈvər-sət-ē\ *n*

per·ver·sion \pər-ˈvər-zhən\ *n* **1** : the action of perverting : the condition of being perverted **2** : a perverted form of something; *esp* : aberrant sexual behavior

¹**per·vert** \pər-ˈvərt\ *vb* **1** : to lead astray : CORRUPT ⟨~ the young⟩ **2** : to divert to a wrong purpose : MISAPPLY ⟨~ evidence⟩ **syn** deprave, debase, debauch, demoralize

²**per·vert** \ˈpər-ˌvərt\ *n* : one that is perverted; *esp* : a person given to sexual perversion

pe·se·ta \pə-ˈsāt-ə\ *n* — see MONEY table

pe·se·wa \pə-ˈsā-wə\ *n* — see *cedi* at MONEY table

pes·ky \ˈpes-kē\ *adj* **pes·ki·er; -est** : causing annoyance : TROUBLESOME

pe·so \ˈpā-sō\ *n, pl* **pesos** — see MONEY table

pes·si·mism \ˈpes-ə-ˌmiz-əm\ *n* [F *pessimisme,* fr. L *pessimus* worst] **:** an inclination to take the least favorable view (as of events) or to expect the worst possible outcome — **pes·si·mist** \-məst\ *n* — **pes·si·mis·tic** \ˌpes-ə-ˈmis-tik\ *adj*

pest \ˈpest\ *n* **1 :** a destructive epidemic disease **:** PLAGUE **2 :** a plant or animal detrimental to man **3 :** one that pesters **:** NUISANCE

pes·ter \ˈpes-tər\ *vb* **pes·tered; pes·ter·ing** \-t(ə-)riŋ\ **:** to harass with petty irritations **:** ANNOY

pes·ti·cide \ˈpes-tə-ˌsīd\ *n* **:** an agent used to kill pests

pes·tif·er·ous \pes-ˈtif-(ə-)rəs\ *adj* **1 :** PESTILENT **2 :** ANNOYING

pes·ti·lence \ˈpes-tə-ləns\ *n* **:** a destructive infectious swiftly spreading disease; *esp* **:** PLAGUE

pes·ti·lent \-lənt\ *adj* **1 :** dangerous to life **:** DEADLY; *also* **:** spreading or causing pestilence **2 :** PERNICIOUS, HARMFUL **3 :** TROUBLESOME

pes·ti·len·tial \ˌpes-tə-ˈlen-chəl\ *adj* **1 :** causing or tending to cause pestilence **:** DEADLY **2 :** morally harmful — **pes·ti·len·tial·ly** \-ē\ *adv*

pes·tle \ˈpes-əl, ˈpes-tᵊl\ *n* **:** an implement for grinding substances in a mortar

[1]**pet** \ˈpet\ *n* **1 :** FAVORITE, DARLING **2 :** a domesticated animal kept for pleasure rather than utility

[2]**pet** *adj* **1 :** kept or treated as a pet ⟨~ dog⟩ **2 :** expressing fondness ⟨~ name⟩ **3 :** particularly liked or favored

[3]**pet** *vb* **pet·ted; pet·ting 1 :** to stroke gently or lovingly **2 :** to make a pet of **:** PAMPER **3 :** to engage in amorous kissing and caressing

[4]**pet** *n* **:** a fit of peevishness, sulkiness, or anger

Pet *abbr* Peter

pet·al \ˈpet-ᵊl\ *n* **:** one of the modified leaves of a flower's corolla

pe·tard \pə-ˈtär(d)\ *n* **:** a case containing an explosive to break down a door or gate or breach a wall

pe·ter \ˈpēt-ər\ *vb* **:** to diminish gradually and come to an end ⟨his energy ~*ed* out⟩

Pe·ter \ˈpēt-ər\ *n* — see BIBLE table

pet·i·ole \ˈpet-ē-ˌōl\ *n* **:** a stalk that supports a leaf

pe·tite \pə-ˈtēt\ *adj* [F] **:** small and trim of figure ⟨a ~ woman⟩

pe·tit four \ˌpet-ē-ˈfōr\ *n, pl* **petits fours** *or* **petit fours** \-ˈfōrz\ [F, lit., small oven] **:** a small cake cut from pound or sponge cake and frosted

[1]**pe·ti·tion** \pə-ˈtish-ən\ *n* **:** an earnest request **:** ENTREATY; *esp* **:** a formal written request made to a superior

[2]**petition** *vb* **-tioned; -tion·ing** \-ˈtish-(ə-)niŋ\ **:** to make a petition — **pe·ti·tion·er** \-(ə-)nər\ *n*

pet·nap·ping \ˈpet-ˌnap-iŋ\ *n* **:** the act of stealing a pet

pe·trel \ˈpe-trəl\ *n* **:** any of various small seabirds that fly far from land

pet·ri·fy \ˈpe-trə-ˌfī\ *vb* **-fied; -fy·ing 1 :** to change into stony material **2 :** to make rigid or inactive (as from fear or awe) — **pet·ri·fac·tion** \ˌpe-trə-ˈfak-shən\ *n*

pet·ro·chem·i·cal \ˌpe-trō-ˈkem-i-kəl\ *n* **:** a chemical isolated or derived from petroleum or natural gas — **pet·ro·chem·is·try** \-ˈkem-ə-strē\ *n*

pet·rol \ˈpe-trəl\ *n, Brit* **:** GASOLINE

pet·ro·la·tum \ˌpe-trə-ˈlāt-əm\ *n* **:** a tasteless, odorless, and oily or greasy substance from petroleum that is used esp. in ointments and dressings

pe·tro·leum \pə-ˈtrō-lē-əm\ *n* [ML, fr. L *petr-* stone, rock (fr. Gk, fr. *petros* stone & *petra* rock) + *oleum* oil] **:** an oily flammable liquid obtained from wells drilled in the ground and refined into gasoline, fuel oils, and other products

petroleum jelly *n* **:** PETROLATUM

[1]**pet·ti·coat** \ˈpet-ē-ˌkōt\ *n* **1 :** a skirt worn under a dress **2 :** an outer skirt

[2]**petticoat** *adj* **:** FEMALE ⟨~ government⟩

pet·ti·fog \ˈpet-ē-ˌfög, -ˌfäg\ *vb* **-fogged; -fog·ging 1 :** to engage in legal trickery **2 :** to quibble over insignificant details — **pet·ti·fog·ger** *n*

pet·tish \ˈpet-ish\ *adj* **:** PEEVISH **syn** irritable, petulant, fretful, huffy, querulous

pet·ty \ˈpet-ē\ *adj* **pet·ti·er; -est** [ME *pety* small, minor, alter. of *petit,* fr. MF, small] **1 :** having secondary rank **:** MINOR ⟨~ prince⟩ **2 :** of little importance **:** TRIFLING ⟨~ faults⟩ **3 :** marked by narrowness or meanness — **pet·ti·ly** \ˈpet-ᵊl-ē\ *adv* — **pet·ti·ness** \-ē-nəs\ *n*

petty officer *n* **:** a subordinate officer in the navy or coast guard appointed from among the enlisted men

petty officer first class *n* **:** a petty officer ranking below a chief petty officer

petty officer second class *n* **:** a petty officer ranking below a petty officer first class

petty officer third class *n* **:** a petty officer ranking below a petty officer second class

pet·u·lant \ˈpech-ə-lənt\ *adj* **:** marked by capricious ill humor **syn** irritable, peevish, fretful, fractious, querulous — **pet·u·lance** \-ləns\ *n* — **pet·u·lant·ly** *adv*

pe·tu·nia \pi-ˈt(y)ün-yə\ *n* **:** a garden plant with bright funnel-shaped flowers

pew \ˈpyü\ *n* [ME *pewe,* fr. MF *puie* balustrade, fr. L *podia,* pl. of *podium* parapet, podium, fr. Gk *podion* base, dim. of *pod-, pous* foot] **:** one of the benches with backs fixed in rows in a church

pe·wee \ˈpē-(ˌ)wē\ *n* **:** any of various small flycatchers

pew·ter \ˈpyüt-ər\ *n* **:** an alloy of tin usu. with lead used esp. for kitchen or table utensils

pey·o·te \pā-ˈōt-ē\ *also* **pey·otl** \-ˈōt-ᵊl\ *n* **:** a stimulant drug derived from an American cactus; *also* **:** this cactus

pf *abbr* **1** pfennig **2** preferred

PFC *abbr* private first class

pfd *abbr* preferred

pfen·nig \ˈfen-ig\ *n, pl* **pfennig** *also* **pfennigs** *or* **pfen·ni·ge** \ˈfen-i-gə\ — see *deutsche mark, mark* at MONEY table

pg *abbr* page

PG *abbr* postgraduate

PGA *abbr* Professional Golfers' Association

pH \(ˈ)pē-ˈāch\ *n* **:** a value used to express acidity and alkalinity; *also* **:** the condition represented by such a value

PH *abbr* **1** pinch hit **2** public health

pha·eton \ˈfā-ət-ᵊn\ *n* [F *phaéton,* fr. Gk *Phaethōn,* son of the sun god who persuaded his father to let him drive the chariot of the sun but who lost control of the horses with disastrous consequences] **1 :** a light 4-wheeled horse-drawn vehicle **2 :** an open automobile with two cross seats

phaeton 1

phage \ˈfāj\ *n* **:** BACTERIOPHAGE

pha·lanx \ˈfā-ˌlaŋks\ *n, pl* **pha·lanx·es** *or* **pha·lan·ges** \fə-ˈlan-ˌjēz\ **1 :** a group or body (as of troops) in com-

\ə\abut \ᵊ\kitten \ər\further \a\ash \ā\ace \ä\cot, cart \aù\out \ch\chin \e\bet \ē\easy \g\go \i\hit \ī\ice \j\job \ŋ\sing \ō\go \ȯ\law \ȯi\boy \th\thin \th\the \ü\loot \ù\foot \y\yet \zh\vision *see also* Pronunciation Symbols page

pact formation 2 *pl phalanges* : one of the digital bones of the hand or foot of a vertebrate

phal·a·rope \ˈfal-ə-ˌrōp\ *n, pl* **-ropes** *also* **-rope** : any of several small shorebirds

phal·lic \ˈfal-ik\ *adj* **1** : of, relating to, or resembling a phallus **2** : relating to or being the stage of psychosexual development in psychoanalytic theory during which children become interested in their own sexual organs

phal·lus \ˈfal-əs\ *n, pl* **phal·li** \ˈfal-ˌī\ *or* **phal·lus·es** : PENIS; *also* : a symbolic representation of the penis

phan·tasm \ˈfan-ˌtaz-əm\ *n* : a product of the imagination : ILLUSION

phan·tas·ma·go·ria \fan-ˌtaz-mə-ˈgōr-ē-ə\ *n* : a constantly shifting complex succession of things seen or imagined; *also* : a scene that constantly changes or fluctuates

phantasy *var of* FANTASY

phan·tom \ˈfant-əm\ *n* [deriv. of L *phantasma*] **1** : something (as a specter) that is apparent to sense but has no substantial existence **2** : a mere show : SHADOW **3** : a representation of something abstract, ideal, or incorporeal — **phantom** *adj* — **phan·tom·like** *adv or adj*

pha·raoh \ˈfe(ə)r-ō, ˈfā-rō\ *n, often cap* : a ruler of ancient Egypt

phar·i·sa·ical \ˌfar-ə-ˈsā-ə-kəl\ *adj* : hypocritically self-righteous — **phar·i·sa·ical·ly** \-k(ə-)lē\ *adv*

phar·i·see \ˈfar-ə-ˌsē\ *n* **1** *cap* : a member of an ancient Jewish sect noted for strict observance of rites and ceremonies of the traditional law **2** : a self-righteous or hypocritical person — **phar·i·sa·ic** \ˌfar-ə-ˈsā-ik\ *adj*

pharm *abbr* pharmaceutical; pharmacist; pharmacy

phar·ma·ceu·ti·cal \ˌfär-mə-ˈsüt-i-kəl\ *adj* **1** : of or relating to pharmacy or pharmacists **2** : MEDICINAL — **pharmaceutical** *n*

phar·ma·col·o·gy \ˌfär-mə-ˈkäl-ə-jē\ *n* **1** : the science of drugs esp. as related to medicinal uses **2** : the reactions and properties of a drug — **phar·ma·co·log·i·cal** \-i-kəl\ *also* **phar·ma·co·log·ic** \-kə-ˈläj-ik\ *adj* — **phar·ma·col·o·gist** \-ˈkäl-ə-jəst\ *n*

phar·ma·co·poe·ia *also* **phar·ma·co·pe·ia** \-kə-ˈpē-(y)ə\ *n* **1** : a book describing drugs and medicinal preparations **2** : a stock of drugs

phar·ma·cy \ˈfär-mə-sē\ *n, pl* **-cies** **1** : the art or practice of preparing and dispensing drugs **2** : DRUGSTORE — **phar·ma·cist** \-səst\ *n*

phar·os \ˈfaər-ˌäs\ *n* : LIGHTHOUSE

phar·ynx \ˈfar-iŋks\ *n, pl* **pha·ryn·ges** \fə-ˈrin-ˌjēz\ *also* **phar·ynx·es** : the space just back of the mouth into which the nostrils, esophagus, and trachea open — **pha·ryn·ge·al** \fə-ˈrin-j(ē-)əl, ˌfar-ən-ˈjē-əl\ *adj*

phase \ˈfāz\ *n* **1** : a particular appearance in a recurring series of changes ⟨~*s* of the moon⟩ **2** : a stage or interval in a process or cycle ⟨first ~ of an experiment⟩ **3** : an aspect or part under consideration

phase in *vb* : to introduce in stages

phase·out \ˈfāz-ˌau̇t\ *n* : a gradual stopping of operations or production

phase out \ˈfāz-ˈau̇t\ *vb* : to stop production or use of in stages

PhD *abbr* [L *philosophiae doctor*] doctor of philosophy

pheas·ant \ˈfez-ᵊnt\ *n, pl* **pheasant** *or* **pheasants** : any of various long-tailed brilliantly colored game birds related to the domestic fowl

phen·cy·cli·dine \ˌfen-ˈsī-klə-ˌdēn\ *n* : a drug used medicinally as an anesthetic and sometimes illicitly to induce vivid mental imagery

phe·no·bar·bi·tal \ˌfē-nō-ˈbär-bə-ˌtȯl\ *n* : a crystalline drug used as a hypnotic and sedative

phe·nol \ˈfē-ˌnōl, -ˌnȯl, fi-ˈnōl, -ˈnȯl\ *n* : a caustic poisonous acidic compound in tar used as a disinfectant

phe·nom·e·non \fi-ˈnäm-ə-ˌnän, -nən\ *n, pl* **-na** \-nə\ *or* **-nons** [LL *phaenomenon*, fr. Gk *phainomenon*, fr. neut. of *phainomenos*, prp. of *phainesthai* to appear] **1** *pl* *-na* : an observable fact or event **2** : an outward sign of the working of a law of nature **3** *pl -nons* : an extraordinary person or thing : PRODIGY — **phe·nom·e·nal** \-ˈnäm-ən-ᵊl\ *adj*

pher·o·mone \ˈfer-ə-ˌmōn\ *n* : a chemical substance that is produced by an animal and serves to stimulate a behavioral response in other individuals of the same species — **pher·o·mon·al** \ˌfer-ə-ˈmōn-ᵊl\ *adj*

phi·al \ˈfī-(-ə)l\ *n* : VIAL

Phil *abbr* Philippians

phi·lan·der \fə-ˈlan-dər\ *vb* **-dered; -der·ing** \-d(ə-)riŋ\ : to make love without serious intent : FLIRT — **phi·lan·der·er** *n*

phi·lan·thro·py \fə-ˈlan-thrə-pē\ *n, pl* **-pies** **1** : goodwill to fellowmen; *esp* : effort to promote human welfare **2** : a charitable act or gift; *also* : an organization that distributes or is supported by donated funds — **phil·an·throp·ic** \ˌfil-ən-ˈthräp-ik\ *adj* — **phi·lan·thro·pist** \fə-ˈlan-thrə-pəst\ *n*

phi·lat·e·ly \fə-ˈlat-ᵊl-ē\ *n* : the collection and study of postage and imprinted stamps — **phi·lat·e·list** \-ᵊl-əst\ *n*

Phi·le·mon \fə-ˈlē-mən, fī-\ *n* — see BIBLE table

Phi·lip·pi·ans \fə-ˈlip-ē-ənz\ *n* — see BIBLE table

phi·lip·pic \fə-ˈlip-ik\ *n* : TIRADE

phi·lis·tine \ˈfil-ə-ˌstēn; fə-ˈlis-tən\ *n, often cap* [*Philistine*, inhabitant of ancient Philistia (Palestine)] : a materialistic person; *esp* : one who is smugly insensitive or indifferent to intellectual or artistic values — **philistine** *adj, often cap*

philo·den·dron \ˌfil-ə-ˈden-drən\ *n, pl* **-drons** *or* **-dra** \-drə\ [NL, fr. Gk, neut. of *philodendros* loving trees, fr. *philos* dear, friendly + *dendron* tree] : any of various arums grown for their showy foliage

phi·lol·o·gy \fə-ˈläl-ə-jē\ *n* **1** : the study of literature and relevant fields **2** : LINGUISTICS; *esp* : historical and comparative linguistics — **phil·o·log·i·cal** \ˌfil-ə-ˈläj-i-kəl\ *adj* — **phi·lol·o·gist** \fə-ˈläl-ə-jəst\ *n*

philos *abbr* philosopher; philosophy

phi·los·o·pher \fə-ˈläs-ə-fər\ *n* **1** : a reflective thinker : SCHOLAR **2** : a student of or specialist in philosophy **3** : one whose philosophical perspective enables him to meet trouble calmly

phi·los·o·phize \fə-ˈläs-ə-ˌfīz\ *vb* **-phized; -phiz·ing** **1** : to reason like a philosopher : THEORIZE **2** : to expound a philosophy esp. superficially

phi·los·o·phy \fə-ˈläs-ə-fē\ *n, pl* **-phies** **1** : a critical study of fundamental beliefs and the grounds for them **2** : sciences and liberal arts exclusive of medicine, law, and theology ⟨doctor of ~⟩ **3** : a system of philosophical concepts ⟨Aristotelian ~⟩ **4** : a basic theory concerning a particular subject or sphere of activity **5** : the sum of the ideas and convictions of an individual or group ⟨his ~ of life⟩ **6** : calmness of temper and judgment — **phil·o·soph·ic** \ˌfil-ə-ˈsäf-ik\ *or* **phil·o·soph·i·cal** \-i-kəl\ *adj* — **phil·o·soph·i·cal·ly** \-k(ə-)lē\ *adv*

phil·ter *or* **phil·tre** \ˈfil-tər\ *n* **1** : a potion, drug, or charm held to arouse sexual passion **2** : a magic potion

phle·bi·tis \fli-ˈbīt-əs\ *n* : inflammation of a vein

phle·bot·o·my \fli-ˈbät-ə-mē\ *n, pl* **-mies** : the opening of a vein for removing or releasing blood

phlegm \ˈflem\ *n* : thick mucus secreted in abnormal quantity esp. in the nose and throat

phleg·mat·ic \fleg-ˈmat-ik\ *adj* : having or showing a slow and stolid temperament **syn** impassive, apathetic, stoic, stolid

phlo·em \ˈflō-ˌem\ *n* : a vascular plant tissue external to the xylem that carries dissolved food material downward

phlox \ˈfläks\ *n, pl* **phlox** *or* **phlox·es** : any of several American herbs; *esp* : one that has tall stalks with showy spreading terminal clusters of flowers

pho·bia \ˈfō-bē-ə\ *n* : an irrational persistent fear or dread

phoe·be \ˈfē-(ˌ)bē\ *n* : a flycatcher of the eastern U.S.

that has a slight crest and is grayish brown above and yellowish white below

phoe·nix \ˈfē-niks\ *n* : a legendary bird held to live for centuries and then to burn itself to death and rise fresh and young from its ashes

phon *abbr* phonetics

[1]**phone** \ˈfōn\ *n* **1** : EARPHONE **2** : TELEPHONE

[2]**phone** *vb* **phoned; phon·ing** : TELEPHONE

pho·neme \ˈfō-ˌnēm\ *n* : one of the smallest units of speech that distinguish one utterance from another — **pho·ne·mic** \fō-ˈnē-mik\ *adj*

pho·net·ics \fə-ˈnet-iks\ *n* : the study and systematic classification of the sounds made in spoken utterance — **pho·net·ic** \-ik\ *adj* — **pho·ne·ti·cian** \ˌfō-nə-ˈtish-ən\ *n*

pho·nic \ˈfän-ik\ *adj* **1** : of, relating to, or producing sound **2** : of or relating to the sounds of speech or to phonics — **pho·ni·cal·ly** \-i-k(ə-)lē\ *adv*

pho·nics \ˈfän-iks\ *n* : a method of teaching people to read and pronounce words by learning the phonetic value of letters, letter groups, and esp. syllables

pho·no·graph \ˈfō-nə-ˌgraf\ *n* : an instrument for reproducing sounds by means of the vibration of a needle following a spiral groove on a revolving disc — **pho·no·graph·ic** \ˌfō-nə-ˈgraf-ik\ *adj* — **pho·no·graph·i·cal·ly** \-i-k(ə-)lē\ *adv*

pho·nol·o·gy \fə-ˈnäl-ə-jē\ *n* : a study and description of the sound changes in a language — **pho·no·log·i·cal** \ˌfōn-ᵊl-ˈäj-i-kəl\ *adj* — **pho·nol·o·gist** \fə-ˈnäl-ə-jəst\ *n*

pho·ny *or* **pho·ney** \ˈfō-nē\ *adj* **pho·ni·er; -est** : marked by empty pretension : FAKE — **phony** *n*

phosph- *or* **phospho-** *comb form* **1** : phosphorus **2** : phosphate

phos·phate \ˈfäs-ˌfāt\ *n* : a salt of a phosphoric acid — **phos·phat·ic** \fäs-ˈfat-ik\ *adj*

phos·phor \ˈfäs-fər\ *also* **phos·phore** \-ˌfōr, -fər\ *n* : a phosphorescent substance

phos·pho·res·cence \ˌfäs-fə-ˈres-ᵊns\ *n* **1** : luminescence caused by radiation absorption that continues after the radiation has stopped **2** : an enduring luminescence without sensible heat — **phos·pho·res·cent** \-ᵊnt\ *adj* — **phos·pho·res·cent·ly** *adv*

phosphoric acid \ˌfäs-ˌfōr-ik-, -ˌfär-\ *n* : any of several oxygen-containing acids of phosphorus

phos·pho·rus \ˈfäs-f(ə-)rəs\ *n* [NL, fr. Gk *phōsphoros* light-bearing, fr. *phōs* light + *pherein* to carry, bring] : a nonmetallic chemical element that has characteristics similar to nitrogen and occurs widely esp. as phosphates — see ELEMENT table — **phos·phor·ic** \fäs-ˈfōr-ik, -ˈfär-\ *adj* — **phos·pho·rous** \ˈfäs-f(ə-)rəs; fäs-ˈfōr-əs, -ˈfōr-\ *adj*

phot- *or* **photo-** *comb form* **1** : light **2** : photograph : photographic **3** : photoelectric

pho·to \ˈfōt-ō\ *n, pl* **photos** : PHOTOGRAPH — **photo** *vb or adj*

pho·to·cell \ˈfōt-ə-ˌsel\ *n* : PHOTOELECTRIC CELL

pho·to·chem·i·cal \ˌfōt-ō-ˈkem-i-kəl\ *adj* : of, relating to, or resulting from the chemical action of radiant energy

pho·to·com·pose \-kəm-ˈpōz\ *vb* : to compose reading matter for reproduction by means of characters photographed on film — **pho·to·com·po·si·tion** \-ˌkäm-pə-ˈzish-ən\ *n*

pho·to·copy \ˈfōt-ə-ˌkäp-ē\ *n* : a photographic reproduction of graphic matter — **photocopy** *vb*

pho·to·elec·tric \ˌfōt-ō-i-ˈlek-trik\ *adj* : relating to an electrical effect due to the interaction of light with matter — **pho·to·elec·tri·cal·ly** \-tri-k(ə-)lē\ *adv*

photoelectric cell *n* : a device in which variations in light are converted into variations in an electric current

pho·to·en·grave \ˌfōt-ō-in-ˈgrāv\ *vb* : to make a photoengraving of

pho·to·en·grav·ing \-ˈgrā-viŋ\ *n* : a process by which an etched printing plate is made from a photograph or drawing; *also* : a print made from such a plate

photo finish *n* : a race finish so close that a photograph of the finish is used to determine the winner

[1]**pho·tog** \fə-ˈtäg\ *n* : PHOTOGRAPHER

[2]**photog** *abbr* photographic; photography

pho·to·ge·nic \ˌfōt-ə-ˈjen-ik\ *adj* : eminently suitable esp. aesthetically for being photographed

pho·to·graph \ˈfōt-ə-ˌgraf\ *n* : a picture taken by photography — **pho·to·graph** *vb* — **pho·tog·ra·pher** \fə-ˈtäg-rə-fər\ *n*

pho·tog·ra·phy \fə-ˈtäg-rə-fē\ *n* : the art or process of producing images on a sensitized surface (as film in a camera) by the action of light — **pho·to·graph·ic** \ˌfōt-ə-ˈgraf-ik\ *adj* — **pho·to·graph·i·cal·ly** \-i-k(ə-)lē\ *adv*

pho·to·gra·vure \ˌfōt-ə-grə-ˈvyu̇r\ *n* : a process for making prints from an intaglio plate prepared by photographic methods

pho·to·li·thog·ra·phy \ˌfōt-ō-lith-ˈäg-rə-fē\ *n* : the process of photographically transferring a pattern to a surface for etching (as in making an integrated circuit)

pho·tom·e·ter \fō-ˈtäm-ət-ər\ *n* : an instrument for measuring luminous intensity — **pho·to·met·ric** \ˌfōt-ə-ˈme-trik\ *adj* — **pho·tom·e·try** \fō-ˈtäm-ə-trē\ *n*

pho·to·mi·cro·graph \ˌfōt-ə-ˈmī-krə-ˌgraf\ *n* : a photograph of a magnified image of a small object — **pho·to·mi·crog·ra·phy** \-mī-ˈkräg-rə-fē\ *n*

pho·ton \ˈfō-ˌtän\ *n* : a quantum of radiant energy

pho·to·play \ˈfōt-ō-ˌplā\ *n* : MOTION PICTURE

pho·to·sen·si·tive \ˌfōt-ə-ˈsen-sət-iv\ *adj* : sensitive or sensitized to the action of radiant energy

pho·to·sphere \ˈfōt-ə-ˌsfiər\ *n* **1** : a sphere of light **2** : the luminous surface of a star — **pho·to·spher·ic** \ˌfōt-ə-ˈsfi(ə)r-ik, -ˈsfer-\ *adj*

pho·to·syn·the·sis \ˌfōt-ō-ˈsin-thə-səs\ *n* : formation of carbohydrates by chlorophyll-containing plants exposed to sunlight — **pho·to·syn·the·size** \-ˌsīz\ *vb* — **pho·to·syn·thet·ic** \-sin-ˈthet-ik\ *adj*

phr *abbr* phrase

[1]**phrase** \ˈfrāz\ *n* **1** : a brief expression **2** : a group of two or more grammatically related words that form a sense unit expressing a thought

[2]**phrase** *vb* **phrased; phras·ing** : to express in words

phrase·ol·o·gy \ˌfrā-zē-ˈäl-ə-jē\ *n, pl* **-gies** : a manner of phrasing : STYLE

phras·ing \ˈfrā-ziŋ\ *n* : style of expression

phre·net·ic \fri-ˈnet-ik\ *adj* : FRENETIC

phren·ic \ˈfren-ik\ *adj* : of or relating to the diaphragm ⟨~ nerves⟩

phre·nol·o·gy \fri-ˈnäl-ə-jē\ *n* : the study of the conformation of the skull as indicative of mental faculties and character traits

phy·lac·tery \fə-ˈlak-t(ə-)rē\ *n, pl* **-ter·ies** **1** : one of two small square leather boxes containing slips inscribed with scripture passages and traditionally worn on the left arm and forehead by Jewish men during morning weekday prayers **2** : AMULET

phy·lum \ˈfī-ləm\ *n, pl* **phy·la** \-lə\ : a major division of the animal and in some classifications the plant kingdom; *also* : a group (as of people) apparently of common origin

phys *abbr* **1** physical **2** physics

[1]**phys·ic** \ˈfiz-ik\ *n* **1** : the profession of medicine **2** : MEDICINE; *esp* : CATHARTIC

[2]**physic** *vb* **phys·icked; phys·ick·ing** : PURGE

[1]**phys·i·cal** \ˈfiz-i-kəl\ *adj* **1** : of or relating to nature or the laws of nature **2** : material as opposed to mental or spiritual **3** : of, relating to, or produced by the forces

and operations of physics **4** : of or relating to the body — **phys·i·cal·ly** \-k(ə-)lē\ *adv*

[2]**physical** *n* : an examination of the bodily functions and condition of an individual

physical education *n* : instruction in the development and care of the body ranging from simple calisthenics to training in hygiene, gymnastics, and the performance and management of athletic games

physical examination *n* : PHYSICAL

physical science *n* : any of the sciences (as physics and astronomy) that deal primarily with nonliving materials — **physical scientist** *n*

physical therapy *n* : the treatment of disease by physical and mechanical means (as massage, exercise, water, or heat) — **physical therapist** *n*

phy·si·cian \fə-ˈzish-ən\ *n* : a doctor of medicine

phys·i·cist \ˈfiz-ə-səst\ *n* : a specialist in physics

phys·ics \ˈfiz-iks\ *n* **1** : the science of matter and energy and their interactions **2** : physical properties and composition

phys·i·og·no·my \ˌfiz-ē-ˈä(g)-nə-mē\ *n, pl* **-mies** : facial appearance esp. as a reflection of inner character

phys·i·og·ra·phy \ˌfiz-ē-ˈäg-rə-fē\ *n* : geography dealing with physical features of the earth — **phys·io·graph·ic** \ˌfiz-ē-ō-ˈgraf-ik\ *adj*

phys·i·ol·o·gy \ˌfiz-ē-ˈäl-ə-jē\ *n* **1** : a science dealing with the functions and functioning of living matter and beings **2** : functional processes in an organism or any of its parts — **phys·i·o·log·i·cal** \-ē-ə-ˈläj-i-kəl\ *or* **phys·i·o·log·ic** \-ik\ *adj* — **phys·i·o·log·i·cal·ly** \-i-k(ə-)lē\ *adv* — **phys·i·ol·o·gist** \-ē-ˈäl-ə-jəst\ *n*

phys·io·ther·a·py \ˌfiz-ē-ō-ˈther-ə-pē\ *n* : treatment of disease by physical means (as massage or exercise) — **phys·io·ther·a·pist** \-pəst\ *n*

phy·sique \fə-ˈzēk\ *n* : the build of a person's body : bodily constitution

phy·to·plank·ton \ˈfīt-ō-ˌplaŋk-tən\ *n* : plant life of the plankton

[1]**pi** *also* **pie** \ˈpī\ *n, pl* **pies** : jumbled type

[2]**pi** *n, pl* **pis** \ˈpīz\ : the symbol π denoting the ratio of the circumference of a circle to its diameter; *also* : the ratio itself

pi·a·nis·si·mo \ˌpē-ə-ˈnis-ə-ˌmō\ *adv or adj* : very softly — used as a direction in music

pi·a·nist \pē-ˈan-əst, ˈpē-ə-nəst\ *n* : one who plays the piano

[1]**pi·a·no** \pē-ˈän-ō\ *adv or adj* : SOFTLY — used as a direction in music

[2]**piano** \pē-ˈan-ō\ *n, pl* **pianos** [It, short for *pianoforte*, fr. *piano e forte* soft and loud, fr. *piano* soft (fr. L *planus* level, flat) + *forte* loud, fr. L *fortis* strong; fr. the fact that its tones could be varied in loudness] : a musical instrument having steel strings sounded by felt-covered hammers operated from a keyboard

pi·ano·forte \pē-ˌan-ō-ˈfōr-ˌtā, -tē; pē-ˈan-ə-ˌfōrt\ *n* : PIANO

pi·as·ter *or* **pi·as·tre** \pē-ˈas-tər\ *n* — see *lira, pound* at MONEY table

pi·az·za \pē-ˈaz-ə, *esp for 1* -ˈat-sə\ *n, pl* **piazzas** *or* **pi·az·ze** \-ˈat-(ˌ)sā, -ˈät-\ [It, fr. L *platea* broad street] **1** : an open square esp. in an Italian town **2** : a long hall with an arched roof; *also, dial* : VERANDA

pi·broch \ˈpē-ˌbräk\ *n* : a set of variations for the bagpipe

pic \ˈpik\ *n, pl* **pics** *or* **pix** \ˈpiks\ **1** : PHOTOGRAPH **2** : MOTION PICTURE

pi·ca \ˈpī-kə\ *n* : a typewriter type providing 10 characters to the inch

pi·ca·resque \ˌpik-ə-ˈresk, ˌpē-kə-\ *adj* : of or relating to rogues ⟨~ fiction⟩

pic·a·yune \ˌpik-ē-ˈ(y)ün\ *adj* [F *picaillon* halfpenny] : of little value : TRIVIAL; *also* : PETTY

pic·ca·lil·li \ˌpik-ə-ˈlil-ē\ *n* : a pungent relish of chopped vegetables and spices

pic·co·lo \ˈpik-ə-ˌlō\ *n, pl* **-los** [It, short for *piccolo flauto* small flute] : a small shrill flute pitched an octave higher than the ordinary flute

pice \ˈpīs\ *n, pl* **pice** : PAISA

[1]**pick** \ˈpik\ *vb* **1** : to pierce or break up with a pointed instrument **2** : to remove bit by bit ⟨~ meat from bones⟩; *also* : to remove covering matter from **3** : to gather by plucking ⟨~ apples⟩ **4** : CULL, SELECT **5** : ROB ⟨~ a pocket⟩ **6** : PROVOKE ⟨~ a quarrel⟩ **7** : to dig into or pull lightly at **8** : to pluck with fingers or a plectrum **9** : to loosen or pull apart with a sharp point ⟨~ wool⟩ **10** : to unlock with a wire **11** : to eat sparingly — **pick·er** *n*

[2]**pick** *n* **1** : the act or privilege of choosing **2** : the best or choicest one **3** : the part of a crop gathered at one time

[3]**pick** *n* **1** : PICKAX **2** : a pointed implement used for picking **3** : a small thin piece (as of metal) used to pluck the strings of a stringed instrument

pick·a·back \ˈpig-ē-ˌbak, ˈpik-ə-\ *var of* PIGGYBACK

pick·ax \ˈpik-ˌaks\ *n* : a tool with a wooden handle and a blade pointed at one end or at both ends that is used by diggers and miners

pick·er·el \ˈpik(-ə)-rəl\ *n, pl* **pickerel** *or* **pickerels** : any of various small pikes; *also* : WALLEYE 2

pick·er·el·weed \-rəl-ˌwēd\ *n* : a blue-flowered American shallow-water herb

[1]**pick·et** \ˈpik-ət\ *n* **1** : a pointed stake (as for a fence) **2** : a detached body of soldiers on outpost duty; *also* : SENTINEL **3** : a person posted by a labor union where workers are on strike; *also* : a person posted for a demonstration

[2]**picket** *vb* **1** : to guard with pickets **2** : TETHER **3** : to post pickets at ⟨~ a factory⟩ **4** : to serve as a picket

pick·ings \ˈpik-iŋz, -ənz\ *n pl* **1** : gleanable or eatable fragments : SCRAPS **2** : yield for effort expended : RETURN; *also* : share of spoils

pick·le \ˈpik-əl\ *n* **1** : a brine or vinegar solution for preserving foods; *also* : a food preserved in a pickle **2** : a difficult situation : PLIGHT — **pickle** *vb*

pick·lock \ˈpik-ˌläk\ *n* **1** : a tool for picking locks **2** : BURGLAR, THIEF

pick·pock·et \ˈpik-ˌpäk-ət\ *n* : one who steals from pockets

pick·up \ˈpik-ˌəp\ *n* **1** : a picking up **2** : revival of activity : IMPROVEMENT **3** : ACCELERATION **4** : a temporary chance acquaintance **5** : the conversion of mechanical movements into electrical impulses in the reproduction of sound; *also* : a device for making such conversion **6** : a light truck having an enclosed cab and an open body with low sides and a tailgate

pick up \(ˈ)pik-ˈəp\ *vb* **1** : to take hold of and lift **2** : IMPROVE **3** : to put in order

picky \ˈpik-ē\ *adj* **pick·i·er; -est** : FUSSY, FINICKY

[1]**pic·nic** \ˈpik-ˌnik\ *n* : an outing with food usu. provided by members of the group and eaten in the open

[2]**picnic** *vb* **pic·nicked; pic·nick·ing** : to go on a picnic : eat in picnic fashion

pi·co·sec·ond \ˈpē-kō-ˌsek-ənd\ *n* : one trillionth of a second

pi·cot \ˈpē-ˌkō\ *n* : one of a series of small loops forming an edging on ribbon or lace

pic·to·ri·al \pik-ˈtōr-ē-əl\ *adj* : of, relating to, or consisting of pictures

[1]**pic·ture** \ˈpik-chər\ *n* **1** : a representation made by painting, drawing, or photography **2** : a vivid description in words **3** : IMAGE, COPY **4** : a transitory visual image or reproduction **5** : MOTION PICTURE **6** : SITUATION

[2]**picture** *vb* **pic·tured; pic·tur·ing** **1** : to paint or draw a picture of **2** : to describe vividly in words **3** : to form a mental image of

pic·tur·esque \ˌpik-chə-ˈresk\ *adj* **1** : resembling a picture ⟨a ~ landscape⟩ **2** : CHARMING, QUAINT ⟨a ~ character⟩ **3** : GRAPHIC, VIVID ⟨a ~ account⟩ — **pic·tur·esque·ness** *n*

picture tube *n* : a cathode-ray tube on which the picture in a television set appears

pid·dle \ˈpid-ᵊl\ *vb* **pid·dled; pid·dling** \ˈpid-(ᵊ-)liŋ\ : to act or work idly : DAWDLE
pid·dling \-(ᵊ-)lən, -(ᵊ-)liŋ\ *adj* : TRIVIAL, PALTRY
pid·gin \ˈpij-ən\ *n* [fr. *Pidgin English,* Pidgin E, modif. of E *business English*] : a simplified speech used for communication between people with different languages; *esp* : an English-based pidgin used in the Orient
[1]**pie** \ˈpī\ *n* : a dish consisting of a pastry crust and a filling (as of fruit or meat)
[2]**pie** *var of* PI
[1]**pie·bald** \ˈpī-ˌbȯld\ *adj* : of different colors; *esp* : blotched with white and black
[2]**piebald** *n* : a piebald animal (as a horse)
[1]**piece** \ˈpēs\ *n* **1** : a part of a whole : FRAGMENT **2** : one of a group, set, or mass ⟨chess ~⟩; *also* : a single item ⟨a ~ of news⟩ **3** : a length, weight, or size in which something is made or sold **4** : a product (as an essay) of creative work **5** : FIREARM **6** : COIN
[2]**piece** *vb* **pieced; piec·ing 1** : to repair or complete by adding pieces : PATCH **2** : to join into a whole
pièce de ré·sis·tance \pē-ˌes-də-rā-ˌzē-ˈstäns\ *n, pl* **pièces de ré·sis·tance** *same*\ **1** : the chief dish of a meal **2** : an outstanding item
piece·meal \ˈpēs-ˌmēl\ *adv or adj* : one piece at a time : GRADUALLY
piece·work \-ˌwərk\ *n* : work done and paid for by the piece — **piece·work·er** *n*
pied \ˈpīd\ *adj* : of two or more colors in blotches : VARIEGATED
pied–à–terre \pē-ˌād-ə-ˈter\ *n, pl* **pieds–à–terre** *same*\ [F, lit., foot to the ground] : a temporary or second lodging
pier \ˈpiər\ *n* **1** : a support for a bridge span **2** : a structure built out into the water for use as a landing place or a promenade or to protect or form a harbor **3** : an upright supporting part (as a pillar) of a building or structure
pierce \ˈpiərs\ *vb* **pierced; pierc·ing 1** : to enter or thrust into sharply or painfully : STAB **2** : to make a hole in or through : PERFORATE **3** : to force or make a way into or through : PENETRATE **4** : to see through : DISCERN
pies *pl of* PI *or of* PIE
pi·ety \ˈpī-ət-ē\ *n, pl* **pi·et·ies 1** : fidelity to natural obligations (as to parents) **2** : dutifulness in religion : DEVOUTNESS **3** : a pious act **syn** allegiance, devotion, loyalty
pif·fle \ˈpif-əl\ *n* : trifling talk or action
pig \ˈpig\ *n* **1** : SWINE; *esp* : a young swine **2** : PORK **3** : one thought to resemble a pig (as in dirtiness or greed) **4** : a casting of metal (as iron or lead) run directly from a smelting furnace into a mold
pi·geon \ˈpij-ən\ *n* : any of numerous stout-bodied short-legged birds with smooth thick plumage
[1]**pi·geon·hole** \ˈpij-ən-ˌhōl\ *n* : a small open compartment (as in a desk) for keeping letters or documents
[2]**pigeonhole** *vb* **1** : to place in or as if in a pigeonhole : FILE **2** : to lay aside **3** : CLASSIFY
pi·geon–toed \ˈpij-ən-ˌtōd\ *adj* : having the toes turned in
pig·gish \ˈpig-ish\ *adj* **1** : GREEDY **2** : STUBBORN
pig·gy·back \ˈpig-ē-ˌbak\ *adv or adj* **1** : up on the back and shoulders **2** : on a railroad flatcar
pig·head·ed \ˈpig-ˈhed-əd\ *adj* : OBSTINATE, STUBBORN
pig latin *n, often cap L* : a jargon that is made by systematic alteration of English
pig·let \ˈpig-lət\ *n* : a small usu. young hog
pig·ment \ˈpig-mənt\ *n* **1** : coloring matter **2** : a powder mixed with a suitable liquid to give color (as in paints and enamels)
pig·men·ta·tion \ˌpig-mən-ˈtā-shən\ *n* : coloration with or deposition of pigment; *esp* : an excessive deposition of bodily pigment
pigmy *var of* PYGMY
pig·nut \ˈpig-ˌnət\ *n* : any of several bitter hickory nuts; *also* : a tree bearing these
pig·pen \-ˌpen\ *n* **1** : a pen for pigs **2** : a dirty place
pig·skin \-ˌskin\ *n* **1** : the skin of a pig; *also* : leather made from it **2** : FOOTBALL 2
pig·sty \-ˌstī\ *n* : PIGPEN
pig·tail \-ˌtāl\ *n* : a tight braid of hair
pi·ka \ˈpī-kə\ *n* : any of various small short-eared mammals of the rocky uplands of Asia and western No. America that are related to the rabbits
[1]**pike** \ˈpīk\ *n* : a sharp point or spike
[2]**pike** *n, pl* **pike** *or* **pikes** : a large slender long-snouted freshwater food fish; *also* : a related fish
[3]**pike** *n* : a long wooden shaft with a pointed steel head formerly used as a foot soldier's weapon
[4]**pike** *n* : TURNPIKE
pik·er \ˈpī-kər\ *n* **1** : one who does things in a small way or on a small scale **2** : TIGHTWAD, CHEAPSKATE
pike·staff \ˈpīk-ˌstaf\ *n* : the staff of a foot soldier's pike
pi·laf *or* **pi·laff** \pi-ˈläf, ˈpē-ˌläf\ *or* **pi·lau** \pi-ˈlō, -ˈlȯ, ˈpē-lō, -lȯ\ *n* : a dish made of seasoned rice often with meat
pi·las·ter \pi-ˈlas-tər, ˈpī-ˌlas-tər\ *n* : a slightly projecting upright column that ornaments or helps to support a wall
pil·chard \ˈpil-chərd\ *n* : any of several fishes related to the herrings and often packed as sardines
[1]**pile** \ˈpīl\ *n* : a long slender column (as of wood or steel) driven into the ground to support a vertical load
[2]**pile** *n* **1** : a quantity of things heaped together **2** : PYRE **3** : a great number or quantity : LOT
[3]**pile** *vb* **piled; pil·ing 1** : to lay in a pile : STACK **2** : to heap up : ACCUMULATE **3** : to press forward in a mass : CROWD
[4]**pile** *n* : a velvety surface of fine short hairs or threads (as on cloth) — **piled** \ˈpīld\ *adj* — **pile·less** *adj*
piles \ˈpīlz\ *n pl* : HEMORRHOIDS
pil·fer \ˈpil-fər\ *vb* **pil·fered; pil·fer·ing** \-f(ə-)riŋ\ : to steal in small quantities
pil·grim \ˈpil-grəm\ *n* [ME, fr. OF *peligrin,* fr. LL *pelegrinus,* alter. of L *peregrinus* foreigner, fr. *peregrinus* foreign, fr. *pereger* being abroad, fr. *per* through + *ager* land] **1** : one who journeys in foreign lands : WAYFARER **2** : one who travels to a shrine or holy place as an act of devotion **3** *cap* : one of the English settlers founding Plymouth colony in 1620
pil·grim·age \-grə-mij\ *n* : a journey of a pilgrim esp. to a shrine or holy place
pil·ing \ˈpī-liŋ\ *n* : a structure of piles
pill \ˈpil\ *n* **1** : a medicine prepared in a little ball to be taken whole **2** : a disagreeable or tiresome person **3** : an oral contraceptive — usu. used with *the*
pil·lage \ˈpil-ij\ *vb* **pil·laged; pil·lag·ing** : to take booty : LOOT, PLUNDER — **pillage** *n*
pil·lar \ˈpil-ər\ *n* **1** : a strong upright support (as for a roof) **2** : a column or shaft standing alone esp. as a monument — **pil·lared** \-ərd\ *adj*
pill·box \ˈpil-ˌbäks\ *n* **1** : a low usu. round box to hold pills **2** : something (as a low concrete emplacement for machine guns) shaped like a pillbox
pil·lion \ˈpil-yən\ *n* **1** : a pad or cushion placed behind a saddle for an extra rider **2** : a motorcycle or bicycle saddle for a passenger
[1]**pil·lo·ry** \ˈpil-(ə-)rē\ *n, pl* **-ries** : a wooden frame for public punishment having holes in which the head and hands can be locked
[2]**pillory** *vb* **-ried; -ry·ing 1** : to set in a pillory **2** : to expose to public scorn
[1]**pil·low** \ˈpil-ō\ *n* : a case filled with springy material (as feathers) and used to support the head of a resting person

---

²**pillow** *vb* : to rest or place on or as if on a pillow; *also* : to serve as a pillow for

pil·low·case \ˈpil-ə-ˌkās, -ō-\ *n* : a removable covering for a pillow

¹**pi·lot** \ˈpī-lət\ *n* **1** : HELMSMAN, STEERSMAN **2** : a person qualified and licensed to take ships into and out of a port **3** : GUIDE, LEADER **4** : one that flies an aircraft or spacecraft **5** : a television show filmed or taped as a sample of a proposed series — **pi·lot·less** *adj*

²**pilot** *vb* : CONDUCT, GUIDE; *esp* : to act as pilot of

³**pilot** *adj* : serving as a guiding or activating device or as a testing or trial unit ⟨a ~ light⟩ ⟨a ~ factory⟩

pi·lot·house \ˈpī-lət-ˌhau̇s\ *n* : an enclosed place forward on the upper deck of a ship that shelters the steering gear and the helmsman

pil·sner *also* **pil·sen·er** \ˈpilz-(ə-)nər\ *n* [G, lit., of Pilsen, city in Czechoslovakia (now Plzeň)] **1** : a light beer with a strong flavor of hops **2** : a tall slender footed glass for beer

pi·men·to \pə-ˈment-ō\ *n, pl* **pimentos** *or* **pimento** [Sp *pimienta* allspice, pepper, fr. LL *pigmenta*, pl. of *pigmentum* plant juice, fr. L, pigment] **1** : PIMIENTO **2** : ALLSPICE

pi·mien·to \pə-ˈm(y)ent-ō\ *n, pl* **-tos** : a mild red sweet pepper fruit that yields paprika

pimp \ˈpimp\ *n* : a man who solicits clients for a prostitute — **pimp** *vb*

pim·per·nel \ˈpim-pər-ˌnel, -pər-nəl\ *n* : any of a genus of herbs related to the primroses and having flowers that close in rainy or cloudy weather

pim·ple \ˈpim-pəl\ *n* : a small inflamed swelling on the skin often containing pus — **pim·ply** \-p(ə-)lē\ *adj*

¹**pin** \ˈpin\ *n* **1** : a piece of wood or metal used esp. for fastening articles together or as a support by which one article may be suspended from another; *esp* : a small pointed piece of wire with a head used for fastening clothes or attaching papers **2** : an ornament or emblem fastened to clothing with a pin **3** : one of the wooden pieces constituting the target (as in bowling); *also* : the staff of the flag marking a hole on a golf course **4** : LEG

²**pin** *vb* **pinned; pin·ning 1** : to fasten with a pin **2** : to press together and hold fast **3** : to make dependent ⟨*pinned* their hopes on one man⟩ **4** : to assign the blame for ⟨~ a crime on someone⟩ **5** : to define clearly : ESTABLISH ⟨~ down an idea⟩ **6** : to hold fast or immobile in a spot or position

pi·ña co·la·da \ˌpēn-yə-kō-ˈläd-ə\ *n* [Sp, lit., strained pineapple] : a tall drink made of rum, cream of coconut, and pineapple juice mixed with ice

pin·afore \ˈpin-ə-ˌfōr\ *n* : a sleeveless dress or apron fastened at the back

pince–nez \paⁿs-ˈnā\ *n, pl* **pince–nez** \-ˈnā(z)\ [F, lit., pinch-nose] : eyeglasses clipped to the nose by a spring

pin·cer \ˈpin-sər\ *n* **1** *pl* : a gripping instrument with two handles and two grasping jaws **2** : a claw (as of a lobster) resembling pincers

¹**pinch** \ˈpinch\ *vb* **1** : to squeeze between the finger and thumb or between the jaws of an instrument **2** : to compress painfully : CRAMP **3** : CONTRACT, SHRIVEL **4** : to be miserly; *also* : to subject to strict economy **5** : STEAL **6** : ARREST

²**pinch** *n* **1** : a critical point **2** : painful effect **3** : an act of pinching **4** : a very small quantity **5** : ARREST

³**pinch** *adj* : SUBSTITUTE ⟨a ~ runner⟩

pinch–hit \(ˈ)pinch-ˈhit\ *vb* **1** : to bat in the place of another player esp. when a hit is particularly needed **2** : to act or serve in place of another — **pinch hit** *n* — **pinch hitter** *n*

pin curl *n* : a curl made usu. by dampening a strand of hair, coiling it, and securing it by a hairpin or clip

pin·cush·ion \ˈpin-ˌku̇sh-ən\ *n* : a cushion for pins not in use

¹**pine** \ˈpīn\ *n* : any of a genus of evergreen cone-bearing trees; *also* : the light durable resinous wood of a pine

²**pine** *vb* **pined; pin·ing 1** : to lose vigor or health through distress **2** : to long for something intensely

pi·ne·al \ˈpī-nē-əl, pī-ˈnē-əl\ *n* : PINEAL GLAND — **pineal** *adj*

pineal gland *n* : a small usu. conical appendage of the brain of all vertebrates with a cranium that is variously postulated to be a vestigial third eye, an endocrine organ, or the seat of the soul

pine·ap·ple \ˈpīn-ˌap-əl\ *n* : a tropical plant bearing an edible juicy fruit; *also* : its fruit

pin·feath·er \ˈpin-ˌfe*th*-ər\ *n* : a new feather just coming through the skin

ping \ˈpiŋ\ *n* **1** : a sharp sound like that of a bullet striking **2** : engine knock

pin·hole \ˈpin-ˌhōl\ *n* : a small hole made by, for, or as if by a pin

¹**pin·ion** \ˈpin-yən\ *n* : the end section of a bird's wing; *also* : WING

²**pinion** *vb* : to restrain by binding the arms; *also* : SHACKLE

³**pinion** *n* : a gear with a small number of teeth designed to mesh with a larger wheel or rack

¹**pink** \ˈpiŋk\ *n* **1** : any of a genus of plants with narrow leaves often grown for their showy flowers **2** : the highest degree : HEIGHT ⟨the ~ of condition⟩

²**pink** *n* : a light tint of red

³**pink** *adj* **1** : of the color pink **2** : holding socialistic views — **pink·ish** *adj*

⁴**pink** *vb* **1** : PIERCE, STAB **2** : to perforate in an ornamental pattern **3** : to cut a saw-toothed edge on

pink elephants *n pl* : any of various hallucinations arising esp. from heavy drinking or use of narcotics

pink·eye \ˈpiŋk-ˌī\ *n* : an acute contagious eye inflammation

pin·kie *or* **pin·ky** \ˈpiŋ-kē\ *n, pl* **pinkies** : the smallest finger of the hand

pin·nace \ˈpin-əs\ *n* **1** : a light sailing ship **2** : a ship's boat

pin·na·cle \ˈpin-i-kəl\ *n* [ME *pinacle*, fr. MF, fr. LL *pinnaculum* gable, fr. dim. of L *pinna* wing, battlement] **1** : a turret ending in a small spire **2** : a lofty peak **3** : the highest point : ACME

pin·nate \ˈpin-ˌāt\ *adj* : having similar parts arranged on each side of an axis — **pin·nate·ly** *adv*

pi·noch·le \ˈpē-ˌnək-əl\ *n* : a card game played with a 48-card deck

pi·ñon *or* **pin·yon** \ˈpin-ˌyōn, -ˌyän\ *n, pl* **pi·ñons** *or* **pinyons** *or* **pi·ño·nes** \pin-ˈyō-nēz\ [AmerSp *piñón*] : any of various low-growing pines of western No. America with edible seeds; *also* : the edible seed of a piñon

pin·point \ˈpin-ˌpȯint\ *vb* : to locate, hit, or aim with great precision

pin·prick \-ˌprik\ *n* **1** : a small puncture made by or as if by a pin **2** : a petty irritation or annoyance

pins and needles *n pl* : a pricking tingling sensation in a limb growing numb or recovering from numbness — **on pins and needles** : in a nervous or jumpy state of anticipation

pin·stripe \ˈpin-ˌstrīp\ *n* : a narrow stripe on a fabric; *also* : a suit with such stripes — **pin–striped** \-ˌstrīpt\ *adj*

pint \ˈpīnt\ *n* — see WEIGHT table

pin·to \ˈpin-ˌtō\ *n, pl* **pintos** *also* **pintoes** : a spotted horse

pinto bean *n* : a mottled kidney bean that is grown in the southwestern U.S. for food and for stock feed

pin·up \ˈpin-ˌəp\ *adj* : suitable for pinning up on an admirer's wall ⟨~ photo⟩; *also* : suited (as by beauty) to be the subject of a pinup photograph

pin·wheel \-ˌhwēl\ *n* **1** : a toy consisting of lightweight vanes that revolve at the end of a stick **2** : a fireworks device in the form of a revolving wheel of colored fire

pin·worm \-ˌwərm\ *n* : a small worm parasitic in the intestines of man

pin·yin \ˈpin-ˈyin\ *n, often cap* : a system for writing

Chinese ideograms by using Roman letters to represent the sounds

[1]**pi·o·neer** \ˌpī-ə-ˈniər\ *n* [MF *pionier,* fr. OF *peonier* foot soldier, fr. *peon* foot soldier, fr. ML *pedon-, pedo,* fr. LL one with broad feet, fr. L *ped-, pes* foot] **1** : one that originates or helps open up a new line of thought or activity **2** : an early settler in a territory

[2]**pioneer** *vb* **1** : to act as a pioneer **2** : to open or prepare for others to follow; *esp* : SETTLE

pi·ous \ˈpī-əs\ *adj* **1** : marked by reverence for deity : DEVOUT **2** : excessively or affectedly religious **3** : SACRED, DEVOTIONAL **4** : marked by sham or hypocrisy **5** : showing loyal reverence for a person or thing : DUTIFUL — **pi·ous·ly** *adv*

[1]**pip** \ˈpip\ *n* **1** : a disease of birds **2** : a usu. minor human ailment

[2]**pip** *n* : one of the dots or figures used chiefly to indicate numerical value (as of a playing card)

[3]**pip** *n* : a small fruit seed (as of an apple)

[1]**pipe** \ˈpīp\ *n* **1** : a musical instrument having a tube played by forcing air through it **2** : BAGPIPE **3** : a tube designed to conduct something (as water, steam, or oil) **4** : a device for smoking having a tube with a bowl at one end and a mouthpiece at the other

[2]**pipe** *vb* **piped; pip·ing 1** : to play on a pipe **2** : to speak in a high or shrill voice **3** : to convey by or as if by pipes — **pip·er** *n*

pipe down *vb* : to stop talking or making noise

pipe dream *n* : an illusory or fantastic hope

pipe·line \ˈpīp-ˌlīn\ *n* **1** : a line of pipe with pumps, valves, and control devices for conveying liquids, gases, or fine solids **2** : a channel for information

pi·pette *or* **pi·pet** \pī-ˈpet\ *n* : a device for measuring and transferring small volumes of liquid

pipe up *vb* : to begin to play, sing, or speak

pip·ing \ˈpī-piŋ\ *n* **1** : the music of pipes **2** : a narrow fold of material used to decorate edges or seams

piping hot *adj* : so hot as to sizzle or hiss : very hot

pip·pin \ˈpip-ən\ *n* : any of several yellowish apples

pip–squeak \ˈpip-ˌskwēk\ *n* : one that is small or insignificant

pi·quant \ˈpē-kənt\ *adj* **1** : pleasantly savory : PUNGENT **2** : engagingly provocative; *also* : having a lively charm — **pi·quan·cy** \-kən-sē\ *n*

[1]**pique** \ˈpēk\ *n* [F] : offense taken by one slighted; *also* : a fit of resentment

[2]**pique** *vb* **piqued; piqu·ing 1** : to offend esp. by slighting **2** : to arouse by a provocation or challenge : GOAD

pi·qué *or* **pi·que** \pi-ˈkā\ *n* : a durable ribbed clothing fabric

pi·quet \pi-ˈkā\ *n* : a 2-handed card game played with 32 cards

pi·ra·cy \ˈpī-rə-sē\ *n, pl* **-cies 1** : robbery on the high seas or in the air **2** : the unauthorized use of another's production or invention

pi·ra·nha \pə-ˈran-yə, -ˈrän-(y)ə\ *n* [Pg] : a small So. American fish that often attacks human beings and large animals

pi·rate \ˈpī-rət\ *n* [ME, fr. MF or L; MF, fr. L *pirata,* fr. Gk *peiratēs,* fr. *peiran* to attempt, attack] : one who commits piracy — **pirate** *vb* — **pi·rat·i·cal** \pə-ˈrat-i-kəl, pī-\ *adj*

pir·ou·ette \ˌpir-ə-ˈwet\ *n* [F] : a full turn on the toe or ball of one foot in ballet; *also* : a rapid whirling about of the body — **pirouette** *vb*

pis *pl of* PI

pis·ca·to·ri·al \ˌpis-kə-ˈtōr-ē-əl\ *adj* : of or relating to fishing

Pi·sces \ˈpī-sēz\ *n* [ME, fr. L, lit., fishes] **1** : a zodiacal constellation between Aquarius and Aries usu. pictured as a fish **2** : the 12th sign of the zodiac in astrology; *also* : one born under this sign

pis·mire \ˈpis-ˌmī(ə)r\ *n* : ANT

pis·ta·chio \pə-ˈstash-(ē-ˌ)ō, -ˈstäsh-\ *n, pl* **-chios** : the greenish edible seed of a small tree related to the sumacs; *also* : the tree

pis·til \ˈpis-tᵊl\ *n* : the female reproductive organ in a flower — **pis·til·late** \ˈpis-tə-ˌlāt\ *adj*

pis·tol \ˈpis-tᵊl\ *n* : a handgun whose chamber is integral with the barrel

pistol–whip \-ˌhwip\ *vb* : to beat with a pistol

pis·ton \ˈpis-tən\ *n* : a sliding piece that receives and transmits motion and that usu. consists of a short cylinder inside a large cylinder

[1]**pit** \ˈpit\ *n* **1** : a hole, shaft, or cavity in the ground **2** : an often sunken area designed for a particular use; *also* : an enclosed place (as for cockfights) **3** : HELL; *also, pl* : WORST ⟨it's the ~*s*⟩ **4** : a hollow or indentation esp. in the surface of the body **5** : a small indented scar (as from smallpox)

[2]**pit** *vb* **pit·ted; pit·ting 1** : to form pits in or become marred with pits **2** : to match for fighting

[3]**pit** *n* : the stony seed of some fruits (as the cherry, peach, and date)

[4]**pit** *vb* **pit·ted; pit·ting** : to remove the pit from

pi·ta \ˈpēt-ə\ *n* [NGk] : a thin flat bread

pit–a–pat \ˌpit-i-ˈpat\ *n* : PITTER-PATTER — **pit–a–pat** *adv or adj*

pit bull *n* : a powerful compact short-haired dog developed for fighting

[1]**pitch** \ˈpich\ *n* **1** : a dark sticky substance left over esp. from distilling tar or petroleum **2** : resin from various conifers — **pitchy** *adj*

[2]**pitch** *vb* **1** : to erect and fix firmly in place ⟨~ a tent⟩ **2** : THROW, FLING **3** : to deliver a baseball to a batter **4** : to toss (as coins) toward a mark **5** : to set at a particular level ⟨~ the voice low⟩ **6** : to fall headlong **7** : to have the front end (as of a ship) alternately plunge and rise **8** : to incline downward : SLOPE

[3]**pitch** *n* **1** : the action or a manner of pitching **2** : degree of slope ⟨~ of a roof⟩ **3** : the relative level of some quality or state ⟨a high ~ of excitement⟩ **4** : highness or lowness of sound **5** : an often high-pressure sales talk **6** : the delivery of a baseball to a batter; *also* : the baseball delivered

pitch·blende \ˈpich-ˌblend\ *n* : a dark mineral that is the chief source of uranium

[1]**pitch·er** \ˈpich-ər\ *n* : a container for liquids that usu. has a lip and a handle

[2]**pitcher** *n* : one that pitches esp. in a baseball game

pitcher plant *n* : a plant with leaves modified to resemble pitchers in which insects are trapped and digested

pitch·fork \ˈpich-ˌfȯrk\ *n* : a long-handled fork used esp. in pitching hay

pitch in *vb* **1** : to begin to work **2** : to contribue to a common effort

pitch·man \ˈpich-mən\ *n* : SALESMAN; *esp* : one who vends novelties on the streets or from a concession

pit·e·ous \ˈpit-ē-əs\ *adj* : arousing pity : PITIFUL — **pit·e·ous·ly** *adv*

pit·fall \ˈpit-ˌfȯl\ *n* **1** : TRAP, SNARE; *esp* : a covered pit used for capturing animals **2** : a hidden danger or difficulty

pith \ˈpith\ *n* **1** : loose spongy tissue esp. in the center of the stem of vascular plants **2** : the essential part : CORE

pithy \ˈpith-ē\ *adj* **pith·i·er; -est 1** : consisting of or filled with pith **2** : being brief and to the point

piti·able \ˈpit-ē-ə-bəl\ *adj* : PITIFUL

piti·ful \ˈpit-i-fəl\ *adj* **1** : arousing or deserving pity ⟨a ~ sight⟩ **2** : MEAN, MEAGER — **piti·ful·ly** \-f(ə-)lē\ *adv*

piti·less \ˈpit-i-ləs\ *adj* : devoid of pity : MERCILESS — **pit·i·less·ly** *adv*
pi·ton \ˈpē-ˌtän\ *n* [F] : a spike, wedge, or peg that can be driven into a rock or ice surface as a support
pit·tance \ˈpit-ᵊns\ *n* : a small portion, amount, or allowance
pit·ter–pat·ter \ˈpit-ər-ˌpat-ər, ˈpit-ē-\ *n* : a rapid succession of light taps or sounds — **pitter–patter** \ˌpit-ər-ˈpat-ər, ˌpit-ē-\ *adv or adj* — **pitter–patter** *like adv*\ *vb*
pi·tu·itary \pə-ˈt(y)ü-ə-ˌter-ē\ *n, pl* **-itar·ies** : PITUITARY GLAND — **pituitary** *adj*
pituitary gland *n* : a small oval endocrine gland attached to the brain which produces various hormones that affect most basic bodily functions
pit viper *n* : any of various mostly New World specialized venomous snakes with a sensory pit on each side of the head and hollow perforated fangs
[1]**pity** \ˈpit-ē\ *n, pl* **pit·ies** [ME *pite*, fr. OF *pité*, fr. L *pietas* piety, pity, fr. *pius* pious] **1** : sympathetic sorrow : COMPASSION **2** : something to be regretted
[2]**pity** *vb* **pit·ied; pity·ing** : to feel pity for
[1]**piv·ot** \ˈpiv-ət\ *n* : a fixed pin on which something turns — **pivot** *adj* — **piv·ot·al** \ˈpiv-ət-ᵊl\ *adj*
[2]**pivot** *vb* : to turn on or as if on a pivot
pix *pl of* PIC
pix·el \ˈpik-səl, -ˌsel\ *n* : any of the small elements that together make up an image (as on a television screen)
pix·ie *or* **pixy** \ˈpik-sē\ *n, pl* **pix·ies** : FAIRY; *esp* : a mischievous sprite
piz·za \ˈpēt-sə\ *n* [It] : an open pie made of rolled bread dough spread with a spiced mixture (as of tomatoes, cheese, and ground meat) and baked
piz·zazz *or* **pi·zazz** \pə-ˈzaz\ *n* **1** : GLAMOUR **2** : VITALITY
piz·ze·ria \ˌpēt-sə-ˈrē-ə\ *n* : an establishment where pizzas are made and sold
piz·zi·ca·to \ˌpit-si-ˈkät-ō\ *adv or adj* [It] : by means of plucking instead of bowing — used as a direction in music
pj's \(ˈ)pē-ˈjāz\ *n pl* : PAJAMAS
pk *abbr* **1** park **2** peak **3** peck **4** pike
pkg *abbr* package
pkt *abbr* **1** packet **2** pocket
pkwy *abbr* parkway
pl *abbr* **1** place **2** plate **3** plural
[1]**plac·ard** \ˈplak-ərd, -ˌärd\ *n* : a notice posted in a public place : POSTER
[2]**plac·ard** \-ˌärd, -ərd\ *vb* **1** : to cover with or as if with placards **2** : to announce by posting
pla·cate \ˈplā-ˌkāt, ˈplak-ˌāt\ *vb* **pla·cat·ed; pla·cat·ing** : to soothe esp. by concessions : APPEASE — **pla·ca·ble** \ˈplak-ə-bəl, ˈplā-kə-\ *adj*
[1]**place** \ˈplās\ *n* [ME, fr. MF, open space, fr. L *platea* broad street, fr. Gk *plateia* (*hodos*), fr. fem. of *platys* broad, flat] **1** : SPACE, ROOM **2** : an indefinite region : AREA **3** : a building or locality used for a speical purpose **4** : a center of population **5** : a particular part of a surface : SPOT **6** : relative position in a scale or sequence; *also* : high and esp. 2d position at the end of a competition **7** : ACCOMMODATION; *esp* : SEAT **8** : the position of a figure in a numeral ⟨12 is a two ~ number⟩ **9** : JOB; *esp* : public office **10** : a public square
[2]**place** *vb* **placed; plac·ing** **1** : to distribute in an orderly manner : ARRANGE **2** : to put in a particular place : SET **3** : IDENTIFY **4** : to give an order for ⟨~ a bet⟩ **5** : to rank high and esp. 2d at the end of a competition
pla·ce·bo \plə-ˈsē-bō\ *n, pl* **-bos** [L, I shall please] : an inert medication used for its psychological effect or for purposes of comparison in an experiment
place·hold·er \ˈplās-ˌhōl-dər\ *n* : a symbol in a mathematical or logical expression that may be replaced by the name of any element of a set
place·kick \-ˌkik\ *n* : the kicking of a ball placed or held on the ground — **placekick** *vb* — **place·kick·er** *n*
place·ment \ˈplās-mənt\ *n* : an act or instance of placing
pla·cen·ta \plə-ˈsent-ə\ *n, pl* **-centas** *or* **-cen·tae** \-ˈsent-(ˌ)ē\ [NL, fr. L, flat cake] : the organ in most mammals by which the fetus is joined to the uterus of the mother and is nourished — **pla·cen·tal** \-ˈsent-ᵊl\ *adj*
plac·er \ˈplas-ər\ *n* : an alluvial or glacial deposit containing particles of valuable mineral
plac·id \ˈplas-əd\ *adj* : UNDISTURBED, PEACEFUL **syn** tranquil, serene, calm — **pla·cid·i·ty** \pla-ˈsid-ət-ē\ *n* — **plac·id·ly** \ˈplas-əd-lē\ *adv*
plack·et \ˈplak-ət\ *n* : a slit in a garment
pla·gia·rize \ˈplā-jə-ˌrīz\ *vb* **-rized; -riz·ing** : to present the ideas or words of another as one's own — **pla·gia·rism** \-ˌriz-əm\ *n* — **pla·gia·rist** \-rəst\ *n*
[1]**plague** \ˈplāg\ *n* **1** : a disastrous evil or influx; *also* : NUISANCE **2** : PESTILENCE; *esp* : a destructive contagious bacterial disease (as bubonic plague)
[2]**plague** *vb* **plagued; plagu·ing** **1** : to afflict with or as if with disease or disaster **2** : TEASE, TORMENT, HARASS
plaid \ˈplad\ *n* **1** : a rectangular length of tartan worn esp. over the left shoulder as part of the Scottish national costume **2** : a twilled woolen fabric with a tartan pattern **3** : a pattern of unevenly spaced repeated stripes crossing at right angles — **plaid** *adj*
[1]**plain** \ˈplān\ *n* : an extensive area of level or rolling treeless country
[2]**plain** *adj* **1** : lacking ornament ⟨a ~ dress⟩ **2** : free of extraneous matter **3** : OPEN, UNOBSTRUCTED ⟨~ view⟩ **4** : EVIDENT, OBVIOUS **5** : easily understood : CLEAR **6** : CANDID, BLUNT **7** : SIMPLE, UNCOMPLICATED ⟨~ cooking⟩ **8** : lacking beauty — **plain·ly** *adv* — **plain·ness** \ˈplān-nəs\ *n*
plain·clothes·man \ˈplān-ˈklō(th)z-mən, -ˌman\ *n* : a police officer who does not wear a uniform while on duty : DETECTIVE
plain·spo·ken \-ˈspō-kən\ *adj* : speaking or spoken plainly and esp. bluntly
plaint \ˈplānt\ *n* **1** : LAMENTATION, WAIL **2** : PROTEST, COMPLAINT
plain·tiff \ˈplānt-əf\ *n* : the complaining party in a lawsuit
plain·tive \ˈplānt-iv\ *adj* : expressive of suffering or woe : MELANCHOLY — **plain·tive·ly** *adv*
plait \ˈplāt, ˈplat\ *n* **1** : PLEAT **2** : a braid esp. of hair or straw — **plait** *vb*
[1]**plan** \ˈplan\ *n* **1** : a drawing or diagram showing the parts or outline of something **2** : a method for accomplishing something **3** : GOAL, AIM — **plan·less** *adj*
[2]**plan** *vb* **planned; plan·ning** **1** : to form a plan of ⟨~ a new city⟩ **2** : INTEND ⟨*planned* to go⟩ — **plan·ner** *n*
[1]**plane** \ˈplān\ *vb* **planed; plan·ing** : to smooth or level off with or as if with a plane — **plan·er** *n*
[2]**plane** *n* : PLANE TREE
[3]**plane** *n* : a tool for smoothing or shaping a wood surface

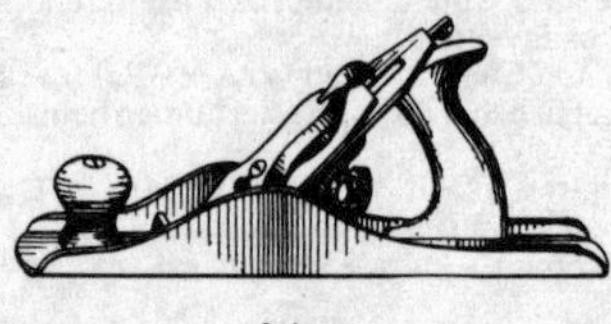

[3]plane

[4]**plane** *n* **1** : a level or flat surface **2** : a level of existence, consciousness, or development **3** : one of the main supporting surfaces of an airplane; *also* : AIRPLANE
[5]**plane** *adj* **1** : FLAT, LEVEL **2** : dealing with flat surfaces or figures ⟨~ geometry⟩
plane·load \ˈplān-ˌlōd\ *n* : a load that fills an airplane
plan·et \ˈplan-ət\ *n* [ME *planete*, fr. OF, fr. LL *planeta*, modif. of Gk *planēt-*, *planēs*, lit., wanderer, fr. *planasthai* to wander] : a celestial body other than a comet,

PLANETS

SYMBOL	NAME	MEAN DISTANCE FROM THE SUN astronomical units	million miles	PERIOD OF REVOLUTION IN DAYS OR YEARS	EQUATORIAL DIAMETER IN MILES
☿	Mercury	0.387	36.0	87.97 d.	3,031
♀	Venus	0.723	67.2	224.70 d.	7,521
⊕	Earth	1.000	92.9	365.26 d.	7,926
♂	Mars	1.524	141.5	686.98 d.	4,216
♃	Jupiter	5.203	483.4	11.86 y.	88,700
♄	Saturn	9.569	889.0	29.46 y.	74,500
⛢	Uranus	19.309	1793.8	84.01 y.	31,600
♆	Neptune	30.284	2813.4	164.79 y.	30,200
♇	Pluto	39.781	3695.7	247.69 y.	1,900

asteroid, or satellite that revolves around the sun — **plan·e·tary** \-ə-ˌter-ē\ *adj*

plan·e·tar·i·um \ˌplan-ə-ˈter-ē-əm\ *n, pl* **-iums** *or* **-ia** \-ē-ə\ : a building or room housing a device to project images of celestial bodies

plan·e·tes·i·mal \ˌplan-ə-ˈtes-ə-məl\ *n* : any of numerous small solid celestial bodies which may have existed during the formation of the solar system

plan·e·toid \ˈplan-ə-ˌtȯid\ *n* : a body resembling a planet; *esp* : ASTEROID

plane tree *n* : SYCAMORE 2; *esp* : one of or introduced from the Old World

plan·gent \ˈplan-jənt\ *adj* **1** : having a loud reverberating sound **2** : having an expressive esp. plaintive quality — **plan·gen·cy** \-jən-sē\ *n*

¹plank \ˈplaŋk\ *n* **1** : a heavy thick board **2** : an article in the platform of a political party

²plank *vb* **1** : to cover with planks **2** : to set or lay down forcibly **3** : to cook and serve on a board

plank·ing \ˈplaŋ-kiŋ\ *n* : a quantity or covering of planks

plank·ton \ˈplaŋk-tən\ *n* : the passively floating or weakly swimming animal and plant life of a body of water — **plank·ton·ic** \plaŋk-ˈtän-ik\ *adj*

¹plant \ˈplant\ *vb* **1** : to set in the ground to grow **2** : ESTABLISH, SETTLE **3** : to stock or provide with something **4** : to place firmly or forcibly **5** : to hide or arrange with intent to deceive

²plant *n* **1** : any of a kingdom of living things that usu. have no locomotor ability or obvious sense organs and have cellulose cell walls and usu. capacity for indefinite growth **2** : the land, buildings, and machinery used in carrying on a trade or business

¹plan·tain \ˈplant-ᵊn\ *n* [ME, fr. OF, fr. L *plantagin-, plantago,* fr. *planta* sole of the foot; fr. its broad leaves] : any of a genus of short-stemmed weedy herbs with spikes of tiny greenish flowers

²plantain *n* [Sp *plántano* plane tree, banana tree, fr. ML *plantanus* plane tree, alter. of L *platanus*] : a banana plant with starchy greenish fruit; *also* : its fruit

plan·tar \ˈplant-ər, ˈplan-ˌtär\ *adj* : of or relating to the sole of the foot

plan·ta·tion \plan-ˈtā-shən\ *n* **1** : a large group of trees under cultivation **2** : an agricultural estate worked by resident laborers

plant·er \ˈplant-ər\ *n* **1** : one that plants or sows; *esp* : an owner or operator of a plantation **2** : a container for a plant

plant louse *n* : APHID

plaque \ˈplak\ *n* [F] **1** : an ornamental brooch **2** : a flat thin piece (as of metal) used for decoration; *also* : a commemorative tablet **3** : a bacteria-containing film on a tooth

plash \ˈplash\ *n* : SPLASH — **plash** *vb*

plas·ma \ˈplaz-mə\ *n* **1** : the watery part of blood, lymph, or milk **2** : a gas composed of ionized particles — **plas·mat·ic** \plaz-ˈmat-ik\ *adj*

¹plas·ter \ˈplas-tər\ *n* **1** : a dressing consisting of a backing spread with an often medicated substance that clings to the skin ⟨adhesive ~⟩ **2** : a paste that hardens as it dries and is used for coating walls and ceilings

²plaster *vb* **plas·tered; plas·ter·ing** \-t(ə-)riŋ\ : to cover with or as if with plaster — **plas·ter·er** *n*

plas·ter·board \ˈplas-tər-ˌbōrd\ *n* : a wallboard consisting of fiberboard, paper, or felt over a plaster core

plaster of par·is \-ˈpar-əs\ *often cap 2d P* : a white powder made from gypsum and used as a quick-setting paste with water for casts and molds

¹plas·tic \ˈplas-tik\ *adj* [L *plasticus* of molding, fr. Gk *plastikos,* fr. *plassein* to mold, form] **1** : capable of being molded ⟨~ clay⟩ **2** : characterized by or using modeling ⟨~ arts⟩ **3** : made or consisting of a plastic **syn** pliable, pliant, ductile, malleable, adaptable — **plas·tic·i·ty** \plas-ˈtis-ət-ē\ *n*

²plastic *n* : a plastic substance; *esp* : a synthetic or processed material that can be formed into rigid objects or into films or filaments

plastic surgery *n* : a branch of surgery concerned with the repair, restoration, or improvement of lost, injured, defective, or misshapen body parts — **plastic surgeon** *n*

¹plat \ˈplat\ *n* **1** : a small plot of ground **2** : a plan of a piece of land with actual or proposed features (as lots)

²plat *vb* **plat·ted; plat·ting** : to make a plat of

¹plate \ˈplāt\ *n* **1** : a flat thin piece of material **2** : domestic hollowware made of or plated with gold, silver, or base metals **3** : DISH **4** : HOME PLATE **5** : the molded metal or plastic cast of a page of type to be printed from **6** : a thin sheet of material (as glass) that is coated with a chemical sensitive to light and is used in photography **7** : the part of a denture that fits to the mouth and holds the teeth **8** : something printed from an engraving **9** : a huge mobile segment of the earth's crust

²plate *vb* **plat·ed; plat·ing** **1** : to arm with armor plate **2** : to overlay with metal (as gold or silver) **3** : to make a printing plate of

pla·teau \pla-ˈtō\ *n, pl* **plateaus** *or* **pla·teaux** \-ˈtōz\ [F] : a large level area raised above adjacent land on at least one side : TABLELAND

plate glass *n* : rolled, ground, and polished sheet glass

plat·en \ˈplat-ən\ *n* **1** : a flat plate of metal; *esp* : one (as the part of a printing press which presses the paper against the type) that exerts or receives pressure **2** : the roller of a typewriter

plat·form \ˈplat-ˌfȯrm\ *n* **1** : a raised flooring or stage for speakers, performers, or workers **2** : a declaration of the principles on which a group of persons (as a political party) stands

plat·ing \ˈplāt-iŋ\ *n* : a coating of metal plates or plate ⟨the ~ of a ship⟩

plat·i·num \ˈplat-(ᵊ-)nəm\ *n* : a heavy silver-white metallic chemical element — see ELEMENT table

plat·i·tude \ˈplat-ə-ˌt(y)üd\ *n* : a flat or trite remark — **plat·i·tu·di·nous** \-ˈt(y)üd-(ᵊ-)nəs\ *adj*

pla·ton·ic love \plə-ˌtän-ik-, plā-\ *n, often cap P* : a close relationship between two persons in which sexual desire has been suppressed or sublimated

pla·toon \plə-ˈtün\ *n* [F *peloton* small detachment, lit., ball, fr. *pelote* little ball] **1** : a subdivision of a company-size military unit usu. consisting of two or more squads or sections **2** : a group of football players trained either for offense or for defense and sent into the game as a body

platoon sergeant *n* : a noncommissioned officer in the army ranking below a first sergeant

plat·ter \ˈplat-ər\ *n* **1** : a large serving plate **2** : a phonograph record

platy \ˈplat-ē\ *n, pl* **platy** *or* **plat·ys** *or* **plat·ies** : any of various small stocky often brilliantly colored fish that are popular for tropical aquariums

platy·pus \ˈplat-i-pəs\ *n, pl* **platy·pus·es** *also* **platy·pi** \-ˌpī\ [NL, fr. Gk *platypous* flat-footed, fr. *platys* broad, flat + *pous* foot] : a small aquatic egg-laying marsupial mammal of Australia with webbed feet and a fleshy bill like a duck's

plau·dit \ˈplȯd-ət\ *n* : an act of applause

plau·si·ble \ˈplȯ-zə-bəl\ *adj* [L *plausibilis* worthy of applause, fr. *plausus*, pp. of *plaudere*] : seemingly worthy of belief : PERSUASIVE — **plau·si·bil·i·ty** \ˌplȯ-zə-ˈbil-ət-ē\ *n* — **plau·si·bly** \ˈplȯ-zə-blē\ *adv*

[1]**play** \ˈplā\ *n* **1** : brisk handling of something (as a weapon) **2** : the course of a game; *also* : a particular act or maneuver in a game **3** : recreational activity; *esp* : the spontaneous activity of children **4** : JEST ⟨said in ~⟩ **5** : the act or an instance of punning **6** : GAMBLING **7** : OPERATION ⟨bring extra force into ~⟩ **8** : a brisk or light movement **9** : free motion (as of part of a machine) **10** : scope for action **11** : PUBLICITY **12** : an effort to arouse liking ⟨made a ~ for her⟩ **13** : a stage representation of a drama; *also* : a dramatic composition — **play·ful** \-fəl\ *adj* — **play·ful·ly** \-ē\ *adv* — **play·ful·ness** *n* — **in play** : in condition or position to be played

[2]**play** *vb* **1** : to engage in recreation : FROLIC **2** : to handle or behave lightly or absentmindedly **3** : to make a pun ⟨~ on words⟩ **4** : to take advantage ⟨~ on fears⟩ **5** : to move or operate in a brisk or irregular manner ⟨a flashlight ~*ed* over the wall⟩ **6** : to perform music ⟨~ on a violin⟩; *also* : to perform (music) on an instrument ⟨~ a waltz⟩ **7** : to perform music upon ⟨~ the piano⟩; *also* : to sound in performance ⟨the organ is ~*ing*⟩ **8** : to cause to emit sounds ⟨~ a radio⟩ **9** : to act in a dramatic medium; *also* : to act in the character of ⟨~ the hero⟩ **10** : GAMBLE **11** : to behave in a specified way ⟨~ safe⟩; *also* : COOPERATE ⟨~ along with him⟩ **12** : to deal with; *also* : EMPHASIZE ⟨~ up her good qualities⟩ **13** : to perform for amusement ⟨~ a trick⟩ **14** : WREAK **15** : to contend with in a game; *also* : to fill (a certain position) on a team **16** : to make wagers on ⟨~ the races⟩ **17** : WIELD, PLY **18** : to keep in action — **play·er** *n*

play·act·ing \ˈplā-ˌak-tiŋ\ *n* **1** : performance in theatrical productions **2** : insincere or artificial behavior

play·back \ˈplā-ˌbak\ *n* : an act of reproducing a sound recording often immediately after recording — **play back** \(ˈ)plā-ˈbak\ *vb*

play·bill \-ˌbil\ *n* : a poster advertising the performance of a play

play·book \-ˌbu̇k\ *n* : a notebook containing diagramed football plays

play·boy \-ˌbȯi\ *n* : a man whose chief interest is the pursuit of pleasure

play·go·er \-ˌgō(-ə)r\ *n* : a person who frequently attends plays

play·ground \-ˌgrau̇nd\ *n* : an area used for games and recreation esp. by children

play·house \-ˌhau̇s\ *n* **1** : THEATER **2** : a small house for children to play in

playing card *n* : one of a set of 24 to 78 cards marked to show its rank and suit and used to play a game of cards

play·let \ˈplā-lət\ *n* : a short play

play·mate \-ˌmāt\ *n* : a companion in play

play–off \-ˌȯf\ *n* : a contest or series of contests to break a tie or determine a championship

play·pen \-ˌpen\ *n* : a portable enclosure in which a young child may play

play·suit \-ˌsüt\ *n* : a sports and play outfit for women and children

play·thing \-ˌthiŋ\ *n* : TOY

play·wright \-ˌrīt\ *n* : a writer of plays

pla·za \ˈplaz-ə, ˈpläz-\ *n* [Sp, fr. L *platea* broad street] **1** : a public square in a city or town **2** : a shopping center

plea \ˈplē\ *n* **1** : a defendant's answer in law to charges made against him **2** : something alleged as an excuse : PRETEXT **3** : ENTREATY, APPEAL

plead \ˈplēd\ *vb* **plead·ed** \ˈplēd-əd\ *or* **pled** \ˈpled\; **plead·ing** **1** : to argue before a court or authority ⟨~ a case⟩ **2** : to answer to a charge or indictment ⟨~ guilty⟩ **3** : to argue for or against something ⟨~ for acquittal⟩ **4** : to appeal earnestly ⟨~*s* for help⟩ **5** : to offer as a plea (as in defense) ⟨~*ed* illness⟩ — **plead·er** *n*

pleas·ant \ˈplez-ᵊnt\ *adj* **1** : giving pleasure : AGREEABLE ⟨a ~ experience⟩ **2** : marked by pleasing behavior or appearance ⟨a ~ person⟩ — **pleas·ant·ly** *adv* — **pleas·ant·ness** *n*

pleas·ant·ry \-ᵊn-trē\ *n, pl* **-ries** : a pleasant and casual act or speech

[1]**please** \ˈplēz\ *vb* **pleased; pleas·ing** **1** : to give pleasure or satisfaction to **2** : LIKE ⟨do as you ~⟩ **3** : to be the will or pleasure of ⟨may it ~ his Majesty⟩

[2]**please** *adv* — used as a function word to express politeness or emphasis in a request ⟨~ come in⟩

pleas·ing \ˈplē-ziŋ\ *adj* : giving pleasure — **pleas·ing·ly** *adv*

plea·sur·able \ˈplezh-(ə-)rə-bəl\ *adj* : PLEASANT, GRATIFYING — **plea·sur·ably** \-blē\ *adv*

plea·sure \ˈplezh-ər\ *n* **1** : DESIRE, INCLINATION ⟨await your ~⟩ **2** : a state of gratification : ENJOYMENT **3** : a source of delight or joy

[1]**pleat** \ˈplēt\ *vb* **1** : FOLD; *esp* : to arrange in pleats **2** : BRAID

[2]**pleat** *n* : a fold (as in cloth) made by doubling material over on itself : PLAIT

plebe \ˈplēb\ *n* : a freshman at a military or naval academy

[1]**ple·be·ian** \pli-ˈbē-ən\ *n* **1** : a member of the Roman plebs **2** : one of the common people

[2]**plebeian** *adj* **1** : of or relating to plebeians **2** : COMMON, VULGAR

pleb·i·scite \ˈpleb-ə-ˌsīt, -sət\ *n* : a vote of the people (as of a country) on a proposal submitted to them

plebs \ˈplebz\ *n, pl* **ple·bes** \ˈplē-bēz\ **1** : the common people of ancient Rome **2** : the general populace

plec·trum \ˈplek-trəm\ *n, pl* **plec·tra** \-trə\ *or* **plec·trums** [L] : [3]PICK 3

[1]**pledge** \ˈplej\ *n* **1** : something given as security for the performance of an act **2** : the state of being held as a security or guaranty **3** : TOAST 3 **4** : PROMISE, VOW

[2]**pledge** *vb* **pledged; pledg·ing** **1** : to deposit as a pledge **2** : TOAST **3** : to bind by a pledge : PLIGHT **4** : PROMISE

Pleis·to·cene \ˈplī-stə-ˌsēn\ *adj* : of, relating to, or being the earlier epoch of the Quaternary — **Pleistocene** *n*

ple·na·ry \ˈplē-nə-rē, ˈplen-ə-\ *adj* **1** : FULL ⟨~ power⟩ **2** : including all entitled to attend ⟨~ session⟩

pleni·po·ten·tia·ry \ˌplen-ə-pə-ˈtench-(ə-)rē, -ˈten-chē-

ˌer-ē\ *n, pl* **-ries** : a diplomatic agent having full authority — **plenipotentiary** *adj*

plen·i·tude \ˈplen-ə-ˌt(y)üd\ *n* **1** : COMPLETENESS **2** : ABUNDANCE

plen·te·ous \ˈplent-ē-əs\ *adj* **1** : FRUITFUL **2** : existing in plenty

plen·ti·ful \ˈplent-i-fəl\ *adj* **1** : containing or yielding plenty **2** : ABUNDANT — **plen·ti·ful·ly** \-ē\ *adv*

plen·ty \ˈplent-ē\ *n* : a more than adequate number or amount

ple·num \ˈplen-əm, ˈplēn-əm\ *n, pl* **-nums** *or* **-na** \-ə\ : a general assembly of all members esp. of a legislative body

pleth·o·ra \ˈpleth-ə-rə\ *n* : an excessive quantity or fullness; *also* : PROFUSION

pleu·ri·sy \ˈplu̇r-ə-sē\ *n* : inflammation of the membrane that lines the chest and covers the lungs

plex·us \ˈplek-səs\ *n* : an interlacing network esp. of blood vessels or nerves

pli·able \ˈplī-ə-bəl\ *adj* **1** : FLEXIBLE **2** : yielding easily to others **syn** plastic, pliant, ductile, malleable, adaptable — **pli·abil·i·ty** \ˌplī-ə-ˈbil-ət-ē\ *n*

pli·ant \ˈplī-ənt\ *adj* **1** : FLEXIBLE **2** : easily influenced : PLIABLE — **pli·an·cy** \-ən-sē\ *n*

pli·ers \ˈplī(-ə)rz\ *n pl* : small pincers for bending wire or handling small objects

¹plight \ˈplīt\ *vb* : to put or give in pledge : ENGAGE

²plight *n* : CONDITION, STATE; *esp* : a bad state

plinth \ˈplinth\ *n* : the lowest part of the base of an architectural column

Plio·cene \ˈplī-ə-ˌsēn\ *adj* : of, relating to, or being the latest epoch of the Tertiary — **Pliocene** *n*

plod \ˈpläd\ *vb* **plod·ded; plod·ding** **1** : to walk heavily or slowly : TRUDGE **2** : to work laboriously and monotonously : DRUDGE — **plod·der** *n* — **plod·ding·ly** \-iŋ-lē\ *adv*

plop \ˈpläp\ *vb* **plopped; plop·ping** **1** : to make or move with a sound like that of something dropping into water **2** : to set, drop, or throw heavily — **plop** *n*

¹plot \ˈplät\ *n* **1** : a small area of ground **2** : a ground plan (as of an area) **3** : the main story (as of a book or movie) **4** : a secret scheme : INTRIGUE

²plot *vb* **plot·ted; plot·ting** **1** : to make a plot or plan of **2** : to mark on or as if on a chart **3** : to plan or contrive esp. secretly — **plot·ter** *n*

plo·ver \ˈpləv-ər, ˈplō-vər\ *n, pl* **plover** *or* **plovers** : any of various shorebirds related to the sandpipers but with shorter stouter bills

¹plow *or* **plough** \ˈplau̇\ *n* **1** : an implement used to cut, turn over, and partly break up soil **2** : a device operating like a plow; *esp* : SNOWPLOW

²plow *or* **plough** *vb* **1** : to open, break up, or work with a plow **2** : to cleave or move through like a plow ⟨a ship ∼*ing* the waves⟩ **3** : to proceed laboriously — **plow·able** *adj* — **plow·er** *n*

plow·boy \ˈplau̇-ˌbȯi\ *n* : a boy who guides a plow or leads the horse drawing it

plow·man \-mən, -ˌman\ *n* **1** : a man who guides a plow **2** : a farm laborer

plow·share \-ˌsheər\ *n* : the part of a plow that cuts the earth

ploy \ˈplȯi\ *n* : a tactic intended to embarrass or frustrate an opponent

¹pluck \ˈplək\ *vb* **1** : to pull off or out : PICK; *also* : to pull something from **2** : to play (an instrument) by pulling the strings **3** : TUG, TWITCH

²pluck *n* **1** : an act or instance of plucking **2** : SPIRIT, COURAGE

plucky \ˈplək-ē\ *adj* **pluck·i·er; -est** : COURAGEOUS, SPIRITED

¹plug \ˈpləg\ *n* **1** : STOPPER; *also* : an obstructing mass **2** : a cake of tobacco **3** : a poor or worn-out horse **4** : a device on the end of a cord for making an electrical connection **5** : a piece of favorable publicity

²plug *vb* **plugged; plug·ging** **1** : to stop, make tight, or secure by inserting a plug **2** : HIT, SHOOT **3** : to publicize insistently **4** : PLOD, DRUDGE

plum \ˈpləm\ *n* [ME, fr. OE *plūme*, fr. L *prunum* plum] **1** : a smooth-skinned juicy fruit borne by trees related to the peach and cherry; *also* : a tree bearing plums **2** : a raisin when used in desserts (as puddings) **3** : something excellent; *esp* : something desirable given in return esp. for a political favor

plum·age \ˈplü-mij\ *n* : the feathers of a bird

¹plumb \ˈpləm\ *n* : a weight on the end of a line (**plumb line**) used esp. by builders to show vertical direction

²plumb *adv* **1** : VERTICALLY **2** : EXACTLY; *also* : IMMEDIATELY **3** : COMPLETELY

³plumb *vb* : to sound, adjust, or test with a plumb ⟨∼ the depth of a well⟩

⁴plumb *adj* **1** : VERTICAL **2** : THOROUGH, COMPLETE

plumb·er \ˈpləm-ər\ *n* [ME, fr. MF *plombier*, fr. L *plumbarius*, deriv. of *plumbum* lead] : a worker who fits or repairs water and gas pipes and fixtures

plumb·ing \ˈpləm-iŋ\ *n* : a system of pipes in a building for supplying and carrying off water

¹plume \ˈplüm\ *n* : FEATHER; *esp* : a large, conspicuous, or showy feather — **plumed** \ˈplümd\ *adj* — **plumy** \ˈplü-mē\ *adj*

²plume *vb* **plumed; plum·ing** **1** : to provide or deck with feathers **2** : to indulge (oneself) in pride

¹plum·met \ˈpləm-ət\ *n* : PLUMB; *also* : PLUMB LINE

²plummet *vb* : to drop or plunge straight down

¹plump \ˈpləmp\ *vb* **1** : to drop or fall suddenly or heavily **2** : to favor something strongly ⟨∼*s* for the new method⟩

²plump *n* : a sudden heavy fall or blow; *also* : the sound made by it

³plump *adv* **1** : straight down; *also* : straight ahead **2** : UNQUALIFIEDLY

⁴plump *adj* : having a full rounded usu. pleasing form : CHUBBY **syn** fleshy, stout, roly-poly, rotund — **plumpness** *n*

¹plun·der \ˈplən-dər\ *vb* **plun·dered; plun·der·ing** \-d(ə-)riŋ\ : to take the goods of by force or wrongfully : PILLAGE — **plun·der·er** *n*

²plunder *n* : something taken by force or theft : LOOT

¹plunge \ˈplənj\ *vb* **plunged; plung·ing** **1** : IMMERSE, SUBMERGE **2** : to enter or cause to enter a state or course of action suddenly or violently ⟨∼ into war⟩ **3** : to cast oneself into or as if into water **4** : to gamble heavily and recklessly **5** : to descend suddenly

²plunge *n* : a sudden dive, leap, or rush

plung·er \ˈplən-jər\ *n* **1** : one that plunges **2** : a sliding piece driven by or against fluid pressure : PISTON **3** : a rubber cup on a handle pushed against an opening to free a waste outlet of an obstruction

plunk \ˈpləŋk\ *vb* **1** : to make or cause to make a hollow metallic sound **2** : to drop heavily or suddenly — **plunk** *n*

plu·per·fect \(ˈ)plü-ˈpər-fikt\ *adj* [modif. of LL *plusquamperfectus*, lit., more than perfect] : of, relating to, or constituting a verb tense that denotes an action or state as completed at or before a past time spoken of — **pluperfect** *n*

plu·ral \ˈplu̇r-əl\ *adj* [ME, fr. MF & L; MF *plurel*, fr. L *pluralis*, fr. *plur-*, *plus* more] : of, relating to, or constituting a word form used to denote more than one — **plural** *n*

plu·ral·i·ty \plu̇-ˈral-ət-ē\ *n, pl* **-ties** **1** : the state of being plural **2** : an excess of votes over those cast for an opposing candidate **3** : the greatest number of votes cast when not a majority

plu·ral·ize \ˈplu̇r-ə-ˌlīz\ *vb* **-ized; -iz·ing :** to make plural or express in the plural form — **plu·ral·iza·tion** \ˌplu̇r-ə-lə-ˈzā-shən\ *n*

[1]**plus** \ˈpləs\ *adj* [L, more] **1 :** requiring addition **2 :** having or being in addition to what is anticipated or specified ⟨∼ values⟩

[2]**plus** *n, pl* **plus·es** \ˈpləs-əz\ *also* **plus·ses 1 :** a sign + (**plus sign**) used in mathematics to require addition or designate a positive quantity **2 :** an added quantity; *also* **:** a positive quantity **3 :** ADVANTAGE

[3]**plus** *prep* **:** increased by **:** with the addition of ⟨3 ∼ 4 equals 7⟩

[1]**plush** \ˈpləsh\ *n* **:** a fabric with a pile longer and less dense than velvet pile — **plushy** *adj*

[2]**plush** *adj* **:** notably luxurious — **plush·ly** *adv*

Plu·to \ˈplüt-ō\ *n* **:** the planet farthest from the sun

plu·toc·ra·cy \plü-ˈtäk-rə-sē\ *n, pl* **-cies 1 :** government by the wealthy **2 :** a controlling class of the wealthy — **plu·to·crat** \ˈplüt-ə-ˌkrat\ *n* — **plu·to·crat·ic** \ˌplüt-ə-ˈkrat-ik\ *adj*

plu·to·ni·um \plü-ˈtō-nē-əm\ *n* **:** a radioactive chemical element formed by the decay of neptunium — see ELEMENT table

plu·vi·al \ˈplü-vē-əl\ *adj* **1 :** of or relating to rain **2 :** characterized by abundant rain

[1]**ply** \ˈplī\ *vb* **plied; ply·ing :** to twist together ⟨∼ yarns⟩

[2]**ply** *n, pl* **plies :** one of the folds, thicknesses, or strands of which something (as plywood or yarn) is made

[3]**ply** *vb* **plied; ply·ing 1 :** to use, practice, or work diligently ⟨*plies* her needle⟩ ⟨∼ a trade⟩ **2 :** to keep supplying something to ⟨*plied* them with liquor⟩ **3 :** to go or travel regularly esp. by sea

Plym·outh Rock \ˌplim-əth-\ *n* **:** any of an American breed of medium-sized single-combed domestic fowls

ply·wood \ˈplī-ˌwu̇d\ *n* **:** material made of thin sheets of wood glued and pressed together

pm *abbr* premium

Pm *symbol* promethium

PM *abbr* **1** paymaster **2** police magistrate **3** postmaster **4** *often not cap* post meridiem **5** postmortem **6** prime minister **7** provost marshal

pmk *abbr* postmark

pmt *abbr* payment

PN *abbr* promissory note

pneu·mat·ic \n(y)u̇-ˈmat-ik\ *adj* **1 :** of, relating to, or using air or wind **2 :** moved by air pressure **3 :** filled with compressed air — **pneu·mat·i·cal·ly** \-i-k(ə-)lē\ *adv*

pneu·mo·co·ni·o·sis \ˈn(y)ü-mō-ˌkō-nē-ˈō-səs\ *n* **:** a disease of the lungs caused by habitual inhalation of irritant mineral or metallic particles

pneu·mo·nia \n(y)u̇-ˈmō-nyə\ *n* **:** an inflammatory disease of the lungs

Po *symbol* polonium

PO *abbr* **1** petty officer **2** post office

[1]**poach** \ˈpōch\ *vb* [ME *pochen,* fr. MF *pocher,* fr. OF *pochier,* lit., to put into a bag, fr. *poche* bag, pocket, of Gmc origin] **:** to cook (as an egg or fish) in simmering liquid

[2]**poach** *vb* **:** to hunt or fish unlawfully — **poach·er** *n*

POC *abbr* port of call

pock \ˈpäk\ *n* **:** a small swelling on the skin (as in smallpox); *also* **:** its scar

[1]**pock·et** \ˈpäk-ət\ *n* **1 :** a small bag open at the top or side inserted in a garment **2 :** supply of money **:** MEANS **3 :** RECEPTACLE, CONTAINER **4 :** a small isolated area or group **5 :** a small body of ore — **pock·et·ful** *n*

[2]**pocket** *vb* **1 :** to put in or as if in a pocket **2 :** STEAL

[3]**pocket** *adj* **1 :** small enough to fit in a pocket; *also* **:** SMALL, MINIATURE **2 :** carried in or paid from one's own pocket

[1]**pock·et·book** \-ˌbu̇k\ *n* **1 :** PURSE; *also* **:** HANDBAG **2 :** financial resources

[2]**pocketbook** *adj* **:** relating to money

pocket gopher *n* **:** GOPHER 2

pock·et·knife \ˈpäk-ət-ˌnīf\ *n* **:** a knife with a folding blade to be carried in the pocket

pocket veto *n* **:** an indirect veto of a legislative bill by an executive through retention of the bill unsigned until after adjournment of the legislature

pock·mark \ˈpäk-ˌmärk\ *n* **:** a pit or scar caused by smallpox or acne — **pock·marked** \-ˌmärkt\ *adj*

po·co \ˌpō-kō, ˌpȯ-\ *adv* [It, little, fr. L *paucus*] **:** SOMEWHAT — used to qualify a direction in music ⟨∼ allegro⟩

po·co a po·co \ˌpō-kō-ä-ˈpō-kō, ˌpȯ-kō-ä-ˈpȯ-\ *adv* **:** little by little **:** by small degrees **:** GRADUALLY

pod \ˈpäd\ *n* **1 :** a dry fruit (as of a pea) that splits open when ripe **2 :** an external streamlined compartment (as for a jet engine) on an airplane **3 :** a detachable compartment (as for personnel, a power unit, or an instrument) on a spacecraft

POD *abbr* pay on delivery

po·di·a·try \pə-ˈdī-ə-trē, pō-\ *n* **:** the care and treatment of the human foot in health and disease — **po·di·a·trist** \pə-ˈdī-ə-trəst, pō-\ *n*

po·di·um \ˈpōd-ē-əm\ *n, pl* **podiums** *or* **po·dia** \-ē-ə\ **1 :** a dais esp. for an orchestral conductor **2 :** LECTERN

POE *abbr* **1** port of embarkation **2** port of entry

po·em \ˈpō-əm\ *n* **:** a composition in verse

po·esy \ˈpō-ə-zē\ *n* **:** POETRY

po·et \ˈpō-ət\ *n* [ME, fr. OF *poete,* fr. L *poeta,* fr. Gk *poiētēs* maker, poet, fr. *poiein* to make, create] **:** a writer of poetry; *also* **:** a creative artist of great sensitivity

po·et·as·ter \ˈpō-ət-ˌas-tər\ *n* **:** an inferior poet

po·et·ess \ˈpō-ət-əs\ *n* **:** a girl or woman who writes poetry

poetic justice *n* **:** an outcome in which vice is punished and virtue rewarded usu. in a manner peculiarly or ironically appropriate

po·et·ry \ˈpō-ə-trē\ *n* **1 :** metrical writing **2 :** POEMS — **po·et·ic** \pō-ˈet-ik\ *or* **po·et·i·cal** \-i-kəl\ *adj*

po·grom \ˈpō-grəm, pō-ˈgräm\ *n* [Yiddish, fr. Russ, lit., devastation] **:** an organized massacre of helpless people and esp. of Jews

poi \ˈpȯi\ *n, pl* **poi** *or* **pois :** a Hawaiian food of taro root cooked, pounded, and kneaded to a paste and often allowed to ferment

poi·gnant \ˈpȯi-nyənt\ *adj* **1 :** painfully affecting the feelings ⟨∼ grief⟩ **2 :** deeply moving ⟨∼ scene⟩ — **poi·gnan·cy** \-nyən-sē\ *n*

poi·lu \pwäl-ˈ(y)ü\ *n* **:** a French soldier

poin·ci·ana \ˌpȯin-sē-ˈan-ə\ *n* **:** any of a genus of ornamental tropical leguminous trees or shrubs with bright orange or red flowers

poin·set·tia \pȯin-ˈset-ə, -ˈset-ē-ə\ *n* **:** a showy tropical American spurge that has scarlet bracts around its small greenish flowers

[1]**point** \ˈpȯint\ *n* **1 :** an individual detail; *also* **:** the most important essential **2 :** PURPOSE **3 :** a geometric element that has position but no size **4 :** a particular place **:** LOCALITY **5 :** a particular stage or degree **6 :** a sharp end **:** TIP **7 :** a projecting piece of land **8 :** a punctuation mark; *esp* **:** PERIOD **9 :** DECIMAL POINT **10 :** one of the divisions of the compass **11 :** a unit of counting (as in a game score) — **point·less** *adj* — **beside the point :** IRRELEVANT — **in point :** to the point — **to the point :** RELEVANT, PERTINENT

[2]**point** *vb* **1 :** to furnish with a point **:** SHARPEN **2 :** PUNCTUATE **3 :** to separate (a decimal fraction) from an integer by a decimal point **4 :** to indicate the position of esp. by extending a finger **5 :** to direct attention to ⟨∼ out an error⟩ **6 :** AIM, DIRECT **7 :** to lie extended, aimed, or turned in a particular direction **:** FACE, LOOK

point–blank \ˈpȯint-ˈblaŋk\ *adj* **1 :** so close to the target that a missile fired will travel in a straight line to the mark **2 :** DIRECT, BLUNT — **point–blank** *adv*

point·ed \ˈpȯint-əd\ *adj* **1 :** having a point **2 :** being to the point : DIRECT **3** : aimed at a particular person or group; *also* : CONSPICUOUS, MARKED — **point·ed·ly** *adv*

point·er \ˈpȯint-ər\ *n* **1** : one that points out : INDICATOR **2** : a large short-haired hunting dog **3** : HINT, TIP

poin·til·lism \ˈpwa^{n}(n)-tē-ˌ(y)iz-əm, ˈpȯint-ᵊl-ˌiz-əm\ *n* [F *pointillisme*, fr. *pointiller* to stipple] : the theory or practice in painting of applying small strokes or dots of color to a surface so that from a distance they blend together — **poin·til·list** *also* **poin·til·liste** \ˌpwa^{n}(n)-tē-ˈ(y)ēst, ˈpȯint-ᵊl-əst\ *n or adj*

point of no return : a critical point (as in a course of action) at which turning back or reversal is not possible

point of view : a position from which something is considered or evaluated

[1]**poise** \ˈpȯiz\ *vb* **poised; pois·ing** : BALANCE

[2]**poise** *n* **1** : BALANCE **2** : self-possessed calmness; *also* : a particular way of carrying oneself

[1]**poi·son** \ˈpȯiz-ᵊn\ *n* [ME, fr. OF, drink, poisonous drink, poison, fr. L *potion-, potio* drink] : a substance that through its chemical action can injure or kill — **poi·son·ous** \-(ᵊ-)nəs\ *adj*

[2]**poison** *vb* **poi·soned; poi·son·ing** \ˈpȯiz-(ᵊ-)niŋ\ **1** : to injure or kill with poison **2** : to treat or taint with poison **3** : to affect destructively : CORRUPT ⟨~*ed* her mind⟩ — **poi·son·er** \ˈpȯiz-(ᵊ-)nər\ *n*

poison hemlock *n* : a large branching poisonous herb with finely divided leaves and white flowers that is related to the carrot

poison ivy *n* : a usu. climbing plant related to sumac that has leaves composed of three shiny leaflets and produces an irritating oil causing a usu. intensely itching skin rash; *also* : any of several related plants

poison oak *n* : any of several plants closely related to poison ivy and with similar properties

poison sumac *n* : a smooth shrubby American swamp plant with pinnate leaves, greenish flowers, greenish white berries, and irritating properties similar to the related poison ivy

[1]**poke** \ˈpōk\ *n* : BAG, SACK

[2]**poke** *vb* **poked; pok·ing** **1** : PROD; *also* : to stir up by prodding **2** : to make a prodding or jabbing movement esp. repeatedly **3** : HIT, PUNCH **4** : to thrust forward obtrusively **5** : RUMMAGE **6** : MEDDLE, PRY **7** : DAWDLE — **poke fun at** : RIDICULE, MOCK

[3]**poke** *n* : a quick thrust; *also* : PUNCH

[1]**pok·er** \ˈpō-kər\ *n* : a metal rod for stirring a fire

[2]**po·ker** \ˈpō-kər\ *n* : any of several card games played with a deck of 52 cards in which each player bets on the superiority of his hand

[2]poker: hands in descending value: *1* five of a kind, *2* royal flush, *3* straight flush, *4* four of a kind, *5* full house, *6* flush, *7* straight, *8* three of a kind, *9* two pairs, *10* one pair

poke·weed \ˈpōk-ˌwēd\ *n* : a coarse American perennial herb with clusters of white flowers and dark purple juicy berries

poky *or* **pok·ey** \ˈpō-kē\ *adj* **pok·i·er; -est** **1** : small and cramped **2** : SHABBY, DULL **3** : annoyingly slow

pol \ˈpäl\ *n* : POLITICIAN

po·lar \ˈpō-lər\ *adj* **1** : of or relating to a geographical pole **2** : of or relating to a pole (as of a magnet)

polar bear *n* : a large creamy-white bear that inhabits arctic regions

Po·lar·is \pə-ˈlar-əs\ *n* : NORTH STAR

po·lar·i·ty \pō-ˈlar-ət-ē, pə-\ *n, pl* **-ties** : the condition of having poles and esp. magnetic or electrical poles

po·lar·iza·tion \ˌpō-lə-rə-ˈzā-shən\ *n* **1** : the action of polarizing : the state of being polarized **2** : concentration about opposing extremes

po·lar·ize \ˈpō-lə-ˌrīz\ *vb* **-ized; -iz·ing** **1** : to cause (light waves) to vibrate in a definite way **2** : to give physical polarity to **3** : to break up into opposing groups

pol·der \ˈpōl-dər, ˈpäl-\ *n* [D] : a tract of low land reclaimed from the sea

[1]**pole** \ˈpōl\ *n* : a long slender piece of wood or metal ⟨telephone ~⟩

[2]**pole** *vb* **poled; pol·ing** : to impel or push with a pole

[3]**pole** *n* **1** : either end of an axis esp. of the earth **2** : either of the terminals of an electric battery **3** : one of two or more regions in a magnetized body at which the magnetism is concentrated

Pole \ˈpōl\ *n* : a native or inhabitant of Poland

pole·ax \ˈpōl-ˌaks\ *n* : a battle-ax with a short handle and a hook or point opposite the blade

pole·cat \ˈpōl-ˌkat\ *n, pl* **polecats** *or* **polecat** **1** : a European carnivorous mammal of which the ferret is considered a domesticated variety **2** : SKUNK

po·lem·ic \pə-ˈlem-ik\ *n* : the art or practice of disputation — usu. used in pl. — **po·lem·i·cal** \-i-kəl\ *also* **po·lem·ic** \-ik\ *adj* — **po·lem·i·cist** \-səst\ *n*

pole·star \ˈpōl-ˌstär\ *n* **1** : NORTH STAR **2** : a directing principle : GUIDE

pole vault *n* : a field contest in which each contestant uses a pole to vault for height over a crossbar — **pole–vault** *vb* — **pole–vault·er** *n*

[1]**po·lice** \pə-ˈlēs\ *vb* **po·liced; po·lic·ing** **1** : to control, regulate, or keep in order esp. by use of police ⟨~ a highway⟩ **2** : to make clean and put in order ⟨~ a camp⟩

[2]**police** *n, pl* **police** [MF, government, fr. LL *politia*, fr. Gk *politeia*, fr. *politeuein* to be a citizen, engage in political activity, fr. *politēs* citizen, fr. *polis* city, state] **1** : the department of government that keeps public order and safety and enforces the laws; *also* : the members of this department **2** : a private organization resembling a police force; *also* : its members **3** : military personnel detailed to clean and put in order

po·lice·man \-mən\ *n* : a member of a police force

police state *n* : a state characterized by repressive, arbitrary, totalitarian rule by means of secret police

po·lice·wom·an \pə-ˈlēs-ˌwu̇-mən\ *n* : a woman who is a member of a police force

[1]**pol·i·cy** \ˈpäl-ə-sē\ *n, pl* **-cies** : a definite course or method of action selected to guide and determine present and future decisions

[2]**policy** *n, pl* **-cies** : a writing whereby a contract of insurance is made

pol·i·cy·hold·er \ˈpäl-ə-sē-ˌhōl-dər\ *n* : one granted an insurance policy

po·lio \ˈpō-lē-ˌō\ *n* : POLIOMYELITIS — **polio** *adj*

po·lio·my·eli·tis \-ˌmī-ə-ˈlīt-əs\ *n* : an acute virus disease marked by inflammation of the nerve cells of the spinal cord

[1]**pol·ish** \ˈpäl-ish\ *vb* **1** : to make smooth and glossy usu.

\ə\abut \ᵊ\kitten \ər\further \a\ash \ā\ace \ä\cot, cart \au̇\out \ch\chin \e\bet \ē\easy \g\go \i\hit \ī\ice \j\job \ŋ\sing \ō\go \ȯ\law \ȯi\boy \th\thin \t͟h\the \ü\loot \u̇\foot \y\yet \zh\vision *see also* Pronunciation Symbols page

by rubbing 2 : to refine or improve in manners, condition, or style
[2]**polish** *n* 1 : a smooth glossy surface : LUSTER 2 : REFINEMENT, CULTURE 3 : the action or process of polishing
Pol·ish \ˈpō-lish\ *n* : the Slavic language of the Poles — **Polish** *adj*
polit *abbr* political; politician
po·lit·bu·ro \ˈpäl-ət-ˌbyu̇r-ō, ˈpō-lət-, pə-ˈlit-\ *n* [Russ *politbyuro*] : the principal policy-making committee of a Communist party
po·lite \pə-ˈlīt\ *adj* **po·lit·er; -est** 1 : REFINED, CULTIVATED ⟨~ society⟩ 2 : marked by correct social conduct : COURTEOUS; *also* : CONSIDERATE, TACTFUL — **po·lite·ly** *adv* — **po·lite·ness** *n*
po·li·tesse \ˌpäl-i-ˈtes\ *n* [F] : formal politeness
pol·i·tic \ˈpäl-ə-ˌtik\ *adj* 1 : wise in promoting a policy ⟨a ~ statesman⟩ 2 : shrewdly tactful ⟨a ~ move⟩
po·lit·i·cal \pə-ˈlit-i-kəl\ *adj* 1 : of or relating to government or politics 2 : involving or charged or concerned with acts against a government or a political system ⟨~ criminals⟩ — **po·lit·i·cal·ly** \-k(ə-)lē\ *adv*
pol·i·ti·cian \ˌpäl-ə-ˈtish-ən\ *n* : a person actively engaged in government or politics
pol·i·tick \ˈpäl-ə-ˌtik\ *vb* : to engage in political discussion or activity
po·lit·i·co \pə-ˈlit-i-ˌkō\ *n, pl* **-cos** *also* **-coes** : POLITICIAN
pol·i·tics \ˈpäl-ə-ˌtiks\ *n sing or pl* 1 : the art or science of government, of guiding or influencing governmental policy, or of winning and holding control over a government 2 : political affairs or business; *esp* : competition between groups or individuals for power and leadership 3 : political opinions
pol·i·ty \ˈpäl-ət-ē\ *n, pl* **-ties** : a politically organized unit; *also* : the form or constitution of such a unit
pol·ka \ˈpōl-kə, ˈpō-kə\ *n* [Czech, fr. Pol *Polka* Polish woman, fem. of *Polak* Pole] : a lively couple dance of Bohemian origin; *also* : music for this dance — **polka** *vb*
pol·ka dot \ˈpō-kə-ˌdät\ *n* : a dot in a pattern of regularly distributed dots — **polka–dot** *or* **polka–dot·ted** \-ˌdät-əd\ *adj*
[1]**poll** \ˈpōl\ *n* 1 : HEAD 2 : the casting and recording of votes; *also* : the total vote cast 3 : the place where votes are cast — usu. used in pl. 4 : a questioning of persons to obtain information or opinions to be analyzed
[2]**poll** *vb* 1 : to cut off or shorten a growth or part of : CLIP, SHEAR 2 : to receive and record the votes of 3 : to receive (as votes) in an election 4 : to question in a poll
pol·lack *or* **pol·lock** \ˈpäl-ək\ *n, pl* **pollack** *or* **pollock** : an important Atlantic food fish that is related to the cods
pol·len \ˈpäl-ən\ *n* [NL fr. L, fine flour] : a mass of male spores of a seed plant usu. appearing as a yellow dust
pol·li·na·tion \ˌpäl-ə-ˈnā-shən\ *n* : the carrying of pollen to the female part of a plant to fertilize the seed — **pol·li·nate** \ˈpäl-ə-ˌnāt\ *vb* — **pol·li·na·tor** \-ər\ *n*
poll·ster \ˈpōl-stər\ *n* : one that conducts a poll or compiles data obtained by a poll
poll tax *n* : a tax of a fixed amount per person levied on adults
pol·lute \pə-ˈlüt\ *vb* **pol·lut·ed; pol·lut·ing** : to make impure; *esp* : to contaminate with man-made waste — **pol·lut·ant** \-ˈlüt-ᵊnt\ *n* — **pol·lut·er** *n* — **pol·lu·tion** \-ˈlü-shən\ *n*
pol·ly·wog *or* **pol·li·wog** \ˈpäl-ē-ˌwäg\ *n* : TADPOLE
po·lo \ˈpō-lō\ *n* : a game played by two teams on horseback using long-handled mallets to drive a wooden ball
po·lo·ni·um \pə-ˈlō-nē-əm\ *n* [NL, fr. ML *Polonia* Poland, birthplace of its discoverer, Mme. Curie] : a radioactive metallic chemical element — see ELEMENT table
pol·ter·geist \ˈpōl-tər-ˌgīst\ *n* [G, fr. *poltern* to knock + *geist* spirit] : a noisy usu. mischievous ghost held to be responsible for unexplained noises
pol·troon \päl-ˈtrün\ *n* : COWARD
poly·chlo·ri·nat·ed bi·phe·nyl \ˌpäl-i-ˈklōr-ə-ˌnāt-əd-ˌbī-ˈfen-ᵊl, -ˈfēn-\ *n* : any of several industrial compounds that are poisonous environmental pollutants
poly·clin·ic \ˌpäl-i-ˈklin-ik\ *n* : a clinic or hospital treating diseases of many sorts
poly·es·ter \ˈpäl-ē-ˌes-tər\ *n* : a polymer composed of ester groups used esp. in making fibers or plastics
poly·eth·yl·ene \ˌpäl-ē-ˈeth-ə-ˌlēn\ *n* : a lightweight plastic resistant to chemicals and moisture and used chiefly in packaging
po·lyg·a·my \pə-ˈlig-ə-mē\ *n* : the practice of having more than one wife or husband at one time — **po·lyg·a·mist** \-məst\ *n* — **po·lyg·a·mous** \-məs\ *adj*
poly·glot \ˈpäl-i-ˌglät\ *adj* 1 : speaking or writing several languages 2 : containing or made up of several languages — **polyglot** *n*
poly·gon \ˈpäl-i-ˌgän\ *n* : a closed plane figure bounded by straight lines — **po·lyg·o·nal** \pə-ˈlig-ən-ᵊl\ *adj*
poly·graph \ˈpäl-i-ˌgraf\ *n* : an instrument for recording variations of several bodily functions (as blood pressure) simultaneously — **po·lyg·ra·pher** \pə-ˈlig-rə-fər, ˈpäl-i-ˌgraf-ər\ *n*
poly·he·dron \ˌpäl-i-ˈhē-drən\ *n* : a solid formed by plane faces — **poly·he·dral** \-drəl\ *adj*
poly·math \ˈpäl-i-ˌmath\ *n* : a person of encyclopedic learning
poly·mer \ˈpäl-ə-mər\ *n* : a chemical compound formed by union of small molecules of the same kind — **poly·mer·ic** \ˌpäl-ə-ˈmer-ik\ *adj*
po·lym·er·iza·tion \pə-ˌlim-ə-rə-ˈzā-shən\ *n* : a chemical reaction in which two or more small molecules combine to form larger molecules with repeating structural units — **po·lym·er·ize** \pə-ˈlim-ə-ˌrīz\ *vb*
Poly·ne·sian \ˌpäl-ə-ˈnē-zhən\ *n* 1 : a member of any of the native peoples of Polynesia 2 : a group of Austronesian languages spoken in Polynesia — **Polynesian** *adj*
poly·no·mi·al \ˌpäl-ə-ˈnō-mē-əl\ *n* : an algebraic expression having two or more terms each of which consists of a constant multiplied by one or more variables raised to a nonnegative integral power — **polynomial** *adj*
pol·yp \ˈpäl-əp\ *n* 1 : an invertebrate animal (as a coral) that is a coelenterate having a hollow cylindrical body closed at one end 2 : a projecting mass of swollen and hypertrophied or tumorous membrane ⟨a rectal ~⟩
po·lyph·o·ny \pə-ˈlif-ə-nē\ *n* : music consisting of two or more melodically independent but harmonizing voice parts — **poly·phon·ic** \ˌpäl-i-ˈfän-ik\ *adj*
poly·sty·rene \ˌpäl-i-ˈstīr-ˌēn\ *n* : a rigid transparent nonconducting thermoplastic used esp. in molded products and foams
poly·syl·lab·ic \ˌpäl-i-sə-ˈlab-ik\ *adj* 1 : having more than three syllables 2 : characterized by polysyllabic words
poly·syl·la·ble \ˈpäl-i-ˌsil-ə-bəl\ *n* : a polysyllabic word
poly·tech·nic \ˌpäl-i-ˈtek-nik\ *adj* : of, relating to, or instructing in many technical arts or applied sciences
poly·the·ism \ˈpäl-i-thē-ˌiz-əm\ *n* : belief in or worship of many gods — **poly·the·ist** \-ˌthē-əst\ *adj or n* — **poly·the·is·tic** \ˌpäl-i-thē-ˈis-tik\ *adj*
poly·un·sat·u·rat·ed \ˈpäl-ē-ˌən-ˈsach-ə-ˌrāt-əd\ *adj, of an oil or fatty acid* : having many unsaturated chemical bonds between carbon atoms
poly·vi·nyl \ˌpäl-i-ˈvīn-ᵊl\ *adj* : of, relating to, or being a polymerized vinyl compound, resin, or plastic — often used in combination
po·made \pō-ˈmād, -ˈmäd\ *n* : a perfumed ointment esp. for the hair or scalp
pome·gran·ate \ˈpäm-(ə-)ˌgran-ət\ *n* [ME *poumgarnet*, fr. MF *pomme grenate*, lit., seedy apple, fr. *pomme* apple (fr. LL *pomum*, fr. L, fruit) + *grenate* seedy, fr. L *granatus*, fr. *granum* grain] : a tropical reddish fruit with many seeds and an edible crimson pulp; *also* : the tree that bears it

[1]pom·mel \ˈpəm-əl, ˈpäm-\ *n* **1** : the knob on the hilt of a sword **2** : the knoblike bulge at the front and top of a saddlebow

[2]pom·mel \ˈpəm-əl\ *vb* **-meled** *or* **-melled; -mel·ing** *or* **-mel·ling** \-(ə-)liŋ\ : PUMMEL

pomp \ˈpämp\ *n* **1** : brilliant display : SPLENDOR **2** : OSTENTATION

pom·pa·dour \ˈpäm-pə-ˌdōr\ *n* : a style of dressing the hair high over the forehead

pom·pa·no \ˈpäm-pə-ˌnō, ˈpəm-\ *n, pl* **-no** *or* **-nos** : a food fish of the southern Atlantic coast

pom–pom \ˈpäm-ˌpäm\ *n* : an ornamental ball or tuft used on a cap or costume

pom·pon \ˈpäm-ˌpän\ *n* **1** : POM-POM **2** : a chrysanthemum or dahlia with small rounded flower heads

pomp·ous \ˈpäm-pəs\ *adj* **1** : suggestive of pomp; *esp* : OSTENTATIOUS **2** : pretentiously dignified **3** : excessively elevated or ornate **syn** arrogant, magisterial, self-important — **pom·pos·i·ty** \päm-ˈpäs-ət-ē\ *n* — **pomp·ous·ly** *adv*

pon·cho \ˈpän-chō\ *n, pl* **ponchos** [AmerSp] **1** : a cloak like a blanket with a slit in the middle for the head **2** : a waterproof garment resembling a poncho

pond \ˈpänd\ *n* : a small body of water

pon·der \ˈpän-dər\ *vb* **pon·dered; pon·der·ing** \-d(ə-)riŋ\ **1** : to weigh in the mind **2** : to consider carefully

pon·der·o·sa pine \ˌpän-də-ˌrō-sə, -zə-\ *n* : a tall timber tree of western No. America with long needles; *also* : its wood

pon·der·ous \ˈpän-d(ə-)rəs\ *adj* **1** : of very great weight ⟨a ~ stone⟩ **2** : UNWIELDY, CLUMSY ⟨a ~ weapon⟩ **3** : oppressively dull ⟨a ~ speech⟩ **syn** cumbrous, cumbersome, weighty

pone \ˈpōn\ *n, Southern & Midland* : an oval-shaped cornmeal cake; *also* : corn bread in the form of pones

pon·gee \pän-ˈjē\ *n* : a thin soft silk, cotton, or rayon fabric

pon·iard \ˈpän-yərd\ *n* : DAGGER

pon·tiff \ˈpänt-əf\ *n* : BISHOP; *esp* : POPE — **pon·tif·i·cal** \pän-ˈtif-i-kəl\ *adj*

pon·tif·i·cals \pän-ˈtif-i-kəlz\ *n pl* : the insignia worn by a bishop when celebrating a pontifical mass

[1]pon·tif·i·cate \pän-ˈtif-i-kət, -ə-ˌkāt\ *n* : the state, office, or term of office of a pontiff

[2]pon·tif·i·cate \pän-ˈtif-ə-ˌkāt\ *vb* **-cat·ed; -cat·ing** : to deliver dogmatic opinions

pon·toon \pän-ˈtün\ *n* **1** : a flat-bottomed boat **2** : a boat or float used in building a floating temporary bridge **3** : a float of an airplane

po·ny \ˈpō-nē\ *n, pl* **ponies** : a small horse

po·ny·tail \-ˌtāl\ *n* : a style of arranging hair to resemble the tail of a pony

pooch \ˈpüch\ *n* : DOG

poo·dle \ˈpüd-ᵊl\ *n* [G *pudel,* short for *pudelhund,* fr. *pudeln* to splash (fr. *pudel* puddle) + *hund* dog] : an active dog with a heavy curly coat

pooh–pooh \ˈpü-ˈpü\ *also* **pooh** \ˈpü\ *vb* **1** : to express contempt or impatience **2** : DERIDE, SCORN

[1]pool \ˈpül\ *n* **1** : a small deep body of usu. fresh water **2** : a small body of standing liquid **3** : SWIMMING POOL

[2]pool *n* **1** : all the money bet on the result of a particular event **2** : any of several games of billiards played on a table having six pockets **3** : the amount contributed by the participants in a joint venture **4** : a combination between competing firms for mutual profit **5** : a readily available supply

[3]pool *vb* : to contribute to a common fund or effort

[1]poop \ˈpüp\ *n* : an enclosed superstructure at the stern of a ship

[2]poop *n, slang* : INFORMATION

poop deck *n* : a partial deck above a ship's main afterdeck

poor \ˈpu̇r\ *adj* **1** : lacking material possessions ⟨~ people⟩ **2** : less than adequate : MEAGER ⟨~ crop⟩ **3** : arousing pity ⟨~ fellows⟩ **4** : inferior in quality or value ⟨~ sportsmanship⟩ **5** : UNPRODUCTIVE, BARREN ⟨~ soil⟩ **6** : fairly unsatisfactory ⟨~ prospects⟩; *also* : UNFAVORABLE ⟨~ opinion⟩ **syn** bad, wrong, unsatisfactory, rotten — **poor·ly** *adv*

poor boy \ˈpō(r)-ˌbȯi\ *n* : SUBMARINE 2

poor·house \ˈpu̇r-ˌhau̇s\ *n* : a publicly supported home for needy or dependent persons

poor–mouth \-ˌmau̇t͟h, -ˌmau̇th\ *vb* : to plead poverty as a defense or excuse

[1]pop \ˈpäp\ *vb* **popped; pop·ping** **1** : to go, come, enter, or issue forth suddenly or quickly ⟨~ into bed⟩ **2** : to put or thrust suddenly ⟨~ questions⟩ **3** : to burst or cause to burst with or make a sharp sound **4** : to protrude from the sockets **5** : SHOOT **6** : to hit a pop-up

[2]pop *n* **1** : a sharp explosive sound **2** : SHOT **3** : a flavored soft drink

[3]pop *n* : FATHER

[4]pop *adj* **1** : POPULAR ⟨~ music⟩ **2** : of or relating to pop music ⟨~ singer⟩ **3** : of or relating to the popular culture disseminated through the mass media ⟨~ psychology⟩ **4** : of, relating to, or imitating pop art ⟨~ painter⟩

[5]pop *n* : pop music, art, or culture

[6]pop *abbr* population

pop art *n* : art in which commonplace objects (as comic strips or soup cans) are used as subject matter — **pop artist** *n*

pop·corn \ˈpäp-ˌkȯrn\ *n* : an Indian corn whose kernels burst open into a white starchy mass when heated; *also* : the burst kernels

pope \ˈpōp\ *n, often cap* : the head of the Roman Catholic Church

pop–eyed \ˈpäp-ˈīd\ *adj* : having eyes that bulge (as from disease)

pop fly *n* : a short high fly in baseball

pop·gun \ˈpäp-ˌgən\ *n* : a toy gun for shooting pellets with compressed air

pop·in·jay \ˈpäp-ən-ˌjā\ *n* [ME *papejay* parrot, fr. MF *papegai, papejai,* fr. Ar *babghā'*] : a strutting supercilious person

pop·lar \ˈpäp-lər\ *n* : any of various slender quick-growing trees related to the willows

pop·lin \ˈpäp-lən\ *n* : a strong plain-woven fabric with crosswise ribs

pop·over \ˈpäp-ˌō-vər\ *n* : a biscuit made from a thin batter rich in egg and expanded by baking into a hollow shell

pop·per \ˈpäp-ər\ *n* : a utensil for popping corn

pop·py \ˈpäp-ē\ *n, pl* **poppies** : any of several herbs that have showy flowers including one that yields opium

pop·py·cock \ˈpäp-ē-ˌkäk\ *n* : empty talk : NONSENSE

pop·u·lace \ˈpäp-yə-ləs\ *n* **1** : the common people **2** : POPULATION

pop·u·lar \ˈpäp-yə-lər\ *adj* **1** : of or relating to the general public ⟨~ government⟩ **2** : easy to understand : PLAIN ⟨~ style⟩ **3** : INEXPENSIVE ⟨~ rates⟩ **4** : frequently encountered or widely accepted ⟨~ notion⟩ **5** : commonly liked or approved ⟨~ teacher⟩ — **pop·u·lar·i·ty** \ˌpäp-yə-ˈlar-ət-ē\ *n* — **pop·u·lar·ize** \ˈpäp-yə-lə-ˌrīz\ *vb* — **pop·u·lar·ly** \-lər-lē\ *adv*

pop·u·late \ˈpäp-yə-ˌlāt\ *vb* **-lat·ed; -lat·ing** **1** : to have a place in : INHABIT **2** : PEOPLE

pop·u·la·tion \ˌpäp-yə-ˈlā-shən\ *n* **1** : the people or number of people in an area **2** : the individuals under consideration (as in statistical sampling)

population explosion *n* : a pyramiding of numbers of a

biological population; *esp* : the recent great increase in human numbers resulting from both increased survival and exponential population growth

pop·u·list \ˈpäp-yə-ləst\ *n* : a believer in or advocate of the rights, wisdom, or virtues of the common people — **pop·u·lism** \-ˌliz-əm\ *n*

pop·u·lous \ˈpäp-yə-ləs\ *adj* **1** : densely populated; *also* : having a large population **2** : CROWDED — **pop·u·lous·ness** *n*

pop–up \ˈpäp-ˌəp\ *n* : a short high fly in baseball

POR *abbr* pay on return

por·ce·lain \ˈpōr-s(ə-)lən\ *n* : a fine-grained translucent ceramic ware

porch \ˈpōrch\ *n* : a covered entrance usu. with a separate roof : VERANDA

por·cine \ˈpȯr-ˌsīn\ *adj* : of, relating to, or suggesting swine

por·cu·pine \ˈpȯr-kyə-ˌpīn\ *n* [ME *porkepin*, fr. MF *porc espin*, fr. It *porcospino*, fr. L *porcus* pig + *spina* spine, prickle] : a mammal having stiff sharp easily detachable spines mingled with its hair

¹pore \ˈpōr\ *vb* **pored; por·ing 1** : to read studiously or attentively ⟨~ over a book⟩ **2** : PONDER, REFLECT

²pore *n* : a tiny hole or space (as in the skin or soil) — **pored** \ˈpōrd\ *adj*

pork \ˈpōrk\ *n* : the flesh of swine dressed for use as food

pork barrel *n* : a government project or appropriation yielding rich patronage benefits

pork·er \ˈpōr-kər\ *n* : HOG; *esp* : a young pig suitable for use as fresh pork

por·nog·ra·phy \pȯr-ˈnäg-rə-fē\ *n* [Gk *pornographos* writing of harlots] : the depiction of erotic behavior designed primarily to cause sexual excitement — **por·no·graph·ic** \ˌpȯr-nə-ˈgraf-ik\ *adj*

po·rous \ˈpōr-əs\ *adj* **1** : full of pores **2** : permeable to fluids : ABSORPTIVE — **po·ros·i·ty** \pə-ˈräs-ət-ē\ *n*

por·phy·ry \ˈpȯr-f(ə-)rē\ *n, pl* **-ries** : a rock consisting of feldspar crystals embedded in a compact fine-grained base material — **por·phy·rit·ic** \ˌpȯr-fə-ˈrit-ik\ *adj*

por·poise \ˈpȯr-pəs\ *n* [ME *porpoys*, fr. MF *porpois*, fr. ML *porcopiscis*, fr. L *porcus* pig + *piscis* fish] **1** : any of several small blunt-snouted whales **2** : any of several dolphins

por·ridge \ˈpȯr-ij\ *n* : a soft food made by boiling meal of grains or legumes in milk or water

por·rin·ger \-ən-jər\ *n* : a low one-handled metal bowl or cup

¹port \ˈpōrt\ *n* **1** : HARBOR **2** : a city with a harbor **3** : AIRPORT

²port *n* **1** : an inlet or outlet (as in an engine) for a fluid **2** : PORTHOLE

³port *n* : BEARING, CARRIAGE

⁴port *vb* : to turn or put a helm to the left

⁵port *n* : the left side of a ship or airplane looking forward — **port** *adj*

⁶port *n* : a sweet fortified wine

por·ta·ble \ˈpōrt-ə-bəl\ *adj* : capable of being carried — **portable** *n*

¹por·tage \ˈpōrt-ij, pȯr-ˈtäzh\ *n* [ME, fr. MF] : the carrying of boats and goods overland between navigable bodies of water; *also* : a route for such carrying

²por·tage \ˈpōrt-ij, pȯr-ˈtäzh\ *vb* **por·taged; por·tag·ing** : to carry gear over a portage

por·tal \ˈpōrt-ᵊl\ *n* : DOOR, ENTRANCE; *esp* : a grand or imposing one

portal–to–portal *adj* : of or relating to the time spent by a worker in traveling from the entrance to his employer's property to his actual working place (as in a mine) and in returning after the work shift

port·cul·lis \pōrt-ˈkəl-əs\ *n* : a grating at the gateway of a castle or fortress that can be let down to stop entrance

porte co·chere \ˌpōrt-kō-ˈsher\ *n* [F *porte cochère*, lit., coach door] : a roofed structure extending from the entrance of a building over an adjacent driveway and sheltering those getting in or out of vehicles

por·tend \pȯr-ˈtend\ *vb* **1** : to give a sign or warning of beforehand **2** : INDICATE, SIGNIFY **syn** augur, prognosticate, foretell, predict, forecast, prophesy

por·tent \ˈpȯr-ˌtent\ *n* **1** : something that foreshadows a coming event : OMEN **2** : MARVEL, PRODIGY

por·ten·tous \pȯr-ˈtent-əs\ *adj* **1** : of, relating to, or constituting a portent **2** : PRODIGIOUS **3** : self-consciously weighty : POMPOUS

¹por·ter \ˈpōrt-ər\ *n, chiefly Brit* : DOORKEEPER

²porter *n* **1** : one that carries burdens; *esp* : one employed (as at a terminal) to carry baggage **2** : an attendant in a railroad car **3** : a dark heavy ale

por·ter·house \ˈpōrt-ər-ˌhau̇s\ *n* : a choice beefsteak with a large tenderloin

port·fo·lio \pōrt-ˈfō-lē-ˌō\ *n, pl* **-li·os 1** : a portable case for papers or drawings **2** : the office and functions of a minister of state **3** : the securities held by an investor

port·hole \ˈpōrt-ˌhōl\ *n* : an opening in the side of a ship or aircraft

por·ti·co \ˈpōrt-i-ˌkō\ *n, pl* **-coes** *or* **-cos** [It] : a row of columns supporting a roof around or at the entrance of a building

por·tiere \pōr-ˈtye(ə)r, -ˈti(ə)r; ˈpōrt-ē-ər\ *n* : a curtain hanging across a doorway

¹por·tion \ˈpōr-shən\ *n* **1** : one's part or share ⟨a ~ of food⟩ **2** : DOWRY **3** : an individual's lot **4** : a part of a whole ⟨a ~ of the sky⟩

²portion *vb* **por·tioned; por·tion·ing** \-sh(ə-)niŋ\ **1** : to divide into portions **2** : to allot to as a portion

port·land cement \ˌpōrt-lən(d)-\ *n* : a cement made by calcining and grinding a mixture of clay and limestone

port·ly \ˈpōrt-lē\ *adj* **port·li·er; -est** : somewhat stout

port·man·teau \pōrt-ˈman-ˌtō\ *n, pl* **-teaus** *or* **-teaux** \-ˌtōz\ [MF *portemanteau*, fr. *porter* to carry + *manteau* mantle, fr. L *mantellum*] : a large traveling bag

port of call : an intermediate port where ships customarily stop for supplies, repairs, or transshipment of cargo

port of entry 1 : a place where foreign goods may be cleared through a customhouse **2** : a place where an alien may enter a country

por·trait \ˈpōr-trət, -ˌtrāt\ *n* : a picture (as a painting or photograph) of a person usu. showing the face

por·trait·ist \-əst\ *n* : a maker of portraits

por·trai·ture \ˈpōr-trə-ˌchu̇r\ *n* : the practice or art of making portraits

por·tray \pōr-ˈtrā\ *vb* **1** : to make a picture of : DEPICT **2** : to describe in words **3** : to play the role of — **por·tray·al** *n*

Por·tu·guese \ˈpōr-chə-ˌgēz, -ˌgēs; ˌpōr-chə-ˈgēz, -ˈgēs\ *n, pl* **Portuguese 1** : a native or inhabitant of Portugal **2** : the language of Portugal and Brazil — **Portuguese** *adj*

Portuguese man–of–war *n* : any of several large colonial invertebrate animals that are related to the jellyfishes and have a large sac resembling a bladder by means of which the colony floats at the surface of the sea

por·tu·laca \ˌpōr-chə-ˈlak-ə\ *n* : a tropical succulent herb cultivated for its showy flowers

pos *abbr* **1** position **2** positive

¹pose \ˈpōz\ *vb* **posed; pos·ing 1** : to assume or cause to assume a posture usu. for artistic purposes **2** : to set forth : PROPOSE ⟨~ a question⟩ **3** : to affect an attitude or character

²pose *n* **1** : a sustained posture; *esp* : one assumed by a model **2** : an attitude assumed for effect : PRETENSE

¹pos·er \ˈpō-zər\ *n* : a puzzling question

²poser *n* : a person who poses

po·seur \pō-ˈzər\ *n* [F, lit., poser] : an affected or insincere person

posh \ˈpäsh\ *adj* : FASHIONABLE

pos·it \ˈpäs-ət\ *vb* : to assume the existence of : POSTULATE

po·si·tion \pə-ˈzish-ən\ *n* **1** : an arranging in order **2** : the stand taken on a question **3** : the point or area occupied by something : SITUATION **4** : the arrangement of parts (as of the body) in relation to one another : POSTURE **5** : RANK, STATUS **6** : EMPLOYMENT, JOB — **position** *vb*

¹pos·i·tive \ˈpäz-ət-iv\ *adj* **1** : expressed definitely ⟨~ views⟩ **2** : CONFIDENT, CERTAIN **3** : of, relating to, or constituting the degree of grammatical comparison that denotes no increase in quality, quantity, or relation **4** : not fictitious : REAL **5** : active and effective in function ⟨~ leadership⟩ **6** : having the light and shade as existing in the original subject ⟨a ~ photograph⟩ **7** : numerically greater than zero ⟨a ~ number⟩ **8** : being, relating to, or charged with electricity of which the proton is the elementary unit **9** : AFFIRMATIVE ⟨a ~ response⟩ — **pos·i·tive·ly** *adv* — **pos·i·tive·ness** *n*

²positive *n* **1** : the positive degree or a positive form in a language **2** : a positive photograph

pos·i·tron \ˈpäz-ə-ˌträn\ *n* : a positively charged particle having the same mass and magnitude of charge as the electron

poss *abbr* possessive

pos·se \ˈpäs-ē\ *n* [ML *posse comitatus*, lit., power or authority of the country] : a body of persons organized to assist a sheriff in an emergency

pos·sess \pə-ˈzes\ *vb* **1** : to have as property : OWN **2** : to have as an attribute, knowledge, or skill **3** : to enter into and control firmly ⟨~*ed* by a devil⟩ — **pos·ses·sor** \-ˈzes-ər\ *n*

pos·ses·sion \-ˈzesh-ən\ *n* **1** : control or occupancy of property **2** : OWNERSHIP **3** : something owned : PROPERTY **4** : domination by something **5** : SELF-CONTROL

pos·ses·sive \pə-ˈzes-iv\ *adj* **1** : of, relating to, or constituting a grammatical case denoting ownership **2** : showing the desire to possess ⟨a ~ nature⟩ — **possessive** *n* — **pos·ses·sive·ness** *n*

pos·si·ble \ˈpäs-ə-bəl\ *adj* **1** : being within the limits of ability, capacity, or realization ⟨a ~ task⟩ **2** : being something that may or may not occur ⟨~ dangers⟩ **3** : able or fitted to become ⟨a ~ site for a bridge⟩ — **pos·si·bil·i·ty** \ˌpäs-ə-ˈbil-ət-ē\ *n* — **pos·si·bly** \ˈpäs-ə-blē\ *adv*

pos·sum \ˈpäs-əm\ *n* : OPOSSUM

¹post \ˈpōst\ *n* **1** : an upright piece of timber or metal serving esp. as a support : PILLAR **2** : a pole or stake set up as a mark or indicator

²post *vb* **1** : to affix to a usual place (as a wall) for public notices ⟨~ no bills⟩ **2** : to publish or announce by or as if by a public notice ⟨~ grades⟩ **3** : to forbid (property) to trespassers by putting up a notice **4** : SCORE 4

³post *n* **1** *obs* : COURIER **2** *chiefly Brit* : MAIL; *also* : POST OFFICE

⁴post *vb* **1** : to ride or travel with haste : HURRY **2** : MAIL ⟨~ a letter⟩ **3** : to enter in a ledger **4** : INFORM ⟨kept him ~*ed* on new developments⟩

⁵post *n* **1** : the place at which a soldier is stationed; *esp* : a sentry's beat or station **2** : a station or task to which a person is assigned **3** : the place at which a body of troops is stationed : CAMP **4** : OFFICE, POSITION **5** : a trading settlement or station

⁶post *vb* **1** : to station in a given place **2** : to put up (as bond)

post·age \ˈpōs-tij\ *n* : the fee for postal service; *also* : stamps representing this fee

post·al \ˈpōs-tᵊl\ *adj* : of or relating to the mails or the post office

postal card *n* : POSTCARD

postal service *n* : a government agency or department handling the transmission of mail

post·boy \ˈpōst-ˌbȯi\ *n* : POSTILION

post·card \-ˌkärd\ *n* : a card on which a message may be written for mailing without an envelope

post chaise *n* : a 4-wheeled closed carriage for two to four persons

post·con·so·nan·tal \ˌpōst-ˌkän-sə-ˈnant-ᵊl\ *adj* : immediately following a consonant

post·date \(ˈ)pōs(t)-ˈdāt\ *vb* : to date with a date later than that of execution

post·doc·tor·al \(ˈ)pōs(t)-ˈdäk-t(ə-)rəl\ *also* **post·doc·tor·ate** \-t(ə-)rət\ *adj* : of, relating to, or engaged in advanced academic or professional work beyond a doctor's degree

post·er \ˈpō-stər\ *n* : a bill or placard for posting in a public place

¹pos·te·ri·or \pō-ˈstir-ē-ər, pä-\ *adj* **1** : later in time **2** : situated behind

²pos·te·ri·or \pä-ˈstir-ē-ər, pō-\ *n* : the hinder parts of the body : BUTTOCKS

pos·ter·i·ty \pä-ˈster-ət-ē\ *n* **1** : the descendants from one ancestor **2** : succeeding generations; *also* : future time

pos·tern \ˈpōs-tərn, ˈpäs-\ *n* **1** : a back door or gate **2** : a private or side entrance

post exchange *n* : a store at a military post that sells to military personnel and authorized civilians

post·grad·u·ate \(ˈ)pōst-ˈgraj-ə-wət\ *adj* : of or relating to studies beyond the bachelor's degree — **postgraduate** *n*

post·haste \ˈpōst-ˈhāst\ *adv* : with all possible speed

post·hole \ˈpōst-ˌhōl\ *n* : a hole for a post and esp. a fence post

post·hu·mous \ˈpäs-chə-məs\ *adj* **1** : born after the death of the father **2** : published after the death of the author

post·hyp·not·ic \ˌpōst-hip-ˈnät-ik\ *adj* : of, relating to, or characteristic of the period following a hypnotic trance

pos·til·ion *or* **pos·til·lion** \pō-ˈstil-yən, pə-\ *n* : a rider on the left-hand horse of a pair drawing a coach

Post·im·pres·sion·ism \ˌpōst-im-ˈpresh-ə-ˌniz-əm\ *n* : a late 19th century French theory or practice of art that stresses variously volume, picture structure, or expressionism

post·lude \ˈpōst-ˌlüd\ *n* : an organ solo played at the end of a church service

post·man \ˈpōst-mən, -ˌman\ *n* : MAILMAN

post·mark \-ˌmärk\ *n* : an official postal marking on a piece of mail; *esp* : the mark canceling the postage stamp — **postmark** *vb*

post·mas·ter \-ˌmas-tər\ *n* : one who has charge of a post office

postmaster general *n, pl* **postmasters general** : an official in charge of a national postal service

post me·ri·di·em \ˈpōst-mə-ˈrid-ē-əm\ *adj* [L] : being after noon

post·mis·tress \-ˌmis-trəs\ *n* : a woman in charge of a post office

¹post·mor·tem \(ˈ)pōst-ˈmȯrt-əm\ *adj* [L *post mortem* after death] **1** : done, occurring, or collected after death **2** : relating to a postmortem examination

²postmortem *n* : AUTOPSY

post·na·sal drip \ˈpōst-ˈnā-zəl-\ *n* : flow of mucous secretion from the posterior part of the nasal cavity onto the wall of the pharynx

post·na·tal \(ˈ)pōst-ˈnāt-ᵊl\ *adj* : subsequent to birth; *also* : of or relating to a newborn child

post office *n* **1** : POSTAL SERVICE **2** : a local branch of a post office department

post·op·er·a·tive \(ˈ)pōst-ˈäp-(ə-)rət-iv, -ˈäp-ə-ˌrāt-\ *adj* : following a surgical operation ⟨~ care⟩

post·paid \ˈpōst-ˈpād\ *adv* : with the postage paid by the sender and not chargeable to the receiver

post·par·tum \(ˈ)pōst-ˈpärt-əm\ *adj* [NL *post partum* after birth] : following parturition — **postpartum** *adv*
post·pone \pōs(t)-ˈpōn\ *vb* **post·poned; post·pon·ing** : to hold back to a later time — **post·pone·ment** *n*
post road *n* : a road over which mail is carried
post·script \ˈpōs(t)-ˌskript\ *n* : a note added esp. to a completed letter
post time *n* : the designated time for the start of a horse race
pos·tu·lant \ˈpäs-chə-lənt\ *n* : a probationary candidate for membership in a religious house
[1]**pos·tu·late** \ˈpäs-chə-ˌlāt\ *vb* **-lat·ed; -lat·ing** : to assume as true
[2]**pos·tu·late** \ˈpäs-chə-lət, -ˌlāt\ *n* : a proposition taken for granted as true and made the starting point in a chain of reasoning
[1]**pos·ture** \ˈpäs-chər\ *n* **1** : the position or bearing of the body or one of its parts **2** : STATE, CONDITION **3** : ATTITUDE
[2]**posture** *vb* **pos·tured; pos·tur·ing** : to strike a pose esp. for effect
post·war \ˈpōst-ˈwȯr\ *adj* : of or relating to the period after a war
po·sy \ˈpō-zē\ *n, pl* **posies 1** : a brief sentiment : MOTTO **2** : a bunch of flowers; *also* : FLOWER
[1]**pot** \ˈpät\ *n* **1** : a rounded container used chiefly for domestic purposes **2** : the total of the bets at stake at one time **3** : RUIN ⟨go to ~⟩ **4** : MARIJUANA — **pot·ful** *n*
[2]**pot** *vb* **pot·ted; pot·ting 1** : to preserve in a pot **2** : SHOOT
po·ta·ble \ˈpōt-ə-bəl\ *adj* : suitable for drinking — **po·ta·bil·i·ty** \ˌpōt-ə-ˈbil-ət-ē\ *n*
po·tage \pȯ-ˈtäzh\ *n* : a thick soup
pot·ash \ˈpät-ˌash\ *n* [sing. of *pot ashes*] : potassium or any of its various compounds
po·tas·si·um \pə-ˈtas-ē-əm\ *n* : a silver-white metallic chemical element that occurs abundantly in nature esp. combined in minerals — see ELEMENT table
potassium bromide *n* : a crystalline salt used as a sedative and in photography
potassium carbonate *n* : a white salt used in making glass and soap
potassium nitrate *n* : a soluble salt used in making gunpowder, in preserving meat, and in medicine
po·ta·tion \pō-ˈtā-shən\ *n* : a usu. alcoholic drink; *also* : the act of drinking
po·ta·to \pə-ˈtāt-ō\ *n, pl* **-toes** : the edible starchy tuber of a plant related to the tomato; *also* : this plant
potato beetle *n* : COLORADO POTATO BEETLE
potato bug *n* : COLORADO POTATO BEETLE
pot·bel·ly \ˈpät-ˌbel-ē\ *n* : a protruding abdomen — **pot·bel·lied** \-ēd\ *adj*
pot·boil·er \-ˌbȯi-lər\ *n* : a usu. inferior work of art or literature produced only to earn money
po·tent \ˈpōt-ᵊnt\ *adj* **1** : having authority or influence : POWERFUL **2** : chemically or medicinally effective **3** : able to copulate **syn** forceful, forcible, mighty, puissant — **po·ten·cy** \-ᵊn-sē\ *n*
po·ten·tate \ˈpōt-ᵊn-ˌtāt\ *n* : one who wields controlling power : RULER
[1]**po·ten·tial** \pə-ˈten-chəl\ *adj* : existing in possibility : capable of becoming actual ⟨a ~ champion⟩ **syn** dormant, latent, quiescent — **po·ten·ti·al·i·ty** \pə-ˌten-chē-ˈal-ət-ē\ *n* — **po·ten·tial·ly** \-ˈtench-(ə-)lē\ *adv*
[2]**potential** *n* **1** : something that can develop or become actual **2** : the work required to move a unit positive charge from infinity to a point in question; *also* : POTENTIAL DIFFERENCE
potential difference *n* : the difference in potential between two points that represents the work involved in the transfer of a unit quantity of electricity from one point to the other
po·ten·ti·ate \pə-ˈten-chē-ˌāt\ *vb* **-at·ed; -at·ing** : to make potent; *esp* : to augment the activity of (as a drug) synergistically — **po·ten·ti·a·tion** \-ˌten-chē-ˈā-shən\ *n*
pot·head \ˈpät-ˌhed\ *n* : an individual who smokes marijuana
poth·er \ˈpäth-ər\ *n* : a noisy disturbance; *also* : FUSS
pot·herb \ˈpät-ˌ(h)ərb\ *n* : an herb whose leaves or stems are boiled for greens or used to season food
pot·hole \ˈpät-ˌhōl\ *n* : a large pit or hole (as in a road surface)
pot·hook \-ˌhu̇k\ *n* : an S-shaped hook for hanging pots and kettles over an open fire
po·tion \ˈpō-shən\ *n* : a mixture of liquids (as liquor or medicine)
pot·luck \ˈpät-ˈlək\ *n* : the regular meal available to a guest for whom no special preparations have been made
pot·pie \-ˈpī\ *n* : pastry-covered meat and vegetables cooked in a deep dish
pot·pour·ri \ˌpō-pu̇-ˈrē\ *n* [F *pot pourri,* lit., rotten pot] : a miscellaneous collection : MEDLEY
pot·sherd \ˈpät-ˌshərd\ *n* : a pottery fragment
pot·shot \-ˌshät\ *n* **1** : a shot taken from ambush or at a random or easy target **2** : a critical remark made in a random or sporadic manner
pot·tage \ˈpät-ij\ *n* : a thick soup of vegetables or vegetables and meat
[1]**pot·ter** \ˈpät-ər\ *n* : one that makes pottery
[2]**potter** *vb* : PUTTER
pot·tery \ˈpät-ə-rē\ *n, pl* **-ter·ies 1** : a place where earthen pots and dishes are made **2** : the art of the potter **3** : dishes, pots, and vases made from clay
[1]**pouch** \ˈpau̇ch\ *n* **1** : a small bag (as for tobacco) carried on the person **2** : a bag for storing or transporting goods ⟨mail ~⟩ ⟨diplomatic ~⟩ **3** : an anatomical sac; *esp* : one for carrying the young on the abdomen of a female marsupial (as a kangaroo)
[2]**pouch** *vb* : to make puffy or protuberant
poult \ˈpōlt\ *n* : a young fowl; *esp* : a young turkey
poul·ter·er \ˈpōl-tər-ər\ *n* : one that deals in poultry
poul·tice \ˈpōl-təs\ *n* : a soft usu. heated and medicated mass spread on cloth and applied to a sore or injury — **poultice** *vb*
poul·try \ˈpōl-trē\ *n* : domesticated birds kept for eggs or meat — **poul·try·man** \-mən\ *n*
pounce \ˈpau̇ns\ *vb* **pounced; pounc·ing** : to spring or swoop upon and seize something
[1]**pound** \ˈpau̇nd\ *n, pl* **pounds** *also* **pound 1** : a unit of avoirdupois, troy, and apothecaries' weight — see WEIGHT table **2** — see MONEY table
[2]**pound** *vb* **1** : to crush to a powder or pulp by beating **2** : to strike or beat heavily or repeatedly **3** : DRILL **4** : to move or move along heavily
[3]**pound** *n* : a public enclosure where stray animals are kept
pound·age \ˈpau̇n-dij\ *n* : POUNDS; *also* : weight in pounds
pound cake *n* : a rich cake made with a large amount of eggs and shortening in proportion to the flour used
pound–fool·ish \ˈpau̇nd-ˈfü-lish\ *adj* : imprudent in dealing with large sums or large matters
pour \ˈpōr\ *vb* **1** : to flow or cause to flow in a stream or flood **2** : to rain hard **3** : to supply freely and copiously
pour·boire \pu̇r-ˈbwär\ *n* [F, fr. *pour boire* for drinking] : TIP, GRATUITY
pout \ˈpau̇t\ *vb* : to show displeasure by thrusting out the lips; *also* : to look sullen — **pout** *n*
pov·er·ty \ˈpäv-ərt-ē\ *n* [ME *poverte,* fr. OF *poverté,* fr. L *paupertat-, paupertas,* fr. *pauper* poor] **1** : lack of money or material possessions : WANT **2** : poor quality (as of soil)
poverty line *n* : a level of personal or family income below which one is classified as poor according to government standards
pov·er·ty–strick·en \ˈpäv-ərt-ē-ˌstrik-ən\ *adj* : very poor : DESTITUTE
POW \ˌpē-(ˌ)ō-ˈdəb-əl-(ˌ)yü\ *abbr* prisoner of war

¹pow·der \ˈpau̇d-ər\ *n* [ME *poudre*, fr. OF, fr. L *pulver-*, *pulvis* dust] **1** : dry material made up of fine particles; *also* : a usu. medicinal or cosmetic preparation in this form **2** : a solid explosive (as gunpowder) — **pow·dery** *adj*

²powder *vb* **pow·dered; pow·der·ing** \ˈpau̇d-(ə-)riŋ\ **1** : to sprinkle or cover with or as if with powder **2** : to reduce to powder

powder room *n* : a rest room for women

¹pow·er \ˈpau̇(-ə)r\ *n* **1** : a position of ascendancy over others : AUTHORITY **2** : the ability to act or produce an effect **3** : one that has control or authority; *esp* : a sovereign state **4** : physical might; *also* : mental or moral vigor **5** : the number of times as indicated by an exponent a number is to be multiplied by itself **6** : force or energy used to do work; *also* : the time rate at which work is done or energy transferred **7** : the amount by which an optical lens magnifies — **pow·er·ful** \-fəl\ *adj* — **pow·er·ful·ly** \-ē\ *adv* — **pow·er·less** *adj*

²power *vb* : to supply with power and esp. motive power

pow·er·boat \-ˌbōt\ *n* : MOTORBOAT

pow·er·house \ˈpau̇(-ə)r-ˌhau̇s\ *n* **1** : POWER PLANT 1 **2** : one having great drive, energy, or ability

power plant *n* **1** : a building in which electric power is generated **2** : an engine and related parts supplying the motive power of a self-propelled vehicle

pow·wow \ˈpau̇-ˌwau̇\ *n* **1** : a No. American Indian ceremony (as for victory in war) **2** : a meeting for discussion : CONFERENCE

pox \ˈpäks\ *n, pl* **pox** *or* **pox·es** : any of various diseases (as smallpox or syphilis) marked by a rash on the skin

pp *abbr* **1** pages **2** pianissimo

PP *abbr* **1** parcel post **2** past participle **3** postpaid **4** prepaid

ppd *abbr* **1** postpaid **2** prepaid

PPS *abbr* [L *post postscriptum*] an additional postscript

ppt *abbr* precipitate

PQ *abbr* Province of Quebec

pr *abbr* **1** pair **2** price

Pr *symbol* praseodymium

PR *abbr* **1** payroll **2** public relations **3** Puerto Rico

prac·ti·ca·ble \ˈprak-ti-kə-bəl\ *adj* : capable of being put into practice, done, or accomplished — **prac·ti·ca·bil·i·ty** \ˌprak-ti-kə-ˈbil-ət-ē\ *n*

prac·ti·cal \ˈprak-ti-kəl\ *adj* **1** : of, relating to, or shown in practice ⟨~ questions⟩ **2** : VIRTUAL ⟨~ control⟩ **3** : capable of being put to use ⟨a ~ knowledge of French⟩ **4** : inclined to action as opposed to speculation ⟨a ~ person⟩ **5** : qualified by practice ⟨a good ~ mechanic⟩ — **prac·ti·cal·i·ty** \ˌprak-ti-ˈkal-ət-ē\ *n* — **prac·ti·cal·ly** \ˈprak-ti-k(ə-)lē\ *adv*

practical joke *n* : a prank intended to trick or embarrass someone or cause him physical discomfort

practical nurse *n* : a nurse who cares for the sick professionally without having the training or experience required of a registered nurse

¹prac·tice *or* **prac·tise** \ˈprak-təs\ *vb* **prac·ticed** *or* **prac·tised; prac·tic·ing** *or* **prac·tis·ing** **1** : to perform or work at repeatedly so as to become proficient ⟨~ tennis strokes⟩ **2** : CARRY OUT, APPLY ⟨~*s* what he preaches⟩ **3** : to do or perform customarily ⟨~ politeness⟩ **4** : to be professionally engaged in ⟨~ law⟩

²practice *also* **practise** *n* **1** : actual performance or application **2** : customary action : HABIT **3** : systematic exercise for proficiency **4** : the exercise of a profession; *also* : a professional business

prac·ti·tio·ner \prak-ˈtish-(ə-)nər\ *n* : one that practices a profession

prae·tor \ˈprēt-ər\ *n* : an ancient Roman magistrate ranking below a consul — **prae·to·ri·an** \prē-ˈtōr-ē-ən, -ˈtȯr-\ *adj*

prag·mat·ic \prag-ˈmat-ik\ *also* **prag·mat·i·cal** \-i-kəl\ *adj* **1** : of or relating to practical affairs **2** : concerned with the practical consequences of actions or beliefs

prag·ma·tism \ˈprag-mə-ˌtiz-əm\ *n* : a practical approach to problems and affairs

prai·rie \ˈprer-ē\ *n* : a broad tract of level or rolling grassland

prairie dog *n* : an American burrowing rodent related to the marmots and living in colonies

prairie schooner *n* : a covered wagon used by pioneers in cross-country travel

prairie schooner

praise \ˈprāz\ *vb* **praised; prais·ing** **1** : to express approval of : COMMEND **2** : to glorify (a divinity or a saint) esp. in song — **praise** *n* — **praise·wor·thy** \-ˌwər-t͟hē\ *adj*

pra·line \ˈprä-ˌlēn, ˈprā-\ *n* [F] : a candy of nut kernels embedded in boiled brown sugar or maple sugar

pram \ˈpram\ *n, chiefly Brit* : PERAMBULATOR

prance \ˈprans\ *vb* **pranced; pranc·ing** **1** : to spring from the hind legs ⟨a *prancing* horse⟩ **2** : SWAGGER; *also* : CAPER — **prance** *n* — **pranc·er** *n*

prank \ˈpraŋk\ *n* : a playful or mildly mischievous act : TRICK — **prank·ster** \-stər\ *n*

pra·seo·dym·i·um \ˌprā-zē-ō-ˈdim-ē-əm\ *n* : a white metallic chemical element — see ELEMENT table

prate \ˈprāt\ *vb* **prat·ed; prat·ing** : to talk long and idly : chatter foolishly

prat·fall \ˈprat-ˌfȯl\ *n* **1** : a fall on the buttocks **2** : a humiliating blunder

¹prat·tle \ˈprat-ᵊl\ *vb* **prat·tled; prat·tling** \ˈprat-(ᵊ-)liŋ\ : PRATE, BABBLE

²prattle *n* : trifling or childish talk

prawn \ˈprȯn\ *n* : any of numerous edible shrimplike crustaceans; *also* : SHRIMP 1

pray \ˈprā\ *vb* **1** : ENTREAT, IMPLORE **2** : to ask earnestly for something **3** : to address a divinity esp. with supplication

prayer \ˈpraər\ *n* **1** : a supplication or expression addressed to God; *also* : a set order of words used in praying **2** : an earnest request or wish **3** : the act or practice of praying to God **4** : a religious service consisting chiefly of prayers — often used in pl. **5** : something prayed for **6** : a slight chance

prayer book *n* : a book containing prayers and often directions for worship

prayer·ful \ˈpraər-fəl\ *adj* **1** : DEVOUT **2** : EARNEST — **prayer·ful·ly** \-ē\ *adv*

praying mantis *n* : MANTIS

preach \ˈprēch\ *vb* **1** : to deliver a sermon **2** : to set forth in a sermon **3** : to advocate earnestly — **preach·er** *n* — **preach·ment** *n*

pre·ad·o·les·cence \ˌprē-ˌad-ᵊl-ˈes-ᵊns\ *n* : the period of human development just preceding adolescence — **pre·ad·o·les·cent** \-ᵊnt\ *adj or n*

pre·am·ble \ˈprē-ˌam-bəl\ *n* [ME, fr. MF *preambule*, fr. ML *preambulum*, fr. LL, neut. of *praeambulus* walking in front of, fr. L *prae* in front of + *ambulare* to walk] : an introductory part ⟨the ~ to a constitution⟩

pre·am·pli·fi·er \(ˈ)prē-ˈam-plə-ˌfī(-ə)r\ *n* : an amplifier that increases extremely weak signals before they are fed to additional amplifier circuits

pre·ar·range \ˌprē-ə-ˈrānj\ *vb* : to arrange beforehand — **pre·ar·range·ment** *n*

pre·as·signed \ˌprē-ə-ˈsīnd\ *adj* : assigned beforehand

prec *abbr* preceding

Pre·cam·bri·an \ˈprē-ˈkam-brē-ən, -ˈkām-\ *adj* : of, relating to, or being the period of geologic history preceding the Paleozoic era — **Precambrian** *n*

1**pre·can·cel** \(ˈ)prē-ˈkan-səl\ *vb* : to cancel (a postage stamp) in advance of use — **pre·can·cel·la·tion** \ˌprē-ˌkan-sə-ˈlā-shən\ *n*

2**precancel** *n* : a precanceled postage stamp

pre·can·cer·ous \(ˈ)prē-ˈkans-(ə-)rəs\ *adj* : likely to become cancerous

pre·car·i·ous \pri-ˈkar-ē-əs\ *adj* : dependent on uncertain conditions : dangerously insecure : UNSTABLE ⟨a ~ foothold⟩ ⟨~ prosperity⟩ **syn** delicate, sensitive, ticklish, touchy, tricky — **pre·car·i·ous·ly** *adv* — **pre·car·i·ous·ness** *n*

pre·cau·tion \pri-ˈkȯ-shən\ *n* : a measure taken beforehand to prevent harm or secure good — **pre·cau·tion·ary** \-shə-ˌner-ē\ *adj*

pre·cede \pri-ˈsēd\ *vb* **pre·ced·ed; pre·ced·ing** : to be, go, or come ahead or in front of (as in rank, sequence, or time)

pre·ce·dence \ˈpres-əd-əns, pri-ˈsēd-ᵊns\ *n* **1** : the act or fact of preceding **2** : consideration based on order of importance : PRIORITY

1**pre·ce·dent** \pri-ˈsēd-ᵊnt, ˈpres-əd-ənt\ *adj* : prior in time, order, or significance

2**prec·e·dent** \ˈpres-əd-ənt\ *n* : something said or done that may serve to authorize or justify further words or acts of the same or a similar kind

pre·ced·ing \pri-ˈsēd-iŋ\ *adj* : that precedes **syn** antecedent, foregoing, prior, former, anterior

pre·cen·tor \pri-ˈsent-ər\ *n* : a leader of the singing of a choir or congregation

pre·cept \ˈprē-ˌsept\ *n* : a command or principle intended as a general rule of action or conduct

pre·cep·tor \pri-ˈsep-tər, ˈprē-ˌsep-\ *n* : TUTOR

pre·ces·sion \prē-ˈsesh-ən\ *n* : a slow gyration of the rotation axis of a spinning body (as the earth) — **pre·cess** \prē-ˈses\ *vb*

pre·cinct \ˈprē-ˌsiŋkt\ *n* **1** : an administrative subdivision (as of a city) : DISTRICT ⟨police ~⟩ ⟨electoral ~⟩ **2** : an enclosure bounded by the limits of a building or place — often used in pl. **3** *pl* : ENVIRONS

pre·ci·os·i·ty \ˌpres(h)-ē-ˈäs-ət-ē\ *n, pl* **-ties** : fastidious refinement

pre·cious \ˈpresh-əs\ *adj* **1** : of great value ⟨~ jewels⟩ **2** : greatly cherished : DEAR ⟨~ memories⟩ **3** : AFFECTED ⟨~ language⟩

prec·i·pice \ˈpres-ə-pəs\ *n* : a steep cliff

pre·cip·i·tan·cy \pri-ˈsip-ət-ən-sē\ *n* : undue hastiness or suddenness

1**pre·cip·i·tate** \pri-ˈsip-ə-ˌtāt\ *vb* **-tat·ed; -tat·ing 1** : to throw violently **2** : to throw down **3** : to cause to happen quickly or abruptly ⟨~ a quarrel⟩ **4** : to cause to separate from solution or suspension **5** : to fall as rain, snow, or hail **syn** speed, accelerate, quicken, hasten, hurry

2**pre·cip·i·tate** \pri-ˈsip-ət-ət, -ə-ˌtāt\ *n* : the solid matter that separates from a solution or suspension

3**pre·cip·i·tate** \pri-ˈsip-ət-ət\ *adj* **1** : showing extreme or unwise haste : RASH **2** : falling with steep descent; *also* : PRECIPITOUS — **pre·cip·i·tate·ly** *adv* — **pre·cip·i·tate·ness** *n*

pre·cip·i·ta·tion \pri-ˌsip-ə-ˈtā-shən\ *n* **1** : rash haste **2** : the process of precipitating or forming a precipitate **3** : water that falls to earth esp. as rain or snow; *also* : the quantity of this water

pre·cip·i·tous \pri-ˈsip-ət-əs\ *adj* **1** : PRECIPITATE **2** : having the character of a precipice : very steep ⟨a ~ slope⟩; *also* : containing precipices ⟨~ trails⟩ — **pre·cip·i·tous·ly** *adv*

pré·cis \prā-ˈsē\ *n, pl* **pré·cis** \-ˈsēz\ [F] : a concise summary of essential points

pre·cise \pri-ˈsīs\ *adj* **1** : exactly defined or stated : DEFINITE **2** : highly accurate : EXACT **3** : conforming strictly to a standard : SCRUPULOUS — **pre·cise·ly** *adv* — **pre·cise·ness** *n*

pre·ci·sion \pri-ˈsizh-ən\ *n* : the quality or state of being precise

pre·clude \pri-ˈklüd\ *vb* **pre·clud·ed; pre·clud·ing** : to make impossible : BAR, PREVENT

pre·co·cious \pri-ˈkō-shəs\ *adj* [L *praecoc-, praecox* early ripening, precocious, fr. *prae-* ahead + *coquere* to cook] : early in development and esp. in mental development — **pre·co·cious·ly** *adv* — **pre·coc·i·ty** \pri-ˈkäs-ət-ē\ *n*

pre·con·ceive \ˌprē-kən-ˈsēv\ *vb* : to form an opinion of beforehand — **pre·con·cep·tion** \-ˈsep-shən\ *n*

pre·con·cert·ed \-ˈsərt-əd\ *adj* : arranged or agreed on in advance

pre·con·di·tion \-ˈdish-ən\ *vb* : to put in proper or desired condition or frame of mind in advance

pre·cook \ˈprē-ˈku̇k\ *vb* : to cook partially or entirely before final cooking or reheating

pre·cur·sor \pri-ˈkər-sər\ *n* : one that precedes and indicates the approach of another : FORERUNNER

pred *abbr* predicate

pre·da·ceous *or* **pre·da·cious** \pri-ˈdā-shəs\ *adj* : living by preying on others : PREDATORY

pre·date \ˈprē-ˈdāt\ *vb* : ANTEDATE

pre·da·tion \pri-ˈdā-shən\ *n* **1** : the act of preying or plundering **2** : a mode of life in which food is primarily obtained by killing and consuming animals

pred·a·tor \ˈpred-ət-ər\ *n* : an animal that lives by killing and consuming other animals

pred·a·to·ry \ˈpred-ə-ˌtōr-ē\ *adj* **1** : of or relating to plunder ⟨~ warfare⟩ **2** : disposed to exploit others **3** : preying upon other animals

pre·de·cease \ˌprē-di-ˈsēs\ *vb* **-ceased; -ceas·ing** : to die before another person

pre·de·ces·sor \ˈpred-ə-ˌses-ər, ˈprēd-\ *n* : one that has previously held a position to which another has succeeded

pre·des·ig·nate \(ˈ)prē-ˈdez-ig-ˌnāt\ *vb* : to designate beforehand

pre·des·ti·na·tion \ˌprē-ˌdes-tə-ˈnā-shən\ *n* : the act of foreordaining to an earthly lot or eternal destiny by divine decree; *also* : the state of being so foreordained — **pre·des·ti·nate** \prē-ˈdes-tə-ˌnāt\ *vb*

pre·des·tine \prē-ˈdes-tən\ *vb* : to settle beforehand : FOREORDAIN

pre·de·ter·mine \ˌprē-di-ˈtər-mən\ *vb* : to determine beforehand

pred·i·ca·ble \ˈpred-i-kə-bəl\ *adj* : capable of being predicated or affirmed

pre·dic·a·ment \pri-ˈdik-ə-mənt\ *n* : a difficult or trying situation **syn** dilemma, pickle, quagmire, jam

1**pred·i·cate** \ˈpred-i-kət\ *n* : the part of a sentence or clause that expresses what is said of the subject

2**pred·i·cate** \ˈpred-ə-ˌkāt\ *vb* **-cat·ed; -cat·ing 1** : AFFIRM **2** : to assert to be a quality or attribute ⟨~ intelligence of man⟩ **3** : FOUND, BASE — **pred·i·ca·tion** \ˌpred-ə-ˈkā-shən\ *n*

pre·dict \pri-ˈdikt\ *vb* : to declare in advance — **pre·dict·able** \-ˈdik-tə-bəl\ *adj* — **pre·dict·ably** \-blē\ *adv* — **pre·dic·tion** \-ˈdik-shən\ *n*

pre·di·ges·tion \ˌprē-dī-ˈjes-chən, -də-\ *n* : artificial partial digestion of food esp. for use in cases of illness or impaired digestion — **pre·di·gest** \-ˈjest\ *vb*

pre·di·lec·tion \ˌpred-ᵊl-ˈek-shən, ˌprēd-\ *n* : a favorable inclination

pre·dis·pose \ˌprē-dis-ˈpōz\ *vb* : to incline in advance : make susceptible — **pre·dis·po·si·tion** \ˌprē-ˌdis-pə-ˈzish-ən\ *n*

pre·dom·i·nant \pri-ˈdäm-ə-nənt\ *adj* : greater in importance, strength, influence, or authority — **pre·dom·i·nance** \-nəns\ *n*

pre·dom·i·nant·ly \-nənt-lē\ *adv* : for the most part : MAINLY

pre·dom·i·nate \pri-ˈdäm-ə-ˌnāt\ *vb* : to be superior esp. in power or numbers : PREVAIL

pree·mie \ˈprē-mē\ *n* : a baby born prematurely

pre·em·i·nent \prē-ˈem-ə-nənt\ *adj* : having highest rank : OUTSTANDING — **pre·em·i·nence** \-nəns\ *n* — **pre·em·i·nent·ly** *adv*

pre·empt \prē-ˈempt\ *vb* **1** : to settle upon (public land) with the right to purchase before others; *also* : to take by such right **2** : to seize upon before someone else can **3** : to take the place of **syn** usurp, confiscate, appropriate, expropriate — **pre·emp·tion** \-ˈemp-shən\ *n*

pre·emp·tive \prē-ˈemp-tiv\ *adj* : marked by the seizing of the initiative : initiated by oneself ⟨∼ attack⟩

preen \ˈprēn\ *vb* **1** : to dress or smooth up : PRIMP **2** : to trim or dress with the beak **3** : to pride (oneself) for achievement

pre·ex·ist \ˌprē-ig-ˈzist\ *vb* : to exist before — **pre·ex·is·tence** \-ˈzis-təns\ *n* — **pre·ex·is·tent** \-tənt\ *adj*

pref *abbr* **1** preface **2** preference **3** preferred **4** prefix

pre·fab \ˈprē-ˈfab, ˈprē-ˌfab\ *n* : a prefabricated structure

pre·fab·ri·cate \ˈprē-ˈfab-rə-ˌkāt\ *vb* : to manufacture the parts of (a structure) beforehand for later assembly — **pre·fab·ri·ca·tion** \ˌprē-ˌfab-ri-ˈkā-shən\ *n*

¹**pref·ace** \ˈpref-əs\ *n* : introductory comments : FOREWORD — **pref·a·to·ry** \ˈpref-ə-ˌtōr-ē\ *adj*

²**preface** *vb* **pref·aced; pref·ac·ing** : to introduce with a preface

pre·fect \ˈprē-ˌfekt\ *n* **1** : a high official; *esp* : a chief officer or magistrate **2** : a student monitor — **pre·fec·ture** \-ˌfek-chər\ *n*

pre·fer \pri-ˈfər\ *vb* **pre·ferred; pre·fer·ring 1** *archaic* : PROMOTE **2** : to like better : choose above another **3** : to bring (as a charge) against a person — **pref·er·a·ble** \ˈpref-(ə-)rə-bəl\ *adj* — **pref·er·a·bly** \-blē\ *adv*

pref·er·ence \ˈpref-(ə-)rəns\ *n* **1** : a special liking for one thing over another **2** : CHOICE, SELECTION — **pref·er·en·tial** \ˌpref-ə-ˈren-chəl\ *adj*

pre·fer·ment \pri-ˈfər-mənt\ *n* : PROMOTION, ADVANCEMENT

pre·fig·ure \prē-ˈfig-yər\ *vb* **1** : FORESHADOW **2** : to imagine beforehand

¹**pre·fix** \ˈprē-ˌfiks, prē-ˈfiks\ *vb* : to place before ⟨∼ a title to a name⟩

²**pre·fix** \ˈprē-ˌfiks\ *n* : an affix occurring at the beginning of a word

pre·flight \ˈprē-ˈflīt\ *adj* : preparing for or preliminary to flight

pre·form \ˈprē-ˈfórm\ *vb* : to form or shape beforehand

preg·na·ble \ˈpreg-nə-bəl\ *adj* : vulnerable to capture ⟨a ∼ fort⟩

preg·nant \ˈpreg-nənt\ *adj* **1** : containing unborn young within the body **2** : rich in significance : MEANINGFUL — **preg·nan·cy** \-nən-sē\ *n*

pre·heat \ˈprē-ˈhēt\ *vb* : to heat beforehand; *esp* : to heat (an oven) to a designated temperature before using

pre·hen·sile \prē-ˈhen-səl, -ˌsīl\ *adj* : adapted for grasping esp. by wrapping around ⟨a monkey with a ∼ tail⟩

pre·his·tor·ic \ˌprē-(h)is-ˈtór-ik\ *or* **pre·his·tor·i·cal** \-i-kəl\ *adj* : of, relating to, or existing in the period before written history began

pre·ig·ni·tion \ˌprē-ig-ˈnish-ən\ *n* : ignition in an internal-combustion engine before the proper time

pre·in·duc·tion \ˌprē-in-ˈdək-shən\ *adj* : occurring prior to induction into military service

pre·judge \ˈprē-ˈjəj\ *vb* : to judge before full hearing or examination

¹**prej·u·dice** \ˈprej-əd-əs\ *n* **1** : DAMAGE; *esp* : detriment to one's rights or claims **2** : an opinion for or against something without adequate basis — **prej·u·di·cial** \ˌprej-ə-ˈdish-əl\ *adj*

²**prejudice** *vb* **-diced; -dic·ing 1** : to damage by a judgment or action esp. at law **2** : to cause to have prejudice

prel·ate \ˈprel-ət\ *n* : an ecclesiastic (as a bishop) of high rank — **prel·a·cy** \-ə-sē\ *n*

pre·launch \ˈprē-ˈlónch\ *adj* : preparing for or preliminary to launch

pre·lim \ˈprē-ˌlim, pri-ˈlim\ *n or adj* : PRELIMINARY

¹**pre·lim·i·nary** \pri-ˈlim-ə-ˌner-ē\ *n, pl* **-nar·ies** : something that precedes or introduces the main business or event

²**preliminary** *adj* : preceding the main discourse or business

pre·lude \ˈprel-ˌ(y)üd, ˈprā-ˌlüd\ *n* **1** : an introductory performance or event **2** : a musical section or movement introducing the main theme; *also* : an organ solo played at the beginning of a church service

prem *abbr* premium

pre·mar·i·tal \(ˈ)prē-ˈmar-ət-ᵊl\ *adj* : existing or occurring before marriage

pre·ma·ture \ˌprē-mə-ˈt(y)ůər, -ˈchů(ə)r\ *adj* : happening, coming, born, or done before the usual or proper time **syn** untimely, early — **pre·ma·ture·ly** *adv*

pre·med \ˈprē-ˈmed\ *adj* : PREMEDICAL — **premed** *n*

pre·med·i·cal \(ˈ)prē-ˈmed-i-kəl\ *adj* : preceding and preparing for the professional study of medicine

pre·med·i·tate \pri-ˈmed-ə-ˌtāt\ *vb* : to consider and plan beforehand — **pre·med·i·ta·tion** \-ˌmed-ə-ˈtā-shən\ *n*

pre·men·stru·al \(ˈ)prē-ˈmen-strə(-wə)l\ *adj* : of, relating to, or occurring in the period just preceding menstruation

¹**pre·mier** \pri-ˈm(y)iər, ˈprē-mē-ər\ *adj* [ME *primier*, fr. MF *premier* first, chief, fr. L *primarius* of the first rank] : first in rank or importance : CHIEF; *also* : first in time : EARLIEST

²**premier** *n* : PRIME MINISTER — **pre·mier·ship** *n*

¹**pre·miere** \pri-ˈmyer, -ˈmiər\ *n* : a first performance

²**premiere** *or* **pre·mier** *like* ¹PREMIERE\ *vb* **pre·miered; pre·mier·ing** : to give or receive a first public performance

prem·ise \ˈprem-əs\ *n* **1** : a statement of fact or a supposition made or implied as a basis of argument **2** *pl* : a piece of land with the structures on it; *also* : the place of business of an enterprise

pre·mi·um \ˈprē-mē-əm\ *n* **1** : REWARD, PRIZE **2** : a sum over and above the stated value **3** : something paid over and above a fixed wage or price **4** : something given with a purchase **5** : the sum paid for a contract of insurance **6** : an unusually high value

pre·mix \ˈprē-ˈmiks\ *vb* : to mix before use

¹**pre·mo·lar** \(ˈ)prē-ˈmō-lər\ *adj* : situated in front of or preceding the molar teeth

²**premolar** *n* : either of two double-pointed premolar teeth behind the canine on each side of each jaw in man

pre·mo·ni·tion \ˌprē-mə-ˈnish-ən, ˌprem-ə-\ *n* : previous notice : FOREWARNING; *also* : PRESENTIMENT — **pre·mon·i·to·ry** \pri-ˈmän-ə-ˌtōr-ē\ *adj*

pre·na·tal \ˈprē-ˈnāt-ᵊl\ *adj* : occurring, existing, or taking place before birth

pre·oc·cu·pa·tion \prē-ˌäk-yə-ˈpā-shən\ *n* : complete absorption of the mind or interests; *also* : something that causes such absorption

pre·oc·cu·pied \prē-ˈäk-yə-ˌpīd\ *adj* **1** : last in thought; *also* : absorbed in some preoccupation **2** : already occupied **syn** abstracted, absent, absentminded

pre·oc·cu·py \-ˌpī\ *vb* **1** : to occupy the attention of beforehand **2** : to take possession of before another

pre·op·er·a·tive \(ˈ)prē-ˈäp-(ə-)rət-iv, -ˈäp-ə-ˌrāt-\ *adj* : occurring before and usu. soon before a surgical operation

pre·or·dain \ˌprē-ȯr-ˈdān\ *vb* : FOREORDAIN

pre–owned \ˈprē-ˈōnd\ *adj* : SECONDHAND

prep *abbr* **1** preparatory **2** preposition

pre·pack·age \(ˈ)prē-ˈpak-ij\ *vb* : to package (as food) before offering for sale to the customer

preparatory school *n* **1** : a usu. private school preparing students primarily for college **2** *Brit* : a private elementary school preparing students primarily for public schools

pre·pare \pri-ˈpaər\ *vb* **pre·pared; pre·par·ing 1** : to make or get ready ⟨~ dinner⟩ ⟨~ a boy for college⟩ **2** : to get ready beforehand : PROVIDE **3** : to put together : COMPOUND ⟨~ a vaccine⟩ — **prep·a·ra·tion** \ˌprep-ə-ˈrā-shən\ *n* — **pre·par·a·to·ry** \pri-ˈpar-ə-ˌtōr-ē\ *adj*

pre·pared·ness \pri-ˈpar-əd-nəs\ *n* : a state of adequate preparation

pre·pay \ˈprē-ˈpā\ *vb* **-paid** \-ˈpād\; **-pay·ing** : to pay or pay the charge on in advance

pre·pon·der·ant \pri-ˈpän-d(ə-)rənt\ *adj* : having greater weight, force, influence, or frequency — **pre·pon·der·ance** \-d(ə-)rəns\ *n* — **pre·pon·der·ant·ly** *adv*

pre·pon·der·ate \pri-ˈpän-də-ˌrāt\ *vb* **-at·ed; -at·ing** [L *praeponderare*, fr. *prae-* ahead + *ponder-*, *pondus* weight] : to exceed in weight, force, influence, or frequency : PREDOMINATE

prep·o·si·tion \ˌprep-ə-ˈzish-ən\ *n* : a word that combines with a noun or pronoun to form a phrase — **prep·o·si·tion·al** \-ˈzish-(ə-)nəl\ *adj*

pre·pos·sess \ˌprē-pə-ˈzes\ *vb* **1** : to influence beforehand for or against someone or something **2** : to induce to a favorable opinion beforehand

pre·pos·sess·ing *adj* : tending to create a favorable impression : ATTRACTIVE ⟨a ~ manner⟩

pre·pos·ses·sion \-ˈzesh-ən\ *n* **1** : PREJUDICE **2** : an exclusive concern with one idea or object

pre·pos·ter·ous \pri-ˈpäs-t(ə-)rəs\ *adj* : contrary to nature or reason : ABSURD

prep·py *or* **prep·pie** \ˈprep-ē\ *n, pl* **preppies 1** : a student at or a graduate of a preparatory school **2** : a person deemed to dress or behave like a preppy

pre·puce \ˈprē-ˌpyüs\ *n* : FORESKIN

pre·re·cord \ˌprē-ri-ˈkȯrd\ *vb* : to record for later broadcast

pre·req·ui·site \prē-ˈrek-wə-zət\ *n* : something required beforehand or for the end in view — **prerequisite** *adj*

pre·rog·a·tive \pri-ˈräg-ət-iv\ *n* : an exclusive or special right, power, or privilege

pres *abbr* **1** present **2** president

[1]**pres·age** \ˈpres-ij\ *n* **1** : something that foreshadows a future event : OMEN **2** : FOREBODING

[2]**pre·sage** \ˈpres-ij, pri-ˈsāj\ *vb* **pre·saged; pre·sag·ing 1** : to give an omen or warning of : FORESHADOW **2** : FORETELL, PREDICT

pres·by·opia \ˌprez-bē-ˈō-pē-ə\ *n* : a visual condition in which loss of elasticity of the lens of the eye causes defective accommodation and inability to focus sharply for near vision — **pres·by·opic** \-ˈō-pik, -ˈäp-ik\ *adj or n*

pres·by·ter \ˈprez-bət-ər\ *n* **1** : PRIEST, MINISTER **2** : an elder in a Presbyterian church

[1]**Pres·by·te·ri·an** \ˌprez-bə-ˈtir-ē-ən\ *adj* **1** *often not cap* : characterized by a graded system of representative ecclesiastical bodies (as presbyteries) exercising legislative and judicial powers **2** : of or relating to a group of Protestant Christian bodies that are presbyterian in government

[2]**Presbyterian** *n* : a member of a Presbyterian church — **Pres·by·te·ri·an·ism** \-ˌiz-əm\ *n*

pres·by·tery \ˈprez-bə-ˌter-ē\ *n, pl* **-ter·ies 1** : the part of a church reserved for the officiating clergy **2** : a ruling body in Presbyterian churches consisting of the ministers and representative elders of a district

pre·school \ˈprē-ˈskül\ *adj* : of, relating to, or constituting the period in a child's life from infancy to the age of five or six — **pre·school·er** \-ˈskü-lər\ *n*

pre·science \ˈpresh-əns, ˈprēsh-\ *n* : foreknowledge of events; *also* : FORESIGHT — **pre·scient** \-(ē-)ənt\ *adj*

pre·scribe \pri-ˈskrīb\ *vb* **pre·scribed; pre·scrib·ing 1** : to lay down as a guide or rule of action **2** : to direct the use of something as a remedy

pre·scrip·tion \pri-ˈskrip-shən\ *n* **1** : the action of prescribing rules or directions **2** : a written direction for the preparation and use of a medicine; *also* : a medicine prescribed

pres·ence \ˈprez-ᵊns\ *n* **1** : the fact or condition of being present **2** : the space immediately around a person **3** : one that is present **4** : the bearing of a person; *esp* : stately bearing

[1]**pres·ent** \ˈprez-ᵊnt\ *n* : something presented : GIFT

[2]**pre·sent** \pri-ˈzent\ *vb* **1** : to bring into the presence or acquaintance of : INTRODUCE **2** : to bring before the public ⟨~ a play⟩ **3** : to make a gift to **4** : to give formally **5** : to lay (as a charge) before a court for inquiry **6** : to aim or direct (as a weapon) so as to face in a particular direction — **pre·sent·able** *adj* — **pre·sen·ta·tion** \ˌprē-ˌzen-ˈtā-shən, ˌprez-ᵊn-\ *n* — **pre·sent·ment** \pri-ˈzent-mənt\ *n*

[3]**pres·ent** \ˈprez-ᵊnt\ *adj* **1** : now existing or in progress ⟨~ conditions⟩ **2** : being in view or at hand ⟨~ at the meeting⟩ **3** : under consideration ⟨the ~ problem⟩ **4** : of, relating to, or constituting a verb tense that expresses present time or the time of speaking

[4]**pres·ent** \ˈprez-ᵊnt\ *n* **1** *pl* : the present legal document **2** : the present tense; *also* : a verb form in it **3** : the present time

pres·ent–day \ˈprez-ᵊnt-ˈdā\ *adj* : now existing or occurring : CURRENT

pre·sen·ti·ment \pri-ˈzent-ə-mənt\ *n* : a feeling that something is about to happen : PREMONITION

pres·ent·ly \ˈprez-ᵊnt-lē\ *adv* **1** : SOON **2** : NOW

present participle *n* : a participle that typically expresses present action and that in English is formed with the suffix *-ing* and is used in the formation of the progressive tenses

[1]**pre·serve** \pri-ˈzərv\ *vb* **pre·served; pre·serv·ing 1** : to keep safe : GUARD, PROTECT **2** : to keep from decaying; *esp* : to process food (as by canning or pickling) to prevent spoilage **3** : MAINTAIN ⟨~ silence⟩ — **pres·er·va·tion** \ˌprez-ər-ˈvā-shən\ *n* — **pre·ser·va·tive** \pri-ˈzər-vət-iv\ *adj or n* — **pre·serv·er** \-ˈzər-vər\ *n*

[2]**preserve** *n* **1** : preserved fruit — often used in pl. **2** : an area for the protection of natural resources (as animals)

pre·set \ˈprē-ˈset\ *vb* **-set; -set·ting** : to set beforehand

pre·shrunk \ˈprē-ˈshrəŋk\ *adj* : of, relating to, or being a fabric subjected to a shrinking process during manufacture usu. to reduce later shrinking

pre·side \pri-ˈzīd\ *vb* **pre·sid·ed; pre·sid·ing** [L *praesidēre* to guard, preside over, lit., to sit in front of, sit at the head of, fr. *prae* in front of + *sedēre* to sit] **1** : to occupy the place of authority; *esp* : to act as chairman **2** : to exercise guidance or control

pres·i·dent \ˈprez-əd-ənt\ *n* **1** : one chosen to preside ⟨~ of the assembly⟩ **2** : the chief officer of an organization (as a corporation or society) **3** : an elected official serving as both chief of state and chief political executive; *also* : a chief of state often with only minimal political powers — **pres·i·den·cy** \-ən-sē\ *n* — **pres·i·den·tial** \ˌprez-ə-ˈden-chəl\ *adj*

pre·si·dio \pri-ˈsēd-ē-ˌō, -ˈsid-\ *n, pl* **-di·os** [Sp] **:** a garrisoned place; *esp* **:** a military post or fortified settlement in areas currently or orig. under Spanish control

pre·sid·i·um \pri-ˈsid-ē-əm\ *n, pl* **-ia** \-ē-ə\ *or* **-iums** [Russ *prezidium,* fr. L *praesidium* garrison] **:** a permanent executive committee selected in Communist countries to act for a larger body

[1]**pre·soak** \(ˈ)prē-ˈsōk\ *vb* **:** to soak beforehand

[2]**pre·soak** \ˈprē-ˌsōk\ *n* **1 :** an instance of presoaking **2 :** a preparation used in presoaking clothes

[1]**press** \ˈpres\ *n* **1 :** a crowded condition **:** THRONG **2 :** a machine for exerting pressure; *esp* **:** PRINTING PRESS **3 :** CLOSET, CUPBOARD **4 :** PRESSURE **5 :** the properly creased condition of a freshly pressed garment **6 :** the act or the process of printing **7 :** a printing or publishing establishment **8 :** the media (as newspapers and magazines) of public news and comment; *also* **:** persons (as reporters) employed in these media **9 :** comment in newspapers and periodicals **10 :** a pressure device (as for keeping a tennis racket from warping)

[2]**press** *vb* **1 :** to bear down upon **:** push steadily against **2 :** ASSAIL, COMPEL **3 :** to squeeze out the juice or contents of ⟨~ grapes⟩ **4 :** to squeeze to a desired density, shape, or smoothness; *esp* **:** IRON **5 :** to try hard to persuade **:** URGE **6 :** to follow through **:** PROSECUTE **7 :** CROWD **8 :** to force one's way **9 :** to require haste or speed in action **10 :** to make (a phonograph record) from a matrix — **press·er** *n*

press agent *n* **:** an agent employed to maintain good public relations through publicity

press·ing \ˈpres-iŋ\ *adj* **:** URGENT

press·man \ˈpres-mən, -ˌman\ *n* **:** the operator of a press and esp. a printing press

press·room \ˈpres-ˌrüm, -ˌru̇m\ *n* **:** a room in a printing plant containing the printing presses; *also* **:** a room for the use of reporters

[1]**pres·sure** \ˈpresh-ər\ *n* **1 :** the burden of physical or mental distress **:** OPPRESSION **2 :** the action of pressing; *esp* **:** the application of force to something by something else in direct contact with it **3 :** the condition of being pressed or of exerting force over a surface **4 :** the stress or urgency of matters demanding attention **syn** stress, strain, tension

[2]**pressure** *vb* **pres·sured; pres·sur·ing** \-(ə-)riŋ\ **:** to apply pressure to

pressure group *n* **:** a group that seeks to influence governmental policy but not to elect candidates to office

pressure suit *n* **:** an inflatable suit for high-altitude or space flight to protect the body from low pressure

pres·sur·ize \ˈpresh-ə-ˌrīz\ *vb* **-ized; -iz·ing 1 :** to maintain normal atmospheric pressure within (an airplane cabin) during high-altitude flight **2 :** to apply pressure to **3 :** to design to withstand pressure — **pres·sur·iza·tion** \ˌpresh-(ə-)rə-ˈzā-shən\ *n*

pres·ti·dig·i·ta·tion \ˌpres-tə-ˌdij-ə-ˈtā-shən\ *n* **:** SLEIGHT OF HAND

pres·tige \pres-ˈtēzh, -ˈtēj\ *n* [F, fr. MF, conjuror's trick, illusion, fr. LL *praestigium,* fr. L *praestigiae,* pl., conjuror's tricks, irreg. fr. *praestringere* to tie up, blindfold, fr. *prae-* in front of + *stringere* to bind tight] **:** standing or estimation in the eyes of people **:** REPUTATION **syn** influence, authority, weight — **pres·ti·gious** \-ˈtij-əs, -ˈtēj-\ *adj*

pres·to \ˈpres-tō\ *adv or adj* [It] **:** suddenly as if by magic **:** IMMEDIATELY

pre·stress \(ˈ)prē-ˈstres\ *vb* **:** to introduce internal stresses into (as a structural beam) to counteract later load stresses

pre·sume \pri-ˈzüm\ *vb* **pre·sumed; pre·sum·ing 1 :** to take upon oneself without leave or warrant **:** DARE **2 :** to take for granted **:** ASSUME **3 :** to act or behave with undue boldness — **pre·sum·able** \-ˈzü-mə-bəl\ *adj* — **pre·sum·ably** \-blē\ *adv*

pre·sump·tion \pri-ˈzəmp-shən\ *n* **1 :** presumptuous attitude or conduct **:** AUDACITY **2 :** an attitude or belief dictated by probability; *also* **:** the grounds lending probability to a belief — **pre·sump·tive** \-tiv\ *adj*

pre·sump·tu·ous \pri-ˈzəmp-chə-(wə)s\ *adj* **:** overstepping due bounds **:** taking liberties **:** OVERBOLD

pre·sup·pose \ˌprē-sə-ˈpōz\ *vb* **1 :** to suppose beforehand **2 :** to require beforehand as a necessary condition **syn** presume, assume — **pre·sup·po·si·tion** \(ˌ)prē-ˌsəp-ə-ˈzish-ən\ *n*

pre·teen \ˈprē-ˈtēn\ *n* **:** a boy or girl not yet 13 years old — **preteen** *adj*

pre·tend \pri-ˈtend\ *vb* **1 :** PROFESS ⟨doesn't ~ to be scientific⟩ **2 :** FEIGN ⟨~ to be angry⟩ **3 :** to lay claim ⟨~ to a throne⟩ — **pre·tend·er** *n*

pre·tense *or* **pre·tence** \ˈprē-ˌtens, pri-ˈtens\ *n* **1 :** CLAIM; *esp* **:** one not supported by fact **2 :** mere display **:** SHOW **3 :** an attempt to attain a certain condition ⟨made a ~ at discipline⟩ **4 :** false show **:** PRETEXT — **pre·ten·sion** \pri-ˈten-chən\ *n*

pre·ten·tious \pri-ˈten-chəs\ *adj* **1 :** making or possessing claims (as to excellence) **:** OSTENTATIOUS ⟨a ~ literary style⟩ **2 :** making demands on one's ability or means **:** AMBITIOUS ⟨too ~ an undertaking⟩ — **pre·ten·tious·ly** *adv* — **pre·ten·tious·ness** *n*

pret·er·it *or* **pret·er·ite** \ˈpret-ə-rət\ *adj* **:** PAST 3 — **preterit** *n*

pre·ter·nat·u·ral \ˌprēt-ər-ˈnach(-ə)-rəl\ *adj* **1 :** exceeding what is natural **2 :** inexplicable by ordinary means — **pre·ter·nat·u·ral·ly** \-ē\ *adv*

pre·text \ˈprē-ˌtekst\ *n* **:** a purpose stated or assumed to cloak the real intention or state of affairs

pret·ti·fy \ˈprit-i-ˌfī, ˈpu̇rt-\ *vb* **-fied; -fy·ing :** to make pretty — **pret·ti·fi·ca·tion** \ˌprit-i-fə-ˈkā-shən, ˌpu̇rt-\ *n*

[1]**pret·ty** \ˈprit-ē, ˈpu̇rt\ *adj* **pret·ti·er; -est** [ME *praty, prety,* fr. OE *prættig* tricky, fr. *prætt* trick] **1 :** pleasing by delicacy or grace **:** superficially appealing rather than strikingly beautiful ⟨~ flowers⟩ **2 :** FINE, GOOD ⟨a ~ profit⟩ — often used ironically ⟨a ~ state of affairs⟩ **syn** comely, fair, beautiful, attractive, lovely — **pret·ti·ly** \ˈprit-ᵊl-ē\ *adv* — **pret·ti·ness** \-ē-nəs\ *n*

[2]**pret·ty** \ˌpu̇rt-ē, pərt-, ˌprit-\ *adv* **:** in some degree **:** MODERATELY

[3]**pret·ty** \ˈprit-ē, ˈpu̇rt-ē\ *vb* **pret·tied; pret·ty·ing :** to make pretty

pret·zel \ˈpret-səl\ *n* [G *brezel,* deriv. of L *brachiatus* having branches like arms, fr. *brachium* arm] **:** a usu. brittle, glazed, salted, and usu. twisted cracker

prev *abbr* previous; previously

pre·vail \pri-ˈvāl\ *vb* **1 :** to win mastery **:** TRIUMPH **2 :** to be or become effective **:** SUCCEED **3 :** to urge successfully ⟨~*ed* upon her to sing⟩ **4 :** to be frequent **:** PREDOMINATE — **pre·vail·ing·ly** \-iŋ-lē\ *adv*

prev·a·lent \ˈprev-ə-lənt\ *adj* **:** generally or widely existent **:** WIDESPREAD — **prev·a·lence** \-ləns\ *n*

pre·var·i·cate \pri-ˈvar-ə-ˌkāt\ *vb* **-cat·ed; -cat·ing :** to deviate from the truth **:** EQUIVOCATE — **pre·var·i·ca·tion** \-ˌvar-ə-ˈkā-shən\ *n* — **pre·var·i·ca·tor** \-ˈvar-ə-ˌkāt-ər\ *n*

pre·vent \pri-ˈvent\ *vb* **1 :** to keep from happening or existing ⟨steps to ~ war⟩ **2 :** to hold back **:** HINDER, STOP ⟨~ us from going⟩ — **pre·vent·able** *also* **pre·vent·ible** \-ə-bəl\ *adj* — **pre·ven·tion** \-ˈven-chən\ *n* — **pre·ven·tive** \-ˈvent-iv\ *or* **pre·ven·ta·tive** \-ˈvent-ət-iv\ *adj or n*

pre·ver·bal \(ˈ)prē-ˈvər-bəl\ *adj* **:** having not yet acquired the faculty of speech

[1]**pre·view** \ˈprē-ˌvyü\ *vb* **:** to see or discuss beforehand; *esp* **:** to view or show in advance of public presentation

[2]**preview** *n* **1 :** an advance showing or viewing **2** *also* **pre·vue** \-ˌvyü\ **:** a showing of snatches from a motion picture advertised for future appearance **3 :** FORETASTE

pre·vi·ous \ˈprē-vē-əs\ *adj* **:** going before **:** EARLIER, FORMER **syn** foregoing, prior, preceding, former, antecedent — **pre·vi·ous·ly** *adv*

pre·vi·sion \prē-ˈvizh-ən\ *n* **1 :** FORESIGHT, PRESCIENCE **2 :** FORECAST, PREDICTION

pre·war \ˈprē-ˈwȯr\ *adj* **:** occurring or existing before a war

[1]**prey** \ˈprā\ *n, pl* **preys 1 :** an animal taken for food by another; *also* **:** VICTIM **2 :** the act or habit of preying

[2]**prey** *vb* **1 :** to raid for booty **2 :** to seize and devour something as prey **3 :** to have a harmful or wearing effect

prf *abbr* proof

[1]**price** \ˈprīs\ *n* **1** *archaic* **:** VALUE **2 :** the amount of money paid or asked for the sale of a specified thing; *also* **:** the cost at which something is obtained

[2]**price** *vb* **priced; pric·ing 1 :** to set a price on **2 :** to ask the price of **3 :** to drive by raising prices ⟨*priced* themselves out of the market⟩

price–fix·ing \ˈprīs-ˌfik-siŋ\ *n* **:** the setting of prices artificially (as by producers or government)

price·less \ˈprīs-ləs\ *adj* **:** having a value beyond any price **:** INVALUABLE **syn** precious, costly, expensive

price support *n* **:** artificial maintenance of prices of a commodity at a level usu. fixed through government action

price war *n* **:** a period of commercial competition in which prices are repeatedly cut by the competitors

pric·ey *also* **pricy** \ˈprī-sē\ *adj* **pric·i·er; -est :** EXPENSIVE

[1]**prick** \ˈprik\ *n* **1 :** a mark or small wound made by a pointed instrument **2 :** something sharp or pointed **3 :** an instance of pricking; *also* **:** a sensation of being pricked

[2]**prick** *vb* **1 :** to pierce slightly with a sharp point; *also* **:** to have or cause a pricking sensation **2 :** to affect with anguish or remorse ⟨∼*s* his conscience⟩ **3 :** to outline with punctures ⟨∼ out a pattern⟩ **4 :** to cause to stand erect ⟨the dog ∼*ed* up his ears⟩ **syn** punch, puncture, perforate, bore, drill

prick·er \ˈprik-ər\ *n* **:** BRIAR, THORN

[1]**prick·le** \ˈprik-əl\ *n* **1 :** a small sharp point (as on a plant) **2 :** a slight stinging pain — **prick·ly** \ˈprik-lē\ *adj*

[2]**prickle** *vb* **prick·led; prick·ling** \-(ə-)liŋ\ **1 :** to prick lightly **2 :** TINGLE

prickly heat *n* **:** a red cutaneous eruption with intense itching and tingling caused by inflammation around the ducts of the sweat glands

prickly pear *n* **:** any of a genus of cacti with usu. yellow flowers and prickly flat or rounded joints; *also* **:** the pulpy pear-shaped edible fruit of a prickly pear

[1]**pride** \ˈprīd\ *n* **1 :** CONCEIT **2 :** justifiable self-respect **3 :** elation over an act or possession **4 :** haughty behavior **:** DISDAIN **5 :** ostentatious display — **pride·ful** *adj*

[2]**pride** *vb* **prid·ed; prid·ing :** to indulge in pride

priest \ˈprēst\ *n* [ME *preist,* fr. OE *prēost,* fr. LL *presbyter,* fr. Gk *presbyteros* elder, priest, fr. compar. of *presbys* old] **:** a person having authority to perform the sacred rites of a religion; *esp* **:** an Anglican, Eastern, or Roman Catholic clergyman ranking below a bishop and above a deacon — **priest·hood** *n* — **priest·li·ness** \-lē-nəs\ *n* — **priest·ly** *adj*

priest·ess \ˈprē-stəs\ *n* **:** a woman authorized to perform the sacred rites of a religion

prig \ˈprig\ *n* **:** one who irritates by rigid or pointed observance of proprieties — **prig·gish** \ˈprig-ish\ *adj* — **prig·gish·ly** *adv*

[1]**prim** \ˈprim\ *adj* **prim·mer; prim·mest :** stiffly formal and precise — **prim·ly** *adv* — **prim·ness** *n*

[2]**prim** *abbr* **1** primary **2** primitive

pri·ma·cy \ˈprī-mə-sē\ *n* **1 :** the state of being first (as in rank) **2 :** the office, rank, or character of an ecclesiastical primate

pri·ma don·na \ˌprim-ə-ˈdän-ə\ *n, pl* **prima donnas** [It, lit., first lady] **1 :** a principal female singer (as in an opera company) **2 :** an extremely sensitive, vain, or undisciplined person

pri·ma fa·cie \ˌprī-mə-ˈfā-shə, -s(h)ē\ *adj or adv* [L, at first view] **1 :** based on immediate impression **:** APPARENT **2 :** SELF-EVIDENT

pri·mal \ˈprī-məl\ *adj* **1 :** ORIGINAL, PRIMITIVE **2 :** first in importance

pri·mar·i·ly \prī-ˈmer-ə-lē\ *adv* **1 :** FUNDAMENTALLY **2 :** ORIGINALLY

[1]**pri·ma·ry** \ˈprī-ˌmer-ē, ˈprīm-(ə-)rē\ *adj* **1 :** first in order of time or development; *also* **:** PREPARATORY **2 :** of first rank or importance; *also* **:** FUNDAMENTAL **3 :** not derived from or dependent on something else ⟨∼ sources⟩

[2]**primary** *n, pl* **-ries :** a preliminary election in which voters nominate or express a preference among candidates usu. of their own party

primary school *n* **1 :** a school usu. including grades 1-3 and sometimes kindergarten **2 :** ELEMENTARY SCHOOL

pri·mate \ˈprī-ˌmāt *or esp for 1* -mət\ *n* **1** *often cap* **:** the highest-ranking bishop of a province or nation **2 :** any of an order of mammals that includes man, the apes, and monkeys

[1]**prime** \ˈprīm\ *n* **1 :** the earliest stage of something; *esp* **:** SPRINGTIME **2 :** the most active, thriving, or successful stage or period (as of one's life) **3 :** the best individual; *also* **:** the best part of something **4 :** any integer that is not 0, +1, or −1 and is divisible by no integer except +1, −1, and plus or minus itself; *esp* **:** any such integer that is positive

[2]**prime** *adj* **1 :** standing first (as in time, rank, significance, or quality) ⟨∼ requisite⟩ **2 :** not capable of being divided without a remainder by any number except itself or 1 ⟨a ∼ number⟩

[3]**prime** *vb* **primed; prim·ing 1 :** FILL, LOAD **2 :** to lay a preparatory coating upon (as in painting) **3 :** to put in working condition **4 :** to instruct beforehand **:** COACH

prime meridian *n* **:** the meridian of 0° longitude from which other longitudes are reckoned east and west

prime minister *n* **1 :** the chief minister of a ruler or state **2 :** the chief executive of a parliamentary government

[1]**prim·er** \ˈprim-ər\ *n* **1 :** a small book for teaching children to read **2 :** a small introductory book on a subject

[2]**prim·er** \ˈprī-mər\ *n* **1 :** one that primes **2 :** a device for igniting an explosive **3 :** material for priming a surface

prime rate *n* **:** an interest rate announced by a bank to be the lowest available to its most credit-worthy customers

prime time *n* **:** the evening period generally from 7 to 11 p.m. during which television has its largest number of viewers

pri·me·val \prī-ˈmē-vəl\ *adj* **:** of or relating to the earliest ages **:** PRIMITIVE

[1]**prim·i·tive** \ˈprim-ət-iv\ *adj* **1 :** ORIGINAL, PRIMEVAL **2 :** of, relating to, or characteristic of an early stage of development or a relatively simple people or culture **3 :** ELEMENTAL, NATURAL **4 :** SELF-TAUGHT; *also* **:** produced by a self-taught artist — **prim·i·tive·ly** *adv* — **prim·i·tive·ness** *n* — **prim·i·tiv·i·ty** \ˌprim-ə-ˈtiv-ət-ē\ *n*

[2]**primitive** *n* **1 :** a primitive artist **2 :** a member of a primitive people

prim·i·tiv·ism \ˈprim-ət-iv-ˌiz-əm\ *n* **:** the style of art of primitive peoples or primitive artists

pri·mo·gen·i·tor \ˌprī-mō-ˈjen-ət-ər\ *n* **:** ANCESTOR, FOREFATHER

pri·mo·gen·i·ture \-ˈjen-ə-ˌchu̇r\ *n* **1 :** the state of being the firstborn of a family **2 :** an exclusive right of inheritance belonging to the eldest son

pri·mor·di·al \prī-ˈmȯrd-ē-əl\ *adj* : first created or developed : existing in its original state : PRIMEVAL

primp \ˈprimp\ *vb* : to dress in a careful or finicky manner

prim·rose \ˈprim-ˌrōz\ *n* : any of a genus of herbs with large leaves arranged at the base of the stem and clusters of showy flowers on leafless stalks

prin *abbr* **1** principal **2** principle

prince \ˈprins\ *n* [ME, fr. OF, fr. L *princeps*, lit., one who takes the first part, fr. *primus* first + *capere* to take] **1** : MONARCH, KING **2** : a male member of a royal family; *esp* : a son of the monarch **3** : a person of high standing (as in a class) ⟨a ~ of poets⟩ — **prince·dom** \-dəm\ *n* — **prince·ly** *adj*

prince·ling \-liŋ\ *n* : a petty prince

prin·cess \ˈprin-səs, -ˌses\ *n* **1** : a female member of a royal family **2** : the consort of a prince

[1]**prin·ci·pal** \ˈprin-sə-pəl\ *adj* : most important — **prin·ci·pal·ly** \-ē\ *adv*

[2]**principal** *n* **1** : a leading person (as in a play) **2** : the chief officer of an educational institution **3** : the person from whom an agent's authority derives **4** : a capital sum placed at interest or used as a fund

prin·ci·pal·i·ty \ˌprin-sə-ˈpal-ət-ē\ *n, pl* **-ties** : the position, territory, or jurisdiction of a prince

principal parts *n pl* : the inflected forms of a verb

prin·ci·ple \ˈprin-sə-pəl\ *n* **1** : a general or fundamental law, doctrine, or assumption **2** : a rule or code of conduct; *also* : devotion to such a code **3** : the laws or facts of nature underlying the working of an artificial device **4** : a primary source : ORIGIN; *also* : an underlying faculty or endowment **5** : the active part (as of a drug)

prin·ci·pled \-sə-pəld\ *adj* : exhibiting, based on, or characterized by principle ⟨high-*principled*⟩

prink \ˈpriŋk\ *vb* : PRIMP

[1]**print** \ˈprint\ *n* **1** : a mark made by pressure **2** : something stamped with an impression **3** : printed state or form **4** : printed matter **5** : a copy made by printing **6** : cloth with a pattern applied by printing

[2]**print** *vb* **1** : to stamp (as a mark) in or on something **2** : to produce impressions of (as from type) **3** : to write in letters like those of printer's type **4** : to make (a positive picture) from a photographic negative — **print·er** *n*

print·able \ˈprint-ə-bəl\ *adj* **1** : capable of being printed or of being printed from **2** : worthy or fit to be published

print·ing \ˈprint-iŋ\ *n* **1** : reproduction in printed form **2** : the art, practice, or business of a printer **3** : IMPRESSION 5

printing press *n* : a machine that produces printed copies

print·out \ˈprint-ˌau̇t\ *n* : a printed record produced by a computer — **print out** \(ˈ)print-ˈau̇t\ *vb*

[1]**pri·or** \ˈprī(-ə)r\ *n* : the superior of a religious house

[2]**pri·or** *adj* **1** : earlier in time or order **2** : taking precedence logically or in importance — **pri·or·i·ty** \prī-ˈȯr-ət-ē\ *n*

pri·or·ess \ˈprī-ə-rəs\ *n* : a nun corresponding in rank to a prior

pri·or·i·tize \prī-ˈȯr-ə-ˌtīz, ˈprī-ə-rə-ˌtīz\ *vb* **-tized; -tiz·ing** : to list or rate in order of priority

prior to *prep* : in advance of : BEFORE

pri·o·ry \ˈprī-(ə-)rē\ *n, pl* **-ries** : a religious house under a prior or prioress

prism \ˈpriz-əm\ *n* [LL *prisma*, fr. Gk, lit., anything sawed, fr. *priein* to saw] **1** : a solid whose sides are parallelograms and whose ends are parallel and alike in shape and size **2** : a usu. 3-sided transparent object that breaks up light into rainbow colors — **pris·mat·ic** \priz-ˈmat-ik\ *adj*

pris·on \ˈpriz-ᵊn\ *n* : a place or state of confinement esp. for criminals

pris·on·er \ˈpriz-(ᵊ-)nər\ *n* : a person deprived of his liberty; *esp* : one on trial or in prison

pris·sy \ˈpris-ē\ *adj* **pris·si·er; -est** : being overly prim and precise : PRIGGISH — **pris·si·ness** \ˈpris-ē-nəs\ *n*

pris·tine \ˈpris-ˌtēn\ *adj* **1** : PRIMITIVE **2** : having the purity of its original state : UNSPOILED

prith·ee \ˈprith-ē\ *interj, archaic* — used to express a wish or request

pri·va·cy \ˈprī-və-sē\ *n, pl* **-cies 1** : the quality or state of being apart from others **2** : SECRECY

[1]**pri·vate** \ˈprī-vət\ *adj* **1** : belonging to or intended for a particular individual or group ⟨~ property⟩ **2** : restricted to the individual : PERSONAL ⟨~ opinion⟩ **3** : carried on by the individual independently ⟨~ study⟩ **4** : not holding public office ⟨a ~ citizen⟩ **5** : withdrawn from company or observation ⟨a ~ place⟩ **6** : not known publicly ⟨~ dealings⟩ — **pri·vate·ly** *adv*

[2]**private** *n* : an enlisted man of the lowest rank in the marine corps or of one of the two lowest ranks in the army — **in private** : not openly or in public

pri·va·teer \ˌprī-və-ˈtiər\ *n* : an armed private ship licensed to attack enemy shipping; *also* : a sailor on such a ship

private first class *n* : an enlisted man ranking next below a corporal in the army and next below a lance corporal in the marine corps

pri·va·tion \prī-ˈvā-shən\ *n* **1** : DEPRIVATION **2** : the state of being deprived; *esp* : lack of what is needed for existence

priv·et \ˈpriv-ət\ *n* : a nearly evergreen shrub related to the olive and widely used for hedges

[1]**priv·i·lege** \ˈpriv(-ə)-lij\ *n* [ME, fr. OF, fr. L *privilegium* law for or against a private person, fr. *privus* private + *leg-, lex* law] : a right or immunity granted as an advantage or favor esp. to some and not others

[2]**privilege** *vb* **-leged; -leg·ing** : to grant a privilege to

priv·i·leged \-lijd\ *adj* **1** : having or enjoying one or more privileges ⟨~ classes⟩ **2** : not subject to disclosure in a court of law ⟨a ~ communication⟩

[1]**privy** \ˈpriv-ē\ *adj* **1** : PERSONAL, PRIVATE **2** : SECRET **3** : admitted as one sharing in a secret ⟨~ to the conspiracy⟩ — **priv·i·ly** \ˈpriv-ə-lē\ *adv*

[2]**privy** *n, pl* **priv·ies** : TOILET; *esp* : OUTHOUSE

[1]**prize** \ˈprīz\ *n* **1** : something offered or striven for in competition or in contests of chance **2** : something exceptionally desirable

[2]**prize** *adj* **1** : awarded or worthy of a prize ⟨a ~ essay⟩; *also* : awarded as a prize ⟨a ~ medal⟩ **2** : OUTSTANDING

[3]**prize** *vb* **prized; priz·ing** : to value highly : ESTEEM **syn** treasure, cherish, appreciate

[4]**prize** *n* : property (as a ship) lawfully captured in time of war

[5]**prize** \ˈprīz\ *vb* **prized; priz·ing** : PRY

prize·fight \ˈprīz-ˌfīt\ *n* : a professional boxing match — **prize·fight·er** *n* — **prize·fight·ing** \-iŋ\ *n*

prize·win·ner \ˈprīz-ˌwin-ər\ *n* : a winner of a prize — **prize·win·ning** \-ˌwin-iŋ\ *adj*

[1]**pro** \ˈprō\ *n, pl* **pros** : a favorable argument, person, or position

[2]**pro** *adv* : in favor : FOR

[3]**pro** *n or adj* : PROFESSIONAL

PRO *abbr* public relations officer

prob *abbr* **1** probable; probably **2** problem

prob·a·ble \ˈpräb-ə-bəl\ *adj* **1** : apparently or presumably true ⟨a ~ hypothesis⟩ **2** : likely to be or become true or real ⟨a ~ result⟩ — **prob·a·bil·i·ty** \ˌpräb-ə-ˈbil-ət-ē\ *n* — **prob·a·bly** \ˈpräb-ə-blē, ˈpräb-lē\ *adv*

[1]**pro·bate** \ˈprō-ˌbāt\ *n* : the judicial determination of the validity of a will

[2]**pro·bate** *vb* **pro·bat·ed; pro·bat·ing** : to establish (a will) by probate as genuine and valid

pro·ba·tion \prō-ˈbā-shən\ *n* **1** : subjection of an individual to a period of testing and trial to ascertain fitness (as for a job) **2** : the action of giving a convicted offender freedom during good behavior under the supervision of a probation officer — **pro·ba·tion·ary** \-shə-ˌner-ē\ *adj*

pro·ba·tion·er \-sh(ə-)nər\ *n* **1** : one (as a newly admitted student nurse) whose fitness is being tested during a trial period **2** : a convicted offender on probation

pro·ba·tive \ˈprō-bət-iv\ *adj* **1** : serving to test or try **2** : serving to prove

[1]**probe** \ˈprōb\ *n* **1** : a slender instrument for examining a cavity (as a wound) **2** : an information-gathering device sent into outer space **3** : a penetrating investigation **syn** inquiry, inquest, research, inquisition

[2]**probe** *vb* **probed; prob·ing** **1** : to examine with a probe **2** : to investigate thoroughly

pro·bi·ty \ˈprō-bət-ē\ *n* : UPRIGHTNESS, HONESTY

prob·lem \ˈpräb-ləm\ *n* **1** : a question raised for consideration or solution **2** : an intricate unsettled question **3** : a source of perplexity or vexation — **problem** *adj*

prob·lem·at·ic \ˌpräb-lə-ˈmat-ik\ *or* **prob·lem·at·i·cal** \-i-kəl\ *adj* **1** : difficult to solve or decide : PUZZLING **2** : DUBIOUS, QUESTIONABLE

pro·bos·cis \prə-ˈbäs-əs, -kəs\ *n, pl* **-bos·cis·es** *also* **-bos·ci·des** \-ˈbäs-ə-ˌdēz\ [L, fr. Gk *proboskis,* fr. *pro-* before + *boskein* to feed] : a long flexible snout (as the trunk of an elephant)

proc *abbr* proceedings

pro·caine \ˈprō-ˌkān\ *n* : a compound used esp. as a local anesthetic

pro·ca·the·dral \ˌprō-kə-ˈthē-drəl\ *n* : a parish church used as a cathedral

pro·ce·dure \prə-ˈsē-jər\ *n* **1** : a particular way of doing something ⟨democratic ~⟩ **2** : a series of steps followed in a regular order ⟨surgical ~⟩ — **pro·ce·dur·al** \-ˈsēj-(ə-)rəl\ *adj*

pro·ceed \prō-ˈsēd\ *vb* **1** : to come forth : ISSUE **2** : to go on in an orderly way; *also* : CONTINUE **3** : to begin and carry on an action **4** : to take legal action **5** : to go forward : ADVANCE

pro·ceed·ing \-iŋ\ *n* **1** : PROCEDURE **2** *pl* : DOINGS **3** *pl* : legal action **4** : TRANSACTION **5** *pl* : an official record of things said or done

pro·ceeds \ˈprō-ˌsēdz\ *n pl* : the total amount or the profit arising from a business deal : RETURN

[1]**pro·cess** \ˈpräs-ˌes, ˈprōs-\ *n, pl* **pro·cess·es** \-ˌes-əz, -ə-səz, -ə-ˌsēz\ **1** : PROGRESS, ADVANCE **2** : something going on : PROCEEDING **3** : a natural phenomenon marked by gradual changes that lead toward a particular result ⟨the ~ of growth⟩ **4** : a series of actions or operations directed toward a particular result ⟨a manufacturing ~⟩ **5** : legal action **6** : a mandate issued by a court; *esp* : SUMMONS **7** : a projecting part of an organism or organic structure

[2]**process** *vb* : to subject to a special process

pro·ces·sion \prə-ˈsesh-ən\ *n* : a group of individuals moving along in an orderly often ceremonial way : PARADE

pro·ces·sion·al \-ˈsesh-(ə-)nəl\ *n* **1** : music for a procession **2** : a ceremonial procession

pro·ces·sor \ˈpräs-ˌes-ər, ˈprōs-\ *n* **1** : one that processes **2** : the part of a computer that operates on data

pro·claim \prō-ˈklām\ *vb* : to make known publicly : DECLARE — **proc·la·ma·tion** \ˌpräk-lə-ˈmā-shən\ *n*

pro·cliv·i·ty \prō-ˈkliv-ət-ē\ *n, pl* **-ties** : an inherent inclination esp. toward something objectionable

pro·con·sul \prō-ˈkän-səl\ *n* **1** : a governor or military commander of an ancient Roman province **2** : an administrator in a modern colony, dependency, or occupied area usu. with wide powers — **pro·con·su·lar** \-sə-lər\ *adj* — **pro·con·su·late** \-sə-lət\ *n* — **pro·con·sul·ship** *n*

pro·cras·ti·nate \prə-ˈkras-tə-ˌnāt\ *vb* **-nat·ed; -nat·ing** [L *procrastinare,* fr. *pro-* forward + *crastinus* of tomorrow, fr. *cras* tomorrow] : to put off usu. habitually the doing of something that should be done **syn** dawdle, delay, loiter, linger — **pro·cras·ti·na·tion** \-ˌkras-tə-ˈnā-shən\ *n* — **pro·cras·ti·na·tor** \-ˈkras-tə-ˌnāt-ər\ *n*

pro·cre·ate \ˈprō-krē-ˌāt\ *vb* **-at·ed; -at·ing** : to beget or bring forth offspring **syn** reproduce, breed, generate, propagate — **pro·cre·ation** \ˌprō-krē-ˈā-shən\ *n* — **pro·cre·ative** \ˈprō-krē-ˌāt-iv\ *adj* — **pro·cre·ator** \-ˌāt-ər\ *n*

pro·crus·te·an \prə-ˈkrəs-tē-ən\ *adj, often cap* [deriv. of *Procrustes,* villain of Greek mythology who made victims fit his bed by stretching them or cutting off their legs] : marked by arbitrary often ruthless disregard of individual differences or special circumstances

proc·tor \ˈpräk-tər\ *n* : one appointed to supervise students (as at an examination) — **proctor** *vb* — **proc·to·ri·al** \präk-ˈtōr-ē-əl\ *adj*

proc·u·ra·tor \ˈpräk-yə-ˌrāt-ər\ *n* : ADMINISTRATOR; *esp* : an official of ancient Rome administering a province

pro·cure \prə-ˈkyu̇(ə)r\ *vb* **pro·cured; pro·cur·ing** **1** : to get possession of : OBTAIN **2** : to make women available for promiscuous sexual intercourse **3** : to cause to happen or be done : ACHIEVE **syn** secure, acquire, gain, win, earn — **pro·cur·able** \-ˈkyu̇r-ə-bəl\ *adj* — **pro·cure·ment** \-ˈkyu̇(ə)r-mənt\ *n* — **pro·cur·er** *n*

[1]**prod** \ˈpräd\ *vb* **prod·ded; prod·ding** **1** : to thrust a pointed instrument into : GOAD **2** : INCITE, STIR — **prod** *n*

[2]**prod** *abbr* product; production

prod·i·gal \ˈpräd-i-gəl\ *adj* **1** : recklessly extravagant; *also* : LUXURIANT **2** : WASTEFUL, LAVISH **syn** profuse, lavish, lush, opulent — **prodigal** *n* — **prod·i·gal·i·ty** \ˌpräd-ə-ˈgal-ət-ē\ *n*

pro·di·gious \prə-ˈdij-əs\ *adj* **1** : exciting wonder **2** : extraordinary in size or degree : ENORMOUS **syn** monstrous, tremendous, stupendous, monumental — **pro·di·gious·ly** *adv*

prod·i·gy \ˈpräd-ə-jē\ *n, pl* **-gies** **1** : something extraordinary : WONDER **2** : a highly talented child

[1]**pro·duce** \prə-ˈd(y)üs\ *vb* **pro·duced; pro·duc·ing** **1** : to present to view : EXHIBIT **2** : to give birth or rise to : YIELD **3** : EXTEND, PROLONG **4** : to give being or form to : BRING ABOUT, MAKE; *esp* : MANUFACTURE **5** : to cause to accrue ⟨~ a profit⟩ — **pro·duc·er** *n*

[2]**pro·duce** \ˈpräd-(ˌ)üs, ˈprōd- *also* -(ˌ)yüs\ *n* : PRODUCT 2; *also* : agricultural products and esp. fresh fruits and vegetables

prod·uct \ˈpräd-(ˌ)əkt\ *n* **1** : the number resulting from multiplication **2** : something produced (as by labor, thought, or growth)

pro·duc·tion \prə-ˈdək-shən\ *n* **1** : something produced : PRODUCT **2** : the act or process of producing — **pro·duc·tive** \-ˈdək-tiv\ *adj* — **pro·duc·tive·ness** *n* — **pro·duc·tiv·i·ty** \(ˌ)prō-ˌdək-ˈtiv-ət-ē, ˌpräd-(ˌ)ək-\ *n*

pro·em \ˈprō-ˌem\ *n* **1** : preliminary comment : PREFACE **2** : PRELUDE

prof *abbr* **1** professional **2** professor

[1]**pro·fane** \prō-ˈfān\ *vb* **pro·faned; pro·fan·ing** **1** : to treat (something sacred) with irreverence or contempt : DESECRATE **2** : to debase by an unworthy use — **prof·a·na·tion** \ˌpräf-ə-ˈnā-shən\ *n*

[2]**profane** *adj* [ME *prophane,* fr. MF, fr. L *profanus,* fr. *pro-* before + *fanum* temple] **1** : not concerned with religion : SECULAR **2** : not holy because unconsecrated, impure, or defiled **3** : serving to debase what is holy : IRREVERENT ⟨~ language⟩ — **pro·fane·ly** *adv* — **pro·fane·ness** \-ˈfān-nəs\ *n*

pro·fan·i·ty \prō-ˈfan-ət-ē\ *n, pl* **-ties** **1** : the quality or state of being profane **2** : the use of profane language **3** : profane language

pro·fess \prə-ˈfes\ *vb* **1** : to declare or admit openly : AF-

FIRM 2 : to declare in words only : PRETEND 3 : to confess one's faith in 4 : to practice or claim to be versed in (a calling or occupation) — **pro·fess·ed·ly** \-əd-lē\ *adv*

pro·fes·sion \prə-ˈfesh-ən\ *n* **1** : an open declaration or avowal of a belief or opinion **2** : a calling requiring specialized knowledge and often long academic preparation **3** : the whole body of persons engaged in a calling

¹pro·fes·sion·al \prə-ˈfesh-(ə-)nəl\ *adj* **1** : of, relating to, or characteristic of a profession **2** : engaged in one of the learned professions **3** : participating for gain in an activity often engaged in by amateurs — **pro·fes·sion·al·ly** \-ē\ *adv*

²professional *n* : one that engages in an activity professionally

pro·fes·sion·al·ism \-ˌiz-əm\ *n* **1** : the conduct, aims, or qualities that characterize or mark a profession or a professional person **2** : the following of a profession (as athletics) for gain or livelihood

pro·fes·sion·al·ize \-ˌīz\ *vb* **-ized; -iz·ing** : to give a professional nature to

pro·fes·sor \prə-ˈfes-ər\ *n* : a teacher at a university or college; *esp* : a faculty member of the highest academic rank — **pro·fes·so·ri·al** \ˌprō-fə-ˈsōr-ē-əl, ˌpräf-ə-\ *adj* — **pro·fes·sor·ship** *n*

prof·fer \ˈpräf-ər\ *vb* **prof·fered; prof·fer·ing** \-(ə-)riŋ\ : to present for acceptance : OFFER — **proffer** *n*

pro·fi·cient \prə-ˈfish-ənt\ *adj* : well advanced in an art, occupation, or branch of knowledge **syn** adept, skillful, expert, masterful, masterly — **pro·fi·cien·cy** \-ən-sē\ *n* — **proficient** *n* — **pro·fi·cient·ly** *adv*

¹pro·file \ˈprō-ˌfīl\ *n* [It *profilo*, fr. *profilare* to draw in outline, fr. *pro-* forward (fr. L) + *filare* to spin, fr. LL, fr. L *filum* thread] **1** : a representation of something in outline; *esp* : a human head seen in side view **2** : a concise biographical sketch **3** : degree or level of public exposure ⟨keep a low ~⟩ **syn** contour, silhouette, outline

²profile *vb* **pro·filed; pro·fil·ing** : to write or draw a profile of

¹prof·it \ˈpräf-ət\ *n* **1** : a valuable return : GAIN **2** : the excess of the selling price of goods over their cost — **prof·it·less** *adj*

²profit *vb* **1** : to be of use : BENEFIT **2** : to derive benefit : GAIN — **prof·it·able** \ˈpräf-ət-ə-bəl, ˈpräf-tə-bəl\ *adj* — **prof·it·ably** \-blē\ *adv*

prof·i·teer \ˌpräf-ə-ˈtiər\ *n* : one who makes what is considered an unreasonable profit — **profiteer** *vb*

prof·li·gate \ˈpräf-li-gət, -lə-ˌgāt\ *adj* **1** : completely given up to dissipation and licentiousness **2** : wildly extravagant — **prof·li·ga·cy** \-gə-sē\ *n* — **profligate** *n* — **prof·li·gate·ly** *adv*

pro for·ma \prō-ˈfȯr-mə\ *adj* : done or existing as a matter of form

pro·found \prə-ˈfau̇nd\ *adj* **1** : marked by intellectual depth or insight ⟨a ~ thought⟩ **2** : coming from or reaching to a depth ⟨a ~ sigh⟩ **3** : deeply felt : INTENSE ⟨~ sympathy⟩ — **pro·found·ly** *adv* — **pro·fun·di·ty** \-ˈfən-dət-ē\ *n*

pro·fuse \prə-ˈfyüs\ *adj* : pouring forth liberally : ABUNDANT **syn** lavish, prodigal, luxuriant, exuberant — **pro·fuse·ly** *adv* — **pro·fu·sion** \-ˈfyü-zhən\ *n*

pro·gen·i·tor \prō-ˈjen-ət-ər\ *n* **1** : a direct ancestor : FOREFATHER **2** : ORIGINATOR, PRECURSOR

prog·e·ny \ˈpräj-ə-nē\ *n, pl* **-nies** : OFFSPRING, CHILDREN, DESCENDANTS

prog·na·thous \ˈpräg-nə-thəs\ *adj* : having the jaws projecting beyond the upper part of the face

prog·no·sis \präg-ˈnō-səs\ *n, pl* **-no·ses** \-ˌsēz\ : a forecast esp. of the course of a disease

prog·nos·tic \präg-ˈnäs-tik\ *n* **1** : PORTENT **2** : PROPHECY — **prognostic** *adj*

prog·nos·ti·cate \präg-ˈnäs-tə-ˌkāt\ *vb* **-cat·ed; -cat·ing** : to foretell from signs or symptoms — **prog·nos·ti·ca·tion** \-ˌnäs-tə-ˈkā-shən\ *n* — **prog·nos·ti·ca·tor** \-ˈnäs-tə-ˌkāt-ər\ *n*

¹pro·gram \ˈprō-ˌgram, -grəm\ *n* **1** : a brief outline of the order to be pursued or the subjects included (as in a public entertainment); *also* : PERFORMANCE **2** : a plan of procedure **3** : coded instructions for a computer — **pro·gram·mat·ic** \ˌprō-grə-ˈmat-ik\ *adj*

²program *also* **programme** *vb* **-grammed** *or* **-gramed; -gram·ming** *or* **-gram·ing** **1** : to enter in a program **2** : to provide (as a computer) with a program — **pro·gram·ma·bil·i·ty** \(ˌ)prō-ˌgram-ə-ˈbil-ət-ē\ *n* — **pro·gram·ma·ble** \ˈprō-ˌgram-ə-bəl\ *adj* — **pro·gram·mer** *or* **pro·gram·er** \ˈprō-ˌgram-ər, -grə-mər\ *n*

programmed instruction *n* : instruction through information given in small steps with each requiring a correct response by the learner before going on to the next step

pro·gram·ming *or* **pro·gram·ing** \-ˌgram-iŋ, -grə-miŋ\ *n* **1** : the process of instructing or learning by means of an instruction program **2** : the process of preparing an instruction program

¹prog·ress \ˈpräg-rəs, -ˌres\ *n* **1** : a forward movement : ADVANCE **2** : a gradual betterment

²pro·gress \prə-ˈgres\ *vb* **1** : to move forward : PROCEED **2** : to develop to a more advanced stage : IMPROVE

pro·gres·sion \prə-ˈgresh-ən\ *n* **1** : an act of progressing : ADVANCE **2** : a continuous and connected series

¹pro·gres·sive \prə-ˈgres-iv\ *adj* **1** : of, relating to, or characterized by progress ⟨a ~ city⟩ **2** : advancing by stages ⟨a ~ disease⟩ **3** *often cap* : of or relating to political Progressives **4** : of, relating to, or constituting a verb form that expresses action in progress at the time of speaking or a time spoken of — **pro·gres·sive·ly** *adv*

²progressive *n* **1** : one that is progressive **2** : a person believing in moderate political change and social improvement by government action; *esp, cap* : a member of a Progressive Party (as in the presidential campaigns of 1912, 1924, and 1948) in the U.S.

pro·hib·it \prō-ˈhib-ət\ *vb* **1** : to forbid by authority **2** : to prevent from doing something

pro·hi·bi·tion \ˌprō-ə-ˈbish-ən\ *n* **1** : the act of prohibiting **2** : the forbidding by law of the sale or manufacture of alcoholic beverages — **pro·hi·bi·tion·ist** \-ˈbish-(ə-)nəst\ *n* — **pro·hib·i·tive** \prō-ˈhib-ət-iv\ *adj* — **pro·hib·i·tive·ly** *adv* — **pro·hib·i·to·ry** \-ˈhib-ə-ˌtōr-ē\ *adj*

¹proj·ect \ˈpräj-ˌekt, -ikt\ *n* **1** : a specific plan or design : SCHEME **2** : a planned undertaking ⟨a research ~⟩

²pro·ject \prə-ˈjekt\ *vb* **1** : to devise in the mind : DESIGN **2** : to throw forward **3** : PROTRUDE **4** : to cause (light or shadow) to fall into space or (an image) to fall on a surface ⟨~ a beam of light⟩ **5** : to attribute (a thought, feeling, or personal characteristic) to a person, group, or object — **pro·jec·tion** \-ˈjek-shən\ *n*

pro·jec·tile \prə-ˈjek-tᵊl\ *n* **1** : a body hurled or projected by external force; *esp* : a missile for a firearm **2** : a self-propelling weapon

pro·jec·tion·ist \prə-ˈjek-sh(ə-)nəst\ *n* : one that operates a motion-picture projector or television equipment

pro·jec·tor \-ˈjek-tər\ *n* : one that projects; *esp* : a device for projecting pictures on a screen

pro·le·gom·e·non \ˌprō-li-ˈgäm-ə-ˌnän, -nən\ *n, pl* **-e·na** \-nə\ : prefatory remarks

pro·le·tar·i·an \ˌprō-lə-ˈter-ē-ən\ *n* : a member of the proletariat — **proletarian** *adj*

pro·le·tar·i·at \-ē-ət\ *n* : the laboring class; *esp* : industrial workers who sell their labor to live

pro·lif·er·ate \prə-ˈlif-ə-ˌrāt\ *vb* **-at·ed; -at·ing** : to grow or increase by rapid production of new units (as cells or offspring) — **pro·lif·er·a·tion** \-ˌlif-ə-ˈrā-shən\ *n*

pro·lif·ic \prə-ˈlif-ik\ *adj* **1** : producing young or fruit abundantly **2** : marked by abundant inventiveness or productivity ⟨a ~ writer⟩ — **pro·lif·i·cal·ly** \-i-k(ə-)lē\ *adv*

pro·lix \prō-ˈliks, ˈprō-ˌliks\ *adj* : VERBOSE **syn** wordy, diffuse, redundant — **pro·lix·i·ty** \prō-ˈlik-sət-ē\ *n*

pro·logue *also* **pro·log** \ˈprō-ˌlȯg, -ˌläg\ *n* : PREFACE ⟨~ of a play⟩

pro·long \prə-ˈlȯŋ\ *vb* **1** : to lengthen in time : CONTINUE ⟨~ a meeting⟩ **2** : to lengthen in extent or range **syn** protract, extend, elongate, stretch — **pro·lon·ga·tion** \ˌprō-ˌlȯŋ-ˈgā-shən\ *n*

prom \ˈpräm\ *n* : a formal dance given by a high school or college class

[1]**prom·e·nade** \ˌpräm-ə-ˈnād, -ˈnäd\ *n* [F, fr. *promener* to take for a walk, fr. L *prominare* to drive forward] **1** : a leisurely walk for pleasure or display **2** : a place for strolling **3** : an opening grand march at a formal ball

[2]**promenade** *vb* **-nad·ed; -nad·ing 1** : to take a promenade **2** : to walk about in or on

pro·me·thi·um \prə-ˈmē-thē-əm\ *n* : a metallic chemical element obtained from uranium or neodymium — see ELEMENT table

prom·i·nence \ˈpräm(-ə)-nəns\ *n* **1** : something prominent **2** : the quality, state, or fact of being prominent or conspicuous **3** : a mass of cloudlike gas that arises from the sun's chromosphere

prom·i·nent \-nənt\ *adj* **1** : jutting out : PROJECTING **2** : readily noticeable : CONSPICUOUS **3** : DISTINGUISHED, EMINENT **syn** remarkable, outstanding, striking, salient — **prom·i·nent·ly** *adv*

pro·mis·cu·ous \prə-ˈmis-kyə-wəs\ *adj* **1** : consisting of various sorts and kinds : MIXED **2** : not restricted to one class or person; *esp* : not restricted to one sexual partner **syn** miscellaneous, assorted, heterogeneous, motley, varied — **prom·is·cu·i·ty** \ˌpräm-is-ˈkyü-ət-ē, ˌprō-ˌmis-\ *n* — **pro·mis·cu·ous·ly** *adv* — **pro·mis·cu·ous·ness** *n*

[1]**prom·ise** \ˈpräm-əs\ *n* **1** : a pledge to do or not to do something specified **2** : ground for expectation of success or improvement **3** : something promised

[2]**promise** *vb* **prom·ised; prom·is·ing 1** : to engage to do, bring about, or provide ⟨~ help⟩ **2** : to suggest beforehand ⟨dark clouds ~ rain⟩ **3** : to give ground for expectation ⟨the book ~*s* to be good⟩

prom·is·ing \ˈpräm-ə-siŋ\ *adj* : likely to succeed or yield good results — **prom·is·ing·ly** *adv*

prom·is·so·ry \ˈpräm-ə-ˌsōr-ē\ *adj* : containing a promise

prom·on·to·ry \ˈpräm-ən-ˌtōr-ē\ *n, pl* **-ries** : a point of land jutting into the sea : HEADLAND

pro·mote \prə-ˈmōt\ *vb* **pro·mot·ed; pro·mot·ing 1** : to advance in station, rank, or honor **2** : to contribute to the growth or prosperity of : FURTHER **3** : LAUNCH — **pro·mo·tion** \-ˈmō-shən\ *n* — **pro·mo·tion·al** \-ˈmōsh-(ə-)nəl\ *adj*

pro·mot·er \-ˈmōt-ər\ *n* : one that promotes; *esp* : one that assumes the financial responsibilities of a sports event

[1]**prompt** \ˈprämpt\ *vb* **1** : INCITE **2** : to assist (one acting or reciting) by suggesting the next words **3** : INSPIRE, URGE — **prompt·er** *n*

[2]**prompt** *adj* **1** : being ready and quick to act; *also* : PUNCTUAL **2** : performed readily or immediately ⟨~ service⟩ — **prompt·ly** *adv* — **prompt·ness** *n*

prompt·book \-ˌbu̇k\ *n* : a copy of a play with directions for performance used by a theater prompter

promp·ti·tude \ˈprämp-tə-ˌt(y)üd\ *n* : the quality or habit of being prompt : PROMPTNESS

pro·mul·gate \ˈpräm-əl-ˌgāt; prō-ˈməl-\ *vb* **-gat·ed; -gat·ing** : to make known or put into force by open declaration — **prom·ul·ga·tion** \ˌpräm-əl-ˈgā-shən, ˌprō-(ˌ)məl-\ *n*

pron *abbr* **1** pronoun **2** pronounced **3** pronunciation

prone \ˈprōn\ *adj* **1** : having a tendency or inclination : DISPOSED **2** : lying face downward; *also* : lying flat or prostrate **syn** subject, exposed, open, liable, susceptible — **prone·ness** \ˈprōn-nəs\ *n*

prong \ˈprȯŋ\ *n* : one of the sharp points of a fork : TINE; *also* : a slender projecting part (as of an antler)

prong·horn \ˈprȯŋ-ˌhȯrn\ *n, pl* **pronghorn** *also* **pronghorns** : a ruminant mammal of treeless parts of western No. America that resembles an antelope

pronghorn

pro·noun \ˈprō-ˌnau̇n\ *n* : a word used as a substitute for a noun

pro·nounce \prə-ˈnau̇ns\ *vb* **pro·nounced; pro·nounc·ing 1** : to utter officially or as an opinion ⟨~ sentence⟩ **2** : to employ the organs of speech in order to produce ⟨~ a word⟩; *esp* : to say or speak correctly ⟨she can't ~ his name⟩ — **pro·nounce·able** *adj* — **pro·nun·ci·a·tion** \-ˌnən-sē-ˈā-shən\ *n*

pro·nounced \-ˈnau̇nst\ *adj* : strongly marked : DECIDED

pro·nounce·ment \prə-ˈnau̇ns-mənt\ *n* : a formal declaration of opinion; *also* : ANNOUNCEMENT

pron·to \ˈprän-ˌtō\ *adv* [Sp, fr. L *promptus* prompt] : QUICKLY

pro·nu·clear \ˈprō-ˈn(y)ü-klē-ər\ *adj* : supporting the use of nuclear-powered electric generating stations

pro·nun·ci·a·men·to \prō-ˌnən-sē-ə-ˈment-ō\ *n, pl* **-tos** *or* **-toes** : PROCLAMATION, MANIFESTO

[1]**proof** \ˈprüf\ *n* **1** : the evidence that compels acceptance by the mind of a truth or fact **2** : a process or operation that establishes validity or truth : TEST **3** : a trial impression (as from type) **4** : a trial print from a photographic negative **5** : alcoholic content (as of a beverage) indicated by a number that is twice the percent by volume of alcohol present ⟨whiskey of 90 ~ is 45% alcohol⟩

[2]**proof** *adj* **1** : successful in resisting or repelling ⟨~ against tampering⟩ **2** : of standard strength or quality or alcoholic content

proof·read \-ˌrēd\ *vb* : to read and mark corrections in (as a printer's proof) — **proof·read·er** *n*

[1]**prop** \ˈpräp\ *n* : something that props

[2]**prop** *vb* **propped; prop·ping 1** : to support by placing something under or against ⟨~ up a wall⟩ **2** : SUSTAIN, STRENGTHEN

[3]**prop** *n* : PROPERTY 4

[4]**prop** *n* : PROPELLER

[5]**prop** *abbr* **1** property **2** proposition **3** proprietor

pro·pa·gan·da \ˌpräp-ə-ˈgan-də, ˌprō-pə-\ *n* [NL, fr. *Congregatio de propaganda fide* Congregation for propagating the faith, organization established by Pope Gregory XV] : the spreading of ideas or information to further or damage a cause; *also* : ideas or allegations spread for such a purpose — **pro·pa·gan·dist** \-dəst\ *n*

pro·pa·gan·dize \-ˌdīz\ *vb* **-dized; -diz·ing** : to subject to or carry on propaganda

prop·a·gate \ˈpräp-ə-ˌgāt\ *vb* **-gat·ed; -gat·ing 1** : to reproduce or cause to reproduce biologically : MULTIPLY **2** : to cause to spread — **prop·a·ga·tion** \ˌpräp-ə-ˈgā-shən\ *n*

pro·pane \ˈprō-ˌpān\ *n* : a heavy flammable gas found in petroleum and natural gas and used as a fuel

pro·pel \prə-ˈpel\ *vb* **pro·pelled; pro·pel·ling** 1 : to drive forward or onward 2 : to urge on : MOTIVATE **syn** push, shove, thrust, drive

pro·pel·lant *also* **pro·pel·lent** \-ˈpel-ənt\ *n* : something (as an explosive or fuel) that propels — **propellant** *or* **propellent** *adj*

pro·pel·ler \prə-ˈpel-ər\ *n* : a device consisting of a hub fitted with blades that is used to propel a vehicle (as a motorboat or an airplane)

pro·pen·si·ty \prə-ˈpen-sət-ē\ *n, pl* **-ties** : an often intense natural inclination or preference

[1]**prop·er** \ˈpräp-ər\ *adj* 1 : referring to one individual only ⟨~ noun⟩ 2 : belonging characteristically to a species or individual : PECULIAR 3 : very satisfactory : EXCELLENT 4 : strictly limited to a specified thing ⟨the city ~⟩ 5 : CORRECT ⟨the ~ way to proceed⟩ 6 : strictly decorous : GENTEEL 7 : marked by suitability or rightness ⟨~ punishment⟩ **syn** meet, appropriate, fitting, seemly — **prop·er·ly** *adv*

[2]**proper** *n* : the parts of the Mass that vary according to the liturgical calendar

prop·er·tied \ˈpräp-ərt-ēd\ *adj* : owning property and esp. much property

prop·er·ty \ˈpräp-ərt-ē\ *n, pl* **-ties** 1 : a quality peculiar to an individual or thing 2 : something owned; *esp* : a piece of real estate 3 : OWNERSHIP 4 : an article or object used in a play other than painted scenery and actor's costumes

proph·e·cy *also* **proph·e·sy** \ˈpräf-ə-sē\ *n, pl* **-cies** *also* **-sies** 1 : an inspired utterance of a prophet 2 : PREDICTION

proph·e·sy \-ˌsī\ *vb* **-sied; -sy·ing** 1 : to speak or utter by divine inspiration 2 : PREDICT — **proph·e·si·er** \-ˌsī(-ə)r\ *n*

proph·et \ˈpräf-ət\ *n* [ME *prophete*, fr. OF, fr. L *propheta*, fr. Gk *prophētēs*, fr. *pro* for + *phanai* to speak] 1 : one who utters divinely inspired revelations 2 : one who foretells future events

proph·et·ess \ˈpräf-ət-əs\ *n* : a woman who is a prophet

pro·phet·ic \prə-ˈfet-ik\ *or* **pro·phet·i·cal** \-i-kəl\ *adj* : of, relating to, or characteristic of a prophet or prophecy — **pro·phet·i·cal·ly** \-i-k(ə-)lē\ *adv*

[1]**pro·phy·lac·tic** \ˌprō-fə-ˈlak-tik, ˌpräf-ə-\ *adj* 1 : preventing or guarding from disease 2 : PREVENTIVE

[2]**prophylactic** *n* : something (as a drug or device) that protects from disease

pro·phy·lax·is \-ˈlak-səs\ *n, pl* **-lax·es** \-ˈlak-ˌsēz\ : measures designed to preserve health and prevent the spread of disease

pro·pin·qui·ty \prə-ˈpiŋ-kwət-ē\ *n* 1 : KINSHIP 2 : nearness in place or time : PROXIMITY

pro·pi·ti·ate \prō-ˈpish-ē-ˌāt\ *vb* **-at·ed; -at·ing** : to gain or regain the favor of : APPEASE — **pro·pi·ti·a·tion** \-ˌpis(h)-ē-ˈā-shən\ *n* — **pro·pi·tia·to·ry** \-ˈpish-(ē-)ə-ˌtōr-ē\ *adj*

pro·pi·tious \prə-ˈpish-əs\ *adj* 1 : favorably disposed ⟨~ deities⟩ 2 : being of good omen ⟨~ circumstances⟩

prop·man \ˈpräp-ˌman\ *n* : one who is in charge of theater or motion-picture stage properties

pro·po·nent \prə-ˈpō-nənt\ *n* : one who argues in favor of something

[1]**pro·por·tion** \prə-ˈpōr-shən\ *n* 1 : the relation of one part to another or to the whole with respect to magnitude, quantity, or degree : RATIO 2 : BALANCE, SYMMETRY 3 : SHARE, QUOTA 4 : SIZE, DEGREE — **in proportion** : PROPORTIONAL

[2]**proportion** *vb* **-tioned; -tion·ing** \-sh(ə-)niŋ\ 1 : to adjust (a part or thing) in size relative to other parts or things 2 : to make the parts of harmonious

pro·por·tion·al \prə-ˈpȯr-sh(ə-)nəl\ *adj* : corresponding in size, degree, or intensity; *also* : having the same or a constant ratio — **pro·por·tion·al·ly** \-ē\ *adv*

pro·por·tion·ate \prə-ˈpȯr-sh(ə-)nət\ *adj* : PROPORTIONAL — **pro·por·tion·ate·ly** *adv*

pro·pose \prə-ˈpōz\ *vb* **pro·posed; pro·pos·ing** 1 : PLAN, INTEND ⟨~*s* to buy a house⟩ 2 : to make an offer of marriage 3 : to offer for consideration : SUGGEST ⟨~ a policy⟩ — **pro·pos·al** \-ˈpō-zəl\ *n* — **pro·pos·er** *n*

[1]**prop·o·si·tion** \ˌpräp-ə-ˈzish-ən\ *n* 1 : something proposed for consideration : PROPOSAL; *esp* : a request for sexual intercourse 2 : a statement of something to be discussed, proved, or explained 3 : SITUATION, AFFAIR ⟨a tough ~⟩ — **prop·o·si·tion·al** \-ˈzish-(ə-)nəl\ *adj*

[2]**proposition** *vb* **-tioned; -tion·ing** \-ˈzish-(ə-)niŋ\ : to make a proposal to; *esp* : to suggest sexual intercourse to

pro·pound \prə-ˈpau̇nd\ *vb* : to set forth for consideration ⟨~ a doctrine⟩

pro·pri·e·tary \prə-ˈprī-ə-ˌter-ē\ *adj* 1 : of, relating to, or characteristic of a proprietor ⟨~ control⟩ 2 : made and sold by one with the sole right to do so ⟨~ medicines⟩

pro·pri·etor \prə-ˈprī-ət-ər\ *n* : OWNER — **pro·pri·etor·ship** *n*

pro·pri·etress \-ˈprī-ə-trəs\ *n* : a woman who is a proprietor

pro·pri·ety \prə-ˈprī-ət-ē\ *n, pl* **-eties** 1 : the standard of what is socially acceptable in conduct or speech 2 *pl* : the customs of polite society

pro·pul·sion \prə-ˈpəl-shən\ *n* 1 : the action or process of propelling 2 : something that propels — **pro·pul·sive** \-siv\ *adj*

pro ra·ta \prō-ˈrāt-ə, -ˈrät-\ *adv* : in proportion to the share of each : PROPORTIONATELY

pro·rate \ˈprō-ˈrāt\ *vb* **pro·rat·ed; pro·rat·ing** : to divide, distribute, or assess proportionately

pro·rogue \prə-ˈrōg\ *vb* **pro·rogued; pro·rogu·ing** : to suspend or end a session of (a legislative body) **syn** adjourn, dissolve, recess — **pro·ro·ga·tion** \ˌprōr-ō-ˈgā-shən\ *n*

pros *pl of* PRO

pro·sa·ic \prō-ˈzā-ik\ *adj* : lacking imagination or excitement : DULL

pro·sce·ni·um \prō-ˈsē-nē-əm\ *n* 1 : the part of a stage in front of the curtain 2 : the wall containing the arch that frames the stage

pro·scribe \prō-ˈskrīb\ *vb* **pro·scribed; pro·scrib·ing** 1 : OUTLAW 2 : to condemn or forbid as harmful — **pro·scrip·tion** \-ˈskrip-shən\ *n*

prose \ˈprōz\ *n* [ME, fr. MF, fr. L *prosa*, fr. fem. of *prorsus, prosus*, straightforward, being in prose, fr. *proversus*, pp. of *provertere* to turn forward] : the ordinary language people use in speaking or writing

pros·e·cute \ˈpräs-i-ˌkyüt\ *vb* **-cut·ed; -cut·ing** 1 : to follow to the end ⟨~ an investigation⟩ 2 : to seek legal punishment of ⟨~ a forger⟩ — **pros·e·cu·tion** \ˌpräs-i-ˈkyü-shən\ *n* — **pros·e·cu·tor** \ˈpräs-i-ˌkyüt-ər\ *n*

[1]**pros·e·lyte** \ˈpräs-ə-ˌlīt\ *n* : a new convert to a religion, belief, or party — **pros·e·lyt·ism** \-ˌlīt-ˌiz-əm\ *n*

[2]**proselyte** *vb* **-lyt·ed; -lyt·ing** : PROSELYTIZE

pros·e·ly·tize \ˈpräs-(ə-)lə-ˌtīz\ *vb* **-tized; -tiz·ing** 1 : to induce someone to convert to one's faith 2 : to recruit someone to join one's party, institution, or cause

pros·o·dy \ˈpräs-əd-ē\ *n, pl* **-dies** : the study of versification and esp. of metrical structure

[1]**pros·pect** \ˈpräs-ˌpekt\ *n* 1 : an extensive view; *also* : OUTLOOK 2 : the act of looking forward 3 : a mental vision of something to come 4 : something that is awaited or expected : POSSIBILITY 5 : a potential buyer or customer; *also* : a likely candidate — **pro·spec·tive** \prə-ˈspek-tiv, ˈpräs-ˌpek-\ *adj* — **pro·spec·tive·ly** *adv*

[2]**pros·pect** \ˈpräs-ˌpekt\ *vb* : to explore esp. for mineral deposits — **pros·pec·tor** \-ˌpek-tər, -ˈpek-\ *n*

pro·spec·tus \prə-ˈspek-təs\ *n* : a preliminary statement that describes an enterprise and is distributed to prospective buyers or participants

pros·per \ˈpräs-pər\ *vb* **pros·pered; pros·per·ing** \-p(ə-)riŋ\ : SUCCEED; *esp* : to achieve economic success

pros·per·i·ty \präs-ˈper-ət-ē\ *n* : thriving condition : SUCCESS; *esp* : economic well-being

pros·per·ous \ˈpräs-p(ə-)rəs\ *adj* **1** : FAVORABLE ⟨~ winds⟩ **2** : marked by success or economic well-being ⟨a ~ business⟩

pros·tate \ˈpräs-ˌtāt\ *also* **pros·tat·ic** \prä-ˈstat-ik\ *adj* : of, relating to, or being the prostate gland — **prostate** *n*

prostate gland *n* : a glandular body about the base of the male urethra that produces a secretion which is a major part of the fluid ejaculated during an orgasm

pros·ta·ti·tis \ˌpräs-tə-ˈtīt-əs\ *n* : inflammation of the prostate gland

pros·the·sis \präs-ˈthē-səs, ˈpräs-thə-\ *n, pl* **-the·ses** \-ˌsēz\ : an artificial replacement for a missing body part — **pros·thet·ic** \präs-ˈthet-ik\ *adj*

pros·thet·ics \-ˈthet-iks\ *n pl* : the surgical and dental specialties concerned with the artificial replacement of missing parts

[1]**pros·ti·tute** \ˈpräs-tə-ˌt(y)üt\ *vb* **-tut·ed; -tut·ing 1** : to offer indiscriminately for sexual intercourse esp. for money **2** : to devote to corrupt or unworthy purposes — **pros·ti·tu·tion** \ˌpräs-tə-ˈt(y)ü-shən\ *n*

[2]**prostitute** *n* : one who engages in promiscuous sexual intercourse for pay

[1]**pros·trate** \ˈpräs-ˌtrāt\ *adj* **1** : stretched out with face on the ground in adoration or submission **2** : lying flat **3** : completely overcome ⟨~ with a cold⟩

[2]**pros·trate** \ˈpräs-ˌtrāt\ *vb* **pros·trat·ed; pros·trat·ing 1** : to throw or put into a prostrate position **2** : to reduce to a weak or powerless condition — **pros·tra·tion** \präs-ˈtrā-shən\ *n*

prosy \ˈprō-zē\ *adj* **pros·i·er; -est 1** : PROSAIC **2** : TEDIOUS

Prot *abbr* Protestant

prot·ac·tin·i·um \ˌprōt-ˌak-ˈtin-ē-əm\ *n* : a metallic radioactive element of relatively short life — see ELEMENT table

pro·tag·o·nist \prō-ˈtag-ə-nəst\ *n* **1** : the principal character in a drama or story **2** : a spokesman for a cause : CHAMPION

pro·te·an \ˈprōt-ē-ən\ *adj* : able to assume different shapes or roles

pro·tect \prə-ˈtekt\ *vb* : to shield from injury : GUARD

pro·tec·tion \prə-ˈtek-shən\ *n* **1** : the act of protecting : the state of being protected **2** : one that protects ⟨wear a helmet as a ~⟩ **3** : the supervision or support of one that is smaller and weaker **4** : the freeing of producers from foreign competition in their home market by high duties on foreign competitive goods — **pro·tec·tive** \-ˈtek-tiv\ *adj*

pro·tec·tion·ist \-sh(ə-)nəst\ *n* : an advocate of government economic protection for domestic producers through restrictions on foreign competitors — **pro·tec·tion·ism** \-shə-ˌniz-əm\ *n*

pro·tec·tor \prə-ˈtek-tər\ *n* **1** : one that protects : GUARDIAN **2** : a device used to prevent injury : GUARD **3** : REGENT 1

pro·tec·tor·ate \-t(ə-)rət\ *n* **1** : government by a protector **2** : the relationship of superior authority assumed by one state over a dependent one; *also* : the dependent political unit in such a relationship

pro·té·gé \ˈprōt-ə-ˌzhā\ *n* [F] : one who is protected, trained, or guided by an influential person

pro·tein \ˈprō-ˌtēn, ˈprōt-ē-ən\ *n* [F *protéine*, fr. LGk *prōteios* primary, fr. Gk *prōtos* first] : any of numerous complex nitrogen-containing substances that consist of chains of amino acids, are present in all living matter, and are an essential part of the human diet

pro tem \prō-ˈtem\ *adv* : PRO TEMPORE

pro tem·po·re \prō-ˈtem-pə-rē\ *adv* [L] : for the time being

Pro·tero·zo·ic \ˌprät-ə-rə-ˈzō-ik, ˌprōt-\ *adj* : of, relating to, or being the era of geologic history between the Archeozoic and the Paleozoic and extending from about 1.4 billion years ago to about 620 million years ago — **Proterozoic** *n*

[1]**pro·test** \ˈprō-ˌtest\ *n* **1** : the act of protesting; *esp* : an organized public demonstration of disapproval **2** : a complaint or objection against an idea, an act, or a course of action

[2]**pro·test** \prə-ˈtest\ *vb* **1** : to assert positively : make solemn declaration of ⟨~*s* his innocence⟩ **2** : to object strongly : make a protest against ⟨~ a ruling⟩ — **prot·es·ta·tion** \ˌprät-əs-ˈtā-shən\ *n* — **pro·test·er** *or* **pro·tes·tor** \-ər\ *n*

Prot·es·tant \ˈprät-əs-tənt, *3 also* prə-ˈtes-\ *n* **1** : a member or adherent of one of the Christian churches deriving from the Reformation **2** : a Christian not of a Catholic or Orthodox church **3** *not cap* : one who makes a protest — **Prot·es·tant·ism** \ˈprät-əs-tənt-ˌiz-əm\ *n*

pro·tha·la·mi·on \ˌprō-thə-ˈlā-mē-ən\ *or* **pro·tha·la·mi·um** \-mē-əm\ *n, pl* **-mia** \-mē-ə\ : a song in celebration of a marriage

pro·to·col \ˈprōt-ə-ˌkȯl\ *n* [MF *prothocole*, fr. ML *protocollum*, fr. LGk *prōtokollon* first sheet of a papyrus roll bearing data of manufacture, fr. Gk *prōtos* first + *kollan* to glue together, fr. *kolla* glue] **1** : an original draft or record **2** : a preliminary memorandum of diplomatic negotiation **3** : a code of diplomatic or military etiquette

pro·ton \ˈprō-ˌtän\ *n* [Gk *prōton*, neut. of *prōtos* first] : a positively charged atomic particle present in all atomic nuclei

pro·to·plasm \ˈprōt-ə-ˌplaz-əm\ *n* : the complex colloidal largely protein substance of living plant and animal cells that is regarded as the only form of matter in which the vital phenomena are manifested — **pro·to·plas·mic** \ˌprōt-ə-ˈplaz-mik\ *adj*

pro·to·type \ˈprōt-ə-ˌtīp\ *n* : an original model : ARCHETYPE

pro·to·zo·an \ˌprōt-ə-ˈzō-ən\ *n* : any of a phylum or subkingdom of lower invertebrate animals that are not divided into cells or are considered as made up of a single cell

pro·tract \prō-ˈtrakt\ *vb* : to prolong in time or space **syn** extend, lengthen, elongate, stretch

pro·trac·tor \-ˈtrak-tər\ *n* : an instrument for drawing and measuring angles

pro·trude \prō-ˈtrüd\ *vb* **pro·trud·ed; pro·trud·ing** : to stick out or cause to stick out : jut out — **pro·tru·sion** \-ˈtrü-zhən\ *n*

pro·tu·ber·ance \prō-ˈt(y)ü-b(ə-)rəns\ *n* : something that protrudes

pro·tu·ber·ant \-b(ə-)rənt\ *adj* : extending beyond the surrounding surface in a bulge

proud \ˈpraủd\ *adj* **1** : having or showing excessive self-esteem : HAUGHTY **2** : highly pleased : EXULTANT **3** : having proper self-respect ⟨too ~ to beg⟩ **4** : GLORIOUS ⟨a ~ occasion⟩ **5** : SPIRITED ⟨a ~ steed⟩ **syn** arrogant, insolent, overbearing, disdainful — **proud·ly** *adv*

prov *abbr* **1** province; provincial **2** provisional

Prov *abbr* Proverbs

prove \ˈprüv\ *vb* **proved; proved** *or* **prov·en** \ˈprü-vən\; **prov·ing** \ˈprü-viŋ\ **1** : to test by experiment or by a standard **2** : to establish the truth of by argument or evidence **3** : to show to be correct, valid, or genuine **4** : to turn out esp. after trial or test ⟨the car *proved* to be a good choice⟩ — **prov·able** \ˈprü-və-bəl\ *adj*

prov·e·nance \ˈpräv-ə-nəns\ *n* : ORIGIN, SOURCE

Pro·ven·çal \ˌprō-ˌvän-ˈsäl, ˌpräv-ən-\ *n* **1** : a native or inhabitant of Provence **2** : a Romance language spoken in southeastern France — **Provençal** *adj*

prov·en·der \ˈpräv-ən-dər\ *n* **1** : dry food for domestic animals : FEED **2** : FOOD, VICTUALS

pro·ve·nience \prə-ˈvē-nyəns\ *n* : ORIGIN, SOURCE
prov·erb \ˈpräv-ˌərb\ *n* : a pithy popular saying : ADAGE
pro·ver·bi·al \prə-ˈver-bē-əl\ *adj* **1** : of, relating to, or resembling a proverb **2** : commonly spoken of
Proverbs *n* — see BIBLE table
pro·vide \prə-ˈvīd\ *vb* **pro·vid·ed; pro·vid·ing** [ME *providen*, fr. L *providēre*, lit., to see ahead, fr. *pro-* forward + *vidēre* to see] **1** : to take measures beforehand ⟨~ against inflation⟩ **2** : to make a proviso or stipulation **3** : to supply what is needed ⟨~ for a family⟩ **4** : EQUIP **5** : to supply for use : YIELD — **pro·vid·er** *n*
pro·vid·ed \prə-ˈvīd-əd\ *conj* : on condition that : IF
prov·i·dence \ˈpräv-əd-əns\ *n* **1** *often cap* : divine guidance or care **2** *cap* : GOD 1 **3** : the quality or state of being provident
prov·i·dent \-əd-ənt\ *adj* **1** : making provision for the future : PRUDENT **2** : FRUGAL — **prov·i·dent·ly** *adv*
prov·i·den·tial \ˌpräv-ə-ˈden-chəl\ *adj* **1** : of, relating to, or determined by Providence **2** : OPPORTUNE, LUCKY
prov·ince \ˈpräv-əns\ *n* **1** : an administrative district or division of a country **2** *pl* : all of a country except the metropolis **3** : proper business or scope : SPHERE
pro·vin·cial \prə-ˈvin-chəl\ *adj* **1** : of or relating to a province **2** : confined to a region : NARROW ⟨~ ideas⟩ — **pro·vin·cial·ism** \-ˌiz-əm\ *n*
proving ground *n* : a place for scientific experimentation or testing
¹**pro·vi·sion** \prə-ˈvizh-ən\ *n* **1** : the act or process of providing; *also* : a measure taken beforehand **2** : a stock of needed supplies; *esp* : a stock of food — usu. used in pl. **3** : PROVISO
²**provision** *vb* **-sioned; -sion·ing** \-ˈvizh-(ə-)niŋ\ : to supply with provisions
pro·vi·sion·al \-ˈvizh-(ə-)nəl\ *adj* : provided for a temporary need : CONDITIONAL
pro·vi·so \prə-ˈvī-zō\ *n, pl* **-sos** *or* **-soes** [ME, fr. ML *proviso quod* provided that] : an article or clause that introduces a condition : STIPULATION
prov·o·ca·tion \ˌpräv-ə-ˈkā-shən\ *n* **1** : the act of provoking **2** : something that provokes
pro·voke \prə-ˈvōk\ *vb* **pro·voked; pro·vok·ing** **1** : to incite to anger : INCENSE **2** : to call forth : EVOKE ⟨a sally that *provoked* laughter⟩ **3** : to stir up on purpose ⟨~ an argument⟩ **syn** irritate, exasperate, aggravate, inflame, rile, pique — **pro·voc·a·tive** \prə-ˈväk-ət-iv\ *adj*
pro·vo·lo·ne \ˌprō-və-ˈlō-nē\ *n* : a hard smooth often smoked Italian cheese that is made from heated and kneaded curd
pro·vost \ˈprō-ˌvōst, ˈpräv-əst\ *n* : a high official : DIGNITARY; *esp* : a high-ranking university administrative officer
provost marshal \ˌprō-ˌvō-ˈmär-shəl\ *n* : an officer who supervises the military police of a command
prow \ˈpraů\ *n* : the bow of a ship
prow·ess \ˈpraů-əs\ *n* **1** : military valor and skill **2** : extraordinary ability
prowl \ˈpraůl\ *vb* : to roam about stealthily — **prowl** *n* — **prowl·er** *n*
prowl car *n* : SQUAD CAR
prox·i·mal \ˈpräk-sə-məl\ *adj* **1** : next to or nearest the point of attachment or origin; *esp* : located toward the center of the body **2** : of, relating to, or being the mesial and distal surfaces of a tooth
prox·i·mate \ˈpräk-sə-mət\ *adj* **1** : very near **2** : DIRECT ⟨the ~ cause⟩
prox·im·i·ty \präk-ˈsim-ət-ē\ *n* : NEARNESS
prox·i·mo \ˈpräk-sə-ˌmō\ *adj* [L *proximo mense* in the next month] : of or occurring in the next month after the present
proxy \ˈpräk-sē\ *n, pl* **prox·ies** : the authority or power to act for another; *also* : a document giving such authorization — **proxy** *adj*
prude \ˈprüd\ *n* : one who shows or affects extreme modesty — **prud·ery** \ˈprüd-ə-rē\ *n* — **prud·ish** \ˈprüd-ish\ *adj*
pru·dent \ˈprüd-ᵊnt\ *adj* **1** : shrewd in the management of practical affairs **2** : CAUTIOUS, DISCREET **3** : PROVIDENT, FRUGAL **syn** judicious, foresighted, sensible, sane — **pru·dence** \-ᵊns\ *n* — **pru·den·tial** \prü-ˈden-chəl\ *adj* — **pru·dent·ly** \ˈprüd-ᵊnt-lē\ *adv*
¹**prune** \ˈprün\ *n* : a dried plum
²**prune** *vb* **pruned; prun·ing** : to cut off unwanted parts (as of a tree)
pru·ri·ent \ˈprůr-ē-ənt\ *adj* : LASCIVIOUS; *also* : exciting to lasciviousness — **pru·ri·ence** \-ē-əns\ *n*
¹**pry** \ˈprī\ *vb* **pried; pry·ing** : to look closely or inquisitively; *esp* : SNOOP
²**pry** *vb* **pried; pry·ing** **1** : to raise, move, or pull apart with a pry or lever **2** : to detach or open with difficulty
³**pry** *n* : a tool for prying
Ps *or* **Psa** *abbr* Psalms
PS *abbr* **1** [L *postscriptum*] postscript **2** public school
psalm \ˈsäm, ˈsälm\ *n, often cap* [ME, fr. OE *psealm*, fr. LL *psalmus*, fr. Gk *psalmos*, lit., twanging of a harp, fr. *psallein* to pluck, play a stringed instrument] : a sacred song or poem; *esp* : one of the hymns collected in the Book of Psalms — **psalm·ist** *n*
psalm·o·dy \ˈsäm-əd-ē, ˈsäl-məd-\ *n* **1** : the singing of psalms in worship **2** : a collection of psalms
Psalms *n* — see BIBLE table
Psal·ter \ˈsȯl-tər\ *n* : the Book of Psalms; *also* : a collection of the Psalms arranged for devotional use
pseud *abbr* pseudonym; pseudonymous
pseu·do \ˈsüd-ō\ *adj* : SPURIOUS, SHAM
pseud·onym \ˈsüd-ᵊn-ˌim\ *n* : a fictitious name — **pseud·on·y·mous** \sü-ˈdän-ə-məs\ *adj*
PSG *abbr* platoon sergeant
psi *abbr* pounds per square inch
psi particle \ˈsī-, ˈpsī-\ *n* [*psi* (Greek letter)] : J PARTICLE
pso·ri·a·sis \sə-ˈrī-ə-səs\ *n* : a chronic skin disease characterized by red patches covered with white scales
PST *abbr* Pacific standard time
¹**psych** *also* **psyche** \ˈsīk\ *vb* **psyched; psych·ing** **1** : OUTGUESS; *also* : to analyze beforehand **2** : INTIMIDATE; *also* : to prepare oneself psychologically ⟨get *psyched* up for the game⟩
²**psych** *abbr* psychology
psy·che \ˈsī-kē\ *n* : SOUL, SELF; *also* : MIND
psy·che·del·ic \ˌsī-kə-ˈdel-ik\ *adj* **1** : of, relating to, or causing abnormal psychic effects ⟨~ drugs⟩ **2** : relating to the taking of psychedelic drugs ⟨~ experience⟩ **3** : imitating, suggestive of, or reproducing the effects of psychedelic drugs ⟨~ art⟩ ⟨~ colors⟩ — **psychedelic** *n* — **psy·che·del·i·cal·ly** \-i-k(ə-)lē\ *adv*
psy·chi·a·try \sə-ˈkī-ə-trē, sī-\ *n* : a branch of medicine dealing with mental disorders — **psy·chi·at·ric** \ˌsī-kē-ˈa-trik\ *adj* — **psy·chi·a·trist** \sə-ˈkī-ə-trəst, sī-\ *n*
¹**psy·chic** \ˈsī-kik\ *also* **psy·chi·cal** \-ki-kəl\ *adj* **1** : of or relating to the psyche **2** : lying outside the sphere of physical science **3** : sensitive to nonphysical or supernatural forces — **psy·chi·cal·ly** \-k(ə-)lē\ *adv*
²**psychic** *n* : a person apparently sensitive to nonphysical forces; *also* : MEDIUM 6
psychic energizer *n* : ANTIDEPRESSANT
psy·cho \ˈsī-kō\ *n, pl* **psychos** : a mentally disturbed person — **psycho** *adj*
psy·cho·ac·tive \ˌsī-kō-ˈak-tiv\ *adj* : affecting the mind or behavior
psy·cho·anal·y·sis \ˌsī-kō-ə-ˈnal-ə-səs\ *n* : a method of dealing with psychic disorders by having the patient talk freely about himself and esp. about dreams, prob-

lems, and early childhood memories and experiences — **psy·cho·an·a·lyst** \-ˈan-ᵊl-əst\ *n* — **psy·cho·an·a·lyt·ic** \-ˌan-ᵊl-ˈit-ik\ *adj* — **psy·cho·an·a·lyze** \-ˈan-ᵊl-ˌīz\ *vb*

psy·cho·dra·ma \ˌsī-kə-ˈdräm-ə, -ˈdram-\ *n* : an extemporized dramatization designed esp. to afford catharsis for one or more of the participants from whose life history the plot is abstracted

psy·cho·gen·ic \-ˈjen-ik\ *adj* : originating in the mind or in mental or emotional conflict

psychol *abbr* psychologist; psychology

psy·chol·o·gy \sī-ˈkäl-ə-jē\ *n, pl* **-gies** **1** : the science of mind and behavior **2** : the mental and behavioral characteristics of an individual or group — **psy·cho·log·i·cal** \ˌsī-kə-ˈläj-i-kəl\ *adj* — **psy·cho·log·i·cal·ly** \-i-k(ə-)lē\ *adv* — **psy·chol·o·gist** \sī-ˈkäl-ə-jəst\ *n*

psy·cho·path \ˈsī-kə-ˌpath\ *n* : a mentally ill or unstable person; *esp* : one who has a poorly balanced personality and does not feel guilty about not living up to normal moral and social responsibilities — **psy·cho·path·ic** \ˌsī-kə-ˈpath-ik\ *adj*

psy·cho·sex·u·al \ˌsī-kō-ˈsek-sh(ə-w)əl\ *adj* **1** : of or relating to the mental, emotional, and behavioral aspects of sexual development **2** : of or relating to the physiological psychology of sex

psy·cho·sis \sī-ˈkō-səs\ *n, pl* **-cho·ses** \-ˌsēz\ : a serious mental illness (as schizophrenia) characterized by defective or lost contact with reality — **psy·chot·ic** \-ˈkät-ik\ *adj or n*

psy·cho·so·mat·ic \ˌsī-kə-sə-ˈmat-ik\ *adj* : of, relating to, or caused by the interaction of mental and bodily phenomena ⟨∼ ulcers⟩

psy·cho·ther·a·py \ˌsī-kō-ˈther-ə-pē\ *n* : treatment of mental or emotional disorder or of related bodily ills by psychological means — **psy·cho·ther·a·pist** \-pəst\ *n*

psy·cho·tro·pic \ˌsī-kə-ˈtrō-pik\ *adj* : acting on the mind ⟨∼ drugs⟩

pt *abbr* **1** part **2** payment **3** pint **4** point **5** port

Pt *symbol* platinum

PT *abbr* **1** Pacific time **2** physical therapy **3** physical training

PTA *abbr* Parent-Teacher Association

ptar·mi·gan \ˈtär-mi-gən\ *n, pl* **-gan** *or* **-gans** : any of various grouses of northern regions with completely feathered feet

PT boat \(ˈ)pē-ˈtē-\ *n* [*p*atrol *t*orpedo] : a fast motorboat usu. armed with torpedos, machine guns, and depth charges

pte *abbr, Brit* private

ptg *abbr* printing

PTO *abbr* **1** Parent-Teacher Organization **2** please turn over

pto·maine \ˈtō-ˌmān\ *n* : any of various chemical substances formed by bacteria in decaying matter (as meat)

ptomaine poisoning *n* : food poisoning caused usu. by bacteria or their products

PTV *abbr* public television

Pu *symbol* plutonium

[1]**pub** \ˈpəb\ *n, chiefly Brit* : PUBLIC HOUSE, TAVERN

[2]**pub** *abbr* **1** public **2** publication **3** published; publisher; publishing

pu·ber·ty \ˈpyü-bərt-ē\ *n* : the condition of being or period of becoming first capable of reproducing sexually — **pu·ber·tal** \-bərt-ᵊl\ *adj*

pu·bes \ˈpyü-bēz\ *n, pl* **pubes** **1** : the hair that appears upon the lower middle region of the abdomen at puberty **2** : the pubic region

pu·bes·cence \pyü-ˈbes-ᵊns\ *n* **1** : the quality or state of being pubescent **2** : a pubescent covering or surface

pu·bes·cent \-ᵊnt\ *adj* **1** : arriving at or having reached puberty **2** : covered with fine soft short hairs

pu·bic \ˈpyü-bik\ *adj* : of, relating to, or situated near the pubes or the pubis

pu·bis \ˈpyü-bəs\ *n, pl* **pu·bes** \-bēz\ : the ventral and anterior of the three principal bones composing either half of the pelvis

publ *abbr* **1** publication **2** published; publisher

[1]**pub·lic** \ˈpəb-lik\ *adj* **1** : of, relating to, or affecting the people as a whole ⟨∼ opinion⟩ **2** : CIVIC, GOVERNMENTAL ⟨∼ expenditures⟩ **3** : of, relating to, or serving the community ⟨∼ officials⟩ **4** : not private : SOCIAL ⟨∼ morality⟩ **5** : open to all ⟨∼ library⟩ **6** : exposed to general view ⟨the story became ∼⟩ **7** : well known : PROMINENT ⟨∼ figures⟩ — **pub·lic·ly** *adv*

[2]**public** *n* **1** : the people as a whole : POPULACE **2** : a group of people having common interests ⟨wrote for his ∼⟩

pub·li·can \ˈpəb-li-kən\ *n* **1** : a Jewish tax collector for the ancient Romans **2** *chiefly Brit* : the licensee of a public house

pub·li·ca·tion \ˌpəb-lə-ˈkā-shən\ *n* **1** : the act or process of publishing **2** : a published work

public house *n* **1** : INN **2** *chiefly Brit* : a licensed saloon or bar

pub·li·cist \ˈpəb-lə-səst\ *n* : one that publicizes; *esp* : PRESS AGENT

pub·lic·i·ty \(ˌ)pə-ˈblis-ət-ē\ *n* **1** : information with news value issued to gain public attention or support **2** : public attention or acclaim

pub·li·cize \ˈpəb-lə-ˌsīz\ *vb* **-cized; -ciz·ing** : to give publicity to

public relations *n sing or pl* : the business of fostering public goodwill toward a person, firm, or institution; *also* : the degree of goodwill and understanding achieved

public school *n* **1** : an endowed secondary boarding school in Great Britain offering a classical curriculum and preparation for the universities or public service **2** : a free tax-supported school controlled by a local governmental authority

pub·lic–spir·it·ed \ˌpəb-lik-ˈspir-ət-əd\ *adj* : motivated by devotion to the general or national welfare

public television *n* : television that provides cultural, informational, and instructive programs without commercials

pub·lish \ˈpəb-lish\ *vb* **1** : to make generally known : announce publicly **2** : to produce or release literature, information, musical scores or sometimes recordings, or art for sale to the public — **pub·lish·er** *n*

[1]**puck** \ˈpək\ *n* : a mischievous sprite — **puck·ish** *adj*

[2]**puck** *n* : a disk used in ice hockey

[1]**puck·er** \ˈpək-ər\ *vb* **puck·ered; puck·er·ing** \-(ə-)riŋ\ : to contract into folds or wrinkles

[2]**pucker** *n* : FOLD, WRINKLE

pud·ding \ˈpu̇d-iŋ\ *n* : a soft, spongy, or thick creamy dessert

pud·dle \ˈpəd-ᵊl\ *n* : a very small pool of usu. dirty or muddy water

pu·den·dum \pyu̇-ˈden-dəm\ *n, pl* **-da** \-də\ [NL, deriv. of L *pudēre* to be ashamed] : the human external genital organs esp. of a woman

pudgy \ˈpəj-ē\ *adj* **pudg·i·er; -est** : being short and plump : CHUBBY

pueb·lo \pü-ˈeb-lō, ˈpweb-\ *n, pl* **-los** [Sp, village, lit., people, fr. L *populus*] **1** : an American Indian village of Arizona or New Mexico consisting of flat-roofed stone or adobe houses **2** *cap* : a member of an American Indian people of the southwestern U.S.

pu·er·ile \ˈpyu̇-ə-rəl\ *adj* : CHILDISH, SILLY — **pu·er·il·i·ty** \ˌpyü-ə-ˈril-ət-ē\ *n*

pu·er·per·al \pyü-ˈər-p(ə-)rəl\ *adj* : of, relating to, or occurring during childbirth or the period immediately following ⟨∼ infection⟩

puerperal fever *n* : an abnormal condition that results from infection of the placental site following childbirth or abortion

Puer·to Ri·can \ˌpōrt-ə-ˈrē-kən, ˌpwert-\ *n* : a native or inhabitant of Puerto Rico — **Puerto Rican** *adj*

[1]**puff** \ˈpəf\ *vb* **1** : to blow in short gusts **2** : PANT **3** : to emit small whiffs or clouds **4** : BLUSTER, BRAG **5** : INFLATE, SWELL **6** : to make proud or conceited **7** : to praise extravagantly

[2]**puff** *n* **1** : a short discharge (as of air or smoke); *also* : a slight explosive sound accompanying it **2** : a light fluffy pastry **3** : a slight swelling **4** : a fluffy mass; *esp* : a small pad for applying cosmetic powder **5** : a laudatory notice or review — **puffy** *adj*

puff·ball \ˈpəf-ˌbȯl\ *n* : any of various globe-shaped and often edible fungi

puf·fin \ˈpəf-ən\ *n* : any of several seabirds having a short neck and a red-tipped triangular bill

[1]**pug** \ˈpəg\ *n* **1** : any of a breed of small stocky short-haired dogs **2** : a close coil of hair

[2]**pug** *n* : [1]BOXER

pu·gi·lism \ˈpyü-jə-ˌliz-əm\ *n* : BOXING — **pu·gi·list** \-ləst\ *n* — **pu·gi·lis·tic** \ˌpyü-jə-ˈlis-tik\ *adj*

pug·na·cious \ˌpəg-ˈnā-shəs\ *adj* : fond of fighting : COMBATIVE **syn** belligerent, quarrelsome, bellicose, contentious, truculent — **pug·nac·i·ty** \-ˈnas-ət-ē\ *n*

puis·sance \ˈpwis-ᵊns, ˈpyü-ə-səns\ *n* : POWER, STRENGTH — **puis·sant** \-ᵊnt, -sənt\ *adj*

puke \ˈpyük\ *vb* **puked; puk·ing** : VOMIT — **puke** *n*

puk·ka \ˈpək-ə\ *adj* [Hindi *pakkā* cooked, ripe, solid, fr. Skt *pakva*] : GENUINE, AUTHENTIC; *also* : FIRST-CLASS, COMPLETE

pul \ˈpül\ *n, pl* **puls** \ˈpülz\ *or* **pul** — see *afghani* at MONEY table

pu·la \ˈp(y)ü-lə\ *n, pl* **pula** — see MONEY table

pul·chri·tude \ˈpəl-krə-ˌt(y)üd\ *n* : BEAUTY — **pul·chri·tu·di·nous** \ˌpəl-krə-ˈt(y)üd-(ᵊ-)nəs\ *adj*

pule \ˈpyül\ *vb* **puled; pul·ing** : WHINE, WHIMPER

[1]**pull** \ˈpu̇l\ *vb* **1** : PLUCK; *also* : EXTRACT ⟨~ a tooth⟩ **2** : to exert force so as to draw (something) toward the force; *also* : MOVE ⟨~ out of a driveway⟩ **3** : STRETCH, STRAIN ⟨~ a tendon⟩ **4** : to draw apart : TEAR **5** : to make (as a proof) by printing **6** : REMOVE **7** : DRAW ⟨~ a gun⟩ **8** : to carry out esp. with daring ⟨~ a robbery⟩ **9** : to be guilty of : PERPETRATE **10** : ATTRACT **11** : to express strong sympathy — **pull·er** *n*

[2]**pull** *n* **1** : the act or an instance of pulling **2** : the effort expended in moving **3** : ADVANTAGE; *esp* : special influence **4** : a device for pulling something or for operating by pulling **5** : a force that attracts or compels

pull·back \ˈpu̇l-ˌbak\ *n* : an orderly withdrawal of troops

pul·let \ˈpu̇l-ət\ *n* : a young hen esp. of the domestic chicken when less than a year old

pul·ley \ˈpu̇l-ē\ *n, pl* **pulleys** **1** : a wheel with a grooved rim that forms part of a tackle for hoisting or for changing the direction of a force **2** : a wheel used to transmit power by means of a band, belt, rope, or chain

Pull·man \ˈpu̇l-mən\ *n* : a railroad passenger car with comfortable furnishings esp. for night travel

pull off *vb* : to accomplish successfully

pull·out \ˈpu̇l-ˌau̇t\ *n* : PULLBACK

pull·over \ˌpu̇l-ˌō-vər\ *adj* : put on by being pulled over the head ⟨~ sweater⟩ — **pull·over** \ˈpu̇l-ˌō-vər\ *n*

pull–up \ˈpu̇l-ˌəp\ *n* : CHIN-UP

pull up \pu̇l-ˈəp\ *vb* : to bring or come to a halt : STOP

pul·mo·nary \ˈpu̇l-mə-ˌner-ē, ˈpəl-\ *adj* : of, relating to, or carried on by the lungs ⟨the ~ circulation⟩

pul·mo·tor \-ˌmōt-ər\ *n* : an apparatus for pumping oxygen or air into and out of the lungs

pulp \ˈpəlp\ *n* **1** : the soft juicy or fleshy part of a fruit or vegetable **2** : a soft moist mass **3** : the soft sensitive tissue that fills the central cavity of a tooth **4** : a material (as from wood or rags) used in making paper **5** : a magazine using rough-surfaced paper and often dealing with sensational material — **pulpy** *adj*

pul·pit \ˈpu̇l-ˌpit\ *n* : a raised platform or high reading desk used in preaching or conducting a worship service

pulp·wood \ˈpəlp-ˌwu̇d\ *n* : wood (as of aspen or pine) used in making pulp for paper

pul·sar \ˈpəl-ˌsär\ *n* : a celestial source of pulsating electromagnetic radiation (as radio waves)

pul·sate \ˈpəl-ˌsāt\ *vb* **pul·sat·ed; pul·sat·ing** : to expand and contract rhythmically : BEAT — **pul·sa·tion** \ˌpəl-ˈsā-shən\ *n*

pulse \ˈpəls\ *n* **1** : the regular throbbing in the arteries caused by the contractions of the heart **2** : a brief change in electrical current or voltage — **pulse** *vb*

pul·ver·ize \ˈpəl-və-ˌrīz\ *vb* **-ized; -iz·ing** **1** : to reduce (as by crushing or grinding) or be reduced to very small particles **2** : DEMOLISH

pu·ma \ˈp(y)ü-mə\ *n, pl* **pumas** *also* **puma** : COUGAR

pum·ice \ˈpəm-əs\ *n* : a light porous volcanic glass used esp. for smoothing and polishing

pum·mel \ˈpəm-əl\ *vb* **-meled** *also* **-melled; -mel·ing** *also* **-mel·ling** \-(ə-)liŋ\ : POUND, BEAT

[1]**pump** \ˈpəmp\ *n* : a device for raising, transferring, or compressing fluids esp. by suction or pressure

[2]**pump** *vb* **1** : to raise (as water) with a pump **2** : to draw water or air from by means of a pump; *also* : to fill by means of a pump ⟨~ up a tire⟩ **3** : to force or propel in the manner of a pump — **pump·er** *n*

[3]**pump** *n* : a low shoe that grips the foot chiefly at the toe and heel

pum·per·nick·el \ˈpəm-pər-ˌnik-əl\ *n* : a dark coarse somewhat sour rye bread

pump·kin \ˈpəm(p)-kən, ˈpəŋ-kən\ *n* : the large usu. orange fruit of a vine of the gourd family that is widely used as food; *also* : this vine

pun \ˈpən\ *n* : the humorous use of a word in a way that suggests two interpretations — **pun** *vb*

[1]**punch** \ˈpənch\ *vb* **1** : PROD, POKE; *also* : DRIVE, HERD ⟨~*ing* cattle⟩ **2** : to strike with the fist **3** : to emboss, perforate, or make with a punch — **punch·er** *n*

[2]**punch** *n* **1** : a quick blow with or as if with the fist **2** : effective energy or forcefulness

[3]**punch** *n* : a tool for piercing, stamping, cutting, or forming

[4]**punch** *n* [perh. fr. Hindi *pạc* five, fr. Skt *pañca:* fr. the number of ingredients] : a drink usu. composed of wine or alcoholic liquor and nonalcoholic beverages; *also* : a drink composed of nonalcoholic beverages (as fruit juices)

punch card *n* : a card with holes punched in particular positions to represent data

pun·cheon \ˈpən-chən\ *n* : a large cask

punch line *n* : the sentence or phrase in a joke that makes the point

punc·til·io \ˌpəŋk-ˈtil-ē-ˌō\ *n, pl* **-i·os** **1** : a nice detail of conduct in a ceremony or in observance of a code **2** : careful observance of forms (as in social conduct)

punc·til·i·ous \ˌpəŋk-ˈtil-ē-əs\ *adj* : marked by precise accordance with codes or conventions **syn** meticulous, scrupulous, careful, punctual

punc·tu·al \ˈpəŋk-chə(-wə)l\ *adj* : acting or habitually acting at an appointed time : PROMPT — **punc·tu·al·i·ty** \ˌpəŋk-chə-ˈwal-ət-ē\ *n* — **punc·tu·al·ly** \ˈpəŋk-chə(-wə)-lē\ *adv*

punc·tu·ate \ˈpəŋk-chə-ˌwāt\ *vb* **-at·ed; -at·ing** **1** : to mark or divide (written matter) with punctuation marks **2** : to break into at intervals **3** : EMPHASIZE

punc·tu·a·tion \ˌpəŋk-chə-ˈwā-shən\ *n* : the act, practice, or system of inserting standardized marks in written matter to clarify the meaning and separate structural units

[1]**punc·ture** \ˈpəŋk-chər\ *n* **1** : an act of puncturing **2** : a small hole made by puncturing

[2]**puncture** *vb* **punc·tured; punc·tur·ing 1** : to make a hole in : PIERCE **2** : to make useless as if by a puncture

pun·dit \ˈpən-dət\ *n* **1** : a learned person : TEACHER **2** : AUTHORITY

pun·gent \ˈpən-jənt\ *adj* **1** : having a sharp incisive quality : CAUSTIC ⟨a ~ editorial⟩ **2** : causing a sharp or irritating sensation; *esp* : ACRID ⟨~ smell of burning leaves⟩ — **pun·gen·cy** \-jən-sē\ *n* — **pun·gent·ly** *adv*

pun·ish \ˈpən-ish\ *vb* **1** : to impose a penalty on for a fault or crime ⟨~ an offender⟩ **2** : to inflict a penalty for ⟨~ treason with death⟩ **3** : to inflict injury on : HURT **syn** chastise, castigate, chasten, discipline, correct — **pun·ish·able** *adj*

pun·ish·ment \-mənt\ *n* **1** : retributive suffering, pain, or loss : PENALTY **2** : rough treatment

pu·ni·tive \ˈpyü-nət-iv\ *adj* : inflicting, involving, or aiming at punishment

[1]**punk** \ˈpəŋk\ *n* **1** : a young inexperienced person **2** : a petty hoodlum

[2]**punk** *adj* : very poor : INFERIOR

[3]**punk** *n* : dry crumbly wood useful for tinder; *also* : a substance made from fungi for use as tinder

pun·kin \ˈpəŋ-kən\ *var of* PUMPKIN

pun·ster \ˈpən-stər\ *n* : one who is given to punning

[1]**punt** \ˈpənt\ *n* : a long narrow flat-bottomed boat with square ends

[2]**punt** *vb* : to propel (as a punt) with a pole

[3]**punt** *vb* : to kick a football or soccer ball dropped from the hands before it touches the ground

[4]**punt** *n* : the act or an instance of punting a ball

pu·ny \ˈpyü-nē\ *adj* **pu·ni·er; -est** [MF *puisné* younger, lit., born afterward, fr. *puis* afterward (fr. L *post*) + *né* born, fr. L *natus*] : slight in power, size, or importance : WEAK

pup \ˈpəp\ *n* : a young dog; *also* : one of the young of some other animals

pu·pa \ˈpyü-pə\ *n, pl* **pu·pae** \-(ˌ)pē\ *or* **pupas** [NL, fr. L *pupa* girl, doll] : a form of some insects (as a bee, moth, or beetle) that occurs between the larva and the adult and is usu. enclosed in a cocoon or case — **pu·pal** \-pəl\ *adj*

[1]**pu·pil** \ˈpyü-pəl\ *n* **1** : a child or young person in school or in the charge of a tutor **2** : DISCIPLE

[2]**pupil** *n* : the dark central opening of the iris of the eye

pup·pet \ˈpəp-ət\ *n* [ME *popet*, fr. MF, deriv. of L *pupa*] **1** : a small figure of a person or animal moved by hand or by strings or wires **2** : DOLL **3** : one whose acts are controlled by an outside force

pup·pe·teer \ˌpəp-ə-ˈtiər\ *n* : one who manipulates puppets

pup·py \ˈpəp-ē\ *n, pl* **puppies** : a young dog

pur·blind \ˈpər-ˌblīnd\ *adj* **1** : partly blind **2** : lacking in insight : OBTUSE

[1]**pur·chase** \ˈpər-chəs\ *vb* **pur·chased; pur·chas·ing** : to obtain by paying money or its equivalent : BUY — **pur·chas·er** *n*

[2]**purchase** *n* **1** : an act or instance of purchasing **2** : something purchased **3** : a secure hold or grasp; *also* : advantageous leverage

pur·dah \ˈpərd-ə\ *n* : seclusion of women from public observation among Muslims and some Hindus esp. in India

pure \ˈpyu̇r\ *adj* **pur·er; pur·est 1** : unmixed with any other matter: : free from taint ⟨~ gold⟩ ⟨~ water⟩ **2** : SHEER, ABSOLUTE ⟨~ nonsense⟩ **3** : ABSTRACT, THEORETICAL ⟨~ mathematics⟩ **4** : free from what vitiates, weakens, or pollutes ⟨speaks a ~ French⟩ **5** : free from moral fault : INNOCENT **6** : CHASTE, CONTINENT — **pure·ly** *adv*

pure–blood·ed \-ˈbləd-əd\ *or* **pure–blood** *adj* : of unmixed ancestry : PUREBRED — **pure·blood** *n*

pure·bred \-ˈbred\ *adj* : bred from members of a recognized breed, strain, or kind without crossbreeding over many generations — **pure·bred** \-ˌbred\ *n*

[1]**pu·ree** \pyu̇-ˈrā, -ˈrē\ *n* [F, fr. MF, fr. fem. of *puré*, pp of *purer* to purify, strain, fr. L *purare* to purify] : a paste or thick liquid suspension usu. produced by rubbing cooked food through a sieve; *also* : a thick soup having vegetables so prepared as a base

[2]**puree** *vb* **pu·reed; pu·ree·ing** : to make a puree of

pur·ga·tion \ˌpər-ˈgā-shən\ *n* : the act or result of purging

[1]**pur·ga·tive** \ˈpər-gət-iv\ *adj* : purging or tending to purge; *also* : being a purgative

[2]**purgative** *n* : a strong laxative : CATHARTIC

pur·ga·to·ry \ˈpər-gə-ˌtōr-ē\ *n, pl* **-ries 1** : an intermediate state after death for expiatory purification **2** : a place or state of temporary punishment — **pur·ga·tor·i·al** \ˌpər-gə-ˈtōr-ē-əl\ *adj*

[1]**purge** \ˈpərj\ *vb* **purged; purg·ing 1** : to cleanse or purify esp. from sin **2** : to have or cause strong and usu. repeated emptying of the bowels **3** : to rid (as a political party) by a purge

[2]**purge** *n* **1** : something that purges; *esp* : PURGATIVE **2** : an act or result of purging; *esp* : a ridding of persons regarded as treacherous or disloyal

pu·ri·fy \ˈpyu̇r-ə-ˌfī\ *vb* **-fied; -fy·ing** : to make or become pure — **pu·ri·fi·ca·tion** \ˌpyu̇r-ə-fə-ˈkā-shən\ *n* — **pu·rif·i·ca·to·ry** \pyu̇-ˈrif-i-kə-ˌtōr-ē\ *adj* — **pu·ri·fi·er** \-ˌfī(-ə)r\ *n*

Pu·rim \ˈpu̇r-(ˌ)im\ *n* : a Jewish holiday celebrated in February or March in commemoration of the deliverance of the Jews from the massacre plotted by Haman

pu·rine \ˈpyu̇r-ˌēn\ *n* **1** : a base that is the parent of compounds of the uric-acid group **2** : a derivative of purine; *esp* : a base (as adenine or guanine) that is a constituent of DNA or RNA

pur·ism \ˈpyu̇r-ˌiz-əm\ *n* : rigid adherence to or insistence on purity or nicety esp. in use of words — **pur·ist** \-əst\ *n*

pu·ri·tan \ˈpyu̇r-ət-ᵊn\ *n* **1** *cap* : a member of a 16th and 17th century Protestant group in England and New England opposing the ceremonies and government of the Church of England **2** : one who practices or preaches a stricter or professedly purer moral code than that which prevails — **pu·ri·tan·i·cal** \ˌpyür-ə-ˈtan-i-kəl\ *adj*

pu·ri·ty \ˈpyu̇r-ət-ē\ *n* : the quality or state of being pure

[1]**purl** \ˈpərl\ *vb* : to knit in purl stitch

[2]**purl** *n* : a stitch in knitting

[3]**purl** *n* : a gentle murmur or movement (as of purling water)

[4]**purl** *vb* **1** : EDDY, SWIRL **2** : to make a soft murmuring sound

pur·lieu \ˈpərl-(y)ü\ *n* **1** : an outlying district : SUBURB **2** *pl* : ENVIRONS

pur·loin \(ˌ)pər-ˈlȯin, ˈpər-ˌlȯin\ *vb* : to appropriate wrongfully : FILCH

[1]**pur·ple** \ˈpər-pəl\ *adj* **pur·pler** \-p(ə-)lər\; **pur·plest** \-p(ə-)ləst\ **1** : of the color purple **2** : highly rhetorical ⟨a ~ passage⟩ **3** : PROFANE ⟨~ language⟩ — **pur·plish** \ˈpər-p(ə-)lish\ *adj*

[2]**purple** *n* **1** : a bluish red color **2** : a purple robe emblematic esp. of regal rank or authority

[1]**pur·port** \ˈpər-ˌpōrt\ *n* : meaning conveyed or implied; *also* : GIST

[2]**pur·port** \(ˌ)pər-ˈpōrt\ *vb* : to convey or profess outwardly as the meaning or intention : CLAIM — **pur·port·ed·ly** \-əd-lē\ *adv*

[1]**pur·pose** \ˈpər-pəs\ *n* **1** : an object or result aimed at : INTENTION **2** : RESOLUTION, DETERMINATION — **pur·pose·ful** \-fəl\ *adj* — **pur·pose·ful·ly** \-ē\ *adv* — **pur·pose·less** *adj* — **pur·pose·ly** *adv*

[2]**purpose** *vb* **pur·posed; pur·pos·ing** : to propose as an aim to oneself

purr \ˈpər\ *n* **:** a low murmur typical of a contented cat — **purr** *vb*

[1]**purse** \ˈpərs\ *n* **1 :** a receptacle (as a pouch) to carry money and often other small objects in **2 :** RESOURCES **3 :** a sum of money offered as a prize or present

[2]**purse** *vb* **pursed; purs·ing :** PUCKER

purs·er \ˈpər-sər\ *n* **:** an official on a ship who keeps accounts and attends to the comfort of passengers

purs·lane \ˈpər-slən, -ˌslān\ *n* **:** a fleshy-leaved weedy trailing plant with tiny yellow flowers that is sometimes used in salads

pur·su·ance \pər-ˈsü-əns\ *n* **:** the act of carrying into effect

pur·su·ant to \-ˈsü-ənt-\ *prep* **:** in carrying out **:** ACCORDING TO ⟨*pursuant to* your instructions⟩

pur·sue \pər-ˈsü\ *vb* **pur·sued; pur·su·ing 1 :** to follow in order to overtake or overcome **:** CHASE **2 :** to seek to accomplish ⟨~*s* his aims⟩ **3 :** to proceed along ⟨~ a course⟩ **4 :** to engage in ⟨~ a vocation⟩ — **pur·su·er** *n*

pur·suit \pər-ˈsüt\ *n* **1 :** the act of pursuing **2 :** OCCUPATION, BUSINESS

pu·ru·lent \ˈpyůr-(y)ə-lənt\ *adj* **:** containing or accompanied by pus — **pu·ru·lence** \-ləns\ *n*

pur·vey \(ˌ)pər-ˈvā\ *vb* **pur·veyed; pur·vey·ing :** to supply (as provisions) usu. as a business — **pur·vey·ance** \-əns\ *n* — **pur·vey·or** \-ər\ *n*

pur·view \ˈpər-ˌvyü\ *n* **1 :** the range or limit esp. of authority, responsibility, or intention **2 :** range of vision, understanding, or cognizance

pus \ˈpəs\ *n* **:** thick yellowish white fluid matter (as in a boil) formed at a place of inflammation and infection (as an abscess) and containing germs, blood cells, and tissue debris

[1]**push** \ˈpůsh\ *vb* [ME *pusshen,* fr. OF *poulser* to beat, push, fr. L *pulsare,* fr. *pulsus,* pp. of *pellere* to drive, strike] **1 :** to press against with force in order to drive or impel **2 :** to thrust forward, downward, or outward **3 :** to urge on **:** press forward **4 :** to urge or press the advancement, adoption, or practice of; *esp* **:** to make aggressive efforts to sell **5 :** to engage in the illicit sale of narcotics

[2]**push** *n* **1 :** a vigorous effort **:** DRIVE **2 :** an act of pushing **:** SHOVE **3 :** vigorous enterprise **:** ENERGY

push–button *adj* **:** using or dependent on complex and more or less automatic mechanisms ⟨~ warfare⟩

push button *n* **:** a small button or knob that when pushed operates something esp. by closing an electric circuit

push·cart \ˈpůsh-ˌkärt\ *n* **:** a cart or barrow pushed by hand

push·er \-ər\ *n* **:** one that pushes; *esp* **:** one that pushes illegal drugs

push·over \-ˌō-vər\ *n* **1 :** an opponent easy to defeat **2 :** SUCKER **3 :** something easily accomplished

push–up \-ˌəp\ *n* **:** a conditioning exercise performed in a prone position by raising and lowering the body with the straightening and bending of the arms while keeping the back straight and supporting the body on the hands and toes

pushy \ˈpůsh-ē\ *adj* **push·i·er; -est :** aggressive often to an objectionable degree

pu·sil·lan·i·mous \ˌpyü-sə-ˈlan-ə-məs\ *adj* [LL *pusillanimis,* fr. L *pusillus* very small (dim. of *pusus* small child) + *animus* spirit] **:** contemptibly timid **:** COWARDLY — **pu·sil·la·nim·i·ty** \ˌpyü-sə-lə-ˈnim-ət-ē\ *n*

[1]**puss** \ˈpůs\ *n* **:** CAT

[2]**puss** *n* **:** FACE

[1]**pussy** \ˈpůs-ē\ *n, pl* **puss·ies :** CAT

[2]**pus·sy** \ˈpəs-ē\ *adj* **pus·si·er; -est :** full of or resembling pus

pussy·cat \ˈpůs-ē-ˌkat\ *n* **:** CAT

pussy·foot \ˈpůs-ē-ˌfůt\ *vb* **1 :** to tread or move warily or stealthily **2 :** to refrain from committing oneself

pussy willow \ˌpůs-ē-\ *n* **:** a willow having large silky catkins

pus·tule \ˈpəs-chül\ *n* **:** a pus-filled pimple

put \ˈpůt\ *vb* **put; put·ting 1 :** to bring into a specified position **:** PLACE ⟨~ the book on the table⟩ **2 :** SEND, THRUST **3 :** to throw with an upward pushing motion ⟨~ the shot⟩ **4 :** to bring into a specified state ⟨~ the plan into effect⟩ **5 :** SUBJECT ⟨~ traitors to death⟩ **6 :** IMPOSE **7 :** to set before one for decision ⟨~ the question⟩ **8 :** EXPRESS, STATE **9 :** TRANSLATE, ADAPT **10 :** APPLY, ASSIGN ⟨~ them to work⟩ **11 :** to give as an estimate ⟨~ the number at 20⟩ **12 :** ATTACH, ATTRIBUTE ⟨~ a high value on it⟩ **13 :** to take a specified course ⟨the ship ~ out to sea⟩

pu·ta·tive \ˈpyüt-ət-iv\ *adj* **1 :** commonly accepted **2 :** INFERRED

put–down \ˈpůt-ˌdaůn\ *n* **:** a belittling remark **:** SQUELCH

put in *vb* **1 :** to come in with **:** INTERPOSE ⟨*put in* a good word for me⟩ **2 :** to spend time at some occupation or job ⟨*put in* eight hours at the office⟩

put off *vb* **:** POSTPONE, DELAY

[1]**put–on** \ˌpůt-ˌȯn, -ˌän\ *adj* **:** PRETENDED, ASSUMED

[2]**put–on** \ˈpůt-ˌȯn, -ˌän\ *n* **:** a deliberate act of misleading someone; *also* **:** PARODY, SPOOF

put·out \ˈpůt-ˌaůt\ *n* **:** the retiring of a base runner or batter in baseball

put out \ˌpůt-ˈaůt\ *vb* **1 :** EXTINGUISH **2 :** ANNOY; *also* **:** INCONVENIENCE **3 :** to cause to be out (as in baseball)

pu·tre·fy \ˈpyü-trə-ˌfī\ *vb* **-fied; -fy·ing :** to make or become putrid **:** ROT — **pu·tre·fac·tion** \ˌpyü-trə-ˈfak-shən\ *n* — **pu·tre·fac·tive** \-tiv\ *adj*

pu·tres·cent \pyü-ˈtres-ᵊnt\ *adj* **:** becoming putrid **:** ROTTING — **pu·tres·cence** \-ᵊns\ *n*

pu·trid \ˈpyü-trəd\ *adj* **1 :** ROTTEN, DECAYED **2 :** VILE, CORRUPT — **pu·trid·i·ty** \pyü-ˈtrid-ət-ē\ *n*

putsch \ˈpůch\ *n* [G] **:** a secretly plotted and suddenly executed attempt to overthrow a government

putt \ˈpət\ *n* **:** a golf stroke made on the green to cause the ball to roll into the hole — **putt** *vb*

put·tee \ˌpə-ˈtē, ˈpət-ē\ *n* [Hindi *paṭṭī* strip of cloth] **1 :** a cloth strip wrapped around the lower leg **2 :** a leather legging

[1]**put·ter** \ˈpůt-ər\ *n* **:** one that puts

[2]**putt·er** \ˈpət-ər\ *n* **1 :** a golf club used in putting **2 :** one that putts

[3]**put·ter** \ˈpət-ər\ *vb* **1 :** to move or act aimlessly or idly **2 :** TINKER

put·ty \ˈpət-ē\ *n, pl* **putties** [F *potée,* lit., potful, fr. OF, fr. *pot,* of Gmc origin] **:** a doughlike cement usu. of whiting and linseed oil used esp. to fasten glass in sashes — **putty** *vb*

[1]**puz·zle** \ˈpəz-əl\ *vb* **puz·zled; puz·zling** \-(ə-)liŋ\ **1 :** to bewilder mentally **:** CONFUSE, PERPLEX **2 :** to solve with difficulty or ingenuity ⟨~ out a mystery⟩ **3 :** to be in a quandary ⟨~ over what to do⟩ **4 :** to attempt a solution of a puzzle ⟨~ over a person's words⟩ **syn** mystify, bewilder, nonplus, confound — **puz·zle·ment** *n* — **puz·zler** \-(ə-)lər\ *n*

[2]**puzzle** *n* **1 :** something that puzzles **2 :** a question, problem, or contrivance designed for testing ingenuity

PVC *abbr* polyvinyl chloride

pvt *abbr* private

PW *abbr* prisoner of war

pwt *abbr* pennyweight

PX *abbr* post exchange

pya \pē-ˈä\ *n* — see *kyat* at MONEY table

pyg·my \ˈpig-mē\ *n, pl* **pygmies** [ME *pigmei,* fr. L *pygmaeus* of a pygmy, dwarfish, fr. Gk *pygmaios,* fr.

pygmē fist, measure of length] **1** *cap* : any of a small people of equatorial Africa **2** : DWARF — **pygmy** *adj*

py·ja·mas \pə-ˈjä-məz\ *chiefly Brit var of* PAJAMAS

py·lon \ˈpī-ˌlän, -lən\ *n* **1** : a usu. massive gateway; *esp* : an Egyptian one flanked by flat-topped pyramids **2** : a tower that supports a long span of wire **3** : a post or tower marking a prescribed course of flight for an airplane

py·or·rhea \ˌpī-ə-ˈrē-ə\ *n* : an inflammation with pus of the sockets of the teeth

[1]**pyr·a·mid** \ˈpir-ə-ˌmid\ *n* **1** : a massive structure with a square base and four triangular faces meeting at a point **2** : a geometrical solid having a polygon for its base and three or more triangles for its sides that meet at a point to form the top — **py·ra·mi·dal** \pə-ˈram-əd-ᵊl, ˌpir-ə-ˈmid-\ *adj*

[2]**pyramid** *vb* **1** : to build up in the form of a pyramid : heap up **2** : to increase rapidly on a broadening base

pyre \ˈpī(ə)r\ *n* : a combustible heap for burning a dead body as a funeral rite

py·re·thrum \pī-ˈrē-thrəm\ *n* : an insecticide consisting of the dried heads of any of several Old World chrysanthemums

py·rim·i·dine \pī-ˈrim-ə-ˌdēn\ *n* : any of a group of bases including several (as cytosine, thymine, or uracil) that are constituents of DNA or RNA

py·rite \ˈpī-ˌrīt\ *n* : a mineral containing sulfur and iron that is brass-yellow in color

py·rol·y·sis \pī-ˈräl-ə-səs\ *n* : chemical change brought about by the action of heat

py·ro·ma·nia \ˌpī-rō-ˈmā-nē-ə\ *n* : an irresistible impulse to start fires — **py·ro·ma·ni·ac** \-nē-ˌak\ *n*

py·ro·tech·nics \ˌpī-rə-ˈtek-niks\ *n pl* **1** : a display of fireworks **2** : a spectacular display (as of oratory) — **py·ro·tech·nic** \-nik\ *also* **py·ro·tech·ni·cal** \-ni-kəl\ *adj*

py·rox·ene \pī-ˈräk-ˌsēn\ *n* : any of various minerals that are silicates and usu. contain aluminum, calcium, sodium, magnesium, or iron

Pyr·rhic victory \ˌpir-ik-\ *n* [*Pyrrhus*, king of Epirus who sustained heavy losses in defeating the Romans] : a victory won at excessive cost

py·thon \ˈpī-ˌthän, -thən\ *n* [L, monstrous serpent killed by the god Apollo, fr. Gk *Pythōn*] : a large snake (as a boa) that squeezes and suffocates its prey; *esp* : any of an Old World genus including the largest snakes living at the present time

pyx \ˈpiks\ *n* : a small case used to carry the Eucharist to the sick

Q

[1]**q** \ˈkyü\ *n, pl* **q's** *or* **qs** \ˈkyüz\ *often cap* : the 17th letter of the English alphabet

[2]**q** *abbr, often cap* **1** quart **2** quarto **3** queen **4** query **5** question

QC *abbr* Queen's Counsel

QED *abbr* [L *quod erat demonstrandum*] which was to be demonstrated

QEF *abbr* [L *quod erat faciendum*] which was to be done

QEI *abbr* [L *quod erat inveniendum*] which was to be found out

qin·tar \kin-ˈtär\ *n, pl* **qin·dar·ka** \kin-ˈdär-kə\ *or* **qintar** — see *lek* at MONEY table

qi·vi·ut \ˈkē-vē-ˌüt\ *n* [Esk] : the wool of the undercoat of the musk-ox

Qld *or* **Q'land** *abbr* Queensland

QM *abbr* quartermaster

QMC *abbr* quartermaster corps

QMG *abbr* quartermaster general

qq v *abbr* [L *quae vide*] which (*pl*) see

qr *abbr* quarter

[1]**qt** \ˈkyü-ˈtē\ *n, often cap Q&T* : QUIET — usu. used in the phrase *on the qt*

[2]**qt** *abbr* **1** quantity **2** quart

qto *abbr* quarto

qty *abbr* quantity

qu *or* **ques** *abbr* question

[1]**quack** \ˈkwak\ *vb* : to make the characteristic cry of a duck

[2]**quack** *n* : the cry of a duck

[3]**quack** *n* **1** : CHARLATAN **2** : a pretender to medical skill **syn** faker, impostor, mountebank — **quack** *adj* — **quack·ery** \-ə-rē\ *n* — **quack·ish** *adj*

[1]**quad** \ˈkwäd\ *n* : QUADRANGLE

[2]**quad** *n* : QUADRUPLET

[3]**quad** *abbr* quadrant

quad·ran·gle \ˈkwäd-ˌraŋ-gəl\ *n* **1** : a flat geometrical figure having four angles and four sides **2** : a 4-sided courtyard or enclosure — **quad·ran·gu·lar** \kwä-ˈdraŋ-gyə-lər\ *adj*

quad·rant \ˈkwäd-rənt\ *n* **1** : an instrument for measuring angular elevation used esp. in astronomy and surveying **2** : one quarter of a circle : an arc of 90° **3** : any of the four quarters into which something is divided by two lines intersecting each other at right angles

quad·ra·phon·ic \ˌkwäd-rə-ˈfän-ik\ *adj* : of or relating to the transmission, recording, or reproduction of sound using four transmission channels

qua·drat·ic \kwä-ˈdrat-ik\ *adj* : having or being a term in which the variable (as *x*) is squared but containing no term in which the variable is raised to a higher power than a square ⟨a ~ equation⟩ — **quadratic** *n*

qua·dren·ni·al \kwä-ˈdren-ē-əl\ *adj* **1** : consisting of or lasting for four years **2** : occurring every four years

qua·dren·ni·um \-ē-əm\ *n, pl* **-ni·ums** *or* **-nia** \-ē-ə\ : a period of four years

[1]**quad·ri·lat·er·al** \ˌkwäd-rə-ˈlat-(ə-)rəl\ *n* : a polygon of four sides

[2]**quadrilateral** *adj* : having four sides

qua·drille \kwä-ˈdril, k(w)ə-\ *n* : a square dance made up of five or six figures in various rhythms

quad·ri·par·tite \ˌkwäd-rə-ˈpär-ˌtīt\ *adj* **1** : consisting of four parts **2** : shared by four parties or persons

quad·ri·phon·ics \-ˈfän-iks\ *n* : QUADRIPHONY

quad·ri·phony \ˈkwäd-rə-ˌfän-ē\ *n* : quadraphonic transmission, recording, or reproduction of sound

qua·driv·i·um \kwä-ˈdriv-ē-əm\ *n* : the four liberal arts of arithmetic, music, geometry, and astronomy in a medieval university

quad·ru·ped \ˈkwäd-rə-ˌped\ *n* : an animal having four feet — **qua·dru·pe·dal** \kwä-ˈdrü-pəd-ᵊl, ˌkwäd-rə-ˈped-\ *adj*

[1]**qua·dru·ple** \kwä-ˈdrüp-əl, -ˈdrəp-; ˈkwäd-rəp-\ *vb* **qua·dru·pled; qua·dru·pling** \-(ə-)liŋ\ : to make or become four times as great or as many

[2]**quadruple** *adj* : FOURFOLD

qua·dru·plet \kwä-ˈdrəp-lət, -ˈdrüp-; ˈkwäd-rəp-\ *n* **1** : one of four offspring born at one birth **2** : a group of four of a kind

[1]**qua·dru·pli·cate** \kwä-ˈdrü-pli-kət\ *adj* **1** : repeated four times **2** : FOURTH

[2]**qua·dru·pli·cate** \-plə-ˌkāt\ *vb* **-cat·ed; -cat·ing** **1** : QUA-

DRUPLE **2** : to provide in quadruplicate — **qua·dru·pli·ca·tion** \-ˌdrü-plə-ˈkā-shən\ *n*

[3]**qua·dru·pli·cate** \-ˈdrü-pli-kət\ *n* **1** : four copies all alike ⟨typed in ~⟩ **2** : one of four like things

quaff \ˈkwäf, ˈkwaf\ *vb* : to drink deeply or repeatedly — **quaff** *n*

quag·mire \ˈkwag-ˌmī(ə)r, ˈkwäg-\ *n* **1** : soft miry land that yields under the foot **2** : a difficult situation from which it is hard to escape

qua·hog \ˈkō-ˌhȯg, ˈkwȯ-, ˈkwō-, -ˌhäg\ *n* : a round thick-shelled American clam

quai \ˈkā\ *n* : QUAY

[1]**quail** \ˈkwāl\ *n, pl* **quail** *or* **quails** [ME *quaille*, fr. MF, fr. ML *quaccula*, of imit. origin] : any of various short-winged stout-bodied game birds (as a bobwhite) related to the domestic chicken

[2]**quail** *vb* [ME *quailen* to curdle, fr. MF *quailler*, fr. L *coagulare*, fr. *coagulum* curdling agent, fr. *cogere* to drive together] : to lose heart : COWER **syn** recoil, shrink, flinch, wince, blanch

quaint \ˈkwānt\ *adj* : unusual or different in character or appearance; *esp* : pleasingly old-fashioned or unfamiliar **syn** odd, queer, curious, strange — **quaint·ly** *adv* — **quaint·ness** *n*

[1]**quake** \ˈkwāk\ *vb* **quaked; quak·ing 1** : to shake usu. from shock or instability **2** : to tremble usu. from cold or fear

[2]**quake** *n* : a shaking or trembling; *esp* : EARTHQUAKE

Quak·er \ˈkwā-kər\ *n* : FRIEND 5

quaking aspen *n* : an aspen of the U.S. and Canada that has small nearly circular leaves with flattened petioles and finely serrate margins

qual *abbr* quality

qual·i·fi·ca·tion \ˌkwäl-ə-fə-ˈkā-shən\ *n* **1** : LIMITATION, MODIFICATION **2** : a special skill that fits a person for some work or position

qual·i·fied \ˈkwäl-ə-ˌfīd\ *adj* **1** : fitted for a given purpose **2** : limited in some way

qual·i·fi·er \ˈkwäl-ə-ˌfī-ər\ *n* **1** : one that satisfies requirements **2** : a word or word group that limits the meaning of another word or word group

qual·i·fy \ˈkwäl-ə-ˌfī\ *vb* **-fied; -fy·ing 1** : to reduce from a general to a particular form : MODIFY **2** : to make less harsh **3** : to limit the meaning of (as a noun) **4** : to fit by skill or training for some purpose **5** : to give or have a legal right to do something **6** : to demonstrate the necessary ability (as in a preliminary race) **syn** moderate, temper

qual·i·ta·tive \ˈkwäl-ə-ˌtāt-iv\ *adj* : of, relating to, or involving quality — **qual·i·ta·tive·ly** *adv*

[1]**qual·i·ty** \ˈkwäl-ət-ē\ *n, pl* **-ties 1** : peculiar and essential character : NATURE **2** : degree of excellence **3** : high social status **4** : a distinguishing attribute

[2]**quality** *adj* : being of high quality

qualm \ˈkwäm\ *n* **1** : a sudden attack (as of nausea) **2** : a sudden misgiving **3** : SCRUPLE

qualm·ish \-ish\ *adj* **1** : feeling qualms : NAUSEATED **2** : overly scrupulous : SQUEAMISH **3** : of, relating to, or producing qualms

quan·da·ry \ˈkwän-d(ə-)rē\ *n, pl* **-ries** : a state of perplexity or doubt

quan·ti·ta·tive \ˈkwän-tə-ˌtāt-iv\ *adj* : of, relating to, or involving quantity — **quan·ti·ta·tive·ly** *adv*

quan·ti·ty \ˈkwän-tət-ē\ *n, pl* **-ties 1** : AMOUNT, NUMBER **2** : a considerable amount

quan·tize \ˈkwän-ˌtīz\ *vb* **quan·tized; quan·tiz·ing** : to subdivide (as energy) into small units

quan·tum \ˈkwänt-əm\ *n, pl* **quan·ta** \-ə\ [L, neut. of *quantus* how much] **1** : QUANTITY, AMOUNT **2** : an elemental unit of energy

quantum mechanics *n sing or pl* : a general mathematical theory dealing with the interactions of matter and radiation in terms of observable quantities only — **quantum mechanical** *adj* — **quantum mechanically** *adv*

quar·an·tine \ˈkwȯr-ən-ˌtēn\ *n* [It *quarantina*, lit., period of forty days, fr. MF *quarantaine*, fr. OF, fr. *quarante* forty, fr. L *quadraginta*] **1** : a period during which a ship suspected of carrying contagious disease is forbidden contact with the shore **2** : a restraint on the movements of persons or goods to prevent the spread of pests or disease **3** : a place or period of quarantine — **quarantine** *vb*

quark \ˈkwȯrk, ˈkwärk\ *n* : a hypothetical particle that carries a fractional charge and is held to be a constituent of heavier particles (as protons and neutrons)

[1]**quar·rel** \ˈkwȯr(-ə)l\ *n* **1** : a ground of dispute **2** : a verbal clash : CONFLICT — **quar·rel·some** \-səm\ *adj*

[2]**quarrel** *vb* **-reled** *or* **-relled; -rel·ing** *or* **-rel·ling 1** : to find fault **2** : to dispute angrily : WRANGLE

[1]**quar·ry** \ˈkwȯr-ē\ *n, pl* **quarries** [ME *querre* entrails of game given to the hounds, fr. MF *cuiree*] **1** : game hunted with hawks **2** : PREY

[2]**quarry** *n, pl* **quarries** [ME *quarey*, alter. of *quarrere*, fr. MF *quarriere*, fr. (assumed) OF *quarre* squared stone, fr. L *quadrum* square] : an open excavation usu. for obtaining building stone, slate, or limestone — **quarry** *vb*

[1]**quart** \ˈkwȯrt\ *n* — see WEIGHT table

[2]**quart** *abbr* quarterly

[1]**quar·ter** \ˈkwȯrt-ər\ *n* **1** : one of four equal parts **2** : a fourth of a dollar; *also* : a coin of this value **3** : a district of a city **4** *pl* : LODGINGS ⟨moved into new ~*s*⟩ **5** : MERCY, CLEMENCY ⟨gave no ~⟩ **6** : a fourth part of the moon's period

[2]**quarter** *vb* **1** : to divide into four equal parts **2** : to provide with shelter

[1]**quar·ter·back** \-ˌbak\ *n* : a football player who calls the signals for his team

[2]**quarterback** *vb* **1** : to direct the offensive play of a football team **2** : LEAD, BOSS

quar·ter·deck \-ˌdek\ *n* : the stern area of a ship's upper deck

quarter horse *n* : a compact muscular saddle horse characterized by great endurance and by high speed for short distances

[1]**quar·ter·ly** \ˈkwȯrt-ər-lē\ *adv* : at 3-month intervals

[2]**quarterly** *adj* : occurring, issued, or payable at 3-month intervals

[3]**quarterly** *n, pl* **-lies** : a periodical published four times a year

quar·ter·mas·ter \-ˌmas-tər\ *n* **1** : a petty officer who attends to a ship's helm, binnacle, and signals **2** : an army officer who provides clothing and subsistence for troops

quar·ter·staff \-ˌstaf\ *n, pl* **-staves** \-ˌstavz, -ˌstāvz\ : a long stout staff formerly used as a weapon

quar·tet *also* **quar·tette** \kwȯr-ˈtet\ *n* **1** : a musical composition for four instruments or voices **2** : a group of four and esp. of four musicians

quar·to \ˈkwȯrt-ō\ *n, pl* **quartos 1** : the size of a piece of paper cut four from a sheet **2** : a book printed on quarto pages

quartz \ˈkwȯrts\ *n* : a common often transparent crystalline mineral that is a form of silica

quartz heater *n* : a portable electric heater whose heating elements are sealed in quartz-glass tubes

quartz·ite \ˈkwȯrt-ˌsīt\ *n* : a compact granular rock composed of quartz and derived from sandstone

qua·sar \ˈkwā-ˌzär, -ˌsär\ *n* : any of various distant starlike celestial objects that are powerful emitters of electromagnetic radiation (as blue light and radio waves)

quash \ˈkwäsh, ˈkwȯsh\ *vb* **1** : to set aside by judicial action : VOID **2** : to suppress or extinguish summarily and completely : QUELL

qua·si \ˈkwā-ˌzī, -ˌsī; ˈkwäz-ē, ˈkwäs-\ *adj* : being in some sense or degree ⟨a ~ corporation⟩

quasi- *comb form* [L, as if, as it were, approximately, fr. *quam* as + *si* if] : in some sense or degree ⟨*quasi*-historical⟩

Qua·ter·na·ry \ˈkwät-ər-ˌner-ē, kwə-ˈtər-nə-rē\ *adj* : of, relating to, or being the geologic period from the end of the Tertiary to the present — **Quaternary** *n*

qua·train \ˈkwä-ˌtrān\ *n* : a unit of four lines of verse

qua·tre·foil \ˈkat-ər-ˌfȯil, ˈkat-rə-\ *n* : a conventionalized representation of a flower with four petals or of a leaf with four leaflets

qua·ver \ˈkwā-vər\ *vb* **qua·vered; qua·ver·ing** \ˈkwāv-(ə-)riŋ\ **1** : TREMBLE, SHAKE **2** : TRILL **3** : to speak in tremulous tones **syn** shudder, quake, twitter, quiver, shiver — **quaver** *n*

quay \ˈkē, ˈk(w)ā\ *n* : WHARF

Que *abbr* Quebec

quean \ˈkwēn\ *n* : PROSTITUTE

quea·sy \ˈkwē-zē\ *adj* **quea·si·er; -est** : NAUSEATED — **quea·si·ly** \-zə-lē\ *adv* — **quea·si·ness** \-zē-nəs\ *n*

queen \ˈkwēn\ *n* **1** : the wife or widow of a king **2** : a female monarch **3** : a woman notable for rank, power, or attractiveness **4** : the most privileged piece in the game of chess **5** : a playing card bearing the figure of a queen **6** : a fertile female of a social insect (as a bee or termite) — **queen·ly** *adj*

Queen Anne's lace \-ˈanz-\ *n* : WILD CARROT

queen consort *n, pl* **queens consort** : the wife of a reigning king

queen mother *n* : a dowager queen who is mother of the reigning sovereign

queen–size *adj* : having dimensions of approximately 60 inches by 80 inches ⟨~ bed⟩; *also* : of a size that fits a queen-size bed

[1]queer \ˈkwiər\ *adj* **1** : differing from the usual or normal : PECULIAR, STRANGE **2** : COUNTERFEIT **syn** weird, bizarre, eccentric, curious — **queer** *n* — **queer·ly** *adv* — **queer·ness** *n*

[2]queer *vb* : to spoil the effect of : DISRUPT ⟨~*ed* our plans⟩

quell \ˈkwel\ *vb* : to put an end to by force : CRUSH ⟨~ a riot⟩

quench \ˈkwench\ *vb* **1** : PUT OUT, EXTINGUISH **2** : SUBDUE **3** : SLAKE, SATISFY ⟨~*ed* his thirst⟩ **4** : to cool (as heated steel) suddenly by immersion esp. in water or oil — **quench·able** *adj* — **quench·less** *adj*

quer·u·lous \ˈkwer-(y)ə-ləs\ *adj* **1** : constantly complaining **2** : FRETFUL, WHINING **syn** petulant, pettish, irritable, peevish, huffy — **quer·u·lous·ly** *adv* — **quer·u·lous·ness** *n*

que·ry \ˈkwi(ə)r-ē, ˈkwe(ə)r-\ *n, pl* **queries** : QUESTION — **query** *vb*

quest \ˈkwest\ *n* : SEARCH — **quest** *vb*

[1]ques·tion \ˈkwes-chən\ *n* **1** : an interrogative expression : QUERY **2** : a subject for discussion or debate; *also* : a proposition to be voted on in a meeting **3** : INQUIRY **4** : DISPUTE

[2]question *vb* **1** : to ask questions **2** : DOUBT, DISPUTE **3** : to subject to analysis : EXAMINE **syn** ask, interrogate, quiz, query — **ques·tion·er** *n*

ques·tion·able \ˈkwes-chə-nə-bəl\ *adj* **1** : not certain or exact : DOUBTFUL **2** : not believed to be true, sound, or moral **syn** dubious, problematical, moot, debatable

question mark *n* : a punctuation mark ? used esp. at the end of a sentence to indicate a direct question

ques·tion·naire \ˌkwes-chə-ˈna(ə)r\ *n* : a set of questions for obtaining information

quet·zal \ket-ˈsäl, -ˈsal\ *n, pl* **quetzals** *or* **quet·za·les** \-ˈsäl-ās, -ˈsal-\ **1** : a Central American bird with brilliant plumage **2** *pl quetzales* — see MONEY table

[1]queue \ˈkyü\ *n* [F, lit., tail, fr. L *cauda, coda*] **1** : a braid of hair usu. worn hanging at the back of the head **2** : a line esp. of persons or vehicles

[2]queue *vb* **queued; queu·ing** *or* **queue·ing** : to line up in a queue

quib·ble \ˈkwib-əl\ *n* **1** : an evasion of or shifting from the point at issue **2** : a minor objection — **quibble** *vb*

[1]quick \ˈkwik\ *adj* **1** *archaic* : LIVING **2** : RAPID, SPEEDY ⟨~ steps⟩ **3** : prompt to understand, think, or perceive : ALERT **4** : easily aroused ⟨a ~ temper⟩ **5** : turning or bending sharply ⟨a ~ turn in the road⟩ **syn** fleet, fast, hasty, expeditious — **quick** *adv* — **quick·ly** *adv* — **quick·ness** *n*

[2]quick *n* **1** : sensitive living flesh **2** : a vital part : HEART

quick bread *n* : a bread made with a leavening agent that permits immediate baking of the dough or batter mixture

quick·en \ˈkwik-ən\ *vb* **quick·ened; quick·en·ing** \-(ə-)niŋ\ **1** : to come to life : REVIVE **2** : AROUSE, STIMULATE **3** : to increase in speed : HASTEN **4** : to show vitality (as by growing or moving) **syn** animate, enliven, liven, vivify

quick–freeze \ˈkwik-ˈfrēz\ *vb* **-froze** \-ˈfrōz\; **-fro·zen** \-ˈfrōz-ᵊn\; **-freez·ing** : to freeze (food) for preservation so rapidly that ice crystals formed are too small to rupture the cells

quick·ie \ˈkwik-ē\ *n* : something hurriedly done or made

quick·lime \ˈkwik-ˌlīm\ *n* : the first solid product obtained by calcining limestone

quick·sand \-ˌsand\ *n* : a deep mass of loose sand mixed with water

quick·sil·ver \-ˌsil-vər\ *n* : MERCURY

quick·step \-ˌstep\ *n* : a spirited march tune esp. accompanying a march in quick time

quick time *n* : a rate of marching in which 120 steps each 30 inches in length are taken in one minute

quick–wit·ted \ˈkwik-ˈwit-əd\ *adj* : mentally alert **syn** clever, bright, smart, intelligent

quid \ˈkwid\ *n* : a cut or wad of something chewable ⟨a ~ of tobacco⟩

quid pro quo \ˌkwid-ˌprō-ˈkwō\ *n* [NL, something for something] : something given or received for something else

qui·es·cent \kwī-ˈes-ᵊnt\ *adj* : being at rest : QUIET **syn** latent, dormant, potential — **qui·es·cence** \-əns\ *n*

[1]qui·et \ˈkwī-ət\ *n* : REPOSE

[2]quiet *adj* **1** : marked by little motion or activity : CALM **2** : GENTLE, MILD ⟨a man of ~ disposition⟩ **3** : enjoyed in peace and relaxation ⟨a ~ cup of tea⟩ **4** : free from noise or uproar **5** : not showy : MODEST ⟨~ clothes⟩ **6** : SECLUDED ⟨a ~ nook⟩ — **quiet** *adv* — **qui·et·ly** *adv* — **qui·et·ness** *n*

[3]quiet *vb* **1** : CALM, PACIFY **2** : to become quiet ⟨~ down⟩

qui·etude \ˈkwī-ə-ˌt(y)üd\ *n* : QUIETNESS, REPOSE

qui·etus \kwī-ˈēt-əs\ *n* [ME *quietus est,* fr. ML, he is quit, formula of discharge from obligation] **1** : final settlement (as of a debt) **2** : DEATH

quill \ˈkwil\ *n* **1** : a large stiff feather; *also* : the hollow tubular part of a feather **2** : one of the hollow sharp spines of a hedgehog or porcupine **3** : a pen made from a feather

[1]quilt \ˈkwilt\ *n* : a padded bed coverlet

[2]quilt *vb* **1** : to fill, pad, or line like a quilt **2** : to stitch or sew in layers with padding in between **3** : to make quilts

quince \ˈkwins\ *n* : a hard yellow applelike fruit; *also* : a tree related to the roses that bears this fruit

qui·nine \ˈkwī-ˌnīn\ *n* : a bitter white drug obtained from cinchona bark and used esp. in treating malaria

quin·sy \ˈkwin-zē\ *n* : a severe inflammation of the throat or adjacent parts with swelling and fever

quint \ˈkwint\ *n* : QUINTUPLET

quin·tal \ˈkwint-ᵊl, ˈkant-\ *n* : HUNDREDWEIGHT

quin·tes·sence \kwin-ˈtes-ᵊns\ *n* **1** : the purest essence of something **2** : the most typical example — **quint·es·sen·tial** \ˌkwint-ə-ˈsen-chəl\ *adj*

quin·tet *also* **quin·tette** \kwin-ˈtet\ *n* **1** : a musical composition for five instruments or voices **2** : a group of five and esp. of five musicians; *also* : a basketball team

¹quin·tu·ple \kwin-ˈt(y)üp-əl, -ˈtəp-; ˈkwint-əp-\ *adj* **1** : having five units or members **2** : being five times as great or as many — **quintuple** *n*

²quintuple *vb* **quin·tu·pled; quin·tu·pling** : to make or become five times as great or as many

quin·tu·plet \kwin-ˈtəp-lət, -ˈt(y)üp-; ˈkwint-əp-\ *n* **1** : a group of five of a kind **2** : one of five offspring born at one birth

¹quin·tu·pli·cate \kwin-ˈt(y)ü-pli-kət\ *adj* **1** : repeated five times **2** : FIFTH

²quintuplicate *n* **1** : one of five like things **2** : five copies all alike ⟨typed in ~⟩

³quin·tu·pli·cate \-plə-ˌkāt\ *vb* **-cat·ed; -cat·ing 1** : QUINTUPLE **2** : to provide in quintuplicate

¹quip \ˈkwip\ *n* : a clever remark : GIBE

²quip *vb* **quipped; quip·ping 1** : to make quips : GIBE **2** : to jest or gibe at

quire \ˈkwī(ə)r\ *n* : a set of 24 or sometimes 25 sheets of paper of the same size and quality

quirk \ˈkwərk\ *n* : a peculiarity of action or behavior — **quirky** *adj*

quirt \ˈkwərt\ *n* : a riding whip with a short handle and a rawhide lash

quis·ling \ˈkwiz-liŋ\ *n* [Vidkun *Quisling* †1945 Norw. politician who collaborated with the Nazis] : a traitor who collaborates with the invaders of his country

quit \ˈkwit\ *vb* **quit** *also* **quit·ted; quit·ting 1** : CONDUCT, BEHAVE ⟨~ themselves well⟩ **2** : to depart from : LEAVE, ABANDON **syn** acquit, comport, deport, demean — **quitter** *n*

quite \ˈkwīt\ *adv* **1** : COMPLETELY, WHOLLY **2** : to an extreme : POSITIVELY **3** : to a considerable extent : RATHER

quits \ˈkwits\ *adj* : even or equal with another ⟨call it ~⟩

quit·tance \ˈkwit-ᵊns\ *n* : REQUITAL

¹quiv·er \ˈkwiv-ər\ *n* : a case for carrying arrows

²quiver *vb* **quiv·ered; quiv·er·ing** \-(ə-)riŋ\ : to shake with a slight trembling motion **syn** shiver, shudder, quaver, quake, tremble

³quiver *n* : the act or action of quivering : TREMOR

qui vive \kē-ˈvēv\ *n* [F *qui-vive,* fr. *qui vive?* long live who?, challenge of a French sentry] : ALERT ⟨on the *qui vive* for prowlers⟩

quix·ot·ic \kwik-ˈsät-ik\ *adj* [fr. Don *Quixote,* hero of the novel *Don Quixote de la Mancha* by Cervantes] : foolishly impractical esp. in the pursuit of ideals

¹quiz \ˈkwiz\ *n, pl* **quiz·zes 1** : an eccentric person **2** : PRACTICAL JOKE **3** : a short oral or written test

²quiz *vb* **quizzed; quiz·zing 1** : MOCK **2** : to look at inquisitively **3** : to question closely : EXAMINE **syn** ask, interrogate, query

quiz·zi·cal \ˈkwiz-i-kəl\ *adj* **1** : slightly eccentric **2** : marked by bantering or teasing **3** : INQUISITIVE, QUESTIONING

quoit \ˈkwāt, ˈk(w)ȯit\ *n* **1** : a flattened ring of iron or circle of rope used in a throwing game **2** *pl* : a game in which quoits are thrown at an upright pin in an attempt to ring the pin

quon·dam \ˈkwän-dəm, -ˌdam\ *adj* [L, at one time, formerly, fr. *quom, cum* when] : FORMER

quo·rum \ˈkwōr-əm\ *n* : the number of members required to be present for business to be legally transacted

quot *abbr* quotation

quo·ta \ˈkwōt-ə\ *n* : a proportional part esp. when assigned : SHARE

quot·able \ˈkwōt-ə-bəl\ *adj* : fit for or worth quoting

quo·ta·tion \kwō-ˈtā-shən\ *n* **1** : the act or process of quoting **2** : the price currently bid or offered for something **3** : something that is quoted

quotation mark *n* : one of a pair of punctuation marks " " or ' ' used esp. to indicate the beginning and end of a quotation in which exact phraseology is directly cited

quote \ˈkwōt\ *vb* **quot·ed; quot·ing** [ML *quotare* to mark the number of, number references, fr. L *quotus* of what number or quantity, fr. *quot* how many, (as) many as] **1** : to speak or write a passage from another usu. with acknowledgment; *also* : to repeat a passage in substantiation or illustration **2** : to state the market price of a commodity, stock, or bond **3** : to inform a hearer or reader that matter following is quoted — **quote** *n*

quoth \(ˈ)kwōth\ *vb past* [ME, past of *quethen* to say, fr. OE *cwethan*] *archaic* : SAID — usu. used in the 1st and 3d persons with the subject following

quo·tid·i·an \kwō-ˈtid-ē-ən\ *adj* **1** : DAILY **2** : COMMONPLACE, ORDINARY

quo·tient \ˈkwō-shənt\ *n* : the number obtained by the division of one number by another

qursh *n, pl* **qursh** \ˈku̇rsh\ — see *riyal* at MONEY table

qv *abbr* [L *quod vide*] which see

qy *abbr* query

R

¹r \ˈär\ *n, pl* **r's** *or* **rs** \ˈärz\ *often cap* : the 18th letter of the English alphabet

²r *abbr, often cap* **1** rabbi **2** radius **3** rare **4** Republican **5** rerun **6** resistance **7** right **8** river **9** roentgen **10** rook **11** run

Ra *symbol* radium

RA *abbr* **1** regular army **2** Royal Academy

¹rab·bet \ˈrab-ət\ *n* : a groove in the edge or face of a board esp. to receive another piece

²rabbet *vb* : to cut a rabbet in; *also* : to join by means of a rabbet

rab·bi \ˈrab-ˌī\ *n* [LL, fr. Gk *rhabbi,* fr. Heb *rabbī* my master, fr. *rabh* master + *-ī* my] **1** : MASTER, TEACHER — used by Jews as a term of address **2** : a Jew trained and ordained for professional religious leadership — **rabbin·ic** \rə-ˈbin-ik\ *or* **rab·bin·i·cal** \-i-kəl\ *adj*

rab·bin·ate \ˈrab-ə-nət, -ˌnāt\ *n* **1** : the office of a rabbi **2** : the whole body of rabbis

rab·bit \ˈrab-ət\ *n, pl* **rabbit** *or* **rabbits** : a long-eared burrowing mammal related to the hare; *also* : its pelt

rabble \ˈrab-əl\ *n* **1** : MOB 2 **2** : the lowest class of people

rab·ble–rous·er \ˈrab-əl-ˌrau̇-zər\ *n* : one that stirs up (as to hatred or violence) the masses of the people

ra·bid \ˈrab-əd\ *adj* **1** : VIOLENT, FURIOUS **2** : being fanatical or extreme **3** : affected with rabies — **ra·bid·ly** *adv*

ra·bies \ˈrā-bēz\ *n, pl* **rabies** [NL, fr. L, madness] : an acute deadly virus disease of the nervous system transmitted by the bite of an affected animal

rac·coon \ra-ˈkün\ *n, pl* **raccoon** *or* **raccoons** : a gray No. American chiefly tree-dwelling mammal with a bushy ringed tail and nocturnal habits; *also* : its fur

¹race \ˈrās\ *n* **1** : a strong current of running water; *also* : its channel **2** : an onward course (as of time or life) **3**

: a contest in speed **4** : a contest for a desired end (as election to office)

[2]race *vb* **raced; rac·ing 1** : to run in a race **2** : to run swiftly : RUSH **3** : to engage in a race with **4** : to drive at high speed — **rac·er** *n*

[3]race *n* **1** : a family, tribe, people, or nation of the same stock; *also* : MANKIND **2** : a group of individuals within a biological species able to breed together — **ra·cial** \ˈrā-shəl\ *adj* — **ra·cial·ly** \-ē\ *adv*

race·course \ˈrās-ˌkōrs\ *n* : a course for racing

race·horse \-ˌhȯrs\ *n* : a horse bred or kept for racing

ra·ceme \rā-ˈsēm\ *n* [L *racemus* bunch of grapes] : a flower cluster with flowers borne along a stem and blooming from the base toward the tip — **rac·e·mose** \ˈras-ə-ˌmōs\ *adj*

race·track \ˈrās-ˌtrak\ *n* : a usu. oval course on which races are run

race·way \-ˌwā\ *n* **1** : a channel for a current of water **2** : RACECOURSE

ra·cial·ism \ˈrā-shə-ˌliz-əm\ *n* : RACISM — **ra·cial·ist** \-ləst\ *n* — **ra·cial·is·tic** \ˌrā-shə-ˈlis-tik\ *adj*

racing form *n* : an information sheet giving data about racehorses for use by bettors

rac·ism \ˈrās-ˌiz-əm\ *n* : a belief that some races are by nature superior to others; *also* : discrimination based on such belief — **rac·ist** \-əst\ *n*

[1]rack \ˈrak\ *n* **1** : an instrument of torture on which a body is stretched **2** : a framework on or in which something may be placed (as for display or storage) **3** : a bar with teeth on one side to mesh with a pinion or worm gear

[2]rack *vb* **1** : to torture with or as if with a rack **2** : to stretch or strain by force **3** : TORMENT **4** : to place on or in a rack

[1]rack·et *also* **rac·quet** \ˈrak-ət\ *n* [MF *raquette*, fr. Ar *rāḥah* palm of the hand] : a light bat made of netting stretched across an oval open frame and used for striking a ball

[2]racket *n* **1** : confused noise : DIN **2** : a fraudulent or dishonest scheme or activity

[3]racket *vb* : to make a racket

rack·e·teer \ˌrak-ə-ˈtiər\ *n* : a person who obtains money by an illegal enterprise usu. involving intimidation — **rack·e·teer·ing** *n*

rack up *vb* : SCORE

ra·con·teur \ˌrak-ˌän-ˈtər\ *n* : one good at telling anecdotes

racy \ˈrā-sē\ *adj* **rac·i·er; -est 1** : having the quality of something in its original or most characteristic form **2** : full of zest **3** : PUNGENT, SPICY **4** : RISQUÉ, SUGGESTIVE — **rac·i·ly** \ˈrā-sə-lē\ *adv* — **rac·i·ness** \-sē-nəs\ *n*

rad *abbr* **1** radical **2** radio **3** radius

ra·dar \ˈrā-ˌdär\ *n* [*ra*dio *d*etecting *a*nd *r*anging] : a device that emits radio waves for detecting and locating an object by the reflection of the radio waves and that may use this reflection to determine the object's direction and speed

ra·dar·scope \ˈrā-ˌdär-ˌskōp\ *n* : a visual display for a radar receiver

[1]ra·di·al \ˈrād-ē-əl\ *adj* : arranged or having parts arranged like rays coming from a common center ⟨the ~ form of a starfish⟩ — **ra·di·al·ly** \-ē\ *adv*

[2]radial *n* : a pneumatic tire with cords laid perpendicular to the center line

radial engine *n* : an internal-combustion engine with cylinders arranged radially like the spokes of a wheel

ra·di·ant \ˈrād-ē-ənt\ *adj* **1** : SHINING, GLOWING **2** : beaming with happiness **3** : transmitted by radiation **syn** brilliant, bright, luminous, lustrous — **ra·di·ance** \-əns\ *n* — **ra·di·ant·ly** *adv*

radiant energy *n* : energy transmitted as electromagnetic waves

ra·di·ate \ˈrād-ē-ˌāt\ *vb* **-at·ed; -at·ing 1** : to send out rays : SHINE, GLOW **2** : to issue in rays ⟨light ~*s*⟩ ⟨heat ~*s*⟩ **3** : to spread around as from a center — **ra·di·a·tion** \ˌrād-ē-ˈā-shən\ *n*

radiation sickness *n* : sickness that results from exposure to radiation and is commonly marked by fatigue, nausea, vomiting, loss of teeth and hair, and in more severe cases by damage to blood-forming tissue

ra·di·a·tor \ˈrād-ē-ˌāt-ər\ *n* : any of various devices (as a set of pipes or tubes) for transferring heat from a fluid within to an area or object outside

[1]rad·i·cal \ˈrad-i-kəl\ *adj* [ME, fr. LL *radicalis*, fr. L *radic-, radix* root] **1** : FUNDAMENTAL, EXTREME, THOROUGHGOING **2** : of or relating to radicals in politics — **rad·i·cal·ism** \-ˌiz-əm\ *n* — **rad·i·cal·ly** \-ē\ *adv*

[2]radical *n* **1** : a person who favors rapid and sweeping changes in laws and methods of government **2** : a group of atoms that is replaceable by a single atom or remains unchanged during reactions **3** : a mathematical expression indicating a root by means of a radical sign; *also* : RADICAL SIGN

rad·i·cal·ize \-kə-ˌlīz\ *vb* **-ized; -iz·ing** : to make radical esp. in politics — **rad·i·cal·iza·tion** \ˌrad-i-kə-lə-ˈzā-shən\ *n*

radical sign *n* : the sign $\sqrt{\ }$ placed over a mathematical expression to indicate that its root is to be taken

radii *pl of* RADIUS

[1]ra·dio \ˈrād-ē-ˌō\ *n, pl* **ra·di·os 1** : transmission or reception of signals using electromagnetic waves without a connecting wire **2** : a radio receiving set **3** : the radio broadcasting industry — **radio** *adj*

[2]radio *vb* : to communicate or send a message to by radio

ra·dio·ac·tiv·i·ty \ˌrād-ē-ō-ˌak-ˈtiv-ət-ē\ *n* : the property that some elements have of spontaneously emitting energetic particles by the disintegration of atomic nuclei — **ra·dio·ac·tive** \-ˈak-tiv\ *adj*

radio astronomy *n* : astronomy dealing with radio waves received from outside the earth's atmosphere

ra·dio·car·bon \ˌrād-ē-ō-ˈkär-bən\ *n* : CARBON 14

radio frequency *n* : an electromagnetic wave frequency intermediate between audio frequency and infrared frequency used esp. in radio and television transmission

ra·dio·gen·ic \ˌrād-ē-ō-ˈjen-ik\ *adj* : produced by radioactivity

ra·dio·gram \ˈrād-ē-ō-ˌgram\ *n* **1** : RADIOGRAPH **2** : a message transmitted by radiotelegraphy

ra·dio·graph \-ˌgraf\ *n* : a photograph made by some form of radiation other than light; *esp* : an X-ray photograph — **radiograph** *vb* — **ra·dio·graph·ic** \ˌrād-ē-ō-ˈgraf-ik\ *adj* — **ra·dio·graph·i·cal·ly** \-i-k(ə-)lē\ *adv* — **ra·di·og·ra·phy** \ˌrād-ē-ˈäg-rə-fē\ *n*

ra·dio·iso·tope \ˌrād-ē-ō-ˈī-sə-ˌtōp\ *n* : a radioactive isotope

ra·di·ol·o·gy \ˌrād-ē-ˈäl-ə-jē\ *n* : the use of radiant energy (as X rays and radium radiations) in medicine — **ra·di·ol·o·gist** \-jəst\ *n*

ra·dio·man \ˈrād-ē-ō-ˌman\ *n* : a radio operator or technician

ra·di·om·e·ter \ˌrād-ē-ˈäm-ət-ər\ *n* : an instrument for measuring the intensity of radiant energy — **ra·di·om·e·try** \-ə-trē\ *n* — **ra·dio·met·ric** \ˌrād-ē-ō-ˈme-trik\ *adj*

ra·dio·phone \ˈrād-ē-ə-ˌfōn\ *n* : RADIOTELEPHONE

ra·dio·sonde \ˈrād-ē-ō-ˌsänd\ *n* : a small radio transmitter carried aloft (as by balloon) and used to transmit meteorological data

ra·dio·tele·graph \ˌrād-ē-ō-ˈtel-ə-ˌgraf\ *n* : wireless telegraphy — **ra·dio·tele·graph·ic** \-ˌtel-ə-ˈgraf-ik\ *adj* — **ra·dio·te·leg·ra·phy** \-tə-ˈleg-rə-fē\ *n*

ra·dio·tele·phone \-ˈtel-ə-ˌfōn\ *n* : a telephone that uses radio waves wholly or partly instead of connecting wires — **ra·dio·te·le·pho·ny** \-tə-ˈlef-ə-nē, -ˈtel-ə-ˌfō-nē\ *n*

radio telescope *n* : a radio receiver-antenna combination used for observation in radio astronomy

ra·dio·ther·a·py \ˌrād-ē-ō-ˈther-ə-pē\ *n* : the treatment of disease by means of X rays or radioactive substances — **ra·dio·ther·a·pist** \-pəst\ *n*

rad·ish \ˈrad-ish\ *n* [ME, alter. of OE *rædic,* fr. L *radic-, radix* root, radish] : a pungent fleshy root usu. eaten raw; *also* : a plant related to the mustards that produces this root

ra·di·um \ˈrād-ē-əm\ *n* : a strongly radioactive metallic chemical element that is used in the treatment of cancer — see ELEMENT table

ra·di·us \ˈrād-ē-əs\ *n, pl* **ra·dii** \-ē-ˌī\ *also* **ra·di·us·es** **1** : the one of the two bones of the human forearm that is on the thumb side; **2** : a straight line extending from the center of a circle or a sphere to the circumference or surface **3** : a circular area defined by the length of its radius **syn** range, reach, scope, compass

RADM *abbr* rear admiral

ra·don \ˈrā-ˌdän\ *n* : a heavy radioactive gaseous chemical element — see ELEMENT table

RAF *abbr* Royal Air Force

raf·fia \ˈraf-ē-ə\ *n* : fiber used esp. for making baskets and hats and obtained from the stalks of the leaves of a Madagascar palm (raffia palm)

raff·ish \ˈraf-ish\ *adj* : jaunty or sporty esp. in a flashy or vulgar manner — **raff·ish·ly** *adv* — **raff·ish·ness** *n*

¹raf·fle \ˈraf-əl\ *n* : a lottery in which the prize is won by one of a number of persons buying chances

²raffle *vb* **raf·fled; raf·fling** \ˈraf-(ə-)liŋ\ : to dispose of by a raffle

¹raft \ˈraft\ *n* **1** : a number of logs or timbers fastened together to form a float **2** : a flat structure for support or transportation on water

²raft *vb* **1** : to travel or transport by raft **2** : to make into a raft

³raft *n* : a large amount or number

raf·ter \ˈraf-tər\ *n* : a usu. sloping timber of a roof

¹rag \ˈrag\ *n* : a waste piece of cloth

²rag *n* : a composition in ragtime

ra·ga \ˈräg-ə\ *n* **1** : an ancient traditional melodic pattern or mode in Indian music **2** : an improvisation based on a raga

rag·a·muf·fin \ˈrag-ə-ˌməf-ən\ *n* [*Ragamoffyn,* a demon in *Piers Plowman* (1393), attributed to William Langland] : a ragged dirty person

¹rage \ˈrāj\ *n* **1** : violent and uncontrolled anger **2** : VOGUE, FASHION

²rage *vb* **raged; rag·ing** **1** : to be furiously angry : RAVE **2** : to be in violent tumult ⟨the storm *raged*⟩ **3** : to continue out of control

rag·ged \ˈrag-əd\ *adj* **1** : TORN, TATTERED; *also* : wearing tattered clothes **2** : done in an uneven way ⟨a ~ performance⟩ — **rag·ged·ly** *adv* — **rag·ged·ness** *n*

rag·lan \ˈrag-lən\ *n* : an overcoat with sleeves (raglan sleeves) sewn in with seams slanting from neck to underarm

ra·gout \ra-ˈgü\ *n* [F *ragoût,* fr. *ragoûter* to revive the taste, fr. *re-* + *a-* to (fr. L *ad-*) + *goût* taste, fr. L *gustus*] : a highly seasoned meat stew with vegetables

rag·pick·er \ˈrag-ˌpik-ər\ *n* : one who collects rags and refuse for a livelihood

rag·time \ˈrag-ˌtīm\ *n* : rhythm in which there is more or less continuous syncopation in the melody

rag·weed \-ˌwēd\ *n* : any of several coarse weedy herbs with allergenic pollen

¹raid \ˈrād\ *n* : a sudden usu. surprise attack or invasion : FORAY

²raid *vb* : to make a raid on — **raid·er** *n*

¹rail \ˈrāl\ *n* [ME *raile,* fr. MF *reille* ruler, bar, fr. L *regula* ruler, fr. *regere* to keep straight, direct, rule] **1** : a bar extending from one support to another as a guard or barrier **2** : a bar forming a track for wheeled vehicles **3** : RAILROAD

²rail *vb* : to provide with a railing : FENCE

³rail *n, pl* **rail** *or* **rails** : any of a family of small wading birds related to the cranes and often hunted as game birds

⁴rail *vb* [ME *railen,* fr. MF *railler* to mock, fr. Old Provençal *ralhar* to babble, joke] : to complain angrily : SCOLD, REVILE — **rail·er** *n*

rail·ing \ˈrā-liŋ\ *n* : a barrier of rails

rail·lery \ˈrā-lə-rē\ *n, pl* **-ler·ies** : good-natured ridicule : BANTER

¹rail·road \ˈrāl-ˌrōd\ *n* : a permanent road with rails fixed to ties providing a track for cars; *also* : such a road and its assets constituting a property

²railroad *vb* **1** : to send by rail **2** : to work on a railroad **3** : to put through (as a law) too hastily **4** : to convict hastily or with insufficient or improper evidence — **rail·road·er** *n* — **rail·road·ing** *n*

rail·way \-ˌwā\ *n* **1** : a line of track providing a runway for wheels **2** : RAILROAD

rai·ment \ˈrā-mənt\ *n* : CLOTHING

¹rain \ˈrān\ *n* **1** : water falling in drops from the clouds **2** : a shower of objects ⟨a ~ of bullets⟩ — **rainy** *adj*

²rain *vb* **1** : to fall as or like rain **2** : to send down rain **3** : to pour down

rain·bow \-ˌbō\ *n* : an arc or circle of colors formed by the refraction and reflection of the sun's rays in rain, spray, or mist

rainbow trout *n* : a large stout-bodied trout of western No. America that usu. has red or pink stripes with black dots along its sides

rain check *n* **1** : a ticket stub good for a later performance when the scheduled one is rained out **2** : an assurance of a deferred extension of an offer

rain·coat \ˈrān-ˌkōt\ *n* : a waterproof or water-repellent coat

rain·drop \-ˌdräp\ *n* : a drop of rain

rain·fall \-ˌfȯl\ *n* **1** : a fall of rain **2** : amount of precipitation ⟨an annual ~ of 50 centimeters⟩

rain forest *n* : a tropical woodland that has an annual rainfall of at least 100 inches and that is marked by lofty broad-leaved evergreen trees forming a continuous canopy

rain·mak·ing \ˈrān-ˌmā-kiŋ\ *n* : the action or process of producing or attempting to produce rain by artificial means — **rain·mak·er** \-kər\ *n*

rain out *vb* : to interrupt or prevent by rain

rain·storm \ˈrān-ˌstȯrm\ *n* : a storm of or with rain

rain·wa·ter \-ˌwȯt-ər, -ˌwät-\ *n* : water fallen as rain

¹raise \ˈrāz\ *vb* **raised; rais·ing** **1** : to cause or help to rise : LIFT ⟨~ a window⟩ **2** : AWAKEN, AROUSE ⟨enough to ~ the dead⟩ **3** : BUILD, ERECT ⟨~ a monument⟩ **4** : PROMOTE ⟨was *raised* to captain⟩ **5** : COLLECT ⟨~ money⟩ **6** : BREED, GROW ⟨~ cattle⟩ ⟨~ corn⟩; *also* : BRING UP ⟨~ a family⟩ **7** : PROVOKE ⟨~ a laugh⟩ **8** : to bring to notice ⟨~ an objection⟩ **9** : INCREASE ⟨~ prices⟩; *also* : to bet more than **10** : to make light and spongy ⟨~ dough⟩ **11** : END ⟨~ a siege⟩ **12** : to cause to form ⟨~ a blister⟩ **syn** lift, hoist, boost, elevate — **rais·er** *n*

²raise *n* : an increase in amount (as of a bid or bet); *also* : an increase in pay

rai·sin \ˈrāz-ᵊn\ *n* [ME, fr. MF, grape, fr. L *racemus* cluster of grapes or berries] : a grape dried for food

rai·son d'être \ˌrā-ˌzōⁿ-ˈdetrᵊ\ *n* : reason or justification for existence

ra·ja *or* **ra·jah** \ˈräj-ə\ *n* [Hindi *rājā,* fr. Skt *rājan* king] : an Indian prince

¹rake \ˈrāk\ *n* : a long-handled garden tool having a crossbar with prongs

²rake *vb* **raked; rak·ing** **1** : to gather, loosen, or smooth with or as if with a rake **2** : to sweep the length of (as a trench or ship) with gunfire

³rake *n* : inclination from either perpendicular or horizontal : SLANT, SLOPE

⁴rake *n* : a dissolute man : LIBERTINE

rake–off \ˈrāk-ˌȯf\ *n* : a percentage or cut taken

¹rak·ish \ˈrā-kish\ *adj* : DISSOLUTE — **rak·ish·ly** *adv* — **rak·ish·ness** *n*

²rakish *adj* **1** : having a smart appearance indicative of speed ⟨a ~ sloop⟩ ⟨~ masts⟩ **2** : JAUNTY, SPORTY — **rak·ish·ly** *adv* — **rak·ish·ness** *n*

¹ral·ly \ˈral-ē\ *vb* **ral·lied; ral·ly·ing 1** : to bring together for a common purpose; *also* : to bring back to order ⟨a leader ~*ing* his forces⟩ **2** : to arouse to activity or from depression or weakness : REVIVE, RECOVER **3** : to come together again to renew an effort **syn** stir, rouse, awaken, waken, kindle

²rally *n, pl* **rallies 1** : an act of rallying **2** : a mass meeting to arouse enthusiasm **3** : a competitive automobile event run over public roads

³rally *vb* **ral·lied; ral·ly·ing** : BANTER

¹ram \ˈram\ *n* **1** : a male sheep **2** : BATTERING RAM

²ram *vb* **rammed; ram·ming 1** : to force or drive in or through **2** : CRAM, CROWD **3** : to strike against violently

¹ram·ble \ˈram-bəl\ *vb* **ram·bled; ram·bling** \-b(ə-)liŋ\ : to go about aimlessly : ROAM, WANDER

²ramble *n* : a leisurely excursion; *esp* : an aimless walk

ram·bler \ˈram-blər\ *n* **1** : a person who rambles **2** : a hardy climbing rose with large clusters of small flowers

ram·bunc·tious \ram-ˈbəŋk-shəs\ *adj* : UNRULY

ra·mie \ˈrā-mē, ˈram-ē\ *n* : a strong lustrous bast fiber from an Asian nettle

ram·i·fy \ˈram-ə-ˌfī\ *vb* **-fied; -fy·ing** : to branch out — **ram·i·fi·ca·tion** \ˌram-ə-fə-ˈkā-shən\ *n*

ramp \ˈramp\ *n* : a sloping passage or roadway connecting different levels

¹ram·page \ˈram-ˌpāj, (ˈ)ram-ˈpāj\ *vb* **ram·paged; ram·pag·ing** : to rush about wildly

²ram·page \ˈram-ˌpāj\ *n* : a course of violent or riotous action or behavior — **ram·pa·geous** \ram-ˈpā-jəs\ *adj*

ram·pan·cy \ˈram-pən-sē\ *n* : the quality or state of being rampant

ram·pant \ˈram-pənt\ *adj* : unchecked in growth or spread : RIFE ⟨fear was ~ in the town⟩ — **ram·pant·ly** *adv*

ram·part \ˈram-ˌpärt\ *n* **1** : a broad embankment raised as a fortification **2** : a protective barrier **3** : a wall-like ridge

¹ram·rod \ˈram-ˌräd\ *n* **1** : a rod used to ram a charge into a muzzle-loading gun **2** : a cleaning rod for small arms **3** : BOSS, OVERSEER

²ramrod *vb* : to direct, supervise, and control

ram·shack·le \ˈram-ˌshak-əl\ *adj* : RICKETY, TUMBLEDOWN

ran *past of* RUN

¹ranch \ˈranch\ *n* [MexSp *rancho* small ranch, fr. Sp, camp, hut & Sp dial., small farm, fr. Old Spanish *ranchear* (*se*) to take up quarters, fr. MF (*se*) *ranger* to take up a position, fr. *ranger* to set in a row] **1** : an establishment for the raising and grazing of livestock (as cattle, sheep, or horses) **2** : a large farm devoted to a specialty

²ranch *vb* : to live or work on a ranch — **ranch·er** *n*

ranch house *n* : a one-story house typically with a low-pitched roof

ran·cho \ˈran-chō, ˈrän-\ *n, pl* **ranchos** : RANCH

ran·cid \ˈran-səd\ *adj* **1** : having a rank smell or taste **2** : ROTTEN, SPOILED — **ran·cid·i·ty** \ran-ˈsid-ət-ē\ *n*

ran·cor \ˈraŋ-kər\ *n* : deep hatred : intense ill will **syn** antagonism, animosity, antipathy, enmity, hostility — **ran·cor·ous** *adj*

rand \ˈrand, ˈränd, ˈränt\ *n, pl* **rand** — see MONEY table

R & B *abbr* rhythm and blues

R & D *abbr* research and development

ran·dom \ˈran-dəm\ *adj* : CHANCE, HAPHAZARD — **ran·dom·ly** *adv* — **ran·dom·ness** *n*

random–access *adj* : allowing access to stored data in any order the user desires

random–access memory \ˌran-dəm-ˈak-ˌses-\ *n* : a computer memory that provides the main internal storage available to the user for programs and data

ran·dom·ize \ˈran-də-ˌmīz\ *vb* **-ized; -iz·ing** : to distribute, treat, or perform in a random way — **ran·dom·iza·tion** \ˌran-də-mə-ˈzā-shən\ *n*

R and R *abbr* rest and recreation; rest and recuperation

rang *past of* RING

¹range \ˈrānj\ *n* **1** : a series of things in a row **2** : the act of ranging or roaming **3** : open land where animals (as livestock) may roam and graze **4** : a cooking stove **5** : a variation within limits **6** : the distance a weapon will shoot or is to be shot **7** : a place where shooting is practiced; *also* : a course over which missiles are tested **8** : the space or extent included, covered, or used : SCOPE **syn** reach, compass, radius, circle

²range *vb* **ranged; rang·ing 1** : to set in a row or in proper order **2** : to set in place among others of the same kind **3** : to roam over or through : EXPLORE **4** : to roam at large or freely **5** : to correspond in direction or line **6** : to vary within limits **7** : to find the range of an object by instrument (as radar)

rang·er \ˈrān-jər\ *n* **1** : a warden who patrols forest lands **2** : a member of a body of troops who range over a region **3** : an expert in close-range fighting and raiding tactics

rangy \ˈrān-jē\ *adj* **rang·i·er; -est** : being long-limbed and slender — **rang·i·ness** \ˈrān-jē-nəs\ *n*

ra·ni *or* **ra·nee** \rä-ˈnē, ˈrän-ˌē\ *n* : a raja's wife

¹rank \ˈraŋk\ *adj* **1** : strong and vigorous and usu. coarse in growth ⟨~ weeds⟩ **2** : unpleasantly strong-smelling — **rank·ly** *adv* — **rank·ness** *n*

²rank *n* **1** : ROW **2** : a line of soldiers ranged side by side **3** *pl* : the body of enlisted men ⟨rose from the ~*s*⟩ **4** : an orderly arrangement **5** : CLASS, DIVISION **6** : a grade of official standing (as in an army) **7** : position in a group **8** : superior position

³rank *vb* **1** : to arrange in lines or in regular formation **2** : to arrange according to classes **3** : to take or have a relative position **4** : to rate above (as in official standing)

rank and file *n* **1** : the enlisted men of an armed force **2** : the general membership of a body as contrasted with its leaders

rank·ing \ˈraŋ-kiŋ\ *adj* **1** : having a high position : FOREMOST **2** : being next to the chairman in seniority

ran·kle \ˈraŋ-kəl\ *vb* **ran·kled; ran·kling** \-k(ə-)liŋ\ [ME *ranclen* to fester, fr. MF *rancler*, fr. OF *draoncler, raoncler*, fr. *draoncle, raoncle* festering sore, fr. (assumed) VL *dracunculus*, fr. L, dim. of *draco* serpent] : to cause anger, irritation, or bitterness

ran·sack \ˈran-ˌsak\ *vb* : to search thoroughly; *esp* : to search through and rob

¹ran·som \ˈran-səm\ *n* [ME *ransoun*, fr. OF *rançon*, fr. L *redemption-, redemptio* act of buying back, fr. *redimere* to buy back, redeem] **1** : something paid or demanded for the freedom of a captive **2** : the act of ransoming

²ransom *vb* : to free from captivity or punishment by paying a price — **ran·som·er** *n*

rant \ˈrant\ *vb* **1** : to talk loudly and wildly **2** : to scold violently — **rant·er** *n* — **rant·ing·ly** \-iŋ-lē\ *adv*

¹rap \ˈrap\ *n* **1** : a sharp blow **2** : a sharp rebuke **3** *slang* : responsibility for or consequences of an action

²rap *vb* **rapped; rap·ping 1** : to strike sharply : KNOCK **2** : to utter sharply **3** : to criticize sharply

³rap *vb* **rapped; rap·ping** : to talk freely and frankly — **rap** *n*

ra·pa·cious \rə-ˈpā-shəs\ *adj* **1** : excessively greedy or covetous **2** : living on prey **3** : RAVENOUS — **ra·pa·cious-**

ly *adv* — **ra·pa·cious·ness** *n* — **ra·pac·i·ty** \-ˈpas-ət-ē\ *n*

¹rape \ˈrāp\ *n* : a European herb related to the mustards that is grown as a forage crop and for its seeds (**rapeseed** \-ˌsēd\)

²rape *vb* **raped; rap·ing** : to commit rape on : RAVISH — **rap·er** *n* — **rap·ist** \ˈrā-pəst\ *n*

³rape *n* **1** : a carrying away by force **2** : sexual intercourse by a man with a woman without her consent and chiefly by force or deception; *also* : unlawful sexual intercourse of any kind by force or threat

¹rap·id \ˈrap-əd\ *adj* [L *rapidus* seizing, sweeping, rapid, fr. *rapere* to seize, sweep away] : very fast : SWIFT **syn** fleet, quick, speedy — **ra·pid·i·ty** \rə-ˈpid-ət-ē\ *n* — **rap·id·ly** \ˈrap-əd-lē\ *adv*

²rapid *n* : a place in a stream where the current flows very fast usu. over obstructions — usu. used in pl.

rapid eye movement *n* : rapid conjugate movement of the eyes associated with REM sleep

rapid transit *n* : fast passenger transportation (as by subway) in urban areas

ra·pi·er \ˈrā-pē-ər\ *n* : a straight 2-edged sword with a narrow pointed blade

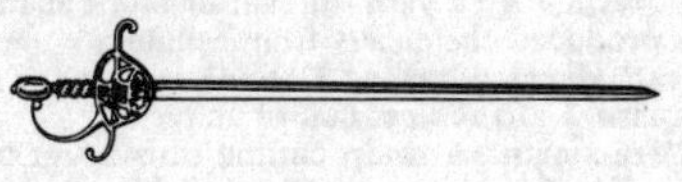

rapier

rap·ine \ˈrap-ən, -ˌīn\ *n* : PILLAGE, PLUNDER

rap·pen \ˈräp-ən\ *n, pl* **rappen** : the centime of Switzerland

rap·port \ra-ˈpōr\ *n* : RELATION; *esp* : relation characterized by harmony

rap·proche·ment \ˌrap-ˌrōsh-ˈmäⁿ, ra-ˈprōsh-ˌmäⁿ\ *n* : the establishment of or a state of having cordial relations

rap·scal·lion \rap-ˈskal-yən\ *n* : RASCAL, SCAMP

rapt \ˈrapt\ *adj* **1** : carried away with emotion **2** : ABSORBED, ENGROSSED — **rapt·ly** \ˈrap-(t)lē\ *adv* — **rapt·ness** \ˈrap(t)-nəs\ *n*

rap·ture \ˈrap-chər\ *n* : spiritual or emotional ecstasy — **rap·tur·ous** \-chə-rəs\ *adj*

rapture of the deep : a confused mental state caused by nitrogen forced into a diver's bloodstream from atmospheric air under pressure

ra·ra avis \ˌrar-ə-ˈā-vəs\ *n* [L, rare bird] : a rare person or thing : RARITY

¹rare \ˈra(ə)r\ *adj* **rar·er; rar·est 1** : not thick or dense : THIN ⟨~ air⟩ **2** : unusually fine : EXCELLENT, SPLENDID **3** : seldom met with — **rare·ly** *adv* — **rare·ness** *n* — **rar·i·ty** \ˈrar-ət-ē\ *n*

²rare *adj* **rar·er; rar·est** : cooked so that the inside is still red ⟨~ beef⟩

rare·bit \ˈra(ə)r-bət\ *n* : WELSH RABBIT

rar·efac·tion \ˌrar-ə-ˈfak-shən\ *n* **1** : the action or process of rarefying **2** : the state of being rarefied **3** : a state or region of minimum pressure in a substance (as air) being traveled through by a wave formed by compression (as sound)

rar·efy *also* **rar·i·fy** \ˈrar-ə-ˌfī\ *vb* **-efied; -efy·ing** : to make or become rare, thin, or less dense

rar·ing \ˈrar-ən, -iŋ\ *adj* : full of enthusiasm or eagerness

ras·cal \ˈras-kəl\ *n* **1** : a mean or dishonest person **2** : a mischievous person — **ras·cal·i·ty** \ras-ˈkal-ət-ē\ *n* — **ras·cal·ly** \ˈras-kə-lē\ *adj*

¹rash \ˈrash\ *adj* : having or showing little regard for consequences : too hasty in decision, action, or speech : RECKLESS **syn** daring, foolhardy, adventurous, venturesome — **rash·ly** *adv* — **rash·ness** *n*

²rash *n* : an eruption on the body

rash·er \ˈrash-ər\ *n* : a thin slice of bacon or ham broiled or fried; *also* : a portion consisting of several such slices

¹rasp \ˈrasp\ *vb* **1** : to rub with or as if with a rough file **2** : to grate harshly on (as one's nerves) **3** : to speak in a grating tone

²rasp *n* : a coarse file with cutting points instead of ridges

rasp·ber·ry \ˈraz-ˌber-ē, -b(ə-)rē\ *n* **1** : an edible red or black berry produced by some brambles; *also* : such a bramble **2** : a sound of contempt made by protruding the tongue through the lips and expelling air forcibly

¹rat \ˈrat\ *n* **1** : any of numerous scaly-tailed rodents larger than the related mice **2** : a contemptible person; *esp* : one that betrays his associates

²rat *vb* **rat·ted; rat·ting 1** : to betray one's associates **2** : to hunt or catch rats

rat cheese *n* : CHEDDAR

ratch·et \ˈrach-ət\ *n* : a device that consists of a bar or wheel having slanted teeth into which a pawl drops so as to allow motion in only one direction

ratchet wheel *n* : a toothed wheel held in position or turned by a pawl

¹rate \ˈrāt\ *vb* **rat·ed; rat·ing** : to scold violently

²rate *n* **1** : quantity, amount, or degree measured by some standard **2** : an amount (as of payment) measured by its relation to some other amount (as of time) **3** : a charge, payment, or price fixed according to a ratio, scale, or standard ⟨tax ~⟩ **4** : RANK, CLASS

³rate *vb* **rat·ed; rat·ing 1** : CONSIDER, REGARD **2** : ESTIMATE **3** : to settle the relative rank or class of **4** : to be classed : RANK **5** : to be of consequence **6** : to have a right to : DESERVE — **rat·er** *n*

rath·er \ˈrat͟h-ər, ˈrät͟h-, ˈrət͟h-\ *adv* [ME, fr. OE *hrathor*, compar. of *hrathe* quickly] **1** : more properly **2** : PREFERABLY **3** : more correctly speaking **4** : to the contrary : INSTEAD **5** : SOMEWHAT

raths·kel·ler \ˈrät-ˌskel-ər, ˈrat(h)-\ *n* [obs. G (now *ratskeller*), city-hall basement restaurant, fr. *rat* council + *keller* cellar] : a usu. basement tavern or restaurant

rat·i·fy \ˈrat-ə-ˌfī\ *vb* **-fied; -fy·ing** : to approve and accept formally — **rat·i·fi·ca·tion** \ˌrat-ə-fə-ˈkā-shən\ *n*

rat·ing \ˈrāt-iŋ\ *n* **1** : a classification according to grade : RANK **2** *Brit* : a naval enlisted man **3** : an estimate of the credit standing and business responsibility of a person or firm

ra·tio \ˈrā-sh(ē-)ō\ *n, pl* **ra·tios 1** : the quotient of two numbers or mathematical expressions **2** : the relation in number, quantity, or degree between things

ra·ti·o·ci·na·tion \ˌrat-ē-ˌōs-ᵊn-ˈā-shən, ˌrash-, -ˌäs-\ *n* : exact thinking : REASONING — **ra·ti·o·ci·nate** \-ˈōs-ᵊn-ˌāt, -ˈäs-\ *vb* — **ra·ti·o·ci·na·tive** \-ˈōs-ᵊn-ˌāt-iv, -ˈäs-\ *adj* — **ra·ti·o·ci·na·tor** \-ˈōs-ᵊn-ˌāt-ər, -ˈäs-\ *n*

¹ra·tion \ˈrash-ən, ˈrā-shən\ *n* **1** : a food allowance for one day **2** : FOOD, PROVISIONS, DIET — usu. used in pl. **3** : SHARE, ALLOTMENT

²ration *vb* **ra·tioned; ra·tion·ing** \ˈrash-(ə-)niŋ, ˈrāsh-\ **1** : to supply with or allot as rations **2** : to use or allot sparingly **syn** apportion, portion, prorate, parcel

¹ra·tio·nal \ˈrash-(ə-)nəl\ *adj* **1** : having reason or understanding; *also* : SANE **2** : of or relating to reason **3** : relating to, consisting of, or being one or more rational numbers — **ra·tio·nal·ly** \-ē\ *adv*

²rational *n* : RATIONAL NUMBER

ra·tio·nale \ˌrash-ə-ˈnal\ *n* **1** : an explanation of principles controlling belief or practice **2** : an underlying reason

ra·tio·nal·ism \ˈrash-(ə-)nə-ˌliz-əm\ *n* : the practice of guiding one's actions and opinions solely by what seems reasonable — **ra·tio·nal·ist** \-ləst\ *n* — **rationalist** *or* **ra·tio·nal·is·tic** \ˌrash-(ə-)nə-ˈlis-tik\ *adj*

ra·tio·nal·i·ty \ˌrash-ə-ˈnal-ət-ē\ *n, pl* **-ties** : the quality or state of being rational

ra·tio·nal·ize \ˈrash-(ə-)nə-ˌlīz\ *vb* **-ized; -iz·ing 1** : to make (something irrational) appear rational or reasonable **2** : to provide a natural explanation of (as a myth) **3** : to justify (as one's behavior or weaknesses) esp. to oneself **4** : to find plausible but untrue reasons for conduct — **ra·tio·nal·iza·tion** \ˌrash-(ə-)nə-lə-ˈzā-shən\ *n*

rational number *n* : an integer or the quotient of two integers

rat·line \ˈrat-lən\ *n* : one of the small transverse ropes fastened to the shrouds of a ship and forming the steps of a rope ladder

rat race *n* : strenuous, tiresome, and usu. competitive activity or rush

rat·tan \ra-ˈtan, rə-\ *n* : an Asian climbing palm with long stems

rat·ter \ˈrat-ər\ *n* : a rat-catching dog or cat

[1]**rat·tle** \ˈrat-ᵊl\ *vb* **rat·tled; rat·tling** \ˈrat-(ᵊ-)liŋ\ **1** : to make or cause to make a series of clattering sounds **2** : to move with a clattering sound **3** : to say or do in a brisk lively fashion ⟨~ off the answers⟩ **4** : CONFUSE, UPSET ⟨~ a witness⟩

[2]**rattle** *n* **1** : a series of clattering and knocking sounds **2** : a toy that produces a rattle when shaken **3** : a rattling organ at the end of a rattlesnake's tail made up of horny joints

rat·tler \ˈrat-lər\ *n* : RATTLESNAKE

rat·tle·snake \ˈrat-ᵊl-ˌsnāk\ *n* : any of various American venomous snakes with a rattle at the end of the tail

rat·tle·trap \ˈrat-ᵊl-ˌtrap\ *n* : something rickety and full of rattles; *esp* : an old car

rat·tling \ˈrat-liŋ\ *adj* **1** : LIVELY, BRISK **2** : FIRST-RATE, SPLENDID

rat·trap \ˈrat-ˌtrap\ *n* **1** : a trap for rats **2** : a dilapidated building

rat·ty \ˈrat-ē\ *adj* **rat·ti·er; -est 1** : infested with rats **2** : of, relating to, or suggestive of rats **3** : SHABBY

rau·cous \ˈrȯ-kəs\ *adj* **1** : HARSH, HOARSE, STRIDENT **2** : boisterously disorderly — **rau·cous·ly** *adv* — **rau·cous·ness** *n*

raun·chy \ˈrȯn-chē, ˈrän-\ *adj* **raun·chi·er; -est 1** : SLOVENLY, DIRTY **2** : OBSCENE, SMUTTY — **raun·chi·ness** \-chē-nəs\ *n*

rau·wol·fia \rau̇-ˈwu̇l-fē-ə, rȯ-\ *n* : a medicinal extract from the root of an Indian tree; *also* : this tree

[1]**rav·age** \ˈrav-ij\ *n* [F] : an act or result of ravaging : DEVASTATION

[2]**ravage** *vb* **rav·aged; rav·ag·ing** : to lay waste : DEVASTATE — **rav·ag·er** *n*

[1]**rave** \ˈrāv\ *vb* **raved; rav·ing** [ME *raven*] **1** : to talk wildly in or as if in delirium : STORM, RAGE **2** : to talk with extreme enthusiasm

[2]**rave** *n* **1** : an act or instance of raving **2** : an extravagantly favorable criticism

[1]**rav·el** \ˈrav-əl\ *vb* **-eled** *or* **-elled; -el·ing** *or* **-el·ling** \-(ə-)liŋ\ **1** : UNRAVEL, UNTWIST **2** : TANGLE, CONFUSE

[2]**ravel** *n* **1** : something tangled **2** : something raveled out; *esp* : a loose thread

[1]**ra·ven** \ˈrā-vən\ *n* : a large black bird related to the crow

[2]**raven** *adj* : black and glossy like a raven's feathers

rav·en·ing \ˈrav-(ə-)niŋ\ *adj* : GREEDY

rav·en·ous \ˈrav-(ə-)nəs\ *adj* **1** : RAPACIOUS, VORACIOUS **2** : eager for food : very hungry — **rav·en·ous·ly** *adv* — **rav·en·ous·ness** *n*

ra·vine \rə-ˈvēn\ *n* : a small narrow steep-sided valley larger than a gully and smaller than a canyon

rav·i·o·li \ˌrav-ē-ˈō-lē\ *n* [It, fr. It dial., pl. of *raviolo*, lit., little turnip, dim. of *rava* turnip, fr. L *rapa*] : small cases of dough with a savory filling (as of meat or cheese)

rav·ish \ˈrav-ish\ *vb* **1** : to seize and take away by violence **2** : to overcome with emotion and esp. with joy or delight **3** : RAPE — **rav·ish·er** *n* — **rav·ish·ment** *n*

[1]**raw** \ˈrȯ\ *adj* **raw·er** \ˈrȯ(-ə)r\; **raw·est** \ˈrȯ-əst\ **1** : not cooked **2** : changed little from the original form : not processed ⟨~ materials⟩ **3** : having the skin abraded or irritated ⟨a ~ sore⟩ **4** : not trained or experienced ⟨~ recruits⟩ **5** : VULGAR, COARSE **6** : disagreeably cold and damp ⟨a ~ day⟩ **7** : UNFAIR ⟨~ deal⟩ — **raw·ness** *n*

[2]**raw** *n* : a raw place or state; *esp* : NUDITY

raw·boned \ˈrȯ-ˈbōnd\ *adj* **1** : LEAN, GAUNT **2** : having a heavy frame that seems to have little flesh

raw·hide \ˈrȯ-ˌhīd\ *n* : the untanned skin of cattle; *also* : a whip made of this

[1]**ray** \ˈrā\ *n* : any of numerous large flat fishes that are related to the sharks and have the eyes on the upper surface and the hind end of the body slender and taillike

[2]**ray** *n* [ME, fr. MF *rai*, fr. L *radius* rod, ray] **1** : one of the lines of light that appear to radiate from a bright object **2** : a thin beam of radiant energy (as light) **3** : light from a beam **4** : a thin line like a beam of light **5** : an animal or plant structure resembling a ray **6** : a tiny bit : PARTICLE ⟨a ~ of hope⟩

ray·on \ˈrā-ˌän\ *n* : a yarn, thread, or fabric made from fibers produced chemically from cellulose

raze \ˈrāz\ *vb* **razed; raz·ing 1** : to destroy to the ground : DEMOLISH **2** : to scrape, cut, or shave off

ra·zor \ˈrā-zər\ *n* : a sharp cutting instrument used to shave off hair

ra·zor–backed \ˌrā-zər-ˈbakt\ *or* **ra·zor·back** \ˈrā-zər-ˌbak\ *adj* : having a sharp narrow back ⟨~ horse⟩

razor clam *n* : any of numerous marine bivalve mollusks having a long narrow curved thin shell

[1]**razz** \ˈraz\ *n* : RASPBERRY 2

[2]**razz** *vb* : RIDICULE, TEASE

Rb *symbol* rubidium

RBC *abbr* red blood cells; red blood count

RBI \ˌär-(ˌ)bē-ˈī, ˈrib-ē\ *n, pl* **RBIs** *or* **RBI** [*r*un *b*atted *i*n] : a run in baseball that is driven in by a batter

RC *abbr* **1** Red Cross **2** Roman Catholic

RCAF *abbr* Royal Canadian Air Force

RCMP *abbr* Royal Canadian Mounted Police

rct *abbr* recruit

rd *abbr* **1** road **2** rod **3** round

RD *abbr* rural delivery

RDA *abbr* recommended daily allowance; recommended dietary allowance

re \(ˈ)rā, (ˈ)rē\ *prep* : with regard to

Re *symbol* rhenium

re- \rē, ˌrē, ˈrē\ *prefix* **1** : again : anew **2** : back : backward

reabsorb
reaccommodate
reacquire
reactivate
reactivation
readapt
readdress
readjust
readjustment
readmission
readmit
readmittance
readopt
reaffirm
reaffirmation
realign
realignment
reallocate
reallocation
reanalysis
reanalyze
reanimate
reanimation
reannex
reannexation
reappear
reappearance
reapplication
reapply
reappoint
reappointment
reapportion
reapportionment
reappraisal
reappraise
rearm
rearmament
rearouse
rearrange
rearrangement
rearrest
reascend
reassail
reassemble
reassembly
reassert

reassess
reassessment
reassign
reassignment
reassume
reattach
reattachment
reattack
reattain
reattempt
reauthorization
reauthorize
reawake
reawaken
rebaptism
rebaptize
rebid
rebind
reboil
rebroadcast
reburial
rebury
recalculate
recalculation
rechannel
recharge
recharter
recheck
rechristen
reclean
recoin
recolonization
recolonize
recolor
recomb
recombine
recommence
recommission
recommit
recompile
recompose
recompress
recompression
recomputation
recompute
reconceive
reconcentrate
reconception
recondensation
recondense
recondition
reconfirm
reconfirmation
reconnect
reconquer
reconquest
reconsecrate
reconsecration
reconsult
reconsultation
recontact
recontaminate
recontamination
recontract
reconvene
reconvert
recook
recopy
recouple
recross
recrystallize
recut
redecorate
redecoration
rededicate
rededication
redefine
redefinition
redeposit
redesign
redetermination
redetermine
redevelop
redevelopment
redigest
redip
redirect
rediscount
rediscover
rediscovery
redissolve
redistill
redistillation
redistribute
redistribution
redouble
redraft
redraw
reecho
reedit
reelect
reelection
reembodiment
reembody
reemerge
reemergence
reemphasis
reemphasize
reemploy
reemployment
reenact
reenactment
reenergize
reenlist
reenlistment
reenter
reequip
reestablish
reestablishment
reevaluate
reevaluation
reexamination
reexamine
reexchange
reexport
refashion
refasten
refight
refigure
refilm
refilter
refinance
refinish
refit
refix
refloat
refly
refold
reforge
reformulate
reformulation
refortify
refound
refreeze
refuel
refurnish
regather
regild
regive
reglue
regrade
regrind
regrowth
rehandle
rehear
reheat
rehouse
reimpose
reimposition
reincorporate
reinsert
reinsertion
reintegrate
reinterpret
reinterpretation
reintroduce
reintroduction
reinvent
reinvention
reinvest
reinvestment
reinvigorate
reinvigoration
reissue
rejudge
rekindle
reknit
relaunch
relearn
reletter
relight
reline
reload
remanufacture
remap
remarriage
remarry
remelt
remigration
remix
remold
rename
renegotiate
renegotiation
renominate
renomination
renumber
reoccupy
reopen
reorder
reorganization
reorganize
reorient
reorientation
repack
repaint
repass
repeople
rephotograph
rephrase
replant
repopulate
reprice
reprocess
republication
republish
repurchase
reradiate
reread
rerecord
resay
rescore
rescreen
reseal
reseed
resell
reset
resettle
resettlement
resew
reshipment
reshow
resow
respell
restaff
restate
restatement
restock
restraighten
restrengthen
restrike
restring
restructure
restudy
restuff
restyle
resubmit
resummon
resupply
resurface
resurvey
resynthesis
resynthesize
retaste
retell
retest
rethink
retool
retrain
retransmission
retransmit
retrial
reunification
reunify
reunite
reusable
reuse
revaluate
revaluation
revalue
reverify
revisit
rewarm
rewash
reweave
rewed
reweigh
reweld
rewind
rewire
rewrite
rezone

[1]**reach** \ˈrēch\ *vb* **1** : to stretch out **2** : to touch or attempt to touch or seize **3** : to extend to **4** : to arrive at **5** : to communicate with **syn** gain, realize, achieve, attain — **reach·able** *adj* — **reach·er** *n*

[2]**reach** *n* **1** : an unbroken stretch or expanse; *esp* : a straight part of a river **2** : the act of reaching **3** : the distance or extent of reaching or of ability to reach **4** : power to comprehend

re·act \rē-ˈakt\ *vb* **1** : to exert a return or counteracting influence **2** : to respond to a stimulus **3** : to act in opposition to a force or influence **4** : to turn back or revert to a former condition **5** : to undergo chemical reaction

re·ac·tant \-tənt\ *n* : a chemically reacting substance

re·ac·tion \rē-ˈak-shən\ *n* **1** : a return or reciprocal action **2** : a counter tendency; *esp* : a tendency toward a former esp. outmoded political or social order or policy **3** : bodily, mental, or emotional response to a stimulus **4** : chemical change **5** : a process involving change in atomic nuclei

[1]**re·ac·tion·ary** \rē-ˈak-shə-ˌner-ē\ *adj* : relating to, marked by, or favoring esp. political reaction

[2]**reactionary** *n, pl* **-ar·ies** : a reactionary person

re·ac·tive \rē-ˈak-tiv\ *adj* : reacting or tending to react

re·ac·tor \rē-ˈak-tər\ *n* **1** : one that reacts **2** : a vessel for a chemical reaction **3** : a device for the controlled release of nuclear energy

[1]**read** \ˈrēd\ *vb* **read** \ˈred\; **read·ing** \ˈrēd-iŋ\ **1** : to understand language by interpreting written symbols for speech sounds **2** : to utter aloud written or printed words **3** : to learn by observing ⟨~ nature's signs⟩ **4** : to discover the meaning of ⟨~ the clues⟩ **5** : to attribute (a meaning) to something ⟨~ guilt in his manner⟩ **6** : INDICATE ⟨thermometer ~*s* 10°⟩ **7** : to study by a course of reading ⟨~*s* law⟩ **8** : to consist in phrasing or meaning ⟨the two versions ~ differently⟩ — **read·abil·i·ty** \ˌrēd-ə-ˈbil-ət-ē\ *n* — **read·able** \ˈrēd-ə-bəl\ *adj* — **read·ably** \-blē\ *adv* — **read·er** *n*

[2]**read** \ˈred\ *adj* : informed by reading ⟨a widely ~ man⟩

read·er·ship \ˈrēd-ər-ˌship\ *n* : the mass or a particular group of readers

read·ing \ˈrēd-iŋ\ *n* **1** : something read or for reading **2** : a particular version **3** : a particular interpretation (as of a law) **4** : a particular performance (as of a musical work) **5** : an indication of a certain state of affairs; *also* : an indication of data made by an instrument ⟨thermometer ~⟩

read–only memory \ˌrēd-ˈōn-lē-\ *n* : a usu. small computer memory that contains special-purpose information (as a program) which cannot be altered

read·out \ˈrēd-ˌau̇t\ *n* : the process of removing information from an automatic device (as a computer) and displaying it in an understandable form; *also* : the information removed from such a device

read out \(ˈ)rēd-ˈau̇t\ *vb* : to expel from an organization

[1]**ready** \ˈred-ē\ *adj* **readi·er; -est** **1** : prepared for use or action **2** : likely to do something indicated; *also* : willingly disposed : INCLINED **3** : spontaneously prompt **4** : notably dexterous, adroit, or skilled **5** : immediately available : HANDY — **read·i·ly** \ˈred-ə-lē\ *adv* — **read·i·ness** \-ē-nəs\ *n*

[2]**ready** *vb* **read·ied; ready·ing** : to make ready : PREPARE

[3]**ready** *n* : the state of being ready

ready–made \ˌred-ē-ˈmād\ *adj* : already made up for general sale : not specially made — **ready–made** *n*

ready room *n* : a room in which pilots are briefed and await orders

re·agent \rē-ˈā-jənt\ *n* : a substance that takes part in or brings about a particular chemical reaction

[1]**re·al** \ˈrē(-ə)l\ *adj* [ME, real, relating to things (in law), fr. MF, fr. ML & LL; ML *realis* relating to things (in law), fr. LL, real, fr. L *res* thing, fact] **1** : actually being or existent **2** : not artificial : GENUINE — **re·al·ness** *n* — **for real 1** : in earnest **2** : GENUINE

[2]**real** *adv* : VERY

real estate *n* : property in buildings and land

real image *n* : an image formed by rays of light coming to a focus

re·al·ism \ˈrē-ə-ˌliz-əm\ *n* **1** : the disposition to face facts and to deal with them practically **2** : true and faithful portrayal of nature and of people in art or literature — **re·al·ist** \-ləst\ *adj or n* — **re·al·is·tic** \ˌrē-ə-ˈlis-tik\ *adj* — **re·al·is·ti·cal·ly** \-ti-k(ə-)lē\ *adv*

re·al·i·ty \rē-ˈal-ət-ē\ *n, pl* **-ties** **1** : the quality or state of being real **2** : something real **3** : the totality of real things and events

re·al·ize \ˈrē-ə-ˌlīz\ *vb* **-ized; -iz·ing** **1** : to make actual : ACCOMPLISH **2** : OBTAIN, GAIN ⟨~ a profit⟩ **3** : to convert into money ⟨~ assets⟩ **4** : to be aware of : UNDERSTAND — **re·al·iz·able** *adj* — **re·al·iza·tion** \ˌrē-ə-lə-ˈzā-shən\ *n*

re·al·ly \ˈrē-(ə-)lē, ˈril-ē\ *adv* : in truth : in fact : ACTUALLY

realm \ˈrelm\ *n* **1** : KINGDOM **2** : SPHERE, DOMAIN

real number *n* : any of the numbers (as −2, 3, ⅞, .25, π) that are rational or irrational

re·al·po·li·tik \rā-ˈäl-ˌpō-li-ˌtēk\ *n* [G] : politics based on practical and material factors rather than on theoretical or ethical objectives

real time *n* : the actual time during which something takes place — **real–time** *adj*

re·al·ty \ˈrē(-ə)l-tē\ *n* : REAL ESTATE

[1]**ream** \ˈrēm\ *n* [ME *reme*, fr. MF *raime*, fr. Ar *rizmah*, lit., bundle] : a quantity of paper that is variously 480, 500, or 516 sheets

[2]**ream** *vb* **1** : to enlarge or shape with a reamer **2** : to clean or clear with a reamer

ream·er \ˈrē-mər\ *n* : a tool with cutting edges that is used to enlarge or shape a hole

reap \ˈrēp\ *vb* **1** : to cut or clear with a scythe, sickle, or machine **2** : to gather by or as if by cutting : HARVEST ⟨~ a reward⟩ — **reap·er** *n*

[1]**rear** \ˈriər\ *vb* **1** : to erect by building **2** : to set or raise upright **3** : to breed and raise for use or market ⟨~ livestock⟩ **4** : BRING UP, FOSTER **5** : to lift or rise up; *esp* : to rise on the hind legs

[2]**rear** *n* **1** : the unit (as of an army) or area farthest from the enemy **2** : BACK; *also* : the position at the back of something

[3]**rear** *adj* : being at the back

rear admiral *n* : a commissioned officer in the navy or coast guard ranking next below a vice admiral

[1]**rear·ward** \ˈriər-wərd\ *adj* **1** : being at or toward the rear **2** : directed toward the rear

[2]**rear·ward** *also* **rear·wards** \-wərdz\ *adv* : at or toward the rear

[1]**rea·son** \ˈrēz-ᵊn\ *n* [ME *resoun*, fr. OF *raison*, fr. L *ration-, ratio* reason, computation] **1** : a statement offered in explanation or justification **2** : GROUND, CAUSE **3** : the power to think : INTELLECT **4** : a sane or sound mind **5** : due exercise of the faculty of logical thought

[2]**reason** *vb* **rea·soned; rea·son·ing** \ˈrēz-(ᵊ-)niŋ\ **1** : to talk with another to cause a change of mind **2** : to use the faculty of reason : THINK **3** : to discover or formulate by the use of reason — **rea·son·er** *n* — **rea·son·ing** *n*

rea·son·able \ˈrēz-(ᵊ-)nə-bəl\ *adj* **1** : being within the bounds of reason : not extreme : MODERATE, FAIR **2** : INEXPENSIVE **3** : able to reason : RATIONAL — **rea·son·able·ness** *n* — **rea·son·ably** \-blē\ *adv*

re·as·sure \ˌrē-ə-ˈshu̇r\ *vb* **1** : to assure again **2** : to restore confidence to : free from fear — **re·as·sur·ance** \-ˈshu̇r-əns\ *n* — **re·as·sur·ing·ly** \-ˈshu̇r-iŋ-lē\ *adv*

[1]**re·bate** \ˈrē-ˌbāt\ *vb* **re·bat·ed; re·bat·ing** : to make or give a rebate

[2]**re·bate** *n* : a return of part of a payment **syn** deduction, abatement, discount

[1]**reb·el** \ˈreb-əl\ *adj* [ME, fr. OF *rebelle*, fr. L *rebellis*, fr.

re- + *bellum* war, fr. OL *duellum*] : of or relating to rebels

²**rebel** *n* : one that rebels against authority

³**re·bel** \ri-ˈbel\ *vb* **re·belled; re·bel·ling 1** : to resist the authority of one's government **2** : to act in or show disobedience **3** : to feel or exhibit anger or revulsion

re·bel·lion \ri-ˈbel-yən\ *n* : resistance to authority; *esp* : defiance against a government through uprising or revolt

re·bel·lious \-yəs\ *adj* **1** : given to or engaged in rebellion **2** : inclined to resist authority — **re·bel·lious·ly** *adv* — **re·bel·lious·ness** *n*

re·birth \ˈrē-ˈbərth\ *n* **1** : a new or 2d birth **2** : RENAISSANCE, REVIVAL

re·born \-ˈbȯrn\ *adj* : born again : REGENERATED, REVIVED

¹**re·bound** \ˈrē-ˈbau̇nd, ri-\ *vb* **1** : to spring back on or as if on striking another body **2** : to recover from a setback or frustration

²**re·bound** \ˈrē-ˌbau̇nd\ *n* **1** : the action of rebounding **2** : a rebounding ball **3** : immediate spontaneous reaction to setback or frustration

re·buff \ri-ˈbəf\ *vb* : to reject or criticize sharply : SNUB — **rebuff** *n*

re·build \(ˈ)rē-ˈbild\ *vb* **-built** \-ˈbilt\; **-build·ing 1** : REPAIR, RECONSTRUCT; *also* : REMODEL **2** : to build again

¹**re·buke** \ri-ˈbyük\ *vb* **re·buked; re·buk·ing** : to reprimand sharply : REPROVE

²**rebuke** *n* : a sharp reprimand

re·bus \ˈrē-bəs\ *n* [L, by things, abl. pl. of *res* thing] : a representation of syllables or words by means of pictures; *also* : a riddle composed of such pictures

re·but \ri-ˈbət\ *vb* **re·but·ted; re·but·ting** : to refute esp. formally (as in debate) by evidence and arguments **syn** disprove, controvert, confute — **re·but·ter** *n*

re·but·tal \ri-ˈbət-ᵊl\ *n* : the act of rebutting

rec *abbr* **1** receipt **2** record; recording **3** recreation

re·cal·ci·trant \ri-ˈkal-sə-trənt\ *adj* [LL *recalcitrant-, recalcitrans*, prp. of *recalcitrare* to be stubbornly disobedient, fr. L, to kick back, fr. *re-* back, again + *calcitrare* to kick, fr. *calc-, calx* heel] **1** : stubbornly resisting authority **2** : resistant to handling or treatment **syn** refractory, headstrong, willful, unruly, ungovernable — **re·cal·ci·trance** \-trəns\ *n*

¹**re·call** \ri-ˈkȯl\ *vb* **1** : to call back **2** : REMEMBER, RECOLLECT **3** : REVOKE, ANNUL

²**re·call** \ri-ˈkȯl, ˈrē-ˌkȯl\ *n* **1** : a summons to return **2** : the procedure of removing an official by popular vote **3** : remembrance of things learned or experienced **4** : the act of revoking

re·cant \ri-ˈkant\ *vb* : to take back (something one has said) publicly : make an open confession of error — **re·can·ta·tion** \ˌrē-ˌkan-ˈtā-shən\ *n*

¹**re·cap** \ˈrē-ˌkap, ri-ˈkap\ *vb* **re·capped; re·cap·ping** : RECAPITULATE — **re·cap** \ˈrē-ˌkap\ *n*

²**re·cap** \ˈrē-ˈkap\ *vb* **re·capped; re·cap·ping** : RETREAD — **re·cap** \ˈrē-ˌkap\ *n*

re·ca·pit·u·late \ˌrē-kə-ˈpich-ə-ˌlāt\ *vb* **-lat·ed; -lat·ing** : to restate briefly : SUMMARIZE — **re·ca·pit·u·la·tion** \-ˌpich-ə-ˈlā-shən\ *n*

re·cap·ture \(ˈ)rē-ˈkap-chər\ *vb* **1** : to capture again **2** : to experience again ⟨~ happy times⟩

re·cast \(ˈ)rē-ˈkast\ *vb* **1** : to cast again **2** : REVISE, REMODEL ⟨~ a sentence⟩

recd *abbr* received

re·cede \ri-ˈsēd\ *vb* **re·ced·ed; re·ced·ing 1** : to move back or away **2** : to slant backward **3** : DIMINISH, CONTRACT

¹**re·ceipt** \ri-ˈsēt\ *n* **1** : RECIPE **2** : the act of receiving **3** : something received — usu. used in pl. **4** : a written acknowledgment of something received

²**receipt** *vb* **1** : to give a receipt for **2** : to mark as paid

re·ceiv·able \ri-ˈsē-və-bəl\ *adj* **1** : capable of being received; *esp* : acceptable as legal ⟨~ certificates⟩ **2** : subject to call for payment ⟨notes ~⟩

re·ceive \ri-ˈsēv\ *vb* **re·ceived; re·ceiv·ing 1** : to take in or accept (as something sent or paid) : come into possession of : GET **2** : CONTAIN, HOLD **3** : to permit to enter : GREET, WELCOME **4** : to be at home to visitors **5** : to accept as true or authoritative **6** : to be the subject of : UNDERGO, EXPERIENCE ⟨~ a shock⟩ **7** : to change incoming radio waves into sounds or pictures

re·ceiv·er \ri-ˈsē-vər\ *n* **1** : one that receives **2** : a person legally appointed to receive and have charge of property or money involved in a lawsuit **3** : a device for converting electromagnetic waves or signals into audio or visual form ⟨telephone ~⟩

re·ceiv·er·ship \-ˌship\ *n* **1** : the office or function of a receiver **2** : the condition of being in the hands of a receiver

re·cen·cy \ˈrēs-ᵊn-sē\ *n* : RECENTNESS

re·cent \ˈrēs-ᵊnt\ *adj* **1** : of the present time or time just past ⟨~ history⟩ **2** : lately made or used : NEW, FRESH **3** *cap* : of, relating to, or being the present geologic epoch — **re·cent·ly** *adv* — **re·cent·ness** *n*

re·cep·ta·cle \ri-ˈsep-ti-kəl\ *n* **1** : something used to receive and hold something else : CONTAINER **2** : the enlarged end of a flower stalk upon which the parts of the flower grow **3** : an electrical fitting containing the live parts of a circuit

re·cep·tion \ri-ˈsep-shən\ *n* **1** : the act of receiving **2** : a social gathering at which guests are formally welcomed

re·cep·tion·ist \-sh(ə-)nəst\ *n* : one employed to greet callers

re·cep·tive \ri-ˈsep-tiv\ *adj* : able or inclined to receive; *esp* : open and responsive to ideas, impressions, or suggestions — **re·cep·tive·ly** *adv* — **re·cep·tive·ness** *n* — **re·cep·tiv·i·ty** \ˌrē-ˌsep-ˈtiv-ət-ē\ *n*

re·cep·tor \ri-ˈsep-tər\ *n* **1** : one that receives; *esp* : SENSE ORGAN **2** : a molecule in the outer cell membrane or in the cell interior that has an affinity for a specific chemical group, molecule, or virus

¹**re·cess** \ˈrē-ˌses, ri-ˈses\ *n* **1** : a secret or secluded place **2** : an indentation in a line or surface (as an alcove in a room) **3** : a suspension of business or procedure for rest or relaxation

²**recess** *vb* **1** : to put into a recess **2** : to make a recess in **3** : to interrupt for a recess **4** : to take a recess

re·ces·sion \ri-ˈsesh-ən\ *n* **1** : the act of receding : WITHDRAWAL **2** : a departing procession (as at the end of a church service) **3** : a period of reduced economic activity

re·ces·sion·al \-(ə-)nəl\ *n* **1** : a hymn or musical piece at the conclusion of a service or program **2** : RECESSION **2**

¹**re·ces·sive** \ri-ˈses-iv\ *adj* **1** : tending to go back : RECEDING **2** : producing or being a bodily characteristic that is masked or not expressed when a contrasting dominant gene or trait is present ⟨~ genes⟩

²**recessive** *n* **1** : a recessive characteristic or gene **2** : an individual that has one or more recessive characteristics

re·cher·ché \rə-ˌsher-ˈshā, -ˈshe(ə)r-ˌshā\ *adj* [F] **1** : CHOICE, RARE **2** : excessively refined

re·cid·i·vism \ri-ˈsid-ə-ˌviz-əm\ *n* : a tendency to relapse into a previous condition; *esp* : relapse into criminal behavior — **re·cid·i·vist** \-vəst\ *n*

recip *abbr* reciprocal; reciprocity

rec·i·pe \ˈres-ə-(ˌ)pē\ *n* [L, take, imperative of *recipere* to receive, fr. *re-* back + *capere* to take] **1** : a set of instructions for making something (as a food dish) from various ingredients **2** : a method of procedure : FORMULA

re·cip·i·ent \ri-ˈsip-ē-ənt\ *n* : one that receives

[1]**re·cip·ro·cal** \ri-ˈsip-rə-kəl\ *adj* **1** : inversely related **2** : MUTUAL, SHARED **3** : so related to each other that one is equivalent to or completes the other **syn** correspondent, complementary — **re·cip·ro·cal·ly** \-k(ə-)lē\ *adv*

[2]**reciprocal** *n* **1** : something in a reciprocal relationship to another **2** : one of a pair of numbers (as ⅔, 3/2) whose product is one

re·cip·ro·cate \-ˌkāt\ *vb* **-cat·ed; -cat·ing 1** : to move backward and forward alternately ⟨a *reciprocating* piston⟩ **2** : to give and take mutually **3** : to make a return for something done or given — **re·cip·ro·ca·tion** \-ˌsip-rə-ˈkā-shən\ *n*

rec·i·proc·i·ty \ˌres-ə-ˈpräs-ət-ē\ *n, pl* **-ties 1** : the quality or state of being reciprocal **2** : mutual exchange of privileges (as trade advantages between countries)

re·cit·al \ri-ˈsīt-ᵊl\ *n* **1** : an act or instance of reciting : ACCOUNT **2** : a public reading or recitation ⟨a poetry ~⟩ **3** : a concert given by a musician, dancer, or dance troupe **4** : a public exhibition of skill given by music or dance pupils — **re·cit·al·ist** \-ᵊl-əst\ *n*

rec·i·ta·tion \ˌres-ə-ˈtā-shən\ *n* **1** : RECITING, RECITAL **2** : delivery before an audience of something memorized **3** : a classroom exercise in which pupils answer questions on a lesson they have studied

re·cite \ri-ˈsīt\ *vb* **re·cit·ed; re·cit·ing 1** : to repeat verbatim (as something memorized) **2** : to recount in some detail : RELATE **3** : to reply to a teacher's questions on a lesson — **re·cit·er** *n*

reck·less \ˈrek-ləs\ *adj* : lacking caution : RASH **syn** hasty, brash, hotheaded, thoughtless — **reck·less·ly** *adv* — **reck·less·ness** *n*

reck·on \ˈrek-ən\ *vb* **reck·oned; reck·on·ing** \-(ə-)niŋ\ **1** : COUNT, CALCULATE, COMPUTE **2** : CONSIDER, REGARD **3** *chiefly dial* : THINK, SUPPOSE, GUESS

reck·on·ing \-iŋ\ *n* **1** : an act or instance of reckoning **2** : a settling of accounts ⟨day of ~⟩

re·claim \ri-ˈklām\ *vb* **1** : to recall from wrong conduct : REFORM **2** : to put into a desired condition (as by labor or discipline) ⟨~ marshy land⟩ **3** : to obtain from a waste product or by-product **4** : to demand or obtain the return of **syn** save, redeem, rescue — **re·claim·able** *adj* — **rec·la·ma·tion** \ˌrek-lə-ˈmā-shən\ *n*

re·cline \ri-ˈklīn\ *vb* **re·clined; re·clin·ing 1** : to lean or incline backward **2** : to lie down : REST

re·clin·er \ri-ˈklī-nər\ *n* : a chair with an adjustable back and footrest

rec·luse \ˈrek-ˌlüs, ri-ˈklüs\ *n* : a person who lives in seclusion or leads a solitary life : HERMIT

rec·og·ni·tion \ˌrek-əg-ˈnish-ən\ *n* **1** : the act of recognizing : the state of being recognized : ACKNOWLEDGMENT **2** : special notice or attention

re·cog·ni·zance \ri-ˈkä(g)-nə-zəns\ *n* : a promise recorded before a court or magistrate to do something (as to appear in court or to keep the peace) usu. under penalty of a money forfeiture

rec·og·nize \ˈrek-əg-ˌnīz\ *vb* **-nized; -niz·ing 1** : to acknowledge (as a speaker in a meeting) as one entitled to be heard at the time **2** : to acknowledge the existence or the independence of (a country or government) **3** : to take notice of **4** : to acknowledge with appreciation **5** : to acknowledge acquaintance with **6** : to identify as previously known **7** : to perceive clearly : REALIZE — **rec·og·niz·able** \ˈrek-əg-ˌnī-zə-bəl\ *adj* — **rec·og·niz·ably** \-blē\ *adv*

[1]**re·coil** \ri-ˈkȯil\ *vb* **1** : to draw back : RETREAT **2** : to spring back to or as if to a starting point **syn** shrink, flinch, wince, quail, blanch

[2]**re·coil** \ˈrē-ˌkȯil, ri-ˈkȯil\ *n* : the action of recoiling (as by a gun or spring)

re·coil·less \-ˌkȯil-ləs, -ˈkȯil-\ *adj* : venting expanding propellant gas before recoil is produced ⟨~ gun⟩

rec·ol·lect \ˌrek-ə-ˈlekt\ *vb* : to recall to mind : REMEMBER **syn** recall, remind, reminisce, bethink

rec·ol·lec·tion \ˌrek-ə-ˈlek-shən\ *n* **1** : the act or power of recollecting **2** : something recollected

re·com·bi·nant DNA \(ˈ)rē-ˈkäm-bə- nənt-\ *n* : DNA prepared in the laboratory by breaking up and splicing together DNA from several different species of organisms

rec·om·mend \ˌrek-ə-ˈmend\ *vb* **1** : to present as deserving of acceptance or trial **2** : to give in charge : COMMIT **3** : to cause to receive favorable attention **4** : ADVISE, COUNSEL — **rec·om·mend·able** \-ˈmen-də-bəl\ *adj*

rec·om·men·da·tion \ˌrek-ə-mən-ˈdā- shən\ *n* **1** : the act of recommending **2** : a thing or a course of action recommended **3** : something that recommends

[1]**rec·om·pense** \ˈrek-əm-ˌpens\ *vb* **-pensed; -pens·ing 1** : to give compensation to : pay for **2** : to return in kind : REQUITE **syn** reimburse, indemnify, repay, compensate

[2]**recompense** *n* : COMPENSATION

rec·on·cile \ˈrek-ən-ˌsīl\ *vb* **-ciled; -cil·ing 1** : to cause to be friendly or harmonious again **2** : ADJUST, SETTLE ⟨~ differences⟩ **3** : to bring to submission or acceptance **syn** conform, accommodate, harmonize, coordinate — **rec·on·cil·able** *adj* — **rec·on·cile·ment** *n* — **rec·on·cil·er** *n* — **rec·on·cil·i·a·tion** \ˌrek-ən-ˌsil-ē-ˈā-shən\ *n*

re·con·dite \ˈrek-ən-ˌdīt\ *adj* **1** : hard to understand : PROFOUND, ABSTRUSE **2** : little known : OBSCURE

re·con·nais·sance \ri-ˈkän-ə-zəns, -səns\ *n* [F, lit., recognition] : a preliminary survey of an area; *esp* : an exploratory military survey of enemy territory

re·con·noi·ter *or* **re·con·noi·tre** \ˌrē-kə-ˈnȯit-ər, ˌrek-ə-\ *vb* **-noi·tered** *or* **-noi·tred; -noi·ter·ing** *or* **-noi·tring** : to make a reconnaissance of : engage in reconnaissance

re·con·sid·er \ˌrē-kən-ˈsid-ər\ *vb* : to consider again with a view to changing or reversing; *esp* : to take up again in a meeting — **re·con·sid·er·a·tion** \-ˌsid-ə-ˈrā-shən\ *n*

re·con·sti·tute \ˈrē-ˈkän-stə-ˌt(y)üt\ *vb* : to restore to a former condition by adding water ⟨~ powdered milk⟩

re·con·struct \ˌrē-kən-ˈstrəkt\ *vb* : to construct again : REBUILD

re·con·struc·tion \ˌrē-kən-ˈstrək-shən\ *n* **1** : the action of reconstructing : the state of being reconstructed **2** *often cap* : the reorganization and reestablishment of the seceded states in the Union after the American Civil War **3** : something reconstructed

[1]**re·cord** \ri-ˈkȯrd\ *vb* **1** : to set down (as proceedings in a meeting) in writing **2** : to register permanently **3** : INDICATE, READ **4** : to give evidence of **5** : to cause (as sound or visual images) to be registered (as on magnetic tape) in a form that permits reproduction

[2]**rec·ord** \ˈrek-ərd\ *n* **1** : the act of recording **2** : a written account of proceedings **3** : known facts about a person **4** : an attested top performance **5** : something on which sound or visual images have been recorded

re·cord·er \ri-ˈkȯrd-ər\ *n* **1** : a judge in some city courts **2** : one who records transactions officially **3** : a recording device **4** : a wind instrument with a whistle mouthpiece and eight fingerholes

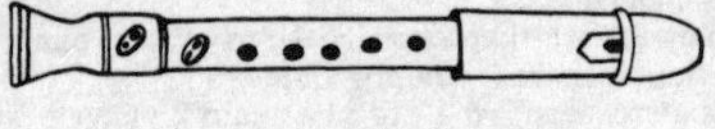

recorder 4

re·cord·ing \ri-ˈkȯrd-iŋ\ *n* : RECORD 5

re·cord·ist \ri-ˈkȯrd-əst\ *n* : one who records sound esp. on film

[1]**re·count** \ri-ˈkaůnt\ *vb* : to relate in detail : TELL **syn** recite, rehearse, narrate, describe, state, report

[2]**re·count** \ˈrē-ˈkaůnt\ *vb* : to count again

[3]**re·count** \ˈrē-ˌkaůnt, (ˈ)rē-ˈkaůnt\ *n* : a second or fresh count

re·coup \ri-ˈküp\ *vb* : to get an equivalent or compensation for : make up for something lost **syn** retrieve, regain, recover

re·course \ˈrē-ˌkōrs, ri-ˈkōrs\ *n* **1** : a turning to someone or something for assistance or protection **2** : a source of aid : RESORT

re·cov·er \ri-ˈkəv-ər\ *vb* **-ered; -er·ing** \-(ə-)riŋ\ **1** : to get back again : REGAIN, RETRIEVE **2** : to regain normal health, poise, or status **3** : to make up for : RECOUP ⟨~*ed* all his losses⟩ **4** : RECLAIM ⟨~ land from the sea⟩ **5** : to obtain a legal judgment in one's favor — **re·cov·er·able** *adj* — **re·cov·ery** \-ˈkəv-(ə-)rē\ *n*

re–cov·er \ˈrē-ˈkəv-ər\ *vb* : to cover again

[1]**rec·re·ant** \ˈrek-rē-ənt\ *adj* [ME, fr. MF, fr. prp. of *recroire* to renounce one's cause in a trial by battle, fr. *re-* back + *croire* to believe, fr. L *credere*] **1** : COWARDLY **2** : UNFAITHFUL

[2]**recreant** *n* **1** : COWARD **2** : DESERTER

rec·re·ate \ˈrek-rē-ˌāt\ *vb* **-at·ed; -at·ing** **1** : to give new life or freshness to **2** : to take recreation — **rec·re·ative** \-ˌāt-iv\ *adj*

re–cre·ate \ˌrē-krē-ˈāt\ *vb* : to create again — **re–cre·ation** \-ˈā-shən\ *n* — **re–cre·ative** \-ˈāt-iv\ *adj*

rec·re·ation \ˌrek-rē-ˈā-shən\ *n* : a refreshing of strength or spirits after work; *also* : a means of refreshment **syn** diversion, entertainment, amusement — **rec·re·ation·al** \-sh(ə-)nəl\ *adj*

recreational vehicle *n* : a vehicle designed for recreational use (as camping)

re·crim·i·nate \ri-ˈkrim-ə-ˌnāt\ *vb* **-nat·ed; -nat·ing** : to make an accusation against an accuser — **re·crim·i·na·tion** \-ˌkrim-ə-ˈnā-shən\ *n* — **re·crim·i·na·to·ry** \-ˈkrim-(ə-)nə-ˌtōr-ē\ *adj*

re·cru·des·cence \ˌrē-krü-ˈdes-ᵊns\ *n* : a new outbreak esp. of something unhealthful or dangerous after a period of abatement or inactivity — **re·cru·desce** \ˌrē-krü-ˈdes\ *vb*

[1]**re·cruit** \ri-ˈkrüt\ *vb* **1** : to form or strengthen with new members ⟨~ an army⟩ **2** : to secure the services of **3** : to restore or increase in health or vigor ⟨resting to ~ his strength⟩ — **re·cruit·er** *n* — **re·cruit·ment** *n*

[2]**recruit** *n* [F *recrute, recrue* fresh growth, new levy of soldiers, fr. MF, fr. *recroistre* to grow up again, fr. L *recrescere*] : a newcomer to an activity or field; *esp* : a newly enlisted member of the armed forces

rec sec *abbr* recording secretary

rect *abbr* **1** receipt **2** rectangle; rectangular **3** rectified

rec·tal \ˈrek-tᵊl\ *adj* : of or relating to the rectum — **rec·tal·ly** \-ē\ *adv*

rect·an·gle \ˈrek-ˌtaŋ-gəl\ *n* : a 4-sided figure with four right angles; *esp* : one with adjacent sides of unequal length — **rect·an·gu·lar** \rek-ˈtaŋ-gyə-lər\ *adj*

rec·ti·fi·er \ˈrek-tə-ˌfī(-ə)r\ *n* : one that rectifies; *esp* : a device for converting alternating current into direct current

rec·ti·fy \ˈrek-tə-ˌfī\ *vb* **-fied; -fy·ing** **1** : to make or set right : CORRECT **2** : to convert alternating current into direct current **syn** emend, amend, mend, right — **rec·ti·fi·ca·tion** \ˌrek-tə-fə-ˈkā-shən\ *n*

rec·ti·lin·ear \ˌrek-tə-ˈlin-ē-ər\ *adj* **1** : moving in a straight line ⟨~ motion⟩ **2** : characterized by straight lines

rec·ti·tude \ˈrek-tə-ˌt(y)üd\ *n* **1** : moral integrity **2** : correctness of procedure **syn** virtue, goodness, morality, probity

rec·to \ˈrek-tō\ *n, pl* **rectos** : a right-hand page

rec·tor \ˈrek-tər\ *n* **1** : a clergyman in charge of a parish **2** : the head of a university or school — **rec·to·ri·al** \rek-ˈtōr-ē-əl\ *adj*

rec·to·ry \ˈrek-t(ə-)rē\ *n, pl* **-ries** : the residence of a rector or a parish priest

rec·tum \ˈrek-təm\ *n, pl* **rectums** *or* **rec·ta** \-tə\ [NL, fr. *rectum intestinum,* lit., straight intestine] : the last part of the intestine joining colon and anus

re·cum·bent \ri-ˈkəm-bənt\ *adj* : lying down : RECLINING

re·cu·per·ate \ri-ˈk(y)ü-pə-ˌrāt\ *vb* **-at·ed; -at·ing** : to get back (as health, strength, or losses) : RECOVER — **re·cu·per·a·tion** \-ˌk(y)ü-pə-ˈrā-shən\ *n* — **re·cu·per·a·tive** \-ˈk(y)ü-pə-ˌrāt-iv\ *adj*

re·cur \ri-ˈkər\ *vb* **re·curred; re·cur·ring** **1** : to go or come back in thought or discussion **2** : to occur or appear again esp. after an interval — **re·cur·rence** \-ˈkər-əns\ *n* — **re·cur·rent** \-ənt\ *adj*

re·cy·cle \rē-ˈsī-kəl\ *vb* **1** : to pass again through a cycle of changes or treatment **2** : to process (as liquid body waste, glass, or cans) in order to regain materials for human use — **recycle** *n*

[1]**red** \ˈred\ *adj* **red·der; red·dest** **1** : of the color red **2** : endorsing radical social or political change esp. by force **3** *often cap* : of or relating to the U.S.S.R. or its allies — **red·ly** *adv* — **red·ness** *n*

[2]**red** *n* **1** : the color of blood or of the ruby **2** : a revolutionary in politics **3** *cap* : COMMUNIST **4** : the condition of showing a loss ⟨in the ~⟩

re·dact \ri-ˈdakt\ *vb* **1** : to put in writing : FRAME **2** : EDIT — **re·dac·tor** \-ˈdak-tər\ *n*

re·dac·tion \-ˈdak-shən\ *n* **1** : an act or instance of redacting **2** : EDITION

red alga *n* : any of several reddish usu. marine algae

red blood cell *n* : one of the hemoglobin-containing cells that carry oxygen from the lungs to the tissues and are responsible for the red color of vertebrate blood

red·breast \ˈred-ˌbrest\ *n* : ROBIN

red·cap \ˈred-ˌkap\ *n* : a baggage porter (as at a railroad station)

red–carpet *adj* : marked by ceremonial courtesy

red cedar *n* : an American juniper with fragrant close-grained red wood; *also* : its wood

red clover *n* : a Eurasian clover with globe-shaped heads of reddish flowers widely cultivated for hay and forage

red·coat \ˈred-ˌkōt\ *n* : a British soldier esp. during the Revolutionary War

red·den \ˈred-ᵊn\ *vb* : to make or become red or reddish : FLUSH, BLUSH

red·dish \ˈred-ish\ *adj* : tinged with red — **red·dish·ness** *n*

re·deem \ri-ˈdēm\ *vb* [ME *redemen,* modif. of MF *redimer,* fr. L *redimere,* fr. *re-, red-* re- + *emere* to take, buy] **1** : to recover (property) by discharging an obligation **2** : to ransom, free, or rescue by paying a price **3** : to free from the consequences of sin **4** : to remove the obligation of by payment ⟨the government ~*s* savings bonds⟩; *also* : to convert into something of value **5** : to make good (a promise) by performing : FULFILL **6** : to atone for — **re·deem·able** *adj* — **re·deem·er** *n*

re·demp·tion \ri-ˈdemp-shən\ *n* : the act of redeeming : the state of being redeemed — **re·demp·tive** \-tiv\ *adj* — **re·demp·to·ry** \-t(ə-)rē\ *adj*

re·de·ploy \ˌrēd-i-ˈplȯi\ *vb* **1** : to transfer from one area or activity to another **2** : to relocate men or equipment — **re·de·ploy·ment** \-mənt\ *n*

red fox *n* : a fox with orange-red to reddish brown fur

red fox

\ə\abut \ᵊ\kitten \ər\further \a\ash \ā\ace \ä\cot, cart \au̇\out \ch\chin \e\bet \ē\easy \g\go \i\hit \ī\ice \j\job \ŋ\sing \ō\go \ȯ\law \ȯi\boy \th\thin \th̲\the \ü\loot \u̇\foot \y\yet \zh\vision *see also* Pronunciation Symbols page

red–hand·ed \ˈred-ˈhan-dəd\ *adv or adj* : in the act of committing a misdeed

red·head \-ˌhed\ *n* : a person having red hair — **red·head·ed** \-ˈhed-əd\ *adj*

red herring *n* : a diversion intended to distract attention from the real issue

red–hot \ˈred-ˈhät\ *adj* **1** : glowing red with heat ⟨~ iron⟩ **2** : EXCITED, FURIOUS **3** : very new ⟨~ news⟩

re·dis·trict \ˈrē-ˈdis-(ˌ)trikt\ *vb* : to organize into new territorial and esp. political divisions

red–let·ter \ˌred-ˌlet-ər\ *adj* : of special significance : MEMORABLE

red–light district *n* : a district with many houses of prostitution

re·do \(ˈ)rē-ˈdü\ *vb* : to do over or again; *esp* : REDECORATE

red oak *n* : any of various American oaks with leaves usu. having spiny-tipped lobes and acorns that take two years to mature; *also* : the wood of a red oak

red·o·lent \ˈred-ᵊl-ənt\ *adj* **1** : FRAGRANT, AROMATIC **2** : having a specified fragrance ⟨a room ~ of cooked cabbage⟩ **3** : REMINISCENT, SUGGESTIVE — **red·o·lence** \-əns\ *n* — **red·o·lent·ly** *adv*

re·doubt \ri-ˈdau̇t\ *n* [F *redoute,* fr. It *ridotto,* fr. ML *reductus* secret place, fr. L, withdrawn, fr. *reducere* to lead back, fr. *re-* back + *ducere* to lead] : a small usu. temporary fortification

re·doubt·able \ri-ˈdau̇t-ə-bəl\ *adj* [ME *redoutable,* fr. MF, fr. *redouter* to dread, fr. *re-* re- + *douter* to doubt] : arousing dread or fear : FORMIDABLE

re·dound \ri-ˈdau̇nd\ *vb* **1** : to have an effect **2** : to become added or transferred : ACCRUE

red pepper *n* : CAYENNE PEPPER

[1]**re·dress** \ri-ˈdres\ *vb* **1** : to set right : REMEDY **2** : COMPENSATE **3** : to remove the cause of (a grievance) **4** : AVENGE

[2]**re·dress** *n* **1** : relief from distress **2** : a means or possibility of seeking a remedy **3** : compensation for loss or injury **4** : an act or instance of redressing

red snapper *n* : any of various fishes including several food fishes

red spider *n* : any of several small web-spinning mites that attack forage and crop plants

red squirrel *n* : a common American squirrel with the upper parts chiefly red

red–tailed hawk \ˌred-ˌtāld-\ *n* : a common hawk of eastern No. America with a rather short typically reddish tail

red tape *n* [fr. the red tape formerly used to bind legal documents in England] : official routine or procedure marked by excessive complexity which results in delay or inaction

red tide *n* : seawater discolored by the presence of large numbers of dinoflagellates which produce a toxin poisonous to many forms of marine life and to human beings who consume infected shellfish

re·duce \ri-ˈd(y)üs\ *vb* **re·duced; re·duc·ing 1** : LESSEN **2** : to bring to a specified state or condition ⟨~ chaos to order⟩ **3** : to put in a lower rank or grade **4** : CONQUER ⟨~ a fort⟩ **5** : to bring into a certain order or classification **6** : to correct (as a fracture) by restoration of displaced parts **7** : to lessen one's weight **syn** decrease, diminish, abate, dwindle, lessen, recede — **re·duc·er** *n* — **re·duc·ible** \-ˈd(y)üs-ə-bəl\ *adj*

re·duc·tion \ri-ˈdək-shən\ *n* **1** : the act of reducing : the state of being reduced **2** : something made by reducing **3** : the amount taken off in reducing something

re·dun·dan·cy \ri-ˈdən-dən-sē\ *n, pl* **-cies 1** : the quality or state of being redundant : SUPERFLUITY **2** : something redundant or in excess **3** : the use of surplus words

re·dun·dant \-dənt\ *adj* : exceeding what is needed or normal : SUPERFLUOUS; *esp* : using more words than necessary — **re·dun·dant·ly** *adv*

red–winged blackbird \ˈred-ˌwiŋd-\ *n* : a No. American blackbird of which the adult male is black with a patch of bright scarlet on the wings

red·wood \ˈred-ˌwu̇d\ *n* : a tall coniferous timber tree of California or its durable wood

reed \ˈrēd\ *n* **1** : any of various tall slender grasses of wet areas; *also* : a stem or growth of reed **2** : a musical instrument made from the hollow stem of a reed **3** : an elastic tongue of cane, wood, or metal by which tones are produced in organ pipes and certain other wind instruments — **reedy** *adj*

re·ed·u·cate \(ˈ)rē-ˈej-ə-ˌkāt\ *vb* : to train again; *esp* : to rehabilitate through education — **re·ed·u·ca·tion** *n*

[1]**reef** \ˈrēf\ *n* **1** : a part of a sail taken in or let out in regulating the sail's size **2** : the reduction in sail area made by reefing

[2]**reef** *vb* : to reduce the area of a sail by rolling or folding part of it

[3]**reef** *n* : a ridge of rocks or sand at or near the surface of the water

[1]**reef·er** \ˈrē-fər\ *n* **1** : one that reefs **2** : a close-fitting thick jacket

[2]**reefer** *n* : a marijuana cigarette

[1]**reek** \ˈrēk\ *n* : a strong or disagreeable fume or odor

[2]**reek** *vb* **1** : to give off or become permeated with a strong or offensive odor **2** : to give a strong impression of some constituent quality ⟨an excuse that ~*ed* of falsehood⟩ — **reek·er** *n* — **reeky** \ˈrē-kē\ *adj*

[1]**reel** \ˈrēl\ *n* : a revolvable device on which something flexible (as film, tape, cord, or wire) may be wound; *also* : a quantity of something wound on such a device

[2]**reel** *vb* **1** : to wind on or as if on a reel **2** : to pull or draw (as a fish) by reeling a line — **reel·able** *adj* — **reel·er** *n*

[3]**reel** *vb* **1** : WHIRL; *also* : to be giddy **2** : to waver or fall back from a blow : RECOIL **3** : to walk or move unsteadily

[4]**reel** *n* : a reeling motion

[5]**reel** *n* : a lively Scottish dance or its music

reel off *vb* : to tell or recite rapidly and easily ⟨*reeled off* the right answers⟩

re·en·force \ˌrē-ən-ˈfōrs\ *var of* REINFORCE

re·en·try \rē-ˈen-trē\ *n* **1** : a second or new entry **2** : the action of reentering the earth's atmosphere from space

reeve \ˈrēv\ *vb* **rove** \ˈrōv\ *or* **reeved; reev·ing** : to pass (as a rope) through a hole in a block or cleat

[1]**ref** \ˈref\ *n* : REFEREE 2

[2]**ref** *abbr* **1** reference **2** referred **3** reformed **4** refunding

re·fec·tion \ri-ˈfek-shən\ *n* **1** : refreshment esp. after hunger or fatigue **2** : food and drink together : REPAST

re·fec·to·ry \ri-ˈfek-t(ə-)rē\ *n, pl* **-ries** : a dining hall (as in a monastery or college)

re·fer \ri-ˈfər\ *vb* **re·ferred; re·fer·ring 1** : to assign to a certain source, cause, or relationship **2** : to direct or send to some person or place (as for information or help) **3** : to submit to someone else for consideration or action **4** : to have recourse (as for information or aid) **5** : to have connection : RELATE **6** : to direct attention : speak of : MENTION, ALLUDE **syn** recur, repair, resort, apply, go, turn — **re·fer·able** \ˈref-(ə-)rə-bəl, ri-ˈfər-ə-\ *adj*

[1]**ref·er·ee** \ˌref-ə-ˈrē\ *n* **1** : a person to whom an issue esp. in law is referred for investigation or settlement **2** : an umpire in certain games

[2]**referee** *vb* **-eed; -ee·ing** : to act as referee

ref·er·ence \ˈref-ərns, ˈref-(ə-)rəns\ *n* **1** : the act of referring **2** : RELATION, RESPECT **3** : ALLUSION, MENTION **4** : a direction of the attention to another passage or book **5** : consultation esp. for obtaining information ⟨books for ~⟩ **6** : a person of whom inquiries as to character or ability can be made **7** : a written recommendation of a person for employment

ref·er·en·dum \ˌref-ə-ˈren-dəm\ *n, pl* **-da** \-də\ *or* **-dums**

[NL, fr. L] : the referring of legislative measures to the voters for approval or rejection; *also* : a vote on a measure so submitted

ref·er·ent \ˈref-(ə-)rənt\ *n* [L *referent-, referens,* prp. of *referre*] : one that refers or is referred to; *esp* : the thing a word stands for — **referent** *adj*

re·fer·ral \ri-ˈfər-əl\ *n* **1** : the act or an instance of referring **2** : one that is referred

[1]**re·fill** \ˈrē-ˈfil\ *vb* : to fill again : REPLENISH — **re·fill·able** *adj*

[2]**re·fill** \ˈrē-ˌfil\ *n* : a new or fresh supply of something

re·fine \ri-ˈfīn\ *vb* **re·fined; re·fin·ing 1** : to free from impurities or waste matter **2** : IMPROVE, PERFECT **3** : to free or become free of what is coarse or uncouth **4** : to make improvements by introducing subtle changes — **re·fin·er** *n*

re·fined \ri-ˈfīnd\ *adj* **1** : freed from impurities **2** : CULTURED, CULTIVATED **3** : SUBTLE

re·fine·ment \ri-ˈfīn-mənt\ *n* **1** : the action of refining **2** : the quality or state of being refined **3** : a refined feature or method; *also* : something intended to improve or perfect

re·fin·ery \ri-ˈfīn-(ə-)rē\ *n, pl* **-er·ies** : a building and equipment for refining metals, oil, or sugar

refl *abbr* reflex; reflexive

re·flect \ri-ˈflekt\ *vb* [ME *reflecten,* fr. L *reflectere* to bend back, fr. *re-* back + *flectere* to bend] **1** : to bend or cast back (as light, heat, or sound) **2** : to give back a likeness or image of as a mirror does **3** : to bring as a result ⟨~*ed* credit on him⟩ **4** : to cast reproach or blame ⟨their bad conduct ~*ed* on their training⟩ **5** : PONDER, MEDITATE — **re·flec·tion** \-ˈflek-shən\ *n* — **re·flec·tive** \-tiv\ *adj* — **re·flec·tiv·ity** \(ˌ)rē-ˌflek-ˈtiv-ət-ē\ *n*

re·flec·tor \ri-ˈflek-tər\ *n* : one that reflects; *esp* : a polished surface for reflecting radiation (as light)

[1]**re·flex** \ˈrē-ˌfleks\ *n* **1** : an automatic and usu. inborn response to a stimulus not involving higher mental centers **2** *pl* : the power of acting or responding with enough speed ⟨an athlete with great ~*es*⟩

[2]**reflex** *adj* **1** : bent or directed back **2** : of or relating to a reflex — **re·flex·ly** *adv*

[1]**re·flex·ive** \ri-ˈflek-siv\ *adj* : of or relating to an action directed back upon the doer or the grammatical subject ⟨a ~ verb⟩ ⟨the ~ pronoun *himself*⟩ — **re·flex·ive·ly** *adv* — **re·flex·ive·ness** *n*

[2]**reflexive** *n* : a reflexive verb or pronoun

re·fo·cus \(ˈ)rē-ˈfō-kəs\ *vb* **1** : to focus again **2** : to change the emphasis or direction of ⟨~*ed* her life⟩

re·for·es·ta·tion \ˌrē-ˌfór-ə-ˈstā-shən\ *n* : the action of renewing a forest by planting seeds or young trees — **re·for·est** \rē-ˈfór-əst\ *vb*

[1]**re·form** \ri-ˈfórm\ *vb* **1** : to make better or improve by removal of faults **2** : to correct or improve one's own character or habits **syn** correct, rectify, emend, remedy, redress, revise — **re·form·able** *adj* — **re·for·ma·tive** \-ˈfór-mət-iv\ *adj*

[2]**reform** *n* : improvement or correction of what is corrupt or defective

re–form \ˈrē-ˈfórm\ *vb* : to form again

ref·or·ma·tion \ˌref-ər-ˈmā-shən\ *n* **1** : the act of reforming : the state of being reformed **2** *cap* : a 16th century religious movement marked by the establishment of the Protestant churches

[1]**re·for·ma·to·ry** \ri-ˈfór-mə-ˌtōr-ē\ *adj* : aiming at or tending toward reformation : REFORMATIVE

[2]**reformatory** *n, pl* **-ries** : a penal institution for reforming young or first offenders or women

re·form·er \ri-ˈfór-mər\ *n* **1** : one that works for or urges reform **2** *cap* : a leader of the Protestant Reformation

refr *abbr* refraction

re·fract \ri-ˈfrakt\ *vb* [L *refractus,* pp. of *refringere* to break open, break up, refract, fr. *re-* back + *frangere* to break] : to subject to refraction

re·frac·tion \ri-ˈfrak-shən\ *n* : the bending of a ray (as of light) when it passes obliquely from one medium into another in which its speed is different — **re·frac·tive** \-tiv\ *adj*

re·frac·to·ry \ri-ˈfrak-t(ə-)rē\ *adj* **1** : OBSTINATE, STUBBORN, UNMANAGEABLE **2** : difficult to melt, corrode, or draw out; *esp* : capable of enduring high temperature ⟨~ bricks⟩ **syn** recalcitrant, intractable, ungovernable, unruly, headstrong, willful — **re·frac·to·ri·ness** \ri-ˈfrak-t(ə-)rē-nəs\ *n* — **refractory** *n*

[1]**re·frain** \ri-ˈfrān\ *vb* : to hold oneself back : FORBEAR — **re·frain·ment** *n*

[2]**refrain** *n* : a phrase or verse recurring regularly in a poem or song

re·fresh \ri-ˈfresh\ *vb* **1** : to make or become fresh or fresher **2** : to revive by or as if by renewal of supplies ⟨~ one's memory⟩ **3** : to freshen up **4** : to supply or take refreshment **syn** restore, rejuvenate, renovate, refurbish — **re·fresh·er** *n* — **re·fresh·ing·ly** *adv*

re·fresh·ment \-mənt\ *n* **1** : the act of refreshing : the state of being refreshed **2** : something that refreshes **3** *pl* : a light meal

re·fried beans \(ˌ)rē-ˌfrīd-\ *n pl* : beans cooked with seasonings, fried, then mashed and fried again

refrig *abbr* refrigerating; refrigeration

re·frig·er·ate \ri-ˈfrij-ə-ˌrāt\ *vb* **-at·ed; -at·ing** : to make cool; *esp* : to chill or freeze (food) for preservation — **re·frig·er·ant** \-(ə-)rənt\ *adj or n* — **re·frig·er·a·tion** \-ˌfrij-ə-ˈrā-shən\ *n* — **re·frig·er·a·tor** \-ˈfrij-ə-ˌrāt-ər\ *n*

ref·uge \ˈref-ˌyüj\ *n* **1** : shelter or protection from danger or distress **2** : a place that provides protection

ref·u·gee \ˌref-yu̇-ˈjē\ *n* : one who flees for safety esp. to a foreign country

re·ful·gence \ri-ˈfu̇l-jəns, -ˈfəl-\ *n* : radiant or shining quality or state — **re·ful·gent** \-jənt\ *adj*

[1]**re·fund** \ri-ˈfənd, ˈrē-ˌfənd\ *vb* : to give or put back (money) : REPAY — **re·fund·able** *adj*

[2]**re·fund** \ˈrē-ˌfənd\ *n* **1** : the act of refunding **2** : a sum refunded

re·fur·bish \ri-ˈfər-bish\ *vb* : to brighten or freshen up : RENOVATE

[1]**re·fuse** \ri-ˈfyüz\ *vb* **re·fused; re·fus·ing 1** : to decline to accept : REJECT **2** : to decline to do, give, or grant : DENY — **re·fus·al** \-ˈfyü-zəl\ *n*

[2]**ref·use** \ˈref-ˌyüs, -ˌyüz\ *n* : rejected or worthless matter : RUBBISH, TRASH

re·fuse·nik *or* **re·fus·nik** \ri-ˈfyüz-nik\ *n* : a Soviet citizen who is refused permission to emigrate

re·fute \ri-ˈfyüt\ *vb* **re·fut·ed; re·fut·ing** [L *refutare,* fr. *re-* back + *-futare* to beat] : to prove to be false by argument or evidence — **ref·u·ta·tion** \ˌref-yu̇-ˈtā-shən\ *n* — **re·fut·er** \ri-ˈfyüt-ər\ *n*

[1]**reg** \ˈreg\ *n* : REGULATION

[2]**reg** *abbr* **1** region **2** register; registered; registration **3** regular

re·gain \ri-ˈgān\ *vb* **1** : to gain or get again : get back ⟨~*ed* his health⟩ **2** : to get back to : reach again ⟨~ the shore⟩ **syn** recover, retrieve, recoup, repossess

re·gal \ˈrē-gəl\ *adj* **1** : of, relating to, or befitting a king : ROYAL **2** : STATELY, SPLENDID — **re·gal·ly** \-ē\ *adv*

re·gale \ri-ˈgāl\ *vb* **re·galed; re·gal·ing 1** : to entertain richly or agreeably **2** : to give pleasure or amusement to **syn** gratify, delight, please, rejoice, gladden

re·ga·lia \ri-ˈgāl-yə\ *n pl* **1** : the emblems, symbols, or paraphernalia of royalty (as the crown and scepter) **2** : the insignia of an office or order **3** : special costume : FINERY

[1]**re·gard** \ri-ˈgärd\ *n* **1** : CONSIDERATION, HEED; *also* : CARE,

CONCERN **2** : GAZE, GLANCE, LOOK **3** : RESPECT, ESTEEM **4** *pl* : friendly greetings implying respect and esteem **5** : an aspect to be considered : PARTICULAR — **re·gard·ful** *adj* — **re·gard·less** *adj*

[2]**regard** *vb* **1** : to pay attention to **2** : to show respect for : HEED **3** : to hold in high esteem : care for **4** : to look at : gaze upon **5** *archaic* : to relate to **6** : to think of : CONSIDER

re·gard·ing \-iŋ\ *prep* : CONCERNING

regardless of \ri-ˈgärd-ləs-\ *prep* : in spite of

re·gat·ta \ri-ˈgät-ə, -ˈgat-\ *n* : a boat race or a series of boat races

regd *abbr* registered

re·gen·cy \ˈrē-jən-sē\ *n, pl* **-cies** **1** : the office or government of a regent or body of regents **2** : a body of regents **3** : the period during which a regent governs

re·gen·er·a·cy \ri-ˈjen-(ə-)rə-sē\ *n* : the state of being regenerated

[1]**re·gen·er·ate** \ri-ˈjen-(ə-)rət\ *adj* **1** : formed or created again **2** : spiritually reborn or converted

[2]**re·gen·er·ate** \ri-ˈjen-ə-ˌrāt\ *vb* **1** : to cause to experience spiritual renewal **2** : to reform completely **3** : to give or gain new life; *also* : to renew by a new growth of tissue — **re·gen·er·a·tion** \-ˌjen-ə-ˈrā-shən\ *n* — **re·gen·er·a·tive** \-ˈjen-ə-ˌrāt-iv\ *adj* — **re·gen·er·a·tor** \-ˌrāt-ər\ *n*

re·gent \ˈrē-jənt\ *n* **1** : a person who rules during the childhood, absence, or incapacity of the sovereign **2** : a member of a governing board (as of a state university)

reg·gae \ˈreg-ˌā\ *n* : popular music that originated in Jamaica and combines indigenous styles with elements of rock and roll and soul music

reg·i·cide \ˈrej-ə-ˌsīd\ *n* **1** : one who murders a king **2** : murder of a king

re·gime *also* **ré·gime** \rā-ˈzhēm, ri-\ *n* **1** : REGIMEN **2** : a form or system of government **3** : a government in power; *also* : a period of rule

reg·i·men \ˈrej-ə-mən\ *n* **1** : a systematic course of treatment or behavior ⟨a strict dietary ~⟩ **2** : GOVERNMENT

[1]**reg·i·ment** \ˈrej-ə-mənt\ *n* : a military unit consisting usu. of a number of battalions — **reg·i·men·tal** \ˌrej-ə-ˈment-ᵊl\ *adj*

[2]**reg·i·ment** \ˈrej-ə-ˌment\ *vb* : to organize rigidly esp. for regulation or central control — **reg·i·men·ta·tion** \ˌrej-ə-mən-ˈtā-shən\ *n*

reg·i·men·tals \ˌrej-ə-ˈment-ᵊlz\ *n pl* **1** : a regimental uniform **2** : military dress

re·gion \ˈrē-jən\ *n* [ME, fr. MF, fr. L *region-*, *regio*, fr. *regere* to rule] : an often indefinitely defined part or area

re·gion·al \ˈrēj-(ə-)nəl\ *adj* **1** : of or relating to a geographical region **2** : of or relating to a bodily region : LOCALIZED — **re·gion·al·ly** \-ē\ *adv*

[1]**reg·is·ter** \ˈrej-ə-stər\ *n* **1** : a record of items or details; *also* : a book or system for keeping such a record **2** : the range of a voice or instrument **3** : a device to regulate ventilation or heating **4** : an automatic device recording a number or quantity

[2]**register** *vb* **-tered; -ter·ing** \-st(ə-)riŋ\ **1** : to enter in a register (as in a list of guests) **2** : to record automatically **3** : to secure special care for (mail matter) by paying additional postage **4** : to show (emotions) by facial expression or gestures **5** : to correspond or adjust so as to correspond exactly

registered nurse *n* : a graduate trained nurse who has been licensed to practice by a state authority after passing qualifying examinations

reg·is·trant \ˈrej-ə-strənt\ *n* : one that registers or is registered

reg·is·trar \-ˌsträr\ *n* : an official recorder or keeper of records (as at an educational institution)

reg·is·tra·tion \ˌrej-ə-ˈstrā-shən\ *n* **1** : the act of registering **2** : an entry in a register **3** : the number of persons registered : ENROLLMENT **4** : a document certifying an act of registering

reg·is·try \ˈrej-ə-strē\ *n, pl* **-tries** **1** : ENROLLMENT, REGISTRATION **2** : the state or fact of being entered in a register **3** : a place of registration **4** : an official record book or an entry in one

reg·nant \ˈreg-nənt\ *adj* **1** : REIGNING **2** : DOMINANT **3** : of common or widespread occurrence : PREVALENT

rego·lith \ˈreg-ə-ˌlith\ *n* : unconsolidated residual or transported material that overlies the solid rock on the earth, moon, or a planet

[1]**re·gress** \ˈrē-ˌgres\ *n* **1** : WITHDRAWAL **2** : RETROGRESSION

[2]**re·gress** \ri-ˈgres\ *vb* : to go or cause to go back or to a lower level — **re·gres·sive** *adj* — **re·gres·sor** \-ˈgres-ər\ *n*

re·gres·sion \ri-ˈgresh-ən\ *n* : the act or an instance of regressing; *esp* : reversion to an earlier mental or behavioral level

[1]**re·gret** \ri-ˈgret\ *vb* **re·gret·ted; re·gret·ting** **1** : to mourn the loss or death of **2** : to be keenly sorry for **3** : to experience regret — **re·gret·ta·ble** \-ə-bəl\ *adj* — **re·gret·ta·bly** \-blē\ *adv* — **re·gret·ter** *n*

[2]**regret** *n* **1** : mental distress caused by something beyond one's power to remedy **2** : an expression of sorrow **3** *pl* : a note or oral message politely declining an invitation — **re·gret·ful** \-fəl\ *adj* — **re·gret·ful·ly** \-ē\ *adv*

re·group \(ˈ)rē-ˈgrüp\ *vb* : to form into a new grouping

regt *abbr* regiment

[1]**reg·u·lar** \ˈreg-yə-lər\ *adj* [ME *reguler*, fr. MF, fr. LL *regularis* regular, fr L, of a bar, fr. *regula* rule, straightedge, fr. *regere* to guide straight, rule] **1** : belonging to a religious order **2** : made, built, or arranged according to a rule, standard, or type; *also* : even or symmetrical in form or structure **3** : ORDERLY, METHODICAL ⟨~ habits⟩; *also* : not varying : STEADY ⟨a ~ pace⟩ **4** : made, selected, or conducted according to rule or custom **5** : properly qualified ⟨not a ~ lawyer⟩ **6** : conforming to the normal or usual manner or inflection **7** : belonging to a permanent standing army and esp. to one maintained by a national government **syn** systematic, orderly, methodical — **reg·u·lar·i·ty** \ˌreg-yə-ˈlar-ət-ē\ *n* — **reg·u·lar·ize** \ˈreg-yə-lə-ˌrīz\ *vb* — **reg·u·lar·ly** *adv*

[2]**regular** *n* **1** : one that is regular (as in attendance) **2** : a member of the regular clergy **3** : a soldier in a regular army **4** : a player on an athletic team who is usu. in the starting lineup

reg·u·late \ˈreg-yə-ˌlāt\ *vb* **-lat·ed; -lat·ing** **1** : to govern or direct according to rule : CONTROL **2** : to bring under the control of law or authority **3** : to put in good order **4** : to fix or adjust the time, amount, degree, or rate of — **reg·u·la·tive** \-ˌlāt-iv\ *adj* — **reg·u·la·tor** \-ˌlāt-ər\ *n* — **reg·u·la·to·ry** \-lə-ˌtōr-ē\ *adj*

reg·u·la·tion \ˌreg-yə-ˈlā-shən\ *n* **1** : the act of regulating : the state of being regulated **2** : a rule dealing with details of procedure **3** : an order issued by an executive authority of a government and having the force of law

re·gur·gi·tate \rē-ˈgər-jə-ˌtāt\ *vb* **-tat·ed; -tat·ing** [ML *regurgitare*, fr. L *re-* re- + LL *gurgitare* to engulf, fr. L *gurgit-*, *gurges* whirlpool] : to throw or be thrown back or out; *esp* : VOMIT — **re·gur·gi·ta·tion** \-ˌgər-jə-ˈtā-shən\ *n*

re·hab \ˈrē-ˌhab\ *n* **1** : REHABILITATION **2** : a rehabilitated building — **rehab** *vb*

re·ha·bil·i·tate \ˌrē-(h)ə-ˈbil-ə-ˌtāt\ *vb* **-tat·ed; -tat·ing** **1** : to restore to a former capacity, rank, or right : REINSTATE **2** : to put into good condition again — **re·ha·bil·i·ta·tion** \-ˌbil-ə-ˈtā-shən\ *n* — **re·ha·bil·i·ta·tive** \-ˌtāt-iv\ *adj*

re·hash \ˈrē-ˈhash\ *vb* : to present again in another form without real change or improvement — **rehash** *n*

re·hear·ing \ˈrē-ˈhi(ə)r-iŋ\ *n* : a second or new hearing by the same tribunal

re·hears·al \ri-ˈhər-səl\ *n* **1** : something told again : RECIT-

AL 2 : a private performance or practice session preparatory to a public appearance

re·hearse \ri-ˈhərs\ *vb* **re·hearsed; re·hears·ing 1** : to say again : REPEAT **2** : to recount in order : ENUMERATE **3** : to give a rehearsal of ⟨~ a play⟩ **4** : to train by rehearsal ⟨~ an actor⟩ **5** : to engage in a rehearsal — **re·hears·er** *n*

¹reign \ˈrān\ *n* **1** : the authority or rule of a sovereign **2** : the time during which a sovereign rules

²reign *vb* **1** : to rule as a sovereign **2** : to be predominant or prevalent

re·im·burse \ˌrē-əm-ˈbərs\ *vb* **-bursed; -burs·ing** [*re-* re- + obs. E *imburse* (to put in the pocket, pay), fr. ML *imbursare* to put into a purse, fr. L *in-* in + ML *bursa* purse, fr. LL, hide of an ox, fr. Gk *byrsa*] : to pay back : make restitution : REPAY **syn** indemnify, recompense, requite, compensate — **re·im·burs·able** *adj* — **re·im·burse·ment** *n*

¹rein \ˈrān\ *n* **1** : a line of a bridle by which a rider or driver directs an animal **2** : a restraining influence : CHECK **3** : position of control or command **4** : complete freedom — usu. used in the phrase *give rein to*

²rein *vb* : to check or direct by reins

re·in·car·na·tion \ˌrē-ˌin-ˌkär-ˈnā-shən\ *n* : rebirth of the soul in a new body — **re·in·car·nate** \ˌrē-in-ˈkär-ˌnāt\ *vb*

rein·deer \ˈrān-ˌdiər\ *n* [ME *reindere,* fr. ON *hreinn* reindeer + ME *deer*] : any of several large deer of northern regions that are used for draft and meat, have antlers in both sexes, and are grouped with the caribou in a single species

reindeer moss *n* : a gray, erect, tufted, and much-branched lichen of northern regions that is consumed by reindeer and sometimes by man

re·in·fec·tion \ˌrē-ən-ˈfek-shən\ *n* : infection following another infection of the same type

re·in·force \ˌrē-ən-ˈfōrs\ *vb* **1** : to strengthen with additional forces (as troops or ships) **2** : to strengthen with new force, aid, material, or support — **re·in·force·ment** *n* — **re·in·forc·er** *n*

re·in·state \ˌrē-ən-ˈstāt\ *vb* **-stat·ed; -stat·ing** : to restore to a former position, condition, or capacity — **re·in·state·ment** *n*

re·it·er·ate \rē-ˈit-ə-ˌrāt\ *vb* **-at·ed; -at·ing** : to state or do over again or repeatedly **syn** repeat, iterate, reprise — **re·it·er·a·tion** \-ˌit-ə-ˈrā-shən\ *n*

¹re·ject \ri-ˈjekt\ *vb* **1** : to refuse to acknowledge or submit to **2** : to refuse to take or accept **3** : to refuse to grant, consider, or accede to **4** : to throw out esp. as useless or unsatisfactory — **re·jec·tion** \-ˈjek-shən\ *n*

²re·ject \ˈrē-ˌjekt\ *n* : a rejected person or thing

re·joice \ri-ˈjȯis\ *vb* **re·joiced; re·joic·ing 1** : to give joy to : GLADDEN **2** : to feel joy or great delight — **re·joic·er** *n*

re·join \ˈrē-ˈjȯin *for 1,* ri- *for 2*\ *vb* **1** : to join again : come together again : REUNITE **2** : to say in answer (as to a plaintiff's plea in court) : REPLY

re·join·der \ri-ˈjoin-dər\ *n* : REPLY; *esp* : an answer to a reply

re·ju·ve·nate \ri-ˈjü-və-ˌnāt\ *vb* **-nat·ed; -nat·ing** : to make young or youthful again : give new vigor to **syn** renew, refresh, renovate, restore — **re·ju·ve·na·tion** \-ˌjü-və-ˈnā-shən\ *n*

rel *abbr* relating; relative

¹re·lapse \ri-ˈlaps, ˈrē-ˌlaps\ *n* : the action or process of relapsing; *esp* : a recurrence of illness after a period of improvement

²re·lapse \ri-ˈlaps\ *vb* **re·lapsed; re·laps·ing** : to slip back into a former condition (as of illness) after a change for the better

re·late \ri-ˈlāt\ *vb* **re·lat·ed; re·lat·ing 1** : to give an account of : TELL, NARRATE **2** : to show or establish logical or causal connection between **3** : to be connected : have reference **4** : to have meaningful social relationships **5** : to respond favorably — **re·lat·able** *adj* — **re·lat·er** *or* **re·la·tor** *n*

re·lat·ed \-əd\ *adj* **1** : connected by some understood relationship **2** : connected through membership in the same family — **re·lat·ed·ness** *n*

re·la·tion \ri-ˈlā-shən\ *n* **1** : NARRATION, ACCOUNT **2** : CONNECTION, RELATIONSHIP **3** : connection by blood or marriage : KINSHIP; *also* : RELATIVE **4** : REFERENCE, RESPECT ⟨in ~ to this matter⟩ **5** : the state of being mutually interested or involved (as in social or commercial matters) **6** *pl* : DEALINGS, AFFAIRS **7** *pl* : SEXUAL INTERCOURSE — **re·la·tion·al** \-sh(ə-)nəl\ *adj*

re·la·tion·ship \-ˌship\ *n* : the state of being related or interrelated

¹rel·a·tive \ˈrel-ət-iv\ *n* **1** : a word referring grammatically to an antecedent **2** : a thing having a relation to or a dependence upon another thing **3** : a person connected with another by blood or marriage; *also* : an animal or plant related to another by common descent

²relative *adj* **1** : introducing a subordinate clause qualifying an expressed or implied antecedent ⟨~ pronoun⟩; *also* : introduced by such a connective ⟨~ clause⟩ **2** : PERTINENT, RELEVANT **3** : not absolute or independent : COMPARATIVE **4** : expressed as the ratio of the specified quantity to the total magnitude or to the mean of all quantities involved **syn** dependent, contingent, conditional — **rel·a·tive·ly** *adv* — **rel·a·tive·ness** *n*

relative humidity *n* : the ratio of the amount of water vapor actually present in the air to the greatest amount possible at the same temperature

rel·a·tiv·is·tic \ˌrel-ət-iv-ˈis-tik\ *adj* **1** : of, relating to, or characterized by relativity **2** : moving at a velocity that is a significant fraction of the speed of light so that effects predicted by the theory of relativity become evident ⟨a ~ electron⟩ — **rel·a·tiv·is·ti·cal·ly** \-ti-k(ə-)lē\ *adv*

rel·a·tiv·i·ty \ˌrel-ə-ˈtiv-ət-ē\ *n, pl* **-ties 1** : the quality or state of being relative **2** : a theory in physics that considers mass and energy to be equivalent and that states that a moving object will experience changes in size and time which are related to its speed but are only noticeable at speeds approaching that of light

re·lax \ri-ˈlaks\ *vb* **1** : to make or become less firm, tense, or rigid **2** : to make less severe or strict **3** : to seek rest or recreation — **re·lax·er** *n*

¹re·lax·ant \ri-ˈlak-sənt\ *adj* : producing relaxation

²relaxant *n* : a relaxing agent; *esp* : a drug that induces muscular relaxation

re·lax·ation \ˌrē-ˌlak-ˈsā-shən\ *n* **1** : the act of relaxing or state of being relaxed : a lessening of tension **2** : DIVERSION, RECREATION **syn** rest, repose, leisure, ease

¹re·lay \ˈrē-ˌlā\ *n* **1** : a fresh supply (as of horses or men) arranged beforehand to relieve or replace others at various stages **2** : a race between teams in which each team member covers a specified part of a course **3** : an electromagnetic device in which the opening or closing of one circuit activates another device (as a switch in another circuit) **4** : the act of passing along by stages

²re·lay \ˈrē-ˌlā, ri-ˈlā\ *vb* **re·layed; re·lay·ing 1** : to place in or provide with relays **2** : to pass along by relays **3** : to control or operate by a relay

³re·lay \ˈrē-ˈlā\ *vb* **-laid** \-ˈlād\; **-lay·ing** : to lay again

¹re·lease \ri-ˈlēs\ *vb* **re·leased; re·leas·ing 1** : to set free from confinement or restraint **2** : to relieve from something (as pain, trouble, or penalty) that oppresses or burdens **3** : RELINQUISH ⟨~ a claim⟩ **4** : to permit publication or performance (as of a news story or a motion picture) on but not before a specified date **syn** emancipate, discharge, free, liberate

²release *n* **1** : relief or deliverance from sorrow, suffering, or trouble **2** : discharge from an obligation or responsibility **3** : an act of setting free : the state of being freed **4** : a document effecting a legal release **5** : a device for holding or releasing a mechanism as required **6** : a releasing for performance or publication; *also* : the matter released (as to the press)

rel·e·gate \ˈrel-ə-ˌgāt\ *vb* **-gat·ed; -gat·ing 1** : to send into exile : BANISH **2** : to remove or dismiss to some less prominent position **3** : to assign to a particular class or sphere **4** : to submit or refer for judgment, decision, or execution : DELEGATE **syn** commit, entrust, consign, commend — **rel·e·ga·tion** \ˌrel-ə-ˈgā-shən\ *n*

re·lent \ri-ˈlent\ *vb* **1** : to become less stern, severe, or harsh **2** : SLACKEN

re·lent·less \-ləs\ *adj* : mercilessly hard or harsh : immovably stern or persistent — **re·lent·less·ly** *adv* — **re·lent·less·ness** *n*

rel·e·vance \ˈrel-ə-vəns\ *n* : relation to the matter at hand : practical and esp. social applicability

rel·e·van·cy \-vən-sē\ *n* : RELEVANCE

rel·e·vant \ˈrel-ə-vənt\ *adj* : bearing on the matter at hand : PERTINENT **syn** germane, material, applicable, apropos — **rel·e·vant·ly** *adv*

re·li·able \ri-ˈlī-ə-bəl\ *adj* : fit to be trusted or relied on : DEPENDABLE, TRUSTWORTHY — **re·li·abil·i·ty** \-ˌlī-ə-ˈbil-ət-ē\ *n* — **re·li·able·ness** *n* — **re·li·ably** \-ˈlī-ə-blē\ *adv*

re·li·ance \ri-ˈlī-əns\ *n* **1** : the act of relying **2** : the state of being reliant **3** : one relied on — **re·li·ant** \-ənt\ *adj*

rel·ic \ˈrel-ik\ *n* **1** : an object venerated because of its association with a saint or martyr **2** : SOUVENIR, MEMENTO **3** *pl* : REMAINS, RUINS **4** : a remaining trace : VESTIGE

rel·ict \ˈrel-ikt\ *n* : WIDOW

re·lief \ri-ˈlēf\ *n* **1** : removal or lightening of something oppressive, painful, or distressing **2** : aid in the form of money or necessities (as for the aged or handicapped) **3** : military assistance in or rescue from a position of difficulty **4** : release from a post or from performance of a duty; *also* : one that relieves another by taking his place **5** : legal remedy or redress **6** : projection of figures or ornaments from the background (as in sculpture) **7** : the elevations of a land surface

relief pitcher *n* : a baseball pitcher who takes over for another during a game

re·lieve \ri-ˈlēv\ *vb* **re·lieved; re·liev·ing 1** : to free partly or wholly from a burden or from distress **2** : to bring about the removal or alleviation of : MITIGATE **3** : to release from a post or duty; *also* : to take the place of **4** : to break the monotony of (as by contrast in color) **5** : to raise in relief **syn** alleviate, lighten, assuage, allay — **re·liev·er** *n*

relig *abbr* religion

re·li·gion \ri-ˈlij-ən\ *n* **1** : the service and worship of God or the supernatural **2** : devotion to a religious faith **3** : an organized system of faith and worship; *also* : a personal set of religious beliefs and practices **4** : a cause, principle, or belief held to with faith and ardor — **re·li·gion·ist** *n*

¹re·li·gious \ri-ˈlij-əs\ *adj* **1** : relating or devoted to the divine or that which is held to be of ultimate importance **2** : of or relating to religious beliefs or observances **3** : scrupulously and conscientiously faithful **4** : FERVENT, ZEALOUS — **re·li·gious·ly** *adv*

²religious *n, pl* **religious** : one (as a monk) bound by vows and devoted to a life of piety

re·lin·quish \ri-ˈliŋ-kwish, -ˈlin-\ *vb* **1** : to withdraw or retreat from : ABANDON, QUIT **2** : GIVE UP ⟨~ a title⟩ **3** : to let go of : RELEASE **syn** yield, leave, resign, surrender, cede, waive — **re·lin·quish·ment** *n*

rel·i·quary \ˈrel-ə-ˌkwer-ē\ *n, pl* **-quar·ies** : a container for religious relics

¹rel·ish \ˈrel-ish\ *n* [ME *reles* aftertaste, fr. OF, release, something left over, fr. *relessier* to relax, release, fr. L *relaxare*] **1** : a characteristic flavor (as of food) : SAVOR **2** : keen enjoyment or delight in something : GUSTO **3** : APPETITE, INCLINATION **4** : a highly seasoned sauce (as of pickles) eaten with other food to add flavor

²relish *vb* **1** : to add relish to **2** : to take pleasure in : ENJOY **3** : to eat with pleasure — **rel·ish·able** *adj*

re·live \(ˈ)rē-ˈliv\ *vb* : to live again or over again; *esp* : to experience again in the imagination

re·lo·cate \(ˈ)rē-ˈlō-ˌkāt, ˌrē-lō-ˈkāt\ *vb* **1** : to locate again **2** : to move to a new location — **re·lo·ca·tion** \ˌrē-lō-ˈkā-shən\ *n*

re·luc·tant \ri-ˈlək-tənt\ *adj* : holding back (as from acting) : UNWILLING; *also* : showing unwillingness ⟨~ obedience⟩ **syn** disinclined, indisposed, hesitant, loath, averse — **re·luc·tance** \-təns\ — **re·luc·tant·ly** *adv*

re·ly \ri-ˈlī\ *vb* **re·lied; re·ly·ing** [ME *relien* to rally, fr. MF *relier* to connect, rally, fr. L *religare* to tie back, fr. *re-* back + *ligare* to tie] : to place faith or confidence : DEPEND **syn** trust, count

REM \ˈrem\ *n* : RAPID EYE MOVEMENT

re·main \ri-ˈmān\ *vb* **1** : to be left after others have been removed, subtracted, or destroyed **2** : to be something yet to be shown, done, or treated ⟨it ~*s* to be seen⟩ **3** : to stay after others have gone **4** : to continue unchanged

re·main·der \ri-ˈmān-dər\ *n* **1** : that which is left over : a remaining group, part, or trace **2** : the number left after a subtraction **3** : the number that is left over from the dividend after division and that is less than the divisor **4** : a book sold at a reduced price by the publisher after sales have slowed **syn** leavings, rest, balance, remnant, residue

re·mains \-ˈmānz\ *n pl* **1** : a remaining part or trace ⟨the ~ of a meal⟩ **2** : writings left unpublished at an author's death **3** : a dead body

¹re·make \(ˈ)rē-ˈmāk\ *vb* **-made** \-ˈmād\; **-mak·ing** : to make anew or in a different form

²re·make \(ˈ)rē-ˌmāk\ *n* : one that is remade; *esp* : a new version of a motion picture

re·mand \ri-ˈmand\ *vb* : to order back; *esp* : to return to custody pending trial or for further detention

¹re·mark \ri-ˈmärk\ *vb* **1** : to take notice of : OBSERVE **2** : to express as an observation or comment : SAY

²remark *n* **1** : the act of remarking : OBSERVATION, NOTICE **2** : a passing observation or comment

re·mark·able \ri-ˈmär-kə-bəl\ *adj* : worthy of being or likely to be noticed : UNUSUAL, EXTRAORDINARY, NOTEWORTHY — **re·mark·able·ness** *n* — **re·mark·ably** \-blē\ *adv*

re·me·di·a·ble \ri-ˈmēd-ē-ə-bəl\ *adj* : capable of being remedied ⟨~ speech defects⟩

re·me·di·al \ri-ˈmēd-ē-əl\ *adj* : intended to remedy or improve

¹rem·e·dy \ˈrem-əd-ē\ *n, pl* **-dies 1** : a medicine or treatment that cures or relieves **2** : something that corrects or counteracts an evil or compensates for a loss

²remedy *vb* **-died; -dy·ing** : to provide or serve as a remedy for

re·mem·ber \ri-ˈmem-bər\ *vb* **-bered; -ber·ing** \-b(ə-)riŋ\ **1** : to have come into the mind again : think of again : RECOLLECT **2** : to keep from forgetting : keep in mind **3** : to convey greetings from **4** : COMMEMORATE

re·mem·brance \-brəns\ *n* **1** : an act of remembering : RECOLLECTION **2** : the ability to remember : MEMORY **3** : the power of remembering; *also* : the period over which one's memory extends **4** : a memory of a person, thing, or event **5** : something that serves to bring to mind : REMINDER, MEMENTO **6** : a greeting or gift recalling or expressing friendship or affection

re·mind \ri-ˈmīnd\ *vb* **:** to put in mind of someone or something **:** cause to remember — **re·mind·er** *n*

rem·i·nisce \ˌrem-ə-ˈnis\ *vb* **-nisced; -nisc·ing :** to indulge in reminiscence

rem·i·nis·cence \-ˈnis-ᵊns\ *n* **1 :** a recalling or telling of a past experience **2 :** an account of a memorable experience

rem·i·nis·cent \-ᵊnt\ *adj* **1 :** of or relating to reminiscence **2 :** marked by or given to reminiscence **3 :** serving to remind **:** SUGGESTIVE — **rem·i·nis·cent·ly** *adv*

re·miss \ri-ˈmis\ *adj* **1 :** negligent or careless in the performance of work or duty **2 :** showing neglect or inattention **syn** lax, neglectful, delinquent, derelict — **re·miss·ly** *adv* — **re·miss·ness** *n*

re·mis·sion \ri-ˈmish-ən\ *n* **1 :** the act or process of remitting **2 :** a state or period during which something is remitted

re·mit \ri-ˈmit\ *vb* **re·mit·ted; re·mit·ting 1 :** FORGIVE, PARDON **2 :** to give or gain relief from (as pain) **3 :** to refer for consideration, report, or decision **4 :** to refrain from exacting or enforcing (as a penalty) **5 :** to send (money) in payment of a bill **syn** excuse, condone

re·mit·tal \ri-ˈmit-ᵊl\ *n* **:** REMISSION

re·mit·tance \ri-ˈmit-ᵊns\ *n* **1 :** a sum of money remitted **2 :** transmittal of money (as to a distant place)

rem·nant \ˈrem-nənt\ *n* **1 :** a usu. small part or trace remaining **2 :** an unsold or unused end of fabrics that are sold by the yard **syn** remainder, residue, rest

re·mod·el \ˈrē-ˈmäd-ᵊl\ *vb* **:** to alter the structure of **:** MAKE OVER

re·mon·strance \ri-ˈmän-strəns\ *n* **:** an act or instance of remonstrating

re·mon·strant \-strənt\ *adj* **:** vigorously objecting or opposing — **remonstrant** *n* — **re·mon·strant·ly** *adv*

re·mon·strate \ri-ˈmän-ˌstrāt\ *vb* **-strat·ed; -strat·ing :** to plead in opposition to something **:** speak in protest or reproof **syn** expostulate, object, protest — **re·mon·stra·tion** \ri-ˌmän-ˈstrā- shən, ˌrem-ən-\ *n* — **re·mon·stra·tive** \ri-ˈmän-strət-iv\ *adj* — **re·mon·stra·tor** \ri-ˈmän-ˌstrāt-ər\ *n*

rem·o·ra \ˈrem-ə-rə\ *n* **:** any of several fishes with sucking organs on the head by means of which they cling to other fishes and ships

re·morse \ri-ˈmȯrs\ *n* [ME, fr. MF *remors,* fr. ML *remorsus,* fr. LL, act of biting again, fr. L *remorsus,* pp. of *remordēre* to bite again, fr. *re-* again + *mordēre* to bite] **:** regret for one's sins or for acts that wrong others **:** distress arising from a sense of guilt **syn** penitence, repentance, contrition — **re·morse·ful** *adj*

re·morse·less \-ləs\ *adj* **1 :** MERCILESS **2 :** PERSISTENT, RELENTLESS

re·mote \ri-ˈmōt\ *adj* **re·mot·er; -est 1 :** far off in place or time **:** not near **2 :** not closely related **:** DISTANT **3 :** located out of the way **:** SECLUDED **4 :** small in degree **:** SLIGHT ⟨a ~ chance⟩ **5 :** distant in manner — **re·mote·ly** *adv* — **re·mote·ness** *n*

¹re·mount \ˈrē-ˈmau̇nt\ *vb* **1 :** to mount again **2 :** to furnish remounts to

²re·mount \ˈrē-ˌmau̇nt\ *n* **:** a fresh horse to replace one disabled or exhausted

¹re·move \ri-ˈmüv\ *vb* **re·moved; re·mov·ing 1 :** to move from one place to another **:** TRANSFER **2 :** to move by lifting or taking off or away **3 :** DISMISS, DISCHARGE **4 :** to get rid of **:** ELIMINATE ⟨~ a fire hazard⟩ **5 :** to change one's residence or location **6 :** to go away **:** DEPART **7 :** to be capable of being removed — **re·mov·able** *adj* — **re·mov·al** \-vəl\ *n* — **re·mov·er** *n*

²remove *n* **1 :** a transfer from one location to another **:** MOVE **2 :** a degree or stage of separation

REM sleep *n* **:** a state of sleep associated with rapid eye movements and occurring at approximately at 90-minute intervals that is characterized by changes in the electrical activity of the brain, changes in heart rhythm, relaxed muscles, vascular congestion of the sex organs, and dreaming

re·mu·ner·ate \ri-ˈmyü-nə-ˌrāt\ *vb* **-at·ed; -at·ing :** to pay an equivalent for or to **:** RECOMPENSE — **re·mu·ner·a·tor** \-ˌrāt-ər\ *n*

re·mu·ner·a·tion \ri-ˌmyü-nə-ˈrā-shən\ *n* **:** COMPENSATION, PAYMENT

re·mu·ner·a·tive \ri-ˈmyü-nə-rət-iv, -ˌrāt-\ *adj* **:** serving to remunerate **:** GAINFUL

re·nais·sance \ˌren-ə-ˈsäns, -ˈzäns\ *n* **1** *cap* **:** the revival of classical influences in art and literature and the beginnings of modern science in Europe in the 14th-17th centuries; *also* **:** the period of the Renaissance **2** *often cap* **:** a movement or period of vigorous artistic and intellectual activity **3 :** REBIRTH, REVIVAL

re·nal \ˈrēn-ᵊl\ *adj* **:** of, relating to, or located in or near the kidneys

re·na·scence \ri-ˈnas-ᵊns, -ˈnās-\ *n, often cap* **:** RENAISSANCE

rend \ˈrend\ *vb* **rent** \ˈrent\; **rend·ing 1 :** to remove by violence **:** WREST **2 :** to tear forcibly apart **:** SPLIT

ren·der \ˈren-dər\ *vb* **ren·dered; ren·der·ing** \-d(ə-)riŋ\ **1 :** to extract (as lard) by heating **2 :** to give to another; *also* **:** YIELD **3 :** to give in return **4 :** to do (a service) for another ⟨~ aid⟩ **5 :** to cause to be or become **:** MAKE **6 :** to reproduce or represent by artistic or verbal means **7 :** TRANSLATE ⟨~ into English⟩

¹ren·dez·vous \ˈrän-di-ˌvü, -dā-\ *n, pl* **ren·dez·vous** \-ˌvüz\ [MF, fr. *rendez vous* present yourselves] **1 :** a place appointed for a meeting; *also* **:** a meeting at an appointed place **2 :** a place of popular resort **3 :** the process of bringing two spacecraft together **syn** tryst, engagement, appointment

²rendezvous *vb* **-voused** \-ˌvüd\; **-vous·ing** \-ˌvü-iŋ\; **-vouses** \-ˌvüz\ **:** to come or bring together at a rendezvous

ren·di·tion \ren-ˈdish-ən\ *n* **:** an act or a result of rendering ⟨first ~ of the work into English⟩

ren·e·gade \ˈren-i-ˌgād\ *n* [Sp *renegado,* fr. ML *renegatus,* fr. pp. of *renegare* to deny, fr. L *re-* re- + *negare* to deny] **:** one who deserts a faith, cause, principle, or party for another

re·nege \ri-ˈnig, -ˈneg, -ˈnēg, -ˈnāg\ *vb* **re·neged; re·neg·ing 1 :** to fail to follow suit when able in a card game in violation of the rules **2 :** to go back on a promise or commitment — **re·neg·er** *n*

re·new \ri-ˈn(y)ü\ *vb* **1 :** to make or become new, fresh, or strong again **2 :** to restore to existence **:** RECREATE, REVIVE **3 :** to make or do again **:** REPEAT ⟨~ a complaint⟩ **4 :** to begin again **:** RESUME ⟨~*ed* his efforts⟩ **5 :** REPLACE ⟨~ the lining of a coat⟩ **6 :** to grant or obtain an extension of or on ⟨~ a lease⟩ ⟨~ a subscription⟩ — **re·new·er** *n*

re·new·able \ri-ˈn(y)ü-ə-bəl\ *adj* **1 :** capable of being renewed **2 :** capable of being replaced by natural ecological cycles or sound management procedures ⟨water, wildlife, and forests are ~ resources⟩

re·new·al \ri-ˈn(y)ü-əl\ *n* **1 :** the act of renewing **:** the state of being renewed **2 :** something renewed

ren·net \ˈren-ət\ *n* **1 :** the contents of the stomach of an unweaned animal (as a calf) or the lining membrane of the stomach used for curdling milk **2 :** rennin or a substitute used to curdle milk

ren·nin \ˈren-ən\ *n* **:** a stomach enzyme that coagulates casein and is used commercially to curdle milk in the making of cheese

re·nounce \ri-ˈnau̇ns\ *vb* **re·nounced; re·nounc·ing 1 :** to give up, refuse, or resign usu. by formal declaration **2 :** to refuse further to follow, obey, or recognize

: REPUDIATE **syn** abdicate, resign — **re·nounce·ment** *n*

ren·o·vate \ˈren-ə-ˌvāt\ *vb* **-vat·ed; -vat·ing 1** : to make like new again : put in good condition : REPAIR **2** : to restore to vigor or activity — **ren·o·va·tion** \ˌren-ə-ˈvā-shən\ *n* — **ren·o·va·tor** \ˈren-ə-ˌvāt-ər\ *n*

re·nown \ri-ˈnau̇n\ *n* : a state of being widely acclaimed and honored : FAME, CELEBRITY **syn** honor, glory, reputation, repute — **re·nowned** \-ˈnau̇nd\ *adj*

1**rent** \ˈrent\ *n* **1** : money or the amount of money paid or due (as monthly) for the use of another's property **2** : property rented or for rent

2**rent** *vb* **1** : to take and hold under an agreement to pay rent **2** : to give possession and use of in return for rent **3** : to be for rent ⟨~*s* for $100 a month⟩ — **rent·er** *n*

3**rent** *n* **1** : a tear in cloth **2** : a split in a party or organized group : SCHISM

1**rent·al** \ˈrent-ᵊl\ *n* **1** : an amount paid or collected as rent **2** : a property rented **3** : an act of renting

2**rental** *adj* : of or relating to rent

re·nun·ci·a·tion \ri-ˌnən-sē-ˈā-shən\ *n* : the act of renouncing : REPUDIATION

rep *abbr* **1** repair **2** report; reporter **3** representative **4** republic

Rep *abbr* Republican

re·pack·age \(ˈ)rē-ˈpak-ij\ *vb* : to package again or anew; *esp* : to put into a more attractive form

1**re·pair** \ri-ˈpaər\ *vb* [ME *repairen*, fr. MF *repairier* to go back to one's country, fr. LL *repatriare*, fr. L *re-* re- + *patria* native country] : to make one's way : GO ⟨~*ed* to his den⟩

2**repair** *vb* [ME *repairen*, fr. MF *reparer*, fr. L *reparare*, fr. *re-* re- + *parare* to prepare] **1** : to restore to good condition **2** : to restore to a healthy state **3** : REMEDY ⟨~ a wrong⟩ — **re·pair·er** *n* — **re·pair·man** \-ˌman\ *n*

3**repair** *n* **1** : an act of repairing **2** : a result of repairing **3** : condition with respect to need of repairing ⟨in bad ~⟩

rep·a·ra·tion \ˌrep-ə-ˈrā-shən\ *n* **1** : the act of making amends for a wrong **2** : amends made for a wrong; *esp* : money paid by a defeated nation in compensation for damages caused during hostilities — usu. used in pl. **syn** redress, restitution, indemnity

re·par·a·tive \ri-ˈpar-ət-iv\ *adj* **1** : of, relating to, or effecting repairs **2** : serving to make amends

rep·ar·tee \ˌrep-ər-ˈtē\ *n* **1** : a witty reply **2** : a succession of clever replies; *also* : skill in making such replies

re·past \ri-ˈpast, ˈrē-ˌpast\ *n* : a supply of food and drink served as a meal

re·pa·tri·ate \rē-ˈpā-trē-ˌāt\ *vb* **-at·ed; -at·ing** : to send or bring back to the country of origin or citizenship ⟨~ profits⟩ ⟨~ prisoners of war⟩ — **re·pa·tri·ate** \-trē-ət, -trē-ˌāt\ *n* — **re·pa·tri·a·tion** \-ˌpā-trē-ˈā-shən\ *n*

re·pay \rē-ˈpā\ *vb* **-paid** \-ˈpād\; **-pay·ing 1** : to pay back : REFUND **2** : to give or do in return or requital **3** : to make a return payment to : RECOMPENSE, REQUITE **syn** remunerate, compensate, reimburse, indemnify — **re·pay·able** *adj* — **re·pay·ment** *n*

re·peal \ri-ˈpēl\ *vb* : to annul by authoritative and esp. legislative action — **repeal** *n* — **re·peal·er** *n*

1**re·peat** \ri-ˈpēt\ *vb* **1** : to say again **2** : to do again **3** : to say over from memory **syn** iterate, reiterate, reprise — **re·peat·able** *adj* — **re·peat·er** *n*

2**re·peat** \ri-ˈpēt, ˈrē-ˌpēt\ *n* **1** : the act of repeating **2** : something repeated or to be repeated (as a radio or television program)

re·peat·ed \ri-ˈpēt-əd\ *adj* : done or recurring again and again : FREQUENT — **re·peat·ed·ly** *adv*

repeating decimal *n* : a decimal in which a particular digit or sequence of digits repeats itself indefinitely

re·pel \ri-ˈpel\ *vb* **re·pelled; re·pel·ling 1** : to drive away : REPULSE **2** : to fight against : RESIST **3** : to turn away : REJECT **4** : to cause aversion in : DISGUST

1**re·pel·lent** *also* **re·pel·lant** \ri-ˈpel-ənt\ *adj* **1** : tending to drive away ⟨a mosquito-*repellent* spray⟩ **2** : causing disgust

2**repellent** *also* **repellant** *n* : something that repels; *esp* : a substance used to prevent insect attacks

re·pent \ri-ˈpent\ *vb* **1** : to turn from sin and resolve to reform one's life **2** : to feel sorry for (something done) : REGRET — **re·pen·tance** \ri-ˈpent-ᵊns\ *n* — **re·pen·tant** \-ᵊnt\ *adj*

re·per·cus·sion \ˌrē-pər-ˈkəsh-ən, ˌrep-ər-\ *n* **1** : REVERBERATION **2** : a reciprocal action or effect **3** : a widespread, indirect, or unforeseen effect of something done or said

rep·er·toire \ˈrep-ə(r)-ˌtwär\ *n* [F] **1** : a list of plays, operas, pieces, or parts which a company or performer is prepared to present **2** : a list of the skills or devices possessed by a person or needed in his occupation

rep·er·to·ry \ˈrep-ə(r)-ˌtōr-ē\ *n, pl* **-ries 1** : REPOSITORY **2** : REPERTOIRE **3** : a company that presents its repertoire in the course of one season at one theater

rep·e·ti·tion \ˌrep-ə-ˈtish-ən\ *n* **1** : the act or an instance of repeating **2** : the fact of being repeated

rep·e·ti·tious \-ˈtish-əs\ *adj* : marked by repetition; *esp* : tediously repeating — **rep·e·ti·tious·ly** *adv* — **rep·e·ti·tious·ness** *n*

re·pet·i·tive \ri-ˈpet-ət-iv\ *adj* : REPETITIOUS — **re·pet·i·tive·ly** *adv* — **re·pet·i·tive·ness** *n*

re·pine \ri-ˈpīn\ *vb* **re·pined; re·pin·ing 1** : to feel or express discontent or dejection **2** : to long for something

repl *abbr* replace; replacement

re·place \ri-ˈplās\ *vb* **1** : to restore to a former place or position **2** : to take the place of : SUPPLANT **3** : to put something new in the place of — **re·place·able** *adj* — **re·plac·er** *n*

re·place·ment \ri-ˈplās-mənt\ *n* **1** : the act of replacing : the state of being replaced : SUBSTITUTION **2** : one that replaces; *esp* : one assigned to a military unit to replace a loss or fill a quota

1**re·play** \ˈrē-ˈplā\ *vb* : to play again or over

2**re·play** \ˈrē-ˌplā\ *n* **1** : an act or instance of replaying **2** : the playing of a tape (as a videotape)

re·plen·ish \ri-ˈplen-ish\ *vb* : to fill or build up again : stock or supply anew — **re·plen·ish·ment** *n*

re·plete \ri-ˈplēt\ *adj* **1** : fully provided **2** : FULL; *esp* : full of food — **re·plete·ness** *n*

re·ple·tion \ri-ˈplē-shən\ *n* : the state of being replete

rep·li·ca \ˈrep-li-kə\ *n* [It, repetition, fr. *replicare* to repeat, fr. LL, fr. L, to fold back, fr. *re-* back + *plicare* to fold] **1** : a close reproduction or facsimile (as of a painting or statue) esp. by the maker of the original **2** : COPY, DUPLICATE

1**rep·li·cate** \ˈrep-lə-ˌkāt\ *vb* **-cat·ed; -cat·ing** : DUPLICATE, REPEAT

2**rep·li·cate** \-li-kət\ *n* : one of several identical experiments or procedures

rep·li·ca·tion \ˌrep-lə-ˈkā-shən\ *n* **1** : ANSWER, REPLY **2** : precise copying or reproduction; *also* : an act or process of this

1**re·ply** \ri-ˈplī\ *vb* **re·plied; re·ply·ing** : to say or do in answer : RESPOND

2**reply** *n, pl* **replies** : ANSWER, RESPONSE

1**re·port** \ri-ˈpōrt\ *n* [ME, fr. MF, fr. OF, fr. *reporter* to report, fr. L *reportare*, fr. *re-* back + *portare* to carry] **1** : common talk : RUMOR **2** : FAME, REPUTATION **3** : a usu. detailed account or statement **4** : an explosive noise

2**report** *vb* **1** : to give an account of : RELATE, TELL **2** : to serve as carrier of (a message) **3** : to prepare or present (as an account of an event) for a newspaper or a broadcast **4** : to make a charge of misconduct against **5** : to present oneself (as for work) **6** : to make known to the authorities ⟨~ a fire⟩ **7** : to return or present (as a matter referred to a committee) with conclusions and recommendations — **re·port·able** *adj*

re·port·age \ri-ˈpōrt-ij, *esp for 2* ˌrep-ər-ˈtäzh, ˌrep-ˌȯr-ˈ\ *n* [F] **1 :** the act or process of reporting news **2 :** writing intended to give an account of observed or documented events

report card *n* **:** a periodic report on a student's grades

re·port·ed·ly \ri-ˈpōrt-əd-lē\ *adv* **:** according to report

re·port·er \ri-ˈpōrt-ər\ *n* **:** one that reports; *esp* **:** a person who gathers and reports news for a news medium — **re·por·to·ri·al** \ˌrep-ə(r)-ˈtōr-ē-əl\ *adj*

[1]**re·pose** \ri-ˈpōz\ *vb* **re·posed; re·pos·ing 1 :** to lay at rest **2 :** to lie at rest **3 :** to lie dead **4 :** to take a rest **5 :** to rest for support **:** LIE

[2]**repose** *n* **1 :** a state of resting (as after exertion); *esp* **:** SLEEP **2 :** CALM, PEACE **3 :** cessation or absence of activity, movement, or animation **4 :** composure of manner **:** POISE — **re·pose·ful** *adj*

[3]**repose** *vb* **re·posed; re·pos·ing 1 :** to place (as trust) in someone or something **2 :** to place for control, management, or use

re·pos·i·to·ry \ri-ˈpäz-ə-ˌtōr-ē\ *n, pl* **-ries 1 :** a place where something is deposited or stored **2 :** a person to whom something is entrusted

re·pos·sess \ˌrē-pə-ˈzes\ *vb* **1 :** to regain possession of **2 :** to resume possession of in default of the payment of installments due — **re·pos·ses·sion** \-ˈzesh-ən\ *n*

rep·re·hend \ˌrep-ri-ˈhend\ *vb* **:** to express disapproval of **:** CENSURE **syn** criticize, condemn, denounce, blame, pan — **rep·re·hen·sion** \-ˈhen-chən\ *n*

rep·re·hen·si·ble \-ˈhen-sə-bəl\ *adj* **:** deserving blame or censure **:** CULPABLE — **rep·re·hen·si·bly** \-blē\ *adv*

rep·re·sent \ˌrep-ri-ˈzent\ *vb* **1 :** to present a picture or a likeness of **:** PORTRAY, DEPICT **2 :** to serve as a sign or symbol of **3 :** to act the role of **4 :** to stand in the place of **:** act or speak for **5 :** to be a member or example of **:** TYPIFY **6 :** to serve as an elected representative of **7 :** to describe as having a specified quality or character **8 :** to state with the purpose of affecting judgment or action

rep·re·sen·ta·tion \ˌrep-ri-ˌzen-ˈtā-shən\ *n* **1 :** the act of representing **2 :** one (as a picture or image) that represents something else **3 :** the state of being represented in a legislative body; *also* **:** the body of persons representing a constituency **4 :** a usu. formal statement made to effect a change

[1]**rep·re·sen·ta·tive** \ˌrep-ri-ˈzent-ət-iv\ *adj* **1 :** serving to represent **2 :** standing or acting for another **3 :** founded on the principle of representation **:** carried on by elected representatives ⟨~ government⟩ — **rep·re·sen·ta·tive·ly** *adv* — **rep·re·sen·ta·tive·ness** *n*

[2]**representative** *n* **1 :** a typical example of a group, class, or quality **2 :** one that represents another; *esp* **:** one representing a district in a legislative body usu. as a member of a lower house

re·press \ri-ˈpres\ *vb* **1 :** CURB, SUBDUE **2 :** RESTRAIN, SUPPRESS; *esp* **:** to exclude from consciousness — **re·pres·sion** \-ˈpresh-ən\ *n* — **re·pres·sive** \-ˈpres-iv\ *adj*

[1]**re·prieve** \ri-ˈprēv\ *vb* **re·prieved; re·priev·ing 1 :** to delay the punishment or execution of **2 :** to give temporary relief to

[2]**reprieve** *n* **1 :** the act of reprieving **:** the state of being reprieved **2 :** a formal temporary suspension of a sentence esp. of death **3 :** a temporary respite

[1]**rep·ri·mand** \ˈrep-rə-ˌmand\ *n* **:** a severe or formal reproof

[2]**reprimand** *vb* **:** to reprove severely or formally

[1]**re·print** \ˈrē-ˈprint\ *vb* **:** to print again

[2]**re·print** \ˈrē-ˌprint\ *n* **:** a reproduction of printed matter

re·pri·sal \ri-ˈprī-zəl\ *n* **:** an act in retaliation for something done by another

re·prise \ri-ˈprēz\ *n* **:** a recurrence, renewal, or resumption of an action; *also* **:** a musical repetition

[1]**re·proach** \ri-ˈprōch\ *n* **1 :** a cause or occasion of blame or disgrace **2 :** DISGRACE, DISCREDIT **3 :** the act of reproaching **:** REBUKE — **re·proach·ful** \-fəl\ *adj* — **re·proach·ful·ly** \-ē\ *adv* — **re·proach·ful·ness** *n*

[2]**reproach** *vb* **1 :** CENSURE, REBUKE **2 :** to cast discredit on **syn** chide, admonish, reprove, reprimand — **re·proach·able** *adj*

rep·ro·bate \ˈrep-rə-ˌbāt\ *n* **1 :** a person foreordained to damnation **2 :** a thoroughly bad person **:** SCOUNDREL — **reprobate** *adj*

rep·ro·ba·tion \ˌrep-rə-ˈbā-shən\ *n* **:** strong disapproval **:** CONDEMNATION

re·pro·duce \ˌrē-prə-ˈd(y)üs\ *vb* **1 :** to produce again or anew **2 :** to bear offspring — **re·pro·duc·ible** \-ˈd(y)ü-sə-bəl\ *adj* — **re·pro·duc·tion** \-ˈdək-shən\ *n* — **re·pro·duc·tive** \-ˈdək-tiv\ *adj*

re·proof \ri-ˈprüf\ *n* **:** blame or censure for a fault

re·prove \ri-ˈprüv\ *vb* **re·proved; re·prov·ing 1 :** to administer a rebuke to **2 :** to express disapproval of **syn** reprimand, admonish, reproach, chide — **re·prov·er** *n*

rept *abbr* report

rep·tile \ˈrep-tᵊl, -ˌtīl\ *n* [ME *reptil,* fr. MF or LL; MF *reptile,* fr. LL *reptile,* fr. L *repere* to creep] **:** any of a large class of air-breathing scaly vertebrates including snakes, lizards, alligators, and turtles — **rep·til·i·an** \rep-ˈtil-ē-ən\ *adj or n*

re·pub·lic \ri-ˈpəb-lik\ *n* [F *république,* fr. MF *republique,* fr. L *respublica,* fr. *res* thing, wealth + *publica,* fem. of *publicus* public] **1 :** a government having a chief of state who is not a monarch and is usu. a president; *also* **:** a nation or other political unit having such a government **2 :** a government in which supreme power is held by the citizens entitled to vote and is exercised by elected officers and representatives governing according to law; *also* **:** a nation or other political unit having such a form of government

[1]**re·pub·li·can** \-li-kən\ *adj* **1 :** of, relating to, or resembling a republic **2 :** favoring or supporting a republic **3** *cap* **:** of, relating to, or constituting one of the two major political parties in the U.S. evolving in the mid-19th century — **re·pub·li·can·ism** *n, often cap*

[2]**republican** *n* **1 :** one that favors or supports a republican form of government **2** *cap* **:** a member of a republican party and esp. of the Republican party of the U.S.

re·pu·di·ate \ri-ˈpyüd-ē-ˌāt\ *vb* **-at·ed; -at·ing** [L *repudiare* to cast off, divorce, fr. *repudium* divorce] **1 :** to cast off **:** DISOWN **2 :** to refuse to have anything to do with **:** refuse to acknowledge, accept, or pay ⟨~ a charge⟩ ⟨~ a debt⟩ **syn** spurn, reject, decline — **re·pu·di·a·tion** \-ˌpyüd-ē-ˈā-shən\ *n* — **re·pu·di·a·tor** \-ˈpyüd-ē-ˌāt-ər\ *n*

re·pug·nance \ri-ˈpəg-nəns\ *n* **1 :** the quality or fact of being contradictory or inconsistent **2 :** strong dislike, distaste, or antagonism

re·pug·nant \-nənt\ *adj* **1 :** marked by repugnance **2 :** contrary to a person's tastes or principles **:** exciting distaste or aversion **syn** repellent, abhorrent, distasteful, obnoxious, revolting, loathsome — **re·pug·nant·ly** *adv*

[1]**re·pulse** \ri-ˈpəls\ *vb* **re·pulsed; re·puls·ing 1 :** to drive or beat back **:** REPEL **2 :** to repel by discourtesy or denial **:** REBUFF **3 :** to cause a feeling of repulsion in **:** DISGUST

[2]**repulse** *n* **1 :** REBUFF, REJECTION **2 :** a repelling or being repelled in hostile encounter

re·pul·sion \ri-ˈpəl-shən\ *n* **1 :** the action of repulsing **:** the state of being repulsed **2 :** the force with which bodies, particles, or like forces repel one another **3 :** a feeling of aversion

re·pul·sive \-siv\ *adj* **1 :** serving or tending to repel or reject **2 :** arousing aversion or disgust **syn** repugnant,

\ə\abut \ᵊ\kitten \ər\further \a\ash \ā\ace \ä\cot, cart \aü\out \ch\chin \e\bet \ē\easy \g\go \i\hit \ī\ice \j\job \ŋ\sing \ō\go \ȯ\law \ȯi\boy \th\thin \t͟h\the \ü\loot \u̇\foot \y\yet \zh\vision *see also* Pronunciation Symbols page

revolting, loathsome, noisome — **re·pul·sive·ly** *adv* — **re·pul·sive·ness** *n*

rep·u·ta·ble \ˈrep-yət-ə-bəl\ *adj* : having a good reputation : ESTIMABLE — **rep·u·ta·bly** \-blē\ *adv*

rep·u·ta·tion \ˌrep-yə-ˈtā-shən\ *n* **1** : overall quality or character as seen or judged by people in general **2** : place in public esteem or regard

[1]**re·pute** \ri-ˈpyüt\ *vb* **re·put·ed; re·put·ing** : CONSIDER, ACCOUNT

[2]**repute** *n* **1** : REPUTATION **2** : the state of being favorably known or spoken of

re·put·ed \ri-ˈpyüt-əd\ *adj* **1** : REPUTABLE **2** : according to reputation : SUPPOSED — **re·put·ed·ly** *adv*

req *abbr* 1 request 2 require; required 3 requisition

[1]**re·quest** \ri-ˈkwest\ *n* **1** : an act or instance of asking for something **2** : a thing asked for **3** : the fact or condition of being asked for ⟨available on ~⟩

[2]**request** *vb* **1** : to make a request to or of **2** : to ask for — **re·quest·er** *n*

re·qui·em \ˈrek-wē-əm, ˈrāk-\ *n* [ME, fr. L (first word of the requiem mass), acc. of *requies* rest, fr. *quies* quiet, rest] **1** : a mass for a dead person; *also* : a musical setting for this **2** : a musical service or hymn in honor of the dead

re·quire \ri-ˈkwī(ə)r\ *vb* **re·quired; re·quir·ing** **1** : to demand as necessary or essential **2** : COMMAND, ORDER

re·quire·ment \-mənt\ *n* **1** : something (as a condition or quality) required ⟨entrance ~⟩ **2** : NECESSITY

req·ui·site \ˈrek-wə-zət\ *adj* : REQUIRED, NECESSARY — **requisite** *n*

req·ui·si·tion \ˌrek-wə-ˈzish-ən\ *n* **1** : formal application or demand (as for supplies) **2** : the state of being in demand or use — **requisition** *vb*

re·quite \ri-ˈkwīt\ *vb* **re·quit·ed; re·quit·ing** **1** : to make return for : REPAY **2** : to make retaliation for : AVENGE **3** : to make return to for a benefit or service or for an injury — **re·quit·al** \-ˈkwīt-ᵊl\ *n*

rere·dos \ˈrer-ə-ˌdäs\ *n* : a usu. ornamental wood or stone screen or partition wall behind an altar

re·run \ˈrē-ˌrən, ˈrē-ˈrən\ *n* : the act or an instance of running again or anew; *esp* : a showing of a motion picture or television program after its first run — **re·run** \ˈrē-ˈrən\ *vb*

res *abbr* 1 research 2 reservation; reserve 3 residence 4 resolution

re·sale \ˈrē-ˌsāl, -ˈsāl\ *n* : the act of selling again usu. to a new party — **re·sal·able** \ˈrē-ˈsā-lə-bəl\ *adj*

re·scind \ri-ˈsind\ *vb* : REPEAL, CANCEL, ANNUL — **re·scind·er** *n* — **re·scis·sion** \-ˈsizh-ən\ *n*

re·script \ˈrē-ˌskript\ *n* : an official or authoritative order or decree

res·cue \ˈres-kyü\ *vb* **res·cued; res·cu·ing** [ME *rescuen*, fr. MF *rescourre*, fr. OF, fr. *re-* re- + *escourre* to shake out, fr. L *excutere*] : to free from danger, harm, or confinement **syn** deliver, save — **rescue** *n* — **res·cu·er** *n*

re·search \ri-ˈsərch, ˈrē-ˌsərch\ *n* **1** : careful or diligent search **2** : studious and critical inquiry and examination aimed at the discovery and interpretation of new knowledge **3** : the collecting of information about a particular subject — **research** *vb* — **re·search·er** *n*

re·sec·tion \ri-ˈsek-shən\ *n* : the surgical removal of part of an organ or structure

re·sem·blance \ri-ˈzem-bləns\ *n* : the quality or state of resembling

re·sem·ble \ri-ˈzem-bəl\ *vb* **-bled; -bling** \-b(ə-)liŋ\ : to be like or similar to

re·sent \ri-ˈzent\ *vb* : to feel or exhibit annoyance or indignation at — **re·sent·ful** \-fəl\ *adj* — **re·sent·ful·ly** \-ē\ *adv* — **re·sent·ment** *n*

re·ser·pine \ri-ˈsər-ˌpēn, -pən\ *n* : a drug obtained from rauwolfia and used in treating high blood pressure and nervous tension

res·er·va·tion \ˌrez-ər-ˈvā-shən\ *n* **1** : an act of reserving **2** : something (as a room in a hotel) arranged for in advance **3** : something reserved; *esp* : a tract of public land set aside for a special use **4** : a limiting condition

[1]**re·serve** \ri-ˈzərv\ *vb* **re·served; re·serv·ing** **1** : to store for future or special use **2** : to hold back for oneself **3** : to set aside or arrange to have set aside or held for special use

[2]**reserve** *n* **1** : something reserved : STOCK, STORE **2** : a military force withheld from action for later use — usu. used in pl. **3** : the military forces of a country not part of the regular services; *also* : RESERVIST **4** : a tract set apart : RESERVATION **5** : an act of reserving **6** : restraint or caution in one's words or bearing **7** : money or its equivalent kept in hand or set apart to meet liabilities

re·served \ri-ˈzərvd\ *adj* **1** : restrained in words and actions **2** : set aside for future or special use — **re·serv·ed·ly** \-ˈzər-vəd-lē\ *adv* — **re·serv·ed·ness** \-vəd-nəs\ *n*

re·serv·ist \ri-ˈzər-vəst\ *n* : a member of a military reserve

res·er·voir \ˈrez-ə(r)v-ˌwär, -ə(r)v-ˌ(w)ȯr\ *n* [F] : a place where something is kept in store; *esp* : an artificial lake where water is collected as a water supply

re·shuf·fle \rē-ˈshəf-əl\ *vb* **1** : to shuffle again **2** : to reorganize usu. by redistribution of existing elements — **reshuffle** *n*

re·side \ri-ˈzīd\ *vb* **re·sid·ed; re·sid·ing** **1** : to make one's home : DWELL **2** : to be present as a quality or vested as a right

res·i·dence \ˈrez-əd-əns\ *n* **1** : the act or fact of residing in a place as a dweller or in discharge of a duty or an obligation **2** : the place where one actually lives **3** : a building used as a home : DWELLING **4** : the period of living in a place

res·i·den·cy \ˈrez-əd-ən-sē\ *n, pl* **-cies** **1** : the residence of or the territory under a diplomatic resident **2** : a period of advanced training in a medical specialty

[1]**res·i·dent** \-ənt\ *adj* **1** : RESIDING **2** : being in residence **3** : not migratory

[2]**resident** *n* **1** : one who resides in a place **2** : a diplomatic representative with governing powers (as in a protectorate) **3** : a physician serving a residency

res·i·den·tial \ˌrez-ə-ˈden-chəl\ *adj* **1** : used as a residence or by residents **2** : occupied by or restricted to residences — **res·i·den·tial·ly** \-ē\ *adv*

[1]**re·sid·u·al** \ri-ˈzij-(ə-w)əl\ *adj* : being a residue or remainder

[2]**residual** *n* **1** : a residual product or substance **2** : a payment (as to an actor or writer) for each rerun after an initial showing (as of a taped TV show)

re·sid·u·ary \ri-ˈzij-ə-ˌwer-ē\ *adj* : of, relating to, or constituting a residue esp. of an estate

res·i·due \ˈrez-ə-ˌd(y)ü\ *n* : a part remaining after another part has been taken away : REMAINDER

re·sid·u·um \ri-ˈzij-ə-wəm\ *n, pl* **re·sid·ua** \-ə-wə\ [L] **1** : something remaining or residual after certain deductions are made **2** : a residual product **syn** remainder, rest, balance, remnant

re·sign \ri-ˈzīn\ *vb* [ME *resignen*, fr. MF *resigner*, fr. L *resignare*, lit., to unseal, cancel, fr. *signare* to sign, seal] **1** : to give up deliberately (as one's position) esp. by a formal act **2** : to give (oneself) over (as to grief or despair) without resistance — **re·sign·ed·ly** \-ˈzī-nəd-lē\ *adv*

re–sign \ˈrē-ˈsīn\ *vb* : to sign again

res·ig·na·tion \ˌrez-ig-ˈnā-shən\ *n* **1** : an act or instance of resigning; *also* : a formal notification of such an act **2** : the quality or state of being resigned

re·sil·ience \ri-ˈzil-yəns\ *n* **1** : the ability of a body to regain its original size and shape after being compressed, bent, or stretched **2** : an ability to recover from or adjust easily to change or misfortune

re·sil·ien·cy \-yən-sē\ *n* : RESILIENCE

re·sil·ient \-yənt\ *adj* : marked by resilience **syn** flexible, supple

res·in \ˈrez-ᵊn\ *n* : a substance obtained from the gum or sap of some trees and used esp. in varnishes, plastics, and medicine; *also* : a comparable synthetic product — **res·in·ous** *adj*

[1]**re·sist** \ri-ˈzist\ *vb* **1** : to fight against : OPPOSE ⟨~ aggression⟩ **2** : to withstand the force or effect of ⟨~ disease⟩ **syn** combat, withstand, repel — **re·sist·ible** \-ˈzis-tə-bəl\ *adj* — **re·sist·less** *adj*

[2]**resist** *n* : something (as a coating) that resists or prevents a particular action

re·sis·tance \ri-ˈzis-təns\ *n* **1** : the act or an instance of resisting : OPPOSITION **2** : the opposition offered by a body to the passage through it of a steady electric current

re·sis·tant \-tənt\ *adj* : giving or capable of resistance

re·sis·tiv·i·ty \ri-ˌzis-ˈtiv-ət-ē, ˌrē-\ *n, pl* **-ties** : capacity for resisting

re·sis·tor \ri-ˈzis-tər\ *n* : a device used to provide resistance to the flow of an electric current

res·o·lute \ˈrez-ə-ˌlüt\ *adj* : firmly determined in purpose : RESOLVED **syn** steadfast, staunch, faithful, true, loyal — **res·o·lute·ly** *adv* — **res·o·lute·ness** *n*

res·o·lu·tion \ˌrez-ə-ˈlü-shən\ *n* **1** : the act or process of resolving **2** : the action of solving; *also* : SOLUTION **3** : the quality of being resolute : FIRMNESS, DETERMINATION **4** : a formal statement expressing the opinion, will, or intent of a body of persons

[1]**re·solve** \ri-ˈzälv\ *vb* **re·solved; re·solv·ing 1** : to break up into constituent parts : ANALYZE **2** : to find an answer to : SOLVE **3** : DETERMINE, DECIDE **4** : to make or pass a formal resolution — **re·solv·able** *adj*

[2]**resolve** *n* **1** : something resolved **2** : fixity of purpose

res·o·nance \ˈrez-ᵊn-əns\ *n* **1** : the quality or state of being resonant **2** : a reinforcement of sound in a vibrating body caused by waves from another body vibrating at nearly the same rate

res·o·nant \ˈrez-ᵊn-ənt\ *adj* **1** : continuing to sound : RESOUNDING **2** : relating to or exhibiting resonance **3** : intensified and enriched by or as if by resonance — **res·o·nant·ly** *adv*

res·o·nate \ˈrez-ᵊn-ˌāt\ *vb* **-nat·ed; -nat·ing 1** : to produce or exhibit resonance **2** : REVERBERATE, RESOUND

res·o·na·tor \-ᵊn-ˌāt-ər\ *n* : something that resounds or exhibits resonance

re·sorp·tion \rē-ˈsȯrp-shən, -ˈzȯrp-\ *n* : the action or process of breaking down and assimilating something (as a tooth or an embryo)

[1]**re·sort** \ri-ˈzȯrt\ *n* [ME, fr. MF, resource, recourse, fr. *resortir* to rebound, resort, fr. OF, fr. *sortir* to escape, sally] **1** : one looked to for help : REFUGE **2** : RECOURSE **3** : frequent or general visiting ⟨place of ~⟩ **4** : a frequently visited place : HAUNT **5** : a place providing recreation esp. to vacationers

[2]**resort** *vb* **1** : to go often or habitually **2** : to have recourse (as for aid)

re·sound \ri-ˈzau̇nd\ *vb* **1** : to become filled with sound : REVERBERATE, RING **2** : to sound loudly

re·sound·ing \-iŋ\ *adj* **1** : RESONATING, RESONANT **2** : impressively sonorous ⟨~ name⟩ **3** : EMPHATIC, UNEQUIVOCAL ⟨a ~ success⟩ — **re·sound·ing·ly** *adv*

re·source \ˈrē-ˌsōrs, ri-ˈsōrs\ *n* [F *ressource*, fr. OF *ressourse* relief, resource, fr. *resourdre* to relieve, lit., to rise again, fr. L *resurgere*, fr. *re-* again + *surgere* to rise] **1** : a source of supply or support — usu. used in pl. **2** *pl* : available funds **3** : a possibility of relief or recovery **4** : a means of spending leisure time **5** : ability to meet and handle situations — **re·source·ful** \ri-ˈsōrs-fəl\ *adj* — **re·source·ful·ness** *n*

resp *abbr* respective; respectively

[1]**re·spect** \ri-ˈspekt\ *n* **1** : relation to something usu. specified : REFERENCE, REGARD **2** : high or special regard : ESTEEM **3** *pl* : an expression of respect or deference **4** : DETAIL, PARTICULAR — **re·spect·ful** \-fəl\ *adj* — **re·spect·ful·ly** \-ē\ *adv* — **re·spect·ful·ness** *n*

[2]**respect** *vb* **1** : to consider deserving of high regard : ESTEEM **2** : to refrain from interfering with ⟨~ another's privacy⟩ **3** : to have reference to : CONCERN — **re·spect·er** *n*

re·spect·able \ri-ˈspek-tə-bəl\ *adj* **1** : worthy of respect : ESTIMABLE **2** : decent or correct in conduct : PROPER **3** : fair in size, quantity, or quality : MODERATE, TOLERABLE **4** : fit to be seen : PRESENTABLE — **re·spect·a·bil·i·ty** \-ˌspek-tə-ˈbil-ət-ē\ *n* — **re·spect·ably** \-ˈspek-tə-blē\ *adv*

re·spect·ing \-tiŋ\ *prep* : with regard to

re·spec·tive \-tiv\ *adj* : PARTICULAR, SEPARATE ⟨returned to their ~ homes⟩

re·spec·tive·ly \-lē\ *adv* **1** : as relating to each **2** : each in the order given

res·pi·ra·tion \ˌres-pə-ˈrā-shən\ *n* **1** : an act or the process of breathing **2** : the physical and chemical processes (as breathing and oxidation) by which a living thing obtains the oxygen and eliminates waste gases (as carbon dioxide) — **re·spi·ra·to·ry** \ˈres-p(ə-)rə-ˌtōr-ē, ri-ˈspī-rə-\ *adj* — **re·spire** \ri-ˈspī(ə)r\ *vb*

res·pi·ra·tor \ˈres-pə-ˌrāt-ər\ *n* **1** : a device covering the mouth or nose esp. to prevent inhaling harmful vapors **2** : a device for artificial respiration

re·spite \ˈres-pət\ *n* **1** : a temporary delay **2** : an interval of rest or relief

re·splen·dent \ri-ˈsplen-dənt\ *adj* : shining brilliantly : gloriously bright : SPLENDID — **re·splen·dence** \-dəns\ *n* — **re·splen·dent·ly** *adv*

re·spond \ri-ˈspänd\ *vb* **1** : ANSWER, REPLY **2** : REACT ⟨~ to a stimulus⟩ **3** : to show favorable reaction ⟨~ to medication⟩ — **re·spond·er** *n*

re·spon·dent \ri-ˈspän-dənt\ *n* : one who responds; *esp* : one who answers in various legal proceedings — **respondent** *adj*

re·sponse \ri-ˈspäns\ *n* **1** : an act of responding **2** : something constituting a reply or a reaction

re·spon·si·bil·i·ty \ri-ˌspän-sə-ˈbil-ət-ē\ *n, pl* **-ties 1** : the quality or state of being responsible **2** : something for which one is responsible

re·spon·si·ble \ri-ˈspän-sə-bəl\ *adj* **1** : liable to be called upon to answer for one's acts or decisions : ANSWERABLE **2** : able to fulfull one's obligations : RELIABLE, TRUSTWORTHY **3** : able to choose for oneself between right and wrong **4** : involving accountability or important duties ⟨~ position⟩ — **re·spon·si·ble·ness** *n* — **re·spon·si·bly** \-blē\ *adv*

re·spon·sive \-siv\ *adj* **1** : RESPONDING **2** : quick to respond : SENSITIVE **3** : using responses ⟨~ readings⟩ — **re·spon·sive·ly** *adv* — **re·spon·sive·ness** *n*

[1]**rest** \ˈrest\ *n* **1** : REPOSE, SLEEP **2** : freedom from work or activity **3** : a state of motionlessness or inactivity **4** : a place of shelter or lodging **5** : a silence in music equivalent in duration to a note of the same value; *also* : a character indicating this **6** : something used as a support — **rest·ful** \-fəl\ *adj* — **rest·ful·ly** \-ē\ *adv*

[1]rest 5

[2]**rest** *vb* **1** : to get rest by lying down; *esp* : SLEEP **2** : to cease from action or motion **3** : to give rest to : set at rest **4** : to sit or lie fixed or supported **5** : to place on or against a support **6** : to remain based or founded **7** : to

cause to be firmly fixed : GROUND **8** : to remain for action : DEPEND

³rest *n* : something that remains over

res·tau·rant \ˈres-t(ə-)rənt, -tə-ˌränt\ *n* [F, fr. prp. of *restaurer* to restore, fr. L *restaurare*] : a public eating place

res·tau·ra·teur \ˌres-tə-rə-ˈtər\ *also* **res·tau·ran·teur** \-ˌrän-\ *n* : the operator or proprietor of a restaurant

rest home *n* : an establishment that gives care for the aged or convalescent

res·ti·tu·tion \ˌres-tə-ˈt(y)ü-shən\ *n* : the act of restoring : the state of being restored; *esp* : restoration of something to its rightful owner **syn** amends, redress, reparation, indemnity, compensation

res·tive \ˈres-tiv\ *adj* [ME, fr. MF *restif,* fr. *rester* to stop behind, remain, fr. L *restare,* fr. *re-* back + *stare* to stand] **1** : BALKY **2** : UNEASY, FIDGETY **syn** restless, impatient, nervous — **res·tive·ly** *adv* — **res·tive·ness** *n*

rest·less \ˈrest-ləs\ *adj* **1** : lacking or denying rest **2** : never resting or ceasing : UNQUIET ⟨the ~ sea⟩ **3** : marked by or showing unrest esp. of mind : DISCONTENTED **syn** restive, impatient, nervous, fidgety — **rest·less·ly** *adv* — **rest·less·ness** *n*

re·stor·able \ri-ˈstōr-ə-bəl\ *adj* : fit for restoring or reclaiming

res·to·ra·tion \ˌres-tə-ˈrā-shən\ *n* **1** : an act of restoring : the state of being restored **2** : something that is restored; *esp* : a reconstruction or representation of an original form (as of a building)

re·stor·ative \ri-ˈstōr-ət-iv\ *n* : something that restores esp. to consciousness or health — **restorative** *adj*

re·store \ri-ˈstōr\ *vb* **re·stored; re·stor·ing 1** : to give back : RETURN **2** : to put back into use or service **3** : to put or bring back into a former or original state : REPAIR, RENEW **4** : to put again in possession of something — **re·stor·er** *n*

re·strain \ri-ˈstrān\ *vb* **1** : to prevent from doing something **2** : to limit, restrict, or keep under control : CURB **3** : to place under restraint or arrest — **re·strain·able** *adj* — **re·strain·er** *n*

re·strained \ri-ˈstrānd\ *adj* : marked by restraint : DISCIPLINED — **re·strain·ed·ly** \-ˈstrā-nəd-lē\ *adv*

re·straint \ri-ˈstrānt\ *n* **1** : an act of restraining : the state of being restrained **2** : a restraining force, agency, or device **3** : deprivation or limitation of liberty : CONFINEMENT **4** : control over one's feelings : RESERVE

re·strict \ri-ˈstrikt\ *vb* **1** : to confine within bounds : LIMIT **2** : to place under restriction as to use — **re·stric·tive** *adj* — **re·stric·tive·ly** *adv*

re·stric·tion \ri-ˈstrik-shən\ *n* **1** : something (as a law or rule) that restricts **2** : an act of restricting : the state of being restricted

rest room *n* : a room or suite of rooms providing personal facilities (as toilets)

¹re·sult \ri-ˈzəlt\ *vb* [ME *resulten,* fr. ML *resultare,* fr. L, to rebound, fr. *re-* re- + *saltare* to leap] : to proceed or come about as an effect or consequence — **re·sul·tant** \-ˈzəlt-ᵊnt\ *adj or n*

²result *n* **1** : something that results : EFFECT, CONSEQUENCE **2** : beneficial or discernible effect **3** : something obtained by calculation or investigation

re·sume \ri-ˈzüm\ *vb* **re·sumed; re·sum·ing 1** : to take or assume again **2** : to return to or begin again after interruption **3** : to take back to oneself — **re·sump·tion** \-ˈzəmp-shən\ *n*

ré·su·mé *or* **re·su·me** *or* **re·su·mé** \ˈrez-ə-ˌmā, ˌrez-ə-ˈmā\ *n* [F *résumé*] : SUMMARY; *esp* : a short account of one's career and qualifications usu. prepared by a job applicant

re·sur·gence \ri-ˈsər-jəns\ *n* : a rising again into life, activity, or prominence — **re·sur·gent** \-jənt\ *adj*

res·ur·rect \ˌrez-ə-ˈrekt\ *vb* **1** : to raise from the dead **2** : to bring to attention or use again

res·ur·rec·tion \ˌrez-ə-ˈrek-shən\ *n* **1** *cap* : the rising of Christ from the dead **2** *often cap* : the rising to life of all human dead before the final judgment **3** : REVIVAL

re·sus·ci·tate \ri-ˈsəs-ə-ˌtāt\ *vb* **-tat·ed; -tat·ing** : to revive from a condition resembling death — **re·sus·ci·ta·tion** \ri-ˌsəs-ə-ˈtā-shən, ˌrē-\ *n* — **re·sus·ci·ta·tor** \-ˌtāt-ər\ *n*

ret *abbr* **1** retain **2** retired **3** return

¹re·tail \ˈrē-ˌtāl, *esp for 2 also* ri-ˈtāl\ *vb* **1** : to sell in small quantities directly to the ultimate consumer **2** : to tell in detail or to one person after another — **re·tail·er** *n*

²re·tail \ˈrē-ˌtāl\ *n* : the sale of goods in small amounts to ultimate consumers — **retail** *adj or adv*

re·tain \ri-ˈtān\ *vb* **1** : to hold in possession or use **2** : to engage (as a lawyer) by paying a fee in advance **3** : to keep in a fixed place or position **syn** detain, withhold, reserve

¹re·tain·er \-ər\ *n* **1** : one that retains **2** : a servant in a wealthy household; *also* : EMPLOYEE

²retainer *n* : a fee paid to secure services (as of a lawyer)

¹re·take \ˈrē-ˈtāk\ *vb* **-took** \-ˈtu̇k\; **-tak·en** \-ˈtā-kən\; **-tak·ing 1** : to take or seize again **2** : to photograph again

²re·take \ˈrē-ˌtāk\ *n* : a second photographing of a motion-picture scene

re·tal·i·ate \ri-ˈtal-ē-ˌāt\ *vb* **-at·ed; -at·ing** : to return like for like; *esp* : to get revenge — **re·tal·i·a·tion** \-ˌtal-ē-ˈā-shən\ *n* — **re·tal·ia·to·ry** \-ˈtal-yə-ˌtōr-ē\ *adj*

re·tard \ri-ˈtärd\ *vb* : to hold back : delay the progress of **syn** slow, slacken, detain — **re·tar·da·tion** \ˌrē-ˌtär-ˈdā-shən, ri-\ *n* — **re·tard·er** *n*

re·tar·date \-ˈtärd-ˌāt, -ət\ *n* : a mentally retarded person

re·tard·ed \ri-ˈtärd-əd\ *adj* : slow or limited in intellectual, emotional, or academic development ⟨a ~ child⟩

retch \ˈrech, ˈrēch\ *vb* : to try to vomit

re·ten·tion \ri-ˈten-chən\ *n* **1** : the act of retaining : the state of being retained **2** : the power of retaining esp. in the mind : RETENTIVENESS

re·ten·tive \-ˈtent-iv\ *adj* : having the power of retaining; *esp* : retaining knowledge easily — **re·ten·tive·ness** *n*

ret·i·cent \ˈret-ə-sənt\ *adj* : inclined to be silent or secretive : UNCOMMUNICATIVE **syn** reserved, taciturn, close-mouthed — **ret·i·cence** \-səns\ *n* — **ret·i·cent·ly** *adv*

ret·i·na \ˈret-ᵊn-ə\ *n, pl* **retinas** *or* **ret·i·nae** \-ᵊn-ˌē\ : the sensory membrane lining the eye and receiving the image formed by the lens — **ret·i·nal** \ˈret-ᵊn-əl\ *adj*

ret·i·nue \ˈret-ᵊn-ˌ(y)ü\ *n* : the body of attendants or followers of a distinguished person

re·tire \ri-ˈtī(ə)r\ *vb* **re·tired; re·tir·ing 1** : RETREAT **2** : to withdraw esp. for privacy **3** : to withdraw from one's occupation or position **4** : to go to bed **5** : to withdraw from circulation or from the market or from usual use or service **6** : to cause to be out in baseball — **re·tire·ment** *n*

re·tired \ri-ˈtī(ə)rd\ *adj* **1** : SECLUDED, QUIET **2** : withdrawn from active duty or from one's occupation **3** : received by or due to one who has retired

re·tir·ee \ri-ˌtī-ˈrē\ *n* : a person who has retired from an occupation

re·tir·ing \ri-ˈtīr-iŋ\ *adj* : SHY, RESERVED

¹re·tort \ri-ˈtȯrt\ *vb* [L *retortus,* pp. of *retorquēre,* lit., to twist back, hurl back, fr. *re-* back + *torquēre* to twist] **1** : to say in reply : answer back usu. sharply **2** : to answer (an argument) by a counter argument **3** : RETALIATE

²retort *n* : a quick, witty, or cutting reply

³re·tort \ri-ˈtȯrt, ˈrē-ˌtȯrt\ *n* [MF *retorte,* fr. ML *retorta,* fr. L, fem. of *retortus,* pp. of *retorquēre* to twist back; fr. its shape] : a vessel in which substances are distilled or broken up by heat

re·touch \ˈrē-ˈtəch\ *vb* : TOUCH UP; *esp* : to change (as a photographic negative) in order to produce a more desirable appearance

re·trace \(ˈ)rē-ˈtrās\ *vb* : to trace again or in a reverse direction ⟨*retraced* his steps⟩

re·tract \ri-ˈtrakt\ *vb* **1** : to draw back or in **2** : to withdraw (as a charge or promise) : DISAVOW — **re·tract·able** *adj* — **re·trac·tion** \-ˈtrak-shən\ *n*

re·trac·tile \ri-ˈtrak-tᵊl, -ˌtīl\ *adj* : capable of being drawn back or in ⟨~ claws⟩

¹re·tread \ˈrē-ˈtred\ *vb* **re·tread·ed; re·tread·ing** : to put a new tread on (a worn tire)

²re·tread \ˈrē-ˌtred\ *n* **1** : a new tread on a tire **2** : a retreaded tire **3** : one pressed into service again; *also* : REMAKE

¹re·treat \ri-ˈtrēt\ *n* **1** : an act of withdrawing esp. from something dangerous, difficult, or disagreeable **2** : a military signal for withdrawal; *also* : a military flag-lowering ceremony **3** : a place of privacy or safety : REFUGE **4** : a period of group withdrawal for prayer, meditation, and study

²retreat *vb* **1** : to make a retreat : WITHDRAW **2** : to slope backward

re·trench \ri-ˈtrench\ *vb* [obs. F *retrencher* (now *retrancher*), fr. MF *retrenchier*, fr. *re-* + *trenchier* to cut] **1** : to cut down or pare away : REDUCE, CURTAIL **2** : to cut down expenses : ECONOMIZE — **re·trench·ment** *n*

ret·ri·bu·tion \ˌre-trə-ˈbyü-shən\ *n* : something administered or exacted in recompense; *esp* : PUNISHMENT **syn** reprisal, vengeance, revenge, retaliation — **re·trib·u·tive** \ri-ˈtrib-yət-iv\ *adj* — **re·trib·u·to·ry** \-yə-ˌtōr-ē\ *adj*

re·trieve \ri-ˈtrēv\ *vb* **re·trieved; re·triev·ing 1** : to search about for and bring in (killed or wounded game) **2** : RECOVER, RESTORE — **re·triev·able** *adj* — **re·triev·al** \-ˈtrē-vəl\ *n*

re·triev·er \ri-ˈtrē-vər\ *n* : one that retrieves; *esp* : a dog of any of several breeds used esp. for retrieving game

ret·ro·ac·tive \ˌre-trō-ˈak-tiv\ *adj* : made effective as of a date prior to enactment ⟨a ~ pay raise⟩ — **ret·ro·ac·tive·ly** *adv*

ret·ro·fire \ˈre-trō-ˌfī(ə)r\ *vb* : to ignite a retro-rocket — **retrofire** *n*

ret·ro·fit \ˌre-trō-ˈfit\ *vb* : to furnish (as an aircraft) with newly available equipment

¹ret·ro·grade \ˈre-trə-ˌgrād\ *adj* **1** : moving or tending backward **2** : tending toward or resulting in a worse condition

²retrograde *vb* **1** : RETREAT **2** : DETERIORATE, DEGENERATE

ret·ro·gres·sion \ˌre-trə-ˈgresh-ən\ *n* : return to a former and less complex level of development or organization — **ret·ro·gress** \ˌre-trə-ˈgres\ *vb* — **ret·ro·gres·sive** \ˌre-trə-ˈgres-iv\ *adj*

ret·ro–rock·et \ˈre-trō-ˌräk-ət\ *n* : an auxiliary rocket (as on a spacecraft) used to slow forward motion

ret·ro·spect \ˈre-trə-ˌspekt\ *n* : a review of past events — **ret·ro·spec·tion** \ˌre-trə-ˈspek-shən\ *n* — **ret·ro·spec·tive** \-ˈspek-tiv\ *adj* — **ret·ro·spec·tive·ly** *adv*

ret·ro·vi·rus \ˈre-trō-ˌvī-rəs\ *n* : any of a group of RNA-containing viruses (as the AIDS virus) that make DNA using RNA instead of the reverse and include numerous viruses causing tumors in animals including man

¹re·turn \ri-ˈtərn\ *vb* **1** : to go or come back **2** : to pass, give, or send back to an earlier possessor **3** : to put back to or in a former place or state **4** : REPLY, ANSWER **5** : to report esp. officially **6** : to elect to office **7** : to bring in (as profit) : YIELD **8** : to give or perform in return — **re·turn·er** *n*

²return *n* **1** : an act of coming or going back to or from a former place or state **2** : RECURRENCE **3** : a report of the results of balloting **4** : a formal statement of taxable income **5** : the profit from labor, investment, or business : YIELD **6** : the act of returning something **7** : something that returns or is returned; *also* : a means (as a pipe) of returning **8** : something given in repayment or reciprocation; *also* : ANSWER, RETORT **9** : an answering play — **return** *adj*

¹re·turn·able \ri-ˈtərn-ə-bəl\ *adj* : capable of being returned (as for reuse or recycling); *also* : permitted to be returned

²returnable *n* : a returnable beverage container

re·turn·ee \ri-ˌtər-ˈnē\ *n* : one who returns

re·union \rē-ˈyü-nyən\ *n* **1** : an act of reuniting : the state of being reunited **2** : a meeting again of persons who have been separated

¹rev \ˈrev\ *n* : a revolution of a motor

²rev *vb* **revved; rev·ving** : to increase the revolutions per minute of (a motor)

³rev *abbr* **1** revenue **2** reverse **3** review; reviewed **4** revised; revision **5** revolution

Rev *abbr* **1** Revelation **2** Reverend

re·vamp \(ˈ)rē-ˈvamp\ *vb* : RECONSTRUCT, REVISE; *esp* : to give a new form to old materials

re·vanche \rə-ˈvänsh\ *n* [F] : REVENGE; *esp* : a usu. political policy designed to recover lost territory or status

re·veal \ri-ˈvēl\ *vb* **1** : to make known **2** : to show plainly : open up to view

rev·eil·le \ˈrev-ə-lē\ *n* [modif. of F *réveillez*, imper. pl. of *réveiller* to awaken, fr. *eveiller* to awaken, fr. (assumed) VL *exvigilare*, fr. L *vigilare* to keep watch, stay awake] : a military signal sounded at about sunrise

¹rev·el \ˈrev-əl\ *vb* **-eled** *or* **-elled; -el·ing** *or* **-el·ling** \-(ə-)liŋ\ **1** : to take part in a revel **2** : to take great delight — **rev·el·er** *or* **rev·el·ler** \-ər\ *n* — **rev·el·ry** \-əl-rē\ *n*

²revel *n* : a usu. wild party or celebration

rev·e·la·tion \ˌrev-ə-ˈlā-shən\ *n* **1** : an act of revealing **2** : something revealed; *esp* : an enlightening or astonishing disclosure

Rev·e·la·tion \ˌrev-ə-ˈlā-shən\ *n* — see BIBLE table

¹re·venge \ri-ˈvenj\ *vb* **re·venged; re·veng·ing** : to inflict harm or injury in return for (a wrong) : AVENGE — **re·veng·er** *n*

²revenge *n* **1** : the act of revenging **2** : a desire to return evil for evil **3** : an opportunity for getting satisfaction **syn** vengeance, retaliation, retribution, reprisal — **re·venge·ful** *adj*

rev·e·nue \ˈrev-ə-ˌn(y)ü\ *n* [ME, fr. MF, fr. *revenir* to return, fr. L *revenire*, fr. *re-* back + *venire* to come] **1** : investment income **2** : money collected by a government (as through taxes)

rev·e·nu·er \ˈrev-ə-ˌn(y)ü-ər\ *n* : a revenue officer or boat

re·verb \ri-ˈvərb, ˈrē-ˌvərb\ *n* : an electronically produced echo effect in recorded music; *also* : a device for producing reverb

re·ver·ber·ate \ri-ˈvər-bə-ˌrāt\ *vb* **-at·ed; -at·ing 1** : REFLECT ⟨~ light or heat⟩ **2** : to resound in or as if in a series of echoes — **re·ver·ber·a·tion** \-ˌvər-bə-ˈrā-shən\ *n*

¹re·vere \ri-ˈviər\ *vb* **re·vered; re·ver·ing** : to show honor and devotion to : VENERATE **syn** reverence, worship, adore

²revere *n* : REVERS

¹rev·er·ence \ˈrev-(ə-)rəns\ *n* **1** : honor and respect mixed with love and awe **2** : a sign (as a bow or curtsy) of respect

²reverence *vb* **-enced; -enc·ing** : to regard or treat with reverence

¹rev·er·end \-rənd\ *adj* **1** : worthy of reverence : REVERED **2** : being a member of the clergy — used as a title

²reverend *n* : a member of the clergy

rev·er·ent \-rənt\ *adj* : expressing reverence — **rev·er·ent·ly** *adv*

rev·er·en·tial \ˌrev-ə-ˈren-chəl\ *adj* : REVERENT

rev·er·ie *also* **rev·ery** \ˈrev-(ə-)rē\ *n, pl* **-er·ies 1** : DAYDREAM **2** : the state of being lost in thought

re·vers \ri-ˈviər, -ˈveər\ *n, pl* **re·vers** \-ˈviərz, -ˈveərz\ [F] : a lapel esp. on a woman's garment

re·ver·sal \ri-ˈvər-səl\ *n* : an act or process of reversing

[1]re·verse \ri-ˈvərs\ *adj* **1** : opposite to a previous or normal condition **2** : acting or operating in a manner opposite or contrary **3** : effecting reverse movement — **re·verse·ly** *adv*

[2]reverse *vb* **re·versed; re·vers·ing 1** : to turn upside down or completely about in position or direction **2** : to set aside or change (as a legal decision) **3** : to change to the contrary ⟨~ a policy⟩ **4** : to go or cause to go in the opposite direction **5** : to put (as a car) in reverse — **re·vers·ible** \-ˈvər-sə-bəl\ *adj*

[3]reverse *n* **1** : something contrary to something else : OPPOSITE **2** : an act or instance of reversing; *esp* : a change for the worse **3** : the back of something **4** : a gear that reverses something

re·ver·sion \ri-ˈvər-zhən\ *n* **1** : the right of succession or future possession (as to a title or property) **2** : return toward some former or ancestral condition; *also* : a product of this — **re·ver·sion·ary** \-zhə-ˌner-ē\ *adj*

re·vert \ri-ˈvərt\ *vb* **1** : to come or go back ⟨~*ed* to savagery⟩ **2** : to return to a proprietor or his or her heirs **3** : to return to an ancestral type

[1]re·view \ri-ˈvyü\ *n* **1** : an act of revising **2** : a formal military inspection **3** : a general survey **4** : INSPECTION, EXAMINATION; *esp* : REEXAMINATION **5** : a critical evaluation (as of a book) **6** : a magazine devoted to reviews and essays **7** : a renewed study of previously studied material **8** : REVUE

[2]re·view \ri-ˈvyü, *1 also* ˈrē-\ *vb* **1** : to examine or study again; *esp* : to reexamine judicially **2** : to hold a review of ⟨~ troops⟩ **3** : to write a critical examination of ⟨~ a novel⟩ **4** : to view retrospectively : look back over ⟨~*ed* his life⟩ **5** : to study material again

re·view·er \ri-ˈvyü-ər\ *n* : one that reviews; *esp* : a writer of critical reviews

re·vile \ri-ˈvīl\ *vb* **re·viled; re·vil·ing** : to abuse verbally : rail at **syn** vituperate, berate, rate, upbraid, scold — **re·vile·ment** *n* — **re·vil·er** *n*

re·vise \ri-ˈvīz\ *vb* **re·vised; re·vis·ing 1** : to look over something written in order to correct or improve **2** : to make a new version of — **re·vis·able** *adj* — **re·vise** *n* — **re·vis·er** *or* **re·vi·sor** \-ˈvī-zər\ *n* — **re·vi·sion** \-ˈvizh-ən\ *n*

re·vi·tal·ize \ˈrē-ˈvīt-ᵊl-ˌīz\ *vb* **-ized; -iz·ing** : to give new life or vigor to — **re·vi·tal·iza·tion** \ˌrē-ˌvīt-ᵊl-ə-ˈzā- shən\ *n*

re·viv·al \ri-ˈvī-vəl\ *n* **1** : an act of reviving : the state of being revived **2** : a new publication or presentation (as of a book or play) **3** : an evangelistic meeting or series of meetings

re·vive \ri-ˈvīv\ *vb* **re·vived; re·viv·ing 1** : to return or restore to consciousness or life : become or make active or flourishing again **2** : to bring back into use **3** : to renew mentally — **re·viv·er** *n*

re·viv·i·fy \rē-ˈviv-ə-ˌfī\ *vb* : REVIVE — **re·viv·i·fi·ca·tion** \-ˌviv-ə-fə-ˈkā-shən\ *n*

re·vo·ca·ble \ˈrev-ə-kə-bəl *also* ri-ˈvō-kə-bəl\ *adj* : capable of being revoked

re·vo·ca·tion \ˌrev-ə-ˈkā-shən\ *n* : an act or instance of revoking

re·voke \ri-ˈvōk\ *vb* **re·voked; re·vok·ing 1** : to annul by recalling or taking back : REPEAL, RESCIND **2** : RENEGE 1 — **re·vok·er** *n*

[1]re·volt \ri-ˈvōlt\ *vb* **1** : to throw off allegiance to a ruler or government : REBEL **2** : to experience disgust or shock **3** : to turn or cause to turn away with disgust or abhorrence — **re·volt·er** *n*

[2]revolt *n* : REBELLION, INSURRECTION

re·volt·ing \-iŋ\ *adj* : extremely offensive — **re·volt·ing·ly** *adv*

rev·o·lu·tion \ˌrev-ə-ˈlü-shən\ *n* **1** : the action by a heavenly body of going round in an orbit **2** : ROTATION **3** : a sudden, radical, or complete change; *esp* : the overthrow or renunciation of one ruler or government and substitution of another by the governed

[1]rev·o·lu·tion·ary \-shə-ˌner-ē\ *adj* **1** : of or relating to revolution **2** : tending to or promoting revolution **3** : constituting or bringing about a major change

[2]revolutionary *n, pl* **-ar·ies** : one who takes part in a revolution or who advocates revolutionary doctrines

rev·o·lu·tion·ist \ˌrev-ə-ˈlü-sh(ə-)nəst\ *n* : REVOLUTIONARY — **revolutionist** *adj*

rev·o·lu·tion·ize \-shə-ˌnīz\ *vb* **-ized; -iz·ing** : to change fundamentally or completely : make revolutionary — **rev·o·lu·tion·iz·er** *n*

re·volve \ri-ˈvälv\ *vb* **re·volved; re·volv·ing 1** : to turn over in the mind : reflect upon : PONDER **2** : to move in an orbit; *also* : ROTATE — **re·volv·able** *adj*

re·volv·er \ri-ˈväl-vər\ *n* : a pistol with a revolving cylinder of several chambers

re·vue \ri-ˈvyü\ *n* : a theatrical production consisting typically of brief often satirical sketches and songs

re·vul·sion \ri-ˈvəl-shən\ *n* **1** : a strong sudden reaction or change of feeling **2** : a feeling of complete distaste or repugnance

revved *past and past part of* REV

revving *pres part of* REV

[1]re·ward \ri-ˈwȯrd\ *vb* **1** : to give a reward to or for **2** : RECOMPENSE

[2]reward *n* **1** : something given in return for good or evil done or received; *esp* : something given or offered for some service or attainment **2** : a stimulus that is administered to an organism after a response and that increases the probability of occurrence of the response **syn** premium, prize, award

re·work \(ˈ)rē-ˈwərk\ *vb* **1** : REVISE **2** : to reprocess for further use

RF *abbr* radio frequency

RFD *abbr* rural free delivery

Rh *symbol* rhodium

RH *abbr* right hand

rhap·so·dy \ˈrap-səd-ē\ *n, pl* **-dies** [L *rhapsodia* portion of an epic poem adapted for recitation, fr. Gk *rhapsōidia* recitation of selections from epic poetry, rhapsody, fr. *rhaptein* to sew, stitch together + *aidein* to sing] **1** : an expression of extravagant praise or ecstasy **2** : an instrumental composition of irregular form — **rhap·sod·ic** \rap-ˈsäd-ik\ *adj* — **rhap·sod·i·cal·ly** \-i-k(ə-)lē\ *adv* — **rhap·so·dize** \ˈrap-sə-ˌdīz\ *vb*

rhea \ˈrē-ə\ *n* : any of several large flightless 3-toed So. American birds that resemble but are smaller than the African ostrich

rhe·ni·um \ˈrē-nē-əm\ *n* : a rare heavy hard metallic chemical element — see ELEMENT table

rheo·stat \ˈrē-ə-ˌstat\ *n* : a resistor for regulating an electric current by means of variable resistances — **rheo·stat·ic** \ˌrē-ə-ˈstat-ik\ *adj*

rhe·sus monkey \ˌrē-səs-\ *n* : a pale brown Indian monkey often used in medical research

rhet·o·ric \ˈret-ə-rik\ *n* [ME *rethorik,* fr. MF *rethorique,* fr. L *rhetorica,* fr. Gk *rhētorikē,* lit., art of oratory] : the art of speaking or writing effectively — **rhe·tor·i·cal** \ri-ˈtȯr-i-kəl\ *adj* — **rhet·o·ri·cian** \ˌret-ə-ˈrish-ən\ *n*

rheum \ˈrüm\ *n* : a watery discharge from the mucous membranes esp. of the eyes or nose — **rheumy** *adj*

rheu·mat·ic fever \rů-ˌmat-ik-\ *n* : an acute disease chiefly of children and young adults that is characterized by fever, by inflammation and pain in and around the joints, and by inflammation of the membranes surrounding the heart and the heart valves

rheu·ma·tism \ˈrü-mə-ˌtiz-əm, ˈrům-ə-\ *n* : any of various conditions marked by stiffness, pain, or swelling in muscles or joints — **rheu·mat·ic** \rů-ˈmat-ik\ *adj*

rheu·ma·toid arthritis \-ˌtȯid-\ *n* : a progressive constitutional disease characterized by inflammation and swelling of joint structures

Rh factor \ˈär-ˈāch-\ *n* [*rh*esus monkey (in which it was first detected)] **:** any of one or more inherited substances in red blood cells that may cause dangerous reactions in some infants or in transfusions

rhine·stone \ˈrīn-ˌstōn\ *n* **:** a colorless imitation stone of high luster made of glass, paste, or gem quartz

rhi·no \ˈrī-nō\ *n, pl* **rhino** *or* **rhinos** **:** RHINOCEROS

rhi·noc·er·os \rī-ˈnäs-(ə-)rəs\ *n, pl* **-noc·er·os·es** *or* **-noc·er·os** *or* **-noc·eri** \-ˈnäs-ə-ˌrī\ [ME *rinoceros,* fr. L *rhinoceros,* fr. Gk *rhinokerōs,* fr. *rhin-, rhis* nose + *keras* horn] **:** a large thick-skinned mammal of Africa and Asia with one or two upright horns of keratin on the snout and three toes on each foot

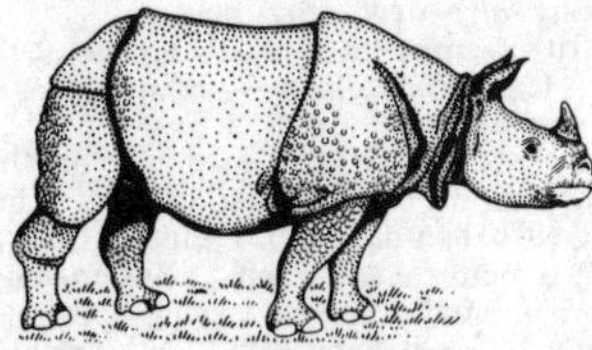

rhinoceros

rhi·zome \ˈrī-ˌzōm\ *n* **:** a specialized rootlike plant stem that forms shoots above and roots below — **rhi·zom·a·tous** \rī-ˈzäm-ət-əs\ *adj*

Rh–neg·a·tive \ˌär-ˌāch-ˈneg-ət-iv\ *adj* **:** lacking Rh factors in the red blood cells

rho·di·um \ˈrōd-ē-əm\ *n* **:** a hard ductile metallic chemical element — see ELEMENT table

rho·do·den·dron \ˌrōd-ə-ˈden-drən\ *n* **:** any of various shrubs or trees of the heath family grown for their clusters of large bright flowers

rhom·boid \ˈräm-ˌbȯid\ *n* **:** a parallelogram with unequal adjacent sides and angles that are not right angles

rhom·bus \ˈräm-bəs\ *n, pl* **rhom·bus·es** *or* **rhom·bi** \-ˌbī\ **:** a parallelogram having all four sides equal

Rh–pos·i·tive \ˌär-ˌāch-ˈpäz-ət-iv\ *adj* **:** containing Rh factors in the red blood cells

rhu·barb \ˈrü-ˌbärb\ *n* [ME *rubarbe,* fr. MF *reubarbe,* fr. ML *reubarbarum,* alter. of *rha barbarum,* lit., barbarian rhubarb] **:** a garden plant related to the buckwheat and having thick juicy edible pink and red stems on the leaves

[1]**rhyme** \ˈrīm\ *n* **1 :** a composition in verse that rhymes; *also* **:** POETRY **2 :** correspondence in terminal sounds (as of two lines of verse)

[2]**rhyme** *vb* **rhymed; rhym·ing 1 :** to make rhymes; *also* **:** to write poetry **2 :** to have rhymes **:** be in rhyme

rhy·o·lite \ˈrī-ə-ˌlīt\ *n* **:** a very acid volcanic rock

rhythm \ˈri*th*-əm\ *n* **1 :** regular rise and fall in the flow of sound in speech **2 :** a movement or activity in which some action or element recurs regularly — **rhyth·mic** \ˈri*th*-mik\ *or* **rhyth·mi·cal** \-mi-kəl\ *adj* — **rhyth·mi·cal·ly** \-k(ə-)lē\ *adv*

rhythm and blues *n* **:** popular music based on blues and Negro folk music

rhythm method *n* **:** a method of birth control in which a couple does not have sexual intercourse during the time when ovulation is most likely to occur

RI *abbr* Rhode Island

ri·al \rē-ˈȯl, -ˈäl\ *n* — see MONEY table

[1]**rib** \ˈrib\ *n* **1 :** any of the series of curved bones of the chest of most vertebrates that are joined to the backbone in pairs and help to support the body wall and protect the organs inside **2 :** something resembling a rib in shape or function **3 :** an elongated ridge

[2]**rib** *vb* **ribbed; rib·bing 1 :** to furnish or strengthen with ribs **2 :** to mark with ridges in knitting

[3]**rib** *vb* **ribbed; rib·bing :** to poke fun at **:** TEASE — **rib·ber** *n*

rib·ald \ˈrib-əld\ *adj* **:** coarse or indecent esp. in language ⟨∼ jokes⟩ — **rib·ald·ry** \-əl-drē\ *n*

rib·and \ˈrib-ənd\ *n* **:** RIBBON

rib·bon \ˈrib-ən\ *n* **1 :** a narrow fabric typically of silk or velvet used for trimming and for badges **2 :** a strip of inked cloth (as in a typewriter) **3 :** TATTER ⟨torn to ∼*s*⟩

ri·bo·fla·vin \ˌrī-bə-ˈflā-vən, ˈrī-bə-ˌflā-vən\ *n* **:** a growth-promoting vitamin of the vitamin B complex occurring in milk and liver

ri·bo·nu·cle·ic acid \ˌrī-bō-n(y)ü-ˌklē-ik-, -ˌklā-\ *n* **:** RNA

ri·bose \ˈrī-ˌbōs\ *n* **:** a sugar with five carbon atoms and five oxygen atoms in each molecule that is part of RNA

ri·bo·some \ˈrī-bə-ˌsōm\ *n* **:** any of the RNA-rich cytoplasmic granules in a cell that are sites of protein synthesis — **ri·bo·som·al** \ˌrī-bə-ˈsō-məl\ *adj*

rice \ˈrīs\ *n* **:** an annual grass grown in warm wet areas for its edible seed; *also* **:** this seed

rich \ˈrich\ *adj* **1 :** possessing or controlling great wealth **:** WEALTHY **2 :** COSTLY, VALUABLE **3 :** deep and pleasing in color or tone **4 :** ABUNDANT **5 :** containing much sugar, fat, or seasoning; *also* **:** high in combustible content **6 :** FRUITFUL, FERTILE — **rich·ly** *adv* — **rich·ness** *n*

rich·es \ˈrich-əz\ *n pl* [ME, sing. or pl., fr. *richesse,* lit., richness, fr. OF, fr. *riche* rich] **:** things that make one rich **:** WEALTH

Rich·ter scale \ˈrik-tər-\ *n* **:** a scale for expressing the magnitude of a seismic disturbance (as an earthquake) in terms of the energy dissipated in it

rick \ˈrik\ *n* **:** a large stack (as of hay) in the open air

rick·ets \ˈrik-əts\ *n* **:** a deficiency disease of children marked esp. by soft deformed bones and caused by inadequate sunlight or inadequate vitamin D

rick·ett·sia \ri-ˈket-sē-ə\ *n, pl* **-si·as** *or* **-si·ae** \-sē-ˌē\ **:** any of a family of rod-shaped microorganisms that cause various diseases (as typhus)

rick·ety \ˈrik-ət-ē\ *adj* **1 :** affected with rickets **2 :** FEEBLE **3 :** SHAKY

rick·sha *or* **rick·shaw** \ˈrik-ˌshȯ\ *n* **:** a small covered 2-wheeled vehicle pulled by one person and used orig. in Japan

[1]**ric·o·chet** \ˈrik-ə-ˌshā, *Brit also* -ˌshet\ *n* **:** a glancing rebound or skipping (as of a bullet off a wall)

[2]**ricochet** *vb* **-cheted** \-ˌshād\ *or* **-chet·ted** \-ˌshet-əd\; **-chet·ing** \-ˌshā-iŋ\ *or* **-chet·ting** \-ˌshet-iŋ\ **:** to skip with or as if with glancing rebounds

rid \ˈrid\ *vb* **rid** *also* **rid·ded; rid·ding :** to make free **:** CLEAR, RELIEVE — **rid·dance** \ˈrid-ᵊns\ *n*

rid·den \ˈrid-ᵊn\ *adj* **1 :** being harassed, oppressed, or obsessed by ⟨debt-*ridden*⟩ ⟨conscience-*ridden*⟩ **2 :** excessively full of or supplied with ⟨slum-*ridden*⟩

[1]**rid·dle** \ˈrid-ᵊl\ *n* **:** a puzzling question to be solved or answered by guessing

[2]**riddle** *vb* **rid·dled; rid·dling** \ˈrid-(ᵊ-)liŋ\ **1 :** EXPLAIN, SOLVE **2 :** to speak in riddles

[3]**riddle** *n* **:** a coarse sieve

[4]**riddle** *vb* **rid·dled; rid·dling** \ˈrid-(ᵊ-)liŋ\ **1 :** to sift with a riddle **2 :** to fill as full of holes as a sieve **3 :** PERMEATE

[1]**ride** \ˈrīd\ *vb* **rode** \ˈrōd\; **rid·den** \ˈrid-ᵊn\; **rid·ing** \ˈrīd-iŋ\ **1 :** to go on an animal's back or in a conveyance (as a boat, car, or airplane); *also* **:** to sit on and control so as to be carried along ⟨∼ a bicycle⟩ **2 :** to float or move on water ⟨∼ at anchor⟩; *also* **:** to move like a floating object **3 :** to bear along **:** CARRY ⟨*rode* her on their shoulders⟩ **4 :** to travel over a surface ⟨car ∼*s* well⟩ **5 :** to proceed

over on horseback **6** : to torment by nagging or teasing

[2]**ride** *n* **1** : an act of riding; *esp* : a trip on horseback or by vehicle **2** : a way (as a lane) suitable for riding **3** : a mechanical device (as a merry-go-round) for riding on **4** : a means of transportation

rid·er \ˈrīd-ər\ *n* **1** : one that rides **2** : an addition to a document often attached on a separate piece of paper **3** : a clause dealing with an unrelated matter attached to a legislative bill during passage — **rid·er·less** *adj*

[1]**ridge** \ˈrij\ *n* **1** : a range of hills **2** : a raised line or strip **3** : the line made where two sloping surfaces meet — **ridgy** *adj*

[2]**ridge** *vb* **ridged; ridg·ing 1** : to form into a ridge **2** : to extend in ridges

ridge·pole \ˈrij-ˌpōl\ *n* : the highest horizontal timber in a sloping roof to which the upper ends of the rafters are fastened

[1]**rid·i·cule** \ˈrid-ə-ˌkyül\ *n* : the act of exposing to laughter : DERISION

[2]**ridicule** *vb* **-culed; -cul·ing** : to laugh at or make fun of mockingly or contemptuously **syn** deride, taunt, twit, mock

ri·dic·u·lous \rə-ˈdik-yə-ləs\ *adj* : arousing or deserving ridicule : ABSURD, PREPOSTEROUS **syn** laughable, ludicrous, farcical, risible — **ri·dic·u·lous·ly** *adv* — **ri·dic·u·lous·ness** *n*

ri·el \rē-ˈel\ *n* — see MONEY table

rife \ˈrīf\ *adj* : WIDESPREAD, PREVALENT, ABOUNDING — **rife** *adv*

riff \ˈrif\ *n* : a repeated phrase in jazz typically supporting a solo improvisation; *also* : a piece based on such a phrase — **riff** *vb*

riff·raff \rif-ˌraf\ *n* [ME *riffe raffe,* fr. *rif and raf* every single one, fr. MF *rif et raf* completely] **1** : RABBLE **2** : REFUSE, RUBBISH

[1]**ri·fle** \ˈrī-fəl\ *vb* **ri·fled; ri·fling** \-f(ə-)liŋ\ : to ransack esp. in order to steal — **ri·fler** \-f(ə-)lər\ *n*

[2]**rifle** *vb* **ri·fled; ri·fling** \-f(ə-)liŋ\ : to cut spiral grooves into the bore of ⟨*rifled* arms⟩ — **rifling** *n*

[3]**rifle** *n* **1** : a shoulder weapon with a rifled bore **2** *pl* : a body of soldiers armed with rifles — **ri·fle·man** \-fəl-mən\ *n*

rift \ˈrift\ *n* **1** : CLEFT, FISSURE **2** : ESTRANGEMENT, SEPARATION — **rift** *vb*

[1]**rig** \ˈrig\ *vb* **rigged; rig·ging 1** : to fit out (as a ship) with rigging **2** : CLOTHE, DRESS **3** : EQUIP **4** : to set up esp. as a makeshift ⟨~ up a shelter⟩

[2]**rig** *n* **1** : the distinctive shape, number, and arrangement of sails and masts of a ship **2** : a carriage with its horse or horses **3** : CLOTHING, DRESS **4** : EQUIPMENT

[3]**rig** *vb* **rigged; rig·ging 1** : to manipulate or control esp. by deceptive or dishonest means **2** : to fix in advance for a desired result — **rig·ger** \ˈrig-ər\ *n*

rig·ging \ˈrig-iŋ, -ən\ *n* **1** : the ropes and chains that hold and move masts, sails, and spars of a ship **2** : a network (as in theater scenery) used for support and manipulation

[1]**right** \ˈrīt\ *adj* **1** : RIGHTEOUS, UPRIGHT **2** : JUST, PROPER **3** : conforming to truth or fact : CORRECT **4** : APPROPRIATE, SUITABLE **5** : STRAIGHT ⟨a ~ line⟩ **6** : GENUINE, REAL **7** : of, relating to, or being the stronger hand in most persons **8** : located nearer to the right hand; *esp* : being on the right when facing in the same direction as the observer **9** : made to be placed or worn outward ⟨~ side of a rug⟩ **10** : NORMAL, SOUND ⟨not in her ~ mind⟩ **syn** correct, accurate, exact, precise, nice — **right·ness** *n*

[2]**right** *n* **1** : qualities that constitute what is correct, just, proper, or honorable **2** : something (as a power or privilege) to which one has a just or lawful claim **3** : just action or decision : the cause of justice **4** : the side or part that is on or toward the right side **5** *cap* : political conservatives **6** *often cap* : a conservative position — **right·ward** \-wərd\ *adj*

[3]**right** *adv* **1** : according to what is right ⟨live ~⟩ **2** : EXACTLY, PRECISELY ⟨~ here and now⟩ **3** : DIRECTLY ⟨went ~ home⟩ **4** : according to fact or truth ⟨guess ~⟩ **5** : all the way : COMPLETELY ⟨~ to the end⟩ **6** : IMMEDIATELY ⟨~ after lunch⟩ **7** : QUITE, VERY ⟨~ nice weather⟩ **8** : on or to the right ⟨looked ~ and left⟩

[4]**right** *vb* **1** : to relieve from wrong **2** : to adjust or restore to a proper state or position **3** : to bring or restore to an upright position **4** : to become upright — **right·er** *n*

right angle *n* : an angle whose measure is 90° : an angle whose sides are perpendicular to each other — **right–an·gled** \ˈrīt-ˈaŋ-gəld\ *or* **right–an·gle** \-gəl\ *adj*

right circular cone *n* : CONE 2

righ·teous \ˈrī-chəs\ *adj* : acting or being in accordance with what is just, honorable, and free from guilt or wrong : UPRIGHT **syn** virtuous, noble, moral, ethical — **righ·teous·ly** *adv* — **righ·teous·ness** *n*

right·ful \ˈrīt-fəl\ *adj* **1** : JUST; *also* : FITTING **2** : having or held by a legally just claim — **right·ful·ly** \-ē\ *adv* — **right·ful·ness** *n*

right–hand \ˈrīt-ˌhand\ *adj* **1** : situated on the right **2** : RIGHT-HANDED **3** : chiefly relied on ⟨his ~ man⟩

right–hand·ed \-ˈhan-dəd\ *adj* **1** : using the right hand habitually or better than the left **2** : designed for or done with the right hand **3** : CLOCKWISE ⟨a ~ twist⟩ — **right–handed** *adv* — **right–hand·ed·ly** *adv* — **right–hand·ed·ness** *n*

right·ly \ˈrīt-lē\ *adv* **1** : FAIRLY, JUSTLY **2** : PROPERLY **3** : CORRECTLY, EXACTLY

right–of–way \ˌrīt-ə(v)-ˈwā\ *n, pl* **rights–of–way 1** : a legal right of passage over another person's ground **2** : the area over which a right-of-way exists **3** : the land on which a public road is built **4** : the land occupied by a railroad **5** : the land used by a public utility **6** : the right of traffic to take precedence over other traffic

right on *interj* — used to express agreement or give encouragement

right–to–life *adj* : opposed to abortion — **right–to–lif·er** \ˈrīt-tə-ˈlī-fər\ *n*

right triangle *n* : a triangle having one right angle

rig·id \ˈrij-əd\ *adj* **1** : lacking flexibility : STIFF **2** : strictly observed **syn** severe, stern, rigorous, stringent — **ri·gid·i·ty** \rə-ˈjid-ət-ē\ *n* — **rig·id·ly** *adv*

rig·ma·role \ˈrig-(ə-)mə-ˌrōl\ *n* [alter. of obs. *ragman roll* (long list, catalog)] **1** : confused or senseless talk **2** : a complex largely meaningless procedure

rig·or \ˈrig-ər\ *n* **1** : the quality of being inflexible or unyielding : STRICTNESS **2** : HARSHNESS, SEVERITY **3** : a tremor caused by a chill **4** : strict precision : EXACTNESS **syn** difficulty, hardship, vicissitude — **rig·or·ous** *adj* — **rig·or·ous·ly** *adv*

rig·or mor·tis \ˌrig-ər-ˈmȯrt-əs\ *n* [NL, stiffness of death] : temporary rigidity of muscles occurring after death

rile \ˈrīl\ *vb* **riled; ril·ing 1** : to make angry **2** : ROIL 1

[1]**rill** \ˈril\ *n* : a very small brook

[2]**rill** \ˈril\ *or* **rille** \ˈril, ˈril-ə\ *n* : a long narrow valley on the moon

[1]**rim** \ˈrim\ *n* **1** : the outer part of a wheel **2** : an outer edge esp. of something curved : BORDER, MARGIN

[2]**rim** *vb* **rimmed; rim·ming 1** : to furnish with a rim **2** : to run around the rim of

[1]**rime** \ˈrīm\ *n* **1** : FROST 2 **2** : frostlike ice tufts formed from fog or cloud on the windward side of exposed objects — **rimy** \ˈrī-mē\ *adj*

[2]**rime** *var of* RHYME

rind \ˈrīnd\ *n* : a usu. hard or tough outer layer ⟨lemon ~⟩

[1]**ring** \ˈriŋ\ *n* **1** : a circular band worn as an ornament or token or used for holding or fastening ⟨wedding ~⟩ ⟨key ~⟩ **2** : something circular in shape ⟨smoke ~⟩ **3** : a place for contest or display ⟨boxing ~⟩; *also* : PRIZEFIGHTING **4** : a group of people who work together for selfish or dishonest purposes — **ring·like** \ˈriŋ-ˌlīk\ *adj*

[2]**ring** *vb* **ringed; ring·ing** \ˈriŋ-iŋ\ **1** : ENCIRCLE **2** : to move

in a ring or spirally **3** : to throw a ring over (a mark) in a game (as quoits)

[3]**ring** *vb* **rang** \ˈraŋ\; **rung** \ˈrəŋ\; **ring·ing** \ˈriŋ-iŋ\ **1** : to sound resonantly when struck; *also* : to feel as if filled with such sound **2** : to cause to make a clear metallic sound by striking **3** : to announce or call by or as if by striking a bell ⟨~ an alarm⟩ **4** : to repeat loudly and persistently **5** : to sound a bell ⟨~ for the butler⟩

[4]**ring** *n* **1** : a set of bells **2** : the clear resonant sound of vibrating metal **3** : resonant tone : SONORITY **4** : a sound or character expressive of a particular quality **5** : an act or instance of ringing; *esp* : a telephone call

[1]**ring·er** \ˈriŋ-ər\ *n* **1** : one that sounds by ringing **2** : one that enters a competition under false representations **3** : one that closely resembles another

[2]**ringer** *n* : one that encircles or puts a ring around

ring·git \ˈriŋ-git\ *n* — see MONEY table

ring·lead·er \ˈriŋ-ˌlēd-ər\ *n* : a leader esp. of a group of troublemakers

ring·let \ˈriŋ-lət\ *n* : a long curl

ring·mas·ter \ˈriŋ-ˌmas-tər\ *n* : one in charge of performances in a circus ring

ring up *vb* **1** : to total and record esp. by means of a cash register **2** : ACHIEVE ⟨*rang up* many triumphs⟩

ring·worm \ˈriŋ-ˌwərm\ *n* : a contagious skin disease caused by fungi and marked by ring-shaped discolored patches

rink \ˈriŋk\ *n* : a level extent of ice marked off for skating or various games; *also* : a similar surface (as of wood) marked off or enclosed for a sport or game ⟨roller-skating ~⟩

[1]**rinse** \ˈrins\ *vb* **rinsed; rins·ing** [ME *rincen*, fr. MF *rincer*, fr. (assumed) VL *recentiare*, fr. L *recent-*, *recens* fresh, recent] **1** : to wash lightly or in water only **2** : to cleanse (as of soap) with clear water **3** : to treat (hair) with a rinse — **rins·er** *n*

[2]**rinse** *n* **1** : an act of rinsing **2** : a liquid used for rinsing **3** : a solution that temporarily tints hair

ri·ot \ˈrī-ət\ *n* **1** *archaic* : disorderly behavior **2** : disturbance of the public peace; *esp* : a violent public disorder **3** : random or disorderly profusion ⟨a ~ of color⟩ — **riot** *vb* — **ri·ot·er** *n* — **ri·ot·ous** *adj*

[1]**rip** \ˈrip\ *vb* **ripped; rip·ping 1** : to cut or tear open **2** : to saw or split (wood) with the grain — **rip·per** *n*

[2]**rip** *n* : a rent made by ripping

RIP *abbr* [L *requiescat in pace*] may he rest in peace, may she rest in peace; [L *requiescant in pace*] may they rest in peace

ri·par·i·an \rə-ˈper-ē-ən\ *adj* : of or relating to the bank of a stream, river, or lake

rip cord *n* : a cord that is pulled to release the pilot parachute which lifts a main parachute out of its container

ripe \ˈrīp\ *adj* **rip·er; rip·est 1** : fully grown and developed : MATURE ⟨~ fruit⟩ **2** : fully prepared for some use or object : READY — **ripe·ly** *adv* — **ripe·ness** *n*

rip·en \ˈrī-pən\ *vb* **rip·ened; rip·en·ing** \ˈrīp-(ə-)niŋ\ **1** : to grow or make ripe **2** : to bring to completeness or perfection; *also* : to age or cure (cheese) to develop characteristic flavor, odor, body, texture, and color

rip–off \ˈrip-ˌȯf\ *n* **1** : an act of stealing : THEFT **2** : a cheap imitation — **rip off** \(ˈ)rip-ˈȯf\ *vb*

ri·poste \ri-ˈpōst\ *n* [F, modif. of It *risposta*, lit., answer] **1** : a fencer's return thrust after a parry **2** : a retaliatory maneuver or response; *esp* : a quick retort — **riposte** *vb*

rip·ple \ˈrip-əl\ *vb* **rip·pled; rip·pling** \-(ə-)liŋ\ **1** : to become lightly ruffled on the surface **2** : to make a sound like that of rippling water — **ripple** *n*

rip·saw \ˈrip-ˌsȯ\ *n* : a coarse-toothed saw used to cut wood in the direction of the grain

rip·stop \ˈrip-ˌstäp\ *adj* : being a fabric woven in such a way that small tears do not spread ⟨~ nylon⟩

[1]**rise** \ˈrīz\ *vb* **rose** \ˈrōz\; **ris·en** \ˈriz-ᵊn\; **ris·ing** \ˈrī-ziŋ\ **1** : to get up from sitting, kneeling, or lying **2** : to get up from sleep or from one's bed **3** : to return from death **4** : to take up arms : go to war; *also* : REBEL **5** : to end a session : ADJOURN **6** : to appear above the horizon **7** : to move upward : ASCEND **8** : to extend above other objects **9** : to attain a higher level or rank **10** : to increase in quantity or in intensity **11** : to come into being : HAPPEN, BEGIN, ORIGINATE

[2]**rise** *n* **1** : an act of rising : a state of being risen **2** : BEGINNING, ORIGIN **3** : the elevation of one point above another **4** : an increase in amount, number, or volume **5** : an upward slope **6** : a spot higher than surrounding ground **7** : an angry reaction

ris·er \ˈrī-zər\ *n* **1** : one that rises **2** : the upright part between stair treads

ris·i·bil·i·ty \ˌriz-ə-ˈbil-ət-ē\ *n, pl* **-ties** : the ability or inclination to laugh — often used in pl.

ris·i·ble \ˈriz-ə-bəl\ *adj* **1** : able or inclined to laugh **2** : arousing laughter : FUNNY **3** : of or relating to laughter ⟨~ muscles⟩

[1]**risk** \ˈrisk\ *n* : exposure to possible loss or injury : DANGER, PERIL — **risk·i·ness** \ˈris-kē-nəs\ *n* — **risky** *adj*

[2]**risk** *vb* **1** : to expose to danger ⟨~*ed* his life⟩ **2** : to incur the danger of

ris·qué \ris-ˈkā\ *adj* [F] : verging on impropriety or indecency

rite \ˈrīt\ *n* **1** : a set form of conducting a ceremony **2** : the liturgy of a church **3** : a ceremonial act or action

rit·u·al \ˈrich-(ə-w)əl\ *n* **1** : the established form esp. for a religious ceremony **2** : a system of rites **3** : a ceremonial act or action **4** : a customarily repeated act or series of acts — **ritual** *adj* — **rit·u·al·ism** \-ˌiz-əm\ *n* — **rit·u·al·is·tic** \ˌrich-(ə-w)əl-ˈis-tik\ *adj* — **rit·u·al·is·ti·cal·ly** \-ti-k(ə-)lē\ *adv* — **rit·u·al·ly** \ˈrich-(ə-w)ə-lē\ *adv*

riv *abbr* river

[1]**ri·val** \ˈrī-vəl\ *n* [MF or L; MF, fr. L *rivalis* one using the same stream as another, rival in love, fr. *rivalis* of a stream, fr. *rivus* stream] **1** : one of two or more trying to get what only one can have **2** : one striving for competitive advantage **3** : one that equals another esp. in desired qualities : MATCH, PEER

[2]**rival** *adj* : COMPETING

[3]**rival** *vb* **-valed** *or* **-valled; -val·ing** *or* **-val·ling** \ˈrīv-(ə-)liŋ\ **1** : to be in competition with **2** : to try to equal or excel **3** : to have qualities that equal another's : MATCH

ri·val·ry \ˈrī-vəl-rē\ *n, pl* **-ries** : COMPETITION

rive \ˈrīv\ *vb* **rived** \ˈrīvd\; **riv·en** \ˈriv-ən\ *also* **rived; riv·ing** \ˈrī-viŋ\ **1** : SPLIT, REND **2** : SHATTER

riv·er \ˈriv-ər\ *n* : a natural stream larger than a brook

riv·er·bank \-ˌbaŋk\ *n* : the bank of a river

riv·er·bed \-ˌbed\ *n* : the channel occupied by a river

riv·er·boat \-ˌbōt\ *n* : a boat for use on a river

riv·er·front \-ˌfrənt\ *n* : the land or area along a river

riv·er·side \ˈriv-ər-ˌsīd\ *n* : the side or bank of a river

[1]**riv·et** \ˈriv-ət\ *n* : a metal bolt with a head at one end used to fasten things together by being put through holes in them and then being flattened on the plain end to make another head

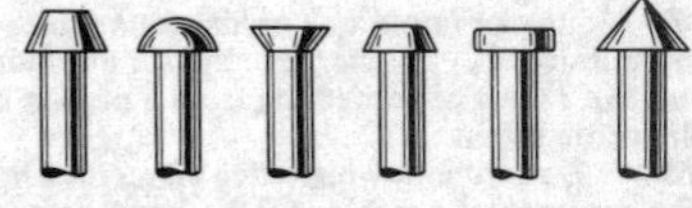

rivet

[2]**rivet** *vb* : to fasten with or as if with a rivet — **riv·et·er** *n*

riv·u·let \ˈriv-(y)ə-lət\ *n* : a small stream
ri·yal \rē-ˈ(y)äl, -ˈ(y)al\ *n* — see MONEY table
rm *abbr* **1** ream **2** room
Rn *symbol* radon
RN *abbr* **1** registered nurse **2** Royal Navy
RNA \ˌär-ˌen-ˈā\ *n* : any of various nucleic acids (as messenger RNA) that are found esp. in the cytoplasm of cells, have ribose as the 5-carbon sugar, and are associated with protein synthesis
rnd *abbr* round
[1]**roach** \ˈrōch\ *n, pl* **roach** *also* **roach·es** : any of various fishes related to the carp; *also* : any of several sunfishes
[2]**roach** *n* **1** : COCKROACH **2** : the butt of a marijuana cigarette
road \ˈrōd\ *n* **1** : ROADSTEAD — often used in pl. **2** : an open way for vehicles, persons, and animals : HIGHWAY **3** : ROUTE, PATH **4** : a series of scheduled visits (as games or performances) in several locations or the travel necessary to make these visits ⟨the team is on the ~⟩
road·abil·i·ty \ˌrōd-ə-ˈbil-ət-ē\ *n* : the qualities (as steadiness and balance) desirable in an automobile on the road
road·bed \ˈrōd-ˌbed\ *n* **1** : the foundation of a road or railroad **2** : the part of the surface of a road on which vehicles travel
road·block \-ˌbläk\ *n* **1** : a barricade on the road ⟨a police ~⟩ **2** : an obstruction to progress
road·run·ner \-ˌrən-ər\ *n* : a largely terrestrial bird of the southwestern U.S. and Mexico that is a speedy runner
road·side \ˈrōd-ˌsīd\ *n* : the strip of land along a road — **roadside** *adj*
road·stead \-ˌsted\ *n* : an anchorage for ships usu. less sheltered than a harbor
road·ster \ˈrōd-stər\ *n* **1** : a driving horse **2** : an open automobile with one cross seat
road·way \ˈrōd-ˌwā\ *n* : ROAD; *esp* : ROADBED
road·work \-ˌwərk\ *n* : conditioning for an athletic contest (as a boxing match) consisting mainly of long runs
roam \ˈrōm\ *vb* **1** : WANDER, ROVE **2** : to range or wander over or about
[1]**roan** \ˈrōn\ *adj* : of dark color (as black, red, or brown) sprinkled with white ⟨a ~ horse⟩
[2]**roan** *n* : an animal (as a horse) with a roan coat; *also* : its color
[1]**roar** \ˈrōr\ *vb* **1** : to utter a full loud prolonged sound **2** : to make a loud confused sound (as of wind or waves) — **roar·er** *n*
[2]**roar** *n* : a sound of roaring
[1]**roast** \ˈrōst\ *vb* **1** : to cook by dry heat (as before a fire or in an oven) **2** : to criticize severely or kiddingly
[2]**roast** *n* **1** : a piece of meat suitable for roasting **2** : an outing at which food is roasted ⟨corn ~⟩ **3** : severe criticism or kidding
[3]**roast** *adj* : ROASTED
roast·er \ˈrō-stər\ *n* **1** : one that roasts **2** : a device for roasting **3** : something adapted to roasting
rob \ˈräb\ *vb* **robbed; rob·bing 1** : to steal from **2** : to commit robbery **3** : to deprive of something due or expected — **rob·ber** *n*
robber fly *n* : any of numerous predaceous flies
rob·bery \ˈräb-(ə-)rē\ *n, pl* **-ber·ies** : the act or practice of robbing; *esp* : theft of something from a person by use of violence or threat
[1]**robe** \ˈrōb\ *n* **1** : a long flowing outer garment; *esp* : one used for ceremonial occasions **2** : a wrap or covering for the lower body (as for sitting outdoors)
[2]**robe** *vb* **robed; rob·ing 1** : to clothe with or as with a robe **2** : DRESS
rob·in \ˈräb-ən\ *n* **1** : a small European thrush with a yellowish red throat and breast **2** : a large No. American thrush with a grayish back, a streaked throat, and a chiefly dull reddish breast
ro·bot \ˈrō-ˌbät, -bət\ *n* [Czech, fr. *robota* work] **1** : a machine that looks and acts like a human being **2** : an efficient but insensitive person **3** : an automatic apparatus **4** : something guided by automatic controls
ro·bust \rō-ˈbəst, ˈrō-(ˌ)bəst\ *adj* [L *robustus* oaken, strong, fr. *robur* oak, strength] : strong and vigorously healthy — **ro·bust·ly** *adv* — **ro·bust·ness** *n*
[1]**rock** \ˈräk\ *vb* **1** : to move back and forth in or as if in a cradle **2** : to sway or cause to sway back and forth
[2]**rock** *n* **1** : a rocking movement **2** : popular music usu. played on electric instruments and characterized by a strong beat and much repetition
[3]**rock** *n* **1** : a mass of stony material; *also* : broken pieces of stone **2** : solid mineral deposits **3** : something like a rock in firmness — **rock** *adj* — **rock·like** *adj* — **rocky** *adj*
rock and roll *n* : [2]ROCK 2
rock·bound \ˈräk-ˌbau̇nd\ *adj* : fringed or covered with rocks
rock·er \ˈräk-ər\ *n* **1** : one of the curved pieces on which something (as a chair or cradle) rocks **2** : a chair that rocks on rockers **3** : a device that works with a rocking motion **4** : a rock performer, song, or enthusiast
[1]**rock·et** \ˈräk-ət\ *n* [It *rocchetta,* lit., small distaff] **1** : a firework that is propelled through the air by the gases produced by a burning substance **2** : a jet engine that operates on the same principle as a firework rocket but carries the oxygen needed for burning its fuel **3** : a rocket-propelled bomb or missile
[2]**rocket** *vb* **1** : to convey by means of a rocket **2** : to rise abruptly and rapidly
rock·et·ry \ˈräk-ə-trē\ *n* : the study or use of rockets
rocket ship *n* : a rocket-propelled spacecraft
rock·fall \ˈräk-ˌfȯl\ *n* : a mass of falling or fallen rocks
rock·fish \ˈräk-ˌfish\ *n* : any of various important market fishes that live among rocks or on rocky bottoms
rock 'n' roll \ˌräk-ən-ˈrōl\ *n* : [2]ROCK 2
rock salt *n* : common salt in rocklike masses or large crystals
rock wool *n* : woollike insulation made from molten rock or slag
Rocky Mountain sheep *n* : BIGHORN
ro·co·co \rə-ˈkō-kō\ *adj* [F, irreg. fr. *rocaille* rock work] : of or relating to an artistic style esp. of the 18th century marked by fanciful curved forms and elaborate ornamentation — **rococo** *n*
rod \ˈräd\ *n* **1** : a straight slender stick **2** : a stick or bundle of twigs used in punishing a person; *also* : PUNISHMENT **3** : a staff borne to show rank **4** — see WEIGHT table **5** *slang* : PISTOL
rode *past of* RIDE
ro·dent \ˈrōd-ᵊnt\ *n* [fr. L *rodent-, rodens,* prp. of *rodere* to gnaw] : any of a large order of relatively small mammals (as mice, squirrels, and beavers) with sharp front teeth used for gnawing
ro·deo \ˈrōd-ē-ˌō, rə-ˈdā-ō\ *n, pl* **ro·de·os** [Sp, fr. *rodear* to surround, fr. *rueda* wheel, fr. L *rota*] **1** : ROUNDUP 1 **2** : a public performance featuring cowboy skills (as riding and roping)
[1]**roe** \ˈrō\ *n, pl* **roe** *or* **roes** : DOE
[2]**roe** *n* : the eggs of a fish esp. while bound together in a mass
roe·buck \ˈrō-ˌbək\ *n, pl* **roebuck** *or* **roebucks** : a male roe deer
roe deer *n* : a small nimble European and Asian deer that is reddish brown in summer and grayish in the winter
roent·gen ray \ˌrent-gən-\ *n, often cap 1st R* : X RAY
rog·er \ˈräj-ər\ *interj* — used esp. in radio and signaling to indicate that a message has been received and understood
rogue \ˈrōg\ *n* **1** : a dishonest person : SCOUNDREL **2** : a mischievous person : SCAMP — **rogu·ery** \ˈrō-gə-rē\ *n* — **rogu·ish** \ˈrō-gish\ *adj* — **rogu·ish·ly** *adv* — **rogu·ish·ness** *n*

roil \ˈrȯil, *for 2 also* ˈrīl\ *vb* **1** : to make cloudy or muddy by stirring up **2** : RILE 1

rois·ter \ˈrȯi-stər\ *vb* **rois·tered; rois·ter·ing** \-st(ə-)riŋ\ : to engage in noisy revelry : CAROUSE — **rois·ter·er** \-stər-ər\ *n*

role *also* **rôle** \ˈrōl\ *n* **1** : an assigned or assumed character; *also* : a part played (as by an actor) **2** : FUNCTION

role model *n* : a person whose behavior in a particular role is imitated by others

¹roll \ˈrōl\ *n* **1** : a document containing an official record **2** : an official list of names **3** : something (as a bun) that is rolled up or rounded as if rolled **4** : something that rolls : ROLLER

²roll *vb* **1** : to move by turning over and over **2** : to press with a roller **3** : to move on wheels **4** : to sound with a full reverberating tone **5** : to make a continuous beating sound (as on a drum) **6** : to move onward as if by completing a revolution ⟨years ~*ed* by⟩ **7** : to flow or seem to flow in a continuous stream or with a rising and falling motion ⟨the river ~*ed* on⟩ **8** : to swing or sway from side to side **9** : to shape or become shaped in rounded form **10** : to utter with a trill

³roll *n* **1** : a sound produced by rapid strokes on a drum **2** : a heavy reverberating sound **3** : a rolling movement or action **4** : a swaying movement (as of a ship) **5** : SOMERSAULT

roll·back \ˈrōl-ˌbak\ *n* : the act or an instance of rolling back

roll back \ˈrōl-ˈbak\ *vb* **1** : to reduce (as a commodity price) on a national scale **2** : to cause to withdraw : push back

roll bar *n* : an overhead metal bar in an automobile designed to protect riders in case the automobile overturns

roll call *n* : the act or an instance of calling off a list of names (as of soldiers); *also* : a time for a roll call

roll·er \ˈrō-lər\ *n* **1** : a revolving cylinder used for moving, pressing, shaping, applying, or smoothing something **2** : a rod on which something is rolled up **3** : a long heavy wave on a coast

roll·er coast·er \ˈrō-lər-ˌkō-stər\ *n* : an elevated railway (as in an amusement park) constructed with sharp curves and steep slopes

roller skate *n* : a skate with wheels instead of a runner — **roller–skate** *vb* — **roller skater** *n*

rol·lick \ˈräl-ik\ *vb* : ROMP, FROLIC

rol·lick·ing \-iŋ\ *adj* : full of fun and good spirits

roly–poly \ˌrō-lē-ˈpō-lē\ *adj* : ROTUND

Rom *abbr* **1** Roman **2** Romance **3** Romania; Romanian **4** Romans

ROM *abbr* read-only memory

ro·maine \rō-ˈmān\ *n* [F, lit., Roman] : a lettuce with a tall loose head of long crisp leaves

¹Ro·man \ˈrō-mən\ *n* **1** : a native or resident of Rome **2** : a citizen of the Roman Empire

²Roman *adj* **1** : of or relating to Rome or the Romans **2** *not cap* : relating to type in which the letters are upright (as in this definition) **3** : of or relating to the Roman Catholic Church

Roman candle *n* : a cylindrical firework that discharges balls of fire

Roman Catholic *adj* : of or relating to the body of Christians in communion with the pope and having a liturgy centered in the Mass — **Roman Catholicism** *n*

¹ro·mance \rō-ˈmans, ˈrō-ˌmans\ *n* [ME *romauns*, fr. OF *romans* French, something written in French, fr. L *romanice* in the Roman manner, fr. *romanicus* Roman, fr. *Romanus*] **1** : a medieval tale of knightly adventure **2** : a prose narrative dealing with heroic or mysterious events set in a remote time or place **3** : a love story **4** : a romantic attachment or episode between lovers — **ro·manc·er** *n*

²romance *vb* **ro·manced; ro·manc·ing** **1** : to exaggerate or invent detail or incident **2** : to have romantic fancies **3** : to carry on a romantic episode with

Ro·mance \rō-ˈmans, ˈrō-ˌmans\ *adj* : of or relating to any of several languages developed from Latin

Ro·ma·nian \rů-ˈmā-nē-ən, rō-, -nyən\ *n* **1** : a native or inhabitant of Romania **2** : RUMANIAN 2

Roman numeral *n* : a numeral in a system of notation that is based on the ancient Roman system

Ro·ma·no \rə-ˈmän-ō, rō-\ *n* : a hard Italian cheese that is sharper than Parmesan

¹ro·man·tic \rō-ˈmant-ik\ *n* : a romantic person; *esp* : a romantic writer, composer, or artist

²romantic *adj* **1** : IMAGINARY **2** : VISIONARY **3** : having an imaginative or emotional appeal **4** : of, relating to, or having the characteristics of romanticism — **ro·man·ti·cal·ly** \-i-k(ə-)lē\ *adv*

ro·man·ti·cism \rō-ˈmant-ə-ˌsiz-əm\ *n, often cap* : a literary movement (as in early 19th century England) marked esp. by emphasis on the imagination and the emotions and by the use of autobiographical material — **ro·man·ti·cist** \-səst\ *n, often cap*

romp \ˈrämp\ *vb* **1** : to play actively and noisily **2** : to win a contest easily — **romp** *n*

romp·er \ˈräm-pər\ *n* **1** : one that romps **2** : a child's one-piece garment with the lower part shaped like bloomers — usu. used in pl.

rood \ˈrüd\ *n* : CROSS, CRUCIFIX

¹roof \ˈrüf, ˈrůf\ *n, pl* **roofs** \ˈrüfs, ˈrůfs; ˈrüvz, ˈrůvz\ **1** : the upper covering part of a building **2** : something suggesting a roof of a building — **roofed** \ˈrüft, ˈrůft\ *adj* — **roof·ing** *n* — **roof·less** *adj*

roof 1: *left* gambrel, *right* mansard

²roof *vb* : to cover with a roof

roof·top \-ˌtäp\ *n* : a roof esp. of a house

roof·tree \-ˌtrē\ *n* : RIDGEPOLE

¹rook \ˈrůk\ *n* : a common Old World bird resembling the related crow

²rook *vb* : CHEAT, SWINDLE

³rook *n* : a chess piece that can move parallel to the sides of the board across any number of unoccupied squares

rook·ery \ˈrůk-ə-rē\ *n, pl* **-er·ies** : a breeding ground or haunt of gregarious birds or mammals; *also* : a colony of such birds or mammals

rook·ie \ˈrůk-ē\ *n* : BEGINNER, RECRUIT; *esp* : a first-year player in a professional sport

¹room \ˈrüm, ˈrům\ *n* **1** : an extent of space occupied by or sufficient or available for something **2** : a partitioned part of a building : CHAMBER; *also* : the people in a room **3** : OPPORTUNITY, CHANCE ⟨~ to develop his talents⟩ — **room·ful** *n* — **roomy** *adj*

²room *vb* : to occupy lodgings : LODGE — **room·er** *n*

room·ette \rü-ˈmet, rům-ˈet\ *n* : a small private room on a railroad sleeping car

room·mate \ˈrüm-ˌmāt, ˈrům-\ *n* : one of two or more persons sharing the same room or dwelling

¹roost \ˈrüst\ *n* : a support on which or a place where birds perch

²roost *vb* : to settle on or as if on a roost

roost·er \ˈrüs-tər, ˈrůs-\ *n* : an adult male domestic fowl : COCK

[1]**root** \ˈrüt, ˈrůt\ *n* **1** : the leafless usu. underground part of a seed plant that functions in absorption, aeration, and storage or as a means of anchorage; *also* : an underground plant part esp. when fleshy and edible **2** : something (as the basal part of a tooth or hair) resembling a root **3** : SOURCE, ORIGIN **4** : the essential core : HEART ⟨get to the ~ of the matter⟩ **5** : a number that when taken as a factor an indicated number of times gives a specified number **6** : the lower part — **root·less** *adj* — **root·like** *adj*

[2]**root** *vb* **1** : to form roots **2** : to fix or become fixed by or as if by roots : ESTABLISH **3** : UPROOT

[3]**root** *vb* **1** : to turn up or dig with the snout ⟨pigs ~*ing*⟩ **2** : to poke or dig around (as in search of something)

[4]**root** \ˈrüt\ *vb* **1** : to applaud or encourage noisily : CHEER **2** : to wish success or lend support to — **root·er** *n*

root beer *n* : a sweetened effervescent beverage flavored with extracts of roots and herbs

root·let \ˈrüt-lət, ˈrůt-\ *n* : a small root

root·stock \-ˌstäk\ *n* : an underground part of a plant that resembles a rhizome

[1]**rope** \ˈrōp\ *n* **1** : a large strong cord made of strands of fiber **2** : a hangman's noose **3** : a thick string (as of pearls) made by twisting or braiding

[2]**rope** *vb* **roped; rop·ing 1** : to bind, tie, or fasten together with a rope **2** : to separate or divide off by means of a rope **3** : LASSO

Ror·schach test \ˈrȯr-ˌshäk-\ *n* : a personality and intelligence test in which a subject interprets ink-blot designs in terms that reveal intellectual and emotional factors

ro·sa·ry \ˈrō-zə-rē\ *n, pl* **-ries 1** *often cap* : a Roman Catholic devotion consisting of meditation on sacred mysteries during recitation of Hail Marys **2** : a string of beads used in praying

[1]**rose** *past of* RISE

[2]**rose** \ˈrōz\ *n* **1** : any of a genus of usu. prickly often climbing shrubs with divided leaves and bright often fragrant flowers; *also* : one of these flowers **2** : something resembling a rose in form **3** : a moderate purplish red color — **rose** *adj*

ro·sé \rō-ˈzā\ *n* [F] : a light pink wine

ro·se·ate \ˈrō-zē-ət, -zē-ˌāt\ *adj* **1** : resembling a rose esp. in color **2** : OPTIMISTIC ⟨a ~ view of the future⟩

rose·bud \ˈrōz-ˌbəd\ *n* : the flower of a rose when it is at most partly open

rose·bush \-ˌbůsh\ *n* : a shrubby rose

rose·mary \ˈrōz-ˌmer-ē\ *n, pl* **-mar·ies** [ME *rosmarine*, fr. L *rosmarinus*, fr. *ros* dew + *marinus* of the sea, fr. *mare* sea] : a fragrant shrubby mint with evergreen leaves used in perfumery and cooking

ro·sette \rō-ˈzet\ *n* [F] **1** : a usu. small badge or ornament of ribbon gathered in the shape of a rose **2** : a circular ornament filled with representations of leaves

rose·wa·ter \ˈrōz-ˌwȯt-ər, -ˌwät-\ *adj* : a watery solution of the fragrant constituents of the rose used as a perfume

rose·wood \-ˌwůd\ *n* : any of various tropical trees with dark red wood streaked with black; *also* : this wood

Rosh Ha·sha·nah \ˌrōsh-(h)ə-ˈshō-nə\ *n* [Heb *rōsh hashshānāh*, lit., beginning of the year] : the Jewish New Year observed as a religious holiday in September or October

ros·in \ˈräz-ᵊn\ *n* : a hard brittle resin obtained esp. from pine trees and used in varnishes and on violin bows

ros·ter \ˈräs-tər\ *n* **1** : a list of personnel; *also* : the persons listed on a roster **2** : an itemized list

ros·trum \ˈräs-trəm\ *n, pl* **rostrums** *or* **ros·tra** \-trə\ [L *Rostra*, pl., a platform for speakers in the Roman Forum decorated with the beaks of captured ships, fr. pl. of *rostrum* beak, ship's beak, fr. *rodere* to gnaw] : a stage or platform for public speaking

rosy \ˈrō-zē\ *adj* **ros·i·er; -est 1** : of the color rose **2** : HOPEFUL, PROMISING — **ros·i·ly** \ˈrō-zə-lē\ *adv* — **ros·i·ness** \-zē-nəs\ *n*

[1]**rot** \ˈrät\ *vb* **rot·ted; rot·ting** : to undergo decomposition : DECAY

[2]**rot** *n* **1** : DECAY **2** : a disease of plants or animals in which tissue breaks down **3** : NONSENSE

[1]**ro·ta·ry** \ˈrōt-ə-rē\ *adj* **1** : turning on an axis like a wheel **2** : having a rotating part

[2]**rotary** *n, pl* **-ries 1** : a rotary machine **2** : a circular road junction

ro·tate \ˈrō-ˌtāt\ *vb* **ro·tat·ed; ro·tat·ing 1** : to turn or cause to turn about an axis or a center : REVOLVE **2** : to alternate in a series **syn** turn, circle, spin, whirl, twirl — **ro·ta·tion** \rō-ˈtā-shən\ *n* — **ro·ta·tor** \ˈrō-ˌtāt-ər\ *n* — **ro·ta·to·ry** \ˈrōt-ə-ˌtōr-ē\ *adj*

ROTC *abbr* Reserve Officers' Training Corps

rote \ˈrōt\ *n* **1** : repetition from memory often without attention to meaning **2** : fixed routine or repetition — **rote** *adj*

ro·tis·ser·ie \rō-ˈtis-(ə-)rē\ *n* [F] **1** : a restaurant specializing in broiled and barbecued meats **2** : an appliance fitted with a spit on which food is rotated before or over a source of heat

ro·to·gra·vure \ˌrōt-ə-grə-ˈvyůr\ *n* : PHOTOGRAVURE

ro·tor \ˈrōt-ər\ *n* **1** : a part that rotates **2** : a system of rotating horizontal blades for supporting a helicopter

rot·ten \ˈrät-ᵊn\ *adj* **1** : having rotted **2** : CORRUPT **3** : extremely unpleasant or inferior — **rot·ten·ness** \-ᵊn-(n)əs\ *n*

rot·ten·stone \ˈrät-ᵊn-ˌstōn\ *n* : a decomposed siliceous limestone used for polishing

ro·tund \rō-ˈtənd\ *adj* : rounded out **syn** plump, chubby, portly, stout — **ro·tun·di·ty** \-ˈtən-dət-ē\ *n*

ro·tun·da \rō-ˈtən-də\ *n* **1** : a round building; *esp* : one covered by a dome **2** : a large round room

rou·ble \ˈrü-bəl\ *var of* RUBLE

roué \rü-ˈā\ *n* [F, lit., broken on the wheel, fr. pp. of *rouer* to break on the wheel, fr. ML *rotare*, fr. L, to rotate; fr. the feeling that such a person deserves this punishment] : a man devoted to a life of sensual pleasure : RAKE

rouge \ˈrüzh, ˈrüj\ *n* [F, lit., red] **1** : a cosmetic used to give a red color to cheeks and lips **2** : a red powder used in polishing glass, gems, and metal — **rouge** *vb*

[1]**rough** \ˈrəf\ *adj* **rough·er; rough·est 1** : uneven in surface : not smooth **2** : SHAGGY **3** : not calm : TURBULENT, TEMPESTUOUS **4** : marked by harshness or violence **5** : DIFFICULT, TRYING **6** : coarse or rugged in character or appearance **7** : marked by lack of refinement **8** : CRUDE, UNFINISHED **9** : done or made hastily or tentatively — **rough·ly** *adv* — **rough·ness** *n*

[2]**rough** *n* **1** : uneven ground covered with high grass esp. along a golf fairway **2** : a crude, unfinished, or preliminary state; *also* : something in such a state **3** : ROWDY, TOUGH

[3]**rough** *vb* **1** : ROUGHEN **2** : MANHANDLE **3** : to make or shape roughly esp. in a preliminary way — **rough·er** *n*

rough·age \ˈrəf-ij\ *n* : coarse bulky food (as bran) whose bulk stimulates the intestine to move its contents along

rough–and–ready \ˌrəf-ən-ˈred-ē\ *adj* : rude or unpolished in nature, method, or manner but effective in action or use

rough–and–tum·ble \-ˈtəm-bəl\ *n* : rough unrestrained fighting or struggling — **rough–and–tumble** *adj*

rough·en \ˈrəf-ən\ *vb* **rough·ened; rough·en·ing** \-(ə-)niŋ\ : to make or become rough

rough–hewn \ˈrəf-ˈhyün\ *adj* **1** : being rough and unfinished ⟨~ beams⟩ **2** : lacking smooth manners or social grace

rough·house \ˈrəf-ˌhaůs\ *vb* **rough·housed; rough·hous·ing** : to participate in rough noisy behavior — **roughhouse** *n*

rough·neck \ˈrəf-ˌnek\ *n* **1** : ROWDY, TOUGH **2** : a worker on a crew drilling oil wells

rough·shod \ˈrəf-ˌshäd\ *adv* : with no consideration for the wishes or feelings of others ⟨rode ~ over the opposition⟩

rou·lette \rü-ˈlet\ *n* [F, lit., small wheel] **1** : a gambling game in which a whirling wheel is used **2** : a wheel or disk with teeth around the outside

¹round \ˈrau̇nd\ *adj* **1** : having every part of the surface or circumference the same distance from the center **2** : CYLINDRICAL **3** : COMPLETE, FULL **4** : approximately correct; *esp* : exact only to a specific decimal or place ⟨use the ~ number 1400 for the exact figure 1411⟩ **5** : liberal or ample in size or amount **6** : BLUNT, OUTSPOKEN **7** : moving in or forming a circle **8** : of or relating to handwriting that is predominantly curved rather than angular — **round·ish** *adj* — **round·ly** \ˈrau̇n-(d)lē\ *adv* — **round·ness** \ˈrau̇n(d)-nəs\ *n*

²round *prep or adv* : AROUND

³round *n* **1** : something round (as a circle, globe, or ring) **2** : a curved or rounded part (as a rung of a ladder) **3** : a circuitous path or course; *also* : an habitually covered route (as of a watchman) **4** : a series or cycle of recurring actions or events **5** : one shot fired by a soldier or a gun; *also* : ammunition for one shot **6** : a period of time or a unit of play in a game or contest **7** : a cut of beef esp. between the rump and the lower leg — **in the round 1** : FREESTANDING **2** : with a center stage surrounded by an audience on all sides ⟨theater *in the round*⟩

⁴round *vb* **1** : to make or become round **2** : to go or pass around or part way around **3** : COMPLETE, FINISH **4** : to become plump or shapely **5** : to express as a round number **6** : to follow a winding course : BEND

¹round·about \ˈrau̇n-də-ˌbau̇t\ *n, Brit* : MERRY-GO-ROUND

²roundabout *adj* : INDIRECT, CIRCUITOUS

roun·de·lay \ˈrau̇n-də-ˌlā\ *n* **1** : a simple song with refrain **2** : a poem with a refrain recurring frequently or at fixed intervals

round·house \ˈrau̇nd-ˌhau̇s\ *n* : a circular building for housing and repairing locomotives

round–shoul·dered \ˈrau̇n(d)-ˈshōl-dərd\ *adj* : having the shoulders stooping or rounded

round–trip *n* : a trip to a place and back

round·up \ˈrau̇nd-ˌəp\ *n* **1** : the gathering together of cattle on the range by riding around them and driving them in; *also* : the men and horses engaged in a roundup **2** : a gathering in of scattered persons or things **3** : SUMMARY ⟨news ~⟩ — **round up** \ˈrau̇nd-ˈəp\ *vb*

round·worm \-ˌwərm\ *n* : NEMATODE

rouse \ˈrau̇z\ *vb* **roused; rous·ing 1** : to wake from sleep **2** : to excite to activity : stir up

roust·about \ˈrau̇s-tə-ˌbau̇t\ *n* : one who does heavy unskilled labor (as on a dock or in an oil field)

¹rout \ˈrau̇t\ *n* **1** : MOB 1, 2 **2** : DISTURBANCE **3** : a fashionable gathering

²rout *vb* **1** : RUMMAGE **2** : to gouge out **3** : to expel by force

³rout *n* **1** : a state of wild confusion or disorderly retreat **2** : a disastrous defeat

⁴rout *vb* **1** : to put to flight **2** : to defeat decisively

¹route \ˈrüt, ˈrau̇t\ *n* **1** : a traveled way **2** : CHANNEL **3** : a line of travel

²route *vb* **rout·ed; rout·ing 1** : to send by a selected route **2** : to arrange and direct the order of

route·man \-mən, -ˌman\ *n* : one who sells and makes deliveries on an assigned route

rou·tine \rü-ˈtēn\ *n* [F, fr. MF, fr. *route* traveled way] **1** : a round (as of work or play) regularly followed **2** : any regular course of action — **routine** *adj* — **rou·tine·ly** *adv* — **rou·tin·ize** \-ˈtēn-ˌīz\ *vb*

¹rove \ˈrōv\ *vb* **roved; rov·ing** : to wander over or through : RAMBLE, ROAM — **rov·er** *n*

²rove *past and past part of* REEVE

¹row \ˈrō\ *vb* **1** : to propel a boat with oars **2** : to travel or convey in a rowboat **3** : to match rowing skill against — **row·er** \ˈrō(-ə)r\ *n*

²row *n* : an act or instance of rowing

³row *n* **1** : a number of objects in an orderly sequence **2** : WAY, STREET

⁴row \ˈrau̇\ *n* : a noisy quarrel

⁵row \ˈrau̇\ *vb* : to engage in a row

row·boat \ˈrō-ˌbōt\ *n* : a small boat designed to be rowed

row·dy \ˈrau̇d-ē\ *adj* **row·di·er; -est** : coarse or boisterous in behavior : ROUGH — **row·di·ness** \ˈrau̇d-ē-nəs\ *n* — **rowdy** *n* — **row·dy·ish** *adj* — **row·dy·ism** *n*

row·el \ˈrau̇(-ə)l\ *n* : a small pointed wheel on a spur used to urge on a horse — **rowel** *vb*

roy·al \ˈrȯi-əl\ *adj* **1** : of or relating to a king or sovereign **2** : resembling or befitting a king — **roy·al·ly** \-ē\ *adv*

royal flush *n* : a straight flush having an ace as the highest card

roy·al·ist \ˈrȯi-ə-ləst\ *n* : an adherent of a king or of monarchical government

roy·al·ty \ˈrȯi-əl-tē\ *n, pl* **-ties 1** : the state of being royal **2** : a royal person : royal persons **3** : a share of a product or profit (as of a mine or oil well) claimed by the owner for allowing another person to use the property **4** : a payment made to an author or composer for each copy of a work sold or to an inventor for each article sold under a patent

RP *abbr* relief pitcher

RPM *abbr* revolutions per minute

RPS *abbr* revolutions per second

rpt *abbr* **1** repeat **2** report

RR *abbr* **1** railroad **2** rural route

RS *abbr* **1** recording secretary **2** revised statutes **3** right side **4** Royal Society

RSV *abbr* Revised Standard Version

RSVP *abbr* [F *répondez s'il vous plaît*] please reply

RSWC *abbr* right side up with care

rt *abbr* right

RT *abbr* radiotelephone

rte *abbr* route

Ru *symbol* ruthenium

¹rub \ˈrəb\ *vb* **rubbed; rub·bing 1** : to use pressure and friction on a body or object **2** : to fret or chafe with friction **3** : to scour, polish, erase, or smear by pressure and friction

²rub *n* **1** : DIFFICULTY, OBSTRUCTION **2** : something grating to the feelings

¹rub·ber \ˈrəb-ər\ *n* **1** : one that rubs **2** : ERASER **3** : a flexible waterproof elastic substance made from the juice of various tropical plants or synthetically; *also* : something made of this material — **rubber** *adj* — **rub·ber·ize** \-ˌīz\ *vb* — **rub·bery** *adj*

²rubber *n* **1** : a contest that consists of an odd number of games and is won by the side that takes a majority **2** : an extra game played to decide a tie

rub·ber·neck \-ˌnek\ *vb* : to look about, stare, or listen with excessive curiosity

rub·ber·neck·er \-ər\ *also* **rubberneck** *n* **1** : an idly or overly inquisitive person **2** : a person on a guided tour

rub·bish \ˈrəb-ish\ *n* **1** : useless waste or rejected matter : TRASH **2** : something worthless or nonsensical

rub·ble \ˈrəb-əl\ *n* : broken stones or bricks used in masonry; *also* : a mass of such material

ru·bel·la \rü-ˈbel-ə\ *n* : GERMAN MEASLES

ru·bi·cund \ˈrü-bi-(ˌ)kənd\ *adj* : RED, RUDDY

ru·bid·i·um \rü-ˈbid-ē-əm\ *n* : a soft silvery metallic chemical element — see ELEMENT table

ru·ble \ˈrü-bəl\ *n* — see MONEY table

---

ru·bric \ˈrü-brik\ *n* [ME *rubrike* red ocher, heading in red letters of part of a book, fr. MF *rubrique*, fr. L *rubrica*, fr. *ruber* red] **1** : HEADING, TITLE; *also* : CLASS, CATEGORY **2** : a rule esp. for the conduct of a religious service

ru·by \ˈrü-bē\ *n, pl* **rubies** : a clear red precious stone

ru·by–throat·ed hummingbird \ˌrü-bē-ˌthrōt-əd-\ *n* : a bright green and whitish hummingbird of eastern No. America with a red throat in the male

ruck·us \ˈrək-əs\ *n* : ROW, DISTURBANCE

rud·der \ˈrəd-ər\ *n* : a movable flat piece attached vertically at the rear of a boat or aircraft for steering

rud·dy \ˈrəd-ē\ *adj* **rud·di·er; -est** : REDDISH; *esp* : of a healthy reddish complexion — **rud·di·ness** \ˈrəd-ē-nəs\ *n*

rude \ˈrüd\ *adj* **rud·er; rud·est 1** : roughly made : CRUDE **2** : UNDEVELOPED, PRIMITIVE **3** : IMPOLITE, DISCOURTEOUS **4** : UNSKILLED — **rude·ly** *adv* — **rude·ness** *n*

ru·di·ment \ˈrüd-ə-mənt\ *n* **1** : an elementary principle or basic skill — usu. used in pl. **2** : something not fully developed — usu. used in pl. — **ru·di·men·ta·ry** \ˌrüd-ə-ˈmen-t(ə-)rē\ *adj*

[1]rue \ˈrü\ *vb* **rued; ru·ing** : to feel regret, remorse, or penitence for

[2]rue *n* : REGRET, SORROW — **rue·ful** \-fəl\ *adj* — **rue·ful·ly** \-ē\ *adv* — **rue·ful·ness** *n*

[3]rue *n* : a European strong-scented woody herb with bitter-tasting leaves

rue anemone *n* : a delicate herb of the buttercup family with white flowers

ruff \ˈrəf\ *n* **1** : a wheel-shaped frilled collar worn about 1600 **2** : a fringe of hair or feathers around the neck of an animal — **ruffed** \ˈrəft\ *adj*

ruf·fi·an \ˈrəf-ē-ən\ *n* [MF *rufian*] : a brutal person — **ruf·fi·an·ly** *adj*

[1]ruf·fle \ˈrəf-əl\ *vb* **ruf·fled; ruf·fling** \-(ə-)liŋ\ **1** : to roughen the surface of **2** : IRRITATE, VEX **3** : to erect (as hair or feathers) in or like a ruff **4** : to draw into or provide with plaits or folds **5** : to flip through (as pages)

[2]ruffle *n* **1** : RIPPLE **2** : a strip of fabric gathered or pleated on one edge **3** : RUFF 2

rug \ˈrəg\ *n* **1** : a piece of heavy fabric usu. with a nap or pile used as a floor covering **2** : a covering for the legs, lap, and feet

rug·by \ˈrəg-bē\ *n, often cap* [*Rugby* School, Rugby, England, where it was first played] : a football game in which play is continuous and interference and forward passing are not permitted

rug·ged \ˈrəg-əd\ *adj* **1** : having a rough uneven surface **2** : TURBULENT, STORMY **3** : HARSH, STERN **4** : ROBUST, STURDY — **rug·ged·ly** *adv* — **rug·ged·ness** *n*

[1]ru·in \ˈrü-ən\ *n* **1** : complete collapse or destruction **2** : the remains of something destroyed — usu. used in pl. **3** : a cause of destruction **4** : the action of destroying

[2]ruin *vb* **1** : DESTROY **2** : to damage beyond repair **3** : BANKRUPT

ru·in·ation \ˌrü-ə-ˈnā-shən\ *n* : RUIN, DESTRUCTION

ru·in·ous \ˈrü-ə-nəs\ *adj* **1** : RUINED, DILAPIDATED **2** : causing ruin — **ru·in·ous·ly** *adv*

[1]rule \ˈrül\ *n* **1** : a guide or principle for governing action : REGULATION **2** : the usual way of doing something **3** : the exercise of authority or control : GOVERNMENT **4** : RULER 2

[2]rule *vb* **ruled; rul·ing 1** : CONTROL, GOVERN **2** : to be preeminent in : DOMINATE, PREVAIL **3** : to give or state as a considered decision **4** : to mark on paper with or as if with a ruler

rul·er \ˈrü-lər\ *n* **1** : SOVEREIGN **2** : a straight strip of material (as wood or metal) marked off in units and used for measuring or as a straightedge

rum \ˈrəm\ *n* **1** : a liquor distilled from a fermented cane product (as molasses) **2** : alcoholic liquor

Rum *abbr* Rumania; Rumanian

Ru·ma·nian \ru̇-ˈmā-nē-ən, -nyən\ *n* **1** : ROMANIAN 1 **2** : the language of the Romanians — **Rumanian** *adj*

rum·ba \ˈrəm-bə, ˈru̇m-\ *n* : a dance of Cuban origin marked by strong rhythmic movements

[1]rum·ble \ˈrəm-bəl\ *vb* **rum·bled; rum·bling** \-b(ə-)liŋ\ : to make a low heavy rolling sound; *also* : to travel or move along with such a sound — **rum·bler** \-b(ə-)lər\ *n*

[2]rumble *n* **1** : a low heavy rolling sound **2** : a street fight esp. among gangs

rumble seat *n* : a folding seat in the back of an automobile that is not covered by the top

rum·bling \ˈrəm-bliŋ\ *n* **1** : RUMBLE **2** : widespread talk or complaints — usu. used in pl.

[1]ru·mi·nant \ˈrü-mə-nənt\ *n* : a ruminant mammal

[2]ruminant *adj* **1** : chewing the cud; *also* : of or relating to a group of hoofed mammals (as cattle, deer, and camels) that chew the cud and have a complex 3- or 4-chambered stomach **2** : given to or engaged in contemplation : MEDITATIVE

ru·mi·nate \ˈrü-mə-ˌnāt\ *vb* **-nat·ed; -nat·ing** [L *ruminari* to chew the cud, muse upon, fr. *rumin-*, *rumen* gullet] **1** : MEDITATE, MUSE **2** : to chew the cud — **ru·mi·na·tion** \ˌrü-mə-ˈnā-shən\ *n*

[1]rum·mage \ˈrəm-ij\ *vb* **rum·maged; rum·mag·ing** : to poke around in all corners looking for something — **rum·mag·er** *n*

[2]rummage *n* **1** : a miscellaneous collection **2** : an act of rummaging

rum·my \ˈrəm-ē\ *n* : any of several card games for two or more players

ru·mor \ˈrü-mər\ *n* **1** : common talk **2** : a statement or report current but not authenticated — **rumor** *vb*

rump \ˈrəmp\ *n* **1** : the rear part of an animal; *also* : a cut of beef behind the upper sirloin **2** : a small remaining fragment : REMNANT

rum·ple \ˈrəm-pəl\ *vb* **rum·pled; rum·pling** \-p(ə-)liŋ\ : TOUSLE, MUSS, WRINKLE — **rumple** *n* — **rum·ply** \ˈrəm-p(ə-)lē\ *adj*

rum·pus \ˈrəm-pəs\ *n* : DISTURBANCE, FRACAS

rumpus room *n* : a room usu. in the basement of a home that is used for games, parties, and recreation

[1]run \ˈrən\ *vb* **ran** \ˈran\; **run; run·ning 1** : to go at a pace faster than a walk **2** : to take to flight : FLEE **3** : to go without restraint ⟨lets his children ~⟩ **4** : to go rapidly or hurriedly : HASTEN, RUSH **5** : to perform or bring about by running **6** : to make a quick or casual trip or visit **7** : to contend in a race; *esp* : to enter an election **8** : to put forward as a candidate for office **9** : to move on or as if on wheels : pass or slide freely **10** : to go back and forth : PLY **11** : to move in schools esp. to a spawning ground ⟨shad are *running*⟩ **12** : FUNCTION, OPERATE ⟨left his car *running*⟩ **13** : to continue in force ⟨two years to ~⟩ **14** : to flow rapidly or under pressure : MELT, FUSE, DISSOLVE; *also* : DISCHARGE **15** : to tend to produce or to recur ⟨family ~*s* to blonds⟩ **16** : to take a certain direction **17** : to be current ⟨rumors *running* wild⟩ **18** : to be worded or written **19** : to cause to run **20** : TRACE ⟨~ down a rumor⟩ **21** : to cause to pass ⟨~ a wire from the antenna⟩ **22** : to cause to collide **23** : SMUGGLE **24** : MANAGE, CONDUCT, OPERATE ⟨~ a business⟩ **25** : INCUR ⟨~ a risk⟩ **26** : to permit to accumulate before settling ⟨~ a charge account⟩

[2]run *n* **1** : an act or the action of running **2** : a school of migrating fish **3** : a score in baseball **4** : BROOK, CREEK **5** : a continuous series esp. of similar things **6** : persistent heavy demands from depositors, creditors, or customers **7** : the quantity of work turned out in a continuous operation; *also* : a period of operation (as of a machine or plant) **8** : the usual or normal kind ⟨the ordinary ~ of students⟩ **9** : the distance covered in continuous travel or sailing **10** : a regular course or route; *also* : TRIP, JOURNEY **11** : freedom of movement in a place or area ⟨has the ~ of the house⟩ **12** : an enclosure for animals **13** : an inclined course (as for skiing) **14** : a lengthwise ravel (as in a stocking) — **run·less** *adj*

run·about \ˈrən-ə-ˌbau̇t\ *n* : a light wagon, automobile, or motorboat

run·a·gate \ˈrən-ə-ˌgāt\ *n* **1** : VAGABOND **2** : FUGITIVE

run·around \ˈrən-ə-ˌrau̇nd\ *n* : evasive or delaying action esp. in reply to a request

[1]**run·away** \ˈrən-ə-ˌwā\ *n* **1** : one that runs away : FUGITIVE **2** : the act of running away or out of control; *also* : something (as a horse) that is running out of control

[2]**runaway** *adj* **1** : FUGITIVE **2** : accomplished by elopement ⟨~ marriage⟩ **3** : won by a long lead **4** : subject to uncontrolled changes ⟨~ inflation⟩ **5** : operating out of control ⟨a ~ locomotive⟩

run·down \ˈrən-ˌdau̇n\ *n* : an item-by-item report : SUMMARY

run–down \ˈrən-ˈdau̇n\ *adj* **1** : EXHAUSTED **2** : completely unwound **3** : being in poor repair : DILAPIDATED

run down \ˈrən-ˈdau̇n\ *vb* **1** : to collide with and knock down **2** : to chase until exhausted or captured **3** : to find by search **4** : DISPARAGE **5** : to cease to operate for lack of motive power **6** : to decline in physical condition

rune \ˈrün\ *n* **1** : any of the characters of any of several alphabets formerly used by the Germanic peoples **2** : MYSTERY, MAGIC **3** : a poem esp. in Finnish or Old Norse — **ru·nic** \ˈrü-nik\ *adj*

[1]**rung** *past part of* RING

[2]**rung** \ˈrəŋ\ *n* **1** : a rounded crosspiece between the legs of a chair **2** : one of the crosspieces of a ladder **3** : a spoke of a wheel

run–in \ˈrən-ˌin\ *n* **1** : something run in **2** : ALTERCATION, QUARREL

run in \ˈrən-ˈin\ *vb* **1** : to insert as additional matter **2** : to arrest esp. for a minor offense **3** : to pay a casual visit

run·nel \ˈrən-ᵊl\ *n* : BROOK, STREAMLET

run·ner \ˈrən-ər\ *n* **1** : one that runs **2** : a baseball player on base or attempting to reach base **3** : BALLCARRIER **4** : a thin piece or part on which something (as a sled or an ice skate) slides **5** : the support of a drawer or a sliding door **6** : a horizontal branch from the base of a plant that produces new plants **7** : a plant producing runners **8** : a long narrow carpet **9** : a narrow decorative cloth cover for a table or dresser top

run·ner–up \ˈrən-ər-ˌəp\ *n, pl* **runners–up** *also* **runner–ups** : the competitor in a contest who finishes next to the winner

[1]**run·ning** \ˈrən-iŋ\ *adj* **1** : FLOWING **2** : FLUID, RUNNY **3** : CONTINUOUS, INCESSANT **4** : measured in a straight line ⟨cost per ~ foot⟩ **5** : of or relating to an act of running **6** : fitted or trained for running ⟨~ horse⟩

[2]**running** *adv* : in succession

running light *n* : one of the lights carried by a vehicle (as a ship) at night

run·ny \ˈrən-ē\ *adj* : having a tendency to run ⟨a ~ nose⟩

run·off \ˈrən-ˌȯf\ *n* : a final contest (as an election) to a previous indecisive contest

run–of–the–mill \ˌrən-ə(v)-t͟hə-ˈmil\ *adj* : not outstanding : AVERAGE

run on \ˈrən-ˈȯn, -ˈän\ *vb* **1** : to continue (matter in type) without a break or a new paragraph **2** : to place or add (as an entry in a dictionary) at the end of a paragraphed item — **run–on** \-ˌȯn, -ˌän\ *n*

runt \ˈrənt\ *n* : an unusually small person or animal : DWARF — **runty** *adj*

run·way \ˈrən-ˌwā\ *n* **1** : a beaten path made by animals; *also* : a passage for animals **2** : a paved strip of ground for the landing and takeoff of aircraft **3** : a narrow platform from a stage into an auditorium **4** : a support on which something runs

ru·pee \rü-ˈpē, ˈrü-ˌpē\ *n* — see MONEY table

ru·pi·ah \rü-ˈpē-ə\ *n, pl* **rupiah** *or* **rupiahs** — see MONEY table

[1]**rup·ture** \ˈrəp-chər\ *n* : a breaking or tearing apart; *also* : HERNIA

[2]**rupture** *vb* **rup·tured; rup·tur·ing** : to cause or undergo rupture

ru·ral \ˈru̇r-əl\ *adj* : of or relating to the country, country people, or agriculture

ruse \ˈrüs, ˈrüz\ *n* : a wily subterfuge : TRICK, ARTIFICE

[1]**rush** \ˈrəsh\ *n* : a hollow-stemmed grasslike marsh plant — **rushy** *adj*

[2]**rush** *vb* [ME *russhen,* fr. MF *ruser* to put to flight, deceive] **1** : to move forward or act with too great haste or eagerness or without preparation **2** : to perform in a short time or at high speed **3** : ATTACK, CHARGE — **rusher** *n*

[3]**rush** *n* **1** : a violent forward motion **2** : unusual demand or activity **3** : a crowding of people to one place **4** : a running play in football

[4]**rush** *adj* : requiring or marked by special speed or urgency ⟨~ orders⟩

rush hour *n* : a time when the amount of traffic or business is at a peak

rusk \ˈrəsk\ *n* : a sweet or plain bread baked, sliced, and baked again until dry and crisp

Russ *abbr* Russia; Russian

rus·set \ˈrəs-ət\ *n* **1** : a coarse reddish brown cloth **2** : a variable reddish brown or yellowish brown color **3** : any of various winter apples with rough russet skins — **russet** *adj*

Rus·sian \ˈrəsh-ən\ *n* **1** : a native or inhabitant of Russia or the U.S.S.R. **2** : the chief language of the U.S.S.R. — **Russian** *adj*

rust \ˈrəst\ *n* **1** : a reddish coating formed on iron when it is exposed to esp. moist air **2** : any of various diseases causing reddish spots on plants **3** : a reddish orange color — **rust** *vb* — **rusty** *adj*

[1]**rus·tic** \ˈrəs-tik\ *adj* **1** : RURAL **2** : made of the rough limbs of trees ⟨~ furniture⟩ **3** : AWKWARD, BOORISH **4** : PLAIN, SIMPLE — **rus·ti·cal·ly** \ˈrəs-ti-k(ə-)lē\ *adv* — **rus·tic·i·ty** \ˌrəs-ˈtis-ət-ē\ *n*

[2]**rustic** *n* : a rustic person

rus·ti·cate \ˈrəs-ti-ˌkāt\ *vb* **-cat·ed; -cat·ing** : to go into or reside in the country — **rus·ti·ca·tion** \ˌrəs-ti-ˈkā-shən\ *n*

[1]**rus·tle** \ˈrəs-əl\ *vb* **rus·tled; rus·tling** \ˈrəs-(ə-)liŋ\ **1** : to make or cause a rustle **2** : to cause to rustle ⟨~ a newspaper⟩ **3** : to act or move with energy or speed; *also* : to procure in this way **4** : to forage food **5** : to steal cattle from the range — **rus·tler** \-(ə-)lər\ *n*

[2]**rustle** *n* : a quick succession or confusion of small sounds ⟨~ of leaves⟩

[1]**rut** \ˈrət\ *n* : state or period of sexual excitement esp. in male deer — **rut** *vb*

[2]**rut** *n* **1** : a track worn by wheels or by habitual passage of something **2** : a usual or fixed routine

ru·ta·ba·ga \ˌrüt-ə-ˈbā-gə, ˌru̇t-\ *n* : a turnip with a large yellowish root

Ruth \ˈrüth\ *n* — see BIBLE table

ru·the·ni·um \rü-ˈthē-nē-əm\ *n* : a hard brittle metallic chemical element — see ELEMENT table

ruth·less \ˈrüth-ləs\ *adj* [fr. *ruth* compassion, pity, fr. ME *ruthe,* fr. *ruen* to rue, fr. OE *hrēowan*] : having no pity : MERCILESS, CRUEL — **ruth·less·ly** *adv* — **ruth·less·ness** *n*

RV *abbr* recreational vehicle

R–value \ˈär-ˌval-yü\ *n* : a measure of the resistance of a substance (as insulation) to heat flow

RW *abbr* **1** right worshipful **2** right worthy

rwy *or* **ry** *abbr* railway

-ry \rē\ *n suffix* : -ERY ⟨bigot*ry*⟩

rye \ˈrī\ *n* **1** : a hardy cereal grass grown for grain or as a cover crop; *also* : its seed **2** : a whiskey distilled from a rye mash

S

[1]s \ˈes\ *n, pl* **s's** *or* **ss** \ˈes-əz\ *often cap* **:** the 19th letter of the English alphabet

[2]s *abbr, often cap* **1** saint **2** second **3** senate **4** series **5** shilling **6** singular **7** small **8** son **9** south; southern

[1]-s \s *after sounds* f, k, k̲, p, t, th; əz *after sounds* ch, j, s, sh, z, zh; z *after other sounds*\ *n pl suffix* — used to form the plural of most nouns that do not end in *s, z, sh, ch,* or postconsonantal *y* ⟨head*s*⟩ ⟨book*s*⟩ ⟨boy*s*⟩ ⟨belief*s*⟩, to form the plural of proper nouns that end in postconsonantal *y* ⟨Mary*s*⟩, and with or without a preceding apostrophe to form the plural of abbreviations, numbers, letters, and symbols used as nouns ⟨MC*s*⟩ ⟨4*s*⟩ ⟨#*s*⟩ ⟨B'*s*⟩

[2]-s *adv suffix* — used to form adverbs denoting usual or repeated action or state ⟨works night*s*⟩

[3]-s *vb suffix* — used to form the third person singular present of most verbs that do not end in *s, z, sh, ch,* or postconsonantal *y* ⟨fall*s*⟩ ⟨take*s*⟩ ⟨play*s*⟩

S *symbol* sulfur

SA *abbr* **1** Salvation Army **2** seaman apprentice **3** sex appeal **4** [L *sine anno* without year] without date **5** South Africa **6** South America **7** subject to approval

Sab·bath \ˈsab-əth\ *n* [ME *sabat,* fr. OF & OE, fr. L *sabbatum,* fr. Gk *sabbaton,* fr. Heb *shabbāth,* lit., rest] **1 :** the 7th day of the week observed as a day of worship by Jews and some Christians **2 :** Sunday observed among Christians as a day of worship

sab·bat·i·cal \sə-ˈbat-i-kəl\ *n* **:** a leave often with pay granted (as to a college professor) usu. every 7th year for rest, travel, or research

sa·ber *or* **sa·bre** \ˈsā-bər\ *n* [F *sabre*] **:** a cavalry sword with a curved blade and thick back

saber saw *n* **:** a light portable electric saw with a pointed reciprocating blade

sa·ble \ˈsā-bəl\ *n, pl* **sables 1 :** the color black **2** *pl* **:** mourning garments **3 :** a dark brown mammal of northern Europe and Asia related to the martens and valued for its fur; *also* **:** this fur

[1]sab·o·tage \ˈsab-ə-ˌtäzh\ *n* [F] **1 :** deliberate destruction of an employer's property or hindering of production by workers **2 :** destructive or hampering action by enemy agents or sympathizers in time of war

[2]sabotage *vb* **-taged; -tag·ing :** to practice sabotage on **:** WRECK

sab·o·teur \ˌsab-ə-ˈtər\ *n* **:** a person who commits sabotage

sac \ˈsak\ *n* **:** a baglike part of an animal or plant

SAC \ˈsak\ *abbr* Strategic Air Command

sac·cha·rin \ˈsak-(ə-)rən\ *n* **:** a white crystalline compound used as an artificial sweetener

sac·cha·rine \ˈsak-(ə-)rən\ *adj* **:** nauseatingly sweet ⟨~ poetry⟩

sac·er·do·tal \ˌsas-ər-ˈdōt-ᵊl, ˌsak-\ *adj* **:** PRIESTLY — **sac·er·do·tal·ism** *n*

sa·chem \ˈsā-chəm\ *n* **:** a No. American Indian chief

sa·chet \sa-ˈshā\ *n* [F, fr. OF, dim. of *sac* bag] **:** a small bag filled with perfumed powder for scenting clothes

[1]sack \ˈsak\ *n* **1 :** a large coarse bag; *also* **:** a small container esp. of paper **2 :** a loose jacket or short coat

[2]sack *vb* **:** DISMISS, FIRE

[3]sack *n* [modif. of MF *sec* dry, fr. L *siccus*] **:** a white wine popular in England in the 16th and 17th centuries

[4]sack *vb* **:** to plunder a captured town

sack·cloth \-ˌklȯth\ *n* **:** a rough garment worn as a sign of penitence

sac·ra·ment \ˈsak-rə-mənt\ *n* **1 :** a formal religious act or rite; *esp* **:** one (as baptism or the Eucharist) held to have been instituted by Christ **2 :** the elements of the Eucharist — **sac·ra·men·tal** \ˌsak-rə-ˈment-ᵊl\ *adj*

sa·cred \ˈsā-krəd\ *adj* **1 :** set apart for the service or worship of deity **2 :** devoted exclusively to one service or use **3 :** worthy of veneration or reverence **4 :** of or relating to religion **:** RELIGIOUS **syn** blessed, divine, hallowed, holy, sanctified — **sa·cred·ly** *adv* — **sa·cred·ness** *n*

sacred cow *n* **:** one that is often unreasonably immune from criticism

[1]sac·ri·fice \ˈsak-rə-ˌfīs\ *n* **1 :** the offering of something precious to deity **2 :** something offered in sacrifice **3 :** LOSS, DEPRIVATION **4 :** a bunt allowing a base runner to advance while the batter is put out; *also* **:** a fly ball allowing a runner to score after the catch — **sac·ri·fi·cial** \ˌsak-rə-ˈfish-əl\ *adj* — **sac·ri·fi·cial·ly** \-ē\ *adv*

[2]sac·ri·fice *vb* **-ficed; -fic·ing 1 :** to offer up or kill as a sacrifice **2 :** to accept the loss or destruction of for an end, cause, or ideal **3 :** to make a sacrifice in baseball

sac·ri·lege \ˈsak-rə-lij\ *n* [ME, fr. OF, fr. L *sacrilegium,* fr. *sacrilegus* one who steals sacred things, fr. *sacr-, sacer* sacred + *legere* to gather, steal] **1 :** violation of something consecrated to God **2 :** gross irreverence toward a hallowed person, place, or thing — **sac·ri·le·gious** \ˌsak-rə-ˈlij-əs, -ˈlē-jəs\ *adj* — **sac·ri·le·gious·ly** *adv*

sac·ris·tan \ˈsak-rə-stən\ *n* **1 :** a church officer in charge of the sacristy **2 :** SEXTON

sac·ris·ty \ˈsak-rə-stē\ *n, pl* **-ties :** VESTRY

sac·ro·il·i·ac \ˌsak-rō-ˈil-ē-ˌak\ *n* **:** the joint between the upper part of the hipbone and the sacrum

sac·ro·sanct \ˈsak-rō-ˌsaŋkt\ *adj* **:** SACRED, INVIOLABLE

sa·crum \ˈsak-rəm, ˈsā-krəm\ *n, pl* **sa·cra** \ˈsak-rə, ˈsā-krə\ **:** the part of the vertebral column that is directly connected with or forms a part of the pelvis and in man consists of five fused vertebrae

sad \ˈsad\ *adj* **sad·der; sad·dest 1 :** GRIEVING, MOURNFUL, DOWNCAST **2 :** causing sorrow **3 :** DULL, SOMBER — **sad·ly** *adv* — **sad·ness** *n*

sad·den \ˈsad-ᵊn\ *vb* **sad·dened; sad·den·ing** \ˈsad-(ᵊ-)niŋ\ **:** to make sad

[1]sad·dle \ˈsad-ᵊl\ *n* **1 :** a usu. padded leather-covered seat (as for a rider on horseback) **2 :** the upper back portion of a carcass (as of mutton)

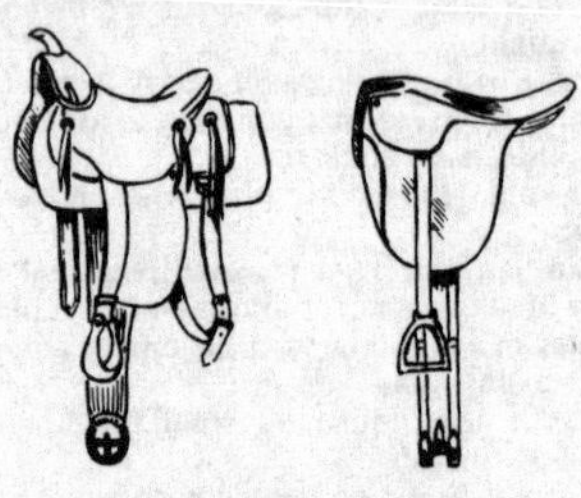

saddle 1

[2]saddle *vb* **sad·dled; sad·dling** \ˈsad-(ᵊ-)liŋ\ **1 :** to put a saddle on **2 :** BURDEN

sad·dle·bow \ˈsad-ᵊl-ˌbō\ *n* **:** the arch in the front of a saddle

saddle horse *n* **:** a horse suited for or trained for riding

Sad·du·cee \ˈsaj-ə-ˌsē, ˈsad-yə-\ *n* **:** a member of an ancient Jewish sect opposed to the Pharisees — **Sad·du·ce·an** \ˌsaj-ə-ˈsē-ən, ˌsad-yə-\ *adj*

sad·iron \ˈsad-ˌī(-ə)rn\ *n* : a flatiron with a removable handle

sa·dism \ˈsā-ˌdiz-əm, ˈsad-ˌiz-\ *n* : a sexual perversion in which gratification is associated with inflicting physical or mental pain on others — **sa·dist** \ˈsād-əst, ˈsad-\ *n* — **sa·dis·tic** \sə-ˈdis-tik\ *adj* — **sa·dis·ti·cal·ly** \-ti-k(ə-)lē\ *adv*

SAE *abbr* **1** self-addressed envelope **2** stamped addressed envelope

sa·fa·ri \sə-ˈfär-ē, -ˈfar-\ *n* [Ar *safarīy* of a trip] **1** : a hunting expedition esp. in eastern Africa **2** : JOURNEY, TRIP

¹safe \ˈsāf\ *adj* **saf·er; saf·est 1** : freed from injury or risk **2** : affording safety; *also* : secure from danger or loss **3** : RELIABLE, TRUSTWORTHY — **safe·ly** *adv*

²safe *n* : a container for keeping articles (as valuables) safe

safe–con·duct \-ˈkän-(ˌ)dəkt\ *n* : a pass permitting a person to go through enemy lines

¹safe·guard \-ˌgärd\ *n* : a measure or device for preventing accident or injury

²safeguard *vb* : to provide a safeguard for : PROTECT

safe·keep·ing \ˈsāf-ˈkē-piŋ\ *n* : a keeping or being kept in safety

safe·ty \ˈsāf-tē\ *n, pl* **safeties 1** : freedom from danger : SECURITY **2** : a protective device **3** : a football play in which the ball is downed by the offensive team behind its own goal line **4** : a defensive football back in the deepest position — **safety** *adj*

safety glass *n* : shatter-resistant material formed of two sheets of glass with a sheet of clear plastic between them

safety match *n* : a match that ignites only when struck on a special surface

saf·flow·er \ˈsaf-ˌlau̇(-ə)r\ *n* : a widely grown Old World herb related to the daisies that has large orange or red flower heads yielding a dyestuff and seeds rich in edible oil

saf·fron \ˈsaf-rən\ *n* : an aromatic deep orange powder from the flower of a crocus used to color and flavor foods

sag \ˈsag\ *vb* **sagged; sag·ging 1** : to bend down at the middle **2** : to become flabby : DROOP — **sag** *n*

sa·ga \ˈsäg-ə\ *n* [ON] : a narrative of heroic deeds; *esp* : one recorded in Iceland in the 12th and 13th centuries

sa·ga·cious \sə-ˈgā-shəs\ *adj* : of keen mind : SHREWD — **sa·gac·i·ty** \-ˈgas-ət-ē\ *n*

sag·a·more \ˈsag-ə-ˌmōr\ *n* : a subordinate No. American Indian chief

¹sage \ˈsāj\ *adj* [ME, fr. OF, fr. (assumed) VL *sapius*, fr. L *sapere* to taste, have good taste, be wise] : WISE, PRUDENT — **sage·ly** *adv*

²sage *n* : a wise man : PHILOSOPHER

³sage *n* [ME, fr. MF *sauge*, fr. L *salvia*, fr. *salvus* healthy; fr. its use as a medicinal herb] **1** : a shrublike mint with leaves used in flavoring **2** : SAGEBRUSH

sage·brush \ˈsāj-ˌbrəsh\ *n* : any of several low shrubby No. American plants related to the daisies; *esp* : one of the western U.S. with a sagelike odor

Sag·it·tar·i·us \ˌsaj-ə-ˈter-ē-əs\ *n* [L, lit., archer] **1** : a zodiacal constellation between Scorpio and Capricorn usu. pictured as a centaur archer **2** : the 9th sign of the zodiac in astrology; *also* : one born under this sign

sa·go \ˈsā-gō\ *n, pl* **sagos** : a dry granulated starch esp. from the pith of an East Indian palm (**sago palm**)

sa·gua·ro \sə-ˈwär-ə\ *n, pl* **-ros** [MexSp] : a desert cactus of the southwestern U.S. and Mexico with a tall columnar simple or sparsely branched trunk of up to 60 feet (20 meters)

said *past and past part of* SAY

¹sail \ˈsāl\ *n* **1** : a piece of fabric by means of which the wind is used to propel a ship **2** : a sailing ship **3** : something resembling a sail **4** : a trip on a sailboat

²sail *vb* **1** : to travel on a sailing ship **2** : to pass over in a ship **3** : to manage or direct the course of a ship **4** : to glide through the air

sail·boat \-ˌbōt\ *n* : a boat usu. propelled by sail

sail·cloth \-ˌklȯth\ *n* : a heavy canvas used for sails, tents, or upholstery

sail·fish \-ˌfish\ *n* : any of a genus of large sea fishes with a very large dorsal fin that are related to the swordfish

sail·ing \ˈsā-liŋ\ *n* : the action, fact, or pastime of cruising or racing in a sailboat

sail·or \ˈsā-lər\ *n* : one that sails; *esp* : a member of a ship's crew

sail·plane \ˈsāl-ˌplān\ *n* : a glider designed to rise in an upward air current

saint \ˈsānt, *before a name* (ˌ)sānt *or* sənt\ *n* **1** : one officially recognized as preeminent for holiness **2** : one of the spirits of the departed in heaven **3** : a holy or godly person — **saint·ed** \-əd\ *adj* — **saint·hood** \-ˌhu̇d\ *n*

Saint Ber·nard \-bər-ˈnärd\ *n* : any of a Swiss alpine breed of tall powerful working dogs used esp. formerly in aiding lost travelers

saint·ly \ˈsānt-lē\ *adj* : relating to, resembling, or befitting a saint — **saint·li·ness** *n*

Saint Val·en·tine's Day \-ˈval-ən-ˌtīnz-\ *n* : February 14 observed in honor of St. Valentine and as a time for exchanging valentines

¹sake \ˈsāk\ *n* **1** : MOTIVE, PURPOSE **2** : personal or social welfare, safety, or well-being

²sa·ke *or* **sa·ki** \ˈsäk-ē\ *n* : a Japanese alcoholic beverage of fermented rice

sa·laam \sə-ˈläm\ *n* [Ar *salām*, lit., peace] **1** : a salutation or ceremonial greeting in the East **2** : an obeisance performed by bowing very low and placing the right palm on the forehead — **salaam** *vb*

sa·la·cious \sə-ˈlā-shəs\ *adj* **1** : arousing sexual desire or imagination **2** : LUSTFUL — **sa·la·cious·ly** *adv* — **sa·la·cious·ness** *n*

sal·ad \ˈsal-əd\ *n* : a cold dish (as of lettuce, vegetables, fish, eggs, or fruit) served with dressing

sal·a·man·der \ˈsal-ə-ˌman-dər\ *n* : any of an order of amphibians that look like lizards but have scaleless usu. smooth moist skin

sa·la·mi \sə-ˈläm-ē\ *n* [It] : a highly seasoned sausage of pork and beef

sal·a·ry \ˈsal(-ə)-rē\ *n, pl* **-ries** [ME *salarie*, fr. L *salarium* salt money, pension, salary, fr. neut. of *salarius* of salt, fr. *sal* salt] : payment made at regular intervals for services

sale \ˈsāl\ *n* **1** : transfer of ownership of property from one person to another in return for money **2** : ready market : DEMAND **3** : AUCTION **4** : a selling of goods at bargain prices — **sal·able** *or* **sale·able** \ˈsā-lə-bəl\ *adj*

sales·girl \ˈsālz-ˌgərl\ *n* : SALESWOMAN

sales·man \-mən\ *n* : a person who sells in a store or to outside customers — **sales·man·ship** *n*

sales·per·son \-ˌpər-sən\ *n* : a salesman or saleswoman

sales·wom·an \-ˌwu̇m-ən\ *n* : a woman who sells merchandise

sal·i·cyl·ic acid \ˌsal-ə-ˌsil-ik-\ *n* : a crystalline organic acid used in the form of its salts to relieve pain and fever

¹sa·lient \ˈsāl-yənt\ *adj* : jutting forward beyond a line; *also* : PROMINENT **syn** conspicuous, striking, noticeable

²salient *n* : a projecting part in a line of defense

¹sa·line \ˈsā-ˌlēn, -ˌlīn\ *adj* : consisting of or containing salt : SALTY — **sa·lin·i·ty** \sā-ˈlin-ət-ē, sə-\ *n*

²saline *n* **1** : a metallic salt esp. with a purgative action **2** : a saline solution

sa·li·va \sə-ˈlī-və\ *n* : a liquid secreted into the mouth that helps digestion — **sal·i·vary** \ˈsal-ə-ˌver-ē\ *adj*

sal·i·vate \ˈsal-ə-ˌvāt\ *vb* **-vat·ed; -vat·ing** : to produce saliva esp. in excess — **sal·i·va·tion** \ˌsal-ə-ˈvā-shən\ *n*

Salk vaccine \ˈsȯ(l)k-\ *n* [after Jonas *Salk* b1914 American physician] : a polio vaccine that contains inactivated virus and is given by injection

sal·low \ˈsal-ō\ *adj* : of a yellowish sickly color ⟨a ∼ liverish skin⟩

sal·ly \ˈsal-ē\ *n, pl* **sallies 1** : a rushing attack on besiegers by troops of a besieged place **2** : a witty remark or retort **3** : a brief excursion — **sally** *vb*

salm·on \ˈsam-ən\ *n, pl* **salmon** *also* **salmons 1** : any of several food fishes with pinkish flesh related to the trouts **2** : a strong yellowish pink

sa·lon \sə-ˈlän, ˈsal-ˌän, sa-ˈlōⁿ\ *n* [F] : an elegant drawing room; *also* : a fashionable shop ⟨beauty ∼⟩

sa·loon \sə-ˈlün\ *n* **1** : a large drawing room or ballroom esp. on a passenger ship **2** : a place where liquors are sold and drunk : BARROOM **3** *Brit* : SEDAN 2

sal soda \ˈsal-ˈsōd-ə\ *n* : SODIUM CARBONATE

¹**salt** \ˈsȯlt\ *n* **1** : a white crystalline substance that consists of sodium and chlorine and is used in seasoning foods **2** : a saltlike cathartic substance (as Epsom salts) **3** : a compound formed usu. by action of an acid on metal **4** : SAILOR — **salt·i·ness** \ˈsȯl-tē-nəs\ *n* — **salty** \ˈsȯl-tē\ *adj*

²**salt** *vb* : to preserve, season, or feed with salt

³**salt** *adj* : preserved or treated with salt; *also* : SALTY

SALT *abbr* Strategic Arms Limitation Talks

salt away *vb* : to lay away safely : SAVE

salt·box \ˈsȯlt-ˌbäks\ *n* : a frame dwelling with two stories in front and one behind and a long sloping roof

salt·cel·lar \ˈsȯlt-ˌsel-ər\ *n* : a small vessel for holding salt at the table

sal·tine \sȯl-ˈtēn\ *n* : a thin crisp cracker sprinkled with salt

salt lick *n* : LICK 5

salt·pe·ter \ˈsȯlt-ˈpēt-ər\ *n* [fr. earlier *saltpeter,* fr. ME, fr. MF *saltpetre,* fr. ML *sal petrae,* lit., salt of the rock] **1** : POTASSIUM NITRATE **2** : SODIUM NITRATE

salt·wa·ter \ˌsȯlt-ˌwȯt-ər, -ˌwät-\ *adj* : of, relating to, or living in salt water

sa·lu·bri·ous \sə-ˈlü-brē-əs\ *adj* : favorable to health

sal·u·tary \ˈsal-yə-ˌter-ē\ *adj* : health-giving; *also* : BENEFICIAL

sal·u·ta·tion \ˌsal-yə-ˈtā-shən\ *n* : an expression of greeting, goodwill, or courtesy usu. by word or gesture

sa·lu·ta·to·ri·an \sə-ˌlüt-ə-ˈtōr-ē-ən\ *n* : the student having the 2nd highest rank in a graduating class who delivers the salutatory address

sa·lu·ta·to·ry \sə-ˈlüt-ə-ˌtōr-ē\ *adj* : relating to or being the welcoming oration delivered at an academic commencement

¹**sa·lute** \sə-ˈlüt\ *vb* **sa·lut·ed; sa·lut·ing 1** : GREET **2** : to honor by special ceremonies **3** : to show respect to (a superior officer) by a formal position of hand, rifle, or sword

²**salute** *n* **1** : GREETING **2** : the formal position assumed in saluting a superior

¹**sal·vage** \ˈsal-vij\ *n* **1** : money paid for saving a ship, its cargo, or passengers when the ship is wrecked or in danger **2** : the saving of a ship **3** : the saving of possessions in danger of being lost **4** : things saved from loss or destruction (as by a wreck or fire)

²**salvage** *vb* **sal·vaged; sal·vag·ing** : to rescue from destruction

sal·va·tion \sal-ˈvā-shən\ *n* **1** : the saving of a person from sin or its consequences esp. in the life after death **2** : the saving from danger, difficulty, or evil **3** : something that saves

¹**salve** \ˈsav, ˈsȧv\ *n* : a medicinal ointment

²**salve** *vb* **salved; salv·ing** : EASE, SOOTHE

sal·ver \ˈsal-vər\ *n* [F *salve,* fr. Sp *salva* sampling of food to detect poison, tray, fr. *salvar* to save, sample food to detect poison, fr. LL *salvare* to save, fr. L *salvus* safe] : a small serving tray

sal·vo \ˈsal-vō\ *n, pl* **salvos** *or* **salvoes** : a simultaneous discharge of guns

Sam *or* **Saml** *abbr* Samuel

SAM \ˈsam, ˌes-ˌā-ˈem\ *n* [*s*urface-to-*a*ir *m*issile] : a guided missile for use against aircraft by ground units

sa·mar·i·um \sə-ˈmer-ē-əm\ *n* : a pale gray lustrous metallic chemical element — see ELEMENT table

¹**same** \ˈsām\ *adj* **1** : being the one referred to : not different **2** : SIMILAR **syn** identical, equivalent, equal, tantamount — **same·ness** *n*

²**same** *pron* : the same one or ones

³**same** *adv* : in the same manner

sam·o·var \ˈsam-ə-ˌvär\ *n* [Russ, fr. *samo-* self + *varit'* to boil] : an urn with a spigot at the base used esp. in Russia to boil water for tea

sam·pan \ˈsam-ˌpan\ *n* : a flat-bottomed skiff of the Far East usu. propelled by two short oars

¹**sam·ple** \ˈsam-pəl\ *n* : a piece or item that shows the quality of the whole from which it was taken : EXAMPLE, SPECIMEN

²**sample** *vb* **sam·pled; sam·pling** \-p(ə-)liŋ\ : to judge the quality of by a sample

sam·pler \ˈsam-plər\ *n* : a piece of needlework; *esp* : one testing skill in embroidering

Sam·u·el \ˈsam-yə(-wə)l\ *n* — see BIBLE table

sam·u·rai \ˈsam-(y)ə-ˌrī\ *n, pl* **samurai** : a member of a Japanese feudal warrior class practicing a chivalric code

san·a·to·ri·um \ˌsan-ə-ˈtōr-ē-əm\ *n, pl* **-riums** *or* **-ria** \-ē-ə\ **1** : a health resort **2** : an establishment for the care esp. of convalescents or the chronically ill

sanc·ti·fy \ˈsaŋk-tə-ˌfī\ *vb* **-fied; -fy·ing 1** : to make holy : CONSECRATE **2** : to free from sin — **sanc·ti·fi·ca·tion** \ˌsaŋk-tə-fə-ˈkā-shən\ *n*

sanc·ti·mo·nious \ˌsaŋk-tə-ˈmō-nē-əs\ *adj* : hypocritically pious — **sanc·ti·mo·nious·ly** *adv*

¹**sanc·tion** \ˈsaŋk-shən\ *n* **1** : authoritative approval **2** : a measure (as a threat or fine) designed to enforce a law or standard ⟨economic ∼*s*⟩

²**sanction** *vb* **sanc·tioned; sanc·tion·ing** \-sh(ə-)niŋ\ : to give approval to : RATIFY **syn** endorse, accredit, certify, approve

sanc·ti·ty \ˈsaŋk-tət-ē\ *n, pl* **-ties 1** : GODLINESS **2** : SACREDNESS

sanc·tu·ary \ˈsaŋk-chə-ˌwer-ē\ *n, pl* **-ar·ies 1** : a consecrated place (as the part of a church in which the altar is placed) **2** : a place of refuge ⟨bird ∼⟩

sanc·tum \ˈsaŋk-təm\ *n, pl* **sanctums** *also* **sanc·ta** \-tə\ : a private office or study : DEN ⟨an editor's ∼⟩

¹**sand** \ˈsand\ *n* : loose particles of hard broken rock — **sandy** *adj*

²**sand** *vb* **1** : to cover or fill with sand **2** : to scour, smooth, or polish with an abrasive (as sandpaper) — **sand·er** *n*

san·dal \ˈsan-dᵊl\ *n* : a shoe consisting of a sole strapped to the foot; *also* : a low or open slipper or rubber overshoe

san·dal·wood \-ˌwu̇d\ *n* : the fragrant yellowish heartwood of a parasitic tree of southeastern Asia that is much used in ornamental carving and cabinetwork; *also* : the tree

sand·bag \ˈsan(d)-ˌbag\ *n* : a bag filled with sand and used in fortifications, as ballast, or as a weapon

sand·bank \-ˌbaŋk\ *n* : a deposit of sand (as in a bar or shoal)

sand·bar \-ˌbär\ *n* : a ridge of sand formed in water by tides or currents

sand·blast \-ˌblast\ *n* : sand blown (as for cleaning stone) by air or steam — **sandblast** *vb* — **sand·blast·er** *n*

sand·hog \ˈsand-ˌhȯg, -ˌhäg\ *n* : a laborer who builds underwater tunnels

sand·lot \ˈsan(d)-ˌlät\ *n* : a vacant lot esp. when used for the unorganized sports of children — **sand·lot** *adj* — **sand·lot·ter** *n*

sand·man \-ˌman\ *n* : the genie of folklore who makes children sleepy

sand·pa·per \-ˌpā-pər\ *n* : paper with abrasive (as sand) glued on one side used in smoothing and polishing surfaces — **sandpaper** *vb*

sand·pip·er \-ˌpī-pər\ *n* : any of numerous shorebirds with a soft-tipped bill longer than that of the related plovers

sand·stone \-ˌstōn\ *n* : rock made of sand held together by a natural cement

sand·storm \-ˌstȯrm\ *n* : a windstorm that drives clouds of sand

sand trap *n* : a hazard on a golf course consisting of a hollow containing sand

[1]**sand·wich** \ˈsand-(ˌ)wich\ *n* [after John Montagu, 4th Earl of *Sandwich* †1792 Eng. diplomat] **1** : two or more slices of bread with a layer (as of meat or cheese) spread between them **2** : something resembling a sandwich

[2]**sandwich** *vb* : to squeeze or crowd in

sane \ˈsān\ *adj* **san·er; san·est** : mentally sound and healthy; *also* : SENSIBLE, RATIONAL — **sane·ly** *adv*

sang *past of* SING

sang·froid \ˈsäⁿ-ˈfrwä\ *n* [F *sang-froid*, lit., cold blood] : self-possession or an imperturbable state esp. under strain

san·gui·nary \ˈsaŋ-gwə-ˌner-ē\ *adj* : BLOODY ⟨~ battle⟩

san·guine \ˈsaŋ-gwən\ *adj* **1** : RUDDY **2** : CHEERFUL, HOPEFUL

sanit *abbr* sanitary; sanitation

san·i·tar·i·an \ˌsan-ə-ˈter-ē-ən\ *n* : a specialist in sanitation and public health

san·i·tar·i·um \ˌsan-ə-ˈter-ē-əm\ *n, pl* **-i·ums** *or* **-ia** \-ē-ə\ : SANATORIUM

san·i·tary \ˈsan-ə-ˌter-ē\ *adj* **1** : of or relating to health : HYGIENIC **2** : free from filth or infective matter

sanitary napkin *n* : a disposable absorbent pad used to absorb uterine flow (as during menstruation)

san·i·ta·tion \ˌsan-ə-ˈtā-shən\ *n* : a making sanitary; *also* : protection of health by maintenance of sanitary conditions

san·i·tize \ˈsan-ə-ˌtīz\ *vb* **-tized; -tiz·ing 1** : to make sanitary **2** : to make more acceptable by removing unpleasant features

san·i·ty \ˈsan-ət-ē\ *n* : soundness of mind

sank *past of* SINK

sans \(ˌ)sanz\ *prep* : WITHOUT

San·skrit \ˈsan-ˌskrit\ *n* : an ancient language that is the classical language of India and of Hinduism — **Sanskrit** *adj*

San·ta Ana \ˌsant-ə-ˈan-ə\ *n* [*Santa Ana* mountains in southern Calif.] : a hot dry wind from the north, northeast, or east in southern California

[1]**sap** \ˈsap\ *n* : a vital fluid; *esp* : a watery fluid that circulates through a vascular plant — **sap·less** *adj*

[2]**sap** *vb* **sapped; sap·ping 1** : UNDERMINE **2** : to weaken gradually

sa·pi·ent \ˈsā-pē-ənt, ˈsap-ē-\ *adj* : WISE, DISCERNING — **sa·pi·ence** \-əns\ *n*

sap·ling \ˈsap-liŋ\ *n* : a young tree

sap·phire \ˈsaf-ˌī(ə)r\ *n* [ME *safir*, fr. OF, fr. L *sapphirus*, fr. Gk *sappheiros*, fr. Heb *sappīr*, fr. Skt *śanipriya*, lit., dear to the planet Saturn, fr. *Śani* Saturn + *priya* dear] : a hard transparent bright blue precious stone

sap·py \ˈsap-ē\ *adj* **sap·pi·er; -est 1** : full of sap **2** : SILLY, FOOLISH

sap·ro·phyte \ˈsap-rə-ˌfīt\ *n* : a living thing and esp. a plant living on dead or decaying organic matter — **sap·ro·phyt·ic** \ˌsap-rə-ˈfit-ik\ *adj*

sap·suck·er \ˈsap-ˌsek-ər\ *n* : any of several small American woodpeckers

sap·wood \-ˌwu̇d\ *n* : the younger active and usu. lighter and softer outer layer of wood (as of a tree trunk)

sar·casm \ˈsär-ˌkaz-əm\ *n* **1** : a cutting or contemptuous remark **2** : ironic criticism or reproach — **sar·cas·tic** \sär-ˈkas-tik\ *adj* — **sar·cas·ti·cal·ly** \-ti-k(ə-)lē\ *adv*

sar·coph·a·gus \sär-ˈkäf-ə-gəs\ *n, pl* **-gi** \-ˌgī, -ˌjī\ *also* **-gus·es** [L *sarcophagus* (*lapis*) limestone used for coffins, fr. Gk (*lithos*) *sarkophagos*, lit., flesh-eating stone, fr. *sark-*, *sarx* flesh + *phagein* to eat] : a large stone coffin

sar·dine \sär-ˈdēn\ *n, pl* **sardines** *also* **sardine** : a young or small fish preserved esp. in oil for use as food

sar·don·ic \sär-ˈdän-ik\ *adj* : expressing scorn or mockery : bitterly disdainful **syn** ironic, satiric, sarcastic — **sar·don·i·cal·ly** \-i-k(ə-)lē\ *adv*

sa·ri *also* **sa·ree** \ˈsär-ē\ *n* [Hindi *sāṛī*] : a garment of southern Asian women that consists of a long cloth draped around the body and head or shoulder

sa·rong \sə-ˈrȯŋ, -ˈräŋ\ *n* : a loose skirt wrapped around the body and worn by men and women of the Malay archipelago and the Pacific islands

sar·sa·pa·ril·la \ˌsas-(ə-)pə-ˈril-ə, ˌsärs-\ *n* **1** : the root of a tropical American smilax used esp. for flavoring; *also* : the plant **2** : a sweetened carbonated beverage flavored with sassafras and an oil from a birch

sar·to·ri·al \sär-ˈtōr-ē-əl\ *adj* : of or relating to a tailor or tailored clothes — **sar·to·ri·al·ly** \-ē\ *adv*

SASE *abbr* self-addressed stamped envelope

[1]**sash** \ˈsash\ *n* : a broad band worn around the waist or over the shoulder

[2]**sash** *n, pl* **sash** *also* **sash·es** : a frame for a pane of glass in a door or window; *also* : the movable part of a window

sa·shay \sa-ˈshā\ *vb* **1** : WALK, GLIDE, GO **2** : to strut or move about in an ostentatious manner **3** : to proceed in a diagonal or sideways manner

Sask *abbr* Saskatchewan

Sas·quatch \ˈsas-ˌkwach, -ˌkwäch\ *n* [from Salish (an American Indian language) *se'sxac* wild men] : a hairy manlike creature reported to exist in the northwestern U.S. and western Canada and said to be a very tall primate

sas·sa·fras \ˈsas-ə-ˌfras\ *n* [Sp *sasafrás*] : a No. American tree related to the laurel; *also* : its dried bark now known to have carcinogenic properties

sassy \ˈsas-ē\ *adj* **sass·i·er; -est** : SAUCY

[1]**sat** *past and past part of* SIT

[2]**sat** *abbr* saturate; saturated; saturation

Sat *abbr* Saturday

Sa·tan \ˈsāt-ᵊn\ *n* : DEVIL

sa·tang \sə-ˈtäŋ\ *n, pl* **satang** *or* **satangs** — see *baht* at MONEY table

sa·tan·ic \sə-ˈtan-ik, sā-\ *adj* **1** : of or resembling Satan **2** : extremely malicious or wicked — **sa·tan·i·cal·ly** \-i-k(ə-)lē\ *adv*

satch·el \ˈsach-əl\ *n* : TRAVELING BAG

sate \ˈsāt\ *vb* **sat·ed; sat·ing** : to satisfy to the full; *also* : SURFEIT, GLUT

sa·teen \sa-ˈtēn, sə-\ *n* : a cotton cloth finished to resemble satin

sat·el·lite \ˈsat-ᵊl-ˌīt\ *n* **1** : an obsequious follower of a prince or distinguished person : TOADY **2** : a celestial body that orbits a larger body **3** : a man-made object that orbits a celestial body

sa·ti·ate \ˈsā-shē-ˌāt\ *vb* **-at·ed; -at·ing** : to satisfy fully or to excess

sa·ti·ety \sə-ˈtī-ət-ē\ *n* : fullness to the point of excess

sat·in \ˈsat-ᵊn\ *n* : a fabric (as of silk) with a glossy surface — **sat·iny** *adj*
sat·in·wood \ˈsat-ᵊn-ˌwu̇d\ *n* : a hard yellowish brown wood of satiny luster; *also* : a tree yielding this wood
sat·ire \ˈsa-ˌtī(ə)r\ *n* : biting wit, irony, or sarcasm used to expose vice or folly; *also* : a literary work having these qualities — **sa·tir·ic** \sə-ˈtir-ik\ *or* **sa·tir·i·cal** \-i-kəl\ *adj* — **sa·tir·i·cal·ly** \-ē\ *adv* — **sat·i·rist** \ˈsat-ə-rəst\ *n* — **sat·i·rize** \-ə-ˌrīz\ *vb*
sat·is·fac·tion \ˌsat-əs-ˈfak-shən\ *n* **1** : payment through penance of punishment incurred by sin **2** : CONTENTMENT, GRATIFICATION **3** : reparation for an insult **4** : settlement of a claim
sat·is·fac·to·ry \-ˈfak-t(ə-)rē\ *adj* : giving satisfaction : ADEQUATE — **sat·is·fac·to·ri·ly** \-ˈfak-t(ə-)rə-lē\ *adv*
sat·is·fy \ˈsat-əs-ˌfī\ *vb* **-fied; -fy·ing 1** : to make happy : GRATIFY **2** : to pay what is due to **3** : to answer or discharge (a claim) in full **4** : CONVINCE **5** : to meet the requirements of — **sat·is·fy·ing·ly** *adv*
sa·trap \ˈsā-ˌtrap, ˈsa-\ *n* [ME, fr. L *satrapes,* fr. Gk *satrapēs,* fr. OPer *xshathrapāvan,* lit., protector of the dominion] : a petty prince : subordinate ruler
sat·u·rate \ˈsach-ə-ˌrāt\ *vb* **-rat·ed; -rat·ing 1** : to soak thoroughly **2** : to treat or charge with something to the point where no more can be absorbed, dissolved, or retained ⟨water *saturated* with salt⟩ — **sat·u·ra·ble** \ˈsach-(ə-)rə-bəl\ *adj* — **sat·u·ra·tion** \ˌsach-ə-ˈrā-shən\ *n*
Sat·ur·day \ˈsat-ər-dē, -ˌdā\ *n* : the 7th day of the week
Saturday night special *n* : a cheap easily concealed handgun
Sat·urn \ˈsat-ərn\ *n* : the planet 6th in order from the sun
sat·ur·nine \ˈsat-ər-ˌnīn\ *adj* : SULLEN, SARDONIC
sa·tyr \ˈsāt-ər\ *n* **1** *often cap* : a woodland deity in Greek mythology having certain characteristics of a horse or goat **2** : a lecherous man
¹**sauce** \ˈsȯs, *3 usu* ˈsas\ *n* **1** : a dressing for salads, meats, or puddings **2** : stewed fruit **3** : IMPUDENCE
²**sauce** \ˈsȯs, *2 usu* ˈsas\ *vb* **sauced; sauc·ing 1** : to add zest to **2** : to be impudent to
sauce·pan \ˈsȯs-ˌpan\ *n* : a cooking pan with a long handle
sau·cer \ˈsȯ-sər\ *n* : a rounded shallow dish for use under a cup
saucy \ˈsas-ē, ˈsȯs-ē\ *adj* **sauc·i·er; -est** : IMPUDENT, PERT — **sauc·i·ly** \-ə-lē\ *adv* — **sauc·i·ness** \-ē-nəs\ *n*
sau·er·kraut \ˈsau̇(-ə)r-ˌkrau̇t\ *n* [G, fr. *sauer* sour + *kraut* cabbage] : finely cut cabbage fermented in brine
sau·na \ˈsau̇-nə\ *n* **1** : a Finnish steam bath in which the steam is provided by water thrown on hot stones **2** : a dry heat bath; *also* : a room or cabinet used for such a bath
saun·ter \ˈsȯnt-ər, ˈsänt-\ *vb* : STROLL
sau·sage \ˈsȯ-sij\ *n* [deriv. of LL *salsicia,* fr. L *salsus* salted] : minced and highly seasoned meat (as pork) usu. enclosed in a tubular casing
S Aust *abbr* South Australia
sau·té \sȯ-ˈtā, sō-\ *vb* **sau·téed** *or* **sau·téd; sau·té·ing** [F] : to fry lightly in a little fat — **sauté** *n*
sau·terne \sō-ˈtərn, sȯ-\ *n, often cap* [F *sauternes*] : a usu. semisweet white wine
¹**sav·age** \ˈsav-ij\ *adj* [ME *sauvage,* fr. MF, fr. ML *salvaticus,* fr. L *silvaticus* of the woods, wild, fr. *silva* wood, forest] **1** : WILD, UNTAMED **2** : UNCIVILIZED, BARBAROUS **3** : CRUEL, FIERCE — **sav·age·ly** *adv* — **sav·age·ness** *n* — **sav·age·ry** \-(ə-)rē\ *n*
²**savage** *n* **1** : a member of a primitive human society **2** : a rude, unmannerly, or brutal person
sa·van·na *or* **sa·van·nah** \sə-ˈvan-ə\ *n* [Sp *zavana*] : grassland containing scattered trees
sa·vant \sa-ˈvänt, sə-, ˈsav-ənt\ *n* : a learned man : SCHOLAR
¹**save** \ˈsāv\ *vb* **saved; sav·ing 1** : to redeem from sin **2** : to rescue from danger **3** : to preserve or guard from destruction or loss **4** : to put aside as a store or reserve — **sav·er** *n*
²**save** *n* : a play that prevents an opponent from scoring or winning
³**save** \(ˌ)sāv\ *prep* : EXCEPT
⁴**save** \(ˌ)sāv\ *conj* : BUT
savings and loan association *n* : a cooperative association that holds savings of members in the form of dividend-bearing shares and that invests chiefly in mortgage loans
savings bank *n* : a bank that holds funds of individual depositors in interest-bearing accounts and makes long-term investments (as in mortgage loans)
savings bond *n* : a registered U.S. bond issued in denominations of $50 to $10,000
sav·ior *or* **sav·iour** \ˈsāv-yər\ *n* **1** : one who saves **2** *cap* : Jesus Christ
sa·voir faire \ˌsav-ˌwär-ˈfar\ *n* [F *savoir-faire,* lit., knowing how to do] : readiness in knowing how to act : TACT
¹**sa·vor** *also* **sa·vour** \ˈsā-vər\ *n* **1** : the taste and odor of something **2** : a special flavor or quality — **sa·vory** *adj*
²**savor** *also* **savour** *vb* **sa·vored; sa·vor·ing** \ˈsāv-(ə-)riŋ\ **1** : to have a specified taste, smell, or quality **2** : to taste with pleasure
sa·vo·ry \ˈsāv(-ə)-rē\ *n, pl* **-ries** : any of several aromatic mints used in cooking
¹**sav·vy** \ˈsav-ē\ *vb* **sav·vied; sav·vy·ing** [modif. of Sp *sabe* he knows] : COMPREHEND, UNDERSTAND
²**savvy** *n* : practical know-how ⟨political ∼⟩
¹**saw** *past of* SEE
²**saw** \ˈsȯ\ *n* : a cutting tool with a blade having a line of teeth along its edge
³**saw** *vb* **sawed** \ˈsȯd\; **sawed** *or* **sawn** \ˈsȯn\; **saw·ing** \ˈsȯ(-)iŋ\ : to cut or divide with or as if with a saw — **saw·yer** \-yər\ *n*
⁴**saw** *n* : a common saying : MAXIM
saw·dust \ˈsȯ-(ˌ)dəst\ *n* : fine particles made by a saw in cutting
saw·fly \ˈsȯ-ˌflī\ *n* : any of numerous insects belonging to the same order as bees and wasps and including many whose larvae are plant-feeding pests
saw·horse \ˈsȯ-ˌhȯrs\ *n* : a rack on which wood is rested while being sawed by hand
saw·mill \-ˌmil\ *n* : a mill for sawing logs
saw palmetto *n* : any of several shrubby palms with spiny-toothed petioles
sax·i·frage \ˈsak-sə-frij, -ˌfrāj\ *n* [deriv. of LL *saxifraga,* fr. L, lit., breaking rocks] : any of a genus of plants with showy 5-parted flowers and usu. with leaves growing in tufts close to the ground
sax·o·phone \ˈsak-sə-ˌfōn\ *n* : a musical instrument consisting of a conical metal tube with a reed mouthpiece and finger keys — **sax·o·phon·ist** \-əst\ *n*
¹**say** \ˈsā\ *vb* **said** \ˈsed\; **say·ing** \ˈsā-iŋ\; **says** \ˈsez\ **1** : to express in words ⟨∼ what you mean⟩ **2** : to state as opinion or belief **3** : PRONOUNCE; *also* : RECITE, REPEAT ⟨∼ your prayers⟩ **4** : INDICATE ⟨the clock ∼*s* noon⟩
²**say** *n, pl* **says** \ˈsāz\ **1** : an expression of opinion **2** : power of decision
say·ing \ˈsā-iŋ\ *n* : a commonly repeated statement
say–so \ˈsā-(ˌ)sō\ *n* : an esp. authoritative assertion or decision; *also* : the right to decide
sb *abbr* substantive
Sb *symbol* [L *stibium*] antimony
SB *abbr* [NL *scientiae baccalaureus*] bachelor of science
SBA *abbr* Small Business Administration
sc *abbr* **1** scale **2** scene **3** science
Sc *symbol* scandium
SC *abbr* **1** South Carolina **2** Supreme Court
¹**scab** \ˈskab\ *n* **1** : scabies of domestic animals **2** : a protective crust over a sore or wound **3** : a worker who replaces a striker or works under conditions not autho-

rized by a union **4** : a plant disease in which crusted spots form on stems or leaves — **scab·by** *adj*

²scab *vb* **scabbed; scab·bing 1** : to become covered with a scab **2** : to work as a scab

scab·bard \ˈskab-ərd\ *n* : a sheath for the blade of a weapon (as a sword)

sca·bies \ˈskā-bēz\ *n* [L] : contagious itch or mange caused by mites living as parasites under the skin

sca·brous \ˈskab-rəs, ˈskāb-\ *adj* **1** : DIFFICULT, KNOTTY **2** : rough to the touch : SCALY, SCURFY ⟨a ∼ leaf⟩ **3** : dealing with suggestive, indecent, or scandalous themes; *also* : SQUALID

scad \ˈskad\ *n* **1** : a large number or quantity **2** *pl* : a great abundance

scaf·fold \ˈskaf-əld, -ˌōld\ *n* **1** : a raised platform for workers to sit or stand on **2** : a platform on which a criminal is executed (as by hanging)

scaf·fold·ing \-iŋ\ *n* : a system of scaffolds; *also* : materials for scaffolds

scal·a·wag \ˈskal-i-ˌwag\ *n* : RASCAL

¹scald \ˈskȯld\ *vb* **1** : to burn with or as if with hot liquid or steam **2** : to heat to just below the boiling point

²scald *n* : a burn caused by scalding

¹scale \ˈskāl\ *n* **1** : either pan of a balance **2** : BALANCE — usu. used in pl. **3** : a weighing instrument

²scale *vb* **scaled; scal·ing** : WEIGH

³scale *n* **1** : one of the small thin plates that cover the body esp. of a fish or reptile **2** : a thin plate **3** : a thin coating, layer, or incrustation **4** : SCALE INSECT — **scaled** \ˈskāld\ *adj* — **scale·less** \ˈskāl-ləs\ *adj* — **scaly** *adj*

⁴scale *vb* **scaled; scal·ing** : to strip of scales

⁵scale *n* [ME, fr. LL *scala* ladder, staircase, fr. L *scalae*, pl., stairs, rungs, ladder] **1** : something divided into regular spaces as a help in drawing or measuring **2** : a graduated series **3** : the size of a sample (as a model) in proportion to the size of the actual thing **4** : a standard of estimation or judgment **5** : a series of musical tones going up or down in pitch according to a specified scheme

⁶scale *vb* **scaled; scal·ing 1** : to go up by or as if by a ladder **2** : to arrange in a graded series

scale insect *n* : any of numerous small insects that live and are often pests on plants and have wingless scale-covered females

scale·pan \ˈskāl-ˌpan\ *n* : ¹SCALE 1

scal·lion \ˈskal-yən\ *n* [deriv. of L *ascalonia* (*caepa*) onion of Ascalon (seaport in Palestine)] : an onion without an enlarged bulb

¹scal·lop \ˈskäl-əp, ˈskal-\ *n* **1** : any of a family of marine mollusks with radially ridged shell valves; *also* : a large edible muscle of this mollusk **2** : one of a continuous series of rounded projections forming an edge (as in lace)

²scallop *vb* **1** : to edge (as lace) with scallops **2** : to bake in a casserole

¹scalp \ˈskalp\ *n* : the part of the skin and flesh of the head usu. covered with hair

²scalp *vb* **1** : to remove the scalp from **2** : to obtain for the sake of reselling at greatly increased prices — **scalp·er** *n*

scal·pel \ˈskal-pəl\ *n* : a small straight knife with a thin blade used esp. in surgery

scam \ˈskam\ *n* : a fraudulent or deceptive act or operation

scamp \ˈskamp\ *n* : RASCAL

scam·per \ˈskam-pər\ *vb* **scam·pered; scam·per·ing** \-p(ə-)riŋ\ : to run nimbly and playfully — **scamper** *n*

scam·pi \ˈskam-pē\ *n, pl* **scampi** [It] : SHRIMP; *esp* : large shrimp prepared with a garlic-flavored sauce

¹scan \ˈskan\ *vb* **scanned; scan·ning 1** : to read (verses) so as to show metrical structure **2** : to examine closely **3** : to move an electromagnetic beam across esp. in a regular pattern **4** : to make a scan of (as the human body) **syn** scrutinize, inspect, examine — **scan·ner** \ˈskan-ər\ *n*

²scan *n* **1** : the act or process of scanning **2** : a picture of the distribution of radioactive material in something; *also* : a picture of part of the body made by combining separate pictures taken from different angles or of different sections

Scand *abbr* Scandinavia; Scandinavian

scan·dal \ˈskan-dᵊl\ *n* [LL *scandalum* stumbling block, offense, fr. Gk *skandalon*] **1** : DISGRACE, DISHONOR **2** : malicious gossip : SLANDER — **scan·dal·ize** *vb* — **scan·dal·ous** *adj* — **scan·dal·ous·ly** *adv*

scan·dal·mon·ger \-ˌməŋ-gər, -ˌmäŋ-\ *n* : a person who circulates scandal

Scan·di·na·vian \ˌskan-də-ˈnā-vē-ən\ *n* : a native or inhabitant of Scandinavia — **Scandinavian** *adj*

scan·di·um \ˈskan-dē-əm\ *n* : a white metallic chemical element — see ELEMENT table

¹scant \ˈskant\ *adj* **1** : barely sufficient **2** : having scarcely enough **syn** scanty, skimpy, meager, sparse, exiguous

²scant *vb* **1** : SKIMP **2** : STINT

scant·ling \ˈskant-liŋ\ *n* : a piece of lumber; *esp* : one used for an upright in building

scanty \ˈskant-ē\ *adj* **scant·i·er; -est** : barely sufficient : SCANT — **scant·i·ly** \ˈskant-ə-lē\ *adv* — **scant·i·ness** \-ē-nəs\ *n*

scape·goat \ˈskāp-ˌgōt\ *n* : one that bears the blame for others

scape·grace \-ˌgrās\ *n* [*scape* (escape)] : an incorrigible rascal

scap·u·la \ˈskap-yə-lə\ *n, pl* **-lae** \-ˌlē\ *or* **-las** [L] : SHOULDER BLADE

scap·u·lar \-lər\ *adj* : of or relating to the shoulder or shoulder blade

scar \ˈskär\ *n* : a mark left after injured tissue has healed — **scar** *vb*

scar·ab \ˈskar-əb\ *n* [MF *scarabee*, fr. L *scarabaeus*] : any of a family of large stout beetles; *also* : an ornament (as a gem) representing such a beetle

scarce \ˈskeərs\ *adj* **scarc·er; scarc·est 1** : not plentiful **2** : RARE — **scar·ci·ty** \ˈsker-sət-ē\ *n*

scarce·ly \ˈskeərs-lē\ *adv* **1** : BARELY **2** : almost not **3** : very probably not

¹scare \ˈskeər\ *vb* **scared; scar·ing** : FRIGHTEN, STARTLE

²scare *n* : FRIGHT — **scary** *adj*

scare·crow \ˈskeər-ˌkrō\ *n* : a crude figure set up to scare birds away from crops

¹scarf \ˈskärf\ *n, pl* **scarves** \ˈskärvz\ *or* **scarfs 1** : a broad band (as of cloth) worn about the shoulders, around the neck, over the head, or about the waist **2** : a long narrow cloth cover for a table or dresser top

²scarf *vb* [alter. of earlier *scoff* eat greedily] : to eat greedily

scar·i·fy \ˈskar-ə-ˌfī\ *vb* **-fied; -fy·ing 1** : to make scratches or small cuts in : wound superficially ⟨∼ skin for vaccination⟩ ⟨∼ seeds to help them germinate⟩ **2** : to lacerate the feelings of : FLAY — **scar·i·fi·ca·tion** \ˌskar-ə-fə-ˈkā-shən\ *n*

scar·la·ti·na \ˌskär-lə-ˈtē-nə\ *n* : SCARLET FEVER

scar·let \ˈskär-lət\ *n* : a bright red — **scarlet** *adj*

scarlet fever *n* : an acute contagious disease marked by fever, sore throat, and red rash and caused by certain streptococci

scarp \ˈskärp\ *n* : a line of cliffs produced by faulting or erosion

scath·ing \ˈskā-t͟hiŋ\ *adj* : bitterly severe

scat·o·log·i·cal \ˌskat-ᵊl-ˈäj-i-kəl\ *adj* : concerned with obscene matters

scat·ter \ˈskat-ər\ *vb* **1** : to distribute or strew about irregularly **2** : DISPERSE

scav·enge \ˈskav-ənj\ *vb* **scav·enged; scav·eng·ing** : to work or function as a scavenger

scav·en·ger \ˈskav-ən-jər\ *n* [alter. of earlier *scavager,* fr. ME *skawager* collector of a toll on goods sold by nonresident merchants, fr. *skawage* toll on goods sold by nonresident merchants, fr. OF *escauwage* inspection] : a person or animal that collects or disposes of refuse or waste

sce·nar·io \sə-ˈnar-ē-ˌō\ *n, pl* **-i·os** : the plot or outline of a dramatic work; *also* : an account of a projected action

scene \ˈsēn\ *n* [MF, stage, fr. L *scena, scaena* stage, scene, fr. Gk *skēnē* temporary shelter, tent, building forming the background for a dramatic performance, stage] **1** : a division of one act of a play **2** : a single situation or sequence in a play or motion picture **3** : a stage setting **4** : VIEW, PROSPECT **5** : the place of an occurrence or action **6** : a display of strong feeling and esp. anger **7** : a sphere of activity ⟨the fashion ~⟩ — **sce·nic** \ˈsēn-ik\ *adj*

scen·ery \ˈsēn-(ə-)rē\ *n, pl* **-er·ies 1** : the painted scenes or hangings of a stage and the fittings that go with them **2** : a picturesque view or landscape

[1]**scent** \ˈsent\ *n* **1** : ODOR, SMELL **2** : sense of smell **3** : course of pursuit : TRACK **4** : PERFUME 2 — **scent·less** *adj*

[2]**scent** *vb* **1** : SMELL **2** : to imbue or fill with odor

scep·ter \ˈsep-tər\ *n* : a staff borne by a sovereign as an emblem of authority

scep·tic \ˈskep-tik\ *var of* SKEPTIC

sch *abbr* school

[1]**sched·ule** \ˈskej-ül, *esp Brit* ˈshed-yül\ *n* **1** : a list of items or details **2** : TIMETABLE

[2]**schedule** *vb* **sched·uled; sched·ul·ing** : to make a schedule of; *also* : to enter on a schedule

sche·mat·ic \ski-ˈmat-ik\ *adj* : of or relating to a scheme or diagram : DIAGRAMMATIC — **schematic** *n* — **sche·mat·i·cal·ly** \-i-k(ə-)lē\ *adv*

[1]**scheme** \ˈskēm\ *n* **1** : a plan for doing something; *esp* : a crafty plot **2** : a systematic design

[2]**scheme** *vb* **schemed; schem·ing** : to form a plot : INTRIGUE — **schem·er** *n* — **schem·ing** *adj*

Schick test \ˈshik-\ *n* : a serological test for susceptibility to diphtheria

schil·ling \ˈshil-iŋ\ *n* — see MONEY table

schism \ˈsiz-əm, ˈskiz-\ *n* **1** : DIVISION, SPLIT; *also* : DISCORD, DISSENSION **2** : a formal division in or separation from a religious body **3** : the offense of promoting schism

schis·mat·ic \siz-ˈmat-ik, skiz-\ *n* : one who creates or takes part in schism — **schismatic** *adj*

schist \ˈshist\ *n* : a metamorphic crystalline rock

schizo·phre·nia \ˌskit-sə-ˈfrē-nē-ə\ *n* [NL, fr. Gk *schizein* to split + *phrēn* diaphragm, mind] : a psychotic disorder that is characterized by a twisted view of the real world, by a greatly reduced ability to carry out one's daily tasks, and by abnormal ways of thinking, feeling, and behaving — **schiz·oid** \ˈskit-ˌsȯid\ *adj or n* — **schizo·phren·ic** \ˌskit-sə-ˈfren-ik\ *adj or n*

schle·miel \shlə-ˈmēl\ *n* : an unlucky bungler : CHUMP

schmaltz *also* **schmalz** \ˈshmȯlts, ˈshmälts\ *n* [Yiddish *shmalts,* lit., rendered fat] : sentimental or florid music or art — **schmaltzy** *adj*

schnau·zer \ˈshnau̇t-sər, ˈs(h)nau̇-zər\ *n* [G, fr. *schnauze* snout] : a dog of any of three breeds that are characterized by a long head, small ears, heavy eyebrows, mustache and beard, and a wiry coat

schol·ar \ˈskäl-ər\ *n* **1** : STUDENT, PUPIL **2** : a learned man : SAVANT — **schol·ar·ly** *adj*

schol·ar·ship \-ˌship\ *n* **1** : the qualities or learning of a scholar **2** : money awarded to a student to help pay for further education

scho·las·tic \skə-ˈlas-tik\ *adj* : of or relating to schools, scholars, or scholarship

[1]**school** \ˈsk̇ül\ *n* **1** : an institution for teaching and learning; *also* : the pupils in attendance **2** : a body of persons of like opinions or beliefs ⟨the radical ~⟩

[2]**school** *vb* : TEACH, TRAIN, DRILL

[3]**school** *n* : a large number of one kind of water animal swimming and feeding together

school·boy \-ˌbȯi\ *n* : a boy attending school

school·fel·low \-ˌfel-ō\ *n* : SCHOOLMATE

school·girl \-ˌgərl\ *n* : a girl attending school

school·house \-ˌhau̇s\ *n* : a building used as a school

school·marm \-ˌmä(r)m\ *or* **school·ma'am** \-ˌmäm, -ˌmam\ *n* **1** : a woman schoolteacher **2** : a person who exhibits characteristics popularly attributed to schoolteachers

school·mas·ter \-ˌmas-tər\ *n* : a male schoolteacher

school·mate \-ˌmāt\ *n* : a school companion

school·mis·tress \-ˌmis-trəs\ *n* : a woman schoolteacher

school·room \-ˌrüm, -ˌru̇m\ *n* : CLASSROOM

school·teach·er \-ˌtē-chər\ *n* : one who teaches in a school

schoo·ner \ˈskü-nər\ *n* : a fore-and-aft rigged sailing ship

schuss \ˈshu̇s, ˈshüs\ *vb* [G] : to ski down a slope at high speed — **schuss** *n*

sci *abbr* science; scientific

sci·at·i·ca \sī-ˈat-i-kə\ *n* : pain in the region of the hips or along the course of the nerve at the back of the thigh

sci·ence \ˈsī-əns\ *n* [ME, fr. MF, fr. L *scientia,* fr. *scient-, sciens* having knowledge, fr. prp. of *scire* to know] **1** : an area of knowledge that is an object of study; *esp* : NATURAL SCIENCE **2** : knowledge covering general truths or the operation of general laws especially as obtained and tested through the scientific method — **sci·en·tif·ic** \ˌsī-ən-ˈtif-ik\ *adj* — **sci·en·tif·i·cal·ly** \-i-k(ə-)lē\ *adv* — **sci·en·tist** \ˈsī-ənt-əst\ *n*

science fiction *n* : fiction dealing principally with the impact of actual or imagined science on society or individuals

scientific method *n* : the rules and methods for the pursuit of knowledge involving the finding and stating of a problem, the collection of facts through observation and experiment, and the making and testing of ideas that need to be proven right or wrong

scim·i·tar \ˈsim-ət-ər\ *n* : a curved sword used chiefly by Arabs and Turks

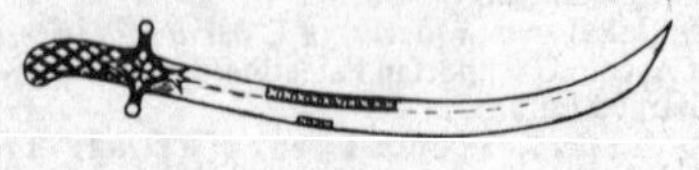

scimitar

scin·til·la \sin-ˈtil-ə\ *n* : SPARK, TRACE

scin·til·late \ˈsint-ᵊl-ˌāt\ *vb* **-lat·ed; -lat·ing** : SPARKLE, GLEAM — **scin·til·la·tion** \ˌsint-ᵊl-ˈā-shən\ *n*

sci·on \ˈsī-ən\ *n* **1** : a shoot of a plant joined to a stock in grafting **2** : DESCENDANT

scis·sors \ˈsiz-ərz\ *n pl* : a cutting instrument like shears but usu. smaller

scissors kick *n* : a swimming kick in which the legs move like scissors

scle·ro·sis \sklə-ˈrō-səs\ *n* : a usu. abnormal hardening of tissue (as of an artery) — **scle·rot·ic** \-ˈrät-ik\ *adj*

scoff \ˈskäf\ *vb* : MOCK, JEER — **scoff·er** *n*

scoff·law \-ˌlȯ\ *n* : a contemptuous law violator

[1]**scold** \ˈskōld\ *n* : a person who scolds

[2]**scold** *vb* : to censure severely or angrily

sconce \ˈskäns\ *n* : a candlestick or an electric light fixture bracketed to a wall

scone \ˈskōn, ˈskän\ *n* : a biscuit (as of oatmeal) baked on a griddle

[1]**scoop** \ˈsküp\ *n* **1** : a large shovel; *also* : a shovellike

utensil ⟨a sugar ~⟩ **2** : an act of scooping **3** : information of immediate interest

[2]**scoop** *vb* **1** : to take out or up or empty with or as if with a scoop **2** : to make hollow **3** : to report a news item in advance of

scoot \ˈsküt\ *vb* : to go suddenly and swiftly

scoot·er \ˈsküt-ər\ *n* **1** : a child's vehicle consisting of a narrow board mounted between two wheels tandem with an upright steering handle attached to the front wheel **2** : MOTOR SCOOTER

[1]**scope** \ˈskōp\ *n* [It *scopo* purpose, goal, fr. Gk *skopos*, fr. *skeptesthai* to watch, look at] **1** : space or opportunity for action or thought **2** : extent covered : RANGE

[2]**scope** *n* : an instrument (as a microscope or radarscope) for viewing

scorch \ˈskȯrch\ *vb* : to burn the surface of; *also* : to dry or shrivel with heat ⟨~*ed* lawns⟩

[1]**score** \ˈskōr\ *n, pl* **scores 1** *or pl* **score** : TWENTY **2** : CUT, SCRATCH, SLASH **3** : a record of points made (as in a game) **4** : DEBT **5** : REASON, GROUND **6** : the music of a composition or arrangement with different parts indicated **7** : success in obtaining something (as drugs) esp. illegally

[2]**score** *vb* **scored; scor·ing 1** : RECORD **2** : to keep score in a game **3** : to mark with lines, grooves, scratches, or notches **4** : to gain or tally in or as if in a game ⟨*scored* a point⟩ **5** : to assign a grade or score to ⟨~ the tests⟩ **6** : to compose a score for **7** : SUCCEED — **score·less** *adj* — **scor·er** *n*

sco·ria \ˈskōr-ē-ə\ *n, pl* **-ri·ae** \-ē-ˌē\ [L] : a rough cindery lava

[1]**scorn** \ˈskȯrn\ *n* : an emotion involving both anger and disgust : CONTEMPT — **scorn·ful** \-fəl\ *adj* — **scorn·ful·ly** \-ē\ *adv*

[2]**scorn** *vb* : to hold in contempt : DISDAIN — **scorn·er** *n*

Scor·pio \ˈskȯr-pē-ˌō\ *n* [L, lit., scorpion] **1** : a zodiacal constellation between Libra and Sagittarius usu. pictured as a scorpion **2** : the 8th sign of the zodiac in astrology; *also* : one born under this sign

scor·pi·on \ˈskȯr-pē-ən\ *n* : any of an order of arthropods related to the spiders and having a poisonous sting at the tip of a long jointed tail

[1]**Scot** \ˈskät\ *n* : a native or inhabitant of Scotland

[2]**Scot** *abbr* Scotland; Scottish

Scotch \ˈskäch\ *n* **1** : SCOTS **2 Scotch** *pl* : the people of Scotland **3** : a whiskey distilled in Scotland esp. from malted barley — **Scotch** *adj* — **Scotch·man** \-mən\ *n* — **Scotch·wom·an** \-ˌwu̇m-ən\ *n*

Scotch pine *n* : a pine that is naturalized in the U.S. from northern Europe and Asia and is a valuable timber tree

scot–free \ˈskät-ˈfrē\ *adj* : free from obligation, harm, or penalty

Scots \ˈskäts\ *n* : the English language of Scotland

Scots·man \ˈskäts-mən\ *n* : SCOTCHMAN

Scots·wom·an \-ˌwu̇-mən\ *n* : SCOTCHWOMAN

Scot·tish \ˈskät-ish\ *adj* : SCOTCH

scoun·drel \ˈskau̇n-drəl\ *n* : a mean or wicked person : VILLAIN

[1]**scour** \ˈskau̇(ə)r\ *vb* **1** : to move rapidly through : RUSH **2** : to examine thoroughly

[2]**scour** *vb* **1** : to rub (as with a gritty substance) in order to clean **2** : to cleanse by or as if by rubbing

[1]**scourge** \ˈskərj\ *n* **1** : LASH, WHIP **2** : PUNISHMENT; *also* : a cause of affliction (as a plague)

[2]**scourge** *vb* **scourged; scourg·ing 1** : LASH, FLOG **2** : to punish severely

[1]**scout** \ˈskau̇t\ *vb* [ME *scouten*, fr. MF *escouter* to listen, fr. L *auscultare*] **1** : to look around : RECONNOITER **2** : to inspect or observe to get information

[2]**scout** *n* **1** : a person sent out to get information; *also* : a soldier, airplane, or ship sent out to reconnoiter **2** : a member of either of two youth organizations **(Boy Scouts, Girl Scouts)** — **scout·mas·ter** \-ˌmas-tər\ *n*

[3]**scout** *vb* : SCORN, SCOFF

scow \ˈskau̇\ *n* : a large flat-bottomed boat with square ends

scowl \ˈskau̇l\ *vb* : to draw down the forehead and make a face in expression of displeasure — **scowl** *n*

SCPO *abbr* senior chief petty officer

scrab·ble \ˈskrab-əl\ *vb* **scrab·bled; scrab·bling** \-(ə-)liŋ\ **1** : SCRAPE, SCRATCH **2** : CLAMBER, SCRAMBLE **3** : to work hard and long **4** : SCRIBBLE — **scrabble** *n* — **scrab·bler** \(ə-)lər\ *n*

scrag·gly \ˈskrag-lē\ *adj* : IRREGULAR; *also* : RAGGED, UNKEMPT

scram \ˈskram\ *vb* **scrammed; scram·ming** : to go away at once

scram·ble \ˈskram-bəl\ *vb* **scram·bled; scram·bling** \-b(ə-)liŋ\ **1** : to clamber clumsily around **2** : to struggle for or as if for possession of something **3** : to spread irregularly **4** : to mix together **5** : to prepare (eggs) by stirring during frying — **scramble** *n*

[1]**scrap** \ˈskrap\ *n* **1** : FRAGMENT, PIECE **2** : discarded material : REFUSE

[2]**scrap** *vb* **scrapped; scrap·ping 1** : to make into scrap ⟨~ a battleship⟩ **2** : to get rid of as useless

[3]**scrap** *n* : FIGHT

[4]**scrap** *vb* **scrapped; scrap·ping** : FIGHT, QUARREL — **scrap·per** *n*

scrap·book \ˈskrap-ˌbu̇k\ *n* : a blank book in which mementos are kept

[1]**scrape** \ˈskrāp\ *vb* **scraped; scrap·ing 1** : to remove by drawing a knife over; *also* : to clean or smooth by rubbing off the covering **2** : GRATE; *also* : to damage or injure the surface of by contact with something rough **3** : to scrape something with a grating sound **4** : to get together (money) by strict economy **5** : to get along with difficulty — **scrap·er** *n*

[2]**scrape** *n* **1** : the act or the effect of scraping **2** : a bow accompanied by a drawing back of the foot **3** : an unpleasant predicament

[1]**scrap·py** \ˈskrap-ē\ *adj* **scrap·pi·er; -est** : DISCONNECTED, FRAGMENTARY

[2]**scrappy** *adj* **scrap·pi·er; -est 1** : QUARRELSOME **2** : having an aggressive and determined spirit

[1]**scratch** \ˈskrach\ *vb* **1** : to scrape, dig, or rub with or as if with claws or nails ⟨a dog ~*ing* at the door⟩ ⟨~*ed* his arm on thorns⟩ **2** : to cause to move or strike roughly and gratingly ⟨~*ed* his nails across the blackboard⟩ **3** : to scrape (as money) together **4** : to cancel or erase by or as if by drawing a line through — **scratchy** *adj*

[2]**scratch** *n* **1** : a mark made by or as if by scratching; *also* : a sound so made **2** : the starting line in a race **3** : a point at the beginning of a project at which nothing has been done ahead of time ⟨built from ~⟩

[3]**scratch** *adj* **1** : made as or used for a trial attempt ⟨~ paper⟩ **2** : made or done by chance ⟨a ~ hit⟩

scrawl \ˈskrȯl\ *vb* : to write hastily and carelessly — **scrawl** *n*

scraw·ny \ˈskrȯ-nē\ *adj* **scraw·ni·er; -est** : very thin : SKINNY

[1]**scream** \ˈskrēm\ *vb* : to cry out loudly and shrilly

[2]**scream** *n* : a loud shrill cry

scream·ing \ˈskrē-miŋ\ *adj* : so striking as to attract notice as if by screaming ⟨~ headlines⟩

screech \ˈskrēch\ *vb* : SHRIEK — **screech** *n* — **screechy** \ˈskrē-chē\ *adj*

[1]**screen** \ˈskrēn\ *n* **1** : a device or partition used to hide, restrain, protect, or decorate ⟨a wire-mesh window ~⟩; *also* : something that shelters, protects, or conceals **2** : a sieve or perforated material for separating finer from

coarser parts (as of sand) **3** : a surface on which an image is made to appear (as in television) **4** : the motion-picture industry

[2]**screen** *vb* **1** : to shield with or as if with a screen **2** : to separate with or as if with a screen **3** : to present (as a motion picture) on the screen **syn** hide, conceal, secrete, cover

screen·ing \-iŋ\ *n* : metal or plastic mesh (as for window screens)

[1]**screw** \ˈskrü\ *n* [ME, fr. MF *escroe* nut, fr. ML *scrofa*, fr. L, sow] **1** : a simple machine consisting of a solid cylinder with a spiral groove around it and a corresponding hollow cylinder into which it fits **2** : a naillike metal piece with a spiral groove and a head with a slot used to fasten pieces of solid material together **3** : PROPELLER

[2]**screw** *vb* **1** : to fasten or close by means of a screw **2** : to operate or adjust by means of a screw **3** : to move or cause to move spirally; *also* : to close or set in position by such an action

screw·ball \ˈskrü-ˌbȯl\ *n* **1** : a baseball pitch breaking in a direction opposite to a curve **2** : a whimsical, eccentric, or crazy person

screw·driv·er \ˈskrü-ˌdrī-vər\ *n* **1** : a tool for turning screws **2** : a drink made of vodka and orange juice

screwy \ˈskrü-ē\ *adj* **screw·i·er; -est 1** : crazily absurd, eccentric, or unusual **2** : : CRAZY, INSANE

scrib·ble \ˈskrib-əl\ *vb* **scrib·bled; scrib·bling** \-(ə-)liŋ\ : to write hastily or carelessly — **scribble** *n* — **scrib·bler** \-(ə-)lər\ *n*

scribe \ˈskrīb\ *n* **1** : one of a learned class in ancient Palestine serving as copyists, teachers, and jurists **2** : a person whose business is the copying of writing **3** : AUTHOR; *esp* : JOURNALIST

scrim \ˈskrim\ *n* : a light loosely woven cotton or linen cloth

scrim·mage \ˈskrim-ij\ *n* : the play between two football teams beginning with the snap of the ball; *also* : practice play between a team's squads — **scrimmage** *vb*

scrimp \ˈskrimp\ *vb* : to be niggardly : economize greatly ⟨~ and save⟩

scrim·shaw \ˈskrim-ˌshȯ\ *n* : carved or engraved articles made esp. by American whalers usu. from whalebone or whale ivory — **scrimshaw** *vb*

scrip \ˈskrip\ *n* **1** : a certificate showing its holder is entitled to something (as stock or land) **2** : paper money issued for temporary use in an emergency

[1]**script** \ˈskript\ *n* **1** : written matter (as lines for a play or broadcast) **2** : HANDWRITING

[2]**script** *abbr* scripture

scrip·ture \ˈskrip-chər\ *n* **1** *cap* : the books of the Bible — often used in pl. **2** : the sacred writings of a religion — **scrip·tur·al** \ˈskrip-chə-rəl\ *adj* — **scrip·tur·al·ly** \-ē\ *adv*

scriv·en·er \ˈskriv-(ə-)nər\ *n* : SCRIBE, WRITER, AUTHOR

scrod \ˈskräd\ *n* : a young fish (as a cod or haddock); *esp* : one split and boned for cooking

scrof·u·la \ˈskrȯf-yə-lə\ *n* : tuberculosis of lymph nodes esp. in the neck

scroll \ˈskrōl\ *n* : a roll of paper or parchment for writing a document; *also* : a spiral or coiled ornamental form suggesting a loosely or partly rolled scroll

scroll saw *n* : JIGSAW

scro·tum \ˈskrōt-əm\ *n, pl* **scro·ta** \-ə\ *or* **scrotums** [L] : a pouch that in most mammals contains the testes

scrounge \ˈskraůnj\ *vb* **scrounged; scroung·ing** : to collect by or as if by foraging

[1]**scrub** \ˈskrəb\ *n* **1** : a thick growth of stunted trees or shrubs; *also* : an area of land covered with scrub **2** : an inferior domestic animal **3** : a person of insignificant size or standing; *esp* : a player not on the first team — **scrub** *adj* — **scrub·by** *adj*

[2]**scrub** *vb* **scrubbed; scrub·bing 1** : to rub in washing ⟨~ clothes⟩ **2** : to wash by rubbing ⟨~ out a spot⟩ **3** : CANCEL

[3]**scrub** *n* : an act or instance of scrubbing ⟨gave the clothes a good ~⟩

scruff \ˈskrəf\ *n* : the loose skin of the back of the neck : NAPE

scruffy \ˈskrəf-ē\ *adj* **scruff·i·er; -est** : UNKEMPT, SLOVENLY

scrump·tious \ˈskrəm(p)-shəs\ *adj* : DELIGHTFUL, EXCELLENT — **scrump·tious·ly** *adv*

[1]**scru·ple** \ˈskrü-pəl\ *n* [MF *scrupule*, fr. L *scrupulus* small sharp stone, cause of mental discomfort, scruple, dim. of *scrupus* sharp stone] **1** : a point of conscience or honor **2** : hesitation due to ethical considerations

[2]**scruple** *vb* **scru·pled; scru·pling** \-p(ə-)liŋ\ : to be reluctant on grounds of conscience : HESITATE

scru·pu·lous \ˈskrü-pyə-ləs\ *adj* **1** : having moral integrity **2** : PAINSTAKING — **scru·pu·lous·ly** *adv* — **scru·pu·lous·ness** *n*

scru·ti·nize \ˈskrüt-ən-ˌīz\ *vb* **-nized; -niz·ing** : to examine closely

scru·ti·ny \ˈskrüt-ᵊn-ē\ *n, pl* **-nies** [L *scrutinium*, fr. *scrutari* to search, examine, fr. *scruta* trash] : a careful looking over **syn** inspection, examination, analysis

scu·ba \ˈsk(y)ü-bə\ *n* [*s*elf-*c*ontained *u*nderwater *b*reathing *a*pparatus] : an apparatus for breathing while swimming under water

scuba diver *n* : one who swims under water with the aid of scuba gear

[1]**scud** \ˈskəd\ *vb* **scud·ded; scud·ding** : to move speedily

[2]**scud** *n* : light clouds driven by the wind

[1]**scuff** \ˈskəf\ *vb* **1** : to scrape the feet while walking : SHUFFLE **2** : to scratch or become scratched or worn away

[2]**scuff** *n* **1** : a mark or injury caused by scuffing **2** : a flat-soled slipper without quarter or heel strap

scuf·fle \ˈskəf-əl\ *vb* **scuf·fled; scuf·fling** \-(ə-)liŋ\ **1** : to struggle confusedly at close quarters **2** : to shuffle one's feet — **scuffle** *n*

[1]**scull** \ˈskəl\ *n* **1** : an oar for use in sculling; *also* : one of a pair of short oars for a single oarsman **2** : a racing shell propelled by one or two persons using sculls

[2]**scull** *vb* : to propel (a boat) by an oar over the stern

scul·lery \ˈskəl-(ə-)rē\ *n, pl* **-ler·ies** [ME, department of household in charge of dishes, fr. MF *escuelerie*, fr. *escuelle* bowl, fr. L *scutella* drinking bowl] : a small room near the kitchen used for cleaning dishes, culinary utensils, and vegetables

scul·lion \ˈskəl-yən\ *n* [ME *sculion*, fr. MF *escouillon* dishcloth, alter. of *escouvillon*, fr. *escouve* broom, fr. L *scopa*, lit., twig] : a kitchen helper

sculpt \ˈskəlpt\ *vb* : CARVE, SCULPTURE

sculp·tor \ˈskəlp-tər\ *n* : one who produces works of sculpture

[1]**sculp·ture** \ˈskəlp-chər\ *n* : the act, process, or art of carving or molding material (as stone, wood, or plastic); *also* : work produced this way — **sculp·tur·al** \ˈskəlp-chə-rəl\ *adj*

[2]**sculpture** *vb* **sculp·tured; sculp·tur·ing** : to form or alter as or as if a work of sculpture

scum \ˈskəm\ *n* **1** : a foul filmy covering on the surface of a liquid **2** : waste matter **3** : RABBLE

scup·per \ˈskəp-ər\ *n* : an opening in the side of a ship through which water on deck is drained overboard

scurf \ˈskərf\ *n* : thin dry scales of skin (as dandruff); *also* : a scaly deposit or covering — **scurfy** \ˈskər-fē\ *adj*

scur·ri·lous \ˈskər-ə-ləs\ *adj* : coarsely jesting : OBSCENE, VULGAR

scur·ry \ˈskər-ē\ *vb* **scur·ried; scur·ry·ing** : SCAMPER

[1]**scur·vy** \ˈskər-vē\ *n* : a disease marked by spongy gums, loosened teeth, and bleeding into the tissues and caused by lack of vitamin C

[2]**scurvy** *adj* : MEAN, CONTEMPTIBLE — **scur·vi·ly** \ˈskər-və-lē\ *adv*

scutch·eon \ˈskəch-ən\ *n* : ESCUTCHEON

[1]**scut·tle** \ˈskət-ᵊl\ *n* : a pail for carrying coal

²**scuttle** *n* : a small opening with a lid esp. in the deck, side, or bottom of a ship
³**scuttle** *vb* **scut·tled; scut·tling** \ˈskət-(ᵊ-)liŋ\ : to cut a hole in the deck, side, or bottom of (a ship) in order to sink
⁴**scuttle** *vb* **scut·tled; scut·tling** \ˈskət-(ᵊ-)liŋ\ : SCURRY, SCAMPER
scut·tle·butt \ˈskət-ᵊl-ˌbət\ *n* : GOSSIP
scythe \ˈsīth\ *n* : an implement for mowing (as grass or grain) by hand — **scythe** *vb*
SD *abbr* **1** South Dakota **2** special delivery
S Dak *abbr* South Dakota
Se *symbol* selenium
SE *abbr* southeast
sea \ˈsē\ *n* **1** : a large body of salt water **2** : OCEAN **3** : rough water; *also* : a heavy wave **4** : something likened to the sea esp. in vastness — **sea** *adj* — **at sea** : LOST, BEWILDERED
sea anemone *n* : any of numerous coelenterate polyps whose form, bright and varied colors, and cluster of tentacles superficially resemble a flower
sea·bird \ˈsē-ˌbərd\ *n* : a bird (as a gull) frequenting the open ocean
sea·board \-ˌbōrd\ *n* : SEACOST; *also* : the land bordering a coast
sea·coast \-ˌkōst\ *n* : the shore of the sea
sea·far·er \-ˌfar-ər\ *n* : SEAMAN
sea·far·ing \-ˌfar-iŋ\ *n* : a mariner's calling — **seafaring** *adj*
sea·food \-ˌfüd\ *n* : edible marine fish and shellfish
sea·go·ing \-ˌgō-iŋ\ *adj* : OCEANGOING
sea horse *n* : any of numerous small sea fishes with the head and forepart of the body sharply flexed like the head and neck of a horse
¹**seal** \ˈsēl\ *n, pl* **seals** *also* **seal 1** : any of various large sea mammals occurring chiefly in cold regions and having limbs adapted for swimming **2** : the pelt of a seal
²**seal** *vb* : to hunt seals
³**seal** *n* **1** : something that fastens or secures; *also* : GUARANTEE, PLEDGE **2** : a device having a raised design that can be stamped on clay or wax; *also* : the impression made by stamping with such a device **3** : a mark acceptable as having the legal effect of an official seal
⁴**seal** *vb* **1** : to affix a seal to; *also* : AUTHENTICATE **2** : to fasten with a seal; *esp* : to enclose securely **3** : to determine irrevocably
sea–lane \ˈsē-ˌlān\ *n* : an established sea route
seal·ant \ˈsē-lənt\ *n* : a sealing agent
seal·er \ˈsē-lər\ *n* : a coat applied to prevent subsequent coats of paint or varnish from sinking in
sea level *n* : the level of the surface of the sea esp. at its mean position midway between mean high and low water
sea lion *n* : any of several large Pacific seals with external ears
seal·skin \ˈsēl-ˌskin\ *n* **1** : ¹SEAL 2 **2** : a garment of sealskin
¹**seam** \ˈsēm\ *n* **1** : the line of junction of two edges and esp. of edges of fabric sewn together **2** : layer of mineral matter ⟨coal ~*s*⟩ **3** : WRINKLE — **seam·less** *adj*
²**seam** *vb* **1** : to join by or as if by sewing **2** : WRINKLE, FURROW
sea·man \ˈsē-mən\ *n* **1** : one who assists in the handling of ships : MARINER **2** : an enlisted man in the navy ranking next below a petty officer third class
seaman apprentice *n* : an enlisted man in the navy ranking next below a seaman
seaman recruit *n* : an enlisted man of the lowest rank in the navy
sea·man·ship \ˈsē-mən-ˌship\ *n* : the art or skill of handling a ship
sea·mount \ˈsē-ˌmaůnt\ *n* : an underwater mountain
seam·stress \ˈsēm-strəs\ *n* : a woman who does sewing
seamy \ˈsē-mē\ *adj* **seam·i·er; -est 1** : UNPLEASANT **2** : DEGRADED, SORDID
sé·ance \ˈsā-ˌäns\ *n* [F] : a spiritualist meeting to receive communications from spirits
sea·plane \ˈsē-ˌplān\ *n* : an airplane that can take off from and land on water
sea·port \-ˌpōrt\ *n* : a port for oceangoing ships
sear \ˈsiər\ *vb* **1** : WITHER **2** : to burn or scorch esp. on the surface; *also* : BRAND
¹**search** \ˈsərch\ *vb* [ME *cerchen,* fr. MF *cerchier* to go about, survey, search, fr. LL *circare* to go about, fr. L *circum* round about] **1** : to look through in trying to find something **2** : SEEK **3** : PROBE — **search·er** *n*
²**search** *n* : the act of searching
search·light \-ˌlīt\ *n* : an apparatus for projecting a beam of light; *also* : the light projected
sea·scape \ˈsē-ˌskāp\ *n* **1** : a view of the sea **2** : a picture representing a scene at sea
sea·shore \-ˌshōr\ *n* : the shore of a sea : SEACOAST
sea·sick \-ˌsik\ *adj* : nauseated by or as if by the motion of a ship — **sea·sick·ness** *n*
sea·side \ˈsē-ˌsīd\ *n* : SEASHORE
¹**sea·son** \ˈsēz-ᵊn\ *n* [ME, fr. OF *saison,* fr. L *sation-, satio* action of sowing, fr. *satus,* pp. of *serere* to sow] **1** : one of the divisions of the year (as spring or summer) **2** : a special period ⟨the Easter ~⟩ — **sea·son·al** \ˈsēz-(ᵊ-)nəl\ *adj* — **sea·son·al·ly** \-ē\ *adv*
²**season** *vb* **sea·soned; sea·son·ing** \ˈsēz-(ᵊ-)niŋ\ **1** : to make pleasant to the taste by use of salt, pepper, or spices **2** : to make (as by aging or drying) suitable for use **3** : to accustom or habituate to something (as hardship) **syn** harden, inure, acclimatize, toughen — **sea·son·er** \ˈsēz-(ᵊ-)nər\ *n*
sea·son·able \ˈsēz-(ᵊ-)nə-bəl\ *adj* : occurring at a fit time **syn** timely, propitious, opportune — **sea·son·ably** \-blē\ *adv*
sea·son·ing \ˈsēz-(ᵊ-)niŋ\ *n* : something that seasons : CONDIMENT
¹**seat** \ˈsēt\ *n* **1** : a chair, bench, or stool for sitting on **2** : a place which serves as a capital or center
²**seat** *vb* **1** : to place in or on a seat **2** : to provide seats for
seat belt *n* : straps designed to hold a person steady in a seat
SEATO \ˈsē-ˌtō\ *abbr* Southeast Asia Treaty Organization
seat–of–the–pants *adj* : employing or based on personal experience, judgment, and effort rather than technological aids ⟨~ navigation⟩
sea urchin *n* : any of a class of oblate spiny marine echinoderms having thin brittle shells
sea·wall \ˈsē-ˌwȯl\ *n* : an embankment to protect the shore from erosion
¹**sea·ward** \ˈsē-wərd\ *n* : the direction or side away from land and toward the open sea
²**seaward** *adj* **1** : directed or situated toward the sea **2** : coming from the sea
³**seaward** *also* **sea·wards** \-wərdz\ *adv* : toward the sea
sea·wa·ter \ˈsē-ˌwȯt-ər, -ˌwät-\ *n* : water in or from the sea
sea·way \-ˌwā\ *n* : an inland waterway that admits ocean shipping
sea·weed \-ˌwēd\ *n* : a marine alga (as a kelp); *also* : a mass of marine algae
sea·wor·thy \ˈsē-ˌwər-thē\ *adj* : fit for a sea voyage
se·ba·ceous \si-ˈbā-shəs\ *adj* : of, relating to, or secreting fatty material
sec *abbr* **1** second; secondary **2** secretary **3** section **4** [L *secundum*] according to
SEC *abbr* Securities and Exchange Commission
se·cede \si-ˈsēd\ *vb* **se·ced·ed; se·ced·ing** : to withdraw

from an organized body and esp. from a political body

se·ces·sion \si-ˈsesh-ən\ *n* : the act of seceding — **se·ces·sion·ist** *n*

se·clude \si-ˈklüd\ *vb* **se·clud·ed; se·clud·ing** : to keep or shut away from others

se·clu·sion \si-ˈklü-zhən\ *n* : the act of secluding : the state of being secluded — **se·clu·sive** \-siv\ *adj*

[1]**sec·ond** \ˈsek-ənd\ *adj* [ME, fr. OF, fr. L *secundus* second, following, favorable, fr. *sequi* to follow] **1** : being number two in a countable series **2** : next after the first **3** : ALTERNATE ⟨every ~ year⟩ — **second** *or* **sec·ond·ly** *adv*

[2]**second** *n* [ME *secunde,* fr. ML *secunda,* fr. L, fem. of *secundus* second; fr. its being the second division of a unit into 60 parts, as a minute is the first] **1** : the 60th part of a minute of time or angular measure **2** : an instant of time

[3]**second** *n* **1** : one that is second **2** : one who assists another (as in a duel) **3** : an inferior or flawed article (as of merchandise) **4** : the second forward gear in a motor vehicle

[4]**second** *vb* **1** : to encourage or give support to **2** : to act as a second to **3** : to support (a motion) by adding one's voice to that of a proposer

sec·ond·ary \ˈsek-ən-ˌder-ē\ *adj* **1** : second in rank, value, or occurrence : INFERIOR, LESSER **2** : belonging to a second or later stage of development **3** : coming after the primary or elementary ⟨~ schools⟩ **syn** subordinate, collateral, dependent

secondary sex characteristic *n* : a physical characteristic (as the breasts of a female mammal or the showy feathers of a male bird) that appears in members of one sex at puberty or in seasonal breeders at breeding season and is not directly concerned with reproduction

second fiddle *n* : one that plays a supporting or subservient role

sec·ond–guess \ˌsek-ᵊŋ-ˈges, -ən-\ *vb* : to think out other strategies or explanations for after the event

sec·ond·hand \ˌsek-ən-ˈhand\ *adj* **1** : not original **2** : not new : USED ⟨~ clothes⟩ **3** : dealing in used goods

second lieutenant *n* : a commissioned officer (as in the army) ranking next below a first lieutenant

sec·ond–rate \ˌsek-ən(d)-ˈrāt\ *adj* : INFERIOR

second–story man *n* : a burglar who enters by an upstairs window

sec·ond–string \ˌsek-ən-ˌstriŋ, ˌsek-ᵊŋ-\ *adj* : being a substitute (as on a ball team)

se·cre·cy \ˈsē-krə-sē\ *n, pl* **-cies 1** : the habit or practice of being secretive **2** : the quality or state of being secret

[1]**se·cret** \ˈsē-krət\ *adj* **1** : HIDDEN, CONCEALED ⟨a ~ panel⟩ **2** : COVERT, STEALTHY; *also* : engaged in detecting or spying ⟨a ~ agent⟩ **3** : kept from general knowledge — **se·cret·ly** *adv*

[2]**secret** *n* **1** : MYSTERY **2** : something kept from the knowledge of others

sec·re·tar·i·at \ˌsek-rə-ˈter-ē-ət\ *n* **1** : the office of a secretary **2** : the body of secretaries in an office **3** : the administrative department of a governmental organization ⟨the UN ~⟩

sec·re·tary \ˈsek-rə-ˌter-ē\ *n, pl* **-tar·ies 1** : a person employed to handle records, correspondence, and routine work for another person **2** : an officer of a corporation or business who is in charge of correspondence and records **3** : an official at the head of a department of government **4** : a writing desk — **sec·re·tari·al** \ˌsek-rə-ˈter-ē-əl\ *adj* — **sec·re·tary·ship** \ˈsek-rə-ˌter-ē-ˌship\ *n*

[1]**se·crete** \si-ˈkrēt\ *vb* **se·cret·ed; se·cret·ing** : to produce and emit as a secretion

[2]**se·crete** \si-ˈkrēt, ˈsē-krət\ *vb* **se·cret·ed; se·cret·ing** : HIDE, CONCEAL

se·cre·tion \si-ˈkrē-shən\ *n* **1** : an act or process of secreting **2** : a product of glandular activity; *esp* : one (as a hormone) useful in the organism — **se·cre·to·ry** \-ˈkrēt-ə-rē\ *adj*

se·cre·tive \ˈsē-krət-iv, si-ˈkrēt-\ *adj* : tending to keep secrets or to act secretly — **se·cre·tive·ly** *adv* — **se·cre·tive·ness** *n*

[1]**sect** \ˈsekt\ *n* **1** : a dissenting religious body **2** : a religious denomination **3** : a group adhering to a distinctive doctrine or to a leader

[2]**sect** *abbr* section

[1]**sec·tar·i·an** \sek-ˈter-ē-ən\ *adj* **1** : of or relating to a sect or sectarian **2** : limited in character or scope — **sec·tar·i·an·ism** *n*

[2]**sectarian** *n* **1** : an adherent of a sect **2** : a narrow or bigoted person

sec·ta·ry \ˈsek-tə-rē\ *n, pl* **-ries** : a member of a sect

[1]**sec·tion** \ˈsek-shən\ *n* **1** : a part cut off or separated **2** : a distinct part **3** : the appearance that a thing has or would have if cut straight through

[2]**section** *vb* **1** : to separate or become separated into sections **2** : to represent in sections

sec·tion·al \ˈsek-sh(ə-)nəl\ *adj* **1** : of, relating to, or characteristic of a section **2** : local or regional rather than general in character **3** : divided into sections — **sec·tion·al·ism** *n*

sec·tor \ˈsek-tər\ *n* **1** : a part of a circle between two radii **2** : an area assigned to a military leader to defend

sec·u·lar \ˈsek-yə-lər\ *adj* **1** : not sacred or ecclesiastical **2** : not bound by monastic vows ⟨~ priest⟩

sec·u·lar·ism \ˈsek-yə-lə-ˌriz-əm\ *n* : indifference to or exclusion of religion — **sec·u·lar·ist** \-rəst\ *n* — **secularist** *or* **sec·u·lar·is·tic** \ˌsek-yə-lə-ˈris-tik\ *adj*

sec·u·lar·ize \ˈsek-yə-lə-ˌrīz\ *vb* **-ized; -iz·ing 1** : to make secular **2** : to transfer from ecclesiastical to civil or lay use, possession, or control — **sec·u·lar·iza·tion** \ˌsek-yə-lə-rə-ˈzā-shən\ *n* — **sec·u·lar·iz·er** \ˈsek-yə-lə-ˌrī-zər\ *n*

[1]**se·cure** \si-ˈkyu̇r\ *adj* **se·cur·er; -est** [L *securus* safe, secure, fr. *se* without + *cura* care] **1** : easy in mind : free from fear **2** : free from danger or risk of loss : SAFE **3** : CERTAIN, SURE — **se·cure·ly** *adv*

[2]**secure** *vb* **se·cured; se·cur·ing 1** : to make safe : GUARD **2** : to assure payment of by giving a pledge or collateral **3** : to fasten safely ⟨~ a door⟩ **4** : GET, ACQUIRE

se·cu·ri·ty \si-ˈkyu̇r-ət-ē\ *n, pl* **-ties 1** : SAFETY **2** : freedom from worry **3** : something (as collateral) given as pledge of payment **4** *pl* : bond or stock certificates **5** : PROTECTION

secy *abbr* secretary

se·dan \si-ˈdan\ *n* **1** : a covered chair borne on poles by two men **2** : an enclosed automobile usu. with front and back seats and a permanent top

se·date \si-ˈdāt\ *adj* : quiet and dignified in behavior **syn** staid, sober, serious, solemn — **se·date·ly** *adv*

[1]**sed·a·tive** \ˈsed-ət-iv\ *adj* : serving or tending to relieve tension — **se·da·tion** \si-ˈdā-shən\ *n*

[2]**sedative** *n* : a sedative drug

sed·en·tary \ˈsed-ᵊn-ˌter-ē\ *adj* : characterized by or requiring much sitting

sedge \ˈsej\ *n* : any of a family of plants that are related to the grasses, grow in marshes, and often have three-sided stems — **sedgy** \ˈsej-ē\ *adj*

sed·i·ment \ˈsed-ə-mənt\ *n* **1** : the material that settles to the bottom of a liquid : LEES, DREGS **2** : material (as stones and sand) deposited by water, wind, or a glacier — **sed·i·men·ta·ry** \ˌsed-ə-ˈment-(ə-)rē\ *adj* — **sed·i·men·ta·tion** \-ˌmən-ˈtā-shən, -ˌmen-\ *n*

se·di·tion \si-ˈdish-ən\ *n* : the causing of discontent, insurrection, or resistance against a government — **se·di·tious** \-əs\ *adj*

se·duce \si-ˈd(y)üs\ *vb* **se·duced; se·duc·ing 1** : to persuade to disobedience or disloyalty **2** : to lead astray **3** : to entice to unlawful sexual intercourse without the use of force **syn** tempt, entice, inveigle, lure — **se·duc·er** *n* — **se·duc·tion** \-ˈdək-shən\ *n* — **se·duc·tive** \-tiv\ *adj*

sed·u·lous \ˈsej-ə-ləs\ *adj* [L *sedulus*, fr. *sedulo* sincerely, diligently, fr. *se* without + *dolus* guile] : DILIGENT, PAINSTAKING

[1]**see** \ˈsē\ *vb* **saw** \ˈsȯ\; **seen** \ˈsēn\; **see·ing** \ˈsē-iŋ\ **1** : to perceive by the eye : have the power of sight **2** : EXPERIENCE **3** : UNDERSTAND **4** : to make sure ⟨~ that order is kept⟩ **5** : to meet with **6** : to keep company with esp. in dating **7** : ACCOMPANY, ESCORT **syn** behold, descry, espy, view, observe, note, discern

[2]**see** *n* : the authority or jurisdiction of a bishop

[1]**seed** \ˈsēd\ *n, pl* **seed** *or* **seeds** **1** : the grains of plants used for sowing **2** : a ripened ovule of a plant that may develop into a new plant; *also* : a plant structure (as a spore or small dry fruit) capable of producing a new plant **3** : DESCENDANTS **4** : SOURCE, ORIGIN — **seed·bed** \-ˌbed\ *n* — **seed·less** *adj* — **go to seed** *or* **run to seed** **1** : to develop seed **2** : DECAY

[2]**seed** *vb* **1** : SOW, PLANT ⟨~ land to grass⟩ **2** : to bear or shed seeds **3** : to remove seeds from — **seed·er** *n*

seed·ling \ˈsēd-liŋ\ *n* **1** : a plant grown from seed **2** : a young plant; *esp* : a tree smaller than a sapling

seed·time \ˈsēd-ˌtīm\ *n* : the season for sowing

seedy \ˈsēd-ē\ *adj* **seed·i·er; -est** **1** : containing or full of seeds **2** : inferior in condition or quality : SHABBY

seek \ˈsēk\ *vb* **sought** \ˈsȯt\; **seek·ing** **1** : to search for **2** : to try to reach or obtain ⟨~ fame⟩ **3** : ATTEMPT — **seek·er** *n*

seem \ˈsēm\ *vb* **1** : to give the impression of being : APPEAR **2** : to appear to the observation or understanding

seem·ing \-iŋ\ *adj* : outwardly apparent — **seem·ing·ly** *adv*

seem·ly \ˈsēm-lē\ *adj* **seem·li·er; -est** : PROPER, DECENT

seep \ˈsēp\ *vb* : to leak through fine pores or cracks : percolate slowly — **seep·age** \ˈsē-pij\ *n*

seer \ˈsiər\ *n* : a person who foresees or predicts events : PROPHET

seer·suck·er \ˈsiər-ˌsək-ər\ *n* [Hindi *śīrśaker*, fr. Per *shīr-o-shakar*, lit., milk and sugar] : a light fabric of linen, cotton, or rayon usu. striped and slightly puckered

see·saw \ˈsē-ˌsȯ\ *n* **1** : a contest in which now one side now the other has the lead **2** : a children's sport of riding up and down on the ends of a plank supported in the middle; *also* : the plank so used — **seesaw** *vb*

seethe \ˈsēth\ *vb* **seethed; seeth·ing** [archaic *seethe* boil] : to become violently agitated

seg·ment \ˈseg-mənt\ *n* **1** : a division of a thing : SECTION ⟨~ of an orange⟩ **2** : a part cut off from a geometrical figure (as a circle) by a line — **seg·ment·ed** \-ˌment-əd\ *adj*

seg·re·gate \ˈseg-ri-ˌgāt\ *vb* **-gat·ed; -gat·ing** [L *segregare*, fr. *se-* apart + *greg-*, *grex* herd, flock] : to cut off from others : ISOLATE — **seg·re·ga·tion** \ˌseg-ri-ˈgā-shən\ *n*

seg·re·ga·tion·ist \ˌseg-ri-ˈgā-sh(ə-)nəst\ *n* : one who believes in or practices the segregation of races

sei·gneur \sān-ˈyər\ *n, often cap* [MF, fr. ML *senior*, fr. L, adj., elder] : a feudal lord

[1]**seine** \ˈsān\ *n* : a large weighted fishing net

[2]**seine** *vb* **seined; sein·ing** : to fish or catch with a seine

seis·mic \ˈsīz-mik, ˈsīs-\ *adj* : of, relating to, resembling, or caused by an earthquake — **seis·mic·i·ty** \sīz-ˈmis-ət-ē, sīs-\ *n*

seis·mo·gram \ˈsīz-mə-ˌgram, ˈsīs-\ *n* : the record of an earth tremor made by a seismograph

seis·mo·graph \-ˌgraf\ *n* : an apparatus for recording earthquake data — **seis·mo·graph·ic** \ˌsīz-mə-ˈgraf-ik, ˌsīs-\ *adj* — **seis·mog·ra·phy** \sīz-ˈmäg-rə-fē, sīs-\ *n*

seis·mol·o·gy \sīz-ˈmäl-ə-jē, sīs-\ *n* : a science that deals with earthquakes — **seis·mo·log·i·cal** \ˌsīz-mə-ˈläj-i-kəl, ˌsīs-\ *adj* — **seis·mol·o·gist** \sīz-ˈmäl-ə-jəst, sīs-\ *n*

seis·mom·e·ter \sīz-ˈmäm-ət-ər, sīs-\ *n* : a seismograph measuring the actual movement of the ground

seize \ˈsēz\ *vb* **seized; seiz·ing** **1** : to lay hold of or take possession of by force **2** : ARREST **3** : UNDERSTAND **4** : to attack or overwhelm physically : AFFLICT **syn** take, grasp, clutch, snatch, grab

sei·zure \ˈsē-zhər\ *n* **1** : the act of seizing : the state of being seized **2** : a sudden attack (as of disease)

sel *abbr* select; selected; selection

sel·dom \ˈsel-dəm\ *adv* : not often : RARELY

[1]**se·lect** \sə-ˈlekt\ *adj* **1** : CHOSEN, PICKED; *also* : CHOICE **2** : judicious or restrictive in choice : DISCRIMINATING

[2]**select** *vb* : to take by preference from a number or group : pick out : CHOOSE

se·lec·tion \sə-ˈlek-shən\ *n* **1** : the act of selecting **2** : something selected : CHOICE **3** : a natural or artificial process that increases the chance of propagation of some organisms and decreases that of others

se·lec·tive \sə-ˈlek-tiv\ *adj* : of or relating to selection : selecting or tending to select ⟨~ shoppers⟩

selective service *n* : a system for calling men up for military service

se·lect·man \si-ˈlek(t)-ˌman, -mən\ *n* : one of a board of officials elected in towns of most New England states to administer town affairs

sel·e·nite \ˈsel-ə-ˌnīt\ *n* [L *selenites*, fr. Gk *selēnitēs (lithos)*, lit., stone of the moon, fr. *selēnē* moon; fr. the belief that it waxed and waned with the moon] : a variety of transparent crystalline gypsum

se·le·ni·um \sə-ˈlē-nē-əm\ *n* : a nonmetallic chemical element that varies in electrical conductivity with the intensity of its illumination — see ELEMENT table

self \ˈself\ *n, pl* **selves** \ˈselvz\ **1** : the essential person distinct from all other persons in identity **2** : a particular side of a person's character **3** : personal interest : SELFISHNESS

self- *comb form* **1** : oneself : itself **2** : of oneself or itself **3** : by oneself; *also* : automatic **4** : to, for, or toward oneself

self-abasement
self-accusation
self-acting
self-addressed
self-adjusting
self-administer
self-advancement
self-aggrandizement
self-aggrandizing
self-analysis
self-appointed
self-asserting
self-assertion
self-assertive
self-assurance
self-assured
self-awareness
self-betrayal
self-closing
self-command
self-complacent
self-conceit
self-concern
self-condemned
self-confessed
self-confidence
self-confident
self-congratulation
self-congratulatory
self-constituted
self-contradiction
self-contradictory
self-control
self-correcting
self-created
self-criticism
self-cultivation
self-deceit
self-deceiving
self-deception
self-defeating
self-defense
self-delusion
self-denial
self-denying
self-depreciation
self-despair
self-destruction
self-destructive
self-determination
self-discipline
self-distrust
self-doubt
self-educated
self-employed
self-employment
self-esteem
self-evident
self-examination
self-explaining
self-explanatory
self-expression
self-forgetful
self-fulfilling

self-giving
self-governing
self-government
self-help
self-hypnosis
self-identity
self-image
self-importance
self-important
self-imposed
self-improvement
self-incrimination
self-induced
self-indulgence
self-inflicted
self-interest
self-limiting
self-love
self-lubricating
self-luminous
self-mastery
self-operating
self-perception
self-perpetuating
self-pity
self-portrait
self-possessed
self-possession
self-preservation
self-proclaimed
self-propelled
self-propelling
self-protection
self-realization
self-regard
self-registering
self-reliance
self-reliant
self-reproach
self-respect
self-respecting
self-restraint
self-rule
self-sacrifice
self-satisfaction
self-satisfied
self-seeking
self-service
self-serving
self-starting
self-styled
self-sufficiency
self-sufficient
self-supporting
self-sustaining
self-taught
self-torment
self-winding
self-worth

self–cen·tered \ˈself-ˈsent-ərd\ *adj* : concerned only with one's own self — **self–cen·tered·ness** *n*

self–com·posed \ˌself-kəm-ˈpōzd\ *adj* : having control over one's emotions

self–con·scious \ˈself-ˈkän-chəs\ *adj* **1** : aware of oneself as an individual **2** : uncomfortably conscious of oneself as an object of observation by others — **self–con·scious·ly** *adv* — **self–con·scious·ness** *n*

self–con·tained \ˌself-kən-ˈtānd\ *adj* **1** : complete in itself **2** : showing self-command; *also* : reserved in manner

self–de·struct \-di-ˈstrəkt\ *vb* : to destroy itself

self–ef·fac·ing \-ə-ˈfā-siŋ\ *adj* : RETIRING, SHY

self–fer·til·iza·tion \ˌself-ˌfərt-ᵊl-ə-ˈzā-shən\ *n* : fertilization of a plant or animal by its own pollen or sperm

self·ish \ˈsel-fish\ *adj* : taking care of one's own comfort, pleasure, or interest excessively or without regard for others — **self·ish·ly** *adv* — **self·ish·ness** *n*

self·less \ˈself-ləs\ *adj* : UNSELFISH — **self·less·ness** *n*

self–made \ˈself-ˈmād\ *adj* : rising from poverty or obscurity by one's own efforts ⟨~ man⟩

self–pol·li·na·tion \ˌself-ˌpäl-ə-ˈnā-shən\ *n* : pollination of a flower by its own pollen or sometimes by pollen from another flower on the same plant

self–reg·u·lat·ing \ˈself-ˈreg-yə-ˌlāt-iŋ\ *adj* : AUTOMATIC

self–righ·teous \-ˈrī-chəs\ *adj* : strongly convinced of one's own righteousness — **self–righ·teous·ly** *adv*

self·same \ˈself-ˌsām\ *adj* : precisely the same : IDENTICAL

self–seal·ing \ˈself-ˈsē-liŋ\ *adj* : capable of sealing itself (as after puncture)

self–start·er \-ˈstärt-ər\ *n* : a person who has initiative

self–will \ˈself-ˈwil\ *n* : OBSTINACY

sell \ˈsel\ *vb* **sold** \ˈsōld\; **sell·ing 1** : to transfer (property) in return for money or something else of value **2** : to deal in as a business **3** : to be sold ⟨cars are ~*ing* well⟩ — **sell·er** *n*

selling climax *n* : a sharp decline in stock prices for a short time on very heavy trading volume followed by a rally

sell out \(ˈ)sel-ˈau̇t\ *vb* **1** : to dispose of entirely by sale; *esp* : to sell one's business **2** : BETRAY — **sell·out** \ˈsel-ˌau̇t\ *n*

selt·zer \ˈselt-sər\ *n* [modif. of G *Selterser (wasser)* water of Selters, fr. Nieder *Selters,* Germany] : an artificially prepared water charged with carbon dioxide

sel·vage *or* **sel·vedge** \ˈsel-vij\ *n* : the edge of a woven fabric so formed as to prevent raveling

selves *pl of* SELF

sem *abbr* **1** semicolon **2** seminar **3** seminary

se·man·tic \si-ˈmant-ik\ *also* **se·man·ti·cal** \-i-kəl\ *adj* : of or relating to meaning

se·man·tics \si-ˈmant-iks\ *n sing or pl* **1** : the study of meanings in language **2** : connotative meaning

sema·phore \ˈsem-ə-ˌfōr\ *n* **1** : a visual signaling apparatus with movable arms **2** : signaling by hand-held flags

semaphore 2: alphabet; 3 positions following Z: error, end of word, numerals follow; numerals 1, 2, 3, 4, 5, 6, 7, 8, 9, 0 same as A through J

sem·blance \ˈsem-bləns\ *n* **1** : outward appearance **2** : IMAGE, LIKENESS

se·men \ˈsē-mən\ *n* [NL, fr. L, seed] : a sticky whitish fluid of the male reproductive tract that contains the sperm

se·mes·ter \sə-ˈmes-tər\ *n* [G, fr. L *semestris* half-yearly, fr. *sex* six + *mensis* month] : half a year; *esp* : one of the two terms into which many colleges divide the school year

semi- \ˌsem-i, ˈsem-, -ˌī\ *prefix* **1** : precisely half of **2** : half in quantity or value; *also* : half of or occurring halfway through a specified period **3** : partly : incompletely **4** : partial : incomplete **5** : having some of the characteristics of

semiannual
semiarid
semicentennial
semicircle
semicircular
semicivilized
semiclassical
semiconscious
semidarkness
semidivine
semiformal
semigloss
semi–independent
semiliquid
semiliterate
semimonthly
semiofficial
semipermanent
semipolitical
semiprecious
semiprivate
semiprofessional
semireligious
semiretired
semiskilled
semisweet
semitransparent
semiweekly
semiyearly

semi·au·to·mat·ic \ˌsem-ē-ˌȯt-ə-ˈmat-ik\ *adj, of a firearm* : employing recoil or gas pressure to eject an empty cartridge case and to load before firing again

semi·co·lon \ˈsem-i-ˌkō-lən\ *n* : a punctuation mark ; used esp. to separate major sentence elements

semi·con·duc·tor \ˌsem-i-kən-ˈdək-tər\ *n* : a substance whose electrical conductivity is between that of a conductor and an insulator — **semi·con·duct·ing** \-ˈdək-tiŋ\ *adj*

semi·dry·ing \ˌsem-i-ˈdrī-iŋ\ *adj* : that dries imperfectly or slowly ⟨a ~ oil⟩

[1]**semi·fi·nal** \ˌsem-i-ˈfīn-ᵊl\ *adj* : being next to the last in an elimination tournament

[2]**semi·fi·nal** \ˈsem-i-ˌfīn-ᵊl\ *n* : a semifinal round or match

semi·flu·id \ˌsem-i-ˈflü-əd, -ˌī-\ *adj* : SEMISOLID

semi·lu·nar \-ˈlü-nər\ *adj* : crescent-shaped

sem·i·nal \ˈsem-ən-ᵊl\ *adj* **1** : of, relating to, or consisting of seed or semen **2** : containing or contributing the seeds of later development : CREATIVE, ORIGINAL — **sem·i·nal·ly** \-ē\ *adv*

sem·i·nar \ˈsem-ə-ˌnär\ *n* **1** : a course of study pursued by a group of advanced students doing original research under a professor **2** : CONFERENCE

sem·i·nary \ˈsem-ə-ˌner-ē\ *n, pl* **-nar·ies** [ME, seedbed, nursery, fr. L *seminarium,* fr. *semen* seed] : an educational institution; *esp* : one that gives theological training — **sem·i·nar·i·an** \ˌsem-ə-ˈner-ē-ən\ *n*

Sem·i·nole \ˈsem-ə-ˌnōl\ *n, pl* **Semi·noles** *or* **Seminole** : a member of an American Indian people of Florida

semi·per·me·able \ˌsem-i-ˈpər-mē-ə-bəl\ *adj* : partially but not freely or wholly permeable; *esp* : permeable to some usu. small molecules but not to other usu. larger particles ⟨a ~ membrane⟩ — **semi·per·me·abil·i·ty** \-ˌpər-mē-ə-ˈbil-ət-ē\ *n*

semi·soft \-ˈsȯft\ *adj* : moderately soft; *esp* : firm but easily cut ⟨~ cheese⟩

semi·sol·id \-ˈsäl-əd\ *adj* : having the qualities of both a solid and a liquid

Sem·ite \ˈsem-ˌīt\ *n* : a member of any of a group of peoples (as the Jews or Arabs) of southwestern Asia — **Se·mit·ic** \sə-ˈmit-ik\ *adj*

semi·trail·er \ˈsem-i-ˌtrā-lər, ˈsem-ˌī-\ *n* : a freight trailer that when attached is supported at its forward end by the truck tractor; *also* : a semitrailer with attached tractor

semi·works \ˈsem-i-ˌwərks, ˈsem-ˌī-\ *n pl* : a manufacturing plant operating on a limited commercial scale to provide final tests of a new product or process

semp·stress \ˈsemp-strəs\ *var of* SEAMSTRESS

[1]**sen** \ˈsen\ *n, pl* **sen** — see *yen* at MONEY table

[2]**sen** *n, pl* **sen** — see *rupiah* at MONEY table

[3]**sen** *n, pl* **sen** — see *dollar, riel* at MONEY table

[4]**sen** *n, pl* **sen** — see *ringgit* at MONEY table

[5]**sen** *abbr* **1** senate; senator **2** senior

sen·ate \ˈsen-ət\ *n* [ME *senat,* fr. OF, fr. L *senatus,* lit., council of elders, fr. *senex* old, old man] : the upper branch of a legislature

sen·a·tor \ˈsen-ət-ər\ *n* : a member of a senate — **sen·a·to·ri·al** \ˌsen-ə-ˈtōr-ē-əl\ *adj*

send \ˈsend\ *vb* **sent** \ˈsent\; **send·ing** **1** : to cause to go **2** : EMIT **3** : to propel or drive esp. with force **4** : to put or bring into a certain condition — **send·er** *n*

send–off \ˈsend-ˌȯf\ *n* : a demonstration of goodwill and enthusiasm for the beginning of a new venture (as a trip)

se·ne \ˈsā-(ˌ)nā\ *n, pl* **sene** — see *tala* at MONEY table

Sen·e·ca \ˈsen-i-kə\ *n, pl* **Seneca** *or* **Senecas** : a member of an American Indian people of western New York

Sen·e·ga·lese \ˌsen-i-gə-ˈlēz, -ˈlēs\ *n, pl* **Senegalese** : a native or inhabitant of Senegal — **Senegalese** *adj*

se·nes·cence \si-ˈnes-ᵊns\ *n* : the state of being old; *also* : the process of becoming old — **se·nes·cent** \-ᵊnt\ *adj*

sen·gi \ˈseŋ-gē\ *n, pl* **sengi** — see *zaire* at MONEY table

se·nile \ˈsēn-ˌīl, ˈsen-\ *adj* : OLD, AGED; *esp* : exhibiting loss of mental ability usu. associated with old age — **se·nil·i·ty** \si-ˈnil-ət-ē\ *n*

[1]**se·nior** \ˈsē-nyər\ *n* **1** : a person older or of higher rank than another **2** : a member of the graduating class of a high school or college

[2]**senior** *adj* [ME, fr. L, older, elder, compar. of *senex* old] **1** : ELDER **2** : more advanced in dignity or rank **3** : belonging to the final year of a school or college course

senior chief petty officer *n* : a petty officer in the navy ranking next below a master chief petty officer

senior citizen *n* : an elderly person; *esp* : one who has retired

senior high school *n* : a school usu. including grades 10 to 12

se·nior·i·ty \sēn-ˈyȯr-ət-ē\ *n* **1** : the quality or state of being senior **2** : a privileged status owing to length of continuous service

senior master sergeant *n* : a noncommissioned officer in the air force ranking next below a chief master sergeant

sen·i·ti \ˈsen-ə-tē\ *n, pl* **seniti** — see *pa'anga* at MONEY table

sen·na \ˈsen-ə\ *n* **1** : any of various cassias **2** : the dried leaflets or pods of a cassia used as a purgative

sen·sa·tion \sen-ˈsā-shən\ *n* **1** : awareness (as of noise or heat) or a mental process (as seeing or hearing) due to stimulation of a sense organ; *also* : an indefinite bodily feeling **2** : a condition of excitement; *also* : the thing that causes this condition

sen·sa·tion·al \-sh(ə-)nəl\ *adj* **1** : of or relating to sensation or the senses **2** : arousing an intense and usu. superficial interest or emotional reaction — **sen·sa·tion·al·ly** \-ē\ *adv*

sen·sa·tion·al·ism \-ˌiz-əm\ *n* : the use or effect of sensational subject matter or treatment

sen·sa·tion·al·ize \-ˌīz\ *vb* **-ized; -iz·ing** : to present in a sensational manner

[1]**sense** \ˈsens\ *n* **1** : semantic content : MEANING **2** : the faculty of perceiving by means of sense organs; *also* : a bodily function or mechanism based on this ⟨the pain ~⟩ **3** : SENSATION, AWARENESS **4** : INTELLIGENCE, JUDGMENT **5** : OPINION ⟨the ~ of the meeting⟩ — **sense·less** *adj* — **sense·less·ly** *adv*

[2]**sense** *vb* **sensed; sens·ing** **1** : to be or become aware of : perceive by the senses **2** : to detect (as radiation) automatically

sense organ *n* : a bodily structure (as an eye or ear) that responds to a stimulus (as heat or light) and sends impulses to the brain where they are interpreted as sensations

sen·si·bil·i·ty \ˌsen-sə-ˈbil-ət-ē\ *n, pl* **-ties** : delicacy of feeling : SENSITIVITY

sen·si·ble \ˈsen-sə-bəl\ *adj* **1** : capable of being perceived by the senses or by reason; *also* : capable of receiving sense impressions **2** : AWARE, CONSCIOUS **3** : REASONABLE, INTELLIGENT — **sen·si·bly** \-blē\ *adv*

sen·si·tive \ˈsen-sət-iv\ *adj* **1** : subject to excitation by or responsive to stimuli **2** : having power of feeling **3** : of such a nature as to be easily affected — **sen·si·tive·ness** *n* — **sen·si·tiv·i·ty** \ˌsen-sə-ˈtiv-ət-ē\ *n*

sensitive plant *n* : any of several mimosas with leaves that fold or droop when touched

sen·si·tize \ˈsen-sə-ˌtīz\ *vb* **-tized; -tiz·ing** : to make or become sensitive or hypersensitive — **sen·si·ti·za·tion** \ˌsen-sət-ə-ˈzā-shən\ *n*

sen·si·tom·e·ter \ˌsen-sə-ˈtäm-ət-ər\ *n* : an instrument for measuring sensitivity of photographic material — **sen·si·to·met·ric** \-sət-ə-ˈme-trik\ *adj* — **sen·si·tom·e·try** \-sə-ˈtäm-ə-trē\ *n*

sen·sor \ˈsen-ˌsȯr, -sər\ *n* : a device that responds to a physical stimulus

sen·so·ry \ˈsens-(ə-)rē\ *adj* : of or relating to sensation or the senses

sen·su·al \ˈsench-(ə-)wəl\ *adj* **1** : relating to the pleasing of the senses **2** : devoted to the pleasures of the senses — **sen·su·al·ist** *n* — **sen·su·al·i·ty** \ˌsen-chə-ˈwal-ət-ē\ *n* — **sen·su·al·ly** \ˈsench-(ə-)wə-lē, ˈsen-shə-lē\ *adv*

sen·su·ous \ˈsench-(ə-)wəs\ *adj* **1** : relating to the senses or to things that can be perceived by the senses **2** : VOLUPTUOUS — **sen·su·ous·ly** *adv* — **sen·su·ous·ness** *n*

sent *past and past part of* SEND

[1]**sen·tence** \ˈsent-ᵊns, -ᵊnz\ *n* [ME, fr. OF, fr. L *sententia,* lit., feeling, opinion, fr. *sentire* to feel] **1** : the punishment set by a court **2** : a grammatically self-contained speech unit that expresses an assertion, a question, a command, a wish, or an exclamation

[2]**sentence** *vb* **sen·tenced; sen·tenc·ing** : to impose a sentence on **syn** condemn, damn, doom

sen·ten·tious \sen-ˈten-chəs\ *adj* : using wise sayings or proverbs; *also* : using pompous language

sen·ti \ˈsent-ē\ *n, pl* **senti** — see *shilling* at MONEY table

sen·tient \ˈsen-ch(ē-)ənt\ *adj* : capable of feeling : having perception

sen·ti·ment \ˈsent-ə-mənt\ *n* **1** : FEELING; *also* : thought and judgment influenced by feeling : emotional attitude **2** : OPINION, NOTION

sen·ti·men·tal \ˌsent-ə-ˈment-ᵊl\ *adj* **1** : influenced by tender feelings **2** : affecting the emotions **syn** bathetic, maudlin, mawkish, mushy — **sen·ti·men·tal·ism** *n* — **sen·ti·men·tal·ist** *n* — **sen·ti·men·tal·i·ty** \-ˌmen-ˈtal-ət-ē, -mən-\ *n* — **sen·ti·men·tal·ly** \-ˈment-ᵊl-ē\ *adv*

sen·ti·men·tal·ize \-ˈment-ᵊl-ˌīz\ *vb* **-ized; -iz·ing 1** : to indulge in sentiment **2** : to look upon or imbue with sentiment — **sen·ti·men·tal·iza·tion** \-ˌment-ᵊl-ə-ˈzā-shən\ *n*

sen·ti·mo \sen-ˈtē-(ˌ)mō\ *n, pl* **-mos** — see *peso* at MONEY table

sen·ti·nel \ˈsent-(ᵊ-)nəl\ *n* [MF *sentinelle,* fr. It *sentinella,* fr. *sentina* vigilance, fr. *sentire* to perceive, fr. L] : one that watches or guards

sen·try \ˈsen-trē\ *n, pl* **sentries** : SENTINEL, GUARD

sep *abbr* separate, separated

Sep *abbr* September

se·pal \ˈsēp-əl, ˈsep-\ *n* : one of the modified leaves comprising a flower calyx

sep·a·ra·ble \ˈsep-(ə-)rə-bəl\ *adj* : capable of being separated

[1]**sep·a·rate** \ˈsep-ə-ˌrāt\ *vb* **-rat·ed; -rat·ing 1** : to set or keep apart : DISUNITE, DISCONNECT, SEVER **2** : to keep apart by something intervening **3** : to cease to be together : PART

[2]**sep·a·rate** \ˈsep-(ə-)rət\ *adj* **1** : not connected **2** : divided from each other **3** : SINGLE, PARTICULAR ⟨the ~ pieces of the puzzle⟩ — **sep·a·rate·ly** *adv*

[3]**sep·a·rate** *n* : an article of dress designed to be worn interchangeably with others to form various combinations

sep·a·ra·tion \ˌsep-ə-ˈrā-shən\ *n* **1** : the act or process of separating : the state of being separated **2** : a point, line, means, or area of division

sep·a·rat·ist \ˈsep-(ə-)rət-əst, ˈsep-ə-ˌrāt-\ *n* : an advocate of separation (as from a political body) — **sep·a·rat·ism** \-rə-ˌtiz-əm\ *n*

sep·a·ra·tive \ˈsep-ə-ˌrāt-iv, ˈsep-(ə-)rət-\ *adj* : tending toward, causing or expressing separation

sep·a·ra·tor \ˈsep-(ə-)ˌrāt-ər\ *n* : one that separates; *esp* : a device for separating cream from milk

se·pia \ˈsē-pē-ə\ *n* : a brownish gray to dark brown

sep·sis \ˈsep-səs\ *n, pl* **sep·ses** \ˈsep-ˌsēz\ : a poisoned condition due to spread of bacteria or their products in the body

Sept *abbr* September

Sep·tem·ber \sep-ˈtem-bər\ *n* : the 9th month of the year having 30 days

sep·tic \ˈsep-tik\ *adj* **1** : PUTREFACTIVE **2** : relating to or characteristic of sepsis

sep·ti·ce·mia \ˌsep-tə-ˈsē-mē-ə\ *n* : BLOOD POISONING

septic tank *n* : a tank in which sewage is disintegrated by bacteria

sep·tu·a·ge·nar·i·an \sep-ˌt(y)ü-ə-jə-ˈner-ē-ən\ *n* : a person who is 70 or more but less than 80 years old — **septuagenarian** *adj*

Sep·tu·a·gint \sep-ˈt(y)ü-ə-jənt, ˈsep-tə-wə-ˌjint\ *n* : a Greek version of the Old Testament used by Greek-speaking Christians

[1]**sep·ul·cher** *or* **sep·ul·chre** \ˈsep-əl-kər\ *n* : burial vault : TOMB

[2]**sepulcher** *or* **sepulchre** *vb* **-chered** *or* **-chred; -cher·ing** *or* **-chring** \-k(ə-)riŋ\ : BURY, ENTOMB

se·pul·chral \sə-ˈpəl-krəl\ *adj* **1** : relating to burial or the grave **2** : GLOOMY

sep·ul·ture \ˈsep-əl-ˌchu̇r\ *n* **1** : BURIAL, INTERMENT **2** : SEPULCHER

seq *abbr* [L *sequens, sequentes, sequentia*] the following

seqq *abbr* [L *sequentia*] the following ones

se·quel \ˈsē-kwəl\ *n* **1** : logical consequence **2** : a literary or cinematic work continuing a story begun in a preceding one

se·quence \ˈsē-kwəns\ *n* **1** : SERIES **2** : chronological order of events **3** : RESULT, SEQUEL **syn** succession, chain, progression, series, train — **se·quen·tial** \si-ˈkwen-chəl\ *adj*

se·quent \ˈsē-kwənt\ *adj* **1** : SUCCEEDING, CONSECUTIVE **2** : RESULTANT

se·ques·ter \si-ˈkwes-tər\ *vb* : to set apart : SEGREGATE

se·ques·trate \ˈsēk-wəs-ˌtrāt, si-ˈkwes-\ *vb* **-trat·ed; -trat·ing** : SEQUESTER — **se·ques·tra·tion** \ˌsēk-wəs-ˈtrā-shən, ˌsek-\ *n*

se·quin \ˈsē-kwən\ *n* **1** : an old gold coin of Turkey and Italy **2** : a small metal or plastic plate used for ornamentation esp. on clothing

se·quoia \si-ˈkwȯi-ə\ *n* : either of two huge California coniferous trees

ser *abbr* **1** serial **2** series

sera *pl of* SERUM

se·ra·glio \sə-ˈral-yō\ *n, pl* **-glios** [It *serraglio*] : HAREM

se·ra·pe \sə-ˈräp-ē\ *n* : a colorful woolen shawl worn over the shoulders esp. by Mexican men

ser·a·phim \ˈser-ə-ˌfim\ *n, pl* **seraphim** : an angel of a high order of celestial beings — **se·raph·ic** \sə-ˈraf-ik\ *adj*

Serb \ˈsərb\ *n* **1** : a native or inhabitant of Serbia, republic, Yugoslavia **2** : a Slavic language of Serbia

sere \ˈsiər\ *adj* : DRY, WITHERED

[1]**ser·e·nade** \ˌser-ə-ˈnād\ *n* [F, fr. It *serenata,* fr. *sereno* clear] : music sung or played as a compliment esp. outdoors at night for a lady

[2]**serenade** *vb* **-nad·ed; -nad·ing** : to entertain with or perform a serenade

ser·en·dip·i·ty \ˌser-ən-ˈdip-ət-ē\ *n* [fr. its possession by the heroes of the Persian fairy tale *The Three Princes of Serendip*] : the gift of finding valuable or agreeable things not sought for — **ser·en·dip·i·tous** \-əs\ *adj*

se·rene \sə-ˈrēn\ *adj* **1** : QUIET, CALM **2** : CLEAR ⟨~ skies⟩ **syn** tranquil, peaceful, placid — **se·rene·ly** *adv* — **se·ren·i·ty** \sə-ˈren-ət-ē\ *n*

serf \ˈsərf\ *n* : a peasant bound to the land and subject in some degree to the owner — **serf·dom** \-dəm\ *n*

serg *or* **sergt** *abbr* sergeant

serge \ˈsərj\ *n* : a twilled woolen cloth

ser·geant \ˈsär-jənt\ *n* [ME, servant, attendant, officer who keeps order, fr. OF *sergent, serjant,* fr. L *servient-, serviens,* prp. of *servire* to serve] **1** : a noncommissioned officer (as in the army) ranking next below a staff sergeant **2** : an officer in a police force

sergeant first class *n* : a noncommissioned officer in the army ranking next below a master sergeant

sergeant major *n, pl* **sergeants major** *or* **sergeant majors 1** : a noncommissioned officer in the army, air force, or marine corps serving as chief administrative assistant in a headquarters **2** : a noncommissioned officer in the marine corps ranking above a first sergeant

[1]**se·ri·al** \ˈsir-ē-əl\ *adj* : appearing in parts that follow regularly ⟨a ~ story⟩ — **se·ri·al·ly** *adv*

[2]**serial** *n* : a serial story or other writing — **se·ri·al·ist** \-ə-ləst\ *n*

se·ries \ˈsi(ə)r-ēz\ *n, pl* **series** : a number of things or events arranged in order and connected by being alike in some way **syn** succession, progression, sequence, chain, train, string

seri·graph \ˈser-ə-ˌgraf\ *n* : an original silk-screen print — **se·rig·ra·pher** \sə-ˈrig-rə-fər\ *n* — **se·rig·ra·phy** \-fē\ *n*

se·ri·ous \ˈsir-ē-əs\ *adj* **1** : thoughtful or subdued in appearance or manner : SOBER **2** : requiring much thought or work **3** : EARNEST, DEVOTED **4** : DANGEROUS, HARMFUL **syn** grave, sedate, sober, staid — **se·ri·ous·ly** *adv* — **se·ri·ous·ness** *n*

ser·mon \ˈsər-mən\ *n* [ME, fr. OF, fr. ML *sermon, sermo,* fr. L, speech, conversation, fr. *serere* to link together] **1** : a religious discourse esp. as part of a worship service **2** : a lecture on conduct or duty

se·rol·o·gy \sə-ˈräl-ə-jē\ *n* : a science dealing with serums and esp. their reactions and properties — **se·ro·log·i·cal** \ˌsir-ə-ˈläj-i-kəl\ *or* **se·ro·log·ic** \-ik\ *adj*

se·rous \ˈsir-əs\ *adj* : of, relating to, resembling, or producing serum; *esp* : thin and watery

ser·pent \ˈsər-pənt\ *n* : SNAKE

[1]**ser·pen·tine** \ˈsər-pən-ˌtēn, -ˌtīn\ *adj* **1** : SLY, CRAFTY **2** : WINDING, TURNING

[2]**ser·pen·tine** \-ˌtēn\ *n* : a dull-green mineral having a mottled appearance

ser·rate \ˈser-ˌāt\ *adj* : having a saw-toothed edge ⟨a ∼ leaf⟩

ser·ried \ˈser-ēd\ *adj* : DENSE

se·rum \ˈsir-əm\ *n, pl* **serums** *or* **se·ra** \-ə\ [L, whey, serum] : the liquid antibody-containing part that can be separated from blood when it clots; *also* : a preparation of animal serum containing specific antibodies and used to prevent or cure disease

serv *abbr* service

ser·vant \ˈsər-vənt\ *n* : a person employed esp. for domestic work

[1]**serve** \ˈsərv\ *vb* **served; serv·ing 1** : to work as a servant **2** : to render obedience and worship to (God) **3** : to comply with the commands or demands of **4** : to work through or perform a term of service (as in the army) **5** : PUT IN ⟨*served* five years in jail⟩ **6** : to be of use : ANSWER ⟨pine boughs *served* for a bed⟩ **7** : BENEFIT **8** : to prove adequate or satisfactory for ⟨a pie that ∼*s* eight people⟩ **9** : to make ready and pass out ⟨∼ drinks⟩ **10** : to furnish or supply with something ⟨one power company *serving* the whole state⟩ **11** : to wait on ⟨∼ a customer⟩ **12** : to treat or act toward in a specified way **13** : to put the ball in play (as in tennis) — **serv·er** *n*

[2]**serve** *n* : the act of serving a ball (as in tennis)

[1]**ser·vice** \ˈsər-vəs\ *n* **1** : the occupation of a servant **2** : HELP, BENEFIT **3** : a meeting for worship; *also* : a form followed in worship or in a ceremony ⟨burial ∼⟩ **4** : the act, fact, or means of serving **5** : performance of official or professional duties **6** : a serving of the ball (as in tennis) **7** : a set of dishes or silverware **8** : a branch of public employment; *also* : the persons in it ⟨civil ∼⟩ **9** : military or naval duty **syn** use, advantage, account, avail

[2]**service** *vb* **ser·viced; ser·vic·ing** : to do maintenance or repair work on or for

ser·vice·able \ˈsər-və-sə-bəl\ *adj* : prepared for service : USEFUL, USABLE

ser·vice·man \ˈsər-vəs-ˌman, -mən\ *n* **1** : a male member of the armed forces **2** : a man employed to repair or maintain equipment

service station *n* : a retail station for servicing motor vehicles

ser·vice·wom·an \ˈsər-vəs-ˌwu̇m-ən\ *n* : a female member of the armed forces

ser·vile \ˈsər-vəl, -ˌvīl\ *adj* **1** : befitting a slave or servant **2** : behaving like a slave : SUBMISSIVE — **ser·vil·i·ty** \ˌsər-ˈvil-ət-ē\ *n*

serv·ing \ˈsər-viŋ\ *n* : HELPING

ser·vi·tor \ˈsər-vət-ər\ *n* : a male servant

ser·vi·tude \ˈsər-və-ˌt(y)üd\ *n* : SLAVERY, BONDAGE

ser·vo \ˈsər-vō\ *n, pl* **servos 1** : SERVOMOTOR **2** : SERVOMECHANISM

ser·vo·mech·a·nism \ˈsər-vō-ˌmek-ə-ˌniz-əm\ *n* : a device for automatically correcting the performance of a mechanism

ser·vo·mo·tor \ˈsər-vō-ˌmōt-ər\ *n* : a motor in a servomechanism that supplements a primary control by correcting position or motion

ses·a·me \ˈses-ə-mē\ *n* : an East Indian annual herb; *also* : its seeds that yield an edible oil (**sesame oil**) and are used in flavoring

ses·qui·cen·ten·ni·al \ˌses-kwi-sen-ˈten-ē-əl\ *n* [L *sesqui-* one and a half, half again] : a 150th anniversary or its celebration — **sesquicentennial** *adj*

ses·qui·pe·da·lian \ˌses-kwə-pə-ˈdāl-yən\ *adj* **1** : having many syllables : LONG **2** : using long words

ses·sile \ˈses-īl, -əl\ *adj* : attached by the base ⟨a ∼ leaf⟩

ses·sion \ˈsesh-ən\ *n* **1** : a meeting or series of meetings of a body (as a court or legislature) for the transaction of business **2** : a meeting or period devoted to a particular activity

[1]**set** \ˈset\ *vb* **set; set·ting 1** : to cause to sit **2** : PLACE **3** : ARRANGE, ADJUST **4** : to cause to be or do **5** : SETTLE, DECREE **6** : to fix in a frame **7** : ESTIMATE **8** : WAGER, STAKE **9** : to make fast or rigid **10** : to adapt (as words) to something (as music) **11** : to become fixed or firm or solid **12** : to be suitable : FIT **13** : BROOD **14** : to have a certain direction **15** : to pass below the horizon **16** : to defeat in bridge — **set about** : to begin to do — **set forth** : to begin a trip — **set off 1** : to start out on a course or a trip **2** : to cause to explode — **set out** : to begin a trip or undertaking — **set sail** : to begin a voyage

[2]**set** *n* **1** : a setting or a being set **2** : DIRECTION, COURSE; *also* : TENDENCY **3** : FORM, BUILD **4** : the fit of something (as a coat) **5** : an artificial setting for the scene of a play or motion picture **6** : a group of tennis games in which one side wins at least six to an opponent's four or less **7** : a group of persons or things of the same kind or having a common characteristic usu. classed together **8** : a collection of things and esp. of mathematical elements (as numbers or points) **9** : an electronic apparatus ⟨a television ∼⟩

[3]**set** *adj* **1** : fixed by authority or custom **2** : DELIBERATE **3** : RIGID **4** : PERSISTENT

set·back \ˈset-ˌbak\ *n* : a temporary defeat : REVERSE

set back \ˈset-ˈbak\ *vb* : HINDER, DELAY; *also* : REVERSE

set·screw \ˈset-ˌskrü\ *n* : a screw screwed through one part tightly upon or into another part to prevent relative movement

set·tee \se-ˈtē\ *n* : a bench or sofa with a back and arms

set·ter \ˈset-ər\ *n* : a large long-coated hunting dog

set·ting \ˈset-iŋ\ *n* **1** : the frame in which a gem is set **2** : BACKGROUND, ENVIRONMENT; *also* : SCENERY **3** : music written for a text (as of a poem) **4** : the eggs that a fowl sits on for hatching at one time

set·tle \ˈset-ᵊl\ *vb* **set·tled; set·tling** \ˈset-(ᵊ-)liŋ\ [ME *settlen* to seat, bring to rest, come to rest, fr. OE *setlan,* fr. *setl* seat] **1** : to put in place **2** : to locate permanently **3** : to make compact **4** : QUIET, CALM **5** : to establish in life, business, or a home **6** : to direct one's efforts **7** : to fix by agreement **8** : to give legally **9** : ADJUST, ARRANGE **10** : DECIDE, DETERMINE **11** : to make a final disposition of ⟨∼ an account⟩ **12** : to come to rest **13** : to reach an agreement on **14** : to sink gradually to a lower level **15** : to become clear by depositing sediment **syn** set, fix, establish, place — **set·tler** \-(ᵊ-)lər\ *n*

set·tle·ment \ˈset-ᵊl-mənt\ *n* **1** : the act or process of settling **2** : BESTOWAL ⟨a marriage ~⟩ **3** : payment of an account **4** : COLONY **5** : a small village **6** : an institution in a poor district of a city to give aid to the community **7** : adjustment of doubts and differences

set–to \ˈset-ˌtü\ *n, pl* **set–tos** : FIGHT

set·up \ˈset-ˌəp\ *n* **1** : the manner or act of arranging **2** : glass, ice, and nonalcoholic beverage for mixing served to patrons who supply their own liquor

set up \ˈset-ˈəp\ *vb* **1** : to place in position; *also* : ASSEMBLE **2** : CAUSE **3** : FOUND, ESTABLISH

sev·en \ˈsev-ən\ *n* **1** : one more than six **2** : the 7th in a set or series **3** : something having seven units — **seven** *adj or pron* — **sev·enth** \-ənth\ *adj or adv or n*

sev·en·teen \ˌsev-ən-ˈtēn\ *n* : one more than 16 — **seventeen** *adj or pron* — **sev·en·teenth** \-ˈtēnth\ *adj or n*

seventeen–year locust *n* : a cicada of the U.S. that has in the North a life of 17 years and in the South of 13 years of which most is spent underground as a nymph and only a few weeks as a winged adult

sev·en·ty \ˈsev-ən-tē\ *n, pl* **-ties** : seven times 10 — **sev·en·ti·eth** \-tē-əth\ *adj or n* — **seventy** *adj or pron*

sev·en·ty–eight \ˌsev-ən-tē-ˈāt\ *n* : a phonograph record designed to be played at 78 revolutions per minute

sev·er \ˈsev-ər\ *vb* **sev·ered; sev·er·ing** \-(ə-)riŋ\ : DIVIDE; *esp* : to separate by force (as by cutting or tearing) — **sev·er·ance** \-(ə-)rəns\ *n*

sev·er·al \ˈsev-(ə-)rəl\ *adj* [ME, fr. ML *separalis,* fr. L *separ* separate, fr. *separare* to separate] **1** : INDIVIDUAL, DISTINCT ⟨federal union of the ~ states⟩ **2** : consisting of an indefinite number but yet not very many — **sev·er·al·ly** \-ē\ *adv*

severance pay *n* : extra pay given an employee upon leaving a job permanently

se·vere \sə-ˈviər\ *adj* **se·ver·er; -est** **1** : marked by strictness or sternness : AUSTERE **2** : strict in discipline **3** : causing distress and esp. physical discomfort or pain ⟨~ weather⟩ ⟨a ~ wound⟩ **4** : hard to endure ⟨~ trials⟩ **syn** stern, ascetic, astringent, austere — **se·vere·ly** *adv* — **se·ver·i·ty** \-ˈver-ət-ē\ *n*

sew \ˈsō\ *vb* **sewed; sewn** \ˈsōn\ *or* **sewed; sew·ing** **1** : to fasten by stitches made with thread and needle **2** : to engage in sewing

sew·age \ˈsü-ij\ *n* : waste materials carried off by sewers

[1]**sew·er** \ˈsō(-ə)r\ *n* : one that sews

[2]**sew·er** \ˈsü-ər\ *n* : an artificial pipe or channel to carry off waste matter

sew·er·age \ˈsü-ə-rij\ *n* **1** : SEWAGE **2** : a system of sewers

sew·ing \ˈsō-iŋ\ *n* **1** : the activity of one who sews **2** : material that has been or is to be sewed

sex \ˈseks\ *n* **1** : either of two groups into which many living things are divided according to their roles in reproduction and which are distinguished as male and female; *also* : the qualities by which these sexes are differentiated and which directly or indirectly function in reproduction involving two parents **2** : sexual activity or intercourse — **sexed** \ˈsekst\ *adj* — **sex·less** *adj*

sex·a·ge·nar·i·an \ˌsek-sə-jə-ˈner-ē-ən\ *n* : a person who is 60 or more but less than 70 years old — **sexagenarian** *adj*

sex cell *n* : an egg cell or sperm cell

sex chromosome *n* : one of usu. a pair of chromosomes that are usu. similar in one sex but different in the other sex and are concerned with the inheritance of sex

sex hormone *n* : a hormone (as from the gonads or adrenal cortex) that affects the growth or function of the reproductive organs or the development of secondary sex characteristics

sex·ism \ˈsek-ˌsiz-əm\ *n* : prejudice or discrimination based on sex; *esp* : discrimination against women — **sex·ist** \ˈsek-səst\ *adj or n*

sex·pot \ˈseks-ˌpät\ *n* : a sexually stimulating woman

sex symbol *n* : a usu. renowned person (as an entertainer) noted and admired for conspicuous attractiveness

sex·tant \ˈsek-stənt\ *n* [NL *sextant-, sextans* sixth part of a circle, fr. L, sixth part, fr. *sextus* sixth] : a navigational instrument for measuring the angle between the horizon and the sun or a star in order to determine latitude

sex·tet \sek-ˈstet\ *n* **1** : a musical composition for six voices or six instruments; *also* : the six performers of such a composition **2** : a group or set of six

sex·ton \ˈsek-stən\ *n* : one who takes care of church property

sex·u·al \ˈsek-sh(ə-w)əl\ *adj* : of, relating to, or involving sex or the sexes ⟨a ~ spore⟩ ⟨~ relations⟩ — **sex·u·al·i·ty** \ˌsek-shə-ˈwal-ət-ē\ *n* — **sex·u·al·ly** \ˈsek-shə-(wə-)lē\ *adv*

sexual intercourse *n* **1** : intercourse between a male and a female in which the penis is inserted into the vagina **2** : intercourse between individuals which involves genital contact but in which the penis is not inserted into the vagina

sexually transmitted disease *n* : a disease (as syphilis, gonorrhea, or the genital form of herpes simplex) usu. or often transmitted by direct sexual contact

sexy \ˈsek-sē\ *adj* **sex·i·er; -est** : sexually suggestive or stimulating : EROTIC

SF *abbr* **1** sacrifice fly **2** science fiction

SFC *abbr* sergeant first class

SG *abbr* **1** senior grade **2** sergeant **3** solicitor general **4** surgeon general

sgd *abbr* signed

Sgt *abbr* sergeant

Sgt Maj *abbr* sergeant major

sh *abbr* share

shab·by \ˈshab-ē\ *adj* **shab·bi·er; -est** **1** : dressed in worn clothes **2** : threadbare and faded from wear **3** : MEAN ⟨~ treatment⟩ — **shab·bi·ly** \ˈshab-ə-lē\ *adv* — **shab·bi·ness** \-ē-nəs\ *n*

shack \ˈshak\ *n* : HUT, SHANTY

[1]**shack·le** \ˈshak-əl\ *n* **1** : something (as a manacle or fetter) that confines the legs or arms **2** : a check on free action made as if by fetters **3** : a device for making something fast or secure

[2]**shackle** *vb* **shack·led; shack·ling** \-(ə-)liŋ\ : to fasten with shackles

shad \ˈshad\ *n, pl* **shad** : any of several sea fishes related to the herrings that swim up rivers to spawn and are important food fish

[1]**shade** \ˈshād\ *n* **1** : partial obscurity **2** : space sheltered from the light esp. of the sun **3** : PHANTOM **4** : something that shelters from or intercepts light or heat; *also, pl* : SUNGLASSES **5** : a dark color or a variety of a color **6** : a small difference — **shady** *adj*

[2]**shade** *vb* **shad·ed; shad·ing** **1** : to shelter from light and heat **2** : DARKEN, OBSCURE **3** : to mark with degrees of light or color **4** : to show slight differences esp. in color or meaning

shad·ing \ˈshād-iŋ\ *n* : the color and lines representing darkness or shadow in a drawing or painting

[1]**shad·ow** \ˈshad-ō\ *n* **1** : partial darkness in a space from which light rays are cut off **2** : SHELTER **3** : shade cast upon a surface by something intercepting rays from a light ⟨the ~ of a tree⟩ **4** : PHANTOM **5** : a shaded portion of a picture **6** : a small portion or degree : TRACE ⟨a ~ of doubt⟩ **7** : a source of gloom or unhappiness — **shad·owy** *adj*

[2]**shadow** *vb* **1** : to cast a shadow on **2** : to represent faintly or vaguely **3** : to follow and watch closely : TRAIL

shad·ow·box \ˈshad-ō-ˌbäks\ *vb* : to box with an imaginary opponent esp. for training

[1]**shaft** \ˈshaft\ *n, pl* **shafts** **1** : the long handle of a spear or lance **2** : SPEAR, LANCE **3** *or pl* **shaves** \ˈshāvz\ : POLE; *esp* : one of two poles between which a horse is hitched to

pull a vehicle **4** : something (as a column) long and slender **5** : a bar to support a rotating piece or to transmit power by rotation **6** : an inclined opening in the ground (as for finding or mining ore) **7** : a vertical opening (as for an elevator) through the floors of a building

[2]**shaft** *vb* : to fit with a shaft

shag \ˈshag\ *n* **1** : a shaggy tangled mat (as of wool) **2** : tobacco cut into fine shreds

shag·gy \ˈshag-ē\ *adj* **shag·gi·er; -est 1** : rough with or as if with long hair or wool **2** : tangled or rough in surface

shah \ˈshä, ˈshȯ\ *n, often cap* : a sovereign of Iran

Shak *abbr* Shakespeare

[1]**shake** \ˈshāk\ *vb* **shook** \ˈshu̇k\; **shak·en** \ˈshā-kən\; **shak·ing 1** : to move or cause to move jerkily or irregularly **2** : BRANDISH, WAVE ⟨*shaking* his fist⟩ **3** : to disturb emotionally ⟨*shaken* by her death⟩ **4** : WEAKEN ⟨*shook* his faith⟩ **5** : to bring or come into a certain position, condition, or arrangement by or as if by moving jerkily **6** : to clasp (hands) in greeting or as a sign of goodwill or agreement **syn** tremble, quake, quaver, shiver, quiver — **shak·able** \ˈshā-kə-bəl\ *adj*

[2]**shake** *n* **1** : the act or a result of shaking **2** : DEAL, TREATMENT ⟨a fair ~⟩

shake·down \ˈshāk-ˌdau̇n\ *n* **1** : an improvised bed **2** : EXTORTION **3** : a process or period of adjustment **4** : a test (as of a new ship or airplane) under operating conditions

shake down \(ˈ)shāk-ˈdau̇n\ *vb* **1** : to take up temporary quarters **2** : to occupy a makeshift bed **3** : to become accustomed esp. to new surroundings or duties **4** : to settle down **5** : to give a shakedown test to **6** : to obtain money from in a dishonest or illegal manner **7** : to bring about a reduction of

shak·er \ˈshā-kər\ *n* **1** : one that shakes ⟨pepper ~⟩ **2** *cap* : a member of a religious sect founded in England in 1747

shake–up \ˈshāk-ˌəp\ *n* : an extensive often drastic reorganization

shaky \ˈshā-kē\ *adj* **shak·i·er; -est** : UNSOUND, WEAK — **shak·i·ly** \ˈshā-kə-lē\ *adv* — **shak·i·ness** \-kē-nəs\ *n*

shale \ˈshāl\ *n* : a rock made up of fine layers and formed from clay, mud, or silt

shall \shəl, (ˈ)shal\ *vb, past* **should** \shəd, (ˈ)shu̇d\; *pres sing & pl* **shall** — used as an auxiliary to express a command, what seems inevitable or likely in the future, simple futurity, or determination

shal·lop \ˈshal-əp\ *n* : a light open boat

shal·lot \shə-ˈlät\ *n* [modif. of F *échalote*] **1** : the bulb of a perennial herb that is produced in clusters, resembles an onion, and is used in seasoning; *also* : this herb **2** : GREEN ONION

[1]**shal·low** \ˈshal-ō\ *adj* **1** : not deep **2** : not intellectually profound **syn** superficial, sketchy

[2]**shallow** *n* : a shallow place in a body of water — usu. used in pl.

[1]**sham** \ˈsham\ *n* **1** : something resembling an article of household linen and used in its place as a decoration ⟨a pillow ~⟩ **2** : COUNTERFEIT, IMITATION

[2]**sham** *vb* **shammed; sham·ming** : FEIGN, PRETEND — **sham·mer** *n*

[3]**sham** *adj* : FALSE ⟨~ pearls⟩

sha·man \ˈshäm-ən, ˈshā-mən\ *n* [Russ, fr. Tungusic (a language of Siberia)] : a priest who uses magic to cure the sick, to divine the hidden, and to control events

sham·ble \ˈsham-bəl\ *vb* **sham·bled; sham·bling** \-b(ə-)liŋ\ : to shuffle along — **sham·ble** *n*

sham·bles \ˈsham-bəlz\ *n* [*shamble* (meat market) & obs. E *shamble* (table for exhibition of meat for sale)] **1** : a scene of great slaughter **2** : a scene or state of great destruction or disorder

[1]**shame** \ˈshām\ *n* **1** : a painful sense of having done something wrong, improper, or immodest **2** : DISGRACE, DISHONOR **3** : a cause of feeling shame — **shame·ful** \-fəl\ *adj* — **shame·ful·ly** \-ē\ *adv* — **shame·less** *adj* — **shame·less·ly** *adv*

[2]**shame** *vb* **shamed; sham·ing 1** : DISGRACE **2** : to make ashamed

shame·faced \ˈshām-ˈfāst\ *adj* : ASHAMED, ABASHED — **shame·faced·ly** \-ˈfā-səd-lē, -ˈfāst-lē\ *adv*

[1]**sham·poo** \sham-ˈpü\ *vb* [Hindi *cāpo*, imper. of *cāpnā* to press, shampoo] : to wash (as the hair) with soap and water or with a special preparation; *also* : to clean (as a rug) similarly

[2]**shampoo** *n, pl* **shampoos 1** : the act or process of shampooing **2** : a preparation for use in shampooing

sham·rock \ˈsham-ˌräk\ *n* [IrGael *seamrōg*, dim. of *seamar* clover, honeysuckle] : a plant with three leaflets used as an Irish floral emblem

shang·hai \shaŋ-ˈhī\ *vb* **shang·haied; shang·hai·ing** [*Shanghai*, China] : to force aboard a ship for service as a sailor; *also* : to trick or force into something

Shan·gri–la \ˌshaŋ-gri-ˈlä\ *n* [*Shangri-La*, imaginary land depicted in the novel *Lost Horizon* (1933) by James Hilton] : a remote idyllic hideaway

shank \ˈshaŋk\ *n* **1** : the part of the leg between the knee and ankle in man or a corresponding part of a quadruped **2** : a cut of meat from the leg **3** : the narrow part of the sole of a shoe beneath the instep **4** : the part of a tool or instrument (as a key or anchor) connecting the functioning part with a part by which it is held or moved

shan·tung \ˈshan-ˈtəŋ\ *n* : a fabric in plain weave having a slightly irregular surface

shan·ty \ˈshant-ē\ *n, pl* **shanties** : a small roughly built shelter or dwelling

[1]**shape** \ˈshāp\ *vb* **shaped; shap·ing 1** : to form esp. in a particular shape **2** : DESIGN **3** : ADAPT, ADJUST **4** : REGULATE **syn** make, fashion, fabricate, manufacture, frame, mold

[2]**shape** *n* **1** : APPEARANCE **2** : surface configuration : FORM **3** : bodily contour apart from the head and face : FIGURE **4** : PHANTOM **5** : CONDITION

shape·less \ˈshāp-ləs\ *adj* **1** : having no definite shape **2** : not shapely — **shape·less·ly** *adv* — **shape·less·ness** *n*

shape·ly \ˈshāp-lē\ *adj* **shape·li·er; -est** : having a pleasing shape — **shape·li·ness** *n*

shard \ˈshärd\ *also* **sherd** \ˈshərd\ *n* : a broken piece : FRAGMENT

[1]**share** \ˈsheər\ *n* **1** : a portion belonging to one person or group **2** : any of the equal interests into which the capital stock of a corporation is divided

[2]**share** *vb* **shared; shar·ing 1** : APPORTION **2** : to use or enjoy with others **3** : PARTICIPATE — **shar·er** *n*

[3]**share** *n* : PLOWSHARE

share·crop·per \-ˌkräp-ər\ *n* : a farmer who works another's land in return for a share of the crop — **share·crop** *vb*

share·hold·er \-ˌhōl-dər\ *n* : STOCKHOLDER

[1]**shark** \ˈshärk\ *n* : any of various active, predaceous, and mostly large marine fishes with skeletons of cartilage

[2]**shark** *n* : a greedy crafty person

shark·skin \-ˌskin\ *n* **1** : the hide of a shark or leather made from it **2** : a fabric (as of cotton or rayon) woven from strands of many fine threads and having a sleek appearance and silky feel

[1]**sharp** \ˈshärp\ *adj* **1** : having a thin cutting edge or fine point : not dull or blunt **2** : COLD, NIPPING ⟨a ~ wind⟩ **3** : keen in intellect, perception, or attention **4** : BRISK, ENERGETIC **5** : IRRITABLE ⟨a ~ temper⟩ **6** : causing intense distress ⟨a ~ pain⟩ **7** : HARSH, CUTTING ⟨~ words⟩ **8** : affecting the senses as if cutting or piercing ⟨a ~ sound⟩ ⟨a ~ smell⟩ **9** : not smooth or rounded ⟨~ fea-

tures⟩ **10** : involving an abrupt or extreme change ⟨a ~ turn⟩ **11** : CLEAR, DISTINCT ⟨mountains in ~ relief⟩; *also* : easy to perceive ⟨a ~ contrast⟩ **12** : higher than the true pitch; *also* : raised by a half step **13** : STYLISH ⟨a ~ dresser⟩ **syn** keen, acute, quick-witted, penetrative — **sharp·ly** *adv* — **sharp·ness** *n*

[2]**sharp** *adv* **1** : in a sharp manner **2** : EXACTLY, PRECISELY ⟨left at 8 ~⟩

[3]**sharp** *n* **1** : a sharp edge or point **2** : a character ♯ indicating a note a half step higher than the note named **3** : SHARPER

[4]**sharp** *vb* : to raise in pitch by a half step

sharp·en \ˈshär-pən\ *vb* **sharp·ened; sharp·en·ing** \ˈshärp-(ə-)niŋ\ : to make or become sharp — **sharp·en·er** \ˈshärp-(ə-)nər\ *n*

sharp·er \ˈshär-pər\ *n* : SWINDLER; *esp* : a cheating gambler

sharp·ie *or* **sharpy** \ˈshär-pē\ *n, pl* **sharp·ies** **1** : SHARPER **2** : a person who is exceptionally keen or alert

sharp·shoot·er \ˈshärp-ˌshüt-ər\ *n* : a good marksman — **sharp·shoot·ing** \-iŋ\ *n*

shat·ter \ˈshat-ər\ *vb* : to dash or burst into fragments — **shat·ter·proof** \ˌshat-ər-ˈprüf\ *adj*

[1]**shave** \ˈshāv\ *vb* **shaved; shaved** *or* **shav·en** \ˈshā-vən\; **shav·ing** **1** : to slice in thin pieces **2** : to make bare or smooth by cutting the hair from **3** : to cut or pare off by the sliding movement of a razor **4** : to skim along or near the surface of

[2]**shave** *n* **1** : any of various tools for cutting thin slices **2** : an act or process of shaving

shav·er \ˈshā-vər\ *n* : an electric-powered razor

shaves *pl of* SHAFT

shav·ing \ˈshā-viŋ\ *n* **1** : the act of one that shaves **2** : something shaved off

shawl \ˈshȯl\ *n* : a square or oblong piece of fabric used esp. by women as a loose covering for the head or shoulders

Shaw·nee \shȯ-ˈnē, shä-\ *n, pl* **Shawnee** *or* **Shawnees** : a member of an American Indian people orig. of the central Ohio valley; *also* : their language

she \(ˈ)shē\ *pron* : that female one ⟨who is ~⟩; *also* : that one regarded as feminine ⟨~'s a fine ship⟩

sheaf \ˈshēf\ *n, pl* **sheaves** \ˈshēvz\ **1** : a bundle of stalks and ears of grain **2** : a group of things bound together

[1]**shear** \ˈshiər\ *vb* **sheared; sheared** *or* **shorn** \ˈshōrn\; **shear·ing** **1** : to cut the hair or wool from : CLIP, TRIM **2** : to deprive by or as if by cutting **3** : to cut or break sharply

[2]**shear** *n* **1** : any of various cutting tools that consist of two blades fastened together so that the edges slide one by the other — usu. used in pl. **2** *chiefly Brit* : the act, an instance, or the result of shearing **3** : an action or stress caused by applied forces that causes two parts of a body to slide on each other

sheath \ˈshēth\ *n, pl* **sheaths** \ˈshēt͟hz, ˈshēths\ **1** : a case for a blade (as of a knife); *also* : an anatomical covering suggesting such a case **2** : a close-fitting dress usu. worn without a belt

sheathe \ˈshēt͟h\ *also* **sheath** \ˈshēth\ *vb* **sheathed; sheath·ing** **1** : to put into a sheath **2** : to cover with something that guards or protects

sheath·ing \ˈshē-t͟hiŋ, -thiŋ\ *n* : material used to sheathe something; *esp* : the first covering of boards or of waterproof material on the outside wall of a frame house or on a timber roof

sheave \ˈshiv, ˈshēv\ *n* : a grooved wheel or pulley (as on a pulley block)

she·bang \shi-ˈbaŋ\ *n* : CONTRIVANCE, AFFAIR, CONCERN ⟨blew up the whole ~⟩

[1]**shed** \ˈshed\ *vb* **shed; shed·ding** **1** : to cause to flow from a cut or wound ⟨~ blood⟩ **2** : to pour down in drops ⟨~ tears⟩ **3** : to give out (as light) : DIFFUSE **4** : to throw off (as a natural covering) : DISCARD

[2]**shed** *n* : a slight structure built for shelter or storage

sheen \ˈshēn\ *n* : a subdued luster

sheep \ˈshēp\ *n, pl* **sheep** **1** : any of a genus of cud-chewing mammals that are stockier than the related goats and lack a beard in the male; *esp* : one raised for meat or for its wool or skin **2** : a timid or defenseless person **3** : SHEEPSKIN

sheep dog *n* : a dog used to tend, drive, or guard sheep

sheep·fold \ˈshēp-ˌfōld\ *n* : a pen or shelter for sheep

sheep·herd·er \ˈshēp-ˌhərd-ər\ *n* : a worker in charge of sheep esp. on open range — **sheep·herd·ing** \-iŋ\ *n*

sheep·ish \ˈshē-pish\ *adj* : BASHFUL, TIMID; *esp* : embarrassed by consciousness of a fault — **sheep·ish·ly** *adv*

sheep·skin \ˈshēp-ˌskin\ *n* **1** : the hide of a sheep or leather prepared from it; *also* : PARCHMENT **2** : DIPLOMA

[1]**sheer** \ˈshiər\ *adj* **1** : very thin or transparent **2** : UNQUALIFIED ⟨~ folly⟩ **3** : very steep **syn** pure, simple, absolute, unadulterated, unmitigated — **sheer** *adv*

[2]**sheer** *vb* : to turn from a course

[1]**sheet** \ˈshēt\ *n* **1** : a broad piece of plain cloth (as for a bed) **2** : a single piece of paper **3** : a broad flat surface ⟨a ~ of water⟩ **4** : something broad and long and relatively thin

[2]**sheet** *n* **1** : a rope that regulates the angle at which a sail is set to catch the wind **2** *pl* : spaces at either end of an open boat

sheet·ing \ˈshēt-iŋ\ *n* : material in the form of sheets or suitable for forming into sheets

sheikh *or* **sheik** \ˈshēk, ˈshāk\ *n* : an Arab chief — **sheikh·dom** *or* **sheik·dom** \-dəm\ *n*

shek·el \ˈshek-əl\ *n* — see MONEY table

shelf \ˈshelf\ *n, pl* **shelves** \ˈshelvz\ **1** : a thin flat usu. long and narrow structure fastened horizontally (as on a wall) above the floor to hold things **2** : something (as a sandbar) that suggests a shelf

shelf life *n* : the period of storage time during which a material will remain useful

[1]**shell** \ˈshel\ *n* **1** : a hard or tough outer covering of an animal (as a beetle, turtle, or mollusk) or of an egg or a seed or fruit (as a nut); *also* : something that resembles a shell ⟨a pastry ~⟩ **2** : a light narrow racing boat propelled by oarsmen **3** : a case holding an explosive and designed to be fired from a cannon; *also* : a case holding the charge of powder and shot or bullet for small arms **4** : a plain usu. sleeveless blouse or sweater — **shelled** \ˈsheld\ *adj* — **shelly** \ˈshel-ē\ *adj*

[2]**shell** *vb* **1** : to remove from a shell or husk **2** : BOMBARD — **shell·er** *n*

[1]**shel·lac** \shə-ˈlak\ *n* **1** : a purified lac used esp. in varnishes **2** : lac dissolved in alcohol and used as a varnish

[2]**shellac** *vb* **shel·lacked; shel·lack·ing** **1** : to coat or treat with shellac **2** : to defeat decisively

shel·lack·ing \shə-ˈlak-iŋ\ *n* : a sound drubbing

shell bean *n* : a bean grown esp. for its edible seeds; *also* : its edible seed

shell·fish \-ˌfish\ *n* : a water animal (as an oyster or lobster) with a shell

shell out *vb* : PAY

shell shock *n* : any of various nervous disorders appearing in soldiers exposed to modern warfare

[1]**shel·ter** \ˈshel-tər\ *n* : something that gives protection : REFUGE

[2]**shelter** *vb* **shel·tered; shel·ter·ing** \-t(ə-)riŋ\ : to give protection or refuge to **syn** harbor, lodge, house

shelve \ˈshelv\ *vb* **shelved; shelv·ing** **1** : to slope gradually **2** : to store on shelves **3** : to dismiss from service or use **4** : to put aside : DEFER ⟨~ a proposal⟩

shelv·ing \ˈshel-viŋ\ *n* : material for shelves

she·nan·i·gan \shə-ˈnan-i-gən\ *n* **1** : an underhand trick **2** : questionable conduct — usu. used in pl. **3** : high-spirited or michievous activity — usu. used in pl.

[1]**shep·herd** \ˈshep-ərd\ *n* : one who tends sheep

[2]**shepherd** *vb* : to tend as or in the manner of a shepherd

shep·herd·ess \ˈshep-ərd-əs\ *n* : a woman who tends sheep

sher·bet \ˈshər-bət\ *n* [Turk *serbet*, fr. Per *sharbat*, fr. Ar *sharbah* drink] **1** : a drink of sweetened diluted fruit juice **2** *or* **sher·bert** \-bərt\ : a frozen dessert of fruit juices, sugar, milk or water, and egg whites or gelatin

sherd *var of* SHARD

sher·iff \ˈsher-əf\ *n* [ME *shirreve*, fr. OE *scīrgerēfa*, lit., shire reeve (local official)] : a county officer charged with the execution of the law and the preservation of order

sher·ry \ˈsher-ē\ *n, pl* **sherries** [alter. of earlier *sherris* (taken as pl.), fr. *Xeres* (now *Jerez*), Spain] : a fortified wine with a nutty flavor

Shet·land pony \ˌshet-lən(d)-\ *n* : any of a breed of small stocky shaggy hardy ponies

shew \ˈshō\ *Brit var of* SHOW

shi·at·su *also* **shi·at·zu** \shē-ˈät-sü\ *n* [short for Jp *Shiatsuryōhō*] : a finger massage of those bodily areas used in acupuncture

shib·bo·leth \ˈshib-ə-ləth\ *n* [Heb *shibbōleth* stream; fr. the use of this word as a test to distinguish the men of Gilead from members of the tribe of Ephraim, who pronounced it *sibbōleth* (Judges 12:5, 6)] **1** : a pet phrase **2** : language that is a criterion for distinguishing members of a group

shied *past and past part of* SHY

[1]**shield** \ˈshēld\ *n* **1** : a broad piece of defensive armor carried on the arm **2** : something that protects or hides

[2]**shield** *vb* : to protect or hide with a shield **syn** protect, guard, safeguard

shier *comparative of* SHY

shiest *superlative of* SHY

[1]**shift** \ˈshift\ *vb* **1** : EXCHANGE, REPLACE **2** : to change place, position, or direction : MOVE; *also* : to change the arrangement of gears transmitting power in an automobile **3** : GET BY, MANAGE **syn** remove, ship, transfer

[2]**shift** *n* **1** : SCHEME, TRICK **2** : a woman's slip or loose-fitting dress **3** : a group working together alternating with other groups **4** : TRANSFER **5** : GEARSHIFT

shift·less \ˈshif(t)-ləs\ *adj* : LAZY, INEFFICIENT — **shift·less·ness** *n*

shifty \ˈshif-tē\ *adj* **shift·i·er; -est 1** : TRICKY; *also* : ELUSIVE **2** : indicative of a tricky nature ⟨~ eyes⟩

Shih Tzu \ˈshēd-ˈzü\ *n* : a small short-legged dog of an ancient Chinese breed that has a short muzzle and a long dense coat

shi·lingi \shil-ˈiŋ-ē\ *n, pl* **shi·lingi** : the shilling of Tanzania

shill \ˈshil\ *n* : one who acts as a decoy (as for a cheater) — **shill** *vb*

shil·le·lagh *also* **shil·la·lah** \shə-ˈlā-lē\ *n* [*Shillelagh*, town in Ireland famed for its oaks] : CUDGEL, CLUB

shil·ling \ˈshil-iŋ\ *n* — see MONEY TABLE

shilly–shally \ˈshil-ē-ˌshal-ē\ *vb* **shilly–shall·ied; shilly–shally·ing 1** : to show hesitation or lack of decisiveness **2** : to waste time

shim \ˈshim\ *n* : a thin often tapered piece of wood, metal, or stone used (as in leveling something) to fill in

shim·mer \ˈshim-ər\ *vb* **shim·mered; shim·mer·ing** \-(ə-)riŋ\ : to shine waveringly or tremulously : GLIMMER **syn** flash, gleam, glint, sparkle, glitter — **shimmer** *n* — **shim·mery** *adj*

shim·my \ˈshim-ē\ *n, pl* **shimmies** : an abnormal vibration esp. in the front wheels of a motor vehicle — **shimmy** *vb*

[1]**shin** \ˈshin\ *n* : the front part of the leg below the knee

[2]**shin** *vb* **shinned; shin·ning** : to climb (as a pole) by gripping alternately with arms or hands and legs

shin·bone \ˈshin-ˈbōn, -ˌbōn\ *n* : TIBIA

[1]**shine** \ˈshīn\ *vb* **shone** \ˈshōn\ *or* **shined; shin·ing 1** : to give light **2** : GLEAM, GLITTER **3** : to be eminent, conspicuous, or distinguished ⟨gave her a chance to ~⟩ **4** : to cause to shed light **5** : POLISH

[2]**shine** *n* **1** : BRIGHTNESS, RADIANCE **2** : LUSTER, BRILLIANCE **3** : fair weather : SUNSHINE ⟨rain or ~⟩ **4** : LIKING, FANCY ⟨took a ~ to them⟩ **5** : a polish given to shoes

shin·er \ˈshī-nər\ *n* **1** : a small silvery fish; *esp* : any of numerous small freshwater American fishes related to the carp **2** : a bruised eye

[1]**shin·gle** \ˈshiŋ-gəl\ *n* **1** : a small thin piece of building material (as wood or an asbestos composition) used in overlapping rows for covering a roof or outside wall **2** : a small sign

[2]**shingle** *vb* **shin·gled; shin·gling** \-g(ə-)liŋ\ : to cover with shingles

[3]**shingle** *n* : a beach strewn with gravel; *also* : coarse gravel (as on a beach)

shin·gles \ˈshiŋ-gəlz\ *n pl* : acute inflammation of the spinal and cranial nerves caused by the chicken pox virus and associated with eruptions and pain along the course of the affected nerves

shin·ny \ˈshin-ē\ *vb* **shin·nied; shin·ny·ing** : SHIN

Shin·to \ˈshin-ˌtō\ *n* : the indigenous religion of Japan consisting esp. in reverence of the spirits of natural forces and imperial ancestors — **Shin·to·ism** *n* — **Shin·to·ist** *n or adj*

shiny \ˈshī-nē\ *adj* **shin·i·er; -est** : BRIGHT, RADIANT; *also* : POLISHED

[1]**ship** \ˈship\ *n* **1** : a large oceangoing boat **2** : a ship's officers and crew **3** : AIRSHIP, AIRCRAFT, SPACECRAFT

[2]**ship** *vb* **shipped; ship·ping 1** : to put or receive on board a ship for transportation **2** : to have transported by a carrier **3** : to take or draw into a boat ⟨~ oars⟩ ⟨~ water⟩ **4** : to engage to serve on a ship — **ship·per** *n*

-ship \ˌship\ *n suffix* **1** : state : condition : quality ⟨friend*ship*⟩ **2** : office : dignity : profession ⟨lord*ship*⟩ ⟨clerk*ship*⟩ **3** : art : skill ⟨horseman*ship*⟩ **4** : something showing, exhibiting, or embodying a quality or state ⟨town*ship*⟩ **5** : one entitled to a (specified) rank, title, or appellation ⟨his Lord*ship*⟩ **6** : the body of persons engaged in a specified activity ⟨reader*ship*⟩

ship·board \ˈship-ˌbōrd\ *n* : SHIP

ship·build·er \ˈship-ˌbil-dər\ *n* : one who designs or builds ships

ship·fit·ter \ˈship-ˌfit-ər\ *n* **1** : one who constructs ships **2** : a naval enlisted man who works as a plumber

ship·mate \-ˌmāt\ *n* : a fellow sailor

ship·ment \-mənt\ *n* : the process of shipping; *also* : the goods shipped

ship·ping \ˈship-iŋ\ *n* **1** : SHIPS; *esp* : ships in one port or belonging to one country **2** : transportation of goods

ship·shape \ˈship-ˈshāp\ *adj* : TRIM, TIDY

ship·worm \-ˌwərm\ *n* : any of various wormlike marine clams that burrow in wood and damage wooden ships and wharves

[1]**ship·wreck** \-ˌrek\ *n* **1** : a wrecked ship **2** : destruction or loss of a ship **3** : total loss or failure : RUIN ⟨save the business from ~⟩

[2]**shipwreck** *vb* : to cause or meet disaster at sea through destruction or foundering

ship·wright \ˈship-ˌrīt\ *n* : a carpenter skilled in ship construction and repair

ship·yard \-ˌyärd\ *n* : a place where ships are built or repaired

shire \ˈshī(ə)r, *in place-name compounds* ˌshiər, shər\ *n* : a county in Great Britain

shirk \ˈshərk\ *vb* : to avoid performing (duty or work) — **shirk·er** *n*

shirr \ˈshər\ *vb* **1** : to make shirring in **2** : to bake (eggs removed from the shell) until set

shirr·ing \ˈshər-iŋ\ *n* : a decorative gathering in cloth made by drawing up parallel lines of stitches

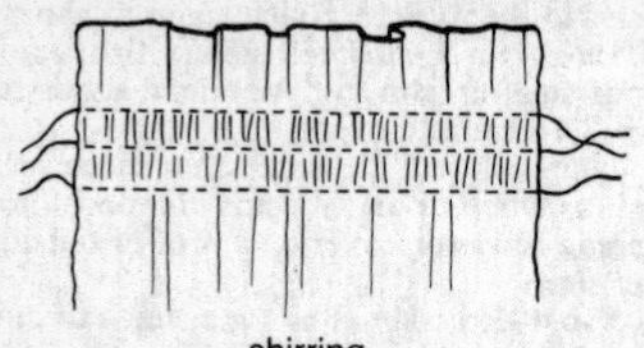

shirring

shirt \ˈshərt\ *n* **1** : a loose cloth garment usu. having a collar, sleeves, a front opening, and a tail long enough to be tucked inside trousers or a skirt **2** : UNDERSHIRT — **shirt·less** *adj*
shirt·ing \-iŋ\ *n* : cloth suitable for making shirts
shish ke·bab \ˈshish-kə-ˌbäb\ *n* : kabob cooked on skewers
shiv \ˈshiv\ *n, slang* : KNIFE
[1]**shiv·er** \ˈshiv-ər\ *vb* **shiv·ered; shiv·er·ing** \-(ə-)riŋ\ : TREMBLE, QUIVER **syn** shudder, quaver, shake, quake
[2]**shiver** *n* : an instance of shivering — **shiv·ery** *adj*
[1]**shoal** \ˈshōl\ *n* **1** : a shallow place in a sea, lake, or river **2** : a sandbank or bar creating a shallow
[2]**shoal** *n* : a large group (as of fish)
shoat \ˈshōt\ *n* : a weaned young pig
[1]**shock** \ˈshäk\ *n* : a pile of sheaves of grain set up in the field
[2]**shock** *n* [MF *choc,* fr. *choquer* to strike against] **1** : a sharp impact or violent shake or jar **2** : a sudden violent mental or emotional disturbance **3** : the effect of a charge of electricity passing through the body **4** : a state of bodily collapse caused esp. by crushing wounds, blood loss, or burns **5** : an attack of apoplexy or heart disease **6** : SHOCK ABSORBER — **shock·proof** \-ˈprüf\ *adj*
[3]**shock** *vb* **1** : to strike with surprise, horror, or disgust **2** : to subject to the action of an electrical discharge
[4]**shock** *n* : a thick bushy mass (as of hair)
shock absorber *n* : any of several devices for absorbing the energy of sudden shocks in machinery
shock·er \ˈshäk-ər\ *n* : one that shocks; *esp* : a sensational work of fiction or drama
shock·ing \-iŋ\ *adj* : extremely startling and offensive — **shock·ing·ly** *adv*
shock therapy *n* : the treatment of mental disorder by induction of coma or convulsion through the use of drugs or electricity
[1]**shod·dy** \ˈshäd-ē\ *n* **1** : wool reclaimed from old rags; *also* : a fabric made from it **2** : inferior or imitation material
[2]**shoddy** *adj* **shod·di·er; -est** **1** : made of shoddy **2** : cheaply imitative : INFERIOR, SHAM — **shod·di·ly** \ˈshäd-ᵊl-ē\ *adv* — **shod·di·ness** \-ē-nəs\ *n*
[1]**shoe** \ˈshü\ *n* **1** : a covering for the human foot **2** : HORSESHOE **3** : the part of a brake that presses on the wheel **4** : the casing of an automobile tire
[2]**shoe** *vb* **shod** \ˈshäd\ *also* **shoed** \ˈshüd\; **shoe·ing** \ˈshü-iŋ\ : to put a shoe or shoes on
shoe·lace \-ˌlās\ *n* : a lace or string for fastening a shoe
shoe·mak·er \-ˌmā-kər\ *n* : one who makes or repairs shoes
shoe·string \ˈshü-ˌstriŋ\ *n* **1** : SHOELACE **2** : a small sum of money
shone *past and past part of* SHINE
shook *past of* SHAKE
shook–up \(ˈ)shu̇k-ˈəp\ *adj* : nervously upset : AGITATED
[1]**shoot** \ˈshüt\ *vb* **shot** \ˈshät\; **shoot·ing** **1** : to drive (as an arrow or bullet) forward quickly or forcibly **2** : to hit, kill, or wound with a missile **3** : to cause a missile to be driven forth or forth from ⟨~ a gun⟩ **4** : to send forth (as a ray of light) **5** : to thrust forward or out **6** : to pass rapidly along ⟨~ the rapids⟩ **7** : PHOTOGRAPH, FILM **8** : to move swiftly : DART **9** : to grow by or as if by sending out shoots; *also* : MATURE, DEVELOP — **shoot·er** *n*
[2]**shoot** *n* **1** : the aerial part of a plant; *also* : a plant part (as a branch) developed from one bud **2** : an act of shooting (as with a bow or a firearm) **3** : a shooting match
shooting iron *n* : FIREARM
shooting star *n* : METEOR 2
shoot up *vb* : to inject a narcotic into a vein
[1]**shop** \ˈshäp\ *n* [ME *shoppe,* fr. OE *sceoppa* booth] **1** : a place where things are made or worked on : FACTORY, MILL **2** : a retail store ⟨dress ~⟩
[2]**shop** *vb* **shopped; shop·ping** : to visit stores for purchasing or examining goods — **shop·per** *n*
shop·keep·er \ˈshäp-ˌkē-pər\ *n* : a retail merchant
shop·lift \-ˌlift\ *vb* : to steal goods on display from a store — **shop·lift·er** \-ˌlif-tər\ *n*
shop·worn \-ˌwōrn\ *adj* : soiled or frayed from much handling in a store
[1]**shore** \ˈshōr\ *n* : land along the edge of a body of water — **shore·less** *adj*
[2]**shore** *vb* **shored; shor·ing** : to give support to : BRACE
[3]**shore** *n* : [1]PROP
shore·bird \-ˌbərd\ *n* : any of a large group of birds (as the plovers and sandpipers) mostly found along the seashore
shore patrol *n* : a branch of a navy that exercises guard and police functions
shor·ing \ˈshōr-iŋ\ *n* : the act of supporting with or as if with a prop
shorn *past part of* SHEAR
[1]**short** \ˈshȯrt\ *adj* **1** : not long or tall **2** : not great in distance **3** : brief in time **4** : not coming up to standard or to an expected amount **5** : CURT, ABRUPT **6** : insufficiently supplied **7** : made with shortening : FLAKY **8** : consisting of or relating to a sale of securities or commodities that the seller does not possess or has not contracted for at the time of the sale ⟨~ sale⟩ — **short·ness** *n*
[2]**short** *adv* **1** : ABRUPTLY, CURTLY **2** : at some point before a goal aimed at
[3]**short** *n* **1** : something shorter than normal or standard **2** *pl* : drawers or trousers of less than knee length **3** : SHORT CIRCUIT
[4]**short** *vb* : SHORT-CIRCUIT
short·age \ˈshȯrt-ij\ *n* : LACK, DEFICIT
short·cake \ˈshȯrt-ˌkāk\ *n* : a dessert consisting of short biscuit spread with sweetened fruit
short·change \-ˈchānj\ *vb* : to cheat esp. by giving less than the correct amount of change
short circuit *n* : a connection made between points in an electric circuit between which current does not normally flow — **short–circuit** *vb*
short·com·ing \ˈshȯrt-ˌkəm-iŋ\ *n* : FAILING, DEFECT
short·cut \-ˌkət\ *n* **1** : a route more direct than that usu. taken **2** : a quicker way of doing something
short·en \ˈshȯrt-ᵊn\ *vb* **short·ened, short·en·ing** \ˈshȯrt-(ᵊ-)niŋ\ : to make or become short **syn** curtail, abbreviate, abridge, retrench
short·en·ing \ˈshȯrt-(ᵊ-)niŋ\ *n* : a substance (as lard or butter) that makes pastry tender and flaky
short·hand \ˈshȯrt-ˌhand\ *n* : a method of writing rapidly by using symbols and abbreviations for letters, words, or phrases : STENOGRAPHY
short·hand·ed \-ˈhan-dəd\ *adj* : short of the needed number of people
short·horn \-ˌhȯrn\ *n, often cap* : any of a breed of mostly red cattle of English origin
short hundredweight *n* — see WEIGHT table
short–lived \ˈshȯrt-ˈlīvd, -ˌlivd\ *adj* : of short life or duration
short·ly \ˈshȯrt-lē\ *adv* **1** : in a few words **2** : in a short time : SOON

short order *n* : an order for food that can be quickly cooked
short shrift *n* **1** : a brief respite from death **2** : little consideration
short·sight·ed \ˈshȯrt-ˈsīt-əd\ *adj* **1** : NEARSIGHTED **2** : lacking foresight — **short·sight·ed·ness** *n*
short·stop \-ˌstäp\ *n* : a baseball player defending the area between second and third base
short story *n* : a short invented prose narrative usu. dealing with a few characters and aiming at unity of effect
short–tem·pered \ˈshȯrt-ˈtem-pərd\ *adj* : having a quick temper
short–term \-ˈtərm\ *adj* **1** : occurring over or involving a relatively short period of time **2** : of or relating to a financial transaction based on a term usu. of less than a year
short ton *n* — see WEIGHT table
short·wave \ˈshȯrt-ˈwāv\ *n* : a radio wave with a wavelength between 10 and 100 meters
Sho·sho·ne *or* **Sho·sho·ni** \shə-ˈshō-nē\ *n, pl* **Shoshones** *or* **Shoshoni** : a member of an American Indian people orig. ranging through California, Colorado, Idaho, Nevada, Utah, and Wyoming
¹shot \ˈshät\ *n* **1** : an act of shooting **2** : a stroke or throw in some games **3** : something that is shot : MISSILE, PROJECTILE; *esp* : small pellets forming a charge for a shotgun **4** : a metal sphere that is thrown for distance in the shot put **5** : RANGE, REACH **6** : MARKSMAN **7** : a single photographic exposure **8** : a single sequence of a motion picture or a television program made by one camera **9** : an injection (as of medicine) into the body **10** : a portion (as of liquor or medicine) taken at one time
²shot *past and past part of* SHOOT
shot·gun \ˈshät-ˈgən\ *n* : a gun with a smooth bore used to fire small shot at short range
shot put *n* : a field event consisting in putting the shot for distance
should \shəd, (ˈ)shu̇d\ *past of* SHALL — used as an auxiliary to express condition, obligation or propriety, probability, or futurity from a point of view in the past
¹shoul·der \ˈshōl-dər\ *n* **1** : the part of the body of a person or animal where the arm or foreleg joins the body **2** : a projecting part resembling a human shoulder
²shoulder *vb* **shoul·dered; shoul·der·ing** \-d(ə-)riŋ\ **1** : to push or thrust with the shoulder **2** : to take upon the shoulder **3** : to take the responsibility of
shoulder belt *n* : an automobile safety belt worn across the torso and over the shoulder
shoulder blade *n* : the flat triangular bone at the back of the shoulder
shout \ˈshau̇t\ *vb* : to utter a sudden loud cry — **shout** *n*
shove \ˈshəv\ *vb* **shoved; shov·ing** : to push along, aside, or away — **shove** *n*
¹shov·el \ˈshəv-əl\ *n* **1** : a broad long-handled scoop used to lift and throw loose material **2** : the amount of something held by a shovel
²shovel *vb* **-eled** *or* **-elled; -el·ing** *or* **-el·ling** \-(ə-)liŋ\ **1** : to take up and throw with a shovel **2** : to dig or clean out with a shovel
¹show \ˈshō\ *vb* **showed** \ˈshōd\; **shown** \ˈshōn\ *or* **showed; show·ing** [ME *shewen, showen,* fr. OE *scēawian* to look, look at, see] **1** : to cause or permit to be seen : EXHIBIT ⟨~ anger⟩ **2** : CONFER, BESTOW ⟨~ mercy⟩ **3** : REVEAL, DISCLOSE ⟨~*ed* courage in battle⟩ **4** : INSTRUCT ⟨~ me how⟩ **5** : PROVE ⟨~*s* he was guilty⟩ **6** : APPEAR **7** : to be noticeable **8** : to be third in a horse race
²show *n* **1** : a demonstrative display **2** : outward appearance ⟨a ~ of resistance⟩ **3** : SPECTACLE **4** : a theatrical presentation **5** : a radio or television program **6** : third place in a horse race
¹show·case \ˈshō-ˌkās\ *n* : a cabinet for displaying items (as in a store)
²showcase *vb* **show·cased; show·cas·ing** : EXHIBIT
show·down \ˈshō-ˌdau̇n\ *n* : the final settlement of a contested issue; *also* : the test of strength by which a contested issue is resolved
¹show·er \ˈshau̇(-ə)r\ *n* **1** : a brief fall of rain **2** : a bath in which water is showered on the person **3** : a party given by friends who bring gifts — **show·ery** *adj*
²shower *vb* **1** : to fall in a shower **2** : to bathe in a shower
show·man \ˈshō-mən\ *n* : one having a gift for dramatization and visual effectiveness — **show·man·ship** *n*
show–off \ˈshō-ˌȯf\ *n* : one that seeks to attract attention by conspicuous behavior
show off \(ˈ)shō-ˈȯf\ *vb* **1** : to display proudly **2** : to act as a show-off
show·piece \ˈshō-ˌpēs\ *n* : an outstanding example used for exhibition
show·place \-ˌplās\ *n* : an estate or building that is a showpiece
show up *vb* : ARRIVE
showy \ˈshō-ē\ *adj* **show·i·er; -est** : superficially impressive or striking — **show·i·ly** \ˈshō-ə-lē\ *adv* — **show·i·ness** \-ē-nəs\ *n*
shpt *abbr* shipment
shrap·nel \ˈshrap-nᵊl\ *n, pl* **shrapnel** [Henry *Shrapnel* †1842 E artillery officer] **1** : a case filled with shot and having a bursting charge which explodes it in flight **2** : bomb, mine, or shell fragments
¹shred \ˈshred\ *n* : a narrow strip cut or torn off : a small fragment
²shred *vb* **shred·ded; shred·ding** : to cut or tear into shreds
shrew \ˈshrü\ *n* **1** : any of numerous very small mammals with velvety fur that are related to the moles **2** : a scolding woman
shrewd \ˈshrüd\ *adj* : KEEN, ASTUTE — **shrewd·ly** *adv* — **shrewd·ness** *n*
shrew·ish \ˈshrü-ish\ *adj* : having an irritable disposition : ILL-TEMPERED
shriek \ˈshrēk\ *n* : a shrill cry : SCREAM, YELL — **shriek** *vb*
shrift \ˈshrift\ *n, archaic* : the act of shriving
shrike \ˈshrīk\ *n* : a grayish or brownish bird that often impales its usu. insect prey upon thorns before devouring it
¹shrill \ˈshril\ *vb* : to make a high-pitched piercing sound
²shrill *adj* : high-pitched : PIERCING ⟨~ whistle⟩ — **shril·ly** \ˈshril-lē\ *adv*
shrimp \ˈshrimp\ *n, pl* **shrimps** *or* **shrimp** **1** : any of various small marine crustaceans related to the lobsters **2** : a small or puny person
shrine \ˈshrīn\ *n* [ME, receptacle for the relics of a saint, fr. OE *scrīn,* fr. L *scrinium* case, chest] **1** : the tomb of a saint; *also* : a place where devotion is paid to a saint or deity **2** : a place or object hallowed by its associations
¹shrink \ˈshriŋk\ *vb* **shrank** \ˈshraŋk\ *also* **shrunk** \ˈshrəŋk\; **shrunk** *or* **shrunk·en** \ˈshrəŋ-kən\ **1** : to draw back or away **2** : to become smaller or more compact **3** : to lessen in value **syn** contract, constrict, compress, condense — **shrink·able** *adj*
²shrink *n* : PSYCHIATRIST
shrink·age \ˈshriŋ-kij\ *n* **1** : the act of shrinking **2** : a decrease in value **3** : the amount by which something contracts or lessens in extent
shrive \ˈshrīv\ *vb* **shrived** *or* **shrove** \ˈshrōv\; **shriv·en** \ˈshriv-ən\ *or* **shrived** : to minister the sacrament of penance to
shriv·el \ˈshriv-əl\ *vb* **-eled** *or* **-elled; -el·ing** *or* **-el·ling** \-(ə-)liŋ\ : to shrink and draw together into wrinkles : wither up
¹shroud \ˈshrau̇d\ *n* **1** : something that covers or screens

---

2 : a cloth placed over a dead body 3 : one of the ropes leading usu. in pairs from the masthead of a ship to the side to support the mast

²**shroud** *vb* : to veil or screen from view

shrub \ˈshrəb\ *n* : a low usu. several-stemmed woody plant — **shrub·by** *adj*

shrub·bery \ˈshrəb-(ə-)rē\ *n, pl* **-ber·ies** : a planting or growth of shrubs

shrug \ˈshrəg\ *vb* **shrugged; shrug·ging** : to hunch (the shoulders) up to express doubt, indifference, or dislike — **shrug** *n*

shrug off *vb* 1 : to brush aside : MINIMIZE 2 : to shake off 3 : to remove (a garment) by wriggling out

sht *abbr* sheet

shtg *abbr* shortage

¹**shuck** \ˈshək\ *n* : SHELL, HUSK

²**shuck** *vb* : to strip of shucks

shud·der \ˈshəd-ər\ *vb* **shud·dered; shud·der·ing** \-(ə-)riŋ\ : TREMBLE, QUAKE — **shudder** *n*

shuf·fle \ˈshəf-əl\ *vb* **shuf·fled; shuf·fling** \-(ə-)liŋ\ 1 : to mix in a disorderly mass 2 : to rearrange the order of (cards in a pack) by mixing two parts of the pack together 3 : to move with a sliding or dragging gait 4 : to shift from place to place 5 : to dance in a slow lagging manner — **shuffle** *n*

shuf·fle·board \ˈshəf-əl-ˌbōrd\ *n* : a game in which players use long-handled cues to shove wooden disks into scoring areas marked on a smooth surface

shun \ˈshən\ *vb* **shunned; shun·ning** : to avoid deliberately or habitually **syn** evade, elude, escape, duck

¹**shunt** \ˈshənt\ *vb* [ME *shunten* to flinch] : to turn off to one side; *esp* : to switch (a train) from one track to another

²**shunt** *n* 1 : a method or device for turning or thrusting aside 2 : a conductor joining two points in an electrical circuit forming a parallel path through which a portion of the current may pass

shut \ˈshət\ *vb* **shut; shut·ting** 1 : CLOSE 2 : to forbid entrance into 3 : to lock up 4 : to fold together ⟨~ a penknife⟩ 5 : to cease or suspend activity ⟨~ down an assembly line⟩

shut·down \-ˌdau̇n\ *n* : a temporary cessation of activity (as in a factory)

shut–in \ˈshət-ˌin\ *n* : an invalid confined to his home, room, or bed

shut·out \ˈshət-ˌau̇t\ *n* : a game or contest in which one side fails to score

shut out \ˌshət-ˈau̇t\ *vb* 1 : EXCLUDE 2 : to prevent (an opponent) from scoring in a game or contest

shut·ter \ˈshət-ər\ *n* 1 : a movable cover for a door or window for privacy or to keep out light or air : BLIND 2 : the part of a camera that opens and closes to expose the film

shut·ter·bug \ˈshət-ər-ˌbəg\ *n* : a photography enthusiast

¹**shut·tle** \ˈshət-ᵊl\ *n* 1 : an instrument used in weaving for passing the horizontal threads between the vertical threads 2 : a vehicle traveling back and forth over a short route ⟨a ~ bus⟩ 3 : SPACE SHUTTLE

²**shuttle** *vb* **shut·tled; shut·tling** \ˈshət-(ᵊ-)liŋ\ : to move back and forth rapidly or frequently

shut·tle·cock \ˈshət-ᵊl-ˌkäk\ *n* : a light feathered object (as of cork or plastic) used in badminton

shut up *vb* : to cease or cause to cease talking

¹**shy** \ˈshī\ *adj* **shi·er** *or* **shy·er** \ˈshī(-ə)r\; **shi·est** *or* **shy·est** \ˈshī-əst\ 1 : easily frightened : TIMID 2 : WARY 3 : BASHFUL 4 : DEFICIENT, LACKING — **shy·ly** *adv* — **shy·ness** *n*

²**shy** *vb* **shied; shy·ing** 1 : to shrink back : RECOIL 2 : to start suddenly aside through fright ⟨the horse *shied*⟩

shy·ster \ˈshī-stər\ *n* : an unscrupulous lawyer or politician

Si *symbol* silicon

Si·a·mese \ˌsī-ə-ˈmēz, -ˈmēs\ *n, pl* **Sia·mese** : THAI — **Siamese** *adj*

Siamese twin *n* [fr. Chang †1874 and Eng †1874 twins born in Siam with bodies united] : one of a pair of twins with bodies joined together at birth

¹**sib·i·lant** \ˈsib-ə-lənt\ *adj* : having, containing, or producing the sound of or a sound resembling that of the *s* or the *sh* in *sash*

²**sibilant** *n* : a sibilant speech sound (as English \s\, \z\, \sh\, \zh\, \ch (=tsh)\, or \j (=dzh)\)

sib·ling \ˈsib-liŋ\ *n* : one of two or more offspring of the same parents

sib·yl \ˈsib-əl\ *n, often cap* : PROPHETESS — **sib·yl·line** \-ə-ˌlīn, -ˌlēn\ *adj*

sic \ˈsik, ˈsēk\ *adv* : intentionally so written — used after a printed word or passage to indicate that it exactly reproduces an original ⟨said he seed [*sic*] it all⟩

sick \ˈsik\ *adj* 1 : not in good health : ILL; *also* : of, relating to, or intended for the sick ⟨~ pay⟩ 2 : NAUSEATED 3 : LANGUISHING, PINING 4 : DISGUSTED 5 : MACABRE, SADISTIC ⟨~ jokes⟩ — **sick·ly** *adj*

sick·bed \ˈsik-ˌbed\ *n* : a bed on which one lies sick

sick·en \ˈsik-ən\ *vb* **sick·ened; sick·en·ing** \-(ə-)niŋ\ : to make or become sick — **sick·en·ing·ly** *adv*

sick·le \ˈsik-əl\ *n* : a cutting tool consisting of a curved metal blade with a short handle

sickle–cell anemia *n* : an inherited anemia in which red blood cells tend to become crescent-shaped and cannot carry oxygen properly and which occurs esp. in blacks

sick·ness \ˈsik-nəs\ *n* 1 : ill health; *also* : a specific disease 2 : NAUSEA

side \ˈsīd\ *n* 1 : a border of an object; *esp* : one of the longer borders as contrasted with an end 2 : an outer surface of an object 3 : the right or left part of the trunk of a body 4 : a place away from a central point or line 5 : a position regarded as opposite to another 6 : a body of contestants — **side** *adj*

side·arm \-ˌärm\ *adj* : made with a sideways sweep of the arm — **sidearm** *adv*

side arm *n* : a weapon worn at the side or in the belt

side·bar \ˈsīd-ˌbär\ *n* : a short news story accompanying a major story and presenting related topics or additional details

side·board \-ˌbōrd\ *n* : a piece of dining-room furniture for holding articles of table service

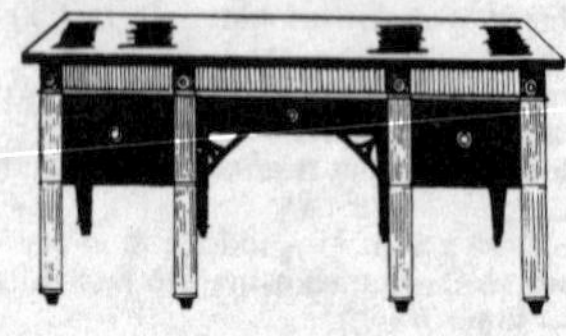

sideboard

side·burns \-ˌbərnz\ *n pl* : whiskers on the side of the face in front of the ears

side·car \-ˌkär\ *n* : a one-wheeled passenger car attached to the side of a motorcycle

side effect *n* : a secondary and usu. adverse effect (as of a drug)

side·kick \ˈsīd-ˌkik\ *n* : PAL, PARTNER

¹**side·long** \ˈsīd-ˌlȯŋ\ *adv* : in the direction of or along the side : OBLIQUELY

²**side·long** \ˌsīd-ˌlȯŋ\ *adj* : directed to one side ⟨~ look⟩

side·man \ˈsīd-ˌman\ *n* : a member of a jazz or swing orchestra

side·piece \-ˌpēs\ *n* : a piece forming or contained in the side of something

si·de·re·al \sī-ˈdir-ē-əl, sə-\ *adj* 1 : of or relating to the stars 2 : measured by the apparent motion of the stars

sid·er·ite \ˈsid-ə-ˌrīt\ *n* : a native carbonate of iron that is a valuable iron ore

side·show \ˈsīd-ˌshō\ *n* **1** : a minor show offered in addition to a main exhibition (as of a circus) **2** : an incidental diversion

side·step \-ˌstep\ *vb* **1** : to step aside **2** : AVOID, EVADE

side·stroke \-ˌstrōk\ *n* : a swimming stroke which is executed on the side and in which the arms are swept backward and downward and the legs do a scissors kick

side·swipe \-ˌswīp\ *vb* : to strike with a glancing blow along the side — **sideswipe** *n*

¹side·track \-ˌtrak\ *n* : SIDING 1

²sidetrack *vb* **1** : to switch from a main railroad line to a siding **2** : to turn aside from a purpose

side·walk \ˈsīd-ˌwȯk\ *n* : a paved walk at the side of a road or street

side·wall \-ˌwȯl\ *n* **1** : a wall forming the side of something **2** : the side of an automobile tire

side·ways \-ˌwāz\ *adv or adj* **1** : from the side **2** : with one side to the front **3** : to, toward, or at one side

side·wind·er \-ˌwīn-dər\ *n* : a small pale-colored desert rattlesnake of the southwestern U.S.

sid·ing \ˈsīd-iŋ\ *n* **1** : a short railroad track connected with the main track **2** : material (as boards) covering the outside of frame buildings

si·dle \ˈsīd-ᵊl\ *vb* **si·dled; si·dling** \ˈsīd-(ᵊ-)liŋ\ : to move sideways or side foremost

SIDS *abbr* sudden infant death syndrome

siege \ˈsēj\ *n* [ME *sege,* fr. OF, seat, blockade] **1** : the placing of an army around or before a fortified place to force its surrender **2** : a persistent attack (as of illness)

sie·mens \ˈsē-mənz, ˈzē-\ *n* : a unit of conductance equivalent to one ampere per volt

si·er·ra \sē-ˈer-ə\ *n* [Sp, lit., saw, fr. L *serra*] : a range of mountains esp. with jagged peaks

si·es·ta \sē-ˈes-tə\ *n* [Sp, fr. L *sexta (hora)* noon, lit., sixth hour] : a midday rest or nap

sieve \ˈsiv\ *n* : a utensil with meshes or holes to separate finer particles from coarser or solids from liquids

sift \ˈsift\ *vb* **1** : to pass through a sieve **2** : to separate with or as if with a sieve **3** : to examine carefully **4** : to scatter by or as if by passing through a sieve — **sift·er** *n*

sig *abbr* **1** signal **2** signature

sigh \ˈsī\ *vb* **1** : to let out a deep audible breath (as in weariness or sorrow) **2** : GRIEVE, YEARN — **sigh** *n*

¹sight \ˈsīt\ *n* **1** : something seen or worth seeing **2** : the process or power of seeing; *esp* : the sense of which the eye is the receptor and by which qualities of appearance (as position, shape, and color) are perceived **3** : INSPECTION **4** : a device (as a small bead on a gun barrel) that aids the eye in aiming **5** : VIEW, GLIMPSE **6** : the range of vision — **sight·less** *adj*

²sight *vb* **1** : to get sight of **2** : to aim by means of a sight

sight·ed \ˈsīt-əd\ *adj* : having sight

sight·ly \-lē\ *adj* : pleasing to the sight

sight–see·ing \ˈsīt-ˌsē-iŋ\ *adj* : engaged in or used for seeing sights of interest — **sight·seer** \-ˌsē-ər\ *n*

¹sign \ˈsīn\ *n* **1** : SYMBOL **2** : a gesture expressing a command, wish, or thought **3** : a notice publicly displayed for advertising purposes or for giving direction or warning **4** : OMEN, PORTENT **5** : TRACE, VESTIGE

²sign *vb* **1** : to mark with a sign **2** : to represent by a sign **3** : to make a sign or signal **4** : to write one's name on in token of assent or obligation **5** : to assign legally **6** : to use sign language — **sign·er** *n*

¹sig·nal \ˈsig-nᵊl\ *n* **1** : a sign agreed on as the start of some joint action **2** : a sign giving warning or notice of something **3** : the message, sound, or image transmitted in electronic communication (as radio)

²signal *vb* **-naled** *or* **-nalled; -nal·ing** *or* **-nal·ling** \-nə-liŋ\ **1** : to communicate by signals **2** : to notify by a signal

³signal *adj* **1** : DISTINGUISHED, OUTSTANDING ⟨a ~ honor⟩ **2** : used in signaling — **sig·nal·ly** \-ē\ *adv*

sig·nal·ize \ˈsig-nə-ˌlīz\ *vb* **-ized; -iz·ing** : to point out or make conspicuous — **sig·nal·iza·tion** \ˌsig-nə-lə-ˈzā-shən\ *n*

sig·nal·man \ˈsig-nᵊl-mən, -ˌman\ *n* : one who signals or works with signals

sig·na·to·ry \ˈsig-nə-ˌtōr-ē\ *n, pl* **-ries** : a person or government that signs jointly with others — **signatory** *adj*

sig·na·ture \ˈsig-nə-ˌchu̇r\ *n* **1** : the name of a person written by himself **2** : the sign placed after the clef to indicate the key or the meter of a piece of music

sign·board \ˈsīn-ˌbōrd\ *n* : a board bearing a sign or notice

sig·net \ˈsig-nət\ *n* : a small intaglio seal (as in a ring)

sig·nif·i·cance \sig-ˈnif-i-kəns\ *n* **1** : something signified : MEANING **2** : SUGGESTIVENESS **3** : CONSEQUENCE, IMPORTANCE

sig·nif·i·cant \-kənt\ *adj* **1** : having meaning; *esp* : having a hidden or special meaning **2** : having or likely to have considerable influence or effect : IMPORTANT — **sig·nif·i·cant·ly** *adv*

sig·ni·fy \ˈsig-nə-ˌfī\ *vb* **-fied; -fy·ing** **1** : to show by a sign **2** : MEAN, IMPORT **3** : to have significance — **sig·ni·fi·ca·tion** \ˌsig-nə-fə-ˈkā-shən\ *n*

sign in *vb* : to make a record of arrival (as by signing a register)

sign language *n* : a formal system of hand gestures used by the deaf to communicate

sign off *vb* : to announce the end (as of a program or broadcast)

sign of the cross : a gesture of the hand forming a cross (as to invoke divine blessing)

sign on *vb* **1** : ENLIST **2** : to announce the start of broadcasting for the day

sign out *vb* : to indicate departure by signing a register or punching a clock

sign·post \ˈsīn-ˌpōst\ *n* : a post bearing a sign

Sikh \ˈsēk\ *n* : an adherent of a religion of India marked by rejection of caste — **Sikh·ism** *n*

si·lage \ˈsī-lij\ *n* : chopped fodder stored in a silo to ferment for use as a rich moist animal feed

¹si·lence \ˈsī-ləns\ *n* **1** : the state of being silent **2** : STILLNESS **3** : SECRECY

²silence *vb* **si·lenced; si·lenc·ing** **1** : to reduce to silence : STILL **2** : to cause to cease hostile firing or criticism

si·lenc·er \ˈsī-lən-sər\ *n* : a device for muffling the noise of a gunshot

si·lent \ˈsī-lənt\ *adj* **1** : not speaking : MUTE; *also* : TACITURN **2** : STILL, QUIET **3** : performed or borne without utterance **syn** reticent, reserved, closemouthed, close — **si·lent·ly** *adv*

¹sil·hou·ette \ˌsil-ə-ˈwet\ *n* [F] **1** : a representation of the outlines of an object filled in with black or some other uniform color **2** : OUTLINE ⟨~ of a ship⟩

²silhouette *vb* **-ett·ed; -ett·ing** : to represent by a silhouette; *also* : to show against a light background

sil·i·ca \ˈsil-i-kə\ *n* : a mineral that consists of silicon and oxygen

sil·i·cate \ˈsil-ə-ˌkāt, ˈsil-i-kət\ *n* : a chemical salt that consists of a metal combined with silicon and oxygen

si·li·ceous *or* **si·li·cious** \sə-ˈlish-əs\ *adj* : of, relating to, or containing silica or a silicate

sil·i·con \ˈsil-i-kən, ˈsil-ə-ˌkän\ *n* : a nonmetallic chemical element that occurs in combination as the most abundant element next to oxygen in the earth's crust and is used esp. in electronics — see ELEMENT table

sil·i·cone \ˈsil-ə-ˌkōn\ *n* : an organic silicon compound used esp. for lubricants and varnishes

sil·i·co·sis \ˌsil-ə-ˈkō-səs\ *n* : a lung disease caused by prolonged inhaling of silica dusts

silk \ˈsilk\ *n* **1** : a fine strong lustrous protein fiber produced by insect larvae for their cocoons; *esp* : one from moth larvae (**silk·worms** \-ˌwərmz\) used for cloth **2** : thread or cloth made from silk — **silk·en** \ˈsil-kən\ *adj* — **silky** *adj*

silk screen *n* : a stencil process in which coloring matter is forced through the meshes of a prepared silk or organdy screen; *also* : a print made by this process — **silk–screen** *vb*

sill \ˈsil\ *n* **1** : a heavy crosspiece (as of wood or stone) that forms the bottom member of a window frame or a doorway; *also* : a horizontal supporting piece at the base of a structure **2** : a flat mass of igneous rock injected while molten between other rocks

sil·ly \ˈsil-ē\ *adj* **sil·li·er; -est** [ME *sely, silly* happy, innocent, pitiable, feeble, fr. OE *sǣlig*] FOOLISH, ABSURD, STUPID — **sil·li·ness** *n*

si·lo \ˈsī-lō\ *n, pl* **silos** [Sp] : a trench, pit, or tall cylinder in which silage is stored

[1]**silt** \ˈsilt\ *n* **1** : fine earth; *esp* : particles of such soil floating in rivers, ponds, or lakes **2** : a deposit (as by a river) of silt — **silty** *adj*

[2]**silt** *vb* : to obstruct or cover with silt — **silt·ation** \sil-ˈtā-shən\ *n*

Si·lu·ri·an \sī-ˈlu̇r-ē-ən\ *adj* : of, relating to, or being the period of the Paleozoic era between the Ordovician and the Devonian — **Silurian** *n*

[1]**sil·ver** \ˈsil-vər\ *n* **1** : a white ductile metallic chemical element that takes a high polish and is a better conductor of heat and electricity than any other substance — see ELEMENT table **2** : coin made of silver **3** : FLATWARE **4** : a grayish white color — **sil·very** *adj*

[2]**silver** *adj* **1** : relating to, made of, or coated with silver **2** : SILVERY

[3]**silver** *vb* **sil·vered; sil·ver·ing** \ˈsilv-(ə-)riŋ\ : to coat with or as if with silver — **sil·ver·er** *n*

silver bromide *n* : a light-sensitive compound used esp. in photography

silver chloride *n* : a light-sensitive compound used esp. in photography

sil·ver·fish \ˈsil-vər-ˌfish\ *n* : a small wingless insect found in houses and sometimes injurious to sized paper and starched clothes

silver iodide *n* : a light-sensitive compound used in photography, rainmaking, and medicine

silver maple *n* : a No. American maple with deeply cut leaves that are green above and silvery white below

silver nitrate *n* : a soluble compound used in photography and as an antiseptic

sil·ver·ware \ˈsil-vər-ˌwaər\ *n* : FLATWARE

sim·i·an \ˈsim-ē-ən\ *n* : MONKEY, APE — **simian** *adj*

sim·i·lar \ˈsim-ə-lər\ *adj* : marked by correspondence or resemblance **syn** alike, akin, comparable, parallel — **sim·i·lar·i·ty** \ˌsim-ə-ˈlar-ət-ē\ *n* — **sim·i·lar·ly** \ˈsim-ə-lər-lē\ *adv*

sim·i·le \ˈsim-ə-(ˌ)lē\ *n* [L, likeness, comparison, fr. neut. of *similis* like, similar] : a figure of speech in which two dissimilar things are compared by the use of *like* or *as* (as in "cheeks like roses")

si·mil·i·tude \sə-ˈmil-ə-ˌt(y)üd\ *n* : LIKENESS, RESEMBLANCE **syn** similarity, semblance

sim·mer \ˈsim-ər\ *vb* **sim·mered; sim·mer·ing** \-(ə-)riŋ\ **1** : to stew at or just below the boiling point **2** : to be on the point of bursting out with violence or emotional disturbance — **simmer** *n*

si·mo·nize \ˈsī-mə-ˌnīz\ *vb* **-nized; -niz·ing** : to polish with or as if with wax

si·mo·ny \ˈsī-mə-nē, ˈsim-ə-\ *n* [LL *simonia,* fr. *Simon* Magus 1st cent. A.D. sorcerer of Samaria (Acts 8:9–24)] : the buying or selling of a church office

sim·pa·ti·co \sim-ˈpät-i-ˌkō, -ˈpat-\ *adj* : CONGENIAL, LIKABLE

sim·per \ˈsim-pər\ *vb* **sim·pered; sim·per·ing** \-p(ə-)riŋ\ : to smile in a silly manner — **simper** *n*

sim·ple \ˈsim-pəl\ *adj* **sim·pler** \-p(ə-)lər\; **sim·plest** \-p(ə-)ləst\ [ME, fr. OF, plain, uncomplicated, artless, fr. L *simplus, simplex,* lit., single; L *simplus* fr. *sim-* one + *-plus* multiplied by; L *simplex* fr. *sim-* + *-plex* -fold] **1** : not combined with anything else **2** : not other than : MERE **3** : not complex : PLAIN **4** : ABSOLUTE ⟨land held in fee ~⟩ **5** : STRAIGHTFORWARD; *also* : ARTLESS **6** : UNADORNED **7** : lacking education, experience, or intelligence **8** : developing from a single ovary ⟨a ~ fruit⟩ **syn** easy, facile, light, effortless — **sim·ple·ness** *n* — **sim·ply** \-plē\ *adv*

sim·ple·ton \ˈsim-pəl-tən\ *n* : FOOL

sim·plic·i·ty \sim-ˈplis-ət-ē\ *n* **1** : lack of complication : CLEARNESS **2** : CANDOR, ARTLESSNESS **3** : plainness in manners or way of life **4** : IGNORANCE, FOOLISHNESS

sim·pli·fy \ˈsim-plə-ˌfī\ *vb* **-fied; -fy·ing** : to make simple : make less complex : CLARIFY — **sim·pli·fi·ca·tion** \ˌsim-plə-fə-ˈkā-shən\ *n*

sim·plis·tic \sim-ˈplis-tik\ *adj* : excessively simple : tending to overlook complexities ⟨a ~ solution⟩

sim·u·late \ˈsim-yə-ˌlāt\ *vb* **-lat·ed; -lat·ing** : to create the effect or appearance of : FEIGN — **sim·u·la·tion** \ˌsim-yə-ˈlā-shən\ *n* — **sim·u·la·tor** \ˈsim-yə-ˌlāt-ər\ *n*

si·mul·ta·ne·ous \ˌsī-məl-ˈtā-nē-əs, ˌsim-əl-\ *adj* : occurring or operating at the same time — **si·mul·ta·ne·ous·ly** *adv* — **si·mul·ta·ne·ous·ness** *n*

[1]**sin** \ˈsin\ *n* **1** : an offense esp. against God **2** : FAULT **3** : a weakened state of human nature in which the self is estranged from God — **sin·less** *adj*

[2]**sin** *vb* **sinned; sin·ning** : to commit a sin — **sin·ner** *n*

[1]**since** \(ˈ)sins\ *adv* **1** : from a past time until now **2** : backward in time : AGO

[2]**since** *prep* **1** : in the period after ⟨changes made ~ the war⟩ **2** : continuously from ⟨has been here ~ 1980⟩

[3]**since** *conj* **1** : from the time when **2** : seeing that : BECAUSE

sin·cere \sin-ˈsiər\ *adj* **sin·cer·er; sin·cer·est** **1** : free from hypocrisy : HONEST **2** : GENUINE, REAL — **sin·cere·ly** *adv* — **sin·cer·i·ty** \-ˈser-ət-ē\ *n*

si·ne·cure \ˈsī-ni-ˌkyu̇ər, ˈsin-i-\ *n* : a well-paid job that requires little work

si·ne die \ˌsī-ni-ˈdī-ˌē, ˌsin-ā-ˈdē-ˌā\ *adv* [L, without day] : INDEFINITELY

si·ne qua non \ˌsin-i-ˌkwä-ˈnän, -ˈnōn\ *n* [LL, without which not] : an indispensable or essential thing

sin·ew \ˈsin-yü\ *n* **1** : TENDON **2** : physical strength — **sin·ewy** *adj*

sin·ful \ˈsin-fəl\ *adj* : marked by or full of sin : WICKED — **sin·ful·ly** \-ē\ *adv* — **sin·ful·ness** *n*

[1]**sing** \ˈsiŋ\ *vb* **sang** \ˈsaŋ\ *or* **sung** \ˈsəŋ\; **sung; sing·ing** \ˈsiŋ-iŋ\ **1** : to produce musical tones with the voice; *also* : to utter with musical tones **2** : to produce harmonious sustained sounds ⟨birds ~*ing*⟩ **3** : CHANT, INTONE **4** : to make a prolonged shrill sound ⟨locusts ~*ing*⟩ **5** : to write poetry; *also* : to celebrate in song or verse **6** : to give information or evidence — **sing·er** *n*

[2]**sing** *abbr* singular

singe \ˈsinj\ *vb* **singed; singe·ing** \ˈsin-jiŋ\ : to scorch lightly the outside of; *esp* : to remove the hair or down from (a plucked fowl) with flame

[1]**sin·gle** \ˈsiŋ-gəl\ *adj* **1** : UNMARRIED **2** : being alone : being the only one **3** : having only one feature or part **4** : made for one person or family **syn** sole, unique, lone, solitary, separate, particular — **sin·gle·ness** *n* — **sin·gly** \-glē\ *adv*

[2]**single** *vb* **sin·gled; sin·gling** \-g(ə-)liŋ\ **1** : to select (one) from a group **2** : to hit a single

[3]**single** *n* **1** : a separate person or thing **2** : a hit in baseball that enables the batter to reach first base **3** *pl* : a tennis match with one player on each side

single bond *n* **:** a chemical bond in which one pair of electrons is shared by two atoms in a molecule

single–lens reflex *n* **:** a camera having a single lens that forms an image which is either reflected to the viewfinder or recorded on film

sin·gle·ton \ˈsiŋ-gəl-tən\ *n* **:** a card that is the only one of its suit orig. held in a hand

sin·gle·tree \-ˌtrē\ *n* **:** WHIFFLETREE

sin·gu·lar \ˈsiŋ-gyə-lər\ *adj* **1 :** of, relating to, or constituting a word form denoting one person, thing, or instance **2 :** of unusual quality **3 :** OUTSTANDING, EXCEPTIONAL **4 :** ODD, STRANGE — **singular** *n* — **sin·gu·lar·i·ty** \ˌsiŋ-gyə-ˈlar-ət-ē\ *n* — **sin·gu·lar·ly** \ˈsiŋ-gyə-lər-lē\ *adv*

sin·is·ter \ˈsin-əs-tər\ *adj* [ME, fr. L on the left side, inauspicious] **1 :** threatening or foreboding evil or disaster **2 :** indicative of lurking evil **syn** baleful, malign, malefic, maleficent

[1]**sink** \ˈsiŋk\ *vb* **sank** \ˈsaŋk\ *or* **sunk** \ˈsəŋk\; **sunk; sink·ing 1 :** SUBMERGE **2 :** to descend lower and lower **3 :** to grow less in volume or height **4 :** to slope downward **5 :** to penetrate downward **6 :** to fail in health or strength **7 :** LAPSE, DEGENERATE **8 :** to cause (a ship) to descend to the bottom **9 :** to make (a hole or shaft) by digging, boring, or cutting **10 :** INVEST — **sink·able** *adj*

[2]**sink** *n* **1 :** DRAIN, SEWER **2 :** a basin connected with a drain **3 :** an extensive depression in the land surface

sink·er \ˈsiŋ-kər\ *n* **:** a weight for sinking a fishing line or net

sink·hole \ˈsiŋk-ˌhōl\ *n* **:** a hollow place in which drainage collects

sin·u·ous \ˈsin-yə-wəs\ *adj* **:** bending in and out **:** WINDING — **sin·u·os·i·ty** \ˌsin-yə-ˈwäs-ət-ē\ *n*

si·nus \ˈsī-nəs\ *n* [NL, fr. L curve, hollow] **1 :** any of several cavities of the skull mostly connecting with the nostrils **2 :** a space forming a channel (as for the passage of blood)

si·nus·itis \ˌsī-nə-ˈsīt-əs\ *n* **:** inflammation of a sinus esp. of the skull

Sioux \ˈsü\ *n, pl* **Sioux** \ˈsü(z)\ [F] **:** DAKOTA

sip \ˈsip\ *vb* **sipped; sip·ping :** to drink in small quantities — **sip** *n*

[1]**si·phon** \ˈsī-fən\ *n* [F] **1 :** a bent tube through which a liquid can be transferred by means of air pressure up and over the edge of one container and into another container placed at a lower level **2** *usu* **sy·phon :** a bottle that ejects soda water through a tube when a valve is opened

[2]**siphon** *vb* **si·phoned; si·phon·ing** \ˈsīf-(ə-)niŋ\ **:** to draw off by means of a siphon

sir \(ˈ)sər\ *n* [ME *sire* sire, fr. OF, fr. L *senior,* compar. of *senex* old, old man] **1 :** a man of rank or position — used as a title before the given name of a knight or baronet **2** — used in addressing a man without using his name

[1]**sire** \ˈsī(ə)r\ *n* **1 :** FATHER; *also, archaic* **:** FOREFATHER **2** *archaic* **:** LORD — used as a title of respect esp. in addressing a sovereign **3 :** the male parent of an animal (as a horse or dog)

[2]**sire** *vb* **sired; sir·ing :** BEGET, PROCREATE

si·ren \ˈsī-rən\ *n* **1 :** a seductive or alluring woman **2 :** an electrically operated device for producing a loud shrill warning signal — **siren** *adj*

sir·loin \ˈsər-ˌlȯin\ *n* [alter. of earlier *surloin,* modif. of MF *surlonge,* fr. *sur* over (fr. L *super*) + *longe* loin] **:** a cut of beef taken from the part in front of the round

sirup *var of* SYRUP

si·sal \ˈsī-səl, -zəl\ *n* **:** a strong cordage fiber from an agave; *also* **:** this agave

sis·sy \ˈsis-ē\ *n, pl* **sissies :** an effeminate boy or man; *also* **:** a timid or cowardly person

sis·ter \ˈsis-tər\ *n* **1 :** a female having one or both parents in common with another individual **2 :** a member of a religious order of women **:** NUN **3** *chiefly Brit* **:** NURSE — **sis·ter·ly** *adj*

sis·ter·hood \-ˌhu̇d\ *n* **1 :** the state of being sisters or a sister **2 :** a community or society of sisters

sis·ter–in–law \ˈsis-t(ə-)rən-ˌlȯ\ *n, pl* **sis·ters–in–law** \-tər-zən-\ **:** the sister of one's husband or wife; *also* **:** the wife of one's brother

sit \ˈsit\ *vb* **sat** \ˈsat\; **sit·ting 1 :** to rest upon the buttocks or haunches **2 :** ROOST, PERCH **3 :** to occupy a seat **4 :** to hold a session **5 :** to cover eggs for hatching **:** BROOD **6 :** to pose for a portrait **7 :** to remain quiet or inactive **8 :** FIT **9 :** to cause (oneself) to be seated **10 :** to place in position **11 :** to keep one's seat on ⟨~ a horse⟩ **12 :** BABY-SIT — **sit·ter** *n*

si·tar \si-ˈtär\ *n* [Hindi] **:** an Indian lute with a long neck and a varying number of strings

site \ˈsīt\ *n* **:** LOCATION

sit–in \ˈsit-ˌin\ *n* **:** an act of sitting in the seats or on the floor of an establishment as a means of organized protest

sit·u·at·ed \ˈsich-ə-ˌwāt-əd\ *adj* **:** LOCATED, PLACED

sit·u·a·tion \ˌsich-ə-ˈwā-shən\ *n* **1 :** LOCATION, SITE **2 :** JOB **3 :** CONDITION, CIRCUMSTANCES

sit–up \ˈsit-ˌəp\ *n* **:** an exercise performed from a supine position by raising the trunk to a sitting position usu. while keeping the legs straight and returning to the original position

six \ˈsiks\ *n* **1 :** one more than five **2 :** the 6th in a set or series **3 :** something having six units; *esp* **:** a 6-cylinder engine or automobile — **six** *adj or pron* — **sixth** \ˈsiksth\ *adj or adv or n*

six–gun \ˈsiks-ˌgən\ *n* **:** a 6-chambered revolver

six–pack \ˈsiks-ˌpak\ *n* **:** six bottles or cans (as of beer) packaged and purchased together; *also* **:** the contents of a six-pack

six·pence \-pəns, *US also* -ˌpens\ *n* **:** the sum of six pence; *also* **:** an English silver coin of this value — **six·pen·ny** \-pən-ē, *US also* -ˌpen-ē\ *adj*

six–shoot·er \ˈsik(s)-ˈshüt-ər\ *n* **:** SIX-GUN

six·teen \ˈsiks-ˈtēn\ *n* **:** one more than 15 — **sixteen** *adj or pron* — **six·teenth** \-ˈtēnth\ *adj or n*

six·ty \ˈsiks-tē\ *n, pl* **sixties :** six times 10 — **six·ti·eth** \ˈsiks-tē-əth\ *adj or n* — **sixty** *adj or pron*

siz·able *or* **size·able** \ˈsī-zə-bəl\ *adj* **:** quite large — **siz·ably** \-blē\ *adv*

[1]**size** \ˈsīz\ *n* **:** physical extent or bulk **:** DIMENSIONS; *also* **:** MAGNITUDE

[2]**size** *vb* **sized; siz·ing :** to grade or classify according to size

[3]**size** *n* **:** a gluey material used for filling the pores in paper, plaster, or textiles — **siz·ing** \ˈsī-ziŋ\ *n*

[4]**size** *vb* **sized; siz·ing :** to cover, stiffen, or glaze with size

siz·zle \ˈsiz-əl\ *vb* **siz·zled; siz·zling** \-(ə-)liŋ\ **:** to fry or shrivel up with a hissing sound — **sizzle** *n*

SJ *abbr* Society of Jesus

SK *abbr* Saskatchewan

[1]**skate** \ˈskāt\ *n, pl* **skates** *also* **skate :** any of numerous rays with thick broad fins

[2]**skate** *n* **1 :** a metal runner with a frame fitting on a shoe used for gliding over ice **2 :** ROLLER SKATE — **skate** *vb* — **skat·er** *n*

skate·board \ˈskāt-ˌbōrd\ *n* **:** a short board mounted on roller-skate wheels — **skate·board·er** \-ər\ *n* — **skate·board·ing** \-iŋ\ *n*

skeet \ˈskēt\ *n* **:** trapshooting in which clay targets are thrown in such a way that their angle of flight simulates that of a flushed game bird

skein \ˈskān\ *n* : a loosely twisted quantity (as of yarn) as it is taken from the reel

skel·e·ton \ˈskel-ət-ᵊn\ *n* **1** : the usu. bony supporting framework of an animal body **2** : a bare minimum **3** : FRAMEWORK — **skel·e·tal** \-ət-ᵊl\ *adj*

skep·tic \ˈskep-tik\ *n* **1** : one who believes in skepticism **2** : one having a critical or doubting attitude **3** : one who doubts or disbelieves in religious tenets — **skep·ti·cal** \-ti-kəl\ *adj*

skep·ti·cism \ˈskep-tə-ˌsiz-əm\ *n* **1** : a doubting state of mind **2** : a doctrine that certainty of knowledge cannot be attained **3** : unbelief in religion

sketch \ˈskech\ *n* **1** : a rough drawing or outline **2** : a short or slight literary composition (as a story or essay); *also* : a vaudeville act — **sketch** *vb* — **sketchy** *adj*

[1]**skew** \ˈskyü\ *vb* : TWIST, SWERVE

[2]**skew** *n* : SLANT

skew·er \ˈskyü-ər\ *n* : a pin for holding meat in form while roasting — **skewer** *vb*

[1]**ski** \ˈskē\ *n, pl* **skis** [Norw, fr. ON *skīth* stick of wood, ski] : one of a pair of long strips (as of wood) bound one on each foot for gliding over snow

[2]**ski** *vb* **skied** \ˈskēd\; **ski·ing** : to glide on skis — **ski·er** *n*

[1]**skid** \ˈskid\ *n* **1** : a plank for supporting something above the ground **2** : a device placed under a wheel to prevent turning **3** : a timber or rail over or on which something is slid or rolled **4** : the action of skidding **5** : a runner on the landing gear of an aircraft **6** : [2]PALLET

[2]**skid** *vb* **skid·ded; skid·ding** **1** : to slide without rotating ⟨a *skidding* wheel⟩ **2** : to slide sideways on the road ⟨the car *skidded* on ice⟩

skid row *n* : a district of cheap saloons frequented by vagrants and alcoholics

skiff \ˈskif\ *n* : a small open boat

ski lift *n* : CHAIR LIFT

skill \ˈskil\ *n* **1** : ability to use one's knowledge effectively in doing something **2** : developed or acquired ability **syn** art, craft, cunning, dexterity, expertise, know-how — **skilled** \ˈskild\ *adj*

skil·let \ˈskil-ət\ *n* : a frying pan

skill·ful *or* **skil·ful** \ˈskil-fəl\ *adj* **1** : having or displaying skill : EXPERT **2** : accomplished with skill — **skill·ful·ly** \-ē\ *adv* — **skill·ful·ness** *n*

[1]**skim** \ˈskim\ *vb* **skimmed; skim·ming** **1** : to take off from the top of a liquid; *also* : to remove (scum or cream) from ⟨~ milk⟩ **2** : to read rapidly and superficially **3** : to pass swiftly over — **skim·mer** *n*

[2]**skim** *adj* **1** : having the cream removed **2** : made of skim milk

skim·ming \ˈskim-iŋ\ *n* : the practice of concealing gambling profits so as to avoid tax payments

ski·mo·bile \ˈskē-mō-ˌbēl\ *n* : SNOWMOBILE

skimp \ˈskimp\ *vb* : to give insufficient attention, effort, or funds; *also* : to save by skimping

skimpy \ˈskim-pē\ *adj* **skimp·i·er; -est** : deficient in supply or execution

[1]**skin** \ˈskin\ *n* **1** : the outer limiting layer of an animal body; *also* : the usu. thin tough tissue of which this is made **2** : an outer or surface layer (as a rind or peel) — **skin·less** *adj* — **skinned** *adj*

[2]**skin** *vb* **skinned; skin·ning** : to free from skin : remove the skin of

[3]**skin** *adj* : devoted to showing nudes ⟨~ magazines⟩

skin–dive \ˈskin-ˌdīv\ *vb* : to swim below the surface of water with a face mask and portable breathing device — **skin diver** *n* — **skin diving** *n*

skin·flint \ˈskin-ˌflint\ *n* : a very stingy person

skin graft *n* : skin that is taken from one area to replace skin in another area — **skin grafting** *n*

skin·ny \ˈskin-ē\ *adj* **skin·ni·er; -est** **1** : resembling skin **2** : very thin

skin·ny–dip·ping \-ˌdip-iŋ\ *n* : swimming in the nude

skin·tight \ˈskin-ˈtīt\ *adj* : closely fitted to the figure

[1]**skip** \ˈskip\ *vb* **skipped; skip·ping** **1** : to move with leaps and bounds **2** : to leap lightly over **3** : to pass from point to point (as in reading) disregarding what is in between **4** : to pass over without notice or mention

[2]**skip** *n* : a light bouncing step; *also* : a gait of alternate hops and steps

skip·jack \ˈskip-ˌjak\ *n* : a small sailboat with bottom similar to a flat V and sides vertical

skip·per \ˈskip-ər\ *n* [ME, fr. Middle Dutch *schipper,* fr. *schip* ship] : the master of a ship — **skipper** *vb*

skir·mish \ˈskər-mish\ *n* : a minor engagement in war; *also* : a minor dispute or contest — **skirmish** *vb*

[1]**skirt** \ˈskərt\ *n* : a free-hanging part of a garment extending from the waist down

[2]**skirt** *vb* **1** : to pass around the outer edge of **2** : BORDER

skit \ˈskit\ *n* : a brief dramatic sketch

ski tow *n* : SKI LIFT

skit·ter \ˈskit-ər\ *vb* : to glide or skip lightly or quickly : skim along a surface

skit·tish \ˈskit-ish\ *adj* **1** : CAPRICIOUS, IRRESPONSIBLE **2** : easily frightened ⟨a ~ horse⟩

skiv·vy \ˈskiv-ē\ *n, pl* **skivvies** : men's underwear; *esp* : a T-shirt and briefs or shorts — usu. used in pl.

ski·wear \ˈskē-ˌwaər\ *n* : clothing suitable for wear while skiing

skulk \ˈskəlk\ *vb* : to move furtively : SNEAK, LURK — **skulk·er** *n*

skull \ˈskəl\ *n* : the bony or cartilaginous case that protects the brain and supports the jaws

skull·cap \ˈskəl-ˌkap\ *n* : a close-fitting brimless cap

[1]**skunk** \ˈskəŋk\ *n, pl* **skunks** *also* **skunk** **1** : any of various No. American mammals related to the weasels that can forcibly eject an ill-smelling fluid when startled **2** : a contemptible person

[2]**skunk** *vb* : to defeat decisively; *esp* : to shut out in a game

skunk cabbage *n* : a perennial herb of eastern No. America with an unpleasant-smelling early spring flower; *also* : a related herb of the Pacific coast region

sky \ˈskī\ *n, pl* **skies** **1** : the upper air **2** : HEAVEN — **sky·ey** \ˈskī-ē\ *adj*

sky·cap \-ˌkap\ *n* : a person employed to carry luggage at an airport

sky·div·ing \-ˌdī-viŋ\ *n* : the sport of jumping from an airplane and executing various body maneuvers before opening a parachute — **sky diver** *n*

sky·jack \-ˌjak\ *vb* : to take control of an airplane in flight by threat of violence — **sky·jack·er** *n* — **sky·jack·ing** *n*

[1]**sky·lark** \-ˌlärk\ *n* : a European lark noted for its song and its steep upward flight

[2]**skylark** *vb* : to frolic boisterously or recklessly

sky·light \ˈskī-ˌlīt\ *n* : a window in a roof or ceiling — **sky·light·ed** \-ˌlīt-əd\ *adj*

sky·line \-ˌlīn\ *n* **1** : HORIZON **2** : an outline against the sky

[1]**sky·rock·et** \-ˌräk-ət\ *n* : [1]ROCKET 1

[2]**skyrocket** *vb* : [2]ROCKET 2

sky·scrap·er \-ˌskrā-pər\ *n* : a very tall building

sky·walk \-ˌwȯk\ *n* : a usu. enclosed aerial walkway connecting two buildings

sky·ward \-wərd\ *adv* : toward the sky

sky·writ·ing \-ˌrīt-iŋ\ *n* : writing in the sky formed by smoke emitted from an airplane — **sky·writ·er** \-ər\ *n*

slab \ˈslab\ *n* : a thick flat piece or slice

[1]**slack** \ˈslak\ *adj* **1** : CARELESS, NEGLIGENT **2** : SLUGGISH, LISTLESS **3** : not taut : LOOSE **4** : not busy or active **syn** lax, remiss, neglectful, delinquent, derelict — **slack·ly** *adv* — **slack·ness** *n*

[2]**slack** *vb* **1** : to make or become slack : LOOSEN, RELAX **2** : SLAKE 2

[3]**slack** *n* **1** : cessation of movement or flow : LETUP **2** : a part that hangs loose without strain ⟨~ of a rope⟩ **3** : trousers for casual wear — usu. used in pl.

slack·en \ˈslak-ən\ *vb* **slack·ened; slack·en·ing** \-(ə-)niŋ\ : to make or become slack

slack·er \ˈslak-ər\ *n* : one that shirks work or evades military duty

slag \ˈslag\ *n* : the waste left after the melting of ores and the separation of metal from them

slain *past part of* SLAY

slake \ˈslāk, *for 2 also* ˈslak\ *vb* **slaked; slak·ing 1** : to cause to subside with or as if with refreshing drink ⟨~ thirst⟩ **2** : to cause (lime) to crumble by mixture with water

sla·lom \ˈsläl-əm\ *n* [Norw, lit., sloping track] : skiing in a zigzag course between obstacles

¹**slam** \ˈslam\ *n* : the winning of every trick or of all tricks but one in bridge

²**slam** *n* : a heavy jarring impact : BANG

³**slam** *vb* **slammed; slam·ming 1** : to shut violently and noisily **2** : to throw or strike with a loud impact

¹**slan·der** \ˈslan-dər\ *n* [ME *sclaundre, slaundre,* fr. OF *esclandre,* fr. LL *scandalum* stumbling block, offense] : a false report maliciously uttered and tending to injure the reputation of a person — **slan·der·ous** *adj*

²**slander** *vb* **slan·dered; slan·der·ing** \-d(ə-)riŋ\ : to utter slander against : DEFAME — **slan·der·er** *n*

slang \ˈslaŋ\ *n* : an informal nonstandard vocabulary composed typically of invented words, arbitrarily changed words, and extravagant figures of speech — **slangy** *adj*

¹**slant** \ˈslant\ *n* **1** : a sloping direction, line, or plane **2** : a particular or personal viewpoint — **slant** *adj* — **slant·wise** \-ˌwīz\ *adv or adj*

²**slant** *vb* **1** : SLOPE **2** : to interpret or present in accordance with a special viewpoint **syn** incline, lean, list, tilt, heel — **slant·ing·ly** *adv*

slap \ˈslap\ *vb* **slapped; slap·ping 1** : to strike sharply with the open hand **2** : REBUFF, INSULT — **slap** *n*

¹**slash** \ˈslash\ *vb* **1** : to cut with sweeping strokes **2** : to cut slits in (a garment) **3** : to reduce sharply

²**slash** *n* **1** : GASH **2** : an ornamental slit in a garment **3** : a clearing in a forest littered with debris; *also* : the debris present

slat \ˈslat\ *n* : a thin narrow flat strip

¹**slate** \ˈslāt\ *n* **1** : a dense fine-grained rock that splits into thin layers **2** : a roofing tile or a writing tablet made from this rock **3** : a list of candidates for election

²**slate** *vb* **slat·ed; slat·ing 1** : to cover with slate **2** : to designate for action or appointment

slath·er \ˈslath-ər\ *vb* **slath·ered; slath·er·ing** \-(ə-)riŋ\ : to spread with or on thickly or lavishly

slat·tern \ˈslat-ərn\ *n* : a slovenly woman — **slat·tern·ly** *adj*

¹**slaugh·ter** \ˈslȯt-ər\ *n* **1** : the butchering of livestock for market **2** : great destruction of lives esp. in battle

²**slaughter** *vb* **1** : to kill (animals) for food : BUTCHER **2** : to kill in large numbers or in a bloody way : MASSACRE

slaugh·ter·house \-ˌhau̇s\ *n* : an establishment where animals are butchered

Slav \ˈsläv, ˈslav\ *n* : a person speaking a Slavic language

¹**slave** \ˈslāv\ *n* [ME *sclave,* fr. OF or ML; OF *esclave,* fr. ML *sclavus,* fr. *Sclavus* Slav; fr. the reduction to slavery of many Slavic peoples of central Europe] **1** : a person held in servitude as property **2** : a device (as the typewriter unit of a computer) that is directly responsive to another — **slave** *adj*

²**slave** *vb* **slaved; slav·ing** : to work like a slave : DRUDGE

¹**sla·ver** \ˈslav-ər, ˈsläv-\ *n* : SLOBBER — **slaver** *vb*

²**slav·er** \ˈslā-vər\ *n* : a ship or a person engaged in transporting slaves

slav·ery \ˈslāv-(ə-)rē\ *n* **1** : wearisome drudgery **2** : the condition of being a slave **3** : the practice of owning slaves **syn** servitude, bondage, enslavement

¹**Slav·ic** \ˈslav-ik, ˈsläv-\ *adj* : of or relating to the Slavs or their languages

²**Slavic** *n* : a branch of the Indo-European language family including various languages (as Russian or Polish) of eastern Europe

slav·ish \ˈslā-vish\ *adj* **1** : SERVILE **2** : obeying or imitating with no freedom of judgment or choice — **slav·ish·ly** *adv*

slaw \ˈslȯ\ *n* : COLESLAW

slay \ˈslā\ *vb* **slew** \ˈslü\; **slain** \ˈslān\; **slay·ing** : KILL — **slay·er** *n*

sleaze \ˈslēz\ *n* : a sleazy quality or appearance

slea·zy \ˈslē-zē, ˈslā-\ *adj* **slea·zi·er; -est 1** : FLIMSY, SHODDY **2** : marked by cheapness of character or quality

¹**sled** \ˈsled\ *n* : a vehicle on runners adapted esp. for sliding on snow

²**sled** *vb* **sled·ded, sled·ding** : to ride or carry on a sled

¹**sledge** \ˈslej\ *n* : SLEDGEHAMMER

²**sledge** *n* : a strong heavy sled

sledge·ham·mer \ˈslej-ˌham-ər\ *n* : a large heavy hammer usu. wielded with both hands — **sledgehammer** *adj or vb*

¹**sleek** \ˈslēk\ *vb* **1** : to make smooth or glossy **2** : to gloss over

²**sleek** *adj* : having a smooth well-groomed look

¹**sleep** \ˈslēp\ *n* **1** : a natural periodic suspension of consciousness **2** : a state (as death or coma) suggesting sleep — **sleep·less** *adj* — **sleep·less·ness** *n*

²**sleep** *vb* **slept** \ˈslept\; **sleep·ing 1** : to rest or be in a state of sleep; *also* : to spend in sleep **2** : to have sexual intercourse **3** : to provide sleeping space for

sleep·er \ˈslē-pər\ *n* **1** : one that sleeps **2** : a horizontal beam to support something on or near ground level **3** : SLEEPING CAR **4** : someone or something unpromising or unnoticed that suddenly attains prominence or value

sleeping bag *n* : a warmly lined bag for sleeping esp. outdoors

sleeping car *n* : a railroad car with berths for sleeping

sleeping pill *n* : a drug in tablet or capsule form taken to induce sleep

sleeping sickness *n* : a serious disease that is prevalent in tropical Africa, is marked by fever, lethargy, tremors, and loss of weight, and is caused by protozoans transmitted by the tsetse fly

sleep·walk·er \ˈslēp-ˌwȯ-kər\ *n* : one who walks in his sleep

sleepy \ˈslē-pē\ *adj* **sleep·i·er; -est 1** : ready for sleep **2** : quietly inactive — **sleep·i·ly** \ˈslē-pə-lē\ *adv* — **sleep·i·ness** \-pē-nəs\ *n*

sleet \ˈslēt\ *n* : frozen or partly frozen rain — **sleet** *vb* — **sleety** *adj*

sleeve \ˈslēv\ *n* **1** : a part of a garment covering an arm **2** : a tubular part designed to fit over another part — **sleeve·less** *adj*

¹**sleigh** \ˈslā\ *n* : an open usu. horse-drawn vehicle on runners for use on snow or ice

²**sleigh** *vb* : to drive or travel in a sleigh

sleight \ˈslīt\ *n* **1** : TRICK **2** : DEXTERITY

sleight of hand : a trick requiring skillful manual manipulation

slen·der \ˈslen-dər\ *adj* **1** : SLIM, THIN **2** : WEAK, SLIGHT **3** : MEAGER, INADEQUATE

slen·der·ize \-də-ˌrīz\ *vb* **-ized; -iz·ing** : to make slender

sleuth \ˈslüth\ *n* [short for *sleuthhound* bloodhound, fr. ME, fr. *sleuth* track of an animal or person, fr. ON *slōth*] : DETECTIVE

¹**slew** \ˈslü\ *past of* SLAY

²**slew** *vb* : TURN, VEER, SKID

¹**slice** \ˈslīs\ *n* **1** : a thin flat piece cut from something **2** : a wedge-shaped blade (as for serving fish) **3** : a flight of a ball (as in golf) that curves in the direction of the dominant hand of the player propelling it

²**slice** *vb* **sliced; slic·ing 1** : to cut a slice from; *also* : to cut into slices **2** : to hit (a ball) so that a slice results

¹**slick** \ˈslik\ *vb* : to make smooth or sleek

²**slick** *adj* **1** : very smooth : SLIPPERY **2** : CLEVER, SMART

³**slick** *n* **1** : a smooth patch of water covered with a film of oil **2** : a popular magazine printed on coated paper

slick·er \ˈslik-ər\ *n* **1** : a long loose raincoat **2** : a sly tricky person **3** : a city dweller esp. of natty appearance or sophisticated mannerisms

¹**slide** \ˈslīd\ *vb* **slid** \ˈslid\; **slid·ing** \ˈslīd-iŋ\ **1** : to move smoothly along a surface **2** : to fall by a loss of support **3** : to slip along quietly

²**slide** *n* **1** : an act or instance of sliding **2** : something (as a cover or fastener) that operates by sliding **3** : a fall of a mass of earth or snow down a hillside **4** : a surface on which something slides **5** : a glass plate on which a specimen is mounted for examination under a microscope **6** : a small transparent image that can be projected on a screen

slid·er \ˈslīd-ər\ *n* **1** : one that slides **2** : a baseball pitch that looks like a fastball but curves slightly

slide rule *n* : an instrument for calculation consisting of a ruler and a medial slide graduated with logarithmic scales

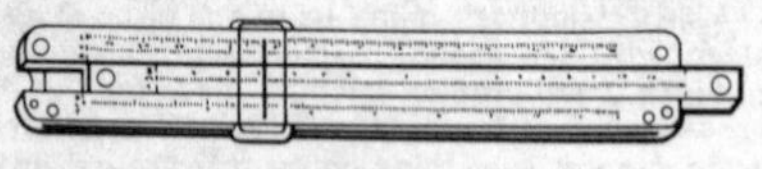

slide rule

slier *comparative of* SLY

sliest *superlative of* SLY

¹**slight** \ˈslīt\ *adj* **1** : SLENDER; *also* : FRAIL **2** : UNIMPORTANT **3** : SCANTY, MEAGER — **slight·ly** *adv*

²**slight** *vb* **1** : to treat as unimportant **2** : to ignore discourteously **3** : to perform or attend to carelessly **syn** neglect, overlook, disregard

³**slight** *n* : a humiliating discourtesy

¹**slim** \ˈslim\ *adj* **slim·mer; slim·mest** [Dutch, bad, inferior, fr. Middle Dutch *slimp* crooked, bad] **1** : SLENDER, SLIGHT, THIN **2** : SCANTY, MEAGER

²**slim** *vb* **slimmed; slim·ming** : to make or become slender

slime \ˈslīm\ *n* **1** : sticky mud **2** : a slippery substance (as on the skin of a slug or catfish) — **slimy** *adj*

slim–jim \ˈslim-ˈjim, -ˌjim\ *adj* : notably slender

¹**sling** \ˈsliŋ\ *vb* **slung** \ˈsləŋ\; **sling·ing** \ˈsliŋ-iŋ\ **1** : to throw forcibly : FLING **2** : to hurl with a sling

²**sling** *n* **1** : a short strap with strings attached for hurling stones or shot **2** : a strap, rope, or chain for holding securely something being lifted, lowered, or carried

sling·shot \ˈsliŋ-ˌshät\ *n* : a forked stick with elastic bands for shooting small stones or shot

slink \ˈsliŋk\ *vb* **slunk** \ˈsləŋk\ *also* **slinked** \ˈsliŋkt\; **slink·ing 1** : to move stealthily or furtively **2** : to move sinuously — **slinky** *adj*

¹**slip** \ˈslip\ *vb* **slipped; slip·ping 1** : to escape quietly or secretly **2** : to slide along or cause to slide along smoothly **3** : to make a mistake **4** : to pass unnoticed or undone **5** : to fall off from a standard or level

²**slip** *n* **1** : a ramp for repairing ships **2** : a ship's berth between two piers **3** : secret or hurried departure, escape, or evasion **4** : BLUNDER **5** : a sudden mishap **6** : a woman's one-piece garment worn under a dress **7** : PILLOWCASE

³**slip** *n* **1** : a shoot or twig from a plant for planting or grafting **2** : a long narrow strip; *esp* : one of paper used for a record ⟨deposit ~⟩

⁴**slip** *vb* **slipped; slip·ping** : to take slips from (a plant)

slip·knot \ˈslip-ˌnät\ *n* : a knot that slips along the rope around which it is made

slipped disk *n* : a protrusion of one of the disks of cartilage between vertebrae with pressure on spinal nerves resulting esp. in low back pain

slip·per \ˈslip-ər\ *n* : a light low shoe that may be easily slipped on and off

slip·pery \ˈslip-(ə-)rē\ *adj* **slip·peri·er; -est 1** : icy, wet, smooth, or greasy enough to cause one to fall or lose one's hold **2** : TRICKY, UNRELIABLE — **slip·peri·ness** *n*

slip·shod \ˈslip-ˈshäd\ *adj* : SLOVENLY, CARELESS ⟨~ work⟩

slip·stream \ˈslip-ˌstrēm\ *n* : the stream of air driven aft by the propeller of an aircraft

slip·up \ˈslip-ˌəp\ *n* **1** : MISTAKE **2** : ACCIDENT

¹**slit** \ˈslit\ *vb* **slit; slit·ting 1** : SLASH **2** : to cut off or away

²**slit** *n* : a long narrow cut or opening

slith·er \ˈslith-ər\ *vb* : to slip or glide along like a snake — **slith·ery** *adj*

sliv·er \ˈsliv-ər\ *n* : SPLINTER

slob \ˈsläb\ *n* : a slovenly or boorish person

slob·ber \ˈsläb-ər\ *vb* **slob·bered; slob·ber·ing** \-(ə-)riŋ\ : to dribble saliva — **slobber** *n*

sloe \ˈslō\ *n* : the fruit of the blackthorn

slog *vb* **slogged; slog·ging 1** : to hit hard : BEAT **2** : to work hard and steadily

slo·gan \ˈslō-gən\ *n* [alter. of earlier *slogorn*, fr. ScGael *sluagh-ghairm* army cry] : a word or phrase expressing the spirit or aim of a party, group, or cause

sloop \ˈslüp\ *n* : a single-masted sailboat with a jib and a fore-and-aft mainsail

¹**slop** \ˈsläp\ *n* **1** : thin tasteless drink or liquid food — usu. used in pl. **2** : food waste or gruel for animal feed **3** : body and toilet waste — usu. used in pl.

²**slop** *vb* **slopped; slop·ping 1** : SPILL **2** : to feed with slop ⟨~ hogs⟩

¹**slope** \ˈslōp\ *vb* **sloped; slop·ing** : SLANT, INCLINE

²**slope** *n* **1** : upward or downward slant or degree of slant **2** : ground that forms an incline **3** : the part of a landmass draining into a particular ocean

slop·py \ˈsläp-ē\ *adj* **slop·pi·er; -est 1** : MUDDY, SLUSHY **2** : SLOVENLY, MESSY

slosh \ˈsläsh\ *vb* **1** : to flounder through or splash about in or with water, mud, or slush **2** : to move with a splashing motion

slot \ˈslät\ *n* **1** : a long narrow opening or groove **2** : a position in a sequence

slot car *n* : an electric toy racing car that runs on a grooved track

sloth \ˈslȯth, ˈslōth\ *n, pl* **sloths** *with* ths *or* t͟hz\ **1** : LAZINESS, INDOLENCE **2** : a slow-moving So. and Central American mammal related to the armadillos — **sloth·ful** *adj*

slot machine *n* **1** : a machine whose operation is begun by dropping a coin into a slot **2** : a coin-operated gambling machine that pays off according to the matching of symbols on wheels spun by a handle

¹**slouch** \ˈslau̇ch\ *n* **1** : a lazy or incompetent person **2** : a loose or drooping gait or posture

²**slouch** *vb* : to walk, stand, or sit with a slouch : SLUMP

¹**slough** \ˈslü, *2 usu* ˈslau̇\ *n* **1** : a wet and marshy or muddy place (as a swamp) **2** : a discouraged state of mind

²**slough** \ˈsləf\ *or* **sluff** *n* : something (as a snake's skin) that may be shed

³**slough** \ˈsləf\ *or* **sluff** *vb* : to cast off

slov·en \ˈsləv-ən\ *n* [ME *sloveyn* rascal, perh. fr. Flem *sloovin* woman of low character] : an untidy person

slov·en·ly \ˈsləv-ən-lē\ *adj* **1** : untidy in dress or person **2** : lazily or carelessly done : SLIPSHOD

¹**slow** \ˈslō\ *adj* **1** : SLUGGISH; *also* : dull in mind : STUPID **2** : moving, flowing, or proceeding at less than the usual speed **3** : taking more than the usual time **4** : registering behind the correct time **5** : not lively : BORING **syn** dilatory, laggard, deliberate, leisurely — **slow** *adv* — **slow·ly** *adv* — **slow·ness** *n*

²**slow** *vb* **1** : to make slow : hold back **2** : to go slower

slow motion *n* : motion-picture action photographed so as

to appear much slower than normal — **slow–motion** *adj*
SLR *abbr* single-lens reflex
sludge \ˈsləj\ *n* : a slushy mass : OOZE; *esp* : solid matter produced by sewage treatment processes
slue *var of* ²SLEW
¹**slug** \ˈsləg\ *n* **1** : a small mass of metal; *esp* : BULLET **2** : a metal disk for use (as in a slot machine) in place of a coin **3** : any of numerous slimy wormlike mollusks related to the snails **4** : a quantity of liquor drunk
²**slug** *vb* **slugged; slug·ging** : to strike forcibly and heavily — **slug·ger** *n*
slug·gard \ˈsləg-ərd\ *n* : a lazy person
slug·gish \ˈsləg-ish\ *adj* **1** : SLOTHFUL, LAZY **2** : slow in movement or flow **3** : STAGNANT, DULL — **slug·gish·ly** *adv* — **slug·gish·ness** *n*
¹**sluice** \ˈslüs\ *n* **1** : an artificial passage for water with a gate for controlling the flow; *also* : the gate so used **2** : a channel that carries off surplus water **3** : an inclined trough or flume for washing ore or floating logs
²**sluice** *vb* **sluiced; sluic·ing 1** : to draw off through a sluice **2** : to wash with running water : FLUSH
sluice·way \ˈslüs-ˌwā\ *n* : an artificial channel into which water is let by a sluice
¹**slum** \ˈsləm\ *n* : a thickly populated area marked by poverty and dirty or deteriorated houses
²**slum** *vb* **slummed; slum·ming** : to visit slums esp. out of curiosity; *also* : to go somewhere or do something that might be considered beneath one's station
¹**slum·ber** \ˈsləm-bər\ *vb* **slum·bered; slum·ber·ing** \-b(ə-)riŋ\ **1** : DOZE; *also* : SLEEP **2** : to be in a sluggish or torpid state
²**slumber** *n* : SLEEP
slum·ber·ous *or* **slum·brous** \ˈsləm-b(ə-)rəs\ *adj* **1** : SLUMBERING, SLEEPY **2** : PEACEFUL, INACTIVE
slum·lord \ˈsləm-ˌlȯrd\ *n* : a landlord who receives unusually large profits from substandard properties
slump \ˈsləmp\ *vb* **1** : to sink down suddenly : COLLAPSE **2** : SLOUCH **3** : to decline sharply — **slump** *n*
slung *past and past part of* SLING
slunk *past and past part of* SLINK
¹**slur** \ˈslər\ *vb* **slurred; slur·ring 1** : to slide or slip over without due mention or emphasis **2** : to perform two or more successive notes of different pitch in a smooth or connected way
²**slur** *n* : a curved line ◡ or ◠ connecting notes to be slurred; *also* : a group of slurred notes
³**slur** *n* : a slighting remark : ASPERSION
slurp \ˈslərp\ *vb* : to eat or drink noisily — **slurp** *n*
slur·ry \ˈslər-ē\ *n, pl* **slur·ries** : a watery mixture of insoluble matter
slush \ˈsləsh\ *n* **1** : partly melted or watery snow **2** : soft mud — **slushy** *adj*
slut \ˈslət\ *n* **1** : a slovenly woman **2** : PROSTITUTE — **slut·tish** \ˈslət-ish\ *adj*
sly \ˈslī\ *adj* **sli·er** *also* **sly·er** \ˈslī(-ə)r\; **sli·est** *also* **sly·est** \ˈslī-əst\ **1** : CRAFTY, CUNNING **2** : SECRETIVE, FURTIVE **3** : ROGUISH **syn** tricky, wily, artful, foxy, guileful — **sly·ly** *adv* — **sly·ness** *n*
sm *abbr* small
Sm *symbol* samarium
SM *abbr* **1** [NL *scientiae magister*] master of science **2** sergeant major
SMA *abbr* sergeant major of the army
¹**smack** \ˈsmak\ *n* : characteristic flavor; *also* : a slight trace
²**smack** *vb* **1** : to have a taste **2** : to have a trace or suggestion
³**smack** *vb* **1** : to move (the lips) so as to make a sharp noise **2** : to kiss or slap with a loud noise
⁴**smack** *n* **1** : a sharp noise made by the lips **2** : a noisy slap
⁵**smack** *adv* : squarely and sharply
⁶**smack** *n* : a sailing ship used in fishing
⁷**smack** *n, slang* : HEROIN
SMaj *abbr* sergeant major
¹**small** \ˈsmȯl\ *adj* **1** : little in size or amount **2** : operating on a limited scale **3** : few in number **4** : made up of little things **5** : TRIFLING, UNIMPORTANT **6** : MEAN, PETTY **syn** diminutive, petite, wee, tiny, minute — **small·ish** *adj* — **small·ness** *n*
²**small** *n* : a small part or product ⟨the ~ of the back⟩
small·pox \ˈsmȯl-ˌpäks\ *n* : a contagious virus disease marked by fever and a skin eruption
small–time \ˈsmȯl-ˈtīm\ *adj* : insignificant in performance and standing : MINOR — **small–tim·er** \-ˈtī-mər\ *n*
¹**smart** \ˈsmärt\ *vb* **1** : to cause or feel a stinging pain **2** : to feel or endure distress — **smart** *n*
²**smart** *adj* **1** : making one smart ⟨a ~ blow⟩ **2** : mentally quick : BRIGHT **3** : WITTY, CLEVER **4** : STYLISH **5** : being a guided missile **6** : containing a microprocessor for limited computing capability ⟨~ terminal⟩ **syn** knowing, quick-witted, intelligent, brainy, sharp — **smart·ly** *adv* — **smart·ness** *n*
smart al·eck \ˈsmärt-ˌal-ik\ *n* : a person given to obnoxious cleverness
¹**smash** \ˈsmash\ *n* **1** : a smashing blow; *esp* : a hard overhand stroke in tennis **2** : the act or sound of smashing **3** : collision of vehicles : CRASH **4** : COLLAPSE, RUIN; *esp* : BANKRUPTCY **5** : a striking success : HIT — **smash** *adj*
²**smash** *vb* **1** : to break or be broken into pieces **2** : to move forward with force and shattering effect **3** : to destroy utterly : WRECK
smat·ter·ing \ˈsmat-ə-riŋ\ *n* **1** : superficial knowledge **2** : a small scattered number or amount
¹**smear** \ˈsmiər\ *n* : a spot left by an oily or sticky substance
²**smear** *vb* **1** : to overspread with something oily or sticky **2** : SMUDGE, SOIL **3** : to injure by slander or insults
¹**smell** \ˈsmel\ *vb* **smelled** \ˈsmeld\ *or* **smelt** \ˈsmelt\; **smell·ing 1** : to perceive the odor of by sense organs of the nose; *also* : to detect or seek with or as if with these organs **2** : to have or give off an odor
²**smell** *n* **1** : the process or power of perceiving odor; *also* : the special sense by which one perceives odor **2** : ODOR, SCENT **3** : an act of smelling — **smelly** *adj*
smelling salts *n pl* : an aromatic preparation used as a stimulant and restorative (as to relieve faintness)
¹**smelt** \ˈsmelt\ *n, pl* **smelts** *or* **smelt** : any of several small food fishes of coastal or fresh waters that are related to the trouts
²**smelt** *vb* : to melt or fuse (ore) in order to separate the metal; *also* : REFINE
smelt·er \ˈsmel-tər\ *n* **1** : one that smelts **2** : an establishment for smelting
smid·gen *also* **smid·geon** *or* **smid·gin** \ˈsmij-ən\ *n* : a small amount : BIT
smi·lax \ˈsmī-ˌlaks\ *n* **1** : any of various mostly climbing and prickly plants related to the lilies **2** : an ornamental plant related to the asparagus
¹**smile** \ˈsmīl\ *vb* **smiled; smil·ing 1** : to look with a smile **2** : to be favorable **3** : to express by a smile
²**smile** *n* : a change of facial expression to express amusement, pleasure, or affection
smirch \ˈsmərch\ *vb* **1** : to make dirty or stained **2** : to bring disgrace on — **smirch** *n*
smirk \ˈsmərk\ *vb* : to wear a self-conscious or conceited smile : SIMPER — **smirk** *n*
smite \ˈsmīt\ *vb* **smote** \ˈsmōt\; **smit·ten** \ˈsmit-ᵊn\ *or* **smote; smit·ing** \ˈsmīt-iŋ\ **1** : to strike heavily; *also* : to kill by striking **2** : to affect as if by a heavy blow
smith \ˈsmith\ *n* : a worker in metals; *esp* : BLACKSMITH

smith·er·eens \ˌsmith-ə-ˈrēnz\ *n pl* [IrGael *smidirīn*] : FRAGMENTS, BITS

smithy \ˈsmith-ē\ *n, pl* **smith·ies** : a smith's workshop

[1]**smock** \ˈsmäk\ *n* : a loose garment worn over other clothes as a protection

[2]**smock** *vb* : to gather (cloth) in regularly spaced tucks — **smock·ing** *n*

smog \ˈsmäg, ˈsmȯg\ *n* [blend of *smoke* and *fog*] : a thick haze caused by the action of sunlight on air polluted by smoke and automobile exhaust fumes — **smog·gy** *adj*

[1]**smoke** \ˈsmōk\ *n* **1** : the gas from burning material (as coal, wood, or tobacco) in which are suspended particles of soot **2** : a mass or column of smoke **3** : something (as a cigarette) to smoke; *also* : the act of smoking — **smoke·less** *adj* — **smoky** *adj*

[2]**smoke** *vb* **smoked; smok·ing 1** : to emit smoke **2** : to inhale and exhale the fumes of burning tobacco; *also* : to use in smoking ⟨~ a pipe⟩ **3** : to stupefy or drive away by smoke **4** : to discolor with smoke **5** : to cure (as meat) with smoke — **smok·er** *n*

smoke detector *n* : an alarm that sounds automatically when it detects smoke

smoke jumper *n* : a forest-fire fighter who parachutes to locations otherwise difficult to reach

smoke·stack \ˈsmōk-ˌstak\ *n* : a pipe or funnel through which smoke and gases are discharged

smol·der *or* **smoul·der** \ˈsmōl-dər\ *vb* **smol·dered** *or* **smoul·dered; smol·der·ing** *or* **smoul·der·ing** \-d(ə-)riŋ\ **1** : to burn and smoke without flame **2** : to burn inwardly — **smolder** *n*

smooch \ˈsmüch\ *vb* : KISS, PET — **smooch** *n*

[1]**smooth** \ˈsmüth\ *adj* **1** : not rough or uneven **2** : not jarring or jolting **3** : BLAND, MILD **4** : fluent in speech and agreeable in manner **syn** even, flat, level, plane — **smooth·ly** *adv* — **smooth·ness** *n*

[2]**smooth** *vb* **1** : to make smooth **2** : to free from trouble or difficulty

smooth muscle *n* : muscle with no cross striations that is typical of visceral organs (as the stomach and bladder) and is not under voluntary control

smor·gas·bord \ˈsmȯr-gəs-ˌbōrd\ *n* [Sw *smörgasbord*, fr. *smörgas* open sandwich + *bord* table] : a luncheon or supper buffet consisting of many foods

smote *past and past part of* SMITE

[1]**smoth·er** \ˈsməth-ər\ *n* **1** : thick stifling smoke **2** : dense fog, spray, foam, or dust **3** : a confused multitude of things : WELTER

[2]**smother** *vb* **smoth·ered; smoth·er·ing** \-(ə-)riŋ\ **1** : to kill by depriving of air **2** : SUPPRESS **3** : to cover thickly

SMSgt *abbr* senior master sergeant

[1]**smudge** \ˈsməj\ *vb* **smudged; smudg·ing** : to soil or blur by rubbing or smearing

[2]**smudge** *n* : a dirty or blurred spot — **smudgy** *adj*

smug \ˈsməg\ *adj* **smug·ger; smug·gest** : conscious of one's virtue and importance : SELF-SATISFIED — **smug·ly** *adv* — **smug·ness** *n*

smug·gle \ˈsməg-əl\ *vb* **smug·gled; smug·gling** \-(ə-)liŋ\ **1** : to import or export secretly, illegally, or without paying the duties required by law **2** : to convey secretly — **smug·gler** \ˈsməg-lər\ *n*

smut \ˈsmət\ *n* **1** : something (as soot) that smudges; *also* : SMUDGE, SPOT **2** : any of various destructive fungous diseases of plants; *also* : a fungus causing smut **3** : indecent language or matter — **smut·ty** *adj*

smutch \ˈsməch\ *n* : SMUDGE

Sn *symbol* [LL *stannum*] tin

snack \ˈsnak\ *n* : a light meal : BITE

snaf·fle \ˈsnaf-əl\ *n* : a simple jointed bit for a horse's bridle

[1]**snag** \ˈsnag\ *n* **1** : a stump or piece of a tree esp. when under water **2** : an unexpected difficulty **syn** obstacle, obstruction, impediment, bar

[2]**snag** *vb* **snagged; snag·ging 1** : to become caught on or as if on a snag **2** : to seize quickly : SNATCH

snail \ˈsnāl\ *n* : a small mollusk with a spiral shell into which it can withdraw

snake \ˈsnāk\ *n* **1** : any of numerous long-bodied limbless crawling reptiles : SERPENT **2** : a treacherous person **3** : something that resembles a snake — **snaky** *adj*

snake·bird \ˈsnāk-ˌbərd\ *n* : any of several fish-eating birds related to the cormorants but having a long slender neck and sharp-pointed bill

snake·bite \-ˌbīt\ *n* : the bite of a snake and esp. a venomous snake

[1]**snap** \ˈsnap\ *vb* **snapped; snapping 1** : to grasp or slash at something with the teeth **2** : to get or buy quickly **3** : to utter sharp or angry words **4** : to break suddenly with a sharp sound **5** : to give a sharp cracking noise **6** : to throw with a quick motion **7** : FLASH ⟨her eyes *snapped*⟩ **8** : to put a football into play — **snap·per** *n* — **snap·pish** *adj* — **snap·py** *adj*

[2]**snap** *n* **1** : the act or sound of snapping **2** : something very easy to do : CINCH **3** : a short period of cold weather **4** : a catch or fastening that closes with a click **5** : a thin brittle cookie **6** : ENERGY, VIM; *also* : smartness of movement **7** : the putting of the ball into play in football

snap bean *n* : a bean grown primarily for its young tender pods that are usu. broken in pieces and cooked as a vegetable

snap·drag·on \ˈsnap-ˌdrag-ən\ *n* : any of several garden plants with long spikes of showy 2-lipped flowers

snapping turtle *n* : either of two large edible American turtles with powerful jaws and a strong musky odor

snap·shot \ˈsnap-ˌshät\ *n* : a photograph taken usu. with an inexpensive hand-held camera

snare \ˈsnaər\ *n* : a trap often consisting of a noose for catching birds or mammals — **snare** *vb*

[1]**snarl** \ˈsnärl\ *n* : TANGLE

[2]**snarl** *vb* : to cause to become knotted and intertwined

[3]**snarl** *vb* : to growl angrily or threateningly

[4]**snarl** *n* : an angry ill-tempered growl

[1]**snatch** \ˈsnach\ *vb* **1** : to try to grasp something suddenly **2** : to seize or take away suddenly **syn** clutch, seize, grab, nab

[2]**snatch** *n* **1** : a short period **2** : an act of snatching **3** : something brief or fragmentary ⟨~*es* of song⟩

[1]**sneak** \ˈsnēk\ *vb* **sneaked** \ˈsnēkt\ *or* **snuck** \ˈsnək\; **sneak·ing** : to move, act, or take in a furtive manner — **sneak·ing·ly** *adv*

[2]**sneak** *n* **1** : one who acts in a furtive or shifty manner **2** : a stealthy or furtive move or escape — **sneaky** *adj*

sneak·er \ˈsnē-kər\ *n* : a usu. canvas sports shoe with a pliable rubber sole

sneer \ˈsniər\ *vb* : to show scorn or contempt by curling the lip or by a jeering tone — **sneer** *n*

sneeze \ˈsnēz\ *vb* **sneezed; sneez·ing** : to force the breath out suddenly and violently as a reflex act — **sneeze** *n*

snick·er \ˈsnik-ər\ *n* : a partly suppressed laugh — **snicker** *vb*

snide \ˈsnīd\ *adj* **1** : MEAN, LOW ⟨a ~ trick⟩ **2** : slyly disparaging ⟨a ~ remark⟩

sniff \ˈsnif\ *vb* **1** : to draw air audibly up the nose **2** : to show disdain or scorn **3** : to detect by or as if by smelling — **sniff** *n*

snif·fle \ˈsnif-əl\ *n* **1** *pl* : a head cold marked by nasal discharge **2** : SNUFFLE — **sniffle** *vb*

[1]**snip** \ˈsnip\ *n* **1** : a fragment snipped off **2** : a simple stroke of the scissors or shears

[2]**snip** *vb* **snipped; snip·ping** : to cut off by bits : CLIP; *also* : to remove by cutting off

[1]**snipe** \ˈsnīp\ *n, pl* **snipes** *or* **snipe** : any of several long-billed game birds that occur esp. in marshy areas and resemble the related woodcocks

[2]**snipe** *vb* **sniped; snip·ing** : to shoot at an exposed enemy

from a concealed position usu. at long range — **snip·er** *n*

snip·py \ˈsnip-ē\ *adj* **snip·pi·er; -est** : CURT, SNAPPISH

snips \ˈsnips\ *n pl* : hand shears used esp. for cutting sheet metal ⟨tin ~⟩

snitch \ˈsnich\ *vb* **1** : INFORM, TATTLE **2** : PILFER, SNATCH

sniv·el \ˈsniv-əl\ *vb* **-eled** *or* **-elled; -el·ing** *or* **-el·ling** \-(ə-)liŋ\ **1** : to have a running nose; *also* : SNUFFLE **2** : to whine in a snuffling manner — **snivel** *n*

snob \ˈsnäb\ *n* [obs. *snob* member of the lower classes, fr. E dial., shoemaker] : one who seeks association with persons of higher social position and looks down on those he considers inferior — **snob·bish** *adj* — **snob·bish·ly** *adv* — **snob·bish·ness** *n*

snob·bery \ˈsnäb-(ə-)rē\ *n, pl* **-ber·ies** : snobbish conduct

[1]**snoop** \ˈsnüp\ *vb* [D *snoepen* to buy or eat on the sly] : to pry in a furtive or meddlesome way

[2]**snoop** *n* : a prying meddlesome person

snooty \ˈsnüt-ē\ *adj* **snoot·i·er; -est** : DISDAINFUL, SNOBBISH

snooze \ˈsnüz\ *vb* **snoozed; snooz·ing** : to take a nap : DOZE — **snooze** *n*

snore \ˈsnōr\ *vb* **snored; snor·ing** : to breathe with a rough hoarse noise while sleeping — **snore** *n*

snor·kel \ˈsnȯr-kəl\ *n* [G *schnorchel*] : a tube projecting above the water used by swimmers for breathing with the face under water — **snorkel** *vb*

snort \ˈsnȯrt\ *vb* : to force air violently and noisily through the nose ⟨his horse ~*ed*⟩ — **snort** *n*

snout \ˈsnau̇t\ *n* **1** : a long projecting muzzle (as of a pig) **2** : a usu. large or grotesque nose

[1]**snow** \ˈsnō\ *n* **1** : crystals of ice formed from the vapor of water in the air **2** : a descent or shower of snow crystals — **snowy** *adj*

[2]**snow** *vb* **1** : to fall or cause to fall in or as snow **2** : to cover or shut in with or as if with snow

snow·ball \ˈsnō-ˌbȯl\ *vb* : to increase or expand at a rapidly accelerating rate

snow·bank \-ˌbaŋk\ *n* : a mound or slope of snow

snow·belt \-ˌbelt\ *n, often cap* : a region that receives an appreciable amount of annual snowfall

snow·blow·er \-ˌblō-ər\ *n* : a machine in which a rotating spiral blade picks up and propels snow aside

snow·drift \-ˌdrift\ *n* : a bank of drifted snow

snow·drop \-ˌdräp\ *n* : a plant with narrow leaves and a nodding white flower that blooms early in the spring

snow·fall \-ˌfȯl\ *n* : a fall of snow

snow fence *n* : a fence across the path of prevailing winds to protect something (as a road) from drifting snow

snow·field \ˈsnō-ˌfēld\ *n* : a mass of perennial snow at the head of a glacier

snow·mo·bile \ˈsnō-mō-ˌbēl\ *n* : any of various automotive vehicles for travel on snow — **snow·mo·bil·er** \-ˌbē-lər\ *n* — **snow·mo·bil·ing** \-liŋ\ *n*

snow pea *n* : any of a variety of the cultivated pea with edible pods

snow·plow \ˈsnō-ˌplau̇\ *n* : a device for clearing away snow

[1]**snow·shoe** \-ˌshü\ *n* : a light frame of wood strung with thongs that is attached to a shoe or boot to prevent sinking down into soft snow

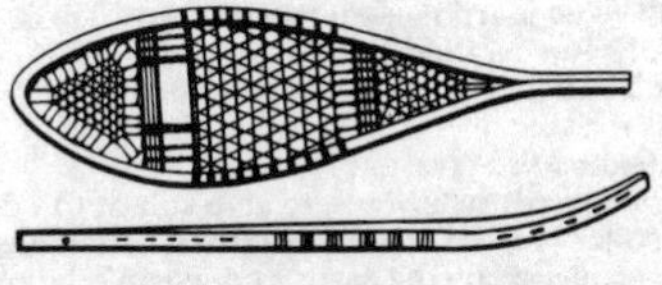

snowshoe

[2]**snowshoe** *vb* **snow·shoed; snow·shoe·ing** : to travel on snowshoes

snow·storm \-ˌstȯrm\ *n* : a storm of falling snow

snow thrower *n* : SNOWBLOWER

snowy \ˈsnō-ē\ *adj* **snow·i·er; -est** **1** : marked by snow **2** : white as snow

snub \ˈsnəb\ *vb* **snubbed; snub·bing** : to treat with disdain : SLIGHT — **snub** *n*

snub–nosed \ˈsnəb-ˈnōzd\ *adj* : having a nose slightly turned up at the end

snuck *past and past part of* SNEAK

[1]**snuff** \ˈsnəf\ *vb* **1** : to pinch off the charred end of (a candle) **2** : to put out (a candle) — **snuff·er** *n*

[2]**snuff** *vb* **1** : to draw forcibly into or through the nose **2** : SMELL

[3]**snuff** *n* : SNIFF

[4]**snuff** *n* : pulverized tobacco

snuf·fle \ˈsnəf-əl\ *vb* **snuf·fled; snuf·fling** \-(ə-)liŋ\ **1** : to snuff or sniff audibly and repeatedly **2** : to breathe with a sniffing sound — **snuf·fle** *n*

snug \ˈsnəg\ *adj* **snug·ger; snug·gest** **1** : fitting closely and comfortably **2** : CONCEALED — **snug·ly** *adv* — **snug·ness** *n*

snug·gle \ˈsnəg-əl\ *vb* **snug·gled; snug·gling** \-(ə-)liŋ\ : to curl up or draw close comfortably : NESTLE

[1]**so** \(ˈ)sō\ *adv* **1** : in the manner indicated **2** : in the same way **3** : THUS **4** : FINALLY **5** : to the extent indicated **6** : THEREFORE

[2]**so** *conj* : for that reason ⟨he wanted it, ~ he took it⟩

[3]**so** \ˌsō, ˈsō\ *pron* **1** : the same ⟨became chairman and remained ~⟩ **2** : approximately that ⟨I'd like a dozen or ~⟩

[4]**so** *abbr* south; southern

SO *abbr* strikeout

[1]**soak** \ˈsōk\ *vb* **1** : to remain in a liquid **2** : WET, SATURATE **3** : to draw in by or as if by absorption **syn** drench, steep, impregnate, saturate

[2]**soak** *n* **1** : the act of soaking **2** : the liquid in which something is soaked **3** : DRUNKARD

soap \ˈsōp\ *n* : a cleansing substance made usu. by action of alkali on fat — **soap** *vb* — **soapy** *adj*

soap opera *n* [fr. its frequently being sponsored by soap manufacturers] : a radio or television daytime serial drama

soap·stone \ˈsōp-ˌstōn\ *n* : a soft stone having a soapy feel and containing talc

soar \ˈsōr\ *vb* : to fly upward or at a height on as if on wings

sob \ˈsäb\ *vb* **sobbed; sob·bing** : to weep with convulsive heavings of the chest or contractions of the throat — **sob** *n*

so·ber \ˈsō-bər\ *adj* **so·ber·er** \-bər-ər\; **so·ber·est** \-b(ə-)rəst\ **1** : temperate in the use of liquor **2** : not drunk **3** : serious or grave in mood or disposition **4** : not affected by passion or prejudice **syn** solemn, earnest, staid, sedate — **so·ber·ly** *adv* — **so·ber·ness** *n*

so·bri·ety \sə-ˈbrī-ət-ē, sō-\ *n* : the quality or state of being sober

so·bri·quet \ˈsō-bri-ˌkā, -ˌket\ *n* [F] : NICKNAME

soc *abbr* social; society

so–called \ˈsō-ˈkȯld\ *adj* : commonly or popularly but often inaccurately so termed

soc·cer \ˈsäk-ər\ *n* [by shortening & alter. fr. *association football*] : a football game played on a field by two teams with a round inflated ball

[1]**so·cia·ble** \ˈsō-shə-bəl\ *adj* **1** : liking companionship : FRIENDLY **2** : characterized by pleasant social relations **syn** gracious, cordial, affable, genial — **so·cia·bil·i·ty** \ˌsō-shə-ˈbil-ət-ē\ *n* — **so·cia·bly** \ˈsō-shə-blē\ *adv*

[2]**sociable** *n* : an informal social gathering

[1]**so·cial** \ˈsō-shəl\ *adj* **1** : marked by pleasant companionship with one's friends **2** : naturally living or growing in groups or communities ⟨~ insects⟩ **3** : of or relating to human society, the interaction of the group and its members, and the welfare of these members ⟨~ behavior⟩ **4** : of, relating to, or based on rank in a particular society ⟨~ circles⟩; *also* : of or relating to fashionable society — **so·cial·ly** \-ē\ *adv*

[2]**social** *n* : a social gathering

social disease *n* : VENEREAL DISEASE

so·cial·ism \ˈsō-shə-ˌliz-əm\ *n* : a theory of social organization based on government ownership, management, and control of the means of production and the distribution and exchange of goods — **so·cial·ist** \ˈsōsh-(ə-)ləst\ *n or adj* — **so·cial·is·tic** \ˌsō-shə-ˈlis-tik\ *adj*

so·cial·ite \ˈsō-shə-ˌlīt\ *n* : a person prominent in fashionable society

so·cial·ize \ˈsō-shə-ˌlīz\ *vb* **-ized; -iz·ing 1** : to regulate according to the theory and practice of socialism **2** : to adapt to social needs or uses **3** : to participate actively in a social gathering — **so·cial·iza·tion** \ˌsōsh-(ə-)lə-ˈzā-shən\ *n*

socialized medicine *n* : medical and hospital services administered by an organized group (as a state agency) and paid for by funds obtained usu. by assessments, taxation, or philanthropy

social science *n* : a science that deals with human society or its elements (as family, state, or race), institutions, and relationships or with a particular aspect of human society — **social scientist** *n*

social work *n* : services, activities, or methods concerned with aiding the economically underprivileged and socially maladjusted — **social worker** *n*

so·ci·ety \sə-ˈsī-ət-ē\ *n, pl* **-et·ies** [MF *societé* fr. L *societat-, societas,* fr. *socius* companion] **1** : COMPANIONSHIP **2** : a voluntary association of persons for common ends **3** : a part of a community bound together by common interests and standards; *esp* : a leisure class indulging in social affairs

sociol *abbr* sociologist; sociology

so·ci·ol·o·gy \ˌsō-s(h)ē-ˈäl-ə-jē\ *n* : the study of the development and structure of society and social relationships — **so·ci·o·log·i·cal** \-ə-ˈläj-i-kəl\ *adj* — **so·ci·ol·o·gist** \-ˈäl-ə-jəst\ *n*

so·cio·re·li·gious \ˌsō-s(h)ē-ō-ri-ˈlij-əs\ *adj* : of, relating to, or involving both social and religious factors

[1]**sock** \ˈsäk\ *n, pl* **socks** *or* **sox** \ˈsäks\ : a stocking with a short leg

[2]**sock** *vb* : to hit, strike, or apply forcefully

[3]**sock** *n* : a vigorous blow : PUNCH

sock·et \ˈsäk-ət\ *n* : an opening or hollow that receives and holds something

socket wrench *n* : a wrench usu. in the form of a bar and removable socket made to fit a bolt or nut

sock in *vb* : to close to takeoffs or landings by aircraft

[1]**sod** \ˈsäd\ *n* : the surface layer of the soil filled with roots (as of grass)

[2]**sod** *vb* **sod·ded; sod·ding** : to cover with sod or turfs

so·da \ˈsōd-ə\ *n* **1** : SODIUM CARBONATE **2** : SODIUM BICARBONATE **3** : SODIUM **4** : SODA WATER **5** : SODA POP **6** : a sweet drink of soda water, flavoring, and often ice cream

soda pop *n* : a carbonated, sweetened, and flavored soft drink

soda water *n* : a beverage of water charged with carbon dioxide

sod·den \ˈsäd-ᵊn\ *adj* **1** : lacking spirit : DULLED **2** : SOAKED, DRENCHED **3** : heavy or doughy from being improperly cooked ⟨~ biscuits⟩

so·di·um \ˈsōd-ē-əm\ *n* : a soft waxy silver white metallic chemical element occurring in nature in combined form (as in salt) — see ELEMENT table

sodium bicarbonate *n* : a white crystalline salt used in cooking and in medicine

sodium carbonate *n* : a carbonate of sodium used esp. in washing and bleaching textiles

sodium chloride *n* : SALT 1

sodium hydroxide *n* : a white brittle caustic substance used in making soap and rayon and in bleaching

sodium nitrate *n* : a crystalline salt used as a fertilizer and in curing meat

sodium thiosulfate *n* : a hygroscopic crystalline salt used as a photographic fixing agent

sod·omy \ˈsäd-ə-mē\ *n* [ME, fr. OF *sodomie,* fr. LL *Sodoma* Sodom; fr. the homosexual proclivities of the men of the city (Gen 19:1–11)] **1** : copulation with a member of the same sex or with an animal **2** : noncoital and esp. anal or oral copulation with a member of the opposite sex — **sod·om·ize** \ˈsäd-ə-ˌmīz\ *vb*

so·ev·er \sō-ˈev-ər\ *adv* **1** : in any degree or manner ⟨how bad ~⟩ **2** : at all : of any kind ⟨any help ~⟩

so·fa \ˈsō-fə\ *n* [Ar *ṣuffah* long bench] : a couch usu. with upholstered back and arms

soft \ˈsȯft\ *adj* **1** : not hard or rough : NONVIOLENT **2** : RESTFUL, GENTLE, SOOTHING **3** : emotionally susceptible **4** : not prepared to endure hardship **5** : not containing certain salts that prevent lathering ⟨~ water⟩ **6** : occurring at such a speed as to avoid destructive impact ⟨~ landing of a spacecraft on the moon⟩ **7** : BIODEGRADABLE ⟨a ~ detergent⟩ **8** : not alcoholic; *also* : less detrimental than a hard narcotic **syn** bland, mild, gentle, balmy — **soft·ly** \ˈsȯft-lē\ *adv* — **soft·ness** \ˈsȯf(t)-nəs\ *n*

soft·ball \ˈsȯf(t)-ˌbȯl\ *n* : a game similar to baseball played with a ball larger and softer than a baseball; *also* : the ball used in this game

soft·bound \-ˌbau̇nd\ *adj* : not bound in hard covers ⟨~ books⟩

soft coal *n* : bituminous coal

soft·en \ˈsȯ-fən\ *vb* **soft·ened; soft·en·ing** \ˈsȯf-(ə-)niŋ\ : to make or become soft — **soft·en·er** \-(ə-)nər\ *n*

soft palate *n* : the fold at the back of the hard palate that partially separates the mouth and the pharynx

soft·ware \ˈsȯft-ˌwaər\ *n* : the entire set of programs, procedures, and related documentation associated with a system; *esp* : computer programs

soft·wood \-ˌwu̇d\ *n* **1** : the wood of a coniferous tree (as a pine or fir) as compared to that of a tree producing enclosed seeds **2** : a tree that yields softwood — **softwood** *adj*

sog·gy \ˈsäg-ē\ *adj* **sog·gi·er; -est** : heavy with moisture : SOAKED, SODDEN — **sog·gi·ly** \ˈsäg-ə-lē\ *adv* — **sog·gi·ness** \-ē-nəs\ *n*

soi·gné *or* **soi·gnée** \swän-ˈyā\ *adj* : elegantly maintained; *esp* : WELL-GROOMED

[1]**soil** \ˈsȯil\ *vb* **1** : CORRUPT, POLLUTE **2** : to make or become dirty **3** : STAIN, DISGRACE

[2]**soil** *n* **1** : STAIN, DEFILEMENT **2** : EXCREMENT, WASTE

[3]**soil** *n* **1** : firm land : EARTH **2** : the loose surface material of the earth in which plants grow **3** : COUNTRY, REGION

soi·ree *or* **soi·rée** \swä-ˈrā\ *n* [F *soirée* evening period, evening party, fr. MF, fr. *soir* evening, fr. L *sero* at a late hour] : an evening party

so·journ \ˈsō-ˌjərn, sō-ˈjərn\ *vb* : to dwell in a place temporarily — **so·journ** *n* — **so·journ·er** *n*

[1]**sol** \ˈsäl, ˈsȯl\ *n* : a fluid colloidal system

[2]**sol** *abbr* **1** solicitor **2** soluble **3** solution

Sol \ˈsäl\ *n* : SUN

[1]**sol·ace** \ˈsäl-əs\ *n* : COMFORT

[2]**solace** *vb* **so·laced; so·lac·ing** : to give solace to : CONSOLE

so·lar \ˈsō-lər\ *adj* **1** : of, derived from, or relating to the sun **2** : measured by the earth's course in relation to the sun ⟨the ~ year⟩ **3** : operated by or utilizing the sun's heat ⟨~ house⟩

solar cell *n* : a photoelectric cell that converts sunlight into electrical energy and is used as a power source

solar collector *n* : any of various devices for the absorption of solar radiation for the heating of water or buildings or the production of electricity

solar flare *n* : a sudden temporary outburst of energy from a small area of the sun's surface

so·lar·i·um \sō-ˈlar-ē-əm, sə-\ *n, pl* **-ia** \-ē-ə\ *also* **-ums** : a room exposed to the sun; *esp* : a room (as in a hospital) for exposure of the body to sunshine

solar plexus \ˈsō-lər-ˈplek-səs\ *n* **1** : a network of nerves situated behind the stomach **2** : the general area of the stomach below the sternum

solar system *n* : the sun with the group of celestial bodies that revolve about it

solar wind *n* : the continuous radiation of charged particles from the sun's surface

sold *past and past part of* SELL

[1]**sol·der** \ˈsäd-ər, ˈsȯd-\ *n* : a metallic alloy used when melted to mend or join metallic surfaces

[2]**solder** *vb* **sol·dered; sol·der·ing** \-(ə-)riŋ\ **1** : to unite or repair with solder **2** : to join securely : CEMENT

soldering iron *n* : a metal device for applying heat in soldering

[1]**sol·dier** \ˈsōl-jər\ *n* [ME *soudier,* fr. OF, fr. *soulde* pay, fr. LL *solidus* a Roman coin, fr. L, solid] : a person in military service; *esp* : an enlisted man — **sol·dier·ly** *adj or adv*

[2]**soldier** *vb* **sol·diered; sol·dier·ing** \ˌsōlj-(ə-)riŋ\ **1** : to serve as a soldier **2** : to pretend to work while actually doing nothing

soldier of fortune : ADVENTURER

sol·diery \ˈsōlj-(ə-)rē\ *n* **1** : a body of soldiers **2** : the profession of soldiering

[1]**sole** \ˈsōl\ *n* **1** : the undersurface of the foot **2** : the bottom of a shoe

[2]**sole** *vb* **soled; sol·ing** : to furnish (a shoe) with a sole

[3]**sole** *n* : any of various mostly small-mouthed flatfishes valued as food

[4]**sole** *adj* : ONLY, SINGLE — **sole·ly** \ˈsō(l)-lē\ *adv*

so·le·cism \ˈsäl-ə-ˌsiz-əm, ˈsō-lə-\ *n* **1** : a mistake in grammar **2** : a breach of etiquette

sol·emn \ˈsäl-əm\ *adj* **1** : marked by or observed with full religious ceremony **2** : FORMAL, CEREMONIOUS **3** : highly serious : GRAVE **4** : SOMBER, GLOOMY **syn** ceremonial, conventional, stately — **so·lem·ni·ty** \sə-ˈlem-nət-ē\ *n* — **sol·emn·ly** \ˈsäl-əm-lē\ *adv* — **sol·emn·ness** *n*

sol·em·nize \ˈsäl-əm-ˌnīz\ *vb* **-nized; -niz·ing** **1** : to observe or honor with solemnity **2** : to celebrate (a marriage) with religious rites — **sol·em·ni·za·tion** \ˈsäl-əm-nə-ˈzā-shən\ *n*

so·le·noid \ˈsō-lə-ˌnȯid, ˈsäl-\ *n* : a coil of wire usu. in cylindrical form that when carrying a current acts like a magnet

so·lic·it \sə-ˈlis-ət\ *vb* **1** : ENTREAT, BEG **2** : to approach with a request or plea **3** : TEMPT, LURE **syn** ask, request, desire — **so·lic·i·ta·tion** \-ˌlis-ə-ˈtā-shən\ *n*

so·lic·i·tor \sə-ˈlis-ət-ər\ *n* **1** : one that solicits **2** : LAWYER; *esp* : a legal official of a city or state

so·lic·i·tous \sə-ˈlis-ət-əs\ *adj* **1** : WORRIED, CONCERNED **2** : EAGER, WILLING **syn** avid, impatient, keen, anxious — **so·lic·i·tous·ly** *adv*

so·lic·i·tude \sə-ˈlis-ə-ˌt(y)üd\ *n* : CONCERN, ANXIETY

[1]**sol·id** \ˈsäl-əd\ *adj* **1** : not hollow; *also* : written as one word without a hyphen ⟨a ~ compound⟩ **2** : having, involving, or dealing with three dimensions or with solids **3** : not loose or spongy : COMPACT ⟨a ~ mass of rock⟩; *also* : neither gaseous nor liquid : HARD, RIGID ⟨~ ice⟩ **4** : of good substantial quality or kind ⟨~ comfort⟩ **5** : thoroughly dependable : RELIABLE ⟨a ~ citizen⟩; *also* : serious in purpose or character ⟨~ reading⟩ **6** : UNANIMOUS, UNITED ⟨~ for pay increases⟩ **7** : of one substance or character — **solid** *adv* — **so·lid·i·ty** \sə-ˈlid-ət-ē\ *n* — **sol·id·ly** \ˈsäl-əd-lē\ *adv* — **sol·id·ness** *n*

[2]**solid** *n* **1** : a geometrical figure (as a cube or sphere) having three dimensions **2** : a solid substance

sol·i·dar·i·ty \ˌsäl-ə-ˈdar-ət-ē\ *n* : unity based on shared interests, objectives, or standards

solid geometry *n* : a branch of geometry that deals with figures of three-dimensional space

so·lid·i·fy \sə-ˈlid-ə-ˌfī\ *vb* **-fied; -fy·ing** : to make or become solid — **so·lid·i·fi·ca·tion** \-ˌlid-ə-fə-ˈkā-shən\ *n*

solid–state *adj* **1** : relating to the structure and properties of solid material **2** : not using vacuum tubes

so·lil·o·quize \sə-ˈlil-ə-ˌkwīz\ *vb* **-quized; -quiz·ing** : to talk to oneself : utter a soliloquy

so·lil·o·quy \sə-ˈlil-ə-kwē\ *n, pl* **-quies** [LL *soliloquium,* fr. L *solus* alone + *loqui* to speak] **1** : the act of talking to oneself **2** : a dramatic monologue that gives the illusion of being a series of unspoken reflections

sol·i·taire \ˈsäl-ə-ˌtaər\ *n* **1** : a single gem (as a diamond) set alone **2** : a card game played by one person alone

sol·i·tary \ˈsäl-ə-ˌter-ē\ *adj* **1** : being or living apart from others **2** : LONELY, SECLUDED **3** : SOLE, ONLY

sol·i·tude \ˈsäl-ə-ˌt(y)üd\ *n* **1** : the state of being alone : SECLUSION **2** : a lonely place **syn** isolation

soln *abbr* solution

[1]**so·lo** \ˈsō-lō\ *n, pl* **solos** [It, fr. *solo* alone, fr. L *solus*] **1** : a piece of music for a single voice or instrument with or without accompaniment **2** : an action in which there is only one performer — **solo** *adj or vb* — **so·lo·ist** *n*

[2]**solo** *adv* : without a companion : ALONE

so·lon \ˈsō-lən\ *n* **1** : a wise and skillful lawgiver **2** : a member of a legislative body

sol·stice \ˈsäl-stəs\ *n* [ME, fr. OF, fr. L *solstitium,* fr. *sol* sun + *status,* pp. of *sistere* to come to a stop, cause to stand] : the time of the year when the sun is farthest north of the equator (**summer solstice**) about June 22 or farthest south (**winter solstice**) about Dec. 22 — **sol·sti·tial** \säl-ˈstish-əl\ *adj*

sol·u·ble \ˈsäl-yə-bəl\ *adj* **1** : capable of being dissolved in or as if in a fluid **2** : capable of being solved or explained — **sol·u·bil·i·ty** \ˌsäl-yə-ˈbil-ət-ē\ *n*

sol·ute \ˈsäl-ˌyüt\ *n* : a dissolved substance

so·lu·tion \sə-ˈlü-shən\ *n* **1** : an action or process of solving a problem; *also* : an answer to a problem **2** : an act or the process by which one substance is homogenously mixed with another usu. liquid substance; *also* : a mixture thus formed

solve \ˈsälv\ *vb* **solved; solv·ing** : to find the answer to or a solution for — **solv·able** *adj*

sol·ven·cy \ˈsäl-vən-sē\ *n* : the condition of being solvent

[1]**sol·vent** \-vənt\ *adj* **1** : able or sufficient to pay all legal debts **2** : dissolving or able to dissolve

[2]**solvent** *n* : a usu. liquid substance capable of dissolving or dispersing one or more other substances

som·ber *or* **som·bre** \ˈsäm-bər\ *adj* **1** : DARK, GLOOMY **2** : GRAVE, MELANCHOLY — **som·ber·ly** *adv*

som·bre·ro \səm-ˈbrer-ō\ *n, pl* **-ros** [Sp, fr. *sombra* shade] : a broad-brimmed felt hat worn esp. in the Southwest and in Mexico

[1]**some** \(ˈ)səm\ *adj* **1** : one unspecified ⟨~ man called⟩ **2** : an unspecified or indefinite number of ⟨~ berries are ripe⟩ **3** : at least a few or a little ⟨~ years ago⟩

[2]**some** \ˈsəm\ *pron* : a certain number or amount ⟨~ of them are here⟩ ⟨~ of it is missing⟩

[1]**-some** \səm\ *adj suffix* : characterized by a (specified) thing, quality, state, or action ⟨awe*some*⟩ ⟨burden*some*⟩

[2]**-some** *n suffix* : a group of (so many) members and esp. persons ⟨four*some*⟩

[1]**some·body** \ˈsəm-ˌbäd-ē, -bəd-\ *pron* : some person

[2]**somebody** *n* : a person of importance

some·day \ˈsəm-ˌdā\ *adv* : at some future time
some·how \-ˌhau̇\ *adv* : by some means
some·one \-(ˌ)wən\ *pron* : some person
som·er·sault \ˈsəm-ər-ˌsȯlt\ *n* [MF *sombresaut* leap, deriv. of L *super* over + *saltus* leap, fr. *salire* to jump] : a leap or roll in which a person turns the heels over the head — **somersault** *vb*
som·er·set \-ˌset\ *n or vb* : SOMERSAULT
some·thing \ˈsəm-thiŋ\ *pron* : some undetermined or unspecified thing
some·time \ˈsəm-ˌtīm\ *adv* **1** : at a future time **2** : at an unknown or unnamed time
some·times \ˈsəm-ˌtīmz\ *adv* : OCCASIONALLY
[1]**some·what** \-ˌhwät, -ˌhwət\ *pron* : SOMETHING
[2]**somewhat** *adv* : in some degree
some·where \-ˌhweər\ *adv* : in, at, or to an unknown or unnamed place
som·nam·bu·lism \säm-ˈnam-byə-ˌliz-əm\ *n* : activity (as walking about) during sleep — **som·nam·bu·list** \-ləst\ *n*
som·no·lent \ˈsäm-nə-lənt\ *adj* : SLEEPY, DROWSY — **som·no·lence** \-ləns\ *n*
son \ˈsən\ *n* **1** : a male offspring or descendant **2** *cap* : Jesus Christ **3** : a person deriving from a particular source (as a country, race, or school)
so·nar \ˈsō-ˌnär\ *n* [*so*und *na*vigation *r*anging] : an apparatus that detects the presence and location of submerged objects (as submarines) by sound waves
so·na·ta \sə-ˈnät-ə\ *n* [It] : an instrumental composition with three or four movements differing in rhythm and mood but related in key
son·a·ti·na \ˌsän-ə-ˈtē-nə\ *n* [It, dim. of *sonata*] : a short usu. simplified sonata
song \ˈsȯŋ\ *n* **1** : vocal music; *also* : a short composition of words and music **2** : poetic composition **3** : a distinctive or characteristic sound (as of a bird) **4** : a small amount ⟨sold for a ~⟩
song·bird \ˈsȯŋ-ˌbərd\ *n* : a bird that utters a series of musical tones
Song of Sol·o·mon \-ˈsäl-ə-mən\ *n* — see BIBLE table
Song of Songs *n* — see BIBLE table
song·ster \-stər\ *n* : one that sings
song·stress \-strəs\ *n* : a female singer
son·ic \ˈsän-ik\ *adj* : of or relating to sound waves or the speed of sound
sonic boom *n* : an explosive sound produced by an aircraft traveling at supersonic speed
son–in–law \ˈsən-ən-ˌlȯ\ *n, pl* **sons–in–law** : the husband of one's daughter
son·net \ˈsän-ət\ *n* : a poem of 14 lines usu. in iambic pentameter with a definite rhyme scheme
so·no·rous \sə-ˈnōr-əs, ˈsän-ə-rəs\ *adj* **1** : giving out sound when struck **2** : loud, deep, or rich in sound : RESONANT **3** : high-sounding : IMPRESSIVE — **so·nor·i·ty** \sə-ˈnȯr-ət-ē\ *n*
soon \ˈsün\ *adv* **1** : before long **2** : PROMPTLY, QUICKLY **3** *archaic* : EARLY **4** : WILLINGLY, READILY
soot \ˈsu̇t, ˈsət, ˈsüt\ *n* : a fine black powder consisting chiefly of carbon that is formed when something burns and that colors smoke — **sooty** *adj*
sooth \ˈsüth\ *n, archaic* : TRUTH
soothe \ˈsüt͟h\ *vb* **soothed; sooth·ing 1** : to please by flattery or attention **2** : to calm down : COMFORT — **sooth·er** *n* — **sooth·ing·ly** *adv*
sooth·say·er \ˈsüth-ˌsā-ər\ *n* : one that foretells events — **sooth·say·ing** \-iŋ\ *n*
[1]**sop** \ˈsäp\ *n* : a conciliatory bribe, gift, or concession
[2]**sop** *vb* **sopped; sop·ping 1** : to steep or dip in or as if in a liquid **2** : to wet thoroughly : SOAK; *also* : to mop up (a liquid)
SOP *abbr* standard operating procedure; standing operating procedure
soph *abbr* sophomore
soph·ism \ˈsäf-ˌiz-əm\ *n* **1** : an argument correct in form but embodying a subtle fallacy **2** : SOPHISTRY
soph·ist \ˈsäf-əst\ *n* : PHILOSOPHER; *esp* : a captious or fallacious reasoner
so·phis·tic \sä-ˈfis-tik, sə-\ *or* **so·phis·ti·cal** \-ti-kəl\ *adj* : of or characteristic of sophists or sophistry **syn** fallacious, illogical, unreasonable, unreasoned
so·phis·ti·cat·ed \-tə-ˌkāt-əd\ *adj* **1** : COMPLEX ⟨~ instruments⟩ **2** : made wise or worldly-wise by experience or disillusionment **3** : intellectually appealing ⟨~ novel⟩ — **so·phis·ti·ca·tion** \-ˌfis-tə-ˈkā-shən\ *n*
soph·ist·ry \ˈsäf-ə-strē\ *n* : subtly deceptive reasoning or argument
soph·o·more \ˈsäf-(ᵊ-)ˌmōr\ *n* : a student in his or her second year of college or secondary school
soph·o·mor·ic \ˌsäf-ə-ˈmōr-ik\ *adj* **1** : being overconfident of knowledge but poorly informed and immature **2** : of, relating to, or characteristic of a sophomore
So·pho·ni·as \ˌsäf-ə-ˈnī-əs, ˌsō-fə-\ *n* — see BIBLE table
sop·o·rif·ic \ˌsäp-ə-ˈrif-ik\ *adj* **1** : causing sleep or drowsiness **2** : LETHARGIC
so·pra·no \sə-ˈpran-ō\ *n, pl* **-nos** [It, fr. *sopra* above, fr. L *supra*] **1** : the highest singing voice; *also* : a part for this voice **2** : a singer with a soprano voice — **soprano** *adj*
sorb \ˈsȯrb\ *vb* : to take up and hold by adsorption or absorption
sor·bet \ˈsȯr-bət\ *n* : ice having a fruit flavor and typically served between courses as a palate refresher
sor·cery \ˈsȯrs-(ə-)rē\ *n* [ME *sorcerie*, fr. OF, fr. *sorcier* sorcerer, fr. (assumed) VL *sortiarius*, fr. L *sort-, sors* chance, lot] : the use of magic : WITCHCRAFT — **sor·cer·er** \-rər\ *n* — **sor·cer·ess** \-rəs\ *n*
sor·did \ˈsȯrd-əd\ *adj* **1** : FILTHY, DIRTY **2** : marked by baseness or grossness : VILE — **sor·did·ly** *adv* — **sor·did·ness** *n*
[1]**sore** \ˈsōr\ *adj* **sor·er; sor·est 1** : causing pain or distress ⟨a ~ bruise⟩ **2** : painfully sensitive ⟨~ eyes⟩ **3** : SEVERE, INTENSE **4** : IRRITATED, ANGRY — **sore·ly** *adv* — **sore·ness** *n*
[2]**sore** *n* **1** : a sore spot on the body; *esp* : one (as an ulcer) with the tissues broken and usu. infected **2** : a source of pain or vexation
sore·head \ˈsō(ə)r-ˌhed, ˈsȯ(ə)r-\ *n* : a person easily angered or discontented
sore throat *n* : painful throat due to inflammation
sor·ghum \ˈsȯr-gəm\ *n* : a tall variable Old World tropical grass grown widely for its edible seed, for forage, or for its sweet juice which yields a syrup
so·ror·i·ty \sə-ˈrȯr-ət-ē\ *n, pl* **-ties** [ML *sororitas* sisterhood, fr. L *soror* sister] : a club of girls or women esp. at a college
sorp·tion \ˈsȯrp-shən\ *n* : the process of sorbing : the state of being sorbed
sor·rel \ˈsȯr-əl\ *n* : any of several sour-juiced herbs
sor·row \ˈsär-ō\ *n* **1** : deep distress and regret **2** : a cause of grief or sadness **3** : a display of grief or sadness — **sor·row** *vb* — **sor·row·ful** \-fəl\ *adj* — **sor·row·ful·ly** \-f(ə-)lē\ *adv*
sor·ry \ˈsär-ē\ *adj* **sor·ri·er; -est 1** : feeling sorrow, regret, or penitence **2** : MOURNFUL, SAD **3** : causing sorrow, pity, or scorn : WRETCHED
[1]**sort** \ˈsȯrt\ *n* **1** : a group of persons or things that have similar characteristics : CLASS **2** : WAY, MANNER **3** : QUALITY, NATURE — **out of sorts 1** : somewhat ill **2** : GROUCHY, IRRITABLE
[2]**sort** *vb* **1** : to put in a certain place according to kind, class, or nature **2** : to be in accord : AGREE
sor·tie \ˈsȯrt-ē, sȯr-ˈtē\ *n* **1** : a sudden issuing of troops from a defensive position against the enemy **2** : one mission or attack by one airplane
SOS \ˌes-(ˌ)ō-ˈes\ *n* : a call or request for help or rescue
so–so \ˈsō-ˈsō\ *adv or adj* : PASSABLY
sot \ˈsät\ *n* : a habitual drunkard — **sot·tish** *adj*

sou·brette \sü-ˈbret\ *n* [F] : a coquettish maidservant or a frivolous young woman in a comedy

souf·flé \sü-ˈflā\ *n* [F, fr. *soufflé*, pp. of *souffler* to blow, puff up, fr. L *sufflare*, fr. *sub-* up + *flare* to blow] : a spongy dish made light in baking by stiffly beaten egg whites

sough \ˈsau̇, ˈsəf\ *vb* : to make a moaning or sighing sound — **sough** *n*

sought *past and past part of* SEEK

¹soul \ˈsōl\ *n* **1** : the immaterial essence of an individual life **2** : the spiritual principle embodied in human beings or the universe **3** : an active or essential part **4** : man's moral and emotional nature **5** : spiritual or moral force **6** : PERSON ⟨a kindly ~⟩ **7** : a strong, positive feeling (as of intense sensitivity and emotional fervor) conveyed esp. by black American performers; *also* : NEGRITUDE — **souled** \ˈsōld\ *adj* — **soul·less** \ˈsōl-ləs\ *adj*

²soul *adj* **1** : of, relating to, or characteristic of black Americans or their culture ⟨~ food⟩ ⟨~ music⟩ **2** : designed for or controlled by blacks ⟨~ radio stations⟩

soul brother *n* : a black male

soul·ful \ˈsōl-fəl\ *adj* : full of or expressing deep feeling — **soul·ful·ly** \-ē\ *adv*

¹sound \ˈsau̇nd\ *adj* **1** : not diseased or sickly **2** : free from flaw or defect **3** : FIRM, STRONG **4** : free from error : RIGHT **5** : LEGAL, VALID **6** : THOROUGH **7** : UNDISTURBED ⟨~ sleep⟩ **8** : showing good judgment — **sound·ly** *adv* — **sound·ness** *n*

²sound *n* **1** : the sensation of hearing; *also* : mechanical energy transmitted by longitudinal pressure waves (as in air) that is the stimulus to hearing **2** : something heard : NOISE, TONE; *also* : hearing distance : EARSHOT **3** : a musical style — **sound·less** *adj* — **sound·proof** \-ˌprüf\ *adj or vb*

³sound *vb* **1** : to make or cause to make a noise **2** : to order or proclaim by a sound ⟨~ the alarm⟩ **3** : to convey a certain impression : SEEM **4** : to examine the condition of by causing to give out sounds

⁴sound *n* : a long passage of water wider than a strait often connecting two larger bodies of water ⟨Long Island ~⟩

⁵sound *vb* **1** : to measure the depth of (water) esp. by a weighted line dropped from the surface : FATHOM **2** : PROBE **3** : to dive down suddenly ⟨the hooked fish ~*ed*⟩ — **sound·ing** *n*

sound·er \ˈsau̇n-dər\ *n* : one that sounds; *esp* : a device for making soundings

sound·stage \ˈsau̇n(d)-ˌstāj\ *n* : the part of a motion-picture studio in which a production is filmed

soup \ˈsüp\ *n* **1** : a liquid food with stock as its base and often containing pieces of solid food **2** : something having the consistency of soup **3** : an unfortunate predicament ⟨in the ~⟩

soup up *vb* : to increase the power of

soup·çon \süp-ˈsōⁿ\ *n* [F] : a little bit : TRACE

soupy \ˈsü-pē\ *adj* **soup·i·er; -est** **1** : having the consistency of soup **2** : densely foggy or cloudy

¹sour \ˈsau̇(ə)r\ *adj* **1** : having an acid or tart taste ⟨~ as vinegar⟩ **2** : SPOILED, PUTRID ⟨a ~ odor⟩ **3** : UNPLEASANT, DISAGREEABLE ⟨~ disposition⟩ — **sour·ish** *adj* — **sour·ly** *adv* — **sour·ness** *n*

²sour *vb* : to become or make sour

source \ˈsōrs\ *n* **1** : ORIGIN, BEGINNING **2** : the beginning of a stream of water **3** : a supplier of information

¹souse \ˈsau̇s\ *vb* **soused; sous·ing** **1** : PICKLE **2** : to plunge into a liquid **3** : DRENCH **4** : to make drunk

²souse *n* **1** : something (as pigs' feet) steeped in pickle **2** : a soaking in liquid **3** : DRUNKARD

¹south \ˈsau̇th\ *adv* : to or toward the south

²south *adj* **1** : situated toward or at the south **2** : coming from the south

³south *n* **1** : the direction to the right of one facing east **2** : the compass point directly opposite to north **3** *cap* : regions or countries south of a specified or implied point; *esp* : the southeastern part of the U.S. — **south·er·ly** \ˈsəth-ər-lē\ *adj or adv* — **south·ern** \ˈsəth-ərn\ *adj* — **South·ern·er** *n* — **south·ern·most** \-ˌmōst\ *adj* — **south·ward** \ˈsau̇th-wərd\ *adv or adj* — **south·wards** \-wərdz\ *adv*

South African *n* : a native or inhabitant of the Republic of South Africa — **South African** *adj*

south·east \sau̇th-ˈēst, *naut* sau̇-ˈēst\ *n* **1** : the general direction between south and east **2** : the compass point midway between south and east **3** *cap* : regions or countries southeast of a specified or implied point — **southeast** *adj or adv* — **south·east·er·ly** *adv or adj* — **south·east·ern** \-ərn\ *adj*

south·paw \ˈsau̇th-ˌpȯ\ *n* : a left-handed baseball pitcher — **southpaw** *adj*

south pole *n, often cap S&P* : the southernmost point of the earth

south·west \sau̇th-ˈwest, *naut* sau̇-ˈwest\ *n* **1** : the general direction between south and west **2** : the compass point midway between south and west **3** *cap* : regions or countries southwest of a specified or implied point — **southwest** *adj or adv* — **south·west·er·ly** *adv or adj* — **south·west·ern** \-ərn\ *adj*

sou·ve·nir \ˌsü-və-ˈnir\ *n* [F] : something serving as a reminder

sou'·west·er \sau̇-ˈwes-tər\ *n* : a waterproof hat worn at sea in stormy weather; *also* : a long waterproof coat

¹sov·er·eign \ˈsäv-(ə-)rən\ *n* **1** : one possessing the supreme power and authority in a state **2** : a gold coin of the United Kingdom

²sovereign *adj* **1** : EXCELLENT, FINE **2** : supreme in power or authority **3** : CHIEF, HIGHEST **4** : having independent authority **syn** dominant, predominant, paramount, preponderant

sov·er·eign·ty \-tē\ *n, pl* **-ties** **1** : supremacy in rule or power **2** : power to govern without external control **3** : the supreme political power in a state

so·vi·et \ˈsōv-ē-ˌet, ˈsäv-, -ē-ət\ *n* **1** : an elected governmental council in a Communist country **2** *pl, cap* : the people and esp. the leaders of the U.S.S.R. — **so·vi·et·ism** *n, often cap* — **so·vi·et·ize** *vb, often cap*

¹sow \ˈsau̇\ *n* : an adult female swine

²sow \ˈsō\ *vb* **sowed; sown** \ˈsōn\ *or* **sowed; sow·ing** **1** : to plant seed for growing esp. by scattering **2** : to strew with or as if with seed **3** : to scatter abroad — **sow·er** \ˈsō(-ə)r\ *n*

sow bug \ˈsau̇-\ *n* : WOOD LOUSE

sox *pl of* SOCK

soy \ˈsȯi\ *n* : a sauce made from soybeans fermented in brine

soy·bean \ˈsȯi-ˌbēn\ *n* : an Asian legume widely grown for forage and for its edible seeds that yield a valuable oil (**soybean oil**); *also* : its seed

sp *abbr* **1** special **2** species **3** specimen **4** spelling **5** spirit

Sp *abbr* Spain

SP *abbr* **1** shore patrol; shore patrolman **2** shore police **3** specialist

spa \ˈspä\ *n* [*Spa*, watering place in Belgium] **1** : a mineral spring; *also* : a resort with mineral springs **2** : a commercial establishment with facilities for healthful exercise

¹space \ˈspās\ *n* **1** : a period of time **2** : some small measurable part of space **3** : the limitless area in which all things exist and move **4** : an empty place **5** : the region beyond the earth's atmosphere **6** : a definite place (as a seat or stateroom on a train or ship)

²space *vb* **spaced; spac·ing** : to place at intervals

\ə\abut \ᵊ\kitten \ər\further \a\ash \ā\ace \ä\cot, cart \au̇\out \ch\chin \e\bet \ē\easy \g\go \i\hit \ī\ice \j\job \ŋ\sing \ō\go \ȯ\law \ȯi\boy \th\thin \t͟h\the \ü\loot \u̇\foot \y\yet \zh\vision *see also* Pronunciation Symbols page

space–age \ˈspās-ˌāj\ *adj* : of, relating to, or befitting the age of space exploration ⟨~ technology⟩

space·craft \-ˌkraft\ *n* : a vehicle for travel beyond the earth's atmosphere

space·flight \-ˌflīt\ *n* : flight beyond the earth's atmosphere

space heater *n* : a device for heating an enclosed space

space·man \ˈspās-ˌman, -mən\ *n* : one who travels outside the earth's atmosphere

space·ship \ˈspās(h)-ˌship\ *n* : a spacecraft designed to carry one or more passengers

space shuttle *n* : a reusable spacecraft designed to transport people and cargo between earth and space

space station *n* : a manned artificial satellite in a fixed orbit serving as a base (as for scientific observation)

space suit *n* : a suit equipped to make life in space possible for its wearer

space walk *n* : a period of movement in space outside a spacecraft by an astronaut — **space walk** *vb* — **space·walk·er** \ˈspās-ˌwȯ-kər\ *n* — **space·walk·ing** \-kiŋ\ *n*

spa·cious \ˈspā-shəs\ *adj* : very large in extent : ROOMY **syn** commodious, capacious, ample — **spa·cious·ly** *adv* — **spa·cious·ness** *n*

[1]**spade** \ˈspād\ *n* : a shovel with a flat blade — **spade·ful** *n*

[2]**spade** *vb* **spad·ed; spad·ing** : to dig with a spade

[3]**spade** *n* : any of a suit of playing cards marked with a black figure resembling an inverted heart with a short stem at the bottom

spa·dix \ˈspād-iks\ *n, pl* **spa·di·ces** \ˈspād-ə-ˌsēz\ : a floral spike with a fleshy or succulent axis usu. enclosed in a spathe

spa·ghet·ti \spə-ˈget-ē\ *n* [It, fr. pl. of *spaghetto,* dim. of *spago* cord, string] : a dough made chiefly from wheat flour and formed in thin solid strings

[1]**span** \ˈspan\ *n* **1** : an English unit of length equal to nine inches (about 23 centimeters) **2** : a limited portion of time **3** : the spread (as of an arch) from one support to another

[2]**span** *vb* **spanned; span·ning 1** : MEASURE **2** : to extend across

[3]**span** *n* : a pair of animals (as mules) driven together

Span *abbr* Spanish

span·dex \ˈspan-ˌdeks\ *n* : an elastic synthetic textile fiber

span·gle \ˈspaŋ-gəl\ *n* : a small disk of shining metal used esp. on a dress for ornament — **spangle** *vb*

Span·iard \ˈspan-yərd\ *n* : a native or inhabitant of Spain

span·iel \ˈspan-yəl\ *n* [ME *spaniell,* fr. MF *espaignol,* lit., Spaniard, fr. L *Hispania* Spain] : any of numerous mostly small and short-legged dogs usu. with long wavy hair and large drooping ears

Span·ish \ˈspan-ish\ *n* **1** : the chief language of Spain and of many countries colonized by the Spanish **2 Spanish** *pl* : the people of Spain — **Spanish** *adj*

Spanish American *n* : a native or inhabitant of one of the countries of America in which Spanish is the national language; *also* : a resident of the U.S. whose native language is Spanish — **Spanish–American** *adj*

Spanish fly *n* : a dried preparation of green European beetles with diuretic and aphrodisiac effects produced by irritating the urinary tract; *also* : this beetle

Spanish moss *n* : a plant related to the pineapple that grows in pendent tufts of grayish green filaments on trees in the southern U.S. and the West Indies

spank \ˈspaŋk\ *vb* : to strike the buttocks of with the open hand — **spank** *n*

spank·ing \ˈspaŋ-kiŋ\ *adj* : BRISK, LIVELY ⟨~ breeze⟩

[1]**spar** \ˈspär\ *n* : a rounded wood or metal piece (as a mast, yard, boom, or gaff) for supporting sail rigging

[2]**spar** *vb* **sparred; spar·ring** : to box for practice without serious hitting; *also* : SKIRMISH, WRANGLE

SPAR \ˈspär\ *n* : a member of the women's reserve of the U.S. Coast Guard

[1]**spare** \ˈspaər\ *vb* **spared; spar·ing 1** : to refrain from punishing or injuring : show mercy to **2** : to exempt from something **3** : to get along without **4** : to use frugally or rarely

[2]**spare** *adj* **spar·er; spar·est 1** : held in reserve **2** : SUPERFLUOUS **3** : not liberal or profuse **4** : LEAN, THIN **5** : SCANTY **syn** meager, sparse, skimpy, exiguous, scant

[3]**spare** *n* **1** : a duplicate kept in reserve; *esp* : a spare tire **2** : the knocking down of all the bowling pins with the first two balls

spar·ing \ˈspar-iŋ\ *adj* : SAVING, FRUGAL **syn** thrifty, economical, provident — **spar·ing·ly** *adv*

[1]**spark** \ˈspärk\ *n* **1** : a small particle of a burning substance or a hot glowing particle struck from a mass (as by steel on flint) **2** : a short bright flash of electricity between two points **3** : SPARKLE **4** : a particle capable of being kindled or developed : GERM

[2]**spark** *vb* **1** : to emit or produce sparks **2** : to stir to activity : INCITE

[3]**spark** *vb* : WOO, COURT

[1]**spar·kle** \ˈspär-kəl\ *vb* **spar·kled; spar·kling** \-k(ə-)liŋ\ **1** : FLASH, GLEAM **2** : to perform brilliantly **3** : EFFERVESCE — **spar·kler** \-k(ə-)lər\ *n*

[2]**sparkle** *n* **1** : GLEAM **2** : ANIMATION

spark plug *n* : a device that produces a spark to ignite the fuel mixture in an engine cylinder

spar·row \ˈspar-ō\ *n* : any of several small dull singing birds

sparrow hawk *n* : any of various small hawks or falcons

sparse \ˈspärs\ *adj* **spars·er; spars·est** : thinly scattered : SCANTY **syn** meager, spare, skimpy, exiguous, scant — **sparse·ly** *adv*

spasm \ˈspaz-əm\ *n* **1** : an involuntary and abnormal muscular contraction **2** : a sudden, violent, and temporary effort or feeling — **spas·mod·ic** \spaz-ˈmäd-ik\ *adj* — **spas·mod·i·cal·ly** \-i-k(ə-)lē\ *adv*

spas·tic \ˈspas-tik\ *adj* : of, relating to, or marked by muscular spasm ⟨~ paralysis⟩ — **spastic** *n*

[1]**spat** \ˈspat\ *past and past part of* SPIT

[2]**spat** *n, pl* **spat** *or* **spats** : a young bivalve mollusk (as an oyster)

[3]**spat** *n* : a gaiter covering instep and ankle

[4]**spat** *n* : a brief petty quarrel : DISPUTE

[5]**spat** *vb* **spat·ted; spat·ting** : to quarrel briefly

spate \ˈspāt\ *n* : a sudden outburst

spathe \ˈspāth\ *n* : a sheathing bract or pair of bracts enclosing an inflorescence (as of the calla lily) and esp. a spadix on the same axis

spa·tial \ˈspā-shəl\ *adj* : of or relating to space — **spa·tial·ly** \-ē\ *adv*

spat·ter \ˈspat-ər\ *vb* **1** : to splash with drops of liquid **2** : to sprinkle around — **spatter** *n*

spat·u·la \ˈspach-ə-lə\ *n* : a flexible knifelike implement for scooping, spreading, or mixing soft substances

spav·in \ˈspav-ən\ *n* : a bony enlargement of the hock of a horse — **spav·ined** \-ənd\ *adj*

[1]**spawn** \ˈspȯn\ *vb* [ME *spawnen,* fr. OF *espandre* to spread out, expand; fr. L *expandere,* fr. *ex-* out + *pandere* to spread] **1** : to produce eggs or offspring esp. in large numbers **2** : GENERATE

[2]**spawn** *n* **1** : the eggs of water animals (as fishes or oysters) that lay many small eggs **2** : offspring esp. when produced in great quantities

spay \ˈspā\ *vb* **spayed; spay·ing** : to remove the ovaries from (a female animal)

SPCA *abbr* Society for the Prevention of Cruelty to Animals

SPCC *abbr* Society for the Prevention of Cruelty to Children

speak \ˈspēk\ *vb* **spoke** \ˈspōk\; **spo·ken** \ˈspō-kən\; **speak·ing 1** : to utter words **2** : to express orally **3** : to mention in speech or writing **4** : to address an audience **5** : to use or be able to use (a language) in speech

speak·easy \ˈspē-ˌkē-zē\ *n, pl* **-eas·ies** : an illicit drinking place

speak·er \ˈspē-kər\ *n* **1** : one that speaks **2** : the presiding officer of a deliberative assembly **3** : LOUDSPEAKER

[1]**spear** \ˈspiər\ *n* **1** : a long-shafted weapon with a sharp point for thrusting or throwing **2** : a sharp-pointed instrument with barbs (as for spearing fish) — **spear·man** \-mən\ *n*

[2]**spear** *vb* : to strike or pierce with or as if with a spear

[3]**spear** *n* : a young shoot (as of asparagus)

spear·head \-ˌhed\ *n* : a leading force, element, or influence — **spearhead** *vb*

spear·mint \-ˌmint\ *n* : a common highly aromatic garden mint

spec *abbr* **1** special **2** specifically

spe·cial \ˈspesh-əl\ *adj* **1** : UNCOMMON, NOTEWORTHY **2** : particularly favored **3** : INDIVIDUAL, UNIQUE **4** : EXTRA, ADDITIONAL **5** : confined to or designed for a definite field of action, purpose, or occasion — **special** *n* — **spe·cial·ly** \-ē\ *adv*

special delivery *n* : delivery of mail by messenger for an extra fee

Special Forces *n pl* : a branch of the army composed of men specially trained in guerrilla warfare

spe·cial·ist \ˈspesh-(ə-)ləst\ *n* **1** : one who devotes himself to some special branch of learning or activity **2** : any of four enlisted ranks in the army corresponding to the grades of corporal through sergeant first class

spe·cial·ize \ˈspesh-ə-ˌlīz\ *vb* **-ized; -iz·ing** : to concentrate one's efforts in a special activity or field; *also* : to change in an adaptive manner — **spe·cial·iza·tion** \ˌspesh-ə-lə-ˈzā-shən\ *n*

spe·cial·ty \ˈspesh-əl-tē\ *n, pl* **-ties** **1** : a particular quality or detail **2** : a product of a special kind or of special excellence **3** : a branch of knowledge, business, or professional work in which one specializes

spe·cie \ˈspē-shē, -sē\ *n* : money in coin

spe·cies \ˈspē-shēz, -sēz\ *n, pl* **spe·cies** [L, appearance, kind, species, fr. *specere* to look] **1** : SORT, KIND **2** : a category of biological classification ranking just below the genus or subgenus and comprising closely related organisms potentially able to breed with one another

specif *abbr* specific; specifically

[1]**spe·cif·ic** \spi-ˈsif-ik\ *adj* **1** : DEFINITE, EXACT **2** : having a unique relation to something ⟨~ antibodies⟩; *esp* : exerting a distinctive and usu. curative or causative influence **3** : of, relating to, or constituting a species — **spe·cif·i·cal·ly** \-i-k(ə-)lē\ *adv*

[2]**specific** *n* : a specific remedy

spec·i·fi·ca·tion \ˌspes-ə-fə-ˈkā-shən\ *n* **1** : the act or process of specifying **2** : a description of work to be done and materials to be used (as in building) — usu. used in pl.

specific gravity *n* : the ratio of the density of a substance to the density of some substance (as water) taken as a standard when both densities are obtained by weighing in air

spec·i·fy \ˈspes-ə-ˌfī\ *vb* **-fied; -fy·ing** : to mention or name explicitly

spec·i·men \ˈspes-ə-mən\ *n* : an item or part typical of a group or whole

spe·cious \ˈspē-shəs\ *adj* : seeming to be genuine, correct, or beautiful but not really so ⟨~ reasoning⟩

speck \ˈspek\ *n* **1** : a small spot or blemish **2** : a small particle : BIT — **speck** *vb*

speck·le \ˈspek-əl\ *n* : a little speck — **speck·le** *vb*

spec·ta·cle \ˈspek-ti-kəl\ *n* **1** : something exhibited to view; *esp* : an impressive public display **2** *pl* : GLASSES — **spec·ta·cled** \-kəld\ *adj*

[1]**spec·tac·u·lar** \spek-ˈtak-yə-lər\ *adj* : SENSATIONAL, STRIKING, SHOWY

[2]**spectacular** *n* : an elaborate spectacle

spec·ta·tor \ˈspek-ˌtāt-ər\ *n* : one who looks on (as at a sports event) **syn** observer, witness, bystander, onlooker, eyewitness

spec·ter *or* **spec·tre** \ˈspek-tər\ *n* : a visible disembodied spirit : GHOST

spec·tral \ˈspek-trəl\ *adj* **1** : of, relating to, or resembling a specter **2** : of, relating to, or made by a spectrum

spec·tro·gram \ˈspek-trə-ˌgram\ *n* : a photograph or diagram of a spectrum

spec·tro·graph \-ˌgraf\ *n* : an instrument for dispersing radiation into a spectrum and photographing or mapping the spectrum — **spec·tro·graph·ic** \ˌspek-trə-ˈgraf-ik\ *adj* — **spec·tro·graph·i·cal·ly** \-i-k(ə-)lē\ *adv*

spec·trom·e·ter \spek-ˈträm-ət-ər\ *n* : a spectroscope fitted for measuring spectra — **spec·tro·met·ric** \ˌspek-trə-ˈme-trik\ *adj*

spec·tro·scope \ˈspek-trə-ˌskōp\ *n* : an optical instrument that produces spectra from or by the use of electromagnetic radiation — **spec·tro·scop·ic** \ˌspek-trə-ˈskäp-ik\ *adj* — **spec·tro·scop·i·cal·ly** \-i-k(ə-)lē\ *adv* — **spec·tros·co·pist** \spek-ˈträs-kə-pəst\ *n* — **spec·tros·co·py** \-pē\ *n*

spec·trum \ˈspek-trəm\ *n, pl* **spec·tra** \-trə\ *or* **spectrums** [NL, fr. L, appearance, specter, fr. *specere* to look] **1** : a series of colors formed when a beam of white light is dispersed (as by a prism) so that its parts are arranged in the order of their wavelengths **2** : a series of radiations arranged in regular order **3** : a continuous sequence or range ⟨a wide ~ of political opinions⟩

spec·u·late \ˈspek-yə-ˌlāt\ *vb* **-lat·ed; -lat·ing** [L *speculari* to spy out, examine, fr. *specula* watchtower, fr. *specere* to look, look at] **1** : REFLECT, MEDITATE **2** : to engage in a business deal where a good profit may be made at considerable risk **syn** reason, think, deliberate, cogitate — **spec·u·la·tion** \ˌspek-yə-ˈlā-shən\ *n* — **spec·u·la·tive** \ˈspek-yə-ˌlāt-iv\ *adj* — **spec·u·la·tive·ly** *adv* — **spec·u·la·tor** \-ˌlāt-ər\ *n*

speech \ˈspēch\ *n* **1** : the act of speaking **2** : TALK, CONVERSATION **3** : a public discourse **4** : LANGUAGE, DIALECT **5** : an individual manner of speaking **6** : the power of speaking — **speech·less** *adj*

[1]**speed** \ˈspēd\ *n* **1** *archaic* : SUCCESS **2** : SWIFTNESS, RAPIDITY **3** : rate of motion or performance **4** : a transmission gear in an automotive vehicle or bicycle **5** : METHAMPHETAMINE; *also* : a related drug **syn** haste, hurry, dispatch, celerity — **speed·i·ly** \ˈspēd-ᵊl-ē\ *adv* — **speedy** *adj*

[2]**speed** *vb* **sped** \ˈsped\ *or* **speed·ed; speed·ing** **1** *archaic* : PROSPER; *also* : GET ALONG, FARE **2** : to go fast; *esp* : to go at an excessive or illegal speed **3** : to cause to go faster — **speed·er** *n*

speed·boat \-ˌbōt\ *n* : a fast motorboat

speed·om·e·ter \spi-ˈdäm-ət-ər\ *n* : an instrument for indicating speed or speed and distance traveled

speed·up \ˈspēd-ˌəp\ *n* **1** : ACCELERATION **2** : an employer's demand for accelerated output without increased pay

speed·way \ˈspēd-ˌwā\ *n* : a racecourse for motor vehicles

speed·well \ˈspēd-ˌwel\ *n* : a low creeping plant that bears spikes of small usu. bluish flowers and is related to the snapdragon

[1]**spell** \ˈspel\ *n* [ME, talk, tale, fr. OE] **1** : a magic formula : INCANTATION **2** : a controlling influence

[2]**spell** *vb* **spelled** \ˈspeld\; **spell·ing** : to take the place of for a time in work or duty : RELIEVE

[3]**spell** *vb* **spelled** \ˈspeld, ˈspelt\; **spell·ing** **1** : to name, write, or print in order the letters of a word **2** : MEAN

[4]**spell** *n* **1** *archaic* : the relief of one person by another in any work or duty **2** : one's turn at work or duty **3** : a

stretch of a specified kind of weather **4** : a period of bodily or mental distress or disorder : ATTACK

spell·bind·er \-ˌbīn-dər\ *n* : a speaker of compelling eloquence

spell·bound \-ˌbau̇nd\ *adj* : held by or as if by a spell : FASCINATED

spell·er \ˈspel-ər\ *n* **1** : one who spells words **2** : a book with exercises for teaching spelling

spe·lunk·er \spi-ˈləŋ-kər, ˈspē-ˌləŋ-kər\ *n* : one who makes a hobby of exploring caves — **spe·lunk·ing** \-kiŋ\ *n*

spend \ˈspend\ *vb* **spent** \ˈspent\; **spend·ing** **1** : to pay out : USE UP **2** : WEAR OUT, EXHAUST; *also* : to consume wastefully **3** : to cause or permit to elapse : PASS **4** : to make use of — **spend·er** *n*

spend·thrift \ˈspen(d)-ˌthrift\ *n* : one who spends wastefully or recklessly

spent \ˈspent\ *adj* : drained of energy

sperm \ˈspərm\ *n, pl* **sperm** *or* **sperms** **1** : SEMEN **2** : a male gamete

sper·ma·to·zo·on \(ˌ)spər-ˌmat-ə-ˈzō-ˌän, -ˈzō-ən\ *n, pl* **-zoa** \-ˈzō-ə\ : a motile male gamete of an animal usu. with a rounded or elongated head and a long posterior flagellum

sperm cell *n* : SPERM 2

sperm whale \ˈspərm-\ *n* : a whale with conical teeth, no whalebone, and a large fluid-containing cavity in the head

sperm whale

spew \ˈspyü\ *vb* : VOMIT

sp gr *abbr* specific gravity

sphag·num \ˈsfag-nəm\ *n* : any of a genus of atypical mosses that grow in wet acid areas where their remains become compacted with other plant debris to form peat; *also* : a mass of these mosses

sphere \ˈsfiər\ *n* [ME *spere* globe, celestial sphere, fr. MF *espere*, fr. L *sphaera*, fr. Gk *sphaira*, lit., ball] **1** : a globular body **2** : a celestial body **3** : a solid figure so shaped that every point on its surface is an equal distance from the center **4** : range of action or influence : FIELD — **spher·i·cal** \ˈsfir-i-kəl, ˈsfer-\ *adj* — **spher·i·cal·ly** \-i-k(ə-)lē\ *adv*

spher·oid \ˈsfi(ə)r-ˌȯid, ˈsfe(ə)r-\ *n* : a figure similar to a sphere but not perfectly round — **sphe·roi·dal** \sfir-ˈȯid-ᵊl\ *adj*

sphinc·ter \ˈsfiŋk-tər\ *n* : a muscular ring that closes a bodily opening

sphinx \ˈsfiŋks\ *n, pl* **sphinx·es** *or* **sphin·ges** \ˈsfin-ˌjēz\ **1** : a winged monster in Greek mythology having a woman's head and a lion's body and noted for killing anyone unable to answer its riddle **2** : an enigmatic or mysterious person **3** : an ancient Egyptian image having the body of a lion and the head of man, ram, or hawk

spice \ˈspīs\ *n* **1** : any of various aromatic plant products (as pepper or nutmeg) used to season or flavor foods **2** : something that adds interest and relish — **spice** *vb* — **spicy** *adj*

spice·bush \ˈspīs-ˌbu̇sh\ *n* : an aromatic shrub related to the laurels that bears dense clusters of small yellow flowers followed by scarlet or yellow berries

spick–and–span *or* **spic–and–span** \ˌspik-ən-ˈspan\ *adj* : quite new; *also* : spotlessly clean

spic·ule \ˈspik-yül\ *n* : a slender pointed body esp. of calcium or silica ⟨sponge ~*s*⟩

spi·der \ˈspīd-ər\ *n* **1** : any of numerous arachnids that have a 2-part body, eight legs, and two or more pairs of abdominal organs for spinning threads of silk used esp. in making webs for catching prey **2** : a cast-iron frying pan — **spi·dery** *adj*

spider plant *n* : a houseplant of the lily family having long green leaves usu. striped with white and producing tufts of small plants on long hanging stems

spiderweb *n* : the web spun by a spider

spiel \ˈspēl\ *vb* : to talk volubly or extravagantly — **spiel** *n*

spig·ot \ˈspig-ət, ˈspik-ət\ *n* : FAUCET

[1]**spike** \ˈspīk\ *n* **1** : a very large nail **2** : any of various pointed projections (as on the sole of a shoe to prevent slipping) — **spiky** *adj*

[2]**spike** *vb* **spiked; spik·ing** **1** : to fasten with spikes **2** : to put an end to : QUASH ⟨~ a rumor⟩ **3** : to pierce with or impale on a spike **4** : to add alcoholic liquor to (a drink)

[3]**spike** *n* **1** : an ear of grain **2** : a long cluster of usu. stemless flowers

[1]**spill** \ˈspil\ *vb* **spilled** \ˈspild, ˈspilt\ *also* **spilt** \ˈspilt\; **spill·ing** **1** : to cause or allow esp. unintentionally to fall, flow, or run out **2** : to lose or allow to be scattered **3** : to cause (blood) to flow **4** : to run out or over with resulting loss or waste — **spill·able** *adj*

[2]**spill** *n* **1** : an act of spilling; *also* : a fall from a horse or vehicle or in running **2** : something spilled **3** : SPILLWAY

spill·way \-ˌwā\ *n* : a passage for surplus water to run over or around an obstruction (as a dam)

[1]**spin** \ˈspin\ *vb* **spun** \ˈspən\; **spin·ning** **1** : to draw out (fiber) and twist into thread; *also* : to form (thread) by such means **2** : to form thread by extruding a sticky quickly hardening fluid; *also* : to construct from such thread ⟨spiders ~ their webs⟩ **3** : to produce slowly and by degrees ⟨~ a story⟩ **4** : TWIRL **5** : WHIRL, REEL ⟨my head is *spinning*⟩ **6** : to move rapidly along — **spin·ner** *n*

[2]**spin** *n* **1** : a rapid rotating motion **2** : an excursion in a wheeled vehicle

spin·ach \ˈspin-ich\ *n* : a dark green herb grown for its edible leaves

spi·nal \ˈspīn-ᵊl\ *adj* : of or relating to the backbone or spinal cord — **spi·nal·ly** \-ē\ *adv*

spinal column *n* : BACKBONE

spinal cord *n* : the thick cord of nervous tissue that extends from the brain along the back in the cavity of the backbone and carries nerve impulses to and from the brain

spinal nerve *n* : any of the paired nerves which arise from the spinal cord and pass to various parts of the body and of which there are normally 31 pairs in human beings

spin·dle \ˈspin-dᵊl\ *n* **1** : a round tapering stick or rod by which fibers are twisted in spinning **2** : a turned part of a piece of furniture ⟨the ~*s* of a chair⟩ **3** : a slender pin or rod which turns or on which something else turns

spin·dling \ˈspin-(d)liŋ\ *adj* : SPINDLY

spin·dly \ˈspin-(d)lē\ *adj* : being long or tall and thin and usu. weak

spin·drift \ˈspin-ˌdrift\ *n* : spray blown from waves

spine \ˈspīn\ *n* **1** : BACKBONE **2** : a stiff sharp process esp. on a plant or animal — **spine·less** *adj* — **spiny** *adj*

spi·nel \spə-ˈnel\ *n* : a hard crystalline mineral of variable color used as a gem

spin·et \ˈspin-ət\ *n* **1** : an early harpsichord having a single keyboard and only one string for each note **2** : a small upright piano

spin·na·ker \ˈspin-i-kər\ *n* : a large triangular sail set on a long light pole

spinning jen·ny \-ˌjen-ē\ *n* : an early multiple-spindle machine for spinning wool or cotton

spinning wheel *n* : a small machine for spinning thread or yarn in which a large wheel drives a single spindle

spin–off \ˈspin-ˌȯf\ *n* **1** : the distribution by a business to its stockholders of particular assets and esp. of stock of another company **2** : a usu. useful by-product ⟨~*s* from missile research⟩ — **spin off** *vb*

spin·ster \ˈspin-stər\ *n* : an unmarried woman past the common age for marrying — **spin·ster·hood** \-ˌhu̇d\ *n*

spiny lobster *n* : an edible crustacean differing from the related lobster in lacking the large front claws and in having a very spiny carapace

[1]**spi·ral** \ˈspī-rəl\ *adj* **1** : circling around a center like the thread of a screw **2** : winding or coiling around a center or pole in gradually enlarging circles — **spi·ral·ly** \-ē\ *adv*

[2]**spiral** *n* **1** : something that has a spiral form; *also* : a single turn in a spiral object **2** : a continuously spreading and accelerating increase or decrease

[3]**spiral** *vb* **-raled** *or* **-ralled; -ral·ing** *or* **-ral·ling 1** : to move in a spiral course **2** : to form into a spiral

spi·rant \ˈspī-rənt\ *n* : a consonant (as \f\, \s\, \sh\) uttered with decided friction of the breath against some part of the oral passage — **spirant** *adj*

spire \ˈspī(ə)r\ *n* **1** : a slender tapering stalk (as of grass) **2** : a pointed tip (as of a tree or antler) **3** : STEEPLE — **spiry** *adj*

spi·rea *or* **spi·raea** \spī-ˈrē-ə\ *n* : any of a genus of shrubs related to the roses with dense clusters of small white or pink flowers

[1]**spir·it** \ˈspir-ət\ *n* [ME, fr. OF or L; OF, fr. L *spiritus*, lit., breath] **1** : a life-giving force; *also* : the animating principle : SOUL **2** *cap* : HOLY SPIRIT **3** : SPECTER, GHOST **4** : PERSON **5** : DISPOSITION, MOOD **6** : VIVACITY, ARDOR **7** : essential or real meaning : INTENT **8** : distilled alcoholic liquor **9** : LOYALTY ⟨school ~⟩ — **spir·it·less** *adj*

[2]**spirit** *vb* : to carry off secretly or mysteriously

spir·it·ed \ˈspir-ət-əd\ *adj* **1** : ANIMATED, LIVELY **2** : COURAGEOUS

[1]**spir·i·tu·al** \ˈspir-ich-(ə-w)əl\ *adj* **1** : of, relating to, consisting of, or affecting the spirit : INCORPOREAL **2** : of or relating to sacred matters **3** : ecclesiastical rather than lay or temporal — **spir·i·tu·al·i·ty** \ˌspir-i-chə-ˈwal-ət-ē\ *n* — **spir·i·tu·al·ize** \ˈspir-ich-(ə-w)ə-ˌlīz\ *vb* — **spir·i·tu·al·ly** \-lē\ *adv*

[2]**spiritual** *n* : a religious song originating among blacks of the southern U.S.

spir·i·tu·al·ism \ˈspir-ich-(ə-w)ə-ˌliz-əm\ *n* : a belief that spirits of the dead communicate with the living usu. through a medium — **spir·i·tu·al·ist** \-ləst\ *n, often cap* — **spir·i·tu·al·is·tic** \ˌspir-ich-(ə-w)ə-ˈlis-tik\ *adj*

spir·i·tu·ous \ˈspir-ich-(ə-w)əs, ˈspir-ət-əs\ *adj* : containing alcohol ⟨~ liquors⟩

spi·ro·chete *also* **spi·ro·chaete** \ˈspī-rə-ˌkēt\ *n* : any of an order of spiral bacteria including one that causes syphilis

spirt *var of* SPURT

[1]**spit** \ˈspit\ *n* **1** : a thin pointed rod for holding meat over a fire **2** : a point of land that runs out into the water

[2]**spit** *vb* **spit·ted; spit·ting** : to pierce with or as if with a spit

[3]**spit** *vb* **spit** *or* **spat** \ˈspat\; **spit·ting 1** : to eject (saliva) from the mouth **2** : to send forth forcefully, defiantly, or disgustedly **3** : to rain or snow lightly

[4]**spit** *n* **1** : SALIVA **2** : perfect likeness ⟨~ and image of his father⟩ **3** : a sprinkle of rain or flurry of snow

spit·ball \ˈspit-ˌbȯl\ *n* **1** : paper chewed and rolled into a ball to be thrown as a missile **2** : a baseball pitch delivered after the ball has been moistened with saliva or sweat

[1]**spite** \ˈspīt\ *n* : ill will with a wish to annoy, anger, or defeat : petty malice **syn** malignity, spleen, grudge, malevolence — **spite·ful** \-fəl\ *adj* — **spite·ful·ly** \-ē\ *adv* — **spite·ful·ness** *n* — **in spite of** : in defiance or contempt of : NOTWITHSTANDING

[2]**spite** *vb* **spit·ed; spit·ing** : to treat maliciously (as by insulting or thwarting)

spit·tle \ˈspit-ᵊl\ *n* : SALIVA

spit·tle·bug \-ˌbəg\ *n* : any of numerous leaping insects with froth-secreting larvae that are related to the aphids

spit·toon \spi-ˈtün\ *n* : a receptacle for spit

splash \ˈsplash\ *vb* **1** : to dash a liquid about **2** : to scatter a liquid on : SPATTER **3** : to fall or strike with a splashing noise **syn** sprinkle, bespatter, douse, splatter — **splash** *n*

splash·down \ˈsplash-ˌdau̇n\ *n* : the landing of a manned spacecraft in the ocean — **splash down** \(ˈ)splash-ˈdau̇n\ *vb*

splat·ter \ˈsplat-ər\ *vb* : SPATTER — **splatter** *n*

[1]**splay** \ˈsplā\ *vb* **1** : to spread out **2** : to slope or slant outward ⟨~*ed* doorway⟩ — **splay** *n*

[2]**splay** *adj* **1** : spread out : turned outward **2** : AWKWARD, CLUMSY

spleen \ˈsplēn\ *n* **1** : a vascular organ located near the stomach in most vertebrates that is concerned esp. with the storage, formation, and destruction of blood cells **2** : SPITE, MALICE **syn** malignity, grudge, malevolence, ill will, spitefulness

splen·did \ˈsplen-dəd\ *adj* [L *splendidus*, fr. *splendēre* to shine] **1** : SHINING, BRILLIANT **2** : SHOWY, GORGEOUS **3** : ILLUSTRIOUS **4** : EXCELLENT **syn** resplendent, glorious, sublime, superb — **splen·did·ly** *adv*

splen·dor \ˈsplen-dər\ *n* **1** : BRILLIANCE **2** : POMP, MAGNIFICENCE

sple·net·ic \spli-ˈnet-ik\ *adj* : marked by bad temper or spite

splen·ic \ˈsplen-ik\ *adj* : of, relating to, or located in the spleen

splice \ˈsplīs\ *vb* **spliced; splic·ing 1** : to unite (as two ropes) by weaving the strands together **2** : to unite (as two timbers or pieces of film) by connecting the ends together — **splice** *n*

splint \ˈsplint\ *n* **1** : a thin strip of wood interwoven with others to make something (as a basket) **2** : material or a device used to protect and keep in place an injured body part (as a broken arm)

[1]**splin·ter** \ˈsplint-ər\ *n* : a thin piece of something split off lengthwise : SLIVER

[2]**splinter** *vb* : to split into splinters

split \ˈsplit\ *vb* **split; split·ting 1** : to divide lengthwise or along a grain or seam **2** : to burst or break in pieces **3** : to divide into parts or sections **4** : LEAVE **syn** rend, cleave, rip, tear — **split** *n*

split–lev·el \ˈsplit-ˈlev-əl\ *n* : a house divided so that the floor in one part is about halfway between two floors in the other

split personality *n* : SCHIZOPHRENIA; *also* : a mental and emotional disorder which is a neurosis and in which the personality becomes separated into two or more parts each of which controls behavior part of the time

split·ting \ˈsplit-iŋ\ *adj* : causing a piercing sensation ⟨~ headache⟩

splotch \ˈspläch\ *n* : BLOTCH

splurge \ˈsplərj\ *n* : a showy display or expense — **splurge** *vb*

splut·ter \ˈsplət-ər\ *n* : SPUTTER — **splutter** *vb*

[1]**spoil** \ˈspȯil\ *n* : PLUNDER, BOOTY

[2]**spoil** *vb* **spoiled** \ˈspȯild, ˈspȯilt\ *or* **spoilt** \ˈspȯilt\; **spoil·ing 1** : ROB, PILLAGE **2** : to damage seriously : RUIN **3** : to impair the quality or effect of **4** : to damage the disposition of by pampering; *also* : INDULGE, CODDLE **5** : DECAY, ROT **6** : to have an eager desire ⟨~*ing* for a fight⟩ **syn** injure, harm, hurt, mar — **spoil·age** \ˈspȯi-lij\ *n*

spoil·er \ˈspȯi-lər\ *n* **1** : one that spoils **2** : a device (as on an airplane or automobile) used to disrupt airflow and decrease lift

spoil·sport \ˈspȯil-ˌspōrt\ *n* : one who spoils the sport or pleasure of others

[1]**spoke** \ˈspōk\ *past & archaic past part of* SPEAK

[2]**spoke** *n* **1** : any of the rods extending from the hub of a wheel to the rim **2** : a rung of a ladder

spo·ken \ˈspō-kən\ *past part of* SPEAK

spokes·man \ˈspōks-mən\ *n* : one who speaks as the representative of another or others

spokes·per·son \-ˌpər-sən\ *n* : SPOKESMAN

spokes·wom·an \-ˌwu̇m-ən\ *n* : a woman who speaks as the representative of another or others

spo·li·a·tion \ˌspō-lē-ˈā-shən\ *n* : the act of plundering : the state of being plundered

[1]**sponge** \ˈspənj\ *n* **1** : the elastic porous mass of fibers that forms the skeleton of any of a phylum of primitive sea animals; *also* : one of the animals **2** : the act of washing or wiping with a sponge **3** : a spongelike or porous mass or material (as used for sponging) — **spongy** \ˈspən-jē\ *adj*

[2]**sponge** *vb* **sponged; spong·ing 1** : to gather sponges **2** : to bathe or wipe with a sponge **3** : to live at another's expense — **spong·er** *n*

sponge cake *n* : a cake made without shortening

sponge rubber *n* : a cellular rubber resembling natural sponge

spon·sor \ˈspän-sər\ *n* [LL, fr. L, guarantor, surety, fr. *sponsus*, pp. of *spondēre* to promise] **1** : one who takes the responsibility for some other person or thing : SURETY **2** : GODPARENT **3** : a business firm that pays the cost of a radio or television program usu. in return for advertising time during its course **syn** patron, guarantor, backer — **sponsor** *vb* — **spon·sor·ship** *n*

spon·ta·ne·ous \spän-ˈtā-nē-əs\ *adj* [LL *spontaneus*, fr. L *sponte* of one's free will, voluntarily] **1** : done or produced freely or naturally **2** : acting or taking place without external force or cause **syn** impulsive, instinctive, automatic, unpremeditated — **spon·ta·ne·ity** \ˌspänt-ən-ˈē-ət-ē\ *n* — **spon·ta·ne·ous·ly** \spän-ˈtā-nē-əs-lē\ *adv*

spontaneous combustion *n* : a bursting into flame of material through heat produced within itself by chemical action (as oxidation)

spoof \ˈspüf\ *vb* **1** : DECEIVE, HOAX **2** : to make good-natured fun of — **spoof** *n*

[1]**spook** \ˈspük\ *n* : GHOST, APPARITION — **spooky** *adj*

[2]**spook** *vb* : FRIGHTEN

spool \ˈspül\ *n* : a cylinder on which flexible material (as thread) is wound

spoon \ˈspün\ *n* [ME, fr. OE *spōn* splinter, chip] **1** : an eating or cooking implement consisting of a shallow bowl with a handle **2** : a metal piece used on a fishing line as a lure — **spoon** *vb* — **spoon·ful** *n*

spoon·bill \ˈspün-ˌbil\ *n* : any of several wading birds related to the ibises that have a bill with a broad flat tip

spoon–feed \ˈspün-ˌfēd\ *vb* **-fed** \-ˌfed\; **-feed·ing 1** : to feed by means of a spoon **2** : to present (information) so completely as to preclude independent thought

spoor \ˈspu̇r, ˈspōr\ *n* : a track, a trail, a scent, or droppings esp. of a wild animal

spo·rad·ic \spə-ˈrad-ik\ *adj* : occurring in scattered single instances **syn** occasional, rare, scarce, infrequent, uncommon — **spo·rad·i·cal·ly** \-i-k(ə-)lē\ *adv*

spore \ˈspōr\ *n* : a primitive usu. one-celled reproductive body produced by plants and some lower animals

[1]**sport** \ˈspōrt\ *vb* [ME *sporten* to divert, disport, short for *disporten*, fr. MF *desporter*, fr. *des-* (fr. L *dis-* apart) + *porter* to carry, fr. L *portare*] **1** : to amuse oneself : FROLIC **2** : to wear or display ostentatiously — **sport·ive** *adj*

[2]**sport** *n* **1** : a source of diversion : PASTIME **2** : physical activity engaged in for pleasure **3** : JEST **4** : MOCKERY ⟨make ~ of his efforts⟩ **5** : BUTT, LAUGHINGSTOCK **6** : one who accepts results cheerfully whether favoring his interests or not **7** : an individual distinguished by a mutation **syn** play, frolic, fun, recreation — **sporty** *adj*

[3]**sport** *or* **sports** *adj* : of, relating to, or suitable for sport or casual wear ⟨~ coats⟩

sport fish *n* : a fish important for the sport it affords anglers

sports·cast \ˈspōrts-ˌkast\ *n* : a broadcast dealing with sports events — **sports·cast·er** \-ˌkas-tər\ *n*

sports·man \ˈspōrts-mən\ *n* **1** : a person who engages in sports and esp. in hunting and fishing **2** : one who plays fairly and wins or loses gracefully — **sports·man·ship** *n*

sports·wom·an \-ˌwu̇m-ən\ *n* : a woman who engages in sports

sports·writ·er \-ˌrīt-ər\ *n* : one who writes about sports esp. for a newspaper — **sports·writ·ing** \-iŋ\ *n*

[1]**spot** \ˈspät\ *n* **1** : STAIN, BLEMISH **2** : a small part different (as in color) from the main part **3** : LOCATION, SITE — **spot·less** *adj* — **spot·less·ly** *adv* — **on the spot** : in difficulty or danger

[2]**spot** *vb* **spot·ted; spot·ting 1** : to mark or disfigure with spots **2** : to pick out : RECOGNIZE, IDENTIFY

[3]**spot** *adj* **1** : being, done, or originating on the spot ⟨a ~ broadcast⟩ **2** : paid upon delivery **3** : made at random or at a few key points ⟨a ~ check⟩

spot–check \ˈspät-ˌchek\ *vb* : to make a spot check of

spot·light \-ˌlīt\ *n* **1** : a circle of brilliant light projected upon a particular area, person, or object (as on a stage); *also* : the device that produces this light **2** : public notice — **spotlight** *vb*

spot·ter \ˈspät-ər\ *n* **1** : one that keeps watch : OBSERVER **2** : one that removes spots

spot·ty \ˈspät-ē\ *adj* **spot·ti·er; -est** : uneven in quality; *also* : sparsely distributed ⟨~ attendance⟩

spou·sal \ˈspau̇-zəl, -səl\ *n* : NUPTIALS — usu. used in pl.

spouse \ˈspau̇s\ *n* : one's husband or wife

[1]**spout** \ˈspau̇t\ *vb* **1** : to eject or issue forth forcibly and freely ⟨wells ~*ing* oil⟩ **2** : to speak pompously

[2]**spout** *n* **1** : a pipe or hole through which liquid spouts **2** : a jet of liquid; *esp* : WATERSPOUT 2

spp *abbr, pl* species

[1]**sprain** \ˈsprān\ *n* : a sudden or severe twisting of a joint with stretching or tearing of ligaments; *also* : a sprained condition

[2]**sprain** *vb* : to subject to sprain

sprat \ˈsprat\ *n* : a small European herring; *also* : a young herring

sprawl \ˈsprȯl\ *vb* **1** : to lie or sit with limbs spread out awkwardly **2** : to spread out irregularly — **sprawl** *n*

[1]**spray** \ˈsprā\ *n* : a usu. flowering branch or a decorative arrangement of flowers and foliage

[2]**spray** *n* **1** : liquid flying in small drops like water blown from a wave **2** : a jet of fine vapor (as from an atomizer) **3** : an instrument (as an atomizer) for scattering fine liquid

[3]**spray** *vb* **1** : to scatter or let fall in a spray **2** : to discharge spray on or into — **spray·er** *n*

spray can *n* : a pressurized container from which aerosols are sprayed

spray gun *n* : a device for spraying liquids (as paint or insecticide)

[1]**spread** \ˈspred\ *vb* **spread; spread·ing 1** : to scatter over a surface **2** : to flatten out : open out **3** : to stretch, force, or push apart **4** : to distribute over a period of time or among many persons **5** : to pass on from person to person **6** : to cover with something ⟨~ a floor with rugs⟩ **7** : to prepare for a meal ⟨~ a table⟩ — **spread·er** *n*

[2]**spread** *n* **1** : the act or process of spreading **2** : EXPANSE, EXTENT **3** : a prominent display in a magazine or newspaper **4** : a food to be spread on bread or crackers **5** : a cloth cover for a bed **6** : distance between two points : GAP

spree \ˈsprē\ *n* : an unrestrained outburst ⟨buying ~⟩; *esp* : a drinking bout
sprig \ˈsprig\ *n* : a small shoot or twig
spright·ly \ˈsprīt-lē\ *adj* **spright·li·er; -est** : LIVELY, SPIRITED **syn** animated, vivacious, gay — **spright·li·ness** *n*
¹**spring** \ˈspriŋ\ *vb* **sprang** \ˈspraŋ\ *or* **sprung** \ˈsprəŋ\; **sprung; spring·ing** \ˈspriŋ-iŋ\ **1** : to move suddenly upward or forward **2** : to shoot up ⟨weeds ~ up overnight⟩ **3** : to move quickly by elastic force **4** : to make lame : STRAIN **5** : WARP **6** : to develop (a leak) through the seams **7** : to make known suddenly ⟨~ a surprise⟩ **8** : to cause to close suddenly ⟨~ a trap⟩
²**spring** *n* **1** : a source of supply; *esp* : an issuing of water from the ground **2** : SOURCE, ORIGIN; *also* : MOTIVE **3** : the season between winter and summer **4** : an elastic body or device that recovers its original shape when it is released after being distorted **5** : the act or an instance of leaping up or forward **6** : RESILIENCE — **springy** *adj*
spring·board \ˈspriŋ-ˌbōrd\ *n* : a springy board used in jumping or vaulting or for diving
spring fever *n* : a lazy or restless feeling often associated with the onset of spring
spring tide *n* : a tide of greater-than-average range that occurs at each new moon and full moon
spring·time \ˈspriŋ-ˌtīm\ *n* : the season of spring
¹**sprin·kle** \ˈspriŋ-kəl\ *vb* **sprin·kled; sprin·kling** \-k(ə-)liŋ\ : to scatter in small drops or particles — **sprin·kler** \-k(ə-)lər\ *n*
²**sprinkle** *n* : a light rainfall
sprin·kling \ˈspriŋ-kliŋ\ *n* : SMATTERING
¹**sprint** \ˈsprint\ *vb* : to run at top speed esp. for a short distance — **sprint·er** *n*
²**sprint** *n* **1** : a short run at top speed **2** : a short distance race
sprite \ˈsprīt\ *n* **1** : GHOST, SPIRIT **2** : ELF, FAIRY
spritz *vb* : SPRAY
sprock·et \ˈspräk-ət\ *n* : a tooth on a wheel (**sprocket wheel**) shaped so as to interlock with a chain
¹**sprout** \ˈspraủt\ *vb* : to send out new growth esp. rapidly ⟨~*ing* seeds⟩
²**sprout** *n* : a usu. young and growing plant shoot
¹**spruce** \ˈsprüs\ *vb* **spruced; spruc·ing** : to make or become spruce
²**spruce** *adj* **spruc·er; spruc·est** : neat and smart in appearance **syn** stylish, fashionable, modish, dapper, natty
³**spruce** *n* : any of a genus of evergreen pyramid-shaped trees related to the pines and having soft light wood; *also* : the wood of a spruce
sprung *past and past part of* SPRING
spry \ˈsprī\ *adj* **spri·er** *or* **spry·er** \ˈsprī(-ə)r\; **spri·est** *or* **spry·est** \ˈsprī-əst\ : NIMBLE, ACTIVE **syn** agile, brisk, lively, sprightly
spud \ˈspəd\ *n* **1** : a sharp narrow spade **2** : POTATO
spume \ˈspyüm\ *n* : frothy matter on liquids : FOAM
spu·mo·ni *or* **spu·mo·ne** \spủ-ˈmō-nē\ *n* [It *spumone*, deriv. of *spuma* foam] : ice cream in layers of different colors, flavors, and textures often with candied fruits and nuts
spun *past and past part of* SPIN
spun glass *n* : FIBERGLASS
spunk \ˈspəŋk\ *n* [fr. *spunk* tinder, fr. ScGael *spong* sponge, tinder, fr. L *spongia* sponge] : PLUCK, COURAGE — **spunky** *adj*
¹**spur** \ˈspər\ *n* **1** : a pointed device fastened to a rider's boot and used to urge on a horse **2** : something that urges to action **3** : a stiffly projecting part or process (as on the leg of a cock or on some flowers) **4** : a ridge extending sideways from a mountain **5** : a branch of railroad track extending from the main line **syn** goad, motive, impulse, incentive, inducement — **spurred** \ˈspərd\ *adj* — **on the spur of the moment** : on hasty impulse
²**spur** *vb* **spurred; spur·ring** **1** : to urge a horse on with spurs **2** : INCITE
spurge \ˈspərj\ *n* : any of various herbs and woody plants with bitter milky juice
spu·ri·ous \ˈspyủr-ē-əs\ *adj* [LL *spurius* false, fr. L, of illegitimate birth, fr. *spurius*, n., bastard] : not genuine : FALSE
spurn \ˈspərn\ *vb* **1** : to kick away or trample on **2** : to reject with disdain **syn** repudiate, refuse, decline
¹**spurt** \ˈspərt\ *vb* : to gush out : spout forth
²**spurt** *n* : a sudden gushing or spouting
³**spurt** *n* **1** : a sudden brief burst of effort or speed **2** : a sharp increase of activity ⟨~ in sales⟩
⁴**spurt** *vb* : to make a spurt
sput·ter \ˈspət-ər\ *vb* **1** : to spit small scattered particles : SPLUTTER **2** : to utter words hastily or explosively in excitement or confusion **3** : to make small popping sounds — **sputter** *n*
spu·tum \ˈspyüt-əm\ *n, pl* **spu·ta** \-ə\ [L] : material that is spit or coughed up and consists of saliva and mucus
¹**spy** \ˈspī\ *vb* **spied; spy·ing** **1** : to watch or search for information secretly : act as a spy **2** : to get a momentary or quick glimpse of : SEE
²**spy** *n, pl* **spies** **1** : one who secretly watches others **2** : one who secretly tries to obtain information for his own country in the territory of an enemy
spy·glass \ˈspī-ˌglas\ *n* : a small telescope
sq *abbr* **1** squadron **2** square
squab \ˈskwäb\ *n, pl* **squabs** *or* **squab** : a young pigeon
squab·ble \ˈskwäb-əl\ *n* : a noisy altercation : WRANGLE **syn** quarrel, spat, row, tiff — **squabble** *vb*
squad \ˈskwäd\ *n* **1** : a small organized group of military personnel **2** : a small group engaged in a common effort
squad car *n* : a police car connected by two-way radio with headquarters
squad·ron \ˈskwäd-rən\ *n* **1** : a body of men in regular formation **2** : any of several units of military organization
squal·id \ˈskwäl-əd\ *adj* **1** : filthy or degraded through neglect or poverty **2** : SORDID, DEBASED **syn** nasty, foul, dirty, grubby
squall \ˈskwȯl\ *n* : a sudden violent gust of wind often with rain or snow — **squally** *adj*
squa·lor \ˈskwäl-ər\ *n* : the quality or state of being squalid
squan·der \ˈskwän-dər\ *vb* **squan·dered; squan·der·ing** \-d(ə-)riŋ\ : to spend wastefully or foolishly
¹**square** \ˈskwaər\ *n* **1** : an instrument used to lay out or test right angles **2** : a rectangle with all four sides equal **3** : something square **4** : the product of a number multiplied by itself **5** : an area bounded by four streets **6** : an open area in a city where streets meet **7** : a highly conventional person
²**square** *adj* **squar·er; squar·est** **1** : having four equal sides and four right angles **2** : forming a right angle ⟨cut a ~ corner⟩ **3** : multiplied by itself : SQUARED ⟨X^2 is the symbol for X ~⟩ **4** : being a unit of square measure equal to a square each side of which measures one unit ⟨a ~ foot⟩ **5** : being of a specified length in each of two dimensions ⟨an area 10 feet ~⟩ **6** : exactly adjusted **7** : JUST, FAIR ⟨a ~ deal⟩ **8** : leaving no balance ⟨make accounts ~⟩ **9** : SUBSTANTIAL ⟨a ~ meal⟩ **10** : highly conservative or conventional — **square·ly** *adv*
³**square** *vb* **squared; squar·ing** **1** : to form with four equal sides and right angles or with flat surfaces ⟨~ a timber⟩ **2** : to multiply a number by itself **3** : CONFORM, AGREE **4** : BALANCE, SETTLE ⟨~ an account⟩

square dance *n* : a dance for four couples arranged to form a square

square measure *n* : a unit or system of units for measuring area — see METRIC SYSTEM table, WEIGHT table

square–rigged \ˈskwaər-ˈrigd\ *adj* : having the chief sails extended on yards that are fastened to the masts horizontally and at their center

square–rig·ger \-ˈrig-ər\ *n* : a square-rigged craft

square root *n* : either of the two numbers whose squares are equal to a given number ⟨either +3 or −3 is the *square root* of 9⟩

[1]**squash** \ˈskwäsh, ˈskwȯsh\ *vb* **1** : to beat or press into a pulp or flat mass **2** : QUASH, SUPPRESS

[2]**squash** *n* **1** : the impact of something soft and heavy; *also* : the sound of such impact **2** : a crushed mass **3** : SQUASH RACQUETS

[3]**squash** *n, pl* **squash·es** *or* **squash** : a fruit of any of various plants related to the gourds that is used esp. as a vegetable; *also* : a plant bearing squashes

squash racquets *n* : a game played on a 4-wall court with a racket and rubber ball

[1]**squat** \ˈskwät\ *vb* **squat·ted; squat·ting** **1** : to sit down upon the hams or heels **2** : to settle on land without right or title; *also* : to settle on public land with a view to acquiring title — **squat·ter** *n*

[2]**squat** *n* : the act or posture of squatting

[3]**squat** *adj* **squat·ter; squat·test** : low to the ground; *also* : short and thick in stature **syn** thickset, stocky, heavyset, stubby

squaw \ˈskwȯ\ *n* : an American Indian woman

squawk \ˈskwȯk\ *n* : a harsh loud cry; *also* : a noisy protest — **squawk** *vb*

squeak \ˈskwēk\ *vb* **1** : to utter or speak in a weak shrill tone **2** : to make a thin high-pitched sound — **squeak** *n* — **squeaky** *adj*

[1]**squeal** \ˈskwēl\ *vb* **1** : to make a shrill sound or cry **2** : COMPLAIN, PROTEST **3** : to betray a secret or turn informer

[2]**squeal** *n* : a shrill sharp somewhat prolonged cry

squea·mish \ˈskwē-mish\ *adj* **1** : easily nauseated; *also* : NAUSEATED **2** : easily disgusted **syn** fussy, nice, dainty, fastidious, persnickety — **squea·mish·ness** *n*

squee·gee \ˈskwē-ˌjē\ *n* : a blade set crosswise on a handle and used for spreading or wiping liquid on, across, or off a surface — **squeegee** *vb*

[1]**squeeze** \ˈskwēz\ *vb* **squeezed; squeez·ing** **1** : to exert pressure on the opposite sides or parts of **2** : to obtain by pressure ⟨∼ juice from a lemon⟩ **3** : to force, thrust, or cause to pass by pressure — **squeez·er** *n*

[2]**squeeze** *n* **1** : an act of squeezing **2** : a quantity squeezed out

squeeze bottle *n* : a flexible plastic bottle that dispenses its contents by being pressed

squelch \ˈskwelch\ *vb* **1** : to suppress completely : CRUSH **2** : to move in soft mud — **squelch** *n*

squib \ˈskwib\ *n* **1** : a small firecracker; *esp* : one that fizzes instead of exploding **2** : a brief witty writing or speech

squid \ˈskwid\ *n, pl* **squid** *or* **squids** : any of numerous 10-armed long-bodied sea mollusks usu. having a slender internal shell

squint \ˈskwint\ *vb* **1** : to look or aim obliquely **2** : to close the eyes partly ⟨the glare made him ∼⟩ **3** : to be cross-eyed — **squint** *n or adj*

[1]**squire** \ˈskwī(ə)r\ *n* [ME *squier,* fr. OF *esquier,* fr. LL *scutarius,* fr. L *scutum* shield] **1** : an armor-bearer of a knight **2** : a man gallantly devoted to a lady **3** : a member of the British gentry ranking below a knight and above a gentleman; *also* : a prominent landowner **4** : a local magistrate

[2]**squire** *vb* **squired; squir·ing** : to attend as a squire or escort

squirm \ˈskwərm\ *vb* : to twist about like a worm : WRIGGLE

squir·rel \ˈskwər(-ə)l\ *n, pl* **squirrels** *also* **squirrel** [ME *squirel,* fr. MF *esquireul,* fr. VL *scurius,* alter. of L *sciurus,* fr. Gk *skiouros,* fr. *skia* shadow + *oura* tail] : any of various rodents usu. with a long bushy tail and strong hind legs; *also* : the fur of a squirrel

[1]**squirt** \ˈskwərt\ *vb* : to eject liquid in a thin spurt

[2]**squirt** *n* **1** : an instrument (as a syringe) for squirting **2** : a small forcible jet of liquid

[1]**Sr** *abbr* **1** senior **2** sister

[2]**Sr** *symbol* strontium

SR *abbr* seaman recruit

SRO *abbr* **1** single-room occupancy **2** standing room only

SS *abbr* **1** saints **2** Social Security **3** steamship **4** sworn statement

SSA *abbr* Social Security Administration

SSE *abbr* south-southeast

SSG *or* **SSgt** *abbr* staff sergeant

ssp *abbr* subspecies

SSR *abbr* Soviet Socialist Republic

SSS *abbr* Selective Service System

SST \ˈes-ˈes-ˈtē\ *n* [*s*uper*s*onic *t*ransport] : a supersonic passenger airplane

SSW *abbr* south-southwest

st *abbr* **1** stanza **2** state **3** stitch **4** stone **5** street

St *abbr* saint

ST *abbr* **1** short ton **2** standard time

-st — see -EST

sta *abbr* station; stationary

[1]**stab** \ˈstab\ *n* **1** : a wound given by a pointed weapon **2** : a quick thrust; *also* : a brief attempt

[2]**stab** *vb* **stabbed; stab·bing** : to pierce or wound with or as if with a pointed weapon; *also* : THRUST, DRIVE

sta·bile \ˈstā-ˌbēl\ *n* : a stable abstract sculpture or construction typically made of sheet metal, wire, and wood

sta·bi·lize \ˈstā-bə-ˌlīz\ *vb* **-lized; -liz·ing** **1** : to make stable **2** : to hold steady ⟨∼ prices⟩ **syn** steady — **sta·bi·li·za·tion** \ˌstā-bə-lə-ˈzā-shən\ *n* — **sta·bi·liz·er** \ˈstā-bə-ˌlī-zər\ *n*

[1]**sta·ble** \ˈstā-bəl\ *n* : a building in which livestock is sheltered and fed — **sta·ble·man** \-mən, -ˌman\ *n*

[2]**stable** *vb* **sta·bled; sta·bling** \-b(ə-)liŋ\ : to put or keep in a stable

[3]**stable** *adj* **sta·bler** \-b(ə-)lər\; **sta·blest** \-b(ə-)ləst\ **1** : firmly established; *also* : mentally healthy and well-balanced **2** : steady in purpose : CONSTANT **3** : DURABLE, ENDURING **4** : resistant to chemical or physical change **syn** lasting, permanent, perpetual, perdurable — **sta·bil·i·ty** \stə-ˈbil-ət-ē\ *n*

stac·ca·to \stə-ˈkät-ō\ *adj* [It] : cut short so as not to sound connected ⟨∼ notes⟩

[1]**stack** \ˈstak\ *n* **1** : a large pile (as of hay) **2** : a large quantity **3** : a vertical pipe : SMOKESTACK **4** : an orderly pile (as of poker chips) **5** : a rack with shelves for storing books

[2]**stack** *vb* **1** : to pile up **2** : to arrange (cards) secretly for cheating

stack up *vb* : MEASURE UP

sta·di·um \ˈstād-ē-əm\ *n, pl* **-dia** \-ē-ə\ *or* **-di·ums** : a structure with tiers of seats for spectators built around a field for sports events

[1]**staff** \ˈstaf\ *n, pl* **staffs** \ˈstafs, ˈstavz\ *or* **staves** \ˈstavz, ˈstāvz\ **1** : a pole, stick, rod, or bar used for supporting, for measuring, or as a symbol of authority; *also* : CLUB, CUDGEL **2** : something that sustains ⟨bread is the ∼ of life⟩ **3** : the five horizontal lines on which music is written **4** : a body of assistants to an executive **5** : a group of officers holding no command but having duties concerned with planning and managing

[2]**staff** *vb* : to supply with a staff or with workers

staff·er \ˈstaf-ər\ *n* : a member of a staff (as of a newspaper)

staff sergeant *n* : a noncommissioned officer ranking in the army next below a sergeant first class, in the air force next below a technical sergeant, and in the marine corps next below a gunnery sergeant

[1]**stag** \ˈstag\ *n, pl* **stags** *or* **stag** : an adult male of various large deer

[2]**stag** *adj* : restricted to or intended for men ⟨a ~ party⟩ ⟨~ movies⟩

[3]**stag** *adv* : unaccompanied by a date

[1]**stage** \ˈstāj\ *n* **1** : a raised platform on which an orator may speak or a play may be presented **2** : the acting profession : THEATER **3** : the scene of a notable action or event **4** : a station or resting place on a traveled road **5** : STAGECOACH **6** : a degree of advance in an undertaking, process, or development **7** : a propulsion unit in a rocket — **stagy** \ˈstā-jē\ *adj*

[2]**stage** *vb* **staged; stag·ing** : to produce or perform on or as if on a stage — **stage·able** *adj*

stage·coach \ˈstāj-ˌkōch\ *n* : a horse-drawn coach that runs regularly between stations

stag·fla·tion \ˌstag-ˈflā-shən\ *n* : inflation with stagnant economic activity and high unemployment

[1]**stag·ger** \ˈstag-ər\ *vb* **stag·gered; stag·ger·ing** \-(ə-)riŋ\ **1** : to reel from side to side : TOTTER **2** : to begin to doubt : WAVER **3** : to cause to reel or waver **4** : to arrange in overlapping or alternating positions or times ⟨~ working hours⟩ **5** : ASTONISH — **stag·ger·ing·ly** *adv*

[2]**stagger** *n* **1** *pl* : an abnormal condition of domestic mammals and birds associated with damage to the central nervous system and marked by lack of coordination and a reeling unsteady gait **2** : a reeling or unsteady gait or stance

stag·ing \ˈstā-jiŋ\ *n* **1** : SCAFFOLDING **2** : the assembling of troops and matériel in transit in a particular place

stag·nant \ˈstag-nənt\ *adj* **1** : not flowing : MOTIONLESS ⟨~ water in a pond⟩ **2** : DULL, INACTIVE ⟨~ business⟩

stag·nate \ˈstag-ˌnāt\ *vb* **stag·nat·ed; stag·nat·ing** : to be or become stagnant — **stag·na·tion** \stag-ˈnā-shən\ *n*

staid \ˈstād\ *adj* : SOBER, SEDATE **syn** grave, serious, earnest

[1]**stain** \ˈstān\ *vb* **1** : DISCOLOR, SOIL **2** : to color (as wood, paper, or cloth) by processes affecting the material itself **3** : TAINT, CORRUPT **4** : DISGRACE

[2]**stain** *n* **1** : SPOT, DISCOLORATION **2** : a taint of guilt : STIGMA **3** : a preparation (as a dye or pigment) used in staining — **stain·less** *adj*

stainless steel *n* : steel alloyed with chromium that is highly resistant to stain, rust, and corrosion

stair \ˈstaər\ *n* **1** : a series of steps or flights of steps for passing from one level to another — often used in pl. **2** : one step of a stairway

stair·case \-ˌkās\ *n* : a flight of steps with their supporting framework, casing, and balusters

stair·way \-ˌwā\ *n* : one or more flights of stairs with connecting landings

stair·well \-ˌwel\ *n* : a vertical shaft in which stairs are located

[1]**stake** \ˈstāk\ *n* **1** : a pointed piece of material (as of wood) driven into the ground as a marker or a support **2** : a post to which a person is bound for death by burning; *also* : such a death **3** : something that is staked for gain or loss **4** : the prize in a contest

[2]**stake** *vb* **staked; stak·ing** **1** : to mark the limits of with stakes **2** : to tether to a stake **3** : to support or secure with stakes **4** : to place as a bet

stake·out \ˈstāk-ˌau̇t\ *n* : a surveillance by police (as of an area)

sta·lac·tite \stə-ˈlak-ˌtīt\ *n* [NL *stalactites,* fr. Gk *stalaktos* dripping] : an icicle-shaped deposit hanging from the roof or sides of a cavern

sta·lag·mite \stə-ˈlag-ˌmīt\ *n* [NL *stalagmites,* fr. Gk *stalagma* drop or *stalagmos* dripping] : a deposit resembling an inverted stalactite rising from the floor of a cavern

stale \ˈstāl\ *adj* **stal·er; stal·est** **1** : flat and tasteless from age ⟨~ beer⟩ **2** : not freshly made ⟨~ bread⟩ **3** : COMMONPLACE, TRITE — **stale** *vb*

stale·mate \ˈstāl-ˌmāt\ *n* : a drawn contest : DEADLOCK — **stalemate** *vb*

[1]**stalk** \ˈstȯk\ *vb* **1** : to approach (game) stealthily **2** : to walk stiffly or haughtily

[2]**stalk** *n* : a plant stem; *also* : any slender usu. upright supporting or connecting part — **stalked** \ˈstȯkt\ *adj*

[1]**stall** \ˈstȯl\ *n* **1** : a compartment in a stable or barn for one animal **2** : a booth or counter where articles may be displayed for sale **3** : a seat in a church choir; *also* : a church pew **4** *Brit* : a front orchestra seat in a theater

[2]**stall** *vb* : to bring or come to a standstill unintentionally ⟨~ an engine⟩

[3]**stall** *n* : the condition of an airfoil or aircraft in which lift is lost and the airfoil or aircraft tends to drop

stal·lion \ˈstal-yən\ *n* : a male horse

stal·wart \ˈstȯl-wərt\ *adj* : STOUT, STRONG; *also* : BRAVE, VALIANT

sta·men \ˈstā-mən\ *n* : an organ of a flower that produces pollen

stam·i·na \ˈstam-ə-nə\ *n* [L, pl. of *stamen* warp, thread of life spun by the Fates] : VIGOR, ENDURANCE

sta·mi·nate \ˈstā-mə-nət, ˈstam-ə-, -ˌnāt\ *adj* **1** : having or producing stamens **2** : having stamens but no pistils

stam·mer \ˈstam-ər\ *vb* **stam·mered; stam·mer·ing** \-(ə-)riŋ\ : to hesitate or stumble in speaking — **stammer** *n* — **stam·mer·er** *n*

[1]**stamp** \ˈstamp; *for 2 also* ˈstämp *or* ˈstȯmp\ *vb* **1** : to pound or crush with a heavy instrument **2** : to strike or beat with the bottom of the foot **3** : to impress or imprint with a mark **4** : to cut out or indent with a stamp or die **5** : to attach a postage stamp to

[2]**stamp** *n* **1** : a device or instrument for stamping **2** : the mark made by stamping; *also* : a distinctive mark or quality **3** : the act of stamping **4** : a paper or a mark put on a thing to show that a required charge has been paid

[1]**stam·pede** \stam-ˈpēd\ *n* : a wild headlong rush or flight esp. of frightened animals

[2]**stampede** *vb* **stam·ped·ed; stam·ped·ing** **1** : to flee or cause to flee in panic **2** : to act or cause to act together suddenly and heedlessly

stance \ˈstans\ *n* : a way of standing

[1]**stanch** \ˈstȯnch, ˈstänch\ *vb* : to check the flowing of (as blood); *also* : to cease flowing or bleeding

[2]**stanch** *var of* [2]STAUNCH

stan·chion \ˈstan-chən\ *n* : an upright bar, post, or support

[1]**stand** \ˈstand\ *vb* **stood** \ˈstu̇d\; **stand·ing** **1** : to take or be at rest in an upright or firm position **2** : to assume a specified position **3** : to remain stationary or unchanged **4** : to be steadfast **5** : to act in resistance ⟨~ against a foe⟩ **6** : to maintain a relative position or rank **7** : to gather slowly and remain briefly ⟨tears *stood* in her eyes⟩ **8** : to set upright **9** : ENDURE, TOLERATE ⟨I won't ~ for that⟩ **10** : to submit to ⟨~ trial⟩ — **stand pat** : to oppose or resist change

[2]**stand** *n* **1** : an act of standing, staying, or resisting **2** : a stop made to give a performance **3** : POSITION, VIEWPOINT **4** : a place taken by a witness to testify in court **5** *pl* : tiered seats for spectators **6** : a raised platform (as for speakers) **7** : a structure for a small retail business **8** : a structure for supporting or holding something up-

right ⟨music ~⟩ **9** : a group of plants growing in a continuous area

stand–alone \ˈstand-ə-ˌlōn\ *adj* : SELF-CONTAINED; *esp* : capable of operation independent of a computer

stan·dard \ˈstan-dərd\ *n* **1** : a figure adopted as an emblem by a people **2** : the personal flag of a ruler; *also* : FLAG **3** : something set up as a rule for measuring or as a model to be followed **4** : an upright support ⟨lamp ~⟩ — **standard** *adj*

stan·dard–bear·er \-ˌbar-ər\ *n* : the leader of a cause

stan·dard·ize \ˈstan-dərd-ˌīz\ *vb* **-ized; -iz·ing** : to make standard or uniform — **stan·dard·iza·tion** \ˌstan-dərd-ə-ˈzā-shən\ *n*

standard of living : the necessities, comforts, and luxuries that a person or group is accustomed to

standard time *n* : the time established by law or by general usage over a region or country

stand·by \ˈstan(d)-ˌbī\ *n, pl* **stand·bys** \-ˌbīz\ **1** : one that can be relied on **2** : a substitute in reserve — **on standby** : ready or available for immediate action or use

stand–in \ˈstan-ˌdin\ *n* **1** : someone employed to occupy an actor's place while lights and camera are readied **2** : SUBSTITUTE

1**stand·ing** \ˈstan-diŋ\ *adj* **1** : ERECT **2** : not flowing : STAGNANT **3** : remaining at the same level or amount for an indefinite period ⟨~ offer⟩ **4** : PERMANENT **5** : done from a standing position ⟨a ~ jump⟩

2**standing** *n* **1** : length of service; *also* : relative position in society or in a profession : RANK **2** : DURATION

stand·off \ˈstand-ˌȯf\ *n* : TIE, DRAW

stand·out \ˈstand-ˌau̇t\ *n* : something conspicuously excellent

stand·pipe \ˈstan(d)-ˌpīp\ *n* : a high vertical pipe or reservoir for water used to produce a uniform pressure

stand·point \-ˌpȯint\ *n* : a position from which objects or principles are judged

stand·still \-ˌstil\ *n* : a state of rest

stank \ˈstaŋk\ *past of* STINK

stan·za \ˈstan-zə\ *n* [It] : a group of lines forming a division of a poem

sta·pes \ˈstā-ˌpēz\ *n, pl* **stapes** *or* **sta·pe·des** \ˈstā-pə-ˌdēz\ : the small innermost bone of the ear of mammals

staph·y·lo·coc·cus \ˌstaf-ə-lō-ˈkäk-əs\ *n, pl* **-coc·ci** \-ˈkäk-ˌ(s)ī\ : any of various spherical bacteria including some that cause purulent infections — **staph·y·lo·coc·cal** \-ˈkäk-əl\ *adj*

1**sta·ple** \ˈstā-pəl\ *n* : a U-shaped piece of metal or wire with sharp points to be driven into or through objects and sometimes bent at the ends to hold or fasten one object to another — **staple** *vb* — **sta·pler** \-p(ə-)lər\ *n*

2**staple** *n* **1** : a chief commodity or product **2** : the main part of a thing : chief item **3** : unmanufactured or raw material **4** : a textile fiber suitable for spinning into yarn

3**staple** *adj* **1** : regularly produced in large quantities **2** : PRINCIPAL, MAIN

1**star** \ˈstär\ *n* **1** : a celestial body that appears as a fixed point of light; *esp* : such a body that is gaseous, self-luminous, and of great mass **2** : a planet or configuration of planets that is held in astrology to influence one's fortune — usu. used in pl. **3** *obs* : DESTINY, FORTUNE **4** : a conventional figure representing a star; *esp* : ASTERISK **5** : an actor or actress playing the leading role **6** : a brilliant performer — **star·dom** \ˈstärd-əm\ *n* — **star·less** *adj* — **star·like** *adj* — **star·ry** *adj*

2**star** *vb* **starred; star·ring** **1** : to adorn with stars **2** : to mark with an asterisk **3** : to play the leading role

star·board \ˈstär-bərd\ *n* [ME *sterbord*, fr. OE *stēorbord*, fr. *stēor-* steering oar + *bord* ship's side] : the right side of a ship or airplane looking forward — **starboard** *adj*

1**starch** \ˈstärch\ *vb* : to stiffen with starch

2**starch** *n* : a complex carbohydrate that is stored in plants, is an important foodstuff, and is used in adhesives and sizes, in laundering, and in pharmacy — **starchy** *adj*

stare \ˈstaər\ *vb* **stared; star·ing** : to look fixedly with wide-open eyes — **stare** *n* — **star·er** *n*

star·fish \ˈstär-ˌfish\ *n* : any of a class of echinoderms usu. having five arms arranged around a central disk and feeding largely on mollusks

stark \ˈstärk\ *adj* **1** *archaic* : STRONG, ROBUST **2** : rigid as if in death; *also* : STRICT **3** : SHEER, UTTER **4** : BARREN, DESOLATE ⟨~ landscape⟩; *also* : UNADORNED ⟨~ realism⟩ **5** : sharply delineated — **stark** *adv* — **stark·ly** *adv*

star·light \ˈstär-ˌlīt\ *n* : the light given by the stars

star·ling \ˈstär-liŋ\ *n* : a dark brown or in summer glossy greenish black European bird related to the crows that is naturalized and often a pest in No. America

1**start** \ˈstärt\ *vb* **1** : to give an involuntary twitch or jerk (as from surprise) **2** : BEGIN, COMMENCE **3** : to set going **4** : to enter (as a horse) in a contest **5** : TAP ⟨~ a cask⟩ — **start·er** *n*

2**start** *n* **1** : a sudden involuntary motion : LEAP **2** : a spasmodic and brief effort or action **3** : BEGINNING; *also* : the place of beginning

star·tle \ˈstärt-ᵊl\ *vb* **star·tled; star·tling** \ˈstärt-(ᵊ-)liŋ\ : to frighten or surprise suddenly : cause to start

star·tling *adj* : causing sudden fear, surprise, or anxiety

starve \ˈstärv\ *vb* **starved; starv·ing** [ME *sterven* to die, fr. OE *steorfan*] **1** : to perish from hunger **2** : to suffer extreme hunger **3** : to kill with hunger; *also* : to distress or subdue by famine — **star·va·tion** \stär-ˈvā-shən\ *n*

starve·ling \ˈstärv-liŋ\ *n* : one that is thin from lack of nourishment

stash \ˈstash\ *vb* : to store in a secret place — **stash** *n*

stat *abbr* **1** [L *statim*] immediately **2** statute

1**state** \ˈstāt\ *n* [ME *stat*, fr. OF & L; OF *estat*, fr. L *status*, fr. *stare* to stand] **1** : mode or condition of being ⟨gaseous ~ of water⟩ **2** : condition of mind **3** : social position **4** : a body of people occupying a definite territory and organized under one government; *also* : the government of such a body of people **5** : one of the constituent units of a nation having a federal government — **state·hood** \-ˌhu̇d\ *n*

2**state** *vb* **stat·ed; stat·ing** **1** : FIX ⟨*stated* intervals⟩ **2** : to express in words

state·craft \ˈstāt-ˌkraft\ *n* : state management : STATESMANSHIP

state·house \-ˌhau̇s\ *n* : the building in which a state legislature meets

state·ly \ˈstāt-lē\ *adj* **state·li·er; -est** **1** : having lofty dignity : HAUGHTY **2** : IMPRESSIVE, MAJESTIC **syn** magnificent, imposing, august — **state·li·ness** *n*

state·ment \ˈstāt-mənt\ *n* **1** : the act or result of presenting in words **2** : a summary of a financial account

state·room \ˈstāt-ˌrüm, -ˌru̇m\ *n* : a private room on a ship or railroad car

state·side \ˈstāt-ˌsīd\ *adj* : of or relating to the U.S. as regarded from outside its continental limits ⟨~ mail⟩ — **stateside** *adv*

states·man \ˈstāts-mən\ *n* : one skilled in government and wise in handling public affairs; *also* : one influential in shaping public policy — **states·man·like** *adj* — **states·man·ship** *n*

1**stat·ic** \ˈstat-ik\ *adj* **1** : acting by mere weight without motion ⟨~ pressure⟩ **2** : relating to bodies or forces at rest or in equilibrium **3** : not moving : not active **4** : of or relating to stationary charges of electricity **5** : of, relating to, or caused by radio static

2**static** *n* : noise produced in a radio or television receiver by atmospheric or other electrical disturbances

1**sta·tion** \ˈstā-shən\ *n* **1** : the place where a person or thing stands or is appointed to remain **2** : a regular stopping place on a transportation route ⟨a railroad ~⟩ ⟨a bus ~⟩; *also* : DEPOT **3** : a place where a fleet is assigned for duty **4** : a stock farm or ranch in Australia or New Zealand **5**

: social standing **6** : a complete assemblage of radio or television equipment for sending or receiving

²station *vb* **sta·tioned; sta·tion·ing** \ˈstā-sh(ə-)niŋ\ : to assign to a station

sta·tion·ary \ˈstā-shə-ˌner-ē\ *adj* **1** : fixed in a certain place or position **2** : not changing condition : neither improving nor getting worse

station break *n* : a pause in a radio or television broadcast for announcement of the identity of the network or station

sta·tio·ner \ˈstā-sh(ə-)nər\ *n* : one that sells stationery

sta·tio·nery \ˈstā-shə-ˌner-ē\ *n* : materials (as paper, pens, or ink) for writing; *esp* : letter paper with envelopes

station wagon *n* : an automobile having an interior longer than a sedan's, one or more folding or removable seats to make carrying light cargo easier, and no trunk

sta·tis·tic \stə-ˈtis-tik\ *n* **1** : a single term or datum in a collection of statistics **2** : a quantity (as the mean) that is computed from a sample

sta·tis·tics \stə-ˈtis-tiks\ *n pl* [G *statistik* study of political facts and figures, fr. NL *statisticus* of politics, fr. L *status* state] **1** : a branch of mathematics dealing with the analysis and interpretation of masses of numerical data **2** : facts collected and arranged in an orderly way for study — **sta·tis·ti·cal** \-ti-kəl\ *adj* — **sta·tis·ti·cal·ly** \-ti-k(ə-)lē\ *adv* — **stat·is·ti·cian** \ˌstat-ə-ˈstish-ən\ *n*

stat·u·ary \ˈstach-ə-ˌwer-ē\ *n, pl* **-ar·ies** **1** : the art of making statues **2** : STATUES

stat·ue \ˈstach-ü\ *n* : a likeness of a living being sculptured in a solid substance

stat·u·esque \ˌstach-ə-ˈwesk\ *adj* : resembling a statue esp. in well-proportioned or massive dignity

stat·u·ette \ˌstach-ə-ˈwet\ *n* : a small statue

stat·ure \ˈstach-ər\ *n* **1** : natural height (as of a person) **2** : quality or status gained (as by achievement)

sta·tus \ˈstāt-əs, ˈstat-\ *n* **1** : the state or condition of a person in the eyes of others **2** : condition of affairs

sta·tus quo \-ˈkwō\ *n* [L, state in which] : the existing state of affairs

stat·ute \ˈstach-üt\ *n* : a law enacted by a legislative body

stat·u·to·ry \ˈstach-ə-ˌtōr-ē\ *adj* : imposed by statute : LAWFUL

¹staunch \ˈstȯnch\ *var of* ¹STANCH

²staunch *adj* **1** : WATERTIGHT ⟨a ~ ship⟩ **2** : FIRM, STRONG; *also* : STEADFAST, LOYAL **syn** resolute, constant, true, faithful — **staunch·ly** *adv*

¹stave \ˈstāv\ *n* **1** : CUDGEL, STAFF **2** : any of several narrow strips of wood placed edge to edge to make something (as a barrel or bucket) **3** : STANZA

²stave *vb* **staved** *or* **stove** \ˈstōv\; **stav·ing** **1** : to break in the staves of; *also* : to break a hole in **2** : to drive or thrust away ⟨~ off trouble⟩

staves *pl of* STAFF

¹stay \ˈstā\ *n* : a strong rope or wire used to support or steady something (as a ship's mast)

²stay *vb* **stayed** \ˈstād\ *also* **staid** \ˈstād\; **stay·ing** **1** : PAUSE, WAIT **2** : to stand firm **3** : LIVE, DWELL **4** : DELAY, POSTPONE **5** : to last out (as a race) **6** : STOP, CHECK **7** : to satisfy (as hunger) for a time **syn** remain, abide, linger, tarry

³stay *n* **1** : STOP, HALT **2** : a residence or sojourn in a place

⁴stay *n* **1** : PROP, SUPPORT **2** : CORSET — usu. used in pl.

⁵stay *vb* : to hold up : PROP

staying power *n* : STAMINA

stbd *abbr* starboard

std *abbr* standard

STD \ˌes-ˈtē-ˈdē\ *n* : SEXUALLY TRANSMITTED DISEASE

Ste *abbr* [F *sainte*] saint (female)

stead \ˈsted\ *n* **1** : ADVANTAGE, AVAIL ⟨stood him in good ~⟩ **2** : the place or function ordinarily occupied or carried out by another ⟨her brother served in her ~⟩

stead·fast \ˈsted-ˌfast\ *adj* **1** : firmly fixed in place **2** : not subject to change **3** : firm in belief, determination, or adherence : LOYAL **syn** resolute, true, faithful, staunch — **stead·fast·ly** *adv* — **stead·fast·ness** *n*

¹steady \ˈsted-ē\ *adj* **steadi·er; -est** **1** : FIRM, FIXED **2** : not faltering or swerving; *also* : CALM **3** : STABLE **4** : CONSTANT, RESOLUTE **5** : REGULAR **6** : RELIABLE, SOBER **syn** uniform, even, stable, constant — **steadi·ly** \ˈsted-ᵊl-ē\ *adv* — **steadi·ness** \-ē-nəs\ *n* — **steady** *adv*

²steady *vb* **stead·ied; steady·ing** : to make or become steady

steak \ˈstāk\ *n* : a slice of meat cut from a fleshy part esp. of a beef carcass

¹steal \ˈstēl\ *vb* **stole** \ˈstōl\; **sto·len** \ˈstō-lən\; **steal·ing** **1** : to come or go secretly or gradually **2** : to take and carry away without right or permission **3** : to get for oneself slyly or secretly **4** : to gain a base in baseball by running without the aid of a hit or an error **syn** pilfer, filch, purloin, swipe

²steal *n* **1** : an act of stealing **2** : BARGAIN

stealth \ˈstelth\ *n* : secret or underhanded procedure : FURTIVENESS

stealthy \ˈstel-thē\ *adj* **stealth·i·er; -est** : done by stealth : FURTIVE, SLY **syn** secret, covert, clandestine, surreptitious, underhanded — **stealth·i·ly** \ˈstel-thə-lē\ *adv*

¹steam \ˈstēm\ *n* **1** : the vapor into which water is changed when heated to the boiling point **2** : water vapor when compressed so that it supplies heat and power **3** : POWER, FORCE, ENERGY — **steamy** *adj*

²steam *vb* **1** : to pass off as vapor **2** : to emit vapor **3** : to move by or as if by the agency of steam — **steam·er** *n*

steam·boat \ˈstēm-ˌbōt\ *n* : a boat driven by steam power

steam engine *n* : a reciprocating engine having a piston driven in a closed cylinder by steam

steam·fit·ter \ˈstēm-ˌfit-ər\ *n* : a workman who puts in or repairs equipment (as steam pipes) for heating, ventilating, or refrigerating systems — **steam fitting** *n*

steam·roll·er \-ˈrō-lər\ *n* : a machine for compacting roads or pavements — **steam·roll·er** *also* **steam·roll** \-ˌrōl\ *vb*

steam·ship \-ˌship\ *n* : a ship driven by steam

steed \ˈstēd\ *n* : HORSE

¹steel \ˈstēl\ *n* **1** : iron treated with intense heat and mixed with carbon to make it hard and tough **2** : an article made of steel **3** : a quality (as hardness of mind) that suggests steel — **steel** *adj* — **steely** *adj*

²steel *vb* **1** : to sheathe, point, or edge with steel **2** : to make able to resist

steel wool *n* : long fine steel shavings used esp. for scouring and smoothing

steel·yard \ˈstēl-ˌyärd\ *n* : a balance in which the object to be weighed is hung from the shorter arm of a lever and is balanced by a weight that slides along the longer arm

¹steep \ˈstēp\ *adj* **1** : having a very sharp slope : PRECIPITOUS **2** : too great or too high ⟨~ prices⟩ — **steep·ly** *adv* — **steep·ness** *n*

²steep *n* : a steep slope

³steep *vb* **1** : to soak in a liquid; *esp* : to extract the essence of by soaking ⟨~ tea⟩ **2** : SATURATE ⟨~*ed* in learning⟩

stee·ple \ˈstē-pəl\ *n* : a tall tapering structure built on top of a church tower; *also* : a church tower

stee·ple·chase \-ˌchās\ *n* [fr. the use of church steeples as landmarks to guide the riders] : a race across country by horsemen; *also* : a race over a course obstructed by hurdles

¹steer \ˈstiər\ *n* : a male bovine animal castrated before sexual maturity and usu. raised for beef

[2]**steer** *vb* **1** : to direct the course of (as by a rudder or wheel) **2** : GUIDE, CONTROL **3** : to pursue a course of action **4** : to be subject to guidance or direction — **steers·man** \ˈstiərz-mən\ *n*

steer·age \ˈsti(ə)r-ij\ *n* **1** : DIRECTION, GUIDANCE **2** : a section in a passenger ship for passengers paying the lowest fares

stein \ˈstīn\ *n* : an earthenware mug

stel·lar \ˈstel-ər\ *adj* : of or relating to stars : resembling a star

[1]**stem** \ˈstem\ *n* **1** : the main stalk of a plant; *also* : a plant part that supports another part (as a leaf or fruit) **2** : the bow of a ship **3** : a line of ancestry : STOCK **4** : that part of an inflected word which remains unchanged throughout a given inflection **5** : something resembling the stem of a plant — **stem·less** *adj*

[2]**stem** *vb* **stemmed; stem·ming** : to have a specified source : DERIVE

[3]**stem** *vb* **stemmed; stem·ming** : to make headway against ⟨~ the tide⟩

[4]**stem** *vb* **stemmed; stem·ming** : to stop or check by or as if by damming

stemmed \ˈstemd\ *adj* : having a stem

stench \ˈstench\ *n* : STINK

sten·cil \ˈsten-səl\ *n* [ME *stanselen* to ornament with sparkling colors, fr. MF *estanceler*, fr. *estancele* spark, fr. (assumed) VL *stincilla*, fr. L *scintilla*] : a piece of thin impervious material (as metal or paper) that is perforated with lettering or a design through which a substance (as ink or paint) is applied to a surface to be printed — **stencil** *vb*

stencil

ste·nog·ra·phy \stə-ˈnäg-rə-fē\ *n* : the art or process of writing in shorthand — **ste·nog·ra·pher** \-fər\ *n* — **steno·graph·ic** \ˌsten-ə-ˈgraf-ik\ *adj*

sten·to·ri·an \sten-ˈtōr-ē-ən\ *adj* : extremely loud

[1]**step** \ˈstep\ *n* **1** : a rest for the foot in ascending or descending : STAIR **2** : an advance made by raising one foot and putting it down in a different spot **3** : manner of walking **4** : a small space or distance **5** : a degree, rank, or plane in a series **6** : a sequential measure leading to a result

[2]**step** *vb* **stepped; step·ping 1** : to advance or recede by steps **2** : to go on foot : WALK **3** : to move along briskly **4** : to press down with the foot **5** : to measure by steps **6** : to construct or arrange in or as if in steps

step·broth·er \ˈstep-ˌbrəth-ər\ *n* : the son of one's stepparent by a former marriage

step·child \-ˌchīld\ *n* : a child of one's husband or wife by a former marriage

step·daugh·ter \-ˌdȯt-ər\ *n* : a daughter of one's wife or husband by a former marriage

step down *vb* **1** : to lower the voltage of (a current) by means of a transformer **2** : RETIRE, RESIGN

step·fa·ther \-ˌfäth-ər\ *n* : the husband of one's mother by a subsequent marriage

step·lad·der \ˈstep-ˌlad-ər\ *n* : a light portable set of steps in a hinged frame

step·moth·er \-ˌməth-ər\ *n* : the wife of one's father by a subsequent marriage

step·par·ent \-ˌpar-ənt\ *n* : the husband or wife of one's mother or father by a subsequent marriage

steppe \ˈstep\ *n* [Russ *step'*] : dry level grass-covered land in regions of wide temperature range esp. in southeastern Europe and Asia

step·sis·ter \ˈstep-ˌsis-tər\ *n* : the daughter of one's stepparent by a former marriage

step·son \-ˌsən\ *n* : a son of one's wife or husband by a former marriage

step up \(ˈ)step-ˈəp\ *vb* **1** : to increase the voltage of (a current) by means of a transformer **2** : INCREASE, ACCELERATE — **step–up** \ˈstep-ˌəp\ *n*

ster *abbr* sterling

ste·reo \ˈster-ē-ˌō, ˈstir-\ *n, pl* **ste·re·os 1** : stereophonic reproduction **2** : a stereophonic sound system — **stereo** *adj*

ste·reo·phon·ic \ˌster-ē-ə-ˈfän-ik, ˌstir-\ *adj* : of or relating to sound reproduction designed to create the effect of listening to the original — **ste·reo·phon·i·cal·ly** \-i-k(ə-)lē\ *adv*

ster·e·o·scope \ˈster-ē-ə-ˌskōp, ˈstir-\ *n* [Gk *stereos* solid + *skopein* to look at] : an optical instrument that blends two slightly different pictures of the same subject to give the effect of depth

ste·reo·scop·ic \ˌster-ē-ə-ˈskäp-ik, ˌstir-\ *adj* **1** : of or relating to the stereoscope **2** : characterized by stereoscopy ⟨~ vision⟩ — **ste·reo·scop·i·cal·ly** \-i-k(ə-)lē\ *adv*

ste·re·os·co·py \ˌster-ē-ˈäs-kə-pē, ˌstir-\ *n* : the seeing of objects in three dimensions

ste·reo·type \ˈster-ē-ə-ˌtīp, ˈstir-\ *n* **1** : a metal printing plate cast from a mold made from set type **2** : something agreeing with a pattern; *esp* : an idea that many people have about a thing or a group and that may often be untrue or only partly true

ste·reo·typed \-ˌtīpt\ *adj* : repeated without variation : lacking originality or individuality **syn** trite, clichéd, commonplace, hackneyed, stale, threadbare

ster·ile \ˈster-əl\ *adj* **1** : unable to bear fruit, crops, or offspring **2** : free from living things and esp. germs — **ste·ril·i·ty** \stə-ˈril-ət-ē\ *n*

ster·il·ize \ˈster-ə-ˌlīz\ *vb* **-ized; -iz·ing** : to make sterile; *esp* : to free from germs — **ster·il·iza·tion** \ˌster-ə-lə-ˈzā-shən\ *n* — **ster·il·iz·er** \ˈster-ə-ˌlī-zər\ *n*

[1]**ster·ling** \ˈstər-liŋ\ *n* **1** : British money **2** : sterling silver

[2]**sterling** *adj* **1** : of, relating to, or calculated in terms of British sterling **2** : having a fixed standard of purity represented by an alloy of 925 parts of silver with 75 parts of copper **3** : made of sterling silver **4** : EXCELLENT

[1]**stern** \ˈstərn\ *adj* **1** : SEVERE, AUSTERE **2** : STOUT, STURDY ⟨~ resolve⟩ — **stern·ly** *adv* — **stern·ness** *n*

[2]**stern** *n* : the rear end of a boat

ster·num \ˈstər-nəm\ *n, pl* **sternums** *or* **ster·na** \-nə\ : a long flat bone or cartilage at the center front of the chest connecting the ribs of the two sides

ste·roid \ˈstir-ˌȯid\ *n* : any of numerous compounds containing a 17-carbon 4-ring system and including various hormones and sugar derivatives — **steroid** *or* **ste·roi·dal** \stə-ˈrȯid-ᵊl\ *adj*

stetho·scope \ˈsteth-ə-ˌskōp\ *n* : an instrument for listening to sounds produced in the body and esp. in the chest

ste·ve·dore \ˈstē-və-ˌdōr\ *n* [Sp *estibador*, fr. *estibar* to pack, fr. L *stipare* to press together] : one who works at loading and unloading ships

[1]**stew** \ˈst(y)ü\ *n* **1** : a dish of stewed meat and vegetables served in gravy **2** : a state of excitement, worry, or confusion

[2]**stew** *vb* **1** : to boil slowly : SIMMER **2** : to become excited or worried

stew·ard \ˈst(y)ü-ərd\ *n* [ME, fr. OE *stīweard*, fr. *stī* hall, sty + *weard* ward] **1** : one employed on a large estate to manage domestic concerns (as keeping accounts and directing servants) **2** : one actively concerned with the direction of the affairs of an organization **3** : one who supervises the provision and distribution of food (as on a ship); *also* : an employee on a ship or airplane who serves passengers — **stew·ard·ship** *n*

stew·ard·ess \-əs\ *n* : a woman who is a steward

stg *abbr* sterling

[1]**stick** \ˈstik\ *n* **1** : a cut or broken branch or twig; *also* : a long slender piece of wood **2** : ROD, STAFF **3** : something resembling a stick **4** : a dull uninteresting person

[2]**stick** *vb* **stuck** \ˈstək\; **stick·ing 1** : STAB, PRICK **2** : IMPALE **3** : ATTACH, FASTEN **4** : to thrust or project in some direction or manner **5** : to be unable to proceed or move freely **6** : to hold fast by or as if by gluing : ADHERE **7** : to hold to something firmly or closely : CLING **8** : to become jammed or blocked

stick·er \ˈstik-ər\ *n* : one that sticks (as a bur) or causes sticking (as glue); *esp* : a gummed label

stick insect *n* : any of various usu. wingless insects (as a walkingstick) with a long round body resembling a stick

stick·ler \ˈstik-(ə-)lər\ *n* : one who insists on exactness or completeness

stick shift *n* : a manually operated gearshift mounted on the steering-wheel column or floor of an automobile

stick–to–it·ive·ness \stik-ˈtü-ət-iv-nəs\ *n* : dogged perseverance : TENACITY

stick up \(ˈ)stik-ˈəp\ *vb* : to rob at gunpoint — **stick·up** \ˈstik-ˌəp\ *n*

sticky \ˈstik-ē\ *adj* **stick·i·er; -est 1** : ADHESIVE **2** : VISCOUS, GLUEY **3** : tending to stick ⟨~ valve⟩

[1]**stiff** \ˈstif\ *adj* **1** : not pliant : RIGID **2** : not limber ⟨~ joints⟩; *also* : TENSE, TAUT **3** : not flowing or working easily ⟨~ paste⟩ **4** : not natural and easy : FORMAL **5** : STRONG, FORCEFUL ⟨~ breeze⟩ **6** : HARSH, SEVERE **syn** inflexible, rigid, inelastic — **stiff·ly** *adv* — **stiff·ness** *n*

[2]**stiff** *vb* : to refrain from tipping ⟨~ a waiter⟩

stiff·en \ˈstif-ən\ *vb* **stiff·ened; stiff·en·ing** \-(ə-)niŋ\ : to make or become stiff — **stiff·en·er** \-(ə-)nər\ *n*

stiff–necked \-ˈnekt\ *adj* : STUBBORN, HAUGHTY

sti·fle \ˈstī-fəl\ *vb* **sti·fled; sti·fling** \-f(ə-)liŋ\ **1** : SUFFOCATE **2** : QUENCH, SUPPRESS **3** : SMOTHER, MUFFLE **4** : to die because of obstruction of the breath

stig·ma \ˈstig-mə\ *n, pl* **stig·ma·ta** \stig-ˈmät-ə, ˈstig-mət-ə\ *or* **stigmas** [L] **1** : a mark of disgrace or discredit **2** *pl* : bodily marks resembling the wounds of the crucified Christ **3** : the upper part of the pistil of a flower that receives the pollen in fertilization — **stig·mat·ic** \stig-ˈmat-ik\ *adj*

stig·ma·tize \ˈstig-mə-ˌtīz\ *vb* **-tized; -tiz·ing 1** : to mark with a stigma **2** : to set a mark of disgrace upon

stile \ˈstīl\ *n* : steps used for crossing a fence or wall

sti·let·to \stə-ˈlet-ō\ *n, pl* **-tos** *or* **-toes** [It, dim. of *stilo* stylus, dagger] : a slender dagger

[1]**still** \ˈstil\ *adj* **1** : MOTIONLESS **2** : making no sound : QUIET, SILENT — **still·ness** *n*

[2]**still** *vb* : to make or become still : QUIET

[3]**still** *adv* **1** : without motion ⟨sit ~⟩ **2** : up to and during this or that time **3** : in spite of that : NEVERTHELESS **4** : EVEN ⟨ran ~ faster⟩ **5** : BESIDES, YET

[4]**still** *n* **1** : STILLNESS, SILENCE **2** : a static photograph esp. of an instant in a motion picture

[5]**still** *n* **1** : DISTILLERY **2** : apparatus used in distillation

still·birth \ˈstil-ˌbərth\ *n* : the birth of a dead fetus

still·born \-ˈbȯrn\ *adj* : born dead

still life *n, pl* **still lifes** : a picture of inanimate objects

stilt \ˈstilt\ *n* : one of a pair of poles for walking with each having a step or loop for the foot; *also* : a polelike support of a structure above ground or water level

stilt·ed \ˈstil-təd\ *adj* : FORMAL, POMPOUS ⟨~ writing⟩

Stil·ton \ˈstilt-ᵊn\ *n* : a blue-veined cheese with wrinkled rind

stim·u·lant \ˈstim-yə-lənt\ *n* **1** : an agent (as a drug) that temporarily increases the activity of an organism or any of its parts **2** : STIMULUS **3** : an alcoholic beverage — **stimulant** *adj*

stim·u·late \-ˌlāt\ *vb* **-lat·ed; -lat·ing** : to make active or more active : ANIMATE, AROUSE **syn** excite, provoke, motivate, quicken — **stim·u·la·tion** \ˌstim-yə-ˈlā-shən\ *n* — **stim·u·la·tive** \ˈstim-yə-ˌlāt-iv\ *adj*

stim·u·lus \ˈstim-yə-ləs\ *n, pl* **-li** \-ˌlī\ [L] : something that stimulates : SPUR

[1]**sting** \ˈstiŋ\ *vb* **stung** \ˈstəŋ\; **sting·ing** \ˈstiŋ-iŋ\ **1** : to prick painfully esp. with a sharp or poisonous process **2** : to cause to suffer acutely — **sting·er** *n*

[2]**sting** *n* **1** : an act of stinging; *also* : a resultant sore, pain, or mark **2** : a pointed often venom-bearing organ (as of a bee)

stin·gy \ˈstin-jē\ *adj* **stin·gi·er; -est** : not generous : SPARING, NIGGARDLY — **stin·gi·ness** *n*

stink \ˈstiŋk\ *vb* **stank** \ˈstaŋk\ *or* **stunk** \ˈstəŋk\; **stunk; stink·ing** : to give forth a strong and offensive smell; *also* : to be extremely bad in quality or repute — **stink** *n* — **stink·er** *n*

stink·bug \ˈstiŋk-ˌbəg\ *n* : any of various true bugs that emit a disagreeable odor

[1]**stint** \ˈstint\ *vb* **1** : to be sparing or frugal **2** : to restrict to a scant allowance : cut short in amount

[2]**stint** *n* **1** : RESTRAINT, LIMITATION **2** : an assigned amount of work **3** : a period of time spent at a particular activity

sti·pend \ˈstī-ˌpend, -pənd\ *n* [alter. of ME *stipendy*, fr. L *stipendium*, fr. *stips* gift + *pendere* to weigh, pay] : a fixed sum of money paid periodically for services or to defray expenses

stip·ple \ˈstip-əl\ *vb* **stip·pled; stip·pling** \-(ə-)liŋ\ **1** : to engrave by means of dots and light strokes instead of by lines **2** : to apply (as paint or ink) with small short touches that together produce an even and softly graded shadow — **stipple** *n*

stip·u·late \ˈstip-yə-ˌlāt\ *vb* **-lat·ed; -lat·ing** : to make an agreement; *esp* : to make a special demand for something as a condition in an agreement — **stip·u·la·tion** \ˌstip-yə-ˈlāsh-ən\ *n*

[1]**stir** \ˈstər\ *vb* **stirred; stir·ring 1** : to move slightly **2** : AROUSE, EXCITE **3** : to mix, dissolve, or make by continued circular movement ⟨~ eggs into cake batter⟩ **4** : to move to activity (as by pushing, beating, or prodding)

[2]**stir** *n* **1** : a state of agitation or activity **2** : an act of stirring

[3]**stir** *n, slang* : PRISON

stir–fry \ˈstər-ˌfrī\ *vb* : to fry quickly over high heat while stirring continuously

stir·ring \ˈstər-iŋ\ *adj* **1** : ACTIVE, BUSTLING **2** : ROUSING, INSPIRING

stir·rup \ˈstər-əp\ *n* [OE *stigrāp*, lit., mounting rope] **1** : a light frame hung from a saddle to support the foot of a horseback rider **2** : STAPES

[1]**stitch** \ˈstich\ *n* **1** : a sudden sharp pain esp. in the side **2** : one of the series of loops formed by or over a needle in sewing **syn** twinge, pang, throe

[2]**stitch** *vb* **1** : to fasten or join with stitches **2** : to decorate with stitches **3** : SEW

stk *abbr* stock

stoat \ˈstōt\ *n, pl* **stoats** *also* **stoat** : the European ermine esp. in its brown summer coat

[1]**stock** \ˈstäk\ *n* **1** *archaic* : a block of wood **2** : a stupid person **3** : a wooden part of a thing serving as its support, frame, or handle **4** *pl* : a device for publicly punishing offenders consisting of a wooden frame with holes in which the feet and hands can be locked **5** : the original from which others derive; *also* : a group having a common origin : FAMILY **6** : farm animals **7** : the supply of goods kept by a merchant **8** : the proprietorship element in a corporation divided to give the owners an interest and usu. voting power **9** : a company of actors playing at a particular theater and presenting a series of

plays **10** : liquid in which meat, fish, or vegetables have been simmered that is used as a basis for soup, gravy, or sauce **11** : raw material

²stock *vb* : to provide with stock

³stock *adj* : kept regularly for sale or use; *also* : used regularly : STANDARD

stock·ade \stä-ˈkād\ *n* [Sp *estacada*, fr. *estaca* stake, pale] : an enclosure of posts and stakes for defense or confinement

stock·bro·ker \-ˌbrō-kər\ *n* : one who executes orders to buy and sell securities

stock car *n* : a racing car having the basic chassis of a commercially produced regular model

stock exchange *n* **1** : a place where trading in securities is accomplished under an organized system **2** : an association of stockbrokers

stock·hold·er \ˈstäk-ˌhōl-dər\ *n* : one who owns corporate stock

stock·i·nette *or* **stock·i·net** \ˌstäk-ə-ˈnet\ *n* : an elastic knitted textile fabric used esp. for infants' wear and bandages

stock·ing \ˈstäk-iŋ\ *n* : a close-fitting knitted covering for the foot and leg

stock market *n* **1** : STOCK EXCHANGE 1 **2** : a market for stocks

stock·pile \ˈstäk-ˌpīl\ *n* : a reserve supply esp. of something essential — **stockpile** *vb*

stocky \ˈstäk-ē\ *adj* **stock·i·er; -est** : being short and relatively thick : STURDY **syn** thickset, squat, heavyset, stubby

stock·yard \ˈstäk-ˌyärd\ *n* : a yard for stock; *esp* : one for livestock about to be slaughtered or shipped

stodgy \ˈstäj-ē\ *adj* **stodg·i·er; -est** : HEAVY, DULL, UNINSPIRED

¹sto·ic \ˈstō-ik\ *n* [ME, fr. L *stoicus*, fr. Gk *stōikos*, lit., of the portico, fr. *Stoa* (*Poikilē*) the Painted Portico, portico at Athens where Zeno taught] : one who suffers without complaining

²stoic *or* **sto·i·cal** \-i-kəl\ *adj* : not affected by passion or feeling; *esp* : showing indifference to pain **syn** impassive, phlegmatic, apathetic, stolid — **sto·ical·ly** \-i-k(ə-)lē\ *adv* — **sto·icism** \ˈstō-ə-ˌsiz-əm\ *n*

stoke \ˈstōk\ *vb* **stoked; stok·ing 1** : to stir up a fire **2** : to tend and supply fuel to a furnace — **stok·er** *n*

STOL *abbr* short takeoff and landing

¹stole \ˈstōl\ *past of* STEAL

²stole *n* **1** : a long narrow band worn round the neck by some clergymen **2** : a long wide scarf or similar covering worn by women

stolen *past part of* STEAL

stol·id \ˈstäl-əd\ *adj* : not easily aroused or excited : showing little or no emotion **syn** phlegmatic, apathetic, impassive, stoic — **sto·lid·i·ty** \stä-ˈlid-ət-ē\ *n* — **stol·id·ly** \ˈstäl-əd-lē\ *adv*

sto·lon \ˈstō-lən, -ˌlän\ *n* : RUNNER 6

¹stom·ach \ˈstəm-ək\ *n* **1** : a saclike digestive organ of a vertebrate into which food goes from the mouth by way of the throat and which opens below into the intestine **2** : a cavity in an invertebrate animal that is analogous to a stomach **3** : ABDOMEN **4** : desire for food caused by hunger : APPETITE **5** : INCLINATION, DESIRE

²stomach *vb* : to bear without overt resentment : BROOK

stom·ach·ache \-ˌāk\ *n* : pain in or in the region of the stomach

stom·ach·er \ˈstəm-i-kər, -i-chər\ *n* : the front of a bodice often appearing between the laces of an outer garment (as in 16th century costume)

¹stomp \ˈstämp, ˈstȯmp\ *vb* : STAMP

²stomp *n* **1** : STAMP 3 **2** : a jazz dance marked by heavy stamping

¹stone \ˈstōn\ *n* **1** : hardened earth or mineral matter : ROCK **2** : a small piece of rock **3** : a precious stone : GEM **4** : a hard abnormal mass in a bodily cavity or duct **5** : a hard stony seed or one (as of a plum) with a stony covering **6** *pl usu* **stone** : a British unit of weight equal to 14 pounds — **stony** *also* **ston·ey** \ˈstō-nē\ *adj*

²stone *vb* **stoned; ston·ing 1** : to pelt or kill with stones **2** : to remove the stones of (a fruit)

Stone Age *n* : the first known period of prehistoric human culture characterized by the use of stone tools

stoned \ˈstōnd\ *adj* **1** : DRUNK **2** : being under the influence of a drug

stood *past and past part of* STAND

stooge \ˈstüj\ *n* **1** : a person who plays a subordinate or compliant role to a principal **2** : STRAIGHT MAN

stool \ˈstül\ *n* **1** : a seat usu. without back or arms **2** : FOOTSTOOL **3** : a seat used while urinating or defecating **4** : a discharge of fecal matter

stool pigeon *n* : DECOY, INFORMER

¹stoop \ˈstüp\ *vb* **1** : to bend over **2** : CONDESCEND **3** : to humiliate or lower oneself socially or morally

²stoop *n* **1** : an act of bending over **2** : a bent position of head and shoulders

³stoop *n* : a porch or platform at a house door

¹stop \ˈstäp\ *vb* **stopped; stop·ping 1** : to close (an opening or hole) by filling or covering closely **2** : BLOCK, HALT **3** : to cease to go on **4** : to cease activity or operation **5** : STAY, TARRY **syn** quit, discontinue, desist, halt, cease

²stop *n* **1** : END, CESSATION **2** : a set of organ pipes of one tone quality; *also* : a control knob for such a set **3** : OBSTRUCTION **4** : PLUG, STOPPER **5** : an act of stopping : CHECK **6** : a delay in a journey : STAY **7** : a place for stopping **8** *chiefly Brit* : any of several punctuation marks

stop·gap \ˈstäp-ˌgap\ *n* : something that serves as a temporary expedient

stop·light \-ˌlīt\ *n* : TRAFFIC LIGHT

stop·page \ˈstäp-ij\ *n* : the act of stopping : the state of being stopped

stop·per \ˈstäp-ər\ *n* : something (as a cork or plug) for sealing an opening

stop·watch \ˈstäp-ˌwäch\ *n* : a watch having a component (as a hand) that can be started or stopped at will for exact timing

stor·age \ˈstōr-ij\ *n* **1** : space for storing; *also* : cost of storing **2** : the act of storing; *esp* : the safekeeping of goods (as in a warehouse)

storage battery *n* : a group of connected cells that converts chemical energy into electrical energy by reversible chemical reactions and that may be recharged by electrical means

¹store \ˈstōr\ *vb* **stored; stor·ing 1** : to provide esp. for a future need **2** : to place or leave in a safe location for preservation or future use

²store *n* **1** : something accumulated and kept for future use **2** : a large or ample quantity **3** : STOREHOUSE **4** : a retail business establishment

store·house \-ˌhau̇s\ *n* : a building for storing goods or supplies; *also* : an abundant source or supply

store·keep·er \-ˌkē-pər\ *n* : one who operates a retail store

store·room \-ˌrüm, -ˌru̇m\ *n* : a room for storing goods or supplies

sto·ried \ˈstōr-ēd\ *adj* : celebrated in story or history

stork \ˈstȯrk\ *n* : any of various large stout-billed Old World wading birds related to the herons and ibises

¹storm \ˈstȯrm\ *n* **1** : a heavy fall of rain, snow, or hail with high wind **2** : a violent outbreak or disturbance **3** : a mass attack on a defended position — **storm·i·ly** \ˈstȯr-mə-lē\ *adv* — **storm·i·ness** \-mē-nəs\ *n* — **stormy** *adj*

²storm *vb* **1** : to blow with violence; *also* : to rain, snow, or hail heavily **2** : to make a mass attack against **3** : to be violently angry : RAGE **4** : to rush along furiously

¹sto·ry \ˈstōr-ē\ *n, pl* **stories 1** : NARRATIVE, ACCOUNT **2** : REPORT, STATEMENT **3** : ANECDOTE **4** : LIE, FALSEHOOD **syn** lie, falsehood, untruth, tale, canard

²story *also* **sto·rey** \ˈstōr-ē\ *n, pl* **stories** *also* **storeys** : a floor of a building or the space between two adjacent floor levels

sto·ry·tell·er \-ˌtel-ər\ *n* : a teller of stories

sto·tin·ka \stō-ˈtiŋ-kə, stə-\ *n, pl* **-tin·ki** \-kē\ — see *lev* at MONEY table

¹stout \ˈstau̇t\ *adj* **1** : BRAVE **2** : FIRM **3** : STURDY **4** : STAUNCH, ENDURING **5** : SOLID **6** : FORCEFUL **7** : BULKY, THICKSET **syn** fleshy, fat, portly, corpulent, obese, plump — **stout·ly** *adv* — **stout·ness** *n*

²stout *n* : a dark heavy alcoholic beverage brewed from roasted malt and hops

¹stove \ˈstōv\ *n* : an apparatus that burns fuel or uses electricity to provide heat (as for cooking or heating)

²stove *past and past part of* STAVE

stow \ˈstō\ *vb* **1** : HIDE, STORE **2** : to pack in a compact mass

stow·away \ˈstō-ə-ˌwā\ *n* : one who hides on a vehicle to ride free

¹STP \ˌes-ˌtē-ˈpē\ *n* : a psychotropic drug chemically related to amphetamine

²STP *abbr* standard temperature and pressure

strad·dle \ˈstrad-ᵊl\ *vb* **strad·dled; strad·dling** \ˈstrad-(ᵊ-)liŋ\ **1** : to stand, sit, or walk with legs spread apart **2** : to favor or seem to favor two apparently opposite sides — **straddle** *n*

strafe \ˈstrāf\ *vb* **strafed; straf·ing** : to fire upon with machine guns from a low-flying airplane

strag·gle \ˈstrag-əl\ *vb* **strag·gled; strag·gling** \-(ə-)liŋ\ **1** : to wander from the direct course : ROVE, STRAY **2** : to become separated from others of the same kind — **strag·gler** \-(ə-)lər\ *n* — **strag·gly** \-(ə-)lē\ *adj*

¹straight \ˈstrāt\ *adj* **1** : free from curves, bends, angles, or irregularities : DIRECT **2** : not wandering from the main point or proper course ⟨~ thinking⟩ **3** : HONEST, UPRIGHT **4** : not marked by confusion : correctly arranged or ordered **5** : UNMIXED, UNDILUTED ⟨~ whiskey⟩ **6** : CONVENTIONAL, SQUARE; *also* : HETEROSEXUAL

²straight *adv* : in a straight manner

³straight *n* **1** : a straight line, course, or arrangement **2** : the part of a racetrack between the last turn and the finish **3** : a sequence of five cards in a poker hand

straight–arm \ˈstrāt-ˌärm\ *vb* : to ward off an opponent with the arm held straight — **straight–arm** *n*

straight·away \ˈstrāt-ə-ˌwā\ *n* : a straight stretch (as at a racetrack)

straight·edge \ˈstrāt-ˌej\ *n* : a piece of material with a straight edge for testing straight lines and surfaces or drawing straight lines

straight·en \ˈstrāt-ᵊn\ *vb* **straight·ened; straight·en·ing** \ˈstrāt-(ᵊ-)niŋ\ : to make or become straight

straight flush *n* : a poker hand containing five cards of the same suit in sequence

straight·for·ward \strāt-ˈfȯr-wərd\ *adj* **1** : CANDID, HONEST **2** : proceeding in a straight course or manner

straight man *n* : an entertainer who feeds lines to a comedian

straight·way \ˈstrāt-ˈwā, -ˌwā\ *adv* : IMMEDIATELY

¹strain \ˈstrān\ *n* [ME *streen* progeny, lineage, fr. OE *strēon* gain, acquisition] **1** : LINEAGE, ANCESTRY **2** : a group (as of people or plants) of presumed common ancestry **3** : an inherited or inherent character or quality ⟨a ~ of madness in the family⟩ **4** : STREAK, TRACE **5** : MELODY **6** : the general style or tone

²strain *vb* [ME *strainen*, fr. MF *estraindre*, fr. L *stringere* to bind or draw tight, press together] **1** : to draw taut **2** : to exert to the utmost **3** : to strive violently **4** : to injure by improper or excessive use **5** : to filter or remove by filtering **6** : to stretch beyond a proper limit — **strain·er** *n*

³strain *n* **1** : excessive tension or exertion (as of body or mind) **2** : bodily injury from excessive tension, effort, or use; *esp* : one in which muscles or ligaments are unduly stretched usu. from a wrench or twist **3** : deformation of a material body under the action of applied forces

¹strait \ˈstrāt\ *adj* [ME, fr. OF *estreit*, fr. L *strictus* strait, strict] **1** *archaic* : NARROW **2** *archaic* : CONSTRICTED **3** *archaic* : STRICT **4** : DIFFICULT, STRAITENED

²strait *n* **1** : a narrow channel connecting two bodies of water **2** *pl* : DISTRESS

strait·en \ˈstrāt-ᵊn\ *vb* **strait·ened; strait·en·ing** \ˈstrāt-(ᵊ-)niŋ\ **1** : to hem in : CONFINE **2** : to make distressing or difficult

strait·jack·et *or* **straight·jack·et** \ˈstrāt-ˌjak-ət\ *n* : a cover or garment of strong material (as canvas) used to bind the body and esp. the arms closely in restraining a violent prisoner or patient — **straitjacket** *or* **straightjacket** *vb*

strait·laced *or* **straight·laced** \-ˈlāst\ *adj* : strict in observing moral or religious laws

¹strand \ˈstrand\ *n* : SHORE; *esp* : a shore of a sea or ocean

²strand *vb* **1** : to run, drift, or drive upon the shore ⟨a ~*ed* ship⟩ **2** : to place or leave in a helpless position

³strand *n* **1** : one of the fibers twisted or plaited together into a cord, rope, or cable; *also* : a cord, rope, or cable made up of such fibers **2** : a twisted or plaited ropelike mass ⟨a ~ of pearls⟩ — **strand·ed** \ˈstran-dəd\ *adj*

strange \ˈstrānj\ *adj* **strang·er; strang·est** [ME, fr. OF *estrange*, fr. L *extraneus*, lit., external, fr. *extra* outside] **1** : of external origin, kind, or character **2** : NEW, UNFAMILIAR **3** : SHY **4** : UNACCUSTOMED, INEXPERIENCED **syn** singular, peculiar, eccentric, erratic, odd, queer, quaint, curious — **strange·ly** *adv* — **strange·ness** *n*

strang·er \ˈstrān-jər\ *n* **1** : FOREIGNER **2** : INTRUDER **3** : a person with whom one is unacquainted

stran·gle \ˈstraŋ-gəl\ *vb* **stran·gled; stran·gling** \-g(ə-)liŋ\ **1** : to choke to death : THROTTLE **2** : STIFLE, SUFFOCATE — **stran·gler** \-g(ə-)lər\ *n*

stran·gu·late \ˈstraŋ-gyə-ˌlāt\ *vb* **-lat·ed; -lat·ing** **1** : STRANGLE, CONSTRICT **2** : to become so constricted as to stop circulation

stran·gu·la·tion \ˌstraŋ-gyə-ˈlā-shən\ *n* : the act or process of strangling or strangulating : the state of being strangled or strangulated

¹strap \ˈstrap\ *n* : a narrow strip of flexible material used esp. for fastening, holding together, or wrapping

²strap *vb* **strapped; strap·ping** **1** : to secure with a strap **2** : BIND, CONSTRICT **3** : to flog with a strap **4** : STROP

strap·less \-ləs\ *adj* : having no straps; *esp* : having no shoulder straps

¹strap·ping \ˈstrap-iŋ\ *adj* : LARGE, STRONG, HUSKY

²strap·ping *n* : material for a strap

strat·a·gem \ˈstrat-ə-jəm, -ˌjem\ *n* **1** : a trick in war to deceive or outwit the enemy; *also* : a deceptive scheme **2** : skill in deception

strat·e·gy \ˈstrat-ə-jē\ *n, pl* **-gies** [Gk *stratēgia* generalship, fr. *stratēgos* general, fr. *stratos* army + *agein* to lead] **1** : the science and art of military command aimed at meeting the enemy under conditions advantageous to one's own force **2** : a careful plan or method esp. for achieving an end — **stra·te·gic** \strə-ˈtē-jik\ *adj* — **strat·e·gist** \ˈstrat-ə-jəst\ *n*

strat·i·fy \ˈstrat-ə-ˌfī\ *vb* **-fied; -fy·ing** : to form or arrange in layers — **strat·i·fi·ca·tion** \ˌstrat-ə-fə-ˈkā-shən\ *n*

stra·tig·ra·phy \strə-ˈtig-rə-fē\ *n* : geology that deals with rock strata — **strati·graph·ic** \ˌstrat-ə-ˈgraf-ik\ *adj*

strato·sphere \ˈstrat-ə-ˌsfiər\ *n* : the portion of the earth's atmosphere higher than 7 miles (11 kilometers) above the earth — **strato·spher·ic** \ˌstrat-ə-ˈsfi(ə)r-ik, -ˈsfer-\ *adj*

stra·tum \ˈstrāt-əm, ˈstrat-\ *n, pl* **stra·ta** \ˈstrāt-ə, ˈstrat-\ [NL, fr. L, spread, bed, fr. neut. of *stratus*, pp. of *sternere* to spread out] **1** : a bed, layer, or sheetlike mass (as of one kind of rock lying between layers of other kinds of rock) **2** : a level of culture; *also* : a group of people representing one stage in cultural development

[1]straw \ˈstrȯ\ *n* **1** : stalks of grain after threshing; *also* : a single coarse dry stem (as of a grass) **2** : a thing of small worth : TRIFLE **3** : a prepared tube for sucking up a beverage

[2]straw *adj* **1** : made of straw **2** : having no real force or validity ⟨a ~ vote⟩

straw·ber·ry \ˈstrȯ-ˌber-ē, -b(ə-)rē\ *n* : an edible juicy usu. red pulpy fruit borne by a low herb with white flowers and long slender runners; *also* : this plant

straw boss *n* : a foreman of a small gang of workers

straw·flow·er \ˈstrȯ-ˌflau̇(-ə)r\ *n* : any of several plants whose flowers can be dried with little loss of form or color

[1]stray \ˈstrā\ *n* **1** : a domestic animal wandering at large or lost **2** : WAIF

[2]stray *vb* **1** : ROVE, ROAM **2** : to wander from a course : DEVIATE

[3]stray *adj* **1** : having strayed : separated from the group or the main body **2** : occurring at random ⟨~ remarks⟩

[1]streak \ˈstrēk\ *n* **1** : a line or mark of a different color or texture from its background **2** : a narrow band of light; *also* : a lightning bolt **3** : a slight admixture : TRACE **4** : a brief run (as of luck); *also* : an unbroken series

[2]streak *vb* **1** : to form streaks in or on **2** : to move very swiftly

[1]stream \ˈstrēm\ *n* **1** : a body of water (as a river) flowing on the earth; *also* : any body of flowing fluid (as water or gas) **2** : a continuous procession ⟨the ~ of history⟩

[2]stream *vb* **1** : to flow in or as if in a stream **2** : to pour out streams of liquid **3** : to trail out in length **4** : to move forward in a steady stream

stream·bed \ˈstrēm-ˌbed\ *n* : the channel occupied or formerly occupied by a stream

stream·er \ˈstrē-mər\ *n* **1** : a long narrow ribbonlike flag **2** : a long ribbon on a dress or hat **3** : a newspaper headline that runs across the entire sheet **4** *pl* : AURORA

stream·let \ˈstrēm-lət\ *n* : a small stream

stream·lined \-ˌlīnd\ *adj* **1** : made with contours to reduce resistance to motion through water or air **2** : SIMPLIFIED **3** : MODERNIZED — **streamline** *vb*

street \ˈstrēt\ *n* [ME *strete*, fr. OE *strǣt*, fr. LL *strata* paved road, fr. L, fem. of *stratus*, pp. of *sternere* to spread out] **1** : a thoroughfare esp. in a city, town, or village **2** : the occupants of the houses on a street

street·car \-ˌkär\ *n* : a passenger vehicle running on rails on city streets

street railway *n* : a company operating streetcars or buses

street·walk·er \ˈstrēt-ˌwȯ-kər\ *n* : PROSTITUTE

strength \ˈstreŋth\ *n* **1** : the quality of being strong : ability to do or endure : POWER **2** : TOUGHNESS, SOLIDITY **3** : power to resist attack **4** : INTENSITY **5** : force as measured in numbers ⟨the ~ of an army⟩

strength·en \ˈstreŋ-thən\ *vb* **strength·ened; strength·en·ing** \ˈstreŋth-(ə-)niŋ\ : to make, grow, or become stronger — **strength·en·er** \ˈstreŋth-(ə-)nər\ *n*

stren·u·ous \ˈstren-yə-wəs\ *adj* **1** : VIGOROUS, ENERGETIC **2** : requiring energetic effort or stamina — **stren·u·ous·ly** *adv*

strep throat \ˈstrep-\ *n* : an inflammatory sore throat cause by streptococci and marked by fever, prostration, and toxemia

strep·to·coc·cus \ˌstrep-tə-ˈkäk-əs\ *n, pl* **-coc·ci** \-ˈkäk-ˌ(s)ī, -ˈkäk-(ˌ)(s)ē\ : any of various spherical bacteria that usu. grow in chains and include some causing serious diseases — **strep·to·coc·cal** \-əl\ *adj*

strep·to·my·cin \-ˈmīs-ᵊn\ *n* : an antibiotic produced by soil bacteria and used esp. in treating tuberculosis

[1]stress \ˈstres\ *n* **1** : PRESSURE, STRAIN; *esp* : a force that tends to distort a body **2** : a factor that induces bodily or mental tension; *also* : a state induced by such a stress **3** : URGENCY, EMPHASIS **4** : relative prominence of sound **5** : ACCENT; *also* : any syllable carrying the accent

[2]stress *vb* **1** : to put pressure or strain on **2** : to put emphasis on : ACCENT

[1]stretch \ˈstrech\ *vb* **1** : to spread or reach out : EXTEND **2** : to draw out in length or breadth : EXPAND **3** : to make tense : STRAIN **4** : EXAGGERATE **5** : to become extended without breaking ⟨rubber ~*es* easily⟩

[2]stretch *n* **1** : an act of extending or drawing out beyond ordinary or normal limits **2** : a continuous extent in length, area, or time **3** : the extent to which something may be stretched **4** : either of the straight sides of a racecourse

[3]stretch *adj* : easily stretched ⟨~ pants⟩

stretch·er \ˈstrech-ər\ *n* **1** : one that stretches **2** : a litter (as of canvas) esp. for carrying a disabled person

stretch·er–bear·er \-ˌbar-ər\ *n* : one who carries one end of a stretcher

strew \ˈstrü\ *vb* **strewed; strewed** *or* **strewn** \ˈstrün\; **strew·ing** **1** : to spread by scattering **2** : to cover by or as if by scattering something over or on **3** : DISSEMINATE

stria \ˈstrī-ə\ *n, pl* **stri·ae** \ˈstrī-ˌē\ **1** : STRIATION 3 **2** : a stripe or line (as in the skin)

stri·at·ed muscle \ˈstrī-ˌāt-əd-\ *n* : muscle tissue made up of long thin cells with many nuclei and alternate light and dark stripes that usually connects to and moves the vertebrate skeleton and is mostly under voluntary control

stri·a·tion \strī-ˈā-shən\ *n* **1** : the state of being marked with stripes or lines **2** : arrangement of striations or striae **3** : a minute groove, scratch, or channel esp. when one of a parallel series

strick·en \ˈstrik-ən\ *adj* **1** : WOUNDED **2** : afflicted with disease, misfortune, or sorrow

strict \ˈstrikt\ *adj* **1** : allowing no evasion or escape : RIGOROUS ⟨~ discipline⟩ **2** : ACCURATE, PRECISE **syn** stringent, rigid, rigorous — **strict·ly** \ˈstrik-(t)lē\ *adv* — **strict·ness** \ˈstrik(t)-nəs\ *n*

stric·ture \ˈstrik-chər\ *n* **1** : an abnormal narrowing of a bodily passage; *also* : the narrowed part **2** : hostile criticism : a critical remark

[1]stride \ˈstrīd\ *vb* **strode** \ˈstrōd\; **strid·den** \ˈstrid-ᵊn\; **strid·ing** \ˈstrīd-iŋ\ : to walk or run with long regular steps — **strid·er** *n*

[2]stride *n* **1** : a long step; *also* : the distance covered by such a step **2** : manner of striding : GAIT

stri·dent \ˈstrīd-ᵊnt\ *adj* : harsh sounding : GRATING, SHRILL

strife \ˈstrīf\ *n* : CONFLICT, FIGHT, STRUGGLE **syn** discord, contention, dissension

[1]strike \ˈstrīk\ *vb* **struck** \ˈstrək\; **struck** *also* **strick·en** \ˈstrik-ən\; **strik·ing** \ˈstrī-kiŋ\ **1** : to take a course : GO ⟨~ out for home⟩ **2** : to touch or hit sharply; *also* : to deliver a blow **3** : to produce by or as if by a blow ⟨*struck* terror in the foe⟩ **4** : to lower (as a flag or sail) **5** : to collide with; *also* : to injure or destroy by collision **6** : DELETE, CANCEL **7** : to produce by impressing ⟨*struck* a medal⟩; *also* : COIN ⟨~ a new cent⟩ **8** : to cause to sound ⟨~ a bell⟩ **9** : to afflict suddenly : lay low ⟨*stricken* with a high fever⟩ **10** : to appear to; *also* : to appear to as remarkable : IMPRESS **11** : to reach by reckoning ⟨~ an average⟩ **12** : to stop work in order to obtain a change in conditions of employment **13** : to cause (a match) to ignite by rubbing **14** : to come upon ⟨~ a detour from the main road⟩ **15** : TAKE ON, ASSUME ⟨~ a pose⟩ — **strik·er** *n*

[2]strike *n* **1** : an act or instance of striking **2** : a sudden discovery of rich ore or oil deposits **3** : a pitched base-

ball recorded against a batter **4** : the knocking down of all the bowling pins with the 1st ball **5** : a military attack
strike·break·er \-ˌbrā-kər\ *n* : one hired to replace a striking worker
strike·out \-ˌau̇t\ *n* : an out in baseball as a result of a batter's being charged with three strikes
strike out \(ˈ)strīk-ˈau̇t\ *vb* **1** : to enter upon a course of action **2** : to start out vigorously **3** : to make an out in baseball by a strikeout
strike up *vb* **1** : to begin or cause to begin to sing or play **2** : BEGIN
strike zone *n* : the area over home plate through which a pitched baseball must pass to be called a strike
strik·ing \ˈstrī-kiŋ\ *adj* : attracting attention : very noticeable **syn** arresting, salient, conspicuous, outstanding, remarkable, prominent — **strik·ing·ly** *adv*
¹string \ˈstriŋ\ *n* **1** : a line usu. composed of twisted threads **2** : a series of things arranged as if strung on a cord **3** : a plant fiber (as a leaf vein) **4** *pl* : the stringed instruments of an orchestra **syn** succession, progression, sequence, chain, train
²string *vb* **strung** \ˈstrəŋ\; **string·ing** \ˈstriŋ-iŋ\ **1** : to provide with strings ⟨~ a racket⟩ **2** : to thread on or as if on a string ⟨~ pearls⟩ **3** : to take the strings out of ⟨~ beans⟩ **4** : to hang, tie, or fasten by a string **5** : to make taut **6** : to extend like a string
string bean *n* : a bean of one of the older varieties of kidney bean that have stringy fibers on the lines of separation of the pods; *also* : SNAP BEAN
stringed instrument *n* : a musical instrument (as a violin, guitar, or piano) sounded by plucking or striking or by drawing a bow across tense strings
strin·gen·cy \ˈstrin-jən-sē\ *n* **1** : STRICTNESS, SEVERITY **2** : SCARCITY ⟨~ of money⟩ — **strin·gent** \-jənt\ *adj*
string·er \ˈstriŋ-ər\ *n* **1** : a long horizontal member in a framed structure or a bridge **2** : a news correspondent paid by the amount of copy
stringy \ˈstriŋ-ē\ *adj* **string·i·er; -est 1** : resembling string esp. in tough, fibrous, or disordered quality ⟨~ meat⟩ ⟨~ hair⟩ **2** : lean and sinewy in build
¹strip \ˈstrip\ *vb* **stripped** \ˈstript\ *also* **stript; strip·ping 1** : to take the covering or clothing from **2** : to take off one's clothes **3** : to pull or tear off **4** : to make bare or clear (as by cutting or grazing) **5** : PLUNDER, PILLAGE **syn** divest, denude, deprive, dismantle — **strip·per** *n*
²strip *n* **1** : a long narrow flat piece **2** : AIRSTRIP
¹stripe \ˈstrīp\ *vb* **striped** \ˈstrīpt\; **strip·ing** : to make stripes on
²stripe *n* **1** : a line or long narrow division having a different color from the background **2** : a strip of braid (as on a sleeve) indicating military rank or length of service **3** : TYPE, CHARACTER **syn** description, nature, kind, sort
striped bass \ˈstrīpt-, ˈstrī-pəd-\ *n* : a large marine food and sport fish of the Atlantic and Pacific coasts of the U.S.
strip·ling \ˈstrip-liŋ\ *n* : YOUTH, LAD
strip mine *n* : a mine that is worked from the earth's surface by the stripping of the topsoil — **strip–mine** *vb*
strip·tease \ˈstrip-ˌtēz\ *n* : a burlesque act in which a performer removes his or her clothing piece by piece — **strip·teas·er** *n*
strive \ˈstrīv\ *vb* **strove** \ˈstrōv\ *also* **strived** \ˈstrīvd\; **striv·en** \ˈstriv-ən\ *or* **strived; striv·ing** \ˈstrī-viŋ\ **1** : to struggle in opposition : CONTEND **2** : to make effort : labor hard **syn** endeavor, attempt, try, assay
strobe \ˈstrōb\ *n* **1** : STROBOSCOPE **2** : a device for high-speed intermittent illumination
stro·bo·scope \ˈstrō-bə-ˌskōp\ *n* : an instrument for studying rapid motion by means of a rapidly flashing light
strode *past of* STRIDE
¹stroke \ˈstrōk\ *vb* **stroked; strok·ing 1** : to rub gently **2** : to flatter in a manner designed to persuade
²stroke *n* **1** : the act of striking : BLOW, KNOCK **2** : a sudden action or process producing an impact ⟨~ of lightning⟩ **3** : sudden weakening or loss of consciousness or the power to feel caused by rupture or obstruction of an artery of the brain **4** : a vigorous effort **5** : the sound of striking (as of a clock) **6** : one of a series of movements against air or water to get through or over it ⟨the ~ of a bird's wing⟩ **7** : a single movement with or as if with a tool or implement (as a pen) **8** : a rower who sets the pace for a crew
stroll \ˈstrōl\ *vb* : to walk in a leisurely or idle manner **syn** saunter, amble, mosey — **stroll** *n* — **stroll·er** *n*
strong \ˈstrȯŋ\ *adj* **stron·ger** \ˈstrȯŋ-gər\; **stron·gest** \ˈstrȯŋ-gəst\ **1** : POWERFUL, VIGOROUS **2** : HEALTHY, ROBUST **3** : of a specified number ⟨an army 10 thousand ~⟩ **4** : not mild or weak **5** : VIOLENT ⟨~ wind⟩ **6** : ZEALOUS **7** : not easily broken **8** : FIRM, SOLID **syn** stout, sturdy, stalwart, tough — **strong·ly** *adv*
strong–arm \ˈstrȯŋ-ˈärm\ *adj* : having or using undue force ⟨~ methods⟩
strong·hold \ˈstrȯŋ-ˌhōld\ *n* : a fortified place : FORTRESS
strong·man \ˈstrȯŋ-ˌman\ *n* : one who leads or controls by force of will and character or by military strength
stron·tium \ˈsträn-ch(ē-)əm, ˈstränt-ē-əm\ *n* : a soft malleable metallic chemical element — see ELEMENT table
¹strop \ˈsträp\ *n* : STRAP; *esp* : one for sharpening a razor
²strop *vb* **stropped; strop·ping** : to sharpen a razor on a strop
stro·phe \ˈstrō-fē\ *n* [Gk *strophē,* lit., act of turning] : a division of a poem — **stroph·ic** \ˈsträf-ik\ *adj*
strove *past of* STRIVE
struck *past and past part of* STRIKE
¹struc·ture \ˈstrək-chər\ *n* [ME, fr. L *structura,* fr. *structus,* pp. of *struere* to heap up, build] **1** : the manner of building : CONSTRUCTION **2** : something built (as a house or a dam); *also* : something made up of interdependent parts in a definite pattern of organization **3** : arrangement or relationship of elements in a substance, body, or system — **struc·tur·al** *adj*
²structure *vb* **struc·tured; struc·tur·ing** : to make into a structure
stru·del \ˈs(h)trüd-ᵊl\ *n* [G] : a pastry made of a thin sheet of dough rolled up with filling and baked ⟨apple ~⟩
¹strug·gle \ˈstrəg-əl\ *vb* **strug·gled; strug·gling** \-(ə-)liŋ\ **1** : to make strenuous efforts against opposition : STRIVE **2** : to proceed with difficulty or with great effort **syn** endeavor, attempt, try, assay
²struggle *n* **1** : CONTEST, STRIFE **2** : a violent effort or exertion
strum \ˈstrəm\ *vb* **strummed; strum·ming** : to play on a stringed instrument by brushing the strings with the fingers ⟨~ a guitar⟩
strum·pet \ˈstrəm-pət\ *n* : PROSTITUTE
strung \ˈstrəŋ\ *past and past part of* STRING
¹strut \ˈstrət\ *vb* **strut·ted; strut·ting** : to walk with an affectedly proud gait **syn** swagger
²strut *n* **1** : a haughty or pompous gait **2** : a bar or rod for resisting lengthwise pressure
strych·nine \ˈstrik-ˌnīn, -nən, -ˌnēn\ *n* : a bitter poisonous alkaloid from some plants used as a poison (as for rats) and medicinally as a stimulant to the central nervous system
¹stub \ˈstəb\ *n* **1** : STUMP 2 **2** : a short blunt end **3** : a small part of each leaf (as of a checkbook) kept as a memorandum of the items on the detached part
²stub *vb* **stubbed; stub·bing** : to strike (as one's toe) against something

stub·ble \ˈstəb-əl\ *n* **1** : the cut stem ends of herbs and esp. grasses left in the soil after harvest **2** : a rough surface or growth resembling stubble — **stub·bly** \-(ə-)lē\ *adj*

stub·born \ˈstəb-ərn\ *adj* **1** : FIRM, DETERMINED **2** : done or continued in a willful, unreasonable, or persistent manner **3** : not easily controlled or remedied ⟨a ~ fever⟩ — **stub·born·ly** *adv* — **stub·born·ness** *n*

stub·by \ˈstəb-ē\ *adj* : short, blunt, and thick like a stub

¹stuc·co \ˈstək-ō\ *n, pl* **stuccos** *or* **stuccoes** [It] : plaster for coating exterior walls

²stucco *vb* : to coat with stucco

stuck *past and past part of* STICK

stuck–up \ˈstək-ˈəp\ *adj* : CONCEITED

¹stud \ˈstəd\ *n* : a male animal and esp. a horse (**stud·horse** \-ˌhȯrs\) kept for breeding

²stud *n* **1** : one of the smaller uprights in a building to which the wall materials are fastened **2** : a removable device like a button used as a fastener or ornament ⟨shirt ~*s*⟩ **3** : a projecting nail, pin, or rod

³stud *vb* **stud·ded; stud·ding 1** : to supply with or adorn with studs **2** : DOT

⁴stud *abbr* student

stud·book \ˈstəd-ˌbu̇k\ *n* : an official record of the pedigree of purebred animals

stud·ding \ˈstəd-iŋ\ *n* **1** : the studs in a building or wall **2** : material for studs

stu·dent \ˈst(y)üd-ᵊnt\ *n* : SCHOLAR, PUPIL; *esp* : one who attends a school

stud·ied \ˈstəd-ēd\ *adj* : INTENTIONAL ⟨a ~ insult⟩ **syn** deliberate, considered, premeditated, designed

stu·dio \ˈst(y)üd-ē-ˌō\ *n, pl* **-dios 1** : a place where an artist works; *also* : a place for the study of an art **2** : a place where motion pictures are made **3** : a place equipped for the transmission of radio or television programs

stu·di·ous \ˈst(y)üd-ē-əs\ *adj* : devoted to study — **stu·di·ous·ly** *adv*

¹study \ˈstəd-ē\ *n, pl* **stud·ies 1** : the use of the mind to gain knowledge **2** : the act or process of learning about something **3** : careful examination **4** : INTENT, PURPOSE **5** : a branch of learning **6** : a room esp. for reading and writing

²study *vb* **stud·ied; study·ing 1** : to engage in study or the study of **2** : to consider attentively or in detail **syn** consider, contemplate, weigh

¹stuff \ˈstəf\ *n* **1** : personal property **2** : raw material **3** : a finished textile fabric; *esp* : a worsted fabric **4** : writing, talk, or ideas of little or transitory worth **5** : an aggregate of matter; *also* : matter of a particular often unspecified kind **6** : fundamental material **7** : special knowledge or capability

²stuff *vb* **1** : to fill by packing something into : CRAM **2** : to eat greedily : GORGE **3** : to prepare (as meat) by filling with seasoned bread crumbs and spices **4** : to stop up : PLUG

stuffed shirt \ˈstəft-\ *n* : a smug, conceited, and usu. pompous and inflexibly conservative person

stuff·ing \ˈstəf-iŋ\ *n* : material used to fill tightly; *esp* : a mixture of bread crumbs and spices used to stuff meat and poultry

stuffy \ˈstəf-ē\ *adj* **stuff·i·er; -est 1** : lacking fresh air : CLOSE; *also* : blocked up ⟨a ~ nose⟩ **2** : STODGY

stul·ti·fy \ˈstəl-tə-ˌfī\ *vb* **-fied; -fy·ing 1** : to cause to appear foolish or stupid **2** : to make untrustworthy; *also* : to make ineffective **3** : to have a dulling effect on — **stul·ti·fi·ca·tion** \ˌstəl-tə-fə-ˈkā-shən\ *n*

stum·ble \ˈstəm-bəl\ *vb* **stum·bled; stum·bling** \-b(ə-)liŋ\ **1** : to trip in walking or running **2** : to walk unsteadily; *also* : to speak or act in a blundering or clumsy manner **3** : to blunder morally; *also* : to come or happen by chance — **stumble** *n*

stumbling block *n* : an obstacle to belief, understanding, or progress

¹stump \ˈstəmp\ *n* **1** : the base of a bodily part (as a leg or tooth) left after the rest is removed **2** : the part of a plant and esp. a tree remaining with the root after the top is cut off **3** : a place or occasion for political public speaking — **stumpy** *adj*

²stump *vb* **1** : to clear (land) of stumps **2** : to tour (a region) making political speeches **3** : BAFFLE, PERPLEX **4** : to walk clumsily and heavily

stun \ˈstən\ *vb* **stunned; stun·ning 1** : to make senseless or dizzy by or as if by a blow **2** : BEWILDER, STUPEFY

stung *past and past part of* STING

stunk *past and past part of* STINK

stun·ning \ˈstən-iŋ\ *adj* : strikingly beautiful — **stun·ning·ly** *adv*

¹stunt \ˈstənt\ *vb* : to hinder the normal growth of : DWARF

²stunt *n* : an unusual or spectacular feat

stu·pe·fy \ˈst(y)ü-pə-ˌfī\ *vb* **-fied; -fy·ing 1** : ASTONISH **2** : to make stupid, groggy, or insensible — **stu·pe·fac·tion** \ˌst(y)ü-pə-ˈfak-shən\ *n*

stu·pen·dous \st(y)u̇-ˈpen-dəs\ *adj* : causing astonishment esp. because of great size or height **syn** tremendous, prodigious, monumental, monstrous — **stu·pen·dous·ly** *adv*

stu·pid \ˈst(y)ü-pəd\ *adj* [MF *stupide*, fr. L *stupidus*, fr. *stupēre* to be benumbed, be astonished] **1** : very dull in mind **2** : showing or resulting from dullness of mind — **stu·pid·i·ty** \st(y)u̇-ˈpid-ət-ē\ *n* — **stu·pid·ly** \ˈst(y)ü-pəd-lē\ *adv*

stu·por \ˈst(y)ü-pər\ *n* **1** : a condition of greatly dulled or completely suspended sense or feeling **2** : a torpid state often following stress or shock — **stu·por·ous** *adj*

stur·dy \ˈstərd-ē\ *adj* **stur·di·er; -est** [ME, reckless, brave, fr. OF *estourdi* stunned, fr. pp. of *estourdir* to stun] **1** : RESOLUTE, UNYIELDING **2** : STRONG, ROBUST **syn** stout, stalwart, tough, tenacious — **stur·di·ly** \ˈstərd-ᵊl-ē\ *adv* — **stur·di·ness** \-ē-nəs\ *n*

stur·geon \ˈstər-jən\ *n* : any of various large food fishes whose roe is made into caviar

sturgeon

stut·ter \ˈstət-ər\ *vb* : to speak with involuntary disruption or blocking of sounds — **stutter** *n*

STV *abbr* subscription television

¹sty \ˈstī\ *n, pl* **sties** : a pen or housing for swine

²sty *or* **stye** \ˈstī\ *n, pl* **sties** *or* **styes** : an inflamed swelling of a skin gland on the edge of an eyelid

¹style \ˈstīl\ *n* **1** : a slender pointed instrument or process; *esp* : STYLUS **2** : a way of speaking or writing; *esp* : one characteristic of an individual, period, school, or nation ⟨ornate ~⟩ **3** : the custom followed in spelling, capitalization, punctuation, and typography **4** : mode of address : TITLE **5** : manner or method of acting, making, or performing; *also* : a distinctive or characteristic manner **6** : a fashionable manner or mode **7** : overall excellence, skill, or grace in performance, manner, or appearance — **sty·lis·tic** \stī-ˈlis-tik\ *adj*

²style *vb* **styled; styl·ing 1** : NAME, DESIGNATE **2** : to make or design in accord with a prevailing mode

styl·ing \ˈstī-liŋ\ *n* : the way in which something is styled

styl·ish \ˈstī-lish\ *adj* : conforming to an accepted standard of style : FASHIONABLE **syn** modish, smart, chic — **styl·ish·ly** *adv* — **styl·ish·ness** *n*

styl·ist \ˈstī-ləst\ *n* **1** : a master of style esp. in writing **2** : a developer or designer of styles

styl·ize \ˈstīl-ˌīz\ *vb* **styl·ized; styl·iz·ing** : to conform to a style; *esp* : to represent or design according to a pattern or style rather than according to nature

sty·lus \ˈstī-ləs\ *n, pl* **sty·li** \ˈstī(ə)l-ˌī\ *also* **sty·lus·es** \ˈstī-lə-səz\ [modif. of L *stilus* stake, stylus] **1** : a pointed implement used by the ancients for writing on wax **2** : a phonograph needle

sty·mie \ˈstī-mē\ *vb* **sty·mied; sty·mie·ing** : BLOCK, FRUSTRATE

styp·tic \ˈstip-tik\ *adj* : tending to check bleeding — **styptic** *n*

suave \ˈswäv\ *adj* [MF, pleasant, sweet, fr. L *suavis*] : persuasively pleasing : smoothly agreeable **syn** urbane, smooth, bland — **suave·ly** *adv* — **sua·vi·ty** \ˈswäv-ət-ē\ *n*

¹sub \ˈsəb\ *n* : SUBSTITUTE — **sub** *vb*

²sub *n* : SUBMARINE

³sub *abbr* **1** subtract **2** suburb

sub- \ˌsəb, ˈsəb\ *prefix* **1** : under : beneath **2** : subordinate : secondary **3** : subordinate portion of : subdivision of **4** : with repetition of a process described in a simple verb so as to form, stress, or deal with subordinate parts or relations **5** : somewhat **6** : falling nearly in the category of : bordering on

subacute	**subminimal**
subagency	**subminimum**
subagent	**suboptimal**
subaqueous	**suborder**
subarctic	**subparagraph**
subarea	**subparallel**
subatmospheric	**subphylum**
subaverage	**subplot**
subbasement	**subpolar**
subcategory	**subprincipal**
subclass	**subproblem**
subclassify	**subprofessional**
subclinical	**subprogram**
subcontract	**subregion**
subcontractor	**subroutine**
subculture	**subsaturated**
subdeacon	**subsection**
subdean	**subsense**
subdiscipline	**subspecies**
subentry	**substage**
subfamily	**subsystem**
subfreezing	**subteen**
subgenus	**subtemperate**
subgroup	**subthreshold**
subhead	**subtopic**
subheading	**subtotal**
subhuman	**subtreasury**
subindex	**subtype**
subinterval	**subunit**
subkingdom	**subvariety**
sublease	**subvisible**
sublethal	**subvocal**
subliterate	**subzero**

sub·al·pine \ˌsəb-ˈal-ˌpīn, ˈsəb-\ *adj* **1** : of or relating to the region about the foot and lower slopes of the Alps **2** *cap* : of, relating to, or growing on high upland slopes

sub·al·tern \sə-ˈbȯl-tərn\ *n* : SUBORDINATE; *also* : a commissioned officer in the British army below the rank of captain

sub·as·sem·bly \ˌsəb-ə-ˈsem-blē\ *n* : an assembled unit to be incorporated with other units in a finished product

sub·atom·ic \ˌsəb-ə-ˈtäm-ik\ *adj* : of or relating to the inside of the atom or to particles smaller than atoms

sub·com·mit·tee \ˈsəb-kə-ˌmit-ē, ˌsəb-kə-ˈmit-ē\ *n* : a subordinate division of a committee

sub·com·pact \ˈsəb-ˈkäm-ˌpakt\ *n* : an automobile smaller than a compact

¹sub·con·scious \ˌsəb-ˈkän-chəs, ˈsəb-\ *adj* : existing in the mind and affecting thought and behavior without entering conscious awareness — **sub·con·scious·ly** *adv* — **sub·con·scious·ness** *n*

²subconscious *n* : mental activities just below the threshold of consciousness

sub·con·ti·nent \ˈsəb-ˈkänt-(ᵊ-)nənt\ *n* : a vast subdivision of a continent — **sub·con·ti·nen·tal** \ˌsəb-ˌkänt-ᵊn-ˈent-ᵊl\ *adj*

sub·cu·ta·ne·ous \ˌsəb-kyu̇-ˈtā-nē-əs\ *adj* : located, made, or used under the skin ⟨~ fat⟩ ⟨~ needle⟩

sub·di·vide \ˌsəb-də-ˈvīd, ˈsəb-də-ˌvīd\ *vb* : to divide into several parts; *esp* : to divide (a tract of land) into building lots — **sub·di·vi·sion** \-ˈvizh-ən, -ˌvizh-\ *n*

sub·duc·tion \səb-ˈdək-shən\ *n* : the descent of the edge of one crustal plate beneath the edge of an adjacent plate

sub·due \səb-ˈd(y)ü\ *vb* **sub·dued; sub·du·ing** **1** : to bring into subjection : VANQUISH **2** : to bring under control : CURB **3** : to reduce the intensity of

subj *abbr* **1** subject **2** subjunctive

¹sub·ject \ˈsəb-jikt\ *n* [ME, fr. MF, fr. L *subjectus* one under authority & *subjectum* subject of a proposition, fr. *subicere* to subject, lit., to throw under, fr. *sub-* under + *jacere* to throw] **1** : a person under the authority of another **2** : a person subject to a sovereign **3** : an individual subjected to an operation or process **4** : the person or thing discussed or treated : TOPIC, THEME **5** : a word or word group denoting that of which something is predicated

²subject *adj* **1** : being under the power or rule of another **2** : LIABLE, EXPOSED ⟨~ to floods⟩ **3** ; dependent on some act or condition ⟨appointment ~ to senate approval⟩ **syn** subordinate, secondary, tributary, collateral, dependent

³sub·ject \səb-ˈjekt\ *vb* **1** : to bring under control : CONQUER **2** : to make liable **3** : to cause to undergo or submit to — **sub·jec·tion** \-ˈjek-shən\ *n*

sub·jec·tive \(ˌ)səb-ˈjek-tiv\ *adj* **1** : of, relating to, or constituting a subject **2** : of, relating to, or arising within one's self or mind in contrast to what is outside : PERSONAL — **sub·jec·tive·ly** *adv* — **sub·jec·tiv·i·ty** \-ˌjek-ˈtiv-ət-ē\ *n*

subject matter *n* : matter presented for consideration, discussion, or study

sub·join \(ˌ)səb-ˈjȯin\ *vb* : APPEND

sub ju·di·ce \(ˈ)su̇b-ˈyüd-i-ˌkā, ˈsəb-ˈjüd-ə-(ˌ)sē\ *adv* [L] : before a judge or court : not yet legally decided

sub·ju·gate \ˈsəb-ji-ˌgāt\ *vb* **-gat·ed; -gat·ing** : CONQUER, SUBDUE; *also* : ENSLAVE **syn** reduce, overcome, overthrow, vanquish, defeat, beat — **sub·ju·ga·tion** \ˌsəb-ji-ˈgā-shən\ *n*

sub·junc·tive \səb-ˈjəŋk-tiv\ *adj* : of, relating to, or constituting a verb form that represents an act or state as contingent or possible or viewed emotionally (as with desire) ⟨~ mood⟩ — **subjunctive** *n*

sub·let \ˈsəb-ˈlet\ *vb* **-let; -let·ting** : to let all or a part of (a leased property) to another; *also* : to rent (a property) from a lessee

sub·li·mate \ˈsəb-lə-ˌmāt\ *vb* **-mat·ed; -mat·ing** **1** : SUBLIME **2** : to direct the expression of (as an instinctual desire or impulse) from a primitive to a more socially and culturally acceptable form — **sub·li·ma·tion** \ˌsəb-lə-ˈmā-shən\ *n*

¹sub·lime \sə-ˈblīm\ *vb* **sub·limed; sub·lim·ing** : to pass or cause to pass directly from the solid to the vapor state

²sublime *adj* **1** : EXALTED, NOBLE **2** : having awe-inspiring beauty or grandeur **syn** glorious, splendid, superb, resplendent, gorgeous — **sub·lim·i·ty** \-ˈblim-ət-ē\ *n*

sub·lim·i·nal \(ˌ)səb-ˈlim-ən-ᵊl, ˈsəb-\ *adj* **1** : inadequate to produce a sensation or a perception ⟨~ stimuli⟩ 2 : existing or functioning below the threshold of conscious awareness ⟨the ~ mind⟩ ⟨~ techniques in advertising⟩

sub·ma·chine gun \ˌsəb-mə-ˈshēn-ˌgən\ *n* : an automatic firearm fired from the shoulder or hip

[1]sub·ma·rine \ˈsəb-mə-ˌrēn, ˌsəb-mə-ˈrēn\ *adj* : UNDERWATER; *esp* : UNDERSEA

[2]submarine *n* **1** : a naval vessel designed to operate underwater **2** : a large sandwich made from a long split roll with any of a variety of fillings

sub·merge \səb-ˈmərj\ *vb* **sub·merged; sub·merg·ing 1** : to put or plunge under the surface of water **2** : INUNDATE **syn** immerse, duck, dip, dunk — **sub·mer·gence** \-ˈmər-jəns\ *n*

sub·merse \səb-ˈmərs\ *vb* **sub·mersed; sub·mers·ing** : SUBMERGE — **sub·mer·sion** \-ˈmər-zhən\ *n*

[1]sub·mers·ible \səb-ˈmər-sə-bəl\ *adj* : capable of being submerged

[2]submersible *n* : something that is submersible; *esp* : SUBMARINE 1

sub·mi·cro·sco·pic \ˌsəb-ˌmī-krə-ˈskäp-ik\ *adj* : too small to be seen in an ordinary microscope

sub·min·ia·ture \ˌsəb-ˈmin-ē-ə-ˌchu̇r, ˈsəb-, -ˈmin-i-ˌchu̇r, -chər\ *adj* : very small

sub·mit \səb-ˈmit\ *vb* **sub·mit·ted; sub·mit·ting 1** : to commit to the discretion or decision of another or of others **2** : YIELD, SURRENDER **3** : to put forward as an opinion — **sub·mis·sion** \-ˈmish-ən\ *n* — **sub·mis·sive** \-ˈmis-iv\ *adj*

sub·nor·mal \ˌsəb-ˈnȯr-məl\ *adj* : falling below what is normal — **sub·nor·mal·i·ty** \ˌsəb-nȯr-ˈmal-ət-ē\ *n*

sub·or·bit·al \ˌsəb-ˈȯr-bət-ᵊl, ˈsəb-\ *adj* : being or involving less than one orbit

[1]sub·or·di·nate \sə-ˈbȯrd-(ᵊ-)nət\ *adj* **1** : of lower class or rank **2** : INFERIOR **3** : submissive to authority **4** : subordinated to other elements in a sentence : DEPENDENT ⟨~ clause⟩ **syn** secondary, subject, tributary, collateral

[2]subordinate *n* : one that is subordinate

[3]sub·or·di·nate \sə-ˈbȯrd-ᵊn-ˌāt\ *vb* **-nat·ed; -nat·ing 1** : to place in a lower rank or class **2** : SUBDUE — **sub·or·di·na·tion** \-ˌbȯrd-ᵊn-ˈā-shən\ *n*

sub·orn \sə-ˈbȯrn\ *vb* **1** : to induce secretly to do an unlawful thing **2** : to induce to commit perjury — **sub·or·na·tion** \ˌsəb-ˌȯr-ˈnā-shən\ *n*

[1]sub·poe·na \sə-ˈpē-nə\ *n* [ME *suppena,* fr. L *sub poena* under penalty] : a writ commanding the person named in it to attend court under penalty for failure to do so

[2]subpoena *vb* **-naed; -na·ing** : to summon with a subpoena

sub·scribe \səb-ˈskrīb\ *vb* **sub·scribed; sub·scrib·ing 1** : to sign one's name to a document **2** : to give consent by or as if by signing one's name **3** : to promise to contribute by signing one's name with the amount promised **4** : to place an order by signing **5** : FAVOR, APPROVE **syn** agree, acquiesce, assent, accede — **sub·scrib·er** *n*

sub·script \ˈsəb-ˌskript\ *n* : a symbol (as a letter or number) immediately below or below and to the right or left of another written character — **subscript** *adj*

sub·scrip·tion \səb-ˈskrip-shən\ *n* **1** : the act of subscribing : SIGNATURE **2** : a purchase by signed order

sub·se·quent \ˈsəb-si-kwənt, -sə-ˌkwent\ *adj* : following after : SUCCEEDING — **sub·se·quent·ly** \-ˌkwent-lē, -kwənt-\ *adv*

sub·ser·vi·ence \səb-ˈsər-vē-əns\ *n* **1** : a subordinate place or condition; *also* : willingness to serve in a subordinate capacity **2** : SERVILITY — **sub·ser·vi·en·cy** \-ən-sē\ *n* — **sub·er·vi·ent** \-ənt\ *adj*

sub·set \ˈsəb-ˌset\ *n* : a set each of whose elements is an element of an inclusive set

sub·side \səb-ˈsīd\ *vb* **sub·sid·ed; sub·sid·ing** [L *subsidere,* fr. *sub-* under + *sidere* to sit down, sink] **1** : to settle to the bottom of a liquid **2** : to tend downward : DESCEND **3** : SINK, SUBMERGE **4** : to become quiet and tranquil **syn** abate, wane, moderate, slacken — **sub·sid·ence** \səb-ˈsīd-ᵊns, ˈsəb-səd-əns\ *n*

[1]sub·sid·iary \səb-ˈsid-ē-ˌer-ē\ *adj* **1** : furnishing aid or support; *also* : owned or controlled by some main company **2** : of or relating to a subsidy **syn** auxiliary, contributory, subservient, accessory

[2]subsidiary *n, pl* **-iar·ies** : one that is subsidiary; *esp* : a company controlled by another

sub·si·dize \ˈsəb-sə-ˌdīz\ *vb* **-dized; -diz·ing** : to aid or furnish with a subsidy

sub·si·dy \ˈsəb-səd-ē\ *n, pl* **-dies** [ME, fr. L *subsidium* reserve troops, support, assistance, fr. *sub-* near + *sedēre* to sit] : a gift of public money to a private person or company or to another government **syn** grant, appropriation, subvention

sub·sist \səb-ˈsist\ *vb* **1** : EXIST, PERSIST **2** : to receive the means (as food and clothing) of maintaining life

sub·sis·tence \səb-ˈsis-təns\ *n* **1** : EXISTENCE **2** : means of subsisting : the minimum (as of food and clothing) necessary to support life

sub·soil \ˈsəb-ˌsȯil\ *n* : a layer of weathered material just under the surface soil

sub·son·ic \ˌsəb-ˈsän-ik, ˈsəb-\ *adj* **1** : being or relating to a speed less than that of sound; *also* : moving at such a speed **2** : INFRASONIC

sub·stance \ˈsəb-stəns\ *n* **1** : essential nature : ESSENCE ⟨divine ~⟩; *also* : the fundamental or essential part or quality ⟨the ~ of his speech⟩ **2** : physical material from which something is made or which has discrete existence; *also* : matter of particular or definite chemical constitution **3** : material possessions : PROPERTY, WEALTH

sub·stan·dard \ˌsəb-ˈstan-dərd, ˈsəb-\ *adj* : falling short of a standard or norm

sub·stan·tial \səb-ˈstan-chəl\ *adj* **1** : existing as or in substance : MATERIAL; *also* : not illusory : REAL **2** : IMPORTANT, ESSENTIAL **3** : NOURISHING, SATISFYING ⟨~ meal⟩ **4** : having means : WELL-TO-DO **5** : CONSIDERABLE ⟨~ profit⟩ **6** : STRONG, FIRM — **sub·stan·tial·ly** \-ē\ *adv*

sub·stan·ti·ate \səb-ˈstan-chē-ˌāt\ *vb* **-at·ed; -at·ing 1** : to give substance or body to **2** : VERIFY, PROVE — **sub·stan·ti·a·tion** \-ˌstan-chē-ˈā-shən\ *n*

sub·stan·tive \ˈsəb-stən-tiv\ *n* : NOUN; *also* : a word or phrase used as a noun

sub·sta·tion \ˈsəb-ˌstā-shən\ *n* : a station (as a post-office branch) subordinate to another station

[1]sub·sti·tute \ˈsəb-stə-ˌt(y)üt\ *n* : a person or thing replacing another — **substitute** *adj*

[2]substitute *vb* **-tut·ed; -tut·ing 1** : to put or use in the place of another **2** : to serve as a substitute — **sub·sti·tu·tion** \ˌsəb-stə-ˈt(y)ü-shən\ *n*

sub·stra·tum \ˈsəb-ˌstrāt-əm, -ˌstrat-\ *n, pl* **-stra·ta** \-ə\ : the layer or structure lying underneath

sub·struc·ture \ˈsəb-ˌstrək-chər\ *n* : FOUNDATION, GROUNDWORK

sub·sur·face \ˈsəb-ˌsər-fəs\ *n* : earth material near the surface of the ground — **subsurface** *adj*

sub·ter·fuge \ˈsəb-tər-ˌfyüj\ *n* : a trick or device used in order to conceal, escape, or evade **syn** fraud, deception, trickery

sub·ter·ra·nean \ˌsəb-tə-ˈrā-nē-ən\ *adj* **1** : lying or being underground **2** : SECRET, HIDDEN

sub·tile \ˈsət-ᵊl\ *adj* **sub·til·er** \ˈsət-lər, -ᵊl-ər\; **sub·til·est** \ˈsət-ləst, -ᵊl-əst\ : SUBTLE

sub·ti·tle \ˈsəb-ˌtīt-ᵊl\ *n* **1** : a secondary or explanatory title (as of a book) **2** : printed matter projected on a motion-picture screen during or between the scenes

sub·tle \ˈsət-ᵊl\ *adj* **sub·tler** \ˈsət-(ᵊ-)lər\; **sub·tlest** \ˈsət-(ᵊ-)ləst\ **1** : hardly noticeable : DELICATE, REFINED **2** : SHREWD, KEEN **3** : CLEVER, SLY — **sub·tle·ty** \-tē\ *n* — **sub·tly** \ˈsət-(ᵊ-)lē\ *adv*

sub·tract \səb-ˈtrakt\ *vb* : to take away (as one number from another); *also* : to perform the operation of deducting one number from another — **sub·trac·tion** \-ˈtrak-shən\ *n*

sub·tra·hend \ˈsəb-trə-ˌhend\ *n* : a number that is to be subtracted from another

sub·trop·i·cal \ˌsəb-ˈträp-i-kəl, ˈsəb-\ *also* **sub·trop·ic** \-ik\ *adj* : of, relating to, or being regions bordering on the tropical zone

sub·urb \ˈsəb-ˌərb\ *n* **1** : an outlying part of a city; *also* : a small community adjacent to a city **2** *pl* : a residential area adjacent to a city — **sub·ur·ban** \sə-ˈbər-bən\ *adj or n*

sub·ur·ban·ite \sə-ˈbər-bə-ˌnīt\ *n* : one living in a suburb

sub·ur·bia \sə-ˈbər-bē-ə\ *n* **1** : SUBURBS **2** : suburban people or customs

sub·ven·tion \səb-ˈven-chən\ *n* : SUBSIDY, ENDOWMENT

sub·vert \səb-ˈvərt\ *vb* **1** : OVERTHROW, RUIN **2** : CORRUPT **syn** sabotage, undermine — **sub·ver·sion** \-ˈvər-zhən\ *n* — **sub·ver·sive** \-ˈvər-siv\ *adj*

sub·way \ˈsəb-ˌwā\ *n* : an underground way; *esp* : an underground electric railway

suc·ceed \sək-ˈsēd\ *vb* **1** : to follow next in order or next after another; *esp* : to inherit sovereignty, rank, title, or property **2** : to attain a desired object or end : be successful

suc·cess \sək-ˈses\ *n* **1** : satisfactory completion of something **2** : the gaining of wealth and fame **3** : one that succeeds — **suc·cess·ful** \-fəl\ *adj* — **suc·cess·ful·ly** \-ē\ *adv*

suc·ces·sion \sək-ˈsesh-ən\ *n* **1** : the order, act, or right of succeeding to a property, title, or throne **2** : the act or process of following in order **3** : a series of persons or things that follow one after another **syn** progression, sequence, chain, train, string

suc·ces·sive \sək-ˈses-iv\ *adj* : following in order : CONSECUTIVE — **suc·ces·sive·ly** *adv*

suc·ces·sor \sək-ˈses-ər\ *n* : one that succeeds (as to a throne, title, estate, or office)

suc·cinct \(ˌ)sək-ˈsiŋkt, sə-ˈsiŋkt\ *adj* : BRIEF, CONCISE **syn** terse, laconic, summary, curt, short — **suc·cinct·ly** *adv* — **suc·cinct·ness** *n*

suc·cor \ˈsək-ər\ *n* [ME *succur*, fr. earlier *sucurs*, taken as pl., fr. OF *sucors*, fr. ML *succursus*, fr. L *succursus*, pp. of *succurrere* to run up, run to help] : AID, HELP, RELIEF — **succor** *vb*

suc·co·tash \ˈsək-ə-ˌtash\ *n* [from an American Indian language] : beans and kernels of sweet corn cooked together

[1]**suc·cu·lent** \ˈsək-yə-lənt\ *adj* : full of juice : JUICY; *also* : having fleshy tissues that conserve moisture — **suc·cu·lence** \-ləns\ *n*

[2]**succulent** *n* : a succulent plant (as a cactus)

suc·cumb \sə-ˈkəm\ *vb* **1** : to give up **2** : DIE **syn** submit, capitulate, relent, defer

[1]**such** \(ˈ)səch, (ˌ)sich\ *adj* **1** : of this or that kind **2** : having a quality just specified or to be specified

[2]**such** *pron* **1** : such a one or ones ⟨he's the boss, and had the right to act as ~⟩ **2** : that or those similar or related thereto ⟨boards and nails and ~⟩

[3]**such** *adv* : to that degree : so

such·like \ˈsəch-ˌlīk\ *adj* : SIMILAR

[1]**suck** \ˈsək\ *vb* **1** : to draw in liquid and esp. mother's milk with the mouth **2** : to draw liquid from by action of the mouth ⟨~ an orange⟩ **3** : to take in or up or remove by or as if by suction

[2]**suck** *n* : the act of sucking : SUCTION

suck·er \ˈsək-ər\ *n* **1** : one that sucks **2** : a part of an animal's body used for sucking or for clinging **3** : a fish with thick soft lips for sucking in food **4** : a shoot from the roots or lower part of a plant **5** : a person easily deceived

suck·le \ˈsək-əl\ *vb* **suck·led; suck·ling** \-(ə-)liŋ\ : to give or draw milk from the breast or udder; *also* : NURTURE, REAR

suck·ling \ˈsək-liŋ\ *n* : a young unweaned mammal

su·cre \ˈsü-(ˌ)krā\ *n* — see MONEY table

su·crose \ˈsü-ˌkrōs, -ˌkrōz\ *n* : a sweet sugar obtained esp. from sugarcane or sugar beets

suc·tion \ˈsək-shən\ *n* **1** : the act of sucking **2** : the act or process of drawing something (as liquid or dust) into a space (as in a vacuum cleaner or a pump) by partially exhausting the air in the space — **suc·tion·al** \-sh(ə-)nəl\ *adj*

sud·den \ˈsəd-ᵊn\ *adj* [ME *sodain*, fr. MF, fr. L *subitaneus*, fr. *subitus* sudden, fr. pp. of *subire* to come up] **1** : happening or coming quickly or unexpectedly ⟨~ shower⟩; *also* : changing angle or character all at once ⟨~ turn in the road⟩ ⟨~ descent to the sea⟩ **2** : HASTY, RASH ⟨~ decision⟩ **3** : made or brought about in a short time : PROMPT ⟨~ cure⟩ **syn** precipitate, headlong, impetuous, hasty — **sud·den·ly** *adv* — **sud·den·ness** *n*

sudden infant death syndrome *n* : death due to unknown causes of an infant in apparently good health that occurs usu. before one year of age

suds \ˈsədz\ *n pl* : soapy water esp. when frothy — **sudsy** \ˈsəd-zē\ *adj*

sue \ˈsü\ *vb* **sued; su·ing 1** : PETITION, SOLICIT **2** : to seek justice or right by bringing legal action **syn** appeal

suede *or* **suède** \ˈswād\ *n* [F *gants de Suède* Swedish gloves] **1** : leather with a napped surface **2** : a fabric with a suedelike nap

su·et \ˈsü-ət\ *n* : the hard fat from beef and mutton that yields tallow

suff *abbr* **1** sufficient **2** suffix

suf·fer \ˈsəf-ər\ *vb* **suf·fered; suf·fer·ing** \-(ə-)riŋ\ **1** : to feel or endure pain **2** : EXPERIENCE, UNDERGO **3** : to bear loss, damage, or injury **4** : ALLOW, PERMIT **syn** endure, abide, tolerate, stand, brook, stomach — **suf·fer·able** \ˈsəf-(ə-)rə-bəl\ *adj* — **suf·fer·er** *n*

suf·fer·ance \ˈsəf-(ə-)rəns\ *n* **1** : consent or approval implied by lack of interference or resistance **2** : ENDURANCE, PATIENCE

suf·fer·ing \-(ə-)riŋ\ *n* : PAIN, MISERY, HARDSHIP

suf·fice \sə-ˈfīs\ *vb* **suf·ficed; suf·fic·ing 1** : to satisfy a need : be sufficient **2** : to be capable or competent

suf·fi·cien·cy \sə-ˈfish-ən-sē\ *n* **1** : a sufficient quantity to meet one's needs **2** : ADEQUACY

suf·fi·cient \sə-ˈfish-ənt\ *adj* : adequate to accomplish a purpose or meet a need — **suf·fi·cient·ly** *adv*

[1]**suf·fix** \ˈsəf-ˌiks\ *n* : an affix occurring at the end of a word

[2]**suf·fix** \ˈsəf-iks, (ˌ)sə-ˈfiks\ *vb* : to attach as a suffix — **suf·fix·ation** \ˌsəf-ˌik-ˈsā-shən\ *n*

suf·fo·cate \ˈsəf-ə-ˌkāt\ *vb* **-cat·ed; -cat·ing** : STIFLE, SMOTHER, CHOKE — **suf·fo·cat·ing·ly** *adv* — **suf·fo·ca·tion** \ˌsəf-ə-ˈkā-shən\ *n*

suf·fra·gan \ˈsəf-ri-gən\ *n* : an assistant bishop; *esp* : one not having the right of succession — **suffragan** *adj*

suf·frage \ˈsəf-rij\ *n* [L *suffragium*] **1** : VOTE **2** : the right to vote : FRANCHISE

suf·frag·ette \ˌsəf-ri-ˈjet\ *n* : a woman who advocates suffrage for her sex

suf·frag·ist \ˈsəf-ri-jəst\ *n* : one who advocates extension of the suffrage esp. to women

suf·fuse \sə-ˈfyüz\ *vb* **suf·fused; suf·fus·ing** : to spread over or through in the manner of a fluid or light **syn** infuse, imbue, ingrain, steep — **suf·fu·sion** \-ˈfyü-zhən\ *n*

[1]**sug·ar** \ˈshu̇g-ər\ *n* **1** : a sweet substance that is colorless or white when pure and is chiefly derived from sugarcane or sugar beets **2** : a water-soluble compound (as glucose) similar to sucrose — **sug·ary** *adj*

---

²**sugar** *vb* **sug·ared; sug·ar·ing** \ˈshu̇g-(ə-)riŋ\ **1** : to mix, cover, or sprinkle with sugar **2** : SWEETEN ⟨~ advice with flattery⟩ **3** : to form sugar ⟨a syrup that ~*s*⟩ **4** : GRANULATE

sugar beet *n* : a large beet with a white root from which sugar is made

sug·ar·cane \ˈshu̇g-ər-ˌkān\ *n* : a tall grass widely grown in warm regions for the sugar in its stalks

sugar daddy *n* **1** : a well-to-do usu. older man who supports or spends lavishly on a mistress or girlfriend **2** : a generous benefactor of a cause

sugar maple *n* : a maple with a sweet sap; *esp* : one of eastern No. America with sap that is the chief source of maple syrup and maple sugar

sugar pea *n* : SNOW PEA

sug·ar·plum \ˈshu̇g-ər-ˌpləm\ *n* : a small ball of candy

sug·gest \sə(g)-ˈjest\ *vb* **1** : to put (as a thought, plan, or desire) into a person's mind **2** : to remind or evoke by association of ideas **syn** imply, hint, intimate, insinuate, connote

sug·gest·ible \sə(g)-ˈjes-tə-bəl\ *adj* : easily influenced by suggestion

sug·ges·tion \-ˈjes-chən\ *n* **1** : an act or instance of suggesting; *also* : something suggested **2** : a slight indication

sug·ges·tive \-ˈjes-tiv\ *adj* : tending to suggest something; *esp* : suggesting something improper or indecent — **sug·ges·tive·ly** *adv* — **sug·ges·tive·ness** *n*

sui·cide \ˈsü-ə-ˌsīd\ *n* **1** : the act of killing oneself purposely **2** : one that commits or attempts suicide — **sui·cid·al** \ˌsü-ə-ˈsīd-ᵊl\ *adj*

sui ge·ner·is \ˌsü-ˌī-ˈjen-ə-rəs; ˌsü-ē-ˈjen-\ *adj* [L, of its own kind] : being in a class by itself : UNIQUE

¹**suit** \ˈsüt\ *n* **1** : an action in court to recover a right or claim **2** : an act of suing or entreating; *esp* : COURTSHIP **3** : a number of things used together ⟨~ of clothes⟩ **4** : one of the four sets of playing cards in a pack **syn** prayer, plea, petition, appeal

²**suit** *vb* **1** : to be appropriate or fitting **2** : to be becoming to **3** : to meet the needs or desires of : PLEASE

suit·able \ˈsüt-ə-bəl\ *adj* : FITTING, PROPER, APPROPRIATE **syn** fit, meet, apt, happy — **suit·abil·i·ty** \ˌsüt-ə-ˈbil-ət-ē\ *n* — **suit·able·ness** \ˈsüt-ə-bəl-nəs\ *n* — **suit·ably** \-ə-blē\ *adv*

suit·case \ˈsüt-ˌkās\ *n* : a flat rectangular traveling bag

suite \ˈswēt, *for 4 also* ˈsüt\ *n* **1** : a personal staff attending a dignitary or ruler : RETINUE **2** : a group of rooms occupied as a unit : APARTMENT **3** : a modern instrumental composition free in its character and number of movements; *also* : a long orchestral concert arrangement in suite form of material drawn from a longer work **4** : a set of matched furniture for a room

suit·ing \ˈsüt-iŋ\ *n* : fabric for suits of clothes

suit·or \ˈsüt-ər\ *n* **1** : one who sues or petitions **2** : one who seeks to marry a woman

su·ki·ya·ki \skē-ˈ(y)äk-ē; ˌsu̇k-ē-ˈ(y)äk-ē, ˌsük-\ *n* : thin slices of meat, bean curd, and vegetables cooked in soy sauce, sake, and sugar

sul·fa \ˈsəl-fə\ *adj* **1** : related chemically to sulfanilamide **2** : of, relating to, or using sulfa drugs ⟨~ therapy⟩

sulfa drug *n* : any of various synthetic organic bacteria-inhibiting drugs that are closely related chemically to sulfanilamide

sul·fa·nil·amide \ˌsəl-fə-ˈnil-ə-ˌmīd\ *n* : a sulfur-containing organic compound that is the parent compound of most sulfa drugs

sul·fate \ˈsəl-ˌfāt\ *n* : a salt or ester of sulfuric acid

sul·fide \ˈsəl-ˈfīd\ *n* : a compound of sulfur

sul·fur *or* **sul·phur** \ˈsəl-fər\ *n* : a nonmetallic element that occurs in nature combined or free in vulcanizing rubber and in medicine — see ELEMENT table

sulfur dioxide *n* : a heavy pungent toxic gas that is used esp. in bleaching, as a preservative, and as a refrigerant, and is a major air pollutant

sul·fu·ric \ˌsəl-ˈfyu̇r-ik\ *adj* : of, relating to, or containing sulfur

sulfuric acid *n* : a heavy corrosive oily strong acid

sul·fu·rous \ˈsəl-f(y)ə-rəs, *also esp for 1* ˌsəl-ˈfyu̇r-əs\ *adj* **1** : of, relating to, or containing sulfur **2** *or* **sul·phu·rous** : of or relating to brimstone or the fire of hell : INFERNAL **3** *or* **sulphurous** : FIERY, INFLAMED ⟨~ sermons⟩

¹**sulk** \ˈsəlk\ *vb* : to be or become moodily silent

²**sulk** *n* : a sulky mood or spell

¹**sulky** \ˈsəl-kē\ *adj* : inclined to sulk : MOROSE, MOODY **syn** surly, glum, sullen, gloomy — **sulk·i·ly** \ˈsəl-kə-lē\ *adv* — **sulk·i·ness** \-kē-nəs\ *n*

²**sulky** *n, pl* **sulkies** : a light 2-wheeled vehicle with a seat for the driver and usu. no body

sul·len \ˈsəl-ən\ *adj* **1** : gloomily silent : MOROSE **2** : DISMAL, GLOOMY ⟨a ~ sky⟩ **syn** glum, surly, dour, saturnine — **sul·len·ly** *adv* — **sul·len·ness** \ˈsəl-ən-(n)əs\ *n*

sul·ly \ˈsəl-ē\ *vb* **sul·lied; sul·ly·ing** : SOIL, SMIRCH, DEFILE

sul·tan \ˈsəlt-ᵊn\ *n* : a sovereign esp. of a Muslim state — **sul·tan·ate** \-ˌāt\ *n*

sul·ta·na \ˌsəl-ˈtan-ə\ *n* **1** : a female member of a sultan's family **2** : a pale seedless grape; *also* : a raisin of this grape

sul·try \ˈsəl-trē\ *adj* **sul·tri·er; -est** [obs. E *sulter* to swelter, alter. of E *swelter*] : very hot and moist : SWELTERING; *also* : burning hot : TORRID

¹**sum** \ˈsəm\ *n* [ME *summe,* fr. OF, fr. L *summa,* fr. fem. of *summus* highest] **1** : a quantity of money **2** : the whole amount **3** : GIST **4** : the result obtained by adding numbers **5** : a problem in arithmetic **syn** aggregate, total, whole

²**sum** *vb* **summed; sum·ming** : to find the sum of by adding or counting

su·mac *also* **su·mach** \ˈs(h)ü-ˌmak\ *n* : any of a genus of trees, shrubs, and woody vines with pinnate compound leaves and spikes of red or whitish berries

sum·ma·rize \ˈsəm-ə-ˌrīz\ *vb* **-rized; -riz·ing** : to tell in a summary

¹**sum·ma·ry** \ˈsəm-ə-rē\ *adj* **1** : covering the main points briefly : CONCISE **2** : done without delay or formality ⟨~ punishment⟩ **syn** terse, succinct, laconic — **sum·mar·i·ly** \(ˌ)sə-ˈmer-ə-lē, ˈsəm-ə-rə-lē\ *adv*

²**sum·ma·ry** *n, pl* **-ries** : a concise statement of the main points

sum·ma·tion \(ˌ)sə-ˈmā-shən\ *n* : a summing up; *esp* : a speech in court summing up the arguments in a case

sum·mer \ˈsəm-ər\ *n* : the season of the year in a region in which the sun shines most directly : the warmest period of the year — **sum·mery** *adj*

sum·mer·house \ˈsəm-ər-ˌhau̇s\ *n* : a covered structure in a garden or park to provide a shady retreat

summer squash *n* : any of various garden squashes (as zucchini) used as a vegetable while immature

sum·mit \ˈsəm-ət\ *n* : the highest point

sum·mon \ˈsəm-ən\ *vb* **sum·moned; sum·mon·ing** \-(ə-)niŋ\ [ME *somonen,* fr. OF *somondre,* fr. (assumed) VL *summonere,* alter. of L *summonēre* to remind secretly] **1** : to call to a meeting : CONVOKE **2** : to send for; *also* : to order to appear in court **3** : to evoke esp. by an act of the will ⟨~ up courage⟩ — **sum·mon·er** *n*

sum·mons \ˈsəm-ənz\ *n, pl* **sum·mons·es** **1** : an authoritative call to appear at a designated place or to attend to a duty **2** : a warning or citation to appear in court at a specified time to answer charges

sump·tu·ous \ˈsəmp-chə(-wə)s\ *adj* : LAVISH, LUXURIOUS

sum up *vb* : SUMMARIZE

¹**sun** \ˈsən\ *n* **1** : the shining celestial body around which the earth and other planets revolve and from which they receive light and heat **2** : a celestial body like the sun **3** : SUNSHINE — **sun·less** *adj* — **sun·ny** *adj*

²**sun** *vb* **sunned; sun·ning 1** : to expose to or as if to the rays of the sun **2** : to sun oneself
Sun *abbr* Sunday
sun·bath \ˈsən-ˌbath, -ˌbàth\ *n* : an exposure to sunlight or a sunlamp — **sun·bathe** \-ˌbāth\ *vb*
sun·beam \-ˌbēm\ *n* : a ray of sunlight
sun·bon·net \-ˌbän-ət\ *n* : a bonnet with a wide brim to shield the face and neck from the sun
¹**sun·burn** \-ˌbərn\ *vb* **-burned** \-ˌbərnd\ *or* **-burnt** \-ˌbərnt\; **-burn·ing** : to burn or discolor by the sun
²**sunburn** *n* : a skin inflammation caused by overexposure to sunlight
sun·dae \ˈsən-dē\ *n* : ice cream served with topping
Sun·day \ˈsən-dē, -ˌdā\ *n* : the 1st day of the week : the Christian Sabbath
sun·der \ˈsən-dər\ *vb* **sun·dered; sun·der·ing** \-d(ə-)riŋ\ : to force apart **syn** sever, part, disjoin, disunite
sun·di·al \-ˌdī(-ə)l\ *n* : a device for showing the time of day from the shadow cast on a plate by an object with a straight edge
sun·down \-ˌdaủn\ *n* : SUNSET 2
sun·dries \ˈsən-drēz\ *n pl* : various small articles or items
sun·dry \ˈsən-drē\ *adj* : SEVERAL, DIVERS, VARIOUS **syn** many, numerous
sun·fish \ˈsən-ˌfish\ *n* **1** : a huge sea fish with a deep flattened body **2** : any of a family of American freshwater fishes that are related to the perches, are often brightly colored, and usu. have the body flattened from side to side
sun·flow·er \-ˌflaủ(-ə)r\ *n* : any of a genus of tall plants related to the daisies and often grown for the oil-rich seeds of their yellow-petaled dark-centered flower heads
sung *past and past part of* SING
sun·glasses \ˈsən-ˌglas-əz\ *n pl* : glasses to protect the eyes from the sun
sunk *past and past part of* SINK
sunk·en \ˈsəŋ-kən\ *adj* **1** : SUBMERGED **2** : fallen in : HOLLOW ⟨~ cheeks⟩ **3** : lying in a depression ⟨~ garden⟩; *also* : constructed below the general floor level ⟨~ living room⟩
sun·lamp \ˈsən-ˌlamp\ *n* : an electric lamp designed to emit radiation of wavelengths from ultraviolet to infrared
sun·light \-ˌlīt\ *n* : SUNSHINE
sun·lit \-ˌlit\ *adj* : lighted by or as if by the sun
sun·rise \-ˌrīz\ *n* **1** : the apparent rising of the sun above the horizon **2** : the time at which the sun rises
sun·roof \-ˌrüf, -ˌrủf\ *n* : an automobile roof having a panel that can be opened
sun·screen \-ˌskrēn\ *n* : a substance used in suntan preparations to protect the skin
sun·set \-ˌset\ *n* **1** : the apparent descent of the sun below the horizon **2** : the time at which the sun sets
sun·shade \ˈsən-ˌshād\ *n* : something (as a parasol or awning) used as a protection from the sun's rays
sun·shine \-ˌshīn\ *n* : the direct light of the sun — **sunshiny** *adj*
sun·spot \-ˌspät\ *n* : one of the dark spots that appear from time to time on the sun's surface
sun·stroke \-ˌstrōk\ *n* : a bodily condition often marked by a high fever and collapse and caused by staying in the sun for too long
sun·tan \-ˌtan\ *n* : a browning of the skin from exposure to the sun's rays
sun·up \-ˌəp\ *n* : SUNRISE 2
¹**sup** \ˈsəp\ *vb* **supped; sup·ping** : to take or drink in swallows or gulps
²**sup** *n* : a mouthful esp. of liquor or broth; *also* : a small quantity of liquid
³**sup** *vb* **supped; sup·ping 1** : to eat the evening meal **2** : to make one's supper ⟨*supped* on roast beef⟩
⁴**sup** *abbr* **1** superior **2** supplement; supplementary **3** supply **4** supra
¹**su·per** \ˈsü-pər\ *n* : SUPERINTENDENT
²**super** *adj* **1** : very fine : EXCELLENT **2** : EXTREME, EXCESSIVE
super- \ˌsü-pər, ˈsü-\ *prefix* **1** : over and above : higher in quantity, quality, or degree than : more than **2** : in addition : extra **3** : exceeding a norm **4** : in excessive degree or intensity **5** : surpassing all or most others of its kind **6** : situated above, on, or at the top of **7** : next above or higher **8** : more inclusive than **9** : superior in status or position

superachiever	**superpower**
superagency	**superrich**
superblock	**supersalesman**
superbomb	**supersecret**
supercity	**supersize**
supereminent	**supersized**
superfine	**supersophisticated**
supergalaxy	**superspectacle**
supergovernment	**superspy**
superheat	**superstar**
superhuman	**superstate**
superhumanly	**superstratum**
superindividual	**superstrength**
superliner	**superstrong**
superman	**supersubtle**
supermom	**supersubtlety**
supernormal	**supersystem**
superpatriot	**supertanker**
superpatriotic	**supertax**
superpatriotism	**superwoman**
superphysical	

su·per·abun·dant \ˌsü-pər-ə-ˈbən-dənt\ *adj* : more than ample — **su·per·abun·dance** \-dəns\ *n*
su·per·an·nu·ate \ˌsü-pər-ˈan-yə-ˌwāt\ *vb* **-at·ed; -at·ing** : to retire and pension because of age or infirmity — **su·per·an·nu·at·ed** *adj*
su·perb \sủ-ˈpərb\ *adj* [L *superbus* excellent, proud, fr. *super* above] : marked to the highest degree by grandeur, excellence, brilliance, or competence **syn** resplendent, glorious, gorgeous, sublime — **su·perb·ly** *adv*
su·per·car·go \ˌsü-pər-ˈkär-gō, ˈsü-pər-ˌkär-gō\ *n* : an officer on a merchant ship who manages the business part of the voyage
su·per·charg·er \ˈsü-pər-ˌchär-jər\ *n* : a device for increasing the amount of air supplied to an internal-combustion engine
su·per·cil·ious \ˌsü-pər-ˈsil-ē-əs\ *adj* [L *superciliosus*, fr. *supercilium* eyebrow, haughtiness] : haughtily contemptuous **syn** disdainful, overbearing, arrogant, lordly, superior
su·per·con·duc·tiv·i·ty \ˈsü-pər-ˌkän-ˌdək-ˈtiv-ət-ē\ *n* : a complete disappearance of electrical resistance in a substance at temperatures near absolute zero — **su·per·con·duc·tive** \ˌsü-pər-kən-ˈdək-tiv\ *adj* — **su·per·con·duc·tor** \-ˈdək-tər\ *n*
su·per·con·ti·nent \ˈsü-pər-ˌkänt-ᵊn-ənt\ *n* : a hypothetical former large continent from which other continents broke off and drifted away
su·per–du·per \ˈsü-pər-ˈdü-pər\ *adj* : of the greatest excellence, size, effectiveness, or impressiveness
su·per·ego \ˌsü-pər-ˈē-gō\ *n* : the one of the three divisions of the psyche in psychoanalytic theory that functions to reward and punish through a system of moral attitudes, conscience, and a sense of guilt
su·per·fi·cial \ˌsü-pər-ˈfish-əl\ *adj* **1** : of or relating to the surface or appearance only **2** : not thorough : SHALLOW

syn cursory, sketchy — **su·per·fi·ci·al·i·ty** \-ˌfish-ē-ˈal-ət-ē\ *n* — **su·per·fi·cial·ly** \-ˈfish-(ə-)lē\ *adv*

su·per·flu·ous \sü-ˈpər-flə-wəs\ *adj* : exceeding what is sufficient or necessary : SURPLUS **syn** extra, spare, supernumerary — **su·per·flu·i·ty** \ˌsü-pər-ˈflü-ət-ē\ *n*

su·per·high·way \ˌsü-pər-ˈhī-ˌwā\ *n* : a broad highway designed for high-speed traffic

su·per·im·pose \-im-ˈpōz\ *vb* : to lay (one thing) over and above something else

su·per·in·tend \ˌsü-p(ə-)rin-ˈtend\ *vb* : to have or exercise the charge and oversight of : DIRECT — **su·per·in·ten·dence** \-ˈten-dəns\ *n* — **su·per·in·ten·den·cy** \-dən-sē\ *n* — **su·per·in·ten·dent** \-dənt\ *n*

[1]**su·pe·ri·or** \sù-ˈpir-ē-ər\ *adj* **1** : situated higher up; *also* : higher in rank or numbers **2** : of greater value or importance **3** : courageously indifferent (as to pain or misfortune) **4** : better than most others of its kind **5** : ARROGANT, HAUGHTY — **su·pe·ri·or·i·ty** \-ˌpir-ē-ˈòr-ət-ē\ *n*

[2]**superior** *n* **1** : one who is above another in rank, office, or station; *esp* : the head of a religious house or order **2** : one higher in quality or merit

[1]**su·per·la·tive** \sù-ˈpər-lət-iv\ *adj* **1** : of, relating to, or constituting the degree of grammatical comparison that denotes an extreme or unsurpassed level or extent **2** : surpassing others : SUPREME **syn** peerless, incomparable, superb — **su·per·la·tive·ly** *adv*

[2]**superlative** *n* **1** : the superlative degree or a superlative form in a language **2** : the utmost degree : ACME

su·per·mar·ket \ˈsü-pər-ˌmär-kət\ *n* : a self-service retail market selling foods and household merchandise

su·per·nal \sù-ˈpərn-əl\ *adj* **1** : of or from on high : TOWERING **2** : of heavenly or spiritual character : ETHEREAL

su·per·nat·u·ral \ˌsü-pər-ˈnach-(ə-)rəl\ *adj* : of or relating to phenomena beyond or outside of nature; *esp* : relating to or attributed to a divinity, ghost, or infernal spirit — **su·per·nat·u·ral·ly** \-ē\ *adv*

su·per·no·va \ˌsü-pər-ˈnō-və\ *n* : the explosion of a very large star

[1]**su·per·nu·mer·ary** \-ˈn(y)ü-mə-ˌrer-ē\ *adj* : exceeding the usual or required number : EXTRA **syn** surplus, superfluous, spare

[2]**supernumerary** *n, pl* **-ar·ies** : an extra person or thing; *esp* : an actor hired for a nonspeaking part

su·per·pose \ˌsü-pər-ˈpōz\ *vb* **-posed; -pos·ing** : SUPERIMPOSE — **su·per·po·si·tion** \-pə-ˈzish-ən\ *n*

su·per·sat·u·rat·ed \ˌsü-pər-ˈsach-ə-ˌrāt-əd\ *adj* : containing an amount of a substance greater than that required for saturation

su·per·scribe \ˈsü-pər-ˌskrīb, ˌsü-pər-ˈskrīb\ *vb* **-scribed; -scrib·ing** : to write on the top or outside : ADDRESS — **su·per·scrip·tion** \ˌsü-pər-ˈskrip-shən\ *n*

su·per·script \ˈsü-pər-ˌskript\ *n* : a symbol (as a numeral or letter) written immediately above or above and to one side of another character

su·per·sede \ˌsü-pər-ˈsēd\ *vb* **-sed·ed; -sed·ing** [MF *superseder* to refrain from, fr. L *supersedēre* to be superior to, refrain from, fr. *super-* above + *sedēre* to sit] : to take the place of : REPLACE **syn** displace, supplant

su·per·son·ic \-ˈsän-ik\ *adj* **1** : ULTRASONIC **2** : being or relating to speeds from one to five times the speed of sound; *also* : capable of moving at such a speed ⟨a ~ airplane⟩

su·per·son·ics \-ˈsän-iks\ *n* : the science of supersonic phenomena

su·per·sti·tion \ˌsü-pər-ˈstish-ən\ *n* **1** : beliefs or practices resulting from ignorance, fear of the unknown, or trust in magic or chance **2** : an irrationally abject attitude of mind toward nature, the unknown, or God resulting from superstition — **su·per·sti·tious** \-əs\ *adj*

su·per·struc·ture \ˈsü-pər-ˌstrək-chər\ *n* : something built on a base or as a vertical extension

su·per·vene \ˌsü-pər-ˈvēn\ *vb* **-vened; -ven·ing** : to occur as something additional or unexpected **syn** follow, succeed, ensue

su·per·vise \ˈsü-pər-ˌvīz\ *vb* **-vised; -vis·ing** : OVERSEE, SUPERINTEND — **su·per·vi·sion** \ˌsü-pər-ˈvizh-ən\ *n* — **su·per·vi·sor** \ˈsü-pər-ˌvī-zər\ *n* — **su·per·vi·so·ry** \ˌsü-pər-ˈvīz-(ə-)rē\ *adj*

su·pine \sù-ˈpīn\ *adj* **1** : lying on the back with face upward **2** : LETHARGIC, SLUGGISH; *also* : ABJECT **syn** inactive, inert, passive, idle

supp *or* **suppl** *abbr* supplement; supplementary

sup·per \ˈsəp-ər\ *n* : the evening meal esp. when dinner is taken at midday — **sup·per·time** \-ˌtīm\ *n*

sup·plant \sə-ˈplant\ *vb* **1** : to take the place of (another) esp. by force or trickery **2** : REPLACE **syn** displace, supersede

sup·ple \ˈsəp-əl\ *adj* **sup·pler** \-(ə-)lər\; **sup·plest** \-(ə-)ləst\ **1** : COMPLIANT, ADAPTABLE **2** : capable of bending without breaking or creasing : LIMBER **syn** resilient, elastic, flexible

[1]**sup·ple·ment** \ˈsəp-lə-mənt\ *n* **1** : something that supplies a want or makes an addition **2** : a continuation (as of a book) containing corrections or additional material — **sup·ple·men·tal** \ˌsəp-lə-ˈment-ᵊl\ *adj* — **sup·ple·men·ta·ry** \-ˈmen-t(ə-)rē\ *adj*

[2]**sup·ple·ment** \ˈsəp-lə-ˌment\ *vb* : to fill up the deficiencies of : add to

sup·pli·ant \ˈsəp-lē-ənt\ *n* : one who supplicates : PETITIONER, PLEADER

sup·pli·cant \ˈsəp-li-kənt\ *n* : SUPPLIANT

sup·pli·cate \ˈsəp-lə-ˌkāt\ *vb* **-cat·ed; -cat·ing** **1** : to make a humble entreaty; *esp* : to pray to God **2** : to ask earnestly and humbly : BESEECH **syn** implore, beg, entreat, plead — **sup·pli·ca·tion** \ˌsəp-lə-ˈkā-shən\ *n*

[1]**sup·ply** \sə-ˈplī\ *vb* **sup·plied; sup·ply·ing** [ME *supplien*, fr. MF *soupleier*, fr. L *supplēre* to fill up, supplement, supply, fr. *sub-* up + *plēre* to fill] **1** : to add as a supplement **2** : to satisfy the needs of **3** : FURNISH, PROVIDE — **sup·pli·er** \-ˈplī(-ə)r\ *n*

[2]**supply** *n, pl* **supplies** **1** : the quantity or amount (as of a commodity) needed or available; *also* : PROVISIONS, STORES — usu. used in pl. **2** : the act or process of filling a want or need : PROVISION **3** : the quantities of goods or services offered for sale at a particular time or at one price

sup·ply–side \sə-ˈplī-ˌsīd\ *adj* : of, relating to, or being an economic theory that recommends the reduction of tax rates to expand economic activity

[1]**sup·port** \sə-ˈpōrt\ *vb* **1** : BEAR, TOLERATE **2** : to take sides with : BACK, ASSIST **3** : to provide with food, clothing, and shelter **4** : to hold up or serve as a foundation for **syn** uphold, advocate, champion — **sup·port·able** *adj* — **sup·port·er** *n*

[2]**support** *n* **1** : the act of supporting : the state of being supported **2** : one that supports : PROP, BASE

sup·pose \sə-ˈpōz\ *vb* **sup·posed; sup·pos·ing** **1** : to assume to be true (as for the sake of argument) **2** : EXPECT ⟨I am *supposed* to go⟩ **3** : to think probable — **sup·pos·al** *n*

sup·posed \sə-ˈpōz(-ə)d\ *adj* : BELIEVED; *also* : mistakenly believed — **sup·pos·ed·ly** \-ˈpō-zəd-lē, -ˈpōz-dlē\ *adv*

sup·pos·ing \sə-ˈpō-ziŋ\ *conj* : if by way of hypothesis : on the assumption that

sup·po·si·tion \ˌsəp-ə-ˈzish-ən\ *n* **1** : something that is supposed : HYPOTHESIS **2** : the act of supposing

sup·pos·i·to·ry \sə-ˈpäz-ə-ˌtōr-ē\ *n, pl* **-ries** [ML *suppositorium*, lit., placed beneath] : a small easily melted mass of usu. medicated material for insertion (as into the rectum)

sup·press \sə-ˈpres\ *vb* **1** : to put down by authority or force : SUBDUE ⟨~ a revolt⟩ **2** : to keep from being known; *also* : to stop the publication or circulation of **3** : to exclude from consciousness : REPRESS — **sup·press·ible** \-ˈpres-ə-bəl\ *adj* — **sup·pres·sion** \-ˈpresh-ən\ *n*

sup·pres·sant \sə-ˈpres-ᵊnt\ *n* : an agent (as a drug) that tends to suppress rather than eliminate something (as appetite)

sup·pu·rate \ˈsəp-yə-ˌrāt\ *vb* **-rat·ed; -rat·ing** : to form or give off pus — **sup·pu·ra·tion** \ˌsəp-yə-ˈrā-shən\ *n*

su·pra \ˈsü-prə, -ˌprä\ *adv* : earlier in this writing : ABOVE

su·pra·na·tion·al \ˌsü-prə-ˈnash-(ə-)nəl, -ˌprä-\ *adj* : transcending national boundaries, authority, or interests ⟨~ organizations⟩

su·prem·a·cist \sü-ˈprem-ə-səst\ *n* : an advocate of group supremacy

su·prem·a·cy \sü-ˈprem-ə-sē\ *n, pl* **-cies** : supreme rank, power, or authority

su·preme \sü-ˈprēm\ *adj* [L *supremus,* superl. of *superus* upper, fr. *super* over, above] **1** : highest in rank or authority **2** : highest in degree or quality ⟨he is ~ among poets⟩ **3** : ULTIMATE ⟨the ~ sacrifice⟩ **syn** superlative, surpassing, peerless, incomparable — **su·preme·ly** *adv* — **su·preme·ness** *n*

Supreme Being *n* : GOD 1

supt *abbr* superintendent

supvr *abbr* supervisor

sur·cease \ˈsər-ˌsēs\ *n* : CESSATION, RESPITE

[1]**sur·charge** \ˈsər-ˌchärj\ *vb* **1** : to fill to excess : OVERLOAD **2** : to print or write a surcharge on (postage stamps)

[2]**surcharge** *n* **1** : an extra fee or cost **2** : an excessive load or burden **3** : something officially printed on a postage stamp to give it a new value or use

sur·cin·gle \ˈsər-ˌsiŋ-gəl\ *n* : a band passing around a horse's body to make something (as a saddle or pack) fast

[1]**sure** \ˈshür\ *adj* **sur·er; sur·est** [ME, fr. MF *sur,* fr. L *securus* secure] **1** : firmly established **2** : TRUSTWORTHY, RELIABLE **3** : CONFIDENT **4** : not to be disputed : UNDOUBTED **5** : bound to happen **6** : careful to remember or attend to something ⟨be ~ to lock the door⟩ **syn** certain, cocksure, positive — **sure·ly** *adv* — **sure·ness** *n*

[2]**sure** *adv* : SURELY

sure·fire \ˌshür-ˌfī(ə)r\ *adj* : certain to get results : DEPENDABLE

sure·ty \ˈshür-ət-ē\ *n, pl* **-ties** **1** : SURENESS, CERTAINTY **2** : something that makes sure : GUARANTEE **3** : one who becomes a guarantor for another person **syn** security, bond, bail

[1]**surf** \ˈsərf\ *n* : waves that break upon the shore; *also* : the sound or foam of breaking waves

[2]**surf** *vb* : to ride the surf (as on a surfboard) — **surf·er** *n* — **surf·ing** *n*

[1]**sur·face** \ˈsər-fəs\ *n* **1** : the outside of an object or body **2** : outward aspect or appearance

[2]**surface** *vb* **sur·faced; sur·fac·ing** **1** : to give a surface to : make smooth **2** : to rise to the surface

surf·board \ˈsərf-ˌbōrd\ *n* : a buoyant board used in riding the crests of waves

[1]**sur·feit** \ˈsər-fət\ *n* **1** : EXCESS, SUPERABUNDANCE **2** : excessive indulgence (as in food or drink) **3** : disgust caused by excess (as in eating and drinking)

[2]**surfeit** *vb* : to feed, supply, or indulge to the point of surfeit : CLOY

surg *abbr* surgeon; surgery; surgical

[1]**surge** \ˈsərj\ *vb* **surged; surg·ing** **1** : to rise and fall actively : TOSS **2** : to move in waves **3** : to rise suddenly to a high value

[2]**surge** *n* **1** : a sweeping onward like a wave of the sea ⟨a ~ of emotion⟩ **2** : a large billow **3** : a transient sudden increase of current in an electrical circuit

sur·geon \ˈsər-jən\ *n* : a physician who specializes in surgery

sur·gery \ˈsərj-(ə-)rē\ *n, pl* **-ger·ies** [ME *surgerie,* fr. OF *cirurgie, surgerie,* fr. L *chirurgia,* fr. Gk *cheirourgia,* fr. *cheirourgos* surgeon, fr. *cheirourgos* working with the hand, fr. *cheir* hand + *ergon* work] **1** : a branch of medicine concerned with the correction of physical defects, the repair of injuries, and the treatment of disease esp. by operations **2** : a surgeon's operating room or laboratory **3** : work done by a surgeon

sur·gi·cal \ˈsər-ji-kəl\ *adj* : of, relating to, or associated with surgeons or surgery — **sur·gi·cal·ly** \-k(ə-)lē\ *adv*

sur·ly \ˈsər-lē\ *adj* **sur·li·er; -est** [alter. of ME *sirly* lordly, imperious, fr. *sir*] : ILL-NATURED, CRABBED **syn** morose, glum, sullen, sulky, gloomy — **sur·li·ness** *n*

sur·mise \sər-ˈmīz\ *vb* **sur·mised; sur·mis·ing** : GUESS **syn** conjecture, presume, suppose — **surmise** *n*

sur·mount \sər-ˈmaůnt\ *vb* **1** : to rise superior to : OVERCOME **2** : to get to or lie at the top of **syn** conquer, lick, master

sur·name \ˈsər-ˌnām\ *n* **1** : NICKNAME **2** : the name borne in common by members of a family

sur·pass \sər-ˈpas\ *vb* **1** : to be superior to in quality, degree, or performance : EXCEL **2** : to be beyond the reach or powers of **syn** transcend, outdo, outstrip, exceed — **sur·pass·ing·ly** *adv*

sur·plice \ˈsər-pləs\ *n* : a loose white outer ecclesiastical vestment usu. of knee length with large open sleeves

sur·plus \ˈsər-(ˌ)pləs\ *n* **1** : quantity left over : EXCESS **2** : the excess of assets over liabilities **syn** superfluity, overabundance, surfeit

[1]**sur·prise** \sə(r)-ˈprīz\ *n* **1** : an attack made without warning **2** : a taking unawares **3** : something that surprises **4** : AMAZEMENT, ASTONISHMENT

[2]**surprise** *also* **sur·prize** *vb* **sur·prised; sur·pris·ing** **1** : to come upon and attack unexpectedly **2** : to take unawares **3** : AMAZE **4** : to effect or accomplish by means of a surprise **syn** astonish, astound, amaze, dumbfound — **sur·pris·ing** *adj* — **sur·pris·ing·ly** *adv*

sur·re·al·ism \sə-ˈrē-ə-ˌliz-əm\ *n* : art, literature, or theater characterized by fantastic or incongruous imagery or effects produced by unnatural juxtapositions and combinations — **sur·re·al·ist** \-ləst\ *n or adj* — **sur·re·al·is·tic** \sə-ˌrē-ə-ˈlis-tik\ *adj* — **sur·re·al·is·ti·cal·ly** \-ti-k(ə-)lē\ *adv*

[1]**sur·ren·der** \sə-ˈren-dər\ *vb* **-dered; -der·ing** \-d(ə-)riŋ\ **1** : to yield to the power of another : give up under compulsion **2** : RELINQUISH

[2]**surrender** *n* : the act of giving up or yielding oneself or the possession of something to another **syn** submission, capitulation

sur·rep·ti·tious \ˌsər-əp-ˈtish-əs\ *adj* : done, made, or acquired by stealth : CLANDESTINE **syn** underhand, covert, furtive — **sur·rep·ti·tious·ly** *adv*

sur·rey \ˈsər-ē\ *n, pl* **surreys** : a 4-wheeled 2-seated horse-drawn carriage

surrey

sur·ro·gate \ˈsər-ə-ˌgāt, -gət\ *n* **1** : DEPUTY, SUBSTITUTE **2** : a law officer in some states with authority in the probate of wills, the settlement of estates, and the appointment of guardians

sur·round \sə-ˈraůnd\ *vb* **1** : to enclose on all sides : ENCIRCLE **2** : to enclose so as to cut off retreat or escape

sur·round·ings \sə-ˈraůn-diŋz\ *n pl* : conditions by which one is surrounded

sur·tax \ˈsər-ˌtaks\ *n* : an additional tax over and above a normal tax

sur·tout \(ˌ)sər-ˈtü\ *n* [F, fr. *sur* over (fr. L *super*) + *tout* all, fr. L *totus* whole] : a man's long close-fitting overcoat

surv *abbr* survey; surveying; surveyor

sur·veil·lance \sər-ˈvā-ləns, -ˈvāl-yəns, -ˈvā-əns\ *n* [F] : close watch; *also* : SUPERVISION

[1]**sur·vey** \sər-ˈvā\ *vb* **sur·veyed; sur·vey·ing 1** : to look over and examine closely **2** : to find and represent the contours, measurements, and position of a part of the earth's surface (as a tract of land) **3** : to view or study something as a whole **syn** scrutinize, examine, inspect, study — **sur·vey·or** \-ər\ *n*

[2]**sur·vey** \ˈsər-ˌvā\ *n, pl* **surveys** : the act or an instance of surveying; *also* : something that is surveyed

sur·vey·ing \sər-ˈvā-iŋ\ *n* : the branch of mathematics that teaches the art of making surveys

sur·vive \sər-ˈvīv\ *vb* **sur·vived; sur·viv·ing 1** : to remain alive or existent **2** : OUTLIVE, OUTLAST — **sur·viv·al** *n* — **sur·vi·vor** \-ˈvī-vər\ *n*

sus·cep·ti·ble \sə-ˈsep-tə-bəl\ *adj* **1** : of such a nature as to permit ⟨words ~ of being misunderstood⟩ **2** : having little resistance to a stimulus or agency ⟨~ to colds⟩ **3** : easily affected or emotionally moved : RESPONSIVE **syn** sensitive, subject, exposed, prone, liable, open — **sus·cep·ti·bil·i·ty** \-ˌsep-tə-ˈbil-ət-ē\ *n*

su·shi \ˈsü-shē\ *n* [Jp] : cold rice shaped into small cakes and topped or wrapped with garnishes (as of raw fish)

[1]**sus·pect** \ˈsəs-ˌpekt, sə-ˈspekt\ *adj* : regarded with suspicion

[2]**sus·pect** \ˈsəs-ˌpekt\ *n* : one who is suspected (as of a crime)

[3]**sus·pect** \sə-ˈspekt\ *vb* **1** : to have doubts of : MISTRUST **2** : to imagine to be guilty without proof **3** : SURMISE

sus·pend \sə-ˈspend\ *vb* **1** : to bar temporarily from a privilege, office, or function **2** : to stop temporarily : make inactive for a time **3** : to withhold (judgment) for a time **4** : HANG; *esp* : to hang so as to be free except at one point; *also* : to keep from falling or sinking by some invisible support **syn** stay, postpone, defer

sus·pend·er \sə-ˈspen-dər\ *n* **1** : one of two supporting straps which pass over the shoulders and to which the trousers are fastened **2** *Brit* : a fastener attached to a garment or garter to hold up a stocking or sock

sus·pense \sə-ˈspens\ *n* **1** : SUSPENSION **2** : mental uncertainty : ANXIETY **3** : excitement as to an outcome — **sus·pense·ful** *adj*

sus·pen·sion \sə-ˈspen-chən\ *n* **1** : the act of suspending : the state or period of being suspended **2** : the state of a substance when its particles are mixed with but undissolved in a fluid or solid; *also* : a substance in this state **3** : something suspended **4** : a device by which something is suspended

sus·pen·so·ry \sə-ˈspens-(ə-)rē\ *adj* **1** : SUSPENDED; *also* : fitted or serving to suspend something **2** : temporarily leaving undetermined

sus·pi·cion \sə-ˈspish-ən\ *n* **1** : the act or an instance of suspecting something wrong without proof **2** : a slight trace **syn** mistrust, uncertainty, doubt, skepticism

sus·pi·cious \sə-ˈspish-əs\ *adj* **1** : open to or arousing suspicion **2** : inclined to suspect **3** : showing suspicion — **sus·pi·cious·ly** *adv*

sus·tain \sə-ˈstān\ *vb* **1** : to provide with nourishment **2** : to keep going : PROLONG ⟨~*ed* effort⟩ **3** : to hold up : PROP **4** : to hold up under : ENDURE **5** : SUFFER ⟨~ a broken arm⟩ **6** : to support as true, legal, or valid **7** : PROVE, CORROBORATE

sus·te·nance \ˈsəs-tə-nəns\ *n* **1** : FOOD, NOURISHMENT **2** : a supplying with the necessities of life **3** : something that sustains or supports

su·ture \ˈsü-chər\ *n* **1** : material or a stitch for sewing a wound together **2** : a seam or line along which two things or parts are joined by or as if by sewing ⟨the ~*s* of the skull⟩

su·zer·ain \ˈsüz-(ə-)rən, -ə-ˌrān\ *n* [F] **1** : a feudal lord **2** : a nation that has political control over another nation — **su·zer·ain·ty** \-tē\ *n*

svc *or* **svce** *abbr* service

svelte \ˈsfelt\ *adj* [F, fr. It *svelto*, fr. *svellere* to pluck out, modif. of L *evellere*, fr. *e-* out + *vellere* to pluck] : SLENDER, LITHE

svgs *abbr* savings

SW *abbr* **1** shortwave **2** southwest

[1]**swab** \ˈswäb\ *n* **1** : MOP **2** : a wad of absorbent material esp. for applying medicine or for cleaning; *also* : a sample taken with a swab **3** : SAILOR

[2]**swab** *vb* **swabbed; swab·bing** : to use a swab on : MOP

swad·dle \ˈswäd-ᵊl\ *vb* **swad·dled; swad·dling** \ˈswäd-(ᵊ-)liŋ\ **1** : to bind (an infant) in bands of cloth **2** : to wrap up : SWATHE

swaddling clothes *n pl* : bands of cloth wrapped around an infant

swag \ˈswag\ *n* : stolen goods : LOOT

swage \ˈswāj, ˈswej\ *n* : a tool used by metal workers for shaping their work — **swage** *vb*

swag·ger \ˈswag-ər\ *vb* **swag·gered; swag·ger·ing** \-(ə-)riŋ\ **1** : to walk with a conceited swing or strut **2** : BOAST, BRAG — **swagger** *n*

Swa·hi·li \swä-ˈhē-lē\ *n, pl* **Swahili** *or* **Swahilis** : a language that is a trade and governmental language over much of East Africa and the Congo region

swain \ˈswān\ *n* [ME *swein* boy, servant, fr. ON *sveinn*] **1** : RUSTIC; *esp* : SHEPHERD **2** : ADMIRER, SUITOR

[1]**swal·low** \ˈswäl-ō\ *n* : any of various small long-winged migratory birds that often have a deeply forked tail

[2]**swallow** *vb* **1** : to take into the stomach through the throat **2** : to envelop or take in as if by swallowing **3** : to accept or believe without question, protest, or anger

[3]**swallow** *n* **1** : an act of swallowing **2** : as much as can be swallowed at one time

swal·low·tail \ˈswäl-ō-ˌtāl\ *n* **1** : a deeply forked and tapering tail like that of a swallow **2** : TAILCOAT **3** : any of various large butterflies with the border of the hind wing drawn out into a process resembling a tail — **swal·low-tailed** \ˌswäl-ō-ˈtāld\ *adj*

swam *past of* SWIM

swa·mi \ˈswäm-ē\ *n* [Hindi *svāmī*, fr. Skt *svāmin* owner, lord] : a Hindu ascetic or religious teacher

[1]**swamp** \ˈswämp\ *n* : wet spongy land — **swamp** *adj* — **swampy** *adj*

[2]**swamp** *vb* **1** : to fill or become filled with or as if with water **2** : OVERWHELM 3

swamp·land \-ˌland\ *n* : SWAMP

swan \ˈswän\ *n, pl* **swans** *also* **swan** : any of several heavy-bodied long-necked mostly pure white swimming birds related to the geese

[1]**swank** \ˈswaŋk\ *or* **swanky** \ˈswaŋ-kē\ *adj* **swank·er** *or* **swank·i·er; -est** : showily smart and dashing; *also* : fashionably elegant

[2]**swank** *n* **1** : PRETENTIOUSNESS **2** : ELEGANCE

swans·down \ˈswänz-ˌdau̇n\ *n* **1** : the very soft down of a swan used esp. for trimming or powder puffs **2** : a soft thick cotton flannel

swan song *n* : a farewell appearance, act, or pronouncement

swap \ˈswäp\ *vb* **swapped; swap·ping** : TRADE, EXCHANGE — **swap** *n*

sward \ˈswȯrd\ *n* : the grassy surface of land

[1]**swarm** \ˈswȯrm\ *n* **1** : a great number of honeybees leaving together from a hive with a queen to start a new colony; *also* : a hive of bees **2** : a large crowd

[2]**swarm** *vb* **1** : to form in a swarm and depart from a hive **2** : to throng together : gather in great numbers

swart \ˈswȯrt\ *adj* : SWARTHY

swar·thy \ˈswȯr-t͟hē, -thē\ *adj* **swar·thi·er; -est** : dark in color or complexion : dark-skinned
swash \ˈswäsh\ *vb* : to move about with a splashing sound — **swash** *n*
swash·buck·ler \-ˌbək-lər\ *n* : a boasting blustering soldier or daredevil — **swash·buck·ling** \-ˌbək-(ə-)liŋ\ *adj*
swas·ti·ka \ˈswäs-ti-kə, swä-ˈstē-\ *n* [Skt *svastika,* fr. *svasti* welfare, fr. *su-* well + *asti* he is] : a symbol or ornament in the form of a cross with the ends of the arms bent at right angles
swat \ˈswät\ *vb* **swat·ted; swat·ting** : to hit sharply ⟨~ a fly⟩ ⟨~ a ball⟩ — **swat** *n* — **swat·ter** *n*
SWAT *abbr* Special Weapons and Tactics
swatch \ˈswäch\ *n* : a sample piece (as of fabric) or a collection of samples
swath \ˈswäth, ˈswȯth\ *or* **swathe** \ˈswät͟h, ˈswȯt͟h, ˈswāt͟h\ *n* [ME, fr. OE *swæth* footstep, trace] **1** : a row of cut grass or grain **2** : the sweep of a scythe or mowing machine or the path cut in mowing
swathe \ˈswät͟h, ˈswȯt͟h, ˈswāt͟h\ *vb* **swathed; swath·ing** : to bind or wrap with or as if with a bandage
[1]**sway** \ˈswā\ *n* **1** : a gentle swinging from side to side **2** : a controlling influence **3** : sovereign power : DOMINION
[2]**sway** *vb* **1** : to swing gently from side to side **2** : RULE, GOVERN **3** : to cause to swing from side to side **4** : BEND, SWERVE; *also* : INFLUENCE **syn** oscillate, fluctuate, vibrate, waver
sway·back \ˈswā-ˈbak, -ˌbak\ *n* : a sagging of the back found esp. in horses — **sway·backed** \-ˈbakt\ *adj*
swear \ˈswaər\ *vb* **swore** \ˈswōr\; **sworn** \ˈswōrn\; **swear·ing** **1** : to make a solemn statement or promise under oath : VOW **2** : to assert emphatically as true with an appeal to God or one's honor **3** : to administer an oath to **4** : to charge or confirm under oath; *also* : to bind by or as if by an oath **5** : to use profane or obscene language — **swear·er** *n*
swear in *vb* : to induct into office by administration of an oath
[1]**sweat** \ˈswet\ *vb* **sweat** *or* **sweat·ed; sweat·ing** **1** : to excrete salty moisture from glands of the skin : PERSPIRE **2** : to form drops of moisture on the surface **3** : to work so that one sweats : TOIL **4** : to cause to sweat **5** : to draw out or get rid of by perspiring **6** : to make a person overwork
[2]**sweat** *n* **1** : perceptible liquid exuded through pores from glands (**sweat glands**) of the skin : PERSPIRATION **2** : moisture issuing from or gathering on the surface in drops — **sweaty** *adj*
sweat·er \ˈswet-ər\ *n* **1** : one that sweats **2** : a knitted or crocheted jacket or pullover
sweat·shop \ˈswet-ˌshäp\ *n* : a shop or factory in which workers are employed for long hours at low wages and under unhealthy conditions
Swed *abbr* Sweden; Swedish
swede \ˈswēd\ *n* **1** *cap* : a native or inhabitant of Sweden **2** : RUTABAGA
Swed·ish \ˈswēd-ish\ *n* **1** : the language of Sweden **2** **Swedish** *pl* : the people of Sweden — **Swedish** *adj*
[1]**sweep** \ˈswēp\ *vb* **swept** \ˈswept\; **sweep·ing** **1** : to remove or clean by brushing **2** : to remove or destroy by vigorous continuous action **3** : to strip or clear by gusts of wind or rain **4** : to move over with speed and force ⟨the tide *swept* over the shore⟩ **5** : to gather in with a single swift movement **6** : to move or extend in a wide curve — **sweep·er** *n* — **sweep·ing** *adj*
[2]**sweep** *n* **1** : something (as a long oar) that operates with a sweeping motion **2** : a clearing off or away **3** : a winning of all the contests or prizes in a competition **4** : a sweeping movement ⟨~ of a scythe⟩ **5** : CURVE, BEND **6** : RANGE, SCOPE
sweep·ing *n* **1** : the act or action of one that sweeps **2** *pl* : things collected by sweeping : REFUSE
sweep–sec·ond \ˈswēp-ˌsek-ənd\ *n* : a hand marking seconds on a timepiece
sweep·stakes \ˈswēp-ˌstāks\ *also* **sweep·stake** \-ˌstāk\ *n, pl* **sweepstakes** **1** : a race or contest in which the entire prize may go to the winner; *esp* : a horse race in which the stakes are contributed at least in part by the owners of the horses **2** : any of various lotteries
[1]**sweet** \ˈswēt\ *adj* **1** : being or causing the one of the four basic taste sensations that is caused esp. by table sugar and is identified esp. by the taste buds at the front of the tongue; *also* : pleasing to the taste **2** : KINDLY, MILD **3** : pleasing to a sense other than taste ⟨a ~ smell⟩ ⟨~ music⟩ **4** : not stale or spoiled : WHOLESOME ⟨~ milk⟩ **5** : not salted ⟨~ butter⟩ — **sweet·ish** *adj* — **sweet·ly** *adv* — **sweet·ness** *n*
[2]**sweet** *n* **1** : something sweet : CANDY **2** : DARLING
sweet·bread \ˈswēt-ˌbred\ *n* : the pancreas or thymus of an animal (as a calf or lamb) used for food
sweet·bri·er *also* **sweet·bri·ar** \-ˌbrī(-ə)r\ *n* : a thorny European rose with fragrant white to deep pink flowers
sweet clover *n* : any of a genus of erect legumes widely grown for soil improvement or hay
sweet corn *n* : an Indian corn with kernels rich in sugar and cooked as a vegetable while immature
sweet·en \ˈswēt-ᵊn\ *vb* **sweet·ened; sweet·en·ing** \ˈswēt-(ᵊ-)niŋ\ : to make sweet — **sweet·en·er** \ˈswēt-(ᵊ-)nər\ *n* — **sweet·en·ing** *n*
sweet fern *n* : a small No. American shrub with sweet-scented or aromatic leaves
sweet·heart \ˈswēt-ˌhärt\ *n* : one who is loved
sweet·meat \ˈswēt-ˌmēt\ *n* : CANDY
sweet pea *n* : a garden plant of the legume family with climbing stems and fragrant flowers of many colors; *also* : its flower
sweet pepper *n* : a large mild thick-walled fruit of a pepper; *also* : a plant related to the potato that bears sweet peppers
sweet potato *n* : a tropical vine related to the morning glory; *also* : its sweet yellow edible root
sweet–talk \ˈswēt-ˌtȯk\ *vb* : FLATTER, COAX — **sweet talk** *n*
sweet tooth *n* : a craving or fondness for sweet food
sweet wil·liam \swēt-ˈwil-yəm\ *n, often cap W* : a widely cultivated Eurasian pink with small white to deep red or purple flowers often showily spotted, banded, or mottled
[1]**swell** \ˈswel\ *vb* **swelled; swelled** *or* **swol·len** \ˈswō-lən\; **swell·ing** **1** : to grow big or make bigger **2** : to expand or distend abnormally or excessively ⟨a *swollen* joint⟩; *also* : BULGE **3** : to fill or be filled with emotion (as pride) **syn** expand, amplify, distend, inflate, dilate — **swell·ing** *n*
[2]**swell** *n* **1** : a long crestless wave or series of waves in the open sea **2** : sudden or gradual increase in size or value **3** : a person dressed in the height of fashion; *also* : a person of high social position or outstanding competence
[3]**swell** *adj* **1** : FASHIONABLE, STYLISH; *also* : socially prominent **2** : EXCELLENT, FIRST-RATE
swelled head *n* : an exaggerated opinion of oneself : SELF-CONCEIT
swell·head \ˈswel-ˌhed\ *n* : one who has a swelled head — **swell·head·ed** \-ˈhed-əd\ *adj*
swel·ter \ˈswel-tər\ *vb* **swel·tered; swel·ter·ing** \-t(ə-)riŋ\ [ME *sweltren,* fr. *swelten* to die, be overcome by heat, fr. OE *sweltan* to die] : to be faint or oppressed with the heat
swept *past and past part of* SWEEP
swerve \ˈswərv\ *vb* **swerved; swerv·ing** : to move abruptly

---

\ə\abut \ᵊ\kitten \ər\further \a\ash \ā\ace \ä\cot, cart \au̇\out \ch\chin \e\bet \ē\easy \g\go \i\hit \ī\ice \j\job \ŋ\sing \ō\go \ȯ\law \ȯi\boy \th\thin \t͟h\the \ü\loot \u̇\foot \y\yet \zh\vision *see also* Pronunciation Symbols page

aside from a straight line or course **syn** digress, deviate, diverge — **swerve** *n*

[1]**swift** \ˈswift\ *adj* **1** : moving or capable of moving with great speed **2** : occurring suddenly **3** : READY, ALERT — **swift·ly** *adv* — **swift·ness** \ˈswif(t)-nəs\ *n*

[2]**swift** *n* : any of numerous small insect-eating birds with long narrow wings

swig \ˈswig\ *vb* **swigged; swig·ging** : to drink in long drafts — **swig** *n*

[1]**swill** \ˈswil\ *vb* **1** : to swallow greedily : GUZZLE **2** : to feed (as hogs) on swill

[2]**swill** *n* **1** : food for animals composed of edible refuse mixed with liquid **2** : GARBAGE

[1]**swim** \ˈswim\ *vb* **swam** \ˈswam\; **swum** \ˈswəm\; **swim·ming 1** : to propel oneself along in water by natural means (as by hands and legs, by tail, or by fins) **2** : to glide smoothly along **3** : FLOAT **4** : to be covered with or as if with a liquid **5** : to be dizzy ⟨his head *swam*⟩ **6** : to cross or go over by swimming — **swim·mer** *n*

[2]**swim** *n* **1** : an act of swimming **2** : the main current of activity or fashion ⟨in the social ~⟩

swim·ming \ˈswim-iŋ\ *n* : the action, art, or sport of swimming and diving

swimming pool *n* : a tank of concrete or plastic designed for swimming

swim·suit \ˈswim-ˌsüt\ *n* : a suit for swimming or bathing

swin·dle \ˈswin-dᵊl\ *vb* **swin·dled; swin·dling** \-(d)liŋ, -dᵊl-iŋ\ [fr. *swindler,* fr. G *schwindler* giddy person, fr. *schwindeln* to be dizzy] : CHEAT, DEFRAUD — **swindle** *n* — **swin·dler** \-d(ᵊ-)lər\ *n*

swine \ˈswīn\ *n, pl* **swine 1** : any of a family of stout short-legged hoofed mammals with bristly skin and a long flexible snout; *esp* : one widely raised as a meat animal **2** : a contemptible person — **swin·ish** \ˈswī-nish\ *adj*

[1]**swing** \ˈswiŋ\ *vb* **swung** \ˈswəŋ\; **swing·ing** \ˈswiŋ-iŋ\ **1** : to move rapidly in an arc **2** : to sway or cause to sway back and forth **3** : to hang so as to move freely back and forth or in a curve **4** : to be executed by hanging **5** : to move or turn on a hinge or pivot **6** : to manage or handle successfully **7** : to march or walk with free swaying movements **8** : to have a steady pulsing rhythm **9** : to be lively and up-to-date; *also* : to engage freely in sex **syn** wield, manipulate, ply, maneuver — **swing·er** *n* — **swing·ing** *adj*

[2]**swing** *n* **1** : the act of swinging **2** : a swinging blow, movement, or rhythm **3** : the distance through which something swings : FLUCTUATION **4** : a seat suspended by a rope or chain for swinging back and forth for pleasure **5** : jazz music played esp. by a large band and marked by a steady lively rhythm, simple harmony, and a basic melody often submerged in improvisation — **swing** *adj*

swing–by \ˈswiŋ-ˌbī\ *n, pl* **swing–bys** : an interplanetary mission in which a spacecraft uses the gravitational field of a planet near which it passes for changing course

[1]**swipe** \ˈswīp\ *vb* **swiped; swip·ing 1** : to strike or wipe with a sweeping motion **2** : PILFER, SNATCH

[2]**swipe** *n* : a strong sweeping blow

swirl \ˈswərl\ *vb* : EDDY — **swirl** *n*

swish \ˈswish\ *n* **1** : a prolonged hissing sound **2** : a light sweeping or brushing sound — **swish** *vb*

Swiss \ˈswis\ *n* **1** *pl* **Swiss** : a native or inhabitant of Switzerland **2** : a hard cheese with large holes

Swiss chard *n* : CHARD

[1]**switch** \ˈswich\ *n* **1** : a slender flexible whip, rod, or twig **2** : a blow with a switch **3** : a shift from one thing to another **4** : a device for adjusting the rails of a track so that a locomotive or train may be turned from one track to another; *also* : a railroad siding **5** : a device for making, breaking, or changing the connections in an electrical circuit **6** : a heavy strand of hair often used in addition to a person's own hair for some coiffures

[2]**switch** *vb* **1** : to punish or urge on with a switch **2** : WHISK ⟨a cow ~*ing* her tail⟩ **3** : to shift or turn by operating a switch **4** : CHANGE, EXCHANGE

switch·back \ˈswich-ˌbak\ *n* : a zig-zag road or arrangement of railroad tracks for climbing a steep grade

switch·blade \-ˌblād\ *n* : a pocket-knife with a spring-operated blade

switch·board \-ˌbōrd\ *n* : a panel on which is mounted a group of electric switches so arranged that a number of circuits may be connected, combined, and controlled

switch–hit·ter \-ˈhit-ər\ *n* : a baseball player who bats either right-handed or left-handed — **switch–hit** \-ˈhit\ *vb*

switch·man \ˈswich-mən\ *n* : one who attends a railroad switch

Switz *abbr* Switzerland

[1]**swiv·el** \ˈswiv-əl\ *n* : a device joining two parts so that one or both can turn freely

[2]**swivel** *vb* **-eled** *or* **-elled; -el·ing** *or* **-el·ling** \-(ə-)liŋ\ : to swing or turn on or as if on a swivel

swiz·zle stick \ˈswiz-əl-\ *n* : a stick used to stir mixed drinks

swollen *past part of* SWELL

swoon \ˈswün\ *vb* : FAINT — **swoon** *n*

swoop \ˈswüp\ *vb* : to descend or pounce swiftly like a hawk on its prey — **swoop** *n*

sword \ˈsōrd\ *n* **1** : a weapon with a long pointed blade and sharp cutting edges **2** : the use of force

sword·fish \-ˌfish\ *n* : a very large ocean food fish with the bones of the upper jaw prolonged in a long swordlike beak

swordfish

sword·play \-ˌplā\ *n* : the art or skill of wielding a sword

swords·man \ˈsōrdz-mən\ *n* : one skilled in wielding a sword; *esp* : FENCER

sword·tail \ˈsōrd-ˌtāl\ *n* : a small brightly marked Central American fish

swore *past of* SWEAR

sworn *past part of* SWEAR

swum *past part of* SWIM

swung *past and past part of* SWING

syb·a·rite \ˈsib-ə-ˌrīt\ *n* : a lover of luxury : VOLUPTUARY

syc·a·more \ˈsik-ə-ˌmōr\ *n* **1** : a Eurasian maple with yellowish green flowers widely planted as a shade tree **2** : a large spreading tree of eastern and central No. America that has light brown flaky bark and small round fruits hanging on long stalks

sy·co·phant \ˈsik-ə-fənt\ *n* : a servile flatterer — **syc·o·phan·tic** \ˌsik-ə-ˈfant-ik\ *adj*

syl *or* **syll** *abbr* syllable

sy·li \ˈsē-lē\ *n, pl* **sylis** — see MONEY table

syl·lab·i·ca·tion \sə-ˌlab-ə-ˈkā-shən\ *n* : the dividing of words into syllables

syl·lab·i·fy \sə-ˈlab-ə-ˌfī\ *vb* **-fied; -fy·ing** : to form or divide into syllables — **syl·lab·i·fi·ca·tion** \-ˌlab-ə-fə-ˈkā-shən\ *n*

syl·la·ble \ˈsil-ə-bəl\ *n* [ME, fr. MF *sillabe,* fr. L *syllaba,* fr. Gk *syllabē,* fr. *syllambanein* to gather together, fr. *syn* with + *lambanein* to take] : a unit of spoken language consisting of an uninterrupted utterance and forming either a whole word (as *cat*) or a commonly recognized division of a word (as *syl* in *syl-la-ble*); *also*

: one or more letters representing such a unit — **syl·lab·ic** \sə-ˈlab-ik\ *adj*

syl·la·bus \ˈsil-ə-bəs\ *n, pl* **-bi** \-ˌbī\ *or* **-bus·es** : a summary containing the heads or main topics of a speech, book, or course of study

syl·lo·gism \ˈsil-ə-ˌjiz-əm\ *n* : a logical scheme of a formal argument consisting of a major and a minor premise and a conclusion which must logically be true if the premises are true — **syl·lo·gis·tic** \ˌsil-ə-ˈjis-tik\ *adj*

sylph \ˈsilf\ *n* **1** : an imaginary being inhabiting the air **2** : a slender graceful woman

syl·van \ˈsil-vən\ *adj* **1** : living or located in a wooded area; *also* : of, relating to, or characteristic of forest **2** : abounding in woods or trees : WOODED

sym *abbr* **1** symbol **2** symmetrical

sym·bi·o·sis \ˌsim-ˌbī-ˈō-səs, -bē-\ *n, pl* **-o·ses** \-ˌsēz\ : the living together in close association of two dissimilar organisms esp. when mutually beneficial — **sym·bi·ot·ic** \-ˈät-ik\ *adj*

sym·bol \ˈsim-bəl\ *n* **1** : something that stands for something else; *esp* : something concrete that represents or suggests another thing that cannot in itself be pictured ⟨the lion is a ~ of bravery⟩ **2** : a letter, character, or sign used in writing or printing relating to a particular field (as mathematics or music) to represent operations, quantities, elements, sounds, or other ideas — **sym·bol·ic** \sim-ˈbäl-ik\ *also* **sym·bol·i·cal** \-i-kəl\ *adj* — **sym·bol·i·cal·ly** \-k(ə-)lē\ *adv*

sym·bol·ism \ˈsim-bə-ˌliz-əm\ *n* : representation of abstract or intangible things by means of symbols or emblems

sym·bol·ize \ˈsim-bə-ˌlīz\ *vb* **-ized; -iz·ing 1** : to serve as a symbol of **2** : to represent by symbols — **sym·bol·iza·tion** \ˌsim-bə-lə-ˈzā-shən\ *n*

sym·me·try \ˈsim-ə-trē\ *n, pl* **-tries 1** : an arrangement marked by regularity and balanced proportions **2** : correspondence in size, shape, and position of parts that are on opposite sides of a dividing line or center **syn** proportion, balance, harmony — **sym·met·ri·cal** \sə-ˈme-tri-kəl\ *or* **sym·met·ric** \sə-ˈme-trik\ *adj* — **sym·met·ri·cal·ly** \-k(ə-)lē\ *adv*

sympathetic nervous system *n* : the part of the autonomic nervous system that is concerned esp. with preparing the body to react to situations of stress or emergency and that tends to depress secretion, decrease the tone and contractility of muscle not under direct voluntary control, and cause the contraction of blood vessels

sym·pa·thize \ˈsim-pə-ˌthīz\ *vb* **-thized; -thiz·ing** : to feel or show sympathy — **sym·pa·thiz·er** *n*

sym·pa·thy \ˈsim-pə-thē\ *n, pl* **-thies 1** : a relationship between persons or things wherein whatever affects one similarly affects the others **2** : harmony of interests and aims **3** : FAVOR, SUPPORT **4** : the capacity for entering into and sharing the feelings or interests of another; *also* : COMPASSION, PITY **5** : an expression of sorrow for another's loss, grief, or misfortune — **sym·pa·thet·ic** \ˌsim-pə-ˈthet-ik\ *adj* — **sym·pa·thet·i·cal·ly** \-i-k(ə-)lē\ *adv*

sym·pho·ny \ˈsim-fə-nē\ *n, pl* **-nies 1** : harmony of sounds **2** : a large and complex composition for a full orchestra **3** : a large orchestra of a kind that plays symphonies — **sym·phon·ic** \sim-ˈfän-ik\ *adj*

sym·po·sium \sim-ˈpō-zē-əm\ *n, pl* **-sia** \-zē-ə\ *or* **-siums** [L, fr. Gk *symposion*, fr. *sympinein* to drink together, fr. *syn-* together + *pinein* to drink] : a conference at which a particular topic is discussed by various speakers; *also* : a collection of opinions about a subject

symp·tom \ˈsimp-təm\ *n* **1** : a change in an organism indicative of disease or abnormality; *esp* : one (as a headache) that can be sensed only by the individual affected **2** : SIGN, INDICATION — **symp·tom·at·ic** \ˌsimp-tə-ˈmat-ik\ *adj*

syn *abbr* synonym; synonymous; synonymy

syn·a·gogue *or* **syn·a·gog** \ˈsin-ə-ˌgäg\ *n* [ME *synagoge*, fr. OF, fr. LL *synagoga*, fr. Gk *synagōgē* assembly, synagogue, fr. *synagein* to bring together] **1** : a Jewish congregation **2** : the house of worship of a Jewish congregation

syn·apse \ˈsin-ˌaps, sə-ˈnaps\ *n* : the point at which a nervous impulse passes from one neuron to another

[1]**sync** *also* **synch** \ˈsiŋk\ *vb* **synced** *also* **synched** \ˈsiŋkt\; **sync·ing** *also* **synch·ing** \ˈsiŋ-kiŋ\ : SYNCHRONIZE

[2]**sync** *also* **synch** *n* : SYNCHRONIZATION, SYNCHRONISM — **sync** *adj*

syn·chro·mesh \ˈsiŋ-krō-ˌmesh, ˈsin-\ *adj* : designed for effecting synchronized shifting of gears — **synchromesh** *n*

syn·chro·nize \ˈsiŋ-krə-ˌnīz, ˈsin-\ *vb* **-nized; -niz·ing 1** : to occur or cause to occur at the same instant **2** : to represent, arrange, or tabulate according to dates or time **3** : to cause to agree in time **4** : to make synchronous in operation — **syn·chro·nism** \-ˌniz-əm\ *n* — **syn·chro·ni·za·tion** \ˌsiŋ-krə-nə-ˈzā-shən, ˌsin-\ *n* — **syn·chro·niz·er** \ˈsiŋ-krə-ˌnī-zər, ˈsin-\ *n*

syn·chro·nous \ˈsiŋ-krə-nəs, ˈsin-\ *adj* **1** : happening at the same time : CONCURRENT **2** : working, moving, or occurring together at the same rate and at the proper time

syn·co·pa·tion \ˌsiŋ-kə-ˈpā-shən, ˌsin-\ *n* : a shifting of the regular musical accent : occurrence of accented notes on the weak beat — **syn·co·pate** \ˈsiŋ-kə-ˌpāt, ˈsin-\ *vb*

syn·co·pe \ˈsiŋ-kə-(ˌ)pē, ˈsin-\ *n* : the loss of one or more sounds or letters in the interior of a word (as in *fo'c'sle* from *forecastle*)

[1]**syn·di·cate** \ˈsin-di-kət\ *n* **1** : a group of persons who combine to carry out a financial or industrial undertaking **2** : a business concern that sells materials for publication in many newspapers and periodicals at the same time

[2]**syn·di·cate** \-də-ˌkāt\ *vb* **-cat·ed; -cat·ing 1** : to combine into or manage as a syndicate **2** : to publish through a syndicate — **syn·di·ca·tion** \ˌsin-də-ˈkā-shən\ *n*

syn·drome \ˈsin-ˌdrōm\ *n* : a group of signs and symptoms that occur together and characterize a particular abnormality

syn·er·gism \ˈsin-ər-ˌjiz-əm\ *n* : interaction of discrete agencies (as industrial firms) or agents (as drugs) such that the total effect is greater than the sum of the individual effects — **syn·er·gist** \-jəst\ *n* — **syn·er·gis·tic** \-ˈjis-tik\ *adj* — **syn·er·gis·ti·cal·ly** \-ti-k(ə-)lē\ *adv*

syn·fuel \ˈsin-ˌfyül\ *n* [*syn*thetic] : a fuel derived from a fossil fuel or from fermentation (as of grain)

syn·od \ˈsin-əd\ *n* : COUNCIL, ASSEMBLY; *esp* : a religious governing body — **syn·od·al** \-əd-ᵊl, -ˌäd-ᵊl\ *adj* **syn·od·ic** \-ik\ *or* **syn·od·i·cal** \sə-ˈnäd-i-kəl\ *adj*

syn·onym \ˈsin-ə-ˌnim\ *n* : one of two or more words in the same language which have the same or very nearly the same meaning — **syn·on·y·mous** \sə-ˈnän-ə-məs\ *adj* — **syn·on·y·my** \-mē\ *n*

syn·op·sis \sə-ˈnäp-səs\ *n, pl* **-op·ses** \-ˌsēz\ : a condensed statement or outline (as of a treatise) : ABSTRACT

syn·op·tic \sə-ˈnäp-tik\ *also* **syn·op·ti·cal** \-ti-kəl\ *adj* : characterized by or affording a comprehensive view

syn·tax \ˈsin-ˌtaks\ *n* : the way in which words are put together to form phrases, clauses, or sentences — **syn·tac·tic** \sin-ˈtak-tik\ *or* **syn·tac·ti·cal** \-ti-kəl\ *adj*

syn·the·sis \ˈsin-thə-səs\ *n, pl* **-the·ses** \-ˌsēz\ : the combination of parts or elements into a whole; *esp* : the production of a substance by union of chemically simpler substances — **syn·the·size** \-ˌsīz\ *vb* — **syn·the·siz·er** *n*

syn·thet·ic \sin-ˈthet-ik\ *adj* : produced artificially esp. by chemical means; *also* : not genuine — **synthetic** *n* — **syn·thet·i·cal·ly** \-i-k(ə-)lē\ *adv*

syph·i·lis \ˈsif-(ə-)ləs\ *n* [NL, fr. poem *Syphilis sive Morbus Gallicus* (*Syphilis or the French disease*) (1530) by Girolamo Fracastoro †1553 Ital. physician] : a destructive contagious usu. venereal disease caused by a spirochete — **syph·i·lit·ic** \ˌsif-ə-ˈlit-ik\ *adj or n*

sy·phon *var of* SIPHON

[1]**sy·ringe** \sə-ˈrinj, ˈsir-inj\ *n* : a device used esp. for injecting liquids into or withdrawing them from the body

[2]**syringe** *vb* **sy·ringed; sy·ring·ing** : to inject or cleanse with or as if with a syringe

syr·up \ˈsər-əp, ˈsir-əp\ *n* **1** : a thick sticky solution of sugar and water often flavored or medicated **2** : the concentrated juice of a fruit or plant — **syr·upy** *adj*

syst *abbr* system

sys·tem \ˈsis-təm\ *n* **1** : a group of units so combined as to form a whole and to operate in unison **2** : the body as a functioning whole; *also* : a group of bodily organs (as the nervous system) that together carry on some vital function **3** : a definite scheme or method of procedure or classification **4** : regular method or order — **sys·tem·at·ic** \ˌsis-tə-ˈmat-ik\ *also* **sys·tem·at·i·cal** \-i-kəl\ *adj* — **sys·tem·at·i·cal·ly** \-k(ə-)lē\ *adv*

sys·tem·atize \ˈsis-tə-mə-ˌtīz\ *vb* **-atized; -atiz·ing** : to make into a system : arrange methodically

[1]**sys·tem·ic** \sis-ˈtem-ik\ *adj* **1** : of, relating to, or affecting the whole body ⟨~ disease⟩ **2** : acting through the bodily systems after absorption or ingestion by making the organism toxic to a pest (as a mite or insect)

[2]**systemic** *n* : a systemic pesticide

systemic lupus erythematosus *n* : a disease characterized by fever, skin rash, and arthritis, often by anemia, by small hemorrhages of the skin and mucous membranes, and in serious cases by involvement of various internal organs

sys·tem·ize \ˈsis-tə-ˌmīz\ *vb* **-ized; -iz·ing** : SYSTEMATIZE

systems analyst *n* : a person who studies a procedure or business to determine its goals or purposes and to discover the best ways to accomplish them — **systems analysis** *n*

sys·to·le \ˈsis-tə-(ˌ)lē\ *n* : a rhythmically recurrent contraction esp. of the heart — **sys·tol·ic** \sis-ˈtäl-ik\ *adj*

Szech·uan *or* **Szech·wan** \ˈsech-ˌwän\ *adj* : of, relating to, or being a style of Chinese cooking that is spicy, oily, and esp. peppery

T

[1]**t** \ˈtē\ *n, pl* **t's** *or* **ts** \ˈtēz\ *often cap* : the 20th letter of the English alphabet

[2]**t** *abbr, often cap* **1** tablespoon **2** teaspoon **3** temperature **4** ton **5** transitive **6** troy **7** true

Ta *symbol* tantalum

TA *abbr* teaching assistant

[1]**tab** \ˈtab\ *n* **1** : a short projecting flap, loop, or tag; *also* : a small insert or addition **2** : close surveillance : WATCH ⟨keep ~*s* on him⟩ **3** : BILL, CHECK

[2]**tab** *vb* **tabbed; tab·bing** : DESIGNATE

tab·bou·leh \tə-ˈbü-lə\ *n* [Ar] : a salad consisting chiefly of wheat, tomatoes, parsley, mint, onions, lemon juice, and olive oil

tab·by \ˈtab-ē\ *n, pl* **tabbies** : a usu. striped or mottled domestic cat; *also* : a female domestic cat

tab·er·na·cle \ˈtab-ər-ˌnak-əl\ *n* [deriv. of L *taberna* hut] **1** *often cap* : a tent sanctuary used by the Israelites during the Exodus **2** : a receptacle for the consecrated elements of the Eucharist **3** : a house of worship

[1]**ta·ble** \ˈtā-bəl\ *n* **1** : a flat slab or plaque : TABLET **2** : a piece of furniture consisting of a smooth flat slab fixed on legs **3** : a supply of food : BOARD, FARE **4** : a group of people assembled at or as if at a table **5** : a systematic arrangement of data for ready reference **6** : a condensed enumeration — **ta·ble·top** \-ˌtäp\ *n*

[2]**table** *vb* **ta·bled; ta·bling** \-b(ə-)liŋ\ **1** *Brit* : to place on the agenda **2** : to remove (a parliamentary motion) from consideration indefinitely

tab·leau \ˈtab-ˌlō\ *n, pl* **tab·leaux** \-ˌlōz\ *also* **tableaus** [F] **1** : a graphic description : PICTURE **2** : a striking or artistic grouping **3** : a static depiction of a scene usu. presented on a stage by costumed participants

ta·ble·cloth \ˈtā-bəl-ˌklȯth\ *n* : a covering spread over a dining table before the table is set

ta·ble d'hôte \ˌtäb-əl-ˈdōt\ *n* [F, lit., host's table] : a complete meal of several courses offered at a fixed price

ta·ble·land \ˈtā-bəl-ˌ(l)and\ *n* : PLATEAU

ta·ble·spoon \-ˌspün\ *n* **1** : a large spoon used esp. for serving **2** : TABLESPOONFUL

ta·ble·spoon·ful \ˈtā-bəl-ˌspün-ˌfu̇l\ *n, pl* **-spoonfuls** \-ˌfu̇lz\ *also* **-spoons·ful** \-ˌspünz-fu̇l\ : a unit of measure equal to one half fluidounce

tab·let \ˈtab-lət\ *n* **1** : a flat slab suited for or bearing an inscription **2** : a collection of sheets of paper glued together at one edge **3** : a compressed or molded block of material; *esp* : a usu. disk-shaped medicated mass

table tennis *n* : a game resembling tennis played on a tabletop with wooden paddles and a small hollow plastic ball

ta·ble·ware \ˈtā-bəl-ˌwaər\ *n* : utensils (as of china or silver) for table use

[1]**tab·loid** \ˈtab-ˌlȯid\ *adj* : condensed into small scope

[2]**tabloid** *n* : a newspaper marked by small pages, condensation of the news, and usu. many photographs; *esp* : one characterized by sensationalism

[1]**ta·boo** *also* **ta·bu** \tə-ˈbü, ta-\ *adj* [fr. Tongan, a Polynesian language] **1** : set apart as charged with a dangerous supernatural power : INVIOLABLE **2** : banned esp. as immoral or dangerous

[2]**taboo** *also* **tabu** *n, pl* **taboos** *also* **tabus** **1** : a prohibition against touching, saying, or doing something for fear of immediate harm from a mysterious superhuman force **2** : a prohibition imposed by social usage or as a protection

ta·bor *also* **ta·bour** \ˈtā-bər\ *n* : a small drum used to accompany a pipe or fife played by the same person

tab·u·lar \ˈtab-yə-lər\ *adj* **1** : having a flat surface **2** : arranged in a table; *esp* : set up in rows and columns **3** : computed by means of a table

tab·u·late \-ˌlāt\ *vb* **-lat·ed; -lat·ing** : to put into tabular form — **tab·u·la·tion** \ˌtab-yə-ˈlā-shən\ *n* — **tab·u·la·tor** \ˈtab-yə-ˌlāt-ər\ *n*

TAC \ˈtak\ *abbr* Tactical Air Command

tach \ˈtak\ *n* : TACHOMETER

ta·chom·e·ter \ta-ˈkäm-ət-ər, tə-\ *n* [deriv. of Gk *tachys* rapid] : a device to indicate speed of rotation

tachy·car·dia \ˌtak-i-ˈkärd-ē-ə\ *n* : rapid heart action

tachy·on \ˈtak-ē-ˌän\ *n* : a hypothetical particle held to travel faster than light

tac·it \ˈtas-ət\ *adj* [F or L; F *tacite*, fr. L *tacitus* silent, fr. *tacēre* to be silent] **1** : expressed without words or speech **2** : implied or indicated but not actually expressed ⟨~ consent⟩ — **tac·it·ly** *adv* — **tac·it·ness** *n*

tac·i·turn \ˈtas-ə-ˌtərn\ *adj* : disinclined to talk : habitually silent **syn** uncommunicative, reserved, reticent, closemouthed — **tac·i·tur·ni·ty** \ˌtas-ə-ˈtər-nət-ē\ *n*

[1]**tack** \ˈtak\ *vb* **1** : to fasten with tacks; *also* : to add on **2** : to change the direction of (a sailing ship) from one tack to another **3** : to follow a zigzag course

[2]**tack** *n* **1** : a small sharp nail with a broad flat head **2** : the direction a ship is sailing as shown by the way the sails are trimmed; *also* : the run of a ship on one tack **3** : a change of course from one tack to another **4** : a zigzag course **5** : a course of action

[3]**tack** *n* : gear for harnessing a horse

[1]**tack·le** \ˈtak-əl, *naut often* ˈtāk-\ *n* **1** : GEAR, APPARATUS, EQUIPMENT **2** : the rigging of a ship **3** : an arrangement of ropes and pulleys for hoisting or pulling heavy objects **4** : the act or an instance of tackling; *also* : a football lineman playing between guard and end

[2]**tackle** *vb* **tack·led; tack·ling** \-(ə-)liŋ\ **1** : to attach and secure with or as if with tackle **2** : to seize, grapple with, or throw down with the intention of subduing or stopping **3** : to set about dealing with ⟨~ a problem⟩

[1]**tacky** \ˈtak-ē\ *adj* **tack·i·er; -est** : sticky to the touch

[2]**tacky** *adj* **tack·i·er; -est** **1** : SHABBY, SEEDY **2** : marked by lack of style or good taste; *also* : cheaply showy : GAUDY

ta·co \ˈtäk-ō\ *n, pl* **tacos** \-ōz, -ōs\ [MexSp] : a tortilla rolled up with or folded over a filling

tact \ˈtakt\ *n* [F, sense of touch, fr. L *tactus*, fr. *tactus*, pp. of *tangere* to touch] : a keen sense of what to do or say to keep good relations with others — **tact·ful** \-fəl\ *adj* — **tact·ful·ly** \-ē\ *adv* — **tact·less** *adj* — **tact·less·ly** *adv*

tac·tic \ˈtak-tik\ *n* : a planned action for accomplishing an end

tac·tics \ˈtak-tiks\ *n sing or pl* **1** : the science of maneuvering forces in combat **2** : the skill of using available means to reach an end — **tac·ti·cal** \-ti-kəl\ *adj* — **tac·ti·cian** \tak-ˈtish-ən\ *n*

tac·tile \ˈtak-tᵊl, -ˌtīl\ *adj* : of, relating to, or perceptible through the sense of touch

tad·pole \ˈtad-ˌpōl\ *n* [ME *taddepol*, fr. *tode* toad + *polle* head] : an aquatic larva of a frog or toad that has a tail and gills

tae kwon do \ˈtī-ˈkwän-ˈdō\ *n* : a Korean martial art resembling karate

taf·fe·ta \ˈtaf-ət-ə\ *n* : a crisp lustrous fabric (as of silk or rayon)

taff·rail \ˈtaf-ˌrāl, -rəl\ *n* : the rail around a ship's stern

taf·fy \ˈtaf-ē\ *n, pl* **taffies** : a candy usu. of molasses or brown sugar stretched until porous and light-colored

[1]**tag** \ˈtag\ *n* **1** : a metal or plastic binding on an end of a shoelace **2** : a piece of hanging or attached material **3** : a hackneyed quotation or saying **4** : a descriptive or identifying epithet

[2]**tag** *vb* **tagged; tag·ging** **1** : to provide or mark with or as if with a tag; *esp* : IDENTIFY **2** : to attach as an addition **3** : to follow closely and persistently ⟨~*s* along everywhere we go⟩ **4** : to hold responsible for something

[3]**tag** *n* : a game in which one player chases others and tries to touch one of them

[4]**tag** *vb* **tagged; tag·ging** **1** : to touch in or as if in a game of tag **2** : SELECT

TAG *abbr* the adjutant general

tag sale *n* : GARAGE SALE

Ta·hi·tian \tə-ˈhē-shən\ *n* **1** : a native or inhabitant of Tahiti **2** : the Polynesian language of the Tahitians — **Tahitian** *adj*

tai·ga \ˈtī-gä\ *n* [Russ] : swampy coniferous northern forest (as of parts of Canada) beginning where the tundra ends

[1]**tail** \ˈtāl\ *n* **1** : the rear end or a process extending from the rear end of an animal **2** : something resembling an animal's tail **3** *pl* : full evening dress for men **4** : the back, last, lower, or inferior part of something; *esp* : the reverse of a coin **5** : one who follows or keeps watch on someone — **tailed** \ˈtāld\ *adj* — **tail·less** \ˈtāl-ləs\ *adj*

[2]**tail** *vb* : FOLLOW; *esp* : to follow for the purpose of surveillance **syn** dog, shadow, trail, tag

tail·coat \-ˈkōt\ *n* : a coat with tails; *esp* : a man's full-dress coat with two long tapering skirts at the back

[1]**tail·gate** \-ˌgāt\ *n* : a board or gate at the back end of a vehicle that can be let down (as for loading)

[2]**tailgate** *adj* : relating to or being a picnic set up on the tailgate esp. of a station wagon

[3]**tailgate** *vb* **tail·gat·ed; tail·gat·ing** : to drive dangerously close behind another vehicle

tail·light \-ˌlīt\ *n* : a usu. red warning light mounted at the rear of a vehicle

[1]**tai·lor** \ˈtā-lər\ *n* [ME *taillour*, fr. OF *tailleur*, fr. *taillier* to cut, fr. LL *taliare*, fr. L *talea* twig, cutting] : one whose occupation is making or altering garments

[2]**tailor** *vb* **1** : to make or fashion as the work of a tailor **2** : to make or adapt to suit a special purpose

tail pipe *n* : an outlet by which the exhaust gases are removed from an engine

tail·spin \ˈtāl-ˌspin\ *n* : a rapid descent or downward spiral

tail wind *n* : a wind blowing in the same general direction as the course of a moving airplane or ship

[1]**taint** \ˈtānt\ *vb* **1** : to affect or become affected with something bad and esp. putrefaction **2** : CORRUPT, CONTAMINATE **syn** pollute, defile, soil

[2]**taint** *n* : a contaminating mark or influence

ta·ka \ˈtäk-ə\ *n* — see MONEY table

[1]**take** \ˈtāk\ *vb* **took** \ˈtu̇k\; **tak·en** \ˈtā-kən\; **tak·ing** **1** : to get into one's hands or possession : GRASP, SEIZE **2** : CAPTURE; *also* : DEFEAT **3** : to obtain or secure for use **4** : to catch or attack through the effect of a sudden force or influence ⟨*taken* ill⟩ **5** : CAPTIVATE, DELIGHT **6** : to bring into a relation ⟨~ a wife⟩ **7** : REMOVE, SUBTRACT **8** : to pick out : CHOOSE **9** : ASSUME, UNDERTAKE **10** : RECEIVE, ACCEPT **11** : to use for transportation ⟨~ a bus⟩ **12** : to become impregnated with : ABSORB ⟨~*s* a dye⟩ **13** : to receive into one's body (as by eating) ⟨~ a pill⟩ **14** : ENDURE, UNDERGO **15** : to lead, carry, or cause to go along to another place **16** : NEED, REQUIRE **17** : to obtain as the result of a special procedure ⟨~ a snapshot⟩ **18** : to undertake and do, make, or perform ⟨~ a walk⟩ **19** : to take effect : ACT, OPERATE **syn** grab, clutch, snatch, seize, nab, grapple — **tak·er** *n* — **take advantage of** **1** : to profit by **2** : EXPLOIT — **take after** : RESEMBLE — **take care** : to be careful — **take care of** : to care for : attend to — **take effect** : to become operative — **take exception** : OBJECT — **take for** : to suppose to be; *esp* : to mistake for — **take place** : HAPPEN — **take to** **1** : to go to **2** : to apply or devote oneself to **3** : to conceive a liking for

[2]**take** *n* **1** : the number or quantity taken; *also* : PROCEEDS, RECEIPTS **2** : an act or the action of taking **3** : a television or movie scene filmed or taped at one time; *also* : a sound recording made at one time **4** : mental response

take·off \-ˌȯf\ *n* **1** : IMITATION; *esp* : PARODY **2** : an act or instance of taking off

take off \ˈtāk-ˈȯf\ *vb* **1** : REMOVE **2** : DEDUCT **3** : to set out : go away **4** : to leave the surface; *esp* : to begin flight

take on *vb* **1** : to begin to perform or deal with; *also* : to contend with as an opponent **2** : ENGAGE, HIRE **3** : to assume or acquire as or as if one's own **4** : to make an unusual show of one's feelings esp. of grief or anger

take over \ˈtāk-ˈō-vər\ *vb* : to assume control or possession of or responsibility for — **take·over** \-ˌō-vər\ *n*

take up *vb* **1** : PICK UP **2** : to begin to occupy **3** : to absorb or incorporate into itself ⟨plants *taking up* nutrients⟩ **4** : to begin to engage in ⟨*took up* jogging⟩ **5** : to make tighter or shorter ⟨*take up* the slack⟩

tak·ings \ˈtā-kiŋz\ *n pl* : receipts esp. of money

ta·la \ˈtäl-ə\ *n, pl* **tala** — see MONEY table

talc \ˈtalk\ *n* : a soft mineral with a soapy feel used esp. in making toilet powder (**tal·cum powder** \ˈtal-kəm-\)

tale \ˈtāl\ *n* **1** : a relation of a series of events **2** : a report of a confidential matter **3** : idle talk; *esp* : harmful gossip **4** : a usu. imaginative narrative **5** : FALSEHOOD **6** : COUNT, TALLY

tal·ent \ˈtal-ənt\ *n* **1** : an ancient unit of weight and value **2** : the natural endowments of a person **3** : a special often creative or artistic aptitude **4** : mental power : ABILITY **5** : a person of talent **syn** genius, gift, faculty, aptitude, knack — **tal·ent·ed** \-əd\ *adj*

ta·ler \ˈtäl-ər\ *n* : any of numerous silver coins issued by German states from the 15th to the 19th centuries

tales·man \ˈtālz-mən\ *n* [ME *tales* talesmen, fr. ML *tales de circumstantibus* such (persons) of the bystanders; fr. the wording of the writ summoning them] : a person summoned for jury duty

tal·is·man \ˈtal-əs-mən, -əz-\ *n, pl* **-mans** [F *talisman* or Sp *talismán* or It *talismano,* fr. Ar *ṭilsam,* fr. MGk *telesma,* fr. Gk, consecration, fr. *telein* to initiate into the mysteries, complete, fr. *telos* end] : an object thought to act as a charm

[1]**talk** \ˈtók\ *vb* **1** : to express in speech : utter words : SPEAK **2** : DISCUSS ⟨~ business⟩ **3** : to influence or cause by talking ⟨~*ed* him into agreeing⟩ **4** : to use (a language) for communicating **5** : CONVERSE **6** : to reveal confidential information; *also* : GOSSIP **7** : to give a talk : LECTURE — **talk·er** *n* — **talk back** : to answer impertinently

[2]**talk** *n* **1** : the act of talking **2** : a way of speaking **3** : a formal discussion **4** : REPORT, RUMOR **5** : the topic of comment or gossip ⟨the ~ of the town⟩ **6** : an informal address or lecture

talk·ative \ˈtó-kət-iv\ *adj* : given to talking **syn** loquacious, chatty, gabby, garrulous — **talk·ative·ly** *adv* — **talk·ative·ness** *n*

talk·ing–to \ˈtó-kiŋ-ˌtü\ *n* : REPRIMAND, REPROOF

tall \ˈtól\ *adj* **1** : high in stature; *also* : of a specified height ⟨six feet ~⟩ **2** : LARGE, FORMIDABLE ⟨a ~ order⟩ **3** : UNBELIEVABLE, IMPROBABLE ⟨a ~ story⟩ **syn** lofty, high — **tall·ness** *n*

tal·low \ˈtal-ō\ *n* : a hard white fat rendered usu. from cattle or sheep tissues and used esp. in soap and lubricants

[1]**tal·ly** \ˈtal-ē\ *n, pl* **tallies** [ME *talye,* fr. ML *talea,* fr. L, twig, cutting] **1** : a device for visibly recording or accounting esp. business transactions **2** : a recorded account **3** : a corresponding part; *also* : CORRESPONDENCE

[2]**tally** *vb* **tal·lied; tal·ly·ing 1** : to mark on or as if on a tally **2** : to make a count of : RECKON; *also* : SCORE **3** : CORRESPOND, MATCH **syn** square, accord, harmonize, conform, jibe

tal·ly·ho \ˌtal-ē-ˈhō\ *n, pl* **-hos 1** : a call of a huntsman at sight of the fox **2** : a four-in-hand coach

Tal·mud \ˈtäl-ˌmůd, ˈtal-məd\ *n* [Heb *talmūdh,* lit., instruction] : the authoritative body of Jewish tradition — **Tal·mu·dic** \tal-ˈm(y)üd-ik, -ˈməd-; täl-ˈmůd-\ *adj* — **Tal·mud·ist** \ˈtäl-ˌmůd-əst, ˈtal-məd-\ *n*

tal·on \ˈtal-ən\ *n* : the claw of an animal and esp. of a bird of prey

ta·lus \ˈtā-ləs, ˈtal-əs\ *n* : rock debris at the base of a cliff

tam \ˈtam\ *n* : TAM-O'-SHANTER

ta·ma·le \tə-ˈmäl-ē\ *n* [MexSp *tamales,* pl. of *tamal* tamale] : ground meat seasoned with chili, rolled in cornmeal dough, wrapped in corn husks, and steamed

tam·a·rack \ˈtam-ə-ˌrak\ *n* : a larch of the northern U.S. and Canada; *also* : its hard resinous wood

tam·a·rind \ˈtam-ə-rənd, -ˌrind\ *n* [Sp & Pg *tamarindo,* fr. Ar *tamr hindī,* lit., Indian date] : a tropical tree of the legume family with hard yellowish wood and feathery leaves; *also* : its acid brown fruit

tam·ba·la \täm-ˈbäl-ə\ *n, pl* **-la** *or* **-las** — see *kwacha* at MONEY table

tam·bou·rine \ˌtam-bə-ˈrēn\ *n* : a small shallow drum with loose disks at the sides played by shaking or striking with the hand

[1]**tame** \ˈtām\ *adj* **tam·er; tam·est 1** : reduced from a state of native wildness esp. so as to be useful to man : DOMESTICATED **2** : made docile : SUBDUED **3** : lacking spirit or interest : INSIPID **syn** submissive, domestic, domesticated — **tame·ly** *adv* — **tame·ness** *n*

[2]**tame** *vb* **tamed; tam·ing 1** : to make or become tame; *also* : to subject (land) to cultivation **2** : HUMBLE, SUBDUE — **tam·able** *or* **tame·able** \ˈtā-mə-bəl\ *adj* — **tame·less** *adj* — **tam·er** *n*

tam–o'–shan·ter \ˈtam-ə-ˌshant-ər\ *n* [fr. poem *Tam o' Shanter* (1790) by Robert Burns †1796 Scot. poet] : a Scottish woolen cap with a wide flat circular crown and usu. a pompon in the center

tamp \ˈtamp\ *vb* : to drive down or in by a series of light blows

tam·per \ˈtam-pər\ *vb* **tam·pered; tam·per·ing** \-p(ə-)riŋ\ **1** : to carry on underhand negotiations (as by bribery) ⟨~ with a witness⟩ **2** : to interfere so as to weaken or change for the worse ⟨~ with a document⟩ **3** : to try foolish or dangerous experiments

tam·pon \ˈtam-ˌpän\ *n* : a plug (as of cotton) introduced into a cavity usu. to check bleeding or absorb secretions

[1]**tan** \ˈtan\ *vb* **tanned; tan·ning 1** : to change (hide) into leather esp. by soaking in a liquid containing tannin **2** : to make or become brown (as by exposure to the sun) **3** : WHIP, THRASH

[2]**tan** *n* **1** : TANBARK; *also* : a tanning material **2** : a brown skin color induced by sun or weather **3** : a light yellowish brown color

[3]**tan** *abbr* tangent

tan·a·ger \ˈtan-i-jər\ *n* : any of numerous American passerine birds with brightly colored males

tan·bark \ˈtan-ˌbärk\ *n* : bark (as of oak or sumac) that is rich in tannin and used in tanning

[1]**tan·dem** \ˈtan-dəm\ *n* [L, at last, at length (taken to mean "lengthwise"), fr. *tam* so] **1** : a 2-seated carriage with horses hitched tandem; *also* : its team **2** : a bicycle for two persons sitting one behind the other — **in tandem** : in a tandem arrangement

[2]**tandem** *adv* : one behind another

[3]**tandem** *adj* **1** : consisting of things arranged one behind the other **2** : working in conjunction with each other

tang \ˈtaŋ\ *n* **1** : a part in a tool that connects the blade with the handle **2** : a sharp distinctive flavor; *also* : a pungent odor — **tangy** *adj*

[1]**tan·gent** \ˈtan-jənt\ *adj* [L *tangent-, tangens,* prp. of *tangere* to touch] : TOUCHING; *esp* : meeting a curve or surface and not cutting it if extended

[2]**tangent** *n* **1** : a tangent line, curve, or surface **2** : an abrupt change of course — **tan·gen·tial** \tan-ˈjen-chəl\ *adj*

tan·ger·ine \ˈtan-jə-ˌrēn, ˌtan-jə-ˈrēn\ *n* : a deep orange loose-skinned citrus fruit; *also* : a tree that bears tangerines

[1]**tan·gi·ble** \ˈtan-jə-bəl\ *adj* **1** : perceptible esp. by the sense of touch : PALPABLE **2** : substantially real : MATERIAL ⟨~ rewards⟩ **3** : capable of being appraised **syn** appreciable, perceptible, sensible, discernible — **tan·gi·bil·i·ty** \ˌtan-jə-ˈbil-ət-ē\ *n*

[2]**tangible** *n* : something tangible; *esp* : a tangible asset

[1]**tan·gle** \ˈtaŋ-gəl\ *vb* **tan·gled; tan·gling** \-g(ə-)liŋ\ **1** : to

involve so as to hamper or embarrass; *also* : ENTRAP **2** : to unite or knit together in intricate confusion : ENTANGLE

²tangle *n* **1** : a tangled twisted mass (as of vines) **2** : a confusedly complicated state : MUDDLE

tan·go \ˈtaŋ-gō\ *n, pl* **tangos** : a dance of Spanish-American origin — **tango** *vb*

tank \ˈtaŋk\ *n* **1** : a large artificial receptacle for liquids **2** : a heavily armed and armored combat vehicle that moves on beltlike tracks — **tank·ful** *n*

tan·kard \ˈtaŋ-kərd\ *n* : a tall one-handled drinking vessel

tank·er \ˈtaŋ-kər\ *n* : a vehicle equipped for transporting a liquid

tank top *n* : a sleeveless collarless pullover shirt with shoulder straps

tank town *n* **1** : a town at which trains stop for water **2** : a small town

tan·ner \ˈtan-ər\ *n* : one that tans hides

tan·nery \ˈtan-(ə-)rē\ *n, pl* **-ner·ies** : a place where tanning is carried on

tan·nic acid \ˌtan-ik-\ *n* : TANNIN

tan·nin \ˈtan-ən\ *n* : any of various substances of plant origin used in tanning and dyeing, in inks, and as astringents

tan·sy \ˈtan-zē\ *n, pl* **tansies** [ME *tanesey*, fr. OF *tanesie*, fr. ML *athanasia*, fr. Gk, immortality, fr. *athanatos* immortal, fr. *a-* not + *thanatos* death] : a common weedy herb related to the daisies with an aromatic odor and very bitter taste

tan·ta·lize \ˈtant-ᵊl-ˌīz\ *vb* **-lized; -liz·ing** [fr. *Tantalus*, mythical Greek king punished in Hades by having to stand up to his chin in water that receded as he bent to drink] : to tease or torment by presenting something desirable but keeping it out of reach — **tan·ta·liz·er** *n* — **tan·ta·liz·ing·ly** *adv*

tan·ta·lum \ˈtant-ᵊl-əm\ *n* : a hard ductile acid-resisting chemical element — see ELEMENT table

tan·ta·mount \ˈtant-ə-ˌmau̇nt\ *adj* : equivalent in value or meaning **syn** same, equal, identical

tan·trum \ˈtan-trəm\ *n* : a fit of bad temper

Tan·za·ni·an \ˌtan-zə-ˈnē-ən\ *n* : a native or inhabitant of Tanzania — **Tanzanian** *adj*

Tao·ism \ˈtau̇-ˌiz-əm, ˈdau̇-\ *n* : a religion developed from a Chinese mystic philosophy and Buddhist religion — **Tao·ist** \-əst\ *adj or n*

¹tap \ˈtap\ *n* **1** : FAUCET, COCK **2** : liquor drawn through a tap **3** : the removing of fluid from a container or cavity by tapping **4** : a tool for forming an internal screw thread **5** : a point in an electric circuit where a connection may be made

²tap *vb* **tapped; tap·ping 1** : to release or cause to flow by piercing or by drawing a plug from a container or cavity **2** : to pierce so as to let out or draw off a fluid **3** : to draw from ⟨~ resources⟩ **4** : to cut in on (a telephone wire) to get information; *also* : to cut in (an electrical circuit) on another circuit **5** : to form an internal screw thread in by means of a tap **6** : to connect (as a gas or water main) with a local supply — **tap·per** *n*

³tap *vb* **tapped; tap·ping 1** : to rap lightly **2** : to make (as a hole) by repeated light blows **3** : to repair by putting a half sole on **4** : SELECT; *esp* : to elect to membership

⁴tap *n* **1** : a light blow or stroke; *also* : its sound **2** : a small metal plate for the sole or heel of a shoe

¹tape \ˈtāp\ *n* **1** : a narrow band of woven fabric **2** : a narrow flexible strip; *esp* : MAGNETIC TAPE

²tape *vb* **taped; tap·ing 1** : to fasten or support with tape **2** : to measure with a tape measure **3** : to record on magnetic tape

tape deck *n* : a device used to play back and often to record on magnetic tapes that usu. has to be connected to a separate audio system

tape measure *n* : a tape marked off in units (as inches) for measuring

tape player *n* : a self-contained device for the playback of recorded magnetic tapes

¹ta·per \ˈtā-pər\ *n* **1** : a slender wax candle; *also* : a long waxed wick **2** : a gradual lessening of thickness or width in a long object ⟨the ~ of a steeple⟩

²taper *vb* **ta·pered; ta·per·ing** \ˈtā-p(ə-)riŋ\ **1** : to make or become gradually smaller toward one end **2** : to diminish gradually

tape–re·cord \ˌtāp-ri-ˈkȯrd\ *vb* : to make a recording of on magnetic tape — **tape recorder** *n* — **tape recording** *n*

tap·es·try \ˈtap-ə-strē\ *n, pl* **-tries** : a heavy reversible textile that has designs or pictures woven into it and is used esp. as a wall hanging

tape·worm \ˈtāp-ˌwərm\ *n* : a long flat segmented worm that lives as a parasite in the intestines

tap·i·o·ca \ˌtap-ē-ˈō-kə\ *n* : a usu. granular preparation of cassava starch used esp. in puddings; *also* : a dish (as pudding) that contains tapioca

ta·pir \ˈtā-pər\ *n, pl* **tapir** *or* **tapirs** : any of several large harmless hoofed mammals of tropical America and southeast Asia related to the horses

tapir

tap·pet \ˈtap-ət\ *n* : a lever or projection moved by some other piece (as a cam) or intended to tap or touch something else to cause a particular motion

tap·room \ˈtap-ˌrüm, -ˌru̇m\ *n* : BARROOM

tap·root \-ˌrüt, -ˌru̇t\ *n* : a large main root growing vertically downward and giving off small lateral roots

taps \ˈtaps\ *n sing or pl* : the last bugle call at night blown as a signal that lights are to be put out; *also* : a similar call blown at military funerals and memorial services

tap·ster \ˈtap-stər\ *n* : BARTENDER

¹tar \ˈtär\ *n* **1** : a thick dark sticky liquid distilled from organic material (as wood or coal) **2** : SAILOR, SEAMAN

²tar *vb* **tarred; tar·ring** : to smear with or as if with tar

tar·an·tel·la \ˌtar-ən-ˈtel-ə\ *n* : a lively folk dance of southern Italy in 6/8 time

ta·ran·tu·la \tə-ˈranch-(ə-)lə, -ˈrant-ᵊl-ə\ *n, pl* **tarantulas** *also* **ta·ran·tu·lae** \-ˈran-chə-ˌlē, -ˈrant-ᵊl-ˌē\ **1** : a large European spider once thought very dangerous **2** : any of a family of large hairy American spiders with a sharp bite that is not very poisonous to human beings

tar·dy \ˈtärd-ē\ *adj* **tar·di·er; -est 1** : moving slowly : SLUGGISH **2** : LATE; *also* : DILATORY **syn** behindhand, overdue, belated — **tar·di·ness** \-ē-nəs\ *n*

¹tare \ˈtaər\ *n* : a weed of fields where grain is grown

²tare *n* : a deduction from the gross weight of a substance and its container made in allowance for the weight of the container — **tare** *vb*

¹tar·get \ˈtär-gət\ *n* [ME, fr. MF *targette*, dim. of *targe* light shield, of Gmc origin] **1** : a mark to shoot at **2** : an object of ridicule or criticism **3** : a goal to be achieved

²target *vb* : to make a target of

tar·iff \ˈtar-əf\ *n* [It *tariffa*, fr. Ar *taʿrīf* notification] **1** : a schedule of duties imposed by a government esp. on imported goods; *also* : a duty or rate of duty imposed in such a schedule **2** : a schedule of rates or charges **syn** duty, toll, tax, levy, assessment

tar·mac \ˈtär-ˌmak\ *n* : a surface paved with crushed stone covered with tar

tarn \ˈtärn\ *n* : a small mountain lake

tar·nish \ˈtär-nish\ *vb* : to make or become dull or discolored — **tarnish** *n*

ta·ro \ˈtär-ō, ˈtar-\ *n, pl* **taros** : a tropical plant grown for its edible starchy fleshy root; *also* : this root

tar·ot \ˈtar-ō\ *n* : one of a set of 22 pictorial playing cards used esp. for fortune-telling

tar·pau·lin \tär-ˈpȯ-lən, ˈtär-pə-\ *n* : a piece of material (as waterproof canvas) used for protecting exposed objects

tar·pon \ˈtär-pən\ *n, pl* **tarpon** *or* **tarpons** : a large silvery sport fish common in warm coastal waters of the Atlantic esp. off Florida

tar·ra·gon \ˈtar-ə-gən\ *n* : a small European perennial wormwood with pungent aromatic foliage used as a flavoring

[1]**tar·ry** \ˈtar-ē\ *vb* **tar·ried; tar·ry·ing 1** : to be tardy : DELAY; *esp* : to be slow in leaving **2** : to stay in or at a place : SOJOURN **syn** remain, wait, linger, abide

[2]**tar·ry** \ˈtär-ē\ *adj* : of, resembling, or smeared with tar

tar sand *n* : sand or sandstone that is naturally soaked with the heavy sticky portions of petroleum

tar·sus \ˈtär-səs\ *n, pl* **tar·si** \-ˌsī\ [NL] : the part of the foot of a vertebrate between the metatarsus and the leg; *also* : the small bones that support this part of the limb — **tar·sal** \-səl\ *adj or n*

[1]**tart** \ˈtärt\ *adj* **1** : agreeably sharp to the taste : PUNGENT **2** : BITING, CAUSTIC **syn** sour, acid, acerb — **tart·ly** *adv* — **tart·ness** *n*

[2]**tart** *n* **1** : a small pie or pastry shell containing jelly, custard, or fruit **2** : PROSTITUTE

tar·tan \ˈtärt-ᵊn\ *n* : a twilled woolen fabric with a plaid design of Scottish origin consisting of stripes of varying width and color against a solid background

tar·tar \ˈtärt-ər\ *n* **1** : a substance in the juice of grapes deposited (as in wine casks) as a reddish crust or sediment **2** : a hard crust of saliva, debris, and calcium salts on the teeth

tar·tar sauce *or* **tar·tare sauce** \ˌtärt-ər-\ *n* : mayonnaise with chopped pickles, olives, or capers

[1]**task** \ˈtask\ *n* [ME *taske*, fr. OF *tasque*, fr. ML *tasca* tax or service imposed by a feudal superior, fr. *taxare* to tax] : a piece of assigned work **syn** job, duty, chore, stint, assignment

[2]**task** *vb* : to oppress with great labor

task force *n* : a temporary grouping to accomplish a particular objective

task·mas·ter \ˈtask-ˌmas-tər\ *n* : one that imposes a task or burdens another with labor

[1]**tas·sel** \ˈtas-əl, ˈtäs-\ *n* **1** : a hanging ornament made of a bunch of cords of even length fastened at one end **2** : something suggesting a tassel; *esp* : a male flower cluster of Indian corn

[2]**tassel** *vb* **-seled** *or* **-selled; -sel·ing** *or* **-sel·ling** \-(ə-)liŋ\ : to adorn with or put forth tassels

[1]**taste** \ˈtāst\ *vb* **tast·ed; tast·ing 1** : EXPERIENCE, UNDERGO **2** : to try or determine the flavor of by taking a bit into the mouth **3** : to eat or drink esp. in small quantities : SAMPLE **4** : to have a specific flavor

[2]**taste** *n* **1** : a small amount tasted **2** : BIT; *esp* : a sample of experience **3** : the special sense that identifies sweet, sour, bitter, or salty qualities and is mediated by receptors in the tongue **4** : a quality perceptible to the sense of taste; *also* : a complex sensation involving true taste, smell, and touch **5** : individual preference **6** : critical judgment, discernment, or appreciation; *also* : aesthetic quality **syn** tang, relish, flavor, savor — **taste·ful** \-fəl\ *adj* — **taste·ful·ly** \-ē\ *adv* — **taste·less** *adj* — **taste·less·ly** *adv* — **tast·er** *n*

taste bud *n* : a sense organ mediating the sensation of taste

tasty \ˈtā-stē\ *adj* **tast·i·er; -est** : pleasing to the taste : SAVORY **syn** palatable, appetizing, toothsome, flavorsome — **tast·i·ness** \ˈtā-stē-nəs\ *n*

tat \ˈtat\ *vb* **tat·ted; tat·ting** : to work at or make by tatting

[1]**tat·ter** \ˈtat-ər\ *vb* : to make or become ragged

[2]**tatter** *n* **1** : a part torn and left hanging **2** *pl* : tattered clothing

tat·ter·de·ma·lion \ˌtat-ərd-i-ˈmāl-yən\ *n* : one that is ragged or disreputable

tat·ter·sall \ˈtat-ər-ˌsȯl, -səl\ *n* : a pattern of colored lines forming squares on solid background; *also* : a fabric in a tattersall pattern

tat·ting \ˈtat-iŋ\ *n* : a delicate handmade lace formed usu. by looping and knotting with a single thread and a small shuttle; *also* : the act or process of making such lace

tat·tle \ˈtat-ᵊl\ *vb* **tat·tled; tat·tling** \ˈtat-(ᵊ-)liŋ\ **1** : CHATTER, PRATE **2** : to tell secrets; *also* : to inform against another — **tat·tler** \ˈtat-(ᵊ-)lər\ *n*

tat·tle·tale \ˈtat-ᵊl-ˌtāl\ *n* : one that tattles : INFORMER

[1]**tat·too** \ta-ˈtü\ *n, pl* **tattoos** [alter. of earlier *taptoo*, fr. D *taptoe*, fr. the phrase *tap toe!* taps shut!] **1** : a call sounded before taps as notice to go to quarters **2** : a rapid rhythmic rapping

[2]**tattoo** *vb* : to mark (the skin) with tattoos

[3]**tattoo** *n, pl* **tattoos** [Tahitian *tatau*] : an indelible figure fixed upon the body esp. by insertion of pigment under the skin

taught *past and past part of* TEACH

[1]**taunt** \ˈtȯnt\ *n* : a sarcastic challenge or insult

[2]**taunt** *vb* : to reproach or challenge in a mocking manner : jeer at **syn** mock, deride, ridicule, twit — **taunt·er** *n*

taupe \ˈtōp\ *n* : a brownish gray

Tau·rus \ˈtȯr-əs\ *n* [L, lit., bull] **1** : a zodiacal constellation between Aries and Gemini usu. pictured as a bull **2** : the 2d sign of the zodiac in astrology; *also* : one born under this sign

taut \ˈtȯt\ *adj* **1** : tightly drawn : not slack **2** : extremely nervous : TENSE **3** : TRIM, TIDY ⟨a ~ ship⟩ — **taut·ly** *adv* — **taut·ness** *n*

tau·tol·o·gy \tȯ-ˈtäl-ə-jē\ *n, pl* **-gies** : needless repetition of an idea, statement, or word; *also* : an instance of such repetition — **tau·to·log·i·cal** \ˌtȯt-ᵊl-ˈäj-i-kəl\ *adj* — **tau·to·log·i·cal·ly** \-i-k(ə-)lē\ *adv* — **tau·tol·o·gous** \tȯ-ˈtäl-ə-gəs\ *adj* — **tau·tol·o·gous·ly** *adv*

tav·ern \ˈtav-ərn\ *n* [ME *taverne*, fr. OF, fr. L *taberna*, lit., hut, shop] **1** : an establishment where alcoholic liquors are sold to be drunk on the premises **2** : INN

taw \ˈtȯ\ *n* **1** : a marble used as a shooter **2** : the line from which players shoot at marbles

taw·dry \ˈtȯ-drē\ *adj* **taw·dri·er; -est** [fr. *tawdry lace* (a tie of lace for the neck), fr. *St. Audrey* (St. Etheldreda) †679 queen of Northumbria] : cheap and gaudy in appearance and quality **syn** garish, flashy, chintzy, meretricious — **taw·dri·ly** *adv*

taw·ny \ˈtȯ-nē\ *adj* **taw·ni·er; -est** : of a brownish orange color

[1]**tax** \ˈtaks\ *vb* **1** : to levy a tax on **2** : CHARGE, ACCUSE **3** : to put under pressure — **tax·able** \ˈtak-sə-bəl\ *adj* — **tax·a·tion** \tak-ˈsā-shən\ *n*

[2]**tax** *n* **1** : a charge usu. of money imposed by authority on persons or property for public purposes **2** : a heavy charge : STRAIN **syn** assessment, levy, duty, tariff

[1]**taxi** \ˈtak-sē\ *n, pl* **tax·is** \-sēz\ *also* **tax·ies** : TAXICAB; *also* : a similarly operated boat or airplane

[2]**taxi** *vb* **tax·ied; taxi·ing** *or* **taxy·ing; tax·is** *or* **tax·ies 1** : to move along the ground or on the water under an airplane's own power when starting or after a landing **2** : to go by taxicab

taxi·cab \ˈtak-sē-ˌkab\ *n* : an automobile that carries passengers for a fare usu. based on the distance traveled

taxi·der·my \ˈtak-sə-ˌdər-mē\ *n* : the art of preparing, stuffing, and mounting skins of animals — **taxi·der·mist** \-məst\ *n*

tax·on·o·my \tak-ˈsän-ə-mē\ *n* : classification esp. of animals or plants according to natural relationships — **tax·o·nom·ic** \ˌtak-sə-ˈnäm-ik\ *adj* — **tax·on·o·mist** \tak-ˈsän-ə-məst\ *n*

tax·pay·er \ˈtaks-ˌpā-ər\ *n* : one who pays or is liable for a tax — **tax·pay·ing** \-iŋ\ *adj*

Tay–Sachs disease \ˈtā-ˈsaks-\ *n* : a fatal hereditary disease caused by the absence of an enzyme needed to break down fatty material and characterized by a build-up of lipids in the nervous tissue

tb *abbr* tablespoon; tablespoonful

Tb *symbol* terbium

TB \(ˈ)tē-ˈbē\ *n* : TUBERCULOSIS

TBA *abbr, often not cap* to be announced

T–bar lift \ˌtē-ˌbär-\ *n* : a chair lift with a series of T-shaped bars

tbs *or* **tbsp** *abbr* tablespoon; tablespoonful

Tc *symbol* technetium

TC *abbr* teachers college

T cell *n* : a lymphocyte specialized esp. for promoting immunity (as against viruses and in the rejection of foreign tissues) or for helping make antibodies

TD *abbr* **1** touchdown **2** Treasury Department

TDY *abbr* temporary duty

Te *symbol* tellurium

tea \ˈtē\ *n* **1** : the cured leaves and leaf buds of a shrub grown chiefly in China, Japan, India, and Sri Lanka; *also* : this shrub **2** : a drink made by steeping tea in boiling water **3** : refreshments usu. including tea served in late afternoon; *also* : a reception at which tea is served

teach \ˈtēch\ *vb* **taught** \ˈtȯt\; **teach·ing** **1** : to cause to know a subject : act as a teacher **2** : to show how ⟨~ a child to swim⟩ **3** : to make to know the disagreeable consequences of an action **4** : to guide the studies of **5** : to impart the knowledge of ⟨~ algebra⟩ — **teach·able** *adj* — **teach·er** *n*

teach·ing \-iŋ\ *n* **1** : the act, practice, or profession of a teacher **2** : something taught; *esp* : DOCTRINE

tea·cup \ˈtē-ˌkəp\ *n* : a small cup used with a saucer for hot beverages

teak \ˈtēk\ *n* : a tall East Indian timber tree; *also* : its hard durable yellowish brown wood

tea·ket·tle \ˈtē-ˌket-ᵊl\ *n* : a covered kettle with a handle and spout for boiling water

teal \ˈtēl\ *n, pl* **teal** *or* **teals** : any of several small short-necked wild ducks

¹team \ˈtēm\ *n* [ME *teme*, fr. OE *tēam* offspring, lineage, group of draft animals] **1** : two or more draft animals harnessed to the same vehicle or implement **2** : a number of persons associated in work or activity; *esp* : a group on one side in a match — **team·mate** \ˈtēm-ˌmāt\ *n*

²team *vb* **1** : to haul with or drive a team **2** : to form a team : join forces

³team *adj* : of or performed by a team

team·ster \ˈtēm-stər\ *n* : one that drives a team or truck

team·work \-ˌwərk\ *n* : the work or activity of a number of persons acting in close association as members of a unit

tea·pot \ˈtē-ˌpät\ *n* : a vessel with a spout for brewing and serving tea

¹tear \ˈtiər\ *n* : a drop of the salty liquid that moistens the eye and inner side of the eyelids — **tear·ful** \-fəl\ *adj* — **tear·ful·ly** \-ē\ *adv*

²tear \ˈtaər\ *vb* **tore** \ˈtōr\; **torn** \ˈtōrn\; **tear·ing** **1** : to separate parts of or pull apart by force : REND **2** : LACERATE **3** : to disrupt by the pull of contrary forces **4** : to remove by force : WRENCH **5** : to move or act with violence, haste, or force **syn** rip, split, cleave, rend

³tear \ˈtaər\ *n* **1** : the act of tearing **2** : a hole or flaw made by tearing : RENT

tear gas \ˈtiər-\ *n* : a substance that on dispersion in the atmosphere blinds the eyes with tears — **tear gas** *vb*

tear·jerk·er \ˈtiər-ˌjər-kər\ *n* : an extravagantly pathetic story, song, play, movie, or broadcast

¹tease \ˈtēz\ *vb* **teased; teas·ing** **1** : to disentangle and lay parallel by combing or carding ⟨~ wool⟩ **2** : to scratch the surface of (cloth) so as to raise a nap **3** : to annoy persistently esp. in fun by goading, coaxing, or tantalizing **4** : to comb (hair) by taking a strand and pushing the short hairs toward the scalp with the comb **syn** harass, worry, pester, annoy

²tease *n* **1** : the act of teasing or state of being teased **2** : one that teases

tea·sel *also* **tea·zel** *or* **tea·zle** \ˈtē-zəl\ *n* : a prickly herb or its flower head covered with stiff bracts and used to raise the nap on cloth; *also* : an artificial device used for this purpose

tea·spoon \ˈtē-ˌspün\ *n* **1** : a small spoon suitable for stirring beverages **2** : TEASPOONFUL

tea·spoon·ful \-ˌfu̇l\ *n, pl* **-spoonfuls** *also* **-spoons·ful** \-ˌspünz-ˌfu̇l\ : a unit of measure equal to one-sixth fluidounce (about 5 milliliters) or one third of a tablespoonful

teat \ˈtit, ˈtēt\ *n* : the protuberance through which milk is drawn from an udder or breast

tech *abbr* **1** technical; technically; technician **2** technological; technology

tech·ne·tium \tek-ˈnē-sh(ē-)əm\ *n* : a metallic chemical element produced in certain nuclear reactions — see ELEMENT table

tech·nic \ˈtek-nik, tek-ˈnēk\ *n* : TECHNIQUE 1

tech·ni·cal \ˈtek-ni-kəl\ *adj* [Gk *technikos* of art, skillful, fr. *technē* art, craft, skill] **1** : having special knowledge esp. of a mechanical or scientific subject ⟨~ experts⟩ **2** : of or relating to a particular and esp. a practical or scientific subject ⟨~ training⟩ **3** : according to a strict interpretation of the rules **4** : of or relating to technique — **tech·ni·cal·ly** \-k(ə-)lē\ *adv*

tech·ni·cal·i·ty \ˌtek-nə-ˈkal-ət-ē\ *n, pl* **-ties** **1** : a detail meaningful only to a specialist **2** : the quality or state of being technical

technical sergeant *n* : a noncommissioned officer in the air force ranking next below a master sergeant

tech·ni·cian \tek-ˈnish-ən\ *n* : a person who has acquired the technique of a specialized skill or subject

tech·nique \tek-ˈnēk\ *n* [F] **1** : the manner in which technical details are treated or basic physical movements are used **2** : technical methods

tech·noc·ra·cy \tek-ˈnäk-rə-sē\ *n* : management of society by technical experts — **tech·no·crat** \ˈtek-nə-ˌkrat\ *n* — **tech·no·crat·ic** \ˌtek-nə-ˈkrat-ik\ *adj*

tech·nol·o·gy \tek-ˈnäl-ə-jē\ *n, pl* **-gies** : applied science; *also* : a technical method of achieving a practical purpose — **tech·no·log·i·cal** \ˌtek-nə-ˈläj-i-kəl\ *adj*

tec·ton·ics \tek-ˈtän-iks\ *n sing or pl* **1** : geological structural features **2** : geology dealing with faulting and folding **3** : DIASTROPHISM — **tec·ton·ic** \-ik\ *adj*

ted·dy bear \ˈted-ē-ˌbaər\ *n* [*Teddy* Roosevelt, fr. a cartoon depicting the president sparing the life of a bear cub while hunting] : a stuffed toy bear

te·dious \ˈtēd-ē-əs, ˈtē-jəs\ *adj* : tiresome because of length or dullness **syn** boring, tiring, irksome — **te·dious·ly** *adv* — **te·dious·ness** *n*

te·di·um \ˈtēd-ē-əm\ *n* : TEDIOUSNESS; *also* : BOREDOM

[1]**tee** \ˈtē\ *n* : a small mound or peg on which a golf ball is placed to be hit at the beginning of play on a hole; *also* : the area from which the ball is hit to begin play

[2]**tee** *vb* **teed; tee·ing** : to place (a ball) on a tee

teem \ˈtēm\ *vb* : to become filled to overflowing : ABOUND **syn** swarm, crawl, flow

teen *adj* : TEENAGE

teen·age \ˈtēn-ˌāj\ *or* **teen·aged** \-ˌājd\ *adj* : of, being, or relating to people in their teens — **teen·ag·er** \-ˌā-jər\ *n*

teens \ˈtēnz\ *n pl* : the numbers 13 to 19 inclusive; *esp* : the years 13 to 19 in a person's life

tee·ny \ˈtē-nē\ *adj* **tee·ni·er; -est** : TINY

tee·pee *var of* TEPEE

tee shirt *var of* T-SHIRT

tee·ter \ˈtēt-ər\ *vb* **1** : to move unsteadily **2** : SEESAW — **teeter** *n*

teeth *pl of* TOOTH

teethe \ˈtēth\ *vb* **teethed; teeth·ing** : to grow teeth : cut one's teeth

teeth·ing \ˈtē-thiŋ\ *n* : the process of growth of the first set of teeth through the gums with its accompanying phenomena

tee·to·tal \ˈtē-ˈtōt-ᵊl, -ˌtōt-\ *adj* : of or relating to the practice of complete abstinence from alcoholic drinks — **tee·to·tal·er** *or* **tee·to·tal·ler** \-ˈtōt-ᵊl-ər\ *n* — **tee·to·tal·ism** \-ᵊl-ˌiz-əm\ *n*

TEFL *abbr* teaching English as a foreign language

tek·tite \ˈtek-ˌtīt\ *n* : a glassy body of probably meteoric origin

tel *abbr* **1** telegram **2** telegraph **3** telephone

tele·cast \ˈtel-i-ˌkast\ *vb* **-cast** *also* **-cast·ed; -cast·ing** : to broadcast by television — **telecast** *n* — **tele·cast·er** *n*

tele·com·mu·ni·ca·tion \ˌtel-i-kə-ˌmyü-nə-ˈkā-shən\ *n* : communication at a distance (as by telephone or radio)

tele·con·fer·ence \ˈtel-i-ˌkän-f(ə-)rəns\ *n* : a conference among people remote from one another held using telecommunications — **tele·con·fer·enc·ing** *n*

teleg *abbr* telegraphy

tele·ge·nic \ˌtel-ə-ˈjen-ik, -ˈjēn-\ *adj* : markedly attractive to television viewers

tele·gram \ˈtel-ə-ˌgram\ *n* : a message sent by telegraph

[1]**tele·graph** \-ˌgraf\ *n* : an electric apparatus or system for sending messages by a code over wires — **tele·graph·ic** \ˌtel-ə-ˈgraf-ik\ *adj*

[2]**telegraph** *vb* : to send or communicate by or as if by telegraph — **te·leg·ra·pher** \tə-ˈleg-rə-fər\ *n*

te·leg·ra·phy \tə-ˈleg-rə-fē\ *n* : the use or operation of a telegraph apparatus or system

te·lem·e·try \tə-ˈlem-ə-trē\ *n* : the transmission esp. by radio of measurements made by automatic instruments to a distant station — **tele·me·ter** \ˈtel-ə-ˌmēt-ər\ *n*

te·lep·a·thy \tə-ˈlep-ə-thē\ *n* : apparent communication from one mind to another by extrasensory means — **tele·path·ic** \ˌtel-ə-ˈpath-ik\ *adj* — **tele·path·i·cal·ly** \-i-k(ə-)lē\ *adv*

[1]**tele·phone** \ˈtel-ə-ˌfōn\ *n* : an instrument for transmitting and receiving sounds over long distances by electricity

[2]**telephone** *vb* **-phoned; -phon·ing** **1** : to send or communicate by telephone **2** : to speak to (a person) by telephone — **tele·phon·er** *n*

te·le·pho·ny \tə-ˈlef-ə-nē, ˈtel-ə-ˌfō-\ *n* : use or operation of apparatus for transmission of sounds between distant points — **tel·e·phon·ic** \ˌtel-ə-ˈfän-ik\ *adj*

tele·pho·to \ˌtel-ə-ˈfōt-ō\ *adj* : being a camera lens giving a large image of a distant object — **tele·pho·to·graph·ic** \-ˌfōt-ə-ˈgraf-ik\ *adj* — **tele·pho·tog·ra·phy** \-fə-ˈtäg-rə-fē\ *n*

tele·play \ˈtel-i-ˌplā\ *n* : a play written for television

tele·print·er \ˈtel-ə-ˌprint-ər\ *n* : TELETYPEWRITER

[1]**tele·scope** \ˈtel-ə-ˌskōp\ *n* : a cylindrical instrument equipped with lenses or mirrors for viewing distant objects

[2]**telescope** *vb* **-scoped; -scop·ing** **1** : to slide or pass or cause to slide or pass one within another like the sections of a hand telescope **2** : COMPRESS, CONDENSE

tele·scop·ic \ˌtel-ə-ˈskäp-ik\ *adj* **1** : of or relating to a telescope **2** : seen only by a telescope **3** : able to discern objects at a distance **4** : having parts that telescope — **tele·scop·i·cal·ly** \-i-k(ə-)lē\ *adv*

tele·text \ˈtel-ə-ˌtekst\ *n* : an electronic system in which printed matter is broadcast by a television station and displayed on a subscriber's television set having a decoder

tele·thon \ˈtel-ə-ˌthän\ *n* : a long television program usu. to solicit funds for a charity

tele·type·writ·er \ˌtel-ə-ˈtīp-ˌrīt-ər\ *n* : a printing device resembling a typewriter used to send and receive signals over telephone lines

tele·vise \ˈtel-ə-ˌvīz\ *vb* **-vised; -vis·ing** : to pick up and usu. broadcast by television

tele·vi·sion \ˈtel-ə-ˌvizh-ən\ *n* [F *télévision,* fr. Gk *tēle* far, at a distance + F *vision* vision] : transmission and reproduction of images by a device that converts light waves into radio waves and then converts these back into visible light rays

tell \ˈtel\ *vb* **told** \ˈtōld\; **tell·ing** **1** : COUNT, ENUMERATE **2** : to relate in detail : NARRATE **3** : SAY, UTTER **4** : to make known : REVEAL **5** : to report to : INFORM **6** : ORDER, DIRECT **7** : to ascertain by observing **8** : to have a marked effect **9** : to serve as evidence **syn** reveal, disclose, discover, betray

tell·er \ˈtel-ər\ *n* **1** : one that relates : NARRATOR **2** : one that counts **3** : a bank employee handling money received or paid out

tell·ing \ˈtel-iŋ\ *adj* : producing a marked effect : EFFECTIVE **syn** cogent, convincing, sound

tell off *vb* : REPRIMAND, SCOLD

tell·tale \ˈtel-ˌtāl\ *n* **1** : INFORMER, TATTLETALE **2** : something that serves to disclose : INDICATION — **telltale** *adj*

tel·lu·ri·um \tə-ˈlu̇r-ē-əm\ *n* : a chemical element that resembles sulfur in properties — see ELEMENT table

te·mer·i·ty \tə-ˈmer-ət-ē\ *n, pl* **-ties** : rash or presumptuous daring : BOLDNESS **syn** audacity, effrontery, gall, nerve, cheek

temp *abbr* **1** temperature **2** temporary

[1]**tem·per** \ˈtem-pər\ *vb* **tem·pered; tem·per·ing** \-p(ə-)riŋ\ **1** : to dilute or soften by the addition of something else ⟨~ justice with mercy⟩ **2** : to bring (as steel) to a desired hardness by reheating and cooling **3** : to toughen (glass) by gradual heating and cooling **4** : TOUGHEN **5** : TUNE

[2]**temper** *n* **1** : characteristic tone : TENDENCY **2** : the hardness or toughness of a substance ⟨~ of a knife blade⟩ **3** : a characteristic frame of mind : DISPOSITION **4** : calmness of mind : COMPOSURE **5** : state of feeling or frame of mind at a particular time **6** : heat of mind or emotion **syn** temperament, character, personality, makeup

tem·pera \ˈtem-pə-rə\ *n* [It] : a painting process using an albuminous or colloidal medium as a vehicle; *also* : a painting done in tempera

tem·per·a·ment \ˈtem-p(ə-)rə-mənt\ *n* **1** : characteristic or habitual inclination or mode of emotional response : DISPOSITION ⟨nervous ~⟩ **2** : excessive sensitiveness or irritability **syn** character, personality, nature, makeup — **tem·per·a·men·tal** \ˌtem-p(ə-)rə-ˈment-ᵊl\ *adj*

tem·per·ance \ˈtem-p(ə-)rəns\ *n* : habitual moderation in the indulgence of the appetites or passions; *esp* : moderation in or abstinence from the use of intoxicating drink

tem·per·ate \ˈtem-p(ə-)rət\ *adj* **1** : not extreme or excessive : MILD **2** : moderate in indulgence of appetite or desire **3** : moderate in the use of intoxicating liquors **4** : having a moderate climate **syn** sober, continent, abstemious

temperate zone *n, often cap T&Z* : the region between the tropic of Cancer and the arctic circle or between the tropic of Capricorn and the antarctic circle

tem·per·a·ture \ˈtem-pər-ˌchu̇r, -p(ə-)rə-ˌchu̇r, -chər\ *n* **1** : degree of hotness or coldness of something (as air, water, or the body) as shown by a thermometer **2** : FEVER

tem·pest \ˈtem-pəst\ *n* [ME, fr. OF *tempeste,* fr. L *tempestas* season, weather, storm, fr. *tempus* time] : a violent wind esp. with rain, hail, or snow

tem·pes·tu·ous \tem-ˈpes-chə-wəs\ *adj* : of, involving, or resembling a tempest : STORMY — **tem·pes·tu·ous·ly** *adv* — **tem·pes·tu·ous·ness** *n*

tem·plate *also* **tem·plet** \ˈtem-plət\ *n* : a gauge, mold, or pattern used as a guide to the form of a piece being made

[1]**tem·ple** \ˈtem-pəl\ *n* **1** : an edifice for the worship of a deity **2** : a place devoted to a special or exalted purpose

[2]**temple** *n* : the flattened space on each side of the forehead esp. of man

tem·po \ˈtem-pō\ *n, pl* **tem·pi** \-(ˌ)pē\ *or* **tempos** [It, lit., time] **1** : the rate of speed of a musical piece or passage **2** : rate of motion or activity : PACE

[1]**tem·po·ral** \ˈtem-p(ə-)rəl\ *adj* **1** : of, relating to, or limited by time ⟨~ and spatial bounds⟩ **2** : of or relating to earthly life or secular concerns ⟨~ power⟩ **syn** profane, secular, lay

[2]**temporal** *adj* : of or relating to the temples or the sides of the skull

[1]**tem·po·rary** \ˈtem-pə-ˌrer-ē\ *adj* : lasting for a time only : TRANSITORY **syn** transient, ephemeral, momentary, impermanent — **tem·po·rar·i·ly** \ˌtem-pə-ˈrer-ə-lē\ *adv*

[2]**temporary** *n, pl* **-rar·ies** : one serving for a limited time

tem·po·rize \ˈtem-pə-ˌrīz\ *vb* **-rized; -riz·ing** **1** : to adapt one's actions to the time or the dominant opinion : COMPROMISE **2** : to draw out matters so as to gain time — **tem·po·riz·er** *n*

tempt \ˈtempt\ *vb* **1** : to entice to do wrong by promise of pleasure or gain **2** : PROVOKE **3** : to risk the dangers of **4** : to induce to do something : INCITE **syn** inveigle, decoy, seduce, lure — **tempt·er** *n* — **tempt·ing·ly** *adv*

temp·ta·tion \temp-ˈtā-shən\ *n* **1** : the act of tempting : the state of being tempted **2** : something that tempts

tempt·ress \ˈtemp-trəs\ *n* : a woman who tempts

ten \ˈten\ *n* **1** : one more than nine **2** : the 10th in a set or series **3** : something having 10 units — **ten** *adj or pron* — **tenth** \ˈtenth\ *adj or adv or n*

ten·a·ble \ˈten-ə-bəl\ *adj* : capable of being held, maintained, or defended — **ten·a·bil·i·ty** \ˌten-ə-ˈbil-ət-ē\ *n*

te·na·cious \tə-ˈnā-shəs\ *adj* **1** : not easily pulled apart : COHESIVE, TOUGH ⟨steel is a ~ metal⟩ **2** : holding fast ⟨~ of his rights⟩ **3** : RETENTIVE ⟨~ memory⟩ — **te·na·cious·ly** *adv* — **te·nac·i·ty** \tə-ˈnas-ət-ē\ *n*

ten·an·cy \ˈten-ən-sē\ *n, pl* **-cies** : the temporary possession or occupancy of something (as a house) that belongs to another; *also* : the period of a tenant's occupancy

ten·ant \ˈten-ənt\ *n* **1** : one who rents or leases (as a house) from a landlord **2** : DWELLER, OCCUPANT — **tenant** *vb* — **ten·ant·less** *adj*

tenant farmer *n* : a farmer who works land owned by another and pays rent either in cash or in shares of produce

ten·ant·ry \ˈten-ən-trē\ *n, pl* **-ries** : the body of tenants esp. on a great estate

Ten Commandments *n pl* : the commandments of God given to Moses on Mount Sinai

[1]**tend** \ˈtend\ *vb* **1** : to apply oneself ⟨~ to your affairs⟩ **2** : to take care of ⟨~ a plant⟩ **3** : to manage the operations of ⟨~ a machine⟩ **syn** mind, watch, attend

[2]**tend** *vb* **1** : to move or develop one's course in a particular direction **2** : to show an inclination or tendency

ten·den·cy \ˈten-dən-sē\ *n, pl* **-cies** **1** : DRIFT, TREND **2** : a proneness to or readiness for a particular kind of thought or action : PROPENSITY **syn** bent, leaning, disposition, inclination

ten·den·tious \ten-ˈden-chəs\ *adj* : marked by a tendency in favor of a particular point of view : BIASED — **ten·den·tious·ly** *adv* — **ten·den·tious·ness** *n*

[1]**ten·der** \ˈten-dər\ *adj* **1** : having a soft texture : easily broken, chewed, or cut **2** : physically weak : DELICATE; *also* : IMMATURE **3** : expressing or responsive to love or sympathy : LOVING, COMPASSIONATE **4** : SENSITIVE, TOUCHY **syn** sympathetic, warm, warmhearted — **ten·der·ly** *adv* — **ten·der·ness** *n*

[2]**tender** *n* **1** : an offer or proposal made for acceptance; *esp* : an offer of a bid for a contract **2** : something (as money) that may be offered in payment

[3]**tender** *vb* : to present for acceptance

[4]**tend·er** \ˈten-dər\ *n* **1** : one that tends or takes care **2** : a boat carrying passengers and freight to a larger ship **3** : a car attached to a steam locomotive for carrying fuel and water

ten·der·foot \ˈten-dər-ˌfu̇t\ *n, pl* **-feet** \-ˌfēt\ *also* **-foots** \-ˌfu̇ts\ **1** : one not hardened to frontier or rough outdoor life **2** : an inexperienced beginner : NEOPHYTE

ten·der·heart·ed \ˌten-dər-ˈhärt-əd\ *adj* : easily moved to love, pity, or sorrow : COMPASSIONATE

ten·der·ize \ˈten-də-ˌrīz\ *vb* **-ized; -iz·ing** : to make (meat) tender — **ten·der·iz·er** \ˈten-də-ˌrī-zər\ *n*

ten·der·loin \ˈten-dər-ˌlȯin\ *n* **1** : a tender strip of beef or pork from near the backbone **2** : a district of a city largely devoted to vice

ten·di·ni·tis *or* **ten·don·itis** \ˌten-də-ˈnīt-əs\ *n* : inflammation of a tendon

ten·don \ˈten-dən\ *n* : a tough cord of dense tissue uniting a muscle with another part (as a bone) — **ten·di·nous** \-də-nəs\ *adj*

ten·dril \ˈten-drəl\ *n* : a slender coiling organ by which some climbing plants attach themselves to a support

ten·e·brous \ˈten-ə-brəs\ *adj* : shut off from the light : GLOOMY, OBSCURE

ten·e·ment \ˈten-ə-mənt\ *n* **1** : a house used as a dwelling **2** : a building divided into apartments for rent to families; *esp* : one meeting only minimum standards of safety and comfort **3** : APARTMENT, FLAT

te·net \ˈten-ət\ *n* [L, he holds, fr. *tenēre* to hold] : one of the principles or doctrines held in common by members of an organized group (as a church or profession) **syn** doctrine, dogma, belief

ten·fold \ˈten-ˌfōld, -ˈfōld\ *adj* : being 10 times as great or as many — **ten·fold** \-ˈfōld\ *adv*

ten–gallon hat *n* : a wide-brimmed hat with a large soft crown

Tenn *abbr* Tennessee

ten·nis \ˈten-əs\ *n* : a game played with a ball and racket on a court divided by a net

ten·on \ˈten-ən\ *n* : a projecting part in a piece of material (as wood) for insertion into a mortise to make a joint

ten·or \ˈten-ər\ *n* **1** : the general drift of something spoken or written : PURPORT **2** : the highest natural adult male voice **3** : TREND, TENDENCY

ten·pen·ny \ˌten-ˌpen-ē\ *adj* : amounting to, worth, or costing 10 pennies

tenpenny nail *n* : a nail three inches (about 7.6 centimeters) long

ten·pin \ˈten-ˌpin\ *n* : a bottle-shaped bowling pin set in groups of 10 and bowled at in a game **(tenpins)**

[1]**tense** \ˈtens\ *n* [ME *tens* time, tense, fr. MF, fr. L *tempus*] : distinction of form of a verb to indicate the time of the action or state

[2]**tense** *adj* **tens·er; tens·est** [L *tensus,* fr. pp. of *tendere* to stretch] **1** : stretched tight : TAUT **2** : feeling or marked by nervous tension **syn** stiff, rigid, inflexible — **tense·ly** *adv* — **tense·ness** *n* — **ten·si·ty** \ˈten-sət-ē\ *n*

[3]**tense** *vb* **tensed; tens·ing** : to make or become tense

ten·sile \ˈten-səl, -ˌsīl\ *adj* : of or relating to tension ⟨~ strength⟩

ten·sion \ˈten-chən\ *n* **1** : the act of straining or stretching; *also* : the condition of being strained or stretched **2** : a state of mental unrest often with signs of bodily stress **3** : a state of latent hostility or opposition **4** : VOLTAGE

ten–speed \ˈten-ˌspēd\ *n* : a bicycle with 10 possible combinations of gears

[1]**tent** \ˈtent\ *n* **1** : a collapsible shelter of material stretched and supported by poles **2** : a canopy placed over the head and shoulders to retain vapors or oxygen being medically administered

[2]**tent** *vb* **1** : to lodge in tents **2** : to cover with or as if with a tent

ten·ta·cle \ˈtent-i-kəl\ *n* : any of the long flexible projections about the head or mouth (as of an insect, mollusk, or fish) — **ten·ta·cled** \-kəld\ *adj* — **ten·tac·u·lar** \ten-ˈtak-yə-lər\ *adj*

ten·ta·tive \ˈtent-ət-iv\ *adj* **1** : not fully worked out or developed ⟨~ plans⟩ **2** : HESITANT, UNCERTAIN ⟨a ~ smile⟩ — **ten·ta·tive·ly** *adv*

ten·u·ous \ˈten-yə-wəs\ *adj* **1** : not dense : RARE ⟨a ~ fluid⟩ **2** : not thick : SLENDER ⟨a ~ rope⟩ **3** : having little substance : FLIMSY, WEAK ⟨~ influences⟩ **syn** thin, slim, slight — **te·nu·i·ty** \te-ˈn(y)ü-ət-ē, tə-\ *n* — **ten·u·ous·ly** \ˈten-yə-wəs-lē\ *adv* — **ten·u·ous·ness** *n*

ten·ure \ˈten-yər\ *n* : the act, right, manner, or period of holding something (as a landed property or a position)

ten·ured \ˈten-yərd\ *adj* : having tenure ⟨~ faculty members⟩

te·o·sin·te \ˌtā-ō-ˈsint-ē\ *n* : a large annual grass of Mexico and Central America closely related to maize

te·pee \ˈtē-(ˌ)pē\ *n* [Dakota *tipi*, fr. *ti* to dwell + *pi* to use for] : an American Indian conical tent usu. of skins

tep·id \ˈtep-əd\ *adj* **1** : moderately warm : LUKEWARM **2** : HALFHEARTED

te·qui·la \tə-ˈkē-lə, tā-\ *n* : a Mexican liquor made from mescal

ter *abbr* **1** terrace **2** territory

ter·bi·um \ˈtər-bē-əm\ *n* : a metallic chemical element — see ELEMENT table

ter·cen·te·na·ry \ˌtər-ˌsen-ˈten-ə-rē, tər-ˈsent-ᵊn-ˌer-ē\ *n, pl* **-ries** : a 300th anniversary; *also* : its celebration — **tercentenary** *adj*

ter·cen·ten·ni·al \ˌtər-ˌsen-ˈten-ē-əl\ *adj or n* : TERCENTENARY

te·re·do \tə-ˈrēd-ō, -ˈrād-\ *n, pl* **teredos** *or* **te·red·i·nes** \-ˈred-ᵊn-ˌēz\ [L] : SHIPWORM

[1]**term** \ˈtərm\ *n* **1** : END, TERMINATION **2** : DURATION; *esp* : a period of time fixed esp. by law or custom **3** : a mathematical expression connected with another by a plus or minus sign; *also* : any of the members of a ratio or of a series **4** : a word or expression that has a precise meaning in some uses or is limited to a particular subject or field **5** *pl* : PROVISIONS, CONDITIONS ⟨~*s* of a contract⟩ **6** *pl* : mutual relationship ⟨on good ~*s*⟩ **7** : AGREEMENT, CONCORD

[2]**term** *vb* : to apply a term to : CALL

ter·ma·gant \ˈtər-mə-gənt\ *n* : an overbearing or nagging woman : SHREW **syn** virago, vixen, scold

[1]**ter·mi·nal** \ˈtər-mən-ᵊl\ *adj* : of, relating to, or forming an end, limit, or terminus **syn** final, concluding, last, latest

[2]**terminal** *n* **1** : EXTREMITY, END **2** : a device at the end of a wire or on electrical equipment for making a connection **3** : either end of a transportation line (as a railroad) with its offices and freight and passenger stations; *also* : a freight or passenger station **4** : a device connected to a communication network used to enter, receive, and display data

ter·mi·nate \ˈtər-mə-ˌnāt\ *vb* **-nat·ed; -nat·ing** : to bring or come to an end **syn** conclude, finish, complete — **ter·mi·na·ble** \-nə-bəl\ *adj* — **ter·mi·na·tion** \ˌtər-mə-ˈnā-shən\ *n* — **ter·mi·na·tor** \ˈtər-mə-ˌnāt-ər\ *n*

ter·mi·nol·o·gy \ˌtər-mə-ˈnäl-ə-jē\ *n, pl* **-gies** : the technical or special terms used in a business, art, science, or special subject

ter·mi·nus \ˈtər-mə-nəs\ *n, pl* **-ni** \-ˌnī\ *or* **-nus·es** [L] **1** : final goal : END **2** : either end of a transportation line, travel route, pipeline, or canal; *also* : the station or city at such a place

ter·mite \ˈtər-ˌmīt\ *n* : any of a large group of pale soft-bodied social insects that feed on wood

tern \ˈtərn\ *n* : any of numerous small seabirds with narrow wings and often a black cap

ter·na·ry \ˈtər-nə-rē\ *adj* **1** : of, relating to, or proceeding by threes **2** : having or consisting of three elements or parts **3** : having a mathematical base of three ⟨a ~ logarithm⟩

terr *abbr* territory

[1]**ter·race** \ˈter-əs\ *n* **1** : a flat roof or open platform **2** : a level area next to a building **3** : an embankment with level top **4** : a bank or ridge on a slope to conserve moisture and soil **5** : a row of houses on raised land; *also* : a street with such a row of houses **6** : a strip of park in the middle of a street

[2]**terrace** *vb* **ter·raced; ter·rac·ing** : to form into a terrace or supply with terraces

ter·ra–cot·ta \ˌter-ə-ˈkät-ə\ *n* [It *terra cotta*, lit., baked earth] : a reddish brown earthenware used for vases and small statues

terra fir·ma \-ˈfər-mə\ *n* [NL] : solid ground

ter·rain \tə-ˈrān\ *n* : the surface features of an area of land ⟨a rough ~⟩

ter·ra in·cog·ni·ta \ˈter-ə-ˌin-ˌkäg-ˈnēt-ə\ *n, pl* **ter·rae in·cog·ni·tae** \ˈter-ˌī-ˌin-ˌkäg-ˈnē-tī\ [L] : an unexplored area or field of knowledge

ter·ra·pin \ˈter-ə-pən\ *n* : any of various No. American edible turtles of fresh or brackish water

terrapin

ter·rar·i·um \tə-ˈrar-ē-əm\ *n, pl* **-ia** \-ē-ə\ *or* **-i·ums** : a vivarium without standing water

ter·res·tri·al \tə-ˈres-t(r)ē-əl\ *adj* **1** : of or relating to the earth or its inhabitants **2** : living or growing on land ⟨~ plants⟩ **syn** mundane, earthly, worldly

ter·ri·ble \ˈter-ə-bəl\ *adj* **1** : exciting terror : FEARFUL, DREADFUL ⟨~ weapons⟩ **2** : hard to bear : DISTRESSING ⟨a ~ situation⟩ **3** : extreme in degree : INTENSE ⟨~ heat⟩ **4** : of very poor quality : AWFUL ⟨a ~ play⟩ **syn** frightful, horrible, shocking, appalling — **ter·ri·bly** \-blē\ *adv*

ter·ri·er \ˈter-ē-ər\ *n* [F *(chien) terrier*, lit., earth dog, fr. *terrier* of earth, fr. ML *terrarius*, fr. L *terra* earth] : any of various usu. small dogs orig. used by hunters to drive small game from holes

ter·rif·ic \tə-ˈrif-ik\ *adj* **1** : exciting terror **2** : EXTRAORDINARY, ASTOUNDING ⟨~ speed⟩ **3** : unusually good ⟨makes ~ chili⟩ **syn** terrible, frightful, dreadful, fearful, horrible, awful

ter·ri·fy \ˈter-ə-ˌfī\ *vb* **-fied; -fy·ing** : to fill with terror : FRIGHTEN **syn** scare, terrorize, startle, alarm — **ter·ri·fy·ing·ly** *adv*

ter·ri·to·ri·al \ˌter-ə-ˈtōr-ē-əl\ *adj* **1** : of or relating to a territory ⟨~ government⟩ **2** : of or relating to an assigned area ⟨~ commanders⟩

ter·ri·to·ry \ˈter-ə-ˌtōr-ē\ *n, pl* **-ries** **1** : a geographical area belonging to or under the jurisdiction of a governmental authority **2** : a part of the U.S. not included within any state but organized with a separate legislature **3** : REGION, DISTRICT; *also* : a region in which one feels at home **4** : a field of knowledge or interest **5** : an assigned area

ter·ror \ˈter-ər\ *n* **1** : a state of intense fear : FRIGHT **2** : one that inspires fear **syn** panic, consternation, dread, alarm, dismay, horror, trepidation

ter·ror·ism \ˈter-ər-ˌiz-əm\ *n* : the systematic use of terror esp. as a means of coercion — **ter·ror·ist** \-əst\ *adj or n*

ter·ror·ize \ˈter-ər-ˌīz\ *vb* **-ized; -iz·ing** **1** : to fill with terror : SCARE **2** : to coerce by threat or violence **syn** terrify, frighten, alarm, startle

ter·ry \ˈter-ē\ *n, pl* **terries** : an absorbent fabric with a loose pile of uncut loops

terse \ˈtərs\ *adj* **ters·er; ters·est** [L *tersus* clean, neat, fr. pp. of *tergēre* to wipe off] : effectively brief : CONCISE — **terse·ly** *adv* — **terse·ness** *n*

ter·tia·ry \ˈtər-shē-ˌer-ē\ *adj* **1** : of third rank, importance, or value **2** *cap* : of, relating to, or being the earlier period of the Cenozoic era **3** : occurring in or being the third stage

Tertiary *n* : the Tertiary period

TESL *abbr* teaching English as a second language

tes·sel·late \ˈtes-ə-ˌlāt\ *vb* **-lat·ed; -lat·ing** : to form into or adorn with mosaic

¹test \ˈtest\ *n* [ME, vessel in which metals were assayed, fr. MF, fr. L *testum* earthen vessel] **1** : a critical examination or evaluation : TRIAL **2** : a means or result of testing

²test *vb* **1** : to put to test : TRY, EXAMINE **2** : to undergo or score on tests ⟨an ore that ~*s* high in gold⟩

tes·ta·ment \ˈtes-tə-mənt\ *n* **1** *cap* : either of two main divisions of the Bible **2** : EVIDENCE, WITNESS **3** : CREDO **4** : an act to determine the disposition of one's property after death : WILL — **tes·ta·men·ta·ry** \ˌtes-tə-ˈment-(ə-)rē\ *adj*

tes·tate \ˈtes-ˌtāt, -tət\ *adj* : having left a valid will

tes·ta·tor \ˈtes-ˌtāt-ər, tes-ˈtāt-\ *n* : a person who dies leaving a valid will

tes·ta·trix \tes-ˈtā-triks\ *n* : a female testator

¹tes·ter \ˈtēs-tər, ˈtes-\ *n* : a canopy over a bed, pulpit, or altar

²test·er \ˈtes-tər\ *n* : one that tests

tes·ti·cle \ˈtes-ti-kəl\ *n* : TESTIS

tes·ti·fy \ˈtes-tə-ˌfī\ *vb* **-fied; -fy·ing** **1** : to make a statement based on personal knowledge or belief : bear witness **2** : to serve as evidence or proof **syn** attest, affirm

tes·ti·mo·ni·al \ˌtes-tə-ˈmō-nē-əl\ *n* **1** : a statement testifying to a person's good character or to the worth of something **2** : an expression of appreciation : TRIBUTE — **testimonial** *adj*

tes·ti·mo·ny \ˈtes-tə-ˌmō-nē\ *n, pl* **-nies** **1** : a solemn declaration made by a witness under oath esp. in a court **2** : evidence based on observation or knowledge **3** : an outward sign : SYMBOL **syn** evidence, confirmation, proof, testament

tes·tis \ˈtes-təs\ *n, pl* **tes·tes** \ˈtes-ˌtēz\ [L, witness, testis] : an oval-shaped male reproductive organ which is usu. located in the scrotum, which produces and secretes various male hormones and esp. testosterone, and in which sperm are produced

tes·tos·ter·one \te-ˈstäs-tə-ˌrōn\ *n* : a male sex hormone that causes development of the male reproductive system and secondary sex character

test tube *n* : a glass tube closed at one end and used esp. in chemistry and biology

tes·ty \ˈtes-tē\ *adj* **tes·ti·er; -est** [ME *testif,* fr. Anglo-French (the French of medieval England), headstrong, fr. OF *teste* head, fr. LL *testa* skull, fr. L, shell] : marked by ill humor : easily annoyed

tet·a·nus \ˈtet-ᵊn-əs\ *n* : a disease caused by bacterial poisons and marked by stiffness and spasms of the muscles with locking of the jaws — **tet·a·nal** \-əl\ *adj*

tetchy \ˈtech-ē\ *adj* **tetchi·er; -est** : irritably or peevishly sensitive

¹tête–à–tête \ˈtāt-ə-ˌtāt\ *n* [F, lit., head to head] : a private conversation between two persons

²tête–à–tête \ˌtāt-ə-ˈtāt\ *adv* : PRIVATELY, FAMILIARLY

³tête–à–tête \ˌtāt-ə-ˌtāt\ *adj* : being face-to-face : PRIVATE

¹teth·er \ˈteth-ər\ *n* **1** : a line by which something (as an animal or balloon) is fastened **2** : the limit of one's strength or resources

²tether *vb* : to fasten or restrain by or as if by a tether

tet·ra·eth·yl lead \ˌte-trə-ˌeth-əl-\ *n* : a heavy oily poisonous liquid used as an antiknock agent in gasoline

tet·ra·he·dron \-ˈhē-drən\ *n, pl* **-drons** *or* **-dra** \-drə\ : a polyhedron that has four faces — **tet·ra·he·dral** \-drəl\ *adj*

tet·ra·hy·dro·can·nab·i·nol \-ˌhī-drə-kə-ˈnab-ə-ˌnȯl, -ˌnōl\ *n* : THC

te·tram·e·ter \te-ˈtram-ət-ər\ *n* : a line consisting of four metrical feet

Teu·ton·ic \t(y)ü-ˈtän-ik\ *adj* : GERMANIC

Tex *abbr* Texas

text \ˈtekst\ *n* **1** : the actual words of an author's work **2** : the main body of printed or written matter on a page **3** : a scriptural passage chosen as the subject esp. of a sermon **4** : THEME, TOPIC **5** : TEXTBOOK — **tex·tu·al** \ˈteks-chə(-wə)l\ *adj*

text·book \ˈteks(t)-ˌbu̇k\ *n* : a book used in the study of a subject

tex·tile \ˈtek-ˌstīl, ˈteks-tᵊl\ *n* : CLOTH; *esp* : a woven or knit cloth

tex·ture \ˈteks-chər\ *n* **1** : the visual or tactile surface characteristics and appearance of something ⟨a coarse ~⟩ **2** : essential part **3** : basic scheme or structure : FABRIC **4** : overall structure

TGIF *abbr* thank God it's Friday

¹Th *abbr* Thursday

²Th *symbol* thorium

¹-th — see ¹-ETH

²-th *or* **-eth** *adj suffix* — used in forming ordinal numbers ⟨hundred*th*⟩

³-th *n suffix* **1** : act or process **2** : state or condition ⟨dear*th*⟩

Thai \ˈtī\ *n, pl* **Thai** *or* **Thais** : a native or inhabitant of Thailand — **Thai** *adj*

thal·a·mus \ˈthal-ə-məs\ *n, pl* **-mi** \-ˌmī\ [NL] : a subdivision of the brain that receives nerve impulses and sends them to appropriate parts of the brain cortex

thal·li·um \ˈthal-ē-əm\ *n* : a poisonous metallic chemical element — see ELEMENT table

¹than \thən, (ˈ)than\ *conj* **1** — used after a comparative adjective or adverb to introduce the second part of a comparison expressing inequality ⟨older ~ I am⟩ **2** — used after *other* or a word of similar meaning to express a difference of kind, manner, or identity ⟨adults other ~ parents⟩

²than *prep* : in comparison with ⟨older ~ me⟩

thane \thān\ *n* **1** : a free retainer of an Anglo-Saxon lord **2** : a Scottish feudal lord

thank \ˈthaŋk\ *vb* : to express gratitude to ⟨~*ed* him for the present⟩

thank·ful \ˈthaŋk-fəl\ *adj* **1** : conscious of benefit received 2 : expressive of thanks 3 : GLAD — **thank·ful·ly** \-ē\ *adv* — **thank·ful·ness** *n*

thank·less \ˈthaŋ-kləs\ *adj* 1 : UNGRATEFUL 2 : UNAPPRECIATED

thanks \ˈthaŋks\ *n pl* : an expression of gratitude

thanks·giv·ing \thaŋks-ˈgiv-iŋ\ *n* 1 : the act of giving thanks 2 : prayer expressing gratitude 3 *cap* : the 4th Thursday in November observed as a legal holiday for giving thanks for divine goodness

[1]**that** \(ˈ)that\ *pron, pl* **those** \(ˈ)thōz\ 1 : the one indicated, mentioned, or understood ⟨~'s my wife⟩ 2 : the one farther away or first mentioned ⟨this is an elm, ~'s a maple⟩ 3 : what has been indicated or mentioned ⟨after ~, we left⟩ 4 : the one or ones : IT, THEY ⟨*those* who wish to leave may do so⟩

[2]**that** *adj, pl* **those** 1 : being the one mentioned, indicated, or understood ⟨~ boy⟩ ⟨*those* people⟩ 2 : being the one farther away or first mentioned ⟨this chair or ~ one⟩

[3]**that** \thət, (ˌ)that\ *conj* 1 : the following, namely ⟨he said ~ he would⟩; *also* : which is, namely ⟨there's a chance ~ it may fail⟩ 2 : to this end or purpose ⟨shouted ~ all might hear⟩ 3 : as to result in the following, namely ⟨so heavy ~ it can't be moved⟩ 4 : for this reason, namely : BECAUSE ⟨we're glad ~ you came⟩ 5 : I wish this, or I am surprised or indignant at this, namely ⟨~ it should come to this⟩

[4]**that** \thət, (ˌ)that\ *pron* 1 : WHO, WHOM, WHICH ⟨the man ~ saw you⟩ ⟨the man ~ you saw⟩ ⟨the money ~ was spent⟩ 2 : in, on, or at which ⟨the way ~ he drives⟩ ⟨the day ~ it rained⟩

[5]**that** \ˈthat\ *adv* : to such an extent or degree ⟨I like it, but not ~ much⟩

[1]**thatch** \ˈthach\ *vb* : to cover with or as if with thatch

[2]**thatch** *n* 1 : plant material (as straw) for use as roofing 2 : a mat of grass clippings accumulated next to the soil on a lawn 3 : a covering of or as if of thatch ⟨a ~ of white hair⟩

thaw \ˈthȯ\ *vb* 1 : to melt or cause to melt 2 : to become so warm as to melt ice or snow 3 : to abandon aloofness or hostility **syn** liquefy — **thaw** *n*

THC \ˌtē-ˌāch-ˈsē\ *n* [*tetrahydrocannabinol*] : a physiologically active chemical from hemp plant resin that is the chief intoxicant in marijuana

[1]**the** \thə, *before vowel sounds usu* thē\ *definite article* 1 : that in particular 2 — used before adjectives functioning as nouns ⟨a word to ~ wise⟩

[2]**the** *adv* 1 : to what extent ⟨~ sooner, the better⟩ 2 : to that extent ⟨the sooner, ~ better⟩

theat *abbr* theater; theatrical

the·ater *or* **the·atre** \ˈthē-ət-ər\ *n* 1 : a building for dramatic performances; *also* : a building or area for showing motion pictures 2 : a place of enactment of significant events ⟨~ of war⟩ 3 : a place (as a lecture room) resembling a theater 4 : dramatic literature or performance

theater–in–the–round *n* : a theater with the stage in the center of the auditorium

the·at·ri·cal \thē-ˈa-tri-kəl\ *also* **the·at·ric** \-trik\ *adj* 1 : of or relating to the theater 2 : marked by artificiality of emotion : HISTRIONIC 3 : marked by extravagant display : SHOWY **syn** dramatic, melodramatic

the·at·ri·cals \-kəlz\ *n pl* : the performance of plays

the·at·rics \thē-ˈa-triks\ *n pl* 1 : THEATRICALS 2 : staged or contrived effects

the·be \ˈthā-bā\ *n, pl* **thebe** — see *pula* at MONEY table

thee \(ˈ)thē\ *pron, objective case of* THOU

theft \ˈtheft\ *n* : the act of stealing

thegn \ˈthān\ *n* : THANE 1

their \thər, (ˌ)theər\ *adj* : of or relating to them or themselves

theirs \ˈtheərz\ *pron* : their one : their ones

the·ism \ˈthē-ˌiz-əm\ *n* : belief in the existence of a god or gods — **the·ist** \-əst\ *n or adj* — **the·is·tic** \thē-ˈis-tik\ *adj*

them \(th)əm, (ˈ)them\ *pron, objective case of* THEY

theme \ˈthēm\ *n* 1 : a subject or topic of discourse or of artistic representation 2 : a written exercise : COMPOSITION 3 : a melodic subject of a musical composition or movement — **the·mat·ic** \thi-ˈmat-ik\ *adj*

them·selves \thəm-ˈselvz, them-\ *pron pl* : THEY, THEM — used reflexively, for emphasis, or in absolute constructions ⟨they govern ~⟩ ⟨they ~ couldn't come⟩ ⟨~ busy, they sent me⟩

[1]**then** \(ˈ)then\ *adv* 1 : at that time 2 : soon after that : NEXT 3 : in addition : BESIDES 4 : in that case 5 : CONSEQUENTLY

[2]**then** \ˈthen\ *n* : that time ⟨since ~⟩

[3]**then** \ˈthen\ *adj* : existing or acting at that time ⟨the ~ king⟩

thence \ˈthens, thens\ *adv* 1 : from that place 2 *archaic* : THENCEFORTH 3 : from that fact : THEREFROM

thence·forth \-ˌfōrth\ *adv* : from that time forward : THEREAFTER

thence·for·ward \thens-ˈfȯr-wərd, thens-\ *also* **thence·for·wards** \-wərdz\ *adv* : onward from that place or time : THENCEFORTH

the·oc·ra·cy \thē-ˈäk-rə-sē\ *n, pl* **-cies** 1 : government by officials regarded as divinely inspired 2 : a state governed by a theocracy — **the·o·crat·ic** \ˌthē-ə-ˈkrat-ik\ *adj*

theol *abbr* theological; theology

the·ol·o·gy \thē-ˈäl-ə-jē\ *n, pl* **-gies** 1 : the study of religion and of religious ideas and beliefs; *esp* : a branch of theology treating of God and his relation to the world 2 : a theory or system of theology — **the·o·lo·gian** \ˌthē-ə-ˈlō-jən\ *n* — **the·o·log·i·cal** \-ˈläj-i-kəl\ *adj*

the·o·rem \ˈthē-ə-rəm, ˈthir-əm\ *n* 1 : a statement in mathematics that has been or is to be proved 2 : an idea accepted or proposed as a demonstrable truth : PROPOSITION

the·o·ret·i·cal \ˌthē-ə-ˈret-i-kəl\ *also* **the·o·ret·ic** \-ik\ *adj* 1 : relating to or having the character of theory 2 : existing only in theory — **the·o·ret·i·cal·ly** \-i-k(ə-)lē\ *adv*

the·o·rize \ˈthē-ə-ˌrīz\ *vb* **-rized; -riz·ing** : to form a theory : SPECULATE — **the·o·rist** \-rəst\ *n*

the·o·ry \ˈthē-ə-rē, ˈthir-ē\ *n, pl* **-ries** 1 : abstract thought 2 : the general principles of a subject 3 : a plausible or scientifically acceptable general principle offered to explain observed facts 4 : HYPOTHESIS, GUESS

theory of games : GAME THEORY

the·os·o·phy \thē-ˈäs-ə-fē\ *n* : belief about God and the world held to be based on mystical insight — **theo·soph·i·cal** \ˌthē-ə-ˈsäf-i-kəl\ *adj* — **the·os·o·phist** \thē-ˈäs-ə-fəst\ *n*

ther·a·peu·tic \ˌther-ə-ˈpyüt-ik\ *adj* [Gk *therapeutikos*, fr. *therapeuein* to attend, treat, fr. *theraps* attendant] : of, relating to, or dealing with healing and esp. with remedies for diseases — **ther·a·peu·ti·cal·ly** \-i-k(ə-)lē\ *adv*

ther·a·peu·tics \ˌther-ə-ˈpyüt-iks\ *n* : a branch of medical science dealing with the use of remedies

ther·a·py \ˈther-ə-pē\ *n, pl* **-pies** : treatment of bodily or mental disorders or maladjustment — **ther·a·pist** \-pəst\ *n*

[1]**there** \ˈthaər, ˈtheər\ *adv* 1 : in or at that place — often used interjectionally 2 : to or into that place : THITHER 3 : in that matter or respect

[2]**there** \(ˌ)thar, (ˌ)ther, thər\ *pron* — used as a function word to introduce a sentence or clause ⟨~'s a man here⟩

[3]**there** \ˈthaər, ˈtheər\ *n* 1 : that place ⟨get away from ~⟩ 2 : that point ⟨you take it from ~⟩

there·abouts *or* **there·about** \ˌthar-ə-ˈbau̇t(s), ˈthar-ə-ˌbau̇t(s), ˌther-ə-ˈbau̇t(s), ˈther-ə-ˌ\ *adv* 1 : near that place or time 2 : near that number, degree, or quantity

there·af·ter \thar-ˈaf-tər, ther-\ *adv* : after that : AFTERWARD

there·at \-ˈat\ *adv* 1 : at that place 2 : at that occurrence : on that account

there·by \thar-ˈbī, ther-, ˈtha(ə)r-ˌbī, ˈthe(ə)r-ˌbī\ *adv* 1

: by that : by that means 2 : connected with or with reference to that

there·for \thar-ˈfȯr, ther-\ *adv* : for or in return for that

there·fore \ˈtha(ə)r-ˌfōr, ˈthe(ə)r-\ *adv* : for that reason : CONSEQUENTLY

there·from \thar-ˈfrəm, ther-\ *adv* : from that or it

there·in \thar-ˈin, ther-\ *adv* **1** : in or into that place, time, or thing **2** : in that respect

there·of \-ˈəv, -ˈäv\ *adv* **1** : of that or it **2** : from that : THEREFROM

there·on \-ˈȯn, -ˈän\ *adv* **1** : on that **2** *archaic* : THEREUPON 3

there·to \thar-ˈtü, ther-\ *adv* : to that

there·un·to \thar-ˈən-(ˌ)tü; ˌthar-ən-ˈtü, ˌther-\ *adv, archaic* : THERETO

there·upon \ˈthar-ə-ˌpȯn, ˈther-, -ˌpän; ˌthar-ə-ˈpȯn, -ˈpän, ˌther-\ *adv* **1** : on that matter : THEREON **2** : THEREFORE **3** : immediately after that : at once

there·with \thar-ˈwith, ther-, -with\ *adv* **1** : with that **2** *archaic* : THEREUPON, FORTHWITH

there·with·al\ˈtha(ə)r-with-ˌȯl, ˈthe(ə)r-, -with-\ *adv* **1** *archaic* : BESIDES **2** : THEREWITH

therm *abbr* thermometer

ther·mal \ˈthər-məl\ *adj* **1** : of, relating to, or caused by heat **2** : designed to prevent the loss of body heat ⟨~ underwear⟩ — **ther·mal·ly** \-ē\ *adv*

thermal pollution *n* : the discharge of liquid (as waste water from a factory) into a natural body of water at a temperature harmful to the environment

therm·is·tor \ˈthər-ˌmis-tər\ *n* : an electrical resistor whose resistance varies sharply with temperature

ther·mo·cline \ˈthər-mə-ˌklīn\ *n* : a transition layer in a thermally stratified body of water that separates zones of widely different temperature

ther·mo·dy·nam·ics \ˌthər-mə-dī-ˈnam-iks\ *n* : physics that deals with the mechanical action or relations of heat — **ther·mo·dy·nam·ic** \-ik\ *adj* — **ther·mo·dy·nam·i·cal·ly** \-i-k(ə-)lē\ *adv*

ther·mom·e·ter \thə(r)-ˈmäm-ət-ər\ *n* [F *thermomètre,* fr. Gk *thermē* heat + *metron* measure] : an instrument for measuring temperature commonly by means of the expansion or contraction of mercury or alcohol as indicated by its rise or fall in a thin glass tube — **ther·mo·met·ric** \ˌthər-mə-ˈme-trik\ *adj* — **ther·mo·met·ri·cal·ly** \-tri-k(ə-)lē\ *adv*

ther·mo·nu·cle·ar \ˌthər-mō-ˈn(y)ü-klē-ər\ *adj* **1** : of or relating to changes in the nucleus of atoms of low atomic weight (as hydrogen) that require a very high temperature (as in the hydrogen bomb) **2** : utilizing or relating to a thermonuclear bomb ⟨~ war⟩

ther·mo·plas·tic \ˌthər-mə-ˈplas-tik\ *adj* : capable of softening when heated and of hardening again when cooled ⟨~ resins⟩ — **thermoplastic** *n*

ther·mo·reg·u·la·tor \ˌthər-mō-ˈreg-yə-ˌlāt-ər\ *n* : a device for the regulation of temperature

ther·mos \ˈthər-məs\ *n* : VACUUM BOTTLE

ther·mo·sphere \ˈthər-mə-ˌsfiər\ *n* : the part of the earth's atmosphere that begins at about 50 miles (about 80 kilometers) above the earth's surface, extends to outer space, and is characterized by steadily increasing temperature with height

ther·mo·stat \ˈthər-mə-ˌstat\ *n* : a device that automatically controls temperature — **ther·mo·stat·ic** \ˌthər-mə-ˈstat-ik\ *adj* — **ther·mo·stat·i·cal·ly** \-i-k(ə-)lē\ *adv*

the·sau·rus \thi-ˈsȯr-əs\ *n, pl* **-sau·ri** \-ˈsȯr-ˌī\ *or* **-sau·rus·es** \-ˈsȯr-ə-səz\ [NL, fr. L, treasure, collection, fr. Gk *thēsauros*] : a book of words and their synonyms — **the·sau·ral** \-ˈsȯr-əl\ *adj*

these *pl of* THIS

the·sis \ˈthē-səs\ *n, pl* **the·ses** \ˈthē-ˌsēz\ **1** : a proposition that a person advances and offers to maintain by argument **2** : an essay embodying results of original research; *esp* : one written for an academic degree

[1]**thes·pi·an** \ˈthes-pē-ən\ *adj, often cap* [fr. *Thespis,* 6th cent. B.C. Greek poet and reputed originator of tragedy] : relating to the drama : DRAMATIC

[2]**thespian** *n* : ACTOR

Thess *abbr* Thessalonians

Thes·sa·lo·nians \ˌthes-ə-ˈlō-nyənz, -nē-ənz\ *n* — see BIBLE table

thew \ˈth(y)ü\ *n* : MUSCLE, SINEW — usu. used in pl.

they \(ˈ)thā\ *pron* **1** : those individuals under discussion : the ones previously mentioned or referred to **2** : unspecified persons : PEOPLE

thi·a·mine \ˈthī-ə-mən, -ˌmēn\ *also* **thi·a·min** \-mən\ *n* : a vitamin of the vitamin B complex that is essential to normal metabolism and nerve function

[1]**thick** \ˈthik\ *adj* **1** : having relatively great depth or extent from one surface to its opposite ⟨a ~ plank⟩; *also* : heavily built : THICKSET **2** : densely massed : CROWDED; *also* : FREQUENT, NUMEROUS **3** : dense or viscous in consistency ⟨~ syrup⟩ **4** : marked by haze, fog, or mist ⟨~ weather⟩ **5** : measuring in thickness ⟨one meter ~⟩ **6** : imperfectly articulated : INDISTINCT ⟨~ speech⟩ **7** : STUPID, OBTUSE **8** : associated on close terms : INTIMATE **9** : EXCESSIVE **syn** compact, close, dense, crowded, tight — **thick·ly** *adv*

[2]**thick** *n* **1** : the most crowded or active part **2** : the part of greatest thickness

thick·en \ˈthik-ən\ *vb* **thick·ened; thick·en·ing** \-(ə-)niŋ\ : to make or become thick — **thick·en·er** \-(ə-)nər\ *n*

thick·et \ˈthik-ət\ *n* : a dense growth of bushes or small trees

thick·ness \-nəs\ *n* **1** : the quality or state of being thick **2** : the smallest of three dimensions ⟨length, width, and ~⟩ **3** : LAYER, SHEET ⟨a single ~ of canvas⟩

thick·set \ˈthik-ˈset\ *adj* **1** : closely placed or planted **2** : having a thick body : BURLY

thick–skinned \-ˈskind\ *adj* **1** : having a thick skin **2** : not easily bothered by criticism or insult

thief \ˈthēf\ *n, pl* **thieves** \ˈthēvz\ : one that steals esp. secretly

thieve \ˈthēv\ *vb* **thieved; thiev·ing** : STEAL, ROB **syn** filch, pilfer, purloin, swipe

thiev·ery \ˈthēv-(ə-)rē\ *n, pl* **-er·ies** : the act of stealing : THEFT

thigh \ˈthī\ *n* : the part of the vertebrate hind limb between the knee and the hip

thigh·bone \ˈthī-ˌbōn\ *n* : FEMUR

thim·ble \ˈthim-bəl\ *n* : a cap or guard used in sewing to protect the finger when pushing the needle — **thim·ble·ful** *n*

[1]**thin** \ˈthin\ *adj* **thin·ner; thin·nest 1** : having little extent from one surface through to its opposite : not thick : SLENDER **2** : not closely set or placed : SPARSE ⟨~ hair⟩ **3** : not dense or not dense enough : more fluid or rarefied than normal ⟨~ air⟩ ⟨~ syrup⟩ **4** : lacking substance, fullness, or strength ⟨~ broth⟩ **5** : FLIMSY **syn** slim, slight, tenuous — **thin·ly** *adv* — **thin·ness** \ˈthin-nəs\ *n*

[2]**thin** *vb* **thinned; thin·ning** : to make or become thin

thine \ˈthīn\ *pron, archaic* : one or the ones belonging to thee

thing \ˈthiŋ\ *n* **1** : a matter of concern : AFFAIR ⟨~*s* to do⟩ **2** *pl* : state of affairs ⟨~*s* are improving⟩ **3** : EVENT, CIRCUMSTANCE ⟨the crime was a terrible ~⟩ **4** : DEED, ACT ⟨expected great ~*s* of him⟩ **5** : a distinct entity : OBJECT **6** : an inanimate object distinguished from a living being **7** *pl* : POSSESSIONS, EFFECTS ⟨packed his ~*s*⟩ **8** : an article of clothing **9** : DETAIL, POINT **10** : IDEA, NOTION **11**

: something one likes to do : SPECIALTY ⟨doing his ~⟩

think \ˈthiŋk\ *vb* **thought** \ˈthȯt\; **think·ing** **1** : to form or have in the mind **2** : to have as an opinion : BELIEVE **3** : to relect on : PONDER **4** : to call to mind : REMEMBER **5** : REASON **6** : to form a mental picture of : IMAGINE **7** : to devise by thinking ⟨*thought* up a plan to escape⟩ **syn** conceive, fancy, realize, envisage — **think·er** *n*

think tank *n* : an institute, corporation, or group organized for interdisciplinary research (as in technological or social problems)

thin·ner \ˈthin-ər\ *n* : a volatile liquid (as turpentine) used to thin paint

thin–skinned \ˈthin-ˈskind\ *adj* **1** : having a thin skin **2** : extremely sensitive to criticism or insult

[1]**third** \ˈthərd\ *adj* : next after the second — **third** *or* **third·ly** *adv*

[2]**third** *n* **1** : one of three equal parts of something **2** : one that is third **3** : the 3d forward gear in an automotive vehicle

third degree *n* : the subjection of a prisoner to mental or physical torture to force a confession

third dimension *n* **1** : thickness, depth, or apparent thickness or depth that confers solidity on an object **2** : a quality that confers reality — **third–dimensional** *adj*

third world *n, often cap T&W* **1** : a group of nations esp. in Africa and Asia that are not aligned with either the Communist or the non-Communist blocs **2** : an aggregate of minority groups within a larger predominant culture **3** : the aggregate of the underdeveloped nations of the world

[1]**thirst** \ˈthərst\ *n* **1** : a feeling of dryness in the mouth and throat associated with a wish to drink; *also* : a bodily condition producing this **2** : an ardent desire : CRAVING ⟨a ~ for knowledge⟩ — **thirsty** *adj*

[2]**thirst** *vb* **1** : to need drink : suffer thirst **2** : to have a strong desire : CRAVE

thir·teen \ˌthər-ˈtēn, ˈthər-\ *n* : one more than 12 — **thirteen** *adj or pron* — **thir·teenth** \-ˈtēnth\ *adj or n*

thir·ty \ˈthərt-ē\ *n, pl* **thirties** : three times 10 — **thir·ti·eth** \-ē-əth\ *adj or n* — **thirty** *adj or pron*

[1]**this** \(ˈ)this\ *pron, pl* **these** \(ˈ)thēz\ **1** : the one close or closest in time or space ⟨~ is your book⟩ **2** : what is in the present or under immediate observation or discussion ⟨~ is a mess⟩; *also* : what is happening or being done now ⟨after ~ we'll leave⟩

[2]**this** *adj, pl* **these** **1** : being the one near, present, just mentioned, or more immediately under observation ⟨~ book⟩ **2** : constituting the immediate past or future ⟨friends all *these* years⟩

[3]**this** \ˈthis\ *adv* : to such an extent or degree ⟨we need a book about ~ big⟩

this·tle \ˈthis-əl\ *n* : any of several tall prickly herbs

this·tle·down \-ˌdau̇n\ *n* : the down from the ripe flower head of a thistle

[1]**thith·er** \ˈthith-ər\ *adv* : to that place

[2]**thither** *adj* : being on the farther side

thith·er·ward \-wərd\ *adv* : toward that place : THITHER

thole \ˈthōl\ *n* : a pin set in the gunwale of a boat against which an oar pivots in rowing

thong \ˈthȯŋ\ *n* **1** : a strip esp. of leather or hide **2** : a sandal held on the foot by a thong between the toes

tho·rax \ˈthōr-ˌaks\ *n, pl* **tho·rax·es** *or* **tho·ra·ces** \ˈthōr-ə-ˌsēz\ **1** : the part of the body of a mammal between the neck and the abdomen; *also* : its cavity **2** : the middle of the three main divisions of the body of an insect — **tho·rac·ic** \thə-ˈras-ik\ *adj*

tho·ri·um \ˈthōr-ē-əm\ *n* : a radioactive metallic chemical element — see ELEMENT table

thorn \ˈthȯrn\ *n* **1** : a woody plant bearing sharp processes **2** : a sharp rigid plant process that is usu. a modified leafless branch **3** : something that causes distress — **thorny** *adj*

thor·ough \ˈthər-ō\ *adj* **1** : COMPLETE, EXHAUSTIVE ⟨a ~ search⟩ **2** : very careful : PAINSTAKING ⟨a ~ scholar⟩ **3** : having full mastery — **thor·ough·ly** *adv* — **thor·ough·ness** *n*

[1]**thor·ough·bred** \ˈthər-ə-ˌbred\ *adj* **1** : bred from the best blood through a long line **2** *cap* : of or relating to the Thoroughbred breed of horses **3** : marked by high-spirited grace

[2]**thoroughbred** *n* **1** *cap* : any of an English breed of light speedy horses kept chiefly for racing **2** : one (as a pedigreed animal) of excellent quality

thor·ough·fare \-ˌfaər\ *n* : a public road or street

thor·ough·go·ing \ˌthər-ə-ˈgō-iŋ\ *adj* : marked by thoroughness or zeal

thorp \ˈthȯrp\ *n, archaic* : village

those *pl of* THAT

[1]**thou** \(ˈ)thau̇\ *pron, archaic* : the person addressed

[2]**thou** \ˈthau̇\ *n, pl* **thou** : a thousand of something (as dollars)

[1]**though** \ˈthō\ *adv* : HOWEVER, NEVERTHELESS ⟨not for long, ~⟩

[2]**though** \(ˌ)thō\ *conj* **1** : despite the fact that ⟨~ the odds are hopeless, they fight on⟩ **2** : granting that ⟨~ it may look bad, still, all is not lost⟩

[1]**thought** \ˈthȯt\ *past and past part of* THINK

[2]**thought** *n* **1** : the process of thinking **2** : serious consideration : REGARD **3** : reasoning power **4** : the power to imagine : CONCEPTION **5** : IDEA, NOTION **6** : OPINION, BELIEF

thought·ful \ˈthȯt-fəl\ *adj* **1** : absorbed in thought **2** : marked by careful thinking ⟨a ~ essay⟩ **3** : considerate of others ⟨a ~ host⟩ — **thought·ful·ly** \-ē\ *adv* — **thought·ful·ness** *n*

thought·less \-ləs\ *adj* **1** : insufficiently alert : CARELESS ⟨a ~ worker⟩ **2** : RECKLESS ⟨a ~ act⟩ **3** : lacking concern for others : INCONSIDERATE ⟨~ remarks⟩ — **thought·less·ly** *adv* — **thought·less·ness** *n*

thou·sand \ˈthau̇z-ᵊnd\ *n, pl* **thousands** *or* **thousand** : 10 times 100 — **thousand** *adj* — **thou·sandth** \-ᵊnth\ *adj or n*

thousands digit *n* : the numeral (as 1 in 1456) occupying the thousands place in a number

thousands place *n* : the place four to the left of the decimal point in an Arabic number

thrall \ˈthrȯl\ *n* **1** : SLAVE, BONDMAN **2** : THRALLDOM

thrall·dom *or* **thral·dom** \ˈthrȯl-dəm\ *n* : the condition of a thrall

thrash \ˈthrash\ *vb* **1** : THRESH 1 **2** : BEAT, WHIP; *also* : DEFEAT **3** : to move about violently **4** : to go over again and again ⟨~ over the matter⟩; *also* : to hammer out ⟨~ out a plan⟩

[1]**thrash·er** \ˈthrash-ər\ *n* : one that thrashes or threshes

[2]**thrasher** *n* : a long-tailed bird resembling a thrush

[1]**thread** \ˈthred\ *n* **1** : a thin continuous strand of spun and twisted textile fibers **2** : something resembling a textile thread **3** : the ridge or groove that winds around a screw **4** : a train of thought **5** : a continuing element

[2]**thread** *vb* **1** : to pass a thread through the eye of (a needle) **2** : to pass (as film) through something **3** : to make one's way through or between **4** : to put together on a thread ⟨~ beads⟩ **5** : to form a screw thread on or in

thread·bare \-ˌbaər\ *adj* **1** : worn so that the thread shows : SHABBY **2** : TRITE

thready \-ē\ *adj* **1** : consisting of or bearing fibers of filaments ⟨a ~ bark⟩ **2** : lacking in fullness, body, or vigor

threat \ˈthret\ *n* **1** : an expression of intent to do harm **2** : one that threatens

threat·en \ˈthret-ᵊn\ *vb* **threat·ened; threat·en·ing** \ˈthret-(ᵊ-)niŋ\ **1** : to utter threats against **2** : to give signs or warning of : PORTEND **3** : to hang over as a threat : MENACE — **threat·en·ing·ly** *adv*

three \ˈthrē\ *n* **1** : one more than two **2** : the 3d in a set or series **3** : something having three units — **three** *adj or pron*

3–D \ˈthrē-ˈdē\ *n* : three-dimensional form

three–dimensional *adj* **1** : relating to or having three dimensions **2** : giving the illusion of varying distances ⟨a ~ picture⟩

three·fold \ˈthrē-ˌfōld, -ˈfōld\ *adj* **1** : having three parts : TRIPLE **2** : being three times as great or as many — **three·fold** \-ˈfōld\ *adv*

three·pence \ˈthrep-əns,ˈthrip-, ˈthrəp-, *US also* ˈthrē-pens\ *n* **1** *pl* **threepence** *or* **three·penc·es** : a coin worth three pennies **2** : the sum of three British pennies

three·score \ˈthrē-ˈskōr\ *adj* : being three times twenty : SIXTY

three·some \ˈthrē-səm\ *n* : a group of three persons or things

thren·o·dy \ˈthren-əd-ē\ *n, pl* **-dies** : a song of lamentation : ELEGY

thresh \ˈthrash, ˈthresh\ *vb* **1** : to separate (as grain from straw) by beating **2** : THRASH — **thresh·er** *n*

thresh·old \ˈthresh-ˌōld\ *n* **1** : the sill of a door **2** : a point or place of beginning or entering : OUTSET **3** : a point at which a physiological or psychological effect begins to be produced

threw *past of* THROW

thrice \ˈthrīs\ *adv* **1** : three times **2** : in a threefold manner or degree

thrift \ˈthrift\ *n* [ME fr. ON, prosperity, fr. *thrīfask* to thrive] : careful management esp. of money : FRUGALITY — **thrift·i·ly** \ˈthrif-tə-lē\ *adv* — **thrift·less** *adj* — **thrifty** *adj*

thrill \ˈthril\ *vb* [ME *thirlen, thrillen* to pierce, fr. OE *thyrlian*, fr. *thyrel* hole, fr. *thurh* through] **1** : to have or cause to have sudden sharp feeling of excitement; *also* : TINGLE, SHIVER **2** : TREMBLE, VIBRATE — **thrill** *n* — **thrill·er** *n* — **thrill·ing·ly** \-iŋ-lē\ *adv*

thrive \ˈthrīv\ *vb* **throve** \ˈthrōv\ *or* **thrived; thriv·en** \ˈthriv-ən\ *also* **thrived; thriv·ing** \ˈthrī-viŋ\ **1** : to grow luxuriantly : FLOURISH **2** : to gain in wealth or possessions : PROSPER

throat \ˈthrōt\ *n* : the part of the neck in front of the spinal column; *also* : the passage through it to the stomach and lungs — **throat·ed** \-əd\ *adj*

throaty \ˈthrōt-ē\ *adj* **throat·i·er; -est** **1** : uttered or produced from low in the throat ⟨a ~ voice⟩ **2** : heavy, thick, or deep as if from the throat ⟨~ notes of a horn⟩ — **throat·i·ly** \ˈthrōt-ᵊl-ē\ *adv* — **throat·i·ness** \-ē-nəs\ *n*

[1]**throb** \ˈthräb\ *vb* **throbbed; throb·bing** : to pulsate or pound esp. with abnormal force or rapidity : BEAT, VIBRATE

[2]**throb** *n* : BEAT, PULSE

throe \ˈthrō\ *n* **1** : PANG, SPASM **2** *pl* : a hard or painful struggle

throm·bo·sis \thräm-ˈbō-səs\ *n, pl* **-bo·ses** \-ˌsēz\ : the formation or presence of a clot in a blood vessel during life — **throm·bot·ic** \-ˈbät-ik\ *adj*

throm·bus \ˈthräm-bəs\ *n, pl* **throm·bi** \-ˌbī\ : a clot of blood formed within a blood vessel and remaining attached to its place of origin

throne \ˈthrōn\ *n* **1** : the chair of state esp. of a king or bishop **2** : royal power : SOVEREIGNTY

[1]**throng** \ˈthrȯŋ\ *n* **1** : MULTITUDE **2** : a crowding together of many persons

[2]**throng** *vb* **thronged; throng·ing** \ˈthrȯŋ-iŋ\ : CROWD

[1]**throt·tle** \ˈthrät-ᵊl\ *vb* **throt·tled; throt·tling** \ˈthrät-(ᵊ-)liŋ\ [ME *throtlen*, fr. *throte* throat] **1** : CHOKE, STRANGLE **2** : SUPPRESS **3** : to reduce the speed of (an engine) by closing the throttle — **throt·tler** \-(ᵊ-)lər\ *n*

[2]**throttle** *n* : a valve regulating the flow of steam or fuel to an engine; *also* : the lever controlling this valve

[1]**through** \(ˈ)thrü\ *prep* **1** : into at one side and out at the other side of ⟨go ~ the door⟩ **2** : by way of ⟨entered ~ a skylight⟩ **3** : AMONG ⟨a path ~ the trees⟩ **4** : by means of ⟨succeeded ~ hard work⟩ **5** : over the whole of ⟨rumors swept ~ the office⟩ **6** : during the whole of ⟨~ the night⟩ **7** : to and including ⟨Monday ~ Friday⟩

[2]**through** \ˈthrü\ *adv* **1** : from one end or side to the other **2** : from beginning to end : to completion ⟨see it ~⟩ **3** : to the core : THOROUGHLY ⟨he was wet ~⟩ **4** : into the open : OUT ⟨break ~⟩

[3]**through** \ˈthrü\ *adj* **1** : permitting free passage ⟨a ~ street⟩ **2** : going from point of origin to destination without change or transfer ⟨~ train⟩ **3** : coming from or going to points outside a local area ⟨~ traffic⟩ **4** : FINISHED ⟨~ with the job⟩

[1]**through·out** \thrü-ˈau̇t\ *adv* **1** : EVERYWHERE **2** : from beginning to end

[2]**throughout** *prep* **1** : in or to every part of **2** : during the whole period of

through·put \ˈthrü-ˌpu̇t\ *n* : OUTPUT, PRODUCTION ⟨the ~ of a computer⟩

through·way *var of* THRUWAY

throve *past of* THRIVE

[1]**throw** \ˈthrō\ *vb* **threw** \ˈthrü\; **thrown** \ˈthrōn\; **throw·ing** **1** : to propel through the air esp. with a forward motion of the hand and arm ⟨~ a ball⟩ **2** : to cause to fall or fall off **3** : to put suddenly in a certain position or condition ⟨~ into panic⟩ **4** : to put on or take off hastily ⟨~ on a coat⟩ **5** : to move (a lever) so as to connect or disconnect parts of something (as a clutch) **6** : to lose intentionally ⟨~ a game⟩ **7** : to act as host for ⟨~ a party⟩ **syn** toss, fling, pitch, sling — **throw·er** \ˈthrō(-ə)r\ *n*

[2]**throw** *n* **1** : an act of throwing, hurling, or flinging; *also* : CAST **2** : the distance a missile may be thrown **3** : a light coverlet **4** : a woman's scarf or light wrap

throw·away \ˈthrō-ə-ˌwā\ *n* : something that is or is designed to be thrown away esp. after one use

throw·back \ˈthrō-ˌbak\ *n* : reversion to an earlier type or phase; *also* : an instance or product of this

throw up *vb* **1** : to build hurriedly **2** : VOMIT

thrum \ˈthrəm\ *vb* **thrummed; thrum·ming** : to play or pluck a stringed instrument idly : STRUM

thrush \ˈthrəsh\ *n* : any of a large family of small or medium-sized songbirds that are mostly of a plain color often with spotted underparts

[1]**thrust** \ˈthrəst\ *vb* **thrust; thrust·ing** **1** : to push or drive with force : SHOVE **2** : STAB, PIERCE **3** : INTERJECT **4** : to press the acceptance of upon someone

[2]**thrust** *n* **1** : a lunge with a pointed weapon **2** : ATTACK **3** : the pressure of one part of a construction against another (as of an arch against an abutment) **4** : the force produced by a propeller or jet or rocket engine that drives a vehicle (as an aircraft) forward **5** : a violent push : SHOVE

thrust·er *also* **thrust·or** \ˈthrəs-tər\ *n* : one that thrusts; *esp* : a rocket engine

thru·way \ˈthrü-ˌwā\ *n* : EXPRESSWAY

[1]**thud** \ˈthəd\ *vb* **thud·ded; thud·ding** : to move or strike so as to make a thud

[2]**thud** *n* **1** : BLOW **2** : a dull sound

thug \ˈthəg\ *n* [Hindi *thag*, lit., thief, fr. Skt *sthaga* rogue] : a brutal ruffian or assassin

thu·li·um \ˈth(y)ü-lē-əm\ *n* : a rare metallic chemical element — see ELEMENT table

[1]**thumb** \ˈthəm\ *n* **1** : the short thick first digit of the human hand or a corresponding digit of a lower animal **2** : the part of a glove or mitten that covers the thumb

[2]**thumb** *vb* **1** : to leaf through (pages) with the thumb **2** : to wear or soil with the thumb by frequent handling **3** : to

request or obtain (a ride) in a passing automobile by signaling with the thumb

thumb index *n* : a series of notches cut in the fore edge of a book to facilitate reference

[1]**thumb·nail** \ˈthəm-ˌnāl\ *n* : the nail of the thumb

[2]**thumb·nail** \ˌthəm-ˌnāl\ *adj* : BRIEF, CONCISE ⟨a ~ description⟩

thumb·print \ˈthəm-ˌprint\ *n* : an impression made by the thumb

thumb·screw \ˈthəm-ˌskrü\ *n* **1** : a screw with a head that may be turned by the thumb and forefinger **2** : a device of torture for squeezing the thumb

thumb·tack \-ˌtak\ *n* : a tack with a broad flat head for pressing with one's thumb into a board or wall

[1]**thump** \ˈthəmp\ *vb* **1** : to strike with or as if with something thick or heavy so as to cause a dull heavy sound **2** : POUND

[2]**thump** *n* : a blow with or as if with something blunt or heavy; *also* : the sound made by such a blow

[1]**thun·der** \ˈthən-dər\ *n* **1** : the sound following a flash of lightning; *also* : a noise like such a sound **2** : a loud utterance or threat

[2]**thunder** *vb* **thun·dered; thun·der·ing** \-d(ə-)riŋ\ **1** : to produce thunder **2** : ROAR, SHOUT

thun·der·bolt \-ˌbōlt\ *n* : a flash of lightning with its accompanying thunder

thun·der·clap \-ˌklap\ *n* : a crash of thunder

thun·der·cloud \-ˌklau̇d\ *n* : a dark storm cloud producing lightning and thunder

thun·der·head \-ˌhed\ *n* : a large cumulus cloud often appearing before a thunderstorm

thun·der·ous \ˈthən-d(ə-)rəs\ *adj* : producing thunder; *also* : making a noise like thunder — **thun·der·ous·ly** *adv*

thun·der·show·er \ˈthən-dər-ˌshau̇(-ə)r\ *n* : a shower accompanied by thunder and lightning

thun·der·storm \-ˌstȯrm\ *n* : a storm accompanied by thunder and lightning

thun·der·struck \-ˌstrək\ *adj* : stunned as if struck by a thunderbolt

Thurs *or* **Thu** *abbr* Thursday

Thurs·day \ˈthərz-dē, -ˌdā\ *n* [deriv. of ON *thōrsdagr*, lit., day of Thor (Norse god)] : the fifth day of the week

thus \ˈt͟həs\ *adv* **1** : in this or that manner **2** : to this degree or extent : so **3** : because of this or that : HENCE

[1]**thwack** \ˈthwak\ *vb* : to strike with something flat or heavy

[2]**thwack** *n* : a heavy blow : WHACK

[1]**thwart** \ˈthwȯrt\ *vb* **1** : BAFFLE **2** : BLOCK, DEFEAT **syn** balk, foil, outwit, frustrate

[2]**thwart** \ˈthwȯrt, *naut often* ˈthȯrt\ *adv* : ATHWART

[3]**thwart** *adj* : situated or placed across something else

[4]**thwart** \ˈth(w)ȯrt\ *n* : a rower's seat extending across a boat

thy \(ˌ)t͟hī\ *adj, archaic* : of, relating to, or done by or to thee or thyself

thyme \ˈtīm, ˈthīm\ *n* [ME, fr. MF *thym*, fr. L *thymum*, fr. Gk *thymon*, fr. *thyein* to make a burnt offering, sacrifice] : any of several mints with aromatic leaves used esp. in seasoning

thy·mine \ˈthī-ˌmēn\ *n* : a pyrimidine base that is one of the four bases coding genetic information in the molecular chain of DNA

thy·mus \ˈthī-məs\ *n* : a glandular organ of the neck that is composed largely of lymphoid tissue, functions esp. in the development of the body's immune system, and tends to disappear or become rudimentary in the adult

thy·ris·tor \thī-ˈris-tər\ *n* : a semiconductor device that acts as a switch, rectifier, or voltage regulator

thy·roid \ˈthī-ˌrȯid\ *also* **thy·roi·dal** \thī-ˈrȯid-ᵊl\ *adj* [NL *thyroides*, fr. Gk *thyreoeidēs* shield-shaped, thyroid, fr. *thyreos* shield shaped like a door, fr. *thyra* door] : of, relating to, or being a large endocrine gland that lies at the base of the neck and produces several iodine-containing hormones that affect growth, development, and metabolism — **thyroid** *n*

thy·rox·ine *or* **thy·rox·in** \thī-ˈräk-ˌsēn, -sən\ *n* : an iodine-containing amino acid that is the active principle of the thyroid gland and is used to treat thyroid disorders

thy·self \t͟hī-ˈself\ *pron, archaic* : YOURSELF

Ti *symbol* titanium

ti·ara \tē-ˈar-ə, -ˈer-, -ˈär-\ *n* **1** : the pope's triple crown **2** : a decorative headband or semicircle for formal wear by women

Ti·bet·an \tə-ˈbet-ᵊn\ *n* : a native or inhabitant of Tibet — **Tibetan** *adj*

tib·ia \ˈtib-ē-ə\ *n, pl* **-i·ae** \-ē-ˌē\ *also* **-i·as** [L] : the inner of the two bones of the vertebrate hind limb between the knee and the ankle

tic \ˈtik\ *n* : a local and habitual twitching of muscles esp. of the face

ti·cal \ti-ˈkäl, ˈtik-əl\ *n, pl* **ticals** *or* **tical** : BAHT

[1]**tick** \ˈtik\ *n* : any of numerous small 8-legged blood-sucking arachnid arthropods

[2]**tick** *n* : the fabric case of a mattress or pillow; *also* : a mattress consisting of a tick and its filling

[3]**tick** *n* **1** : a light rhythmic audible tap or beat **2** : a small mark used to draw attention to or check something

[4]**tick** *vb* **1** : to make the sound of a tick or series of ticks **2** : to mark, count, or announce by or as if by ticking beats **3** : to function as an operating mechanism : RUN **4** : to mark or check with a tick

[5]**tick** *n* : CREDIT; *also* : a credit account

tick·er \ˈtik-ər\ *n* **1** : something (as a watch) that ticks **2** : a telegraph instrument that prints information (as stock prices) on paper tape **3** *slang* : HEART

ticker tape *n* : the paper ribbon on which a telegraphic ticker prints

[1]**tick·et** \ˈtik-ət\ *n* **1** : CERTIFICATE, LICENSE, PERMIT; *esp* : a certificate or token showing that a fare or admission fee has been paid **2** : TAG, LABEL **3** : SLATE 3 **4** : a summons issued to a traffic offender

[2]**ticket** *vb* **1** : to attach a ticket to **2** : to furnish or serve with a ticket

tick·ing \ˈtik-iŋ\ *n* : a strong fabric used in upholstering and as a mattress covering

tick·le \ˈtik-əl\ *vb* **tick·led; tick·ling** \-(ə-)liŋ\ **1** : to have a tingling sensation **2** : to excite or stir up agreeably : PLEASE, AMUSE **3** : to touch (as a body part) lightly so as to cause uneasiness, laughter, or spasmodic movements — **tickle** *n*

tick·lish \ˈtik-(ə-)lish\ *adj* **1** : OVERSENSITIVE, TOUCHY **2** : UNSTABLE ⟨a ~ foothold⟩ **3** : requiring delicate handling ⟨~ subject⟩ **4** : sensitive to tickling — **tick·lish·ly** *adv* — **tick·lish·ness** *n*

tid·al wave \ˈtīd-ᵊl-\ *n* **1** : an unusually high sea wave that sometimes follows an earthquake **2** : an unusual rise of water alongshore due to strong winds

tid·bit \ˈtid-ˌbit\ *n* : a choice morsel

[1]**tide** \ˈtīd\ *n* [ME, time, fr. OE *tīd*] **1** : the alternate rising and falling of the surface of the ocean **2** : something that fluctuates like the tides of the sea — **tid·al** \ˈtīd-ᵊl\ *adj*

[2]**tide** *vb* **tid·ed; tid·ing** : to carry through or help along as if by the tide ⟨a loan to ~ him over⟩

tide·land \ˈtīd-ˌland, -lənd\ *n* **1** : land overflowed during flood tide **2** : land under the ocean within a nation's territorial waters — often used in pl.

tide·wa·ter \-ˌwȯt-ər, -ˌwät-\ *n* **1** : water overflowing land at flood tide **2** : low-lying coastal land

tid·ings \ˈtīd-iŋz\ *n pl* : NEWS, MESSAGE

[1]**ti·dy** \ˈtīd-ē\ *adj* **ti·di·er; -est** **1** : well ordered and cared for : NEAT **2** : LARGE, SUBSTANTIAL ⟨a ~ sum⟩ — **ti·di·ness** \ˈtīd-ē-nəs\ *n*

[2]**tidy** *vb* **ti·died; ti·dy·ing** **1** : to put in order **2** : to make things tidy

[3]**tidy** *n, pl* **tidies** : a piece of decorated cloth or needlework

used to protect the back or arms of a chair from wear or soil

[1]**tie** \ˈtī\ *n* **1** : a line, ribbon, or cord used for fastening, uniting, or closing **2** : a structural element (as a beam or rod) holding two pieces together **3** : one of the cross supports to which railroad rails are fastened **4** : a connecting link : BOND ⟨family ~*s*⟩ **5** : an equality in number (as of votes or scores); *also* : an undecided or deadlocked contest **6** : NECKTIE

[2]**tie** *vb* **tied; ty·ing** \ˈtī-iŋ\ *or* **tie·ing 1** : to fasten, attach, or close by means of a tie **2** : to bring together firmly : UNITE **3** : to form a knot or bow in ⟨~ a scarf⟩ **4** : to restrain from freedom of action : CONSTRAIN **5** : to make or have an equal score with

tie·back \ˈtī-ˌbak\ *n* : a decorative strip for draping a curtain to the side of a window

tie–dye·ing \ˈtī-ˌdī-iŋ\ *n* : a method of producing patterns in textiles by tying parts of the fabric so that they will not absorb the dye — **tie–dyed** \-ˌdīd\ *adj*

tie–in \ˈtī-ˌin\ *n* : CONNECTION

tier \ˈtiər\ *n* : ROW, LAYER; *esp* : one of two or more rows arranged one above another

tie–rod \ˈtī-ˌräd\ *n* : a rod used as a connecting member or brace

tie–up \ˈtī-ˌəp\ *n* **1** : a slowing or stopping of traffic or business **2** : CONNECTION

tiff \ˈtif\ *n* : a petty quarrel — **tiff** *vb*

tif·fin \ˈtif-ən\ *n, chiefly Brit* : LUNCHEON

ti·ger \ˈtī-gər\ *n* : a large tawny black-striped Asian flesh-eating mammal related to the cat — **ti·ger·ish** \-g(ə-)rish\ *adj*

tiger

[1]**tight** \ˈtīt\ *adj* **1** : so close in structure as not to permit passage of a liquid or gas **2** : fixed or held very firmly in place **3** : TAUT **4** : fitting usu. too closely ⟨~ shoes⟩ **5** : set close together : COMPACT ⟨a ~ formation⟩ **6** : DIFFICULT, TRYING ⟨get in a ~ spot⟩ **7** : STINGY, MISERLY **8** : evenly contested : CLOSE **9** : INTOXICATED **10** : low in supply : hard to get ⟨money is ~⟩ — **tight·ly** *adv* — **tight·ness** *n*

[2]**tight** *adv* **1** : TIGHTLY, FIRMLY **2** : SOUNDLY ⟨sleep ~⟩

tight·en \ˈtīt-ᵊn\ *vb* **tight·ened; tight·en·ing** \ˈtīt-(ᵊ-)niŋ\ : to make or become tight

tight·fist·ed \ˈtīt-ˈfis-təd\ *adj* : STINGY

tight·rope \ˈtīt-ˌrōp\ *n* : a taut rope or wire for acrobats to perform on

tights \ˈtīts\ *n pl* : skintight garments covering the body esp. below the waist

tight·wad \ˈtīt-ˌwäd\ *n* : a stingy person

ti·gress \ˈtī-grəs\ *n* : a female tiger

til·de \ˈtil-də\ *n* [Sp, fr. ML *titulus* tittle] : a mark ˜ placed esp. over the letter *n* (as in Spanish *señor* sir) to denote the sound \nʸ\ or over vowels (as in Portuguese *irmã* sister) to indicate nasal quality

[1]**tile** \ˈtīl\ *n* **1** : a thin piece of fired clay, stone, or concrete used for roofs, floors, or walls; *also* : a hollow or concave earthenware or concrete piece used for a drain **2** : a thin piece (as of a rubber composition) used for covering walls or floors — **til·ing** \-iŋ\ *n*

[2]**tile** *vb* **tiled; til·ing 1** : to cover with tiles **2** : to install drainage tile in — **til·er** *n*

[1]**till** \(ˌ)til\ *prep or conj* : UNTIL

[2]**till** \ˈtil\ *vb* : to work by plowing, sowing, and raising crops : CULTIVATE — **till·able** *adj* — **till·er** *n*

[3]**till** \ˈtil\ *n* : DRAWER; *esp* : a money drawer in a store or bank

till·age \ˈtil-ij\ *n* **1** : the work of tilling land **2** : cultivated land

[1]**til·ler** \ˈtil-ər\ *n* [OE *telgor, telgra* twig, shoot] : a sprout or stalk esp. from the base or lower part of a plant

[2]**til·ler** \ˈtil-ər\ *n* [ME *tiler* stock of a crossbow, fr. MF *telier,* lit., beam of a loom, fr. ML *telarium,* fr. L *tela* web] : a lever used for turning a boat's rudder from side to side

[1]**tilt** \ˈtilt\ *n* **1** : a military exercise in which two combatants charging usu. with lances try to unhorse each other : JOUST; *also* : a tournament of tilts **2** : a verbal contest **3** : SLANT, TIP

[2]**tilt** *vb* **1** : to move or shift so as to incline : TIP **2** : to engage in or as if in combat with lances : JOUST

tilth \ˈtilth\ *n* **1** : TILLAGE 2 **2** : the state of aggregation of the soil esp. in relation to its suitability for crop growth

Tim *abbr* Timothy

[1]**tim·ber** \ˈtim-bər\ *n* [ME, fr. OE, building, wood] **1** : wooded land or growing trees from which timber may be obtained **2** : wood for use in making something **3** : a usu. large squared or dressed piece of wood — **tim·ber·land** \-bər-ˌland\ *n*

[2]**timber** *vb* **tim·bered; tim·ber·ing** \-b(ə-)riŋ\ : to cover, frame, or support with timbers

tim·bered \ˈtim-bərd\ *adj* **1** : having walls framed by exposed timbers **2** : covered with growing timber

tim·ber·ing \ˈtim-b(ə-)riŋ\ *n* : a set or arrangement of timbers

tim·ber·line \ˈtim-bər-ˌlīn\ *n* : the upper limit of tree growth on mountains or in high latitudes

timber rattlesnake *n* : a moderate-sized rattlesnake widely distributed through the eastern half of the U.S.

timber wolf *n* : a large usu. gray No. American wolf

tim·bre *also* **tim·ber** \ˈtam-bər, ˈtim-\ *n* [F, fr. MF, bell struck by a hammer, fr. OF, drum, fr. MGk *tymbanon* kettledrum, fr. Gk *tympanon*] : the distinctive quality given to a sound by its overtones

tim·brel \ˈtim-brəl\ *n* : a small hand drum or tambourine

[1]**time** \ˈtīm\ *n* **1** : a period during which an action, process, or condition exists or continues ⟨gone a long ~⟩ **2** : LEISURE ⟨found ~ to read⟩ **3** : a point or period when something occurs : OCCASION ⟨the last ~ we met⟩ **4** : a set or customary moment or hour for something to occur ⟨arrived on ~⟩ **5** : AGE, ERA **6** : state of affairs : CONDITIONS ⟨hard ~*s*⟩ **7** : a rate of speed : TEMPO **8** : a moment, hour, day, or year as indicated by a clock or calendar ⟨what ~ is it⟩ **9** : a system of reckoning time ⟨solar ~⟩ **10** : one of a series of recurring instances; *also, pl* : added or accumulated quantities or examples ⟨five ~*s* greater⟩ **11** : a person's experience during a particular period ⟨had a good ~ at the beach⟩

[2]**time** *vb* **timed; tim·ing 1** : to arrange or set the time of : SCHEDULE ⟨~*s* his calls conveniently⟩ **2** : to set the tempo or duration of ⟨~ a performance⟩ **3** : to cause to keep time with ⟨~*s* her steps to the music⟩ **4** : to determine or record the time, duration, or rate of ⟨~ a sprinter⟩ — **tim·er** *n*

time bomb *n* **1** : a bomb so made as to explode at a predetermined time **2** : something having the potential of a dangerous delayed reaction

time clock *n* : a clock that records the times of arrival and departure of workers

time frame *n* : a period of time esp. with respect to some action or project

time–hon·ored \ˈtīm-ˌän-ərd\ *adj* : honored because of age or long usage

time·keep·er \ˈtīm-ˌkē-pər\ *n* **1** : a clerk who keeps records of the time worked by employees **2** : one appointed to mark and announce the time in an athletic game or contest

time·less \ˈtīm-ləs\ *adj* **1** : UNENDING **2** : not limited or affected by time ⟨~ works of art⟩ — **time·less·ly** *adv* — **time·less·ness** *n*

time·ly \ˈtīm-lē\ *adj* **time·li·er; -est** **1** : coming early or at the right time : OPPORTUNE ⟨a ~ arrival⟩ **2** : appropriate to the time ⟨a ~ book⟩ — **time·li·ness** *n*

time–out \ˈtīm-ˈau̇t\ *n* : a brief suspension of activity esp. in an athletic game

time·piece \ˈtīm-ˌpēs\ *n* : a device (as a clock) to show the passage of time

times \ˌtīmz\ *prep* : multiplied by ⟨2 ~ 2 is 4⟩

time–shar·ing \ˈtīm-ˌsheər-iŋ\ *n* : simultaneous access to a computer by many users

times sign *n* : the symbol × used to indicate multiplication

time·ta·ble \ˈtīm-ˌtā-bəl\ *n* **1** : a table of the departure and arrival times (as of trains) **2** : a schedule showing a planned order or sequence

time warp *n* : an anomaly, discontinuity, or suspension held to occur in the progress of time

time·worn \-ˌwōrn\ *adj* **1** : worn by time **2** : HACKNEYED, STALE

tim·id \ˈtim-əd\ *adj* : lacking in courage or self-confidence : FEARFUL — **ti·mid·i·ty** \tə-ˈmid-ət-ē\ *n* — **tim·id·ly** \ˈtim-əd-lē\ *adv*

tim·o·rous \ˈtim-(ə-)rəs\ *adj* : of a timid disposition : AFRAID — **tim·o·rous·ly** *adv* — **tim·o·rous·ness** *n*

tim·o·thy \ˈtim-ə-thē\ *n* : a grass with long cylindrical spikes widely grown for hay

Tim·o·thy \ˈtim-ə-thē\ *n* — see BIBLE table

tim·pa·ni \ˈtim-pə-nē\ *n pl* [It] : a set of kettledrums played by one performer in an orchestra — **tim·pa·nist** \-nəst\ *n*

[1]tin \ˈtin\ *n* **1** : a soft white crystalline metallic element malleable at ordinary temperatures but brittle when heated that is used in solders and alloys — see ELEMENT table **2** : a container (as a can) made of tinplate

[2]tin *vb* **tinned; tin·ning** **1** : to cover or plate with tin **2** *chiefly Brit* : to pack in tins : CAN

tinct \ˈtiŋkt\ *n* : TINCTURE, TINGE

[1]tinc·ture \ˈtiŋk-chər\ *n* **1** : a substance that colors or dyes **2** : a slight admixture : TRACE **3** : an alcoholic solution of a medicinal substance **syn** touch, suggestion, suspicion, soupçon

[2]tincture *vb* **tinc·tured; tinc·tur·ing** : COLOR, TINGE

tin·der \ˈtin-dər\ *n* : something that catches fire easily; *esp* : a substance used to kindle a fire from a slight spark

tin·der·box \ˈtin-dər-ˌbäks\ *n* **1** : a metal box for holding tinder and usu. flint and steel for striking a spark **2** : a highly flammable object or place

tine \ˈtīn\ *n* : a slender pointed part (as of a fork or an antler) : PRONG

tin·foil \ˈtin-ˌfȯil\ *n* : a thin metal sheeting usu. of aluminum or tin-lead alloy

[1]tinge \ˈtinj\ *vb* **tinged; tinge·ing** *or* **ting·ing** \ˈtin-jiŋ\ **1** : to color slightly : TINT **2** : to affect or modify esp. with a slight odor or taste

[2]tinge *n* : a slight coloring, flavor, or quality : TRACE **syn** touch, suggestion, suspicion, tincture

tin·gle \ˈtiŋ-gəl\ *vb* **tin·gled; tin·gling** \-g(ə-)liŋ\ **1** : to feel a prickling or thrilling sensation **2** : TINKLE — **tingle** *n*

[1]tin·ker \ˈtiŋ-kər\ *n* **1** : a usu. itinerant mender of household utensils **2** : an unskillful mender : BUNGLER

[2]tinker *vb* **tin·kered; tin·ker·ing** \-k(ə-)riŋ\ : to repair or adjust something in an unskillful or experimental manner — **tin·ker·er** *n*

[1]tin·kle \ˈtiŋ-kəl\ *vb* **tin·kled; tin·kling** \-k(ə-)liŋ\ : to make or cause to make a tinkle

[2]tinkle *n* : a series of short high ringing or clinking sounds

tin·ny \ˈtin-ē\ *adj* **tin·ni·er; -est** **1** : abounding in or yielding tin **2** : resembling tin; *also* : LIGHT, CHEAP **3** : thin in tone ⟨a ~ voice⟩ — **tin·ni·ly** \ˈtin-ᵊl-ē\ *adv* — **tin·ni·ness** \-ē-nəs\ *n*

tin·plate \ˈtin-ˈplāt\ *n* : thin sheet iron or steel coated with tin — **tin–plate** *vb*

tin·sel \ˈtin-səl\ *n* [MF *etincelle* spark, glitter] **1** : a thread, strip, or sheet of metal, paper, or plastic used to produce a glittering appearance (as in fabrics) **2** : something superficially attractive but of little worth

tin·smith \ˈtin-ˌsmith\ *n* : one that works with sheet metal (as tinplate)

[1]tint \ˈtint\ *n* **1** : a slight or pale coloration : HUE **2** : any of various shades of a color

[2]tint *vb* : to impart a tint to : COLOR

tin·tin·nab·u·la·tion \ˌtin-tə-ˌnab-yə-ˈlā-shən\ *n* **1** : the ringing of bells **2** : a tingling sound as if of bells

tin·ware \ˈtin-ˌwaər\ *n* : articles made of tinplate

ti·ny \ˈtī-nē\ *adj* **ti·ni·er; -est** : very small : MINUTE **syn** miniature, diminutive, wee, lilliputian

[1]tip \ˈtip\ *vb* **tipped; tip·ping** **1** : OVERTURN, UPSET **2** : LEAN, SLANT; *also* : TILT

[2]tip *n* : the act or an instance of tipping

[3]tip *n* **1** : the usu. pointed end of something **2** : a small piece or part serving as an end, cap, or point

[4]tip *vb* **tipped, tip·ping** **1** : to furnish with a tip **2** : to cover or adorn the tip of

[5]tip *n* : a light touch or blow

[6]tip *vb* **tipped; tip·ping** : to strike lightly : TAP

[7]tip *n* : a piece of expert of confidential information : HINT

[8]tip *vb* **tipped; tip·ping** : to impart a piece of information about or to

[9]tip *vb* **tipped; tip·ping** : to give a gratuity to

[10]tip *n* : a gift or small sum given for a service performed or anticipated

tip–off \ˈtip-ˌȯf\ *n* : WARNING, TIP

tip·pet \ˈtip-ət\ *n* : a long scarf or shoulder cape

tip·ple \ˈtip-əl\ *vb* **tip·pled; tip·pling** \-(ə-)liŋ\ : to drink intoxicating liquor esp. habitually or excessively — **tip·pler** \-(ə-)lər\ *n*

tip·ster \ˈtip-stər\ *n* : one who gives or sells tips esp. for gambling

tip·sy \ˈtip-sē\ *adj* **tip·si·er; -est** : unsteady or foolish from the effects of alcohol

[1]tip·toe \ˈtip-ˌtō\ *n* : the tip of a toe; *also* : the ends of the toes

[2]tiptoe *adv or adj* : on or as if on tiptoe

[3]tiptoe *vb* **tip·toed; tip·toe·ing** : to walk or proceed on or as if on tiptoe

[1]tip–top \ˈtip-ˈtäp\ *n* : the highest point

[2]tip–top *adj* : EXCELLENT, FIRST-RATE

ti·rade \tī-ˈrād, ˈtī-ˌrād\ *n* [F, shot, tirade, fr. MF, fr. It *tirata*, fr. *tirare* to draw, shoot] : a prolonged speech of abuse or condemnation

[1]tire \ˈtī(ə)r\ *vb* **tired; tir·ing** **1** : to make or become weary : FATIGUE **2** : to wear out the patience of : BORE

[2]tire *n* **1** : a wheel band that forms the tread of a wheel **2** : a rubber cushion usu. containing compressed air that encircles a wheel (as of an automobile)

tired \ˈtī(ə)rd\ *adj* **1** : WEARY, FATIGUED **2** : HACKNEYED

tire·less \ˈtī(ə)r-ləs\ *adj* : not tiring : UNTIRING, INDEFATIGABLE —**tire·less·ly** *adv* — **tire·less·ness** *n*

tire·some \ˈtī(ə)r-səm\ *adj* : tending to bore : WEARISOME, TEDIOUS — **tire·some·ly** *adv* — **tire·some·ness** *n*

tis·sue \ˈtish-ü\ *n* [ME *tissu*, a rich fabric, fr. OF, fr. *tistre* to weave, fr. L *texere*] **1** : a fine lightweight often sheer fabric **2** : NETWORK, WEB **3** : a soft absorbent paper **4** : a mass or layer of cells forming a basic structural element of an animal or plant body

[1]**tit** \ˈtit\ *n* : TEAT

[2]**tit** *n* : TITMOUSE

Tit *abbr* Titus

ti·tan \ˈtīt-ᵊn\ *n* **1** *cap* : one of a family of giants overthrown by the gods of ancient Greece **2** : one gigantic in size or power

ti·tan·ic \tī-ˈtan-ik, tə-\ *adj* : enormous in size, force, or power **syn** immense, huge, gigantic, giant, colossal, mammoth

ti·ta·ni·um \tī-ˈtān-ē-əm, tə-\ *n* : a gray light strong metallic chemical element used in alloys — see ELEMENT table

tit·bit \ˈtit-ˌbit\ *var of* TIDBIT

tithe \ˈtīth\ *n* : a 10th part paid or given esp. for the support of a church — **tithe** *vb* — **tith·er** *n*

tit·il·late \ˈtit-ᵊl-ˌāt\ *vb* **-lat·ed; -lat·ing** **1** : TICKLE **2** : to excite pleasurably — **tit·il·la·tion** \ˌtit-ᵊl-ˈā-shən\ *n*

tit·i·vate *or* **tit·ti·vate** \ˈtit-ə-ˌvāt\ *vb* **-vat·ed; -vat·ing** : to dress up : spruce up

ti·tle \ˈtīt-ᵊl\ *n* **1** : CLAIM, RIGHT; *esp* : a legal right to the ownership of property **2** : the distinguishing name esp. of an artistic production (as a book) **3** : an appellation of honor, rank, or office **4** : CHAMPIONSHIP **syn** designation, denomination, appellation

ti·tled \ˈtīt-ᵊld\ *adj* : having a title esp. of nobility

title page *n* : a page of a book bearing the title and usu. the names of the author and publisher

tit·mouse \ˈtit-ˌmau̇s\ *n, pl* **tit·mice** \-ˌmīs\ : any of numerous small long-tailed insect-eating birds

tit·ter \ˈtit-ər\ *vb* : to laugh in an affected or in a nervous or half-suppressed manner — **titter** *n*

tit·tle \ˈtit-ᵊl\ *n* : a tiny piece : JOT

tit·tle–tat·tle \ˈtit-ᵊl-ˌtat-ᵊl\ *n* : idle talk : GOSSIP

tit·u·lar \ˈtich-(ə-)lər\ *adj* **1** : existing in title only : NOMINAL ⟨~ ruler⟩ **2** : of, relating to, or bearing a title ⟨~ role⟩

Ti·tus \ˈtīt-əs\ *n* — see BIBLE table

tiz·zy \ˈtiz-ē\ *n, pl* **tizzies** : a highly excited and distracted state of mind

tk *abbr* **1** tank **2** truck

TKO \ˈtē-ˈkā-ˈō\ *n* [*t*echnical *k*nock*o*ut] : the termination of a boxing match when a boxer is declared unable to continue the fight

tkt *abbr* ticket

Tl *symbol* thallium

TLC *abbr* tender loving care

T lymphocyte *n* : T CELL

Tm *symbol* thulium

TM *abbr* trademark

T-man \ˈtē-ˌman\ *n* : a special agent of the U.S. Treasury Department

tn *abbr* **1** ton **2** town

TN *abbr* Tennessee

tng *abbr* training

tnpk *abbr* turnpike

TNT \ˌtē-ˌen-ˈtē\ *n* : a flammable toxic compound used as a high explosive

[1]**to** \tə, (ˈ)tü\ *prep* **1** : in the direction of and reaching ⟨drove ~ town⟩ **2** : in the direction of : TOWARD ⟨walking ~ school⟩ **3** : ON, AGAINST ⟨apply salve ~ a burn⟩ **4** : as far as ⟨can pay up ~ a dollar⟩ **5** : so as to become or bring about ⟨beaten ~ death⟩ ⟨broken ~ pieces⟩ **6** : BEFORE ⟨it's five minutes ~ six⟩ **7** : UNTIL ⟨from May ~ December⟩ **8** : fitting or being a part of : FOR ⟨key ~ the lock⟩ **9** : with the accompaniment of ⟨sing ~ the music⟩ **10** : in relation or comparison with ⟨similar ~ that one⟩ ⟨won 10 ~ 6⟩ **11** : in accordance with ⟨add salt ~ taste⟩ **12** : within the range of ⟨~ my knowledge⟩ **13** : contained, occurring, or included in ⟨two pints ~ a quart⟩ **14** : as regards ⟨agreeable ~ everyone⟩ **15** : affecting as the receiver or beneficiary ⟨whispered ~ her⟩ ⟨gave it ~ me⟩ **16** : for no one except ⟨a room ~ myself⟩ **17** : into the action of ⟨we got ~ talking⟩ **18** — used for marking the following verb as an infinitive ⟨wants ~ go⟩ ⟨easy ~ like⟩ ⟨the man ~ beat⟩ and often used by itself at the end of a clause in place of an infinitive suggested by the preceding context ⟨goes to town whenever he wants ~⟩ ⟨can leave if you'd like ~⟩

[2]**to** \ˈtü\ *adv* **1** : in a direction toward ⟨run ~ and fro⟩ ⟨wrong side ~⟩ **2** : into contact esp. with the frame of a door ⟨the door slammed ~⟩ **3** : to the matter in hand ⟨fell ~ and ate heartily⟩ **4** : to a state of consciousness or awareness ⟨came ~ hours after the accident⟩

TO *abbr* turn over

toad \ˈtōd\ *n* : a leaping amphibian differing typically from the related frogs in shorter stockier build, rough dry warty skin, and less aquatic habits

toad·stool \-ˌstül\ *n* : MUSHROOM; *esp* : one that is poisonous or inedible

toady \ˈtōd-ē\ *n, pl* **toad·ies** : one who flatters in the hope of gaining favors : SYCOPHANT — **toady** *vb*

to–and–fro \ˌtü-ən-ˈfrō\ *adj* : forward and backward

[1]**toast** \ˈtōst\ *vb* **1** : to warm thoroughly **2** : to make (as bread) crisp, hot, and brown by heat

[2]**toast** *n* **1** : sliced toasted bread **2** : someone or something in whose honor persons drink **3** : an act of drinking in honor of a toast

[3]**toast** *vb* : to propose or drink to as a toast

toast·er \ˈtō-stər\ *n* : one that toasts; *esp* : an electrical appliance for toasting

toaster oven *n* : a small electrical appliance that bakes, toasts, and usu. broils

toast·mas·ter \ˈtōst-ˌmas-tər\ *n* : one that presides at a banquet and introduces the after-dinner speakers — **toast·mis·tress** \-ˌmis-trəs\ *n*

to·bac·co \tə-ˈbak-ō\ *n, pl* **-cos** [Sp *tabaco*] **1** : a tall broad-leaved herb related to the potato; *also* : its leaves prepared for smoking or chewing or as snuff **2** : manufactured tobacco products

to·bac·co·nist \tə-ˈbak-ə-nəst\ *n* : a dealer in tobacco

To·bi·as \tə-ˈbī-əs\ *n* — see BIBLE table

To·bit \ˈtō-bət\ *n* — see BIBLE table

[1]**to·bog·gan** \tə-ˈbäg-ən\ *n* [CanF *tobogan*] : a long flat-bottomed light sled made of thin boards curved up at one end

[2]**toboggan** *vb* **1** : to coast on a toboggan **2** : to decline suddenly (as in value)

toc·sin \ˈtäk-sən\ *n* **1** : an alarm bell **2** : a warning signal

[1]**to·day** \tə-ˈdā\ *adv* **1** : on or for this day **2** : at the present time

[2]**today** *n* : the present day, time, or age

tod·dle \ˈtäd-ᵊl\ *vb* **tod·dled; tod·dling** \ˈtäd-(ᵊ-)liŋ\ : to walk with short tottering steps in the manner of a young child — **toddle** *n* — **tod·dler** \-(ᵊ-)lər\ *n*

tod·dy \ˈtäd-ē\ *n, pl* **toddies** [Hindi *tāṛī* juice of a palm, fr. *tāṛ* a palm, fr. Skt *tāla*] : a drink made of liquor, sugar, spices, and hot water

to–do \tə-ˈdü\ *n, pl* **to–dos** \-ˈdüz\ : BUSTLE, STIR

[1]**toe** \ˈtō\ *n* **1** : one of the jointed parts of the front end of a foot **2** : the front part of a foot or hoof

[2]**toe** *vb* **toed; toe·ing** : to touch, reach, or drive with the toes

toea \ˈtoi-ə\ *n* — see *kina* at MONEY table

toe·hold \ˈtō-ˌhōld\ *n* **1** : a place of support for the toes **2** : a slight footing

toe·nail \ˈtō-ˌnāl\ *n* : a nail of a toe

tof·fee *or* **tof·fy** \ˈtȯ-fē, ˈtäf-ē\ *n, pl* **toffees** *or* **toffies** : candy of brittle but tender texture made by boiling sugar and butter together

tog \ˈtäg, ˈtȯg\ *vb* **togged; tog·ging** : to put togs on : DRESS

to·ga \ˈtō-gə\ *n* : the loose outer garment worn in public by citizens of ancient Rome — **to·gaed** \-gəd\ *adj*

[1]**to·geth·er** \tə-ˈgeth-ər\ *adv* **1** : in or into one place or group **2** : in or into contact or association ⟨mix ~⟩ **3** : at one time : SIMULTANEOUSLY ⟨talk and work ~⟩ **4** : in succession ⟨for days ~⟩ **5** : in or into harmony or coherence ⟨get ~ on a plan⟩ **6** : as a group : JOINTLY — **to·geth·er·ness** *n*

[2]**together** *adj* : composed in mind or manner

tog·gery \ˈtäg-(ə-)rē, ˈtȯg-\ *n* : CLOTHING

tog·gle switch \ˈtäg-əl-\ *n* : an electric switch operated by pushing a projecting lever through a small arc

togs \ˈtägz, ˈtȯgz\ *n pl* : CLOTHING; *esp* : clothes for a specified use ⟨riding ~⟩

[1]**toil** \ˈtȯil\ *n* **1** : laborious effort **2** : long fatiguing labor : DRUDGERY — **toil·some** *adj*

[2]**toil** *vb* [ME *toilen* to argue, struggle, fr. OF *toeillier* to stir, disturb, dispute, fr. L *tudiculare* to crush, grind, fr. *tudicula* machine for crushing olives, dim. of *tudes* hammer] **1** : to work hard and long **2** : to proceed with laborious effort : PLOD — **toil·er** *n*

[3]**toil** *n* [ME *toile* cloth, net, fr. L *tela* web, fr. *texere* to weave, construct] : NET, TRAP — usu. used in pl.

toi·let \ˈtȯi-lət\ *n* **1** : the act or process of dressing and grooming oneself **2** : BATHROOM **3** : a fixture for use in urinating and defecating; *esp* : one consisting essentially of a water-flushed bowl and seat

toi·let·ry \ˈtȯi-lə-trē\ *n, pl* **-ries** : an article or preparation used in making one's toilet — usu. used in pl.

toi·lette \twä-ˈlet\ *n* **1** : TOILET 1 **2** : formal attire; *also* : a particular costume

toilet training *n* : the process of training a child to control bladder and bowel movements and to use the toilet — **toilet train** *vb*

toil·worn \ˈtȯil-ˌwōrn\ *adj* : showing the effects of toil

To·kay \tō-ˈkā\ *n* : naturally sweet wine from Hungary

toke \ˈtōk\ *n, slang* : a puff on a marijuana cigarette

[1]**to·ken** \ˈtō-kən\ *n* **1** : an outward sign **2** : SYMBOL, EMBLEM **3** : SOUVENIR, KEEPSAKE **4** : a small part representing the whole **5** : a piece resembling a coin issued as money or for use by a particular group on specified terms

[2]**token** *adj* **1** : done or given as a token esp. in partial fulfillment of an obligation **2** : MINIMAL, PERFUNCTORY

to·ken·ism \ˈtō-kə-ˌniz-əm\ *n* : the policy or practice of making only a token effort (as to desegregate)

told *past and past part of* TELL

tole \ˈtōl\ *n* : sheet metal and esp. tinplate for use in domestic and ornamental wares

tol·er·a·ble \ˈtäl-(ə-)rə-bəl\ *adj* **1** : capable of being borne or endured **2** : moderately good : PASSABLE — **tol·er·a·bly** \-blē\ *adv*

tol·er·ance \ˈtäl(-ə)-rəns\ *n* **1** : the act or practice of tolerating; *esp* : sympathy or indulgence for beliefs or practices differing from one's own **2** : the allowable deviation from a standard (as of size) **3** : capacity for enduring or adapting (as to a poor environment) **syn** forbearance, leniency, clemency — **tol·er·ant** *adj* — **tol·er·ant·ly** *adv*

tol·er·ate \ˈtäl-ə-ˌrāt\ *vb* **-at·ed; -at·ing 1** : to allow to be or to be done without hindrance **2** : to endure or resist the action of (as a drug) **syn** abide, bear, suffer, stand, brook — **tol·er·a·tion** \ˌtäl-ə-ˈrā-shən\ *n*

[1]**toll** \ˈtōl\ *n* **1** : a tax paid for a privilege (as for passing over a bridge) **2** : a charge for a service (as for a long-distance telephone call) **3** : the cost in loss or suffering at which something is achieved **syn** levy, assessment, duty, tariff

[2]**toll** *vb* **1** : to give signal of : SOUND **2** : to cause the slow regular sounding of (a bell) esp. by pulling a rope **3** : to sound with slow measured strokes **4** : to announce by tolling

[3]**toll** *n* : the sound of a tolling bell

toll·booth \ˈtōl-ˌbüth\ *n* : a booth where tolls are paid

toll·gate \ˈtōl-ˌgāt\ *n* : a point where vehicles stop to pay a toll

toll·house \-ˌhau̇s\ *n* : a house or booth where tolls are paid

tol·u·ene \ˈtäl-yə-ˌwēn\ *n* : a liquid hydrocarbon used as a solvent and as an antiknock agent

tom \ˈtäm\ *n* : the male of various animals; *esp* : TOMCAT

[1]**tom·a·hawk** \ˈtäm-ə-ˌhȯk\ *n* : a light ax used as a missile and as a hand weapon by No. American Indians

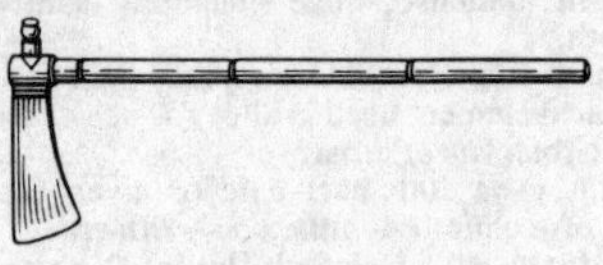

tomahawk

[2]**tomahawk** *vb* : to strike or kill with a tomahawk

to·ma·to \tə-ˈmāt-ō, -ˈmät-\ *n, pl* **-toes** : a usu. large, rounded, and red or yellow pulpy edible berry of a widely grown tropical herb related to the potato; *also* : this herb

tomb \ˈtüm\ *n* **1** : a place of burial : GRAVE **2** : a house, chamber, or vault for the dead

tom·boy \ˈtäm-ˌbȯi\ *n* : a girl of boyish behavior

tomb·stone \ˈtüm-ˌstōn\ *n* : a stone marking a grave

tom·cat \ˈtäm-ˌkat\ *n* : a male cat

Tom Col·lins \ˈtäm-ˈkäl-ənz\ *n* : a tall iced drink with a base of gin

tome \ˈtōm\ *n* : BOOK; *esp* : a large or weighty one

tom·fool·ery \täm-ˈfül-(ə-)rē\ *n* : foolish trifling : NONSENSE

tom·my gun \ˈtäm-ē-ˌgən\ *n* : SUBMACHINE GUN

to·mog·ra·phy \tō-ˈmäg-rə-fē\ *n* : a diagnostic technique using X-ray photographs in which the shadows of structures before and behind the section under study do not show — **to·mo·graph·ic** \ˌtō-mə-ˈgraf-ik\ *adj*

to·mor·row \tə-ˈmär-ō\ *adv* : on or for the day after today — **tomorrow** *n*

tom·tit \ˈtäm-ˌtit, täm-ˈtit\ *n* : any of several small active birds

tom–tom \ˈtäm-ˌtäm\ *n* : a small-headed drum beaten with the hands

ton \ˈtən\ *n, pl* **tons** *also* **ton 1** — see WEIGHT table **2** : a unit equal to the volume of a long-ton weight of seawater or 35 cubic feet used in reckoning the displacement of ships

to·nal·i·ty \tō-ˈnal-ət-ē\ *n, pl* **-ties** : tonal quality

[1]**tone** \ˈtōn\ *n* [ME, fr. L *tonus* tension, tone, fr. Gk *tonos*, lit., act of stretching; fr. the dependence of the pitch of a musical string on its tension] **1** : vocal or musical sound; *esp* : sound quality **2** : a sound of definite pitch **3** : WHOLE STEP **4** : accent or inflection expressive of an emotion **5** : the pitch of a word often used to express differences of meaning **6** : style or manner of expression **7** : color quality; *also* : SHADE, TINT **8** : the effect in painting of light and shade together with color **9** : the healthy and vigorous condition of a living body or bodily part **10** : general character, quality, or trend **syn** atmosphere, feeling, mood, vein — **ton·al** \ˈtōn-ᵊl\ *adj*

[2]**tone** *vb* **toned; ton·ing 1** : to give a particular intonation or inflection to **2** : to impart tone to **3** : SOFTEN, MELLOW **4** : to harmonize in color : BLEND

tone·arm *n* : the movable part of a record player that carries the pickup and the needle

tong \ˈtäŋ, ˈtȯŋ\ *n* : a Chinese secret society in the U.S.

tongs \ˈtäŋz, ˈtȯŋz\ *n pl* : a grasping device consisting of two pieces joined at one end by a pivot or hinged like scissors

[1]**tongue** \ˈtəŋ\ *n* **1** : a fleshy movable process of the floor of the mouth used in tasting and in taking and swallow-

ing food and in man as a speech organ **2** : the flesh of a tongue (as of the ox) used as food **3** : the power of communication **4** : LANGUAGE 1 **5** : manner or quality of utterance; *also* : intended meaning **6** : ecstatic usu. unintelligible utterance accompanying religious excitation — usu. used in pl. **7** : something resembling an animal's tongue in being elongated and fastened at one end only — **tongued** \ˈtəŋd\ *adj* — **tongue·less** *adj*

²**tongue** *vb* **tongued; tongu·ing** \ˈtəŋ-iŋ\ **1** : to touch or lick with the tongue **2** : to articulate notes on a wind instrument

tongue–in–cheek *adj* : with insincerity, irony, or whimsical exaggeration — **tongue in cheek** *adv*

tongue–lash \ˈtəŋ-ˌlash\ *vb* : CHIDE, REPROVE — **tongue–lash·ing** \-iŋ\ *n*

tongue–tied \ˈtəŋ-ˌtīd\ *adj* : unable to speak clearly or freely usu. from shortness of the membrane under the tongue or from shyness

tongue twister *n* : an utterance that is difficult to articulate because of a succession of similar consonants

¹**ton·ic** \ˈtän-ik\ *adj* **1** : of, relating to, or producing a healthy physical or mental condition : INVIGORATING **2** : relating to or based on the 1st tone of a scale

²**tonic** *n* **1** : something (as a drug) that invigorates, restores, or refreshes **2** : the 1st degree of a musical scale

¹**to·night** \tə-ˈnīt\ *adv* : on this present night or the night following this present day

²**tonight** *n* : the present or the coming night

ton·nage \ˈtən-ij\ *n* **1** : a duty on ships based on tons carried **2** : ships in terms of the number of tons registered or carried **3** : total weight in tons shipped, carried, or mined

ton·sil \ˈtän-səl\ *n* : either of a pair of oval masses of spongy tissue that lie one on each side of the throat at the back of the mouth

ton·sil·lec·to·my \ˌtän-sə-ˈlek-tə-mē\ *n, pl* **-mies** : the surgical removal of the tonsils

ton·sil·li·tis \-ˈlīt-əs\ *n* : inflammation of the tonsils

ton·so·ri·al \tän-ˈsōr-ē-əl\ *adj* : of or relating to a barber or his work

ton·sure \ˈtän-chər\ *n* [ME, fr. ML *tonsura,* fr. L, act of shearing, fr. *tonsus,* pp. of *tondēre* to shear] **1** : the rite of admission to the clerical state by the clipping or shaving of the head **2** : the shaven crown or patch worn by clerics (as monks)

too \(ˈ)tü\ *adv* **1** : in addition : ALSO **2** : EXCESSIVELY **3** : to such a degree as to be regrettable **4** : VERY

took *past of* TAKE

¹**tool** \ˈtül\ *n* **1** : a hand instrument used to aid in mechanical operations **2** : the cutting or shaping part in a machine; *also* : a machine for shaping metal in any way **3** : something used in doing a job ⟨a scholar's books are his ∼*s*⟩; *also* : a means to an end **4** : a person used by another : DUPE

²**tool** *vb* **1** : to shape, form, or finish with a tool; *esp* : to letter or decorate (as a book cover) by means of hand tools **2** : to equip a plant or industry with machines and tools for production **3** : DRIVE, RIDE ⟨∼*ing* along at 60⟩

¹**toot** \ˈtüt\ *vb* **1** : to sound or cause to sound esp. in short blasts **2** : to blow a wind instrument (as a horn)

²**toot** *n* : a short blast (as on a horn)

tooth \ˈtüth\ *n, pl* **teeth** \ˈtēth\ **1** : one of the hard bony structures borne esp. on the jaws of vertebrates and used for seizing and chewing food and as weapons; *also* : a hard sharp structure esp. around the mouth of an invertebrate **2** : something resembling an animal's tooth **3** : one of the projections on the edge of a wheel that fits into corresponding projections on another wheel — **toothed** \ˈtütht\ *adj* — **tooth·less** *adj*

tooth·ache \ˈtüth-ˌāk\ *n* : pain in or about a tooth

tooth·brush \-ˌbrəsh\ *n* : a brush for cleaning the teeth

tooth·paste \-ˌpāst\ *n* : a paste for cleaning the teeth

tooth·pick \-ˌpik\ *n* : a pointed instrument for removing substances caught between the teeth

tooth powder *n* : a powder for cleaning the teeth

tooth·some \ˈtüth-səm\ *adj* **1** : ATTRACTIVE ⟨a ∼ blond⟩ **2** : pleasing to the taste : DELICIOUS **syn** palatable, appetizing, savory, tasty

toothy \ˈtü-thē\ *adj* **tooth·i·er; -est** : having or showing prominent teeth

¹**top** \ˈtäp\ *n* **1** : the highest part, point, or level of something **2** : the stalks and leaves of a plant with edible roots ⟨beet ∼*s*⟩ **3** : the upper end, edge, or surface ⟨the ∼ of a page⟩ **4** : an upper piece, lid, or covering **5** : a platform around the head of the lower mast **6** : the highest degree, pitch, or rank

²**top** *vb* **topped; top·ping** **1** : to remove or trim the top of : PRUNE ⟨∼ a tree⟩ **2** : to cover with a top or on the top : CROWN, CAP **3** : to be superior to : EXCEL, SURPASS **4** : to go over the top of **5** : to strike (a golf ball) above the center **6** : to make an end or conclusion ⟨∼ off a meal with coffee⟩

³**top** *adj* : of, relating to, or being at the top : HIGHEST

⁴**top** *n* : a child's toy that has a tapering point on which it is made to spin

to·paz \ˈtō-ˌpaz\ *n* : a hard silicate mineral that when occurring as perfect yellow crystals is valued as a gem

top·coat \ˈtäp-ˌkōt\ *n* : a lightweight overcoat

top–dress \ˈtäp-ˌdres\ *vb* : to apply material to (as land) without working it in; *esp* : to scatter fertilizer over

top·dress·ing \-iŋ\ *n* : a material used to top-dress soil

tope \ˈtōp\ *vb* **toped; top·ing** : to drink intoxicating liquor to excess

top·er \ˈtō-pər\ *n* : one that topes; *esp* : DRUNKARD

top flight *n* : the highest level of excellence or rank — **top·flight** *adj*

top hat *n* : a man's tall-crowned hat usu. of beaver or silk

top–heavy \ˈtäp-ˌhev-ē\ *adj* : having the top part too heavy for the lower part

top·ic \ˈtäp-ik\ *n* **1** : a heading in an outlined argument **2** : the subject of a discourse or a section of it : THEME

top·i·cal \-i-kəl\ *adj* **1** : of, relating to, or arranged by topics ⟨a ∼ outline⟩ **2** : relating to current or local events — **top·i·cal·ly** \-k(ə-)lē\ *adv*

top·knot \ˈtäp-ˌnät\ *n* **1** : an ornament (as a knot of ribbons) forming a headdress **2** : a crest of feathers or hair on the top of the head

top·less \-ləs\ *adj* **1** : wearing no clothing on the upper body **2** : featuring topless waitresses or entertainers

top·mast \ˈtäp-ˌmast, -məst\ *n* : the 2d mast above a ship's deck

top·most \ˈtäp-ˌmōst\ *adj* : highest of all : UPPERMOST

top–notch \-ˈnäch\ *adj* : of the highest quality : FIRST-RATE

topog *abbr* topography

to·pog·ra·phy \tə-ˈpäg-rə-fē\ *n* **1** : the art of showing in detail on a map or chart the physical features of a place or region **2** : the outline of the form of a place showing its relief and the position of features (as rivers, roads, or cities) — **to·pog·ra·pher** \-fər\ *n* — **top·o·graph·ic** \ˌtäp-ə-ˈgraf-ik\ *or* **top·o·graph·i·cal** \-i-kəl\ *adj*

top·ping \ˈtäp-iŋ\ *n* : something (as a garnish or sauce) that forms a top

top·ple \ˈtäp-əl\ *vb* **top·pled; top·pling** \-(ə-)liŋ\ **1** : to fall from or as if from being top-heavy **2** : to push over : OVERTURN; *also* : OVERTHROW

tops \ˈtäps\ *adj* : topmost in quality or eminence ⟨is considered ∼ in his field⟩

top·sail \ˈtäp-ˌsāl, -səl\ *also* **top·s'l** \-səl\ *n* : the sail next above the lowest sail on a mast in a square-rigged ship

top secret *adj* : demanding inviolate secrecy among those concerned

top·side \ˈtäp-ˈsīd\ *adv or adj* **1** : to or on the top or surface **2** : on deck

top·sides \-ˈsīdz\ *n pl* : the top portion of the outer surface of a ship on each side above the waterline

top·soil \ˈtäp-ˌsȯil\ *n* : surface soil usu. including the organic layer in which plants have most of their roots

top·sy–tur·vy \ˌtäp-sē-ˈtər-vē\ *adv* **1** : in utter confusion **2** : UPSIDE DOWN — **topsy–turvy** *adj*

toque \ˈtōk\ *n* : a woman's small hat without a brim

tor \ˈtȯr\ *n* : a high craggy hill

To·rah \ˈtōr-ə\ *n* **1** : a scroll of the first five books of the Old Testament used in a synagogue; *also* : these five books **2** : the body of divine knowledge and law found in the Jewish scriptures and tradition

torch \ˈtȯrch\ *n* **1** : a flaming light made of something that burns brightly and usu. carried in the hand **2** : something that resembles a torch in giving light, heat, or guidance **3** *chiefly Brit* : FLASHLIGHT — **torch·bear·er** \-ˌbar-ər\ *n* — **torch·light** \-ˌlīt\ *n*

torch song *n* : a popular sentimental song of unrequited love

tore *past of* TEAR

to·re·ador \ˈtȯr-ē-ə-ˌdȯr\ *n* : BULLFIGHTER

to·re·ro \tə-ˈrer-ō\ *n, pl* **-ros** [Sp] : BULLFIGHTER

[1]**tor·ment** \ˈtȯr-ˌment\ *n* **1** : extreme pain or anguish of body or mind **2** : a source of vexation or pain

[2]**tor·ment** \tȯr-ˈment\ *vb* **1** : to cause severe suffering of body or mind to **2** : VEX, HARASS **syn** rack, afflict, try, torture — **tor·men·tor** \-ər\ *n*

torn *past part of* TEAR

tor·na·do \tȯr-ˈnād-ō\ *n, pl* **-does** *or* **-dos** [modif of Sp *tronada* thunderstorm, fr. *tronar* to thunder, fr. L *tonare*] : a violent destructive whirling wind accompanied by a funnel-shaped cloud that moves over a narrow path

[1]**tor·pe·do** \tȯr-ˈpēd-ō\ *n, pl* **-does** : a thin cylindrical self-propelled submarine weapon

[2]**torpedo** *vb* **tor·pe·doed; tor·pe·do·ing** \-ˈpēd-ə-wiŋ\ : to hit or destroy with or as if with a torpedo

torpedo boat *n* : a small very fast boat for firing torpedoes

tor·pid \ˈtȯr-pəd\ *adj* **1** : having lost motion or the power of exertion **2** : SLUGGISH **3** : lacking vigor : DULL — **tor·pid·i·ty** \tȯr-ˈpid-ət-ē\ *n*

tor·por \ˈtȯr-pər\ *n* **1** : DULLNESS, APATHY **2** : extreme sluggishness : STAGNATION **syn** stupor, lethargy, languor, lassitude

[1]**torque** \ˈtȯrk\ *n* : a force that produces or tends to produce rotation or torsion

[2]**torque** *vb* **torqued; torqu·ing** : to impart torque to : cause to twist (as about an axis)

tor·rent \ˈtȯr-ənt\ *n* [F, fr. L *torrent-, torrens,* fr. *torrent-, torrens* burning, seething, rushing, fr. prp. of *torrēre* to parch, burn] **1** : a rushing stream (as of water) **2** : a tumultuous outburst

tor·ren·tial \tȯ-ˈren-chəl, tə-\ *adj* : relating to or resembling a torrent ⟨~ rains⟩

tor·rid \ˈtȯr-əd\ *adj* **1** : parched with heat esp. of the sun : HOT **2** : ARDENT

torrid zone *n* : the region of the earth between the tropic of Cancer and the tropic of Capricorn

tor·sion \ˈtȯr-shən\ *n* **1** : a twisting of a bodily organ on its own axis **2** : a wrenching by which one part of a body is under pressure to turn about a longitudinal axis while the other part is held fast or is under pressure to turn in the opposite direction — **tor·sion·al** \ˈtȯr-sh(ə-)nəl\ *adj* — **tor·sion·al·ly** \-ē\ *adv*

tor·so \ˈtȯr-sō\ *n, pl* **torsos** *or* **tor·si** \ˈtȯr-ˌsē\ [It, lit., stalk] : the trunk of the human body

tort \ˈtȯrt\ *n* : a wrongful act which does not involve a breach of contract and for which the injured party can recover damages in a civil action

tor·ti·lla \tȯr-ˈtē-(y)ə\ *n* : a round thin cake of unleavened cornmeal bread usu. eaten hot with a topping of ground meat or cheese

tor·toise \ˈtȯrt-əs\ *n* : TURTLE; *esp* : a land turtle

[1]**tor·toise·shell** \ˈtȯrt-ə-ˌshel, -əs(h)-ˌshel\ *n* **1** : the mottled horny substance of the shell of some turtles used in inlaying and in making various ornamental articles **2** : any of several showy butterflies

[2]**tortoiseshell** *adj* : made of or resembling tortoiseshell esp. in spotted brown and yellow coloring

tor·to·ni \tȯr-ˈtō-nē\ *n* : ice cream made of heavy cream often with minced almonds and chopped cherries and flavored with rum

tor·tu·ous \ˈtȯrch-(ə-)wəs\ *adj* **1** : marked by twists or turns : WINDING **2** : DEVIOUS, TRICKY

[1]**tor·ture** \ˈtȯr-chər\ *n* **1** : anguish of body or mind : AGONY **2** : the infliction of severe pain esp. to punish or coerce

[2]**torture** *vb* **tor·tured; tor·tur·ing** \ˈtȯrch-(ə-)riŋ\ **1** : to cause intense suffering to : TORMENT **2** : to punish or coerce by inflicting severe pain **3** : TWIST, DISTORT **syn** rack, harrow, afflict, try — **tor·tur·er** *n*

To·ry \ˈtōr-ē\ *n, pl* **Tories** [IrGael *tōraidhe* pursued man, robber] **1** : a member of a chiefly 18th century British party upholding the established church and the traditional political structure **2** : an American supporter of the British during the American Revolution **3** *often not cap* : an extreme conservative — **Tory** *adj*

[1]**toss** \ˈtȯs, ˈtäs\ *vb* **1** : to fling to and fro or up and down **2** : to throw with a quick light motion; *also* : BANDY **3** : to fling or lift with a sudden motion ⟨~*ed* her head angrily⟩ **4** : to move restlessly or turbulently ⟨~*es* on the waves⟩ **5** : to twist and turn repeatedly **6** : FLOUNCE **7** : to accomplish readily ⟨~ off an article⟩ **8** : to decide an issue by flipping a coin

[2]**toss** *n* : an act or instance of tossing; *esp* : TOSS-UP 1

toss–up \-ˌəp\ *n* **1** : a deciding by flipping a coin **2** : an even chance **3** : something that offers no clear basis for choice

[1]**tot** \ˈtät\ *n* **1** : a small child **2** : a small drink of alcoholic liquor : SHOT

[2]**tot** *vb* **tot·ted; tot·ting** : to add up

[3]**tot** *abbr* total

[1]**to·tal** \ˈtōt-ᵊl\ *adj* **1** : making up a whole : ENTIRE ⟨~ amount⟩ **2** : COMPLETE, UTTER ⟨a ~ failure⟩ **3** : involving a complete and unified effort esp. to achieve a desired effect — **to·tal·ly** \-ē\ *adv*

[2]**total** *n* **1** : SUM 4 **2** : the entire amount **syn** aggregate, whole, gross, totality

[3]**total** *vb* **to·taled** *or* **to·talled; to·tal·ing** *or* **to·tal·ling** **1** : to add up : COMPUTE **2** : to amount to : NUMBER **3** : to make a total wreck of (a car)

to·tal·i·tar·i·an \tō-ˌtal-ə-ˈter-ē-ən\ *adj* : of or relating to a political regime based on subordination of the individual to the state and strict control of all aspects of life esp. by coercive measures; *also* : advocating, constituting, or characteristic of such a regime — **totalitarian** *n* — **to·tal·i·tar·i·an·ism** \-ē-ə-ˌniz-əm\ *n*

to·tal·i·ty \tō-ˈtal-ət-ē\ *n, pl* **-ties** **1** : an aggregate amount : SUM, WHOLE **2** : ENTIRETY, WHOLENESS

to·tal·iza·tor *or* **to·tal·isa·tor** \ˈtōt-ᵊl-ə-ˌzāt-ər\ *n* : a machine for registering and indicating the number of bets and the odds on a horse or dog race

[1]**tote** \ˈtōt\ *vb* **tot·ed; tot·ing** : CARRY

[2]**tote** *vb* **tot·ed; tot·ing** : ADD, TOTAL — usu. used with *up*

to·tem \ˈtōt-əm\ *n* : an object (as an animal or plant) serving as the emblem of a family or clan and often as a reminder of its ancestry; *also* : something usu. carved or painted to represent such an object

totem pole *n* : a pole that is carved with a series of totems and is erected before the houses of some northwest American Indians

tot·ter \ˈtät-ər\ *vb* **1** : to tremble or rock as if about to fall : SWAY **2** : to move unsteadily : STAGGER

tou·can \ˈtü-ˌkan\ *n* : any of a family of fruit-eating birds of tropical America with brilliant coloring and a very large beak

[1]**touch** \ˈtəch\ *vb* **1** : to bring a bodily part (as the hand) into contact with so as to feel **2** : to be or cause to be in contact **3** : to strike or push lightly esp. with the hand or foot **4** : DISTURB, HARM **5** : to make use of ⟨never ~*es* alcohol⟩ **6** : to induce to give or lend **7** : to get to : REACH **8** : to refer to in passing : MENTION **9** : to affect the interest of : CONCERN **10** : to leave a mark on; *also* : BLEMISH **11** : to move to sympathetic feeling **12** : to come close : VERGE **13** : to have a bearing : RELATE **14** : to make a usu. brief or incidental stop in port **syn** affect, influence, impress, strike, sway

[2]**touch** *n* **1** : a light stroke or tap **2** : the act or fact of touching or being touched **3** : the sense by which pressure or traction on the skin or mucous membrane is perceived; *also* : a particular sensation conveyed by this sense **4** : mental or moral sensitiveness : TACT **5** : a small quantity : HINT **6** : a manner of striking or touching esp. the keys of a keyboard instrument **7** : an improving detail ⟨add a few ~*es* to the painting⟩ **8** : distinctive manner or skill ⟨~ of a master⟩ **9** : the state of being in contact ⟨keep in ~⟩ **syn** suggestion, suspicion, tincture, tinge

touch·down \ˈtəch-ˌdau̇n\ *n* : the act of scoring six points in American football by being lawfully in possession of the ball on, above, or behind an opponent's goal line

tou·ché \tü-ˈshā\ *interj* [F] — used to acknowledge a hit in fencing or the success of an argument, an accusation, or a witty point

touch football *n* : football played informally and chiefly characterized by the substitution of touching for tackling

touch·ing \ˈtəch-iŋ\ *adj* : capable of stirring emotions **syn** moving, impressive, poignant, affecting

touch off *vb* **1** : to describe with precision **2** : to cause to explode **3** : to release or initiate with sudden intensity

touch·stone \ˈtəch-ˌstōn\ *n* : a test or criterion of genuineness or quality **syn** standard, gauge, benchmark, yardstick

touch up \(ˈ)təch-ˈəp\ *vb* : to improve or perfect by small additional strokes or alterations

touchy \ˈtəch-ē\ *adj* **touch·i·er; -est 1** : easily offended : PEEVISH **2** : calling for tact in treatment ⟨a ~ subject⟩ **syn** irascible, cranky, cross, tetchy, testy

[1]**tough** \ˈtəf\ *adj* **1** : strong or firm in texture but flexible and not brittle **2** : not easily chewed **3** : characterized by severity and determination ⟨a ~ policy⟩ **4** : capable of enduring strain or hardship : ROBUST **5** : hard to influence : STUBBORN **6** : difficult to accomplish, resolve, or cope with ⟨a ~ problem⟩ **7** : ROWDYISH **syn** tenacious, stout, sturdy, stalwart — **tough·ly** *adv* — **tough·ness** *n*

[2]**tough** *n* : a tough person : ROWDY

tough·en \ˈtəf-ən\ *vb* **tough·ened; tough·en·ing** \-(ə-)niŋ\ : to make or become tough

tou·pee \tü-ˈpā\ *n* [F *toupet* forelock] : a small wig for a bald spot

[1]**tour** \ˈtu̇r, *1 is also* ˈtau̇(ə)r\ *n* **1** : one's turn : SHIFT **2** : a journey in which one returns to the starting point

[2]**tour** *vb* : to travel over as a tourist

tour de force \ˌtu̇rd-ə-ˈfōrs\ *n, pl* **tours de force** *same*\ [F] : a feat of strength, skill, or ingenuity

tour·ist \ˈtu̇r-əst\ *n* : one that makes a tour for pleasure or culture

tourist class *n* : economy accommodation on a ship, airplane, or train

tour·ma·line \ˈtu̇r-mə-lən, -ˌlēn\ *n* : a mineral that when transparent is valued as a gem

tour·na·ment \ˈtu̇r-nə-mənt, ˈtər-\ *n* **1** : a medieval sport in which mounted armored knights contended with blunted lances or swords; *also* : the whole series of knightly sports, jousts, and tilts occurring at one time and place **2** : a championship series of games or athletic contests

tour·ney \-nē\ *n, pl* **tourneys** : TOURNAMENT

tour·ni·quet \ˈtu̇r-ni-kət, ˈtər-\ *n* : a device (as a bandage twisted tight with a stick) for stopping bleeding or blood flow

tou·sle \ˈtau̇-zəl\ *vb* **tou·sled; tou·sling** \ˈtau̇z-(ə-)liŋ\ : to disorder by rough handling : DISHEVEL, MUSS

[1]**tout** \ˈtau̇t\ *vb* : to give a tip or solicit bets on a racehorse — **tout** *n*

[2]**tout** \ˈtau̇t, ˈtüt\ *vb* : to praise or publicize loudly

[1]**tow** \ˈtō\ *vb* : to draw or pull along behind **syn** tug, haul, drag, lug

[2]**tow** *n* **1** : an act of towing or condition of being towed **2** : something (as a barge) that is towed

[3]**tow** *n* : short or broken fiber (as of flax or hemp) used esp. for yarn, twine, or stuffing

to·ward *or* **to·wards** \(ˈ)tō(-ə)rd(z), tə-ˈwȯrd(z)\ *prep* **1** : in the direction of ⟨heading ~ the river⟩ **2** : along a course leading to ⟨efforts ~ reconciliation⟩ **3** : in regard to ⟨tolerance ~ minorities⟩ **4** : FACING ⟨the gun's muzzle was ~ him⟩ **5** : close upon ⟨it was getting along ~ sundown⟩ **6** : for part payment of ⟨paid $100 ~ his tuition⟩

tow·boat \ˈtō-ˌbōt\ *n* : TUGBOAT

tow·el \ˈtau̇(-ə)l\ *n* : an absorbent cloth or paper for wiping or drying

tow·el·ing *or* **tow·el·ling** \ˈtau̇-(ə-)liŋ\ *n* : a cotton or linen fabric often used for making towels

[1]**tow·er** \ˈtau̇(-ə)r\ *n* **1** : a tall structure either isolated or built upon a larger structure ⟨an observation ~⟩ ⟨a bell ~ of a church⟩ **2** : a towering citadel — **tow·ered** \ˈtau̇(-ə)rd\ *adj*

[2]**tower** *vb* : to reach or rise to a great height **syn** overlook, dominate

tow·er·ing \-iŋ\ *adj* **1** : LOFTY ⟨~ pines⟩ **2** : reaching high intensity ⟨a ~ rage⟩ **3** : EXCESSIVE ⟨~ ambition⟩

tow·head \ˈtō-ˌhed\ *n* : a person having flaxen hair — **tow·head·ed** \-ˌhed-əd\ *adj*

to·whee \ˈtō-ˌhē, ˈtō-(ˌ)ē, tō-ˈhē\ *n* : a common finch of eastern No. America having the male black, white, and reddish; *also* : any of several related finches

to wit \tə-ˈwit\ *adv* : NAMELY

town \ˈtau̇n\ *n* **1** : a compactly settled area usu. larger than a village but smaller than a city **2** : CITY **3** : the inhabitants of a town **4** : a New England territorial and political unit usu. containing both rural and urban areas; *also* : a New England community in which matters of local government are decided by a general assembly (**town meeting**) of qualified voters

town house *n* **1** : the city residence of a person having a country home **2** : a single-family house of two or sometimes three stories connected to another house by a common wall

town·ie *or* **towny** \ˈtau̇-nē\ *n, pl* **townies** : a permanent resident of a town as distinguished from a member of another group

towns·folk \ˈtau̇nz-ˌfōk\ *n pl* : TOWNSPEOPLE

town·ship \ˈtau̇n-ˌship\ *n* **1** : TOWN 4 **2** : a unit of local government in some states **3** : an unorganized subdivision of a county; *also* : an administrative division **4** : a division of territory in surveys of U.S. public land containing 36 square miles

towns·man \ˈtau̇nz-mən\ *n* **1** : a native or resident of a town or city **2** : a fellow citizen of a town

towns·peo·ple \-ˌpē-pəl\ *n pl* **1** : the inhabitants of a town or city **2** : town-bred persons

tow·path \ˈtō-ˌpath, -ˌpȧth\ *n* : a path (as along a canal) traveled by men or animals towing boats

tow truck *n* : WRECKER 2

tox·emia \täk-ˈsē-mē-ə\ *n* : a bodily disorder associated with the presence of toxic matter in the blood

tox·ic \ˈtäk-sik\ *adj* [LL *toxicus*, fr. L *toxicum* poison, fr. Gk *toxikon* arrow poison, fr. neut. of *toxikos* of a bow, fr. *toxon* bow, arrow] : of, relating to, or caused by poison or a toxin : POISONOUS — **tox·ic·i·ty** \täk-ˈsis-ət-ē\ *n*

tox·i·col·o·gy \ˌtäk-sə-ˈkäl-ə-jē\ *n* : a science that deals with poisons and esp. with problems of their use and control — **tox·i·co·log·i·cal** \-ˈläj-i-kəl\ *or* **tox·i·co·log·ic** \ˌtäk-si-kə-ˈläj-ik\ *adj* — **tox·i·col·o·gist** \-ˈkäl-ə-jəst\ *n*

toxic shock syndrome *n* : an acute disease probably of bacterial origin that is characterized by fever, sore throat, and diffuse erythema and occurs esp. in menstruating females using tampons

tox·in \ˈtäk-sən\ *n* : a substance produced by a living organism that is very poisonous when introduced into the tissues but is usu. destroyed by digestive processes when taken by mouth

[1]**toy** \ˈtȯi\ *n* **1** : something trifling **2** : a small ornament : BAUBLE **3** : something for a child to play with

[2]**toy** *vb* **1** : FLIRT **2** : to deal with something lightly : TRIFLE **3** : to amuse oneself as if with a plaything

[3]**toy** *adj* **1** : DIMINUTIVE **2** : designed for use as a toy

tp *abbr* **1** title page **2** township

tpk *or* **tpke** *abbr* turnpike

tr *abbr* **1** translated; translation; translator **2** transpose **3** troop

[1]**trace** \ˈtrās\ *n* **1** : a mark (as a footprint or track) left by something that has passed : VESTIGE **2** : a minute or barely detectable amount

[2]**trace** *vb* **traced; trac·ing 1** : to mark out : SKETCH **2** : to form (as letters) carefully **3** : to copy (a drawing) by marking lines on transparent paper laid over the drawing to be copied **4** : to follow the trail of : track down **5** : to study out and follow the development of — **trace·able** *adj* — **trac·er** *n*

[3]**trace** *n* : either of two lines of a harness for fastening a draft animal to a vehicle

trac·ery \ˈtrās(-ə)-rē\ *n, pl* **-er·ies** : ornamental work having a design with branching or interlacing lines

tra·chea \ˈtrā-kē-ə\ *n, pl* **-che·ae** \-kē-ˌē\ *also* **-che·as** : the main tube by which air enters the lungs : WINDPIPE — **tra·che·al** \-kē-əl\ *adj*

trac·ing \ˈtrā-siŋ\ *n* **1** : the act of one that traces **2** : something that is traced **3** : a graphic record made by an instrument for measuring vibrations or pulsations

[1]**track** \ˈtrak\ *n* **1** : a mark left in passing **2** : PATH, ROUTE, TRAIL **3** : a course laid out for racing; *also* : track-and-field sports **4** : one of a series of paths along which material (as music) is recorded (as on magnetic tape) **5** : the course along which something moves; *esp* : a way made by two parallel lines of metal rails **6** : awareness of a fact or progression ⟨lost ~ of his movements⟩ **7** : either of two endless metal belts on which a vehicle (as a tractor) travels

[2]**track** *vb* **1** : to follow the tracks or traces of : TRAIL **2** : to make tracks on **3** : to carry on the feet and deposit ⟨~*ed* mud on the floor⟩ — **track·er** *n*

track·age \ˈtrak-ij\ *n* : lines of railway track

track–and–field \ˌtrak-ən-ˈfēld\ *adj* : of or relating to athletic contests held on a running track or on the adjacent field

[1]**tract** \ˈtrakt\ *n* **1** : a stretch of land without precise boundaries ⟨broad ~*s* of prairie⟩ **2** : a defined area of land ⟨a garden ~⟩ **3** : a system of body parts or organs together serving some special purpose ⟨the digestive ~⟩

[2]**tract** *n* : a pamphlet of political or religious propaganda

trac·ta·ble \ˈtrak-tə-bəl\ *adj* **1** : easily controlled : DOCILE **2** : easily wrought : MALLEABLE **syn** amenable, obedient, biddable

trac·tate \ˈtrak-ˌtāt\ *n* : TREATISE

tract house *n* : any of many similarly designed houses built on a tract of land

trac·tion \ˈtrak-shən\ *n* **1** : the act of drawing : the state of being drawn **2** : the drawing of a vehicle by motive power; *also* : the particular form of motive power used **3** : the adhesive friction of a body on a surface on which it moves **4** : a pulling force applied to a skeletal structure (as a broken bone) by using a special device; *also* : a state of tension created by such a pulling force ⟨a leg in ~⟩ — **trac·tion·al** \-sh(ə-)nəl\ *adj* — **trac·tive** \ˈtrak-tiv\ *adj*

trac·tor \ˈtrak-tər\ *n* **1** : an automotive vehicle that is borne on four wheels or beltlike metal tracks and is used esp. for drawing farm equipment **2** : a motortruck with short chassis for hauling a trailer

[1]**trade** \ˈtrād\ *n* **1** : one's regular business or work : OCCUPATION **2** : an occupation requiring manual or mechanical skill **3** : the persons engaged in a business or industry **4** : the business of buying and selling or bartering commodities **5** : an act of trading : TRANSACTION **syn** craft, profession, calling, vocation

[2]**trade** *vb* **trad·ed; trad·ing 1** : to give in exchange for another commodity : BARTER **2** : to engage in the exchange, purchase, or sale of goods **3** : to deal regularly as a customer — **trade on** : EXPLOIT ⟨*trades on* his family name⟩

trade–in \ˈtrād-ˌin\ *n* : an item of merchandise taken as part payment of a purchase

trade in \(ˈ)trād-ˈin\ *vb* : to turn in as part payment for a purchase

[1]**trade·mark** \ˈtrād-ˌmärk\ *n* : a device (as a word or mark) that points distinctly to the origin or ownership of merchandise to which it is applied and that is legally reserved for the exclusive use of the owner

[2]**trademark** *vb* : to secure the trademark rights for

trade name *n* : a name that is given by a manufacturer or merchant to a product to distinguish it as made or sold by him and that may be used and protected as a trademark

trad·er \ˈtrād-ər\ *n* **1** : a person whose business is buying or selling **2** : a ship engaged in trade

trades·man \ˈtrādz-mən\ *n* **1** : one who runs a retail store : SHOPKEEPER **2** : CRAFTSMAN

trades·peo·ple \-ˌpē-pəl\ *n pl* : people engaged in trade

trade wind *n* : a wind blowing almost constantly in one direction

trading stamp *n* : a printed stamp of value given as a premium to a retail customer and when accumulated in numbers redeemed in merchandise

tra·di·tion \trə-ˈdish-ən\ *n* **1** : an inherited, established, or customary pattern of thought or action **2** : the handing down of beliefs and customs by word of mouth or by example without written instruction; *also* : a belief or custom thus handed down — **tra·di·tion·al** \-ˌdish(ə-)nəl\ *adj* — **tra·di·tion·al·ly** \-ē\ *adv*

tra·duce \trə-ˈd(y)üs\ *vb* **tra·duced; tra·duc·ing** : to lower the reputation of : DEFAME, SLANDER **syn** malign, libel, calumniate — **tra·duc·er** *n*

[1]**traf·fic** \ˈtraf-ik\ *n* **1** : the business of bartering or buying and selling **2** : communication or dealings between individuals or groups **3** : the movement (as of vehicles) along a route **4** : the passengers or cargo carried by a transportation system

[2]**traffic** *vb* **traf·ficked; traf·fick·ing** : to carry on traffic — **traf·fick·er** *n*

traffic circle *n* : ROTARY 2

traffic light *n* : an electrically operated visual signal for controlling traffic

tra·ge·di·an \trə-ˈjēd-ē-ən\ *n* **1** : a writer of tragedies **2** : an actor who plays tragic roles

tra·ge·di·enne \trə-ˌjēd-ē-ˈen\ *n* [F] : an actress who plays tragic roles

trag·e·dy \ˈtraj-əd-ē\ *n, pl* **-dies** [ME *tragedie,* fr. MF, fr. L *tragoedia,* fr. Gk *tragōidia,* fr. *tragos* goat + *aeidein* to sing] **1** : a serious drama describing a conflict between the protagonist and a superior force (as destiny) and having a sad end that excites pity or terror **2** : a disastrous event : CALAMITY; *also* : MISFORTUNE **3** : tragic quality or element

trag·ic \ˈtraj-ik\ *also* **trag·i·cal** \-i-kəl\ *adj* **1** : of, relating to, or expressive of tragedy **2** : appropriate to tragedy **3** : LAMENTABLE, UNFORTUNATE — **trag·i·cal·ly** \-i-k(ə-)lē\ *adv*

[1]**trail** \ˈtrāl\ *vb* **1** : to hang down so as to drag along or sweep the ground **2** : to draw or drag along behind **3** : to extend over a surface in a straggling manner **4** : to follow slowly : lag behind **5** : to follow upon the track of : PURSUE **6** : DWINDLE ⟨her voice ~*ed* off⟩ **syn** tag, tail, dog, shadow

[2]**trail** *n* **1** : something that trails or is trailed ⟨a ~ of smoke⟩ **2** : a trace or mark left by something that has passed or been drawn along : TRACK ⟨a ~ of blood⟩ **3** : a beaten path; *also* : a marked path through woods **4** : SCENT

trail bike *n* : a small motorcycle for use other than on highways

trail·blaz·er \-ˌblā-zər\ *n* : PATHFINDER, PIONEER — **trail·blaz·ing** \-ziŋ\ *adj or n*

trail·er \ˈtrā-lər\ *n* **1** : one that trails; *esp* : a creeping plant (as an ivy) **2** : a vehicle that is hauled by another (as a tractor) **3** : a vehicle equipped to serve wherever parked as a dwelling or as a place of business

trailing arbutus *n* : a trailing spring-flowering plant of the heath family with fragrant pink or white flowers; *also* : its flower

[1]**train** \ˈtrān\ *n* **1** : a part of a gown that trails behind the wearer **2** : RETINUE **3** : a moving file of persons, vehicles, or animals **4** : a connected series ⟨a ~ of thought⟩ **5** : AFTERMATH **6** : a connected line of railroad cars usu. hauled by a locomotive **syn** succession, sequence, procession, chain

[2]**train** *vb* **1** : to cause to grow as desired ⟨~ a vine on a trellis⟩ **2** : to form by instruction, discipline, or drill **3** : to make or become prepared (as by exercise) for a test of skill **4** : to aim or point at an object ⟨~ guns on a fort⟩ **syn** discipline, school, educate, instruct — **train·er** *n*

train·ee \trā-ˈnē\ *n* : one who is being trained for a job

train·ing \ˈtrā-niŋ\ *n* **1** : the act, process, or method of one who trains **2** : the knowledge or experience gained by one who trains

train·load \ˈtrān-ˈlōd\ *n* : the full freight or passenger capacity of a railroad train

train·man \-mən\ *n* : a member of a train crew

traipse \ˈtrāps\ *vb* **traipsed; traips·ing** : TRAMP, WALK

trait \ˈtrāt\ *n* : a distinguishing quality (as of personality) : CHARACTERISTIC

trai·tor \ˈtrāt-ər\ *n* [ME *traitre,* fr. OF, fr. L *traditor,* fr. *traditus,* pp. of *tradere* to hand over, deliver, betray, fr. *trans-* across + *dare* to give] **1** : one who betrays another's trust or is false to an obligation **2** : one who commits treason — **trai·tor·ous** *adj*

tra·jec·to·ry \trə-ˈjek-t(ə-)rē\ *n, pl* **-ries** : the curve that a body (as a planet in its orbit) describes in space

tram \ˈtram\ *n* **1** *chiefly Brit* : STREETCAR **2** : a boxlike car running on a railway (**tram·way** \-ˌwā\) in a mine or a logging camp

[1]**tram·mel** \ˈtram-əl\ *n* [ME *tramayle,* a kind of net, fr. MF *tremail,* fr. LL *tremaculum,* fr. L *tres* three + *macula* mesh, spot] : something impeding activity, progress, or freedom

[2]**trammel** *vb* **-meled** *or* **-melled; -mel·ing** *or* **-mel·ling** \-(ə-)liŋ\ **1** : to catch and hold in or as if in a net **2** : HAMPER **syn** clog, fetter, shackle, hobble

[1]**tramp** \ˈtramp, *1 & 3 are also* ˈträmp, ˈtrȯmp\ *vb* **1** : to walk, tread, or step heavily **2** : to walk about or through; *also* : HIKE **3** : to tread on forcibly and repeatedly

[2]**tramp** \ˈtramp, *5 is also* ˈträmp, ˈtrȯmp\ *n* **1** : a foot traveler **2** : a begging or thieving vagrant **3** : an immoral woman; *esp* : PROSTITUTE **4** : a walking trip : HIKE **5** : the succession of sounds made by the beating of feet on a road **6** : a ship that does not follow a regular course but takes cargo to any port

tram·ple \ˈtram-pəl\ *vb* **tram·pled; tram·pling** \-p(ə-)liŋ\ **1** : to tread heavily so as to bruise, crush, or injure **2** : to inflict injury or destruction **3** : to press down or crush by or as if by treading : STAMP — **trample** *n* — **tram·pler** \-p(ə-)lər\ *n*

tram·po·line \ˌtram-pə-ˈlēn, ˈtram-pə-ˌlēn\ *n* [Sp *trampolín*] : a resilient canvas sheet or web supported by springs in a metal frame used as a springboard in tumbling — **tram·po·lin·ist** \-nəst\ *n*

trance \ˈtrans\ *n* [ME, fr. MF *transe,* fr. *transir* to pass away, swoon, fr. L *transire* to pass, pass away, fr. *trans-* across + *ire* go] **1** : DAZE, STUPOR **2** : a prolonged and profound sleeplike condition (as of deep hypnosis) **3** : a state of mystical absorption

tran·quil \ˈtraŋ-kwəl, ˈtran-\ *adj* : free from agitation or disturbance : QUIET **syn** serene, placid, peaceful — **tran·quil·li·ty** *or* **tran·quil·i·ty** \tran-ˈkwil-ət-ē, traŋ-\ *n* — **tran·quil·ly** \ˈtraŋ-kwə-lē, ˈtran-\ *adv*

tran·quil·ize *also* **tran·quil·lize** \ˈtraŋ-kwə-ˌlīz, ˈtran-\ *vb* **-ized** *also* **-lized; -iz·ing** *also* **-liz·ing** : to make or become tranquil; *esp* : to relieve of mental tension and anxiety

tran·quil·iz·er *also* **tran·quil·liz·er** \-ˌlī-zər\ *n* : a drug used to relieve tension and anxiety

trans *abbr* **1** transaction **2** transitive **3** translated; translation; translator **4** transportation **5** transverse

trans·act \trans-ˈakt, tranz-\ *vb* : CARRY OUT, PERFORM; *also* : CONDUCT

trans·ac·tion \-ˈak-shən\ *n* **1** : something transacted; *esp* : a business deal **2** : an act or process of transacting **3** *pl* : the records of the proceedings of a society or organization

trans·at·lan·tic \ˌtrans-ət-ˈlant-ik, ˌtranz-\ *adj* : crossing or extending across or situated beyond the Atlantic ocean

trans·ceiv·er \trans-ˈē-vər, tranz-\ *n* : a radio transmitter-receiver that uses many of the same components for transmission and reception

tran·scend \trans-ˈend\ *vb* **1** : to rise above the limits of **2** : SURPASS **syn** exceed, outdo, outshine, outstrip

tran·scen·dent \-ˈen-dənt\ *adj* **1** : exceeding usual limits : SURPASSING **2** : transcending material existence **syn** superlative, supreme, peerless, incomparable

tran·scen·den·tal \ˌtrans-ˌen-ˈdent-ᵊl, -ən-\ *adj* **1** : TRANSCENDENT **2** : of, relating to, or characteristic of transcendentalism; *also* : ABSTRUSE

tran·scen·den·tal·ism \-ᵊl-ˌiz-əm\ *n* : a philosophy holding that ultimate reality is unknowable or asserting the primacy of the spiritual over the material and empirical — **tran·scen·den·tal·ist** \-ᵊl-əst\ *adj or n*

trans·con·ti·nen·tal \ˌtrans-ˌkänt-ᵊn-ˈent-ᵊl\ *adj* : extending or going across a continent

tran·scribe \trans-ˈkrīb\ *vb* **tran·scribed; tran·scrib·ing** **1** : to write a copy of **2** : to make a copy of (dictated or recorded matter) in longhand or on a typewriter **3** : to represent (speech sounds) by means of phonetic symbols; *also* : to make a musical transcription of

tran·script \ˈtrans-ˌkript\ *n* **1** : a written, printed, or typed copy **2** : an official copy esp. of a student's educational record

tran·scrip·tion \trans-ˈkrip-shən\ *n* **1** : an act or process of transcribing **2** : COPY, TRANSCRIPT **3** : an arrangement of a musical composition for some instrument or voice other than the original

trans·duc·er \-ˈd(y)ü-sər\ *n* : a device that is actuated by power from one system and supplies power usu. in another form to a second system

tran·sept \ˈtrans-ˌept\ *n* : the part of a cruciform church that crosses at right angles to the greatest length; *also* : either of the projecting ends

[1]trans·fer \trans-ˈfər, ˈtrans-ˌfər\ *vb* **trans·ferred; trans·fer·ring 1** : to pass or cause to pass from one person, place, or situation to another : TRANSPORT, TRANSMIT **2** : to make over the possession of : CONVEY **3** : to print or copy from one surface to another by contact **4** : to change from one vehicle or transportation line to another — **trans·fer·able** \trans-ˈfər-ə-bəl\ *adj* — **trans·fer·al** \-əl\ *n*

[2]trans·fer \ˈtrans-ˌfər\ *n* **1** : conveyance of right, title, or interest in property from one person to another **2** : an act or process of transferring **3** : one that transfers or is transferred **4** : a ticket entitling a passenger to continue a journey on another route

trans·fer·ence \trans-ˈfər-əns\ *n* : an act, process, or instance of transferring

trans·fig·ure \trans-ˈfig-yər\ *vb* **-ured; -ur·ing 1** : to change the form or appearance of **2** : EXALT, GLORIFY — **trans·fig·u·ra·tion** \ˌtrans-ˌfig-(y)ə-ˈrā-shən\ *n*

trans·fix \trans-ˈfiks\ *vb* **1** : to pierce through with or as if with a pointed weapon **2** : to hold motionless by or as if by piercing

trans·form \trans-ˈfȯrm\ *vb* **1** : to change in structure, appearance, or character **2** : to change (an electric current) in potential or type **syn** transmute, transfigure, transmogrify — **trans·for·ma·tion** \ˌtrans-fər-ˈmā- shən\ *n* — **trans·form·er** \trans-ˈfȯr-mər\ *n*

trans·fuse \trans-ˈfyüz\ *vb* **trans·fused; trans·fus·ing 1** : to cause to pass from one to another **2** : to diffuse into or through **3** : to transfer (as blood) into a vein of a person or animal — **trans·fu·sion** \-ˈfyü-zhən\ *n*

trans·gress \trans-ˈgres, tranz-\ *vb* [F *transgresser,* fr. L *transgressus,* pp. of *transgredi* to step beyond or across, fr. *trans-* across + *gradi* to step] **1** : to go beyond the limits set by ⟨~ the divine law⟩ **2** : to go beyond : EXCEED **3** : SIN — **trans·gres·sion** \-ˈgresh-ən\ *n* — **trans·gres·sor** \-ˈgres-ər\ *n*

[1]tran·sient \ˈtranch-ənt\ *adj* **1** : not lasting long : SHORT-LIVED **2** : passing through a place with only a brief stay **syn** transitory, passing, momentary, fleeting — **tran·sient·ly** *adv*

[2]transient *n* : one that is transient; *esp* : a transient guest

tran·sis·tor \tranz-ˈis-tər, trans-\ *n* [*trans*fer + re*sistor:* fr. its transferring an electrical signal across a resistor] **1** : a small electronic semiconductor device similar in use to a vacuum tube **2** : a radio having transistors

tran·sis·tor·ize \-tə-ˌrīz\ *vb* **-ized; -iz·ing** : to equip (a device) with transistors

tran·sit \ˈtrans-ət, ˈtranz-\ *n* **1** : a passing through, across, or over : PASSAGE **2** : conveyance of persons or things from one place to another **3** : usu. local transportation esp. of people by public conveyance **4** : a surveyor's instrument for measuring angles

tran·si·tion \trans-ˈish-ən, tranz-\ *n* : passage from one state, place, stage, or subject to another : CHANGE — **tran·si·tion·al** \-ˈish-(ə-)nəl\ *adj*

tran·si·tive \ˈtrans-ət-iv, ˈtranz-\ *adj* **1** : having or containing an object required to complete the meaning **2** : TRANSITIONAL — **tran·si·tive·ly** *adv* — **tran·si·tive·ness** *n* — **tran·si·tiv·i·ty** \ˌtrans-ə-ˈtiv-ət-ē, ˌtranz-\ *n*

tran·si·to·ry \ˈtrans-ə-ˌtōr-ē, ˈtranz-\ *adj* : of brief duration : SHORT-LIVED, TEMPORARY **syn** transient, passing, momentary, fleeting

transl *abbr* translated; translation

trans·late \trans-ˈlāt, tranz-\ *vb* **trans·lat·ed; trans·lat·ing 1** : to bear or change from one place, state, or form to another **2** : to convey to heaven without death **3** : to transfer (a bishop) from one see to another **4** : to turn into one's own or another language — **trans·lat·able** *adj* — **trans·la·tion** \-ˈlā-shən\ *n* — **trans·la·tor** \-ˈlāt-ər\ *n*

trans·lit·er·ate \trans-ˈlit-ə-ˌrāt, tranz-\ *vb* **-at·ed; -at·ing** : to represent or spell in the characters of another alphabet — **trans·lit·er·a·tion** \ˌtrans-ˌlit-ə-ˈrā-shən, ˌtranz-\ *n*

trans·lu·cent \trans-ˈlüs-ᵊnt, tranz-\ *adj* : admitting and diffusing light so that objects beyond cannot be clearly distinguished : partly transparent — **trans·lu·cence** \-ᵊns\ *n* — **trans·lu·cen·cy** \-ᵊn-sē\ *n* — **trans·lu·cent·ly** *adv*

trans·mi·grate \-ˈmī-ˌgrāt\ *vb* : to pass at death from one body or being to another — **trans·mi·gra·tion** \ˌtrans-mī-ˈgrā-shən, ˌtranz-\ *n* — **trans·mi·gra·to·ry** \trans-ˈmī-grə-ˌtōr-ē\ *adj*

trans·mis·sion \-ˈmish-ən\ *n* **1** : an act or process of transmitting **2** : the passage of radio waves between transmitting stations and receiving stations **3** : the gears by which power is transmitted from the engine of an automobile to the axle that propels the vehicle **4** : something transmitted

trans·mit \-ˈmit\ *vb* **trans·mit·ted; trans·mit·ting 1** : to transfer from one person or place to another : FORWARD **2** : to pass on by or as if by inheritance **3** : to cause or allow to spread abroad or to another ⟨~ a disease⟩ **4** : to cause (as light, electricity, or force) to pass through space or a medium **5** : to send out (radio or television signals) **syn** convey, communicate, impart — **trans·mis·si·ble** \-ˈmis-ə-bəl\ *adj* — **trans·mit·ta·ble** \-ˈmit-ə-bəl\ *adj* — **trans·mit·tal** \-ˈmit-ᵊl\ *n*

trans·mit·ter \-ˈmit-ər\ *n* **1** : one that transmits **2** : the part of a telephone into which one speaks **3** : an apparatus for transmitting telegraph, radio, or television signals

trans·mog·ri·fy \trans-ˈmäg-rə-ˌfī, tranz-\ *vb* **-fied; -fy·ing** : to change or alter often with grotesque or humorous effect — **trans·mog·ri·fi·ca·tion** \-ˌmäg-rə-fə-ˈkā-shən\ *n*

trans·mute \-ˈmyüt\ *vb* **trans·muted; trans·mut·ing** : to change or alter in form, appearance, or nature **syn** transform, convert, transfigure, metamorphose — **trans·mu·ta·tion** \ˌtrans-myu̇-ˈtā-shən, ˌtranz-\ *n*

trans·na·tion·al \-ˈnash-(ə-)nəl\ *adj* : extending beyond national boundaries

trans·oce·an·ic \ˌtrans-ˌō-shē-ˈan-ik, ˌtranz-\ *adj* **1** : lying or dwelling beyond the ocean **2** : crossing or extending across the ocean

tran·som \ˈtran-səm\ *n* **1** : a piece (as a crossbar in the frame of a window or door) that lies crosswise in a structure **2** : a window above an opening (as a door) built on and often hinged to a horizontal crossbar

tran·son·ic *also* **trans–son·ic** \tran(s)-ˈsän-ik\ *adj* : being, relating to, or moving at a speed that is about that of sound in air or about 741 miles (1185 kilometers) per hour

transp *abbr* transportation

trans·pa·cif·ic \ˌtrans-pə-ˈsif-ik\ *adj* : crossing, extending across, or situated beyond the Pacific ocean

trans·par·ent \trans-ˈpar-ənt\ *adj* **1** : transmitting light : clear enough to be seen through **2** : SHEER, DIAPHANOUS ⟨a ~ fabric⟩ **3** : readily understood : CLEAR; *also* : easily detected ⟨a ~ lie⟩ **syn** lucid, translucent, lucent — **trans·par·en·cy** \-ən-sē\ *n* — **trans·par·ent·ly** *adv*

tran·spire \trans-ˈpī(ə)r\ *vb* **trans·pired; trans·pir·ing** [MF *transpirer,* fr. L *trans-* across + *spirare* to breathe] **1** : to pass off (as watery vapor) through pores or a membrane **2** : to become known : come to light **3** : to take place : OCCUR — **tran·spi·ra·tion** \ˌtrans-pə-ˈrā-shən\ *n*

[1]**trans·plant** \trans-ˈplant\ *vb* **1** : to take up and set again in another soil or location **2** : to remove from one place and settle or introduce elsewhere : TRANSPORT **3** : to transfer (an organ or tissue) from one part or individual to another **4** : to tolerate or adapt to being transplanted — **trans·plan·ta·tion** \ˌtrans-ˌplan-ˈtā-shən\ *n*

[2]**trans·plant** \ˈtrans-ˌplant\ *n* **1** : something transplanted **2** : the act or process of transplanting

trans·po·lar \trans-ˈpō-lər\ *adj* : going or extending across either of the polar regions

[1]**trans·port** \trans-ˈpōrt\ *vb* **1** : to convey from one place to another : CARRY **2** : to carry away by strong emotion : ENRAPTURE **3** : to send to a penal colony overseas **syn** bear, carry, convey, ferry — **trans·por·ta·tion** \ˌtrans-pər-ˈtā-shən\ *n* — **trans·port·er** \trans-ˈpōrt-ər\ *n*

[2]**trans·port** \ˈtrans-ˌpōrt\ *n* **1** : an act of transporting : TRANSPORTATION **2** : strong or intensely pleasurable emotion : RAPTURE **3** : a ship used in transporting troops or supplies; *also* : a vehicle (as a truck or plane) used to transport persons or goods

trans·pose \trans-ˈpōz\ *vb* **trans·posed; trans·pos·ing 1** : to change the position or sequence of ⟨∼ the letters in a word⟩ **2** : to write or perform (a musical composition) in a different key **syn** reverse, invert — **trans·po·si·tion** \ˌtrans-pə-ˈzish-ən\ *n*

trans·ship \tran(ch)-ˈship, trans-\ *vb* : to transfer for further transportation from one ship or conveyance to another — **trans·ship·ment** *n*

tran·sub·stan·ti·a·tion \ˌtrans-əb-ˌstan-chē-ˈā-shən\ *n* : the change in the eucharistic elements from the substance of bread and wine to the substance of the body of Christ with only the appearances of bread and wine remaining

trans·verse \trans-ˈvərs, tranz-\ *adj* : lying across : set crosswise — **transverse** \ˈtrans-ˌvərs, ˈtranz-\ *n* — **trans·verse·ly** *adv*

trans·ves·tite \trans-ˈves-ˌtīt, tranz-\ *n* : a person and esp. a male who adopts the dress and often the behavior of the opposite sex — **transvestite** *adj* — **trans·ves·tism** \-ˌtiz-əm\ *n*

[1]**trap** \ˈtrap\ *n* **1** : a device for catching animals **2** : something by which one is caught unawares **3** : a machine for throwing objects into the air to be targets for shooters; *also* : a hazard on a golf course consisting of a depression containing sand **4** : a light one-horse carriage on springs **5** : a device to allow some one thing to pass through while keeping other things out ⟨a ∼ in a drainpipe⟩ **6** *pl* : a group of percussion instruments used in a jazz or dance orchestra

[2]**trap** *vb* **trapped; trap·ping 1** : to catch in or as if in a trap; *also* : CONFINE **2** : to provide or set (a place) with traps **3** : to set traps for animals esp. as a business **syn** snare, entrap, ensnare, bag, lure, decoy — **trap·per** *n*

[3]**trap** *n* : any of various dark fine-grained igneous rocks used esp. in making roads

trap·door \ˈtrap-ˈdōr\ *n* : a lifting or sliding door covering an opening in a floor or roof

tra·peze \tra-ˈpēz\ *n* : a gymnastic apparatus consisting of a horizontal bar suspended by two parallel ropes

trap·e·zoid \ˈtrap-ə-ˌzȯid\ *n* [NL *trapezoïdes,* fr. Gk *trapezoeidēs* trapezoid-shaped, fr. *trapeza* table, fr. *tra-* four + *peza* foot] : a plane 4-sided figure with two and only two sides parallel — **trap·e·zoi·dal** \ˌtrap-ə-ˈzȯid-ᵊl\ *adj*

trap·pings \ˈtrap-iŋz\ *n pl* **1** : an ornamental covering esp. for a horse **2** : outward decoration or dress

trap·rock \ˈtrap-ˈräk\ *n* : [3]TRAP

traps \ˈtraps\ *n pl* : personal belongings : LUGGAGE

trap·shoot·ing \ˈtrap-ˌshüt-iŋ\ *n* : shooting at clay pigeons sprung from a trap into the air away from the shooter

trash \ˈtrash\ *n* **1** : something of little worth : RUBBISH **2** : a worthless person; *also* : such persons as a group : RIFFRAFF — **trashy** *adj*

trau·ma \ˈtrau̇-mə, ˈtrȯ-\ *n, pl* **trau·ma·ta** \-mət-ə\ *or* **traumas** [Gk] : a bodily or mental injury usu. caused by an external agent; *also* : a cause of trauma — **trau·mat·ic** \trə-ˈmat-ik, trȯ-, trau̇-\ *adj*

[1]**tra·vail** \trə-ˈvāl, ˈtrav-ˌāl\ *n* **1** : painful work or exertion : TOIL **2** : AGONY, TORMENT **3** : CHILDBIRTH, LABOR **syn** work, drudgery, grind

[2]**travail** *vb* : to labor hard : TOIL

[1]**trav·el** \ˈtrav-əl\ *vb* **-eled** *or* **-elled; -el·ing** *or* **-el·ling** \-(ə-)liŋ\ **1** : to go on or as if on a trip or tour : JOURNEY **2** : to move as if by traveling : PASS ⟨news ∼*s* fast⟩ **3** : ASSOCIATE **4** : to go from place to place as a salesman **5** : to move from point to point ⟨light waves ∼ very fast⟩ **6** : to journey over or through ⟨∼*ing* the highways⟩ — **trav·el·er** *or* **trav·el·ler** *n*

[2]**travel** *n* **1** : the act of traveling : PASSAGE **2** : JOURNEY, TRIP — often used in pl. **3** : the number traveling : TRAFFIC **4** : the motion of a piece of machinery and esp. when to and fro; *also* : length of motion (as of a piston)

traveling bag *n* : a bag carried by hand and designed to hold a traveler's clothing and personal articles

trav·el·ogue *or* **trav·el·og** \ˈtrav-ə-ˌlȯg, -ˌläg\ *n* : a usu. illustrated lecture on travel

[1]**tra·verse** \ˈtrav-ərs\ *n* : something (as a crosswise beam) that crosses or lies across

[2]**tra·verse** \trə-ˈvərs, tra-ˈvərs *or* ˈtra-vərs\ *vb* **tra·versed; tra·vers·ing 1** : to pass through : PENETRATE **2** : to go or travel across or over **3** : to extend over **4** : SWIVEL

[3]**tra·verse** \ˈtra-ˌvərs\ *adj* : TRANSVERSE

trav·er·tine \ˈtrav-ər-ˌtēn, -tən\ *n* : a crystalline mineral formed by deposition from spring waters

[1]**trav·es·ty** \ˈtrav-ə-stē\ *vb* **-tied; -ty·ing** : to make a travesty of

[2]**travesty** *n, pl* **-ties** [obs. E *travesty,* disguised, parodied, fr. F *travesti,* pp. of *travestir* to disguise, fr. It *travestire,* fr. *tra-* across (fr. L *trans-*) + *vestire* to dress] : a burlesque and usu. grotesque translation or imitation

[1]**trawl** \ˈtrȯl\ *vb* : to fish or catch with a trawl — **trawl·er** *n*

[2]**trawl** *n* **1** : a large conical net dragged along the sea bottom in fishing **2** : a long fishing line anchored at both ends and equipped with many hooks

tray \ˈtrā\ *n* : an open receptacle with flat bottom and low rim for holding, carrying, or exhibiting articles

treach·er·ous \ˈtrech-(ə-)rəs\ *adj* **1** : characterized by treachery **2** : UNTRUSTWORTHY, UNRELIABLE **3** : providing insecure footing or support **syn** traitorous, faithless, false, disloyal — **treach·er·ous·ly** *adv*

treach·ery \ˈtrech-(ə-)rē\ *n, pl* **-er·ies** : violation of allegiance or trust

trea·cle \ˈtrē-kəl\ *n* [ME *triacle* a medicinal compound, fr. MF, fr. L *theriaca,* fr. Gk *thēriakē* antidote against a poisonous bite, fr. *thērion* wild animal] **1** *chiefly Brit* : MOLASSES **2** : something heavily sweet and cloying

[1]**tread** \ˈtred\ *vb* **trod** \ˈträd\; **trod·den** \ˈträd-ᵊn\ *or* **trod; tread·ing 1** : to step or walk on or over **2** : to move on foot : WALK; *also* : DANCE **3** : to beat or press with the feet

[2]**tread** *n* **1** : a mark made by or as if by treading **2** : the manner or sound of stepping **3** : the part of a wheel that makes contact with a road **4** : the horizontal part of a step

trea·dle \ˈtred-ᵊl\ *n* : a lever device pressed by the foot to drive a machine

tread·mill \ˈtred-ˌmil\ *n* **1** : a mill worked by persons who tread on steps around the edge of a wheel or by animals that walk on an endless belt **2** : a wearisome routine

treas *abbr* treasurer; treasury

trea·son \ˈtrēz-ᵊn\ *n* : the offense of attempting to overthrow the government of one's country or of assisting its enemies in war — **trea·son·able** \-(ᵊ-)nə-bəl\ *adj* — **trea·son·ous** \-(ᵊ-)nəs\ *adj*

[1]trea·sure \ˈtrezh-ər, ˈtrāzh-\ *n* **1** : wealth stored up or held in reserve **2** : something of great value

[2]treasure *vb* **trea·sured; trea·sur·ing** \-(ə-)riŋ\ **1** : HOARD **2** : to keep as precious : CHERISH **syn** prize, value, appreciate, esteem

trea·sur·er \ˈtrezh-rər, ˈtrezh-ər-ər, ˈtrāzh-\ *n* : an officer entrusted with the receipt, care, and disbursement of funds

treasure trove \-ˌtrōv\ *n* **1** : treasure (as money in gold) which is found hidden and whose ownership is unknown **2** : a valuable discovery

trea·sury \ˈtrezh-(ə-)rē, ˈtrāzh-\ *n, pl* **-sur·ies** **1** : a place in which stores of wealth are kept **2** : the place of deposit and disbursement of collected funds; *esp* : one where public revenues are deposited, kept, and disbursed **3** *cap* : a governmental department in charge of finances

[1]treat \ˈtrēt\ *vb* **1** : NEGOTIATE **2** : to deal with esp. in writing; *also* : HANDLE **3** : to pay for the food or entertainment of **4** : to behave or act toward ⟨~ them well⟩ **5** : to regard in a specified manner ⟨~ as inferiors⟩ **6** : to care for medically or surgically **7** : to subject to some action (as of a chemical) ⟨~ soil with lime⟩

[2]treat *n* **1** : food or entertainment paid for by another **2** : a source of joy or amusement

trea·tise \ˈtrēt-əs\ *n* : a systematic written exposition or argument

treat·ment \ˈtrēt-mənt\ *n* : the act or manner or an instance of treating someone or something; *also* : a substance or method used in treating

trea·ty \ˈtrēt-ē\ *n, pl* **treaties** : an agreement made by negotiation or diplomacy esp. between two or more states or governments **syn** contract, bargain, pact, convention

[1]tre·ble \ˈtreb-əl\ *n* **1** : the highest of the four voice parts in vocal music : SOPRANO **2** : a high-pitched or shrill voice or sound **3** : the upper half of the musical pitch range

[2]treble *adj* **1** : triple in number or amount **2** : relating to or having the range of a musical treble **3** : high-pitched : SHRILL — **tre·bly** \ˈtreb-(ə-)lē\ *adv*

[3]treble *vb* **tre·bled; tre·bling** \ˈtreb-(ə-)liŋ\ : to make or become three times the size, amount, or number

[1]tree \ˈtrē\ *n* **1** : a woody perennial plant usu. with a single main stem and a head of branches and leaves at the top **2** : a piece of wood adapted to a particular use ⟨a shoe ~⟩ **3** : something resembling a tree ⟨a genealogical ~⟩ — **tree·less** *adj*

[2]tree *vb* **treed; tree·ing** : to drive to or up a tree ⟨~ a raccoon⟩

tree farm *n* : an area of forest land managed to ensure continuous commercial production

tree line *n* : TIMBERLINE

tree of heaven : an Asian ailanthus that is widely grown as a shade and ornamental tree

tree surgery *n* : operative treatment of diseased trees esp. for control of decay — **tree surgeon** *n*

tre·foil \ˈtrē-ˌfȯil, ˈtref-ˌȯil\ *n* **1** : a clover or related herb with leaves with three leaflets **2** : a decorative design with three leaflike parts

[1]trek \ˈtrek\ *vb* **trekked; trek·king** **1** : to travel or migrate by ox wagon **2** : to make one's way arduously

[2]trek *n* **1** : a migration esp. of settlers by ox wagon **2** : TRIP; *esp* : one involving difficulties or complex organization

[1]trel·lis \ˈtrel-əs\ *n* [ME *trelis,* fr. MF *treliz* fabric of coarse weave, trellis, fr. (assumed) VL *trilicius* woven with triple thread, fr. L *tres* three + *liceum* thread] : a structure of latticework

[2]trellis *vb* : to train (as a vine) on a trellis

trem·a·tode \ˈtrem-ə-ˌtōd\ *n* : any of a class of parasitic worms

[1]trem·ble \ˈtrem-bəl\ *vb* **trem·bled; trem·bling** \-b(ə-)liŋ\ **1** : to shake involuntarily (as with fear or cold) : SHIVER **2** : to move, sound, pass, or come to pass as if shaken or tremulous **3** : to be affected with fear or doubt

[2]tremble *n* : a spell of shaking or quivering : TREMOR

tre·men·dous \tri-ˈmen-dəs\ *adj* **1** : such as may excite trembling : TERRIFYING **2** : astonishingly large, powerful, great, or excellent **syn** stupendous, monumental, monstrous — **tre·men·dous·ly** *adv*

trem·o·lo \ˈtrem-ə-ˌlō\ *n, pl* **-los** [It] : a rapid fluttering of a tone or alternating tones to produce a tremulous effect

trem·or \ˈtrem-ər\ *n* **1** : a trembling or shaking esp. from weakness or disease **2** : a quivering motion of the earth (as during an earthquake)

trem·u·lous \ˈtrem-yə-ləs\ *adj* **1** : marked by trembling or tremors : QUIVERING **2** : TIMOROUS, TIMID — **trem·u·lous·ly** *adv*

[1]trench \ˈtrench\ *n* [ME *trenche* track cut through a wood, fr. MF, act of cutting, fr. *trenchier* to cut] **1** : a long narrow cut in the ground : DITCH; *esp* : a ditch protected by banks of earth and used to shelter soldiers **2** : a long narrow steep-sided depression in the ocean floor

[2]trench *vb* **1** : to cut or dig trenches in; *also* : to drain by trenches **2** : to protect (troops) with trenches **3** : to come close : VERGE

tren·chant \ˈtren-chənt\ *adj* **1** : vigorously effective; *also* : CAUSTIC **2** : sharply perceptive : KEEN **3** : CLEAR-CUT, DISTINCT **syn** incisive, biting, crisp

tren·cher \ˈtren-chər\ *n* : a wooden platter for serving food

tren·cher·man \ˈtren-chər-mən\ *n* : a hearty eater

trench foot *n* : a painful foot disorder resembling frostbite and resulting from exposure to cold and wet

trench mouth *n* : a contagious infection of the mouth and adjacent parts that is marked by ulceration and caused by bacteria

[1]trend \ˈtrend\ *vb* **1** : to have or take a general direction : TEND **2** : to show a tendency : INCLINE

[2]trend *n* **1** : a general direction taken (as by a stream or mountain range) **2** : a prevailing tendency : DRIFT **3** : a current style or preference : VOGUE

tre·pan \tri-ˈpan\ *vb* **tre·panned; tre·pan·ning** : to remove surgically a disk of bone from (the skull) — **trep·a·na·tion** \ˌtrep-ə-ˈnā-shən\ *n*

tre·phine \ˈtrē-ˌfīn\ *n* : a surgical instrument for cutting out circular sections (as of bone or corneal tissue) — **trephine** *vb*

trep·i·da·tion \ˌtrep-ə-ˈdā-shən\ *n* : nervous agitation : APPREHENSION **syn** horror, terror, panic, consternation, dread, fright, dismay

[1]tres·pass \ˈtres-pəs, -ˌpas\ *n* **1** : SIN, OFFENSE **2** : wrongful entry on real property **syn** transgression, violation, infraction, infringement

[2]trespass *vb* **1** : to commit an offense : ERR, SIN **2** : INTRUDE, ENCROACH; *esp* : to enter unlawfully upon the land of another — **tres·pass·er** *n*

tress \ˈtres\ *n* : a long lock of hair — usu. used in pl.

tres·tle *also* **tres·sel** \ˈtres-əl\ *n* **1** : a supporting framework consisting usu. of a horizontal piece with spreading legs at each end **2** : a braced framework of timbers, piles, or steel for carrying a road or railroad over a depression

trey \ˈtrā\ *n, pl* **treys** : a card or the side of a die with three spots

tri·ad \ˈtrī-ˌad, -əd\ *n* : a union or group of three usu. closely related persons or things

tri·age \trē-ˈäzh, ˈtrē-ˌäzh\ *n* [F, sifting] : the sorting of and allocation of treatment to patients and esp. battle and disaster victims according to a system of priorities designed to maximize the number of survivors

[1]**tri·al** \ˈtrī(-ə)l\ *n* **1** : the action or process of trying or putting to the proof : TEST **2** : the hearing and judgment of a matter in issue before a competent tribunal **3** : a source of vexation or annoyance **4** : a temporary use or experiment to test quality or usefulness **5** : EFFORT, ATTEMPT **syn** cross, ordeal, tribulation, affliction

[2]**trial** *adj* **1** : of, relating to, or used in a trial **2** : made or done as a test

tri·an·gle \ˈtrī-ˌaŋ-gəl\ *n* **1** : a figure that has three sides and three angles : a polygon having three sides **2** : something shaped like a triangle — **tri·an·gu·lar** \trī-ˈaŋ-gyə-lər\ *adj* — **tri·an·gu·lar·ly** *adv*

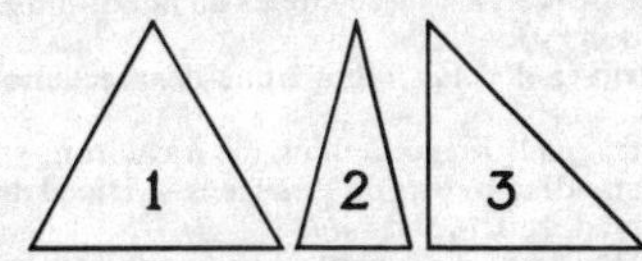

triangle 1: *1* equilateral, *2* isosceles, *3* right-angled

tri·an·gu·la·tion \(ˌ)trī-ˌaŋ-gyə-ˈlā-shən\ *n* : a trigonometric operation for finding a position using bearings from two fixed points a known distance apart — **tri·an·gu·late** \trī-ˈaŋ-gyə-ˌlāt\ *vb*

Tri·as·sic \trī-ˈas-ik\ *adj* : of, relating to, or being the earliest period of the Mesozoic era — **Triassic** *n*

trib *abbr* tributary

tribe \ˈtrīb\ *n* **1** : a social group comprising numerous families, clans, or generations **2** : a group of persons having a common character, occupation, or interest **3** : a group of related plants or animals ⟨the cat ~⟩ — **trib·al** \ˈtrī-bəl\ *adj*

tribes·man \ˈtrībz-mən\ *n* : a member of a tribe

trib·u·la·tion \ˌtrib-yə-ˈlā-shən\ *n* [ME *tribulacion,* fr. OF, fr. L *tribulatio,* fr. *tribulare* to press, oppress, fr. *tribulum* drag used in threshing] : distress or suffering resulting from oppression or persecution; *also* : a trying experience **syn** trial, affliction, cross, ordeal

tri·bu·nal \trī-ˈbyün-ᵊl, trib-ˈyün-\ *n* **1** : the seat of a judge **2** : a court of justice **3** : something that decides or determines ⟨the ~ of public opinion⟩

tri·bune \ˈtrib-ˌyün, trib-ˈyün\ *n* **1** : an official in ancient Rome with the function of protecting the interests of plebeian citizens from the patricians **2** : a defender of the people

[1]**trib·u·tary** \ˈtrib-yə-ˌter-ē\ *adj* **1** : paying tribute : SUBJECT **2** : flowing into a larger stream or a lake **syn** subordinate, secondary, dependent

[2]**tributary** *n, pl* **-tar·ies 1** : a ruler or state that pays tribute **2** : a tributary stream

trib·ute \ˈtrib-(ˌ)yüt, -yət\ *n* **1** : a payment by one ruler or nation to another as an act of submission or price of protection **2** : a usu. excessive tax, rental, or levy exacted by a sovereign or superior **3** : a gift or service showing respect, gratitude, or affection; *also* : PRAISE **syn** eulogy, citation, encomium, panegyric

trice \ˈtrīs\ *n* : INSTANT, MOMENT

tri·ceps \ˈtrī-ˌseps\ *n, pl* **tri·ceps·es** *also* **triceps** : a large muscle along the back of the upper arm that is attached at its upper end by three main parts and acts to extend the arm at the elbow joint

tri·chi·na \trik-ˈī-nə\ *n, pl* **-nae** \-(ˌ)nē\ *also* **-nas** : a small slender nematode worm that in the larval state is parasitic in the voluntary muscles of flesh-eating mammals (as the hog and human beings)

trich·i·no·sis \ˌtrik-ə-ˈnō-səs\ *n* : a disease caused by infestation of muscle tissue by trichinae and marked by pain, fever, and swelling

[1]**trick** \ˈtrik\ *n* **1** : a crafty procedure meant to deceive **2** : a mischievous action : PRANK **3** : a childish action **4** : a deceptive or ingenious feat designed to puzzle or amuse **5** : PECULIARITY, MANNERISM **6** : a quick or artful way of getting a result : KNACK **7** : the cards played in one round of a card game **8** : a tour of duty : SHIFT **syn** ruse, maneuver, artifice, wile, feint

[2]**trick** *vb* **1** : to deceive by cunning or artifice : CHEAT **2** : to dress ornately

trick·ery \ˈtrik-(ə-)rē\ *n* : deception by tricks and stratagems

trick·le \ˈtrik-əl\ *vb* **trick·led; trick·ling** \-(ə-)liŋ\ **1** : to run or fall in drops **2** : to flow in a thin gentle stream — **trickle** *n*

trick·ster \ˈtrik-stər\ *n* : one who tricks or cheats

tricky \ˈtrik-ē\ *adj* **trick·i·er; -est 1** : inclined to trickery ⟨a ~ person⟩ **2** : requiring skill or caution ⟨a ~ situation to handle⟩ **3** : UNRELIABLE

tri·col·or \ˈtrī-ˌkəl-ər\ *n* : a flag of three colors ⟨the French ~⟩

tri·cy·cle \ˈtrī-(ˌ)sik-əl\ *n* : a 3-wheeled vehicle usu. propelled by pedals

tri·dent \ˈtrīd-ᵊnt\ *n* [L *trident-, tridens,* fr. *tres* three + *dent-, dens* tooth] : a 3-pronged spear

tried \ˈtrīd\ *adj* **1** : found trustworthy through testing **2** : subjected to trials **syn** reliable, dependable, trusty

tri·en·ni·al \ˈtrī-ˈen-ē-əl\ *adj* **1** : lasting for three years **2** : occurring or being done every three years — **triennial** *n*

[1]**tri·fle** \ˈtrī-fəl\ *n* : something of little value or importance; *esp* : an insignificant amount (as of money)

[2]**trifle** *vb* **tri·fled; tri·fling** \-f(ə-)liŋ\ **1** : to talk in a jesting or mocking manner **2** : to act frivolously or playfully **3** : DALLY, FLIRT **4** : to handle idly : TOY — **tri·fler** \-f(ə-)lər\ *n*

tri·fling \ˈtrī-fliŋ\ *adj* **1** : FRIVOLOUS **2** : TRIVIAL, INSIGNIFICANT **syn** petty, paltry, measly, inconsequential

tri·fo·cals \trī-ˈfō-kəlz\ *n pl* : eyeglasses with lenses having one part for close focus, one for intermediate focus, and one for distant focus

tri·fo·li·ate \trī-ˈfō-lē-ət\ *adj* : having three leaves or leaflets

[1]**trig** \ˈtrig\ *adj* : stylishly trim : SMART **syn** tidy, spruce, shipshape

[2]**trig** *n* : TRIGONOMETRY

[1]**trig·ger** \ˈtrig-ər\ *n* [alter. of earlier *tricker,* fr. Dutch *trekker,* fr. Middle Dutch *trecker* one that pulls, fr. *trecken* to pull] : a movable lever that activates a device when it is squeezed; *esp* : the part of a firearm lock moved by the finger to release the hammer in firing — **trigger** *adj* — **trig·gered** \-ərd\ *adj*

[2]**trigger** *vb* **1** : to fire by pulling a trigger **2** : to initiate, actuate, or set off as if by a trigger

trig·o·nom·e·try \ˌtrig-ə-ˈnäm-ə-trē\ *n* : the branch of mathematics dealing with the relations of the sides and angles of triangles and of methods of deducing from given parts other required parts — **trig·o·no·met·ric** \-nə-ˈme-trik\ *also* **trig·o·no·met·ri·cal** \-trik-əl\ *adj*

[1]**trill** \ˈtril\ *n* **1** : the alternation of two musical tones a scale degree apart **2** : WARBLE **3** : the rapid vibration of one speech organ against another (as of the tip of the tongue against the teeth)

[2]**trill** *vb* : to utter as or with a trill

tril·lion \ˈtril-yən\ *n* **1** : a thousand billions **2** *Brit* : a million billions — **trillion** *adj* — **tril·lionth** \-yənth\ *adj or n*

tril·li·um \ˈtril-ē-əm\ *n* : any of a genus of herbs of the lily family with an erect stem bearing a whorl of three leaves and a large solitary flower with three petals

tril·o·gy \ˈtril-ə-jē\ *n, pl* **-gies** : a series of three dramas or literary or musical compositions that are closely related and develop one theme

[1]**trim** \ˈtrim\ *vb* **trimmed; trim·ming** [OE *trymian, trymman* to strengthen, arrange, fr. *trum* strong, firm] **1** : to put ornaments on : ADORN **2** : to defeat esp. resoundingly **3** : to make trim, neat, regular, or less bulky by or as if by cutting ⟨~ a beard⟩ ⟨~ a budget⟩ **4** : to cause (a boat) to assume a desired position in the water by arrangement of ballast, cargo, or passengers; *also* : to adjust (as a submarine or airplane) esp. for horizontal motion **5** : to adjust (a sail) to a desired position **6** : to change one's views for safety or expediency — **trim·ly** *adv* — **trim·mer** *n* — **trim·ness** *n*

[2]**trim** *adj* **trim·mer; trim·mest** : showing neatness, good order, or compactness ⟨~ figure⟩ **syn** tidy, trig, smart, spruce, shipshape

[3]**trim** *n* **1** : good condition : FITNESS **2** : material used for ornament or trimming; *esp* : the woodwork in the finish of a house esp. around doors and windows **3** : the position of a ship or boat esp. with reference to the horizontal; *also* : the relation between the plane of a sail and the direction of a ship **4** : the position of an airplane at which it will continue in level flight with no adjustments to the controls **5** : something that is trimmed off

tri·ma·ran \ˈtrī-mə-ˌran, ˌtrī-mə-ˈran\ *n* : a fast pleasure sailboat with three hulls side by side

tri·mes·ter \trī-ˈmes-tər, ˈtrī-ˌmes-tər\ *n* **1** : a period of three or about three months **2** : one of three terms into which an academic year is sometimes divided

trim·e·ter \ˈtrim-ət-ər\ *n* : a line consisting of three metrical feet

trim·ming \ˈtrim-iŋ\ *n* **1** : DEFEAT **2** : the action of one that trims **3** : something that trims, ornaments, or completes

tri·month·ly \trī-ˈmənth-lē\ *adj* : occurring every three months

trine \ˈtrīn\ *adj* : THREEFOLD, TRIPLE

Trin·i·da·di·an \ˌtrin-ə-ˈdād-ē-ən, -ˈdad-\ *n* : a native or inhabitant of the island of Trinidad — **Trinidadian** *adj*

Trin·i·tar·i·an \ˌtrin-ə-ˈter-ē-ən\ *n* : a believer in the doctrine of the Trinity — **Trin·i·tar·i·an·ism** \-ē-ə-ˌniz-əm\ *n*

Trin·i·ty \ˈtrin-ət-ē\ *n* **1** : the unity of Father, Son, and Holy Spirit as three persons in one Godhead **2** *not cap* : TRIAD

trin·ket \ˈtriŋ-kət\ *n* **1** : a small ornament (as a jewel or ring) **2** : TRIFLE

trio \ˈtrē-ō\ *n, pl* **tri·os** **1** : a musical composition for three voices or three instruments **2** : the performers of a musical or dance trio **3** : a group or set of three

tri·ode \ˈtrī-ˌōd\ *n* : a vacuum tube with three electrodes

[1]**trip** \ˈtrip\ *vb* **tripped; trip·ping** **1** : to move with light quick steps **2** : to catch the foot against something so as to stumble or cause to stumble **3** : to make a mistake : SLIP; *also* : to detect in a misstep : EXPOSE **4** : to release (as a spring or switch) by moving a catch; *also* : ACTIVATE **5** : to get high on a psychedelic drug

[2]**trip** *n* **1** : JOURNEY, VOYAGE **2** : a quick light step **3** : a false step : STUMBLE; *also* : ERROR **4** : the action of tripping mechanically; *also* : a device for tripping **5** : an intense drug-induced hallucinatory experience **6** : pursuit of an obsessive interest ⟨an ego ~⟩

tri·par·tite \trī-ˈpär-ˌtīt\ *adj* **1** : divided into three parts **2** : having three corresponding parts or copies **3** : made between three parties ⟨a ~ treaty⟩

tripe \ˈtrīp\ *n* **1** : stomach tissue of a ruminant and esp. an ox used as food **2** : something poor, worthless, or offensive : TRASH

[1]**tri·ple** \ˈtrip-əl\ *vb* **tri·pled; tri·pling** \-(ə-)liŋ\ **1** : to make or become three times as great or as many **2** : to hit a triple

[2]**triple** *n* **1** : a triple quantity **2** : a group of three **3** : a hit in baseball that lets the batter reach third base

[3]**triple** *adj* **1** : being three times as great or as many **2** : having three units or members **3** : repeated three times

triple bond *n* : a chemical bond in which three pairs of electrons are shared by two atoms in a molecule

triple point *n* : the condition of temperature and pressure under which the gaseous, liquid, and solid forms of a substance can exist in equilibrium

trip·let \ˈtrip-lət\ *n* **1** : a unit of three lines of verse **2** : a group of three of a kind **3** : one of three offspring born at one birth

tri·plex \ˈtrip-ˌleks, ˈtrī-ˌpleks\ *adj* : THREEFOLD, TRIPLE

[1]**trip·li·cate** \ˈtrip-li-kət\ *adj* : made in three identical copies

[2]**trip·li·cate** \-lə-ˌkāt\ *vb* **-cat·ed; -cat·ing** **1** : TRIPLE **2** : to provide three copies of ⟨~ a document⟩

[3]**trip·li·cate** \-li-kət\ *n* : three copies all alike — used with *in* ⟨typed in ~⟩

tri·ply \ˈtrip-(ə-)lē\ *adv* : in a triple degree, amount, or manner

tri·pod \ˈtrī-ˌpäd\ *n* : something (as a caldron, stool, or camera stand) that rests on three legs — **tripod** *or* **tri·po·dal** \ˈtrip-əd-ᵊl, ˈtrī-ˌpäd-\ *adj*

trip·tych \ˈtrip-tik\ *n* : a picture or carving (as an altarpiece) in three panels side by side

tri·reme \ˈtrī-ˌrēm\ *n* : an ancient galley having three banks of oars

tri·sect \ˈtrī-ˌsekt, trī-ˈsekt\ *vb* : to divide into three usu. equal parts — **tri·sec·tion** \ˈtrī-ˌsek-shən\ *n*

trite \ˈtrīt\ *adj* **trit·er; trit·est** [L *tritus*, fr. pp. of *terere* to rub, wear away] : used so commonly that the novelty is worn off : STALE **syn** hackneyed, stereotyped, commonplace, clichéd

tri·ti·um \ˈtrit-ē-əm, ˈtrish-ē-\ *n* : a radioactive form of hydrogen with atoms of three times the mass of ordinary hydrogen atoms

tri·ton \ˈtrīt-ᵊn\ *n* : any of various large marine mollusks with a heavy elongated conical shell; *also* : the shell of a triton

trit·u·rate \ˈtrich-ə-ˌrāt\ *vb* **-rat·ed; -rat·ing** : to rub or grind to a fine powder

[1]**tri·umph** \ˈtrī-əmf\ *n, pl* **tri·umphs** \-əmfs, -əm(p)s\ **1** : the joy or exultation of victory or success **2** : VICTORY, CONQUEST — **tri·um·phal** \trī-ˈəm-fəl\ *adj*

[2]**triumph** *vb* **1** : to celebrate victory or success exultantly **2** : to obtain victory : PREVAIL — **tri·um·phant** \trī-ˈəm-fənt\ *adj* — **tri·um·phant·ly** *adv*

tri·um·vir \trī-ˈəm-vər\ *n, pl* **-virs** *also* **-vi·ri** \-və-ˌrī\ : a member of a triumvirate

tri·um·vi·rate \-və-rət\ *n* : a ruling body of three persons

tri·une \ˈtrī-ˌ(y)ün\ *adj, often cap* : being three in one ⟨the ~ God⟩

triv·et \ˈtriv-ət\ *n* **1** : a 3-legged stand : TRIPOD **2** : a metal stand with short feet for use under a hot dish

triv·ia \ˈtriv-ē-ə\ *n sing or pl* : unimportant matters : TRIFLES

triv·i·al \ˈtriv-ē-əl\ *adj* [L *trivialis* found everywhere, commonplace, trivial, fr. *trivium* crossroads, fr. *tres* three + *via* way] : of little importance — **triv·i·al·i·ty** \ˌtriv-ē-ˈal-ət-ē\ *n*

triv·i·um \ˈtriv-ē-əm\ *n, pl* **triv·ia** \-ē-ə\ : the three liberal arts of grammar, rhetoric, and logic in a medieval university

tri·week·ly \trī-ˈwē-klē\ *adj* **1** : occurring or appearing three times a week **2** : occurring or appearing every three weeks — **triweekly** *adv*

tro·che \ˈtrō-kē\ *n* : a medicinal lozenge

tro·chee \ˈtrō-(ˌ)kē\ *n* : a metrical foot of one accented syllable followed by one unaccented syllable — **tro·cha·ic** \trō-ˈkā-ik\ *adj*

trod *past and past part of* TREAD

trodden *past part of* TREAD

troi·ka \ˈtrȯi-kə\ *n* [Russ *troĭka* a vehicle drawn by three horses, fr. *troe* three] : a group of three; *esp* : an administrative or ruling body of three

[1]**troll** \ˈtrōl\ *vb* **1** : to sing the parts of (a song) in succession **2** : to angle for with a hook and line drawn through the water **3** : to sing or play jovially

[2]**troll** *n* : a lure used in trolling; *also* : the line with its lure

[3]**troll** *n* : a dwarf or giant in Teutonic folklore inhabiting caves or hills

trol·ley *or* **trol·ly** \ˈträl-ē\ *n, pl* **trolleys** *or* **trollies** **1** : a device (as a grooved wheel on the end of a pole) to carry current from a wire to an electrically driven vehicle **2** : TROLLEY CAR **3** : a wheeled carriage running on an overhead rail or track

trol·ley·bus \ˈträl-ē-ˌbəs\ *n* : a bus powered electrically from two overhead wires

trolley car *n* : a streetcar powered electrically through a trolley

trol·lop \ˈträl-əp\ *n* **1** : a slovenly woman **2** : a loose woman : WANTON

trom·bone \träm-ˈbōn, ˈträm-ˌbōn\ *n* [It, lit., big trumpet, fr. *tromba* trumpet] : a brass wind instrument that consists of a long metal tube with two turns and a flaring end and that has a movable slide to vary the pitch — **trom·bon·ist** \-ˈbō-nəst, -ˌbō-\ *n*

trombone

tromp \ˈträmp, ˈtrómp\ *vb* **1** : TRAMP, MARCH **2** : to stamp with the foot **3** : DEFEAT

[1]**troop** \ˈtrüp\ *n* **1** : a cavalry unit corresponding to an infantry company **2** *pl* : armed forces : SOLDIERS **3** : a collection of people or things **4** : a unit of Girl Scouts or Boy Scouts under an adult leader **syn** band, troupe, party, corps

[2]**troop** *vb* : to move or gather in crowds

troop·er \ˈtrü-pər\ *n* **1** : an enlisted cavalryman; *also* : a cavalry horse **2** : a mounted or state policeman

troop·ship \ˈtrüp-ˌship\ *n* : a ship for carrying troops

trope \ˈtrōp\ *n* : the use of a word or expression in a figurative sense

tro·phy \ˈtrō-fē\ *n, pl* **trophies** : something gained or given in conquest or victory esp. when preserved or mounted as a memorial

trop·ic \ˈträp-ik\ *n* [ME *tropik,* fr. L *tropicus* of the solstice, fr. Gk *tropikos,* fr. *tropē* turn] **1** : either of the two parallels of latitude one approximately 23½ degrees north of the equator (**tropic of Cancer** \-ˈkan-sər\) and one approximately 23½ degrees south of the equator (**tropic of Capricorn** \-ˈkap-rə-ˌkórn\) where the sun is directly overhead when apparently at its greatest distance north or south of the equator **2** *pl, often cap* : the region lying between the tropics of Cancer and Capricorn — **trop·i·cal** \-i-kəl\ *or* **tropic** *adj*

tro·pism \ˈtrō-ˌpiz-əm\ *n* : involuntary orientation of an organism in response to a source of stimulation; *also* : a reflex reaction involving this

tro·po·sphere \ˈtrōp-ə-ˌsfiər, ˈträp-\ *n* : the portion of the atmosphere which extends outward about 10 miles (16 kilometers) from the earth's surface and in which most weather occurs — **tro·po·spher·ic** \ˌtrōp-ə-ˈsfi(ə)r-ik, ˌträp-, -ˈsfer-\ *adj*

[1]**trot** \ˈträt\ *n* **1** : a moderately fast gait of a 4-footed animal (as a horse) in which the legs move in diagonal pairs **2** : a jogging gait of a man between a walk and a run

[2]**trot** *vb* **trot·ted; trot·ting** **1** : to ride, drive, or go at a trot **2** : to proceed briskly : HURRY — **trot·ter** *n*

troth \ˈträth, ˈtróth, ˈtrōth\ *n* **1** : pledged faithfulness : FIDELITY **2** : one's pledged word; *also* : BETROTHAL

trou·ba·dour \ˈtrü-bə-ˌdōr\ *n* [F, fr. Old Provençal *trobador*] : one of a class of poet-musicians flourishing esp. in southern France and northern Italy during the 11th, 12th, and 13th centuries

[1]**trou·ble** \ˈtrəb-əl\ *vb* **trou·bled; trou·bling** \ˈtrəb-(ə-)liŋ\ **1** : to agitate mentally or spiritually : DISTURB, WORRY **2** : to produce physical disorder in : AFFLICT **3** : to put to inconvenience **4** : RUFFLE ⟨~ the waters⟩ **5** : to make an effort **syn** distress, ail, upset, worry — **trou·ble·some** *adj* — **trou·ble·some·ly** *adv* — **trou·blous** \-(ə-)ləs\ *adj*

[2]**trouble** *n* **1** : the quality or state of being troubled esp. mentally **2** : an instance of distress or annoyance **3** : DISEASE, AILMENT ⟨heart ~⟩ **4** : EXERTION, PAINS ⟨took the ~ to phone⟩ **5** : a cause of disturbance or distress

trou·ble·mak·er \-ˌmā-kər\ *n* : a person who causes trouble

trou·ble·shoot·er \-ˌshüt-ər\ *n* **1** : a worker employed to locate trouble and make repairs in equipment **2** : an expert in resolving disputes or problems — **trou·ble·shoot** *vb*

trough \ˈtróf, ˈtróth, *by bakers often* ˈtrō\ *n, pl* **troughs** \ˈtrófs, ˈtróvz; ˈtróths, ˈtró(th)z; ˈtrōz\ **1** : a long shallow open boxlike container esp. for water or feed for livestock **2** : a gutter along the eaves of a house **3** : a long channel or depression (as between waves or hills)

trounce \ˈtraůns\ *vb* **trounced; trounc·ing** **1** : to thrash or punish severely **2** : to defeat decisively

troupe \ˈtrüp\ *n* : COMPANY; *esp* : a group of performers on the stage — **troup·er** *n*

trou·sers \ˈtraů-zərz\ *n pl* [alter. of earlier *trouse,* fr. ScGael *triubhas*] : an outer garment extending from the waist to the ankle or sometimes only to the knee, covering each leg separately, and worn esp. by males — **trouser** *adj*

trous·seau \ˈtrü-sō, trü-ˈsō\ *n, pl* **trous·seaux** \-sōz, -ˈsōz\ *or* **trous·seaus** [F] : the personal outfit of a bride

trout \ˈtraůt\ *n, pl* **trout** *also* **trouts** [ME, fr. OE *trūht,* fr. LL *tructa,* a fish with sharp teeth, fr. Gk *trōktēs,* lit., gnawer] : any of various mostly freshwater food and game fishes usu. smaller than the related salmons

trout lily *n* : DOGTOOTH VIOLET

trow \ˈtrō\ *vb, archaic* : THINK, SUPPOSE

trow·el \ˈtraů(-ə)l\ *n* **1** : any of various hand implements used for spreading, shaping, or smoothing loose or plastic material (as mortar or plaster) **2** : a small flat or scooplike implement used in gardening — **trowel** *vb*

troy \ˈtrói\ *adj* : expressed in troy weight ⟨~ ounce⟩

troy weight *n* : a system of weights based on a pound of 12 ounces and an ounce of 480 grains and used in the U.S. esp. for precious metals and gems — see WEIGHT table

tru·ant \ˈtrü-ənt\ *n* [ME, vagabond, idler, fr. OF, vagrant] : one who shirks duty; *esp* : one who stays out of school without permission — **tru·an·cy** \-ən-sē\ *n* — **truant** *adj*

truce \ˈtrüs\ *n* **1** : ARMISTICE **2** : a respite esp. from a disagreeable state or action

[1]**truck** \ˈtrək\ *vb* **1** : EXCHANGE, BARTER **2** : to have dealings : TRAFFIC

[2]**truck** *n* **1** : BARTER **2** : small goods or merchandise; *esp* : vegetables grown for market **3** : DEALINGS

[3]**truck** *n* **1** : a vehicle (as a strong heavy automobile) designed for carrying heavy articles or hauling a trailer **2** : a swiveling frame with springs and one or more pairs of wheels used to carry and guide one end of a locomotive or of a railroad or electric car — **truck·load** \-ˌlōd\ *n*

[4]**truck** *vb* **1** : to transport on a truck **2** : to be employed in driving a truck — **truck·er** *n*

truck·age \ˈtrək-ij\ *n* : transportation by truck; *also* : the cost of such transportation
truck farm *n* : a farm growing vegetables for market — **truck farmer** *n*
truck garden *n* : a garden where vegetables are raised for market
truck·le \ˈtrək-əl\ *vb* **truck·led; truck·ling** \-(ə-)liŋ\ : to yield slavishly to the will of another : SUBMIT **syn** fawn, toady, cringe, cower
truc·u·lent \ˈtrək-yə-lənt\ *adj* **1** : feeling or showing ferocity : SAVAGE **2** : aggressively self-assertive : PUGNACIOUS — **truc·u·lence** \-ləns\ *n* — **truc·u·len·cy** \-lən-sē\ *n* — **truc·u·lent·ly** *adv*
trudge \ˈtrəj\ *vb* **trudged; trudg·ing** : to walk or march steadily and usu. laboriously
[1]**true** \ˈtrü\ *adj* **tru·er; tru·est 1** : STEADFAST, LOYAL **2** : conformable to fact or reality ⟨a ~ description⟩ **3** : CONSISTENT ⟨~ to expectations⟩ **4** : properly so called ⟨the ~ stomach⟩ **5** : RIGHTFUL ⟨~ and lawful king⟩ **6** : conformable to a standard or pattern; *also* : placed or formed accurately **syn** constant, staunch, resolute, steadfast
[2]**true** *adv* **1** : TRUTHFULLY **2** : ACCURATELY ⟨the bullet flew straight and ~⟩; *also* : without variation from type ⟨breed ~⟩
[3]**true** *n* **1** : TRUTH, REALITY — usu. used with *the* **2** : the state of being accurate (as in alignment) ⟨out of ~⟩
[4]**true** *vb* **trued; true·ing** *also* **tru·ing** : to make level, square, balanced, or concentric
true–blue *adj* : marked by unswerving loyalty
true bug *n* : BUG 2
true·heart·ed \ˈtrü-ˈhärt-əd\ *adj* : FAITHFUL, LOYAL
truf·fle \ˈtrəf-əl, ˈtrüf-\ *n* **1** : a European underground fungus; *also* : its dark wrinkled edible fruit **2** : a candy made of chocolate, butter, and sugar shaped into balls and coated with cocoa
tru·ism \ˈtrü-ˌiz-əm\ *n* : an undoubted or self-evident truth **syn** commonplace, platitude, bromide, cliché
tru·ly \ˈtrü-lē\ *adv* **1** : in all sincerity **2** : in agreement with fact **3** : ACCURATELY **4** : in a proper or suitable manner
[1]**trump** \ˈtrəmp\ *n* : TRUMPET
[2]**trump** *n* : a card of a designated suit any of whose cards will win over a card that is not of this suit; *also* : the suit itself — often used in pl.
[3]**trump** *vb* : to take with a trump
trumped–up \ˈtrəm(p)t-ˈəp\ *adj* : fraudulently concocted : SPURIOUS
trum·pery \ˈtrəm-p(ə-)rē\ *n* **1** : NONSENSE **2** : trivial articles : JUNK
[1]**trum·pet** \ˈtrəm-pət\ *n* **1** : a wind instrument consisting of a long curved metal tube flaring at one end and with a cup-shaped mouthpiece at the other **2** : something that resembles a trumpet or its tonal quality **3** : a funnel-shaped instrument for collecting, directing, or intensifying sound
[2]**trumpet** *vb* **1** : to blow a trumpet **2** : to proclaim on or as if on a trumpet — **trum·pet·er** *n*
[1]**trun·cate** \ˈtrəŋ-ˌkāt, ˈtrən-\ *adj* : having the end square or blunt
[2]**truncate** *vb* **trun·cat·ed; trun·cat·ing** : to shorten by or as if by cutting : LOP — **trun·ca·tion** \ˌtrəŋ-ˈkā-shən\ *n*
trun·cheon \ˈtrən-chən\ *n* : a policeman's club
trun·dle \ˈtrən-dᵊl\ *vb* **trun·dled; trun·dling** : to roll along : WHEEL
trundle bed *n* : a low bed that can be slid under a higher bed when not in use
trunk \ˈtrəŋk\ *n* **1** : the main stem of a tree **2** : the body of a person or animal apart from the head and limbs **3** : the main or basal part of something **4** : a box or chest used to hold usu. clothes or personal effects (as of a traveler); *also* : the enclosed luggage space in the rear of an automobile **5** : the long muscular nose of an elephant **6** *pl* : men's shorts worn chiefly for sports **7** : a usu. major channel or passage **8** : a circuit between telephone exchanges
trunk line *n* : a system handling long-distance through traffic
[1]**truss** \ˈtrəs\ *vb* **1** : to secure tightly : BIND **2** : to arrange for cooking by binding close the wings or legs of (a fowl) **3** : to support, strengthen, or stiffen by a truss
[2]**truss** *n* **1** : a collection of structural parts (as beams) forming a rigid framework (as in bridge or building construction) **2** : a device worn to reduce a hernia by pressure
[1]**trust** \ˈtrəst\ *n* **1** : assured reliance on the character, strength, or truth of someone or something **2** : a basis of reliance, faith, or hope **3** : confident hope **4** : financial credit **5** : a property interest held by one person for the benefit of another **6** : a combination of firms formed by a legal agreement; *esp* : one that reduces competition **7** : something entrusted to one to be cared for in the interest of another **8** : CARE, CUSTODY **syn** confidence, dependence, faith, reliance
[2]**trust** *vb* **1** : to place confidence : DEPEND **2** : to be confident : HOPE **3** : ENTRUST **4** : to permit to stay or go or to do something without fear or misgiving **5** : to rely on or on the truth of : BELIEVE **6** : to extend credit to
trust·ee \ˌtrəs-ˈtē\ *n* **1** : a person to whom property is legally committed in trust **2** : a country charged with the supervision of a trust territory
trust·ee·ship \ˌtrəs-ˈtē-ˌship\ *n* **1** : the office or function of a trustee **2** : supervisory control by one or more nations over a trust territory
trust·ful \ˈtrəst-fəl\ *adj* : full of trust : CONFIDING — **trust·ful·ly** \-ē\ *adv* — **trust·ful·ness** *n*
trust territory *n* : a non-self-governing territory placed under a supervisory authority by the Trusteeship Council of the United Nations
trust·wor·thy \-ˌwər-t͟hē\ *adj* : worthy of confidence : DEPENDABLE **syn** trusty, tried, reliable — **trust·wor·thi·ness** *n*
[1]**trusty** \ˈtrəs-tē\ *adj* **trust·i·er; -est** : TRUSTWORTHY, DEPENDABLE
[2]**trusty** \ˈtrəs-tē, ˌtrəs-ˈtē\ *n, pl* **trust·ies** : a trusted person; *esp* : a convict considered trustworthy and allowed special privileges
truth \ˈtrüth\ *n, pl* **truths** \ˈtrü͟thz, ˈtrüths\ **1** : TRUTHFULNESS, HONESTY **2** : the real state of things : FACT **3** : the body of real events or facts : ACTUALITY **4** : a true or accepted statement or proposition ⟨the ~*s* of science⟩ **5** : agreement with fact or reality : CORRECTNESS **syn** veracity, verity, truthfulness
truth·ful \ˈtrüth-fəl\ *adj* : telling or disposed to tell the truth — **truth·ful·ly** \-ē\ *adv* — **truth·ful·ness** *n*
truth serum *n* : a drug held to induce a subject under questioning to talk freely
[1]**try** \ˈtrī\ *vb* **tried; try·ing 1** : to examine or investigate judicially **2** : to conduct the trial of **3** : to put to test or trial **4** : to subject to strain, affliction, or annoyance **5** : to extract or clarify (as lard) by melting **6** : to make an effort to do something : ATTEMPT, ENDEAVOR **syn** essay, assay, strive, struggle
[2]**try** *n, pl* **tries** : an experimental trial
try·ing \ˈtrī-iŋ\ *adj* : severely straining the powers of endurance
try on *vb* : to put on (a garment) to test the fit and looks
try out \(ˈ)trī-ˈau̇t\ *vb* : to participate in competition esp. for a position on an athletic team or a part in a play — **try·out** \ˈtrī-ˌau̇t\ *n*
tryst \ˈtrist, ˌtrīst\ *n* : an agreement (as between lovers) to meet; *also* : an appointed place of meeting **syn** rendezvous, engagement, assignation
tsar \ˈzär, ˈ(t)sär\ *var of* CZAR
tset·se fly \ˈt(s)et-sē-, ˈt(s)ēt-sē-\ *n* : any of several flies that occur in Africa south of the Sahara desert and include the vector of sleeping sickness

TSgt *abbr* technical sergeant

T–shirt \ˈtē-ˌshərt\ *n* : a collarless short-sleeved or sleeveless cotton undershirt for men; *also* : an outer shirt of similar design

tsp *abbr* teaspoon; teaspoonful

T square *n* : a ruler with a crosspiece at one end for making parallel lines

tsu·na·mi \(t)sü-ˈnäm-ē\ *n* [Jp] : a tidal wave caused by an earthquake or volcanic eruption

TT *abbr* Trust Territories

Tu *abbr* Tuesday

tub \ˈtəb\ *n* **1** : a wide low bucketlike vessel **2** : BATHTUB; *also* : BATH **3** : the amount that a tub will hold

tu·ba \ˈt(y)ü-bə\ *n* : a large low-pitched brass wind instrument

tube \ˈt(y)üb\ *n* **1** : a hollow cylinder to convey fluids : CHANNEL, DUCT **2** : any of various usu. cylindrical structures or devices **3** : a round metal container from which a paste is squeezed **4** : a tunnel for vehicular or rail travel **5** : an airtight tube of rubber inside a tire to hold air under pressure **6** : ELECTRON TUBE **7** : TELEVISION — **tubed** \ˈt(y)übd\ *adj* — **tube·less** *adj*

tu·ber \ˈt(y)ü-bər\ *n* : a short fleshy usu. underground stem (as of a potato plant) bearing minute scalelike leaves each with a bud at its base

tu·ber·cle \ˈt(y)ü-bər-kəl\ *n* **1** : a small knobby prominence or outgrowth esp. on an animal or plant **2** : a small abnormal lump in an organ or on the skin; *esp* : one caused by tuberculosis

tubercle bacillus *n* : a bacterium that is the cause of tuberculosis

tu·ber·cu·lar \t(y)u̇-ˈbər-kyə-lər\ *adj* **1** : of, resembling, or being a tubercle : TUBERCULATED **2** : TUBERCULOUS

tu·ber·cu·lat·ed \t(y)u̇-ˈbər-kyə-ˌlāt-əd\ *also* **tu·ber·cu·late** \-lət\ *adj* : having or covered with tubercles

tu·ber·cu·lin \t(y)u̇-ˈbər-kyə-lən\ *n* : a sterile liquid extracted from the tubercle bacillus and used in the diagnosis of tuberculosis esp. in children and cattle

tu·ber·cu·lo·sis \t(y)u̇-ˌbər-kyə-ˈlō-səs\ *n, pl* **-lo·ses** \-ˌsēz\ : a communicable bacterial disease typically marked by wasting, fever, and formation of cheesy tubercles often in the lungs — **tu·ber·cu·lous** \-ˈbər-kyə-ləs\ *adj*

tube·rose \ˈt(y)üb-ˌrōz\ *n* : a bulbous herb related to the amaryllis and often grown for its spike of fragrant waxy-white flowers

tu·ber·ous \ˈt(y)ü-b(ə-)rəs\ *adj* : of, resembling, or being a plant tuber

tub·ing \ˈt(y)ü-biŋ\ *n* **1** : material in the form of a tube; *also* : a length of tube **2** : a series of tubes

tu·bu·lar \ˈt(y)ü-byə-lər\ *adj* : having the form of or consisting of a tube; *also* : made with tubes

tu·bule \ˈt(y)ü-byül\ *n* : a small tube

[1]**tuck** \ˈtək\ *n* : a fold stitched into cloth to shorten, decorate, or control fullness

[2]**tuck** *vb* **1** : to pull up into a fold ⟨~*ed* up her skirt⟩ **2** : to make tucks in **3** : to put into a snug often concealing place ⟨~ a book under the arm⟩ **4** : to secure in place by pushing the edges under ⟨~ in a blanket⟩ **5** : to cover by tucking in bedclothes

tuck·er \ˈtək-ər\ *vb* **tuck·ered; tuck·er·ing** \ˈtək-(ə-)riŋ\ : EXHAUST, FATIGUE

Tues *or* **Tue** *abbr* Tuesday

Tues·day \ˈt(y)üz-dē\ *n* : the 3d day of the week

tu·fa \ˈt(y)ü-fə\ *n* : a porous rock formed as a deposit from springs or streams

tuff \ˈtəf\ *n* : a rock composed of volcanic detritus

[1]**tuft** \ˈtəft\ *n* **1** : a small cluster of long flexible outgrowths (as hairs); *also* : a bunch of soft fluffy threads cut off short and used as ornament **2** : CLUMP, CLUSTER — **tuft·ed** \ˈtəf-təd\ *adj*

[2]**tuft** *vb* **1** : to provide or adorn with a tuft **2** : to make (as a mattress) firm by stitching at intervals and sewing on tufts

[1]**tug** \ˈtəg\ *vb* **tugged; tug·ging** **1** : to pull hard **2** : to struggle in opposition : CONTEND **3** : to move by pulling hard : HAUL **4** : to tow with a tugboat

[2]**tug** *n* **1** : a harness trace **2** : an act of tugging : PULL **3** : a straining effort **4** : a struggle between opposing people or forces **5** : TUGBOAT

tug·boat \-ˌbōt\ *n* : a strongly built boat used for towing or pushing

tug–of–war \ˌtəg-ə(v)-ˈwȯr\ *n, pl* **tugs–of–war** **1** : a struggle for supremacy **2** : an athletic contest in which two teams pull against each other at opposite ends of a rope

tu·grik *or* **tu·ghrik** \ˈtü-grik\ *n* — see MONEY table

tu·ition \t(y)u̇-ˈish-ən\ *n* **1** : INSTRUCTION **2** : the price of or payment for instruction

tu·la·re·mia \ˌt(y)ü-lə-ˈrē-mē-ə\ *n* : an infectious bacterial disease esp. of wild rabbits, rodents, humans, and some domestic animals that in humans is marked by symptoms (as fever) of toxemia

tu·lip \ˈt(y)ü-ləp\ *n* [NL *tulipa*, fr. Turk *tülbend* turban] : any of a genus of Eurasian bulbous herbs related to the lilies and grown for their large showy erect cup-shaped flowers; *also* : a flower or bulb of a tulip

tulip tree *n* : a tall American timber tree with greenish tulip-shaped flowers and soft white wood

tulle \ˈtül\ *n* : a sheer silk, rayon, or nylon net ⟨a bridal veil of ~⟩

[1]**tum·ble** \ˈtəm-bəl\ *vb* **tum·bled; tum·bling** \-b(ə-)liŋ\ [ME *tumblen*, fr. *tumben* to dance, fr. OE *tumbian*] **1** : to perform gymnastic feats of rolling and turning **2** : to fall or cause to fall suddenly and helplessly **3** : to fall into ruin **4** : to roll over and over : TOSS **5** : to issue forth hurriedly and confusedly **6** : to come to understand **7** : to throw together in a confused mass

[2]**tumble** *n* **1** : a disorderly state **2** : an act or instance of tumbling

tum·ble·down \ˌtəm-bəl-ˌdau̇n\ *adj* : DILAPIDATED, RAMSHACKLE

tum·bler \ˈtəm-blər\ *n* **1** : one that tumbles; *esp* : ACROBAT **2** : a drinking glass without foot or stem **3** : a movable obstruction in a lock that must be adjusted to a particular position (as by a key) before the bolt can be thrown

tum·ble·weed \ˈtəm-bəl-ˌwēd\ *n* : a plant that breaks away from its roots in autumn and is driven about by the wind

tum·bril *also* **tum·brel** \ˈtəm-brəl\ *n* **1** : CART **2** : a vehicle carrying condemned persons (as political prisoners during the French Revolution) to a place of execution

tu·mid \ˈt(y)ü-məd\ *adj* **1** : SWOLLEN, DISTENDED **2** : BOMBASTIC, TURGID

tum·my \ˈtəm-ē\ *n, pl* **tummies** : BELLY, ABDOMEN, STOMACH

tu·mor \ˈt(y)ü-mər\ *n* : an abnormal and functionless mass of tissue that is not inflammatory and arises from preexistent tissue — **tu·mor·ous** *adj*

tu·mult \ˈt(y)ü-ˌməlt\ *n* **1** : disorderly agitation of a crowd usu. with uproar and confusion of voices **2** : DISTURBANCE, RIOT **3** : a confusion of loud noise and usu. turbulent movement **4** : violent agitation of mind or feelings

tu·mul·tu·ous \t(y)u̇-ˈməlch-(ə-)wəs, -ˈməl-chəs\ *adj* **1** : marked by tumult **2** : tending to incite a tumult **3** : marked by violent upheaval

tun \ˈtən\ *n* : a large cask

tu·na \ˈt(y)ü-nə\ *n, pl* **tuna** *or* **tunas** [Sp] : any of several mostly large sea fishes related to the mackerels and important for food and sport

tun·able \ˈt(y)ü-nə-bəl\ *adj* : capable of being tuned — **tun·abil·i·ty** \ˌt(y)ü-nə-ˈbil-ət-ē\ *n*

tun·dra \ˈtən-drə\ *n* : a treeless plain of arctic and subarctic regions

[1]**tune** \ˈt(y)ün\ *n* **1** : an easily remembered melody **2** : correct musical pitch **3** : harmonious relationship : AGREEMENT ⟨in ~ with the times⟩ **4** : general attitude ⟨changed his ~⟩ **5** : AMOUNT, EXTENT ⟨in debt to the ~ of millions⟩

[2]**tune** *vb* **tuned; tun·ing 1** : to adjust in musical pitch **2** : to bring or come into harmony : ATTUNE **3** : to adjust a radio or television receiver so as to receive a broadcast **4** : to put in good working order **5** : to adjust the frequency of the output of (a device) to a chosen frequency — **tun·er** *n*

tune·ful \-fəl\ *adj* : MELODIOUS, MUSICAL — **tune·ful·ly** \-ē\ *adv* — **tune·ful·ness** *n*

tune·less \-ləs\ *adj* **1** : UNMELODIOUS **2** : not producing music — **tune·less·ly** *adv*

tune–up \ˈt(y)ün-ˌəp\ *n* : an adjustment to ensure efficient functioning ⟨an engine ~⟩

tung·sten \ˈtəŋ-stən\ *n* [Sw, fr. *tung* heavy + *sten* stone] : a white hard heavy ductile metallic element used for electrical purposes and in hardening alloys (as steel) — see ELEMENT table

tu·nic \ˈt(y)ü-nik\ *n* **1** : a usu. knee-length belted under or outer garment worn by ancient Greeks and Romans **2** : a hip-length or longer blouse or jacket

tuning fork *n* : a 2-pronged metal implement that gives a fixed tone when struck and is useful for tuning musical instruments

Tu·ni·sian \t(y)ü-ˈnē-zh-ən, -ˈnizh-\ *n* : a native or inhabitant of Tunisia — **Tunisian** *adj*

[1]**tun·nel** \ˈtən-ᵊl\ *n* : an enclosed passage (as a tube or conduit); *esp* : one underground (as in a mine)

[2]**tunnel** *vb* **-neled** *or* **-nelled; -nel·ing** *or* **-nel·ling** \ˈtən-(ᵊ-)liŋ\ : to make a tunnel through or under

tun·ny \ˈtən-ē\ *n, pl* **tunnies** *also* **tunny** : TUNA

-tu·ple \ˌtəp-əl, ˌtüp-\ *n comb form* : set of (so many) elements

tuque \ˈt(y)ük\ *n* [CanF] : a warm knitted cone-shaped cap with a tassel or pom-pom worn esp. for winter sports or play

tur·ban \ˈtər-bən\ *n* **1** : a headdress worn esp. by Muslims and made of a cap around which is wound a long cloth **2** : a headdress resembling a Muslim turban; *esp* : a woman's close-fitting hat without a brim

tur·bid \ˈtər-bəd\ *adj* [L *turbidus* confused, turbid, fr. *turba* confusion, crowd] **1** : thick with roiled sediment ⟨a ~ stream⟩ **2** : heavy with smoke or mist : DENSE **3** : CONFUSED, MUDDLED — **tur·bid·i·ty** \ˌtər-ˈbid-ət-ē\ *n*

tur·bine \ˈtər-bən, -ˌbīn\ *n* [F, fr. L *turbin-*, *turbo* top, whirlwind, whirl] : an engine whose central drive shaft is fitted with curved vanes whirled by the pressure of water, steam, or gas

tur·bo·elec·tric \ˈtər-bō-i-ˈlek-trik\ *adj* : involving or depending as a power source on electricity produced by turbine generators

tur·bo·fan \-ˌfan\ *n* **1** : a fan that is directly connected to and driven by a turbine and is used to supply air for cooling, ventilation, or combustion **2** : a jet engine having a turbofan

tur·bo·jet \-ˌjet\ *n* : an airplane powered by a jet engine (**turbojet engine**) having a turbine-driven air compressor supplying compressed air to the combustion chamber

tur·bo·prop \-ˌpräp\ *n* : an airplane powered by a jet engine (**turbo–propeller engine**) having a turbine-driven propeller but usu. obtaining additional thrust from the discharge of a jet of hot gases

tur·bot \ˈtər-bət\ *n, pl* **turbot** *also* **turbots** : a European flatfish that is a popular food fish; *also* : any of several similar flatfishes

tur·bu·lence \ˈtər-byə-ləns\ *n* : the quality or state of being turbulent

tur·bu·lent \-lənt\ *adj* **1** : causing violence or disturbance **2** : marked by agitation or tumult : TEMPESTUOUS — **tur·bu·lent·ly** *adv*

tu·reen \tə-ˈrēn, tyu̇-\ *n* [F *terrine*, fr. MF, fr. fem. of *terrin* of earth, fr. L *terra* earth] : a deep bowl from which foods (as soup) are served at table

[1]**turf** \ˈtərf\ *n, pl* **turfs** \ˈtərfs\ *also* **turves** \ˈtərvz\ **1** : the upper layer of soil bound by grass and roots into a close mat; *also* : a piece of this **2** : an artificial substitute for turf (as on a playing field) **3** : a piece of peat dried for fuel **4** : a track or course for horse racing; *also* : horse racing as a sport or business

[2]**turf** *vb* : to cover with turf

tur·gid \ˈtər-jəd\ *adj* **1** : marked by distension : SWOLLEN **2** : excessively embellished in style or language : BOMBASTIC — **tur·gid·i·ty** \ˌtər-ˈjid-ət-ē\ *n*

[1]**Turk** \ˈtərk\ *n* : a native or inhabitant of Turkey

[2]**Turk** *abbr* Turkey; Turkish

tur·key \ˈtər-kē\ *n, pl* **turkeys** [*Turkey*, country in western Asia and southeastern Europe; fr. confusion with the guinea fowl, supposed to be imported from Turkish territory] : a large American bird related to the domestic chicken and widely raised for food; *also* : its flesh

turkey buzzard *n* : TURKEY VULTURE

turkey vulture *n* : an American vulture common in South and Central America and in the U.S.

Turk·ish \ˈtər-kish\ *n* : the language of Turkey — **Turkish** *adj*

tur·mer·ic \ˈtər-mə-rik\ *n* : a spice or dyestuff obtained from the large aromatic deep-yellow rhizome of an East Indian perennial herb; *also* : this herb

tur·moil \ˈtər-ˌmȯil\ *n* : an extremely confused or agitated condition

[1]**turn** \ˈtərn\ *vb* **1** : to move or cause to move around an axis or center : ROTATE, REVOLVE ⟨~ a wheel⟩ **2** : to twist so as to effect a desired end ⟨~ a key⟩ **3** : WRENCH ⟨~ an ankle⟩ **4** : to change or cause to change position by moving through an arc of a circle ⟨~*ed* his chair to the fire⟩ **5** : to cause to move around a center so as to show another side of ⟨~ a page⟩ **6** : to revolve mentally : PONDER **7** : to become dizzy : REEL **8** : to reverse the sides or surfaces of ⟨~ a pancake⟩ **9** : UPSET, DISORDER ⟨things ~*ed* topsy-turvy⟩ ⟨~*ed* his stomach⟩ **10** : to set in another esp. contrary direction **11** : to change one's course or direction **12** : TRANSFER ⟨~ the task over to him⟩ **13** : to go around ⟨~ a corner⟩ **14** : to reach or pass beyond ⟨~*ed* twenty-one⟩ **15** : to direct toward or away from something; *also* : DEVOTE, APPLY **16** : to have recourse **17** : to become or make hostile **18** : to cause to become of a specified nature or appearance ⟨~*s* the leaves yellow⟩ **19** : to make or become spoiled : SOUR **20** : to pass from one state to another ⟨water ~*s* to ice⟩ **21** : CONVERT, TRANSFORM **22** : TRANSLATE, PARAPHRASE **23** : to give a rounded form to; *esp* : to shape by means of a lathe **24** : to gain by passing in trade ⟨~ a quick profit⟩ — **turn color 1** : BLUSH **2** : to become pale — **turn loose** : to set free

[2]**turn** *n* **1** : a turning about a center or axis : REVOLUTION, ROTATION **2** : the action or an act of giving or taking a different direction ⟨make a left ~⟩ **3** : a change of course or tendency ⟨a ~ for the better⟩ **4** : a place at which something turns : BEND, CURVE **5** : a short walk or trip round about ⟨take a ~ around the deck⟩ **6** : an act affecting another ⟨did him a good ~⟩ **7** : a place, time, or opportunity accorded in a scheduled order ⟨waited his ~ to be served⟩ **8** : a period of duty : SHIFT **9** : a short act esp. in a variety show **10** : a special purpose or requirement ⟨the job serves his ~⟩ **11** : a skillful fashioning ⟨neat ~ of phrase⟩ **12** : a single round (as of rope passed around an object) **13** : natural or special

aptitude **14** : a usu. sudden and brief disorder of body or spirits; *esp* : a spell of nervous shock or faintness

turn·about \ˈtər-nə-ˌbau̇t\ *n* **1** : a reversal of direction, trend, or policy **2** : RETALIATION

turn·buck·le \ˈtərn-ˌbək-əl\ *n* : a link with a screw thread at one or both ends for tightening a rod or stay

turn·coat \-ˌkōt\ *n* : one who forsakes his party or principles : RENEGADE

turn down \ˌtərn-ˈdau̇n, ˈtərn-\ *vb* : to decline to accept : REJECT — **turn·down** \ˈtərn-ˌdau̇n\ *n*

turn·er \ˈtər-nər\ *n* **1** : one that turns or is used for turning **2** : one that forms articles with a lathe

turn·ery \ˈtər-nə-rē\ *n, pl* **-er·ies** : the work, products, or shop of a turner

turn in *vb* **1** : to deliver up **2** : to inform on **3** : to acquit oneself of ⟨*turn in* a good job⟩ **4** : to go to bed

turn·ing \ˈtər-niŋ\ *n* **1** : the act or course of one that turns **2** : a place of a change of direction

tur·nip \ˈtər-nəp\ *n* **1** : a garden herb related to the cabbage with hairy leaves and an edible usu. white root **2** : RUTABAGA **3** : the root of a turnip

turn·key \ˈtərn-ˌkē\ *n, pl* **turnkeys** : one who has charge of a prison's keys

turn·off \ˈtərn-ˌȯf\ *n* : a place for turning off esp. from an expressway

turn off \ˌtərn-ˈȯf, ˈtərn-\ *vb* **1** : to deviate from a straight course or a main road **2** : to stop the functioning or flow of **3** : to cause to lose interest; *also* : to evoke a negative feeling in

turn on *vb* **1** : to get high or cause to get high as a result of using a drug (as marijuana) **2** : EXCITE, STIMULATE

turn·out \ˈtərn-ˌau̇t\ *n* **1** : an act of turning out **2** : a gathering of people for a special purpose **3** : a widened place in a highway for vehicles to pass or park **4** : manner of dress **5** : net yield : OUTPUT

turn out \ˌtərn-ˈau̇t, ˈtərn-\ *vb* **1** : EXPEL, EVICT **2** : PRODUCE **3** : to come forth and assemble **4** : to get out of bed **5** : to prove to be in the end

[1]**turn·over** \ˈtərn-ˌō-vər\ *n* **1** : UPSET **2** : SHIFT, REVERSAL **3** : a filled pastry made by turning half of the crust over the other half **4** : the volume of business done **5** : movement (as of goods or people) into, through, and out of a place; *esp* : a cycle of purchase, sale, and replacement of a stock of goods **6** : the number of persons hired within a period to replace those leaving or dropped; *also* : the ratio of this number to that of the average force maintained

[2]**turn·over** \ˌtərn-ˌō-vər\ *adj* : capable of being turned over

turn·pike \ˈtərn-ˌpīk\ *n* [ME *turnepike* revolving frame bearing spikes and serving as a barrier, fr. *turnen* to turn + *pike*] **1** : TOLLGATE; *also* : an expressway on which tolls are charged **2** : a main road

turn·spit \-ˌspit\ *n* : a device for turning a spit

turn·stile \-ˌstīl\ *n* : a post with arms pivoted on the top set in a passageway so that persons can pass through only on foot one by one

turn·ta·ble \-ˌtā-bəl\ *n* : a circular platform that revolves (as for turning a locomotive or a phonograph record)

turn to *vb* : to apply oneself to work

turn up *vb* **1** : to come to light or bring to light : DISCOVER, APPEAR **2** : to arrive at an appointed time or place **3** : to happen unexpectedly

tur·pen·tine \ˈtər-pən-ˌtīn\ *n* **1** : a mixture of oil and resin obtained from various cone-bearing trees (as pines) **2** : an oil obtained from various turpentines by distillation and used as a solvent and paint thinner; *also* : a similar oil obtained from distillation of pine wood

tur·pi·tude \ˈtər-pə-ˌt(y)üd\ *n* : inherent baseness : DEPRAVITY

turps \ˈtərps\ *n* : TURPENTINE

tur·quoise *also* **tur·quois** \ˈtər-ˌk(w)ȯiz\ *n* [ME *turkeis, turcas,* fr. MF *turquoyse,* fr. fem. of *turquoys* Turkish, fr. OF, fr. *Turc* Turk] **1** : a blue, bluish green, or greenish gray mineral that contains a little copper and is valued as a gem **2** : a light greenish blue color

tur·ret \ˈtər-ət\ *n* **1** : a little tower often at an angle of a larger structure and merely ornamental **2** : a revolvable holder in a machine tool **3** : a low usu. revolving structure (as on a tank, warship, or airplane) in which one or more guns are mounted

[1]**tur·tle** \ˈtərt-ᵊl\ *n, archaic* : TURTLEDOVE

[2]**turtle** *n, pl* **turtles** *also* **turtle** : any of an order of horny-beaked land, freshwater, or sea reptiles with the trunk enclosed in a bony shell

tur·tle·dove \ˈtərt-ᵊl-ˌdəv\ *n* : any of several small wild pigeons; *esp* : an Old World bird noted for plaintive cooing

tur·tle·neck \-ˌnek\ *n* : a high close-fitting turnover collar used esp. for sweaters; *also* : a sweater with a turtleneck

turves *pl of* TURF

Tus·ca·ro·ra \ˌtəs-kə-ˈrōr-ə\ *n, pl* **Tuscarora** *or* **Tuscaroras** : a member of an American Indian people of No. Carolina and later of New York and Ontario

tusk \ˈtəsk\ *n* **1** : a long enlarged protruding tooth (as of an elephant, walrus, or boar) used to dig up food or as a weapon **2** : a long projecting tooth — **tusked** \ˈtəskt\ *adj*

tusk·er \ˈtəs-kər\ *n* : an animal with tusks; *esp* : a male elephant with two normally developed tusks

[1]**tus·sle** \ˈtəs-əl\ *n* **1** : a physical struggle : SCUFFLE **2** : an intense argument, controversy, or struggle

[2]**tussle** *vb* **tus·sled; tus·sling** \-(ə-)liŋ\ : to struggle roughly

tus·sock \ˈtəs-ək\ *n* : a dense tuft esp. of grass or sedge; *also* : a hummock in marsh bound together by roots — **tus·socky** *adj*

tussock moth *n* : any of numerous dull-colored moths that usu. have wingless females and larvae with long tufts of hair

tu·te·lage \ˈt(y)üt-ᵊl-ij\ *n* **1** : an act of guarding or protecting **2** : the state of being under a guardian or tutor **3** : instruction esp. of an individual

tu·te·lary \ˈt(y)üt-ᵊl-ˌer-ē\ *adj* : acting as a guardian ⟨~ deity⟩ ⟨a ~ power⟩

[1]**tu·tor** \ˈt(y)üt-ər\ *n* **1** : a person charged with the instruction and guidance of another **2** : a private teacher

[2]**tutor** *vb* **1** : to have the guardianship of **2** : to teach or guide individually : COACH ⟨~*ed* the boy in Latin⟩ **3** : to receive instruction esp. privately

tu·to·ri·al \t(y)ü-ˈtōr-ē-əl\ *n* : a class conducted by a tutor for one student or a small number of students

tut·ti–frut·ti \ˌtüt-i-ˈfrüt-ē, ˌtu̇t-\ *n* [It, lit., all fruits] : a confection or ice cream containing chopped usu. candied fruits

tux·e·do \ˌtək-ˈsēd-ō\ *n, pl* **-dos** *or* **-does** [*Tuxedo* Park, N.Y.] **1** : a usu. black or blackish blue jacket **2** : semiformal evening clothes for men

TV \ˈtē-ˈvē\ *n* : TELEVISION

TVA *abbr* Tennessee Valley Authority

TV dinner \ˌtē-ˌvē-\ *n* : a frozen packaged dinner that needs only heating before serving

twad·dle \ˈtwäd-ᵊl\ *n* : silly idle talk : DRIVEL — **twaddle** *vb*

twain \ˈtwān\ *n* **1** : TWO **2** : PAIR

[1]**twang** \ˈtwaŋ\ *n* **1** : a harsh quick ringing sound like that of a plucked bowstring **2** : nasal speech or resonance **3** : the characteristic speech of a region

[2]**twang** *vb* **twanged; twang·ing** \ˈtwaŋ-iŋ\ **1** : to sound or cause to sound with a twang **2** : to speak with a nasal twang

tweak \ˈtwēk\ *vb* : to pinch and pull with a sudden jerk and twitch — **tweak** *n*

tweed \ˈtwēd\ *n* [alter. of Sc *tweel* twill, fr. ME *twyll*] **1** : a rough woolen fabric made usu. in twill weaves **2** *pl* : tweed clothing; *esp* : a tweed suit

tweedy \ˈtwēd-ē\ *adj* **tweed·i·er; -est 1** : of or resembling tweed **2** : given to wearing tweeds **3** : suggestive of the outdoors in taste or habits

tween \(ˈ)twēn\ *prep* : BETWEEN

tweet \ˈtwēt\ *n* : a chirping note — **tweet** *vb*

tweet·er \ˈtwēt-ər\ *n* : a small loudspeaker that reproduces sounds of high pitch

twee·zers \ˈtwē-zərz\ *n pl* [obs. E *tweeze,* n. (case for small implements) short for obs. E *etweese,* fr. pl. of obs. E *etwee,* fr. F *étui*] : a small pincerlike implement held between the thumb and forefinger for grasping something

twelve \ˈtwelv\ *n* **1** : one more than 11 **2** : the 12th in a set or series **3** : something having 12 units — **twelfth** \ˈtwelfth\ *adj or n* — **twelve** *adj or pron*

twelve·month \-ˌmənth\ *n* : YEAR

twen·ty \ˈtwent-ē\ *n, pl* **twenties** : two times 10 — **twen·ti·eth** \-ē-əth\ *adj or n* — **twenty** *adj or pron*

twenty–twenty *or* **20/20** \ˌtwent-ē-ˈtwent-ē\ *adj* : having a visual capacity to see detail that is normal for the human eye ⟨~ vision⟩

twice \ˈtwīs\ *adv* **1** : on two occasions **2** : two times ⟨~ two is four⟩

[1]**twid·dle** \ˈtwid-ᵊl\ *vb* **twid·dled; twid·dling** \ˈtwid-(ᵊ-)liŋ\ **1** : to be busy with trifles; *also* : to play idly with something **2** : to rotate lightly or idly

[2]**twiddle** *n* : TURN, TWIST

twig \ˈtwig\ *n* : a small branch — **twig·gy** *adj*

twi·light \ˈtwī-ˌlīt\ *n* **1** : the light from the sky between full night and sunrise or between sunset and full night **2** : a state of imperfect clarity; *also* : a period of decline — **twilight** *adj*

twill \ˈtwil\ *n* [ME *twyll,* fr. OE *twilic* having a double thread, modif. of L *bilic-, bilix,* fr. *bi-* two + *licium* thread] **1** : a fabric with a twill weave **2** : a textile weave that gives an appearance of diagonal lines in the fabric

twilled \ˈtwild\ *adj* : made with a twill weave

[1]**twin** \ˈtwin\ *adj* **1** : born with one another or as a pair at one birth ⟨~ brother⟩ ⟨~ girls⟩ **2** : made up of two similar or related members or parts **3** : being one of a pair ⟨~ city⟩

[2]**twin** *vb* **twinned; twin·ning 1** : to bring forth twins **2** : to be coupled with another

[3]**twin** *n* **1** : either of two offspring produced at a birth **2** : one of two persons or things closely related to or resembling each other

[1]**twine** \ˈtwīn\ *n* **1** : a strong thread of two or three strands twisted together **2** : an act of entwining or interlacing — **twiny** *adj*

[2]**twine** *vb* **twined; twin·ing 1** : to twist together; *also* : to form by twisting **2** : INTERLACE, WEAVE **3** : to coil about a support **4** : to stretch or move in a sinuous manner — **twin·er** *n*

[1]**twinge** \ˈtwinj\ *vb* **twinged; twing·ing** \ˈtwin-jiŋ\ *or* **twinge·ing** : to affect with or feel a sharp sudden pain

[2]**twinge** *n* : a sudden sharp stab (as of pain or distress)

[1]**twin·kle** \ˈtwiŋ-kəl\ *vb* **twin·kled; twin·kling** \-k(ə-)liŋ\ **1** : to shine or cause to shine with a flickering or sparkling light **2** : to appear bright with merriment **3** : to flutter or flit rapidly — **twin·kler** \-k(ə-)lər\ *n*

[2]**twinkle** *n* **1** : a wink of the eyelids; *also* : the duration of a wink **2** : an intermittent radiance **3** : a rapid flashing motion

twin·kling \ˈtwiŋ-kliŋ\ *n* : the time occupied by a single wink : INSTANT **syn** instant, moment, minute, second, flash

[1]**twirl** \ˈtwərl\ *vb* **1** : to whirl round **2** : to pitch in a baseball game **syn** turn, revolve, rotate, circle, spin, swirl, pirouette — **twirl·er** \ˈtwər-lər\ *n*

[2]**twirl** *n* **1** : an act of twirling **2** : COIL, WHORL

[1]**twist** \ˈtwist\ *vb* **1** : to unite by winding one thread or strand round another **2** : WREATHE, TWINE **3** : to turn so as to hurt ⟨~*ed* her ankle⟩ **4** : to twirl into spiral shape **5** : to subject (as a shaft) to torsion **6** : to turn from the true form or meaning **7** : to pull off or break by torsion **8** : to follow a winding course **9** : to turn around

[2]**twist** *n* **1** : something formed by twisting or winding **2** : an act of twisting : the state of being twisted **3** : a spiral turn or curve; *also* : SPIN **4** : a turning aside **5** : ECCENTRICITY **6** : a distortion of meaning **7** : an unexpected turn or development **8** : DEVICE, TRICK **9** : a variant approach or method

twist·er \ˈtwis-tər\ *n* **1** : one that twists; *esp* : a ball with a forward and spinning motion **2** : TORNADO; *also* : WATERSPOUT 2

twit \ˈtwit\ *vb* **twit·ted; twit·ting** : to reproach, taunt, or tease esp. by reminding of a fault or defect **syn** ridicule, deride, mock, razz

[1]**twitch** \ˈtwich\ *vb* **1** : to move or pull with a sudden motion : JERK **2** : to move jerkily : QUIVER

[2]**twitch** *n* **1** : an act or movement of twitching **2** : a short sharp contraction of muscle fibers

[1]**twit·ter** \ˈtwit-ər\ *vb* **1** : to make a succession of chirping noises **2** : to talk in a chattering fashion; *also* : TITTER **3** : to have a slight trembling of the nerves : FLUTTER

[2]**twitter** *n* **1** : a slight agitation of the nerves **2** : a small tremulous intermittent noise (as made by a swallow) **3** : a light chattering; *also* : TITTER

twixt \(ˈ)twikst\ *prep* : BETWEEN

two \ˈtü\ *n, pl* **twos 1** : one more than one **2** : the second in a set or series **3** : something having two units — **two** *adj or pron*

two cents *n* **1** : a sum or object of very small value **2** *or* **two cents worth** : an opinion offered on a topic under discussion

two–faced \ˈtü-ˈfāst\ *adj* **1** : DOUBLE-DEALING, FALSE **2** : having two faces

two·fold \ˈtü-ˌfōld, -ˈfōld\ *adj* **1** : having two units or members **2** : being twice as much or as many — **twofold** \-ˈfōld\ *adv*

2,4–D \ˌtü-ˌfōr-ˈdē\ *n* : a white crystalline compound used as a weed killer

2,4,5–T \-ˌfīv-ˈtē\ *n* : an irritant compound used in brush and weed control

two·pence \ˈtəp-əns, *US also* ˈtü-ˌpens\ *n* : the sum of two pence

two·pen·ny \ˈtəp-(ə-)nē, *US also* ˈtü-ˌpen-ē\ *adj* : of the value of or costing twopence

two–ply \ˈtü-ˈplī\ *adj* **1** : woven as a double cloth **2** : consisting of two strands or thicknesses

two·some \ˈtü-səm\ *n* **1** : a group of two persons or things : COUPLE **2** : a golf match between two players

two–step \ˈtü-ˌstep\ *n* : a ballroom dance performed with a sliding step in march or polka time; *also* : a piece of music for this dance — **two–step** *vb*

two–time \ˈtü-ˌtīm\ *vb* : to betray (a spouse or lover) by secret lovemaking with another — **two–tim·er** *n*

two–way *adj* : involving two elements or allowing movement or use in two directions or manners

two–winged fly \ˌtü-ˌwiŋd-\ *n* : any of a large order of insects mostly with one pair of functional wings and another pair that if present are reduced to balancing organs and often with larvae without a head, eyes, or legs

twp *abbr* township

TWX *abbr* teletypewriter exchange

TX *abbr* Texas

-ty *n suffix* : quality : condition : degree ⟨real*ty*⟩

ty·coon \tī-ˈkün\ *n* [Jp *taikun,* fr. Chin *ta*[4] great + *chün*[1] ruler] **1** : a masterful leader (as in politics) **2** : a powerful businessman or industrialist

tying *pres part of* TIE

tyke \ˈtīk\ *n* : a small child

tym·pan·ic membrane \tim-ˈpan-ik-\ *n* : EARDRUM

tym·pa·num \ˈtim-pə-nəm\ *n, pl* **-na** \-nə\ *also* **-nums** : EARDRUM; *also* : MIDDLE EAR — **tym·pan·ic** \tim-ˈpan-ik\ *adj*

[1]**type** \ˈtīp\ *n* [LL *typus,* fr. L & Gk; L *typus* image, fr. Gk *typos* blow, impression, model, fr. *typtein* to strike, beat] **1** : a person, thing, or event that foreshadows another to come : TOKEN, SYMBOL **2** : MODEL, EXAMPLE **3** : a distinctive stamp, mark, or sign : EMBLEM **4** : rectangular blocks usu. of metal each having a face so shaped as to produce a character when printed **5** : the letters or characters printed from or as if from type **6** : general character or form common to a number of individuals and setting them off as a distinguishable class ⟨horses of draft ~⟩ **7** : a class, kind, or group set apart by common characteristics ⟨a seedless ~ of orange⟩; *also* : something distinguishable as a variety ⟨reactions of this ~⟩ **syn** sort, nature, character, description

[2]**type** *vb* **typed; typ·ing** **1** : to represent beforehand as a type **2** : to produce a copy of; *also* : REPRESENT, TYPIFY **3** : TYPEWRITE **4** : to identify as belonging to a type **5** : TYPECAST

type·cast \-ˌkast\ *vb* **-cast; -cast·ing** **1** : to cast (an actor) in a part calling for characteristics possessed by the actor himself **2** : to cast repeatedly in the same type of role

type·face \-ˌfās\ *n* : all type of a single design

type·found·er \-ˌfau̇n-dər\ *n* : one engaged in the design and production of metal printing type for hand composition — **type·found·ing** \-diŋ\ *n*

type·script \ˈtīp-ˌskript\ *n* : typewritten matter

type·set \-ˌset\ *vb* **-set; -set·ting** : to set in type : COMPOSE — **type·set·ter** \-ˌset-ər\ *n*

type·write \-ˌrīt\ *vb* **-wrote** \-ˌrōt\; **-writ·ten** \-ˌrit-ᵊn\ : to write with a typewriter

type·writ·er \-ˌrīt-ər\ *n* **1** : a machine for writing in characters similar to those produced by printers' types by means of types striking through an inked ribbon **2** : TYPIST

type·writ·ing \-ˌrīt-iŋ\ *n* : the use of a typewriter ⟨teach ~⟩; *also* : the printing done with a typewriter

[1]**ty·phoid** \ˈtī-ˌfȯid, tī-ˈfȯid\ *adj* : of, relating to, or being a communicable bacterial disease **(typhoid fever)** marked by fever, diarrhea, prostration, and intestinal inflammation

[2]**typhoid** *n* : TYPHOID FEVER

ty·phoon \tī-ˈfün\ *n* : a tropical cyclone in the region of the Philippines or the China sea

ty·phus \ˈtī-fəs\ *n* : a severe infectious disease transmitted esp. by body lice, caused by a rickettsia, and marked by high fever, stupor and delirium, intense headache, and a dark red rash

typ·i·cal \ˈtip-i-kəl\ *adj* **1** : being or having the nature of a type **2** : exhibiting the essential characteristics of a group **3** : conforming to a type — **typ·i·cal·i·ty** \ˌtip-ə-ˈkal-ət-ē\ *n* — **typ·i·cal·ly** \-ē\ *adv* — **typ·i·cal·ness** *n*

typ·i·fy \ˈtip-ə-ˌfī\ *vb* **-fied; -fy·ing** **1** : to represent by an image, form, model, or resemblance **2** : to embody the essential or common characteristics of

typ·ist \ˈtī-pəst\ *n* : one who operates a typewriter

ty·po \ˈtī-pō\ *n, pl* **typos** : an error in typing or in setting type

ty·pog·ra·pher \tī-ˈpäg-rə-fər\ *n* : one who designs or arranges printing

ty·pog·ra·phy \tī-ˈpäg-rə-fē\ *n* : the art of printing with type; *also* : the style, arrangement, or appearance of matter printed from type — **ty·po·graph·ic** \ˌtī-pə-ˈgraf-ik\ *or* **ty·po·graph·i·cal** \-i-kəl\ *adj* — **ty·po·graph·i·cal·ly** \-ē\ *adv*

ty·ran·ni·cal \tə-ˈran-i-kəl, tī-\ *also* **ty·ran·nic** \-ik\ *adj* : of or relating to a tyrant : DESPOTIC **syn** arbitrary, absolute, autocratic — **ty·ran·ni·cal·ly** \-i-k(ə-)lē\ *adv*

tyr·an·nize \ˈtir-ə-ˌnīz\ *vb* **-nized; -niz·ing** : to act as a tyrant : rule with unjust severity — **tyr·an·niz·er** *n*

ty·ran·no·saur \tə-ˈran-ə-ˌsȯr\ *n* : TYRANNOSAURUS

ty·ran·no·sau·rus \tə-ˌran-ə-ˈsȯr-əs\ *n* : a very large American flesh-eating dinosaur of the Cretaceous that had small forelegs and walked on its hind legs

tyr·an·nous \ˈtir-ə-nəs\ *adj* : TYRANNICAL — **tyr·an·nous·ly** *adv*

tyr·an·ny \ˈtir-ə-nē\ *n, pl* **-nies** **1** : oppressive power **2** : the rule or authority of a tyrant : government in which absolute power is vested in a single ruler **3** : a tyrannical act

ty·rant \ˈtī-rənt\ *n* **1** : an absolute ruler : DESPOT **2** : a ruler who governs oppressively or brutally **3** : one who uses authority or power harshly

ty·ro \ˈtī-rō\ *n, pl* **tyros** [ML, fr. L *tiro* young soldier, tyro] : a beginner in learning : NOVICE

tzar \ˈzär, ˈ(t)sär\ *var of* CZAR

U

[1]**u** \ˈyü\ *n, pl* **u's** *or* **us** \ˈyüz\ *often cap* : the 21st letter of the English alphabet

[2]**u** *abbr, often cap* unit

[1]**U** \ˈyü\ *adj* : characteristic of the upper classes

[2]**U** *abbr* **1** [abbr. of *Union of Orthodox Hebrew Congregations*] kosher certification **2** university

[3]**U** *symbol* uranium

UAE *abbr* United Arab Emirates

UAR *abbr* United Arab Republic

UAW *abbr* United Automobile Workers

ubiq·ui·tous \yü-ˈbik-wət-əs\ *adj* : existing or being everywhere at the same time : OMNIPRESENT — **ubiq·ui·tous·ly** *adv* — **ubiq·ui·ty** \-wət-ē\ *n*

U–boat \ˈyü-ˌbōt\ *n* [trans. of G *u-boot,* short for *unterseeboot,* lit., undersea boat] : a German submarine

ud·der \ˈəd-ər\ *n* : an organ (as of a cow) consisting of two or more milk glands enclosed in a large hanging sac and each provided with a nipple

UFO \ˌyü-ˌef-ˈō\ *n, pl* **UFO's** *or* **UFOs** \-ˈōz\ : an unidentified flying object; *esp* : FLYING SAUCER

ug·ly \ˈəg-lē\ *adj* **ug·li·er; -est** [ME, fr. ON *uggligr,* fr. *uggr* fear] **1** : FRIGHTFUL, DIRE **2** : offensive to the sight : HIDEOUS **3** : offensive or unpleasing to any sense **4** : morally objectionable : REPULSIVE **5** : likely to cause inconvenience or discomfort **6** : SURLY, QUARRELSOME ⟨an ~ disposition⟩ — **ug·li·ness** \-lē-nəs\ *n*

UHF *abbr* ultrahigh frequency

UK *abbr* United Kingdom

ukase \yü-ˈkās, -ˈkāz\ *n* [F & Russ; F, fr. Russ *ukaz,* fr. *ukazat'* to show, order] : an edict esp. of a Russian emperor or government

Ukrai·ni·an \yü-ˈkrā-nē-ən\ *n* **:** a native or inhabitant of the Ukraine, U.S.S.R. — **Ukrainian** *adj*

uku·le·le \ˌyü-kə-ˈlā-lē\ *n* [Hawaiian *ʻukulele,* fr. *ʻuku* flea + *lele* jumping] **:** a small usu. 4-stringed guitar popularized in Hawaii

ul·cer \ˈəl-sər\ *n* **1 :** an eroded sore often discharging pus **2 :** something that festers and corrupts like an open sore — **ul·cer·ous** *adj*

ul·cer·ate \ˈəl-sə-ˌrāt\ *vb* **-at·ed; -at·ing :** to cause or become affected with an ulcer — **ul·cer·ative** \ˈəl-sə-ˌrāt-iv\ *adj*

ul·cer·ation \ˌəl-sə-ˈrā-shən\ *n* **1 :** the process of forming or state of having an ulcer **2 :** ULCER 1

ul·lage \ˈəl-ij\ *n* [ME *ulage,* fr. MF *eullage* act of filling a cask, fr. *eullier* to fill a cask, fr. OF *ouil* eye, bunghole, fr. L *oculus* eye] **:** the amount that a container (as a cask) lacks of being full

ul·na \ˈəl-nə\ *n* **:** the one of the two bones of the human forearm that is on the little-finger side; *also* **:** a corresponding bone of the forelimb of vertebrates above fishes

ul·ster \ˈəl-stər\ *n* **:** a long loose overcoat

ult *abbr* **1** ultimate **2** ultimo

ul·te·ri·or \ˌəl-ˈtir-ē-ər\ *adj* **1 :** lying farther away **:** more remote **2 :** situated beyond or on the farther side **3 :** going beyond what is openly said or shown **:** HIDDEN ⟨~ motives⟩

[1]**ul·ti·mate** \ˈəl-tə-mət\ *adj* **1 :** most remote in space or time **:** FARTHEST **2 :** last in a progression **:** FINAL **3 :** EXTREME, UTMOST **4 :** finally reckoned **5 :** FUNDAMENTAL, ABSOLUTE, SUPREME ⟨~ reality⟩ **6 :** incapable of further analysis or division **:** ELEMENTAL **7 :** MAXIMUM — **ul·ti·mate·ly** *adv*

[2]**ultimate** *n* **:** something ultimate

ul·ti·ma·tum \ˌəl-tə-ˈmāt-əm, -ˈmät-\ *n, pl* **-tums** *or* **-ta** \-ə\ **:** a final condition or demand whose rejection will bring about a resort to forceful action

ul·ti·mo \ˈəl-tə-ˌmō\ *adj* [L *ultimo mense* in the last month] **:** of or occurring the month preceding the present

[1]**ul·tra** \ˈəl-trə\ *adj* **:** going beyond others or beyond due limits **:** EXTREME

[2]**ultra** *n* **:** EXTREMIST

ul·tra·cen·tri·fuge \ˌəl-trə-ˈsen-trə-ˌfyüj\ *n* **:** a high-speed centrifuge able to separate small particles (as from colloidal suspension)

ul·tra·con·ser·va·tive \-kən-ˈsər-vət-iv\ *adj* **:** extremely conservative

ul·tra·fash·ion·able \-ˈfash-(ə-)nə-bəl\ *adj* **:** extremely fashionable

ul·tra·high \-ˈhī\ *adj* **:** very high **:** exceedingly high ⟨~ vacuum⟩

ultrahigh frequency *n* **:** a radio frequency between 300 and 3000 megahertz

ul·tra·ma·rine \ˌəl-trə-mə-ˈrēn\ *n* **1 :** a deep blue pigment **2 :** a very bright deep blue color

ul·tra·mi·cro·scop·ic \-ˌmī-krə-ˈskäp-ik\ *adj* **:** too small to be seen with an ordinary microscope

ul·tra·mod·ern \-ˈmäd-ərn\ *adj* **:** extremely or excessively modern in idea, style, or tendency

ul·tra·mon·tane \-ˈmän-ˌtān, -ˌmän-ˈtān\ *adj* **1 :** of or relating to countries or peoples beyond the mountains (as the Alps) **2 :** favoring greater or absolute supremacy of papal over national or diocesan authority in the Roman Catholic Church — **ultramontane** *n, often cap* — **ul·tra·mon·tan·ism** \-ˈmänt-ᵊn-ˌiz-əm\ *n*

ul·tra·pure \-ˈpyu̇r\ *adj* **:** of the utmost purity

ul·tra·short \-ˈsho̊rt\ *adj* **1 :** very short in duration **2 :** having a wavelength below 10 meters

ul·tra·son·ic \ˌəl-trə-ˈsän-ik\ *adj* **:** having a frequency too high to be heard by the human ear — **ul·tra·son·i·cal·ly** \-i-k(ə-)lē\ *adv*

ul·tra·son·ics \-ˈsän-iks\ *n* **1 :** ultrasonic vibrations **2 :** the science of ultrasonic phenomena

ul·tra·sound \-ˌsau̇nd\ *n* **1 :** ultrasonic vibrations **2 :** a diagnostic or therapeutic procedure or technique using ultrasound to form a two-dimensional image of internal body structures

ul·tra·vi·o·let \-ˈvī-ə-lət\ *adj* **:** having a wavelength shorter than those of visible light and longer than those of X rays ⟨~ radiation⟩; *also* **:** producing or employing ultraviolet radiation — **ultraviolet** *n*

ul·tra vi·res \ˌəl-trə-ˈvī-rēz\ *adv or adj* [NL, lit., beyond power] **:** beyond the scope of legal power or authority

ul·u·late \ˈəl-yə-ˌlāt\ *vb* **-lat·ed; -lat·ing :** HOWL, WAIL

um·bel \ˈəm-bəl\ *n* **:** a flat-topped or ball-shaped flower cluster in which the individual flower stalks all arise at one point on the main stem

um·ber \ˈəm-bər\ *n* **:** a brown earthy substance valued as a pigment either in its raw state or burnt — **umber** *adj*

umbilical cord *n* **:** a cord arising from the navel that connects the fetus with the placenta

um·bi·li·cus \ˌəm-bə-ˈlī-kəs, ˌəm-ˈbil-i-\ *n, pl* **um·bi·li·ci** \ˌəm-bə-ˈlī-ˌkī, -ˌsī; ˌəm-ˈbil-ə-ˌkī\ *or* **um·bi·li·cus·es** **:** NAVEL — **um·bil·i·cal** \ˌəm-ˈbil-i-kəl\ *adj*

um·bra \ˈəm-brə\ *n, pl* **umbras** *or* **um·brae** \-(ˌ)brē, -ˌbrī\ **1 :** SHADE, SHADOW **2 :** the conical part of the shadow of a celestial body from which the sun's light is completely blocked

um·brage \ˈəm-brij\ *n* **1 :** SHADE; *also* **:** FOLIAGE **2 :** RESENTMENT, OFFENSE ⟨take ~ at a remark⟩

um·brel·la \ˌəm-ˈbrel-ə\ *n* **1 :** a collapsible shade for protection against weather consisting of fabric stretched over hinged ribs radiating from a center pole **2 :** something that resembles an umbrella in shape or purpose

umi·ak \ˈü-mē-ˌak\ *n* **:** an open Eskimo boat made of a wooden frame covered with skins

umiak

um·pire \ˈəm-ˌpī(ə)r\ *n* [ME *oumpere,* alter. of *noumpere* (the phrase *a noumpere* being understood as *an oumpere*), fr. MF *nomper* not equal, not paired, fr. *non* not + *per* equal, fr. L *par*] **1 :** one having authority to decide finally a controversy or question between parties **2 :** an official in a sport who rules on plays — **umpire** *vb*

ump·teen \ˈəmp-ˈtēn\ *adj* **:** very many **:** indefinitely numerous — **ump·teenth** \-ˈtēnth\ *adj*

UN *abbr* United Nations

un- \ˌən, ˈən\ *prefix* **1 :** not **:** IN-, NON- **2 :** opposite of **:** contrary to

unabashed
unabated
unabsorbed
unabsorbent
unacademic
unaccented
unacceptable
unacclimatized
unaccommodating
unaccredited
unacknowledged
unacquainted
unadapted
unadjusted
unadorned
unadventurous
unadvertised
unaesthetic
unaffiliated
unafraid
unaggressive
unaided
unalike
unallied
unalterable
unalterably
unaltered
unambiguous
unambiguously
unambitious
unanchored
unanimated
unannounced
unanswerable
unanswered
unanticipated

unapologetic
unapparent
unappealing
unappeased
unappetizing
unappreciated
unappreciative
unapproachable
unappropriated
unapproved
unarmored
unartistic
unashamed
unasked
unassertive
unassisted
unathletic
unattainable
unattempted
unattended
unattested
unattractive
unauthentic
unauthenticated
unauthorized
unavailable
unavenged
unavowed
unawakened
unbaked
unbaptized
unbeloved
unblamed
unbleached
unblemished
unblinking
unbound
unbranched
unbranded
unbreakable
unbridgeable
unbrotherly
unbruised
unbrushed
unbudging
unburied
unburned
unburnished
uncanceled
uncanonical
uncap
uncapitalized
uncared-for
uncataloged
uncaught
uncensored
uncensured
unchallenged
unchangeable
unchanged
unchanging
unchaperoned
uncharacteristic
unchecked
unchivalrous
unchristened
unclad
unclaimed
unclassified
uncleaned
unclear
uncleared
unclouded
uncluttered
uncoated
uncollected
uncolored
uncombed
uncombined
uncomely
uncomic
uncommercial
uncompensated
uncomplaining
uncompleted
uncomplicated
uncomplimentary
uncompounded
uncomprehending
unconcealed
unconfined
unconfirmed
unconformable
uncongenial
unconnected
unconquered
unconsecrated
unconsidered
unconsolidated
unconstrained
unconsumed
uncontaminated
uncontested
uncontradicted
uncontrolled
unconverted
unconvincing
uncooked
uncooperative
uncoordinated
uncordial
uncorrected
uncorroborated
uncorrupted
uncountable
uncreative
uncredited
uncropped
uncrowded
uncrowned
uncrystallized
uncultivated
uncultured
uncurbed
uncured
uncurious
uncurtained
uncustomary
undamaged
undamped
undated
undazzled
undecided
undecipherable
undecked
undeclared
undecorated
undefeated
undefended
undefiled
undefinable
undefined
undemanding
undemocratic
undenominational
undependable
undeserved
undeserving
undetected
undetermined
undeterred
undeveloped
undifferentiated
undigested
undignified
undiluted
undiminished
undimmed
undiplomatic
undirected
undiscerning
undisciplined
undisclosed
undiscovered
undiscriminating
undisguised
undismayed
undisputed
undissolved
undistinguished
undistributed
undisturbed
undivided
undogmatic
undomesticated
undone
undoubled
undramatic
undraped
undrawn
undreamed
undressed
undrinkable
undulled
undutiful
undyed
uneager
uneatable
uneaten
uneconomic
uneconomical
unedifying
uneducated
unembarrassed
unemotional
unemphatic
unenclosed
unencumbered
unendorsed
unendurable
unenforceable
unenforced
unengaged
unenjoyable
unenlightened
unenterprising
unentertaining
unenthusiastic
unenviable
unequipped
unessential
unethical
unexaggerated
unexcelled
unexceptional
unexcited
unexciting
unexperienced
unexpired
unexplained
unexploded
unexplored
unexposed
unexpressed
unexpurgated
unextinguished
unfading
unfaltering
unfashionable
unfashionably
unfathomable
unfeasible
unfed
unfeminine
unfenced
unfermented
unfertilized
unfilled
unfiltered
unfitted
unflagging
unflattering
unflavored
unfocused
unfolded
unforced
unforeseeable
unforeseen
unforgivable
unforgiving
unformulated
unfortified
unframed
unfree
unfulfilled
unfunded
unfunny
unfurnished
ungentle
ungentlemanly
ungerminated
unglazed
ungoverned
ungraceful
ungraded
ungrammatical
ungrounded
ungrudging
unguided
unhackneyed
unhampered
unhardened
unharmed
unharvested
unhatched
unhealed
unhealthful
unheeded
unhelpful
unheralded
unheroic
unhesitating

unhindered
unhonored
unhoused
unhurried
unhurt
unhygienic
unidentified
unidiomatic
unimaginable
unimaginative
unimpaired
unimpassioned
unimpeded
unimportant
unimposing
unimpressive
unimproved
unincorporated
uninfluenced
uninformative
uninformed
uninhabitable
uninhabited
uninitiated
uninjured
uninspired
uninstructed
uninstructive
uninsured
unintended
uninteresting
uninvested
uninvited
uninviting
unjointed
unjustifiable
unjustified
unkept
unknowable
unknowledgeable
unlabeled
unladylike
unlamented
unleavened
unlicensed
unlighted
unlikable
unlimited
unlined
unlisted
unlit
unliterary
unlivable
unlobed
unlovable
unloved
unloving
unmade
unmalicious
unmanageable
unmanned
unmanufactured
unmapped
unmarked
unmarketable
unmarred
unmarried
unmasculine
unmatched
unmeant
unmeasured
unmeditated
unmelodious
unmentioned
unmerited
unmilitary
unmilled
unmixed
unmolested
unmounted
unmovable
unmoved
unmusical
unnameable
unnamed
unnecessary
unneighborly
unnewsworthy
unnoticeable
unnoticed
unobjectionable
unobliging
unobservant
unobserved
unobserving
unobstructed
unobtainable
unofficial
unofficially
unopened
unopposed
unoriginal
unorthodox
unostentatious
unowned
unpaged
unpaid
unpainted
unpaired
unpalatable
unpardonable
unpasteurized
unpatriotic
unpaved
unperceived
unperceptive
unperformed
unperturbed
unpitied
unplanned
unplanted
unpleasing
unplowed
unpoetic
unpolished
unpolitical
unpolluted
unposed
unpractical
unpracticed
unpredictable
unprejudiced
unpremeditated
unprepared
unpreparedness
unprepossessing
unpressed
unpretending
unpretty
unprivileged
unprocessed
unproductive
unprofessed
unprofessional
unprogrammed
unprogressive
unpromising
unprompted
unpronounceable
unpropitious
unprotected
unproven
unprovided
unprovoked
unpublished
unpunished
unquenchable
unquestioned
unraised
unratified
unreachable
unreadable
unready
unrealistic
unrealized
unrecognizable
unrecompensed
unrecorded
unrecoverable
unredeemable
unrefined
unreflecting
unreflective
unregistered
unregulated
unrehearsed
unrelated
unreliable
unrelieved
unreluctant
unremarkable
unremembered
unremovable
unrepentant
unreported
unrepresentative
unrepressed
unrequited
unresistant
unresisting
unresolved
unresponsive
unrestful
unrestricted
unreturnable
unreturned
unrewarding
unrhymed
unrhythmic
unripened
unromantic
unromantically
unsafe
unsaid
unsalable
unsalted
unsanitary
unsatisfactory
unsatisfied
unscented
unscheduled
unscholarly
unsealed
unseasoned
unseaworthy
unsegmented
unsensational
unsentimental
unserviceable
unsexual
unshaded
unshakable
unshaken
unshapely
unshaven
unshed
unshorn
unsifted
unsigned
unsinkable
unsmiling
unsociable
unsoiled
unsold
unsoldierly
unsolicited
unsolvable
unsolved
unsorted
unspecified
unspectacular
unspent
unspiritual
unspoiled
unspoken
unsportsmanlike
unstained
unstated
unsterile
unstoppable
unstructured
unstylish
unsubdued
unsubstantiated
unsubtle
unsuccessful
unsuccessfully
unsuitable
unsuited
unsullied
unsupervised
unsupportable
unsupported
unsuppressed
unsure
unsurpassed
unsuspected
unsuspecting
unsuspicious
unsweetened
unsymmetrical
unsympathetic
unsystematic
untactful
untainted
untalented
untamed
untanned
untapped
untarnished
untaxed
unteachable
untenable
untenanted
untested
unthankful
unthoughtful
unthrifty
untidy
untilled
untitled
untouched

untraceable
untrained
untrammeled
untranslatable
untraveled
untraversed
untrimmed
untrod
untroubled
untrustworthy
untruthful
unusable
unvaried
unvarying
unventilated
unverifiable
unverified
unversed
unvisited
unwanted
unwarranted
unwary
unwashed
unwatched
unwavering
unweaned
unwearable
unwearied
unweathered
unwed
unwelcome
unwished
unwitnessed
unwomanly
unworkable
unworn
unworried
unwounded
unwoven
unwrinkled

un·able \ˌən-ˈā-bəl, ˈən-\ *adj* **1** : not able **2** : UNQUALIFIED, INCOMPETENT

un·abridged \ˌən-ə-ˈbrijd\ *adj* **1** : not abridged ⟨an ~ edition of Shakespeare⟩ **2** : complete of its class : not based on one larger ⟨an ~ dictionary⟩

un·ac·com·pa·nied \ˌən-ə-ˈkəmp-(ə-)nēd\ *adj* : not accompanied; *esp* : being without instrumental accompaniment

un·ac·count·able \ˌən-ə-ˈkau̇nt-ə-bəl\ *adj* **1** : not to be accounted for : INEXPLICABLE **2** : not responsible — **un·ac·count·ably** \-blē\ *adv*

un·ac·count·ed \-əd\ *adj* : not accounted ⟨the loss was ~ for⟩

un·ac·cus·tomed \ˌən-ə-ˈkəs-təmd\ *adj* **1** : not customary : not usual or common **2** : not accustomed or habituated ⟨~ to noise⟩

un·adul·ter·at·ed \ˌən-ə-ˈdəl-tə-ˌrāt-əd\ *adj* : PURE, UNMIXED

un·ad·vised \ˌən-əd-ˈvīzd\ *adj* **1** : done without due consideration : RASH **2** : not prudent — **un·ad·vis·ed·ly** \-ˈvī-zəd-lē\ *adv*

un·af·fect·ed \ˌən-ə-ˈfek-təd\ *adj* **1** : not influenced or changed mentally, physically, or chemically **2** : free from affectation : NATURAL, GENUINE — **un·af·fect·ed·ly** *adv*

un·alien·able \-ˈāl-yə-nə-bəl, -ˈā-lē-ə-\ *adj* : INALIENABLE

un·aligned \ˌən-əl-ˈīnd\ *adj* : not associated with any one of competing international blocs ⟨~ nations⟩

un·al·loyed \ˌən-əl-ˈȯid\ *adj* : UNMIXED, UNQUALIFIED, PURE ⟨~ metals⟩

un–Amer·i·can \ˌən-ə-ˈmer-ə-kən\ *adj* : not characteristic of or consistent with American customs, principles, or traditions

unan·i·mous \yu̇-ˈnan-ə-məs\ *adj* [L *unanimus*, fr. *unus* one + *animus* mind] **1** : being of one mind : AGREEING **2** : formed with or indicating the agreement of all — **una·nim·i·ty** \yü-nə-ˈnim-ət-ē\ *n* — **unan·i·mous·ly** \yu̇-ˈnan-ə-məs-lē\ *adv*

un·arm \ˌən-ˈärm, ˈən-\ *vb* : DISARM

un·armed \-ˈärmd\ *adj* : not armed or armored

un·as·sail·able \ˌən-ə-ˈsā-lə-bəl\ *adj* : not assailable : not liable to doubt, attack, or question

un·as·sum·ing \ˌən-ə-ˈsü-miŋ\ *adj* : MODEST, RETIRING

un·at·tached \ˌən-ə-ˈtacht\ *adj* **1** : not married or engaged **2** : not joined or united

un·avail·ing \ˌən-ə-ˈvā-liŋ\ *adj* : being of no avail — **un·avail·ing·ly** *adv*

un·avoid·able \ˌən-ə-ˈvȯid-ə-bəl\ *adj* : not avoidable : INEVITABLE — **un·avoid·ably** \-blē\ *adv*

[1]un·aware \ˌən-ə-ˈwaər\ *adv* : UNAWARES

[2]unaware *adj* : not aware : IGNORANT — **un·aware·ness** *n*

un·awares \-ˈwaərz\ *adv* **1** : without knowing : UNINTENTIONALLY **2** : without warning : by surprise ⟨taken ~⟩

un·bal·anced \ˌən-ˈbal-ənst\ *adj* **1** : not equally poised or balanced **2** : mentally disordered **3** : not adjusted so as to make credits equal to debits

un·bar \-ˈbär\ *vb* : UNBOLT, OPEN

un·bear·able \ˌən-ˈbar-ə-bəl\ *adj* : greater than can be borne ⟨~ pain⟩ — **un·bear·ably** \-blē\ *adv*

un·beat·able \-ˈbēt-ə-bəl\ *adj* : not capable of being defeated

un·beat·en \-ˈbēt-ən\ *adj* **1** : not pounded, beaten, or whipped **2** : UNTROD **3** : UNDEFEATED

un·be·com·ing \ˌən-bi-ˈkəm-iŋ\ *adj* : not becoming : UNSUITABLE, IMPROPER — **un·be·com·ing·ly** *adv*

un·be·knownst \ˌən-bi-ˈnōnst\ *also* **un·be·known** \-ˈnōn\ *adj* : happening without one's knowledge

un·be·lief \ˌən-bə-ˈlēf\ *n* : the withholding or absence of belief : DOUBT — **un·be·liev·ing** \-ˈlē-viŋ\ *adj*

un·be·liev·able \-ˈlē-və-bəl\ *adj* : too improbable for belief : INCREDIBLE — **un·be·liev·ably** \-blē\ *adv*

un·be·liev·er \-ˈlē-vər\ *n* **1** : DOUBTER **2** : INFIDEL

un·bend \-ˈbend\ *vb* **-bent** \-ˈbent\; **-bend·ing** **1** : to free from being bent : make or become straight **2** : UNTIE **3** : to make or become less stiff or more affable : RELAX

un·bend·ing \-ˈben-diŋ\ *adj* : formal and distant in manner : INFLEXIBLE

un·bi·ased \ˌən-ˈbī-əst, ˈən-\ *adj* : free from bias; *esp* : UNPREJUDICED

un·bid·den \-ˈbid-ən\ *also* **un·bid** \-ˈbid\ *adj* : not bidden : UNASKED

un·bind \-ˈbīnd\ *vb* **-bound** \-ˈbau̇nd\; **-bind·ing** **1** : to remove bindings from : UNTIE **2** : RELEASE

un·blessed *also* **un·blest** \ˌən-ˈblest, ˈən-\ *adj* **1** : not blessed **2** : EVIL

un·block \-ˈbläk\ *vb* : to free from being blocked

un·blush·ing \-ˈbləsh-iŋ\ *adj* **1** : not blushing **2** : SHAMELESS — **un·blush·ing·ly** *adv*

un·bod·ied \-ˈbäd-ēd\ *adj* **1** : having no body; *also* : DISEMBODIED **2** : FORMLESS

un·bolt \ˌən-ˈbōlt, ˈən-\ *vb* : to open or unfasten by withdrawing a bolt

un·bolt·ed \-ˈbōl-təd\ *adj* : not fastened by bolts

un·born \-ˈbȯrn\ *adj* : not yet born

un·bo·som \-ˈbu̇z-əm, -ˈbüz-\ *vb* **1** : DISCLOSE, REVEAL ⟨~*ed* his secrets⟩ **2** : to disclose the thoughts or feelings of oneself

un·bound·ed \-ˈbau̇n-dəd\ *adj* : having no bounds or limits ⟨~ enthusiasm⟩

un·bowed \ˌən-ˈbau̇d, ˈən-\ *adj* **1** : not bowed down **2** : UNSUBDUED

un·bri·dled \-ˈbrīd-əld\ *adj* **1** : UNRESTRAINED **2** : not confined by a bridle

un·bro·ken \-ˈbrō-kən\ *adj* **1** : not damaged **2** : not subdued or tamed **3** : not interrupted : CONTINUOUS

un·buck·le \-ˈbək-əl\ *vb* : to loose the buckle of : UNFASTEN ⟨~ a belt⟩

un·bur·den \-ˈbərd-ən\ *vb* **1** : to free or relieve from a burden **2** : to relieve oneself of (as cares or worries) : cast off

un·but·ton \-ˈbət-ən\ *vb* : to unfasten the buttons of ⟨~ your coat⟩

un·called–for \ˌən-ˈkȯld-ˌfȯr\ *adj* : not called for, needed, or wanted

un·can·ny \-ˈkan-ē\ *adj* **1** : GHOSTLY, MYSTERIOUS, EERIE **2** : suggesting superhuman or supernatural powers — **un·can·ni·ly** \-ˈkan-əl-ē\ *adv*

un·ceas·ing \-ˈsē-siŋ\ *adj* : never ceasing — **un·ceas·ing·ly** *adv*

un·cer·e·mo·ni·ous \ˌən-ˌser-ə-ˈmō-nē-əs\ *adj* : acting

---

without or lacking ordinary courtesy : ABRUPT — **un·cer·e·mo·ni·ous·ly** *adv*

un·cer·tain \ˌən-ˈsərt-ᵊn, ˈən-\ *adj* **1** : not determined or fixed ⟨an ~ quantity⟩ **2** : subject to chance or change : not dependable **3** : not definitely known **4** : not sure ⟨~ of the truth⟩ — **un·cer·tain·ly** *adv*

un·cer·tain·ty \-ᵊn-tē\ *n* **1** : lack of certainty : DOUBT **2** : something that is uncertain

un·chain \ˌən-ˈchān, ˈən-\ *vb* : to free by or as if by removing a chain

un·charged \ˌən-ˈchärjd\ *adj* : having no electrical charge

un·char·i·ta·ble \-ˈchar-ət-ə-bəl\ *adj* : not charitable; *esp* : severe in judging others — **un·char·i·ta·ble·ness** *n* — **un·char·i·ta·bly** \-blē\ *adv*

un·chart·ed \-ˈchärt-əd\ *adj* **1** : not recorded on a map, chart, or plan **2** : UNKNOWN

un·chaste \-ˈchāst\ *adj* : not chaste — **un·chaste·ly** *adv* — **un·chaste·ness** \-ˈchās(t)-nəs\ *n* — **un·chas·ti·ty** \-ˈchas-tət-ē\ *n*

un·chris·tian \-ˈkris-chən\ *adj* **1** : not of the Christian faith **2** : contrary to the Christian spirit

un·churched \-ˈchərcht\ *adj* : not belonging to or connected with a church

un·cial \ˈən-shəl, -chəl; ˈən-sē-əl\ *adj* [L *uncialis* inch-high, fr. *uncia* twelfth part, ounce, inch] : relating to or written in a form of script with rounded letters used esp. in early Greek and Latin manuscripts — **uncial** *n*

un·cir·cu·lat·ed \ˌən-ˈsər-kyə-ˌlāt-əd\ *adj* : issued for use as money but kept out of circulation

un·cir·cum·cised \ˌən-ˈsər-kəm-ˌsīzd, ˈən-\ *adj* : not circumcised; *also* : HEATHEN

un·civ·il \ˌən-ˈsiv-əl, ˈən-\ *adj* **1** : not civilized : BARBAROUS **2** : DISCOURTEOUS, ILL-MANNERED, IMPOLITE

un·civ·i·lized \-ˈsiv-ə-ˌlīzd\ *adj* **1** : not civilized : BARBAROUS **2** : remote from civilization : WILD

un·clasp \-ˈklasp\ *vb* : to open by or as if by loosing the clasp

un·cle \ˈəŋ-kəl\ *n* [ME, fr. OF, fr. L *avunculus* mother's brother] : the brother of one's father or mother; *also* : the husband of one's aunt

un·clean \ˌən-ˈklēn, ˈən-\ *adj* **1** : morally or spiritually impure **2** : prohibited by ritual law for use or contact **3** : DIRTY, FILTHY — **un·clean·ness** \-ˈklēn-nəs\ *n*

un·clean·ly \-ˈklen-lē\ *adj* : morally or physically unclean — **un·clean·li·ness** \-lē-nəs\ *n*

un·clench \-ˈklench\ *vb* : to open from a clenched position : RELAX

Uncle Tom \ˌəŋ-kəl-ˈtäm\ *n* [fr. *Uncle Tom*, faithful Negro slave in Harriet Beecher Stowe's novel *Uncle Tom's Cabin* (1851-52)] : a black who is overeager to win the approval of whites

un·cloak \ˌən-ˈklōk, ˈən-\ *vb* **1** : to remove a cloak or cover from **2** : UNMASK, REVEAL

un·clog \-ˈkläg\ *vb* : to remove an obstruction from

un·close \-ˈklōz\ *vb* : OPEN — **un·closed** \-ˈklōzd\ *adj*

un·clothe \-ˈklōth\ *vb* : to strip of clothes or a covering — **un·clothed** \-ˈklōthd\ *adj*

un·coil \ˌən-ˈkȯil, ˈən-\ *vb* : to release or become released from a coiled state

un·com·fort·able \ˌən-ˈkəm(p)f-tə-bəl, ˈən-, -ˈkəm(p)-fərt-ə-\ *adj* **1** : causing discomfort **2** : feeling discomfort : UNEASY — **un·com·fort·ably** \-blē\ *adv*

un·com·mit·ted \ˌən-kə-ˈmit-əd\ *adj* : not committed; *esp* : not pledged to a particular belief, allegiance, or program

un·com·mon \ˌən-ˈkäm-ən, ˈən-\ *adj* **1** : not ordinarily encountered : UNUSUAL, RARE **2** : REMARKABLE, EXCEPTIONAL — **un·com·mon·ly** *adv*

un·com·mu·ni·ca·tive \ˌən-kə-ˈmyü-nə-ˌkāt-iv, -ni-kət-\ *adj* : not inclined to talk or impart information : RESERVED

un·com·pro·mis·ing \ˈən-ˈkäm-prə-ˌmī-ziŋ\ *adj* : not making or accepting a compromise : UNYIELDING

un·con·cern \ˌən-kən-ˈsərn\ *n* **1** : lack of care or interest : INDIFFERENCE **2** : freedom from excessive concern or anxiety

un·con·cerned \-ˈsərnd\ *adj* **1** : not having any part or interest **2** : not anxious or upset : free of worry — **un·con·cern·ed·ly** \-ˈsər-nəd-lē\ *adv*

un·con·di·tion·al \ˌən-kən-ˈdish-(ə-)nəl\ *adj* : not limited in any way — **un·con·di·tion·al·ly** \-ē\ *adv*

un·con·di·tioned \-ˈdish-ənd\ *adj* **1** : not subject to conditions **2** : not acquired or learned : INHERENT, NATURAL **3** : producing an unconditioned response ⟨~ stimuli⟩

un·con·quer·able \ˌən-ˈkäŋ-k(ə-)rə-bəl, ˈən-\ *adj* : incapable of being conquered or overcome : INDOMITABLE

un·con·scio·na·ble \-ˈkänch-(ə-)nə-bəl\ *adj* **1** : not guided or controlled by conscience **2** : not in accordance with what is right or just — **un·con·scio·na·bly** \-blē\ *adv*

[1]**un·con·scious** \ˌən-ˈkän-chəs, ˈən-\ *adj* **1** : deprived of consciousness or awareness **2** : not realized by oneself : not consciously done **3** : of or relating to the unconscious — **un·con·scious·ly** *adv* — **un·con·scious·ness** *n*

[2]**unconscious** *n* : the part of one's mental life of which one is not ordinarily aware and which is revealed esp. in spontaneous behavior (as slips of the tongue) or in dreams

un·con·sti·tu·tion·al \ˌən-ˌkän-stə-ˈt(y)üsh-(ə-)nəl\ *adj* : not according to or consistent with the constitution of a state or society — **un·con·sti·tu·tion·al·i·ty** \-t(y)ü-shə-ˈnal-ət-ē\ *n* — **un·con·sti·tu·tion·al·ly** \-ˈt(y)üsh-(ə-)nə-lē\ *adv*

un·con·trol·la·ble \ˌən-kən-ˈtrō-lə-bəl\ *adj* : incapable of being controlled : UNGOVERNABLE — **un·con·trol·la·bly** \-blē\ *adv*

un·con·ven·tion·al \-ˈvench-(ə-)nəl\ *adj* : not conventional : being out of the ordinary — **un·con·ven·tion·al·i·ty** \-ˌven-chə-ˈnal-ət-ē\ *n* — **un·con·ven·tion·al·ly** \-ˈvench-(ə-)nə-lē\ *adv*

un·cork \ˌən-ˈkȯrk, ˈən-\ *vb* **1** : to draw a cork from **2** : to release from a sealed or pent-up state; *also* : to let go

un·count·ed \-ˈkaunt-əd\ *adj* **1** : not counted **2** : INNUMERABLE

un·cou·ple \-ˈkəp-əl\ *vb* : DISCONNECT

un·couth \-ˈküth\ *adj* [OE *uncūth* unknown, unfamiliar, fr. *un-* + *cūth* known] **1** : strange, awkward, and clumsy in shape or appearance **2** : vulgar in conduct or speech : RUDE

un·cov·er \-ˈkəv-ər\ *vb* **1** : to make known : DISCLOSE, REVEAL **2** : to expose to view by removing some covering **3** : to take the cover from **4** : to remove the hat from; *also* : to take off the hat as a token of respect — **un·covered** \-ərd\ *adj*

un·crit·i·cal \ˌən-ˈkrit-i-kəl, ˈən-\ *adj* **1** : not critical : lacking in discrimination **2** : showing lack or improper use of critical standards or procedures

un·cross \-ˈkrȯs\ *vb* : to change from a crossed position ⟨~*ed* his legs⟩

unc·tion \ˈəŋk-shən\ *n* **1** : the act of anointing as a rite of consecration or healing **2** : exaggerated, assumed, or superficial earnestness of language or manner

unc·tu·ous \ˈəŋk-chə(-wə)s\ *adj* [ME, fr. MF or ML; MF *unctueux*, fr. ML *unctuosus*, fr. L *unctum* ointment, fr. *unguere* to anoint] **1** : FATTY, OILY **2** : full of unction in speech and manner; *esp* : insincerely smooth — **unc·tu·ous·ly** *adv*

un·curl \ˌən-ˈkərl, ˈən-\ *vb* : to make or become straightened out from a curled or coiled position

un·cut \ˌən-ˈkət, ˈən-\ *adj* **1** : not cut down or into **2** : not shaped by cutting ⟨an ~ diamond⟩ **3** : not having the folds of the leaves slit ⟨an ~ book⟩ **4** : not abridged or curtailed

un·daunt·ed \-ˈdȯnt-əd\ *adj* : not daunted : not discouraged or dismayed — **un·daunt·ed·ly** *adv*

un·de·ceive \ˌən-di-ˈsēv\ *vb* : to free from deception, illusion, or error

un·de·mon·stra·tive \ˌən-di-ˈmän-strət-iv\ *adj* : restrained in expression of feeling : RESERVED
un·de·ni·able \ˌən-di-ˈnī-ə-bəl\ *adj* **1** : plainly true : INCONTESTABLE **2** : unquestionably excellent or genuine — **un·de·ni·ably** \-blē\ *adv*
[1]**un·der** \ˈən-dər\ *adv* **1** : in or into a position below or beneath something **2** : below some quantity, level, or norm ⟨$10 or ~⟩ **3** : in or into a condition of subjection, subordination, or unconsciousness ⟨the ether put him ~⟩
[2]**un·der** \ˌən-dər, ˈən-\ *prep* **1** : lower than and overhung, surmounted, or sheltered by ⟨~ a tree⟩ **2** : subject to the authority or guidance of ⟨served ~ him⟩ ⟨had the man ~ contract⟩ **3** : subject to the action or effect of ⟨~ an anesthetic⟩ **4** : within the division or grouping of ⟨items ~ this head⟩ **5** : less or lower than (as in size, amount, or rank) ⟨makes ~ $5000⟩
[3]**under** \ˈən-dər\ *adj* **1** : lying below, beneath, or on the ventral side **2** : facing or protruding downward **3** : SUBORDINATE **4** : lower than usual, proper, or desired in amount, quality, or degree
un·der·achiev·er \ˌən-dər-ə-ˈchē-vər\ *n* : one who performs below an expected level of proficiency
un·der·act \-ˈakt\ *vb* : to perform feebly or with restraint
un·der·ac·tive \-ˈak-tiv\ *adj* : characterized by abnormally low activity ⟨~ glands⟩ — **un·der·ac·tiv·i·ty** \-ˌak-ˈtiv-ət-ē\ *n*
un·der·age \-ˈāj\ *adj* : of less than mature or legal age
un·der·arm \-ˈärm\ *adj* **1** : UNDERHAND 2 ⟨an ~ throw⟩ **2** : placed under or on the underside of the arms ⟨~ seams⟩ — **underarm** *adv or n*
un·der·bel·ly \ˈən-dər-ˌbel-ē\ *n* **1** : the underside of a body or mass **2** : a vulnerable area
un·der·bid \ˌən-dər-ˈbid\ *vb* **-bid; -bid·ding 1** : to bid less than another **2** : to bid too low
un·der·body \ˈən-dər-ˌbäd-ē\ *n* : the lower parts of the body of a vehicle
un·der·bred \ˌən-dər-ˈbred\ *adj* : marked by lack of good breeding
un·der·brush \ˈən-dər-ˌbrəsh\ *n* : shrubs and small trees growing beneath large trees
un·der·car·riage \-ˌkar-ij\ *n* **1** : a supporting framework (as of an automobile) **2** : the landing gear of an airplane

1 undercarriage 2

un·der·charge \ˌən-dər-ˈchärj\ *vb* : to charge (as a person) too little — **undercharge** \ˈən-dər-ˌchärj\ *n*
un·der·class·man \ˌən-dər-ˈklas-mən\ *n* : a member of the freshman or sophomore class
un·der·clothes \ˈən-dər-ˌklō(th)z\ *n pl* : UNDERWEAR
un·der·cloth·ing \-ˌklō-thiŋ\ *n* : UNDERWEAR
un·der·coat \-ˌkōt\ *n* **1** : a coat worn under another **2** : a growth of short hair or fur partly concealed by a longer growth ⟨a dog's ~⟩ **3** : a coat of paint under another
un·der·coat·ing \-ˌkōt-iŋ\ *n* : a special waterproof coating applied to the underside of a vehicle
un·der·cov·er \ˌən-dər-ˈkəv-ər\ *adj* : acting or executed in secret; *esp* : employed or engaged in secret investigation ⟨~ agent⟩
un·der·croft \ˈən-dər-ˌkrȯft\ *n* [ME, fr. *under* + *crofte* crypt, fr. Middle Dutch, fr. ML *crupta*, fr. L *crypta*] : a vaulted chamber under a church
un·der·cur·rent \-ˌkər-ənt\ *n* **1** : a current below the surface **2** : a hidden tendency of feeling or opinion
un·der·cut \ˌən-dər-ˈkət\ *vb* **-cut; -cut·ting 1** : to cut away the underpart of **2** : to offer to sell or to work at a lower rate than **3** : to strike (the ball) obliquely downward so as to give a backward spin or elevation to the shot — **un·der·cut** \ˈən-dər-ˌkət\ *n*
un·der·de·vel·oped \ˌən-dər-di-ˈvel-əpt\ *adj* **1** : not normally or adequately developed ⟨~ muscles⟩ **2** : having a relatively low level of economic development ⟨the ~ nations⟩
un·der·dog \ˈən-dər-ˌdȯg\ *n* **1** : the loser or predicted loser in a struggle **2** : a victim of injustice or persecution
un·der·done \ˌən-dər-ˈdən\ *adj* : not thoroughly done or cooked : RARE
un·der·draw·ers \ˈən-dər-ˌdrȯ(-ə)rz\ *n pl* : UNDERPANTS
un·der·em·pha·size \ˌən-dər-ˈem-fə-sīz\ *vb* : to emphasize inadequately — **un·der·em·pha·sis** \-səs\ *n*
un·der·em·ployed \-im-ˈplȯid\ *adj* : having less than full-time or adequate employment
un·der·es·ti·mate \-ˈes-tə-ˌmāt\ *vb* : to set too low a value on
un·der·ex·pose \-ik-ˈspōz\ *vb* : to expose (a photographic plate or film) for less time than is needed — **un·der·ex·po·sure** \-ˈspō-zhər\ *n*
un·der·feed \ˌən-dər-ˈfēd\ *vb* **-fed** \-ˈfed\; **-feed·ing** : to feed inadequately
un·der·foot \-ˈfu̇t\ *adv* **1** : under the feet ⟨flowers trampled ~⟩ **2** : close about one's feet : in the way
un·der·fur \ˈən-dər-ˌfər\ *n* : the thick soft undercoat of fur lying beneath the longer and coarser hair of a mammal
un·der·gar·ment \-ˌgär-mənt\ *n* : a garment to be worn under another
un·der·gird \ˌən-dər-ˈgərd\ *vb* **1** : to make secure underneath **2** : to brace up : STRENGTHEN
un·der·go \ˌən-dər-ˈgō\ *vb* **-went** \-ˈwent\; **-gone** \-ˈgȯn, -ˈgän\; **-go·ing** \-ˈgō-iŋ, -ˈgȯ(-)iŋ\ **1** : to be subjected to : ENDURE **2** : to pass through : EXPERIENCE
un·der·grad·u·ate \ˌən-dər-ˈgraj-(ə-)wət, -ə-ˌwāt\ *n* : a student at a university or college who has not taken a first degree
[1]**un·der·ground** \ˌən-dər-ˈgrau̇nd\ *adv* **1** : beneath the surface of the earth **2** : in secret
[2]**un·der·ground** \ˈən-dər-ˌgrau̇nd\ *n* **1** : a space under the surface of the ground; *esp* : SUBWAY **2** : a secret political movement or group; *esp* : an organized body working in secret to overthrow a government or an occupying power **3** : an avant-garde group or movement that operates outside the establishment
[3]**underground** \ˈən-dər-ˌgrau̇nd\ *adj* **1** : being or growing under the surface of the ground ⟨~ stems⟩ **2** : conducted by secret means **3** : produced or published outside the establishment esp. by the avant-garde ⟨~ movies⟩; *also* : of or relating to the avant-garde underground
un·der·growth \ˈən-dər-ˌgrōth\ *n* : low growth (as of herbs and shrubs) on the floor of a forest
[1]**un·der·hand** \ˈən-dər-ˌhand\ *adv* **1** : in an underhanded or secret manner **2** : with an underhand motion
[2]**underhand** *adj* **1** : UNDERHANDED **2** : made with the hand kept below the level of the shoulder
[1]**un·der·hand·ed** \ˌən-dər-ˈhan-dəd\ *adv* : UNDERHAND
[2]**underhanded** *adj* : marked by secrecy and deception — **un·der·hand·ed·ly** *adv* — **un·der·hand·ed·ness** *n*
un·der·lie \-ˈlī\ *vb* **-lay** \-ˈlā\; **-lain** \-ˈlān\; **-ly·ing** \-ˈlī-iŋ\ **1** : to lie or be situated under **2** : to be at the basis of : form the foundation of : SUPPORT
un·der·line \ˈən-dər-ˌlīn\ *vb* **1** : to draw a line under **2** : EMPHASIZE, STRESS — **underline** *n*

un·der·ling \ˈən-dər-liŋ\ *n* : SUBORDINATE, INFERIOR
un·der·lip \ˌən-dər-ˈlip\ *n* : the lower lip
un·der·ly·ing \ˌən-dər-ˌlī-iŋ\ *adj* **1** : lying under or below **2** : FUNDAMENTAL, BASIC ⟨~ principles⟩
un·der·mine \-ˈmīn\ *vb* **1** : to excavate beneath **2** : to weaken or wear away secretly or gradually
un·der·most \ˈən-dər-ˌmōst\ *adj* : lowest in relative position — **undermost** *adv*
[1]**un·der·neath** \ˌən-dər-ˈnēth\ *prep* **1** : directly under **2** : under subjection to
[2]**underneath** *adv* **1** : below a surface or object : BENEATH **2** : on the lower side
un·der·nour·ished \ˌən-dər-ˈnər-isht\ *adj* : supplied with insufficient nourishment — **un·der·nour·ish·ment** \-ˈnər-ish-mənt\ *n*
un·der·pants \ˈən-dər-ˌpants\ *n pl* : short or long pants worn under an outer garment : DRAWERS
un·der·part \-ˌpärt\ *n* **1** : a part lying on the lower side esp. of a bird or mammal **2** : a subordinate or auxiliary part or role
un·der·pass \-ˌpas\ *n* : a passage underneath something ⟨a railroad ~⟩
un·der·pay \ˌən-dər-ˈpā\ *vb* : to pay too little
un·der·pin·ning \ˈən-dər-ˌpin-iŋ\ *n* : the material and construction (as a foundation) used for support of a structure — **un·der·pin** \ˌən-dər-ˈpin\ *vb*
un·der·play \ˌən-dər-ˈplā\ *vb* : to treat or handle with restraint; *esp* : to play a role with subdued force
un·der·pop·u·lat·ed \ˌən-dər-ˈpäp-yə-ˌlāt-əd\ *adj* : having a lower than normal or desirable density of population
un·der·priv·i·leged \-ˈpriv-(ə-)lijd\ *adj* : having fewer esp. economic and social privileges than others
un·der·pro·duc·tion \ˌən-dər-prə-ˈdək-shən\ *n* : the production of less than enough to satisfy the demand or of less than the usual supply
un·der·rate \ˌən-də(r)-ˈrāt\ *vb* : to rate or value too low
un·der·rep·re·sent·ed \-ˌrep-ri-ˈzent-əd\ *adj* : inadequately represented
un·der·score \ˈən-dər-ˌskōr\ *vb* **1** : to draw a line under : UNDERLINE **2** : EMPHASIZE — **underscore** *n*
[1]**un·der·sea** \ˌən-dər-ˌsē\ *adj* : being, carried on, or used beneath the surface of the sea
[2]**un·der·sea** \ˌən-dər-ˈsē\ *or* **un·der·seas** \-ˈsēz\ *adv* : beneath the surface of the sea
under secretary *n* : a secretary immediately subordinate to a principal secretary ⟨~ of state⟩
un·der·sell \-ˈsel\ *vb* **-sold** \-ˈsōld\; **-sell·ing** : to sell articles cheaper than
un·der·sexed \-ˈsekst\ *adj* : deficient in sexual desire
un·der·shirt \ˈən-dər-ˌshərt\ *n* : a collarless undergarment with or without sleeves
un·der·shoot \ˌən-dər-ˈshüt\ *vb* **-shot** \-ˈshät\; **-shoot·ing** **1** : to shoot short of or below (a target) **2** : to fall short of (a runway) in landing an airplane
un·der·shorts \ˈən-dər-ˌshȯrts\ *n pl* : SHORT 2
un·der·shot \ˌən-dər-ˌshät\ *adj* **1** : having the lower front teeth projecting beyond the upper when the mouth is closed **2** : moved by water passing beneath ⟨an ~ waterwheel⟩
un·der·side \ˈən-dər-ˌsīd, ˌən-dər-ˈsīd\ *n* : the side or surface lying underneath
un·der·signed \ˈən-dər-ˌsīnd\ *n, pl* **undersigned** : one who signs his name at the end of a document
un·der·sized \ˌən-dər-ˈsīzd\ *also* **un·der·size** \-ˈsīz\ *adj* : of a size less than is common, proper, or normal
un·der·skirt \ˈən-dər-ˌskərt\ *n* : a skirt worn under an outer skirt; *esp* : PETTICOAT
un·der·slung \ˌən-dər-ˈsləŋ\ *adj* : suspended so as to extend below the axles ⟨an ~ automobile frame⟩
un·der·stand \ˌən-dər-ˈstand\ *vb* **-stood** \-ˈstu̇d\; **-stand·ing** **1** : to grasp the meaning of : COMPREHEND **2** : to have thorough or technical acquaintance with or expertness in ⟨~ finance⟩ **3** : GATHER, INFER ⟨I ~ that you spread this rumor⟩ **4** : INTERPRET ⟨we ~ this to be a refusal⟩ **5** : to have a sympathetic attitude **6** : to accept as settled ⟨it is *understood* that he will pay the expenses⟩ — **un·der·stand·able** \-ˈstan-də-bəl\ *adj* — **un·der·stand·ably** \-blē\ *adv*
[1]**un·der·stand·ing** \ˌən-dər-ˈstan-diŋ\ *n* **1** : knowledge and ability to apply judgment : INTELLIGENCE **2** : ability to comprehend and judge ⟨a man of ~⟩ **3** : agreement of opinion or feeling **4** : a mutual agreement informally or tacitly entered into
[2]**understanding** *adj* : endowed with understanding : TOLERANT, SYMPATHETIC
un·der·state \ˌən-dər-ˈstāt\ *vb* **1** : to represent as less than is the case **2** : to state with restraint esp. for greater effect — **un·der·state·ment** *n*
un·der·stood \ˌən-dər-ˈstu̇d\ *adj* **1** : agreed upon **2** : IMPLICIT
un·der·sto·ry \ˈən-dər-ˌstōr-ē, -ˌstȯr-\ *n* : the plants of a forest undergrowth
un·der·study \ˈən-dər-ˌstəd-ē, ˌən-dər-ˈstəd-ē\ *vb* : to study another actor's part in order to be his substitute in an emergency — **understudy** \ˈən-dər-ˌstəd-ē\ *n*
un·der·sur·face \ˈən-dər-ˌsər-fəs\ *n* : UNDERSIDE
un·der·take \ˌən-dər-ˈtāk\ *vb* **-took** \-ˈtu̇k\; **-tak·en** \-ˈtā-kən\; **-tak·ing** **1** : to take upon oneself as a task : set about **2** : to put oneself under obligation **3** : GUARANTEE, PROMISE
un·der·tak·er \ˈən-dər-ˌtā-kər\ *n* : one whose business is to prepare the dead for burial and to take charge of funerals
un·der·tak·ing \ˈən-dər-ˌtā-kiŋ, ˌən-dər-ˈtā-kiŋ; *2 is* ˈən-dər-ˌtā-kiŋ *only*\ *n* **1** : the act of one who undertakes or engages in any project **2** : the business of an undertaker **3** : something undertaken **4** : PROMISE, GUARANTEE
under–the–counter *adj* : UNLAWFUL, ILLICIT ⟨~ sale of drugs⟩
un·der·tone \ˈən-dər-ˌtōn\ *n* **1** : a low or subdued tone or utterance **2** : a subdued color (as seen through and modifying another color)
un·der·tow \-ˌtō\ *n* : the current beneath the surface that sets seaward when waves are breaking upon the shore
un·der·trick \-ˌtrik\ *n* : a trick by which a declarer in bridge falls short of making his contract
un·der·val·ue \ˌən-dər-ˈval-yü\ *vb* **1** : to value or estimate below the real worth **2** : to esteem lightly
un·der·wa·ter \ˌən-dər-ˌwȯt-ər, -ˌwät-\ *adj* : lying, growing, worn, or operating below the surface of the water — **un·der·wa·ter** \-ˈwȯt-, -ˈwät-\ *adv*
under way \-ˈwā\ *adv* **1** : into motion from a standstill **2** : in progress
un·der·wear \ˈən-dər-ˌwa(ə)r\ *n* : clothing or a garment worn next to the skin and under other clothing
un·der·weight \ˌən-dər-ˈwāt\ *n* : weight below what is normal, average, or necessary — **underweight** *adj*
un·der·wood \ˈən-dər-ˌwu̇d\ *n* : UNDERBRUSH, UNDERGROWTH
un·der·world \-ˌwərld\ *n* **1** : the place of departed souls : HADES **2** : a social sphere below the level of ordinary life; *esp* : the world of organized crime
un·der·write \ˈən-də(r)-ˌrīt, ˌən-də(r)-ˈrīt\ *vb* **-wrote** \-ˌrōt, -ˈrōt\; **-writ·ten** \-ˌrit-ᵊn, -ˈrit-ᵊn\; **-writ·ing** \-ˌrīt-iŋ, -ˈrīt-\ **1** : to write under or at the end of something else **2** : to set one's name to an insurance policy and thereby become answerable for a designated loss or damage **3** : to subscribe to : agree to **4** : to agree to purchase (as bonds) usu. on a fixed date at a fixed price; *also* : to guarantee financial support of — **un·der·writ·er** *n*
un·de·sign·ing \ˌən-di-ˈzī-niŋ\ *adj* : having no artful, ulterior, or fraudulent purpose : SINCERE

un·de·sir·able \-ˈzī-rə-bəl\ *adj* : not desirable — **unde-sirable** *n*

un·de·vi·at·ing \ˌən-ˈdē-vē-ˌāt-iŋ, ˈən-\ *adj* : keeping a true course

un·dies \ˈən-dēz\ *n pl* : UNDERWEAR; *esp* : women's underwear

un·do \ˌən-ˈdü, ˈən-\ *vb* **-did** \-ˈdid\; **-done** \-ˈdən\; **-do·ing** \-ˈdü-iŋ\ **1** : to make or become unfastened or loosened : OPEN **2** : to make null or as if not done : REVERSE **3** : to bring to ruin; *also* : UPSET

un·do·ing \-ˈdü-iŋ\ *n* **1** : LOOSING, UNFASTENING **2** : RUIN; *also* : a cause of ruin **3** : REVERSAL

un·doubt·ed \-ˈdau̇t-əd\ *adj* : not doubted or called into question : CERTAIN — **un·doubt·ed·ly** *adv*

[1]**un·dress** \ˌən-ˈdres, ˈən-\ *vb* : to remove the clothes or covering of : STRIP, DISROBE

[2]**undress** *n* **1** : informal dress; *esp* : a loose robe or dressing gown **2** : ordinary dress **3** : NUDITY

un·due \-ˈd(y)ü\ *adj* **1** : not due **2** : exceeding or violating propriety or fitness

un·du·lant \ˈən-jə-lənt, ˈən-d(y)ə-\ *adj* : UNDULATING

undulant fever *n* : a human disease caused by bacteria and marked by intermittent fever, pain and swelling in the joints, and great weakness

un·du·late \-ˌlāt\ *vb* **-lated; -lating** [LL *undula* small wave, fr. L *unda* wave] **1** : to have a wavelike motion or appearance **2** : to rise and fall in pitch or volume

un·du·la·tion \ˌən-jə-ˈlā-shən, ˌən-d(y)ə-\ *n* **1** : wavy or wavelike motion **2** : pulsation of sound **3** : a wavy appearance or outline — **un·du·la·to·ry** \ˈən-jə-lə-ˌtōr-ē, ˈən-d(y)ə-\ *adj*

un·du·ly \ˌən-ˈd(y)ü-lē, ˈən-\ *adv* : in an undue manner; *esp* : EXCESSIVELY

un·dy·ing \-ˈdī-iŋ\ *adj* : not dying : IMMORTAL, PERPETUAL

un·earned \-ˈərnd\ *adj* : not earned by labor, service, or skill ⟨~ income⟩

un·earth \ˌən-ˈərth, ˈən-\ *vb* **1** : to draw from the earth : dig up ⟨~ buried treasure⟩ **2** : to bring to light : DISCOVER ⟨~ a secret⟩

un·earth·ly \-lē\ *adj* **1** : not of or belonging to the earth **2** : SUPERNATURAL, WEIRD, TERRIFYING

un·easy \ˈən-ˈē-zē\ *adj* **1** : AWKWARD, EMBARRASSED ⟨~ among strangers⟩ **2** : disturbed by pain or worry; *also* : RESTLESS — **un·eas·i·ly** \-ˈē-zə-lē\ *adv* — **un·eas·i·ness** \-ˈē-zē-nəs\ *n*

un·em·ployed \ˌən-im-ˈplȯid\ *adj* : not employed; *esp* : not engaged in a gainful occupation

un·em·ploy·ment \-ˈplȯi-mənt\ *n* : lack of employment

un·end·ing \ˌən-ˈen-diŋ, ˈən-\ *adj* : having no ending : ENDLESS

un·equal \ˌən-ˈē-kwəl, ˈən-\ *adj* **1** : not alike (as in size, amount, number, or value) **2** : not uniform : VARIABLE **3** : badly balanced or matched **4** : INADEQUATE, INSUFFICIENT — **un·equal·ly** \-ē\ *adv*

un·equaled *or* **un·equalled** \-kwəld\ *adj* : not equaled : UNPARALLELED

un·equiv·o·cal \ˌən-i-ˈkwiv-ə-kəl\ *adj* : leaving no doubt : CLEAR — **un·equiv·o·cal·ly** \-ē\ *adv*

un·err·ing \ˌən-ˈe(ə)r-iŋ, ˌən-ˈər-\ *adj* : making no errors : CERTAIN, UNFAILING — **un·err·ing·ly** *adv*

UNES·CO \yu̇-ˈnes-kō\ *abbr* United Nations Educational, Scientific, and Cultural Organization

un·even \ˌən-ˈē-vən, ˈən-\ *adj* **1** : ODD 3 **2** : not even : not level or smooth : RUGGED, RAGGED **3** : IRREGULAR; *also* : varying in quality — **un·even·ly** *adv* — **un·even·ness** \-vən-nəs\ *n*

un·event·ful \ˌən-i-ˈvent-fəl\ *adj* : not eventful : lacking interesting or noteworthy incidents

un·ex·am·pled \ˌən-ig-ˈzam-pəld\ *adj* : UNPRECEDENTED, UNPARALLELED

un·ex·cep·tion·able \ˌən-ik-ˈsep-sh(ə-)nə-bəl\ *adj* : not open to exception or objection : beyond reproach

un·ex·pect·ed \ˌən-ik-ˈspek-təd\ *adj* : not expected : UNFORESEEN — **un·ex·pect·ed·ly** *adv*

un·fail·ing \ˌən-ˈfā-liŋ, ˈən-\ *adj* **1** : not failing, flagging, or waning : CONSTANT **2** : INEXHAUSTIBLE **3** : INFALLIBLE, SURE — **un·fail·ing·ly** *adv*

un·fair \-ˈfaər\ *adj* **1** : marked by injustice, partiality, or deception : UNJUST, DISHONEST **2** : not equitable in business dealings — **un·fair·ly** *adv* — **un·fair·ness** *n*

un·faith·ful \ˌən-ˈfāth-fəl, ˈən-\ *adj* **1** : not observant of vows, allegiance, or duty : DISLOYAL **2** : INACCURATE, UNTRUSTWORTHY — **un·faith·ful·ly** \-ē\ *adv* — **un·faith·ful·ness** *n*

un·fa·mil·iar \ˌən-fə-ˈmil-yər\ *adj* **1** : not well-known : STRANGE ⟨an ~ place⟩ **2** : not well acquainted ⟨~ with the subject⟩ — **un·fa·mil·iar·i·ty** \-ˌmil-ˈyar-ət-ē, -ˌmil-ē-ˈ(y)ar-\ *n*

un·fas·ten \ˌən-ˈfas-ᵊn, ˈən-\ *vb* : to make or become loose : UNDO, DETACH

un·fa·vor·able \ˌən-ˈfāv-(ə-)rə-bəl, ˈən-\ *adj* : not favorable — **un·fa·vor·ably** \-blē\ *adv*

un·feel·ing \-ˈfē-liŋ\ *adj* **1** : lacking feeling : INSENSATE **2** : HARDHEARTED, CRUEL — **un·feel·ing·ly** *adv*

un·feigned \-ˈfānd\ *adj* : not feigned : not hypocritical : GENUINE

un·fet·ter \-ˈfet-ər\ *vb* **1** : to free from fetters **2** : LIBERATE

un·fil·ial \ˌən-ˈfil-ē-əl, ˈən-, -ˈfil-yəl\ *adj* : not observing the obligations of a child to a parent : UNDUTIFUL

un·fin·ished \ˌən-ˈfin-isht\ *adj* **1** : not brought to an end **2** : being in a rough or unpolished state

[1]**un·fit** \-ˈfit\ *adj* : not fit or suitable; *esp* : physically or mentally unsound — **un·fit·ness** *n*

[2]**unfit** *vb* : DISABLE, DISQUALIFY

un·fix \-ˈfiks\ *vb* **1** : to loosen from a fastening : DETACH **2** : UNSETTLE

un·flap·pa·ble \-ˈflap-ə-bəl\ *adj* : not easily upset or panicked — **un·flap·pa·bly** *adv*

un·fledged \ˌən-ˈflejd\ *adj* : not feathered or ready for flight; *also* : IMMATURE, CALLOW

un·flinch·ing \-ˈflin-chiŋ\ *adj* : not flinching or shrinking : STEADFAST — **un·flinch·ing·ly** *adv*

un·fold \-ˈfōld\ *vb* **1** : to open the folds of : open up **2** : to lay open to view : DISCLOSE **3** : BLOSSOM, DEVELOP

un·for·get·ta·ble \ˌən-fər-ˈget-ə-bəl\ *adj* : not to be forgotten — **un·for·get·ta·bly** \-blē\ *adv*

un·formed \-ˈfȯrmd\ *adj* : not regularly formed : SHAPELESS

un·for·tu·nate \-ˈfȯrch-(ə-)nət\ *adj* **1** : not fortunate : UNLUCKY **2** : attended with misfortune **3** : UNSUITABLE — **unfortunate** *n* — **un·for·tu·nate·ly** *adv*

un·found·ed \ˌən-ˈfau̇n-dəd, ˈən-\ *adj* : lacking a sound basis : GROUNDLESS

un·freeze \-ˈfrēz\ *vb* **-froze** \-ˈfrōz\; **-fro·zen** \-ˈfrōz-ᵊn\; **-freez·ing** **1** : to cause to thaw **2** : to remove from a freeze ⟨~ prices⟩

un·fre·quent·ed \ˌən-frē-ˈkwent-əd; ˌən-ˈfrē-kwənt-, ˈən-\ *adj* : seldom visited or traveled over

un·friend·ly \ˌən-ˈfren-(d)lē, ˈən-\ *adj* **1** : not friendly or kind : HOSTILE **2** : UNFAVORABLE — **un·friend·li·ness** \-ˈfren-(d)lē-nəs\ *n*

un·frock \-ˈfräk\ *vb* : to deprive (as a priest) of the right to exercise the functions of his office

un·fruit·ful \-ˈfrüt-fəl\ *adj* **1** : not producing fruit or offspring : UNPRODUCTIVE **2** : yielding no desired or valuable result ⟨~ efforts⟩ — **un·fruit·ful·ness** *n*

un·furl \-ˈfərl\ *vb* : to loose from a furled state : UNFOLD

un·gain·ly \-ˈgān-lē\ *adj* [*un-* + *gainly* graceful, fr. *gain* direct, handy, fr. ME *geyn*, fr. OE *gēn*, fr. ON *gegn*] : CLUMSY, AWKWARD — **un·gain·li·ness** \-lē-nəs\ *n*

\ə\abut \ᵊ\kitten \ər\further \a\ash \ā\ace \ä\cot, cart \au̇\out \ch\chin \e\bet \ē\easy \g\go \i\hit \ī\ice \j\job \ŋ\sing \ō\go \ȯ\law \ȯi\boy \th\thin \t͟h\the \ü\loot \u̇\foot \y\yet \zh\vision *see also* Pronunciation Symbols page

un·gen·er·ous \ˌən-ˈjen-(ə-)rəs, ˈən-\ *adj* : not generous or liberal : STINGY

un·gird \-ˈgərd\ *vb* : to divest of a restraining band or girdle : UNBIND

un·glued \ˌən-ˈglüd\ *adj* : UPSET, DISORDERED

un·god·ly \ˌən-ˈgäd-lē, -ˈgȯd-; ˈən-\ *adj* **1** : IMPIOUS, IRRELIGIOUS **2** : SINFUL, WICKED **3** : OUTRAGEOUS — **un·god·li·ness** \-lē-nəs\ *n*

un·gov·ern·able \-ˈgəv-ər-nə-bəl\ *adj* : not capable of being governed, guided, or restrained : UNRULY

un·gra·cious \-ˈgrā-shəs\ *adj* **1** : not courteous : RUDE **2** : not pleasing : DISAGREEABLE

un·grate·ful \ˌən-ˈgrāt-fəl, ˈən-\ *adj* **1** : not thankful for favors **2** : not pleasing — **un·grate·ful·ly** \-ē\ *adv* — **un·grate·ful·ness** *n*

un·guard·ed \-ˈgärd-əd\ *adj* **1** : UNPROTECTED **2** : DIRECT, INCAUTIOUS

un·guent \ˈəŋ-gwənt, ˈən-\ *n* : a soothing or healing salve : OINTMENT

[1]**un·gu·late** \ˈəŋ-gyə-lət, ˈən-, -ˌlāt\ *adj* [LL *ungulatus,* fr. L *ungula* hoof, fr. *unguis* nail, hoof] : having hoofs

[2]**ungulate** *n* : a hoofed mammal (as a cow, horse, or rhinoceros)

Unh *symbol* unnilhexium

un·hal·lowed \ˌən-ˈhal-ōd, ˈən-\ *adj* **1** : not consecrated : UNHOLY **2** : IMPIOUS, PROFANE **3** : contrary to accepted standards : IMMORAL

un·hand \ˌən-ˈhand\ *vb* : to remove the hand from : let go

un·hand·some \-ˈhan-səm\ *adj* **1** : not beautiful or handsome : HOMELY **2** : UNBECOMING **3** : DISCOURTEOUS, RUDE

un·handy \-ˈhan-dē\ *adj* : INCONVENIENT; *also* : AWKWARD

un·hap·py \-ˈhap-ē\ *adj* **1** : UNLUCKY, UNFORTUNATE **2** : SAD, MISERABLE **3** : INAPPROPRIATE — **un·hap·pi·ly** \-ˈhap-ə-lē\ *adv* — **un·hap·pi·ness** \-ē-nəs\ *n*

un·har·ness \-ˈhär-nəs\ *vb* : to remove the harness from (as a horse)

un·healthy \-ˈhel-thē\ *adj* **1** : not conducive to health : UNWHOLESOME **2** : SICKLY, DISEASED

un·heard \-ˈhərd\ *adj* **1** : not heard **2** : not granted a hearing

un·heard–of \-ˌəv, -ˌäv\ *adj* : previously unknown : UNPRECEDENTED

un·hinge \ˌən-ˈhinj, ˈən-\ *vb* **1** : to take from the hinges **2** : to make unstable (as one's mind)

un·hitch \-ˈhich\ *vb* : UNFASTEN, LOOSE

un·ho·ly \-ˈhō-lē\ *adj* : not holy : PROFANE, WICKED — **un·ho·li·ness** \-lē-nəs\ *n*

un·hook \-ˈhu̇k\ *vb* : to loose from a hook

un·horse \-ˈhȯrs\ *vb* : to dislodge from or as if from a horse : UNSEAT

uni·ax·i·al \ˌyü-nē-ˈak-sē-əl\ *adj* : having only one axis

uni·cam·er·al \ˌyü-ni-kam-(ə-)rəl\ *adj* : having a single legislative house or chamber

UNI·CEF \ˈyü-nə-ˌsef\ *abbr* [*United Nations International Children's Emergency Fund,* its former name] United Nations Children's Fund

uni·cel·lu·lar \ˌyü-ni-ˈsel-yə-lər\ *adj* : of or having a single cell

uni·corn \ˈyü-nə-ˌkȯrn\ *n* [ME *unicorne,* fr. OF, fr. LL *unicornis,* fr. L, having one horn, fr. *unus* one + *cornu* horn] : a mythical animal with one horn in the middle of the forehead

uni·cy·cle \ˈyü-ni-ˌsī-kəl\ *n* : a vehicle that has a single wheel and is usu. propelled by pedals

uni·di·rec·tion·al \ˌyü-ni-də-ˈrek-sh(ə-)nəl, -dī-\ *adj* : having, moving in, or responsive in a single direction ⟨a ~ current⟩ ⟨a ~ microphone⟩

uni·fi·ca·tion \ˌyü-nə-fə-ˈkā-shən\ *n* : the act, process, or result of unifying : the state of being unified

[1]**uni·form** \ˈyü-nə-ˌfȯrm\ *adj* **1** : having always the same form, manner, or degree : not varying **2** : of the same form with others : conforming to one rule — **uni·form·ly** *adv*

[2]**uniform** *vb* : to clothe with a uniform

[3]**uniform** *n* : distinctive dress worn by members of a particular group (as an army or a police force)

uni·for·mi·ty \ˌyü-nə-ˈfȯr-mət-ē\ *n, pl* **-ties** : the state of being uniform

uni·fy \ˈyü-nə-ˌfī\ *vb* **-fied; -fy·ing** : to make into a unit or a coherent whole : UNITE

uni·lat·er·al \ˌyü-nə-ˈlat-(ə-)rəl\ *adj* : of, having, affecting, or done by one side only — **uni·lat·er·al·ly** \-ē\ *adv*

un·im·peach·able \ˌən-im-ˈpē-chə-bəl\ *adj* : exempt from liability to accusation : BLAMELESS; *also* : not doubtable ⟨an ~ authority⟩

un·in·hib·it·ed \ˌən-in-ˈhib-ət-əd\ *adj* : free from inhibition; *also* : boisterously informal — **un·in·hib·it·ed·ly** *adv*

un·in·tel·li·gent \-ˈtel-ə-jənt\ *adj* : lacking intelligence

un·in·tel·li·gi·ble \-jə-bəl\ *adj* : not intelligible : OBSCURE — **un·in·tel·li·gi·bly** \-blē\ *adv*

un·in·ten·tion·al \ˌən-in-ˈtench-(ə-)nəl\ *adj* : not intentional — **un·in·ten·tion·al·ly** \-ē\ *adv*

un·in·ter·est·ed \ˌən-ˈin-t(ə-)rəs-təd, -tə-ˌres-; ˈən-\ *adj* : not interested : not having the mind or feelings engaged or aroused

un·in·ter·rupt·ed \ˌən-ˌint-ə-ˈrəp-təd\ *adj* : not interrupted : CONTINUOUS

union \ˈyü-nyən\ *n* **1** : an act or instance of uniting two or more things into one : the state of being so united : COMBINATION, JUNCTION **2** : a uniting in marriage **3** : something formed by a combining of parts or members; *esp* : a confederation of independent individuals (as nations or persons) for some common purpose **4** : an organization of workers (as a labor union or a trade union) formed to advance its members' interests esp. in respect to wages and working conditions **5** : a device emblematic of union used on or as a national flag; *also* : the upper inner corner of a flag **6** : a device for connecting parts (as of a machine); *esp* : a coupling for pipes

union·ism \ˈyü-nyə-ˌniz-əm\ *n* **1** : the principle or policy of forming or adhering to a union; *esp, cap* : adherence to the policy of a firm federal union prior to or during the U.S. Civil War **2** : the principles or system of trade unions — **union·ist** *n*

union·ize \ˈyü-nyə-ˌnīz\ *vb* **-ized; -iz·ing** : to form into or cause to join a labor union — **union·iza·tion** \ˌyü-nyən-ə-ˈzā-shən\ *n*

union jack *n* **1** : a flag consisting of the part of a national flag that signifies union **2** *cap U&J* : the national flag of the United Kingdom

unique \yu̇-ˈnēk\ *adj* **1** : being the only one of its kind : SINGLE, SOLE **2** : very unusual : NOTABLE — **unique·ly** *adv* — **unique·ness** *n*

uni·sex \ˈyü-nə-ˌseks\ *adj* : not distinguishable as male or female; *also* : suitable or designed for both males or females — **unisex** *n*

uni·sex·u·al \ˌyü-nə-ˈsek-sh(ə-w)əl\ *adj* **1** : having only male or only female sex organs **2** : UNISEX

uni·son \ˈyü-nə-sən, -nə-zən\ *n* [MF, fr. ML *unisonus* having the same sound, fr. L *unus* one + *sonus* sound] **1** : sameness or identity in musical pitch **2** : the condition of being tuned or sounded at the same pitch or at an octave ⟨sing in ~ rather than in harmony⟩ **3** : harmonious agreement or union : ACCORD

unit \ˈyü-nət\ *n* **1** : the least whole number : ONE **2** : a definite amount or quantity used as a standard of measurement **3** : a single thing or person or group that is a constituent of a whole; *also* : a part of a military establishment that has a prescribed organization — **unit** *adj*

Uni·tar·i·an \ˌyü-nə-ˈter-ē-ən\ *n* : a member of a religious denomination stressing individual freedom of belief — **Uni·tar·i·an·ism** *n*

uni·tary \ˈyü-nə-ˌter-ē\ *adj* **1** : of or relating to a unit

: characterized by unity **2** : not divided — **uni·tar·i·ly** \ˌyü-nə-ˈter-ə-lē\ *adv*

unite \yü-ˈnīt\ *vb* **unit·ed; unit·ing 1** : to put or join together so as to make one : COMBINE, COALESCE **2** : to join by a legal or moral bond (as nations by treaty); *also* : to join in interest or fellowship **3** : AMALGAMATE, CONSOLIDATE **4** : to join in an act

unit·ed \yü-ˈnīt-əd\ *adj* **1** : made one : COMBINED **2** : relating to or produced by joint action **3** : being in agreement : HARMONIOUS

unit·ize \ˈyü-nət-ˌīz\ *vb* **-ized; -iz·ing 1** : to form or convert into a unit **2** : to divide into units

uni·ty \ˈyü-nət-ē\ *n, pl* **-ties 1** : the quality or state of being one : ONENESS, SINGLENESS **2** : a definite quantity or combination of quantities taken as one or for which 1 is made to stand in calculation **3** : CONCORD, ACCORD, HARMONY **4** : continuity without change ⟨~ of purpose⟩ **5** : reference of all the parts of a literary or artistic composition to a single main idea **6** : totality of related parts **syn** solidarity, union, integrity

univ *abbr* **1** universal **2** university

uni·va·lent \ˌyü-ni-ˈvā-lənt\ *adj* : having a valence of one

uni·valve \ˈyü-ni-ˌvalv\ *n* : a mollusk (as a snail or whelk) having a shell with one valve — **univalve** *adj*

uni·ver·sal \ˌyü-nə-ˈvər-səl\ *adj* **1** : including, covering, or affecting the whole without limit or exception : UNLIMITED, GENERAL ⟨a ~ rule⟩ **2** : present or occurring everywhere **3** : used or for use among all ⟨a ~ language⟩ — **uni·ver·sal·ly** \-ē\ *adv*

Uni·ver·sal·ist \ˌyü-nə-ˈvər-s(ə-)ləst\ *n* : a member of a religious denomination now united with Unitarians that upholds the belief that all men will be saved

uni·ver·sal·i·ty \-vər-ˈsal-ət-ē\ *n* : the quality or state of being universal

uni·ver·sal·ize \-ˈvər-sə-ˌlīz\ *vb* **-ized; -iz·ing** : to make universal : GENERALIZE — **uni·ver·sal·iza·tion** \-ˌvər-sə-lə-ˈzā-shən\ *n*

universal joint *n* : a shaft coupling for transmitting rotation from one shaft to another not in a straight line with it

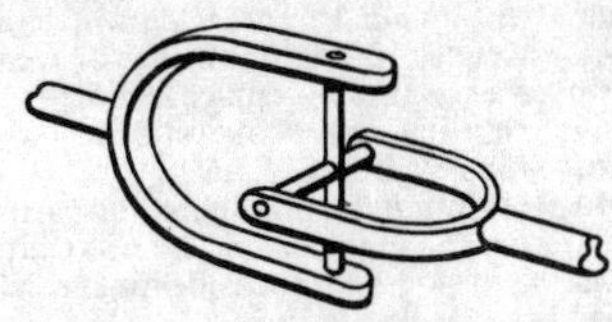

universal joint

Universal Product Code *n* : a bar code that identifies a product's type and price for entry into a computer or cash register (as at a supermarket checkout)

uni·verse \ˈyü-nə-ˌvərs\ *n* [L *universum,* fr. neut. of *universus* entire, whole, fr. *unus* one + *versus* turned toward, fr. pp. of *vertere* to turn] : all created things and phenomena viewed as constituting one system or whole

uni·ver·si·ty \ˌyü-nə-ˈvər-s(ə-)tē\ *n, pl* **-ties** : an institution of higher learning authorized to confer degrees in various special fields (as theology, law, and medicine) as well as in the arts and sciences generally

un·just \ˌən-ˈjəst, ˈən-\ *adj* : characterized by injustice — **un·just·ly** *adv*

un·kempt \-ˈkempt\ *adj* **1** : ROUGH, UNPOLISHED **2** : not combed : DISHEVELED

un·kind \-ˈkīnd\ *adj* : wanting in kindness or sympathy : CRUEL, HARSH — **un·kind·ly** \-ˈkīn-(d)lē\ *adv* — **un·kind·ness** \-ˈkīn(d)-nəs\ *n*

un·kind·ly \-ˈkīn-(d)lē\ *adj* : UNKIND — **un·kind·li·ness** *n*

un·know·ing \ˌən-ˈnō-iŋ, ˈən-\ *adj* : not knowing : IGNORANT — **un·know·ing·ly** *adv*

un·known \-ˈnōn\ *adj* : not known : UNFAMILIAR; *also* : not ascertained — **unknown** *n*

un·lace \ˌən-ˈlās, ˈən-\ *vb* : to loose by undoing a lace

un·lade \-ˈlād\ *vb* **-lad·ed; -laded** *or* **-lad·en** \-ˈlād-ᵊn\; **-lad·ing** : to take the load or cargo from : UNLOAD

un·latch \-ˈlach\ *vb* **1** : to open or loose by lifting the latch **2** : to become loosed or opened

un·law·ful \ˌən-ˈlȯ-fəl, ˈən-\ *adj* **1** : not lawful : ILLEGAL **2** : ILLEGITIMATE — **un·law·ful·ly** \-ē\ *adv*

un·lead·ed \-ˈled-əd\ *adj* : not treated or mixed with lead or lead compounds

un·learn \-ˈlərn\ *vb* : to put out of one's knowledge or memory

un·learned \-ˈlər-nəd *for 1, 2;* -ˈlərnd *for 3*\ *adj* **1** : UNEDUCATED, ILLITERATE **2** : not learned by study : not known **3** : not learned by previous experience

un·leash \-ˈlēsh\ *vb* : to free from or as if from a leash

un·less \ən-ˌles, ˌən-\ *conj* : except on condition that ⟨won't go ~ you do⟩

un·let·tered \ˌən-ˈlet-ərd, ˈən-\ *adj* : not educated : ILLITERATE

[1]**un·like** \-ˈlīk\ *adj* **1** : not like : DISSIMILAR, DIFFERENT **2** : UNEQUAL — **un·like·ness** *n*

[2]**unlike** *prep* **1** : different from ⟨he's quite ~ his brother⟩ **2** : unusual for ⟨it's ~ him to be late⟩ **3** : differently from ⟨behaves ~ his brother⟩

un·like·li·hood \ˌən-ˈlī-klē-ˌhu̇d, ˈən-\ *n* : IMPROBABILITY

un·like·ly \-ˈlī-klē\ *adj* **1** : not likely : IMPROBABLE **2** : likely to fail

un·lim·ber \ˌən-ˈlim-bər, ˈən-\ *vb* : to get ready for action

un·list·ed \ˌən-ˈlis-təd, ˈən-\ *adj* **1** : not appearing on a list; *esp* : not appearing in a telephone book **2** : being or involving a security not listed formally on an organized exchange

un·load \-ˈlōd\ *vb* **1** : to take away or off : REMOVE ⟨~ cargo from a hold⟩; *also* : to get rid of **2** : to take a load from; *also* : to relieve or set free : UNBURDEN ⟨~ one's mind of worries⟩ **3** : to get rid of or be relieved of a burden **4** : to sell in volume

un·lock \-ˈläk\ *vb* **1** : to unfasten through release of a lock **2** : RELEASE ⟨~*ed* her emotions⟩ **3** : DISCLOSE, REVEAL

un·looked–for \-ˈlu̇kt-ˌfȯr\ *adj* : UNEXPECTED

un·loose \ˌən-ˈlüs\ *vb* : to relax the strain of : set free; *also* : UNTIE

un·loos·en \-ˈlüs-ᵊn\ *vb* : UNLOOSE

un·love·ly \-ˈləv-lē\ *adj* : having no charm or appeal : not amiable

un·lucky \-ˈlək-ē\ *adj* **1** : UNFORTUNATE, ILL-FATED **2** : likely to bring misfortune : INAUSPICIOUS **3** : REGRETTABLE — **un·luck·i·ly** \-ˈlək-ə-lē\ *adv*

un·man \ˌən-ˈman, ˈən-\ *vb* **1** : to deprive of manly courage **2** : CASTRATE

un·man·ly \-ˈman-lē\ *adj* : not manly : COWARDLY; *also* : EFFEMINATE

un·man·ner·ly \-ˈman-ər-lē\ *adj* : RUDE, IMPOLITE — **unmannerly** *adv*

un·mask \ˌən-ˈmask\ *vb* **1** : to strip of a mask or a disguise : EXPOSE **2** : to remove one's own disguise (as at a masquerade)

un·mean·ing \-ˈmē-niŋ\ *adj* : having no meaning : SENSELESS

un·meet \-ˈmēt\ *adj* : not meet or fit : UNSUITABLE, IMPROPER

un·men·tion·able \-ˈmench-(ə-)nə-bəl\ *adj* : not fit or proper to be talked about

un·mer·ci·ful \-ˈmər-si-fəl\ *adj* : not merciful : CRUEL, MERCILESS — **un·mer·ci·ful·ly** \-ē\ *adv*

un·mind·ful \-ˈmīnd-fəl\ *adj* : not mindful : CARELESS, UNAWARE
un·mis·tak·able \ˌən-mə-ˈstā-kə-bəl\ *adj* : not capable of being mistaken or misunderstood : CLEAR, OBVIOUS — **un·mis·tak·ably** \-blē\ *adv*
un·mit·i·gat·ed \ˌən-ˈmit-ə-ˌgāt-əd, ˈ-ən-\ *adj* **1** : not softened or lessened **2** : ABSOLUTE, DOWNRIGHT ⟨an ~ liar⟩
un·moor \-ˈmu̇r\ *vb* **1** : to loose from or as if from moorings **2** : to cast off moorings
un·mor·al \-ˈmȯr-əl\ *adj* : having no moral perception or quality : being neither moral nor immoral — **un·mo·ral·i·ty** \ˌən-mə-ˈral-ət-ē\ *n*
un·muz·zle \-ˈməz-əl\ *vb* : to remove a muzzle from
un·nat·u·ral \ˌən-ˈnach-(ə-)rəl, ˈən-\ *adj* : contrary to or acting contrary to nature or natural instincts : ARTIFICIAL, IRREGULAR; *also* : ABNORMAL — **un·nat·u·ral·ly** \-ē\ *adv* — **un·nat·u·ral·ness** *n*
un·nec·es·sar·i·ly \ˌən-ˌnes-ə-ˈser-ə-lē\ *adv* **1** : not by necessity ⟨spent more money ~⟩ **2** : to an unnecessary degree ⟨~ harsh⟩
un·nerve \ˌən-ˈnərv, ˈən-\ *vb* : to deprive of nerve, courage, or self-control
un·nil·hex·i·um \ˌyün-ᵊl-ˈhek-sē-əm\ *n* [NL *unnil-* (fr. L *unus* one + *nil* zero) + Gk *hex* six + NL *-ium*] : the chemical element of atomic number 106 — see ELEMENT table
un·nil·pen·ti·um \-ˈpent-ē-əm\ *n* : the chemical element of atomic number 105 — see ELEMENT table
un·nil·qua·di·um \-ˈkwäd-ē-əm\ *n* : the chemical element of atomic number 104 — see ELEMENT table
un·num·bered \-ˈnəm-bərd\ *adj* : not numbered or counted : INNUMERABLE
un·ob·tru·sive \ˌən-əb-ˈtrü-siv\ *adj* : not obtrusive or forward : not bold : INCONSPICUOUS — **un·ob·tru·sive·ly** *adv*
un·oc·cu·pied \ˌən-ˈäk-yə-ˌpīd, ˈən-\ *adj* **1** : not busy : UNEMPLOYED **2** : not occupied : EMPTY, VACANT
un·or·ga·nized \-ˈȯr-gə-ˌnīzd\ *adj* **1** : not formed or brought into an integrated or ordered whole **2** : not organized into unions ⟨~ labor⟩
unp *abbr* unpaged
Unp *symbol* unnilpentium
un·pack \ˌən-ˈpak, ˈən-\ *vb* **1** : to separate and remove things packed **2** : to open and remove the contents of
un·par·al·leled \ˌən-ˈpar-ə-ˌleld\ *adj* : having no parallel; *esp* : having no equal or match
un·par·lia·men·ta·ry \ˌən-ˌpär-lə-ˈment-ə-rē, -ˌpärl-yə-, -ˈmen-trē\ *adj* : contrary to parliamentary practice
un·peg \ˌən-ˈpeg, ˈən-\ *vb* : to remove a peg from : UNFASTEN
un·per·son \ˈən-ˈpərs-ᵊn, -ˌpərs-\ *n* : a person who usu. for political or ideological reasons is removed from recognition, consideration, or memory
un·pile \ˌən-ˈpīl, ˈən-\ *vb* : to take or disentangle from a pile
un·pin \-ˈpin\ *vb* : to remove a pin from : UNFASTEN
un·pleas·ant \-ˈplez-ᵊnt\ *adj* : not pleasant : DISAGREEABLE — **un·pleas·ant·ly** *adv* — **un·pleas·ant·ness** *n*
un·plug \ˌən-ˈpləg, ˈən-\ *vb* **1** : UNCLOG **2** : to remove (a plug) from a receptacle; *also* : to disconnect from an electric circuit by removing a plug
un·plumbed \-ˈpləmd\ *adj* **1** : not tested or measured with a plumb line **2** : not thoroughly explored
un·pop·u·lar \ˌən-ˈpäp-yə-lər, ˈən-\ *adj* : not popular : looked upon or received unfavorably — **un·pop·u·lar·i·ty** \ˌən-ˌpäp-yə-ˈlar-ət-ē\ *n*
un·prec·e·dent·ed \ˌən-ˈpres-ə-ˌdent-əd, ˈən-\ *adj* : having no precedent : NOVEL, NEW
un·pre·ten·tious \ˌən-pri-ˈten-chəs\ *adj* : not pretentious or pompous : MODEST ⟨~ homes⟩
un·prin·ci·pled \ˌən-ˈprin-sə-pəld, ˈən-\ *adj* : lacking sound or honorable principles : UNSCRUPULOUS
un·print·able \-ˈprint-ə-bəl\ *adj* : unfit to be printed
un·prof·it·able \ˌən-ˈpräf-ət-ə-bəl, ˈən-, -ˈpräf-tə-bəl\ *adj* : not profitable : USELESS, VAIN
Unq *symbol* unnilquadium
un·qual·i·fied \ˌən-ˈkwäl-ə-ˌfīd, ˈən-\ *adj* **1** : not having requisite qualifications **2** : not modified or restricted by reservations — **un·qual·i·fied·ly** \-ˌfī(-ə)d-lē\ *adv*
un·ques·tion·able \-ˈkwes-chə-nə-bəl\ *adj* **1** : acknowledged as beyond doubt **2** : INDISPUTABLE — **un·ques·tion·ably** \-blē\ *adv*
un·ques·tion·ing \-chə-niŋ\ *adj* : not questioning : accepting without examination or hesitation — **un·ques·tion·ing·ly** *adv*
un·qui·et \-ˈkwī-ət\ *adj* **1** : not quiet : AGITATED, DISTURBED **2** : physically, emotionally, or mentally restless : UNEASY
un·quote \ˈən-ˌkwōt\ *n* — used orally to indicate the end of a direct quotation
un·rav·el \ˌən-ˈrav-əl, ˈən-\ *vb* **1** : to separate the threads of **2** : SOLVE ⟨~ a mystery⟩ **3** : to become unraveled
un·read \-ˈred\ *adj* **1** : not read **2** : not well informed through reading **3** : UNEDUCATED
un·re·al \-ˈrē(-ə)l\ *adj* : lacking in reality, substance, or genuineness — **un·re·al·i·ty** \ˌən-rē-ˈal-ət-ē\ *n*
un·rea·son·able \-ˈrēz-(ᵊ-)nə-bəl\ *adj* **1** : not governed by or acting according to reason; *also* : not conformable to reason : ABSURD **2** : exceeding the bounds of reason or moderation — **un·rea·son·able·ness** *n* — **un·rea·son·ably** *adv*
un·rea·soned \-ˈrēz-ᵊnd\ *adj* : not based on reason or reasoning
un·rea·son·ing \-ˈrēz-(ᵊ-)niŋ\ *adj* : not using or showing the use of reason as a guide or control
un·re·con·struct·ed \ˌən-ˌrē-kən-ˈstrək-təd\ *adj* : not reconciled to some political, economic, or social change; *esp* : holding stubbornly to principles, beliefs, or views that are or are held to be outmoded
un·reel \ˌən-ˈrēl, ˈən-\ *vb* **1** : to unwind from or as if from a reel **2** : perform successfully
un·re·gen·er·ate \ˌən-ri-ˈjen-(ə-)rət\ *adj* : not regenerated or reformed
un·re·lent·ing \-ˈlent-iŋ\ *adj* **1** : not yielding in determination : STERN ⟨~ leader⟩ **2** : not letting up or weakening in vigor or pace : CONSTANT — **un·re·lent·ing·ly** *adv*
un·re·mit·ting \-ˈmit-iŋ\ *adj* : CONTINUOUS, INCESSANT, PERSEVERING — **un·re·mit·ting·ly** *adv*
un·re·served \-ˈzərvd\ *adj* **1** : not limited or partial : ENTIRE, UNQUALIFIED ⟨~ enthusiasm⟩ **2** : not cautious or reticent : FRANK, OPEN **3** : not set aside for special use — **un·re·serv·ed·ly** \-ˈzər-vəd-lē\ *adv*
un·rest \ˌən-ˈrest, ˈən-\ *n* : a disturbed or uneasy state : TURMOIL
un·re·strained \ˌən-ri-ˈstrānd\ *adj* **1** : IMMODERATE, UNCONTROLLED **2** : SPONTANEOUS
un·re·straint \-ri-ˈstrānt\ *n* : lack of restraint
un·rid·dle \ˌən-ˈrid-ᵊl, ˈən-\ *vb* : to read the riddle of : SOLVE
un·righ·teous \-ˈrī-chəs\ *adj* **1** : SINFUL, WICKED **2** : UNJUST — **un·righ·teous·ness** *n*
un·ripe \-ˈrīp\ *adj* : not ripe : IMMATURE
un·ri·valed *or* **un·ri·valled** \ˌən-ˈrī-vəld, ˈən-\ *adj* : having no rival : INCOMPARABLE
un·robe \-ˈrōb\ *vb* : DISROBE, UNDRESS
un·roll \-rōl\ *vb* **1** : to unwind a roll of : open out **2** : DISPLAY, DISCLOSE **3** : to become unrolled or spread out
un·roof \-ˈrüf, -ˈru̇f\ *vb* : to strip off the roof or covering of
un·ruf·fled \ˌən-ˈrəf-əld, ˈən-\ *adj* **1** : not agitated or upset **2** : not ruffled : SMOOTH ⟨~ water⟩
un·ruly \-ˈrü-lē\ *adj* [ME *unreuly*, fr. *un-* + *reuly* disciplined, fr. *reule* rule, fr. OF, fr. L *regula* straightedge, rule, fr. *regere* to lead straight] : not submissive to rule or restraint : TURBULENT ⟨~ passions⟩ — **un·rul·i·ness** \-ˈrü-lē-nəs\ *n*

UNRWA *abbr* United Nations Relief and Works Agency
un·sad·dle \ˌən-ˈsad-ᵊl, ˈən-\ *vb* **1** : to remove the saddle from a horse **2** : UNHORSE
un·sat·u·rat·ed \-ˈsach-ə-ˌrāt-əd\ *adj* **1** : capable of absorbing or dissolving more of something **2** : containing double or triple bonds between carbon atoms ⟨~ fats or oils⟩ — **un·sat·u·rate** \-rət\ *n*
un·saved \ˌən-ˈsāvd, ˈən-\ *adj* : not saved; *esp* : not rescued from eternal punishment
un·sa·vory \-ˈsāv-(ə-)rē\ *adj* **1** : TASTELESS **2** : unpleasant to taste or smell **3** : morally offensive
un·say \-ˈsā\ *vb* **-said** \-ˈsed\; **-say·ing** \-ˈsā-iŋ\ : to take back (something said) : RETRACT, WITHDRAW
un·scathed \-ˈskāt͟hd\ *adj* : wholly unharmed : not injured
un·schooled \-ˈsküld\ *adj* : not schooled : UNTAUGHT, UNTRAINED
un·sci·en·tif·ic \ˌən-ˌsī-ən-ˈtif-ik\ *adj* : not scientific : not in accord with the principles and methods of science
un·scram·ble \ˌən-ˈskram-bəl, ˈən-\ *vb* **1** : RESOLVE, CLARIFY **2** : to restore (as a radio message) to intelligible form
un·screw \-ˈskrü\ *vb* **1** : to draw the screws from **2** : to loosen by turning
un·scru·pu·lous \-ˈskrü-pyə-ləs\ *adj* : not scrupulous : UNPRINCIPLED — **un·scru·pu·lous·ly** *adv* — **un·scru·pu·lous·ness** *n*
un·seal \-ˈsēl\ *vb* : to break or remove the seal of : OPEN
un·search·able \-ˈsər-chə-bəl\ *adj* : not capable of being searched or explored
un·sea·son·able \-ˈsēz-(ᵊ-)nə-bəl\ *adj* : not seasonable : happening or coming at the wrong time : UNTIMELY — **un·sea·son·ably** \-blē\ *adv*
un·seat \-ˈsēt\ *vb* **1** : to throw from one's seat esp. on horseback **2** : to remove from political office
un·seem·ly \-ˈsēm-lē\ *adj* : not according with established standards of good form or taste; *also* : not suitable — **un·seem·li·ness** *n*
un·seen \ˌən-ˈsēn, ˈən-\ *adj* : not seen : INVISIBLE
un·seg·re·gat·ed \-ˈseg-ri-ˌgāt-əd\ *adj* : not segregated; *esp* : free from racial segregation
un·self·ish \-ˈsel-fish\ *adj* : not selfish : GENEROUS — **un·self·ish·ly** *adv* — **un·self·ish·ness** *n*
un·set·tle \ˌən-ˈset-ᵊl, ˈən-\ *vb* : to move or loosen from a settled position : DISPLACE, DISTURB
un·set·tled \-ˈset-ᵊld\ *adj* **1** : not settled : not fixed (as in position or character) **2** : not calm : DISTURBED **3** : not decided in mind : UNDETERMINED **4** : not paid ⟨~ accounts⟩ **5** : not occupied by settlers
un·shack·le \-ˈshak-əl\ *vb* : to free from shackles
un·shaped \-ˈshāpt\ *adj* : not shaped : RUDE ⟨~ ideas⟩ ⟨~ timber⟩
un·sheathe \ˌən-ˈshēt͟h, ˈən-\ *vb* : to draw from or as if from a sheath
un·ship \-ˈship\ *vb* **1** : to remove from a ship **2** : to remove or become removed from position ⟨~ an oar⟩
un·shod \ˌən-ˈshäd, ˈən-\ *adj* : not shod : not wearing shoes
un·sight·ly \ˌən-ˈsīt-lē, ˈən-\ *adj* : unpleasant to the sight : UGLY
un·skilled \-ˈskild\ *adj* **1** : not skilled; *esp* : not skilled in a specified branch of work **2** : not requiring skill ⟨~ labor⟩
un·skill·ful \-ˈskil-fəl\ *adj* : lacking in skill or proficiency — **un·skill·ful·ly** \-ē\ *adv*
un·sling \-ˈsliŋ\ *vb* **-slung** \-ˈsləŋ\; **-sling·ing** \-ˈsliŋ-iŋ\ **1** : to remove from being slung **2** : to take off the slings of esp. aboard ship
un·snap \-ˈsnap\ *vb* : to loosen or free by or as if by undoing a snap
un·snarl \-ˈsnärl\ *vb* : to remove snarls from : UNTANGLE
un·so·phis·ti·cat·ed \ˌən-sə-ˈfis-tə-ˌkāt-əd\ *adj* **1** : not worldly-wise : lacking sophistication **2** : SIMPLE
un·sought \ˌən-ˈsȯt, ˈən-\ *adj* : not sought : not searched for or asked for : not obtained by effort
un·sound \-ˈsau̇nd\ *adj* **1** : not healthy or whole; *also* : not mentally normal **2** : not valid **3** : not firmly made or fixed — **un·sound·ly** *adv* — **un·sound·ness** *n*
un·spar·ing \-ˈspa(ə)r-iŋ\ *adj* **1** : HARD, RUTHLESS **2** : not frugal : LIBERAL, PROFUSE
un·speak·able \-ˈspē-kə-bəl\ *adj* **1** : impossible to express in words **2** : extremely bad — **un·speak·ably** \-blē\ *adv*
un·spot·ted \-ˈspät-əd\ *adj* : free from spot or stain; *esp* : free from moral stain
un·sprung \-ˈsprəŋ\ *adj* : not sprung; *esp* : not equipped with springs
un·sta·ble \-ˈstā-bəl\ *adj* **1** : not stable **2** : FICKLE, VACILLATING; *also* : having defective emotional control **3** : readily changing (as by decomposing) in chemical or physical composition or in biological activity ⟨an ~ atomic nucleus⟩
un·steady \ˌən-ˈsted-ē\ *adj* : not steady : UNSTABLE — **un·steadi·ly** \-ˈsted-ᵊl-ē\ *adv* — **un·steadi·ness** \-ˈsted-ē-nəs\ *n*
un·stint·ing \-ˈstint-iŋ\ *adj* : giving or being given freely or generously ⟨~ praise⟩
un·stop \-ˈstäp\ *vb* **1** : UNCLOG **2** : to remove a stopper from
un·strap \-ˈstrap\ *vb* : to remove or loose a strap from
un·stressed \ˌən-ˈstrest, ˈən-\ *adj* : not stressed; *esp* : not bearing a stress or accent
un·strung \-ˈstrəŋ\ *adj* **1** : having the strings loose or detached **2** : nervously tired or anxious
un·stud·ied \-ˈstəd-ēd\ *adj* **1** : not acquired by study **2** : NATURAL, UNFORCED
un·sub·stan·tial \ˌən-səb-ˈstan-chəl\ *adj* : INSUBSTANTIAL
un·sung \ˌən-ˈsəŋ, ˈən-\ *adj* **1** : not sung **2** : not celebrated in song or verse ⟨~ heroes⟩
un·swerv·ing \ˌən-ˈswer-viŋ, ˈən-\ *adj* **1** : not swerving or turning aside **2** : STEADY
un·tan·gle \-ˈtaŋ-gəl\ *vb* **1** : DISENTANGLE **2** : to straighten out : RESOLVE ⟨~ a problem⟩
un·taught \-ˈtȯt\ *adj* **1** : not instructed or taught : IGNORANT **2** : NATURAL, SPONTANEOUS
un·think·able \-ˈthiŋ-kə-bəl\ *adj* : not to be thought of or considered as possible : INCREDIBLE
un·think·ing \ˌən-ˈthiŋ-kiŋ, ˈən-\ *adj* : not thinking; *esp* : THOUGHTLESS, HEEDLESS — **un·think·ing·ly** *adv*
un·thought \ˈən-ˈthȯt\ *adj* : not anticipated : UNEXPECTED ⟨*unthought*-of development⟩
un·tie \-ˈtī\ *vb* **-tied; -ty·ing** *or* **-tie·ing** **1** : to free from something that ties, fastens, or restrains : UNBIND **2** : DISENTANGLE, RESOLVE **3** : to become loosened or unbound
[1]**un·til** \(ˌ)ən-ˌtil\ *prep* : up to the time of ⟨worked ~ 5 o'clock⟩
[2]**until** *conj* **1** : up to the time that ⟨wait ~ he calls⟩ **2** : to the point or degree that ⟨ran ~ he was breathless⟩
[1]**un·time·ly** \ˌən-ˈtīm-lē, ˈən-\ *adv* : at an inopportune time : UNSEASONABLY; *also* : PREMATURELY
[2]**untimely** *adj* : PREMATURE ⟨~ death⟩; *also* : INOPPORTUNE, UNSEASONABLE
un·tir·ing \ˌən-ˈtī-riŋ\ *adj* : not becoming tired : INDEFATIGABLE — **un·tir·ing·ly** *adv*
un·to \ˌən-tə, ˈən-(ˌ)tü\ *prep* : TO
un·told \ˌən-ˈtōld, ˈən-\ *adj* **1** : not counted : VAST, NUMBERLESS **2** : not told : not revealed
[1]**un·touch·able** \ˌən-ˈtəch-ə-bəl, ˈən-\ *adj* : forbidden to the touch
[2]**untouchable** *n* : a member of the lowest social class in

India having in traditional Hindu belief the quality of defiling by contact a member of a higher caste

un·tow·ard \ən-ˈtō(-ə)rd\ *adj* **1** : difficult to manage : STUBBORN, WILLFUL ⟨an ~ child⟩ **2** : INCONVENIENT, TROUBLESOME ⟨an ~ encounter⟩

un·tried \ˌən-ˈtrīd, ˈən-\ *adj* : not tested or proved by experience or trial; *also* : not tried in court

un·true \-ˈtrü\ *adj* **1** : not faithful : DISLOYAL **2** : not according with a standard of correctness **3** : FALSE

un·truth \ˌən-ˈtrüth, ˈən-\ *n* **1** : lack of truthfulness **2** : FALSEHOOD

un·tune \-ˈt(y)ün\ *vb* **1** : to put out of tune **2** : DISARRANGE, DISCOMPOSE

un·tu·tored \-ˈt(y)üt-ərd\ *adj* : UNTAUGHT, UNLEARNED, IGNORANT

un·twine \-ˈtwīn\ *vb* : UNWIND, DISENTANGLE

un·twist \ˌən-ˈtwist, ˈən-\ *vb* **1** : to separate the twisted parts of : UNTWINE **2** : to become untwined

un·used \-ˈyüst, -ˈyüzd *for 1;* -ˈyüzd *for 2*\ *adj* **1** : UNACCUSTOMED **2** : not used

un·usu·al \-ˈyü-zhə(-wə)l\ *adj* : not usual : UNCOMMON, RARE — **un·usu·al·ly** \-ē\ *adv*

un·ut·ter·able \ˌən-ˈət-ə-rə-bəl, ˈən-\ *adj* : being beyond the powers of description : INEXPRESSIBLE — **un·ut·ter·ably** \-blē\ *adv*

un·var·nished \-ˈvär-nisht\ *adj* **1** : not varnished **2** : not embellished : PLAIN ⟨the ~ truth⟩

un·veil \ˌən-ˈvāl, ˈən-\ *vb* **1** : to remove a veil or covering from : DISCLOSE **2** : to remove a veil : reveal oneself

un·voiced \-ˈvȯist\ *adj* **1** : not verbally expressed : UNSPOKEN **2** : VOICELESS 2

un·war·rant·able \-ˈwȯr-ənt-ə-bəl\ *adj* : not justifiable : INEXCUSABLE — **un·war·rant·ably** \-blē\ *adv*

un·weave \-ˈwēv\ *vb* **-wove** \-ˈwōv\; **-wo·ven** \-ˈwō-vən\; **-weav·ing** : DISENTANGLE, RAVEL

un·well \ˌən-ˈwel\ *adj* **1** : SICK, AILING **2** : MENSTRUATING

un·whole·some \-ˈhōl-səm\ *adj* **1** : harmful to physical, mental, or moral well-being **2** : CORRUPT, UNSOUND; *also* : offensive to the senses : LOATHSOME

un·wieldy \-ˈwēl-dē\ *adj* : not easily managed or handled because of size or weight : AWKWARD ⟨an ~ tool⟩

un·will·ing \-ˈwil-iŋ\ *adj* : not willing — **un·will·ing·ly** *adv* — **un·will·ing·ness** *n*

un·wind \-ˈwīnd\ *vb* **-wound** \-ˈwau̇nd\; **-wind·ing** **1** : to undo something that is wound : loose from coils **2** : to become unwound : be capable of being unwound **3** : RELAX

un·wise \ˌən-ˈwīz, ˈən-\ *adj* : not wise : FOOLISH — **un·wise·ly** *adv*

un·wit·ting \-ˈwit-iŋ\ *adj* **1** : not intended : INADVERTENT ⟨~ mistake⟩ **2** : not knowing : UNAWARE — **un·wit·ting·ly** *adv*

un·wont·ed \-ˈwȯnt-əd, -ˈwōnt-, -ˈwənt-\ *adj* **1** : RARE, UNUSUAL **2** : not accustomed by experience — **un·wont·ed·ly** *adv*

un·world·ly \-ˈwərl-(d)lē\ *adj* **1** : not of this world; *esp* : SPIRITUAL **2** : NAIVE **3** : not swayed by worldly considerations — **un·world·li·ness** \-ˈwərl-(d)lē-nəs\ *n*

un·wor·thy \ˌən-ˈwər-t͟hē, ˈən-\ *adj* **1** : BASE, DISHONORABLE **2** : not meritorious : not worthy : UNDESERVING **3** : not deserved : UNMERITED ⟨~ treatment⟩ **un·wor·thi·ly** \-t͟hə-lē\ *adv* — **un·wor·thi·ness** \-t͟hē-nəs\ *n*

un·wrap \-ˈrap\ *vb* : to free from wrappings : DISCLOSE

un·writ·ten \-ˈrit-ᵊn\ *adj* **1** : not in writing : ORAL, TRADITIONAL ⟨an ~ law⟩ **2** : containing no writing : BLANK

un·yield·ing \ˌən-ˈyēl-diŋ, ˈən-\ *adj* **1** : characterized by lack of softness or flexibility **2** : characterized by firmness or obduracy

un·yoke \-ˈyōk\ *vb* : to free from a yoke; *also* : SEPARATE, DISCONNECT

un·zip \-ˈzip\ *vb* : to zip open : open by means of a zipper

¹up \ˈəp\ *adv* **1** : in or to a higher position or level; *esp* : away from the center of the earth **2** : from beneath a surface (as ground or water) **3** : from below the horizon **4** : in or into an upright position; *esp* : out of bed **5** : with greater intensity ⟨speak ~⟩ **6** : in or into a better or more advanced state or a state of greater intensity or activity ⟨stir ~ a fire⟩ **7** : into existence, evidence, or knowledge ⟨the missing book turned ~⟩ **8** : into consideration ⟨brought the matter ~⟩ **9** : to or at bat **10** : into possession or custody ⟨gave himself ~⟩ **11** : ENTIRELY, COMPLETELY ⟨eat it ~⟩ **12** — used for emphasis ⟨clean ~ a room⟩ **13** : ASIDE, BY ⟨lay ~ supplies⟩ **14** : so as to arrive or approach ⟨ran ~ the path⟩ **15** : in a direction opposite to down **16** : in or into parts ⟨tear ~ paper⟩ **17** : to a stop ⟨pull ~ at the curb⟩ **18** : for each side ⟨the score was 15 ~⟩

²up *adj* **1** : risen above the horizon ⟨the sun is ~⟩ **2** : being out of bed ⟨~ by 6 o'clock⟩ **3** : relatively high ⟨prices are ~⟩ **4** : RAISED, LIFTED ⟨windows are ~⟩ **5** : BUILT, CONSTRUCTED ⟨the house is ~⟩ **6** : grown above a surface ⟨the corn is ~⟩ **7** : moving, inclining, or directed upward **8** : marked by agitation, excitement, or activity **9** : READY; *esp* : highly prepared **10** : going on : taking place ⟨find out what is ~⟩ **11** : EXPIRED, ENDED ⟨the time is ~⟩ **12** : well informed ⟨~ on the news⟩ **13** : being ahead or in advance of an opponent ⟨one hole ~ in a match⟩ **14** : presented for or being under consideration **15** : charged before a court ⟨~ for robbery⟩

³up *prep* **1** : to, toward, or at a higher point of ⟨~ a ladder⟩ **2** : to or toward the source of ⟨~ the river⟩ **3** : to or toward the northern part of ⟨~ the coast⟩ **4** : to or toward the interior of ⟨traveling ~ the country⟩ **5** : ALONG ⟨walk ~ the street⟩

⁴up *n* **1** : an upward course or slope **2** : a period or state of prosperity or success ⟨he had his ~*s* and downs⟩

⁵up *vb* **upped** *or in 2* **up; upped; up·ping; ups** *or in 2* **up 1** : to rise from a lying or sitting position **2** : to act abruptly or surprisingly ⟨she *upped* and left home⟩ **3** : to move or cause to move upward : ASCEND ⟨*upped* prices⟩

Upa·ni·shad \ü-ˈpän-i-ˌshäd\ *n* : one of a set of Vedic philosophical treatises

¹up·beat \ˈəp-ˌbēt\ *n* : an unaccented beat in a musical measure; *esp* : the last beat of the measure

²upbeat *adj* : OPTIMISTIC, CHEERFUL

up·braid \ˌəp-ˈbrād\ *vb* : to criticize, reproach, or scold severely

up·bring·ing \ˈəp-ˌbriŋ-iŋ\ *n* : the process of bringing up and training

UPC *abbr* Universal Product Code

up·chuck \ˈə-ˌchək\ *vb* : VOMIT

up·com·ing \ˌəp-ˌkəm-iŋ\ *adj* : FORTHCOMING, APPROACHING

up–coun·try \ˌəp-ˌkən-trē\ *adj* : of or relating to the interior of a country or a region — **up–country** \ˈəp-ˈkən-\ *adv*

up·date \ˌəp-ˈdāt\ *vb* : to bring up to date — **update** \ˈəp-ˌdāt\ *n*

up·draft \ˈəp-ˌdraft, -ˌdrȧft\ *n* : an upward movement of gas (as air)

up·end \ˌəp-ˈend\ *vb* : to set, stand, or rise on end

up–front \ˈəp-ˈfrənt\ *adj* **1** : HONEST, CANDID **2** : ADVANCE ⟨~ payment⟩

up front *adv* : in advance ⟨paid *up front*⟩

¹up·grade \ˈəp-ˌgrād\ *n* **1** : an upward grade or slope **2** : INCREASE, RISE

²up·grade \ˈəp-ˌgrād, ˌəp-ˈgrād\ *vb* : to raise to a higher grade or position; *esp* : to advance to a job requiring a higher level of skill

up·growth \ˈəp-ˌgrōth\ *n* : the process or result of growing up : upward growth : DEVELOPMENT

up·heav·al \ˌəp-ˈhē-vəl\ *n* **1** : the action or an instance of uplifting esp. of part of the earth's crust **2** : a violent agitation or change

¹up·hill \ˈəp-ˈhil\ *adv* : upward on a hill or incline; *also* : against difficulties

[2]**up·hill** \-ˌhil\ *adj* **1** : situated on elevated ground **2** : ASCENDING **3** : DIFFICULT, LABORIOUS

up·hold \ˌəp-ˈhōld\ *vb* **-held** \-ˈheld\; **-hold·ing** **1** : to give support to **2** : to support against an opponent **3** : to keep elevated — **up·hold·er** *n*

up·hol·ster \ˌəp-ˈhōl-stər\ *vb* **-stered; -ster·ing** \-st(ə-)riŋ\ : to furnish with or as if with upholstery — **up·hol·ster·er** *n*

up·hol·stery \-st(ə-)rē\ *n, pl* **-ster·ies** [ME *upholdester* upholsterer, fr. *upholden* to uphold, fr. *up* + *holden* to hold] : materials (as fabrics, padding, and springs) used to make a soft covering esp. for a seat

UPI *abbr* United Press International

up·keep \ˈəp-ˌkēp\ *n* : the act or cost of keeping up or maintaining; *also* : the state of being maintained

up·land \ˈəp-lənd, -ˌland\ *n* : high land esp. at some distance from the sea — **upland** *adj*

[1]**up·lift** \ˌəp-ˈlift\ *vb* **1** : to lift or raise up : ELEVATE **2** : to improve the condition of esp. morally, socially, or intellectually

[2]**up·lift** \ˈəp-ˌlift\ *n* **1** : a lifting up; *esp* : an upheaval of the earth's surface **2** : moral or social improvement; *also* : a movement to make such improvement

up·mar·ket \ˌəp-ˈmär-kət\ *adj* : appealing to wealthy consumers

up·most \ˈep-ˌmōst\ *adj* : UPPERMOST

up·on \ə-ˈpȯn, -ˈpän\ *prep* : ON

[1]**up·per** \ˈəp-ər\ *adj* **1** : higher in physical position, rank, or order **2** : constituting the smaller and more restricted branch of a bicameral legislature **3** *cap* : being a later part or formation of a specific geological period **4** : being toward the interior ⟨the ~ Amazon⟩ **5** : NORTHERN ⟨~ New York State⟩

[2]**upper** *n* : one that is upper; *esp* : the parts of a shoe or boot above the sole

up·per·case \ˌəp-ər-ˈkās\ *adj* : CAPITAL 5 — **uppercase** *n*

upper class *n* : a social class occupying a position above the middle class and having the highest status in a society — **upper–class** *adj*

up·per·class·man \ˌəp-ər-ˈklas-mən\ *n* : a junior or senior in a college or high school

upper crust *n* : the highest social class or group; *esp* : the highest circle of the upper class

up·per·cut \ˈəp-ər-ˌkət\ *n* : a short swinging punch delivered (as in boxing) in an upward direction usu. with a bent arm

upper hand *n* : MASTERY, ADVANTAGE

up·per·most \ˈəp-ər-ˌmōst\ *adv* : in or into the highest or most prominent position — **uppermost** *adj*

up·pish \ˈəp-ish\ *adj* : UPPITY

up·pi·ty \ˈəp-ət-ē\ *adj* : ARROGANT, PRESUMPTUOUS

up·raise \ˌəp-ˈrāz\ *vb* : to lift up : ELEVATE

[1]**up·right** \ˈəp-ˌrīt\ *adj* **1** : PERPENDICULAR, VERTICAL **2** : erect in carriage or posture **3** : morally correct : JUST — **upright** *adv* — **up·right·ly** *adv* — **up·right·ness** *n*

[2]**upright** *n* **1** : the state of being upright : a vertical position **2** : something that stands upright

upright piano *n* : a piano whose strings run vertically

up·ris·ing \ˈəp-ˌrī-ziŋ\ *n* : INSURRECTION, REVOLT, REBELLION

up·riv·er \ˈəp-ˈriv-ər\ *adv or adj* : toward or at a point nearer the source of a river

up·roar \ˈəp-ˌrōr\ *n* [Dutch *oproer*, fr. Middle Dutch, fr. *op* up + *roer* motion] : a state of commotion, excitement, or violent disturbance

up·roar·i·ous \ˌəp-ˈrōr-ē-əs\ *adj* **1** : marked by uproar **2** : extremely funny — **up·roar·i·ous·ly** *adv*

up·root \ˌəp-ˈrüt, -ˈrůt\ *vb* : to remove by or as if by pulling up by the roots

[1]**up·set** \ˌəp-ˈset\ *vb* **-set; -set·ting** **1** : to force or be forced out of the usual upright, level, or proper position **2** : to disturb emotionally : WORRY; *also* : to make somewhat ill **3** : UNSETTLE, DISARRANGE **4** : to defeat unexpectedly

[2]**up·set** \ˈəp-ˌset\ *n* **1** : an upsetting or being upset; *esp* : a minor physical disorder **2** : a derangement of plans or ideas

up·shot \ˈəp-ˌshät\ *n* : final result

up·side \ˈəp-ˌsīd\ *n* : the upper side

up·side down \ˌəp-ˌsīd-ˈdaůn\ *adv* **1** : with the upper and the lower parts reversed in position **2** : in or into confusion or disorder — **upside–down** *adj*

up·si·lon particle \ˈyüp-sə-ˌlän-, ˈəp-\ *n* : any of a group of unstable electrically neutral elementary particles that have a mass about 10 times that of a proton

[1]**up·stage** \ˈəp-ˈstāj\ *adv or adj* : toward or at the rear of a theatrical stage

[2]**up·stage** \ˌəp-ˈstāj\ *vb* : to steal the show from

[1]**up·stairs** \ˈəp-ˈstaərz\ *adv* **1** : up the stairs : to or on a higher floor **2** : to or at a higher position

[2]**up·stairs** \ˌəp-ˌstaərz\ *adj* : situated above the stairs esp. on an upper floor ⟨~ bedroom⟩

[3]**up·stairs** \ˈəp-ˈstaərz, ˈəp-ˌstaərs\ *n sing or pl* : the part of a building above the ground floor

up·stand·ing \ˌəp-ˈstan-diŋ, ˈəp-ˌstan-diŋ\ *adj* **1** : ERECT **2** : STRAIGHTFORWARD, HONEST

[1]**up·start** \ˌəp-ˈstärt\ *vb* : to jump up suddenly

[2]**up·start** \ˈəp-ˌstärt\ *n* : one that has risen suddenly; *esp* : one that claims more personal importance than he warrants — **up·start** \ˌəp-\ *adj*

up·state \ˈəp-ˈstāt\ *adj* : of, relating to, or characteristic of a part of a state away from a large city and esp. to the north — **upstate** *adv* — **upstate** *n*

up·stream \ˈəp-ˈstrēm\ *adv* : at or toward the source of a stream — **upstream** *adj*

up·stroke \ˈəp-ˌstrōk\ *n* : an upward stroke (as of a pen)

up·surge \-ˌsərj\ *n* : a rapid or sudden rise

up·swept \ˈəp-ˌswept\ *adj* : swept upward ⟨~ hairdo⟩

up·swing \ˈəp-ˌswiŋ\ *n* : an upward swing; *esp* : a marked increase or rise (as in activity)

up·take \ˈəp-ˌtāk\ *n* **1** : UNDERSTANDING, COMPREHENSION ⟨quick on the ~⟩ **2** : the process of absorbing and incorporating esp. into a living organism ⟨~ of iodine by the thyroid gland⟩

up·thrust \ˈəp-ˌthrəst\ *n* : an upward thrust; *esp* : an uplift of part of the earth's crust — **upthrust** *vb*

up·tight \ˈəp-ˈtīt\ *adj* **1** : TENSE, NERVOUS, UNEASY; *also* : ANGRY, INDIGNANT **2** : rigidly conventional

up–to–date *adj* **1** : extending up to the present time **2** : abreast of the times : MODERN — **up–to–date·ness** *n*

up·town \ˈəp-ˌtaůn\ *n* : the upper part of a town or city; *esp* : the residential district — **up·town** \ˈəp-ˈtaůn\ *adj or adv*

[1]**up·turn** \ˈəp-ˌtərn, ˌəp-ˈtərn\ *vb* **1** : to turn (as earth) up or over **2** : to turn or direct upward

[2]**up·turn** \ˈəp-ˌtərn\ *n* : an upward turn esp. toward better conditions or higher prices

[1]**up·ward** \ˈəp-wərd\ *or* **up·wards** \-wərdz\ *adv* **1** : in a direction from lower to higher **2** : toward a higher or better condition **3** : toward a greater amount or higher number, degree, or rate

[2]**upward** *adj* : directed or moving toward or situated in a higher place or level : ASCENDING

upwards of *also* **upward of** *adv* : more than : in excess of ⟨they cost *upwards of* $25 each⟩

up·well \ˌəp-ˈwel\ *vb* : to move or flow upward

up·well·ing \-ˈwel-iŋ\ *n* : a rising or an appearance of rising to the surface and flowing outward; *esp* : the movement of deep cold usu. nutrient-rich ocean water to the surface

up·wind \ˈəp-ˈwind\ *adv or adj* : in the direction from which the wind is blowing

---

ura·cil \ˈyu̇r-ə-ˌsil\ *n* : a pyrimidine base that is one of the four bases coding genetic information in the molecular chain of RNA

ura·ni·um \yu̇-ˈrā-nē-əm\ *n* : a silvery heavy radioactive metallic chemical element used as a source of atomic energy — see ELEMENT table

Ura·nus \ˈyu̇r-ə-nəs, yu̇-ˈrā-\ *n* [LL, heaven personified as a god, fr. Gk *Ouranos*, fr. *ouranos* sky, heaven] : the planet 7th in order from the sun

ur·ban \ˈər-bən\ *adj* : of, relating to, characteristic of, or constituting a city

ur·bane \ˌər-ˈbān\ *adj* [L *urbanus* urban, urbane, fr. *urbs* city] : very polite and polished in manner : SUAVE

ur·ban·ite \ˈər-bə-ˌnīt\ *n* : one living in a city

ur·ban·i·ty \ˌər-ˈban-ət-ē\ *n, pl* **-ties** : the quality or state of being urbane

ur·ban·ize \ˈər-bə-ˌnīz\ *vb* **-ized; -iz·ing** : to cause to take on urban characteristics — **ur·ban·iza·tion** \ˌər-bə-nə-ˈzā-shən\ *n*

ur·chin \ˈər-chən\ *n* [ME, hedgehog, fr. MF *herichon*, fr. L *ericius*] : a pert or mischievous youngster

Ur·du \ˈu̇r-dü, ˈər-\ *n* [Hindi *urdū-zabān*, lit., camp language] : a language that is an official literary language of Pakistan and is widely used in India

urea \yu̇-ˈrē-ə\ *n* : a soluble nitrogenous compound that is the chief solid constituent of mammalian urine

ure·mia \yu̇-ˈrē-mē-ə\ *n* : accumulation in the blood of materials normally passed off in the urine resulting in a poisoned condition — **ure·mic** \-mik\ *adj*

ure·ter \ˈyu̇r-ət-ər\ *n* : a duct that carries the urine from a kidney to the bladder

ure·thra \yu̇-ˈrē-thrə\ *n, pl* **-thras** *or* **-thrae** \-(ˌ)thrē\ : the canal that in most mammals carries off the urine from the bladder and in the male also serves as a genital duct — **ure·thral** \-thrəl\ *adj*

ure·thri·tis \ˌyu̇r-i-ˈthrīt-əs\ *n* : inflammation of the urethra

[1]**urge** \ˈərj\ *vb* **urged; urging 1** : to present, advocate, or demand earnestly **2** : to try to persuade or sway ⟨~ a guest to stay⟩ **3** : to serve as a motive or reason for **4** : to impress or impel to some course or activity ⟨the dog *urged* the sheep onward⟩

[2]**urge** *n* **1** : the act or process of urging **2** : a force or impulse that urges or drives

ur·gent \ˈər-jənt\ *adj* **1** : calling for immediate attention : PRESSING **2** : urging insistently — **ur·gen·cy** \-jən-sē\ *n* — **ur·gent·ly** *adv*

uric \ˈyu̇r-ik\ *adj* : of, relating to, or found in urine

uric acid *n* : a nearly insoluble acid that is the chief nitrogenous excretory product of birds but is present in only small amounts in mammalian urine

uri·nal \ˈyu̇r-ən-ᵊl\ *n* **1** : a receptacle for urine **2** : a place for urinating

uri·nal·y·sis \ˌyu̇r-ə-ˈnal-ə-səs\ *n* : analysis of urine usu. for medical purposes

uri·nary \ˈyu̇r-ə-ˌner-ē\ *adj* **1** : relating to, occurring in, or being organs for the formation and discharge of urine **2** : of, relating to, or found in urine

urinary bladder *n* : a membranous sac in many vertebrates that serves for the temporary retention of urine and discharges by the urethra

uri·nate \ˈyu̇r-ə-ˌnāt\ *vb* **-nat·ed; -nat·ing** : to discharge urine — **uri·na·tion** \ˌyu̇r-ə-ˈnā-shən\ *n*

urine \ˈyu̇r-ən\ *n* : a waste material from the kidneys that is usu. a yellowish watery liquid in mammals but is highly viscous in birds and reptiles

urn \ˈərn\ *n* **1** : a vessel that typically has the form of a vase on a pedestal and often is used to hold the ashes of the dead **2** : a closed vessel usu. with a spout for serving a hot beverage

uro·gen·i·tal \ˌyu̇r-ō-ˈjen-ə-tᵊl\ *adj* : of, relating to, or being the organs or functions of excretion and reproduction

urol·o·gy \yu̇-ˈräl-ə-jē\ *n* : a branch of medical science dealing with the urinary or urogenital tract and its disorders — **uro·log·ic** \ˌyu̇r-ə-ˈläj-ik\ *also* **uro·log·i·cal** \-i-kəl\ *adj* — **urol·o·gist** \yu̇-ˈräl-ə-jəst\ *n*

Ur·sa Ma·jor \ˌər-sə-ˈmā-jər\ *n* [L, lit., greater bear] : the most conspicuous of the northern constellations that contains the stars which form the Big Dipper

Ursa Mi·nor \-ˈmī-nər\ *n* [L, lit., lesser bear] : the constellation including the north pole of the heavens and the stars that form the Little Dipper with the North Star at the tip of the handle

ur·sine \ˈər-ˌsīn\ *adj* : of, relating to, or resembling a bear

ur·ti·car·ia \ˌərt-ə-ˈkar-ē-ə\ *n* [NL, fr. L *urtica* nettle] : HIVES

us \(ˈ)əs\ *pron, objective case of* WE

US *abbr* United States

USA *abbr* **1** United States Army **2** United States of America

us·able *also* **use·able** \ˈyü-zə-bəl\ *adj* : suitable or fit for use — **us·abil·i·ty** \ˌyü-zə-ˈbil-ət-ē\ *n*

USAF *abbr* United States Air Force

us·age \ˈyü-sij, -zij\ *n* **1** : habitual or customary practice or procedure **2** : the way in which words and phrases are actually used **3** : the action or mode of using **4** : manner of treating

USCG *abbr* United States Coast Guard

USDA *abbr* United States Department of Agriculture

[1]**use** \ˈyüs\ *n* **1** : the act or practice of using or employing something : EMPLOYMENT, APPLICATION **2** : the fact or state of being used **3** : the way of using **4** : USAGE, CUSTOM **5** : the privilege or benefit of using something **6** : the ability or power to use something (as a limb) **7** : the legal enjoyment of property that consists in its employment, occupation, or exercise; *also* : the benefit or profit esp. from property held in trust **8** : USEFULNESS, UTILITY; *also* : the end served : OBJECT, FUNCTION **9** : the occasion or need to employ ⟨he had no more ~ for it⟩ **10** : ESTEEM, LIKING ⟨had no ~ for modern art⟩

[2]**use** \ˈyüz\ *vb* **used** \ˈyüzd; "*used to*" *usu* ˈyüs-tə\; **us·ing** \ˈyü-ziŋ\ **1** : to put into action or service : EMPLOY **2** : to consume or take (as drugs) regularly **3** : UTILIZE ⟨~ tact⟩ ; *also* : MANIPULATE ⟨*used* his friends to get ahead⟩ **4** : to expend or consume by putting to use **5** : to behave toward : TREAT ⟨*used* the horse cruelly⟩ **6** : to benefit from ⟨house could ~ a coat of paint⟩ **7** — used in the past with *to* to indicate a former practice, fact, or state ⟨we *used* to work harder⟩ — **us·er** *n*

used \ˈyüzd\ *adj* **1** : having been used by another : SECONDHAND ⟨~ cars⟩ **2** : ACCUSTOMED, HABITUATED ⟨~ to the heat⟩

use·ful \ˈyüs-fəl\ *adj* : capable of being put to use : ADVANTAGEOUS; *esp* : serviceable for a beneficial end — **use·ful·ly** \-ē\ *adv* — **use·ful·ness** *n*

use·less \ˈyüs-ləs\ *adj* : having or being of no use : WORTHLESS — **use·less·ly** *adv* — **use·less·ness** *n*

USES *abbr* United States Employment Service

use up *vb* : to consume completely

[1]**ush·er** \ˈəsh-ər\ *n* [ME *ussher*, fr. MF *ussier*, fr. (assumed) VL *ustiarius* doorkeeper, fr. L *ostium*, *ustium* door, mouth of a river] **1** : an officer who walks before a person of rank **2** : one who escorts people to their seats (as in a church or theater)

[2]**usher** *vb* **1** : to conduct to a place **2** : to precede as an usher, forerunner, or harbinger **3** : INAUGURATE, INTRODUCE ⟨~ in a new era⟩

ush·er·ette \ˌəsh-ə-ˈret\ *n* : a female usher (as in a theater)

USIA *abbr* United States Information Agency

USM *abbr* United States mail

USMC *abbr* United States Marine Corps

USN *abbr* United States Navy

USO *abbr* United Service Organizations

USP *abbr* United States Pharmacopeia

USPS *abbr* United States Postal Service

USS *abbr* United States ship
USSR *abbr* Union of Soviet Socialist Republics
usu *abbr* usual; usually
usu·al \ˈyü-zhə(-wə)l\ *adj* **1** : accordant with usage, custom, or habit : NORMAL **2** : commonly or ordinarily used **3** : ORDINARY **syn** customary, habitual, accustomed, routine — **usu·al·ly** \ˈyüzh-(ə-)wə-lē, ˈyüzh-(ə-)lē\ *adv*
usu·fruct \ˈyü-zə-ˌfrəkt\ *n* [L *ususfructus*, fr. *usus et fructus* use and enjoyment] : the legal right to use and enjoy the benefits and profits of something belonging to another
usu·rer \ˈyü-zhər-ər\ *n* : one that lends money esp. at an exorbitant rate
usu·ri·ous \yu̇-ˈzhu̇r-ē-əs\ *adj* : practicing, involving, or constituting usury ⟨a ~ rate of interest⟩
usurp \yu̇-ˈsərp, -ˈzərp\ *vb* [ME *usurpen*, fr. MF *usurper*, fr. L *usurpare*, lit., to take possession of by use, fr. *usu* (abl. of *usus* use) + *rapere* to seize] : to seize and hold by force or without right ⟨~ a throne⟩ — **usur·pa·tion** \ˌyü-sər-ˈpā-shən, -zər-\ *n* — **usurp·er** \yu̇-ˈsər-pər, -ˈzər-\ *n*
usu·ry \ˈyüzh-(ə-)rē\ *n, pl* **-ries** [ME, fr. ML *usuria*, alter. of L *usura*, fr. *usus*, pp. of *uti* to use] **1** : the lending of money with an interest charge for its use **2** : an excessive rate or amount of interest charged; *esp* : interest above an established legal rate
UT *abbr* Utah
Ute \ˈyüt\ *n, pl* **Ute** *or* **Utes** : a member of an American Indian people orig. ranging through Utah, Colorado, Arizona, and New Mexico
uten·sil \yu̇-ˈten-səl\ *n* [ME, vessels for domestic use, fr. MF *utensile*, fr. L *utensilia*, fr. neut. pl. of *utensilis* useful, fr. *uti* to use] **1** : an instrument or vessel used in a household and esp. a kitchen **2** : an article serving a useful purpose
uter·us \ˈyüt-ə-rəs\ *n, pl* **uteri** \ˈyüt-ə-ˌrī\ *also* **uter·us·es** : the muscular organ of a female mammal in which the young develop before birth — **uter·ine** \-ˌrīn, -rən\ *adj*
utile \ˈyüt-ᵊl, ˈyü-ˌtīl\ *adj* : USEFUL
¹**util·i·tar·i·an** \yu̇-ˌtil-ə-ˈter-ē-ən\ *n* : a person who believes in utilitarianism
²**utilitarian** *adj* **1** : of or relating to utilitarianism **2** : of or relating to utility : aiming at usefulness rather than beauty; *also* : serving a useful purpose
util·i·tar·i·an·ism \-ē-ə-ˌniz-əm\ *n* : a theory that the greatest good for the greatest number should be the main consideration in making a choice of actions
¹**util·i·ty** \yü-ˈtil-ət-ē\ *n, pl* **-ties** **1** : USEFULNESS **2** : something useful or designed for use **3** : a business organization performing a public service and subject to special governmental regulation **4** : a public service or a commodity (as electricity or water) provided by a public utility; *also* : equipment to provide such or a similar service
²**utility** *adj* **1** : capable of serving esp. as a substitute in various uses or positions ⟨a ~ outfielder⟩ ⟨a ~ knife⟩ **2** : being of a usable but inferior grade ⟨~ beef⟩
uti·lize \ˈyüt-ᵊl-ˌīz\ *vb* **-lized; -liz·ing** : to make use of : turn to profitable account or use — **uti·li·za·tion** \ˌyüt-ᵊl-ə-ˈzā-shən\ *n*
ut·most \ˈət-ˌmōst\ *adj* **1** : situated at the farthest or most distant point : EXTREME **2** : of the greatest or highest degree, quantity, number, or amount — **utmost** *n*
uto·pia \yu̇-ˈtō-pē-ə\ *n* [fr. *Utopia*, imaginary island described in Sir Thomas More's *Utopia*, fr. Gk *ou* not, no + *topos* place] **1** *often cap* : a place of ideal perfection esp. in laws, government, and social conditions **2** : an impractical scheme for social improvement
¹**uto·pi·an** \-pē-ən\ *adj, often cap* **1** : of, relating to, or resembling a utopia **2** : proposing ideal social and political schemes that are impractical : VISIONARY
²**utopian** *n* **1** : a believer in the perfectibility of human society **2** : one that proposes or advocates utopian schemes
¹**ut·ter** \ˈət-ər\ *adj* [ME, remote, fr. OE *ūtera* outer, compar. adj. fr. *ūt* out, adv.] : ABSOLUTE, TOTAL ⟨~ ruin⟩ — **ut·ter·ly** *adv*
²**utter** *vb* [ME *uttren*, fr. *utter* outside, adv., fr. OE *ūtor*, compar. of *ūt* out] **1** : to send forth as a sound : express in usu. spoken words : PRONOUNCE, SPEAK **2** : to put (as currency) into circulation
ut·ter·ance \ˈət-ə-rəns, ˈə-trəns\ *n* **1** : something uttered; *esp* : an oral or written statement **2** : the action of uttering with the voice : SPEECH **3** : power, style, or manner of speaking
ut·ter·most \ˈət-ər-ˌmōst\ *adj* : EXTREME, UTMOST ⟨the ~ parts of the earth⟩ — **uttermost** *n*
U–turn \ˈyü-ˈtərn\ *n* : a turn resembling the letter U; *esp* : a 180-degree turn made by a vehicle in a road
UV *abbr* ultraviolet
U–val·ue \ˈyü-ˌval-yü\ *n* : a measure of the heat transmission through a building part (as a wall) or a given thickness of insulating material a low value of which indicates high insulating effectiveness
uvu·la \ˈyü-vyə-lə\ *n, pl* **-las** *or* **-lae** \-ˌlē, -ˌlī\ : the fleshy lobe hanging at the back of the palate — **uvu·lar** \-lər\ *adj*
UW *abbr* underwriter
ux·o·ri·ous \ˌək-ˈsōr-ē-əs, ˌəg-ˈzōr-\ *adj* : excessively devoted or submissive to a wife

¹**v** \ˈvē\ *n, pl* **v's** *or* **vs** \ˈvēz\ *often cap* : the 22d letter of the English alphabet
²**v** *abbr, often cap* **1** vector **2** velocity **3** verb **4** verse **5** versus **6** victory **7** vide **8** voice **9** volt; voltage **10** volume **11** vowel
V *symbol* vanadium
Va *abbr* Virginia
VA *abbr* **1** Veterans Administration **2** vice admiral **3** Virginia
va·can·cy \ˈvā-kən-sē\ *n, pl* **-cies** **1** : a vacating esp. of an office, position, or piece of property **2** : the state of being vacant **3** : a vacant office, position, or tenancy; *also* : the period during which it stands vacant **4** : empty space : VOID
va·cant \ˈvā-kənt\ *adj* **1** : not occupied ⟨~ seat⟩ ⟨~ room⟩ **2** : EMPTY ⟨~ space⟩ **3** : free from business or care ⟨a few ~ hours⟩ **4** : devoid of thought, reflection, or expression ⟨a ~ smile⟩ — **va·cant·ly** *adv*
va·cate \ˈvā-ˌkāt\ *vb* **va·cat·ed; va·cat·ing** **1** : to make void : ANNUL **2** : to make vacant (as an office or house); *also* : to give up the occupancy of
¹**va·ca·tion** \vā-ˈkā-shən, və-\ *n* : a period of rest from work : HOLIDAY
²**vacation** *vb* **-tioned; -tion·ing** \-sh(ə-)niŋ\ : to take or spend a vacation — **va·ca·tion·er** \-sh(ə-)nər\ *n*

va·ca·tion·ist \-sh(ə-)nəst\ *n* : a person taking a vacation

va·ca·tion·land \-shən-ˌland\ *n* : an area with recreational attractions and facilities for vacationists

vac·ci·nate \ˈvak-sə-ˌnāt\ *vb* **-nat·ed; -nat·ing** : to inoculate with a related harmless virus to produce immunity to smallpox; *also* : to administer a vaccine to usu. by injection

vac·ci·na·tion \ˌvak-sə-ˈnā-shən\ *n* **1** : the act of vaccinating **2** : the scar left by vaccinating

vac·cine \vak-ˈsēn, ˈvak-ˌsēn\ *n* [L *vaccinus* of or from cows, fr. *vacca* cow; so called from the derivation of smallpox vaccine from cows] : material (as a preparation of killed or weakened virus or bacteria) used in vaccinating to induce immunity to a disease

vac·cin·ia \vak-ˈsin-ē-ə\ *n* : COWPOX

vac·il·late \ˈvas-ə-ˌlāt\ *vb* **-lat·ed; -lat·ing** **1** : SWAY, TOTTER; *also* : FLUCTUATE **2** : to incline first to one course or opinion and then to another : WAVER — **vac·il·la·tion** \ˌvas-ə-ˈlā-shən\ *n*

va·cu·ity \va-ˈkyü-ət-ē, və-\ *n, pl* **-ities** **1** : an empty space **2** : the state, fact, or quality of being vacuous **3** : something that is vacuous

vac·u·ole \ˈvak-yə-ˌwōl\ *n* : a usu. fluid-filled cavity in tissues or in the protoplasm of an individual cell — **vac·u·o·lar** \ˌvak-yə-ˈwō-lər, -ˌlär\ *adj*

vac·u·ous \ˈvak-yə-wəs\ *adj* **1** : EMPTY, VACANT, BLANK **2** : DULL, STUPID, INANE — **vac·u·ous·ly** *adv* — **vac·u·ous·ness** *n*

[1]**vac·u·um** \ˈvak-yü-əm, -(ˌ)yüm, -yəm\ *n, pl* **vacuums** *or* **vac·ua** \-yə-wə\ [L, fr. neut. of *vacuus* empty] **1** : a space entirely empty of matter **2** : a space from which most of the air has been removed (as by a pump) **3** : VOID, GAP **4** : VACUUM CLEANER — **vacuum** *adj*

[2]**vacuum** *vb* : to use a vacuum device (as a vacuum cleaner) on

vacuum bottle *n* : a cylindrical container with a vacuum between an inner and an outer wall used to keep liquids hot or cold

vacuum cleaner *n* : an electrical appliance for cleaning (as floors or rugs) by suction

vac·u·um–packed \ˌvak-yüm-ˈpakt, -yəm-\ *adj* : having much of the air removed before being hermetically sealed

vacuum tube *n* : an electron tube from which most of the air has been removed

va·de me·cum \ˌvād-ē-ˈmē-kəm\ *n, pl* **vade mecums** [L, go with me] : something (as a handbook or manual) carried as a constant companion

VADM *abbr* vice admiral

[1]**vag·a·bond** \ˈvag-ə-ˌbänd\ *adj* **1** : WANDERING, HOMELESS **2** : of, characteristic of, or leading the life of a vagrant or tramp **3** : leading an unsettled or irresponsible life

[2]**vagabond** *n* : one leading a vagabond life; *esp* : TRAMP

va·gar·i·ous \vā-ˈger-ē-əs, və-\ *adj* : marked by vagaries : CAPRICIOUS — **va·gar·i·ous·ly** *adv*

va·ga·ry \ˈvā-gə-rē, və-ˈger-ē\ *n, pl* **-ries** : an odd or eccentric idea or action : WHIM, CAPRICE

va·gi·na \və-ˈjī-nə\ *n, pl* **-nae** \-(ˌ)nē\ *or* **-nas** [L, lit., sheath] : a canal that leads from the uterus to the external opening of the female sex organs — **vag·i·nal** \ˈvaj-ən-ᵊl\ *adj*

vag·i·ni·tis \ˌvaj-ə-ˈnīt-əs\ *n* : inflammation of the vagina

va·gran·cy \ˈvā-grən(t)-sē\ *n, pl* **-cies** **1** : the quality or state of being vagrant; *also* : a vagrant act or notion **2** : the offense of being a vagrant

[1]**va·grant** \ˈvā-grənt\ *n* : a person who has no job and wanders from place to place

[2]**vagrant** *adj* **1** : of, relating to, or characteristic of a vagrant **2** : following no fixed course : RANDOM, CAPRICIOUS ⟨~ thoughts⟩ — **va·grant·ly** *adv*

vague \ˈvāg\ *adj* **vagu·er; vagu·est** [MF, fr. L *vagus,* lit., wandering] **1** : not clear, definite, or distinct **2** : not clearly felt or analyzed ⟨a ~ unrest⟩ **syn** obscure, dark, enigmatic, ambiguous, equivocal — **vague·ly** *adv* — **vague·ness** *n*

vain \ˈvān\ *adj* [ME, fr. OF, fr. L *vanus* empty, vain] **1** : of no real value : IDLE, WORTHLESS **2** : FUTILE, UNSUCCESSFUL **3** : proud of one's looks or abilities **syn** conceited, narcissistic, vainglorious — **vain·ly** *adv*

vain·glo·ri·ous \(ˈ)vān-ˈglōr-ē-əs\ *adj* : marked by vainglory : BOASTFUL

vain·glo·ry \ˈvān-ˌglōr-ē\ *n* **1** : excessive or ostentatious pride esp. in one's own achievements **2** : vain display : VANITY

val *abbr* value; valued

va·lance \ˈval-əns, ˈvāl-\ *n* **1** : drapery hanging from an edge (as of an altar, table, or bed) **2** : a drapery or a decorative frame across the top of a window

vale \ˈvāl\ *n* : VALLEY, DALE

vale·dic·tion \ˌval-ə-ˈdik-shən\ *n* [L *valedictus,* pp. of *valedicere* to say farewell, fr. *vale* farewell + *dicere* to say] : an act or utterance of leave-taking : FAREWELL

vale·dic·to·ri·an \-ˌdik-ˈtōr-ē-ən\ *n* : the student usu. of the highest rank in a graduating class who pronounces the valedictory oration at commencement

vale·dic·to·ry \-ˈdik-t(ə-)rē\ *adj* : bidding farewell : delivered as a valediction ⟨a ~ address⟩ — **valedictory** *n*

va·lence \ˈvā-ləns\ *n* [LL *valentia* power, capacity, fr. L *valēre* to be strong] : the combining power of an atom as shown by the number of electrons in its outermost energy level that are lost, gained, or shared in the formation of chemical bonds

valence electron *n* : an electron in the outer shell of an atom that determines the atom's chemical properties

Va·len·ci·ennes \və-ˌlen-sē-ˈen(z), ˌval-ən-sē-\ *n* : a fine handmade lace

val·en·tine \ˈval-ən-ˌtīn\ *n* : a sweetheart chosen or complimented on St. Valentine's Day; *also* : a greeting card sent on this day

Valentine Day *or* **Valentine's Day** *n* : SAINT VALENTINE'S DAY

[1]**va·let** \ˈval-ət, ˈval-(ˌ)ā, va-ˈlā\ *n* **1** : a male servant who takes care of a man's clothes and performs personal services **2** : an attendant in a hotel who performs personal services for customers

[2]**valet** *vb* : to serve as a valet

val·e·tu·di·nar·i·an \ˌval-ə-ˌt(y)üd-ᵊn-ˈer-ē-ən\ *n* : a person of a weak or sickly constitution; *esp* : one whose chief concern is his invalidism — **val·e·tu·di·nar·i·an·ism** \-ē-ə-ˌniz-əm\ *n*

val·iant \ˈval-yənt\ *adj* : having or showing valor : BRAVE, HEROIC **syn** valorous, doughty, courageous, bold, audacious, dauntless, undaunted, intrepid — **val·iant·ly** *adv*

val·id \ˈval-əd\ *adj* **1** : having legal force ⟨a ~ contract⟩ **2** : founded on truth or fact : capable of being justified or defended : SOUND ⟨a ~ argument⟩ ⟨~ reasons⟩ — **va·lid·i·ty** \və-ˈlid-ət-ē, va-\ *n* — **val·id·ly** \ˈval-əd-lē\ *adv*

val·i·date \ˈval-ə-ˌdāt\ *vb* **-dat·ed; -dat·ing** **1** : to make legally valid **2** : to confirm the validity of **3** : VERIFY — **val·i·da·tion** \ˌval-ə-ˈdā-shən\ *n*

va·lise \və-ˈlēs\ *n* [F] : TRAVELING BAG

val·ley \ˈval-ē\ *n, pl* **valleys** : a long depression between ranges of hills or mountains

val·or \ˈval-ər\ *n* [ME, fr. MF *valour,* fr. ML *valor* value, valor, fr. L *valēre* to be strong] : personal bravery **syn** heroism, prowess, gallantry — **val·or·ous** \ˈval-ə-rəs\ *adj*

val·o·ri·za·tion \ˌval-ə-rə-ˈzā-shən\ *n* : the support of commodity prices by any of various forms of government subsidy — **val·o·rize** \ˈval-ə-ˌrīz\ *vb*

valse \väls\ *n* [F] : WALTZ; *esp* : a concert waltz

[1]**valu·able** \ˈval-yə-(wə-)bəl\ *adj* **1** : having money value **2** : having great money value **3** : of great use or service **syn** invaluable, priceless, costly, expensive, dear, precious

[2]**valuable** *n* : a usu. personal possession of considerable value ⟨their ~*s* were stolen⟩

val·u·ate \ˈval-yə-ˌwāt\ *vb* **-at·ed; -at·ing** : to place a value on : APPRAISE — **val·u·a·tor** \-ˌwāt-ər\ *n*

val·u·a·tion \ˌval-yə-ˈwā-shən\ *n* **1** : the act or process of valuing; *esp* : appraisal of property **2** : the estimated or determined market value of a thing

[1]**val·ue** \ˈval-yü\ *n* **1** : a fair return or equivalent in money, goods, or services for something exchanged **2** : the worth of a thing : market price, purchasing power, or estimated worth **3** : an assigned or computed numerical quantity ⟨the ~ of *x* in an equation⟩ **4** : precise meaning ⟨~ of a word⟩ **5** : distinctive quality of sound in speech **6** : luminosity of a color : BRILLIANCE; *also* : the relation of one detail in a picture to another with respect to lightness or darkness **7** : the relative length of a tone or note **8** : something (as a principle or ideal) intrinsically valuable or desirable ⟨human rather than material ~*s*⟩ — **val·ue·less** *adj*

[2]**value** *vb* **val·ued; valu·ing** **1** : to estimate the monetary worth of : APPRAISE **2** : to rate in usefulness, importance, or general worth **3** : to consider or rate highly : PRIZE, ESTEEM — **val·u·er** *n*

val·ue–add·ed tax *n* : an incremental excise tax that is levied on the value added at each stage of the processing of a raw material or the production and distribution of a commodity

val·ued \ˈval-yüd\ *adj* : highly esteemed : PRIZED

valve \ˈvalv\ *n* **1** : a structure (as in a vein) that temporarily closes a passage or that permits movement in one direction only **2** : one of the pieces into which a ripe seed capsule or pod separates **3** : a device by which the flow of liquid, gas, or loose material in bulk may be regulated by a movable part; *also* : the movable part of such a device **4** : a device in a brass wind instrument for quickly varying the tube length in order to change the fundamental tone by some definite interval **5** : one of the separable usu. hinged pieces of which the shell of some animals and esp. bivalve mollusks consists — **valved** \ˈvalvd\ *adj* — **valve·less** *adj*

val·vu·lar \ˈval-vyə-lər\ *adj* **1** : resembling or functioning as a valve; *also* : opening by valves **2** : of or relating to a valve esp. of the heart

va·moose \və-ˈmüs, va-\ *vb* **va·moosed; va·moos·ing** [Sp *vamos* let us go] *slang* : to leave or go away quickly

[1]**vamp** \ˈvamp\ *vb* **1** : to provide with a new vamp **2** : to patch up with a new part **3** : INVENT, IMPROVISE ⟨~ up an excuse⟩

[2]**vamp** *n* **1** : the part of a boot or shoe upper covering esp. the front part of the foot **2** : a short introductory musical passage often repeated

[3]**vamp** *n* : a woman who uses her charm and allurements to seduce and exploit men

[4]**vamp** *vb* : to practice seductive wiles on

vam·pire \ˈvam-ˌpī(ə)r\ *n* **1** : a night-wandering bloodsucking ghost **2** : a person who preys on other people; *esp* : a woman who exploits and ruins her lover **3** : any of various bats of Mexico and Central and South America that feed on the blood of animals including man; *also* : any of several bats believed to suck blood

[1]**van** \ˈvan\ *n* : VANGUARD

[2]**van** *n* : a usu. enclosed wagon or motortruck for moving goods or animals; *also* : a versatile enclosed boxlike motor vehicle with side or rear doors and side panels that often have windows

va·na·di·um \və-ˈnād-ē-əm\ *n* : a soft ductile metallic chemical element used to form alloys — see ELEMENT table

Van Al·len belt \van-ˈal-ən-\ *n* : a belt of intense ionizing radiation in the earth's magnetosphere

van·dal \ˈvan-dᵊl\ *n* **1** *cap* : a member of a Germanic people who sacked Rome in A.D. 455 **2** : one who willfully mars or destroys property

van·dal·ism \-ˌiz-əm\ *n* : willful or malicious destruction or defacement of public or private property

van·dal·ize \-ˌīz\ *vb* **-ized; -iz·ing** : to subject to vandalism : DAMAGE

Van·dyke \van-ˈdīk\ *n* : a trim pointed beard

vane \ˈvān\ *n* [ME, fr. OE *fana* banner] **1** : a movable device attached to a high object to show the way the wind blows **2** : a thin flat or curved object that is rotated about an axis by a flow of fluid or that rotates to cause a fluid to flow or that redirects a flow of fluid ⟨the ~*s* of a windmill⟩

van·guard \ˈvan-ˌgärd\ *n* **1** : the troops moving at the front of an army : VAN **2** : the forefront of an action or movement

va·nil·la \və-ˈnil-ə\ *n* [NL, genus name, fr. Sp *vainilla* vanilla (plant and fruit), dim. of *vaina* sheath, fr. L *vagina* sheath, vagina] : a tropical American climbing orchid with beanlike pods; *also* : its pods or a flavoring extract made from these

van·ish \ˈvan-ish\ *vb* : to pass from sight or existence : disappear completely — **van·ish·er** *n*

van·i·ty \ˈvan-ət-ē\ *n, pl* **-ties** **1** : something that is vain, empty, or useless **2** : the quality or fact of being useless or futile : FUTILITY **3** : undue pride in oneself or one's appearance : CONCEIT **4** : a small case for cosmetics : COMPACT

vanity plate *n* : an automobile license plate bearing distinctive letters or numbers designated by the owner

van·quish \ˈvaŋ-kwish, ˈvan-\ *vb* **1** : to overcome in battle or in a contest **2** : to gain mastery over (as an emotion)

van·tage \ˈvant-ij\ *n* **1** : superiority in a contest **2** : a position giving a strategic advantage or a commanding perspective

van·ward \ˈvan-wərd\ *adj* : being in or toward the vanguard : ADVANCED — **vanward** *adv*

va·pid \ˈvap-əd, ˈvā-pəd\ *adj* : lacking spirit, liveliness, or zest : FLAT, INSIPID — **va·pid·i·ty** \va-ˈpid-ət-ē\ *n* — **vap·id·ly** \ˈvap-əd-lē\ *adv* — **vap·id·ness** *n*

[1]**va·por** \ˈvā-pər\ *n* **1** : fine separated particles (as fog or smoke) floating in the air and clouding it **2** : a substance in the gaseous state; *esp* : one that is liquid under ordinary conditions **3** : something insubstantial or fleeting **4** *pl* : a depressed or hysterical nervous condition

[2]**vapor** *vb* **1** : to rise or pass off in vapor **2** : to emit vapor

va·por·ing \ˈvā-p(ə-)riŋ\ *n* : an idle, boastful, or high-flown expression or speech — usu. used in pl.

va·por·ish \ˈvā-p(ə-)rish\ *adj* **1** : resembling or suggestive of vapor **2** : given to fits of depression or hysteria — **va·por·ish·ness** *n*

va·por·ize \ˈvā-pə-ˌrīz\ *vb* **-ized; -iz·ing** : to convert into vapor — **va·por·iza·tion** \ˌvā-pə-rə-ˈzā-shən\ *n*

va·por·iz·er \-ˌrī-zər\ *n* : a device that vaporizes something (as a medicated liquid)

vapor lock *n* : a partial or complete interruption of flow of a fluid (as fuel in an internal-combustion engine) caused by the formation of bubbles of vapor in the feeding system

va·por·ous \ˈvā-p(ə-)rəs\ *adj* **1** : consisting of or characteristic of vapor **2** : producing vapors : VOLATILE **3** : full of vapors : FOGGY, MISTY — **va·por·ous·ly** *adv* — **va·por·ous·ness** *n*

va·pory \ˈvā-p(ə-)rē\ *adj* : VAPOROUS, VAGUE

va·que·ro \vä-ˈker-ō\ *n, pl* **-ros** [Sp, fr. *vaca* cow, fr. L *vacca*] : a ranch hand : COWBOY

var *abbr* **1** variable **2** variant; variation **3** variety **4** various

[1]**vari·able** \ˈver-ē-ə-bəl\ *adj* **1** : able or apt to vary

: CHANGEABLE **2** : FICKLE **3** : not true to type : ABERRANT ⟨a ~ wheat⟩ — **vari·abil·i·ty** \ˌver-ē-ə-ˈbil-ət-ē\ *n* — **vari·able·ness** \ˈver-ē-ə-bəl-nəs\ *n* — **vari·ably** \-blē\ *adv*

²variable *n* **1** : something that is variable **2** : a quantity that may assume a succession of values; *also* : a symbol standing for any one of a class of things

vari·ance \ˈver-ē-əns\ *n* **1** : variation or a degree of variation : DEVIATION **2** : DISAGREEMENT, DISPUTE **3** : a license to do something contrary to the usual rule ⟨a zoning ~⟩ **syn** discord, contention, dissension, strife, conflict

¹vari·ant \ˈver-ē-ənt\ *adj* **1** : differing from others of its kind or class **2** : varying usu. slightly from the standard or type

²variant *n* **1** : one that exhibits variation from a type or norm **2** : one of two or more different spellings or pronunciations of a word

vari·a·tion \ˌver-ē-ˈā-shən\ *n* **1** : an act or instance of varying : a change in form, position, or condition : MODIFICATION, ALTERATION **2** : extent of change or difference **3** : divergence in qualities from those typical or usual to a group; *also* : one exhibiting such variation **4** : repetition of a musical theme with modifications in rhythm, tune, harmony, or key

vari·col·ored \ˈver-i-ˌkəl-ərd\ *adj* : having various colors : VARIEGATED

var·i·cose \ˈvar-ə-ˌkōs\ *adj* : abnormally and irregularly swollen ⟨~ veins⟩

var·i·cos·i·ty \ˌvar-ə-ˈkäs-ət-ē\ *n, pl* **-ties 1** : the quality or state of being varicose **2** : a varicose part or lesion (as of a vein)

var·ied \ˈver-ēd\ *adj* **1** : having many forms or types : DIVERSE **2** : VARIEGATED — **var·ied·ly** *adv*

var·ie·gate \ˈver-ē-ə-ˌgāt, ˈver-i-ˌgāt\ *vb* **-gat·ed; -gat·ing 1** : to diversify in external appearance esp. with different colors **2** : to introduce variety into : DIVERSIFY — **var·ie·gat·ed** *adj* — **var·ie·ga·tion** \ˌver-ē-ə-ˈgā-shən, ˌver-i-ˈgā-\ *n*

va·ri·etal \və-ˈrī-ət-ᵊl\ *adj* : of or relating to a variety; *also* : being a variety rather than an individual or species

va·ri·ety \və-ˈrī-ət-ē\ *n, pl* **-et·ies 1** : the state of being varied or various : DIVERSITY **2** : a collection of different things **3** : something varying from other things of the same general kind **4** : any of various groups of plants or animals within a species distinguished by characteristics not constant enough or too unimportant to separate species **5** : entertainment such as is given in a stage presentation comprising a series of performances (as songs, dances, or acrobatic acts)

var·i·o·rum \ˌver-ē-ˈōr-əm\ *n* : an edition or text of a work containing notes by various persons or variant readings of the text

var·i·ous \ˈver-ē-əs\ *adj* **1** : VARICOLORED **2** : of differing kinds : MULTIFARIOUS **3** : UNLIKE ⟨animals as ~ as the jaguar and the sloth⟩ **4** : having a number of different aspects **5** : NUMEROUS, MANY **6** : INDIVIDUAL, SEPARATE **syn** divergent, disparate, different, dissimilar, diverse, unalike — **var·i·ous·ly** *adv*

va·ris·tor \va-ˈris-tər\ *n* : a voltage-dependent electrical resistor

var·let \ˈvär-lət\ *n* [ME, fr. MF *vaslet, varlet* young nobleman, page] **1** : ATTENDANT **2** : SCOUNDREL, KNAVE

var·mint \ˈvär-mənt\ *n* [alter. of *vermin*] **1** : an animal considered a pest; *esp* : a mammal or bird classed as vermin and unprotected by game law **2** : a contemptible person : RASCAL

¹var·nish \ˈvär-nish\ *n* **1** : a liquid preparation that is spread on a surface and dries into a hard glossy coating; *also* : the glaze of this coating **2** : something suggesting varnish by its gloss **3** : outside show : GLOSS

²varnish *vb* **1** : to cover with varnish **2** : to cover or conceal with something that gives a fair appearance : gloss over

var·si·ty \ˈvär-sət-ē, -stē\ *n, pl* **-ties** [by shortening & alter. fr. *university*] **1** *Brit* : UNIVERSITY **2** : the principal team representing a college, school, or club

vary \ˈver-ē\ *vb* **var·ied; vary·ing 1** : ALTER, CHANGE **2** : to make or be of different kinds : introduce or have variety : DIVERSIFY, DIFFER **3** : DEVIATE, SWERVE **4** : to diverge structurally or physiologically from typical members of a group

vas·cu·lar \ˈvas-kyə-lər\ *adj* [NL *vascularis,* fr. L *vasculum* small vessel, dim. of *vas* vase, vessel] : of or relating to a channel or system of channels for the conveyance of a body fluid (as blood or sap); *also* : supplied with or containing such vessels and esp. blood vessels

vascular plant *n* : a plant having a specialized conducting system that includes xylem and phloem

vase \ˈvās, ˈvāz\ *n* : a usu. round vessel of greater depth than width used chiefly for ornament or for flowers

va·sec·to·my \və-ˈsek-tə-mē, vā-ˈzek-\ *n, pl* **-mies** : surgical excision of all or part of the sperm-carrying ducts of the testis usu. to induce permanent sterility

va·so·con·stric·tion \ˌvas-ō-kən-ˈstrik-shən, ˌvāz-\ *n* : narrowing of the interior diameter of blood vessels

va·so·con·stric·tor \-tər\ *n* : an agent (as a nerve fiber or a drug) that initiates or induces vasoconstriction

vas·sal \ˈvas-əl\ *n* **1** : a person under the protection of a feudal lord to whom he owes homage and loyalty : a feudal tenant **2** : one occupying a dependent or subordinate position — **vassal** *adj*

vas·sal·age \-ə-lij\ *n* **1** : the state of being a vassal **2** : the homage and loyalty due from a vassal **3** : SERVITUDE, SUBJECTION

¹vast \ˈvast\ *adj* : very great in size, amount, degree, intensity, or esp. extent **syn** enormous, huge, gigantic, colossal, mammoth — **vast·ly** *adv* — **vast·ness** *n*

²vast *n* : a great expanse : IMMENSITY

vasty \ˈvas-tē\ *adj* : VAST, IMMENSE

vat \ˈvat\ *n* : a large vessel (as a tub or barrel) esp. for holding liquids in manufacturing processes

VAT *abbr* value-added tax

vat·ic \ˈvat-ik\ *adj* : PROPHETIC, ORACULAR

Vat·i·can \ˈvat-i-kən\ *n* **1** : the papal headquarters in Rome **2** : the papal government

va·tu \ˈvä-ˌtü\ *n, pl* **vatu** — see MONEY table

vaude·ville \ˈvȯd-(ə-)vəl, ˈväd-, ˈvōd-, -(ə-)ˌvil\ *n* [F, fr. MF, popular satirical song, alter. of *vaudevire,* fr. *vau-de-Vire* valley of Vire, fr. *Vire,* town in northwest France where such songs were composed] : a stage entertainment consisting of unrelated acts (as of acrobats, comedians, dancers, or singers)

¹vault \ˈvȯlt\ *n* **1** : an arched masonry structure usu. forming a ceiling or roof; *also* : something (as the sky) resembling a vault **2** : a room or space covered by a vault esp. when underground and used for a special purpose (as for storage of valuables or wine supplies) **3** : a burial chamber; *also* : a usu. metal or concrete case in which a casket is enclosed at burial — **vaulty** *adj*

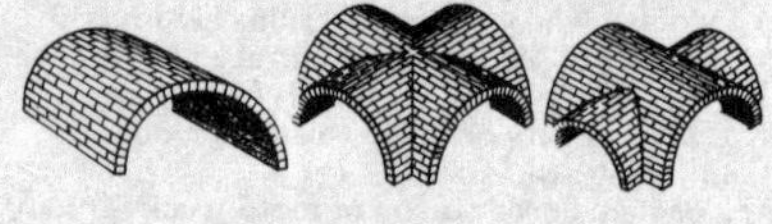

¹vault 1

²vault *vb* : to form or cover with a vault

³vault *vb* : to leap vigorously esp. by aid of the hands or a pole — **vault·er** *n*

⁴vault *n* : an act of vaulting : LEAP

vault·ed \ˈvȯl-təd\ *adj* **1** : built in the form of a vault : ARCHED **2** : covered with a vault

vault·ing \-tiŋ\ *adj* : leaping upward : reaching for the heights ⟨~ ambition⟩

vaunt \ˈvȯnt\ *vb* [ME *vaunten,* fr. MF *vanter,* fr. LL

vanitare, fr. L *vanitas* vanity] : BRAG, BOAST — **vaunt** *n*
vb *abbr* verb
VCR \ˈvē-ˈsē-ˈär\ *n* [*v*ideo*c*assette *r*ecorder] : a videotape recorder that uses videocassettes
VD *abbr* venereal disease
veal \ˈvēl\ *n* : the flesh of a young calf
vec·tor \ˈvek-tər\ *n* **1** : a quantity that has magnitude and direction **2** : an organism (as a fly) that transmits disease germs
Ve·da \ˈvād-ə\ *n* [Skt, lit., knowledge] : any of a class of Hindu sacred writings — **Ve·dic** \ˈvād-ik\ *adj*
Ve·dan·ta \vā-ˈdänt-ə, və-, -ˈdant-\ *n* : an orthodox Hindu philosophy based on the Upanishads
veep \ˈvēp\ *n* : VICE PRESIDENT
veer \ˈviər\ *vb* : to shift from one direction or course to another **syn** turn, avert, deflect, divert — **veer** *n*
vee·ry \ˈvi(ə)r-ē\ *n, pl* **veeries** : a tawny brown thrush of the woods of the eastern U.S.
veg·an \ˈvej-ən, ˈvē-gən\ *n* : a strict vegetarian; *esp* : one who consumes no animal food or dairy products — **veg·an·ism** \ˈvej-ə-ˌniz-əm, ˈvē-gə-\ *n*
[1]**veg·e·ta·ble** \ˈvej-(ə-)tə-bəl\ *adj* [ME, fr. ML *vegetabilis* vegetative, fr. *vegetare* to grow, fr. L, to animate, fr. *vegetus* lively, fr. *vegēre* to rouse, excite] **1** : of, relating to, or growing like plants **2** : made or obtained from plants ⟨~ oils⟩ ⟨the ~ kingdom⟩ **3** : suggesting that of a plant ⟨a ~ existence⟩
[2]**vegetable** *n* **1** : PLANT 1 **2** : a usu. herbaceous plant grown for an edible part that is usu. eaten with the principal course of a meal; *also* : such an edible part
veg·e·tal \ˈvej-ət-ᵊl\ *adj* **1** : VEGETABLE **2** : VEGETATIVE
veg·e·tar·i·an \ˌvej-ə-ˈter-ē-ən\ *n* : one that believes in or practices living solely on plant products — **vegetarian** *adj* — **veg·e·tar·i·an·ism** \-ē-ə-ˌniz-əm\ *n*
veg·e·tate \ˈvej-ə-ˌtāt\ *vb* **-tat·ed; -tat·ing** : to grow in the manner of a plant; *esp* : to lead a dull inert life
veg·e·ta·tion \ˌvej-ə-ˈtā-shən\ *n* **1** : the act or process of vegetating; *also* : a dull inert existence **2** : plant life or cover (as of an area) — **veg·e·ta·tion·al** \-sh(ə-)nəl\ *adj*
veg·e·ta·tive \ˈvej-ə-ˌtāt-iv\ *adj* **1** : of or relating to nutrition and growth esp. as contrasted with reproduction **2** : of, relating to, or composed of vegetation **3** : leading or marked by a passive, stupid, and dull existence
ve·he·mence \ˈvē-ə-məns\ *n* : the quality or state of being vehement : INTENSITY, VIOLENCE
ve·he·ment \-mənt\ *adj* **1** : marked by great force or energy **2** : marked by strong feeling or expression : PASSIONATE **3** : strong in effect : INTENSE — **ve·he·ment·ly** *adv*
ve·hi·cle \ˈvē-ˌ(h)ik-əl, ˈvē-ə-kəl\ *n* **1** : a medium by which a thing is applied or administered ⟨linseed oil is a ~ for pigments⟩ **2** : a medium through or by means of which something is conveyed or expressed **3** : a means of carrying or transporting something : CONVEYANCE **syn** means, instrument, agent, agency, organ, channel — **ve·hic·u·lar** \vē-ˈhik-yə-lər\ *adj*
[1]**veil** \ˈvāl\ *n* **1** : a piece of often sheer or diaphanous material used to screen or curtain something or to cover the head or face **2** : the state accepted when a woman becomes a nun ⟨take the ~⟩ **3** : something that hides or obscures like a veil
[2]**veil** *vb* : to cover with or as if with a veil : wear a veil
veil·ing \ˈvā-liŋ\ *n* **1** : VEIL **2** : any of various sheer fabrics (as net or chiffon)
[1]**vein** \ˈvān\ *n* **1** : a fissure in rock filled with mineral matter; *also* : a bed of useful mineral matter **2** : one of the tubular branching vessels that carry blood from the capillaries toward the heart **3** : one of the vascular bundles forming the framework of a leaf **4** : one of the thickened ribs that stiffen the wings of an insect **5** : something (as a wavy variegation in marble) suggesting veins **6** : a distinctive mode of expression : STYLE **7** : something of distinctive character considered as running through something else : STRAIN **8** : MOOD, HUMOR — **veined** \ˈvānd\ *adj*
[2]**vein** *vb* : to form or mark with or as if with veins — **vein·ing** *n*
vel *abbr* velocity
ve·lar \ˈvē-lər\ *adj* : of or relating to a velum and esp. that of the soft palate
veld *or* **veldt** \ˈvelt, ˈfelt\ *n* [Afrikaans *veld*, fr. Middle Dutch, field] : open grassland esp. in Africa usu. with scattered shrubs or trees
vel·lum \ˈvel-əm\ *n* [ME *velim*, fr. MF *veelin*, fr. *veelin*, adj., of a calf, fr. *veel* calf] **1** : a fine-grained lambskin, kidskin, or calfskin prepared for writing on or for binding books **2** : a paper manufactured to resemble vellum — **vellum** *adj*
ve·loc·i·pede \və-ˈläs-ə-ˌpēd\ *n* : an early bicycle
ve·loc·i·ty \və-ˈläs-(ə-)tē\ *n, pl* **-ties** : quickness of motion : SPEED ⟨the ~ of light⟩
ve·lour *or* **ve·lours** \və-ˈlu̇r\ *n, pl* **velours** \-ˈlu̇rz\ : any of various textile fabrics with pile like that of velvet
ve·lum \ˈvē-ləm\ *n, pl* **ve·la** \-lə\ : a membranous partition (as the soft palate) resembling a veil
[1]**vel·vet** \ˈvel-vət\ *n* [ME *veluet, velvet*, fr. MF *velu* shaggy, fr. L *villus* shaggy hair] **1** : a fabric characterized by a short soft dense warp pile **2** : something resembling or suggesting velvet (as in softness or luster) **3** : soft skin covering the growing antlers of deer **4** : the winnings of a player in a gambling game — **velvety** *adj*
[2]**velvet** *adj* **1** : made of or covered with velvet **2** : resembling or suggesting velvet : SMOOTH, SOFT, SLEEK
vel·ve·teen \ˌvel-və-ˈtēn\ *n* **1** : a fabric woven usu. of cotton in imitation of velvet **2** *pl* : clothes made of velveteen
Ven *abbr* venerable
ve·nal \ˈvēn-ᵊl\ *adj* : capable of being bought esp. by underhanded means : MERCENARY, CORRUPT — **ve·nal·i·ty** \vi-ˈnal-ət-ē\ *n* — **ve·nal·ly** \ˈvēn-ᵊl-ē\ *adv*
ve·na·tion \ve-ˈnā-shən, vē-\ *n* : an arrangement or system of veins ⟨the ~ of the hand⟩ ⟨leaf ~⟩
vend \ˈvend\ *vb* : SELL; *esp* : to sell as a hawker or peddler — **vend·ible** *adj*
vend·ee \ven-ˈdē\ *n* : one to whom a thing is sold : BUYER
vend·er \ˈven-dər\ *n* : VENDOR
ven·det·ta \ven-ˈdet-ə\ *n* : a feud between clans or families
vending machine *n* : a coin-operated machine for vending merchandise
ven·dor \ˈven-dər, *for 1 also* ven-ˈdȯr\ *n* **1** : one that vends : SELLER **2** : VENDING MACHINE
[1]**ve·neer** \və-ˈniər\ *n* [G *furnier*, fr. *furnieren* to veneer, fr. F *fournir* to furnish] **1** : a thin usu. superficial layer of material ⟨brick ~⟩; *esp* : a thin layer of fine wood glued over a cheaper wood **2** : superficial display : GLOSS
[2]**veneer** *vb* : to overlay with a veneer
ven·er·a·ble \ˈven-ər-(ə-)bəl, ˈven-rə-bəl\ *adj* **1** : deserving to be venerated — often used as a religious title **2** : made sacred by association
ven·er·ate \ˈven-ə-ˌrāt\ *vb* **-at·ed; -at·ing** : to regard with reverential respect **syn** adore, revere, reverence, worship — **ven·er·a·tion** \ˌven-ə-ˈrā-shən\ *n*
ve·ne·re·al \və-ˈnir-ē-əl\ *adj* : of or relating to sexual intercourse or to diseases transmitted by it ⟨a ~ infection⟩
venereal disease *n* : a contagious disease (as gonorrhea or syphilis) that is usu. acquired by having sexual intercourse with someone who already has it
ve·ne·tian blind \və-ˌnē-shən-\ *n* : a blind having thin horizontal parallel slats that can be adjusted to admit a desired amount of light

---

Ven·e·zue·lan \ˌven-əz-ˈwā-lən\ *n* : a native or inhabitant of Venezuela — **Venezuelan** *adj*

ven·geance \ˈven-jəns\ *n* : punishment inflicted in retaliation for an injury or offense : RETRIBUTION

venge·ful \ˈvenj-fəl\ *adj* : filled with a desire for revenge : VINDICTIVE — **venge·ful·ly** \-ē\ *adv*

ve·nial \ˈvē-nē-əl, -nyəl\ *adj* : capable of being forgiven : EXCUSABLE ⟨~ sin⟩

ven·i·punc·ture \ˈvēn-ə-ˌpəŋk-chər, ˈven-ə-\ *n* : surgical puncture of a vein esp. for withdrawal of blood or for intravenous medication

ve·ni·re \və-ˈnī-rē\ *n* : a panel from which a jury is drawn

ve·ni·re fa·ci·as \-ˈfā-shē-əs\ *n* [ME, fr. ML, you should cause to come] : a writ summoning persons to appear in court to serve as jurors

ve·ni·re·man \və-ˈnī-rē-mən, -ˈnir-ē-\ *n* : a member of a venire

ven·i·son \ˈven-ə-sən, -ə-zən\ *n, pl* **venisons** *also* **venison** [ME, fr. OF *veneison* hunting, game, fr. L *venatio,* fr. *venari* to hunt, pursue] : the edible flesh of a deer

ven·om \ˈven-əm\ *n* [ME *venim, venom,* fr. OF *venim,* deriv. of L *venenum* magic charm, drug, poison] **1** : poisonous material secreted by some animals (as snakes, spiders, or bees) and transmitted usu. by biting or stinging **2** : something that poisons or embitters the mind or spirit : MALIGNITY, MALICE

ven·om·ous \ˈven-ə-məs\ *adj* **1** : full of venom : POISONOUS **2** : MALIGNANT, SPITEFUL, MALICIOUS **3** : secreting and using venom ⟨~ snakes⟩ — **ven·om·ous·ly** *adv*

ve·nous \ˈvē-nəs\ *adj* **1** : of, relating to, or full of veins **2** : being purplish red oxygen-deficient blood present in most veins

¹vent \ˈvent\ *vb* **1** : to provide with a vent **2** : to serve as a vent for **3** : EXPEL, DISCHARGE **4** : to give expression to

²vent *n* **1** : an opportunity or way of escape or passage : OUTLET **2** : an opening for passage or escape (as of a fluid, gas, or smoke) or for relieving pressure

³vent *n* : a slit in a garment esp. in the lower part of a seam (as of a jacket or skirt)

ven·ti·late \ˈvent-ᵊl-ˌāt\ *vb* **-lat·ed; -lat·ing 1** : to discuss freely and openly ⟨~ a question⟩ **2** : to give vent to ⟨~ one's grievances⟩ **3** : to cause fresh air to circulate through (as a room or mine) so as to replace foul air **4** : to provide with a vent or outlet **syn** express, vent, air, utter, voice, broach — **ven·ti·la·tor** \-ᵊl-ˌāt-ər\ *n*

ven·ti·la·tion \ˌvent-ᵊl-ˈā-shən\ *n* **1** : the act or process of ventilating **2** : circulation of air (as in a room) **3** : a system or means of providing fresh air

ven·tral \ˈven-trəl\ *adj* **1** : of or relating to the belly : ABDOMINAL **2** : of, relating to, or located on or near the surface of the body that in humans is the front but in most other animals is the lower surface — **ven·tral·ly** \-ē\ *adv*

ven·tri·cle \ˈven-tri-kəl\ *n* **1** : a chamber of the heart that receives blood from the atrium of the same side and pumps it into the arteries **2** : any of the communicating cavities of the brain that are continuous with the central canal of the spinal cord

ven·tril·o·quism \ven-ˈtril-ə-ˌkwiz-əm\ *n* [LL *ventriloquus* ventriloquist, fr. L *venter* belly + *loqui* to speak; fr. the belief that the voice is produced from the ventriloquist's stomach] : the production of the voice in such a manner that the sound appears to come from a source other than the speaker — **ven·tril·o·quist** \-kwəst\ *n*

ven·tril·o·quy \-kwē\ *n* : VENTRILOQUISM

¹ven·ture \ˈven-chər\ *vb* **ven·tured; ven·tur·ing** \ˈvench-(ə-)riŋ\ **1** : to expose to hazard : RISK **2** : to undertake the risks of : BRAVE **3** : to advance or put forward or expose to criticism or argument ⟨~ an opinion⟩ **4** : to make a venure : run a risk : proceed despite danger : DARE

²venture *n* **1** : an undertaking involving chance or risk; *esp* : a speculative business enterprise **2** : something risked in a speculative venture : STAKE

ven·ture·some \ˈven-chər-səm\ *adj* **1** : involving risk : DANGEROUS, HAZARDOUS **2** : inclined to venture : BOLD, DARING **syn** adventurous, venturous, rash, reckless, foolhardy — **ven·ture·some·ly** *adv* — **ven·ture·some·ness** *n*

ven·tur·ous \ˈvench-(ə-)rəs\ *adj* : VENTURESOME — **ven·tur·ous·ly** *adv* — **ven·tur·ous·ness** *n*

ven·ue \ˈven-yü\ *n* : the place in which the alleged events from which a legal action arises took place; *also* : the place from which the jury is taken and where the trial is held

Ve·nus \ˈvē-nəs\ *n* : the planet second in order from the sun

Ve·nu·sian \vi-ˈn(y)ü-zhən\ *adj* : of or relating to the planet Venus

Ve·nus's–fly·trap \ˌvē-nəs(-əz)-ˈflī-ˌtrap\ *or* **Venus fly·trap** *n* : an insectivorous plant of the Carolina coast that has the leaf tip modified into an insect trap

ve·ra·cious \və-ˈrā-shəs\ *adj* **1** : TRUTHFUL, HONEST **2** : TRUE, ACCURATE — **ve·ra·cious·ly** *adv*

ve·rac·i·ty \və-ˈras-ət-ē\ *n, pl* **-ties 1** : devotion to truth : TRUTHFULNESS **2** : conformity with fact : ACCURACY **3** : something true

ve·ran·da *or* **ve·ran·dah** \və-ˈran-də\ *n* : a long open usu. roofed porch

verb \ˈvərb\ *n* : a word that is the grammatical center of a predicate and expresses an act, occurrence, or mode of being

¹ver·bal \ˈvər-bəl\ *adj* **1** : of, relating to, or consisting of words; *esp* : having to do with words rather than with the ideas to be conveyed **2** : expressed in usu. spoken words : not written : ORAL ⟨a ~ contract⟩ **3** : of, relating to, or formed from a verb **4** : LITERAL, VERBATIM — **ver·bal·ly** \-ē\ *adv*

²verbal *n* : a word that combines characteristics of a verb with those of a noun or adjective

verbal auxiliary *n* : an auxiliary verb

ver·bal·ize \ˈvər-bə-ˌlīz\ *vb* **-ized; -iz·ing 1** : to speak or write in wordy or empty fashion **2** : to express something in words : describe verbally **3** : to convert into a verb — **ver·bal·iza·tion** \ˌvər-bə-lə-ˈzā-shən\ *n*

verbal noun *n* : a noun derived directly from a verb or verb stem and in some uses having the sense and constructions of a verb

ver·ba·tim \(ˌ)vər-ˈbāt-əm\ *adv or adj* : in the same words : word for word

ver·be·na \(ˌ)vər-ˈbē-nə\ *n* : VERVAIN; *esp* : any of several garden plants with showy spikes of bright often fragrant flowers

ver·biage \ˈvər-bē-ij\ *n* **1** : superfluity of words or words with little meaning : WORDINESS **2** : DICTION, WORDING

ver·bose \(ˌ)vər-ˈbōs\ *adj* : using more words than are needed : WORDY **syn** prolix, diffuse, redundant, windy — **ver·bos·i·ty** \-ˈbäs-ət-ē\ *n*

ver·bo·ten \vər-ˈbōt-ᵊn\ *adj* [G] : forbidden usu. by authority and often unreasonably

ver·dant \ˈvərd-ᵊnt\ *adj* **1** : green with growing plants **2** : unripe in experience : GREEN — **ver·dant·ly** *adv*

ver·dict \ˈvər-(ˌ)dikt\ *n* [alter. of ME *verdit,* fr. Anglo-French (the French of medieval England), fr. OF *ver* true (fr. L *verus*) + *dit* saying, dictum, fr. L *dictum,* fr. *dicere* to say] **1** : the finding or decision of a jury on the matter submitted to it in trial **2** : DECISION, JUDGMENT

ver·di·gris \ˈvərd-ə-ˌgrēs, -ˌgris\ *n* : a green or bluish deposit that forms on copper, brass, or bronze surfaces when exposed to the weather

ver·dure \ˈvər-jər\ *n* : the greenness of growing vegetation; *also* : green vegetation

¹verge \ˈvərj\ *n* **1** : a staff carried as an emblem of authority or office **2** : something that borders or bounds : EDGE, MARGIN **3** : BRINK, THRESHOLD

²verge *vb* **verged; verg·ing 1 :** to be contiguous **2 :** to be on the verge or border

³verge *vb* **verged; verg·ing 1 :** to move or extend in some direction or toward some condition **:** INCLINE **2 :** to be in transition or change

verg·er \ˈvər-jər\ *n* **1** *chiefly Brit* **:** an attendant who carries a verge (as before a bishop) **2 :** SEXTON

ve·rid·i·cal \və-ˈrid-i-kəl\ *adj* **1 :** TRUTHFUL **2 :** not illusory **:** GENUINE

ver·i·fy \ˈver-ə-ˌfī\ *vb* **-fied; -fy·ing 1 :** to confirm in law by oath **2 :** to establish the truth, accuracy, or reality of **syn** authenticate, confirm, corroborate, substantiate, validate — **ver·i·fi·able** *adj* — **ver·i·fi·ca·tion** \ˌver-ə-fə-ˈkā-shən\ *n*

ver·i·ly \ˈver-ə-lē\ *adv* **1 :** in very truth **:** CERTAINLY **2 :** TRULY, CONFIDENTLY

veri·si·mil·i·tude \ˌver-ə-sə-ˈmil-ə-ˌt(y)üd\ *n* **:** the quality or state of appearing to be true **:** PROBABILITY; *also* **:** a statement that is apparently true **syn** plausibility

ver·i·ta·ble \ˈver-ət-ə-bəl\ *adj* **:** ACTUAL, GENUINE, TRUE — **ver·i·ta·bly** *adv*

ver·i·ty \ˈver-ət-ē\ *n, pl* **-ties 1 :** the quality or state of being true or real **:** TRUTH, REALITY **2 :** something (as a statement) that is true **3 :** HONESTY, VERACITY

ver·meil *n* [MF] **1** \ˈvər-məl, -ˌmāl\ **:** VERMILION **2** \ver-ˈmā\ **:** gilded silver

ver·mi·cel·li \ˌvər-mə-ˈchel-ē, -ˈsel-\ *n* [It, lit., little worms] **:** a dough made in long solid strings smaller in diameter than spaghetti

ver·mic·u·lite \vər-ˈmik-yə-ˌlīt\ *n* **:** any of various minerals that result usu. from the expansion of mica granules at high temperatures to give a lightweight highly water-absorbent material

ver·mi·form appendix \ˈvər-mə-ˌform-\ *n* **:** APPENDIX 2

ver·mi·fuge \ˈvər-mə-ˌfyüj\ *n* **:** a medicine for destroying or expelling intestinal worms

ver·mil·ion *also* **ver·mil·lion** \vər-ˈmil-yən\ *n* **:** any of a number of very bright red colors not quite as bright as scarlet; *also* **:** a pigment yielding one of these colors

ver·min \ˈvər-mən\ *n, pl* **vermin** [ME, fr. MF, deriv. of L *vermis* worm] **:** small common harmful or disgusting animals (as lice or mice) that are difficult to get rid of — **ver·min·ous** *adj*

ver·mouth \vər-ˈmüth\ *n* [F *vermout*, fr. G *wermut* wormwood] **:** a white wine flavored with herbs and often used in combination with other beverages

¹ver·nac·u·lar \və(r)-ˈnak-yə-lər\ *adj* [L *vernaculus* native, fr. *verna* slave born in his master's house] **1 :** of, relating to, or being a language or dialect native to a region or country rather than a literary, cultured, or foreign language **2 :** of, relating to, or being the normal spoken form of a language **3 :** applied to a plant or animal in common speech as distinguished from biological nomenclature ⟨~ names⟩

²vernacular *n* **1 :** a vernacular language **2 :** the mode of expression of a group or class **3 :** a vernacular name of a plant or animal

ver·nal \ˈvərn-ᵊl\ *adj* **:** of, relating to, or occurring in the spring

ver·nal·iza·tion \ˌvərn-ᵊl-ə-ˈzā-shən\ *n* **:** the act or process of hastening the flowering and fruiting of plants by treating seeds, bulbs, or seedlings so as to shorten the vegetative period — **ver·nal·ize** \ˈvərn-ᵊl-ˌīz\ *vb*

ver·ni·er \ˈvər-nē-ər\ *n* **:** a short scale made to slide along the divisions of a graduated instrument to indicate parts of divisions

ve·ron·i·ca \və-ˈrän-i-kə\ *n* **:** SPEEDWELL

ver·sa·tile \ˈvər-sət-ᵊl\ *adj* **:** turning with ease from one thing or position to another; *esp* **:** having many aptitudes — **ver·sa·til·i·ty** \ˌvər-sə-ˈtil-ət-ē\ *n*

verse \ˈvərs\ *n* **1 :** a line of poetry; *also* **:** STANZA **2 :** metrical writing distinguished from poetry esp. by its lower level of intensity **3 :** POETRY **4 :** POEM **5 :** one of the short divisions of a chapter in the Bible

versed \vərst\ *adj* **:** familiar from experience, study, or practice **:** SKILLED

ver·si·cle \ˈvər-si-kəl\ *n* **:** a verse or sentence said or sung by a clergyman and followed by a response from the people

ver·si·fi·ca·tion \ˌvər-sə-fə-ˈkā-shən\ *n* **1 :** the making of verses **2 :** metrical structure

ver·si·fy \ˈvər-sə-ˌfī\ *vb* **-fied; -fy·ing 1 :** to write verse **2 :** to turn into verse — **ver·si·fi·er** \-ˌfī(-ə)r\ *n*

ver·sion \ˈvər-zhən\ *n* **1 :** TRANSLATION; *esp* **;** a translation of the Bible **2 :** an account or description from a particular point of view esp. as contrasted with another **3 :** a form or variant of a type or original

vers li·bre \ˌver-ˈlēbrᵊ\ *n, pl* **vers li·bres** *same*\ [F] **:** FREE VERSE

ver·so \ˈvər-sō\ *n, pl* **versos :** a left-hand page

ver·sus \ˈvər-səs\ *prep* **1 :** AGAINST 2 ⟨the champion ~ the challenger⟩ **2 :** in contrast or as an alternative to ⟨free trade ~ protection⟩

vert *abbr* vertical

ver·te·bra \ˈvərt-ə-brə\ *n, pl* **-brae** \-ˌbrā, -(ˌ)brē\ *or* **-bras** [L] **:** one of the segments of bone or cartilage making up the backbone

ver·te·bral \(ˌ)vər-ˈtē-brəl, ˈvərt-ə-\ *adj* **:** of, relating to, or made up of vertebrae **:** SPINAL

vertebral column *n* **:** BACKBONE

¹ver·te·brate \ˈvərt-ə-brət, -ˌbrāt\ *adj* **1 :** having a backbone **2 :** of or relating to the vertebrates

²vertebrate *n* **:** any of a large group of animals (as mammals, birds, reptiles, amphibians, or fishes) that have a backbone or in some primitive forms a flexible rod of cells and that have a tubular nervous system arranged along the back and divided into a brain and spinal cord

ver·tex \ˈvər-ˌteks\ *n, pl* **ver·ti·ces** \ˈvərt-ə-ˌsēz\ *also* **ver·tex·es** [L *vertex, vortex* whirl, whirlpool, top of the head, summit, fr. *vertere* to turn] **1 :** the point opposite to and farthest from the base of a geometrical figure **2 :** the termination or intersection of lines or curves ⟨the ~ of an angle⟩ **3 :** ZENITH 1 **4 :** the highest point **:** TOP, SUMMIT

ver·ti·cal \ˈvərt-i-kəl\ *adj* **1 :** of, relating to, or located at the vertex **:** directly overhead **2 :** rising perpendicularly from a level surface **:** UPRIGHT — **vertical** *n* — **ver·ti·cal·i·ty** \ˌvərt-ə-ˈkal-ət-ē\ *n* — **ver·ti·cal·ly** \-k(ə-)lē\ *adv*

ver·tig·i·nous \(ˌ)vər-ˈtij-ə-nəs\ *adj* **:** marked by, suffering from, or tending to cause dizziness

ver·ti·go \ˈvərt-i-ˌgō\ *n, pl* **-goes** *or* **-gos :** DIZZINESS, GIDDINESS

ver·vain \ˈvər-ˌvān\ *n* **:** any of a genus of herbs or low woody plants with often showy heads or spikes of tubular flowers

verve \ˈvərv\ *n* **:** liveliness of imagination; *also* **:** VIVACITY

¹very \ˈver-ē\ *adj* **veri·er; -est** [ME *verray, verry*, fr. OF *verai*, fr. L *verax* truthful, fr. *verus* true] **1 :** EXACT, PRECISE ⟨the ~ heart of the city⟩ **2 :** exactly suitable ⟨the ~ tool for the job⟩ **3 :** ABSOLUTE, UTTER ⟨the *veriest* nonsense⟩ **4** — used as an intensive esp. to emphasize identity ⟨made the ~ walls shake⟩ **5 :** MERE, BARE ⟨the ~ idea scared him⟩ **6 :** SELFSAME, IDENTICAL ⟨the ~ man I saw⟩

²very *adv* **1 :** in actual fact **:** TRULY **2 :** to a high degree **:** EXTREMELY

very high frequency *n* **:** a radio frequency of between 30 and 300 megahertz

ves·i·cant \ˈves-i-kənt\ *n* **:** an agent that causes blistering — **vesicant** *adj*

ves·i·cle \ˈves-i-kəl\ *n* **:** a membranous and usu. fluid-filled cavity in a plant or animal; *also* **:** BLISTER — **ve·sic·u·lar** \və-ˈsik-yə-lər\ *adj*

[1]**ves·per** \ˈves-pər\ *n* **1** *cap* **:** EVENING STAR **2 :** a vesper bell **3** *archaic* **:** EVENING, EVENTIDE

[2]**vesper** *adj* **:** of or relating to vespers or to the evening

ves·pers \-pərz\ *n pl, often cap* **:** a late afternoon or evening worship service

ves·per·tine \ˈves-pər-ˌtīn\ *adj* **1 :** of, relating to, or taking place in the evening **2 :** active, flowering, or flourishing in the evening

ves·sel \ˈves-əl\ *n* **1 :** a hollow or concave utensil (as a barrel, bottle, bowl, or cup) for holding something **2 :** a person held to be the recipient of a quality (as grace) **3 :** a craft bigger than a rowboat for navigation of the water **4 :** a tube in which a body fluid (as blood) is contained and circulated

[1]**vest** \ˈvest\ *vb* **1 :** to place or give into the possession or discretion of some person or authority **2 :** to clothe with a particular authority, right, or property **3 :** to become legally vested **4 :** to clothe with or as if with a garment; *esp* **:** to garb in ecclesiastical vestments

[2]**vest** *n* **1 :** a man's sleeveless garment for the upper body usu. worn under a suit coat; *also* **:** a similar garment for women **2** *chiefly Brit* **:** a man's sleeveless undershirt **3 :** a front piece of a dress resembling the front of a vest

[1]**ves·tal** \ˈves-tᵊl\ *adj* **:** CHASTE — **ves·tal·ly** \-ē\ *adv*

[2]**vestal** *n* **:** a chaste woman

vestal virgin *n* **:** a virgin consecrated to the Roman goddess Vesta and to the service of watching the sacred fire perpetually kept burning on her altar

vest·ed \ˈves-təd\ *adj* **:** fully and unconditionally guaranteed as a legal right, benefit, or privilege

vested interest *n* **:** an interest (as in an existing political, economic, or social arrangement) to which the holder has a strong commitment; *also* **:** one (as a corporation) having a vested interest

ves·ti·bule \ˈves-tə-ˌbyül\ *n* **1 :** any of various bodily cavities forming or suggesting an entrance to some other part **2 :** a passage or room between the outer door and the interior of a building — **ves·tib·u·lar** \ve-ˈstib-yə-lər\ *adj*

ves·tige \ˈves-tij\ *n* [F, fr. L *vestigium* footprint, track, vestige] **:** a trace or visible sign left by something lost or vanished; *also* **:** a minute remaining amount — **ves·ti·gial** \ve-ˈstij-(ē-)əl\ *adj* — **ves·ti·gial·ly** \-ē\ *adv*

vest·ing \ˈves-tiŋ\ *n* **:** the conveying to an employee of inalienable rights to share in a pension fund; *also* **:** the right so conveyed

vest·ment \ˈves(t)-mənt\ *n* **1 :** an outer garment; *esp* **:** a ceremonial or official robe **2** *pl* **:** CLOTHING, GARB **3 :** a garment or insignia worn by a clergyman when officiating or assisting at a religious service

vest–pocket *adj* **:** very small ⟨a ~ park⟩

ves·try \ˈves-trē\ *n, pl* **vestries 1 :** a room in a church for vestments, altar linens, and sacred vessels **2 :** a room used for church meetings and classes **3 :** a body administering the temporal affairs of an Episcopal parish

ves·try·man \-mən\ *n* **:** a member of a vestry

ves·ture \ˈves-chər\ *n* **1 :** a covering garment (as a robe) **2 :** CLOTHING, APPAREL

[1]**vet** \ˈvet\ *n* **:** VETERINARIAN, VETERINARY

[2]**vet** *adj or n* **:** VETERAN

vetch \ˈvech\ *n* **:** any of several herbs related to the pea including some valued for fodder

vet·er·an \ˈvet-(ə-)rən\ *n* [L *veteranus,* fr. *veteranus* old, of long experience, fr. *veter-, vetus* old] **1 :** an old soldier of long service **2 :** a former member of the armed forces **3 :** a person of long experience in an occupation or skill — **veteran** *adj*

Veterans Day *n* **:** November 11 observed as a legal holiday in commemoration of the end of hostilities in 1918 and 1945

vet·er·i·nar·i·an \ˌvet-(ə-)rən-ˈer-ē-ən, ˌvet-ᵊn-\ *n* **:** one qualified and authorized to treat injuries and diseases of animals

[1]**vet·er·i·nary** \ˈvet-(ə-)rən-ˌer-ē, ˈvet-ᵊn-\ *adj* **:** of, relating to, or being the medical care of animals and esp. domestic animals

[2]**veterinary** *n, pl* **-nar·ies :** VETERINARIAN

[1]**ve·to** \ˈvēt-ō\ *n, pl* **vetoes** [L, I forbid] **1 :** an authoritative prohibition **2 :** a power of one part of a government to forbid the carrying out of projects attempted by another part; *esp* **:** a power vested in a chief executive to prevent the carrying out of measures adopted by a legislature **3 :** the exercise of the power of veto; *also* **:** a document or message stating the reasons for a specific use of this power

[2]**veto** *vb* **1 :** FORBID, PROHIBIT **2 :** to refuse assent to (a legislative bill) so as to prevent enactment or cause reconsideration — **ve·to·er** *n*

vex \ˈveks\ *vb* **vexed** *also* **vext; vex·ing 1 :** to bring trouble, distress, or agitation to **2 :** to irritate or annoy by petty provocations **3 :** to shake or toss about

vex·a·tion \vek-ˈsā-shən\ *n* **1 :** the act of vexing **2 :** the quality or state of being vexed **:** IRRITATION **3 :** a cause of trouble or annoyance

vex·a·tious \-shəs\ *adj* **1 :** causing vexation **:** ANNOYING, DISTRESSING **2 :** full of distress or annoyance **:** TROUBLED — **vex·a·tious·ly** *adv* — **vex·a·tious·ness** *n*

vexed \ˈvekst\ *adj* **:** fully debated or discussed ⟨a ~ question⟩

VF *abbr* **1** video frequency **2** visual field

VFD *abbr* volunteer fire department

VFW *abbr* Veterans of Foreign Wars

VG *abbr* **1** very good **2** vicar-general

VHF *abbr* very high frequency

VI *abbr* Virgin Islands

via \ˌvī-ə, ˌvē-ə\ *prep* **:** by way of ⟨goods shipped ~ the Panama Canal⟩

vi·a·ble \ˈvī-ə-bəl\ *adj* **1 :** capable of living; *esp* **:** capable of surviving outside the mother's womb without artificial support ⟨a ~ fetus⟩ **2 :** capable of being put into practice **:** WORKABLE **3 :** having a reasonable chance of succeeding ⟨a ~ candidate⟩ — **vi·a·bil·i·ty** \ˌvī-ə-ˈbil-ət-ē\ *n* — **vi·a·bly** \ˈvī-ə-blē\ *adv*

via·duct \ˈvī-ə-ˌdəkt\ *n* **:** a bridge with high supporting towers or piers for carrying a road or railroad over something (as a valley, river, or road)

vi·al \ˈvī(-ə)l\ *n* **:** a small vessel for liquids

vi·and \ˈvī-ənd\ *n* **:** an article of food

vi·at·i·cum \vī-ˈat-i-kəm, vē-\ *n, pl* **-cums** *or* **-ca** \-kə\ **1 :** the Christian Eucharist given to a person in danger of death **2 :** an allowance esp. in money for traveling needs and expenses

vibes \ˈvībz\ *n pl* **1 :** VIBRAPHONE **2 :** VIBRATIONS

vi·brant \ˈvī-brənt\ *adj* **1 :** VIBRATING, PULSATING **2 :** pulsating with vigor or activity **3 :** readily set in vibration **:** RESPONSIVE, SENSITIVE **4 :** sounding from vibration — **vi·bran·cy** \-brən-sē\ *n*

vi·bra·phone \ˈvī-brə-ˌfōn\ *n* **:** a percussion instrument like the xylophone but with metal bars and motor-driven resonators

vi·brate \ˈvī-ˌbrāt\ *vb* **vi·brat·ed; vi·brat·ing 1 :** OSCILLATE **2 :** to set in vibration **3 :** to be in vibration **4 :** to respond sympathetically **:** THRILL **5 :** WAVER, FLUCTUATE

vi·bra·tion \vī-ˈbrā-shən\ *n* **1 :** a rapid to-and-fro motion of the particles of an elastic body or medium (as a stretched cord) that produces sound **2 :** an act of vibrating **:** a state of being vibrated **:** OSCILLATION **3 :** a trembling motion **4 :** VACILLATION **5 :** a distinctive usu. emotional emanation or atmosphere that can be instinctively sensed — usu. used in pl. — **vi·bra·tion·al** \-sh(ə-)nəl\ *adj*

vi·bra·to \vi-ˈbrät-ō\ *n, pl* **-tos** [It] **:** a slightly tremulous effect imparted to vocal or instrumental music

vi·bra·tor \ˈvī-ˌbrāt-ər\ *n* : one that vibrates or causes vibration; *esp* : a vibrating electrical device used in massage or for sexual stimulation

vi·bra·to·ry \ˈvī-brə-ˌtōr-ē\ *adj* : consisting in, capable of, or causing vibration

vi·bur·num \vī-ˈbər-nəm\ *n* : any of a genus of widely distributed shrubs or trees related to the honeysuckle and bearing small usu. white flowers in broad clusters

vic *abbr* vicinity

Vic *abbr* Victoria

vic·ar \ˈvik-ər\ *n* **1** : an administrative deputy **2** : an Anglican clergyman in charge of a dependent parish — **vi·car·i·ate** \vī-ˈker-ē-ət\ *n*

vic·ar·age \ˈvik-ə-rij\ *n* : the benefice or house of a vicar

vicar–general *n, pl* **vicars–general** : an administrative deputy (as of a Roman Catholic or Anglican bishop)

vi·car·i·ous \vī-ˈker-ē-əs, -ˈkar-\ *adj* **1** : acting for another **2** : done or suffered by one person on behalf of another or others ⟨a ~ sacrifice⟩ **3** : realized or experienced by one person through sympathetic sharing in the experience of another — **vi·car·i·ous·ly** *adv* — **vi·car·i·ous·ness** *n*

¹vice \ˈvīs\ *n* **1** : DEPRAVITY, WICKEDNESS **2** : a moral fault; *esp* : an immoral habit **3** : a physical imperfection : BLEMISH **4** : an undesirable behavior pattern in a domestic animal

²vice *chiefly Brit var of* VISE

³vi·ce \ˈvī-sē\ *prep* : in the place of : SUCCEEDING

vice admiral *n* : a commissioned officer in the navy or coast guard ranking above a rear admiral

vice·ge·rent \ˈvīs-ˈjir-ənt\ *n* : an administrative deputy of a king or magistrate — **vice·ge·ren·cy** \-ən-sē\ *n*

vi·cen·ni·al \vī-ˈsen-ē-əl\ *adj* : occurring once every 20 years

vice presidency *n* : the office of vice president

vice president *n* **1** : an officer ranking next to a president and usu. empowered to act for the president during an absence or disability **2** : a president's deputy in charge of a particular location or function

vice·re·gal \ˈvīs-ˈrē-gəl\ *adj* : of or relating to a viceroy

vice·roy \ˈvīs-ˌrȯi\ *n* : the governor of a country or province who rules as representative of the sovereign — **vice·roy·al·ty** \-əl-tē\ *n*

vice ver·sa \ˌvī-si-ˈvər-sə, (ˈ)vīs-ˈvər-\ *adv* : with the order reversed : CONVERSELY

vi·chys·soise \ˌvish-ē-ˈswäz, ˌvē-shē-\ *n* [F] : a thick soup made esp. from leeks or onions and potatoes, cream, and chicken stock and usu. served cold

Vi·chy water \ˈvish-ē-\ *n* : carbonated water

vic·i·nage \ˈvis-ᵊn-ij\ *n* : a neighboring or surrounding district : VICINITY

vi·cin·i·ty \və-ˈsin-ət-ē\ *n, pl* **-ties** [MF *vicinité*, fr. L *vicinitas*, fr. *vicinus* neighboring, fr. *vicus* row of houses, village] **1** : NEARNESS, PROXIMITY **2** : a surrounding area : NEIGHBORHOOD

vi·cious \ˈvish-əs\ *adj* **1** : addicted to vice : WICKED, DEPRAVED **2** : DEFECTIVE, FAULTY; *also* : INVALID **3** : IMPURE, FOUL **4** : having a savage disposition **5** : MALICIOUS, SPITEFUL **6** : worsened by internal causes that augment each other ⟨~ wage-price spiral⟩ — **vi·cious·ly** *adv* — **vi·cious·ness** *n*

vi·cis·si·tude \və-ˈsis-ə-ˌt(y)üd, vī-\ *n* **1** : the quality or state of being changeable **2** : a change or succession from one thing to another; *esp* : an irregular, unexpected, or surprising change

vic·tim \ˈvik-təm\ *n* **1** : a living being offered as a sacrifice in a religious rite **2** : an individual injured or killed (as by disease or accident) **3** : a person cheated, fooled, or injured ⟨a ~ of circumstances⟩

vic·tim·ize \ˈvik-tə-ˌmīz\ *vb* **-ized; -iz·ing** : to make a victim of — **vic·tim·iza·tion** \ˌvik-tə-mə-ˈzā-shən\ *n* — **vic·tim·iz·er** \ˈvik-tə-ˌmī-zər\ *n*

vic·tim·less *adj* : having no victim ⟨considered gambling to be a ~ crime⟩

vic·tor \ˈvik-tər\ *n* : WINNER, CONQUEROR

vic·to·ria \vik-ˈtōr-ē-ə\ *n* : a low 4-wheeled carriage with a folding top and a raised seat in front for the driver

¹Vic·to·ri·an \vik-ˈtōr-ē-ən\ *adj* **1** : of or relating to the reign of Queen Victoria of England or the art, letters, or tastes of her time **2** : typical of the standards, attitudes, or conduct of the age of Victoria esp. when considered prudish or narrow

²Victorian *n* : a person and esp. an author of the Victorian period

vic·to·ri·ous \vik-ˈtōr-ē-əs\ *adj* **1** : having won a victory : CONQUERING **2** : of, relating to, or characteristic of victory — **vic·to·ri·ous·ly** *adv*

vic·to·ry \ˈvik-t(ə-)rē\ *n, pl* **-ries** **1** : the overcoming of an enemy or an antagonist **2** : achievement of mastery or success in a struggle or endeavor against odds

¹vict·ual \ˈvit-ᵊl\ *n* **1** : food usable by man **2** *pl* : food supplies : PROVISIONS

²victual *vb* **-ualed** *or* **-ualled; -ual·ing** *or* **-ual·ling** **1** : to supply with food **2** : to store up provisions

vict·ual·ler *or* **vict·ual·er** \ˈvit-ᵊl-ər\ *n* : one that supplies provisions (as to an army or a ship)

vi·cu·ña *or* **vi·cu·na** \vi-ˈkün-yə, vī-; vī-ˈk(y)ü-nə\ *n* **1** : a So. American wild mammal related to the llama and alpaca; *also* : its wool **2** : a soft fabric woven from the wool of the vicuña; *also* : a sheep's wool imitation of this

vi·de \ˈvīd-ē, ˈvē-ˌdā\ *vb imper* [L] : SEE — used to direct a reader to another item

vi·de·li·cet \və-ˈdel-ə-ˌset, vī-; vi-ˈdā-li-ˌket\ *adv* [ME, fr. L, fr. *vidēre* to see + *licet* it is permitted] : that is to say : NAMELY

¹vid·eo \ˈvid-ē-ˌō\ *n* **1** : TELEVISION **2** : VIDEOTAPE

²video *adj* **1** : relating to or used in transmission or reception of the television image **2** : relating to or being images on a television screen or computer display ⟨a ~ terminal⟩

vid·eo·cas·sette \ˈvid-ē-ō-kə-ˌset\ *n* **1** : a case containing videotape for use with a VCR **2** : a recording (as of a movie) on a videocassette

videocassette recorder *n* : VCR

vid·eo·disc *or* **vid·eo·disk** \-ˌdisk\ *n* **1** : a disc similar in appearance and use to a phonograph record on which programs have been recorded for playback on a television set; *also* : OPTICAL DISC **2** : a recording (as of a movie) on a videodisc

video game *n* : an electronic game played on a video screen

vid·eo·phone \ˈvid-ē-ə-ˌfōn\ *n* : a telephone for transmitting both audio and video signals

¹vid·eo·tape \ˈvid-ē-ō-ˌtāp\ *n* : a recording of visual images and sound made on magnetic tape; *also* : the magnetic tape used for such a recording

²videotape *vb* : to make a videotape of ⟨~ a show⟩

videotape recorder *n* : a device for recording and playing back videotapes

vid·eo·tex \-ˌteks\ *also* **vid·eo·text** \-ˌtekst\ *n* : an interactive electronic communications system in which data transmitted by a computer appears on a subscriber's video display

vie \ˈvī\ *vb* **vied; vy·ing** \ˈvī-iŋ\ : to strive for superiority : CONTEND — **vi·er** \ˈvī(-ə)r\ *n*

Viet·cong \vē-ˈet-ˈkäŋ, ˌvē-ət-, -ˈkȯŋ\ *n, pl* **Vietcong** : an adherent of the Vietnamese communist movement

Viet·nam·ese \vē-ˌet-nə-ˈmēz, ˌvē-ət-, -ˈmēs\ *n, pl*

Viet·nam·ese : a native or inhabitant of Vietnam — **Vietnamese** *adj*

[1]**view** \ˈvyü\ *n* **1** : the act of seeing or examining : INSPECTION; *also* : SURVEY **2** : a way of looking at or regarding something **3** : ESTIMATE, JUDGMENT ⟨stated his ∼*s*⟩ **4** : a sight (as of a landscape) regarded for its pictorial quality **5** : extent or range of vision ⟨within ∼⟩ **6** : OBJECT, PURPOSE ⟨done with a ∼ to promotion⟩ **7** : a picture of a scene

[2]**view** *vb* **1** : to look at attentively : EXAMINE **2** : SEE, BEHOLD **3** : to examine mentally : CONSIDER — **view·er** *n*

view·er·ship \-ˌship\ *n* : a television audience esp. with respect to size or makeup

view·find·er \ˈvyü-ˌfīn-dər\ *n* : a device on a camera for showing the view to be included in the picture

view·point \-ˌpȯint\ *n* : a position from which something is considered : POINT OF VIEW, STANDPOINT

vi·ges·i·mal \vī-ˈjes-ə-məl\ *adj* : based on the number 20

vig·il \ˈvij-əl\ *n* **1** : a religious observance formerly held on the night before a religious feast **2** : the day before a religious feast observed as a day of spiritual preparation **3** : evening or nocturnal devotions or prayers — usu. used in pl. **4** : an act or a time of keeping awake when sleep is customary; *esp* : WATCH 1

vig·i·lance \ˈvij-ə-ləns\ *n* : the quality or state of being vigilant

vigilance committee *n* : a committee of vigilantes

vig·i·lant \ˈvij-ə-lənt\ *adj* : alertly watchful esp. to avoid danger — **vig·i·lant·ly** *adv*

vig·i·lan·te \ˌvij-ə-ˈlant-ē\ *n* : a member of a volunteer committee organized to suppress and punish crime summarily (as when the processes of law appear inadequate)

[1]**vi·gnette** \vin-ˈyet\ *n* [F, fr. MF *vignete*, fr. dim. of *vigne* vine] **1** : a small decorative design on or just before the title page of a book or at the beginning or end of a chapter **2** : a picture (as an engraving or a photograph) that shades off gradually into the surrounding ground **3** : a short descriptive literary sketch

[2]**vignette** *vb* **vi·gnett·ed; vi·gnett·ing** : to finish (as a photograph) in the manner of a vignette

vig·or \ˈvig-ər\ *n* **1** : active strength or energy of body or mind **2** : INTENSITY, FORCE

vig·or·ous \ˈvig-(ə-)rəs\ *adj* **1** : having vigor : ROBUST **2** : done with vigor : carried out forcefully and energetically — **vig·or·ous·ly** *adv* — **vig·or·ous·ness** *n*

Vi·king \ˈvī-kiŋ\ *n* [ON *vīkingr*] : one of the pirate Norsemen plundering the coasts of Europe in the 8th to 10th centuries

vil *abbr* village

vile \ˈvīl\ *adj* **vil·er; vil·est** **1** : morally despicable **2** : physically repulsive : FOUL **3** : of little worth **4** : DEGRADING, IGNOMINIOUS **5** : utterly bad or inferior ⟨∼ weather⟩ — **vile·ly** \ˈvīl-lē\ *adv* — **vile·ness** *n*

vil·i·fy \ˈvil-ə-ˌfī\ *vb* **-fied; -fy·ing** : to blacken the character of with abusive language : DEFAME **syn** malign, calumniate, slander, libel, traduce — **vil·i·fi·ca·tion** \ˌvil-ə-fə-ˈkā-shən\ *n* — **vil·i·fi·er** \ˈvil-ə-ˌfī(-ə)r\ *n*

vil·la \ˈvil-ə\ *n* **1** : a country estate **2** : the rural or suburban residence of a wealthy person

vil·lage \ˈvil-ij\ *n* **1** : a settlement usu. larger than a hamlet and smaller than a town **2** : an incorporated minor municipality **3** : the people of a village

vil·lag·er \ˈvil-ij-ər\ *n* : an inhabitant of a village

vil·lain \ˈvil-ən\ *n* **1** : VILLEIN **2** : a deliberate scoundrel or criminal

vil·lain·ess \-ə-nəs\ *n* : a woman who is a villain

vil·lain·ous \-ə-nəs\ *adj* **1** : befitting a villain : WICKED, EVIL **2** : highly objectionable : DETESTABLE **syn** vicious, iniquitous, nefarious, infamous, corrupt, degenerate — **vil·lain·ous·ly** *adv* — **vil·lain·ous·ness** *n*

vil·lainy \-ə-nē\ *n, pl* **-lain·ies** **1** : villainous conduct; *also* : a villainous act **2** : villainous character or nature : DEPRAVITY

vil·lein \ˈvil-ən, ˈvil-ˌān\ *n* **1** : a free villager of Anglo-Saxon times **2** : an unfree peasant having the status of a slave to a feudal lord

vil·len·age \ˈvil-ə-nij\ *n* **1** : the holding of land at the will of a feudal lord **2** : the status of a villein

vil·lous \ˈvil-əs\ *adj* : covered with fine hairs or villi

vil·lus \ˈvil-əs\ *n, pl* **vil·li** \ˈvil-ˌī, -(ˌ)ē\ : a slender usu. vascular process; *esp* : one of the tiny projections of the mucous membrane of the small intestine that function in the absorption of food

vim \ˈvim\ *n* : robust energy and enthusiasm : VITALITY

vin·ai·grette \ˌvin-i-ˈgret\ *n* [F] **1** : a sauce made typically of oil and vinegar, onions, parsley, and herbs **2** : a small box or bottle for holding aromatic preparations (as smelling salts)

vin·ci·ble \ˈvin-sə-bəl\ *adj* : capable of being overcome or subdued

vin·di·cate \ˈvin-də-ˌkāt\ *vb* **-cat·ed; -cat·ing** **1** : AVENGE **2** : EXONERATE, ABSOLVE **3** : CONFIRM, SUBSTANTIATE **4** : to provide defense for : JUSTIFY **5** : to maintain a right to : ASSERT — **vin·di·ca·tor** \-ˌkāt-ər\ *n*

vin·di·ca·tion \ˌvin-də-ˈkā-shən\ *n* : a vindicating or being vindicated; *esp* : justification against denial or censure

vin·dic·tive \vin-ˈdik-tiv\ *adj* **1** : disposed to revenge **2** : intended for or involving revenge **3** : VICIOUS, SPITEFUL — **vin·dic·tive·ly** *adv* — **vin·dic·tive·ness** *n*

vine \ˈvīn\ *n* [ME, fr. OF *vigne*, fr. L *vinea* vine, vineyard, fr. fem. of *vineus* of wine, fr. *vinum* wine] **1** : GRAPE 2 **2** : a plant whose stem requires support and which climbs (as by tendrils) or trails along the ground; *also* : the the stem of such a plant

vin·e·gar \ˈvin-i-gər\ *n* [ME *vinegre*, fr. OF *vinaigre*, fr. *vin* wine + *aigre* keen, sour] : a sour liquid obtained by fermentation (as of cider, wine, or malt) and used in cookery and pickling

vin·e·gary \ˈvin-i-g(ə-)rē\ *adj* **1** : resembling vinegar : SOUR **2** : disagreeable in manner or disposition : CRABBED

vine·yard \ˈvin-yərd\ *n* **1** : a plantation of grapevines **2** : an area of physical or mental occupation

vi·nous \ˈvī-nəs\ *adj* **1** : of, relating to, or made with wine ⟨∼ medications⟩ **2** : showing the effects of the use of wine

[1]**vin·tage** \ˈvint-ij\ *n* **1** : a season's yield of grapes or wine **2** : WINE; *esp* : a usu. superior wine which comes from a single year **3** : the act or period of gathering grapes or making wine **4** : a period of origin ⟨clothes of 1890 ∼⟩

[2]**vintage** *adj* **1** : of, relating to, or produced in a particular vintage **2** : of old, recognized, and enduring interest, importance, or quality : CLASSIC ⟨∼ cars⟩ **3** : of the best and most characteristic — used with a proper noun

vint·ner \ˈvint-nər\ *n* : a dealer in wines

vi·nyl \ˈvīn-ᵊl\ *n* **1** : a chemical derived from ethylene by the removal of one hydrogen atom **2** : a polymer of a vinyl compound or a product (as a textile fiber) made from one

vinyl chloride *n* : a flammable gaseous carcinogenic compound used esp. to make vinyl resins

vi·ol \ˈvī(-ə)l\ *n* : a bowed stringed instrument chiefly of the 16th and 17th centuries having a fretted neck and usu. six strings

[1]**vi·o·la** \vī-ˈō-lə, ˈvī-ə-lə\ *n* : VIOLET 1; *esp* : any of various hybrid garden plants with white, yellow, purple, or variously colored flowers that resemble but are smaller than the related pansies

[2]**vi·o·la** \vē-ˈō-lə\ *n* : an instrument of the violin family slightly larger and tuned lower than a violin — **vi·o·list** \-ləst\ *n*

vi·o·la·ble \ˈvī-ə-lə-bəl\ *adj* : capable of being violated

vi·o·late \ˈvī-ə-ˌlāt\ *vb* **-lat·ed; -lat·ing** **1** : BREAK, DISREGARD ⟨∼ a law⟩ ⟨∼ a frontier⟩ **2** : RAPE **3** : PROFANE,

DESECRATE **4** : INTERRUPT, DISTURB ⟨*violated* his privacy⟩ — **vi·o·la·tor** \-ˌlāt-ər\ *n*

vi·o·la·tion \ˌvī-ə-ˈlā-shən\ *n* : an act or instance of violating : the state of being violated **syn** breach, infraction, trespass, infringement, transgression

vi·o·lence \ˈvī-ə-ləns\ *n* **1** : exertion of physical force so as to injure or abuse **2** : injury by or as if by infringement or profanation **3** : intense or furious often destructive action or force **4** : vehement feeling or expression : INTENSITY **5** : jarring quality : DISCORDANCE **syn** compulsion, coercion, duress, constraint

vi·o·lent \-lənt\ *adj* **1** : marked by extreme force or sudden intense activity; *esp* : marked by improper use of such force **2** : caused by or showing strong feeling ⟨~ words⟩ **3** : EXTREME, INTENSE **4** : caused by force : not natural ⟨~ death⟩ — **vi·o·lent·ly** *adv*

vi·o·let \ˈvī-ə-lət\ *n* **1** : any of a genus of herbs or woody-stemmed plants usu. with heart-shaped leaves and both aerial and underground flowers; *esp* : one with small solid-colored flowers **2** : a variable color averaging a reddish blue

vi·o·lin \ˌvī-ə-ˈlin\ *n* : a bowed stringed instrument with four strings that has a shallower body and a more curved bridge than a viol — **vi·o·lin·ist** \-əst\ *n*

violin

vi·o·lon·cel·lo \ˌvī-ə-lən-ˈchel-ō\ *n* [It] : CELLO — **vi·o·lon·cel·list** \-əst\ *n*

VIP \ˌvē-ˌī-ˈpē\ *n, pl* **VIPs** \-ˈpēz\ [*v*ery *i*mportant *p*erson] : a person of great influence or prestige; *esp* : a high official with special privileges

vi·per \ˈvī-pər\ *n* **1** : any of various sluggish heavy-bodied Old World venomous snakes **2** : PIT VIPER **3** : any venomous or reputedly venomous snake **4** : a vicious or treacherous person — **vi·per·ine** \-pə-ˌrīn\ *adj*

vi·ra·go \və-ˈräg-ō, -ˈrāg-\ *n, pl* **-goes** *or* **-gos** [L, manlike heroic woman, fr. *vir* man] : a scolding, quarrelsome, or loud overbearing woman **syn** amazon, termagant, scold, shrew, vixen

vi·ral \ˈvī-rəl\ *adj* : of, relating to, or caused by a virus

vir·eo \ˈvir-ē-ˌō\ *n, pl* **-e·os** [L, a small bird, fr. *virēre* to be green] : any of various small insect-eating American songbirds mostly olive green and grayish in color

[1]**vir·gin** \ˈvər-jən\ *n* **1** : an unmarried woman devoted to religion **2** : an unmarried girl or woman **3** *cap* : the mother of Jesus **4** : a person who has not had sexual intercourse

[2]**virgin** *adj* **1** : free from stain : PURE, SPOTLESS **2** : CHASTE **3** : befitting a virgin : MODEST **4** : FRESH, UNSPOILED; *esp* : not altered by human activity ⟨~ forest⟩ **5** : INITIAL, FIRST

[1]**vir·gin·al** \ˈvər-jən-ᵊl\ *adj* : of, relating to, or characteristic of a virgin or virginity — **vir·gin·al·ly** \-ē\ *adv*

[2]**virginal** *n* : a small rectangular spinet without legs popular in the 16th and 17th centuries

Vir·gin·ia creeper \vər-ˌjin-yə-\ *n* : a No. American vine having leaves with five leaflets and bluish black berries

Virginia reel *n* : an American country-dance

vir·gin·i·ty \vər-ˈjin-ət-ē\ *n, pl* **-ties** **1** : the quality or state of being virgin; *esp* : MAIDENHOOD **2** : the unmarried life : CELIBACY

Vir·go \ˈvər-ˌgō\ *n* [L, lit., virgin] **1** : a zodiacal constellation between Leo and Libra usu. pictured as a young woman **2** : the 6th sign of the zodiac in astrology; *also* : one born under this sign

vir·gule \ˈvər-gyül\ *n* : a mark / used typically to denote "or" (as in *and/or*) or "per" (as in *feet/second*)

vir·i·des·cent \ˌvir-ə-ˈdes-ᵊnt\ *adj* : slightly green : GREENISH

vir·ile \ˈvir-əl\ *adj* **1** : having the nature, powers, or qualities of a man **2** : MASCULINE, MALE **3** : MASTERFUL, FORCEFUL — **vi·ril·i·ty** \və-ˈril-ət-ē\ *n*

vi·ri·on \ˈvī-rē-ˌän, ˈvir-ē-\ *n* : a complete virus particle consisting of an RNA or DNA core with a protein coat

vi·rol·o·gy \vī-ˈräl-ə-jē\ *n* : a branch of science that deals with viruses — **vi·rol·o·gist** \-jəst\ *n*

vir·tu \ˌvər-ˈtü, vir-\ *n* **1** : a love of or taste for objects of art **2** : objects of art (as curios and antiques)

vir·tu·al \ˈvər-chə(-wə)l\ *adj* : being in essence or in effect though not formally recognized or admitted ⟨a ~ dictator⟩ — **vir·tu·al·ly** \-ē\ *adv*

vir·tue \ˈvər-chü\ *n* [ME *virtu*, fr. OF, fr. L *virtus* strength, manliness, virtue, fr. *vir* man] **1** : conformity to a standard of right : MORALITY **2** : a particular moral excellence **3** : manly strength or courage : VALOR **4** : a commendable quality : MERIT **5** : active power to accomplish a given effect : POTENCY, EFFICACY **6** : chastity esp. in a woman

vir·tu·os·i·ty \ˌvər-chə-ˈwäs-ət-ē\ *n, pl* **-ties** : great technical skill in the practice of a fine art

vir·tu·o·so \ˌvər-chə-ˈwō-sō, -zō\ *n, pl* **-sos** *or* **-si** \-sē, -zē\ [It] **1** : one skilled in or having a taste for the fine arts **2** : one who excels in the technique of an art; *esp* : a highly skilled musical performer **syn** expert, adept, artist, doyen, master — **virtuoso** *adj*

vir·tu·ous \ˈvərch-(ə-)wəs\ *adj* **1** : having or showing virtue and esp. moral virtue **2** : CHASTE — **vir·tu·ous·ly** *adv*

vir·u·lent \ˈvir-(y)ə-lənt\ *adj* **1** : highly infectious ⟨a ~ germ⟩; *also* : marked by a rapid and very severe course ⟨a ~ disease⟩ **2** : extremely poisonous or venomous : NOXIOUS **3** : bitterly hostile : MALIGN — **vir·u·lence** \-ləns\ *n* — **vir·u·lent·ly** *adv*

vi·rus \ˈvī-rəs\ *n* [L, slimy liquid, poison, stench] **1** : any of a large group of submicroscopic infectious agents that have an outside coat of protein around a core of RNA or DNA, that can grow and multiply only in living cells, and that cause important diseases in human beings, lower animals, and plants; *also* : a disease caused by a virus **2** : something (as a corrupting influence) that poisons the mind or spirit

vis *abbr* **1** visibility **2** visual

[1]**vi·sa** \ˈvē-zə, -sə\ *n* [F] **1** : an endorsement by the proper authorities on a passport to show that it has been examined and the bearer may proceed **2** : a signature by a superior official signifying approval of a document

[2]**visa** *vb* **vi·saed** \-zəd, -səd\; **vi·sa·ing** \-zə-iŋ, -sə-\ : to give a visa to (a passport)

vis·age \ˈviz-ij\ *n* : the face or countenance of a person or sometimes an animal; *also* : LOOK, APPEARANCE

[1]**vis–à–vis** \ˌvēz-ə-ˈvē, ˌvēs-\ *prep* [F, lit., face-to-face] **1** : face-to-face with : OPPOSITE **2** : in relation to **3** : as compared with

[2]**vis–à–vis** *n, pl* **vis–à–vis** \-ə-ˈvē(z)\ **1** : one that is face-to-face with another **2** : ESCORT **3** : COUNTERPART **4** : TÊTE-À-TÊTE

[3]**vis–à–vis** *adv* : in company : TOGETHER

viscera *pl of* VISCUS

vis·cer·al \ˈvis-ə-rəl\ *adj* **1** : felt in or as if in the viscera **2** : of or relating to the viscera — **vis·cer·al·ly** \-ē\ *adv*

vis·cid \ˈvis-əd\ *adj* : VISCOUS — **vis·cid·i·ty** \vis-ˈid-ət-ē\ *n*

vis·cos·i·ty \vis-ˈkäs-ət-ē\ *n, pl* **-ties** : the quality of being viscous; *esp* : the property of a fluid that causes it to resist flow

vis·count \ˈvī-ˌkau̇nt\ *n* : a member of the British peerage ranking below an earl and above a baron

vis·count·ess \-ˌkau̇nt-əs\ *n* **1** : the wife or widow of a viscount **2** : a woman who holds the rank of viscount in her own right

vis·cous \ˈvis-kəs\ *adj* [ME *viscouse*, fr. LL *viscosus* full of birdlime, viscous, fr. L *viscum* mistletoe, birdlime] **1** : having the sticky consistency of glue **2** : having or characterized by viscosity

vis·cus \ˈvis-kəs\ *n, pl* **vis·cera** \ˈvis-ə-rə\ : an internal organ of the body; *esp* : one (as the heart or liver) located in the cavity of the trunk

vise \ˈvīs\ *n* [MF *vis* something winding, fr. L *vitis* vine] : a tool with two jaws for holding or clamping work that typically close by a screw or lever

vis·i·bil·i·ty \ˌviz-ə-ˈbil-ət-ē\ *n, pl* **-ties 1** : the quality, condition, or degree of being visible **2** : the degree of clearness of the atmosphere

vis·i·ble \ˈviz-ə-bəl\ *adj* : capable of being seen ⟨~ stars⟩; *also* : MANIFEST, APPARENT ⟨has no ~ means of support⟩ — **vis·i·bly** *adv*

[1]**vi·sion** \ˈvizh-ən\ *n* **1** : something seen otherwise than by ordinary sight (as in a dream or trance) **2** : a vivid picture created by the imagination **3** : the act or power of imagination **4** : unusual wisdom in foreseeing what is going to happen **5** : the act or power of seeing : SIGHT **6** : something seen; *esp* : a lovely sight

[2]**vision** *vb* **vi·sioned; vi·sion·ing** \ˈvizh-(ə-)niŋ\ : to see in or as if in a vision : IMAGINE, ENVISION

[1]**vi·sion·ary** \ˈvizh-ə-ˌner-ē\ *adj* **1** : of the nature of a vision : ILLUSORY, UNREAL **2** : seeing or likely to see visions : given to dreaming or imagining **3** : not practical : UTOPIAN **syn** imaginary, fantastic, chimerical, quixotic

[2]**visionary** *n, pl* **-ar·ies 1** : one whose ideas or projects are impractical : DREAMER **2** : one who sees visions

[1]**vis·it** \ˈviz-ət\ *vb* **1** : to go to see in order to comfort or help **2** : to call upon either as an act of courtesy or in a professional capacity **3** : to dwell with for a time as a guest **4** : to come to or upon as a reward, affliction, or punishment **5** : INFLICT **6** : to make a visit or regular or frequent visits **7** : CHAT, CONVERSE — **vis·it·able** *adj*

[2]**visit** *n* **1** : a short stay : CALL **2** : a brief residence as a guest **3** : a journey to and stay at a place **4** : a formal or professional call (as by a doctor)

vis·i·tant \ˈviz-ət-ənt\ *n* : VISITOR

vis·i·ta·tion \ˌviz-ə-ˈtā-shən\ *n* **1** : VISIT; *esp* : an official visit **2** : a special dispensation of divine favor or wrath; *also* : a severe trial

visiting nurse *n* : a nurse employed to visit sick persons or perform public-health services in a community

vis·i·tor \ˈviz-ət-ər\ *n* : one that visits

vi·sor \ˈvī-zər\ *n* **1** : the front piece of a helmet; *esp* : a movable upper piece **2** : VIZARD **3** : a projecting part (as on a cap) to shade the eyes — **vi·sored** \-zərd\ *adj*

vis·ta \ˈvis-tə\ *n* **1** : a distant view through or along an avenue or opening **2** : an extensive mental view over a series of years or events

VISTA *abbr* Volunteers in Service to America

[1]**vi·su·al** \ˈvizh-(ə-w)əl\ *adj* **1** : of, relating to, or used in sight ⟨~ organs⟩ **2** : perceived by vision ⟨a ~ impression⟩ **3** : VISIBLE **4** : done by sight only ⟨~ navigation⟩ **5** : of or relating to instruction by means of sight ⟨~ aids⟩ — **vi·su·al·ly** \-ē\ *adv*

[2]**visual** *n* : something (as a picture, chart, or film) that appeals to the sight and is used for illustration, demonstration, or promotion — usu. used in pl.

vi·su·al·ize \ˈvizh-(ə-)wə-ˌlīz\ *vb* **-ized; -iz·ing** : to make visible; *esp* : to form a mental image of — **vi·su·al·iza·tion** \ˌvizh-ə-(wə-)lə-ˈzā-shən\ *n* — **vi·su·al·iz·er** \ˈvizh-ə-(wə-)ˌlī-zər\ *n*

vi·ta \ˈvēt-ə, ˈvīt-ə\ *n, pl* **vi·tae** \ˈvē-ˌtī, ˈvīt-ē\ [L, lit., life] : a brief autobiographical sketch

vi·tal \ˈvīt-ᵊl\ *adj* **1** : concerned with or necessary to the maintenance of life **2** : full of life and vigor : ANIMATED **3** : of, relating to, or characteristic of life **4** : FATAL, MORTAL ⟨~ wound⟩ **5** : FUNDAMENTAL, BASIC, INDISPENSABLE — **vi·tal·ly** \-ē\ *adv*

vi·tal·i·ty \vī-ˈtal-ət-ē\ *n, pl* **-ties 1** : the peculiarity distinguishing the living from the nonliving; *also* : capacity to live : mental and physical vigor **2** : enduring quality **3** : ANIMATION, LIVELINESS

vi·tal·ize \ˈvīt-ᵊl-ˌīz\ *vb* **-ized; -iz·ing** : to impart life or vigor to : ANIMATE, ENERGIZE — **vi·tal·iza·tion** \ˌvīt-ᵊl-ə-ˈzā-shən\ *n*

vi·tals \ˈvīt-ᵊlz\ *n pl* **1** : vital organs **2** : essential parts

vital signs *n pl* : the pulse rate, respiratory rate, body temperature, and sometimes blood pressure of a person

vital statistics *n pl* : statistics dealing with births, deaths, marriages, health, and disease

vi·ta·min \ˈvīt-ə-mən\ *n* : any of various organic substances that are essential in tiny amounts to most animals and some plants and are mostly obtained from foods

vitamin A *n* : any of several vitamins (as from egg yolk or fish-liver oils) required for healthy epithelium and sight

vitamin B *n* **1** : VITAMIN B COMPLEX **2** *or* **vitamin B_1** : THIAMINE

vitamin B complex *n* : a group of vitamins that are found widely in foods and are essential for normal function of certain enzymes and for growth

vitamin B_6 \-ˈbē-ˈsiks\ *n* : any of several compounds that are considered essential to vertebrate nutrition

vitamin B_{12} \-ˈbē-ˈtwelv\ *n* : a complex cobalt-containing compound that occurs esp. in liver and is essential to normal blood formation, neural function, and growth; *also* : any of several compounds of similar action

vitamin C *n* : a vitamin found esp. in fruits and vegetables and needed by the body to prevent scurvy

vitamin D *n* : any or all of several vitamins that are needed for normal bone and tooth structure and are found esp. in fish-liver oils, egg yolk, and milk or are produced in response to ultraviolet light

vitamin E *n* : any of various oily fat-soluble liquid compounds that are found esp. in plants and are necessary in the body to prevent such ailments as infertility, the breakdown of muscles, and vascular problems

vitamin K *n* [Dan *koagulation* coagulation] : any of several vitamins that are needed in order for blood to clot properly

vi·ti·ate \ˈvish-ē-ˌāt\ *vb* **-at·ed; -at·ing 1** : CONTAMINATE, POLLUTE; *also* : DEBASE, PERVERT **2** : to make legally without force : INVALIDATE — **vi·ti·a·tion** \ˌvish-ē-ˈā-shən\ *n* — **vi·ti·a·tor** \ˈvish-ē-ˌāt-ər\ *n*

vi·ti·cul·ture \ˈvit-ə-ˌkəl-chər\ *n* : the growing of grapes — **vi·ti·cul·tur·al** \ˌvit-ə-ˈkəlch(-ə)-rəl\ *adj* — **vi·ti·cul·tur·ist** \-rəst\ *n*

vit·re·ous \ˈvi-trē-əs\ *adj* **1** : of, relating to, or resembling glass **2** : GLASSY ⟨~ rocks⟩ **3** : of, relating to, or being the clear colorless transparent jelly (**vitreous humor**) behind the lens in the eyeball

vit·ri·ol \ˈvi-trē-əl\ *n* : something resembling acid in being caustic, corrosive, or biting — **vit·ri·ol·ic** \ˌvi-trē-ˈäl-ik\ *adj*

vit·tles \ˈvit-ᵊlz\ *n pl* : VICTUALS

vi·tu·per·ate \vī-ˈt(y)ü-pə-ˌrāt, və-\ *vb* **-at·ed; -at·ing** : to abuse in words : SCOLD **syn** revile, berate, rate, upbraid, rail, lash — **vi·tu·per·a·tive** \-ˈt(y)ü-p(ə-)rət-iv, -pə-ˌrāt-\ *adj* — **vi·tu·per·a·tive·ly** *adv*

vi·tu·per·a·tion \(ˌ)vī-t(y)ü-pə-ˈrā-shən, və-\ *n* : lengthy harsh criticism or abuse

vi·va \ˈvē-və\ *interj* [It, long live, fr. *vivere* to live, fr. L] — used to express goodwill or approval

vi·va·ce \vē-ˈväch-ā\ *adv or adj* [It] : in a brisk spirited manner — used as a direction in music

vi·va·cious \və-ˈvā-shəs, vī-\ *adj* : lively in temper or conduct : ANIMATED, SPRIGHTLY — **vi·va·cious·ly** *adv* — **vi·va·cious·ness** *n*

vi·vac·i·ty \-ˈvas-ət-ē\ *n* : the quality or state of being vivacious

vi·var·i·um \vī-ˈvar-ē-əm, -ˈver-\ *n, pl* **-ia** \-ē-ə\ *or* **-iums** : an enclosure for keeping or raising and observing animals or plants indoors; *esp* : one for terrestrial animals

vi·va vo·ce \ˌvī-və-ˈvō-sē\ *adj* [ML, with the living voice] : expressed or conducted by word of mouth : ORAL ⟨*viva voce* examination⟩ ⟨*viva voce* voting⟩ — **viva voce** *adv*

viv·id \ˈviv-əd\ *adj* **1** : having the appearance of vigorous life or freshness : LIVELY **2** : BRILLIANT, INTENSE ⟨a ~ red⟩ **3** : producing a strong impression on the senses : SHARP **4** : calling forth lifelike mental images — **viv·id·ly** *adv* — **viv·id·ness** *n*

viv·i·fy \ˈviv-ə-ˌfī\ *vb* **-fied; -fy·ing 1** : to endue with life : ANIMATE **2** : to make vivid — **viv·i·fi·ca·tion** \ˌviv-ə-fə-ˈkā-shən\ *n* — **viv·i·fi·er** \ˈviv-ə-ˌfī(-ə)r\ *n*

vi·vip·a·rous \vī-ˈvip-(ə-)rəs, və-\ *adj* : producing living young from within the body rather than from eggs — **vi·vi·par·i·ty** \ˌvī-və-ˈpar-ət-ē, ˌviv-ə-\ *n*

vivi·sec·tion \ˌviv-ə-ˈsek-shən, ˈviv-ə-ˌsek-shən\ *n* : the cutting of or operation on a living animal; *also* : animal experimentation

vix·en \ˈvik-sən\ *n* **1** : a female fox **2** : an ill-tempered scolding woman **syn** shrew, scold, termagant, virago

viz \ˈnām-lē, ˈviz, və-ˈdel-ə-ˌset\ *abbr* videlicet

viz·ard \ˈviz-ərd\ *n* : a mask for disguise or protection

vi·zier \və-ˈziər\ *n* : a high executive officer of many Muslim countries and esp. of the former Turkish empire

vi·zor *var of* VISOR

VOA *abbr* Voice of America

voc *abbr* **1** vocational **2** vocative

vocab *abbr* vocabulary

vo·ca·ble \ˈvō-kə-bəl\ *n* : TERM, NAME; *esp* : a word composed of various sounds or letters without regard to its meaning

vo·cab·u·lary \vō-ˈkab-yə-ˌler-ē\ *n, pl* **-lar·ies 1** : a list or collection of words usu. alphabetically arranged and defined or explained : LEXICON **2** : a stock of words used in a language by a class or individual or in relation to a subject

vocabulary entry *n* : a word (as the noun *book*), hyphened or open compound (as the verb *cross-refer* or the noun *boric acid*), word element (as the affix *-an*), abbreviation (as *agt*), verbalized symbol (as *Na*), or term (as *master of ceremonies*) entered alphabetically in a dictionary for the purpose of definition or identification or expressly included as an inflected form (as the noun *mice* or the verb *saw*) or as a derived form (as the noun *godlessness* or the adverb *globally*) or related phrase (as *in spite of*) run on at its base word and usu. set in a type (as boldface) readily distinguishable from that of the lightface running text which defines, explains, or identifies the entry

¹vo·cal \ˈvō-kəl\ *adj* **1** : uttered by the voice : ORAL **2** : relating to, composed or arranged for, or sung by the human voice ⟨~ music⟩ **3** : of, relating to, or having the power of producing voice **4** : full of voices : RESOUNDING **5** : given to expressing one's feelings or opinions in speech : TALKATIVE; *also* : OUTSPOKEN **syn** articulate, fluent, eloquent

²vocal *n* **1** : a vocal sound **2** : a vocal composition or its performance

vocal cords *n pl* : either of two pairs of elastic folds of mucous membrane that project into the cavity of the larynx and function in the production of vocal sounds

vo·cal·ic \vō-ˈkal-ik\ *adj* : of, relating to, or functioning as a vowel

vo·cal·ist \ˈvō-kə-ləst\ *n* : SINGER

vo·cal·ize \-ˌlīz\ *vb* **-ized; -iz·ing 1** : to give vocal expression to : UTTER; *esp* : SING **2** : to make voiced rather than voiceless — **vo·cal·iz·er** *n*

vo·ca·tion \vō-ˈkā-shən\ *n* **1** : a summons or strong inclination to a particular state or course of action ⟨religious ~⟩ **2** : regular employment : OCCUPATION, PROFESSION — **vo·ca·tion·al** \-sh(ə-)nəl\ *adj*

vo·ca·tion·al·ism \-sh(ə-)nəl-ˌiz-əm\ *n* : emphasis on vocational training in education

voc·a·tive \ˈväk-ət-iv\ *adj* : of, relating to, or constituting a grammatical case marking the one addressed — **vocative** *n*

vo·cif·er·ate \vō-ˈsif-ə-ˌrāt\ *vb* **-at·ed; -at·ing** [L *vociferari*, fr. *voc-*, *vox* voice + *ferre* to bear] : to cry out loudly : CLAMOR, SHOUT — **vo·cif·er·a·tion** \-ˌsif-ə-ˈrā-shən\ *n*

vo·cif·er·ous \vō-ˈsif-(ə-)rəs\ *adj* : making or given to loud outcry : CLAMOROUS — **vo·cif·er·ous·ly** *adv* — **vo·cif·er·ous·ness** *n*

vod·ka \ˈväd-kə\ *n* [Russ, fr. *voda* water] : a colorless liquor of neutral spirits distilled from a mash (as of rye or wheat)

vogue \ˈvōg\ *n* [MF, action of rowing, course, fashion, fr. It *voga*, fr. *vogare* to row] **1** : popular acceptance or favor : POPULARITY **2** : a period of popularity **3** : something or someone in fashion at a particular time **syn** mode, fad, rage, craze, trend, fashion

vogu·ish \ˈvō-gish\ *adj* **1** : FASHIONABLE, SMART **2** : suddenly or temporarily popular

¹voice \ˈvȯis\ *n* **1** : sound produced through the mouth by vertebrates and esp. by human beings in speaking or shouting **2** : musical sound produced by the vocal cords : the power to produce such sound; *also* : one of the melodic parts in a vocal or instrumental composition **3** : the vocal organs as a means of tone production ⟨train the ~⟩ **4** : sound produced by vibration of the vocal cords as heard in vowels and some consonants **5** : the faculty of speech **6** : a sound suggesting vocal utterance ⟨the ~ of the sea⟩ **7** : an instrument or medium of expression **8** : a choice, opinion, or wish openly expressed; *also* : right of expression **9** : distinction of form of a verb to indicate the relation of the subject to the action expressed by the verb

²voice *vb* **voiced; voic·ing 1** : to give voice or expression to : UTTER; *also* : ANNOUNCE **2** : to regulate the tone of ⟨~ the pipes of an organ⟩ **syn** express, vent, air, ventilate

voice box *n* : LARYNX

voiced \ˈvȯist\ *adj* **1** : furnished with a voice ⟨soft-*voiced*⟩ **2** : uttered with voice — **voiced·ness** \ˈvȯis(t)-nəs, ˈvȯi-səd-nəs\ *n*

voice·less \ˈvȯis-ləs\ *adj* **1** : having no voice **2** : not pronounced with voice — **voice·less·ly** *adv* — **voice·less·ness** *n*

voice·print \ˈvȯis-ˌprint\ *n* : an individually distinctive pattern of voice characteristics that is spectrographically produced

¹void \ˈvȯid\ *adj* **1** : containing nothing : EMPTY **2** : UNOCCUPIED, VACANT **3** : LACKING, DEVOID ⟨proposals ~ of sense⟩ **4** : VAIN, USELESS **5** : of no legal force or effect : NULL

²void *n* **1** : empty space : EMPTINESS, VACUUM **2** : a feeling of want or hollowness

³void *vb* **1** : to make or leave empty; *also* : VACATE, LEAVE **2** : DISCHARGE, EMIT ⟨~ urine⟩ **3** : to render void : ANNUL, NULLIFY — **void·able** *adj* — **void·er** *n*

voi·là \vwä-ˈlä\ *interj* [F] — used to call attention or to express satisfaction or approval

voile \ˈvȯil\ *n* : a sheer fabric from various fibers used for women's clothing and curtains

vol *abbr* **1** volume **2** volunteer

vol·a·tile \ˈväl-ət-ᵊl\ *adj* **1** : readily becoming a vapor at a relatively low temperature ⟨a ~ liquid⟩ **2** : LIGHTHEART-

ED **3** : easily erupting into violent action **4** : CHANGEABLE — **vol·a·til·i·ty** \ˌväl-ə-ˈtil-ət-ē\ *n* — **vol·a·til·ize** \ˈväl-ət-ᵊl-ˌīz\ *vb*

vol·ca·nic \väl-ˈkan-ik\ *adj* **1** : of or relating to a volcano **2** : explosively violent : VOLATILE ⟨~ emotions⟩

volcanic glass *n* : natural glass produced by cooling of molten lava

vol·ca·nism \ˈväl-kə-ˌniz-əm\ *n* : volcanic power or action

vol·ca·no \väl-ˈkā-nō\ *n, pl* **-noes** *or* **-nos** [It *vulcano,* fr. L *Volcanus, Vulcanus* Roman god of fire and metalworking] : an opening in the earth's crust from which molten rock and steam issue; *also* : a hill or mountain composed of the ejected material

vol·ca·nol·o·gy \ˌväl-kə-ˈnäl-ə-jē\ *n* : a branch of geology that deals with volcanic phenomena — **vol·ca·nol·o·gist** \-kə-ˈnäl-ə-jəst\ *n*

vole \ˈvōl\ *n* : any of various mouselike or ratlike rodents that are closely related to the lemmings and muskrats

vo·li·tion \vō-ˈlish-ən\ *n* **1** : the act or the power of making a choice or decision : WILL **2** : a choice or decision made — **vo·li·tion·al** \-ˈlish-(ə-)nəl\ *adj*

[1]**vol·ley** \ˈväl-ē\ *n, pl* **volleys** **1** : a flight of missiles (as arrows or bullets) **2** : simultaneous discharge of a number of missile weapons **3** : a pouring forth of many things at the same instant ⟨a ~ of oaths⟩

[2]**volley** *vb* **vol·leyed; vol·ley·ing** **1** : to discharge or become discharged in or as if in a volley **2** : to hit an object of play in the air before it touches the ground

vol·ley·ball \-ˌbȯl\ *n* : a game played by volleying an inflated ball over a net; *also* : the ball used in this game

volt \ˈvōlt\ *n* : the mks unit of potential difference and electromotive force equal to the difference in potential between two points in a conducting wire carrying a constant current of one ampere when the power dissipated between the points is equal to one watt

volt·age \ˈvōl-tij\ *n* : potential difference measured in volts

vol·ta·ic \väl-ˈtā-ik, vōl-\ *adj* : of, relating to, or producing direct electric current by chemical action ⟨~ current⟩

volte–face \ˌvȯlt-(ə-)ˈfäs\ *n* : a reversal in policy : ABOUT-FACE

volt·me·ter \ˈvōlt-ˌmēt-ər\ *n* : an instrument for measuring in volts the difference in potential between different points of an electrical circuit

vol·u·ble \ˈväl-yə-bəl\ *adj* : fluent and smooth in speech : GLIB **syn** garrulous, loquacious, talkative — **vol·u·bil·i·ty** \ˌväl-yə-ˈbil-ət-ē\ *n* — **vol·u·bly** \ˈväl-yə-blē\ *adv*

vol·ume \ˈväl-yəm\ *n* [ME, fr. MF, fr. L *volumen* roll, scroll, fr. *volvere* to roll] **1** : a series of printed sheets bound typically in book form; *also* : an arbitrary number of issues of a periodical **2** : space occupied as measured by cubic units ⟨the ~ of a cylinder⟩ **3** : sufficient matter to fill a book ⟨her glance spoke ~*s*⟩ **4** : AMOUNT ⟨increasing ~ of business⟩ ; *also* : an aggregate forming a body or unit **5** : the degree of loudness of a sound **syn** body, bulk, mass

vo·lu·mi·nous \və-ˈlü-mə-nəs\ *adj* **1** : consisting of many folds or windings **2** : BULKY, LARGE **3** : filling or sufficient to fill a large volume or several volumes — **vo·lu·mi·nous·ly** \-ˈlü-mə-nəs-lē\ *adv* — **vo·lu·mi·nous·ness** *n*

[1]**vol·un·tary** \ˈväl-ən-ˌter-ē\ *adj* **1** : done, made, or given freely and without compulsion ⟨a ~ sacrifice⟩ **2** : not accidental : INTENTIONAL ⟨a ~ slight⟩ **3** : of, relating to, or regulated by the will ⟨~ behavior⟩ **4** : having power of free choice ⟨man is a ~ agent⟩ **5** : provided or supported by voluntary action ⟨a ~ hospital⟩ **syn** deliberate, willful, willing, witting — **vol·un·tari·ly** \ˌväl-ən-ˈter-ə-lē\ *adv*

[2]**voluntary** *n, pl* **-tar·ies** : an organ solo played in a religious service

voluntary muscle *n* : muscle (as most striated muscle) under voluntary control

[1]**vol·un·teer** \ˌväl-ən-ˈtiər\ *n* **1** : a person who of his own free will offers himself for a service or duty **2** : a plant growing spontaneously esp. from seeds lost from a previous crop

[2]**volunteer** *vb* **1** : to offer or give voluntarily **2** : to offer oneself as a volunteer

vo·lup·tu·ary \və-ˈləp-chə-ˌwer-ē\ *n, pl* **-ar·ies** : one whose chief interest in life is the indulgence of sensual appetites

vo·lup·tuous \-chə(-wə)s\ *adj* **1** : giving sensual gratification ⟨~ furnishings⟩ **2** : given to or spent in enjoyment of luxury or pleasure **syn** luxurious, epicurean, sensuous, sensual — **vo·lup·tuous·ly** *adv* — **vo·lup·tuous·ness** *n*

vo·lute \və-ˈlüt\ *n* : a spiral or scroll-shaped decoration

[1]**vom·it** \ˈväm-ət\ *n* : an act or instance of throwing up the contents of the stomach through the mouth; *also* : the matter discharged

[2]**vomit** *vb* **1** : to throw up the contents of the stomach as vomit **2** : to belch forth : GUSH

voo·doo \ˈvüd-ü\ *n, pl* **voodoos** [LaF *voudou*] **1** : VOODOOISM **2** : one who practices voodooism **3** : a charm or a fetish used in voodooism — **voodoo** *adj*

voo·doo·ism \-ˌiz-əm\ *n* **1** : a religion derived from African ancestor worship and consisting largely of sorcery **2** : the practice of sorcery

vo·ra·cious \vȯ-ˈrā-shəs, və-\ *adj* **1** : greedy in eating : RAVENOUS **2** : excessively eager : INSATIABLE ⟨a ~ reader⟩ **syn** gluttonous, ravening, rapacious — **vo·ra·cious·ly** *adv* — **vo·ra·cious·ness** *n* — **vo·rac·i·ty** \-ˈras-ət-ē\ *n*

vor·tex \ˈvȯr-ˌteks\ *n, pl* **vor·ti·ces** \ˈvȯrt-ə-ˌsēz\ *also* **vor·tex·es** \ˈvȯr-ˌtek-səz\ : a mass of whirling liquid forming a cavity in the center toward which things are drawn : WHIRLPOOL

vo·ta·ry \ˈvōt-ə-rē\ *n, pl* **-ries** **1** : ENTHUSIAST, DEVOTEE; *also* : a devoted adherent or admirer **2** : a devout or zealous worshiper

[1]**vote** \ˈvōt\ *n* [ME, fr. L *votum* vow, wish, fr. *vovēre* to vow] **1** : a choice or opinion of a person or body of persons expressed usu. by a ballot, spoken word, or raised hand; *also* : the ballot, word, or gesture used to express a choice or opinion **2** : the decision reached by voting **3** : the right of suffrage **4** : a group of voters with some common characteristics ⟨the big city ~⟩ — **vote·less** *adj*

[2]**vote** *vb* **vot·ed; vot·ing** **1** : to cast a vote **2** : to choose, endorse, authorize, or defeat by vote **3** : to express an opinion **4** : to adjudge by general agreement : DECLARE **5** : to offer as a suggestion : PROPOSE **6** : to cause to vote esp. in a given way — **vot·er** *n*

vo·tive \ˈvōt-iv\ *adj* : offered or performed in fulfillment of a vow or in petition, gratitude, or devotion

vou *abbr* voucher

vouch \ˈvau̇ch\ *vb* **1** : PROVE, SUBSTANTIATE **2** : to verify by examining documentary evidence **3** : to give a guarantee **4** : to supply supporting evidence or testimony; *also* : to give personal assurance

vouch·er \ˈvau̇-chər\ *n* **1** : an act of vouching **2** : one that vouches for another **3** : a documentary record of a business transaction **4** : a written affidavit or authorization **5** : a form indicating a credit against future purchases or expenditures

vouch·safe \vau̇ch-ˈsāf\ *vb* **vouch·safed; vouch·saf·ing** **1** : to grant or give often in a condescending manner **2** : to grant as a privilege or as a special favor — **vouch·safe·ment** *n*

[1]**vow** \ˈvau̇\ *n* : a solemn promise or assertion; *esp* : one by which a person binds himself or herself to an act, service, or condition

[2]**vow** *vb* **1** : to make a vow or as a vow **2** : to bind or commit by a vow — **vow·er** \ˈvaú(-ə)r\ *n*
vow·el \ˈvaú(-ə)l\ *n* **1** : a speech sound produced without obstruction or friction in the mouth **2** : a letter representing such a sound
vox po·pu·li \ˈväks-ˈpäp-yə-ˌlī\ *n* [L, voice of the people] : popular sentiment
[1]**voy·age** \ˈvȯi-ij\ *n* [ME, fr. OF *voiage*, fr. LL *viaticum*, fr. L, traveling money, fr. neut. of *viaticus* of a journey, fr. *via* way] : a journey esp. by water from one place or country to another
[2]**voyage** *vb* **voy·aged; voy·ag·ing** : to take or make a voyage — **voy·ag·er** *n*
voya·geur \ˌvȯi-ə-ˈzhər, ˌvwä-yä-\ *n* [CanF] : a person employed by a fur company to transport goods and men to and from remote stations esp. in the Canadian Northwest
voy·eur \vwä-ˈyər, vȯi-ˈər\ *n* : one who habitually seeks sexual stimulation by visual means — **voy·eur·ism** \-ˌiz-əm\ *n*
VP *abbr* **1** verb phrase **2** vice president
vs *abbr* **1** verse **2** versus
vss *abbr* **1** verses **2** versions
V/STOL *abbr* vertical short takeoff and landing
Vt *or* **VT** *abbr* Vermont
VTOL *abbr* vertical takeoff and landing
VTR *abbr* videotape recorder
vul·ca·nism \ˈvəl-kə-ˌniz-əm\ *n* : VOLCANISM
vul·ca·nize \ˈvəl-kə-ˌnīz\ *vb* **-nized; -niz·ing** : to treat rubber or rubberlike material chemically to give useful properties (as elasticity and strength) — **vul·ca·ni·za·tion** \ˌvəl-kə-nə-ˈzā-shən\ *n*
Vulg *abbr* Vulgate
vul·gar \ˈvəl-gər\ *adj* [ME, fr. L *vulgaris* of the mob, vulgar, fr. *vulgus* mob, common people] **1** : VERNACULAR ⟨the ~ tongue⟩ **2** : of or relating to the common people : GENERAL, COMMON **3** : lacking cultivation or refinement : BOORISH; *also* : offensive to good taste or refined feelings **syn** gross, obscene, ribald, dirty, indecent, profane — **vul·gar·ly** *adv*
vul·gar·i·an \ˌvəl-ˈgar-ē-ən\ *n* : a vulgar person
vul·gar·ism \ˈvəl-gə-ˌriz-əm\ *n* **1** : a word or expression originated or used chiefly by illiterate persons **2** : a coarse expression : OBSCENITY **3** : VULGARITY
vul·gar·i·ty \ˌvəl-ˈgar-ət-ē\ *n, pl* **-ties 1** : an instance of coarseness of manners or language **2** : the quality or state of being vulgar
vul·gar·ize \ˈvəl-gə-ˌrīz\ *vb* **-ized; -iz·ing** : to make vulgar — **vul·gar·iza·tion** \ˌvəl-gə-rə-ˈzā-shən\ *n* — **vul·gar·iz·er** \ˈvəl-gə-ˌrī-zər\ *n*
Vul·gate \ˈvəl-ˌgāt\ *n* [ML *vulgata*, fr. LL *vulgata editio* edition in general circulation] : a Latin version of the Bible used by the Roman Catholic Church
vul·ner·a·ble \ˈvəln-(ə-)rə-bəl\ *adj* **1** : capable of being wounded : susceptible to wounds **2** : open to attack **3** : liable to increased penalties in contract bridge — **vul·ner·a·bil·i·ty** \ˌvəln-(ə-)rə-ˈbil-ət-ē\ *n* — **vul·ner·a·bly** \ˈvəln-(ə-)rə-blē\ *adv*
vul·pine \ˈvəl-ˌpīn\ *adj* : of, relating to, or resembling a fox esp. in cunning
vul·ture \ˈvəl-chər\ *n* **1** : any of various large birds (as a turkey vulture) related to hawks and eagles but having weaker claws and the head usu. naked and living chiefly on carrion **2** : a rapacious person
vul·va \ˈvəl-və\ *n, pl* **vul·vae** \-ˌvē\ [L] : the external parts of the female genital organs
vv *abbr* **1** verses **2** vice versa
vying *pres part of* VIE

[1]**w** \ˈdəb-əl-(ˌ)yü\ *n, pl* **w's** *or* **ws** *often cap* : the 23d letter of the English alphabet
[2]**w** *abbr, often cap* **1** water **2** watt **3** week **4** weight **5** west **6** western **7** wide; width **8** wife **9** with
W *symbol* [G *Wolfram*] tungsten
WA *abbr* **1** Washington **2** Western Australia
Wac \ˈwak\ *n* [*W*omen's *A*rmy *C*orps] : a member of the Women's Army Corps
wacky \ˈwak-ē\ *adj* **wacki·er; -est** : ECCENTRIC, CRAZY
[1]**wad** \ˈwäd\ *n* **1** : a little mass, bundle, or tuft ⟨~*s* of clay⟩ **2** : a soft mass of usu. light fibrous material **3** : a pliable plug (as of felt) used to retain a powder charge (as in a cartridge) **4** : a considerable amount (as of money) **5** : a roll of paper money
[2]**wad** *vb* **wad·ded; wad·ding 1** : to push a wad into ⟨~ a gun⟩ **2** : to form into a wad **3** : to hold in by a wad ⟨~ a bullet in a gun⟩ **4** : to stuff or line with a wad : PAD
wad·ding \ˈwäd-iŋ\ *n* **1** : WADS; *also* : material for making wads **2** : a soft mass or sheet of short loose fibers used for stuffing or padding
wad·dle \ˈwäd-ᵊl\ *vb* **wad·dled; wad·dling** \ˈwäd-(ᵊ-)liŋ\ : to walk with short steps swaying from side to side like a duck — **waddle** *n*
wade \ˈwād\ *vb* **wad·ed; wad·ing 1** : to step in or through a medium (as water) more resistant than air **2** : to move or go with difficulty or labor and often with determined vigor ⟨~ through a dull book⟩ — **wad·able** *or* **wade·able** \ˈwād-ə-bəl\ *adj* — **wade** *n*
wad·er \ˈwād-ər\ *n* **1** : one that wades **2** : WADING BIRD **3** *pl* : high waterproof rubber boots or trousers for wading
wa·di \ˈwäd-ē\ *n* [Ar] : a watercourse dry except in the rainy season esp. in southwestern Asia and northern Africa
wading bird *n* : any of many long-legged birds (as sandpipers, cranes, or herons) that wade in water in search of food
Waf \ˈwaf\ *n* [*W*omen in the *A*ir *F*orce] : a member of the women's component of the Air Force
wa·fer \ˈwā-fər\ *n* **1** : a thin crisp cake or cracker **2** : a thin round piece of unleavened bread used in the Eucharist **3** : something (as a piece of candy or an adhesive seal) that resembles a wafer
waf·fle \ˈwäf-əl\ *n* : a soft but crisped cake of batter cooked in a special hinged metal utensil (**waffle iron**)
[1]**waft** \ˈwäft, ˈwaft\ *vb* : to cause to move or go lightly by or as if by the impulse of wind or waves
[2]**waft** *n* **1** : a slight breeze : PUFF **2** : the act of waving
[1]**wag** \ˈwag\ *vb* **wagged; wag·ging 1** : to sway or swing shortly from side to side or to-and-fro ⟨the dog *wagged* his tail⟩ **2** : to move in chatter or gossip ⟨scandal caused tongues to ~⟩
[2]**wag** *n* : an act of wagging : a wagging movement
[3]**wag** *n* : WIT, JOKER
[1]**wage** \ˈwāj\ *vb* **waged; wag·ing 1** : to engage in : CARRY ON ⟨~ a war⟩ **2** : to be in process of being waged
[2]**wage** *n* **1** : payment for labor or services usu. according to contract **2** *pl* : RECOMPENSE, REWARD

[1]**wa·ger** \ˈwā-jər\ *n* **1** : BET, STAKE **2** : something on which bets are laid : GAMBLE

[2]**wager** *vb* : BET — **wa·ger·er** *n*

wag·gery \ˈwag-ə-rē\ *n, pl* **-ger·ies 1** : mischievous merriment : PLEASANTRY **2** : JEST, TRICK

wag·gish \ˈwag-ish\ *adj* **1** : SPORTIVE, HUMOROUS **2** : resembling or characteristic of a wag : MISCHIEVOUS, ROGUISH, FROLICSOME

wag·gle \ˈwag-əl\ *vb* **wag·gled; wag·gling** \-(ə-)liŋ\ : to move backward and forward or from side to side : WAG — **waggle** *n*

wag·on \ˈwag-ən\ *n* **1** : a 4-wheeled vehicle; *esp* : one drawn by animals and used for freight or merchandise **2** : PATROL WAGON **3** : a child's 4-wheeled cart **4** : STATION WAGON

wag·on·er \ˈwag-ə-nər\ *n* : the driver of a wagon

wag·on·ette \ˌwag-ə-ˈnet\ *n* : a light wagon with two facing seats along the sides behind a cross seat in front

wa·gon–lit \ˌvá-gō^{n}-ˈlē\ *n, pl* **wagons–lits** *or* **wagon–lits** \-gō^{n}-ˈlē(z)\ [F, fr. *wagon* railroad car + *lit* bed] : a railroad sleeping car

wagon train *n* : a group of wagons traveling overland

wag·tail \ˈwag-ˌtāl\ *n* : any of various slender-bodied mostly Old World birds with a long tail that jerks up and down

wa·hi·ne \wä-ˈhē-nā\ *n* **1** : a Polynesian woman **2** : a female surfer

wa·hoo \ˈwä-ˌhü\ *n, pl* **wahoos** : a large vigorous food and sport fish related to the mackerel and found in warm seas

waif \ˈwāf\ *n* **1** : something found without an owner and esp. by chance **2** : a stray person or animal; *esp* : a homeless child

wail \ˈwāl\ *vb* **1** : LAMENT, WEEP **2** : to make a sound suggestive of a mournful cry **3** : COMPLAIN — **wail** *n*

wail·ful \-fəl\ *adj* : SORROWFUL, MOURNFUL — **wail·ful·ly** \-ē\ *adv*

wain \ˈwān\ *n* : a usu. large heavy farm wagon

wain·scot \ˈwān-skət, -ˌskōt, -ˌskät\ *n* **1** : a usu. paneled wooden lining of an interior wall of a room **2** : the lower part of an interior wall when finished differently from the rest — **wainscot** *vb*

wain·scot·ing *or* **wain·scot·ting** \-ˌskōt-iŋ, -ˌskät-, -skət-\ *n* : material for a wainscot; *also* : WAINSCOT

wain·wright \ˈwān-ˌrīt\ *n* : a builder and repairer of wagons

waist \ˈwāst\ *n* **1** : the narrowed part of the body between the chest and hips **2** : a part resembling the human waist esp. in narrowness or central position ⟨the ~ of a ship⟩ **3** : a garment or part of a garment (as a blouse or bodice) for the upper part of the body

waist·band \ˈwās(t)-ˌband\ *n* : a band (as on trousers or a skirt) that fits around the waist

waist·coat \ˈwes-kət, ˈwās(t)-ˌkōt\ *n, chiefly Brit* : VEST 1

waist·line \ˈwāst-ˌlīn\ *n* **1** : a line thought of as surrounding the waist at its narrowest part; *also* : the length of this **2** : the line at which the bodice and skirt of a dress meet

[1]**wait** \ˈwāt\ *vb* **1** : to remain inactive in readiness or expectation : AWAIT ⟨~ for orders⟩ **2** : POSTPONE, DELAY ⟨~ dinner for late guests⟩ **3** : to act as attendant or servant ⟨~ on customers⟩ **4** : to attend as a waiter : SERVE ⟨~ tables⟩ ⟨~ at a banquet⟩ **5** : to be ready

[2]**wait** *n* **1** : a position of concealment usu. with intent to attack or surprise ⟨lie in ~⟩ **2** : an act or period of waiting

wait·er \ˈwāt-ər\ *n* **1** : one that waits upon another; *esp* : a man who waits on table **2** : TRAY

waiting game *n* : a strategy in which one or more participants withhold action in the hope of an opportunity for more effective action later

waiting room *n* : a room (as at a doctor's office) for the use of persons waiting

wait·ress \ˈwā-trəs\ *n* : a girl or woman who waits on table

waive \ˈwāv\ *vb* **waived; waiv·ing** [ME *weiven,* fr. OF *weyver,* fr. *waif* lost, unclaimed] **1** : to give up claim to ⟨*waived* his right to a trial⟩ **2** : POSTPONE

waiv·er \ˈwā-vər\ *n* : the act of waiving right, claim, or privilege; *also* : a document containing a declaration of such an act

[1]**wake** \ˈwāk\ *vb* **woke** \ˈwōk\ *also* **waked** \ˈwākt\; **wo·ken** \ˈwō-kən\ *also* **waked** *or* **woke; wak·ing 1** : to be or remain awake; *esp* : to keep watch (as over a corpse) **2** : AWAKE, AWAKEN ⟨the baby *waked* up early⟩ ⟨the thunder *waked* him up⟩

[2]**wake** *n* **1** : the state of being awake **2** : a watch held over the body of a dead person prior to burial

[3]**wake** *n* : the track left by a ship in the water; *also* : a track left behind

wake·ful \ˈwāk-fəl\ *adj* : not sleeping or able to sleep : SLEEPLESS, ALERT — **wake·ful·ness** *n*

wak·en \ˈwā-kən\ *vb* **wak·ened; wak·en·ing** \ˈwāk-(ə-)niŋ\ : WAKE

wake–rob·in \ˈwāk-ˌräb-ən\ *n* : TRILLIUM

wak·ing \ˈwā-kiŋ\ *adj* : passed in a conscious or alert state ⟨every ~ hour⟩

wale \ˈwāl\ *n* : a ridge esp. on cloth; *also* : the texture esp. of a fabric

[1]**walk** \ˈwȯk\ *vb* [partly fr. ME *walken,* fr. OE *wealcan* to roll, toss and partly fr. ME *walkien,* fr. OE *wealcian* to roll up, muffle up] **1** : to move or cause to move on foot usu. at a natural unhurried gait ⟨~ to town⟩ ⟨~ a horse⟩ **2** : to pass over, through, or along by walking ⟨~ the streets⟩ **3** : to perform or accomplish by walking ⟨~ guard⟩ **4** : to follow a course of action or way of life ⟨~ humbly in the sight of God⟩ **5** : to receive a base on balls; *also* : to give a base on balls to — **walk·er** *n*

[2]**walk** *n* **1** : a going on foot ⟨go for a ~⟩ **2** : a place, path, or course for walking **3** : distance to be walked ⟨a 10-minute ~ from here⟩ **4** : manner of living : CONDUCT, BEHAVIOR; *also* : social or economic status ⟨various ~*s* of life⟩ **5** : manner of walking : GAIT; *esp* : a slow 4-beat gait of a horse **6** : BASE ON BALLS

walk·away \ˈwȯk-ə-ˌwā\ *n* : an easily won contest

walk·ie–talk·ie \ˈwȯ-kē-ˈtȯ-kē\ *n* : a small portable radio transmitting and receiving set

[1]**walk–in** \ˈwȯk-ˌin\ *adj* : large enough to be walked into ⟨a ~ refrigerator⟩

[2]**walk–in** \ˈwȯk-ˌin\ *n* **1** : an easy election victory **2** : one that walks in

walking papers *n pl* : DISMISSAL, DISCHARGE

walking stick *n* **1** : a stick used in walking **2** *usu* **walk·ing·stick** : STICK INSECT; *esp* : one common in parts of the U.S.

walk–on \ˈwȯk-ˌȯn, -ˌän\ *n* : a small part or brief appearance in a dramatic production

walk·out \-ˌau̇t\ *n* **1** : a labor strike **2** : the action of leaving a meeting or organization as an expression of disapproval

walk·over \-ˌō-vər\ *n* : a one-sided contest : an easy victory

walk–up \ˈwȯk-ˌəp\ *n* : a building or apartment house without an elevator — **walk–up** *adj*

walk·way \-ˌwā\ *n* : a passage for walking

[1]**wall** \ˈwȯl\ *n* [ME, fr. OE *weall,* fr. L *vallum* rampart, fr. *vallus* stake, palisade] **1** : a structure (as of stone or brick) intended for defense or security or for enclosing something **2** : one of the upright enclosing parts of a building or room **3** : the inside surface of a cavity or vessel ⟨the ~ of a boiler⟩ **4** : something like a wall in appearance or function ⟨a tariff ~⟩ — **walled** \ˈwȯld\ *adj*

[2]**wall** *vb* **1** : to provide, separate, or surround with or as if with a wall ⟨~ in a garden⟩ **2** : to close (an opening) with or as if with a wall ⟨~ up a door⟩

wal·la·by \ˈwäl-ə-bē\ *n, pl* **wallabies** *also* **wallaby** : any of various small or medium-sized kangaroos

wall·board \ˈwȯl-ˌbōrd\ *n* : a structural material (as of wood pulp or plaster) made in large sheets and used for sheathing interior walls and ceilings

wal·let \ˈwäl-ət\ *n* **1** : a bag or sack for carrying things on a journey **2** : a pocketbook with compartments (as for personal papers and usu. unfolded money) : BILLFOLD

wall·eye \ˈwȯl-ˌī\ *n* **1** : an eye with whitish iris or an opaque white cornea **2** : a large vigorous No. American food and sport fish related to the perches — **wall·eyed** \-ˌīd\ *adj*

wall·flow·er \ˈwȯl-ˌflau̇(-ə)r\ *n* **1** : any of several Old World plants related to the mustards; *esp* : one with showy fragrant flowers **2** : a person who usu. from shyness or unpopularity remains alone (as at a dance)

Wal·loon \wä-ˈlün\ *n* : a member of a chiefly Celtic people of southern and southeastern Belgium and adjacent parts of France — **Walloon** *adj*

1**wal·lop** \ˈwäl-əp\ *vb* [ME, gallop, fr. Old Northern French *waloper* to gallop] **1** : to beat soundly : TROUNCE **2** : to hit hard : SOCK

2**wallop** *n* **1** : a powerful blow or impact **2** : the ability to hit hard **3** : emotional or psychological force : IMPACT

wal·lop·ing \ˈwäl-ə-piŋ\ *adj* **1** : LARGE, WHOPPING **2** : exceptionally fine or impressive

1**wal·low** \ˈwäl-ō\ *vb* **1** : to roll oneself about in or as if in deep mud : FLOUNDER ⟨hogs ~*ing* in the mire⟩ **2** : to live in or be filled with excessive pleasure ⟨~ in luxury⟩

2**wallow** *n* : a muddy or dust-filled area where animals wallow

wall·pa·per \ˈwȯl-ˌpā-pər\ *n* : decorative paper for the walls of a room — **wallpaper** *vb*

wall–to–wall *adj* **1** : covering the entire floor ⟨*wall-to-wall* carpeting⟩ **2** : covering or filling one entire space or time ⟨crowds of *wall-to-wall* people⟩

wal·nut \ˈwȯl-(ˌ)nət\ *n* [ME *walnot,* fr. OE *wealhhnutu,* lit., foreign nut, fr. *Wealh* Welshman, foreigner + *hnutu* nut] **1** : an edible nut with a furrowed usu. rough shell and an adherent husk from any of a genus of trees related to the hickories; *esp* : the large edible nut of a Eurasian tree **2** : a tree that bears walnuts **3** : the usu. reddish to dark brown wood of a walnut used esp. in cabinetwork and veneers

wal·rus \ˈwȯl-rəs, ˈwäl-\ *n, pl* **walrus** *or* **wal·rus·es** : either of two large mammals of northern seas related to the seals and having ivory tusks

walrus

1**waltz** \ˈwȯlts\ *vb* [G *walzer,* fr. *walzen* to roll, dance, fr. Old High German *walzan* to turn, roll] **1** : to dance a waltz **2** : to move or advance easily, successfully, or conspicuously ⟨he ~*ed* through customs⟩

2**waltz** *n* **1** : a gliding dance done to music having three beats to the measure **2** : music for or suitable for waltzing

wam·ble \ˈwäm-bəl\ *vb* **wam·bled; wam·bling** \-b(ə-)liŋ\ : to progress unsteadily or with a lurching shambling gait

wam·pum \ˈwäm-pəm\ *n* [short for *wampumpeag,* fr. Narraganset (a North American Indian language) *wampompeag,* fr. *wampan* white + *api* string + *-ag* pl. suffix] **1** : beads made of shells strung in strands, belts, or sashes and used by No. American Indians as money and ornaments **2** *slang* : MONEY

wan \ˈwän\ *adj* **wan·ner; wan·nest 1** : SICKLY, PALLID; *also* : FEEBLE **2** : DIM, FAINT **3** : LANGUID ⟨a ~ smile⟩ — **wan·ly** *adv* — **wan·ness** \ˈwän-nəs\ *n*

wand \ˈwänd\ *n* **1** : a slender staff carried in a procession **2** : the staff of a fairy, diviner, or magician

wan·der \ˈwän-dər\ *vb* **wan·dered; wan·der·ing** \-d(ə-)riŋ\ **1** : to move about aimlessly or without a fixed course or goal : RAMBLE **2** : STRAY **3** : to go astray in conduct or thought; *esp* : to become delirious — **wan·der·er** *n*

Wan·der·ing Jew *n* : any of several trailing or creeping plants some of which are often planted in hanging baskets

wan·der·lust \ˈwän-dər-ˌləst\ *n* : strong longing for or impulse toward wandering

1**wane** \ˈwān\ *vb* **waned; wan·ing 1** : to grow gradually smaller or less ⟨the moon ~*s*⟩ ⟨his strength *waned*⟩ **2** : to lose power, prosperity, or influence **3** : to draw near an end ⟨summer is *waning*⟩

2**wane** *n* : a waning (as in size or power); *also* : a period in which something is waning

wan·gle \ˈwaŋ-gəl\ *vb* **wan·gled; wan·gling** \-g(ə-)liŋ\ **1** : to obtain by sly or roundabout means; *also* : to use trickery or questionable means to achieve an end **2** : MANIPULATE; *also* : FINAGLE

Wan·kel engine \ˈväŋ-kəl-, ˈwaŋ-\ *n* : an internal-combustion rotary engine with a rounded triangular rotor functioning as a piston

1**want** \ˈwȯnt\ *vb* **1** : to fail to possess : LACK ⟨they ~ the necessities of life⟩ **2** : to fall short by ⟨it ~*s* three minutes to six⟩ **3** : to feel or suffer the need of **4** : NEED, REQUIRE ⟨the house ~*s* painting⟩ **5** : to desire earnestly : WISH

2**want** *n* **1** : a lack of a required or usual amount : SHORTAGE **2** : dire need : DESTITUTION **3** : something wanted : DESIRE **4** : personal defect : FAULT

1**want·ing** \-iŋ\ *adj* **1** : not present or in evidence : ABSENT **2** : falling below standards or expectations **3** : lacking in ability or capacity : DEFICIENT ⟨~ in common sense⟩

2**wanting** *prep* **1** : WITHOUT ⟨a book ~ a cover⟩ **2** : LESS, MINUS ⟨a month ~ two days⟩

1**wan·ton** \ˈwȯnt-ᵊn\ *adj* [ME, undisciplined, fr. *wan-* deficient, wrong + *towen,* pp. of *teen* to draw, train, discipline] **1** : UNCHASTE, LEWD, LUSTFUL; *also* : SENSUAL **2** : having no regard for justice or for other persons' feelings, rights, or safety : MERCILESS, INHUMANE ⟨~ cruelty⟩ **3** : having no just cause ⟨a ~ attack⟩ — **wan·ton·ly** *adv* — **wan·ton·ness** *n*

2**wanton** *n* : a wanton individual; *esp* : a lewd or immoral person

3**wanton** *vb* **1** : to be wanton : act wantonly **2** : to pass or waste wantonly

wa·pi·ti \ˈwäp-ət-ē\ *n, pl* **wapiti** *or* **wapitis** : ELK 2

1**war** \ˈwȯr\ *n* **1** : a state or period of usu. open and declared armed fighting between states or nations **2** : the art or science of warfare **3** : a state of hostility, conflict, or antagonism **4** : a struggle between opposing forces or for a particular end ⟨~ against disease⟩ — **war·less** \-ləs\ *adj*

2**war** *vb* **warred; war·ring** : to engage in warfare : be in conflict

3**war** *abbr* warrant

1**war·ble** \ˈwȯr-bəl\ *n* **1** : a melodious succession of low pleasing sounds **2** : a musical trill

²warble *vb* **war·bled; war·bling** \-b(ə-)liŋ\ **1** : to sing or utter in a trilling manner or with variations **2** : to express by or as if by warbling

³warble *n* : a swelling under the hide esp. of the back of cattle, horses, and wild mammals caused by the maggot of a fly (**warble fly**); *also* : its maggot

war·bler \ˈwȯr-blər\ *n* **1** : SONGSTER **2** : any of various small slender-billed Old World singing birds related to the thrushes and noted for their song **3** : any of various small bright-colored American insect-eating birds with a usu. weak and unmusical song

war·bon·net \ˈwȯr-ˌbän-ət\ *n* : a feathered American Indian ceremonial headdress

war cry *n* **1** : a cry used by fighters in war **2** : a slogan used esp. to rally people to a cause

¹ward \ˈwȯrd\ *n* **1** : a guarding or being under guard or guardianship; *esp* : CUSTODY **2** : a body of guards **3** : a division of a prison **4** : a division in a hospital **5** : a division of a city for electoral or administrative purposes **6** : a person (as a child) under the protection of a guardian or a law court **7** : a person or body of persons under the protection or tutelage of a government **8** : a means of defense : PROTECTION

²ward *vb* : to turn aside : DEFLECT — usu. used with *off* ⟨~ off a blow⟩

¹-ward \wərd\ *also* **-wards** \wərdz\ *adj suffix* **1** : that moves, tends, faces, or is directed toward ⟨wind*ward*⟩ **2** : that occurs or is situated in the direction of ⟨sea*ward*⟩

²-ward *or* **-wards** *adv suffix* **1** : in a (specified) direction ⟨up*wards*⟩ ⟨after*ward*⟩ **2** : toward a (specified) point, position, or area ⟨sky*ward*⟩

war dance *n* : a dance performed by primitive peoples before going to war or in celebration of victory

war·den \ˈwȯrd-ᵊn\ *n* **1** : GUARDIAN, KEEPER **2** : the governor of a town, district, or fortress **3** : an official charged with special supervisory or enforcement duties ⟨game ~⟩ ⟨air raid ~⟩ **4** : an official in charge of the operation of a prison **5** : one of two ranking lay officers of an Episcopal parish **6** : any of various British college officials

ward·er \ˈwȯrd-ər\ *n* : WATCHMAN, WARDEN

ward heeler \-ˌhē-lər\ *n* : a local worker for a political boss

ward·robe \ˈwȯrd-ˌrōb\ *n* [ME *warderobe,* fr. OF, fr. *warder* to guard + *robe* robe] **1** : a room or closet where clothes are kept; *also* : CLOTHESPRESS **2** : a collection of wearing apparel ⟨his summer ~⟩

ward·room \-ˌrüm, -ˌru̇m\ *n* : the quarters in a warship allotted to the commissioned officers except the captain; *esp* : the room allotted to these officers for meals

ward·ship \ˈwȯrd-ˌship\ *n* **1** : GUARDIANSHIP **2** : the state of being under care of a guardian

ware \ˈwaər\ *n* **1** : manufactured articles or products of art or craft : GOODS **2** : an article of merchandise ⟨a peddler hawking his ~*s*⟩ **3** : items (as dishes) of fired clay : POTTERY

ware·house \-ˌhau̇s\ *n* : a place for the storage of merchandise or commodities : STOREHOUSE — **warehouse** *vb* — **ware·house·man** \-mən\ *n* — **ware·hous·er** \-hau̇-zər, -sər\ *n*

ware·room \ˈwaər-ˌrüm, -ˌru̇m\ *n* : a room in which goods are exhibited for sale

war·fare \ˈwȯr-ˌfaər\ *n* **1** : military operations between enemies : WAR; *also* : an activity undertaken by one country to weaken or destroy another ⟨economic ~⟩ **2** : STRUGGLE, CONFLICT

war·fa·rin \ˈwȯr-fə-rən\ *n* : an anticoagulant used as a rodent poison and in medicine

war·head \-ˌhed\ *n* : the section of a missile containing the charge

war–horse \-ˌhȯrs\ *n* **1** : a horse for use in war **2** : a veteran soldier or public person (as a politician)

war·like \-ˌlīk\ *adj* **1** : fond of war ⟨~ peoples⟩ **2** : of, relating to, or useful in war : MILITARY, MARTIAL ⟨~ supplies⟩ **3** : befitting or characteristic of war or of soldiers ⟨~ attitudes⟩

war·lock \-ˌläk\ *n* [ME *warloghe,* fr. OE *wǣrloga* one that breaks faith, the Devil, fr. *wǣr* faith, troth + *-loga* (fr. *lēogan* to lie)] : SORCERER, WIZARD

war·lord \-ˌlȯrd\ *n* **1** : a high military leader **2** : a military commander exercising local civil power by force ⟨former Chinese ~*s*⟩

¹warm \ˈwȯrm\ *adj* **1** : having or giving out heat to a moderate or adequate degree ⟨~ milk⟩ ⟨a ~ stove⟩ **2** : serving to retain heat ⟨~ clothes⟩ **3** : feeling or inducing sensations of heat ⟨~ from exercise⟩ ⟨a ~ climb⟩ **4** : showing or marked by strong feeling : ARDENT ⟨~ support⟩ **5** : marked by tense excitement or hot anger ⟨a ~ campaign⟩ **6** : giving a pleasant impression of warmth, cheerfulness, or friendliness ⟨~ colors⟩ ⟨a ~ tone of voice⟩ **7** : marked by or tending toward injury, distress, or pain ⟨made things ~ for the enemy⟩ **8** : newly made : FRESH ⟨a ~ scent⟩ **9** : near to a goal ⟨getting ~ in a search⟩ — **warm·ly** *adv*

²warm *vb* **1** : to make or become warm **2** : to give a feeling of warmth or vitality to **3** : to experience feelings of affection or pleasure ⟨she ~*ed* to her guest⟩ **4** : to reheat for eating ⟨~*ed* over the roast⟩ **5** : to make ready for operation or performance by preliminary exercise or operation ⟨~ up the motor⟩ **6** : to become increasingly ardent, interested, or competent ⟨the speaker ~*ed* to his topic⟩ — **warm·er** *n*

warm–blood·ed \-ˈbləd-əd\ *adj* : able to maintain a relatively high and constant body temperature essentially independent of that of the surroundings

warmed–over \ˈwȯrmd-ˈō-vər\ *adj* **1** : REHEATED ⟨~ cabbage⟩ **2** : not fresh or new ⟨~ ideas⟩

warm·heart·ed \ˈwȯrm-ˈhärt-əd\ *adj* : marked by warmth of feeling : CORDIAL — **warm·heart·ed·ness** *n*

warming pan *n* : a long-handled covered pan filled with live coals and formerly used to warm a bed

war·mon·ger \ˈwȯr-ˌməŋ-gər, -ˌmäŋ-\ *n* : one who urges or attempts to stir up war

warmth \ˈwȯrmth\ *n* **1** : the quality or state of being warm **2** : ZEAL, ARDOR, FERVOR

warm up \(ˈ)wȯrm-ˈəp\ *vb* : to engage in exercise or practice esp. before entering a game or contest — **warm–up** \ˈwȯrm-ˌəp\ *n*

warn \ˈwȯrn\ *vb* **1** : to put on guard : CAUTION; *also* : ADMONISH, COUNSEL **2** : to notify esp. in advance : INFORM **3** : to order to go or keep away

¹warn·ing \-iŋ\ *n* **1** : the act of warning : the state of being warned **2** : something that warns or serves to warn

²warning *adj* : serving as an alarm, signal, summons, or admonition ⟨~ bell⟩ — **warn·ing·ly** *adv*

¹warp \ˈwȯrp\ *n* **1** : the lengthwise threads on a loom or in a woven fabric **2** : a twist out of a true plane or straight line ⟨a ~ in a board⟩

²warp *vb* [ME *warpen,* fr. OE *weorpan* to throw] **1** : to turn or twist out of shape; *also* : to become so twisted **2** : to lead astray : PERVERT; *also* : FALSIFY, DISTORT

war paint *n* : paint put on the face and body by American Indians as a sign of going to war

war·path \ˈwȯr-ˌpath, -ˌpa̐th\ *n* : the course taken by a party of American Indians going on a hostile expedition — **on the warpath** : ready to fight or argue

war·plane \-ˌplān\ *n* : a military airplane; *esp* : one armed for combat

¹war·rant \ˈwȯr-ənt, ˈwär-\ *n* **1** : AUTHORIZATION; *also* : JUSTIFICATION, GROUND **2** : evidence (as a document) of authorization; *esp* : a legal writ authorizing an officer to take action (as in making an arrest, seizure, or search) **3** : a certificate of appointment issued to an officer of lower rank than a commissioned officer

²warrant *vb* **1** : to guarantee security or immunity to : SECURE **2** : to declare or maintain positively ⟨I ~ this is so⟩

3 : to assure (a person) of the truth of what is said 4 : to guarantee to be as it appears or as it is represented ⟨~ goods as of the first quality⟩ 5 : SANCTION, AUTHORIZE 6 : to give proof of : ATTEST; *also* : GUARANTEE 7 : JUSTIFY ⟨his need ~*s* the expenditure⟩

warrant officer *n* 1 : an officer in the armed forces ranking next below a commissioned officer 2 : a commissioned officer ranking below an ensign in the navy or coast guard and below a second lieutenant in the marine corps

war·ran·ty \ˈwȯr-ənt-ē, ˈwär-\ *n, pl* **-ties** : an expressed or implied statement that some situation or thing is as it appears to be or is represented to be; *esp* : a usu. written guarantee of the integrity of a product and of the maker's responsibility for the repair or replacement of defective parts

war·ren \ˈwȯr-ən, ˈwär-\ *n* 1 : an area for the keeping of small game and esp. rabbits; *also* : an area where rabbits breed 2 : a crowded tenement or district

war·rior \ˈwȯr-yər, ˈwȯr-ē-ər; ˈwär-ē-, ˈwär-yər\ *n* : a man engaged or experienced in warfare

war·ship \ˈwȯr-ˌship\ *n* : a military ship armed for combat

wart \ˈwȯrt\ *n* 1 : a small usu. horny projection on the skin; *esp* : one caused by a virus 2 : a protuberance resembling a wart (as on a plant) — **warty** *adj*

wart·hog \ˈwȯrt-ˌhȯg, -ˌhäg\ *n* : an African wild hog with large tusks and two pairs of rough warty protuberances below the eyes

war·time \ˈwȯr-ˌtīm\ *n* : a period during which a war is in progress

wary \ˈwa(ə)r-ē\ *adj* **wari·er; -est** : very cautious; *esp* : careful in guarding against danger or deception

was *past 1st & 3d sing of* BE

[1]**wash** \ˈwȯsh, ˈwäsh\ *vb* 1 : to cleanse with or as if with a liquid (as water) 2 : to wet thoroughly with water or other liquid 3 : to flow along the border of ⟨waves ~ the shore⟩ 4 : to pass (a gas or gaseous mixture) through or over a liquid for purifying 5 : to pour or flow in a stream or current 6 : to move or remove by or as if by the action of water 7 : to cover or daub lightly with a liquid (as whitewash) 8 : to run water over (as gravel or ore) in order to separate valuable matter from refuse ⟨~ sand for gold⟩ 9 : to undergo laundering ⟨a dress that doesn't ~ well⟩ 10 : to stand a test ⟨that story will not ~⟩ 11 : to be worn away by water

[2]**wash** *n* 1 : the act or process or an instance of washing or being washed 2 : articles to be washed or being washed 3 : the flow or action of a mass of water (as a wave) 4 : erosion by waves (as of the sea) 5 *West* : the dry bed of a stream 6 : worthless esp. liquid waste : REFUSE, SWILL 7 : a thin coat of paint (as watercolor) 8 : a disturbance in the air caused by the passage of a wing or propeller

[3]**wash** *adj* : WASHABLE

Wash *abbr* Washington

wash·able \-ə-bəl\ *adj* : capable of being washed without damage

wash–and–wear *adj* : of, relating to, or constituting a fabric or garment that needs little or no ironing after washing

wash·ba·sin \ˈwȯsh-ˌbās-ᵊn, ˈwäsh-\ *n* : WASHBOWL

wash·board \-ˌbōrd\ *n* : a grooved board to scrub clothes on

wash·bowl \-ˌbōl\ *n* : a large bowl for water for washing hands and face

wash·cloth \-ˌklȯth\ *n* : a cloth used for washing one's face and body

wash drawing *n* : watercolor painting in or chiefly in washes

washed–out \ˈwȯsht-ˈau̇t, ˈwäsht-\ *adj* 1 : faded in color 2 : EXHAUSTED ⟨felt ~ after working all night⟩

washed–up \ˈwȯsht-ˈəp, ˈwäsht-\ *adj* : no longer successful, popular, or needed

wash·er \ˈwȯsh-ər, ˈwäsh-\ *n* 1 : a ring or perforated plate used around a bolt or screw to ensure tightness or relieve friction 2 : one that washes; *esp* : a machine for washing

wash·er·wom·an \-ˌwu̇m-ən\ *n* : a woman who works at washing clothes

wash·house \ˈwȯsh-ˌhau̇s, ˈwäsh-\ *n* : a house or building used or equipped for washing and esp. for washing clothes

wash·ing \ˈwȯsh-iŋ, ˈwäsh-\ *n* 1 : material obtained by washing 2 : a thin covering or coat ⟨a ~ of silver⟩ 3 : articles washed or to be washed

washing soda *n* : SODIUM CARBONATE

Wash·ing·ton's Birthday \ˌwȯsh-iŋ-tənz-, ˌwäsh-\ *n* : the 3d Monday in February observed as a legal holiday

wash·out \ˈwȯsh-ˌau̇t, ˈwäsh-\ *n* 1 : the washing away of earth (as from a road); *also* : a place where earth is washed away 2 : FAILURE; *esp* : one who fails in a course of training or study

wash·room \-ˌrüm, -ˌru̇m\ *n* : a room equipped with washing and toilet facilities : LAVATORY

wash·stand \-ˌstand\ *n* 1 : a stand holding articles needed for washing face and hands 2 : a washbowl permanently set in place

wash·tub \-ˌtəb\ *n* : a tub for washing clothes or for soaking them before washing

wash·wom·an \ˈwȯsh-ˌwu̇m-ən, ˈwäsh-\ *n* : WASHERWOMAN

washy \ˈwȯsh-ē, ˈwäsh-\ *adj* **wash·i·er; -est** 1 : WEAK, WATERY 2 : PALLID 3 : lacking in vigor, individuality, or definiteness

wasp \ˈwäsp, ˈwȯsp\ *n* : any of numerous social or solitary winged insects related to the bees and ants with biting mouthparts and in females and workers a formidable sting

WASP *or* **Wasp** *n* [*w*hite *A*nglo-*S*axon *P*rotestant] : an American of northern European and esp. British stock and of Protestant background

wasp·ish \ˈwäs-pish, ˈwȯs-\ *adj* 1 : SNAPPISH, IRRITABLE 2 : resembling a wasp in form; *esp* : slightly built

wasp waist *n* : a very slender waist

[1]**was·sail** \ˈwäs-əl, wä-ˈsāl\ *n* [ME *wæs hæil,* fr. ON *ves heill* be well] 1 : an early English toast to someone's health 2 : a hot drink made with wine, beer, or cider, spices, sugar, and usu. baked apples and that is traditionally served at Christmas 3 : riotous drinking : REVELRY

[2]**wassail** *vb* 1 : CAROUSE 2 : to drink to the health or thriving of — **was·sail·er** *n*

Was·ser·mann test \ˌwäs-ər-mən-, ˌväs-\ *n* : a blood test for infection with syphilis

wast·age \ˈwā-stij\ *n* : loss by use, decay, erosion, or leakage or through wastefulness

[1]**waste** \ˈwāst\ *n* 1 : a sparsely settled or barren region : DESERT; *also* : uncultivated land 2 : the act or an instance of wasting : the state of being wasted 3 : gradual loss or decrease by use, wear, or decay 4 : material left over, rejected, or thrown away; *also* : an unwanted product of a manufacturing or chemical process 5 : refuse (as garbage or rubbish) that accumulates about habitations; *also* : material (as feces) produced but not used by a living body — **waste·ful** \-fəl\ *adj* — **waste·ful·ly** \-ē\ *adv* — **waste·ful·ness** *n*

[2]**waste** *vb* **wast·ed; wast·ing** 1 : DEVASTATE 2 : to wear away or diminish gradually : CONSUME 3 : to spend money or use property carelessly or uselessly : SQUANDER; *also* : to allow to be used inefficiently or become dissipated 4 : to lose or cause to lose weight, strength, or vitality

⟨*wasting* away from fever⟩ **5** : to become diminished in bulk or substance : DWINDLE — **wast·er** *n*

[3]**waste** *adj* **1** : being wild and uninhabited : BARREN, DESOLATE; *also* : UNCULTIVATED **2** : RUINED, DEVASTATED ⟨bombs laid ~ the city⟩ **3** : discarded as worthless after being used ⟨~ water⟩ **4** : excreted from or stored in inert form in a living body as a byproduct of vital activity ⟨~ matter from birds⟩ **5** : serving to conduct or hold refuse material; *esp* : carrying off superfluous water

waste·bas·ket \ˈwās(t)-ˌbas-kət\ *n* : a receptacle for refuse

waste·land \ˈwāst-ˌland, -lənd\ *n* : land that is barren or unfit for cultivation

waste·pa·per \ˈwās(t)-ˈpā-pər\ *n* : paper discarded as used, superfluous, or not fit for use

waste product *n* : material resulting from a process (as of metabolism or manufacture) that is of no further use to the system producing it

wast·rel \ˈwā-strəl\ *n* : one that wastes : SPENDTHRIFT

[1]**watch** \ˈwäch, ˈwȯch\ *vb* **1** : to be or stay awake intentionally : keep vigil ⟨~*ed* by the patient's bedside⟩ ⟨~ and pray⟩ **2** : to be on the lookout for danger : be on one's guard **3** : to keep guard ⟨~ outside the door⟩ **4** : OBSERVE ⟨~ a game⟩ **5** : to keep in view so as to prevent harm or warn of danger ⟨~ a brush fire carefully⟩ **6** : to keep oneself informed about ⟨~ his progress⟩ **7** : to lie in wait for esp. so as to take advantage of ⟨~*ed* his opportunity⟩ — **watch·er** *n*

[2]**watch** *n* **1** : the act of keeping awake to guard, protect, or attend; *also* : a state of alert and continuous attention **2** : close observation **3** : one that watches : LOOKOUT, WATCHMAN, GUARD **4** : an allotted period for being on nautical duty; *also* : the members of a ship's company operating the vessel during such a period **5** : a portable timepiece carried on the person

watch·band \ˈwäch-ˌband, ˈwȯch-\ *n* : the bracelet or strap of a wristwatch

watch·case \-ˌkās\ *n* : the outside metal covering of a watch

watch·dog \-ˌdȯg\ *n* **1** : a dog kept to guard property **2** : one that guards or protects

watch·ful \ˈwäch-fəl, ˈwȯch-\ *adj* : steadily attentive and alert esp. to danger : VIGILANT — **watch·ful·ly** \-ē\ *adv* — **watch·ful·ness** *n*

watch·mak·er \-ˌmā-kər\ *n* : one that makes or repairs watches — **watch·mak·ing** \-ˌmā-kiŋ\ *n*

watch·man \-mən\ *n* : a person assigned to watch : GUARD

watch night *n* : a devotional service lasting until after midnight esp. on New Year's Eve

watch·tow·er \ˈwäch-ˌtau̇(-ə)r, ˈwȯch-\ *n* : a tower for a lookout

watch·word \-ˌwərd\ *n* **1** : a secret word used as a signal or sign of recognition **2** : a motto used as a slogan or rallying cry

[1]**wa·ter** \ˈwȯt-ər, ˈwät-\ *n* **1** : the liquid that descends as rain and forms rivers, lakes, and seas **2** : a natural mineral water — usu. used in pl. **3** *pl* : the water occupying or flowing in a particular bed; *also* : a band of seawater bordering on and under the control of a country ⟨sailing Canadian ~*s*⟩ **4** : any of various liquids containing or resembling water; *esp* : a watery fluid (as tears, urine, or sap) formed or circulating in a living body **5** : a specified degree of thoroughness or completeness ⟨a scoundrel of the first ~⟩ **6** : a wavy lustrous pattern (as of a textile)

[2]**water** *vb* **1** : to supply with or get or take water ⟨~ horses⟩ ⟨the ship ~*ed* at each port⟩ **2** : to treat (as cloth) so as to give a lustrous appearance in wavy lines **3** : to dilute by or as if by adding water to **4** : to form or secrete water or watery matter ⟨his eyes ~*ed*⟩ ⟨my mouth ~*ed*⟩

water ballet *n* : a synchronized sequence of movements performed by a group of swimmers

water bed *n* : a bed whose mattress is a plastic bag filled with water

wa·ter·borne \-ˌbōrn\ *adj* : supported or carried by water

water buffalo *n* : a common oxlike often domesticated Asian bovine

water buffalo

water chestnut *n* : any of several aquatic plants (as a Chinese sedge) with edible underground parts or fruits; *also* : the edible part

water closet *n* : a compartment or room for defecation and urination into a toilet bowl : BATHROOM; *also* : a toilet bowl along with its accessories

wa·ter·col·or \ˈwȯt-ər-ˌkəl-ər, ˈwät-\ *n* **1** : a paint whose liquid part is water **2** : the art of painting with watercolors **3** : a picture made with watercolors

wa·ter·course \-ˌkōrs\ *n* : a stream of water; *also* : the bed of a stream

wa·ter·craft \-ˌkraft\ *n* : a craft for water transport : SHIP, BOAT

wa·ter·cress \-ˌkres\ *n* : a perennial plant with white flowers related to the cabbage, found chiefly in clear running water, and used esp. in salads

wa·ter·fall \-ˌfȯl\ *n* : a very steep descent of the water of a stream

water flea *n* : any of various tiny active freshwater crustaceans

wa·ter·fowl \ˈwȯt-ər-ˌfau̇l, ˈwät-\ *n* **1** : a bird that frequents the water **2 waterfowl** *pl* : wild ducks and geese hunted as game

wa·ter·front \-ˌfrənt\ *n* : land or a section of a town fronting or abutting on a body of water

water gap *n* : a pass in a mountain ridge through which a stream runs

water gas *n* : a poisonous flammable gaseous mixture of chiefly hydrogen and carbon monoxide made by forcing air and steam over red-hot coke or coal that is used as a fuel

water glass *n* : a drinking glass

watering place *n* : a resort that features mineral springs or bathing

water lily *n* : any of a family of aquatic plants with floating roundish leaves and showy solitary flowers

wa·ter·line \ˈwȯt-ər-ˌlīn, ˈwät-\ *n* : any of several lines that are marked on the outside of a ship and correspond with the surface of the water when the ship is afloat on an even keel

wa·ter·logged \-ˌlȯgd, -ˌlägd\ *adj* : so filled or soaked with water as to be heavy or unmanageable ⟨a ~ boat⟩

wa·ter·loo \ˌwȯt-ər-ˈlü, ˌwät-\ *n, pl* **-loos** [*Waterloo,* Belgium, scene of Napoleon's defeat in 1815] : a decisive defeat

[1]**wa·ter·mark** \ˈwȯt-ər-ˌmärk, ˈwät-\ *n* **1** : a mark indicating height to which water has risen **2** : a marking in paper visible when the paper is held up to the light

[2]**watermark** *vb* : to mark (paper) with a watermark

wa·ter·mel·on \-ˌmel-ən\ *n* : a large roundish or oblong fruit with sweet juicy usu. red pulp; *also* : an African vine related to the squashes that produces watermelons

water moccasin *n* : a venomous snake of the southern U.S. that is a pit viper related to the copperhead

water ouzel *n* : DIPPER 1

water pipe *n* : a tobacco-smoking device so arranged that the smoke is drawn through water

water polo *n* : a team game played in a swimming pool with a ball resembling a soccer ball

wa·ter·pow·er \ˈwȯt-ər-ˌpau̇(-ə)r, ˈwät-\ *n* : the power of moving water used to run machinery

[1]**wa·ter·proof** \ˌwȯt-ər-ˈprüf, ˌwät-\ *adj* : not letting water through; *esp* : covered or treated with a material to prevent permeation by water — **wa·ter·proof·ing** \-iŋ\ *n*

[2]**waterproof** \ˈwȯt-ər-ˌprüf, ˈwät-\ *n* **1** : a waterproof fabric **2** *chiefly Brit* : RAINCOAT

[3]**waterproof** \ˌwȯt-ər-ˈprüf, ˌwät-\ *vb* : to make waterproof

wa·ter–re·pel·lent \ˌwȯt-ə(r)-ri-ˈpel-ənt, ˌwät-\ *adj* : treated with a finish that is resistant to penetration by water

wa·ter–re·sis·tant \-ri-ˈzis-tənt\ *adj* : WATER-REPELLENT

wa·ter·shed \ˈwȯt-ər-ˌshed, ˈwät-\ *n* **1** : a dividing ridge between two drainage areas **2** : the region or area drained by a particular body of water

wa·ter·side \-ˌsīd\ *n* : the land bordering a body of water

water ski *n* : a ski used on water when the wearer is towed — **wa·ter–ski** *vb* — **wa·ter–ski·er** \-ˌskē-ər\ *n*

wa·ter·spout \ˈwȯt-ər-ˌspau̇t, ˈwät-\ *n* **1** : a pipe for carrying off water from a roof **2** : a funnel-shaped cloud extending from a cumulus cloud down to a cloud of spray torn up by whirling winds from an ocean or lake

water strider *n* : any of various long-legged bugs that move about swiftly on the surface of the water

water table *n* : the upper limit of the portion of the ground wholly saturated with water

wa·ter·tight \ˌwȯt-ər-ˈtīt, ˌwät-\ *adj* **1** : constructed so as to keep water out **2** : so worded that its meaning cannot be misunderstood or its purpose defeated ⟨a ~ contract⟩

wa·ter·way \ˈwȯt-ər-ˌwā, ˈwät-\ *n* : a navigable body of water

wa·ter·wheel \-ˌhwēl\ *n* : a wheel rotated by direct action of water flowing against it

water wings *n pl* : an air-filled device to give support to a person's body when he is swimming or learning to swim

wa·ter·works \ˈwȯt-ər-ˌwərks, ˈwät-\ *n pl* : a system of reservoirs, pipes, and machinery for supplying water (as to a city)

wa·tery \ˈwȯt-ə-rē, ˈwät-\ *adj* **1** : containing, full of, or giving out water ⟨~ clouds⟩ **2** : being like water : THIN, WEAK ⟨~ lemonade⟩; *also* : being soft and soggy ⟨~ turnips⟩

WATS \ˈwäts\ *abbr* Wide Area Telephone Service

watt \ˈwät\ *n* [after James *Watt* †1819 Scottish engineer and inventor] : the metric unit of power equal to the work done at the rate of one joule per second or to the power produced by a current of one ampere across a potential difference of one volt

watt·age \ˈwät-ij\ *n* : amount of power expressed in watts

wat·tle \ˈwät-ᵊl\ *n* **1** : a framework of rods with flexible branches or reeds interlaced used for fencing and esp. formerly in building; *also* : material for this framework **2** : a naked fleshy process hanging usu. from the head or neck (as of a bird) — **wat·tled** \-ᵊld\ *adj*

W Aust *abbr* Western Australia

[1]**wave** \ˈwāv\ *vb* **waved; wav·ing 1** : FLUTTER ⟨flags *waving* in the breeze⟩ **2** : to motion with the hands or with something held in them in signal or salute **3** : to become moved or brandished to-and-fro; *also* : BRANDISH, FLOURISH ⟨~ a sword⟩ **4** : to move before the wind with a wavelike motion ⟨fields of *waving* grain⟩ **5** : to curve up and down like a wave : UNDULATE

[2]**wave** *n* **1** : a moving ridge or swell on the surface of water **2** : a wavelike formation or shape ⟨a ~ in the hair⟩ **3** : the action or process of making wavy or curly **4** : a waving motion; *esp* : a signal made by waving something **5** : FLOW, GUSH ⟨a ~ of color swept her face⟩ **6** : a rapid increase : SURGE ⟨a ~ of buying⟩ ⟨a heat ~⟩ **7** : a disturbance somewhat similar to a wave in water that transfers energy progressively from point to point ⟨a light ~⟩ ⟨a sound ~⟩ — **wave·like** *adj*

Wave \ˈwāv\ *n* [*W*omen *A*ccepted for *V*olunteer *E*mergency Service] : a woman serving in the navy

wave·length \ˈwāv-ˌleŋth\ *n* **1** : the distance in the line of advance of a wave from any one point (as a crest) to the next corresponding point **2** : a particular line of thought esp. as related to mutual understanding

wave·let \-lət\ *n* : a little wave : RIPPLE

wa·ver \ˈwā-vər\ *vb* **wa·vered; wa·ver·ing** \ˈwāv-(ə-)riŋ\ **1** : to vacillate between choices : fluctuate in opinion, allegiance, or direction **2** : REEL, TOTTER; *also* : QUIVER, FLICKER ⟨~*ing* flames⟩ **3** : FALTER **4** : to give an unsteady sound : QUAVER — **waver** *n* — **wa·ver·er** *n* — **wa·ver·ing·ly** *adv*

wavy \ˈwā-vē\ *adj* **wav·i·er; -est** : having waves : moving in waves

[1]**wax** \ˈwaks\ *n* **1** : a yellowish plastic substance secreted by bees for constructing the honeycomb **2** : any of various substances resembling beeswax

[2]**wax** *vb* : to treat or rub with wax

[3]**wax** *vb* **1** : to increase in size, numbers, strength, volume, or duration **2** : to increase in apparent size ⟨the moon ~*es* toward the full⟩ **3** : to pass from one state to another : BECOME ⟨~*ed* indignant⟩ ⟨the party ~*ed* merry⟩

wax bean *n* : a kidney bean with pods that turn creamy yellow to bright yellow when mature enough to use as a snap bean

wax·en \ˈwak-sən\ *adj* **1** : made of or covered with wax **2** : resembling wax (as in color or consistency)

wax myrtle *n* : any of various shrubs or trees with aromatic leaves; *esp* : an American evergreen shrub that produces small hard berries with a thick coating of white wax used for candles

wax·wing \ˈwaks-ˌwiŋ\ *n* : any of a genus of singing birds that are mostly brown with a showy crest and velvety plumage

wax·work \-ˌwərk\ *n* **1** : an effigy usu. of a person in wax **2** *pl* : an exhibition of wax figures

waxy \ˈwak-sē\ *adj* **wax·i·er; -est 1** : made of or full of wax **2** : WAXEN 2

way \ˈwā\ *n* **1** : a thoroughfare for travel or passage : ROAD, PATH, STREET **2** : ROUTE **3** : a course of action ⟨chose the easy ~⟩; *also* : opportunity, capability, or fact of doing as one pleases ⟨always had his own ~⟩ **4** : a possible course : POSSIBILITY ⟨no two ~*s* about it⟩ **5** : METHOD, MODE ⟨this ~ of thinking⟩ ⟨a new ~ of painting⟩ **6** : FEATURE, RESPECT ⟨a good worker in many ~*s*⟩ **7** : the usual or characteristic state of affairs ⟨as is the ~ with old people⟩; *also* : individual characteristic or peculiarity ⟨used to his ~*s*⟩ **8** : DISTANCE ⟨a short ~ from here⟩ ⟨a long ~ from success⟩ **9** : progress along a course ⟨working his ~ through college⟩ **10** : something having direction : LOCALITY ⟨out our ~⟩ **11** : STATE, CONDITION ⟨that is the ~ things are⟩ **12** *pl* : an inclined structure upon which a ship is built or is supported in launching **13** : CATEGORY, KIND ⟨get what you need in the ~ of supplies⟩ **14** : motion or speed of a boat through the water — **by way of 1** : for the purpose of ⟨*by way of* illustration⟩ **2** : by the route through : VIA — **out of the way 1** : WRONG, IMPROPER **2** : SECLUDED, REMOTE — **under way 1** : in motion through the water **2** : in progress

way·bill \ˈwā-ˌbil\ *n* : a paper that accompanies a freight shipment and gives details of goods, route, and charges

way·far·er \ˈwā-ˌfar-ər\ *n* : a traveler esp. on foot — **way·far·ing** \-ˌfar-iŋ\ *adj*

way·lay \ˈwā-ˌlā\ *vb* **-laid** \-ˌlād\; **-lay·ing** : to lie in wait for often in order to seize, rob, or kill

way–out \ˈwā-ˈau̇t\ *adj* : FAR-OUT

-ways \ˌwāz\ *adv suffix* : in (such) a way, course, direction, or manner ⟨side*ways*⟩

ways and means *n pl* : methods and resources for accomplishing something and esp. for raising revenues needed by a state; *also* : a legislative committee concerned with this function

way·side \ˈwā-ˌsīd\ *n* : the side of or land adjacent to a road or path

way station *n* : an intermediate station on a line of travel (as a railroad)

way·ward \ˈwā-wərd\ *adj* [ME, short for *awayward* turned away, fr. *away*, adv. + *-ward* directed toward] **1** : taking one's own and usu. irregular or improper way : DISOBEDIENT ⟨~ children⟩ **2** : UNPREDICTABLE, IRREGULAR **3** : opposite to what is desired or expected ⟨~ fate⟩

WBC *abbr* white blood cells

WC *abbr* **1** water closet **2** without charge

WCTU *abbr* Women's Christian Temperance Union

we \(ˈ)wē\ *pron* **1** — used of a group that includes the speaker or writer **2** — used for the singular *I* by sovereigns and by writers (as of editorials)

weak \ˈwēk\ *adj* **1** : lacking strength or vigor : FEEBLE **2** : not able to sustain or resist much weight, pressure, or strain **3** : deficient in vigor of mind or character; *also* : resulting from or indicative of such deficiency ⟨a ~ policy⟩ ⟨a ~ will⟩ ⟨*weak*-minded⟩ **4** : not supported by truth or logic ⟨a ~ argument⟩ **5** : not able to function properly **6** : lacking skill or proficiency; *also* : indicative of a lack of skill or aptitude **7** : wanting in vigor of expression or effect **8** : deficient in the usual or required ingredients : of less than usual strength ⟨~ tea⟩ **9** : not having or exerting authority ⟨~ government⟩; *also* : INEFFECTIVE, IMPOTENT **10** : of, relating to, or constituting a verb or verb conjugation that forms the past tense and past participle by adding *-ed* or *-d* or *-t* — **weak·ly** *adv*

weak·en \ˈwē-kən\ *vb* **weak·ened; weak·en·ing** \ˈwēk-(ə-)niŋ\ : to make or become weak **syn** enfeeble, debilitate, undermine, sap, cripple, disable

weak·fish \ˈwēk-ˌfish\ *n* [obs. Dutch *weekvis*, fr. D *week* soft + *vis* fish; fr. its tender flesh] : a common sport and market fish of the Atlantic coast of the U.S. related to the perches; *also* : any of several related food fishes

weak–kneed \ˈwēk-ˈnēd\ *adj* : lacking willpower or resolution

weak·ling \-liŋ\ *n* : a person who is physically, mentally, or morally weak

weak·ly \ˈwēk-lē\ *adj* : FEEBLE, WEAK

weak·ness \-nəs\ *n* **1** : the quality or state of being weak; *also* : an instance or period of being weak ⟨in a moment of ~ he agreed to go⟩ **2** : FAULT, DEFECT **3** : an object of special desire or fondness ⟨coffee is her ~⟩

[1]**weal** \ˈwēl\ *n* : WELL-BEING, PROSPERITY

[2]**weal** *n* : WELT

weald \ˈwēld\ *n* [The *Weald*, wooded district in England, fr. ME *Weeld* the Weald, fr. OE *weald* wood, forest] **1** : FOREST **2** : a wild or uncultivated usu. upland region : WOLD

wealth \ˈwelth\ *n* [ME *welthe*, welfare, prosperity, fr. *wele* weal] **1** : abundance of possessions or resources : AFFLUENCE, RICHES **2** : abundant supply : PROFUSION ⟨a ~ of detail⟩ **3** : all property that has a money or an exchange value; *also* : all objects or resources that have economic value

wealthy \ˈwel-thē\ *adj* **wealth·i·er; -est** : having wealth : RICH, AFFLUENT, OPULENT

wean \ˈwēn\ *vb* **1** : to accustom (a young mammal) to take food otherwise than by nursing **2** : to free from a cause of dependence or preoccupation

weap·on \ˈwep-ən\ *n* **1** : something (as a gun, knife, or club) that may be used to fight with **2** : a means by which one contends against another

weap·on·less \ˈwep-ən-ləs\ *adj* : lacking weapons : UNARMED

weap·on·ry \-rē\ *n* **1** : WEAPONS **2** : the science of designing and making weapons

[1]**wear** \ˈwaər\ *vb* **wore** \ˈwōr\; **worn** \ˈwōrn\; **wear·ing** **1** : to bear on the person or use habitually for clothing or adornment ⟨~ a coat⟩ ⟨~ a wig⟩; *also* : to carry on the person ⟨~ a gun⟩ **2** : to have or show an appearance of ⟨~ a smile⟩ **3** : to impair, diminish, or decay by use or by scraping or rubbing ⟨clothes *worn* to shreds⟩ ⟨letters on the stone *worn* away by weathering⟩; *also* : to produce gradually by friction, rubbing, or wasting away ⟨~ a hole in the rug⟩ **4** : to exhaust or lessen the strength of : WEARY, FATIGUE ⟨*worn* by care and toil⟩ **5** : to endure use : last under use or the passage of time ⟨this cloth ~*s* well⟩ **6** : to diminish or fail with the passage of time ⟨the day ~*s* on⟩ ⟨the effect of the drug *wore* off⟩ **7** : to grow or become by attrition, use, or age ⟨the coin was *worn* thin⟩ — **wear·able** \ˈwar-ə-bəl\ *adj* — **wear·er** *n*

[2]**wear** *n* **1** : the act of wearing : the state of being worn ⟨clothes for everyday ~⟩ **2** : clothing usu. of a particular kind or for a special occasion or use ⟨children's ~⟩ **3** : wearing or lasting quality ⟨the coat still has lots of ~ in it⟩ **4** : the result of wearing or use : impairment resulting from use ⟨her suit shows ~⟩

wear and tear \ˌwar-ən-ˈtaər\ *n* : the loss or injury to which something is subjected in the course of use; *esp* : normal depreciation

wear down *vb* : to weary and overcome by persistent resistance or pressure

wea·ri·some \ˈwir-ē-səm\ *adj* : causing weariness : TIRESOME — **wea·ri·some·ly** *adv* — **wea·ri·some·ness** *n*

wear out *vb* **1** : TIRE **2** : to make or become useless by wear

[1]**wea·ry** \ˈwi(ə)r-ē\ *adj* **wea·ri·er; -est** **1** : worn out in strength, endurance, vigor, or freshness **2** : expressing or characteristic of weariness ⟨a ~ sigh⟩ **3** : having one's patience, tolerance, or pleasure exhausted ⟨~ of war⟩ — **wea·ri·ly** \ˈwir-ə-lē\ *adv* — **wea·ri·ness** \-ē-nəs\ *n*

[2]**weary** *vb* **wea·ried; wea·ry·ing** : to become or make weary : TIRE

wea·sel \ˈwē-zəl\ *n, pl* **weasels** : any of various small slender flesh-eating mammals related to the minks

weasel word *n* [fr. the weasel's reputed habit of sucking the contents out of an egg while leaving the shell superficially intact] : a word used in order to evade or retreat from a direct or forthright statement or position

[1]**weath·er** \ˈweth-ər\ *n* **1** : condition of the atmosphere with respect to heat or cold, wetness or dryness, calm or storm, clearness or cloudiness **2** : a particular and esp. a disagreeable atmospheric state : RAIN, STORM

[2]**weather** *vb* **1** : to expose to or endure the action of weather; *also* : to alter (as in color or texture) by such exposure **2** : to sail or pass to the windward of **3** : to bear up against successfully ⟨~ a storm⟩ ⟨~ troubles⟩

[3]**weather** *adj* : WINDWARD

weath·er–beat·en \ˈweth-ər-ˌbēt-ᵊn\ *adj* : altered by exposure to the weather; *also* : toughened or tanned by the weather ⟨~ face⟩

weath·er·board \-ˌbōrd\ *n* : CLAPBOARD

weath·er·board·ing \-ˌbōrd-iŋ\ *n* : CLAPBOARDS, SIDING

weath·er–bound \-ˌbau̇nd\ *adj* : kept in port or at anchor or from travel or sport by bad weather

weath·er·cock \-ˌkäk\ *n* **1** : a weather vane shaped like a rooster **2** : a fickle person

weath·er·glass \ˈweth-ər-ˌglas\ *n* : BAROMETER

weath·er·ing \ˈweth-(ə-)riŋ\ *n* : the action of the weather in altering the color, texture, composition, or form of exposed objects; *also* : alteration thus effected

weath·er·ize \ˈweth-ə-ˌrīz\ *vb* **-ized; -iz·ing** : to make (as a house) better protected against winter weather esp. by adding insulation and by caulking joints — **weath·er·iza·tion** \ˌweth-ə-rə-ˈzā-shən\ *n*

weath·er·man \-ˌman\ *n* : one who reports and forecasts the weather : METEOROLOGIST

weath·er·proof \ˌweth-ər-ˈprüf\ *adj* : able to withstand exposure to weather without appreciable harm — **weatherproof** *vb*

weather strip *n* : a strip of material to make a seal where a door or window joins the sill or casing — **weath·er–strip** *vb*

weather vane *n* : VANE 1

weath·er·worn \ˈweth-ər-ˌwōrn\ *adj* : worn by exposure to the weather

¹**weave** \ˈwēv\ *vb* **wove** \ˈwōv\ *or* **weaved; wo·ven** \ˈwō-vən\ *or* **weaved; weav·ing** **1** : to form by interlacing strands of material; *esp* : to make on a loom by interlacing warp and filling threads ⟨~ cloth⟩ **2** : to interlace (as threads) into a fabric and esp. cloth **3** : SPIN 2 **4** : CONTRIVE **5** : to unite in a coherent whole **6** : to work in ⟨*wove* the episodes into a story⟩ **7** : to direct or move in a winding or zigzag course esp. to avoid obstacles ⟨we *wove* our way through the crowd⟩ — **weav·er** *n*

²**weave** *n* : a pattern or method of weaving ⟨a loose ~⟩

¹**web** \ˈweb\ *n* **1** : a fabric on a loom or coming from a loom **2** : COBWEB; *also* : SNARE, ENTANGLEMENT ⟨caught in a ~ of deceit⟩ **3** : an animal or plant membrane; *esp* : one uniting the toes (as in many birds) **4** : NETWORK ⟨a ~ of highways⟩ **5** : the series of barbs on each side of the shaft of a feather

²**web** *vb* **webbed; web·bing** **1** : to cover or provide with webs or a network **2** : ENTANGLE, ENSNARE **3** : to make a web

webbed \ˈwebd\ *adj* : having or being toes or fingers united by a web ⟨the ~ feet of ducks⟩

web·bing \ˈweb-iŋ\ *n* : a strong closely woven tape designed for bearing weight and used esp. for straps, harness, or upholstery

web–foot·ed \ˈweb-ˈfu̇t-əd\ *adj* : having webbed feet

wed \ˈwed\ *vb* **wed·ded** *also* **wed; wed·ding** **1** : to take, give, or join in marriage : enter into matrimony : MARRY **2** : to unite firmly

Wed *abbr* Wednesday

wed·ding \ˈwed-iŋ\ *n* **1** : a marriage ceremony usu. with accompanying festivities : NUPTIALS **2** : a joining in close association **3** : a wedding anniversary or its celebration

¹**wedge** \ˈwej\ *n* **1** : a solid triangular piece of wood or metal that tapers to a thin edge and is used to split logs or rocks or to raise heavy weights **2** : something (as an action or policy) that serves to open up a way for a breach, change, or intrusion **3** : a wedge-shaped object or part ⟨a ~ of pie⟩

²**wedge** *vb* **wedged; wedg·ing** **1** : to hold firm by or as if by driving in a wedge **2** : to force (something) into a narrow space **3** : to split apart with or as if with a wedge

wed·lock \ˈwed-ˌläk\ *n* [ME *wedlok*, fr. OE *wedlāc* marriage bond, fr. *wedd* pledge + *-lāc*, suffix denoting activity] : the state of being married : MARRIAGE, MATRIMONY

Wednes·day \ˈwenz-dē\ *n* [ME, fr. OE *wōdensdæg*, lit., day of Odin (supreme god of Norse mythology)] : the 4th day of the week

wee \ˈwē\ *adj* [ME *we*, fr. *we*, n., little bit, fr. OE *wǣge* weight] **1** : very small : TINY **2** : very early ⟨~ hours of the morning⟩

¹**weed** \ˈwēd\ *n* : a plant that is not valued where it is growing and is usu. of rank growth; *esp* : one growing in cultivated ground to the damage of a crop

²**weed** *vb* **1** : to clear of or remove weeds or something harmful, inferior, or superfluous ⟨~ a garden⟩ **2** : to get rid of (unwanted items) ⟨~ out the loafers from the crew⟩ — **weed·er** *n*

³**weed** *n* : GARMENT; *esp* : dress worn (as by a widow) as a sign of mourning — usu. used in pl.

weedy \ˈwēd-ē\ *adj* **1** : full of weeds **2** : resembling a weed esp. in vigor of growth or spread **3** : noticeably lean and scrawny : LANK

week \ˈwēk\ *n* **1** : seven successive days; *esp* : a calendar period of seven days beginning with Sunday and ending with Saturday **2** : the working or school days of the calendar week

week·day \ˈwēk-ˌdā\ *n* : a day of the week except Sunday or sometimes except Saturday and Sunday

¹**week·end** \-ˌend\ *n* : the period between the close of one working or business or school week and the beginning of the next

²**weekend** *vb* : to spend the weekend

¹**week·ly** \ˈwēk-lē\ *adj* **1** : occurring, done, produced, or issued every week **2** : computed in terms of one week — **weekly** *adv*

²**weekly** *n, pl* **weeklies** : a weekly publication

ween \ˈwēn\ *vb, archaic* : IMAGINE, SUPPOSE

wee·ny \ˈwē-nē\ *also* **ween·sy** \ˈwēn(t)-sē\ *adj* : exceptionally small

weep \ˈwēp\ *vb* **wept** \ˈwept\; **weep·ing** **1** : to express emotion and esp. sorrow by shedding tears : BEWAIL, CRY **2** : to drip or exude (liquid) — **weep·er** *n*

weep·ing \ˈwē-piŋ\ *adj* **1** : TEARFUL **2** : having slender drooping branches

weeping willow *n* : an Asian willow with weeping branches

weepy \ˈwē-pē\ *adj* : inclined to weep : TEARFUL

wee·vil \ˈwē-vəl\ *n* : any of a suborder of mostly small beetles with a long head usu. curved into a snout and larvae that feed esp. in fruits or seeds — **wee·vily** *or* **wee·vil·ly** \ˈwēv-(ə-)lē\ *adj*

weft \ˈweft\ *n* **1** : WOOF 1 **2** : WEB, FABRIC; *also* : something woven

¹**weigh** \ˈwā\ *vb* [ME *weyen*, fr. OE *wegan* to move, carry, weigh] **1** : to ascertain the heaviness of by a balance **2** : to have weight or a specified weight **3** : to consider carefully : PONDER **4** : to merit consideration as important : COUNT ⟨evidence ~*ing* against him⟩ **5** : to heave up (an anchor) **6** : to press down with or as if with a heavy weight

²**weigh** *n* [alter. of *way*] : WAY — used in the phrase *under weigh*

weigh in *vb* : to have something weighed; *esp* : to have oneself weighed preliminary to participation in a sports event

¹**weight** \ˈwāt\ *n* **1** : the amount that something weighs; *also* : the standard amount that something should weigh **2** : a quantity or portion weighing usu. a certain amount **3** : a unit (as a pound or kilogram) of weight or mass; *also* : a system of such units **4** : a heavy object for holding or pressing something down; *also* : a heavy object for throwing or lifting in an athletic contest **5** : BURDEN ⟨a ~ of grief⟩ **6** : IMPORTANCE; *also* : INFLUENCE ⟨threw his ~ around⟩ **7** : overpowering force **8** : relative heaviness (as of a textile) **syn** significance, moment, consequence, import, authority, prestige, credit

☞ see next page

²**weight** *vb* **1** : to load with or as if with a weight **2** : to oppress with a burden ⟨~*ed* down with cares⟩

weight·less \ˈwāt-ləs\ *adj* : having little weight : lacking apparent gravitational pull — **weight·less·ly** *adv* — **weight·less·ness** *n*

WEIGHTS AND MEASURES[1]

UNIT	ABBREVIATION OR SYMBOL	EQUIVALENT IN OTHER U.S. UNITS	METRIC EQUIVALENT
		WEIGHT	
		avoirdupois (ordinary commodities)	
ton			
short ton		200 short hundredweight, 2000 pounds	0.907 metric ton
long ton		200 long hundredweight, 2240 pounds	1.016 metric tons
hundredweight	cwt		
short hundredweight		100 pounds, 0.05 short ton	45.359 kilograms
long hundredweight		112 pounds, 0.05 long ton	50.802 kilograms
pound	lb *or* lb avdp *also* #	16 ounces, 7000 grains (1.215 apothecaries' or troy pound)	0.454 kilograms
ounce	oz *or* oz avdp	16 drams, 437.5 grains (0.911 apothecaries' or troy ounce)	28.350 grams
dram	dr *or* dr avdp	27.344 grains, 0.0625 ounce	1.772 grams
grain	gr	0.037 dram, 0.002286 ounce (1.0 apothecaries' or troy grain)	0.0648 gram
		troy (precious metals, jewels)	
pound	lb t	12 ounces, 240 pennyweight, 5760 grains (0.822 avoirdupois pound, 1.0 apothecaries' pound)	0.0373 kilogram
ounce	oz t	20 pennyweight, 480 grains (1.097 avoirdupois ounce, 1.0 apothecaries' ounce)	31.103 grams
pennyweight	dwt *also* pwt	24 grains, 0.05 ounce	1.555 grams
grain	gr	0.042 pennyweight, 0.002083 ounce (1.0 avoirdupois or apothecaries' grain)	0.0648 gram
		apothecaries' (drugs)	
pound	lb ap	12 ounces, 5760 grains (0.822 avoirdupois pound, 1.0 troy pound)	0.373 kilogram
ounce	oz ap *or* ℥	8 drams, 480 grains (1.097 avoirdupois ounce, 1.0 troy ounce)	31.103 grams
dram	dr ap *or* ʒ	0.125 ounce, 60 grains	3.888 grams
grain	gr	0.0166 dram, 0.002083 ounce (1.0 avoirdupois or troy grain)	0.0648 gram
		CAPACITY	
		U.S. liquid measure	
gallon	gal	4 quarts (231 cubic inches)	3.785 liters
quart	qt	2 pints (57.75 cubic inches)	0.946 liter
pint	pt	4 gills (28.875 cubic inches)	0.473 liter
gill	gi	4 fluidounces (7.219 cubic inches)	118.294 milliliters
fluidounce	fl oz *or* *f*℥	8 fluidrams (1.805 cubic inches)	29.573 milliliters
fluidram	fl dr *or* *f*ʒ	60 minims (0.226 cubic inch)	3.697 milliliters
minim	min *or* ♏	1/60 fluidram (0.003760 cubic inch)	0.061610 milliliter
		U.S. dry measure	
bushel	bu	4 pecks (2150.42 cubic inches)	35.239 liters
peck	pk	8 quarts (537.605 cubic inches)	8.10 liters
quart	qt	2 pints (67.201 cubic inches)	1.101 liters
pint	pt	½ quart (33.600 cubic inches)	0.551 liter
		LENGTH	
mile	mi	5280 feet, 320 rods, 1760 yards	1.609 kilometers
rod	rd	5.50 yards, 16.5 feet	5.029 meters
yard	yd	3 feet, 36 inches	0.9144 meter
foot	ft *or* ′	12 inches, 0.333 yard	30.48 centimeters
inch	in *or* ″	0.083 feet, 0.028 yard	2.54 centimeters
		AREA	
square mile	sq mi *or* mi^2	640 acres, 102,400 square rods	2.590 square kilometers
acre		4840 square yards, 43,560 square feet	4047 square meters
square rod	sq rd *or* rd^2	30.25 square yards, 0.00625 acres	25.293 square meters
square yard	sq yd *or* yd^2	1296 square inches, 9 square feet	0.836 square meter
square foot	sq ft *or* ft^2	144 square inches, 0.111 square yard	0.093 square meter
square inch	sq in *or* in^2	0.0069 square foot, 0.00077 square yard	6.452 square centimeters
		VOLUME	
cubic yard	cu yd *or* yd^3	27 cubic feet, 46,656 cubic inches	0.765 cubic meter
cubic foot	cu ft *or* ft^3	1728 cubic inches, 0.0370 cubic yard	0.028 cubic meter
cubic inch	cu in *or* in^3	0.00058 cubic foot, 0.00021 cubic yard	16.387 cubic centimeters

[1]For U.S. equivalents of metric units see Metric System table

weighty \ˈwāt-ē\ *adj* **weight·i·er; -est 1** : of much importance or consequence : MOMENTOUS, SERIOUS ⟨~ problems⟩ **2** : SOLEMN ⟨a ~ manner⟩ **3** : HEAVY **4** : exerting force, influence, or authority ⟨~ arguments⟩

weir \ˈwaər, ˈwiər\ *n* **1** : a fence set in a waterway for catching fish **2** : a dam in a river for the purpose of directing water to a mill or making a pond

weird \ˈwiərd\ *adj* [ME *wird, werd* fate, destiny, fr. OE *wyrd*] **1** : MAGICAL **2** : UNEARTHLY, MYSTERIOUS **3** : ODD, UNUSUAL, FANTASTIC **syn** eerie, uncanny, spooky — **weird·ly** *adv* — **weird·ness** *n*

Welch \ˈwelch\ *var of* WELSH

[1]**wel·come** \ˈwel-kəm\ *vb* **wel·comed; wel·com·ing 1** : to greet cordially or courteously **2** : to accept, meet, or face with pleasure ⟨he ~*s* criticism⟩

[2]**welcome** *adj* **1** : received gladly into one's presence ⟨a ~ visitor⟩ **2** : giving pleasure : PLEASING ⟨~ news⟩ **3** : willingly permitted or admitted ⟨all are ~ to use the books⟩ **4** — used in the phrase "You're welcome" as a reply to an expression of thanks

[3]**welcome** *n* : a cordial greeting or reception

[1]**weld** \ˈweld\ *vb* **1** : to unite (metal or plastic parts) either by heating and allowing the parts to flow together or by hammering or pressing together **2** : to unite closely or intimately ⟨~*ed* together in friendship⟩ — **weld·er** *n*

[2]**weld** *n* **1** : a welded joint **2** : union by welding

wel·fare \ˈwel-ˌfaər\ *n* **1** : the state of doing well esp. in respect to happiness, well-being, or prosperity ⟨the ~ of mankind⟩ **2** : organized efforts for the social betterment of a group in society **3** : RELIEF 2

welfare state *n* : a nation or state that assumes primary responsibility for the individual and social welfare of its citizens

wel·kin \ˈwel-kən\ *n* : SKY; *also* : AIR

[1]**well** \ˈwel\ *n* **1** : a spring with its pool : FOUNTAIN; *also* : a source of supply ⟨a ~ of information⟩ **2** : a hole sunk in the earth to obtain a natural deposit (as of water, oil, or gas) **3** : an open space (as for a staircase) extending vertically through floors of a structure **4** : something suggesting a well

[2]**well** *vb* : to rise up and flow forth : RUN

[3]**well** *adv* **bet·ter** \ˈbet-ər\; **best** \ˈbest\ **1** : in a good or proper manner : RIGHTLY; *also* : EXCELLENTLY, SKILLFULLY **2** : SATISFACTORILY, FORTUNATELY ⟨the party turned out ~⟩ **3** : ABUNDANTLY ⟨eat ~⟩ **4** : with reason or courtesy : PROPERLY ⟨I cannot ~ refuse⟩ **5** : COMPLETELY, FULLY, QUITE ⟨~ worth the price⟩ ⟨*well*-hidden⟩ **6** : INTIMATELY, CLOSELY ⟨I know him ~⟩ **7** : CONSIDERABLY, FAR ⟨~ over a million⟩ ⟨~ ahead⟩ **8** : without trouble or difficulty ⟨he could ~ have gone⟩ **9** : EXACTLY, DEFINITELY ⟨remember it ~⟩

[4]**well** *adj* **1** : PROSPEROUS; *also* : being in satisfactory condition or circumstances **2** : SATISFACTORY, PLEASING ⟨all is ~⟩ **3** : ADVISABLE, DESIRABLE ⟨it is not ~ to anger him⟩ **4** : free or recovered from infirmity or disease : HEALTHY **5** : FORTUNATE ⟨it is ~ that this has happened⟩

well–ad·vised \ˌwel-əd-ˈvīzd\ *adj* **1** : PRUDENT **2** : resulting from, based on, or showing careful deliberation or wise counsel ⟨~ plans⟩

well–ap·point·ed \-ə-ˈpȯint-əd\ *adj* : having good and complete equipment

well–be·ing \ˈwel-ˈbē-iŋ\ *n* : the state of being happy, healthy, or prosperous

well·born \-ˈbȯrn\ *adj* : born of good stock either socially or physically

well–bred \-ˈbred\ *adj* : having or indicating good breeding : REFINED

well–con·di·tioned \ˌwel-kən-ˈdish-ənd\ *adj* **1** : characterized by proper disposition, morals, or behavior **2** : having a good physical condition : SOUND ⟨a ~ animal⟩

well–de·fined \-di-ˈfīnd\ *adj* : having clearly distinguishable limits or boundaries ⟨a ~ scar⟩

well–dis·posed \-dis-ˈpōzd\ *adj* : disposed to be friendly, favorable, or sympathetic

well–done \ˈwel-ˈdən\ *adj* **1** : rightly or properly performed **2** : cooked thoroughly

well–fa·vored \-ˈfā-vərd\ *adj* : GOOD-LOOKING, HANDSOME

well–fixed \-ˈfikst\ *adj* : financially well-off

well–found·ed \-ˈfau̇n-dəd\ *adj* : based on sound information, reasoning, judgment, or grounds ⟨~ rumors⟩

well–groomed \-ˈgrümd, -ˈgru̇md\ *adj* : well and neatly dressed or cared for ⟨~ men⟩ ⟨a ~ lawn⟩

well–ground·ed \-ˈgrau̇n-dəd\ *adj* : having a firm foundation

well·head \-ˌhed\ *n* **1** : the source of a spring or a stream **2** : principal source **3** : the top of or a structure built over a well

well–heeled \-ˈhēld\ *adj* : financially well-off

well–knit \-ˈnit\ *adj* : well and firmly formed or framed ⟨a ~ argument⟩

well–known \-ˈnōn\ *adj* : fully or widely known

well–mean·ing \-ˈmē-niŋ\ *adj* : having or based on excellent intentions

well–nigh \-ˈnī\ *adv* : ALMOST, NEARLY

well–off \-ˈȯf\ *adj* : being in good condition or circumstances; *esp* : WELL-TO-DO

well–or·dered \-ˈȯrd-ərd\ *adj* : having an orderly procedure or arrangement

well–read \-ˈred\ *adj* : well informed through reading

well–round·ed \-ˈrau̇n-dəd\ *adj* **1** : broadly trained, educated, and experienced **2** : COMPREHENSIVE ⟨a ~ program of activities⟩

well–spo·ken \ˈwel-ˈspō-kən\ *adj* **1** : speaking well and esp. courteously **2** : spoken with propriety ⟨~ words⟩

well·spring \-ˌspriŋ\ *n* : FOUNTAINHEAD, SPRING

well–timed \-ˈtīmd\ *adj* : coming or happening at an opportune moment : TIMELY

well–to–do \ˌwel-tə-ˈdü\ *adj* : having more than adequate material resources : PROSPEROUS

well–turned \ˈwel-ˈtərnd\ *adj* **1** : pleasingly rounded : SHAPELY ⟨a ~ ankle⟩ **2** : pleasingly and appropriately expressed ⟨a ~ phrase⟩

well–wish·er \ˈwel-ˌwish-ər, -ˈwish-\ *n* : one that wishes well to another — **well–wish·ing** \-iŋ\ *adj or n*

well–worn \-ˈwōrn\ *adj* **1** : worn by much use ⟨~ shoes⟩ **2** : TRITE **3** *archaic* : worn well or properly ⟨~ honors⟩

welsh \ˈwelsh, ˈwelch\ *vb* **1** : to cheat by avoiding payment of bets **2** : to break one's word ⟨~*ed* on his promises⟩

Welsh \ˈwelsh\ *n* **1 Welsh** *pl* : the people of Wales **2** : the Celtic language of Wales — **Welsh** *adj* — **Welsh·man** \-mən\ *n*

Welsh cor·gi \-ˈkȯr-gē\ *n* [W *corgi,* fr. *cor* dwarf + *ci* dog] : a short-legged long-backed dog with foxy head of either of two breeds of Welsh origin

Welsh rabbit *n* : melted often seasoned cheese poured over toast or crackers

Welsh rare·bit \-ˈraər-bət\ *n* : WELSH RABBIT

[1]**welt** \ˈwelt\ *n* **1** : the narrow strip of leather between a shoe upper and sole to which other parts are stitched **2** : a doubled edge, strip, insert, or seam for ornament or reinforcement **3** : a ridge or lump raised on the skin usu. by a blow; *also* : a heavy blow

[2]**welt** *vb* **1** : to furnish with a welt **2** : to hit hard

[1]**wel·ter** \ˈwel-tər\ *vb* **1** : WRITHE, TOSS; *also* : WALLOW **2** : to rise and fall or toss about in or with waves **3** : to become deeply sunk, soaked, or involved **4** : to be in turmoil

[2]**welter** *n* **1** : TURMOIL **2** : a chaotic mass or jumble

wel·ter·weight \ˈwel-tər-ˌwāt\ *n* : a boxer weighing more than 135 but not over 147 pounds

wen \ˈwen\ *n* : a cyst formed by blocking of a skin gland and filled with fatty material

wench \ˈwench\ *n* [ME *wenche,* short for *wenchel* child, fr. OE *wencel*] **1** : a young woman : GIRL **2** : a female servant

wend \ˈwend\ *vb* : to direct one's course : proceed on (one's way)

went *past of* GO

wept *past and past part of* WEEP

were *past 2d sing, past pl, or past subjunctive of* BE

were·wolf \ˈwer-ˌwu̇lf, ˈwir-\ *n, pl* **were·wolves** \-ˌwu̇lvz\ [ME, fr. OE *werwulf,* fr. *wer* man + *wulf* wolf] : a person transformed into a wolf or capable of assuming a wolf's form

wes·kit \ˈwes-kət\ *n* : VEST 1

¹**west** \ˈwest\ *adv* : to or toward the west

²**west** *n* **1** : the general direction of sunset **2** : the compass point directly opposite to east **3** *cap* : regions or countries west of a specified or implied point **4** *cap* : Europe and the Americas — **west·er·ly** \ˈwes-tər-lē\ *adv or adj* — **west·ward** *adv or adj* — **west·wards** *adv*

³**west** *adj* **1** : situated toward or at the west **2** : coming from the west

¹**west·ern** \ˈwes-tərn\ *adj* **1** *cap* : of, relating to, or characteristic of a region conventionally designated West **2** : lying toward or coming from the west **3** *cap* : of or relating to the Roman Catholic or Protestant segment of Christianity — **West·ern·er** *n*

²**western** *n* **1** : one that is produced in or is characteristic of a western region and esp. the western U.S. **2** *often cap* : a novel, story, motion picture, or broadcast dealing with life in the western U.S. during the latter half of the 19th century

west·ern·ize \ˈwes-tər-ˌnīz\ *vb* **-ized; -iz·ing** : to give western characteristics to

¹**wet** \ˈwet\ *adj* **wet·ter; wet·test 1** : consisting of or covered or soaked with liquid (as water) **2** : RAINY **3** : not dry ⟨~ paint⟩ **4** : permitting or advocating the manufacture and sale of intoxicating liquor ⟨a ~ town⟩ ⟨a ~ candidate⟩ **syn** damp, dank, moist, humid — **wet·ly** *adv* — **wet·ness** *n*

²**wet** *n* **1** : WATER; *also* : WETNESS, MOISTURE **2** : rainy weather : RAIN **3** : an advocate of a wet liquor policy

³**wet** *vb* **wet** *or* **wet·ted; wet·ting** : to make or become wet

wet blanket *n* : one that quenches or dampens enthusiasm or pleasure

weth·er \ˈwet͟h-ər\ *n* : a male sheep castrated while immature

wet·land \ˈwet-ˌland, -lənd\ *n* : land or areas containing much soil moisture

wet nurse *n* : one who cares for and suckles young not her own

wet suit *n* : a rubber suit for swimmers that acts to retain body heat by keeping a layer of water against the body as insulation

wh *abbr* **1** which **2** white

WHA *abbr* World Hockey Association

¹**whack** \ˈhwak\ *vb* **1** : to strike with a smart or resounding blow **2** : to cut with or as if with a whack

²**whack** *n* **1** : a smart or resounding blow; *also* : the sound of such a blow **2** : PORTION, SHARE **3** : CONDITION, STATE ⟨the machine is out of ~⟩ **4** : an opportunity or attempt to do something : CHANCE **5** : a single action or occasion : TIME ⟨made three pies at a ~⟩

¹**whale** \ˈhwāl\ *n, pl* **whales 1** *or pl* **whale** : any of an order of marine mammals that lack hind limbs and have the front limbs modified into flippers; *esp* : one of the larger members of the order **2** : a person or thing impressive in size or quality ⟨a ~ of a story⟩

²**whale** *vb* **whaled; whal·ing** : to fish or hunt for whales

³**whale** *vb* **whaled; whal·ing 1** : THRASH **2** : to strike or hit vigorously

whale·boat \-ˌbōt\ *n* : a long narrow rowboat made with both ends sharp and sloping and formerly used by whalers

whale·bone \-ˌbōn\ *n* : a horny substance attached in plates to the upper jaw of some large whales (**whalebone whales**)

whal·er \ˈhwā-lər\ *n* **1** : a person or ship that hunts whales **2** : WHALEBOAT

wham·my \ˈhwam-ē\ *n, pl* **wham·mies** : JINX, HEX

wharf \ˈhwȯrf\ *n, pl* **wharves** \ˈhwȯrvz\ *also* **wharfs** : a structure alongside which ships lie to load and unload

wharf·age \ˈhwȯr-fij\ *n* : the provision or use of a wharf; *also* : the charge for using a wharf

wharf·in·ger \ˈhwȯr-fən-jər\ *n* : the operator or manager of a wharf

¹**what** \(ˈ)hwät, (ˈ)hwət\ *pron* **1** — used to inquire about the identity or nature of a being, an object, or some matter or situation ⟨~ is he, a salesman⟩ ⟨~*'s* that⟩ ⟨~ happened⟩ **2** : that which ⟨I know ~ you want⟩ **3** : WHATEVER 1 ⟨take ~ you want⟩

²**what** *adv* **1** : in what respect : HOW ⟨~ does he care⟩ **2** — used with *with* to introduce a prepositional phrase that expresses cause ⟨kept busy ~ with school and work⟩

³**what** *adj* **1** — used to inquire about the identity or nature of a person, object, or matter ⟨~ books does he read⟩ **2** : how remarkable or surprising ⟨~ an idea⟩ **3** : WHATEVER

¹**what·ev·er** \hwät-ˈev-ər\ *pron* **1** : anything or everything that ⟨does ~ he wants to⟩ **2** : no matter what ⟨~ you do, don't cheat⟩ **3** : WHAT 1 — used as an intensive ⟨~ do you mean⟩

²**whatever** *adj* : of any kind at all ⟨no food ~⟩

¹**what·not** \ˈhwät-ˌnät\ *pron* : any of various other things that might also be mentioned ⟨paper clips, pins, and ~⟩

²**whatnot** *n* : a light open set of shelves for small ornaments

what·so·ev·er \ˌhwät-sə-ˈwev-ər\ *pron or adj* : WHATEVER

wheal \ˈhwēl\ *n* : a wale or welt on the skin; *also* : a suddenly-appearing itching or burning raised patch of skin

wheat \ˈhwēt\ *n* : a cereal grain that yields a fine white flour and is the chief breadstuff of temperate regions; *also* : any of several grasses whose white to dark red grains are wheat — **wheat·en** *adj*

wheat germ *n* : the vitamin-rich wheat embryo separated in milling

whee·dle \ˈhwēd-ᵊl\ *vb* **whee·dled; whee·dling** \ˈhwēd-(ᵊ-)liŋ\ **1** : to coax or entice by flattery **2** : to gain or get by wheedling

¹**wheel** \ˈhwēl\ *n* **1** : a disk or circular frame that turns on a central axis **2** : a device whose main part is a wheel **3** : something resembling a wheel (as in being round or turning) **4** : a curving or circular movement **5** : machinery that imparts motion : moving power ⟨the ~*s* of government⟩ **6** : a person of importance **7** *pl, slang* : AUTOMOBILE — **wheeled** \ˈhwēld\ *adj* — **wheel·less** \ˈhwēl-ləs\ *adj*

²**wheel** *vb* **1** : ROTATE, REVOLVE **2** : to change direction as if turning on a pivot **3** : to convey or move on wheels or in a vehicle

wheel·bar·row \-ˌbar-ō\ *n* : a vehicle with handles and usu. one wheel for conveying small loads

wheel·base \-ˌbās\ *n* : the distance in inches between the front and rear axles of an automotive vehicle

wheel·chair \-ˌcheər\ *n* : a chair mounted on wheels esp. for the use of invalids

wheel·er \ˈhwē-lər\ *n* **1** : one that wheels **2** : something that has wheels — used in combination ⟨a side-*wheeler*⟩ **3** : WHEELHORSE

wheel·er–deal·er \ˌhwē-lər-ˈdē-lər\ *n* : a shrewd operator esp. in business or politics

wheel·horse \ˈhwēl-ˌhȯrs\ *n* **1** : a horse in a position nearest the wheels in a tandem or similar arrangement **2** : a steady and effective worker esp. in a political body

wheel·house \-ˌhau̇s\ *n* : PILOTHOUSE

wheel·wright \-ˌrīt\ *n* : a maker and repairer of wheels and wheeled vehicles

[1]**wheeze** \ˈhwēz\ *vb* **wheezed; wheez·ing** : to breathe with difficulty usu. with a whistling sound

[2]**wheeze** *n* **1** : a sound of wheezing **2** : an often repeated and well-known joke **3** : a trite saying

wheezy \ˈhwē-zē\ *adj* **wheez·i·er; -est** **1** : inclined to wheeze **2** : having a wheezing sound

whelk \ˈhwelk\ *n* : a large sea snail; *esp* : one much used as food in Europe

whelm \ˈhwelm\ *vb* : to overcome or engulf completely : OVERWHELM

[1]**whelp** \ˈhwelp\ *n* **1** : one of the young of various carnivorous mammals (as a dog) **2** : a low contemptible fellow

[2]**whelp** *vb* : to give birth to (whelps) : bring forth whelps

[1]**when** \(ˈ)hwen, hwən\ *adv* **1** : at what time ⟨~ will he return⟩ **2** : at or during which time ⟨a time ~ things were upset⟩

[2]**when** *conj* **1** : at or during the time that ⟨leave ~ I do⟩ **2** : every time that ⟨they all laughed ~ he sang⟩ **3** : in the event that : IF ⟨disqualified ~ he cheats⟩ **4** : ALTHOUGH ⟨quit politics ~ he might have had a great career in it⟩

[3]**when** \ˌhwen\ *pron* : what or which time ⟨since ~ have you been the boss⟩

[4]**when** \ˈhwen\ *n* : the time of a happening

whence \(ˈ)hwens\ *adv* **1** : from what place, source, or cause ⟨asked ~ the gifts came⟩ **2** : from or out of which ⟨the land ~ he came⟩

when·ev·er \hwen-ˈev-ər, hwən-\ *conj or adv* : at whatever time

when·so·ev·er \ˈhwen-sə-ˌwev-ər\ *conj* : at whatever time

[1]**where** \(ˈ)hweər\ *adv* **1** : at, in, or to what place ⟨~ is he⟩ ⟨~ did he go⟩ **2** : at, in, or to what situation, position, direction, circumstances, or respect ⟨~ does this road lead⟩

[2]**where** *conj* **1** : at, in, or to what place ⟨knows ~ the house is⟩ **2** : at, in, or to what situation, position, direction, circumstances, or respect ⟨shows ~ the road leads⟩ **3** : WHEREVER ⟨goes ~ he likes⟩ **4** : at, in, or to which place ⟨the town ~ she lives⟩ **5** : at, in, or to the place at, in, or to which ⟨stay ~ you are⟩ **6** : in a case, situation, or respect in which ⟨outstanding ~ endurance is called for⟩

[3]**where** \ˈhweər\ *n* **1** : PLACE, LOCATION ⟨the ~ and how of the accident⟩ **2** : what place ⟨~ is he from⟩

[1]**where·abouts** \-ə-ˌbau̇ts\ *also* **where·about** \-ˌbau̇t\ *adv* : about where ⟨~ does he live⟩

[2]**whereabouts** *n sing or pl* : the place where a person or thing is ⟨his present ~ are unknown⟩

where·as \hwer-ˈaz\ *conj* **1** : when in fact : while on the contrary **2** : in view of the fact that : SINCE

where·at \-ˈat\ *conj* **1** : at or toward which **2** : in consequence of which : WHEREUPON

where·by \-ˈbī\ *conj* : by, through, or in accordance with which ⟨the means ~ he achieved his goal⟩

[1]**where·fore** \ˈhweər-ˌfōr\ *adv* **1** : for what reason or purpose : WHY **2** : THEREFORE

[2]**wherefore** *n* : CAUSE, REASON

[1]**where·in** \hwer-ˈin\ *adv* : in what : in what respect ⟨~ was he wrong⟩

[2]**wherein** *conj* **1** : in which : WHERE ⟨the city ~ he lives⟩ **2** : during which **3** : in what way : HOW ⟨showed him ~ he was wrong⟩

where·of \-ˈəv, -ˈäv\ *conj* **1** : of what ⟨knows ~ he speaks⟩ **2** : of which or whom ⟨books ~ the best are lost⟩

where·on \-ˈȯn, -ˈän\ *conj* : on which ⟨the base ~ it rests⟩

where·so·ev·er \ˈhwer-sə-ˌwev-ər\ *conj* : WHEREVER

where·to \ˈhweər-ˌtü\ *conj* : to which

where·up·on \ˈhwer-ə-ˌpȯn, -ˌpän\ *conj* **1** : on which **2** : closely following and in consequence of which

[1]**wher·ev·er** \hwer-ˈev-ər\ *adv* : where in the world ⟨~ did she get that hat⟩

[2]**wherever** *conj* **1** : at, in, or to whatever place **2** : in any circumstance in which

where·with \ˈhweər-ˌwit͟h, -ˌwith\ *conj* : with or by means of which

where·with·al \ˈhwer-wit͟h-ˌȯl, -with-\ *n* : MEANS, RESOURCES; *esp* : MONEY

wher·ry \ˈhwer-ē\ *n, pl* **wherries** : a light boat; *esp* : a long light rowboat sharp at both ends

whet \ˈhwet\ *vb* **whet·ted; whet·ting** **1** : to sharpen by rubbing against or with a hard substance (as a whetstone) **2** : to make keen : STIMULATE ⟨~ the appetite⟩

wheth·er \ˈhwet͟h-ər\ *conj* **1** : if it is or was true that ⟨ask ~ he is going⟩ **2** : if it is or was better ⟨uncertain ~ to go or stay⟩ **3** : whichever is or was the case, namely that ⟨~ we succeed or fail, we must try⟩ **4** : EITHER ⟨turned out well ~ by accident or design⟩

whet·stone \ˈhwet-ˌstōn\ *n* : a stone for sharpening blades

whey \ˈhwā\ *n* : the watery part of milk that separates after the milk sours and thickens

[1]**which** \(ˈ)hwich\ *adj* **1** : being what one or ones out of a group ⟨~ tie should I wear⟩ **2** : WHICHEVER

[2]**which** *pron* **1** : which one or ones ⟨~ is yours⟩ ⟨~ are his⟩ ⟨he's a Swede or a Dane, I don't remember ~⟩ **2** : WHICHEVER ⟨we have all kinds of them; take ~ you like⟩ **3** — used to introduce a relative clause and to serve as a substitute therein for the substantive modified by the clause ⟨give me the money ~ is coming to me⟩

[1]**which·ev·er** \hwich-ˈev-ər\ *adj* : no matter which ⟨~ way you go⟩

[2]**whichever** *pron* : whatever one or ones

which·so·ev·er \ˌhwich-sə-ˈwev-ər\ *pron or adj* : WHICHEVER

whick·er \ˈhwik-ər\ *vb* : NEIGH, WHINNY — **whicker** *n*

[1]**whiff** \ˈhwif\ *n* **1** : a quick puff or slight gust esp. of air, gas, smoke, or spray **2** : an inhalation of odor, gas, or smoke **3** : a slight trace : HINT

[2]**whiff** *vb* **1** : to expel, puff out, or blow away in or as if in whiffs **2** : to inhale an odor

whif·fle·tree \ˈhwif-əl-(ˌ)trē\ *n* [alter. of *whippletree*] : the pivoted swinging bar to which the traces of a harness are fastened

Whig \ˈhwig\ *n* [short for *Whiggamore* (member of a Scottish group that marched to Edinburgh in 1648 to oppose the court party)] **1** : a member or supporter of a British political group of the 18th and early 19th centuries seeking to limit royal authority and increase parliamentary power **2** : an American favoring independence from Great Britain during the American Revolution **3** : a member or supporter of an American political party formed about 1834 to oppose the Democrats

[1]**while** \ˈhwīl\ *n* **1** : a period of time ⟨stay a ~⟩ **2** : the time and effort used : TROUBLE ⟨worth your ~⟩

[2]**while** \(ˌ)hwīl\ *conj* **1** : during the time that ⟨she called ~ you were out⟩ **2** : AS LONG AS ⟨~ there's life there's hope⟩ **3** : ALTHOUGH ⟨~ he's respected, he's not liked⟩

[3]**while** \ˈhwīl\ *vb* **whiled; whil·ing** : to cause to pass esp. pleasantly ⟨~ away an hour⟩

[1]**whi·lom** \ˈhwī-ləm\ *adv* [ME, lit., at times, fr. OE *hwīlum*, dat. pl. of *hwīl* time, while] *archaic* : FORMERLY

[2]**whilom** *adj* : FORMER ⟨his ~ friends⟩

whilst \ˈhwīlst\ *conj, chiefly Brit* : WHILE

whim \ˈhwim\ *n* : a sudden wish, desire, or change of mind : NOTION, FANCY, CAPRICE

whim·per \ˈhwim-pər\ *vb* **whim·pered; whim·per·ing**

\-p(ə-)riŋ\ : to make a low whining plaintive or broken sound — **whimper** *n*

whim·si·cal \'hwim-zi-kəl\ *adj* **1** : full of whims : CAPRICIOUS **2** : resulting from or characterized by whim or caprice : ERRATIC — **whim·si·cal·i·ty** \ˌhwim-zə-'kal-ət-ē\ *n* — **whim·si·cal·ly** \'hwim-zi-k(ə-)lē\ *adv*

whim·sy *or* **whim·sey** \'hwim-zē\ *n, pl* **whimsies** *or* **whimseys 1** : WHIM, CAPRICE **2** : a fanciful or fantastic device, object, or creation esp. in writing or art

whine \'hwīn\ *vb* **whined; whin·ing** [ME *whinen,* fr. OE *hwīnan* to whiz] **1** : to utter a usu. high-pitched plaintive or distressed cry; *also* : to make a sound similar to such a cry **2** : to utter a complaint with or as if with a whine — **whine** *n*

[1]**whin·ny** \'hwin-ē\ *vb* **whin·nied; whin·ny·ing** : to neigh usu. in a low or gentle manner

[2]**whinny** *n, pl* **whinnies** : NEIGH

[1]**whip** \'hwip\ *vb* **whipped; whip·ping 1** : to move, snatch, or jerk quickly or forcefully ⟨~ out a gun⟩ **2** : to strike with a slender lithe implement (as a lash) esp. as a punishment; *also* : SPANK **3** : to drive or urge on by or as if by using a whip **4** : to bind or wrap (as a rope or rod) with cord in order to protect and strengthen; *also* : to wind or wrap around something **5** : DEFEAT **6** : to stir up : INCITE ⟨~ up enthusiasm⟩ **7** : to produce in a hurry ⟨~ up a meal⟩ **8** : to beat (as eggs or cream) into a froth **9** : to gather together or hold together for united action **10** : to proceed nimbly or briskly; *also* : to thrash about like a whiplash — **whip·per** *n* — **whip into shape** : to bring forcefully to a desired state or condition

[2]**whip** *n* **1** : a flexible instrument used for whipping **2** : a stroke or cut with or as if with a whip **3** : a dessert made by whipping a portion of the ingredients ⟨prune ~⟩ **4** : a person who handles a whip; *esp* : a driver of horses **5** : a member of a legislative body appointed by his party to enforce party discipline and to secure the attendance of party members at important sessions **6** : a whipping or thrashing motion ⟨a ~ of his tail⟩

[2]whip 1

whip·cord \-ˌkȯrd\ *n* **1** : a thin tough cord made of braided or twisted hemp or catgut **2** : a cloth that is made of hard-twisted yarns and has fine diagonal cords or ribs

whip hand *n* : positive control : ADVANTAGE

whip·lash \'hwip-ˌlash\ *n* **1** : the lash of a whip **2** : WHIPLASH INJURY

whiplash injury *n* : injury resulting from a sudden sharp movement of the neck and head (as of a person in a vehicle that is struck from the front or rear)

whip·per·snap·per \'hwip-ər-ˌsnap-ər\ *n* : a small, insignificant, or presumptuous person

whip·pet \'hwip-ət\ *n* : any of a breed of small swift slender dogs that are widely used for racing

whipping boy *n* : SCAPEGOAT

whip·ple·tree \'hwip-əl-(ˌ)trē\ *n* : WHIFFLETREE

whip·poor·will \'hwip-ər-ˌwil\ *n* : an American bird with dull variegated plumage whose call is heard at nightfall and just before dawn

[1]**whip·saw** \'hwip-ˌsȯ\ *n* **1** : a narrow tapering saw that has hook teeth **2** : a 2-man crosscut saw

[2]**whipsaw** *vb* **1** : to saw with a whipsaw **2** : to worst in two opposite ways at once, by a 2-phase operation, or by the collusive action of two opponents

[1]**whir** *also* **whirr** \'hwər\ *vb* **whirred; whir·ring** : to move, fly, or revolve with a whizzing sound : WHIZ

[2]**whir** *also* **whirr** *n* : a continuous fluttering or vibratory sound made by something in rapid motion

[1]**whirl** \'hwərl\ *vb* **1** : to move or drive in a circle or similar curve esp. with force or speed **2** : to turn or cause to turn on or around an axis : SPIN **3** : to turn abruptly : WHEEL **4** : to pass, move, or go quickly **5** : to become dizzy or giddy : REEL

[2]**whirl** *n* **1** : a rapid rotating or circling movement; *also* : something undergoing such a movement **2** : COMMOTION, BUSTLE ⟨the social ~⟩ **3** : a state of mental confusion

whirl·i·gig \'hwər-li-ˌgig\ *n* [ME *whirlegigg,* fr. *whirlen* to whirl + *gigg* top] **1** : a child's toy having a whirling motion **2** : MERRY-GO-ROUND **3** : something that continuously whirls or changes; *also* : a whirling course (as of events)

whirl·pool \'hwərl-ˌpül\ *n* : water moving rapidly in a circle so as to produce a depression in the center into which floating objects may be drawn

whirl·wind \-ˌwind\ *n* **1** : a small whirling windstorm **2** : a confused rush : WHIRL

whirly·bird \'hwər-lē-ˌbərd\ *n* : HELICOPTER

[1]**whish** \'hwish\ *vb* : to move with a whizzing of swishing sound

[2]**whish** *n* : a rushing sound : SWISH

[1]**whisk** \'hwisk\ *n* **1** : a quick light sweeping or brushing motion **2** : a small usu. wire kitchen implement for hand beating of food **3** : a flexible bunch (as of twigs, feathers, or straw) attached to a handle for use as a brush

[2]**whisk** *vb* **1** : to move nimbly and quickly **2** : to move or convey briskly ⟨~ out a knife⟩ ⟨~*ed* the children off to bed⟩ **3** : to beat or whip lightly ⟨~ eggs⟩ **4** : to brush or wipe off lightly ⟨~ a coat⟩

whisk broom *n* : a small broom with a short handle used esp. as a clothes brush

whis·ker \'hwis-kər\ *n* **1** *pl* : the part of the beard that grows on the sides of the face or on the chin **2** : one hair of the beard **3** : one of the long bristles or hairs growing near the mouth of an animal (as a cat or bird) — **whiskered** \-kərd\ *adj*

whis·key *or* **whis·ky** \'hwis-kē\ *n, pl* **whiskeys** *or* **whiskies** [IrGael *uisce beathadh* & ScGael *uisge beatha,* lit., water of life] : a liquor distilled from the fermented mash of grain (as rye, corn, or barley)

[1]**whis·per** \'hwis-pər\ *vb* **whis·pered; whis·per·ing** \-p(ə-)riŋ\ **1** : to speak very low or under the breath; *also* : to tell or utter by whispering ⟨~ a secret⟩ **2** : to make a low rustling sound ⟨~*ing* leaves⟩

[2]**whisper** *n* **1** : something communicated by or as if by whispering : HINT, RUMOR **2** : an act or instance of whispering; *esp* : speech without vibration of the vocal cords

whist \'hwist\ *n* : a card game played by four players in two partnerships with a deck of 52 cards

[1]**whis·tle** \'hwis-əl\ *n* **1** : a device by which a shrill sound is produced ⟨steam ~⟩ ⟨tin ~⟩ **2** : a shrill clear sound made by forcing breath out or air in through the puckered lips **3** : the sound or signal produced by a whistle or as if by whistling **4** : the shrill clear note of an animal (as a bird)

[2]**whistle** *vb* **whis·tled; whis·tling** \-(ə-)liŋ\ **1** : to utter a shrill clear sound by blowing or drawing air through the puckered lips **2** : to utter a shrill note or call resembling a whistle **3** : to make a shrill clear sound esp. by rapid movements ⟨bullets *whistled* by him⟩ **4** : to blow or sound a whistle **5** : to signal or call by a whistle **6** : to produce, utter, or express by whistling ⟨~ a tune⟩ — **whis·tler** \-(ə-)lər\ *n*

whis·tle–blow·er \'hwis-əl-ˌblō-ər\ *n* : INFORMER

whis·tle–stop \'hwis-əl-ˌstäp\ *n* **1** : a small station at which trains stop only on signal **2** : a small community **3** : a brief personal appearance by a political candidate orig. on the rear platform of a touring train

whit \'hwit\ *n* [prob. alter. of ME *wiht, wight* creature, thing, bit, fr. OE *wiht*] : the smallest part or particle imaginable : BIT

[1]white \ˈhwīt\ *adj* **whit·er; whit·est 1 :** free from color **2 :** of the color of new snow or milk; *esp* **:** of the color white **3 :** light or pallid in color ⟨lips ~ with fear⟩ **4 :** SILVERY; *also* **:** made of silver **5 :** of, relating to, or being a member of a group or race characterized by light-colored skin **6 :** free from spot or blemish **:** PURE, INNOCENT **7 :** BLANK 3 ⟨~ space in printed matter⟩ **8 :** not intended to cause harm ⟨a ~ lie⟩ **9 :** wearing white ⟨~ friars⟩ **10 :** SNOWY ⟨~ Christmas⟩ **11 :** ARDENT, PASSIONATE ⟨~ fury⟩ **12 :** conservative or reactionary in politics

[2]white *n* **1 :** the color of maximal lightness that characterizes objects which both reflect and transmit light **:** the opposite of black **2 :** a white or light-colored part or thing ⟨the ~ of an egg⟩; *also, pl* **:** white garments **3 :** the light-colored pieces in a 2-player board game; *also* **:** the person by whom these are played **4 :** one that is or approaches the color white **5 :** a member of a light-skinned race **6 :** a member of a conservative or reactionary political group

white ant *n* **:** TERMITE

white·bait \ˈhwīt-ˌbāt\ *n* **:** the young of a herring or a similar small fish used for food

white blood cell *n* **:** a blood cell that does not contain hemoglobin **:** LEUKOCYTE

white·cap \ˈhwīt-ˌkap\ *n* **:** a wave crest breaking into foam

white–col·lar \ˈhwīt-ˈkäl-ər\ *adj* **:** of, relating to, or constituting the class of salaried workers whose duties do not require the wearing of work clothes or protective clothing

white dwarf *n* **:** a small very dense whitish star of low luminosity

white elephant *n* [so called because white elephants were venerated in parts of Asia and maintained without being required to work] **1 :** an Indian elephant of a pale color that is sometimes venerated in India, Sri Lanka, Thailand, and Burma **2 :** something requiring much care and expense and yielding little profit **3 :** an object no longer wanted by its owner though not without value to others

white–faced \ˈhwīt-ˈfāst\ *adj* **1 :** having a wan pale face **2 :** having the face white in whole or in part ⟨~ cattle⟩

white feather *n* [fr. the superstition that a white feather in the plumage of a gamecock is a mark of a poor fighter] **:** a mark or symbol of cowardice

white·fish \ˈhwīt-ˌfish\ *n* **:** any of various freshwater food fishes related to the salmons and trouts

white flag *n* **:** a flag of plain white used as a flag of truce or as a token of surrender

white·fly \ˈhwīt-ˌflī\ *n* **:** any of numerous small insects that are injurious plant pests related to the scale insects

white gold *n* **:** a pale alloy of gold esp. with nickel or palladium resembling platinum in appearance

white goods *n pl* **:** white fabrics or articles (as sheets or towels) typically made of cotton or linen

White·hall \ˈhwīt-ˌhȯl\ *n* **:** the British government

white·head \-ˌhed\ *n* **:** a small whitish lump in the skin due to retention of secretion in an oil gland duct

white heat *n* **:** a temperature higher than red heat at which a body becomes brightly incandescent so as to appear white

white–hot *adj* **1 :** being at or radiating white heat **2 :** FERVID

White House \-ˌhau̇s\ *n* **1 :** the executive department of the U.S. government **2 :** a residence of the president of the U.S.

white lead *n* **:** a heavy white poisonous carbonate of lead used as a pigment in exterior paints

white matter *n* **:** the whitish part of nervous tissue consisting mostly of nerve-cell processes

whit·en \ˈhwīt-ᵊn\ *vb* **whit·ened; whit·en·ing** \ˈhwīt(ᵊ-)niŋ\ **:** to make or become white **syn** blanch, bleach — **whit·en·er** \ˈhwīt-(ᵊ-)nər\ *n*

white·ness \ˈhwīt-nəs\ *n* **:** the quality or state of being white

white pine *n* **:** a tall-growing pine of eastern No. America with leaves in clusters of five; *also* **:** its wood

white–pine blister rust *n* **:** a destructive disease of white pine caused by a rust fungus that passes part of its complex life cycle on currant or gooseberry bushes; *also* **:** this fungus

white sale *n* **:** a sale on white goods

white shark *n* **:** a large and dangerous shark of warm seas that is light colored below and darker above becoming dirty white in older and larger specimens

white slave *n* **:** a woman or girl held unwillingly for purposes of prostitution — **white slavery** *n*

white·tail \ˈhwīt-ˌtāl\ *n* **:** WHITE-TAILED DEER

white–tailed deer \ˌhwīt-ˌtāl-ˈdiər\ *n* **:** a No. American deer with a rather long tail white on the underside and with forward-arching antlers

white·wall \ˈhwīt-ˌwȯl\ *n* **:** an automobile tire having a white band on the sidewall

[1]white·wash \-ˌwȯsh, -ˌwäsh\ *vb* **1 :** to whiten with whitewash **2 :** to clear of a charge of wrongdoing by offering excuses, hiding facts, or conducting a perfunctory investigation **3 :** to prevent (an opponent) from scoring in a game or contest

[2]whitewash *n* **1 :** a liquid mixture (as of lime and water) for whitening a surface **2 :** a clearing of wrongdoing by whitewashing

white·wood \-ˌwu̇d\ *n* **:** any of various trees and esp. a tulip tree having light-colored wood; *also* **:** the wood of such a tree

[1]whith·er \ˈhwith-ər\ *adv* **1 :** to what place **2 :** to what situation, position, degree, or end ⟨~ will this drive him⟩

[2]whither *conj* **1 :** to the place at, in, or to which; *also* **:** to which place **2 :** to whatever place

whith·er·so·ev·er \ˌhwith-ər-sə-ˈwev-ər\ *conj* **:** to whatever place

[1]whit·ing \ˈhwīt-iŋ\ *n* **:** any of several usu. light or silvery food fishes (as a hake) found mostly near seacoasts

[2]whiting *n* **:** calcium carbonate in the form of pulverized chalk or limestone used as a pigment and in putty

whit·ish \ˈhwīt-ish\ *adj* **:** somewhat white

whit·low \ˈhwit-ˌlō\ *n* **:** a deep inflammation of a finger or toe with pus formation

Whit·sun·day \ˈhwit-ˈsən-dē, -sən-ˌdā\ *n* [ME *Whitsonday,* fr. OE *hwīta sunnandaeg,* lit., white Sunday, prob. fr. the custom of wearing white robes by those newly baptized at this season] **:** PENTECOST

whit·tle \ˈhwit-ᵊl\ *vb* **whit·tled; whit·tling** \ˈhwit-(ᵊ-)liŋ\ **1 :** to pare or cut off chips from the surface of (wood) with a knife; *also* **:** to cut or shape by such paring **2 :** to reduce, remove, or destroy gradually as if by paring down **:** PARE ⟨~ down expenses⟩

[1]whiz *or* **whizz** \ˈhwiz\ *vb* **whizzed; whiz·zing :** to hum, whir, or hiss like a speeding object (as an arrow or ball) passing through air

[2]whiz *or* **whizz** *n, pl* **whiz·zes :** a hissing, buzzing, or whirring sound

[3]whiz *n, pl* **whiz·zes :** WIZARD 2

who \(ˈ)hü\ *pron* **1 :** what or which person or persons ⟨~ did it⟩ ⟨~ is he⟩ ⟨~ are they⟩ **2 :** the person or persons that ⟨knows ~ did it⟩ **3** \(ˌ)hü, ü\ — used to introduce a relative clause and to serve as a substitute therein for the substantive modified by the clause ⟨the man ~ lives there is rich⟩ ⟨the people ~ did it were caught⟩

WHO *abbr* World Health Organization

whoa \ˈwō, ˈhwō, ˈhō\ *vb imper* — a command (as to a draft animal) to stand still

who·dun·it *also* **who·dun·nit** \hü-ˈdən-ət\ *n* : a detective story or mystery story presented as a novel, play, or motion picture

who·ev·er \hü-ˈev-ər\ *pron* : whatever person : no matter who

[1]**whole** \ˈhōl\ *adj* [ME *hool* healthy, unhurt, entire, fr. OE *hāl*] **1** : being in healthy or sound condition : free from defect or damage : WELL, INTACT **2** : having all its proper parts or elements ⟨~ milk⟩ **3** : constituting the total sum of : ENTIRE ⟨~ continental landmasses⟩ **4** : each or all of the ⟨the ~ family⟩ **5** : not scattered or divided : CONCENTRATED ⟨gave me his ~ attention⟩ **6** : seemingly complete or total ⟨the ~ idea is to help, not hinder⟩ **syn** entire, perfect, intact, sound — **whole·ness** *n*

[2]**whole** *n* **1** : a complete amount or sum : a number, aggregate, or totality lacking no part, member, or element **2** : something constituting a complex unity : a coherent system or organization of parts fitting or working together as one — **on the whole 1** : in view of all the circumstances or conditions **2** : in general

whole·heart·ed \hōl-ˈhärt-əd\ *adj* : undivided in purpose, enthusiasm, or will : HEARTY, ZESTFUL, SINCERE

whole note *n* : a musical note equal to one measure of four beats

whole number *n* : INTEGER

[1]**whole·sale** \ˈhōl-ˌsāl\ *n* : the sale of goods in quantity usu. for resale by a retail merchant

[2]**wholesale** *adj* **1** : performed on a large scale without discrimination ⟨~ slaughter⟩ **2** : of, relating to, or engaged in wholesaling — **wholesale** *adv*

[3]**wholesale** *vb* **whole·saled; whole·sal·ing** : to sell at wholesale — **whole·sal·er** *n*

whole·some \ˈhōl-səm\ *adj* **1** : promoting mental, spiritual, or bodily health or well-being ⟨~ advice⟩ ⟨a ~ environment⟩ **2** : sound in body, mind, or morals : HEALTHY **3** : PRUDENT ⟨~ respect for the law⟩ — **whole·some·ness** *n*

whole step *n* : a musical interval comprising two half steps (as C–D or F♯–G♯)

whole wheat *adj* : made of ground entire wheat kernels

whol·ly \ˈhōl-(l)ē\ *adv* **1** : COMPLETELY, TOTALLY **2** : SOLELY, EXCLUSIVELY

whom \(ˈ)hüm\ *pron, objective case of* WHO

whom·ev·er \hüm-ˈev-ər\ *pron, objective case of* WHOEVER

whom·so·ev·er \ˌhüm-sə-ˈwev-ər\ *pron, objective case of* WHOSOEVER

[1]**whoop** \ˈh(w)üp, ˈh(w)u̇p\ *vb* **1** : to shout or call loudly and vigorously **2** : to make the sound that follows a fit of coughing in whooping cough **3** : to go or pass with a loud noise **4** : to utter or express with a whoop; *also* : to urge, drive, or cheer with a whoop

[2]**whoop** *n* **1** : a whooping sound or utterance : SHOUT, HOOT **2** : a crowing sound accompanying the intake of breath after a fit of coughing in whooping cough

whooping cough *n* : an infectious disease esp. of children marked by convulsive coughing fits sometimes followed by a whoop

whooping crane *n* : a large white nearly extinct No. American crane noted for its loud whooping note

whoop·la \ˈh(w)üp-ˌlä, ˈh(w)u̇p-\ *n* **1** : a noisy commotion **2** : boisterous merrymaking

whop·per \ˈhwäp-ər\ *n* : something unusually large or extreme of its kind; *esp* : a monstrous lie

whop·ping \ˈhwäp-iŋ\ *adj* : extremely large

whore \ˈhōr\ *n* : PROSTITUTE

whorl \ˈhwȯrl, ˈhwərl\ *n* **1** : a row of parts (as leaves or petals) encircling an axis and esp. a plant stem **2** : something that whirls or coils around a center : COIL, SPIRAL **3** : one of the turns of a snail shell

whorled \ˈhwȯrld, ˈhwərld\ *adj* : having or arranged in whorls

[1]**whose** \(ˈ)hüz\ *adj* : of or relating to whom or which esp. as possessor or possessors, agent or agents, or object or objects of an action ⟨asked ~ bag it was⟩

[2]**whose** *pron* : whose one or ones ⟨~ is this car⟩ ⟨~ are those books⟩

who·so \ˈhü-ˌsō\ *pron* : WHOEVER

who·so·ev·er \ˌhü-sə-ˈwev-ər\ *pron* : WHOEVER

whs *or* **whse** *abbr* warehouse

whsle *abbr* wholesale

[1]**why** \(ˈ)hwī\ *adv* : for what reason, cause, or purpose ⟨~ did you do it⟩

[2]**why** *conj* **1** : the cause, reason, or purpose for which ⟨that is ~ you did it⟩ **2** : for which : on account of which ⟨knows the reason ~ you did it⟩

[3]**why** \ˈhwī\ *n, pl* **whys** : REASON, CAUSE ⟨the ~*s* of racial prejudice⟩

[4]**why** \(ˌ)wī, (ˌ)hwī\ *interj* — used to express surprise, hesitation, approval, disapproval, or impatience ⟨~, here's what I was looking for⟩

WI *abbr* **1** West Indies **2** Wisconsin

WIA *abbr* wounded in action

wick \ˈwik\ *n* : a loosely bound bundle of soft fibers that draws up oil, tallow, or wax to be burned in a candle, oil lamp, or stove

wick·ed \ˈwik-əd\ *adj* **1** : morally bad : EVIL, SINFUL **2** : FIERCE, VICIOUS **3** : ROGUISH ⟨a ~ glance⟩ **4** : REPUGNANT, VILE ⟨a ~ odor⟩ **5** : HARMFUL, DANGEROUS ⟨a ~ attack⟩ — **wick·ed·ly** *adv* — **wick·ed·ness** *n*

wick·er \ˈwik-ər\ *n* **1** : a small pliant branch (as an osier or a withe) **2** : WICKERWORK — **wicker** *adj*

wick·er·work \-ˌwərk\ *n* : work made of osiers, twigs, or rods : BASKETRY

wick·et \ˈwik-ət\ *n* **1** : a small gate or door; *esp* : one forming a part of or placed near a larger one **2** : a windowlike opening usu. with a grille or grate (as at a ticket office) **3** : a set of three upright rods topped by two crosspieces bowled at in cricket **4** : an arch through which the ball is driven in croquet

wick·i·up \ˈwik-ē-ˌəp\ *n* : a hut used by nomadic Indians of the western and southwestern U.S. with a usu. oval base and a rough frame covered with reed mats, grass, or brushwood

wid *abbr* widow, widower

[1]**wide** \ˈwīd\ *adj* **wider; wid·est 1** : covering a vast area **2** : measured across or at right angles to the length **3** : not narrow : BROAD; *also* : ROOMY **4** : opened to full width ⟨eyes ~ with wonder⟩ **5** : not limited : EXTENSIVE ⟨~ experience⟩ **6** : far from the goal, mark, or truth ⟨a ~ guess⟩ — **wide·ly** *adv*

[2]**wide** *adv* **wid·er; wid·est 1** : over a great distance or extent : WIDELY ⟨searched far and ~⟩ **2** : over a specified distance, area, or extent **3** : so as to leave a wide space between ⟨~ apart⟩ **4** : so as to clear by a considerable distance ⟨ran ~ around left end⟩ **5** : COMPLETELY, FULLY ⟨opened her eyes ~⟩

wide–awake \ˌwīd-ə-ˈwāk\ *adj* : fully awake; *also* : KNOWING, ALERT ⟨a group of ~ young men⟩

wide–eyed \ˈwīd-ˈīd\ *adj* **1** : having the eyes wide open esp. with wonder or astonishment **2** : NAIVE

wide·mouthed \ˈwīd-ˈmau̇t͟hd, -ˈmau̇tht\ *adj* **1** : having one's mouth opened wide (as in awe) **2** : having a wide mouth ⟨~ jars⟩

wid·en \ˈwīd-ᵊn\ *vb* **wid·ened; wid·en·ing** \ˈwīd-(ᵊ-)niŋ\ : to make or become wide : BROADEN

wide·spread \ˈwīd-ˈspred\ *adj* **1** : widely scattered or prevalent ⟨~ fear⟩ **2** : widely extended or spread out ⟨~ wings⟩

[1]**wid·ow** \ˈwid-ō\ *n* : a woman who has lost her husband by death and has not married again — **wid·ow·hood** *n*

[2]**widow** *vb* : to cause to become a widow

wid·ow·er \ˈwid-ə-wər\ *n* : a man who has lost his wife by death and has not married again

width \ˈwidth\ *n* **1** : a distance from side to side : the measurement taken at right angles to the length : BREADTH **2** : largeness of extent or scope; *also* : FULLNESS **3** : a measured and cut piece of material ⟨a ~ of calico⟩ ⟨a ~ of lumber⟩

wield \ˈwēld\ *vb* **1** : to use or handle esp. effectively ⟨~ a broom⟩ ⟨~ a pen⟩ **2** : to exert authority by means of : EMPLOY ⟨~ influence⟩ — **wield·er** *n*

wie·ner \ˈwē-nər\ *n* [short for *wienerwurst,* fr. G, lit., Vienna sausage] : FRANKFURTER

wife \ˈwīf\ *n, pl* **wives** \ˈwīvz\ **1** *dial* : WOMAN **2** : a woman acting in a specified capacity — used in combination **3** : a married woman — **wife·hood** *n* — **wife·less** *adj* — **wife·ly** *adj*

wig \ˈwig\ *n* [short for *periwig,* fr. MF *perruque,* fr. It *perrucca* hair, wig] : a manufactured covering of natural or synthetic hair for the head; *also* : TOUPEE

wi·geon *or* **wid·geon** \ˈwij-ən\ *n, pl* **wigeon** *or* **wigeons** *or* **widgeon** *or* **widgeons** : any of several freshwater ducks between the teal and the mallard in size

wig·gle \ˈwig-əl\ *vb* **wig·gled; wig·gling** \-(ə-)liŋ\ **1** : to move to and fro with quick jerky or shaking movements : JIGGLE **2** : WRIGGLE — **wiggle** *n*

wig·gler \ˈwig-(ə-)lər\ *n* **1** : a larva or pupa of a mosquito **2** : one that wiggles

wig·gly \-(ə-)lē\ *adj* **1** : tending to wiggle ⟨a ~ worm⟩ **2** : WAVY ⟨~ lines⟩

wight \ˈwīt\ *n* : a living being : CREATURE

wig·let \ˈwig-lət\ *n* : a small wig used esp. to enhance a hairstyle

[1]**wig·wag** \ˈwig-ˌwag\ *vb* **1** : to signal by or as if by a flag or light waved according to a code **2** : to make or cause to make a signal (as with the hand or arm)

[2]**wigwag** *n* **1** : the art or practice of wigwagging **2** : the act of wigwagging

wig·wam \ˈwig-ˌwäm\ *n* : a hut of the Indians of the eastern U.S. having typically an arched framework of poles overlaid with bark, rush mats, or hides

wigwam

[1]**wild** \ˈwīld\ *adj* **1** : living in a state of nature and not ordinarily tamed ⟨~ ducks⟩ **2** : growing or produced without human aid or care ⟨~ honey⟩ ⟨~ plants⟩ **3** : WASTE, DESOLATE ⟨~ country⟩ **4** : UNCONTROLLED, UNRESTRAINED, UNRULY ⟨~ passions⟩ ⟨a ~ young stallion⟩ **5** : TURBULENT, STORMY ⟨a ~ night⟩ **6** : EXTRAVAGANT, FANTASTIC, CRAZY ⟨~ ideas⟩ **7** : indicative of strong passion, desire, or emotion ⟨a ~ stare⟩ **8** : UNCIVILIZED, SAVAGE **9** : deviating from the natural or expected course : ERRATIC ⟨a ~ throw⟩ **10** : having a denomination determined by the holder ⟨deuces ~⟩ — **wild·ly** *adv* — **wild·ness** \ˈwīl(d)-nəs\ *n*

[2]**wild** *adv* **1** : WILDLY **2** : without regulation or control ⟨running ~⟩

[3]**wild** *n* **1** : WILDERNESS **2** : a natural or undomesticated state or existence

wild boar *n* : an Old World wild hog from which most domestic swine are descended

wild carrot *n* : a widely naturalized Eurasian weed that is probably the original of the cultivated carrot

[1]**wild·cat** \ˈwīl(d)-ˌkat\ *n, pl* **wildcats** **1** : any of various small or medium-sized cats (as a lynx or ocelot) **2** : a quick-tempered hard-fighting person

[2]**wildcat** *adj* **1** : not sound or safe ⟨~ schemes⟩ **2** : initiated by a group of workers without formal union approval ⟨~ strike⟩

[3]**wildcat** *vb* **wild·cat·ted; wild·cat·ting** : to drill an oil or gas well in a region not known to be productive

wil·de·beest \ˈwil-də-ˌbēst\ *n, pl* **wildebeests** *also* **wildebeest** [Afrikaans *wildebees,* fr. *wilde* wild + *bees* ox] : GNU

wil·der·ness \ˈwil-dər-nəs\ *n* [ME, fr. *wildern* wild, fr. OE *wilddēoren* of wild beasts] : an uncultivated and uninhabited region

wild·fire \ˈwīl(d)-ˌfī(ə)r\ *n* : an uncontrollable fire — **like wildfire** : very rapidly

wild·fowl \-ˌfau̇l\ *n* : a bird and esp. a waterfowl (as a wild duck) hunted as game

wild–goose chase *n* : the pursuit of something unattainable

wild·life \ˈwīl(d)-ˌlīf\ *n* : nonhuman living things and esp. wild animals living in their natural environment

wild oat *n* **1** : any of several wild grasses **2** *pl* : offenses and indiscretions attributed to youthful exuberance ⟨was just sowing his *wild oats*⟩

wild rice *n* : a No. American aquatic grass; *also* : its edible seed

wild·wood \ˈwīld-ˌwu̇d\ *n* : a wild or unfrequented wood

[1]**wile** \ˈwīl\ *n* **1** : a trick or stratagem intended to ensnare or deceive; *also* : a playful trick **2** : TRICKERY, GUILE

[2]**wile** *vb* **wiled; wil·ing** : LURE, ENTICE

[1]**will** \wəl, (ə)l, (ˈ)wil\ *vb, past* **would** \wəd, (ə)d, (ˈ)wu̇d\; *pres sing & pl* **will** **1** : WISH, DESIRE ⟨call it what you ~⟩ **2** — used as an auxiliary verb to express (1) desire, willingness, or in negative constructions refusal ⟨~ you have another⟩ ⟨he *won't* do it⟩, (2) customary or habitual action ⟨~ get angry over nothing⟩, (3) simple futurity ⟨tomorrow we ~ go shopping⟩, (4) capability or sufficiency ⟨the back seat ~ hold three⟩, (5) determination or willfulness ⟨I ~ go despite them⟩, (6) probability ⟨that ~ be the mailman⟩, (7) inevitability ⟨accidents ~ happen⟩, or (8) a command ⟨you ~ do as I say⟩

[2]**will** \ˈwil\ *n* **1** : wish or desire often combined with determination ⟨the ~ to win⟩ **2** : something desired; *esp* : a choice or determination of one having authority or power **3** : the act, process, or experience of willing : VOLITION **4** : the mental powers manifested as wishing, choosing, desiring, or intending **5** : a disposition to act according to principles or ends **6** : power of controlling one's own actions or emotions ⟨a man of iron ~⟩ **7** : a legal document in which a person declares to whom his possessions are to go after his death

[3]**will** \ˈwil\ *vb* **1** : to dispose of by or as if by a will : BEQUEATH **2** : to determine by an act of choice; *also* : DECREE, ORDAIN **3** : INTEND, PURPOSE; *also* : CHOOSE

will·ful *or* **wil·ful** \ˈwil-fəl\ *adj* **1** : governed by will without regard to reason : OBSTINATE, STUBBORN **2** : INTENTIONAL ⟨~ murder⟩ — **will·ful·ly** \-lē\ *adv*

wil·lies \ˈwil-ēz\ *n pl* : a fit of nervousness : JITTERS

will·ing \ˈwil-iŋ\ *adj* **1** : inclined or favorably disposed in mind : READY ⟨~ to go⟩ **2** : prompt to act or respond ⟨~ workers⟩ **3** : done, borne, or accepted voluntarily or without reluctance : VOLUNTARY **4** : of or relating to the will : VOLITIONAL — **will·ing·ly** *adv* — **will·ing·ness** *n*

wil·li·waw \ˈwil-ē-ˌwȯ\ *n* : a sudden violent gust of cold land air common along mountainous coasts of high latitudes

will–o'–the–wisp \ˌwil-ə-t͟hə-ˈwisp\ *n* **1** : a light that appears at night over marshy grounds **2** : a misleading or elusive goal or hope

wil·low \ˈwil-ō\ *n* **1** : any of numerous quick-growing shrubs and trees with tough pliable shoots used in basketry **2** : an object made of willow wood

wil·low·ware \-ˌwaər\ *n* : dinnerware that is usu. blue and white and that is decorated with a story-telling design featuring a large willow tree by a little bridge

wil·lowy \ˈwil-ə-wē\ *adj* : PLIANT; *also* : gracefully tall and slender ⟨a ~ young woman⟩

will·pow·er \ˈwil-ˌpaů(-ə)r\ *n* : energetic determination : RESOLUTENESS

wil·ly–nil·ly \ˌwil-ē-ˈnil-ē\ *adv or adj* [alter. of *will I nill I* or *will ye nill ye* or *will he nill he*; *nill* fr. archaic *nill* to be unwilling, fr. ME *nilen*, fr. OE *nyllan*, fr. *ne* not + *wyllan* to wish] : without regard for one's choice : by compulsion ⟨they rushed us along ~⟩

[1]**wilt** \ˈwilt\ *vb* **1** : to lose or cause to lose freshness and become limp : DROOP **2** : to grow weak or faint : LANGUISH

[2]**wilt** *n* : any of various plant disorders marked by wilting and often shriveling

wily \ˈwī-lē\ *adj* **wil·i·er; -est** : full of guile : TRICKY — **wil·i·ness** \ˈwī-lē-nəs\ *n*

wimp \ˈwimp\ *n* : a weak or ineffectual person — **wimpy** \ˈwim-pē\ *adj*

[1]**wim·ple** \ˈwim-pəl\ *n* : a cloth covering worn over the head and around the neck and chin by women esp. in the late medieval period and by some nuns

[2]**wimple** *vb* **wim·pled; wim·pling** \-p(ə-)liŋ\ **1** : to cover with or as if with a wimple **2** : to ripple or cause to ripple

[1]**win** \ˈwin\ *vb* **won** \ˈwən\; **win·ning** [ME *winnen*, fr. OE *winnan* to struggle] **1** : to gain the victory in or as if in a contest : SUCCEED **2** : to get possession of esp. by effort : GAIN **3** : to gain in or as if in battle or contest; *also* : to be the victor in ⟨*won* the war⟩ **4** : to obtain by work : EARN **5** : to solicit and gain the favor of; *esp* : to induce to accept oneself in marriage

[2]**win** *n* : VICTORY; *esp* : 1st place at the finish (as of a horse race)

wince \ˈwins\ *vb* **winced; winc·ing** : to shrink back involuntarily (as from pain) : FLINCH — **wince** *n*

winch \ˈwinch\ *n* **1** : a machine that has a drum on which a rope or cable is wound for hauling or hoisting — **winch** *vb*

[1]**wind** \ˈwind\ *n* **1** : a movement of the air **2** : a force or agency that carries along or influences : TENDENCY, TREND **3** : BREATH ⟨he had the ~ knocked out of him⟩ **4** : gas generated in the stomach or intestines **5** : something insubstantial; *esp* : idle words **6** : air carrying a scent (as of game) **7** : INTIMATION ⟨they got ~ of our plans⟩ **8** : WIND INSTRUMENTS; *also, pl* : players of wind instruments

[2]**wind** *vb* **1** : to get a scent of ⟨the dogs ~*ed* the game⟩ **2** : to cause to be out of breath ⟨he was ~*ed* from the climb⟩ **3** : to allow (as a horse) to rest so as to recover breath

[3]**wind** \ˈwīnd, ˈwind\ *vb* **wind·ed** \ˈwīn-dəd, ˈwin-\ *or* **wound** \ˈwaůnd\; **wind·ing** : to sound by blowing ⟨~ a horn⟩

[4]**wind** \ˈwīnd\ *vb* **wound** \ˈwaůnd\ *also* **wind·ed; wind·ing 1** : to have a curving course or shape ⟨a river ~*ing* through the valley⟩ **2** : to move or lie so as to encircle **3** : ENTANGLE, INVOLVE **4** : to introduce stealthily : INSINUATE **5** : to encircle or cover with something pliable : WRAP, COIL, TWINE, TWIST ⟨~ a bobbin⟩ **6** : to hoist or haul by a rope or chain and a winch ⟨~ a ship to the wharf⟩ **7** : to tighten the spring of; *also* : CRANK **8** : to raise to a high level (as of excitement) **9** : to cause to move in a curving line or path **10** : to traverse on a curving course

[5]**wind** \ˈwīnd\ *n* : COIL, TURN

wind·age \ˈwin-dij\ *n* : the influence of the wind in deflecting the course of a projectile through the air; *also* : the amount of such deflection

wind·bag \ˈwin(d)-ˌbag\ *n* : an idly talkative person

wind·blown \-ˌblōn\ *adj* : blown by the wind; *also* : having the appearance of being blown by the wind

wind·break \-ˌbrāk\ *n* : something (as a growth of trees) serving as a shelter from the wind

wind–bro·ken \-ˌbrō-kən\ *adj, of a horse* : having the power of breathing impaired by disease

wind·burn \-ˌbərn\ *n* : skin irritation caused by wind

wind·chill \ˈwin(d)-ˌchil\ *n* : a still-air temperature that would have the same cooling effect on exposed human flesh as a given combination of temperature and wind speed

windchill factor *n* : WINDCHILL

wind·er \ˈwīn-dər\ *n* : one that winds

wind·fall \ˈwin(d)-ˌfȯl\ *n* **1** : something (as a tree or fruit) blown down by the wind **2** : an unexpected or sudden gift, gain, or advantage

wind·flow·er \-ˌflaů(-ə)r\ *n* : ANEMONE

[1]**wind·ing** \ˈwīn-diŋ\ *n* : material (as wire) wound or coiled about an object

[2]**winding** *adj* **1** : having a pronounced curve; *esp* : SPIRAL ⟨~ stairs⟩ **2** : having a course that winds ⟨a ~ road⟩

wind·ing–sheet \-ˌshēt\ *n* : SHROUD

wind instrument *n* : a musical instrument (as a flute or horn) sounded by wind and esp. by the breath

wind·jam·mer \ˈwin(d)-ˌjam-ər\ *n* : a sailing ship; *also* : one of its crew

wind·lass \ˈwin-dləs\ *n* [ME *wyndlas*, alter. of *wyndas*, fr. ON *vindāss*, fr. *vinda* to wind + *āss* pole] : a winch used esp. on ships for hoisting or hauling

wind·mill \ˈwin(d)-ˌmil\ *n* : a mill or machine worked by the wind turning sails or vanes that radiate from a central shaft

win·dow \ˈwin-dō\ *n* [ME *windowe*, fr. ON *vindauga*, fr. *vindr* wind + *auga* eye] **1** : an opening in the wall of a building to let in light and air; *also* : the framework with fittings that closes such an opening **2** : WINDOWPANE **3** : an opening resembling or suggesting that of a window in a building — **win·dow·less** *adj*

window dressing *n* **1** : display of merchandise in a store window **2** : a showing made to create a good but sometimes false impression

win·dow·pane \ˈwin-dō-ˌpān\ *n* : a pane in a window

win·dow–shop \-ˌshäp\ *vb* : to look at the displays in store windows without going inside the stores to make purchases — **win·dow–shop·per** *n*

win·dow·sill \-ˌsil\ *n* : the horizontal member at the bottom of a window

wind·pipe \ˈwin(d)-ˌpīp\ *n* : the passage for the breath from the larynx to the lungs

wind·proof \-ˈprüf\ *adj* : impervious to wind ⟨a ~ jacket⟩

wind·row \ˈwin-ˌ(d)rō\ *n* **1** : hay raked up into a row to dry **2** : a row of something (as dry leaves) swept up by or as if by the wind

wind shear *n* : a radical shift in wind speed and direction between slightly different altitudes

wind·shield \ˈwin(d)-ˌshēld\ *n* : a transparent screen in front of the occupants of a vehicle

wind sock *n* : an open-ended truncated cloth cone mounted in an elevated position to indicate the direction of the wind

wind·storm \-ˌstȯrm\ *n* : a storm with high wind and little or no precipitation

wind·swept \ˈwin(d)-ˌswept\ *adj* : swept by or as if by wind ⟨~ plains⟩

wind tunnel *n* : an enclosed passage through which air is blown to determine the effects of wind pressure on an object

wind·up \ˈwīn-ˌdəp\ *n* **1** : CONCLUSION, FINISH **2** : a series of regular and distinctive motions made by a pitcher preliminary to delivering a pitch

wind up \(ˈ)wīn-ˈdəp\ *vb* **1** : to bring or come to a conclusion : END **2** : SETTLE **3** : to arrive in a place, situation, or condition at the end or as a result of a course of action ⟨*wound up* as paupers⟩ **4** : to give a preliminary swing to the arm

[1]**wind·ward** \ˈwin-(d)wərd\ *n* : the point or side from which the wind is blowing

[2]**windward** *adj* : being in or facing the direction from which the wind is blowing

windy \ˈwin-dē\ *adj* **wind·i·er; -est 1** : having wind : exposed to winds ⟨a ~ day⟩ ⟨a ~ prairie⟩ **2** : STORMY **3** : FLATULENT **4** : indulging in or characterized by useless talk : VERBOSE

[1]**wine** \ˈwīn\ *n* **1** : fermented grape juice used as a beverage **2** : the usu. fermented juice of a plant product (as fruit) used as a beverage ⟨rice ~⟩

[2]**wine** *vb* **wined; win·ing** : to treat to or drink wine

wine cellar *n* : a room for storing wines; *also* : a stock of wines

wine·grow·er \-ˌgrō(-ə)r\ *n* : one that cultivates a vineyard and makes wine

wine·press \ˈwīn-ˌpres\ *n* : a vat in which juice is expressed from grapes by treading or by means of a plunger

[1]**wing** \ˈwiŋ\ *n* **1** : one of the movable feathered or membranous paired appendages by means of which a bird, bat, or insect is able to fly **2** : something suggesting a wing in position, appearance, or function **3** : a plant or animal appendage or part likened to a wing; *esp* : one that is flat or broadly extended **4** : a turned-back or extended edge on an article of clothing **5** : a means of flight or rapid progress **6** : the act or manner of flying : FLIGHT **7** *pl* : the area at the side of the stage out of sight **8** : one of the positions or players on either side of a center position or line **9** : either of two opposing groups within an organization : FACTION **10** : a unit in military aviation consisting of two or more squadrons — **wing·less** *adj* — **on the wing** : in flight : FLYING — **under one's wing** : in one's charge or care

[2]**wing** *vb* **1** : to fit with wings; *also* : to enable to fly easily **2** : to pass through in flight : FLY ⟨~ the air⟩ ⟨swallows ~*ing* southward⟩ **3** : to achieve or accomplish by flying **4** : to let fly : DISPATCH ⟨~ an arrow through the air⟩ **5** : to wound in the wing ⟨~ a bird⟩; *also* : to wound without killing

wing·ding \ˈwiŋ-ˌdiŋ\ *n* : a wild, lively, or lavish party

winged \ˈwiŋd, *also except for "esp." sense of 1* ˈwiŋ-əd\ *adj* **1** : having wings esp. of a specified character **2** : soaring with or as if with wings : ELEVATED **3** : SWIFT, RAPID

wing·span \ˈwiŋ-ˌspan\ *n* : WINGSPREAD; *esp* : the distance between the tips of an airplane's wings

wing·spread \-ˌspred\ *n* : the spread of the wings; *esp* : the distance between the tips of the fully extended wings of a winged animal

[1]**wink** \ˈwiŋk\ *vb* **1** : to close and open one eye quickly as a signal or hint **2** : to close and open the eyes quickly : BLINK **3** : to avoid seeing or noticing something ⟨~ at a violation of the law⟩ **4** : TWINKLE, FLICKER **5** : to affect or influence by or as if by blinking the eyes ⟨he ~*ed* back his tears⟩ — **wink·er** \ˈwiŋ-kər\ *n*

[2]**wink** *n* **1** : a brief period of sleep : NAP **2** : an act of winking; *esp* : a hint or sign given by winking **3** : INSTANT ⟨dries in a ~⟩

win·ner \ˈwin-ər\ *n* : one that wins

[1]**win·ning** \ˈwin-iŋ\ *n* **1** : VICTORY **2** : something won; *esp* : money won at gambling ⟨large ~*s*⟩

[2]**winning** *adj* **1** : successful esp. in competition **2** : ATTRACTIVE, CHARMING

win·now \ˈwin-ō\ *vb* **1** : to remove (as chaff from grain) by a current of air; *also* : to free (as grain) from waste in this manner **2** : to get rid of (something unwanted) or to separate, sift, or sort (something) as if by winnowing

wino \ˈwī-nō\ *n, pl* **win·os** : one who is chronically addicted to drinking wine

win·some \ˈwin-səm\ *adj* [ME *winsum,* fr. OE *wynsum,* fr. *wynn* joy] **1** : generally pleasing and engaging ⟨a ~ lass⟩ **2** : CHEERFUL, GAY — **win·some·ly** *adv* — **win·some·ness** *n*

[1]**win·ter** \ˈwint-ər\ *n* **1** : the season of the year in any region in which the noonday sun shines most obliquely : the coldest period of the year **2** : YEAR ⟨a man of 70 ~*s*⟩ **3** : a time or season of inactivity or decay

[2]**winter** *adj* : occurring in or surviving winter; *esp* : sown in autumn for harvesting in the following spring or summer ⟨~ wheat⟩

[3]**winter** *vb* **win·tered; win·ter·ing** \ˈwin-t(ə-)riŋ\ **1** : to pass or survive the winter **2** : to keep, feed, or manage through the winter ⟨~ cattle on silage⟩

win·ter·green \ˈwint-ər-ˌgrēn\ *n* **1** : a low evergreen plant of the heath family with white bell-shaped flowers and spicy red berries **2** : any of several plants related to the wintergreen **3** : an aromatic oil from the common wintergreen or its flavor or something flavored with it

win·ter·ize \ˈwint-ə-ˌrīz\ *vb* **-ized; -iz·ing** : to make ready for winter

win·ter–kill \ˈwint-ər-ˌkil\ *vb* : to kill or die by exposure to winter weather

winter squash *n* : any of various squashes or pumpkins that keep well in storage

win·ter·tide \-ˌtīd\ *n* : WINTER

win·ter·time \-ˌtīm\ *n* : WINTER

win·try \ˈwin-trē\ *also* **win·tery** \ˈwin-t(ə-)rē\ *adj* **win·tri·er; -est 1** : of, relating to, or characteristic of winter : coming in winter ⟨~ weather⟩ **2** : CHILLING, CHEERLESS ⟨a ~ welcome⟩

[1]**wipe** \ˈwīp\ *vb* **wiped; wip·ing 1** : to clean or dry by rubbing ⟨~ dishes⟩ **2** : to remove by or as if by rubbing or cleaning ⟨~ away tears⟩ **3** : to erase completely : OBLITERATE **4** : DESTROY, ANNIHILATE ⟨the platoon was *wiped* out⟩ **5** : to pass or draw over a surface ⟨*wiped* his hand across his face⟩ — **wip·er** *n*

[2]**wipe** *n* **1** : an act or instance of wiping; *also* : BLOW, STRIKE, SWIPE **2** : something used for wiping

[1]**wire** \ˈwī(ə)r\ *n* **1** : metal in the form of a thread or slender rod; *also* : a thread or rod of metal **2** *usu pl* : hidden or secret influences controlling the action of a person or body of persons ⟨pull ~*s* to get a nomination⟩ **3** : a line of wire for conducting electric current **4** : a telegraph or telephone wire or system; *esp* : WIRE SERVICE **5** : TELEGRAM, CABLEGRAM **6** : the finish line of a race

[2]**wire** *vb* **wired; wir·ing 1** : to provide or equip with wire ⟨~ a house⟩ **2** : to bind, string, or mount with wire **3** : to telegraph or telegraph to

wire·hair \ˈwī(ə)r-ˌhaər\ *n* : a wirehaired fox terrier

wire·haired \-ˈhaərd\ *adj* : having a stiff wiry outer coat of hair

[1]**wire·less** \-ləs\ *adj* **1** : having no wire or wires **2** *chiefly Brit* : RADIO

[2]**wireless** *n* **1** : wireless telegraphy **2** *chiefly Brit* : RADIO

wire–pull·er \ˈwī(ə)r-ˌpu̇l-ər\ *n* : one who uses secret or underhanded means to influence the acts of a person or organization — **wire–pull·ing** \-ˌpu̇l-iŋ\ *n*

wire service *n* : a news agency that sends out syndicated news copy by wire to subscribers

wire·tap \-ˌtap\ *vb* : to tap a telephone or telegraph wire to get information — **wiretap** *n* — **wire·tap·per** \-ˌtap-ər\ *n*

wire·worm \-ˌwərm\ *n* : the slender hard-coated larva of certain beetles that is esp. destructive to plant roots

wir·ing \ˈwī(ə)r-iŋ\ *n* **:** a system of wires; *esp* **:** one for distributing electricity through a building

wiry \ˈwī(ə)r-ē\ *adj* **wir·i·er** \ˈwī-rē-ər\; **-est 1 :** made of or resembling wire **2 :** slender yet strong and sinewy — **wir·i·ness** \ˈwī-rē-nəs\ *n*

Wis *or* **Wisc** *abbr* Wisconsin

Wisd *abbr* Wisdom

wis·dom \ˈwiz-dəm\ *n* [ME, fr. OE *wīsdom,* fr. *wīs* wise] **1 :** accumulated philosophic or scientific learning **:** KNOWLEDGE; *also* **:** INSIGHT **2 :** good sense **:** JUDGMENT **3 :** a wise attitude or course of action

Wisdom *n* — see BIBLE table

wisdom tooth *n* **:** the last tooth of the full set on each half of each jaw in man

[1]**wise** \ˈwīz\ *n* **:** WAY, MANNER, FASHION ⟨in no ~⟩ ⟨in this ~⟩

[2]**wise** *adj* **wis·er; wis·est 1 :** having wisdom **:** SAGE **2 :** having or showing good sense or good judgment **:** SENSIBLE, SOUND, PRUDENT **3 :** aware of what is going on **:** KNOWING; *also* **:** CRAFTY, SHREWD **4 :** possessing inside information — **wise·ly** *adv*

wise·acre \ˈwī-ˌzā-kər\ *n* [Middle Dutch *wijssegger* soothsayer, fr. Old High German *wīzzago*] **:** SMART ALECK

[1]**wise·crack** \ˈwīz-ˌkrak\ *n* **:** a clever, smart, or flippant remark

[2]**wisecrack** *vb* **:** to make a wisecrack

[1]**wish** \ˈwish\ *vb* **1 :** to have a desire **:** long for **:** CRAVE, WANT ⟨~ you were here⟩ ⟨~ for a puppy⟩ **2 :** to form or express a wish concerning ⟨~*ed* him a happy birthday⟩ **3 :** BID ⟨he ~*ed* me good morning⟩ **4 :** to request by expressing a desire ⟨I ~ you to go now⟩

[2]**wish** *n* **1 :** an act or instance of wishing or desire **:** WANT; *also* **:** GOAL **2 :** an expressed will or desire **:** MANDATE

wish·bone \-ˌbōn\ *n* **:** a forked bone in front of the breastbone in most birds

wish·ful \ˈwish-fəl\ *adj* **1 :** expressive of a wish **:** HOPEFUL, LONGING; *also* **:** DESIROUS **2 :** according with wishes rather than fact ⟨~ thinking⟩

wishy–washy \ˈwish-ē-ˌwȯsh-ē, -ˌwäsh-\ *adj* **:** WEAK, INSIPID; *also* **:** morally feeble

wisp \ˈwisp\ *n* **1 :** a small handful (as of hay or straw) **2 :** a thin strand, strip, or fragment ⟨a ~ of hair⟩; *also* **:** a thready streak ⟨a ~ of smoke⟩ **3 :** something frail, slight, or fleeting ⟨a ~ of a girl⟩ ⟨a ~ of a smile⟩ — **wispy** *adj*

wis·te·ria \wis-ˈtir-ē-ə\ *or* **wis·ter·ia** \-ˈtir-ē-ə *also* -ˈter-\ *n* **:** any of a genus of chiefly Asian mostly woody vines related to the peas and widely grown for their long showy clusters of blue, white, purple, or rose flowers

wist·ful \ˈwist-fəl\ *adj* **:** full of longing and unfulfilled desire **:** YEARNING ⟨a ~ expression⟩ — **wist·ful·ly** \-ē\ *adv* — **wist·ful·ness** *n*

wit \ˈwit\ *n* **1 :** reasoning power **:** INTELLIGENCE **2 :** mental soundness **:** SANITY — usu. used in pl. **3 :** RESOURCEFULNESS, INGENUITY; *esp* **:** quickness and cleverness in handling words and ideas **4 :** a talent for making clever remarks; *also* **:** one noted for making witty remarks — **at one's wit's end :** at a loss for a means of solving a problem

[1]**witch** \ˈwich\ *n* **1 :** a person believed to have magic power; *esp* **:** SORCERESS **2 :** an ugly old woman **:** HAG **3 :** a charming or alluring girl or woman

[2]**witch** *vb* **:** BEWITCH

witch·craft \ˈwich-ˌkraft\ *n* **:** the power or practices of a witch **:** SORCERY

witch doctor *n* **:** a practitioner of magic in a primitive society

witch·ery \ˈwich-(ə-)rē\ *n, pl* **-er·ies 1 :** SORCERY **2 :** FASCINATION, CHARM

witch·grass \ˈwich-ˌgras\ *n* **:** any of several grasses that are weeds in cultivated areas

witch ha·zel \ˈwich-ˌhā-zəl\ *n* **1 :** a No. American shrub bearing small yellow flowers in the fall **2 :** an alcoholic solution of material from witch hazel bark used as a soothing astringent lotion

witch–hunt \ˈwich-ˌhənt\ *n* **1 :** a searching out and persecution of persons accused of witchcraft **2 :** the searching out and deliberate harassment of those (as political opponents) with unpopular views

witch·ing \ˈwich-iŋ\ *adj* **:** of, relating to, or suitable for sorcery or supernatural occurrences

wi·te·na·ge·mot *or* **wi·te·na·ge·mote** \ˈwit-ᵊn-ə-gə-ˌmōt\ *n* [OE *witena gemōt,* fr. *witena* (gen. pl. of *wita* sage, adviser) + *gemōt* assembly] **:** an Anglo-Saxon council of nobles, prelates, and officials to advise the king on administrative and judicial matters

with \(ˈ)with, (ˈ)with\ *prep* **1 :** AGAINST ⟨a fight ~ his wife⟩ **2 :** FROM ⟨parting ~ friends⟩ **3 :** in mutual relation to ⟨talk ~ a friend⟩ **4 :** in the company of ⟨a professor ~ her students⟩ **5 :** AS REGARDS, TOWARD ⟨is patient ~ the children⟩ **6 :** compared to ⟨on equal terms ~ another⟩ **7 :** in support of ⟨I'm ~ you all the way⟩ **8 :** in the presence of **:** CONTAINING ⟨tea ~ sugar⟩ **9 :** in the opinion of **:** as judged by ⟨their arguments had weight ~ him⟩ **10 :** BECAUSE OF, THROUGH ⟨pale ~ anger⟩ **11 :** in a manner indicating ⟨work ~ a will⟩ **12 :** GIVEN, GRANTED ⟨~ your permission I'll leave⟩ **13 :** HAVING ⟨came ~ good news⟩ ⟨stood there ~ his mouth open⟩ **14 :** at the time of **:** right after ⟨~ that he left⟩ **15 :** DESPITE ⟨~ all her cleverness, she failed⟩ **16 :** so as not to cross or oppose ⟨swim ~ the tide⟩

with·al \wi-ˈthȯl, with-\ *adv* **1 :** together with this **:** BESIDES **2** *archaic* **:** THEREWITH **3 :** on the other hand **:** NEVERTHELESS

with·draw \with-ˈdrȯ, with-\ *vb* **-drew** \-ˈdrü\; **-drawn** \-ˈdrȯn\; **-draw·ing** \-ˈdrȯ(-)iŋ\ **1 :** to take back or away **:** draw away **:** REMOVE **2 :** to call back (as from consideration) **:** RECALL, RESCIND; *also* **:** RETRACT ⟨~ an accusation⟩ **3 :** to go away **:** RETREAT, LEAVE **4 :** to terminate one's participation in or use of something

with·draw·al \-ˈdrȯ(-ə-)l\ *n* **1 :** an act or instance of withdrawing **2 :** the discontinuance of the use or administration of a drug and esp. a habit-forming drug; *also* **:** the often painful physiological and psychological symptoms produced by withdrawal **3 :** a pathological retreat from the real world (as in some schizophrenic states)

with·drawn \with-ˈdrȯn\ *adj* **1 :** ISOLATED, SECLUDED **2 :** socially detached and unresponsive

withe \ˈwith\ *n* **:** a slender flexible twig or branch; *esp* **:** one used as a band or rope

with·er \ˈwith-ər\ *vb* **with·ered; with·er·ing** \-(ə-)riŋ\ **1 :** to become dry and shrunken; *esp* **:** to shrivel from or as if from loss of bodily moisture **2 :** to lose or cause to lose vitality, force, or freshness **3 :** to cause to feel shriveled or blighted **:** STUN ⟨~*ed* him with a glance⟩

with·ers \ˈwith-ərz\ *n pl* **:** the ridge between the shoulder bones of a horse; *also* **:** the corresponding part in other 4-footed animals

with·hold \with-ˈhōld, with-\ *vb* **-held** \-ˈheld\; **-hold·ing 1 :** to hold back **:** RESTRAIN; *also* **:** RETAIN **2 :** to refrain from granting, giving, or allowing ⟨~ permission⟩ ⟨~ names⟩

withholding tax *n* **:** a tax on income withheld at the source

[1]**with·in** \with-ˈin, with-\ *adv* **1 :** in or into the interior **:** INSIDE **2 :** inside oneself **:** INWARDLY ⟨calm without but furious ~⟩

[2]**within** *prep* **1 :** inside the limits or influence of ⟨~ call⟩ **2 :** in the limits or compass of ⟨~ a mile⟩ **3 :** in or to the inner part of ⟨~ the room⟩

[3]**within** *n* **:** an inner place or area ⟨revolt from ~⟩

with–it \ˈwith-ət\ *adj* **:** socially or culturally up-to-date

[1]**with·out** \with-ˈau̇t, with-\ *prep* **1 :** OUTSIDE **2 :** LACKING ⟨she's ~ hope⟩; *also* **:** not accompanied by or showing ⟨spoke ~ thinking⟩ ⟨took his punishment ~ flinching⟩

[2]**without** *adv* **1** : on the outside : ETERNALLY **2** : with something lacking or absent ⟨has learned to do ∼⟩

with·stand \with-ˈstand, wit͟h-\ *vb* **-stood** \-ˈstu̇d\; **-stand·ing** : to stand against : RESIST; *esp* : to oppose (as an attack) successfully

wit·less \ˈwit-ləs\ *adj* : lacking wit or understanding : mentally defective : FOOLISH — **wit·less·ly** *adv* — **wit·less·ness** *n*

[1]**wit·ness** \ˈwit-nəs\ *n* [ME *witnesse,* fr. OE *witnes* knowledge, testimony, witness, fr. *wit* mind, intelligence] **1** : TESTIMONY ⟨bear ∼ to the fact⟩ **2** : one that gives evidence; *esp* : one who testifies in a cause or before a court **3** : one present at a transaction so as to be able to testify that it has taken place **4** : one who has personal knowledge or experience of something **5** : something serving as evidence or proof : SIGN

[2]**witness** *vb* **1** : to bear witness : TESTIFY **2** : to act as legal witness of **3** : to furnish proof of : BETOKEN **4** : to be a witness of **5** : to be the scene of ⟨this region has ∼*ed* many wars⟩

wit·ted \ˈwit-əd\ *adj* : having wit or understanding ⟨dull-*witted*⟩

wit·ti·cism \ˈwit-ə-ˌsiz-əm\ *n* : a witty saying or phrase

wit·ting \ˈwit-iŋ\ *adj* : done knowingly : INTENTIONAL — **wit·ting·ly** *adv*

wit·ty \ˈwit-ē\ *adj* **wit·ti·er; -est** : marked by or full of wit : AMUSING ⟨a ∼ writer⟩ ⟨a ∼ remark⟩ **syn** humorous, facetious, jocular, jocose — **wit·ti·ly** \ˈwit-ᵊl-ē\ *adv* — **wit·ti·ness** \-ē-nəs\ *n*

wive \ˈwīv\ *vb* **wived; wiv·ing 1** : to marry a woman **2** : to take for a wife

wives *pl of* WIFE

wiz·ard \ˈwiz-ərd\ *n* [ME *wysard* wise man, fr. *wys* wise] **1** : MAGICIAN, SORCERER **2** : a very clever or skillful person ⟨a ∼ at chess⟩

wiz·ard·ry \ˈwiz-ə(r)-drē\ *n, pl* **-ries 1** : magic skill : SORCERY, WITCHCRAFT **2** : great skill or cleverness in an activity

wiz·ened \ˈwiz-ᵊnd\ *adj* : dried up : SHRIVELED, WITHERED

wk *abbr* **1** week **2** work

WL *abbr* wavelength

wmk *abbr* watermark

WNW *abbr* west-northwest

WO *abbr* warrant officer

w/o *abbr* without

woad \ˈwōd\ *n* : a European herb related to the mustards; *also* : a blue dyestuff made from its leaves

wob·ble \ˈwäb-əl\ *vb* **wob·bled; wob·bling** \-(ə-)liŋ\ **1** : to move or cause to move with an irregular rocking or side-to-side motion **2** : TREMBLE, QUAVER **3** : WAVER, VACILLATE — **wobble** *n* — **wob·bly** \ˈwäb-(ə-)lē\ *adj*

woe \ˈwō\ *n* **1** : a condition of deep suffering from misfortune, affliction, or grief **2** : CALAMITY, MISFORTUNE ⟨economic ∼*s*⟩

woe·be·gone \ˈwō-bi-ˌgȯn\ *adj* : exhibiting woe, sorrow, or misery; *also* : DISMAL, DESOLATE

woe·ful *also* **wo·ful** \ˈwō-fəl\ *adj* **1** : full of woe : AFFLICTED **2** : involving, bringing, or relating to woe **3** : PALTRY, DEPLORABLE — **woe·ful·ly** \-ē\ *adv*

wok \ˈwäk\ *n* : a bowl-shaped cooking utensil used esp. in the preparation of Chinese food

woke *past of* WAKE

woken *past part of* WAKE

wold \ˈwōld\ *n* : an upland plain or stretch of rolling land without woods

[1]**wolf** \ˈwu̇lf\ *n, pl* **wolves** \ˈwu̇lvz\ **1** : any of several large erect-eared bushy-tailed doglike predatory mammals that often hunt in packs **2** : a fierce or destructive person **3** : a man forward, direct, and zealous in amatory attentions to women — **wolf·ish** *adj*

[2]**wolf** *vb* : to eat greedily : DEVOUR

wolf·hound \-ˌhau̇nd\ *n* : any of several large dogs orig. used in hunting wolves

wol·fram \ˈwu̇l-frəm\ *n* : TUNGSTEN

wol·ver·ine \ˌwu̇l-və-ˈrēn\ *n, pl* **wolverines** *also* **wolverine** : a dark shaggy-coated flesh-eating mammal of northern forests and associated tundra that is related to the weasels and sables

wom·an \ˈwu̇m-ən\ *n, pl* **wom·en** \ˈwim-ən\ [ME, fr. OE *wīfman,* fr. *wīf* woman, wife + *man* human being, man] **1** : an adult female person **2** : WOMANKIND **3** : feminine nature : WOMANLINESS **4** : a female servant or attendant

wom·an·hood \ˈwu̇m-ən-ˌhu̇d\ *n* **1** : the state of being a woman : the distinguishing qualities of a woman or of womankind **2** : WOMEN, WOMANKIND

wom·an·ish \ˈwu̇m-ə-nish\ *adj* **1** : of, relating to, or characteristic of a woman **2** : suitable to a woman rather than to a man : EFFEMINATE

wom·an·kind \ˈwu̇m-ən-ˌkīnd\ *n* : the females of the human race : WOMEN

wom·an·like \-ˌlīk\ *adj* : WOMANLY

wom·an·ly \-lē\ *adj* : having qualities characteristic of a woman — **wom·an·li·ness** \-lē-nəs\ *n*

woman suffrage *n* : possession and exercise of suffrage by women

womb \ˈwüm\ *n* **1** : UTERUS **2** : a place where something is generated or developed

wom·bat \ˈwäm-ˌbat\ *n* : any of several stocky burrowing Australian marsupials that resemble small bears

wom·en·folk \ˈwim-ən-ˌfōk\ *also* **wom·en·folks** \-ˌfōks\ *n pl* : WOMEN

[1]**won** \ˈwən\ *past and past part of* WIN

[2]**won** \ˈwȯn\ *n, pl* **won** — see MONEY table

[1]**won·der** \ˈwən-dər\ *n* **1** : a cause of astonishment or surprise : MARVEL; *also* : MIRACLE **2** : the quality of exciting wonder ⟨the charm and ∼ of the scene⟩ **3** : a feeling (as of awed astonishment or uncertainty) aroused by something extraordinary or affecting

[2]**wonder** *vb* **won·dered; won·der·ing** \-d(ə-)riŋ\ **1** : to feel surprise or amazement **2** : to feel curiosity or doubt

wonder drug *n* : MIRACLE DRUG

won·der·ful \ˈwən-dər-fəl\ *adj* **1** : exciting wonder : MARVELOUS, ASTONISHING **2** : unusually good : ADMIRABLE — **won·der·ful·ly** \-f(ə-)lē\ *adv* — **won·der·ful·ness** \-fəl-nəs\ *n*

won·der·land \-ˌland, -lənd\ *n* **1** : an imaginary place of delicate beauty or magical charm **2** : a place that excites admiration or wonder

won·der·ment \-mənt\ *n* **1** : ASTONISHMENT, SURPRISE **2** : a cause of or occasion for wonder **3** : curiosity about something

won·drous \ˈwən-drəs\ *adj* : WONDERFUL, MARVELOUS — **wondrous** *adv, archaic* — **won·drous·ly** *adv* — **won·drous·ness** *n*

[1]**wont** \ˈwȯnt, ˈwōnt\ *adj* [ME *woned, wont,* fr. pp. of *wonen* to dwell, be used to, fr. OE *wunian*] **1** : ACCUSTOMED, USED ⟨as he was ∼ to do⟩ **2** : INCLINED, APT

[2]**wont** *n* : CUSTOM, USAGE, HABIT ⟨according to her ∼⟩

wont·ed \ˈwȯnt-əd, ˈwōnt-\ *adj* : ACCUSTOMED, CUSTOMARY ⟨his ∼ courtesy⟩

woo \ˈwü\ *vb* **1** : to try to gain the love of and usu. marriage with : COURT **2** : SOLICIT, ENTREAT **3** : to try to gain or bring about ⟨∼ public favor⟩ — **woo·er** *n*

[1]**wood** \ˈwu̇d\ *n* **1** : a dense growth of trees usu. larger than a grove and smaller than a forest — often used in pl. **2** : a hard fibrous substance that is basically xylem and forms the bulk of trees and shrubs beneath the bark; *also* : this material fit or prepared for some use (as burning or building) **3** : something made of wood

[2]**wood** *adj* **1** : WOODEN **2** : suitable for holding, cutting, or

working with wood **3** *or* **woods** \ˈwu̇dz\ : living or growing in woods

[3]**wood** *vb* **1** : to supply or load with wood esp. for fuel **2** : to cover with a growth of trees

wood alcohol *n* : METHANOL

wood·bine \ˈwu̇d-ˌbīn\ *n* : any of several climbing vines (as a honeysuckle or Virginia creeper)

wood·block \-ˌbläk\ *n* **1** : a block of wood **2** : WOODCUT

wood·chop·per \-ˌchäp-ər\ *n* : one engaged esp. in chopping down trees

wood·chuck \-ˌchək\ *n* : any of several No. American marmots; *esp* : a thickset grizzled marmot of the northeastern U.S. and Canada

wood·cock \ˈwu̇d-ˌkäk\ *n, pl* **woodcocks** : a brown No. American game bird with a short neck and long bill that is related to the snipe; *also* : a related and similar bird widespread in the Old World

wood·craft \-ˌkraft\ *n* **1** : skill and practice in matters relating to the woods esp. in maintaining oneself and making one's way or in hunting or trapping **2** : skill in shaping or constructing articles from wood

wood·cut \-ˌkət\ *n* **1** : a relief printing surface engraved on wood **2** : a print from a woodcut

wood·cut·ter \-ˌkət-ər\ *n* : a person who cuts wood esp. as an occupation

wood·ed \ˈwu̇d-əd\ *adj* : covered with woods or trees ⟨~ slopes⟩

wood·en \ˈwu̇d-ᵊn\ *adj* **1** : made of wood **2** : lacking resilience : STIFF **3** : AWKWARD, CLUMSY — **wood·en·ly** *adv* — **wood·en·ness** \-ᵊn-(n)əs\ *n*

wood·en·ware \ˈwu̇d-ᵊn-ˌwaər\ *n* : articles made of wood for domestic use

wood·land \ˈwu̇d-lənd, -ˌland\ *n* : land covered with trees : FOREST

wood·lot \ˈwu̇d-ˌlät\ *n* : a relatively small area of trees kept usu. to meet fuel and timber needs ⟨a farm ~⟩

wood louse *n* : a small flat grayish crustacean that lives esp. under stones and bark

wood·man \ˈwu̇d-mən\ *n* : WOODSMAN

wood·note \-ˌnōt\ *n* : verbal expression that is natural and artless

wood nymph *n* : a nymph living in the woods

wood·peck·er \ˈwu̇d-ˌpek-ər\ *n* : any of various usu. brightly marked climbing birds with stiff spiny tail feathers and a chisellike bill used to drill into trees for insects

wood·pile \-ˌpīl\ *n* : a pile of wood and esp. firewood

wood·shed \-ˌshed\ *n* : a shed for storing wood and esp. firewood

woods·man \ˈwu̇dz-mən\ *n* : a person who frequents or works in the woods; *esp* : one skilled in woodcraft

woodsy \ˈwu̇d-zē\ *adj* : relating to or suggestive of woods

wood·wind \ˈwu̇d-ˌwind\ *n* : one of a group of wind instruments including flutes, clarinets, oboes, bassoons, and sometimes saxophones

wood·work \-ˌwərk\ *n* **1** : work made of wood; *esp* : interior fittings (as moldings or stairways) of wood **2** : a place of hiding or seclusion ⟨came out of the ~ to claim the lost money⟩

woody \ˈwu̇d-ē\ *adj* **wood·i·er; -est 1** : abounding or overgrown with woods **2** : of or containing wood or wood fibers **3** : resembling or characteristic of wood — **wood·i·ness** \ˈwu̇d-ē-nəs\ *n*

woof \ˈwu̇f\ *n* [alter. of ME *oof,* fr. OE *ōwef,* fr. *ō-* (fr. *on* on) + *wefan* to weave] **1** : the threads in a woven fabric that cross the warp **2** : a woven fabric; *also* : its texture

woof·er \ˈwu̇f-ər\ *n* : a loudspeaker that reproduces sounds of low pitch

wool \ˈwu̇l\ *n* **1** : the soft wavy or curly hair of some mammals and esp. the domestic sheep; *also* : something (as a textile or garment) made of wool **2** : material that resembles a mass of wool — **wooled** \ˈwu̇ld\ *adj*

[1]**wool·en** *or* **wool·len** \ˈwu̇l-ən\ *adj* **1** : made of wool **2** : of or relating to the manufacture or sale of woolen products ⟨~ mills⟩

[2]**woolen** *or* **woollen** *n* **1** : a fabric made of wool **2** : garments of woolen fabric — usu. used in pl.

wool·gath·er·ing \-ˌgath-(ə-)riŋ\ *n* : the act of indulging in idle daydreaming

[1]**wool·ly** *also* **wooly** \ˈwu̇l-ē\ *adj* **wool·li·er; -est 1** : of, relating to, or bearing wool **2** : consisting of or resembling wool **3** : CONFUSED, BLURRY ⟨~ thinking⟩ **4** : marked by a lack of order or restraint ⟨the wild and ~ West of frontier times⟩

[2]**wool·ly** *also* **wool·ie** *or* **wooly** \ˈwu̇l-ē\ *n, pl* **wool·lies** : a garment made from wool; *esp* : underclothing of knitted wool

woolly aphid *n* : a plant louse covered with a dense coat of white filaments

woolly aphis *n* : WOOLLY APHID

woolly bear *n* : any of numerous very hairy caterpillars

wool·sack \ˈwu̇l-ˌsak\ *n* **1** *archaic* : a sack of or for wool **2** : the seat of the Lord Chancellor in the House of Lords

woo·zy \ˈwü-zē\ *adj* **woo·zi·er; -est 1** : BEFUDDLED **2** : somewhat dizzy, nauseated, or weak — **woo·zi·ness** \ˈwü-zē-nəs\ *n*

[1]**word** \ˈwərd\ *n* **1** : something that is said; *esp* : a brief remark **2** : a speech sound or series of speech sounds that communicates a meaning; *also* : a graphic representation of such a sound or series of sounds **3** : ORDER, COMMAND **4** *often cap* : the 2d person of the Trinity; *also* : GOSPEL **5** : NEWS, INFORMATION **6** : PROMISE **7** *pl* : QUARREL, DISPUTE **8** : a verbal signal : PASSWORD — **word·less** *adj*

[2]**word** *vb* : to express in words : PHRASE

word·age \ˈwərd-ij\ *n* **1** : WORDS **2** : number of words **3** : WORDING

word·book \ˈwərd-ˌbu̇k\ *n* : VOCABULARY, DICTIONARY

word·ing \ˈwərd-iŋ\ *n* : verbal expression : PHRASEOLOGY

word of mouth : oral communication

word·play \ˈwərd-ˌplā\ *n* : verbal wit

word processing *n* : the production of typewritten documents with automated and usu. computerized text-editing equipment

word processor *n* : a keyboard-operated terminal with a video display and a magnetic storage device for use in word processing; *also* : software to perform word processing

wordy \ˈwərd-ē\ *adj* **word·i·er; -est** : using many words : VERBOSE **syn** prolix, diffuse, redundant — **word·i·ness** \ˈwərd-ē-nəs\ *n*

wore *past of* WEAR

[1]**work** \ˈwərk\ *n* **1** : TOIL, LABOR; *also* : EMPLOYMENT ⟨out of ~⟩ **2** : TASK, JOB ⟨have ~ to do⟩ **3** : the transference of energy when a force produces movement of a body **4** : DEED, ACHIEVEMENT **5** : a fortified structure of any kind **6** *pl* : engineering structures **7** *pl* : the buildings, grounds, and machinery of a factory **8** *pl* : the moving parts of a mechanism **9** : something produced by mental effort or physical labor; *esp* : an artistic production (as a book or needlework) **10** : WORKMANSHIP ⟨careless ~⟩ **11** : material in the process of manufacture **12** *pl* : everything possessed, available, or belonging ⟨the whole ~*s* went overboard⟩; *also* : subjection to drastic treatment ⟨gave him the ~*s*⟩ **syn** occupation, employment, business, pursuit, calling — **in the works** : in process of preparation

[2]**work** *adj* **1** : used for work ⟨~ elephants⟩ **2** : suitable or styled for wear while working ⟨~ clothes⟩

[3]**work** *vb* **worked** \ˈwərkt\ *or* **wrought** \ˈrȯt\; **work·ing 1** : to bring to pass : EFFECT **2** : to fashion or create a useful or desired product through labor or exertion **3** : to prepare for use (as by kneading) **4** : to bring into a desired form by a process of cutting, hammering, scraping, pressing, or stretching ⟨~ cold steel⟩ **5** : to set or

keep in operation : OPERATE ⟨a pump ~*ed* by hand⟩ **6** : to solve by reasoning or calculation ⟨~ a problem⟩ **7** : to cause to toil or labor ⟨~*ed* his men hard⟩; *also* : EXPLOIT **8** : to pay for with labor or service ⟨~ off a debt⟩ **9** : to bring into some (specified) position or condition by stages ⟨the stream ~*ed* itself clear⟩ **10** : CONTRIVE, ARRANGE ⟨we'll go if we can ~ it⟩ **11** : to practice trickery or cajolery on for some end ⟨~*ed* the management for a free ticket⟩ **12** : EXCITE, PROVOKE ⟨~*ed* himself into a rage⟩ **13** : to exert oneself physically or mentally; *esp* : to perform work regularly for wages **14** : to function according to plan or design **15** : to produce a desired effect : SUCCEED **16** : to make way slowly and with difficulty ⟨he ~*ed* forward through the crowd⟩ **17** : to permit of being worked ⟨this wood ~*s* easily⟩ **18** : to be in restless motion; *also* : FERMENT 1 **19** : to move slightly in relation to another part; *also* : to get into a specified condition slowly or imperceptibly ⟨the knot ~*ed* loose⟩ — **work on 1** : AFFECT **2** : to try to influence or persuade — **work upon** : to have effect upon : operate on : PERSUADE, INFLUENCE

work·able \ˈwər-kə-bəl\ *adj* **1** : capable of being worked **2** : PRACTICABLE, FEASIBLE — **work·able·ness** *n*

work·a·day \ˈwərk-ə-ˌdā\ *adj* **1** : relating to or suited for working days **2** : PROSAIC, ORDINARY

work·a·hol·ic \ˌwərk-ə-ˈhȯl-ik, -ˈhäl-\ *n* : a compulsive worker

work·bag \ˈwərk-ˌbag\ *n* : a bag for holding implements or materials for work; *esp* : a bag for needlework

work·bas·ket \-ˌbas-kət\ *n* : a basket for needlework

work·bench \-ˌbench\ *n* : a bench on which work esp. of mechanics, machinists, and carpenters is performed

work·book \-ˌbu̇k\ *n* **1** : a booklet outlining a course of study **2** : a worker's manual **3** : a record of work done **4** : a student's book of problems to be answered directly on the pages

work·box \-ˌbäks\ *n* : a box for work instruments and materials

work·day \ˈwərk-ˌdā\ *n* **1** : a day on which work is done as distinguished from a day off **2** : the period of time in a day when work is performed

work·er \ˈwər-kər\ *n* **1** : one that works; *esp* : a person who works for wages **2** : one of the sexually undeveloped individuals of a colony of social insects (as bees, ants, or termites) that perform the work of the community

work ethic *n* : belief in work as a moral good

work farm *n* : a farm on which persons guilty of minor law violations are confined

work·horse \ˈwərk-ˌhȯrs\ *n* **1** : a horse used chiefly for labor **2** : a person who undertakes arduous labor

work·house \-ˌhau̇s\ *n* **1** *Brit* : POORHOUSE **2** : a house of correction where persons who have committed minor offenses are confined

[1]**work·ing** \ˈwər-kiŋ\ *adj* **1** : adequate to allow work to be done ⟨a ~ majority⟩ ⟨a ~ knowledge of French⟩ **2** : adopted or assumed to help further work or activity ⟨a ~ draft of a treaty⟩ **3** : engaged in work ⟨a ~ journalist⟩ **4** : spent at work ⟨~ life⟩

[2]**working** *n* **1** : manner of functioning : OPERATION **2** *pl* : an excavation made in mining or tunneling

work·ing·man \ˈwər-kiŋ-ˌman\ *n* : one who works for wages usu. at manual labor

work·man \ˈwərk-mən\ *n* **1** : WORKINGMAN **2** : ARTISAN, CRAFTSMAN

work·man·like \-ˌlīk\ *adj* : worthy of a good workman : SKILLFUL

work·man·ship \-ˌship\ *n* : the art or skill of a workman : CRAFTSMANSHIP; *also* : the quality imparted to something in the process of making it ⟨a vase of exquisite ~⟩

work·out \ˈwərk-ˌau̇t\ *n* **1** : a practice or exercise to test or improve one's fitness esp. for athletic competition, ability, or performance **2** : a test or trial to determine ability or capacity or suitability

work out \ˌwərk-ˈau̇t, ˈwərk-\ *vb* **1** : to bring about esp. by resolving difficulties **2** : DEVELOP, ELABORATE **3** : to prove effective, practicable, or suitable **4** : to amount to a total or calculated figure — used with *at* **5** : to engage in a workout

work·room \ˈwərk-ˌrüm, -ˌru̇m\ *n* : a room used esp. for manual work

work·shop \-ˌshäp\ *n* **1** : a small establishment where manufacturing or handicrafts are carried on **2** : a seminar emphasizing exchange of ideas and practical methods and given mainly for adults already employed in the field

work·sta·tion \-ˌstā-shən\ *n* : an area with equipment for a single worker; *also* : a usu. intelligent terminal connected to a computer network

work·ta·ble \-ˌtā-bəl\ *n* : a table for holding working materials and implements (as for needlework)

world \ˈwərld\ *n* [ME, fr. OE *woruld* human existence, this world, age, fr. a prehistoric compound whose first constituent is represented by OE *wer* man and whose second constituent is akin to OE *eald* old] **1** : the earth with its inhabitants and all things upon it **2** : people in general : MANKIND **3** : the affairs of men ⟨withdraw from the ~⟩ **4** : UNIVERSE, CREATION **5** : a state of existence : scene of life and action ⟨the ~ of the future⟩ **6** : a distinctive class of persons or their sphere of interest ⟨the musical ~⟩ **7** : a part or section of the earth or its inhabitants by itself **8** : a great number or quantity ⟨a ~ of troubles⟩ **9** : a celestial body esp. if inhabited

world–beat·er \-ˌbēt-ər\ *n* : one that excels all others of its kind : CHAMPION

world·ling \-liŋ\ *n* : a person absorbed in the affairs and pleasures of the present world

world·ly \ˈwərld-lē\ *adj* **1** : of, relating to, or devoted to this world and its pursuits rather than to religion or spiritual affairs **2** : WORLDLY-WISE, SOPHISTICATED — **world·li·ness** \-lē-nəs\ *n*

world·ly–wise \-ˌwīz\ *adj* : possessing a practical and often shrewd understanding of human affairs

world·wide \ˈwərld-ˈwīd\ *adj* : extended throughout the entire world ⟨~ fame⟩

[1]**worm** \ˈwərm\ *n* **1** : any of various small long usu. naked and soft-bodied round or flat invertebrate animals (as an earthworm, nematode, tapeworm, or maggot) **2** : a human being who is an object of contempt, loathing, or pity : WRETCH **3** : something that inwardly torments or devours **4** *pl* : infestation with or disease caused by parasitic worms **5** : a spiral or wormlike thing (as the thread of a screw) — **wormy** *adj*

[2]**worm** *vb* **1** : to free from worms ⟨~ a dog⟩ **2** : to move or cause to move or proceed slowly and deviously **3** : to obtain or extract by artful or insidious pleading, asking, or persuading ⟨~*ed* the truth out of him⟩ **4** : to insinuate or introduce (oneself) by devious or subtle means

worm–eat·en \ˈwərm-ˌēt-ᵊn\ *adj* **1** : eaten or burrowed by worms **2** : PITTED **3** : WORN-OUT, ANTIQUATED ⟨tried to update the ~ regulations⟩

worm gear *n* : a mechanical linkage consisting of a short rotating screw whose threads mesh with the teeth of a gear wheel

worm·hole \ˈwərm-ˌhōl\ *n* : a hole or passage burrowed by a worm

worm·wood \ˈwərm-ˌwu̇d\ *n* **1** : any of a genus of aromatic woody plants including the sagebrush and related plants; *esp* : one of Europe used in making absinthe **2** : something bitter or grievous : BITTERNESS

worn *past part of* WEAR
worn–out \ˈwōrn-ˈau̇t\ *adj* : exhausted or used up by or as if by wear ⟨an old ~ suit⟩ ⟨a ~ automobile⟩
wor·ri·some \ˈwər-ē-səm\ *adj* **1** : causing distress or worry **2** : inclined to worry or fret
[1]**wor·ry** \ˈwər-ē\ *vb* **wor·ried; wor·ry·ing 1** : to shake and mangle with the teeth ⟨a terrier ~*ing* a rat⟩ **2** : to make anxious or upset ⟨his poor health *worries* his parents⟩ **3** : to feel or express great care or anxiety : FRET — **wor·ri·er** *n*
[2]**worry** *n, pl* **worries 1** : ANXIETY **2** : a cause of anxiety : TROUBLE
wor·ry·wart \ˈwər-ē-ˌwȯrt\ *n* : one who is inclined to worry unduly
[1]**worse** \ˈwərs\ *adj, comparative of* BAD *or of* ILL **1** : bad or evil in a greater degree : less good; *esp* : more unwell **2** : more unfavorable, unpleasant, or painful
[2]**worse** *n* **1** : one that is worse **2** : a greater degree of ill or badness
[3]**worse** *adv, comparative of* BAD *or of* ILL : in a worse manner : to a worse extent or degree
wors·en \ˈwərs-ᵊn\ *vb* **wors·ened; wors·en·ing** \ˈwərs-(ᵊ-)niŋ\ : to make or become worse
[1]**wor·ship** \ˈwər-shəp\ *n* [ME *worshipe* worthiness, repute, respect, reverence paid to a divine being, fr. OE *weorthscipe* worthiness, repute, respect, fr. *weorth* worthy, worth + *-scipe* -ship, suffix denoting quality or condition] **1** *chiefly Brit* : a person of importance — used as a title for officials (as magistrates and some mayors) **2** : reverence toward a divine being or supernatural power; *also* : the expression of such reverence **3** : extravagant respect or admiration for or devotion to an object of esteem ⟨~ of the dollar⟩
[2]**worship** *vb* **-shiped** *or* **-shipped; -ship·ing** *or* **-ship·ping 1** : to honor or reverence as a divine being or supernatural power **2** : IDOLIZE **3** : to perform or take part in worship — **wor·ship·er** *or* **wor·ship·per** *n*
wor·ship·ful \ˈwər-shəp-fəl\ *adj* **1** *archaic* : NOTABLE, DISTINGUISHED **2** *chiefly Brit* — used as a title for various persons or groups of rank or distinction **3** : VENERATING, WORSHIPING
[1]**worst** \ˈwərst\ *adj, superlative of* BAD *or of* ILL **1** : most bad, evil, ill, or corrupt **2** : most unfavorable, unpleasant, or painful; *also* : most unsuitable, faulty, or unattractive **3** : least skillful or efficient **4** : most wanting in quality, value, or condition
[2]**worst** *adv, superlative of* ILL *or of* BAD *or* BADLY : to the extreme degree of badness or inferiority : in the worst manner
[3]**worst** *n* : one that is worst
[4]**worst** *vb* : DEFEAT
wor·sted \ˈwu̇s-təd, ˈwər-stəd\ *n* [ME, fr. *Worsted* (now *Worstead*), England] : a smooth compact yarn from long wool fibers used esp. for firm napless fabrics, carpeting, or knitting; *also* : a fabric made from such yarn
wort \ˈwərt, ˈwȯrt\ *n* : a solution obtained by infusion from malt and fermented to form beer
[1]**worth** \ˈwərth\ *prep* **1** : equal in value to; *also* : having possessions or income equal to **2** : deserving of ⟨well ~ the effort⟩
[2]**worth** *n* **1** : monetary value : the equivalent of a specified amount or figure **2** : the value of something measured by its qualities or by the esteem in which it is held **3** : moral or personal value : MERIT, EXCELLENCE **4** : WEALTH, RICHES
worth·less \ˈwərth-ləs\ *adj* **1** : lacking worth : VALUELESS; *also* : USELESS **2** : LOW, DESPICABLE — **worth·less·ness** *n*
worth·while \ˈwərth-ˈhwīl\ *adj* : being worth the time or effort spent
[1]**wor·thy** \ˈwər-t͟hē\ *adj* **wor·thi·er; -est 1** : having worth or value : ESTIMABLE **2** : HONORABLE, MERITORIOUS **3** : having sufficient worth ⟨a man ~ of the honor⟩ — **wor·thi·ly** \ˈwər-t͟hə-lē\ *adv* — **wor·thi·ness** \-t͟hē-nəs\ *n*
[2]**worthy** *n, pl* **worthies** : a worthy person
would \wəd, əd, d, (ˈ)wu̇d\ *past of* WILL **1** *archaic* : wish for : WANT **2** : strongly desire : WISH ⟨I ~ I were young again⟩ **3** — used as an auxiliary to express (1) preference ⟨~ rather run than fight⟩, (2) wish, desire, or intent ⟨those who ~ forbid gambling⟩, (3) habitual action ⟨we ~ meet often for lunch⟩, (4) a contingency or possibility ⟨if he were coming, he ~ be here by now⟩, (5) probability ⟨~ have won if he hadn't tripped⟩, or (6) a request ⟨~ you help us⟩ **4** : COULD **5** : SHOULD
would–be \ˌwu̇d-ˌbē\ *adj* : desiring, professing, or having the potential to be ⟨a ~ artist⟩
[1]**wound** \ˈwünd\ *n* **1** : an injury involving cutting or breaking of bodily tissue (as by violence, accident, or surgery) **2** : an injury or hurt to feelings or reputation
[2]**wound** *vb* : to inflict a wound to or in
[3]**wound** \ˈwau̇nd\ *past and past part of* WIND
wove *past of* WEAVE
woven *past part of* WEAVE
[1]**wow** \ˈwau̇\ *n* : a striking success : HIT
[2]**wow** *vb* : to arouse enthusiastic approval
[3]**wow** *n* : a distortion in reproduced sound consisting of a slow rise and fall of pitch caused by speed variation in the reproducing system
WP *abbr* word processing; word processor
WPM *abbr* words per minute
wpn *abbr* weapon
[1]**wrack** \ˈrak\ *n* **1** : a wrecked ship; *also* : WRECKAGE, WRECK **2** : sea vegetation (as kelp) esp. when cast up on the shore
[2]**wrack** *n* [ME, fr. OE *wræc* misery, punishment, something driven by the sea] **1** : RUIN, DESTRUCTION **2** : a remnant of something destroyed
wraith \ˈrāth\ *n, pl* **wraiths** \ˈrāths, ˈrāt͟hz\ **1** : APPARITION; *also* : GHOST, SPECTER **2** : an insubstantial appearance : SHADOW
[1]**wran·gle** \ˈraŋ-gəl\ *vb* **wran·gled; wran·gling** \-g(ə-)liŋ\ **1** : to quarrel angrily or peevishly : BICKER **2** : ARGUE **3** : to obtain by persistent arguing **4** : to herd and care for (livestock) on the range — **wran·gler** *n*
[2]**wrangle** *n* : an angry, noisy, or prolonged dispute or quarrel; *also* : CONTROVERSY
[1]**wrap** \ˈrap\ *vb* **wrapped; wrap·ping 1** : to cover esp. by winding or folding **2** : to envelop and secure for transportation or storage : BUNDLE **3** : to enclose wholly : ENFOLD **4** : to coil, fold, draw, or twine about something **5** : SURROUND, ENVELOP; *also* : SUFFUSE **6** : INVOLVE, ENGROSS ⟨*wrapped* up in a hobby⟩ **7** : to conceal as if by enveloping or enfolding : HIDE **8** : to put on clothing : DRESS **9** : to be subject to covering or enclosing ⟨~*s* up into a small package⟩
[2]**wrap** *n* **1** : WRAPPER, WRAPPING **2** : an article of clothing that may be wrapped around a person; *esp* : an outer garment (as a coat or shawl) **3** *pl* : SECRECY ⟨kept under ~*s*⟩
wrap·around \ˈrap-ə-ˌrau̇nd\ *n* : a garment (as a dress) made with a full-length opening and adjusted to the figure by wrapping around
wrap·per \ˈrap-ər\ *n* **1** : that in which something is wrapped **2** : one that wraps **3** : an article of clothing worn wrapped around the body
wrap·ping \ˈrap-iŋ\ *n* : something used to wrap an object : WRAPPER
wrap–up \ˈrap-ˌəp\ *n* : a summarizing report
wrap up \(ˈ)rap-ˈəp\ *vb* **1** : SUMMARIZE, SUM UP **2** : to bring to a usu. successful conclusion
wrasse \ˈras\ *n* : any of various usu. brightly colored sea fishes including many food fishes
wrath \ˈrath\ *n* **1** : violent anger : RAGE **2** : retributory punishment for an offense or a crime : divine chastisement **syn** indignation, ire, fury, anger
wrath·ful \-fəl\ *adj* **1** : filled with wrath : very angry **2**

: showing, marked by, or arising from anger — **wrath·ful·ly** \-ē\ *adv* — **wrath·ful·ness** *n*

wreak \ˈrēk\ *vb* **1** : to exact as a punishment : INFLICT ⟨~ vengeance on an enemy⟩ **2** : to give free scope or rein to ⟨~*ed* his wrath⟩ **3** : BRING ABOUT, CAUSE ⟨~ havoc⟩

wreath \ˈrēth\ *n, pl* **wreaths** \ˈrēt͟hz, ˈrēths\ : something (as boughs or flowers) intertwined into a circular shape

wreathe \ˈrēt͟h\ *vb* **wreathed; wreath·ing 1** : to shape or take on the shape of a wreath : move or extend in circles or spirals **2** : to twist or become twisted esp. so as to show folds or creases ⟨a face *wreathed* in smiles⟩ **3** : to fold or coil around : ENTWINE

¹wreck \ˈrek\ *n* **1** : something (as goods) cast up on the land by the sea after a shipwreck **2** : SHIPWRECK **3** : the action of breaking up or destroying something : WRECKING **4** : broken remains (as of a ship or vehicle after heavy damage) **5** : something disabled or in a state of ruin; *also* : an individual broken in health or strength

²wreck *vb* **1** : SHIPWRECK **2** : to ruin or damage by breaking up : involve in disaster or ruin

wreck·age \ˈrek-ij\ *n* **1** : the act of wrecking : the state of being wrecked : RUIN **2** : the remains of a wreck

wreck·er \ˈrek-ər\ *n* **1** : one that searches for or works upon the wrecks of ships **2** : a truck equipped to remove disabled cars **3** : one that salvages junked automobile parts **4** : one that wrecks; *esp* : one that razes buildings

wren \ˈren\ *n* : any of various small mostly brown singing birds with short wings and tail

¹wrench \ˈrench\ *vb* **1** : to move with a violent twist **2** : to pull, strain, or tighten with violent twisting or force **3** : to injure or disable by a violent twisting or straining **4** : to change (as the meaning of a word) violently : DISTORT **5** : to snatch forcibly : WREST **6** : to cause to suffer mental anguish

²wrench *n* **1** : a forcible twisting; *also* : an injury (as to one's ankle) by twisting **2** : a tool for holding, twisting, or turning an object (as a nut or bolt)

¹wrest \ˈrest\ *vb* **1** : to pull or move by a forcible twisting movement **2** : to gain with difficulty by or as if by force or violence ⟨~ a living from the barren land⟩ ⟨~ control of government from the dictator⟩

²wrest *n* : a forcible twist : WRENCH

¹wres·tle \ˈres-əl, ˈras-\ *vb* **wres·tled; wres·tling** \-(ə-)liŋ\ **1** : to scuffle with an opponent in an attempt to trip him or throw him down **2** : to contend against in wrestling **3** : to struggle for mastery (as with something difficult) ⟨~ with a problem⟩ — **wres·tler** \ˈres-lər, ˈras-\ *n*

²wrestle *n* : the action or an instance of wrestling : STRUGGLE

wres·tling \ˈres-liŋ\ *n* : the sport of hand-to-hand combat between two opponents who seek to throw and pin each other

wretch \ˈrech\ *n* [ME *wrecche,* fr. OE *wrecca* outcast, exile] **1** : a miserable unhappy person **2** : a base, despicable, or vile person

wretch·ed \ˈrech-əd\ *adj* **1** : deeply afflicted, dejected, or distressed : MISERABLE **2** : WOEFUL, GRIEVOUS ⟨a ~ accident⟩ **3** : DESPICABLE ⟨a ~ trick⟩ **4** : poor in quality or ability : INFERIOR ⟨~ workmanship⟩ — **wretch·ed·ness** *n*

wrig·gle \ˈrig-əl\ *vb* **wrig·gled; wrig·gling** \-(ə-)liŋ\ **1** : to twist and turn restlessly : SQUIRM ⟨*wriggled* in his chair⟩; *also* : to move or advance by twisting and turning ⟨a snake *wriggled* along the path⟩ **2** : to extricate oneself or bring into a state or place by maneuvering, twisting, or dodging ⟨~ out of a difficulty⟩ — **wriggle** *n*

wrig·gler \ˈrig-(ə-)lər\ *n* **1** : one that wriggles **2** : WIGGLER 1

wring \ˈriŋ\ *vb* **wrung** \ˈrəŋ\; **wring·ing** \ˈriŋ-iŋ\ **1** : to squeeze or twist esp. so as to make dry or to extract moisture or liquid ⟨~ clothes⟩ **2** : to get by or as if by forcible exertion or pressure : EXTORT ⟨~ the truth out of him⟩ **3** : to twist so as to strain or sprain : CONTORT ⟨~ his neck⟩ **4** : to twist together as a sign of anguish ⟨*wrung* her hands⟩ **5** : to affect painfully as if by wringing : TORMENT ⟨her plight *wrung* my heart⟩

wring·er \ˈriŋ-ər\ *n* : one that wrings; *esp* : a device for squeezing out liquid or moisture ⟨clothes ~⟩

¹wrin·kle \ˈriŋ-kəl\ *n* **1** : a crease or small fold on a surface (as in the skin or in cloth) **2** : METHOD, TECHNIQUE **3** : INNOVATION, NOVELTY ⟨the latest ~ in hairdos⟩ — **wrin·kly** \-k(ə-)lē\ *adj*

²wrinkle *vb* **wrin·kled; wrin·kling** \-k(ə-)liŋ\ : to develop or cause to develop wrinkles

wrist \ˈrist\ *n* : the joint or region between the hand and the arm; *also* : a corresponding part in a lower animal

wrist·band \ˈris(t)-ˌband\ *n* **1** : the part of a sleeve covering the wrist **2** : a band encircling the wrist

wrist·let \ˈris(t)-lət\ *n* : a band encircling the wrist; *esp* : a close-fitting knitted band attached to the top of a glove or the end of a sleeve

wrist·watch \-ˌwäch\ *n* : a small watch attached to a bracelet or strap to fasten about the wrist

writ \ˈrit\ *n* **1** : something written **2** : a legal order in writing issued in the name of the sovereign power or in the name of a court or judicial authority commanding the performance or nonperformance of a specified act **3** : a written order constituting a symbol of the power and authority of the issuer

write \ˈrīt\ *vb* **wrote** \ˈrōt\; **writ·ten** \ˈrit-ᵊn\ *also* **writ** \ˈrit\; **writ·ing** \ˈrīt-iŋ\ [ME *writen,* fr. OE *wrītan* to scratch, draw, inscribe] **1** : to form characters, letters, or words on a surface (as with a pen) ⟨learn to read and ~⟩ **2** : to form the letters or the words of (as on paper) : INSCRIBE ⟨*wrote* his name⟩ **3** : to put down on paper : give expression to in writing **4** : to make up and set down for others to read : COMPOSE ⟨~ music⟩ **5** : to pen, typewrite, or dictate a letter to **6** : to communicate by letter : CORRESPOND **7** : to be fitted for writing ⟨this pen ~*s* easily⟩

write–in \ˈrīt-ˌin\ *n* : a vote cast by writing in the name of a candidate; *also* : a candidate whose name is written in

write in \(ˈ)rīt-ˈin\ *vb* : to insert (a name not listed on a ballot) in an appropriate space; *also* : to cast (a vote) in this manner

write off *vb* **1** : to reduce the estimated value of : DEPRECIATE **2** : CANCEL ⟨*write off* a bad debt⟩

writ·er \ˈrīt-ər\ *n* : one that writes esp. as a business or occupation : AUTHOR

writer's cramp *n* : a painful spasmodic cramp of muscles of the hand or fingers brought on by excessive writing

write–up \ˈrīt-ˌəp\ *n* : a written account (as in a newspaper); *esp* : a flattering article

writhe \ˈrīt͟h\ *vb* **writhed; writh·ing 1** : to move or proceed with twists and turns ⟨~ in pain⟩ **2** : to suffer with shame or confusion : SQUIRM

writ·ing \ˈrīt-iŋ\ *n* **1** : the act of one that writes; *also* : HANDWRITING **2** : something (as a letter, book, or document) that is written or printed **3** : INSCRIPTION **4** : a style or form of composition **5** : the occupation of a writer

wrnt *abbr* warrant

¹wrong \ˈrȯŋ\ *n* **1** : an injurious, unfair, or unjust act **2** : a violation of the legal rights of another person **3** : something that is contrary to justice, goodness, equity, or law ⟨know right from ~⟩ **4** : the state, position, or fact of being or doing wrong; *also* : the state of being guilty ⟨in the ~⟩

²wrong *adj* **wrong·er** \ˈrȯŋ-ər\; **wrong·est** \ˈrȯŋ-əst\ **1** : SINFUL, IMMORAL **2** : not right according to a standard or code : IMPROPER **3** : INCORRECT ⟨a ~ solution⟩ **4** : UNSATISFACTORY **5** : UNSUITABLE, INAPPROPRIATE **6** : constituting a surface that is considered the back, bottom, inside, or reverse of something ⟨iron only on the ~ side of the fabric⟩ **syn** false, erroneous, incorrect, inaccurate, untrue — **wrong·ly** *adv*

[3]**wrong** *adv* **1** : INCORRECTLY **2** : in a wrong direction, manner, position, or relation

[4]**wrong** *vb* **wronged; wrong·ing** \ˈrȯŋ-iŋ\ **1** : to do wrong to : INJURE, HARM **2** : to treat unjustly : DISHONOR, MALIGN **syn** oppress, persecute, aggrieve

wrong·do·er \ˈrȯŋ-ˈdü-ər\ *n* : a person who does wrong and esp. moral wrong — **wrong·do·ing** \-ˈdü-iŋ\ *n*

wrong·ful \ˈrȯŋ-fəl\ *adj* **1** : WRONG, UNJUST **2** : UNLAWFUL — **wrong·ful·ly** \-ē\ *adv* — **wrong·ful·ness** *n*

wrong·head·ed \ˈrȯŋ-ˈhed-əd\ *adj* : obstinately wrong : PERVERSE — **wrong·head·ed·ly** *adv* — **wrong·head·ed·ness** *n*

wrote *past of* WRITE

wroth \ˈrȯth, ˈrōth\ *adj* : filled with wrath : ANGRY

wrought \ˈrȯt\ *adj* [ME, fr. pp. of *worken* to work] **1** : FASHIONED, FORMED ⟨carefully ~ essays⟩ **2** : ORNAMENTED **3** : beaten into shape by tools : HAMMERED ⟨~ silver dishes⟩ **4** : deeply stirred : EXCITED ⟨gets easily ~ up over nothing⟩

wrought iron *n* : a commercial form of iron that contains less than 0.3 percent carbon and is tough, malleable, and relatively soft — **wrought–iron** *adj*

wrung *past and past part of* WRING

wry \ˈrī\ *adj* **wry·er** \ˈrī(-ə)r\; **wry·est** \ˈrī-əst\ **1** : having a bent or twisted shape ⟨a ~ smile⟩; *esp* : turned abnormally to one side : CONTORTED ⟨a ~ neck⟩ **2** : cleverly and often ironically humorous — **wry·ly** *adv* — **wry·ness** *n*

wry·neck \ˈrī-ˌnek\ *n* **1** : any of several birds related to the woodpeckers that have a peculiar manner of twisting the head and neck **2** : a disorder marked by a twisting of the neck and head

WSW *abbr* west-southwest

wt *abbr* weight

wurst \ˈwərst, ˈwu̇rst\ *n* : SAUSAGE

WV *or* **W Va** *abbr* West Virginia

WW *abbr* World War

w/w *abbr* wall-to-wall

WY *or* **Wyo** *abbr* Wyoming

[1]**x** \ˈeks\ *n, pl* **x's** *or* **xs** \ˈek-səz\ *often cap* **1** : the 24th letter of the English alphabet **2** : an unknown quantity

[2]**x** *vb* **x-ed** *also* **x'd** *or* **xed; x-ing** *or* **x'ing** : to cancel or obliterate with a series of *x*'s — usu. used with *out*

[3]**x** *abbr, often cap* experimental

[4]**x** *symbol* **1** times ⟨3 *x* 2 is 6⟩ **2** by ⟨a 3 *x* 5 index card⟩ **3** *often cap* power of magnification

Xan·thip·pe \zan-ˈt(h)ip-ē\ *or* **Xan·tip·pe** \-ˈtip-ē\ *n* [Gk *Xanthippē*, shrewish wife of Socrates] : an ill-tempered woman

x–ax·is \ˈeks-ˌak-səs\ *n* : the axis of a graph or a system of coordinates in a plane parallel to which abscissas are measured

X chromosome *n* : a sex chromosome that usually occurs paired in each female cell and single in each male cell in organisms (as human beings) in which the male normally has two unlike sex chromosomes

Xe *symbol* xenon

xe·bec \ˈzē-ˌbek\ *n* : a usu. 3-masted Mediterranean sailing ship with long overhanging bow and stern

xe·non \ˈzē-ˌnän, ˈzen-ˌän\ *n* [Gk, neut. of *xenos* strange] : a heavy gaseous chemical element occurring in minute quantities in air — see ELEMENT table

xe·no·pho·bia \ˌzen-ə-ˈfō-bē-ə, ˌzēn-\ *n* : fear and hatred of strangers or foreigners or of what is strange or foreign — **xe·no·phobe** \ˈzen-ə-ˌfōb, ˈzēn-\ *n*

xe·ric \ˈzir-ik, ˈzer-\ *adj* : low or deficient in moisture for the support of life

xe·rog·ra·phy \zə-ˈräg-rə-fē, zir-ˈäg-\ *n* : a process for copying printed matter by the action of light on an electrically charged surface in which the latent image usu. is developed with powders — **xe·ro·graph·ic** \ˌzir-ə-ˈgraf-ik\ *adj*

xe·ro·phyte \ˈzir-ə-ˌfīt\ *n* : a plant adapted for growth with a limited water supply — **xe·ro·phyt·ic** \ˌzir-ə-ˈfit-ik\ *adj*

XL *abbr* **1** extra large **2** extra long

Xmas \ˈkris-məs *also* ˈeks-məs\ *n* [*X* (symbol for *Christ*, fr. the Gk letter chi (X), initial of *Christos* Christ) + *-mas* (in *Christmas*)] : CHRISTMAS

Xn *abbr* Christian

Xnty *abbr* Christianity

x–ra·di·a·tion \ˌeks-ˌrād-ē-ˈā-shən\ *n, often cap* **1** : exposure to X rays **2** : radiation consisting of X rays

x–ray \ˈeks-ˌrā\ *vb, often cap* : to examine, treat, or photograph with X rays

X ray \ˈeks-ˌrā\ *n* **1** : a radiation of the same nature as light rays but of extremely short wavelength that is generated by the striking of a stream of electrons against a metal surface in a vacuum and that is able to penetrate through various thicknesses of solids **2** : a photograph taken with X rays — **X–ray** *adj*

XS *abbr* extra small

xu \ˈsü\ *n, pl* **xu** — see *dong* at MONEY table

xy·lem \ˈzī-ləm, -ˌlem\ *n* : woody tissue of higher plants that transports water and dissolved materials upward, functions also in support and storage, and lies central to the phloem

xy·lo·phone \ˈzī-lə-ˌfōn\ *n* [Gk *xylon* wood + *phōnē* voice, sound] : a musical instrument consisting of a series of wooden bars graduated in length to produce the musical scale, supported on belts of straw or felt, and sounded by striking with two small wooden hammers — **xy·lo·phon·ist** \-ˌfō-nəst\ *n*

Y

[1]**y** \ˈwī\ *n, pl* **y's** *or* **ys** \ˈwīz\ *often cap* **:** the 25th letter of the English alphabet

[2]**y** *abbr* **1** yard **2** year

[1]**Y** \ˈwī\ *n* **:** YMCA

[2]**Y** *symbol* yttrium

[1]**-y** *also* **-ey** \ē\ *adj suffix* **1 :** characterized by **:** full of ⟨dirty⟩ ⟨clayey⟩ **2 :** having the character of **:** composed of ⟨icy⟩ **3 :** like **:** like that of ⟨homey⟩ ⟨wintry⟩ ⟨stagy⟩ **4 :** devoted to **:** addicted to **:** enthusiastic over ⟨horsy⟩ **5 :** tending or inclined to ⟨sleepy⟩ ⟨chatty⟩ **6 :** giving occasion for (specified) action ⟨teary⟩ **7 :** performing (specified) action ⟨curly⟩ **8 :** somewhat **:** rather **:** -ISH ⟨chilly⟩ **9 :** having (such) characteristics to a marked degree or in an affected or superficial way ⟨Frenchy⟩

[2]**-y** \ē\ *n suffix, pl* **-ies 1 :** state **:** condition **:** quality ⟨beggary⟩ **2 :** activity, place of business, or goods dealt with ⟨laundry⟩ **3 :** whole body or group ⟨soldiery⟩

[3]**-y** *n suffix, pl* **-ies :** instance of a (specified) action ⟨entreaty⟩ ⟨inquiry⟩

YA *abbr* young adult

[1]**yacht** \ˈyät\ *n* [obs. D *jaght,* fr. Middle Low German *jacht,* short for *jachtschiff,* lit., hunting ship] **:** any of various relatively small ships used for pleasure cruising or racing

[2]**yacht** *vb* **:** to race or cruise in a yacht

yacht·ing \-iŋ\ *n* **:** the action, fact, or pastime of racing or cruising in a yacht

yachts·man \ˈyäts-mən\ *n* **:** one who owns or sails a yacht

ya·hoo \ˈyā-hü, ˈyä-\ *n, pl* **yahoos** [fr. *Yahoo* one of a race of brutes having the form of men in Jonathan Swift's *Gulliver's Travels*] **:** a boorish, crass, or stupid person

Yah·weh \ˈyä-ˌwā\ *also* **Yah·veh** \-ˌvā\ *n* **:** the God of the Hebrews

[1]**yak** \ˈyak\ *n, pl* **yaks** *also* **yak :** a large long-haired wild or domesticated ox of Tibet and adjacent Asian uplands

[1]yak

[2]**yak** *also* **yack** \ˈyak\ *n* **:** persistent or voluble talk — **yak** *also* **yack** *vb*

yam \ˈyam\ *n* **1 :** the edible starchy root of a twining vine that largely replaces the potato as food in the tropics; *also* **:** a plant distantly related to the lilies that produces yams **2 :** a usu. deep orange sweet potato

yam·mer \ˈyam-ər\ *vb* **yam·mered; yam·mer·ing** \-(ə-)riŋ\ [alter. of ME *yomeren* to murmur, be sad, fr. OE *gēomrian*] **1 :** WHIMPER **2 :** CHATTER — **yammer** *n*

[1]**yank** \ˈyaŋk\ *n* **:** a strong sudden pull **:** JERK

[2]**yank** *vb* **:** to pull with a quick vigorous movement

Yank \ˈyaŋk\ *n* **:** YANKEE

Yan·kee \ˈyaŋ-kē\ *n* **1 :** a native or inhabitant of New England; *also* **:** a native or inhabitant of the northern U.S. **2 :** AMERICAN 2

yan·qui \ˈyäŋ-kē\ *n, often cap* [Sp] **:** a citizen of the U.S. as distinguished from a Latin American

[1]**yap** \ˈyap\ *vb* **yapped; yap·ping 1 :** BARK, YELP **2 :** GAB

[2]**yap** *n* **1 :** a quick sharp bark **2 :** CHATTER

[1]**yard** \ˈyärd\ *n* [ME, fr. OE *geard* enclosure, yard] **1 :** a small enclosed area open to the sky and adjacent to a building **2 :** the grounds of a building **3 :** an enclosure for livestock **4 :** an area set aside for a particular business or activity **5 :** a system of railroad tracks for storing cars and making up trains

[2]**yard** *n* [ME *yarde,* fr. OE *gierd* twig, measure, yard] **1** — see WEIGHT table **2 :** a long spar tapered toward the ends that supports and spreads the head of a sail

yard·age \-ij\ *n* **:** an aggregate number of yards; *also* **:** the length, extent, or volume of something as measured in yards

yard·arm \ˈyärd-ˌärm\ *n* **:** either end of the yard of a square-rigged ship

yard·man \ˈyärd-mən, -ˌman\ *n* **:** a man employed in or about a yard

yard·mas·ter \-ˌmas-tər\ *n* **:** the person in charge of a railroad yard

yard·stick \ˈyärd-ˌstik\ *n* **1 :** a graduated measuring stick three feet long **2 :** a standard for making a critical judgment **:** CRITERION **syn** gauge, touchstone, benchmark, measure

yarn \ˈyärn\ *n* **1 :** a continuous often plied strand composed of fibers or filaments and used in weaving and knitting to form cloth **2 :** STORY; *esp* **:** a tall tale

yar·row \ˈyar-ō\ *n* **:** a strong-scented herb related to the daisies that has white or pink flowers in flat clusters

yaw \ˈyȯ\ *vb* **:** to deviate erratically from a course ⟨the ship ~*ed* in the heavy seas⟩ — **yaw** *n*

yawl \ˈyȯl\ *n* **:** a 2-masted fore-and-aft rigged sailboat with the shorter mast aft of the rudder

[1]**yawn** \ˈyȯn\ *vb* **:** to open wide; *esp* **:** to open the mouth wide usu. as an involuntary reaction to fatigue or boredom — **yawn·er** *n*

[2]**yawn** *n* **:** a deep usu. involuntary intake of breath through the wide-open mouth

yawp *or* **yaup** \ˈyȯp\ *vb* **1 :** to make a raucous noise **:** SQUAWK **2 :** CLAMOR, COMPLAIN — **yawp·er** *n*

yaws \ˈyȯz\ *n pl* **:** an infectious tropical disease caused by a spirochete closely resembling the causative agent of syphilis

y–ax·is \ˈwī-ˌak-səs\ *n* **:** the axis of a graph or a system of coordinates in a plane parallel to which the ordinates are measured

Yb *symbol* ytterbium

YB *abbr* yearbook

Y chromosome *n* **:** a sex chromosome that is characteristic of male zygotes and cells in species in which the male typically has two unlike sex chromosomes

yd *abbr* yard

[1]**ye** \(ˈ)yē\ *pron* YOU 1

[2]**ye** \yē, yə, *or like* THE\ *definite article, archaic* **:** THE — used by early printers to represent the manuscript word þe (*the*)

[1]**yea** \ˈyā\ *adv* **1 :** YES — used in oral voting **2 :** INDEED, TRULY

[2]**yea** *n* **:** an affirmative vote; *also* **:** a person casting such a vote

year \ˈyiər\ *n* **1 :** the period of about 365¼ solar days required for one revolution of the earth around the sun **2 :** a cycle of 365 or 366 days beginning with January 1; *also* **:** a calendar year specified usu. by a number **3** *pl* **:** a time of special significance ⟨~*s* of plenty⟩ **4** *pl* **:** AGE

\ə\abut \ᵊ\kitten \ər\further \a\ash \ā\ace \ä\cot, cart \au̇\out \ch\chin \e\bet \ē\easy \g\go \i\hit \ī\ice \j\job \ŋ\sing \ō\go \ȯ\law \ȯi\boy \th\thin \th̲\the \ü\loot \u̇\foot \y\yet \zh\vision *see also* Pronunciation Symbols page

⟨advanced in ~*s*⟩ **5** : a period of time other than a calendar year ⟨the school ~⟩

year·book \-ˌbu̇k\ *n* **1** : a book published annually esp. as a report **2** : a school publication recording the history and activities of a graduating class

year·ling \ˈyiər-liŋ, ˈyər-lən\ *n* : one that is or is rated as a year old

year·long \ˈyiər-ˈlȯŋ\ *adj* : lasting through a year

[1]**year·ly** \ˈyiər-lē\ *adj* : ANNUAL

[2]**yearly** *adv* : every year

yearn \ˈyərn\ *vb* **1** : to feel a longing or craving **2** : to feel tenderness or compassion **syn** long, pine, hanker, hunger, thirst

yearn·ing \-iŋ\ *n* : a tender or urgent longing

year–round \ˈyiər-ˈrau̇nd\ *adj* : effective, employed, or operating for the full year : not seasonal ⟨a ~ resort⟩

yeast \ˈyēst\ *n* **1** : a surface froth or a sediment in sugary liquids (as fruit juices) that consists largely of cells of a tiny fungus and is used in making alcoholic liquors and as a leaven in baking **2** : a commercial product containing yeast plants in a moist or dry medium **3** : any of various usu. one-celled fungi that reproduce by budding and promote alcoholic fermentation **4** : the foam of waves : SPUME **5** : something that causes ferment or activity

yeasty \ˈyē-stē\ *adj* **yeast·i·er; -est 1** : of, relating to, or resembling yeast **2** : UNSETTLED **3** : full of vitality; *also* : FRIVOLOUS

yegg \ˈyeg\ *n* : one that breaks open safes to steal; *also* : ROBBER

[1]**yell** \ˈyel\ *vb* : to utter a loud cry or scream : SHOUT

[2]**yell** *n* **1** : SHOUT **2** : a cheer used esp. to encourage an athletic team (as at a college)

[1]**yel·low** \ˈyel-ō\ *adj* **1** : of the color yellow **2** : having a yellow complexion or skin **3** : SENSATIONAL ⟨~ journalism⟩ **4** : COWARDLY — **yel·low·ish** \ˈyel-ə-wish\ *adj*

[2]**yellow** *n* **1** : a color between green and orange in the spectrum : the color of ripe lemons or sunflowers **2** : something yellow; *esp* : the yolk of an egg **3** *pl* : any of several plant virus diseases marked by stunted growth and yellowing of foliage

[3]**yellow** *vb* : to make or turn yellow

yellow birch *n* : a No. American birch with thin lustrous gray or yellow bark; *also* : its strong hard pale wood

yellow fever *n* : an acute destructive virus disease marked by prostration, jaundice, fever, and often hemorrhage and transmitted by a mosquito

yellow jack *n* : YELLOW FEVER

yellow jacket *n* : any of various small social wasps having the body barred with bright yellow

yelp \ˈyelp\ *vb* [ME *yelpen* to boast, cry out, fr. OE *gielpan* to boast, exult] : to utter a sharp quick shrill cry — **yelp** *n*

[1]**yen** \ˈyen\ *n, pl* **yen** — see MONEY table

[2]**yen** *n* [obs. E slang *yen-yen* craving for opium, fr. Chin *in-yan,* fr. *in* opium + *yan* craving] : a strong desire : LONGING

yeo·man \ˈyō-mən\ *n* **1** : an attendant or officer in a royal or noble household **2** : a naval petty officer who performs clerical duties **3** : a small farmer who cultivates his own land; *esp* : one of a class of English freeholders below the gentry

yeo·man·ry \ˈyō-mən-rē\ *n* : the body of yeomen and esp. of small landed proprietors

-yer — see -ER

yer·ba ma·té \ˌyer-bə-ˈmä-ˌtā\ *n* : MATÉ

[1]**yes** \ˈyes\ *adv* — used as a function word esp. to express assent or agreement or to introduce a more emphatic or explicit phrase

[2]**yes** *n* : an affirmative reply

ye·shi·va *or* **ye·shi·vah** \yə-ˈshē-və\ *n, pl* **yeshivas** *or* **ye·shi·voth** \-ˌshē-ˈvōt(h)\ : a Jewish school esp. for religious instruction

yes–man \ˈyes-ˌman\ *n* : a person who endorses uncritically every opinion or proposal of a superior

[1]**yes·ter·day** \ˈyes-tərd-ē\ *adv* **1** : on the day preceding today **2** : only a short time ago

[2]**yesterday** *n* **1** : the day last past **2** : time not long past

yes·ter·year \ˈyes-tər-ˌyiər\ *n* **1** : last year **2** : the recent past

[1]**yet** \(ˈ)yet\ *adv* **1** : in addition : BESIDES; *also* : EVEN 5 **2** : up to now; *also* : STILL **3** : so soon as now ⟨not time to go ~⟩ **4** : EVENTUALLY **5** : NEVERTHELESS, HOWEVER

[2]**yet** *conj* : despite the fact that : BUT

ye·ti \ˈyet-ē, ˈyāt-\ *n* [Tibetan] : ABOMINABLE SNOWMAN

yew \ˈyü\ *n* **1** : any of a genus of evergreen trees or shrubs with dark stiff poisonous needles and fleshy fruits **2** : the fine-grained wood of a yew; *esp* : that of an Old World yew

Yid·dish \ˈyid-ish\ *n* [Yiddish *yidish,* short for *yidish daytsh,* lit., Jewish German] : a language derived from German and spoken by Jews esp. of eastern Europe — **Yiddish** *adj*

[1]**yield** \ˈyēld\ *vb* **1** : to give as fitting, owed, or required **2** : GIVE UP; *esp* : to give up possession of on claim or demand **3** : to bear as a natural product **4** : PRODUCE, SUPPLY **5** : to bring in : RETURN **6** : to give way (as to force or influence) **7** : to give place **syn** relinquish, cede, waive, surrender

[2]**yield** *n* : something yielded; *esp* : the amount or quantity produced or returned

yield·ing \ˈyēl-diŋ\ *adj* **1** : not rigid or stiff : FLEXIBLE **2** : SUBMISSIVE, COMPLIANT

YMCA \ˌwī-ˌem-(ˌ)sē-ˈā\ *n* : Young Men's Christian Association

YMHA \ˌwī-ˌem-ˌā-ˈchā\ *n* : Young Men's Hebrew Association

YOB *abbr* year of birth

yo·del \ˈyōd-ᵊl\ *vb* **yo·deled** *or* **yo·delled; yo·del·ing** *or* **yo·del·ling** \ˈyōd-(ᵊ-)liŋ\ : to sing by suddenly changing from chest voice to falsetto and the reverse; *also* : to shout or call in this manner — **yodel** *n* — **yo·del·er** \ˈyōd-(ᵊ-)lər\ *n*

yo·ga \ˈyō-gə\ *n* [Skt, lit., yoking, fr. *yunakti* he yokes] **1** *cap* : a Hindu theistic philosophy teaching the suppression of all activity of body, mind, and will in order that the self may realize its distinction from them and attain liberation **2** : a system of exercises for attaining bodily or mental control and well-being

yo·gi \ˈyō-gē\ *also* **yo·gin** \-gən, -ˌgin\ *n* **1** : a person who practices yoga **2** *cap* : an adherent of Yoga philosophy

yo·gurt *also* **yo·ghurt** \ˈyō-gərt\ *n* [Turk] : a soured slightly acid often flavored semisolid milk food made of skimmed cow's milk and milk solids to which cultures of bacteria have been added

[1]**yoke** \ˈyōk\ *n, pl* **yokes 1** : a wooden bar or frame by which two draft animals (as oxen) are coupled at the heads or necks for working together; *also* : a frame fitted to a person's shoulders to carry a load in two equal portions **2** : a clamp that embraces two parts to hold or unite them in position **3** *pl usu* **yoke** : two animals yoked together **4** : SERVITUDE, BONDAGE **5** : TIE, LINK ⟨the ~ of matrimony⟩ **6** : a fitted or shaped piece esp. at the shoulder of a garment **syn** couple, pair, brace

[2]**yoke** *vb* **yoked; yok·ing 1** : to put a yoke on : couple with a yoke **2** : to attach a draft animal to ⟨~ a plow⟩ **3** : JOIN; *esp* : MARRY

yo·kel \ˈyō-kəl\ *n* : BUMPKIN

yolk \ˈyō(l)k\ *n* **1** : the yellow rounded inner mass of the egg of a bird or reptile **2** : the stored food material of an egg consisting chiefly of proteins, lecithin, and cholesterol — **yolked** \ˈyō(l)kt\ *adj*

Yom Kip·pur \ˌyōm-ki-ˈpu̇r, ˌyäm-, -ˈkip-ər\ *n* [Heb *yōm kippūr,* fr. *yōm* day + *kippūr* atonement] : a Jewish holiday observed in September or October with fasting and prayer as a day of atonement

[1]yon \ˈyän\ *adj* : YONDER
[2]yon *adv* 1 : YONDER 2 : THITHER ⟨ran hither and ~⟩
[1]yon·der \ˈyän-dər\ *adv* : at or to that place
[2]yonder *adj* 1 : more distant ⟨the ~ side of the river⟩ 2 : being at a distance within view ⟨~ hills⟩
yore \ˈyōr\ *n* [ME, fr. *yore,* adv., long ago, fr. OE *geāra,* fr. *gēar* year] : time long past ⟨in days of ~⟩
you \(ˈ)yü, yə\ *pron* 1 : the person or persons addressed ⟨~ are a nice person⟩ ⟨~ are nice people⟩ 2 : ONE 2 ⟨~ turn this knob to open it⟩
[1]**young** \ˈyəŋ\ *adj* **youn·ger** \ˈyəŋ-gər\; **youn·gest** \ˈyəŋ-gəst\ 1 : being in the first or an early stage of life, growth, or development 2 : having little experience 3 : recently come into being 4 : YOUTHFUL 5 *cap* : belonging to or representing a new or revived usu. political group or movement — **young·ish** \ˈyəŋ-ish\ *adj*
[2]**young** *n, pl* **young** : young persons or lower animals
young·ling \ˈyəŋ-liŋ\ *n* : one that is young — **youngling** *adj*
young·ster \-stər\ *n* 1 : a young person 2 : CHILD
your \yər, (ˈ)yu̇r, (ˈ)yōr\ *adj* : of or relating to you or yourself
yours \ˈyu̇rz, ˈyōrz\ *pron* : one or the ones belonging to you
your·self \yər-ˈself\ *pron, pl* **yourselves** \-ˈselvz\ : YOU — used reflexively, for emphasis, or in absolute constructions ⟨you'll hurt ~⟩ ⟨do it ~⟩ ⟨~ a man, you should understand⟩
youth \ˈyüth\ *n, pl* **youths** \ˈyüt͟hz, ˈyüths\ 1 : the period of life between childhood and maturity 2 : a young man; *also* : young persons 3 : YOUTHFULNESS
youth·ful \ˈyüth-fəl\ *adj* 1 : of, relating to, or appropriate to youth 2 : being young and not yet mature 3 : FRESH, VIGOROUS — **youth·ful·ly** \-ē\ *adv* — **youth·ful·ness** *n*
youth hostel *n* : HOSTEL 2
yowl \ˈyau̇l\ *vb* : to utter a loud long mournful cry : WAIL — **yowl** *n*
yo–yo \ˈyō-(ˌ)yō\ *n, pl* **yo–yos** : a thick grooved double disk with a string attached to its center which is made to fall and rise to the hand by unwinding and rewinding on the string
yr *abbr* 1 year 2 your
yrbk *abbr* yearbook
YT *abbr* Yukon Territory
yt·ter·bi·um \i-ˈtər-bē-əm\ *n* : a rare metallic chemical element — see ELEMENT table
yt·tri·um \ˈi-trē-əm\ *n* : a rare metallic chemical element — see ELEMENT table
yu·an \ˈyü-ən, yu̇-ˈän\ *n, pl* **yuan** 1 — see MONEY table 2 : the dollar of the Republic of China (Taiwan)
yuc·ca \ˈyək-ə\ *n* : any of a genus of plants related to the lilies that grow in dry regions and have white cup-shaped flowers in erect clusters; *also* : the flower of this plant
yuck \ˈyək\ *interj* — used to express rejection or disgust
Yu·go·slav \ˌyü-gō-ˈsläv, -ˈslav\ *n* : a native or inhabitant of Yugoslavia — **Yugoslav** *adj* — **Yu·go·sla·vi·an** \-ˈsläv-ē-ən\ *adj or n*
yule \ˈyül\ *n, often cap* : CHRISTMAS
Yule log *n* : a large log formerly put on the hearth on Christmas Eve as the foundation of the fire
yule·tide \ˈyül-ˌtīd\ *n, often cap* : CHRISTMASTIDE
yum·my \ˈyəm-ē\ *adj* **yum·mi·er; -est** : highly attractive or pleasing
yup·pie \ˈyəp-ē\ *n* [young *u*rban *p*rofessional + *-ie* (as in hipp*ie*)] : a young college-educated adult employed in a well-paying profession and living and working in or near a large city
yurt \ˈyu̇rt\ *n* : a light round tent of skins or felt stretched over a lattice framework used by various nomadic tribes in Siberia, U.S.S.R.
YWCA \ˌwī-ˌdəb-əl-yü-(ˌ)sē-ˈā\ *n* : Young Women's Christian Association
YWHA \-ˌā-ˈchā\ *n* : Young Women's Hebrew Association

Z

[1]**z** \ˈzē\ *n, pl* **z's** *or* **zs** *often cap* : the 26th letter of the English alphabet
[2]**z** *abbr* 1 zero 2 zone
Z *symbol* atomic number
Zach *abbr* Zacharias
Zach·a·ri·as \ˌzak-ə-ˈrī-əs\ *n* — see BIBLE table
zaire \zä-ˈir, ˈzīr\ *n, pl* **zaires** *or* **zaire** — see MONEY table
Zair·ian \zä-ˈir-ē-ən\ *n* : a native or inhabitant of Zaire — **Zairian** *adj*
Zam·bi·an \ˈzam-bē-ən\ *n* : a native or inhabitant of Zambia — **Zambian** *adj*
[1]**za·ny** \ˈzā-nē\ *n, pl* **zanies** [It *zanni,* a traditional masked clown, fr. It (dial.) *Zanni,* nickname for *Giovanni* John] 1 : CLOWN, BUFFOON 2 : a silly or foolish person
[2]**zany** *adj* **za·ni·er; -est** 1 : characteristic of a zany 2 : CRAZY, FOOLISH — **za·ni·ly** \ˈzā-nə-lē, ˈzān-ᵊl-ē\ *adv* — **za·ni·ness** \ˈzā-nē-nəs\ *n*
zap \ˈzap\ *vb* **zapped; zap·ping** : DESTROY, KILL
zeal \ˈzēl\ *n* : eager and ardent interest in the pursuit of something : FERVOR **syn** enthusiasm, passion, ardor
zeal·ot \ˈzel-ət\ *n* : a zealous person; *esp* : a fanatical partisan **syn** enthusiast, bigot, fanatic
zeal·ous \ˈzel-əs\ *adj* : filled with, characterized by, or due to zeal — **zeal·ous·ly** *adv* — **zeal·ous·ness** *n*
ze·bra \ˈzē-brə\ *n, pl* **zebras** *also* **zebra** : any of several African mammals related to the horse but conspicuously striped with black or brown and white or buff
ze·bu \ˈzē-b(y)ü\ *n* : an Asian domesticated ox that differs from European cattle with which it crosses freely by a large fleshy hump over the shoulders and a loose skin with hanging folds
Zech *abbr* Zechariah
Zech·a·ri·ah \ˌzek-ə-ˈrī-ə\ *n* — see BIBLE table
zed \ˈzed\ *n, chiefly Brit* : the letter *z*
zeit·geist \ˈtsīt-ˌgīst, ˈzīt-\ *n* [G, fr. *zeit* time + *geist* spirit] : the general intellectual, moral, and cultural state of an era
Zen \ˈzen\ *n* : a Japanese Buddhist sect that teaches self-discipline, meditation, and attainment of enlightenment through direct intuitive insight
ze·na·na \zə-ˈnän-ə\ *n* : HAREM, SERAGLIO
ze·nith \ˈzē-nəth\ *n* 1 : the point in the heavens directly overhead 2 : the highest point : ACME **syn** culmination, pinnacle, apex
ze·o·lite \ˈzē-ə-ˌlīt\ *n* : any of various feldsparlike silicates used as water softeners

Zeph *abbr* Zephaniah

Zeph·a·ni·ah \ˌzef-ə-ˈnī-ə\ *n* — see BIBLE table

zeph·yr \ˈzef-ər\ *n* **1** : a breeze from the west; *also* : a gentle breeze **2** : any of various lightweight fabrics and articles of clothing

zep·pe·lin \ˈzep-(ə-)lən\ *n* [after Count Ferdinand von *Zeppelin* †1917 Ger. airship manufacturer] : a rigid airship consisting of a cylindrical trussed and covered frame

[1]**ze·ro** \ˈzē-rō\ *n, pl* **zeros** *also* **zeroes** [deriv. of Ar *ṣifr*] **1** : the numerical symbol 0 **2** : the number represented by the symbol 0 **3** : the point at which the graduated degrees or measurements on a scale (as of a thermometer) begin **4** : the lowest point

[2]**zero** *adj* **1** : of, relating to, or being a zero **2** : having no magnitude or quantity **3** : ABSENT, LACKING; *esp* : having no modified inflectional form

[3]**zero** *vb* : TRAIN ⟨~ in artillery on the crossroads⟩

zero hour *n* : the time at which an event (as a military operation) is scheduled to begin

zest \ˈzest\ *n* **1** : a quality of enhancing enjoyment : PIQUANCY **2** : keen enjoyment : RELISH, GUSTO — **zest·ful** \-fəl\ *adj* — **zest·ful·ly** \-ē\ *adv* — **zest·ful·ness** *n*

[1]**zig·zag** \ˈzig-ˌzag\ *n* : one of a series of short sharp turns, angles, or alterations in a course; *also* : something marked by such a series

[2]**zigzag** *adv* : in or by a zigzag path

[3]**zigzag** *adj* : having short sharp turns or angles

[4]**zigzag** *vb* **zig·zagged; zig·zag·ging** : to form into or proceed along a zigzag

zil·lion \ˈzil-yən\ *n* : a large indeterminate number

Zim·ba·bwe·an \zim-ˈbäb-wē-ən\ *n* : a native or inhabitant of Zimbabwe — **Zimbabwean** *adj*

zinc \ˈziŋk\ *n* : a bluish white crystalline metallic chemical element that is commonly found in minerals and is used esp. as a protective coating for iron and steel — see ELEMENT table

zinc ointment *n* : ZINC OXIDE OINTMENT

zinc oxide *n* : a white solid used as a pigment, in compounding rubber, and in ointments

zinc oxide ointment *n* : an ointment containing 20 percent of zinc oxide and used for skin disorders

zing \ˈziŋ\ *n* **1** : a shrill humming noise **2** : VITALITY — **zing** *vb*

zing·er \ˈziŋ-ər\ *n* **1** : a pointed witty remark or retort **2** : something causing or meant to cause interest, surprise, or shock

zin·nia \ˈzin-ē-ə, ˈzēn-yə\ *n* : any of a small genus of tropical American herbs related to the daisies and widely grown for their showy long-lasting flower heads

Zi·on \ˈzī-ən\ *n* **1** : the Jewish people **2** : the Jewish homeland as a symbol of Judaism or of Jewish national aspiration **3** : HEAVEN **4** : UTOPIA

Zi·on·ism \ˈzī-ə-ˌniz-əm\ *n* : an international movement orig. for the establishment of a Jewish national or religious community in Palestine and later for the support of modern Israel — **Zi·on·ist** \-nəst\ *adj or n*

[1]**zip** \ˈzip\ *vb* **zipped; zip·ping** : to move or act with speed or vigor

[2]**zip** *n* **1** : a sudden sharp hissing sound **2** : ENERGY, VIM

[3]**zip** *vb* **zipped; zip·ping** : to close or open with a zipper

zip code *n, often cap Z&I&P* [zone *i*mprovement *p*lan] : a 5-digit number that identifies each postal delivery area in the U.S.

zip·per \ˈzip-ər\ *n* : a fastener consisting of two rows of metal or plastic teeth on strips of tape and a sliding piece that closes an opening by drawing the teeth together

zip·py \ˈzip-ē\ *adj* **zip·pi·er; -est** : BRISK, SNAPPY

zir·con \ˈzər-ˌkän\ *n* : a zirconium-containing mineral several transparent varieties of which are used as gems

zir·co·ni·um \ˌzər-ˈkō-nē-əm\ *n* : a corrosion-resistant metallic element with a high melting point that occurs widely in combination and is used in alloys and ceramics — see ELEMENT table

zith·er \ˈzith-ər, ˈzith-\ *n* : a musical instrument having 30 to 40 strings played with plectrum and fingers

zi·ti \ˈzēt-ē\ *n, pl* **ziti** [It] : tubular pasta of medium size

zlo·ty \ˈzlȯt-ē\ *n, pl* **zlo·tys** \-ēz\ *or* **zloty** — see MONEY table

Zn *symbol* zinc

zo·di·ac \ˈzōd-ē-ˌak\ *n* [ME, fr. MF *zodiaque*, fr. L *zodiacus*, fr. Gk *zōidiakos*, fr. *zōidion* carved figure, sign of the zodiac, fr. dim. of *zōion* living being, figure] **1** : an imaginary belt in the heavens that encompasses the paths of most of the planets and that is divided into 12 constellations or signs **2** : a figure representing the signs of the zodiac and their symbols — **zo·di·a·cal** \zō-ˈdī-ə-kəl\ *adj*

zom·bi *also* **zom·bie** \ˈzäm-bē\ *n* **1** : the voodoo snake deity **2** : the supernatural power held in voodoo belief to enter into and reanimate a dead body

zon·al \ˈzōn-ᵊl\ *adj* : of, relating to, or having the form of a zone — **zon·al·ly** \-ē\ *adv*

[1]**zone** \ˈzōn\ *n* [L *zona* belt, zone, fr. Gk *zōnē*] **1** : any of five great divisions of the earth's surface made according to latitude and temperature and including the torrid zone about the equator, the two temperate zones lying between the torrid zone and the polar circles, and the two frigid zones lying between the polar circles and the poles **2** *archaic* : GIRDLE, BELT **3** : an encircling band or girdle ⟨a ~ of trees⟩ **4** : an area or region set off or distinguished in some way from adjoining parts

[2]**zone** *vb* **zoned; zon·ing 1** : ENCIRCLE **2** : to arrange in or mark off into zones; *esp* : to divide (as a city) into sections reserved for different purposes — **zo·na·tion** \zō-ˈnā-shən\ *n*

zonked \ˈzäŋkt\ *adj* : being or acting as if under the influence of alcohol or a drug : HIGH

zoo \ˈzü\ *n, pl* **zoos** : a zoological garden or collection of living animals usu. for public display

zoo·ge·og·ra·phy \ˌzō-ə-jē-ˈäg-rə-fē\ *n* : a branch of biogeography concerned with the geographical distribution of animals — **zoo·ge·og·ra·pher** \-fər\ *n* — **zoo·geo·graph·ic** \-ˌjē-ə-ˈgraf-ik\ *also* **zoo·geo·graph·i·cal** \-i-kəl\ *adj*

zoo·keep·er \ˈzü-ˌkē-pər\ *n* : a person who keeps or cares for animals in a zoo

zool *abbr* zoological; zoology

zoological garden *n* : a garden or park where wild animals are kept for exhibition

zo·ol·o·gy \zō-ˈäl-ə-jē\ *n* : a branch of biology that deals with animals and the animal kingdom — **zo·o·log·i·cal** \ˌzō-ə-ˈläj-i-kəl\ *adj* — **zo·ol·o·gist** \zō-ˈäl-ə-jəst\ *n*

zoom \ˈzüm\ *vb* **1** : to move with a loud hum or buzz **2** : to gain altitude quickly **3** : to focus a camera or microscope using a special lens that permits the apparent distance of the object to be varied — **zoom** *n*

zoom lens *n* : a camera lens in which the image size can be varied continuously while the image remains in focus

zoo·mor·phic \ˌzō-ə-ˈmȯr-fik\ *adj* **1** : having the form of an animal **2** : of, relating to, or being the representation of a deity in the form or with the attributes of an animal

zoo·plank·ton \ˌzō-ə-ˈplaŋk-tən, -ˌtän\ *n* : animal life of the plankton

zoo·spore \ˈzō-ə-ˌspōr\ *n* : a motile spore

zoot suit \ˈzüt-\ *n* : a flashy suit of extreme cut typically consisting of a thigh-length jacket with wide padded shoulders and trousers that are wide at the top and narrow at the bottom — **zoot·suit·er** \-ˌsüt-ər\ *n*

Zo·ro·as·tri·an·ism \ˌzōr-ə-ˈwas-trē-ə-ˌniz-əm\ *n* : a religion founded by the Persian prophet Zoroaster — **Zo·ro·as·tri·an** \-trē-ən\ *adj or n*

Zou·ave \zü-ˈäv\ *n* : a member of a French infantry unit orig. composed of Algerians wearing a brilliant uniform and conducting a quick spirited drill; *also* : a member of a military unit modeled on the Zouaves

zounds \ˈzau̇n(d)z\ *interj* [euphemism for *God's wounds*] — used as a mild oath

zoy·sia \ˈzȯi-shə, -zhə, -sē-ə, -zē-ə\ *n* : any of a genus of creeping perennial grasses having fine wiry leaves and including some used as lawn grasses

ZPG *abbr* zero population growth

Zr *symbol* zirconium

zuc·chet·to \zü-ˈket-ō, tsü-\ *n, pl* **-tos** [It] : a small round skullcap worn by Roman Catholic ecclesiastics

zuc·chi·ni \zu̇-ˈkē-nē\ *n, pl* **-ni** *or* **-nis** [It] : a summer squash of bushy growth with smooth cylindrical dark green fruits; *also* : its fruit

Zu·lu \ˈzü-ˌlü\ *n, pl* **Zulu** *or* **Zulus** : a member of a Bantu-speaking people of South Africa; *also* : a Bantu language of the Zulus

Zu·ni \ˈzü-nē\ *or* **Zu·ñi** \-nyē\ *n, pl* **Zuni** *or* **Zunis** *or* **Zuñi** *or* **Zuñis** : a member of an American Indian people of northeastern Arizona; *also* : the language of the Zuni people

zwie·back \ˈswē-bak, ˈswī-, ˈzwē-, ˈzwī-\ *n* [G, lit., twice baked, fr. *zwie-* twice + *backen* to bake] : a usu. sweetened bread that is baked and then sliced and toasted until dry and crisp

Zwing·li·an \ˈzwiŋ-(g)lē-ən, ˈswiŋ-\ *adj* : of or relating to the Swiss religious reformer Ulrich Zwingli or his teachings — **Zwinglian** *n*

zy·gote \ˈzī-ˌgōt\ *n* : a cell formed by the union of two sexual cells; *also* : the developing individual produced from such a cell — **zy·got·ic** \zī-ˈgät-ik\ *adj*

Common English Given Names

The following vocabulary presents given names that are most frequent in English use. The list is not exhaustive either of the names themselves or the variant spellings of those names which are entered. Compound or double names and surnames used as given names are not entered except in cases where long-continued or common use gives them an independent character.

Besides the pronunciations of the names, the list usually provides at least one of the following kinds of information at each entry: (1) etymology, indicating the language source but not the original form of the name, and (2) meaning where known or ascertainable with reasonable certainty.

Names of Men

Aar·on \ˈar-ən, ˈer-\ [Heb]
Abra·ham \ˈā-brə-ˌham\ [Heb]
Ad·am \ˈad-əm\ [Heb] man
Ad·di·son \ˈad-ə-sən\ [fr. a surname]
Adolph \ˈad-ˌälf, ˈā-ˌdälf\ [Gmc] noble wolf, *i.e.*, noble hero
Adri·an \ˈā-drē-ən\ [L] of Hadria, ancient town in central Italy
Al \al\ *dim of* ALAN, ALBERT, *etc.*
Al·an \ˈal-ən\ [Celt]
Al·bert \ˈal-bərt\ [Gmc] illustrious through nobility
Al·den \ˈȯl-dən\ [OE] old friend
Al·ex \ˈal-iks\ *or* **Al·ec** \ˈal-ik\ *dim of* ALEXANDER
Al·ex·an·der \ˌal-ig-ˈzan-dər\ [Gk] a defender of men
Al·fred \ˈal-frəd, -fərd\ [OE] elf counsel, *i.e.*, good counsel
Al·len *or* **Al·lan** *or* **Al·lyn** \ˈal-ən\ *var of* ALAN
Al·ton \ˈȯlt-ᵊn, ˈalt-\ [prob. fr. a surname]
Al·va *or* **Al·vah** \ˈal-və\ [Heb]
Al·vin \ˈal-vən\ [Gmc]
Amos \ˈā-məs\ [Heb]
An·dre \ˈän-(ˌ)drā\ [F] *var of* ANDREW
An·drew \ˈan-(ˌ)drü\ [Gk] manly
An·dy \ˈan-dē\ *dim of* ANDREW
An·ge·lo \ˈan-jə-ˌlō\ [It, fr. Gk] angel, messenger
An·gus \ˈaŋ-gəs\ [Celt]
An·tho·ny \ˈan(t)-thə-nē, *chiefly Brit* ˈan-tə-\ [L]
An·ton \ˈant-ᵊn, ˈan-ˌtän\ [G & Slav] *var of* ANTHONY
An·to·nio \an-ˈtō-nē-ˌō\ [It] *var of* ANTHONY
Ar·chi·bald \ˈär-chə-ˌbȯld, -bəld\ [Gmc]
Ar·chie \ˈär-chē\ *dim of* ARCHIBALD
Ar·den \ˈärd-ᵊn\ [prob. fr. a surname]
Ar·len *or* **Ar·lin** \ˈär-lən\ [prob. fr. a surname]
Ar·lo \ˈär-(ˌ)lō\
Ar·mand \ˈär-ˌmänd, -mənd\ [F] *var of* HERMAN
Arne \ˈärn\ [Scand] eagle
Ar·nold \ˈärn-ᵊld\ [Gmc] power of an eagle
Art \ˈärt\ *dim of* ARTHUR
Ar·thur \ˈär-thər\ [prob. L]
Au·brey \ˈȯ-brē\ [Gmc] elf ruler
Au·gust \ˈȯ-gəst\ [L] August, majestic
Aus·tin \ˈȯs-tən, ˈäs-\ *alter of* Augustine

Bai·ley \ˈbā-lē\ [fr. a surname]
Bar·clay \ˈbär-klē\ [fr. a surname]
Bar·net *or* **Bar·nett** \bär-ˈnet\ [fr. a surname]
Bar·ney \ˈbär-nē\ *dim of* BERNARD
Bar·rett \ˈbar-ət\ [fr. a surname]
Bar·ry *or* **Bar·rie** \ˈbar-ē\ [Ir]
Bart \ˈbärt\ *dim of* Bartholomew
Bar·ton \ˈbärt-ᵊn\ [fr. a surname]
Ba·sil \ˈbaz-əl, ˈbäs-, ˈbās-, ˈbāz-\ [Gk] kingly, royal
Ben \ˈben\ *or* **Ben·nie** *or* **Ben·ny** \ˈben-ē\ *dim of* BENJAMIN
Ben·e·dict \ˈben-ə-ˌdikt\ [L] blessed
Ben·ja·min \ˈbenj-(ə-)mən\ [Heb] son of the right hand
Ben·nett \ˈben-ət\ [OF] *var of* BENEDICT
Ben·ton \ˈbent-ᵊn\ [fr. a surname]
Ber·nard \ˈbər-nərd, (ˌ)bər-ˈnärd\ *or* **Bern·hard** \ˈbərn-ˌhärd\ [Gmc] bold as a bear
Ber·nie \ˈbər-nē\ *dim of* BERNARD
Bert *or* **Burt** \ˈbərt\ *dim of* BERTRAM, ALBERT, etc.
Ber·tram \ˈbər-trəm\ [Gmc] bright raven
Bill \ˈbil\ *or* **Bil·ly** *or* **Bil·lie** \ˈbil-ē\ *dim of* WILLIAM
Blaine \ˈblān\ [fr. a surname]
Blair \ˈbla(ə)r, ˈble(ə)r\ [fr. a surname]
Bob·by \ˈbäb-ē\ *or* **Bob** \ˈbäb\ *dim of* ROBERT
Bo·ris \ˈbōr-əs, ˈbȯr-, ˈbär-\ [Russ]
Boyd \ˈbȯid\ [fr. a surname]
Brad·ford \ˈbrad-fərd\ [fr. a surname]
Brad·ley \ˈbrad-lē\ [fr. a surname]
Bran·don \ˈbran-dən\ [fr. a surname]
Bren·dan \ˈbren-dən\ [Celt]
Brent \ˈbrent\ [fr. a surname]
Brett *or* **Bret** \ˈbret\ [IrGael]
Bri·an *or* **Bry·an** \ˈbrī-ən\ [Celt]
Brooks \ˈbru̇ks\ [fr. a surname]
Bruce \ˈbrüs\ [fr. a surname]
Bru·no \ˈbrü-(ˌ)nō\ [It, fr. Gmc] brown
Bryce *or* **Brice** \ˈbrīs\ [fr. a surname]
Bud·dy \ˈbəd-ē\ [prob. alter. of *brother*]
Bu·ford \ˈbyü-fərd\ [fr. a surname]
Burke \ˈbərk\ [fr. a surname]
Bur·ton \ˈbərt-ᵊn\ [fr. a surname]
By·ron \ˈbī-rən\ [fr. a surname]

Cal·vin \ˈkal-vən\ [fr. a surname]
Cam·er·on \ˈkam-(ə-)rən\ [fr. a surname]
Carl \ˈkär(-ə)l\ *var of* KARL
Car·los \ˈkär-ləs, -ˌlōs\ [Sp] *var of* CHARLES
Carl·ton *or* **Carle·ton** \ˈkär(-ə)l-tən, ˈkärlt-ᵊn\ [fr. a surname]
Car·lyle \kär-ˈlī(ə)l, ˈkär-ˌ\ [fr. a surname]
Car·men \ˈkär-mən\ [Sp, fr. L] song
Car·roll \ˈkar-əl\ [fr. a surname]
Car·son \ˈkärs-ᵊn\ [fr. a surname]
Car·ter \ˈkärt-ər\ [fr. a surname]
Cary *or* **Car·ey** \ˈka(ə)r-ē, ˈke(ə)r-ē\ [fr. a surname]
Ce·cil \ˈsē-səl, ˈses-əl\ [L]
Chad \ˈchad\ [Gmc]
Charles \ˈchär(-ə)lz\ [Gmc] man of the common people
Ches·ter \ˈches-tər\ [fr. a surname]
Chris \ˈkris\ *dim of* CHRISTOPHER
Chris·tian \ˈkris(h)-chən\ [Gk] Christian (the believer)
Chris·to·pher \ˈkris-tə-fər\ [Gk] Christ bearer
Clar·ence \ˈklar-ən(t)s\ [fr. the English dukedom]
Clark *or* **Clarke** \ˈklärk\ [fr. a surname]
Claude *or* **Claud** \ˈklȯd\ [L]
Clay \ˈklā\ *dim of* CLAYTON

Clay•ton \ˈklāt-ᵊn\ [fr. a surname]
Clem \ˈklem\ *dim of* CLEMENT
Clem•ent \ˈklem-ənt\ [L] mild, merciful
Clif•ford \ˈklif-ərd\ [fr. a surname]
Clif•ton \ˈklif-tən\ [fr. a surname]
Clint \ˈklint\ *dim of* CLINTON
Clin•ton \ˈklint-ᵊn\ [fr. a surname]
Clyde \ˈklīd\ [fr. a surname]
Cole \ˈkōl\ [fr. a surname]
Co•lin \ˈkäl-ən, ˈkō-lən\ *or* **Col•lin** \ˈkäl-ən\ *dim of* NICHOLAS
Con•rad \ˈkän-ˌrad, -rəd\ [Gmc] bold counsel
Con•stan•tine \ˈkän(t)-stən-ˌtēn, -ˌtīn\ [L]
Cor•ey \ˈkȯr-ē\ [fr. a surname]
Cor•ne•lius \kȯr-ˈnēl-yəs\ [L]
Craig \ˈkrāg\ [fr. a surname]
Cur•tis \ˈkərt-əs\ [OF] courteous
Cyr•il \ˈsir-əl\ [Gk] lordly
Cy•rus \ˈsī-rəs\ [OPer]

Dale \ˈdā(ə)l\ [fr. a surname]
Dal•las \ˈdal-əs\ [fr. a surname]
Dal•ton \ˈdȯlt-ᵊn\ [fr. a surname]
Dan \ˈdan\ [Heb] judge
Da•na \ˈdā-nə\ [fr. a surname]
Dan•iel \ˈdan-yəl *also* ˈdan-ᵊl\ [Heb] God has judged
Dan•ny \ˈdan-ē\ *dim of* DANIEL
Dar•old \ˈdar-əld\ *perh alter of* DARRELL
Dar•rell *or* **Dar•rel** *or* **Dar•ryl** *or* **Dar•yl** \ˈdar-əl\ [fr. a surname]
Dar•win \ˈdär-wən\ [fr. a surname]
Dave \ˈdāv\ *dim of* DAVID
Da•vid \ˈdā-vəd\ [Heb] beloved
Da•vis \ˈdā-vəs\ [fr. a surname]
Dean *or* **Deane** \ˈdēn\ [fr. a surname]
Del•a•no \ˈdel-ə-ˌnō\ [fr. a surname]
Del•bert \ˈdel-bərt\ *dim of* Adalbert
Del•mar \ˈdel-mər, -ˌmär\ *or* **Del•mer** \-mər\ [fr. a surname]
Den•nis *or* **Den•is** \ˈden-əs\ [OF, fr. Gk] belonging to Dionysus, god of wine
Den•ny \ˈden-ē\ *dim of* DENNIS
Den•ton \ˈdent-ᵊn\ [fr. a surname]
Der•ek \ˈder-ik\ [Middle Dutch, fr. Gmc] ruler of the people
Dew•ey \ˈd(y)ü-ē\ [fr. a surname]
De•witt \di-ˈwit\ [fr. a surname]
Dex•ter \ˈdek-stər\ [L] on the right hand, fortunate
Dick \ˈdik\ *dim of* RICHARD
Dirk \ˈdərk\ [Dutch] *var of* DEREK
Dom•i•nic *or* **Dom•i•nick** \ˈdäm-ə-(ˌ)nik\ [L] belonging to the Lord
Don *or* **Donn** \ˈdän\ *dim of* DONALD
Don•al \ˈdän-ᵊl\ *var of* DONALD
Don•ald \ˈdän-ᵊld\ [ScGael] world ruler
Don•nie \ˈdän-ē\ *dim of* DON
Don•o•van \ˈdän-ə-vən, ˈdən-\ [fr. a surname]
Doug \ˈdəg\ *dim of* DOUGLAS
Doug•las *or* **Doug•lass** \ˈdəg-ləs\ [fr. a surname]
Duane \dü-ˈän, ˈdwān\ [fr. a surname]
Dud•ley \ˈdəd-lē\ [fr. a surname]
Dun•can \ˈdəŋ-kən\ [ScGael] brown head
Dur•ward \ˈdər-wərd\ [fr. a surname]
Dwayne *or* **Dwaine** \ˈdwān\ [fr. a surname]
Dwight \ˈdwīt\ [fr. a surname]
Dy•lan \ˈdil-ən\ [W]

Earl *or* **Earle** \ˈər(-ə)l\ [OE] warrior, noble
Ed \ˈed\ *dim of* EDWARD, EDGAR, etc.
Ed•die *or* **Ed•dy** \ˈed-ē\ *dim of* ED
Ed•gar \ˈed-gər\ [OE] spear of wealth
Ed•mund *or* **Ed•mond** \ˈed-mənd\ [OE] protector of wealth
Ed•son \ˈed-sən\ [fr. a surname]
Ed•ward \ˈed-wərd\ [OE] guardian of wealth
Ed•win \ˈed-wən\ [OE] friend of wealth
El•bert \ˈel-bərt\ *var of* ALBERT
Eli \ˈē-ˌlī\ [Heb] high
E•li•as \i-ˈlī-əs\ [Gk] *var of* Elijah
El•liott *or* **El•liot** *or* **El•iot** \ˈel-ē-ət, ˈel-yət\ [fr. a surname]
El•lis \ˈel-əs\ *var of* ELIAS
Ells•worth \ˈelz-(ˌ)wərth\ [fr. a surname]
El•mer \ˈel-mər\ [fr. a surname]
El•mo \ˈel-(ˌ)mō\ [It, fr. Gk] lovable
El•ton \ˈelt-ᵊn\ [fr. a surname]
El•vin \ˈel-vən\ [fr. a surname]
El•wood *or* **Ell•wood** \ˈel-ˌwu̇d\ [fr. a surname]
Em•man•u•el *or* **Eman•u•el** \i-ˈman-yə(-wə)l\ [Heb] God with us
Em•er•son \ˈem-ər-sən\ [fr. a surname]
Emil \ˈā-məl\ *or* **Emile** \ā-ˈmē(ə)l\ [L]
Em•mett \ˈem-ət\ [fr. a surname]
Em•o•ry *or* **Em•ery** \ˈem-(ə-)rē\ [Gmc]
Er•ic *or* **Er•ich** *or* **Er•ik** \ˈer-ik\ [Scand]
Er•nest *or* **Ear•nest** \ˈər-nəst\ [G] earnestness
Er•nie \ˈər-nē\ *dim of* ERNEST
Ernst \ˈərn(t)st, ˈe(ə)rn(t)st\ [G] *var of* ERNEST
Er•rol \ˈer-əl\ [prob. fr. a surname]
Ethan \ˈē-thən\ [Heb] strength
Eu•gene \yü-ˈjēn, ˈyü-ˌ\ [Gk] wellborn
Ev•an \ˈev-ən\ [W] *var of* JOHN
Ev•er•ett \ˈev-(ə-)rət\ [fr. a surname]

Fe•lix \ˈfē-liks\ [L] happy, prosperous
Fer•di•nand \ˈfərd-ᵊn-ˌand\ [Gmc]
Fer•nan•do \fər-ˈnan-(ˌ)dō\ [Sp] *var of* FERDINAND
Fletch•er \ˈflech-ər\ [fr. a surname]
Floyd \ˈflȯid\ [fr. a surname]
For•rest *or* **For•est** \ˈfȯr-əst, ˈfär-\ [fr. a surname]
Fos•ter \ˈfȯs-tər, ˈfäs-\ [fr. a surname]
Fran•cis \ˈfran(t)-səs\ [OIt & OF] Frenchman
Fran•cis•co \fran-ˈsis-(ˌ)kō\ [Sp] *var of* FRANCIS
Frank \ˈfraŋk\ [Gmc] freeman, Frank
Frank•lin *or* **Frank•lyn** \ˈfraŋ-klən\ [fr. a surname]
Fred \ˈfred\ *dim of* FREDERICK, ALFRED
Fred•die \ˈfred-ē\ *dim of* FREDERICK
Fred•er•ick *or* **Fred•er•ic** *or* **Fred•rick** *or* **Fred•ric** \ˈfred-(ə-)rik\ [Gmc] peaceful ruler
Free•man \ˈfrē-mən\ [fr. a surname]
Fritz \ˈfrits\ [G] *dim of* Friedrich

Ga•bri•el \ˈgā-brē-əl\ [Heb] man of God
Gar•land \ˈgär-lənd\ [fr. a surname]
Gar•rett \ˈgar-ət\ [fr. a surname]
Garth \ˈgärth\ [fr. a surname]
Gary \ˈgar-ē, ˈger-ē\ *or* **Gar•ry** \ˈgar-\ [prob. fr. a surname]
Gay•lord \ˈgā-ˌlȯ(ə)rd\ [fr. a surname]
Gene \ˈjēn\ *dim of* EUGENE
Geof•frey \ˈjef-rē\ [OF, fr. Gmc]
George \ˈjȯ(ə)rj\ [Gk] of or relating to a farmer
Ger•ald \ˈjer-əld\ [Gmc] spear dominion
Ge•rard \jə-ˈrärd, *chiefly Brit* ˈjer-ˌärd, -ərd\ *or* **Ger•hard** \ˈge(ə)r-ˌhärd\ [Gmc] strong with the spear
Ger•ry \ˈjer-ē\ *var of* JERRY
Gil•bert \ˈgil-bərt\ [Gmc] *prob* illustrious through hostages
Giles \ˈjī(ə)lz\ [OF, fr. LL]
Glenn *or* **Glen** \ˈglen\ [fr. a surname]
Gor•don \ˈgȯrd-ᵊn\ [fr. a surname]
Gra•ham \ˈgrā-əm, ˈgra(-ə)m\ [fr. a surname]
Grant \ˈgrant\ [fr. a surname]
Gran•ville \ˈgran-ˌvil\ [fr. a surname]
Gray \ˈgrā\ [fr. a surname]
Gregg *or* **Greg** \ˈgreg\ *dim of* GREGORY
Greg•o•ry \ˈgreg-(ə-)rē\ [LGk] vigilant
Gro•ver \ˈgrō-vər\ [fr. a surname]
Gus \ˈgəs\ *dim of* Gustav *or* Augustus

Guy \ˈgī\ [OF, fr. Gmc]

Hal \ˈhal\ *dim of* HENRY
Hall \ˈhȯl\ [fr. a surname]
Ham•il•ton \ˈham-əl-tən, -əlt-ᵊn\ [fr. a surname]
Hans \ˈhanz, ˈhän(t)s\ [G] *dim of* Johannes
Har•lan \ˈhär-lən\ *or* **Har•land** \-lənd\ [fr. a surname]
Har•ley \ˈhär-lē\ [fr. a surname]
Har•low \ˈhär-(ˌ)lō\ [fr. a surname]
Har•mon \ˈhär-mən\ [fr. a surname]
Har•old \ˈhar-əld\ [OE] army dominion
Har•ris \ˈhar-əs\ [fr. a surname]
Har•ri•son \ˈhar-ə-sən\ [fr. a surname]
Har•ry \ˈhar-ē\ *dim of* HENRY
Har•vey \ˈhär-vē\ [fr. a surname]
Hec•tor \ˈhek-tər\ [Gk] holding fast
Hel•mut \ˈhel-mət, -ˌmüt\ [G] helmet courage
Hen•ry \ˈhen-rē\ [Gmc] ruler of the home
Her•bert \ˈhər-bərt\ [Gmc] illustrious by reason of an army
Her•man *or* **Her•mann** \ˈhər-mən\ [Gmc] warrior
Her•schel *or* **Her•shel** \ˈhər-shəl\ [fr. a surname]
Hi•ram \ˈhī-rəm\ [Phoenician]
Ho•bart \ˈhō-bərt, -ˌbärt\ [fr. a surname]
Hol•lis \ˈhäl-əs\ [fr. a surname]
Ho•mer \ˈhō-mər\ [Gk]
Hor•ace \ˈhȯr-əs, ˈhär-\ [L]
How•ard \ˈhau̇(-ə)rd\ [fr. a surname]
How•ell \ˈhau̇(-ə)l\ [W]
Hu•bert \ˈhyü-bərt\ [Gmc] bright in spirit
Hud•son \ˈhəd-sən\ [fr. a surname]
Hugh \ˈhyü\ *or* **Hu•go** \ˈhyü-(ˌ)gō\ [Gmc] *prob* mind, spirit

Ian \ˈē-ən\ [ScGael] *var of* JOHN
Ira \ˈī-rə\ [Heb]
Ir•ving \ˈər-viŋ\ *or* **Ir•vin** \-vən\ [fr. a surname]
Ir•win \ˈər-wən\ [fr. a surname]
Isaac \ˈī-zik, -zək\ [Heb] he laughs
Ivan \ˈī-vən\ [Russ] *var of* JOHN

Jack \ˈjak\ *dim of* JOHN
Jack•son \ˈjak-sən\ [fr. a surname]
Ja•cob \ˈjā-kəb, -kəp\ [Heb] one who supplants
Jacques *or* **Jacque** \ˈzhäk\ [F] *var of* JAMES
Jake \ˈjāk\ *dim of* JACOB
James \ˈjāmz\ [OF, fr. LL *Jacobus*] *var of* JACOB
Ja•mie \ˈjā-mē\ *dim of* JAMES
Jan \ˈjan\ [Dutch & LG] *var of* JOHN
Jar•ed \ˈjar-əd, ˈjer-\ [Heb] descent
Ja•son \ˈjās-ᵊn\ [Gk]
Jay \ˈjā\ [prob. fr. a surname]
Jed \ˈjed\ *dim of* Jedidiah
Jef•frey *or* **Jeff•ery** *or* **Jef•fry** \ˈjef-(ə-)rē\ *var of* GEOFFREY
Jer•ald *or* **Jer•old** *or* **Jer•rold** \ˈjer-əld\ *var of* GERALD
Jer•e•my \ˈjer-ə-mē\ *or* **Jer•e•mi•ah** \ˌjer-ə-ˈmī-ə\ [Heb] *prob* Yahweh exalts
Je•rome \jə-ˈrōm, *Brit also* ˈjer-əm\ [Gk] bearing a holy name
Jer•ry *or* **Jere** \ˈjer-ē\ *dim of* GERALD
Jes•se \ˈjes-ē\ [Heb]
Jim \ˈjim\ *or* **Jim•my** *or* **Jim•mie** \ˈjim-ē\ *dim of* JAMES
Jo•dy \ˈjō-dē\ *perh alter of* JOSEPH
Joe \ˈjō\ *dim of* JOSEPH
Jo•el \ˈjō-əl\ [Heb] Yahweh is God
John \ˈjän\ [Heb] Yahweh is gracious
Jon \ˈjän\ *var of* JOHN
Jo•nah \ˈjō-nə\ [Heb]
Jon•a•than \ˈjän-ə-thən\ [Heb] Yahweh has given
Jor•dan \ˈjȯrd-ᵊn\ [fr. a surname]
Jo•seph *or* **Jósef** \ˈjō-zəf *also* -səf\ [Heb] he shall add
Josh•u•a \ˈjäsh-(ə-)wə\ [Heb] Yahweh saves
Judd \ˈjəd\ [fr. a surname]
Jud•son \ˈjəd-sən\ [fr. a surname]
Jules \ˈjülz\ [F] *var of* JULIUS
Ju•lian *or* **Ju•lien** \ˈjül-yən\ [L] sprung from or belonging to Julius
Ju•lius \ˈjül-yəs\ *or* **Ju•lio** \-(ˌ)yō\ [L]
Jus•tin \ˈjəs-tən\ *or* **Jus•tus** \-təs\ [L] just

Karl \ˈkär(-ə)l\ [G & Scand] *var of* CHARLES
Keith \ˈkēth\ [fr. a surname]
Kel•ly \ˈkel-ē\ [fr. a surname]
Ken \ˈken\ *dim of* KENNETH
Ken•dall \ˈken-dᵊl\ [fr. a surname]
Ken•neth \ˈken-əth\ [ScGael]
Kent \ˈkent\ [prob. fr. a surname]
Ken•ton \ˈkent-ᵊn\ [fr. a surname]
Ker•mit \ˈkər-mət\ [prob. fr. a surname]
Ker•ry \ˈker-ē\ [prob. fr. the county of Ireland]
Kev•in \ˈkev-ən\ [OIr]
Kir•by \ˈkər-bē\ [fr. a surname]
Kirk \ˈkərk\ [fr. a surname]
Klaus \ˈklau̇s, ˈklȯs\ [G] *dim of* Nikolaus
Kurt \ˈkərt, ˈku̇(ə)rt\ [G] *dim of* CONRAD
Kyle \ˈkī(ə)l\ [Celt]

La•mar \lə-ˈmär\ [fr. a surname]
Lance \ˈlan(t)s\ *dim of* Lancelot
Lane \ˈlān\ [fr. a surname]
Lan•ny \ˈlan-ē\ *prob dim of* LAWRENCE
Lar•ry \ˈlar-ē\ *dim of* LAWRENCE
Lars \ˈlärz\ [Sw] *var of* LAWRENCE
Law•rence *or* **Lau•rence** \ˈlȯr-ən(t)s, ˈlär-\ [L] of Laurentum, ancient city in central Italy
Lee *or* **Leigh** \ˈlē\ [fr. a surname]
Leigh•ton *or* **Lay•ton** \ˈlāt-ᵊn\ [fr. a surname]
Le•land \ˈlē-lənd\ [fr. a surname]
Len \ˈlen\ *dim of* LEONARD
Leo \ˈle-(ˌ)ō\ [L] lion
Le•on \ˈlē-ˌän, -ən\ [Sp] *var of* LEO
Leon•ard \ˈlen-ərd\ [G] strong or brave as a lion
Le•roy \li-ˈrȯi, ˈlē-ˌ\ [OF] royal
Les•lie \ˈles-lē, ˈlez-\ [fr. a surname]
Les•ter \ˈles-tər\ [fr. a surname]
Lew•is \ˈlü-əs\ *var of* LOUIS
Li•am \ˈlē-əm\ [Ir]
Lin•coln \ˈliŋ-kən\ [fr. a surname]
Li•o•nel \ˈlī-ən-ᵊl, -ə-ˌnel\ [OF] young lion
Lloyd *or* **Loyd** \ˈlȯid\ [W] gray
Lo•gan \ˈlō-gən\ [fr. a surname]
Lon \ˈlän\ *dim of* Alonzo
Lon•nie *or* **Lon•ny** \ˈlän-ē\ *dim of* LON
Lo•ren \ˈlōr-ən, ˈlȯr-\ *dim of* Lorenzo
Lou•ie \ˈlü-ē\ *var of* LOUIS
Lou•is *or* **Lu•is** \ˈlü-əs, ˈlü-ē\ [Gmc] famous warrior
Low•ell \ˈlō-əl\ [fr. a surname]
Lu•cian \ˈlü-shən\ [Gk]
Lud•wig \ˈləd-(ˌ)wig, ˈlüd-\ [G] *var of* LOUIS
Luke \ˈlük\ [Gk] *prob dim of* Lucius
Lu•ther \ˈlü-thər\ [fr. a surname]
Lyle \ˈlī(ə)l\ [fr. a surname]
Ly•man \ˈlī-mən\ [fr. a surname]
Lynn \ˈlin\ [fr. a surname]

Mack *or* **Mac** \ˈmak\ [fr. surnames beginning with *Mc* or *Mac*, fr. Gael *mac* son]
Mal•colm \ˈmal-kəm\ [ScGael] servant of (St.) Columba
Man•fred \ˈman-frəd\ [Gmc] peace among men
Man•u•el \ˈman-yə(-wə)l\ [Sp & Pg] *var of* EMMANUEL
Mar•cus \ˈmär-kəs\ [L]
Ma•rio \ˈmär-ē-ˌō\ [It] *var of* Marius
Mar•i•on \ˈmer-ē-ən, ˈmar-\ [fr. a surname]
Mark *or* **Marc** \ˈmärk\ *var of* MARCUS
Mar•lin \ˈmär-lən\ [prob. fr. a surname]
Mar•shall *or* **Mar•shal** \ˈmär-shəl\ [fr. a surname]
Mar•tin \ˈmärt-ᵊn\ [LL] of Mars

Mar•vin \ˈmär-vən\ [prob. fr. a surname]
Ma•son \ˈmās-ᵊn\ [fr. a surname]
Matt \ˈmat\ *dim of* MATTHEW
Mat•thew \ˈmath-(ˌ)yü *also* ˈmath-(ˌ)ü\ [Heb] gift of Yahweh
Mau•rice \ˈmȯr-əs, ˈmär-; mȯ-ˈrēs\ [LL] *prob* Moorish
Max \ˈmaks\ *dim of* Maximilian
Max•well \ˈmak-ˌswel, -swəl\ [fr. a surname]
May•nard \ˈmā-nərd\ [Gmc] bold in strength
Mel•ville \ˈmel-ˌvil\ [fr. a surname]
Mel•vin *or* **Mel•vyn** \ˈmel-vən\ [prob. fr. a surname]
Mer•e•dith \ˈmer-əd-əth\ [W]
Merle \ˈmər(-ə)l\ [F] blackbird
Mer•lin *or* **Mer•lyn** \ˈmər-lən\ [Celt]
Mer•rill \ˈmer-əl\ [fr. a surname]
Mi•chael \ˈmī-kəl\ [Heb] who is like God?
Mick•ey \ˈmik-ē\ *dim of* MICHAEL
Mike \ˈmīk\ *dim of* MICHAEL
Mi•lan \ˈmī-lən\ [prob. fr. the city in Italy]
Miles *or* **Myles** \ˈmī(ə)lz\ [Gmc]
Mil•ford \ˈmil-fərd\ [fr. a surname]
Mil•lard \ˈmil-ərd, mil-ˈärd\ [fr. a surname]
Mi•lo \ˈmī-(ˌ)lō\ [prob. L]
Mil•ton \ˈmilt-ᵊn\ [fr. a surname]
Mitch•ell \ˈmich-əl\ [fr. a surname]
Mon•roe \mən-ˈrō, ˈmən-ˌ\ [fr. a surname]
Mon•te *or* **Mon•ty** \ˈmänt-ē\ *dim of* Montague
Mor•gan \ˈmȯr-gən\ [W] *prob* dweller on the sea
Mor•ris \ˈmȯr-əs, ˈmär-\ *var of* MAURICE
Mor•ton \ˈmȯrt-ᵊn\ [fr. a surname]
Mur•ray \ˈmər-ē, ˈmə-rē\ [fr. a surname]
My•ron \ˈmī-rən\ [Gk]

Na•than \nā-thən\ [Heb] given, gift
Na•than•iel \nə-ˈthan-yəl\ [Heb] gift of God
Ned \ˈned\ *dim of* EDWARD, EDWIN
Neil *or* **Neal** \ˈnē(ə)l\ [Celt]
Nel•son \ˈnel-sən\ [fr. a surname]
Nev•ille \ˈnev-əl\ [fr. a surname]
Nev•in \ˈnev-ən\ [fr. a surname]
New•ell \ˈn(y)ü-əl\ [fr. a surname]
New•ton \ˈn(y)üt-ᵊn\ [fr. a surname]
Nich•o•las \ˈnik-(ə-)ləs\ [Gk] victorious among the people
Nick \ˈnik\ *dim of* NICHOLAS
Niles \ˈnī(ə)lz\ [fr. a surname]
Nils \ˈnils, ˈnē(ə)ls\ [Scand]
No•ah \ˈnō-ə\ [Heb] rest
No•el \ˈnō-əl\ [F, fr. L] Christmas
No•lan \ˈnō-lən\ [fr. a surname]
Nor•man \ˈnȯr-mən\ [Gmc] Norseman, Norman
Nor•ris \ˈnȯr-əs, ˈnär-\ [fr. a surname]
Nor•ton \ˈnȯrt-ᵊn\ [fr. a surname]

Ol•i•ver \ˈäl-ə-vər\ [OF]
Ol•lie \ˈäl-ē\ *dim of* OLIVER
Or•lan•do \ȯr-ˈlan-(ˌ)dō\ [It] *var of* ROLAND
Or•rin \ˈȯr-ən, ˈär-\ *or* **Orin** *or* **Oren** \ˈȯr-, ˈär-, ˈōr-\ [prob. fr. a surname]
Or•ville *or* **Or•val** \ˈȯr-vəl\ [prob. fr. a surname]
Os•car \ˈäs-kər\ [OE] spear of a deity
Otis \ˈōt-əs\ [fr. a surname]
Ot•to \ˈät-(ˌ)ō\ [Gmc]
Ow•en \ˈō-ən\ [OW]

Palm•er \ˈpäm-ər, ˈpäl-mər\ [fr. a surname]
Par•ker \ˈpär-kər\ [fr. a surname]
Pat \ˈpat\ *dim of* PATRICK
Pat•rick \ˈpa-trik\ [L] patrician
Paul \ˈpȯl\ [L] little
Pe•dro \ˈpē-(ˌ)drō, ˈpā-\ [Sp] *var of* PETER
Per•cy \ˈpər-sē\ [fr. a surname]
Per•ry \ˈper-ē\ [fr. a surname]
Pete \ˈpēt\ *dim of* PETER
Pe•ter \ˈpēt-ər\ [Gk] rock
Phil \ˈfil\ *dim of* PHILIP
Phil•ip *or* **Phil•lip** \ˈfil-əp\ [Gk] lover of horses
Pierre \pē-ˈe(ə)r\ [F] *var of* PETER
Por•ter \ˈpōrt-ər, ˈpȯrt-\ [fr. a surname]
Pres•ton \ˈpres-tən\ [fr. a surname]

Quen•tin \ˈkwent-ᵊn\ [LL] of or relating to the fifth

Ra•fa•el *or* **Ra•pha•el** \ˈraf-ē-əl, ˈrā-fē-\ [Heb] God has healed
Ra•leigh \ˈrȯl-ē, ˈräl-\ [fr. a surname]
Ralph \ˈralf, *Brit also* ˈrāf\ [Gmc] wolf in counsel
Ra•mon \rə-ˈmōn, ˈrā-mən\ [Sp] *var of* RAYMOND
Ran•dall *or* **Ran•dal** \ˈran-dᵊl\ *var of* RANDOLPH
Ran•dolph \ˈran-ˌdälf\ [Gmc] shield wolf
Ran•dy \ˈran-dē\ *dim of* RANDOLPH
Ray \ˈrā\ *dim of* RAYMOND
Ray•mond \ˈrā-mənd\ [Gmc] wise protection
Reed *or* **Reid** \ˈrēd\ [fr. a surname]
Reg•gie \ˈrej-ē\ *dim of* REGINALD
Reg•i•nald \ˈrej-ən-ᵊld\ [Gmc] wise dominion
Re•gis \ˈrē-jəs\ [fr. a proper name]
Re•ne \ˈren-(ˌ)ā, rə-ˈnā, ˈrā-nē, ˈrē-nē\ [F, fr. L] reborn
Reu•ben *or* **Ru•ben** \ˈrü-bən\ [Heb]
Rex \ˈreks\ [L] king
Reyn•old \ˈren-ᵊld\ *var of* REGINALD
Rich•ard \ˈrich-ərd\ [Gmc] strong in rule
Rob•ert \ˈräb-ərt\ [Gmc] bright in fame
Ro•ber•to \rə-ˈbərt-(ˌ)ō, rō-, -ˈbert-\ [Sp & It] *var of* ROBERT
Rob•in \ˈräb-ən\ *dim of* ROBERT
Rod•er•ick \ˈräd-(ə-)rik\ [Gmc] famous ruler
Rod•ney \ˈräd-nē\ [fr. a surname]
Rog•er *or* **Rod•ger** \ˈräj-ər\ [Gmc] famous spear
Rog•ers \ˈräj-ərz\ [fr. a surname]
Ro•land \ˈrō-lənd\ *or* **Rol•land** \ˈräl-ənd\ *or* **Row•land** \ˈrō-lənd\ [Gmc] famous land
Rolf \ˈrälf\ *var of* RUDOLPH
Rol•lin \ˈräl-ən\ *var of* ROLAND
Ron \ˈrän\ *dim of* RONALD
Ron•al \ˈrän-ᵊl\ *var of* RONALD
Ron•ald \ˈrän-ᵊld\ [ON] *var of* REGINALD
Ron•nie *or* **Ron•ny** \ˈrän-ē\ *dim of* RONALD
Ros•coe \ˈräs-(ˌ)kō, ˈrȯs-\ [fr. a surname]
Ross \ˈrȯs\ [fr. a surname]
Roy \ˈrȯi\ [ScGael]
Roy•al \ˈrȯi(-ə)l\ [prob. fr. a surname]
Royce \ˈrȯis\ [fr. a surname]
Ru•dolph *or* **Ru•dolf** \ˈrü-ˌdälf\ [Gmc] famous wolf
Ru•dy \ˈrüd-ē\ *dim of* RUDOLPH
Ru•fus \ˈrü-fəs\ [L] red, red-haired
Ru•pert \ˈrü-pərt\ *var of* ROBERT
Rus•sell *or* **Rus•sel** \ˈrəs-əl\ [fr. a surname]
Ry•an \ˈrī-ən\ [IrGael]

Sal•va•tore \ˈsal-və-ˌtō(ə)r, -ˌtȯ(ə)r; ˌsal-və-ˈtōr-ē, -ˈtȯr-\ [It] savior
Sam \ˈsam\ *dim of* SAMUEL
Sam•my *or* **Sam•mie** \ˈsam-ē\ *dim of* SAM
Sam•u•el \ˈsam-yə(-wə)l\ [Heb] name of God
San•ford \ˈsan-fərd\ [fr. a surname]
Saul \ˈsȯl\ [Heb] asked for
Scott \ˈskät\ [fr. a surname]
Sean \ˈshȯn\ [Ir] *var of* JOHN
Seth \ˈseth\ [Heb]
Sey•mour \ˈsē-ˌmō(ə)r, -ˌmȯ(ə)r\ [fr. a surname]
Shel•by \ˈshel-bē\ [fr. a surname]
Shel•don \ˈshel-dən\ [fr. a surname]
Sher•i•dan \ˈsher-əd-ᵊn\ [fr. a surname]
Sher•man \ˈshər-mən\ [fr. a surname]
Sher•win \ˈshər-wən\ [fr. a surname]
Sher•wood \ˈshər-ˌwu̇d, ˈshe(ə)r-\ [fr. a surname]

Sid•ney *or* **Syd•ney** \ˈsid-nē\ [fr. a surname]
Sieg•fried \ˈsig-ˌfrēd, ˈsēg-\ [Gmc] victorious peace
Sig•mund \ˈsig-mənd\ [Gmc] victorious protection
Si•mon \ˈsī-mən\ [Heb]
Sol•o•mon \ˈsäl-ə-mən\ [Heb] peaceable
Spen•cer \ˈspen(t)-sər\ [fr. a surname]
Sta•cy *or* **Sta•cey** \ˈstā-sē\ [ML]
Stan \ˈstan\ *dim of* STANLEY
Stan•ford \ˈstan-fərd\ [fr. a surname]
Stan•ley \ˈstan-lē\ [fr. a surname]
Stan•ton \ˈstant-ᵊn\ [fr. a surname]
Ste•fan \ˈstef-ən, -ˌän\ [Pol] *var of* STEPHEN
Ste•phen *or* **Ste•ven** *or* **Ste•phan** \ˈstē-vən\ [Gk] crown
Ster•ling \ˈstər-liŋ\ [fr. a surname]
Steve \ˈstēv\ *dim of* STEVEN
Stu•art *or* **Stew•art** \ˈst(y)ü-ərt, ˈst(y)ü(-ə)rt\ [fr. a surname]
Syl•ves•ter \sil-ˈves-tər\ [L] woodsy, of the woods

Tay•lor \ˈtā-lər\ [fr. a surname]
Ted \ˈted\ *or* **Ted•dy** \ˈted-ē\ *dim of* EDWARD, THEODORE
Ter•ence *or* **Ter•rance** *or* **Ter•rence** \ˈter-ən(t)s\ [L]
Ter•rell *or* **Ter•rill** \ˈter-əl\ [fr. a surname]
Ter•ry \ˈter-ē\ *dim of* TERENCE
Thad \ˈthad\ *dim of* THADDEUS
Thad•de•us \ˈthad-ē-əs\ [Gk]
The•o•dore \ˈthē-ə-ˌdō(ə)r, -ˌdȯ(ə)r, -əd-ər\ [Gk] gift of God
Thom•as \ˈtäm-əs\ [Aram] twin
Thur•man \ˈthər-mən\ [fr. a surname]
Tim \ˈtim\ *dim of* TIMOTHY
Tim•o•thy \ˈtim-ə-thē\ [Gk] revering God
To•by \ˈtō-bē\ *dim of* Tobias
Todd \ˈtäd\ [prob. fr. a surname]
Tom \ˈtäm\ *or* **Tom•my** *or* **Tom•mie** \ˈtäm-ē\ *dim of* THOMAS
To•ny \ˈtō-nē\ *dim of* ANTHONY
Tra•cy \ˈtrā-sē\ [fr. a surname]
Trav•is \ˈtrav-əs\ [fr. a surname]
Trent \ˈtrent\ [fr. a surname]
Tre•vor \ˈtrev-ər\ [Celt]
Troy \ˈtrȯi\ [prob. fr. a surname]
Tru•man \ˈtrü-mən\ [fr. a surname]
Ty•ler \ˈtī-lər\ [fr. a surname]
Ty•rone \ˈtī-ˌrōn, tī-ˈ; tir-ˈōn\ [prob. fr. the county in Ireland]

Val \ˈval\ *dim of* Valentine
Van \ˈvan\ [fr. surnames beginning with *Van,* fr. Dutch *van* of]
Vance \ˈvan(t)s\ [fr. a surname]
Vaughn \ˈvȯn, ˈvän\ [fr. a surname]
Verne *or* **Vern** \ˈvərn\ *prob alter of* VERNON
Ver•non \ˈvər-nən\ [prob. fr. a surname]
Vic•tor \ˈvik-tər\ [L] conqueror
Vin•cent \ˈvin(t)-sənt\ [LL] of or relating to the conquering one
Vir•gil \ˈvər-jəl\ [L]

Wade \ˈwād\ [fr. a surname]
Wal•lace *or* **Wal•lis** \ˈwäl-əs\ [fr. a surname]
Walt \ˈwȯlt\ *dim of* WALTER
Wal•ter \ˈwȯl-tər\ [Gmc] army of dominion
Wal•ton \ˈwȯlt-ᵊn\ [fr. a surname]
Ward \ˈwȯ(ə)rd\ [fr. a surname]
War•ner \ˈwȯr-nər\ [fr. a surname]
War•ren \ˈwȯr-ən, ˈwär-\ [fr. a surname]
Wayne \ˈwān\ [fr. a surname]
Wel•don \ˈwel-dən\ [fr. a surname]
Wen•dell \ˈwen-dᵊl\ [fr. a surname]
Wer•ner \ˈwər-nər, ˈwe(ə)r-\ [Gmc] army of the Varini, a Germanic people
Wes•ley \ˈwes-lē *also* ˈwez-\ [fr. a surname]
Wil•bur *or* **Wil•ber** \ˈwil-bər\ [fr. a surname]
Wi•ley *or* **Wy•lie** \ˈwī-lē\ [fr. a surname]
Wil•ford \ˈwil-fərd\ [fr. a surname]
Wil•fred \ˈwil-frəd\ [OE] desired peace
Will \ˈwil\ *or* **Wil•lie** \-ē\ *dim of* WILLIAM
Wil•lard \ˈwil-ərd\ [fr. a surname]
Wil•liam \ˈwil-yəm\ [Gmc] desired helmet
Wil•lis \ˈwil-əs\ [fr. a surname]
Wil•mer \ˈwil-mər\ [fr. a surname]
Wil•son \ˈwil-sən\ [fr. a surname]
Wil•ton \ˈwilt-ᵊn\ [fr. a surname]
Win•field \ˈwin-ˌfēld\ [fr. a surname]
Win•fred \ˈwin-frəd\ [OE] *prob* joyous peace
Win•ston \ˈwin(t)-stən\ [fr. a surname]
Win•ton \ˈwint-ᵊn\ [fr. a surname]
Wood•row \ˈwu̇d-(ˌ)rō\ [fr. a surname]
Wy•att \ˈwī-ət\ [fr. a surname]

Yale \ˈyā(ə)l\ [fr. a surname]

Zach•a•ry \ˈzak-ə-rē\ *dim of* Zachariah
Zane \ˈzān\ [fr. a surname]

Names of Women

Ab•by \ˈab-ē\ *dim of* ABIGAIL
Ab•i•gail \ˈab-ə-ˌgāl\ [Heb] *prob* source of joy
Ada \ˈād-ə\ [Heb] *prob* ornament
Ad•di•son \ˈad-ə-sən\ [fr. a surname]
Ad•e•laide \ˈad-ᵊl-ˌād\ [Gmc] of noble rank
Adele \ə-ˈdel\ [Gmc] noble
Adri•enne \ˈā-drē-ˌen, -ən\ [F] *fem of* Adrien
Ag•nes \ˈag-nəs\ [LL]
Ai•leen \ī-ˈlēn\ [IrGael] *var of* HELEN
Al•ber•ta \al-ˈbərt-ə\ *fem of* ALBERT
Al•ex•an•dra \ˌal-ig-ˈzan-drə\ [Gk] *fem of* ALEXANDER
Alex•is \ə-ˈlek-səs\ [Gk]
Al•ice *or* **Al•yce** \ˈal-əs\ [OF] *var of* ADELAIDE
Ali•cia \ə-ˈlish-ə\ [ML] *var of* ADELAIDE
Al•i•son *or* **Al•li•son** \ˈal-ə-sən\ [OF] *dim of* ALICE
Al•ma \ˈal-mə\ [L] nourishing, cherishing
Al•va \ˈal-və\ [Sp, fr. L] white
Aman•da \ə-ˈman-də\ [L] worthy to be loved
Am•ber \ˈam-bər\ [E]
Ame•lia \ə-ˈmēl-yə\ [Gmc]
Amy \ˈā-mē\ [L] beloved
An•as•ta•sia \ˌan-ə-ˈstā-zh(ē-)ə\ [LGk] of the resurrection
An•drea \ˈan-drē-ə, an-ˈdrā-ə\ *fem of* ANDREW
An•ge•la \ˈan-jə-lə\ [It, fr. Gk] angel
An•gel•i•ca \an-ˈjel-i-kə\ *var of* ANGELA
An•ge•line \ˈan-jə-ˌlīn, -ˌlēn\ *dim of* ANGELA
Ani•ta \ə-ˈnēt-ə\ [Sp] *dim of* ANN
Ann *or* **Anne** \ˈan\ *or* **An•na** \ˈan-ə\ [Heb] grace
An•na•belle \ˈan-ə-ˌbel\ *prob var of* MABEL
An•nette \a-ˈnet, ə-\ *or* **An•net•ta** \-ˈnet-ə\ [F] *dim of* ANN
An•nie \ˈan-ē\ *dim of* ANN
An•toi•nette \ˌan-t(w)ə-ˈnet\ [F] *dim of* Antonia
April \ˈā-prəl\ [E] April (the month)
Ar•dell *or* **Ar•delle** \är-ˈdel\ *var of* ADELE
Ar•lene *or* **Ar•leen** *or* **Ar•line** \är-ˈlēn\
Ash•ley \ˈash-lē\ [OE] ash-tree meadow
As•trid \ˈas-trəd\ [Scand] beautiful as a deity
Au•dra \ˈȯ-drə\ *var of* AUDREY
Au•drey \ˈȯ-drē\ [OE] noble strength

Ba•bette \ba-ˈbet\ [F] *dim of* ELIZABETH
Bar•ba•ra \ˈbär-b(ə-)rə\ [Gk] foreign

Be•atrice \'bē-ə-trəs\ [It, fr. ML] she that makes happy
Becky \'bek-ē\ *dim of* REBECCA
Ber•na•dette \ˌbər-nə-'det\ [F] *fem of* BERNARD
Ber•na•dine \'bər-nə-ˌdēn\ *fem of* BERNARD
Ber•nice \(ˌ)bər-'nēs, 'bər-nəs\ [Gk] bringing victory
Ber•tha \'bər-thə\ [Gmc] bright
Ber•yl \'ber-əl\ [Gk] beryl (the mineral)
Bes•sie \'bes-ē\ *dim of* ELIZABETH
Beth \'beth\ *dim of* ELIZABETH
Bet•sy *or* **Bet•sey** \'bet-sē\ *dim of* ELIZABETH
Bet•ty *or* **Bet•te** *or* **Bet•tye** *or* **Bet•tie** \'bet-ē\ *dim of* ELIZABETH
Beu•lah \'byü-lə\ [Heb] married
Bev•er•ly *or* **Bev•er•ley** \'bev-ər-lē\ [prob. fr. a surname]
Bil•lie \'bil-ē\ *fem of* BILLY
Blair \'ble(ə)r\ [fr. a surname]
Blake \'blāk\ [fr. a surname]
Blanche \'blanch\ [OF, fr. Gmc] white
Bob•bie \'bäb-ē\ *dim of* ROBERTA
Bo•ni•ta \bə-'nēt-ə\ [Sp] pretty
Bon•nie \'bän-ē\ [ME] pretty
Bran•dy \'bran-dē\ [E]
Bren•da \'bren-də\ [Scand]
Bri•gitte \'brij-ət, brə-'jit\ [G] *var of* Bridget
Brit•tany \'brit-ᵊn-ē\ [E]
Brooke \'brůk\ [OE] brook

Cait•lin \'kāt-lin\ [Ir] *var of* CATHERINE
Ca•mil•la \kə-'mil-ə\ [L] freeborn girl attendant at a sacrifice
Ca•mille \kə-'mē(ə)l\ [F] *var of* CAMILLA
Can•da•ce \'kan-dəs, kan-'dā-sē\ [Gk]
Car•la \'kär-lə\ [It] *fem of* Carlo
Car•lene \kär-'lēn\ *var of* CARLA
Car•lot•ta \kär-'lät-ə\ [It] *var of* CHARLOTTE
Car•men \'kär-mən\ *or* **Car•mine** \kär-'mēn, 'kär-mən\ [Sp, fr. L] song
Car•ol *or* **Car•ole** *or* **Car•yl** \'kar-əl\ *dim of* CAROLYN
Car•o•lyn \'kar-ə-lən\ *or* **Car•o•line** \-lən, -ˌlīn\ [It] *fem of* CHARLES
Car•rie \'kar-ē\ *dim of* CAROLINE
Cath•er•ine *or* **Cath•a•rine** \'kath-(ə-)rən\ [LGk]
Cath•leen \kath-'lēn\ [IrGael] *var of* CATHERINE
Cath•ryn \'kath-rən\ *var of* CATHERINE
Cathy *or* **Cath•ie** \'kath-ē\ *dim of* CATHERINE
Ce•cile \sə-'sē(ə)l\ *var of* CECILIA
Ce•ci•lia \sə-'sēl-yə, -'sil-\ *or* **Ce•ce•lia** \-'sēl-\ [L] *fem of* CECIL
Ce•leste \sə-'lest\ [L] heavenly
Ce•lia \'sēl-yə\ *dim of* CECILIA
Char•lene \shär-'lēn\ *fem of* CHARLES
Char•lotte \'shär-lət\ [F] *fem dim of* CHARLES
Cher•ie \'sher-ē\ [F] dear
Cher•ry \'cher-ē\ [E] cherry
Cher•yl \'cher-əl, 'sher-\ *prob var of* CHERRY
Chloe \'klō-ē\ [Gk] young verdure
Chris•tie \'kris-tē\ *dim of* CHRISTINE
Chris•tine \kris-'tēn\ *or* **Chris•ti•na** \-'tē-nə\ [Gk] Christian
Cin•dy \'sin-dē\ *dim of* LUCINDA
Claire *or* **Clare** \'kla(ə)r, 'kle(ə)r\ *var of* CLARA
Clara \'klar-ə\ [L] bright
Cla•rice \'klar-əs, klə-'rēs\ *dim of* CLARA
Clau•dette \klo̊-'det\ [F] *fem of* CLAUDE
Clau•dia \'klo̊d-ē-ə\ [L] *fem of* CLAUDE
Clau•dine \klo̊-'dēn\ [F] *fem of* CLAUDE
Cleo \'klē-(ˌ)ō\ *dim of* Cleopatra
Co•lette \kä-'let\ [OF] *fem dim of* NICHOLAS
Col•leen \kä-'lēn\ [IrGael] girl
Con•nie \'kän-ē\ *dim of* CONSTANCE
Con•stance \'kän(t)-stən(t)s\ [L] constancy
Co•ra \'kōr-ə, 'ko̊r-\ [Gk] maiden
Cor•ey \'ko̊r-ē\ [Ir]
Co•rinne *or* **Cor•rine** \kə-'rin, -'rēn\ [Gk] *dim of* CORA
Cor•ne•lia \ko̊r-'nēl-yə\ [L] *fem of* CORNELIUS
Court•ney \'kō(ə)rt-nē, 'ko̊(ə)rt-\ [OE] of the court
Crys•tal \'kris-tᵊl\ [E]
Cyn•thia \'sin(t)-thē-ə\ [Gk] she of Mount Cynthus on the island of Delos

Dai•sy \'dā-zē\ [E] daisy
Dale \'dā(ə)l\ [E] valley
Da•na \'dā-nə\ [fr. a surname]
Dan•ielle \dan-'yel\ [F] *fem of* DANIEL
Daph•ne \'daf-nē\ [Gk] laurel
Dar•la \'där-lə\ [deriv. of *darling*]
Dar•lene \där-'lēn\ [deriv. of *darling*]
Dawn \'do̊n, 'dän\ [E] dawn
De•an•na \dē-'an-ə\ *or* **De•anne** \-'an\ *var of* DIANA
Deb•bie *or* **Deb•by** \'deb-ē\ *dim of* DEBORAH
Deb•o•rah *or* **Deb•o•ra** \'deb-(ə-)rə\ [Heb] bee
Deb•ra \'deb-rə\ *var of* DEBORAH
Dee \'dē\ *prob dim of* EDITH
Deir•dre \'di(ə)r-drē, 'de(ə)r-\ [IrGael]
De•lia \'dēl-yə\ [Gk] she of Delos (i.e. the goddess Artemis)
Del•la \'del-ə\ *dim of* ADELAIDE, DELIA
De•lo•res \də-'lōr-əs, -'lo̊r-\ *var of* DOLORES
De•na *or* **Dee•na** \'dē-nə\ *dim of* GERALDINE
De•nise \də-'nēz, -'nēs\ [F] *fem of* DENIS
Di•ana *or* **Di•an•na** \dī-'an-ə\ [L]
Di•ane *or* **Di•anne** *or* **Di•an** *or* **Di•ann** \dī-'an\ [F] *var of* DIANA
Di•na *or* **Di•nah** \'dī-nə\ [Heb] judged
Dix•ie \'dik-sē\ [E] *prob* Dixie (nickname for the southern states of the U.S.)
Do•lo•res \də-'lōr-əs, -'lo̊r-\ [Sp, fr. L] sorrows (i.e. those of the Virgin Mary)
Don•na \'dän-ə\ *or* **Do•na** \'dän-ə, 'dō-nə\ [It, fr. L] lady
Do•ra \'dōr-ə, 'do̊r-\ *dim of* THEODORA, Eudora
Do•reen \do̊-'rēn, də-\ [IrGael]
Dor•is \'do̊r-əs, 'där-\ [Gk] *prob* Dorian (a member of an ancient Hellenic race)
Dor•o•thy \'do̊r-ə-thē, 'där-\ *or* **Dor•o•thea** \ˌdo̊r-ə-'thē-ə, ˌdär-\ [LGk] goddess of gifts
Dot•tie *or* **Dot•ty** \'dät-ē\ *dim of* DOROTHY

Edith *or* **Edythe** \'ēd-əth\ [OE]
Ed•na \'ed-nə\ [Aram]
Ed•wi•na \e-'dwē-nə, -'dwin-ə\ *fem of* EDWIN
Ef•fie \'ef-ē\ *dim of* Euphemia
Ei•leen \ī-'lēn\ [IrGael] *var of* HELEN
Elaine \i-'lān\ [OF] *var of* HELEN
El•ea•nor *or* **El•i•nor** *or* **El•ea•nore** \'el-ə-nər, -ˌno̊(ə)r, -ˌnō(ə)r\ [OProv] *var of* HELEN
Ele•na \'el-ə-nə, ə-'lē-nə\ [It] *var of* HELEN
Elise \ə-'lēz, -'lēs\ [F] *var of* ELIZABETH
Eliz•a•beth *or* **Elis•a•beth** \i-'liz-ə-bəth\ [Heb] God has sworn
El•la \'el-ə\ [OF]
El•len *or* **El•lyn** \'el-ən\ *var of* HELEN
El•o•ise \'el-ə-ˌwēz, ˌel-ə-'\ [OF, fr. Gmc]
El•sa \'el-sə\ [G] *dim of* ELIZABETH
El•sie \'el-sē\ *dim of* ELIZABETH
El•va \'el-və\ [Gmc] elf
Em•i•ly *or* **Em•i•lie** \'em-(ə-)lē\ [L] *fem of* EMIL
Em•ma \'em-ə\ [Gmc] *var of* ERMA
Enid \'ē-nəd\ [W]
Er•i•ka \'er-i-kə\ *fem of* ERIC
Er•in \'er-ən\ [IrGael]
Er•ma \'ər-mə\ [Gmc]
Er•nes•tine \'ər-nə-ˌstēn\ *fem of* ERNEST
Es•telle \e-'stel\ *or* **Es•tel•la** \e-'stel-ə\ [OProv, fr. L] star
Es•ther \'es-tər\ [prob. fr. Per] *prob* star
Eth•el \'eth-əl\ [OE] noble
Et•ta \'et-ə\ *dim of* HENRIETTA

Eu•ge•nia \yu̇-ˈjēn-yə\ *or* **Eu•ge•nie** \-ˈjē-nē\ *fem of* EUGENE
Eu•nice \ˈyü-nəs\ [Gk] having (i.e. bringing) happy victory
Eva \ˈē-və\ *var of* EVE
Evan•ge•line \i-ˈvan-jə-lən, -ˌlēn, -ˌlīn\ [Gk] bringing good news
Eve \ˈēv\ [Heb] life, living
Ev•e•lyn \ˈev-(ə-)lən, *chiefly Brit* ˈēv-\ [OF, fr. Gmc]

Faith \ˈfāth\ [E] faith
Faye *or* **Fay** \ˈfā\ *dim of* FAITH
Fe•lice \fə-ˈlēs\ [L] happiness
Fern *or* **Ferne** \ˈfərn\ [E] fern
Flo•ra \ˈflōr-ə, ˈflȯr-\ [L] goddess of flowers
Flor•ence \ˈflȯr-ən(t)s, ˈflär-\ [L] bloom, prosperity
Fran•ces \ˈfran(t)-səs, -səz\ *fem of* FRANCIS
Fran•cine \fran-ˈsēn\ [F] *prob dim of* FRANCES
Fre•da *or* **Frie•da** \ˈfrēd-ə\ *dim of* WINIFRED
Fred•er•ic•ka *or* **Fred•er•i•ca** \ˌfred-(ə-)ˈrē-kə, -ˈrik-ə\ *fem of* FREDERICK

Gail *or* **Gayle** *or* **Gale** \ˈgā(ə)l\ *dim of* ABIGAIL
Gay \ˈgā\ [E] gay
Ge•ne•va \jə-ˈnē-və\ *var of* GENEVIEVE
Gen•e•vieve \ˈjen-ə-ˌvēv\ [prob. fr. Celt]
George•ann \jȯr-ˈjan\ [*George* + *Ann*]
Geor•gette \jȯr-ˈjet\ *fem of* GEORGE
Geor•gia \ˈjȯr-jə\ *fem of* GEORGE
Geor•gi•na \jȯr-ˈjē-nə\ *fem of* GEORGE
Ger•al•dine \ˈjer-əl-ˌdēn\ *fem of* GERALD
Ger•trude \ˈgər-ˌtrüd\ [Gmc] spear strength
Gil•li•an \ˈjil-ē-ən\ *var of* JULIANA
Gin•ger \ˈjin-jər\ [E] ginger
Gi•sela \jə-ˈsel-ə, -ˈzel-\ [Gmc] pledge
Gi•selle \jə-ˈzel\ *var of* GISELA
Glad•ys \ˈglad-əs\ [W]
Glen•da \ˈglen-də\ *prob var of* GLENNA
Glen•na \ˈglen-ə\ *fem of* GLENN
Glo•ria \ˈglōr-ē-ə, ˈglȯr-\ [L] glory
Grace \ˈgrās\ [L] favor, grace
Gre•ta \ˈgrēt-ə, ˈgret-\ *dim of* MARGARET
Gretch•en \ˈgrech-ən\ [G] *dim of* MARGARET
Gwen \ˈgwen\ *dim of* GWENDOLYN
Gwen•do•lyn \ˈgwen-də-lən\ [W]

Han•nah \ˈhan-ə\ [Heb] *var of* ANN
Har•ri•et *or* **Har•ri•ett** *or* **Har•ri•ette** \ˈhar-ē-ət\ *var of* HENRIETTA
Hat•tie \ˈhat-ē\ *dim of* HARRIET
Ha•zel \ˈhā-zəl\ [E] hazel
Heath•er \ˈheth-ər\ [ME] heather (the shrub)
Hei•di \ˈhīd-ē\ [G] *dim of* ADELAIDE
He•laine \hə-ˈlān\ *var of* HELEN
Hel•en \ˈhel-ən\ *or* **He•le•na** \ˈhel-ə-nə, hə-ˈlē-nə\ [Gk]
He•lene \hə-ˈlēn\ [F] *var of* HELEN
Hel•ga \ˈhel-gə\ [Scand] holy
Hen•ri•et•ta \ˌhen-rē-ˈet-ə\ [MF] *fem of* HENRY
Her•mine \ˈhər-ˌmēn\ [G] *prob fem of* HERMAN
Hes•ter \ˈhes-tər\ *var of* ESTHER
Hil•ary *or* **Hil•la•ry** \ˈhil-ə-rē\ [L] cheerful
Hil•da \ˈhil-də\ [OE] battle
Hil•de•gard *or* **Hil•de•garde** \ˈhil-də-ˌgärd\ [Gmc] *prob* battle enclosure
Hol•ly \ˈhäl-ē\ [E] holly
Hope \ˈhōp\ [E] hope

Ida \ˈīd-ə\ [Gmc]
Ilene \ī-ˈlēn\ *var of* EILEEN
Imo•gene \ˈim-ə-ˌjēn, ˈī-mə-\
Ina \ˈī-nə\
Inez \ī-ˈnez, ˈī-nəz\ [Sp] *var of* AGNES
In•grid \ˈiŋ-grəd\ [Scand] beautiful as Ing (an ancient Germanic god)

Irene \ī-ˈrēn\ [Gk] peace
Iris \ˈī-rəs\ [Gk] rainbow
Ir•ma \ˈər-mə\ *var of* ERMA
Is•a•bel *or* **Is•a•belle** \ˈiz-ə-ˌbel\ [OProv] *var of* ELIZABETH

Jack•ie *or* **Jacky** \ˈjak-ē\ *dim of* JACQUELINE
Jac•que•line *or* **Jac•que•lyn** *or* **Jac•que•lin** \ˈjak-(w)ə-lən, -ˌlēn\ [OF] *fem of* JACOB
Ja•mie \ˈjā-mē\ *fem of* JAMES
Jan \ˈjan\ *dim of* JANET
Jane *or* **Jayne** \ˈjān\ [OF] *var of* JOAN
Ja•net *or* **Ja•nette** \ˈjan-ət, jə-ˈnet\ *dim of* JANE
Ja•nice \ˈjan-əs, jə-ˈnēs\ *or* **Jan•is** \ˈjan-əs\ *prob dim of* JANE
Ja•nie \ˈjā-nē\ *dim of* JANE
Jean *or* **Jeanne** \ˈjēn\ [OF] *var of* JOAN
Jea•nette *or* **Jean•nette** \jə-ˈnet\ [F] *dim of* JEANNE
Jean•nie *or* **Jean•ie** \ˈjē-nē\ *dim of* JEAN
Jean•nine *or* **Jea•nine** \jə-ˈnēn\ [F] *dim of* JEANNE
Jen•nie *or* **Jen•ny** \ˈjen-ē\ *dim of* JANE
Jen•ni•fer \ˈjen-ə-fər\ [Celt]
Jer•al•dine \ˈjer-əl-ˌdēn\ *var of* GERALDINE
Jer•i•lyn \ˈjer-ə-lən\ *var of* GERALDINE
Jer•ry *or* **Jeri** *or* **Jer•rie** \ˈjer-ē\ *dim of* GERALDINE
Jes•si•ca \ˈjes-i-kə\ [prob. Heb]
Jes•sie \ˈjes-ē\ [Sc] *dim of* JANET
Jew•el *or* **Jew•ell** \ˈjü(-ə)l, ˈju̇(-ə)l\ [E] jewel
Jill \ˈjil\ *dim of* JULIANA
Jo \ˈjō\ *dim of* JOSEPHINE
Joan *or* **Joann** *or* **Joanne** \ˈjō(-ə)n, jō-ˈan\ [Gk] *fem of* JOHN
Jo•an•na \jō-ˈan-ə\ *or* **Jo•han•na** \-ˈ(h)an-ə\ *var of* JOAN
Joc•e•lyn \ˈjäs-(ə-)lən\ [OF, fr. Gmc]
Jo•dy *or* **Jo•die** \ˈjō-dē\ *alter of* JUDITH
Jo•lene \jō-ˈlēn\ *prob dim of* JO
Jo•se•phine \ˈjō-zə-ˌfēn *also* ˈjō-sə-\ *fem of* JOSEPH
Joy \ˈjȯi\ [E] joy
Joyce \ˈjȯis\ [OF]
Jua•ni•ta \wä-ˈnēt-ə\ [Sp] *fem dim of* JOHN
Ju•dith \ˈjüd-əth\ [Heb] Jewess
Ju•dy *or* **Ju•di** *or* **Ju•die** \ˈjüd-ē\ *dim of* JUDITH
Ju•lia \ˈjül-yə\ [L] *fem of* JULIUS
Ju•li•ana \ˌjü-lē-ˈan-ə\ [LL] *fem of* JULIAN
Ju•li•anne *or* **Ju•li•ann** \ˌjü-lē-ˈan, jül-ˈyan\ *var of* JULIANA
Ju•lie \ˈjü-lē\ [MF] *var of* JULIA
Ju•liet \ˈjül-yət, -ē-ˌet, -ē-ət; ˌjül-ē-ˈet, jül-ˈyet, ˈjül-ˌyet\ [It] *dim of* JULIA
June \ˈjün\ [E] June (the month)
Jus•tine \ˌjəs-ˈtēn\ [F] *fem of* JUSTIN

Ka•ra \ˈkär-ə, ˈkar-ə\ *var of* CATHERINE
Kar•en *or* **Kar•in** *or* **Kaa•ren** \ˈkar-ən, ˈkär-\ [Scand] *var of* CATHERINE
Kar•la \ˈkär-lə\ *var of* CARLA
Kar•ol \ˈkar-əl\ *var of* CAROL
Kar•o•lyn \ˈkar-ə-lən\ *var of* CAROLYN
Kate \ˈkāt\ *dim of* CATHERINE
Kath•er•ine *or* **Kath•a•rine** *or* **Kath•ryn** \ˈkath-(ə-)rən\ *var of* CATHERINE
Kath•leen \kath-ˈlēn\ [IrGael] *var of* CATHERINE
Kathy \ˈkath-ē\ *dim of* CATHERINE
Ka•tie \ˈkāt-ē\ *dim of* KATE
Kay *or* **Kaye** \ˈkā\ *dim of* CATHERINE
Kel•ly \ˈkel-ē\ [fr. a surname]
Ker•ry \ˈker-ē\ [prob. fr. the county of Ireland]
Kim \ˈkim\ *prob dim of* KIMBERLY
Kim•ber•ly \ˈkim-bər-lē\ [OE]
Kit•ty \ˈkit-ē\ *dim of* CATHERINE
Kris•tin \ˈkris-tən\ [Scand] *var of* CHRISTINE
Kris•tine \kris-ˈtēn\ *var of* CHRISTINE

La•na \ˈlan-ə, ˈlän-ə, ˈlā-nə\
Lau•ra \ˈlȯr-ə, ˈlär-\ [ML] *prob fem dim of* LAWRENCE
Lau•rel \ˈlȯr-əl, ˈlär-\ [E] laurel

Lau•ren \ˈlȯr-ən, ˈlär-\ *var of* LAURA
Lau•rie \ˈlȯr-ē, ˈlär-\ *dim of* LAURA
La•verne *or* **La•vern** \lə-ˈvərn\
Le•ah \ˈlē-ə\ [Heb] *prob* wild cow
Le•anne \lē-ˈan\ [prob. fr. *Lee* + *Ann*]
Lee \ˈlē\ [fr. a surname]
Leigh \ˈlē\ *var of* LEE
Lei•la *or* **Le•la** \ˈlē-lə\ [Per] dark as night
Le•lia \ˈlēl-yə\ [L]
Le•na \ˈlē-nə\ [G] *dim of* HELENA, Magdalena
Le•nore \lə-ˈnō(ə)r, -ˈnȯ(ə)r\ *or* **Le•no•ra** \lə-ˈnōr-ə, -ˈnȯr-\ *var of* LEONORA
Le•o•na \lē-ˈō-nə\ *fem of* LEON
Le•o•no•ra \ˌlē-ə-ˈnōr-ə, -ˈnȯr-\ *var of* ELEANOR
Les•lie *or* **Les•ley** \ˈles-lē *also* ˈlez-\ [fr. a surname]
Le•ti•tia \li-ˈtish-ə, -ˈtē-shə\ [L] gladness
Lib•by \ˈlib-ē\ *dim of* ELIZABETH
Li•la \ˈlī-lə\ *var of* LEILA
Lil•lian \ˈlil-yən, ˈlil-ē-ən\ *prob dim of* ELIZABETH
Lil•lie \ˈlil-ē\ *dim of* LILLIAN
Lily \ˈlil-ē\ [E] lily
Lin•da *or* **Lyn•da** \ˈlin-də\ *dim of* MELINDA, Belinda
Lind•sey *or* **Lind•say** \ˈlin-zē\ [OE] linden isle
Li•sa \ˈlī-zə, ˈlē-\ *dim of* ELIZABETH
Lo•is \ˈlō-əs\ [Gk]
Lo•la \ˈlō-lə\ [Sp] *dim of* DOLORES
Lon•na \ˈlän-ə\ *fem of* LON
Lo•ra \ˈlōr-ə, ˈlȯr-\ *var of* LAURA
Lo•re•lei \ˈlōr-ə-ˌlī, ˈlȯr-\ [G]
Lo•rene \lȯ-ˈrēn\ *dim of* LORA
Lo•ret•ta \lə-ˈret-ə, lȯ-\ [ML] *var of* Lauretta
Lo•ri \ˈlōr-ē, ˈlȯr-\ *var of* LAURA
Lor•na \ˈlȯr-nə\
Lor•raine *or* **Lo•raine** \lə-ˈrān, lȯ-\ [prob. fr. *Lorraine*, region in northeast France]
Lou \ˈlü\ *dim of* LOUISE
Lou•ise \lu̇-ˈēz\ *or* **Lou•i•sa** \-ˈē-zə\ *fem of* LOUIS
Lu•anne \lü-ˈan\ [*Lu-* + *Anne*]
Lu•cille *or* **Lu•cile** \lü-ˈsē(ə)l\ [L] *prob dim of* LUCIA
Lu•cin•da \lü-ˈsin-də\ [L] *var of* LUCY
Lu•cre•tia \lü-ˈkrē-shə\ [L]
Lu•cy \ˈlü-sē\ *or* **Lu•cia** \ˈlü-shə\ [L] *fem of* Lucius
Lu•el•la \lu̇-ˈel-ə\ [prob. fr. *Lou* (dim. of *Louise*) + *Ella*]
Lyd•ia \ˈlid-ē-ə\ [Gk] woman of Lydia, ancient country in Asia Minor
Ly•nette \lə-ˈnet\ [W]
Lynne *or* **Lynn** \ˈlin\ *dim of* CAROLYN, JACQUELYN, etc.

Ma•bel \ˈmā-bəl\ [L] lovable
Mac•ken•zie \mə-ˈken-zē\ [fr. a surname]
Mad•e•line *or* **Mad•e•leine** *or* **Mad•e•lyn** \ˈmad-ᵊl-ən\ [Gk] woman of Magdala, ancient town in northern Palestine
Madge \ˈmaj\ *dim of* MARGARET
Mal•lory \ˈmal-(ə-)rē\ [fr. a surname]
Ma•mie \ˈmā-mē\ *dim of* MARGARET
Ma•ra \ˈmär-ə\ *var of* MARY
Mar•cel•la \mär-ˈsel-ə\ [L] *fem of* Marcellus
Mar•cia \ˈmär-shə\ [L] *fem of* MARCUS
Mar•ga•ret \ˈmär-g(ə-)rət\ [Gk] pearl
Mar•gery \ˈmärj-(ə-)rē\ [OF] *var of* MARGARET
Mar•gie \ˈmär-jē\ *dim of* MARGARET
Mar•go \ˈmär-(ˌ)gō\ *var of* MARGOT
Mar•got \ˈmär-(ˌ)gō, -gət\ *dim of* MARGARET
Mar•gue•rite \ˌmär-g(y)ə-ˈrēt\ [OF] *var of* MARGARET
Ma•ria \mə-ˈrē-ə *also* -ˈrī-\ *var of* MARY
Mar•i•an \ˈmer-ē-ən, ˈmar-\ *var of* MARIANNE
Mar•i•anne \ˌmer-ē-ˈan, ˌmar-\ *or* **Mar•i•an•na** \-ˈan-ə\ [F] *dim of* MARY
Ma•rie \mə-ˈrē\ [OF] *var of* MARY
Mar•i•et•ta \ˌmer-ē-ˈet-ə, ˌmar-\ *dim of* MARY
Mar•i•lee \ˈmer-ə-(ˌ)lē, ˈmar-\ [prob. fr. *Mary* + *Lee*]
Mar•i•lyn *or* **Mar•i•lynn** *or* **Mar•y•lyn** \ˈmer-ə-lən, ˈmar-\ [prob. fr. *Mary* + *-lyn*]
Ma•ri•na \mə-ˈrē-nə\ [LGk]
Mar•i•on \ˈmer-ē-ən, ˈmar-\ *dim of* MARY
Mar•jo•rie *or* **Mar•jo•ry** \ˈmärj-(ə-)rē\ *var of* MARGERY
Mar•la \ˈmär-lə\ *prob dim of* MARLENE
Mar•lene \mär-ˈlēn(-ə), -ˈlā-nə\ [G] *dim of* Magdalene
Mar•lyn \ˈmär-lən\ *prob var of* MARLENE
Mar•sha \ˈmär-shə\ *var of* MARCIA
Mar•ta \ˈmärt-ə\ [It] *var of* MARTHA
Mar•tha \ˈmär-thə\ [Aram] lady
Mar•va \ˈmär-və\ *prob fem of* MARVIN
Mary \ˈme(ə)r-ē, ˈmā-rē\ [Gk, fr. Heb]
Mary•ann *or* **Mary•anne** \ˌmer-ē-ˈan, ˌmā-rē-\ [*Mary* + *Ann*]
Mary•el•len \ˌmer-ē-ˈel-ən, ˌmā-rē-\ [*Mary* + *Ellen*]
Mar•y•lon \ˈmer-ə-lən, ˈmar-\ *var of* MARILYN
Maude \ˈmȯd\ [OF] *var of* Matilda
Mau•reen *or* **Mau•rine** \mȯ-ˈrēn\ [Ir] *dim of* MARY
Max•ine \mak-ˈsēn\ [F] *fem dim of* Maximilian
May *or* **Mae** \ˈmā\ *dim of* MARY
Me•gan \ˈmeg-ən, ˈmē-gən\ [Ir]
Mel•a•nie \ˈmel-ə-nē\ [Gk] blackness
Mel•ba \ˈmel-bə\ [E] woman of Melbourne, Australia
Me•lin•da \mə-ˈlin-də\ *prob alter of* Belinda
Me•lis•sa \mə-ˈlis-ə\ [Gk] bee
Mel•va \ˈmel-və\ *prob fem of* MELVIN
Mer•e•dith \ˈmer-əd-əth\ [W]
Merle \ˈmər(-ə)l\ [F] blackbird
Mer•ri•ly \ˈmer-ə-lē\ *alter of* MARILEE
Mer•ry \ˈmer-ē\ [E] merry
Mia \ˈmē-ə\ [It]
Mi•chele *or* **Mi•chelle** \mi-ˈshel\ [F] *fem of* MICHAEL
Mil•dred \ˈmil-drəd\ [OE] gentle strength
Mil•li•cent \ˈmil-ə-sənt\ [Gmc]
Mil•lie \ˈmil-ē\ *dim of* MILDRED
Min•nie \ˈmin-ē\ [Sc] *dim of* MARY
Mir•an•da \mə-ˈran-də\ [L] admirable
Mir•i•am \ˈmir-ē-əm\ [Heb] *var of* MARY
Mit•zi \ˈmit-sē\ *prob dim of* MARGARET
Mol•ly *or* **Mol•lie** \ˈmäl-ē\ *dim of* MARY
Mo•na \ˈmō-nə\ [IrGael]
Mon•i•ca \ˈmän-i-kə\ [LL]
Mu•ri•el \ˈmyu̇r-ē-əl\ [prob. Celt]
My•ra \ˈmī-rə\
Myr•na \ˈmər-nə\
Myr•tle \ˈmərt-ᵊl\ [Gk] myrtle

Na•dine \nā-ˈdēn, nə-\ [F, fr. Russ] hope
Nan \ˈnan\ *dim of* ANN
Nan•cy \ˈnan(t)-sē\ *dim of* ANN
Nan•nette *or* **Na•nette** \na-ˈnet, nə-\ [F] *dim of* ANN
Na•o•mi \nā-ˈō-mē\ [Heb] pleasant
Nat•a•lie \ˈnat-ᵊl-ē\ [LL] of or relating to Christmas
Nel•lie \ˈnel-ē\ *or* **Nell** \ˈnel\ *dim of* ELLEN, HELEN, ELEANOR
Net•tie \ˈnet-ē\ [Sc] *dim of* JANET
Ni•cole \nē-ˈkōl\ [F] *fem of* NICHOLAS
Ni•na \ˈnē-nə\ [Russ] *dim of* ANN
Ni•ta \ˈnēt-ə\ [Sp] *dim of* JUANITA
No•na \ˈnō-nə\ [L] ninth
No•ra \ˈnōr-ə, ˈnȯr-\ *dim of* LEONORA, ELEANOR, Honora
No•reen \nȯ-ˈrēn\ [IrGael] *dim of* NORA
Nor•ma \ˈnȯr-mə\ [It]

Ol•ga \ˈäl-gə, ˈōl-\ [Russ] *var of* HELGA
Ol•ive \ˈäl-iv, -əv\ *or* **O•liv•ia** \ə-ˈliv-ē-ə, ō-\ [L] olive
Opal \ˈō-pəl\ [E] opal

Pam \ˈpam\ *dim of* PAMELA
Pa•me•la \ˈpam-ə-lə; pə-ˈmē-lə, pa-\
Pa•tri•cia \pə-ˈtrish-ə, -ˈtrē-shə\ [L] *fem of* PATRICK
Pat•sy \ˈpat-sē\ *dim of* PATRICIA
Pat•ty *or* **Pat•ti** *or* **Pat•tie** \ˈpat-ē\ *dim of* PATRICIA
Pau•la \ˈpȯ-lə\ [L] *fem of* PAUL
Pau•lette \pȯ-ˈlet\ *fem dim of* PAUL

Pau•line \pȯ-ˈlēn\ *fem dim of* PAUL
Pearl \ˈpər(-ə)l\ [E] pearl
Peg•gy \ˈpeg-ē\ *dim of* MARGARET
Pe•nel•o•pe \pə-ˈnel-ə-pē\ [Gk]
Pen•ny \ˈpen-ē\ *dim of* PENELOPE
Phoe•be \ˈfē-bē\ [Gk] shining
Phyl•lis \ˈfil-əs\ [Gk] green leaf
Pol•ly \ˈpäl-ē\ *dim of* MARY
Por•tia \ˈpōr-shə, ˈpȯr-\ [L]
Pris•cil•la \prə-ˈsil-ə\ [L]
Pru•dence \ˈprüd-ᵊn(t)s\ [E] prudence

Ra•chel \ˈrā-chəl\ [Heb] ewe
Rae \ˈrā\ *dim of* RACHEL
Ra•mo•na \rə-ˈmō-nə\ [Sp] *fem of* RAMON
Re•ba \ˈrē-bə\ *dim of* REBECCA
Re•bec•ca \ri-ˈbek-ə\ [Heb]
Re•gi•na \ri-ˈjē-nə, -ˈjī-\ [L] queen
Re•nee \rə-ˈnā, ˈren-(ˌ)ā, ˈrā-nē, ˈrē-nē\ [F] reborn
Rhea \ˈrē-ə\ [Gk]
Rho•da \ˈrōd-ə\ [Gk] rose
Ri•ta \ˈrēt-ə\ [It] *dim of* MARGARET
Ro•ber•ta \rə-ˈbərt-ə, rō-\ *fem of* ROBERT
Rob•in *or* **Rob•yn** \ˈräb-ən\ [E] robin
Ro•chelle \rō-ˈshel\ [prob. fr. a surname]
Ro•na *or* **Rho•na** \ˈrō-nə\
Ron•da \ˈrän-də\ *var of* Rhonda
Ron•nie \ˈrän-ē\ *dim of* VERONICA
Ro•sa•lie \ˈrō-zə-(ˌ)lē, ˈräz-ə-\ [L] festival of roses
Ro•sa•lind \ˈräz-(ə-)lənd, ˈrō-zə-lənd\ [Sp]
Rose \ˈrōz\ *or* **Ro•sa** \ˈrō-zə\ [L] rose
Rose•anne \rō-ˈzan\ [*Rose* + *Anne*]
Rose•mary \ˈrōz-ˌmer-ē\ *or* **Rose•ma•rie** \ˌrōz-mə-ˈrē\ [E] rosemary
Ro•set•ta \rō-ˈzet-ə\ *dim of* ROSE
Ros•lyn \ˈräz-lən\ *or* **Ro•sa•lyn** *or* **Ro•se•lyn** \ˈräz-(ə-)lən, ˈrō-zə-lən\ *var of* ROSALIND
Ro•we•na \rə-ˈwē-nə\ [perh. fr. OE]
Rox•anne \räk-ˈsan\ [OPer]
Ru•by \ˈrü-bē\ [E] ruby
Ruth \ˈrüth\ [Heb]
Ruth•ann \rü-ˈthan\ [*Ruth* + *Ann*]

Sa•bra \ˈsā-brə\ *dim of* Sabrina
Sa•die \ˈsād-ē\ *dim of* SARA
Sal•ly *or* **Sal•lie** \ˈsal-ē\ *dim of* SARA
Sa•man•tha \sə-ˈman-thə\ [Aram]
San•dra \ˈsan-drə, ˈsän-\ *dim of* ALEXANDRA
San•dy \ˈsan-dē\ *dim of* ALEXANDRA
Sar•ah *or* **Sara** \ˈser-ə, ˈsar-ə, ˈsā-rə\ [Heb] princess
Sara•lee \ˈser-ə-(ˌ)lē, ˈsar-\ [prob. fr. *Sara* + *Lee*]
Saun•dra \ˈsȯn-drə, ˈsän-\ *var of* SANDRA
Sel•ma \ˈsel-mə\ [Sw] *fem dim of* Anselm
Shari \ˈsha(ə)r-ē, ˈshe(ə)r-\ *dim of* SHARON
Shar•lene \shär-ˈlēn\ *var of* CHARLENE
Shar•on *or* **Shar•ron** \ˈshar-ən, ˈsher-\ [Heb]
Shei•la \ˈshē-lə\ [IrGael] *var of* CECILIA
She•lia \ˈshēl-yə\ *var of* SHEILA
Shel•ley \ˈshel-ē\ [fr. a surname]
Sher•rill *or* **Sher•yl** \ˈsher-əl\ [prob. fr. a surname]
Sher•ry *or* **Sher•rie** *or* **Sheri** \ˈsher-ē\
Shir•ley \ˈshər-lē\ [fr. a surname]
Sig•rid \ˈsig-rəd\ [Scand] beautiful as victory
Son•dra \ˈsän-drə\ *var of* SANDRA
So•nia *or* **So•nya** *or* **So•nja** \ˈsō-nyə, ˈsȯ-\ [Russ] *dim of* SOPHIA
So•phia \sə-ˈfē-ə, -ˈfī-\ *or* **So•phie** \ˈsō-fē\ [Gk] wisdom
Sta•cy *or* **Sta•cey** \ˈstā-sē\ *dim of* ANASTASIA
Stel•la \ˈstel-ə\ [L] star
Steph•a•nie \ˈstef-ə-nē\ *fem of* STEPHEN
Sue \ˈsü\ *or* **Su•sie** \ˈsü-zē\ *dim of* SUSAN
Su•el•len \sü-ˈel-ən\ [*Sue* + *Ellen*]
Su•san *or* **Su•zan** \ˈsüz-ᵊn\ *dim of* SUSANNA
Su•san•na *or* **Su•san•nah** \sü-ˈzan-ə\ [Heb] lily
Su•zanne *or* **Su•sanne** *or* **Su•zann** \sü-ˈzan\ [F] *var of* SUSAN
Syb•il \ˈsib-əl\ [Gk] sibyl
Syl•via \ˈsil-vē-ə\ [L] she of the forest

Ta•mara \tə-ˈmar-ə\ [prob. fr. Georgian (language of the Soviet republic of Georgia)]
Tan•ya \ˈtan-yə\ [Russ] *dim of* TATIANA
Ta•ra \ˈtȧr-ə\ [IrGael]
Tat•i•ana \ˌtät-ē-ˈän-ə\ [Russ]
Te•re•sa \tə-ˈrē-sə\ *var of* THERESA
Ter•ry *or* **Ter•ri** \ˈter-ē\ *dim of* THERESA
Thel•ma \ˈthel-mə\
The•o•do•ra \ˌthē-ə-ˈdōr-ə, -ˈdȯr-\ [LGk] *fem of* THEODORE
The•re•sa *or* **Te•re•sa** \tə-ˈrē-sə\ [LL]
The•rese \tə-ˈrēs\ *var of* THERESA
Tif•fa•ny \ˈtif-ə-nē\ [Gk]
Ti•na \ˈtē-nə\ *dim of* CHRISTINA
To•by \ˈtō-bē\
To•ni \ˈtō-nē\ *dim of* Antonia
Tra•cy \ˈtrā-sē\ [fr. a surname]
Tru•dy \ˈtrüd-ē\ *dim of* GERTRUDE

Ur•su•la \ˈər-sə-lə\ [LL] little she-bear

Val•er•ie \ˈval-ə-rē\ [L] *prob* strong
Van•es•sa \və-ˈnes-ə\
Vel•ma \ˈvel-mə\
Ve•ra \ˈvir-ə\ [Russ] faith
Ver•na \ˈvər-nə\ *prob fem of* VERNON
Ve•ron•i•ca \və-ˈrän-i-kə\ [LL]
Vicki *or* **Vicky** *or* **Vick•ie** \ˈvik-ē\ *dim of* VICTORIA
Vic•to•ria \vik-ˈtōr-ē-ə, -ˈtȯr-\ [L] victory
Vi•da \ˈvēd-ə, ˈvīd-\ *fem dim of* DAVID
Vi•o•la \vī-ˈō-lə, vē-ˈō-, ˈvī-ə-, ˈvē-ə-\ [L] violet
Vi•o•let \ˈvī-ə-lət\ [OF, fr. L] violet
Vir•gin•ia \vər-ˈjin-yə, -ˈjin-ē-ə\ [L]
Viv•i•an \ˈviv-ē-ən\ [LL]

Wan•da \ˈwän-də\ [Pol]
Wen•dy \ˈwen-dē\
Whit•ney \ˈhwit-nē, ˈwit-\ [OE]
Wil•da \ˈwil-də\ *var of* WILLA
Wil•la \ˈwil-ə\ *or* **Wil•lie** \ˈwil-ē\ *prob fem dim of* WILLIAM
Wil•ma \ˈwil-mə\ *prob fem dim of* WILLIAM
Win•i•fred \ˈwin-ə-frəd\ [W]

Yvette \i-ˈvet\ [F]
Yvonne \i-ˈvän\ [F]

Zel•da \ˈzel-də\ *dim of* Griselda

Foreign Words and Phrases

ab·eunt stu·dia in mo·res \ˈäb-e-ˌu̇nt-ˈstüd-ē-ˌä-ˌin-ˈmō-ˌrās\ [L] : practices zealously pursued pass into habits
à bien·tôt \á-byaⁿ-tō\ [F] : so long : farewell
ab in·cu·na·bu·lis \ˌäb-ˌiŋ-kə-ˈnäb- ə-ˌlēs\ [L] : from the cradle : from infancy
à bon chat, bon rat \á-bōⁿ-ˈshá- bōⁿ-ˈrá\ [F] : to a good cat, a good rat : retaliation in kind
à bouche ou·verte \á-bü-shü-vert\ [F] : with open mouth : eagerly : uncritically
ab ovo us·que ad ma·la \äb-ˈō-vō-ˌu̇s-kwe- ˌäd-ˈmäl-ä\ [L] : from egg to apples : from soup to nuts : from beginning to end
à bras ou·verts \á-brá-zü-ver\ [F] : with open arms : cordially
ab·sit in·vi·dia \ˈäb-ˌsit-in-ˈwid-ē-ˌä\ [L] : let there be no envy or ill will
ab uno dis·ce om·nes \äb-ˈü-nō-ˌdis-ke-ˈȯm-ˌnās\ [L] : from one learn to know all
ab ur·be con·di·ta \äb-ˈu̇r-be-ˈkȯn-də-ˌtä\ [L] : from the founding of the city (Rome, founded 753 B.C.) — used by the Romans in reckoning dates
ab·usus non tol·lit usum \ˈäb-ˌü-səs-ˌnōn-ˌtȯ-lət-ˈü-səm\ [L] : abuse does not take away use, i.e., is not an argument against proper use
à compte \á-kōⁿt\ [F] : on account
à coup sûr \á-kü-sūr\ [F] : with sure stroke : surely
acte gra·tuit \ák-tə-grá-twʸē\ [F] : gratuitous impulsive act
ad ar·bi·tri·um \ˌad-är-ˈbit-rē-əm\ [L] : at will : arbitrarily
ad as·tra per as·pe·ra \ad-ˈas-trə-ˌpər-ˈas-pə-rə\ [L] : to the stars by hard ways — motto of Kansas
ad ex·tre·mum \ˌad-ik-ˈstrē-məm\ [L] : to the extreme : at last
ad ka·len·das Grae·cas \ˌäd-kə-ˈlen-dəs- ˈgrī-ˌkäs\ [L] : at the Greek calends : never (since the Greeks had no calends)
ad ma·jo·rem Dei glo·ri·am \äd-mä-ˈyōr-ˌem-ˈde-ˌē-ˈglōr-ē-ˌäm\ [L] : to the greater glory of God — motto of the Society of Jesus
ad pa·tres \äd-ˈpä-ˌtrās\ [L] : (gathered) to his fathers : deceased
à droite \á-drwät\ [F] : to or on the right hand
ad un·guem \äd-ˈu̇ŋ-ˌgwem\ [L] : to the fingernail : to a nicety : exactly (from the use of the fingernail to test the smoothness of marble)
ad utrum·que pa·ra·tus \ˌäd-ü-ˈtrüm-kwe-pə-ˈrät-əs\ [L] : prepared for either (event)
ad vi·vum \äd-ˈwē-ˌwu̇m\ [L] : to the life
ae·gri som·nia \ˈī-grē-ˈsȯm-nē-ˌä\ [L] : a sick man's dreams
ae·quam ser·va·re men·tem \ˈī-ˌkwäm-sər-ˌwä-rā-ˈmen-ˌtem\ [L] : to preserve a calm mind
ae·quo ani·mo \ˈī-ˌkwō-ˈän-ə-ˌmō\ [L] : with even mind : calmly
ae·re per·en·ni·us \ˈī-rā-pə-ˈren-ē-ˌu̇s\ [L] : more lasting than bronze
à gauche \á-gōsh\ [F] : to or on the left hand
age quod agis \ˈäg-e-ˌkwȯd-ˈäg-is\ [L] : do what you are doing : to the business at hand
à grands frais \á-gräⁿ-fre\ [F] : at great expense
à huis clos \á-wʸē-klō\ [F] : with closed doors
aide–toi, le ciel t'ai·dera \ed-twá lə-ˈsyel-te-drá\ [F] : help yourself (and) heaven will help you
ai·né \e-nā\ [F] : elder : senior (masc.)
ai·née \e-nā\ [F] : elder : senior (fem.)
à l'aban·don \á-lá-bäⁿ-dōⁿ\ [F] : carelessly : in disorder
à la belle étoile \á-lá-bel-ā-twál\ [F] : under the beautiful star : in the open air at night
à la bonne heure \á-lá-bȯ-nœr\ [F] : at a good time : well and good : all right
à la fran·çaise \á-lá-fräⁿ-sez\ [F] : in the French style
à l'an·glaise \á-läⁿ-glez\ [F] : in the English style
alea jac·ta est \ˈäl-ē-ˌä-ˌyäk-tə-ˈest\ [L] : the die is cast
à l'im·pro·viste \á-laⁿ-prȯ-vēst\ [F] : unexpectedly
ali·quan·do bo·nus dor·mi·tat Ho·me·rus \ˌäl-i-ˌkwän- dō-ˈbȯ-nəs-dȯr-ˈmē-tät-hō-ˈmer-əs\ [L] : sometimes (even) good Homer nods
alis vo·lat pro·pri·is \ˈäl-ˌēs- ˈwȯ-ˌlät-ˈprō-prē-ˌēs\ [L] : she flies with her own wings — motto of Oregon
al–ki \ˈal-ˌkī\ [Chinook Jargon] : by and by — motto of Washington
alo·ha oe \ä-ˌlō-hä-ˈȯi, -ˈō-ē\ [Hawaiian] : love to you : greetings : farewell
al·ter idem \ˌȯl-tər-ˈī-ˌdem, ˌäl-tər-ˈē-\ [L] : second self
a max·i·mis ad mi·ni·ma \ä-ˈmäk-sə-ˌmēs-ˌäd-ˈmin-ə-ˌmä\ [L] : from the greatest to the least
ami·cus hu·ma·ni ge·ne·ris \ä-ˈmē-kəs- hü-ˌmän-ē-ˈgen-ə-rəs\ [L] : friend of the human race
ami·cus us·que ad aras \-ˌu̇s-kwe-ˌäd-ˈär-ˌäs\ [L] : a friend as far as to the altars, i.e., except in what is contrary to one's religion; *also* : a friend to the last extremity
ami de cour \á-ˌmēd-ə-ˈku̇r\ [F] : court friend : insincere friend
amor pa·tri·ae \ˌäm-ˌȯr-ˈpä-trē-ˌī\ [L] : love of one's country
amor vin·cit om·nia \ˈä-ˌmȯr-ˌwiŋ-kət-ˈȯm-nē-ə\ [L] : love conquers all things
an·cienne no·blesse \äⁿ-syen-nȯ-bles\ [F] : old-time nobility : the French nobility before the Revolution of 1789
an·guis in her·ba \ˌäŋ-gwis-in-ˈher-ˌbä\ [L] : snake in the grass
ani·mal bi·pes im·plu·me \ˈän-i-ˌmäl-ˌbip-ˌās-im-ˈplü-me\ [L] : two-legged animal without feathers (i.e., man)
ani·mis opi·bus·que pa·ra·ti \ˈän-ə-ˌmēs-ˌō-pi-ˈbu̇s-kwe-pə-ˈrät-ē\ [L] : prepared in mind and resources — one of the mottoes of South Carolina
an·no ae·ta·tis su·ae \ˈän-ō-ī-ˌtät-is-ˈsü-ˌī\ [L] : in the (specified) year of his (or her) age
an·no mun·di \ˌän-ō-ˈmu̇n-dē\ [L] : in the year of the world — used in reckoning dates from the supposed period of the creation of the world, esp. as fixed by James Ussher at 4004 B.C. or by the Jews at 3761 B.C.
an·no ur·bis con·di·tae \ˌän-ō-ˌu̇r-bis- ˈkȯn-də-ˌtī\ [L] : in the year of the founded city (Rome, founded 753 B.C.)
an·nu·it coep·tis \ˌän-ə-ˌwit-ˈkȯip-ˌtēs\ [L] : He (God) has smiled on our undertakings — motto on the reverse of the Great Seal of the United States
à peu près \á-pœ-pre\ [F] : nearly : approximately
à pied \á-pyā\ [F] : on foot
après moi le dé·luge \á-pre-mwá-lə-dā-lʸüzh\ [F] : after me the deluge (at-tributed to Louis XV)
à pro·pos de bottes \á-prə-pōd-ə-bȯt\ [F] : apropos of boots — used to change the subject
à pro·pos de rien \-ryaⁿ\ [F] : apropos of nothing
aqua et ig·ni in·ter·dic·tus \ˌäk-wä-et-ˈig-nē-ˌint-ər-ˈdik-təs\ [L] : forbidden to be furnished with water and fire : outlawed
Ar·ca·des am·bo \ˌär-kə-ˌdes-ˈäm-bō\ [L] : both Arcadi-

ans : two persons of like occupations or tastes; *also* : two rascals
ar·rec·tis au·ri·bus \ä-ˈrek-ˌtēs-ˈau̇-ri-ˌbu̇s\ [L] : with ears pricked up : attentively
ar·ri·ve·der·ci \ä-ˌrē-ve-ˈder-chē\ [It] : till we meet again : farewell
ars est ce·la·re ar·tem \ˌärs-ˌest-kä-ˌlär-ē-ˈär-ˌtem\ [L] : it is (true) art to conceal art
ars lon·ga, vi·ta bre·vis \ärs-ˈlȯŋ-ˌgä- ˌwē-ˌtä-ˈbre-wis\ [L] : art is long, life is short
a ter·go \ä-ˈter-(ˌ)gō\ [L] : from behind
à tort et à tra·vers \ȧ-tȯr-ā-ȧ-trȧ-ver\ [F] : wrong and crosswise : at random : without rhyme or reason
au bout de son la·tin \ō-büd-(ə-)sōⁿ-lȧ-taⁿ\ [F] : at the end of one's Latin : at the end of one's mental resources
au con·traire \ō-kōⁿ-trer\ [F] : on the contrary
au·de·mus ju·ra nos·tra de·fen·de·re \au̇-ˈdā-məs-ˌyu̇r-ə-ˈnȯ-strə-dā-ˈfen-də-rā\ [L] : we dare defend our rights — motto of Alabama
au·den·tes for·tu·na ju·vat \au̇-ˈden-ˌtās-fȯr-ˌtü-nə-ˈyü-ˌwät\ [L] : fortune favors the bold
au·di al·ter·am par·tem \ˈau̇-ˌdē-ˌäl-tə-ˌräm-ˈpär-ˌtem\ [L] : hear the other side
au fait \ō-fet, -fe\ [F] : to the point : fully competent : fully informed : socially correct
au fond \ō-fōⁿ\ [F] : at bottom : fundamentally
au grand sé·rieux \ō-gräⁿ-sā-ryœ\ [F] : in all seriousness
au pays des aveugles les borgnes sont rois \ō-pā-ē-dā-zȧ-vœglᵊ-lā-bȯrnʸ-ə-sōⁿ-rwä\ [F] : in the country of the blind the one-eyed men are kings
au pied de la lettre \ō-pyād-lȧ-letrᵊ\ [F] : literally
au·rea me·di·o·cri·tas \ˈau̇-rē-ə-ˌmed-ē-ˈō-krə-ˌtäs\ [L] : the golden mean
au reste \ō-rest\ [F] : for the rest : besides
aus·si·tôt dit, aus·si·tôt fait \ō-sē-tō-dē ō-sē-tō-fe\ [F] : no sooner said than done
aut Cae·sar aut ni·hil \au̇t-ˈkī-sär-ˌau̇t-ˈni-ˌhil\ [L] : either a Caesar or nothing
aut Caesar aut nul·lus \-ˈnu̇l-əs\ [L] : either a Caesar or a nobody
au·tres temps, au·tres mœurs \ō-trə-täⁿ ō-trə-mœrs\ [F] : other times, other customs
aut vin·ce·re aut mo·ri \au̇t-ˈwiŋ-kə-rē-ˌau̇t-ˈmȯ-ˌrē\ [L] : either to conquer or to die
aux armes \ō-zȧrm\ [F] : to arms
ave at·que va·le \ˈä-ˌwā-ˌät-kwe-ˈwä-ˌlā\ [L] : hail and farewell
à vo·tre san·té \ȧ-vȯt-säⁿ-tā, -vȯ-trə-\ [F] : to your health — used as a toast
beaux yeux \bō-zyǿ\ [F] : beautiful eyes : beauty of face
bien en·ten·du \byaⁿ-näⁿ-täⁿ-dǖ\ [F] : well understood : of course
bien–pen·sant \byaⁿ-päⁿ-säⁿ\ [F] : right-minded : one who holds orthodox views
bien·sé·ance \byaⁿ-sā-äⁿs\ [F] : propriety
bis dat qui ci·to dat \ˌbis-ˌdät-kwē-ˈki-tō-ˌdät\ [L] : he gives twice who gives promptly
bon ap·pé·tit \bȯ-nȧ-pā-tē\ [F] : good appetite : enjoy your meal
bon gré, mal gré \ˈbōⁿ-ˌgrā- ˈmȧl-ˌgrā\ [F] : whether with good grace or bad : willy-nilly
bo·nis avi·bus \ˌbȯ-ˌnēs-ˈä-wi-ˌbu̇s\ [L] : under good auspices
bon jour \bōⁿ-zhür\ [F] : good day : good morning
bonne foi \bȯn-fwä\ [F] : good faith
bon soir \bōⁿ-swȧr\ [F] : good evening
bru·tum ful·men \ˌbrüt-əm-ˈfu̇l-men\ [L] : insensible thunderbolt : a futile threat or display of force
buon gior·no \bwȯn-ˈjȯr-nō\ [It] : good day
ca·dit quae·stio \ˌkäd-ət-ˈkwī-stē-ˌō\ [L] : the question drops : the argument collapses
cau·sa si·ne qua non \ˈkau̇-ˌsä-ˌsin-ē-kwä-ˈnōn\ [L] : an indispensable cause or condition
ca·ve ca·nem \ˌkä-wā-ˈkän-ˌem\ [L] : beware the dog
ce·dant ar·ma to·gae \ˈkā-ˌdänt-ˌär-mə-ˈtō-ˌgī\ [L] : let arms yield to the toga : let military power give way to civil power — motto of Wyoming
ce n'est que le pre·mier pas qui coûte \snek-lə-prə-myā-pä-kē-küt\ [F] : it is only the first step that costs
c'est a dire \se-tȧ-dēr\ [F] : that is to say : namely
c'est au·tre chose \se-tōt-shōz, -tō-trə-\ [F] : that's a different thing
c'est la guerre \se-lȧ-ger\ [F] : that's war : it cannot be helped
c'est la vie \se-lȧ-vē\ [F] : that's life : that's how things happen
c'est plus qu'un crime, c'est une faute \se-plǖ-kœⁿ-krēm se-tǖn-fōt\ [F] : it is worse than a crime, it is a blunder
ce·te·ra de·sunt \ˌkāt-ə-ˌrä-ˈdā-ˌsu̇nt\ [L] : the rest is missing
cha·cun à son goût \shȧ-kœⁿ- nȧ-sōⁿ-gü\ [F] : everyone to his taste
châ·teau en Es·pagne \shä-tō-äⁿ-nes-pȧnʸ\ [F] : castle in Spain : a visionary project
cher·chez la femme \sher-shā-lȧ-fȧm\ [F] : look for the woman
che sa·rà, sa·rà \ˌkā-sä-ˌrä- sä-ˈrä\ [It] : what will be, will be
che·val de ba·taille \shə-vȧl-də-bȧ-täʸ\ [F] : war-horse : argument constantly relied on : favorite subject
co·gi·to, er·go sum \ˈkō-gi-ˌtō ˌer-gō-ˈsu̇m\ [L] : I think, therefore I exist
co·mé·die hu·maine \kȯ-mā-dē-ǖ-men\ [F] : human comedy : the whole variety of human life
comme ci, comme ça \kȯm-sē-kȯm-sȧ\ [F] : so-so
com·pa·gnon de voy·age \kōⁿ-pȧ-nʸōⁿ-də-vwȧ-yȧzh\ [F] : traveling companion
compte ren·du \kōⁿt-räⁿ-dǖ\ [F] : report (as of proceedings in an investigation)
con·cor·dia dis·cors \kän-kȯrd-ē-ä-ˈdis-ˌkōrs\ [L] : discordant harmony
cor·rup·tio op·ti·mi pes·si·ma \kə-ˈru̇p-tē-ˌō-ˈäp-tə-ˌmē-ˈpes-ə-ˌmä\ [L] : the corruption of the best is the worst of all
coup de maî·tre \küd-(ə-)metrᵊ\ [F] : masterstroke
coup d'es·sai \kü-dā-se\ [F] : experiment : trial
coûte que coûte \küt-kə-küt\ [F] : cost what it may
cre·do quia ab·sur·dum est \ˌkrād-ō-ˈkwē-ä-äp-ˌsu̇rd-əm-ˈest\ [L] : I believe it because it is absurd
cres·cit eun·do \ˌkres-kət-ˈeu̇n-dō\ [L] : it grows as it goes — motto of New Mexico
crise de nerfs *or* **crise des nerfs** \krēz-də-ner\ [F] : crisis of nerves : nervous collapse : hysterical fit
crux cri·ti·co·rum \ˈkru̇ks-ˌkrit-ə-ˈkōr-əm\ [L] : crux of critics
cum gra·no sa·lis \ku̇m-ˌgrän-ō-ˈsäl-is\ [L] : with a grain of salt
cus·tos mo·rum \ˌku̇s-tōs-ˈmōr-əm\ [L] : guardian of manners or morals : censor
d'ac·cord \dȧ-kȯr\ [F] : in accord : agreed
dame d'hon·neur \dȧm-dȯ-nœr\ [F] : lady-in-waiting
dam·nant quod non in·tel·li·gunt \ˈdäm-ˌnänt-ˌkwȯd-ˌnōn-in-ˈtel-ə-ˌgu̇nt\ [L] : they condemn what they do not understand
de bonne grâce \də-bȯn-gräs\ [F] : with good grace : willingly
de gus·ti·bus non est dis·pu·tan·dum \dā-ˈgu̇s-tə-ˌbu̇s-ˌnōn-ˌest-ˌdis-pu̇-ˈtän-ˌdu̇m\ [L] : there is no disputing about tastes
Dei gra·tia \ˈde-ˌē-ˈgrät-ē-ˌä\ [L] : by the grace of God
de in·te·gro \dā-ˈint-ə-ˌgrō\ [L] : anew : afresh
de l'au·dace, en·core de l'au·dace, et tou·jours de l'au·dace \də-lō-ˈdȧs äⁿ-ˈkȯr-də-lō-dȧs ā-tü-ˈzhür-də-lō-dȧs\ [F] : audacity, more audacity, and ever more audacity
de·len·da est Car·tha·go \dā-ˈlen-dä-ˌest-kär-ˈtäg-ō\ [L] : Carthage must be destroyed

de·li·ne·a·vit \dā-ˌlē-nā-ˈä-wit\ [L] : he (or she) drew it
de mal en pis \də-mȧ-lä^n-pē\ [F] : from bad to worse
de mi·ni·mis non cu·rat lex \dā-ˈmin-ə-ˌmēs-ˌnōn-ˌkü-ˌrät-ˈleks\ [L] : the law takes no account of trifles
de mor·tu·is nil ni·si bo·num \dā-ˈmȯrt-ə-ˌwēs-ˌnēl-ˌnis-ē-ˈbȯ-ˌnu̇m\ [L] : of the dead (say) nothing but good
de nos jours \də-nō-zhür\ [F] : of our time : contemporary — used postpositively esp. after a proper name
Deo fa·ven·te \ˌdā-ō-fä-ˈvent-ā\ [L] : with God's favor
Deo gra·ti·as \ˌdā-ō-ˈgrät-ē-ˌäs\ [L] : thanks (be) to God
de pro·fun·dis \ˌdā-prō-ˈfu̇n-dēs\ [L] : out of the depths
der Geist der stets ver·neint \dər-ˈgīst-dər-ˌshtāts-fer-ˈnīnt\ [G] : the spirit that ever denies — applied originally to Mephistopheles
de·si·pe·re in lo·co \dā-ˈsip-ə-rē-in-ˈlō- kō\ [L] : to indulge in trifling at the proper time
Deus vult \ˌdā-əs-ˈwu̇lt\ [L] : God wills it — rallying cry of the First Crusade
di·es fau·stus \ˌdē-ˌās-ˈfau̇-stəs\ [L] : lucky day
dies in·fau·stus \-ˈin-ˌfau̇-stəs\ [L] : unlucky day
dies irae \-ˈē-ˌrī\ [L] : day of wrath — used of the Judgment Day
Dieu et mon droit \dyœ-ā-mō^n-drwä\ [F] : God and my right — motto on the British royal arms
Dieu vous garde \dyœ-vü-gȧrd\ [F] : God keep you
di·ri·go \ˈdē-ri-ˌgō\ [L] : I direct — motto of Maine
dis ali·ter vi·sum \ˌdēs-ˌäl-ə-ˌter-ˈwē-ˌsu̇m\ [L] : the Gods decreed otherwise
di·tat De·us \ˌdē-ˌtät-ˈdā-ˌu̇s\ [L] : God enriches — motto of Arizona
di·vi·de et im·pe·ra \ˈdē-wi-ˌde-ˌet-ˈim-pə-ˌrä\ [L] : divide and rule
do·cen·do dis·ci·mus \dō-ˌken-dō-ˈdis-ki-ˌmu̇s\ [L] : we learn by teaching
Do·mi·ne di·ri·ge nos \ˈdō-mi-ˌne-ˌdē-ri-ge-ˈnōs\ [L] : Lord, direct us — motto of the City of London
Do·mi·nus vo·bis·cum \ˌdō-mi-ˌnu̇s-wō-ˈbēs-ˌku̇m\ [L] : the Lord be with you
dul·ce et de·co·rum est pro pa·tria mo·ri \ˌdu̇l-ˌket-de-ˈkōr-ˌest-prō-ˌpä-trē-ˌä- ˈmō-ˌrē\ [L] : it is sweet and seemly to die for one's country
dum spi·ro, spe·ro \du̇m-ˈspē-rō-ˈspā-rō\ [L] : while I breathe I hope — one of the mottoes of South Carolina
dum vi·vi·mus vi·va·mus \du̇m-ˈwē-wē-ˌmu̇s-wē-ˈwäm-u̇s\ [L] : while we live, let us live
dux fe·mi·na fac·ti \ˌdu̇ks-ˌfā-mi-nä-ˈfäk-ˌtē\ [L] : a woman was leader of the exploit
ec·ce sig·num \ˌek-e-ˈsig-ˌnu̇m\ [L] : behold the sign : look at the proof
e con·tra·rio \ˌā-kōn-ˈträr-ē-ˌō\ [L] : on the contrary
écra·sez l'in·fâme \ā-krä-zā-la^n-fäm\ [F] : crush the infamous thing
eheu fu·ga·ces la·bun·tur an·ni \ˌā-ˌheu̇-fu̇-ˈgä-ˌkās-lä-ˌbu̇n-ˌtu̇r-ˈän-ˌē\ [L] : alas! the fleeting years glide on
ein' fes·te Burg ist un·ser Gott \īn-ˌfes-tə-ˈbu̇rk-ist-ˌu̇n-zər-ˈgōt\ [G] : a mighty fortress is our God
em·bar·ras de ri·chesses \ä^n-bȧ-räd-(ə-)rē-shes\ [F] : embarrassing surplus of riches : confusing abundance
em·bar·ras du choix \ä^n-bȧ-rä-dᵫ-shwȧ\ [F] : embarrassing variety of choice
en ami \ä^n-nȧ-mē\ [F] : as a friend
en ef·fet \ä^n-nā-fe\ [F] : in fact : indeed
en fa·mille \ä^n-fä-mēy\ [F] : in or with one's family : at home : informally
en·fant gâ·té \ä^n-fä^n-gä-tā\ [F] : spoiled child
en·fants per·dus \ä^n-fä^n-per-dᵫ\ [F] : lost children : soldiers sent to a dangerous post
en·fin \ä^n-fa^n\ [F] : in conclusion : in a word
en gar·çon \ä^n-gȧr-sō^n\ [F] : as or like a bachelor
en pan·tou·fles \ä^n-pä^n-tüfl^ə\ [F] : in slippers : at ease : informally
en plein air \ä^n-plen-er\ [F] : in the open air
en plein jour \ä^n-pla^n-zhür\ [F] : in broad day
en règle \ä^n-regl^ə\ [F] : in order : in due form
en re·tard \ä^nr-(ə-)tȧr\ [F] : behind time : late
en re·traite \ä^n-rə-tret\ [F] : in retreat : in retirement
en re·vanche \ä^nr-(ə-)vä^nsh\ [F] : in return : in compensation
en se·condes noces \ä^ns-(ə-)gō^nd-nȯs\ [F] : in a second marriage
en·se pe·tit pla·ci·dam sub li·ber·ta·te qui·e·tem \ˈen-se-ˌpet-ət-ˈpläk-i-ˌdäm-su̇b-ˌlē-ber-ˌtä-te-kwē-ˈā-ˌtem\ [L] : with the sword she seeks calm repose under liberty — motto of Massachusetts
épa·ter les bour·geois \ā-pȧ-tā-lā-bür-zhwȧ\ [F] : to shock the middle classes
e plu·ri·bus unum \ˌē-ˌplu̇r-ə-bəs-ˈ(y)ü-nəm, ˌā-ˌplu̇r-\ [L] : one out of many — used on the seal of the U.S. and on several U.S. coins
ep·pur si muo·ve \āp-ˌpür-sē-ˈmwȯ-vā\ [It] : and yet it does move — attributed to Galileo after recanting his assertion of the earth's motion
Erin go bragh \ˌer-ən-gə-ˈbrȯ, -gō-ˈbrä\ [IrGael *go brāth*, lit., till doomsday] : Ireland forever
er·ra·re hu·ma·num est \e-ˈrär-e-hü-ˌmän-əm-ˈest\ [L] : to err is human
es·prit de l'es·ca·lier \es-prēd-les-kȧ-lyā\ *or* **es·prit d'es·ca·lier** \-prē-des-\ [F] : staircase wit : repartee thought of only too late
es·se quam vi·de·ri \ˈes-ē-ˌkwäm-wi-ˈdā-rē\ [L] : to be rather than to seem — motto of North Carolina
est mo·dus in re·bus \est-ˈmō-ˌdu̇s-in-ˈrā-ˌbu̇s\ [L] : there is a proper measure in things, i.e., the golden mean should always be observed
es·to per·pe·tua \ˈes-ˌtō-pər-ˈpet-ə-ˌwä\ [L] : may she endure forever — motto of Idaho
et hoc ge·nus om·ne \et-ˌhōk-ˌgen-əs-ˈōm-ne\ *or* **et id genus omne** \et-ˌid-\ [L] : and everything of this kind
et in Ar·ca·dia ego \ˌet-in-är-ˌkäd-ē-ə-ˈeg-ō\ [L] : I too (lived) in Arcadia
et sic de si·mi·li·bus \et-ˌsēk-dā-si-ˈmil-ə-ˌbu̇s\ [L] : and so of like things
et tu Bru·te \et-ˈtü-ˈbrü-te\ [L] : thou too, Brutus — exclamation attributed to Julius Caesar on seeing his friend Brutus among his assassins
eu·re·ka \yu̇-ˈrē-kə\ [Gk] : I have found it — motto of California
Ewig–Weib·li·che \ˌā-vik-ˈvīp-li-kə\ [G] : eternal feminine
ex ani·mo \ek-ˈsän-ə-ˌmō\ [L] : from the heart : sincerely
ex·cel·si·or \ik-ˈsel-sē-ər, eks-ˈkel-sē-ˌȯr\ [L] : still higher — motto of New York
ex·cep·tio pro·bat re·gu·lam de re·bus non ex·cep·tis \eks-ˈkep-tē-ˌō-ˌprō-bät-ˈrā-gə-ˌläm-dā-ˈrā- ˌbu̇s-ˌnōn-eks-ˈkep-ˌtēs\ [L] : an exception establishes the rule as to things not excepted
ex·cep·tis ex·ci·pi·en·dis \eks-ˈkep-ˌtēs-eks-ˌkip-ē-ˈen-ˌdēs\ [L] : with the proper or necessary exceptions
ex·i·tus ac·ta pro·bat \ˈek-sə-ˌtu̇s-ˌäk-tə-ˈprō-ˌbät\ [L] : the event justifies the deed
ex li·bris \eks-ˈlē-bris\ [L] : from the books of — used on bookplates
ex me·ro mo·tu \ˌeks-ˌmer-ō-ˈmō-tü\ [L] : out of mere impulse : of one's own accord
ex ne·ces·si·ta·te rei \ˌeks-ne-ˌkes-i-ˈtä-te-ˈrā(-ˌē)\ [L] : from the necessity of the case
ex ni·hi·lo ni·hil fit \eks-ˈni-hi-ˌlō-ni-ˌhil-ˈfit\ [L] : from nothing nothing is produced
ex pe·de Her·cu·lem \eks-ˌped-e-ˈher-kə-ˌlem\ [L] : from the foot (we may judge of the size of) Hercules : from a part we may judge of the whole
ex·per·to cre·di·te \eks-ˌpert-ō-ˈkrād-ə-ˌte\ [L] : believe one who has had experience
ex un·gue le·o·nem \eks-ˈu̇ŋ-gwe-le-ˈō-ˌnem\ [L] : from the claw (we may judge of) the lion : from a part we may judge of the whole

ex vi ter·mi·ni \eks-ˌwē-ˈter-mə-ˌnē\ [L] : from the force of the term

fa·ci·le prin·ceps \ˌfäk-i-le-ˈpriŋ-ˌkeps\ [L] : easily first

fa·ci·lis de·scen·sus Aver·no \ˈfäk-i-ˌlis-dā-ˌskän-ˌsu̇s-ä-ˈwer-nō\ *or* **facilis descensus Aver·ni** \-(ˌ)nē\ [L] : the descent to Avernus is easy : the road to evil is easy

fa·çon de par·ler \fȧ-sōⁿ-də-pȧr-lā\ [F] : manner of speaking : figurative or conventional expression

faire suivre \fer-swʸēvrᵊ\ [F] : have forwarded : please forward

fas est et ab ho·ste do·ce·ri \fäs-ˈest-et- äb-ˈhȯ-ste-dȯ-ˈkā-(ˌ)rē\ [L] : it is right to learn even from an enemy

Fa·ta vi·am in·ve·ni·ent \ˌfä-tä-ˈwē-ˌäm-in-ˈwen-ē-ˌent\ [L] : the Fates will find a way

fat·ti mas·chii, pa·ro·le fe·mi·ne \ˌfät-tē-ˈmäs-ˌkē pä-ˌrȯ-lā-ˈfā- mē-ˌnā\ [It] : deeds are males, words are females : deeds are more effective than words — motto of Maryland, where it is generally interpreted as meaning "manly deeds, womanly words"

faux bon·homme \fō-bȯ-nȯm\ [F] : pretended good fellow

faux–naïf \fō-nȧ-ēf\ [F] : pretending to be childlike

femme de cham·bre \fäm-də-shäⁿbrᵊ\ [F] : chambermaid : lady's maid

fe·sti·na len·te \fe-ˌstē-nə-ˈlen-ˌtā\ [L] : make haste slowly

feux d'ar·ti·fice \fœ̄-dȧr-tē-fēs\ [F] : fireworks : display of wit

fi·at ex·pe·ri·men·tum in cor·po·re vi·li \ˈfē-ˌät-ek-ˌsper-ē-ˈmen-ˌtu̇m-in-ˌkȯr-pə-re-ˈwē-lē\ [L] : let experiment be made on a worthless body

fi·at ju·sti·tia, ru·at cae·lum \ˌfē-ät-yu̇s-ˈtit-ē-ä,ˌrü-ˌät- ˈkī-ˌlu̇m\ [L] : let justice be done though the heavens fall

fi·at lux \ˌfē-ˌät-ˈlu̇ks\ [L] : let there be light

Fi·dei De·fen·sor \ˌfid-e-ˌē-dā-ˈfān-ˌsȯr\ [L] : Defender of the Faith — a title of the sovereigns of England

fi·dus Acha·tes \ˌfēd-əs-ä-ˈkä-ˌtās\ [L] : faithful Achates : trusty friend

fille de cham·bre \fēy-də-shäⁿbrᵊ\ [F] : lady's maid

fille d'hon·neur \fēy-dȯ-nœr\ [F] : maid of honor

fils \fēs\ [F] : son — used after French proper names to distinguish a son from his father

fi·nem re·spi·ce \ˌfē-ˌnem-ˈrā-spi-ˌke\ [L] : consider the end

fi·nis co·ro·nat opus \ˌfē-nəs-kə-ˈrō-ˌnät-ˈō-ˌpu̇s\ [L] : the end crowns the work

fluc·tu·at nec mer·gi·tur \ˈflu̇k-tə-ˌwät-ˌnek-ˈmer-gə-ˌtu̇r\ [L] : it is tossed by the waves but does not sink — motto of Paris

fo·lie de gran·deur *or* **fo·lie des gran·deurs** \fȯ-lē-də-gräⁿ-dœr\ [F] : delusion of greatness : megalomania

fors·an et haec olim me·mi·nis·se ju·va·bit \ˌfȯr-ˌsän-ˌet-ˈhīk-ˌō-lim-ˌmem-ə-ˈnis-e-yü-ˈwä-bit\ [L] : perhaps this too will be a pleasure to look back on one day

for·tes for·tu·na ju·vat \ˈfȯr-ˌtās-fȯr-ˌtü- nə-ˈyü-ˌwät\ [L] : fortune favors the brave

fron·ti nul·la fi·des \ˈfrȯn-ˌtē-ˌnu̇l- ə-ˈfid-ˌās\ [L] : no reliance can be placed on appearance

fu·it Ili·um \ˈfu̇-ət-ˈil-ē-əm\ [L] : Troy has been (i.e., is no more)

fu·ror lo·quen·di \ˌfu̇r-ˌȯr-lȯ-ˈkwen-(ˌ)dē\ [L] : rage for speaking

furor po·e·ti·cus \-pȯ-ˈāt-i-ku̇s\ [L] : poetic frenzy

furor scri·ben·di \-skrē-ˈben-(ˌ)dē\ [L] : rage for writing

Gal·li·ce \ˈgäl-ə-ˌke\ [L] : in French : after the French manner

gar·çon d'hon·neur \gȧr-sōⁿ-dȯ-nœr\ [F] : bridegroom's attendant

garde du corps \gȧrd-dꟹ-kȯr\ [F] : bodyguard

gar·dez la foi \gȧr-dā-lȧ-fwä\ [F] : keep faith

gau·de·a·mus igi·tur \ˌgau̇d-ē-ˈäm-əs-ˈig-ə-ˌtu̇r\ [L] : let us then be merry

gens d'é·glise \zhäⁿ-dā-glēz\ [F] : church people : clergy

gens de guerre \zhäⁿ-də-ger\ [F] : military people : soldiery

gens du monde \zhäⁿ-dꟹ- mōⁿd\ [F] : people of the world : fashionable people

gno·thi se·au·ton \gə-ˈnō-thē-ˌse-au̇-ˈtȯn\ [Gk] : know thyself

grand monde \gräⁿ-mōⁿd\ [F] : great world : high society

guerre à ou·trance \ger-ȧ-ü-träⁿs\ [F] : war to the uttermost

gu·ten Tag \ˌgüt-ᵊn-ˈtäk\ [G] : good day

has·ta la vis·ta \ˌäs-tä-lä-ˈvēs-tä\ [Sp] : good-bye

haut goût \ō-gü\ [F] : high flavor : slight taint of decay

hic et ubi·que \ˌhēk-et-u̇-ˈbē-kwe\ [L] : here and everywhere

hic ja·cet \hik-ˈjā-sət, hēk-ˈyäk-ət\ [L] : here lies — used preceding a name on a tombstone

hinc il·lae la·cri·mae \ˌhiŋk-ˌil-ˌī-ˈläk- ri-ˌmī\ [L] : hence those tears

hoc age \hōk-ˈäg-e\ [L] : do this : apply yourself to what you are about

hoc opus, hic la·bor est \hōk-ˈō-ˌpu̇s-ˌhēk-ˌlä-ˌbȯr-ˈest\ [L] : this is the hard work, this is the toil

homme d'af·faires \ȯm-dȧ-fer\ [F] : man of business : business agent

homme d'es·prit \-des-prē\ [F] : man of wit

homme moyen sen·suel \ȯm-mwȧ-yaⁿ-säⁿ-swʸel\ [F] : the average nonintellectual man

ho·mo sum: hu·ma·ni nil a me ali·e·num pu·to \ˈhȯ-mō-ˌsu̇m hü-ˌmän-ē-ˈnēl-ä-ˌmā-ˌäl-ē-ˈā-nəm-ˈpu̇-tō\ [L] : I am a man: I regard nothing that concerns man as foreign to my interests

ho·ni soit qui mal y pense \ȯ-nē-swȧ-kē-mȧl-ē-päⁿs\ [F] : shamed be he who thinks evil of it — motto of the Order of the Garter

hu·ma·num est er·ra·re \hü-ˌmän-əm-ˌest-e-ˈrär-e\ [L] : to err is human

ich dien \ik̲-ˈdēn\ [G] : I serve — motto of the Prince of Wales

ici on parle fran·cais \ē-sē-ōⁿ-pȧrl-(-ə)-fräⁿ-se\ [F] : French is spoken here

id est \id-ˈest\ [L] : that is

ig·no·ran·tia ju·ris ne·mi·nem ex·cu·sat \ˌig-nə-ˌränt-ē-ä-ˈyu̇r-əs-ˈnā-mə-ˌnem-eks-ˈkü-ˌsät\ [L] : ignorance of the law excuses no one

ig·no·tum per ig·no·ti·us \ig-ˈnōt-əm-ˌper-ig-ˈnōt-ē-ˌu̇s\ [L] : (explaining) the unknown by means of the more unknown

il faut cul·ti·ver no·tre jar·din \ēl-fō-kꟹl-tē-vā-nȯt-zhȧr-daⁿ, -nȯ-trə-zhȧr-\ [F] : we must cultivate our garden : we must tend to our own affairs

in ae·ter·num \ˌin-ī-ˈter-ˌnu̇m\ [L] : forever

in du·bio \in-ˈdu̇b-ē-ˌō\ [L] : in doubt : undetermined

in fu·tu·ro \ˌin-fə-ˈtu̇r-ō\ [L] : in the future

in hoc sig·no vin·ces \in-hōk-ˈsig-nō-ˈviŋ-ˌkās\ [L] : by this sign (the Cross) you will conquer

in li·mi·ne \in-ˈlē-mə-ˌne\ [L] : on the threshold : at the beginning

in om·nia pa·ra·tus \in-ˈȯm-nē-ə-pə-ˈrä-ˌtu̇s\ [L] : ready for all things

in par·ti·bus in·fi·de·li·um \in-ˈpärt-ə-ˌbu̇s-ˌin-fə-ˈdā-lē-ˌu̇m\ [L] : in the regions of the infidels — used of a titular bishop having no diocesan jurisdiction, usu. in non-Christian countries

in prae·sen·ti \ˌin-prī-ˈsen-ˌtē\ [L] : at the present time

in sae·cu·la sae·cu·lo·rum \in-ˈsī-ku̇-ˌlä-ˌsī-kə-ˈlōr-əm, -ˈsā-ku̇-ˌlä- ˌsā-\ [L] : for ages of ages : forever and ever

insh·al·lah \ˌin-shä-ˈlä\ [Ar] : if Allah wills : God willing

in sta·tu quo an·te bel·lum \in-ˈstä-ˌtü-kwō-ˌänt-ē-ˈbel-əm\ [L] : in the same state as before the war

in·te·ger vi·tae sce·le·ris·que pu·rus \ˌin-tə-ˌger-ˈwē-ˌtī-ˌskel-ə-ˈris-kwe-ˈpü-rəs\ [L] : upright of life and free from wickedness

in·ter nos \ˌint-ər-ˈnōs\ [L] : between ourselves

in·tra mu·ros \ˌin-trä-ˈmü-ˌrōs\ [L] : within the walls
in usum Del·phi·ni \in-ˈü-səm-del-ˈfē- nē\ [L] : for the use of the Dauphin : expurgated
in utrum·que pa·ra·tus \ˌin-ü-ˈtrùm-kwe-pə-ˈrä-ˌtùs\ [L] : prepared for either (event)
in·ve·nit \in-ˈwā-nit\ [L] : he (or she) devised it
in vi·no ve·ri·tas \in-ˈwē-nō-ˈwā-rə-ˌtäs\ [L] : there is truth in wine
in·vi·ta Mi·ner·va \in-ˈwē-ˌtä-mi-ˈner-ˌwä\ [L] : Minerva being unwilling : without natural talent or inspiration
ip·sis·si·ma ver·ba \ip-ˌsis-ə-ˌmä-ˈwer-ˌbä\ [L] : the very words
ira fu·ror bre·vis est \ˌē-rä-ˈfùr-ˌòr-ˈbre-wis-ˌest\ [L] : anger is a brief madness
j'ac·cuse \zhä-kᵫz\ [F] : I accuse
jac·ta alea est \ˈyäk-ˌtä-ˌä- lē-ˌä-ˈest\ [L] : the die is cast
j'adoube \zhà-düb\ [F] : I adjust — used in chess when touching a piece without intending to move it
ja·nu·is clau·sis \ˌyän-ə-ˌwēs-ˈklaù-ˌsēs\ [L] : behind closed doors
je main·tien·drai \zhə-maⁿ-tyaⁿ-drā\ [F] : I will maintain — motto of the Netherlands
jeu de mots \zhœ̄d-(ə-)mō\ [F] : play on words : pun
Jo·an·nes est no·men eius \yō-ˈän-ās-est-ˌnō-men-ˈā-yùs\ [L] : John is his name — motto of Puerto Rico
jo·lie laide \zhò-lē-led\ [F] : good-looking ugly woman : woman who is attractive though not conventionally pretty
jour·nal in·time \zhür-nàl-aⁿ-tēm\ [F] : intimate journal : private diary
jus di·vi·num \ˌyüs-di-ˈwē-ˌnùm\ [L] : divine law
jus·ti·tia om·ni·bus \yùs-ˌtit-ē-ˌä-ˈòm-ni-ˌbùs\ [L] : justice for all — motto of the District of Columbia
j'y suis, j'y reste \zhē-swʸē-zhē-rest\ [F] : here I am, here I remain
la belle dame sans mer·ci \là-bel-dàm-säⁿ-mer-sē\ [F] : the beautiful lady without mercy
la·bo·ra·re est ora·re \ˈläb-ō-ˌrär-ā-ˌest-ˈō-ˌrär-ā\ [L] : to work is to pray
la·bor om·nia vin·cit \ˈlä-ˌbòr-ˌòm-nē-ˌä-ˈwiŋ-kit\ [L] : labor conquers all things — motto of Oklahoma
la·cri·mae re·rum \ˌläk-ri-ˌmī-ˈrā-ˌrùm\ [L] : tears for things : pity for misfortune; *also* : tears in things : tragedy in life
lais·sez–al·ler *or* **lais·ser–al·ler** \le-sā-à-lā\ [F] : letting go : lack of restraint
lap·sus ca·la·mi \ˌläp-sùs-ˈkäl-ə-ˌmē\ [L] : slip of the pen
lap·sus lin·guae \-ˈliŋ-ˌgwī\ [L] : slip of the tongue
la reine le veut \là-ren-lə-vœ̄\ [F] : the queen wills it
la·scia·te ogni spe·ran·za, voi ch'en·tra·te \läsh-ˈshä-tā- ˌō-nʸē-spā-ˈrän-tsä- ˌvō-ē-kān-ˈträ-tā\ [It] : abandon all hope, ye who enter
lau·da·tor tem·po·ris ac·ti \laù-ˈdä-ˌtòr-ˌtem-pə-ris-ˈäk-ˌtē\ [L] : one who praises past times
laus Deo \laùs-ˈdā-ō\ [L] : praise (be) to God
le cœur a ses rai·sons que la rai·son ne con·nait point \lə-kœr-à-sā-re-zōⁿk-là-re-zōⁿn-(ə-)kò- ne-pwaⁿ\ [F] : the heart has its reasons that reason knows nothing of
le roi est mort, vive le roi \lə-rwä-e-mòr vēv-lə-rwä\ [F] : the king is dead, long live the king
le roi le veut \-lə-vœ̄\ [F] : the king wills it
le roi s'avi·se·ra \-sà-vēz-rà\ [F] : the king will consider
le style, c'est l'homme \lə-stēl-se-lòm\ [F] : the style is the man
l'état, c'est moi \lā-tà-se-mwà\ [F] : the state, it is I
l'étoile du nord \lā-twàl-dᵫ-nòr\ [F] : the star of the north — motto of Minnesota
Lie·der·kranz \ˈlēd-ər-ˌkräns\ [G] : wreath of songs : German singing society
lit·tera scrip·ta ma·net \ˌlit-ə-ˌrä-ˌskrip-tə-ˈmän-et\ [L] : the written letter abides
lo·cus in quo \ˌlò-kəs-in-ˈkwō\ [L] : place in which
l'union fait la force \lᵫ-nyōⁿ-fe-là-fòrs\ [F] : union makes strength — motto of Belgium
lu·sus na·tu·rae \ˌlü-səs-nə-ˈtùr-ē, -ˈtùr-ˌī\ [L] : freak of nature
ma foi \mà-fwä\ [F] : my faith! : indeed
mag·na est ve·ri·tas et prae·va·le·bit \ˌmäg-nä-ˌest-ˈwā-ri-ˌtäs-et-ˌprī-wä-ˈlā-bit\ [L] : truth is mighty and will prevail
mag·ni no·mi·nis um·bra \ˌmäg-nē-ˌnō-mə-nis-ˈùm-brä\ [L] : the shadow of a great name
mai·son de san·té \mā-zōⁿd-(ə-)säⁿ-tā\ [F] : private hospital : asylum
ma·lade ima·gi·naire \mà-làd-ē-mà-zhē-ner\ [F] : imaginary invalid : hypochondriac
ma·lis avi·bus \ˌmäl-ˌēs-ˈä-wi-ˌbùs\ [L] : under evil auspices
ma·no a ma·no \ˌmän-ō-ä-ˈmän-ō\ [Sp] : hand to hand : in direct competition or confrontation
man spricht Deutsch \män-shpriḵt-ˈdòich\ [G] : German spoken
ma·riage de con·ve·nance \mà-ryàzh-də-kōⁿv-näⁿs\ [F] : marriage of convenience
mau·vaise honte \mò-vez-ōⁿt\ [F] : bad shame : bashfulness
mau·vais quart d'heure \mò-ve-kàr-dœr\ [F] : bad quarter hour : an uncomfortable though brief experience
me·dio tu·tis·si·mus ibis \ˈmed-ē-ˌō-tü-ˌtis-ə-mùs-ˈē-bis\ [L] : you will go most safely by the middle course
me ju·di·ce \mā-ˈyüd-ə-ke\ [L] : I being judge : in my judgment
mens sa·na in cor·po·re sa·no \māns-ˈsän-ə-in-ˌkòr- pə-re-ˈsän-ō\ [L] : a sound mind in a sound body
me·um et tu·um \ˌmē-əm-ˌet-ˈtü-əm, ˌmā-əm-\ [L] : mine and thine : distinction of private property
mi·ra·bi·le vi·su \mi-ˌräb-ə-lā-ˈwē-sü\ [L] : wonderful to behold
mi·ra·bi·lia \ˌmir-ə-ˈbil-ē-ə\ [L] : wonders : miracles
mœurs \mœr(s)\ [F] : mores : attitudes, customs, and manners of a society
mo·le ru·it sua \ˈmō-le-ˌrù-it-ˈsù-ä\ [L] : it collapses from its own bigness
monde \mōⁿd\ [F] : world : fashionable world : society
mon·ta·ni sem·per li·be·ri \mòn-ˈtän-ē-ˌsem-pər-ˈlē-bə-ˌrē\ [L] : mountaineers are always free men — motto of West Virginia
mo·nu·men·tum ae·re per·en·ni·us \ˌmò-nə-ˈmen-tùm-ˌī-re-pə-ˈren-ē-ùs\ [L] : a monument more lasting than bronze — used of an immortal work of art or literature
mo·ri·tu·ri te sa·lu·ta·mus \ˌmòr-ə-ˈtùr-ē-ˌtā-ˌsäl-ə-ˈtäm-ùs\ *or* **morituri te sa·lu·tant** \-ˈsäl-ə-ˌtänt\ [L] : we (or those) who are about to die salute thee
mul·tum in par·vo \ˌmùl-təm-in-ˈpär-vō\ [L] : much in little
mu·ta·to no·mi·ne de te fa·bu·la nar·ra·tur \mü-ˌtät-ō-ˈnō-mə-ne-dā-ˈtā-ˌfäb-ə-lä-nä-ˈrä-ˌtùr\ [L] : with the name changed the story applies to you
na·tu·ram ex·pel·las fur·ca, ta·men us·que re·cur·ret \nä-ˈtü-ˌräm-ek-ˌspel-äs-ˈfùr-ˌkä ˌtä-mən-ˈùs-kwe-re-ˈkùr-et\ [L] : you may drive nature out with a pitchfork, but she will keep coming back
na·tu·ra non fa·cit sal·tum \nä-ˈtü-rä-ˌnōn-ˌfäk-ət-ˈsäl-ˌtùm\ [L] : nature makes no leap
ne ce·de ma·lis \nā-ˌkā-de-ˈmäl-ˌēs\ [L] : yield not to misfortunes
ne·mo me im·pu·ne la·ces·sit \ˈnā-mō-ˈmā-im-ˌpü-nā-lä-ˈkes-ət\ [L] : no one attacks me with impunity — motto of Scotland and of the Order of the Thistle
ne quid ni·mis \ˌnā-ˌkwid-ˈnim-əs\ [L] : not anything in excess
n'est–ce pas? \nes-pä\ [F] : isn't it so?
nicht wahr? \niḵt-ˈvär\ [G] : not true? : isn't it so?
nil ad·mi·ra·ri \ˈnēl-ˌäd-mə-ˈrär-ē\ [L] : to be excited by nothing : equanimity

nil de·spe·ran·dum \ˈnēl-ˌdā-spā-ˈrän-dům\ [L] : never despair
nil si·ne nu·mi·ne \ˈnēl-ˌsin-e-ˈnü-mə-ne\ [L] : nothing without the divine will — motto of Colorado
n'im·porte \naⁿ-pȯrt\ [F] : it's no matter
no·lens vo·lens \ˌnō-ˌlenz-ˈvō-ˌlenz\ [L] : unwilling (or) willing : willy-nilly
non om·nia pos·su·mus om·nes \nōn-ˈȯm-nē-ä-ˌpȯ-sə-mu̇s-ˈȯm-ˌnās\ [L] : we can't all (do) all things
non om·nis mo·ri·ar \nōn-ˈȯm-nis-ˈmȯr-ē-ˌär\ [L] : I shall not wholly die
non sans droict \nōⁿ-säⁿ-drwä\ [OF] : not without right — motto on Shakespeare's coat of arms
non sum qua·lis eram \ˌnōn-ˌsu̇m-ˌkwäl-əs-ˈer-ˌäm\ [L] : I am not what I used to be
nos·ce te ip·sum \ˌnȯs-ke-ˌtā-ˈip-ˌsu̇m\ [L] : know thyself
nos·tal·gie de la boue \nȯs-tȧl-zhē-(ə-)lȧ-bü\ [F] : nostalgia for the mud : homesickness for the gutter
nous avons chan·gé tout ce·la \nü-zȧ-vōⁿ-shäⁿ-zhā-tü-slȧ\ [F] : we have changed all that
nous ver·rons ce que nous ver·rons \nü-ve-rōⁿs-(ə-)kə-nü-ve-rōⁿ\ [F] : we shall see what we shall see
no·vus ho·mo \ˌnȯ-wəs-ˈhȯ-mō\ [L] : new man : man newly ennobled : upstart
no·vus or·do se·clo·rum \-ˈȯr-ˌdō-sā-ˈklōr-əm\ [L] : a new cycle of the ages — motto on the reverse of the Great Seal of the United States
nu·gae \ˈnü-ˌgī\ [L] : trifles
nuit blanche \nwʸē-bläⁿsh\ [F] : white night : a sleepless night
nyet \ˈnyet\ [Russ] : no
ob·iit \ˈō-bē-ˌit\ [L] : he (or she) died
ob·scu·rum per ob·scu·ri·us \əb-ˈskyu̇r-əm-ˌper-əb-ˈskyu̇r-ē-əs\ [L] : (explaining) the obscure by means of the more obscure
ode·rint dum me·tu·ant \ˈōd-ə-ˌrint-ˌdu̇m-ˈmet-ə-ˌwänt\ [L] : let them hate, so long as they fear
odi et amo \ˈō-ˌdē-et-ˈäm-(ˌ)ō\ [L] : I hate and I love
om·ne ig·no·tum pro mag·ni·fi·co \ˌȯm-ne-ig-ˈnō-ˌtu̇m-prō-mäg-ˈnif-i-ˌkō\ [L] : everything unknown (is taken) as grand : the unknown tends to be exaggerated in importance or difficulty
om·nia mu·tan·tur, nos et mu·ta·mur in il·lis \ˌȯm-nē-ä-mü-ˈtän-ˌtu̇r ˌnōs-ˌet-mü-ˌtäm-ər-in-ˈil-ˌēs\ [L] : all things are changing, and we are changing with them
om·nia vin·cit amor \ˈȯm-nē-ä-ˈwiŋ-kət-ˈäm-ˌȯr\ [L] : love conquers all
onus pro·ban·di \ˌō-nəs-prō-ˈban-ˌdī, -dē\ [L] : burden of proof
ora pro no·bis \ˌō-rä-prō-ˈnō-ˌbēs\ [L] : pray for us
ore ro·tun·do \ˌōr-ā-rō-ˈtu̇n-dō\ [L] : with round mouth : eloquently
oro y pla·ta \ˌōr-ō-ē-ˈplät-ə\ [Sp] : gold and silver — motto of Montana
o tem·pora! o mo·res! \ō-ˈtem-pə-rä-ō-ˈmō-ˌrās\ [L] : oh the times! oh the manners!
oti·um cum dig·ni·ta·te \ˈōt-ē-ˌu̇m-ku̇m-ˌdig-nə-ˈtä-te\ [L] : leisure with dignity
où sont les neiges d'an·tan? \ü-sōⁿ-lā-nezh-däⁿ-täⁿ\ [F] : where are the snows of yesteryear?
pal·li·da Mors \ˌpal-id-ə-ˈmȯrz\ [L] : pale Death
pa·nem et cir·cen·ses \ˈpän-ˌem-et-kir-ˈkān-ˌsās\ [L] : bread and circuses : provision of the means of life and recreation by government to appease discontent
pan·ta rhei \ˌpän-ˌtä-ˈ(h)rā\ [Gk] : all things are in flux
par avance \pȧr-ȧ-väⁿs\ [F] : in advance : by anticipation
par avion \pȧr-ȧ-vyōⁿ\ [F] : by airplane — used on airmail
par ex·em·ple \pȧr-äg-zäⁿplᵊ\ [F] : for example
par·tu·ri·unt mon·tes, nas·ce·tur ri·di·cu·lus mus \pär-ˌtu̇r-ē-ˌu̇nt-ˈmȯn-ˌtās näs-ˈkā-ˌtu̇r-ri-ˌdik-ə-lu̇s-ˈmüs\ [L] : the mountains are in labor, and a ridiculous mouse will be brought forth
pa·ter pa·tri·ae \ˈpä-ˌter-ˈpä-trē-ˌī\ [L] : father of his country
pau·cis ver·bis \ˌpau̇-ˌkēs-ˈwer-ˌbēs\ [L] : in a few words
pax vo·bis·cum \ˌpäks-vō-ˈbēs-ˌku̇m\ [L] : peace (be) with you
peine forte et dure \pen-fȯr-tā-dᵫr\ [F] : strong and hard punishment : torture
per an·gus·ta ad au·gus·ta \per-ˈän-ˌgu̇s-tə-äd-ˈau̇-ˌgu̇s-tə\ [L] : through difficulties to honors
père \per\ [F] : father — used after French proper names to distinguish a father from his son
per·eant qui an·te nos nos·tra dix·e·runt \ˈper-e-ˌänt-kwē-ˌän-te-ˈnōs-ˈnȯs-trä-dēk-ˈsā-ˌru̇nt\ [L] : may they perish who have expressed our bright ideas before us
per·fide Al·bion \per-fēd-ȧl-byōⁿ\ [F] : perfidious Albion (England)
peu a peu \pœ-ȧ-pœ\ [F] : little by little
peu de chose \pœd-(ə-)shōz\ [F] : a trifle
pièce d'oc·ca·sion \pyes-dȯ-kä-zyōⁿ\ [F] : piece for a special occasion
pinx·it \ˈpiŋk-sət\ [L] : he (or she) painted it
place aux dames \plȧs-ō-dȧm\ [F] : (make) room for the ladies
ple·no ju·re \ˌplā-nō-ˈyu̇r-e\ [L] : with full right
plus ça change, plus c'est la même chose \plᵫ-sȧ-shäⁿzh plᵫ-se-lȧ-mem-shōz\ [F] : the more that changes, the more it's the same thing
plus roy·a·liste que le roi \plᵫ-rwȧ-yȧ-lēst-kəl-rwȧ\ [F] : more royalist than the king
po·cas pa·la·bras \ˌpō-käs-pä-ˈläb-räs\ [Sp] : few words
po·eta nas·ci·tur, non fit \pȯ-ˌā-tä-ˈnäs-kə-ˌtu̇r nōn-ˈfit\ [L] : a poet is born, not made
pol·li·ce ver·so \ˌpȯ-li-ke-ˈver-sō\ [L] : with thumb turned : with a gesture or expression of condemnation
post hoc, er·go prop·ter hoc \ˈpōst-ˌhōk ˌer-gō-ˈprȯp-ter-ˌhōk\ [L] : after this, therefore on account of it (a fallacy of argument)
post ob·itum \pōst-ˈō-bə-ˌtu̇m\ [L] : after death
pour ac·quit \pür-ȧ-kē\ [F] : received payment
pour le mé·rite \pür-lə-mā-rēt\ [F] : for merit
pro aris et fo·cis \prō-ˌä-ˌrēs-et-ˈfō-ˌkēs\ [L] : for altars and firesides
pro bo·no pu·bli·co \prō-ˌbō-nō-ˈpü-bli-ˌkō\ [L] : for the public good
pro hac vi·ce \prō-ˌhäk-ˈwik-e\ [L] : for this occasion
pro pa·tria \prō-ˈpä-trē-ˌä\ [L] : for one's country
pro re·ge, le·ge, et gre·ge \prō-ˈrā-ˌge-ˈlā-ˌge-et-ˈgreg-ˌe\ [L] : for the king, the law, and the people
pro re na·ta \ˌprō-ˌrā-ˈnät-ə\ [L] : for an occasion that has arisen : as needed — used in medical prescriptions
quand même \käⁿ-mem\ [F] : even though : whatever may happen
quan·tum mu·ta·tus ab il·lo \ˌkwänt-əm-mü-ˈtät-əs-äb-ˈil-ō\ [L] : how changed from what he once was
quan·tum suf·fi·cit \ˌkwänt-əm-ˈsəf-ə-ˌkit\ [L] : as much as suffices : a sufficient quantity — used in medical prescriptions
¿quién sa·be? \kyān-ˈsä-bā\ [Sp] : who knows?
qui fa·cit per ali·um fa·cit per se \kwē-ˌfäk-it-ˌper-ˈäl-ē-ˌu̇m-ˌfäk-it-ˌper-ˈsā\ [L] : he who does (anything) through another does it through himself
quis cus·to·di·et ip·sos cus·to·des? \ˌkwis-ku̇s-ˈtōd-ē-ˌet-ip-ˌsōs-ku̇s-ˈtō-ˌdās\ [L] : who will keep the keepers themselves?
qui s'ex·cuse s'ac·cuse \kē-ˈsek-ˌskᵫz-ˈsȧ-ˌkᵫz\ [F] : he who excuses himself accuses himself
quis se·pa·ra·bit? \ˌkwis-ˌsā-pə-ˈräb-it\ [L] : who shall separate (us)? — motto of the Order of St. Patrick
qui trans·tu·lit sus·ti·net \kwē-ˈträns-tə-ˌlit-ˈsu̇s-tə-ˌnet\ [L] : He who transplanted sustains (us) — motto of Connecticut
qui va là? \kē-vȧ-lȧ\ [F] : who goes there?

quo·ad hoc \ˌkwō-ˌäd-ˈhōk\ [L] : as far as this : to this extent

quod erat de·mon·stran·dum \ˌkwōd-ˈer-ˌät-ˌdem-ən-ˈsträn-dəm\ [L] : which was to be proved

quod erat fa·ci·en·dum \-ˌfäk-ē-ˈen-ˌdu̇m\ [L] : which was to be done

quod sem·per, quod ubi·que, quod ab om·ni·bus \kwōd-ˈsem-ˌper kwōd-ˈu̇b-i-ˌkwā ˌkwōd-äb-ˈōm-ni-ˌbu̇s\ [L] : what (has been held) always, everywhere, by everybody

quod vi·de \kwōd-ˈwid-ˌe\ [L] : which see

quo·rum pars mag·na fui \ˈkwōr-əm-ˌpärs-ˌmäg-nə-ˈfu̇-ē\ [L] : in which I played a great part

quos de·us vult per·de·re pri·us de·men·tat \kwōs-ˈde-u̇s-ˌwu̇lt-ˈperd-ə-ˌre-ˌprē-u̇s-dā-ˈmen-ˌtät\ [L] : those whom a god wishes to destroy he first drives mad

quot ho·mi·nes, tot sen·ten·ti·ae \kwōt-ˈhō-mə-ˌnās-ˌtōt-sen-ˈten-tē-ˌī\ [L] : there are as many opinions as there are men

quo va·dis? \kwō-ˈväd-is, -ˈwäd-\ [L] : whither are you going?

rai·son d'état \re-zōⁿ-dā-tä\ [F] : reason of state

re·cu·ler pour mieux sau·ter \rə-kǣ-lā-pür-myœ-sō-tā\ [F] : to draw back in order to make a better jump

reg·nat po·pu·lus \ˈreg-ˌnät-ˈpō-pə-ˌlu̇s\ [L] : the people rule — motto of Arkansas

re in·fec·ta \ˌrā-in-ˈfek-ˌtä\ [L] : the business being unfinished : without accomplishing one's purpose

re·li·gio lo·ci \re-ˌlig-ē-ˌō-ˈlō-ˌkē\ [L] : religious sanctity of a place

rem acu te·ti·gis·ti \rem-ˈä-ˌkü-ˌtet-ə-ˈgis-tē\ [L] : you have touched the point with a needle : you have hit the nail on the head

ré·pon·dez s'il vous plait \rā-pōⁿ-dā-sēl-vü-ple\ [F] : reply, if you please

re·qui·es·cat in pa·ce \ˌrek-wē-ˈes-ˌkät-in-ˈpäk-ˌe, ˌrā-kwē-ˈes-ˌkät-in-ˈpäch-ˌā\ [L] : may he (or she) rest in peace — used on tombstones

re·spi·ce fi·nem \ˌrā-spi-ˌke-ˈfē-ˌnem\ [L] : look to the end : consider the outcome

re·sur·gam \re-ˈsu̇r-ˌgäm\ [L] : I shall rise again

re·te·nue \rət-nǣ\ [F] : self-restraint : reserve

re·ve·nons à nos mou·tons \rəv-nōⁿ-ä-nō-mü-tōⁿ\ [F] : let us return to our sheep : let us get back to the subject

ruse de guerre \rǣz-də-ger\ [F] : war stratagem

rus in ur·be \ˌrüs-in-ˈu̇r-ˌbe\ [L] : country in the city

sae·va in·dig·na·tio \ˌsī-wä-ˌin-dig-ˈnät-ē-ō\ [L] : fierce indignation

sal At·ti·cum \ˌsal-ˈat-i-kəm\ [L] : Attic salt : wit

salle à man·ger \säl-ä-mäⁿ-zhā\ [F] : dining room

sa·lus po·pu·li su·pre·ma lex es·to \ˌsäl-ˌüs-ˈpō-pə-ˌlē- su̇-ˌprā-mə-ˌleks- ˈes-tō\ [L] : let the welfare of the people be the supreme law — motto of Missouri

sans doute \säⁿ-düt\ [F] : without doubt

sans gêne \säⁿ-zhen\ [F] : without embarrassment or constraint

sans peur et sans re·proche \säⁿ-pœr-ā-säⁿ-rə-ˈprōsh\ [F] : without fear and without reproach

sans sou·ci \säⁿ-sü-sē\ [F] : without worry

sa·yo·na·ra \ˌsä-yə-ˈnär-ə\ [Jp] : good-bye

sculp·sit \ˈsku̇lp-sit\ [L] : he (or she) carved it

scu·to bo·nae vo·lun·ta·tis tu·ae co·ro·nas·ti nos \ˈskü- ˌtō-ˈbō-ˌnī-ˌvō-lu̇n-ˌtät-əs-ˈtü-ˌī-ˌkōr-ə-ˌnäs-tē-ˈnōs\ [L] : Thou hast crowned us with the shield of Thy good will — a motto on the Great Seal of Maryland

se·cun·dum ar·tem \se-ˌku̇n-dəm-ˈär-ˌtem\ [L] : according to the art : according to the accepted practice of a profession or trade

secundum na·tu·ram \-nä-ˈtü-ˌräm\ [L] : according to nature : naturally

se de·fen·den·do \ˈsā-ˌdā-ˌfen-ˈden-dō\ [L] : in self-defense

se ha·bla es·pa·ñol \sā-ˌäb-lä-ˌās-pä-ˈnʸōl\ [Sp] : Spanish spoken

sem·per ea·dem \ˌsem-ˌper-ˈe-ä-ˌdem\ [L] : always the same (fem.) — motto of Queen Elizabeth I

sem·per fi·de·lis \ˌsem-pər-fi-ˈdā-lis\ [L] : always faithful — motto of the U.S. Marine Corps

sem·per idem \ˌsem-ˌper-ˈē-ˌdem\ [L] : always the same (masc.)

sem·per pa·ra·tus \ˌsem-pər-pä-ˈrät-əs\ [L] : always prepared — motto of the U.S. Coast Guard

se non è ve·ro, è ben tro·va·to \sā-ˌnōn-e-ˈvā-rō-e-ˌben-trō-ˈvä-tō\ [It] : even if it is not true, it is well conceived

sic itur ad as·tra \sēk-ˈi-ˌtu̇r-ˌäd-ˈäs- trə\ [L] : thus one goes to the stars : such is the way to immortality

sic sem·per ty·ran·nis \ˌsik-ˌsem-pər-ti- ˈran-is\ [L] : thus ever to tyrants — motto of Virginia

sic trans·it glo·ria mun·di \sēk-ˈträn-sət-ˌglōr-ē-ä-ˈmu̇n-dē\ [L] : so passes away the glory of the world

si jeu·nesse sa·vait, si vieil·lesse pou·vait! \sē-ˈzhœ-nes-ˈsä-ve sē-ˈvye-yes-ˈpü-ve\ [F] : if youth only knew, if age only could!

si·lent le·ges in·ter ar·ma \ˌsil-ˌent-ˈlā-ˌgās-ˌint-ər-ˈär-mä\ [L] : the laws are silent in the midst of arms

s'il vous plait \sēl-vü-ple\ [F] : if you please

si·mi·lia si·mi·li·bus cu·ran·tur \sim-ˈil-ē-ä-sim-ˈil-ə-bu̇s-kü-ˈrän-ˌtu̇r\ [L] : like is cured by like

si·mi·lis si·mi·li gau·det \ˈsim-ə-lis-ˈsim-ə-lē-ˈgau̇-ˌdet\ [L] : like takes pleasure in like

si mo·nu·men·tum re·qui·ris, cir·cum·spi·ce \ˌsē- ˌmō-nə-ˌment-əm-re-ˈkwē-rəs kir-ˈku̇m-spi-ke\ [L] : if you seek his monument, look around — epitaph of Sir Christopher Wren in St. Paul's, London, of which he was architect

si quae·ris pen·in·su·lam amoe·nam, cir·cum·spi·ce \sē-ˌkwī-rəs-pā-ˌnin-sə-ˌläm-ə-ˈmōi-ˌnäm kir-ˈku̇m-spi- ke\ [L] : if you seek a beautiful peninsula, look around — motto of Michigan

sis·te vi·a·tor \ˌsis-te-wē-ˈä-ˌtōr\ [L] : stop, traveler — used on Roman roadside tombs

si vis pa·cem, pa·ra bel·lum \sē-ˌwēs-ˈpä-ˌkem ˌpä-rä-ˈbel-ˌu̇m\ [L] : if you wish peace, prepare for war

sol·vi·tur am·bu·lan·do \ˈsōl-wi-ˌtu̇r-ˌäm-bə-ˈlän-dō\ [L] : it is solved by walking : the problem is solved by a practical experiment

splen·di·de men·dax \ˈsplen-də-ˌdā- ˈmen-ˌdäks\ [L] : nobly untruthful

spo·lia opi·ma \ˈspō-lē-ə-ō-ˈpē-mə\ [L] : rich spoils : the arms taken by the victorious from the vanquished general

sta·tus in quo \ˈstät-əs-ˌin-ˈkwō\ [L] : state in which : the existing state

status quo an·te bel·lum \-kwō-ˌänt-ə-ˈbel-u̇m\ [L] : the state existing before the war

sua·vi·ter in mo·do, for·ti·ter in re \ˈswä-wə-ˌter-in- ˈmōd-ō ˈfȯrt-ə-ˌter-in-ˈrā\ [L] : gently in manner, strongly in deed

sub ver·bo \su̇b-ˈwer-bō\ *or* **sub vo·ce** \su̇b-ˈwō-ke\ [L] : under the word — introducing a cross-reference in a dictionary or index

sunt la·cri·mae re·rum \su̇nt-ˌläk-ri-ˌmī-ˈrā-ru̇m\ [L] : there are tears for things

suo ju·re \ˌsu̇-ō-ˈyu̇r-e\ [L] : in his (or her) own right

suo lo·co \-ˈlō-kō\ [L] : in its proper place

suo Mar·te \-ˈmär-te\ [L] : by one's own exertions

su·um cui·que \ˌsu̇-əm-ˈkwik-we\ [L] : to each his own

tant mieux \täⁿ-myœ\ [F] : so much the better

tant pis \-pē\ [F] : so much the worse

tem·po·ra mu·tan·tur, nos et mu·ta·mur in il·lis \ˌtem-pə-rä-mü-ˈtän-ˌtu̇r ˌnōs-ˌet-mü-ˌtäm-ər-in-ˈil-ˌēs\ [L] : the times are changing, and we are changing with them

tem·pus edax re·rum \ˈtem-pu̇s-ˌed-ˌäks-ˈrā-ru̇m\ [L] : time, that devours all things

tem·pus fu·git \ˌtem-pəs-ˈfyü-jət, -ˈfü-git\ [L] : time flies

ti·meo Da·na·os et do·na fe·ren·tes \ˌtim-ē-ˌō-ˈdän-ä-ˌōs-ˌet-ˌdō-nä-fe-ˈren- ˌtās\ [L] : I fear the Greeks even when they bring gifts
to·ti·dem ver·bis \ˌtōt-ə-ˌdem-ˈwer- ˌbēs\ [L] : in so many words
to·tis vi·ri·bus \ˌtō-ˌtēs-ˈwē-ri-ˌbu̇s\ [L] : with all one's might
to·to cae·lo \ˌtō-tō-ˈkī-lō\ *or* **toto coe·lo** \-ˈkȯi-lō\ [L] : by the whole extent of the heavens : diametrically
tou·jours per·drix \tü-zhür-per-drē\ [F] : always partridge : too much of a good thing
tour d'ho·ri·zon \tür-dȯ-rē-zōⁿ\ [F] : circuit of the horizon : general survey
tous frais faits \tü-fre-fe\ [F] : all expenses defrayed
tout à fait \tü-tȧ-fe\ [F] : altogether : quite
tout au con·traire \tü-tō-kōⁿ-trer\ [F] : quite the contrary
tout à vous \tü-tȧ-vü\ [F] : wholly yours : at your service
tout bien ou rien \tü-ˈbyaⁿ- nü-ˈryaⁿ\ [F] : everything well (done) or nothing (attempted)
tout com·pren·dre c'est tout par·don·ner \ˈtü-kōⁿ- präⁿ-drə se-ˈtü-pȧr-dȯ-nā\ [F] : to understand all is to forgive all
tout court \tü-kür\ [F] : quite short : simply; *also* : brusquely
tout de même \tüt-mem\ [F] : all the same : nevertheless
tout de suite \tüt-swʸēt\ [F] : immediately; *also* : all at once : consecutively
tout en·sem·ble \tü-täⁿ-säⁿblᵊ\ [F] : all together : general effect
tout est per·du fors l'hon·neur \tü-te-per-dᵫ-fȯr-lȯ-nœr\ *or* **tout est perdu hors l'honneur** \-dᵫ-ȯr-\ [F] : all is lost save honor
tout le monde \tül-mōⁿd\ [F] : all the world : everybody
tranche de vie \träⁿsh-də-ˈvē\ [F] : slice of life
trist·esse \trē-stes\ [F] : melancholy
tru·di·tur di·es die \ˈtrüd-ə-ˌtu̇r-ˌdi-ˌās- ˈdi-ˌā\ [L] : day is pushed forth by day : one day hurries on another
tu·e·bor \tu̇-ˈā-ˌbȯr\ [L] : I will defend — a motto on the Great Seal of Michigan
ua mau ke ea o ka ai·na i ka po·no \ˌu̇-ä-ˈmä-u̇-ke-ˈe-ä-ō-kä-ˈä-ē-nä-ˌē-kä-ˈpō-nō\ [Hawaiian] : the life of the land is established in righteousness — motto of Hawaii
ue·ber·mensch \ˈᵫ-bər-ˌmensh\ [G] : superman
ul·ti·ma ra·tio re·gum \ˈu̇l-ti-mä-ˌrät-ē-ō-ˈrā-gu̇m\ [L] : the final argument of kings, i.e., war
und so wei·ter \u̇nt-zō-ˈvī-tər\ [G] : and so on
uno ani·mo \ˌü-nō-ˈän-ə-ˌmō\ [L] : with one mind : unanimously
ur·bi et or·bi \ˌu̇r-bē-ˌet-ˈȯr-bē\ [L] : to the city (Rome) and the world
uti·le dul·ci \ˌüt-ᵊl-e-ˈdu̇l-ˌkē\ [L] : the useful with the agreeable
ut in·fra \u̇t-ˈin-frä\ [L] : as below
ut su·pra \u̇t-ˈsü-prä\ [L] : as above
va·de re·tro me, Sa·ta·na \ˌwä-de-ˈrā-trō-ˌmā-ˈsä-tə-ˌnä\ [L] : get thee behind me, Satan
vae vic·tis \wī-ˈwik-ˌtēs\ [L] : woe to the vanquished
va·ria lec·tio \ˌwär-ē-ä-ˈlek-tē-ˌō\ *pl* **va·ri·ae lec·ti·o·nes** \ˈwär-ē-ˌī-ˌlek-tē-ˈō-ˌnās\ [L] : variant reading
va·ri·um et mu·ta·bi·le sem·per fe·mi·na \ˌwär-ē-ˌet-ˌmü-ˈtä-bə-le-ˌsem-ˌper-ˈfā-mə-nä\ [L] : woman is ever a fickle and changeable thing
ve·di Na·po·li e poi mo·ri \ˌvā-dē-ˈnä-pō-lē-ā-ˌpȯ- ē-ˈmȯ-rē\ [It] : see Naples, and then die
ve·ni, vi·di, vi·ci \ˌwā-nē-ˌwēd-ē-ˈwē- kē\ [L] : I came, I saw, I conquered
ven·tre à terre \väⁿ-trȧ-ter\ [F] : belly to the ground : at very great speed
ver·ba·tim ac lit·te·ra·tim \wer-ˈbä-tim- ˌäk-ˌlit-ə-ˈrä-tim\ [L] : word for word and letter for letter
ver·bum sat sa·pi·en·ti est \ˌwer-bu̇m-ˈsät-ˌsäp-ē-ˈent-ē-ˌest\ [L] : a word to the wise is sufficient
vin·cit om·nia ve·ri·tas \ˌwiŋ-ket-ˈȯm-nē-ä-ˈwā-rə-ˌtäs\ [L] : truth conquers all things
vin·cu·lum ma·tri·mo·nii \ˌwiŋ-kə-lu̇m-ˌmä-trə-ˈmō-nē-ˌē\ [L] : bond of marriage
vir·gi·ni·bus pu·e·ris·que \wir-ˈgin-ə- bu̇s-ˌpu̇-ə-ˈrēs-kwe\ [L] : for girls and boys
vir·tu·te et ar·mis \wir-ˈtü-te-ˌet-ˈär-mēs\ [L] : by valor and arms — motto of Mississippi
vis me·di·ca·trix na·tu·rae \ˈwēs-ˌmed-i-ˈkä-triks-nä-ˈtü-ˌrī\ [L] : the healing power of nature
vive la dif·fé·rence \vēv(-ə)-lä-dē-fā-räⁿs\ [F] : long live the difference (between the sexes)
vive la reine \vēv-lȧ-ren\ [F] : long live the queen
vive le roi \vēv-lə-rwä\ [F] : long live the king
vix·e·re for·tes an·te Aga·mem·no·na \wik-ˌsā-re-ˈfȯr-ˌtās-ˌänt-ˌäg-ə-ˈmem-nə-ˌnä\ [L] : brave men lived before Agamemnon
vogue la ga·lère \vȯg-lȧ-gȧ-ler\ [F] : let the galley be kept rowing : keep on, whatever may happen
voi·là \vwȧ-lȧ\ [F] : there you are : there you see (it)
voi·là tout \vwȧ-lȧ-tü\ [F] : that's all
vox et prae·te·rea ni·hil \ˈwōks-et-prī-ˌter-e-ä-ˈni-ˌhil\ [L] : voice and nothing more
vox po·pu·li vox Dei \wōks-ˈpȯ-pə-ˌlē-ˌwōks-ˈde-ē\ [L] : the voice of the people is the voice of God
Wan·der·jahr \ˈvän-dər-ˌyär\ [G] : year of wandering
wie geht's? \vē-ˈgāts\ [G] : how goes it?

Nations of the World

name and pronunciation	population
Afghanistan \af-ˈgan-ə-ˌstan\	13,051,000
Albania \al-ˈbā-nē-ə\	2,841,000
Algeria \al-ˈjir-ē-ə\	16,948,000
Andorra \an-ˈdȯr-ə\	40,000
Angola \aŋ-ˈgō-lə, an-\	6,761,000
Antigua and Barbuda \an-ˈtē-gə-ən-bär-ˈbüd-ə\	77,000
Argentina \ˌär-jen-ˈtē-nə\	27,947,000
Australia \ȯ-ˈstrāl-yə\	14,574,000
Austria \ˈȯs-trē-ə\	7,555,000
Bahamas \bə-ˈhäm-əz\	223,000
Bahrain \bä-ˈrān\	359,000
Bangladesh \ˌbäŋ-glə-ˈdesh, -ˈdäsh\	87,052,000
Barbados \bär-ˈbād-əs, -(ˌ)ōz, -(ˌ)äs\	249,000
Belgium \ˈbel-jəm\	9,849,000
Belize \bə-ˈlēz\	145,000
Benin \bə-ˈnin\	3,338,000
Bhutan \bü-ˈtan, -ˈtän\	1,333,000
Bolivia \bə-ˈliv-ē-ə\	4,613,000
Botswana \bät-ˈswän-ə\	937,000
Brazil \brə-ˈzil\	118,675,000
Brunei \brü-ˈnī\	193,000
Bulgaria \ˌbəl-ˈgar-ē-ə, bu̇l-\	8,730,000
Burkina Faso \bu̇r-ˈkē-nə-ˈfä-sō\	5,638,000
Burma \ˈbər-mə\	35,314,000
Burundi \bu̇-ˈrün-dē\	3,638,000
Cambodia \kam-ˈbōd-ē-ə\	6,646,000
Cameroon \ˌkam-ə-ˈrün\	7,090,000
Canada \ˈkan-əd-ə\	24,098,000
Cape Verde \-ˈvərd\	303,000
Central African Republic \-ˈaf-ri-kən-\	2,055,000
Chad \ˈchad\	4,681,000
Chile \ˈchil-ē\	11,275,000
China, People's Republic of \-ˈchī-nə\	1,031,882,000
Colombia \kə-ˈləm-bē-ə\	26,929,000
Comoro Islands \ˈkäm-ə-ˌrō-\	421,000
Congo \ˈkäŋ-gō\	1,300,000
Costa Rica \ˌkäs-tə-ˈrē-kə\	2,435,000
Cuba \ˈkyü-bə\	9,706,000
Cyprus \ˈsī-prəs\	613,000
Czechoslovakia \ˌchek-ə-slō-ˈväk-ē-ə\	15,283,000
Denmark \ˈden-ˌmärk\	5,119,000
Djibouti \jə-ˈbüt-ē\	323,000
Dominica \ˌdäm-ə-ˈnē-kə\	74,000
Dominican Republic \də-ˌmin-i-kən-\	5,648,000
East Germany \-ˈjər-mən-ē\	16,706,000
Ecuador \ˈek-wə-ˌdȯr\	6,522,000
Egypt \ˈē-jəpt\	36,626,000
El Salvador \el-ˈsal-və-ˌdȯr\	4,813,000
Equatorial Guinea \-ˈgin-ē\	300,000
Ethiopia \ˌē-thē-ˈō-pē-ə\	32,775,000

name and pronunciation	population
Fiji \ˈfē-(ˌ)jē\	588,000
Finland \ˈfin-lənd\	4,718,000
France \ˈfrans\	52,656,000
Gabon \ga-ˈbōn\	1,108,000
Gambia \ˈgam-bē-ə\	696,000
Ghana \ˈgän-ə\	12,244,000
Greece \ˈgrēs\	9,707,000
Grenada \grə-ˈnād-ə\	110,000
Guatemala \ˌgwät-ə-ˈmäl-ə\	6,044,000
Guinea \ˈgin-ē\	5,057,000
Guinea-Bissau \-bis-ˈau̇\	768,000
Guyana \gī-ˈan-ə\	900,000
Haiti \ˈhāt-ē\	5,054,000
Honduras \hän-ˈd(y)u̇r-əs\	3,955,000
Hungary \ˈhəŋ-g(ə-)rē\	10,709,000
Iceland \ˈīs-lənd, -ˌland\	235,000
India \ˈin-dē-ə\	685,185,000
Indonesia \ˌin-də-ˈnē-zhə, -shə\	147,490,000
Iran \i-ˈran, -ˈrän\	33,592,000
Iraq \i-ˈräk, -ˈrak\	12,000,000
Ireland (Irish Republic) \ˈī(ə)r-lənd\	3,443,000
Israel \ˈiz-rē-əl\	4,112,000
Italy \ˈit-ə-lē\	56,244,000
Ivory Coast \ˈīv-(ə-)rē-\	6,710,000
Jamaica \jə-ˈmā-kə\	2,096,000
Japan \jə-ˈpan\	117,057,000
Jordan \ˈjȯrd-ən\	2,152,000
Kenya \ˈken-yə, ˈkēn-\	15,327,000
Kuwait \kə-ˈwāt\	1,356,000
Laos \ˈlau̇s, ˈlä-ōs\	4,104,000
Lebanon \ˈleb-ə-nən\	3,161,000
Lesotho \lə-ˈsü-ˌtü\	1,214,000
Liberia \lī-ˈbir-ē-ə\	1,503,000
Libya \ˈlib-ē-ə\	3,224,000
Liechtenstein \ˈlik-tən-ˌs(h)tīn\	26,000
Luxembourg \ˈlək-səm-ˌbərg, ˈlu̇k-səm-ˌbu̇rg\	365,000
Madagascar \ˌmad-ə-ˈgas-kər\	7,604,000
Malawi \mə-ˈlä-wē\	5,547,000
Malaysia \mə-ˈlā-zh(ē-)ə\	13,700,000
Maldives \ˈmȯl-ˌdēvz, -ˌdīvz\	143,000
Mali \ˈmäl-ē\	6,525,000
Malta \ˈmȯl-tə\	366,000
Mauritania \ˌmȯr-ə-ˈtā-nē-ə\	1,420,000
Mauritius \mȯ-ˈrish-(ē-)əs\	993,000
Mexico \ˈmek-si-ˌkō\	67,396,000
Monaco \ˈmän-ə-ˌkō\	27,000
Mongolia \män-ˈgōl-yə\	1,595,000
Morocco \mə-ˈräk-ō\	21,392,000
Mozambique \ˌmō-zəm-ˈbēk\	11,674,000
Nauru \nä-ˈü-(ˌ)rü\	7,000
Nepal \nə-ˈpȯl\	15,020,000
Netherlands \ˈneth-ər-lən(d)z\	14,386,000
New Zealand \-ˈzē-lənd\	3,176,000
Nicaragua \ˌnik-ə-ˈräg-wə\	2,824,000

Niger \ˈnī-jər\ 5,098,000
Nigeria \nī-ˈjir-ē-ə\ 86,126,000
North Korea \-kə-ˈrē-ə\ 18,747,000
Norway \ˈnȯr-ˌwā\ 4,091,000
Oman \ō-ˈmän\ 1,079,000
Pakistan \ˈpak-i-ˌstan, ˌpäk-i-ˈstän\ 83,782,000
Panama \ˈpan-ə-ˌmä\ 1,825,000
Papua New Guinea \ˈpäp-ə-wə-\ 3,011,000
Paraguay \ˈpar-ə-ˌgwī, -ˌgwā\ 3,026,000
Peru \pə-ˈrü\ 17,031,000
Philippines \ˌfil-ə-ˈpēnz, ˈfil-ə-ˌpēnz\ 48,098,000
Poland \ˈpō-lənd\ 35,061,000
Portugal \ˈpōr-chi-gəl\ 9,784,000
Qatar \ˈkät-ər\ 270,000
Romania \rü-ˈmā-nē-ə\ 21,560,000
Rwanda \rü-ˈän-də\ 4,819,000
St. Christopher-Nevis \sānt-ˈkris-tə-fər-ˈnē-vəs\ 44,000
St. Lucia \-ˈlü-shə\ 122,000
St. Vincent and the Grenadines .... \-ˈvin-sənt . . . ˌgren-ə-ˈdēnz\ 124,000
San Marino \ˌsan-mə-ˈrē-nō\ 19,000
Sao Tome and Principe \ˌsaü-tə-ˈmā-ən-ˈprin-sə-pə\ 89,000
Saudi Arabia \ˌsaüd-ē-ə-ˈrā-bē-ə, sä-ˌüd-ē-\ 10,025,000
Senegal \ˌsen-i-ˈgȯl\ 5,811,000
Seychelles \sā-ˈchel(z)\ 62,000
Sierra Leone \sē-ˌer-ə-lē-ˈōn\ 2,735,000
Singapore \ˈsiŋ-(g)ə-ˌpōr\ 2,414,000
Solomon Islands \ˈsäl-ə-mən-\ 197,000
Somalia \sō-ˈmäl-ē-ə\ 5,085,000
South Africa, Republic of 26,129,000
South Korea \-kə-ˈrē-ə\ 37,436,000
Spain \ˈspān\ 37,746,000
Sri Lanka \(ˈ)srē-ˈläŋ-kə, (ˈ)shrē-\ 14,850,000
Sudan \sü-ˈdan\ 20,564,000
Suriname \ˌsu̇r-ə-ˈnäm-ə\ 352,000
Swaziland \ˈswäz-ē-ˌland\ 494,000
Sweden \ˈswēd-ən\ 8,208,000
Switzerland \ˈswit-sər-lənd\ 6,366,000
Syria \ˈsir-ē-ə\ 9,172,000
Taiwan (Republic of China) \tī-ˈwän\ 14,811,000
Tanzania \ˌtan-zə-ˈnē-ə\ 17,528,000
Thailand \ˈtī-ˌland, -lənd\ 44,278,000
Togo \ˈtō-gō\ 2,703,000
Trinidad and Tobago \ˈtrin-ə-ˌdad-ən-tə-ˈbā-gō\ 1,060,000
Tunisia \t(y)ü-ˈnē-zh(ē-)ə\ 6,966,000
Turkey \ˈtər-kē\ 44,737,000
Uganda \yü-ˈgan-də\ 12,630,000
Union of Soviet Socialist Republics (U.S.S.R.) .... \-ˈsō-vē-ˌet-, (ˌyü-ˌes-ˌes-ˈär)\ 262,436,000
United Arab Emirates \-ˈem-ə-rəts\ 1,043,000
United Kingdom of Great Britain and Northern Ireland .... \-ˈbrit-ən. . . ˈī(ə)r-lənd\ 55,671,000
England \ˈiŋ-glənd\ ....
Northern Ireland ....
Scotland \ˈskät-lənd\ ....
Wales \ˈwālz\ ....
United States of America \-ə-ˈmer-i-kə\ 226,504,825
Uruguay \ˈ(y)u̇r-ə-ˌgwī, ˈyu̇r-ə-ˌgwā\ 2,788,000
Vanuatu \ˌvan-ə-ˈwät-ü\ 112,000
Vatican City State \ˌvat-i-kən-\ 700
Venezuela \ˌven-əz(-ə)-ˈwā-lə\ 14,517,000
Vietnam \vē-ˈet-ˈnäm\ 52,742,000
Western Samoa \-sə-ˈmō-ə\ 156,000
West Germany \-ˈjər-mə-nē\ 61,371,000
Yemen, People's Democratic Republic of \-ˈyem-ən\ 2,158,000
Yemen Arab Republic 5,238,000
Yugoslavia \ˌyü-gō-ˈsläv-ē-ə\ 22,839,000
Zaire \zä-ˈi(ə)r\ 30,261,000
Zambia \ˈzam-bē-ə\ 5,680,000
Zimbabwe \zim-ˈbäb-wā\ 7,550,000

Population of Places in the United States

Having 16,500 or More Inhabitants in 1980

A

Aberdeen, S. Dak.	25,956
Aberdeen, Wash.	18,739
Abilene, Tex.	98,315
Acton, Mass.	17,544
Addison, Ill.	29,759
Adrian, Mich.	21,186
Agawam, Mass.	26,271
Aiea, Hawaii	32,879
Akron, Ohio	237,177
Alameda, Calif.	63,852
Alamogordo, N. Mex.	24,024
Albany, Ga.	74,059
Albany, N.Y.	101,727
Albany, Oreg.	26,546
Albert Lea, Minn.	19,200
Albuquerque, N. Mex.	331,767
Alexandria, La.	51,565
Alexandria, Va.	103,217
Alhambra, Calif.	64,615
Alice, Tex.	20,961
Aliquippa, Pa.	17,094
Allen Park, Mich.	34,196
Allentown, Pa.	103,758
Alliance, Ohio	24,315
Alsip, Ill.	17,134
Altamonte Springs, Fla.	22,028
Alton, Ill.	34,171
Altoona, Pa.	57,078
Altus, Okla.	23,101
Alvin, Tex.	16,515
Amarillo, Tex.	149,230
Ames, Iowa	45,775
Amherst, Mass.	33,229
Amsterdam, N.Y.	21,872
Anaheim, Calif.	221,847
Anchorage, Alaska	174,431
Anderson, Ind.	64,695
Anderson, S.C.	27,313
Andover, Mass.	26,370
Annapolis, Md.	31,740
Ann Arbor, Mich.	107,966
Anniston, Ala.	29,523
Ansonia, Conn.	19,039
Antioch, Calif.	43,559
Appleton, Wis.	59,032
Apple Valley, Minn.	21,818
Arcadia, Calif.	45,994
Ardmore, Okla.	23,689
Arlington, Mass.	48,219
Arlington, Tex.	160,113
Arlington Heights, Ill.	66,116
Arnold, Mo.	19,141
Arvada, Colo.	84,576
Asbury Park, N.J.	17,015
Asheville, N.C.	53,583
Ashland, Ky.	27,064
Ashland, Ohio	20,326
Ashtabula, Ohio	23,449
Athens, Ga.	42,549
Athens, Ohio	19,743
Atlanta, Ga.	425,022
Atlantic City, N.J.	40,199
Attleboro, Mass.	34,196
Atwater, Calif.	17,530
Auburn, Ala.	28,471
Auburn, Me.	23,128
Auburn, N.Y.	32,548
Auburn, Wash.	26,417
Augusta, Ga.	47,532
Augusta, Me.	21,819
Aurora, Colo.	158,588
Aurora, Ill.	81,293
Austin, Minn.	23,020
Austin, Tex.	345,496
Azusa, Calif.	29,380

B

Bakersfield, Calif.	105,611
Baldwin, Pa.	24,598
Baldwin Park, Calif.	50,554
Baltimore, Md.	786,775
Bangor, Me.	31,643
Barberton, Ohio	29,751
Barnstable, Mass.	30,898
Barstow, Calif.	17,690
Bartlesville, Okla.	34,568
Bartlett, Tenn.	17,170
Batavia, N.Y.	16,703
Baton Rouge, La.	219,419
Battle Creek, Mich.	35,724
Bay City, Mich.	41,593
Bay City, Tex.	17,837
Bayonne, N.J.	65,047
Baytown, Tex.	56,923
Bay Village, Ohio	17,846
Beaumont, Tex.	118,102
Beavercreek, Ohio	31,589
Beaverton, Oreg.	30,582
Beckley, W. Va.	20,492
Bedford, Tex.	20,821
Bell, Calif.	25,450
Belle Glade, Fla.	16,535
Belleville, Ill.	41,580
Belleville, N.J.	35,367
Bellevue, Nebr.	21,813
Bellevue, Wash.	73,903
Bellflower, Calif.	53,441
Bell Gardens, Calif.	34,117
Bellingham, Wash.	45,794
Bellwood, Ill.	19,811
Belmont, Calif.	24,505
Belmont, Mass.	26,100
Beloit, Wis.	35,207
Bend, Oreg.	17,263
Benton, Ark.	17,717
Berea, Ohio	19,567
Bergenfield, N.J.	25,568
Berkeley, Calif.	103,328
Berkley, Mich.	18,637
Berwyn, Ill.	46,849
Bessemer, Ala.	31,729
Bethany, Okla.	22,130
Bethel Park, Pa.	34,755
Bethlehem, Pa.	70,419
Bettendorf, Iowa	27,381
Beverly, Mass.	37,655
Beverly Hills, Calif.	32,367
Biddeford, Me.	19,638
Big Spring, Tex.	24,804
Billerica, Mass.	36,727
Billings, Mont.	66,798
Biloxi, Miss.	49,311

Place	Population
Binghamton, N.Y.	55,860
Birmingham, Ala.	284,413
Birmingham, Mich.	21,689
Bismarck, N. Dak.	44,485
Blacksburg, Va.	30,638
Blaine, Minn.	28,558
Bloomfield, Conn.	18,608
Bloomfield, N.J.	47,792
Bloomington, Ill.	44,189
Bloomington, Ind.	52,044
Bloomington, Minn.	81,831
Blue Island, Ill.	21,853
Blue Springs, Mo.	25,927
Blytheville, Ark.	23,844
Boca Raton, Fla.	49,505
Bogalusa, La.	16,976
Boise, Idaho	102,451
Bolingbrook, Ill.	37,261
Bossier City, La.	50,817
Boston, Mass.	562,994
Boulder, Colo.	76,685
Bountiful, Utah	32,877
Bowie, Md.	33,695
Bowling Green, Ky.	40,450
Bowling Green, Ohio	25,728
Boynton Beach, Fla.	35,624
Bozeman, Mont.	21,645
Bradenton, Fla.	30,170
Braintree, Mass.	36,337
Branford, Conn.	23,363
Brea, Calif.	27,913
Bremerton, Wash.	36,208
Bridgeport, Conn.	142,546
Bridgeton, Mo.	18,445
Bridgeton, N.J.	18,795
Bristol, Conn.	57,370
Bristol, R.I.	20,128
Bristol, Tenn.	23,986
Bristol, Va.	19,042
Brockton, Mass.	95,172
Broken Arrow, Okla.	35,761
Brookfield, Ill.	19,395
Brookfield, Wis.	34,035
Brookline, Mass.	55,062
Brooklyn Center, Minn.	31,230
Brooklyn Park, Minn.	43,332
Brook Park, Ohio	26,195
Broomfield, Colo.	20,730
Brownsville, Tex.	84,997
Brownwood, Tex.	19,396
Brunswick, Ga.	17,605
Brunswick, Me.	17,366
Brunswick, Ohio	28,104
Bryan, Tex.	44,337
Buena Park, Calif.	64,165
Buffalo, N.Y.	357,870
Burbank, Calif.	84,625
Burbank, Ill.	28,462
Burlingame, Calif.	26,173
Burlington, Iowa	29,529
Burlington, Mass.	23,486
Burlington, N.C.	37,266
Burlington, Vt.	37,712
Burnsville, Minn.	35,674
Burton, Mich.	29,976
Butler, Pa.	17,026
Butte, Mont.	36,817

C

Place	Population
Cahokia, Ill.	18,904
Caldwell, Idaho	17,699
Calumet City, Ill.	39,697
Camarillo, Calif.	37,732
Cambridge, Mass.	95,322
Camden, N.J.	84,910
Campbell, Calif.	27,067
Canton, Mass.	18,182
Canton, Ohio	94,730
Cape Coral, Fla.	32,103
Cape Girardeau, Mo.	34,361
Carbondale, Ill.	26,287
Carlisle, Pa.	18,314
Carlsbad, Calif.	35,490
Carlsbad, N. Mex.	25,496
Carmel, Ind.	18,272
Carpentersville, Ill.	23,272
Carrollton, Tex.	40,595
Carson, Calif.	81,221
Carson City, Nev.	32,022
Carteret, N.J.	20,598
Cary, N.C.	21,763
Casper, Wyo.	51,016
Cedar Falls, Iowa	36,322
Cedar Rapids, Iowa	110,243
Centerville, Ohio	18,886
Central Falls, R.I.	16,995
Cerritos, Calif.	53,020
Champaign, Ill.	58,133
Chandler, Ariz.	29,673
Chapel Hill, N.C.	32,421
Charleston, Ill.	19,355
Charleston, S.C.	69,510
Charleston, W. Va.	63,968
Charlotte, N.C.	314,447
Charlottesville, Va.	39,916
Chattanooga, Tenn.	169,565
Chelmsford, Mass.	31,174
Chelsea, Mass.	25,431
Chesapeake, Va.	114,486
Cheshire, Conn.	21,788
Chester, Pa.	45,794
Cheyenne, Wyo.	47,283
Chicago, Ill.	3,005,072
Chicago Heights, Ill.	37,026
Chico, Calif.	26,601
Chicopee, Mass.	55,112
Chillicothe, Ohio	23,420
Chino, Calif.	40,165
Chula Vista, Calif.	83,927
Cicero, Ill.	61,232
Cincinnati, Ohio	385,457
Claremont, Calif.	30,950
Clarksburg, W. Va.	22,371
Clarksdale, Miss.	21,137
Clarksville, Tenn.	54,777
Clearfield, Utah	17,982
Clearwater, Fla.	85,528
Cleburne, Tex.	19,218
Cleveland, Ohio	573,822
Cleveland, Tenn.	26,415
Cleveland Heights, Ohio	56,438
Cliffside Park, N.J.	21,464
Clifton, N.J.	74,388
Clinton, Iowa	32,828
Clovis, Calif.	33,021
Clovis, N. Mex.	31,194
Coeur d'Alene, Idaho	20,054
Cohoes, N.Y.	18,144
College Park, Ga.	24,632
College Park, Md.	23,614
College Station, Tex.	37,272
Collinsville, Ill.	19,613
Colonial Heights, Va.	16,509
Colorado Springs, Colo.	215,150
Colton, Calif.	21,310
Columbia, Mo.	62,061
Columbia, S.C.	99,296
Columbia, Tenn.	26,372
Columbia Heights, Minn.	20,029
Columbus, Ga.	169,441
Columbus, Ind.	30,614
Columbus, Miss.	27,383
Columbus, Nebr.	17,328
Columbus, Ohio	564,871
Compton, Calif.	81,286
Concord, Calif.	103,255

Concord, N.H. 30,400
Concord, N.C. 16,942
Connersville, Ind. 17,023
Conroe, Tex. 18,034
Conway, Ark. 20,375
Cookeville, Tenn. 20,535
Coon Rapids, Minn. 35,826
Copperas Cove, Tex. 19,469
Coral Gables, Fla. 43,241
Coral Springs, Fla. 37,349
Corona, Calif. 37,791
Coronado, Calif. 16,859
Corpus Christi, Tex. 231,999
Corsicana, Tex. 21,712
Cortland, N.Y. 20,138
Corvallis, Oreg. 40,960
Costa Mesa, Calif. 82,562
Cottage Grove, Minn. 18,994
Council Bluffs, Iowa 56,449
Coventry, R.I. 27,065
Covina, Calif. 33,751
Covington, Ky. 49,563
Cranston, R.I. 71,992
Crystal, Minn. 25,543
Crystal Lake, Ill. 18,590
Cudahy, Calif. 17,984
Cudahy, Wis. 19,547
Culver City, Calif. 38,139
Cumberland, Md. 25,933
Cumberland, R.I. 27,069
Cupertino, Calif. 34,015
Cuyahoga Falls, Ohio 43,890
Cypress, Calif. 40,391

D

Dallas, Tex. 904,078
Dalton, Ga. 20,939
Daly City, Calif. 78,519
Danbury, Conn. 60,470
Danvers, Mass. 24,100
Danville, Ill. 38,985
Danville, Va. 45,642
Darien, Conn. 18,892
Dartmouth, Mass. 23,966
Davenport, Iowa 103,264
Davie, Fla. 20,877
Davis, Calif. 36,640
Dayton, Ohio 203,371
Daytona Beach, Fla. 54,176
Dearborn, Mich. 90,660
Dearborn Heights, Mich. 67,706
Decatur, Ala. 42,002
Decatur, Ga. 18,404
Decatur, Ill. 94,081
Dedham, Mass. 25,298
Deerfield, Ill. 17,430
Deerfield Beach, Fla. 39,193
Deer Park, Tex. 22,648
Defiance, Ohio 16,810
De Kalb, Ill. 33,099
Delaware, Ohio 18,780
Del City, Okla. 28,424
Delray Beach, Fla. 34,325
Del Rio, Tex. 30,034
Denison, Tex. 23,884
Denton, Tex. 48,063
Denver, Colo. 492,365
Depew, N.Y. 19,819
Derry, N.H. 18,875
Des Moines, Iowa 191,003
Des Plaines, Ill. 53,568
Detroit, Mich. 1,203,339
Dodge City, Kans. 18,001
Dolton, Ill. 24,766
Dothan, Ala. 48,750
Dover, Del. 23,512
Dover, N.H. 22,377
Downers Grove, Ill. 42,572
Downey, Calif. 82,602
Dracut, Mass. 21,249
Duarte, Calif. 16,766
Dubuque, Iowa 62,321
Duluth, Minn. 92,811
Dumont, N.J. 18,334
Duncan, Okla. 22,517
Duncanville, Tex. 27,781
Dunedin, Fla. 30,203
Dunmore, Pa. 16,781
Durham, N.C. 100,831

E

Eagan, Minn. 20,700
Eagle Pass, Tex. 21,407
East Chicago, Ind. 39,786
East Cleveland, Ohio 36,957
East Detroit, Mich. 38,280
East Hartford, Conn. 52,563
East Haven, Conn. 25,028
Eastlake, Ohio 22,104
East Lansing, Mich. 51,392
East Liverpool, Ohio 16,687
East Moline, Ill. 20,907
Easton, Mass. 16,623
Easton, Pa. 26,027
East Orange, N.J. 77,690
East Peoria, Ill. 22,385
East Point, Ga. 37,486
East Providence, R.I. 50,980
East Ridge, Tenn. 21,236
East St. Louis, Ill. 55,200
Eau Claire, Wis. 51,509
Edina, Minn. 46,073
Edinburg, Tex. 24,075
Edmond, Okla. 34,637
Edmonds, Wash. 27,679
El Cajon, Calif. 73,892
El Centro, Calif. 23,996
El Cerrito, Calif. 22,731
El Dorado, Ark. 25,270
Elgin, Ill. 63,798
Elizabeth, N.J. 106,201
Elk Grove Village, Ill. 28,907
Elkhart, Ind. 41,305
Elmhurst, Ill. 44,276
Elmira, N.Y. 35,327
El Monte, Calif. 79,494
Elmwood Park, Ill. 24,016
Elmwood Park, N.J. 18,377
El Paso, Tex. 425,259
Elyria, Ohio 57,538
Emporia, Kans. 25,287
Enfield, Conn. 42,695
Englewood, Colo. 30,021
Englewood, N.J. 23,701
Enid, Okla. 50,363
Enterprise, Ala. 18,033
Erie, Pa. 119,123
Escondido, Calif. 64,355
Euclid, Ohio 59,999
Eugene, Oreg. 105,624
Euless, Tex. 24,002
Eureka, Calif. 24,153
Evanston, Ill. 73,706
Evansville, Ind. 130,496
Everett, Mass. 37,195
Everett, Wash. 54,413
Evergreen Park, Ill. 22,260

F

Fairbanks, Alaska 22,645
Fairborn, Ohio 29,702
Fairfax, Va. 19,390
Fairfield, Calif. 58,099
Fairfield, Conn. 54,849
Fairfield, Ohio 30,777
Fair Lawn, N.J. 32,229

Fairmont, W. Va.	23,863
Fairview Park, Ohio	19,311
Fall River, Mass.	92,574
Falmouth, Mass.	23,640
Fargo, N. Dak.	61,383
Farmers Branch, Tex.	24,863
Farmington, N. Mex.	31,222
Farmington Hills, Mich.	58,056
Fayetteville, Ark.	36,608
Fayetteville, N.C.	59,507
Ferguson, Mo.	24,740
Ferndale, Mich.	26,227
Findlay, Ohio	35,594
Fitchburg, Mass.	39,580
Flagstaff, Ariz.	34,743
Flint, Mich.	159,611
Floral Park, N.Y.	16,805
Florence, Ala.	37,029
Florence, S.C.	30,062
Florissant, Mo.	55,372
Fond du Lac, Wis.	35,863
Fontana, Calif.	37,111
Forest Park, Ga.	18,782
Forest Park, Ohio	18,675
Fort Collins, Colo.	65,092
Fort Dodge, Iowa	29,423
Fort Lauderdale, Fla.	153,279
Fort Lee, N.J.	32,449
Fort Myers, Fla.	36,638
Fort Pierce, Fla.	33,802
Fort Smith, Ark.	71,626
Fort Walton Beach, Fla.	20,829
Fort Wayne, Ind.	172,196
Fort Worth, Tex.	385,164
Foster City, Calif.	23,287
Fountain Valley, Calif.	55,080
Framingham, Mass.	65,113
Frankfort, Ky.	25,973
Franklin, Mass.	18,217
Franklin, Wis.	16,871
Franklin Park, Ill.	17,507
Frederick, Md.	28,086
Freeport, Ill.	26,266
Freeport, N.Y.	38,272
Fremont, Calif.	131,945
Fremont, Nebr.	23,979
Fremont, Ohio	17,834
Fresno, Calif.	218,202
Fridley, Minn.	30,228
Fullerton, Calif.	102,034

G

Gadsden, Ala.	47,565
Gahanna, Ohio	18,001
Gainesville, Fla.	81,371
Gaithersburg, Md.	26,424
Galesburg, Ill.	35,305
Gallatin, Tenn.	17,191
Gallup, N. Mex.	18,161
Galveston, Tex.	61,902
Gardena, Calif.	45,165
Garden City, Kans.	18,256
Garden City, Mich.	35,640
Garden City, N.Y.	22,927
Garden Grove, Calif.	123,351
Gardner, Mass.	17,900
Garfield, N.J.	26,803
Garfield Heights, Ohio	34,938
Garland, Tex.	138,857
Gary, Ind.	151,953
Gastonia, N.C.	47,333
Germantown, Tenn.	20,459
Gilroy, Calif.	21,641
Gladstone, Mo.	24,990
Glastonbury, Conn.	24,327
Glen Cove, N.Y.	24,618
Glendale, Ariz.	97,172
Glendale, Calif.	139,060
Glendale Heights, Ill.	23,163
Glendora, Calif.	38,654
Glen Ellyn, Ill.	23,649
Glenview, Ill.	32,060
Gloucester, Mass.	27,768
Gloversville, N.Y.	17,836
Golden Valley, Minn.	22,775
Goldsboro, N.C.	31,871
Goose Creek, S.C.	17,811
Goshen, Ind.	19,665
Grand Forks, N. Dak.	43,765
Grand Island, Nebr.	33,180
Grand Junction, Colo.	28,144
Grand Prairie, Tex.	71,462
Grand Rapids, Mich.	181,843
Grandview, Mo.	24,502
Granite City, Ill.	36,815
Great Bend, Kans.	16,608
Great Falls, Mont.	56,725
Greeley, Colo.	53,006
Green Bay, Wis.	87,899
Greenbelt, Md.	17,332
Greendale, Wis.	16,928
Greenfield, Mass.	18,436
Greenfield, Wis.	31,467
Greensboro, N.C.	155,642
Greensburg, Pa.	17,558
Greenville, Miss.	40,613
Greenville, N.C.	35,740
Greenville, S.C.	58,242
Greenville, Tex.	22,161
Greenwich, Conn.	59,578
Greenwood, Ind.	19,327
Greenwood, Miss.	20,115
Greenwood, S.C.	21,613
Gresham, Oreg.	33,005
Gretna, La.	20,615
Griffin, Ga.	20,728
Griffith, Ind.	17,026
Grosse Pointe Woods, Mich.	18,886
Groton, Conn.	41,062
Grove City, Ohio	16,816
Groves, Tex.	17,090
Guilford, Conn.	17,375
Gulfport, Miss.	39,676

H

Hackensack, N.J.	36,039
Hagerstown, Md.	34,132
Hallandale, Fla.	36,517
Haltom City, Tex.	29,014
Hamden, Conn.	51,071
Hamilton, Ohio	63,189
Hammond, Ind.	93,714
Hampton, Va.	122,617
Hamtramck, Mich.	21,300
Hanford, Calif.	20,958
Hannibal, Mo.	18,811
Hanover Park, Ill.	28,850
Harlingen, Tex.	43,543
Harrisburg, Pa.	53,264
Harrison, N.Y.	23,046
Harrisonburg, Va.	19,671
Hartford, Conn.	136,392
Harvey, Ill.	35,810
Hastings, Nebr.	23,045
Hattiesburg, Miss.	40,829
Havelock, N.C.	17,718
Haverhill, Mass.	46,865
Hawthorne, Calif.	56,447
Hawthorne, N.J.	18,200
Hayward, Calif.	94,167
Hazel Park, Mich.	20,914
Hazleton, Pa.	27,318
Helena, Mont.	23,938
Hemet, Calif.	22,454

Hempstead, N.Y.	40,404
Henderson, Ky.	24,834
Henderson, Nev.	24,363
Hendersonville, Tenn.	26,561
Hermosa Beach, Calif.	18,070
Hialeah, Fla.	145,254
Hibbing, Minn.	21,193
Hickory, N.C.	20,757
Highland, Ind.	25,935
Highland Park, Ill.	30,611
Highland Park, Mich.	27,909
High Point, N.C.	63,380
Hillsboro, Oreg.	27,664
Hilo, Hawaii	35,269
Hingham, Mass.	20,339
Hinsdale, Ill.	16,726
Hobart, Ind.	22,987
Hobbs, N. Mex.	29,153
Hoboken, N.J.	42,460
Hoffman Estates, Ill.	37,272
Holland, Mich.	26,281
Hollywood, Fla.	121,323
Holyoke, Mass.	44,678
Homestead, Fla.	20,668
Homewood, Ala.	21,412
Homewood, Ill.	19,724
Honolulu, Hawaii	365,048
Hoover, Ala.	19,792
Hopewell, Va.	23,397
Hopkinsville, Ky.	27,318
Hot Springs, Ark.	35,781
Houma, La.	32,602
Houston, Tex.	1,595,138
Huber Heights, Ohio	35,480
Huntington, W. Va.	63,684
Huntington Beach, Calif.	170,505
Huntington Park, Calif.	46,223
Huntsville, Ala.	142,513
Huntsville, Tex.	23,936
Hurst, Tex.	31,420
Hutchinson, Kans.	40,284
I	
Idaho Falls, Idaho	39,590
Imperial Beach, Calif.	22,689
Independence, Mo.	111,806
Indianapolis, Ind.	700,807
Indio, Calif.	21,611
Inglewood, Calif.	94,245
Inkster, Mich.	35,190
Inver Grove Heights, Minn.	17,171
Iowa City, Iowa	50,508
Irvine, Calif.	62,134
Irving, Tex.	109,943
Irvington, N.J.	61,493
Ithaca, N.Y.	28,732
J	
Jackson, Mich.	39,739
Jackson, Miss.	202,895
Jackson, Tenn.	49,131
Jacksonville, Ark.	27,589
Jacksonville, Fla.	540,920
Jacksonville, Ill.	20,284
Jacksonville, N.C.	17,056
Jamestown, N.Y.	35,775
Janesville, Wis.	51,071
Jefferson City, Mo.	33,619
Jeffersonville, Ind.	21,220
Jennings, Mo.	17,026
Jersey City, N.J.	223,532
Johnson City, N.Y.	17,126
Johnson City, Tenn.	39,753
Johnston, R.I.	24,907
Johnstown, Pa.	35,496
Joliet, Ill.	77,956
Jonesboro, Ark.	31,530
Joplin, Mo.	38,893
Junction City, Kans.	19,305
Juneau, Alaska	19,528
K	
Kailua, Hawaii	35,812
Kalamazoo, Mich.	79,722
Kaneohe, Hawaii	29,919
Kankakee, Ill.	30,141
Kansas City, Kans.	161,087
Kansas City, Mo.	448,159
Kearney, Nebr.	21,158
Kearny, N.J.	35,735
Keene, N.H.	21,449
Kenmore, N.Y.	18,474
Kenner, La.	66,382
Kennewick, Wash.	34,397
Kenosha, Wis.	77,685
Kent, Ohio	26,164
Kent, Wash.	23,152
Kentwood, Mich.	30,438
Kettering, Ohio	61,186
Key West, Fla.	24,382
Killeen, Tex.	46,296
Kingsport, Tenn.	32,027
Kingston, N.Y.	24,481
Kingsville, Tex.	28,808
Kinston, N.C.	25,234
Kirkland, Wash.	18,779
Kirksville, Mo.	17,167
Kirkwood, Mo.	27,987
Klamath Falls, Oreg.	16,661
Knoxville, Tenn.	175,030
Kokomo, Ind.	47,808
L	
La Canada Flintridge, Calif.	20,153
Lackawanna, N.Y.	22,701
La Crosse, Wis.	48,347
Lafayette, Calif.	20,879
Lafayette, Ind.	43,011
Lafayette, La.	81,961
La Grange, Ga.	24,204
Laguna Beach, Calif.	17,901
La Habra, Calif.	45,232
Lake Charles, La.	75,226
Lake Jackson, Tex.	19,102
Lakeland, Fla.	47,406
Lake Oswego, Oreg.	22,868
Lakewood, Calif.	74,654
Lakewood, Colo.	112,860
Lakewood, Ohio	61,963
Lake Worth, Fla.	27,048
La Mesa, Calif.	50,308
La Mirada, Calif.	40,986
Lancaster, Calif.	48,027
Lancaster, Ohio	34,953
Lancaster, Pa.	54,725
Lansdale, Pa.	16,526
Lansing, Ill.	29,039
Lansing, Mich.	130,414
La Porte, Ind.	21,796
La Puente, Calif.	30,882
Laramie, Wyo.	24,410
Laredo, Tex.	91,449
Largo, Fla.	58,977
Las Cruces, N. Mex.	45,086
Las Vegas, Nev.	164,674
Lauderdale Lakes, Fla.	25,426
Lauderhill, Fla.	37,271
Laurel, Miss.	21,897
La Verne, Calif.	23,508
Lawndale, Calif.	23,460
Lawrence, Ind.	25,591
Lawrence, Kans.	52,738
Lawrence, Mass.	63,175
Lawton, Okla.	80,054

Place	Population
Layton, Utah	22,862
League City, Tex.	16,578
Leavenworth, Kans.	33,656
Lebanon, Pa.	25,711
Lee's Summit, Mo.	28,741
Lemon Grove, Calif.	20,780
Lenexa, Kans.	18,639
Leominster, Mass.	34,508
Lewiston, Idaho	27,986
Lewiston, Me.	40,481
Lewisville, Tex.	24,273
Lexington, Ky.	204,165
Lexington, Mass.	29,479
Libertyville, Ill.	16,520
Lima, Ohio	47,381
Lincoln, Nebr.	171,932
Lincoln, R.I.	16,949
Lincoln Park, Mich.	45,105
Linden, N.J.	37,836
Lindenhurst, N.Y.	26,919
Lindenwold, N.J.	18,196
Little Rock, Ark.	158,461
Littleton, Colo.	28,631
Livermore, Calif.	48,349
Livonia, Mich.	104,814
Lockport, N.Y.	24,844
Lodi, Calif.	35,221
Lodi, N.J.	23,956
Logan, Utah	26,844
Logansport, Ind.	17,899
Lombard, Ill.	37,295
Lomita, Calif.	18,807
Lompoc, Calif.	26,267
Long Beach, Calif.	361,334
Long Beach, N.Y.	34,073
Long Branch, N.J.	29,819
Longmont, Colo.	42,942
Longview, Tex.	62,762
Longview, Wash.	31,052
Lorain, Ohio	75,416
Los Altos, Calif.	25,769
Los Angeles, Calif.	2,966,763
Los Gatos, Calif.	26,593
Louisville, Ky.	298,451
Loveland, Colo.	30,244
Lowell, Mass.	92,418
Lubbock, Tex.	173,979
Ludlow, Mass.	18,150
Lufkin, Tex.	28,562
Lumberton, N.C.	18,241
Lynbrook, N.Y.	20,424
Lynchburg, Va.	66,743
Lyndhurst, Ohio	18,092
Lynn, Mass.	78,471
Lynnwood, Wash.	22,641
Lynwood, Calif.	48,548

M

Place	Population
McAlester, Okla.	17,255
McAllen, Tex.	66,281
McKeesport, Pa.	31,012
Macomb, Ill.	19,863
Macon, Ga.	116,896
Madera, Calif.	21,732
Madison, Wis.	170,616
Madison Heights, Mich.	35,375
Madisonville, Ky.	16,979
Malden, Mass.	53,386
Mamaroneck, N.Y.	17,616
Manchester, Conn.	49,761
Manchester, N.H.	90,936
Manhattan, Kans.	32,644
Manhattan Beach, Calif.	31,542
Manitowoc, Wis.	32,547
Mankato, Minn.	28,651
Mansfield, Conn.	20,634
Mansfield, Ohio	53,927
Manteca, Calif.	24,925
Maple Grove, Minn.	20,525
Maple Heights, Ohio	29,735
Maplewood, Minn.	26,990
Marblehead, Mass.	20,126
Margate, Fla.	36,044
Marietta, Ga.	30,829
Marina, Calif.	20,647
Marion, Ind.	35,874
Marion, Iowa	19,474
Marion, Ohio	37,040
Marlborough, Mass.	30,617
Marquette, Mich.	23,288
Marshall, Tex.	24,921
Marshalltown, Iowa	26,938
Marshfield, Mass.	20,916
Marshfield, Wis.	18,290
Martinez, Calif.	22,582
Martinsville, Va.	18,149
Maryville, Tenn.	17,480
Mason City, Iowa	30,144
Massapequa Park, N.Y.	19,779
Massillon, Ohio	30,557
Mattoon, Ill.	19,055
Mayfield Heights, Ohio	21,550
Maywood, Calif.	21,810
Maywood, Ill.	27,998
Medford, Mass.	58,076
Medford, Oreg.	39,603
Melbourne, Fla.	46,536
Melrose, Mass.	30,055
Melrose Park, Ill.	20,735
Memphis, Tenn.	646,356
Menlo Park, Calif.	25,673
Menomonee Falls, Wis.	27,845
Mentor, Ohio	42,065
Merced, Calif.	36,499
Mercer Island, Wash.	21,522
Meriden, Conn.	57,118
Meridian, Miss.	46,577
Merrillville, Ind.	27,677
Mesa, Ariz.	152,453
Mesquite, Tex.	67,053
Methuen, Mass.	36,701
Miami, Fla.	346,865
Miami Beach, Fla.	96,298
Michigan City, Ind.	36,850
Middletown, Conn.	39,040
Middletown, N.Y.	21,454
Middletown, Ohio	43,719
Middletown, R.I.	17,216
Midland, Mich.	37,250
Midland, Tex.	70,525
Midwest City, Okla.	49,559
Milford, Conn.	50,898
Milford, Mass.	23,390
Mililani, Hawaii	21,365
Millbrae, Calif.	20,058
Millington, Tenn.	20,236
Millville, N.J.	24,815
Milpitas, Calif.	37,820
Milton, Mass.	25,860
Milwaukee, Wis.	636,212
Milwaukie, Oreg.	17,931
Mineola, N.Y.	20,757
Minneapolis, Minn.	370,951
Minnetonka, Minn.	38,683
Minot, N. Dak.	32,843
Miramar, Fla.	32,813
Mishawaka, Ind.	40,201
Mission, Tex.	22,589
Missoula, Mont.	33,388
Missouri City, Tex.	24,533
Mobile, Ala.	200,452
Modesto, Calif.	106,105
Moline, Ill.	45,709
Monroe, La.	57,597
Monroe, Mich.	23,531
Monroeville, Pa.	30,977

Monrovia, Calif.	30,531
Montclair, Calif.	22,628
Montclair, N.J.	38,321
Montebello, Calif.	52,929
Monterey, Calif.	27,558
Monterey Park, Calif.	54,338
Montgomery, Ala.	177,857
Moore, Okla.	35,063
Moorhead, Minn.	29,998
Morgan Hill, Calif.	17,060
Morgantown, W. Va.	27,605
Morristown, N.J.	16,614
Morristown, Tenn.	19,683
Morton Grove, Ill.	23,747
Moscow, Idaho	16,513
Moss Point, Miss.	18,998
Mountain Brook, Ala.	19,718
Mountain View, Calif.	58,655
Mount Clemens, Mich.	18,806
Mountlake Terrace, Wash.	16,534
Mount Pleasant, Mich.	23,746
Mount Prospect, Ill.	52,634
Mount Vernon, Ill.	17,193
Mount Vernon, N.Y.	66,713
Muncie, Ind.	77,216
Mundelein, Ill.	17,053
Munster, Ind.	20,671
Murfreesboro, Tenn.	32,845
Murray, Utah	25,750
Muscatine, Iowa	23,467
Muskegon, Mich.	40,823
Muskogee, Okla.	40,011
Myrtle Beach, S.C.	18,446

N

Nacogdoches, Tex.	27,149
Nampa, Idaho	25,112
Napa, Calif.	50,879
Naperville, Ill.	42,330
Naples, Fla.	17,581
Nashua, N.H.	67,865
Nashville, Tenn.	446,027
Natchez, Miss.	22,015
Natchitoches, La.	16,664
Natick, Mass.	29,461
National City, Calif.	48,772
Naugatuck, Conn.	26,456
Nederland, Tex.	16,855
Needham, Mass.	27,901
Neenah, Wis.	22,432
New Albany, Ind.	37,103
Newark, Calif.	32,126
Newark, Del.	25,247
Newark, N.J.	329,248
Newark, Ohio	41,200
New Bedford, Mass.	98,478
New Berlin, Wis.	30,529
New Braunfels, Tex.	22,402
New Brighton, Minn.	23,269
New Britain, Conn.	73,840
New Brunswick, N.J.	41,442
Newburgh, N.Y.	23,438
New Canaan, Conn.	17,931
New Castle, Ind.	20,056
New Castle, Pa.	33,621
New Haven, Conn.	126,109
New Hope, Minn.	23,087
New Iberia, La.	32,766
Newington, Conn.	28,841
New Kensington, Pa.	17,660
New London, Conn.	28,842
New Milford, Conn.	19,420
New Milford, N.J.	16,876
New Orleans, La.	557,515
New Philadelphia, Ohio	16,883
Newport, Ky.	21,587
Newport, R.I.	29,259
Newport Beach, Calif.	62,556
Newport News, Va.	144,903
New Rochelle, N.Y.	70,794
Newton, Mass.	83,622
Newtown, Conn.	19,107
New York City, N.Y.	7,071,639
Bronx	1,168,972
Brooklyn	2,230,936
Manhattan	1,428,285
Queens	1,891,325
Richmond	352,121
Niagara Falls, N.Y.	71,384
Niles, Ill.	30,363
Niles, Ohio	23,088
Norco, Calif.	21,126
Norfolk, Nebr.	19,449
Norfolk, Va.	266,979
Normal, Ill.	35,672
Norman, Okla.	68,020
Norristown, Pa.	34,684
North Adams, Mass.	18,063
Northampton, Mass.	29,286
North Andover, Mass.	20,129
North Arlington, N.J.	16,587
North Attleboro, Mass.	21,095
Northbrook, Ill.	30,778
North Charleston, S.C.	62,534
North Chicago, Ill.	38,774
Northglenn, Colo.	29,847
North Haven, Conn.	22,080
North Kingstown, R.I.	21,938
North Las Vegas, Nev.	42,739
North Lauderdale, Fla.	18,479
North Little Rock, Ark.	64,288
North Miami, Fla.	42,566
North Miami Beach, Fla.	36,553
North Olmsted, Ohio	36,486
North Plainfield, N.J.	19,108
North Platte, Nebr.	24,479
North Providence, R.I.	29,188
North Richland Hills, Tex.	30,592
North Ridgeville, Ohio	21,522
North Royalton, Ohio	17,671
North Tonawanda, N.Y.	35,760
Norton Shores, Mich.	22,025
Norwalk, Calif.	85,286
Norwalk, Conn.	77,767
Norwich, Conn.	38,074
Norwood, Mass.	29,711
Norwood, Ohio	26,342
Novato, Calif.	43,916
Novi, Mich.	22,525
Nutley, N.J.	28,998

O

Oak Creek, Wis.	16,932
Oak Forest, Ill.	26,096
Oakland, Calif.	339,288
Oakland Park, Fla.	23,035
Oak Lawn, Ill.	60,590
Oak Park, Ill.	54,887
Oak Park, Mich.	31,537
Oak Ridge, Tenn.	27,662
Ocala, Fla.	37,170
Oceanside, Calif.	76,698
Odessa, Tex.	90,027
Ogden, Utah	64,407
Oklahoma City, Okla.	403,213
Olathe, Kans.	37,258
Olean, N.Y.	18,207
Olympia, Wash.	27,447
Omaha, Nebr.	314,255
Ontario, Calif.	88,820
Opelika, Ala.	21,896
Opelousas, La.	18,903
Orange, Calif.	91,788
Orange, N.J.	31,136
Orange, Tex.	23,628
Oregon, Ohio	18,675

Place	Population
Orem, Utah	52,399
Orlando, Fla.	128,291
Orland Park, Ill.	23,045
Ormond Beach, Fla.	21,378
Oshkosh, Wis.	49,620
Ossining, N.Y.	20,196
Oswego, N.Y.	19,793
Ottawa, Ill.	18,166
Ottumwa, Iowa	27,381
Overland, Mo.	19,620
Overland Park, Kans.	81,784
Owatonna, Minn.	18,632
Owensboro, Ky.	54,450
Oxford, Ohio	17,655
Oxnard, Calif.	108,195

P

Place	Population
Pacifica, Calif.	36,866
Paducah, Ky.	29,315
Palatine, Ill.	32,166
Palm Bay, Fla.	18,560
Palm Springs, Calif.	32,271
Palo Alto, Calif.	55,225
Palos Hills, Ill.	16,654
Pampa, Tex.	21,396
Panama City, Fla.	33,346
Paradise, Calif.	22,571
Paramount, Calif.	36,407
Paramus, N.J.	26,474
Paris, Tex.	25,498
Parkersburg, W. Va.	39,967
Park Forest, Ill.	26,222
Park Ridge, Ill.	38,704
Parma, Ohio	92,548
Parma Heights, Ohio	23,112
Pasadena, Calif.	119,374
Pasadena, Tex.	112,560
Pascagoula, Miss.	29,318
Pasco, Wash.	17,944
Passaic, N.J.	52,463
Paterson, N.J.	137,970
Pawtucket, R.I.	71,204
Peabody, Mass.	45,976
Pearl, Miss.	20,778
Pearl City, Hawaii	42,575
Peekskill, N.Y.	18,236
Pekin, Ill.	33,967
Pembroke Pines, Fla.	35,776
Pensacola, Fla.	57,619
Peoria, Ill.	124,160
Perth Amboy, N.J.	38,951
Petaluma, Calif.	33,834
Petersburg, Va.	41,055
Pharr, Tex.	21,381
Phenix City, Ala.	26,928
Philadelphia, Pa.	1,688,210
Phillipsburg, N.J.	16,647
Phoenix, Ariz.	789,704
Pico Rivera, Calif.	53,459
Pine Bluff, Ark.	56,636
Pinellas Park, Fla.	32,811
Piqua, Ohio	20,480
Pittsburg, Calif.	33,034
Pittsburg, Kans.	18,770
Pittsburgh, Pa.	423,938
Pittsfield, Mass.	51,974
Placentia, Calif.	35,041
Plainfield, N.J.	45,555
Plainview, Tex.	22,187
Plano, Tex.	72,331
Plantation, Fla.	48,501
Plant City, Fla.	19,270
Plattsburgh, N.Y.	21,057
Pleasant Hill, Calif.	25,124
Pleasanton, Calif	35,160
Plum, Pa.	25,390
Plymouth, Mass.	35,913
Plymouth, Minn.	31,615
Pocatello, Idaho	46,340
Point Pleasant, N.J.	17,747
Pomona, Calif.	92,742
Pompano Beach, Fla.	52,618
Ponca City, Okla.	26,238
Pontiac, Mich.	76,715
Poplar Bluff, Mo.	17,139
Portage, Ind.	27,409
Portage, Mich.	38,147
Port Angeles, Wash.	17,311
Port Arthur, Tex.	61,251
Port Chester, N.Y.	23,565
Porterville, Calif.	19,707
Port Hueneme, Calif.	17,803
Port Huron, Mich.	33,981
Portland, Me.	61,572
Portland, Oreg.	366,383
Port Orange, Fla.	18,756
Portsmouth, N.H.	26,254
Portsmouth, Ohio	25,943
Portsmouth, Va.	104,577
Pottstown, Pa.	22,729
Pottsville, Pa.	18,195
Poughkeepsie, N.Y.	29,757
Prairie Village, Kans.	24,657
Prattville, Ala.	18,647
Prescott, Ariz.	20,055
Prichard, Ala.	39,541
Providence, R.I.	156,804
Provo, Utah	73,907
Pueblo, Colo.	101,686
Pullman, Wash.	23,579
Puyallup, Wash.	18,251

Q

Place	Population
Quincy, Ill.	42,554
Quincy, Mass.	84,743

R

Place	Population
Racine, Wis.	85,725
Rahway, N.J.	26,723
Raleigh, N.C.	150,255
Rancho Cucamonga, Calif.	55,250
Rancho Palos Verdes, Calif.	36,577
Randolph, Mass.	28,218
Rantoul, Ill.	20,161
Rapid City, S. Dak.	46,492
Raytown, Mo.	31,759
Reading, Mass.	22,678
Reading, Pa.	78,686
Redding, Calif.	41,995
Redlands, Calif.	43,619
Redmond, Wash.	23,318
Redondo Beach, Calif.	57,102
Redwood City, Calif.	54,951
Reno, Nev.	100,756
Renton, Wash.	30,612
Revere, Mass.	42,423
Reynoldsburg, Ohio	20,661
Rialto, Calif.	37,474
Richardson, Tex.	72,496
Richfield, Minn.	37,851
Richland, Wash.	33,578
Richmond, Calif.	74,676
Richmond, Ind.	41,349
Richmond, Ky.	21,705
Richmond, Va.	219,214
Ridgefield, Conn.	20,120
Ridgewood, N.J.	25,208
Riverside, Calif.	170,876
Riviera Beach, Fla.	26,489
Roanoke, Va.	100,220
Rochester, Minn.	57,890
Rochester, N.H.	21,560
Rochester, N.Y.	241,741
Rockford, Ill.	139,712
Rock Hill, S.C.	35,344
Rock Island, Ill.	47,036

Rock Springs, Wyo.	19,458
Rockville, Md.	43,811
Rockville Centre, N.Y.	25,412
Rocky Mount, N.C.	41,283
Rocky River, Ohio	21,084
Rogers, Ark.	17,429
Rohnert Park, Calif.	22,965
Rolling Meadows, Ill.	20,167
Rome, Ga.	29,654
Rome, N.Y.	43,826
Romulus, Mich.	24,857
Roseburg, Oreg.	16,644
Roselle, Ill.	16,948
Roselle, N.J.	20,641
Rosemead, Calif.	42,604
Rosenberg, Tex.	17,995
Roseville, Calif.	24,347
Roseville, Mich.	54,311
Roseville, Minn.	35,820
Roswell, Ga.	23,337
Roswell, N. Mex.	39,676
Roy, Utah	19,694
Royal Oak, Mich.	70,893
Ruston, La.	20,585
Rutherford, N.J.	19,068
Rutland, Vt.	18,436

S

Sacramento, Calif.	275,741
Saginaw, Mich.	77,508
St. Charles, Ill.	17,492
St. Charles, Mo.	37,379
St. Clair Shores, Mich.	76,210
St. Cloud, Minn.	42,566
St. Joseph, Mo.	76,691
St. Louis, Mo.	453,085
St. Louis Park, Minn.	42,931
St. Paul, Minn.	270,230
St. Petersburg, Fla.	238,647
Salem, Mass.	38,220
Salem, N.H.	24,124
Salem, Oreg.	89,233
Salem, Va.	23,958
Salina, Kans.	41,843
Salinas, Calif.	80,479
Salisbury, N.C.	22,677
Salt Lake City, Utah	163,033
San Angelo, Tex.	73,240
San Antonio, Tex.	785,880
San Benito, Tex.	17,988
San Bernardino, Calif.	117,490
San Bruno, Calif.	35,417
San Carlos, Calif.	24,710
San Clemente, Calif.	27,325
San Diego, Calif.	875,538
San Dimas, Calif.	24,014
Sandusky, Ohio	31,360
Sandy City, Utah	50,546
San Fernando, Calif.	17,731
Sanford, Fla.	23,176
Sanford, Me.	18,020
San Francisco, Calif.	678,974
San Gabriel, Calif.	30,072
San Jose, Calif.	636,550
San Juan Capistrano, Calif.	18,959
San Leandro, Calif.	63,952
San Luis Obispo, Calif.	34,252
San Marcos, Calif.	17,479
San Marcos, Tex.	23,420
San Mateo, Calif.	77,561
San Pablo, Calif.	19,750
San Rafael, Calif.	44,700
Santa Ana, Calif.	203,713
Santa Barbara, Calif.	74,542
Santa Clara, Calif.	87,746
Santa Cruz, Calif.	41,483
Santa Fe, N. Mex.	48,953
Santa Maria, Calif.	39,685
Santa Monica, Calif.	88,314
Santa Paula, Calif.	20,552
Santa Rosa, Calif.	83,205
Sarasota, Fla.	48,868
Saratoga, Calif.	29,261
Saratoga Springs, N.Y.	23,906
Saugus, Mass.	24,746
Savannah, Ga.	141,390
Sayreville, N.J.	29,969
Scarsdale, N.Y.	17,650
Schaumburg, Ill.	53,305
Schenectady, N.Y.	67,972
Schofield Barracks, Hawaii	18,851
Scituate, Mass.	17,317
Scottsdale, Ariz.	88,412
Scranton, Pa.	88,117
Seal Beach, Calif.	25,975
Seaside, Calif.	36,567
Seattle, Wash.	493,846
Sedalia, Mo.	20,927
Seguin, Tex.	17,854
Selma, Ala.	26,684
Shaker Heights, Ohio	32,487
Sharon, Pa.	19,057
Shawnee, Kans.	29,653
Shawnee, Okla.	26,506
Sheboygan, Wis.	48,085
Shelton, Conn.	31,314
Sherman, Tex.	30,413
Shively, Ky.	16,819
Shoreview, Minn.	17,300
Shreveport, La.	205,820
Shrewsbury, Mass.	22,674
Sidney, Ohio	17,657
Sierra Vista, Ariz.	24,937
Sikeston, Mo.	17,431
Simi Valley, Calif.	77,500
Simsbury, Conn.	21,161
Sioux City, Iowa	82,003
Sioux Falls, S. Dak.	81,343
Skokie, Ill.	60,278
Slidell, La.	26,718
Smithfield, R.I.	16,886
Smyrna, Ga.	20,312
Somerset, Mass.	18,813
Somerville, Mass.	77,372
South Bend, Ind.	109,727
Southbridge, Mass.	16,665
South El Monte, Calif.	16,623
South Euclid, Ohio	25,713
Southfield, Mich.	75,568
South Gate, Calif.	66,784
Southgate, Mich.	32,058
South Holland, Ill.	24,977
Southington, Conn.	36,879
South Kingstown, R.I.	20,414
South Lake Tahoe, Calif.	20,681
South Milwaukee, Wis.	21,069
South Pasadena, Calif.	22,681
South Plainfield, N.J.	20,521
South Portland, Me.	22,712
South St. Paul, Minn.	21,235
South San Francisco, Calif.	49,393
South Windsor, Conn.	17,198
Sparks, Nev.	40,780
Spartanburg, S.C.	43,968
Spokane, Wash.	171,300
Springdale, Ark.	23,458
Springfield, Ill.	99,637
Springfield, Mass.	152,319
Springfield, Mo.	133,116
Springfield, Ohio	72,563
Springfield, Oreg.	41,621
Spring Valley, N.Y.	20,537
Stamford, Conn.	102,453
Stanton, Calif.	23,723
State College, Pa.	36,130
Statesville, N.C.	18,622

Place	Population
Staunton, Va.	21,857
Sterling Heights, Mich.	108,999
Steubenville, Ohio	26,400
Stevens Point, Wis.	22,970
Stillwater, Okla.	38,268
Stockton, Calif.	149,779
Stoneham, Mass.	21,424
Stoughton, Mass.	26,710
Stow, Ohio	25,303
Stratford, Conn.	50,541
Streamwood, Ill.	23,456
Strongsville, Ohio	28,577
Suffolk, Va.	47,621
Sulphur, La.	19,709
Summit, N.J.	21,071
Sumter, S.C.	24,890
Sunnyvale, Calif.	106,618
Sunrise, Fla.	39,681
Superior, Wis.	29,571
Syracuse, N.Y.	170,105

T

Place	Population
Tacoma, Wash.	158,501
Talladega, Ala.	19,128
Tallahassee, Fla.	81,548
Tamarac, Fla.	29,376
Tampa, Fla.	271,523
Taunton, Mass.	45,001
Taylor, Mich.	77,568
Tempe, Ariz.	106,743
Temple, Tex.	42,483
Temple City, Calif.	28,972
Terre Haute, Ind.	61,125
Tewksbury, Mass.	24,635
Texarkana, Ark.	21,459
Texarkana, Tex.	31,271
Texas City, Tex.	41,403
Thomasville, Ga.	18,463
Thornton, Colo.	40,343
Thousand Oaks, Calif.	77,072
Tiffin, Ohio	19,549
Tinley Park, Ill.	26,171
Titusville, Fla.	31,910
Toledo, Ohio	354,635
Tonawanda, N.Y.	18,693
Topeka, Kans.	115,266
Torrance, Calif.	131,497
Torrington, Conn.	30,987
Tracy, Calif.	18,428
Trenton, Mich.	22,762
Trenton, N.J.	92,124
Troy, Mich.	67,102
Troy, N.Y.	56,638
Troy, Ohio	19,086
Trumbull, Conn.	32,989
Tucson, Ariz.	330,537
Tulare, Calif.	22,475
Tulsa, Okla.	360,919
Tupelo, Miss.	23,905
Turlock, Calif.	26,287
Tuscaloosa, Ala.	75,211
Tustin, Calif.	32,317
Twin Falls, Idaho	26,209
Tyler, Tex.	70,508

U

Place	Population
Union City, Calif.	39,406
Union City, N.J.	55,593
University City, Mo.	42,738
University Park, Tex.	22,254
Upland, Calif.	47,647
Upper Arlington, Ohio	35,648
Urbana, Ill.	35,978
Urbandale, Iowa	17,869
Utica, N.Y.	75,632

V

Place	Population
Vacaville, Calif.	43,367
Valdosta, Ga.	37,596
Vallejo, Calif.	80,303
Valley Stream, N.Y.	35,769
Valparaiso, Ind.	22,247
Vancouver, Wash.	42,834
Ventura (San Buenaventura), Calif.	74,474
Vernon, Conn.	27,974
Vicksburg, Miss.	25,434
Victoria, Tex.	50,695
Villa Park, Ill.	23,185
Vincennes, Ind.	20,857
Vineland, N.J.	53,753
Virginia Beach, Va.	262,199
Visalia, Calif.	49,729
Vista, Calif.	35,834

W

Place	Population
Waco, Tex.	101,261
Wahiawa, Hawaii	16,911
Waipahu, Hawaii	29,139
Wakefield, Mass.	24,895
Walla Walla, Wash.	25,618
Wallingford, Conn.	37,274
Walnut Creek, Calif.	53,643
Walpole, Mass.	18,859
Waltham, Mass.	58,200
Wareham, Mass.	18,457
Warner Robins, Ga.	39,893
Warren, Mich.	161,134
Warren, Ohio	56,629
Warrensville Heights, Ohio	16,565
Warwick, R.I.	87,123
Washington, D.C.	637,651
Washington, Pa.	18,363
Waterbury, Conn.	103,266
Waterford, Conn.	17,843
Waterloo, Iowa	75,985
Watertown, Conn.	19,489
Watertown, Mass.	34,384
Watertown, N.Y.	27,861
Watertown, Wis.	18,113
Waterville, Me.	17,779
Watsonville, Calif.	23,543
Waukegan, Ill.	67,653
Waukesha, Wis.	50,319
Wausau, Wis.	32,426
Wauwatosa, Wis.	51,308
Waycross, Ga.	19,371
Wayne, Mich.	21,159
Webster Groves, Mo.	23,097
Weirton, W. Va.	24,736
Wellesley, Mass.	27,209
Wenatchee, Wash.	17,257
Weslaco, Tex.	19,331
West Allis, Wis.	63,982
West Bend, Wis.	21,484
Westchester, Ill.	17,730
West Chester, Pa.	17,435
West Covina, Calif.	80,291
West Des Moines, Iowa	21,894
Westerly, R.I.	18,580
Westerville, Ohio	23,414
Westfield, Mass.	36,465
Westfield, N.J.	30,447
West Hartford, Conn.	61,301
West Haven, Conn.	53,184
West Jordan, Utah	27,192
West Lafayette, Ind.	21,247
Westlake, Ohio	19,483
Westland, Mich.	84,603
West Memphis, Ark.	28,138
West Mifflin, Pa.	26,279
Westminster, Calif.	71,133
Westminster, Colo.	50,211
Westmont, Ill.	16,718
West New York, N.J.	39,194
West Orange, N.J.	39,510

West Palm Beach, Fla.	63,305
Westport, Conn.	25,290
West St. Paul, Minn.	18,527
West Springfield, Mass.	27,042
West Warwick, R.I.	27,026
Wethersfield, Conn.	26,031
Weymouth, Mass.	55,601
Wheaton, Ill.	43,043
Wheat Ridge, Colo.	30,293
Wheeling, Ill.	23,266
Wheeling, W. Va.	43,070
White Bear Lake, Minn.	22,538
Whitehall, Ohio	21,299
White Plains, N.Y.	46,999
Whittier, Calif.	69,717
Wichita, Kans.	279,272
Wichita Falls, Tex.	94,201
Wickliffe, Ohio	16,790
Wilkes-Barre, Pa.	51,551
Wilkinsburg, Pa.	23,669
Williamsport, Pa.	33,401
Willoughby, Ohio	19,329
Willowick, Ohio	17,834
Wilmette, Ill.	28,229
Wilmington, Del.	70,195
Wilmington, Mass.	17,471
Wilmington, N.C.	44,000
Wilson, N.C.	34,424
Winchester, Mass.	20,701
Winchester, Va.	20,217
Windham, Conn.	21,062
Windsor, Conn.	25,204
Winona, Minn.	25,075
Winston-Salem, N.C.	131,885
Winter Haven, Fla.	21,119
Winter Park, Fla.	22,339
Winthrop, Mass.	19,294
Wisconsin Rapids, Wis.	17,995
Woburn, Mass.	36,626
Woodland, Calif.	30,235
Woodridge, Ill.	22,322
Woonsocket, R.I.	45,914
Wooster, Ohio	19,289
Worcester, Mass.	161,799
Wyandotte, Mich.	34,006
Wyoming, Mich.	59,616

X

Xenia, Ohio	24,653

Y

Yakima, Wash.	49,826
Yarmouth, Mass.	18,449
Yonkers, N.Y.	195,351
Yorba Linda, Calif.	28,254
York, Pa.	44,619
Youngstown, Ohio	115,436
Ypsilanti, Mich.	24,031
Yuba City, Calif.	18,736
Yukon, Okla.	17,112
Yuma, Ariz.	42,433

Z

Zanesville, Ohio	28,655
Zion, Ill.	17,861

Population of the United States in 1980

Summary by States and Dependencies

(Figures in parentheses give rank of states in population)

The States and the District of Columbia

Alabama	(22)	3,893,888
Alaska	(50)	401,851
Arizona	(29)	2,718,215
Arkansas	(33)	2,286,435
California	(1)	23,667,902
Colorado	(28)	2,889,964
Connecticut	(25)	3,107,576
Delaware	(47)	594,338
District of Columbia		638,333
Florida	(7)	9,746,324
Georgia	(13)	5,463,105
Hawaii	(39)	964,691
Idaho	(41)	943,935
Illinois	(5)	11,426,518
Indiana	(12)	5,490,224
Iowa	(27)	2,913,808
Kansas	(32)	2,363,679
Kentucky	(23)	3,660,777
Louisiana	(19)	4,205,900
Maine	(38)	1,124,660
Maryland	(18)	4,216,975
Massachusetts	(11)	5,737,037
Michigan	(8)	9,262,078
Minnesota	(21)	4,075,970
Mississippi	(31)	2,520,638
Missouri	(15)	4,916,686
Montana	(44)	786,690
Nebraska	(35)	1,569,825
Nevada	(43)	800,493
New Hampshire	(42)	920,610
New Jersey	(9)	7,364,823
New Mexico	(37)	1,302,894
New York	(2)	17,558,072
North Carolina	(10)	5,881,766
North Dakota	(46)	652,717
Ohio	(6)	10,797,630
Oklahoma	(26)	3,025,290
Oregon	(30)	2,633,105
Pennsylvania	(4)	11,863,895
Rhode Island	(40)	947,154
South Carolina	(24)	3,121,820
South Dakota	(45)	690,768
Tennessee	(17)	4,591,120
Texas	(3)	14,229,191
Utah	(36)	1,461,037
Vermont	(48)	511,456
Virginia	(14)	5,356,818
Washington	(20)	4,132,156
West Virginia	(34)	1,949,644
Wisconsin	(16)	4,705,767
Wyoming	(49)	469,557
Total		226,545,805

Dependencies

American Samoa	32,297
Guam	105,979
Puerto Rico	3,196,520
Virgin Islands of the U.S.	96,569
Other (Trust Territory of the Pacific Islands, etc.)	132,929
Total	3,564,294
Total U.S. & Dependencies	230,110,099

Population of Places in Canada

Having 16,500 or More Inhabitants in 1981

Ajax, Ont.	25,475
Alma, Que.	26,322
Anjou, Que.	37,346
Aylmer, Que.	26,695
Barrie, Ont.	38,423
Beaconsfield, Que.	19,613
Beauport, Que.	60,447
Belleville, Ont.	34,881
Beloeil, Que.	17,540
Boucherville, Que.	29,704
Brampton, Ont.	149,030
Brandon, Man.	36,242
Brantford, Ont.	74,315
Brockville, Ont.	19,896
Brossard, Que.	52,232
Burlington, Ont.	114,853
Burnaby, B.C.	136,494
Caledon, Ont.	26,645
Calgary, Alta.	592,743
Cambridge, Ont.	77,183
Cap-de-la-Madeleine, Que.	32,626
Charlesbourg, Que.	68,326
Châteauguay, Que.	36,928
Chatham, Ont.	40,952
Chicoutimi, Que.	60,064
Chilliwack, B.C.	40,642
Corner Brook, Nfld.	24,339
Cornwall, Ont.	46,144
Côte-St-Luc, Que.	27,531
Dartmouth, N.S.	62,277
Delta, B.C.	74,692
Dollard-des-Ormeaux, Que.	39,940
Dorval, Que.	17,722
Drummondville, Que.	27,347
Dundas, Ont.	19,586
East York, Ont.	101,974
Edmonton, Alta.	532,246
Elliot Lake, Ont.	16,723
Etobicoke, Ont.	298,713
Fort Erie, Ont.	24,096
Fort McMurray, Alta.	31,000
Fredericton, N.B.	43,723
Gaspé, Que.	17,261
Gatineau, Que.	74,988
Glace Bay, N.S.	21,466
Gloucester, Ont.	72,859
Granby, Que.	38,069
Grande Prairie, Alta.	24,263
Greenfield Park, Que.	18,527
Guelph, Ont.	71,207
Haldimand, Ont.	16,866
Halifax, N.S.	114,594
Halton Hills, Ont.	35,190
Hamilton, Ont.	306,434
Hull, Que.	56,225
Joliette, Que.	16,987
Jonquière, Que.	60,354
Kamloops, B.C.	64,048
Kanata, Ont.	19,728
Kelowna, B.C.	59,196
Kingston, Ont.	52,616
Kitchener, Ont.	139,734
La Baie, Que.	20,935
Lachine, Que.	37,521
LaSalle, Que.	76,299
Laval, Que.	268,335
Lethbridge, Alta.	54,072
Lévis, Que.	17,895
London, Ont.	254,280
Longueuil, Que.	124,320
Markham, Ont.	77,037
Mascouche, Que.	20,345
Medicine Hat, Alta.	40,380
Milton, Ont.	28,067
Mississauga, Ont.	315,056
Moncton, N.B.	54,743
Montreal, Que.	980,354
Montreal-Nord, Que.	94,914
Mont-Royal, Que.	19,247
Moose Jaw, Sask.	33,941
Nanaimo, B.C.	47,069
Nanticoke, Ont.	19,816
Nepean, Ont.	84,361
Newcastle, Ont.	32,229
Newmarket, Ont.	29,753
New Westminster, B.C.	38,550
Niagara Falls, Ont.	70,960
North Bay, Ont.	51,268
North Vancouver, B.C.	33,952
North York, Ont.	559,521
Oakville, Ont.	75,773
Orillia, Ont.	23,955
Oshawa, Ont.	117,519
Ottawa, Ont.	295,163
Outremont, Que.	24,338
Owen Sound, Ont.	19,883
Penticton, B.C.	23,181
Peterborough, Ont.	60,620
Pickering, Ont.	37,754
Pierrefonds, Que.	38,390
Pointe-aux-Trembles, Que.	36,270
Pointe-Claire, Que.	24,571
Port Alberni, B.C.	19,892
Port Colborne, Ont.	19,225
Port Coquitlam, B.C.	27,535
Prince Albert, Sask.	31,380
Prince George, B.C.	67,559
Quebec, Que.	166,474
Red Deer, Alta.	46,393
Regina, Sask.	162,613
Repentigny, Que.	34,419
Richmond Hill, Ont.	37,778
Rimouski, Que.	29,120
Rouyn, Que.	17,224
St. Albert, Alta.	31,996
St-Bruno-de-Montarville, Que.	22,880
St. Catharines, Ont.	124,018
Ste-Foy, Que.	68,883
Ste-Thérèse, Que.	18,750
St. Eustache, Que.	29,716
St-Hubert, Que.	60,573
St-Hyacinthe, Que.	38,246
St-Jean, Que.	35,640
St-Jerôme, Que.	25,123
Saint John, N.B.	80,521
St. John's, Nfld.	83,770
St-Lambert, Que.	20,557
St-Laurent, Que.	65,900
St-Léonard, Que.	79,429
St. Thomas, Ont.	28,165
Sarnia, Ont.	50,892
Saskatoon, Sask.	154,210
Sault Ste. Marie, Ont.	82,697
Scarborough, Ont.	443,353

Sept-Iles, Que.	29,262
Shawinigan, Que.	23,011
Sherbrooke, Que.	74,075
Sorel, Que.	20,347
Stoney Creek, Ont.	36,762
Stratford, Ont.	26,262
Sudbury, Ont.	91,829
Sydney, N.S.	29,444
Thetford Mines, Que.	19,965
Thunder Bay, Ont.	112,486
Timmins, Ont.	46,114
Toronto, Ont.	599,217
Trois-Rivières, Que.	50,466
Val-d'Or, Que.	21,371
Valley East, Ont.	20,433
Valleyfield, Que.	29,574
Vancouver, B.C.	414,281
Vanier, Ont.	18,792
Vaughan, Ont.	29,674
Verdun, Que.	61,287
Vernon, B.C.	19,987
Victoria, B.C.	64,379
Victoriaville, Que.	21,838
Waterloo, Ont.	49,428
Welland, Ont.	45,448
Westmount, Que.	20,480
Whitby, Ont.	36,698
Windsor, Ont.	192,083
Winnipeg, Man.	564,473
Woodstock, Ont.	26,603
York, Ont.	134,617

Population of Canada in 1981

Summary by Provinces and Territories

Alberta	2,237,724
British Columbia	2,744,467
Manitoba	1,026,241
New Brunswick	696,403
Newfoundland	567,681
Nova Scotia	847,442
Ontario	8,625,107
Prince Edward Island	122,506
Quebec	6,438,403
Saskatchewan	948,313
Yukon Territory	21,836
Northwest Territories	45,741
Total	24,098,473

Signs and Symbols

Astronomy

- ☉ the sun; Sunday
- ◐, ☾, *or* ☽ the moon; Monday
- ● new moon
- ☽, ◐, ☽, ☽ first quarter
- ○ *or* ☺ full moon
- ☾, ◑, ☾, ☾ last quarter
- ☿ Mercury; Wednesday
- ♀ Venus; Friday
- ⊕, ⊖, *or* ♁ the earth
- ♂ Mars; Tuesday
- ♃ Jupiter; Thursday
- ♄ *or* ♄ Saturn; Saturday
- ♅, ♅, *or* ♅ Uranus
- ♆, ♆, *or* ♆ Neptune
- ♇ Pluto
- ☄ comet
- * *or* ✳ fixed star

Business

- a/c account ⟨in a/c with⟩
- @ at; each ⟨4 apples @ 5¢=20¢⟩
- ⅌ per
- c/o care of
- # number if it precedes a numeral ⟨track #3⟩; pounds if it follows ⟨a 5# sack of sugar⟩
- ℔ pound; pounds
- % percent
- ‰ per thousand
- $ dollars
- ¢ cents
- £ pounds
- / shillings
- © copyrighted
- ® registered trademark

Mathematics

- + plus; positive ⟨a+b=c⟩—used also to indicate omitted figures or an approximation
- − minus; negative
- ± plus of minus ⟨the square root of $4a^2$ is ± 2a⟩
- × multiplied by; times ⟨6×4=24⟩—also indicated by placing a dot between the factors ⟨6·4=24⟩ or by writing factors other than numerals without signs
- ÷ *or* : divided by ⟨24÷6=4⟩—also indicated by writing the divisor under the dividend with a line between ⟨$\frac{24}{6}=4$⟩ or by writing the divisor after the dividend with an oblique line between ⟨3/8⟩
- = equals ⟨6+2=8⟩
- ≠ *or* ≠ is not equal to
- > is greater than ⟨6>5⟩
- >> is much greater than
- < is less than ⟨3<4⟩
- << is much less than
- ≧ *or* ≥ is greater than or equal to
- ≦ *or* ≤ is less than or equal to
- ≯ is not greater than
- ≮ is not less than
- ≈ is approximately equal to
- ≡ is identical to
- ∽ equivalent; similar
- ≅ is congruent to
- ∝ varies directly as; is proportional to
- : is to; the ratio of
- ∴ therefore
- ∞ infinity
- ∠ angle; the angle ⟨∠ABC⟩
- ∟ right angle ⟨∟ABC⟩
- ⊥ the perpendicular; is perpendicular to ⟨AB⊥CD⟩
- ∥ parallel; is parallel to ⟨AB ∥ CD⟩
- ⊙ *or* ○ circle
- ⌒ arc of a circle
- △ triangle
- □ square
- ▭ rectangle
- √ *or* √ radical—used without a figure to indicate a square root (as in √4=) or

with an index above the sign to indicate the root to be taken (as $\sqrt[3]{x}$) if the root is not a square root

( ) parentheses, [ ] brackets, { } braces — indicate that the quantities enclosed by them are to be taken together

π pi; the number 3.14159265+; the ratio of the circumference of a circle to its diameter

° degree ⟨60°⟩

′ minute; foot ⟨30′⟩

″ second; inch ⟨30″⟩

! factorial—used to indicate the product of all the whole numbers up to and including a given preceding number

∪ union of two sets

∩ intersection of two sets

⊂ is included in, is a subset of

⊃ contains as a subset

∈ *or* ϵ is an element of

∉ is not an element of

Λ *or* 0 *or* ϕ or { } empty set, null set

Medicine

$\overline{AA}$, Ā, *or* āā of each

℞ take—used on prescriptions; prescription; treatment

☠ poison

APOTHECARIES' MEASURES

℥ ounce

f℥ fluidounce

*f*ʒ fluidram

♏, ♍, ♏ *or* min minim

APOTHECARIES' WEIGHTS

℔ pound

℥ ounce (as ℥ i or ℥ j, one ounce; ℥ ss, half an ounce; ℥ iss *or* ℥ jss, one ounce and a half; ℥ ij, two ounces)

ʒ dram

℈ scruple

Miscellaneous

& and

&c et cetera; and so forth

" *or* " ditto marks

/ virgule; used to mean "or" (as in *and/or*), "and/or" (as in *dead/wounded*), "per" (as in *feet/second*), indicates end of a line of verse; separates the figures of a date (4/8/74)

☞ index *or* fist

< derived from, > whence derived, + and, * assumed — used in etymologies

† died—used esp. in genealogies

✚ cross

☧ monogram from Greek XP signifying Christ

卐 swastika

✡ Judaism

☥ ankh

℣ versicle

℟ response

* —used in Roman Catholic and Anglican service books to divide each verse of a psalm, indicating where the response begins

✠ *or* +—used in some service books to indicate where the sign of the cross is to be made; also used by certain Roman Catholic and Anglican prelates as a sign of the cross preceding their signatures

LXX Septuagint

f/ or f: relative aperture of a photographic lens

civil defense

☮ peace

Reference marks

* asterisk *or* star
† dagger
‡ double dagger
§ section *or* numbered clause
‖ parallels
¶ *or* ⁋ paragraph

Stamps and stamp collecting

★ unused
○ used
⊞ block of four or more
⊠ entire cover or card

Weather

barometer, changes of
^ Rising, then falling
⁄‾ Rising, then steady; or rising, then rising more slowly
/ Rising steadily, or unsteadily
✓ Falling or steady, then rising; or rising, then rising more quickly
— Steady, same as 3 hours ago
v Falling, then rising, same or lower than 3 hours ago
_ Falling, then steady; or falling then falling more slowly
\\ Falling steadily, or unsteadily
^ Steady or rising, then falling; or falling, then falling more quickly
◎ calm
○ clear
◐ cloudy (partly)
● cloudy (completely overcast)
+ drifting or blowing snow
, drizzle
▬ fog
freezing rain
▲▲▲▲ cold front
warm front
stationary front
)(funnel clouds
∞ haze
hurricane
tropical storm
• rain
: rain and snow
frost
sandstorm or dust storm
▿ shower(s)
shower of rain
shower of hail
△ sleet
• snow
thunderstorm
visibility reduced by smoke

A Handbook of Style

Punctuation

The English writing system uses punctuation marks to separate groups of words for meaning and emphasis; to convey an idea of the variations of pitch, volume, pauses, and intonations of speech; and to help avoid ambiguity. English punctuation marks, together with general rules and examples of their use, follow.

Apostrophe ’

1. indicates the possessive case of nouns and indefinite pronouns

   <Mrs. Cenacci's office>
   <the boy's mother>
   <the boys' mothers>
   <It is anyone's guess how much it will cost.>
   <her mother-in-law's car>

   NOTE: The use of an *'s* with words ending in \s\ or \z\ sounds usually depends on whether a pronounceable final syllable is thus formed: if the syllable is pronounced, the *'s* is usually used; if no final pronounceable syllable is formed, the apostrophe is retained but the *s* is usually not added.

   <Knox's products>
   <the bus's brakes>
   <Aristophanes' play>
   <for righteousness' sake>

2. marks omissions in contracted words

   <didn't> <o'clock>

3. marks omission of numerals

   <class of '91>

4. often forms plurals of letters, figures, and words referred to as words

   <You should dot your *i*'s and cross your *t*'s.>
   <His *l*'s and his *7*'s looked alike.>
   <She has trouble pronouncing her *the*'s.>

Brackets [ ]

1. set off extraneous data such as editorial interpolations especially within quoted material

   <He wrote, "I ain't [sic] going.">
   <"But there's one thing to be said for it [his apprenticeship with Samuels]: it started me thinking about architecture in a new way.">

2. function as parentheses within parentheses

   <Bowman Act (22 Stat., ch. 4, § [or sec.] 4, p. 50)>

Colon :

1. introduces a clause or phrase that explains, illustrates, amplifies, or restates what has gone before

   <The sentence was poorly constructed: it lacked both unity and coherence.>

2. directs attention to an appositive

   <He had only one pleasure: eating.>

3. introduces a series

   <Three countries were represented: England, France, and Belgium.>

4. introduces lengthy quoted material set off from the rest of a text by indentation but not by quotation marks

   <I quote from the text of Chapter One:>

5. separates elements in page references, bibliographical and biblical citations, and in set formulas used to express ratios and time

   <*Journal of the American Medical Association* 48:356>
   <Springfield, Mass.: Merriam-Webster Inc.>
   <John 4:10> <8:30 a.m.> <a ratio of 3:5>

6. separates titles and subtitles (as of books)

   <*The Tragic Dynasty: A History of the Romanovs*>

7. follows the salutation in formal correspondence

   <Dear Sir or Madam:> <Dear Dean Alvarez:>
   <Dear Ms. North:>

8. punctuates memorandum and government correspondence headings, and some subject lines in general business letters

   <TO:> <VIA:>
   <SUBJECT:>
   <REFERENCE:>

Comma ,

1. separates main clauses joined by a coordinating conjunction (as *and, but, or, nor*, or *for*) and very short clauses not so joined

   <She knew very little about him, and he volunteered nothing.>
   <I came, I saw, I conquered.>

2. sets off an adverbial clause (or long phrase) that precedes or interrupts the main clause

   <When she discovered the answer, she reported it to us.>
   <The report, after being read aloud, was put up for consideration.>

3. sets off from the rest of the sentence transitional words and expressions (as *on the contrary, on the other hand*), conjunctive adverbs (as *consequently, furthermore, however*), and expressions that introduce an illustration or example (as *namely, for example*)

   <Your second question, on the other hand, remains unanswered.>
   <They will travel through two countries, namely, France and England.>
   <He responded as completely as he could; that is, he answered each individual question specifically.>

4. sets off contrasting and opposing expressions within sentences

   <The cost is not $65.00, but $56.65.>
   <He changed his style, not his ethics.>

5. separates words, phrases, or clauses in series

   <He was young, eager, and restless.>
   <Her job required her to travel often, to dress expensively, and to be self-sufficient.>

   NOTE: Commas separate coordinate adjectives modifying a noun.

   <She spoke in a calm, reflective manner.>

6. sets off from the rest of the sentence parenthetical elements (as nonrestrictive modifiers and nonrestrictive appositives)

   <Our guide, who wore a blue beret, was an experienced traveler.>
   <We visited Gettysburg, the site of a famous battle.>
   <The author, Marie Jones, was an accomplished athlete.>

7. introduces a direct quotation, terminates a direct quotation that is neither a question nor an exclamation, and encloses split quotations

<Mary said, "I am leaving.">
<"I am leaving," Mary said.>
<"I am leaving," Mary said with determination, "even if you want me to stay.">

NOTE: If the quotation is used as a subject or as a noun phrase that follows a linking verb or if it is not being presented as actual dialogue, a comma is not used.

<"The computer is down" was the reply she feared.>
<The fact that he said he was about to "leave this instant" doesn't mean he actually left.>

8. sets off words in direct address, absolute phrases, and mild interjections

<You may go, John, if you wish.>
<Our business concluded, we adjourned for lunch.>
<Ah, that's my idea of an excellent dinner.>

9. introduces a direct question that starts in the middle of a sentence

<It's a fine day, isn't it?>
<I wondered, What is going on here?>
<The question is, How do we get out of here?>

10. indicates the omission of a word or words, and especially a word or words used earlier in the sentence

<Common stocks are preferred by some investors; bonds, by others.>

NOTE: When the meaning of the sentence is quite clear without the comma, the comma is omitted.

<He was in love with her and she with him.>

11. is used to avoid ambiguity and also to emphasize a particular phrase

<To Mary, Jane was someone special.>
<The more embroidery on a dress, the higher the price.>

12. is used to group numbers into units of three in separating thousands, millions, etc; however, it is generally not used in numbers of four figures, in pagination, in dates, or in street numbers

<Smithville, pop. 100,000>
but
<3600 rpm> <the year 1983>
<page 1411> <27509 Alameda Drive>

13. punctuates an inverted name

<Morton, William A.>

14. separates a proper name from a following corporate, academic, honorary, governmental, or military title

<Sandra H. Cobb, Vice President>

15. sets off geographical names (as state or country from city), items in dates, and addresses from the rest of a text

<Shreveport, Louisiana, is the site of a large air base.>
<On Sunday, June 23, 1940, he was wounded.>
<Number 10 Downing Street, London, is a famous address.>

NOTE: When just the month and the year are given, the comma is usually omitted.

<She began her career in April 1983 at a modest salary.>

16. follows the salutation in informal correspondence and follows the complimentary close of a formal or informal letter

<Dear Mark,>
<Affectionately,>
<Very truly yours,>

Dash —

1. usually marks an abrupt change or break in the continuity of a sentence

<When they heard about it, they—well, let's just say they weren't too pleased.>

2. is sometimes used in place of other punctuation (as the comma) when special emphasis is required

<The presentations—and especially the one by Ms. Dow—impressed the audience.>

3. introduces a summary statement that follows a series of words or phrases

   <Oil, steel, and wheat—these are the sinews of industrialization.>

4. often precedes the attribution of a quotation

   <My foot is on my native heath . . .—Sir Walter Scott>

5. may be used with the exclamation point or the question mark

   <The faces of the crash victims—how bloody!—were shown on TV.>
   <Your question—it was *your* question, wasn't it, Mr. Jones?—just can't be answered.>

6. removes the need for a comma if the dash falls where a comma would ordinarily separate two clauses

   <If we don't succeed—and the critics say we won't—then the whole project is in jeopardy.>

Ellipsis . . . .

1. indicates the omission of one or more words within a quoted passage

   <I never knew any man . . . who could not bear another's misfortunes—Alexander Pope>

2. indicates the omission of one or more sentences within a quoted passage or the omission of words at the end of a sentence by using four dots the first of which represents the period

   <That recovering the manuscripts would be worth almost any effort is without question. . . . The monetary value of a body of Shakespeare's manuscripts would be almost incalculable—Charlton Ogburn>
   <It will take scholars years to determine conclusively the origins, the history, and, most importantly, the significance of the finds. . . .—Robert Morse>

3. usually indicates omission of one or more lines of poetry when ellipsis is extended the length of the line

   <It little profits that an idle king,
   . . . .
   Matched with an aged wife, I mete and dole
   Unequal laws unto a savage race,
   That hoard, and sleep, and feed,
   and know not me.
   —Alfred Tennyson>

4. indicates halting speech or an unfinished sentence in dialogue

   <"I'd like to . . . that is . . . if you're sure you don't mind. . . .">

Exclamation Point !

1. terminates an emphatic phrase or sentence

   <Get out of here!>

2. terminates an emphatic interjection

   <Encore!>

Hyphen -

1. marks end-of-line division of a word when part of the word is to be carried down to the next line

   <mill-
   stone>

   <pas-
   sion>

2. is used between some prefix and root combinations, as

   prefix + proper name;

   <pre-Renaissance>

prefix ending with a vowel + root word beginning often with the same vowel;
stressed prefix + root word, especially when this combination is similar to a different word

<co-opted> <re-ink>
<re-cover a sofa>
but
<recover from an illness>

3. is used in some compounds, especially those containing prepositions

   <president-elect> <sister-in-law>
   <attorney-at-law> <good-for-nothing>

4. is often used between elements of an attributive compound modifier in order to avoid ambiguity

   <traveling in a fast-moving van>
   <She has gray-green eyes.>
   <He looked at her with a know-it-all expression.>

5. suspends the first part of a hyphenated compound when used with another hyphenated compound

   <a six- or eight-cylinder engine>

6. is used in writing out compound numbers between 21 and 99

   <thirty-four>
   <one hundred and thirty-eight>

7. is used between the numerator and the denominator in writing out fractions especially when they are used as modifiers; however, fractions used as nouns are often styled as open compounds especially when either the numerator or the denominator already contains a hyphen

   <a two-thirds majority of the vote>
   <one seventy-second of an inch>

8. serves as an arbitrary equivalent of the phrase "(up) to and including" when used between numbers and dates

   <pages 40–98>
   <the decade 1980–89>

9. is used between capitalized names to replace the word "to" or to indicate linkages

   <the New York–Paris flight>
   <the Dempsey–Tunney fight>

Hyphen, Double

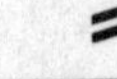

is used in dictionaries at the end-of-line division of a hyphenated compound to indicate that the compound would be hyphenated at that point if it were not being broken at the end of the line

self= [end of line] seeker (self-seeker)
but
self- [end of line] same (selfsame)

The styling of compounds varies: they may be open, hyphenated, or solid. When in doubt, consult the main vocabulary of this dictionary for the most commonly used styling.

Parentheses ( )

1. set off supplementary, parenthetic, or explanatory material when the interruption is more than that indicated by commas and when the inclusion of such material does not essentially alter the meaning of the sentence

   <Three old destroyers (all now out of commission) will be scrapped.>

2. enclose Arabic numerals which confirm a written number in a text

   <Delivery will be made in thirty (30) days.>

3. enclose numbers or letters in a series

   <We must set forth (1) our long-term goals, (2) our immediate objectives, and (3) the means at our disposal.>

4. enclose an abbreviation that immediately follows its spelled-out form or may enclose a spelled-out form that follows its abbreviation

   <a ruling by the Federal Communications Commission (FCC)>
   <the manufacture and disposal of PVC (polyvinyl chloride)>

5. indicate alternative terms and omissions (as in form letters)

   <Please indicate the lecture(s) you would like to attend.>

6. are used with other punctuation marks in the following ways:

   if the parenthetic expression is an independent sentence standing alone, its first word is capitalized and a period is included *inside* the last parenthesis; however, if the parenthetic expression, even if it could stand alone as a sentence, occurs within a sentence, it needs neither capitalization nor a final period but may have an exclamation point or question mark

   <The discussion was held in the boardroom. (The results are still confidential.)>
   <Although we liked the restaurant (their Italian food was the best), we seldom went there.>
   <After waiting in line for an hour (why do we do these things?), we finally left.>

   parenthetic material within a sentence may be internally punctuated by a question mark, a period after an abbreviation only, an exclamation point, or a set of quotation marks

   <Years ago, someone (who was it?) told me about it.>
   <The conference was held in Vancouver (that's in B.C.).>
   <He was depressed ("I must resign") and refused to do anything.>

   no punctuation mark should be placed directly before parenthetical material in a sentence; if a break is required, punctuation should be placed *after* the final parenthesis

   <I'll get back to you tomorrow (Friday), when I have more details.>

Period

1. terminates sentences or sentence fragments that are neither interrogatory nor exclamatory

   <Give it your best.> <I gave it my best.>
   <He asked if she had given it her best.>

2. follows some abbreviations and contractions

   <Dr.> <A.D.> <ibid.> <i.e.>
   <Jr.> <etc.> <cont.>

3. is used with an individual's initials

   <F. Scott Fitzgerald>
   <T.S. Eliot>

4. is used after Roman and Arabic numerals and after letters when they are used in outlines and enumerations

   <I. Objectives
   A. Economy
   1. low initial cost
   2. low maintenance cost
   B. Ease of operation>

   <Required skills are:
   1. Shorthand
   2. Typing
   3. Transcription>

Question Mark ?

1. terminates a direct question

   <How did she do it?>
   <"How did she do it?" he asked.>

2. terminates an interrogative element that is part of a sentence; however, indirect questions should not be followed by a question mark

   <How did she do it? was the question on each person's mind.>
<He wondered, Will it work?>
<He wondered whether it would work.>

3. punctuates each element of an interrogative series that is neither numbered nor lettered; however, only one such mark punctuates a numbered or lettered interrogative series

   <Can you give us a reasonable forecast? back up your predictions? compare them with last quarter's earnings?>
<Can you (1) give us a reasonable forecast, (2) back up your predictions, (3) compare them with last quarter's earnings?>

4. indicates the writer's ignorance or uncertainty

   <Geoffrey Chaucer, English poet (1340?-1400)>

Quotation Marks, Double " "

1. enclose direct quotations in conventional usage, but not indirect quotations

   <He said, "I am leaving.">
<He said that he was leaving.>

2. enclose words or phrases borrowed from others, words used in a special way, and often slang words when introduced into formal writing

   <As the leader of a gang of "droogs," he is altogether frightening, as is this film.—Liz Smith>
<He called himself "emperor," but he was really just a dictator.>

3. enclose titles of poems, short stories, articles, lectures, chapters of books, short musical compositions, and radio and TV programs

   <Robert Frost's "Dust of Snow">
<Katherine Anne Porter's "That Tree">
<The third chapter of *Treasure Island* is entitled "The Black Spot.">
<"America the Beautiful">
<Ravel's "Bolero">
<NBC's "Today Show">

4. are used with other punctuation marks in the following ways:

   the period and the comma fall *within* the quotation marks

   <"I am leaving," he said>
<Her camera was described as "waterproof," but "moisture-resistant" would have been a better description.>

   the colon and semicolon fall *outside* the quotation marks

   <There was only one thing to do when he said, "I may not run": promise him a large campaign contribution.>
<He spoke of his "little cottage in the country"; he might better have called it a mansion.>

   the dash, the question mark, and the exclamation point fall *within* the quotation marks when they refer to the quoted matter only; they fall *outside* when they refer to the whole sentence

   <He asked, "When did she leave?">
<What is the meaning of "the open door"?>
<The sergeant shouted "Halt!">
<Save us from his "mercy"!>

5. are not used with *yes* or *no* except in direct discourse

   <She said yes to all our requests.>

6. are not used with lengthy quotations set off from the text

   <He took the title for his biography of Thoreau from a passage in *Walden*:

   > I long ago lost a hound, a bay horse, and a turtle-dove, and am still on their trail. . . . I have met one or two who had heard the hound, and the tramp of the horse, and even seen the dove dis-

appear behind a cloud, and they seemed as anxious to recover them as if they had lost them themselves.

However, the title *A Hound, a Bay Horse, and a Turtle-Dove* probably puzzled some readers.>

Quotation Marks, Single ‘ ’

1. enclose a quotation within a quotation in American usage

   <The witness said, “I distinctly heard him say, ‘Don’t be late,’ and then heard the door close.”>

2. are sometimes used in place of double quotation marks especially in British usage

   <The witness said, ‘I distinctly heard him say, “Don’t be late,” and then heard the door close.’>

   NOTE: When both single and double quotation marks occur at the end of a sentence, the period typically falls *within* both sets of marks.

   <The witness said, “I distinctly heard him say, ‘Don’t be late.’ ”>

Semicolon ;

1. links main clauses not joined by a coordinating conjunction

   <Some people have the ability to write well; others do not.>

2. links main clauses joined by conjunctive adverbs (as *consequently, furthermore, however*)

   <Speeding is illegal; furthermore, it is very dangerous.>

3. separates phrases and clauses which themselves contain commas

   <The country’s resources consist of large ore deposits; lumber, waterpower, and fertile soils; and a strong, rugged people.>
   <Send copies to our offices in Portland, Maine; Springfield, Illinois; and Savannah, Georgia.>

4. often occurs before phrases or abbreviations (as *for example, for instance, that is, that is to say, namely, e.g.*, or *i.e.*) that introduce expansions or series

   <As a manager she tried to do the best job she could; that is, to keep her project on schedule and under budget.>

Virgule /

1. separates alternatives

   <Each applicant should have this form signed by his/her parent.>

2. separates successive divisions (as months or years) of an extended period of time

   <the fiscal year 1991/1992>
   <the May/June issue>

3. serves as a dividing line between one line of poetry and the next when each is not set on its own line

   <Say, sages, what’s the charm on earth/Can turn death’s dart aside?—Robert Burns>

4. often represents *per* in abbreviations

   <9 ft/sec> <20 km/hr>

Italicization

The following are usually italicized in print and underlined in manuscript and typescript.

1. titles of books, magazines, newspapers, plays, movies, works of art, and long musical compositions (but not musical compositions identified by the nature of the musical form in which they were written)

   <Eliot's *The Waste Land*>
   <*Saturday Review*>
   <*Christian Science Monitor*>
   <Shakespeare's *Othello*>
   <the movie *High Noon*>
   <Gainsborough's *Blue Boy*>
   <Mozart's *Don Giovanni*>
   but
   <Fantasy in C Minor>

   NOTE: Plurals of such italicized titles have roman, not italic, inflectional endings.

   <hidden under a stack of *Saturday Review*s>

2. names of ships and aircraft, and often spacecraft

   <M. V. *West Star*>
   <Lindbergh's *Spirit of St. Louis*>
   <*Apollo 13*>

3. words, letters, and figures when referred to as words, letters, and figures

   <The word *receive* is often misspelled.>
   <The *g* in *align* is silent.>
   <You should dot your *i*'s and cross your *t*'s.>
   <The first *2* and the last *0* are barely legible.>

4. foreign words and phrases that have not become established as part of English

   <*aere perennius*>
   <*che sarà, sarà*>
   <*sans peur et sans reproche*>
   <*ich dien*>
   but
   <pasta> <ad hoc>
   <ex officio>

   NOTE: The decision as to whether or not a word or phrase has become established in English will vary according to the subject matter and the expected audience of the passage in which it appears. In general, any word entered in the main A-Z vocabulary of this dictionary need not be italicized.

5. New Latin scientific names of genera, species, subspecies, and varieties (but not groups of higher rank, as phyla, classes, or orders) in botanical or zoological names

   <a thick-shelled American clam *(Mercenaria mercenaria)*>
   <a cardinal *(Richmondena cardinalis)*>
   but
   <the family Hominidae>

6. case titles in legal citations, both in full and shortened form ("v" for "versus" is set in roman, though)

   <*Jones* v. *Massachusetts*>
   <the *Jones* case> <*Jones*>

Capitalization

Capitals are used for two broad purposes in English: they mark a beginning (as of a sentence) and they signal a proper noun, pronoun, or adjective. The following principles, each with bracketed examples, describe the most common uses of capital letters.

Beginnings

1. The first word of a sentence or sentence fragment is capitalized.

<The play lasted nearly three hours.>
<How are you feeling?>
<Bravo!>
<"Have you hand grenades?"
"Plenty."
"How many rounds per rifle?"
"Plenty."
"How many?"
"One hundred fifty. More maybe."
—Ernest Hemingway>

2. The first word of a sentence contained within parentheses is capitalized if it does not occur within another sentence; however, a parenthetical sentence occurring in the midst of another sentence does not begin with a capital.

<The discussion was held in the boardroom. (The results are still confidential.)>
<Although we liked the restaurant (their Italian food was the best), we seldom ate there.>
<After waiting in line for an hour (why do we do these things?), we finally left.>

3. The first word of a direct quotation is capitalized; however, if the quotation is interrupted in the middle of a sentence, the second part does not begin with a capital.

<The President said, "We have rejected this report entirely.">
<"We have rejected this report entirely," the President said, "and we will not comment on it further.">

NOTE: When a quotation, whether a sentence fragment or a complete sentence, is syntactically dependent on the sentence in which it occurs, the quotation does not begin with a capital.

<The President made it clear "that there is no room for compromise.">

4. The first word of a direct question within a sentence is capitalized.

<That question is: Is man an ape or an angel?
—Benjamin Disraeli>
<My first thought was, How can I avoid this assignment?>

5. The first word of a line of poetry is conventionally capitalized.

<The best lack all conviction, while the worst
Are full of passionate intensity.
—W. B. Yeats>

6. The first word following a colon may be lowercased or capitalized if it introduces a complete sentence; while the former is the more usual styling, the latter is common when the sentence introduced by the colon is fairly lengthy and distinctly separate from the preceding clause.

<The advantage of this particular system is clear: it's inexpensive.>
<The situation is critical: This company cannot hope to recoup the fourth-quarter losses that were sustained in five operating divisions.>

7. When a sentence or phrase introduces a listing of items, the first word in each item is capitalized if the items are complete sentences themselves or if each item is set on its own line. Otherwise, the first word of each item is not capitalized.

<Do the following tasks at the end of the day: 1. Clean your typewriter. 2. Clear your desktop of papers. 3. Cover office machines. 4. Straighten the contents of your desk drawers, cabinets, and bookcases.>

<This is the agenda:
Call to order
Roll call
Minutes of the previous meeting
Treasurer's report>

<On the agenda will be (1) call to order, (2) roll call, (3) minutes of the previous meeting, (4) treasurer's report. . . .>

8. The first word in an outline heading is capitalized.

<I. Editorial tasks
II. Production responsibilities
A. Cost estimates
B. Bids>

9. The first word of the salutation of a letter and the first word of a complimentary close are capitalized.

<Dear Mary,>
<Ladies and Gentlemen:>
<Sincerely yours,>
<Cordially,>

Proper Nouns, Pronouns, and Adjectives

The essential distinction in the use of capitals and lowercase letters beginning words lies in the particularizing or individualizing significance of capitals as against the generic or generalizing significance of lowercase. A capital is used with proper nouns, that is, nouns that distinguish some individual person, place, or thing from others of the same class, and with proper adjectives, that is, adjectives that take their descriptive meaning from what is named by the noun.

ARMED FORCES

1. Branches and units of the armed forces are capitalized, as are easily recognized short forms of full branch and unit designations; however, the words *army, navy*, etc., are lowercased when standing alone, when used collectively in the plural, or when they are not part of an official title.

<United States Army>
<a contract with the Army>
<Corps of Engineers>
<a bridge built by the Engineers>
<allied armies>

AWARDS

2. The names of awards and prizes are capitalized.

<the Nobel Prize in medicine>
<Distinguished Service Cross>
<Academy Award>

DERIVATIVES OF PROPER NAMES

3. Derivatives of proper names are capitalized when used in their primary sense. However, if the derived term has taken on a specialized meaning, it is usually not capitalized.

<Roman customs>
<Shakespearean comedies>
<Edwardian era>
but
<quixotic> <pasteurized milk>
<cesarean section>

GEOGRAPHICAL REFERENCES

4. Divisions of the earth's surface and names of distinct areas, regions, places, or districts are capitalized, as are derivative adjectives and some derivative nouns and verbs.

<the Eastern Hemisphere>
<Midwest> <Tropic of Cancer>
<Springfield, Massachusetts>
<the Middle Eastern situation>
<an Americanism>
but
<a japan finish>
<a green jersey>

5. Popular names of localities are capitalized.

<the Corn Belt> <the Loop>
<The Big Apple> <the Gold Coast>
<the Eastern Shore>

6. Words designating global, national, regional, or local political divisions are capitalized when they are essential elements of specific names; however, they are usually lowercased when they precede a proper name or stand alone.

<the British Empire> <Washington State>
<Bedford County> <New York City>
<Ward 1>
but
<the fall of the empire>
<the state of Washington>
<the county of Bedford>
<the city of New York>
<fires in three wards>

NOTE: In legal documents, these words are often capitalized regardless of position.

<the State of New York>
<the County of Bedford>
<the City of New York>

7. Generic geographical terms (as *lake, mountain, river, valley*) are capitalized if they are part of a specific proper name.

<Hudson Bay> <Long Island>
<Niagara Falls> <Crater Lake>

8. Generic terms preceding names are usually capitalized.

<Lakes Michigan and Superior>
<Mounts Whitney and Rainier>

9. Generic terms following names are usually lowercased, as are singular or plural generic terms that are used descriptively or alone.

<the Himalaya and Andes mountains>
<the Missouri and Platte rivers>
<the Atlantic coast of Labrador>
<the Hudson valley> <the Arizona desert>
<the river valley> <the valley>

10. Compass points are capitalized when they refer to a geographical region or when they are part of a street name, but they are lowercased when they refer to simple direction.

<up North> <back East> <the Northwest>
<West Columbus Avenue>
but
<west of the Rockies>
<the west coast of Florida>

11. Adjectives derived from compass points and nouns designating the inhabitants of some geographical regions are capitalized; when in doubt consult the main vocabulary portion of this dictionary.

<a Southern accent>
<Northerners>

12. Terms designating public places are capitalized if they are part of a proper name.

<Brooklyn Bridge> <Lincoln Park>
<the Dorset Hotel> <Independence Hall>
but
<Fifth and Park avenues>
<the Dorset and Drake hotels>

GOVERNMENTAL AND JUDICIAL BODIES

13. Full names of legislative, deliberative, executive, and administrative bodies are capitalized, as are easily recognized short forms of these names; however, nonspecific noun and adjective references to them are usually lowercased.

<the U.S. House of Representatives>
<the House>
<the Federal Bureau of Investigation>
but
<both houses of Congress>
<a federal agency>

14. Names of international courts, the U.S. Supreme Court, and other higher courts are capitalized; however, names of city and county courts are usually lowercased.

<The International Court of Arbitration>
<the Supreme Court of the United States>
<the Supreme Court>
<the United States Court of Appeals for the Second Circuit>
<the Michigan Court of Appeals>
<Lawton municipal court>
<Newark night court>

HISTORICAL PERIODS AND EVENTS

15. The names of congresses, councils, and expositions are capitalized.

<the Yalta Conference>
<the Republican National Convention>

16. The names of historical events, some historical periods, and some cultural periods and movements are capitalized.

<the Boston Tea Party>
<Renaissance> <Prohibition>
<Augustan Age>
<the Enlightenment>
but
<space age> <cold war>
<neoclassicism>

17. Numerical designations of historical time periods are capitalized when they are part of a proper name; otherwise they are lowercased.

<the Third Reich>
<Roaring Twenties>
but
<eighteenth century>
<the eighties>

18. Names of treaties, laws, and acts are capitalized.

<Treaty of Versailles>
<The Controlled Substances Act of 1970>

ORGANIZATIONS

19. Names of firms, corporations, schools, and organizations and their members are capitalized; however, common nouns used descriptively and occurring after the names of two or more organizations are lowercased.

<Merriam-Webster Inc.>
<University of Wisconsin>
<European Economic Community>
<Rotary International>
<Kiwanians>
<American and United airlines>

NOTE: The word *the* at the beginning of such names is only capitalized when the legal name is referred to.

20. Words such as *group, division, department, office*, or *agency* that designate corporate and organizational units are capitalized only when used with a specific name.

<while working for the Editorial Department of this company>
but
<a notice to all department heads>

PEOPLE

21. The names of persons are capitalized.

<Noah Webster>
<Sir Arthur Thomas Quiller-Couch>

NOTE: The capitalization of particles (as *de, della, der, du, l', la, ten, van*) varies widely especially in names of people in English-speaking countries.

<Thomas De Quincey> <Willem de Kooning>
<Werner Von Braun>
<Gerald ter Hoerst>

22. Titles preceding the name of a person and epithets used instead of a name are capitalized; however, titles following a name or used alone are usually lowercased.

<President Roosevelt>
<Professor Harris>
<Queen Elizabeth>
<Old Hickory> <the Iron Chancellor>
but
<Henry VIII, king of England>

23. Corporate titles are capitalized when referring to specific individuals; when used in general or plural contexts, they are lowercased.

<Laura Jones, Vice President>
<The sales manager called me.>

24. Words of family relationship preceding or used in place of a person's name are capitalized; however, these words are lowercased if they are part of a noun phrase that is being used in place of a name.

<Cousin Julia>
<Grandfather Jones>
<I know when Mother's birthday is.>
but
<I know when my mother's birthday is.>

25. Words designating peoples, tribes, races, and languages are capitalized.

<Canadians> <Iroquois>
<Afro-American>
<Latin> <Indo-European>

NOTE: Designations based on color or local usage are variously capitalized or lowercased by different writers; however, style manuals usually recommend lowercasing such words.

<black> <white>

PERSONIFICATIONS

26. Personifications are capitalized.

<She dwells with Beauty—Beauty, that must die;
And Joy, whose hand is ever at his lips
Bidding adieu.
—John Keats>

<obey the commands of Nature>

PRONOUNS

27. The pronoun I is capitalized. For pronouns referring to the Deity, see rule 29 below.

<. . . no one but I myself had yet printed any of my work—Paul Bowles>

RELIGIOUS TERMS

28. Words designating the Deity are capitalized.

<An anthropomorphic, vengeful Jehovah became a spiritual, benevolent Supreme Being.—A. R. Katz>

29. Personal pronouns referring to the Deity are capitalized by some authors only when such words are not closely preceded by their antecedents; other writers capitalize these words regardless of their distance from their antecedents.

<The principal group that disagreed with them . . . did so only in an even greater faith—that when God chose to save the heathen He could do it by Himself.—Elmer Davis>
<Allah will not subject any believer to eternal punishment because of His readiness to yield to the Prophet's intercession.—G. E. Grunebaum>
<The Almighty has his own purposes.—Abraham Lincoln>
<so lonely 'twas, that God himself scarce seemed there to be.—S. T. Coleridge>
<all Thy works, O Lord, shall bless Thee.—*Oxford Amer. Hymnal*>
<God's in His heaven—all's right with the world!—Robert Browning>

30. Traditional designations of revered persons, as prophets, apostles, and saints are often capitalized.

<our Lady>
<the Prophet>
<the Lawgiver>

31. Names of creeds and confessions, religious denominations, and monastic orders are capitalized, as is the word *Church* when used to designate a specific body or edifice.

<Apostles' Creed>
<the Thirty-nine Articles of the Church of England>
<Society of Jesus>
<Hunt Memorial Church>
but
<the Baptist church>

32. Names for the Bible or parts, versions, or editions of it and names of other sacred books are capitalized.

<Authorized Version> <New English Bible>
<Old Testament>
<Apocrypha>
<Gospel of Saint Mark>
<Koran> <Talmud>

NOTE: Adjectives derived from the names of sacred books are irregularly capitalized or lowercased; when in doubt, consult the main vocabulary portion of this dictionary.

SCIENTIFIC TERMS

33. Names of planets and their satellites, asteroids, stars, constellations, and groups of stars and other unique celestial objects are capitalized; however, the words *sun, earth*, and *moon* are usually lowercased unless they occur with other astronomical names.

<Venus>
<Ganymede>
<Sirius>
<Pleiades>
<the Milky Way>
<probes heading for the Moon and Mars>

34. Genera in binomial scientific names in zoology and botany are capitalized; names of species are not.

<a cabbage butterfly *(Pieris rapae)*>
<a common buttercup *(Ranunculus acris)*>
<a robin *(Turdus migratorius)*>

35. New Latin names of classes, families, and all groups above genera in zoology and botany are capitalized; however, their derivative adjectives and nouns are not.

<Gastropoda> *but* <gastropod>
<Thallophyta> *but* <thallophyte>

36. Geological eras, periods, epochs, strata, and names of prehistoric divisions are capitalized.

<Silurian period>
<Pleistocene epoch>
<Age of Reptiles>
<Neolithic age>

TIME PERIODS AND ZONES

37. The names of days of the week, months of the year, and holidays and holy days are capitalized.

<Tuesday> <June> <Thanksgiving>
<Independence Day> <Easter>
<Yom Kippur>

38. The names of time zones are capitalized when abbreviated but usually lowercased when spelled out except for words that are proper names. See also rules 16 and 17 above.

<CST>
<central standard time>
<Pacific standard time>

TITLES OF PRINTED MATTER

39. Words in titles are capitalized with the exception of internal conjunctions, prepositions, and articles.

NOTE: In some publications, prepositions of five or more letters (as *about, toward*) are capitalized also.

<*The Lives of a Cell*>
<*Of Mice and Men*>
<"The Man Who Would Be King">
<"To His Coy Mistress">
<"Acquainted with the Night">

40. Major sections (as a preface, introduction, or index) of books, long articles, or reports are capitalized when they are specifically referred to within the same material. The word *chapter* is usually capitalized when used with a cardinal number.

Capitalization of the titles of movies, plays, and musical compositions follows similar conventions. For more details, see the Italicization section above.

<See the Appendix for further information.>
<The Introduction explains the scope of this book.>
<discussed later in Chapter 4>
but
<discussed in a later chapter>

TRADEMARKS

41. Registered trademarks are capitalized.

<Dubonnet> <Orlon>

VEHICLES

42. The names of ships, aircraft, and spacecraft are capitalized.

<M. V. *West Star*>
<Lindbergh's *Spirit of St. Louis*>
<*Apollo 13*>

[illegible]

Names of plants and [illegible]

[illegible]

[illegible] and [illegible] capitalized [illegible]

[illegible]

TITLES OF [illegible]

[illegible] names of [illegible] and periodicals [illegible]

[illegible]

[illegible]

[illegible] capitalized [illegible]

[illegible]

[illegible] trademarks [illegible] capitalized

[illegible]

Documentation of Sources

Authors and editors often need to let their readers know the sources of information and quotations in a space-saving way that does not make a major interruption to the flow of the text. This type of documentation is usually provided by a note, and there are various forms that a note may take. In works related to the humanities, the footnote form has traditionally been preferred. In this form, full bibliographical information including author, title, publisher, date, and page is keyed to specific text passages by means of notes set aside from the rest of the text. In works related to the social and natural sciences, a system relying on parenthetical notes that appear in the text and that refer the reader to a list of sources elsewhere in the work has traditionally been used. Details relating to both these systems of documentation, as well as to modified system that uses elements of each, are explained in the following pages. For more detailed information, *Webster's Standard American Style Manual* may be consulted.

Footnotes

Footnotes to a text are indicated by superscript Arabic numerals placed after a quotation or after material containing information that the author obtained from another source. When the reference material is not a quotation, the numeral is usually placed at the end of a sentence or clause, or at some other natural break in the sentence. There should be no space between the quotation or text and the superscript numeral that follows it.

The text of the note itself is introduced by the applicable Arabic numeral, which may be a superior numeral, unpunctuated and separated from the first word of the footnote by one space, or a full-size numeral set on the line and followed by a period and one or two spaces. The latter styling has become more popular recently and is much easier to type; it is the styling used in the examples below.

The indentation of footnote text varies according to individual preference. Indenting the first line of the footnote and having continuation lines return to flush left on the page is probably the most common styling and is the styling used in the examples below. However, stylings in which the first line is flush left and continuation lines are indented or in which all lines are flush left are also common.

In typewritten works, the notes themselves are usually single-spaced, but double spacing is used between notes. When a manuscript is being typed prior to typesetting, however, the notes should be double-spaced internally with triple spacing between the notes.

The numbering of footnotes may be consecutive throughout a paper, article, or book, or, especially in longer works, may start over with each new chapter or major section of the text. The footnotes may appear at the end of the complete text, at the end of each chapter, or at the bottom of each page. Notes appearing at the end of the chapter or the work are often called endnotes, and they are generally preferred over notes appearing at the bottom of the page because they are easier to handle when preparing manuscript or printed pages. Endnotes are, however, much less convenient for the reader to use than are notes that appear on the same page as the text with which they are associated. The disadvantages of footnotes and endnotes have prompted some style books to urge writers in the humanities to adopt parenthetical references (described on the following pages), which are somewhat less cumbersome than footnotes. Despite their disadvantages, however, footnotes and endnotes are still widely used.

The following examples illustrate the basic types of footnotes.

Sample Footnotes

BOOKS

one author

1. Albert H. Marckwardt, *American English* (New York: Oxford University Press, 1958), p. 94.

multiple authors

2. De Witt T. Starnes and Gertrude E. Noyes, *The English Dictionary from Cawdrey to Johnson 1604–1775* (Chapel Hill: University of North Carolina Press, 1946), p. 119.

translation and/or edition

3. Simone de Beauvoir, *The Second Sex*, trans. and ed. H. M. Parshley (New York: Alfred A. Knopf, 1953), p. 600.

4. William Shakespeare, *The Complete Works of Shakespeare*, ed. George Lyman Kittredge (Boston: Ginn and Company, 1936), p. 801.

second or later edition

5. Albert C. Baugh, *A History of the English Language*, 2nd ed. (New York: Appleton-Century-Crofts, 1957), p. 300.

a work in a collection

6. Kemp Malone, "The Phonemes of Current English," *Studies for William A. Read*, ed. Nathaniel M. Caffee and Thomas A. Kirby (Baton Rouge: Louisiana State University Press, 1940), pp. 133–65.

author is a group or organization

7. President's Commission on Higher Education, *Higher Education for American Democracy* (Washington, D.C.: GPO, 1947), I:26.

ARTICLES

from a journal with pagination throughout the annual volume

8. James M. Kusack and John S. Bowers, "Public Microcomputers in Public Libraries," *Library Journal* 107 (1982): 2137–41.

from a journal paging each issue separately

9. Roseann Duenas Gonzalez, "Teaching Mexican American Students to Write: Capitalizing on the Culture," *English Journal* 71.7 (November 1982): 22–24.

from a monthly magazine

10. Shirley Abbot, "Southern Women," *Harper's*, July 1982, pp. 44–47.

from a weekly magazine

11. Walter Clemons, "Cheever's Triumph," *Newsweek*, 14 March 1977, pp. 61–67.

from a newspaper

12. Nancy Bauer, "Housing and the Native: A Sore Spot on Nantucket," *Boston Globe*, 20 June 1982, News section, p. 29, col. 2–4.

letter to the editor

13. Charles H. Percy, "Letters to the Editor," *The Wall Street Journal*, 4 November 1982, p. 31.

a signed review

14. Jane H. Hill, rev. of *Language and Learning: The Debate between Jean Piaget and Noam Chomsky*, ed. Massimo Piattelli-Palmarini, *Language* 57 (1981): 948–53.

Style and Content for Subsequent Footnotes

There are two systems that are currently used to refer to a source that has already been cited. One makes use of a shortened footnote styling and is especially useful when the same source is cited repeatedly with intervening footnotes. The other system uses the traditional Latin abbreviations *ibid., loc. cit.*, and *op. cit.* as space-savers in repeated references to sources cited earlier. Both systems are illustrated below.

Shortened Footnotes

first reference	1. Albert H. Marckwardt, *American English* (New York: Oxford University Press, 1980), p. 94.
repeated reference when the author's name appears in the text	2. *American English*, p. 95.
repeated reference when the author's name does not appear in the text	3. Marckwardt, *American English*, p. 95. *or* 4. Marckwardt, p. 95.
first reference to a work by more than one author	5. De Witt T. Starnes and Gertrude E. Noyes, *The English Dictionary from Cawdrey to Johnson 1604–1775* (Chapel Hill: University of North Carolina Press, 1946), p. 120.
repeated reference to a work by more than one author	6. Starnes and Noyes, *The English Dictionary from Cawdrey to Johnson 1604–1775*, p. 126. *or* 7. Starnes and Noyes, p. 126.
a long title may be shortened in a repeated reference	8. Starnes and Noyes, *The English Dictionary*, p. 126.
a repeated reference to an article in a periodical can be shortened	9. Gonzalez, "Teaching Mexican American Students," p. 22.

Latin Abbreviations

Note: *Ibid.* is used when a footnote refers to the same source as the previous footnote. *Loc. cit.* and *op. cit.* are used when the previous footnote does not refer to the same source; *loc. cit.* refers to the same page(s) cited earlier, and *op. cit.* refers to different pages in a source cited earlier. These Latin abbreviations are generally not italicized when used in footnotes, and the comma before the page number is optional.

first reference	10. Simone de Beauvoir, *The Second Sex*, trans. and ed. H. M. Parshley (New York: Alfred A. Knopf, 1953), p. 600.
repeated reference to a work cited in the previous footnote	11. Ibid., p. 609.
repeated reference to the page cited in the previous footnote	12. Ibid.
repeated reference to the same page(s) of a work cited earlier	13. Starnes and Noyes, loc. cit.
repeated reference to a different page of a work cited earlier	14. Starnes and Noyes, op. cit., p. 133.

Bibliographies

A bibliography differs from a list of references in that it lists all of the works that a writer has found relevant in writing the text. A list of references, on the other hand, includes only those works that are specifically mentioned in the text of from which a particular quotation or piece of information was taken. In all other respects, however, bibliographies and lists of references are quite similar. They both appear at the end of an article, chapter, or book, where they list sources of information that are relevant to the text. They differ from a section of endnotes in that their entries are arranged alphabetically, and they share patterns of indentation, punctuation, and capitalization that are different from those of footnotes and endnotes. Because the entries in a bibliography are styled in the same way as entries in a list of references, the list of references (shown in two versions, one for the humanities and the other for social and natural sciences) given in the section below may be used as a guide to styling entries in a bibliography.

Parenthetical References

A parenthetical reference, like a shortened footnote, is a highly abbreviated reference to a source. Unlike a footnote, it is included in the main body of the text and is set off from the text by parentheses. Such a reference directs readers to a bibliography or list of references with full information that is usually placed at the end of the work. A parenthetical reference usually includes the name of the author, the date of the work, and a page reference. If an entire work in the list of references is being cited, the page reference may be omitted. To distinguish among works published by the same author in a single year, an additional designation in the form of a lowercase letter (as 1980a or 1980b) is used.

Parenthetical formats have the advantage of providing essential and useful information within the text, without providing so much information that reading the text is impeded. They can help the reader decide whether to turn to the list of references for further information.

The following parenthetical references are keyed to the list of references that follows them and refer to some of the same sources used in the Footnotes section above. The two different versions of the list of references show how such a list might be styled, respectively, in the humanities and in the social and natural sciences; however, numerous variations of these basic forms are in use throughout the academic disciplines and professional specialty fields.

Sample References

one author	(Chapman 1969)
multiple authors	(Starnes and Noyes 1946, 119)
translation and/or edition	(Beauvoir 1953, 600)
second or later edition	(Baugh 1957, 300)
a work in a collection	(Malone 1940) [entire article being cited]
author is a group or organization	(President's Commission on Higher Education 1947, I:26)
journal article	(Webb 1977) [entire article being cited]
signed review	(Hill 1981) [entire review being cited]

Sample Lists of References

representative style for the humanities

Baugh, Albert C. *A History of the English Language*, 2nd ed. New York: Appleton-Century-Crofts, 1957.

Beauvoir, Simone de. *The Second Sex*. Translated and edited by H. M. Parshley. New York: Alfred A. Knopf, 1953.

Chapman, R. F. *The Insects*. New York: American Elsevier, 1969.

Hill, Jane H. Review of *Language and Learning: The Debate between Jean Piaget and Noam Chomsky*, ed. Massimo Piattelli-Palmarini. *Language* 57 (December 1981): 948–53.

Malone, Kemp. "The Phonemes of Current English." In *Studies for William A. Read*, edited by Nathaniel M. Caffee and Thomas A. Kirby, pp. 133–65. Baton Rouge: Louisiana State University Press, 1940.

President's Commission on Higher Education. *Higher Education for American Democracy*. Washington, D.C.: GPO, 1947.

Starnes, De Witt T., and Gertrude E. Noyes. *The English Dictionary from Cawdrey to Johnson 1604–1775*. Chapel Hill: University of North Carolina Press, 1946.

Webb, Karen E. "An Evolutionary Aspect of Social Structure and a Verb 'Have.' " *American Anthropologist* 79 (1977): 42–49.

representative style for the social and natural sciences

Baugh, Albert C. 1957. *A history of the English language*. 2nd ed. New York: Appleton-Century-Crofts.

Beauvoir, Simone de. 1953. *The second sex*. Trans and ed. H. M. Parshley. New York: Alfred A. Knopf.

Chapman, R. F. 1969. *The insects*. New York: American Elsevier.

Hill, Jane H. 1981. Review of *Language and Learning: The Debate between Jean Piaget and Noam Chomsky*, ed. Massimo Piattelli-Palmarini. *Language* 57: 948–53.

Malone, Kemp. 1940. The phonemes of current English. In *Studies for William A. Read*, ed. Nathaniel M. Caffee and Thomas A. Kirby, pp. 133–65. Baton Rouge: Louisiana State University Press.

President's Commission on Higher Education. 1947. *Higher education for American democracy*. Washington, D.C.: GPO.

Starnes, De Witt T., and Gertrude E. Noyes. 1946. *The English dictionary from Cawdrey to Johnson 1604–1775*. Chapel Hill: University of North Carolina Press.

Webb, Karen E. 1977. An evolutionary aspect of social structure and a verb "have." *American Anthropologist* 79: 42–49.

A Modified System

There are many modifications and combinations of the two basic documentation methods outlined above that are followed by various publishing houses and professional journals and societies. The modified system described here is fairly common among scholarly publications. The first reference to a work gives complete bibliographical information in the form of a footnote either at the bottom of the page or in a notes section. Such a note can also include an author's comment on the work cited and may indicate a shortened form by which the work will be cited elsewhere in the text. Subsequent references to that work are given in the form of parenthetical references which may rely on the shortened form indicated in the first note or may include the name of the author, a shortened form of the title, and a page reference. Even if no shortened form is indicated in the first note, subsequent parenthetical references need not repeat any element of the reference that is clear from the context.

first reference

1. Albert H. Marckwardt, *American English* (New York: Oxford University Press, 1958), 94.

2. De Witt T. Starnes and Gertrude E. Noyes, *The English Dictionary from Cawdrey to Johnson 1604–1775* (Chapel Hill: University of North Carolina Press, 1946), 119; hereafter cited parenthetically in the text as *English Dictionary*.

subsequent references

(Marckwardt 101) [appropriate if only one of Marckwardt's works will be cited in text]

(*American English 101*) [appropriate if more than one of Marckwardt's works will be cited and if the author's name is clear from the context]

(101) [appropriate if both author and title can be easily established]

(*English Dictionary* 201)